CHAMBERS

Dictionary of QUOTATIONS

CHAMBERS

This edition published 2005
By BCA
By arrangement with CHAMBERS
An imprint of Chambers Harrap Publishers Ltd
7 Hopetoun Crescent
Edinburgh
EH7 4AY

CN 139029

Previous edition published 1996

Designed and typeset by Chambers Harrap Publishers Ltd, Edinburgh
Printed and bound in Italy by
NIIAG - Bergamo

Contributors

Editor
Una McGovern

Contributors
Don Currie
David Pickering
Alan Taylor
Wilson J Wall
Tim Winter

Consultants
Paul Edmondson
Susan Shatto

Editorial assistance
Hazel Norris
Elaine O'Donoghue

Proofreaders
Hilary Bates
Sheila Ferguson
Rosalind Fergusson
Graham Frankland
Ingalo Thomson

Publishing manager
Patrick White

Prepress manager
Sharon McTeir

Prepress
David Reid

The editors would also like to thank the following members of the public who have contributed quotations to this edition of the dictionary: Ross Beresford, S S Chubbs, Ivy Chung, Sue Flavell, Ambrose Kennedy, Richard Little, Jayne Loughry, Cairns McDevitte, Irving Rosenwater, Mark Snegg, Hugh Tyler

Contributors to the previous edition

Editors
Alison Jones
Stephanie Pickering
Megan Thomson

Contributors
Katherine Acheson
Julia Carlson
John Robert Colombo
Ingrid Cranfield
Wendy Dossett
José Garcia
Graham Giles
W Eric Gustafson
Bruce Henstell
David Horspool
Dean Juniper
Victoria Keller
Grace Kenny
Michael Kinsella
Paul Maloney
Kenny Mathieson
Kevin McGinley
Jim Orton
Patricia Perilli
Michael Petheram
David Pickering
James Robertson
Adrian Room
Donald Rutherford
D W D Shaw
Sean Sheehan
Jane Stewart
Susan Stiles
Onno van Nijf

Political consultant
Kenneth Baker

North American consultant
Rev James B Simpson

Introduction

A quotation can come from any notable source, spoken or written, and from any language at any time. Quotations interest us especially when they express an idea or thought in an interesting or memorable way, or simply amuse us with their sharp wit. Thus this collection contains not only literary quotations from important authors both past and present, but also quotations from people in many other walks of life. As well as writers, critics, politicians and journalists, we have sought out memorable phrases from scientists, industrialists, entertainers, sportspeople, and many more, to reflect the diversity of modern life. And just as the world has changed since the last edition of this dictionary, so many of the hundreds of new quotations we have selected reflect these changes, and important global and local events.

The coverage is truly international, extending to other varieties of English and to other languages where these provide material that is readily quotable in English. Where appropriate, quotations from languages using the Roman alphabet are given in their original form and are followed by a translation. Where no specific translation has been used, we have aimed to give a good working English version.

Quotations are arranged alphabetically by author, and chronologically (as far as possible) within each author entry, with the year of the quotation put first when this is known. This enables the reader to browse through the quotes of a particular person, and see their thoughts or works as they developed over time. This chronological arrangement is specific to this dictionary, and it makes this dictionary much more than a collection of *bons mots*. Where possible, each entry also includes a brief biography of the author, and many quotations are supplemented by contextual notes. These will help the reader to understand and appreciate the quotations more fully.

A dependable source is given for each quotation where possible. Where quotations are known from many secondary sources with no traceable primary source they are given as 'attributed'.

The comprehensive index is arranged by keyword. This allows the reader to find quotations on a particular subject. Once you have located your keyword, each entry in the index refers the user to the author, the page number on which the quotation occurs, and the number of the quotation on the page. Quotations are numbered from 1 to 99 and then start again at 1. So a reference to BACON 47:58 points to the quotation by Francis Bacon numbered 58 on page 47. Cross-references within the text use the same system.

Our aim has been to present the most memorable comments on all aspects of human experience, but we appreciate that no selection can be definitive, and the editors would appreciate suggestions for inclusion in future editions.

Abbreviations

b.	born
bk.	book
c	century (in dates, eg 18c)
c.	circa
ch.	chapter
d.	died
fl.	floruit
l.	line
pt.	part
sc.	scene

Names of months are shortened to their first three letters.

QUOTATIONS

Abbott, Diane Julie 1953–

British Labour politician, who became the first black woman Member of Parliament in 1987.

1 Forests of middle-aged men in dark suits…all slightly redfaced from eating and drinking too much…a nightmare of elderly white males.
1988 Of the House of Commons. In the *New York Times*, 3 Jun.

Abelard, Peter 1079–1142

French ecclesiast and theologian. At the age of 38, he fell in love with his 17-year-old pupil Héloïse; when the affair was discovered, he was castrated by her relatives. He became a monk and went on to found the monastic school of the Paraclete and to serve as Abbot of St Gildas-de-Rhuys, Brittany. Declared a heretic by his adversaries, he died on his way to defend himself.

2 *Non enim facile de his, quos plurimum diligimus, turpitudinem suspicamur.*
We do not easily suspect evil of those whom we love most.
c.1132 *Historia Calamitatum*, ch.6.

3 *Cum itaque membris his vilissimis, quæ pro summæ turpitudinis exercitio pudenda vocantur, nec proprium sustinent nomen, me divina gratia mundavit potius quam privavit, quid aliud egit quam ad puritatem munditiæ conservandam sordida removit et vitia.*
When divine grace cleansed rather than deprived me of those most vile members which from their grossly depraved activity are called 'pudenda' ['shameful'], having no proper name of their own, what else did it do but remove filth and foulness so as to preserve unblemished purity?
c.1135 Of his castration. Second letter to Héloïse.

4 *O quanta qualia sunt illa sabbata,*
Quae semper celebrat superna curia.
O what their joy and their glory must be,
Those endless sabbaths the blessèd ones see.
Hymnarius Paraclitensis, bk.1, no.29, 'Sabbato. Ad Vesperas' (translated by J M Neale).

Abercrombie, Lascelles 1881–1938

English poet and critic. He wrote several volumes of poetry in the Georgian manner, and a number of works of academic literary criticism.

5 The poet's business is not to describe things to us, or to tell us about things, but to create in our minds the very things themselves.
1932 *Poetry: Its Music and Meaning*, introduction.

Abse, Dannie 1923–

Welsh writer and physician, specialist at a London chest clinic from 1954 to 1989. Best known as a poet, he has also written novels, plays and autobiographical works, including *A Poet in the Family* (1974) and *Goodbye, Twentieth Century* (2001).

6 I know the colour rose, and it is lovely,
But not when it ripens in a tumour;
And healing greens, leaves and grass, so springlike,
In limbs that fester are not springlike.
1968 'Pathology of Colours'.

7 So in the simple blessing of a rainbow,
In the bevelled edge of a sunlit mirror,
I have seen visible, Death's artifact
Like a soldier's ribbon on a tunic tacked.
1968 'Pathology of Colours'.

8 The theme of Death is to Poetry what Mistaken Identity is to Drama.
1984 Journal entry, Feb, collected in *Journals from the Ant-Heap* (1986).

9 We British are an aggressive nation. We seem to have become more violent this last decade: look how we drive fast and furious, with fists clenched; listen, at the stadiums, how the crowds shout, 'Kick his fuckin' head in,' or to the sirens of police cars and ambulances in the shoddy streets of Brixton or Liverpool.
1986 *Journals from the Ant-Heap*, 'Appendix 1: Authors Take Sides'.

Abu'l-'Ala Al-Ma'arri 973–1058

Syrian poet and scholar. He was blinded by smallpox in childhood and devoted himself to study, memorizing the manuscripts of Syrian libraries. As well as poems, he wrote philosophical and mystical works.

10 We live ignorant and die in errancy as we lived.
c.1000 *Luzùmiyyàt*, stanza 4 (translated by R A Nicholson in *Studies in Islamic Poetry*, 1921).

11 The world's best moment is a calm hour passed
In listening to a friend who can talk well.
c.1000 *Luzùmiyyàt*, stanza 32 (translated by R A Nicholson in *Studies in Islamic Poetry*, 1921).

12 We flee from Death's bitter cup; he follows, loving and fain.
c.1000 *Luzùmiyyàt*, stanza 36 (translated by R A Nicholson in *Studies in Islamic Poetry*, 1921).

13 Life is a malady whose one medicine is Death.
c.1000 *Luzùmiyyàt*, stanza 41 (translated by R A Nicholson in *Studies in Islamic Poetry*, 1921).

14 Consider every moment past
A thread from life's frayed mantle cast.
c.1000 *Luzùmiyyàt*, stanza 57 (translated by R A Nicholson in *Studies in Islamic Poetry*, 1921).

Abzug, Bella *originally* ***Bella Savitzky*** 1920–98

US feminist, lawyer, writer and Congresswoman. She was one of the key figures of the modern feminist movement.

15 Richard Nixon self-impeached…[and] gave us General Ford as his revenge.
1976 In *Rolling Stone*, 2 Dec.

Accius 170–c.86 BC

Roman poet and playwright.

16 *Oderint, dum metuant.*
Let them hate, so long as they fear.
Quoted in Seneca *Dialogues*, 'De Ira'.

Ace, Goodman 1899–1982

US humorist, best known for his radio shows such as *The Easy*

Aces (1928–45), with his wife Jane Epstein Ace. He also wrote for television comedians from 1952.

17 Derived from the words Terrible Vaudeville… We call it a medium because nothing's well done.
1954 Of T V. Letter to Groucho Marx. Collected in *The Groucho Letters* (1967).

Achebe, Chinua *originally* Albert Chinualumogo 1930–

Nigerian novelist, poet and essayist. His novel *Things Fall Apart* (1958) explores tensions in 19c African society. Other works include *Anthills of the Savannah* (1987, shortlisted for the Booker Prize).

18 Among the Ibo the art of conversation is regarded very highly, and proverbs are the palm-oil with which words are eaten.
1958 *Things Fall Apart*, ch.1. The title is taken from Yeats's poem 'The Second Coming'.

19 Even now they have not found the mouth with which to tell of their suffering.
1958 *Things Fall Apart*, ch.20.

20 Whenever people have asked me which among my novels is my favourite I have always evaded a direct answer, being strongly of the mind that in sheer invidiousness that question is fully comparable to asking a man to list his children in the order in which he loves them. A paterfamilias worth his salt will, if he must, speak about the peculiar attractiveness of each child.
1974 *Arrow of God*, preface to 2nd edn.

Acheson, Dean Gooderham 1893–1971

US lawyer and politician. As Under-Secretary (1945–7) and then Secretary of State (1949–53) in the Truman administration, he helped to establish the Marshall Plan (1947) and the North Atlantic Treaty Organization.

21 I will undoubtedly have to seek what is happily known as gainful employment, which I am glad to say does not describe holding public office.
1952 On resigning as Secretary of State to resume his career as a lawyer. In *Time*, 22 Dec.

22 Diplomatic problems used to be discussed by ambassadors… Foreign Ministers were called…somebody thought of the summit meetings… We are nearing the moment when political meetings will be held at a divine level.
1959 Comment to reporters in Florence, Sep. Recalled in *This Vast External Realm* (1973).

23 The institution of the throne is an anachronistic, feudal institution perfectly adapted to the use of anachronistic feudal-minded groups.
Opposing US Ambassador Joseph Grew's recommendation for the Emperor's retention in postwar Japan. Quoted in Lee Giovanitti and Fred Freed *The Decision to Drop the Atomic Bomb* (1960).

24 He still had his glorious sense of words drawn from the special reservoir from which Lincoln also drew, fed by Shakespeare and those Tudor critics who wrote the first Prayer Book of Edward VI and their Jacobean successors who translated the Bible.
1961 Of Winston Churchill. *Sketches from Life of Men I Have Known.*

25 The old house carried an assurance, typically Portuguese, that nothing was urgent.
1961 On the US Embassy residence in Lisbon. *Sketches from Life of Men I Have Known.*

26 He wanted to be independent of the vagaries of butlers.
1961 Of Winston Churchill, who liked to keep a champagne bottle next to his plate. *Sketches from Life of Men I Have Known.*

27 He smiled with the spontaneity of a mechanical tiger.
1961 Of Soviet Foreign Minister V M Molotov. *Sketches from Life of Men I Have Known.*

28 He struck me as looking like a pear on top of two toothpicks.
1962 Of Charles de Gaulle, 22 Oct, after a visit during the Cuban missile crisis. Quoted in David S McLellan and David C Acheson (eds) *Among Friends: Personal Letters of Dean Gooderham Acheson* (1980).

29 Great Britain has lost an Empire and not yet found a role. The attempt to play a separate power role—that is, a role apart from Europe, based on a special relationship with the United States, on being the head of the Commonwealth—is about to be played out. Her Majesty's Government is now attempting, wisely in my opinion, to re-enter Europe.
1962 Speech at West Point military academy, 5 Dec. According to the *New York Times*, 23 Nov 1969, Prime Minister Harold Wilson later countered, 'Mr Acheson is a distinguished figure who has lost a State Department and not yet found himself a role'.

30 Fumbling silence in the White House seeps out over the country like a cold fog over a river bed where no stream runs.
1963 Letter to Harry S Truman, 28 May, alluding to the Eisenhower administration. Quoted in David S McLellan and David C Acheson (eds) *Among Friends: Personal Letters of Dean Gooderham Acheson* (1980).

31 A real Centaur—part man, part horse's ass. A rough appraisal, but curiously true.
1968 Of President Johnson. 13 Apr.

32 Like finding oneself pregnant and trying to fall in love as quickly as possible.
On the weekend of Richard M Nixon's inauguration. Quoted in Douglas Brinkley *Dean Acheson: The Cold War Years 1953–71* (1992).

33 I had shown my colors. Those who took their red straight, without a chaser of white and blue, were not mollified.
1969 *Present at the Creation.*

34 The enormity of the task…[was] just a bit less formidable than that described in the first chapter of Genesis.
1969 Of postwar restructuring. *Present at the Creation.*

35 The first requirement of a statesman is that he be dull.
1970 In the *Observer*, 21 Jun.

36 Much in life cannot be affected…but must be borne…without complaint, because complaints are a bore…and undermine the serenity essential to endurance.
Quoted in Gaddis Smith *American Secretaries of State* (1972).

37 Neither action nor style could have accomplished the result alone. Both were needed.
1975 Of Winston Churchill's charisma. *Grapes from Thorns.*

38 His speeches were prepared with that infinite capacity for taking pains, which is said to be genius.
1975 Of Winston Churchill. *Grapes from Thorns.*

39 Courageous and loyal to the tips of his stubby fingers.
1975 Of British Foreign Secretary Ernest Bevin. *Grapes from Thorns.*

40 Breathless and bewildered like an old lady at a busy intersection.
On the State Dept under Cordell Hull. Quoted in David S McLellan *Dean Acheson: The State Department Years* (1976).

41 Our name for problems is significant. We call them headaches. You take a powder and they are gone.
Quoted in David S McLellan *Dean Acheson: The State Department Years* (1976).

42 You can't argue with a river, it is going to flow. You can dam it up…put it to useful purposes…deflect it, but you can't argue with it.
On the fruitlessness of keeping Russian fishermen from waters that should be off limits. Quoted in David S McLellan *Dean Acheson: The State Department Years* (1976).

43 A memorandum is written not to inform the reader but to protect the writer.
1977 In the *Wall Street Journal*, 8 Sep.

44 The Canadians seem to be held together with string and safety pins.
Quoted in David S McLellan and David C Acheson (eds) *Among Friends: Personal Letters of Dean Gooderham Acheson* (1980).

45 Trust him as much as you would a rattlesnake with a silencer on its rattle.
1980 Advice to President Truman on J Edgar Hoover. Quoted in David S McLellan and David C Acheson (eds) *Among Friends: Personal Letters of Dean Gooderham Acheson* (1980).

46 How gently, wisely, and justly G M Young deals with him. That is not the way to write biography.
Collected in David S McClellan and David C Acheson (eds) *Among Friends: Personal Letters of Dean Gooderham Acheson* (1980). On Young's biography *Stanley Baldwin* (1952).

47 Homage to plain dumb luck.
Of the effectiveness of the US blockade of Soviet ships bringing missiles to Cuba. Quoted in Walter Isaacson and Evan Thomas *The Wise Men* (1986).

48 The Iraqi is really not whacky
Toady, perhaps, even tacky.
When they gave *him* the word
He gave *us* the bird
And joined with the Arabs, by cracky!
Limerick written during dull meeting of Foreign Ministers. Quoted in Walter Isaacson and Evan Thomas *The Wise Men* (1986).

49 Charm never made a rooster.
Of poorly-organized attempts to maintain peace by good intentions. Quoted in James B Reston *Deadline* (1991).

50 It is just as full of propaganda as a dog is full of fleas. In fact, I say it's all fleas and no dog.
Of Russian Foreign Minister Andre Vishinsky's proposal that the US should withdraw from postwar Europe. Quoted in James B Reston *Deadline* (1991).

51 With a nation, as with a boxer, one of the greatest assurances of safety is to add reach to power.
Alluding to US bases in Europe. Quoted in James B Reston *Deadline* (1991).

52 If the best minds in the world had set out to find us the worst possible location in the world to fight this damnable war, politically and militarily, the unanimous choice would have been Korea.
On the Korean War. Quoted in Joseph Goulden *Korea* (1992).

Ackerman, Diane 1948–

US poet and writer. Her poetry is published in many journals and books, which include *Wife of Light* (1978) and *Lady Faustus* (1983). She has published non-fiction and was a staff writer at the *New Yorker* from 1988 to 1994.

53 An occasion, catalyst, or tripwire…permits the poet to reach into herself and haul up whatever nugget of the human condition distracts her at the moment, something that can't be reached in any other way.
Quoted in the *New York Times*, 10 Mar 1991.

Ackroyd, Peter 1949–

English novelist, biographer and critic. He has written a number of erudite and playful novels and scholarly biographies, including studies of Dickens and T S Eliot.

54 And the smell of the library was always the same—the musty odour of old clothes mixed with the keener scent of unwashed bodies, creating what the chief librarian had once described as 'the steam of the social soup'.
1987 *Chatterton*, ch.5.

55 No poet is ever completely lost. He has the secret of his childhood safe with him, like some secret cave in which he can kneel. And, when we read his poetry, we can join him there.
1987 *Chatterton*, ch.10.

56 He had a fear of the dead, and of all inanimate things, rising up around him to claim him; it is the fear of the pre-eminently solitary child and solitary man.
1990 Of Charles Dickens. *Dickens*, prologue.

57 Is it possible to be nostalgic about old fears?
1992 *English Music*, ch.1.

58 Yes, I have inherited the past because I have acknowledged it at last… And, now that I have come to understand it, I no longer need to look back.
1992 *English Music*, ch.19.

Acton, John Emerich Edward Dalberg, 1st Baron Acton of Aldenham 1834–1902

English historian. He sat as a Liberal MP (1859–64) and was created baron by Gladstone in 1869. In 1895 he was appointed Professor of Modern History at Cambridge.

59 Power tends to corrupt, and absolute power corrupts absolutely. Great men are almost always bad men. There is no worse heresy than that the office sanctifies the holder of it.
1887 Letter to Bishop Mandell Creighton, 3 Apr.

Adamov, Arthur 1908–70

Russian-born French playwright. A leading exponent of the Theatre of the Absurd, he was the author of such plays as *Le Professeur Taranne* (1953), *Le Ping Pong* (1955) and *Le Printemps '71* (1961).

60 The reason why Absurdist plays take place in No Man's Land with only two characters is primarily financial.
1962 Speech at Edinburgh, 13 Sep.

Adams, Abigail 1744–1818

US first lady, wife of President John Adams, and early feminist.

61 In the new code of laws which I suppose it will be necessary for you to make I desire you would remember

the ladies, and be more generous and favourable to them than your ancestors. Do not put such unlimited power into the hands of the husbands. Remember all men would be tyrants if they could.
1776 Letter to John Adams, 31 Mar.

62 It is not in the still calm of life, or the repose of a pacific station, that great characters are formed... Great necessities call out great virtues.
1780 Letter to John Quincy Adams, 19 Jan.

Adams, Arthur Henry 1872–1936

New Zealand-born journalist, poet and playwright, whose first collection was *Maoriland: and Other Verses* (1899). His *London Streets* (1906) is a colonist's portrayal of the city. He returned to Sydney, Australia, as editor of *Bulletin* and *Lone Hand*.

63 The land lies desolate and stripped;
Across its waste has thinly strayed
A tattered host of eucalypt.
From whose gaunt uniform is made
A ragged penury of shade.
1913 'Written in Australia', in *The Collected Verses of Arthur H Adams*.

Adams, Charles Francis 1807–86

US diplomat and writer, congressman from Massachusetts (1858–61) and Minister to Britain during the American Civil War (1861–8).

64 It would be superfluous in me to point out to your lordship that this is war.
1863 Despatch to Earl Russell during the Civil War, 5 Sep. Quoted in C F Adams *Charles Francis Adams* (1900), ch.17.

Adams, Douglas Noël 1952–2001

English novelist and scriptwriter. His radio serial *The Hitch-Hiker's Guide to the Galaxy* (1978–80) was a cult success, and it and its sequels were also successful novels.

65 Don't Panic.
1979 *The Hitch-Hiker's Guide to the Galaxy*, preface. These words are said to be written in large friendly letters on the cover of the Guide.

66 The Answer to the Great Question Of...Life, the Universe and Everything...Is...Forty-two.
1979 *The Hitch-Hiker's Guide to the Galaxy*, ch.27.

67 'The first ten million years were the worst,' said Marvin, 'and the second ten million years, they were the worst too. The third ten million I didn't enjoy at all. After that I went into a bit of a decline.'
1980 Marvin, the paranoid android. *The Restaurant at the End of the Universe*, ch.18.

68 So Long, and Thanks for All the Fish.
1984 Title of novel.

69 It can hardly be a coincidence that no language on earth has ever produced the expression 'as pretty as an airport'.
1988 *The Long Dark Tea-Time of the Soul*, ch.1.

70 Kate's spirits sank to the very bottom of her being and began to prowl around there making a low growling noise.
1988 *The Long Dark Tea-Time of the Soul*, ch.1.

71 I love deadlines. I love the whooshing noise they make as they go by.
2001 In *The Guardian*, 14 May.

Adams, Gerry (Gerard) 1948–

Northern Irish politician. He has been President of Sinn Féin since 1983 (Vice-President 1978–83).

72 We want him to be the last British Prime Minister with jurisdiction in Ireland.
1997 On Tony Blair. In *The Irish Times*, 8 Oct.

73 Peace cannot be built on exclusion. That has been the price of the last 30 years.
1998 In the *Daily Telegraph*, 11 Apr.

Adams, Henry Brooks 1838–1918

US historian, son of Charles Francis Adams and grandson of John Quincy Adams. His historical works include *Mont Saint Michel and Chartres* (1904), and his autobiography *The Education of Henry Adams* (published privately 1907, publicly 1918) won the 1919 Pulitzer Prize.

74 Some day science may have the existence of mankind in its power and the human race commit suicide by blowing up the race.
1862 Letter to Charles Francis Adams, Jr, 11 Apr.

75 Politics, as a practice, whatever its professions, has always been the systematic organization of hatreds.
1907 *The Education of Henry Adams*, ch.1.

76 All experience is an arch to build on.
1907 *The Education of Henry Adams*, ch.6.

77 A friend in power is a friend lost.
1907 *The Education of Henry Adams*, ch.7.

78 These questions of taste, of feeling, of inheritance, need no settlement. Everyone carries his own inch-rule of taste, and amuses himself by applying it, triumphantly, wherever he travels.
1907 *The Education of Henry Adams*, ch.12.

79 Chaos often breeds life, when order breeds habit.
1907 *The Education of Henry Adams*, ch.16.

80 A teacher affects eternity; he can never tell where his influence stops.
1907 *The Education of Henry Adams*, ch.20, 'Failure'.

81 One friend in a lifetime is much; two are many; three are hardly possible. Friendship needs a certain parallelism of life, a community of thought, a rivalry of aim.
1907 *The Education of Henry Adams*, ch.20.

82 What one knows is, in youth, of little moment; they know enough who know how to learn.
1907 *The Education of Henry Adams*, ch.21.

83 He had often noticed that six months' oblivion amounts to newspaper death, and that resurrection is rare. Nothing is easier, if a man wants it, than rest, profound as the grave.
1907 *The Education of Henry Adams*, ch.22.

84 Practical politics consists in ignoring the facts.
1907 *The Education of Henry Adams*, ch.22.

85 American art, like the American language and American education, was as far as possible sexless.
1907 *The Education of Henry Adams*, ch.25, 'The Dynamo and the Virgin'.

86 No one means all he says, and yet very few say all they mean, for words are slippery and thought is viscous.
1907 *The Education of Henry Adams*, ch.31, 'The Grammar of Science'.

Adams, John 1735–1826

US statesman and second President, a leader of resistance to Britain and central figure in the Declaration of Independence (1776). He became the first US Vice-President under Washington (1789), and later President (1796–1800).

87 A government of laws, and not of men.
1774 In the *Boston Gazette*, no.7. The phrase was later incorporated into the Massachusetts Constitution (1780).

88 I agree with you that in politics the middle way is none at all.
1776 Letter to Horatio Gates, 23 Mar.

89 The second day of July 1776 will be the most
memorable epoch in the history of America. It
ought to be solemnised with pomp and parade,
with shows, games, sports, guns, bells, bonfires
and illuminations from one end of this continent
to the other—from this time forward, for ever
more.
1776 Letter to his wife, 3 Jul, on the vote of Congress for independence from Britain.

90 You and I ought not to die before we have explained ourselves to each other.
1813 Letter to Thomas Jefferson, 15 Jul.

91 What a poor, ignorant, malicious, short-sighted, crapulous mass is Tom Paine's common sense.
1819 Letter to Thomas Jefferson, 22 Jun, referring to the Republican's treatise on independence entitled *Common Sense*.

Adams, John Quincy 1767–1848

US politician and sixth President. Ambassador to Europe and Secretary of State under Monroe, he negotiated the acquisition of Florida from Spain, before becoming President (1825). He failed to win re-election but continued to oppose slavery as a congressman.

92 *Fiat justitia, pereat coelum.* My toast would be, may our country be always successful, but whether successful or otherwise, always right.
1816 Letter to John Adams, 1 Aug.
➸ *See Decatur 258:8, Ferdinand I 320:1.*

93 The American continents, by the free and independent condition that they have assumed and maintain, are henceforth not to be considered as subjects for future colonisation by any European powers... In the wars of the European powers in matters relating to ourselves, we have never taken any part; nor does it comport with our policy to do so.
1823 The Monroe Doctrine, 2 Dec.

94 I inhabit a weak, frail, decayed tenement; battered by the winds and broken in on by the storms, and, from all I can learn, the landlord does not intend to repair.
1848 Attributed, as he lay on his deathbed. Quoted in Clifton Fadiman *The Faber Book of Anecdotes* (1985).

Adams, Judge Richard 1846–1908

Irish judge. After a Law degree, he became a journalist in Cork until he was called to the Irish Bar in 1873. From 1894 he was Judge of the County Court, Limerick.

95 Look here, sir, tell me no more unnecessary lies. Such lies as your attorney advised you are necessary for the presentation of your fraudulent case I will listen to though I shall decide against you whatever you swear, but if you tell me another unnecessary lie, I'll put you in the dock.
Presiding over Limerick County Court. Quoted in A M Sullivan *Old Ireland*.

96 You have been acquitted by a Limerick jury, and you may now leave the dock without any other stain upon your character.
Quoted in Maurice Healy *The Old Munster Circuit*.

Adams, Samuel 1722–1803

Political leader in the American Revolution, who signed the Declaration of Independence. Clerk of the lower house of Massachusetts legislature, he was involved in the Boston Tea Party.

97 What a glorious morning is this.
1775 On hearing gunfire at Lexington, 19 Apr. Quoted in J K Hosmer *Samuel Adams* (1886), ch.19.

Adamson, Harold 1906–80

US lyricist.

98 Comin' in on a wing and a prayer.
1943 Title of song. The phrase was taken from the words of a fighter pilot from his battered jet to ground control.

Adcock, (Karen) Fleur 1934–

New Zealand poet who settled in Britain in 1963. Her works include *The Eye of the Hurricane* (1964), *Selected Poems* (1983) and *Poems 1960–2000* (2000).

99 Do not ask me for charity now:
Go away until your bones are clean.
1983 *Selected Poems*, 'Advice to a Discarded Lover'.

Addison, Joseph 1672–1719

English poet, playwright and essayist. After a Grand Tour of Europe (1699–1704), he entered Parliament as a Whig in 1708. He contributed numerous essays to the *Tatler* and was co-founder with Richard Steele of the *The Spectator* (1711).

1 Music, the greatest good that mortals know,
And all of heaven we have below.
1694 'A Song for St Cecilia's Day'.

2 For wheresoe'er I turn my ravished eyes,
Gay gilded scenes and shining prospects rise,
Poetic fields encompass me around,
And still I seem to tread on classic ground.
1704 *A Letter from Italy*.

3 A painted meadow, or a purling stream.
1704 *A Letter from Italy*.

4 'Twas then great Marlbro's mighty soul was proved.
1705 *The Campaign*, l.279.

5 And, pleased th'Almighty's orders to perform,
Rides in the whirl-wind, and directs the storm.
1705 *The Campaign*, l.291–2.

6 And those who paint 'em truest praise 'em most.
1705 *The Campaign*, l.476.

7 This republic has been much more powerful than it is at present, as it is still likelier, to sink than increase in its dominions.
1705 On Venice. *Remarks on Several parts of Italy*.

8 I remember when our whole island was shaken with an earthquake some years ago, there was an impudent

mountebank who sold pills which (as he told the country people) were very good against an earthquake.
1710 In *The Tatler*, no.240, 21 Oct.

9 A reader seldom peruses a book with pleasure until he knows whether the writer of it be a black man or a fair man, of a mild or choleric disposition, married or a bachelor.
1711 In *The Spectator*, no.1, 1 Mar.

10 Thus I live in the world rather as a Spectator of mankind, than as one of the species, by which means I have made myself a speculative statesman, soldier, merchant, and artisan, without ever meddling with any practical part of life.
1711 In *The Spectator*, no.1, 1 Mar.

11 Nothing is capable of being well set to music that is not nonsense.
1711 In *The Spectator*, no.18.

12 A perfect tragedy is the noblest production of human nature.
1711 In *The Spectator*, no.39.

13 In all thy humours, whether grave or mellow,
Thou'rt such a touchy, testy, pleasant fellow;
Hast so much wit, and mirth, and spleen about thee,
There is no living with thee, nor without thee.
1711 In *The Spectator*, no.68, 18 May.

14 As Sir Roger is landlord to the whole congregation, he keeps them in very good order, and will suffer nobody to sleep in it [the church] besides himself; for if by chance he has been surprised into a short nap at sermon, upon recovering out of it, he stands up, and looks about him; and if he sees anybody else nodding, either wakes them himself, or sends his servant to them.
1711 In *The Spectator*, no.112, 9 Jul.

15 Sir Roger told them, with the air of a man who would not give his judgement rashly, that much might be said on both sides.
1711 In *The Spectator*, no.122, 20 Jul.

16 It was a saying of an ancient philosopher, which I find some of our writers have ascribed to Queen Elizabeth, who perhaps might have taken occasion to repeat it, that a good face is a letter of recommendation.
1711 In *The Spectator*, no.221, 13 Nov.

17 I have often thought, says Sir Roger, it happens very well that Christmas should fall out in the Middle of Winter.
1712 In *The Spectator*, no.269, 8 Jan.

18 A true critic ought to dwell rather upon excellencies than imperfections, to discover the concealed beauties of a writer, and communicate to the world such things as are worth their observation.
1712 In *The Spectator*, no.291, 2 Feb.

19 These widows, Sir, are the most perverse creatures in the world.
1712 In *The Spectator*, no.335, 25 Mar.

20 Mirth is short and transient, cheerfulness fixed and permanent… Mirth is like a flash of lightning that breaks through a gloom of clouds, and glitters for a moment: cheerfulness keeps up a kind of day-light in the mind, and fills it with a steady and perpetual serenity.
1712 In *The Spectator*, no.381, 17 May.

21 The Knight in the triumph of his heart made several reflections on the greatness of the British Nation; as, that one Englishman could beat three Frenchmen; that we could never be in danger of Popery so long as we took care of our fleet; that the Thames was the noblest river in Europe; that London Bridge was a greater piece of work than any of the Seven Wonders of the World; with many other honest prejudices which naturally cleave to the heart of a true Englishman.
1712 In *The Spectator*, no.383, 20 May.

22 Wide and undetermined prospects are as pleasing to the fancy, as the speculations of eternity or infinitude are to the understanding.
1712 In *The Spectator*, no.412, 23 Jun.

23 An account of it would have been thought fabulous, were not the Wall itself extant.
1712 Commenting on the Great Wall of China, *The Spectator*, no.415, 26 Jun.

24 Through all Eternity to Thee
A joyful Song I'll raise,
For oh! Eternity's too short
To utter all thy Praise.
1712 In *The Spectator*, no.453, 9 Aug.

25 We have in England a particular bashfulness in every thing that regards religion.
1712 In *The Spectator*, no.458, 15 Aug.

26 The spacious firmament on high,
With all the blue ethereal sky,
And spangled heavens, a shining frame,
Their great Original proclaim.
Th' unwearied sun from day to day
Does his Creator's power display;
And publishes to every land
The work of an Almighty hand.
1712 In *The Spectator*, no.465, 23 Aug.

27 In Reason's ear they all rejoice,
And utter forth a glorious voice,
For ever singing, as they shine:
'The hand that made us is divine.'
1712 In *The Spectator*, no.465, 23 Aug.

28 A woman seldom asks advice before she has bought her wedding clothes.
1712 In *The Spectator*, no.475, 4 Sep.

29 Our disputants put me in mind of the skuttle fish, that when he is unable to extricate himself, blackens all the water about him, till he becomes invisible.
1712 In *The Spectator*, no.476, 5 Sept.

30 If we may believe our logicians, man is distinguished from all other creatures by the faculty of laughter.
1712 In *The Spectator*, no.494, 26 Sep.

31 'Tis not in mortals to command success,
But we'll do more, Sempronius; we'll deserve it.
1713 *Cato*, act 1, sc.2, l.43–4.

32 'Tis pride, rank pride, and haughtiness of soul;
I think the Romans call it stoicism.
1713 *Cato*, act 1, sc.4, l.82–3.

33 Were you with these, my prince, you'd soon forget
The pale, unripened beauties of the north.
1713 *Cato*, act 1, sc.4, l.134–5.

34 The woman that deliberates is lost.
1713 *Cato*, act 4, sc.1, l.31.

35 Curse on his virtues! they've undone his country.
Such popular humanity is treason.
1713 *Cato*, act 4, sc.1, l.205–6.

36 What a pity is it
That we can die but once to serve our country!
1713 *Cato*, act 4, sc.1, l.258–9.

37 Content thyself to be obscurely good.
When vice prevails, and impious men bear sway,
The post of honour is a private station.
1713 *Cato*, act 4, sc.1, l.319–21.

38 It must be so—Plato, thou reason'st well!—
Else whence this pleasing hope, this fond desire,
This longing after immortality?
Or whence this secret dread, and inward horror,
Of falling into naught? Why shrinks the soul
Back on herself, and startles at destruction
'Tis the divinity that stirs within us;
'Tis heaven itself, that points out an hereafter,
And intimates eternity to man.
Eternity! thou pleasing, dreadful thought!
1713 *Cato*, act 5, sc.1, l.1–10.

39 From hence, let fierce contending nations know
What dire effects from civil discord flow.
1713 *Cato*, act 5, sc.1, closing words.

40 'We are always doing,' says he, 'something for Posterity, but I would fain see Posterity do something for us.'
1714 In *The Spectator* no.583, 20 Aug.

41 There is sometimes a greater judgement shewn in deviating from the rules of art, than in adhering to them; and...there is more beauty in the works of a great genius who is ignorant of all the rules of art, than in the works of a little genius, who not only knows but scrupulously observes them.
1714 In *The Spectator*, no.592, 10 Sep.

42 I should think myself a very bad woman, if I had done what I do for a farthing less.
1716 *The Drummer*, act 1, sc.1.

43 See in what peace a Christian can die.
1719 Last words, to his stepson Lord Warwick. Quoted in Edward Young *Conjectures on Original Composition* (1759).

44 Hunting is not a proper employment for a thinking man.
Quoted in Colin Jarman *The Guinness Dictionary of Sports Quotations* (1990).

Ade, George 1866–1944

US humorist and dramatist.

45 R-E-M-O-R-S-E!
Those dry Martinis did the work for me;
Last night at twelve I felt immense,
Today I feel like thirty cents.
My eyes are blurred, my coppers hot,
I'll try to eat, but I cannot.
It is no time for mirth and laughter,
The cold, grey dawn of the morning after.
1903 *The Sultan of Sulu*, act 2.

Adelman, Kenneth Lee 1946–

US political scientist, director of the US Arms Control and Disarmament Agency (1983–8). His works include *The Great Universal Embrace: Arms Summitry—a skeptic's account* (1989).

46 The history of arms control is a history of great visions eventually mugged by reality.
1986 In *Newsweek*, 1 Dec.

Adenauer, Konrad 1876–1967

German statesman. Dismissed by the Nazis (1933), he founded the Christian Democratic Union (1945) and became first Chancellor of the Federal Republic of Germany (1949–63).

47 We must free ourselves from thinking in terms of nation states. The countries of western Europe are no longer in a position to protect themselves individually. Not one of them is any longer in a position to salvage Europe's culture.
1953 Speech, May.

Adler, Jerry 1949–

US journalist, a senior editor at *Newsweek*.

48 She...happens to stick out a foot just as history is rushing by.
1988 Of Fawn Hall, the secretary who helped Col Oliver North to dispose of top-secret papers, 'the archetype of the Accidental Celebrity'. In *Newsweek*, 9 Mar.

49 Norman Rockwell, the Brueghel of the 20th century bourgeoisie, the Holbein of Jell-O ads and magazine covers; by common assent, the most American artist of all.
1993 On the opening of the Norman Rockwell Museum at Stockbridge, Massachusetts. In *Newsweek*, 12 Apr.

50 The widespread belief that Yuppies as a class would perish from Brie-cheese poisoning turned out to be over-optimistic.
1995 'The Rise of the Overclass', in *Newsweek*, 31 Jul.

Adler, Larry (Lawrence Cecil) 1914–2001

US musician and virtuoso on the harmonica. He emigrated to Britain after being blacklisted in the US.

51 His first choice had been Yehudi Menuhin; he was lucky he got me. Menuhin on the mouth-organ is a mess.
1984 On Henry Koster's casting for the film *Music for Millions* (1944)

Adler, Polly 1900–62

US writer.

52 A House is not a Home.
1954 Title of a book.

Adorno, Theodor 1903–69

German social philosopher and musicologist, who emigrated to the US in 1934. His *Negative Dialectics* (1966) expounds his complex theories, but he also wrote more accessible mass-culture works.

53 In psychoanalysis nothing is true except the exaggerations.
1966 *Negative Dialectics*.

Aelius Aristides AD 117–189

Greek orator. He spent much of his life giving rhetorical demonstrations throughout Asia Minor. He is best known for his encomium of Rome and his 'Sacred Teachings', an account of his dreams while seeking a cure in the temple of Asclepius.

54 As the character is, such is the speech.
Pros Platona Peri Rhetorikes, bk.2, l.392.

St Aelred of Riveaulx d.1167

English writer, historian and Cistercian monk. Raised at the court of David I of Scotland, he became Abbot of Revesby (1143) and Riveaulx (1147). He aided the England–France alliance in support of Pope Alexander II against Emperor Frederick III.

55 *Inveni fateor in rege monachum, claustrum in curia, in palatio monasterii disciplinam.*
I confess that I found in the king a monk, in the court a cloister, and in the palace the discipline of a monastery.
?c.1160 Lament for David I, King of Scotland. Quoted in John Fordoun *Chronicle of Scotland* (c.1384), bk.5, ch.43.

Aeschylus c.525–c.456 BC

Greek dramatist, who served in the Athenian army at Marathon (490 BC) and probably in the navy at Salamis (480 BC). He won 13 first prizes in the dramatic contests of Athens from 484 to 458 BC, but only seven of his many works have survived.

56 Ship-destroyer, man-destroyer, city-destroyer.
Of Helen. *Agamemnon*, l.689.

57 Unworthy was what he did to her, worthy was what he suffered.
Clytemnestra speaks of Agamemnon's sacrifice of their daughter Iphigeneia. *Agamemnon*, l.1527–8 (translated by H Lloyd-Jones).

58 For by the will of the gods Fate hath held sway since ancient days.
Persae, l.102 (translated by H Weir Smyth).

59 Now you battle for your all.
Persae, l.402–5 (translated by H Weir Smyth).

60 Once to die is better than length of days in sorrow without end.
Prometheus Vinctus, l.750–1.

61 It's a man's job—no place for women's plans here!—what lies outside. Stay home and cause no trouble.
Septem contra Thebas, l.200–1 (translated by C M Dawson).

62 Obedience, you know, is Good Luck's mother, wedded to Salvation, they say.
Septem contra Thebas, l.224–5 (translated by C M Dawson).

63 Remember to be submissive, thou art an alien, a fugitive, and in need.
Supplices, l.202 (translated by H Weir Smyth).

Agassi, Andre 1970–

US tennis player who won the men's singles at Wimbledon in 1992.

64 You expect to leave the dance with the ones you came with.
2003 On his surprise at being the last star of his generation still playing. Quoted in *The Independent*, 29 Dec.

Agassiz, (Jean) Louis (Rodolphe) 1807–73

Swiss-born US zoologist and geologist. A professor of natural history at Neuchâtel, he came to the US (1846) to teach at Harvard University. His works include a study of fossil fish and a *Natural History of the United States* (1857–62).

65 The student must remember, for his consolation…that his failures are almost as important to the cause of science and to those who follow him in the same road, as his successes. It is much to know what we cannot do in any given direction—the first step, indeed, toward the accomplishment of what we can do.
1896 *Geological Sketches*.

66 The study of nature is interwoven with the highest mind. You should never trifle with nature.
Attributed.

Agate, James 1877–1947

English theatre critic. He wrote for the *Sunday Times* from 1923 until his death and also published a notable nine-part autobiography, *Ego* (1935–47).

67 Happy is the country which has no history, and happier still is that musical comedy about which one can find nothing to say.
1920 In the *Sunday Times*.

68 I don't know very much, but what I do know I know better than anybody, and I don't want to argue about it. I know what I think about an actor or an actress, and am not interested in what anybody else thinks. My mind is not a bed to be made and re-made.
1943 Journal entry, 9 Jun. Collected in *Ego 6* (1944).

69 Long experience has taught me that in England nobody goes to the theatre unless he or she has bronchitis.
Attributed.

70 She had a heart as big as Waterloo Station.
Of Marie Lloyd. Attributed.

Agawa, Hiroyuki 1920–

Japanese novelist. His *Citadel in Spring* (1949) is the semi-autobiographical story of a young man fighting on the losing side of World War II. Much of the story is set in Hiroshima, the city of his birth.

71 It quickly swelled into the shape of a gigantic question mark, the middle of which was a vivid crimson, and as this thunderhead-like column billowed upward through the sky, she could see a red ball of fire at its core.
1949 Of the atomic explosion, Hiroshima. *Haru no shiro* (*Citadel in Spring*, translated by Lawrence Rogers), ch.9.

Agnew, Spiro T(heodore) 1918–96

US Republican politician. As liberal Governor of Maryland he introduced anti-racial-discrimination legislation, but by 1968 had become much more conservative. He was Nixon's running mate in the 1968 election, and Vice-President (1969–73).

72 To some extent, if you've seen one city slum, you've seen them all.
1968 Election campaign speech, Detroit, 18 Oct.

73 A spirit of national masochism prevails, encouraged by an effete corps of impudent snobs who characterize themselves as intellectuals.
1969 Of media pundits. Speech, New Orleans, 19 Oct.

74 In the United States today we have more than our fair share of the nattering nabobs of negativism. They have formed their own Four H Club—the hopeless, hysterical, hypochondriacs of history.
1970 Of media pundits. Speech, San Diego, 11 Sep.

75 I was…one of the worst complications he could have had.
1980 On the effect of his no-contest plea to income-tax evasion and subsequent resignation upon Richard M Nixon. *Go Quietly or Else*.

Agustini, Delmira 1886–1914

Uruguayan poet, who was murdered by her estranged husband, who then committed suicide. Her bold sincerity and impassioned lyrics rank her among the most outstanding early modernist poets.

76 *Por todos los senderos de la noche han venido*
a llorar en mi lecho.
¡Fueron tantos, son tantos!
Yo no sé cuáles viven, yo no sé cuál ha muerto.
Me lloraré a mí misma para llorarlos todos.
They have come from all of night's pathways
to cry in my bed.
They were so many, they are so many!
I don't know who lives, I don't know who has died.
I'll cry for myself so that I can cry for all.
1924 *El rosario de Eros*, 'Mis amores' ('My lovers').

St Aidan c.600–651

Irish monk, known as the Apostle of Northumbria. He was summoned from Iona by King Oswald to evangelize the north and established a community on Lindisfarne. He died in the church he had built in Bamburgh.

77 *Nam tibi carior est ille filius equae quam ille filius Dei?*
Is this son of a mare dearer to you, then, than that son of God?
c.645 To King Oswin of Deira, who had objected when Aidan gave to a beggar a horse which he had received as a gift from the king. Quoted in Bede *Historia Ecclesiastica Gentis Anglorum* (731), bk.3, ch.14.

Aitken, Jonathan William Patrick 1942–

British Conservative politician. In 1995 he sued *The Guardian* for libel following articles relating to his dealings with Saudi arms dealers. In 1999 he served a prison sentence for perjury after it was revealed he had lied repeatedly.

78 If it falls to me to start a fight to cut out the cancer of bent and twisted journalism in our country with the simple sword of truth and the trusting shield of British fair play, so be it.
1995 Press statement, 10 Apr.

Akers, John Fellows 1934–

American businessman. He joined IBM as a sales trainee in 1960 and rose to become Chairman 1986–93.

79 Each school can, once again, become what it was always meant to be—a building that has four walls with tomorrow inside.
1991 In the *Wall Street Journal*, 20 Mar.

Akins, Zoë 1886–1958

US poet and playwright. Her works include the play *The Greeks Had a Word for It* (1930) and the Pulitzer Prize-winning stage adaptation of Edith Wharton's novel *The Old Maid* (1935).

80 The Greeks Had a Word for It.
1930 Title of play.

Alain (Émile-Auguste Chartier) 1868–1951

French philosopher, writer and poet.

81 *Rien n'est plus dangereux qu'une idée, quand on n'a qu'une idée.*
Nothing is more dangerous than an idea, when you have only one idea.
1938 Propos sur la religion, no.74.

Alan of Lille *also known as 'Alanus de Insulis'* c.1114–1202

French writer and scholar. His major literary works include *De Planctu Natura* and *Anticlaudianus*.

82 *Omnis mundi creatura*
Quasi liber et pictura
Nobis est, et speculum.
Each creature of the world
Is as a book, a picture,
And a mirror to us.
c.1170 *De Incarnatione Christi* (*Rhythmus Alter*), l.1–3.

83 *Post nubila maxima, Phoebus.*
After the greatest clouds, the sun.
1175 *Liber Parabolarum*, ch.1, l.33.

84 *Qui jacet in terra non habet unde cadat.*
He who is lying on the ground has nowhere to fall.
1175 *Liber Parabolarum*, ch.2, l.18.

85 *Mille viae ducunt homines per sæcula Romam.*
Throughout the ages, a thousand roads lead to Rome.
1175 *Liber Parabolarum*, ch.3, l.56.

Alba, Duke of, Ferdinand Alvarez de Toledo 1508–82

Spanish soldier, made a general at 26 and Commander-in-Chief at 30. He led successful campaigns against the Netherlands and Portugal.

86 I have tamed men of iron in my day, shall I not easily crush these men of butter?
1567 On his appointment as Lieutenant-General to the Netherlands. Quoted in J L Motley *The Rise of the Dutch Republic* (1889), vol.2.

Albee, Edward Franklin, III 1928–

US dramatist, influenced by the Theatre of the Absurd, whose plays address the moral ambiguities of US middle-class life. His best-known work is *Who's Afraid of Virginia Woolf?* (1962), but *A Delicate Balance* (1966), *Seascape* (1975) and *Three Tall Women* (1991) all won Pulitzer Prizes.

87 JERRY: I have learned that neither kindness or cruelty by themselves, or independent of each other, create any effect beyond themselves.
1958 *The Zoo Story*.

88 JERRY: When you're a kid you use the cards as a substitute for a real experience, and when you're older you use real experience as a substitute for the fantasy.
1958 On pornographic playing cards. *The Zoo Story*.

89 BESSIE: I am sick of the disparity between things as they are and as they should be. I'm tired. I'm tired of the truth and I'm tired of lying about the truth.
1960 *The Death of Bessie Smith*.

90 Who's Afraid of Virginia Woolf?
1962 Title of play.

91 MARTHA: I have a fine sense of the ridiculous, but no sense of humour.

1962 *Who's Afraid of Virginia Woolf?*, act 1.

92 GEORGE: By God, you gotta have a swine to show you where the truffles are.
1962 *Who's Afraid of Virginia Woolf?*, act 2.

93 I am a Doctor. A.B.… M.A.… PH.D.… ABMAPHID!… a wasting disease of the frontal lobes.
1962 Spoken by a college professor. *Who's Afraid of Virginia Woolf?*

94 American critics are like American universities… both have dull and half-dead faculties.
1969 Speech to the New York Cultural League. Reported in news summaries, 6 Nov.

95 People would rather sleep their way through life than stay awake for it.
Quoted in Joseph F McCrindle (ed) *Behind the Scenes* (1971).

Prince Albert 1819–61

Prince Consort of Queen Victoria, son of the Duke of Saxe-Coburg-Gotha. A patron of the arts and science, he planned the Great Exhibition of 1851. He died of typhoid.

96 I have had wealth, rank and power, but, if these were all I had, how wretched I should be.
1861 Attributed last words.

Alberti, Leon Battista 1404–72

Italian architect, musician, painter and humanist, dubbed 'Alberti the all-sided' by the historian Burckhardt. His work *De re aedificatoria* (c.1450), is considered the first modern work on architecture.

97 Perhaps the artist who seeks dignity above all in his 'historia', ought to represent very few figures; for as paucity of words imparts majesty to a prince, provided his thoughts and orders are understood, so the presence of only the strictly necessary numbers of bodies confers dignity on a picture.
1436 *On Painting* (translated by Cecil Grayson).

98 I prefer you to take as your model a mediocre sculpture rather than an excellent painting, for from painted objects we train our hand only to make a likeness, whereas from sculptures we learn to represent both likeness and correct incidence of light.
1436 *On Painting* (translated by Cecil Grayson).

99 I am really persuaded that if we were to inquire of all the Cities which… have fallen by Siege into the Power of new Masters, who it was that subjected and overcame them, they would tell you, the Architect; and that they were strong enough to have despised the armed Enemy, but not to withstand the Shocks of the Engines, the Violence of the Machines and the Force of other Instruments of War with which the Architect, distressed, demolished and ruinated them. On the contrary, they would inform you that their greatest Defense lay in the Art and Assistance of the Architect.
1451–2 *Architecttura* (translated by James Leoni, 1755).

Alcaeus c.620–c.580 BC

Greek lyric poet. He lived in Mytilene on Lesbos, and was a contemporary of Sappho. Only fragments remain of his ten books of *Odes*.

1 Brave men are a city's strongest tower of defence.
c.600 BC Attributed.

Alcott, Louisa May 1832–88

US writer. Her children's classic *Little Women* (1868) drew on her own experiences. She completed a sequel, *Good Wives*, in 1869 and wrote other novels, including *Little Men* (1871) and *Jo's Boys* (1886).

2 Christmas won't be Christmas without any presents.
1868 *Little Women*, pt.1, ch.1.

3 Conceit spoils the finest genius… and the great charm of all power is modesty.
1868 *Little Women*, pt.1, ch.7.

4 Housekeeping ain't no joke.
1868 *Little Women*, pt.1, ch.11.

5 She had a womanly instinct that clothes possess an influence more powerful over many than the worth of character or the magic of manners.
1869 *Little Women*, pt.2, ch.34.

6 Girls are so queer you never know what they mean. They say no when they mean yes, and drive a man out of his wits just for the fun of it.
1869 *Little Women*, pt.2, ch.35.

7 What *do* girls do who haven't any mothers to help them through their troubles?
1869 *Little Women*, pt.2, ch.46.

Alcuin 735–804

English cleric and scholar. In 771 Charlemagne summoned him to his court as tutor of the royal family. In 778 he became master of his old school at York. His numerous works include treatises on rhetoric, ethics, and theology.

8 *Nec audiendi qui solent dicere, vox populi, vox Dei, quum tumultuositas vulgi semper insaniae proxima sit.*
We should not listen to those who like to affirm that the voice of the people is the voice of God, for the tumult of the masses is truly close to madness.
800 Letter to Charlemagne.

Aldington, Richard *pseudonym of* Edward Godfree 1892–1962

English poet, novelist and biographer. He married fellow Imagist poet Hilda Doolittle ('H.D.'). His best-known work is the novel *Death of a Hero* (1929).

9 Patriotism is a lively sense of collective responsibility. Nationalism is a silly cock crowing on its own dunghill.
1931 *The Colonel's Daughter*, pt.1, ch.6.

Aldiss, Brian Wilson 1925–

English science-fiction writer and novelist. Early novels include *The Hand-Reared Boy* (1970) and *A Soldier Erect* (1971), but his major work has been in science fiction, as a writer, critic and compiler of anthologies.

10 Science fiction is no more written for scientists than ghost stories are written for ghosts.
1961 *Penguin Science Fiction*, introduction.

11 Keep violence in the mind
Where it belongs.
1969 *Barefoot in the Head*, 'Charteris'.

12 The feat represents immense achievement for the neotenic ape, species Homo sapiens. But behind this lie two old attributes of the ape—tribalism and inquisitiveness.
1969 On space flight, in *The Guardian*.

13 Hubris clobbered by Nemesis.
1975 His definition of science fiction. *Science Fiction Art*, introduction.

Aldrich, Henry 1647–1710

English cleric, Dean of Christ Church, Oxford. He designed the Peckwater Quadrangle and wrote the popular catch 'Hark, the bonny Christ-Church Bells', but is best remembered for his *Artis Logicae Compendium* (1691).

14 If all be true that I do think,
There are five reasons why men drink,
Good wine, a friend, or being dry,
Or lest we should be by-and-by,
Or any other reason why.
1689 'Five Reasons for Drinking'.

Aldrin, Edwin E(ugene) Jr *known as* *'Buzz'* 1930–

US astronaut, a crew member on Apollo 11 and the second man to walk on the moon.

15 Houston, Tranquillity Base here. The Eagle has landed.
1969 Radio transmission from the moon, 20 Jul. These were the first words uttered by a human on the moon's surface.

16 Beautiful! Beautiful! Magnificent desolation.
1969 Spoken as he stepped out of the Eagle to join Neil Armstrong on the first moon walk, 20 Jul.

Alembert, Jean le Rond d' 1717–83

French mathematician and philosopher. He wrote a major work on *Dynamics* (1743) and pioneered studies on the mechanics of rigid bodies, the motions of fluids and vibrating strings.

17 Day by day natural science accumulates new riches… The true system of the World has been recognized, developed and perfected… Everything has been discussed and analyzed, or at least mentioned.
1759 *Elements of Philosophy.*

Alexander the Great 356–323 BC

King of Macedonia. He succeeded his father Philip at the age of 20, and set out to conquer the Persian Empire, campaigning as far as Afghanistan and the Indus valley. He died of a fever in Babylon, and his empire was divided between his generals.

18 Truly, if I were not Alexander, I would be Diogenes.
Quoted in Plutarch *Alexander*, 14.3.
► *See Diogenes of Sinope 275:21.*

19 The end and object of conquest is to avoid doing the same thing as the conquered.
Quoted in Plutarch *Alexander*, 40.2.

Alexander I 1777–1825

Tsar of Russia (1801–25), grandson of Catherine the Great. He spent much of his reign fighting Napoleon and founded the Holy Alliance (1815) to exclude the House of Bonaparte from power in France.

20 Napoleon thinks that I am a fool, but he who laughs last laughs longest.
1808 Letter to his sister, 8 Oct.

Alexander II *known as* *'the Liberator'* 1818–81

Tsar of Russia (1855–81). His reign was marked by the emancipation of the serfs (1861), political and military reform, the expansion of the Russian Empire into Asia and the defeat of Turkey (1877–8). He was assassinated.

21 It is better to abolish serfdom from above than to wait for it to abolish itself from below.
1856 Speech, 30 Mar.

Alexander, Cecil Frances 1818–95

Irish hymnwriter and poet.

22 All things bright and beautiful,
All creatures great and small,
All things wise and wonderful,
The Lord God made them all.
1848 'All Things Bright and Beautiful'.

23 The rich man in his castle,
The poor man at his gate,
God made them, high or lowly,
And ordered their estate.
1848 'All Things Bright and Beautiful'.

24 Once in royal David's city
Stood a lowly cattle-shed,
Where a mother laid her baby
In a manger for his bed.
Mary was that mother mild,
Jesus Christ her little child.
1848 'Once in Royal David's City'.

25 There is a green hill far away,
Without a city wall,
Where the dear Lord was crucified,
Who died to save us all.
1848 'There is a Green Hill Far Away'

26 I bind into myself today
The strong name of the Trinity,
By invocation of the same
The Three in One and One in Three.
1889 'St Patrick's Breastplate', his translation from the Irish.

Alexander, Sir William c.1567–1640

Scottish courtier and poet.

27 The weaker sex, to piety more prone.
1637 Of women. 'Doomsday', Fifth Hour.

Algren, Nelson 1909–81

US novelist, a journalist in Chicago and a migrant worker during the Depression. His hard-bitten, realist novels include *The Man with the Golden Arm* (1949).

28 A Walk on the Wild Side.
1956 Title of novel.

29 Never play cards with a man called Doc. Never eat at a place called Mom's. And never, ever, no matter what else you do in your whole life, never sleep with anyone whose troubles are worse than your own.
1956 In *Newsweek*, 2 Jul. Algren claimed that these were his only principles, taught him by 'a nice old Negro lady'.

30 I went out there for a thousand a week, and I worked Monday, and I got fired Wednesday. The guy that hired me was out of town Tuesday.
In Malcolm Crowley (ed) *Writers at Work* (1958).

31 The hard necessity of bringing the judge on the bench down into the dock has been the peculiar responsibility

of the writer in all ages of man.
1961 Preface to reprint of *Chicago: City On The Make* (first published 1951).

Ali, Muhammad *formerly* *Cassius Clay* 1942–

US boxer. World heavyweight champion in 1964, he was stripped of his title after refusing military service on religious grounds (he was a Black Muslim). His title was restored in 1970, lost to Joe Frazier the next year and regained in 1974 and 1978. He retired in 1981.

32 I am the greatest!
1962 In the *Louisville Times*, 16 Nov. This became his catchphrase.

33 Float like a butterfly, sting like a bee.
c.1964 Of his boxing style. Quoted in G Sullivan *Cassius Clay* (1964), ch.8.

Allainval, Abbé d' 1700–53

French dramatist.

34 *L'embarras des richesses.*
The Embarrassment of Riches.
1726 Title of play.

Allen, Henry Southworth 1941–

US journalist. He is a feature writer and editor for the *Washington Post* (1970–).

35 They are a great tradition...gliding in and out of the corridors of power with the opulent calm of angelfish swimming through an aquarian castle.
1989 Of presidential advisers. In the *Washington Post*, 3 Jan.

36 He long ago learned to eschew the little turf-dances of human encounter.
1989 Of Brent Scowcroft, National Security Council adviser to George Bush. In the *Washington Post*, 3 Jan.

37 It is unlikely that anyone will write his biography, but he will be enshrined in 10,000 indexes.
1989 Of Brent Scowcroft, National Security Council adviser to George Bush. In the *Washington Post*, 3 Jan.

38 Doesn't she know that numberless women have walked past mirrors hoping for a hint of Bacall's slinkiness?
1994 Of Lauren Bacall at age 70. In the *Washington Post*, 27 Oct.

39 Edward Hopper is the great painter of American hell in the 20th century, the limner-laureate of the beauty, poignance, eternity and bone-ache disquietude of life.
1995 In the *Washington Post*, 25 Jun.

Allen, Tim 1953–

US actor and comedian.

40 To infinity and beyond!
1995 As the voice of Buzz Lightyear in *Toy Story* (1995, screenplay by Joss Whedon, Andrew Stanton, Joel Cohen, Joe Ranft, John Lasseter and Pete Docter).

Allen, Woody *pseudonym of* *Allen Stewart Konigsberg* 1935–

US film-maker and writer. He is best known for his comic films, which focus on the neuroses of urban life and relationships, and he has also published collections of essays and stories.

41 I think crime pays. The hours are good, you travel a lot.
1969 *Take the Money and Run.*

42 Not only is there no God, but try getting a plumber on weekends.
1969 'My Philosophy', in the *New Yorker*, 27 Dec.

43 TB or not TB, that is the congestion.
1972 *Everything You Always Wanted to Know about Sex.*

44 The lion and the calf shall lie down together but the calf won't get much sleep.
1974 'The Scrolls', in *The New Republic*, 31 Aug.

45 It's not that I'm afraid to die. I just don't want to be there when it happens.
1975 *Death: A Comedy in One Act.*

46 It immediately doubles your chances for a date on Saturday night.
1975 On bisexuality. In the *New York Times*, 1 Dec.

47 My one regret in life is that I am not someone else.
Quoted as epigraph in Eric Lax *Woody Allen and His Comedy* (1975).

48 Death is an acquired trait.
Quoted in Eric Lax *Woody Allen and His Comedy* (1975), ch.11.

49 I don't want to achieve immortality through my work... I want to achieve it through not dying.
Quoted in Eric Lax *Woody Allen and His Comedy* (1975), ch.12.

50 And my parents finally realize that I'm kidnapped and they snap into action immediately: they rent out my room.
Quoted in Eric Lax *Woody Allen and His Comedy* (1975).

51 On the plus side, death is one of the few things that can be done as easily lying down.
1976 *Without Feathers*, 'Early Essays'.

52 Money is better than poverty, if only for financial reasons.
1976 *Without Feathers*, 'Early Essays'.

53 That was the most fun I ever had without laughing.
1977 Of sex. *Annie Hall* (with Marshall Brickman).

54 Don't knock masturbation. It's sex with someone I love.
1977 *Annie Hall* (with Marshall Brickman).

55 I'm old fashioned. I don't believe in extra-marital relationships. I think people should mate for life, like pigeons or Catholics.
1979 *Manhattan* (with Marshall Brickman).

56 More than at any other time in history, mankind faces a crossroads. One path leads to despair and utter hopelessness. The other, to total extinction. Let us pray we have the wisdom to choose correctly.
1980 *Side Effects*, 'My Speech to the Graduates'.

57 Eighty percent of success is showing-up.
Quoted in Thomas J Peters and Robert H Waterman *Among Friends* (1982).

58 I recently turned sixty. Practically a third of my life is over.
Quoted in the *Observer*, 'Sayings of the Week', 10 Mar 1996.

59 Life does not imitate art. It imitates bad television.
2000 In *The Guardian*, 31 Dec.

Allingham, Margery Louise 1904–66

English writer, creator of the fictional detective Albert Campion. She wrote a series of elegant and witty detective novels, such as *Flowers for the Judge* (1936) and *The China Governess* (1963).

60 Once sex rears its ugly 'ead it's time to steer clear.
1936 *Flowers for the Judge*, ch.4.

Allingham, William 1824–89

Irish poet and editor of *Fraser's Magazine* (from 1874). His *Diary* (published 1907) is a rich recollection of Victorian literary life. Other works include *Day and Night Songs* (1855), illustrated by Dante Gabriel Rossetti and Millais.

61 Up the airy mountain,
Down the rushy glen,
We daren't go a-hunting,
For fear of little men;
Wee folk, good folk,
Trooping all together;
Green jacket, red cap,
And white owl's feather!
1850 'The Fairies'.

62 Four ducks on a pond,
A grass-bank beyond,
A blue sky of spring,
White clouds on the wing;
What a little thing
To remember for years—
To remember with tears!
1888 'A Memory'.

Allsop, (Harold) Bruce 1912–2000

English architect, author, publisher and artist. His many books include *A Modern Theory of Architecture* (1977) and *Should Man Survive?* (1982).

63 For the normal business of living man is most at ease on the ground.
1977 *A Modern Theory of Architecture*.

64 The phenomenon of architecture is a development of the phenomenon of man.
1977 *A Modern Theory of Architecture*.

Almeida, Manuel Antônio de 1831–61

Brazilian writer, translator and journalist, killed in a shipwreck off the Brazilian coast while on a newspaper assignment. His *Memórias de um sargento de milícias* (1853) is considered the first great novel in Brazilian literature.

65 *Espiar a vida alheia, inquirir dos escravos o que se passava no interior das casas, era naquele tempo coisa tão comum e enraizada nos costumes, que ainda hoje, depois de passados tantos anos, restam grandes vestígios dêsse belo hábito.*
Spying on other people's lives, asking slaves what was going on inside their houses was then so common and such a part of our customs that today, after so many years have passed, we have many remnants of such a beautiful habit.
1853 *Memórias de um sargento de milícias* (*Memoirs of a Militia Sergeant*, 1959), ch.3.

Almodóvar, Pedro 1951–

Spanish film director. His first film to attain worldwide success was *Mujeres al Borde de un Ataque de Nervios* (1988, *Women on the Verge of a Nervous Breakdown*).

66 When I was 10, I expressly gave God one year to manifest himself. He didn't.
2004 In *The Guardian*, 7 May.

Alsop, Stewart 1914–74

US political columnist.

67 A fashionable gentleman who much concerns himself with the fashions of gentlemen is neither fashionable nor a gentleman.
1975 In *Newsweek*, 30 Jun.

Alther, Lisa *née Reed* 1944–

US novelist. She achieved success with her comic novel *Kinflicks* (1976), and explored the themes of personal and sexual identity in several subsequent books.

68 If this was adulthood, the only improvement she could detect in her situation was that now she could eat dessert without eating her vegetables.
1976 *Kinflicks*, ch.2.

69 There was nothing wrong with her that a vasectomy of the vocal chords wouldn't fix.
1976 *Kinflicks*, ch.4.

70 I happen to feel that the degree of a person's intelligence is directly reflected by the number of conflicting attitudes she can bring to bear on the same topic.
1976 *Kinflicks*, ch.7.

71 He picked her up out of the dirt and turned her into the clod she was today.
1981 *Original Sins*, pt.4, ch.1.

Altman, Robert 1925–

US film director. His first critical and commercial success was *M*A*S*H* (1970).

72 What's a cult? It just means not enough people to make a minority.
1981 Interview in the *Observer*, 11 Apr.

73 You will never see 'Altman's Great Film of the Seventies: The Director's Cut' because you have never seen a film of mine that wasn't the director's cut. I have never permitted it.
2004 In *The Independent*, 14 May.

Amado, Jorge 1912–2001

Brazilian novelist, born on a cacao plantation in Ferradas. He was imprisoned several times and exiled for leftist activities. Most of his novels are picaresque, ribald tales of lower-class Bahian city life.

74 *Ninguém no cais tem um nome só. Todos têm também um apelido ou abreviam o nome, ou o aumentam, ou lhe acrescentam qualquer coisa que recorde uma história, uma luta, um amor.*
No one on the docks has just one name. Everybody has a nickname too, or the name is shortened, or lengthened, or something is added that recalls a tale, a fight, a woman.
1936 *Mar morto* (*Sea of Death*, 1984), 'Iemanjá'.

St Ambrose c.339–397 AD

Bishop of Milan. He was much admired by St Augustine.

75 *Ubi Petrus, ibi ergo ecclesia.*
Where Peter is, there, accordingly, is the Church.
Explanatio psalmi 40.

American Library Association

76 The computer is a fast idiot, it has no imagination; it cannot originate action. It is, and will remain, only a tool to man.

1964 Statement of the American Library Association regarding the Univac computer exhibited at the New York World's Fair, 1964.

Amerine, Maynard Andrew 1911–98

US oenologist, Professor at the University of California. His works on viniculture include *Wine: An Introduction for Americans* (1965) and *Introduction to Food Science and Technology* (1973).

77 The fine wine leaves you with something pleasant; the ordinary wine just leaves.
Quoted in Clifton Fadiman *The New Joy of Wine* (1990).

Amery, Leo(pold) Charles Maurice Stennett 1873–1955

English Conservative politician. After working on *The Times* for 10 years he became an MP and served as Colonial Secretary (1919–29) and Secretary of State for India and Burma.

78 For twenty years he has held a season ticket on the line of least resistance and has gone wherever the train of events has carried him, lucidly justifying his position at whatever point he happened to find himself.
1914 Of Herbert Asquith, in *Quarterly Review*, Jul.

79 Speak for England, Arthur!
1939 Shouted to Arthur Greenwood, Labour Opposition spokesman, 2 Sep, as Greenwood began a House of Commons speech calling for the resignation of Prime Minister Neville Chamberlain, immediately preceding the declaration of World War II.

80 Cromwell said to the Long Parliament when he thought it was no longer fit to conduct the affairs of the nation, 'You have sat too long here for any good you have been doing. Depart, I say, and let us have done with you. In the name of God, go!'
1940 Remark addressed to Prime Minister Neville Chamberlain, House of Commons, 7 May.

Amin (Dada), Idi 1925–2003

Ugandan soldier and politician, an army commander who seized power in 1971 and was proclaimed President. He was deposed by exiled Ugandans with the help of the Tanzanian army in 1979 and fled to Libya.

81 Your experience will be a lesson to all of us men to be careful not to marry ladies in very high positions.
1978 Unsolicited advice to Lord Snowdon on the ending of his marriage to Princess Margaret, quoted in A Barrow *International Gossip* (1983).

Amis, Sir Kingsley 1922–95

English novelist and poet. He achieved success with his irreverent novel *Lucky Jim* (1954), and went on to write a substantial body of novels, poetry and non-fiction.

82 The light did him harm, but not as much as looking at things did; he resolved, having done it once, never to move his eyeballs again. A dusty thudding in his head made the scene before him beat like a pulse. His mouth had been used as a latrine by some small creature of the night, and then as its mausoleum.
1953 *Lucky Jim*, ch.6.

83 He thought what a pity it was that all his faces were designed to express rage or loathing. Now that something had happened that really deserved a face, he'd none to celebrate it with. As a kind of token, he made his Sex Life in Ancient Rome face.
1953 *Lucky Jim*, ch.25.

84 Man's love is of man's life a thing apart;
Girls aren't like that.
1956 'A Bookshop Idyll'.
► *See Byron 181:73.*

85 Politics is a thing that only the unsophisticated can really go for.
1957 'Socialism and the Intellectuals'.

86 Work was like cats were supposed to be: if you disliked and feared it and tried to keep out if its way, it knew at once and sought you out and jumped on your lap and climbed all over you to show how much it loved you. Please God, he thought, don't let me die in harness.
1960 *Take A Girl Like You*, ch.5.

87 More will mean worse.
1960 On expanding university intake, in *Encounter*, Jul.

88 Outside every fat man there was an even fatter man trying to close in.
1963 *One Fat Englishman*, ch.3.
► *See also Connolly 233:82.*

89 He was of the faith chiefly in the sense that the church he currently did not attend was Catholic.
1963 *One Fat Englishman*, ch.8.

90 It was no wonder that people were so horrible when they started life as children.
1963 *One Fat Englishman*, ch.14.

91 I was never an Angry Young Man. I am angry only when I hit my thumb with a hammer.
1979 Dissociating himself from that literary grouping, in *The Eton College Chronicle*, Jun.

92 The rewards for being sane may not be very many but knowing what's funny is one of them.
1984 *Stanley and the Women*, ch.2.

93 Alun's life was coming to consist more and more exclusively of being told at dictation speed what he knew.
1986 *The Old Devils*, ch.7.

94 Booze, of course, and then curtains.
1986 His response to being asked how he would spend his Booker Prize cheque, 22 Oct.

95 I wish he'd *shut up* about Flaubert.
Said about Julian Barnes. Quoted in Julian Barnes *Something to Declare* (2002).

Amis, Martin Louis 1949–

English novelist, son of Kingsley Amis. His novels include *The Rachel Papers* (1974), *London Fields* (1989), *Time's Arrow* (1991) and *The Information* (1995).

96 The middle-management of Manhattan stared on, their faces as thin as credit cards.
1984 *Money.*

97 His name was Shadow, short for Shadow That Comes in Sight, an old Indian name, Apache or Cheyenne. I very much approved of this. You don't want dogs called Spot or Pooch. You don't want dogs called Nigel or Keith. The names of dogs should salute the mystical drama of the animal life. *Shadow*—that's a *good* name.
1984 *Money.*

98 My theory is—we don't really go that far into other people, even when we think we do. We hardly ever go in and bring them out. We just stand at the jaws of the cave, and strike a match, and ask quickly if anybody's there.
1984 *Money.*

99 New York is a jungle, they tell you. You could go further, and say that New York is a jungle. New York *is a jungle*. Beneath the columns of the old rain forest, made of melting macadam, the mean Limpopo of swamped Ninth Avenue bears an angry argosy of crocs and dragons, tiger fish, noise machines, sweating rainmakers.
1984 *Money.*

1 My belief is that everything that's written about you is actually secondary showbiz nonsense, and you shouldn't take any notice of it.
1985 Quoted in John Haffenden *Novelists in Interview* (1985).

2 When success happens to an English writer, he acquires a new typewriter. When success happens to an American writer, he acquires a new life.
1986 *The Moronic Inferno*, 'Kurt Vonnegut'.

3 Most writers need a wound, either physical or spiritual.
1987 In the *Observer*, 30 Aug.

4 How do we prevent the use of nuclear weapons? By threatening to use nuclear weapons. And we can't get rid of nuclear weapons, because of nuclear weapons.
1987 *Einstein's Monsters*, introduction.

5 Someone watches over us when we write. Mother. Teacher. Shakespeare. God.
1989 *London Fields*, ch.1.

6 And meanwhile time goes about its immemorial work of making everyone look and feel like shit.
1989 *London Fields*, ch.2.

7 But we mustn't go too far back...in anybody's life... Because if we do...then nobody is to blame for anything, and nothing matters, and everything is allowed.
1989 *London Fields*, ch.10.

8 Insects are what neurosis would sound like, if neurosis could make a noise with its nose.
1995 *The Information*, pt.3.

9 You see tragedy requires persons of heroic stature. It works on the principle of people being more than human—super-human—and also being only too human. But there just aren't many great figures around now, so the tragic mechanisms can't work.
1995 Explaining why only comedy can reflect contemporary reality. Quoted in an interview in *The Scotsman*, 7 Apr.

10 We live in the age of mass loquacity. We are all writing it or at any rate talking it: the memoir, the apologia, the c.v., the *cri de coeur*.
2000 *Experience.*

Ammianus Marcellinus c.330–390 AD

Roman historian, born of Greek parents in Antioch. After a military career he moved to Rome, and devoted himself to literature. He wrote in Latin a history of the Roman Empire.

11 *Etiam parietes arcanorum soli conscii timebantur.*
Even the walls, the only sharers of secrets, were feared.
History, 14.1.7 (translated by J C Rolfe). This became a proverbial expression in the medieval tradition: 'parietes habent aures' (the walls have ears).

Amundsen, Roald Engelbregt Gravning 1872–1928

Norwegian explorer. In 1903–6 he sailed the Northwest Passage in the smack *Gjöa*. Hearing of a British expedition to the South Pole, he made as if sailing for the Arctic but instead turned south. His party beat that of Captain Scott to the South Pole by one month.

12 Beg leave to inform you proceeding Antarctica. Amundsen.
1910 Cable sent from Madeira to Captain Robert F Scott in Melbourne, 12 Oct.

Anaxagoras c.500–428 BC

Greek philosopher. He taught in Athens, and Pericles and Euripides were among his pupils. He denied the divine nature of the celestial bodies, was banned from Athens for impiety, and died in Lampsacus.

13 The sun provides the moon with its brightness.
Fragment in Plutarch *De facie in orbe lunae*, 929b.

Ancona, Ronni 1968–

Scottish comedienne and impressionist.

14 You're sitting in a room with male writers and you say something and it's ignored. You say it again and it's ignored. Then a man will say it and everyone goes 'That's brilliant'.
2004 In the *Observer*, 25 Apr.

Anderson, Admiral George, Jr c.1907–1992

US Chief of Naval Operations in the Cuban missile crisis, 1962. On retirement from the Navy he served as US Ambassador to Portugal.

15 Now, Mr Secretary, if you and your deputy will go back to your offices, the Navy will run the blockade.
1962 On brandishing a manual of procedures to Pentagon officials at the time of the Cuban missile crisis. Recalled on his death, 4 Mar 1992.

Anderson, John Edward 1917–

US businessman.

16 You need enough cash cows to feed your pigs.
1994 On financing. In *Forbes*, 17 Oct.

Anderson, Dame Judith *originally* ***Frances Margaret Anderson*** 1898–1992

Australian actress. She achieved fame in the theatre, but is best remembered for her screen role as Mrs Danvers in Alfred Hitchcock's *Rebecca* (1940). In 1984 a Broadway theatre was named after her.

17 I find myself wearing gloves more often.
On how being made a Dame of the British Empire had changed her. Attributed.

Anderson, Lindsay 1932–94

Indian-born British stage and film director. During the 1950s he made documentary films and won an Oscar for his short film *Thursday's Children* (1953). His feature film credits include *This Sporting Life* (1963), *If* (1968) and *The Whales of August* (1987).

18 Perhaps the tendency is to treat the films of one's own country like the prophets—with less than justice.
1947 Comment, quoted in Ian Christie *Arrows of Desire*.

Anderson, Maxwell 1888–1959

US dramatist. He wrote a large number of plays in both prose and verse, many on historical subjects.

19 What Price Glory?
1924 Title of play (with Lawrence Stallings).

20 But it's a long, long while
From May to December;
And the days grow short
When you reach September.
1938 'September Song' (music by Kurt Weill).

Anderson, Poul William 1926–2001

US science fiction and fantasy writer, author of numerous novels and short stories.

21 I have yet to see any problem, however complicated, which, when you looked at it in the right way, did not become still more complicated.
1969 In the *New Scientist*, 25 Sep.

Anderson, Robert Woodruff 1917–

US dramatist and novelist. His plays, confronting the difficulties of human relationships, include *Tea and Sympathy* (1953) and *I Never Sang for My Father* (1968), and he also wrote several screenplays.

22 All you're supposed to do is every once in a while give the boys a little tea and sympathy.
1953 On the duties of a headmaster's wife. *Tea and Sympathy*, act 1.

Anderson, Sherwood 1876–1941

US author, who left a lucrative job as manager of a paint factory to write full-time. His *Winesburg, Ohio* (1919) is a naturalistic study of small-town America in 23 stories.

23 The moment one of the people took one of the truths to himself, called it his truth, and tried to live his life by it, he became a grotesque and the truth he embraced a falsehood.
1919 *Winesburg, Ohio*, 'The Book of the Grotesque'.

Andrade, Carlos Drummond de 1902–87

Brazilian modernist poet. Although trained in pharmacy, he turned to writing and journalism. A friend of Neruda, he shared his devotion to socialism. His writing is characteristically low-key and ironic, focusing on everyday subjects.

24 *O marciano encontrou-me na rua*
e teve miedo de minha impossibilidade humana.
Como pode existir, penseu consigo, um ser
que no existir põe sem tamanha anulação de existência?
The Martian met me in the streets
and was frightened by my human impossibility.
He wondered how such a being could exist
who could not exist without unmaking so much existence.
1961 *Lição de coisas*, 'Science Fiction'.

Andrade, Mário de 1893–1945

Brazilian modernist writer. His works reflect a deep interest in Brazilian folk culture, and his highly individual prose style imitates colloquial Brazilian speech.

25 *Os guerreiros de cá não buscam mavórticas damas para o enlace epitalâmico; mas antes as preferem dóceis e facilmente trocáveis por pequeninas e voláteis folhas de papel a que o vulgo chamará dinheiro—o 'curriculum vitae' da Civilização.*
The warriors here do not seek out mettlesome women for epithalamic conjunction, but prefer them docile and willing to exchange with ease their favours for those small and deliquescent leaves of paper which the masses call money—the *curriculum vitae* of Civilization.
1928 *Macunaíma* (*O Herói sem nenhum caráter*) (*Macunaima*, 1984), ch.9.

Andreas Capellanus fl. late 12c

French priest and writer, possibly chaplain to the court of Champagne. *De Amore* is his only known work.

26 *Liquide constet inter virum et uxorem amorem sibi locum vindicare non posse.*
It is clearly certain that between man and wife love can claim no place.
c.1185 *De Amore*, bk.1, ch.6, section 7.

Andrewes, Lancelot 1555–1626

English ecclesiastic, renowned for his memorable sermons. He became Bishop of Chichester, then Ely and finally Winchester.

27 It was no summer progress. A cold coming they had of it, at this time of the year; just, the worst time of the year, to take a journey, and specially a long journey, in. The ways deep, the weather sharp, the days short, the sun farthest off *in solstitio brumali*, the very dead of winter.
1622 *Of the Nativity*, sermon 15.
► *See Eliot 306:73.*

28 The nearer the Church, the further from God.
1622 *Of the Nativity*, sermon 15.

Andrews, Julie *originally* Julia Elizabeth Wells 1935–

British singer and actress. She starred in several long-running Broadway musicals, notably *My Fair Lady* (1956) and *Camelot* (1960). Her most popular films have been *Mary Poppins* (1964) and *The Sound of Music* (1965).

29 I'd like to thank all those who made this possible—especially Jack Warner
1965 Speech at the Oscar ceremony when she won an Academy Award for her role in *Mary Poppins*, 5 Apr. Warner had rejected her for the screen role of Eliza in *My Fair Lady*, although she had played it to great acclaim on the stage, preferring Audrey Hepburn whose singing had to be dubbed. Andrews had instead taken the part in *Mary Poppins*.

Angell, Roger 1920–

US journalist. Fiction editor at the *New Yorker*, he is also known for his baseball writing.

30 Such days and moments pass, in ways that this one has not, but there's a weary strength in experience, even in the midst of horror.
2001 Reflecting on the terrorist attacks on 11 Sep. In the *New Yorker*.

Angelou, Maya *originally Maya Johnson* 1928–

US writer. A sexual assault on her in childhood left her mute for several years. She became a successful writer with her multi-volume autobiography. She has also published several volumes of verse.

31 If growing up is painful for the Southern Black girl, being aware of her displacement is the rust on the razor that threatens the throat.
1969 *I Know Why The Caged Bird Sings*, opening section.

32 Children's talent to endure stems from their ignorance of alternatives.
1969 *I Know Why The Caged Bird Sings*, ch.17.

33 The quality of strength lined with tenderness is an unbeatable combination, as are intelligence and necessity when unblunted by formal education.
1970 *I Know Why The Caged Bird Sings*, ch.29.

34 At fifteen life had taught me undeniably that surrender, in its place, was as honorable as resistance, especially if one had no choice.
1970 *I Know Why The Caged Bird Sings*, ch.31.

35 The fact that the adult American Negro female emerges a formidable character is often met with amazement, distaste and even belligerence. It is seldom accepted as an inevitable outcome of the struggle won by survivors, and deserves respect if not enthusiastic acceptance.
1970 *I Know Why The Caged Bird Sings*, ch.34

36 Most plain girls are virtuous because of the scarcity of opportunity to be otherwise.
1970 *I Know Why The Caged Bird Sings*, ch.35

37 It is a historical truth. No man can know where he is going unless he knows exactly where he has been and exactly how he arrived at his present place.
1972 On Africa. In the *New York Times*, 16 Apr.

38 There is a kind of strength that is almost frightening in black women. It's as if a steel rod runs right through the head down to the feet.
1973 Television interview, 21 Nov. Collected in *Conversations with Maya Angelou* (1989).

39 We had won… I thought if war did not include killing, I'd like to see one every year. Something like a festival.
1974 On the end of World War II. *Gather Together In My Name*, prologue.

40 Self-pity in its early stage is as snug as a feather mattress. Only when it hardens does it become uncomfortable.
1974 *Gather Together In My Name*, ch.6.

41 The sadness of the women's movement is that they don't allow the necessity of love. See, I don't personally trust any revolution where love is not allowed.
1975 Interview in *California Living*, 14 May. Collected in *Conversations with Maya Angelou* (1989).

42 Oh, the holiness of always being the injured party. The historically oppressed can find not only sanctity but safety in the state of victimization.When access to a better life has been denied often enough, and successfully enough, one can use the rejection as an excuse to cease all efforts.
1976 *Singin' and Swingin' and Getting Merry Like Christmas*, ch.9.

43 Life loves the liver of it.
1977 Interview in *Black Scholar*, Jan–Feb. Collected in *Conversations with Maya Angelou* (1989).

44 Something made greater by ourselves and in turn that makes us greater.
1977 Defining work. Interview in *Black Scholar*, Jan–Feb. Collected in *Conversations with Maya Angelou* (1989).

45 There is an awesome reality to Rent Day. It comes trumpeting, forcing the days before it into a wild scramble.
1981 *The Heart of a Woman*, ch.3.

46 The cliché of whites being ignorant of blacks was not only true, but understandable. Oh, but we knew them with the intimacy of a surgeon's scalpel.
1981 *The Heart of a Woman*, ch.12.

47 Genet had been right at least about one thing. Blacks should be used to play whites. For centuries we had probed their faces, the angles of their bodies, the sounds of their voices and even their odors. Often our survival had depended on the accurate reading of a white man's chuckle or the disdainful wave of a white woman's hand.
1981 *The Heart of a Woman*, ch.12.

48 Poetry is music written for the human voice.
1989 In 'The Power of the Word', Public Broadcasting Service, 15 Sep.

49 Wouldn't Take Nothing for my Journey Now.
1994 Title of book.

Angle, Colin

US businessman. Co-founder and Chief Executive Officer of iRobot.

50 We're not using these robots to hand out flowers.
2004 On the possibility of arming military robots.

Annan, Noël Gilroy, Baron 1916–2000

English scholar, Chair of the Board of Trustees of the National Gallery (1980–5). His works include *Our Age: portrait of a generation* (1990).

51 He cultivated to perfection the sneer which he used like an oyster-knife, inserting it into the shell of his victim, exposing him with a quick-turn of the wrist, and finally flipping him over and inviting his audience to discard him as tainted and inedible.
1991 On the critic F R Leavis. *English Intellectuals Between the World Wars.*

Anne, Queen 1665–1714

Queen of Great Britain and Ireland (1702–14), the last Stuart monarch. Her reign was marked by the union of England and Scotland (1707) and the War of the Spanish Succession. After quarrelling with the Marlboroughs (Whigs), she appointed a Tory government in 1710.

52 Cricket is not illegal, for it is a manly game.
1710 Quoted in Colin Jarman *The Guinness Dictionary of Sports Quotations* (1990).

53 I have changed my Ministers but I have not changed my measures. I am still for moderation, and I will govern by it.
1711 Addressing her new Tory administration, Jan.

Anne Elizabeth Alice Louise 1950–

HRH The Princess Royal, daughter of Queen Elizabeth II and Prince Philip. She has worked on behalf of various charities, notably as President of the Save the Children Fund.

54 It could be said that the AIDS pandemic is a classic own-goal scored by the human race against itself.
1988 In the *Daily Telegraph*, 27 Jan.

Annenberg, Walter H 1908–2002

US publishing tycoon, philanthropist and former US Ambassador to Great Britain and Northern Ireland, a noted art enthusiast and collector.

55 Only when you are moved by a painting should you buy it. Being moved is what collecting is all about.
1991 In *Connoisseur*, Feb.

56 You are asking me to sell members of my family.
1991 In the *New York Times*, 12 Mar. Rejecting a billion-dollar Japanese offer for his art collection.

Anonymous

57 Either with it or upon it.
Traditionally said by a Spartan mother while handing her son his shield when he went to war; he should either return with it (ie as a victor) or on it (ie dead). Plutarch *Lacaenarum Apophthegmata*, 241f.

58 *Cave canem!*
Beware of the dog!
Famous expression, found in mosaics and inscriptions in Pompeii and other Roman towns. See also Petronius *Satyricon*, 29.1: *Ad sinistram enim intrantibus non longe ab ostiarii cella canis ingens, catena vinctus, in pariete erat pictus superque quadrata littera scriptum cave canem* (For on the left hand as you went in, not far from the porter's office, a great dog on a chain was painted on the wall, and over him was written in large letters: 'Beware of the dog'. Translation by W H D Rouse).

59 Not everyone can sail to Corinth.
ie, not everybody has the same opportunities. Greek proverb, which is also mentioned by Horace *Epistulae*, 1.17.36: 'Non cuivis homini contingit adire Corinthum'.

60 Nothing in excess.
Famous motto in Antiquity. According to Plato, the text was a temple inscription in Delphi (*Hipparchus*, 228e).

61 *Patria est ubicumque est bene.*
One's country is wherever one does well.
Quoted as proverbial by Cicero in *Tusculanes Disputationes*, 5.108. The saying was attributed to the mythical figure Teucer, ancestor of the Trojans, by the Roman tragedian Pacuvius (220–c.130 BC).

62 *Ave Caesar, morituri te salutant!*
Hail Caesar, we who are about to die salute you!
Traditional formula for gladiators saluting the emperor. One source for the expression is Suetonius *Claudius* 21: 'Ave Imperator, morituri te salutant', ('Hail Emperor, we salute you, we who are about to die!').

63 *Candida me docuit nigras odisse puellas. Odero si potero. Si non, invitus amabo.*
A white girl instructed me to hate black girls. I shall hate them if I can. If not, I shall love them—against my will.
c.1c AD Graffito found in Pompeii. In *Corpus Inscriptionum Latinarum* I V, 1520.

64 *Fures fores, frugi intro!*
Thieves out, profit in!
c.1c AD Graffito found in Pompeii. In *Corpus Inscriptionum Latinarum* I V, 4278.

65 *Fullones ululamque cano, non arma virumque.*
Of fullers and their wailing, I sing, not of arms and the man.
c.1c AD Graffito found in Pompeii. In *Corpus Inscriptionum Latinarum* I V, 9131. This is a parody of the famous opening line of Virgil's *Aeneid* 1.1: 'Arma virumque cano'.

66 Enjoy another glass, for you see what the end is.
c.2c AD Epitaph from Cos for a certain Chrysogonos. Quoted in W Peek *Griechische Versinschriften*, vol.1, no.378.

67 The glory of God is man, and the glory of man is his dress.
c.450 *Babylonian Talmud*. Quoted in Barton Stevenson (ed) *The Macmillan Book of Proverbs, Maxims, and Famous Phrases* (1948).

68 *Gæth a wyrd swa hio scel.*
Fate always goes as it must.
c.800 *Beowulf*, l.455.

69 *Wyrd oft nereth*
unfægne eorl thonne his ellen deah.
Fate often preserves
the undoomed warrior when his courage holds firm.
c.800 *Beowulf*, l.572–3.

70 *Oft seldan hwær*
æfter leodhyre lytle hwile
bongar bugeth.
It is very rare that,
after the fall of a prince,
the deadly spear rests for long.
c.800 *Beowulf*, l.2029–31.

71 He is joyful with swift movement when a mouse sticks in his sharp paw.
I too am joyful when I understand a dearly loved difficult problem.
c.820 'Me and Pangur Bán', by an unidentified cat-owning scholar, translated in Gerard Murphy *Early Irish Lyrics* (1956), no.1.

72 *Lytle hwile leof beoth grene*
thonne hie eft fealewiath, feallath on eorthan
and forweorniath weorthiath to duste.
For a little while the leaves are green.
Then they turn yellow, fall to the ground,
and perish, turning to dust.
c.900 *Second Dialogue of Solomon and Saturn*, l.136–8.

73 *Widgongel wif word gespringeth.*
A roving woman gives rise to gossip.
c.900 *Maxims I*, l.64.

74 *Feoh byth frofur fira gehwylcum*
Sceal theah manna gehwylc miclun hyt dælan.
Money is a comfort to each man,
But everyone should nevertheless give it away freely.
?c.900 *The Rune Poem*, l.1–2.

75 *Ear byth egle eorla gehwylcun.*
The grave is ghastly to every man.
?c.900 *The Rune Poem*, l.90.

76 Thought shall be the harder, heart the keener, courage the greater, as our might lessens.
c.1000 *The Battle of Maldon* (translated by R K Gordon).

77 *La flur de France as perdut.*
The flower of France is lost.
c.1110 *Chanson de Roland*, l.2445.

78 *Mult ad apris ki bien conuist ahan.*
He who has suffered much learns much.
c.1110 *Chanson de Roland*, l.2524.

79 *Man sol sô vrouwen ziehen…*
das si üppeclîche sprüche lasen under wegen.

Women should be trained in such a way
that they avoid idle chatter.
c.1200 *Das Nibelungenlied*, ch.14, l.193–4.

80 And nowe in the winter, when men kill the fat swine
They get the bladder and blow it great and thin,
With many beans and peason put within:
It ratleth, soundeth, and shineth clere and fayre
While it is throwen and caste up in the ayre,
Each one contendeth and hath a great delite
With foote and with hands the bladder for to smite;
If it fall to grounde, they lifte it up agayne,
But this waye to labour they count in no payne.
Medieval verse, one of the earliest descriptions of football in England.

81 *Graeca non leguntur.*
Things in Greek are not read.
Term used by medieval 'glossatores' (commentators) of the *Corpus Iuris*, indicating that the parts in Greek should be skipped. It became a traditional comment to indicate ignorance.

82 Al night by the rose, rose,
Al night by the rose I lay,
Dorst ich nought the rose stele,
And yet I bar the flour away.
c.1210–1240 Untitled lyric.

83 Sumer is icumen in,
Lhude sing cuccu!
Groweth sed, and bloweth med,
And springth the wude nu.
c.1250 'Sumer is icumen in', l.1–4.
► *See also Pound 664:27.*

84 Quhen Alysaunder oure kyng wes dede,
That Scotland led in lauche and le,
Away wes sons of alle and brede,
Off wyne and wax, of gamyn and gle;
Oure gold wes changyd in to lede.
Cryst, borne in to virgynyte,
Succour Scotland, and remede,
That stad is in perplexyte.
c.1286 Lines said to have been written after the death of Alexander II of Scotland, the earliest extant piece of Scottish verse. Quoted in the *Original Chronicle of Andrew Wyntoun* (c.1420), bk.7.

85 Lenten is come with love to toune.
c.1300 'Lenten is come', l.1.

86 *Quamdiu centum viui remanserint, nuncquam Anglorum dominio aliquatenus volumus subjugari.*
As long as one hundred of us shall remain alive, we shall never consent to subject ourselves in any degree to English dominion.
1320 *Declaration of Arbroath*, a letter sent by the barons of Scotland to Pope John XXII, asserting Scotland's independence from England and their right to defend that independence with or without the support of their sovereign.

87 Not what thou arte, ne what thou hast ben, beholdeth God with his mercyful iye; bot that thou woldest be.
c.1370 *The Cloud of Unknowing*, ch.75.

88 *Patience is a poynt, thagh it displese ofte.*
Patience is a virtue, though it often displeases.
c.1370 *Patience*, l.1.

89 *Ay wolde man of happe more hente*
Then moghte by ryght upon hem cleven.
Man always desires to seize more of happiness,
Than rightfully belongs to him.
c.1370 *Pearl*, l.1195–6.

90 *Of alle chevalry to chose, the chef thyng alosed*
Is the lel layk of luf, the lettrure of armes.
Choosing from all chivalrous actions, the chief things to praise
Are the loyal sport of love and the lore of arms.
c.1370 *Sir Gawain and the Green Knight*, l.1512–3.

91 Yif thou wolte lyve frely, lerne to dye gladly.
c.1375 *The Art of Dieing.*

92 Young men a wooing, for God that you bought,
Be well ware of wedding and think in your thought:
'Had I wist' is a thing, it serves of nought.
c.1425 *The Second Shepherd's Play*, part of the York cycle of Mystery Plays, l.91–3.

93 *Now why that erthe luves erthe, wondere me thinke,*
Or why that erthe for erthe sholde other swete or swinke:
For when that erthe upon erthe es broghte within brinke,
Thane shall erthe of erthe have a foulle stinke.
Now, why earth loves earth, I wonder to think,
Or why earth for earth should either sweat or labour:
For when earth upon earth comes within the grave's brink,
Then earth upon earth shall have a foul stink.
c.1450 'Erthe oute of erthe', l.19–22.

94 I wyll that my son manhede take
For reson wyll that there be thre—
A man, a madyn, and a tre.
Man for man, tre for tre,
Madyn for madyn; thus shall it be.
?c.1450 God the Father explains how Christ will atone for Adam's sin. *Towneley Annunciation Play*, l.30–5.

95 *Pees maketh plente;*
Plente maketh pride;
Pride make plee;
Plee maketh povert;
Povert maketh pees.
Peace makes plenty;
Plenty makes pride;
Pride makes lawsuits;
Lawsuits make poverty;
Poverty makes peace.
c.1470 Untitled lyric.

96 O God in Heaven, on you we call,
Kyrie eleison,
Help us seize our priests and kill them all,
Kyrie eleison.
1476 Satirical chant. Quoted in Gerald Strauss *Manifestations of Discontent in Germany on the Eve of the Reformation* (1971).

97 Everyman, I will go with thee, and be thy guide.
In thy most need to go by thy side.
c.1485 Knowledge speaks to Everyman. *Everyman*, l.522–3.

98 In youth open your mind, And let all learning in;
Words the head does not shape Are worthless, out and in.
Words wit has not salted, No nearer the heart than the lip,
Are nothing more than wind, A puppy's insolent yelp.
c.1500 'To a Boy'. Translated from the Irish by Michael O'Donovan ('Frank O'Connor').

99 Westron winde, when wilt thou blow,
The smalle raine downe can raine?
Christ if my love were in my armes,
And I in my bed againe.
c.1500 Untitled lyric.

1 Back and side go bare, go bare,
Both foot and hand go cold;
But, belly, God send thee good ale enough,
Whether it be new or old.
c.1575 Song, included in the play *Gammer Gurton's Needle*, act 2. William Stevenson (c.1530–75) and John Still (1543–1608) have both been credited with authorship of the play, but the song probably predates it.

2 I cannot eat but little meat,
My stomach is not good;
But sure I think that I can drink
With him that wears a hood.
c.1575 Song, included in the play *Gammer Gurton's Needle*, act 2. 'Him that wears a hood' is either a monk or a scholar.

3 And Tib my wife, that as her life
Loveth well good ale to seek,
Full oft drinks she, till ye may see
The tears run down her cheeks.
c.1575 Song, included in the play *Gammer Gurton's Needle*, act 2.

4 Though raging stormes movis us to shake,
And wind makis waters overflow;
We yield thereto bot dois not break
And in the calm bent up we grow.

So baneist men, though princes rage,
And prisoners, be not despairit.
Abide the calm, whill that it 'suage,
For time sic causis has repairit.
1582 *The Maitland Manuscript*, 'The Reeds in the Loch Sayis'.

5 Brissit brawnis and broken banis
Stryfe discorde and waistis wanis
Crukit in eild, syne halt withal,
This are the bewteis of the fute-ball.
1582 *The Maitland Manuscript*, 'The Bewteis of the Fute-ball'.

6 *Flavit deus et dissipati sunt*
God blew and they were scattered.
1588 Inscription on medallion to commemorate the English defeat of the Spanish Armada.

7 The rose is red, the leaves are green,
God save Elizabeth, our noble queen.
1589 Lines written by a Westminster schoolboy in the margin of his copy of *Julius Caesar*. Quoted in P W Hasler (ed) *The House of Commons, 1558–1603* (vol.1), p.474.

8 My Love in her attire doth show her wit,
It doth so well become her;
For every season she hath dressings fit,
For winter, spring, and summer.
No beauty she doth miss
When all her robes are on;
But beauty's self she is
When all her robes are gone.
'Madrigal'. Collected in F Davison (ed) *Poetical Rhapsody* (1602).

9 Nose, nose, jolly red nose,
Who gave thee this jolly red nose?...
Nutmegs and ginger, cinnamon and cloves,
And they gave me this jolly red nose.
Quoted in Francis Beaumont and John Fletcher *The Knight of the Burning Pestle* (1609) but thought to be a rhyme of earlier origin.

10 Even when the courtesan farts
She does it as a favour
c.1616–1853 Collected in R H Blyth *Senryō: Japanese Satirical Verses Translated and Explained* (1949).

11 Possession is nine points of the law.
Proverb, quoted in T Draxe *Adages* (1616) no.163.

12 Too many cooks spoil the broth.
Quoted in Sir Balthazar Gerbier *Three Chief Principles of Magnificent Building* (1665).

13 O he's a ranting roving blade!
O he's a brisk and a bonnie lad!
Betide what may, my heart is glad
To see my lad wi' his white cockade.
18c 'The White Cockade'.

14 O this is no my ain house,
I ken by the biggin o't.
18c 'This is no my ain house'.

15 A good rider may often be thrown from his horse,
And climb on once again to face forward his course,
Which is how I went forward myself on my way,
And come, Christ, and give me my true judgment day.
18c Traditional Irish poem. Translated by Owen Dudley Edwards.

16 And wasna he a roguey,
A roguey, a roguey,
And wasna he a roguey,
The piper o' Dundee?
18c 'The Piper o' Dundee'.

17 The Campbells are comin', O-ho, O-ho!
c.1715 'The Campbells are comin''. Although its origins are uncertain, this song may date from John Campbell, Duke of Argyll's attack on the Jacobite army at Sheriffmuir (1715).

18 Cam ye ower frae France?
Cam ye doun by Lunnon?
Saw ye Geordie Whelps
And his bonnie woman?
Were ye at the place
Ca'd the Kittle Housie?
Saw ye Geordie's grace
Ridin' on a goosie?
c.1715 'Cam Ye Ower Frae France?', stanza 1. This Jacobite song alludes to George I and his reputed fondness for visiting brothels.

19 It made Gay Rich and Rich Gay.
c.1728 Alluding to the phenomenal success of *The Beggar's Opera*, written by John Gay and produced by John Rich.

20 O ye'll tak the high road, and I'll tak the low road,
And I'll be in Scotland afore ye,
But me and my true love will never meet again
On the bonnie, bonnie banks o' Loch Lomond
By yon bonnie banks and by yon bonnie braes,
Where the sun shines bright on Loch Lomond.
1746 'The Bonnie Banks o' Loch Lomond', chorus and stanza 1. The author was a Jacobite imprisoned in Carlisle.

21 Whaur's yer Wullie Shakespeare noo?
1756 Shout from an enthusiastic member of the audience at the first production of John Home's *Douglas* at the Canongate Theatre, Edinburgh.

22 Boston, Boston, Boston!
Thou hast naught to boast on,
But a Grand Sluice, and a high steeple;

A proud conceited ignorant people,
And a coast where souls are lost on.

1766 Comment by visitor at the opening of the Grand Sluice, Boston, Lincolnshire, 15 Oct. Quoted in Jennifer Westwood *Albion* (1985), ch. 6, 'English Shires'.

23 Some hae meat and canna eat
And some wad eat that want it;
But we hae meat and we can eat,
And sae the Lord be thankit.

c.1790 'The Selkirk Grace', sometimes attributed to Robert Burns.

24 I challenge all the men alive
To say they e'er were gladder,
Than boys all striving,
Who should kick most wind out of the bladder.

1794 Charterhouse public school song, celebrating football.

25 Here's tae us; wha's like us?
Gey few, and they're a' deid.

19c Scottish toast of uncertain origin. 'Damn' and other variations are sometimes substituted for 'gey'.

26 This stone commemorates the exploit of William Webb Ellis, who, with a fine disregard for the rules of football as played in his time, first took the ball in his arms and ran with it, thus originating the distinctive feature of the Rugby game. AD 1823.

Plaque at Rugby School.

27 What can be more palpably absurd than the prospect held out of locomotives travelling twice as fast as stagecoaches?

1825 *Quarterly Review*, Mar.

28 There was a girl in our town,
Silk an' satin was her gown,
Silk an' satin, gold an' velvet,
Guess her name, three times I've telled it.

Quoted in James Orchard Halliwell *The Nursery Rhymes of England* (1842). The answer, of course, is 'Ann'.

29 The deceased Gentleman was, we are informed, a native of Ashbourn, Derbyshire, at which place he was born in the Year of Grace, 217, and was consequently in the 1643rd year of his age. For some months the patriotic Old Man had been suffering from injuries sustained in his native town, so far back as Shrovetide in last year; he was at once removed (by appeal) to London, where he lingered in suspense till the law of death put its icy hand upon him, and claimed as another trophy to magisterial interference one who had long lived in the hearts of the people.

1860 'Death of the Right Honourable Game Football', as published in a court circular. There had been recent attempts in the courts to ban the riotous custom of 'Shrovetide football' pursued at Ashbourne, Derbyshire, and other villages.

30 What happens when a game of football is proposed at Christmas among a party of young men assembled from different schools? Alas!... The Eton man is enamoured of his own rules, and turns up his nose at Rugby as not sufficiently aristocratic; while the Rugbeian retorts that 'bullying' and 'sneaking' are not to his taste, and he is not afraid of his shins, or of a 'maul' or 'scrimmage'. On hearing this the Harrovian pricks up his ears, and though he might previously have sided with Rugby, the insinuation against the courage of those who do not allow 'shinning' arouses his ire, and causes him to refuse to lay with one who has offered it. Thus it is found impossible to get up a game.

1861 Editorial in *The Field* newspaper, illustrating the confusion before the codification of the rules of football and rugby.

31 Well-informed people know it is impossible to transmit the voice over wires and that were it possible to do so, the thing would be of no practical value.

1865 Editorial in the *Boston Post*.

32 It is a good plan, if it can previously be so arranged, to have one side with striped jerseys of one colour, say red; and the other with another, say blue. This prevents confusion and wild attempts to run after and wrest the ball from your neighbour. I have often seen this done, and the invariable apology 'I beg your pardon, I thought you were on the opposite side'.

1867 In *Routledge's Handbook of Football*.

33 In affectionate remembrance of English cricket, which died at the Oval on 29th August, 1882. Deeply lamented by a large circle of sorrowing friends and acquaintances. RIP. NB The body will be cremated and the ashes taken to Australia.

1882 Notice in *The Sporting Times*, 2 Sep, after the England cricket team's defeat by the Australians.

34 The climate of Manitoba consists of seven months of Arctic weather and five months of cold weather.

1882 *Settler's Guide to the North-West*, issued by the Northern Pacific Railway Company, New York.

35 The British 'Sphere of Influence'—the cricket ball.

Mr Punch's Book of Sport.

36 £1 per week should be ample remuneration for the best professional footballer that ever existed.

1886 In *The Field* newspaper.

37 To the Glorious, Pious, and Immortal Memory of King William the Third, Prince of Orange, who delivered us from Popes and Popery, Knaves and Knavery, Slaves and Slavery, Brass Money, and Wooden Shoes, and He that Will Not Take this Toast May He Be Damn'd, Cramm'd, and Jamm'd Down the Great Gun of Athlone, and the Gun Fired in the Pope's Belly, and the Pope Fired in the Devil's Belly, and the Devil Fired into Hell, and the Door Lock'd, and the Key Forever in the Pocket of a Stout Orangeman. And Here's a Fart for the Bishop of Cork!

c.1890 'The Orange Toast', traditional Protestant Irish.

38 These Ibsen creatures are 'neither men nor women, they are ghouls', vile, unlovable, morbid monsters, and it were well indeed for society if all such went and drowned themselves at once.

1891 In *The Gentlewoman*. Review of Henrik Ibsen's *Rosmersholm*.

39 How different, how very different, from the home life of our own dear Queen!

c.1892 Overheard from a member of the audience when Sarah Bernhardt appeared in the role of Cleopatra.

40 I don't know, darlin', but I think it was somethin' he did against the English.

1895 Unidentified Irish nurse in the US answering an infant's question on the cause of Oscar Wilde's imprisonment, reported by Kenneth Wiggins Porter.

41 The ordinary 'horseless-carriage' is at present a luxury for the wealthy; and although the price will probably fall in the future, it will never, of course, come into as

common use as the bicycle.
1899 *Literary Digest*, 14 Oct.

42 Far away from where I am now there is a little gap in the hills, and beyond it the sea; and 'tis there I do be looking the whole day long, for it's the nearest thing to yourself that I can see.
c.1900 Letter from an unidentified Irish postboy to his beloved, quoted in Maurice Healy *The Old Munster Circuit*.

43 *Citius, altius, fortius.*
Swifter, higher, stronger.
Motto of the Olympic Games, c.1908. It was apparently adopted by Baron de Coubertin after he spotted it over the doorway of a French lycée, though it has also been attributed to Reverend Father Didon.

44 Skegness is so bracing.
from 1909 Slogan in railway advertisements promoting Skegness, Lincolnshire, as a holiday resort. Quoted in Nigel Rees *Dictionary of Popular Phrases* (1990).

45 That the automobile has practically reached the limit of its development is suggested by the fact that during the past year no improvements of a radical nature have been introduced.
1909 *Scientific American*, 2 Jan.

46 Your country needs you!
1914 First use of British World War I recruiting slogan.

47 Berlin by Christmas.
1914 British press.

48 Say it ain't so, Joe.
1919 Attributed words of a young fan, to US baseball star 'Shoeless Joe' Jackson (1887–1951) who was accused of accepting bribes to throw the 1919 World Series (the 'Black Sox' scandal). Jackson always maintained his innocence, but he and seven other players were barred from baseball for life.

49 Four and twenty Yankees, feeling very dry,
Went across the border to get a drink of rye.
When the rye was opened, the Yanks began to sing,
'God bless America, but God save the King!'
c.1919 Ditty current in Canada, referring to Americans crossing the border to drink during Prohibition. The Duke of Windsor, later Edward VIII, heard it during his tour of Canada (1919) and repeated it to his father, George V, on his return, as he recalled in *A King's Story* (1951).

50 The cure of the id by the odd.
c.1920 Popular definition of psychoanalysis.

51 Dear Sir, your astonishment's odd:
I am always about in the Quad.
And that's why the tree
Will continue to be
Since observed by Yours faithfully, God.
c.1924 Reply to Ronald Knox's limerick. The limericks summarize Bishop George Berkeley's philosophy that everything is dependent at all times on the will of God.
➡ *See Knox 476:22.*

52 There is no woman who does not dream of being dressed in Paris.
1925 Catalogue of the 1925 Paris Exhibition. Quoted in Colin McDowell *McDowell's Directory of Twentieth Century Fashion* (1984), ch.1.

53 There was a faith-healer of Deal
Who said, 'Although pain isn't real,
If I sit on a pin
And it punctures my skin,
I dislike what I fancy I feel.'
Collected in *The Week-End Book* (1925).

54 Let's get out of these wet clothes and into a dry martini.
c.1925 The origin of this line is disputed; it has been attributed to Billy Wilder, Charles Butterworth, Alexander Woollcott and Robert Benchley's press agent. It was used by Mae West in *Every Day's a Holiday* (1937 film) and by Benchley in *The Major and the Minor* (1942 film).

55 Can't act. Can't sing. Slightly bald. Can dance a little.
c.1930 Studio executive's assessment of Fred Astaire on his first screen test.

56 *Ein Reich, ein Volk, ein Führer.*
One realm, one people, one leader.
1934 German Nazi slogan.

57 Sticks nix hick pix
1935 Headline from *Variety*, 17 Jul. A famous example of the US trade paper's idiosyncratic form of English, referring to the unpopularity of films with rural themes in rural areas.

58 A bayonet is a weapon with a worker at each end.
1940 British pacifist slogan during World War II.

59 A neurotic builds castles in the air, but a psychotic lives in them.
c.1940 Popular saying.

60 *Arbeit macht frei.*
Work liberates.
c.1940 Legend over the gates of the concentration camp at Auschwitz, Poland.

61 Who dares, wins.
1940s Motto of the British Special Air Service regiment.

62 Export or die.
1940s British Board of Trade.

63 Walls have ears.
1940s British war slogan.

64 Coughs and sneezes spread diseases. Trap the germs in your handkerchief.
1942 British Government health slogan, quoted in J Darracott and B Loftus *Second World War Posters* (1972).

65 Went the day well?
Title of an anthology of tributes to men and women killed in the war, used for the title of Cavalcanti's 1942 film about German soldiers invading an English village.

66 No girls, no legs, no jokes, no chance.
1943 Review of the Rodgers and Hammerstein musical *Oklahoma!* wired to theatre critic Walter Winchell by one of his informants after its pre-Broadway tryout in New Haven. Quoted in Peter Hay *Broadway Anecdotes* (1989).

67 If only we might fall
Like cherry blossoms in the spring
So pure and radiant.
c.1945 Quoted in Ivan Morris *The Nobility of Failure* (1975).

68 I like Ike.
1947 Campaign slogan for Dwight D Eisenhower's presidential bid. Irving Berlin presented a song with this title, based on *They Like Ike* from his Broadway musical *Call Me Madam*, to an Eisenhower rally at Madison Square Garden, 8 Feb 1952.

69 Whose finger do you want on the trigger?
1952 Headline in the *Daily Mirror*, 21 Sep, reflecting popular mistrust of both Labour and Conservative leadership in the light of the new destructive potential of the atomic bomb.

70 Massermann, the cat man,
Makes cats neurotic.

Are cats and humans
Similarly symptotic?
1952 Popular jingle. Dr Jules Massermann conducted some bizarre, behavioural experiments into animal neurosis.

71 No pain—no gain.
Bodybuilding motto. The catchphrase may have had its origins in Adlai Stevenson's slogan 'There are no gains without pain', first voiced when accepting the Democratic nomination in 1952.

72 Piping Pebworth, Dancing Marston,
Haunted Hillborough, Hungry Grafton,
Dodging Exhall, Papist Wixford,
Beggarly Broom, and Drunken Bidford.
'Traditional Rhyme on the Vale of Avon Place-Names', quoted in Arnold Silcock, *Verse and Worse* (1952), 'Whimsies'.

73 Madly for Adlai.
1952 Campaign slogan for Adlai Stevenson's presidential bid.

74 Ban the Bomb.
1953 Used by US nuclear disarmament movement from 1953.

75 Psychology? When my daughter needs psychology I fetch her a skelp across her backside, which lifts her nigh six inches in t'air.
1955 Young Yorkshire mother's response on being asked by a local education psychologist how she felt psychology might assist her in the upbringing of her difficult daughter.

76 Cambridge has always tried to be more typical and less exotic than the other place.
1958 In *The Listener*, 14 Aug. 'The other place' has traditionally come to be used of Cambridge from an Oxford viewpoint and vice versa.

77 Life's better with the Conservatives...don't let Labour ruin it.
1959 Conservative Party general election slogan.

78 A chair should be judged by one's pants, a jewel by the light in a lady's eyes, a typewriter by the hovering fingers.
1959 On good design. In *Time*, 12 Jan.

79 Nature's way of telling you to slow down.
Of death. Quoted in *Newsweek*, 25 Apr 1960.

80 Let's get America moving again.
1960 John F Kennedy's presidential election slogan.

81 Would you buy a used car from this man?
1960 Democratic slogan to disparage Richard M Nixon in the 1960 presidential campaign. Nixon had come across badly in television debates, in contrast to the charismatic John F Kennedy.

82 Never again.
1960 Jewish Defence League.

83 GIGO: Garbage in, garbage out.
c.1960 The great and seemingly most basic principle of the computer, coined anonymously sometime early in its development.

84 I have to say Miss Brown, that your methods are outdated and incorrect. But the children love you and are learning well. Do not on any account make any changes.
c.1960 Unknown school inspector, quoted in Antony Garrard Newton Flew *Shephard's Warning. Setting schools back on course* (1994).

85 Stop The World, I Want to Get Off.
1961 From the musical by Leslie Bricusse and Anthony Newley.

86 Stretch pants—the garment that made skiing a spectator sport.
1961 In *Time*, 23 Feb.

87 All the egg heads are in one basket.
1961 Of President Kennedy's advisers. Quoted by Harold Macmillan in a letter to the Queen, 12 Apr.

88 That Was The Week That Was.
1962–3 Title of satirical BBC TV series.

89 Our little bit of grandeur is gone.
1963 Heard on a Dublin bus shortly after the assassination of John Fitzgerald Kennedy, 22 Nov, reported by Sheila O'Sullivan.

90 Make love, not war.
Flower Power movement, mid-1960s.

91 Thirteen wasted years.
1964 Labour Party general election slogan.

92 Don't report what he says, report what he means.
1964 Unwritten reporters' rule for covering Senator Barry Goldwater's campaign for presidential nomination. Quoted in Robert MacNeil *The Right Place at the Right Time* (1982).

93 Hearts and minds.
c.1965 Used by US Defense Department official with regard to winning public support for its Vietnam policy.

94 An important senior faun
Description of Prime Minister Harold Macmillan's appearance. Quoted in John Gunther *Procession* (1965).

95 Hey, hey, LBJ! How many kids did you kill today?
1966 US anti- Vietnam war demonstrators.

96 Black is beautiful.
1966 US black civil rights movement.

97 Black power.
1966 US black civil rights slogan coined by Stokely Carmichael.

98 Magnificent magpiety.
1966 Of the art collection of cosmetic manufacturer Helena Rubinstein. *Time*, 29 Apr.

99 Bombs away with Curtis LeMay.
1967 Used by US anti- Vietnam demonstrators.

1 Burn, baby, burn!
1967 Radical cry in racial riots and fire-raising in Watts, California and Newark, New Jersey. Quoted in *Time*, 11 Aug.

2 It became necessary to destroy the town to save it.
1968 Statement issued by the US army, referring to Ben Tre in Vietnam. In the *New York Times*, 8 Feb.

3 I'm Backing Britain.
1968 Coined by publisher Robert Maxwell to encourage the public to buy British-made goods.

4 Culture is dead, now let us start creating.
1968 Graffito by Parisian students on the School of Architecture walls, May.

5 Who Else but Nelse?
1968 Campaign slogan for Nelson Rockefeller's presidential bid.

6 My mother thinks Vietnam is somewhere near Panama.
c.1968 The last words of a US soldier fatally wounded during the Vietnam War, quoted by Australian film-maker John Pilger in his 1978 film *Do you remember Vietnam?*

7 When you've got it, flaunt it.
1969 Braiff Airlines slogan.

8 Power to the people.
1969 US Black Panther movement slogan.

9 Out of the closets and into the streets.
1969 US Gay rights movement slogan.

10 Here men from the planet Earth first set foot upon the moon, July 1969 AD. We came in peace for all mankind.
1969 Text of the plaque left on the moon by the first astronauts to walk there, Buzz Aldrin and Neil Armstrong, 20 Jul.

11 Burn your bra!
1970 US feminists' slogan.

12 Yesterday's men.
1970 Labour Party general election slogan, referring to the Conservative leadership.

13 Send them a message.
1972 Governor George Wallace's presidential election slogan.

14 Nice one, Cyril.
1972 Buy-line in TV advertisement for Wonderloaf. It was adopted in 1973 as the title of a pop song by the Cockerel Chorus, addressed to Tottenham Hotspur left-back Cyril Knowles.

15 The abominable no-man.
Of Sherman Adams, Eisenhower's Chief of Staff. Quoted in William Safire *Before the Fall* (1975).

16 The Grin Will Win.
1976 Campaign slogan for Jimmy Carter's presidential bid.

17 He who has not travelled does not know the value of a man.
Arab proverb. Quoted in Ingrid Cranfield *The Challengers* (1976), preface.

18 Hypochondria is the only disease I haven't got.
1978 Graffito seen in New York.

19 Just when you thought it was safe to get back into the water.
c.1978 Publicity slogan for *Jaws 2*.

20 Sick as a parrot.
c.1978 Football cliché. The phrase may have started life as 'sick as a pierrot', an allusion to the sadfaced French Pierrot character of the 18th century, but similar phrases appear in literature as early as the 17th century.

21 To err is human; to blame it on the other party is politics.
1979 In the *Washingtonian*, Nov.

22 Labour isn't working.
1979 Used by the Conservative Party in its general election campaign, referring to high unemployment under the then Labour Government.

23 On yer bike!
1981 Catchphrase derived from Norman Tebbit's Conservative Party conference speech.

24 The Great Communicator.
1981 Tag coined for President Reagan, who was renowned for his ability to put a good spin on speeches prepared for him.

25 Britain is a Morris Minor country, but with Rolls Royce diplomacy.
1982 Remark made during the Falklands crisis by a UN delegate, Apr. Quoted in The Sunday Times Insight Team *The Falklands War* (1982).

26 See Freddy before he sees you!
1984 Publicity for the film *A Nightmare on Elm Street*.

27 It's morning again in America.
1984 Campaign slogan for Ronald Reagan's presidential campaign. Quoted in Hedrick Smith *The Power Game* (1988).

28 A desk is a dangerous place from which to view the world.
1985 Sign on desk of American Express president Louis Gerstner. Quoted in the *New York Times*, 26 Jun.

29 Cannes…is 10,000 people looking for 10 people who really count.
1986 Unknown French publicist speaking on the Cannes Film Festival. Quoted in the *New York Times*, 17 May.

30 Art comes to you proposing to give nothing but the highest quality to your moments as they pass.
Inscription on wall of entrance gallery at Dallas' Lloyd Paxton Art and Antiques. Quoted in *Architectural Digest*, May 1986.

31 Save something for the Third Act.
Show business adage applied by President Reagan to his final months in the White House. Quoted in *Time*, 16 Mar 1987.

32 The future ain't what it used to be.
1987 Anonymous Iowa farmer quoted by President Bush on NBC TV, 10 May.

33 There are checks and balances in government—the checks go to candidates and the balance to the people.
Quoted in *Sunday Morning*, CBS TV broadcast, 17 May 1987.

34 Bill was a tropical fish. His native habitat was hot water.
1987 Of William J Casey of the CIA and his role in the Iran arms sales. Quoted in the *New York Times*, 19 Jul.

35 I know one thing we did right
Was the day we started to fight,
Keep your eye on the prize,
Hold on, hold on!
Civil rights song, quoted in Juan Williams *Eye on the Prize* (1987).

36 Skinny cooks can't be trusted.
1987 Quoted by David Cobb Craig in 'Home Cooking Away From Home', *Life*, Jul.

37 Global double zero.
1987 In *Time*, 3 Aug. This arms control term was applied to Mikhail Gorbachev's agreement for mutual elimination of intermediate and shorter-range missiles in Asia and Europe.

38 Don't die of ignorance.
1987 AIDS awareness campaign slogan.

39 To go to school and finish my schooling without getting pregnant.
1987 15-year-old Detroit girl's definition of the American dream. Reported in *Newsweek*, 29 Jan.

40 Mr Elbows and Knees.
1988 Of Democratic presidential nominee Michael S Dukakis. Quoted in *Time*, 21 Nov.

41 We loved your play. We only have problems with your main character, the second act and the ending.
1988 Fan's comment to playwright Wendy Wasserstein on *The Heidi Chronicles*. Quoted in the *New York Times*, 24 Jan 1991.

42 No duties, only opportunities.
Motto of Princeton, NJ, Institute for Advanced Study. Quoted in Ed Regis *Who Got Einstein's Office?* (1988).

43 Before you save the world, you've got to save your seat.
1989 On the need for legislators to keep in close touch with their constituents. Quoted in the *New York Times*, 2 Jan.

44 Life is a sexually transmitted disease.
Graffito, quoted in D J Enright *Faber Book of Fevers and Frets* (1989).

45 We're kuwaiting.
1990 NBC TV broadcast, 16 Aug. The speaker was a US serviceman posted to the Gulf after Iraq's invasion of Kuwait.

46 All the 'isms are wasms.
Attributed comment of a Foreign Office spokesman on the signing of the Molotov–Ribbentrop Pact in Aug 1939. In Peter Hennessy *Whitehall* (1990).

47 Don't iron while the strike is hot.
1991 Women's liberation slogan, quoted in PBS broadcast, 26 Jan.

48 We're here,
We're queer.

Get used to it.
1991 Motto of the homosexual liberation movement, Queer Nation, which rejected use of the term 'gay'. Quoted in the *New York Times*, 6 Apr.

49 Twelve drawers full of political cancer.
1991 FBI agent referring to the files of J Edgar Hoover. Quoted in *Newsweek*, 23 Sep.

50 A fatheaded, boneheaded, dunderheaded, blunderheaded, muttonheaded, knuckleheaded, chuckleheaded, puddingheaded, jobernowled wash-out of a cock-up.
1991 Journalist speaking of the poll tax introduced by Margaret Thatcher. Quoted in *The Economist*, 3 Dec 1994.

51 He who hath the gold maketh the rule.
1991 Inscription on plaque in Armand Hammer's bedroom. Quoted in *Regardie's*, Feb.

52 Polyester...the most valuable word to come out of the 70s, the one that defines tacky for all time.
1991 'Prettier Poly', *New York Times* editorial, 21 Mar.

53 The heraldic equivalent of a pair of furry dice bouncing around in the back of a state coach.
1992 On the title of Countess of Finchley bestowed on former Prime Minister Margaret Thatcher. In the *New Yorker*, 6 Jan.

54 The economy, stupid!
1992 Sign in the Clinton campaign headquarters which became a by-word for the central issue of the 1992 presidential campaign. Quoted in *Fortune*, 19 Oct.

55 It's easier to get a photograph of the Pope in the shower than a picture of her.
1993 On Hillary Rodham Clinton's low profile in the period between her husband's election and inauguration. In *Newsweek*, 25 Jan.

56 Behold the turtle, it only makes progress when it sticks its neck out.
Favourite saying of Harvard's president James B Conant. Quoted in James G Hershberg *James B Conant* (1993).

57 From the cradle to the grave,
Even if I misbehave,
There's a place for me
On government subsidy.
Quoted by a caller from Baltimore on Station WAMU, Washington, 15 Jun 1993.

58 Artists and poets are the raw nerve ends of humanity. By themselves they can do little to save humanity. Without them there would be little worth saving.
Inscription on headstone in Green River Cemetery, Springs NY where Jackson Pollock, Elaine de Kooning, and other artists are buried. Quoted in the *New York Times*, 17 Aug 1993.

59 To have one's credit cards cancelled is now akin to being excommunicated by the medieval church.
1993 In *Reader's Digest*, Sep.

60 Complete the mission, though I be the lone survivor. Never leave a fallen comrade to fall into the hands of the enemy.
1993 *The Ranger's Creed*, quoted in the *New York Times*, 25 Oct. The Rangers, a US Army unit, had stayed to guard the body of a pilot fatally caught in a downed helicopter in Somalia.

61 A potato candidate. The best part of him is underground.
1994 Of Adlai Stevenson and his respectable ancestors. In the *Washington Post*, 9 Jan.

62 I don't know if Mr Kissinger is a great writer, but anyone finishing this book is a great reader.
1994 Unidentified book reviewer quoted by Henry Kissinger on the publication of his 900-page *Diplomacy*. In the *Washington Post*, 11 Apr.

63 The castor oil of the Palestinian peace movement.
1994 Of PLO Chair Yassir Arafat. In NPR broadcast, 4 Jul.

64 He looks like a homeless man in a thousand dollar suit.
1994 On Senator Edward M Kennedy's campaign for re-election at age 62. In the *Washington Post*, 1 Oct.

65 If you are not the lead dog, the view never changes.
Paperweight on the desk of Richard Scott, chief executive officer, Hospital Corp of America. Quoted in *Forbes*, 10 Oct 1994.

66 The President is a walking dead man. He just doesn't know it yet.
1994 Senior legislator on President Clinton's political future as he entered the second half of his term of office. In *Nightline*, ABC TV broadcast, 6 Dec.

67 Running a cemetery is just like being President: you got a lot of people under you and nobody's listening.
Quoted by Bill Clinton, 10 Jan 1995.

68 Has he reconnected with the angry middle?
1995 Listener's question on Clinton's rapport with the middle class after the State of the Union speech. In NPR broadcast, 26 Jan.

69 I'm spending my children's inheritance.
Bumper sticker alluding to the economics of Social Security. Quoted in the *New York Times*, 24 Feb 1995.

70 Louisianans don't tolerate corruption; they demand it.
1995 In the *New York Times*, 5 Mar.

71 Welfare should be a safety-net, not a hammock.
1995 In NPR broadcast, 12 Mar.

72 To avoid criticism, say nothing, do nothing, be nothing.
Inscription on a pillow given Claudia ('Lady Bird') Johnson by her staff. Quoted in *Life*, Apr 1995.

73 Hussein isn't just sitting on the fence; he *is* the fence.
1995 Unknown US diplomat on Jordan's King Hussein prior to making peace with Palestine. Quoted in *The Times*, 22 Jul.

74 The French want to attack, the Americans want to bomb, and the British want to have another meeting.
1995 US diplomat commenting on the war in Bosnia. Quoted by William Safire in the *New York Times*, 27 Jul.

75 You can't expect the Rapid Reaction Force to be ready immediately.
1995 On the British force being sent to Bosnia. Military spokesperson interviewed on BBC Radio 4's *Today* programme.

76 Craft is the handprint of all culture.
1995 On exhibit of metal and ceramic work displayed at the White House. In *Sunday Morning*, CBS TV, 30 Apr.

77 The future's bright, the future's Orange.
1996 Advertising slogan for Orange telecommunications.

78 He may be a minister of the British Government but we are the Walt Disney Corporation and we don't roll over for anyone.
1998 An unidentified Disneyland executive commenting on reports that Peter Mandelson might use the theme park's ideas in the Millennium Dome without permission. In the *Sunday Telegraph*, 18 Jan.

79 Prudence is the other woman in Gordon's life.
1998 On Gordon Brown. Comment from unidentified aide, quoted on BBC News online, 20 Mar.

80 Hear ye! Hear ye! All persons are commanded to keep silent, on pain of imprisonment, while the House of Representatives is exhibiting to the Senate of the United

States articles of impeachment against William Jefferson Clinton, President of the United States.
1999 Formal announcement. Quoted in *The Guardian*, 8 Jan.

81 He who dies with the most shoes wins.
c.2000 Advertising slogan for Nike running shoes, inspired by the earlier T-shirt slogan 'he who has the most stuff when he dies, wins'.

82 The plan is called 'shock and awe', and its goal is 'the psychological destruction of the enemy's will to frighten'.
2003 In the *New Yorker*, 10 Feb.

83 An apple a day keeps the doctor away.
Proverb.

84 It's 105 degrees in Saigon and rising.
Prearranged coded signal for US citizens and their dependents to assemble at evacuation points during Vietnam War. Quoted in Walter Isaacson *Kissinger* (1992).

85 It's what's in the grooves that counts.
Slogan of Tamla Motown Records.

86 Let no-one enter who does not know his geometry.
Inscription at the entrance of Plato's Academy. Reported by commentators on Aristotle (Elias *In Aristotelis categorias commentarium*, 18, 118, 18).

87 Twelve Highlanders and a bagpipe make a rebellion.
Scottish proverb.

88 Wha daur meddle wi' me?
Scots paraphrase of the Scottish royal motto, 'Nemo me impune lacessit' ('No one provokes me with impunity').

89 When the world was made, the rubbish was sent to Stockport.
Quoted in Wolfgang Mieder *Investigations of Proverbs, Proverbial Expressions, Quotations and Clichés* (1984), in turn taken from *Notes and Queries* (1871).

90 *Resta viator et lege!*
Stand still, traveller, and read!
Corpus Inscriptionum Latinarum III, 371 (From Cyzicus in Mysia).

91 *Salud, Dinero, Amor…y Tiempo.*
Health, Wealth, Love…and Time to enjoy them.
Traditional Spanish wedding toast.

Anouilh, Jean 1910–87

French playwright. The author of light comedies, historical pieces and tragedies, his plays include *Antigone* (1944), *Ring Round the Moon* (1947) and *Becket, or the Honour of God* (1959).

92 *Faire l'amour avec une femme qui ne vous plaît pas, c'est aussi triste que de travailler.*
To make love with a woman whom you do not like is as sad as going to work.
1931 *L'Hermine*, act 1.

93 *Je sais de quelles petitesses meurent les plus grandes amours.*
I know how pettiness ruins the greatest loves.
1931 *L'Hermine*, act 2.

94 *Nous voulons tous louer à l'année et nous ne pouvons jamais louer que pour une semaine ou pour un jour. C'est l'image de la vie.*
We would all like to lease for a year and we can only lease for a week or from day to day. That is the image of life.
1937 *Le Rendez-vous de Senlis*, act 1.

95 *Il y aura toujours un chien perdu quelque part qui m'empêchera d'être heureux.*
There will always be a lost dog somewhere that will prevent me being happy.
1938 *La Sauvage*, act 3.

96 *La mort ne fait jamais mal. La mort est douce… Ce qui fait souffrir avec certains poisons, certaines blessures maladroites, c'est la vie. C'est le reste de vie. Il faut se confier franchement à la mort comme une amie.*
Death never hurts. Death is sweet… Life is what makes us suffer with its poisons and awkward injuries. That's what remains of life. We must confide freely in death as we would in a friend.
1941 *Eurydice*, act 1.

97 *C'est bon pour les hommes de croire aux idées et de mourir pour elles.*
It is good for people to believe in ideas and die for them.
1944 *Antigone*.

98 *C'est plein de disputes, un bonheur.*
Happiness is full of strife.
1944 *Antigone*.

99 *Rien n'est vrai que ce qu'on ne dit pas.*
Nothing is true except that which is unsaid.
1944 *Antigone*.

1 *Chacun de nous a un jour, plus ou moins triste, plus ou moins lointain, où il doit enfin accepter d'être un homme.*
There will come a day for each of us, more or less sad, more or less distant, when we must accept the condition of being human.
1944 *Antigone*.

2 *Mourir, ce n'est rien. Commence donc par vivre. C'est moins drôle et c'est plus long.*
To die is nothing. Begin by living. It's less funny and lasts longer.
1946 *Roméo et Jeannette*, act 3.

3 *Vous savez bien que l'amour, c'est avant tout le don de soi!*
Above all, you must understand that love is the gift of oneself!
1949 *Ardèle*.

4 *Dieu est avec tout le monde… Et, en fin de compte, il est toujours avec ceux qui ont beaucoup d'argent et de grosses armées.*
God is on everyone's side… And, in the last analysis, he is on the side with plenty of money and large armies.
1953 *L'Alouette (The Lark)*.

St Anselm 1033–1109

Italian cleric, scholar and scholastic philosopher, author of numerous philosophical and devotional treatises. In 1078 he became Abbot of Bec, in Normandy, and in 1093 was appointed Archbishop of Canterbury.

5 *Neque enim quaero ut credem, sed credo ut intelligam.*
For I do not seek to understand so that I may believe; but I believe so that I may understand.
1078 *Proslogion*, ch.1 (translated by M J Charlesworth).

6 *Id quo maius non cogitari potest.*
That than which a greater cannot be thought.
1078 Of God. *Proslogion*, ch.3. His famous ontological argument for the existence of God. Since a being that exists is necessarily greater than a being that does not, God must by this definition exist.

Antheil, George 1900–59

US composer, of Polish descent. His controversial modernistic works included the *Jazz Symphony* (1925) and the *Ballet Mécanique* (1927), written for ten pianos and a variety of eccentric percussion instruments.

7 Art cannot hold its breath too long without dying.
1945 *Bad Boy of Music.*

Anthony, Susan B(rownell) 1820–1906

US social reformer and women's suffrage leader. A campaigner in temperance and anti-slavery movements, she co-founded the National Women's Suffrage Association with Elizabeth Cady (1869).

8 The true Republic: men, their rights and nothing more; women, their rights and nothing less.
1868–70 On the front of her newspaper, *The Revolution.*

9 There will never be complete equality until women themselves help to make laws and to elect lawmakers.
In *The Arena.*

Antiphon 5c BC

Greek philosopher and sophist. Only fragments survive of his works.

10 The greatest cost, namely time.
Quoted in Plutarch *Antonius*, 28.

Apelles 4c BC

Greek painter, probably born in Colophon on the Ionian coast of Asia Minor.

11 *Ne supra crepidam sutor iudicaret.*
Let the cobbler stick to his last.
Quoted in Pliny *Naturalis Historia*, 35.36.85. A cobbler who had criticized Apelles' way of rendering a sandal in one of his paintings, proceeded to criticize the rest of the painting as well. The expression became proverbial.

Apollinaire, Guillaume *originally* ***Wilhelm Apollinaris de Kostrowitzki*** 1880–1918

French poet and author of Polish–Italian parentage. Associated with avant-garde literary groups, he is said to have invented the word 'surrealism'.

12 *Et toi mon coeur pourquoi bats-tu*
Comme un guetteur mélancolique
J'observe la nuit et la mort.
And you my heart why do you pound
Like some melancholy watchman
I watch the night and death.
1899 *Le Guetteur mélancolique*, préface.

13 *Avant tout, les artistes sont des hommes qui veulent devenir inhumains.*
Above all, artists are men who want to become inhuman.
1913 *Les Peintres cubistes; Méditations esthétiques*, 'Sur la peinture, 1'.

14 *Un Picasso étudie un objet comme un chirurgien dissèque un cadavre.*
A Picasso studies an object like a surgeon dissects a corpse.
1913 *Les Peintres cubistes; Méditations esthétiques*, 'Sur la peinture, 2'.

15 *La géométrie est aux arts plastiques ce que la grammaire est à l'art de l'écrivain.*
Geometry is to sculpture what grammar is to the art of the writer.
1913 *Les Peintres cubistes; Méditations esthétiques*, 'Sur la peinture, 3'.

16 *Sous le pont Mirabeau coule la Seine.*
Et nos amours, faut-il qu'il m'en souvienne?
La joie venait toujours après la peine.
Under Mirabeau Bridge flows the Seine.
And our loves, must I remember them?
Joy always came after pain.
1913 *Les Alcools*, 'Le Pont Mirabeau'.

17 *Vienne la nuit sonne l'heure*
Les jours s'en vont je demeure.
Let night come, ring out the hour,
The days go by, I remain.
1913 *Les Alcools*, 'Le Pont Mirabeau'.

18 *Je connais gens de toutes sortes*
Ils n'égalent pas leur destin.
I know people of all sorts
They do not measure up to their destiny.
1913 *Les Alcools*, 'Marizibill'.

19 *L'art, de plus en plus, aura une patrie.*
Art, more and more, will have a country.
1913 'L'Esprit nouveau et les poètes', *Mercure de France.*

20 *Il est grand temps de rallumer les étoiles.*
It's high time we relit the stars.
1917 *Les Mamelles de Tirésias*, prologue.

21 *Perdre*
Mais perdre vraiment
Pour laisser place à la trouvaille
Perdre
La vie pour trouver la Victoire.
To lose
But really to lose
And make room for discovery
To lose
Life so as to discover Victory.
1918 *Calligrammes*, 'Toujours'.

Appleton, Sir Edward Victor 1892–1965

English physicist, Professor at London University (1924) and Cambridge (1936). He discovered the Appleton layer of electrically charged particles in the Earth's upper atmosphere, and was awarded the 1947 Nobel prize for physics.

22 You must not miss Whitehall. At one end you will find a statue of one of our kings who was beheaded; at the other, a monument to the man who did it. That is just one example of our attempts to be fair to everybody.
1948 Speech, Stockholm, 1 Jan.

23 I do not mind what language an opera is sung in so long as it is a language I don't understand.
1955 In the *Observer*, 28 Aug.

Appleton, Thomas Gold 1812–84

US man of letters and wit, the brother-in-law of Henry Wadsworth Longfellow. His own literary output consisted of formal poetry and pleasant essays and is collected in *Faded Leaves* (1872) and *A Sheaf of Papers* (1875).

24 Good Americans, when they die, go to Paris.
Quoted in Oliver Wendell Holmes *The Autocrat at the Breakfast*

Table (1858), ch.6. Although the speaker in Holmes's book is not identified by name, he is generally identified as Appleton.

25 Boston is a state of mind.
Attributed. This quotation has also been attributed to Ralph Waldo Emerson and Mark Twain.

26 A Boston man is the east wind made flesh.
Attributed.

Aquinas, St Thomas 1225–74

Italian Dominican monk and leading scholastic theologian, known as The Angelic Doctor. He was the first to attempt a complete theological system, and as Doctor of the Church his work is particularly respected in the Roman Catholic tradition.

27 *Pulchritudo enim creaturae nihil est aliud quam similitudo divinae pulchritudinis in rebus participata.*
The beauty of creatures is nothing other than an image of the divine beauty in which things participate.
c.1260 *Commentarium in Dionysii De Divinibus Nominibus*, bk.4, ch.5.

28 *Pange, lingua, gloriosi*
Corporis mysterium,
Sanguinisque pretiosi,
Quem in mundi pretium
Fructus ventris generosi
Rex effudit gentium.
Now, my tongue, the mystery telling
Of the glorious Body sing,
And the Blood, all price excelling,
Which the Gentiles' Lord and King,
In a Virgin's womb once dwelling,
Shed for this world's ransoming.
1263 *Pange Lingua Gloriosi*, known as the Corpus Christi hymn (translated by J M Neale et al).

29 *Tantum ergo sacramentum*
Veneremur cernui;
Et antiquum documentum
Novo cedat ritui.
Therefore we, before him bending,
This great Sacrament revere;
Types and shadows have their ending,
For the newer rite is here.
1263 *Pange Lingua Gloriosi*, known as the Corpus Christi hymn (translated by J M Neale et al).

30 *Solus homo delectatur in ipsa pulchritudine sensibilium secundum seipsam.*
Only man delights in the beauty of sense objects for their own sake.
c.1268 *Summa Theologia*, bk.1, question 91, article 3.

31 *Ars autem deficit ab operatione naturae.*
Art pales when compared to the workings of nature.
c.1272 *Summa Theologia*, bk. 3, question 66, article 4.

Arbuthnot, John 1667–1735

Scottish physician and writer, who published five satirical pamphlets against the Duke of Marlborough in 1712, under the title *The History of John Bull*.

32 Law is a bottomless pit.
1712 *The History of John Bull*, title of pamphlet.

33 Hame's hame, be it never so hamely.
1712 *The History of John Bull*, 'John Bull Still in His Senses', ch.3.

34 Curle (who is one of the new terrors of Death) has been writing letters to every body for memoirs of his life.
1733 Letter to Jonathan Swift, 13 Jan.

Archer, Jeffrey Howard, Lord 1940–

English politician and writer. A Conservative MP (1969–74), he resigned from the Commons after a financial disaster and turned to fiction, becoming a best-selling author of political potboilers. In 2001 he received a four-year jail sentence on charges of perjury and perverting the course of justice.

35 Not a Penny More, Not a Penny Less.
1975 Title of novel.

36 First Among Equals.
1984 Title of novel.

37 I am innocent of the charge, and nothing you will say however clever you are in the wording of out-of-context pieces, however clever you are in letting people know what 'on and off the record' means, there is only one thing that matters in this court of law, sir: I have never had sexual intercourse with her. And that is the truth!
Giving evidence at a libel trial in 1987. Quoted in Michael Crick *Jeffrey Archer: Stranger than Fiction* (1996).

Archer, Mary 1944–

English scientist. She is married to Jeffrey Archer.

38 I am cross with Jeffrey, but I have formed the judgement that he is a decent and generous spirited man over 35 years and that will not change over one weekend.
Following the revelation that her husband planned to establish a false alibi in his 1987 libel case. In the *Observer*, 'They said what…?', 28 Nov 1999.

Archimedes c.287–212 BC

Greek mathematician, whose innovations included siege-engines and the Archimedean screw for water raising. He was killed at the Roman siege of Syracuse.

39 Give me a firm spot on which to stand, and I shall move the earth.
Traditionally attributed to Archimedes; a variation can be found in Plutarch *Marcellus*, 14.

40 Eureka, Eureka! (I found it, I found it!).
Vitruvius 9.9.10. Attributed, on discovering the principle of upthrust on a floating body while having a bath. Archimedes had been given the task of establishing whether there was the proper weight of gold in the crown of Hieron of Syracuse. One day when entering his bath he noticed the water which flowed over the sides as he entered and he correctly perceived that the weight of the water displaced was that of the weight of his body.

Arenas, Reinaldo 1943–90

Cuban novelist. He held several minor positions in Cuba before leaving the country in 1980 for the US. He committed suicide in New York while suffering from AIDS.

41 *Nuestro portero descubrió, o creyó descubrir, que su labor no se podía limitar a abrir la puerta del edificio, sino que él, el portero, era el señalado, el elegido, el indicado…para mostrarles a todas aquellas personas una puerta más amplia y hasta entonces invisible o inaccesible; puerta que era la de sus propias vidas.*
Our doorman discovered (or thought he had discovered) that his tasks could not be limited to just opening the door of the building—but that he, the doorman, was the one *chosen, elected, singled out*…to

show everyone who lived there a wider door, until then either invisible or inaccessible: the door to their own lives.
1989 *El portero* (*The Doorman*, 1961), pt.1, ch.1.

Aretino, Pietro 1492–1557

Italian poet, illegitimate son of a nobleman. Banished from his native town, he wandered through Italy. His wit secured the favour of Pope Leo X, subsequently lost with the salacious *Sonetti Lussuriosi.* Later patrons included Giovanni de Medici, Francis I and Charles V. He reputedly died by falling from a stool while laughing.

42 I am a free man, I do not need to copy Petrarch or Boccaccio. My own genius is enough. Let others worry themselves about style and so cease to be themselves. Without a master, without a model, without a guide, without artifice, I go to work and earn my living, my well-being, and my fame. What do I need more? With a goose quill and a few sheets of paper I mock the universe.
Quoted in J H Plumb (ed) *The Horizon Book of the Renaissance* (1961, new edn by Penguin, 1982).

Arguedas, José María 1911–69

Peruvian fiction writer and ethnologist. His works reflect the tensions that underlie Peruvian society, in the marginalization of native peoples. He committed suicide.

43 *Dónde está la patria, amigo? Ni en el corazón ni en la saliva.*
Where is the country, my friend? It is not in the heart or in the saliva.
1971 *El zorro de arriba y el zorro de abajo* ('The Upper and the Lower Fox'), ch.3.

Ariosto, Ludovico 1474–1533

Italian poet. He joined the court of Cardinal Ippolito d'Este at Ferrara in 1503, where he produced his most famous work, the Roland epic, *Orlando Furioso* (completed 1516, enlarged 1532). He also wrote comedies, satires and sonnets.

44 *Natura il fece, e poi roppe la stampa.*
Nature made him, and then broke the mould.
1516 *Orlando Furioso*, canto 10, stanza 84.

Aristophanes c.448–c.388 BC

Greek comic poet. Only 11 comedies survive of his 54 plays; they are characterized by exaggeration, parody and satire of contemporary political and cultural life.

45 Who brings owls to Athens?
Avae (The Birds), l.301. This ancient proverb, quoted by various authors, is the equivalent of 'to carry coals to Newcastle'.

46 Old age is second childhood.
Nubes (The Clouds), l.1417.

47 Till the wolf and the lamb be united.
On the impossibility of peace between sworn enemies. *Pax*, l.1076.

Aristotle 384–322 BC

Greek philosopher, scientist and physician, a student of Plato and tutor to Alexander the Great. His philosophical works include *Metaphysics, Politics, Rhetoric* and *Poetics*. His influence has been incalculable; in medieval Europe he was known simply as 'The Philosopher'.

48 All men naturally desire knowledge.
Metaphysics, bk.1, ch.1, 980a (translated by H Tredennick).

49 It is through wonder that men now begin and originally began to philosophize; wondering in the first place at obvious perplexities, and then by gradual progression raising questions about the greater matters too.
Metaphysics, bk.1, ch.2, 982 (translated by H Tredennick).

50 Every art and every inquiry, and similarly every action and pursuit, is thought to aim at some good; and for this reason the good has rightly been declared to be that at which all things aim.
Nicomachean Ethics, bk.1, ch.1, 1093 (translated by Sir David Ross).

51 Human good turns out to be activity of soul exhibiting excellence, and if there is more than one sort of excellence, in accordance with the best and most complete. For one swallow does not make a summer, nor does one day; and so too one day, or a short time, does not make a man blessed and happy.
Nicomachean Ethics, bk.1, ch.7, 1098 (translated by Sir David Ross).

52 Virtue, then, is a state of character concerned with choice, lying in a mean…it is a mean between two vices, that which depends on excess and that which depends on defect.
Nicomachean Ethics, bk.2, ch.6, 1006 (translated by Sir David Ross).

53 For man, therefore, the life according to reason is best and pleasantest, since reason more than anything else *is* man.
Nicomachean Ethics, bk.10, ch.7, 1178 (translated by Sir David Ross).

54 Tragedy is thus a representation of an action that is worth serious attention, complete in itself and of some amplitude…by means of pity and fear bringing about the purgation of such emotions.
c.330 BC *Poetics*, ch.6.

55 Now a whole is that which has a beginning, a middle, and an end.
c.330 BC *Poetics*, ch.7, referring to tragedy.

56 Man is by nature a political animal; it is his nature to live in a state.
c.330 BC *Politics*, bk.1, ch.2, 1253a (translated by T A Sinclair).

57 Nature, as we say, does nothing without some purpose; and for the purpose of making man a political animal she has endowed him alone among the animals with the power of reasoned speech.
c.330 BC *Politics*, bk.1, ch.2, 1253b (translated by T A Sinclair).

58 It is a bad thing that many from being rich should become poor; for men of ruined fortunes are sure to stir up revolutions.
c.330 BC *Politics*, bk.4.

59 The flute is not an instrument that has a good moral effect—it is too exciting.
c.330 BC *Politics*.

60 For that which has become habitual, becomes as it were natural.
Rhetorica, 1370a (translated by J H Freese).

61 *Amicus Plato, sed magis amica veritas.*
Plato is dear to me, but dearer still is truth.
Proverbial expression, traditionally attributed to Aristotle, going back to a passage in the *Ethica Nicomachea*, 1069a.

Arlott, (Leslie Thomas) John 1914–91

English cricket commentator and writer, a police detective before joining the BBC in 1945. His voice became the epitome of radio cricket commentary.

62 The Master: records prove the title good:
Yet figures fail you, for they cannot say
How many men whose names you never knew
Are proud to tell their sons they saw you play.

They share the sunlight of your summer day
Of thirty years; and they, with you, recall
How, through those well-wrought centuries, your hand
Reshaped the history of bat and ball.

1952 'To John Berry Hobbs on his Seventieth Birthday'.

63 Cricket, like the novel, is great when it presents men in the round, when it shows the salty quality of human nature.

1953 Quoted in Colin Jarman *The Guinness Dictionary of Sports Quotations* (1990).

64 Most games are skin-deep, but cricket goes to the bone.

1977 *Arlott and Trueman on Cricket*.

65 Cricket is a game of the most terrifying stresses with more luck about it than any other game I know. They call it a team game, but in fact it is the loneliest game of all.

Another Word from Arlott.

Arlt, Roberto 1900–42

Argentinian fiction writer, dramatist and journalist. The son of German immigrants, his works emphasize the anger and disillusionment of the urban middle class.

66 *¡Y yo, yo, Señor, no tendré nunca una querida tan linda como esa querida que lucen los cromos de los libros viciosos!*
And I, Sir, I'll never have a mistress as beautiful as those in the pictures of obscene books!

1926 *El juguete rabioso* ('The Rabid Toy'), ch.2.

Armani, Giorgio 1935–

Italian fashion designer.

67 I believe that style is the only real luxury that is really desirable.

Attributed.

Armey, Dick (Richard Keith) 1940–

US Congressman and former economics lecturer.

68 It is like relying on the Flintstones for an understanding of the Stone Age.

1994 On economic data from the Congressional Budget Office. In *Time*, 25 Nov.

69 Entitlement spending—the politics of greed wrapped in the language of love.

1994 On President Johnson's legacy to his party. In the *US News & World Report*, 12 Dec.

Armistead, Lewis Addison 1817–63

Confederate general. Commissioned in the US army from Virginia, he resigned when that state seceded. He took part in Picket's charge at Gettysburg, where he was killed.

70 Give them the cold steel, boys!

1863 Attributed, during the American Civil War.

Armstrong, Lance 1971–

US cyclist. He won the Tour de France a record six times from 1999 to 2004.

71 My illness was also my antidote: it cured me of laziness.

2003 Referring to his recovery from cancer in *Every Second Counts*.

72 You know when I need to die? When I'm done living. When I can't walk, can't eat, can't see, when I'm a crotchety old bastard, mad at the world. Then I can die.

2003 *Every Second Counts*.

73 I'm on my bike.

When, during a furore about drug-taking by professional cyclists, he was asked: 'What are you on?'. Quoted in Graeme Fife *Tour de France—the History, the Legend, the Riders* (2000).

Armstrong, Louis *known as* Satchmo 1900–71

US jazz trumpeter and singer, the first major jazz virtuoso. He led studio groups such as the Hot Five and the Hot Seven as well as working with many big bands, and as a singer introduced the scat style. He toured extensively and appeared in over 50 films as a musician and entertainer.

74 Musicians don't retire; they stop when there's no more music in them.

1968 Quoted in the *Observer*, 21 Apr.

75 If you still have to ask…shame on you.

Habitual response when asked what is jazz? Quoted in M Jones *Salute to Satchmo* (1970).

76 All music is folk music. I ain't never heard no horse sing a song.

Quoted in the *New York Times*, 7 Jul 1971.

77 A lotta cats copy the Mona Lisa, but people still line up to see the original.

Alluding to his many imitators. Quoted in David Pickering *Brewer's Twentieth Century Music* (1994).

Armstrong, Neil A(lden) 1930–

US astronaut. A former fighter pilot, he commanded Gemini 8 (1966) and in 1969 was a crew member of Apollo 11, and the first man to walk on the moon.

78 That's one small step for a man, one giant leap forward for mankind.

1969 His words on becoming the first man to walk on the moon, 20 Jul. Armstrong claimed to have said 'That's one small step for a man…', but tape-recordings seem to confirm that he omitted the 'a', thereby causing some confusion among his listeners.

79 I believe every human has a finite number of heart-beats. I don't intend to waste any of mine running around doing exercises.

Quoted in Colin Jarman *The Guinness Dictionary of Sports Quotations* (1990).

Armstrong, Robert, Baron Armstrong of Ilminster 1927–

English civil servant. In 1970 he became principal private secretary to Prime Minister Edward Heath, and later Secretary to the Cabinet and Head of the Home Civil Service under Margaret Thatcher.

80 It contains a misleading impression, not a lie. It was being economical with the truth.

1986 On a letter, during cross-examination at the 'Spycatcher' trial, New South Wales, Australia, quoted in the *Daily Telegraph*, 19 Nov.

Arnald Amaury d.1225

French clergyman. Abbot of Citeaux (1202–12), he was the first inquisitor against the Albigensian heresy. In 1212 as Bishop of Narbonne he crusaded against the Moors in Spain.

81 Kill them all. God will recognize his own.

1209 Quoted in Caeserius of Heisterbach *Dialogus Miraculorum* (c.1233), bk.5, ch.21. Cited and translated in Jonathon Sumpton *The Albigensian Crusade* (1978), ch.6.

Arnold, Matthew 1822–88

English poet and critic. His poems, mainly elegiac in mood and on pastoral themes, include 'The Forsaken Merman' (1849), 'The Scholar-Gipsy' (1853) and 'Thyrsis' (1867). His critical works include *Essays in Criticism* (1865, 1888) and *Culture and Anarchy* (1869).

82 Come, dear children, let us away;
Down and away below!

1849 *The Strayed Reveller, and Other Poems*, 'The Forsaken Merman', l.1–2.

83 Now the great winds shorewards blow;
Now the salt tides seawards flow;
Now the wild white horses play,
Champ and chafe and toss in the spray.

1849 *The Strayed Reveller, and Other Poems*, 'The Forsaken Merman', l.4–7.

84 Sand-strewn caverns, cool and deep,
Where the winds are all asleep;
Where the spent lights quiver and gleam;
Where the salt weed sways in the stream.

1849 *The Strayed Reveller, and Other Poems*, 'The Forsaken Merman', l.35–8.

85 Where great whales come sailing by,
Sail and sail, with unshut eye,
Round the world for ever and aye.

1849 *The Strayed Reveller, and Other Poems*, 'The Forsaken Merman', l.43–5.

86 Not deep the Poet sees, but wide.

1849 *The Strayed Reveller, and Other Poems*, 'Resignation', l.214.

87 Yet they, believe me, who await
No gifts from chance, have conquered fate.

1849 *The Strayed Reveller, and Other Poems*, 'Resignation', l.247–8.

88 Not milder is the general lot
Because our spirits have forgot,
In action's dizzying eddy whirled,
The something that infects the world.

1849 *The Strayed Reveller, and Other Poems*, 'Resignation', l.275–8.

89 Others abide our question. Thou art free.
We ask and ask: Thou smilest and art still,
Out-topping knowledge.

1849 *The Strayed Reveller, and Other Poems*, 'Shakespeare'.

90 And thou, who didst the stars and sunbeams know,
Self-schooled, self-scanned, self-honoured, self-secure,
Didst tread on Earth unguessed at.—Better so!
All pains the immortal spirit must endure,
All weakness which impairs, all griefs which bow,
Find their sole speech in that victorious brow.

1849 *The Strayed Reveller, and Other Poems*, 'Shakespeare'.

91 Who saw life steadily, and saw it whole:
The mellow glory of the Attic stage;
Singer of sweet Colonus, and its child.

1849 Of Sophocles. *The Strayed Reveller, and Other Poems*, 'To a Friend'.

92 France, famed in all great arts, in none supreme.

1849 *The Strayed Reveller, and Other Poems*, 'To a Republican Friend—Continued'.

93 The sea of faith
Lay like the folds of a bright girdle furled.
But now I only hear
Its melancholy, long, withdrawing roar,
Retreating, to the breath
Of the night-wind, down the vast edges drear
And naked shingles of the world.

1851 'Dover Beach', stanza 3.

94 And we are here as on a darkling plain
Swept with confused alarms of struggle and flight,
Where ignorant armies clash by night.

1851 'Dover Beach', stanza 4.

95 Be neither saint nor sophist-led, but be a man.

1852 'Empedocles on Etna', act 1, sc.2, l.136.

96 Is it so small a thing
To have enjoyed the sun,
To have lived light in the spring,
To have loved, to have thought, to have done.

1852 'Empedocles on Etna', act 1, sc.2, l.397–400.

97 Because thou must not dream, thou needst not then despair!

1852 'Empedocles on Etna', act 1, sc.2, l.426.

98 And we forget because we must
And not because we will.

1852 *Empedocles on Etna and Other Poems*, 'Absence'.

99 Only—but this is rare—
When a beloved hand is laid in ours,
When, jaded with the rush and glare
Of the interminable hours,
Our eyes can in another's eyes read clear,
When our world-deafened ear
Is by the tones of a loved voice caressed—
A bolt is shot back somewhere in our breast,
And a lost pulse of feeling stirs again.
The eye sinks inward, and the heart lies plain,
And what we mean, we say, and what we would, we know.

1852 *Empedocles on Etna and Other Poems*, 'The Buried Life', l.77–87.

1 Come to me in my dreams, and then
By day I shall be well again!
For then the night will more than pay
The hopeless longing of the day.

1852 *Empedocles on Etna and Other Poems*, 'Longing' (later published as 'Faded Leaves' in *Poems: Second Series*, 1855).

2 Calm soul of all things! make it mine
To feel, amid the city's jar,
That there abides a peace of thine,
Man did not make, and cannot mar.

1852 *Empedocles on Etna and Other Poems*, 'Lines written in Kensington Garden'.

3 He spoke, and loosed our heart in tears.
He laid us as we lay at birth

On the cool flowery lap of earth.
1852 Of William Wordsworth. *Empedocles on Etna and Other Poems*, 'Memorial Verses, April 1850', l.47–9.

4 With aching hands and bleeding feet
We dig and heap, lay stone on stone;
We bear the burden and the heat
Of the long day, and wish 'twere done.
Not till the hours of light return,
All we have built do we discern.
1852 *Empedocles on Etna and Other Poems*, 'Morality'.

5 Say, has some wet bird-haunted English lawn
Lent it the music of its trees at dawn?
1852 *Empedocles on Etna and Other Poems*, 'Parting', l.19–20.

6 Resolve to be thyself: and know, that he
Who finds himself, loses his misery.
1852 *Empedocles on Etna and Other Poems*, 'Self-Dependence', l.31–2.

7 Ah! two desires toss about
The poet's feverish blood.
One drives him to the world without,
And one to solitude.
1852 *Empedocles on Etna and Other Poems*, 'Stanzas in Memory of the Author of "Obermann"', l.93–6.

8 Still bent to make some port he knows not where,
Still standing for some false impossible shore.
1852 *Empedocles on Etna and Other Poems*, 'A Summer Night', l.68–9.

9 Yes! in the sea of life enisled,
With echoing straits between us thrown,
Dotting the shoreless watery wild,
We mortal millions live alone.
1852 *Empedocles on Etna and Other Poems*, 'To Marguerite—Continued', l.1–4.

10 A God, a God their severance ruled!
And bade betwixt their shores to be
The unplumbed, salt, estranging sea.
1852 *Empedocles on Etna and Other Poems*, 'To Marguerite—Continued', l.22–4.

11 I am past thirty, and three parts iced over.
1853 Letter to Arthur Hugh Clough, 12 Feb

12 Hark! ah, the Nightingale!
The tawny-throated!
Hark! from that moonlit cedar what a burst!
What triumph! hark—what pain!
1853 *Poems: A New Edition*, 'Philomela', l.1–4.

13 Eternal Passion!
Eternal Pain!
1853 *Poems: A New Edition*, 'Philomela', l.31–2.

14 Her cabined ample Spirit,
It fluttered and failed for breath.
Tonight it doth inherit
The vasty hall of death.
1853 *Poems: A New Edition*, 'Requiescat'.

15 Go, for they call you, Shepherd, from the hill.
1853 *Poems: A New Edition*, 'The Scholar-Gipsy', l.1.

16 All the live murmur of a summer's day.
1853 *Poems: A New Edition*, 'The Scholar-Gipsy', l.20.

17 Tired of knocking at Preferment's door.
1853 *Poems: A New Edition*, 'The Scholar-Gipsy', l.35.

18 Crossing the stripling Thames at Bab-lock-hithe,
Trailing in the cool stream thy fingers wet,
As the slow punt swings round.
1853 *Poems: A New Edition*, 'The Scholar-Gipsy', l.74–6.

19 Rapt, twirling in thy hand a withered spray,
And waiting for the spark from heaven to fall.
1853 *Poems: A New Edition*, 'The Scholar-Gipsy', l.119–20.

20 The line of festal light in Christ-Church hall.
1853 *Poems: A New Edition*, 'The Scholar-Gipsy', l.129.

21 Thou waitest for the spark from heaven! and we,
Light half-believers in our casual creeds...
Who hesitate and falter life away,
And lose tomorrow the ground won today—
Ah, do not we, Wanderer, await it too?
1853 *Poems: A New Edition*, 'The Scholar-Gipsy', l.171–4.

22 O born in days when wits were fresh and clear,
And life ran gaily as the sparkling Thames:
Before this strange disease of modern life,
With its sick hurry, its divided aims,
Its heads o'ertaxed, its palsied hearts, was rife—
Fly hence, our contact fear!
1853 *Poems: A New Edition*, 'The Scholar-Gipsy', l.201–6.

23 Still nursing the unconquerable hope,
Still clutching the inviolable shade.
1853 *Poems: A New Edition*, 'The Scholar-Gipsy', l.211–12.

24 Curled minion, dancer, coiner of sweet words!
1853 *Poems: A New Edition*, 'Sohrab and Rustum', l.458.

25 No horse's cry was that, most like the roar
Of some pained desert lion, who all day
Hath trailed the hunter's javelin in his side,
And comes at night to die upon the sand.
1853 *Poems: A New Edition*, 'Sohrab and Rustum', l.501–4.

26 Truth sits upon the lips of dying men.
1853 *Poems: A New Edition*, 'Sohrab and Rustum', l.656.

27 But the majestic river floated on,
Out of the mist and hum of that low land,
Into the frosty starlight.
1853 *Poems: A New Edition*, 'Sohrab and Rustum', l.875–7.

28 Oxus, forgetting the bright speed he had
In his high mountain cradle in Pamere,
A foiled circuitous wanderer—till at last
The longed-for dash of waves is heard, and wide
His luminous home of waters opens, bright
And tranquil, from whose floor the new-bathed stars
Emerge, and shine upon the Aral Sea.
1853 *Poems: A New Edition*, 'Sohrab and Rustrum', l.886–92.

29 Cruel, but composed and bland,
Dumb, inscrutable and grand,
So Tiberius might have sat,
Had Tiberius been a cat.
1855 *Poems: Second Series*, 'Poor Matthias', l.40–3.

30 For rigorous teachers seized my youth,
And other its faith, and trimmed its fire,
Showed me the high, white star of Truth,
There bade me gaze, and there aspire.
1855 *Poems: Second Series*, 'Stanzas from the Grande Chartreuse', l.67–70.

31 Wandering between two worlds, one dead,
The other powerless to be born,
With nowhere yet to rest my head,
Like these, on earth I wait forlorn.
1855 *Poems: Second Series*, 'Stanzas from the Grande Chartreuse', l.85–8.

32 What helps it now, that Byron bore,
With haughty scorn which mocked the smart,
Through Europe to the Aetolian shore
The pageant of his bleeding heart?
That thousands counted every groan,
And Europe made his woe her own?
1855 *Poems: Second Series*, 'Stanzas from the Grande Chartreuse', l.133–8.

33 This truth—to prove, and make thine own:
'Thou hast been, shalt be, art, alone.'
1857 'Isolation. To Marguerite', l.29-30.

34 Wordsworth says somewhere that wherever Virgil seems to have composed 'with his eye on the object', Dryden fails to render him. Homer invariably composes 'with his eye on the object', whether the object be moral or a material one: Pope composes with his eye on his style, into which he translates his object, whatever it is.
1861 *On Translating Homer*, lecture 1.

35 Of these two literatures [French and German], as of the intellect of Europe in general, the main effort, for now many years, has been a critical effort; the endeavours, in all branches of knowledge—theology, philosophy, history, art, science—to see the object as in itself it really is.
1861 *On Translating Homer*, lecture 2.

36 [The translator] will find one English book and one only, where, as in the *Iliad* itself, perfect plainness of speech is allied with perfect nobleness; and that book is the Bible.
1861 *On Translating Homer*, lecture 3.

37 Nothing has raised more questioning among my critics than these words—noble, the grand style… I think it will be found that the grand style arises in poetry, when a noble nature, poetically gifted, treats with simplicity or with severity a serious subject.
1862 *On Translating Homer; Last Words*.

38 Nothing could moderate, in the bosom of the great English middle class, their passionate, absorbing, almost blood-thirsty clinging to life.
1865 *Essays in Criticism First Series*, preface.

39 Beautiful city! so venerable, so lovely, so unravaged by the fierce intellectual life of our century, so serene!…whispering from her towers the last enchantments of the Middle Age… Home of lost causes, and forsaken beliefs, and unpopular names, and impossible loyalties!
1865 Of Oxford. *Essays in Criticism First Series*, preface.

40 I am bound by my own definition of criticism: a disinterested endeavour to learn and propagate the best that is known and thought in the world.
1865 *Essays in Criticism First Series*, 'The Function of Criticism at the Present Time'.

41 Philistinism!—We have not the expression in English. Perhaps we have not the word because we have so much of the thing.
1865 *Essays in Criticism First Series*, 'Heinrich Heine'.

42 The great apostle of the Philistine, Lord Macaulay.
1865 *Essays in Criticism First Series*, 'Joubert'.

43 The signal-elm, that looks on Ilsley downs,
The Vale, the three lone weirs, the youthful Thames.
1866 *New Poems*, 'Thyrsis', l.14–15. The poem is an elegy for his friend Arthur Hugh Clough, who drowned in 1861.

44 And that sweet City with her dreaming spires,
She needs not June for beauty's heightening.
1866 Of Oxford. *New Poems*, 'Thyrsis', l.19–20.

45 So have I heard the cuckoo's parting cry,
From the wet field, through the vext garden trees,
Come with the volleying rain and tossing breeze:
'The bloom is gone, and with the bloom go I.'
1866 *New Poems*, 'Thyrsis', l.57–60.

46 Too quick despairer, wherefore wilt thou go?
Soon will the high Midsummer pomps come on,
Soon will the musk carnations break and swell.
1866 *New Poems*, 'Thyrsis', l.61–3.

47 For Time, not Corydon, hath conquered thee.
1866 *New Poems*, 'Thyrsis', l.80.

48 The foot less prompt to meet the morning dew,
The heart less bounding at emotion new,
And hope, once crushed, less quick to spring again.
1866 *New Poems*, 'Thyrsis', l.138–40.

49 It is not in the outward and visible world of material life that the Celtic genius of Wales or Ireland can at this day hope to count for much; it is in the inward world of thought and science. What it *has* been, what is *has* done, what it will be or will do, as a matter of modern politics.
1867 'On the Study of Celtic Literature'

50 Let us reunite ourselves with our better mind and with the world through science; and let it be one of our angelic revenges on the Philistines, who among their other sins are the guilty authors of Fenianism, to found at Oxford a chair of Celtic, and to send, through the gentle ministration of science, a message of peace to Ireland.
1867 'On the Study of Celtic Literature'.

51 Creep into thy narrow bed,
Creep, and let no more be said!
Vain thy onset! all stands fast.
Thou thyself must break at last.
Let the long contention cease!
Geese are swans, and swans are geese.
Let them have it how they will!
Thou art tired; best be still.
1867 *New Poems*, 'The Last Word'.

52 Coldly, sadly descends
The autumn evening. The field
Strewn with its dank yellow drifts
Of withered leaves, and the elms,
Fade into dimness apace,
Silent;—hardly a shout
From a few boys late at their play!
1867 *New Poems*, 'Rugby Chapel, November 1857'.

53 Our society distributes itself into Barbarians, Philistines, and Populace; and America is just ourselves, with the Barbarians quite left out, and the Populace nearly.
1869 *Culture and Anarchy*, preface.

54 The pursuit of perfection, then, is the pursuit of sweetness and light… He who works for sweetness and light united, works to make reason and the will of God prevail.
1869 *Culture and Anarchy*, ch.1.

55 The men of culture are the true apostles of equality.
1869 *Culture and Anarchy*, ch.1.

56 That vast portion…of the working-class which, raw and

half-developed has long lain half-hidden amidst its poverty and squalor, and is now issuing from its hiding-place to assert an Englishman's heaven-born privilege of doing as he likes, and is beginning to perplex us by marching where it likes, meeting where it likes, bawling what it likes, breaking what it likes—to this vast residuum we may with great propriety give the name of Populace.
1869 *Culture and Anarchy*, ch.3.

57 Hebraism and Hellenism—between these two points of influence moves our world.
1869 *Culture and Anarchy*, ch.4.

58 'He knows' says Hebraism, 'his Bible!'—whenever we hear this said, we may, without any elaborate defence of culture, content ourselves with answering simply: 'No man, who knows nothing else, knows even his Bible.'
1869 *Culture and Anarchy*, ch.5.

59 Culture, the acquainting ourselves with the best that has been known and said in the world, and thus with the history of the human spirit.
1873 *Literature and Dogma*, preface.

60 Culture is the passion for sweetness and light, and (what is more) the passion for making them prevail.
1873 *Literature and Dogma*, preface.

61 The true meaning of religion is thus not simply morality, but morality touched with emotion.
1873 *Literature and Dogma*, ch.1.

62 Conduct is three-fourths of our life and its largest concern.
1873 *Literature and Dogma*, ch.1.

63 The eternal *not ourselves* that makes for righteousness.
1873 *Literature and Dogma*, ch.8.

64 But there remains the question: what righteousness really is. The method and secret and sweet reasonableness of Jesus.
1873 *Literature and Dogma*, ch.12.

65 So we have the Philistine of genius in religion—Luther; the Philistine of genius in politics—Cromwell; the Philistine of genius in literature—Bunyan.
1879 *Mixed Essays*, 'Lord Falkland'.

66 The theatre is irresistible: organise the theatre.
1882 *Irish Essays*, 'The French Play in London'.

67 In poetry, no less than in life, he is 'a beautiful and ineffectual angel, beating in the void his luminous wings in vain'.
1888 Of Shelley. *Essays in Criticism Second Series*, 'Shelley'. The phrase is a quotation from his own work on Byron.

68 More and more mankind will discover that we have to turn to poetry to interpret life for us, to console us, to sustain us. Without poetry, our science will appear incomplete; and most of what now passes with us for religion and philosophy will be replaced by poetry.
1888 *Essays in Criticism Second Series*, 'The Study of Poetry'.

69 The difference between genuine poetry and the poetry of Dryden, Pope, and all their school, is briefly this: their poetry is conceived and composed in their wits, genuine poetry is conceived and composed in the soul.
1888 *Essays in Criticism Second Series*, 'Thomas Gray'.

70 Poetry is at bottom a criticism of life.
1888 *Essays in Criticism Second Series*, 'Wordsworth'.

71 His expression may often be called bald…but it is bald as the bare mountain tops are bald, with a baldness full of grandeur.
1888 *Essays in Criticism Second Series*, 'Wordsworth'.

Arnold, Thomas 1795–1842

British educator and historian, educational reformer who introduced mathematics, modern languages, and modern history into the curriculum of his day.

72 My object will be, if possible, to form Christian men, for Christian boys I can scarcely hope to make.
1828 Letter to Rev John Tucker, 2 Mar, on being appointed headmaster of Rugby School.

73 Rather than have it the principal thing in my son's mind, I would gladly have him think that the sun went around the earth, and that the stars were so many spangles set in the bright blue firmament.
1836 Letter to Dr Greenhill, 9 May.

Arnold, Thurman Wesley 1891–1969

US lawyer, Professor at Yale (1930–8), Assistant Attorney General in charge of anti-trust enforcement (1938–43) and Associate Justice at the Court of Appeals (1943–5).

74 We must protect big business from domination by fat-minded men whose principal business policy is to avoid a competitive race for efficiency… They believe in a system of soft enterprise,—soft in the way that an octopus is soft, with tentacles that stifle and suffocate.
1942 'The Abuse of Patents', in *Atlantic Monthly*, Jul.

Aron, Raymond Claude Ferdinand 1905–83

French sociologist and journalist, editor of *La France Libre* in London (1940–4).

75 To customs and beliefs, the very ones we hold sacred, sociology ruthlessly attaches the adjective 'arbitrary'.
1971 *Politics and History.*

76 In a way, all sociologists are akin to Marxists because of their inclination to settle everyone's accounts but their own.
1971 *Politics and History.*

Arras, Jean d' *also known as* Jean Blondel fl.c.1375

French writer. He collaborated with Antoine du Val and Fouquart de Cambrai on the *Évangile des Quenouilles*, which provides much information on life at the time.

77 *Bonté vaut mieux que beauté.*
Kindness is worth more than beauty.
c.1393 *Melusine.*

Asahi Shimbun

Leading mass-circulation newspaper in Japan.

78 Are we correct to have changed as much as we have? Or is Yokoi correct not to have changed at all?
1972 Editorial comment, 28 Jan, on the discovery of World War II survivor Sergeant Yokoi in the Pacific jungles.

Ascham, Roger 1515–68

English humanist, Protestant and scholar, reader in Greek at Cambridge, and tutor to Princess Elizabeth. He published a defence of archery, *Toxophilus*, in 1545, and is most famous for his treatise on humanist education, *The Schoolmaster* (1570).

79 He that will write well in any tongue, must follow this counsel of Aristotle, to speak as the common people do, to think as wise men do; and so should every man understand him, and the judgment of wise men allow him.
1545 *Toxophilus*, 'To all Gentlemen and Yeomen of England'.

80 Young children [are] sooner allured by love than driven by beating to attain good learning.
1570 *The Schoolmaster*, 'A Preface to the Reader'.

81 For [the] quick in wit and light in manners be either seldom troubled or very soon weary, in carrying a very heavy purse.
1570 *The Schoolmaster*, bk.2.

Ashbery, John Lawrence 1927–

US poet, critic and novelist. Poetry collections include the award-winning *Self-Portrait in a Convex Mirror* (1976).

82 Darkness falls like a wet sponge.
1956 *Some Trees*, 'The Picture of Little J. A. in a Prospect of Flowers', opening line.

83 And it is the colour of sand,
The darkness, as it sifts through your hand.
1962 *The Tennis Court Oath*, 'How Much Longer Will I Be Able To Inhabit The Divine Sepulcher...'.

84 Self-portrait in a Convex Mirror.
1976 Title of book.

85 Slated for demolition.
1979 Complete text of poem entitled 'The Cathedral Is', in *As We Know*.

86 Still I enjoy
The long sweetness of the simultaneity, yours and mine, ours and mine,
The mosquitoey summer night light.
1981 *Shadow Train*, 'Here Everything Is Still Floating'.

87 My name has gotten to be a household word — at least in certain households. I think there are now people who know my name, but don't know what I do. I'm famous for being famous.
1985 Interview in *PN Review*, no.46.

88 There is the view that poetry should improve your life. I think people confuse it with the Salvation Army.
1989 In the *International Herald Tribune*, 2 Oct.

Ashdown (of Norton-sub-Hamdon), Paddy Ashdown, Baron 1941–

British politician. After working with the Royal Marines (1959–71) and the diplomatic service (1971–6), he was an MP (1983–2001) and leader of the Liberal Democrats (1988–99).

89 Neil Kinnock has travelled the road to Damascus so often, I hear that he has decided to buy himself a season ticket.
1990 At the Liberal Democratic Party conference, Sep.

90 The ringmaster has altered, but the circus remains the same.
1990 On John Major's election as Conservative Party leader, in the *Observer*, 2 Dec.

91 I have learnt from bitter experience that when the armchair theorists and the Whitehall generals start talking of a surgical war, it is time to run for cover.
1991 Referring to plans for the Gulf War. In the *Sunday Times*, 27 Jan.

92 There can be no place in a 21st-century parliament for people with 15th-century titles upholding 19th-century prejudices.
1998 In *The Independent*, 24 Nov.

Ashford, Daisy Mary Margaret 1881–1972

English writer. She wrote her only book, *The Young Visiters*, in 1890, and published the manuscript in 1919. Its childish idiosyncrasies made it a best-seller, and it was adapted for the stage in 1920, and as a musical in 1968.

93 Mr Salteena was an elderly man of 42 and was fond of asking peaple to stay with him.
1890 *The Young Visiters, or Mr Salteena's Plan*, ch.1.

94 You look rather rash my dear your colors don't quite match your face.
1890 *The Young Visiters, or Mr Salteena's Plan*, ch.2.

95 Bernard always had a few prayers in the hall and some whiskey afterwards as he was rather pious but Mr Salteena was not very addicted to prayers so he marched up to bed.
1890 *The Young Visiters, or Mr Salteena's Plan*, ch.3.

96 Oh I see said the Earl but my own idear is that these things are as piffle before the wind.
1890 *The Young Visiters, or Mr Salteena's Plan*, ch.5.

97 I am very fond of fresh air and royalties.
1890 *The Young Visiters, or Mr Salteena's Plan*, ch.5.

98 The bearer of this letter is an old friend of mine not quite the right side of the blanket as they say in fact he is the son of a first rate butcher but his mother was a decent family called Hyssopps of the Glen so you see he is not so bad and is desireus of being the correct article.
1890 *The Young Visiters, or Mr Salteena's Plan*, ch.5.

99 My life will be sour grapes and ashes without you.
1890 *The Young Visiters, or Mr Salteena's Plan*, ch.8.

1 Oh Bernard muttered Ethel this is so sudden. No no cried Bernard and taking the bull by both horns he kissed her violently on her dainty face.
1890 *The Young Visiters, or Mr Salteena's Plan*, ch.9.

2 She had very nice feet and plenty of money.
1890 *The Young Visiters, or Mr Salteena's Plan*, ch.12.

Asimov, Isaac 1920–92

Russian-born US science-fiction novelist and popular scientist. A distinguished biochemist and hugely popular writer, he became a familiar media figure. His works include the 'Foundation' series (1951–3). He coined the term 'robotics'.

3 How many people is the earth able to sustain?
1971 *Der Spiegel*.

4 Science fiction writers foresee the inevitable, and although problems and catastrophes may be inevitable, solutions are not.
1975 'How Easy To See The Future', in *Natural History*, Apr.

5 If there is a category of human being for whom his work ought to speak for itself, it is the writer.
1976 Comment in D L Fitzpatrick (ed) *Contemporary Novelists*.

6 It is change, continuing change, inevitable change, that is the dominant factor in our society today... This, in turn, means that our statesmen, our businessmen, our everyman must take on a science fictional way of thinking.

1978 'My Own View', in R Holdstock (ed) *Encyclopedia of Science Fiction* (1978).

Aslet, Clive William 1955–

English journalist, editor of *Country Life* (1993–).

7 Biography is now more or less a branch of psychiatry.
1994 In *Country Life*, 10 Nov, reviewing Jonathan Dimbleby *The Prince of Wales: A Biography* (1994).

8 We expect the ticking movement of the human timepiece to be revealed.
1994 In *Country Life*, 10 Nov, reviewing Jonathan Dimbleby *The Prince of Wales: A Biography* (1994).

Asquith, Herbert Henry, 1st Earl of Oxford and Asquith 1852–1928

British Liberal politician and Prime Minister. He became an MP (1886), Home Secretary (1892–5), Chancellor (1906) and Prime Minister (1908–16). His period in office was marked by the introduction of old age pensions, the Parliament Act of 1911, the declaration of war (1914) and the Sinn Féin rebellion (1916). A coalition with Conservatives hastened his resignation. He wrote *Memories and Reflections* (1928).

9 We shall never sheath the sword which we have not lightly drawn until Belgium recovers in full measure all and more than all that she has sacrificed, until France is adequately assured against the menace of aggression, until the rights of the smaller nationalities of Europe are placed upon an unassailable foundation and until the military domination of Prussia is wholly and finally destroyed.
1914 Speech at the Guildhall, London, 9 Nov.

10 It is fitting that we should have buried the unknown Prime Minister by the side of the Unknown Soldier.
1923 Remark at the Westminster Abbey funeral of Bonar Law, 5 Nov.

11 One to mislead the public, another to mislead the Cabinet, and the third to mislead itself.
Of the three sets of figures kept by the War Office. Quoted in Alistair Horne *Price of Glory* (1962).

Asquith, Margot 1864–1945

Scottish society figure and wit, wife of Herbert Asquith (married 1894). Her group 'The Souls' advocated greater freedom for women. She continued her extravagant lifestyle through the war, and when Asquith was forced to resign (1916) wrote two sensational autobiographies.

12 If Kitchener is not a great man, he is, at least, a great poster.
Quoted in P Magnus *Kitchener: Portrait of an Imperialist*. Lady Asquith uses the phrase in her *Memories* (1933), but attributes it to her daughter Elizabeth.

13 She tells enough white lies to ice a wedding cake.
Of Lady Desborough. Quoted in *The Listener*, 11 Jun 1953.

14 David Lloyd George could not see a belt without hitting underneath it.
Quoted in *The Listener*, 11 Jun 1953.

15 Stafford Cripps has a brilliant mind, until he makes it up.
Quoted in *The Wit of the Asquiths* (published 1974).

16 F E Smith is very clever, but sometimes he lets his brains go to his head.
Quoted in *The Wit of the Asquiths* (published 1974).

17 The t is silent, as in Harlow.
Attributed riposte to Jean Harlow who was having trouble pronouncing her name. The line may actually have been spoken by Margot Grahame, an English actress in Hollywood in the 1930s.

18 I have no face, only two profiles clapped together.
Attributed.

Asquith of Yarnbury, (Helen) Violet Bonham-Carter, Baroness 1887–1969

English Liberal politician and publicist, daughter of Herbert Asquith. A prominent society figure, she was president of the Liberal Party Organization (1944–5) and governor of the BBC (1941–6).

19 Harold Macmillan held his party together by not allowing his left wing to see what his right wing was doing.
Attributed.

Astell, Mary 1668–1731

English writer, the 'first British feminist'. Orphaned in 1684, she moved alone to London in about 1686. In *A Serious Proposal to the Ladies* (1694) she argues for the education of women. *Some Reflections Upon Marriage* (1700, 2nd edn 1706) highlights the disadvantages of marriage for women.

20 Your glass will not do you half so much service as a serious reflection of your own minds.
1694 *A Serious Proposal to the Ladies For the Advancement of their True and Greatest Interest*, 'By a Lover of Her Sex', pt.1.

21 Women are from their very Infancy debarred those advantages, with the want of which they are afterwards reproached, and nursed up in those vices which will hereafter be upbraided to them. So partial are men as to expect brick where they afford no straw.
1694 *A Serious Proposal to the Ladies For the Advancement of their True and Greatest Interest*, 'By a Lover of Her Sex', pt.1.

22 Fetters of gold are still fetters, and the softest lining can never make them so easy as liberty.
1696 An Essay in Defence of the Female Sex.

23 If absolute sovereignty be not necessary in a State, how comes it to be so in a family?
1706 *Some Reflections upon Marriage Occasion'd by the Duke and Duchess of Mazarine's Case which is also consider'd*, preface (1706 edn).

24 If all men are born free, how is it that all women are born slaves? as they must be if the being subjected to the inconsistent, uncertain, unknown, arbitrary will of men, be the perfect condition of slavery? and if the essence of freedom consists, as our masters say it does, in having a standing rule to live by? And why is slavery so much condemned and strove against in one case, and so highly applauded, and held so necessary and so sacred in another?
1706 *Some Reflections upon Marriage Occasion'd by the Duke and Duchess of Mazarine's Case which is also consider'd*, preface (1706 edn).

25 But if marriage be such a blessed state, how comes it, may you say, that there are so few happy marriages? Now in answer to this, is it not to be wondered that so few succeed, we should rather be surprized to find so many do, considering how imprudently men engage, the

motive they act by, and the very strange conduct they observe throughout.
1706 *Some Reflections upon Marriage Occasion'd by the Duke and Duchess of Mazarine's Case which is also consider'd*, preface (1706 edn).

26 A woman indeed can't properly be said to choose, all that is allowed her, is to refuse or accept what is offered.
1706 *Some Reflections upon Marriage Occasion'd by the Duke and Duchess of Mazarine's Case which is also consider'd*, preface (1706 edn).

Astley, Sir Jacob 1579–1652

English Royalist commander, leader of Charles I's last remaining army which surrendered in March 1646.

27 O Lord! Thou knowest how busy I must be this day: if I forget thee, do not thou forget me.
1642 Prayer before the Battle of Edgehill, 23 Oct. Quoted in Sir Philip Warwick *Memoires* (1702).

28 You have now done your work and may go play, unless you will fall out amongst yourselves.
1646 Remark to his Parliamentarian captors, Mar. Quoted in Samuel Rawson Gardiner *History of the Great Civil War, 1642–9* (1911), vol.3.

Astor (of Hever Castle), Nancy Witcher Astor, Viscountess *née Langhorne* 1879–1964

US-born British politician, the first woman MP to sit in the House of Commons. She was especially interested in social problems, including women's rights and temperance.

29 I married beneath me. All women do.
1951 Speech, Oldham.

30 You will never get on in politics, my dear, with *that* hair.
Attributed remark addressed to Shirley Williams.

Asturias, Miguel Ángel 1889–1974

Guatemalan poet, novelist and diplomat, winner of the Nobel prize for literature in 1967 and the Soviet Union's Lenin Peace Prize in 1966.

31 *Como te decía al principio, nadie hace nada y, naturalmente, soy yo, es el Presidente de la República el que lo tiene que hacer todo, aunque salga como el cohetero. Con decir que si no fuera por mí no existiría la fortuna, ya que hasta de diosa ciega tengo que hacer en la lotería.*
But, as I told you, nobody ever does a thing, and so naturally it is I, the President of the Republic, who has to do everything, and take all the blame as well. You might almost say that if it weren't for me Fortune wouldn't exist, as I have even to take the part of the blind goddess in the lottery.
1946 *El señor presidente* (*The President*, 1963), pt.3, ch.37.

Atatürk, Mustapha Kemal 1880–1938

Turkish soldier and statesman, founder and first President (1923–38) of the Turkish Republic. In the subsequent social and political revolution he encouraged westernization. He took the title Atatürk, 'Father of the Turks', in 1935.

32 It was necessary to abolish the fez, emblem of ignorance, negligence, fanaticism and hatred of progress and civilization, to accept in its place the hat—the headgear worn by the whole civilized world.
1927 From his six-day speech to the Turkish Assembly, Oct.

Atkinson, Brooks 1894–1984

US journalist and theatre critic.

33 After each war there is a little less democracy to save.
1951 *Once Around the Sun*.

34 Thanks for tomorrow, thanks for last week, thanks for next Friday—in fact thanks for everything except last night.
Reviewing Le Roy Bailey's *Thanks for Tomorrow*. Quoted in the *New York Times*, 14 Jan 1984.

Atkinson, Ron 1939–

English football manager. He played for Oxford United until 1971 and subsequently managed teams including West Bromwich Albion, Atlético Madrid, Manchester United, Sheffield Wednesday, Aston Villa and Coventry City, before becoming a commentator.

35 It's bloody tough being a legend.
1983 Quoted in Peter Ball and Phil Shaw *The Book of Football Quotations* (1989).

Atlas, Charles 1894–1972

US bodybuilder.

36 You too can have a body like mine!
c.1922 Advertising slogan.

Atlas, James 1949–

US writer and critic, contributor to the *New Yorker* and former editor at the *New York Times Magazine*.

37 A penumbra of somber dignity has descended over his reputation.
1985 Of Edmund Wilson. In the *New York Times*, 28 Jul, reviewing David Castronovo *Edmund Wilson* (1984).

38 To read Wilson…is to be instructed and amused in the highest sense—that is educated.
1985 Of Edmund Wilson. In the *New York Times*, 28 Jul, reviewing David Castronovo *Edmund Wilson* (1984).

Attenborough, Sir David Frederick 1923–

English naturalist and broadcaster, a respected and popular wildlife documentary maker. His series include *Life on Earth* (1979), *The Living Planet* (1984) and *Life in the Freezer* (1993).

39 Most of the animals that appeared on British television screens in 1950 did so sitting on door-mats.
1982 *The Zoo Quest Expeditions*.

Attlee (of Walthamstow), Clement (Richard) Attlee, 1st Earl 1883–1967

English Labour politician, Deputy Prime Minister in Churchill's war cabinet (1942–5) and Prime Minister (1945–51). During his administration the National Health Service was established and India and Burma were given independence.

40 We believe in a League system in which the whole world should be ranged against an aggressor… We do not think that you can deal with national armaments by piling up national armaments in other countries.
1935 House of Commons, 11 Mar.

41 We have seen today a gallant, civilized and democratic people betrayed and handed over to a ruthless despotism.
1938 House of Commons speech on Czechoslovakia, 3 Oct.

42 I count our progress by the extent to which what we cried in the wilderness five and thirty years ago has now become part of the assumptions of the ordinary man and woman… It is better to argue from what has been done to what may be done, rather than to suggest that very little has been accomplished.
1944 Of the Labour Party. Letter to Harold J Laski, 1 May.

43 I have been very happy…serving in a state of life to which I had never expected to be called.
1954 *As It Happened.*

44 Few thought he was even a starter
There were many who thought themselves smarter
But he ended PM
CH and OM
An earl and a knight of the garter.
1956 A limerick on himself, in a letter to Tom Attlee, 8 Apr.

45 Russian communism is the illegitimate child of Karl Marx and Catherine the Great.
1956 Speech, Aarhus University, 11 Apr.

46 Democracy means government by discussion, but it is only effective if you can stop people talking.
1957 Speech, Oxford, 14 Jun.

47 The House of Lords is like a glass of champagne that has stood for five days.
Attributed.

Atwood, Margaret Eleanor 1939–

Canadian writer, poet and critic. Her first book of poetry, *The Circle Game* (1966), won the Governor General's Award. Her novels include *The Edible Woman* (1969) and *The Robber Bride* (1993). She won the Booker Prize in 2000 for *The Blind Assassin.*

48 (The photograph was taken
the day after I drowned.
I am in the lake, in the center
of the picture, just under the surface.)
1966 *The Circle Game*, 'This is a Photograph of Me'.

49 we flounder, the air
ungainly in our new lungs
with sunlight streaming merciless on the shores of morning
1966 *The Circle Game*, 'Pre- Amphibian'.

50 He stood, a point
on a sheet of green paper
proclaiming himself the center,
with no walls, no borders
anywhere; the sky no height
above him, totally un-
enclosed
and shouted:
Let me out!
1968 *The Animals in that Country*, 'Progressive Insanities of a Pioneer'.

51 Marriage is not
a house or even a tent
it is before that, and colder.
1970 *Procedures from Underground*, 'Habitation'.

52 If the national mental illness of the United States is megalomania, that of Canada is paranoid schizophrenia.
1970 *The Journals of Susanna Moodie: Poems by Margaret Atwood*, afterword.

53 We are all immigrants to this place even if we were born here: the country is too big for anyone to inhabit completely, and in the parts unknown to us we move in fear, exiles and invaders.
1970 Writing of Canada and Canadians in *The Journals of Susanna Moodie: Poems by Margaret Atwood*, afterword.

54 Possibly the symbol for America is the Frontier… The corresponding symbol for England is the Island… The central symbol for Canada…is undoubtedly Survival, *la Survivance.*
1972 *Survival: a Thematic Guide to Canadian Literature*, ch.1, 'Survival'.

55 This above all, to refuse to be a victim. Unless I can do that I am nothing.
1972 *Surfacing.*

56 Mirrors
are the perfect lovers.
1974 *You are Happy*, 'Tricks with Mirrors'.

57 You are suspended in me
beautiful and frozen, I
preserve you, in me you are safe.
1974 *You Are Happy*, 'Tricks with Mirrors'.

58 To live in prison is to live without mirrors. To live without mirrors is to live without the self.
1978 *Two-headed Poems*, 'Marrying the Hangman'.

59 I would like to be the air
that inhabits you for a moment
only. I would like to be that unnoticed
and that necessary.
1981 *True Stories*, 'Variation on the Word *Sleep*'.

60 At some time during that hour, though not for the whole hour, I forgot what things were called and saw instead what they are.
1983 *Murder in the Dark*, 'Strawberries'.

61 Canada was open for business. And closed for everything else.
1988 Essay on censorship in *The Globe and Mail*, 'The Porn Patrol', 18 Feb. Collected in Douglas Fetherling (ed) *Best Canadian Essays* (1989).

62 Who knows what evil lurks in the hearts of men? An older woman knows. But how much older do you have to get before you acquire that kind of wisdom?
1993 *The Robber Bride*, ch.48.

63 His father was self-made, but his mother was constructed by others, and such edifices are notoriously fragile.
1996 *Alias Grace.*

64 Publishing a book is often very much like being put on trial for some offence which is quite other than the one you know in your heart you've committed.
2002 *Negotiating with the Dead: A Writer on Writing.*

Auber, Daniel-François-Esprit 1782–1871

French composer of operas. His best-known works are *La Muette de Portici*, usually entitled *Masaniello* (1828), and *Fra Diavolo* (1830).

65 Well, there's no help for it. Ageing seems to be the only available way to live a long time.
Attributed, when a friend lamented that they were both getting older. Quoted in Clifton Fadiman *The Faber Book of Anecdotes* (1985).

Aubrey, John 1626–97

English antiquary. Only his credulous *Miscellanies* (1696) of folklore and ghost stories were printed in his lifetime, and his colourful biographical anecdotes were later collected as *Letters by Eminent Persons* (1813), better known as *Brief Lives*.

66 How these curiosities would be quite forgot, did not such idle fellows as I am put them down.
1693 *Brief Lives* (published 1813), 'Venetia Digby'.

67 He had read much, if one considers his long life; but his contemplation was much more than his reading. He was wont to say that if he had read as much as other men, he should have known no more than other men.
1693 Of Thomas Hobbes. *Brief Lives* (published 1813), 'Thomas Hobbes'.

68 His harmonical and ingenious soul did lodge in a beautiful and well proportioned body. He was a spare man.... He was so fair that they called him the *lady* of Christ's College.
1693 Of Milton. *Brief Lives* (published 1813), 'John Milton'.

69 Sir Walter, being strangely surprised and put out of his countenance at so great a table, gives his son a damned blow over the face. His son, as rude as he was, would not strike his father, but strikes over the face the gentleman that sat next to him and said 'Box about: 'twill come to my father anon.'
1693 *Brief Lives* (published 1813), 'Sir Walter Raleigh'.

70 When he killed a calf he would do it in a high style, and make a speech.
1693 *Brief Lives* (published 1813), 'William Shakespeare'. Aubrey had been misinformed that Shakespeare's father was a butcher. He was in fact a glover.

71 The first sense he had of God was when he was eleven years old at Chigwell being retired into a chamber alone: he was so suddenly surprised with a sense of inward comfort and (as he thought) an external glory in the room that he had many times said that from thence he has the Seal of Divinity and Immortality, that there was a God and that the soul of man was capable of enjoying his divine communications.
1693 Of William Penn, early Quaker. *Brief Lives* (published 1813).

Auchincloss, Louis Stanton 1917–

US writer and critic, who studied law. His works chronicle the life of New York City and its inhabitants, particularly the aristocracy. His works include *Venus in Sparta* (1958) and *Pursuit of the Prodigal* (1960).

72 Perfection irritates as well as it attracts, in fiction as in life.
1965 *Pioneers and Caretakers: A Study of Nine American Women Novelists*.

73 A neurotic can perfectly well be a literary genius, but his greatest danger is always that he will not recognize when he is dull.
1965 *Pioneers and Caretakers: A Study of Nine American Women Novelists*.

74 The glittering structure of her cultivation sits on her novels like a rather showy icing that detracts from the cake beneath.
1965 Of Edith Wharton. *Pioneers and Caretakers: A Study of Nine American Women Novelists*.

75 I would rather see the old reservoir on Forty-second Street or the original Madison Square Garden than I would any of the lost wonders of the ancient world.
Quoted in Carol Gelderman *Louis Auchincloss* (1993).

Auden, W(ystan) H(ugh) 1907–73

English born US poet. His early work reflects his concern with social problems of the 1930s and his left-wing commitment. His conversion from liberal humanism to Anglo-Catholicism informs his later work. He collaborated with Christopher Isherwood in three plays and *Journey to a War* (1939).

76 Harrow the house of the dead; look shining at
New styles of architecture, a change of heart.
1930 'Sir, No Man's Enemy'.

77 Private faces in public places
Are wiser and nicer
Than public faces in private places.
1932 *The Orators*, dedication.

78 What do you think about England, this country of ours where nobody is well?
1932 *The Orators*, 'Address for a Prize Day'.

79 To ask the hard question is simple.
1933 *Poems*, no.27.

80 The sky is darkening like a stain;
Something is going to fall like rain,
And it won't be flowers.
1935 'The Witness'.

81 This is the Night Mail crossing the border
Bringing the cheque and the postal order.
1936 'Night Mail', pt.1, written to accompany a documentary by the Post Office Film Unit.

82 And none will hear the postman's knock
Without a quickening of the heart.
For who can bear to feel himself forgotten?
1936 'Night Mail', written to accompany a documentary by the Post Office Film Unit.

83 Out on the lawn I lie in bed,
Vega conspicuous overhead.
1936 *Look, Stranger*, no.2.

84 August for the people and their favourite islands.
Daily the steamers sidle up to meet
The effusive welcome of the pier.
1936 *Look, Stranger*, no.30.

85 I dread this like the dentist, rather more so:
To me Art's subject is the human clay,
And landscape but a background to a torso;
All Cézanne's apples I would give away
For one small Goya or a Daumier.
1936 'Letter to Byron', pt.3, stanza 20, collected in *Poems, Essays, Dramatic Writings 1927–1939* (1977).

86 The stars are dead. The animals will not look:
We are left alone with our day, and the time is short, and
History to the defeated
May say Alas but cannot help nor pardon.
1937 *Spain*.

87 The desires of the heart are as crooked as corkscrews,
Not to be born is the best for man;
The second-best is a formal order,
The dance's pattern; dance while you can.
1937 'Letter to William Coldstream, Esq', in *Letter from Iceland* (with Louis MacNeice).

88 All the others translate: the painter sketches

A visible world to love or reject.
1938 'The Composer' (XXXI V), collected in *The English Auden. Poems 1936–39* (1977).

89 Stop all the clocks, cut off the telephone,
Prevent the dog from barking with a juicy bone,
Silence the pianos and with muffled drum
Bring out the coffin, let the mourners come.
1939 'Stop all the clocks', *Collected Poems*. Featured in the 1994 film *Four Weddings and a Funeral*.

90 About suffering they were never wrong,
The Old Masters: how well they understood
Its human position; how it takes place
While someone else is eating or opening a window or just walking dully along.
1940 'Musée des Beaux Arts'.

91 I'll love you dear, I'll love you
Till China and Africa meet
And the river jumps over the mountain
And the salmon sing in the street,
I'll love you till the ocean
Is folded and hung up to dry
And the seven stars go squawking
Like geese about the sky.
1940 'As I Walked Out One Evening'.

92 But all the clocks in the city
Began to whirr and chime:
'O let not Time deceive you,
You cannot conquer Time.'
1940 'As I Walked Out One Evening'.

93 O tell me the truth about love.
When it comes, will it come without warning
Just as I'm picking my nose?
Will it knock on my door in the morning,
Or tread in the bus on my toes?
1940 'Twelve Poems', section 12.

94 Encased in talent like a uniform,
The rank of every poet is well known;
They can amaze us like a thunderstorm,
Or die so young, or live for years alone.
1940 'The Novelist'.

95 When there was peace, he was for peace; when there was war, he went.
1940 'The Unknown Citizen'.

96 Was he free? Was he happy? The question is absurd:
Had anything been wrong, we should certainly have heard.
1940 'The Unknown Citizen'.

97 Perfection, of a kind, was what he was after,
And the poetry he invented was easy to understand.
1940 'Epitaph On A Tyrant'.

98 When he laughed, respectable senators burst with laughter,
And when he cried the little children died in the streets.
1940 'Epitaph On A Tyrant'.

99 To us he is no more a person
Now but a whole climate of opinion.
1940 'In Memory of Sigmund Freud', stanza 17.

1 O all the instruments agree
The day of his death was a dark cold day.
1940 'In Memory of W.B. Yeats', pt.1.

2 You were silly like us: your gift survived it all;
The parish of rich women, physical decay,
Yourself; mad Ireland hurt you into poetry.
Now Ireland has her madness and her weather still,
For poetry makes nothing happen.
1940 'In Memory of W.B. Yeats', pt.2.

3 Earth receive an honoured guest;
William Yeats is laid to rest:
Let the Irish vessel lie
Emptied of its poetry.
1940 'In Memory of W.B. Yeats', pt.3.

4 In the nightmare of the dark
All the dogs of Europe bark,
And the living nations wait,
Each sequestered in its hate.
1940 'In Memory of W.B. Yeats', pt.3.

5 In the deserts of the heart
Let the healing fountain start,
In the prison of his days
Teach the free man how to praise.
1940 'In Memory of W.B. Yeats', pt.3.

6 Lay your sleeping head, my love,
Human on my faithless arm.
1940 'Lullaby'.

7 I and the public know
What all schoolchildren learn,
Those to whom evil is done
Do evil in return.
1940 'September 1, 1939'.

8 There is no such thing as the State
And no one exists alone;
Hunger allows no choice
To the citizen or the police;
We must love one another or die.
1940 'September 1, 1939'.

9 To the man-in-the-street, who, I'm sorry to say,
Is a keen observer of life,
The word 'Intellectual' suggests straight away
A man who's untrue to his wife.
1940 *New Year Letter* (published 1941), note to l.1277.

10 Blessed Cecilia, appear in visions
To all musicians, appear and inspire:
Translated Daughter, come down and startle
Composing mortals with immortal fire.
1941 'Anthem for St Cecilia's Day'.

11 Sob, heavy world,
Sob as you spin
Mantled in mist, remote from the happy.
1944–6 *The Age of Anxiety*, pt.4, 'The Dirge'.

12 In our anguish we struggle
To elude Him, to lie to Him, yet His love observes
His appalling promise; His predilection
As we wander and weep is with us to the end,
Minding our meanings, our least matter dear to Him.
1944–6 *The Age of Anxiety*, pt.6, Epilogue.

13 There is no love;
There are only the various envies, all of them sad.
1951 'In Praise of Limestone', l.58–9.

14 To save your world you asked this man to die:
Would this man, could he see you now, ask why?
1955 'Epitaph for the Unknown Soldier'.

15 No good opera plot can be sensible, for people do not sing when they are feeling sensible.
Quoted in *Time*, 29 Dec 1961.

16 It is a sad fact about our culture that a poet can earn much more money writing or talking about his art than he can by practising it.
1963 *The Dyer's Hand*, foreword.

17 Pleasure is by no means an infallible critical guide, but it is the least fallible.
1963 *The Dyer's Hand*, 'Reading'.

18 Some books are undeservedly forgotten; none are undeservedly remembered.
1963 *The Dyer's Hand*, 'Reading'.

19 No poet or novelist wishes he were the only one who ever lived, but most of them wish they were the only one alive, and quite a number fondly believe that their wish has been granted.
1963 *The Dyer's Hand*, 'Writing'.

20 The true men of action in our time, those who transform the world, are not the politicians and statesmen, but the scientists… When I find myself in the company of scientists, I feel like a shabby curate who has strayed by mistake into a drawing room full of dukes.
1963 *The Dyer's Hand*, 'The Poet and the City'.

21 Man is a history-making creature who can neither repeat his past nor leave it behind.
1963 *The Dyer's Hand*, 'D.H. Lawrence'.

22 The image of myself which I try to create in my own mind in order that I may love myself is very different from the image which I try to create in the minds of others in order that they may love me.
1963 *The Dyer's Hand*, 'Hic et Ille'.

23 Among those whom I like or admire, I can find no common denominator, but among those whom I love, I can: all of them make me laugh.
1963 *The Dyer's Hand*, 'Notes on the Comic'.

24 Geniuses are the luckiest of mortals because what they must do is the same as what they most want to do.
1964 Foreword to Dag Hammarskjöld, *Markings*.

25 Some thirty inches from my nose
The frontier of my Person goes,
And all the untilled air between
Is private *pagus* or demesne.
Stranger, unless with bedroom eyes
I beckon you to fraternize,
Beware of rudely crossing it:
I have no gun, but I can spit.
1966 'Prologue: The Birth of Architecture', postscript.

26 Youth may be forgiven when it is brash or noisy, but this does not mean that brashness and noise are virtues.
1966 *Collected Shorter Poems 1927–1957*, introduction.

27 Political history is far too criminal and pathological to be a fit subject of study for the young. Children should acquire their heroes and villains from fiction.
1970 *A Certain World*.

28 All sin tends to be addictive, and the terminal point of addiction is what is called damnation.
1970 *A Certain World*, 'Hell'.

29 Of course, Behaviourism 'works'. So does torture.
1970 *A Certain World*, 'Behaviourism'

30 To my generation no other English poet seemed so perfectly to express the sensibility of a male adolescent. If I do not now turn to him very often, I am eternally grateful to him for the joy he gave me in my youth.
1972 Of A E Housman. 'A Worcestershire Lad', collected in *Forewords and Afterwords* (1973).

31 Music is the best means we have of digesting time.
Quoted in Robert Craft *Stravinsky: Chronicle of a Friendship* (1972).

32 That singular command,
I do not understand,
Bless what there is for being,
What else am I for,
Agreeing or disagreeing?
'Precious Fire', in *Collected Poems* (1976).

33 Thou shall not sin
With statisticians nor commit
A social science.
'Under Which Lyre'.

34 My face looks like a wedding-cake left out in the rain.
Quoted in Humphrey Carpenter *W H Auden* (1981), pt.2, ch.6.

St Augustine *originally* ***Aurelius Augustinus*** AD 354–430

Bishop of Hippo from 395. The son of Numidian Roman citizens (from modern Tunisia), he was converted to Christianity in 386. His works include his *Confessions* and *The City of God*.

35 *Da mihi castitatem et continentiam, sed noli modo.*
Grant me chastity and continence, but not yet.
AD 397 *Confessions*, bk.8, ch.7 (translated by Henry Chadwick).

36 *Tolle, lege, tolle, lege.*
Pick up and read, pick up and read.
AD 397 *Confessions*, bk.8, ch.12.

37 *Sero te amavi, pulchritudo tam antiqua et tam nova, sero te amavi!*
Late have I loved you, beauty so old and so new: late have I loved you.
AD 397 *Confessions*, bk.10, ch.27.

38 *Continentiam iubes; da quod iubes et iube quod vis.*
You command continence; give what you command and command what you will.
AD 397 *Confessions*, bk.10, ch.29.

39 *Quid est ergo tempus? Si nemo ex me quaerat, scio; si quaerenti explicare velim, nescio.*
What, then, is time? I know well enough what it is, provided that nobody asks me; but if I am asked what it is and try to explain, I am baffled.
AD 397 *Confessions*, bk.11, ch.14 (translated by R S Pine-Coffin).

40 *Multi quidem facilius se abstinent ut non utantur, quam temperent ut bene utantur.*
For many, total abstinence is easier than perfect moderation.
AD 401 *On the Good of Marriage*, ch.21.

41 *Dilige et quod vis fac.*
Love, and do what you like
AD 413 *In Epistolam Joannis ad Parthos*, tractatus 7, section 8.

42 What varieties man has found out in buildings, attires, husbandry, navigation, sculpture and imagery! What perfection has he shown, in the shows of theatres, in taming, killing, and catching wild beasts! What millions of inventions has he against others, and for himself in

poisons, arms, engines, stratagems, and the like! What thousands of medicines for the health, of meats for the throat, of means and figures to persuade, of elegant phrases to delight, of verses for pleasure, of musical inventions and instruments! What excellent inventions are geography, arithmetic, astrology, and the rest! How large is the capacity of man, if we should stand upon particulars!
AD 427 *The City of God.*

43 All the devastation, the butchery, the plundering, the conflagrations, and all the anguish which accompanied the recent disaster at Rome were in accordance with the general practice of warfare.
AD 427 *City of God*, vol.1, ch.1, section 8.

44 If you don't believe it, you won't understand it.
Quoted in Erasmus *De Libero Arbitrio* (1523).

45 Do not plan long journeys, because whatever you believe in you have already seen. When a thing is everywhere, the way to find it is not to travel but to love.
Quoted in Ingrid Cranfield *The Challengers* (1976).

Augustus *originally* *Gaius Iulius Caesar Octavianus* 63 BC–AD 14

First Roman emperor, a senator's son adopted by Caesar in his will (44 BC). With Marcus Antonius and Lepidus he secured power after the battle of Philippi (42 BC) but the triumvirate collapsed and after Actium (31 BC) Caesar was sole ruler of the Roman Empire. He took the title Augustus in 27 BC and expanded the empire until the loss of three legions in Germany (AD 9).

46 *Quintili Vare, legiones redde.*
Quintilius Varus, give me back my legions.
Quoted in Suetonius, *Augustus*, section 23.

47 *Festina lente.*
Hurry slowly.
Quoted in Suetonius *Augustus*, section 25 (originally quoted in Greek, but better known in the Latin form).

48 *Acta est fabula.*
The play is over.
AD 14 Last words, attributed. In Suetonius *Augustus*, section 99.1, the scene of his death-bed is described: 'He summoned a group of friends and asked: 'Have I played my part in the farce of life well enough?' adding the verse: 'If it was any good, please applaud for the play, and send us with pleasure on our way'.'

Aung San Suu Kyi 1945–

Burmese human rights activist and a leading campaigner for the National League for Democracy before being detained in 1989 by the country's ruling military junta. She has since spent long periods under house arrest. She was awarded the Nobel peace prize in 1991.

49 There is nothing new in Third World governments seeking to justify and perpetuate authoritarian rule by denouncing liberal democratic principles as alien.
1989 *Freedom From Fear*, 'In Quest of Democracy'.

50 Regimented minds cannot grasp the concept of confrontation as an open exchange of major differences with a view to settlement through genuine dialogue.
1989 *Freedom From Fear*, 'In Quest of Democracy'.

51 In societies where men are truly confident of their own worth women are not merely tolerated, they are valued.
1995 Videotaped address at the NGO Forum on Women, Beijing, China, 31 Aug.

Aurelius, Marcus Aurelius Antoninus AD 121–80

Roman emperor. He was consul from 140 to 161, when he succeeded Antoninus Pius to the throne. His *Meditations*, written in Greek, consist of notes made throughout his life.

52 A little flesh, a little breath, and a Reason to rule all—that is myself.
c. AD 170–180 *Meditations*, bk.2, no.2 (translated by M Staniforth).

53 Nowhere can a man find a quieter or more untroubled retreat than in his own soul.
c. AD 170–180 *Meditations*, bk.4, no.3 (translated by M Staniforth).

54 Soon you will have forgotten the world, and the world will have forgotten you.
c. AD 170–180 *Meditations*, bk.7, no.21 (translated by M Staniforth).

55 To live each day as though one's last, never flustered, never apathetic, never attitudinizing—here is perfection of character.
c. AD 170–180 *Meditations*, bk.7, no.69 (translated by M Staniforth).

Austen, Jane 1775–1817

English novelist. Her works satirized fashionable society, exploring the role of women. *Sense and Sensibility* (1811), *Pride and Prejudice* (1813), *Mansfield Park* (1814) and *Emma* (1815) were published anonymously; *Persuasion* and *Northanger Abbey* were both published posthumously (1818).

56 It was too pathetic for the feelings of Sophia and myself—we fainted alternately on the sofa.
1790 *Love and Freindship*, 'Letter the 8th'.

57 She was nothing more than a mere good-tempered, civil and obliging young woman; as such we could scarcely dislike her—she was only an Object of Contempt.
1790 *Love and Freindship*, 'Letter the 13th'.

58 We met…Dr Hall in such very deep mourning that either his mother, his wife, or himself must be dead.
1799 Letter to Cassandra Austen, 17 May.

59 On every formal visit a child ought to be of the party, by way of provisions for discourse.
1811 *Sense and Sensibility*, vol.2, ch.6.

60 It is not time or opportunity that is to determine intimacy; it is disposition alone. Seven years would be insufficient to make some people acquainted with each other, and seven days are more than enough for others.
1811 *Sense and Sensibility*, vol.2, ch.12.

61 It is a truth universally acknowledged, that a single man in possession of a good fortune, must be in want of a wife.
1813 *Pride and Prejudice*, ch.1, opening lines.

62 Her mind was less difficult to develop. She was a woman of mean understanding, little information, and uncertain temper.
1813 Of Mrs Bennet. *Pride and Prejudice*, ch.1.

63 Happiness in marriage is entirely a matter of chance.
1813 *Pride and Prejudice*, ch.6.

64 May I ask whether these pleasing attentions proceed from the impulse of the moment, or are the result of previous study?
1813 *Pride and Prejudice*, ch.14.

65 Mr Wickham is blessed with such happy manners as may ensure his making friends—whether he may be equally capable of retaining them, is less certain.
1813 *Pride and Prejudice*, ch.18.

66 From this day you must be a stranger to one of your parents.—Your mother will never see you again if you do *not* marry Mr Collins, and I will never see you again if you *do*.
1813 *Pride and Prejudice*, ch.20.

67 Without thinking highly either of men or matrimony, marriage had always been her object; it was the only honourable provision for well-educated young women of small fortune, and however uncertain of giving happiness, must be their pleasantest preservative from want.
1813 *Pride and Prejudice*, ch.22.

68 Next to being married, a girl likes to be crossed in love a little now and then. It is something to think of, and gives her a sort of distinction among her companions.
1813 *Pride and Prejudice*, ch.24.

69 What are men to rocks and mountains? Oh! what hours of transport we shall spend! And when we do return, it shall not be like other travellers, without being able to give one accurate idea of anything. We will know where we have gone—we will recollect what we have seen. Lakes, mountains, and rivers, shall not be jumbled together in our imaginations; nor, when we attempt to describe any particular scene, will we begin quarrelling about its relative situation.
1813 *Pride and Prejudice*, ch.27.

70 You ought certainly to forgive them as a Christian, but never to admit them in your sight, or allow their names to be mentioned in your hearing.
1813 *Pride and Prejudice*, ch.57.

71 For what do we live, but to make sport for our neighbours, and laugh at them in our turn?
1813 *Pride and Prejudice*, ch.57.

72 There is not one in a hundred of either sex who is not taken in when they marry. Look where I will, I see that it is so; and I feel that it must be so, when I consider that it is, of all transactions, the one in which people expect most from others, and are least honest themselves.
1814 *Mansfield Park*, ch.5.

73 Selfishness must always be forgiven you know, because there is no hope for a cure.
1814 *Mansfield Park*, ch.7.

74 We do not look in great cities for our best morality.
1814 *Mansfield Park*, ch.9.

75 Let us have no ranting tragedies. Too many characters—Not a tolerable woman's part in the play.
1814 *Mansfield Park*, ch.14.

76 A large income is the best recipe for happiness I ever heard of. It certainly may secure all the myrtle and turkey part of it.
1814 *Mansfield Park*, ch.22.

77 Shakespeare one gets acquainted with without knowing how. It is part of an Englishman's constitution. His thoughts and beauties are so spread abroad that one touches them everywhere, one is intimate with him by instinct.
1814 *Mansfield Park*, ch.34.

78 I must have a London audience. I could never preach, but to the educated; to those who were capable of estimating my composition.
1814 *Mansfield Park*, ch.34.

79 I think I may boast myself to be, with all possible vanity, the most unlearned and uninformed female who ever dared to be an authoress.
1815 Letter to Rev James Clarke, quoted in Justin Wintle and Richard Kenin (eds) *The Dictionary of Biographical Quotation* (1978).

80 She would not have him really suspect such a circumstance as her not being thought perfect by every body.
1816 *Emma*, ch.1.

81 A real, honest, old-fashioned Boarding-school, where a reasonable quantity of accomplishments were sold at a reasonable price, and where girls might be sent to be out of the way and scramble themselves into a little education, without any danger of coming back prodigies.
1816 *Emma*, ch.3.

82 One half of the world cannot understand the pleasures of the other.
1816 *Emma*, ch.9.

83 The sooner every party breaks up the better.
1816 *Emma*, ch.25.

84 I do not know whether it ought to be so, but certainly silly things do cease to be silly if they are done by sensible people in an impudent way. Wickedness is always wickedness, but folly is not always folly. It depends upon the character of those who handle it.
1816 *Emma*, ch.26.

85 Surprises are foolish things. The pleasure is not enhanced, and the inconvenience is often considerable.
1816 *Emma*, ch.26.

86 One has no great hopes from Birmingham. I always say there is something direful in the sound.
1816 Mrs Elton speaking. *Emma*, ch. 36.

87 Goldsmith tells us, when a lovely woman stoops to folly, she has nothing to do but die; and when she stoops to be disagreeable, it is equally to be recommended as a clearer of ill-fame.
1816 *Emma*, ch.45.
► *See Goldsmith 361:47.*

88 What should I do with your strong, manly, spirited sketches, full of variety and glow?—How could I possibly join them on to the little bit (two inches wide) of ivory on which I work with so fine a brush, as produces little effect after much labour?
1816 Letter to J Edward Austen, 16 Dec.

89 Single women have a dreadful propensity for being poor—which is one very strong argument in favour of matrimony.
1817 Letter to Fanny Knight, 13 Mar.

90 Pictures of perfection as you know make me sick and wicked.
1817 Of heroines in novels. Letter to Fanny Knight, 23 Mar.

91 Oh! it is only a novel!...only some work in which the most thorough knowledge of human nature, the happiest delineation of its varieties, the liveliest effusions of wit and humour are conveyed to the world in the best chosen language.
1818 *Northanger Abbey*, ch.5.

92 But history, real solemn history, I cannot be interested in…it tells me nothing that does not vex or weary me…the men all so good for nothing, and hardly any women at all.
1818 *Northanger Abbey*, vol.1, ch.14.

93 Where people wish to attach, they should always be ignorant. To come with a well informed mind, is to come with an inability of administering to the vanity of others, which a sensible person would always wish to avoid. A woman especially, if she have the misfortune of knowing anything, should conceal it as well she can…imbecility in females is a great enhancement of their personal charms.
1818 *Northanger Abbey*, ch.14.

94 Vanity was the beginning and the end of Sir Walter Elliot's character; vanity of person and of situation.
1818 *Persuasion*, ch.1.

95 'My idea of good company, Mr Elliot, is the company of clever, well-informed people, who have a great deal of conversation; that is what I call good company.' 'You are mistaken,' said he gently, 'that is not good company, that is the best.'
1818 *Persuasion*, ch.16.

96 We cannot help ourselves. We live at home, quiet, confined, and our feelings prey upon us. You are forced on exertion. You have always a profession, pursuits, business of some sort or other, to take you back into the world immediately, and continual occupation and change soon weaken impressions.
1818 Of the difference between women and men. *Persuasion*, ch.23.

97 Men have every advantage of us in telling their story. Education has been theirs in so much higher a degree; the pen has been in their hands.
1818 *Persuasion*, ch.23.

98 All the privilege I claim for my own sex (it is not a very enviable one, you need not covet it) is that of loving longest, when existence or when hope is gone.
1818 *Persuasion*, ch.23.

Auster, Paul *pseudonym of* ***Paul Benjamin*** 1947–

US novelist, poet and essayist. He is best known for his novels, which include the *New York Trilogy* (1985–7) and *Mr Vertigo* (1994).

99 We construct a narrative for ourselves, and that's the thread we follow from one day to the next. People who disintegrate as personalities are the ones who lose that thread.
1989 In the *Sunday Times*, 16 Apr.

1 More often than not, our lives resemble the stuff of eighteenth-century novels.
2003 *Collected Prose*, 'The National Story Project'.

Austin, Alfred 1835–1913

English poet. Appointed Poet Laureate in 1896, he was the author of *The Season; a Satire* (1861), *The Human Tragedy* (1862), *The Conversion of Winckelmann* (1862), several volumes of poetry and an autobiography (1911).

2 Along the electric wires the message came:
'He is no better, he is much the same.'
1910 'On the Illness of the Prince of Wales'. There is some doubt about the authorship of this satiric poem, but it is usually credited to Austin.

Austin, Mary Hunter 1868–1934

US novelist, short-story writer and suffragist, best known for her fiction about the American West and portraits of Native American life. Her works include *The Land of Little Rain* (1903), *A Woman of Genius* (1912) and her autobiography, *Earth Horizon* (1932).

3 When a woman ceases to alter the fashion of her hair, you guess that she has passed the crisis of her experience.
1903 *The Land of Little Rain*, 'The Basket Maker'.

Austin, Warren R(obinson) 1877–1962

US lawyer and diplomat, a Senator (1931–46) and subsequently US representative at the United Nations (1947–53).

4 It is better that aged diplomats be bored than for young men to die.
On soporifically lengthy debates at the United Nations.

5 Jews and Arabs should settle their differences like good Christians.
Attributed.

Avison, Margaret 1918–

Canadian poet. She has worked as a librarian, lecturer, social worker and embassy secretary. Her first book of poems was *Winter Sun* (1960). Her sixth collection, *Concrete and Wild Carrot*, was published in 2002.

6 Purpose apart, perched like an umpire, dozes,
Dreams golden balls whirring through indigo.
Clay blurs the whitewash but day still encloses
The albinos, bonded in their flick and flow.
Playing in musicked gravity, the pair
Score liquid Euclids in foolscaps of air.
1960 *Winter Sun*, 'Tennis'.

Ayckbourn, Sir Alan 1939–

English playwright. Recognized as a master of farce, his plays often shrewdly observe the English class-structure

7 My mother used to say, Delia, if S-E-X ever rears its ugly head, close your eyes before you see the rest of it.
1977 *Bedroom Farce*, act 2.

Ayer, Sir Alfred Jules 1910–89

English philosopher, professor at Oxford (1947–59). His first book *Language, Truth and Logic* (1936) was an iconoclastic attack on metaphysical speculation. He wrote many more works, and was knighted in 1970.

8 The traditional disputes of philosophers are, for the most part, as unwarranted as they are unfruitful.
1936 *Language, Truth and Logic*, ch.1.

9 We shall maintain that no statement which refers to a 'reality' transcending the limits of all possible sense-experience can possibly have any literal significance.
1936 *Language, Truth and Logic*, ch.1.

10 The criterion which we use to test the genuineness of apparent statements of fact is the criterion of verifiability. We say that a sentence is factually significant to any given person, if, and only if, he knows how to

verify the proposition which it purports to express — that is, if he knows what observations would lead him, under certain conditions, to accept the proposition as being true, or reject it as being false.
1936 *Language, Truth and Logic*, ch.1

11 Sentences which simply express moral judgements do not say anything. They are pure expressions of feeling and as such do not come under the category of truth and falsehood.
1936 *Language, Truth and Logic*, ch.6.

12 It appears, then, that ethics, as a branch of knowledge, is nothing more than a department of psychology and sociology.
1936 *Language, Truth and Logic*, ch.6.

13 But if science may be said to be blind without philosophy, it is true also that philosophy is virtually empty without science.
1936 *Language, Truth and Logic*, ch.8.

Ayres, Pam 1947–

English poet and broadcaster. She established a reputation as a popular versifier, reading her own poems on everyday themes on British television in the 1970s.

14 Medicinal discovery,
It moves in mighty leaps,
It leapt straight past the common cold
And gave it us for keeps.
1976 *Some of Me Poetry*, 'Oh no, I got a cold'.

Aytoun, Sir Robert 1570–1638

Scottish poet and courtier at the court of James VI and I in London. He wrote lyrics in English and Latin, and is credited with the prototype of 'Auld Lang Syne'.

15 I loved thee once; I'll love no more—
Thine be the grief as is the blame;
Thou art not what thou wast before,
What reason I should be the same?
'To an Inconstant Mistress', stanza 1.

Aytoun, William Edmonstoune 1813–65

Scottish lawyer and humorist, who contributed many parodies and burlesque reviews to *Blackwood's*. His best-known work was *Lays of the Scottish Cavaliers and other Poems* (1848).

16 Fhairshon swore a feud
Against the clan M'Tavish;
Marched into their land
To murder and to ravish;
For he did resolve
To extirpate the vipers,
With four-and-twenty men
And five-and-thirty pipers.
1845 'The Massacre of the Macpherson', stanza 1.

17 'He is coming! he is coming!'
Like a bridegroom from his room,
Came the hero from his prison
To the scaffold and the doom.
1848 *Lays of the Scottish Cavaliers and other Poems*, 'The Execution of Montrose', stanza 14.

18 They bore within their breasts the grief
That fame can never heal—
The deep, unutterable woe
Which none save exiles feel.
1848 *Lays of the Scottish Cavaliers and other Poems*, 'The Island of the Scots', stanza 12.

Babbage, Charles 1792–1871

English mathematician, inventor and scientific theoretician, who developed the programmable 'analytical engine', which was able to perform computations.

19 Perhaps the most important principle on which the economy of a manufacture depends, is the division of labour amongst the persons who perform the work.
1832 *On the Economy of Machinery and Manufactures*.

Babbitt, Bruce Edward 1938–

US lawyer, Governor of Arizona (1978–87), a Democrat and noted conservationist.

20 There is room in the west for wolves.
1995 Statement at Yellowstone National Park in Wyoming, 12 Jan, to the House of Representatives Natural Resources Committee, on the controversial restoration of wildlife.

Babel, Isaac 1894–c.1939

Russian short-story writer.

21 No iron can stab the heart with such force as a full stop put just at the right place.
1932 *Guy de Maupassant*.

Babeuf, François Noël 1760–97

French communist. As 'Gracchus Babeuf' during the French Revolution, he plotted to destroy the Directory (1796) and institute a communist state, but he was discovered and guillotined.

22 The French Revolution is merely the herald of a far greater and much more solemn revolution, which will be the last... The hour has come for founding the Republic of equals—that great refuge open to every man.
Conjuration des Égaux.

Bacall, Lauren *originally* Betty Perske 1924–

US film actress who married Humphrey Bogart in 1945.

23 I think your whole life shows in your face and you should be proud of that.
1988 In the *Daily Telegraph*, 2 Mar.

Bach, Johann Sebastian 1685–1750

German composer and organist, whose polyphonic works greatly influenced the course of Western music. He composed over 200 cantatas, the *Saint John Passion* (1723), the *Saint Matthew Passion* (1729), the *Mass in B Minor* (1733), and Christmas and Easter Oratorios, as well as much keyboard and instrumental music.

24 There is nothing to it. You only have to hit the right notes at the right time and the instrument plays itself.
Of the organ. Quoted in K Geiringer *The Bach Family* (1954).

25 An agreeable harmony for the honour of God and the permissible delights of the soul.
His definition of music. Quoted in Derek Watson *Music Quotations* (1991).

Bach, Richard 1936–

US author, formerly a military pilot. He is best known for *Jonathan Livingston Seagull* (1970).

26 Heaven is not a place, and it is not a time. Heaven is being perfect.
1970 *Jonathan Livingston Seagull.*

27 The gull sees farthest who sees highest.
1970 *Jonathan Livingston Seagull.*

28 'To begin with,' he said heavily, 'you've got to understand that a seagull is an unlimited idea of freedom, an image of the Great Gull, and your whole body, from wingtip to wingtip, is nothing more than your thought itself.'
1970 *Jonathan Livingston Seagull.*

29 There is no such thing as a problem without a gift for you in its hands. You seek problems because you need their gifts.
1977 *Illusions.*

30 Argue for your limitations, and sure enough, they're yours.
1977 *Illusions.*

31 'I don't know they're true,' he said. 'I believe them because it's fun to believe them.'
1977 *Illusions.*

Bacon, Francis, Viscount St Albans 1561–1626

English philosopher and statesman. Educated as a scholar and a lawyer, he entered the service of the crown and eventually became Lord Chancellor. Key works include *Essays* (1597–1625), *The Advancement of Learning* (1605), *Novum Organum* (1620) and *The New Atlantis* (1627).

32 I have taken all knowledge to be my province.
1592 Letter to Lord Burghley.

33 Knowledge is power
1597 *Meditationes sacrae*, 'De Haresibus' (Of Heresies).

34 Opportunity makes a thief.
1598 Letter to the Earl of Essex.

35 For all knowledge and wonder (which is the seed of knowledge) is an impression of pleasure in itself.
1605 *The Advancement of Learning*, bk.1, ch.1, section 3.

36 So let great authors have their due, as time, which is the author of authors, be not deprived of his due, which is further and further to discover the truth.
1605 *The Advancement of Learning*, bk.1, ch.4, section 12.

37 If a man will begin with certainties, he shall end in doubts; but if he will be content to begin with doubts, he shall end in certainties.
1605 *The Advancement of Learning*, bk.1, ch.5, section 8.

38 Learned men...do many times fail to observe decency and discretion in their behaviour and carriage, so as the vulgar sort of capacities do make a judgment of them in greater matters by that which they find them wanting in smaller.
1605 *The Advancement of Learning*, bk.1.

39 Martin Luther...was enforced to awake all antiquity and to call former times to his succour to make a party against the present time, so that the ancient authors both in divinity and in humanity which had long time slept in libraries began generally to be read and revolved.
1605 *The Advancement of Learning*, bk.1.

40 Vain matter is worse than vain words.
1605 *The Advancement of Learning*, bk.1.

41 Time seemeth to be of the nature of a river or stream, which carrieth down to us that which is light and blown up, and sinketh and drowneth that which is weighty and solid.
1605 *The Advancement of Learning*, bk.1.

42 Antiquities are history defaced, or some remnants of history which have casually escaped the shipwreck of time.
1605 *The Advancement of Learning*, bk.2, ch.2, section 1.

43 [Poesy] was ever thought to have some participation of divineness, because it doth raise and erect the mind, by submitting the shows of things to the desires of the mind; whereas reason doth buckle and bow the mind unto the nature of things.
1605 *The Advancement of Learning*, bk.2, ch.4, section 2.

44 The knowledge of man is as the waters, some descending from above, and some springing from beneath; the one informed by the light of nature, the other inspired by divine revelation.
1605 *The Advancement of Learning*, bk.2, ch.5, section 1.

45 They are ill discoverers that think there is no land, when they can see nothing but sea.
1605 *The Advancement of Learning*, bk.2, ch.7, section 5.

46 A dance is a measured pace, as a verse is a measured speech.
1605 *The Advancement of Learning*, bk.2, ch.16, section 5.

47 But men must know, that in this theatre of man's life it is reserved only for God and angels to be lookers on.
1605 *The Advancement of Learning*, bk.2, ch.20, section 8.

48 We are much beholden to Machiavel and others, that write what men do, and not what they ought to do.
1605 *The Advancement of Learning*, bk.2, ch.21, section 9.

49 Did not one of the fathers in great indignation call poesy *vinum daemonum*?
1605 *The Advancement of Learning*, bk.2, ch.22, section 13. The Latin translates as 'the wine of the devils'.

50 All good moral philosophy is but an handmaid to religion.
1605 *The Advancement of Learning*, bk.2, ch.22, section 14.

51 Of knowledge there is no satiety.
1605 *The Advancement of Learning*, bk.2.

52 It is not granted to man to love and to be wise.
1605 *The Advancement of Learning*, bk.2.

53 Tennis is a game of no use in itself.
1605 *The Advancement of Learning*, bk.2.

54 Man seeketh in society comfort, use, and protection.
1605 *The Advancement of Learning*, bk.2.

55 Fortunes...come tumbling into some men's laps.
1605 *The Advancement of Learning*, bk.2.

56 It is in life as it is in ways, the shortest way is most

commonly the foulest, and surely the fairer way is not much about.
1605 *The Advancement of Learning*, bk.2, ch.23, section 45.

57 Empires and old women are more happy many times in their cures than learned physicians, because they are more exact and religious in holding to the composition and confection of tried medicines.
1605 *The Advancement of Learning*, bk.4, ch.2.

58 The subtlety of nature is greater many times over than the subtlety of the senses and understanding.
1620 *Novum Organum*, bk.1, aphorism 10.

59 *Quod enim mavult homo verum esse, id potius credit.*
For what a man would like to be true, that he more readily believes.
1620 *Novum Organum*, bk.1, aphorism 49.

60 Those who have handled sciences have been either men of experiment or men of dogmas. The men of experiment are like the ant; they only collect and use; the reasoners resemble spiders, who make cobwebs out of their own substance. But the bee takes a middle course; it gathers its material from the flowers of the garden and of the field, but transforms and digests by a power of its own. Not unlike this is the true business of philosophy.
1620 *Novum Organum* bk.1, aphorism 95.

61 *Vim et virtutem et consequentias rerum inventarum notare juvat; quae non in aliis manifestius occurrunt, quam in illis tribus quae antiquis incognitae, et quarum primordia, licet recentia, obscura et ingloria sunt: Artis nimirum Imprimendi, Pulveris Tormentarii, et Acus Nauticae. Haec enim tria rerum faciem et statum in orbe terrarum mutaverunt.*
It is well to observe the force and virtue and consequence of discoveries, and these are to be seen nowhere more conspicuously than in those three which were unknown to the ancients, and of which the origin, though recent, is obscure and inglorious; namely, printing, gunpowder and the magnet [ie the compass]. For these three have changed the whole face and state of things throughout the world.
1620 *Novum Organum*, bk.1, aphorism 129 (translated by James Spedding).

62 *Natura enim non imperatur, nisi parendo.*
For we cannot command Nature except by obeying her.
1620 *Novum Organum*, bk.1, aphorism 129.

63 It would be unsound fancy and self-contradictory to expect that things which have never yet been done can be done except by means which have never yet been tried.
1620 *Novum Organum.*

64 The lame man who keeps the right road outstrips the runner who takes a wrong one. Nay, it is obvious that when a man runs the wrong way, the more active and swift he is the further he will go astray.
1620 *Novum Organum.*

65 *Divitiae bona ancilla, pessima domina.*
Riches are a good handmaid, but the worst mistress.
1623 *De Dignitiate et Augmentis Scientiarum*, Antitheta no.6 (translated by Gilbert Watts, 1640).

66 The voice of the people hath some divineness in it, else how should so many men agree to be of one mind?
1623 *De Dignitiate et Augmentis Scientiarum*, Antitheta no.9 (translated by Gilbert Watts, 1640).

67 *Silentium, stultorum virtus.*
Silence is the virtue of fools.
1623 *De Dignitiate et Augmentis Scientiarum*, Antitheta no.31 (translated by Gilbert Watts, 1640).

68 The end of our foundation is the knowledge of causes, and secret motions of things; and the enlarging of the bounds of human Empire, to the effecting of all things possible.
1624 *New Atlantis* (published posthumously, 1627).

69 Wise nature did never put her precious jewels into a garret four stories high: and therefore...exceeding tall men had ever very empty heads.
1625 *Apophthegms.*

70 Hope is a good breakfast, but it is a bad supper.
1625 *Apophthegms.*

71 What is truth? said jesting Pilate; and would not stay for an answer.
1625 *Essays*, no.1, 'Of Truth'.

72 The inquiry of truth, which is the love-making, or wooing of it, the knowledge of truth, which is the presence of it, and the belief of truth, which is the enjoying of it, is the sovereign good of human nature.
1625 *Essays*, no.1, 'Of Truth'.

73 Men fear death as children fear to go in the dark; and as that natural fear in children is increased with tales, so is the other.
1625 *Essays*, no.2, 'Of Death'.

74 There is no passion in the mind of man so weak, but it mates and masters the fear of death. And therefore death is no such terrible enemy, when a man hath so many attendants about him that can win the combat of him. Revenge triumphs over death; love slights it; honour aspireth to it; grief flieth to it.
1625 *Essays*, no.2, 'Of Death'.

75 It is as natural to die as to be born; and to a little infant, perhaps, the one is as painful as the other.
1625 *Essays*, no.2, 'Of Death'.

76 Death...openeth the gate to good fame, and extinguisheth envy.
1625 *Essays*, no.2, 'Of Death'.

77 All colours will agree in the dark.
1625 *Essays*, no.3, 'Of Unity in Religion'.

78 Revenge is a kind of wild justice, which the more man's nature runs to, the more ought law to weed it out.
1625 *Essays*, no.4, 'Of Revenge'.

79 The virtue of prosperity, is temperance; the virtue of adversity, is fortitude.
1625 *Essays*, no.5, 'Of Adversity'.

80 Prosperity is the blessing of the Old Testament, adversity is the blessing of the New.
1625 *Essays*, no.5, 'Of Adversity'.

81 Prosperity is not without many fears and distastes; and adversity is not without comforts and hopes.
1625 *Essays*, no.5, 'Of Adversity'.

82 Prosperity doth best discover vice, but adversity doth best discover virtue.
1625 *Essays*, no.5, 'Of Adversity'.

83 Let judges also remember that Solomon's throne was

supported by lions on both sides; let them be lions, but yet lions under the throne.
1625 *Essays*, no.6, 'Of Judicature'.

84 The joys of parents are secret, and so are their griefs and fears.
1625 *Essays*, no.7, 'Of Parents and Children'.

85 Children sweeten labours, but they make misfortunes more bitter.
1625 *Essays*, no.7, 'Of Parents and Children'.

86 He that hath wife and children hath given hostages to fortune; for they are impediments to great enterprises, either of virtue or mischief. Certainly the best works, and of greatest merit for the public, have proceeded from the unmarried or childless men, which both in affection and means have married and endowed the public.
1625 *Essays*, no.8, 'Of Marriage and the Single Life'.

87 There are some others that account wife and children but as bills of charge.
1625 *Essays*, no.8, 'Of Marriage and the Single Life'.

88 The most ordinary cause of a single life is liberty, especially in certain self-pleasing and humorous minds, which are so sensible of every restraint, as they will go near to think their girdles and garters to be bonds and shackles.
1625 *Essays*, no.8, 'Of Marriage and the Single Life'.

89 Unmarried men are best friends, best masters, best servants, but not always best subjects, for they are light to run away, and almost all fugitives are of that condition.
1625 *Essays*, no.8, 'Of Marriage and the Single Life'.

90 Certainly wife and children are a kind of discipline of humanity; and single men, though they be many times more charitable, because their means are less exhaust, yet…they are more cruel and hardhearted (good to make severe inquisitors), because their tenderness is not so oft called upon.
1625 *Essays*, no.8, 'Of Marriage and the Single Life'.

91 Wives are young men's mistresses, companions for middle age, and old men's nurses.
1625 *Essays*, no.8, 'Of Marriage and the Single Life'.

92 He was reputed one of the wise men that made answer to the question when a man should marry? 'A young man not yet, an elder man not at all.'
1625 *Essays*, no.8, 'Of Marriage and the Single Life'.

93 It is often seen that bad husbands have very good wives; whether it be that it raiseth the price of their husband's kindness when it comes, or that the wives take a pride in their patience. But this never fails, if the bad husbands were of their own choosing, against their friends' consent; for then they will be sure to make good their own folly.
1625 *Essays*, no.8, 'Of Marriage and the Single Life'.

94 I had rather believe all the fables in the legend, and the Talmud, and the Alcoran, than that this universal frame is without a mind.
1625 *Essays*, no.9, 'Of Atheism'.

95 It is true, that a little philosophy inclineth Man's mind to atheism; but depth in philosophy bringeth men's minds about to religion.
1625 *Essays*, no.9 'Of Atheism'.
► *See Berkeley 79:7.*

96 For it is a true Rule that Love is ever rewarded, either with the reciproque, or with an inward and secret contempt.
1625 *Essays*, no.10, 'Of Love'.

97 The speaking in perpetual hyperbole is comely in nothing but love.
1625 *Essays*, no.10, 'Of Love'.

98 All rising to great place is by a winding stair.
1625 *Essays*, no.11, 'Of Great Place'.

99 Men in great place are thrice servants: servants of the sovereign or state, servants of fame, and servants of business.
1625 *Essays*, no.11, 'Of Great Place'.

1 It is a strange desire to seek power and to lose liberty.
1625 *Essays*, no.11, 'Of Great Place'.

2 The rising unto place is laborious, and by pains men come to greater pains; and it is sometimes base, and by indignities men come to dignities. The standing is slippery, and the regress is either a downfall, or at least an eclipse, which is a melancholy thing: *Cum non sis qui fueris, non esse cur velis vivere.*
1625 *Essays*, no.11, 'Of Great Place'. The Latin is taken from Cicero's *Familiar Letters*, and translates as: 'When you are not what you were, there is no reason to live.'

3 Certainly great persons had need to borrow other men's opinions to think themselves happy; for if they judge by their own feeling, they cannot find it; but if they think with themselves what other men think of them, and that other men would fain be as they are, then they are happy.
1625 *Essays*, no.11, 'Of Great Place'.

4 Men in great fortunes are strangers to themselves.
1625 *Essays*, no.11, 'Of Great Place'.

5 Merit and good works is the end of man's motion, and conscience of the same is the accomplishment of man's rest.
1625 *Essays*, no.11, 'Of Great Place'.

6 The vices of authority are chiefly four: delays, corruption, roughness, and facility.
1625 *Essays*, no.11, 'Of Great Place'.

7 In civil business; What first? Boldness; What second, and third? Boldness. And yet boldness is a child of ignorance and baseness.
1625 *Essays*, no.12, 'Of Boldness'.

8 There is in human nature generally more of the fool than of the wise.
1625 *Essays*, no.12, 'Of Boldness'.

9 Mahomet made the people believe that he would call a hill to him, and from the top of it offer up his prayers for the observers of his law. The people assembled: Mahomet called the hill to come to him again and again; and when the hill stood still he was never a whit abashed, but said, 'If the hill will not come to Mahomet, Mahomet will go to the hill.'
1625 *Essays*, no.12, 'Of Boldness'.

10 New nobility is but the act of power, but ancient nobility is the act of time.
1625 *Essays*, no.14, 'Of Nobility'.

11 The surest way to prevent seditions…is to take away the matter of them.
1625 *Essays*, no.15, 'Of Seditions and Troubles'.

12 Money is like muck, not good except it be spread.
1625 *Essays*, no.15, 'Of Seditions and Troubles'.

13 The remedy is worse than the disease.
1625 *Essays*, no.15, 'Of Seditions and Troubles'.

14 It were better to have no opinion of God at all than such an opinion as is unworthy of him.
1625 *Essays*, no.17, 'Of Superstition'.

15 In all superstition wise men follow fools.
1625 *Essays*, no.17, 'Of Superstition'.

16 There is a superstition in avoiding superstition.
1625 *Essays*, no.17, 'Of Superstition'. This is directed against Puritan reformers, who decried both Catholic and Anglican rites as 'superstitious'.

17 It is a miserable state of mind to have few things to desire and many things to fear.
1625 *Essays*, no.19, 'Of Empire'.

18 In things that are tender and unpleasing, it is good to break the ice by some whose words are of less weight, and to reserve the more weighty voice to come in as by chance.
1625 *Essays*, no.22, 'Of Cunning'.

19 Nothing doth more hurt in a state than that cunning men pass for wise.
1625 *Essays*, no.22, 'Of Cunning'.

20 Be so true to thyself as thou be not false to others.
1625 *Essays*, no.23, 'Of Wisdom for a Man's Self'.

21 It is a poor centre of a man's actions, himself.
1625 *Essays*, no.23, 'Of Wisdom for a Man's Self'.

22 It is the nature of extreme self-lovers, as they will set a house on fire, and it were but to roast their eggs.
1625 *Essays*, no.23, 'Of Wisdom for a Man's Self'.

23 It is the wisdom of the crocodiles, that shed tears when they would devour.
1625 *Essays*, no.23, 'Of Wisdom for a Man's Self'.

24 As the births of living creatures at first are ill-shapen, so are all innovations, which are the births of time.
1625 *Essays*, no.24, 'Of Innovations'.

25 He that will not apply new remedies must expect new evils; for time is the greatest innovator.
1625 *Essays*, no.24, 'Of Innovations'.

26 To choose time is to save time.
1625 *Essays*, no.25, 'Of Dispatch'.

27 The French are wiser than they seem, and the Spaniards seem wiser than they are.
1625 *Essays*, no.26, 'Of Seeming Wise'.

28 It had been hard for him that spake it to have put more truth and untruth together, in a few words, than in that speech: 'Whosoever is delighted in solitude is either a wild beast, or a god.'
1625 *Essays*, no.27, 'Of Friendship'.

29 A crowd is not company, and faces are but a gallery of pictures, and talk but a tinkling cymbal, where there is no love.
1625 *Essays*, no.27, 'Of Friendship'.
➤ *See Bible 121:9.*

30 [Friendship] redoubleth joys, and cutteth griefs in half.
1625 *Essays*, no.27, 'Of Friendship'.

31 As if you would call a physician, that is thought good for the cure of the disease you complain of but is unacquainted with your body, and therefore may put you in the way for a present cure but overthroweth your health in some other kind; and so cure the disease and kill the patient.
1625 *Essays*, no.27, 'Of Friendship'.

32 Riches are for spending; and spending for honour and good actions.
1625 *Essays*, no.28, 'Of Expense'.

33 Neither will it be, that a people overlaid with taxes should ever become valiant and martial.
1625 *Essays*, no.29, 'Of the True Greatness of Kingdoms'.

34 Suspicions amongst thoughts are like bats amongst birds, they ever fly by twilight.
1625 *Essays*, no.31, 'Of Suspicion'.

35 There is nothing makes a man suspect much, more than to know little.
1625 *Essays*, no.31, 'Of Suspicion'.

36 If you dissemble sometimes your knowledge of that you are thought to know, you shall be thought, another time, to know that you know not.
1625 *Essays*, no.32, 'Of Discourse'.

37 When the world was young it begat more children; but now it is old it begets fewer: for I may justly account new plantations to be the children of former kingdoms.
1625 *Essays*, no.33, 'Of Plantations'.

38 If you plant where savages are, do not only entertain them with trifles and jingles, but use them justly and graciously.
1625 *Essays*, no.33, 'Of Plantations'.

39 Nature is often hidden, sometimes overcome, seldom extinguished.
1625 *Essays*, no.38, 'Of Nature in Men'.

40 Chiefly the mould of a man's fortune is in his own hands.
1625 *Essays*, no.40, 'Of Fortune'.

41 If a man look sharply, and attentively, he shall see Fortune; for though she be blind, yet she is not invisible.
1625 *Essays*, no.40, 'Of Fortune'.

42 Beauty is as summer-fruits, which are easy to corrupt, and cannot last.
1625 *Essays*, no.43, 'Of Beauty'.

43 Virtue is like a rich stone, best plain set.
1625 *Essays*, no.43, 'Of Beauty'.

44 That is the best part of beauty, which a picture cannot express.
1625 *Essays*, no.43, 'Of Beauty'.

45 There is no excellent beauty that hath not some strangeness in the proportion.
1625 *Essays*, no.43, 'Of Beauty'.

46 God Almighty first planted a garden; and indeed, it is the purest of human pleasures.
1625 *Essays*, no.46, 'Of Gardens'.

47 It is generally better to deal by speech than by letter.
1625 *Essays*, no.47, 'Of Negotiating'.

48 It is better dealing with men in appetite, than with those that are where they would be.
1625 *Essays*, no.47, 'Of Negotiating'.

49 If you would work any man, you must either know his nature and fashions, and so lead him; or his ends, and so persuade him; or his weakness and disadvantages, and

so awe him, or those that have interest in him, and so govern him.
1625 *Essays*, no.47, 'Of Negotiating'.

50 There is little friendship in the world, and least of all between equals.
1625 *Essays*, no.48, 'Of Followers and Friends'.

51 To spend too much time in studies is sloth; to use them too much for ornament is affectation; to make judgment wholly by their rules is the humour of a scholar.
1625 *Essays*, no.50, 'Of Studies'.

52 Read not to contradict and confute, nor to believe and take for granted, nor to find talk and discourse, but to weigh and consider.
1625 *Essays*, no.50, 'Of Studies'.

53 Some books are to be tasted, others to be swallowed, and some few to be chewed and digested; that is, some books are to be read only in parts; others to be read but not curiously; and some few to be read wholly, and with diligence and attention. Some books also may be read by deputy, and extracts made of them by others.
1625 *Essays*, no.50, 'Of Studies'.

54 If a man write little, he had need have a great memory; if he confer little, he had need have a present wit; and if he read little he had need have much cunning, to seem to know that he doth not.
1625 *Essays*, no.50, 'Of Studies'.

55 Histories make men wise; poets, witty; the mathematics, subtle; natural philosophy, deep; moral, grave; logic and rhetoric, able to contend.
1625 *Essays*, no.50, 'Of Studies'.

56 Light gains make heavy purses.
1625 *Essays*, no.52, 'Of Ceremonies and Respects'.

57 A wise man will make more opportunities than he finds.
1625 *Essays*, no.52, 'Of Ceremonies and Respects'.

58 It was prettily devised of Aesop, 'The fly sat upon the axletree of the chariot-wheel and said, what a dust do I raise.'
1625 *Essays*, no.54, 'Of Vain-Glory'.

59 In the youth of a state arms do flourish; in the middle age of a state, learning; and then both of them together for a time; in the declining age of a state, mechanical arts and merchandise.
1625 *Essays*, no.58, 'Of Vicissitude of Things'.

60 I bequeath my soul to God... For my name and memory, I leave it to men's charitable speeches, and to foreign nations, and the next age.
1626 From his will.

61 God's first Creature, which was Light.
New Atlantis (published 1627).

62 The end of our foundation is the knowledge of causes, and secret motions of things; and the enlarging of the bounds of human Empire, to the effecting of all things possible.
1627 Of Solomon's House, the centre of Bacon's scientific utopia. *New Atlantis* (published 1627).

63 No man can tickle himself.
Sylva Sylvarum (published 1627), bk.8.

64 Generally music feedeth that disposition of the spirits which it findeth.
Sylva Sylvarum (published 1627).

65 The world's a bubble; and the life of man
Less than a span.
The World (published 1629).

66 Books must follow sciences, and not sciences books.
A Proposition... Touching Amendment of the Laws of England (published 1657).

67 The government of a woman has been a rare thing at all times; felicity in such government a rarer thing still; felicity and long continuance together the rarest thing of all.
Quoted in J E Neale *The Age of Catherine de Medici and Essays in Elizabethan History* (1963), p.217.

Bacon, Francis 1909–92

Irish-born painter, who settled in England in 1928 and began painting without formal training. His work draws on surrealism and motion photography, often evoking angst. He was a technical perfectionist, and destroyed much of his work.

68 I think of myself as a kind of pulverizing machine into which everything I look at and feel is fed. I believe that I am different from the mixed-media jackdaws who use photographs etc. more or less literally.
On the use of photographs in his art. Quoted in John Russell *Francis Bacon* (1979).

69 Who can I tear to pieces, if not my friends?... If they were not my friends, I could not do such violence to them.
Quoted in John Russell *Francis Bacon* (1979).

Bacon, Martha 1917–81

US educator and author

70 She soothed and solaced and celebrated, destroying her gift by maiming it to suit her hearers.
1965 On Phillis Wheatley. In *Christian Science Monitor*, 24 Jun.

Bacon, Roger *known as* ***Doctor Mirabilis*** c.1214–c.1292

English philosopher, scientist and alchemist, closely associated with Oxford. His major works include the *Opus Majus*, *Opus Minor* and *Opus Tertium*. He became a Franciscan, but was rejected and persecuted for heresy.

71 All science requires mathematics...the knowledge of mathematical things is almost innate in us...this is the easiest of sciences. A fact which is obvious in that no one's brain rejects it. For laymen and people who are utterly illiterate know how to count and reckon.
1267 *Opus Majus*, pt.4, ch.1 (translated by Robert Belle Burke, 1928).

72 Mathematics is the door and key to the sciences.
1267 *Opus Majus*, pt.4, ch.1 (translated by Robert Belle Burke, 1928).

73 There are two modes of acquiring knowledge, namely, by reasoning and experience. Reasoning draws a conclusion and makes us grant the conclusion, but does not make the conclusion certain, nor does it remove doubt so that the mind may rest on the intuition of truth unless the mind discovers it by the path of experience.
1267 *Opus Majus* (translated by Robert Belle Burke, 1928).

Baden-Powell, Robert Stephenson Smyth, 1st Baron 1857–1941

English soldier. He became a hero for his defence of Mafeking

(1899–1900) during the Boer War but is usually remembered as the founder of the Boy Scout movement in 1908 and for his book *Scouting for Boys* (1908).

74 The scouts' motto is founded on my initials, it is: BE PREPARED, which means, you are always to be in a state of readiness in mind and body to do your DUTY.
1908 *Scouting for Boys.*

75 Football, in itself, is a grand game for developing a lad physically and also morally...but it is a vicious game when it draws crowds of lads away from playing the game themselves to be merely onlookers at a few paid players.
1908 *Scouting for Boys.*

Baedeker, Karl 1801–59

German editor and publisher, famous for his foreign travel guides. The first, for Coblenz, appeared in 1829, and they continued to be published after his death.

76 On arrival at a Syrian port the traveller's passport is sometimes asked for, but an ordinary visiting-card will answer the purpose equally well.
1876 *Palestine and Syria*, 'Passports and Custom House'.

77 Oxford is on the whole more attractive than Cambridge to the ordinary visitor; and the traveller is therefore recommended to visit Cambridge first, or to omit it altogether if he cannot visit both.
1887 *Great Britain*, Route 30: 'From London to Oxford'.

Baer, George Frederick 1842–1914

US lawyer and industrialist, who led the resistance to the strike by the United Mine Workers of America in 1902.

78 The rights and interests of the laboring man will be protected and cared for, not by the labor agitators, but by the Christian men to whom God, in his infinite wisdom, has given control of the property interests of the country.
1902 Letter to the press during the Pennsylvanian miners' strike.

Bagehot, Walter 1826–77

British economist and journalist. His *English Constitution* (1867) is still considered a standard work, and *Physics and Politics* (1872), applying evolution theories to politics, greatly influenced 19c thought.

79 The essence of Toryism is enjoyment...but as far as communicating and establishing your creed are concerned—try a little pleasure. The way to keep up old customs is, to enjoy old customs; the way to be satisfied with the present state of things is, to enjoy that state of things.
1856 Essay on *Macaulay.*

80 No real English gentleman, in his secret soul, was ever sorry for the death of a political economist.
1858 *Estimates of Some Englishmen and Some Scotchmen*, 'The First Edinburgh Reviewers'.

81 Writers, like teeth, are divided into incisors and grinders.
1858 *Estimates of Some Englishmen and Some Scotchmen*, 'The First Edinburgh Reviewers'.

82 It is said that England invented the phrase, 'Her Majesty's Opposition'; that it was the first government which made a criticism of administration as much a part of the polity as administration itself.
1867 *The English Constitution*, ch.2, 'The Cabinet'.

83 *The Times* has made many ministries.
1867 *The English Constitution*, ch.2, 'The Cabinet'.

84 The fancy of the mass of men is incredibly weak; it can see nothing without a visible symbol, and there is much that it can scarcely make out with a symbol.
1867 *The English Constitution*, ch.4, 'The House of Lords'.

85 The order of nobility is of great use, too, not only in what it creates, but in what it prevents. It prevents the rule of wealth—the religion of gold. This is the obvious and natural idol of the Anglo-Saxon... From this our aristocracy preserves us.
1867 *The English Constitution*, ch.4, 'The House of Lords'.

86 A severe though not unfriendly critic of our institutions said that the cure for admiring the House of Lords was to go and look at it.
1867 *The English Constitution*, ch.4, 'The House of Lords'.

87 The great offices, whether permanent or parliamentary, which require mind now give social prestige, and almost only those. An Under-Secretary of State with £2,000 a year is a much greater man than the director of a finance company with £5,000, and the country saves the difference.
1867 *The English Constitution*, ch.4, 'The House of Lords'.

88 Nations touch at their summits.
1867 *The English Constitution*, ch.4, 'The House of Lords'.

89 The best reason why monarchy is a strong government is, that it is an intelligible government. The mass of mankind understand it, and they hardly anywhere in the world understand any other.
1867 *The English Constitution*, ch.6, 'The Monarchy'.

90 Throughout the greater part of his life George III was a kind of 'consecrated obstruction'.
1867 *The English Constitution*, ch.6, 'The Monarchy'.

91 Above all things our royalty is to be reverenced, and if you begin to poke about it you cannot reverence it... Its mystery is its life. We must not let in daylight upon magic.
1867 *The English Constitution*, ch.6, 'The Monarchy (continued)'.

92 Political economy traces in an abstract way the effects of the desire to be rich; and nations must nowadays abound in that passion if they are to have much power or respect in the world.
1876 'Preliminaries of Political Economy', collected in *Economic Studies* (1880).

93 Men of business have a solid judgment, a wonderful guessing power of what is going to happen, each in his own trade, but they have never practised themselves in reasoning out their judgments and in supporting their guesses by argument; probably if they did so, some of the finer and correcter parts of their anticipations would vanish.
1876 'Postulates of English Political Economy', in *Economic Studies* (1880).

94 Who can tell without instruction what is likely to be the effect of the new loans of England to foreign nations? We press upon half-finished and half-civilized communities incalculable sums; we are to them what the London money-dealers are to students at Oxford and Cambridge.
1876 'Postulates of English Political Economy', in *Economic Studies* (1880).

95 No man has come so near to our definition of a

constitutional statesman—the powers of a first-rate man and the creed of a second-rate man.
1881 *Biographical Studies*, 'The Character of Sir Robert Peel'.

96 A constitutional statesman is in general a man of common opinion and uncommon abilities.
1881 *Biographical Studies*, 'The Character of Sir Robert Peel'.

Bailey, David 1938–

English photographer known particularly for his striking pictures of cultural icons.

97 I never cared for fashion much. Amusing little seams and witty little pleats. It was the girls I liked.
1990 In *The Independent*, 5 Nov.

98 I grew up scared of Hitler. I wanted to kill him because he spent all my childhood trying to kill me.
2001 In *The Mail on Sunday*, 14 Oct.

99 It's funny: you hate authority and then your photography takes on an authority.
2001 In *The Mail on Sunday*, 14 Oct.

Bailey, F(rancis) Lee 1933–

US criminal lawyer, who founded his own detective agency at Harvard. He defended the Boston Strangler and, more recently, he defended O J Simpson at his 1995 murder trial.

1 When you see a lawyer trying to pick a smart jury, you know he's got a strong case.
1972 In the *Los Angeles Times*, 9 Jan.

2 The guilty never escape unscathed. My fees are sufficient punishment for anyone.
1972 In the *Los Angeles Times*, 9 Jan.

3 I think my grandmother actually smelled like a cookie and that's enough to get any child's attention.
Quoted by Phyllis Hanes in *Christian Science Monitor*, 15 Jun 1988.

Bailey, Nathan d.1742

English lexicographer, best known for *An Universal Etymological English Dictionary* (1721), which gives word origins as well as definitions.

4 LONDON…the Metropolis of *Great-Britain*, founded before the City of *Rome*, walled by *Constantine* the Great, no ways inferior to the greatest in *Europe* for Riches and Greatness.
1721 *An Universal Etymological English Dictionary.*

Bailey, Philip James 1816–1902

English poet, father of the Spasmodic school. His great work *Festus* (1839) was expanded in 1889 to incorporate previously published volumes: *The Angel World* (1850), *The Mystic* (1855) and *Universal Hymn* (1867).

5 America, thou half-brother of the world;
With something good and bad of every land.
1839 *Festus*, sc.10.

Baillie, Robert 1599–1662

Scottish Presbyterian leader, an opponent of Archbishop Laud and of episcopacy. He was selected by the Scottish Church to invite Charles II to accept the covenant and crown of Scotland.

6 The Parliament of England cannot have on earth so strong pillars and pregnant supporters of all their privileges as free protestant assemblies established by law, and kept in their full freedom from the lowest to the highest—from the congregational eldership to the general synod of the nation.
A Dissuasive from the Errors of Time, 1645–6.

Bainbridge, Dame Beryl Margaret 1934–

English novelist and playwright. She worked as an actress and publisher's clerk before publishing *A Weekend with Claude* (1967). Her work is marked by a caustic wit and a finely turned prose style.

7 I am of the firm belief that everybody could write books and I never understand why they don't. After all, everybody speaks. Once the grammar has been learnt it is simply talking on paper and in time learning what not to say.
1976 In D L Kirkpatrick (ed) *Contemporary Novelists*.

8 Being constantly with children was like wearing a pair of shoes that were expensive and too small. She couldn't bear to throw them out, but they gave her blisters.
1977 *Injury Time*, ch.4.

9 We are essentially fragile. We don't have to wait for the sword or some other equally sensational weapon to strike us down… There are so many ways of us dying it's astonishing any of us choose old age.
1978 *Young Adolf*, ch.12.

10 I haven't the humility to find anything beneath me.
1989 *An Awfully Big Adventure*, ch.3.

11 It's all changed now, which is why it mattered to those young men from Liverpool that they should be there to support their team. What other group is going to troop their colours for them, present them with scarves and emblems?
1989 After the Hillsborough football disaster. Quoted in David Pickering *The Cassell Soccer Companion* (1994).

12 The vital accessories to my work are my reference books, such as the complete Shakespeare and a prayer book, and a large refuse bin.
1991 In *The Guardian*, 8 Aug.

13 Women are programmed to love completely, and men are programmed to spread it around.
1996 Interview in the *Daily Telegraph*, 10 Sep.

14 Bugger the writing, I'd have given anything to have had a long-lasting relationship.
2004 In *The Times*, 7 Apr.

Bairnsfather, Bruce 1888–1959

British cartoonist, a soldier in World War I and cartoonist with US troops in World War II. His works include *Fragments from France* (1916), *Bullets and Billets* (1917) and *Jeeps and Jests* (1943).

15 Well, if you knows of a better 'ole, go to it.
1915 Caption to cartoon in *Fragments from France*. The speaker, Ol' Bill, is waist-deep in mud on the Somme. The phrase was used as the title for a 1926 US film based on the character, *The Better 'Ole*.

Baker, Colin 1943–

English actor who played Doctor Who from 1984 to 1986.

16 Love is a human emotion and the doctor isn't human. We

were always told there is one golden rule: no hanky panky in the Tardis.
2004 On playing Doctor Who. Quoted in the *Sunday Times*, 7 Mar.

Baker, Howard Henry, Jr 1925–

US public official, Republican senator from Tennessee and a member of the Watergate Committee (1973). He became Senate Leader and White House Chief of Staff (1987–8) under Reagan.

17 Never speak more clearly than you think.
1987 On becoming President Reagan's third Chief of Staff. In the *New York Times*, 6 Sep.

Baker, James Addison, III 1930–

US lawyer and government official. He managed the campaigns of Ford (1976) and Bush (1980, 1988). As Secretary of State (1989–92) he initiated a round of Middle East peace talks.

18 Sometimes you move publicly, sometimes privately. Sometimes quietly, sometimes at the top of your voice. And sometimes an active policy is best advanced by doing nothing until the right time—or never.
1990 Of statesmanship. In *Time*, 19 Mar.

Baker, John Austin 1928–

English cleric and theologian, Bishop of Salisbury (1982–93).

19 The crucified Jesus is the only accurate picture of God the world has ever seen.
1970 *The Foolishness of God.*

Baker (of Dorking), Kenneth Baker, Baron 1934

English Conservative politician and writer. He was Secretary of State for the Environment (1985) and introduced a controversial education reform bill as Secretary of State for Education (1986–9) under Margaret Thatcher. He was Home Secretary under John Major (1990–2).

20 If Conservative Backbench MPs want to get on in politics they will have to find a foothold in the narrow strip of land that lies between sycophancy and rebellion.
1979 Queen's Speech in the House of Commons.

21 Why should Scottish and Welsh nationalism be seen as a noble thing, when in England it is seen as something dirty?
2000 In the *Sunday Times*, 'Talking Heads', 6 Jan.

Baker, Russell Wayne 1925–

US newspaper columnist and humorist. In 1979 won a Pulitzer Prize for distinguished commentary.

22 So there he is at last. Man on the moon. The poor magnificent bungler! He can't even get to the office without undergoing the agonies of the damned, but give him a little metal, a few chemicals, some wire and twenty or thirty billion dollars and vroom! there he is, up on a rock a quarter of a million miles up in the sky.
1969 Editoral pages, the *New York Times*, 21 Jul.

23 What is it about sociology that instantly bogs us down in fens of jargon?
1990 In the *New York Times*, 15 Dec.

24 California's power to cloud men's minds must never be forgot. Under its spell we submitted for eight years to the governance of Ronald Reagan, who had trouble distinguishing history from old movie plots.
1995 'Don't Look Back', in the *New York Times*, 1 Aug.

Bakunin, Mikhail Alekseyevich 1814–76

Russian anarchist. He was sent to Siberia in 1855 but escaped, and became an advocate of anarchism, speaking against Marx at the First Communist International (1868), until he was outvoted and expelled at the Hague Congress (1872).

25 From each according to his faculties, to each according to his needs; that is what we wish, sincerely and energetically.
1870 Anarchists' declaration, signed by the 47 defendants after the failed uprising in Lyons.
➤ *See Marx 558:14.*

Balazs, Bela *originally* Hubert Bauer 1884–1949

Hungarian writer who wrote *Theory of the Film: Character and Growth of a New Art* (1953).

26 Film art has a greater influence on the minds of the general public than any other art.
1953 *Theory of the Film: Character and Growth of a New Art* (translated by Edith Bone).

Balcon, Michael 1896–1977

British film producer.

27 In the absence of money, we'll have to make do with talent.
Quoted in David Puttnam *Michael Balcon: The Pursuit of British Cinema* (1984), preface.

28 Well if you fellows feel so strongly in favour, on my head be it.
Quoted in David Puttnam *Michael Balcon: The Pursuit of British Cinema* (1984), preface.

Baldwin, James Arthur 1924–87

US writer and civil rights activist. His often autobiographical novels include *Go Tell it on the Mountain* (1954) and *Just Above My Head* (1979).

29 At the root of the American Negro problem is the necessity of the American white man to find a way of living with the Negro in order to be able to live with himself.
1953 'Stranger in a Village', in *Harper's*, Oct.

30 It seems to be typical of life in America, where opportunities, real and fancied, are thicker than anywhere else on the globe, that the second generation has no time to talk to the first.
1955 *Notes of a Native Son*, 'Notes of a Native Son'.

31 I learned in New Jersey that to be a Negro meant, precisely, that one was never looked at but was simply at the mercy of the reflexes the color of one's skin caused in other people.
1955 *Notes of a Native Son*, 'Notes of a Native Son'.

32 The writer's greed is appalling. He wants, or seems to want, everything and practically everybody; in another sense, and at the same time, he needs no one at all.
1961 *Nobody Knows My Name*, 'Alas, Poor Richard'.

33 Children have never been very good at listening to their

elders, but they have never failed to imitate them. They must, they have no other models.
1961 *Nobody Knows My Name*, 'Fifth Avenue, Uptown'.

34 Anyone who has ever struggled with poverty knows how extremely expensive it is to be poor.
1961 *Nobody Knows My Name*, 'Fifth Avenue, Uptown'.

35 Freedom is not something that anybody can be given; freedom is something people take and people are as free as they want to be.
1961 *Nobody Knows My Name*, 'Notes for a Hypothetical Novel'.

36 Money, it turned out, was exactly like sex, you thought of nothing else if you didn't have it and thought of other things if you did.
1961 'Black Boy Looks at the White Boy', in *Esquire*, May.

37 If the concept of God has any validity or any use, it can only be to make us larger, freer, and more loving. If God cannot do this, then it is time we got rid of Him.
1962 'Down at the Cross', in the *New Yorker*, 17 Nov.

38 The Fire Next Time.
1963 Title of book of essays. Baldwin took the phrase from the traditional spiritual, 'Home in the Rock'.

39 It comes as a great shock around the age of five, six or seven to discover that the flag to which you have pledged your allegiance, along with everybody else, has not pledged its allegiance to you. It comes as a shock to see Gary Cooper killing off the Indians and, although you are rooting for Gary Cooper, that the Indians are you.
1965 Speech at Cambridge Union, 17 Feb, arguing for the motion that 'The American Dream is at the expense of the American Negro'.

40 If they take you in the morning, they will be coming for us that night.
1971 'Open Letter to my Sister, Angela Davis', in *The New York Review of Books*, 7 Jan.

Baldwin (of Bewdley), Stanley Baldwin, 1st Earl
1867–1947

English Conservative politician, Chancellor (1922–3) and Prime Minister (1923, 1924–9 and 1935–7). His period of office was marked by the abdication of Edward VIII in 1936.

41 A lot of hard-faced men who look as if they had done very well out of the war.
1918 Of the first post- World War I Parliament. Quoted in J M Keynes *Economic Consequences of the Peace* (1919).

42 I met Curzon in Downing Street, and received the sort of greeting a corpse would give an undertaker.
1923 Of his rival for the premiership, Lord Curzon, on the death of Bonar Law. Attributed.

43 A platitude is simply a truth repeated until people get tired of hearing it.
1924 Speech in the House of Commons, 29 May.

44 There are three classes which need sanctuary more than others—birds, wild flowers, and Prime Ministers.
1925 In the *Observer*, 24 May.

45 The work of a Prime Minister is the loneliest job in the world.
1927 Speech, 9 Jan.

46 The papers conducted by Lord Rothermere and Lord Beaverbrook are not newspapers in the ordinary acceptance of the term. They are engines of propaganda for the constantly-changing policies, desires, personal wishes, and personal likes and dislikes of two men… What the proprietorship of those papers is aiming at is power, and power without responsibility—the prerogative of the harlot throughout the ages.
1931 Speech, 18 Mar. Rudyard Kipling, Baldwin's cousin, is alleged to be the original author of this famous phrase. Harold Macmillan claimed that the Duke of Devonshire (his father-in-law) responded 'Good God, that's done it, he's lost us the tarts.'

47 I think it is well also for the man in the street to realize that there is no power on earth that can protect him from being bombed. Whatever people will tell him, the bomber will always get through. The only defence is in offence, which means that you have to kill more women and children more quickly than the enemy if you want to save yourselves.
1932 Speech in the House of Commons, 10 Nov.

48 When you think about the defence of England, you no longer think of the chalk cliffs of Dover. You think of the Rhine. That is where our frontier lies today.
1934 House of Commons, 30 Jul.

49 There is a wind of nationalism and freedom blowing round the world, and blowing as strongly in Asia as elsewhere.
1934 Speech, Dec.

50 I shall be but a short time tonight. I have seldom spoken with greater regret, for my lips are not yet unsealed. Were these troubles over I would make a case, and I guarantee that not a man would go into the lobby against us.
1935 Speech in the House of Commons, 10 Dec, speaking on the Abyssinian crisis. This is often misquoted as 'My lips are sealed'.

51 You will find in politics that you are much exposed to the attribution of false motives. Never complain and never explain.
1943 Advice to Harold Nicholson.

52 When the call came for me to form a Government, one of my first thoughts was that it should be a Government of which Harrow would not be ashamed.
Attributed.

Balfour, Arthur James Balfour, 1st Earl 1848–1930

Scottish Conservative politician and Prime Minister (1902–5). As Chief Secretary for Ireland (1887–91) his policy of suppression earned him the name 'Bloody Balfour', and as Foreign Secretary (1916–19) he was responsible for the Balfour Declaration, which promised Zionists a national home in Palestine.

53 I look forward to a time when Irish patriotism will as easily combine with British patriotism as Scottish patriotism combines now.
1889 Speech, Glasgow, Dec.

54 His Majesty's Government looks with favour upon the establishment in Palestine of a national home for the Jews.
1917 The Balfour Declaration, made in a letter to Lord Rothschild, 2 Nov.

55 The General Strike has taught the working classes more in four days than years of talking could have done.
1926 Speech in the House of Commons, 7 May.

56 I thought that he was a young man of promise, but it appears that he is a young man of promises.
Of Winston Churchill. Quoted in Churchill *My Early Life* (1930), ch. 17.

57 Herbert Asquith's clarity is a great liability because he has nothing to say.
Quoted by George Will in *Newsweek*, 9 Sep 1991.

58 Nothing matters very much, and very few things matter at all.
Attributed.

59 I would rather be an opportunist and float, than go to the bottom with my principles around my neck.
Attributed.

60 It has always been desirable to tell the truth, but seldom if ever necessary to tell the whole truth.
Attributed.

Ball, George Wildman 1909–94

US lawyer and diplomat. As Under-Secretary of State (1961–6) he played a major part in foreign policy, particularly in the Trade Agreements of 1962. He opposed the war in Vietnam, and left government for banking in 1966.

61 Once on the tiger's back, we cannot be sure of picking the place to dismount.
1964 Memo to Secretary of Defense Robert S McNamara, 5 Oct, on the escalation of the Vietnam War. It became known as 'the tiger's back memo'. Quoted in Deborah Shapley *Promise and Power* (1993).

62 Like giving the keys of the world's largest liquor store to a confirmed alcoholic.
On oil profiteering that permitted an arms-buying spree by Mohammed Reza Pahlavi, last shah of Iran. Quoted in William Shawcross *The Shah's Last Ride* (1988).

63 Never to be bored, never to be frustrated, never to be alone.
Defining what John F Kennedy wanted from the presidency. *President Kennedy* (1993).

Ball, John d.1381

English priest, one of the leaders of the Peasants' Revolt of 1381. He was executed for his part in these events.

64 When Adam delved and Eve span,
Who was then a gentleman?
1381 Sermon on the eve of the Peasants' Revolt. Quoted in George Holmes *The Later Middle Ages, 1272–1485* (1962), ch.7.

Ballads

65 'Oh, mother, mother, mak my bed,
And mak it saft and narrow;
My love has died for me to-day,
I'll die for him tomorrow.'
'Barbara Allen'.

66 It fell about the Lammas tide,
When the muir-men win their hay,
The doughty Douglas bound him to ride
Into England, to drive a prey.
'The Battle of Otterbourne', opening lines.

67 There was twa sisters in a bower,
Binnorie, O Binnorie;
There came a knight to be their wooer,
By the bonnie mill-dams o' Binnorie.
'Binnorie', stanza 1.

68 Ye Highlands and ye Lawlands,
O where hae ye been?
They hae slain the Earl of Murray
And laid him on the green.
'The Bonnie Earl of Murray', stanza 1.

69 He was a braw gallant,
And he play'd at the ba';
And the bonnie Earl of Murray
Was the flower amang them a'.

He was a braw gallant,
And he play'd at the glove;
And the bonnie Earl of Murray,
O he was the Queen's luve.

O lang will his lady
Look owre the castle Doune,
Ere she sees the Earl of Murray
Come sounding thro' the toun.
'The Bonnie Earl of Murray'.

70 O the broom, the bonnie, bonnie broom,
The broom of Cowdenknowes;
I wish I were with my dear swain,
With his pipe and my yowes.
'The Broom of Cowdenknowes', opening lines.

71 'A bed, a bed,' Clerk Sanders said,
'A bed for you and me!'
'Fye na, fye na,' said may Margaret,
'Till anes we married be!'
'Clerk Sanders'

72 Is there any room at your head, Sanders?
Is there any room at your feet?
Or any room at your twa sides,
Where fain, fain I would sleep?

There is nae room at my head, Margaret,
There is nae room at my feet;
My bed it is the cold, cold grave;
Among the hungry worms I sleep.
'Clerk Sanders'.

73 She hadna sailed a league, a league,
A league but barely three,
When dismal grew his countenance
And drumlie grew his e'e.
They hadna sailed a league, a league,
A league but barely three,
Until she espied his cloven foot,
And she wept right bitterlie.
'The Demon Lover'.

74 Late at e'en, drinkin' the wine,
And ere they paid the lawin',
They set a combat them between,
To fight it at the dawin'.

'O stay at hame, my noble lord,
O stay at hame, my marrow!
My cruel brother will you betray
On the dowie houms o' Yarrow!'
'The Dowie Houms o' Yarrow'.

75 'Yestreen I dreamed a dolefu' dream;
I ken'd here wad be sorrow!
I dreamed I pu'd the heather green,
On the dowie banks o' Yarrow.'

She gaed up yon high, high hill—
I wat she gaed wi' sorrow—
An' in the den spied nine dead men,
On the dowie houms o' Yarrow.
'The Dowie Houms o' Yarrow'.

76 'Why dois your brand sae drap wi' bluid,
Edward, Edward,
Why dois your brand sae drap wi' bluid,
And why sae sad gang ye O?'
'Edward', opening lines.

77 Then up and started our gudewife,
Gied three skips on the floor:
'Gudeman, ye've spoken the foremost word,
Get up and bar the door.'
'Get Up and Bar the Door'.

78 I wish I were where Helen lies,
Night and day on me she cries;
O that I were where Helen lies,
On fair Kirkconnell lea!
'Helen of Kirkconnell', opening lines.

79 'It's I, Jamie Telfer o' the fair Dodhead,
And a harried man I think I be!
There's naething left at the fair Dodhead
But a waefu' wife and bairnies three.'
'Jamie Telfer'.

80 'Will ye gang wi' me, Lizzy Lindsay,
Will ye gang to the Highlands wi' me?
Will ye gang wi' me, Lizzy Lindsay,
My bride and my darling to be?'
'Lizzy Lindsay', opening lines.

81 This ae nighte, this ae nighte,
—*Every nighte and alle*,
Fire and fleet and candle-lighte,
And Christe receive thy saule.
'A Lyke-Wake Dirge', opening lines.

82 Marie Hamilton's to the kirk gane,
Wi' ribbons in her hair;
The king thought mair o' Marie Hamilton
Than ony that were there.
'Marie Hamilton', opening lines.

83 'Yestreen the queen had four Maries,
The night she'll hae but three;
There was Marie Seaton, and Mari Beaton,
And Marie Carmichael, and me.'
'Marie Hamilton'.

84 The king sits in Dunfermline town,
Drinking the blude-red wine;
'O whare will I get a skeely skipper,
To sail this new ship of mine?'
'Sir Patrick Spens', opening lines.

85 'I saw the new moon late yestreen,
Wi' the auld moon in her arm;
And if we gang to sea, master,
I fear we'll come to harm.'
'Sir Patrick Spens'.

86 And lang, lang may the ladyes sit,
Wi' their fans into their hand,
Before they see Sir Patrick Spens
Come sailing to the strand!
'Sir Patrick Spens'.

87 Half-owre, half-owre to Aberdour,
'Tis fifty fathoms deep,
And there lies gude Sir Patrick Spens,
Wi' the Scots lords at his feet.
'Sir Patrick Spens'.

88 'O I forbid you, maidens a',
That wear gowd on your hair,
To come or gae by Carterhaugh,
For young Tam Lin is there.

'There's nane that gaes by Carterhaugh,
But they leave him a wad.
Either their rings or green mantles,
Or else their maidenhead.'

Janet has kilted her green kirtle
A little aboon her knee,
And she has braided her yellow hair
A little aboon her bree,
And she's awa' to Carterhaugh
As fast as she can hie.
'Tam Lin', opening stanzas.

89 True Thomas lay on Huntlie bank,
A ferlie he spied wi' his e'e,
And there he saw a ladye bright,
Come riding down by the Eildon Tree.
'Thomas the Rhymer', opening lines.

90 And see ye not yon braid, braid road,
That lies across the lily leven?
That is the path of Wickedness,
Though some call it the Road to Heaven.
'Thomas the Rhymer'.

91 There were three ravens sat on a tree,
They were as black as they might be.
The one of them said to his make,
'Where shall we our breakfast take?'
'The Three Ravens'.

92 As I was walking all alane,
I heard twa corbies making a mane;
The tane unto the tother say,
'Where sall we gang and dine to-day?'

'In behint yon auld fail dye,
I wot there lies a new-slain knight;
And naebody kens that he lies there,
But his hawk, his hound, and his lady fair.

'His hound is to the hunting gane,
His hawk to fetch the wild-fowl hame,
His lady's ta'en another mate,
So we may mak our dinner sweet.'
'The Twa Corbies', opening stanzas.

93 O'er his white banes, when they are bare,
The wind sall blaw for evermair.
'The Twa Corbies'.

94 O waly, waly up the bank,
And waly, waly doun the brae,
And waly, waly yon burn-side
Where I and my love wont to gae.

I lean'd my back unto an aik,

I thocht it was a trustie tree;
But first it bow'd, and syne it brake—
Sae my true love did lichtlie me.

O waly, waly, gin love be bonnie
A little time while it is new;
But when 'tis auld it waxeth cauld
And fades awa' like morning dew.

O wherefore should I busk my heid,
O wherefore should I kame my hair?
For my true love has me forsook,
And says he'll never lo'e me mair.
pre-1566 'Waly, Waly', opening stanzas

95 But had I wist, before I kiss'd,
That love had been sae ill to win.
I'd lock'd my heart in a case o' gowd,
And pinn'd it wi' a siller pin.
pre-1566 'Waly, Waly', stanza 4.

96 Tom Pearce, Tom Pearce, lend me your grey mare,
All along, down along, out along lee.
For I want for to go to Widdicombe Fair,
Wi' Bill Brewer, Jan Stewer, Peter Gurney, Peter Davey,
Dan'l Whiddon, Harry Hawk,
Old Uncle Tom Cobleigh and all.
'Widdicombe Fair'.

97 There lived a wife at Usher's Well,
And a wealthy wife was she;
She had three stout and stalwart sons,
And sent them o'er the sea.
'The Wife of Usher's Well', opening lines.

98 The cock doth craw, the day doth daw,
The channerin' worm doth chide.
'The Wife of Usher's Well'.

Ballard, J(ames) G(raham) 1930–

British novelist and science-fiction writer, born in China. His best-known work, the novel *Empire of the Sun* (1984), draws on his childhood experiences in wartime Shanghai, then occupied by Japan.

99 The only truly alien planet is Earth.
1962 'Which Way to Inner Space', in *New Worlds*, May.

1 He believes that science fiction is the apocalyptic literature of the 20th century, the authentic language of Auschwitz, Eniwetok and Aldermaston. He also believes that inner space, not outer, is the real subject of science fiction.
1965 Author's statement contained in a biographical note to *The Drowned World*.

2 Science and technology multiply around us. To an increasing extent they dictate the languages in which we speak and think. Either we use those languages, or we remain mute.
1974 *Crash*.

Balliett, Whitney 1926–

US writer. He became jazz critic of the *New Yorker* in 1957, and has written several books on music.

3 The Sound of Surprise.
1959 Title of book, much cited as a definition of jazz.

4 A bundle of biases held loosely together by a sense of taste.
1962 His definition of a critic. *Dinosaurs in the Morning*, introductory note.

Balzac, Honoré de 1799–1850

French writer, one of the great 19c realist novelists. He created a world of characters whose lives are interwoven in his *Comédie humaine* (1842).

5 *Un homme n'a jamais pu élever sa maîtresse jusqu'à lui; mais une femme place toujours son amant aussi haut qu'elle.*
A man can never elevate his mistress to his rank, but a woman can always place her lover as high as she.
1829 *Physiologie du mariage*.

6 *Le mariage doit incessamment combattre un monstre qui dévore tout: l'habitude.*
Marriage should always combat the monster that devours everything: habit.
1829 *Physiologie du mariage*.

7 *La femme mariée est un esclave qu'il faut savoir mettre sur un trône.*
A married woman is a slave whom one must put on a throne.
1829 *Physiologie du mariage*.

8 *Un mari, comme un gouvernement, ne doit jamais avouer de faute.*
A husband, like a government, never needs to admit a fault.
1829 *Physiologie du mariage*.

9 *En toute chose, nous ne pouvons être jugés que par nos pairs.*
In all things, we should only be judged by our peers.
1830 *La Maison du chat-qui-pelote*.

10 *Dans ces grandes crises, le coeur se brise ou se bronze.*
In times of crisis, the heart either breaks or boldens.
1830 *La Maison du chat-qui-pelote*.

11 *Le bonheur engloutit nos forces, comme le malheur éteint nos vertus.*
Happiness engulfs our strength, just as misfortune extinguishes our virtues.
1831 *La Peau de chagrin*.

12 *La haine est un tonique, elle fait vivre, elle inspire la vengeance; mais la pitié tue, elle affaiblit encore notre faiblesse.*
Hatred is a tonic, it makes one live, it inspires vengeance; but pity kills, it weakens our weaknesses still further.
1831 *La Peau de chagrin*.

13 *Beaucoup d'hommes ont un orgueil qui les pousse à cacher leurs combats et à ne se montrer que victorieux.*
Many men have pride that causes them to hide their combats and to only show themselves victorious.
1831 *La Recherche de l'absolu*.

14 *À lui la foi, à elle le doute, à elle le fardeau le plus lourd: la femme ne souffre-t-elle pas toujours pour deux?*
For him, faith; for her, doubt and for her the heavier load: does not the woman always suffer for both?
1831 *La Recherche de l'absolu*.

15 *L'amour n'est pas seulement un sentiment, il est un art aussi.*
Love is not only a feeling; it is also an art.
1831 *La Recherche de l'absolu*.

16 *L'amour a son instinct, il sait trouver le chemin du coeur comme le plus faible insecte marche à sa fleur avec une irrésistible volonté qui ne s'épouvante de rien.*
Love has its own instinct. It knows how to find the road to the heart just as the weakest insect moves toward its flower by an irresistible will which fears nothing.
1832 *La Femme de trente ans*.

17 *Le coeur d'une mère est un abîme au fond duquel se trouve toujours un pardon.*
A mother's heart is an abyss at the bottom of which there is always forgiveness.
1832 *La Femme de trente ans*.

18 *Les faits ne sont rien, ils n'existent pas, il ne subsiste de nous que des Idées.*
Deeds are nothing. They do not exist. Only our ideas survive.
1832 *Louis Lambert*.

19 *Nos beaux sentiments ne sont-ils pas les poésies de la volonté?*
Aren't our best feelings poetry of the will?
1835 *Le Père Goriot*.

20 *La passion est toute l'humanité. Sans elle, la religion, l'histoire, le roman, l'art seraient inutiles.*
Passion is all of humanity. Without it, religion, history, the novel and art would be useless.
1842 *La Comédie humaine*, foreword.

21 *L'homme n'est ni bon ni méchant, il naît avec des instincts et des aptitudes.*
Man is neither good nor evil; he is born with instincts and abilities.
1842 *La Comédie humaine*, foreword.

22 *L'avarice commence où la pauvreté cesse.*
Greed begins where poverty ends.
1843 *Illusions perdues*, 'Les deux poètes'.

23 *Les dettes sont jolies chez les jeunes gens de vingt-cinq ans, plus tard, personne ne les leur pardonne.*
Debts are becoming for 25-year-olds; after this, no one forgives them.
1843 *Illusions perdues*, 'Un Grand homme de province'.

Banda, Hastings Kamuzu 1898–1997

Malawian statesman, Prime Minister (1963) and President (1966; Life President from 1971).

24 I wish that I could bring Stonehenge to Nyasaland, to show that there was a time when Britain had a savage culture.
1963 In the *Observer*, 10 Mar.

Bandeira, Manuel 1886–1968

Brazilian poet, literary historian, translator and educator. He achieved enormous popularity and national acclaim.

25 *Estou farto do lirismo comedido*
Do lirismo bem comportado
Do lirismo funcionário público com livro de ponto expediente protocolo e manifestações de apreço ao Sr Diretor.
Estou farto do lirismo que pára e vai averiguar no dicionário o cunho vernáculo de um vocábulo.

Abaixo os puristas

I'm sick of cautious lyricism
of well-behaved lyricism
of a civil servant lyricism complete with time card office hours set procedures and expressions of esteem for Mr Boss, Sir.
I'm sick of the lyricism that has to stop in midstream to look up the precise meaning of a word.

Down with purists!
1930 *Libertinagem*, 'Poética' (translated as 'Poetics', 1989).

Bankhead, Tallulah 1903–68

US actress. She made her New York debut in 1918 and subsequently played a range of classical and contemporary roles, attracting notoriety for her scandalous private life. She wrote an autobiography, *Tallulah* (1952).

26 There is less in this than meets the eye.
1922 Attending a revival of Maeterlinck's play *Aglavaine and Selysette*. Quoted in Alexander Woollcott *Shouts and Murmurs* (1923), ch.4.

27 Cocaine habit-forming? Of course not. I ought to know. I've been using it for years.
1939 In conversation at the first night party of Lillian Hellman's *Little Foxes*. Recalled in *Tallulah* (1952), ch.4.

28 I'm as pure as the driven slush.
Quoted by Maurice Zolotow, in *The Saturday Evening Post*, 12 Apr 1947.

29 Darling, they've absolutely ruined your perfectly dreadful play!
1957 Greeting Tennessee Williams at the film première of his play *Orpheus Descending*. Quoted in Peter Hay *Broadway Anecdotes*.

30 Only good girls keep diaries. Bad girls don't have time.
Recalled on her death, 12 Dec 1968.

31 Nobody can be exactly like me. Sometimes even I have trouble doing it.
Attributed.

Banks, Iain Menzies 1954–

Scottish novelist and science-fiction writer. His works include *The Wasp Factory* (1984) and *Complicity* (1993). He writes science-fiction novels using the name Iain M Banks.

32 They are, after all, a language; they do not so much say things about as, they are what is said.
1986 Of clothes. *The Bridge*, ch.2.

33 'You're not upset, are you, Orr?' Brooke says, pouring wine into my glass.
'Merely sober. The symptoms are similar.'
1986 *The Bridge*, ch.3.

34 The choice is not between dream and reality; it is between two different dreams.
1986 *The Bridge*, coda.

35 It was the day my grandmother exploded.
1992 *The Crow Road*, ch.1, opening words.

36 Mr Blawke always reminded me of a heron; I'm not sure why. Something to do with a sense of rapacious stillness, perhaps, and also the aura of one who knows time is on his side.
1992 Of the family lawyer. *The Crow Road*, ch.1.

37 The belief that we somehow moved on to something else—whether still recognisably ourselves, or quite

thoroughly changed—might be a tribute to our evolutionary tenacity and our animal thirst for life, but not to our wisdom.
1992 On the idea of life after death. *The Crow Road*, ch.18.

Banks, Lynne Reid 1929–

English novelist and playwright. Her best-known novel is her first, *The L-Shaped Room* (1960). She has also written plays for radio and television and fiction for children.

38 Jane Austen is the only novelist I know whose peculiar genius lies in taking perfectly ordinary people through ordinary situations, and transmogrifying them into fascinating fiction.
1991 In her entry in *Contemporary Novelists*, 5th edn.

Bannister, Sir Roger Gilbert 1929–

English athlete and neurologist. In 1954 he ran the first 'four-minute mile' (3 mins 59.4 secs). He was knighted in 1975. After a distinguished medical career, he was appointed Master of Pembroke College, Oxford (1985–93).

39 I leapt at the tape like a man taking his last spring to save himself from the chasm that threatens to engulf him.
1955 Of the end of his record-breaking run. *First Four Minutes*.

40 I sometimes think that running has given me a glimpse of the greatest freedom a man can ever know, because it results in the simultaneous liberation of both body and mind.
1955 *First Four Minutes*.

Banting, Frederick Grant 1891–1941

Canadian physician and discoverer of insulin.

41 Diabetus. Ligate pancreatic ducts of dog. Keep dogs alive till acini degenerate leaving Islets. Try to isolate the internal secretion of these to relieve glycosuria.
1920 Note scribbled in his journal, 2.00am, 31 Oct. This led to the discovery of insulin for the treatment of diabetes, as recorded in Michael Bliss *The Discovery of Insulin* (1982).

Barach, Alvan Leroy 1895–1977

US physician. He was Professor of Medicine at Columbia University and a pioneer in respiratory therapy.

42 An alcoholic has been lightly defined as a man who drinks more than his own doctor.
1962 In the *Journal of the American Medical Association*, vol.181, p.393.

Baraka, Amiri *adopted name of* LeRoi (Everett Leroy) Jones 1934–

US poet, playwright and prose writer. He adopted a Muslim identity in 1967 after establishing his reputation as a radical and outspoken black voice.

43 Preface to a Twenty Volume Suicide Note.
1961 Title of poetry collection.

44 A rich man told me recently that a liberal is a man who tells other people what to do with their money.
1962 'Tokenism', in *Kulchur*, spring issue.

45 A man is either free or he is not. There cannot be any apprenticeship for freedom.
1962 'Tokenism', in *Kulchur*, spring issue.

46 But when a man who sees the world one way becomes the slave of a man who interprets the world in exactly the opposite way, the result is, to my mind, the *worst* possible kind of slavery.
1963 *Blues People*, ch.1.

Barbellion, W(illiam) N(ero) P(ilate) *pseudonym of* Bruce Frederick Cummings 1889–1919

English diarist. He was a self-taught biologist, and worked for the British Museum. His principal work is the self-critical *Journal of A Disappointed Man* (1919).

47 I can remember wondering as a child if I were a young Macaulay or Ruskin and secretly deciding that I was. My infant mind even was bitter with those who insisted on regarding me as a normal child and not as a prodigy.
1919 *Journal of A Disappointed Man*, 23 Oct.

48 Give me the man who will surrender the whole world for a moss or a caterpillar, and impracticable visions for a simple human delight.
1919 *Enjoying Life and Other Literary Remains*, 'Crying for the Moon'.

Barbirolli, Sir John 1899–1970

British conductor and cellist, conductor of the New York Philharmonic in 1937 and of the Hallé Orchestra in Manchester (1943–58). In 1950 he was awarded the Gold Medal of the Royal Philharmonic Society, and he became principal conductor of the Hallé in 1958.

49 Three farts and a raspberry, orchestrated.
Of modern music. Quoted in M Kennedy *Barbirolli, Conductor Laureate* (1971).

50 I want you to sound like 22 women having babies without chloroform.
To a chorus. Quoted in M Kennedy *Barbirolli, Conductor Laureate* (1971).

Barbour, John c.1316–1395

Scottish poet, prelate and scholar, the 'father of Scottish poetry'. His national epic, *The Brus*, is a narrative poem on the life of Robert I, the Bruce. He served as Archdeacon of Aberdeen from c.1357 until his death.

51 Storyss to rede ar delitabill,
Supposs that thai be nocht but fabill.
c.1375 *The Brus*, bk.1, l.1–2.

52 A! fredome is a noble thing!
Fredome mayss man to haiff liking,
Fredome all solace to man giffis:
He levys at ess that frely levys!
c.1375 *The Brus*, bk.1, l.225–8.

53 Luff is off sae mekill mycht,
That it all paynis makis lycht.
c.1375 *The Brus*, bk.2, l.520–1.

Barker, George Granville 1913–91

English poet, novelist and playwright. He was associated with Dylan Thomas and the New Apocalyptic group, but his poetry retained a distinctively individual quality.

54 Sitting as huge as Asia, seismic with laughter,
Gin and chicken helpless in her Irish hand.
1944 'To My Mother'.

55 Honouring itself the clay rears up
To praise its pottering purposes,

But, oh, much sorrow shall it sup
Before fulfilment is.
1954 'Goodman Jacksin and the Angel'.

56 When the guns begin to rattle
And the men to die
Does the Goddess of the Battle
Smile or sigh?
1962 'Battle Hymn of the New Republic'.

Barkley, Alben William 1877–1956

US lawyer and Democratic politician, Vice-President under Truman (1949–53).

57 The best audience is intelligent, well-educated and a little drunk.
Recalled on his death, 30 Apr 1956.

Barlow, Joel 1754–1812

US poet. He is best remembered for his mock-heroic salute to the humble hasty-pudding (a dish of boiled Indian meal), although he considered his turgid epic *The Colombiad* (1807) his major work.

58 I sing the sweets I know, the charms I feel,
My morning incense, and my evening meal,
The sweets of Hasty-Pudding. Come, dear bowl,
Glide o'er my palate, and inspire my soul.
1796 'The Hasty-Pudding', canto 1

Barnard, Frederick R

59 One picture is worth ten thousand words.
1927 In *Printer's Ink*, 10 Mar.

Barnes, Clive Alexander 1927–

English theatre critic. He has written for the *New York Post* since 1977, directing much of his venom against the commercial Broadway stage.

60 This is the kind of show to give pornography a bad name.
1969 Reviewing *Oh, Calcutta!*, *New York Times*, 18 Jun.

Barnes, Djuna 1892–1982

US writer, who spent a large part of her life in Europe. She is best known for her novel *Nightwood* (1936).

61 New York is the meeting place of the peoples, the only city where you can hardly find a typical American.
1916 'Greenwich Village As It Is', in *Pearson's Magazine*, Oct.

62 After all, it is not where one washes one's neck that counts but where one moistens one's throat.
1916 'Greenwich Village As It Is', in *Pearson's Magazine*, Oct.

63 Sleep demands of us a guilty immunity. There is not one of us who, given an eternal incognito, a thumbprint nowhere set against our souls, would not commit rape, murder and all abominations.
1936 Doctor. *Nightwood*, ch.5.

64 Dreams have only the pigmentation of fact.
1936 Doctor. *Nightwood*, ch.5.

65 I'm a fart in a gale of wind, a humble violet under a cow pat.
1936 Doctor. *Nightwood*, ch.5.

Barnes, Julian Patrick 1946–

English novelist, formerly a lexicographer and journalist. His best-known work is *Flaubert's Parrot* (1984), a meditation on fiction and biography.

66 We'd both been to the country and found it disappointingly empty.
1981 *Metroland*, pt.1, ch.4.

67 You can have your cake and eat it: the only trouble is you get fat.
1984 *Flaubert's Parrot*, ch.7.

68 The writer must be universal in sympathy and an outcast by nature: only then can he see clearly.
1984 *Flaubert's Parrot*, ch.10.

69 Do not imagine that Art is something which is designed to give gentle uplift and self-confidence. Art is not a *brassière*. At least, not in the English sense. But do not forget that *brassière* is the French for life-jacket.
1984 *Flaubert's Parrot*, ch.10.

70 Books are where things are explained to you; life is where things aren't… Books make sense of life. The only problem is that the lives they make sense of are other people's lives, never your own.
1984 *Flaubert's Parrot*, ch.13.

71 Women were brought up to believe that men were the answer. They weren't. They weren't even one of the questions.
1986 *Staring At The Sun*, pt.2.

72 Does history repeat itself, the first time as tragedy, the second time as farce? No, that's too grand, too considered a process. History just burps, and we taste again that raw-onion sandwich it swallowed centuries ago.
1989 *A History of the World in 10½ Chapters*, 'Parenthesis'.

73 I've always thought you are what you are and you shouldn't pretend to be anyone else. But Oliver used to correct me and explain that you are whoever it is you're pretending to be.
1991 *Talking It Over*, ch.2.

74 Love is just a system for getting someone to call you darling after sex.
1991 *Talking It Over*, ch.16.

75 Remember that cookery writers are no different from other writers: many have only one book in them (and some shouldn't have let it out in the first place).
2003 *The Pedant in the Kitchen*.

Barnum, P(hineas) T(aylor) 1810–91

US showman. He introduced freak shows, including General Tom Thumb (1842), in his New York museum, and in 1881 co-founded the Barnum and Bailey Circus, 'the greatest show on earth'.

76 There's a sucker born every minute.
Attributed.

Barr, Alfred Hamilton, Jr 1902–81

US art historian, first Director of the Museum of Modern Art, New York. His many works include *Cubism and Abstract Art* (1936).

77 Except the American woman, nothing interests the eye of American man more than the automobile, or seems so important to him as an object of aesthetic appreciation.
1963 In news summaries, 31 Dec.

Barrer, Bruce

78 She endured a five-year marriage to Ernest Hemingway that roughly coincided with and bore more than a passing resemblance to World War II.
1993 Of Martha Gelhorn. In the *Wall Street Journal*, 9 Mar.

Barrie, Sir J(ames) M(atthew) 1860–1937

Scottish novelist and dramatist. After journalism and several autobiographical works, he turned to playwriting in 1890, with such works as *The Admirable Crichton* (1902), *Peter Pan* (1904) and *What Every Woman Knows* (1908, published 1918).

79 The life of every man is a diary in which he means to write one story, and writes another; and his humblest hour is when he compares the volume as it is with what he vowed to make it.
1891 *The Little Minister*, vol.1, ch.1.

80 That is ever the way. 'Tis all jealousy to the bride and good wishes to the corpse.
1901 *Quality Street* (published 1913), act 1.

81 When the first baby laughed for the first time, the laugh broke into a thousand pieces and they all went skipping about, and that was the beginning of fairies.
1904 *Peter Pan* (published 1928), act 1.

82 Every time a child says 'I don't believe in fairies' there is a little fairy somewhere that falls down dead.
1904 *Peter Pan* (published 1928), act 1.

83 To die will be an awfully big adventure.
1904 *Peter Pan* (published 1928), act 3.

84 Charm...it's a sort of a bloom on a woman. If you have it, you don't need to have anything else; and if you don't have it, it doesn't much matter what else you have.
1908 *What Every Woman Knows* (published 1918), act 1.

85 My lady, there are few more impressive sights in the world than a Scotsman on the make.
1908 *What Every Woman Knows* (published 1918), act 2.

86 I have always found that the man whose second thoughts are good is worth watching.
1908 *What Every Woman Knows* (published 1918), act 3.

87 Every man who is high up loves to think that he has done it all himself; and the wife smiles, and lets it go at that. It's our only joke. Every woman knows that.
1908 *What Every Woman Knows* (published 1918), act 4.

88 One's religion is whatever he is most interested in, and yours is Success.
1921 *The Twelve-Pound Look*.

89 I bowl so slow that if after I have delivered the ball and don't like the look of it, I can run after it and bring it back.
Quoted in Colin Jarman *The Guinness Dictionary of Sports Quotations* (1990).

90 What a polite game tennis is. The chief word in it seems to be 'sorry' and admiration of each other's play crosses the net as frequently as the ball.
Quoted in Colin Jarman *The Guinness Dictionary of Sports Quotations* (1990).

91 I am glad you have asked me. I should like you to convey when you are acting it that the man you portray has a brother in Shropshire who drinks port.
Responding to a young actor's urgent request for advice as to how he should play a minor part in one of Barrie's plays. Attributed.

Barrington, Jonah 1941–

English squash player. He was British Open Champion 1967–8 and 1970–3.

92 Squash is boxing with racquets.
Quoted in Colin Jarman *The Guinness Dictionary of Sports Quotations* (1990).

Barry, Marion Shepilov, Jr 1936–

US politician, Mayor of Washington, DC (1979–91). He was arrested and charged with possession of cocaine in 1990.

93 There are two kinds of truth...real truths and made-up truths.
1990 Of the drug charges lodged against him. In the *Washington Post*, 13 May.

Barrymore, Ethel 1879–1959

US actress, one of the most prominent members of the Drew-Barrymore acting dynasty. She made her New York debut in 1901 and went on to excel both in contemporary dramas and in Shakespearean roles. New York's Barrymore Theatre was opened in her honour in 1928.

94 For an actress to be a success she must have the face of Venus, the brains of Minerva, the grace of Terpsichore, the memory of Macaulay, the figure of Juno, and the hide of a rhinoceros.
Quoted in George Jean Nathan *The Theatre in the Fifties* (1953).

95 I never let them cough. They wouldn't dare.
1956 Of her audiences. In the *New York Post*, 7 Jun.

Barrymore, John 1882–1942

US actor of the Drew-Barrymore dynasty. He made his stage debut in 1903 and distinguished himself in Shakespearean and other roles before turning to films. Renowned for his chaotic private life, he suffered increasingly from alcoholism.

96 Die? I should say not, old fellow. No Barrymore would allow such a conventional thing to happen to him.
1942 Quoted in Lionel Barrymore *We Barrymores* (1951), ch.26.

97 My only regret in the theatre is that I could never sit out front and watch me.
Quoted in Eddie Cantor *The Way I See It* (1959), ch.2.

98 Method acting? There are quite a few methods. Mine involves a lot of talent, a glass, and some cracked ice.
Quoted in *Actors about Acting, Loving, Living, Life* (1972).

Barrymore, Lionel 1878–1954

US actor, brother of Ethel and John Barrymore. He gave up a successful stage career for the cinema in 1925, finding fame as Dr Gillespie in a series of *Dr Kildare* films (from 1938).

99 How like father—a curtain call!
1905 Attributed comment, when his father's coffin had to be raised up again after it had snagged on being lowered into the grave.

1 I've played everything but the harp.
Attributed, when asked to suggest his own epitaph.

Barth, John Simmons 1930–

US novelist. His books are much concerned with the processes of story-telling and the making of myths.

2 Everyone is necessarily the hero of his own life story.
1958 *The End of the Road*, ch.1.

3 Every life has a Scheherazadesworth of stories.
1994 *Once Upon A Time*, 'Program Note'.

Barth, Karl 1886–1968

Swiss Reformed theologian, champion of neo-orthodoxy and influential in founding the German Confessing Church, which opposed Nazism. His extensive theological output proved highly influential in 20c Christian theology.

4 Jesus Christ, as he is attested to us in Holy Scripture, is the one Word of God whom we have to hear, and whom we have to trust and obey in life and in death.
1934 *The Barmen Declaration* adopted by the Confessing Church in Germany (translated by D S Bax, 1984).

5 Humanity in its basic form is co-humanity.
1948 *Kirchliche Dogmatik* vol.3, pt.2 (translated by H Knight as *Church Dogmatics*, 1960).

6 Basically and comprehensively, therefore, to be human is *to be with God*.
1948 *Kirchliche Dogmatik* vol.3, pt.2 (translated by H Knight as *Church Dogmatics*, 1960).

7 It is a bad sign when Christians are frightened by 'political' sermons—as if Christian preaching could be anything but political.
1954 *Gegen den Strom* (translated by E M Delacourt and S Godwin as 'The Christian Community and the Civil Community' in *Against the Stream*, 1954).

8 Whether the angels play only Bach in praising God I am not quite sure; I am sure, however, that *en famille* they play Mozart.
1968 Quoted in the *New York Times*.

Barthelme, Donald 1931–89

US novelist and short story writer.

9 The distinction between children and adults, while probably useful for some purposes, is at bottom a specious one, I feel. There are only individual egos, crazy for love.
1964 *Come Back, Dr Caligari*, 'Me and Miss Mandible'.

10 We like books that have a lot of *dreck* in them, matter which presents itself as not wholly relevant (or indeed, at all relevant), but which, carefully attended to, can supply a kind of 'sense' of what is going on. This 'sense' is not to be obtained by reading between the lines (for there is nothing there, in those white spaces), but by reading the lines themselves.
1967 *Snow White*.

11 'Some people', Miss R. said, 'run to conceits or wisdom but I hold to the hard, brown, nutlike word. I might point out that there is enough aesthetic excitement here to satisfy anyone but a damned fool.'
1968 *Unspeakable Practices, Unnatural Acts*, 'The Indian Uprising'.

12 Endings are elusive, middles are nowhere to be found, but worst of all is to begin, to begin, to begin.
1968 *Unspeakable Practices, Unnatural Acts*, 'The Dolt'.

13 Doubt is a necessary precondition to meaningful action. Fear is the great mover in the end.
1972 *Sadness*, 'The Rise of Capitalism'.

14 The self cannot be escaped, but it can be, with ingenuity and hard work, distracted.
1972 *Sadness*, 'Daumier'.

15 Let me point out, if it has escaped your notice, that what an artist does, is fail.
1972 *Sadness*, 'The Sandman'.

16 The world is sagging, snagging, scaling, spalling, pilling, pinging, pitting, warping, checking, fading, chipping, cracking, yellowing, leaking, stalling, shrinking, and in dynamic unbalance.
1974 *Guilty Pleasures*, 'Down the Line with the Annual'.

17 No tale ever happened in the way we tell it. But the moral is always correct.
1975 *The Dead Father*, ch.6.

Barthes, Roland 1915–80

French literary critic, and major theorist of semiology. He developed a modernist school of criticism which argues for the 'death' of the author, and the need for the reader to recreate the text.

18 *Je crois que l'automobile est aujourd'hui l'équivalent assez exact des grandes cathédrales gothiques: je veux dire une grande création d'époque, conçue passionnément par des artistes inconnus, consommée dans son image, sinon dans son usage, par un peuple entier qui s'approprie en elle un objet parfaitement magique.*
Cars today are almost the exact equivalent of the great Gothic cathedrals...the supreme creation of an era, conceived with passion by unknown artists, and consummated in image if not in usage by a whole population which appropriates them as a purely magical object.
1957 *Mythologies*, 'La nouvelle Citroën'.

19 *Le toucher est le plus démystificateur de tous les sens, à la différence de la vue, qui est le plus magique.*
Touch is the most demystifying of all senses, different from sight which is the most magical.
1957 *Mythologies*, 'La nouvelle Citroën'.

20 *Tout refus du langage est une mort.*
Any refusal of language is a death.
1957 *Mythologies*, 'Le mythe, aujourd'hui'.

21 *L'endroit le plus érotique d'un corps n'est-il pas là où le vêtement bâille?*
Is not the most erotic part of the body wherever the clothing affords a glimpse?
1973 *Le Plaisir du texte*.

22 *L'amoureux qui n'oublie pas quelquefois meurt par excès, fatigue et tension de mémoire (tel Werther).*
The lover who does not forget *sometimes* dies from excess, fatigue, and the strain of memory (like Werther).
1977 *Fragments d'un discours amoureux*.

23 *Le langage est une peau: je frotte mon langage contre l'autre.*
Language is a skin; I rub my language against another language.
1977 *Fragments d'un discours amoureux*, 'Déclaration'.

24 *Tout ce qui est anachronique est obscène.*
Everything anachronistic is obscene.
1977 *Fragments d'un discours amoureux*, 'Obscène'.

Bartley, Robert Leroy 1937–2003

US journalist. He joined the *Wall Street Journal* in 1962 as a staff writer, and rose to become Editor and Vice-President. He won a Pulitzer Prize for editorial writing in 1980.

25 You can't beat the market because it's smarter than you are. Intellectually, the only task is trying to determine what the market is telling you.
1992 *The Seven Fat Years*, ch.3.

26 The mystery is why we even collect these figures; if we kept similar statistics for Manhattan Island, Park Avenue could lay awake at night worrying about its trade deficit.
1992 On the balance of payments record. *The Seven Fat Years*.

Bartók, Béla 1881–1945

Hungarian composer and pianist. Much influenced by European folk music, he wrote works for piano and strings as well as music for ballet and opera. He died in poverty in the US, having emigrated in 1940.

27 The trouble is that I have to go with so much still to say.
1945 Spoken on his deathbed. Quoted in David Pickering *Brewer's Twentieth Century Music* (1994).

28 I cannot conceive of music that expresses absolutely nothing.
Quoted in Machlis *Introduction to Contemporary Music* (1963).

Baruch, Bernard Mannes 1870–1965

US financier and statesman. He became a powerful political influence, 'the adviser of presidents', and served on many commissions, including the American Atomic Energy Commission.

29 Let us not be deceived—we are today in the midst of a cold war.
1947 Address to the South Carolina legislature, 16 Apr, using an expression suggested to him by editor Herbert Bayard Swope.

30 The cold war is getting warmer.
1948 Address to a Senate committee.

31 To me old age is always fifteen years older than I am.
1955 In *Newsweek*, 29 Aug.

Barzun, Jacques 1907–

French-born US scholar, Professor of History at Columbia University (1945) and Dean and Provost there (1958–67). His works include *Darwin, Marx, Wagner* (1941) and *The Use and Abuse of Art* (1974).

32 Teaching is not a lost art, but the regard for it is a lost tradition.
1955 In *Newsweek*, 5 Dec.

33 The test and use of man's education is that he finds pleasure in the exercise of the mind.
1958 'Science and the Humanities', in the *Saturday Evening Post*, 3 May.

34 If it were possible to talk to the unborn, one could never explain to them how it feels to be alive, for life is washed in the speechless real.
1959 *The House of Intellect*.

35 Science is an all-pervasive energy, for it is at once a mode of thought, a source of strong emotion, and a faith as fanatical as any in history.
1964 *Science, The Glorious Entertainment*.

36 Whoever wants to know the heart and mind of America had better learn baseball.
Quoted in Michael Novak *The Joy of Sport* (1976), pt 1.

37 Baseball is a kind of collective chess with arms and legs in full play under sunlight.
Quoted in Colin Jarman *The Guinness Dictionary of Sports Quotations* (1990).

38 To watch a football game is to be in prolonged neurotic doubt as to what you're seeing. It's more like an emergency happening at a distance than a game.
Quoted in Colin Jarman *The Guinness Dictionary of Sports Quotations* (1990).

Baselitz, Georg 1938–

German avant-garde artist.

39 I have trouble with beauty.
1995 On the effects of witnessing suffering as a child in Dresden during the war. In the *New York Times*, 21 May.

Basho, Matsuo 1644–94

Japanese poet, regarded as the founder of *haiku* as a significant poetic form, and influenced by Zen Buddhism.

40 An old pond
A frog jumps in
The sound of water
c.1689 Quoted in Hugh Cortazzi *The Japanese Achievement* (1990).

41 Year by year,
the monkey's mask
reveals the monkey
c.1689 *On Love and Barley: Haiku of Basho*, no.3 (translated by Lucien Stryk).

42 Year's end—
still in straw hat
and sandals
c.1689 *On Love and Barley: Haiku of Basho*, no.126 (translated by Lucien Stryk).

43 Orchid—breathing
incense into
butterfly's wings
c.1689 *On Love and Barley: Haiku of Basho*, no.166 (translated by Lucien Stryk).

44 Friends part
forever—wild geese
lost in cloud
c.1689 *On Love and Barley: Haiku of Basho*, no.219 (translated by Lucien Stryk).

45 Learn about a pine tree from a pine tree, and about a bamboo stalk from a bamboo stalk.
Attributed, quoted in *On Love and Barley: Haiku of Basho* (translated by Lucien Stryk), introduction.

Baskin, Leonard 1922–2000

US sculptor and graphic artist, also an influential teacher. His powerful works include *Man with a Dead Bird*.

46 Pop art is the inedible raised to the unspeakable.
1965 In *Publisher's Weekly*, 5 Apr.
► *See Wilde 909:22.*

Bastard, Thomas 1566–1618

English poet.

47 Age is deformed, youth unkind,
We scorn their bodies, they our mind.
1598 *Chrestoleros*, bk.7, epigram 9.

Bates, H(erbert) E(rnest) 1905–74

English novelist, playwright and short-story writer. His most popular publications include *Fair Stood the Wind for France* (1944), *The Jacaranda Tree* (1949) and *The Darling Buds of May* (1958).

48 Perfick.
1958 Pa Larkin's characteristic summation. *The Darling Buds of May*, ch.1 and passim.

Bates, Katharine Lee 1859–1929

US educator, author and poet. Her works include *College Beautiful and Other Poems* (1887), *Sunshine and Other Verses for Children* (1890), *Hermit Island* (1891) and *Fairy Gold* (1916).

49 O beautiful for spacious skies,
For amber waves of grain,
For purple mountain majesties
Above the fruited plain!
America! America!
God shed His grace on thee.
And crown thy good with brotherhood
From sea to shining sea.
1893 'America the Beautiful', opening lines.

Bateson, Gregory 1904–80

English-born US social scientist, with interests in anthropology and psychology.

50 Information is any difference that makes a difference.
1984 Quoted in *Scientific American*, no.41, Sep.

Batman, John 1801–39

Australian explorer, generally accepted as the founder of Melbourne, the site of which he bought from a local Aboriginal group for trinkets.

51 This will be the place for a Village.
1835 Journal entry, Jun. The phrase is often quoted as 'a fine place for a Village'.

Battelle, Phyllis 1922–

US columnist.

52 Where great-grandmothers dread to grow old.
1958 Of Hollywood. In the New York *Journal-American*, 15 Mar.

Baudelaire, Charles 1821–67

French Symbolist poet and critic. He is best known for his collection *Les Fleurs du mal* (1857), for which author, printer and publisher were prosecuted for impropriety, but was praised by critics and has exerted an influence far into the 20c.

53 *Hypocrite lecteur,—mon semblable,—mon frère!*
Hypocrite reader—my fellow man—my brother!
1857 *Les Fleurs du mal*, 'Au lecteur'.
► *See Eliot 306:55.*

54 *Je sais la douleur est la noblesse unique*
Où ne mordront jamais la terre et les enfers.
I know that pain is the one nobility
upon which Hell itself cannot encroach.
1857 *Les Fleurs du mal*, 'Bénédiction' (translated by Richard Howard, 1982).

55 *Le Poète est semblable au prince des nuées*
Qui hante la tempête et se rit de l'archer;
Exilé sur le sol au milieu des huées,
Ses ailes de géant l'empêchent de marcher.
The Poet is like that prince of the clouds
Who haunts the storms and laughs at the archer;
Exiled to the ground in the midst of jeers,
His giant wings prevent him from walking.
1857 *Les Fleurs du mal*, 'L'Albatros'—'Spleen et idéal', no.2.

56 *Les parfums, les couleurs et les sons se répondent.*
Scents, colours, and sounds echo one another.
1857 *Les Fleurs du mal*, 'Correspondances'.

57 *Ô douleur! ô douleur! Le Temps mange ma vie.*
Oh pain! Oh pain! time is eating away my life.
1857 *Les Fleurs du mal*, 'L'Ennemi'.

58 *Homme libre, toujours tu chériras la mer.*
Free man! You shall always cherish the sea.
1857 *Les Fleurs du mal*, 'L'Homme et la mer'.

59 *Quand notre coeur a fait une fois sa vendange,*
Vivre est un mal.
Once our heart has been harvested once,
Life becomes miserable.
1857 *Les Fleurs du mal*, 'Semper eadem'.

60 *Ne cherchez plus mon coeur; les bêtes l'ont mangé.*
Don't search any further for my heart; wild beasts ate it.
1857 *Les Fleurs du mal*, 'Causerie'.

61 *Là, tout n'est qu'ordre et beauté,*
Luxe, calme et volupté.
There where all is order and beauty.
Lush, calm and voluptuous.
1857 *Les Fleurs du mal*, 'L'Invitation au Voyage'.

62 *J'ai plus de souvenirs que si j'avais mille ans.*
I have more memories than if I were one thousand years old.
1857 *Les Fleurs du mal*, 'Spleen'.

63 *Souviens-toi que le Temps est un joueur avide*
Qui gagne sans tricher, à tout coup! c'est la loi.
Remember! Time, that tireless gambler, wins
on every turn of the wheel: that is the law.
1857 *Les Fleurs du mal*, 'L'Horloge' (translated by Richard Howard, 1982).

64 *Certes, je sortirai quant à moi satisfait*
D'un monde où l'action n'est pas la soeur du rêve.
Indeed, for my part, I shall be happy to leave
A world where action is not sister to the dream.
1857 *Les Fleurs du mal*, 'Le Reniement de Saint-Pierre'.

65 *Ah! Seigneur! donnez-moi la force et le courage*
De contempler mon coeur et mon corps sans dégoût.
Lord! give me the strength and the courage
To see my heart and my body without disgust.
1857 *Les Fleurs du mal*, 'Un Voyage à Cythère'.

66 *Amer savoir, celui qu'on tire du voyage!*
Bitter is the knowledge gained in travelling.
1857 *Les Fleurs du mal*, 'Le Voyage'.

67 If photography is allowed to stand in for art in some of its functions it will soon supplant or corrupt it completely thanks to the natural support it will find in the stupidity of the multitude. It must return to its real task, which is to be the servant of the sciences and the arts, but the very humble servant, like printing and shorthand which have neither created nor supplanted literature.
1859 'Salon of 1859', section 2, in *Curiosités Esthétiques* (1868).

68 Woe betide the man who goes to antiquity for the study of anything other than ideal art, logic and general method!
c.1860 Letter, published in *The Painter of Modern Life* (1863).

69 *Il est l'heure de s'enivrer! Pour n'être pas les esclaves martyrisés du Temps, enivrez-vous sans cesse! De vin, de poésie ou de vertu, à votre guise.*
This is the time for drunkenness! Be not the martyred slaves of Time, drink without stopping! Drink wine, poetry, or virtue, as you please.
1869 *Le Spleen de Paris*, 'Enivrez-vous'.

70 *Parce que le Beau est toujours étonnant, il serait absurde de supposer que ce qui est étonnant est toujours beau.*
Just because the beautiful is *always* shocking, it would be absurd to suppose that that which is shocking is *always* beautiful.
1869 *Le Spleen de Paris*, 'Salon de 1859', pt.2.

71 *L'imagination est la reine du vrai, et le possible est une des provinces du vrai.*
Imagination is the queen of the truth and the *possible* is one of the provinces of the truth.
1869 *Le Spleen de Paris*, 'Salon de 1859', pt.3.

72 *Comme l'imagination a créé le monde, elle le gouverne.*
Because imagination created the world, it governs it.
1869 *Le Spleen de Paris*, 'Salon de 1859', pt.4.

73 *Le mal se fait sans effort, naturellement, par fatalité; le bien est toujours le produit d'un art.*
Evil is done without effort, *naturally*, it's destiny; good is always a product of art.
1869 *Le Spleen de Paris*, 'Le Peintre de la vie moderne', pt.11.

74 *L'art moderne a une tendance essentiellement démoniaque.*
Modern art tends towards the demonic.
1869 *L'Art romantique*.

75 *Quand même Dieu n'existerait pas, la religion serait encore sainte et divine. Dieu est le seul être qui, pour régner, n'ait même pas besoin d'exister.*
Even if God did not exist, religion would still be holy and divine. God is the only being who, in order to reign, need not even exist.
1875 *Journaux intimes*. 'Fusées', no.1.

76 *La volupté unique et suprême de l'amour gît dans la certitude de faire le mal.*
The unique, supreme pleasure of love consists in the certainty of doing evil.
1875 *Journaux intimes*. 'Fusées', no.2.

77 *La femme est naturelle, c'est-à-dire abominable.*
Woman is *natural*, that is, abominable.
1887 *Mon coeur mis à nu*, pt.5.

78 *Le Dandy doit aspirer à être sublime, sans interruption. Il doit vivre et dormir devant un miroir.*
The dandy must aspire to be sublime at all times. He must live and sleep in front of a mirror.
1887 *Mon coeur mis à nu*, pt.5.

79 *Etre un homme utile m'a paru toujours quelque chose de bien hideux.*
To be useful has always seemed to me quite hideous.
1887 *Mon coeur mis à nu*, pt.9.

80 *Il faut travailler sinon par goût, au moins par désespoir, puisque, tout bien vérifié, travailler est moins ennuyeux que s'amuser.*
We should work: if not by preference, at least out of despair. All things considered, work is less boring than amusement.
1887 *Mon coeur mis à nu*, pt.18.

81 *Il y a dans tout homme, à toute heure, deux postulations simultanées, l'une vers Dieu, l'autre vers Satan.*
Every man at every moment has two simultaneous tendencies: one toward God, the other toward Satan.
1887 *Mon coeur mis à nu*, pt.19.

82 *Il n'existe que trois êtres respectables: le prêtre, le guerrier, le poète. Savoir, tuer et créer.*
There are only three respectable beings: priest, warrior, poet. To know, to kill and to create.
1887 *Mon coeur mis à nu*, pt.22.

83 *L'être le plus prostitué, c'est l'être par excellence, c'est Dieu, puisqu'il est*
l'ami suprême pour chaque individu, puisqu'il est le réservoir commun,
inépuisable de l'amour.
The most prostituted being, the Being par excellence, is God, since he is
supreme friend to every individual, since he is the common, inexhaustible
reservoir of love.
1887 *Mon coeur mis à nu*, pt.16.

84 *Je ne comprends pas qu'une main pure puisse toucher un journal sans une convulsion de dégoût.*
I cannot imagine how a pure hand can touch a newspaper without disgust.
1887 *Mon coeur mis à nu*, pt.81.

85 At its best a poem full of space and reverie.
Of portraits. Quoted in the *New York Times*, 1 Jan 1995.

86 *Il faut épater le bourgeois.*
One must astound the bourgeois.
Attributed.

Baughan, Blanche Edith 1870–1958

New Zealand writer and penal reformer, born in England where she published *Verses* (1898). She emigrated in 1900 and wrote popular verse with an increasingly local flavour.

87 Well, I'm leaving the poor old place, and it cuts as keen as a knife;
The place that's broken my heart—the place where I've lived my life.
1903 *Reuben and Other Poems*, 'The Old Place'.

Baxter, Sir Beverley (Arthur) 1891–1964

British politician and journalist. Canadian-born, he joined the Daily Express in London in 1920 and was editor-in-chief from 1929–33. He became MP for Wood Green 1935–45, and 1945–50 and MP for Southgate from 1950 until his death.

88 Beaverbrook is so pleased to be in the Government that he is like the town tart who has finally married the mayor.
1940 Remark attributed to Baxter in Sir Henry Channon *Chips: the Diaries* (1967), entry for 12 Jun.

89 A great many persons are able to become Members of this House without losing their insignificance.
1946 Speech, House of Commons.

Baxter, Richard 1615–91

English Nonconformist clergyman. Chaplain to Cromwell's army in the English Civil War, he became Royal Chaplain in 1660, but was imprisoned in 1685 for sedition in his *Paraphrase on the New Testament*.

90 Watch against inordinate sensual delight in even the

lawfullest of sports. Excess of pleasure in any such vanity doth very much corrupt and befool the mind.
1678 *A Christian Directory.*

Beachcomber

► See J B Morton

Beamer, Todd 1968–2001

US businessman, passenger on the hijacked United Airlines Flight 93 on 11 September 2001.

91 Let's roll.
2001 Last known words before he and other passengers tackled the hijackers.

Bearden, Romare 1914–88

US painter, whose bright, bold works deal with the experience of black Americans.

92 The canvas was always saying no to me.
Of early attempts to perfect his medium. Recalled on his death in the *Washington Post*, 14 Mar 1988.

Beasant, Dave 1959–

English goalkeeper, he has played for teams including Wimbledon, Newcastle United and Chelsea. He became the first goalkeeper to captain a team to victory in the FA Cup, 1988.

93 I was a bit disappointed. I should have caught it really.
1988 Of the save that made him the first goalkeeper to stop a penalty in an FA Cup Final. Quoted in Peter Ball and Phil Shaw *The Book of Football Quotations* (1989).

Beattie, Ann 1947–

US short-story writer and novelist.

94 There are things that get whispered about that writers are there to overhear.
1987 *Best American Short Stories*, introduction.

Beattie, James 1735–1803

Scottish philosopher and poet, professor of moral philosophy at Aberdeen. He attacked Hume's scepticism in his *Essay on the Nature and Immutability of Truth* (1770), and wrote an autobiographical poem, *The Minstrel* (1771–4).

95 Some deemed him wondrous wise, and some believed him mad.
1771 *The Minstrel*, bk.1, stanza 16.

96 In the deep windings of the grove no more
The hag obscene, and grisly phantom dwell;
Nor in the fall of mountain-stream, or roar
Of winds, is heard the angry spirit's yell.
1774 *The Minstrel*, bk.2, stanza 47.

Beatty, David, 1st Earl Beatty 1871–1936

British Admiral. After serving in Egypt and Sudan he became Rear Admiral in 1910. Early successes in World War I were followed by a major role in the Battle of Jutland. He commanded the fleet (1916–19) and was First Sea Lord (1919–27).

97 There's something wrong with our bloody ships today, Chatfield.
1916 Comment at the Battle of Jutland, which ended in stalemate, 31 May. Quoted in Winston Churchill *The World Crisis 1916–1918* (1927), pt.1.

Beaumarchais, Pierre Augustin Caron de 1732–99

French writer who led a colourful life as artisan, member of the royal household, music teacher to Louis XV's daughter, speculator, secret agent in England, and munitions runner for the American colonies.

98 *Aujourd'hui, ce qui ne vaut pas la peine d'être dit, on le chante.*
Today, what is not worth being said is sung.
1775 *Le Barbier de Séville*, act 1, sc.2.

99 *Je me presse de rire de tout, de peur d'être obligé d'en pleurer.*
I am quick to laugh at everything so as not to be obliged to cry.
1775 *Le Barbier de Séville*, act 1, sc.2.

1 *On s'intéresse guère aux affaires des autres que lorsqu'on est sans inquiétude sur les siennes.*
We hardly interest ourselves in the affairs of others when things are going well for ourselves.
1775 *Le Barbier de Séville.*

2 *Les vices, les abus, voilà ce qui ne change point, mais se déguise en mille formes sous le masque des moeurs dominantes: leur arracher ce masque et les montrer à découvert, telle est la noble tâche de l'homme qui se voue au théâtre.*
Vices, indulgences, these are the things which never change but which disguise themselves in a thousand forms beneath the mask of prevailing morals: to lift off this mask and expose them, this is the noble task of the person who devotes himself to the theatre.
1784 *Le Mariage de Figaro*, préface.

3 *De toutes les choses sérieuses, le mariage étant la plus bouffonne.*
Of all serious things, marriage is the most farcical.
1784 *Le Mariage de Figaro*, act 1, sc.9.

4 *Boire sans soif et faire l'amour en tout temps, Madame, il n'y a que ça qui nous distingue des autres bêtes.*
We drink when we are not thirsty and make love at any time, Madam. These are the only things which distinguish us from other animals.
1784 *Le Mariage de Figaro*, act 2, sc.21.

5 *Les Anglais, à la vérité, ajoutent par ci, par là, quelques autres mots en conversant; mais il est bien aisé de voir que* God-dam *est le fond de la langue.*
In truth, the English do add here and there other words when speaking, but it is obvious that *Goddamn* is the basis of their language.
1784 *Le Mariage de Figaro*, act 3, sc.5.

Beaumont, Francis c.1584–1616

English dramatist, a friend of Ben Jonson and his circle, particularly John Fletcher, with whom he wrote at least 10 plays. *The Woman Hater* (1605) and *The Knight of the Burning Pestle* (c.1607) are thought to be mainly Beaumont's work.

6 What things have we seen,
Done at the Mermaid! heard words that have been
So nimble, and so full of subtil flame,
As if that every one from whence they came,
Had meant to put his whole wit in a jest,
And had resolv'd to live a fool, the rest
Of his dull life.
1605 *Letter to Ben Jonson*, verses prefacing Jonson's *Volpone*.

7 She's private to herself, and best of knowledge
Whom she will make so happy as to sigh for.
c.1607 *The Knight of the Burning Pestle*, act 1.

Beaumont, Francis and Fletcher, John c.1584–1616, c.1578–1625

English dramatists.

8 It is always good
When a man has two irons in the fire.
1608 *The Faithful Friends*, act 1.

9 PHILASTER: Oh, but thou dost not know
What 'tis to die.
BELLARIO: Yes, I do know, my Lord:
'Tis less than to be born; a lasting sleep;
A quiet resting from all jealousy,
A thing we all pursue; I know besides,
It is but giving over of a game,
That must be lost.
1609 *Philaster* (published 1620), act 3, sc.1.

10 All your better deeds
Shall be in water writ, but this in marble.
1609 *Philaster* (published 1620), act 5.

11 Kiss till the cow comes home.
c.1610 *The Scornful Lady* (published 1616), act 2, sc.2.

12 There is no other purgatory but a woman.
c.1610 *The Scornful Lady* (published 1616), act 3.

13 Upon my buried body lay
Lightly gentle earth
1610–11 *The Maid's Tragedy*, act 2, sc.1.

14 Those have most power to hurt us that we love.
1610–11 *The Maid's Tragedy*, act 5

15 The terror of his name has stretched itself
Wherever there is sun.
1611 *A King and No King*, act 2, sc.2.

16 What art thou that dost creep into my breast
And dar'st not see my face? Show forth thyself.
I feel a pair of fiery wings displayed
Hither, from thence. You shall not tarry there;
Up and begone. If thou beest love, begone.
1611 *A King and No King*, act 3, sc.1.

17 I see there's truth in no man, nor obedience
But for his own ends.
1611 *A King and No King*, act 4, sc.2.

18 You are no better than you should be.
1612 *The Coxcomb*, act 4, sc.3.

Beaverbrook, Max (William Maxwell Aitken), 1st Baron 1879–1964

Canadian-born British newspaper magnate and politician. After entering politics in 1910, he bought the *Daily Express* (1916) and made it the world's most widely read newspaper, founding the *Sunday Express* (1921). He was Minister of Supply and Lord Privy Seal during World War II.

19 Churchill on top of the wave has in him the stuff of which tyrants are made.
1928–32 *Politicians and the War*.

20 He has all the qualities that go to the making of a leader of the Conservative Party. He is not stupid, but he is very dull. He is not eloquent, but he talks well. He is not honest, politically, but he is most evangelical. He has a little money, but not much. He always conforms to the party policy.
1935 Commenting on Sir Samuel Hoare's appointment as Foreign Secretary.

21 Our cock won't fight.
1936 Of Edward VIII. Comment to Winston Churchill during the abdication crisis. Quoted in Francis Donaldson *Edward VIII* (1974).

22 I run the paper purely for the purpose of making propaganda, and with no other motive.
1947 Evidence to the Royal Commission on the Press.

23 With the publication of his private papers in 1952, he committed suicide 25 years after his death.
1956 Of Earl Haig. *Men and Power: 1917–1918*.

24 He did not seem to care which way he travelled providing he was in the driver's seat.
1963 Of Lloyd George. *The Decline and Fall of Lloyd George*, ch.7.

25 I am now in my eighty-fourth year and that is approaching the moment when I must bring out my Late Night Final.
c.1963 Quoted in A J P Taylor *Beaverbrook* (1972), ch.13.

26 Here I must say, in my eighty-sixth year, I do not feel greatly different from when I was eighty-five. This is my final word. It is time for me to become an apprentice once more. I have not settled in which direction. But somewhere, sometime soon.
1964 Address at a farewell banquet in London, hosted for him by Roy Thomson, Lord Thomson of Fleet, 25 May. He died two weeks later.

27 *News, Opinion and Advertisment must all come under the head of Entertainment to a reasonable extent—or they will not be read.* People do not read to be bored. Unless a newspaper can make its material in every department interesting it simply is not read.
Publicity handout for the *Daily Express*, quoted in A J P Taylor *Beaverbrook* (1972), ch.8.

28 Success never depended on pandering to the public taste. It has always been founded on simplicity.
Quoted in A J P Taylor *Beaverbrook* (1972), ch.13.

Beckenbauer, Franz 1945–

German footballer who captained the West German national side to European Nations Cup success in 1972 and to World Cup triumph in 1974.

29 We used to get our old players coming to watch training with football magazines in their hands. Now, more often than not, they're checking their share prices.
2001 In *World Soccer*, Nov.

Becker, Gary Stanley 1930–

US economist, Professor of Economics and Sociology at the University of Chicago. He won the Nobel prize for economics (1992).

30 They talk a good game, but economists hardly know enough about business cycles to figure out where they come from, let alone where they're going.
1989 'How Bad Will the Next Downturn Be?', in *Business Week*, 10 Apr.

Beckett, Margaret (Mary) 1943–

English Labour politician.

31 Being effective is more important to me than being recognized.
2000 In the *Independent on Sunday*, 2 Jan.

Beckett, Samuel 1906–89

Irish author and playwright who lived mostly in France. His best-known play, *En Attendant Godot* (*Waiting for Godot*, 1955), exemplifies his absurdist view of the human condition. He was awarded the Nobel prize for literature (1969).

32 *Je ne supporterai plus d'être un homme, je n'essaierai plus.*
I can no longer bear to be human and I will no longer try.
1951 *Molloy, Malone Meurt.*

33 There is man in his entirety, blaming his shoe when his foot is guilty.
1955 *Waiting for Godot*, act 1.

34 Nothing happens, nobody comes, nobody goes, it's awful!
1955 *Waiting for Godot*, act 1.

35 He can't think without his hat.
1955 Of Lucky. *Waiting for Godot*, act 1.

36 VLADIMIR: That passed the time.
ESTRAGON: It would have passed in any case.
VLADIMIR: Yes, but not so rapidly.
1955 *Waiting for Godot*, act 1.

37 I am like that. I either forget right away or I never forget.
1955 *Waiting for Godot*, act 2.

38 You overdo it with your carrots.
1955 *Waiting for Godot*, act 2.

39 We are not saints, but we have kept our appointment. How many people can boast as much?
1955 *Waiting for Godot*, act 2.

40 We are all born crazy. Some remain that way.
1955 *Waiting for Godot*, act 2.

41 They give birth astride of a grave, the light gleams an instant, then it's night once more.
1955 *Waiting for Godot*, act 2.

42 If I had the use of my body, I would throw it out of the window.
1958 *Malone Dies.*

43 *Tout est faux, il n'y a personne...il n'y a rien.*
Everything is false. There is no one...there is nothing.
1958 *Nouvelles et textes pour rien.*

44 CLOV: Do you believe in the life to come?
HAMM: Mine was always that.
1958 *Endgame.*

45 *Bien choisir son moment et se taire, serait-ce le seul moyen d'avoir être et habitat?*
To carefully choose one's moment and keep quiet, is this the only way one can be and live?
1958 *Nouvelles et textes pour rien.*

46 Joyce was a synthesizer, trying to bring in as much as he could. I am an analyzer, trying to leave out as much as I can.
1981 In the *New York Times*, 19 Apr.

47 Ever tried. Ever failed. No matter. Try again. Fail again. Fail better.
1983 *Worstward Ho.*

48 I was in hospital once. There was a man in another ward, dying of throat cancer. In the silence, I could hear his screams continually. That's the only kind of form my work has.
Attributed, in conversation with Harold Pinter.

Becket, Thomas à, Saint 1118–70

English churchman and martyr. Appointed Chancellor of England by Henry II in 1155, in 1162 he became Archbishop of Canterbury. He proved troublesome to Henry, opposing his remarriage, and was murdered in Canterbury Cathedral by four of the king's soldiers.

49 You will soon hate me as much as you love me now, for you assume an authority in the affairs of the church to which I shall never assent.
c.1160 Remark to Henry II. Quoted in J R Green *A Short History of the English People* (1915), vol.1, ch.2, section 8.

Beckham, David 1975–

English footballer. He was appointed captain of the English national side in 2000, and is a popular icon.

50 It's not easy when someone pulls your ponytail.
2003 In *The Independent*, 29 Dec.

51 I'm very honoured to be given this honour.
2003 On being awarded the OBE. Quoted on bbc.co.uk.

52 I showed that I wasn't just at Real Madrid to sell shirts.
2004 On his first season at the Spanish club, 25 May.

Beckham, Victoria 1975–

English pop singer and former member of The Spice Girls. She is married to the footballer David Beckham.

53 David and I will never split. We're a business.
2004 In *The Scotsman*.

Bede *known as 'the Venerable'* 673–735

English Benedictine monk, scholar and historian. His numerous works include saints' lives, hymns, grammatical treatises and biblical commentaries. His *Historia Ecclesiastica Gentis Anglorum* (731) is the single most valuable source for early English history.

54 *Talis, inquiens, mihi videtur, rex, vita hominum praesens in terris, ad comparationem eius, quod nobis incertum est, temporis, quale cum te residente, ad caenam cum ducibus ac ministris tuis tempore brumale...adveniens unus passerum domum citissime, pervolaverit; qui cum per unum ostium ingrediens, mox per aliud exierit. Ipso quidem tempore, quo intus est, hiemis tempestate non tangitur, sed tamen parvissimo spatio serenitatis ad momentum excurso, mox de hieme in hiemem regrediens, tuis oculis elabitur. Ita haec vita hominum ad modicum apparet; quid autem sequatur, quidve praecesserit, prorsus ignoramus.*
'Such,' he said, 'O King, seems to me the present life of men on earth, in comparison with that time which to us is uncertain, as if when on a winter's night you sit feasting with your ealdormen and thegns—a single sparrow should fly swiftly into the hall, and coming in at one door, instantly fly out through another. In that time in which it is indoors it is indeed not touched by the fury of the winter, and yet, this smallest space of calmness being passed almost in a flash, from winter going into winter again, it is lost to your eyes. Somewhat like this appears the life of

man; but of what follows or what went before, we are utterly ignorant.'
731 *Historia Ecclesiastica Gentis Anglorum* (*Ecclesiastical History of the English People*, translated by B Colgrave, 1969), bk.2, ch.13.

Bee, Barnard Elliot 1823–61

Confederate General, killed at the First Battle of Bull Run.

55 There is Jackson with his Virginians, standing like a stone wall. Let us determine to die here, and we will conquer.
1861 Of General Thomas J Jackson, whose resistance stopped the Union advance at Bull Run, 21 Jul. Quoted in B Perley Poore *Perley's Reminiscences* (1886), vol.2, ch.7. 'Stonewall Jackson' became a popular nickname for the General.

Beecham, Sir Thomas 1879–1961

British conductor and impresario, famed for his outspokenness and wit, and for a dashing and romantic style of performance. He conducted frequently at Covent Garden from 1910, and founded several orchestras, including the London Philharmonic (1932) and the Royal Philharmonic (1947), with whom he made many recordings

56 A musicologist is a man who can read music but can't hear it.
1930 Quoted in H Proctor-Gregg *Beecham Remembered* (1976).

57 The English may not like music—but they absolutely love the noise it makes.
Quoted in L Ayre *The Wit of Music* (1930).

58 It is far too large. It ought to be removed.
1940 On his first visit to Sydney, in 1940, being asked by a local journalist his opinion of the Harbour Bridge. Quoted in Gerald Moore *Am I too Loud?* (1962).

59 Good music is that which penetrates the ear with facility and quits the memory with difficulty. Magical music never leaves the memory.
1953 Television broadcast, 17 Nov.

60 Hark! The herald angels sing!
Beecham's Pills are just the thing,
Two for a woman, one for a child,
Peace on earth and mercy mild!
Quoted in Neville Cardus *Sir Thomas Beecham* (1961). Sir Thomas was heir to the Beecham pharmaceutical company.

61 The musical equivalent of the towers of St Pancras Station.
Of Elgar's First Symphony. Quoted in Neville Cardus *Sir Thomas Beecham* (1961).

62 There are two golden rules for an orchestra: start together and finish together. The public doesn't give a damn what goes on in between.
Quoted in Harold Atkins and Archie Newman *Beecham Stories* (1978).

63 Like two skeletons copulating on a corrugated tin roof.
Of the harpsichord's sound. Quoted in Harold Atkins and Archie Newman *Beecham Stories* (1978).

64 British music is in a state of perpetual promise. It might almost be said to be one long promissory note.
Quoted in Harold Atkins and Archie Newman *Beecham Stories* (1978).

65 The function of music is to release us from the tyranny of conscious thought.
Quoted in Harold Atkins and Archie Newman *Beecham Stories* (1978).

66 You have between your legs the most sensitive instrument known to man, and all you can do is scratch it.
Attributed rebuke to a female cellist. Quoted in Ian Crofton and Donald Fraser *A Dictionary of Musical Quotations* (1985).

Beerbohm, Sir (Henry) Max(imilian) 1872–1956

English writer, caricaturist and theatre critic, of Lithuanian extraction, who succeeded George Bernard Shaw as drama critic of the *Saturday Review*. His criticism was collected in *Around Theatre* (1953) and *More Theatres* (1968). He also wrote a novel, *Zuleika Dobson* (1911), an ironic romance about Oxford student life.

67 Most women are not so young as they are painted.
1894 *The Yellow Book*, vol.1.

68 Fate wrote her a most tremendous tragedy, and she played it in tights.
1894 Of Queen Caroline of Brunswick. *The Yellow Book*, vol.3.

69 There is always something rather absurd about the past.
1895 *The Yellow Book*, vol.4

70 To give an accurate and exhaustive account of the period would need a far less brilliant pen than mine.
1895 *The Yellow Book*, vol.4.

71 I have the satiric temperament: when I am laughing at anyone I am generally rather amusing, but when I am praising anyone, I am always deadly dull.
1898 In *The Saturday Review*, 28 May.

72 [At school] I was a modest, good-humoured boy. It is Oxford that has made me insufferable.
1899 *More*, 'Going Back To School'.

73 When a public man lays his hand on his heart and declares that his conduct needs no apology, the audience hastens to put up its umbrellas against the particularly severe downpour of apologies in store for it. I won't give the customary warning. My conduct shrieks aloud for apology, and you are in for a thorough drenching.
1906 'A Straight Talk' (parody of George Bernard Shaw), in the *Saturday Review*, 22 Dec.

74 She was one of those born to make chaos cosmic.
1911 *Zuleika Dobson*, ch.2.

75 Zuleika, on a desert island, would have spent most of her time in looking for a man's footprint.
1911 *Zuleika Dobson*, ch.2.

76 The dullard's envy of brilliant men is always assuaged by the suspicion that they will come to a bad end.
1911 *Zuleika Dobson*, ch.4.

77 Women who love the same man have a kind of bitter freemasonry.
1911 *Zuleika Dobson*, ch.4.

78 You will find that the woman who is really kind to dogs is always one who has failed to inspire sympathy in men.
1911 *Zuleika Dobson*, ch.6.

79 Beauty and the lust for learning have yet to be allied.
1911 *Zuleika Dobson*, ch.7.

80 You will think me lamentably crude: my experience of life has been drawn from life itself.
1911 *Zuleika Dobson*, ch.7.

81 She was one of the people who say 'I don't know anything about music really, but I know what I like.'
1911 *Zuleika Dobson*, ch.9.

82 You cannot make a man by standing a sheep on its hind-

legs. But by standing a flock of sheep in that position you can make a crowd of men.
1911 *Zuleika Dobson*, ch.9.

83 The Socratic method is not a game at which two can play.
1911 *Zuleika Dobson*, ch.15.

84 I looked out for what the metropolitan reviewers would have to say. They seemed to fall into two classes: those who had little to say and those who had nothing.
1919 *Seven Men*, 'Enoch Soames'.

85 I have known no man of genius who had not to pay, in some affliction or defect either physical or spiritual, for what the gods had given him.
1920 *And Even Now*, 'The Pines'.

86 Not philosophy, after all, not humanity, just sheer joyous power of song, is the primal thing in poetry.
1920 *And Even Now*, 'The Pines'.

87 One might well say that mankind is divisible into two great classes: hosts and guests.
1920 *And Even Now*, 'Hosts and Guests'.

88 I maintain that though you would often in the fifteenth century have heard the snobbish Roman say, in a would-be off-hand tone, 'I am dining with the Borgias tonight,' no Roman ever was able to say, 'I dined last night with the Borgias.'
1920 *And Even Now*, 'Hosts and Guests'.

89 The critic who justly admires all kinds of things simultaneously cannot love any one of them.
1946 'George Moore', in the *Saturday Review*, c.1912.

90 The thought of him has always slightly irritated me. Of course he was a wonderful all-round man, but the act of walking round him has always tired me.
1956 Of William Morris. Letter to Sam Behrman, Feb.

91 Only mediocrity can be trusted to be always at its best.
Quoted in S N Behrman *Conversations with Max* (1960), but also attributed elsewhere to Jean Giraudoux and W Somerset Maugham.

92 The one art-form that has been invented in England.
Of the pantomime. Attributed.

93 Reminds me of a Christmas-tree decorated by a Pre-Raphaelite.
Of the actress Ellen Terry. Attributed.

94 They were a tense and peculiar family, the Oedipuses, weren't they?
Attributed.

Beethoven, Ludwig van 1770–1827

German composer. His prolific output included two masses, the opera *Fidelio*, nine symphonies, five piano concertos, piano sonatas and string quartets. Increasing deafness affected him and his music deeply. His influence, especially on the Romantics, was immense.

95 The immortal god of harmony.
1801 Of Bach. Letter to Christoph Breitkopf.

96 I must confess that I live a miserable life… I live entirely in my music.
1801 Letter to F G Wegeler.

97 *Muss es sein? Es muss sein! Es muss sein!*
Must it be? It must be! It must be!
1826 Written above the opening bars of the String Quartet in F Major, Op 135, his last work.

98 I still hope to create a few great works and then like an old child to finish my earthly course somewhere among kind people.
1826 Letter to F G Wegeler.

99 *Plaudite, amici, comedia finita est.*
Applaud, my friends, the comedy is over.
1827 Quoted in Ian Crofton and Donald Fraser *A Dictionary of Musical Quotations* (1985), quoting the last words of Augustus as he lay dying.
➡ *See Augustus 42:48.*

1 I shall hear in heaven.
1827 Attributed last words. Quoted in Ian Crofton and Donald Fraser *A Dictionary of Musical Quotations* (1985).

Beeton, Isabella Mary *née Mayson* 1836–65

English writer on cookery. Her *Book of Household Management* (1859–60) was published in serial form in a woman's magazine founded by her husband, the publisher Samuel Orchard Beeton.

2 There is no more fruitful source of family discontent than a housewife's badly-cooked dinners and untidy ways.
1861 *The Book of Household Management*, preface.

3 A place for everything and everything in its place.
1861 *The Book of Household Management*, ch.2.

Behan, Brendan Francis 1923–64

Irish playwright, twice imprisoned for IRA activities. He was released by general amnesty (1946), but was rearrested and deported in 1952. His works include *The Quare Fellow* (1956), *The Hostage* (1958) and an autobiography, *Borstal Boy* (1958).

4 When I came back to Dublin, I was courtmartialled in my absence and sentenced to death in my absence, so I said they could shoot me in my absence.
1958 *The Hostage*, act 1.

5 My name is Behan, Brendan Behan, after Saint Brendan, who got into one of our little Irish boats called a curragh one day in the sixth century and sailed across the Atlantic and found America, and when he'd found it, like a sensible man he turned around and sailed back and left it where it fuckin' well was.
1962 Speech in New York.

6 Bless you, Sister. May all your sons be bishops!
1964 Addressing a nursing nun taking his pulse shortly before he died. Attributed.

7 Critics are like eunuchs in a harem. They're in there every night, they see how it should be done every night, but they can't do it themselves.
Quoted in Gyles Brandreth *Great Theatrical Disasters* (1983).

8 I am a daylight atheist.
Quoted in Daniel Farson *Sacred Monsters*, 'Rousting in Dublin' (1988).

9 Other people have a nationality. The Irish and the Jews have a psychosis.
Richard's Cork Leg (1961).

Behn, Aphra *née Amis* 1640–89

English writer. She had an adventurous life, growing up in Surinam and acting as a professional spy in Antwerp. Perhaps the first professional woman author in England, her works include *Oroonoko* (1688), *The Forced Marriage* (1670) and *The Rover* (1678).

10 Variety is the soul of pleasure.
1678 *The Rover*, pt.2, act 1.

11 Come away; poverty's catching.
1678 *The Rover*, pt.2, act 1.

12 Money speaks sense in a language all nations understand.
1678 *The Rover*, pt.2, act 3, sc.1.

13 A brave world, Sir, full of religion, knavery, and change: we shall shortly see better days.
1682 *The Roundheads*, act 1, sc.1.

14 Be just, my lovely swain, and do not take
Freedoms you'll not to me allow;
Or give Amynta so much freedom back
That she may rove as well as you.

Let us then love upon the honest square,
Since interest neither have designed.
For the sly gamester, who ne'er plays me fair,
Must trick for trick expect to find.
1684 *Poems upon Several Occasions*, 'To Lysander, on some Verses he writ, and asking more for his Heart than 'twas worth'.

15 Faith, Sir, we are here to-day, and gone to-morrow.
1686 *The Lucky Chance*, act 4.

16 Love ceases to be a pleasure, when it ceases to be a secret.
1686 *The Lover's Watch*, 'Four o'Clock. General Conversation'.

17 Oh, what a dear ravishing thing is the beginning of an Amour!
1687 *The Emperor of the Moon*, act 1, sc.1.

18 They represented to me an absolute idea of the first state of innocence, before man knew how to sin.
1688 Of the Indians of Surinam. *Oroonoko, or the Royal Slave*.

19 Simple Nature is the most harmless, inoffensive, and virtuous mistress.
1688 *Oroonoko, or the Royal Slave*.

20 And though she had some decays in the face, she had none in her sense and wit.
1688 *Oroonoko, or the Royal Slave*.

21 Since Man with that inconstancy was born,
To love the absent, and the present scorn.
Why do we deck, why do we dress
For such a short-liv'd happiness?
1688 *Lycidus*, 'To Alexis in Answer to his Poem against Fruition,' stanza 3.

22 The soft, unhappy sex.
1698 *The Wandering Beauty*.

Behrman, S(amuel) N(athaniel) 1893–1973

US playwright, known for sophisticated comedies such as *No Time for Comedy* (1939) and *Lord Pengo* (1962). Other works include screenplays and biographies.

23 Early in life, Duveen…noticed that Europe had plenty of art and America had plenty of money, and his entire astonishing career was the product of that simple observation.
1952 *Duveen*, ch.1. Joseph Duveen was a highly successful US art dealer.

Belasco, David *stagename of* *David Valasco* 1859–1931

US actor-manager and dramatist. Nicknamed the 'Bishop of Broadway', he adapted many successful plays for the theatres he managed in New York.

24 Boxing is show-business with blood.
Quoted in Colin Jarman *The Guinness Dictionary of Sports Quotations* (1990).

Bell, Alexander Melville 1819–1905

Language instructor, father of Alexander Graham Bell.

25 Yes, Alec, it is I, your father, speaking.
1876 The first words spoken and heard on the world's first long-distance telephone call, from Alexander Melville Bell in Brantford, Ontario, Canada, to his son Alexander Graham Bell in nearby Paris, 13 km away, 10 Aug.

Bell, Bernard Iddings 1886–1958

US cleric, chaplain at the University of Chicago.

26 A good education is not so much one which prepares a man to succeed in the world, as one which enables him to sustain a failure.
1950 In *Life*, 16 Oct.

Bell, (Arthur) Clive Howard 1881–1964

English critic of art and literature, an influential member of the Bloomsbury set, husband of Vanessa Bell. His aesthetic theory emphasized form over content in art.

27 It would follow that 'significant form' was form behind which we catch a sense of ultimate reality.
1914 *Art*, pt.1, ch.3.

28 Art and Religion are, then, two roads by which men escape from circumstance to ecstasy.
1914 *Art*, pt.2, ch.1.

29 I will try to account for the degree of my aesthetic emotion. That, I conceive, is the function of the critic.
1914 *Art*, pt.3, ch.3.

30 Materially make the life of the artist sufficiently miserable to be unattractive, and no one will take to art save those in whom the divine daemon is absolute.
1914 *Art*, pt.5, ch.1.

31 Comfort came in with the middle classes.
1928 *Civilization*, ch.4.

32 Only reason can convince us of those three fundamental truths without a recognition of which there can be no effective liberty: that what we believe is not necessarily true; that what we like is not necessarily good; and that all questions are open.
1928 *Civilization*, ch.5.

Bell, Martin 1938–

English journalist and MP. After a career as a television news reporter he stood as an Independent candidate for Tatton in the 1997 general election.

33 I knew when Sir Alec Guinness endorsed my campaign that the force was with us.
1997 Victory speech on winning the Tatton constituency. In *The Oxford Mail*, 2 May.

34 The great American tradition of telling truth to power was incinerated in New York on 11 September 2001.
2003 *Through Gates of Fire*.

Bell, Vanessa *née* ***Stephen*** 1879–1961

English painter and designer, sister of Virginia Woolf. She married the critic Clive Bell (1907) but left him in 1916 to live with Duncan Grant.

35 Rather lovely descriptions of scenery, don't you think?
1928 Remark to Robert Medley and Rupert Doone, when asked what she thought of D H Lawrence's *Lady Chatterley's Lover*. Recalled in Robert Medley *Drawn from the Life: a Memoir* (1983), p.91.

Bellay, Joachim du 1522–60

French poet famous for his sonnets. He was a founding member of the Pléiade and wrote its manifesto, *La défense et illustration de la langue française* (1549).

36 *Rome de Rome est le seul monument,*
Et Rome Rome a vaincu seulement.
Rome is the only monument left of Rome,
And only Rome vanquished Rome.
1558 *Antiquitez de Rome*, no.5.

37 *Rome seule pouvait à Rome ressembler,*
Rome seule pouvait Rome fait trembler.
Only Rome can resemble Rome,
And Rome alone can make Rome fall.
1558 *Antiquitez de Rome*, no.6.

38 *France, mère des arts, des armes et des lois.*
France, mother of arts, of weapons and of laws.
1558 *Les Regrets*, no.9.

39 *Heureux, qui comme Ulysse, a fait un beau voyage,*
Ou comme cestuy là qui conquit la toison,
Et puis est retourné, plein d'usage et raison,
Vivre entre ses parents le reste de son âge!
Happy is he who, like Ulysses, has taken a wondrous journey
Or has won the Golden Fleece,
And then returns home wise and useful
To live in his homeland the rest of his days.
1558 *Les Regrets*, no.31.

40 *Celuy vit seulement, lequel vit aujourdhuy.*
Only the person who lives for today lives at all.
1558 *Les Regrets*, no.65.

41 *Je n'écris point d'amour, n'estant point amoureux,*
Je n'écris de beauté, n'aiant belle maistresse,
Je n'écris de douceur, n'esprouvant que rudesse,
Je n'écris de plaisir, me trouvant douloureux.
I cannot write of love, as I am not in love,
I cannot write of beauty, as I have no beautiful mistress,
I cannot write of sweetness, as I experience nothing but hardship,
I cannot write of pleasure, as I am always in pain.
1558 *Les Regrets*, no.79.

Belli, Carlos Germán 1927–

Peruvian poet, translator and journalist. He travelled widely in South America, Spain, Italy and the United States. His poems are noted for their nihilistic outlook and an orderly precision of language.

42 *De los libros el luminoso plectro*
diríase que pasa
a ser lía del recto,
pues después de tanto leer sin tasa
nada ha quedado en casa.
The luminous plectrum of books
can be said to become
a portion of the rectum,
since after so much eager reading
not a thing remains at home.
1961 *¡Oh hada cibernética!*, 'Cuando el seso tiene la altura de un grano de arena' ('When the brain is as high as a grain of sand').

Bellini, Mario 1935–

Italian architect.

43 A design career is a process of learning better and better what you know instinctively.
1987 In the *New York Times*, 25 Jun.

44 I designed a bench in a few moments. But, of course, it took me 25 years to do it.
1987 In the *New York Times*, 25 Jun.

Belloc, (Joseph) Hilaire Pierre 1870–1953

French-born British writer, poet, Roman Catholic apologist and Liberal MP (1906–10). His works include *The Servile State* (1912), travel books, historical studies and religious books. He is best known for his comic and nonsensical verse for children.

45 Child! do not throw this book about;
Refrain from the unholy pleasure
Of cutting all the pictures out!
Preserve it as your chiefest treasure.
1896 *The Bad Child's Book of Beasts*, dedication.

46 A manner rude and wild
Is common at your age.
1896 *The Bad Child's Book of Beasts*, introduction.

47 When people call this beast to mind,
They marvel more and more
At such a little tail behind,
So large a trunk before.
1896 *The Bad Child's Book of Beasts*, 'The Elephant'.

48 I shoot the Hippopotamus
With bullets made of platinum,
Because if I use the leaden ones
His hide is sure to flatten 'em.
1896 *The Bad Child's Book of Beasts*, 'The Hippopotamus'.

49 Mothers of large families (who claim to common sense)
Will find a Tiger will repay the trouble and expense.
1896 *The Bad Child's Book of Beasts*, 'The Tiger'.

50 The Microbe is so very small
You cannot make him out at all.
1897 *More Beasts for Worse Children*, 'The Microbe'.

51 Whatever happens, we have got
The Maxim Gun, and they have not.
1898 *The Modern Traveller*, bk.6.

52 I am a Catholic. As far as possible I go to Mass every day. As far as possible I kneel down and tell these beads every day. If you reject me on account of my religion, I shall thank God that he has spared me the indignity of being your representative.
1906 Election campaign speech, Salford.

53 The chief defect of Henry King
Was chewing little bits of string.
1907 *Cautionary Tales*, 'Henry King'.

54 Physicians of the utmost fame
Were called at once, but when they came

They answered, as they took their fees,
'There is no cure for this disease.'
1907 *Cautionary Tales*, 'Henry King'.

55 'Oh, my friends, be warned by me,
That breakfast, dinner, lunch, and tea
Are all the human frame requires…'
With that the wretched child expires.
1907 *Cautionary Tales*, 'Henry King'.

56 And always keep a hold of Nurse
For fear of finding something worse.
1907 *Cautionary Tales*, 'Jim'.

57 We had intended you to be
The next Prime Minister but three:
The stocks were sold; the Press was squared;
The Middle Class was quite prepared.
But as it is!… My language fails!
Go out and govern New South Wales!
1907 *Cautionary Tales*, 'Jim'.

58 Matilda told such Dreadful Lies,
It made one Gasp and Stretch one's Eyes,
Her Aunt, who, from her Earliest Youth,
Had kept a Strict Regard for Truth,
Attempted to Believe Matilda:
The effort very nearly killed her.
1907 *Cautionary Tales*, 'Matilda'.

59 She was not really bad at heart,
But only rather rude and wild;
She was an aggravating child.
1907 *Cautionary Tales*, 'Rebecca'.

60 Her funeral sermon (which was long
And followed by a sacred song)
Mentioned her virtues, it is true,
But dwelt upon her vices too.
1907 *Cautionary Tales*, 'Rebecca'.

61 It is the best of trades, to make songs, and the second best to sing them.
1909 *On Everything*.

62 I said to Heart, 'How goes it?' Heart replied:
'Right as a Ribstone Pippin!' But it lied.
1910 'The False Heart'.

63 When I am living in the Midlands
That are sodden and unkind.
1910 'The South Country'.

64 Everywhere the sea is a teacher of truth. I am not sure that the best thing I find in sailing is not this salt of reality.
c.1910 *The Cruise of the Nona*.

65 Do you remember an Inn,
Miranda?
Do you remember an Inn,
And the tedding and the spreading
Of the straw for a bedding,
And the fleas that tease in the High Pyrenees
And the wine that tasted of the tar?
1923 'Tarantella'.

66 When I am dead, I hope it may be said,
'His sins were scarlet, but his books were read.'
1923 'On His Books'.

67 And even now, at twenty-five,
He has to WORK to keep alive!
Yes! All day long from 10 till 4!
For half the year or even more;
With but an hour or two to spend
At luncheon with a city friend.
1930 *New Cautionary Tales*, 'Peter Goole'.

68 I am a sundial, and I make a botch
Of what is done much better by a watch.
1938 'On a Sundial'.

69 Statistics are the triumph of the quantitative method, and the quantitative method is the victory of sterility and death.
1940 *The Silence of the Sea*.

Bellow, Saul 1915–

Canadian-born US writer. He moved to Chicago in 1924, and was educated there. His best novels examine Jewish-American identity and the dilemma of liberal humanist values in a fast-changing world. He won the Nobel prize for literature in 1976.

70 Everyone knows there is no fineness or accuracy of suppression. If you hold down one thing you hold down the adjoining.
1953 *The Adventures of Augie March*.

71 I am an American, Chicago born—Chicago, that somber city—and go at things as I have taught myself, free-style, and will make the record in my own way: first to knock, first admitted; sometimes an innocent knock, sometimes a not so innocent.
1953 *The Adventures of Augie March*.

72 Of course, in an age of madness, to expect to be untouched by madness is a form of madness. But the pursuit of sanity can be a form of madness, too.
1959 *Henderson The Rain King*, ch.3.

73 If I am out of my mind, it's all right with me, thought Moses Herzog.
1961 *Herzog*, opening words.

74 A man may say, 'From now on I'm going to speak the truth.' But the truth hears him and runs away and hides before he's even done speaking.
1961 *Herzog*.

75 I feel that art has something to do with the achievement of stillness in the midst of chaos.
1965 Interview in *The Paris Review*, no.37, winter issue.

76 No wonder the really powerful men in our society, whether politicians or scientists, hold writers in contempt. They do it because they get no evidence from modern literature that anybody is thinking about any significant question.
1965 Interview in *The Paris Review*, no.37, winter issue.

77 I am more stupid about some things than about others; not equally stupid in all directions; I am not a well-rounded person.
1969 *Mr Sammler's Planet*, ch.2.

78 Conquered people tend to be witty.
1969 *Mr Sammler's Planet*, ch.2.

79 Mr Sammler with his screwy visions! He saw the increasing triumph of Enlightenment—Liberty, Equality, Adultery!
1969 *Mr Sammler's Planet*, ch.3.

80 There is much to be said for exotic marriages. If your husband is a bore, it takes years longer to discover.
1969 *Mr Sammler's Planet*, ch.6.

81 I think that New York is not the cultural centre of America, but the business and administrative centre of American culture.
1969 In radio interview, reported in *The Listener*, 22 May.

82 The idea, anyway, was to ward off trouble. But now the moronic inferno had caught up with me.
1975 *Humboldt's Gift*. Martin Amis used the phrase *The Moronic Inferno* as the title for a book of essays on the US (1986).

83 The only real distinction at this dangerous moment in human history and cosmic development has nothing to do with medals and ribbons. Not to fall asleep is distinguished. Everything else is mere popcorn.
1975 *Humboldt's Gift*.

84 After all these years wallowing in low seriousness—low seriousness, you understand, is high seriousness that's failed.
1975 Interview in the *Sunday Times*, 12 Jan.

85 The feeling individual appeared weak—he felt only his own weakness. But if he accepted his weakness and his separateness and descended into himself, intensifying his loneliness, he discovered his solidarity with other isolated creatures.
1976 Nobel prize lecture, Stockholm, 12 Dec.

86 A novel is balanced between a few true impressions and the multitude of false ones that make up most of what we call life.
1976 Nobel prize lecture, Stockholm, 12 Dec.

87 Tears may be intellectual, but they can never be political. They save no man from being shot, no child from being thrown alive into the furnace.
1982 *The Dean's December*, ch.12.

88 As a rule Corde avoided cemeteries and never went near the graves of his parents. He said it was just as easy for your dead to visit you, only by now he would have to hire a hall.
1982 *The Dean's December*, ch.15.

89 The secret motive of the absent-minded is to be innocent while guilty. Absent-mindedness is spurious innocence.
1987 *More Die of Heartbreak*.

90 Erotic practices have become diversified. Sex used to be a single-crop farming, like cotton or wheat; now people raise all kinds of things.
1987 *More Die of Heartbreak*.

91 The modern reader (or viewer, or listener: let's include everybody) is perilously overloaded. His attention is, to use the latest lingo, 'targeted' by powerful forces… Our consciousness is a staging area, a field of operations for all kinds of enterprises, which make free use of it.
1989 *Something To Remember Me By*, preface.

92 But Fonstein belonged to an even more advanced category…their aim is to convert weaknesses and secrets into burnable energy. A first-class man subsists on the matter he destroys, just as the stars do.
1989 *Something To Remember Me By*, 'The Bellarosa Connection'.

Bemelmans, Ludwig 1898–1962

US writer and restaurateur. He wrote food and travel books, and is best remembered for his 'Madeline' series for children.

93 In an old house in Paris
that was covered with vines
lived twelve little girls in two straight lines.
1939 *Madeline*.

94 And nobody knew so well
How to frighten Miss Clavell.
1939 *Madeline*.

95 Serves you right, you horrid brat
For what you did to that poor cat.
1956 *Madeline and the Bad Hat*.

Benaud, Richie (Richard) 1930–

Australian cricketer and broadcaster. He played in 63 Test matches (28 as captain), scoring 2201 Test runs and taking 248 wickets.

96 Cricket is a batsman's game.
1961 *Way of Cricket*.

Benchley, Robert Charles 1889–1945

US humorist and critic, a member of the famous circle of New York wits and writers known as the Algonquin Round Table. He was drama critic of *Life* and the *New Yorker*, and appeared in cameo roles in many films.

97 In America there are two classes of travel—first class, and with children.
1925 *Pluck and Luck*.

98 The surest way to make a monkey of a man is to quote him.
1936 *My Ten Years in a Quandary*.

99 I haven't been abroad in so long that I almost speak English without an accent now.
1938 *After 1903— What?*

1 One square foot less and it would be adulterous.
On the tiny office he shared with Dorothy Parker, quoted in the *New Yorker*, 5 Jan 1946.

2 My only solution for the problem of habitual accidents…is to stay in bed all day. Even then, there is always the chance that you will fall out.
1949 *Chips Off the Old Benchley*, 'Safety Second'.

3 A great many people have come up to me and asked how I manage to get so much work done and still keep looking so dissipated.
1949 *Chips Off the Old Benchley*, 'How To Get Things Done'.

4 So who's in a hurry?
On being told that the particular drink he was drinking was slow poison. Quoted in Nathaniel Benchley *Robert Benchley* (1955), ch.1.

5 STREETS FLOODED. PLEASE ADVISE.
Telegraph message to the US on arriving in Venice. Quoted in R E Drennan (ed) *Wits End* (1973).

6 Opera is where a guy gets stabbed in the back, and instead of dying, he sings.
Quoted in Ian Crofton and Donald Fraser *A Dictionary of Musical Quotations* (1985).

Bendix, Reinhard 1916–91

German-born US sociologist, Professor at the University of California, Berkeley.

7 In retrospect it always seems as if everything had to develop just the way it did. I call this view the fallacy of retrospective determinism—which looks at the modern world as a victory of the children of light over the

children of darkness if we approve of the development, and of darkness over light if we condemn it.
1984 *Force, Fate, and Freedom: On Historical Sociology.*

Benedetti, Mario 1920–

Uruguayan fiction writer, poet and essayist, who lived in Cuba in the late 1960s. After returning to Uruguay, he helped establish a leftist coalition for future elections. With the military takeover of 1973 he was forced to leave the country.

8 *está demás decirte que a esta altura*
no creo en predicadores ni en generales
ni en las nalgas de miss universo
ni en el arrepentimiento de los verdugos
ni en el catecismo del confort
ni en el flaco perdón de dios.
It's not useless to tell you that, at this stage,
I don't believe in preachers or generals
or in Miss Universe's buttocks
or in the executioner's repentance
or in the catechism of comfort
or in God's slim forgiving.
1974 *Poemas de otros*, 'Credo' ('Creed').

Benét, Stephen Vincent 1898–1943

US poet and novelist. He wrote many evocative poems on the history and national identity of America, of which 'American Names' is the most famous.

9 I have fallen in love with American names,
The sharp, gaunt names that never get fat,
The snakeskin-titles of mining-claims,
The plumed war-bonnet of Medicine Hat,
Tucson and Deadwood and Lost Mule Flat.
1927 'American Names'.

10 There are English counties like hunting-tunes
Played on the keys of a postboy's horn,
But I will remember where I was born.
1927 'American Names'.

11 I will get me a bottle of Boston sea
And a blue-gum nigger to sing me blues.
I am tired of loving a foreign muse.
1927 'American Names'.

12 I shall not rest quiet in Montparnasse.
I shall not lie easy at Winchelsea.
You may bury my body in Sussex grass,
You may bury my tongue at Champmédy.
I shall not be there, I shall rise and pass.
Bury my heart at Wounded Knee.
1927 'American Names'. *Bury My Heart At Wounded Knee* was used by Dee Brown as the title of a book on the Indian genocide (1971).

13 One cannot balance tragedy in the scales
Unless one weighs it with the tragic heart.
1928 'John Brown's Body'.

14 We thought we were done with these things but we were wrong.
We thought, because we had power, we had wisdom.
1935 'A Litany for Dictatorships'.

Benn, Tony (Anthony Neil Wedgwood) 1925–

English Labour politician. He became an MP (1950–60), and renounced his hereditary title to be re-elected to the Commons (1963–83, 1984–2001). He held various government posts, and as a left-wing representative unsuccessfully challenged Neil Kinnock for the leadership of the Labour Party in 1988.

15 The House of Lords is the British Outer Mongolia for retired politicians.
1962 Speech made during his campaign to disclaim his hereditary peerage, 11 Feb.

16 It is as wholly wrong to blame Marx for what was done in his name, as it is to blame Jesus for what was done in his.
Quoted in Alan Freeman *The Benn Heresy* (1982).

17 It is beginning to dawn on people that the influence of a nation is not measured by the size of its military budget, but by its industrial strength.
1991 In *The Independent*, 18 Apr.

18 The dependence of London on Washington for the supply of our so-called independent nuclear weapons is all that remains of the 'special relationship' and...it is really a ball and chain limiting our capacity to play a more positive role in the world.
1991 In *The Independent*, 18 Apr.
➡ *See Churchill 217:93.*

19 It is the same each time with progress. First they ignore you, then they say you are mad, then dangerous, then there's a pause, and then you can't find anyone who disagrees.
1991 Speech at the Labour Party Conference, Oct.

20 It will be Blair, Blair, Blair just as it was Thatcher, Thatcher, Thatcher.
1997 Replying to a student's question on the supremacy of prime ministerial power.

21 We should put the spin-doctors in spin clinics, where they can meet other spin patients and be treated by spin consultants. The rest of us can get on with the proper democratic process.
1997 In *The Independent*, 'Quote Unquote', 25 Oct.

22 The Weetabix Years.
2004 Book title.

Bennard, George 1873–1958

US clergyman and hymn-writer.

23 I will cling to the old rugged cross,
And exchange it some day for a crown.
1913 'The Old Rugged Cross'.

Bennett, Alan 1934–

English writer. He came to prominence as an actor and writer in *Beyond the Fringe* (1960), and went on to write wry, mordant plays and monologues for stage and screen. He adapted his play *The Madness of George III* (1991) as an Oscar-winning film (*The Madness of King George*, 1995).

24 Life is rather like a tin of sardines—we're all of us looking for the key.
1960 *Beyond the Fringe.*

25 I've never understood this liking for war. It panders to instincts already catered for within the scope of any respectable domestic establishment.
1968 *Forty Years On* (published 1969), act 1.

26 Memories are not shackles, Franklin, they are garlands.
1968 *Forty Years On* (published 1969), act 2.

27 The Breed never dies. Sapper, Buchan, Dornford Yates, practitioners in that school of Snobbery with Violence that runs like a thread of good-class tweed through twentieth-century literature.
1968 *Forty Years On* (published 1969), act 2. *Snobbery With Violence* was used as a book title by Colin Wilson (1971).

28 It's the one species I wouldn't mind seeing vanish from the face of the earth. I wish they were like the White Rhino—six of them left in the Serengeti National Park, and all males.
1971 Of dogs. *Getting On* (published 1972), act 1.

29 The longer I practise medicine, the more convinced I am there are only two types of cases: those that involve taking the trousers off and those that don't.
1973 *Habeas Corpus*.

30 One of the few things I have learned in life is that there is invariably something odd about women who wear ankle socks.
1977 *The Old Country*, act 1.

31 We were put to Dickens as children but it never took. That unremitting humanity soon had me cheesed off.
1977 *The Old Country*, act 2.

32 There is no such thing as a good script, only a good film, and I'm conscious that my scripts often read better than they play.
1984 *A Private Function*, introduction to published screenplay.

33 I'm going to throw caution to the winds and have a sweet sherry.
1984 Spoken by Maggie Smith as Joyce Chilvers in *A Private Function*.

34 I want a future that will live up to my past.
1984 Spoken by Maggie Smith as Joyce Chilvers in *A Private Function*.

35 They're going to have to be made to sit up and take notice. They're going to have to be made to realise who we are. My father had a chain of dry cleaners.
1984 *A Private Function*.

36 I'm not good at precise, coherent argument. But plays are suited to incoherent argument, put into the mouths of fallible people.
1991 In the *Sunday Times*, 24 Nov.

37 My claim to literary fame is that I used to deliver meat to a woman who became T. S. Eliot's mother-in-law.
1992 In the *Observer*, 26 Apr. The lady in question was the mother of Eliot's wife Valerie Fletcher; Bennett's father was the butcher in the same Yorkshire village.

Bennett, (Enoch) Arnold 1867–1931

English novelist. He was also a journalist, and lived in Paris for ten years. His best-known books are those set in the pottery-making heartland of the Five Towns in the Midlands, notably the *Clayhanger* trilogy (1910–16).

38 Essential characteristic of the really great novelist: a Christ-like, all-embracing compassion.
1896 Journal entry, 15 Oct.

39 'Bah!', she said, 'With people like you, love only means one thing.' 'No,' he replied. 'It means twenty things, but it doesn't mean nineteen.'
1904 Journal entry, 20 Nov.

40 My general impression is that Englishmen act better than Frenchmen, and Frenchwomen better than Englishwomen.
1909 *Cupid and Commonsense*, preface.

41 His opinion of himself, having once risen, remained at 'set fair'.
1911 *The Card*, ch.1.

42 'Ye can call it influenza if ye like,' said Mrs Machin. 'There was no influenza in my young days. We called a cold a cold.'
1911 *The Card*, ch.8.

43 A cause may be inconvenient, but it's magnificent. It's like champagne or high heels, and one must be prepared to suffer for it.
1918 *The Title*, act 1.

44 Being a husband is a whole-time job. That is why so many husbands fail. They cannot give their entire attention to it.
1918 *The Title*, act 1.

45 Journalists say a thing that they know isn't true, in the hope that if they keep on saying it long enough it will be true.
1918 *The Title*, act 2.

46 Mr Lloyd George spoke for 17 minutes, in which period he was detected only once in the use of an argument.
1921 *Things That Have Interested Me*.

47 A test of a first-rate work, and a test of your sincerity in calling it a first-rate work, is that you finish it.
1921 *Things That Have Interested Me*, 'Finishing Books'.

48 In the meantime alcohol produces a delightful social atmosphere that nothing else can produce.
1921 *Things That Have Interested Me*, 'For and Against Prohibition'.

49 Pessimism, when you get used to it, is just as agreeable as optimism.
1921 *Things That Have Interested Me*, 'Slump Into Pessimism'.

50 The price of justice is eternal publicity.
1923 *Things That Have Interested Me* (2nd series), 'Secret Trials'.

51 Between thirty and forty a man may have reached the height of discretion without having tumbled over the top and into the feather-bed of correctitude.
1930 In the *Evening Standard*, 29 May.

52 Good taste is better than bad taste, but bad taste is better than no taste, and men without individuality have no taste—at any rate no taste that they can impose on their publics.
1930 In the *Evening Standard*, 21 Aug.

53 The thing is to produce an impression on the reader—the best you can, the truest you can, but some impression. The newest despisers of form and conventionalization produce no impression at all.
1931 Journal entry, 11 Sep.

54 The saxophone is the embodied spirit of beer.
Quoted in Derek Watson *Music Quotations* (1991).

Bennett, James Gordon, Snr 1795–1872

Scots-born US journalist. In 1835 he started the *New York Herald*, pioneering many journalistic innovations.

55 The Press is the living Jury of the Nation.
1831 In the *Courier and Enquirer*, 6 Aug.

56 An editor must always be with the people—think with

them—feel with them—and he need fear nothing, he will always be right—always be strong—always *free*.
1831 In the *Courier and Enquirer*, 12 Nov.

57 This is the editorial age, and the most intellectual of all ages.
1831 In the *Courier and Enquirer*, 12 Nov.

58 What is to prevent a daily newspaper from being made the greatest organ of social life? Books have had their day—the theatres have had their day—the temple of religion has had its day. A newspaper can be made to take the lead of all these in the great movements of human thought and of human civilisation. A newspaper can send more souls to Heaven, and save more from Hell, than all the churches or chapels in New York—besides making money at the same time.
1836 In the *New York Herald*, 19 Aug.

59 I have infused life, glowing eloquence, philosophy, taste, sentiment, wit, and humor into the daily newspaper… Shakespeare is the great genius of the drama—Scott of the novel—Milton and Byron of the poem—and I mean to be the genius of the daily newspaper press.
c.1836 Quoted in Oliver Carlson *The Man Who Made News: James Gordon Bennett* (1942), ch.10.

Bennis, Warren Gameliel 1925–

US economist and business administrator.

60 Leaders are people who do the right things. Managers are people who do things right…a profound difference.
1994 In *Fortune*, 19 Sep.

Benson, A(rthur) C(hristopher) 1862–1925

English academic writer. He wrote a number of critical studies and biographies of eminent literary Victorians, and is remembered now for his patriotic poem 'Land of Hope and Glory', set to music by Elgar.

61 Land of Hope and Glory, Mother of the Free,
How shall we extol thee who are born of thee?
Wider still and wider shall thy bounds be set;
God who made thee mighty, make thee mightier yet.
1902 'Land of Hope and Glory'.

62 If the dullest person in the world would only put down sincerely what he or she thought about his or her life, about work and love, religion and emotion, it would be a fascinating document.
1906 'From A College Window'.

Benson, Stella 1892–1933

English novelist. Her diary was published long after her death from tuberculosis.

63 Call no man foe, but never love a stranger.
1917 *This is the End*.

Bentham, Jeremy 1748–1832

English philosopher, jurist and writer. His works include *A Fragment of Government* (1776) and *Introduction to the Principles of Morals and Legislation* (1789), which expounds his theory of hedonistic utilitarianism.

64 The community is a fictitious *body*, composed of the individual persons who are considered as constituting as it were its *members*. The interest of the community then, is what? The sum of the interests of the several members who compose it.
1789 *An Introduction to the Principles of Morals and Legislation*, ch.1.

65 The greatest happiness of the greatest number is the foundation of morals and legislation.
1789 *An Introduction to the Principles of Morals and Legislation*, ch.1.
► *See Hutcheson 424:52.*

66 All punishment is mischief: all punishment in itself is evil.
1789 *An Introduction to the Principles of Morals and Legislation*, ch.13.

67 Every law is an evil, for every law is an infraction of liberty.
1789 *An Introduction to the Principles of Morals and Legislation*.

68 An absolute and unlimited right over any object of property would be the right to commit nearly every crime. If I had such a right over the stick I am about to cut, I might employ it as a mace to knock down the passengers, or I might convert it into a sceptre as an emblem of royalty, or into an idol to offend the national religion.
Principles of the Civil Code, pt.1, ch.13, final note. Collected in John Bowring (ed) *Works* (1838–43), vol.1.

69 Natural rights is simple nonsense: natural and imprescriptable rights, rhetorical nonsense—nonsense upon stilts.
Anarchical Fallacies. Collected in J Bowring (ed) *Works* (1838–43), vol.2.

70 Publicity is the very soul of justice. It is the keenest spur to exertion, and the surest of all guards against improbity.
Draught of a code for the organization of the judicial establishment in France. Collected in John Bowring (ed) *Works* (1838–43), vol.4.

71 He rather hated the ruling few than loved the suffering many.
Of James Mill. Quoted in *Memories of Old Friends, being Extracts from the Journals and Letters of Caroline Fox* (1882).

72 Prose is when all the lines except the last go on to the end. Poetry is when some of them fall short of it.
Quoted in M St J Packe *The Life of John Stuart Mill* (1954), bk.1, ch.2.

73 To be the most effectively benevolent man who ever lived.
His ambition. Quoted in Mary Peter Mack *International Encyclopedia of the Social Sciences* (1968), vol.2.

Bentley, Edmund Clerihew 1875–1956

English writer and journalist. His books include *Biography for Beginners* (1905), *Baseless Biography* (1939) and the classic detective novel *Trent's Last Case* (1913). He is best known for his humorous verse form, named the clerihew after him.

74 The art of Biography
Is different from Geography.
Geography is about Maps,
But Biography is about Chaps.
1905 *Biography for Beginners*, introduction.

75 What I like about Clive
Is that he is no longer alive.
There is a great deal to be said
For being dead.
1905 *Biography for Beginners*, 'Clive'.

76 Sir Christopher Wren
said, 'I am going to dine with some men.
If anybody calls
Say I am designing St Paul's.'
1905 *Biography for Beginners*, 'Sir Christopher Wren'.

77 Sir Humphrey Davy
Abominated gravy.
He lived in the odium
Of having discovered sodium.
1905 *Biography for Beginners*, 'Sir Humphrey Davy'.

78 John Stuart Mill,
By a mighty effort of will,
Overcame his natural *bonhomie*
And wrote 'Principles of Political Economy'.
1905 *Biography for Beginners*, 'John Stuart Mill'.

79 Henry the Eighth
Took a thuctheththion of mateth.
He inthithted that the monkth
Were a lathy lot of thkunkth.
1929 *More Biography*, 'Henry the Eighth'.

80 George the Third
Ought never to have occurred.
One can only wonder
At so grotesque a blunder.
1929 *More Biography*, 'George the Third'.

81 When their lordships asked Bacon
How many bribes he had taken
He had at least the grace
To get very red in the face.
1939 *Baseless Biography*, 'Bacon'.

Bentley, Nicholas Clerihew 1907–78

English artist and writer, son of Edmund Clerihew Bentley. He was best known for his cartoons, and illustrations to works such as T S Eliot's *Old Possum's Book of Practical Cats* (1939). He edited several editions of *Pick of Punch* (1955–60).

82 Henry Campbell-Bannerman is remembered chiefly as the man about whom all is forgotten.
1974 *An Edwardian Album*.

Bentsen, Lloyd Millard, Jr 1921–

US politician, senator for Texas (1971–93). He was the Democratic nominee for Vice-President in the 1988 elections.

83 America has just passed through...an eight-year coma in which slogans were confused with solutions and rhetoric passed for reality.
1988 Recalling the Reagan administration as he accepted the Democratic nomination for Vice-President, 21 Jul.

84 Senator, I served with Jack Kennedy. I knew Jack Kennedy. Jack Kennedy was a friend of mine. Senator, you're no Jack Kennedy.
1988 On his opponent Dan Quayle's contention that his congressional experience equalled that of President Kennedy when he sought the presidency. Reported in the *New York Times*, 9 Oct.

Benuzzi, Felice 1910–88

Italian diplomat, lawyer and athlete. In Jan 1943 he and two friends escaped from a POW camp at Nanyuki to climb Mt Kenya with minimal equipment and provisions, before breaking back into the camp again and giving themselves up to the British commandant.

85 I emerged at last, stumbled a few steps in the mud and then I saw it: an ethereal mountain emerging from a tossing sea of clouds framed between two dark barracks—a massive, blue-black tooth of sheer rock inlaid with azure glaciers, austere yet floating fairy-like on the near horizon. It was the first 17,000-foot peak I had ever seen.
I stood gazing until the vision disappeared among the shifting cloud banks.
For hours afterwards I remained spell-bound.
I had definitely fallen in love.
1952 *No Picnic on Mount Kenya*.

86 To remember is far worse than to forget.
1952 On being a Prisoner of War. *No Picnic on Mount Kenya*.

Berdyaev, Nicholas 1874–1948

Russian philosopher. He originally supported the communist revolution but subsequently found that Marxism lacked a spiritual element and abandoned it. He founded the Academy of the Philosophy of Religion in Berlin (later transferred to Paris).

87 Man found his form and his identity under the action of religious principles and energies; the confusion in which he is losing them cannot be re-ordered by purely human efforts.
1923 'Konets Rennesansa' in *Sofiya* (translated as 'The End of the Renaissance' in the *Slavonic Review*, Jun/Dec 1925).

Berendt, John 1939–

US writer, journalist and editor. He was a Pulitzer Prize finalist for general non-fiction in 1995 for *Midnight in the Garden of Good and Evil* (1994).

88 In Atlanta, the first question is 'What's your business?' In Macon, it is 'Where do you go to church?' In Augusta they want your grandmother's maiden name. But in Savannah, the first question is 'What would you like to drink?'
1994 *Midnight in the Garden of Good and Evil*.

Berenson, Bernard 1865–1959

Lithuanian-born US art critic. An authority on the Renaissance, he could identify Italian masterworks by style and technique. His works include *Venetian Painters of the Renaissance* (1894) and *Rumor and Reflection* (1952).

89 I earn it by enjoying such authority and prestige that people will not buy expensive Italian pictures without my approval.
Comment on his income, addressed to the Internal Revenue Service. Quoted in *The Making of a Legend* (1987).

Beresford, Lord Charles 1846–1919

British politician.

90 Very sorry can't come. Lie follows by post.
Telegraph to the Prince of Wales, declining a dinner invitation. Quoted in Ralph Nevill *The World of Fashion 1837–1922* (1923), ch.5.

Berg, Alban 1885–1935

Austrian composer, best known for his opera *Wozzeck* (1925), his violin concerto (1935) and the *Lyric Suite* (1926) for string quartet.

91 Why is Schoenberg's Music so Hard to Understand?
1924 Title of essay.

Berger, Bennett Maurice 1926–

US sociologist, Professor at the University of California, San Diego (1973–91, then emeritus).

92 Oversimplification is now a common term of reproach in academic discussions; everyone is against oversimplification. But there is no parallel term nearly as frequently used to describe the opposite phenomenon, which surely occurs as often, if not more so.
1990 *Authors of their Own Lives* (edited by Berger), introduction.

Berger, Gerhard 1959–

Austrian Formula One racing driver.

93 There was something supernatural about him. An aura, as if he came from another planet and therefore had more insight, more brain cells, more power, more energy.
1997 On Ayrton Senna. In his autobiography, *Zielgerade*.

Berger, John Peter 1926–

English writer and art critic. His writing has been strongly influenced by Marxism, and he caused a sensation by denouncing the Booker Corporation in his acceptance speech when awarded the Booker Prize for his novel *G* in 1972.

94 The five senses within whose pentagon each man is alone.
1972 *G*, pt.3, ch.5.

95 If we could all live a thousand years...we would each, at least once during that period, be considered a genius.
1972 *G*, pt.3, ch.6.

96 The camera relieves us of the burden of memory.
1978 *New Statesman*, 17 Aug.

97 It is not usually possible in a poem or a story to make the relationship between particular and universal fully explicit. Those who try to do so end up writing parables.
1979 *Pig Earth*, 'Historical Afterward'.

98 Photography, because it stops the flow of life, is always flirting with death.
1983 In the *New Statesman*, 22/29 Dec.

99 All weddings are similar but every marriage is different. Death comes to everyone but one mourns alone.
1985 *The White Bird*, 'The Storyteller'.

1 Every city has a sex and age which have nothing to do with demography.
1987 In *The Guardian*, 27 Mar.

2 Every painted image of something is also about the absence of the real thing. All painting is about the presence of absence.
1988 In *New Statesman and Society*, 15 Jul.

Bergreen, Laurence 1950–

US journalist and biographer.

3 He was not fit for marriage, only for work. A major writer, he conceded, required major torment.
1984 Of James Agee. *James Agee*.

Berkeley, George 1685–1753

Irish idealist philosopher and Anglican Bishop of Cloyne (1734–52). His philosophical works, such as *A Treatise Concerning the Principles of Human Knowledge* (1710), argue that things in the material world only exist when perceived in the mind.

4 I am inclined to think that the far greater part, if not all, of those difficulties which have hitherto amused philosophers, and blocked up the way to knowledge, are entirely owing to ourselves—that we have first raised a dust and then complain we cannot see.
1710 *A Treatise Concerning the Principles of Human Knowledge*, Introduction.

5 Some truths there are so near and obvious to the mind that a man need only open his eyes to see them. Such I take this important one to be, viz. that all the choir of heaven and furniture of the earth, in a word all those bodies which compose the mighty frame of the world, have not any subsistence without a mind—that their *being is to be perceived or known*.
1710 *A Treatise Concerning The Principles Of Human Knowledge*, pt.1, section 6.

6 Whatever is immediately perceived is an idea: and can any *idea* exist out of the mind?
1713 *Three Dialogues between Hylas And Philonous*, first dialogue.

7 The same principles which at first lead to scepticism, pursued to a certain point bring men back to common sense.
1734 *Three Dialogues between Hylas and Philonous*, dialogue 3.
► See Bacon 48:95.

8 Whose fault is it if poor Ireland still continues poor?
1737 *The Querist*, pt.3.

9 Truth is the cry of all, but the game of the few.
1744 *Siris*.

10 It is impossible that a man who is false to his friends and neighbours should be true to the public.
1750 *Maxims Concerning Patriotism*.

Berlin, Irving *originally* ***Israel Baline*** 1888–1989

Russian-born US composer, who began as a singing waiter. He wrote lyrics and music for over 900 songs including 'Alexander's Ragtime Band' and 'White Christmas'. The musical *Annie Get Your Gun* (1946) marked the peak of his career.

11 Come on and hear,
Come on and hear
Alexander's Ragtime Band
1911 'Alexander's Ragtime Band', opening lines, featured in the 1938 film of the same title.

12 A pretty girl is like a melody
That haunts you night and day.
1919 'A Pretty Girl is Like a Melody'.

13 The song is ended
But the melody lingers on.
1927 Song from *Ziegfeld Follies*.

14 I'm puttin' on my top hat
Tyin' up my white tie
Brushin' off my tails
1935 'Top Hat, White Tie and Tails', performed by Fred Astaire in *Top Hat*.

15 There may be trouble ahead

But while there's moonlight and music and love and romance
Let's face the music and dance
1936 'Let's Face the Music and Dance', in the film *Follow the Fleet*.

16 I'm dreaming of a white Christmas,
Just like the ones I used to know,
Where the tree-tops glisten
And children listen
To hear sleigh bells in the snow.
1942 'I'm Dreaming of a White Christmas', in the film *Holiday Inn*.

17 There's No Business Like Show Business.
1946 Title of song from the film *Annie Get Your Gun*.

18 Listen kid, take my advice—never hate a song that has sold half a million copies.
Comment to the young Cole Porter, attributed.

19 No, for prosperity.
Attributed, when asked whether he wrote his songs for posterity.

Berlin, Sir Isaiah 1907–97

Russian-born British philosopher and historian of ideas. He was Professor of Social and Political Theory at Oxford (1957–67) and President of Wolfson College (1966–75). He served as a diplomat to Russia and the US in World War II.

20 Liberty is liberty, not equality or fairness or justice or human happiness or a quiet conscience.
1958 *Two Concepts of Liberty*, note.

21 The desire not to be impinged upon, to be left to oneself, has been the mark of high civilisation both on the part of individuals and communities.
1959 *Four Essays on Liberty*.

22 Man cannot live without seeking to describe and explain the universe.
1962 In the *Sunday Times*.

23 No perfect solution is, not merely in practice, but in principle, possible in human affairs, and any determined attempt to produce it is likely to lead to suffering, disillusionment and failure.
1978 *The Crooked Timber of Humanity*, 'The Decline of Utopian Ideals in the West'.

24 Pluralism—that is, the conception that there are many different ends that men may seek and still be fully rational, fully men, capable of understanding each other and sympathising and deriving light from each other.
1978 *The Crooked Timber of Humanity*, 'The Pursuit of the Ideal'.

Berlusconi, Silvio 1936–

Italian businessman and politician who has at times been criticized for the conflict of interest between his business empire and the office of Prime Minister and who is a controversial figure in European politics.

25 I heard that the game was getting dangerous, and that it was being played in the two penalty areas, with midfield being left desolately empty… And we decided to fill that immense space.
On why he founded Forza Italia, a new political party. Quoted in Paul Ginsberg *Italy and Its Discontents* (2001).

26 Let's talk about football or women.
2003 Comment at a formal lunch at an abortive summit meeting of EU leaders, Brussels, Dec.

Bernanos, Georges 1888–1948

French novelist who explored the role of the devil and sin in modern society. A fervent opponent of Fascism, he lost favour with conservative Catholics after publishing polemical tracts against Franco.

27 *Le désir de la prière est déjà une prière.*
The wish for prayer is already a prayer.
1936 *Le Journal d'un curé de campagne*, ch.2 (translated by P Morris as *Diary of a Country Priest*, 1937).

28 *L'enfer, Madame, c'est de ne plus aimer.*
Hell, Madam, is to no longer love.
1936 *Journal d'un curé de campagne*, ch.2.

Bernard of Chartres d. c.1130

French divine and scholar. He taught logic and grammar at Chartres school from 1114, becoming Chancellor in 1119. In 1124 he began teaching at Paris. Only fragments of his three philosophical treatises survive.

29 *Nanos gigantium humeris insidentes.*
Dwarfs standing on the shoulders of giants.
c.1128 Of modern scholars in relation to their ancient predecessors. Quoted in John of Salisbury *Metalogicon* (1159), bk.3, ch.4.

St Bernard of Clairvaux 1090–1153

Theologian and reformer, first abbot (1115) of the newly-founded Cistercian monastery of Clairvaux, Champagne. Renowned for his studious, ascetic life and eloquence (he spoke in support of the Second Crusade, 1146), he founded over 70 monasteries.

30 *Omnes nimirum, ex quo monachi sumus, infirmos stomachos habemus, et tam necessarium Apostoli de utendo vino consilium merito non negligimus. Modico, tamen quod ille praemissit, nescio cur praetermisso.*
Being monks, we all naturally have a weak stomach, and we therefore justly attend to the Apostle's advice to use wine. He adds, however, the words 'a little'; I can't think why I have omitted them.
c.1124 *Apologia ad Guillelmum*, ch.9, section 21.

31 You have been called to hold a high position, but not a safe one; a sublime position, but not a secure one. How terrible, how very terrible is the place you hold!
c.1145 Letter to Eugenius III shortly after he had became Pope, on the dangers of the growth of papal power. Collected in B S James (ed and trans) *The Letters of St Bernard of Clairvaux* (1953).

32 *Aiunt non vos esse papam, sed me.*
They say it is not you who are pope, but me.
c.1145 Of his own influence within the Cistercian order. Letter to Pope Eugenius III.

33 You ordered. I obeyed… I opened my mouth; I spoke; and at once the Crusaders have multiplied to infinity. Villages and towns are now deserted. You will scarcely find one man for every seven women. Everywhere you see widows whose husbands are still alive.
1146 Letter to Pope Eugenius III describing the effects of preaching the Second Crusade. Collected in J P Migne (ed) *Patrologia Latina*, vol.182, letter no.247.

34 *Liberavi animam meam.*
I have freed my soul.
c.1147 Letter to Abbot Suger.

Bernard, Claude 1813–78

French scientist, considered the founder of contemporary experimental medicine on account of his work on the digestive process and on the vasomotor mechanism.

35 Science does not permit exceptions.
1855–6 *Lessons of Experimental Pathology.*

36 In science, the best precept is to alter and exchange our ideas as fast as science moves ahead.
1865 *An Introduction to the Study of Experimental Medicine*, vol.1, ch.1, section 3 (translated by H C Greene).

37 Science rejects the indeterminate.
1865 *An Introduction to the Study of Experimental Medicine*, vol.1, ch.1, section 3 (translated by H C Greene).

38 True science teaches us to doubt and, in ignorance, to refrain.
1865 *An Introduction to the Study of Experimental Medicine*, vol.1, ch.1, section 3 (translated by H C Greene).

39 Particular facts are never scientific; only generalization can establish science.
1865 *An Introduction to the Study of Experimental Medicine*, vol.1, ch.1, section 3 (translated by H C Greene).

Bernardin de Saint-Pierre, Jacques-Henri 1737–1814

French novelist, friend of Rousseau and enemy of many others, naturalist and precursor of the Romantics. He travelled widely in Martinique, Russia and Madagascar.

40 *Les hommes ne veulent connaître que l'histoire des grands et des rois, qui ne sert à personne.*
Men wish to hear no stories but those about the great and powerful, which are no use to anyone.
1788 *Paul et Virginie.*

41 *Après le rare bonheur de trouver une compagne qui nous soit bien assortie, l'état le moins malheureux de la vie est sans doute de vivre seul.*
After the rare happiness of finding a companion with whom we are well matched, the least unpleasant state of life is without doubt to live alone.
1788 *Paul et Virginie.*

42 *La solitude rétablit aussi bien les harmonies du corps que celles de l'âme.*
Solitude restores the harmonies of the body no less than those of the soul.
1788 *Paul et Virginie.*

43 *On se fait une idée précise de l'ordre, mais non pas du désordre. La beauté, la vertu, le bonheur, ont des proportions; la laideur, le vice, et le malheur, n'en ont point.*
We can form a precise idea of order, but not of disorder. Beauty, virtue, happiness, all have their proportions; ugliness, vice and unhappiness have none.
1788 *Paul et Virginie.*

44 *Le parfum de mille roses ne plaît qu'un instant; mais la douleur que cause une seule de leurs épines dure longtemps après la piqûre.*
The perfume of a thousand roses pleases only for an instant; but the pain caused by a single one of their thorns lasts a long time after the prick.
1788 *Paul et Virginie.*

45 *La mort, mon fils, est un bien pour tous les hommes; elle est la nuit de ce jour inquiet qu'on appelle la vie.*
Death, my son, is a good for all; it is the night of this worrisome day that one calls life.
1788 *Paul et Virginie.*

46 *Artistes, poètes, écrivains, si vous copiez toujours, on ne vous copiera jamais.*
Artists, poets, writers, if you copy others all the time, no one will copy you.
1790 *Mémoires sur la ménagerie.*

Bernays, Edward 1891–1995

US pioneer public relations consultant, born in Vienna. His many books include *Crystallizing Public Opinion* (1923) and *The Engineering of Consent* (1955).

47 The engineering of consent.
1955 His definition of public relations, the field he was credited with founding. *The Engineering of Consent.*

Berners, Dame Juliana *or* *Juliana Barnes* fl.14c

English nun, traditionally Prioress of Sopwell convent, St Albans. She was the author of the *Treatyse perteynynge to Hawkynge, Huntynge, Fyshynge, and Coote Armiris* (1486).

48 A greyhound should be heeded lyke a snake,
And neckyd lyke a drake,
Backed lyke a bream,
Footed lyke a catte,
Taylled lyke a ratte.
1486 *Treatyse perteynynge to Hawkynge, Huntynge, Fyshynge, and Coote Armiris.*

49 The Salmon is the most stately fish that any man may angle to in fresh water.
1486 *Treatyse perteynyne to Hawkynge, Huntynge, Fyshynge, and Coote Armiris.*

Bernhardt, Sarah *stage-name of* *Sarah Henriette Rosine Bernard* 1844–1923

French actress. Hailed internationally as one of the leading theatrical performers of her generation, she made her stage debut in 1862 and went on to play many of the great tragic roles in Shakespeare, Racine, Hugo, Rostand, Sardou and others.

50 *J'adore ce cricket; c'est tellement Anglais.*
I do so love cricket—it's so very English.
c.1905 On being taken to see a game of football in Manchester. Quoted in R Buckle *Nijinsky* (1971).

51 For the theatre one needs long arms; it is better to have them too long than too short. An *artiste* with short arms can never, never make a fine gesture.
1907 *Memories of My Life.*

Bernini, Gianlorenzo 1598–1680

Italian sculptor, painter and architect, one of the key figures of Italian Baroque art.

52 Sometimes, in order to imitate the original, it is necessary to put something that is not in the original into a portrait in marble.
Attributed remark made to Paul Fréart, in *Diary of Cavalier Bernini's Journey in France* (1665).

Bernstein, Leonard 1918–90

US conductor, pianist and composer. He achieved fame in 1943 as conductor with the New York Philharmonic. His compositions include three symphonies, a television opera and the musical *West Side Story* (1958).

53 It would be nice to hear someone accidentally whistle
something of mine, somewhere, just once.
1960 *The Joy of Music*.

Berra, Yogi Lawrence Peter 1925–

US baseball player and coach. A star with the New York Yankees, he took part in a record 14 World Series (1946–63). He went on to manage the New York Yankees, the New York Mets and the Houston Astros.

54 If the people don't want to come out to the park,
nobody's gonna stop them.
Quoted in Colin Jarman *The Guinness Dictionary of Sports Quotations* (1990).

55 He made too many wrong mistakes.
Quoted in Colin Jarman *The Guinness Dictionary of Sports Quotations* (1990).

56 You can observe a lot just by watching.
Quoted in Colin Jarman *The Guinness Dictionary of Sports Quotations* (1990).

57 You can't think and hit at the same time.
Quoted in Colin Jarman *The Guinness Dictionary of Sports Quotations* (1990).

58 It ain't over 'til it's over.
Attributed.

Berry, Chuck (Charles Edward Anderson) 1926–

US black rock 'n' roll singer, whose influential hits included 'Maybelline' (1955), 'School Days' (1957), and 'Johnny B Goode' (1958). In 1959 he was charged with transporting a minor over state lines for immoral purposes and jailed for two years (1962).

59 You know my temperature's risin',
The juke box's blowin' a fuse,
My heart's beatin' rhythm,
My soul keeps a singin' the blues—
Roll over Beethoven,
Tell Tchaikovsky the news.
1956 'Roll over Beethoven'.

Berryman, John *originally* John Allyn Smith 1914–72

US poet and novelist. His reputation rests on his complex, often obscure poetry, collected in *The Dispossessed* (1948), *Homage to Mistress Bradstreet* (1953) and the extended sequence of *Dream Songs* (1964).

60 We must travel in the direction of our fears.
1942 'A Point of Age'.

61 Headstones stagger under great draughts of time
after heads pass out, and their world must reel
speechless, blind in the end
about its chilling star
1953 'Homage to Mistress Bradstreet', stanza 55.

62 Life, friends, is boring. We must not say so.
1964 'Dream Song No.14'.

63 And moreover my mother taught me as a boy
(repeatingly) 'Ever to confess you're bored
means you have no
Inner Resources.' I conclude now I have no
inner resources, because I am heavy bored.
1964 'Dream Song No.14'.

64 I seldom go to films. They are too exciting
said the Honourable Possum.
1964 'Dream Song No.53'.

65 Bats have no bankers and they do not drink
and cannot be arrested and pay no tax
and, in general, bats have it made.
1964 'Dream Song No.63'.

66 A lone letter from a young man: that is fame.
1968 'Dream Song No.342'.

67 My girls suffered during this month or so,
so did my seminars & lectures &
my poetry even. To be a *critic*, ah,
how deeper and more scientific.
1971 'Olympus'.

68 The artist is extremely lucky who is presented with the
worst possible ordeal which will not actually kill him.
1972 Interview in *The Paris Review*, winter issue.

Berton, Pierre 1920–

Canadian writer, journalist and broadcaster. His many works include *The Mysterious North* (1956) and *Why We Act Like Canadians* (1982).

69 A Canadian is somebody who knows how to make love
in a canoe.
1973 Interviewed by Dick Brown in *The Canadian*, 22 Dec.

Best, George 1946–

Northern Irish footballer who was the leading scorer for Manchester United in the Football League First Division in 1967–8, and in 1968 won a European Cup medal and the title of European Footballer of the Year.

70 Alcoholics Anonymous might have worked for me if I
had been anonymous, but I was not. People kept asking
me for my autograph.
2001 In the *Observer*, 30 Dec.

71 I *will* respect this liver. After all, it's not mine.
Referring to his liver transplant. In *Scoring at Half Time* (2003).

72 I told the assembled media that I was not the White Pele
and that Pele was in fact the Black George Best.
On his arrival in the United States in 1975. In *Blessed* (2003).

Bethell, (Mary) Ursula 1874–1945

New Zealand poet, born in England. Her works, celebrating detail in nature, include *From a Garden in the Antipodes* (1929) and *Day and Night: Poems 1924–1935* (1939).

73 But beside it I have planted a green Bay-tree,
—A sweet Bay, an Olive, and a Turkey Fig,
—A Fig, an Olive, and a Bay.
1929 *From a Garden in the Antipodes*, 'Detail'.

Bethmann Hollweg, Theobald von 1856–1921

German statesman, Imperial Chancellor (1909–17), who played an important part in events leading to war in 1914. Anxious for a negotiated peace, he was forced from office in 1917.

74 Just for a word 'neutrality'—a word which in wartime has
so often been disregarded—just for a scrap of paper
Great Britain is going to make war on a kindred nation
who desires nothing better than to be friends with her.
1914 On Britain's reaction to the German invasion of neutral

Belgium, 4 Aug. Quoted in *British Documents on the Origins of the War 1898–1914* (1926), vol.11.

75 If the iron dice roll, may God help us.
1914 Speech in the Reichstag.

Bethune, Norman 1890–1939

Canadian physician and revolutionary.

76 The function of the artist is to disturb. His duty is to arouse the sleeper, to shake the complacent pillars of the world. He reminds the world of its dark ancestry, and shows the world its present, and points the way to its new birth. He is at once the product and the preceptor of his time.
1937 Letter from Madrid, 5 May. Quoted in Ted Allen and Sydney Gordon *The Scalpel, The Sword* (1952).

Betjeman, Sir John 1906–84

English poet, writer and broadcaster, whose nostalgic light verse, often masking an underlying melancholy, achieved great popularity. Appointed Poet Laureate in 1972, he was also a defender of traditional architecture and a perceptive social critic.

77 Oh! Chintzy, chintzy cheeriness,
Half dead and half alive.
1930 'Death in Leamington', first published in the *London Mercury*.

78 Sing on, with hymns uproarious,
Ye humble and aloof,
Look up! and oh, how glorious
He has restored the roof!
1931 *Mount Zion*, 'Hymn'.

79 Broad of Church and broad of Mind,
Broad before and broad behind,
A keen ecclesiologist,
A rather dirty Wykehamist.
1931 *Mount Zion*, 'The Wykehamist'.

80 Ghastly Good Taste, or a depressing story of the rise and fall of English architecture.
1933 Title and sub-title of book.

81 He sipped at the weak hock and seltzer
As he gazed at the London skies
Through the Nottingham lace of the curtains
Or was it his bees-winged eyes?
1937 *Continual Dew*, 'The Arrest of Oscar Wilde at The Cadogan Hotel'.

82 Spirits of well-shot woodcock, partridge, snipe,
Flutter and bear him up the Norfolk sky:
In that red house in a red mahogany book-case
The stamp collection waits with mounts long dry.
1937 *Continual Dew*, 'Death of King George V'.

83 Come, friendly bombs, and fall on Slough
It isn't fit for humans now
There isn't grass to graze a cow
Swarm over, Death!
1937 *Continual Dew*, 'Slough'.

84 Pam, I adore you, Pam, you great mountainous
sports girl,
Whizzing them over the net, full of the strength of five:
That old Malvernian brother, you zephyr and khaki
shorts girl,
Although he's playing for Woking,
Can't stand up to your wonderful backhand drive.
1940 *Old Lights for New Chancels*, 'Pot Pourri from a Surrey Garden'.

85 Think of what our Nation stands for,
Books from Boots' and country lanes,
Free speech, free passes, class distinction,
Democracy and proper drains.
Lord, put beneath Thy special care
One-eighty-nine Cadogan Square.
1940 *Old Lights for New Chancels*, 'In Westminster Abbey'.

86 The test of an abstract picture, for me, is not my first reaction to it, but how long I can stand it hanging on the wall of a room where I am living.
1944 *John Piper*.

87 Miss J. Hunter Dunn, Miss J. Hunter Dunn,
Furnish'd and burnish'd by Aldershot sun,
What strenuous singles we played after tea,
We in the tournament—you against me!
1945 *New Bats in Old Belfries*, 'A Subaltern's Love-Song'.

88 Miss Joan Hunter Dunn, Miss Joan Hunter Dunn,
I can hear from the car-park the dance has begun.
Oh! full Surrey twilight! importunate band!
Oh! strongly adorable tennis-girl's hand!
1945 *New Bats in Old Belfries*, 'A Subaltern's Love-Song'.

89 For a full spring-tide of blossom seethed and departed
hence,
Leaving land-locked pools of jonquils by sunny garden
fence.
1945 *New Bats in Old Belfries*, 'May-Day Song for North Oxford'.

90 And low the mists of evening lie
And lightly skims the midge.
1945 *New Bats in Old Belfries*, 'Henley-on-Thames'.

91 Rumbling under blackened girders, Midland, bound for
Cricklewood,
Puffed its sulphur to the sunset where that Land of
laundries stood.
1945 *New Bats in Old Belfries*, 'Parliament Hill Fields'.

92 Up the hill where stucco houses in Virginia creeper
drown—
And my childish wave of pity, seeing children carrying
down
Sheaves of drooping dandelions to the courts of Kentish
Town.
1945 *New Bats in Old Belfries*, 'Parliament Hill Fields'.

93 Bournemouth is one of the few English towns one can safely call 'her'.
1949 Radio talk, later collected in *First and Last Loves* (1952), 'Bournemouth'.

94 St Endellion! St Endellion! The name is like a ring of bells.
1950 Radio talk, later collected in *First and Last Loves* (1952), 'St Endellion'.

95 Imagine the position of the modern architect. Picture the young fellow to be put into a 'profession' because trade is considered beneath him (another antiquarian prejudice). The young fellow hasn't exactly got a legal mind, like father; he's not much good at essays, so he can't write; he faints at the sight of blood so can't be a doctor. What is there for him to do? Architecture of course.
1952 *First and Last Loves*.

96 Oh prams on concrete balconies, what will your children
see?
1952 *First and Last Loves*.

97 History must not be written with bias, and both sides must be given, even if there is only one side.
1952 *First and Last Loves.*

98 And girls in slacks remember Dad,
And oafish louts remember Mum.
1954 *A Few Late Chrysanthemums*, 'Christmas'.

99 And is it true? And is it true,
This most tremendous tale of all,
Seen in a stained-glass window's hue,
A Baby in an ox's stall?
The Maker of the stars and sea
Become a Child on earth for me?
1954 *A Few Late Chrysanthemums*, 'Christmas'.

1 Gaily into Ruislip Gardens
Runs the red electric train
With a thousand Ta's and Pardon's
Daintily alights Elaine.
1954 *A Few Late Chrysanthemums*, 'Middlesex'.

2 Then Harrow-on-the-Hill's a rocky island
And Harrow churchyard full of sailor's graves,
And the constant click and kissing of the trolley busses hissing
Is the level to the Wealdstone turned to waves.
1954 *A Few Late Chrysanthemums*, 'Harrow-on-the-Hill'.

3 But I'm dying now and done for,
What on earth was all the fun for?
I am ill and old and terrified and tight.
1954 *A Few Late Chrysanthemums*, 'Sun and Fun—Song of a Night-club Proprietress'.

4 Does Mum, the Persil-user, still believe
That there's no Devil and that youth is bliss?
As certain as the sun behind the Downs
And quite as plain to see, the Devil walks.
1954 *A Few Late Chrysanthemums*, 'Original Sin on the Sussex Coast'.

5 Phone for the fish knives, Norman
As Cook is a little unnerved;
You kiddies have crumpled the serviettes
And I must have things daintily served.
1954 *A Few Late Chrysanthemums*, 'How To Get On In Society'.

6 In the licorice fields at Pontefract
My love and I did meet
And many a burdened licorice bush
Was blooming round our feet;
Red hair she had and golden skin,
Her sulky lips were shaped for sin,
Her sturdy legs were flannel-slack'd,
The strongest legs in Pontefract.
1954 *A Few Late Chrysanthemums*, 'The Licorice Fields at Pontefract'.

7 In the Garden City Café with its murals on the wall
Before a talk on 'Sex and Civics' I meditated on the Fall.
1954 *A Few Late Chrysanthemums*, 'Huxley Hall'.

8 It's awf'lly bad luck on Diana
Her ponies have swallowed their bits;
She fished down their throats with a spanner
And frightened them all into fits.
1954 *A Few Late Chrysanthemums*, 'Hunter Trails'.

9 Oh wasn't it naughty of Smudges?
Oh, Mummy, I'm sick with disgust.
She threw me in front of the Judges
And my silly old collarbone's bust.
1954 *A Few Late Chrysanthemums*, 'Hunter Trails'.

10 I heard the church bells hollowing out the sky
Deep beyond deep, like never-ending stars.
1960 *Summoned By Bells*, ch.1.

11 Childhood is measured out by sounds and smells
And sights, before the dark of reason grows.
1960 *Summoned By Bells*, ch.4.

12 The dread of beatings! Dread of being late!
And, greatest dread of all, the dread of games!
1960 *Summoned by Bells*, ch.7.

Beuys, Joseph 1921–86

German avant-garde artist. Professor of Sculpture at Düsseldorf Academy (1961–71), his works were typically 'assemblages' of rubbish, deliberately anti-formal. He co-founded the German Green Party.

13 A total work of art is only possible in the context of the whole of society. Everyone will be a necessary co-creator of a social architecture, and, so long as anyone cannot participate, the ideal form of democracy has not been reached. Whether people are artists, assemblers of machines or nurses, it is a matter of participating in the whole.
1972 From an interview with G Jappe (translated by J Wheelwright), in *Studio International*, vol.184, no.950, Dec. Quoted in C Harrison and P Wood (eds) *Art in Theory 1900–1990* (1992).

Bevan, Aneurin 1897–1960

Welsh Labour politician, a miner who took a leading part in the 1926 General Strike, and a brilliant, irreverent orator. He entered politics in 1929 and joined the Labour Party (1931). As Minister of Health (1945–51), he introduced the National Health Service (1948).

14 The worst thing I can say about democracy is that it has tolerated the right honourable gentleman [Neville Chamberlain] for four and a half years.
1929 House of Commons, 23 Jul.

15 We have been the dreamers. We have been the sufferers. Now we are the builders. We want the complete political extinction of the Tory Party—and 25 years of Labour Government, for we cannot do in five years what requires to be done.
1945 Labour Party conference, Blackpool, 18 May.

16 This island is made mainly of coal and surrounded by fish. Only an organizing genius could produce a shortage of coal and a shortage of fish at the same time.
1945 Speech at Blackpool. Reported in the *Daily Herald*, 25 May.

17 No amount of cajolery, and no attempts at ethical or social seduction, can eradicate from my heart a deep and burning hatred for the Tory Party that inflicted those experiences on me. So far as I am concerned, they are lower than vermin.
1948 Speech on the inter-war depression, made at the inauguration of the National Health Service, 5 Jul.

18 In Place of Fear.
1952 Title of his book about disarmament.

19 We know what happens to people who stay in the middle of the road. They get run over.
1953 In the *Observer*, Dec.

20 A man suffering from petrified adolescence.
Of Winston Churchill. Quoted in Vincent Brome *Aneurin Bevan* (1953).

21 I am not going to spend any time whatsoever attacking the Foreign Secretary. Quite honestly, I am beginning to feel extremely sorry for him. If we complain about the tune, there is no reason to attack the monkey when the organ grinder is present.
1957 Expressing his wish to address Prime Minister Harold Macmillan rather than Selwyn Lloyd on the Suez crisis in the House of Commons, May.

22 If you carry this resolution, you will send a Foreign Secretary—whoever he may be—naked into the conference chamber. You call that statesmanship. I call it an emotional spasm.
1957 Labour Party conference speech against unilateral disarmament, Oct.

23 I read the newspapers avidly. It is my one form of continuous fiction.
1960 In *The Times*, 29 Mar.

24 Politics is a blood sport.
Quoted in Jennie Lee *My Life with Nye* (1980).

Beveridge, William Henry Beveridge, 1st Baron
1879–1963

British economist, administrator and social reformer, Director of the London School of Economics (1919–37). His *Report on Social Insurance and Allied Services* (The Beveridge Report, 1942) helped to create the Welfare State.

25 The trouble in modern democracy is that men do not approach to leadership until they have lost the desire to lead anyone.
1934 In the *Observer*, 15 Apr.

26 The object of government in peace and in war is not the glory of rulers or of races, but the happiness of the common man.
1942 *Social Insurance and Allied Services*, pt.7.

27 The most urgent tasks in Britain, once war is over, are, on the one hand, the making of a common attack on the giant evils of Want, Disease, Ignorance and Squalor, and on the other hand, the re-equipping of British industry.
1944 *Full Employment in a Free Society.*

28 The state is or can be master of money, but in a free society it is master of very little else.
1948 *Voluntary Action*, ch.12.

Bevin, Ernest 1881–1951

English Labour politician. He formed the National Transport and General Workers' Union, becoming its General Secretary (1921–40), then entered politics. He was appointed Minister of Labour and National Service in the coalition, and later Foreign Secretary (1945–51).

29 The most conservative man in the world is the British trade unionist, when you want to change him.
1927 Speech to Trade Union Congress, 8 Sep.

30 If you open that Pandora's box, you never know what Trojan 'orses will appear.
1948 Expressing doubts about the value of the newly formed Council of Europe. Recalled by his secretary Sir Roderick Barclay in Michael Charlton *The Price of Victory* (1983).

31 Well you know, Chris, we've got to give them something and I think we'll give them this talking shop in Strasbourg—the Council of Europe.
1948 Comment to Christopher Mayhew. Quoted in Michael Charlton *The Price of Victory* (1983).

32 A turn-up in a million.
On himself. Quoted in his entry by Baron Francis Williams in the *Dictionary of National Biography* (1951–60).

33 Anything you make a mistake about, I will get you out of, and anything you do well I will take the credit for.
Attributed, to a subordinate. Quoted in A J P Taylor *From the Boer War to the Cold War: Essays on Twentieth-Century Europe* (1995).

Bhagavad Gita

A sacred Hindu text, part of the Mahabharata. All translations are from J Mascaro (1978).

34 As the Spirit of our mortal body wanders on in childhood and youth and old age, the Spirit wanders on to a new body: of this the sage has no doubts.
Ch.2, v.13.

35 As a man leaves an old garment and puts on one that is new, the spirit leaves his mortal body and puts on one that is new.
Ch.2, v.22.

36 Leave all things behind, and come unto me for thy salvation. I will make thee free from the bondage of sins. Fear no more.
Ch.18, v.66.

Bible (Old Testament)

All quotations are taken from the King James, or Authorized, translation of the Bible (1611).

37 In the beginning God created the heaven and the earth. And the earth was without form, and void; and darkness was upon the face of the deep. And the spirit of God moved upon the face of the waters.
Genesis 1:1–2.

38 And God said, Let there be light: and there was light.
Genesis 1:3.

39 And God called the light Day and the darkness he called Night. And the evening and morning were the first day.
Genesis 1:5.

40 And God saw that it was good.
Genesis 1:10.

41 And God said, Let us create man in our image, after our likeness: and let them have dominion over the fish of the sea, and over the fowl of the air, and over the cattle, and over all the earth, and over every creeping thing that creepeth upon the earth. So God created man in his own image, in the image of God created he him; male and female created he them. And God blessed them, and God said unto them, Be fruitful and multiply, and replenish the earth, and subdue it: and have dominion over the fish of the sea, and over the fowl of the air, and over every living thing that moveth upon the earth.
Genesis 1:26–8.

42 And on the seventh day God ended his work which he had made, and he rested on the seventh day from all his work which he had made. And God blessed the seventh day and sanctified it: because that in it he had rested

from all his work which God created and made.
Genesis 2:2–3.

43 And the LORD God formed man out of the dust of the ground, and breathed into his nostrils the breath of life; and man became a living soul.
Genesis 2:7.

44 And the LORD God planted a garden eastwards in Eden; and there he put the man whom he had formed. And out of the ground made the LORD God to grow every tree that is pleasant for the sight, and good for food; the tree of life also in the midst of the garden, and the tree of knowledge of good and evil.
Genesis 2:8–9.

45 And the LORD God took the man and put him into the garden of Eden to dress it and to keep it. And the LORD God commanded the man, saying, Of every tree of the garden thou mayest freely eat: But of the tree of the knowledge of good and evil, thou shalt not eat of it: for in the day that thou eatest thereof thou shalt surely die.
Genesis 2:15–17.

46 And the LORD God said, It is not good that the man should be alone; I will make him an help meet for him.
Genesis 2:18.

47 And the LORD God caused a deep sleep to fall on Adam, and he slept: and he took one of his ribs, and closed up the flesh instead thereof; And the rib, which the LORD God had taken from man, made he a woman, and brought her unto the man. And Adam said, This is now bone of my bones, and flesh of my flesh: she shall be called Woman, because she was taken out of Man. Therefore shall a man leave his father and his mother, and shall cleave unto his wife: and they shall be one flesh.
Genesis 2:21–4.

48 Now the serpent was more subtil than any beast of the field which the LORD God had made.
Genesis 3:1.

49 And the serpent said unto the woman, Ye shall not surely die: For God doth know that in the day ye eat thereof, then your eyes shall be opened, and ye shall be as gods, knowing good and evil.
Genesis 3:4–5.

50 And when the woman saw that the tree was good for food, and that it was pleasant to the eyes, and a tree to be desired to make one wise she took of the fruit thereof, and did eat, and gave also to her husband with her; and he did eat. And the eyes of them both were opened, and they knew that they were naked; and they sewed fig leaves together, and made themselves aprons. And they heard the voice of the LORD God walking in the garden in the cool of the day: and Adam and his wife hid themselves from the presence of the LORD God amongst the trees of the garden.
Genesis 3:6–8. In the Geneva Bible of 1560, the word 'aprons' was rendered 'breeches', and the version was therefore known as the Breeches Bible.

51 And he said, I heard thy voice in the garden, and I was afraid, because I was naked; and I hid myself. And he said, Who told thee that thou wast naked? Hast thou eaten of the tree, whereof I commanded thee that thou shouldst not eat?
Genesis 3:10–11.

52 And the man said, The woman whom thou gavest to be with me, she gave me of the tree, and I did eat. And the LORD God said unto the woman, What is this that thou hast done? And the woman said, The serpent beguiled me, and I did eat.
Genesis 3:12–13.

53 And the LORD God said unto the serpent, Because thou hast done this, thou art cursed above all cattle, and above every beast of the field; upon thy belly thou shalt go, and dust shalt thou eat all the days of thy life: And I will put enmity between thy seed and her seed; it shall bruise thy head, and thou shalt bruise his heel.
Genesis 3:14–15.

54 Unto the woman he said, I will greatly multiply thy sorrow and conception; in sorrow thou shalt bring forth children; and thy desire shall be for thy husband, and he shall rule over thee.
Genesis 3:16.

55 And unto Adam he said, Because thou hast hearkened unto the voice of thy wife, and hast eaten of the tree, of which I commanded thee, saying, Thou shalt not eat of it: cursed is the ground for thy sake; in sorrow shalt thou eat of it all the days of thy life.
Genesis 3:17.

56 In the sweat of thy face shalt thou eat bread, till thou return to the ground; for out of it wast thou taken: for dust thou art, and unto dust shall return.
Genesis 3:19.

57 And the LORD God said, Behold, the man is become as one of us, to know good and evil: and now, lest he put forth his hand, and take also of the tree of life, and eat, and live for ever: Therefore the LORD God sent him forth from the garden of Eden, to till the ground from whence he was taken. So he drove out the man; and he placed at the east of the garden of Eden Cherubims, and a flaming sword which turned every way, to keep the tree of life.
Genesis 3:21–4.

58 And Adam knew Eve his wife; and she conceived and bare Cain, and said, I have gotten a man from the LORD.
Genesis 4:1.

59 And the LORD said unto Cain, Where is Abel thy brother? And he said, I know not: Am I my brother's keeper? And he said, What hast thou done? the voice of thy brother's blood crieth unto me from the ground.
Genesis 4:9.

60 My punishment is greater than I can bear.
Cain. Genesis 4:10.

61 And the LORD said unto him, Therefore whoever slayeth Cain, vengeance shall be taken on him sevenfold. And the LORD set a mark upon Cain lest any finding him should kill him.
Genesis 4:15.

62 And Cain went out from the presence of the LORD, and dwelt in the land of Nod, on the east of Eden.
Genesis 4:16.

63 And all the days of Methuselah were nine hundred sixty and nine years; and he died.
Genesis 5:27.

64 They went in two and two unto Noah into the ark, the male and the female, as God had commanded Noah.
Genesis 7:9.

65 But the dove found no rest for the sole of her foot.
Genesis 8:9.

66 And the dove came to him in the evening; and, lo, in her mouth was an olive leaf pluckt off: so Noah knew that the waters were abated from off the earth.
Genesis 8:11.

67 I will not again curse the ground any more for man's sake; for the imagination of man is evil from his youth; neither will I again smite any more every thing living, as I have done.While the earth remaineth, seedtime and harvest, and cold and heat, and summer and winter, and day and night shall not cease.
Genesis 8:21–2.

68 At the hand of every man's brother will I require the life of man.Whoso sheddeth man's blood, by man shall his blood be shed: for in the image of God made he man.
Genesis 9:5–6.

69 I do set my bow in the cloud, and it shall be for a token of a covenant between me and the earth.
Genesis 9:13.

70 He was a mighty hunter before the LORD: wherefore it is said, Even as Nimrod the mighty hunter before the LORD.
Genesis 10:9.

71 Therefore is the name of it called Babel; because the LORD did there confound the language of all the earth: and from thence did the LORD scatter them abroad upon the face of all the earth.
Genesis 11:9.

72 Now the LORD had said unto Abram, Get thee out of thy country, and from thy kindred, and from thy father's house, unto a land that I will shew thee: And I will make of thee a great nation, and I will bless thee, and make thy name great; and thou shalt be a blessing: And I will bless them that bless thee, and curse him that curseth thee: and in thee shall all families of the earth be blessed.
Genesis 12:1–3.

73 But the men of Sodom were wicked and sinners before the LORD exceedingly.
Genesis 13:13.

74 Thou shalt be buried in a good old age.
Genesis 15:15.

75 Behold, thou art with child, and shalt bear a son, and shalt call his name Ishmael; because the LORD hath heard thy affliction. And he will be a wild man; his hand will be against every man, and every man's hand against him; and he shall dwell in the presence of all his brethren.
Genesis 16:11–12.

76 And when Abram was ninety years old and nine, the LORD appeared to Abram, and said unto him, I am the Almighty God: walk before me, and be thou perfect.
Genesis 17:1.

77 And I will establish my covenant between me and thee and thy seed after thee in their generations for an everlasting covenant, to be a God unto thee, and to thy seed after thee. And I will give unto thee, and to thy seed after thee, the land wherein thou art a stranger, all the land of Canaan, for an everlasting possession; and I will be their God… Every man child among you shall be circumcised.
Genesis 17:7–10.

78 Shall not the Judge of all the earth do right.
Genesis 18:25.

79 Then the LORD rained upon Sodom and upon Gomorrah brimstone and fire from the LORD out of heaven.
Genesis 19:24.

80 But his wife looked back from behind him, and she became a pillar of salt.
Genesis 19:26.

81 Take now thy son, thine only son Isaac, whom thou lovest.
Genesis 22:2.

82 My son, God will provide himself a lamb for a burnt offering.
Genesis 22:8.

83 Esau sells his birthright for a mess of pottage.
1560 Chapter heading for Genesis 25 (in the Geneva Bible).

84 And the boys grew: and Esau was a cunning hunter, a man of the field; and Jacob was a plain man, dwelling in tents.
Genesis 25:27.

85 Esau said, Behold, I am at the point to die: and what profit shall this birthright do to me? And Jacob said, Swear to me this day: and he sware unto him: and he sold his birthright unto Jacob. Then Jacob gave Esau bread and pottage of lentiles; and he did eat and drink, and rose up, and went his way: thus Esau despised his birthright.
Genesis 25:32–4.

86 And Jacob said to Rebekah his mother, Behold, Esau my brother is a hairy man, and I am a smooth man.
Genesis 27:11.

87 Thy brother came with subtilty, and hath taken away thy blessing.
Genesis 27:35.

88 And he dreamed and behold a ladder set up on the earth, and the top of it reached to heaven: and behold the angels of God ascending and descending on it.
Genesis 28:12.

89 And Jacob awaked out of his sleep, and he said, Surely the LORD is in this place; and I knew it not.
Genesis 28:16.

90 And Jacob served seven years for Rachel; and they seemed unto him but a few days, for the love he had to her.
Genesis 29:20.

91 The LORD watch between me and thee, when we are absent one from another.
Genesis 31:49.

92 I will not let thee go, except thou bless me.
Genesis 32:26.

93 Now Israel loved Joseph more than all his children, because he was the son of his old age: and he made him a coat of many colours.
Genesis 37:3.

94 And they said to one another, Behold, this dreamer cometh.
Genesis 37:19.

95 And all his sons and all his daughters rose up to comfort him; but he refused to be comforted; and he said, For I will go down into the grave unto my son mourning. Thus his father wept for him.
Genesis 37:35.

96 And Onan knew that the seed should not be his; and it came to pass, when he went in unto his brother's wife, that he spilled it on the ground, lest that he should give seed to his brother.
Genesis 38:9.

97 And she caught him by his garment, saying, Lie with me: and he left his garment in her hand, and fled, and got him out.
Genesis 39:12.

98 And the seven thin ears devoured the seven rank and full ears. And Pharaoh awoke, and, behold, it was a dream.
Genesis 41:7.

99 Ye are spies; to see the nakedness of the land ye are come.
Genesis 42:9.

1 And he said, My son shall not go down with you; for his brother is dead, and he is left alone: if mischief befall him by the way in the which ye go, then shall ye bring down my gray hairs with sorrow to the grave.
Genesis 42:38.

2 And the famine was sore in the land.
Genesis 43:1.

3 I will give you the good of the land of Egypt, and ye shall eat the fat of the land.
Genesis 45:18.

4 So he sent his brethren away, and they departed: and he said unto them, See that ye fall not out by the way.
Genesis 45:24.

5 And Jacob said unto Pharaoh, The days of the years of my pilgrimage are an hundred and thirty years: few and evil have the days of the years of my life been, and have not attained unto the days of the years of the life of my fathers in the days of their pilgrimage.
Genesis 47:9.

6 Unstable as water, thou shalt not excel.
Genesis 49:4.

7 And he said, Who made thee a prince and a judge over us? intendest thou to kill me, as thou killedst the Egyptian?
Exodus 2:14.

8 And the angel of the LORD appeared unto him in a flame of fire out of the midst of a bush: and he looked, and, behold, the bush burned with fire, and the bush was not consumed.
Exodus 3:2.

9 And he said, Draw not nigh hither: put off thy shoes from off thy feet, for the place whereon thou standest is holy ground.
Exodus 3:5.

10 And Moses hid his face; for he was afraid to look upon God.
Exodus 3:6.

11 And I am come down to deliver them out of the hand of the Egyptians, and to bring them up out of that land unto a good land and a large, unto a land flowing with milk and honey.
Exodus 3:8.

12 And God said unto Moses, I AM THAT I AM.
Exodus 3:14.

13 But I am slow of speech, and of a slow tongue.
Exodus 4:10.

14 Let my people go.
Exodus 7:16.

15 Your lamb shall be without blemish, a male of the first year.
Exodus 12:5.

16 And thus shall ye eat it; with your loins girded, your shoes on your feet, and your staff in your hand; and ye shall eat it in haste: it is the LORD's passover. For I will pass through the land of Egypt this night, and will smite all the firstborn in the land of Egypt, both man and beast; and against all the gods of Egypt I will execute judgment: I am the LORD.
Exodus 12:11–12.

17 And Pharaoh rose up in the night, he and all his servants, and all the Egyptians; and there was a great cry in Egypt; for there was not a house where there was not one dead.
Exodus 12:30.

18 And the Egyptians were urgent upon the people, that they might send them out of the land in haste; for they said, We be all dead men.
Exodus 12:33.

19 And the LORD went before them by day in a pillar of a cloud, to lead them the way; and by night in a pillar of fire, to give them light; to go by day and night.
Exodus 13:21.

20 The LORD is a man of war: the LORD is his name.
Exodus 15:3.

21 And the children of Israel said unto them, Would to God we had died by the hand of the LORD in the land of Egypt, when we sat by the flesh pots, and when we did eat bread to the full; for ye have brought us forth to this wilderness, to kill this whole assembly with hunger.
Exodus 16:3.

22 And it came to pass, when Moses held up his hand, that Israel prevailed: and when he let down his hand, Amalek prevailed.
Exodus 17:11.

23 And God spake all these words, saying, I am the LORD thy God, which have brought thee out of the land of Egypt, out of the house of bondage.
Thou shalt have no other gods before me.
Thou shalt not make unto thee any graven image, or any likeness of any thing that is in heaven above, or that is in the earth beneath, or that is in the water under the earth:
Thou shalt not bow down thyself to them, nor serve them: for I the LORD thy God am a jealous God, visiting the iniquity of the fathers upon the children unto the third and fourth generation of them that hate me;
And shewing mercy unto thousands of them that love me, and keep my commandments.
Thou shalt not take the name of the LORD thy God in vain; for the LORD will not hold him guiltless that taketh his name in vain.
Remember the sabbath day, to keep it holy. Six days thou shalt labour and do all thy work: But the seventh day is the sabbath of the LORD thy God: in it thou shalt not do any work, thou, nor thy son, nor thy daughter, thy manservant, nor thy maidservant, nor thy cattle, nor thy stranger that is within thy gates:
For in six days the LORD made heaven and earth, the sea,

and all that in them is, and rested the seventh day:
wherefore the LORD blessed the sabbath day, and hallowed it.
Honour thy father and thy mother: that thy days may be long upon the land which the LORD thy God giveth thee.
Thou shalt not kill.
Thou shalt not commit adultery.
Thou shalt not steal.
Thou shalt not bear false witness against thy neighbour.
Thou shalt not covet thy neighbour's house, thou shalt not covet thy neighbour's wife, nor his manservant, nor his maidservant, nor his ox, nor his ass, nor any thing that is thy neighbour's.
Exodus 20:1–17.

24 And if any mischief follow, then thou shalt give life for life, Eye for eye, tooth for tooth, hand for hand, foot for foot, Burning for burning, wound for wound, stripe for stripe.
Exodus 21:23–4.

25 And thou shalt put in the breastplate of judgment the Urim and the Thummim; and thy shall be upon Aaron's heart, when he goeth in before the LORD: and Aaron shall bear the judgment of the children of Israel upon his heart before the LORD continually.
Exodus 28:30.

26 And he received them at their hand, and fashioned it with a graving tool, after he had made it a molten calf: and they said, These be thy gods, O Israel, which brought thee up out of the land of Egypt.
Exodus 32:4.

27 And the LORD said unto Moses, I have seen this people, and, behold, it is a stiffnecked people.
Exodus 32:9.

28 Who is on the LORD's side? let him come unto me.
Exodus 32:26.

29 And the LORD spake unto Moses face to face, as a man speaketh unto his friend.
Exodus 33:11.

30 And he said, My presence shall go with thee, and I will give thee rest. And he said unto him, If thy presence go not with me carry us not up hence.
Exodus 33:14–15.

31 And he said, I beseech thee, shew me thy glory.
Exodus 33:18.

32 And he said, I will make all my goodness pass before thee… And he said, Thou canst not see my face: for there shall no man see me, and live.
Exodus 33:19–20.

33 For I am the LORD your God: ye shall therefore sanctify yourselves, and ye shall be holy; for I am holy: neither shall ye defile yourselves with any manner of creeping thing that creepeth upon the earth.
Leviticus 11:44.

34 But the goat, on which the lot fell to be the scapegoat, shall be presented alive before the LORD, to make an atonement with him, and to let him go for a scapegoat into the wilderness.
Leviticus 16:10.

35 Thou shalt not avenge, nor bear any grudge against the children of thy people, but thou shalt love thy neighbour as thyself: I am the LORD.
Leviticus 19:18.

36 The LORD bless thee, and keep thee:
The LORD make his face shine upon thee, and be gracious unto thee:
The LORD lift up his countenance upon thee, and give thee peace.
Numbers 6:24–6.

37 And there we saw the giants, the sons of Anak, which come of the giants: and we were in our own sight as grasshoppers, and so we were in their sight.
Numbers 13:33.

38 The rod of Aaron for the house of Levi was budded, and brought forth buds, and bloomed blossoms, and yielded almonds.
Numbers 17:8.

39 And Moses made a serpent of brass, and put it upon a pole, and it came to pass, that if a serpent had bitten any man, when he beheld the serpent of brass, he lived.
Numbers 21:9.

40 And the LORD opened the mouth of the ass, and she said unto Balaam, What have I done unto thee, that thou hast smitten me these three times?
Numbers 22:28.

41 God is not a man, that he should lie; neither the son of man, that he should repent: hath he said, and shall he not do it? or hath he spoken, and shall he not make it good?
Numbers 23:19.

42 What hath God wrought!
Numbers 23:23. These words were transmitted by Samuel Morse on 24 May 1844, the first electronic telegraph message.

43 Be sure your sin will find you out.
Numbers 32:23.

44 I call heaven and earth to witness against you this day.
Deuteronomy 4:26.

45 Hear, O Israel: the LORD our God is one LORD. And thou shalt love the LORD thy God with all thy soul, and with all thy might.
Deuteronomy 6:4–5.

46 Ye shall not go after other gods, of the gods of the people which are round about you; (For the LORD thy God is a jealous God among you).
Deuteronomy 6:14–15.

47 And he humbled thee, and suffered thee to hunger, and fed thee with manna, which thou knewest not, neither did thy fathers know; that he might make thee know that man doth not live by bread only, but by every word that proceedeth out of the mouth of the LORD doth man live.
Deuteronomy 8:3.

48 Speak not thou in thine heart, after that the LORD thy God hath cast them out from before thee, saying, For my righteousness the LORD hath brought me in to possess this land: but for the wickedness of these nations the LORD doth drive them out from before thee.
Deuteronomy 9:4.

49 If there arise among you a prophet, or a dreamer of dreams, and giveth thee a sign or a wonder… Thou shalt not hearken.
Deuteronomy 13:1–3.

50 When thou cuttest down thine harvest in thy field, and

hast forgot a sheaf in the field, thou shalt not go again to fetch it: it shall be for the stranger, for the fatherless, and for the widow: that the LORD thy God may bless thee in all the work of thine hands.
Deuteronomy 24:19.

51 Thou shalt not muzzle the ox when he treadeth out the corn.
Deuteronomy 25:4.

52 Cursed be he that removeth his neighbour's landmark. And all the people shall say, Amen.
Deuteronomy 27:17.

53 The secret things belong unto the LORD our God; but those things which are revealed belong unto us and our children for ever, that we may do all the words of this law.
Deuteronomy 29:29.

54 I call heaven and earth to record this day against you, that I have set before you life and death, blessing and cursing: therefore choose life, that both thou and thy seed may live.
Deuteronomy 30:19.

55 Give ear, O ye heavens, and I will speak: and hear, O earth, the words of my mouth. My doctrine shall drop as the rain, my speech shall distil as the dew, as the small rain upon the tender herb, and as the showers upon the grass.
Deuteronomy 32:1–2.

56 He found him in a desert land, and in the waste howling wilderness; he led him about, he instructed him, he kept him as the apple of his eye.
Deuteronomy 32:10.

57 Thou art waxen fat, thou art grown thick, thou art covered with fatness.
Deuteronomy 32:15.

58 As thy days, so shall thy strength be.
Deuteronomy 33:25.

59 The eternal God is thy refuge, and underneath are the everlasting arms.
Deuteronomy 33:27.

60 So Moses the servant of the LORD died there in the land of Moab… but no man knoweth of his sepulchre unto this day.
Deuteronomy 34:5–6.

61 There shall not any man be able to stand before thee all the days of thy life: as I was with Moses, so I will be with thee: I will not fail thee, nor forsake thee.
Joshua 1:5.

62 Have I not commanded thee? Be strong and of a good courage: be not afraid, neither be thou dismayed: for the LORD thy God is with thee whithersoever thou goest.
Joshua 1:9.

63 Behold, when we come into the land, thou shalt bind this line of scarlet thread in the window which thou didst let us down by.
Joshua 2:18.

64 So the people shouted when the priests blew with the trumpets: and it came to pass, when the people heard the sound of the trumpet, and the people shouted with a great shout, that the wall fell down flat, so that the people went up into the city, every man straight before him, and they took the city.
Joshua 6:20.

65 I am going the way of all the earth.
Joshua 23:14.

66 Choose you this day whom ye will serve… but as for me and my house, we will serve the LORD.
Joshua 24:15.

67 Then Jael Heber's wife took a nail of the tent, and took an hammer in her hand, and went softly unto him and smote the nail into his temples, and fastened it into the ground: for he was fast asleep and weary. So he died.
Judges 4:21.

68 He asked for water, and she brought him milk; she brought forth butter in a lordly dish. She put her hand to the nail, and her right hand to the workmen's hammer; and with the hammer she smote Sisera, she smote off his head, when she had pierced and stricken through his temples. At her feet he bowed, he fell, he lay down: at her feet he bowed he fell: where he bowed, there he fell down dead. The mother of Sisera looked out at a window, and cried through the lattice, Why is his chariot so long in coming? why tarry the wheels of his chariots?
Judges 5:25–8.

69 The sword of the LORD, and of Gideon.
Judges 7:18.

70 Then said they unto him, Say now Shibboleth: and he said Sibboleth: for he could not frame to pronounce it right. Then they took him, and slew him.
Judges 12:6.

71 And he said unto them, Out of the eater came forth meat, and out of the strong came forth sweetness. And they could not in three days expound the riddle.
Judges 14:14.

72 If ye had not plowed with my heifer, ye had not found out my riddle.
Judges 14:18.

73 He smote them hip and thigh.
Judges 15:8.

74 With the jawbone of an ass, heaps upon heaps, with the jaw of an ass have I slain a thousand men.
Judges 15:16.

75 And she said, The Philistines be upon thee, Samson. And he awoke out of his sleep, and said, I will go out as at other times before, and shake myself. And he wist not that the LORD was departed from him. But the Philistines took him, and put out his eyes, and brought him down to Gaza, and bound him with fetters of brass; and he did grind in the prison house.
Judges 16:20–21.

76 And Samson said, Let me die with the Philistines. And he bowed himself with all his might; and the house fell upon the lords, and upon all the people that were therein. So the dead which he slew at his death were more than they which he slew in his life.
Judges 16:30.

77 In those days there was no king in Israel, but every man did that which was right in his own eyes.
Judges 17:6.

78 The people arose as one man.
Judges 20:8.

79 Intreat me not to leave thee, or to return from following after thee: for whither thou goest, I will go; and where

thou lodgest, I will lodge: thy people shall be my people, and thy God my God:
Where thou diest, will I die, and there will I be buried: the LORD do so to me, and more also, if ought but death part thee and me.
Ruth 1:16–17

80 Now the Lord saith, Be it far from me; for them that honour me I will honour, and they that despise me shall be lightly esteemed.
1 Samuel 2:30.

81 The LORD called Samuel: and he answered, Here am I. And he ran unto Eli, and said, Here am I; for thou calledst me. And he said, I called not; lie down again.
1 Samuel 3:4–5

82 Speak, LORD; for thy servant heareth.
1 Samuel 3:9.

83 Behold, I will do a thing in Israel, at which both the ears of every one that heareth it shall tingle.
1 Samuel 3:11.

84 Be strong, and quit yourselves like men.
1 Samuel 4:9.

85 And it came to pass, when he made mention of the ark of God, that he fell from off the seat backward by the side of the gate, and his neck brake, and he died: for he was an old man, and heavy.
1 Samuel 4:18.

86 Behold, thou art old, and thy sons walk not in thy ways: now make us a king to judge us like all the nations.
1 Samuel 8:5.

87 God save the king.
1 Samuel 10:24.

88 But now thy kingdom shall not continue: the LORD hath sought him a man after his own heart, and the LORD hath commanded him to be captain over his people.
1 Samuel 13:14.

89 Hath the LORD as great delight in burnt offerings and sacrifices, as in obeying the voice of the LORD? Behold, to obey is better than sacrifice, and to hearken than the fat of rams. For rebellion is as the sin of witchcraft, and stubbornness is as iniquity and idolatry.
1 Samuel 15:22–3.

90 Look not on his countenance, or on the height of his stature; because I have refused him: for the LORD seeth not as man seeth; for man looketh on the outward appearance, but the LORD looketh on the heart.
1 Samuel 16:7.

91 Now he was ruddy, and withal of a beautiful countenance, and goodly to look to. And the LORD said, Arise, anoint him: for this is he.
1 Samuel 16:12.

92 I know thy pride, and the naughtiness of thine heart.
1 Samuel 17:28.

93 David said moreover, The LORD that delivered me out of the paw of the lion, and out of the paw of the bear, he will deliver me out of the hand of this Philistine. And Saul said unto David, Go, and the LORD be with thee.
1 Samuel 17:37.

94 And he took his staff in his hand, and chose him five smooth stones out of the brook.
1 Samuel 17:40.

95 And the Philistine said unto David, Am I a dog, that thou comest to me with staves?
1 Samuel 17:43.

96 Saul hath slain his thousands, and David his ten thousands.
1 Samuel 18:7.

97 Behold, I have played the fool, and have erred exceedingly.
1 Samuel 26:21.

98 Saul and Jonathan were lovely and pleasant in their lives, and in their death they were not divided: they were swifter than eagles, they were stronger than lions… I am distressed for thee, my brother Jonathan: very pleasant hast thou been unto me: thy love to me was wonderful, passing the love of women. How are the mighty fallen, and the weapons of war perished!
2 Samuel 1:23–7.

99 And David danced before the LORD with all his might.
2 Samuel 6:14

1 Set ye Uriah in the forefront of the hottest battle, and retire ye from him, that he may be smitten, and die.
2 Samuel 11:15.

2 But the poor man had nothing, save one little ewe lamb
2 Samuel 12:3.

3 Thou art the man.
2 Samuel 12:7.

4 For we must needs die, and are as water spilt on the ground, which cannot be gathered up again: neither doth God respect any person.
2 Samuel 14:14.

5 And when Ahithophel saw that his counsel was not followed, he saddled his ass, and arose, and gat him home to his house, to his city, and put his household in order, and hanged himself.
2 Samuel 17:23.

6 And the king was much moved, and went up to the chamber over the gate, and wept: and as he went, thus he said, O my son Absalom, my son, my son Absalom! would God I had died for thee, O Absalom, my son, my son!
2 Samuel 18:33.

7 Nay: but I will surely buy it of thee at a price: neither will I offer burnt offerings unto the Lord my God of that which dost cost me nothing.
2 Samuel 24:24.

8 Now king David was old and stricken in years; and they covered him with clothes, but he gat no heat.
1 Kings 1:1.

9 I go the way of all the earth: be thou strong therefore, and shew thyself a man.
1 Kings 2:2.

10 I am but a little child: I know not how to go out or come in.
1 Kings 3:7.

11 But if ye shall at all turn from following me… Then will I cut off Israel out of the land which I have given them; and this house, which I have hallowed for my name, will I cast out of my sight; and Israel shall be a proverb and a byword among all people.
1 Kings 9:6–7.

12 And when the queen of Sheba heard of the fame of Solomon concerning the name of the LORD, she came to prove him with hard questions.
1 Kings 10:1.

13 I believed not the words, until I came, and mine eyes had seen it: and, behold, the half was not told me.
1 Kings 10:7.

14 But king Solomon loved many strange women.
1 Kings 11:1.

15 My little finger shall be thicker than my father's loins. And now whereas my father did lade you with a heavy yoke, I will add to your yoke: my father hath chastised you with whips, but I will chastise you with scorpions.
1 Kings 12:10–11.

16 He slept with his fathers.
1 Kings 14:20.

17 And the ravens brought him bread and flesh in the morning, and bread and flesh in the evening; and he drank of the brook.
Of Elijah. 1 Kings 17:6.

18 Elijah came unto all the people, and said, How long halt ye between two opinions? if the LORD be God, follow him: but if Baal, then follow him. And the people answered him not a word.
1 Kings 18:21.

19 Cry aloud: for he is a god; either he is talking, or he is pursuing, or he is in a journey, or peradventure he sleepeth, and must be wakened.
1 Kings 18:27.

20 There is a sound of abundance of rain.
1 Kings 18:41.

21 Behold, there ariseth a little cloud out of the sea, like a man's hand.
1 Kings 18:44.

22 Elijah...girded up his loins, and ran before Ahab.
1 Kings 18:46.

23 But he himself went a day's journey into the wilderness, and came and sat down under a juniper tree: and he requested for himself that he might die; and said, It is enough, now, O LORD, take away my life; for I am not better than my fathers.
1 Kings 19:4.

24 And, behold, the LORD passed by, and a great and strong wind rent the mountains, and brake in pieces the rocks before the LORD; but the LORD was not in the wind: and after the wind an earthquake; but the LORD was not in the earthquake: And after the earthquake a fire; but the LORD was not in the fire: and after the fire a still small voice.
1 Kings 19:11–12.

25 Elijah passed by him and cast his mantle upon him.
1 Kings 19:19.

26 In the place where dogs licked the blood of Naboth shall dogs lick thy blood, even thine. And Ahab said to Elijah, Hast thou found me, O mine enemy?
1 Kings 21:19–20.

27 A certain man drew a bow at a venture, and smote the king of Israel between the joints of the harness.
1 Kings 22:34.

28 Behold there appeared a chariot of fire, and horses of fire, and parted them both asunder; and Elijah went up by a whirlwind into heaven. And Elisha saw it, and he cried, My father, my father, the chariot of Israel, and the horsemen thereof.
2 Kings 2:11–12.

29 The spirit of Elijah doth rest on Elisha.
2 Kings 2:15.

30 Go up, thou bald head.
2 Kings 2:23.

31 Say unto her, Is it well with thee? is it well with thy husband? is it well with the child? And she answered, It is well.
2 Kings 4:26.

32 Let him come now to me, and he shall know that there is a prophet in Israel.
2 Kings 5:8.

33 Is it peace? and Jehu said, What hast thou to do with peace? turn thee behind me.
2 Kings 9:18.

34 The driving is like the driving of Jehu the son of Nimshi; for he driveth furiously.
2 Kings 9:20.

35 And when Jehu was come to Jezreel, Jezebel heard of it; and she painted her face, and tired her head, and looked out at a window.
2 Kings 9:30.

36 And he lifted up his face to the window, and said, Who is on my side? who? And there looked out to him two or three eunuchs.
2 Kings 9:32.

37 So they threw her down: and some of her blood was sprinkled on the wall, and on the horses: and he trode her under foot.
2 Kings 9:33.

38 And they went to bury her: but they found no more of her than the skull, and the feet, and the palms of her hands.
2 Kings 9:35.

39 Now, behold, thou trustest upon the staff of this bruised reed, even upon Egypt, on which if a man lean, it will go into his hand, and pierce it: so is Pharaoh king of Egypt unto all that trust on him.
2 Kings 18:21.

40 For we are strangers before thee, and soujourners, as were all our fathers: our days on the earth are as a shadow, and there is none abiding.
1 Chronicles 29:15.

41 And he died in a good old age, full of days, riches, and honour: and Solomon his son reigned in his stead.
1 Chronicles 29:28.

42 And king Solomon gave to the queen of Sheba all her desire, whatsoever she asked, beside that which she had brought unto the king.
2 Chronicles 9:12.

43 For the eyes of the LORD run to and fro throughout the whole earth, to shew himself strong in the behalf of them whose heart is perfect toward him. Herein thou hast done foolishly: therefore from henceforth thou shalt have wars.
2 Chronicles 16:9.

44 Be not afraid nor dismayed by reason of this great multitude; for the battle is not yours, but God's.
2 Chronicles 20:15.

45 Every one with one of his hands wrought in the work, and with the other hand held a weapon.
Nehemiah 4:17.

46 So will I go in unto the king, which is not according to the law: and if I perish, I perish.
Esther 4:16.

47 And the LORD said unto Satan, Whence comest thou? Then Satan answered the LORD, and said, From going to and fro in the earth, and from walking up and down in it.
Job 1:7.

48 Naked came I out of my mother's womb, and naked shall I return thither: the LORD gave, and the LORD hath taken away; blessed be the name of the LORD.
Job 1:21.

49 Skin for skin, yea, all that a man hath will he give for his life. But put forth thine hand now, and touch his bone and his flesh, and he will curse thee to thy face.
Job 2:4–5.

50 And he took him a potsherd to scrape himself withal; and he sat down among the ashes. Then said his wife unto him, Dost thou still retain thine integrity? curse God, and die.
Job 2:8–9.

51 Let the day perish wherein I was born, and the night in which it was said, There is a man child conceived.
Job 3:3.

52 There the wicked cease from troubling, and there the weary be at rest.
Job 3:17.

53 Shall mortal man be more just than God? shall a man be more pure than his maker?
Job 4:17.

54 Yet man is born unto trouble, as the sparks fly upward.
Job 5:7.

55 My days are swifter than a weaver's shuttle
Job 7:6.

56 Wherefore then hast thou brought me forth out of the womb? Oh that I had given up the ghost, and no eye had seen me!
Job 10:18.

57 Canst thou by searching find out God? canst thou find out the Almighty unto perfection? It is as high as heaven; what canst thou do? deeper than hell; what canst thou know? The measure thereof is longer than the earth, and broader than the sea.
Job 11:7–9.

58 No doubt but ye are the people, and wisdom shall die with you.
Job 12:2.

59 With the ancient is wisdom; and in length of days understanding.
Job 12:12.

60 Though he slay me, yet will I trust in him: but I will maintain mine own ways before him.
Job 13:15.

61 Man that is born of a woman is of few days, and full of trouble. He cometh forth like a flower, and is cut down: he fleeth also as a shadow, and continueth not.
Job 14:1–2.

62 I have heard many such things: miserable comforters are ye all.
Job 16:2.

63 I am escaped with the skin of my teeth.
Job 19:20.

64 For I know that my redeemer liveth, and that he shall stand at the latter day upon the earth: And though after my skin worms destroy this body, yet in my flesh shall I see God.
Job 19:25–6.

65 But ye should say, Why persecute we him, seeing the root of the matter is found in me?
Job 19:28.

66 Behold, my desire is, that the Almighty would answer me, and that mine adversary had written a book.
Job 31:35.

67 Great men are not always wise: neither do the aged understand judgment.
Job 32:9.

68 Therefore doth Job open his mouth in vain; he multiplieth words without knowledge.
Job 35:16.

69 Who is this that darkeneth counsel by words without knowledge? Gird up now thy loins like a man; for I will demand of thee, and answer thou me. Where wast thou when I laid the foundations of the earth? declare, if thou hast understanding.
Job 38:2–4.

70 When the morning stars sang together, and all the sons of God shouted for joy.
Job 38:7.

71 Hitherto shalt thou come, but no further: and here shall thy proud waves be stayed.
Job 38:11.

72 Hath the rain a father? or who hath begotten the drops of dew?
Job 38:28.

73 Canst thou bind the sweet influences of Pleiades, or loose the bands of Orion?
Job 38:31.

74 Hast thou given the horse strength? hast thou clothed his neck with thunder? Canst thou make him afraid as a grasshopper? the glory of his nostrils is terrible. He paweth in the valley and rejoiceth in his strength: he goeth on to meet the armed men.
Job 39:19–21.

75 He swalloweth the ground with fierceness and rage: neither believeth he that it is the sound of the trumpet. He saith among the trumpets, Ha, ha, and he smelleth the battle afar off, the thunder of the captains, and the shouting.
Job 39:24–5.

76 Behold now behemoth, which I made with thee; he eateth grass as an ox.
Job 40:15.

77 The shady trees cover him with their shadow; the willows of the brook compass him about. Behold, he drinketh up a river, and hasteth not: he trusteth that he

can draw up Jordan into his mouth.
Job 40:22–3.

78 Canst thou draw out leviathan with an hook?
Job 41:1.

79 I have heard of thee by the hearing of the ear: but now mine eye seeth thee. Wherefore I abhor myself, and repent in dust and ashes.
Job 42:5–6.

80 So the LORD blessed the latter end of Job more than his beginning.
Job 42:12.

81 Blessed is the man that walketh not in the counsel of the ungodly, nor standeth in the way of sinners, nor sitteth in the seat of the scornful. But his delight is in the law of the LORD; and in his law doth he meditate day and night. And he shall be like a tree planted by the rivers of water, that bringeth forth his fruit in his season; his leaf also shall not wither; and whatsoever he doeth shall prosper. The ungodly are not so: but are like the chaff which the wind driveth away.
Psalms 1:1–4.

82 Why do the heathen rage, and the people imagine a vain thing?
Psalms 2:1.

83 He that sitteth in the heavens shall laugh: the LORD shall have them in derision.
Psalms 2:4.

84 Thou art my Son: this day have I begotten thee. Ask of me, and I shall give thee the heathen for thine inheritance, and the uttermost parts of the earth for thy possession. Thou shalt break them with a rod of iron; thou shalt dash them in pieces like a potter's vessel.
Psalms 2:7–9.

85 Stand in awe, and sin not: commune with your own heart upon your bed, and be still.
Psalms 4:4.

86 O LORD our Lord, how excellent is thy name in all the earth! who hast set thy glory above the heavens. Out of the mouth of babes and sucklings hast thou ordained strength because of thine enemies, that thou mightest still the enemy and the avenger.
Psalms 8:1–2.

87 When I consider thy heavens, the work of thy fingers, the moon and the stars, which thou hast ordained; What is man, that thou art mindful of him? and the son of man, that thou visitest him? For thou hast made him a little lower than the angels, and hast crowned him with glory and honour. Thou madest him to have dominion over the works of thy hands; thou hast put all things under his feet.
Psalms 8:3–6.

88 The fool hath said in his heart, There is no God.
Psalms 14:1.

89 They are all gone aside, they are all together become filthy: there is none that doeth good, no, not one.
Psalms 14:3.

90 LORD, who shall abide in thy tabernacle? who shall dwell in thy holy hill? He that walketh uprightly, and worketh righteousness, and speaketh the truth in his heart.
Psalms 15:1–2.

91 The lines are fallen unto me in pleasant places; yea, I have a goodly heritage.
Psalms 16:6.

92 For thou wilt not leave my soul in hell; neither wilt thou suffer thine Holy One to see corruption.
Psalms 16:10.

93 Keep me as the apple of the eye, hide me under the shadow of thy wings.
Psalms 17:8.

94 For by thee I have run through a troop; and by my God have I leaped over a wall.
Psalms 18:29.

95 He maketh my feet like hinds' feet, and setteth me upon my high places.
Psalms 18:33.

96 Some trust in chariots, and some in horses: but we will remember the name of the LORD our God.
Psalms 20:7.

97 My God, my God, why hast thou forsaken me? why art thou so far from helping me, and from the words of my roaring?
Psalms 22:1.

98 But I am a worm, and no man; a reproach of men, and despised of the people. All they that see me laugh me to scorn: they shoot out the lip, they shake the head, saying, He trusted on the LORD that he would deliver him: let him deliver him, seeing he delighted in him.
Psalms 22:6–8.

99 I am poured out like water, and all my bones are out of joint: my heart is like wax; it is melted in the midst of my bowels.
Psalms 22:14.

1 They pierced my hands and my feet. I may tell all my bones: they look *and* stare upon me. They part my garments among them, and cast lots upon my vesture.
Psalms 22:16–18.

2 The LORD is my shepherd; I shall not want. He maketh me to lie down in green pastures: he leadeth me beside the still waters. He restoreth my soul: he leadeth me in the paths of righteousness for his name's sake. Yea, though I walk through the valley of the shadow of death, I will fear no evil: for thou art with me; thy rod and thy staff they comfort me. Thou preparest a table before me in the presence of mine enemies: thou anointest my head with oil; my cup runneth over. Surely goodness and mercy shall follow me all the days of my life: and I will dwell in the house of the LORD for ever.
Psalms 23:1–6.

3 The earth is the LORD's, and the fulness thereof; the world, and they that dwell therein.
Psalms 24:1.

4 Lift up your heads, O ye gates; and be ye lift up, ye everlasting doors; and the King of glory shall come in. Who is this King of glory? The LORD strong and mighty, the LORD mighty in battle.
Psalms 24:7–8.

5 Remember not the sins of my youth, nor my transgressions.
Psalms 25:7.

6 The LORD is my light and my salvation; whom shall I fear?

the LORD is the strength of my life; of whom shall I be afraid?
Psalms 27:1.

7 Though an host should encamp against me, my heart shall not fear: though war should rise against me, in this will I be confident. One thing have I desired of the LORD, that will I seek after; that I may dwell in the house of the LORD all the days of my life, to behold the beauty of the LORD, and to inquire in his temple.
Psalms 27:3–4.

8 Thou hast turned for me my mourning into dancing: thou hast put off my sackcloth, and girded me with gladness.
Psalms 30:11.

9 Into thine hand I commit my spirit: thou hast redeemed me, O LORD God of truth.
Psalms 31:5.

10 For this shall every one that is godly pray unto thee in a time when thou mayest be found: surely in the floods of great waters they shall not come nigh unto him. Thou *art* my hiding place; thou shalt preserve me from trouble; thou shalt compass me about with songs of deliverance. Selah.
Psalms 32:6–7.

11 I will instruct thee and teach thee in the way which thou shalt go: I will guide thee with mine eye. Be ye not as the horse, or as the mule, which have no understanding: whose mouth must be held in with bit and bridle, lest they come near unto thee.
Psalms 32:8–9.

12 I sought the LORD, and he heard me, and delivered me from all my fears.
Psalms 34:4

13 O taste and see that the LORD is good: blessed is the man that trusteth in him. O fear the LORD, ye his saints: for there is no want to them that fear him. The young lions do lack, and suffer hunger: but they that seek the LORD shall not want any good thing.
Psalms 34:8–10.

14 The children of men put their trust under the shadow of thy wings.
Psalms 36:7.

15 Delight thyself also in the LORD, and he shall give thee the desires of thine heart. Commit thy way unto the LORD; trust also in him; and he shall bring *it* to pass.
Psalms 37:4–5.

16 But the meek shall inherit the earth; and shall delight themselves in the abundance of peace.
Psalms 37:11.

17 I have been young and now am old; yet have I not seen the righteous forsaken, nor his seed begging bread.
Psalms 37:25.

18 I waited patiently for the LORD, and he inclined unto me, and heard my cry. He brought me up also out of an horrible pit, out of the miry clay, and set my feet upon a rock, and established my goings.
Psalms 40:1–2.

19 Yea, mine own familiar friend, in whom I trusted, which did eat of my bread, hath lifted up his heel against me.
Psalms 41:9.

20 As the hart panteth after the water brooks, so panteth my soul after thee, O God. My soul thirsteth for God, for the living God: when shall I come and appear before God?
Psalms 42:1–2.

21 Why art thou cast down, O my soul? and why art thou disquieted in me? hope thou in God: for I shall yet praise him for the help of his countenance.
Psalms 42:5.

22 Deep calleth unto deep at the noise of thy waterspouts: all thy waves and thy billows are gone over me.
Psalms 42:7.

23 Yea, for thy sake are we killed all the day long; we are counted as sheep for the slaughter.
Psalms 44:22.

24 God is our refuge and strength, a very present help in trouble. Therefore will not we fear, though the earth be removed, and though the mountains be carried into the midst of the sea.
Psalms 46:1–2.

25 There is a river, the streams whereof shall make glad the city of God, the holy place of the tabernacles of the most High. God is in the midst of her; she shall not be moved: God shall help her, and that right early.
Psalms 46:4–5.

26 He maketh wars to cease unto the end of the earth; he breaketh the bow, and cutteth the spear in sunder; he burneth the chariot in the fire.
Be still, and know that I am God: I will be exalted among the heathen, I will be exalted in the earth.
Psalms 46:9–10.

27 Great is the LORD, and greatly to be praised in the city of our God, in the mountain of his holiness. Beautiful for situation, the joy of the whole earth, is mount Zion, on the sides of the north, the city of the great King.
Psalms 48:1–2.

28 For I acknowledge my transgressions: and my sin is ever before me. Against thee, thee only, have I sinned, and done this evil in thy sight: that thou mightest be justified when thou speakest, and be clear when thou judgest. Behold, I was shapen in iniquity; and in sin did my mother conceive me.
Psalms 51:3–5.

29 Behold, thou desirest truth in the inward parts: and in the hidden part thou shalt make me to know wisdom. Purge me with hyssop, and I shall be clean: wash me, and I shall be whiter than snow.
Psalms 51:6–7.

30 Create in me a clean heart, O God; and renew a right spirit within me. Cast me not away from thy presence; and take not thy holy spirit from me. Restore unto me the joy of thy salvation; and uphold me with thy free spirit. Then will I teach transgressors thy ways; and sinners shall be converted unto thee.
Psalms 51:10–13.

31 Deliver me from bloodguiltiness, O God, thou God of my salvation: and my tongue shall sing aloud of thy righteousness. O Lord, open thou my lips; and my mouth shall shew forth thy praise. For thou desirest not sacrifice; else would I give it: thou delightest not in burnt offering. The sacrifices of God are a broken spirit: a

broken and a contrite heart, O God, thou wilt not despise.
Psalms 51:14–17.

32 Oh that I had wings like a dove! for then would I fly away, and be at rest.
Psalms 55:6.

33 Lead me to the rock that is higher than I.
Psalms 61:2.

34 Truly my soul waiteth upon God: from him cometh my salvation. He only is my rock and my salvation; he is my defence; I shall not be greatly moved.
Psalms 62:1–2.

35 O God, thou art my God; early will I seek thee: my soul thirsteth for thee, my flesh longeth for thee in a dry and thirsty land, where no water is.
Psalms 63:1.

36 Thou crownest the year with thy goodness; and thy paths drop fatness.
Psalms 65:11.

37 God be merciful unto us, and bless us; and cause his face to shine upon us; Selah. That thy way may be known upon earth, thy saving health among all nations. Let the people praise thee, O God; let all the people praise thee.
Psalms 67:1–3.

38 Sing unto God, sing praises to his name: extol him that rideth upon the heavens by his name JAH, and rejoice before him. A father of the fatherless, and a judge of the widows, is God in his holy habitation. God setteth the solitary in families: he bringeth out those which are bound with chains: but the rebellious dwell in a dry land.
Psalms 68:4–6.

39 Thou hast ascended on high, thou hast led captivity captive: thou hast received gifts for men; yea, for the rebellious also, that the LORD God might dwell among them.
Psalms 68:18.

40 In thee, O LORD, do I put my trust: let me never be put to confusion.
Psalms 71:1.

41 Truly God is good to Israel, even to such as are of a clean heart. But as for me, my feet were almost gone; my steps had well nigh slipped. For I was envious at the foolish, when I saw the prosperity of the wicked.
Psalms 73:1–3.

42 When I thought to know this, it was too painful for me; Until I went into the sanctuary of God; then understood I their end.
Psalms 73:16–17.

43 Nevertheless I am continually with thee: thou hast holden me by my right hand. Thou shalt guide me with thy counsel, and afterward receive me to glory.Whom have I in heaven but thee? and there is none upon earth that I desire beside thee. My flesh and my heart faileth: but God is the strength of my heart, and my portion for ever.
Psalms 73:23–6.

44 I am the LORD thy God, which brought thee out of the land of Egypt: open thy mouth wide, and I will fill it.
Psalms 81:10.

45 How amiable are thy tabernacles, O LORD of hosts!
My soul longeth, yea, even fainteth for the courts of the LORD: my heart and my flesh crieth out for the living God.
Yea, the sparrow hath found an house, and the swallow a nest for herself, where she may lay her young, even thine altars, O LORD of hosts, my King, and my God.
Psalms 84:1–3.

46 Who passing through the valley of Baca make it a well; the rain also filleth the pools.
They go from strength to strength, every one of them in Zion appeareth before God.
Psalms 84:6–7.

47 For a day in thy courts is better than a thousand.
I had rather be a doorkeeper in the house of my God, than to dwell in the tents of wickedness.
Psalms 84:10.

48 Glorious things are spoken of thee, O city of God.
Psalms 87:3.

49 Lord, thou hast been our dwelling place in all generations. Before the mountains were brought forth, or ever thou hadst formed the earth and the world, even from everlasting to everlasting, thou art God.
Psalms 90:1–2.

50 For a thousand years in thy sight are but as yesterday when it is past, and as a watch in the night.
Psalms 90:4.

51 The days of our years are threescore years and ten; and if by reason of strength they be fourscore years, yet is their strength labour and sorrow; for it is soon cut off, and we fly away.
Psalms 90:10.

52 So teach us to number our days that we may apply our hearts unto wisdom.
Psalms 90:12.

53 Surely he shall deliver thee from the snare of the fowler, and from the noisome pestilence.
He shall cover thee with his feathers, and under his wings shalt thou trust: his truth shall be thy shield and buckler.
Thou shalt not be afraid for the terror by night; nor for the arrow that flieth by day;
Nor for the pestilence that walketh in darkness; nor for the destruction that wasteth at noonday.
A thousand shall fall at thy side, and ten thousand at thy right hand, but it shall not come nigh thee.
Psalms 91:3–7.

54 Because thou hast made the LORD, which is my refuge, even the most high, thy habitation.
Psalms 91:9.

55 They shall still bring forth fruit in old age; they shall be fat and flourishing.
Psalms 92:14.

56 He that planted the ear, shall he not hear? he that formed the eye, shall he not see?
Psalms 94:9.

57 O come let us sing unto the LORD: let us make a joyful noise to the rock of our salvation. Let us come before his presence with thanksgiving, and make a joyful noise unto him with psalms.
Psalms 95:1–2.

58 Harden not your heart, as in the provocation, and as in the day of temptation in the wilderness: When your fathers tempted me, proved me, and saw my work. Forty years long was I grieved with this generation, and said, It is a people that do err in their heart, and they have not known my ways: Unto whom I sware in my wrath that they should not enter into my rest.
Psalms 95:8–11.

59 O worship the LORD in the beauty of holiness: fear before him, all the earth.
Psalms 96:9.

60 Make a joyful noise unto the LORD, all ye lands. Serve the LORD with gladness: come before his presence with singing. Know ye that the LORD he is God: it is he that hath made us, and not we ourselves; we are his people, and the sheep of his pasture.
Psalms 100:1–3.

61 Of old hast thou laid the foundation of the earth: and the heavens are the work of thy hands.
Psalms 102:25.

62 Bless the LORD, O my soul: and all that is within me, bless his holy name. Bless the LORD, O my soul, and forget not all his benefits: Who forgiveth all thine iniquities; who healeth all thy diseases; Who redeemeth thy life from destruction; who crowneth thee with loving kindness and tender mercies; Who satisfieth thy mouth with good things; so that thy youth is renewed like the eagle's.
Psalms 103:1–5.

63 The LORD is merciful and gracious, slow to anger, and plenteous in mercy. He will not always chide: neither will he keep his anger for ever. He hath not dealt with us after our sins; nor rewarded us according to our iniquities.
Psalms 103:8–10.

64 For as the heaven is high above the earth, so great is his mercy toward them that fear him. As far as the east is from the west, so far hath he removed our transgressions from us.
Psalms 103:11–12.

65 Like as a father pitieth his children, so the LORD pitieth them that fear him. For he knoweth our frame; he remembereth that we are dust.
Psalms 103:13–14.

66 As for man, his days are as grass: as a flower of the field, so he flourisheth. For the wind passeth over it, and it is gone; and the place thereof shall know it no more.
Psalms 103:15–16.

67 He causeth the grass to grow for the cattle, and herb for the service of man: that he may bring forth food out of the earth; And wine that maketh glad the heart of man, and oil to make his face to shine, and bread which strengtheneth man's heart.
Psalms 104:14–15.

68 Man goeth forth unto his work and to his labour until the evening.
Psalms 104:23.

69 So is this great and wide sea, wherein are things creeping innumerable, both small and great beasts.
There go the ships: there is that leviathan, whom thou hast made to play therein.
These wait all upon thee; that thou mayest give them their meat in due season.
Psalms 104:25–7.

70 Their soul abhorreth all manner of meat; and they draw near unto the gates of death.
Psalms 107:18.

71 They that go down to the sea in ships, that do business in great waters;
These see the works of the LORD, and his wonders in the deep.
Psalms 107:23–4.

72 They reel to and fro, and stagger like a drunken man, and are at their wits' end.
Psalms 107:27.

73 The LORD said unto my Lord, Sit thou at my right hand, until I make thine enemies thy footstool.
Psalms 110:1.

74 The LORD hath sworn, and will not repent, Thou art a priest for ever after the order of Melchizedek.
Psalms 110:4.

75 The fear of the LORD is the beginning of wisdom.
Psalms 111:10.

76 For thou hast delivered my soul from death, mine eyes from tears, and my feet from falling. I will walk before the LORD in the land of the living. I believed, therefore have I spoken: I was greatly afflicted: I said in my haste, All men are liars.
Psalms 116:8–11.

77 Precious in the sight of the LORD is the death of his saints.
Psalms 116:15.

78 The stone which the builders refused is become the head stone of the corner. This is the LORD's doing; it is marvellous in our eyes. This is the day which the LORD hath made; we will rejoice and be glad in it.
Psalms 118:22–4.

79 Blessed be he that cometh in the name of the LORD: we have blessed you out of the house of the LORD.
Psalms 118:26.

80 Wherewithal shall a young man cleanse his way? by taking heed thereto according to thy word.
Psalms 119:9.

81 Thy word have I hid in mine heart, that I might not sin against thee.
Psalms 119:11.

82 I have more understanding than all my teachers: for thy testimonies are my meditation.
Psalms 119:99.

83 How sweet are thy words unto my taste! yea, sweeter than honey to my mouth!
Psalms 119:103.

84 Thy word is a lamp unto my feet, and a light unto my path.
Psalms 119:105.

85 The entrance of thy words giveth light; it giveth understanding unto the simple.
Psalms 119:130.

86 Great peace have they which love thy law: and nothing shall offend them.
Psalms 119:165.

87 I will lift up mine eyes unto the hills, from whence

cometh my help. My help cometh from the LORD, which made heaven and earth. He will not suffer thy foot to be moved: he that keepeth thee will not slumber. Behold, he that keepeth Israel shall neither slumber nor sleep. The LORD is thy keeper: the LORD is thy shade upon thy right hand. The sun shall not smite thee by day, nor the moon by night. The LORD shall preserve thee from all evil: he shall preserve thy soul. The LORD shall preserve thy going out and thy coming in from this time forth, and even for evermore.
Psalms 121:1–8.

88 I was glad when they said unto me, Let us go into the house of the LORD.
Psalms 122:1.

89 Pray for the peace of Jerusalem: they shall prosper that love thee. Peace be within thy walls, and prosperity within thy palaces.
Psalms 122:6–7.

90 They that trust in the LORD shall be as mount Zion, which cannot be removed, but abideth for ever.
Psalms 125:1.

91 They that sow in tears shall reap in joy. He that goeth forth and weepeth, bearing precious seed, shall doubtless come again with rejoicing, bringing his sheaves with him.
Psalms 126:5–6.

92 Except the LORD build the house, they labour in vain that build it: except the LORD keep the city, the watchman waketh but in vain. It is vain for you to rise up early, to sit up late, to eat the bread of sorrows: for so he giveth his beloved sleep.
Psalms 127:1–2.

93 Lo, children are an heritage of the LORD: and the fruit of the womb is his reward. As arrows are in the hand of a mighty man; so are children of the youth. Happy is the man that hath his quiver full of them: they shall not be ashamed, but they shall speak with the enemies in the gate.
Psalms 127:3–5.

94 Thy wife shall be as a fruitful vine by the sides of thine house: thy children like olive plants round about thy table.
Psalms 128:3.

95 Out of the depths have I cried unto thee, O LORD. Lord, hear my voice: let thine ears be attentive to the voice of my supplications. If thou, LORD, shouldest mark iniquities, O LORD, who shall stand? But, there is forgiveness with thee, that thou mayest be feared.
Psalms 130:1–4.

96 Behold, how good and how pleasant it is for brethren to dwell together in unity! It is like the precious ointment upon the head, that ran down upon the beard, even Aaron's beard: that went down to the skirts of his garments; As the dew of Hermon, and as the dew that descended upon the mountains of Zion: for there the LORD commanded the blessing, even life for evermore.
Psalms 133:1–3.

97 O give thanks unto the LORD; for he is good: for his mercy endureth for ever.
Psalms 136:1.

98 By the rivers of Babylon, there we sat down, yea, we wept, when we remembered Zion. We hanged our harps upon the willows in the midst thereof. For there they that carried us away captive required of us a song; and they that wasted us required of us mirth, saying, Sing us one of the songs of Zion. How shall we sing the LORD's song in a strange land?
Psalms 137:1–4.

99 O LORD, thou hast searched me, and known me. Thou knowest my downsitting and mine uprising, thou understandest my thought afar off. Thou compassest my path and my lying down, and art acquainted with all my ways. For there is not a word in my tongue, but, lo, O LORD, thou knowest it altogether. Thou hast beset me behind and before, and laid thine hand upon me. Such knowledge is too wonderful for me; it is high, I cannot attain unto it.
Psalms 139:1–6.

1 Whither shall I go from thy spirit? or whither shall I flee from thy presence?
If I ascend up into heaven, thou art there: if I make my bed in hell, behold, thou art there.
If I take the wings of the morning, and dwell in the uttermost parts of the sea;
Even there shall thy hand lead me, and thy right hand shall hold me.
If I say, Surely the darkness shall cover me; even the night shall be light about me.
Yea, the darkness hideth not from thee; but the night shineth as the day: the darkness and the light are both alike to thee.
Psalms 139:7–12.

2 I will praise thee; for I am fearfully and wonderfully made: marvellous are thy works; and that my soul knoweth right well. My substance was not hid from thee, when I was made in secret, and curiously wrought in the lowest parts of the earth. Thine eyes did see my substance, yet being unperfect; and in thy book all my members were written, which in continuance were fashioned, when as yet there was none of them.
Psalms 139:14–16.

3 Search me, O God, and know my heart: try me, and know my thoughts: And see if there be any wicked way in me, and lead me in the way everlasting.
Psalms 139:23–4.

4 Set a watch, O LORD, before my mouth; keep the door of my lips.
Psalms 141:3.

5 The eyes of all wait upon thee; and thou givest them their meat in due season. Thou openest thine hand, and satisfiest the desire of every living thing.
Psalms 145:15–16.

6 He telleth the number of the stars; he calleth them all by their names.
Psalms 147:4.

7 Let the high praises of God be in their mouth, and a two-edged sword in their hand.
Psalms 149:6.

8 Wisdom crieth without; she uttereth her voice in the streets.
Proverbs 1:20.

9 Trust in the LORD with all thine heart; and lean not unto

thine own understanding. In all thy ways acknowledge him, and he shall direct thy paths.
Proverbs 3:5–6.

10 For whom the LORD loveth he correcteth; even as a father the son in whom he delighteth.
Proverbs 3:12.

11 Wisdom is the principal thing; therefore get wisdom: and with all thy getting get understanding.
Proverbs 4:7.

12 Happy is the man that findeth wisdom, and the man that getteth understanding. For the merchandise of it is better than the merchandise of silver, and the gain thereof than fine gold. She is more precious than rubies: and all the things thou canst desire are not to be compared unto her. Length of days is in her right hand; and in her left hand riches and honour. Her ways are ways of pleasantness, and all her paths are peace. She is a tree of life to them that lay hold upon her: and happy is every one that retaineth her.
Proverbs 3:13–18.

13 For the lips of a strange woman drop as an honeycomb, and her mouth is smoother than oil: But her end is bitter as wormwood, sharp as a two-edged sword. Her feet go down to death; her steps take hold on hell.
Proverbs 5:3–5.

14 Let thy fountain be blessed: and rejoice with the wife of thy youth. Let her be as the loving hind and pleasant roe; let her breasts satisfy thee at all times; and be thou ravished always with her love.
Proverbs 5:18–19.

15 Go to the ant, thou sluggard; consider her ways, and be wise.
Proverbs 6:6.

16 Yet a little sleep, a little slumber, a little folding of the hands to sleep: So shall thy poverty come as one that travelleth, and thy want as an armed man.
Proverbs 6:10–11.

17 Can a man take fire in his bosom and his clothes not be burned? Can one go upon hot coals, and his feet not be burned?
Proverbs 6:27–8.

18 Wisdom hath builded her house, she hath hewn out her seven pillars.
Proverbs 9:1.

19 Stolen waters are sweet, and bread eaten in secret is pleasant.
Proverbs 9:17.

20 The rich man's wealth is his strong city: the destruction of the poor is their poverty.
Proverbs 10:15.

21 A false balance is abomination to the LORD: but a just weight is his delight.
Proverbs 11:1.

22 He that is surety for a stranger shall smart for it: and he that hateth suretiship is sure.
Proverbs 11:15.

23 A virtuous woman is a crown to her husband: but she that maketh ashamed is as rottenness in his bones.
Proverbs 12:4.

24 A wise son heareth his father's instruction: but a scorner heareth not rebuke.
Proverbs 13:1.

25 Hope deferred maketh the heart sick: but when the desire cometh, it is a tree of life.
Proverbs 13:12.

26 He that spareth his rod hateth his son: but he that loveth him chasteneth him betimes.
Proverbs 13:24.

27 There is a way which seemeth right unto a man, but the end thereof are the ways of death.
Proverbs 14:12.

28 The poor is hated even of his own neighbour: but the rich hath many friends.
Proverbs 14:20.

29 In all labour there is profit: but the talk of the lips tendeth only to penury.
Proverbs 14:23.

30 A soft answer turneth away wrath: but grievous words stir up anger.
Proverbs 15:1.

31 A merry heart maketh a cheerful countenance.
Proverbs 15:13.

32 Better is little with the fear of the LORD than great treasure and trouble therewith. Better is a dinner of herbs where love is, than a stalled ox and hatred therewith.
Proverbs 15:16–17.

33 A word spoken in due season, how good is it!
Proverbs 15:23.

34 A good report maketh the bones fat.
Proverbs 15:30.

35 Commit thy works unto the LORD, and thy thoughts shall be established.
Proverbs 16:3.

36 Pride goeth before destruction, and an haughty spirit before a fall.
Proverbs 16:18.

37 Children's children are the crown of old men; and the glory of children are their fathers.
Proverbs 17:6.

38 A friend loveth at all times, and a brother is born for adversity.
Proverbs 17:17.

39 A merry heart doeth good like a medicine: but a broken spirit drieth the bones.
Proverbs 17:22.

40 The name of the LORD is a strong tower: the righteous runneth into it, and is safe.
Proverbs 18:10.

41 A man that hath friends must shew himself friendly: and there is a friend that sticketh closer than a brother.
Proverbs 18:24.

42 He that hath pity upon the poor lendeth unto the LORD; and that which he hath given will he pay him again.
Proverbs 19:17.

43 The king's heart is in the hand of the LORD, as the rivers of water: he turneth it whithersoever he will.
Proverbs 21:1.

44 Every way of a man is right in his own eyes: but the LORD

pondereth the hearts.
Proverbs 21:2.

45 It is better to dwell in a corner of the housetop, than with a brawling woman in a wide house.
Proverbs 21:9.

46 Train up a child in the way he should go: and when he is old, he will not depart from it.
Proverbs 22:6.

47 Wilt thou set thine eyes upon that which is not? for riches certainly make themselves wings; they fly away as an eagle toward heaven.
Proverbs 23:5.

48 Remove not the old landmark; and enter not into the fields of the fatherless.
Proverbs 23:10.

49 If thou faint in the day of adversity, thy strength is small.
Proverbs 24:10.

50 A word fitly spoken is like apples of gold in pictures of silver.
Proverbs 25:11.

51 Confidence in an unfaithful man in time of trouble is like a broken tooth, and a foot out of joint.
Proverbs 25:19.

52 If thine enemy be hungry, give him bread to eat; and if he be thirsty, give him water to drink: For thou shalt heap coals of fire upon his head, and the LORD shall reward thee.
Proverbs 25:21–2.

53 As a dog returneth to his vomit, so a fool returneth to his folly.
Proverbs 26:11.

54 The slothful man saith, There is a lion in the way; a lion is in the streets.
Proverbs 26:13.

55 Where no wood is, there the fire goeth out: so where there is no talebearer, the strife ceaseth.
Proverbs 26:20.

56 Boast not thyself of tomorrow; for thou knowest not what a day may bring forth.
Proverbs 27:1.

57 Wrath is cruel, and anger is outrageous; but who is able to stand before envy?
Proverbs 27:4.

58 Open rebuke is better than secret love. Faithful are the wounds of a friend; but the kisses of an enemy are deceitful.
Proverbs 27:5–6.

59 A continual dropping in a very rainy day and a contentious woman are alike.
Proverbs 27:15.

60 Hell and destruction are never full; so the eyes of man are never satisfied.
Proverbs 27:20.

61 A fool uttereth all his mind: but a wise man keepeth it in till afterwards.
Proverbs 29:11.

62 Where there is no vision, the people perish: but he that keepeth the law, happy is he.
Proverbs 29:18.

63 Who can find a virtuous woman? for her price is far above rubies.
Proverbs 31:10.

64 Favour is deceitful, and beauty is vain: but a woman that feareth the LORD, she shall be praised.
Proverbs 31:30.

65 Vanity of vanities, saith the Preacher, vanity of vanities; all is vanity. What profit hath a man of all his labour which he taketh under the sun? One generation passeth away, and another generation cometh: but the earth abideth for ever.
Ecclesiastes 1:2–4.

66 All the rivers run into the sea; yet the sea is not full; unto the place from whence the rivers come, thither they return again.
Ecclesiastes 1:7.

67 The thing that hath been, it is that which shall be; and that which is done is that which shall be done: and there is no new thing under the sun.
Ecclesiastes 1:9.

68 For in much wisdom is much grief: and he that increaseth knowledge increaseth sorrow.
Ecclesiastes 1:18.

69 I said of laughter, It is mad: and of mirth, What doeth it?
Ecclesiastes 2:2.

70 To every thing there is a season, and a time to every purpose under the heaven:
A time to be born, and a time to die; a time to plant, and a time to pluck up that which is planted;
A time to kill, and a time to heal; a time to break down, and a time to build up;
A time to weep, and a time to laugh; a time to mourn, and a time to dance:
A time to cast away stones, and a time to gather stones together; a time to embrace, and a time to refrain from embracing;
A time to get, and a time to lose; a time to keep, and a time to cast away;
A time to rend, and a time to sew; a time to keep silence, and a time to speak;
A time to love, and a time to hate; a time of war, and a time of peace.
Ecclesiastes 3:1–8.

71 Wherefore I perceive that there is nothing better, than that a man should rejoice in his own works; for that is his portion: for who shall bring him to see what shall be after him?
Ecclesiastes 3:22.

72 Wherefore I praise the dead which are already dead more than the living which are yet alive.
Ecclesiastes 4:2.

73 Two are better than one; because they have a good reward for their labour. For if they fall, the one will lift up his fellow: but woe to him that is alone when he falleth; for he hath not another to help him up.
Ecclesiastes 4:9–10.

74 And if one prevail against him, two shall withstand him; and a threefold cord is not quickly broken.
Ecclesiastes 4:12.

75 Better is a poor and a wise child than an old and foolish

king, who will no more be admonished.
Ecclesiastes 4:13.

76 Be not rash with thy mouth, and let not thine heart be hasty to utter any thing before God: for God is in heaven, and thou upon earth: therefore let thy words be few.
Ecclesiastes 5:2.

77 For as the crackling of thorns under a pot, so is the laughter of a fool: this also is vanity.
Ecclesiastes 7:6.

78 Better is the end of a thing than the beginning thereof: and the patient in spirit is better than the proud in spirit.
Ecclesiastes 7:8.

79 Say not thou, What is the cause that the former days were better than these? for thou dost not inquire wisely concerning this.
Ecclesiastes 7:10.

80 There is no man that hath power over the spirit to retain the spirit; neither hath he power in the day of death: and there is no discharge in that war; neither shall wickedness deliver those that are given to it.
Ecclesiastes 8:8.

81 Then I commended mirth, because a man hath no better thing under the sun, than to eat, and to drink, and to be merry: for that shall abide with him of his labour the days of his life, which God giveth him under the sun.
Ecclesiastes 8:15.

82 For to him that is joined to all the living there is hope: for a living dog is better than a dead lion. For the living know that they shall die: but the dead know not any thing, neither have they any more a reward; for the memory of them is forgotten.
Ecclesiastes 9:4–5.

83 Go thy way, eat thy bread with joy, and drink thy wine with a merry heart; for God now accepteth thy works.
Ecclesiastes 9:7.

84 Whatsoever thy hand findeth to do; do it with thy might; for there is no work, nor device, nor knowledge, nor wisdom, in the grave, whither thou goest.
Ecclesiastes 9:10.

85 I returned, and saw under the sun, that the race is not to the swift, nor the battle to the strong, neither yet bread to the wise, nor yet riches to men of understanding, nor yet favour to men of skill; but time and chance happeneth to them all.
Ecclesiastes 9:11

86 Dead flies cause the ointment of the apothecary to send forth a stinking savour: so doth a little folly him that is in reputation for wisdom and honour.
Ecclesiastes 10:1.

87 He that diggeth a pit shall fall into it; and whoso breaketh an hedge, a serpent shall bite him.
Ecclesiastes 10:8.

88 A feast is made for laughter, and wine maketh merry: but money answereth all things.
Ecclesiastes 10:19.

89 Curse not the king, no not in thy thought; and curse not the rich in thy bedchamber: for a bird of the air shall carry the voice, and that which hath wings shall tell the matter.
Ecclesiastes 10:20.

90 Cast thy bread upon the waters: for thou shalt find it after many days.
Ecclesiastes 11:1.

91 Rejoice, O young man, in thy youth; and let thy heart cheer thee in the days of thy youth, and walk in the ways of thine heart, and in the sight of thine eyes: but know thou, that for all these things God will bring thee into judgment.
Ecclesiastes 11:9.

92 Remember now thy Creator in the days of thy youth, while the evil days come not, nor the years draw nigh, when thou shalt say, I have no pleasure in them;
While the sun, or the light, or the moon, or the stars, be not darkened, nor the clouds return after the rain:
In the day when the keepers of the house shall tremble, and the strong men shall bow themselves, and the grinders cease because they are few, and those that look out of the windows be darkened,
And the doors shall be shut in the streets, when the sound of the grinding is low, and he shall rise up at the voice of the bird, and all the daughters of musick shall be brought low:
Also when they shall be afraid of that which is high, and fears shall be in the way, and the almond tree shall flourish, and the grasshopper shall be a burden, and desire shall fail: because man goeth to his long home, and mourners go about the streets:
Or ever the silver cord be loosed, or the golden bowl be broken, or the pitcher be broken at the fountain, or the wheel broken at the cistern.
Then shall the dust return to the earth as it was: and the spirit shall return unto God who gave it.
Ecclesiastes 12:1–7.

93 And further, by these, my son, be admonished: of making many books there is no end; and much study is a weariness of the flesh.
Ecclesiastes 12:12.

94 Fear God, and keep his commandments: for this is the whole duty of man.
Ecclesiastes 12:13.

95 The song of songs, which is Solomon's.
Song of Solomon 1:1.

96 I am the rose of Sharon, and the lily of the valleys. As the lily among thorns, so is my love among the daughters.
Song of Solomon 2:1–2.

97 He brought me to the banqueting house, and his banner over me was love.
Song of Solomon 2:4.

98 I charge you, O ye daughters of Jerusalem, by the roes, and by the hinds of the field, that ye stir not up, nor awake my love, till he please.
Song of Solomon 2:7.

99 My beloved spake, and said unto me, Rise up, my love, my fair one, and come away. For lo, the winter is past, the rain is over and gone.
Song of Solomon 2:10–11.

1 My beloved is mine, and I am his: he feedeth among the lilies.
Song of Solomon 2:16.

2 Behold, thou art fair, my love; behold, thou art fair; thou hast doves' eyes within thy locks: thy hair is as a flock of

goats, that appear from mount Gilead. Thy teeth are like a flock of sheep that are even shorn, which came up from the washing; whereof every one bear twins, and none is barren among them. Thy lips are like a thread of scarlet, and thy speech is comely: thy temples are like a piece of a pomegranate within thy locks. Thy neck is like the tower of David builded for an armoury, whereon there hang a thousand bucklers, all shields of mighty men. Thy two breasts are like two young roes that are twins, which feed among the lilies. Until the day break, and the shadows flee away, I will get me to the mountain of myrrh, and to the hill of frankincense. Thou art all fair, my love; there is no spot in thee.
Song of Solomon 4:1–7.

3 A garden inclosed is my sister, my spouse; a spring shut up, a fountain sealed.
Song of Solomon 4:12.

4 My beloved put in his hand by the hole of the door, and my bowels were moved for him.
Song of Solomon 5:4.

5 How fair and how pleasant art thou, O love, for delights!
Song of Solomon 7:6.

6 Love is strong as death; jealousy is cruel as the grave: the coals thereof are coals of fire, which hath a most vehement flame. Many waters cannot quench love, neither can the floods drown it: if a man would give all the substance of his house for love, it would utterly be contemned.
Song of Solomon 8:6–7.

7 Come now, and let us reason together, saith the LORD: though your sins be as scarlet, they shall be as white as snow; though they be red like crimson, they shall be as wool.
Isaiah 1:18.

8 They shall beat their swords into plowshares, and their spears into pruninghooks: nation shall not lift up sword against nation, neither shall they learn war any more.
Isaiah 2:4.

9 What mean ye that ye beat my people to pieces, and grind the faces of the poor? saith the Lord GOD of hosts.
Isaiah 3:15.

10 Woe unto them that rise up early in the morning, that they may follow strong drink; that continue until night, till wine inflame them!
Isaiah 5:11.

11 In the year that king Uzziah died I saw also the Lord sitting upon a throne, high and lifted up, and his train filled the temple. Above it stood the seraphims: each one had six wings; with twain he covered his face, and with twain he covered his feet, and with twain he did fly. And one cried unto another, and said, Holy, holy, holy, is the LORD of hosts: the whole earth is full of his glory. And the posts of the door moved at the voice of him that cried, and the house was filled with smoke.
Isaiah 6:1–4.

12 Then said I, Woe is me! for I am undone; because I am a man of unclean lips, and I dwell in the midst of a people of unclean lips; for mine eyes have seen the King, the LORD of hosts. Then flew one of the seraphims unto me, having a live coal in his hand, which he had taken with the tongs from off the altar: And he laid it upon my mouth, and said, Lo, this hath touched thy lips; and thine iniquity is taken away, and thy sin purged. Also I heard the voice of the Lord, saying, Whom shall I send, and who will go for us? Then said I, Here am I; send me.
Isaiah 6:5–8.

13 Then said I, Lord, how long?
Isaiah 6:11.

14 Therefore the Lord himself shall give you a sign; Behold, a virgin shall conceive, and bear a son, and shall call his name Immanuel.
Isaiah 7:14.

15 And he shall be for a sanctuary; but for a stone of stumbling and for a rock of offence to both the houses of Israel, for a gin and for a snare to the inhabitants of Jerusalem.
Isaiah 8:14.

16 The people that walked in darkness have seen a great light: they that dwell in the land of the shadow of death, upon them hath the light shined.
Isaiah 9:2.

17 For unto us a child is born, unto us a son is given: and the government shall be upon his shoulder: and his name shall be called Wonderful, Counseller, The mighty God, The everlasting Father, The Prince of Peace. Of the increase of his government and peace there shall be no end, upon the throne of David, and upon his kingdom, to order it, and to establish it with judgment and with justice from henceforth even for ever. The zeal of the LORD of hosts will perform this.
Isaiah 9:6–7.

18 And there shall come forth a rod out of the stem of Jesse, and a Branch shall grow out of his roots: And the spirit of the LORD shall rest upon him, the spirit of wisdom and understanding, the spirit of counsel and might, the spirit of knowledge and of the fear of the LORD.
Isaiah 11:1–2.

19 The wolf also shall dwell with the lamb, and the leopard shall lie down with the kid; and the calf and the young lion and the fatling together; and a little child shall lead them. And the cow and the bear shall feed; their young ones shall lie down together: and the lion shall eat straw like the ox. And the sucking child shall play on the hole of the asp, and the weaned child shall put his hand on the cockatrice' den. They shall not hurt nor destroy in all my holy mountain for the earth shall be full of the knowledge of the LORD, as the waters cover the sea.
Isaiah 11:6–9.

20 Therefore with joy shall ye draw water out of the wells of salvation.
Isaiah 12:3.

21 How art thou fallen from heaven, O Lucifer, son of the morning!
Isaiah 14:12.

22 And behold joy and gladness, slaying oxen, and killing sheep, eating flesh, and drinking wine: let us eat and drink; for to morrow we shall die.
Isaiah 22:13.

23 The earth shall reel to and fro like a drunkard, and shall be removed like a cottage; and the transgression thereof shall be heavy upon it; and it shall fall, and not rise again.
Isaiah 24:20.

24 He will swallow up death in victory; and the Lord GOD will wipe away tears from off all faces; and the rebuke of his people shall he take away from off all the earth: for the LORD hath spoken it.
Isaiah 25:8.

25 Thou wilt keep him in perfect peace, whose mind is stayed on thee.
Isaiah 26:3.

26 For precept must be upon precept, precept upon precept; line upon line, line upon line; here a little, and there a little:
For with stammering lips and another tongue will he speak to this people.
Isaiah 28:10–11.

27 We have made a covenant with death, and with hell are we at agreement.
Isaiah 28:15.

28 Behold, I lay in Zion for a foundation a stone, a tried stone, a precious corner stone, a sure foundation: he that believeth shall not make haste. Judgment also will I lay to the line, and righteousness to the plummet: and the hail shall sweep away the refuge of lies, and the waters shall overflow the hiding place.
Isaiah 28:16–17.

29 Forasmuch as this people draw near me with their mouth, and with their lips do honour me, but have removed their heart far from me, and their fear toward me is taught by the precept of men.
Isaiah 29:13.

30 In returning and rest shall ye be saved; in quietness and in confidence shall be your strength: and ye would not.
Isaiah 30:15.

31 And thine ears shall hear a word behind thee, saying, This is the way, walk ye in it, when ye turn to the right hand, and when ye turn to the left.
Isaiah 30:21.

32 And a man shall be as an hiding place from the wind, and a covert from the tempest; as rivers of water in a dry place, as the shadow of a great rock in a weary land.
Isaiah 32:2

33 Then the eyes of the blind shall be opened, and the ears of the deaf shall be unstopped. Then shall the lame man leap as an hart, and the tongue of the dumb sing: for in the wilderness shall waters break out, and streams in the desert. And the parched ground shall become a pool, and the thirsty land springs of water: in the habitation of dragons, where each lay, shall be grass with reeds and rushes.
Isaiah 35:5–7.

34 And an highway shall be there, and a way, and it shall be called The way of holiness; the unclean shall not pass over it; but it shall be for those: the wayfaring men, though fools shall not err therein.
Isaiah 35:8.

35 Lo, thou trusted in the staff of this broken reed, on Egypt; whereon if a man lean, it will go into his hand, and pierce it: so is Pharaoh king of Egypt to all that trust in him.
Isaiah 36:6.

36 Comfort ye, comfort ye my people, saith your God. Speak ye comfortably to Jerusalem, and cry unto her, that her warfare is accomplished, that her iniquity is pardoned: for she hath received of the LORD'S hand double for all her sins.
The voice of him that crieth in the wilderness, Prepare ye the way of the LORD, make straight in the desert a highway for our God.
Every valley shall be exalted, and every mountain and hill shall be made low: and the crooked shall be made straight, and the rough places plain:
And the glory of the LORD shall be revealed, and all flesh shall see it together: for the mouth of the LORD hath spoken it.
The voice said, Cry. And he said, What shall I cry? All flesh is grass, and all the goodliness thereof is as the flower of the field:
The grass withereth, the flower fadeth: because the spirit of the LORD bloweth upon it: surely the people is grass. The grass withereth, the flower fadeth: but the word of our God shall stand for ever.
Isaiah 40:1–8.

37 He shall feed his flock like a shepherd: he shall gather the lambs with his arm, and carry them in his bosom, and shall gently lead those that are with young.
Isaiah 40:11.

38 Who hath measured the waters in the hollow of his hand, and meted out heaven with the span, and comprehended the dust of the earth in a measure, and weighed the mountains in scales, and the hills in a balance?
Isaiah 40:12.

39 Behold, the nations are as a drop of a bucket, and are counted as the small dust of the balance: behold, he taketh up the isles as a very little thing.
Isaiah 40:15.

40 To whom then will ye liken God? or what likeness will ye compare unto him?
Isaiah 40:18.

41 Have ye not known? have ye not heard? hath it not been told you from the beginning? have ye not understood from the foundations of the earth?
Isaiah 40:21.

42 Even the youths shall faint and be weary, and the young men shall utterly fall: But they that wait upon the LORD shall renew their strength; they shall mount up with wings as eagles; they shall run, and not be weary; and they shall walk, and not faint.
Isaiah 40:30–31.

43 A bruised reed shall he not break, and the smoking flax shall he not quench: he shall bring forth judgment unto truth.
Isaiah 42:3.

44 Fear not: for I have redeemed thee, I have called thee by thy name; thou art mine. When thou passest through the waters, I will be with thee; and through the rivers, they shall not overflow thee: when thou walkest through the fire, thou shalt not be burned; neither shall the flame kindle upon thee.
Isaiah 43:1–2.

45 Woe unto him that striveth with his Maker! Let the potsherd strive with the potsherds of the earth. Shall the clay say to him that fashioneth it, What makest thou? or

thy work, He hath no hands?
Isaiah 45:9.

46 Can a woman forget her suckling child, that she should not have compassion on the son of her womb? yea, they may forget, yet will I not forget thee.
Isaiah 49:15.

47 How beautiful upon the mountains are the feet of him that bringeth good tidings, that publisheth peace; that bringeth good tidings of good, that publisheth salvation; that saith unto Zion, Thy God reigneth! Thy watchmen shall lift up the voice; with the voice together shall they sing: for they shall see eye to eye, when the LORD shall bring again Zion.
Isaiah 52:7–8.

48 Break forth into joy, sing together, ye waste places of Jerusalem: for the LORD hath comforted his people, he hath redeemed Jerusalem. The LORD hath made bare his holy arm in the eyes of all the nations; and all the ends of the earth shall see the salvation of our God.
Isaiah 52:9–10.

49 As many were astonished at thee; his visage was so marred more than any man, and his form more than the sons of men: So shall he sprinkle many nations; the kings shall shut their mouths at him: for that which had not been told them shall they see; and that which they had not heard shall they consider.
Isaiah 52:14–15.

50 Who hath believed our report? and to whom is the arm of the LORD revealed? For he shall grow up before him as a tender plant, and as a root out of a dry ground: he hath no form nor comeliness; and when we shall see him, there is no beauty that we should desire him. He is despised and rejected of men; a man of sorrows, and acquainted with grief: and we hid as it were our faces from him; he was despised, and we esteemed him not. Surely he hath borne our griefs, and carried our sorrows.
Isaiah 53:1–4.

51 But he was wounded for our transgressions, he was bruised for our iniquities: the chastisement of our peace was upon him; and with his stripes we are healed. All we like sheep have gone astray; we have turned every one to his own way; and the LORD hath laid on him the iniquity of us all. He was oppressed, and he was afflicted, yet he opened not his mouth: he is brought as a lamb to the slaughter, and as a sheep before her shearers is dumb, so he openeth not his mouth.
Isaiah 53:5–7.

52 He was cut off out of the land of the living: for the transgression of my people was he stricken. And he made his grave with the wicked, and with the rich in his death; because he had done no violence, neither was any deceit in his mouth.
Isaiah 53:8–9.

53 Ho, every one that thirsteth, come ye to the waters, and he that hath no money; come ye, buy, and eat; yea, come, buy wine and milk without money and without price. Wherefore do ye spend money for that which is not bread? and your labour for that which satisfieth not? hearken diligently unto me, and eat ye that which is good, and let your soul delight itself in fatness.
Isaiah 55:1–2.

54 Seek ye the LORD while he may be found, call ye upon him while he is near.
Isaiah 55:6.

55 For my thoughts are not your thoughts, neither are your ways my ways, saith the LORD. For as the heavens are higher than the earth, so are my ways higher than your ways, and my thoughts than your thoughts.
Isaiah 55:8–9.

56 For as the rain cometh down, and the snow from heaven, and returneth not thither, but watereth the earth, and maketh it bring forth and bud, that it may give seed to the sower, and bread to the eater: So shall my word be that goeth forth out of my mouth: it shall not return unto me void, but it shall accomplish that which I please, and it shall prosper in the thing whereto I sent it.
Isaiah 55:10–11.

57 For ye shall go out with joy, and be led forth with peace: the mountains and the hills shall break forth before you into singing, and all the trees of the field shall clap their hands.
Isaiah 55:12.

58 Instead of the thorn shall come up the fir tree, and instead of the brier shall come up the myrtle tree: and it shall be to the LORD for a name, for an everlasting sign that shall not be cut off.
Isaiah 55:13.

59 Peace, peace to him that is far off, and to him that is near, saith the LORD; and I will heal him.
Isaiah 57:19.

60 There is no peace, saith my God, to the wicked.
Isaiah 57:21.

61 Arise, shine; for thy light is come, and the glory of the LORD is risen upon thee.
Isaiah 60:1.

62 The Spirit of the Lord GOD is upon me; because the LORD hath anointed me to preach good tidings unto the meek; he hath sent me, to bind up the brokenhearted, to proclaim liberty to the captives, and the opening of the prison to them that are bound; To proclaim the acceptable year of the LORD, and the day of vengeance of our God; to comfort all that mourn; To appoint unto them that mourn in Zion, to give unto them beauty for ashes, the oil of joy for mourning, the garment of praise for the spirit of heaviness; that they might be called trees of righteousness, the planting of the LORD, that he might be glorified.
Isaiah 61:1–3.

63 But we are all as an unclean thing, and all our righteousnesses are as filthy rags; and we all do fade as a leaf; and our iniquities, like the wind, have taken us away.
Isaiah 64:6.

64 Stand by thyself, come not near to me; for I am holier than thou.
Isaiah 65:5.

65 For, behold, I create new heavens and a new earth: and the former shall not be remembered, nor come into mind.
Isaiah 65:17.

66 The wolf and the lamb shall feed together, and the lion shall eat straw like the bullock: and dust shall be the

serpent's meat. They shall not hurt nor destroy in all my holy mountain, saith the LORD.
Isaiah 65:25.

67 Behold, I have put my words in thy mouth. See, I have this day set thee over the nations and over the kingdoms, to root out, and to pull down, and to destroy, and to throw down, to build, and to plant.
Jeremiah 1:9–10.

68 They have forsaken me the fountain of living waters, and hewed them out cisterns, broken cisterns, that can hold no water.
Jeremiah 2:13.

69 They were as fed horses in the morning: every one neighed after his neighbour's wife.
Jeremiah 5:8.

70 But this people hath a revolting and a rebellious heart; they are revolted and gone.
Jeremiah 5:23.

71 Saying, Peace, peace; when there is no peace.
Jeremiah 6:14.

72 Is this house, which is called by my name, become a den of robbers in your eyes?
Jeremiah 7:11.

73 The harvest is past, the summer is ended, and we are not saved.
Jeremiah 8:20.

74 Is there no balm in Gilead; is there no physician there?
Jeremiah 8:22.

75 Can the Ethiopian change his skin, or the leopard his spots? then may ye also do good, that are accustomed to do evil.
Jeremiah 13:23.

76 The heart is deceitful above all things, and desperately wicked: who can know it? I the LORD search the heart, I try the reins.
Jeremiah 17:9–10

77 The LORD hath appeared of old unto me, saying, Yea, I have loved thee with an everlasting love: therefore with lovingkindness have I drawn thee.
Jeremiah 31:3.

78 A voice was heard in Ramah, lamentation, and bitter weeping; Rachel weeping for her children refused to be comforted for her children, because they were not.
Jeremiah 31:15.

79 How doth the city sit solitary, that was full of people! how is she become as a widow! she that was great among the nations, and princess among the provinces, how is she become tributary!
Lamentations 1:1.

80 Is it nothing to you, all ye that pass by? behold, and see if there be any sorrow like unto my sorrow.
Lamentations 1:12.

81 And I said, My strength and my hope is perished from the LORD: Remembering mine affliction and my misery, the wormwood and the gall.
Lamentations 3:18–19.

82 It is of the LORD'S mercies that we are not consumed, because his compassions fail not. They are new every morning: great is thy faithfulness.
Lamentations 3:22–3.

83 It is good for a man that he bear the yoke in his youth.
Lamentations 3:27.

84 The appearance of the wheels and their work was like unto the colour of a beryl: and they four had one likeness: and their appearance and their work was as it were a wheel in the middle of a wheel.
Of his vision in exile. Ezekiel 1:16.

85 For thou art not sent to a people of a strange speech and of an hard language, but to the house of Israel; Not many people of a strange speech and of an hard language, whose words thou canst not understand. Surely, had I sent thee to them, they would have hearkened unto thee.
Ezekiel 3:5–6.

86 And I will give them one heart, and I will put a new spirit within you; and I will take the stony heart out of their flesh, and will give them an heart of flesh.
Ezekiel 11:19.

87 Son of man, eat thy bread with quaking, and drink thy water with trembling and with carefulness.
Ezekiel 12:18.

88 The fathers have eaten sour grapes, and the children's teeth are set on edge.
Ezekiel 18:2.

89 I will accept you with your sweet savour, when I bring you out from the people, and gather you out of the countries wherein you have been scattered; and I will be sanctified in you before the heathen. And ye shall know that I am the LORD, when I shall bring you into the land of Israel, into the country for the which I lifted up mine hand to give it to your fathers. And there shall ye remember your ways, and all your doings, wherein ye have been defiled; and ye shall loath yourselves in your own sight for all your evils that ye have committed.
Ezekiel 20:41–3.

90 As I live, saith the Lord GOD, I have no pleasure in the death of the wicked; but that the wicked turn from his way and live: turn ye, turn ye from your evil ways; for why will ye die, O house of Israel?
Ezekiel 33:11.

91 The hand of the LORD was upon me, and carried me out in the spirit of the LORD, and set me down in the midst of the valley which was full of bones.
Ezekiel 37:1.

92 Son of man, can these bones live?
Ezekiel 37:3.

93 Prophesy upon these bones, and say unto them, O ye dry bones, hear the word of the LORD. Thus saith the Lord GOD unto these bones; Behold, I will cause breath to enter into you, and ye shall live: And I will lay sinews upon you, and will bring up flesh upon you, and cover you with skin, and put breath in you, and ye shall live; and ye shall know that I am the LORD.
Ezekiel 37:4–6.

94 Thou, O king, sawest, and behold a great image. This great image, whose brightness was excellent, stood before thee; and the form thereof was terrible. This image's head was of fine gold, his breast and his arms of silver, his belly and his thighs of brass. His legs of iron, his feet part of iron and part of clay. Thou sawest till that a stone was cut out without hands, which smote the image

upon his feet that were of iron and clay, and brake them to pieces.
Daniel 2:31–34.

95 Then Nebuchadnezzar came near to the mouth of the burning fiery furnace, and spake, and said, Shadrach, Meshach, and Abednego, ye servants of the most high God, come forth, and come hither. Then Shadrach, Meshach, and Abednego, came forth of the midst of the fire.
Daniel 3:26.

96 The same hour was the thing fulfilled upon Nebuchadnezzar: and he was driven from men, and did eat grass as oxen, and his body was wet with the dew of heaven, till his hairs were grown like eagles' feathers, and his nails like birds' claws.
Daniel 4:33.

97 In the same hour came forth fingers of a man's hand, and wrote over against the candlestick upon the plaister of the wall of the king's palace: and the king saw the part of the hand that wrote.
Daniel 5:5.

98 And this is the writing that was written, MENE, MENE, TEKEL, UPHARSIN. This is the interpretation of the thing: MENE; God hath numbered thy kingdom, and finished it, TEKEL; Thou art weighed in the balances, and art found wanting. PERES; Thy kingdom is divided, and given to the Medes and Persians.
Daniel 5:25–8.

99 I saw in the night visions and, behold, one like the Son of man came with the clouds of heaven, and came to the Ancient of days, and they brought him near before him.
Daniel 7:13.

1 And they that be wise shall shine as the brightness of the firmament; and they that turn many to righteousness as the stars for ever and ever. But thou, O Daniel, shut up the words, and seal the book, even to the time of the end: many shall run to and fro, and knowledge shall be increased.
Daniel 12:3–4.

2 For they have sown the wind, and they shall reap the whirlwind.
Hosea 8:7.

3 When Israel was a child, then I loved him, and called my son out of Egypt.
Hosea 11:1.

4 And I will restore to you the years that the locust hath eaten, the cankerworm, and the caterpiller, and the palmerworm, my great army which I sent among you.
Joel 2:25.

5 And it shall come to pass afterward, that I will pour out my spirit upon all flesh, and your sons and your daughters shall prophesy, your old men shall dream dreams, your young men shall see visions.
Joel 2:28.

6 Beat your plowshares into swords, and your pruninghooks into spears: let the weak say, I am strong.
Joel 3:10.

7 Can two walk together, except they be agreed?
Amos 3:3.

8 The lion hath roared, who will not fear? the Lord GOD hath spoken, who can but prophesy?
Amos 3:8.

9 Therefore thus will I do unto thee, O Israel: and because I will do this unto thee, prepare to meet thy God, O Israel.
Amos 4:12.

10 Shall not the day of the LORD be darkness, and not light? even very dark, and no brightness in it?
Amos 5:20.

11 Behold, the days come, saith the Lord GOD, that I will send a famine in the land, not a famine of bread, nor a thirst for water, but of hearing the words of the LORD: And they shall wander from sea to sea, and from the north even to the east, they shall run to and fro to seek the word of the LORD, and shall not find it.
Amos 8:11–12.

12 But thou, Bethlehem, Ephratah, though thou be little among the thousands of Judah, yet out of thee shall he come forth unto me that is to be ruler in Israel.
Micah 5:2.

13 O LORD, revive thy work in the midst of the years, in the midst of the years make known; in wrath remember mercy.
Habakkuk 3:2.

14 He that earneth wages earneth wages to put it into a bag with holes.
Haggai 1:6.

15 I lifted up mine eyes again, and looked, and behold a man with a measuring line in his hand. Then said I, Whither goest thou? And he said unto me, To measure Jerusalem, to see what is the breadth thereof, and what is the length thereof.
Zechariah 2:1–2.

16 For thus saith the LORD of hosts; After the glory hath he sent me unto the nations which spoiled you: for he that toucheth you toucheth the apple of his eye.
Zechariah 2:8.

17 Then he answered and spake unto me, saying, This is the word of the LORD unto Zerubbabel, saying, Not by might, nor by power, but by my spirit, saith the LORD of hosts.
Zechariah 4:6.

18 And I said unto them, If ye think good, give me my price; and if not, forbear. So they weighed for my price thirty pieces of silver.
Zechariah 11:12.

19 Have we not all one father, hath not one God created us? why do we deal treacherously every man against his brother, by profaning the covenant of our fathers?
Malachi 2:10.

20 Bring ye all the tithes into the storehouse, that there may be meat in mine house, and prove me now herewith, saith the LORD of hosts, if I will not open you the windows of heaven, and pour you out a blessing, that there shall not be room enough to receive it.
Malachi 3:10.

21 Then they that feared the LORD spake often one to another: and the LORD hearkened, and heard it, and a book of remembrance was written before him for them that feared the LORD, and that thought upon his name.
Malachi 3:16.

22 For, behold, the day cometh, that shall burn as an oven;

and all the proud, yea, and all that do wickedly, shall be stubble: and the day that cometh shall burn them up, saith the LORD of hosts, that it shall leave them neither root nor branch. But unto you that fear my name shall the Sun of righteousness arise with healing in his wings; and ye shall go forth, and grow up as calves of the stall.
Malachi 4:1–2.

23 Behold, I will send you Elijah the prophet before the coming of the great and dreadful day of the LORD: And he shall turn the heart of the fathers to the children, and the heart of the children to their fathers, lest I come and smite the earth a curse.
Malachi 4:5–6.

Bible (Apocrypha)

24 The first wrote, Wine is the strongest. The second wrote, The king is strongest. The third wrote, Women are strongest: but above all things Truth beareth away the victory.
1 Esdras 3:10–12.

25 By this also ye must know that women have dominion over you: do ye not labour and toil, and give and bring all to the woman? Yea, a man taketh his sword, and goeth his way to rob and to steal, to sail upon the sea and upon rivers; And looketh upon a lion, and goeth in the darkness; and when he hath stolen, spoiled, and robbed, he bringeth it to his love.
1 Esdras 4:22–4.

26 Then were the entrances of this world made narrow, full of sorrow and travail: they are but few and evil, full of perils, and very painful. For the entrances of the elder world were wide and sure, and brought immortal fruit. If then they that live labour not to enter these strait and vain things, they can never receive those that are laid up for them.
2 Esdras 7:12–14.

27 For the world hath lost his youth, and the times begin to wax old.
2 Esdras 14:10.

28 Be not greedy to add money to money: but let it be as refuse in respect of our child.
Tobit 5:18.

29 For the ear of jealousy heareth all things: and the noise of murmurings is not hid.
Wisdom of Solomon 1:10.

30 Nevertheless through envy of the devil came death into the world: and they that do hold of his side do find it.
Wisdom of Solomon 2:24.

31 But the souls of the righteous are in the hand of God, and there shall no torment touch them. In the sight of the unwise they seemed to die: and their departure is taken for misery, And their going from us to be utter destruction: but they are in peace. For though they be punished in the sight of men, yet is their hope full of immortality. And having been a little chastised, they shall be greatly rewarded: for God proved them, and found them worthy for himself.
Wisdom of Solomon 3:1–5.

32 And in the time of their visitation they shall shine, and run to and fro like sparks among the stubble.
Wisdom of Solomon 3:7.

33 For the bewitching of naughtiness doth obscure things that are honest; and the wanderings of concupiscence doth undermine the simple mind. He being made perfect in a short time, fulfilled a long time.
Wisdom of Solomon 4:12–13.

34 Even so we in like manner, as soon as we were born, began to draw to our end, and had no sign of virtue to shew; but were consumed in our own wickedness. For the hope of the ungodly is like dust that is blown away with the wind; like a thin froth that is driven away with the storm; like as the smoke which is dispersed here and there with a tempest, and passeth away as the remembrance of a guest that tarrieth but a day.
Wisdom of Solomon 5:13–14.

35 For all men have one entrance into life, and the like going out.
Wisdom of Solomon 7:6.

36 For thou hast power of life and death: thou leadest to the gates of hell, and bringest up again.
Wisdom of Solomon 16:13.

37 My son, if thou come to serve the Lord, prepare thy soul for temptation.
Ecclesiasticus 2:1.

38 Saying, We will fall into the hands of the Lord, and not into the hands of men: for as his majesty is, so is his mercy.
Ecclesiasticus 2:18.

39 Be not curious in unnecessary matters: for more things are shewed unto thee than men understand.
Ecclesiasticus 3:23.

40 Be not ignorant of any thing in a great matter or a small.
Ecclesiasticus 5:15.

41 A faithful friend is the medicine of life; and they that fear the Lord shall find him.
Ecclesiasticus 6:16.

42 Laugh no man to scorn in the bitterness of his soul: for there is one which humbleth and exalteth.
Ecclesiasticus 7:11.

43 Miss not the discourse of the elders: for they also learned of their fathers, and of them thou shalt learn understanding, and to give answer as need requireth.
Ecclesiasticus 8:9.

44 Open not thine heart to every man, lest he requite thee with a shrewd turn.
Ecclesiasticus 8:19.

45 Give not thy soul unto a woman to set her foot upon thy substance.
Ecclesiasticus 9:2.

46 Forsake not an old friend; for the new is not comparable to him: a new friend is as new wine; when it is old, thou shalt drink it with pleasure.
Ecclesiasticus 9:10.

47 Many kings have sat down upon the ground; and one that was never thought of hath worn the crown.
Ecclesiasticus 11:5.

48 Judge none blessed before his death: for a man shall be known in his children.
Ecclesiasticus 11:28.

49 He that toucheth pitch shall be difiled therewith; and he

that hath fellowship with a proud man shall be like unto him.
Ecclesiasticus 13:1.

50 Burden not thyself above thy power while thou livest; and have no fellowship with one that is mightier and richer than thyself: for how agree the kettle and the earthen pot together? for if the one be smitten against the other, it shall be broken.
Ecclesiasticus 13:2.

51 All flesh waxeth old as a garment: for the covenant from the beginning is, Thou shalt die the death.
Ecclesiasticus 14:17.

52 Desire not a multitude of unprofitable children, neither delight in ungodly sons.
Ecclesiasticus 16:1.

53 Be not made a beggar by banqueting upon borrowing, when thou hast nothing in thy purse: for thou shalt lie in wait for thine own life, and be talked on.
Ecclesiasticus 18:33.

54 A labouring man that is given to drunkenness shall not be rich: and he that contemneth small things shall fall by little and little.
Ecclesiasticus 19:1.

55 Wine and women will make men of understanding to fall away: and he that cleaveth to harlots will become impudent.
Ecclesiasticus 19:2.

56 If thou hast heard a word, let it die with thee; and be bold, it will not burst thee.
Ecclesiasticus 19:10.

57 As the climbing up a sandy way is to the feet of the aged, so is a wife full of words to a quiet man.
Ecclesiasticus 25:20.

58 The stroke of the whip maketh marks in the flesh: but the stroke of the tongue breaketh the bones. Many have fallen by the edge of the sword: but not so many as have fallen by the tongue.
Ecclesiasticus 28:17–18.

59 Envy and wrath shorten the life, and carefulness bringeth age before the time.
Ecclesiasticus 30:24.

60 Leave off first for manners' sake; and be not unsatiable, lest thou offend.
Ecclesiasticus 31:17.

61 Wine is as good as life to a man, if it be drunk moderately: what life is then to a man that is without wine? for it was made to make men glad.
Ecclesiasticus 31:27.

62 Let thy speech be short, comprehending much in few words; be as one that knoweth and yet holdeth his tongue.
Ecclesiasticus 32:8.

63 In all thy works keep to thyself the preeminence; leave not a stain in thine honour.
Ecclesiasticus 33:22.

64 Honour a physician with the honour due unto him for the uses which ye may have of him: for the Lord hath created him. For of the most High cometh healing, and he shall receive honour of the king.
Ecclesiasticus 38:1–2.

65 The wisdom of a learned man cometh by opportunity of leisure: and he that hath little business shall become wise. How can he get wisdom that holdeth the plough, and that glorieth in the goad, that driveth oxen, and is occupied in their labours, and whose talk is of bullocks?
Ecclesiasticus 38:24–5.

66 Let us now praise famous men, and our fathers that begat us.
Ecclesiasticus 44:1.

67 Their bodies are buried in peace; but their name liveth for evermore.
Ecclesiasticus 44:14.

68 Here then will we begin the story: only adding thus much to that which hath been said, that it is a foolish thing to make a long prologue, and to be short in the story itself.
Maccabees 2:32.

69 And when he was at the last gasp, he said, Thou like a fury takest us out of this present life, but the King of the world shall raise us up, who have died for his laws, unto everlasting life.
Maccabees 7:9.

Bible (New Testament)

70 And she shall bring forth a son, and thou shalt call his name JESUS: for he shall save his people from their sins.
St Matthew 1:21.

71 Now all this was done, that it might be fulfilled which was spoken of the Lord by the prophet, saying, Behold, a virgin shall be with child, and shall bring forth a son, and they shall call his name Emmanuel, which being interpreted is, God with us.
St Matthew 1:22–3

72 Now when Jesus was born in Bethlehem of Judaea in the days of Herod the king, behold, there came wise men from the east to Jerusalem, Saying, Where is he that is born King of the Jews? for we have seen his star in the east, and are come to worship him.
St Matthew 2:1–2.

73 And when they were come into the house, they saw the young child with Mary his mother, and fell down, and worshipped him: and when they had opened their treasures, they presented unto him gifts; gold, and frankincense, and myrrh.
St Matthew 2:11.

74 And saying, Repent ye: for the kingdom of heaven is at hand. For this is he that was spoken of by the prophet Esaias, saying, The voice of one crying in the wilderness, Prepare ye the way of the Lord, make his paths straight.
St Matthew 3:2–3.

75 And the same John had his raiment of camel's hair, and a leathern girdle about his loins; and his meat was locusts and wild honey.
St Matthew 3:4.

76 But when he saw many of the Pharisees and Sadducees come to his baptism, he said unto them, O generation of vipers, who hath warned you to flee from the wrath to come?
St Matthew 3:7.

77 And Jesus, when he was baptized, went up straightway

out of the water: and, lo, the heavens were opened unto him, and he saw the Spirit of God descending like a dove, and lighting upon him: And lo a voice from heaven, saying, This is my beloved Son, in whom I am well pleased.
St Matthew 3:16–17.

78 Then was Jesus led up of the spirit into the wilderness to be tempted of the devil. And when he had fasted forty days and forty nights, he was afterward an hungred. And when the tempter came to him, he said, If thou be the Son of God, command that these stones be made bread. But he answered and said, It is written, Man shall not live by bread alone, but by every word that proceedeth out of the mouth of God.
St Matthew 4:1–4.

79 Jesus said unto him, It is written again, Thou shalt not tempt the Lord thy God.
St Matthew 4:7.

80 Again, the devil taketh him up into an exceeding high mountain, and sheweth him all the kingdoms of the world, and the glory of them; And saith unto him, All these things will I give thee, if thou wilt fall down and worship me. Then saith Jesus unto him, Get thee hence, Satan: for it is written, Thou shalt worship the Lord thy God, and him only shalt thou serve.
St Matthew 4:8–10.

81 The people which sat in darkness saw great light; and to them which sat in the region and shadow of death light is sprung up.
St Matthew 4:16.

82 And he saith unto them, Follow me, and I will make you fishers of men.
St Matthew 4:19.

83 And seeing the multitudes, he went up into a mountain: and when he was set, his disciples came unto him:
And he opened his mouth, and taught them, saying,
Blessed are the poor in spirit: for theirs is the kingdom of heaven.
Blessed are they that mourn: for they shall be comforted.
Blessed are the meek: for they shall inherit the earth.
Blessed are they which do hunger and thirst after righteousness: for they shall be filled.
Blessed are the merciful: for they shall obtain mercy.
Blessed are the pure in heart: for they shall see God.
Blessed are the peacemakers: for they shall be called the children of God.
Blessed are they which are persecuted for righteousness' sake: for theirs is the kingdom of heaven.
Blessed are ye, when men shall revile you, and persecute you, and shall say all manner of evil against you falsely, for my sake.
Rejoice, and be exceeding glad: for great is your reward in heaven: for so persecuted they the prophets which were before you.
St Matthew 5:1–12.

84 Ye are the salt of the earth: but if the salt have lost his savour, wherewith shall it be salted? it is thenceforth good for nothing, but to be cast out, and to be trodden under foot of men.
St Matthew 5:13.

85 Ye are the light of the world. A city that is set on an hill cannot be hid. Neither do men light a candle, and put it under a bushel, but on a candlestick; and it giveth light unto all that are in the house. Let your light so shine before men, that they may see your good works and glorify your Father which is in heaven.
St Matthew 5:14–16.

86 Think not that I am come to destroy the law, or the prophets: I am not come to destroy, but to fulfil. For verily I say unto you, Till heaven and earth pass, one jot or one tittle shall in no wise pass from the law, till all be fulfilled.
St Matthew 5:17–18.

87 For I say unto you, That except your righteousness shall exceed the righteousness of the scribes and Pharisees, ye shall in no case enter into the kingdom of heaven.
St Matthew 5:20.

88 But I say unto you, That whosoever is angry with his brother without a cause shall be in danger of the judgment: and whosoever shall say to his brother, Raca, shall be in danger of the council: but whosoever shall say, Thou fool, shall be in danger of hell fire.
St Matthew 5:22.

89 Ye have heard that it was said by them of old time. Thou shalt not commit adultery: But I say unto you. That whosoever looketh on a woman to lust after her hath committed adultery with her already in his heart.
St Matthew 5:27–8.

90 And if thy right eye offend thee, pluck it out, and cast it from thee: for it is profitable for thee that one of thy members should perish, and not that thy whole body should be cast into hell. And if thy right hand offend thee, cut it off, and cast it from thee: for it is profitable for thee that one of thy members should perish, and not that thy whole body should be cast into hell.
St Matthew 5:29–30.

91 Ye have heard that it hath been said, An eye for an eye, and a tooth for a tooth. But I say unto you, That ye resist not evil: but whosoever shall smite thee on thy right cheek, turn to him the other also.
St Matthew 5:38–9.

92 And whosoever shall compel thee to go a mile, go with him twain.
St Matthew 5:41.

93 Ye have heard that it hath been said, Thou shalt love thy neighbour, and hate thine enemy. But I say unto you, Love your enemies, bless them that curse you, do good to them that hate you, and pray for them which despitefully use you, and persecute you.
St Matthew 5:43–4.

94 That ye may be the children of your Father which is in heaven: for he maketh his sun to rise on the evil and on the good, and sendeth rain on the just and on the unjust.
St Matthew 5:45.

95 Be ye therefore perfect, even as your Father which is in heaven is perfect.
St Matthew 5:48.

96 Therefore when thou doest thine alms, do not sound a trumpet before thee, as the hypocrites do in the synagogues and in the streets, that they may have glory of men, Verily I say unto you, They have their reward. But when thou doest alms, let not thy left hand know what

thy right hand doeth: That thine alms may be in secret: and thy Father which seeth in secret himself shall reward thee openly.
St Matthew 6:2–4.

97 But thou, when thou prayest, enter into thy closet, and when thou hast shut thy door, pray to thy Father which is in secret; and thy Father which seeth in secret shall reward thee openly. But when ye pray, use not vain repetitions, as the heathen do: for they think that they shall be heard for their much speaking.
St Matthew 6:6–7.

98 After this manner therefore pray ye: Our Father which art in heaven, Hallowed be thy name. Thy kingdom come. Thy will be done in earth, as it is in heaven. Give us this day our daily bread. And forgive us our debts, as we forgive our debtors. And lead us not into temptation, but deliver us from evil: For thine is the kingdom, and the power, and the glory, for ever. Amen.
St Matthew 6:9–13

99 Lay not up for yourselves treasures upon earth, where moth and rust doth corrupt, and where thieves break through and steal: But lay up for yourselves treasures in heaven, where neither moth nor rust doth corrupt, and where thieves do not break through nor steal: For where your treasure is, there will your heart be also.
St Matthew 6:19–21.

1 No man can serve two masters: for either he will hate the one, and love the other; or else he will hold to the one, and despise the other. Ye cannot serve God and mammon.
St Matthew 6:24.

2 Behold the fowls of the air: for they sow not, neither do they reap, nor gather into barns; yet your heavenly Father feedeth them. Are ye not much better than they? Which of you by taking thought can add one cubit unto his stature? And why take ye thought for raiment? Consider the lilies of the field, how they grow; they toil not, neither do they spin: And yet I say unto you, That even Solomon in all his glory was not arrayed like one of these.
St Matthew 6:26–9.

3 But seek ye first the kingdom of God, and his righteousness; and all these things shall be added unto you. Take therefore no thought for the morrow: for the morrow shall take thought for the things of itself. Sufficient unto the day is the evil thereof.
St Matthew 6:33–4

4 Judge not, that ye be not judged. For with what judgment ye judge, ye shall be judged: and with what measure ye mete, it shall be measured to you again.
St Matthew 7:1–2.

5 And why beholdest thou the mote that is in thy brother's eye, but considerest not the beam that is in thine own eye?
St Matthew 7:3.

6 Give not that which is holy unto the dogs, neither cast ye your pearls before swine, lest they trample them under their feet, and turn again and rend you.
St Matthew 7:6.

7 Ask, and it shall be given you; seek, and ye shall find; knock, and it shall be opened unto you: For every one that asketh receiveth; and he that seeketh findeth; and to him that knocketh it shall be opened.
St Matthew 7:7–8.

8 Or what man is there of you, whom if his son ask bread, will he give him a stone? Or if he ask a fish, will he give him a serpent? If ye then, being evil, know how to give good gifts unto your children, how much more shall your Father which is in heaven give good things to them that ask him?
St Matthew 7:9–11.

9 Enter ye in at the strait gate: for wide is the gate, and broad is the way, that leadeth to destruction, and many there be which go in thereat: Because strait is the gate, and narrow is the way, which leadeth unto life, and few there be that find it.
St Matthew 7:13–14.

10 Beware of false prophets, which come to you in sheep's clothing, but inwardly they are ravening wolves.
St Matthew 7:15.

11 Wherefore by their fruits ye shall know them.
St Matthew 7:20.

12 Not every one that saith unto me, Lord, Lord, shall enter into the kingdom of heaven; but he that doeth the will of my Father which is in heaven.
St Matthew 7:21.

13 Therefore whosoever heareth these sayings of mine, and doeth them, I will liken him unto a wise man, which built his house upon a rock: And the rain descended, and the floods came, and the winds blew, and beat upon that house; and it fell not: for it was founded upon a rock. And every one that heareth these sayings of mine, and doeth them not, shall be likened unto a foolish man, which built his house upon the sand: And the rain descended, and the floods came, and the winds blew, and beat upon that house; and it fell: and great was the fall of it.
St Matthew 7:24–7.

14 The centurion answered and said, Lord, I am not worthy that thou shouldest come under my roof: but speak the word only, and my servant shall be healed. For I am a man under authority, having soldiers under me: and I say to this man, Go, and he goeth; and to another, Come, and he cometh; and to my servant, Do this, and he doeth it. When Jesus heard it, he marvelled, and said to them that followed, Verily I say unto you, I have not found so great faith, no, not in Israel.
St Matthew 8:8–10.

15 But the children of the kingdom shall be cast out into outer darkness: there shall be weeping and gnashing of teeth.
St Matthew 8:12.

16 And Jesus saith unto him, The foxes have holes, and the birds of the air have nests; but the Son of man hath not where to lay his head.
St Matthew 8:20.

17 But Jesus said unto him, Follow me; and let the dead bury their dead.
St Matthew 8:22.

18 And his disciples came to him, and awoke him, saying, Lord, save us: we perish. And he saith unto them, Why are ye fearful, O ye of little faith? Then he arose, and rebuked

the winds and the sea; and there was a great calm. But the men marvelled, saying, What manner of man is this, that even the winds and the sea obey him!
St Matthew 8:25–7.

19 And as Jesus passed forth from thence, he saw a man, named Matthew, sitting at the receipt of custom: and he saith unto him, Follow me. And he arose, and followed him.
St Matthew 9:9.

20 But when Jesus heard that, he said unto them, They that be whole need not a physician, but they that are sick. But go ye and learn what that meaneth, I will have mercy, and not sacrifice: for I am not come to call the righteous, but sinners to repentance.
St Matthew 9:12–13.

21 No man putteth a piece of new cloth unto an old garment, for that which is put in to fill it up taketh from the garment, and the rent is made worse. Neither do men put new wine into old bottles: else the bottles break, and the wine runneth out, and the bottles perish: but they put new wine into new bottles, and both are preserved.
St Matthew 9:16–17.

22 But the Pharisees said, He casteth out devils through the prince of the devils.
St Matthew 9:34.

23 But go rather to the lost sheep of the house of Israel.
St Matthew 10:6.

24 Heal the sick, cleanse the lepers, raise the dead, cast out devils: freely ye have received, freely give.
St Matthew 10:8.

25 And whosoever shall not receive you, nor hear your words, when ye depart out of that house or city, shake off the dust of your feet.
St Matthew 10:14.

26 Behold, I send you forth as sheep in the midst of wolves: be ye therefore wise as serpents, and harmless as doves.
St Matthew 10:16.

27 The disciple is not above his master, nor the servant above his lord.
St Matthew 10:24.

28 Are not two sparrows sold for a farthing? and one of them shall not fall on the ground without your Father. But the very hairs of your head are all numbered. Fear ye not therefore, ye are of more value than many sparrows.
St Matthew 10:29–31.

29 Think not that I am come to send peace on earth: I came not to send peace, but a sword.
St Matthew 10:34.

30 He that loveth father or mother more than me is not worthy of me: and he that loveth son or daughter more than me is not worthy of me. And he that taketh not his cross, and followeth after me, is not worthy of me. He that findeth his life shall lose it: and he that loseth his life for my sake shall find it.
St Matthew 10:37–9.

31 And whosoever shall give to drink unto one of these little ones a cup of cold water only in the name of a disciple, verily I say unto you, he shall in no wise lose his reward.
St Matthew 10:42.

32 And said unto him, Art thou he that should come, or do we look for another?
St Matthew 11:3.

33 Jesus answered and said unto them, Go and shew John again those things which ye do hear and see: The blind receive their sight, and the lame walk, the lepers are cleansed, and the deaf hear, the dead are raised up, and the poor have the gospel preached to them.
St Matthew 11:4–5.

34 And as they departed, Jesus began to say unto the multitudes concerning John, What went ye out into the wilderness to see? A reed shaken with the wind? But what went ye out for to see? A man clothed in soft raiment? behold, they that wear soft clothing are in kings' houses. But what went ye out for to see? A prophet? yea, I say unto you, and more than a prophet.
St Matthew 11:7–9.

35 He that hath ears to hear, let him hear.
St Matthew 11:15.

36 And saying, We have piped unto you, and ye have not danced; we have mourned unto you, and ye have not lamented.
St Matthew 11:17.

37 But wisdom is justified of her children.
St Matthew 11:19.

38 Come unto me, all ye that labour and are heavy laden, and I will give you rest. Take my yoke upon you, and learn of me; for I am meek and lowly in heart: and ye shall find rest unto your souls. For my yoke is easy, and my burden is light.
St Matthew 11:28–30.

39 A bruised reed shall he not break, and smoking flax shall he not quench, till he send forth judgment unto victory.
St Matthew 12:20.

40 He that is not with me is against me: and he that gathereth not with me scattereth abroad.
St Matthew 12:30.

41 Wherefore I say unto you, All manner of sin and blasphemy shall be forgiven unto men: but the blasphemy against the Holy Ghost shall not be forgiven unto men.
St Matthew 12:31.

42 O generation of vipers, how can ye, being evil, speak good things? for out of the abundance of the heart the mouth speaketh.
St Matthew 12:34.

43 But he answered and said unto them, An evil and adulterous generation seeketh after a sign; and there shall no sign be given to it, but the sign of the prophet Jonas: For Jonas was three days and three nights in the whale's belly; so shall the Son of man be three days and three nights in the heart of the earth.
St Matthew 12:39–40.

44 The queen of the south shall rise up in the judgment with this generation, and shall condemn it: for she came from the uttermost parts of the earth to hear the wisdom of Solomon; and, behold, a greater than Solomon is here.
St Matthew 12:42.

45 When the unclean spirit is gone out of a man, he walketh through dry places, seeking rest, and findeth none. Then

he saith, I will return into my house from whence I came out; and when he is come, he findeth it empty, swept, and garnished. Then goeth he, and taketh with himself seven other spirits more wicked than himself, and they enter in and dwell there: and the last state of that man is worse than the first. Even so shall it be also unto this wicked generation.
St Matthew 12:43–5.

46 And he stretched forth his hand toward his disciples, and said, Behold my mother and my brethren! For whosoever shall do the will of my Father which is in heaven, the same is my brother, and sister, and mother.
St Matthew 12:49–50.

47 And he spake many things unto them in parables, saying, Behold, a sower went forth to sow; And when he sowed, some seeds fell by the wayside, and the fowls came and devoured them up: Some fell upon stony places, where they had not much earth: and forthwith they sprung up, because they had no deepness of earth: And when the sun was up, they were scorched; and because they had no root, they withered away. And some fell among thorns; and the thorns sprung up, and choked them: But others fell into good ground, and brought forth fruit, some an hundredfold, some sixtyfold, some thirtyfold.
St Matthew 13:3–8.

48 He also that received seed among the thorns is he that heareth the word; and the care of this world, and the deceitfulness of riches, choke the word, and he becometh unfruitful.
St Matthew 13:22.

49 But he that received seed into the good ground is he that heareth the word, and understandeth it; which also beareth fruit, and bringeth forth, some an hundredfold, some sixty, some thirty.
St Matthew 13:23.

50 But while men slept, his enemy came and sowed tares among the wheat, and went his way.
St Matthew 13:25.

51 He said unto them, An enemy hath done this. The servants said unto him, Wilt thou then that we go and gather them up?
St Matthew 13:28.

52 Another parable put he forth unto them, saying, The kingdom of heaven is like to a grain of mustard seed which a man took, and sowed in his field: Which indeed is the least of all seeds: but when it is grown, it is the greatest among herbs, and becometh a tree, so that the birds of the air come and lodge in the branches thereof.
St Matthew 13:31–2.

53 Again the kingdom of heaven is like unto a merchant man, seeking goodly pearls: Who, when he had found one pearl of great price, went and sold all that he had, and bought it.
St Matthew 13:45–6.

54 And they were offended in him. But Jesus said unto them, A prophet is not without honour, save in his own country, and in his own house.
St Matthew 13:57.

55 And they say unto him, We have here but five loaves, and two fishes.
St Matthew 14:17.

56 And in the fourth watch of the night Jesus went unto them, walking on the sea. And when the disciples saw him walking on the sea, they were troubled, saying, It is a spirit; and they cried out for fear. But straightway Jesus spake unto them, saying, Be of good cheer; it is I; be not afraid.
St Matthew 14:25–7.

57 And immediately Jesus stretched forth his hand, and caught him, and said unto him, O thou of little faith, wherefore didst thou doubt?
St Matthew 14:31.

58 Not that which goeth into the mouth defileth a man; but that which cometh out of the mouth, this defileth a man.
St Matthew 15:11.

59 Let them alone: they be blind leaders of the blind. And if the blind lead the blind, both shall fall into the ditch.
St Matthew 15:14.

60 And she said, Truth, Lord: yet the dogs eat of the crumbs which fall from their masters' table.
St Matthew 15:27.

61 He answered and said unto them, When it is evening, ye say, It will be fair weather: for the sky is red. And in the morning, It will be foul weather to day: for the sky is red and lowring. O ye hypocrites, ye can discern the face of the sky; but can ye not discern the signs of the times?
St Matthew 16:2–3.

62 Thou art Peter, and upon this rock I will build my church; and the gates of hell shall not prevail against it. And I will give unto thee the keys of the kingdom of heaven: and whatsoever thou shalt loose on earth shall be loosed in heaven.
St Matthew 16:18–19.

63 But he turned, and said unto Peter, Get thee behind me, Satan: thou art an offence unto me: for thou savourest not the things that be of God, but those that be of men.
St Matthew 16:23.

64 For whosoever will save his life shall lose it: and whosoever will lose his life for my sake shall find it. For what is a man profited, if he shall gain the whole world, and lose his own soul? or what shall a man give in exchange for his soul?
St Matthew 16:25–6.

65 And Jesus said unto them, Because of your unbelief: for verily I say unto you, If ye have faith as a grain of mustard seed, ye shall say unto this mountain, Remove hence to yonder place; and it shall remove; and nothing shall be impossible unto you.
St Matthew 17:20.

66 And said, Verily I say unto you, Except ye be converted, and become as little children, ye shall not enter into the kingdom of heaven.
St Matthew 18:3

67 And whoso shall receive one such little child in my name receiveth me. But whoso shall offend one of these little ones which believe in me, it were better for him that a millstone were hanged about his neck, and that he were drowned in the depth of the sea.
St Matthew 18:5–6.

68 And if thine eye offend thee, pluck it out, and cast it from thee: it is better for thee to enter into life with one eye,

rather than having two eyes to be cast into hell fire.
St Matthew 18:9.

69 For where two or three are gathered together in my name, there am I in the midst of them.
St Matthew 18:20.

70 Then came Peter to him, and said, Lord, how oft shall my brother sin against me, and I forgive him? till seven times? Jesus saith unto him, I say not unto thee, Until seven times: but, Until seventy times seven.
St Matthew 18:21–2.

71 What therefore God hath joined together, let not man put asunder.
St Matthew 19:6.

72 Then were there brought unto him little children, that he should put his hands on them, and pray: and the disciples rebuked them. But Jesus said, Suffer little children, and forbid them not, to come unto me: for of such is the kingdom of heaven.
St Matthew 19:13–14.

73 Jesus said unto him, If thou wilt be perfect, go and sell that thou hast, and give to the poor, and thou shalt have treasure in heaven: and come and follow me. But when the young man heard that saying, he went away sorrowful: for he had great possessions.
St Matthew 19:21–2.

74 And again I say unto you, It is easier for a camel to go through the eye of a needle, than for a rich man to enter into the kingdom of God.
St Matthew 19:24.

75 When his disciples heard it, they were exceedingly amazed, saying, Who then can be saved? But Jesus beheld them, and said unto them, With men this is impossible; but with God all things are possible.
St Matthew 19:25–6.

76 But many that are first shall be last; and the last shall be first.
St Matthew 19:30.

77 And about the eleventh hour he went out, and found others standing idle, and saith unto them, Why stand ye here all the day idle?
St Matthew 20:6.

78 Is it not lawful for me to do what I will with mine own? Is thine eye evil, because I am good? So the last shall be first, and the first last: for many be called, but few chosen.
St Matthew 20:15–16.

79 And Jesus went into the temple of God, and cast out all them that sold and bought in the temple, and overthrew the tables of the moneychangers, and the seats of them that sold doves, And said unto them, It is written, My house shall be called the house of prayer; but ye have made it a den of thieves.
St Matthew 21:12–13.

80 Render therefore unto Caesar the things which are Caesar's; and unto God the things that are God's.
St Matthew 22:21.

81 For in the resurrection they neither marry, nor are given in marriage, but are as the angels of God in heaven.
St Matthew 22:30.

82 Jesus said unto him, Thou shalt love the Lord Thy God with all thy heart, and with all thy soul, and with all thy mind. This is the first and great commandment. And the second is like unto it, Thou shalt love thy neighbour as thyself. On these two commandments hang all the law and the prophets.
St Matthew 22:37–40.

83 Ye blind guides, which strain at a gnat, and swallow a camel.
St Matthew 23:24.

84 Woe unto you, scribes and Pharisees, hypocrites! for ye are like unto whited sepulchres, which indeed appear beautiful outward, but are within full of dead men's bones, and of all uncleanness.
St Matthew 23:27.

85 And ye shall hear of wars and rumours or wars: see that ye be not troubled: for all these things must come to pass, but the end is not yet. For nation shall rise against nation, and kingdom against kingdom: and there shall be famines, and pestilences, and earthquakes, in divers places.
St Matthew 24:6–7.

86 Verily I say unto you. This generation shall not pass, till all these things be fulfilled. Heaven and earth shall pass away, but my words shall not pass away.
St Matthew 24:34–5.

87 For as in the days that were before the flood they were eating and drinking, marrying and giving in marriage, until the day that Noe entered into the ark.
St Matthew 24:38.

88 Watch therefore: for ye know not what hour your Lord doth come. But know this, that if the goodman of the house had known in what watch the thief would come, he would have watched, and would not have suffered his house to be broken up.
St Matthew 24:42–3.

89 His lord said unto him, Well done, thou good and faithful servant: thou hast been faithful over a few things, I will make thee ruler over many things: enter thou into the joy of thy lord.
St Matthew 25:21.

90 For unto every one that hath shall be given, and he shall have abundance: but from him that hath not shall be taken away even that which he hath. And cast ye the unprofitable servant into outer darkness: there shall be weeping and gnashing of teeth.
St Matthew 25:29–30.

91 When the Son of man shall come in his glory, and all the holy angels with him, then shall he sit upon the throne of his glory: And before him shall be gathered all nations: and he shall separate them one from another, as a shepherd divideth his sheep from the goats: And he shall set the sheep on his right hand, but the goats on the left.
St Matthew 25:31–3.

92 For I was an hungred, and ye gave me meat: I was thirsty, and ye gave me drink: I was a stranger, and ye took me in: Naked, and ye clothed me: I was sick, and ye visited me: I was in prison, and ye came unto me.
St Matthew 25:35–6.

93 And the King shall answer and say unto them, Verily I say unto you, Inasmuch as ye have done it unto one of the

least of these my brethren, ye have done it unto me.
St Matthew 25:40.

94 For ye have the poor always with you; but me ye have not always.
St Matthew 26:11.

95 Then one of the twelve, called Judas Iscariot, went unto the chief priests, And said unto them, What will ye give me, and I will deliver him unto you? And they covenanted with him for thirty pieces of silver.
St Matthew 26:14–15.

96 And as they were eating, Jesus took bread, and blessed it, and brake it, and gave it to the disciples, and said, Take, eat; this is my body. And he took the cup, and gave thanks, and gave it to them, saying, Drink ye all of it; For this is my blood of the new testament, which is shed for many for the remission of sins.
St Matthew 26:26–8.

97 Jesus said unto him, Verily I say unto thee, That this night, before the cock crow, thou shalt deny me thrice. Peter said unto him, Though I should die with thee yet will I not deny thee. Likewise also said all the disciples.
St Matthew 26:34–5.

98 And he went a little further, and fell on his face, and prayed, saying, O my Father, if it be possible, let this cup pass from me: nevertheless not as I will, but as thou wilt.
St Matthew 26:39.

99 Watch and pray, that ye enter not into temptation: the spirit indeed is willing, but the flesh is weak.
St Matthew 26:41.

1 Then said Jesus unto him, Put up again thy sword into his place: for all they that take the sword shall perish with the sword.
St Matthew 26:52.

2 When Pilate saw that he could prevail nothing, but that rather a tumult was made, he took water, and washed his hands before the multitude, saying I am innocent of the blood of this just person: see ye to it.
St Matthew 27:24.

3 He saved others; himself he cannot save. If he be the King of Israel, let him now come down from the cross, and we will believe him.
St Matthew 27:42.

4 And about the ninth hour Jesus cried with a loud voice, saying Eli, Eli, lama sabachthani? that is to say, My God, my God, why hast thou forsaken me?
St Matthew 27:46.

5 Jesus, when he had cried again with a loud voice, yielded up the ghost. And behold, the veil of the temple was rent in twain from the top to the bottom; and the earth did quake, and the rocks rent; And the graves were opened; and many bodies of the saints which slept arose.
St Matthew 27:50–2.

6 And, lo, I am with you alway, even unto the end of the world. Amen.
St Matthew 28:20.

7 When Jesus heard it, he saith unto them, They that are whole have no need of the physician, but they that are sick: I came not to call the righteous, but sinners to repentance.
St Mark 2:17.

8 And he said unto them, The sabbath was made for man, and not man for the sabbath: Therefore the Son of man is Lord also of the sabbath.
St Mark 2:27–8.

9 And if a kingdom be divided against itself, that kingdom cannot stand. And if a house be divided against itself, that house cannot stand.
St Mark 3:24–5.

10 And he said unto them, He that hath ears to hear, let him hear.
St Mark 4:9.

11 And he said unto them, Take heed what ye hear: with what measure ye mete, it shall be measured to you: and unto you that hear shall more be given.
St Mark 4:24.

12 And he asked him, What is thy name? And he answered, saying, My name is Legion: for we are many.
St Mark 5:9.

13 And Jesus, immediately knowing in himself that virtue had gone out of him, turned him about in the press, and said, Who touched my clothes?
St Mark 5:30.

14 And were beyond measure astonished, saying, He hath done all things well: he maketh both the deaf to hear, and the dumb to speak.
St Mark 7:37.

15 And he looked up, and said, I see men as trees, walking.
St Mark 8:24.

16 And straightway the father of the child cried out, and said with tears, Lord, I believe; help thou mine unbelief.
St Mark 9:24.

17 But when Jesus saw it, he was much displeased, and said unto them, Suffer the little children to come unto me, and forbid them not: for of such is the kingdom of God.
St Mark 10:14.

18 And there came a certain poor widow, and she threw in two mites, which make a farthing. And he called unto him his disciples, and saith unto them, Verily I say unto you, That this poor widow hath cast more in, than all they which have cast into the treasury: For all they did cast in of their abundance; but she of her want did cast in all that she had, even all her living.
St Mark 12:42–4.

19 And when the centurion, which stood over against him, saw that he so cried out, and gave up the ghost, he said, Truly this man was the Son of God.
St Mark 15:39.

20 And he said unto them, Go ye into all the world, and preach the gospel to every creature.
St Mark 16:15.

21 And the angel came in unto her, and said, Hail, thou that art highly favoured, the Lord is with thee: blessed art thou among women. And when she saw him, she was troubled at his saying, and cast in her mind what manner of salutation this should be.
St Luke 1:28–9.

22 And Mary said, Behold the handmaid of the Lord; be it unto me according to thy word. And the angel departed from her.
St Luke 1:38.

23 And Mary said,
My soul doth magnify the Lord,
And my spirit hath rejoiced in God my Saviour.
For he hath regarded the low estate of his handmaiden: for, behold, from henceforth all generations shall call me blessed.
For he that is mighty hath done to me great things; and holy is his name.
And his mercy is on them that fear him from generation to generation.
He hath shewed strength with his arm; he hath scattered the proud in the imagination of their hearts.
He hath put down the mighty from their seats, and exalted them of low degree.
He hath filled the hungry with good things; and the rich he hath sent empty away.
St Luke 1:46–53.

24 And it came to pass in those days, that there went out a decree from Caesar Augustus, that all the world should be taxed.
St Luke 2:1.

25 And so it was, that, while they were there, the days were accomplished that she should be delivered. And she brought forth her firstborn son, and wrapped him in swaddling clothes, and laid him in a manger; because there was no room for them in the inn.
St Luke 2:6–7.

26 And there were in the same country shepherds abiding in the field, keeping watch over their flock by night. And, lo, the angel of the Lord came upon them, and the glory of the Lord shone round about them: and they were sore afraid. And the angel said unto them, Fear not: for, behold, I bring you good tidings of great joy, which shall be to all people. For unto you is born this day in the city of David a Saviour, which is Christ the Lord. And this shall be a sign unto you; Ye shall find the babe wrapped in swaddling clothes, lying in a manger. And suddenly there was with the angel a multitude of the heavenly host praising God, and saying, Glory to God in the highest, and on earth peace, good will toward men. And it came to pass, as the angels were gone away from them into heaven, the shepherds said one to another, Let us now go even unto Bethlehem, and see this thing which is come to pass, which the Lord hath made known unto us.
St Luke 2:8–15.

27 Lord, now lettest thou thy servant depart in peace, according to thy word: For mine eyes have seen thy salvation, Which thou hast prepared before the face of all people; A light to lighten the Gentiles, and the glory of thy people Israel.
St Luke 2:29–32.

28 And Jesus increased in wisdom and stature, and in favour with God and man.
St Luke 2:52.

29 And he said unto them, Ye will surely say unto me this proverb, Physician, heal thyself: whatsoever we have heard done in Capernaum, do also here in thy country.
St Luke 4:23.

30 Woe unto you, when all men shall speak well of you! for so did their fathers to the false prophets.
St Luke 6:26.

31 Give, and it shall be given unto you; good measure, pressed down, and shaken together, and running over, shall men give into your bosom. For with the same measure that ye mete withal it shall be measured to you again.
St Luke 6:38

32 Wherefore I say unto thee, Her sins, which are many, are forgiven; for she loved much: but to whom little is forgiven, the same loveth little.
St Luke 7:47.

33 And he said to them all, If any man will come after me, let him deny himself, and take up his cross daily, and follow me.
St Luke 9:23.

34 And Jesus said unto him, No man, having put his hand to the plough, and looking back, is fit for the kingdom of God.
St Luke 9:62.

35 And into whatsoever house ye enter, first say, Peace be to this house. And if the son of peace be there, your peace shall rest upon it: if not, it shall turn to you again. And in the same house remain, eating and drinking such things as they give: for the labourer is worthy of his hire.
St Luke 10:5–7.

36 And he said unto them, I beheld Satan as lightning fall from heaven.
St Luke 10:18.

37 And Jesus answering said, A certain man went down from Jerusalem to Jericho, and fell among thieves, which stripped him of his raiment, and wounded him, and departed, leaving him half dead. And by chance there came down a certain priest that way: and when he saw him, he passed by on the other side.
St Luke 10.30–31.

38 But a certain Samaritan, as he journeyed, came where he was: and when he saw him, he had compassion on him, And went to him, and bound up his wounds, pouring in oil and wine, and set him on his own beast, and brought him to an inn, and took care of him. And on the morrow when he departed, he took out two pence, and gave them to the host, and said unto him, Take care of him; and whatsoever thou spendest more, when I come again, I will repay thee.
St Luke 10:33–5.

39 And he said, He that shewed mercy on him. Then said Jesus unto him, Go, and do thou likewise.
St Luke 10:37

40 But Martha was cumbered about much serving, and came to him, and said, Lord, dost thou not care that my sister hath left me to serve alone? bid her therefore that she help me.
And Jesus answered and said unto her, Martha, Martha, thou art careful and troubled about many things:
But one thing is needful: and Mary hath chosen that good part, which shall not be taken away from her.
St Luke 10:40–2.

41 Woe unto you, lawyers! for ye have taken away the key of knowledge.
St Luke 11:52.

42 And I will say to my soul, Soul, thou hast much goods laid up for many years; take thine ease, eat, drink, and be

merry. But God said unto him, Thou fool, this night thy soul shall be required of thee.
St Luke 12:19–20.

43 For which of you, intending to build a tower, sitteth not down first, and counteth the cost, whether he have sufficient to finish it?
St Luke 14:28.

44 What man of you, having an hundred sheep, if he lose one of them, doth not leave the ninety and nine in the wilderness, and go after that which is lost, until he find it? And when he hath found it, he layeth it on his shoulders, rejoicing.
St Luke 15:4–5.

45 Either what woman having ten pieces of silver, if she lose one piece, doth not light a candle, and sweep the house, and seek diligently till she find it? And when she hath found it, she calleth her friends and her neighbours together, saying, Rejoice with me; for I have found the piece which I had lost. Likewise, I say unto you, there is joy in the presence of the angels of God over one sinner that repenteth.
St Luke 15:8–10.

46 And not many days after the younger son gathered all together, and took his journey into a far country, and there wasted his substance with riotous living.
St Luke 15:13.

47 And he would fain have filled his belly with the husks that the swine did eat: and no man gave unto him. And when he came to himself, he said, How many hired servants of my father's have bread enough and to spare, and I perish with hunger! I will arise and go to my father, and will say unto him, Father, I have sinned against heaven, and before thee, And am no more worthy to be called thy son: make me as one of thy hired servants.
St Luke 15:16–19.

48 And he arose, and came to his father. But when he was yet a great way off, his father saw him, and had compassion, and ran, and fell on his neck, and kissed him. And the son said unto him, Father, I have sinned against heaven, and in thy sight, and am no more worthy to be called thy son. But the father said to his servants, Bring forth the best robe, and put it on him; and put a ring on his hand, and shoes on his feet: And bring hither the fatted calf, and kill it: and let us eat, and be merry: For this my son was dead, and is alive again; he was lost, and is found. And they began to be merry.
St Luke 15:20–4.

49 It was meet that we should make merry, and be glad: for this thy brother was dead, and is alive again; and was lost, and is found.
St Luke 15:32.

50 And the lord commended the unjust steward, because he had done wisely: for the children of this world are in their generation wiser than the children of light.
St Luke 16:8.

51 And I say unto you, Make to yourselves friends of the mammon of unrighteousness; that, when ye fail, they may receive you into everlasting habitations.
St Luke 16:9.

52 He that is faithful in that which is least is faithful also in much: and he that is unjust in the least is unjust also in much.
St Luke 16:10.

53 There was a certain rich man, which was clothed in purple and fine linen, and fared sumptuously every day: And there was a certain beggar named Lazarus, which was laid at his gate, full of sores, And desiring to be fed with the crumbs which fell from the rich man's table: moreover the dogs came and licked his sores.
St Luke 16:19–21.

54 And it came to pass, that the beggar died, and was carried by the angels into Abraham's bosom: the rich man also died, and was buried; And in hell he lift up his eyes, being in torments, and seeth Abraham afar off, and Lazarus in his bosom.
St Luke 16:22–3.

55 And beside all this, between us and you there is a great gulf fixed: so that they which would pass from hence to you cannot; neither can they pass to us, that would come from thence.
St Luke 16:26.

56 Neither shall they say, Lo here! or, lo there! for, behold, the kingdom of God is within you.
St Luke 17:21.

57 Remember Lot's wife.
St Luke 17:32.

58 For every one that exalteth himself shall be abased; and he that humbleth himself shall be exalted.
St Luke 18:14.

59 And he answered and said unto them, I tell you that, if these should hold their peace, the stones would immediately cry out.
St Luke 19:40.

60 In your patience possess ye your souls.
St Luke 21:19.

61 Saying, Father, if thou be willing, remove this cup from me: nevertheless not my will, but thine, be done.
St Luke 22:42.

62 And the Lord turned, and looked upon Peter. And Peter remembered the word of the Lord, how he had said unto him, Before the cock crow, thou shalt deny me thrice.
St Luke 22:61.

63 Then said Jesus, Father, forgive them; for they know not what they do. And they parted his raiment, and cast lots.
St Luke 23:34.

64 And he said unto Jesus, Lord, remember me when thou comest into thy kingdom. And Jesus said unto him, Verily I say unto thee, To day shalt thou be with me in paradise.
St Luke 23:42–3.

65 And the sun was darkened, and the veil of the temple was rent in the midst.
St Luke 23:45.

66 And when Jesus had cried with a loud voice, he said, Father, into thy hands I commend my spirit: and having said thus, he gave up the ghost.
St Luke 23:46.

67 And as they were afraid, and bowed down their faces to the earth, they said unto them, Why seek ye the living among the dead? He is not here, but is risen: remember

how he spake unto you when he was yet in Galilee.
St Luke 24:5–6.

68 And their words seemed to them as idle tales, and they believed them not.
St Luke 24:11.

69 And they said one to another, Did not our heart burn within us, while he talked with us by the way, and while he opened to us the scriptures?
St Luke 24:32.

70 And they gave him a piece of a broiled fish, and of an honeycomb.
St Luke 24:42.

71 In the beginning was the Word, and the Word was with God, and the Word was God. The same was in the beginning with God. All things were made by him; and without him was not anything made that was made.
St John 1:1–3.

72 In him was life; and the life was the light of men. And the light shineth in darkness; and the darkness comprehended it not.
St John 1:4–5.

73 That was the true Light, which lighteth every man that cometh into the world. He was in the world, and the world was made by him, and the world knew him not.
St John 1:9–10.

74 And the Word was made flesh, and dwelt among us, (and we beheld his glory, the glory as of the only begotten of the Father,) full of grace and truth.
St John 1:14.

75 The next day John seeth Jesus coming unto him, and saith, Behold the Lamb of God, which taketh away the sin of the world.
St John 1:29.

76 And Nathanael said unto him, Can there any good thing come out of Nazareth? Philip saith unto him, Come and see.
St John 1:46.

77 Jesus saith unto her, Woman, what have I to do with thee? mine hour is not yet come.
St John 2:4.

78 When the ruler of the feast had tasted the water that was made wine, and knew not whence it was: (but the servants which drew the water knew;) the governor of the feast called the bridegroom, And saith unto him, Every man at the beginning doth set forth good wine; and when men have well drunk, then that which is worse: but thou hast kept the good wine until now.
St John 2:9–10.

79 Jesus answered and said unto him, Verily, verily, I say unto thee, Except a man be born again, he cannot see the kingdom of God.
St John 3:3.

80 The wind bloweth where it listeth, and thou hearest the sound thereof, but canst not tell whence it cometh, and whither it goeth: so is every one that is born of the Spirit.
St John 3:8.

81 For God so loved the world, that he gave his only begotten Son, that whosoever believeth in him should not perish, but have everlasting life.
St John 3:16.

82 And this is the condemnation, that light is come into the world, and men loved darkness rather than light, because their deeds were evil.
St John 3:19.

83 He must increase, but I must decrease.
St John 3:30.

84 God is a Spirit: and they that worship him must worship him in spirit and in truth.
St John 4:24.

85 Say not ye, There are yet four months, and then cometh harvest? behold, I say unto you, Lift up your eyes, and look on the fields; for they are white already to harvest.
St John 4:35.

86 Jesus saith unto him, Rise, take up thy bed, and walk.
St John 5:8.

87 He was a burning and a shining light; and ye were willing for a season to rejoice in his light.
Of John the Baptist. St John 5:35.

88 Search the scriptures; for in them ye think ye have eternal life: and they are they which testify of me.
St John 5:39.

89 There is a lad here, which hath five barley loaves, and two small fishes: but what are they among so many?
St John 6:9.

90 And Jesus said unto them, I am the bread of life: he that cometh to me shall never hunger; and he that believeth on me shall never thirst.
St John 6:35.

91 All that the Father giveth me shall come to me; and him that cometh to me I will in no wise cast out.
St John 6:37.

92 Verily, verily, I say unto you, He that believeth on me hath everlasting life. I am that bread of life.
St John 6:47–8.

93 It is the spirit that quickeneth; the flesh profiteth nothing: the words that I speak unto you, they are spirit, and they are life.
St John 6:63.

94 So when they continued asking him, he lifted up himself, and said unto them, He that is without sin among you, let him first cast a stone at her.
St John 8:7.

95 Then spake Jesus again unto them, saying, I am the light of the world: he that followeth me shall not walk in darkness, but shall have the light of life.
St John 8:12.

96 And ye shall know the truth, and the truth shall make you free.
St John 8:32.

97 If the Son therefore shall make you free, ye shall be free indeed.
St John 8:36.

98 Ye are of your father the devil, and the lusts of the father ye will do. He was a murderer from the beginning, and abode not in the truth, because there is no truth in him. When he speaketh a lie, he speaketh of his own: for he is a liar, and the father of it.
St John 8:44.

99 Whether he be a sinner or no, I know not: one thing I know, that, whereas I was blind, now I see.
St John 9:25.

1 The thief cometh not, but for to steal, and to kill, and to destroy: I am come that they might have life, and that they might have it more abundantly.
St John 10:10.

2 I am the good shepherd: the good shepherd giveth his life for the sheep. But he that is an hireling, and not the shepherd, whose own the sheep are not, seeth the wolf coming, and leaveth the sheep, and fleeth: and the wolf catcheth them, and scattereth the sheep. The hireling fleeth, because he is an hireling, and careth not for the sheep. I am the good shepherd, and know my sheep, and am known of mine. As the Father knoweth me, even so know I the Father: and I lay down my life for the sheep. And other sheep I have which are not of this fold: them also must I bring, and they shall hear my voice; and there shall be one fold, and one shepherd.
St John 10:11–16.

3 I am the resurrection, and the life: he that believeth in me, though he were dead, yet shall he live.
St John 11:25.

4 Jesus wept.
This is the shortest verse in the Bible. St John 11:35.

5 For the poor always ye have with you; but me ye have not always.
St John 12:8.

6 That thou doest, do quickly.
Jesus to Judas. St John 13:27.

7 A new commandment I give unto you, That ye love one another; as I have loved you, that ye also love one another. By this shall all men know that ye are my disciples, if ye have love one to another.
St John 13:34–5.

8 Let not your heart be troubled: ye believe in God, believe also in me.
St John 14:1.

9 In my Father's house are many mansions: if it were not so, I would have told you. I go to prepare a place for you. And if I go and prepare a place for you, I will come again, and receive you unto myself; that where I am, there ye may be also.
St John 14:2–3.

10 Jesus saith unto him, I am the way, the truth, and the life: no man cometh unto the Father, but by me.
St John 14:6.

11 Peace I leave with you, my peace I give unto you: not as the world giveth, give I unto you, Let not your heart be troubled, neither let it be afraid.
St John 14:27.

12 This is my commandment, That ye love one another, as I have loved you. Greater love hath no man than this, that a man lay down his life for his friends.
St John 15:12–13.

13 I have yet many things to say unto you, but ye cannot bear them now.
St John 16:12.

14 These things I have spoken unto you, that in me ye might have peace. In the world ye shall have tribulation: but be of good cheer; I have overcome the world.
St John 16:33.

15 While I was with them in the world, I kept them in thy name: those that thou gavest me I have kept, and none of them is lost, but the son of perdition; that the scripture might be fulfilled.
St John 17:12.

16 Pilate saith unto him, What is truth?
St John 18:38.

17 Then said the chief priests of the Jews to Pilate, Write not, The King of the Jews; but that he said, I am King of the Jews. Pilate answered, What I have written I have written.
St John 19:21–2.

18 When Jesus therefore saw his mother, and the disciple standing by, whom he loved, he saith unto his mother, Woman, behold thy son! Then saith he to the disciple, Behold thy mother! And from that hour that disciple took her unto his own home.
St John 19:26–7.

19 He said It is finished: and he bowed his head, and gave up the ghost.
St John 19:30.

20 But one of the soldiers with a spear pierced his side, and forthwith came there out blood and water.
St John 19:34.

21 The first day of the week cometh Mary Magdalene early, when it was yet dark, unto the sepulchre, and seeth the stone taken away from the sepulchre.
St John 20:1.

22 So they ran both together: and the other disciple did outrun Peter, and came first to the sepulchre.
St John 20:4.

23 Jesus saith unto her, Woman, why weepest thou? whom seekest thou? She, supposing him to be the gardener, saith unto him, Sir, if thou have borne him hence, tell me where thou hast laid him, and I will take him away. Jesus saith unto her, Mary. She turned herself, and saith unto him, Rabboni; which is to say, Master. Jesus saith unto her, Touch me not; for I am not yet ascended to my Father: but go to my brethren, and say unto them, I ascend unto my Father, and your Father; and to my God, and your God.
St John 20:15–17. The Latin Vulgate translation of the Bible, ascribed to St Jerome, famously renders the phrase 'Do not touch me' as 'Noli me tangere'.

24 Except I shall see in his hands the print of the nails, and put my finger into the print of the nails, and thrust my hand into his side, I will not believe.
Thomas. St John 20:25.

25 Be not faithless, but believing. And Thomas answered and said unto him, My Lord and my God. Jesus saith unto him, Thomas, because thou hast seen me, thou hast believed: blessed are they that have not seen, and yet have believed.
St John 20:27–9.

26 When thou wast young, thou girdest thyself, and walkedst whither thou wouldest: but when thou shalt be old, thou shalt stretch forth thy hands, and another shall gird thee, and carry thee whither thou wouldest not.
St John 21:18.

27 It is not for you to know the times or the seasons, which

the Father hath put in his own power. But ye shall receive power, after that the Holy Ghost is come upon you: and ye shall be witnesses unto me both in Jerusalem, and in all Judea, and in Samaria, and unto the uttermost part of the earth.
Acts of the Apostles 1:7–8.

28 Ye men of Galilee, why stand ye gazing up into heaven? this same Jesus, which is taken up from you into heaven, shall so come in like manner as ye have seen him go into heaven.
Acts of the Apostles 1:11.

29 And when the day of Pentecost was fully come, they were all with one accord in one place. And suddenly there came a sound from heaven as of a rushing mighty wind, and it filled all the house where they were sitting. And there appeared unto them cloven tongues like as of fire, and it sat upon each of them. And they were all filled with the Holy Ghost, and began to speak with other tongues, as the Spirit gave them utterance.
Acts of the Apostles 2:1–4.

30 Silver and gold have I none; but such as I have give I thee: In the name of Jesus Christ of Nazareth rise up and walk.
Acts of the Apostles 3:6.

31 And he leaping up stood, and walked, and entered with them into the temple, walking, and leaping, and praising God.
Acts of the Apostles 3:8.

32 Neither is there salvation in any other: for there is none other name under heaven given among men, whereby we must be saved.
Acts of the Apostles 4:12.

33 We ought to obey God rather than men.
Acts of the Apostles 5:29.

34 Then the twelve called the multitude of the disciples unto them, and said, It is not reason that we should leave the word of God, and serve tables.
Acts of the Apostles 6:2–4.

35 And the witnesses laid down their clothes at a young man's feet, whose name was Saul.
Acts of the Apostles 7:57–8.

36 Understandest thou what thou readest? And he said, How can I, except some man should guide me?
Acts of the Apostles 8:30–1.

37 Saul, Saul, why persecutest thou me? And he said, Who art thou, Lord? And the Lord said, I am Jesus whom thou persecutest: it is hard for thee to kick against the pricks.
Acts of the Apostles 9:3–5.

38 Tabitha, which by interpretation is called Dorcas: this woman was full of good works.
Acts of the Apostles 9:36.

39 And saw heaven opened, and a certain vessel descending unto him, as it had been a great sheet knit at the four corners, and let down to the earth:
Wherein were all manner of fourfooted beasts of the earth, and wild beasts, and creeping things, and fowls of the air. And there came a voice to him, Rise, Peter; kill, and eat.
Acts of the Apostles 10:11–13.

40 What God hath cleansed, that call not thou common.
Acts of the Apostles 10:15.

41 Of a truth I perceive that God is no respecter of persons: But in every nation he that feareth Him, and worketh righteousness, is accepted with Him.
Acts of the Apostles 10:34–5.

42 The gods are come down to us in the likeness of men.
Acts of the Apostles 14:11.

43 Sirs, why do ye these things? We also are men of like passions with you, and preach unto you that ye should turn from these vanities unto the living God, which made heaven, and earth, and the sea, and all things that are therein.
Acts of the Apostles 14:15.

44 Sirs, what must I do to be saved? And they said, Believe on the Lord Jesus Christ, and thou shalt be saved, and thy house.
Acts of the Apostles 16:30–1.

45 But the Jews which believeth not, moved with envy, took unto them certain lewd fellows of the baser sort, and gathered a company, and set all the city on an uproar.
Acts of the Apostles 17:5.

46 These that have turned the world upside down are come hither also.
Acts of the Apostles 17:6.

47 What will this babbler say?
Acts of the Apostles 17:18.

48 Ye men of Athens, I perceive that in all things ye are too superstitious. For as I passed by, and beheld your devotions, I found an altar with this inscription, TO THE UNKNOWN GOD. Whom therefore ye ignorantly worship, him declare I unto you.
Acts of the Apostles 17:22–3.

49 God that made the world and all things therein, seeing that he is Lord of heaven and earth, dwelleth not in temples made with hands.
Acts of the Apostles 17:24.

50 For in him we live, and move and have our being.
Acts of the Apostles 17:28.

51 And the times of this ignorance God winked at; but now commandeth all men every where to repent.
Acts of the Apostles 17:30.

52 Have ye received the Holy Ghost since ye believed? And they said unto him, We have not so much as heard whether there be any Holy Ghost.
Acts of the Apostles 19:2.

53 It is more blessed to give than to receive.
Acts of the Apostles 20:35.

54 I am a man which am a Jew of Tarsus, a city in Cilicia, a citizen of no mean city.
Acts of the Apostles 21:39.

55 The chief captain answered, With a great sum obtained I this freedom. And Paul said, But I was free born.
Acts of the Apostles 22:27–8.

56 Paul, thou art beside thyself; much learning doth make thee mad.
Acts of the Apostles 26:24.

57 Almost thou persuadest me to be a Christian.
Acts of the Apostles 26:28.

58 The just shall live by faith.
Romans 1:17.

59 Who changed the truth of God into a lie, and worshipped and served the creature more than the Creator.
Romans 1:25.

60 For when the Gentiles, which have not the law, do by nature the things contained in the law, these, having not the law, are a law unto themselves.
Romans 2:14.

61 God forbid: yea, let God be true, but every man a liar.
Romans 3:4.

62 For all have sinned, and come short of the glory of God.
Romans 3:23.

63 Because the law worketh wrath: for where no law is, there is no transgression.
Romans 4:15.

64 Who against hope believed in hope, that he might become the father of many nations.
Romans 4:18.

65 While we were yet sinners, Christ died for us.
Romans 5:8.

66 Where sin abounded, grace did much more abound.
Romans 5:20.

67 What shall we say then? Shall we continue in sin, that grace may abound? God forbid. How shall we, that are dead to sin, live any longer therein?
Romans 6:1–2.

68 Knowing that Christ being raised from the dead dieth no more; death hath no more dominion over him.
Romans 6:9.

69 For the wages of sin is death; but the gift of God is eternal life through Jesus Christ our Lord.
Romans 6:23.

70 To will is present with me; but how to perform that which is good I find not. For the good that I would I do not: but the evil which I would not, that I do.
Romans 7:19.

71 O wretched man that I am! who shall deliver me from the body of this death?
Romans 7:24.

72 There is therefore now no condemnation to them which are in Christ Jesus, who walk not after the flesh, but after the Spirit.
Romans 8:1.

73 For they that are after the flesh do mind the things of the flesh; but they that are after the Spirit the things of the Spirit. For to be carnally minded is death; but to be spiritually minded is life and peace.
Romans 8:5–6.

74 For ye have not received the spirit of bondage again to fear; but ye have received the Spirit of adoption, whereby we cry, Abba, Father. The Spirit itself beareth witness with our spirit, that we are the children of God: And if children, then heirs; heirs of God, and joint-heirs with Christ; if so be that we suffer with him, that we may be also glorified together.
Romans 8:15–17.

75 For we know that the whole creation groaneth and travaileth in pain together until now.
Romans 8:22.

76 And we know that all things work together for good to them that love God, to them who are the called according to his purpose.
Romans 8:28.

77 If God be for us, who can be against us?
Romans 8:31.

78 I am persuaded, that neither death, nor life, nor angels, nor principalities, nor powers, nor things present, nor things to come, Nor height, nor depth, nor any other creature, shall be able to separate us from the love of God, which is in Christ Jesus our Lord.
Romans 8:38–9.

79 Nay but, O man, who art thou that repliest against God? Shall the thing formed say to him that formed it, Why hast thou made me thus? Hath not the potter power over the clay, of the same lump to make one vessel unto honour, and another unto dishonour?
Romans 9:20–1.

80 I beseech you therefore, brethren, by the mercies of God, that ye present your bodies a living sacrifice, holy, acceptable unto God, which is your reasonable service.
Romans 12:1.

81 Not slothful in business; fervent in spirit; serving the Lord.
Romans 12:11.

82 Rejoice with them that do rejoice, and weep with them that weep.
Romans 12:15.

83 Mind not high things, but condescend to men of low estate. Be not wise in your own conceits. Recompense to no man evil for evil. Provide things honest in the sight of all men. If it be possible, as much as lieth in you, live peaceably with all men. Dearly beloved, avenge not yourselves, but rather give place unto wrath: for it is written, Vengeance is mine; I will repay, saith the Lord.
Romans 12:16–19.

84 Be not overcome of evil, but overcome evil with good.
Romans 12:21.

85 Let every soul be subject unto the higher powers. For there is no power but of God: the powers that be are ordained of God.
Romans 13:1.

86 Render therefore to all their dues: tribute to whom tribute is due; custom to whom custom; fear to whom fear; honour to whom honour. Owe no man any thing, but to love one another: for he that loveth another hath fulfilled the law.
Romans 13:7–8.

87 Love worketh no ill to his neighbour: therefore love is the fulfilling of the law.
Romans 13:10.

88 Doubtful disputations.
Romans 14:1.

89 Whether we live therefore, or die, we are the Lord's.
Romans 14:8.

90 Salute one another with an holy kiss.
Romans 16:16.

91 For after that in the wisdom of God the world by wisdom knew not God, it pleased God by the foolishness of preaching to save them that believe.
1 Corinthians 1:21.

92 But God hath chosen the foolish things of the world to confound the wise; and God hath chosen the weak things of the world to confound the things which are mighty.
1 Corinthians 1:27.

93 I have planted, Apollos watered; but God gave the increase.
1 Corinthians 3:6.

94 We are made a spectacle unto the world, and to angels, and to men.
1 Corinthians 4:9.

95 What? know ye not that your body is the temple of the Holy Ghost which is in you, which ye have of God, and ye are not your own?
1 Corinthians 6:19.

96 It is better to marry than to burn.
1 Corinthians 7:9.

97 For the unbelieving husband is sanctified by the wife.
1 Corinthians 7:14

98 But he that is married careth for the things that are of the world, how he may please his wife.
1 Corinthians 7:33.

99 I am made all things to all men, that I might by all means save some.
1 Corinthians 9:22.

---

1 Know ye not that they which run in a race run all, but one receiveth the prize? So run, that ye may obtain.
1 Corinthians 9:24.

2 Wherefore let him that thinketh he standeth take heed lest he fall.
1 Corinthians 10:12.

3 All things are lawful for me, but all things are not expedient: all things are lawful for me, but all things edify not.
1 Corinthians 10:23.

4 For the earth is the Lord's, and the fulness thereof
1 Corinthians 10:26.

5 If a man have long hair, it is a shame unto him.
But if a woman have long hair, it is a glory to her: for her hair is given her for a covering.
1 Corinthians 11:15.

6 The Lord Jesus the same night in which he was betrayed took bread: And when he had given thanks, he brake it, and said, Take, eat: this is my body, which is broken for you: this do in remembrance of me. After the same manner also he took the cup, when he had supped, saying, This cup is the new testament in my blood: this do ye, as oft as ye drink it, in remembrance of me. For as often as ye eat this bread, and drink this cup, ye do shew the Lord's death till he come.
1 Corinthians 11:23–6.

7 No man can say that Jesus is the Lord, but by the Holy Ghost.
1 Corinthians 12:3.

8 Now there are diversities of gifts, but the same Spirit. And there are differences of administrations, but the same Lord. And there are diversities of operations, but it is the same God which worketh all in all.
1 Corinthians 12:4–6.

9 Though I speak with the tongues of men and of angels, and have not charity, I am become as sounding brass, or a tinkling cymbal. And though I have the gift of prophecy, and understand all mysteries, and all knowledge; and though I have all faith, so that I could remove mountains, and have not charity, I am nothing. And though I bestow all my goods to feed the poor, and though I give my body to be burned, and have not charity, it profiteth me nothing. Charity suffereth long, and is kind; charity envieth not; charity vaunteth not itself, is not puffed up, Doth not behave itself unseemly, seeketh not her own, is not easily provoked, thinketh no evil; Rejoiceth not in iniquity, but rejoiceth in the truth; Beareth all things, believeth all things, hopeth all things, endureth all things. Charity never faileth: but whether there be prophecies, they shall fail; whether there be tongues, they shall cease; whether there be knowledge, it shall vanish away. For we know in part, and we prophesy in part. But when that which is perfect is come, then that which is in part shall be done away. When I was a child, I spake as a child, I understood as a child, I thought as a child: but when I became a man, I put away childish things. For now we see through a glass, darkly; but then face to face: now I know in part; but then shall I know even as also I am known. And now abideth faith, hope, charity, these three; but the greatest of these is charity.
1 Corinthians 13:1–13.

10 For if the trumpet give an uncertain sound, who shall prepare himself to the battle?
1 Corinthians 14:8.

11 Let all things be done decently and in order.
1 Corinthians 14:40.

12 And last of all he was seen of me also, as of one born out of due time. For I am the least of the apostles, that am not meet to be called an apostle, because I persecuted the church of God.
But by the grace of God I am what I am.
1 Corinthians 15:8–9.

13 If in this life only we have hope in Christ, we are of all men most miserable.
1 Corinthians 15:19.

14 But now is Christ risen from the dead, and become the first-fruits of them that slept.
For since by man came death, by man came also the resurrection of the dead.
For as in Adam all die, even so in Christ shall all be made alive.
1 Corinthians 15:20–2.

15 He must reign, till he hath put all enemies under his feet.
The last enemy that shall be destroyed is death.
1 Corinthians 15:26.

16 What advantageth it me, if the dead rise not? let us eat and drink; for tomorrow we die.
1 Corinthians 15:32.
► *See Parker 638:61.*

17 Evil communications corrupt good manners.
1 Corinthians 15:33.

18 The first man is of the earth, earthy.
1 Corinthians 15:47.

19 Behold, I shew you a mystery; We shall not all sleep, but we shall all be changed, In a moment, in the twinkling of an eye, at the last trump: for the trumpet shall sound, and

the dead shall be raised incorruptible, and we shall be changed.
1 Corinthians 15:51–2.

20 O death, where is thy sting? O grave, where is thy victory?
1 Corinthians 15:55.

21 Watch ye, stand fast in the faith, quit you like men, be strong.
1 Corinthians 16:13.

22 Not that we are sufficient of ourselves to think any thing as of ourselves; but our sufficiency is of God; Who also hath made us able ministers of the new testament; not of the letter, but of the spirit: for the letter killeth, but the spirit giveth life.
2 Corinthians 3:5–6.

23 But we have this treasure in earthen vessels.
2 Corinthians 4:7.

24 We are troubled on every side, yet not distressed; we are perplexed, but not in despair.
2 Corinthians 4:8.

25 For we know that if our earthly house of this tabernacle were dissolved, we have a building of God, an house not made with hands, eternal in the heavens.
2 Corinthians 5:1.

26 For we walk by faith, not by sight.
2 Corinthians 5:7.

27 Therefore if any man be in Christ, he is a new creature: old things are passed away; behold, all things are become new.
2 Corinthians 5:17.

28 Now then we are ambassadors for Christ.
2 Corinthians 5:20.

29 For he saith, I have heard thee in a time accepted, and in the day of salvation have I succoured thee: behold, now is the accepted time; behold, now is the day of salvation.
2 Corinthians 6:2.

30 As unknown, and yet well known; as dying, and, behold, we live; as chastened, and not killed; As sorrowful, yet alway rejoicing; as poor, yet making many rich; as having nothing, and yet possessing all things.
2 Corinthians 6:9–10.

31 So let him give; not grudgingly, or of necessity: for God loveth a cheerful giver.
2 Corinthians 9:7.

32 For ye suffer fools gladly, seeing ye yourselves are wise.
2 Corinthians 11:19.

33 And lest I should be exalted above measure through the abundance of the revelations, there was given to me a thorn in the flesh, the messenger of Satan to buffet me.
2 Corinthians 12:7.

34 My grace is sufficient for thee: for my strength is made perfect in weakness.
2 Corinthians 12:9.

35 They gave to me and Barnabas the right hands of fellowship.
Galatians 2:9.

36 There is neither Jew nor Greek, there is neither bond nor free, there is neither male nor female: for ye are all one in Christ Jesus.
Galatians 3:28.

37 Ye are fallen from grace.
Galatians 5:4.

38 But the fruit of the Spirit is love, joy, peace, longsuffering, gentleness, goodness, faith,
Meekness, temperance: against such there is no law.
Galatians 5:22–3.

39 Be not deceived; God is not mocked: for whatsoever a man soweth, that shall he also reap.
Galatians 6:7.

40 Let us not be weary in well doing: for in due season we shall reap, if we faint not.
Galatians 6:9.

41 See what a large letter I have written unto you with mine own hand.
Galatians 6:11.

42 And came and preached peace to you which were afar off, and to them that were nigh.
Ephesians 2:17.

43 Now therefore ye are no more strangers and foreigners, but fellow citizens with the saints, and of the household of God.
Ephesians 2:19.

44 Unto me, who am less than the least of all saints, is this grace given, that I should preach among the Gentiles the unsearchable riches of Christ.
Ephesians 3:8.

45 That he would grant you, according to the riches of his glory, to be strengthened with might by his Spirit in the inner man; That Christ may dwell in your hearts by faith; that ye, being rooted and grounded in love, May be able to comprehend with all saints what is the breadth, and length, and depth, and height; And to know the love of Christ, which passeth knowledge, that ye might be filled with all the fulness of God.
Ephesians 3:16–19.

46 Now unto him that is able to do exceeding abundantly above all that we ask or think, according to the power that worketh in us, Unto him be glory in the church by Christ Jesus throughout all ages, world without end. Amen.
Ephesians 3:20–1.

47 Wherefore putting away lying, speak every man truth with his neighbour: for we are members one of another. Be ye angry, and sin not: let not the sun go down upon your wrath.
Ephesians 4:25–6.

48 Redeeming the time, because the days are evil.
Ephesians 5:16.

49 Be not drunk with wine, wherein is excess; but be filled with the Spirit.
Ephesians 5:18.

50 Ye fathers, provoke not your children to wrath.
Ephesians 6:4.

51 Not with eyeservice, as menpleasers; but as the servants of Christ, doing the will of God from the heart;
With good will doing service, as to the Lord, and not to men.
Ephesians 6:6–7.

52 Put on the whole armour of God, that ye may be able to stand against the wiles of the devil. For we wrestle not

against flesh and blood, but against principalities, against powers, against the rulers of the darkness of this world, against spiritual wickedness in high places. Wherefore take unto you the whole armour of God, that ye may be able to withstand in the evil day, and having done all, to stand. Stand therefore, having your loins girt about with truth, and having on the breastplate of righteousness; And your feet shod with the preparation of the gospel of peace; Above all, taking the shield of faith, wherewith ye shall be able to quench all the fiery darts of the wicked. And take the helmet of salvation, and the sword of the Spirit, which is the word of God.
Ephesians 6:11–17.

53 For to me to live is Christ, and to die is gain.
Philippians 1:21.

54 Let this mind be in you, which was also in Christ Jesus: Who, being in the form of God, thought it not robbery to be equal with God: But made himself of no reputation, and took upon him the form of a servant, and was made in the likeness of men: And being found in fashion as a man, he humbled himself, and became obedient unto death, even the death of the cross. Wherefore God also hath highly exalted him, and given him a name which is above every name: That at the name of Jesus every knee should bow, of things in heaven, and things in earth, and things under the earth; And that every tongue should confess that Jesus Christ is Lord, to the glory of God the Father.
Philippians 2:5–11.

55 Work out your own salvation with fear and trembling.
Philippians 2:12.

56 Circumcised the eighth day, of the stock of Israel, of the tribe of Benjamin, an Hebrew of the Hebrews; as touching the law, a Pharisee.
Paul lists his religious credentials. Philippians 3:5

57 But what things were gain to me, those I counted loss for Christ.
Philippians 3:7.

58 Forgetting those things which are behind, and reaching forth unto those things which are before, I press toward the mark for the prize of the high calling of God in Christ Jesus.
Philippians 3:13–14.

59 Whose end is destruction, whose God is their belly, and whose glory is in their shame, who mind earthly things.
Philippians 3:19.

60 Rejoice in the Lord alway: and again I say, Rejoice. Let your moderation be known unto all men. The Lord is at hand. Be careful for nothing; but in every thing by prayer and supplication with thanksgiving let your requests be made known unto God. And the peace of God, which passeth all understanding, shall keep your hearts and minds through Christ Jesus.
Philippians 4:4–7.

61 Finally, brethren, whatsoever things are true, whatsoever things are honest, whatsoever things are just, whatsoever things are pure, whatsoever things are lovely, whatsoever things are of good report; if there be any virtue, and if there be any praise, think on these things.
Philippians 4:8.

62 I have learned, in whatsoever state I am, therewith to be content.
Philippians 4:11.

63 I can do all things through Christ which strengtheneth me.
Philippians 4:13.

64 My God shall supply all your need according to his riches in glory by Christ Jesus.
Philippians 4:19.

65 Beware lest any man spoil you through philosophy and vain deceit, after the tradition of men, after the rudiments of the world, and not after Christ.
Colossians 2:8.

66 Set your affection on things above, not on things on the earth.
Colossians 3:2.

67 Lie not one to another, seeing that ye have put off the old man with his deeds; And have put on the new man, which is renewed in knowledge after the image of him that created him. Where there is neither Greek nor Jew, circumcision nor uncircumcision, Barbarian, Scythian, bond nor free: but Christ is all, and in all.
Colossians 3:9–11.

68 Husbands, love your wives, and be not bitter against them.
Colossians 3:19.

69 Let your speech be alway with grace, seasoned with salt, that ye may know how ye ought to answer every man.
Colossians 4:6.

70 Study to be quiet, and to do your own business, and to work with your own hands, as we commanded you.
1 Thessalonians 4:11.

71 Prove all things; hold fast that which is good.
1 Thessalonians 5:21.

72 If any would not work, neither should he eat.
2 Thessalonians 3:10.

73 This is a faithful saying, and worthy of all acceptation, that Christ Jesus came into the world to save sinners; of whom I am chief.
1 Timothy 1:15.

74 If a man desire the office of a bishop, he desireth a good work. A bishop then must be blameless, the husband of one wife, vigilant, sober, of good behaviour, given to hospitality, apt to teach; Not given to wine, no striker, not greedy of filthy lucre; but patient, not a brawler, not covetous.
1 Timothy 3:1–3.

75 But refuse profane and old wives' fables, and exercise thyself rather unto godliness.
1 Timothy 4:7–8.

76 Let no man despise thy youth.
1 Timothy 4:12.

77 Drink no longer water, but use a little wine for thy stomach's sake and thine often infirmities.
1 Timothy 5:23.

78 For we brought nothing into this world, and it is certain we can carry nothing out. And having food and raiment let us be therewith content.
1 Timothy 6:7–8.

79 For the love of money is the root of all evil.
1 Timothy 6:10.

80 Fight the good fight of faith.
1 Timothy 6:12.

81 For God hath not given us the spirit of fear; but of power, and of love, and of a sound mind.
2 Timothy 1:7.

82 I know whom I have believed, and am persuaded that he is able to keep that which I have committed unto him against that day.
2 Timothy 1:12.

83 Hold fast the form of sound words, which thou hast heard of me.
2 Timothy 1:13.

84 All scripture is given by inspiration of God, and is profitable of doctrine, for reproof, for correction, for instruction in righteousness.
2 Timothy 3:16.

85 Preach the word; be instant in season, out of season.
2 Timothy 4:2.

86 I have fought a good fight, I have finished my course, I have kept the faith.
2 Timothy 4:7.

87 The Cretans are always liars, evil beasts, slow bellies.
Titus 1:12.

88 Unto the pure all things are pure: but unto them that are defiled and unbelieving is nothing pure; but even their mind and conscience is defiled.
Titus 1:15.

89 God, who at sundry times and in divers manners spake in time past unto the fathers by the prophets, Hath in these last days spoken unto us by his Son, whom he hath appointed heir of all things, by whom he also made the worlds: Who being the brightness of his glory, and the express image of his person, and upholding all things by the word of his power, when he had by himself purged our sins, sat down on the right hand of the Majesty on high.
Hebrews 1:1–3.

90 For the word of God is quick, and powerful, and sharper than any two-edged sword, piercing even to the dividing asunder of soul and spirit.
Hebrews 4:12.

91 Ye have need that one teach you again which be the first principles of the oracles of God; and are become such as have need of milk, and not of strong meat.
Hebrews 5:12.

92 Without shedding of blood is no remission.
Hebrews 9:22.

93 It is appointed unto men once to die, but after this the judgment.
Hebrews 9:27.

94 It is a fearful thing to fall into the hands of the living God.
Hebrews 10:31.

95 Now faith is the substance of things hoped for, the evidence of things not seen.
Hebrews 11:1.

96 These all died in faith, not having received the promises, but having seen them afar off, and were persuaded of them, and embraced them, and confessed that they were strangers and pilgrims on the earth.
Hebrews 11:13.

97 But now they desire a better country, that is, an heavenly: wherefore God is not ashamed to be called their God: for he hath prepared for them a city.
Hebrews 11:16.

98 Of whom the world was not worthy.
Hebrews 11:38.

99 Wherefore seeing we also are compassed about with so great a cloud of witnesses, let us lay aside every weight, and the sin which doth so easily beset us, and let us run with patience the race that is set before us, Looking unto Jesus the author and finisher of our faith; who for the joy that was set before him endured the cross, despising the shame, and is set down at the right hand of the throne of God.
Hebrews 12:1–2.

1 For whom the Lord loveth he chasteneth.
Hebrews 12:6.

2 For our God is a consuming fire.
Hebrews 12:29.

3 Be not forgetful to entertain strangers: for thereby some have entertained angels unawares.
Hebrews 13:1–2.

4 Jesus Christ the same yesterday, and to day, and for ever.
Hebrews 13:8.

5 He that wavereth is like a wave of the sea driven with the wind and tossed. For let not that man think that he shall receive any thing of the Lord. A double minded man is unstable in all his ways.
James 1:7–8.

6 Every good gift and every perfect gift is from above, and cometh down from the Father of lights, with whom is no variableness, neither shadow of turning.
James 1:17.

7 Be ye doers of the word, and not hearers only, deceiving your own selves. For if any be a hearer of the word, and not a doer, he is like unto a man beholding his natural face in a glass: For he beholdeth himself, and goeth his way, and straightway forgetteth what manner of man he was.
James 1:22–4.

8 If any man among you seem to be religious, and bridleth not his tongue, but deceiveth his own heart, this man's religion is vain.
James 1:26.

9 Pure religion and undefiled before God and the Father is this, To visit the fatherless and widows in their affliction, and to keep himself unspotted from the world.
James 1:27.

10 Thou believest that there is one God; thou doest well: the devils also believe, and tremble.
James 2:19.

11 Faith without works is dead.
James 2:20.

12 Even so the tongue is a little member, and boasteth great things. Behold, how great a matter a little fire kindleth!
James 3:5.

13 And the tongue is a fire, a world of iniquity: so is the tongue among our members, that it defileth the whole

body, and setteth on fire the course of nature; and it is set on fire of hell.
James 3:6.

14 Out of the same mouth proceedeth blessing and cursing. My brethren, these things ought not so to be. Doth a fountain send forth at the same place sweet water and bitter?
James 3:10–11.

15 Submit yourselves therefore to God, Resist the devil, and he will flee from you. Draw nigh to God, and he will draw nigh to you.
James 4:7–8.

16 What is your life? It is even a vapour, that appeareth for a little time, and then vanisheth away. For that ye ought to say, If the Lord will, we shall live, and do this, or that.
James 4:14–15.

17 Grudge not one against another, brethren, lest ye be condemned: behold, the judge standeth before the door.
James 5:9.

18 Swear not, neither by heaven, neither by the earth, neither by any other oath: but let your yea be yea; and your nay, nay.
James 5:12.

19 The effectual fervent prayer of a righteous man availeth much.
James 5:16.

20 He which converteth the sinner from the error of his way shall save a soul from death, and shall hide a multitude of sins.
James 5:20.

21 Wherefore gird up the loins of your mind, be sober, and hope to the end for the grace that is to be brought unto you at the revelation of Jesus Christ.
1 Peter 1:13.

22 For all flesh is as grass, and all the glory of man as the flower of grass. The grass withereth, and the flower thereof falleth away.
1 Peter 1:24.

23 As newborn babes, desire the sincere milk of the word, that ye may grow thereby: If so be you have tasted that the Lord is gracious.
1 Peter 2:2.

24 But ye are a chosen generation, a royal priesthood, an holy nation, a peculiar people; that ye should shew forth the praises of him who hath called you out of darkness into his marvellous light.
1 Peter 2:9.

25 Honour all men. Love the brotherhood. Fear God. Honour the king.
1 Peter 2:17.

26 For ye were as sheep going astray; but are now returned unto the Shepherd and Bishop of your souls.
1 Peter 2:25.

27 Giving honour unto the wife, as unto the weaker vessel.
1 Peter 3:7.

28 And above all things have fervent charity among yourselves: for charity shall cover the multitude of sins.
1 Peter 4:8.

29 Casting all your care upon him; for he careth for you.
1 Peter 5:6–7.

30 Be sober, be vigilant; because your adversary the devil, as a roaring lion, walketh about, seeking whom he may devour.
1 Peter 5:8.

31 The dog is turned to his own vomit again; and the sow that was washed to her wallowing in the mire.
2 Peter 2:22.

32 One day is with the Lord as a thousand years, and a thousand years as one day.
2 Peter 3:8–9.

33 But the day of the Lord will come as a thief in the night.
2 Peter 3:10–11.

34 If we say that we have no sin, we deceive ourselves, and the truth is not in us. If we confess our sins, he is faithful and just to forgive us our sins, and to cleanse us from all unrighteousness.
1 John 1:8–9.

35 If any man sin, we have an advocate with the Father, Jesus Christ the righteous.
1 John 2:1.

36 Behold, what manner of love the Father hath bestowed upon us, that we should be called the sons of God.
1 John 3:1.

37 But whoso hath this world's good, and seeth his brother have need, and shutteth up his bowels of compassion from him, how dwelleth the love of God in him?
1 John 3:17.

38 Beloved, let us love one another: for love is of God; and every one that loveth is born of God, and knoweth God. He that loveth not knoweth not God; for God is love.
1 John 4:7–8.

39 Herein is love, not that we loved God, but that he loved us, and sent his Son to be the propitiation for our sins.
1 John 4:10.

40 There is no fear in love; but perfect love casteth out fear.
1 John 4:18.

41 If a man say, I love God, and hateth his brother, he is a liar: for he that loveth not his brother whom he hath seen, how can he love God whom he hath not seen?
1 John 4:20.

42 John to the seven churches which are in Asia: Grace be unto you, and peace, from him which is, and which was, and which is to come.
Revelation 1:4.

43 Behold, he cometh with clouds; and every eye shall see him, and they also which pierced him: and all kindreds of the earth shall wail because of him. Even so, Amen.
Revelation 1:7.

44 I was in the Spirit on the Lord's day, and heard behind me a great voice, as of a trumpet, Saying, I am Alpha and Omega, the first and the last: and, What thou seest, write in a book, and send it unto the seven churches which are in Asia.
Revelation 1:10–11.

45 And in the midst of the seven candlesticks one like unto the Son of man, clothed with a garment down to the foot, and girt about the paps with golden girdle. His head and his hairs were white like wool, as white as

snow; and his eyes were as a flame of fire;
And his feet like unto fine brass, as if they burned in a furnace; and his voice as the sound of many waters.
And he had in his right hand seven stars: and out of his mouth went a sharp two-edged sword: and his countenance was as the sun shineth in his strength.
And when I saw him, I fell as his feet as dead.
Revelation 1:13–17.

46 I am he that liveth, and was dead; and, behold, I am alive for evermore, Amen; and have the keys of hell and of death.
Revelation 1:18.

47 I have somewhat against thee, because thou hast left thy first love.
Revelation 2:4.

48 Be thou faithful unto death, and I will give thee a crown of life.
Revelation 2:10.

49 And he shall rule them with a rod of iron; as the vessels of a potter shall they be broken to shivers.
Revelation 2:27.

50 Behold, I have set before thee an open door, and no man can shut it: for thou hast a little strength, and hast kept my word, and hast not denied my name.
Revelation 3:8.

51 I know thy works, that thou art neither cold nor hot: I would thou wert cold or hot. So then because thou art lukewarm, and neither cold nor hot, I will spew thee out of my mouth.
Revelation 3:15–16.

52 Behold, I stand at the door, and knock: if any man hear my voice, and open the door, I will come in to him, and will sup with him, and he with me.
Revelation 3:20.

53 And before the throne there was a sea of glass like unto crystal: and in the midst of the throne, and round about the throne, were four beasts full of eyes before and behind.
Revelation 4:6–7.

54 And the four beasts had each of them six wings about him; and they were full of eyes within: and they rest not day and night, saying, Holy, holy, holy, Lord God Almighty, which was, and is, and is to come.
Revelation 4:8.

55 Cast their crowns before the throne, saying, Thou art worthy, O Lord, to receive glory and honour and power: for thou hast created all things, and for thy pleasure they are and were created.
Revelation 4:10–11.

56 Who is worthy to open the book, and to loose the seals thereof? And no man in heaven, nor in earth, neither under the earth, was able to open the book, neither to look thereon.
Revelation 5:2–3.

57 And I looked, and behold a pale horse: and his name that sat on him was Death, and Hell followed with him.
Revelation 6:8.

58 And said to the mountains and rocks, Fall on us, and hide us from the face of him that sitteth on the throne, and from the wrath of the Lamb: For the great day of his wrath is come; and who shall be able to stand?
Revelation 6:16–17.

59 A great multitude, which no man could number, of all nations, and kindreds, and people, and tongues, stood before the throne, and before the Lamb, clothed with white robes, and palms in their hands.
Revelation 7:9.

60 These are they which came out of great tribulation, and have washed their robes, and made them white in the blood of the Lamb. Therefore are they before the throne of God, and serve him day and night in his temple: and he that sitteth on the throne shall dwell among them. They shall hunger no more, neither thirst any more; neither shall the sun light on them nor any heat. For the Lamb which is in the midst of the throne shall feed them, and shall lead them unto living fountains of waters: and God shall wipe away all tears from their eyes.
Revelation 7:14–17.

61 And when he had opened the seventh seal, there was silence in heaven about the space of half an hour.
Revelation 8:1.

62 I saw a star fall from heaven unto the earth: and to him was given the key of the bottomless pit.
Revelation 9:1.

63 And there were stings in their tails.
Revelation 9:10.

64 I took the little book out of the angel's hand, and ate it up; and it was in my mouth sweet as honey: and as soon as I had eaten it, my belly was bitter.
Revelation 10:9–10.

65 And there appeared a great wonder in heaven; a woman clothed with the sun, and the moon under her feet, and upon her head a crown of twelve stars.
Revelation 12:1.

66 And there was war in heaven: Michael and his angels fought against the dragon; and the dragon fought and his angels, And prevailed not; neither was their place found any more in heaven. And the great dragon was cast out, that old serpent, called the Devil, and Satan, which deceiveth the whole world: he was cast out into the earth, and his angels were cast out with him.
Revelation 12:7–9.

67 And that no man might buy or sell, save he that had the mark, or the name of the beast, or the number of his name. Here is wisdom. Let him that hath understanding count the number of the beast: for it is the number of a man; and his number is Six hundred threescore and six.
Revelation 13:17–18.

68 And the smoke of their torment ascendeth up for ever and ever: and they have no rest day nor night, who worship the beast and his image, and whosoever receiveth the mark of his name.
Revelation 14:11.

69 Blessed are the dead which die in the Lord from henceforth: Yea, saith the Spirit, that they may rest from their labours; and their works do follow them.
Revelation 14:13.

70 And I saw as it were a sea of glass mingled with fire.
Revelation 15:2.

71 Behold, I come as a thief. Blessed is he that watcheth, and keepeth his garments, lest he walk naked, and they see his shame. And he gathereth them together into a place called in the Hebrew tongue Armageddon.
Revelation 16:15–16.

72 Come hither; I will shew unto thee the judgment of the great whore that sitteth upon many waters.
Revelation 17:1.

73 And upon her forehead was a name written, MYSTERY, BABYLON THE GREAT, THE MOTHER OF HARLOTS AND ABOMINATIONS OF THE EARTH.
Revelation 17:5.

74 And a mighty angel took up a stone like a great millstone, and cast it into the sea, saying, Thus with violence shall that great city Babylon be thrown down, and shall be found no more at all.
Revelation 18:21.

75 And I saw heaven opened, and behold a white horse; and he that sat upon him was called Faithful and True, and in righteousness he doth judge and make war.
Revelation 19:11.

76 And he hath on his vesture and on his thigh a name written, KING OF KINGS, AND LORD OF LORDS.
Revelation 19:16.

77 And he laid hold on the dragon, that old serpent, which is the Devil, and Satan, and bound him a thousand years, And cast him into the bottomless pit, and shut him up, and set a seal upon him, that he should deceive the nations no more, till the thousand years should be fulfilled: and after that he must be loosed a little season.
Revelation 20:2–3.

78 And I saw a great white throne, and him that sat on it, from whose face the earth and the heaven fled away; and there was found no place for them. And I saw the dead, small and great, stand before God; and the books were opened: and another book was opened, which is the book of life: and the dead were judged out of those things which were written in the books, according to their works. And the sea gave up the dead which were in it; and death and hell delivered up the dead which were in them: and they were judged every man according to their works. And death and hell were cast into the lake of fire.
Revelation 20:11–14.

79 And I saw a new heaven and a new earth: for the first heaven and the first earth were passed away; and there was no more sea. And I John saw the holy city, new Jerusalem, coming down from God out of heaven, prepared as a bride adorned for her husband.
Revelation 21:1–2.

80 And God shall wipe away all tears from their eyes; and there shall be no more death, neither sorrow, nor crying, neither shall there be any more pain: for the former things are passed away. And he that sat upon the throne said, Behold, I make all things new. And he said unto me, Write: for these words are true and faithful.
Revelation 21:4–5.

81 I will give unto him that is athirst of the fountain of the water of life freely.
Revelation 21:6.

82 And the street of the city was pure gold, as it were transparent glass.
Revelation 21:21.

83 And the gates of it shall not be shut at all by day: for there shall be no night there.
Revelation 21:25.

84 And he shewed me a pure river of water of life, clear as crystal, proceeding out of the throne of God and of the Lamb. In the midst of the street of it, and on either side of the river, was there the tree of life, which bare twelve manner of fruits, and yielded her fruit every month: and the leaves of the tree were for the healing of the nations.
Revelation 22:1–2.

85 He which testifieth these things saith, Surely I come quickly. Amen. Even so, come, Lord Jesus. The grace of our Lord Jesus Christ be with you all. Amen.
Revelation 22:20–1.

Bible (Vulgate)

A 4c translation of the Bible into Latin, commissioned by Pope Damasus and undertaken by Jerome (382–405). It became known as the *versio vulgata*, the 'common translation', and is still an official text of the Roman Catholic Church. The quotations given here are those that are well known in their Latin form.

86 *Dominus illuminatio mea, et salus mea, quem timebo?*
The Lord is the source of my light and my safety, so whom shall I fear?
Psalm 26:1.

87 *Asperges me hyssopo, et mundabor; lavabis me, et super nivem dealbabor.*
You will sprinkle me with hyssop, and I shall be made clean; you will wash me and I shall be made whiter than snow.
Psalm 50:9 (Psalm 51:7 Authorized Version).

88 *Cantate Domino canticum novum, quia mirabilia fecit.*
Sing to the Lord a new song, because he has done marvellous things.
Psalm 97:1 (Psalm 98:1 Authorized Version).
➤ *See Book of Common Prayer 143:46.*

89 *Jubilate Deo, omnis terra; servite Domino in laetitia.*
Sing joyfully to God, all the earth; serve the Lord with gladness.
Psalm 99:2 (Psalm 100:2 Authorized Version).
➤ *See Book of Common Prayer 143:66.*

90 *Beatus vir qui timet Dominum, in mandatis ejus volet nimis!*
Happy is the man who fears the Lord, who is only too willing to follow his orders.
Psalm 111:1 (Psalm 112:1 Authorized Version).

91 *Non nobis, Domine, non nobis; sed nomini tuo da gloriam.*
Not unto us, Lord, not unto us; but to thy name give glory.
Psalm 113 (2nd part):1 (Psalm 115:1 Authorized Version).

92 *Laudate Dominum, omnes gentes; laudate eum, omnes populi.*
Praise the Lord, all nations; praise him, all people.
Psalm 116:1 (Psalm 117:1 Authorized Version).

93 *Nisi Dominus aedificaverit domum, in vanum laboraverunt qui aedificant eam.*
Nisi Dominus custodierit civitatem, frustra vigilat qui custodit eam.

Unless the Lord has built the house, its builders have laboured in vain. Unless the Lord guards the city, the watchman watches in vain.
Psalm 126:1 (Psalm 127:1 Authorized Version).

94 *De profundis clamavi ad te, Domine; Domine exaudi vocem meam.*
Up from the depths I have cried to thee, Lord; Lord, hear my voice.
Psalm 129:1 (Psalm 130:1 Authorized Version).

95 *Vanitas vanitatum, dixit Ecclesiastes; vanitas vanitatum, et omnia vanitas.*
Vanity of vanities, said the preacher; vanity of vanities, and everything is vanity.
Ecclesiastes 1:2.
► *See Bible (Old Testament) 100:65.*

96 *Rorate, coeli, desuper, et nubes pluant Justum; aperiatur terra, et germinet Salvatorem.*
Drop down dew, heavens, from above, and let the clouds rain down righteousness; let the earth be opened, and a saviour spring to life.
Isaiah 45:8.

97 *Benedicite, omnia opera Domini, Domino; laudate et superexaltate eum in secula.*
Bless the Lord, all the works of the Lord; praise him and exalt him above all things for ever.
Daniel 3:57.

98 *Magnificat anima mea Dominum; et exsultavit spiritus meus in Deo salvatore meo.*
My soul doth magnify the Lord: and my spirit hath rejoiced in God my Saviour.
St Luke 1:46.
► *See Bible (New Testament) 115:23.*

99 *Esurientes implevit bonis, et divites dimisit inanes.*
He hath filled the hungry with good things: and the rich he hath sent empty away.
St Luke 1.53.
► *See Bible (New Testament) 115:23.*

1 *Nunc dimittis servum tuum, Domine, secundum verbum tuum in pace.*
Lord, now lettest thou thy servant depart in peace: according to thy word.
St Luke 2:29.
► *See Bible (New Testament) 115:27.*

2 *Pax Vobis.*
Peace be unto you.
St Luke 24:36.

3 *Quo vadis?*
Where are you going?
St John 16:5.

4 *Ecce homo.*
Behold the man.
St John 19:5.

5 *Noli me tangere.*
Do not touch me.
St John 20:17.
► *See Bible (New Testament) 118:23.*

Bickerstaffe, Isaac c.1735–c.1812

Irish playwright. An officer of marines, he was dismissed from the service and later forced to flee the country. He is credited with establishing the comic opera in English theatre.

6 And this the burthen of his song,
For ever used to be,
I care for nobody, not I,
If no one cares for me.
1762 *Love in a Village*, act 1, sc.2.

7 'Tis a sure sign that work goes on merrily, when folks sing at it.
1765 *The Maid of the Mill*, act 1, sc.1.

8 Perhaps it was right to dissemble your love,
But—why did you kick me downstairs?
1789 'An Expostulation'.

Biddle, Francis Beverley 1886–1968

US lawyer, Solicitor General (1940) and Attorney General (1941–5). He served as US judge on the Nuremberg trials of war criminals.

9 The Constitution has never greatly bothered any wartime President.
1962 *In Brief Authority.*

Bierce, Ambrose Gwinett 1842–c.1914

US writer and journalist, best known for his *Cynic's Word Book* (1906, retitled *The Devil's Dictionary*, 1911). His collection of stories *Tales of Soldiers and Civilians* (1892) coincided with his divorce and the death of his son in a gunfight. He is thought to have died in Mexico.

10 That sovereign of insufferables.
1882 *Wasp*, alluding to Oscar Wilde.

11 Accordion, n. An instrument in harmony with the sentiments of an assassin.
1906 *The Cynic's Word Book*. Retitled *The Devil's Dictionary* (1911).

12 Acquaintance, n. A person whom we know well enough to borrow from, but not well enough to lend to.
1906 *The Cynic's Word Book*. Retitled *The Devil's Dictionary* (1911).

13 Advice, n. The smallest current coin.
1906 *The Cynic's Word Book*. Retitled *The Devil's Dictionary* (1911).

14 Alliance, n. In international politics, the union of two thieves who have their hands so deeply inserted in each other's pocket that they cannot separately plunder a third.
1906 *The Cynic's Word Book*. Retitled *The Devil's Dictionary* (1911).

15 Ambition, n. An overmastering desire to be vilified by enemies while living and made ridiculous by friends when dead.
1906 *The Cynic's Word Book*. Retitled *The Devil's Dictionary* (1911).

16 Applause, n. The echo of a platitude.
1906 *The Cynic's Word Book*. Retitled *The Devil's Dictionary* (1911).

17 Battle, n. A method of untying with the teeth a political knot that would not yield to the tongue.
1906 *The Cynic's Word Book*. Retitled *The Devil's Dictionary* (1911).

18 Bore, n. A person who talks when you wish him to listen.
1906 *The Cynic's Word Book*. Retitled *The Devil's Dictionary* (1911).

19 Brain, n. An apparatus with which we think that we think.

1906 *The Cynic's Word Book*. Retitled *The Devil's Dictionary* (1911).

20 Calamity, n. A more than commonly plain and unmistakable reminder that the affairs of this life are not of our own ordering. Calamities are of two kinds: misfortune to ourselves, and good fortune to others.
1906 *The Cynic's Word Book*. Retitled *The Devil's Dictionary* (1911).

21 Circumlocution, n. A literary trick whereby the writer who has nothing to say breaks it gently to the reader.
1906 *The Cynic's Word Book*. Retitled *The Devil's Dictionary* (1911).

22 Conservative, n. A statesman who is enamoured of existing evils, as distinguished from the Liberal, who wishes to replace them with others.
1906 *The Cynic's Word Book*. Retitled *The Devil's Dictionary* (1911).

23 Consult, v.t. To seek another's approval of a course already decided upon.
1906 *The Cynic's Word Book*. Retitled *The Devil's Dictionary* (1911).

24 Corporation, n. An ingenious device for obtaining individual profit without individual responsibility.
1906 *The Cynic's Word Book*. Retitled *The Devil's Dictionary* (1911).

25 Cynic, n. A blackguard whose faulty vision sees things as they are, not as they ought to be.
1906 *The Cynic's Word Book*. Retitled *The Devil's Dictionary* (1911).

26 Diplomacy, n. The patriotic art of lying for one's country.
1906 *The Cynic's Word Book*. Retitled *The Devil's Dictionary* (1911).

27 Education, n. That which discloses to the wise and disguises from the foolish their lack of understanding.
1906 *The Cynic's Word Book*. Retitled *The Devil's Dictionary* (1911).

28 Egotist, n. A person of low taste, more interested in himself than in me.
1906 *The Cynic's Word Book*. Retitled *The Devil's Dictionary* (1911).

29 Faith, n. Belief without evidence in what is told by one who speaks, without knowledge, of things without parallel.
1906 *The Cynic's Word Book*. Retitled *The Devil's Dictionary* (1911).

30 Fashion, n. A despot whom the wise ridicule and obey.
1906 *The Cynic's Word Book*. Retitled *The Devil's Dictionary* (1911).

31 Future, n. That period of time in which our affairs prosper, our friends are true and our happiness is assured.
1906 *The Cynic's Word Book*. Retitled *The Devil's Dictionary* (1911).

32 History, n. An account, mostly false, of events, mostly unimportant, which are brought about by rulers, mostly knaves, and soldiers, mostly fools.
1906 *The Cynic's Word Book*. Retitled *The Devil's Dictionary* (1911).

33 Ink, n. A villainous compound…chiefly used to facilitate the infection of idiocy and promote intellectual crime.
1906 *The Cynic's Word Book*. Retitled *The Devil's Dictionary* (1911).

34 Marriage, n. The state or condition of a community consisting of a master, a mistress and two slaves, making in all, two.
1906 *The Cynic's Word Book*. Retitled *The Devil's Dictionary* (1911).

35 Mayonnaise, n. One of the sauces which serve the French in place of a state religion.
1906 *The Cynic's Word Book*. Retitled *The Devil's Dictionary* (1911).

36 Painting, n. The art of protecting flat surfaces from the weather and exposing them to the critic.
1906 *The Cynic's Word Book*. Retitled *The Devil's Dictionary* (1911).

37 Patience, n. A minor form of despair, disguised as a virtue.
1906 *The Cynic's Word Book*. Retitled *The Devil's Dictionary* (1911).

38 Peace, n. In international affairs, a period of cheating between two periods of fighting.
1906 *The Cynic's Word Book*. Retitled *The Devil's Dictionary* (1911).

39 Philosophy, n. A route of many roads leading from nowhere to nothing.
1906 *The Cynic's Word Book*. Retitled *The Devil's Dictionary* (1911).

40 Piano, n. A parlour utensil for subduing the impenitent visitor. It is operated by depressing the keys of the machine and the spirits of the audience.
1906 *The Cynic's Word Book*. Retitled *The Devil's Dictionary* (1911).

41 Positive, adj. Mistaken at the top of one's voice.
1906 *The Cynic's Word Book*. Retitled *The Devil's Dictionary* (1911).

42 Prejudice, n. A vagrant opinion without visible means of support.
1906 *The Cynic's Word Book*. Retitled *The Devil's Dictionary* (1911).

43 Saint, n. A dead sinner revised and edited.
1906 *The Cynic's Word Book*. Retitled *The Devil's Dictionary* (1911).

44 Talk, v.t. To commit an indiscretion without temptation, from an impulse without purpose.
1906 *The Cynic's Word Book*. Retitled *The Devil's Dictionary* (1911).

45 Vote, n. The instrument and symbol of a freeman's power to make a fool of himself and a wreck of his country.
1906 *The Cynic's Word Book*. Retitled *The Devil's Dictionary* (1911).

Biko, Stephen 1946–77

South African black civil rights activist, founder of the Black Consciousness Movement. In 1973 he was placed under a banning order, and detained four times. He died in police custody, allegedly as a result of beatings.

46 Whites must be made to realise that they are only human, not superior. It's the same with Blacks. They must be made to realise that they are also human, not inferior.
1977 In the *Boston Globe*, 26 Oct.

Billings, Josh *pseudonym of* Henry Wheeler Shaw 1818–85

US humorist. He became a popular success with *Josh Billings, His Sayings* (1865).

47 Man was kreated a little lower than the angells and has bin gittin a little lower ever since.
1865 *Josh Billings, His Sayings*, ch.28.

48 It ain't often that a man's reputashun outlasts his munny.
1865 *Josh Billings, His Sayings*, ch.39.

49 Mi advise to them who are about tu begin, in arnest, the jurney ov life, is tu take their harte in one hand and a club in the other.
1865 *Josh Billings, His Sayings*, ch.71.

50 Love iz like the meazles; we kant have it bad but onst, and the latter in life we hav it the tuffer it goes with us.
1874 *Josh Billings' Wit and Humour.*

Binyon, (Robert) Laurence 1869–1943

English poet and art critic. He worked at the British Museum (1913–33) and was Norton Professor of Poetry at Harvard (1933–4). He is best remembered for his patriotic elegy 'For the Fallen', which Elgar set to music.

51 With proud thanksgiving, a mother for her children,
England mourns for her dead across the sea.
Flesh of her flesh they were, spirit of her spirit,
Fallen in the cause of the free.
1914 'For the Fallen', in *The Times*, 21 Sep.

52 They shall grow not old, as we that are left grow old:
Age shall not weary them, nor the years condemn.
At the going down of the sun and in the morning
We will remember them.
1914 'For the Fallen', in *The Times*, 21 Sep.

53 Now is the time for the burning of the leaves.
1942 'The Burning of the Leaves'.

54 Rootless hope and fruitless desire are there;
Let them go to the fire, with never a look behind.
The world that was ours is a world that is ours no more.
1942 'The Burning of the Leaves'.

55 Earth cares for her own ruins, naught for ours.
Nothing is certain, only the certain spring.
1942 'The Burning of the Leaves'.

Bioy Casares, Adolfo 1914–99

Argentinian fiction writer, known for his lifelong association with Jorge Luis Borges, with whom he published several anthologies and works of fiction. His own writings are examples of fantastic literature.

56 *La eternidad rotativa puede parecer atroz al espectador; es satisfactoria para sus individuos. Libres de malas noticias y de enfermedades, viven siempre como si fuera la primera vez, sin recordar las anteriores.*
A circular eternity may seem atrocious to the spectator, but it is satisfactory to individuals inside. Free from bad news and disease, they always live as if it were the first time, and do not remember previous times.
1940 *La invención de Morel* (*The Invention of Morel*, 1964).

Bird, Isabella *married name* ***Isabella Bishop*** 1831–1904

English traveller. She travelled and climbed in Australasia, America and the East; then returned to England to marry. When her husband died in 1886, she set off for Tibet and in 1890 travelled between Persia and the Black Sea. In 1894–7 she again visited the Far East, founding hospitals and orphanages, and her last journey was to Africa.

57 A man who any woman might love, but who no sane woman would marry.
1879 Of Rocky Mountain Jim, her guide on her travels on horseback through the Rockies. *A Lady's Life in the Rocky Mountains.*

58 One eye was entirely gone, and the loss made one side of the face repulsive, while the other might have been modelled in marble. 'Desperado' was written in large letters all over him. I almost repented of having sought his acquaintance.
1879 Of Rocky Mountain Jim, her guide on her travels on horseback through the Rockies. *A Lady's Life in the Rocky Mountains.*

59 I am well as long as I live on horseback…sleep out-of-doors, or in a log cabin, and lead in all respects a completely unconventional life. But each time for a few days…I have become civilised, I have found myself rapidly going down again.
1879 *A Lady's Life in the Rocky Mountains.*

60 Japan offers as much novelty perhaps as an excursion to another planet.
1880 *Unbeaten Tracks in Japan: An Account of Travels on Horseback in the Interior 1880* (published 1885).

61 Appropriating the fruits of Christian civilisation, but rejecting the tree from which they spring.
1880 *Unbeaten Tracks in Japan: An Account of Travels on Horseback in the Interior 1880* (published 1885).

62 It is singular that the Japanese, who rarely commit a solecism in taste in their national costume, architecture, or decorative art, seem to be perfectly destitute of perception when they borrow ours.
1880 *Unbeaten Tracks in Japan: An Account of Travels on Horseback in the Interior 1880* (published 1885).

Birkenhead, F(rederick) E(dwin) Smith, 1st Earl of 1872–1930

English Conservative politician and lawyer, a brilliant orator. In the Irish crisis (1914) he opposed Home Rule, but helped to negotiate the Settlement of 1921. He resigned after criticism over his conduct as Secretary of State for India (1924–8) to pursue commerce.

63 The world continues to offer glittering prizes to those who have stout hearts and stout swords.
1923 Rectorial address, Glasgow University, 7 Nov.

64 We have the highest authority for believing that the meek shall inherit the Earth; though I have never found any particular corroboration of this aphorism in the records of Somerset House.
1924 *Contemporary Personalities*, 'Marquess Curzon'.

65 As a matter of fact, we both are, and the only difference between us is that I am trying to be, and you can't help it.
In response to a judge's observation that Smith was being 'extremely offensive'. Quoted in 2nd Earl of Birkenhead *Frederick Edwin Earl of Birkenhead* (1933), vol.1, ch.9.

66 It is not for me, Your Honour, to attempt to fathom the inscrutable workings of Providence.
In reply to a judge's testy inquiry 'What do you suppose I am on the Bench for, Mr Smith?'. Quoted in 2nd Earl of Birkenhead *F. E.: The Life of F. E. Smith, First Earl of Birkenhead* (1959), ch.9.

67 Possibly not, My Lord, but far better informed.

In reply to a judge who had complained 'I have read your case, Mr Smith, and I am no wiser now than I was when I started'. Quoted in 2nd Earl of Birkenhead *F. E.: The Life of F. E. Smith, First Earl of Birkenhead* (1959), ch.9.

68 I do not deal with subtleties; I am only a lawyer.
Quoted in Richard Fountain *The Wit of the Wig* (1968).

69 He has devoted the best years of his life to preparing his impromptu speeches.
Of Winston Churchill. Attributed.

Birney, Earle 1904–95

Canadian poet, professor at the universities of Toronto and, after World War II, British Columbia. His first work was *David and Other Poems* (1942).

70 And now he could only
bar himself in and wait
for the great flint to come singing into his heart.
1952 'Bushed'.

71 Through the cold time
she holds me
with evergreen
devotion
she bears up my whiteness.
1977 'She Is'.

Birns, Harold

New York City Buildings Commissioner (1962–5).

72 OG = PLR × AEB: the opportunity for graft equals the plethora of legal requirements multiplied by the number of architects, engineers and builders.
1963 Formula for bribery in building and housing codes. In the *New York Times*, 2 Oct.

Biro, Lajos 1880–1948

Hungarian screenwriter. He worked for Alexander Korda during the 1930s on various films, including *The Private Life of Henry VIII* (1933) and *The Four Feathers* (1939).

73 The things I've done for England.
1933 Line delivered by Charles Laughton as Henry VIII to Else Lanchester as Anne of Cleves in *The Private Life of Henry VIII* (with Arthur Wimperis).

Bishop, Elizabeth 1911–79

US poet. Her work is highly regarded for its precision, elegance and imagination.

74 The ship's ignored. The iceberg rises
and sinks again; its glassy pinnacles
correct elliptics in the sky.
This is a scene where he who treads the boards
is artlessly rhetorical.
1946 'The Imaginary Iceberg'.

75 The armoured cars of dreams, contrived to let us do
so many a dangerous thing.
1946 'Sleeping Standing Up'.

76 All the untidy activity continues,
awful but cheerful.
1955 'The Bight'.

77 Come like a light in the white mackerel sky,
come like a daytime comet
with a long unnebulous train of words,
from Brooklyn, over the Brooklyn Bridge, on this fine
morning,
please come flying.
1955 'Invitation to Miss Marianne Moore'.

78 What childishness is it that while there's breath of life
in our bodies, we are determined to rush
to see the sun the other way round?
1965 'Questions of Travel'.

79 Oh, must we dream our dreams
and have them, too?
1965 'Questions of Travel'.

80 The art of losing isn't hard to master;
so many things seem filled with the intent
to be lost that their loss is no disaster.
1969 'One Art'.

Bishop, Jim 1907–87

US syndicated columnist.

81 A good writer is not, per se, a good book critic. No more so than a good drunk is automatically a good bartender.
1957 In the New York *Journal-American*, 26 Nov.

82 The peeping Tom of the sciences…men who care not where they are going: they merely want to know where everyone else has been.
1961 Of archaeology. In the New York *Journal-American*, 14 Mar.

Bismarck, Otto Edward Leopold, Fürst von (Prince of) 1815–98

Prussian statesman, Prime Minister of Prussia. He expanded territory at the expense of Denmark and Austria, forming a new German Empire of which he was Chancellor (1871–90) until he resigned, disapproving of the policies of the new Kaiser, Wilhelm II.

83 The great questions of our day cannot be solved by speeches and majority votes but by iron and blood.
1862 Speech to the Prussian Chamber, 30 Sep. He later altered the concluding words to the more commonly quoted 'blood and iron'.

84 Politics is not an exact science.
1863 Speech to the Prussian Chamber, 18 Dec.

85 Anyone who has ever looked into the glazed eyes of a soldier dying on the battlefield will think hard before starting a war.
1867 Speech, Berlin, Aug.

86 If we are to negotiate, I envisage that we shall play an essentially modest role; that of an honest broker who really intends to do business.
1878 Speech to the Reichstag, 19 Feb, on preventing war in Europe.

87 If there is ever another war in Europe, it will come out of some damned silly thing in the Balkans.
1898 Attributed deathbed remark. Quoted in the House of Commons, 16 Aug 1945.

88 My map of Africa lies in Europe. Here lies Russia and here lies France, and we are in the middle. That is my map of Africa.
Remarking on his preoccupation with European, as opposed to colonial, territorial concerns. Quoted in A J P Taylor *The Struggle for Mastery in Europe 1848–1918* (1954), p.294.

Bissell, Claude T(homas) 1916–2000

Canadian scholar and university administrator, President of the University of Toronto (1958–71).

89 It's ironical that the first people to demand free speech are the first people to deny it to others.
1969 Of student protesters who disrupted the appearance of Clark Kerr, former President of Berkeley, at the University of Toronto, 5 Feb. Recalled in *Halfway up Parnassus* (1974).

Black, Arthur 1943–

Canadian broadcaster and humorist.

90 I predict that ashtrays will become as obsolete as spitoons in our lifetime.
1989 *That Old Black Magic*, 'Smoking Can be Dangerous to Your Health'.

Black (of Crossharbour), Conrad Black, Baron 1944–

Canadian newspaper proprietor, Chairman and Chief Executive Officer of Hollinger Inc (1985–2003).

91 Journalists as a group, unlike all other powerful groups, require some protection from themselves, and from their own excesses.
1988 Speech, Annual Dinner of the Canadian Press, 20 Apr, reported in the *Globe and Mail* the following day.

Black, Hugo LaFayette 1886–1971

US lawyer, senator (1927–37) and Associate Justice of the US Supreme Court (1937–71). He strongly supported civil liberties.

92 Without deviation, without exception, without any ifs, buts, or whereases, freedom of speech means you shall not do something to people for views they have, express, speak, or write.
Quoted in Irving Dillard (ed) *One Man's Stand for Freedom* (1963).

Blacker, Valentine 1728–1823

Anglo-Irish soldier.

93 Put your trust in God, my boys, and keep your powder dry.
'Oliver's Advice', collected in E Hayes *Ballads of Ireland* (1856), vol.1, p.192. The words are sometimes attributed to Oliver Cromwell.
► *See Forgy 330:25.*

Blackstone, Sir William 1723–80

English jurist. Called to the bar in 1746, he became King's Counsel and MP (both 1761), Solicitor-General (1763) and a judge of the court of common pleas (1770). He published *Commentaries on the Laws of England* (1765–9).

94 It is better that ten guilty persons escape than one innocent suffer.
1769 *Commentaries on the Laws of England*, vol.4, ch.27. A puzzled visitor is apocryphally said to have remarked, 'Better for whom?'

Blainey, Geoffrey Norman 1930–

Australian economic historian and social commentator. He showed in *The Tyranny of Distance* (1966) how geographical isolation had shaped Australian history and people.

95 The Tyranny of Distance.
1966 Title of book.

Blair, Cherie 1954–

English barrister. She is married to Prime Minister Tony Blair.

96 I am not superwoman. The reality of my daily life is that I am juggling a lot of balls in the air… And sometimes some of the balls get dropped.
2002 Statement following revelations of her links to the convicted conman Peter Foster, 10 Dec.

Blair, Hamish *pseudonym of* Andrew James Fraser Blair 1872–1935

Scottish author and journalist. He moved from England to India where he founded *Empire* (1906) and the *Eastern Bureau* (1912). He wrote a number of short stories as well as articles, sketches and light verse.

97 This bloody town's a bloody cuss—
No bloody trains, no bloody bus,
And no one cares for bloody us—
In bloody Orkney.
1952 'The Bloody Orkneys', stanza 1. First published in Arnold Silcock *Verse and Worse*, 'Queer People'.

98 Best bloody place is bloody bed,
With bloody ice on bloody head,
You might as well be bloody dead,
In bloody Orkney.
1952 'The Bloody Orkneys', last stanza. First published in Arnold Silcock *Verse and Worse*, 'Queer People'.

Blair, Tony (Anthony Charles Lynton) 1953–

Scottish-born Labour politician and barrister, elected Prime Minister in 1997.

99 Labour is the Party of law and order in Britain today—tough on crime and tough on the causes of crime.
1993 Speech as Shadow Home Secretary, Labour Party Conference, Sep.

1 The art of leadership is saying no, not yes. It is very easy to say yes.
1994 In *The Mail on Sunday*, 2 Oct.

2 I didn't come into politics to change the Labour Party. I came into politics to change the country.
1995 Speech at the Labour Party Conference, 30 Sep.

3 Ask me my three main priorities for Government, and I tell you: education, education and education.
1996 Speech at the Labour Party Conference, 1 Oct.

4 People have to know that we will run from the centre and govern from the centre.
1997 Speech given to The Newspaper Society, London, 16 Mar.

5 We are not the masters. The people are the masters. We are the servants of the people… What the electorate gives, the electorate can take away.
1997 Addressing Labour MPs on the first day of the new Parliament, 7 May.

6 Sometimes I forget I'm Prime Minister. To me, I'm just Tony Blair.
1997 In *The Sun*, 29 Jul.

7 She was the people's princess and this is how she will stay.
1997 On the death of Diana, Princess of Wales. In a press statement, 1 Sep.

8 This is not the time for soundbites. I can feel the hand of

history on our shoulders.
1998 On peace talks in Northern Ireland. In the *Daily Telegraph*, 8 Apr.

9 In future, welfare will be a hand-up, not a hand-out.
1999 Lecture, London, 18 Mar.

10 Britain must, and I am sure will, stand shoulder-to-shoulder with the United States of America and peaceful nations across the world in deploying every possible resource to bring to justice the people responsible, and make sure terrorism never prevails.
2001 Statement, 11 Sep.

11 Jesus was a moderniser.
Quoted in John Rentoul *Tony Blair: Prime Minister* (2001).

12 Every time I have asked us to go to war, I have hated it. I spent months trying to get Milosevic to stop ethnic cleansing in Kosovo, delaying action while we negotiated endlessly.
2003 Speech at the Labour Party Conference, 15 Feb.

13 At every stage, we should seek to avoid war. But if the threat cannot be removed peacefully, please let us not fall for the delusion that it can be safely ignored.
2003 Speech at the Labour Party Conference, 15 Feb.

14 To retreat now, I believe, would put at hazard all that we hold dearest, turn the United Nations back into a talking shop, stifle the first steps of progress in the Middle East; leave the Iraqi people to the mercy of events on which we would have relinquished all power to influence for the better.
2003 Speech to the House of Commons, 18 Mar.

15 I somehow feel I am not being entirely persuasive in certain quarters.
2004 Following protests from the public gallery during a debate on the Iraq war in the House of Commons, 4 Feb.

16 The good news is that it is easy to describe the problem in Iraq today, the bad news is it's tough to tackle it.
2004 Press conference, 22 Apr.

17 There will be no cutting and running in Iraq.
2004 Press conference, 17 May.

18 Now is not the time for a change in direction…but a change in gear.
2004 Press conference, 15 Jun.

Blake, Eubie James Hubert 1883–1983

US jazz musician.

19 If I'd known I was gonna live this long, I'd have taken better care of myself.
1983 Quoted in the *Observer*, 13 Feb. He died 5 days after his 100th birthday.

Blake, Peter 1932–

English painter. A pioneer of the pop art movement in Britain, his most widely-known work is the cover design for the Beatles' album *Sergeant Pepper's Lonely Hearts Club Band* (1967).

20 Most artists go potty as they get older: dafter and madder as they get more celibate. So I am consciously going to do that.
2004 In *The Guardian*, 3 Jun.

Blake, William 1757–1827

English poet, painter, engraver and mystic. His works range from the lyrical *Songs of Innocence* (1789) and *Songs of Experience* (1794) to the mystical poems of *The Marriage of Heaven and Hell* (1791). His best-known engravings are in *The Illustrations to the Book of Job* (1826).

21 Whether on Ida's shady brow,
Or in the chambers of the East,
The chambers of the sun that now
From ancient melody have ceased.
1783 *Poetical Sketches*, 'To The Muses'.

22 How have you left the ancient love
That bards of old enjoyed in you!
The sound is forced, the notes are few!
1783 *Poetical Sketches*, 'To The Muses'.

23 The hills tell each other, and the listening
Valleys hear; all our longing eyes are turned
Up to thy holy feet visit our clime.
Come o'er the eastern hills and let our winds
Kiss thy perfumed garments; let us taste
Thy morn and evening breath. Scatter thy pearls
Upon our love-sick land that mourns for thee.
1783 *Poetical Sketches*, 'To Spring'.

24 O thou who passest through our valleys in
Thy strength, curb thy fierce steeds, ally the heat
That flames from their large nostrils! thou, O Summer,
Beneath our oaks hast slept while we beheld
With joy thy ruddy limbs and flourishing hair.
1783 *Poetical Sketches*, 'To Summer'.

25 O Autumn, laden with fruit, and stained
With the blood of grape, pass not, but sit
Beneath my shady roof; there thou may'st rest,
And tune thy jolly voice to my fresh pipe,
And all the daughters of the year shall dance!
Sing now the lusty song of fruits and flowers.
1783 *Poetical Sketches*, 'To Autumn'.

26 O Winter! bar thine adamantine doors.
The north is thine—there hast thou built thy dark
Deep-founded habitation. Shake not thy roofs,
Nor bend thy pillars with thine iron car.
1783 *Poetical Sketches*, 'To Winter'.

27 Does the eagle know what's in the pit
Or wilt thou go ask the mole?
Can wisdom be put in a silver rod,
Or Love in a golden bowl.
1789 Thel's Motto. *The Book of Thel*.

28 Piping down the valleys wild,
Piping songs of pleasant glee,
On a cloud I saw a child,
And he laughing said to me,
'Pipe a song about a lamb!'
So I piped with merry cheer.
'Piper, pipe that song again!'
So I piped. He wept to hear.
1789 *Songs of Innocence*, 'Introduction'.

29 Little lamb, who made thee?
Dost thou know who made thee?
Gave thee life and bid thee feed
By the stream and o'er the mead;
Gave thee clothing of delight,
Softest clothing, woolly, bright;
Gave thee such a tender voice,
Making all the vales rejoice?

Little lamb, who made thee?
Dost thou know who made thee?
1789 *Songs of Innocence*, 'The Lamb'.

30 My mother bore me in the southern wild,
And I am black, but O! my soul is white;
White as an angel is the English child,
But I am black as if bereaved of light.
1789 *Songs of Innocence*, 'The Little Black Boy'.

31 For Mercy has a human heart
Pity a human face:
And Love, the human form divine,
And Peace, the human dress.
1789 *Songs of Innocence*, 'The Divine Image'.

32 And all must love the human form,
In heathen, Turk or Jew;
Where mercy, Love and Pity dwell
There God is dwelling too.
1789 *Songs of Innocence*, 'The Divine Image'.

33 When my mother died I was very young,
And my father sold me while yet my tongue
Could scarcely cry weep weep weep weep.
So your chimneys I sweep, and in soot I sleep.
1789 *Songs of Innocence*, 'The Chimney Sweep'.

34 'Father! father! where are you going?
O do not walk so fast.
Speak, father, speak to your little boy,
Or else I shall be lost.'
1789 *Songs of Innocence*, 'The Little Boy Lost'.

35 He kissed the hand and by the hand led
And to his mother brought,
Who in sorrow pale, through the lonely dale,
Her little boy weeping sought.
1789 *Songs of Innocence*, 'The Little Boy Found'.

36 Then cherish pity, lest you drive an angel from your door.
1789 *Songs of Innocence*, 'Holy Thursday'.

37 Without contraries is no progression. Attraction and repulsion, reason and energy, love and hate, are necessary to human existence.
1790 *The Marriage of Heaven and Hell*, 'The Argument'.

38 Energy is Eternal Delight.
1790 *The Marriage of Heaven and Hell*, 'The Voice of the Devil'.

39 The road of excess leads to the palace of wisdom.
1790 *The Marriage of Heaven and Hell*, 'Proverbs of Hell'.

40 He who desires and acts not, breeds pestilence.
1790 *The Marriage of Heaven and Hell*, 'Proverbs of Hell'.

41 Eternity is in love with the productions of time.
1790 *The Marriage of Heaven and Hell*, 'Proverbs of Hell'.

42 Prisons are built with stones of Law, brothels with bricks of Religion.
1790 *The Marriage of Heaven and Hell*, 'Proverbs of Hell'.

43 The tygers of wrath are wiser than the horses of instruction.
1790 *The Marriage of Heaven and Hell*, 'Proverbs of Hell'.

44 The Pride of the peacock is the glory of God.
The lust of the goat is the bounty of God.
The wrath of the lion is the wisdom of God.
The nakedness of woman is the work of God.
1790 *The Marriage of Heaven and Hell*, 'Proverbs of Hell'.

45 Sooner murder an infant in its cradle than nurse unacted desires.
1790 *The Marriage of Heaven and Hell*, 'Proverbs of Hell'.

46 If the doors of perception were cleansed everything would appear to man as it is, infinite.
1790 *The Marriage of Heaven and Hell*, 'A Memorable Fancy', plate 14. Aldous Huxley used this phrase as the title of his work *The Doors of Perception* (1954).

47 Mutual forgiveness of each vice,
Such are the Gates of Paradise.
1793 *The Gates of Paradise*, prologue.

48 He who binds to himself a Joy
Doth the winged life destroy;
But he who kisses the Joy as it flies
Lives in Eternity's sunrise.
1793 *MS Notebooks*, p.105.

49 Never pain to tell thy love
Love that never told can be;
For the gentle wind does move
Silently, invisibly.
1793 *MS Notebooks*, p.115.

50 Hear the voice of the Bard!
Who present, past and future sees.
1794 *Songs of Experience*, 'Introduction'.

51 Love seeketh not itself to please,
Nor for itself hath any care,
But for another gives its ease,
And builds a heaven in hell's despair.
1794 *Songs of Experience*, 'The Clod and the Pebble'.

52 Love seeketh only self to please,
To bind another to its delight,
Joys in another's loss of ease
And builds a hell in heaven's despite.
1794 *Songs of Experience*, 'The Clod and the Pebble'.

53 Ah, sunflower, weary of time,
Who countest the steps of the sun,
Seeking after that sweet golden clime
Where the traveller's journey is done;
Where the youth pined away with desire
And the pale virgin shrouded in snow
Arise from their graves, and aspire
Where my sunflower wishes to go.
1794 *Songs of Experience*, 'Ah! Sunflower'.

54 O rose, thou art sick!
The invisible worm
That flies in the night,
In the howling storm,
Has found out thy bed
Of crimson joy,
And his dark secret love
Does thy life destroy.
1794 *Songs of Experience*, 'The Sick Rose'.

55 Is this a holy thing to see
In a rich fruitful land,
Babes reduced to misery,
Fed with cold and usurous hand?
1794 *Songs of Experience*, 'Holy Thursday'.

56 I went to the Garden of Love,
And saw what I never had seen:
A chapel was built in the midst
Where I used to play on the green.
1794 *Songs of Experience*, 'The Garden of Love'.

57 And I saw it was filled with graves,

And tomb-stones where flowers should be;
And priests in black gowns were walking their rounds,
And blinding with briars my joys and desires.
1794 *Songs of Experience*, 'The Garden of Love'.

58 I wander through each charter'd street,
Near where the charter'd Thames does flow,
And mark in every face I meet
Marks of weakness, marks of woe.
1794 *Songs of Experience*, 'London'.

59 I was angry with my friend:
I told my wrath, my wrath did end.
I was angry with my foe:
I told it not, my wrath did grow.
1794 *Songs of Experience*, 'A Poison Tree'.

60 My mother groaned! my father wept.
Into the dangerous world I leapt,
Helpless, naked, piping loud
Like a fiend hid in a cloud.
1794 *Songs of Experience*, 'Infant Sorrow'.

61 Tyger! Tyger! burning bright
In the forests of the night,
What immortal hand or eye
Could frame thy fearful symmetry?
1794 *Songs of Experience*, 'The Tyger'.

62 When the stars threw down their spears,
And watered heaven with their tears,
Did he smile his work to see?
Did he who made the Lamb make thee?
1794 *Songs of Experience*, 'The Tyger'.

63 Dear Mother, dear Mother, the Church is cold,
But the Ale-house is healthy and pleasant and warm.
1794 *Songs of Experience*, 'The Little Vagabond'.

64 Mock on, mock on, Voltaire Rousseau;
Mock on, mock on, 'tis all in vain!
You throw the sand against the wind,
And the wind blows it back again.
1800–3 *MS Notebooks*, p.7.

65 O why was I born with a different face?
Why was I not born like the rest of my race?
1803 Letter to Thomas Butts, 16 Aug.

66 To see a world in a grain of sand,
And heaven in a wild flower,
Hold infinity in the palm of your hand,
And eternity in an hour.
c.1803 *Auguries of Innocence*, l.1–4.

67 A robin red breast in a cage
Puts all Heaven in a rage.
c.1803 *Auguries of Innocence*, l.5–6.

68 Man was made for Joy and Woe,
And when this we rightly know,
Thro' the world we safely go.
Joy and Woe are woven fine,
A clothing for the soul divine.
c.1803 *Auguries of Innocence*, l.56–60.

69 The strongest poison ever known
Came from Ceasar's laurel crown.
c.1803 *Auguries of Innocence*, l.97–8.

70 The whore and gambler, by the state
Licensed build that nation's fate.
The harlot's cry from street to street
Shall weave old England's winding sheet.
c.1803 *Auguries of Innocence*, l.113–6

71 We are led to believe a Lie
When we see with, not thro' the Eye.
c.1803 *Auguries of Innocence*, l.125–6

72 The fields from Islington to Marybone,
To Primrose Hill and Saint John's Wood,
Were builded over with pillars of gold;
And there Jerusalem's pillars stood.
c.1804–1807 *Jerusalem*, plate 27.

73 He who would do good to another man must do it in Minute Particulars.
General Good is the plea of the scoundrel, hypocrite, and flatterer;
For Art and Science cannot exist but in minutely organized Particulars.
c.1804–1807 *Jerusalem*, plate 55.

74 I gave you the end of the golden string;
Only wind it into a ball,
It will lead you in at Heaven's gate,
Built in Jerusalem's wall.
c.1804–1807 *Jerusalem*, plate 77.

75 I care not whether a man is good or evil; all that I care
Is whether he is a wise man or a fool. Go! put off Holiness,
And put on intellect, or my thunderous hammer shall drive thee,
To wrath which thou condemnest, till thou obey my voice.
c.1804–1807 *Jerusalem*, plate 91.

76 Painters are noted for being dissipated and wild.
c.1808 *Annotations to Sir Joshua Reynolds' Discourses*.

77 The man who never in his mind and thoughts travelled to heaven is no artist.
c.1808 *Annotations to Sir Joshua Reynolds' Discourses*.

78 What has Reasoning to do with the Art of Painting?
c.1808 *Annotations to Sir Joshua Reynolds' Discourses*.

79 Knowledge of ideal beauty is not to be acquired. It is born with us. Innate ideas are in every man, born with him; they are truly himself.
c.1808 *Annotations to Sir Joshua Reynolds' Discourses*.

80 When Sir Joshua Reynolds died
All Nature was degraded;
The King dropp'd a tear into the Queen's ear,
And all his pictures faded.
c.1808 *Annotations to Sir Joshua Reynolds' Discourses*.

81 Thy friendship oft has made my heart to ache:
Do be my enemy—for friendship's sake.
1808–11 *MS Notebooks*, 'To H[ayley]', p.37.

82 And did those feet in ancient time
Walk upon England's mountains green?
And was the holy Lamb of God
On England's pleasant pastures seen?
1809 *Milton*, preface. Stanza 1.

83 And did the Countenance Divine
Shine forth upon our clouded hills?
And was Jerusalem builded here
Among these dark Satanic mills?
1809 *Milton*, preface. Stanza 2.

84 Bring me my bow of burning gold!

Bring me my arrows of desire!
Bring me my spear! O clouds, unfold!
Bring me my chariot of fire!
1809 *Milton*, preface. Stanza 3.

85 I will not cease from mental fight,
Nor shall my sword sleep in my hand,
Till we have built Jerusalem
In England's green and pleasant land.
1809 *Milton*, preface. Stanza 4.

86 God appears and God is light
To those poor souls who dwell in night,
But does a human form display
To those who dwell in realms of day.
1809 *Milton*, 'And Did Those Feet In Ancient Time'.

Blanch, Lesley 1904–

English biographer, traveller and cookery writer.

87 She was an Amazon. Her whole life was spent riding at breakneck speed towards the wilder shores of love.
1954 *The Wilder Shores of Love*, pt.2, ch.1.

Blanchflower, Danny (Robert Dennio) 1926–93

Northern Ireland-born footballer. He won numerous titles as captain of Tottenham Hotspur in the early 1960s and collected a total of 56 caps playing for Northern Ireland before retiring to become a noted football commentator and columnist.

88 We try to equalize before the others have scored.
1958 Explaining his tactics as captain of Northern Ireland. Quoted in Colin Jarman *The Guinness Dictionary of Sports Quotations* (1990).

89 The great fallacy is that the game is first and last about winning. It's nothing of the kind. The game is about glory. It's about doing things in style, with a flourish, about going out and beating the other lot, not waiting for them to die of boredom.
Quoted in Hunter Davis *The Glory Game* (1972).

Blass, Bill (William Ralph) 1922–2002

US fashion designer.

90 When in doubt wear red.
1982 In news summaries, 31 Dec.

Blavatsky, Helena Petrovna 1831–91

Russian-born mystic, founder of the Theosophical Society. Her works include *Isis Unveiled* (1877).

91 'Theosophy' is the essence of all religion and of absolute truth, a drop of which only underlies every creed.
1889 *The Key to Theosophy.*

92 Theosophy, on earth, is like the white ray of the spectrum, and each religion only one of the seven colours.
1889 *The Key to Theosophy.*

Blest Gana, Alberto 1830–1920

Chilean novelist and Ambassador to France and England. He lived in Paris until the end of his career. He pioneered the documentary social novel in Spanish American literature.

93 *Entre nosotros el dinero ha hecho desaparecer más preocupaciones de familia que en las viejas sociedades europeas. En éstas hay lo que llaman aristocracia de dinero, que jamás alcanza con su poder…a hacer olvidar enteramente la oscuridad de la cuna, al paso que en Chile…todo va cediendo su puesto a la riqueza.*
Among us, money has dissolved more worries than among ancient European societies. The latter have what they call the moneyed aristocracy, which, despite all its power, never gets to forget its humble origins; on the other hand, in Chile everything yields to wealth.
1862 *Martín Rivas*, ch.2 (translated 1918).

Blinder, Alan 1945–

US economist, Professor at Princeton University (1982–) and Vice Chair of the Federal Reserve System Board (1994–6).

94 Economists have the least influence on policy where they know the most and are most agreed…the most influence on policy where they know the least and disagree most.
1987 *Hard Heads, Soft Hearts.*

95 If you try to give an on-the-one-hand-or-the-other-hand answer, only one of the hands tends to get quoted.
1995 On economic forecasting. In the *Wall Street Journal*, 23 Jun.

Bliss, Sir Arthur 1891–1975

English composer, Music Director of the BBC (1942–4) and Master of the Queen's Music (from 1953). His compositions, sometimes avant-garde, included ballets, an opera, chamber music and film scores.

96 The jazz band can be used for artificial excitement and aphrodisiac purposes, but not for spreading eternal truths.
1941 'Music Policy'.

Blix, Hans 1928–

Swedish diplomat. He was appointed Executive Chairman of the UN Monitoring, Verification and Inspection Commission for Iraq in 2000.

97 We have not found any smoking guns.
2003 Of weapons inspections in Iraq. To reporters, 9 Jan.

98 Iraq appears not to have come to a genuine acceptance—not even today—of the disarmament which was demanded of it and which it needs to carry out to win the confidence of the world and to live in peace.
2003 Security Council update on weapons inspections in Iraq, 27 Jan.

99 These reports do not contend that weapons of mass destruction remain in Iraq, but nor do they exclude that possibility. They point to lack of evidence and inconsistencies, which raise question marks, which must be straightened out, if weapons dossiers are to be closed and confidence is to arise.
2003 Security Council update on weapons inspections in Iraq, 27 Jan.

Blixen, Karen, Baroness *pseudonym* *Isak Dinesen* 1885–1962

Danish novelist and story teller. Her book *Out of Africa* (1938) is set on the Kenyan coffee plantation she managed with her husband (also cousin) Baron Bror Blixen. She was divorced in 1921, and returned to Denmark in 1931.

1 What is man, when you come to think upon him, but a minutely set, ingenious machine for turning, with infinite artfulness, the red wine of Shiraz into urine?
1934 *Seven Gothic Tales*, 'The Dreamers'.

2 The true aristocracy and the true proletariat of the world are both in understanding with tragedy. To them it is the fundamental principle of God, and the key, the minor key, to existence. They differ in this way from the bourgeoisie of all classes, who deny tragedy, who will not tolerate it, and to whom the word tragedy means in itself unpleasantness.
1937 *Out of Africa*, pt.5, ch.1.

Bloom, Allan 1930–92

US writer and educator, Professor of Political Science at the University of Chicago. His best-known work is *The Closing of the American Mind* (1987).

3 The liberally educated person is one who is able to resist the easy and preferred answers, not because he is obstinate but because he knows others worthy of consideration.
1987 *The Closing of the American Mind*, preface.

4 Education is the taming or demonstration of the soul's raw passions—not suppressing them or excising them, which would deprive the soul of its energy—but forming and informing them as art.
1987 *The Closing of the American Mind*.

Bloom, André Borisovich, Anthony, Metropolitan of Sourozh 1914–2003

Russian churchman and writer, Head of the Russian Orthodox Church in Great Britain and Ireland.

5 It is not the constant thought of their sins, but the vision of the holiness of God that makes the saints aware of their own sinfulness.
1966 *Living Prayer*.

6 A miracle is not the breaking of the laws of the fallen world. It is the re-establishment of the laws of the kingdom.
1966 *Living Prayer*.

Bloom, Harold 1930–

US literary critic and writer, Professor of English (1965–77) and Humanities (1974–) at Yale. His many works include *The Breaking of the Vessels* (1981).

7 The most beautiful prose paragraph yet written by any American.
1991 On the opening of ch.19 of Mark Twain's *Huckleberry Finn*. *The Western Canon*.

Blough, Roger M(iles) 1904–85

US industrialist.

8 Steel prices cause inflation like wet sidewalks cause rain.
1967 In *Forbes*, 1 Aug.

Blunden, Edmund Charles 1896–1974

English poet and critic. He served in World War I, an experience reflected both in his poetry and in his prose work *Undertones of War* (1928), but is essentially a nature poet.

9 All things they have in common, being so poor,
And their one fear, Death's shadow at the door.
Each sundown makes them mournful, each sunrise
Brings back the brightness in their failing eyes.
1920 'Almswomen'.

10 And night this toppling reed, still as the dead
The great pike lies, the murderous patriarch,
Watching the water-pit shelving and dark
Where through the plash his lithe bright vassals tread.
1920 'The Pike'.

11 Unrecorded, unrenowned,
Men from whom my ways begin,
Here I know you by your ground
But I know you not within—
There is silence, there survives
Not a moment of your lives.
1922 'Forefathers'.

12 Then is not death at watch
Within those secret waters?
What wants he but to catch
Earth's heedless sons and daughters?
1925 'The Midnight Skaters'.

13 Dance on this ball-floor thin and wan,
Use him as though you love him;
Court him, elude him, reel and pass,
And let him hate you through the glass.
1925 'The Midnight Skaters'.

14 Cuinchy...was a slaughter yard... Who that had been there for but a few hours could ever forget the sullen sorcery and mad lineaments of Cuinchy?
1928 *Undertones of War*, 'IV. The Sudden Depths'. Cuinchy, near Arras, was the scene of heavy fighting in 1914.

15 This was my country and it may be yet,
But something flew between me and the sun.
1928 'The Resignation'.

16 I have been young, and now am not too old;
And I have seen the righteous forsaken,
His health, his honour and his quality taken.
This is not what we were formerly told.
1929 'Report On Experience'.

17 Mastery in poetry consists largely in the instinct for not ruining or smothering or tinkering with moments of vision.
1930 'Leigh Hunt'.

18 I am for the woods against the world,
But are the woods for me?
1931 'The Kiss'.

19 Cricket to us was more than play,
It was a worship in the summer sun.
'Pride of the Village'. Quoted in Alan Ross (ed) *The Penguin Cricketer's Companion* (1978).

Blunkett, David 1947–

English Labour politician. Blind from birth, he has been MP for Sheffield (Brightside) since 1987 and Home Secretary since 2001.

20 Let me say this very slowly indeed. Watch my lips: no selection by examination or interview under a Labour Government.
1995 Speech at the Labour Party Conference, 5 Oct.

21 They should go back home and re-create their countries

which we have freed from tyranny, whether it be Kosovo or now Afghanistan. I have no sympathy whatsoever with young men in their twenties who do not get back home and rebuild their countries.
2002 On asylum seekers, 18 Sep.

22 I haven't given up on the idea that we're going to nail this individual.
2004 On the convicted football hooligan Garry Mann, who escaped his sentence when he was repatriated from Portugal before the paperwork was complete, 20 Jun.

Blythe, Ronald George 1922–

English writer. He is best known for his book *Akenfield* (1963), a portrait of an English village told in interviews with linking commentary.

23 As for the British churchman, he goes to church as he goes to the bathroom, with the minimum of fuss and with no explanation if he can help it.
1963 *The Age of Illusion*, ch.12.

24 An industrial worker would sooner have a £5 note but a countryman must have praise.
1969 *Akenfield*, ch.5.

25 Suffolk used to worship Sunday, not God.
1969 *Akenfield*, ch.6.

26 One of the reasons why old people make so many journeys into the past is to satisfy themselves that it is still there.
1979 *The View in Winter*, introduction.

Boccioni, Umberto 1882–1916

Italian artist, futurist painter and sculptor. A key figure in the drafting of the Futurist Manifesto (1910), he later turned to sculpture, attempting to convey motion and light in three-dimensional form.

27 It is necessary to destroy the pretended nobility, entirely literary and traditional, of marble and bronze... The sculptor can use twenty different materials, or even more, in a single work, provided that the plastic emotion requires it.
1912 In the *Technical Manifesto of Futurist Sculpture* (11 Apr, Milan).

Bodenheim, Maxwell 1892–1954

US writer and critic.

28 Poetry is the impish attempt to paint the color of the wind.
Quoted in Ben Hecht's play *Winkelberg* (1958).

Boethius, Anicius Manlius Severinus c.480–524 AD

Roman philosopher and statesman. Under Theodoric he became consul and later chief minister, but was accused of treason and executed. While in prison he wrote *De con-solatione philosophiae* (*The Consolation of Philosophy*, 523).

29 *Nam in omni adversitate fortunae infelicissimum est genus infortunii, fuisse felicem.*
In all adversity of fortune, the most wretched kind is once to have been happy.
523 *De consolatione philosophiae*, bk.2, pt.4 (translated by V E Watts).

Bogan, Louise 1897–1970

US poet and critic, poetry editor of the *New Yorker* for many years. Her work is intense and deeply personal.

30 Women have no wideness in them
They are provident instead,
Content in the tight hot cell of their hearts
To eat dusty bread.
1923 'Women'.

31 But childhood prolonged cannot remain a fairy-land. It becomes a hell.
1940 On Katherine Mansfield. 'Childhood's False Eden'.

32 The intellectual...is the fine nervous flower of the bourgeoisie.
1943 'Some Notes on Popular and Unpopular Poetry'.

Bogarde, Sir Dirk *originally* ***Derek Jules Ulric Niven van den Bogaerde*** 1921–99

English actor and novelist.

33 It's always full of all the people I'd hoped were dead.
On the Cannes Film Festival. Quoted in Barry Norman *And Why Not?* (2002).

Bogart, John B 1848–1921

US journalist, an early editor of the *New York Sun*.

34 When a dog bites a man, that is not news, because it happens so often. But if a man bites a dog, that is news.
Quoted in F M O'Brien *The Story of the Sun* (1918), ch.10. The phrase is often attributed to Charles A Dana.

Bohlen, Charles Eustis 1904–74

US diplomat and Soviet specialist, Ambassador to Russia (1953–7, 1959–61).

35 A non-Communist premier with Communist ministers would be like a woman trying to stay half pregnant.
Of Winston Churchill's suggestion that the West share spheres of influence with Joseph Stalin in the post-war development of the Balkans. Quoted in Walter Isaacson and Evan Thomas *The Wise Men* (1986).

36 There are two ways you can tell when a man is lying...when he says he can drink champagne all night and not get drunk...[and] when he says he understands Russians.
Quoted in the *New York Times*, 26 Dec 1993.

Boileau (Despréaux), Nicolas 1636–1711

French critic. His works include satires (1660–6), epistles, critical dissertations (particularly the influential *L'Art poétique*, 'The Art of Poetry', 1674), epigrams and translations.

37 *Si j'écris quatre mots, j'en effacerai trois.*
If I write four words, I strike out three of them.
1665 *Satire no.2 A M Molière*.

38 Often, the fear of one evil leads us into inflicting one that is worse.
1674 *L'Art poétique*.

Bok, Derek 1930–

US educator, President of Harvard University (1971–91) and Professor Emeritus there from 1991. His works include *Beyond the Ivory Tower: Social Responsibilities of the Modern University* (1982).

39 If you think education is expensive—try ignorance.
1979 In *Town and Country*, May.

Bold, Alan 1943–98

Scottish poet, biographer and critic, a prolific full-time writer and anthologizer since 1967. He wrote an award-winning biography of Hugh MacDiarmid (1989).

40 In Scotland, land of the omnipotent No.
1969 'A Memory of Death'.

41 That which once united man
Now drives him apart. We are not helpless
Creatures crashing onwards irresistibly to doom.
There is time for everything and time to choose
For everything. We are that time, that choice.
Everybody gets what he deserves.
1969 'June 1967 at Buchenwald'.

42 The poet lives as long as his lines are imprinted on the minds of his readers.
1989 *MacDiarmid*, epilogue.

Bolingbroke, Henry St John, 1st Viscount 1678–1751

English Jacobite statesman, joint leader of the Tory Party. On the death of Queen Anne he fled to France, where he wrote *Reflections on Exile* (1714). He also wrote the influential *Idea of a Patriot King* (1749).

43 What a world is this, and how does fortune banter us!
1714 Letter to Jonathan Swift, 3 Aug.

44 Faction is to party what the superlative is to the positive. Party is a political evil, and faction is the worst of all parties.
1738 *Idea of a Patriot King*. Published in 1749.

Bolívar, Simón 1783–1830

Venezuelan soldier and statesman. He led revolutions against Spanish rule in New Granada (Colombia), Peru and Upper Peru (Bolivia). He became President of Colombia (1821–30) and of Peru (1823–9), and was a gifted prose writer.

45 *Más grande es el odio que nos ha inspirado la Península, que el mar que nos separa de ella; menos difícil es unir los dos continentes, que reconciliar los espíritus de ambos países.*
The hate that the Iberian peninsula has inspired in us is broader than the sea which separates us from it; it is less difficult to join both continents than to join both countries' souls.
1815 'Carta de Jamaica' (translated as *The Jamaica Letter*, 1977).

Bolles, Richard Nelson 1927–

US writer, famous for his manual for job hunters.

46 What Color is Your Parachute?
1972 Title of a vocational guidance book published annually.

Bolt, Robert Oxton 1924–95

English playwright and screenwriter. His best-known work is the play *A Man for All Seasons* (1960). His screenplays include *Dr Zhivago* (1965) and *The Mission* (1986).

47 A Man for All Seasons.
1960 Play title, originally said by Robert Whittington about his contemporary Sir Thomas More, the central character in Bolt's play.

48 It profits a man nothing to give his soul for the whole world…
But for Wales—!
1960 Thomas More. *A Man for All Seasons*.

49 To be human at all… we must stand fast a little—even at the risk of being heroes.
1960 Thomas More. *A Man for All Seasons*.

50 The courts of Europe are a jungle, compared to which your jungles here are a well-kept garden.
1986 Line delivered by Ray Mc Anally as Cardinal Altamirano in *The Mission*.

Bonavia, David 1940–88

British journalist and Editor of the *Far East Economic Review*. His main field of interest was China.

51 Their civilization is based on the most forthrightly materialistic value system in the history of mankind. If they see pie in the sky, they immediately start figuring out how to get it down onto the dinner table.
1961 *The Chinese*.

Bond, Carrie Jacobs 1862–1946

US songwriter and lyricist.

52 When you come to the end of a perfect day,
And you sit alone with your thought,
While the chimes ring out with a carol gay
For the joy that the day has brought,
Do you think what the end of a perfect day
Can mean to a tired heart,
When the sun goes down with a flaming ray,
And the dear friends have to part?
1910 'A Perfect Day'.

Bonds, Barry Lamar 1964–

US baseball player.

53 Don't talk about him no more.
2003 On the legendary Babe Ruth, whose slugging record he broke. Quoted by Associated Press, 16 Jul.

Bone, Sir David 1874–1959

Scottish novelist. He was a high-ranking sailor, and wrote novels about the sea.

54 It's 'Damn you, Jack—I'm all right!' with you chaps.
1910 *The Brassbounder*, ch.3.

Bonham Carter, Helena 1966–

English actress.

55 It is acting in its purest form. You have to act with your eyes.
2001 On playing a chimp in *Planet of the Apes*. In the *Observer*, 30 Dec.

Bonhoeffer, Dietrich 1906–45

German Lutheran pastor and theologian, executed for implication in a plot against Hitler. His theology, especially his plea for 'religionless Christianity', was influential in mid- and late-20c theology.

56 The Church knows nothing of a sacredness of war. The Church which prays 'Our Father' asks God only for peace.
1932 Draft of a new Catechism with F Hildebrandt, in

Gesammelte Schriften, vol.3 (1947, translated by E Robinson and J Bowden in *No Rusty Sword*, 1965).

57 The cross is God's truth about us, and therefore it is the only power that can make us truthful. When we know the cross we are no longer afraid of the truth.
1937 *Nachfolge* (translated as *The Cost of Discipleship*).

58 *Billige Gnade ist Gnade ohne Nachfolge, Gnade ohne Kreuz, Gnade ohne den lebendigen, menschgewordenen Jesus Christus.*
Cheap grace is grace without discipleship, grace without the cross, grace without Jesus Christ, living and incarnate.
1937 *Nachfolge* (translated as *The Cost of Discipleship*).

59 If religion is only a garment of Christianity—and even this garment has looked very different at different times—then what is religionless Christianity?
1944 Letter to Eberhardt Bethge, 30 Apr. Collected in *Widerstand und Ergebung* (1951, translated 1953).

60 Death is the supreme Festival on the road to freedom.
1945 Letter, collected in *Widerstand und Ergebung* (1951, translated 1953).

61 *Es ist der Vorzug und das Wesen der Starken, dass sie die großen Entscheidungsfragen stellen und zu ihnen klar Stellung nehmen können. Die Schwachen müssen sich immer zwischen Alternativen entscheiden, die nicht die ihren sind.*
It is the nature, and the advantage, of strong people that they can bring out the crucial questions and form a clear opinion about them. The weak always have to decide between alternatives that are not their own.
1951 *Widerstand und Ergebung*, 'Ein paar Gedanken über Verschiedenes' (translated 1953).

62 *Ein Gott, der sich von uns beweisen ließe, wäre ein Götze.*
A God who let us prove his existence would be an idol.
'Glaubst du, so hast du'. Versuch eines Lutherischen Katchismus ('If you believe it, you have it'. Attempt at a Lutheran Catechism). Quoted in E Robinson and J Bowden *No Rusty Sword* (1965).

Bono *real name* ***Paul Hewson*** 1960–

Irish rock singer with the band U2. He is also known for his charity campaigning and political views.

63 They didn't have Kalashnikovs but U2 tickets in their hands.
1997 Of the audience at the U2 concert in Sarajevo, 24 Sep.

64 Elvis ate America before America ate him.
2004 On Elvis Presley. In *Rolling Stone*, 15 Apr.

Book of Common Prayer

The idea of a new prayer book was developed initially by Thomas Cranmer during the reigns of Edward VI and Elizabeth I. The final text was published in 1662.

65 Dearly beloved brethren, the Scripture moveth us in sundry places to acknowledge and confess our manifold sins and wickedness.
Morning Prayer, Sentences of the Scriptures.

66 We have erred and strayed from thy ways like lost sheep. We have followed too much the devices and desires of our own hearts. We have offended against thy holy laws. We have left undone those things which we ought to have done. And we have done those things which we ought not to have done. And there is no health in us.
Morning Prayer, General Confession.

67 A godly, righteous, and sober life.
Morning Prayer, General Confession.

68 And forgive us our trespasses, As we forgive them that trespass against us.
Morning Prayer, the Lord's Prayer.

69 Glory be to the Father, and to the Son: and to the Holy Ghost;
As it was in the beginning, is now and ever shall be: world without end. Amen.
Morning Prayer, Gloria.

70 Lord God of Sabaoth.
Morning Prayer, Te Deum.

71 I believe in God the Father Almighty, Maker of heaven and earth: And in Jesus Christ his only Son our Lord, Who was conceived by the Holy Ghost, Born of the Virgin Mary, Suffered under Pontius Pilate, Was crucified, dead, and buried: He descended into hell; The third day he rose again from the dead; He ascended into heaven, And sitteth on the right hand of God the Father Almighty; From thence he shall come to judge the quick and the dead. I believe in the Holy Ghost; The holy Catholick Church; The Communion of Saints; The Forgiveness of sins; The Resurrection of the body, And the life everlasting. Amen.
Morning Prayer, Apostle's Creed.

72 Give peace in our time, O Lord.
Morning Prayer, versicle.

73 The author of peace and lover of concord, in knowledge of whom standeth our eternal life, whose service is perfect freedom.
Morning Prayer, Second Collect, for Peace.

74 Neither run into any kind of danger.
Morning Prayer, Third Collect, for Grace.

75 Pour upon them the continual dew of thy blessing.
Morning Prayer, Prayer for the Clergy and People.

76 O God, from whom all holy desires, all good counsels, and all just works do proceed: Give unto thy servants that peace which the world cannot give.
Evening Prayer, Second Collect.

77 Lighten our darkness, we beseech thee, O Lord; and by thy great mercy defend us from all perils and dangers of this night.
Evening Prayer, Third Collect, for Aid against Perils.

78 Whosoever will be saved: before all things it is necessary that he hold the Catholic Faith.
Athanasian Creed.

79 And yet they are not three Gods: but one God.
Athanasian Creed.

80 O God the Father of heaven: have mercy upon us miserable sinners.
Litany.

81 From envy, hatred, and malice, and all uncharitableness, Good Lord, deliver us.
Litany.

82 All sorts and conditions of men.
Prayer for all Conditions of Men.

83 All who profess and call themselves Christians.
Prayer for all Conditions of Men.

84 We bless thee for our creation, preservation, and all the blessings of this life; but above all for thine inestimable love in the redemption of the world by our Lord Jesus Christ; for the means of grace, and for the hope of glory.
General Thanksgiving.

85 Almighty God, give us grace that we may cast away the works of darkness, and put upon us the armour of light, now in the time of this mortal life.
Collects, 1st Sunday in Advent.

86 Hear them, read, mark, learn, and inwardly digest them.
Of all the holy Scriptures. *Collects*, 2nd Sunday in Advent.

87 Have mercy upon all Jews, Turks, Infidels, and Hereticks, and take from them all ignorance, hardness of heart, and contempt of thy word.
Collects, Good Friday.

88 Lord of all power and might, who art the author and giver of all good things.
Collects, 7th Sunday after Trinity.

89 Serve thee with a quiet mind.
Collects, 21st Sunday after Trinity.

90 Lord, we beseech thee to keep thy household the Church in continual godliness.
Collects, 22nd Sunday after Trinity.

91 The glory that shall be revealed.
Collects, St Stephen's Day.

92 Almighty God, unto whom all hearts be open, all desires known, and from whom no secrets are hid: Cleanse the thoughts of our hearts by the inspiration of thy Holy Spirit, that we may perfectly love thee, and worthily magnify thy holy Name; through Christ our Lord. Amen.
Holy Communion, Collect.

93 For I the Lord thy God am a jealous God, and visit the sins of the fathers upon the children unto the third and fourth generation of them that hate me, and shew mercy unto thousands in them that love me and keep my commandments.
Holy Communion, Second Commandment.

94 All things visible and invisible.
Holy Communion, Nicene Creed.

95 Very God of very God, Begotten, not made, Being of one substance with the Father, By whom all things were made: Who for us men and for our salvation came down from heaven.
Holy Communion, Nicene Creed.

96 And I believe in the Holy Ghost, The Lord and giver of life, Who proceedeth from the Father and Son, Who with the Father and the Son together is worshipped and glorified, Who spake by the Prophets.
Holy Communion, Nicene Creed.

97 And I believe in one Catholick and Apostolick Church.
Holy Communion, Nicene Creed.

98 Let us pray for the whole state of Christ's Church militant here in earth.
Holy Communion, Introduction to Prayer for the Church militant.

99 Draw near with faith.
Holy Communion, Invitation.

1 Ye that do truly and earnestly repent you of your sins, and are in love and charity with your neighbours, and intend to lead a new life.
Holy Communion, Invitation.

2 We acknowledge and bewail our manifold sins and wickedness, Which we from time to time most grievously have committed, By thought, word, and deed, Against thy Divine Majesty, Provoking most justly thy wrath and indignation against us.
Holy Communion, General Confession.

3 Hear what comfortable words our Saviour Christ saith unto all that truly turn to him.
Holy Communion, Words of Encouragement.

4 It is meet and right so to do.
Holy Communion, versicles and responses.

5 Therefore with Angels, and Archangels, and with all the company of heaven, we laud and magnify thy glorious Name; evermore praising thee, and saying: Holy, holy, holy, Lord God of hosts, heaven and earth are full of thy glory: Glory be to thee, O Lord most High. Amen.
Holy Communion, Praise.

6 A full, perfect, and sufficient sacrifice, oblation, and satisfaction, for the sins of the whole world.
Holy Communion, Prayer of Consecration.

7 We do not presume to come to this thy Table, O merciful Lord, trusting in our own righteousness, but in thy manifold and great mercies. We are not worthy so much as to gather up the crumbs under thy Table. But thou art the same Lord, whose property is always to have mercy: Grant us therefore, gracious Lord, so to eat the flesh of thy dear Son Jesus Christ, and to drink his blood, that our sinful bodies may be made clean by his body, and our souls washed through his most precious blood, and that we may evermore dwell in him, and he in us. Amen.
Holy Communion, Prayer of Humble Access.

8 The Body of our Lord Jesus Christ, which was given for thee, preserve thy body and soul unto everlasting life: Take and eat this in remembrance that Christ died for thee, and feed on him in thy heart by faith with thanksgiving.
Holy Communion.

9 The Blood of our Lord Jesus Christ, which was shed for thee, preserve thy body and soul unto everlasting life: Drink this in remembrance that Christ's Blood was shed for thee, and be thankful.
Holy Communion.

10 The peace of God, which passeth all understanding, keep your hearts and minds in the knowledge and love of God, and of his Son Jesus Christ our Lord: And the blessing of God Almighty, the Father, the Son, and the Holy Ghost, be amongst you and remain with you always. Amen.
Holy Communion, Blessing.

11 O merciful God, grant that the old Adam in this Child may be so buried, that the new man may be raised up in him. Amen.
Publick Baptism of Infants, Blessing.

12 We receive this Child into the Congregation of Christ's flock, and do sign him with the sign of the Cross, in token that hereafter he shall not be ashamed to confess the faith of Christ crucified, and manfully to fight under his banner against sin, the world, and the devil, and to

continue Christ's faithful soldier and servant unto his life's end. Amen.
Publick Baptism of Infants, Reception of the Child.

13 I should renounce the devil and all his works, the pomps and vanity of this wicked world, and all the sinful lusts of the flesh.
Catechism.

14 To keep my hands from picking and stealing, and my tongue from evil-speaking, lying, and slandering.
Catechism.

15 To learn and labour truly to get mine own living, and to do my duty in that state of life, unto which it shall please God to call me.
Catechism.

16 An outward and visible sign of an inward and spiritual grace given unto us.
Catechism.

17 Children being now come to the years of discretion.
Confirmation, Preface.

18 If any of you know cause or just impediment, why these two persons should not be joined together in holy Matrimony, ye are to declare it. This is the first time of asking.
Solemnization of Matrimony, the Banns.

19 Dearly beloved, we are gathered together here in the sight of God, and in the face of this Congregation, to join together this man and this woman in holy Matrimony; which is an honourable estate, instituted of God.
Solemnization of Matrimony, Exhortation.

20 Therefore is not by any to be enterprized, nor taken in hand, unadvisedly, lightly, or wantonly, to satisfy men's carnal lusts and appetites, like brute beasts that have no understanding; but reverently, discreetly, advisedly, soberly, and in the fear of God.
Solemnization of Marriage, Exhortation.

21 First, It was ordained for the procreation of children, to be brought up in the fear and nurture of the Lord, and to the praise of his holy Name.
Solemnization of Marriage, Exhortation.

22 Thirdly, It was ordained for the mutual society, help, and comfort, that the one ought to have of the other, both in prosperity and adversity. Into which holy estate these two persons present come now to be joined.
Solemnization of Marriage, Exhortation.

23 Therefore if any man can shew any just cause, why they may not lawfully be joined together, let him now speak, or else hereafter for ever hold his peace.
Solemnization of Marriage, Exhortation.

24 Wilt thou have this woman to thy wedded wife, to live together after God's ordinance in the holy estate of Matrimony? Wilt thou love her, comfort her, honour, and keep her, in sickness and in health; and, forsaking all other, keep thee only unto her, so long as ye both shall live?
Solemnization of Marriage, Betrothal.

25 Wilt thou have this man to thy wedded husband, to live together after God's ordinance in the holy estate of Matrimony? Wilt thou obey him, and serve him, love, honour and keep him, in sickness and in health; and, forsaking all other, keep thee only unto him, so long as ye both shall live?
Solemnization of Marriage, Betrothal.

26 To have and to hold from this day forward, for better for worse, for richer for poorer, in sickness and in health, to love and to cherish, till death us do part, according to God's holy ordinance; and thereto I plight thee my troth.
Solemnization of Marriage, Betrothal.

27 To love, cherish, and to obey.
Solemnization of Marriage, Betrothal. This is the bride's form of the oath.

28 With this ring I thee wed, with my body I thee worship, and with all my worldly goods I thee endow.
Solemnization of Marriage, Wedding.

29 Those whom God hath joined together let no man put asunder.
Solemnization of Marriage, Priest's Declaration.

30 Consented together in holy wedlock.
Solemnization of Marriage, Minister's Declaration.

31 Peace be to this house.
Visitation of the Sick.

32 Almighty God, the fountain of all goodness.
Morning Prayer, Prayer for the Royal Family.

33 Man that is born of a woman hath but a short time to live, and is full of misery.
Burial of the Dead, Anthem.

34 In the midst of life we are in death.
Burial of the Dead, Anthem.

35 We therefore commit his body to the ground; earth to earth, ashes to ashes, dust to dust; in sure and certain hope of the Resurrection to eternal life, through our Lord Jesus Christ.
Burial of the Dead, Committal.

36 Why do the heathen so furiously rage together, and why do the people imagine a vain thing? The kings of the earth stand up, and the rulers take counsel together, against the Lord, and against his Anointed.
Psalm 2:1–2.

37 The Lord will abhor both the blood-thirsty and deceitful man.
Psalm 5:6.

38 Make thy way plain before my face.
Psalm 5:8.

39 Let them perish through their own imaginations.
Psalm 5:11.

40 Up, Lord, and let not man have the upper hand.
Psalm 9:19.

41 But they are all gone out of the way, they are altogether become abominable: there is none that doeth good, no not one.
Psalm 14:4.

42 The lot is fallen unto me in a fair ground: yea, I have a goodly heritage.
Psalm 16:7.
➥ *See Kipling 473:53.*

43 The heavens declare the glory of God: and the firmament sheweth his handywork. One day telleth another: and one night certifieth another. There is neither speech nor language: but their voices are heard among them. Their sound is gone out into all lands: and

their words into the ends of the world.
Psalm 19:1–4.

44 Thou shalt prepare a table before me against them that trouble me: thou hast anointed my head with oil, and my cup shall be full.
Psalm 23:5.

45 Into thy hands I commend my spirit.
Psalm 31:6.

46 Sing unto the Lord a new song: sing praises lustily unto him with a good courage.
Psalm 33:3.

47 I myself have seen the ungodly in great power, and flourishing like a green bay-tree. I went by, and lo, he was gone: I sought him, but his place could no where be found. Keep innocency, and take heed unto the thing that is right: for that shall bring a man peace at the last.
Psalm 37:36–8.

48 Lord, let me know mine end, and the number of my days: that I may be certified how long I have to live.
Psalm 39:5.

49 My bones are smitten asunder as with a sword: while mine enemies that trouble me cast me in the teeth; Namely, while they say daily unto me: Where is now thy God?
Psalm 42:12–13.

50 Instead of thy fathers thou shalt have children, whom thou mayest make princes in all lands.
Psalm 45:17.

51 He maketh wars to cease in all the world: he breaketh the bow, and knappeth the spear in sunder, and burneth the chariots in the fire. Be still then, and know that I am God.
Psalm 46:9–10.

52 God is gone up with a merry noise: and the Lord with the sound of the trump.
Psalm 47:5.

53 And I said, O that I had wings like a dove: for then would I flee away, and be at rest.
Psalm 55:6.

54 Be merciful unto me, O God, be merciful unto me, for my soul trusteth in thee: and under the shadow of thy wings shall be my refuge, until this tyranny be over-past.
Psalm 57:1.

55 They are as venomous as the poison of a serpent: even like the deaf adder that stoppeth her ears; Which refuseth to hear the voice of the charmer: charm he never so wisely.
Psalm 58:4–5.

56 They go to and fro in the evening: they grin like a dog, and run about through the city.
Psalm 59:6.

57 He is the God that maketh men to be of one mind in an house, and bringeth the prisoners out of captivity: but letteth the runagates continue in scarceness.
Psalm 68:6.

58 Why hop ye so, ye high hills? this is God's hill, in the which it pleaseth him to dwell: yea, the Lord will abide in it for ever.
Psalm 68:16.

59 Thou art gone up on high, thou hast led captivity captive, and received gifts for men.
Psalm 68:18.

60 Thy rebuke hath broken my heart; I am full of heaviness: I looked for some to have pity on me, but there was no man, neither found I any to comfort me. They gave me gall to eat: and when I was thirsty they gave me vinegar to drink.
Psalm 69:21–2.

61 So the Lord awaked as one out of sleep: and like a giant refreshed with wine.
Psalm 78:66.

62 O how amiable are thy dwellings, thou Lord of hosts!
Psalm 84:1.

63 Lord, thou hast been our refuge from one generation to another. Before the mountains were brought forth, or ever the earth and the world were made: thou art God from everlasting, and world without end.
Psalm 90:1–2.

64 O come, let us sing unto the Lord: let us heartily rejoice in the strength of our salvation. Let us come before his presence with thanksgiving; and shew ourselves glad in him with psalms. For the Lord is a great God; and a great King above all gods. In his hand are all the corners of the earth; and the strength of the hills is his also. The sea is his, and he made it; and his hands prepared the dry land. O come, let us worship and fall down, and kneel before the Lord our Maker. For he is the Lord our God; and we are the people of his pasture, and the sheep of his hand.
Psalm 95:1–7.

65 Today if ye will hear his voice, harden not your hearts: as in the provocation, and as in the day of temptation in the wilderness; When your fathers tempted me: proved me, and saw my works.
Psalm 95:8–9.

66 O be joyful in the Lord, all ye lands: serve the Lord with gladness, and come before his presence with a song.
Psalm 100:1.

67 Whose feet they hurt in the stocks: the iron entered into his soul.
Psalm 105:18.

68 Their soul abhorred all manner of meat: and they were even hard at death's door.
Psalm 107:18.

69 Lord, I am not high-minded: I have no proud looks.
Psalm 131:1.

70 Such knowledge is too wonderful and excellent for me: I cannot attain unto it.
Psalm 139:5.

71 I will give thanks unto thee, for I am fearfully and wonderfully made: marvellous are thy works, and that my soul knoweth right well.
Psalm 139:13.

72 O put not your trust in princes, nor in any child of man: for there is no help in them.
Psalm 146:2.

73 We therefore commit his body to the deep, to be turned into corruption, looking for the resurrection of the body, (when the Sea shall give up her dead).
Forms of Prayer to be Used at Sea, At the Burial of their Dead at Sea.

74 Holy Scripture containeth all things necessary to salvation.
Articles of Religion, VI Of the Sufficiency of the holy Scriptures for Salvation.

75 A fond thing vainly invented.
Articles of Religion, XXII Of Purgatory.

76 The Bishop of *Rome* hath no jurisdiction in this Realm of *England*.
Articles of Religion, XXXVII Of the Civil Magistrates.

77 It is lawful for Christian men, at the commandment of the Magistrate, to wear weapons, and serve in the wars.
Articles of Religion, XXXVII Of the Civil Magistrates.

78 A Man may not marry his Grandmother.
Table of Kindred and Affinity.

Bookchin, Murray *pseudonym of* Lewis Herber 1921–

US writer on social, ecological and environmental issues.

79 Once regarded as the herald of enlightenment in all spheres of knowledge, science is now increasingly seen as a strictly instrumental system of control. Its use as a system of manipulation and its role in restricting human freedom now parallel in every detail its use as a means of natural manipulation.
1982 *The Ecology of Freedom.*

Booth, John Wilkes 1839–65

US actor, usually remembered as the assassin of President Abraham Lincoln. He was hunted down and shot several days after the killing.

80 *Sic semper tyrannis!* The South is avenged!
1865 Attributed, as he shot Lincoln at Ford's Theatre, Washington DC, 14 Apr. 'Sic semper tyrannis', *Thus always to tyrants*, is the motto of the Commonwealth of Virginia.

Booth, Junius Brutus 1796–1852

English-born US actor, a leading rival of Edmund Kean in London, particularly admired as Shylock and Richard III. He continued his success after emigrating in 1821, but succumbed to alcohol-induced melancholia.

81 Where's the stage and what's the play?
Attributed, on being found drunk backstage shortly before making his first entrance.

Booth, Martin 1944–2004

English writer educated in Hong Kong. *The Dragon and the Pearl* (1994) is an account of life there.

82 At any one time, 15 per cent of the buildings of Hong Kong are being either demolished or rebuilt, renovated or restructured.
1994 *The Dragon and the Pearl*, foreword.

Boothby, Sir Robert John Graham, 1st Baron Boothby of Buchan and Rattray Head 1900–86

Scottish Conservative politician, Parliamentary Secretary to Winston Churchill (1926–9) and an original member of the Council of United Europe. His works include *The New Economy* (1943) and *I Fight to Live* (1947).

83 Of all the pygmies, Samuel Hoare was the pygmiest.
Attributed.

Boothroyd, Betty Boothroyd, Baroness 1929–

English Labour politician and first woman Speaker of the House of Commons (1992–2000).

84 My desire to get here [Parliament] was like miners' coal dust, it was under my fingers and I couldn't scrub it out.
Quoted in Glenys Kinnock and Fiona Millar (eds) *By Faith and Daring* (1993).

85 Good temper and moderation are the characteristics of parliamentary language.
1995 In *The Independent*, 9 Feb.

86 Time's up!
2000 On retiring as Speaker of the House of Commons, 26 Jul.

Borah, William Edgar 1865–1940

US Republican politician. Elected Senator for Idaho in 1906, he advocated disarmament and, as a convinced isolationist, was instrumental in blocking US entry into the League of Nations.

87 A democracy must remain at home in all matters that affect the nature of her institutions. They are of a nature to call for the undivided attention and devotion of the entire nation. We do not want the racial antipathies or national antagonisms of the Old World transformed to this continent—as they will, should we become a part of European politics. The people of this country are overwhelmingly for a policy of neutrality.
1936 Radio broadcast, 22 Feb.

Borelli, Giovanni Alfonso 1608–79

Italian mathematician and astronomer, who reasoned that celestial objects follow parabolic paths.

88 No sensible person will deny that the works of Nature are in the highest degree simple, necessary and as economical as possible. Therefore machines devised by mankind will doubtlessly likewise attain most success if they are as far as possible modelled on works of Nature.
1680 *De moto animalium.*

Borges, Jorge Luis 1899–1986

Argentinian writer. He returned to Argentina from Europe in 1921, introducing avant-garde Ultraist theories in essays and poems before publishing his intricate and fantasy-woven short stories in the 1940s. He lost his sight in the 1950s.

89 *Los metafísicos de Tlön no buscan la verdad ni siquiera la verosimilitud: buscan el asombro. Juzgan que la metafísica es una rama de la literatura fantástica.*
The metaphysicians of Tlön do not seek for the truth or even for verisimilitude, but rather for the astounding. They judge that metaphysics is a branch of fantastic literature.
1941 *Ficciones*, 'Tlön, Uqbar, Orbis Tertius' (1963).

90 *Quizá la historia universal es la historia de la diversa entonación de algunas metáforas.*
It may be that universal history is the history of the different intonations given a handful of metaphors.
1952 *Otras inquisiciones*, 'La esfera de Pascal' (translated as *The Fearful Sphere of Pascal*, 1964).

91 *En vano te hemos prodigado el océano,*
En vano el sol, que vieron los maravillados ojos de Whitman;
Has gastado los años y te has gastado,

Y todavía no has escrito el poema.
We have lavished the ocean on you in vain,
In vain the sun that was seen by Whitman's astounded eyes;
You have spent your years and you have spent yourself,
But you haven't written the poem yet.
1964 *El otro, el mismo*, 'Mateo XX V, 30' ('Matthew 25:30').

92 While we are asleep in this world, we are awake in another one; in this way, every man is two men.
Quoted in John Russell *The Meaning of Modern Art* (1974).

93 Canada is so far away it hardly exists.
1974 Response to the question, 'What do you think of when you think of Canada?', when interviewed in Buenos Aires by Canadian poet and broadcaster Robert Zend, 4 Oct.

94 The Falklands thing was a fight between two bald men over a comb.
1983 In *Time*, 14 Feb.

Borgia, Cesare 1476–1507

Italian soldier, illegitimate son of Pope Alexander VI. He served in the papal army and was created Duke of Romagna, but was defeated in 1506 under Pope Julius II. Macchiavelli praised him as a model prince, but he was commonly perceived as a cruel dictator.

95 *Aut Caesar, aut nihil.*
Either Caesar or nothing.
Motto. It goes back to a couplet composed in 1507, after Borgia's death, by Fausto Maddalena Romano: 'Borgia Caesar erat, factis et nomine Caesar, /aut nihil, aut Caesar dixit: utrumque fuit.' (Borgia was Caesar: he was Caesar in name and in fact. He said / Either Caesar, or nothing: he was both.)

Borman, Frank 1928–

US astronaut, later President of Eastern Airlines.

96 Capitalism without bankruptcy is like Christianity without hell.
1986 In *US*, 21 Apr.

Born, Max 1882–1970

German-born British physicist, Professor of Physics at Göttingen until forced to leave by the Nazis. He won the Nobel prize (1954) for his insights into quantum mechanics.

97 There are two objectionable types of believers: those who believe the incredible and those who believe that 'belief' must be discarded and replaced by 'the scientific method'.
1951 *Natural Philosophy of Cause and Chance*.

98 Science...is so greatly opposed to history and tradition that it cannot be absorbed by our civilization.
1968 *My Life and Views*.

Borotra, Jean 1898–1994

French tennis player. His wins included the men's singles title at Wimbledon in 1924.

99 The only possible regret I have is the feeling that I will die without having played enough tennis.
Quoted in Colin Jarman *The Guinness Dictionary of Sports Quotations* (1990).

Borovoy, A Alan 1932–

General Counsel of the Canadian Civil Liberties Association.

1 I would renounce, therefore, the attempt to create heaven on earth, and focus instead on reducing the hell.
1988 *When Freedoms Collide: A Case for Our Civil Liberties*. His personal maxim.

2 I don't ask employers, for example, to *like* blacks or Jews or native people; I ask employers to *hire* the qualified members of these groups whether they like them or not.
1988 *When Freedoms Collide: A Case for Our Civil Liberties*.

Borrow, George Henry 1803–81

English writer and traveller. His part fictional, part factual books reflect his interest in languages and his love of Romany lore. They include *The Bible in Spain* (1843), *Lavengro* (1851), *The Romany Rye* (1857) and *Wild Wales* (1862).

3 There's night and day, brother, both sweet things; sun, moon, and stars, brother, all sweet things: there's likewise a wind on the heath. Life is very sweet, brother; who would wish to die?
1851 *Lavengro*, ch.25.

4 Fear God, and take your own part.
1857 *The Romany Rye*, ch.16.

5 I never saw such a place for merched anllad [wanton women] as Northampton.
1862 *Wild Wales*, ch.34.

6 'Scotland! a queer country that, your honour!' 'So it is,' said I; 'a queerer country I never saw in all my life.' 'And a queer set of people, your honour.' 'So they are,' said I; 'a queerer set of people than the Scotch you would scarcely see in a summer's day.'
1862 *Wild Wales*, ch.83.

Bosquet, Pierre 1810–61

French soldier, General during the Crimean War.

7 *C'est magnifique, mais ce n'est pas la guerre.*
It is magnificent, but it isn't war.
1854 On seeing the Charge of the Light Brigade at the Battle of Balaclava, 25 Oct. Quoted in Cecil Woodham Smith *The Reason Why* (1953), ch.12.

Bossidy, John Collins 1860–1928

US doctor and versifier.

8 And this is good old Boston,
The home of the bean and the cod,
Where the Lowells talk to the Cabots
And the Cabots talk only to God.
1910 Toast delivered at Holy Cross alumni dinner, Boston.

Boswell, James 1740–95

Scottish man of letters and biographer of Dr Johnson, whom he first met in 1763. Their great friendship led, after Johnson's death, to Boswell's literary masterpiece, the *Life of Samuel Johnson* (1791).

9 I think there is a blossom about me of something more distinguished than the generality of mankind.
1763 Journal entry, 20 Jan. Collected in F A Pottle (ed) *Boswell's London Journal* (1950).

10 JOHNSON: Well, we had a good talk.
BOSWELL: Yes, Sir; you tossed and gored several persons.
1768 Conversation, summer, recorded in *The Life of Samuel Johnson* (1791), vol.2.

11 I am, I flatter myself, completely a citizen of the world. In my travels through Holland, Germany, Switzerland, Italy, Corsica, France, I never felt myself from home.
1773 *Journal of a Tour to the Hebrides* (ed F A Pottle, 1936), entry for 14 Aug.

12 A man, indeed, is not genteel when he gets drunk; but most vices may be committed very genteelly: a man may debauch his friend's wife genteelly: he may cheat at cards genteelly.
1775 *The Life of Samuel Johnson* (1791), vol.2, entry for 6 Apr.

Botha, P(ieter) W(illem) 1932–

South African statesman, Prime Minister (1978–84) and President (1984–9). His attempts at limited constitutional reform were met with a right-wing defection from his ruling National Party (1982).

13 We simply could not go on with policies that were a failure economically and internationally, and which we could not morally justify. To allocate rights and privileges on the basis of a physical characteristic was tantamount to sinning against God.
1991 Interviewed by Donald Woods, BBC TV, Feb.

Botham, Ian Terence 1955–

English cricketer. He established a record number of Test wickets (373) and scored 5,057 runs in Tests for England, including 14 Test centuries.

14 Cricket is full of theorists who can ruin your game in no time.
1980 *Ian Botham on Cricket*.

15 I want to stress again one aspect of the game which is most important. *Never argue with an umpire*.
1980 *Ian Botham on Cricket*.

Bottomley, Gordon 1874–1948

English poet and playwright. His interest in Celtic folklore is reflected in much of his work, and he is best remembered for his *Poetry of Thirty Years* (1925) and some of his plays.

16 When you destroy a blade of grass
You poison England at her roots;
Remember no man's foot can pass
Where evermore no green life shoots.
1912 'To Ironfounders and Others'.

17 Your worship is your furnaces
Which, like old idols, lost obscenes,
Have molten bowels; your vision is
Machines for making more machines.
1912 'To Ironfounders and Others'.

Boucicault, Dion(ysus Lardner) *originally* Dionysius Lardner Bursiquot c.1820–1890

Irish playwright, actor and director. His many works include popular melodramas such as *The Corsican Brothers* (1852), *The Colleen Bawn* (1860) and *The Shaughraun* (1875). He also promoted theatrical reforms, including the box set.

18 Men talk of killing time, while time quietly kills them.
1841 *London Assurance*, act 2, sc.1.

19 It's a mighty pleasant thing to die like this, once in a way, and hear all the good things said about ye afther you're dead and gone, when they can do you no good.
1874 Aside by Conn. *The Shaughraun*, act 3, sc.2.

20 His first holiday.
His own suggested epitaph. Attributed.

Boulanger, Nadia 1887–1979

French musician and teacher. She studied at the Paris Conservatoire (1879–1904) and wrote many vocal and instrumental works.

21 Do not take up music unless you would rather die than not do so.
Advice to her pupils. Quoted in Alan Kendall *The Tender Tyrant: Nadia Boulanger* (1976).

Boulding, Kenneth Ewart 1910–93

British-born US economist and social philosopher (or 'social ecologist'), president of the American Economic Association and professor at the Universities of Michigan and Colorado.

22 We know very little about what it is that moves great masses of men to action, and until we know more about this it is fitting for the social scientist to maintain a becoming modesty in the presence of a great deal to be modest about.
1966 *The Impact of the Social Sciences*.

23 Science might almost be redefined as the process of substituting unimportant questions which can be answered for important questions which cannot.
1969 *The Image*.

24 Almost the whole pollution–environmental problem is summed up in the proposition that all goods are generally produced jointly with bads.
1972 In Sam H Schurr (ed) *Energy, Economic Growth, and the Environment* (1972).

Boulton, Sir Harold Edwin 1859–1935

English songwriter. He compiled and wrote many collections of national songs, including the well-known 'Glorious Devon' (1902) and 'Skye Boat Song' (1908).

25 When Adam and Eve were dispossessed
Of the garden hard by Heaven,
They planted another one down in the west,
'Twas Devon, glorious Devon!
1902 'Glorious Devon'.

26 Speed, bonnie boat, like a bird on the wing,
'Onward!' the sailors cry;
Carry the lad that's born to be king
Over the sea to Skye.
1908 'Skye Boat Song'. The date and authorship of the original song are uncertain, but this is now the most famous version.

Bourassa, Henri 1868–1952

Canadian politician. He entered the Commons as an Independent Liberal (1896) and founded the Quebec Nationalist party, opposing involvement with Britain and the US. He was founding editor of *Le Devoir*, a Montreal newspaper.

27 Our special task, as French Canadians, is to insert into America the spirit of Christian France.
1918 *La Langue, Gardienne de la Foi*.

Bourdillon, F(rancis) W(illiam) 1852–1951

English poet.

28 The night has a thousand eyes,
And the day but one;
Yet the light of the bright world dies,
With the dying sun.

The mind has a thousand eyes,
And the heart but one;
Yet the light of a whole life dies,
When love is done.

1878 *Among the Flowers*, 'Light'.

➤ *See Lyly 523:12.*

Bowen, Catherine Shober *née Drinker* 1897–1973

US writer, biographer and essayist, whose many books include *The Lion and the Throne* (biography of Sir Edward Coke, 1957) and *Miracle at Philadelphia* (1966).

29 In writing biography, fact and fiction shouldn't be mixed. And if they are, the fiction parts should be printed in red ink, the fact parts in black ink.

1950 In *Publisher's Weekly*, 24 Mar. Bowen's biographies were frequently partly fictionalized.

Bowen, Frank Charles 1894–

30 *Irish hurricane*, a flat calm with drizzling rain.

1929 *Sea Slang, a Dictionary of the Old-Timers' Expressions and Epithets.*

Bowie, David *real name David Robert Jones* 1947–

English rock singer and actor. His career blossomed throughout the 1970s as he adopted a range of extreme stage images to suit a variety of musical styles and concepts.

31 You must understand that this is not a woman's dress I'm wearing. It's a man's dress.

Quoted in Maxim Jakubowski *The Wit and Wisdom of Rock and Roll* (1983).

Bowles, Paul Frederick 1910–99

US novelist, poet, travel writer, translator and composer. He studied music in Paris, and began writing fiction after World War II. He lived in Tangier from 1952, and much of his work is set there.

32 The Sheltering Sky.

1947 Title of novel.

33 Too much importance is given the writer and not enough to his work. What difference does it make who he is and what he feels, since he's merely a machine for transmission of ideas. In reality he doesn't exist—he's a cipher, a blank. A spy sent into life by the forces of death. His main objective is to get the information across the border, back into death.

1966 Letter to James Leo Herlihy, 30 Apr.

34 The wind howls and the countryside is the colour of a lion. For a week the cicadas have been screaming; I think by now most of them have burst, for there are far fewer.

1969 Letter to Ned Rorem, 20 Aug.

35 It was an experiment, and I think a successful one, in communal living. It worked largely because Auden ran it; he was exceptionally adept at getting the necessary money out of us when it was due.

1972 On an artist's house in New York. *Without Stopping: An Autobiography*, ch.12.

36 My curiosity about alien cultures was avid and obsessive. I had a placid belief that it was good for me to live in the midst of people whose motives I did not understand; this unreasoned conviction was clearly an attempt to legitimize my curiosity.

1972 *Without Stopping: An Autobiography*, ch.14.

37 The act of living had been enjoyable; at some point when I was not paying attention, it had turned into a different sort of experience, to whose grimness I had grown so accustomed that I now took it for granted.

1972 *Without Stopping: An Autobiography*, ch.17.

38 I envy you if you're able to sustain a uniform degree of interest throughout *Ulysses*. People are always saying they do. People also claim to be clairvoyant and to levitate.

1981 Letter to Millicent Dillon, 1 Jul.

39 The only effort worth making is the one it takes to learn the geography of one's own nature.

1989 In the *Sunday Times*, 23 Jul.

Boycott, Geoffrey 1940–

English cricketer, who made 108 appearances for England. He scored a total of 8,114 Test runs.

40 To have some idea what it's like, stand in the outside lane of a motorway, get your mate to drive his car at you at 95 mph and wait until he's 12 yards away, before you decide which way to jump.

1989 Of the experience of facing fast bowlers. Quoted in Helen Exley *Cricket Quotations* (1992).

Boyd, L(ouis) M(alcolm) 1927–

US journalist.

41 Most business meetings are staged to supply people who'd rather talk than work with people who'd rather listen than work.

1990 'Grab Bag', in the *San Francisco Chronicle*, 7 Apr.

Boyd, William Andrew Murray 1952–

Scottish writer, born in Ghana. A lecturer in English at Oxford (1980–3) and TV critic with the *New Statesman*, he then concentrated on fiction and screenplays. His novels include *A Good Man in Africa* (1981), *Brazzaville Beach* (1990) and *Any Human Heart* (2002).

42 Like Rome, Nkongsamba was built on seven hills, but there all similarity ended. Set in undulating tropical rain forest, from the air it resembled nothing so much as a giant pool of crapulous vomit on somebody's expansive unmown lawn.

1981 *A Good Man in Africa*, ch.1.

43 Morgan liked to imagine the town as some immense yeast culture, left in a deep cupboard by an absent-minded lab technician, festering uncontrolled, running rampant in the ideal growing conditions.

1981 *A Good Man in Africa*, ch.1.

44 My first act on entering this world was to kill my mother.

1988 *The New Confessions*, opening words.

45 The natural world is full of irregularity and random alteration, but in the antiseptic, dust-free, shadowless, brightly lit, abstract realm of the mathematicians they

like their cabbages spherical, please.
1990 *Brazzaville Beach*, 'Cabbages Are Not Spheres'.

46 It seems to me that there are statements about the world and our lives that have no need of formal proof procedures.
1990 *Brazzaville Beach*, 'Fermat's Last Theorem II'.

Boyer, Charles 1899–1978

French actor who moved to Hollywood in 1929 and was particularly successful in romantic roles. His appearances include *The Garden of Allah* (1936), *Mayerling* (1937), *Love Affair* (1939) and *All This and Heaven Too* (1940).

47 Come with me to the Casbah.
1938 Although he never actually spoke this line, it was popularly associated with him as Pepe in the film *Algiers*.

Boyer, Dr Ernest L 1928–95

US educationalist, president of the Carnegie Foundation for the Advancement of Teaching (1979–95).

48 A poor surgeon hurts one person at a time. A poor teacher hurts 30.
1986 In *People*, 17 Mar.

Boyle, Peter G(erard) 1941–

Scottish academic historian.

49 They are the last drops of vintage wine from a musty old bottle.
Of Winston Churchill's letters to President Eisenhower. Quoted in Peter G Boyle (ed) *The Churchill–Eisenhower Correspondence 1953–1955* (1990).

Bracken, Peg 1918–

US writer and humorist. Her books include *The I Hate to Cook Book* (1960) and *I Didn't Come Here to Argue* (1969).

50 Cheese for dessert is rather like *Paradise Lost* in that everyone thinks he *ought* to like it, but still you don't notice too many people actually curling up with it.
1960 *The I Hate to Cook Book*, ch.9.

Bracken, Thomas 1843–98

New Zealand poet, journalist and politician, born in Ireland. He emigrated in 1869. His work, characterized by Victorian sentimentality, includes *Lays and Lyrics: God's Own Country and Other Poems* (1893).

51 Oh, God! that men would see a little clearer,
Or judge less harshly where they cannot see;
Oh, God! that men would draw a little nearer
To one another, they'd be nearer Thee,
And understood.
1905 *Not Understood, and Other Poems*, 'Not Understood'.

Bradbury, Malcolm Stanley 1932–2000

English novelist, critic and teacher. His novels include *The History Man* (1975) and *Rates of Exchange* (1982).

52 It had always seemed to Louis that a fundamental desire to take postal courses was being sublimated by other people into sexual activity.
1959 *Eating People Is Wrong*, ch.5.

53 I like the English. They have the most rigid code of immorality in the world.
1959 *Eating People Is Wrong*, ch.5.

54 Reading someone else's newspaper is like sleeping with someone else's wife. Nothing seems to be precisely in the right place, and when you find what you are looking for, it is not clear then how to respond to it.
1965 *Stepping Westward*, bk.1, ch.1.

55 My experience of ships is that on them one makes an interesting discovery about the world. One finds one can do without it completely.
1965 *Stepping Westward*, bk.1, ch.2.

56 They don't spend themselves in relationships until they know what the odds are; long hours spent as babies lying in the rain outside greengrocers' shops have made them tough.
1965 *Stepping Westward*, bk.2, ch.4.

57 English history is all about men liking their fathers, and American history is all about men hating their fathers and trying to burn down everything they ever did.
1965 *Stepping Westward*, bk.2, ch.5.

58 The English are polite by telling lies. The Americans are polite by telling the truth.
1965 *Stepping Westward*, bk.2, ch.5.

59 'We stay together, but we distrust each other.'
'Ah, yes,... but isn't that a definition of marriage?'
1975 *The History Man*, ch.3.

60 If God had meant us to have group sex, I guess he'd have given us all more organs.
1976 *Who Do You Think You Are?*, 'A Very Hospitable Person'.

61 The British have long had a taste for bad books, but they like them well written.
1981 In the *Observer*, 25 Oct.

62 In Slaka, sex is just politics with the clothes off.
1983 *Rates of Exchange*, pt.4, ch.3.

63 Here we have a saying: a good friend is someone who visits you when you are in prison. But a *really* good friend is someone who comes to hear your lectures.
1983 *Rates of Exchange*, pt.4, ch.3.

64 Conversation is never easy for the British, who are never keen to express themselves to strangers or, for that matter, anyone, even themselves.
1983 *Rates of Exchange*, pt.5, ch.3.

65 You probably know, the better class of Briton likes to send his children away to school until they're old and intelligent enough to come home again. Then they're too old and intelligent to want to.
1983 *Rates of Exchange*, pt.5, ch.3.

66 There were moments when Henry was glad he was a writer, for writers could live in their own minds and didn't have to go out at all.
1987 *Cuts*.

67 The modern novel has been many things, and functioned at many levels. It would keep D.H. Lawrence poor, and make Jilly Cooper and Jeffrey Archer rich.
1993 *The Modern British Novel*, preface.

68 The post-war period has not been marked by a great aesthetic debate about the novel comparable to that of the earlier half of the century, in part because the role of the writer and critic divided, the writer going off to the marketplace and the critic to the university (which eventually turned out to be much the same thing).
1993 *The Modern British Novel*, preface.

Bradbury, Ray(mond Douglas) 1920–

US science-fiction writer, one of the earliest writers in the genre to be recognized for his literary merits. His short-story collections include *The Martian Chronicles* (1950) and *The Illustrated Man* (1951); novels include *Fahrenheit 451* (1953) and *Something Wicked This Way Comes* (1962).

69 The Day it Rained Forever.
1959 Title of story.

70 Where robot mice and robot men, I said, run round in robot towns.
1977 *Where Robot Mice and Robot Men Run Round In Robot Towns*, prologue.

Bradley, Francis Herbert 1846–1924

Welsh philosopher, who spent most of his life at Oxford, a central figure of the 19c British Idealist movement. His important works are *Ethical Studies* (1876) and *Appearance and Reality* (1893).

71 Metaphysics is the finding of bad reasons for what we believe upon instinct, but to find these reasons is no less an instinct.
1893 *Appearance and Reality*, preface.

72 Where everything is bad it must be good to know the worst.
1893 *Appearance and Reality*, preface.

Bradley, Omar Nelson 1893–1981

US soldier. He played a prominent part in World War II, especially in Tunisia and Sicily. Chairman of the joint Chiefs-of-Staff in 1949, he was promoted to General in 1950.

73 We have grasped the mystery of the atom and rejected the Sermon on the Mount.
1948 Speech, 10 Nov, commemorating Armistice Day.

74 The wrong war, at the wrong place, at the wrong time—and with the wrong enemy.
1951 At the Senate inquiry into proposals to escalate the Korean war into China, May.

Bradman, Sir Don(ald George) 1908–2001

Australian cricketer and stockbroker. He played for Australia (1928–48, Captain 1936–48), scoring the highest aggregate and largest number of centuries in Tests against England. In 1949 he became the first Australian cricketer to be knighted.

75 It's hard to bat with tears in your eyes.
1948 When bowled for a duck in his final Test innings. Quoted in Colin Jarman *The Guinness Dictionary of Sports Quotations* (1990).

76 There is probably a greater premium on temperament for a batsman than for any player in any branch of sport.
1958 *The Art of Cricket*.

77 May cricket continue to flourish and spread its wings. The world can only be richer for it.
1958 *The Art of Cricket*.

78 Every ball is for me the first ball, whether my score is 0 or 200, and I never visualize the possibility of anybody getting me out.
Quoted in Colin Jarman *The Guinness Dictionary of Sports Quotations* (1990).

Bradstreet, Anne *née Dudley* 1612–72

English-born American Puritan poet. She emigrated to New England with her husband, a nonconformist minister, later Governor of Massachusetts. Her first collection was published in London by her brother-in-law without her knowledge.

79 In Criticks hands, beware thou dost not come;
And take thy way where yet thou art not known,
If for thy Father askt, say, thou hadst none:
And for thy Mother, she alas is poor,
Which caus'd her thus to send thee out of door.
1650 *The Tenth Muse Lately Sprung Up In America*, 'The Author to Her Book'.

80 I am obnoxious to each carping tongue
Who says my hand a needle better fits,
A poet's pen all scorn I should thus wrong
For such despite they cast on female wits;
If what I do prove well, it won't advance,
They'll say it's stolen, or else, it was by chance.
1678 *Several Poems Compiled with Great Variety of Wit and Learning*, 'The Prologue'.

81 If ever two were one, then surely we.
1678 *Several Poems Compiled with Great Variety of Wit and Learning*, 'To My Dear and Loving Husband'.

Brady, Nicholas F(rederick) 1930–

US financier and politician, Secretary of the Treasury (1988–93) under Presidents Reagan and Bush.

82 If you want to be vice-president, stand out here in the rain in your underwear and let everybody see what you're made of.
1988 On the need to strip the secrecy from selection of vice-presidential candidates instead of having surprise choices such as Dan Quayle. In the *Washington Post*, 28 Aug.

83 We have a habit in this country of correcting things just as they are about to correct themselves.
1989 In the *New York Times*, 1 Feb.

Bragg, Melvyn Bragg, Baron 1939–

English novelist and television arts presenter. He has written a number of novels in the realist tradition, and is well known as a television presenter, notably of the long-running arts series *The South Bank Show*.

84 Patriotism is seen not only as the last refuge of the scoundrel but as the first bolt-hole of the hypocrite.
1976 *Speak For England*, introduction.
► See Johnson 444:8.

85 There is nothing left to envy about America.
Quoted in Jonathan Freedland *Bringing Home the Revolution: How Britain Can Live in the American Dream* (1998).

Brahms, Johannes 1833–97

German Romantic composer. His compositions include four symphonies and several concertos, a large body of songs, chamber music and music for piano, and *A German Requiem* (1869).

86 When I feel the urge to compose, I begin by appealing directly to my Maker and I first ask Him the three most important questions pertaining to our life here in this world—whence, wherefore, whither.
Quoted in A Hopkins *Music All Around Me* (1967).

Bramante, Donato 1444–1514

Italian High Renaissance architect.

87 The dome of the Pantheon over the vault of the Temple of Peace.
c.1505 Description of his design for St Peter's, Rome. Quoted in Vincent Cronin *The Flowering of the Renaissance* (1969).

Bramston, James c.1694–1744

English cleric and poet.

88 What's not destroyed by Time's devouring hand?
Where's Troy, and where's the Maypole in the Strand?
1729 *The Art of Politics*.

Brando, Marlon 1924–2004

US film and stage actor. He found fame in stage (1947) and screen (1951) productions of *A Streetcar Named Desire*. Subsequent films include *The Wild One* (1953), *On the Waterfront* (1954), for which he won an Academy Award, *Last Tango in Paris* (1972) and *The Godfather* (1972), for which he refused to accept an Academy Award.

89 Sometimes you just get the feeling that here it is 11 o'clock in the morning and you're not in school.
1959 On playing in Western films. In the *New York Post*, 11 May.

90 An actor is a kind of guy who if you ain't talking about him ain't listening.
Quoted in Bob Thomas *Brando* (1973), ch.8.

91 He's the kind of guy that when he dies, he gives God a bad time for making him bald.
1977 On Frank Sinatra. In the *Daily Mail*, 30 Mar.

Braque, Georges 1882–1963

French painter, a developer of Fauvism, and later under the influence of Picasso, of Cubism. He was badly injured in World War I.

92 *L'Art est fait pour troubler, la Science rassure.*
Art was made to disturb, science reassures.
Notebook entry. Collected in *Le Jour et la nuit: Cahiers 1917–52*.

93 *La vérité existe; on n'invente que le mensonge.*
Truth exists; only lies are invented.
Notebook entry. Collected in *Le Jour et la nuit: Cahiers 1917–52*.

Brasch, Charles 1909–73

New Zealand poet. His works include *The Land and Other People* (1939), *Ambulando* (1964) and *Home Ground* (1974). A posthumous book of *Collected Poems* was published in 1984.

94 The ruby and amethyst eyes of anemones
Glow through me, fiercer than stars.
Home Ground (1974), 'Night Cries, Wakari Hospital: Winter Anemones'.

Brathwaite, Edward Kamau *originally* *Lawson Edward Brathwaite* 1930–

West Indian poet and historian, born in Barbados. His best-known work *The Arrivants: A New World Trilogy* (1973) consists of three earlier long poems, exploring different aspects of Caribbean culture and identity.

95 It is not enough
to be pause, to be hole
to be void, to be silent
to be semicolon, to be semicolony;
1969 *Islands*, no.3 'Rebellion', pt.6 'Negus', collected as *The Arrivants: A New World Trilogy* (1973).

Bratton, John W

British songwriter.

96 If you go down in the woods today
You're sure of a big surprise
If you down in the woods today
You'd better go in disguise.
For every Bear that ever there was
Will gather there for certain because,
Today's the day the Teddy Bears have their Picnic.
1932 'The Teddy Bears' Picnic' (with James B Kennedy).

Braudy, Leo Beal 1941–

US academic. He became Bing Professor of Literature at the University of Southern California in 1985, and University Professor in 1997.

97 People are looking to other lives for answers to questions about their own.
1987 On the increasing popularity of biography. Quoted by Alvin P Sarnoff in *US News and World Report*, 3 Aug.

Braun, Wernher von 1912–77

German-born US rocket scientist and engineer who helped develop the liquid-fuel rocket for the Nazis, and later switched his allegiance to the US. He became technical adviser to the US rocket program and later director of development operations at NASA where he was responsible for development of the Saturn V launch vehicle.

98 Our sun is one of 100 billion stars in our galaxy. Our galaxy is one of billions of galaxies populating the universe. It would be the height of presumption to think that we are the only living things in that enormous immensity.
1960 In the *New York Times*, 29 Apr.

Brautigan, Richard 1935–84

US fabulist and poet, an icon of the 1960s counter-culture movement. His seemingly whimsical fables were also literary experiments. He committed suicide.

99 Language does not leave fossils, at least not until it has become written.
1967 *Trout Fishing In America*, 'Prelude to the Mayonnaise Chapter'.

1 The time is right to mix sentences with dirt and the sun with punctuation and rain with verbs.
1968 *Please Plant This Book*, 'Squash'.

2 If you get hung up on everybody else's hangups, then the whole world's going to be nothing more than one huge gallows.
1970 *The Abortion: An Historical Romance*.

3 Loading Mercury with a Pitchfork.
1976 Title of poetry collection.

4 They used language concentrating emotion, detail and image until they arrived at a form of dew-like steel.
1978 On Japanese poets. *June 30th – June 30th*.

Brecher, Irving 1914–

US screenwriter and director. He wrote the scripts for two of the Marx Brothers' later films—*At the Circus* (1939) and *Go West* (1940).

5 I'll bet your father spent the first year of your life

throwing rocks at the stork.
1939 *At the Circus.*

Brecht, Bertolt Eugen Friedrich 1898–1956

German poet, playwright and theatre director, an innovator of epic theatre and the alienation effect. He fled Nazi Germany when Hitler came to power and returned to settle in East Berlin in 1947, where he directed the *Berliner Ensemble* theatre. His works include *The Threepenny Opera* (1928, with Kurt Weill), *The Life of Galileo* (1938), *Mother Courage and her Children* (1939) and *The Caucasian Chalk Circle* (1945).

6 *Und der Haifisch, der hat Zähne*
Und die trägt er im Gesicht
Und Macheath, der hat ein Messer
Doch das Messer sieht man nicht.
Oh, the shark has pretty teeth, dear,
And he shows them pearly white.
Just a jack-knife has Macheath, dear,
And he keeps it out of sight.
1928 *Die Dreigroschenoper* ('The Threepenny Opera'), prologue (translated by Ralph Manheim and John Willett, 1970).

7 *Erst kommt das Fressen, dann kommt die Moral.*
Food comes first, then morals.
1928 *Die Dreigroschenoper* ('The Threepenny Opera'), act 2, sc.3 (translated by Ralph Manheim and John Willett, 1970).

8 *Von der Wiege bis zur Bahre, zuerst die Wäsche.*
From the cradle to the grave, underwear first, last and all the time.
1928 *Die Dreigroschenoper* ('The Threepenny Opera'), act 2, sc.5 (translated by Ralph Manheim and John Willet, 1970).

9 ANDREA: *Unglücklich das Land das keine Helden hat.*
GALILEI: *Unglücklich das Land das Helden nötig hat.*
ANDREA: Unlucky the land that has no heroes.
GALILEI: Unlucky the land that has need of heroes.
1938 *Leben des Galilei* ('The Life of Galileo'), sc.13.

10 *Angesichts von Hindernissen mag die kürzeste Linie zwischen zwei Punkten die krumme sein.*
When it comes to obstacles, the shortest line between two points may be the crooked one.
1938 *Leben des Galilei* ('The Life of Galileo'), sc. 14 (translated by Howard Benton, 1980).
➡ *See Lessing 505:47.*

11 *Die Wissenschaft kennt nur ein Gebot: den wissenschaftlichen Beitrag.*
Science knows only one commandment: contribute to science.
1938 *Leben des Galilei* ('The Life of Galileo'), sc.14 (translated by Howard Brenton, 1980).

12 *Weil ich ihm nicht traue, sind wir befreundet.*
Because I don't trust him, we are friends.
1939 *Mutter Courage und ihre Kinder* ('Mother Courage and her Children'), sc.3.

13 *Die schönsten Pläne sind schon zuschanden geworden durch die Kleinlichkeit von denen, wo sie ausführen sollten, denn die Kaiser selber können ja nix machen.*
The finest plans have always been spoiled by the pettiness of those who should carry them out. Even emperors cannot do it all by themselves.
1939 *Mutter Courage und ihre Kinder* ('Mother Courage and her Children'), sc.6.

14 *Der Krieg findet immer einen Ausweg.*
War always finds a way.
1939 *Mutter Courage und ihre Kinder* ('Mother Courage and her Children'), sc.6.

Brenan, Gerald 1894–1987

English travel writer, born in Malta. After an itinerant early life he settled in Spain, producing *South from Granada* (1957) and *The Spanish Labyrinth* (1943) among other works.

15 Religions are kept alive by heresies, which are really sudden explosions of faith. Dead religions do not produce them.
1978 *Thoughts in a Dry Season.*

Brennan, William J(oseph), Jr 1906–97

US jurist, Associate Justice of the US Supreme Court (1956–90). He took an active role in liberal decisions handed down under Chief Justice Earl Warren.

16 Sex and obscenity are not synonymous.
1967 Ruling that established a new legal standard for obscenity, 24 Jun.

17 Death is an unusually severe and degrading punishment.
1972 Ruling to outlaw states' right to impose capital punishment, 29 Jun.

Brennus

Gallic king who captured Rome, 390 BC.

18 *Vae victis.*
Down with the defeated!
390 BC His cry on capturing Rome. Quoted in Livy *Ab urbe condita*, bk.5, ch.48, section 9.

Breslin, Jimmy 1930–

US sports journalist, writer and broadcaster. His works include *Can't Anybody Here Play This Game?* (1963). He won a Pulitzer Prize for outstanding commentary (1986).

19 They're killing the game with this phoney mystique—telling people that a guy needs the abilities of a brain surgeon to play left-guard for the Colts. Football is simply a game to keep the coalminers off the streets.
Quoted in Colin Jarman *The Guinness Dictionary of Sports Quotations* (1990).

20 Rage is the only quality which has kept me, or anybody I have ever studied, writing columns for newspapers.
1990 In *The Times*, 9 May.

Brewster, Kingman, Jr 1919–88

US educator, Professor of Law at Harvard (1950–60) and President of Yale (1963–77). He was US Ambassador to Britain (1977–81), and stayed on there as the representative of a US law firm.

21 The most fundamental value of a liberal education is that it makes life more interesting.
Recalled on his death in the *New York Times*, 9 Nov 1988.

Brezhnev, Leonid Ilyich 1906–82

Russian politician. As General Secretary of the Soviet Communist Party Central Committee after Khrushchev (1964), he became the most powerful Soviet leader, the first to hold simultaneously the position of General Secretary and President of the Supreme Soviet (1977–82).

22 She is trying to wear the trousers of Winston Churchill.
1979 Of Margaret Thatcher. Speech.

23 Whatever may divide us, Europe is our common home. A common fate has linked us through the centuries, and it continues to link us today.
1981 Speech while visiting the Federal Republic of Germany, 23 Nov.

Bricker, John W(illiam) 1893–1986

US Senator. He was Governor of Ohio (1939–45) and then Senator (1945–49). He ran as Republican vice-presidential candidate in 1944.

24 Joe, you're a dirty son of a bitch but there are times when you've got to have a son of a bitch around, and this is one of them.
c.1953 Comment to Senator Joseph R McCarthy on rescuing Republic prominence by pressing charges of Communism in government. Recalled in *This Fabulous Century* (1970).

Bridges, Robert Seymour 1844–1930

English Poet Laureate and hymn writer who qualified and practised as a doctor, and a friend of Gerard Manley Hopkins. As wartime Poet Laureate he compiled an anthology *The Spirit of Man* (1916) to lift the nation's spirits.

25 So sweet love seemed that April morn,
When first we kissed beside the thorn,
So strangely sweet, it was not strange
We thought that love could never change.

But I can tell—let truth be told—
That love will change in growing old;
Though day by day is nought to see,
So delicate his motions be.
1894 'So Sweet Loved Seemed'.

26 All my hope on God is founded
He does still my trust renew,
Me through change and chance he guideth,
Only good and only true.
God unknown,
He alone
Calls my heart to be his own.
1899 Hymn.

27 And I replied unto all these things which encompass the door of my flesh, 'Ye have told me of my god, that ye are not he: tell me something of him'. And they cried all with a great voice, 'He made us'. My questioning them was my mind's desire, and their Beauty was their answer.
1916 *The Spirit of Man: The Confessions of St Augustine.*

Bridges, (Henry) Styles 1898–1961

US Senator. He was Republican Governor of New Hampshire (1935–37) and then Senator (1937–61). He opposed the New Deal and was a supporter of Joseph McCarthy.

28 China asked for a sword, and we gave her a dull paring knife.
Of China's collapse to Communism. Quoted in David Halberstam *The Fifties* (1993).

Bridie, James *pseudonym of* *Osborne Henry Mavor* 1888–1951

Scottish playwright and doctor. Founder of the Glasgow Citizens' Theatre, he enjoyed considerable success with such plays as *The Anatomist* (1930) and *Daphne Laureola* (1949).

29 I sat through the first act and heard my lovely lines falling like cold porridge on a damp mattress.
1939 *One Way of Living*, alluding to a performance of his play *Marriage is no Joke.*

Bright, John 1811–89

British radical statesman and orator, a leading member of the Anti-Corn League (1839), MP from 1843 and an enormous influence on the Unionist party. A member of the Peace Society, he denounced the Crimean War (1854).

30 The Angel of Death has been abroad throughout the land. You may almost hear the beating of his wings.
1855 Of the Crimean War. Speech, House of Commons, 23 Feb.

31 This regard for the liberties of Europe, this care at one time for the protestant interest, this excessive love for the balance of power, is neither more nor less than a gigantic system of outdoor relief for the aristocracy of Great Britain.
1858 Speech, Birmingham, 29 Oct.

32 England is the mother of Parliaments.
1865 Speech, Birmingham, 18 Jan.

33 There is no nation on the continent of Europe that is less able to do harm to England, and there is no nation on the continent of Europe to whom we are less able to do harm, than Russia. We are so separate that it seems impossible that the two nations, by the use of reason or common sense at all, could possibly be brought into conflict with each other.
1878 Speech, Birmingham, 13 Jan.

Brillat-Savarin, Jean Anthelme 1755–1826

French politician, gastronome and writer, Mayor of Belley in 1793. During the French Revolution he took refuge in Switzerland and America. His *Physiologie du goût* (1825) is an elegant and witty compendium of the art of dining.

34 *Dis-moi ce que tu manges, je te dirai ce que tu es.*
Tell me what you eat and I will tell you what you are.
1825 *Physiologie du goût*, aphorism 4 (translated by Anne Drayton, 1970).

35 *La découverte d'un mets nouveau fait plus pour le bonheur du genre humain que la découverte d'une étoile.*
The discovery of a new dish does more for the happiness of mankind than the discovery of a star.
1825 *Physiologie du goût*, aphorism 9 (translated by Anne Drayton, 1970).

36 *La volaille est pour la cuisine ce qu'est la toile pour les peintres.*
Fowls are to the kitchen what his canvas is to the painter.
1825 *Physiologie du goût*, pt.1, ch.6, section 34 (translated by Anne Drayton, 1970).

37 *La truffe n'est point un aphrodisiaque positif; mais elle peut, en certaines occasions, rendre les femmes plus tendres et les hommes plus aimables.*
The truffle is not a true aphrodisiac; but in certain circumstances it can make women more affectionate and men more attentive.
1825 *Physiologie du goût*, pt.1, ch.6, section 44 (translated by Anne Drayton, 1970).

38 *L'alcool est le monarque des liquides, et porte au dernier degré l'exaltation palatale.*
Alcohol is the prince of liquids, and carries the palate to its highest pitch of exaltation.
1825 *Physiologie du goût*, pt.1, ch.9, section 53 (translated by Anne Drayton, 1970).

39 *C'est aussi de tous les arts celui qui nous a rendu le service le plus important pour la vie civile.*
It is also of all arts the one which has done the most to advance the cause of civilization.
1825 Of cooking. *Physiologie du goût*, pt.1, ch.27, section 123 (translated by Anne Drayton, 1970).

Brinkley, David McClure 1920–2003

US news commentator who is best known for the nightly *Huntley–Brinkley Report* (1956–70), co-hosted with Chet Huntley.

40 If you turn on your set and see nothing is happening...do not call a serviceman. You have tuned in the US Senate.
1986 On ABC TV broadcast, 1 Jun.

41 A cavalry commander...said he had just been given a thousand new men who had never seen a horse and a thousand horses who had never seen a man.
1988 On World War II. *Washington Goes to War.*

42 [They] will fearlessly commit both parties to favor mother love and the protection of the whooping crane, and to oppose the man-eating shark and the more unpopular forms of sin.
Of party platforms. Quoted in Marc Gunther *The House That Roone Built* (1994).

Brisbane, Arthur 1864–1936

US newspaper editor and writer. Editor of the *New York Herald*, which was owned by William Randolph Hearst, he was a proponent of 'sensationalist' journalism.

43 Never forget that if you don't hit a newspaper reader between the eyes with your first sentence, there is no need of writing a second one.
c.1900 Quoted in Oliver Carlson *Brisbane: a Candid Biography* (1937), ch.5.

44 Hang your idea on a peg that all can read.
c.1907 Quoted in Oliver Carlson *Brisbane: a Candid Biography* (1937), ch.7.

Britten, Baron (Edward) Benjamin, of Aldeburgh 1913–76

English composer, pianist and conductor, a student of John Ireland and Frank Bridge. His extensive output includes the opera *Peter Grimes* (1945) and other operas, songs, chamber music and orchestral works, and the *War Requiem* (1961), written for the reopening of Coventry Cathedral. With Peter Pears, he founded the Aldeburgh Festival (1948), at which much of his work was first performed.

45 I remember the first time I tried the result looked rather like the Forth Bridge.
1964 Of his first attempts at composition. Quoted in the *Sunday Telegraph*.

Brock, Sir Isaac 1768–1812

British soldier, commander of the British and militia forces in the War of 1812.

46 Push on, brave York Volunteers!
1812 Last command before succumbing to a sniper's bullet in the Battle of Queenston Heights, Upper Canada (modern Ontario), 13 Oct. Quoted in C P Stacey 'Brock's Muniments', in *Books in Canada* (Aug–Sep 1980).

Brodber, Erna 1940–

Jamaican writer, critic and academic. Her works include sociological studies on women and children in Jamaica, books on Caribbean literature, and novels including *Jane and Louisa Will Soon Come Home* (1980) and *Myal* (1988).

47 Different rhymes for different times
Different styles for different climes
Someday them rogues in Whitehall
Be forced to change their tune.
1988 *Myal*, ch.15.

Brodkey, Harold 1930–96

US writer and journalist. He died of AIDS.

48 I have AIDS. I am surprised that I do. I have not been exposed since 1977, which is to say that my experience, my adventures in homosexuality took place largely in the 1960s and '70s, and back then I relied on time and abstinence to indicate my degree of freedom from infection—and to protect others and myself.
1996 *This Wild Darkness: The Story of My Death.*

49 I'm sixty-two, and it's ecological sense to die while you're still productive, die and clear a space for others, old and young.
1996 *This Wild Darkness: The Story of My Death.*

50 Death is not soft-mouthed, vague-footed, nearby. It is in the hall.
1996 *This Wild Darkness: The Story of My Death.*

51 Nothing I have ever written has been admired as much as the announcement of my death.
Remark about his articles tracing the course of his illness in the *New Yorker*. Quoted in his obituary in *The Scotsman*, 29 Jan 1996.

Brodsky, Joseph 1940–96

Russian-born US poet. Exiled from Russia as a 'social parasite', he took US citizenship in 1977 and was awarded the Nobel prize in 1987. He latterly wrote in English, and translated his earlier Russian poems.

52 Illness and death...the only things that a tyrant has in common with his subjects... In this sense alone, a nation profits from being run by an old man.
1986 *Less Than One*, 'On Tyranny'.

53 The dusty catastrophe of Asia. Green only on the banner of the Prophet. Nothing grows here except mustaches.
1986 *Less Than One*, 'Flight From Byzantium'.

54 Racism? But isn't it only a form of misanthropy?
1986 *Less Than One*, 'Flight From Byzantium'.

55 Snobbery? But it's only a form of despair.
1986 *Less Than One*, 'Flight From Byzantium'.

56 A big step for me, and a small step for mankind.
1987 Response on hearing of his Nobel prize award. Quoted in his obituary in *The Scotsman*, 29 Jan 1996.
➤ *See Armstrong 30:78.*

57 Were we to choose our leaders on the basis of their reading experience and not their political programs, there would be much less grief on earth. I believe—not

empirically, alas, but only theoretically—that for someone who has read a lot of Dickens to shoot his like in the name of an idea is harder than for someone who has read no Dickens.
1987 Nobel prize acceptance speech.

58 There are worse crimes than burning books. One of them is not reading them.
1991 Comment at a press conference in Washington, DC, 15 May, on accepting the US poet laureateship.

59 Russia is my home…and for everything that I have in my soul I am obligated to Russia and its people. And—this is the main thing—obligated to its language.
1992 In the *New York Times*, 1 Oct.

60 They should be in every room in every motel in the land.
1992 Of poetry books. In the *New York Times*, 1 Oct.

Brody, Hugh 1943–

Canadian explorer, anthropologist and writer.

61 Resources left in the ground are saved, not lost.
1981 *Maps and Dreams: Indians and the British Columbia Frontier.*

Bronowski, Jacob 1908–74

Polish-born British mathematician, poet and humanist. He was a popular broadcaster, particularly on the BBC's *Brains Trust* and *The Ascent of Man* (1973).

62 Dissent is the native activity of the scientist, and it has got him into a good deal of trouble in the last years. But if that is cut off, what is left will not be a scientist. And I doubt whether it will be a man.
1953 'The Sense of Human Dignity', lecture at Massachusetts Institute of Technology, 19 Mar.

63 Science has nothing to be ashamed of, even in the ruins of Nagasaki. The shame is theirs who appeal to other values than the human imaginative values which science has evolved.
1953 'The Sense of Human Dignity', lecture at Massachusetts Institute of Technology, 19 Mar.

64 At bottom, the society of scientists is more important than their discoveries. What science has to teach us here is not its techniques but its spirit: the irresistible need to explore.
1956 *Science and Human Values.*

65 Man masters nature not by force but by understanding. This is why science has succeeded where magic failed: because it has looked for no spell to cast on nature.
1956 *Universities Quarterly*, vol.10, issue 3.

66 Sooner or later every one of us breathes an atom that has been breathed before by anyone you can think of who has lived before us—Michelangelo or George Washington or Moses.
1966 Quoted in the *New York Times*, 13 Oct 1969.

67 No science is immune to the infection of politics and the corruption of power.
1971 In *The Listener.*

68 The world can only be grasped by action, not by contemplation… The hand is the cutting edge of the mind.
1973 *The Ascent of Man*, ch.3.

69 That is the essence of science: ask an impertinent question and you are on the way to a pertinent answer.
1973 *The Ascent of Man*, ch.4.

70 Man is a singular creature. He has a set of gifts which make him unique among the animals, so that unlike them he is not a figure in the landscape—he is the shaper of the landscape.
1979 In *The Listener.*

Brontë, Anne 1820–49

English novelist and poet, younger sister of Charlotte and Emily. Her first novel *Agnes Grey* (1847) was published under the pseudonym Acton Bell. She also wrote *The Tenant of Wildfell Hall* (1848).

71 To think a soul so near divine,
Within a form, so angel fair,
United to a heart like thine,
Has gladdened once our humble sphere.
1846 'A Reminiscence', in *Poems by Currer, Ellis and Acton Bell.*

72 My soul is awakened, my spirit is soaring
And carried aloft on the wings of the breeze;
For above and around me the wild wind is roaring,
Arousing to rapture the earth and the seas.
1846 'Line Composed in a Wood on a Windy Day', in *Poems by Currer, Ellis and Acton Bell.*

73 All true histories contain instruction; though in some, the treasure may be hard to find, and when found, so trivial in quantity that the dry, shrivelled kernel scarcely compensates for the trouble of cracking the nut.
1847 *Agnes Grey*, ch.1.

74 He'll be all right when he's married, as Mama says; and reformed rakes make the best husbands, everybody knows. I only wish he were not so ugly—that's all I think about—but then there's no choice here in the country.
1847 *Agnes Grey*, ch.13.

75 What is it that constitutes virtue, Mrs Graham? Is it the circumstance of being able and willing to resist temptation; or that of having no temptation to resist?
1848 *The Tenant of Wildfell Hall*, ch.3.

Brontë, Charlotte 1816–55

English novelist and poet, elder sister of Emily and Anne. Her four novels are *Jane Eyre* (1847), *Shirley* (1849), *Villette* (1853) and *The Professor* (1857).

76 We wove a web in childhood,
A web of sunny air;
We dug a spring in infancy
Of water pure and fair;
We sowed in youth a mustard seed,
We cut an almond rod;
We are now grown up to riper age—
Are they withered in the sod?
1835 'We Wove a Web in Childhood'.

77 But two miles more and then we rest!
Well, there is still an hour of day,
And long the brightness of the west
Sit then, awhile, here in this wood
So total is the solitude,
We safely may delay.
1846 'Regret', in *Poems by Currer, Ellis and Acton Bell.*

78 Women are supposed to be very calm generally: but women feel just as men feel: they need exercise for their faculties, and a field for their efforts as much as their brothers do; they suffer from too rigid a restraint, too

absolute a stagnation, precisely as men would suffer...it is thoughtless to condem them, or laugh at them, if they seek to do more than custom has pronounced necessary for their sex.
1847 *Jane Eyre*, ch.12.

79 I grant an ugly woman is a blot on the fair face of creation; but as to the gentleman, let them be solicitous to possess only strength and valour: let their motto be:—Hunt, shoot, and fight: the rest is not worth a flip.
1847 *Jane Eyre* ch.17.

80 The soul fortunately, has an interpreter—often an unconscious, but still a truthful interpreter—in the eye.
1847 *Jane Eyre*, ch.28.

81 Reader, I married him.
1847 *Jane Eyre*, ch.38.

82 Conventionality is not morality. Self-righteousness is not religion. To attack the first is not to assail the last. To pluck the mask from the face of the Pharisee, is not to lift an impious hand to the Crown of Thorns.
1848 *Jane Eyre* (2nd edn), preface.

83 Of late years an abundant shower of curates has fallen upon the north of England.
1849 *Shirley*, ch.1.

84 I describe imperfect characters. Every character in this book will be found to be more or less imperfect, my pen refusing to draw anything in the model line.
1849 *Shirley*, ch.5.

85 Old maids like the houseless and unemployed poor, should not ask for a place and an occupation in the world: the demand disturbs the happy and the rich.
1849 *Shirley*, ch.22.

86 Liberty lends us her wings and Hope guides us by her star.
1853 *Villette*, ch.6.

87 Out of association grows adhesion, and out of adhesion amalgamation.
1853 *Villette*, ch.25.

88 What animal magnetism drew thee and me together—I know not.
1857 *The Professor*, ch.1.

89 Unlawful pleasure, trenching on another's rights, is delusive and envenomed pleasure—its hollowness disappoints at the time, its poison cruelly tortures afterwards, its effects deprave forever.
1857 *The Professor*, ch.20.

Brontë, Emily Jane 1818–48

English novelist and poet, sister of Anne and Charlotte. Her poems were first published under the pseudonym Ellis Bell. Her only novel is the intense and powerful *Wuthering Heights* (1847).

90 The night is darkening round me,
The wild winds coldly blow;
But a tyrant spell has bound me
And I cannot, cannot go.
1837 'The Night is Darkening Round Me'.

91 The winter wind is loud and wild,
Come close to me, my darling child;
Forsake thy books, and mateless play;
And, while the night is gathering grey,
We'll talk its pensive hours away.
1846 'Faith and Despondency', in *Poems by Currer, Ellis and Acton Bell.*

92 No coward soul is mine,
No trembler in the world's storm-troubled sphere:
I see Heaven's glories shine,
And faith shines equal, arming me from fear.
1846 'No Coward Soul is Mine', in *Poems by Currer, Ellis and Acton Bell.*

93 Cold in the earth—and the deep snow piled above thee,
Far, far, removed, cold in the dreary grave!
Have I forgot, my only Love, to love thee,
Severed at last by Time's all-serving wave?
1846 'Remembrance', in *Poems by Currer, Ellis and Acton Bell.*

94 I've dreamt in my life dreams that have stayed with me ever after, and changed my ideas; they've gone through and through me, like wine through water, and altered the colour of my mind.
1847 *Wuthering Heights*, ch.9.

95 As different as a moonbeam from lightning, or frost from fire.
1847 *Wuthering Heights*, ch.9.

96 My love for Linton is like the foliage in the woods. Time will change it, I'm well aware, as winter changes the trees. My Love for Heathcliff resembles the eternal rocks beneath—a source of little visible delight but necessary. Nelly, I *am* Heathcliff.
1847 *Wuthering Heights*, ch.9.

97 He might as well plant an oak in a flower-pot, and expect it to thrive, as imagine he can restore her to vigour in the soil of his shallow cares!
1847 *Wuthering Heights*, ch.14.

98 The more the worms writhe, the more I yearn to crush out their entrails!
1847 Heathcliff. *Wuthering Heights*, ch.14.

99 I lingered around them, under the benign sky; watched the moths fluttering among the heath and hare-bells; listened to the soft wind breathing through the grass; and wondered how anyone could ever imagine unquiet slumbers, for the sleepers in that quiet earth.
1847 *Wuthering Heights*, ch.34, closing words.

Brooke, Frances *née Moore* 1724–89

English writer. In Canada (1763–8) with her minister husband, she produced 'Canada's first novel', *The History of Emily Montague* (1769). She wrote other novels and plays, and edited a periodical, *The Old Maid.*

1 I no longer wonder the elegant arts are unknown here; the rigor of the climate suspends the very powers of the understanding; what then must become of those of the imagination?... Genius will never mount high, where the faculties of the mind are benumbed half the year.
1769 *The History of Emily Montague*, 'Letter 49'.

Brooke, Rupert Chawner 1887–1915

English poet, icon of the World War I 'lost generation'. His early verse was published in 1911, and his reputation was established by the posthumous publication of *1914 and Other Poems* (1915). He died of blood poisoning on Skyros.

2 Breathless, we flung us on the windy hill.
Laughed in the sun, and kissed the lovely grass.
1910 'Sonnet'.

3 But there's wisdom in women, of more than they have known,
And thoughts go blowing through them, are wiser than their own.
1913 'There's Wisdom in Women'.

4 Then, the cool kindliness of sheets, that soon
Smooth away trouble; and the rough male kiss
Of blankets.
1914 'The Great Lover'.

5 The benison of hot water; furs to touch;
The good smell of old clothes.
1914 'The Great Lover'.

6 If I should die, think only this of me:
That there's some corner of a foreign field
That is for ever England.
There shall be
In that rich dust a richer dust concealed;
A dust whom England bore, shaped, made aware,
Gave, once, her flowers to love, her ways to roam,
A body of England's, breathing English air,
Washed by the rivers, blest by suns of home.
1914 'The Soldier'.

7 In hearts at peace, under an English heaven.
1914 'The Soldier'.

8 Blow out, you bugles, over the rich Dead!
There's none of these so lonely and poor of old,
But, dying, has made us rarer gifts than gold.
1914 'The Dead'.

9 Naught broken save this body, lost but breath;
Nothing to shake the laughing heart's long peace there
But only agony, and that has ending;
And the worst friend and enemy is but Death.
1914 'Peace'.

10 Here tulips bloom as they are told;
Unkempt about those hedges blows
An English unofficial rose.
1915 'The Old Vicarage, Grantchester'.

11 And spectral dance, before the dawn,
A hundred Vicars down the lawn;
Curates, long dust, will come and go
On lissom, clerical, printless toe;
And oft between the boughs is seen
The sly shade of a Rural Dean.
1915 'The Old Vicarage, Grantchester'.

12 God! I will pack, and take a train,
And get me to England once again!
For England's the one land, I know,
Where men with Splendid Hearts may go.
1915 'The Old Vicarage, Grantchester'.

13 For Cambridge people rarely smile,
Being urban, squat, and packed with guile.
1915 'The Old Vicarage, Grantchester'.

14 They love the Good; they worship Truth;
They laugh uproariously in youth;
(And when they get to feeling old,
They up and shoot themselves, I'm told).
1915 'The Old Vicarage, Grantchester'.

15 Stands the Church clock at ten to three?
And is there honey still for tea?
1915 'The Old Vicarage, Grantchester'.

16 Fish (fly-replete, in depth of June,
Dawdling away their wat'ry noon).
1915 'Heaven'.

17 Fish say, they have their stream and pond;
But is there anything beyond?
1915 'Heaven'.

18 But somewhere, beyond Space and Time
Is wetter water, slimier slime!
1915 'Heaven'.

19 Unfading moths, immortal flies,
And the worm that never dies.
And in that heaven of all their wish,
There shall be no more land, say fish.
1915 'Heaven'.

Brookner, Anita 1928–

English novelist and art historian. A spare, elegant stylist, she won the Booker Prize in 1984 for her novel *Hôtel du Lac*.

20 It is best to marry for purely selfish reasons.
1981 *A Start in Life*.

21 It is my contention that Aesop was writing for the tortoise market…hares have no time to read.
1984 *Hôtel du Lac*, ch.2.

22 Good women always think it is their fault when someone else is being offensive. Bad women never take the blame for anything.
1984 *Hôtel du Lac*, ch.7.

23 Blanche Vernon occupied her time most usefully in keeping feelings at bay.
1986 *Misalliance*, ch.1.

24 I think you always feel braver in another language.
1988 In the *Observer*, 7 Aug.

25 They were privileged children…they would always expect to be greeted with smiles.
1989 *Lewis Percy*, ch.9.

26 Satire is dependent on strong beliefs, and on strong beliefs wounded.
1989 In *The Spectator*, 23 Mar.

27 I reflected how easy it is for a man to reduce women of a certain age to imbecility. All he has to do is give an impersonation of desire, or better still, of secret knowledge, for a woman to feel herself a source of power.
1993 *A Family Romance*, ch.7.

28 In youth Beatrice had been attractive, but what was attractive about her was not her appearance but her disposability.
1998 *Falling Slowly*.

Brooks, Louise 1906–85

US film actress, embodiment of the flapper age, renowned for her innocent sexuality and natural screen presence.

29 Every actor has a natural animosity toward every other actor, present or absent, living or dead.
1982 *Lulu in Hollywood*.

Brooks, Mel *pseudonym of* ***Melvin Kaminsky*** 1926–

US director, writer and actor. His successful comedies have included *The Producers* (1968), *Blazing Saddles* (1974) and *Young Frankenstein* (1974).

30 That's it baby. If you've got it, flaunt it.
1968 *The Producers*.

31 Tragedy is if I cut my finger. Comedy is if I walk into an open sewer and die.
Attributed.

Brooks, Van Wyck 1886–1963

US author and critic. He wrote biographical studies of Mark Twain (1920), Henry James (1925) and Emerson (1932). His works, which attacked materialism, also include *The Flowering of New England* (1936, Pulitzer Prize).

32 It is not that the French are not profound, but they all express themselves so well that we are led to take their geese for swans.
1958 *From A Writer's Notebook*.

Brougham, Henry Peter, 1st Baron Brougham and Vaux 1778–1868

Scottish jurist and politician. He was called to the English bar in 1808 and entered parliament in 1810. Noted for his eloquence, he became Lord Chancellor in 1830 and promoted the passage of the Reform Bill.

33 A legal gentleman who rescues your estate from your enemies, and keeps it himself.
His definition of a lawyer. Quoted in Richard Fountain *The Wit of the Wig* (1968).

Broun, (Matthew) Heywood Campbell 1888–1939

US journalist, humorist and novelist.

34 Except that right side is up is best, there is not much to learn about holding a baby. There are one hundred and fifty-two distinctly different ways—and all are right! At least, all will do.
1921 *Seeing Things at Night*, 'Holding a Baby'.

35 The tragedy of life is not that man loses, but that he almost wins.
1922 *Pieces of Hate, and Other Enthusiasms*, 'Sport for Art's Sake'.

36 Just as every conviction begins as a whim so does every emancipator serve his apprenticeship as a crank. A fanatic is a great leader who is just entering the room.
1928 In *New York World*, 6 Feb.

37 The tradition of baseball always has been agreeably free of chivalry. The rule is 'Do anything you can get away with'.
Quoted in Colin Jarman *The Guinness Dictionary of Sports Quotations* (1990).

38 Sports do not build character. They reveal it.
Quoted in Colin Jarman *The Guinness Dictionary of Sports Quotations* (1990).

Brown, (James) Gordon 1951–

Scottish Labour politician, Chancellor of the Exchequer since 1997.

39 We have been prudent for a purpose: a stronger, fairer Britain.
2000 Budget speech, 21 Mar.

40 It is about time we had an end to the old Britain, where all that matters is the privileges you were born with, rather than the potential you actually have.
2000 Speech, 25 May.

41 I'm a father, that's what matters most. Nothing matters more.
2003 Following the birth of his son. Quoted in the *Observer*, 19 Oct.

Brown, John 1800–59

US militant abolitionist. In 1859 he led an unsuccessful raid on the US Armory at Harper's Ferry, Virginia, and was convicted of treason and hanged. He was twice married and had 20 children.

42 I am as content to die for God's eternal truth on the scaffold as in any other way.
1859 Letter to his children on the eve of his execution, 2 Dec.

Brown, John Mason 1900–69

US theatre critic. He wrote long-running theatre columns in the *New York Post* and *Saturday Review* as well as publishing several books on the theatre.

43 Tallulah Bankhead barged down the Nile last night as Cleopatra—and sank.
1937 In the *New York Post*, 11 Nov.

44 To many, dramatic criticism must seem like an attempt to tattoo soap bubbles.
1963 *Stagebill*.

45 He has ears he likes to bathe in sound.
1963 Of playwright Maxwell Anderson. *Dramatis Personae*.

Brown, Olympia 1835–1900

US religious leader, the first woman ordained in the US.

46 The more we learn of science, the more we see that its wonderful mysteries are all explained by a few simple laws so connected together and so dependent upon each other, that we see the same mind animating them all.
1895 Sermon in Wisconsin, c.13 Jan.

Brown, Pat (Edmund Gerald, Sr) 1905–96

US lawyer and politician, Governor of California (1959–66).

47 Why, this is the worst disaster since my election.
1965 Of the Watts riots. Recalled in the *New York Times*, 21 Aug 1994.

Brown, Rita Mae 1944–

US writer and feminist, a campaigner for gay rights. She is the author of a number of popular novels.

48 No government has the right to tell its citizens when or whom to love. The only queer people are those who don't love anybody.
1982 Speech, 28 Aug, at the opening ceremony of the Gay Olympics, San Francisco.

49 If Michaelangelo were a heterosexual, the Sistine Chapel would have been painted basic white and with a roller.
1988 In the *New York Times*, 15 May.

50 I think the reward for conformity is that everyone likes you except yourself.
1988 *Bingo*, ch.35.

Brown, Thomas 1663–1704

English satirical writer.

51 I do not love thee, Dr Fell.

The reason why I cannot tell;
But this I know, and know full well,
I do not love thee, Dr Fell.
Composed while an undergraduate at Christ Church, Oxford, under the Deanship of Dr Fell.

Brown, Walter fl.15c

Scottish poet. *Letters of Gold* is his only known surviving poem.

52 Grit riches and prosperitie
Upfosteris vyce.
15c *Letters of Gold*, l.131–2.

Browne, Sir Thomas 1605–82

English writer and physician. His meditative *Religio Medici* appeared in an authorized version in 1643. Other works include *Pseudodoxia Epidemica, or Enquiries into…Vulgar and Common Errors* (1646) and *Hydriotaphia* (Urn Burial) (1658).

53 For my religion, though there be several circumstances that might persuade the world I have none at all—as the general scandal of my profession, the natural course of my studies, the indifferency of my behaviour and discourse in matters of religion, neither violently defending one, nor with that common ardour and contention opposing another—yet in despite hereof I dare without usurpation assume the honourable style of a Christian.
1634–5 *Religio Medici* (published 1643), pt.1, section 1.

54 My common conversation I do acknowledge austere, my behaviour full of rigor, sometimes not without morosity; yet at my devotion I love to use the civility of my knee, my hat, and hand, with all those outward and sensible motions which may express or promote my invisible devotion.
1634–5 *Religio Medici* (published 1643), pt.1, section 3.

55 Those vulgar heads that look asquint on the face of truth.
1634–5 *Religio Medici* (published 1643), pt.1, section 3.

56 In brief, where the Scripture is silent, the church is my text; where that speaks, 'tis but my comment; where there is a joint silence of both, I borrow not the rules of my religion from Rome or Geneva, but the dictates of my own reason.
1634–5 *Religio Medici* (published 1643), pt.1, section 5.

57 Where we desire to be informed, 'tis good to contest with men above ourselves; but to confirm and establish our opinions, 'tis best to argue with judgements below our own, that the frequent spoils and victories over their reasons may settle in ourselves an esteem and confirmed opinion of our own.
1634–5 *Religio Medici* (published 1643), pt.1, section 6.

58 Every man is not a proper champion for truth, nor fit to take up the gauntlet in the cause of verity.
1634–5 *Religio Medici* (published 1643), pt.1, section 6.

59 Every man's own reason is his best Oedipus.
1634–5 Oedipus here means riddle-solver. *Religio Medici* (published 1643), pt.1, section 6.

60 For indeed heresies perish not with their authors, but like the river Arethusa, though they lose their currents in one place, they rise up again in another.
1634–5 *Religio Medici* (published 1643), pt.1, section 6.

61 Men are lived over again; the world is now as it was in ages past.
1634–5 *Religio Medici* (published 1643), pt.1, section 6.

62 Methinks there be not impossibilities enough in religion for an active faith.
1634–5 *Religio Medici* (published 1643), pt.1, section 6.

63 I desire to exercise my faith in the difficultest points, for to credit ordinary and visible objects is not faith but persuasion.
1634–5 *Religio Medici* (published 1643), pt.1, section 6.

64 I love to lose myself in a mystery, to pursue my reason to an *O altitudo!*
1634–5 *Religio Medici* (published 1643), pt.1, section 9.

65 Who can speak of eternity without a solecism, or think thereof without an ecstasy? Time we may comprehend, 'tis but five days elder than ourselves.
1634–5 *Religio Medici* (published 1643), pt.1, section 11.

66 We carry with us the wonders we seek without us: there is all Africa and her prodigies in us.
1634–5 *Religio Medici* (published 1643), pt.1, section 15.

67 We are that bold and adventurous piece of nature which he that studies wisely learns in a compendium what others labour at in a divided piece and endless volume.
1634–5 *Religio Medici* (published 1643), pt.1, section 15.

68 Nature is not at variance with art nor art with nature, they both being the servants of his providence: art is the perfection of nature.
1634–5 *Religio Medici* (published 1643), pt.1, section 16.

69 All things are artificial, for nature is the art of God.
1634–5 *Religio Medici* (published 1643), pt.1, section 16.

70 Obstinacy in a bad cause, is but constancy in a good.
1634–5 *Religio Medici* (published 1643), pt.1, section 25.

71 Persecution is a bad and indirect way to plant religion.
1634–5 *Religio Medici* (published 1643), pt.1, section 25.

72 There are many…canonized on earth, that shall never be Saints in Heaven.
1634–5 *Religio Medici* (published 1643), pt.1, section 26.

73 I am not so much afraid of death, as ashamed thereof.
1634–5 *Religio Medici* (published 1643), pt.1, section 40.

74 Certainly there is no happiness within this circle of flesh, nor is it in the optics of these eyes to behold felicity; the first day of our Jubilee is death.
1634–5 *Religio Medici* (published 1643), pt.1, section 44.

75 I have tried if I could reach that great resolution…to be honest without a thought of Heaven or Hell.
1634–5 *Religio Medici* (published 1643), pt.1, section 47.

76 To believe only in possibilities, is not faith, but mere Philosophy.
1634–5 *Religio Medici* (published 1643), pt.1, section 48.

77 There is no road or ready way to virtue.
1634–5 *Religio Medici* (published 1643), pt.1, section 55.

78 The world was before the creation and at an end before it had a beginning; and thus was I dead before I was alive. Though my grave be England, my dying place was Paradise, and Eve miscarried of me before she conceived of Cain.
1634–5 *Religio Medici* (published 1643), pt.1, section 59.

79 All places, all airs make unto me one country; I am in England, everywhere, and under any meridian.
1634–5 *Religio Medici* (published 1643), pt.2, section 1.

80 It is the common wonder of all men, how among so many

millions of faces, there should be none alike.
1634–5 *Religio Medici* (published 1643), pt.2, section 1.

81 I could be content that we might procreate like trees, without conjunction, or that there were any way to perpetuate the World without this trivial and vulgar way of coition: it is the foolishest act a wise man commits in all his life.
1634–5 *Religio Medici* (published 1643), pt.2, section 9.

82 We all labour against our own cure, for death is the cure of all diseases.
1634–5 *Religio Medici* (published 1643), pt.2, section 9.

83 Whilst I study to find how I am a microcosm of little world, I find myself something more than the great. There is surely a piece of divinity in us; something that was before the elements, and owes no homage unto the sun.
1634–5 *Religio Medici* (published 1643), pt.2, section 11.

84 Old mortality, the ruins of forgotten times.
1658 *Hydriotaphia* (Urn Burial), Epistle Dedicatory.

85 Were the happiness of the next world as closely apprehended as the felicities of this, it were a martyrdom to live.
1658 *Hydriotaphia* (Urn Burial), ch.4.

86 The long habit of living indisposeth us for dying.
1658 *Hydriotaphia* (Urn Burial), ch.5.

87 Adversity stretcheth our days.
1658 *Hydriotaphia* (Urn Burial), ch.5.

88 We cannot hope to live so long in our names as some have done in their persons.
1658 *Hydriotaphia* (Urn Burial), ch.5.

89 'Tis too late to be ambitious.
1658 *Hydriotaphia* (Urn Burial), ch.5.

90 There is no antidote against the opium of time.
1658 *Hydriotaphia* (Urn Burial), ch.5.

91 To be nameless in worthy deeds exceeds an infamous history... Who would not rather have been the good thief than Pilate?
1658 *Hydriotaphia* (Urn Burial), ch.5.

92 Man is a noble animal, splendid in ashes, and pompous in the grave.
1658 *Hydriotaphia* (Urn Burial), ch.5.

93 Life is a pure flame, and we live by an invisible sun within us.
1658 *Hydriotaphia* (Urn Burial), ch.5.

94 Life itself is but the shadow of death, and souls departed but the shadows of the living. All things fall under this name. The sun itself is but the dark *simulacrum*, and light but the shadow of God.
1658 *The Garden of Cyrus*, ch.2.

95 The quincunx of heaven runs low, and 'tis time to close the five parts of knowledge.
1658 *The Garden of Cyrus*, ch.5.

96 All things began in order, so shall they end, and so shall they begin again; according to the ordainer of order and mystical mathematics of the city of heaven.
1658 *The Garden of Cyrus*, ch.5.

97 Nor will the sweetest delight of gardens afford much comfort in sleep; wherein the dullness of that sense shakes hands with delectable odours; and though in the bed of Cleopatra, can hardly with any delight raise up the ghost of a rose.
1658 *The Garden of Cyrus*, ch.5.

Browne, William 1692–1774

English physician and poet.

98 The King to Oxford sent a troop of horse,
For Tories own no argument but force;
With equal skill to Cambridge books he sent,
For Whigs admit no force but argument.
Literary Anecdotes.

Browning, Elizabeth *née Barrett* 1806–61

English poet, who married Robert Browning (1846). Her early work includes her *Essay on Mind, and other Poems* which was published anonymously when she was 19. Her other writings include *Poems* (1884), translations of Aeschylus's *Prometheus Bound* (1833 and a new translation in her *Poems* of 1850), the long narrative poem *Aurora Leigh* (1856), *Sonnets from the Portuguese* (also published in *Poems*, 1850) which were not translations but express her own love, and *Casa Guidi Windows* (1851) on the theme of Italian Liberation. *Last Poems* was published posthumously in 1862.

99 Thou large-brained woman and large-hearted man.
1844 *Poems*, 'To George Sand. A Desire', l.1.

1 And because I was a poet, and because the public praised me,
With their critical deductions for the modern writer's fault;
I could sit at rich men's tables,—though the courtesies that raise me,
Still suggested clear between us, the pale spectrum of the salt.
1844 *Poems*, 'Lady Geraldine's Courtship', stanza 9.

2 And the rolling anapaestic
Curled, like vapour over shrines.
1844 *Poems*, 'Wine of Cyprus', stanza 10.

3 I am floated along, as if I should die
Of Liberty's exquisite pain.
1849 'The Runaway Slave at Pilgrim's Point', stanza 36.

4 Straightway I was 'ware
So weeping, how a mystic shape did move
Behind me, and drew me backward by the hair
And a voice said in mastery while I strove...
'Guess now who holds thee!'—'*Death*', I said, but there
The silver answer rang... 'Not Death, but Love.'
1850 *Poems*, 'Sonnets from the Portuguese', sonnet 1.

5 If thou must love me, let it be for naught
Except for love's sake only.
1850 *Poems*, 'Sonnets from the Portuguese', sonnet 14.

6 When our two souls stand up erect and strong,
Face to face, silent, drawing nigh and nigher,
Until their lengthening wings break into fire
At either curvèd point,... what bitter wrong,
Can the earth do to us, that we should not long
Be here contented?
1850 *Poems*, 'Sonnets from the Portuguese', sonnet 22.

7 Let the world's sharpness like a clasping knife
Shut in upon itself, and do no harm
In this close hand of love.
1850 *Poems*, 'Sonnets from the Portuguese', sonnet 24.

8 First time he kissed me, but only kissed

The fingers of this hand wherewith I write,
And ever since it grew more clean and white...
1850 *Poems*, 'Sonnets from the Portuguese', sonnet 38.

9 How do I love thee? Let me count the ways!—
I love thee to the depth and breadth and height
My soul can reach, when feeling out of sight
For the ends of Being and Ideal Grace.
1850 *Poems*, 'Sonnets from the Portuguese', sonnet 43.

10 I love thee with the love I seemed to lose
With my lost Saints,—I love thee with the breath
Smiles, tears, of all my life!—and, if God choose,
I shall but love thee better after death.
1850 *Poems*, 'Sonnets from the Portuguese', sonnet 43.

11 God answers sharp and sudden on some prayers,
And thrusts the thing we have prayed for in our face,
A gauntlet with a gift in't.
1856 *Aurora Leigh*, bk.2.

12 The music soars within the little lark,
And the lark soars.
1856 *Aurora Leigh*, bk.3.

13 Since when was genius found respectable?
1856 *Aurora Leigh*, bk.6.

14 Earth's crammed with heaven,
And every common bush afire with God.
1856 *Aurora Leigh*, bk.7.

Browning, Guy 1964–

English writer and broadcaster.

15 A shoal of a million fish might not be able to write *Romeo and Juliet* but they can change direction as one in the blink of an eye. Using language a human team leader can giver an order to a team of six and have it interpreted in six completely different ways.
1999 In *The Guardian*, 24 Jul.

16 Major cities are divided into two parts; the bits that are in the guidebook and the bits that aren't. If you don't take a guidebook, you'll see a different city.
2002 In *The Guardian*, 21 May.

17 Maths is the purest science in that you don't need any test tubes or animal testing to do it. All the other sciences eventually boil down to maths, apart from biology, which boils down to soup.
2004 In *The Guardian*, 19 Jun.

Browning, Robert 1812–89

English poet, who married Elizabeth Browning (1846). His poetry offers a wide range of characters, dramatic situations, and a rich variety of forms and rhythms. His work includes *Men and Women* (1855), *Dramatis Personae* (1864) and *The Ring and the Book* (1868–9).

18 God is the perfect poet,
Who in his person acts his own creations.
1835 *Paracelsus*, pt.2, l.648–9.

19 The year's at the spring,
And days at the morn;
Morning's at seven;
The hill-side's dew-pearled;
The lark's on the wing;
The snail's on the thorn;
God's in His heaven—
All's right with the world.
1841 *Pippa Passes*, pt.1.

20 Like a god going thro' his world there stands
One mountain, for a moment in the dusk,
Whole brotherhoods of cedars on its brow
1841 *Pippa Passes*, pt.2.

21 There's a great text in Galatians,
Once you trip on it, entails
Twenty-nine distinct damnations,
One sure, if another fails.
1842 *Dramatic Lyrics*, 'Soliloquy of the Spanish Cloister'.

22 My scrofulous French novel
On grey paper with blunt type!
1842 *Dramatic Lyrics*, 'Soliloquy of the Spanish Cloister'.

23 The moth's kiss, first!
Kiss me as if you made believe
You were not sure, this eve,
How my face, your flower, had pursed
Its petals up.
1842 *Dramatic Lyrics*, 'In a Gondola'.

24 What's become of Waring
Since he gave us all the slip?
1842 *Dramatic Lyrics*, 'Waring'. The first line was used as the title of a novel by Anthony Powell.

25 Hamelin Town's in Brunswick,
By famous Hanover city;
The river Weser, deep and wide,
Washes its wall on the southern side;
A pleasanter spot you never spied.
1842 *Dramatic Lyrics*, 'The Pied Piper of Hamlin'.

26 Rats!
They fought the dogs and killed the cats,
And bit the babies in the cradles.
And ate the cheeses out of the vats.
1842 *Dramatic Lyrics*, 'The Pied Piper of Hamlin'.

27 I sprang to the stirrup, and Joris, and he;
I galloped, Dirck galloped, we galloped all three.
1845 *Dramatic Romances and Lyrics*, 'How they brought the Good News from Ghent to Aix'.

28 Just for a handful of silver he left us,
Just for a riband to stick in his coat.
1845 Of Wordsworth. *Dramatic Romances and Lyrics*, 'The Lost Leader'.

29 Never glad confident morning again!
1845 *Dramatic Romances and Lyrics*, 'The Lost Leader'.

30 Oh, to be in England
Now that April's there,
And whoever wakes in England
Sees, some morning, unaware,
That the lowest boughs and the brushwood sheaf
Round the elm-tree bole are in tiny leaf,
While the chaffinch sings on the orchard bough
In England—now!
1845 *Dramatic Romances and Lyrics*, 'Home-Thoughts, from Abroad'.

31 That's the wise thrush; he sings each song twice over,
Lest you think he never could recapture
The first fine careless rapture!
1845 *Dramatic Romances and Lyrics*, 'Home-Thoughts, from Abroad'.

32 'Here and here did England help me: how can I help England?'—say.
1845 *Dramatic Romances and Lyrics*, 'Home-Thoughts, from the Sea'.

33 And then how I shall lie through centuries,
And hear the blessed mutter of the mass,
And see God made and eaten all day long,
And feel the steady candle-flame, and taste
Good strong thick stupefying incense-smoke!
1845 *Dramatic Romances and Lyrics*, 'The Bishop Orders his Tomb'.

34 A tap at the pane, the quick sharp scratch
And blue spurt of a lighted match,
And a voice less loud, through its joys and fears,
Than the two hearts beating each to each!
1845 *Dramatic Romances and Lyrics*, 'Meeting at Night'.

35 There may be heaven; there must be hell.
1845 *Dramatic Romances and Lyrics*, 'Time's Revenges'.

36 In the natural fog of the good man's mind.
1850 'Christmas Eve'.

37 Where the quiet-coloured end of evening smiles,
Miles and miles.
1855 *Men and Women*, 'Love among the Ruins'.

38 If you get simple beauty and naught else,
You get about the best thing God invents.
1855 *Men and Women*, 'Fra Lippo Lippi'.

39 This world's no blot for us
Nor blank; it means intensely, and means good:
To find its meaning is my meat and drink.
1855 *Men and Women*, 'Fra Lippo Lippi'.

40 Hark—the dominant's persistence till it must be answered to!
1855 *Men and Women*, 'A Toccata of Galuppi's'.

41 What of soul was left, I wonder, when the kissing had to stop?
1855 *Men and Women*, 'A Toccata of Galuppi's'.

42 Dear, dead woman, with such hair, too—what's become of all the gold
Used to hang and brush their bosoms? I feel chilly and grown old.
1855 *Men and Women*, 'A Toccata of Galuppi's'.

43 'Tis the Last Judgement's fire must cure this place,
Calcine its clods and set my prisoners free.
1855 *Men and Women*, 'Childe Roland to the Dark Tower Came'.

44 As for the grass, it grew as scant as hair in leprosy—thin
dried blades pricked the mud which underneath looked
kneaded up with blood.
One stiff blind horse, his every bone a-stare, stood
stupefied.
1855 *Men and Women*, 'Childe Roland to the Dark Tower Came'.

45 I never saw a brute I hated so;
He must be wicked to deserve such pain.
1855 *Men and Women*, 'Childe Roland to the Dark Tower Came'.

46 It was roses, roses, all the way.
1855 *Men and Women*, 'The Patriot'.

47 And find a poor devil has ended his cares
At the foot of your rotten-runged rat-riddled stairs?
Do I carry the moon in my pocket?
1855 *Men and Women*, 'Master Huges of Saxe-Gotha'.

48 Just when we are safest, there's a sunset-touch,
A fancy from a flower-bell, some one's death,
A chorus-ending from Euripides,—
And that's enough for fifty hopes and fears
As old and new at once as Nature's self,
To rap and knock and enter in our soul.
Take hands and dance there, a fantastic ring,
Round the ancient idol, on his base again,—
The grand Perhaps.
1855 *Men and Women*, 'Bishop Blougram's Apology'.

49 All we have gained then by our unbelief
Is a life of doubt diversified by faith,
For one of faith diversified by doubt:
We called the chess-board white,—we call it black.
1855 *Men and Women*, 'Bishop Blougram's Apology'.

50 You, for example, clever to a fault,
The rough and ready man who write apace,
Read somewhat seldomer, think perhaps even less.
1855 *Men and Women*, 'Bishop Blougram's Apology'.

51 No, when the fight begins within himself,
A man's worth something.
1855 *Men and Women*, 'Bishop Blougram's Apology'.

52 He said true things but called them by wrong names.
1855 *Men and Women*, 'Bishop Blougram's Apology'.

53 Ah, did you once see Shelley plain,
And did he stop to speak to you
And did you speak to him again?
How strange it seems, and new!
1855 *Men and Women*, 'Memorabilia'.

54 So free we seem, so fretted fast we are!
1855 *Men and Women*, 'Andrea del Sarto'.

55 Ah, but a man's reach should exceed his grasp,
Or what's a heaven for?
1855 *Men and Women*, 'Andrea del Sarto', l.97–8.

56 Your ghost will walk, you lover of trees,
(If love remains)
In an English lane.
1855 *Men and Women*, 'De Gustibus'.

57 Open your heart and you will see
graved inside of it, 'Italy.'
Such lovers old are I and she;
So it always was, so it still shall be!
1855 *Men and Women*, 'De Gustibus'.

58 Stand still, true poet that you are!
I know you; let me try and draw you.
Some night you'll fail us: when afar
You rise, remember one man saw you,
Knew you, and named a star!
1855 *Men and Women*, 'Popularity'.

59 I would that you were all to me,
You that are just so much, no more.
1855 *Men and Women*, 'Two in the Campagna'.

60 Only I discern—
Infinite passion, and the pain
Of finite hearts that yearn.
1855 *Men and Women*, 'Two in the Campagna'.

61 There they are, my fifty men and women
Naming me the fifty poems finished!
Take them, Love, the book and me together.
Where the heart lies, let the brain lie also.
1855 *Men and Women*, 'One Word More. To E.B.B.', stanza 1.

62 Suddenly, as rare things will, it vanished.
1855 *Men and Women*, 'One Word More. To E.B.B.', stanza 4.

63 Dante, who loved well because he hated,
Hated wickedness that hinders loving.
1855 *Men and Women*, 'One Word More. To E.B.B.', stanza 5.

64 Proves she like some portent of an iceberg
Swimming full upon the ship it founders
Hungry with huge teeth of splintered crystals?
1855 *Men and Women*, 'One Word More. To E.B.B.', stanza 17.

65 What's come to perfection perishes.
Things learned on earth, we shall practise in heaven.
Work done least rapidly, Art most cherishes.
1855 *Men and Women*, 'One Word More. To E.B.B.', stanza 17.

66 God be thanked, the meanest of his creatures
Boasts two soul-sides, one to face the world with,
One to show a woman when he loves her!
1855 *Men and Women*, 'One Word More. To E.B.B.', stanza 18.

67 Wrote one song—and in my brain I sing it,
Drew one angel—borne, see, on my bosom!
1855 *Men and Women*, 'One Word More. To E.B.B.', closing lines.

68 But God has a few of us to whom he whispers in the ear;
The rest may reason and welcome; 'tis we musicians know.
1864 *Dramatis Personae*, 'Abt Vogler'.

69 Grow old along with me!
The best is yet to be,
The last of life, for which the first was made:
Our times are in His hand
Who saith, 'A whole I planned,
Youth shows but half; trust God:
See all nor be afraid!'
1864 *Dramatis Personae*, 'Rabbi ben Ezra', stanza 1.

70 Time's wheels runs back or stops: Potter and clay endure.
1864 *Dramatis Personae*, 'Rabbi ben Ezra', stanza 27.

71 My times be in Thy hand!
Perfect the cup as planned!
Let age approve of youth, and
Death complete the same!
1864 *Dramatis Personae*, 'Rabbi ben Ezra', stanza 32.

72 Stung by the splendour of a sudden thought.
1864 *Dramatis Personae*, 'A Death in the Desert'.

73 For I say, this is death and the sole death,
When a man's loss comes to him from his gain,
Darkness from light, from knowledge ignorance,
And lack of love from love made manifest.
1864 *Dramatis Personae*, 'A Death in the Desert'.

74 Progress, man's distinctive mark alone,
Not God's, and not the beasts'; God is, they are,
Man partly is and wholly hopes to be.
1864 *Dramatis Personae*, 'A Death in the Desert'.

75 And it is good to cheat the pair, and gibe,
Letting the rank tongue blossom into speech.
Setebos, Setebos, and Setebos!
Thinketh, He dwelleth i' the cold o' the moon.
Thinketh He made it, with the sun to match,
But not the stars; the stars came otherwise.
1864 *Dramatis Personae*, 'Caliban upon Setebos', stanza 1.

76 Let twenty pass, and stone the twenty-first,
Loving not, hating not, just choosing so.
1864 *Dramatis Personae*, 'Caliban upon Setebos', stanza 1.

77 We loved, sir—used to meet:
How sad and bad and mad it was—
But then, how it was sweet!
1864 *Dramatis Personae*, 'Confessions', stanza 9.

78 There's more hateful form of foolery—
The social sage's, Solomon of saloons
And philosophic diner-out.
1864 *Dramatis Personae*, 'Mr Sludge, The Medium', stanza 1.

79 Well, British Public, ye who like me not,
(God love you!)
1868–9 *The Ring and the Book*, bk.1, l.410

80 'Go get you manned by Manning and new-manned
By Newman and, mayhap, wise-manned to boot
By Wiseman.'
1868–9 *The Ring and the Book*, bk.1, l.444–6.

81 Youth means love,
Vows can't change nature, priests are only men.
1868–9 *The Ring and the Book*, bk.1, l.1056–7.

82 O lyric love half angel and half bird
And all a wonder and a wild desire.
1868–9 *The Ring and the Book*, bk.1, l.1391–2.

83 In the great right of an excessive wrong.
1868–9 *The Ring and the Book*, bk.3, l.1055.

84 Faultless to a fault.
1868–9 *The Ring and the Book*, bk.9, l.1175.

85 Why comes temptation but for a man to meet
And master and make crouch beneath his foot,
And so be pedestalled in triumph?
1868–9 *The Ring and the Book*, bk.10, l.1184–6.

86 White shall not neutralize the black, nor good
Compensate bad in man, absolve him so:
Life's business being just the terrible choice.
1868–9 *The Ring and the Book*, bk.10, l.1235–7.

87 There's a new tribunal now
Higher than God's,—the educated man's!
1868–9 *The Ring and the Book*, bk.10, l.1975–6.

88 Into that sad obscure sequestered state
Where God unmakes but to remake the soul
He else made first in vain; which must not be.
1868–9 *The Ring and the Book*, bk.10, l.2129–31.

89 It is the glory and good of Art,
That Art remains the one way possible
Of speaking truth, to mouths like mine, at least.
1868–9 *The Ring and the Book*, bk.12, l.838–40.

90 But, thanks to wine-less and democracy,
We've still our stage where truth calls spade a spade!
1875 'Aristophanes' Apology', stanza 1.

91 Ignorance is not innocence but sin.
1875 *The Inn Album*, canto 5.

92 I want to know a butcher paints,
A baker rhymes for his pursuit,
Candlestick-maker much acquaints
His soul with song, or, haply mute,
Blows out his brains upon the flute.
1876 'Shop', stanza 21.

93 Good, to forgive;
Best, to forget!
Living, we fret;
Dying, we live.
1878 *La Saisiaz*, prologue.

94 At midnight in the silence of the sleep-time,
When you set your fancies free.
1889 *Asolando*, epilogue.

95 One who never turned his back but marched breast forward,
Never doubted clouds would break,
Never dreamed, though right were worsted, wrong would triumph,
Held we fall to rise, are baffled to fight better,
Sleep to wake.
1889 *Asolando*, epilogue.

96 Greet the unseen with a cheer!
1889 *Asolando*, epilogue.

Broyard, Anatole 1920–90

Literary critic, writer and editor at the *New York Times*.

97 She has always ridden the passions as if they were a magnificent horse.
1978 On Edna O'Brien. In the *New York Times*, 1 Jan.

98 Such a fatigue of adjectives, a drone of alliterations, a huffing of hyphenated words hurdling the meter like tired horses. Such a faded upholstery of tears, stars, bells, bones, flood and blood...a thud of consonants in tongue, night, dark, dust, seed, wound and wind.
1974 On Dylan Thomas's poetry. *Aroused by Books*.

99 I remember a table in *Barchester Towers* that had more character than the combined heroes of three recent novels I've read.
1974 *Aroused by Books*.

1 When Harriet goes to bed with a man, she always takes her wet blanket with her.
1974 On a character in Iris Owen's *After Claude* (1973). *Aroused by Books*.

2 Chic is a convent for unloved women.
1988 In the *New York Times*, 10 Jan.

Brummel, George Bryan *called* *Beau Brummell* 1778–1840

English dandy, a leader of 19c fashionable society. A close friend of the Prince Regent (later George IV), he quarrelled with him in 1813, and was later forced to flee to Calais with gambling debts. He died a pauper in a lunatic asylum.

3 Who's your fat friend?
c.1813 Of the Prince Regent. Remark addressed to his companion, whom the Prince had acknowledged while studiously ignoring Brummell. Quoted in Jesse *Life of George Brummell* (1844), vol.1.

Brunet, Michel 1917–85

Canadian historian.

4 The thing which amazes me is that I know perfectly well, as a historian, that there is corruption in any government—there's always corruption. It's bad when it's more than fifteen percent.
Interviewed by Ramsay Cook in Eleanor Cook (ed) *The Craft of History* (1973).

Brunner, John Kilian Houston 1934–95

English science-fiction writer, an important contributor to the more literary aspirations of the genre. *Stand On Zanzibar* (1969) is his best-known work.

5 POPULATION EXPLOSION Unique in human experience, an event which happened yesterday but which everyone swears won't happen until tomorrow.
1969 *Stand On Zanzibar*, 'The Hipcrime Vocab'.

Bruno, Frank(lin Roy) 1961–

English boxer. He won the European heavyweight title in 1985, and the World Championship in 1995.

6 Know what I mean, Harry?
Catchphrase, addressed to sports commentator Harry Carpenter.

Bryan, Richard H(udson) 1937–

US politician, Governor of Nevada (1983–9) and Senator (1989–2001).

7 Being chairman of the Senate Ethics Committee is like jumping off a cliff. The thrill is very short.
1993 NPR broadcast, 2 Nov.

Bryan, William Jennings 1860–1925

US lawyer, Democratic politician and pacifist. Elected to Congress in 1890, he ran unsuccessfully in two presidential elections (1896, 1900). Appointed Secretary of State by Woodrow Wilson (1913), he resigned in 1915 over the USA's second *Lusitania* note to Germany.

8 There are two ideas of government. There are those who believe that, if you will only legislate to make the well-to-do prosperous, their prosperity will leak through on those below. The Democratic idea, however, has been that if you legislate to make the masses prosperous, their prosperity will find its way up through every class which rests upon them.
1896 Speech at the Democratic National Convention, 10 Jul.

9 What shall we say of the intelligence, not to say religion, of those who are so particular to distinguish between fishes and reptiles and birds, but put a man with an immortal soul in the same circle with the wolf, the hyena, and the skunk? What must be the impression made upon children by such a degradation of man?
Statement issued in Dayton, Tennessee, 28 Jul 1925, by Mrs W J Bryan, shortly after the end of the Scopes trial and her husband's death.

Bryant, David 1931–

English bowls player. He was the World Singles Champion in 1966, 1980 and 1988.

10 I'm not an athlete, more a gymnast and golfer, soldered together.
Quoted in Colin Jarman *The Guinness Dictionary of Sports Quotations* (1990).

11 Bowls is a young man's game which old men can play.
Quoted in Colin Jarman *The Guinness Dictionary of Sports Quotations* (1990).

Bryant, William Cullen 1794–1878

US writer and journalist. Originally a lawyer, after the success of *Thanatopsis* (1817) he turned increasingly to prose and verse writing, becoming editor of the New York *Evening Post* (1829).

12 All that tread
The globe are but a handful to the tribes
That slumber in its bosom.
1817 'Thanatopsis', in the *North American Review*, Sep.

13 These are the gardens of the Desert, these
The unshorn fields, boundless and beautiful,
For which the speech of England has no name—
The Prairies.
1832 *Poems*, 'The Prairies'.

Bryson, Bill 1951–

US author, particularly known for his humorous travel memoirs.

14 My mother only ever said two things. She said, 'I don't know, dear.' And she said, 'Can I get you a sandwich, honey?'
1989 *The Lost Continent*, ch.1.

15 There are three things you just can't do in life. You can't beat the phone company, you can't make a waiter see you until he's ready to see you, and you can't go home again.
1989 *The Lost Continent*, ch.2.

16 It sometimes occurs to me that the British have more heritage than is good for them.
1995 *Notes from a Small Island.*

17 I have a small tattered clipping that I sometimes carry with me and pull out for purposes of private amusement. It's a weather forecast from the *Western Daily Mail* and it says, in toto: 'Outlook: Dry and warm, but cooler with some rain.'
1995 *Notes from a Small Island.*

18 Hunters will tell you that a moose is a wily and ferocious forest creature. In fact, a moose is a cow drawn by a three-year-old.
1998 *Notes from a Big Country.*

19 He was the only person in American history for whom attaining the White House was a bad career move.
1998 On Herbert Hoover. *Notes from a Big Country.*

20 In the first three months of this year the US edition of *Time* did not have a single report from France, Italy, Spain or Japan, to name just a few of the countries that seem to have escaped its notice.
1998 *Notes from a Big Country.*

21 According to an opinion poll, 13 per cent of women in the United States cannot say whether they wear their tights under their knickers or over them. That's something like a million women walking around in a state of chronic foundation garment uncertainty.
1998 *Notes from a Big Country.*

Buber, Martin 1878–1965

Austrian Jewish theologian and philosopher, founding editor of *Der Jude* (1916–24, 'The Jew'), known for his important studies in Hasidism and Existentialism. Professor at Frankfurt (1923–33), he fled Germany for Palestine in 1938, becoming Professor of the Sociology of Religion in Jerusalem.

22 Egos appear by setting themselves apart from other egos. Persons appear by entering into relation with other persons.
1923 *Ich und Du* (translated by R G Smith as *I and Thou*, 1936).

23 *Jedes geeinzelte Du ist ein Durchblick zu ihm. Durch jedes geeinzelte Du spricht das Grundwort das Ewige an.*
Every particular *Thou* is a glimpse through to the eternal *Thou*; by means of every particular *Thou* the primary word addresses the eternal *Thou.*
1923 *Ich und Du* (translated by R G Smith as *I and Thou*, 1936).

Buchan, John, 1st Baron Tweedsmuir 1875–1940

Scottish author and statesman, best known for his fast-moving adventure stories, particularly *The Thirty-Nine Steps* (1915). He was Governor-General of Canada from 1935 until his death.

24 You think that a wall as solid as the earth separates civilisation from barbarism. I tell you the division is a thread, a sheet of glass.
1916 *The Power-House*, ch.3, 'Tells of a Midsummer Night'.

25 Civilisation is a conspiracy.
1916 *The Power-House*, ch.3, 'Tells of a Midsummer Night'.

26 It's a great life if you don't weaken.
1919 *Mr Standfast*, ch.5.

27 Look at the Irish! They are the cleverest propagandists extant, and managed to persuade most people that they were a brave, generous, humorous, talented, warm-hearted race, cruelly yoked to a dull mercantile England, when, God knows, they were exactly the opposite.
1924 *The Three Hostages.*

28 To live for a time close to great minds is the best kind of education.
1940 *Memory Hold-the-Door*, ch.2.

29 An atheist is a man who has no invisible means of support.
1943 Quoted in H E Fosdick *On Being a Real Person*, ch.10.

Buchanan, James 1791–1868

US statesman and 15th President (1857–61). A Democrat, he tried to maintain a balance between pro-slavery and anti-slavery factions, but was unable to avert the Civil War (1861–5).

30 All the friends that I loved and wanted to reward are dead, and all the enemies that I hated and I had marked out for punishment are turned to my friends.
1857 On finally achieving his country's highest political office at the age of 65.

31 If you are as happy, my dear Sir, on entering this house as I am on leaving it and returning home, you are the happiest man in the country.
1861 Said on welcoming his successor, Abraham Lincoln, to the White House.

Buchman, Sidney 1902–75

US film writer and producer. His films include *Mr Smith Goes to Washington* (1939), *Here Comes Mr Jordan* (1941) and *The Group* (1966).

32 I wouldn't give you two cents for all your fancy rules if, behind them, they didn't have a little bit of plain, ordinary kindness—and a little looking out for the other fella, too.
1939 Line delivered by James Stewart in *Mr Smith Goes to Washington.*

Buchwald, Art 1925–

US writer and humorist. He won a Pulitzer Prize for outstanding commentary (1982).

33 This is not an easy time for humorists because the government is far funnier than we are.
1987 Speech to international meeting of satirists and cartoonists. Reported in the *New York Times*, 28 Jun.

Buck, Gene (Edward Eugene) 1885–1957

US songwriter.

34 That Shakespearian rag,—
Most intelligent, very elegant.
1912 'That Shakespearian Rag' (with Herman Ruby).
► See Eliot 306:57.

Buck, Pearl *née Sydenstricker* 1892–1973

US novelist, brought up in China and later a teacher and missionary there. Her works include *The Good Earth* (1931), set in China. She won the Nobel prize for literature in 1938.

35 Race prejudice is not only a shadow over the colored—it is a shadow over all of us, and the shadow is darkest over those who feel it least and allow its evil effects to go on.
1943 *What America Means To Me*, ch.1.

36 None who have always been free can understand the terrible fascinating power of the hope of freedom to those who are not free.
1943 *What America Means To Me*, ch.4.

37 Every great mistake has a halfway moment, a split second when it can be recalled and perhaps remedied.
1943 *What America Means To Me*, ch.10.

38 Praise out of season, or tactlessly bestowed, can freeze the heart as much as blame.
1967 *To My Daughters, With Love*, 'First Meeting'.

39 Nothing and no one can destroy the Chinese people. They are relentless survivors… They yield, they bend to the wind, but they never break.
1972 *China, Past and Present*, ch.1.

Bucke, Richard Maurice 1837–1902

Canadian psychiatrist and author. His works include *Cosmic Consciousness: A Study in the Evolution of the Human Mind* (1901).

40 Cosmic consciousness.
1894 Phrase first used in a paper read by Bucke to the American Medico-Psychological Association, Philadelphia, 18 May. He defined it as 'a higher form of consciousness than that possessed by the ordinary man'.

Buckingham, George Villiers, 2nd Duke of 1628–87

English statesman, exiled after the Royalist defeat in the Civil War. He became a member of Charles II's cabal after the Restoration, and was instrumental in Clarendon's downfall (1667), but lost power and was dismissed in 1674.

41 Ay, now the plot thickens very much upon us.
1672 *The Rehearsal*, act 3, sc.1.

42 The world is made up for the most part of fools and knaves.
'To Mr Clifford, on his *Humane Reason*', collected in *The Dramatic Works* (1715), vol.2.

Buechner, (Carl) Frederick 1926–

US clergyman, novelist, poet and essayist. His works include *Lion Country* (1971) and *Godric* (1980).

43 Glory is to God what style is to an artist… To behold God's glory, to sense his style, is the closest you can get this side of Paradise, just as to read King Lear is the closest you can get to Shakespeare.
1973 *Wishful Thinking*.

44 There is no event so commonplace but that God is present in it, always hiddenly, always leaving you room to recognize him or not to recognize him… Listen to your life. See it for the fathomless mystery it is. In the boredom and pain of it no less than in the excitement and gladness: touch, taste, smell your way to the heavenly and hidden heart of it because in the last analysis all moments are key moments, and life itself is grace.
1983 *Now and Then*.

Buffett, Warren Edward 1930–

US investment broker and corporate executive.

45 It is better to be approximately right than precisely wrong.
1994 In *Fortune*, 4 Apr.

Buford, Bill (William Holmes) 1954–

US-born editor and writer who has spent much of his career in Britain. He edited *Granta* (1979–95), then moved to the *New Yorker* as Fiction and Literary Editor (1995–2002) and became its European Correspondent in 2002.

46 I found myself growing increasingly irritated with the notion of a British novel, which was really an irritation with the word British, a grey, unsatisfactory, bad-weather kind of word, a piece of linguistic compromise.
1994 Editorial, *Granta*, no.43.

Bukowski, Charles 1920–94

German-born US poet and writer. His spare, sardonic writing evoked a seamy, low-life urban netherworld in poems, short stories and novels.

47 Show me a man who lives alone and has a perpetually clean kitchen, and 8 times out of 9 I'll show you a man with detestable spiritual qualities.
1967 *Tales of Ordinary Madness*, 'Too Sensitive'.

48 You begin saving the world by saving one man at a time; all else is grandiose romanticism or politics.
1967 *Tales of Ordinary Madness*, 'Too Sensitive'.

49 Erections, Ejaculations, Exhibitions and General Tales of Ordinary Madness.
1972 Title of book.

50 Love is a Dog from Hell.
1977 Title of book.

51 Play the Piano Drunk Like a Percussion Instrument Until the Fingers Begin to Bleed a Bit.
1979 Title of book.

Buller, A(rthur) H(enry) Reginald 1874–1944

Canadian botanist, Professor of Botany at the University of Manitoba.

52 There was a young lady named Bright
Whose speed was far faster than light;
She set out one day
In a relative way
And returned on the previous night.
1923 'Relativity', published anonymously in *Punch*, 19 Dec. Buller's claim to authorship is recorded in W S Baring-Gould *The Lure of the Limerick* (1968).

Bullock, Alan Louis Charles, Baron Bullock
1914–2004

British historian, notably of 20c Europe. He was Master of St Catherine's College, Oxford (1960–80).

53 Hitler showed surprising loyalty to Mussolini, but it never extended to trusting him.
1952 *Hitler: A Study in Tyranny.*

54 The people Hitler never understood, and whose actions continued to exasperate him to the end of his life, were the British.
1952 *Hitler: A Study in Tyranny.*

Bulmer-Thomas, Ivor 1905–93

British politician and writer. He joined *The Times* (1930–7) and was later deputy editor of the *Daily Telegraph* (1953–4). He entered parliament as a Labour MP in 1942, turning Conservative in 1949.

55 If he ever went to school without any boots, it was because he was too big for them.
1949 At the Conservative Party conference, responding to remarks by Harold Wilson about his humble upbringing.
➥ *See Wilson 915:89.*

Bülow, Prince Bernhard Heinrich von 1849–1929

German statesman, Chancellor (1900–9), Foreign Secretary (1897), Count (1899) and Prince (1905). He wrote *Imperial Germany* (translated 1916) and *Memoirs* (translated 1931–2).

56 *Mit einem Worte: wir wollen niemand in den Schatten stellen aber wir verlangen auch unseren Platz an der Sonne.*
In a word, we desire to throw no one into the shade, but we also demand our own place in the sun.
1897 Speech to the Reichstag, 6 Dec.

Bulwer-Lytton, Edward George Lytton, 1st Baron Lytton 1803–73

English writer and politician, known for historical novels such as *The Last Days of Pompeii* (1834), poetry and several plays. A Reform MP (1831–41), he returned as a Conservative in 1852.

57 It was a dark and stormy night.
1830 Opening words of *Paul Clifford.*

58 Beneath the rule of men entirely great, the pen is mightier than the sword.
1839 *Richelieu*, act 2, sc.2.

Bunting, Basil 1900–85

English poet. He was encouraged by Pound and worked with Ford Madox Ford on *The Transatlantic Review*, but never found a wide audience. The long poem *Briggflatts* (1966) is his best-known work.

59 Our doom
is, to be sifted by the wind,

heaped up, smoothed down like silly sands.
We are less permanent than thought.
1925 *Villon*, pt.1.

60 Name and date
split in soft slate
a few months obliterate.
1966 *Briggflatts.*

61 It looks well enough on the page, but never
well enough.
1966 *Briggflatts.*

62 Clear Cymric voices carry well this Autumn night,
Aneurin and Taliesin, cruel owls
for whom it is never altogether dark
before the rules made poetry a pedant's game.
1966 *Briggflatts.*

63 Who
swinging his axe
to fell kings,
guesses
where we go?
1966 *Briggflatts*, coda.

Buñuel, Luis 1900–83

Spanish film director, who was successful with early surrealist experiments in collaboration with Dalí. His work is characterized by a poetic, often erotic, use of imagery, black humour and a hatred of Catholicism.

64 *Grâce à Dieu, je suis toujours athée.*
Thanks be to God, I am still an atheist.
1959 In *Le Monde*, 16 Dec.

65 *Le Charme discret de la bourgeoisie.*
The Discreet Charm of the Bourgeoisie.
1972 Title of film.

Bunyan, John 1628–88

English writer and preacher. His father was a tinker and he received little formal education. His works, including an autobiography *Grace Abounding to the Chief of Sinners* (1666) and probably most of *The Pilgrim's Progress* (1st part 1678, 2nd part 1684), were written while imprisoned for nonconformity.

66 Oh, the diligence of Satan! Oh, the desperateness of man's heart!
1666 *Grace Abounding to the Chief of Sinners.*

67 This miry slough, is such a place as cannot be mended: It is the descent whither the scum and filth that attends conviction for sin doth continually run, and therefore is it called the Slough of Despond.
1678 *The Pilgrim's Progress*, pt.1.

68 The valley of Humiliation.
1678 *The Pilgrim's Progress*, pt.1.

69 It beareth the name of Vanity-Fair, because the town where 'tis kept, is lighter than vanity.
1678 *The Pilgrim's Progress*, pt.1.

70 Hanging is too good for him, said Mr Cruelty.
1678 *The Pilgrim's Progress*, pt 1.

71 Now Giant Despair had a wife, and her name was Diffidence.
1678 *The Pilgrim's Progress*, pt.1.

72 Sleep is sweet to the labouring man.
1678 *The Pilgrim's Progress*, pt.1.

73 So I awoke, and behold it was a dream.
1678 *The Pilgrim's Progress*, pt.1.

74 A man that could look no way but downwards, with a muckrake in his hand.
1684 *The Pilgrim's Progress*, pt.2.

75 For though when he was here, he was Fool in every man's mouth, yet now he is gone he is highly

commended of all.
1684 *The Pilgrim's Progress*, pt.2.

76 He that is down needs fear no fall,
He that is low no pride.
He that is humble ever shall
Have God to be his guide.
1684 *The Pilgrim's Progress*, pt.2.

77 My Sword, I give to him that shall succeed me in my Pilgrimage, and my Courage and Skill, to him that can get it. My Marks and Scars I carry with me, to be a witness for me, that I have fought his Battles, who now will be my Rewarder… As he went, he said, Death, where is thy Sting? And as he went down deeper, he said, Grave where is thy Victory? So he passed over, and the Trumpets sounded for him on the other side.
1684 Mr Valiant-for-Glory. *The Pilgrim's Progress*, pt.2.

78 He that lives in sin and looks for happiness hereafter is like him that soweth cockle and thinks to fill his barn with wheat or barley.
1684 *The Pilgrim's Progress*, pt.2.

Burbank, Luther 1849–1926

US plant breeder and natural scientist.

79 Science is knowledge arranged and classified according to truth, facts, and the general laws of nature.
1926 Interview in the *San Francisco Bulletin*, 22 Jan.

Burchard, Samuel Dickinson 1812–91

US Presbyterian minister and staunch Republican supporter.

80 The party whose antecedents are rum, Romanism, and rebellion.
1884 Of the Democratic party. Speech at the Fifth Avenue Hotel, New York City, 29 Oct.

Burgess, Anthony *real name John Anthony Burgess Wilson* 1917–94

English writer. He is widely regarded as among the most important novelists of his generation, notably for his controversial dystopian novel *A Clockwork Orange* (1962).

81 Who ever heard of a clockwork orange? Then I read a malenky bit out loud in a sort of very high type preaching goloss: 'The attempt to impose upon man, a creature of growth and capable of sweetness, to ooze juicily at the last round the bearded lips of God, to attempt to impose, I say, laws and conditions appropriate to a mechanical creation, against this I raise my sword-pen.'
1962 *A Clockwork Orange*.

82 He said it was artificial respiration, but now I find I am to have his child.
1963 *Inside Mr Enderby*, pt.1, ch.4.

83 Bath twice a day to be really clean, once a day to be passably clean, once a week to avoid being a public menace.
1963 *Inside Mr Enderby*, pt.2, ch.1.

84 Rome's just a city like anywhere else. A vastly overrated city, I'd say. It trades on belief just as Stratford trades on Shakespeare.
1963 *Inside Mr Enderby*, pt.2, ch.1.

85 *Pax Romana*. Where they made a desolation they called it a peace. What absolute nonsense! It was a nasty, vulgar sort of civilization, only dignified by being hidden under a lot of declensions.
1963 *Inside Mr Enderby*, pt.2, ch.2.

86 Keep away from physicians. It is all probing and guessing and pretending to them. They leave it to Nature to cure in her own time, but they take the credit. As well as very fat fees.
1964 *Nothing Like the Sun*.

87 The possession of a book becomes a substitute for reading it.
1966 In the *New York Times Book Review*, 4 Dec.

88 A sure sign of an amateur is too much detail to compensate for too little life.
1971 In the *Times Literary Supplement*, 18 Jun.

89 Death comes along like a gas bill one can't pay—and that's all one can say about it.
1974 Interview in *Playboy*.

90 There is usually something wrong with writers the young like.
1974 Interview in *Playboy*.

91 It was the afternoon of my eighty-first birthday, and I was in bed with my catamite when Ali announced that the archbishop had come to see me.
1980 *Earthly Powers*, opening lines.

92 Reality is what I see, not what you see.
1983 In the *Sunday Times Magazine*, 18 Dec.

93 God was good on the physical and emotional sides and a great one for hate. He generously spilled his own hate into his dearest creation.
1984 *Enderby's Dark Lady*.

94 If Freud had worn a kilt in the prescribed Highland manner he might have had a very different attitude to genitals.
1986 In the *Observer*, 24 Aug.

95 Death, like the quintessence of otherness, is for others.
1987 *Little Wilson and Big God*, ch.6.

96 Music says nothing to the reason: it is a kind of closely structured nonsense.
1989 In the *Observer*, 23 Jul.

97 I could see now that a literary education did not fit one for the popular novelist's trade. Once you had started using words like flavicomous or acroamatic, because you liked the sound of them, you were lost.
1990 *You've Had Your Time*, ch.1.

Burgon, John William 1813–88

English cleric, Dean of Chichester from 1876.

98 Match me such marvel, save in Eastern clime,—
A rose-red city—'half as old as Time'!
1845 *Petra*.

Burke, Edmund 1729–97

Anglo-Irish statesman and political philosopher. He became Secretary for Ireland (1759) and an MP (1765). His works include *Reflections on the French Revolution* (1790).

99 No passion so effectually robs the mind of all its powers of acting than fear.
1757 *On the Sublime and Beautiful*, pt.2, section 2.

1 Custom reconciles us to everything.
1757 *On the Sublime and Beautiful*, pt.4, section 18.

2 It is a general popular error to imagine the loudest complainers for the public to be the most anxious for its welfare.
1769 *Observations on a Late Publication on the Present State of the Nation*, 2nd edn.

3 To complain of the age we live in, to murmur at the present possessors of power, to lament the past, to conceive extravagant hopes of the future, are the common dispositions of the greatest part of mankind.
1770 *Thoughts on the Cause of the Present Discontents*.

4 When bad men combine, the good must associate; else they will fall, one by one, an unpitied sacrifice in a contemptible struggle.
1770 *Thoughts on the Cause of the Present Discontents*.

5 It is therefore our business carefully to cultivate in our minds, to rear to the most perfect vigour and maturity, every sort of generous and honest feeling that belongs to our nature. To bring the dispositions that are loved in private life into the service and conduct of the commonwealth; so to be patriots, as not to forget we are gentlemen.
1770 *Thoughts on the Cause of the Present Discontents*.

6 The greater the power, the more dangerous is the abuse.
1771 Speech on the Middlesex Election, House of Commons, 7 Feb.

7 Parliament is a deliberative assembly of one nation. You choose a Member indeed; but when you have chosen him, he is not the Member for Bristol, but he is a Member of Parliament.
1774 Speech to Bristol voters.

8 The concessions of the weak are the concessions of fear.
1775 *On Conciliation with America*.

9 The use of force alone is but temporary. It may subdue for a moment; but it does not remove the necessity of subduing again; and a nation is not governed, which is perpetually to be conquered.
1775 *On Conciliation with America*.

10 Nothing less will content me, than *whole America*.
1775 *On Conciliation with America*.

11 All Protestantism, even the most cold and passive, is a sort of dissent. But the religion most prevalent in our northern colonies is a refinement on the principle of resistance; it is the dissidence of dissent, and the Protestantism of the Protestant religion.
1775 *On Conciliation with America*.

12 It is not, what a lawyer tells me I may do; but what humanity, reason, and justice, tells me I ought to do.
1775 *On Conciliation with America*.

13 Freedom and not servitude is the cure of anarchy; as religion, and not atheism, is the true remedy for superstition.
1775 *On Conciliation with America*.

14 Slavery they can have anywhere. It is a weed that grows in every soil.
1775 *On Conciliation with America*.

15 It is the love of the people; it is their attachment to their government, from the sense of the deep stake they have in such a glorious institution, which gives you your army and your navy, and infuses into both that liberal obedience, without which your army would be a base rabble, and your navy nothing but rotten timber.
1775 *On Conciliation with America*.

16 A great empire and little minds go ill together.
1775 *On Conciliation with America*.

17 All government, indeed every human benefit and enjoyment, every virtue and every prudent act, is founded on compromise and barter.
1775 *On Conciliation with America*.

18 Between craft and credulity, the voice of reason is stifled.
1777 *Letter to the Sheriffs of Bristol*.

19 Liberty too must be limited in order to be possessed.
1777 *Letter to the Sheriffs of Bristol*.

20 Among a people generally corrupt, liberty cannot long exist.
1777 *Letter to the Sheriffs of Bristol*.

21 If any man ask me what a free government is, I answer that for any practical purpose, it is what the people think it so.
1777 *Letter to the Sheriffs of Bristol*.

22 People crushed by law have no hope but from power. If laws are their enemies, they will be enemies to laws; and those, who have much to hope and nothing to lose, will always be dangerous, more or less.
1777 Letter to Charles James Fox, 8 Oct.

23 Individuals pass like shadows, but the Commonwealth is fixed and stable.
1780 Speech, House of Commons, 11 Feb.

24 The people are the masters.
1780 Speech, House of Commons, 11 Feb.

25 Bad laws are the worst sort of tyranny.
1780 Speech, Bristol.

26 He was not merely a chip off the old block, but the old block itself.
1781 Commenting on William Pitt the Younger's maiden speech in the House of Commons, 26 Feb.

27 The people never give up their liberties but under some delusion.
1784 Speech, Buckinghamshire.

28 Whenever our neighbour's house is on fire, it cannot be amiss for the engines to play a little on our own.
1790 *Reflections on the Revolution in France*.

29 A state without the means of some change is without the means of its conservation.
1790 *Reflections on the Revolution in France*.

30 People will not look forward to posterity, who never look backward to their ancestors.
1790 *Reflections on the Revolution in France*.

31 Those who attempt to level never equalize.
1790 *Reflections on the Revolution in France*.

32 Whatever each man can separately do, without trespassing upon others, he has a right to do for himself; and he has a right to a fair portion of all which society, with all its combination of skill and force, can do in his favour.
1790 *Reflections on the Revolution in France*.

33 Government is a contrivance of human wisdom to provide for human wants.
1790 *Reflections on the Revolution in France*.

34 The age of chivalry is gone.—That of sophisters, economists, and calculators, has succeeded; and the glory of Europe is extinguished for ever.
1790 *Reflections on the Revolution in France.*

35 The unbought grace of life, the cheap defence of nations, the nurse of manly sentiment and heroic enterprise is gone! it is gone, that sensibility of principle, that chastity of honour, which felt a stain like a wound, which ennobled whatever it touched, and under which vice itself lost half its evil, by losing all its grossness.
1790 *Reflections on the Revolution in France.*

36 In the groves of their academy, at the end of every vista, you see nothing but the gallows.
1790 *Reflections on the Revolution in France.*

37 Kings will be tyrants from policy when subjects are rebels from principle.
1790 *Reflections on the Revolution in France.*

38 Man is by his constitution a religious animal; atheism is against not only our reason, but our instincts.
1790 *Reflections on the Revolution in France.*

39 Society is indeed a contract…it becomes a partnership not only between those who are living, but between those who are living, those who are dead, and those who are to be born.
1790 *Reflections on the Revolution in France.*

40 Superstition is the religion of feeble minds.
1790 *Reflections on the Revolution in France.*

41 Our patience will achieve more than our force.
1790 *Reflections on the Revolution in France.*

42 By hating vices too much, they come to love men too little.
1790 *Reflections on the Revolution in France.*

43 We begin our public affection in our families. No cold relation is a zealous citizen.
1790 *Reflections on the Revolution in France.*

44 Good order is the foundation of all good things.
1790 *Reflections on the Revolution in France.*

45 The only infallible criterion of wisdom to vulgar judgements—success.
1791 *Letter to a Member of the National Assembly.*

46 Tyrants seldom want pretexts.
1791 *Letter to a Member of the National Assembly.*

47 Somebody has said, that a king may make a nobleman but he cannot make a gentleman.
1795 Letter to William Smith, 29 Jan.

48 And having looked to government for bread, on the very first scarcity they will turn and bite the hand that fed them. To avoid that evil, government will redouble the causes of it; and then it will become inveterate and incurable.
1795 *Thoughts and Details on Scarcity*, Nov (published 1800).

49 To innovate is not to reform.
1796 *A Letter to a Noble Lord.*

50 All men that are ruined are ruined on the side of their natural propensities.
1796 *Two Letters on the Proposals for Peace with the Regicide Directory*, 9th edn.

51 Example is the school of mankind, and they will learn at no other.
1796 *Two Letters on the Proposals for Peace with the Regicide Directory*, 9th edn.

52 It is necessary only for the good man to do nothing for evil to triumph.
Attributed.

Burke, Johnny 1908–64

US lyricist.

53 Every time it rains, it rains
Pennies from heaven.
1936 'Pennies from Heaven'.
➨ *See also Thatcher 850:18.*

54 Like Webster's dictionary, we're Morocco bound.
1942 Title song in *Road to Morocco*, sung by Bing Crosby and Bob Hope. Music by Jimmy Van Heusen.

55 Or would you like to swing on a star
Carry moonbeams home in a jar
And be better off than you are
Or would you rather be a fish?
1944 *Swinging on a Star*, sung by Bing Crosby in the film *Going My Way.* Music by Jimmy Van Heusen.

Burke, Kathy 1964–

English actress.

56 If they want rough, then I get the phone call.
1997 In the *Observer*, 5 Jan.

Burke, Kenneth 1897–1986

US music and literary critic. His theory of literature as 'symbolic action' was very influential.

57 Any performance is discussable from the standpoint of what it *attains* or what it *misses*. Comprehensiveness can be discussed as superficiality, intensiveness as stricture, tolerance as uncertainty—and the poor *pedestrian* abilities of a fish are clearly explainable in terms of his excellence as a *swimmer*. A way of seeing is also a way of not seeing.
1936 *Permanence and Change.*

Burke, Tim(othy) c.1942–

Canadian newspaper columnist.

58 There are no lapsed Catholics after a Christmas concert by Pavarotti.
1987 In *The Montreal Gazette*, 8 Dec.

Burns, Ken Lauren 1953–

US film-maker and historian. He has won numerous awards for documentary and historical films on aspects of American life.

59 We are a people starved for self-definition.
1991 On the success of his 11-hour television documentary *The Civil War*. In *People*, 7 Jan.

Burns, Robert 1759–96

Scottish poet and songwriter, the son of a farmer. The Kilmarnock edition (1786) of his poems made his name, and his skill at providing lyrics for old Scottish airs assured his place as one of the world's most popular poets and as his country's national bard. His influence in promoting Scots in literature was enormous.

60 Green grow the rashes, O;
Green grow the rashes, O;
The sweetest hours that e'er I spend,
Are spent amang the lasses, O.
1784 'Green grow the Rashes. A Fragment', chorus.

61 What signifies the life o' man,
An 'twere na for the lasses, O.
1784 'Green grow the Rashes. A Fragment', stanza 1.

62 If honest Nature made you *fools*,
What sairs your grammars.
1785 'Epistle to J. Lapraik, An Old Scotch Bard, 1 April 1785', stanza 11.

63 They *gang* in Stirks, and *come out* Asses,
Plain truth to speak;
An' syne they think to climb Parnassus
By dint o' Greek!
1785 'Epistle to J. Lapraik, An Old Scotch Bard, 1 April 1785', stanza 12.

64 Gie me ae spark o' Nature's fire,
That's a' the learning I desire.
1785 'Epistle to J. Lapraik, An Old Scotch Bard, 1 April 1785', stanza 13.

65 O Thou that in the heavens does dwell!
Wha, as it pleases best Thysel,
Sends ane to heaven, an' ten to hell,
A' for Thy glory,
And no for ony gude or ill
They've done before Thee!
1785 'Holy Willie's Prayer', stanza 1.

66 My curse upon your whunstane hearts,
Ye Enbrugh Gentry!
The tythe o' what ye waste at *cartes*
Wad stow'd his pantry!
1785 'To W. Simpson, Ochiltree', stanza 4, referring to the poet Robert Fergusson, who died a pauper in the Edinburgh bedlam in 1774 at the age of 24, and whom Burns considered 'my elder brother in misfortune, by far my elder brother in the muse'.

67 Some books are lies frae end to end,
And some great lies were never penn'd.
1785 'Death and Doctor Hornbook. A True Story', stanza 1.

68 I was na fou, but just had plenty.
1785 'Death and Doctor Hornbook. A True Story', stanza 3.

69 There's some are fou o' *love divine*;
There's some are fou o' *brandy*.
1785 'The Holy Fair', stanza 27.

70 From scenes like these, old SCOTIA's grandeur springs,
That makes her lov'd at home, rever'd abroad:
Princes and lords are but the breath of kings,
'An honest man's the noble work of GOD'.
1785 'The Cotter's Saturday Night', stanza 19. The last line is in fact a misquotation of Pope; 'noble' was corrected to 'noblest' in the 1794 edition of Burns's poems.
► *See Pope 660:25.*

71 Wee, sleeket, cowrin, tim'rous *beastie*,
O, what a panic's in thy breastie!
Thou need na start awa sae hasty
Wi' bickering brattle!
I wad be laith to rin an' chase thee,
Wi' murd'ring *pattle!*
1785 'To A Mouse, On turning her up in her Nest with the Plough, November, 1785', stanza 1.

72 The best-laid schemes o' *Mice* an' *Men*
Gang aft a-gley.
1785 'To A Mouse, On turning her up in her Nest with the Plough, November, 1785', stanza 7.

73 A fig for those by law protected!
Liberty's a glorious feast!
Courts for Cowards were erected,
Churches built to please the Priest.
c.1786 'The Jolly Beggars', or 'Love and Liberty, a Cantata', chorus to a song to the tune 'Jolly Mortals, fill your glasses'.

74 His lockèd, letter'd, braw brass-collar,
Show'd him the *gentleman* an' *scholar*.
1786 'The Twa Dogs'.

75 The tither was a *ploughman's collie*,
A rhyming, ranting, raving billie.
1786 'The Twa Dogs'.

76 FREEDOM and WHISKY gang thegither,
Tak aff your *dram!*
1786 'The Author's Earnest Cry and Prayer, to the Right Honorable and Honorable, the Scotch Representatives in the House of Commons', stanza 30.

77 O Thou, whatever title suit thee!
Auld Hornie, Satan, Nick, or Clootie.
1786 'Address to the Deil', stanza 1.

78 An' now, auld *Cloots*, I ken ye're thinkan,
A certain *Bardie's* rantin, drinkin,
Some luckless hour will send him linkan,
To your black pit;
But faith! he'll turn a corner jinkan,
An' cheat you yet.
1786 'Address to the Deil', stanza 20.

79 But *Facts* are cheels that winna ding,
And downa be disputed.
1786 'A Dream', stanza 4.

80 Man's inhumanity to Man
Makes countless thousands mourn!
1786 'Man was made to Mourn, A Dirge', stanza 7.

81 O wad some Pow'r the giftie gie us
To see oursels as ithers see us!
It wad frae monie a blunder free us
An' foolish notion.
1786 'To a Louse, On Seeing one on a Lady's Bonnet at Church', stanza 8.

82 It was upon a Lammas night,
When corn rigs are bonie,
Beneath the moon's unclouded light,
I held awa to Annie.
1786 'Song, The Rigs o' Barley', or 'Corn Rigs Are Bonie', stanza 1.

83 I hae been blythe wi' Comrades dear;
I hae been merry drinking.
1786 'Song, The Rigs o' Barley', or 'Corn Rigs Are Bonie', stanza 4.

84 Corn rigs, an' barley rigs,
An' corn rigs are bonie:
I'll ne'er forget that happy night,
Amang the rigs wi' Annie.
1786 'Song, The Rigs o' Barley', or 'Corn Rigs Are Bonie', chorus.

85 Now westlin winds, and slaught'rin guns
Bring Autumn's pleasant weather.
1786 'Song, composed in August', stanza 1.

86 O ye wha are sae guid yoursel,
Sae pious and sae holy,
Ye've nought to do but mark and tell

Your Neebours' fauts an folly!
1786 'Address to the Unco Guid, or the Rigidly Righteous', stanza 1.

87 Then gently scan your brother Man,
Still gentler sister Woman;
Tho' they may gang a kennin wrang,
To step aside is human.
1786 'Address to the Unco Guid, or the Rigidly Righteous', stanza 7.

88 Fair fa' your honest, sonsie face,
Great Chieftain o' the Puddin-race!
Aboon them a' ye tak your place,
Painch, tripe, or thairm:
Weel are ye wordy of a *grace*
As lang's my arm.
1786 'To a Haggis', stanza 1.

89 Auld Scotland wants nae skinking ware That jaups in luggies;
But, if ye wish her gratefu' prayer,
Gie her a *Haggis!*
1786 'To a Haggis', stanza 8.

90 Edina! *Scotia's* darling seat,
All hail thy palaces and tow'rs,
Where once beneath a monarch's feet
Sat Legislation's sov'reign pow'rs.
1786 'Address to Edinburgh', stanza 1.

91 There was a lad was born in Kyle,
But what na day o' what na style.
I doubt it's hardly worth the while
To be sae nice wi' Robin.
1787 'There was a lad', or 'Rantin' Rovin' Robin', stanza 1.

92 Robin was a rovin' Boy,
Rantin' rovin', rantin', rovin',
Robin was a rovin' Boy,
Rantin' rovin' Robin.
1787 'There was a lad', or 'Rantin' Rovin' Robin', chorus.

93 There was three kings into the east,
Three kings both great and high,
And they hae sworn a solemn oath
John Barleycorn should die.
1787 'John Barleycorn. A Ballad', stanza 1.

94 Bony lassie will ye go
To the birks of Aberfeldey.
1787 'The Birks of Aberfeldey', chorus.

95 Sae rantingly, sae wantonly,
Sae dauntingly gae'd he:
He play'd a spring, and danc'd it round
Below the gallows-tree.
1788 'McPherson's Farewell', chorus.

96 O rattlin, roarin Willie,
O he held to the fair;
An' for to sell his fiddle
And buy some other ware.
1788 'Rattlin, roarin Willie', stanza 1.

97 Rattlin, roarin Willie,
Ye're welcome hame to me!
1788 'Rattlin, roarin Willie', stanza 3.

98 Should auld acquaintance be forgot
And never brought to mind?
Should auld acquaintance be forgot,
And auld lang syne!
1788 'Auld Lang Syne', stanza 1. This is the most familiar version of an older, traditional song, reworked by Burns.

99 For auld lang syne, my jo,
For auld lang syne,
We'll tak a cup o' kindness yet
For auld lang syne.
1788 'Auld Lang Syne', chorus. This is the most familiar version of an older, traditional song, reworked by Burns.

1 And there's a hand, my trusty fiere!
And gie's a hand o' thine!
1788 'Auld Lang Syne', stanza 5. This is the most familiar version of an older, traditional song, reworked by Burns.

2 Go fetch to me a pint o' wine,
And fill it in a silver tassie,
That I may drink, before I go,
A service to my bonie lassie.
1788 'My Bonie Mary', stanza 1.

3 Of a' the airts the wind can blaw,
I dearly like the West;
For there the bonie Lassie lives,
The Lassie I lo'e best.
1788 'Of a' the airts the wind can blaw', or 'I Love my Jean', stanza 1.

4 Flow gently, sweet Afton, among thy green braes,
Flow gently, I'll sing thee a song in thy praise.
1789 'Afton Water', stanza 1.

5 The golden Hours, on angel wings,
Flew o'er me and my Dearie;
For dear to me as light and life
Was my sweet Highland Mary.
1789 'Highland Mary', stanza 2.

6 We are na fou, we're nae that fou,
But just a drappie in our e'e;
The cock may craw, the day may daw,
And ay we'll taste the barley bree.
1789 'Willie brew'd a peck o' maut', chorus.

7 Ay waukin, O,
Waukin still and weary:
Sleep I can get nane,
For thinkin on my Dearie.
1790 'Ay waukin O', chorus.

8 My love she's but a lassie yet,
My love she's but a lassie yet;
We'll let her stand a year or twa,
She'll no be half sae saucy yet.
1790 'My love she's but a lassie yet', chorus.

9 My heart's in the Highlands, my heart is not here,
My heart's in the Highlands a chasing the deer;
Chasing the wild deer, and following the roe;
My heart's in the Highlands, wherever I go.
1790 'My heart's in the Highlands', chorus.

10 John Anderson my jo, John,
When we were first acquent;
Your locks were like the raven,
Your bonie brow was brent;
But now your brow is beld, John,
Your locks are like the snaw;
But blessings on your frosty pow,
John Anderson my jo.
1790 'John Anderson my Jo', stanza 1.

11 An ye had been whare I hae been,
Ye wad na been sae canty, O;
An ye had seen what I hae seen,
I' th' braes o' Killiecrankie, O.
1790 'Killiecrankie', chorus.

12 When chapman billies leave the street,
And drouthy neebors, neebors meet,
As market-days are wearing late,
An' folk begin to tak the gate.
1790 'Tam o' Shanter. A Tale'.

13 Whare sits our sulky sullen dame,
Gathering her brows like gathering storm,
Nursing her wrath to keep it warm.
1790 'Tam o' Shanter. A Tale'.

14 Auld Ayr, wham ne'er a town surpasses,
For honest men and bonny lasses.
1790 'Tam o' Shanter. A Tale'.

15 Ah! gentle dames! it gars me greet,
To think how mony counsels sweet,
How mony lengthen'd sage advices,
The husband frae the wife despises!
1790 'Tam o' Shanter. A Tale'.

16 Tam lo'ed him like a vera brither;
They had been fou for weeks thegither.
1790 'Tam o' Shanter. A Tale'.

17 The storm without might rair and rustle,
Tam did na mind the storm a whistle.
1790 'Tam o' Shanter. A Tale'.

18 Kings may be blest but Tam was glorious,
O'er a' the ills o' life victorious!
1790 'Tam o' Shanter. A Tale'.

19 But pleasures are like poppies spread,
You seize the flower, its bloom is shed;
Or like the snow falls in the river,
A moment white—then melts for ever.
1790 'Tam o' Shanter. A Tale'.

20 Nae man can tether time or tide;
The hour approaches Tam maun ride;
That hour, o' night's black arch the key-stane,
That dreary hour Tam mounts his beast in.
1790 'Tam o' Shanter. A Tale'.

21 Inspiring, bold John Barleycorn!
What dangers thou canst make us scorn!
Wi' tippenny, we fear nae evil;
Wi' usquabae, we'll face the devil!
1790 'Tam o' Shanter. A Tale'. 'Usquabae' = whisky.

22 Five tomahawks, wi' blude red-rusted;
Five scymitars, wi' murder crusted.
1790 'Tam o' Shanter. A Tale'.

23 As Tammie glowr'd, amaz'd, and curious,
The mirth and fun grew fast and furious:
The piper loud and louder blew;
The dancers quick and quicker flew.
1790 'Tam o' Shanter. A Tale'.

24 Ah, Tam! Ah, Tam! thou'll get thy fairin!
In hell they'll roast thee like a herrin!
1790 'Tam o' Shanter. A Tale'.

25 Whene'er to drink you are inclin'd,
Or cutty sarks run in your mind,
Think, ye may buy the joys o'er dear—
Remember Tam o' Shanter's mare.
1790 'Tam o' Shanter. A Tale'.

26 Ye banks and braes o' bonie Doon,
How can ye bloom sae fresh and fair;
How can ye chant, ye little birds,
And I sae weary fu' o' care!
1791 'The Banks o' Doon' (2nd version), stanza 1.

27 And my fause Luver staw my rose,
But, ah! he left the thorn wi' me.
1791 'The Banks o' Doon' (2nd version), stanza 2.

28 Ae fond kiss, and then we sever!
Ae fareweel, and then for ever!
Deep in heart-wrung tears I'll pledge thee,
Warring sighs and groans I'll wage thee.
1791 'Ae Fond Kiss', stanza 1.

29 Had we never lov'd sae kindly,
Had we never lov'd sae blindly!
Never met—or never parted,
We had ne'er been broken-hearted.
1791 'Ae Fond Kiss', stanza 4.

30 Fare-thee-weel, thou first and fairest!
Fare-thee-weel, thou best and dearest!
Thine be ilka joy and treasure,
Peace, Enjoyment, Love and Pleasure!
1791 'Ae Fond Kiss', stanza 5.

31 Ye Jacobites by name, give an ear, give an ear!
Ye Jacobites by name, give an ear.
1792 'Ye Jacobites by name', stanza 1.

32 Sic a wife as Willie's wife,
I wad na gie a button for her.
1792 'Willie Wastle', or 'Sic a wife as Willie's wife', stanza 1.

33 Willie Wastle dwalt on Tweed,
The spot they ca'd it Linkumdoddie.
1792 'Willie Wastle', or 'Sic a wife as Willie's wife', stanza 1.

34 Fareweel to a' our Scottish fame,
Fareweel our ancient glory.
1792 'Such a parcel of rogues in a nation', stanza 1.

35 Now Sark rins o'er the Solway sands,
An' Tweed rins to the ocean,
To mark where England's province stands,
Such a parcel of rogues in a nation!
1792 'Such a parcel of rogues in a nation', stanza 1.

36 We're bought and sold for English gold,
Such a parcel of rogues in a nation!
1792 'Such a parcel of rogues in a nation', stanza 3.

37 The deil cam fiddlin thro' the town,
And danc'd awa wi' th' Exciseman;
And ilka wife cries, auld Mahoun,
I wish you luck o' the prize, man!
1792 'The Deil's awa wi' th' Exciseman', stanza 1.

38 There's threesome reels, there's foursome reels,
There's hornpipes and strathspeys, man,
But the ae best dance e'er cam to the Land
Was, the deil's awa wi' th' Exciseman.
1792 'The Deil's awa wi' th' Exciseman', stanza 3.

39 When o'er the hill the eastern star
Tells bughtin-time is near, my jo,
And owsen frae the furrowed field
Return sae dowf and weary O.
1792 'My ain kind dearie', or 'The Lea-rig', stanza 1.

40 I'll meet thee on the lea-rig,
My ain kind Dearie, O.
1792 'My ain kind dearie', or 'The Lea-rig', stanza 1.

41 Scots, wha hae wi' Wallace bled,
Scots, wham Bruce has aften led,
Welcome to your gory bed,—
Or to victorie!—
Now's the day, and now's the hour;
See the front o' battle lour;
See approach proud Edward's power,
Chains and Slaverie!
1793 'Bruce's Address at Bannockburn', stanza 1.

42 Liberty's in every blow!
Let us do or die!
1793 'Bruce's Address at Bannockburn', stanza 3.

43 Though this was fair, and that was braw,
And yon the toast of a' the town,
I sigh'd, and said amang them a',
'Ye are na Mary Morison.'
1793 'Mary Morison', stanza 2.

44 O my Luve's like a red, red rose
That's newly sprung in June;
O my luve's like the melodie
That's sweetly play'd in tune.
As fair art thou, my bonie lass,
So deep in luve am I;
And I will luve thee still, my Dear,
Till a' the seas gang dry.
Till a' the seas gang dry, my Dear,
And the rocks melt wi' the sun:
O I will love thee still, my Dear,
While the sands o' life shall run.
1794 'A red, red rose'.

45 Ca' the yowes to the knowes,
Ca' them whare the heather grows,
Ca' them whare the burnie rowes,
My bonie Dearie!
1794 'Ca' the yowes to the knowes' (2nd version), chorus.

46 Is there for honest Poverty
That hings his head, and a' that;
The coward-slave, we pass him by,
We dare be poor for a' that!
For a' that, and a' that,
Our toils obscure, and a' that,
The rank is but the guinea's stamp,
The man's the gowd for a' that.
1795 'For a' that and a' that', stanza 1.

47 A man's a man for a' that.
1795 'For a' that and a' that', stanza 2.

48 For a' that, and a' that,
It's comin' yet for a' that,
That Man to Man the warld o'er
Shall brothers be, for a' that.
1795 'For a' that and a' that', stanza 5.

49 Gin a body meet a body
Comin thro' the rye,
Gin a body kiss a body
Need a body cry?
1796 'Comin thro' the rye', stanza 2.

50 An' Charlie he's my darling, my darling, my darling,
Charlie he's my darling, the young Chevalier.
1796 'Charlie he's my darling', chorus.

51 It was a' for our rightfu' king,
We left fair Scotland's strand.
1796 'It was a' for our rightfu' king', stanza 1.

52 Now a' is done that men can do,
And a' is done in vain.
1796 'It was a' for our rightfu' king', stanza 2.

53 He turn'd him right and round about,
Upon the Irish shore,
And gae his bridle reins a shake,
With, Adieu for evermore, my dear,
And Adieu for evermore!
1796 'It was a' for our rightfu' king', stanza 3.

54 Oh wert thou in the cauld blast,
On yonder lea, on yonder lea;
My plaidie to the angry airt,
I'd shelter thee, I'd shelter thee.
1796 'Oh wert thou in the cauld blast', stanza 1.

55 There's death in the cup—sae beware!
Nay, more—there is danger in touching;
But wha can avoid the fell snare?
The man and his wine's sae bewitching!
1796 'Inscription on a Goblet'.

Burroughs, Edgar Rice 1875–1950

US novelist. He was a hugely successful writer of popular fiction, much of it in the science-fiction and fantasy genres, and is best known as the creator of Tarzan. The much-quoted line 'Me Tarzan, you Jane', does not appear in any story, and is a misattribution by actor Johnny Weissmuller.

56 Tarzan of the Apes.
1912 Title of story.

Burroughs, William S(eward) 1914–97

US writer. He wandered through the USA and Europe after graduating from Harvard, becoming a heroin addict in New York (1944). His novels draw on his experiences, establishing him as a spokesman of the 'beat' generation.

57 The face of 'evil' is always the face of total need.
1959 *The Naked Lunch*, introduction.

58 I think there are innumerable gods. What we on earth call God is a little tribal God who has made an awful mess.
1965 In *Paris Review*, Fall.

59 After one look at this planet any visitor from outer space would say 'I WANT TO SEE THE MANAGER.'
1985 *The Adding Machine*, 'Women: A Biological Mistake'.

60 You can't fake quality any more than you can fake a good meal.
1987 *The Western Lands*, ch.2.

61 No problems can be solved, and all solutions lead to more problems.
Comment to Allen Ginsberg. Quoted in Barry Miles *Ginsberg* (1989), ch.17.

62 Nothing exists until or unless it is observed. An artist is making something exist by observing it.
1992 *Painting and Guns*, 'The Creative Observer'.

63 Virtue is simply happiness, and happiness is a by-product of function. You are happy when you are functioning.
1992 *Painting and Guns*, 'The Creative Observer'.

Burt, Benjamin Hapgood 1880–1950

US songwriter.

64 All Dressed Up and No Place to Go.
1913 Song title, *The Beauty Shop* (music by Silvio Hein).

65 One evening in October, when I was one-third sober,
An' taking home a 'load' with manly pride;
My poor feet began to stutter, so I lay down in the gutter,
And a pig came up an' lay down by my side.
Then we sang 'It's all fair weather when good fellows get together,'
Till a lady passing by was heard to say:
'You can tell a man who boozes by the company he chooses',
And the pig got up and slowly walked away.
1933 'The Pig Got Up and Slowly Walked Away'.

Burton, C(harles) L(uther) 1876–1961

Canadian businessman.

66 I hold no brief for private enterprise. But I have unshakeable faith in individual enterprise.
1952 *A Sense of Urgency: Memoirs of a Canadian Merchant.*

67 Life, if you have a bent for it, is a beautiful thing. It consists, I do believe, of having a sense of urgency.
1952 *A Sense of Urgency: Memoirs of a Canadian Merchant.*

Burton, Robert *pseudonym* ***Democritus Junior*** 1577–1640

English writer and clergyman. Educated at Oxford, he remained at Christ Church for life. His *Anatomy of Melancholy* (1621) is a vast, witty compendium of Jacobean knowledge and superstition about the 'disease' of melancholy; it went through several editions in his lifetime.

68 All my joys to this are folly,
Naught so sweet as melancholy.
1621 *Anatomy of Melancholy,* 'The Author's Abstract of Melancholy'.

69 A loose, plain, rude writer…I call a spade a spade.
1621 *Anatomy of Melancholy,* 'Democritus to the Reader'.

70 All poets are mad.
1621 *Anatomy of Melancholy,* 'Democritus to the Reader'.

71 I may not here omit those two main plagues, and common dotages of human kind, wine and women, which have infatuated and besotted myriads of people. They go commonly together.
1621 *Anatomy of Melancholy,* pt.1, section 2, member 3, subsection 13.

72 *Hinc quam sit calamus saevior ense patet.*
From this it is clear how much the pen is worse than the sword.
1621 *Anatomy of Melancholy,* pt.1, section 2, member 4, subsection 4.

73 See one promontory (said Socrates of old), one mountain, one sea, one river, and see all.
1621 *Anatomy of Melancholy,* pt.1, section 2, member 4, subsection 7.

74 One was never married, and that's his hell; another is, and that's his plague.
1621 *Anatomy of Melancholy,* pt.1, section 2, member 4, subsection 7.

75 Who cannot give good counsel? 'tis cheap, it costs them nothing.
1621 *Anatomy of Melancholy,* pt.2, section 3, member 1, subsection 1.

76 What is a ship but a prison?
1621 *Anatomy of Melancholy,* pt.2, section 3, member 4, subsection 1.

77 Tobacco, divine, rare, superexcellent tobacco, which goes far beyond all their panaceas, potable gold, and philosopher's stones, a sovereign remedy to all diseases… But, as it is commonly abused by most men, which take it as tinkers do ale, 'tis a plague, a mischief, a violent purger of goods, lands, health, hellish, devilish, and damned tobacco, the ruin and overthrow of body and soul.
1621 *Anatomy of Melancholy,* pt.2, section 4, member 2, subsection 1.

78 But this love of ours is immoderate, inordinate, and not to be comprehended in any bounds. It will not contain itself within the union of marriage or apply to one object, but is a wandering, extravagant, a domineering, a boundless, an irrefragable, a destructive passion.
1621 *Anatomy of Melancholy,* pt.3, section 2, member 1, subsection 2.

79 No cord nor cable can so forcibly draw, or hold so fast, as love can do with a twined thread. The scorching beams under the equinoctial or extremity of cold within the circle Arctic, where the very seas are frozen, cold or torrid zone cannot avoid or expel this heat, fury, and rage of mortal men.
1621 *Anatomy of Melancholy,* pt.3, section 2, member 1, subsection 2.

80 Of women's unnatural, unsatiable lust, what country, what village doth not complain?
1621 *Anatomy of Melancholy,* pt.3, section 2, member 1, subsection 2.

81 A passion of the brain, as all other melancholy, by reason of corrupt imagination.
1621 Of love. *Anatomy of Melancholy,* pt.3, section 2, member 1, subsection 2.

82 One religion is as true as another.
1621 *Anatomy of Melancholy,* pt.3, section 4, member 2, subsection 1.

83 Be not solitary, be not idle.
1621 *Anatomy of Melancholy,* closing words.

Buruma, Ian 1951–

British writer. His works include *The Wages of Guilt* (1994).

84 Isherwood did not so much find himself in Berlin as reinvent himself; Isherwood became a fiction, a work of art.
1986 Of Christopher Isherwood. In the *New Republic*, 4 Nov.

85 A nation of people longing to be 12-year-olds or even younger.
1994 Of Japan. *The Wages of Guilt.*

86 German memory was like a massive tongue seeking out, over and over, a sore tooth.
1994 *The Wages of Guilt.*

Busby, Sir Matt(hew) 1909–94

Scottish football player and manager. He led Manchester United to glory in the 1950s, and successfully rebuilt the team after the Munich air crash in 1958 to win the European Cup in 1968.

87 The theory that the League and Cup double will never be done in modern times is nonsense. I realize no one has done it for sixty years, but there is a simple explanation for that. No club has been good enough.
1957 Attributed, four years before Tottenham Hotspur won both the League Championship and the FA Cup.

Bush, Barbara Pierce 1925–

Former US First Lady. The daughter of a wealthy New York publisher, she married George Bush (1945), who became President in 1989.

88 No other single building is so much a part of the American consciousness.
1992 At the 200th anniversary of the laying of the White House cornerstone. Reported in the *Washington Times*, 24 Jan.

89 I wrote in my diaries about...good meals that I have eaten and am wearing today.
1994 *Barbara Bush: A Memoir.*

90 I am advising the former President, the governor of Florida and the President of the United States. I guess you could say I rule the world.
2003 On her political power. Quoted in *Newsweek*, 31 Mar.

Bush, George Herbert Walker 1924–

US Republican politician and 41st President. After losing to Reagan for the Republican candidacy in the 1980 elections, he became his Vice-President and later President (1989–92). He presided over the US-led UN coalition to defeat Iraq in the Gulf War.

91 The United States is the best and fairest and most decent nation on the face of the earth.
1988 Speech, May.

92 Read my lips: no new taxes.
1988 Accepting the Republican presidential nomination, 19 Aug.

93 It's amazing how many people beat you at golf now that you're no longer president.
1996 In the *Sunday Times*, 22 Dec.

Bush, George W(alker) 1948–

US Republican politician and 43rd President. The son of George Herbert Walker Bush, he was Governor of Texas (1995–2000) before becoming President in 2001.

94 I've inherited 100 per cent of his enemies and only 50 per cent of his friends.
1994 Of the influence of his father, former President George Bush, on his campaign for governor. In the *Washington Times*, 12 Oct.

95 I'm not going to talk about what I did as a child.
1999 On being asked if he ever used marijuana or cocaine. Quoted in *Time*, 22 Feb.

96 Keep good relations with the Grecians.
1999 Quoted in *The Economist*, 12 Jun.

97 New Hampshire has long been known as the bump in the road for front runners—and this year is no exception.
2000 After being defeated in the New Hampshire primary. In the *Sunday Times*, 6 Feb.

98 Reading is the basics for all learning.
2000 Announcing his 'Reading First' initiative in Reston, Virginia, 28 Mar.

99 It's no sign of weakness to talk to your dad.
2000 Denying that he is too much under his father's influence. In the *Sunday Telegraph*, 30 Jul.

1 Well, I think if you say you're going to do something and don't do it, that's trustworthiness.
2000 CNN online chat, 30 Aug.

2 I know the human being and fish can coexist peacefully.
2000 Speaking in Saginaw, Michigan, 29 Sep.

3 I am mindful not only of preserving executive powers for myself, but for my predecessors as well.
2001 Speaking in Washington, 29 Jan.

4 You teach a child to read, and he or her will be able to pass a literacy test.
2001 Speaking in Townsend, Tennessee, 21 Feb.

5 According to the *Oxford English Dictionary*, Mr Jefferson contributed more new words to the language than any other US President. I especially like his term for barbaric pirates: barbaresques. I'm also impressed by his words, debarrass and graffage. The other day I tried a new word for our press corps: misunderestimate. It's not quite in Jefferson's league, but I am giving it my best shot.
2001 Speaking in Washington, 12 Apr.

6 We spent a lot of time talking about Africa, as we should. Africa is a nation that suffers from incredible disease.
2001 Speaking in Gothenburg, Sweden, 14 Jun.

7 We cannot let terrorist and rogue nations hold this nation hostile or hold our allies hostile.
2001 Speaking in Des Moines, Iowa, 21 Aug.

8 Whether we bring our enemies to justice, or bring justice to our enemies, justice will be done.
2001 Address to a joint session of Congress, 20 Sep.

9 Every nation, in every region, now has a decision to make. Either you are with us, or you are with the terrorists. From this day forward, any nation that continues to harbor or support terrorism will be regarded by the United States as a hostile regime.
2001 Address to a joint session of Congress, 20 Sep.

10 States like these, and their terrorist allies, constitute an axis of evil, arming to threaten the peace of the world. By seeking weapons of mass destruction, these regimes pose a grave and growing danger.
2002 State of the Union Address, 29 Jan.

11 Our war on terror is well begun, but it is only begun. This campaign may not be finished on our watch—yet it must be and it will be waged on our watch.
2002 State of the Union Address, 29 Jan.

12 For a century and a half now, America and Japan have formed one of the great and enduring alliances of modern times.
2002 Speaking in Tokyo, Japan, 18 Feb.

13 If this is not evil, then evil has no meaning.
2003 On torture in Iraq. State of the Union Address, 28 Jan.

14 The Columbia is gone. There are no survivors.
2003 On the loss of the space shuttle. Quoted in *Newsweek*, 10 Feb.

15 You're free. And freedom is beautiful. And, you know, it'll take time to restore chaos and order—order out of chaos. But we will.
2003 Speaking in Washington, 13 Apr.

16 Our country puts $1 billion a year up to help feed the hungry. And we're by far the most generous nation in the

world when it comes to that, and I'm proud to report that. This isn't a contest of who's the most generous. I'm just telling you as an aside. We're generous. We shouldn't be bragging about it. But we are. We're very generous.
2003 Speaking in Washington, 16 Jul.

17 The best way to get news is from objective sources. And the most objective sources I have are people on my staff who tell me what's happening in the world.
2003 On Fox News, 22 Sep.

18 See, free nations are peaceful nations. Free nations don't attack each other. Free nations don't develop weapons of mass destruction.
2003 Speaking in Milwaukee, Wisconsin, 3 Oct.

19 The illiteracy level of our children are appalling.
2004 Speaking in Washington, 23 Jan.

20 Iraqis are sick of foreign people coming in their country and trying to destabilize their country. And we will help them rid Iraq of these killers.
2004 Interview on Al Arabiya Television, 4 May.

21 When I speak about the blessings of liberty, coarse videos and crass commercialism are not what I have in mind.
2004 Speaking in Istanbul, 29 Jun.

22 See if Saddam did this. See if he's linked in any way.
In the wake of the 11 September 2001 attacks. Quoted in Richard A Clarke *Against All Enemies: Inside America's War on Terror* (2004).

Bush, Vannevar 1890–1974

US electrical engineer and physicist, Dean of Engineering at the Massachusetts Institute of Technology. He later led the US Office of Scientific Research.

23 To pursue science is not to disparage things of the spirit.
1953 Speech at the Massachusetts Institute of Technology, 5 Oct.

24 It was through the Second World War that most of us suddenly appreciated for the first time the power of man's concentrated efforts to understand and control the forces of nature. We were appalled by what we saw.
1967 *Science is Not Enough.*

25 Knowledge for the sake of understanding, not merely to prevail, that is the essence of our being. None can define its limits, or set its ultimate boundaries.
1967 *Science is Not Enough.*

Bushnell, Candace 1958–

US journalist and author.

26 Let's face it, the unmarried guys in New York suck.
1996 *Sex in the City.*

27 Modelizers are a particular breed. They're a step beyond womanizers, who will sleep with just about anything in a skirt. Modelizers are obsessed not with women but with models. They love them for their beauty and hate them for everything else.
1996 *Sex in the City.*

Busoni, Ferruccio Benvenuto 1866–1924

Italian pianist and composer. An infant prodigy, he taught and played throughout Europe and wrote four operas among other works, mainly for piano. His pupils included Kurt Weill.

28 Music is the art of sounds in the movement of time.
1923 *The Essence of Music.*

Bussy-Rabutin, Comte de 1618–93

French soldier and poet.

29 *L'absence est à l'amour ce qu'est au feu le vent;*
Il éteint le petit, il allume le grand.
Absence is to love what wind is to fire;
It extinguishes the small, it kindles the great.
1665 *Histoire Amoureuse des Gaules. Maximes d'Amour*, pt.2.

30 *Comme vous savez, Dieu est d'ordinaire pour les gros escadrons contre les petits.*
As you know, God is usually on the side of the big squadrons against the small.
1677 Letter to the Comte de Limoges, 18 Oct.

Butler, Joseph 1692–1752

English moral philosopher, cleric and Christian apologist. Originally a dissenter, he joined the Church of England and became Bishop of Bristol, and later of Durham.

31 But to us, probability is the very guide of life.
1736 *The Analogy of Religion*, introduction.

32 Sir, the pretending to extraordinary revelations and gifts of the Holy Ghost is a horrid thing, a very horrid thing.
Comment to John Wesley. Quoted in John Wesley *Works*, pt.13.

Butler (of Saffron Walden), R(ichard) A(usten) Butler, Baron 1902–82

British Conservative politician. He became Chancellor of the Exchequer, Home Secretary and Deputy Prime Minister, and narrowly lost the premiership to Alec Douglas-Home, becoming Foreign Secretary (1963–4).

33 After all, it is not every man who nearly becomes Prime Minister of England.
1957 On being passed over as Harold Macmillan's successor in favour of Alec Douglas-Home, Jan.

34 Politics is the art of the possible.
1971 *The Art of the Possible.*
► *See Galbraith 343:94.*

35 The best Prime Minister we've got.
Attributed comment on Harold Macmillan, made on a train going to the Party Conference in Brighton.

Butler, Samuel 1612–80

English satirist, who served in noble households and in government. His *Hudibras* (1663–78), a burlesque satire on Puritanism, was a special favourite of Charles II. Despite royal favour, he died in penury.

36 A client is fain to hire a lawyer to keep from the injury of other lawyers—as Christians that travel in Turkey are forced to hire Janissaries, to protect them from the insolencies of other Turks.
1660 *Prose Observations.*

37 But here our authors make a doubt
Whether he were more wise or stout.
Some hold the one and some the other;
But howsoe'er they make a pother,
The difference was so small his brain
Outweighed his rage but half a grain;
Which made some take him for a tool

That knaves do work with, called a fool.
1663 *Hudibras*, pt.1, canto 1, l.29–36.

38 We grant, although he had much wit,
He was very shy of using it;
As being loath to wear it out,
And therefore bore it not about,
Unless on holidays, or so,
As men their best apparel do.
1663 *Hudibras*, pt.1, canto 1, l.45–50.

39 'Tis known he could speak Greek
As naturally as pigs squeak.
1663 *Hudibras*, pt.1, canto 1, l.51–2.

40 He was in logic a great critic,
Profoundly skilled in analytic.
He could distinguish and divide
A hair 'twixt south and southwest side.
1663 *Hudibras*, pt.1, canto 1, l.65–8.

41 For every *why* he had a *wherefore*.
1663 *Hudibras*, pt.1, canto 1, l.132.

42 He knew what's what, and that's as high
As metaphysic wit can fly.
1663 *Hudibras*, pt.1, canto 1, l.149–50.

43 And with as delicate a hand
Could twist as tough a rope of sand;
And weave fine cobwebs, fit for skull
That's empty when the moon is full;
Such as take lodgings in a head
That's to be let unfurnished.
1663 *Hudibras*, pt.1, canto 1, l.155–60.

44 And still be doing, never done:
As if Religion were intended
For nothing else but to be mended.
1663 *Hudibras*, pt.1, canto 1, l.202–4.

45 For rhyme the rudder is of verses,
With which like ships they steer their courses.
1663 *Hudibras*, pt.1, canto 1, l.457–8.

46 Great actions are not always true sons
Of great and mighty resolutions.
1663 *Hudibras*, pt.1, canto 1, l.877–8.

47 Ay me! what perils do environ
The man that meddles with cold iron!
1663 *Hudibras*, pt.1, canto 3, l.1–2.

48 I'll make the fur
Fly 'bout the ears of the old cur.
1663 *Hudibras*, pt.1, canto 3, l.277–8.

49 I am not now in fortune's power
He that is down can fall no lower.
1663 *Hudibras*, pt.1, canto 3, l.871–2.

50 Learning, that cobweb of the brain,
Profane, erroneous, and vain.
1663 *Hudibras*, pt.1, canto 3, l.1339–40.

51 She that with poetry is won
Is but a desk to write upon.
1664 *Hudibras*, pt.2, canto 1, l.591–2.

52 Love is a boy, by poets styled,
Then spare the rod, and spoil the child.
1664 *Hudibras*, pt.2, canto 1, l.843–4.

53 Oaths are but words, and words but wind.
1664 *Hudibras*, pt.2, canto 2, l.107.

54 For saints may do the same things by
The spirit, in sincerity,
Which other men are tempted to.
1664 *Hudibras*, pt.2, canto 2, l.235–7.

55 Doubtless the pleasure is as great
Of being cheated, as to cheat.
As lookers-on feel most delight,
That least perceive a juggler's sleight,
And still the less they understand,
The more th' admire his sleight of hand.
1664 *Hudibras*, pt.2, canto 3, l.1–6.

56 For in what stupid age or nation
Was marriage ever out of fashion?
1678 *Hudibras*, pt.3, canto 1, l.817–18.

57 What makes all doctrines plain and clear?
About two hundred pounds a year.
And that which was prov'd true before,
Prove false again? Two hundred more.
1678 *Hudibras*, pt.3, canto 1, l.1277–80.

58 For if it be but half denied,
'Tis half as good as justified.
1678 *Hudibras*, pt.3, canto 2, l.803–4.

59 For, those that fly, may fight again,
Which he can never do that's slain.
1678 *Hudibras*, pt.3, canto 3, l.243–4.

60 He that complies against his will
Is of his own opinion still.
1678 *Hudibras*, pt.3, canto 3, l.547.

61 Neither have the heart to stay,
Nor wit enough to run away.
1678 *Hudibras*, pt.3, canto 3, l.569–60.

62 For money has a power above
The stars and fate, to manage love.
1678 *Hudibras*, pt.3, canto 3, l.1279–80.

Butler, Samuel 1835–1902

English writer and parliamentary secretary. His Utopian satire *Erewhon* (1872) and its supplement *Erewhon Revisited* (1901) deal with the origins of religious belief. His autobiographical novel *The Way of All Flesh* was published posthumously (1903).

63 I am forgetting myself into admiring a mountain which is of no use for sheep. This is wrong. A mountain here is only beautiful if it has good grass on it.
1863 Of Mt Cook. *A First Year in Canterbury Settlement*.

64 The wish to spread those opinions that we hold conducive to our own welfare is so deeply rooted in the English character that few of us can escape its influence.
1872 *Erewhon*.

65 Exploring is delightful to look forward to and back upon, but it is not comfortable at the time, unless it be of such an easy nature as not to deserve the name.
1872 *Erewhon*.

66 A hen is only an egg's way of making another egg.
1877 *Life and Habit*, ch.8.

67 It was very good of God to let Carlyle and Mrs Carlyle marry one another and so make only two people miserable instead of four.
1884 Letter to Miss E M A Savage, 21 Nov.

68 Life is like playing a violin solo in public and learning the

instrument as one goes on.
1895 Speech at the Somerville Club, 27 Feb.

69 It has been said that although God cannot alter the past, historians can; it is perhaps because they can be useful to Him in this respect that He tolerates their existence.
1901 *Erewhon Revisited*, ch.14.

70 All animals, except man, know that the principal business of life is to enjoy it.
1903 *The Way of All Flesh*, ch.19.

71 The advantage of doing one's praising for oneself is that one can lay it on so thick and exactly in the right places.
1903 *The Way of All Flesh*, ch.34.

72 Young as he was, his instinct told him that the best liar is he who makes the smallest amount of lying go the longest way.
1903 *The Way of All Flesh*, ch.39.

73 A man's friendships are, like his will, invalidated by marriage.
1903 *The Way of All Flesh*, ch.75.

74 'Getting into the key of C sharp,' he said, 'is like an unprotected female travelling on the Metropolitan Railway, and finding herself at Shepherd's Bush, without quite knowing where she wants to go to. How is she ever to get safe back to Clapham Junction?'
1903 *The Way of All Flesh*.

75 There's many a good tune played on an old fiddle.
1903 *The Way of All Flesh*.

76 As soon as any art is pursued with a view to money, then farewell, in ninety-nine cases out of a hundred, all hope of genuine good work.
Collected in H F Jones (ed) *The Notebooks of Samuel Butler* (1912).

77 Justice is being allowed to do whatever I like. Injustice is whatever prevents my doing it.
Collected in H F Jones (ed) *The Notebooks of Samuel Butler* (1912).

78 An apology for the Devil: It must be remembered that we have only heard one side of the case. God has written all the books.
Collected in H F Jones (ed) *The Notebooks of Samuel Butler* (1912), ch.14.

79 Handel is so great and so simple that no one but a professional musician is unable to understand him.
Collected in H F Jones (ed) *The Notebooks of Samuel Butler* (1912).

80 The healthy stomach is nothing if not conservative. Few radicals have good digestions.
Collected in H F Jones (ed) *The Notebooks of Samuel Butler* (1912).

81 Science, after all, is only an expression for our ignorance of our own ignorance.
Collected in H F Jones (ed) *The Notebooks of Samuel Butler* (1912).

82 To live is like to love—all reason is against it, and all healthy instinct for it.
Collected in H F Jones (ed) *The Notebooks of Samuel Butler* (1912).

83 The three most important things a man has are, briefly, his private parts, his money, and his religious opinions.
Collected in *Further Extracts from the Notebooks* (1934).

84 Jesus! with all thy faults I love thee still.
Collected in *Further Extracts from the Notebooks* (1934).

85 A lawyer's dream of heaven: every man reclaimed his own property at the resurrection, and each tried to recover it from all his forefathers.
Collected in *Further Extracts from the Notebooks* (1934).

Butler, William 1535–1618

English royal physician.

86 Doubtless God could have made a better berry, but doubtless God never did.
Of the strawberry. Quoted in Izaak Walton *The Compleat Angler* (3rd edn, 1661), pt.1, ch.5.

Butterfield, Sir Herbert 1900–79

English historian, Professor of Modern History at Cambridge.

87 We can do worse than remember the principle which both gives us a firm Rock and leaves us the maximum elasticity for our minds—Hold to Christ, and for the rest be totally uncommitted.
1949 *Christianity and History*.

88 In a profound sense we may say that the crucifixion, however else we may interpret it, accuses human nature, accuses all of us in the very things that we think are our righteousness.
1951 *History and Human Relations*.

Byatt, Dame A(ntonia) S(usan) *née Drabble* 1936–

English writer and critic, sister of Margaret Drabble. Her works include critical studies, short stories and novels, such as *Possession* (Booker Prize, 1990), which explores the experience of women in 20c society, and *The Biographer's Tale* (2000).

89 There is something both gratifying and humiliating in watching a man who has taken you for a routinely silly woman begin to take you seriously.
1985 *Still Life*, ch.18, 'Hic Ille Raphael'.

90 Autobiographies tell more lies than all but the most self-indulgent fiction.
1987 'The Day That E.M. Forster Died'.

91 He's one of those men who argues by increments of noise—so that as you open your mouth he says another, cleverer, louder thing.
1990 *Possession*, ch.15.

92 [J K] Rowling speaks to an adult generation that hasn't known and doesn't care about mystery. They are inhabitants of urban jungles, not of the real wild. They don't have the skills to tell ersatz magic from the real thing, for as children they daily invested the ersatz with what imagination they had.
2003 In the *New York Times*, 8 Jul.

Byrd, William 1543–1623

English composer and organist. A firm Catholic, prosecuted as a recusant, he wrote music for both Catholic and Anglican services, as well as madrigals, songs and music for strings.

93 The exercise of singing is delightful to nature and good to preserve the health of Man.
1588 *Psalmes, Sonets and Songs*.

Byrne, David 1952–

Scottish rock singer and guitarist, member of Talking Heads.

94 Book learning, or intelligence of one sort, doesn't guarantee you intelligence of another sort. You can behave just as stupidly with a good college education.
2004 In *Scotland on Sunday*, 29 Feb.

Byron, George Gordon, 6th Baron Byron of Rochdale 1788–1824

English Romantic poet. Lame from birth, he later dramatized himself as a gloomy, romantic man of mystery, the 'Byronic hero'. Suspected of an incestuous affair with his half-sister, he left for Venice, where he wrote *Beppo* (1818) and *Don Juan* (1819–24). He died fervently supporting the Greek war of independence against the Turks.

95 Yet, when confinement's lingering hour was done,
Our sport, our studies, and our souls were one:
Together we impell'd the flying ball;
Together waited in our tutor's hall;
Together join'd in cricket's manly toil.
1807 *Hours of Idleness*, 'Childish Recollections'. Of his childhood days at Harrow public school.

96 I'll publish, right or wrong:
Fools are my theme, let satire be my song.
1809 *English Bards and Scotch Reviewers*, l.5–6.

97 A man must serve his time to every trade
Save censure—critics all are ready made.
Take hackneyed jokes from Miller, got by rote,
With just enough of learning to misquote.
1809 *English Bards and Scotch Reviewers*, l.63–6.

98 Be warm, but pure; be amorous, but be chaste.
1809 *English Bards and Scotch Reviewers*, l.306.

99 The petrifactions of a plodding brain.
1809 *English Bards and Scotch Reviewers*, l.416.

1 Then let Ausonia, skilled in every art
To soften manners, but corrupt the heart,
Pour her exotic follies o'er the town,
To sanction Vice, and hunt Decorum down.
1809 *Engish Bards and Scotch Reviewers*, l.618–21.

2 Let simple Wordsworth chime his childish verse,
And brother Coleridge lull the babe at nurse.
1809 *English Bards and Scotch Reviewers*, l.917–18.

3 And glory, like the phoenix midst her fires,
Exhales her odours, blazes, and expires.
1809 *English Bards and Scotch Reviewers*, l.959–60.

4 Never under the most despotic of infidel Governments did I behold such squalid wretchedness as I have seen since my return, in the very heart of a Christian country. And what are your remedies? After months of inaction, and months of action worse than inactivity, at length comes forth the grand specific—the never-failing nostrum of all state physicians from the days of Draco to the present time; death. Is there not blood enough upon your penal code that more must be poured forth to ascend to Heaven and testify against you?
1812 Maiden speech, House of Lords, 27 Feb, against a proposal to introduce the death penalty for machine-wrecking.

5 A land of meanness, sophistry and mist.
1812 Of Scotland. 'The Curse of Minerva', l.138.

6 Each breeze from foggy mount and marshy plain
Dilutes with drivel every drizzly brain,
Till, burst at length, each wat'ry head o'er flows,
Foul as their soil, and frigid as their snows.
1812 Of Scotland and the Scots. 'The Curse of Minerva', l.139–42.

7 The laughing dames in who he did delight,
Whose large blue eyes, fair locks, and snowy hands,
Might shake the saintship of an anchorite.
1812–18 *Childe Harold's Pilgrimage*, canto 1, stanza 11.

8 Adieu, adieu! my native shore
Fades o'er the waters blue.
1812–18 *Childe Harold's Pilgrimage*, canto 1, stanza 13.

9 Here all were noble, save Nobility.
1812–18 *Childe Harold's Pilgrimage*, canto 1, stanza 85.

10 None are so desolate but something dear,
Dearer than self, possesses or possessed
A thought, and claims the homage of a tear.
1812–18 *Childe Harold's Pilgrimage*, canto 2, stanza 24.

11 Oh, lovely Spain! renown'd, romantic land!
1812–18 *Childe Harold's Pilgrimage*, canto 2, stanza 35.

12 Dark Sappho! could not verse immortal save
That beast imbued with such immortal fire?
Could she not live who life eternal gave?
1812–18 *Childe Harold's Pilgrimage*, canto 2, stanza 39.

13 Fair Greece! sad relic of departed worth!
Immortal, though no more! though fallen, great!
1812–18 *Childe Harold's Pilgrimage*, canto 2, stanza 73.

14 Hereditary bondsmen! know ye not
Who would be free themselves must strike the blow?
1812–18 *Childe Harold's Pilgrimage*, canto 2, stanza 76.

15 And yet how lovely in thine age of woe,
Land of lost gods and godlike men! art thou!
1812–18 Of Greece. *Childe Harold's Pilgrimage*, canto 2, stanza 85.

16 Art, Glory, Freedom fail, but Nature still is fair.
1812–18 *Childe Harold's Pilgrimage*, canto 2, stanza 87.

17 What is the worst of woes that wait on age?
What stamps the wrinkle deeper on the brow?
To view each loved one blotted from life's page,
And be alone on earth, as I am now.
1812–18 *Childe Harold's Pilgrimage*, canto 2, stanza 98.

18 Once more upon the waters! yet once more!
And the waves bound beneath me as a steed
That knows his rider.
1812–18 *Childe Harold's Pilgrimage*, canto 3, stanza 2.

19 The wandering outlaw of his own dark mind.
1812–18 *Childe Harold's Pilgrimage*, canto 3, stanza 3.

20 Years steal
Fire from the mind as vigour from the limb;
And life's enchanted cup but sparkles near the brim.
1812–18 *Childe Harold's Pilgrimage*, canto 3, stanza 8.

21 Where rose the mountains, there to him were friends;
Where rolled the ocean, thereon was his home;
Where a blue sky, and glowing clime, extends,
He had the passion and the power to roam.
1812–18 *Childe Harold's Pilgrimage*, canto 3, stanza 13.

22 The very knowledge that he lived in vain,
That all was over on this side the tomb,
Had made Despair a smilingness assume.
1812–18 *Childe Harold's Pilgrimage*, canto 3, stanza 16.

23 There was a sound of revelry by night,
And Belgium's capital had gathered then
Her beauty and her chivalry, and bright

The lamps that shone o'er fair women and brave men;
A thousand hearts beat happily; and when
Music arose with its voluptuous swell,
Soft eyes looked love to eyes which spake again,
And all went merry as a marriage bell;
But hush! hark! a deep sound strikes like a rising knell!
1812–18 *Childe Harold's Pilgrimage*, canto 3, stanza 21.

24 He rushed into the field, and, foremost fighting, fell.
1812–18 *Childe Harold's Pilgrimage*, canto 3, stanza 23.

25 Quiet to quick bosoms is a hell.
1812–18 *Childe Harold's Pilgrimage*, canto 3, stanza 42.

26 I live not in myself, but I become
Portion of that around me; and to me,
High mountains are a feeling, but the hum
Of human cities torture.
1812–18 *Childe Harold's Pilgrimage*, canto 3, stanza 72.

27 His love was passion's essence:—as a tree
On fire by lightning, with ethereal flame
Kindled he was, and blasted.
1812–18 *Childe Harold's Pilgrimage*, canto 3, stanza 78.

28 Sapping a solemn creed with solemn sneer.
1812–18 Of Edward Gibbon. *Childe Harold's Pilgrimage*, canto 3, stanza 107.

29 I have not loved the world, nor the world me.
1812–18 *Childe Harold's Pilgrimage*, canto 3, stanza 113.

30 I stood
Among them, but not of them; in a shroud
Of thoughts which were not their thoughts.
1812–18 *Childe Harold's Pilgrimage*, canto 3, stanza 113.

31 I stood in Venice, on the Bridge of Sighs;
A palace and a prison on each hand:
I saw from out the wave her structures rise
As from the stroke of the enchanter's wand:
A thousand years their cloudy wings expand
Around me, and a dying Glory smiles
O'er the far times, when many a subject land
Look'd to the winged Lion's marble piles,
Where Venice sate in state, thron'd on her hundred isles!
1812–18 *Childe Harold's Pilgrimage*, canto 4, stanza 1.

32 Fair Italy!
Thou art the garden of the world, the home
Of all Art yields, and Nature can decree;
Even in thy desert, what is like to thee?
1812–18 *Childe Harold's Pilgrimage*, canto 4, stanza 26.

33 The moon is up, and yet it is not night;
Sunset divides the sky with her—a sea
Of glory streams along the Alpine height
Of blue Friuli's mountains; Heaven is free
From clouds, but of all colours seems to be
Melted to one vast Iris of the West,
Where the day joins the past eternity.
1812–18 *Childe Harold's Pilgrimage*, canto 4, stanza 27.

34 Italia! oh Italia! thou who hast
The fatal gift of beauty.
1812–18 *Childe Harold's Pilgrimage*, canto 4, stanza 42.

35 Oh Rome! my country! city of the soul!
1812–18 *Childe Harold's Pilgrimage*, canto 4, stanza 78.

36 From mighty wrongs to petty perfidy
Have I not seen what human things could do?
From the loud roar of foaming calumny
To the small whisper of the asp paltry few,
And subtler venom of the reptile crew,
The Janus glance of whose significant eye,
Learning to lie with silence, would seem true,
And without utterance, save the shrug or sigh,
Deal round to happy fools its speechless obloquy.
1812–18 *Childe Harold's Pilgrimage*, canto 4, stanza 136.

37 But I have lived, and have not lived in vain:
My mind may loose its force, my blood its fire,
And my frame perish even in conquering pain;
But there is that within me which shall tire
Torture and Time, and breathe when I expire.
Something unearthly, which they deem not of,
Like the remembered tone of a mute lyre,
Shall on their softened spirits sink, and move
In hearts all rocky now the late remorse of love.
1812–18 *Childe Harold's Pilgrimage*, canto 4, stanza 137.

38 The seal is set.—Now welcome, thou dread power!
Nameless, yet thus omnipotent, which here
Walk'st in the shadow of the midnight hour
With a deep awe, yet all distinct from fear;
Thy haunts are ever where the dead walls rear
Their ivy mantles, and the solemn scene
Derives from thee a sense so deep and clear
That we become a part of what has been,
And grow unto the spot, all-seeing but unseen.
1812–18 *Childe Harold's Pilgrimage*, canto 4, stanza 138.

39 There were his young barbarians all at play,
There was their Dacian mother—he, their sire,
Butchered to make a Roman holiday.
1812–18 *Childe Harold's Pilgrimage*, canto 4, stanza 141.

40 A ruin—yet what ruin! from its mass
Walls, palaces, half-cities, have been reared.
1812–18 *Childe Harold's Pilgrimage*, canto 4, stanza 143.

41 While stands the Coliseum, Rome shall stand;
When falls the Coliseum, Rome shall fall;
And when Rome falls—the World.
1812–18 *Childe Harold's Pilgrimage*, canto 4, stanza 145.

42 Oh! that desert were my dwelling-place,
With one fair spirit for my minister,
That I might all forget the human race,
And, hating no one, love but only her!
1812–18 *Childe Harold's Pilgrimage*, canto 4, stanza 177.

43 There is a pleasure in the pathless woods,
There is a rapture on the lonely shore,
There is society, where none intrudes,
By the deep sea, and music in its roar:
I love not man less, but nature more.
1812–18 *Childe Harold's Pilgrimage*, canto 4, stanza 178.

44 Roll on, thou deep and dark blue Ocean—roll!
Ten thousand fleets sweep over thee in vain;
Man marks the earth with ruin—his control
Stops with the shore.
1812–18 *Childe Harold's Pilgrimage*, canto 4, stanza 179.

45 When for a moment, like a drop of rain,
He sinks into thy depths with bubbling groan,
Without a grave, unknelled, uncoffined, and unknown.
1812–18 *Childe Harold's Pilgrimage*, canto 4, stanza 179.

46 Dark-heaving;—boundless, endless, and sublime—
The image of eternity.
1812–18 Of the sea. *Childe Harold's Pilgrimage*, canto 4, stanza 183.

47 Such hath it been—shall be—beneath the sun
The many still must labour for the one.
1814 *The Corsair*, canto 1, stanza 8.

48 There was a laughing devil in sneer,
That raised emotions both of rage and fear;
And where his frown of hatred darkly fell,
Hope withering fled, and Mercy sighed farewell!
1814 *The Corsair*, canto 1, stanza 9.

49 Deep in my soul that tender secret dwells,
Lonely and lost to light for evermore,
Save when to thine my heart responsive swells,
Then trembles into silence as before.
1814 *The Corsair*,'Medora's Song', canto 1, stanza 14.

50 The spirit burning but unbent
May writhe, rebel—the weak alone repent!
1814 *The Corsair*, canto 2, stanza 10.

51 Oh! too convincing—dangerously dear—
In woman's eye the unanswerable tear!
1814 *The Corsair*, canto 2, stanza 15.

52 Shakespeare's name, you may depend upon it, stands absurdly too high and will go down. He had no invention as to stories, none whatever. He took all his plots from old novels, and threw their stories into dramatic shape… That he threw over whatever he did write some flashes of genius, nobody can deny; but this was all.
1814 Letter to James Hogg, 24 Mar.

53 She walks in beauty like the night
Of cloudless climes and starry skies;
And all that's best of dark and bright
Meet in her aspect and her eyes:
Thus mellowed to that tender light
Which heaven to gaudy day denies.
1815 'She Walks in Beauty'.

54 There's not a joy the world can give like that it takes away.
1816 'Stanzas for Music'.

55 The mind can make
Substance, and people planets of its own
With beings brighter than have been, and give
A breath to forms which can outlive all flesh.
1816 *The Dream*, stanza 1.

56 Sorrow is knowledge: they who know the most
Must mourn the deepest o'er the fatal truth,
The tree of knowledge is not that of Life.
1817 *Manfred*, act 1, sc.1.

57 How beautiful is all this visible world!
How glorious in its action and itself!
But we, who name ourselves its sovereigns, we,
Half dust, half deity, alike unfit
To sink or soar, with our mixed essence make
A conflict of its elements, and breathe
The breath of degradation and of pride.
1817 *Manfred*, act 1, sc.2.

58 In short he was a perfect cavaliero,
And to his very valet seemed a hero.
1818 *Beppo*, stanza 33.

59 His heart was one of those which most enamour us,
Wax to receive, and marble to retain.
1818 *Beppo*, stanza 34.

60 Our cloudy climate, and our chilly women.
1818 *Beppo*, stanza 49.

61 Old man! 'tis not so difficult to die.
1819 *Manfred* (2nd edn), act 3, sc.4.

62 And Coleridge, too, has lately taken wing,
But, like a hawk encumbered with his hood,
Explaining metaphysics to the nation—
I wished he would explain his explanation.
1819–24 *Don Juan*, canto 1, dedication, stanza 2.

63 But—Oh! ye lords of ladies intellectual,
Inform us truly, have they not hen-pecked you all?.
1819–24 *Don Juan*, canto 1, stanza 22.

64 Married, charming, chaste, and twenty-three.
1819–24 *Don Juan*, canto 1, stanza 59.

65 What men call gallantry, and gods adultery,
Is much more common where the climate's sultry.
1819–24 *Don Juan*, canto 1, stanza 63.

66 Christians have burnt each other, quite persuaded
That all the Apostles would have done as they did.
1819–24 *Don Juan*, canto 1, stanza 83.

67 He thought about himself, and the whole earth,
Of man the wonderful, and of the stars,
And how the deuce they ever could have birth;
And then he thought of earthquakes, and of wars,
How many miles the moon might have in girth,
Of air-balloons, and of the many bars
To perfect knowledge of the boundless skies;
And then he thought of Donna Julia's eyes.
1819–24 *Don Juan*, canto 1, stanza 92.

68 A little still she strove, and much repented,
And whispering 'I will ne'er consent'—consented.
1819–24 *Don Juan*, canto 1, stanza 117.

69 Sweet is revenge—especially to women.
1819–24 *Don Juan*, canto 1, stanza 124.

70 'Tis sweet to win, no matter how, one's laurels
By blood or ink; 'tis sweet to put an end
To strife; 'tis sometimes sweet to have our quarrels,
Particularly with a tiresome friend;
Sweet is old wine in bottles, ale in barrels;
Dear is the helpless creature we defend
Against the world; and dear the schoolboy spot
We ne'er forget, though there we are forgot.
1819–24 *Don Juan*, canto 1, stanza 126.

71 But sweeter still than this, than these, than all,
Is first and passionate love—it stands alone,
Like Adam's recollection of his fall;
The tree of knowledge hath been pluck'd—all's known
And life yields nothing further to recall
Worthy of this ambrosial sin, so shown,
No doubt in fable, as the unforgiven
Fire which Prometheus filch'd for us from heaven.
1819–24 *Don Juan*, canto 1, stanza 127.

72 Pleasure's a sin, and sometimes sin is a pleasure.
1819–24 *Don Juan*, canto 1, stanza 133.

73 Man's love is of man's life a thing apart,
'Tis woman's whole existence.
1819–24 *Don Juan*, canto 1, stanza 194.
► *See Amis 14:84.*

74 If ever I should condescend to prose,
I'll write poetical commandments, which
Shall supersede beyond all doubt all those
That went before; in these I shall enrich

My text with many things that no one knows,
And carry precept to the highest pitch:
I'll call the work 'Longinus o'er a Bottle,
Or, Every Poet his own Aristotle'.
1819–24 *Don Juan*, canto 1, stanza 204.

75 Thou shalt believe in Milton, Dryden, Pope;
Thou shalt not set up Wordsworth, Coleridge, Southey;
Because the first is crazed beyond all hope,
The second drunk, the third so quaint and mouthey:
With Crabbe it may be difficult to cope,
And Campbell's Hippocrene is somewhat drouthy:
Thou shalt not steal from Samuel Rogers, nor
Commit flirtation with the muse of Moore.
1819–24 *Don Juan*, canto 1, stanza 205.

76 So for a good old-gentlemanly vice,
I think I must take up with avarice.
1819–24 *Don Juan*, canto 1, stanza 216.

77 There's nought, no doubt, so much the spirit calms
As rum and true religion.
1819–24 *Don Juan*, canto 2, stanza 34.

78 It was a wild and breaker-beaten coast,
With cliffs above, and a broad sandy shore,
Guarded by shoals and rocks as by an host,
With here and there a creek, whose aspect wore
A better welcome to the tempest-tost;
And rarely ceased the haughty billow's roar,
Save on the dead long summer days, which make
The outstretch'd ocean glitter like a lake.
1819–24 *Don Juan*, canto 2, stanza 177.

79 Few things surpass old wine; and they may preach
Who please,—the more because they preach in vain,
Let us have wine and woman, mirth and laughter,
Sermons and soda water the day after.
1819–24 *Don Juan*, canto 2, stanza 178.

80 Man, being reasonable, must get drunk;
The best of Life is but intoxication.
Glory, the grape, love, gold, in these are sunk
The hopes of all men, and of every nation.
1819–24 *Don Juan*, canto 2, stanza 179.

81 They looked up to the sky, whose floating glow
Spread like a rosy ocean, vast and bright;
They gazed upon the glittering sea below,
Whence the broad moon rose circling into sight;
They heard the wave's splash, and the wind so low,
And saw each other's dark eyes darting light
Into each other—and, beholding this,
Their lips drew near, and clung to a kiss.
1819–24 *Don Juan*, canto 2, stanza 185.

82 In her first passion woman loves her lover,
In all the others all she loves is love.
1819–24 *Don Juan*, canto 3, stanza 3.

83 'Tis melancholy, and a fearful sign
Of human frailty, folly, also crime,
That love and marriage rarely can combine,
Although they both are born in the same clime;
Marriage from love, like vinegar from wine
A sad, sour, sober beverage—by time
Is sharpened from its high celestial flavour,
Down to a very homely household savour.
1819–24 *Don Juan*, canto 3, stanza 5.

84 Think you, if Laura had been Petrach's wife,
He would have written sonnets all his life?
1819–24 *Don Juan*, canto 3, stanza 8.

85 All tragedies are finished by a death,
All comedies are ended by a marriage;
The future states of both are left to faith.
1819–24 *Don Juan*, canto 3, stanza 9.

86 He was the mildest mannered man
That ever scuttled ship or cut a throat,
With such true breeding of a gentleman,
You never could divine his real thought.
1819–24 *Don Juan*, canto 3, stanza 41.

87 The mountains look on Marathon—
And Marathon looks on the sea;
And musing there an hour alone,
I dreamed that Greece might still be free.
1819–24 *Don Juan*, canto 3, stanza 86.

88 And if I laugh at any mortal thing
'Tis that I may not weep.
1819–24 *Don Juan*, canto 4, stanza 4.

89 But after being fired at once or twice,
The ear becomes more Irish, and less nice.
1819–24 *Don Juan*, canto 4, stanza 41.

90 I have a passion for the name of 'Mary,'
For once it was a magic sound to me;
And still it half calls up the realms of fairy,
Where I beheld what never was to be.
1819–24 *Don Juan*, canto 5, stanza 4.

91 There is a tide in the affairs of women,
Which taken at the flood, leads—God knows where.
1819–24 *Don Juan*, canto 6, stanza 2.

92 Gaunt Famine never shall approach the throne.
Though Ireland starve, great George weighs twenty stone.
1819–24 *Don Juan*, canto 8, stanza 126.

93 And, after all what is a lie? 'Tis but
The truth in masquerade.
1819–24 *Don Juan*, canto 11, stanza 37.

94 Now hatred is by far the longest pleasure;
Men love in haste, but they detest at leisure.
1819–24 *Don Juan*, canto 13, stanza 4.

95 The English winter—ending in July,
To recommence in August.
1819–24 *Don Juan*, canto 13, stanza 42.

96 Society is now one polished horde,
Formed of two mighty tribes, the Bores and Bored.
1819–24 *Don Juan*, canto 13, stanza 95.

97 'Tis strange but true; for truth is always stranger;
Stranger than fiction.
1819–24 *Don Juan*, canto 14, stanza 101.

98 All present life is but an interjection,
An 'Oh!' or 'Ah!' of joy or misery,
Or a 'Ha! ha!' or 'Bah!'—a yawn or 'Pooh!'
Of which perhaps the latter is most true.
1819–24 *Don Juan*, canto 15, stanza 1.

99 There's music in the sighing of a reed;
There's music in the gushing of a rill;
There's music in all things, if men had ears:
Their earth is but an echo of the spheres.
1819–24 *Don Juan*, canto 15, stanza 5.

1 Between two worlds life hovers like a star,
'Twixt night and morn, upon the horizon's verge.

How little do we know that which we are!
How less what we may be!
1819–24 *Don Juan*, canto 15, stanza 99.

2 Eat, drink, and love; the rest's not worth a fillip.
1821 *Sardanapalus*, act 1, sc.2.

3 Oh, talk not to me of a name great in story;
The days of our youth are the days of our glory;
And the myrtle and ivy of sweet two-and-twenty
Are worth all your laurels, though ever so plenty.
1821 'Stanzas Written on the Road between Florence and Pisa, November 1821'.

4 The angels all were singing out of tune,
And hoarse with having little else to do,
Excepting to wind up the sun and moon,
Or curb a runaway young star or two.
1822 *The Vision of Judgement*, stanza 2.

5 As he drew near, he gazed upon the gate
Ne'er to be entered more by him or Sin,
With such a glance of supernatural hate,
As made Saint Peter wish himself within;
He pattered with his keys at a great rate,
And sweated through his apostolic skin:
Of course his perspiration was but ichor,
Or some such other spiritual liquor.
1822 *The Vision of Judgement*, stanza 25.

6 And when the tumult dwindled to a calm,
I left him practising the hundredth psalm.
1822 *The Vision of Judgement*, stanza 106.

7 For what were all these country patriots born?
To hunt, and vote, and raise the price of corn?
1823 *The Age of Bronze*, stanza 14.

8 I awoke one morning and found myself famous.
Of the instant popularity of *Childe Harolde*. Quoted in Thomas Moore *Letters and Journals of Lord Byron* (1830), vol.1.

Byron, Henry James 1834–84

English playwright and actor. His most successful plays included *Our Boys* (1874) and the comedies *War to the Knife* (1865) and *A Hundred Thousand Pounds* (1866), as well as numerous burlesques and extravaganzas.

9 Life's too short for chess.
1874 *Our Boys*.

Byron, Robert 1905–41

English traveller, critic of art and architecture and historian, who travelled extensively in Europe and Asia. His best-known book is *The Road to Oxiana* (1937). He drowned in 1941 when his ship to the Mediterranean was torpedoed.

10 The existence of St Sophia is atmospheric; that of St Peter's, overpowering, imminently substantial. One is a church to God; the other a salon for his agents. One is consecrated to reality, the other to illusion. St Sophia, in fact, is large, and St Peter's is vilely, tragically small.
1929 *The Byzantine Achievement*.

11 *Herat, 8 December.* What a day it was! God save me from any more adventures on a drained stomach.
1937 *The Road to Oxiana*.

12 I shall have warmonger put on my passport.
c.1938 Comment in response to the rise of Nazism, opposing the policy of appeasement. Quoted in Bruce Chatwin's introduction to *The Road to Oxiana* (1980 edn).

C

Cabell, James Branch 1879–1958

US novelist and critic. *Jurgen* (1919) is the best known of a sequence of 18 novels, collectively known as *Biography of Michael*. His *Preface to the Past* (1936) is a book of criticism.

13 I am willing to taste any drink once.
1919 *Jurgen*, ch.1.

14 A man possesses nothing certainly save a brief loan of his own body.
1919 *Jurgen*, ch.20.

15 I shall marry in haste and repeat at leisure.
1919 *Jurgen*, ch.26.
➤ *See Congreve 231:1.*

16 Drunkenness is a joy reserved for the Gods: so do men partake of it impiously, and so are they very properly punished for their audacity.
1919 *Jurgen*, ch.28.

17 Poetry is man's rebellion against being what he is.
1919 *Jurgen*.

18 The optimist proclaims that we live in the best of all possible worlds; and the pessimist fears this is true.
1926 *The Silver Stallion*, bk.4, ch.26.

Cabrera Infante, Guillermo 1929–

Cuban novelist, scriptwriter, film critic and diplomat. He supported Castro's revolutionary forces initially, but later left the country and settled in London (1965), becoming a British subject. *Tres tristes tigres* (1967, translated as *Three Trapped Tigers*, 1971) is full of puns, neologisms and humorous word play.

19 *Hablando siempre y siempre contando chismes y haciendo chistes y siempre y también filosofando o estetizando o moralizando, siempre: la cuestión era hacer ver como que no trabajábamos porque en La Habana, Cuba, esa es la única manera de ser gente bien.*
Talking all the time and telling jokes or gossiping all the time and always and also philosophizing or aestheticizing or moralizing, but always: the thing was to make it look like we didn't have to work because in Havana, Cuba, this is the only way to be high society...
1967 *Tres tristes tigres* (*Three Trapped Tigers*, 1971), 'Bachata'.

Cadoria, Brigadier General Sherian G(race) 1940–

US soldier. In 1985 she became the highest-ranking black woman in the US military. She retired in 1990.

20 By act of Congress, male officers are gentlemen, but by act of God, we are ladies.
1989 In *US News and World Report*, 13 Feb.

Caesar, Irving 1895–1996

US librettist and lyricist.

21 Tea for two, and two for tea.
1924 *No! No! Nanette*, 'Tea for Two' (with Otto Harbach. Music by Vincent Youmans).

Caesar, Gaius Julius 100/102–44 BC

Roman general and statesman. As consul (59 BC) and proconsul (58–50 BC) he extended Roman power in Gaul and Britain. Refusing to disband his army, he came into conflict with the Senate, supported by Pompey, whom Caesar defeated in the civil war that followed. He became dictator for life, but was assassinated in 44 BC. His works include the *Commentarii* ('War Commentaries'), *De Bello Gallico* ('On the Gallic War', 7 vols) and *De Bello Civili* ('On the Civil War', 3 vols).

22 *Gallia est omnis divisa in partes tres.*
Gaul as a whole is divided into three parts.
51 BC *De Bello Gallico*, bk.1, section 1, opening words.

23 *Fere libenter homines id quod volunt credunt.*
Men are nearly always willing to believe what they wish.
51 BC *De Bello Gallico*, bk.3, section 18.

24 *Iacta est alea.*
The die is cast.
49 BC Comment on crossing the river Rubicon (the border between his province and Italy) with his troops, thereby committing himself to civil war. Quoted in Suetonius *Lives of the Twelve Caesars*, 'Divus Iulius', section 32.

25 *Veni, vidi, vici.*
I came, I saw, I conquered.
46 BC Said to have been written on a *titulus* (placard) carried along in Caesar's triumph after a campaign in Pontus (Asia Minor) during the civil war (46 BC). Quoted in Suetonius *Lives of the Twelve Caesars*, 'Divus Iulius', section 37. Another source reports that Caesar used this expression in a letter to the Senate after the same campaign (cf Plutarch, *Caesar* 50, 3–4).

26 Caesar's wife must be above suspicion.
Attributed. Based on an episode in Plutarch *Caesar* 10.6, which tells that Caesar divorced his wife after accusations of impiety, although he defended her in court.

27 *Et tu, Brute?*
You too, Brutus?
Attributed last words, when struck by his murderers, Cassius and Brutus. The tradition is based on Suetonius *Lives of the Twelve Caesars*, 'Divus Iulius', section 82: 'Some say that when he saw Marcus Brutus about to deliver the second blow, he reproached him in Greek with: 'You too, my son?' (the Greek is *kai su, teknon*).

Cage, John 1912–92

US ultra-modernist composer. His experiments included 'aleatory' music, in which the role of chance determines how a piece will develop. *Silence* (1961), *M* (1973), and *Empty Works* (1979) are among his books.

28 Which is more musical, a truck passing by a factory or a truck passing by a music school?
1961 *Silence.*

29 I have nothing to say
and I am saying it and that is poetry.
1961 'Lecture on Nothing'.

Cagney, James 1899–1986

US film actor. A leading role in *Public Enemy* (1931) established him as the quintessential screen gangster. He won an Academy Award for his performance in *Yankee Doodle Dandy* (1942).

30 Look Ma—top of the world.
1949 Line delivered in *White Heat* (screenplay by Ivan Goff and Ben Roberts).

Cain, James M(allahan) 1892–1977

US crime writer.

31 The Postman Always Rings Twice.
1934 Title of novel.

32 Double Indemnity.
1943 Title of novel.

Calas, Nicolas 1907–88

Greek-born art critic and poet, who associated with the Surrealists in Paris in the 1930s. He moved to the United States in 1939.

33 Art is a form of communication that insinuates. We *expect* the artist to have more to say than what he communicated and *suspect* that what he said was a subterfuge for hiding something.
1968 *Art in the Age of Risk.*

Caldwell, Philip 1920–

US company executive, Chairman of the Ford Motor Co (1980–5).

34 We redesigned everything but the air in the tires.
1995 Of the development of the Taurus, which was to become America's best-selling car. In *Fortune*, 3 Apr.

Calhoun, John Caldwell 1782–1850

US statesman and orator, Vice-President under John Q Adams and then Andrew Jackson. His *Address to the People of South Carolina* (1831) set forth his theory of state rights.

35 The Government of the absolute majority, instead of the Government of the people, is but the Government of the strongest interests; and when not efficiently checked, it is the most tyrannical and oppressive that can be devised.
1833 Speech, US Senate, 15 Feb.

Caligiuri, Paul 1964–

US footballer.

36 The world knows the American athlete is superior. It's only a matter of time before we develop the world's best soccer teams.
2002 In *The Times*, 28 Dec.

Caligula *properly* *Gaius Julius Caesar Germanicus* AD 12–41

Roman Emperor (AD 37–41), nicknamed Caligula as a child from his little soldier's boots (*caligae*). His extravagant, autocratic, vicious and mentally unstable behaviour resulted in his assassination.

37 *Utinam populus Romanus unam cervicem haberet!*
Would that the Roman people had but one neck!
c.40 AD Quoted in Suetonius *Lives of the Twelve Caesars*, 'Gaius Caligula', section 30.

Callaghan (of Cardiff), (Leonard) James Callaghan, Baron 1912–

English Labour politician. As Chancellor of the Exchequer he introduced controversial corporation and selective employment taxes. He was Home Secretary (1967–70), Foreign Secretary (1974–6) and Prime Minister (1976–9).

38 Britain has lived for too long on borrowed time,

borrowed money, and even borrowed ideas.
1976 Quoted in the *Observer*, 3 Oct.

39 There is no virtue in producing socially well adjusted members of society who are unemployed because they do not have the skills. Nor at the other extreme must they be technically efficient robots.
1976 Speech at Ruskin College, Oxford, reprinted in the *Times Higher Education Supplement*, 15 Oct. This speech began the so-called 'Great Debate' on education.

40 A lie can travel halfway round the world before the truth has got its boots on.
1976 Speech in the House of Commons, Nov.
➡ *See Spurgeon 811:41.*

41 Either back us or sack us.
1977 Speech, Labour Party Conference, 5 Oct.

42 Crisis? What crisis?
1979 Headline in *The Sun*, 11 Jan, alluding to his remark on returning from the Guadaloupe summit to be confronted by widespread strikes. His actual words were, 'I don't think that other people in the world would share the view that there is mounting chaos.'

Callanan, Jeremiah John 1795–1829

Irish poet. Born in Cork and sent by his parents to study for the priesthood, he developed instead his interest in lyrical poetry. He supported himself by teaching and writing. He gained general celebrity with 'Gougane Barra' (1826).

43 There grows the wild ash; and a time-stricken willow
Looks chidingly down on the mirth of the billow,
As, like some gay child that sad monitor scorning,
It lightly laughs back to the laugh of the morning.
1826 'Gougane Barra'.

Callow, Simon Phillip Hugh 1949–

English actor and director.

44 When he speaks, I hear Shakespeare think.
On Sir John Gielgud. Quoted in *The Guardian*, 14 Apr 2004.

Calonne, Charles Alexandre de 1734–1802

French politician. Appointed Controller-General in 1783, he was exiled in 1787 when he failed to provide a statement of accounts to explain the treasury deficit. Napoleon I permitted his return in 1802.

45 *Madame, si c'est possible, c'est fait; impossible? cela se fera.*
Madam, if a thing is possible, consider it done; the impossible? that will be done.
Quoted in J Michelet *Histoire de la Révolution Française* (1847), vol.1, pt.2. This has been adapted as the slogan of the US army: 'The difficult we do immediately; the impossible takes a little longer.'

Calvino, Italo 1923–85

Italian modernist writer and journalist, born in Cuba. A fascist under compulsion, he later joined the Resistance (1943) and wrote for the Communist *L'unità* in the 1940s. His novels combine fantasy with a hard satirical wit.

46 *Lo sguardo dei cani che non capiscono e non sanno che possono aver ragione a non capire.*
The gaze of dogs who don't understand and who don't know that they may be right not to understand.
1957 *Il Barone Rampante*, ch.10.

Cambronne, Pierre, Baron de 1770–1842

French general in the Napoleonic wars.

47 *La Garde meurt, mais ne se rend pas.*
The Guards die but do not surrender.
1815 Attributed, when called upon to surrender at the Battle of Waterloo, 18 Jun.

Cameron, James 1954–

Canadian film director. His film *Titanic* (1997) won eleven Academy Awards, equalling the record set by *Ben Hur* in 1959.

48 I'm king of the world.
1998 Accepting his Best Director Oscar for *Titanic* (1997), 23 Mar, an allusion to a line in *Titanic*.

Campbell, Donald Malcolm 1921–67

English speedboat racer. Son of Sir Malcolm Campbell, he broke all his father's land and water speed records, but was killed when his hydroplane *Bluebird* crashed on Lake Coniston at about 300mph.

49 There is no hope of bailing out of a speedboat. You hit the water and become so much pulp.
Quoted in Douglas Young-James *Donald Campbell: An Informal Biography* (1968).

Campbell, Kim *originally* *Avril Phaedra Campbell* 1947–

Canadian politician. She entered the Commons in 1988 as a Progressive Conservative, becoming Canada's first woman Prime Minister (Jun–Dec, 1993); she lost her parliamentary seat in the 1993 election.

50 Charisma without substance is a dangerous thing.
1986 Speech, while unsuccessfully contesting the leadership of the Social Credit Party of British Columbia, 22 Oct.

Campbell, Mrs Patrick *née* *Beatrice Rose Stella Tanner* 1865–1940

English actress. Famed for her stage presence and incisive wit, she made her debut in 1888. She corresponded with George Bernard Shaw, who wrote *Pygmalion* especially for her.

51 When you were quite a little boy somebody ought to have said 'hush' just once.
1912 Letter to George Bernard Shaw, 1 Nov.

52 The deep, deep peace of the double-bed after the hurly-burly of the chaise-longue.
Her definition of marriage, quoted in Alexander Woollcott *While Rome Burns* (1934), 'The First Mrs Tanqueray'.

53 It doesn't matter what you do in the bedroom as long as you don't do it in the street and frighten the horses.
Quoted in Daphne Fielding *The Duchess of Jermyn Street* (1964), ch.2. Sometimes attributed to Edward VII.

54 Watching Tallulah Bankhead on the stage is like watching somebody skating on very thin ice—and the English want to be there when she falls through.
Quoted in *The Times*, 13 Dec 1968.

Campbell, (Ignatius) Roy Dunnachie 1901–57

South African poet, who spent much of his life in Britain. He moved from an early liberalism to outspoken right-wing Catholicism, and is best remembered for his early lyric poems.

55 South Africa, renowned both far and wide

For politics and little else besides.
1928 'The Wayzgoose'.

56 You praise the firm restraint with which they write—
I'm with you there, of course:
They use the snaffle and the curb all right,
But where's the bloody horse?
1930 'On Some South African Novelists'.

57 Of all the clever people round me here
I most delight in Me—
Mine is the only voice I care to hear,
And mine the only face I like to see.
1930 'Home Thoughts in Bloomsbury'.

58 Write with your spade, and garden with your pen,
Shove your couplets to their long repose.
And type your turnips down the field in rows.
1931 'The Georgiad', pt.2.

59 Burn, with Athens and with Rome,
A sacred city of the mind.
1936 'Toledo, July 1936'.

60 I will go stark: and let my meanings show
Clear as a milk-white feather in a crow
Or a black stallion on a field of snow.
1936 'A Good Resolution'.

61 He shouldered high his voluntary Cross,
Wrestled his hardships into forms of beauty,
And taught his gorgon destinies to sing.
1943 'Luis de Camões'.

62 Giraffes!—a People
Who live between the earth and skies,
Each in his own religious steeple,
Keeping a light-house with his eyes.
1946 'Dreaming Spires'.

63 Translations, like wives, are seldom faithful if they are in the least attractive.
1949 *The Poetry Review*, Jun/ Jul.

64 I hate 'Humanity' and all such abstracts: but I love *people*. Lovers of 'Humanity' generally hate *people and children*, and keep parrots or puppy dogs.
1951 *Light On A Dark Horse*, ch.13.

Campbell, Thomas 1777–1844

Scottish poet and journalist, Editor from 1820 to 1830 of *The New Monthly Magazine*, to which he contributed many poems. He is buried in Westminster Abbey.

65 On the green banks of Shannon, when Sheelah was nigh,
No blithe Irish lad was so happy as I;
No harp like my own could so cheerily play,
And wherever I went was my poor dog Tray.
1799 'The Harper', stanza 1.

66 'Tis distance lends enchantment to the view,
And robes the mountain in its azure hue.
1799 *The Pleasures of Hope*, pt.1, l.7–8.

67 Hope, for a season, bade the world farewell,
And Freedom shrieked—as Kosciusko fell!
1799 *The Pleasures of Hope*, pt.1, l.381–2.

68 What millions died—that Caesar might be great!
1799 *The Pleasures of Hope*, pt.2, l.174.

69 What though my wingèd hours of bliss have been,
Like angel-visits, few and far between?
1799 *The Pleasures of Hope*, pt.2, l.375–6.

70 A chieftain to the Highlands bound
Cries 'Boatman, do not tarry!
And I'll give thee a silver pound
To row us o'er the ferry.'
1809 'Lord Ullin's Daughter', stanza 1.

71 And yet, amidst that joy and uproar,
Let us think of them that sleep,
Full many a fathom deep,
By thy wild and stormy steep,
Elsinore!
1809 'The Battle of the Baltic', stanza 8.

72 To-morrow let us do or die!
1809 'Gertrude of Wyoming', pt.3, stanza 37.

73 An original something, fair maid you would win me
To write—but how shall I begin?
For I fear I have nothing original in me—
Excepting Original Sin.
1843 'To a Young Lady, Who Asked Me to Write Something Original for Her Album'.

74 Now Barabbas was a publisher.
Attributed. Quoted in Samuel Smiles *A Publisher and his Friends: Memoir and Correspondence of the late John Murray* (1891), vol.1, ch.14. The quote is sometimes attributed to Byron.

Campion, Jane 1954–

New Zealand film director and writer. She dramatized Janet Frame's autobiography *An Angel at My Table* for television (1990) and won an Academy Award for her screenplay for *The Piano* (1993), which she also directed.

75 Remember your own childhood. That complete certainty you had, looking at the grown-ups, that you would never be like that. It was a lonely feeling, but euphoric, too.
1994 Interview with Sarah Gristwood in *The Times Magazine*, 'Jane Campion: A Childhood', 1 Jan.

Campion, Thomas 1567–1620

English physician, poet and composer. As well as poetry in Latin and English he wrote four *Books of Airs* for voice and lute (1601–17) and *Observations in the Art of English Poesie* (1602), defending classical structures.

76 My sweetest Lesbia, let us live and love,
And though the sager sort our deeds reprove,
Let us not weigh them. Heaven's great lamps do dive
Into their west, and straight again revive,
But soon as once set is our little light,
Then must we sleep one ever-during night.
1601 *A Book of Airs*, no.1, 'My Sweetest Lesbia', translation of a song by Catullus.
► *See Catullus 200:5.*

77 As her lute doth live or die,
Led by her passion, so must I:
For when of pleasure she doth sing,
My thoughts enjoy a sudden spring,
But if she doth of sorrow speak,
Ev'n from my heart the strings do break.
1601 *A Book of Airs*, no.6, 'When to Her Lute Corinna Sings'.

78 I care not for these ladies that must be wooed and prayed.
Give me kind Amaryllis, the wanton country maid.
1601 *A Book of Airs*, 'I Care Not for These Ladies'.

79 Rose-cheeked Laura, come,
Sing thou smoothly with thy beauty's
Silent music, either other
Sweetly gracing.
1602 *Second Book of Airs*, 'Rose-Cheeked Laura'.

80 There is a garden in her face,
Where roses and white lilies grow,
A heavenly paradise is that place,
Wherein all pleasant fruits do flow.
There cherries grow, which none may buy
Till 'Cherry ripe!' themselves do cry.
1617 *Fourth Book of Airs*, 'There is a Garden in her Face'.

81 Fain would I wed a fair young man that night and day could please me,
When my mind or body grieved that had the power to ease me.
Maids are full of longing thoughts that breed a bloodless sickness,
And that, oft I hear men say, is only cured by quickness.
1617 *Fourth Book of Airs*, 'Fain Would I Wed'.

82 Yet I would not die a maid, because I had a mother,
As I was by one brought forth, I would bring forth another.
1617 *Fourth Book of Airs*, 'Fain Would I Wed'.

Campo, Estanislao de 1834–80

Argentinian soldier, political journalist and *gaucho* (pampas cowboy) poet. *Fausto*, a long poetic dialogue in six episodes, relates a *gaucho's* impressions of a performance of Gounod's *Faust* in Buenos Aires.

83 *Por hembras yo no me pierdo.*
La que me empaca su amor
pasa por el cernidor
y...si te vi, no me acuerdo.
I make no fuss about females.
The one who gives me her love
Gets sifted in my private sieve
and...I don't think we ever met.
1866 *Fausto* (translated as *Faust*, 1943), pt.3.

Camus, Albert 1913–60

French writer. Active in the French Resistance, he found fame with his Existentialist novel *L'Étranger* (1942). Other works include *La Peste* (1947), *La Chute* (1956), plays and political writings. He was awarded a Nobel prize in 1957 and he died in a car accident.

84 *Intellectuel = celui qui se dédouble.*
Intellectual: someone whose mind watches itself.
Carnets, 1935–42 (published 1962).

85 *La politique et le sort des hommes sont formés par des hommes sans idéal et sans grandeur. Ceux qui ont une grandeur en eux ne font pas de politique.*
Politics and the fate of mankind are shaped by men without ideals and without greatness. Those who have greatness within them do not go in for politics.
Carnets, 1935–42 (published 1962).

86 *L'absurde est la notion essentielle et la première vérité.*
The absurd is the fundamental idea and the first truth.
1942 *Le Mythe de Sisyphe* (*The Myth of Sisyphus*, 1955).

87 *Il n'y a qu'un problème philosophique vraiment sérieux: c'est le suicide. Juger que la vie vaut ou ne vaut pas la peine d'être vécue, c'est répondre à la question fondamentale de la philosophie.*
There is but one truly serious philosophical problem, and that is suicide. Judging whether life is or is not worth living amounts to answering the fundamental question of philosophy.
1942 *Le Mythe de Sisyphe* (*The Myth of Sisyphus*, 1955), 'Absurdity and Suicide'.

88 *L'homme se trouve devant l'irrationnel. Il sent en lui son désir de bonheur et de raison. L'absurde naît de cette confrontation entre l'appel humain et le silence déraisonnable du monde.*
Man stands face to face with the irrational. He feels within him his longing for happiness and for reason. The absurd is born of this confrontation between the human need and the unreasonable silence of the world.
1942 *Le Mythe de Sisyphe* (*The Myth of Sisyphus*, 1955), 'The Absurd Walls'.

89 *Il n'est pas de destin que ne se surmonte par le mépris.*
There is no fate that cannot be surmounted by scorn.
1942 *Le Mythe de Sisyphe* (*The Myth of Sisyphus*, 1955).

90 *La lutte elle-même vers les sommets suffit à remplir un coeur d'homme. Il faut imaginer Sisyphe heureux.*
The struggle itself towards the heights is enough to fill a human heart. One must imagine that Sisyphus is happy.
1942 *Le Mythe de Sisyphe* (*The Myth of Sisyphus*, 1955).

91 *Aujourd'hui, maman est morte. Ou peut-être hier, je ne sais pas.*
Mother died today. Or perhaps it was yesterday, I don't know.
1942 *L'Etranger.*

92 *Peut-on être un saint sans Dieu: C'est le seul problème concret que je connaisse aujourd'hui.*
Can one become a saint without God? That is the only concrete problem I know of today.
1947 *La Peste.*

93 *Il y a dans les hommes plus de choses à admirer que de choses à mépriser.*
There are more things to admire in people than to despise.
1947 *La Peste.*

94 *Qu'est-ce qu'un homme révolté? Un homme qui dit non.*
What is a rebel? A man who says no.
1951 *L'Homme révolté.*

95 *Toutes les révolutions modernes ont abouti à un renforcement de l'Etat.*
All modern revolutions have ended in a reinforcement of the State.
1951 *L'Homme révolté.*

96 *Tout révolutionnaire finit en oppresseur ou en hérétique.*
Every revolutionary ends as an oppressor or a heretic.
1951 *L'Homme révolté.*

97 *Le style, comme la popeline, dissimule trop souvent de l'eczéma.*
Style, like sheer silk, too often hides eczema.
1956 *La Chute*, ch.1 (translated by Stuart Gilbert).

98 *Vous savez ce qu'est le charme: une manière de s'entendre répondre oui sans avoir posé aucune question claire.*
You know what charm is: a way of getting the answer yes

without having asked any clear question.
1956 *La Chute* (translated by Stuart Gilbert).

99 *Chacun exige d'être innocent, à tout prix, même si, pour cela, il faut accuser le genre humain et le ciel.*
Everyone insists on his or her innocence, at all costs, even if it means accusing the rest of the human race and heaven.
1956 *La Chute* (translated by Stuart Gilbert).

1 *C'est si vrai que nous nous confions rarement à ceux qui sont meilleurs que nous.*
It is true that we seldom confide in those who are better than ourselves.
1956 *La Chute* (translated by Stuart Gilbert).

2 *N'attendez pas le jugement dernier. Il a lieu tous les jours.*
Do not wait for the last judgment. It happens every day.
1956 *La Chute* (translated by Stuart Gilbert).

3 *Combien de crimes commis simplement parce que leur auteur ne pouvait supporter d'être en faute!*
How many crimes are committed merely because their authors could not endure being wrong!
1956 *La Chute* (translated by Stuart Gilbert).

4 *La vérité, comme la lumière, aveugle. Le mensonge, au contraire, est un beau crépuscule qui met chaque objet en valeur.*
Truth, like light, blinds. A lie, on the contrary, is a beautiful twilight which shows the value of each object.
1956 *La Chute* (translated by Stuart Gilbert).

5 All that I know surely about morality and the obligations of man, I owe to football.
1957 'What I owe to Football', in *France Football*. In his youth, Camus kept goal for the Oran football club in Algiers.

6 A novel is never anything but a philosophy put into images.
Recalled on his death, 4 Jan 1960.

Canmore, Malcolm d.1093

King of Scotland. The son of Duncan (who was killed by Macbeth), he spent his youth in Northumbria and returned in 1057 to take the throne after Macbeth's death.

7 *Excellentioris personæ semper casus in vitium, minoris lapsum, comparatione scandali multe longius antecedit.*
The scandal of an exalted person's fall into vice, when compared to the lapse of one lesser, always far exceeds it.
c.1057 Quoted in John Fordun's *Chronicle of Scotland* (c.1384), bk.5, ch.4.

Cannadine, David 1950–

English historian and academic.

8 Prince Albert...discovered the impotence of being earnest.
1991 Of Queen Victoria's consort. *The Pleasure of the Past.*

9 Neville Chamberlain had greatness thrust upon him—and in trying to prove he could bear it, collapsed under the weight.
1991 *The Pleasure of the Past.*

Cannan, Edwin 1861–1935

English economist, Professor at the London School of Economics. He was editor of the standard edition of Adam Smith's *Wealth of Nations* in 1904.

10 It often happens that a man of considerable eminence in his own profession, but without the smallest acquaintance with the fundamentals of economics, will make a suggestion which is precisely on a level with the proposition that the locomotive would be much more efficient if its weight were taken off the driving wheels so that they could revolve more easily. The editor of an important magazine accepts with joy the contribution in which he develops his ideas, and the public feebly thinks that there may be something in it, and is confirmed in this view by the fact that professional economists are as disinclined to publish a refutation of it as the Astronomer Royal is to answer the theorists who declare that the world is flat.
1914 *Wealth*, ch.6.

Canning, George 1770–1827

English statesman. He became Foreign Secretary in 1822 on the death of his political opponent Castlereagh, and began a programme of liberalization. On Liverpool's resignation in 1827, he formed his own administration but died the same year.

11 Pitt is to Addington
As London is to Paddington.
c.1803 'The Oracle'. Henry Addington, 1st Viscount Sidmouth (1757–1844) was Prime Minister (1801–4) and a political rival of Pitt, who served in his administration.

12 And finds, with keen discriminating sight,
Black's not so black;—nor white so very white.
1821 'New Morality', l.199–200.

13 Give me the avowed, erect and manly foe;
Firm I can meet, perhaps return the blow;
But of all plagues, good Heaven, thy wrath can send,
Save me, oh, save me, from the candid friend.
1821 'New Morality', l.207–8.

14 In matters of commerce
The fault of the Dutch
Is offering too little
And asking too much.
1826 Dispatch enciphered to Sir Charles Bagehot, English ambassador at The Hague, 31 Jan.

15 I called the New World into existence, to redress the balance of the Old.
1826 Speech to the Commons, on Portugal, 12 Dec.

Cantillon, Richard c.1680–1734

Irish-born banker and economist who made a fortune in Paris after the collapse of the Mississippi Company. His single surviving work is *Essai sur la nature du Commerce en Général* ('Essay on the Nature of Trade', published 1755).

16 If all the Labourers in a Village breed up several Sons to the same work there will be too many Labourers to cultivate the Lands belonging to the Village, and the surplus Adults must go to seek a livelihood elsewhere, which they generally do in Cities.
1730–4 *Essay on the Nature of Trade.*

17 The Crafts which require the most Time in training or most Ingenuity and Industry must necessarily be the best paid.
1730–4 *Essay on the Nature of Trade.*

18 Men multiply like Mice in a barn if they have unlimited Means of Subsistence.
1730–4 *Essay on the Nature of Trade.*

Cantona, Eric 1966–

French footballer. He retired from football in 1997 to develop an acting career.

19 When the seagulls follow a trawler, it is because they think sardines will be thrown into the sea.
1995 At a press conference, 31 Mar.

20 I was always being creative. I could never have played a defensive role because I would have been forced to destroy the other player's creativity.
2003 In *The Guardian*, 26 Sep.

Capote, Truman 1924–84

US novelist. His best-known works include the semi-documentary novel *In Cold Blood* (1966), *Breakfast at Tiffany's* (1958) and *Music for Chameleons* (1980).

21 Other Voices, Other Rooms.
1948 Title of novel.

22 None of these people have anything interesting to say, and none of them can write, not even Mr Kerouac. What they do isn't writing at all—it's typing.
1959 On the Beat novelists. Television discussion, reported in the *New Republic*, 9 Feb.

23 Venice is like eating an entire box of chocolate liqueurs in one go.
1961 In the *Observer*, 26 Nov.

24 Even an attorney of modest talent can postpone doomsday year after year, for the system of appeals that pervades American jurisprudence amounts to a legalistic wheel of fortune, a game of chance, somewhat fixed in the favor of the criminal, that the participants play interminably.
1965 *In Cold Blood*, ch.4.

25 Buddy, it's fruitcake weather!
1966 Of December in Alabama. *A Christmas Memory.*

26 I don't care what anybody says about me as long as it isn't true.
Quoted in David Frost *The Americans* (1970), 'When Does A Writer Become A Star'.

27 Writing has laws of perspective, of light and shade, just as painting does, or music. If you are born knowing them, fine. If not, learn them. Then rearrange the rules to suit yourself.
1974 Interview in *Paris Review*, Summer.

28 When God hands you a gift, he also hands you a whip; and the whip is intended for self-flagellation solely.
1979 In *Vogue*, Dec. Collected in *Music for Chameleons* (1980), 'Music for Chameleons'.

29 Writing stopped being fun when I discovered the difference between good writing and bad, and then made an even more terrifying discovery—the difference between very good writing and true art: it is subtle, but savage.
1979 In *Vogue*, Dec.

30 Great fury, like great whisky, requires long fermentation.
1980 *Music for Chameleons*, 'Handcarved Coffins'.

31 Finishing a book is just like you took a child out in the yard and shot it.
Quoted in Linda Botts (ed) *Loose Talk* (1980).

32 The chic old blue-haired ladies…chew in mute chandeliered isolation.
Of elderly residents of the Ritz. *Answered Prayers* (1986).

33 The morals of a baboon and the guts of a butterfly.
Of Kenneth Tynan. Quoted in Gerald Clarke *Capote* (1988).

34 The better the actor the more stupid he is.
Attributed.

Capp, Al *originally Alfred Gerald Caplin* 1909–79

US cartoonist, best known for his strip 'L'il Abner' (1934–77), which satirized current affairs with a hillbilly cast of characters in Dogpatch.

35 A product of the untalented, sold by the unprincipled to the utterly bewildered.
1963 Of abstract art. In the *National Observer*, 1 Jul.

Capra, Frank 1897–1991

Italian-born US film director. He became renowned for his films celebrating the common man, such as *You Can't Take It With You* (1938).

36 There are no rules in filmmaking. Only sins. And the cardinal sin is dullness.
Recalled on his death in *People*, 16 Sep 1991.

Caraway, Hattie Wyatt 1878–1950

US politician. In 1932, she was the first woman to be elected to the US Senate.

37 The windows need washing.
1932 On arriving in the Senate. Recalled on her death, 21 Dec 1950.

38 I haven't the heart to take a minute from the men. The poor dears love it so.
Explaining why she never made a speech during 13 years as the first woman in the US Senate. Quoted in David Brinkley *Washington Goes to War* (1988).

Carballido, Emilio 1925–

Mexican short-story writer and dramatist. He is one of the most popular Latin American playwrights.

39 *Es usted un homo sapiens, mamífero vertebrado… Se encuentra en el periodo de domesticación, y sería colocado en una jaula al menor síntoma de ferocidad. En la escuela, en los laboratorios o en las oficinas de gobierno sabemos todo cuanto puede saberse de usted, de sus semejantes o de los otros seres en la escala zoológica.*
You are a homo sapiens, a vertebrate mammal… You are currently being tamed, and you would be put in a cage if you showed any sign of fierceness. At school, in the laboratories and in government offices we know as much as can be known about you, about your fellow beings and about the other beings in the zoological scale.
1960 *El día que se soltaron los leones* ('The Day When They Let the Lions Loose'), act 1.

Cardus, Sir Neville 1889–1975

English critic and journalist. He joined the *Manchester Guardian* as a music critic (1916), later becoming a cricket writer, and wrote several books on his two passions.

40 Pussycats.
1938 Of Bruch's violin concertos. In the *Manchester Guardian*.

41 Sawdust and spangles.
1938 Of Liszt's Second Piano Concerto. In the *Manchester Guardian*.

42 Like the British constitution, cricket was not made: it has 'grown'.
1945 *English Cricket.*

43 The opera...is the only one in existence that might conceivably have been composed by God.
1961 Of Mozart's *The Magic Flute*. In the *Manchester Guardian.*

44 The laws of cricket tell of the English love of compromise between a particular freedom and a general orderliness, or legality.
Quoted in Sir Rupert Hart-Davis *Cardus on Cricket* (1977).

45 Cricket more than any other game is inclined towards sentimentalism and cant.
Quoted in Sir Rupert Hart-Davis *Cardus on Cricket* (1977).

46 There ought to be some other means of reckoning quality in this the best and loveliest of games; the scoreboard is an ass.
1981 *A Fourth Innings with Cardus.*

47 It is far more than a game, this cricket.
1981 *A Fourth Innings with Cardus.*

48 The elements are cricket's presiding geniuses.
1981 *A Fourth Innings with Cardus.*

Carew, Thomas 1595–1639

English Cavalier poet, courtier and statesman. His most notable works include 'Rapture', 'To Ben Jonson' and an elegy for John Donne.

49 Why should the follies of this dull age
Draw from thy pen such an immodest rage
As seems to blast thy else-immortal bays,
When thine own tongue proclaims thy itch of praise?
Such thirst will argue drought.
1631 'To Ben Jonson, Upon occasion of his Ode of Defiance annexed to his play of *The New Inn*'.

50 The wiser world doth greater thee confess
Than all men else, than thy self only less.
1631 'To Ben Jonson, Upon occasion of his Ode of Defiance annexed to his play of *The New Inn*'.

51 Can we not force from widowed poetry,
Now thou art dead, great Donne, one elegy
To crown thy hearse?
1633 'An Elegy upon the Death of the Dean of Paul's, Dr. John Donne'.

52 Unkneaded dough-baked prose.
1633 'An Elegy upon the Death of the Dean of Paul's, Dr. John Donne'.

53 You committed holy rapes upon our will.
1633 'An Elegy upon the Death of the Dean of Paul's, Dr. John Donne'.

54 The Muses' garden, with pedantic weeds
O'erspread, was purged by thee; the lazy seeds
Of servile imitation thrown away,
And fresh invention planted.
1633 'An Elegy upon the Death of the Dean of Paul's, Dr. John Donne'.

55 Here lies a king, that ruled as he thought fit
The universal monarchy of wit.
1633 'An Elegy upon the Death of the Dean of Paul's, Dr. John Donne'.

56 And so our souls that cannot be embraced
Shall the embraces of our bodies taste.
1640 'A Rapture'.

57 I'll seize the rosebuds in their perfumed bed,
The violet knots, like curious mazes spread
O'er all the garden, taste the ripened cherry,
The warm, firm apple, tipped with coral berry.
Then will I visit with a wandering kiss
The vale of lilies and the bower of bliss,
And where the beauteous region doth divide
Into two milky ways, my lips shall slide
Down those smooth alleys, wearing as I go
A track for lovers on the printed snow.
1640 'A Rapture'.

58 All things are lawful there that may delight
Nature or unrestrainèd appetite.
1640 'A Rapture'.

59 Then tell me why
This goblin Honour which the world adores
Should make men atheists and not women whores.
1640 'A Rapture'.

60 Ask me no more whither dost haste
The nightingale when May is past;
For in your sweet dividing throat
She winters, and keeps warm her note.
1640 'A Song'.

61 Ask me no more if east or west
The Phoenix builds her spicy nest;
For unto you at last she flies,
And in your fragrant bosom dies.
1640 'A Song'.

62 Give me more love or more disdain;
The torrid or the frozen zone:
Bring equal ease unto my pain;
The temperate affords me none.
1640 'Mediocrity in Love Rejected'.

63 So though a virgin, yet a bride
To every Grace, she justified
A chaste polygamy, and died.
1640 'Inscription on the Tomb of Lady Mary Wentworth'.

Carey, John 1934–

English literary critic, Professor of English Literature at Oxford (1976–2001).

64 Given the state of the planet, humans, or some humans, must now be categorized as vermin.
1992 *The Intellectuals and the Masses*, postscript.

Carey, Peter 1943–

Australian novelist and short-story writer, twice winner of the Booker Prize for *Oscar and Lucinda* (1988) and *True History of the Kelly Gang* (2001).

65 Glass is a thing in disguise, an actor, is not solid at all, but a liquid...an old sheet of glass will not only take on a royal and purplish tinge but will reveal its true liquid nature by having grown fatter at the bottom and thinner at the top, and... It is invisible, solid, in short a joyous and paradoxical thing, as good a material as any to build a life from.
1988 *Oscar and Lucinda*, ch.32, 'Prince Rupert's Drops'.

66 The declared meaning of a spoken sentence is only its overcoat, and the real meaning lies underneath its scarves and buttons.
1988 *Oscar and Lucinda*, ch.43, 'Leviathan'.

67 Writers are always envious, mean-minded, filled with rage and envy at other's good fortune. There is nothing like the failure of a close friend to cheer us up.
2002 In the *Observer*, 18 Aug.

Carleton, William 1794–1869

Irish writer, the youngest of 14 children born to peasant parents. His sketches were collected as *Traits and Stories of the Irish Peasantry* (1830, 2nd series 1833). Other works include *The Squanders of Castle Squander* (1852).

68 I remember on one occasion, when she was asked to sing the English version of the touching melody 'The Red-Haired Man's Wife', she replied, 'I will sing it for you; but the English words and the air are like a quarrelling man and wife; *the Irish melts into the tune*, but the English doesn't.'
1830 *Traits and Stories of the Irish Peasantry*, introduction.

Carlyle, Jane Baillie *née Jane Baillie Welsh* 1801–66

Wife of Thomas Carlyle. She married Carlyle in 1826, supporting him loyally through his depressions and ill-health, though resisting his suggestions that she write herself. After her death, Carlyle wrote a memoir of her in *Reminiscences* (1881) and edited her letters and diaries.

69 I am not at all the sort of person you and I took me for.
1822 Letter to Thomas Carlyle, 2 May.

70 Medical men all over the world having merely entered into a tacit agreement to call all sorts of maladies people are liable to, in cold weather, by one name; so that one sort of treatment may serve for all, and their practice thereby be greatly simplified.
1837 Letter to John Welsh, 4 Mar.

71 When I think of what I is
And what I used to was,
I gin to think I've sold myself
For very little cas.
1855 Journal entry, 5 Nov. Collected in James Anthony Froude (ed) *Letters and Memorials of Jane Welsh Carlyle* (1883), vol.2.

72 I scorched my intellect into a cinder of stolidity.
Quoted in Alexander Carlyle (ed) *New Letters and Memorials of Jane Welsh Carlyle* (1903), 'Mrs Carlyle's Notebook'.

73 If you hate a man, though only in secret, never trust him, because hate is hardly to be hidden.
Quoted in Alexander Carlyle (ed) *New Letters and Memorials of Jane Welsh Carlyle* (1903), 'Mrs Carlyle's Notebook'.

Carlyle, Thomas 1795–1881

Scottish historian and essayist. His best-known work, *Sartor Resartus*, on social philosophy, appeared in 1833–4. In 1834 he moved to London, where his major works included *The French Revolution* (3 vols, 1837) and *Frederick the Great* (6 vols, 1858–65).

74 His fellow creatures are still objects of reverence and love, though their basenesses are plainer to no eye than to his. To reconcile these contradictions is the task of all good men.
1824 *Goethe*, vol.4, 'Introduction to German Romance'.

75 A mind that has seen, and suffered, and done, speaks to us of what it has tried and conquered.
1824 *Goethe*, vol.4, 'Introduction to German Romance'.

76 The true Church of England, at this moment, lies in the Editors of the newspapers.
1829 *Signs of the Times*.

77 It is no very good symptom either of nations or individuals, that they deal much in vaticination.
1829 *Signs of the Times*.

78 Seldom can the unhappy be persuaded that the evil of the day is sufficient for it; and the ambitious will not be content with the present splendour, but paints yet more glorious triumphs, on the cloud curtain of the future.
1829 *Signs of the Times*.

79 Meanwhile, we too admit that the present is an important time... We were wise indeed, could we discern truly the signs of our own time; and by knowledge of its wants and advantages, wisely adjust our own position in it.
1829 *Signs of the Times*.

80 Were we required to characterise this age of ours by any single epithet, we should be tempted to call it, not an Heroical, Devotional, Philosophical, or Moral Age, but above all others, the Mechanical Age. It is the Age of Machinery, in every outward and inward sense of the word.
1829 *Signs of the Times*.

81 We remove mountains, and make seas our smooth highway; nothing can resist us. We war with rude Nature; and, by our resistless engines, come off always victorious, and loaded with spoils.
1829 *Signs of the Times*.

82 Wealth has more and more increased, and at the same time gathered itself more and more into masses, strangely altering the old relations, and increasing the distance between the rich and the poor.
1829 *Signs of the Times*.

83 Men are grown mechanical in head and in the heart, as well as in the hand. They have lost faith in individual endeavour, and in natural force of any kind.
1829 *Signs of the Times*.

84 By our skill in Mechanism, it has come to pass, that in the management of external things we excel all other ages; while in whatever respects the pure mortal nature, in true dignity of soul and character, we are perhaps inferior to most civilised ages.
1829 *Signs of the Times*.

85 We are Giants in physical power: in a deeper than metaphorical sense, we are Titans, that strive, by heaping mountain on mountain, to conquer Heaven also.
1829 *Signs of the Times*.

86 Philosophers...stand among us not to do, nor to create anything, but as a sort of Logic-mill to grind out the true causes and effects of all that is done and created.
1829 *Signs of the Times*.

87 We have a faith in the imperishable dignity of man; in the high vocation to which, throughout this his earthly history, he has been appointed.
1829 *Signs of the Times*.

88 To reform a world, to reform a nation no wise man will undertake; and all but foolish men know, that the only solid, though a far slower reformation, is what each begins and perfects on himself.
1829 *Signs of the Times*.

89 No man who has once heartily and wholly laughed can be altogether irreclaimably bad.
1833–4 *Sartor Resartus*, bk.1, ch.4.

90 He who first shortened the labour of copyists by device of *Movable Types* was disbanding hired armies, and cashiering most Kings and Senates, and creating a whole new democratic world: he had invented the art of printing.
1833–4 *Sartor Resartus*, bk.1, ch.5.

91 Man is a tool-using animal… Without tools he is nothing, with tools he is all.
1833–4 *Sartor Resartus*, bk.1, ch.5.

92 Whoso has sixpence is sovereign (to the length of sixpence) over all men; commands cooks to feed him, philosophers to teach him, kings to mount guard over him,—to the length of sixpence.
1833–4 *Sartor Resartus*, bk.1, ch.5.

93 Man's earthly interests, 'are all hooked and buttoned together, and held up, by Clothes.'
1833–4 *Sartor Resartus*, bk.1, ch.8.

94 Be not the slave of words.
1833–4 *Sartor Resartus*, bk.1, ch.8.

95 Language is called the garment of thought: however, it should rather be, language is the flesh-garment, the body, of thought.
1833–4 *Sartor Resartus*, bk.1, ch.11.

96 The end of man is an action and not a thought, though it were the noblest.
1833–4 *Sartor Resartus*, bk.2, ch.6.

97 The everlasting No.
1833–4 *Sartor Resartus*, bk.2, ch.7, title.

98 Most true it is, as a wise man teaches us, that 'doubt of any sort cannot be removed except by Action.' On which ground, too, let him who gropes painfully in darkness or in uncertain light, and prays vehemently that the dawn may ripen into day, lay this other precept well to heart, which to me was of invaluable service: *'Do the Duty which lies nearest thee'*, which thou knowest to be a Duty! Thy second duty will already have become clearer.
1833–4 *Sartor Resartus*, bk.2, ch.9.

99 Man's unhappiness, as I construe, comes of his greatness; it is because there is an Infinite in him, which with all his cunning he cannot quite bury under the Finite.
1833–4 *Sartor Resartus*, bk.2, ch.9.

1 Be no longer a chaos, but a world, or even worldkin. Produce! Produce! Were it but the pitifullest infinitesimal fraction of a product, produce it in God's name! 'Tis the utmost thou hast in thee: out with it, then.
1833–4 *Sartor Resartus*, bk.2, ch.9.

2 Friends! trust not the heart of that man for whom Old Clothes are not venerable.
1833–4 *Sartor Resartus*, bk.3, ch.6.

3 How great a Possibility, how small a realized Result.
1834 Of Samuel Taylor Coleridge. Letter to Emerson, 12 Aug.

4 The public is an old woman. Let her maunder and mumble.
1835 Journal entry.

5 Hope ushers in a Revolution—as earthquakes are preceded by bright weather.
1837 *History of the French Revolution*, vol.1, bk.2, ch.1.

6 A whiff of grapeshot.
1837 *History of the French Revolution*, vol.1, bk.5, ch.3.

7 Under all the roofs of this distracted City is the nodus of a drama, not untragical, crowding towards solution.
1837 *History of the French Revolution*, vol.1, bk.5, ch.6.

8 How true it is, that there is nothing dead in this Universe; that what we call dead is only changed, its forces working in inverse order! 'The leaf that lies rotting in moist winds,' says one, 'has still force; else how could it rot?'
1837 *History of the French Revolution*, vol.2, bk.3, ch.1.

9 The difference between Orthodoxy or My-doxy and Heterodoxy or Thy-doxy.
1837 *History of the French Revolution*, vol.2, bk.4, ch.2.

10 The seagreen Incorruptible.
1837 Of Robespierre. *History of the French Revolution*, vol.2, bk.4, ch.4.

11 Pity is lost in rage and fear.
1837 *History of the French Revolution*, vol.3, bk.2, ch.7.

12 France was long a despotism tempered by epigrams.
1837 *History of the French Revolution*, vol.3, bk.7, ch.7.

13 Aristocracy of the Moneybag.
1837 *History of the French Revolution*, vol.3, bk.7, ch.7.

14 The 'golden-calf of self-love'.
1838 *Critical and Miscellaneous Essays*, 'Burns'.

15 For, strictly considered, what is all knowledge too but recorded experience, and a product of history; of which, therefore, reasoning and belief, no less than action and passion are essential materials?
1838 *Critical and Miscellaneous Essays*, 'History'.

16 History is the essence of innumerable biographies.
1838 *Critical and Miscellaneous Essays*, 'History'.

17 When the oak-tree is fallen, the whole forest echoes with it; but a hundred acorns are planted silently by some unnoticed breeze.
1838 *Critical and Miscellaneous Essays*, 'History'.

18 Laws themselves, political Constitutions, are not our Life; but only the house wherein our Life is led.
1838 *Critical and Miscellaneous Essays*, 'History'.

19 History is philosophy teaching by experience.
1838 *Critical and Miscellaneous Essays*, 'History'.

20 A well-written life is almost as rare as a well-spent one.
1838 *Critical and Miscellaneous Essays*, 'Jean Paul Fredrich Richter'.

21 There is no life of a man, faithfully recorded, but is a heroic poem of its sort, rhymed or unrhymed.
1838 *Critical and Miscellaneous Essays*, 'Sir Walter Scott'.

22 Under all speech there lies a silence that is better. Silence is deep as Eternity; speech is shallow as Time.
1838 *Critical and Miscellaneous Essays*, 'Sir Walter Scott'.

23 A feeling generally exists that the condition and disposition of the Working Class is a rather ominous matter at present; that something ought to be said, something ought to be done, in regard to it.
1839 *Chartism*, ch.1.

24 A witty statesman said, you might prove anything by figures.
1839 *Chartism*, ch.2.

25 To believe practically that the poor and luckless are here

only as a nusiance to be abraded and abated, and in some permissable manner made away with, and swept out of sight, is not an amiable faith.
1839 *Chartism*, ch.3.

26 A man willing to work, and unable to find work, is perhaps the saddest sight that fortune's inequality exhibits under the sun.
1839 *Chartism*, ch.4.

27 Surely of all 'rights of man', this right of the ignorant man to be guided by the wiser, to be, gently or forcibly, held in the true course by him, is the indisputablest.
1839 *Chartism*, ch.6.

28 In epochs when cash payment has become the sole nexus of man to man.
1839 *Chartism*, ch.6.

29 The English are used to suffrage; it is their panacea for all that goes wrong with them.
1839 *Chartism*, ch.9.

30 Books are written by martyr-men, not for rich men alone but for all men. If we consider it, every human being has, by the nature of the case, a *right* to hear what other wise human beings have spoken to him. It is one of the Rights of Men; a very cruel injustice if you deny it to a man!
1840 Letter to John Sterling, collected in *New Letters of Carlyle* (1904), vol.1.

31 It is well said, in every sense, that a man's religion is the chief fact with regard to him.
1841 *On Heroes, Hero-Worship, and the Heroic*, 'The Hero as Divinity' (published 1897).

32 Worship is transcendent wonder.
1841 *On Heroes, Hero-Worship, and the Heroic*, 'The Hero as King'.

33 I hope we English will long maintain our *grand talent pour le silence*.
1841 *On Heroes, Hero-Worship, and the Heroic*, 'The Hero as King'.

34 In books lies the soul of the whole Past Time; the articulate audible voice of the Past, when the body and material substance of it has altogether vanished like a dream.
1841 *On Heroes, Hero-Worship, and the Heroic*, 'The Hero as Man of Letters'.

35 The true University these days is a collection of books.
1841 *On Heroes, Hero-Worship, and the Heroic*, 'The Hero as Man of Letters'.

36 Adversity is sometimes hard upon a man; but for one man who can stand prosperity, there are a hundred that will stand adversity.
1841 *On Heroes, Hero-Worship, and the Heroic*, 'The Hero as Man of Letters'.

37 Heaven's splendour over his head, Hell's darkness under his feet.
1843 *Past and Present*, bk.2, ch.15.

38 Work earnestly at anything, you will by degrees learn to work at all things.
1843 *Past and Present*, bk.3, ch.2.

39 Captains of Industry.
1843 *Past and Present*, bk.4, ch.4, title.

40 Respectable Professors of the Dismal Science.
1850 *Latter-Day Pamphlets*, no.1, 'The Present Time'.

41 Nature admits no lie.
1850 *Latter-Day Pamphlets*, no.5.

42 A Parliament speaking through reporters to Buncombe and the twenty-seven millions mostly fools.
1850 *Latter-Day Pamphlets*, no.6, 'Parliaments'.

43 Transcendental moonshine.
1851 Of the romantic impulses that had led Sterling to the priesthood. *The Life of John Sterling*, pt.1, ch.15.

44 Maid-servants, I hear people complaining, are getting instructed in the 'ologies'.
1866 Inaugural address as Rector of Edinburgh University, 2 Apr.

45 All reform except a moral one will prove unavailing.
1872 *Critical and Miscellaneous Essays*, 'Corn Law Rhymes'.

46 If Jesus Christ were to come today, people would not even crucify him. They would ask him to dinner, and hear what he had to say, and make fun of it.
Quoted in D A Wilson *Carlyle at his Zenith* (1927).

Carman, (William) Bliss 1861–1929

Canadian poet. His vivid and optimistic poetry includes *Songs from Vagabondia* (with Richard Hovey, 1894, 1896 and 1901) and *Pipes of Pan* (1902–5).

47 Have little care that Life is brief,
And less that art is long.
Success is in the silences,
Though fame is in the song.
1923 *Ballads and Lyrics*, 'Envoi'. These lines are reproduced on the plaque erected in his honour at the University of New Brunswick, Fredericton, Canada.

Carnegie, Andrew 1835–1919

Scottish-born US steel magnate and philanthropist. He emigrated with his family in 1848, investing his savings in oil lands as a youth and amassing a vast fortune, with which he endowed numerous institutions and good causes.

48 The man who dies rich...dies disgraced.
1889 'The Gospel of Wealth', in the *North American Review*, Jun.

49 While the law [of competition] may be sometimes hard for the individual, it is best for the race, because it insures the survival of the fittest in every department. We accept and welcome, therefore, as conditions to which we must accommodate ourselves, great inequality of environment, the concentration of business, industrial and commercial, in the hands of a few, and the law of competition between these, as being not only beneficial, but essential to the future progress of the race.
1889 'The Gospel of Wealth', in the *North American Review*, Jun.

Carnegie, Dale *originally* ***Dale Carnagey*** 1888–1955

US lecturer and writer, a pioneer of self-help psychology.

50 How to Win Friends and Influence People.
1930 Title of book.

Carpentier, Alejo 1904–80

Cuban novelist, musicologist and journalist, Ambassador to Europe for a considerable period of Castro's regime. His style has been called neo-Baroque.

51 *A tal punto me hunden mis palabras, como dichas por*

otro, por un juez que yo llevara dentro sin saberlo y se valiera de mis propios medios físicos para expresarse, que me aterro, al oírme, de lo difícil que es volver a ser hombre cuando se ha dejado de ser hombre.
As though they were coming from the lips of another, from a judge I carried within me without knowing it, and who made use of my own faculties to express himself, my words took such hold upon me that it frightened me to realize, as I listened to myself, how hard it is to become a man when one has ceased to be a man.
1953 *Los pasos perdidos* (translated as *The Lost Steps*, 1956), ch.1, pt.2.

Carr, E(dward) H(allet) 1892–1982

English political scientist and historian. In the diplomatic service until 1936, he was Assistant Editor of *The Times* (1941–6) and wrote several important historical texts, including biographies of Marx (1934) and Bakunin (1937).

52 The unending dialogue between the present and the past.
Of biography. Quoted in James G Hershberg *James B Conant* (1993).

Carr, Emily 1871–1945

Canadian painter and writer, who recorded the lives of west-coast native Canadians in words and paintings. Her first book *Klee Wyck* (1941) won the Governor-General's Award.

53 The outstanding event was the *doing* which I am still at. Don't pickle me away as done.
c.1940 Quoted in Ira Dilworth's foreword to *Klee Wyck* (1951 edn).

54 There was neither horizon, cloud, nor sound; of that pink, spread silence even I had become part, belonging as much to sky as to earth.
1941 *Klee Wyck*, ch.17, 'Salt Water'.

Carr, J(ames) L(loyd) 1912–94

English novelist. His best-known work is *A Month in the Country* (1980), which was also filmed.

55 'I've never been spoken to like this before in all my thirty years' experience,' she wails. '*You* have not had thirty years' experience, Mrs Grindle-Jones,' he says witheringly. '*You* have had one year's experience 30 times.'
1972 *The Harpole Report*, ch.21.

56 In rural England, people live wrapped tight in a cocoon; only their eyes move to make sure that nobody gets more than themselves.
1975 *How Steeple Sinderby Wanderers Won the FA Cup*, pt.2.

57 You must understand, James, that their English God is not so dominant a business institution as ours.
1985 On the US version of God. *The Battle of Pollocks Crossing*.

Carrà, Carlo 1881–1966

Italian painter, involved first in *Pittura metafisica* and then in Futurism.

58 *The painting of sounds, noises and smells calls for:*
1. Reds, rrrrreds, the rrrrrreddest rrrrrrreds that shouuuuuuut.
2. Greens, that can never be greener, greeeeeeeeeeeens that screeeeeeam, yellows, as violent as can be: polenta yellows, saffron yellows, brass yellows.
1913 In the *Manifesto of Futurist Painting*, quoted in *Futurismo e Futurismi* (1986).

59 This is the truth! In order to achieve this *total painting*, which requires the active cooperation of all the senses, a *painting which is a plastic state of mind of the universal*, you must paint, as drunkards sing and vomit, sounds, noises and smells!
1913 In the *Manifesto of Futurist Painting*, quoted in *Futurismo e Futurismi* (1986).

Carracci, Annibale 1560–1609

Italian painter, one of a family of artists from Bologna.

60 Poets paint with words, painters speak with works.
Attributed rebuke to his brother Agostino. Quoted in G P Bellori *Vite* (1672).

Carrigan, Jim R(ichard) 1929–

US lawyer, judge at the US Court of Appeals.

61 It is all too rare today to hear the clear, clean ring of a really original insult.
1987 In *Time*, 28 Aug.

Carroll, Lewis *pseudonym of* Rev Charles Lutwidge Dodgson 1832–98

English poet, mathematician and logician. A shy man with a stammer, he was most comfortable in the company of children. He is best known for his children's books *Alice's Adventures in Wonderland* (1865) and *Through the Looking-Glass* (1871).

62 'And what is the use of a book,' thought Alice, 'without pictures or conversations?'
1865 *Alice's Adventures in Wonderland*, ch.1, 'Down the Rabbit-Hole'.

63 'Even if my head *would* go through,' thought poor Alice, 'it would be of very little use without my shoulders.'
1865 *Alice's Adventures in Wonderland*, ch.1, 'Down the Rabbit-Hole'.

64 'Curiouser and curiouser!' cried Alice (she was so much surprised, that for the moment she quite forgot how to speak good English).
1865 *Alice's Adventures in Wonderland*, ch.2, 'The Pool of Tears'.

65 How doth the little crocodile
Improve his shining tail,
And pour the waters of the Nile
On every golden scale!

How cheerfully he seems to grin,
How neatly spreads his claws,
And welcomes little fishes in,
With gently smiling jaws!
1865 *Alice's Adventures in Wonderland*, ch.2, 'The Pool of Tears'.

66 'I'll be judge, I'll be jury,' said cunning old Fury;
'I'll try the whole cause, and condemn you to death.'
1865 *Alice's Adventures in Wonderland*, ch.3, 'A Caucus-Race and a Long Tale', told by the Dormouse.

67 'You are old, Father William,' the young man said,
'And your hair has become very white;
And yet you incessantly stand on your head—
Do you think, at your age, it is right?'

'In my youth,' Father William replied to his son,

'I feared it might injure the brain;
But now that I'm perfectly sure I have none,
Why, I do it again and again.'
1865 *Alice's Adventures in Wonderland*, ch.5, 'Advice from a Caterpillar'.
➥ *See Southey 805:96.*

68 'If everybody minded their own business,' the Duchess said, in a hoarse growl, 'the world would go round a deal faster than it does.'
1865 *Alice's Adventures in Wonderland*, ch.6, 'Pig and Pepper'.

69 Speak roughly to your little boy,
And beat him when he sneezes:
He only does it to annoy,
Because he knows it teases.
1865 The Duchess's lullaby. *Alice's Adventures in Wonderland*, ch.6, 'Pig and Pepper'.

70 'All right,' said the Cat; and this time it vanished quite slowly, beginning with the end of the tail, and ending with the grin, which remained some time after the rest of it had gone.
1865 The disappearance of the Cheshire Cat. *Alice's Adventures in Wonderland*, ch.6, 'Pig and Pepper'.

71 'Then you should say what you mean,' the March Hare went on.
'I do,' Alice hastily replied; 'at least—at least I mean what I say—that's the same thing, you know.'
'Not the same thing a bit!' said the Hatter. 'Why, you might just as well say that "I see what I eat" is the same thing as "I eat what I see!"'
1865 *Alice's Adventures in Wonderland*, ch.7, 'A Mad Tea-Party'.

72 Twinkle, twinkle, little bat!
How I wonder what you're at!
Up above the world you fly!
Like a teatray in the sky.
1865 *Alice's Adventures in Wonderland*, Ch. 7, 'A Mad Tea-Party'.

73 'Take some more tea,' the March Hare said to Alice, very earnestly.
'I've had nothing yet,' Alice replied in an offended tone, 'so I can't take more.'
'You mean you can't take *less*,' said the Hatter; 'It's very easy to take *more* than nothing.'
1865 *Alice's Adventures in Wonderland*, ch.7, 'A Mad Tea-Party'.

74 Off with her head!
1865 The Queen of Hearts. *Alice's Adventures in Wonderland*, ch.8, 'The Queen's Croquet Ground'.

75 Everything's got a moral, if only you can find it.
1865 The Duchess. *Alice's Adventures in Wonderland*, ch.9, 'The Mock Turtle's Story'.

76 Take care of the sense, and the sounds will take care of themselves.
1865 The Duchess. *Alice's Adventures in Wonderland*, ch.9, 'The Mock Turtle's Story'.

77 'Just about as much right,' said the Duchess, 'as pigs have to fly.'
1865 *Alice's Adventures in Wonderland*, ch.9, 'The Mock Turtle's Story'.

78 'That's the reason they're called lessons,' the Gryphon remarked: 'because they lessen from day to day.'
1865 *Alice's Adventures in Wonderland*, ch.9, 'The Mock Turtle's Story'.

79 'I only took the regular course.'
'What was that?' inquired Alice.
'Reeling and Writhing, of course, to begin with,' the Mock Turtle replied; 'and then the different branches of Arithmetic—Ambition, Distraction, Uglification, and Derision.'
1865 *Alice's Adventures in Wonderland*, ch.9, 'The Mock Turtle's Story'

80 The Drawling-master was an old conger-eel, that used to come once a week: *he* taught us Drawling, Stretching, and Fainting in Coils.
1865 *Alice's Adventures in Wonderland*, ch.9, 'The Mock Turtle's Story'.

81 'Will you walk a little faster?' said a whiting to a snail, 'There's a porpoise close behind us and he's treading on my tail.'
1865 *Alice's Adventures in Wonderland*, ch.10, 'The Lobster-Quadrille'.

82 Will you, won't you, will you, won't you, will you join the dance?
1865 *Alice's Adventures in Wonderland*, ch.10, 'The Lobster-Quadrille'.

83 Beautiful Soup, so rich and green,
Waiting in a hot tureen!
Who for such dainties would not stoop?
Soup of the evening, beautiful Soup!
1865 Song of the Mock Turtle. *Alice's Adventures in Wonderland*, ch.10.

84 'Tis the voice of the lobster; I heard him declare,
'You have baked me too brown, I must sugar my hair.'
1865 *Alice's Adventures in Wonderland*, ch.10, 'The Lobster-Quadrille'.

85 The Queen of Hearts, she made some tarts,
All of a summer day:
The Knave of Hearts, he stole those tarts
And took them quite away!
1865 *Alice's Adventures in Wonderland*, ch.11, 'Who Stole the Tarts?'

86 'Where shall I begin, please your Majesty?' he asked.
'Begin at the beginning,' the King said, gravely, 'and go on till you come to the end; then stop.'
1865 *Alice's Adventures in Wonderland*, ch.12, 'Alice's Evidence'.

87 'That's not a regular rule; you invented it just now.'
'It's the oldest rule in the book,' said the King.
'Then it ought to be Number One,' said Alice.
1865 *Alice's Adventures in Wonderland*, ch.12, 'Alice's Evidence'.

88 'No, no!' said the Queen. 'Sentence first—verdict afterwards.'
1865 *Alice's Adventures in Wonderland*, ch.12, 'Alice's Evidence'.

89 'Why,' said the Dodo, 'the best way to explain it is to do it.'
1865 *Alice's Adventures in Wonderland*, ch.3, 'A Caucus-Race and a Long Tale'.

90 'Twas brillig, and the slithy toves
Did gyre and gimble in the wabe;
All mimsy were the borogoves,
And the mome raths outgrabe.

'Beware the Jabberwock, my son!
The jaws that bite, the claws that catch!
Beware the Jubjub bird, and shun
The frumious Bandersnatch!'
1871 *Through the Looking-Glass*, ch.1, 'Looking-Glass House'.

91 And, as in uffish thought he stood,

The Jabberwock, with eyes of flame,
Came whiffling through the tulgey wood,
And burbled as it came!

One, two! One, two! And through and through
The vorpal blade went snicker-snack!
He left it dead and with its head
He went galumphing back.

'And hast thou slain the Jabberwock?
Come to my arms, my beamish boy!
Oh frabjous day! Callooh! Callay!'
He chortled in his joy.

1871 *Through the Looking-Glass*, ch.1, 'Looking-Glass House'.

92 Curtsey while you're thinking what to say. It saves time.
1871 *Through the Looking-Glass*, ch.2, 'The Garden of Live Flowers'.

93 'When you say "hill",' the Queen interrupted, 'I could show you hills, in comparison with which you'd call that a valley.'
'No, I shouldn't,' said Alice, surprised into contradicting her at last: 'a hill *can't* be a valley, you know. That would be nonsense—'
The Red Queen shook her head. 'You may call it "nonsense" if you like,' she said, 'but *I've* heard nonsense, compared with which that would be as sensible as a dictionary!'
1871 *Through the Looking-Glass*, ch.2, 'The Garden of Live Flowers'.

94 Now, *here*, you see, it takes all the running *you* can do, to keep in the same place. If you want to get somewhere else, you must run at least twice as fast as that!
1871 *Through the Looking-Glass*, ch.2, 'The Garden of Live Flowers'.

95 Speak in French when you can't think of the English for a thing—turn out your toes as you walk—and remember who you are!
1871 The Red Queen's advice to Alice as she begins the chess game. *Through the Looking-Glass*, ch.2, 'The Garden of Live Flowers'.

96 'You shouldn't make jokes,' Alice said, 'if it makes you so unhappy.'
1871 Alice to the gnat. *Through the Looking-Glass*, ch.3, 'Looking-Glass Insects'.

97 Tweedledum and Tweedledee
Agreed to have a battle;
For Tweedledum said Tweedledee
Had spoilt his nice new rattle.
1871 *Through the Looking-Glass*, ch.4, 'Tweedledum and Tweedledee'.

98 'Contrariwise,' continued Tweedledee, 'if it was so, it might be; and if it were so, it would be: but as it isn't it ain't. That's logic.'
1871 *Through the Looking-Glass*, ch.4, 'Tweedledum and Tweedledee'.

99 The sun was shining on the sea,
Shining with all his might:
He did his very best to make
The billows smooth and bright—
And this was odd, because it was
The middle of the night.
1871 Tweedledee. *Through the Looking-Glass*, ch.4, 'Tweedledum and Tweedledee'.

1 The Walrus and the Carpenter
Were walking close at hand;
They wept like anything to see
Such quantities of sand:
'If this were only cleared away,'
They said, 'it would be grand!'
1871 Tweedledee. *Through the Looking-Glass*, ch.4, 'Tweedledum and Tweedledee'.

2 'The time has come,' the Walrus said,
'To talk of many things:
Of shoes—and ships—and sealing-wax—
Of cabbages—and kings—
And why the sea is boiling hot—
And whether pigs have wings.'
1871 Tweedledee. *Through the Looking-Glass*, ch.4, 'Tweedledum and Tweedledee'.

3 'You know,' he said very gravely, 'it's one of the most serious things that can possibly happen to one in a battle—to get one's head cut off.'
1871 *Through the Looking-Glass*, ch.4, 'Tweedledum and Tweedledee'.

4 The rule is, jam to-morrow and jam yesterday—but never jam to-day.
1871 The White Queen. *Through the Looking-Glass*, ch.5, 'Wool and Water'.

5 'It's a poor sort of memory that only works backwards,' the Queen remarked.
1871 *Through the Looking-Glass*, ch.5, 'Wool and Water'.

6 Consider anything, only don't cry!
1871 *Through the Looking-Glass*, ch.5, 'Wool and Water'.

7 Alice laughed. 'There's no use trying,' she said: 'one can't believe impossible things.'
'I daresay you haven't had much practice,' said the Queen. 'When I was your age, I always did it for half-an-hour a day. Why, sometimes I've believed as many as six impossible things before breakfast.'
1871 *Through the Looking-Glass*, ch. 5, 'Wool and Water'.

8 'It's *very* provoking,' Humpty Dumpty said after a long silence, looking away from Alice as he spoke, 'to be called an egg—*very!*'
1871 *Through the Looking-Glass*, ch.6, 'Humpty Dumpty'.

9 With a name like yours you might be any shape, almost.
1871 *Through the Looking-Glass*, ch.6, 'Humpty Dumpty'.

10 'They gave it me,' Humpty Dumpty continued thoughtfully... 'for an un-birthday present.'
1871 *Through the Looking-Glass*, ch.6, 'Humpty Dumpty'.

11 'The question is,' said Humpty Dumpty, 'which is to be master—that's all.'
1871 *Through the Looking-Glass*, ch.6, 'Humpty Dumpty'.

12 'That's a great deal to make one word mean,' Alice said in a thoughtful tone.
'When I make a word do a lot of work like that,' said Humpty Dumpty, 'I always pay it extra.'
1871 *Through the Looking-Glass*, ch.6, 'Humpty Dumpty'.

13 'Slithy' means 'lithe and slimy'... You see it's like a portmanteau—there are two meanings packed up into one word.
1871 Humpty Dumpty explaining the *Jabberwock* poem. *Through the Looking-Glass*, ch.6, 'Humpty Dumpty'.

14 'I can repeat poetry as well as other folk if it comes to that—'

'Oh, it needn't come to that!' Alice hastily said.
1871 *Through the Looking-Glass*, ch.6, 'Humpty Dumpty'.

15 'There's glory for you!'
'I don't know what you mean by "glory",' Alice said.
'I meant, "there's a nice knock-down argument for you!"'
'But "glory" doesn't mean "a nice knock-down argument",' Alice objected.
'When I use a word,' Humpty Dumpty said in a rather scornful tone, 'it means just what I choose it to mean—neither more nor less.'
1871 *Through the Looking-Glass*, ch.6, 'Humpty Dumpty'.

16 The Lion and the Unicorn were fighting for the crown:
The Lion beat the Unicorn all round the town.
Some gave them white bread, some gave them brown;
Some gave them plum-cake and drummed them out of town.
1871 *Through the Looking Glass*, ch.7, 'The Lion and the Unicorn'.

17 He's an Anglo-Saxon Messenger—and those are Anglo-Saxon attitudes.
1871 *Through the Looking Glass*, ch.7, 'The Lion and the Unicorn'.

18 The Lion looked at Alice wearily. 'Are you animal—or vegetable—or mineral?' he said, yawning at every other word.
1871 *Through the Looking-Glass*, ch.7, 'The Lion and the Unicorn'.

19 I must have *two* you know—to come and go. One to come, and one to go.
1871 The King speaking of his messengers. *Through the Looking-Glass*, ch.7, 'The Lion and the Unicorn'.

20 It's as large as life and twice as natural!
1871 *Through the Looking-Glass*, ch.7, 'The Lion and the Unicorn'.

21 'It's long,' said the Knight, 'but it's very, *very* beautiful. Everybody that hears me sing it—either it brings the *tears* into their eyes, or else—'
'Or else what?' said Alice, for the Knight had made a sudden pause.
'Or else it doesn't, you know.'
1871 *Through the Looking-Glass*, ch.8, 'It's My Own Invention'.

22 I'll tell thee everything I can:
There's little to relate.
I saw an aged, aged man,
A-sitting on a gate.
1871 *Through the Looking-Glass*, ch.8, 'It's My Own Invention'.

23 Or madly squeeze a right-hand foot
Into a left-hand shoe.
1871 *Through the Looking-Glass*, ch.8, 'It's My Own Invention'.

24 Un-dish-cover the fish, or dishcover the riddle.
1871 *Through the Looking-Glass*, ch.9, 'Queen Alice'.

25 'Fan her head!' the Red Queen anxiously interrupted. 'She'll be feverish after so much thinking.'
1871 *Through the Looking-Glass*, ch.9, 'Queen Alice'.

26 'Do you know Languages? What's the French for fiddle-de-dee?'
'Fiddle-de-dee's not English,' Alice replied gravely.
'Who ever said it was?' said the Red Queen.
Alice thought she saw a way out of the difficulty this time. 'If you'll tell me what language 'fiddle-de-dee' is, I'll tell you the French for it!' she exclaimed triumphantly.
But the Red Queen drew herself up rather stiffly, and said 'Queens never make bargains.'
1871 *Through the Looking-Glass*, ch.9, 'Queen Alice'.

27 What I tell you three times is true.
1876 *The Hunting of the Snark*, 'Fit the First: The Landing'.

28 He would answer to 'Hi!' or to any loud cry,
Such as 'Fry me!' or 'Fritter-my-wig!'
1876 *The Hunting of the Snark*, 'Fit the First: The Landing'.

29 His intimate friends called him 'Candle-ends',
And his enemies, 'Toasted-cheese'.
1876 *The Hunting of the Snark*, 'Fit the First: The Landing'.

30 'What's the good of Mercator's North Poles and Equators,
Tropics, Zones and Meridian lines?'
So the Bellman would cry: and the crew would reply,
'They are merely conventional signs!'
1876 *The Hunting of the Snark*, 'Fit the Second: The Bellman's Speech'.

31 But the principal failing occurred in the sailing,
And the Bellman, perplexed and distressed,
Said he *had* hoped, at least, when the wind blew due East,
That the ship would *not* travel due West!
1876 *The Hunting of the Snark*, 'Fit the Second: The Bellman's Speech'.

32 They sought it with thimbles, they sought it with care;
They pursued it with forks and hope;
They threatened its life with a railway-share;
They charmed it with smiles and soap.
1876 *The Hunting of the Snark*, 'Fit the Fifth: The Beaver's Lesson'.

33 He thought he saw an Elephant,
That practised on a fife:
He looked again, and found it was
A letter from his wife.
'At length I realize,' he said
'The bitterness of life!'
1889 *Sylvie and Bruno*, ch.5.

34 He thought he saw a Rattlesnake
That questioned him in Greek,
He looked again and found it was
The Middle of Next Week.
'The one thing I regret,' he said,
'Is that it cannot speak!'
1889 *Sylvie and Bruno*, ch.6.

Carson, Edward Henry, Baron 1854–1935

Irish Unionist politician, Solicitor General in the Conservative Government (1900–5). He successfully defended the Marquis of Queensberry against Oscar Wilde's libel suit in 1895. In 1912, he forced the Government to exclude Ulster from the Home Rule settlement. During World War I, he served as Attorney General (1915), First Lord of the Admiralty (1916–17) and a member of the war cabinet (1917–18).

35 A sentence of death with a stay of execution for six years.
1914 On the British Government's compromise terms by which Ireland was to be allowed to defer Home Rule for six years. Speech, Mar.

36 My only great qualification for being put at the head of the navy is that I am wholly at sea.
c.1916 Quoted in I Colvin *Life of Lord Carson* (1936), vol.3, ch.23.

Carter, Angela Olive 1940–92

English novelist and essayist, whose works combine fantasy and genre pastiche. They include *The Magic Toyshop* (1967) and *The Sadeian Woman* (1979).

37 Clothes are our weapons, our challenges, our visible insults.
1967 'Notes for a Theory of Sixties Style', in *New Society* (1967). Collected in *Nothing Sacred* (1982).

38 Solitude and melancholy, that is a woman's life.
1977 *The Passion of New Eve*, ch.9.

39 Myth deals in false universals, to dull the pain of particular circumstances.
1979 *The Sadeian Woman*, 'Polemical Preface'.

40 What is marriage but prostitution to one man instead of many?
1985 *Nights at the Circus*, 'London 2'.

41 I notice that I'm getting more sentimental as I get older; I feel I owe it to myself somehow.
Quoted in John Haffenden *Novelists in Interview* (1985).

42 He was a man with a great future behind him, already.
1991 *Wise Children*, ch.3.

43 She looked like a million dollars, I must admit, even if in well-used notes.
1991 *Wise Children*, ch.5.

Carter, Jimmy (James Earl) 1924–

US Democratic politician and 39th President (1977–81). He helped to effect the Egypt–Israel peace treaties (1979), but after the Iran hostage crisis and the Soviet invasion of Afghanistan he was defeated by Reagan in 1980. Latterly he has been a prolific human rights campaigner and negotiator. He won the Nobel peace prize in 2002.

44 Why not the best?
1976 Presidential campaign slogan.

45 I am convinced that UFOs exist, because I have seen one.
1976 T V interview, 16 Jun.

46 We become not a melting pot but a beautiful mosaic. Different people, different beliefs, different yearnings, different hopes, different dreams.
1976 Speech at Pittsburgh, 27 Oct.

47 I have looked on a lot of women with lust. I have committed adultery in my heart many times. God recognizes I will do that, and forgives me.
1976 *Playboy* interview, Nov.

48 The experience of democracy is like the experience of life itself—always changing, infinite in its variety, sometimes turbulent and all the more valuable for having been tested by adversity.
1978 Address to the Parliament of India, 2 Jun.

49 If you fear making anyone mad, then you ultimately probe for the lowest common denominator of human achievement.
1978 Address to the Future Farmers of America, Kansas City, 9 Nov.

50 All of you have met another Democratic President. I've never had that opportunity yet.
1991 On greeting former Presidents Bush, Reagan, Ford and Nixon at the dedication of the Reagan Library. Reported in the *New York Times*, 5 Nov.

51 My role is one of filling vacuums.
1994 On his work with 105 countries since leaving the White House. Broadcast on ABC TV, 13 Dec.

52 I feel truer to myself…more of a missionary than a politician.
1995 On the Carter Library as a centre for the study of international issues. In *Life*, Nov.

Carter, Lillian 1898–1983

Mother of US President Jimmy Carter.

53 Sometimes when I look at my children, I say to myself, 'Lillian, you should have stayed a virgin.'
1977 In *Woman* magazine, 9 Apr.

Cartier, Jacques 1491–1557

French navigator and explorer in North America, discoverer of the St Lawrence river.

54 In fine I am rather inclined to believe that this is the land God gave to Cain.
1534 Of Canada, as he sailed past the bleak northern shore of the Gulf of St Lawrence. Journal entry, summer. Quoted in H P Biggar (ed) *The Voyages of Jacques Cartier* (1924).

Cartland, Dame (Mary) Barbara Hamilton 1901–2000

English romantic novelist. A prolific writer of popular romances, she became a media celebrity for her garish dress and well-honed sense of social status.

55 At fifty you have the choice of keeping your face or your figure and it's *much* better to keep your face.
1981 In the *Daily Mail*, 10 Jul.

56 I answer 20,000 letters a year and so many couples are having problems because they are not getting the right proteins and vitamins.
1986 Quoted in the *Observer*, 31 Aug.

Cartwright, John 1740–1824

English reformer, 'The Father of Reform', and political writer.

57 One man shall have one vote.
1780 *The People's Barrier Against Undue Influence*, ch.1, 'Principles, maxims, and primary rules of politics'.

Caruso, Enrico 1873–1921

Italian operatic tenor renowned for the power and musical purity of his voice.

58 You know whatta you do when you shit? Singing, it's the same thing, only up!
Quoted in H Brown *Whose Little Boy Are You?* (1983).

Cary, (Arthur) Joyce Lunel 1888–1957

English novelist. His best-known books are *Mister Johnston* (1939), set in Africa, and *The Horse's Mouth* (1944), the final work in a trilogy exploring the pretensions of the art world.

59 This is not to pretend that reading is a passive act. On the contrary, it is highly creative, or re-creative; itself an art.
1939 *Mister Johnston*, preface.

60 I ain't complaining—it's a duty laid down upon us by God—but the Pax Britania takes a bit of keeping up—with 'arf the world full of savages and 'arf the other 'arf just getting in the way.
1939 *Mister Johnston*.

61 She had a mannish manner of mind and face, able to feel hot and think cold.
1940 *Herself Surprised*, ch.7.

62 It is the misfortune of an old man that though he can put things out of his head he can't put them out of his feelings.
1942 *To Be A Pilgrim*, ch.8.

63 Sara could commit adultery at one end and weep for her sins at the other, and enjoy both at once.
1944 *The Horse's Mouth*, ch.8.

64 Remember I'm an artist. And you know what that means in a court of law. Next worse to an actress.
1944 *The Horse's Mouth*, ch.14.

65 To a real anarchist a poke in the eye is better than a bunch of flowers. It makes him see stars.
1944 *The Horse's Mouth*, ch.16.

66 The only good government...is a bad one in a hell of a fright.
1944 *The Horse's Mouth*, ch.32.

67 It is the tragedy of the world that no one knows what he doesn't know; and the less a man knows, the more sure he is that he knows everything.
1956 *Art and Reality*, introduction.

Casal, Julián del 1863–93

Cuban poet, forerunner of the *modernista* movement, influenced by Baudelaire and the Parnassian poets. He was a chronic invalid and frequently took a morbid view of life.

68 *Tengo el impuro amor de las ciudades,*
y a este sol que ilumina las edades
prefiero yo del gas las claridades.
I have an impure love for cities,
and I prefer the light coming from gaslamps
rather than this sun that lights the ages.
1893 *Bustos y rimas*, 'En el campo' ('In the Countryside').

Casals, Pablo 1876–1973

Spanish cellist, conductor and composer. In 1936 he emigrated because of the Civil War.

69 The most perfect technique is that which is not noticed at all.
Quoted in Julian Lloyd Webber *The Song of the Birds* (1985).

Cassini, Oleg Lolewski 1913–

French-born US fashion designer, raised in Italy.

70 I imagined her as an ancient Egyptian princess.
1987 On designing for Jacqueline Kennedy as First Lady. *In My Own Fashion.*

71 Fashion anticipates, and elegance is a state of mind.
1987 *In My Own Fashion.*

Casson, Sir Hugh Maxwell 1910–99

English architect and artist, Director of Architecture for the Festival of Britain (1948–51). Among his works are *Homes by the Million* (1947) and a series, *Hugh Casson's London* (1983), *Oxford* (1988) and *Cambridge* (1992).

72 Architecture cannot be understood without some knowledge of the society it serves.
1948 *An Introduction to Victorian Architecture.*

73 The Victorians expected every building, like every painting, to tell a story, and preferably to point to a moral as well.
1948 *An Introduction to Victorian Architecture.*

Castle (of Blackburn), Barbara Anne Castle, Baroness 1910–2002

English Labour politician.

74 Dogs make you walk. Politics make you think. Only boredom makes you old.
1997 In the *Daily Mail*, 11 Jan.

Castle (of Islington), Ted (Edward Cyril) Castle, Baron 1907–79

English journalist, Assistant Editor (1944–50) and Editor (1951–2) of *Picture Post*.

75 In Place of Strife.
1969 Title of a White Paper on industrial relations, 17 Jan. Suggested by Castle to his wife Barbara Castle, Secretary of State for Employment and Productivity.

Castro (Ruz), Fidel 1927–

Cuban revolutionary. He landed in Cuba in 1956 with a small band of insurgents. In 1958 Batista was forced to flee and Castro became Prime Minister (1959–76) and President (1976–), instituting a Marxist–Leninist programme.

76 *La historia me absolverá.*
History will absolve me.
1953 Title of propaganda pamphlet.

77 We are not politicians. We made our revolution to get the politicians out.
1961 Speech on assuming the presidency, two years after overthrowing the Batista regime.

78 A man who does not believe in human beings is not a revolutionary.
1967 Speech, 29 Jan.

79 I was a man lucky enough to have discovered a political theory, a man who was caught up in the whirlpool of Cuba's political crisis long before becoming a fully-fledged communist. Discovering Marxism was like finding a map in a forest.
1971 Speech, Chile, 18 Nov.

Caswall, Edward 1814–78

English hymnwriter and translator.

80 Jesu, the very thought of Thee
With sweetness fills the breast.
1849 *Hymns and Poems*, 'Jesu, the Very Thought of Thee' (a translation from 12c Latin, often attributed to St Bernard).

81 When morning gilds the skies.
1854 Title and first line of hymn.

82 See amid the winter's snow,
Born for us on earth below,
See, the Lamb of God appears,
Promised from eternal years!

Hail thou ever-blessèd morn!
Hail, redemption's happy dawn!
Sing through all Jerusalem:
Christ is born in Bethlehem!
1858 'See Amid the Winter's Snow'.

Cather, Willa Sibert 1873–1947

US novelist, poet and journalist. Her best-known books are the trilogy on pioneering life, *O Pioneers!* (1913), *The Song of the*

Lark (1915) and *My Antonia* (1918).

83 The history of every country begins in the heart of a man or a woman.
1913 *O Pioneers!*, pt.1, ch.5.

84 Isn't it queer: there are only two or three human stories, and they go on repeating themselves as fiercely as if they had never happened before; like the larks in this country, that have been singing the same five notes over for thousands of years.
1913 *O Pioneers!*, p.2, ch.4.

85 I like trees because they seem more resigned to the way they have to live than other things do.
1913 *O Pioneers!*, pt.2, ch.8.

86 Artistic growth is, more than it is anything else, a refining of the sense of truthfulness.
1915 *The Song of the Lark*, pt.6, ch.11.

87 Winter lies too long in country towns; hangs on until it is stale and shabby, old and sullen.
1918 *My Antonia*, bk.2, ch.7.

88 The dead might as well speak to the living as the old to the young.
1922 *One of Ours*, bk.2, ch.6.

89 When it has left a place where we have always found it, it is like shipwreck; we drop from security into something malevolent and bottomless.
1926 Of kindness. *My Mortal Enemy.*

90 Oh, the Germans classify, but the French arrange.
1927 *Death Comes to the Archbishop*, prologue.

91 The irregular and intimate quality of things made entirely by the human hand.
1927 *Death Comes to the Archbishop*, bk.1, ch.3.

92 Most of the basic material a writer works with is acquired before the age of fifteen.
Quoted in René Rapin *Willa Cather* (1930).

93 Only solitary men know the full joys of friendship. Others have their family—but to a solitary and an exile his friends are everything.
1931 *Shadows On The Rock*, bk.3, ch.5.

94 Religion and art spring from the same root and are close kin. Economics and art are strangers.
1936 In *Commonweal*, 17 Apr.

95 Every fine story must leave in the mind of the sensitive reader an intangible residuum of pleasure, a cadence, a quality of voice that is exclusively the writer's own, individual, unique.
1936 *Not Under Forty*, 'Miss Jewett'.

Catiline *full name* ***Lucius Sergius Catilina*** c.108–62 BC

Roman conspirator, from an obscure senatorial family. In 63 BC, he plotted to murder Cicero and other hostile senators, and to seize power, but was arrested and executed.

96 *Idem velle atque idem nolle, ea demum firma amicitia est.*
Agreements in likes and dislikes—this, and only this is what constitutes true friendship.
Quoted in Sallust *De Catilinae coniuratione*, bk.20, pt.4 (translated by J C Rolfe).

Cato *full name* ***Marcus Porcius Cato*** *known as* ***'the Elder'*** *or* ***'the Censor'*** 234–149 BC

Roman statesman and orator, renowned for his strict morality and conservatism. Appointed censor in 184 BC, he discharged his duties rigorously. He was sent on a mission to Carthage in 175 BC.

97 All mankind rules its women, and we rule all mankind, but our women rule us.
Criticizing the prevalent domination of women. Quoted (in Greek) in Plutarch *Regum et imperatorum apophthegmata*, pt.198d (translated by F C Babbitt).

98 *Orator vir bonus dicendi peritus.*
An orator is a good man, skilled in speaking.
Quoted in Quintilian *Institutio Oratoria*, bk.12, pt.1, section 1 (translated by H E Butler).

99 *Rem tene, verba sequentur.*
Stick to your subject, and words will follow.
Attributed advice to orators. Quoted in Gaius Julius Victor *Ars Rhetorica*, 'De inventione'.

1 *Delenda est Carthago.*
Carthage must be destroyed.
Attributed. Quoted in Florus *Epitome*, bk.1, pt.31 (*Cato inexpiabili odio delendam esse Carthaginem, et cum de alio consuletur, pronuntiabat*, Cato bore an unquenchable hatred to Carthage and used to announce that Carthage had to be destroyed, even when he was consulted on a different subject) and Pliny *Naturalis Historia*, bk.15, ch.74.

Cattell, Raymond B(ernard) 1905–98

British psychologist, designer of intelligence and personality tests. Associated with the eugenics movement in the 1930s, he believed that the large size and low IQs of lower-class families would undermine the nation's intellect.

2 The Fight for our National Intelligence.
1937 Title of book.

Catto, Henry E(dward) 1930–

US government official, chief of protocol at the White House (1974–6), Ambassador to the UK (1989–91) and Director of the US Information Agency (1991–3).

3 Like being the captain of a mine-sweeper, if you do your job well, nobody notices. If you don't, there's a hell of an explosion.
1988 On his role as chief of protocol. In the *Washington Post*, 22 Mar.

Catullus *full name* ***Gaius Valerius Catullus*** c.84–c.54 BC

Latin poet, mainly known for his passionate love poems for Lesbia. Her true name was Clodia, and she was probably the sister of Cicero's enemy P Clodius Pulcher.

4 *Cui dono lepidum novum libellum*
arida modo pumice expolitum?
Corneli, tibi.
Who shall I give my nice new little book to,
my little book polished with dry pumice? To you,
Cornelius.
Dedication to Cornelius Nepos, the biographer.
Carmina, no.1.

5 *Vivamus, mea Lesbia, atque amemus,*
rumoresque senum severiorum
omnes unius aestimemus assis.
Let us live, my Lesbia, and let us love!
Let us not give one penny if old men
protest and disapprove.

Carmina, no.5.
➤ *See Campion 186:76.*

6 *Quaeris, quot mihi basiationes*
tuae, Lesbia, sint satis superque?
You ask me, Lesbia, how many kisses
it will take to make me fully satisfied?
Carmina, no.7.

7 *Nam risu inepto res ineptior nulla est.*
For there is nothing more ridiculous than a ridiculous laugh.
Carmina, no.39.

8 *Ille mi par esse Deo videtur,*
ille, si fas est, superare Divos,
qui sedens adversus identidem te
spectat et audit
dulce ridentem.
He seems to me to be like a god,
even superior to the Gods, if it is
permitted to say so, the man who sits
gazing on you all day and listens to
your sweet laughter.
Carmina, no.51.

9 *Otium et reges prius et beatas*
perdidit urbes.
Often has leisure ruined great kings and fine cities.
Carmina, no.51.

10 *Odi et amo. quare id faciam, fortasse requiris.*
nescio sed fieri sentio et excrucior.
I hate and I love. You ask me to explain, perhaps.
I don't know. But I feel it happen and the pain is dreadful.
Carmina, no.85.

Caulfield, Sir Bernard 1914–94

English high court judge.

11 Remembering Mary Archer in the witness box. Your vision of her probably will never disappear. Has she elegance? Has she fragrance? Would she have, without the strain of this trial, radiance?
Summing up in 1987 libel trial in which Jeffrey Archer contested a newspaper's claim that he had sex with a prostitute. Quoted in Michael Crick *Jeffrey Archer: Stranger than Fiction* (1996).

Causley, Charles 1917–2003

English poet of verse for adults and children, much of it set in his native Cornwall.

12 You must take off your clothes for the doctor
And stand as straight as a pin,
His hand of stone on your white breastbone
Where the bullets all go in.
1953 'Recruiting Drive'.

13 Timothy Winters comes to school
With eyes as wide as a football pool,
Ears like bombs and teeth like splinters:
A blitz of a boy is Timothy Winters.
1957 'Timothy Winters'.

14 Who is the smiling stranger
With hair as white as gin,
What is he doing with the children
And who could have let him in?
1961 'Innocent's Song'.

Cavafy, Constantine *pseudonym of* Konstantínos Pétron Kaváfis 1863–1933

Egyptian-born Greek poet who spent much of his life working as a civil servant in Alexandria. Most of his work was published posthumously, including in English translation *Poems* (1951) and *Complete Poems* (1961).

15 And now, what will become of us without any barbarians?
Those people were a kind of solution.
1904 'Waiting for the Barbarians' (translated by E Keeley and P Sherrard).

16 Have Ithaka always in your mind
Your arrival there is what you are destined for.
1911 'Ithaka' (translated by E Keeley and P Sherrard).

17 New places you will not find, you will not find another sea
The city will follow you.
1911 'The Town' (translated by E Keeley and P Sherrard).

Cavell, Edith Louisa 1865–1915

English nurse, matron of a Red Cross hospital in Brussels during World War I. She was arrested by the Germans in 1915, charged with helping Allied soldiers escape to Holland, and executed when she did not deny the charges.

18 Standing, as I do, in view of God and eternity, I realize that patriotism is not enough. I must have no hatred or bitterness towards anyone.
1915 On the eve of her execution. Reported in *The Times*, 23 Oct.

Cavendish, Margaret, Duchess of Newcastle 1624–74

English writer and playwright. She was a maid of honour at the court of Charles I, and married the Duke of Newcastle in 1645. They lived in exile in Europe during the Civil War.

19 Marriage is the grave or tomb of wit.
1662 *Plays*, 'Nature's Three Daughters', pt.2, act 5, sc.20.

20 If Nature had not befriended us with beauty, and other good graces, to help us to insinuate our selves into men's affections, we should have been more enslaved than any other of Nature's creatures she hath made.
1664 *Sociable Letters.*

Caxton, William c.1422–c.1491

English printer responsible for printing the first book in English.

21 I, according to my copy, have done set it in imprint, to the intent that noble men may see and learn the noble acts of chivalry, the gentle and virtuous deeds that some knights used in those days.
1485 Thomas Malory *Le Morte D'Arthur*, prologue.

Cecil, Lord (Edward Christian) David Gascoyne 1902–86

English literary critic and essayist, Professor of English Literature at Oxford (1948-70) and a respected literary biographer. His traditional approach to literary criticism earned him the scorn of F R Leavis.

22 It does not matter that Dickens's world is not life-like; it is alive.
1934 *Early Victorian Novelists.*

23 The primary object of a student of literature is to be delighted.
1949 *Reading as One of the Fine Arts.*

24 Funny you should ask. As a matter of fact I did have a light temperature when I set out.
Response to a Berlin nightclubber's ambiguous question, 'Sind Sie normal?'. Quoted in Jonathan Keates 'The Delightful Lord David', in the *Times Literary Supplement*, 1 Mar 1991. Keates also describes how Cecil had confessed that, had he visited Sodom and Gomorrah, he would probably only have noticed the cathedral.

Cecil, Robert Arthur James Gascoyne, 5th Marquis of Salisbury 1893–1972

English Conservative statesman. Opposition Leader in the Lords (1945–51), he became Secretary of State for Commonwealth Relations in Churchill's Government and Leader of the Lords (1951–7).

25 The Colonial Secretary [Iain Macleod] has been too clever by half. I believe that he is a very fine bridge player. It is not considered immoral, or even bad form, to outwit one's opponent at bridge. It almost seems to me as if the Colonial Secretary, when he abandoned the sphere of bridge for the sphere of politics, brought his bridge technique with him.
1961 Speech, House of Lords.

Cecil, Robert Arthur Talbot Gascoyne, 3rd Marquis of Salisbury 1830–1903

English Conservative statesman and three times Prime Minister (1885–6, 1886–92, 1895–1902), often serving as his own Foreign Secretary. He remained as head of government during the Boer War (1899–1902), and then retired.

26 Peace without honour is not only a disgrace, but, except as a temporary respite, it is a chimera.
1864 In the *Quarterly Review*, Apr.

27 Under a more heroic Minister, and in a less self-seeking age, it is probable that England would have preferred the risk, whatever its extent, to the infamy of betraying an ally whom she had enticed into peril. But our Ministry is not heroic; and our generation, though not indifferent to glory, prefers it when it is safe and cheap.
1864 On Palmerston's failure to defend Denmark against Prussia, in the *Quarterly Review*, Jul.

28 Horny-handed sons of toil.
1873 In the *Quarterly Review*, Oct.

29 English policy is to float lazily downstream, occasionally putting out a diplomatic boathook to avoid collisions.
1877 Letter to Lord Lytton, 9 Mar.

30 The commonest error in politics is sticking to the carcasses of old policies.
1877 Speech, Hatfield, 25 May.

31 Randolph and the Mahdi have occupied my thoughts about equally. The Mahdi pretends to be half mad, but is very sane in reality. Randolph occupies exactly the converse position.
1884 Of Lord Randolph Churchill. Letter to Lady John Manners, May.

32 We are part of the community of Europe, and we must do our duty as such.
1888 Speech, Caernarvon, 10 Apr.

33 It is a superstition of an antiquated diplomacy that there is any necessary antagonism between Russia and Great Britain.
1896 Speech, London Guildhall, 9 Nov.

Céline, Louis-Ferdinand *pseudonym of* *Louis Ferdinand Destouches* 1894–1961

French novelist, author of *Journey to the End of Night* (1932), and other misanthropic works. He wrote anti-Semitic tracts before World War II and collaborated with the Germans. He escaped to Denmark after the war, but returned to France in 1951.

34 *Entre le pénis et les mathématiques...il n'existe rien. Rien!*
Between the penis and mathematics...there's nothing. Nothing!
1932 *Voyage au bout de la nuit* (*Journey to the End of Night*, translated by John H P Marks, 1960).

35 *Voyager, c'est bien utile, ça fait travailler l'imagination. Tout le reste n'est que déceptions et fatigues. Notre voyage à nous est entièrement imaginaire. Voilà sa force.*
To travel is useful. It engages the imagination. Everything else is deceitful and boring. Our own voyage is entirely imaginary. And therein lies its force.
1932 *Voyage au bout de la nuit* (*Journey to the End of Night*, translated by John H P Marks, 1960).

36 *Quand on a pas d'imagination, mourir c'est peu de chose, quand on en a, mourir c'est trop.*
For those who have no imagination, death means little. For those who have one, death is often too much.
1932 *Voyage au bout de la nuit* (*Journey to the End of Night*, translated by John H P Marks, 1960).

37 *C'est l'actuel qui compte. Invoquer sa postérité, c'est faire un discours aux asticots.*
It is the present that counts. To invoke one's posterity is to make a speech to maggots.
1932 *Voyage au bout de la nuit* (*Journey to the End of Night*, translated by John H P Marks, 1960).

38 *La plupart des gens ne meurent qu'au dernier moment; d'autres commencent et s'y prennent vingt ans d'avance et parfois davantage. Ce sont les malheureux de la terre.*
Most people only die at the last moment; others begin early and take twenty years and sometimes more. These are the most miserable people on earth.
1932 *Voyage au bout de la nuit* (*Journey to the End of Night*, translated by John H P Marks, 1960).

39 *Des pauvres, c'est-à-dire des gens dont la mort n'intéresse personne.*
The poor—that is, the people whose death interests no one.
1932 *Voyage au bout de la nuit* (*Journey to the End of Night*, translated by John H P Marks, 1960).

40 *Les Anglais, c'est drôle quand même comme dégaine, c'est mi-curé, mi-garçonnet.*
The English are funny and peculiar, half-clergymen and half-little boys.
1936 *Mort à crédit*.

Cellini, Benvenuto 1500–71

Italian goldsmith and sculptor, known for his autobiography as much as for his art.

41 A painting is merely the image of a tree, a man, or any other object reflected in a fountain. The difference between a painting and sculpture is the difference between a shadow and the thing which casts it.
1547 Letter to Benedetto Varchi.

Cennini, Cennino c.1370–c.1440

Florentine painter and writer, best remembered for his *Il Libro dell'Arte*, a practical guide for the art student.

42 Do not fail, as you go on, to draw something every day, for no matter how little it is it will be well worth while, and it will do you a world of good.
c.1400 *Il Libro dell'Arte* ('The Craftsman's Handbook').

43 There is another cause which, if you indulge it, can make your hand so unsteady that it will waver more, and flutter far more, than leaves do in the wind, and this is indulging too much in the company of women.
c.1400 *Il Libro dell'Arte* ('The Craftsman's Handbook').

Cervantes, Miguel de 1547–1616

Spanish writer, best known for his novel *Don Quixote* (in two parts 1605, 1615), the first part of which is thought to have been written in prison in La Mancha. Other works include *La Galatea* (1585), a pastoral romance, and many plays, only two of which survive.

44 *La mejor salsa del mundo es el hambre.*
Hunger is the best sauce in the world.
1615 *Don Quixote*, pt.2, ch.5.

45 *El pan comido y la compañía deshecha.*
With the bread eaten, the company breaks up.
1615 *Don Quixote*, pt.2, ch.7.

46 *Para todo hay remedio, si no es para la muerte.*
There's a remedy for everything except death.
1615 *Don Quixote*, pt.2, ch.10.

47 *Dos linajes sólo hay en el mundo, como decía una abuela mía, que son el tener y el no tener.*
There are but two families in the world, as my grandmother used to say—the Haves and the Havenots.
1615 *Don Quixote*, pt.2, ch.20.

48 *Digo, paciencia y barajar.*
What I say is, patience, and shuffle the cards.
1615 *Don Quixote*, pt.2, ch.23.

Césaire, Aimé Fernand 1913–

Caribbean poet known for his visionary, surrealist style and as a Marxist and anti-colonialist.

49 *Ma bouche sera la bouche des malheurs qui n'ont point de bouche, ma voix, la liberté de celles qui s'affaissent au cachot du désespoir.*
My voice will be the voice of those who suffer and have no voice. My voice, the freedom of those weakened in the dungeon of despair.
1939 *Cahier d'un retour au pays natal.*

50 *Je vois l'Afrique multiple et une*
verticale dans la tumultueuse péripétie
avec ses bourrelets, ses nodules,
un peu à part, mais à portée
du siècle, comme un coeur de réserve.
I see several Africas and one
vertical in the tumultuous event
with its screens and nodules,
a little separated, but within
the century, like a heart in reserve.
1960 *Ferrements*, 'Pour saluer le Tiers-Monde'.

Cézanne, Paul 1839–1906

French Post-Impressionist painter, a friend of Zola who persuaded him to go to Paris to paint in 1862. His paintings foreshadow Cubism, emphasizing underlying forms with glowing colours.

51 May I repeat what I told you here: treat nature by the cylinder, the sphere, the cone, everything in perspective.
1904 Letter to Émile Bernard, 15 Apr.

52 The Louvre is the book in which we learn to read.
1905 Letter to Émile Bernard.

53 Monet is only an eye, but my God what an eye!
Attributed, in conversation with Ambroise Vollard. Quoted in Cooper *Claude Monet* (1957).

54 I wished to copy nature but I could not. But I was satisfied when I discovered that the sun could not be reproduced but that it must be represented by something else—colour.
Quoted in D Hooker (ed) *Art of the Western World* (1989).

Chalmers, Patrick Reginald 1872–1942

English writer and banker, an authority on field sports.

55 What's lost upon the roundabouts we pulls up on the swings!
1912 *Green Days and Blue Days*, 'Roundabouts and Swings'.

Chamberlain, Sir (Joseph) Austen 1863–1937

English Conservative politician, successively Chancellor of the Exchequer, Secretary for India, Unionist leader, Foreign Secretary and First Lord of the Admiralty. He received the 1925 Nobel peace prize for negotiating the Locarno Pact.

56 I yield to no one in my devotion to this great League of Nations, but not even for this will I destroy that smaller but older league of which my own country was the birthplace, and of which it remains the centre… Beware how you so draw tight the bonds, how you so pile obligation on obligation and sanction on sanction, lest at last you find that you are not living nations but dead states.
1927 Speech, League of Nations Assembly, Geneva, 9 Sep.

Chamberlain, Joseph 1836–1914

English Liberal politician. He was President of the Board of Trade, but resigned over Gladstone's Home Rule bill (1880). Leader of the Liberal Unionists from 1889, he was also Secretary of State for the Colonies (1895), and retired in 1903.

57 Lord Salisbury constitutes himself the spokesman of a class, of the class to which he himself belongs, who 'toil not neither do they spin'.
1883 Speech, 30 Mar.

58 Provided that the City of London remains, as it is at present, the clearing-house of the world, any other nation may be its workshop.
1904 Speech at the Guildhall, 19 Jan.

59 The day of small nations has passed away. The day of Empires has come.
1904 Speech at Birmingham, 12 May, advocating preferential trade within the British Empire as a means of ensuring Britain's security.

Chamberlain, (Arthur) Neville 1869–1940

English politician, who played a leading part in the formation of the National Government (1931). As Prime Minister (1937–40) he advocated appeasement of Italy and Germany. He resigned as a result of criticism of his war leadership.

60 In war, whichever side may call itself the victor, there are no winners, but all are losers.
1938 Speech at Kettering, 3 Jul.

61 How horrible, fantastic, incredible it is that we should be digging trenches and trying on gas-masks here because of a quarrel in a far away country between people of whom we know nothing.
1938 Radio broadcast, 27 Sep, referring to Germany's annexation of the Sudetenland.

62 This morning I had another talk with the German Chancellor, Herr Hitler, and here is the paper that bears his name upon it as well as mine: 'We regard the agreement signed last night and the Anglo-German naval agreement, as symbolic of the desire of our two people never to go to war with one another again.'
1938 Speech on the signing of the Munich Agreement, Heston airport, 30 Sep.

63 My good friends, this is the second time in our history that there has come back from Germany to Downing Street peace with honour. I believe it is peace for our time. Go home and have a nice, quiet sleep.
1938 Speech from the window of No. 10 Downing Street to the crowds outside, 30 Sep, having returned that day from signing the Munich Agreement. The earlier peace referred to was the Treaty of Berlin which Beaconsfield brought back in 1878.
► *See also Disraeli 277:85.*

64 We should seek by all means in our power to avoid war, by analysing possible causes, by trying to remove them, by discussion in a spirit of collaboration and good will. I cannot believe that such a programme would be rejected by the people of this country, even if it does mean the establishment of personal contact with the dictators.
1938 Speech in the House of Commons, 6 Oct.

65 This morning, the British ambassador in Berlin handed the German Government a final note stating that, unless we heard from them by 11 o'clock, that they were prepared at once to withdraw their troops from Poland, a state of war would exist between us. I have to tell you that no such undertaking has been received, and that consequently this country is at war with Germany.
1939 Radio broadcast, 3 Sep.

66 Whatever may be the reason—whether it was that Hitler thought he might get away with what he had got without fighting for it, or whether it was that after all the preparations were not sufficiently complete—however, one thing is certain—he missed the bus.
1940 Speech at Central Hall, Westminster, 4 Apr.

Chamberlain, Wilt(on Norman) 1936–99

US basketball player. Over seven feet tall, he set many individual scoring records.

67 Nobody roots for Goliath.
1967 Quoted in Colin Jarman *The Guinness Dictionary of Sports Quotations* (1990).

Chamfort, Sébastien-Roch Nicolas 1741–94

French writer. He joined the Jacobins at the outbreak of the French Revolution, but his remarks on the terror brought him into disfavour. Threatened with arrest, he attempted suicide, dying several days later.

68 *Guerre aux châteaux, paix aux chaumières.*
War to the castles, peace to the cottages.
1790 Motto for the Revolution.

69 Society is composed of two large classes; those who have more dinners than appetites, and those with more appetites than dinners.
Maximes et Pensées (1795), ch.1.

70 *Vivre est une maladie dont le sommeil nous soulage toutes les 16 heures. C'est un palliatif. La mort est le remède.*
Living is an illness to which sleep provides relief every 16 hours. It's a palliative. Death is the remedy.
Maximes et Pensées (1795), ch.2.

71 *Sois mon frère, ou je te tue.*
Be my brother, or I kill you.
His interpretation of the motto 'Fraternité ou la mort'. Quoted in P R Angus (ed) *Oeuvres Complètes* (1824), vol.1.

Chandler, Raymond 1888–1959

US crime writer, brought up in England. He returned to America and lived in California. He is best known for his creation of Philip Marlowe, a cynically philosophical, wise-cracking private detective whose career is closely involved with a series of beautiful and seductive *femmes fatales*.

72 I was neat, clean, shaved and sober, and I didn't care who knew it.
1939 Philip Marlowe. *The Big Sleep*, ch.1.

73 The General spoke again, slowly, using his strength as carefully as an out-of-work showgirl uses her last good pair of stockings.
1939 *The Big Sleep*, ch.2.

74 He looked about as inconspicuous as a tarantula on a slice of angel food.
1940 Of Moose Malloy. *Farewell, My Lovely*, ch.1.

75 It was a blonde. A blonde to make a bishop kick a hole in a stained glass window.
1940 *Farewell, My Lovely*, ch.13.

76 She gave me a smile I could feel in my hip pocket.
1940 *Farewell, My Lovely*, ch.18

77 Down these mean streets a man must go who is not himself mean, who is neither tarnished nor afraid.
1944 'The Simple Art of Murder'. In *Atlantic Monthly*, Dec.

78 The English may not always be the best writers in the world, but they are incomparably the best dull writers.
1944 'The Simple Art of Murder'. In *Atlantic Monthly*, Dec.

79 If my books had been any worse, I should not have been invited to Hollywood, and if they had been any better, I should not have come.
1945 Letter to Charles W Morton, 12 Dec.

80 Just don't get too complicated Eddie. When a guy gets too complicated he's unhappy. And when he's unhappy—his luck runs out.
1945 *The Blue Dahlia*.

81 Would you convey my compliments to the purist who reads your proofs and tell him or her that I write in a sort of broken-down patois which is something like the way a Swiss waiter talks, and that when I split an infinitive, God damn it, I split it so it will stay split.
1947 Letter to Edward Weeks at *Atlantic Monthly*, 18 Jan.

82 By the way, do you ever read the Bible? I suppose not

very often, but I had occasion to the other night and believe me it is a lesson in how not to write for the movies. The worst kind of overwriting. Whole chapters that could have been said in one paragraph. And the dialogue!
1947 Letter to Edgar Carter, 28 Mar.

83 It wasn't exactly carelessness; her knowledge of literate English contained such vast areas of desert that she took it for granted that half of what she wrote would be meaningless to her.
1947 On the shortcomings of his ex-secretary. Letter to Erle Stanley Gardner, 1 Jul.

84 California, the department-store state. The most of everything and the best of nothing.
1949 *The Little Sister*, ch.13.

85 A big hard-boiled city with no more personality than a paper cup.
1949 Of Los Angeles. *The Little Sister*, ch.26.

86 It is pretty obvious that the debasement of the human mind caused by a constant flow of fraudulent advertising is no trivial thing. There is more than one way to conquer a country.
1951 Letter to Carl Barndt, 15 Nov.

87 Some people are better off dead—like your wife and my father for instance.
1951 Line delivered by Robert Walker as Bruno in the film *Strangers on a Train* (with Czenzi Ormonde), based on the novel by Patricia Highsmith.

88 A preoccupation with words for their own sake is fatal to good film-making. It's not what films are for.
1951 To Dale Warren, 7 Nov.

89 If people could deal with each other honestly, they would not need agents.
1952 'Ten Per Cent of Your Life', in *Atlantic Monthly*, Feb.

90 Alcohol is like love... The first kiss is magic, the second is intimate, the third is routine. After that you take the girl's clothes off.
1953 *The Long Good-Bye*, ch.4.

91 A dead man is the best fall guy in the world. He never talks back.
1953 *The Long Good-Bye*, ch.10.

92 By his standards anyone who noticed how many walls the room had would be observant.
1953 On an interviewer. Letter to Roger Machell, 15 Mar.

93 I suppose all writers are crazy, but if they are any good, I believe they have a terrible honesty.
1957 Letter to Edgar Carter, 3 Jun.

94 Dashiell Hammett took murder out of the Venetian vase and dropped it into the alley.
On the moving of murder mysteries from the English country house to more realistic areas. Quoted in *Contemporary Authors* (1979).

95 As elaborate a waste of human intelligence as you can find outside an advertising agency.
Of chess. Quoted in Colin Jarman *The Guinness Dictionary of Sports Quotations* (1990).

96 The streets were dark with something more than night.
Quoted in the *Smithsonian*, May 1994.

Chanel, Gabrielle *known as* Coco 1883–1971

French couturier. In the 1920s she came to prominence with designs notable for simple elegance and comfort, such as her 'chemise' dress and collarless cardigan jacket. She also developed a perfume, Chanel No.5.

97 Fashion is made to become unfashionable.
1957 In *Life*, 19 Aug.

98 Youth is something very new: twenty years ago no one mentioned it.
Quoted in Marcel Haedrich *Coco Chanel: Her Life, Her Secrets* (1972), ch.1 (translated by Charles Lam Markmann).

99 A fashion for the young? That is a pleonasm: there is no fashion for the old.
Quoted in Marcel Haedrich *Coco Chanel: Her Life, Her Secrets* (1972), ch.1 (translated by Charles Lam Markmann).

1 Nature gives you the face you have when you are twenty. Life shapes the face you have at thirty. But it is up to you to earn the face you have at fifty.
Quoted in Marcel Haedrich *Coco Chanel: Her Life, Her Secrets* (1972), ch.1 (translated by Charles Lam Markmann).
► *See Orwell 630:7, Cartland 198:55.*

2 Fashion is architecture: it is a matter of proportions.
Quoted in Marcel Haedrich *Coco Chanel: Her Life, Her Secrets* (1972), ch.1 (translated by Charles Lam Markmann).

3 You ask if they were happy. This is not a characteristic of a European. To be contented—that's for the cows.
Quoted in A Madsen *Coco Chanel* (1990), ch.35.

Channing, Carol Elaine 1921–

US comedienne. A star of US cabaret, she has made occasional appearances in films, notably in *Thoroughly Modern Millie* (1967).

4 Laughter is much more important than applause. Applause is almost a duty. Laughter is a reward. Laughter means they trust and like you.
Attributed.

5 I am terribly shy, but of course no one believes me. Come to think of it, neither would I.
Attributed.

Channon, Sir Henry 1897–1958

English Conservative politician. He became an MP in 1935, becoming a parliamentary private secretary in 1938. He kept a witty diary recording the political and society figures of the time.

6 This afternoon I slept for two hours in the Library of the House of Commons. A deep House of Commons sleep. There is no sleep to compare with it—rich, deep, and guilty.
Attributed.

7 I love the House of Commons so passionately that were I to be offered a peerage, I should be tempted to refuse it. Only tempted, of course.
Attributed.

Chao AD 168–89

Chinese poet. Little is known of him and only fragments of his poetry have survived.

8 Obsequiousness is glorified:
While honest worth must wait outside.
c.180 AD 'Poems of Disgust, no.1', collected in *A Golden Treasury of Chinese Poetry* (translated by John Turner, 1976).

Chaplin, Charlie (Sir Charles Spencer) 1889–1977

English film actor and director. He developed his skill in comedy under Fred Karno and moved to Hollywood in 1914. His early short comedies were extremely popular. His feature films included *Modern Times* (1936), *The Great Dictator* (1940) and *Limelight* (1952).

9 They are spoiling the oldest art in the world—the art of pantomime. They are ruining the great beauty of silence.
1929 Of the advent of talking pictures. Interview in *Motion Picture Magazine*, May.

10 All I need to make a comedy is a park, a policeman and a pretty girl.
1964 *My Autobiography*, ch.10.

Chapman, Arthur 1873–1935

US poet and author, best known for his long poem *Out Where The West Begins* (1916).

11 Out where the handclasp's a little stronger,
Out where the smile dwells a little longer,
That's where the West begins.
1916 *Out Where the West Begins*, stanza 1.

Chapman, (Anthony) Colin Bruce 1928–82

English motor racing manager, founder of the Lotus racing team.

12 Money is how we keep the score in motor racing nowadays.
1974 Quoted in Colin Jarman *The Guinness Dictionary of Sports Quotations* (1990).

Chapman, Dinos 1962–

English installation artist, who works with his brother Jake under the name the Chapman Brothers.

13 We will just make it again—it's only art.
2004 After the installation *Hell* was destroyed in a fire in east London. Quoted in *The Scotsman*, 5 Jun.

Chapman, George c.1559–1634

English dramatist, poet and translator. His plays include *The Blind Beggar of Alexandria* (1595) and *Bussy d'Ambois* (1607). In 1598 he wrote a continuation of Marlowe's unfinished *Hero and Leander*, and he made important translations of Homer (1598–1624).

14 Man is a torch borne in the wind; a dream
But of a shadow, summed with all his substance.
1607 *Bussy d'Ambois*, act 1, sc.1.

15 Who to himself is law, no law doth need,
Offends no law, and is a king indeed.
1607 *Bussy d'Ambois*, act 1, sc.1.

16 Perfect happiness, by princes sought,
Is not with birth born, nor exchequers bought.
1611 *The Iliads of Homer Prince of Poets*, 'Epistle Dedicatory'.

17 Fate's such a shrewish thing.
1611 *The Iliads of Homer Prince of Poets*, bk.4, l.21.

18 We have watered our houses in Helicon.
1611 *May-Day*, act 3, sc.3. This is sometimes misquoted as 'We have watered our horses in Helicon'.

19 A poem, whose subject is not truth, but things like truth.
1613 *The Revenge of Bussy d'Ambois*, dedication.

20 Danger, the spur of all great minds.
1613 *The Revenge of Bussy d'Ambois*, act 5, sc.1.

21 I know an Englishman
Being flattered, is a lamb; threatened, a lion.
Alphonsus, Emperor of Germany (published posthumously, 1654), act 1. Although this is credited to Chapman, his authorship is doubtful.

22 I am ashamed the law is such an ass.
Revenge for Honour (published posthumously, 1654), act 3, sc.2. Although this is credited to Chapman, his authorship is doubtful.
➥ *See Dickens 267:96.*

Chapman, Jake 1966–

English installation artist, who works with his brother Dinos under the name the Chapman Brothers.

23 I hold God personally responsible.
2004 After the installation *Hell* was destroyed in a fire in east London. In the *London Evening Standard*, 26 May.

Chapman, John 1900–72

US theatre critic.

24 It is three and a half hours long, four characters wide, and a cesspool deep.
1962 In the *New York Daily News*, 15 Oct, reviewing Edward Albee's *Who's Afraid of Virginia Woolf?*

Chardin, Jean-Baptiste-Siméon 1699–1779

French painter of genre scenes and still-life.

25 The man who has not realized the difficulty of art never does anything worthwhile; the man who realizes it too soon does nothing at all.
1765 Quoted in Frank Elgar *Mondrian* (1968).

Chargaff, Erwin 1905–2002

Czech-born US biochemist. He settled at Columbia University in 1935, where his pioneering research on nucleic acids laid the foundations for modern molecular biology.

26 What counts…in science is to be not so much the first as the last.
1971 In *Science*, vol.172.

Charles, Elizabeth 1828–96

British writer.

27 To know how to say what others only know how to think is what makes men poets or sages; and to dare to say what others only dare to think makes men martyrs or reformers—or both.
Chronicle of the Schönberg-Cotta Family.

Charles I 1600–49

King of Scotland and England. His marriage to the Catholic French princess, Henrietta Maria, his expensive foreign wars and his high-handed treatment of Parliament (he dismissed three parliaments and ruled for 11 years without one) culminated in the Civil War and his execution.

28 A rule that may serve for a statesman, a courtier, or a lover—never make a defence or an apology before you be accused.
1636 Letter to Lord Wentworth, 3 Sep.

29 I see all the birds are flown.
1642 After his unsuccessful attempt to arrest the Five Members in the House of Commons, 4 Jan.

30 I tell you (and I pray God it be not laid to your charge) that I am the martyr of the people.
1649 Speech upon the scaffold.

Charles II 1630–85

King of Scotland and England. Exiled during the Civil War, on the execution of his father Charles I (1649) he was proclaimed king in Edinburgh but was not recalled as king to England until 1660. His childless marriage produced a succession crisis and contributed to much political and religious tension.

31 Whereas, women's parts in plays have hitherto been acted by men in the habits of women...we do permit and give leave for the time to come that all women's parts be acted by women.
1662 Royal licence, sanctioning the appearance of actresses on the English stage.

32 Better than a play.
1670 Commenting on the debates in the House of Lords over the Divorce Bill. Quoted in A Bryant *King Charles II* (1931).

33 This is very true—for my words are my own, and my actions are my Ministers'.
Riposte to 'The King's Epitaph'.
► *See Rochester 692:72.*

34 Let not poor Nelly starve.
c.1685 Worrying on his deathbed about his mistress, Nell Gwynn. Quoted in Bishop Gilbert Burney *History of My Own Time* (1724), vol.1, bk.2.

Charles V 1500–58

Holy Roman Emperor (1519–58) and King of Spain (1516–56), founder of the Habsburg dynasty. His wars against France led to the formation of the Holy League against him. After numerous wars, he divided his Empire between his son and brother and retired to a monastery in Spain.

35 I came, I saw, God conquered.
1547 Attributed remark after the Battle of Muhlberg, 23 Apr.
► *See also Caesar 184:25, John III Sobieski 438:59.*

36 Remember, the prince is like a mirror exposed to the eyes of all his subjects who continually look to him as a pattern on which to model themselves, and who in consequence without much trouble discover his vices and virtues.
1555 *Instructions à Philippe II son Fils* (*Advice To His Son*, translated 1788). Quoted in G R Elton *Renaissance and Reformation, 1300–1648* (2nd edn, 1968), p.137.

37 To God I speak Spanish, to women Italian, to men French, and to my horse—German.
Attributed.

Charles, Prince of Wales 1948–

HRH The Prince of Wales, son of Elizabeth II.

38 Yes...whatever that may mean.
1981 On being asked whether he was in love, after the announcement of his engagement, 24 Feb.

39 What is proposed is like a monstrous carbuncle on the face of a much-loved and elegant friend.
1984 On the proposed extension to the National Gallery, London. Speech at the 150th anniversary of the Royal Institute of British Architects, 30 May.

40 I just come and talk to the plants, really—very important to talk to them, they respond I find.
1986 In a television interview, 21 Sep.

41 Both myself and the Respondent recognized there were irreconcilable differences and that accordingly we could no longer live together.
1996 On why he and Diana, Princess of Wales, were getting a divorce. Quoted in *The Times*, 16 Jul.

42 It's really the result of talking to trees too often.
2001 Explaining his appearance in public wearing an eyepatch.

Charlton, Sir Bobby (Robert) 1937–

English footballer. He won 106 caps for England and played in the victorious World Cup team of 1966.

43 Some people tell me that we professional players are soccer slaves. Well, if this is slavery, give me a life sentence.
1960 Quoted in Peter Ball and Phil Shaw *The Book of Football Quotations* (1989).

44 They know on the Continent that European football without the English is like a hot dog without the mustard.
1988 Quoted in Peter Ball and Phil Shaw *The Book of Football Quotations* (1989). There was at the time a European ban in force against English clubs.

Charlton, Jack (John) 1935–

English footballer, brother of Sir Bobby Charlton. He played in the victorious World Cup team of 1966, and later managed the Republic of Ireland team (1986–95).

45 Soccer is a man's game; not an outing for mamby-pambies.
1967 *For Leeds and England.*

46 I have a little black book with two players in it, and if I get a chance to do them I will. I will make them suffer before I pack this game in. If I can kick them four years over the touch-line, I will.
1970 Remark to reporters, which led to severe trouble with the soccer authorities. Quoted in Colin Jarman *The Guinness Dictionary of Sports Quotations* (1990).

Charpak, Georges 1924–

French physicist, born in Poland. He was awarded the Nobel prize for physics in 1992.

47 I can buy a new pair of shoes this afternoon.
1992 On being awarded $1.2 million for his work on atom smashers. In the *Washington Post*, 15 Oct.

Chase, Edna Woolman 1877–1954

US fashion journalist, editor of *Vogue* (1914–52).

48 Fashion can be bought. Style one must possess.
1954 *Always in Vogue*, ch.12.

Chatwin, Bruce 1940–89

English travel writer and novelist. His travels in the Sudan, Patagonia and Australia converted him to nomadic asceticism. His prize-winning books are a mixture of documentary, fiction, anthropology and philosophy.

49 That will not bring back the things we love: the high, clear days and the blue icecaps on the mountains; the lines of white poplars fluttering in the wind, and the long

white prayer flags… Nor shall we get back the smell of the beanfields; the sweet, resinous smell of deodar wood burning, or the whiff of a snow leopard at 14,000 feet. Never. Never. Never.
1980 Introduction to Robert Byron's *The Road to Oxiana*.

50 Being lost in Australia gives you a lovely feeling of security.
1987 *The Songlines*, ch.10.

51 Tyranny sets up its own echo-chamber.
1988 *Utz*.

52 Like all self-possessed people, he was prey to doubt.
1989 *What Am I Doing Here*, 'Heavenly Horses'.

Chaucer, Geoffrey c.1345–1400

English poet. He served in the King's household, travelling extensively on state business. Much influenced by Boccaccio, his spirited and often humorous poetry established the literary language of English. He lost his offices in 1386 and fell on hard times, but in 1399 was awarded a pension.

53 Ful craftier to pley she was
Than Athalus, that made the game
First of the ches, so was his name.
c.1370 *The Book of the Duchess*, l.662–4.

54 That lyf so short, the craft so long to lerne,
Th'assay so hard, so sharp the conquerynge.
c.1380 *The Parliament of Fowls*, l.1–2.

55 But love a womman that she woot it nought,
And she wol quyte it that thow shalt nat fele;
Unknowe, unkist, and lost, that is unsought.
c.1385 *Troilus and Criseyde*, bk.1, l.807–9.

56 So longe mote ye lyve, and alle proude,
Til crowes feet be growen under youre y'.
c.1385 *Troilus and Criseyde*, bk 2, l.402–3.

57 It is nought good a slepyng hound to wake.
c.1385 *Troilus and Criseyde*, bk.3, l.764.

58 For I have seyn of a ful misty morwe
Folowen ful ofte a myrie someris day.
c.1385 *Troilus and Criseyde*, bk.3, l.1060–1.

59 Right as an aspes leef she gan to quake.
c.1385 *Troilus and Criseyde*, bk.3, l.1200.

60 For of fortunes sharpe adversitee
The worst kynde of infortune is this,
A man to han ben in prosperitee,
And it remembren, whan it passed is.
c.1385 *Troilus and Criseyde*, bk.3, l.1625–8.

61 Oon ere it herde, at tother out it went.
c.1385 *Troilus and Criseyde*, bk.4, l.434.

62 For tyme ylost may nought recovered be.
c.1385 *Troilus and Criseyde*, bk.4, l.1283.

63 Ek gret effect men write in place lite;
Th'entente is al, and nat the lettres space.
c.1385 *Troilus and Criseyde*, bk.5, l.1629–30.

64 Go, litel bok, go, litel myn tragedye,
Ther God thi makere yet, er that he dye,
So sende myght to make in som comedye!
c.1385 *Troilus and Criseyde*, bk.5, l.1786–8.

65 And for ther is so gret diversite
In Englissh and in writing of oure tonge,
So prey I God that non myswrite the,
Ne the mysmetre for defaute of tonge.
And red wherso thow be, or elles songe,
That thow be understonde, God I biseche!
c.1385 *Troilus and Criseyde*, bk.5, l.1793–8.

66 Whan that Aprill with his shoures soote
The droghte of March hath perced to the roote.
1387 *Canterbury Tales*, 'General Prologue', l.1–2.

67 And smale foweles maken melodye,
That slepen al the nyght with open ye
(So priketh hem nature in hir corages);
Thanne longen folk to goon on pilgrimages.
1387 *Canterbury Tales*, 'General Prologue', l.9–12.

68 He loved chivalrie,
Trouthe and honour, fredom and curteisie.
1387 *Canterbury Tales*, 'General Prologue', l.45–6.

69 He was a verray, parfit gentil knyght.
1387 *Canterbury Tales*, 'General Prologue', l.72.

70 Ful weel she soong the service dyvyne,
Entuned in hir nose ful semely,
And Frenssh she spak ful faire and fetisly,
After the scole of Stratford atte Bowe,
For Frenssh of Parys was to hire unknowe.
1387 *Canterbury Tales*, 'General Prologue', l.122–6.

71 A Clerk ther was of Oxenford also,
That unto logyk hadde longe ygo.
As leene was his hors as is a rake.
1387 *Canterbury Tales*, 'General Prologue', l.285–7.

72 But al be that he was a philosophre,
Yet hadde he but litel gold in cofre.
1387 *Canterbury Tales*, 'General Prologue', l.298–9.

73 Nowher so bisy a man as he ther nas,
And yet he semed bisier than he was.
1387 *Canterbury Tales*, 'General Prologue', l.321–2.

74 And thries hadde she been at Jerusalem;
She hadde passed many a straunge strem;
At Rome she hadde been, and at Boloigne,
In Galice at Seint-Jame, and at Coloigne.
1387 *Canterbury Tales*, 'General Prologue', l.463–6.

75 If gold ruste, what shall iren do?
1387 *Canterbury Tales*, 'General Prologue', l.500.

76 But Cristes lore, and his apostles twelve,
He taughte, but first he folwed it him-selve.
1387 *Canterbury Tales*, 'General Prologue', l.527–8.

77 And therefore, at the kynges court, my brother,
Ech man for hymself, ther is noon oother.
1387 *Canterbury Tales*, 'The Knight's Tale', l.1181–2.

78 Ther is no newe gyse that it nas old.
1387 *Canterbury Tales*, 'The Knight's Tale', l.1267.

79 The bisy larke, messager of day.
1387 *Canterbury Tales*, 'The Knight's Tale', l.1491.

80 Pitee renneth soone in gentil herte.
1387 *Canterbury Tales*, 'The Knight's Tale', l.1761.

81 The smylere with the knyf under the cloke.
1387 *Canterbury Tales*, 'The Knight's Tale', l.1999.

82 What is this world? what asketh men to have?
Now with his love, now in his colde grave.
1387 *Canterbury Tales*, 'The Knight's Tale', l.2777–8.

83 This world nys but a thurghfare ful of wo,
And we been pilgrymes, passynge to and fro.
1387 *Canterbury Tales*, 'The Knight's Tale', l. 2847–8.

84 'The gretteste clerkes been noght wisest men.'
1387 *Canterbury Tales*, 'The Reeve's Tale', l.4054.

85 Yblessed be god that I have wedded fyve!
Welcome the sixte, whan that evere he shal.
1387 *Canterbury Tales*, 'The Wife of Bath's Prologue', l.44–5.

86 Crist wole we clayme of hym oure gentillesse,
Nat of oure eldres for hire old richesse.
1387 *Canterbury Tales*, 'The Wife of Bath's Tale', l.1117–8.

87 Love wol nat been constreyned by maistrye.
Whan maistrie comth, the God of Love anon
Beteth his wynges, and farewel he is gon!
1387 *Canterbury Tales*, 'The Franklin's Tale', l.764–6.

88 Wommen, of kynde, desiren libertee,
And nat to been constreyned as a thral;
And so doon men, if I sooth seyen shal.
1387 *Canterbury Tales*, 'The Franklin's Tale', l.768–70.

89 Til that the brighte sonne loste his hewe;
For th'orisonte hath reft the sonne his lyght;
This is as muche to seye as it was nyght!
1387 *Canterbury Tales*, 'The Franklin's Tale', l.1016–8.

90 Trouthe is the hyest thyng that man may kepe.
1387 *Canterbury Tales*, 'The Franklin's Tale', l.1479.

91 O wombe! O bely! O stynkyng cod
Fulfilled of dong and of corrupcioun!
1387 *Canterbury Tales*, 'The Pardoner's Tale', l.534–5.

92 'By God,' quod he, 'for pleynly, at a word,
Thy drasty rymyng is nat worth a toord!'
1387 *Canterbury Tales*, 'Sir Thopas', l.929–30.

93 What is bettre than gold? Jaspre. What is bettre than jaspre? Wisedoom.
1387 *Canterbury Tales*, 'The Tale of Melibee', l.1106–7.

94 And what is bettre than wisedoom? Womman. And what is bettre than a good womman? Nothyng.
1387 *Canterbury Tales*, 'The Tale of Melibee', l.1107–8.

95 His coomb was redder than the fyn coral,
And batailled as it were a castle wal;
His byle was blak, and as the jeet it shoon;
Lyk asure were his legges and his toon;
His nayles whitter than the lylye flour,
And lyk the burned gold was his colour.
1387 Of Chauntecleer. *Canterbury Tales*, 'The Nun's Priest's Tale', l.2859–64.

96 Mordre wol out, that see we day by day.
1387 *Canterbury Tales*, 'The Nun's Priest's Tale', l.3052.

97 Thou shalt make castels thanne in Spayne
And dreme of joye, all but in vayne.
The Romaunt of the Rose, l.2573–4. This translation of the *Roman de la Rose* has been attributed to Chaucer but it is thought now to be the work of several authors, including Chaucer.

Cheever, John William 1912–82

US short-story writer and novelist. He sold his first short story, 'Expelled', after being thrown out of school at the age of 17, and became a regular contributor to the *New Yorker*, writing lyrical tales of alcoholism, adultery and loss. His novels include *The Wapshot Chronicle* (1957) and *Falconer* (1977).

98 The city is old, out of step with the century, but age only seems to have quickened its elements... Relics from the past continually pierce the present. Some dream of love survives the sandstone apartment houses.
1934 Of Boston. Letter to Elizabeth Ames.

99 When the beginnings of self-destruction enter the heart it seems no bigger than a grain of sand.
1952 Collected in *The Journals*, 'The Late Forties and Fifties'.

1 Wisdom we know is the knowledge of good and evil—not the strength to choose between the two.
1956 Collected in *The Journals*, 'The Late Forties and Fifties'.

2 Neither you nor I nor anyone else can describe the volcanic landscapes a poor girl strays into when she marries a literary man.
1965 Letter to Frederick Exley, 16 Jun.

3 A lonely man is a lonesome thing, a stone, a bone, a stick, a receptacle for Gilbey's gin, a stooped figure sitting at the edge of a hotel bed, heaving copious sighs like the autumn wind.
1966 Collected in *The Journals*, 'The Sixties'.

4 We travel by plane, oftener than not, and yet the spirit of our country seems to have remained a country of railroads.
1969 On the US. *Bullet Park*, pt.1, ch.1.

5 My veins are filled once a week with a Neapolitan carpet cleaner distilled from the Adriatic and I am as bald as an egg. However I still get around and am mean to cats.
1982 On his cancer treatment. Letter to Philip Roth, 10 May.

6 Yevtushenko has... an ego that can crack crystal at a distance of 20 feet.
Recalled on Cheever's death, 18 Jun 1982.

7 Trust your editor, and you'll sleep on straw.
Favourite axiom, quoted in Susan Cheever *Home Before Dark* (1984).

Chekhov, Anton 1860–1904

Russian playwright and short-story writer. His first play, *The Seagull* (1896), failed initially but was revived in Moscow in 1898. Others include *Uncle Vanya* (1897), *The Three Sisters* (1901) and *The Cherry Orchard* (1904).

8 Brevity is the sister of talent.
1889 Letter to Alexander Chekhov, 11 Apr.

9 MEDVEDENKO: Why do you wear black all the time?
MASHA: I'm in mourning for my life.
1896 *The Seagull*, act 1.

10 Women can't forgive failure.
1896 *The Seagull*, act 2.

11 The chief thing, my dear fellows, is to play it simply, without any theatricality: just very simply. Remember that they are all ordinary people.
1896 Attributed advice to actors, during a rehearsal of *The Seagull*.

12 A woman can become a man's friend only in the following stages—first an acquaintance, next a mistress, and only then a friend.
1897 *Uncle Vanya*, act 2.

13 When a woman isn't beautiful, people always say, 'You have lovely eyes, you have lovely hair.'
1897 *Uncle Vanya*, act 3.

14 If a lot of cures are suggested for a disease, it means that the disease is incurable.
1904 *The Cherry Orchard*, act 1 (translated by Elisaveta Fen).

15 To begin to live in the present, we must first atone for our past and be finished with it, and we can only atone for it by suffering, by extraordinary, unceasing exertion.
1904 *The Cherry Orchard*, act 2 (translated by Elisaveta Fen).

Chelmsford, Frederick John Napier Thesiger, 1st Viscount 1868–1933

English colonial administrator, Governor of Queensland (1905–9) and of New South Wales (1909–13), Viceroy of India (1916–21) and First Lord of the Admiralty (1924).

16 We have here an educated class 95 per cent of whom hate us.
1918 Of the situation in India. Letter to George V.

Cheney, Dick (Richard Bruce) 1946–

US politician. He was Secretary of Defense under George Bush from 1989 to 1993 and in 2001 was sworn in as Vice-President under George W Bush.

17 Except for the occasional heart attack, I never felt better.
2003 In *Newsweek*, 16 Jun.

18 The days of looking the other way while despotic regimes trample human rights, rob their nations' wealth, and then excuse their failings by feeding their people a steady diet of anti-Western hatred are over.
2004 Speaking at the World Economic Forum in Davos, Switzerland, 24 Jan.

19 When diplomacy fails, we must be prepared to face our responsibilities and be willing to use force if necessary. Direct threats require decisive action.
2004 Speaking at the World Economic Forum in Davos, Switzerland, 24 Jan.

Cher *originally* ***Cheryl Sarkisian La Pier*** 1946–

US pop singer and film actress.

20 Do I enjoy getting older? No. I'm thrilled and delighted for those people who enjoy the experience. I just don't happen to be one of them.
2004 In *The Scotsman*, 11 May.

Chereskin, Alvin 1928–

US advertising executive, founder and president of AC & R Advertising (later affiliated with Saatchi & Saatchi).

21 Sex! What is that but *life*, after all? We're all of us selling sex, because we're all selling life.
1986 In the *New Yorker*, 15 Sep.

Chernow, Ron 1949–

US journalist, a columnist with *The Wall Street Journal* (1990–).

22 Capitalism requires people to be pious souls in the workplace, wild pagans at the cash register.
1993 In *The Wall Street Journal*, 31 Aug.

Cherry-Garrard, Apsley 1886–1959

Polar explorer and a member of Scott's last expedition. His group found the bodies of Scott and his companions in 1912.

23 At once the cleanest and most isolated way of having a bad time which has ever been devised.
1952 Of polar exploration. Recalled in *The Worst Journey in the World*.

Chesnut, Mary Boykin Miller 1823–86

US diarist, daughter of a South Carolina senator and wife of the heir to a large plantation. Her diary of the Civil War, *A Diary from Dixie*, was published in 1905.

24 Mrs. Stowe did not hit the sorest spot. She makes Legree a bachelor.
1861 Diary entry, 26 Aug, recording the conversation of a group of southern white women on the subject of men and slavery. The reference is to the principal slaveholder in Harriet Beecher Stowe's *Uncle Tom's Cabin*.

Chesnutt, Charles Waddell 1858–1932

US writer, the first black fiction writer to gain national acclaim when his stories were published in the *Atlantic Monthly* in the 1880s. He also wrote a biography of Frederick Douglass (1899).

25 Those who set in motion the forces of evil cannot always control them afterwards.
1901 *The Marrow of Tradition*, ch.35.

Chesterfield, Philip Dormer Stanhope, 4th Earl of 1694–1773

English statesman and orator, a member of the Pelham ministry (1744), Irish Lord-Lieutenant (1745) and Secretary of State (1746–8). His *Letters to his Son* (published 1774) are a worldly guide to manners and success.

26 The difference in this case between a man of sense and a fop, is, that the fop values himself upon his dress; the man of sense laughs at it, at the same time that he knows he must not neglect it.
1745 Letter to his son, 19 Nov.

27 Whatever is worth doing at all is worth doing well.
1746 Letter to his son, 10 Mar.

28 An injury is much sooner forgotten than an insult.
1746 Letter to his son, 9 Oct.

29 I recommend you to take care of the minutes, for hours will take care of themselves.
1747 Letter to his son, 6 Nov.

30 Advice is seldom welcome; and those who want it the most always like it the least.
1748 Letter to his son, 29 Jan.

31 Wear your learning, like your watch in a private pocket: and do not merely pull it out and strike it, merely to show that you have one.
1748 Letter to his son, 22 Feb.

32 There is nothing so illiberal and so ill-bred, as audible laughter.
1748 Letter to his son, 9 Mar.

33 It must be owned, that the Graces do not seem to be natives of Great Britain; and I doubt, the best of us here have more of rough than polished diamond.
1748 Letter to his son, 11 Nov.

34 Style is the dress of thoughts.
1749 Letter to his son, 24 Nov.

35 Fashion is more tyrannical at Paris than in any other place in the world; it governs even more absolutely than their king, which is saying a great deal. The least revolt against it is punished by proscription. You must observe and conform to all the minutiae of it, if you will be in fashion there yourself; and if you are not in fashion, you are nobody.
1750 Letter to his son, 30 Apr.

36 The chapter of knowledge is very short, but the chapter of accidents is a very long one.
1753 Letter to Solomon Dayrolles, 16 Feb.

37 In matters of religion and matrimony I never give any advice; because I will not have anybody's torments in this world or the next laid to my charge.
1765 Letter to Arthur Charles Stanhope, 12 Oct.

38 In case my godson Philip Stanhope shall at anytime keep or be concerned in keeping any racehorse or pack of hounds, or reside one night at Newmarket, that infamous seminary of iniquity and ill-manners, during the course of the races there, or shall resort to the said races or shall lose in one day at any game or bet whatsoever the sum of £500 then in any of the cases aforesaid it is my express will that he, my said godson, shall forfeit and pay out of my estate the sum of £50,000 to and for the use of the Dean and Chapter of Westminster.
1773 Clause in his will.

39 David, you are an actor everywhere but upon the stage.
Attributed, in conversation with the actor David Garrick.

40 The pleasure is momentary, the position ridiculous, and the expense damnable.
Of sex. Attributed.

Chesterton, G(ilbert) K(eith) 1874–1936

English critic, novelist and poet, one of the most colourful and provocative writers of his day. His amiable detective-priest Father Brown first appeared in *The Innocence of Father Brown* (1911). Many of his essays and articles were published in his own *G.K.'s Weekly*.

41 I share all your antipathy to the noisy Plebeian excursionist. A visit to Ramsgate during the season and the vision of the crowded, howling sands has left in me feelings which all my Radicalism cannot allay. At the same time I think that the lower orders are seen unfavourably when enjoying themselves. In labour and trouble they are more dignified and less noisy.
1891 Letter to E C Bentley. Collected in Maisie Ward *Gilbert Keith Chesterton* (1943).

42 With monstrous head and sickening cry
And ears like errant wings,
The devil's walking parody
Of all four-footed things.
1900 'The Donkey'.

43 Fools! For I also had my hour;
One far fierce hour and sweet:
There was a shout about my ears,
And palms before my feet.
1900 'The Donkey'.

44 Literature is a luxury; fiction is a necessity.
1901 *The Defendant*, 'Defence of Penny Dreadfuls'.

45 All slang is metaphor, and all metaphor is poetry.
1901 *The Defendant*, 'Defence of Slang'.

46 'My country right or wrong', is a thing that no patriot would think of saying except in a desperate case. It is like saying, 'My mother, drunk or sober'.
1901 *The Defendant*, 'Defence of Patriotism'.
➡ *See Decatur 258:8.*

47 The human race, to which so many of my readers belong, has been playing at children's games from the beginning, and will probably do it till the end, which is a nuisance for the few people who grow up.
1904 *The Napoleon of Notting Hill*, ch.1.

48 The word 'orthodoxy' not only no longer means being right; it practically means being wrong.
1905 *Heretics*, ch.1.

49 There is no such thing on earth as an uninteresting subject; the only thing that can exist is an uninterested person.
1905 *Heretics*, ch.3.

50 In the case of Smith, the name is so poetical that it must be an arduous and heroic matter for the man to live up to it... The name shouts poetry at you.
1905 *Heretics*, ch.3.

51 Charity is the power of defending that which we know to be indefensible. Hope is the power of being cheerful in circumstances which we know to be desperate.
1905 *Heretics*, ch.12.

52 Science in the modern world has many uses; its chief use, however, is to provide long words to cover the errors of the rich.
1905 *Heretics*, ch.13.

53 A good novel tells us the truth about its hero; but a bad novel tells us the truth about its author.
1905 *Heretics*, ch.15.

54 The artistic temperament is a disease that afflicts amateurs. It is a disease which arises from men not having sufficient power of expression to utter and get rid of the element of art in their being.
1905 *Heretics*, ch.17.

55 Bigotry may be roughly defined as the anger of men who have no opinions.
1905 *Heretics*, ch.20.

56 There is a great man who makes every man feel small. But the real great man is the man who makes every man feel great.
1906 *Charles Dickens*, ch.1.

57 The madman is not the man who has lost his reason. The madman is the one who has lost everything except his reason.
1908 *Orthodoxy*, ch.2.

58 Poets do not go mad; but chess players do.
1908 *Orthodoxy*, ch.2.

59 The men who really believe in themselves are all in lunatic asylums.
1908 *Orthodoxy*, ch.2.

60 It is an act of faith to assert that our thoughts have any relation to reality at all.
1908 *Orthodoxy*, ch.3.

61 Tradition means giving votes to the most obscure of all classes, our ancestors. It is the democracy of the dead.
1908 *Orthodoxy*, ch.4.

62 All conservatism is based upon the idea that if you leave things alone you leave them as they are. But you do not. If you leave a thing alone you leave it to a torrent of change.
1908 *Orthodoxy*, ch.7.

63 Angels can fly because they take themselves lightly.
1908 *Orthodoxy*, ch.7.

64 Thieves respect property. They merely wish the property to become their property that they may more perfectly respect it.
1908 *The Man who was Thursday*, ch.4.

65 An adventure is only an inconvenience rightly

considered. An inconvenience is only an adventure wrongly considered.
1908 *All Things Considered*, 'On Running After One's Hat'.

66 No animal ever invented anything so bad as drunkenness—or so good as drink.
1908 *All Things Considered*, 'Wine When It Is Red'.

67 Lying in bed would be an altogether perfect and supreme experience if only one had a coloured pencil long enough to draw on the ceiling.
1909 'On Lying In Bed'.

68 He desired all beautiful things—even God.
1909 Of Oscar Wilde. In the *Daily News*, 19 Oct.

69 The Christian ideal has not been tried and found wanting. It has been found difficult; and left untried.
1910 *What's Wrong with the World*, ch.1, 'The Unfinished Temple'.

70 Compromise used to mean that half a loaf was better than no bread. Among modern statesmen, it really seems to mean that half a loaf is better than a whole loaf.
1910 *What's Wrong with the World*, ch.3.

71 She was maintaining the prime truth of woman, the universal mother…that if a thing is worth doing, it is worth doing badly.
1910 *What's Wrong with the World*, pt.4, 'Folly and Female Education'.

72 I tell you naught for your comfort,
Yea, naught for your desire,
Save that the sky grows darker yet
And the sea rises higher.
1911 *Ballad of the White Horse*, bk.1.

73 For the great Gaels of Ireland
Are the men that God made mad,
For all their wars are merry,
And all their songs are sad.
1911 *Ballad of the White Horse*, bk.2.

74 There is always a forgotten thing,
And love is not secure.
1911 *Ballad of the White Horse*, bk.3.

75 When all philosophies shall fail,
This word alone shall fit;
That a sage feels too small for life,
And a fool too large for it.
1911 *Ballad of the White Horse*, bk.8.

76 He could not think up to the height of his own towering style.
1912 Of Tennyson. *The Victorian Age in Literature*, ch.3.

77 And Noah he often said to his wife when he sat down to dine.
'I don't care where the water goes if it doesn't get into the wine.'
1914 *The Flying Inn*, ch.5, stanza 1. Collected as 'Wine and Water' in *Wine, Water and Song* (1915).

78 The rich are the scum of the earth in every country.
1914 *The Flying Inn*, ch.15.

79 Tea is like the East he grows in,
A great yellow Mandarin
With urbanity of manner
And unconsciousness of sin.
1914 *The Flying Inn*, ch.18, stanza 2. Collected as 'The Song of Right and Wrong' in *Wine, Water and Song* (1915).

80 Tea, although an Oriental,
Is a gentleman at least;
Cocoa is a cad and coward,
Cocoa is a vulgar beast.
1914 *The Flying Inn*, ch.18, stanza 3. Collected as 'The Song of Right and Wrong' in *Wine, Water and Song* (1915).

81 When red wine had brought red ruin
And the death-dance of our times,
Heaven sent us Soda Water
As a torment for our crimes.
1914 *The Flying Inn*, ch.18, stanza 4. Collected as 'The Song of Right and Wrong' in *Wine, Water and Song* (1915).

82 The folk that live in Liverpool, their heart is in their boots;
They go to hell like lambs, they do, because the hooter hoots.
1914 'Me Heart'.

83 They haven't got no noses,
The fallen sons of Eve.
1914 'Song of Quoodle'.

84 And goodness only knowses
The Noselessness of Man.
1914 'Song of Quoodle'.

85 Before the Roman came to Rye or out to Severn strode,
The rolling English drunkard made the rolling English road.
1914 'The Rolling English Road'.

86 A merry road, a mazy road, and such as we did tread
The night we went to Birmingham by way of Beachy Head.
1914 'The Rolling English Road'.

87 For there is good news yet to hear and fine things to be seen,
Before we go to Paradise by way of Kensal Green.
1914 'The Rolling English Road'.

88 To be clever enough to get all that money, one must be stupid enough to want it.
1914 *The Wisdom of Father Brown*, 'Paradise of Thieves'.

89 Journalism largely consists in saying 'Lord Jones Dead' to people who never knew Lord Jones was alive.
1914 *The Wisdom of Father Brown*, 'The Purple Wig'.

90 We only know the last sad squires ride slowly towards the sea,
And a new people takes the land: and still it is not we.
1915 'The Secret People'.

91 The souls most fed with Shakespeare's flame
Still sat unconquered in a ring,
Remembering him like anything.
1915 'Shakespeare Memorial'.

92 John Grubby, who was short and stout
And troubled with religious doubt,
Refused about the age of three
To sit upon the curate's knee.
1915 'The New Freethinker'.

93 And I dream of the days when work was scrappy,
And rare in our pockets the mark of the mint,
When we were angry and poor and happy,
And proud of seeing our names in print.
1915 'Song of Defeat'.

94 The gallows in my garden, people say,
Is new and neat and adequately tall.
1915 'Ballade of Suicide'.

95 The strangest whim has seized me... After all
I think I will not hang myself today.
1915 'Ballade of Suicide'.

96 They died to save their country and they only saved the world.
1922 'English Graves'.

97 Democracy means government by the uneducated, while aristocracy means government by the badly educated.
1931 In the *New York Times*, 1 Feb.

98 A great deal of contemporary criticism reads to me like a man saying: 'Of course I do not like green cheese: I am very fond of brown sherry'.
1933 *All I Survey*, 'On Jonathan Swift'.

99 Why do you rush through the fields in trains,
Guessing so much and so much.
Why do you flash through the flowery meads,
Fat-head poet that nobody reads;
And why do you know such a frightful lot
About people in gloves and such?
1933 'The Fat White Woman Speaks', a response to Frances Cornford's poem.
➤ *See Cornford 237:69.*

1 It isn't that they can't see the solution. It is that they can't see the problem.
1935 *The Scandal of Father Brown*, 'Point of a Pin'.

2 Am in Market Harborough. Where ought I to be?
Attributed. Chesterton remarks in his *Autobiography* (1936), ch.16, 'I cannot remember whether this story is true; but it is not unlikely, or, I think, unreasonable.'

3 Music with dinner is an insult both to the cook and the violinist.
Quoted in *The New York Times*, 16 Nov 1967.

4 I regard golf as an expensive way of playing marbles.
Quoted in Colin Jarman *The Guinness Dictionary of Sports Quotations* (1990).

Chiang Kai-Shek 1887–1975

Chinese general and nationalist, defeated by Mao Zedong's forces. In 1948 he was forced to withdraw to Taiwan where he retained the office of President.

5 The sky cannot have two suns.
c.1945 Quoted in Ross Merrill *Mao* (1993) ch.10.

Chilcott, Gareth 1956–

English rugby union player.

6 I thought I would have a quiet pint...and about 17 noisy ones.
1993 On playing his last game of rugby for Bath.

Child, Julia McWilliams 1912–2004

US cookery expert.

7 Life itself is the proper binge.
1980 In *Time*, 7 Jan.

8 The view of history that we get through the kitchen window is a more gentle view, not of war and politics, but of family and community and sharing.
1993 On studying cookbooks dating back to the 1400s in the Library of Congress. In *Memory and Imagination*, PBS TV, 15 Aug.

Ch'in Chia c.150 BC

Chinese poet and civil servant about whom very little is known. He wrote a series of three poems on his separation from his wife, the result of a posting to Beijing.

9 I sent a carriage to bring you back
But it went empty, and empty it returned.
c.150 BC 'To My Wife 1', collected in *A Book of Chinese Verse* (translated by N L Smith and R H Kotewall).

10 Sorrow comes as in a circle
And cannot be rolled up like a map.
c.150 BC 'To My Wife 2', collected in *A Book of Chinese Verse* (translated by N L Smith and R H Kotewall).

11 One separation breeds ten thousand regrets.
c.150 BC 'To My Wife 2', collected in *A Book of Chinese Verse* (translated by N L Smith and R H Kotewall).

Chirac, Jacques René 1932–

French Conservative politician, Prime Minister (1974–6, 1986–8) and President (1995–) of France.

12 What's it for?
On being shown a scale model of the Millennium Dome. Quoted in *Servants of the People: The Inside Story of New Labour* (2000).

13 Tony Blair is very convincing, he will sway public opinion.
2004 On the proposed British referendum on the EU Constitution, 9 May.

14 This cuisine here in America was certainly on a par with French cuisine.
2004 At the G8 meeting on Sea Island, Georgia, 10 Jun.

Chirico, Giorgio de 1888–1978

Italian painter, born in Greece, the developer of 'metaphysical painting' based on semi-abstract geometric figures. In the 1930s he renounced his earlier work and returned to an academic style.

15 If a work of art is to be truly immortal, it must pass quite beyond the limits of the human world, without any sign of common sense and logic. In this way the work will draw nearer to dream and to the mind of a child.
Quoted in Saranne Alexandrian *Surrealist Art* (1970).

Chisholm, Caroline *née Jones* 1808–77

English-born Australian social worker and philanthropist. She married an army officer and settled in New South Wales in 1838, where she worked with impoverished immigrant women and children. Her petition to Earl Grey helped persuade the British Government to grant free passage to the families of convicts.

16 If Her Majesty's Government be really desirous of seeing a well-conducted community spring up in these Colonies, the social wants of the people must be considered... For all the clergy you can despatch, all the schoolmasters you can appoint, all the churches you can build, and all the books you can export, will never do much good without what a gentleman in that Colony very appropriately called 'God's police'—wives and little children—good and virtuous women.
1847 *Emigration and Transportation Relatively Considered; in a Letter, Dedicated, by Permission, to Earl Grey*, 17 Jun. The phrase 'God's police' was adopted by Australian feminist Anne

Summers in her feminist critique of Australian culture, *Damned Whores and God's Police* (1975).
➥ *See Clark 219:54.*

Chocano, José Santos 1875–1934

Peruvian poet, teacher, editor and diplomat. He visited almost every Central and South American country, often being expelled for political intrigue. He was assassinated in Chile.

17 *Soy el cantor de América autóctono y salvaje;*
mi lira tiene un alma, mi canto un ideal.
Mi verso no se mece colgado de un ramaje
con un vaivén pausado de hamaca tropical.
I am the aboriginal and savage singer of America;
my lyre has a soul, my song has an ideal.
My poetry does not swing from the branches
with the slow movement of a tropical hammock.
1906 *Alma América*, 'Blasón' (translated as 'Blazon', 1935).

Chomsky, (Avram) Noam 1928–

US linguist and social critic. His theories revolutionized the study of language and remain controversial. In the political arena, he has criticized many aspects of US foreign policy.

18 An obscenity, a depraved act by weak and miserable men, including all of us, who have allowed it to go on and on with endless fury.
1969 Of US involvement in the war in Vietnam. *American Power and the New Mandarins.*

19 As soon as questions of will or decision arise, human science is at a loss.
1978 Television interview, 30 Mar, reported in *The Listener*, 6 Apr.

20 The military system is, to a substantial extent, a method whereby the population provides a subsidy to the high technology industry.
1988 Interview, Public Broadcasting System, 4 Nov.

Chopin, Kate (Katherine) *née O'Flaherty* 1851–1904

US novelist and short-story writer. After the death of her husband she began to write sketches of Creole life, including *Bayou Folk* (1894). Her novel *The Awakening* (1899) was harshly condemned for its frank treatment of female sexuality.

21 The voice of the sea speaks to the soul. The touch of the sea is sensuous, enfolding the body in its soft, close embrace.
1899 *The Awakening*, ch.6.

22 The past was nothing to her… The future was a mystery which she never attempted to penetrate. The present alone was significant.
1899 *The Awakening*, ch.15.

23 She was becoming herself and daily casting aside that fictitious self which we assume like a garment with which to appear before the world.
1899 *The Awakening*, ch.19.

24 The artist must possess the courageous soul that dares and defies.
1899 *The Awakening*, ch.39.

25 I trust I will not be giving away professional secrets to say that many readers would be surprised, perhaps shocked, at the questions which some newspaper editors will put to a defenseless woman under the guise of flattery.
1899 'On Certain Brisk Days', in the *St Louis Post–Dispatch*, 26 Nov.

Christiansen, Arthur 1904–63

British journalist, Editor of the *Daily Express* (1933–58).

26 Whenever possible print a woman's age.
1957 Quoted in Francis Williams *Dangerous Estate*.

27 The people who lived behind those clean lace curtains in row after row of identical boxes were newspaper readers, and every word in at any rate *my* newspaper must be clear and comprehensible to them, must be interesting to them, must encourage them to break away from littleness, stimulate their ambition, help them to want to build a better land.
1961 *Headlines all my Life*, ch.1.

28 Remember the people in the back streets of Derby.
1961 *Headlines all my Life*, ch.1.

29 Show me a contented newspaper editor and I will show you a bad newspaper.
1961 *Headlines all my Life*, ch.15.

30 No matter how many media for the dissemination of news are created, there is one rule that should never be broken: TELL THE PEOPLE!
1961 *Headlines all my Life*, ch.18.

31 My approach to newspapers was based on the idea that when you looked at the front page you said: 'Good heavens', when you looked at the middle page you said: 'Holy smoke', and by the time you got to the back page—well, I'd have to utter a profanity to show how exciting it was.
1961 *Headlines all my Life*, ch.19.

Christie, Dame Agatha Mary Clarissa *née Miller* 1890–1976

English author, who wrote more than 70 classic detective novels including *The Mysterious Affair at Styles* (1920), *Murder on the Orient Express* (1934) and *Death on the Nile* (1937).

32 He tapped his forehead. 'These little grey cells. It is up to them—as you say over here.'
1920 *The Mysterious Affair at Styles*, ch.10.

33 Life nowadays is dominated and complicated by the remorseless Zip. Blouses zip up, skirts zip down, ski-ing suits zip everywhere… Why? Is there anything more deadly than a Zip that turns nasty on you?
1946 *Come, Tell Me How You Live*, ch.1.

34 Here, in the west of Ireland, the Romans had never marched, tramp, tramp, tramp: had never fortified a camp: had never built a well-ordered, sensible, useful road. It was a land where common sense and an orderly way of life were unknown.
Hercule Poirot looked down at the tips of his patent-leather shoes and sighed. He felt forlorn and very much alone. The standards by which he lived were here not appreciated.
1947 *The Labours of Hercules*.

35 War settles *nothing*…to *win* a war is as disastrous as to lose one.
1977 *An Autobiography*, ch.10.

Christie, Linford 1960–

English athlete who won an Olympic gold medal for the 100m at the 1992 games in Barcelona.

36 I could have been a god, but people only allow you to get so far in this country.
2002 In *The Independent*, 20 Dec.

Christine de Pisan 1364–1430

Italian-born French writer. Taken to the court of Charles V as a child, married at 15 and widowed at 25, she became the first professional woman poet and official biographer of Charles V. Other works include lyrics and essays on politics and the status of women in society.

37 *En la hauteur ou abaissement des gens ne gist mie es corps selonc le sexe, mais en la perfeccion des meurs et vertus.*
The dignity or baseness of a person lies not in their body according to the sex, but in the perfection of behaviour and virtues.
1405 *Le livre de la Cité des Dames*, bk.1, ch.9.

38 *De tant comme femmes ont le corps plus delie que les hommes, plus foible et moins habille a plusieurs choses faire, de tant ont elles l'entendement plus a delivre et plus agu ou elles s'appliquent.*
Just as women's bodies are more delicate than men's, weaker and less able for many things, so, where they apply themselves, their understanding is freer and sharper.
1405 *Le livre de la Cité des Dames*, bk.1, ch.27.

Christopher, Warren Minor 1925–

US lawyer and government official, Secretary of State (1993–6). In 1980 he negotiated for the release of US hostages in Iran.

39 I wish the meeting had been as good as the lunch.
1994 On beginning talks in Beijing with China's Prime Minister. In the *New York Times*, 13 Mar.

40 Sometimes you have to learn how to give the right answer to the wrong question.
1994 On Syrian President Hafez Assad's complaint that he had been put off by a hostile question in a news conference shared with President Clinton. In *US News and World Report*, 19 Dec.

Church, Richard 1893–1972

English author, known for his poems, novels, literary criticism, travel books and children's stories.

41 We have to accept the verbal portraits, as indeed we have to accept paintings and sculptures, as well as photographs, of the immortals whose influence on our lives is often greater than that of our own family members.
In praise of biography. Quoted in *Christian Science Monitor*, 30 Apr 1963.

42 He delights to expose the raw nerves of evil, showing it as a force in the world, a skeletonlike figure working visible mischief in the ordinary everyday affairs of men and women and children.
Of Graham Greene. Recalled on Greene's death in the *New York Times*, 4 Apr 1991.

Churchill, Charles 1731–64

English satirical poet. His works savagely attacked many well-known figures of his time, including Samuel Johnson, Tobias Smollett and William Hogarth. He is best known for *The Rosciad* (1761).

43 A pert, prim Prater of the northern race,
Guilt in his heart, and famine in his face.
1761 Of the Scottish-born judge Alexander Wedderburn, later Lord Loughborough. *The Rosciad*, l.75–6.

44 Fashion—a word which knaves and fools may use,
Their knavery and folly to excuse.
1761 *The Rosciad*, l.455–6.

45 So much they talked, so very little said.
1761 *The Rosciad*, l.550.

46 But, spite of all the criticizing elves,
Those who would make us feel, must feel themselves.
1761 *The Rosciad*, l.961–2.

47 Keep up appearances; there lies the test;
The world will give thee credit for the rest.
Outward be fair, however foul within;
Sin if thou wilt, but then in secret sin.
1762 *Night*, l.311–12.

48 Just to the windward of the law.
1763 *The Ghost*, bk.3, l.56.

49 A joke's a very serious thing.
1763 *The Ghost*, bk.3, l.1386.

50 Apt Alliteration's artful aid.
1763 *The Prophecy of Famine*, l.86.

51 The danger chiefly lies in acting well;
No crime's so great as daring to excel.
1763 *An Epistle to William Hogarth*, l.51–2.

52 Be England what she will,
With all her faults, she is my country still.
1764 *The Farewell*, l.27–8.

53 It can't be Nature, for it is not sense.
1764 *The Farewell*, l.200.

Churchill, Jeanette *née Jeanette Jerome* 1852–1921

US-born wife of Lord Randolph Henry Spencer Churchill, daughter of a prominent New York businessman.

54 There is no such thing as a moral dress... It's people who are moral or immoral.
1921 'That Moral Dress', in the *Daily Chronicle*, 16 Feb.

Churchill, Lord Randolph Henry Spencer 1849–95

English politician, the leader of a guerrilla band of Conservatives known as the 'Fourth Party' (from 1880) and father of Sir Winston Churchill. He was Chancellor of the Exchequer and leader of the House of Commons (1886).

55 Ulster will not be a consenting party. Ulster, at the proper time, will resort to the supreme arbitrament of force; Ulster will fight and Ulster will be right.
1886 Public letter, 7 May.

56 This monstrous mixture of imbecility, extravagance and political hysteria, better known as the Bill for the future government of Ireland—this farrago of superlative nonsense, is to be put in motion for this reason and no other: to gratify the ambition of an old man in a hurry.
1886 Pamphlet attacking Gladstone's Home Rule Bill, Jun.

57 I could never make out what those damned dots meant.
Of decimal points. Quoted in Winston Churchill *Lord Randolph Churchill* (1906).

58 The duty of an Opposition is to oppose.
Remark attributed by his son, Winston Churchill. The phrase

was used earlier by Edward Stanley, 14th Earl of Derby, who attributed it to Mr Tierney (4 Jun 1841).

Churchill, Sir Winston Leonard Spencer 1874–1965

English statesman, Prime Minister (1940–5, 1951–2) and writer. He became a Conservative MP in 1900 but turned Liberal in 1904 and was made First Lord of the Admiralty (1911) and Chancellor of the Exchequer (1924–9). He returned to the Conservative Party in 1929 and on Chamberlain's defeat formed a coalition government to pursue the war with Germany.

59 Business carried on as usual during alterations on the map of Europe.
1914 Of the British people's view of World War I. Speech at the Guildhall, London, 9 Nov.

60 In war: resolution. In defeat: defiance. In victory: magnanimity. In peace: goodwill.
c.1918 *The Second World War* (1948), vol.1, epigraph. According to Sir Edward Marsh, in *A Number of People* (1939), the phrase occurred to Churchill shortly after the end of World War I. Some sources attribute it to Marsh himself.

61 Of all tyrannies in history, the Bolshevik tyranny is the worst, the most destructive, the most degrading. Every British and French soldier killed last year was really done to death by Lenin and Trotsky—not in fair war, but by the treacherous desertion of an ally without parallel in the history of the world.
1919 Speech, London, 11 Apr.

62 The community lacks goods and a million and a quarter people lack work. It is certainly one of the highest functions of national finance and credit to bridge the gap between the two.
1925 Letter to Otto Niemeyer, 22 Feb. Collected in D E Moggridge *Maynard Keynes* (1992).

63 The day must come when the nation's whole scale of living must be reduced. If that day comes, Parliament must lay the burden equally on all classes.
1925 Speech as Chancellor of the Exchequer, House of Commons, 7 Aug.

64 Jellicoe was the only man on either side who could lose the war in an afternoon.
1927 On Admiral Jellicoe, commander of the Grand Fleet in World War I. *The World Crisis*, pt.1, ch.5.

65 The loss of India would mark and consummate the downfall of the British Empire. That great organism would pass at a stroke out of life into history. From such a catastrophe there could be no recovery.
1930 Speech to the Indian Empire Society, London, 12 Dec.

66 Mr Gladstone read Homer for fun, which I thought served him right.
1930 *My Early Life*.

67 Those who can win a war well can rarely make a good peace, and those who could make a good peace would never have won the war.
1930 *My Early Life*.

68 The War was decided in the first twenty days of fighting, and all that happened afterwards consisted in battles which, however formidable and devastating, were but desparate and vain appeals against the decision of Fate.
1930 His preface to E L Spears *Liaison 1914*.

69 I remember, when I was a child, being taken to the celebrated Barnum's circus, which contained an exhibition of freaks and monstrosities, but the exhibit on the programme which I most desired to see was the one described as 'The Boneless Wonder'. My parents judged that the spectacle would be too revolting and demoralizing for my youthful eyes, and I have waited 50 years to see the boneless wonder sitting on the Treasury Bench.
1931 Alluding to Ramsay MacDonald. Speech in the House of Commons, 28 Jan.

70 It is alarming and odious to see Mr Gandhi, a seditious Middle Temple lawyer, now posing as a fakir of a type well-known in the East, striding half-naked up the steps of the vice-regal palace, while he is still conducting a defiant campaign of civil disobedience, to parley on equal terms with the representative of the King-Emperor.
1931 Speech, 23 Feb.

71 That long frontier from the Atlantic to the Pacific oceans, guarded only by neighbourly respect and honourable obligations, is an example to every country and a pattern for the future of the world.
1939 Address at the Canada Club, London, 20 Apr.

72 This is no war for domination or imperial aggrandisement or material gain… It is a war…to establish, on impregnable rocks, the rights of the individual and it is a war to establish and revive the stature of man.
1939 Speech in the House of Commons, 3 Sep, on the declaration of war against Germany by Britain and France.

73 I cannot forecast to you the action of Russia. It is a riddle wrapped inside a mystery inside an enigma. But perhaps there is a key; that key is Russian national interest.
1939 Radio broadcast, 1 Oct.

74 You ask what is our aim. I can answer in one word—victory. Victory at all costs, victory in spite of all terror, victory, however long and hard the road may be.
1939 Radio broadcast, 1 Oct.

75 I have nothing to offer but blood, toil, tears and sweat.
1940 Speech in the House of Commons on assuming the premiership, 13 May.

76 We shall not flag or fail. We shall go on to the end. We shall fight in France, we shall fight on the seas and oceans, we shall fight with growing confidence and growing strength in the air, we shall defend our island whatever the cost may be. We shall fight on the beaches, we shall fight on the landing grounds, we shall fight in the fields and in the streets, we shall fight in the hills. We shall never surrender.
1940 Speech in the House of Commons, 4 Jun, after the Dunkirk evacuation.

77 Let us therefore brace ourselves to our duties, and so bear ourselves that, if the British Empire and its Commonwealth last for a thousand years, men will still say: 'This was their finest hour.'
1940 Speech, 18 Jun. Quoted in A J P Taylor *English History 1914–45*, p.491.

78 Never in the field of human conflict has so much been owed by so many, to so few.
1940 On the Battle of Britain pilots. Speech, House of Commons, 20 Aug.

79 No one can guarantee success in war, but only deserve it.
1940 Letter to Lord Wavell, 26 Nov. Quoted in Winston Churchill *The Second World War*, vol.2 (1949), ch.27.

80 Here is the answer that I will give to President Roosevelt… Give us the tools, and we will finish the job.
1941 Radio broadcast, 9 Feb.

81 No one has been a more consistent opponent of Communism than I have for the last 25 years. I will unsay no word that I have spoken about it, but all that fades away before the spectacle that is now unfolding. The past, with its crimes, its follies, and its tragedies, flashes away. I see the Russian soldiers standing on the threshold of their native land, guarding the fields that their fathers have tilled from time immemorial. Any man or state who fights on against Nazidom will have our aid. Any man or state who marches with Hitler is our foe.
1941 Radio broadcast on the German invasion of Russia, 22 Jun.

82 When I warned the French that Britain would fight on alone, General Weygand told their Prime Minister and his divided Cabinet that in three weeks England will have her neck wrung like a chicken. Some chicken, some neck!
1941 Speech to the Canadian Parliament, 30 Dec.

83 What kind of people do they think we are?
1941 Of the Japanese. Speech to Congress, Dec.

84 Commanders and senior officers should die with troops. The honour of the British Empire and the British Army is at stake.
1942 Telegram to Wavell, the commander in chief of armed forces in Singapore, 10 Feb, after being told that a Japanese victory was inevitable. Recalled in *The Second World War*, vol.4 (1951).

85 The latest refinements of science are linked with the cruelties of the Stone Age.
1942 Speech, 26 Mar, in devastated war-time London.

86 Now this is not the end. It is not even the beginning of the end. But it is, perhaps, the end of the beginning.
1942 Speech at the Mansion House, London, 10 Nov, referring to the Battle of Egypt.

87 I have not become the King's First Minister in order to preside over the liquidation of the British Empire.
1942 Speech at the Mansion House, London, 10 Nov.

88 We make this wide encircling movement in the Mediterranean, having for its primary object the recovery of the command of that vital sea, but also having for its object the exposure of the under-belly of the Axis, especially Italy, to heavy attack.
1942 Speech in the House of Commons, 11 Nov.

89 There is no finer investment for any community than putting milk into babies. Healthy citizens are the greatest asset any country can have.
1943 Speech on BBC radio, 21 Mar.

90 The Bomb brought peace, but man alone can keep that peace.
1945 Speech in the House of Commons, 16 Aug.

91 If this is a blessing, it is certainly very well disguised.
1945 On his defeat in the first post-war general election, quoted in Richard Nixon *Memoirs* (1978).

92 From Stettin in the Baltic to Trieste in the Adriatic, an iron curtain has descended across the Continent.
1946 Speech at Fulton, Missouri, 5 Mar. He had used the phrase in a telegraph to President Truman, 12 May 1945, when he said of the Russian-held territories that 'An iron curtain is drawn down upon their front'.

93 Would a special relationship between the United States and the British Commonwealth be inconsistent with our overriding loyalty to the world organization?
1946 Speech at Fulton, Missouri, Mar.

94 No one pretends that democracy is perfect or all-wise. Indeed, it has been said that democracy is the worst form of Government except all those other forms that have been tried from time to time.
1947 Speech in the House of Commons, 11 Nov.

95 Science bestowed immense new powers on man, and, at the same time, created conditions which were largely beyond his comprehension and still more beyond his control.
1949 Speech, Massachusetts Institute of Technology, 31 Mar.

96 I am ready to meet my maker. Whether my maker is ready for the ordeal of meeting me is another matter.
1949 Speech, Nov.

97 I have only one purpose—the destruction of Hitler, and my life is much simplified thereby. If Hitler invaded Hell, I would at least make a favourable reference to the Devil in the House of Commons.
Recalled in *The Second World War*, vol.3 (1950), ch.20.

98 Perhaps it is better to be irresponsible and right than to be responsible and wrong.
1950 Radio broadcast, 26 Aug.

99 If you recognize anyone, it does not mean that you like him. We all, for instance, recognize the honourable Member for Ebbw Vale.
1952 Of Ernest Bevin, in a House of Commons debate on 1 Jul on British recognition of communist China.

1 I have lived 78 years without hearing of bloody places like Cambodia.
1953 Comment, 28 Apr. Quoted in Lord Moran *Winston Churchill, The Struggle for Survival* (1966).

2 Talking jaw is better than going to war.
1954 White House speech, 26 Jun. His comment is often rendered 'To jaw-jaw is always better than to war-war.'

3 I have never accepted what many people have kindly said—that I inspired the nation. It was the nation and the race living around the globe that had the lion heart. I had the luck to be called upon to give the roar.
1954 Speech to both Houses of Parliament in Westminster Hall, Nov, on the occasion of his 80th birthday.

4 An appeaser is someone who feeds a crocodile, hoping it will eat him last.
Attributed. Quoted in *Reader's Digest*, Dec 1954.

5 In defeat unbeatable: in victory unbearable.
Of Montgomery. Quoted in Sir Edward Howard Marsh *Ambrosia and Small Beer* (1964), ch.5.

6 Scientists should be on tap, but not on top.
Quoted in Randolph S Churchill *Twenty-One Years* (1965).

7 An empty taxi arrived at 10 Downing Street, and when the door was opened Attlee got out.
Attributed. Quoted in Kenneth Harris *Attlee* (1982), ch.16.

8 An ineffectual attempt to direct an uncontrollable sphere into an inaccessible hole with instruments ill-adapted for the purpose.
Quoted in Michael Hobbs *The Golf Quotations Book* (1992).

9 All I wanted was compliance with my wishes after reasonable discussion.

Attributed. Quoted in A J P Taylor *From the Boer War to the Cold War: Essays on Twentieth-Century Europe* (1995).

10 Do not criticize your Government when out of the country. Never cease to do so when at home.
Attributed.

11 There, but for the grace of God, goes God.
Of Sir Stafford Cripps. Attributed.

12 I am so bored with it all.
Attributed last words.

Ciardi, John 1916–85

US poet, critic and translator. His translation of Dante's *Inferno* is much admired.

13 This island rock in space turns flowering endlessly
To peaks of cloud still mounting where you took
Your last high passage and your faltering luck.
1947 'Elegy for Kurt Porjescz, Missing in Action, 1 April, 1945'.

14 At the next vacancy for God, if I am elected,
I shall forgive last the delicately wounded
who, having been slugged no harder than anyone else,
never got up again, neither to fight back,
nor to finger their jaws in painful admiration.
1959 'In Place of a Curse'.

15 You don't have to suffer to be a poet. Adolescence is enough.
1962 In the *Saturday Review*, Fall issue.

Cibber, Colley 1671–1757

English actor and dramatist. He worked for most of his career at theTheatre Royal in Drury Lane, and in 1696 established himself as both playwright and actor with his first comedy, *Love's Last Shift*. From 1730 he was Poet Laureate.

16 One had as good be out of the World, as out of the Fashion.
1696 *Love's Last Shift: or, The Fool in Fashion*, act 2, sc.1.

17 Perish the thought!
1700 *Richard III*, act 5 (his adaptation of Shakespeare's play).

18 Stolen sweets are best.
1709 *The Rival Fools*, act 1.

Cicero *full name* Marcus Tullius Cicero 106–43 BC

Roman orator and statesman, exiled after his unconstitutional execution of the Catiline conspirators. Although recalled by the people (57 BC) he lost the respect of both Caesar and Pompey by his vacillations. He wrote most of his major works on rhetoric and philosophy in retirement in Rome. His speeches against Mark Antony after Caesar's death (*The Philippics*) cost him his life.

19 *Quo usque tandem abutere, Catilina, patientia nostra?*
In heaven's name, Catiline, how long will you abuse our patience?
63 BC Opening line of the first of four speeches against the conspirator L Sergius Catilina, 8 Nov. *In Catilinam* 1.1.

20 *Salus populi suprema est lex.*
The good of the people is the chief law.
52 BC *De Legibus*, bk.3, ch.3.

21 *Silent enim leges inter arma.*
For laws are silent in time of war.
51 BC *Pro Milone*, ch.11.

22 *Cui bono?*
Who benefits?
51 BC *Pro Milone*, ch.12 (and elsewhere).

23 *Nervos belli, pecuniam infinitam.*
The sinews of war, unlimited money.
44 BC *Fifth Philippic*, ch.5.

24 *Nihil tam absurde dici potest quo non dicatur ab aliquo philosophorum.*
There is nothing so absurd that it has not been said by some philosopher.
c.44 BC *De Divinatione*, bk.2, section 58.

25 *Civis Romanus sum.*
I am a Roman citizen.
In Verrem 5.147. This is a reference to the tradition that Roman citizens in foreign courts could often expect preferential treatment. The Roman governor Verres, whom Cicero was prosecuting, had ignored this fact altogether, even executing Roman citizens.

26 *Cedant arma togae, concedant laurea laudi.*
Let war yield to peace, laurels to paeans.
De Officiis, bk.1, ch.77.

27 *Mens cuiusque is est quisque: non ea figura quae digito demonstrari potest.*
The mind is the true self, not the person that can be pointed to with the finger.
De Republica bk.6, ch.24.

28 *O fortunatam natam me consule Romam!*
O lucky Rome, born when I was consul!
Cicero was consul in 63 BC. His only extant line of poetry, quoted in Juvenal, *Satires* 10, l.122.

29 *O tempora, o mores!*
What times! what morals!
Favourite phrase, used on various occasions. See *In Catilinam* 1.1, *In Verrem* 4.25 and *Pro rege Deiotaro* 11.31.

Cisneros, Henry 1947–

US politician, Secretary of Housing and Urban Development (1993–7).

30 Like piles of dry wood with red-hot coals underneath.
1993 Of US cities, rife with racial tension. In *US News and World Report*, 19 Apr.

31 We have to be honest, we have to be truthful and speak to the one dirty secret in American life, and that is racism.
1993 In *US News and World Report*, 19 Apr.

Cixous, Hélène 1937–

French feminist author and critic who has argued that women write differently from men by virtue of their bodies.

32 *On dit que la vie et la mort sont au pouvoir de la langue.*
It is said that life and death are under the power of language.
1969 *Dedans*.

33 *La seule différence incontestable n'est pas celle des sexes ou des âges ou des forces, mais celle des vifs et des morts.*
The only incontestable difference is not that of sex or age or strength, but that of the living and the dead.
1969 *Dedans*.

34 *J'ai peu de mots. Mon père qui les avait tous, est parti si précipitamment, qu'il n'a pas eu le temps de me les donner.*

I have few words. My father, who had all of them, left so suddenly that he did not have the time to give them all to me.
1969 *Dedans.*

35 *Le temps et le monde et la personne ne se rencontrent qu'une seule fois.*
Time, the world and the person only encounter one another once.
1969 *Dedans.*

36 *Je me cherche à travers les siècles et je ne me vois nulle part.*
I have searched for myself across time and have not found myself anywhere.
1974 *Prénoms du soleil* (translated by Morag Shiach in *Hélène Cixous: A Politics of Writing*).

37 *Des mots sont arrachés vivants à la langue défunte.*
Words are taken alive from a defunct language.
1976 *La.*

38 *On ne s'éveille qu'au contact de l'amour. Et avant ce temps, on n'est que jardins sans douleurs, espaces fourmillant de corps érotiques, champs de mers poissonneuses, chairs sans soucis.*
One wakes only to the touch of love. Before then, we are only gardens without sorrows, spaces swarming with erotic bodies, landscapes of seas full of fish, flesh without cares.
1976 *La.*

39 *Quand je n'écris pas, c'est comme si j'étais morte.*
When I do not write, it's as though I'm dead.
Quoted in Jean-Louis Rambures *Comment travaillent les écrivains* (1978).

40 *Je ne suis pas innocente. L'innocence est une science du sublime. Et je ne suis qu'au tout début de l'apprentissage.*
I am not innocent. Innocence is a science of the sublime. And I am only at the very beginning of the apprenticeship.
1979 *Vivre l'orange/ To Live the Orange* (bilingual text, translated by Ann Liddle and Sarah Cornell).

41 *Je voudrais tant être une femme sans y penser.*
I would like so much to be a woman without thinking about it.
1983 *Le Livre de Promethea.*

Clare, John 1793–1864

English poet, whose work reflects the harsh rural world of the 19c. He became mentally unstable in 1823 and spent the last 23 years of his life in a lunatic asylum.

42 When badgers fight and everyone's a foe.
1836 'Badger'.

43 A quiet, pilfering, unprotected race.
1841 'The Gipsy Camp'.

44 The present is the funeral of the past,
And man the living sepulchre of life.
1845 'The Present is the Funeral of the Past'.

45 I am—yet what I am, none cares or knows;
My friends forsake me like a memory lost:
I am the self-consumer of my woes.
1848 'I Am'.

46 I long for scenes where man hath never trod
A place where woman never smiled or wept
There to abide with my Creator God
And sleep as I in childhood sweetly slept,
Untroubling and untroubled where I lie
The grass below, above, the vaulted sky.
1848 'I Am'.

47 He could not die when the trees were green,
For he loved the time too well.
'The Dying Child' (published 1873).

Clark, Alan Kenneth McKenzie 1928–99

English Conservative politician, noted for his diaries, which were published from 1993. He was the son of the art historian Kenneth Clark.

48 There are no true friends in politics. We are all sharks circling, and waiting, for traces of blood to appear in the water.
1990 Diary entry, 30 Nov.

49 Safe is spelled D-U-L-L. Politics has got to be a fun activity.
1997 On being selected as parliamentary candidate for Kensington and Chelsea, 24 Jan. In the *Daily Telegraph*, 25 Jan.

50 If I can comport myself with the dignity and competence of Ms Mo Mowlam, I shall be very satisfied.
1999 After surgery for a brain tumour. In the *Sunday Times*,'Talking Heads', 6 Jun.

Clark, Eleanor 1913–

US writer, wife of Robert Penn Warren. Her works include *Eyes, Etc.* (1977), on her experience of blindness. She won the National Book Award, 1965, for *The Oysters of Locmariaquer.*

51 If you don't love life you can't enjoy an oyster.
1964 *The Oysters of Locmariaquer*, ch.1.

Clark, Kenneth Mackenzie Clark, Baron 1903–83

English art historian, particularly remembered for his pioneering television series, *Civilisation* (1969).

52 All great civilisations, in their early stages, are based on success in war.
1969 *Civilisation*, ch.1.

53 Medieval marriages were entirely a matter of property, and, as everyone knows, marriage without love means love without marriage.
1969 *Civilisation*, ch.3.

Clark, Ralph c.1755–1794

British lieutenant of the First Fleet to Australia.

54 The damned whores the moment that they got below fell a fighting amongst one and another and Capt Meridith order the Sergt. not to part them but to let them fight it out.
c.1789 *The Journal and Letters of Lt Ralph Clark 1787–1792.* The phrase 'damned whores' was adopted by Australian feminist Anne Summers in her feminist critique of Australian culture, *Damned Whores and God's Police* (1975).
➤ *See Chisholme 213:16.*

Clark, Ramsey 1927–

US lawyer, appointed Attorney General (1967–9), known for his staunch defence of civil liberties and his opposition to the Vietnam War.

55 A right is not what someone gives you; it's what no one

can take from you.
1977 In the *New York Times*, 2 Oct.

Clark, William R and Michael Grunstein

US scientists.

56 Why are human beings so different from one another?
2000 *Are We Hardwired? The Role of Genes in Human Behaviour.*

Clarke, Sir Arthur C(harles) 1917–

English author, a prolific and entertaining writer of works of science fiction, popular science, mysticism and speculative thought. His story 'The Sentinel' was the basis of Stanley Kubrick's film *2001: A Space Odyssey* (1968).

57 Overhead without any fuss the stars were going out.
1958 'The Nine Billion Names of God'.

58 Any sufficiently advanced technology is indistinguishable from magic.
1962 *Profiles of the Future*, introduction.

59 When a distinguished but elderly scientist states that something is possible he is almost certainly right. When he states that something is impossible, he is very probably wrong.
1962 *Profiles of the Future*.

60 For the radiance of eternity is not white: it is infra-red.
1993 *By Space Possessed*.

Clarke, Kenneth Harry 1940–

English Conservative politician.

61 I do not wear a bleeper. I can't speak in soundbites. I refuse to repeat slogans… I hate focus groups. I absolutely hate image consultants.
1999 In the *New Statesman*, 12 Feb.

Claudel, Paul 1868–1955

French dramatist, poet and diplomat, whose writing reflects his mystical Catholicism. He was ambassador to Japan (1921–7), the US (1927–33) and Belgium (1933–35). His works include the play *Tidings Brought to Mary* (1912) and *Five Great Odes* (1910).

62 You explain nothing, O poet, but thanks to you all things become explicable.
Recalled on his death, 23 Feb 1955.

63 A cocktail is to a glass of wine as rape is to love.
Quoted by William Grimes in 'The American Cocktail', *Americana*, Dec 1992.

Claudius Caecus, Appius 4c–3c BC

Roman statesman and lawgiver. He oversaw the construction of Rome's first aqueduct, the Aqua Appia. He later became blind, hence his surname, Caecus.

64 *Faber est suae quisque fortunae.*
Each man is the architect of his own fate.
Quoted in Sallust *Ad Caesarem Senem de Re Publica Oratio*, ch.1, section 2.

Clausewitz, Karl von 1780–1831

Prussian general, Director of the Prussian army school in Berlin (1818–30) and Gneisenau's Chief-of-Staff. His treatise *Vom Kriege* ('On War', 1833) had a major impact on strategic studies.

65 Battles decide everything.
1812 *Principles of War* (translated by J J Graham).

66 Only the study of military history is capable of giving those who have no experience of their own a clear picture of what I have just called the friction of the whole machine.
1812 *Principles of War* (translated by J J Graham).

67 *Der Krieg ist nichts als eine Fortsetzung des politischen Verkehrs mit Einmischung anderer Mittel.*
War is merely the continuation of policy with the admixture of other means.
1833 *Vom Kriege*, bk.8, ch.6, section b. The phrase is commonly rendered 'War is the continuation of politics by other means.'

Clavell, James du Maresq 1924–94

Australian-born US novelist. His first novel, *King Rat* (1962), is set in Singapore's Changi prison, where the Japanese kept prisoners of war (1942–5). Clavell was himself a prisoner of war in Java.

68 These men too were criminals. Their crime was vast. They had lost a war. And they had lived.
1962 *King Rat*.

Cleaver, Eldridge 1935–98

US political activist.

69 You're either part of the solution, or you're part of the problem.
1968 Speech, San Francisco.

Cleese, John 1939–

British actor, comedian and writer, best known for his contribution to the satirical television series, *Monty Python's Flying Circus* (1969–74).

70 I wish to complain about this parrot what I have purchased not half an hour ago from this very boutique.
1968 As Mr Praline in the 'Dead Parrot' sketch, *Monty Python's Flying Circus*.

71 Don't mention the war. I mentioned it once but I think I got away with it.
1975 As Basil Fawlty in *Fawlty Towers*, 'The Germans'.

72 Loving your neighbour as much as yourself is practically bloody impossible… You might as well have a commandment that states, 'Thou shalt fly'.
1993 In *The Times*.

Clemenceau, Georges 1841–1929

French statesman, leader of the extreme left, known as 'The Tiger'. He was Premier (1906–9, 1917–20) and presided at the 1919 Peace Conference.

73 *La guerre, c'est une chose trop grave pour la confier à des militaires.*
War is too serious a business to be left to generals.
Quoted in Hampden Jackson *Clemenceau and the Third Republic* (1946), but also attributed elsewhere to others.

74 He died as he had lived—like a second lieutenant.
1891 On the death of General Boulanger, who had shot himself on the grave of his mistress, who had died two months earlier. In *La Justice*. Quoted in Edgar Holt *The Tiger: The Life of Georges Clemenceau 1841–1929* (1976).

75 Your verdict, gentlemen, will be less upon us than upon yourselves. We appear before you. You appear before history.

1898 Addressing the jury as a member of the defence at Zola's trial, 22 Feb, following the publication of *J'Accuse*.

76 *Politique intérieure, je fais la guerre; politique extérieure, je fais toujours la guerre. Je fais toujours la guerre.*
My home policy? I wage war. My foreign policy? I wage war. Always, everywhere, I wage war.
1918 Speech to the Chamber of Deputies, 8 Mar.

77 *Il est plus facile de faire la guerre que la paix.*
It is far easier to make war than to make peace.
1919 Speech at Verdun, 20 Jul.

78 America is the only country in history that miraculously has gone directly from barbarism to decadence without the usual interval of civilization.
Attributed. This has also been attributed to George Bernard Shaw.

79 We have won the war. Now we have to win the peace—and that may be more difficult.
Quoted in David R Watson *George Clemenceau; A Political Biography* (1974).

Cleveland, (Stephen) Grover 1837–1908

22nd and 24th US President (1885–9, 1893–7). He supported civil service reform and lower tariffs, and in his second term he took a strong stance against Britain in its boundary dispute with Venezuela.

80 I have considered the pension list of the republic a roll of honour.
1888 Veto of the Dependent Pension Bill, 5 Jul.

Cleveland, John 1613–1658

English poet, a satirical propagandist for the Royalists in the Civil War, and for a time a political prisoner. Two collections of his poems were published during his lifetime, one in 1651 and the other in 1653.

81 Had Cain been Scot, God would have changed his doom
Nor forced him wander, but confined him home.
1647 'The Rebel Scot'.

82 Mystical grammar of amorous glances,
Feeling of pulses the physic of love,
Rhetorical courtings, and musical dances;
Numbering of kisses arithmetic prove.
1651 'Mark Antony'.

83 Virtue's no more in womankind
But the green sickness of the mind.
Philosophy, their new delight,
A kind of charcoal appetite.
1653 'The Antiplatonic'.

84 Give me a lover bold and free,
Not eunuched with formality.
1653 'The Antiplatonic'.

85 Like an ambassador that beds a queen
With the nice caution of a sword between.
1653 'The Antiplatonic'.

Clifford, Clark M(cAdams) 1906–98

US lawyer, adviser to Truman and Kennedy and later Secretary of Defense (1968–9) under Johnson.

86 The amiable dunce.
Of Ronald Reagan. Quoted in Haynes Johnson *Sleep-Walking Through History* (1991).

Clinton, Bill (William) 1946–

US Democratic politician and 42nd President. He became Governor of Arkansas in 1978 and served for five terms (1979–81, 1983–92). In 1992 he became the first Democrat President for twelve years and in 1996 the first Democrat to gain re-election since Roosevelt in 1936. In 1998 his initial denial of an affair with White House intern Monica Lewinsky was followed by charges of perjury and obstruction of justice, although he was subsequently acquitted by the Senate. He is married to Hillary Rodham Clinton.

87 Cash for trash.
1992 On tabloid payments to his alleged mistress Gennifer Flowers. On ABC TV, 23 Jan.

88 I experimented with marijuana a time or two. And I didn't like it, and I didn't inhale.
1992 In the *Washington Post*, 30 Mar.

89 On this day with high hopes and brave hearts, in massive numbers, the American people have voted to make a new beginning.
1992 Accepting victory in the election, 3 Nov.

90 When somebody tells you it is not a money problem, they're talking about somebody else's money.
1992 In *USA Today*, 20 Dec.

91 That hallowed piece of earth, that land of light and revelation, is the home to the memories and dreams of Jews, Muslims and Christians throughout the world.
1993 On the signing of Palestinian–Israeli peace accord at the White House, 13 Sep.

92 I have had a drill to the tooth of America for the last two years.
1994 Of painful political decisions. In the *US News & World Report*, 13 Feb.

93 I can't stop being President.
1994 Comment after a suicide plane attack and two incidents of gunfire on the White House. Reported in the *New York Times*, 18 Dec.

94 If something makes you cry, you have to do something about it. That's the difference between politics and guilt.
On what makes a liberal. Quoted in Meredith Oakley *On the Make* (1994).

95 Half the time when I see the evening news, I wouldn't be for me, either.
1995 Comment, 2 Jun.

96 Hillary was born 40, and she'll always be 40... I was born 16, and I'll always be 16.
Quoted in Gore Vidal *Virgin Islands: Essays 1992–1997* (1997).

97 I did not have sexual relations with that woman.
1998 On Monica Lewinsky, in a television interview. Quoted in the *Daily Telegraph*, 27 Jan.

98 I did have a relationship with Ms Lewinsky that was not appropriate. In fact, it was wrong.
1998 Television broadcast to America, 18 Aug. In *The Times*, 19 Aug.

99 It depends on what the meaning of 'is' is.
1998 Evidence to the grand jury. Quoted in *The Guardian*, 2 Sep.

1 I believe any person who asks for forgiveness has to be prepared to give it.
1999 Statement after being acquitted by the Senate, 12 Feb.

2 Golf is like life in a lot of ways. The most important competition is the one against yourself.
2000 Quoted in *The Independent*, 23 Dec.

3 A terrible moral error.
2004 On his affair with Monica Lewinsky. In an interview on CBS television programme *60 Minutes*, 20 Jun.

4 I did something for the worst possible reason. Just because I could.
2004 On his affair with Monica Lewinsky. In an interview on CBS television programme *60 Minutes*, 20 Jun.

5 Don't ask, don't tell.
2004 The Clinton family motto. In *My Life*.

6 Do I have regrets? Sure, both private and public ones.
2004 *My Life*.

7 During the government shutdowns I was engaged in two titanic struggles: a public one with Congress over the future of our country, and a private one to hold the old demons at bay. I had won the public fight and lost the private one.
2004 *My Life*.

Clinton, Hillary Rodham 1947–

US politician and lawyer, wife of President Bill Clinton. As a lawyer she specialized in family issues and children's rights, and after her husband's election she served as chief presidential adviser. In 2001 she became Senator for New York, the first First Lady to be elected to public office.

8 I suppose I could have stayed home, baked cookies, and had teas.
1992 Rejecting charges of a conflict of interest between politics and her legal career. In the *New York Times*, 18 May.

9 I'd be a terrific governor…a terrific president.
1992 Statement during her husband's presidential campaign. Reported in the *Washington Post*, 22 Feb 1995.

10 It is time for us to say here in Beijing, and the world to hear, that it is no longer acceptable to discuss women's rights as separate from human rights.
1995 Addressing the 4th World Conference on Women. Reported in the *New York Times*, 6 Sep.

11 I was talking to one of the Secret Service men about security the other day, and he said that as far as they were concerned, they'd be happier if we lived in a bunker and travelled the streets in a tank.
Quoted in Gore Vidal *Virgin Islands: Essays 1992–1997* (1997).

12 The great story here…is this vast right-wing conspiracy that has been conspiring against my husband since the day he announced for president.
1998 Interview on NBC television's *Today*, 27 Jan.

13 A hard dog to keep on the porch.
1999 On her husband. In *The Guardian*, 2 Aug.

Clive, Kitty 1711–85

English comic actress. Though she longed to be a tragic actress, she excelled in light comedy under the management of David Garrick at Drury Lane. She retired in 1769.

14 Damn him, he could act a gridiron.
On watching a performance by David Garrick. Quoted in William Archer's introduction to *Dramatic Essays of Leigh Hunt* (1894).

Clive, Robert, 1st Baron of Plassey 1725–74

English soldier and administrator in India, who defeated a large Indian–French force at Plassey (1757). After a spell in Parliament in Britain he returned to Calcutta (1765) to reform the civil service and the military, but was criticized for his drastic measures.

15 It is scarcely hyperbole to say that tomorrow the whole Moghul Empire is in our power.
1757 Letter, 24 Jun, following victory at Plassey the previous day.

16 By God, Mr Chairman—at this moment I stand astonished at my own moderation!
1773 At a parliamentary inquiry into his rapacious policies on India.

Clough, Arthur Hugh 1819–61

English poet. A friend of Ruskin, Arnold and Carlyle, he experienced a religious crisis in Oxford which pervades much of his writing.

17 Sesquipedalian blackguard.
1848 *The Bothie of Tober-na-Vuolich*, pt.2, l.223.

18 Grace is given of God, but knowledge is bought in the market.
1848 *The Bothie of Tober-na-Vuolich*, pt.4, l.159.

19 What shall we do without you? Think where we are. Carlyle has led us all out into the desert, and he has left us there.
1848 Parting words to Ralph Waldo Emerson, 15 Jul. Quoted in E E Hale *James Russell Lowell and His Friends* (1898), ch.9.

20 Say not the struggle naught availeth
The labour and the wounds are vain,
The enemy faints not, nor faileth,
And as things have been, things remain.
1849 'Say Not the Struggle Naught Availeth'.

21 If hopes were dupes, fears may be liars.
1849 'Say Not the Struggle Naught Availeth'.

22 And not by eastern windows only,
When daylight comes, comes in the light,
In front the sun climbs slow, how slowly,
But westward, look, the land is bright.
1849 'Say Not the Struggle Naught Availeth'.

23 Afloat. We move: Delicious! Ah,
What else is like the gondola?
1850 *Dipsychus* (published 1865), sc.5.

24 This world is bad enough maybe;
We do not comprehend it;
But in one fact can all agree
God won't, and we can't mend it.
1850 *Dipsychus* (published 1865), sc.5.

25 'There is no God', the wicked saith,
'And truly it's a blessing,
For what he might have done with us
It's better only guessing.'
1850 *Dipsychus* (published 1865), sc.6.

26 And almost every one when age,
Disease, or sorrow strike him,
Inclines to think there is a God,
Or something very like him.
1850 *Dipsychus* (published 1865), sc.6.

27 'Tis better to have fought and lost,
Than never to have fought at all.
1854 'Peschiera'.
► *See Tennyson 843:34.*

28 Rome, believe me, my friend, is like its own Monte Testaceo,

Merely a marvellous mass of broken and castaway
wine-pots.
1858 *Amours de Voyage*, canto 1, pt.2.

29 The horrible pleasure of pleasing inferior people.
1858 *Amours de Voyage*, canto 1, pt.11.

30 Am I prepared to lay down my life for the British female?
Really, who knows?...
Ah, for a child in the street I could strike; for the full-blown lady—
Somehow, Eustace, alas! I have not felt the vocation.
1858 *Amours de Voyage*, canto 2, pt.4.

31 I do not like being moved: for the will is excited; and action
Is a most dangerous thing: I tremble for something factitious,
Some malpractice of heart and illegitimate process;
We are so prone to these things with our terrible notions of duty.
1858 *Amours de Voyage*, canto 2, pt.11.

32 But for his funeral train which the bridegroom sees in the distance,
Would he so joyfully, think you, fall in with the marriage-procession?
1858 *Amours de Voyage*, canto 3, pt.6.

33 Allah is great, no doubt, and Juxtaposition his prophet.
1858 *Amours de Voyage*, canto 3, pt.6.

34 Mild monastic faces in quiet collegiate cloisters.
1858 *Amours de Voyage*, canto 3, pt.9.

35 Whither depart the souls of the brave that die in the battle,
Die in the lost, lost fight, for the cause that perishes with them?
1858 *Amours de Voyage*, canto 5, pt.6.

36 Thou shalt have one God only: who
Would be at the expense of two?
1862 *The Latest Decalogue*.

37 Thou shalt not kill; but need'st not strive
Officiously to keep alive.
1862 *The Latest Decalogue*.

38 Do not adultery commit;
Advantage rarely comes of it.
1862 *The Latest Decalogue*.

39 Thou shalt not steal; an empty feat,
When it's so lucrative to cheat.
1862 *The Latest Decalogue*.

40 Thou shalt not covet; but tradition
Approves all forms of competition.
1862 *The Latest Decalogue*.

Clough, Brian 1935–2004

English football player and manager. As a player, he set a postwar goal-scoring record of 254 goals, and also won two England caps. He went on to become a controversial and outspoken but successful manager.

41 Football hooligans? Well, there are 92 club chairmen for a start.
Quoted in Colin Jarman *The Guinness Dictionary of Sports Quotations* (1990).

42 Say nowt, win it, then—talk your head off.
Quoted in Colin Jarman *The Guinness Dictionary of Sports Quotations* (1990).

43 My wife says OBE stands for Old Big 'Ead.
Quoted in Phil Shaw *The Book of Football Quotations* (2003).

44 Resignations are for Prime Ministers and those caught with their trousers down, not for me.
Quoted in Phil Shaw *The Book of Football Quotations* (2003).

Cobain, Kurt (Donald) 1967–94

US singer and guitarist, founder member of the band Nirvana.

45 Here we are now, entertain us.
1991 'Smells Like Teen Spirit'.

46 Here's the one who likes all our pretty songs
And he likes to sing along
And he likes to shoot his gun
But he don't know what it means.
1991 'In Bloom'.

Cobbett, William 1762–1835

English radical politician and journalist. His pioneering essays on the the conditions of the rural poor were collected in his best-known work, *Rural Rides* (1830).

47 Protestations of impartiality I shall make none. They are always useless and are besides perfect nonsense, when used by a news-monger.
1797 In the first issue of *Porcupine's Gazette*, 4 Mar, 'Address to the public'.

48 All Middlesex is *ugly*, notwithstanding the millions upon millions which it is continually sucking up from the rest of the kingdom.
1822 *Rural Rides* (published 1830), entry for 25 Sep.

49 DEAL is a most villainous place. It is full of filthy-looking people. Great desolation of abomination has been going on here.
1823 On Deal, Kent. *Rural Rides* (published 1830), entry for 3 Sep.

50 The town of GUILDFORD, which (taken with its environs) I, who have seen so many, many towns, think the prettiest, and, taken all together, the most agreeable and most happy-looking, that I ever saw in my life.
1825 On Guildford, Surrey. *Rural Rides* (published 1830), entry for 23 Oct.

51 WESTBURY, a nasty odious *rotten-borough*, a really *rotten* place.
1826 On Westbury, Wiltshire. *Rural Rides* (published 1830), entry for 3 Sep.

52 From a very early age, I had imbibed the opinion, that it was every man's duty to do all that lay in his power to leave his country as good as he had found it.
1832 *Political Register*, 22 Dec.

Cobden, Richard 1804–65

English economist and politician, known as 'The Apostle of Free Trade'. In 1838 he co-founded the Anti-Corn League, and as MP from 1841 he spoke in support of the cause, bringing about the repeal of the Corn Laws in 1846.

53 Are we to be the Don Quixotes of Europe—to go about fighting for every cause where we find that someone has been wronged?
1854 Referring to the Crimean War, House of Commons, 22 Dec.

Cockburn, Alison *née* ***Rutherford*** 1713–94

Scottish poet, whose best-known lyric 'The Flowers of the Forest' commemorates a calamity in Ettrick Forest. Walter Scott was her protégé.

54 I've seen the smiling of Fortune beguiling,
I've felt all its favours and found its decay;
Sweet was its blessing, kind its caressing,
But now it is fled, fled far, far away.
1765 'The Flowers of the Forest'.

55 O fickle Fortune, why this cruel sporting?
Why thus torment us poor sons of day?
Nae mair your smiles can cheer me, nae mair your frowns can fear me,
For the flowers of the forest are a' wade away.
1765 'The Flowers of the Forest'. wade = weeded. The last line is often rendered 'For the flowers of the forest are withered away'.

Cocker, Jarvis 1963–

English singer, member of the band Pulp.

56 Let's all meet up in the year 2000
Won't it be strange when we're all fully grown?
1995 'Disco 2000'.

Cocteau, Jean 1889–1963

French poet, playwright and film director, a key figure in Surrealism and Dadaism, elected to the French Academy in 1955. His works explore the problems of adolescence and family relationships.

57 *Le tact dans l'audace c'est de savoir jusqu'où on peut aller trop loin.*
Being tactful in audacity is knowing how far one can go too far.
1918 *Le Coq et l'Arlequin.*

58 *Le pire drame pour un poète, c'est d'être admiré par malentendu.*
The worst tragedy for a poet is to be admired through being misunderstood.
1918 *Le Coq et l'Arlequin.*

59 *S'il faut choisir un crucifié, la foule sauve toujours Barabbas.*
If it has to choose who is to be crucified, the crowd will always save Barabbas.
1918 *Le Coq et l'Arlequin.*

60 *Vivre est une chute horizontale.*
Life is a horizontal fall.
1930 *Opium.*

61 Art produces ugly things which frequently become beautiful with time. Fashion, on the other hand, produces beautiful things which always become ugly with time.
1960 In the *New York World-Telegram and Sun*, 21 Aug.

Coen, Joel 1954–

US film director and screenwriter who often works in collaboration with his brother Ethan Coen.

62 We'll gladly enter the mainstream any time the mainstream will have us.
2004 In *The Guardian*, 15 Jun.

Coffee, Lenore 1900–84

US screenwriter, Oscar-nominated for *Four Daughters* (1938).

63 What a dump!
1949 Spoken by Bette Davis in *Beyond the Forest.*

Coffinhal, Jean Baptiste 1754–94

Presiding judge at the trial of chemist Antoine Lavoisier.

64 The Republic has no need for scientists.
1794 Quoted in the *Encyclopedia Britannica* (1911), vol.16.

Cohan, George M(ichael) 1878–1942

US actor-manager and playwright. Having started out in vaudeville, he became one of the great Broadway personalities, appearing in plays by himself and others at his own George M Cohan Theatre from 1911.

65 I'm a Yankee Doodle Dandy
A Yankee Doodle, do or die;
A real live nephew of my Uncle Sam's,
Born on the fourth of July.
1904 'Yankee Doodle Boy'.

66 I don't care what you say about me, as long as you say *something* about me, and as long as you spell my name right.
Quoted in John McCabe *George M Cohan, The Man Who Owned Broadway* (1973), ch.13.

Cohen, Sacha Baron 1972–

English comedian, best known for the character Ali G.

67 Is it because I is black?
1998 Frequently, as comic character Ali G.

Coke, Sir Edward 1552–1634

English jurist, prosecutor of Essex, Raleigh and the Gunpowder conspirators. After 1606 he vindicated national liberties against the royal prerogative. Dismissed in 1617, he led the popular party in Parliament from 1620 and instigated the Petition of Right (1628).

68 How long soever it hath continued, if it be against reason, it is of no force in law.
1628 *The First Part of the Institutes of the Laws of England*, bk.1, ch.10, section 80.

69 We have a saying in the House of Commons; that old ways are the safest and surest ways.
1628 Speech, London, 8 May.

70 A man's house is his castle.
1628 *The Third Part of the Institutes of the Laws of England*, ch.73.

Coke, F T Desmond 1879–1931

English novelist. A schoolmaster, he wrote several popular novels set in English public schools and universities, notably *The Bending of a Twig* (1906) and *Sandford of Merton* (1908).

71 His blade struck the water a full second before any other…until, as the boats began to near the winning post his own was dipping in the water twice as fast as any other.
1908 *Sandford of Merton*, ch.12. Often misquoted as 'All rowed fast but none so fast as stroke'.

Cole, Mac

Founder, Cole Carnival Shows.

72 The first carnival person was Christopher Columbus.
When he sailed, he didn't know where he was going.
When he got there, he didn't know where he was. And
when he got back, he didn't know where he'd been.
1989 In the *Washington Times*, 18 Aug.

Cole, W Sterling 1904–88

Chair, Joint Committee on Atomic Energy.

73 It is more sinful to conceal the power of the atom than it is to reveal it.
1954 Statement, 9 Mar, endorsed by Winston Churchill in a letter to President Eisenhower. Quoted in Peter G Boyle (ed) *The Churchill–Eisenhower Correspondence 1953–55*.

Cole, William 1919–2000

US children's writer. His output consisted chiefly of humorous verse, such as *A Boy Named Mary Jane* (1975). He also edited many poetry and verse collections.

74 Said Jerome K. Jerome to Ford Madox Ford,
'There's something, old boy, that I've always abhorred:
When people address me and call me 'Jerome',
Are they being standoffish, or too much at home?'
Said Ford, 'I agree;
It's the same thing with me.'
'Mutual Problem', collected in *The Oxford Book of American Light Verse* (1979).

Coleman, Ornette 1930–

US jazz saxophonist and composer. A controversial figure when he first appeared in New York in the late 1950s, he went on to become a key figure in the development of Free Jazz, and beyond.

75 The creation of music is just as natural as the air we breathe. I believe music is really a free thing, and any way you can enjoy it, you should.
1958 Sleeve-note, *Something Else!*

76 Many people apparently don't trust their reactions to art or to music unless there is a verbal *explanation* for it. In music the only thing that matters is whether you *feel* it or not.
1959 Sleeve-note, *Change of the Century*.

77 When I have them working together, it's like a beautiful kaleidoscope.
1981 On the music of his band Prime Time. Quoted in John Litweiler *The Freedom Principle* (1984).

Coleridge, Samuel Taylor 1772–1834

English poet, with Wordsworth one of the founders of the Romantic movement. Among his best-known poems are 'The Rime of the Ancient Mariner' (1798), 'Christabel' (1816) and 'Kubla Khan' (1816).

78 So for the mother's sake the child was dear,
And dearer was the mother for the child.
1797 'Sonnet to a Friend Who Asked Me How I Felt When the Nurse First Presented My Infant to Me'.

79 No sound is dissonant which tells of life.
1797 'This Lime-Tree Bower my Prison'.

80 It is an ancient Mariner,
And he stoppeth one of three.
'By thy long grey beard and glittering eye,
Now wherefore stopp'st thou me?'
1798 'The Rime of the Ancient Mariner', pt.1.

81 He holds him with his glittering eye—
The Wedding-Guest stood still,
And listens like a three years' child:
The Mariner hath his will.
The Wedding-Guest sat on a stone:
He cannot choose but hear;
And thus spake on that ancient man,
The bright-eyed Mariner.
1798 'The Rime of the Ancient Mariner', pt.1.

82 'God save thee, ancient Mariner!
From the fiends that plague thee thus!
Why look'st thou so?'—With my cross-bow
I shot the Albatross.
1798 'The Rime of the Ancient Mariner', pt.1.

83 We were the first that ever burst
Into that silent sea.
1798 'The Rime of the Ancient Mariner', pt.2.

84 As idle as a painted ship
Upon a painted ocean.
1798 'The Rime of the Ancient Mariner', pt.2.

85 Water, water, everywhere,
Nor any drop to drink.
The very deep did rot: O Christ!
That ever this should be!
Yes, slimy things did crawl with legs
Upon the slimy sea.
1798 'The Rime of the Ancient Mariner', pt.2.

86 I fear thee ancient Mariner!
I fear thy skinny hand!
And thou art long, and lank, and brown,
As is the ribbed sea-sand.
1798 'The Rime of the Ancient Mariner', pt.4.

87 And a thousand thousand slimy things
Lived on; and so did I.
1798 'The Rime of the Ancient Mariner', pt.4.

88 A spring of love gushed from my heart,
And I blessed them unaware.
1798 'The Rime of the Ancient Mariner', pt.4.

89 We were a ghastly crew.
1798 'The Rime of the Ancient Mariner', pt.5.

90 Like one, that on a lonesome road
Doth walk in fear and dread,
And having once turned round walks on,
And turns no more his head;
Because he knows, a frightful fiend
Doth close behind him tread.
1798 'The Rime of the Ancient Mariner', pt.6.

91 No voice, but oh! the silence sank
Like music on my heart.
1798 'The Rime of the Ancient Mariner', pt.6.

92 He prayeth well, who loveth well
Both man and bird and beast.
He prayeth best, who loveth best
All things both great and small.
1798 'The Rime of the Ancient Mariner', pt.7.

93 He went like one that hath been stunned,
And is of sense forlorn:
A sadder and wiser man,
He rose the morrow morn.
1798 'The Rime of the Ancient Mariner', pt.7.

94 O let me be awake, my God!
Or let me sleep alway.
1798 'The Rime of the Ancient Mariner', pt.7.

95 The frost performs its secret ministry,
Unhelped by any wind.
1798 'Frost at Midnight'.

96 Bells, the poor man's only music.
1798 'Frost at Midnight'.

97 And hark! the Nightingale begins its song,
'Most musical, most melancholy' bird!
A melancholy bird?...his song
Should make all Nature lovelier, and itself
Be loved like Nature!
1798 'The Nightingale'.

98 Belovèd, what are names but air?
Choose thou whatever suits the line;
Call me Sappho, call me Chloris,
Call me Lalage or Doris,
Only, only call me Thine.
1799 'Names', a translation from G E Lessing's German original (first published in the *Morning Post*, 1803).

99 All thoughts, all passions, all delights
Whatever stirs this mortal frame,
All are but ministers of Love,
And feed his sacred flame.
1799 'Love'.

1 Those sounds which oft have raised me, whilst they awed,
And sent my soul abroad,
Might now perhaps their wonted impulse give,
Might startle this dull pain, and make it move and live!
1802 'Dejection: An Ode', stanza 1.

2 I may not hope from outward forms to win
The passion and the life, whose fountains are within.
1802 'Dejection: An Ode', stanza 3.

3 Ah! from the soul itself must issue forth
A light, a glory, a fair luminous cloud
Enveloping the Earth—
And from the soul itself must there be sent
A sweet and potent voice, of its own birth
Of all sweet sounds the life and element!
1802 'Dejection: An Ode', stanza 4.

4 O pure of heart! thou need'st not ask of me
What this strong music in the soul may be!
What, and wherein it doth exist,
This light, this glory, this fair luminous mist,
This beautiful and beauty-making power.
1802 'Dejection: An Ode', stanza 5.

5 'Alas!' said she, 'we ne'er can be
Made happy by compulsion!'
1809 'The Three Graves', pt.4, stanza 12.

6 What is an Epigram? a dwarfish whole,
Its body brevity, and wit its soul.
1809 'Epigram'.

7 Alas! they had been friends in youth;
But whispering tongues can poison truth;
And constancy lives in realms above;
And life is thorny; and youth is vain;
And to be wroth with one we love
Doth work like madness on the brain.
1816 'Christabel', pt.2.

8 On awaking he...instantly and eagerly wrote down the lines that are here preserved. At this moment he was unfortunately called out by a person on business from Porlock.
1816 Preliminary note to 'Kubla Khan', explaining the reasons for the fragmented end of the poem.

9 In Xanadu did Kubla Khan
A stately pleasure-dome decree:
Where Alph, the sacred river, ran
Through caverns measureless to man
Down to a sunless sea.
1816 'Kubla Khan', opening lines.

10 A savage place! as holy and enchanted
As e'er beneath a waning moon was haunted
By woman wailing for her demon-lover!
1816 'Kubla Khan'.

11 And from this chasm, with ceaseless turmoil seething,
As if this earth in fast thick pants were breathing,
A mighty fountain momently was forced.
1816 'Kubla Khan'.

12 It was a miracle of rare device,
A sunny pleasure-dome with caves of ice!
1816 'Kubla Khan'.

13 Through wood and dale the sacred river ran,
Then reached the caverns measureless to man,
And sank in tumult to a lifeless ocean:
And 'mid this tumult Kubla heard from far
Ancestral voices prophesying war!
1816 'Kubla Khan'.

14 A damsel with a dulcimer
In a vision once I saw:
It was an Abyssinian maid,
And on her dulcimer she played,
Singing of Mount Abora.
1816 'Kubla Khan'.

15 And all who heard should see them there,
And all should cry, Beware! Beware!
His flashing eyes, his floating hair!
Weave a circle round him thrice,
And close your eyes with holy dread,
For he on honey-dew hath fed,
And drunk the milk of Paradise.
1816 'Kubla Khan'.

16 Until you understand a writer's ignorance, presume yourself ignorant of his understanding.
1817 *Biographia Literaria*, ch.12.

17 That willing suspension of disbelief for the moment, which constitutes poetic faith.
1817 *Biographia Literaria*, ch.14.

18 Kean is original; but he copies from himself. His rapid descents from the hyper-tragic to the infra-colloquial, though sometimes productive of great effect, are often unreasonable. To see him act, is like reading Shakespeare by flashes of lightning.
1823 Of Edmund Kean. *Table Talk* (published 1835), entry for 27 Apr.

19 He who begins by loving Christianity better than Truth will proceed by loving his own sect or church better than Christianity, and end by loving himself better than all.
1825 *Aids to Reflection: Moral and Religious Aphorisms.*

20 Summer has set in with its usual severity.
1826 Letter to Vincent Novello, 9 May.

21 Prose = words in their best order;—poetry = the *best* words in the best order.
1827 *Table Talk* (published 1835), entry for 12 Jul.

22 The man's desire is for the woman; but the woman's desire is rarely other than for the desire of the man.
1827 *Table Talk* (published 1835), entry for 23 Jul.

23 In Köhln, a town of monks and bones,
And pavements fang'd with murderous stones
And rags, and hags, and hideous wenches;
I counted two and seventy stenches,
All well defined, and several stinks!
Ye Nymphs that reign o'er sewers and sinks,
The river Rhine, it is well known,
Doth wash your city of Cologne;
But tell me, Nymphs, what power divine
Shall henceforth wash the river Rhine?
1828 'Cologne', first published in *Friendship's Offering* (1834), as 'Lightheartedness in Rhyme', no.4.

24 If men could learn from history, what lessons it might teach us! But passion and party blind our eyes, and the light which experience gives is a lantern on the stern, which shines only on the waves behind us!
1831 *Table Talk* (published 1835), entry for 18 Dec.

25 Farce is nearer tragedy in its essence than comedy is.
1833 *Table Talk* (published 1835), entry for 25 Aug.

26 Of no age—nor of any religion, or party or profession. The body and substance of his works came out of the unfathomable depths of his own oceanic mind.
1834 Of Shakespeare. *Table Talk* (published 1835), entry for 15 Mar.

27 Iago's soliloquy—the motive-hunting of motiveless malignity.
The Literary Remains of Samuel Taylor Coleridge (published 1836), bk.2, 'Notes on the Tragedies of Shakespeare: Othello'.

Colette *full name* *Sidonie Gabrielle Colette* 1873–1954

French writer. Her first husband, Henri Gauthier-Villars, published her early *Claudine* series under his pen-name 'Willy'. Her writing is marked by its exploration of the sensual. Later works include *Chéri* (1920) and *Gigi* (1944).

28 *Quand elle lève ses paupières, on dirait qu'elle se déshabille.*
When she raises her eyelids it's as if she were taking off all her clothes.
1903 *Claudine et Annie*, ch.3 (translated by Antonia White).

29 *Il découvrait…le monde des émotions qu'on nomme, à la légère, physiques.*
He was discovering…the world of the emotions that are so lightly called physical.
1923 *Le Blé en herbe.*

30 *Ne porte jamais de bijoux artistiques, ça déconsidère complètement une femme.*
Don't ever wear artistic jewellery; it wrecks a woman's reputation.
1944 *Gigi.*

Collingwood, Cuthbert, Baron 1748–1810

English admiral. He rose from midshipman to become second-in-command to Nelson at Trafalgar, on board the *Royal Sovereign*.

31 Now, gentlemen, let us do something today which the world may talk of hereafter.
1805 Remark to troops before the Battle of Trafalgar, 21 Oct. Quoted in G L Newnham Collingwood (ed) *A Selection from the Correspondence of Lord Collingwood* (1828), vol.1.

Collingwood, R(obin) G(eorge) 1889–1943

English philosopher and historian, with a strong archaeological interest. He wrote widely on the philosophy of history although his work was not well known until well after his death.

32 Perfect freedom is reserved for the man who lives by his own work and in that work does what he wants to do.
1924 *Speculum Mentis.*

33 A man ceases to be a beginner in any given science and becomes a master in that science when he has learned that…he is going to be a beginner all his life.
1942 *New Leviathan*, pt.1 ch.1.

Collins, Billy 1941–

US poet.

34 The name of the author is the first to go
followed obediently by the title, the plot,
the heartbreaking conclusion, the entire novel
which suddenly becomes one you have never read,
never even heard of.
2000 *Taking off Emily Dickinson's Clothes: Selected Poems*, 'Forgetfulness'.

Collins, Charles 1874–1926

English songwriter. He wrote rapid patter songs for use by music-hall stars of the day such as Harry Champion.

35 Any old iron, any old iron,
Any any old old iron?
You look neat
Talk about a treat,
You look dapper from your napper to your feet.
Dressed in style, brand new tile,
And your father's old green tie on,
But I wouldn't give you tuppence for your old watch chain;
Old iron, old iron?
1911 'Any Old Iron' (with E A Sheppard and Fred Terry). The second line is commonly rendered 'Any any any old iron?'.

36 My old man said, 'Follow the van,
Don't dilly-dally on the way!'
Off went the cart with the home packed in it,
I walked behind with my old cock linnet.
But I dillied and dallied, dallied and dillied,
Lost the van and don't know where to roam.
You can't trust the 'specials' like the old time 'coppers'
When you can't find your way home.
1919 'Don't Dilly-Dally on the Way' (with Fred Leigh).

Collins, Michael 1890–1922

Irish patriot and leader of the IRA. He signed the treaty of 1921 giving Ireland dominion status, believing it the best possible at the time, and after attempting to form a government under the terms of the treaty was killed in an ambush by hardline republicans.

37 Think—what I have got for Ireland? Something which she has wanted these past seven hundred years. Will anyone be satisfied with the bargain? Will anyone? I tell you this—early this morning I signed my death warrant. I thought at the time how odd, how ridiculous—a bullet may just as well have done the job five years ago.

1921 Letter, written after signing the peace treaty with Great Britain, 6 Dec.

Collins, Michael 1930–

Italian-born US astronaut who as a crew member of Apollo 11 piloted the spacecraft during its historic mission to the moon (1969). He orbited the moon alone in the command unit while Neil Armstrong and Buzz Aldrin made the first manned lunar landing.

38 I knew I was alone in a way that no earthling has ever been before.

1972 In *Time*, Dec 11.

Collins, Phil 1951–

English singer, drummer and songwriter. He joined Genesis as drummer in 1970, and took over as lead vocalist when Peter Gabriel left the group (1985). He has also had a successful solo career.

39 I suppose Phil Collins offers something for everybody,
and in hipdom that's not cool. But in the real world,
there's no shame in that at all.

Quoted in *Guinness Rockopedia* (1998).

Collins, William 1721–59

English poet, first published at the age of 17. His poetry, which is original and even experimental for the day, includes the 'Ode to Simplicity', 'Dirge in Cymbeline', 'Ode to Evening' and 'How Sleep the Brave'.

40 Too nicely Jonson knew the critic's part,
Nature in him was almost lost in Art.

1743 'Verses addressed to Sir Thomas Hanmer'.

41 To fair Fidele's grassy tomb
Soft maids and village hinds shall bring
Each opening sweet of earliest bloom,
And rifle all the breathing spring.

1744 'Dirge in Cymbeline'.

42 How sleep the brave, who sink to rest,
By all their country's wishes blest!

1746 'How Sleep the Brave' (published 1748), no.1.

43 By fairy hands their knell is rung,
By forms unseen their dirge is sung.

1746 'How Sleep the Brave' (published 1748), no.2.

44 O thou, the friend of man assigned,
With balmy hands his wounds to bind,
And charm his frantic woe:
When first Distress with dagger keen
Broke forth to waste his destined scene,
His wild unsated foe!

1747 *Odes on Several Descriptive and Allegoric Subjects*, 'Ode to Pity', no.1.

45 Ah Fear! Ah frantic Fear!
I see, I see thee near.

1747 *Odes on Several Descriptive and Allegoric Subjects*, 'Ode to Fear', l.5–6.

46 Though taste, though genius bless
To some divine excess,
Faints the cold work till thou inspire the whole;
What each, what all supply
May court, may charm our eye,
Thou, only thou can't raise the meeting soul!

1747 *Odes on Several Descriptive and Allegoric Subjects*, 'Ode to Simplicity', no.8.

47 Now air is hushed, save where the weak-eyed bat
With short shrill shriek flits by on leathern wing,
Or where the beetle winds
His small but sullen horn,
As oft he rises midst the twilight path,
Against the pilgrim borne in heedless hum.

1747 *Odes on Several Descriptive and Allegoric Subjects*, 'Ode to Evening', l.9–14.

48 While Spring shall pour his showers, as oft he wont,
And bathe thy breathing tresses, meekest Eve!
While Summer loves to sport
Beneath thy lingering light;
While sallow Autumn fills thy lap with leaves,
Or Winter, yelling through the troublous air,
Affrights thy shrinking train,
And rudely rends thy robes.

1747 *Odes on Several Descriptive and Allegoric Subjects*, 'Ode to Evening', l.41–8.

49 With eyes up-raised, as one inspired,
Pale Melancholy sate retired,
And from her wild sequestered seat,
In notes by distance made more sweet,
Poured thro' the mellow horn her pensive soul.

1747 'The Passions, An Ode for Music', l.57–61.

50 Love of peace, and lonely musing,
In hollow murmurs died away.

1747 'The Passions, An Ode for Music', l.67–8.

Colombo, John Robert 1936–

Canadian editor and poet.

51 Canada could have enjoyed:
English government,
French culture,
And American know-how.
Instead it ended up with:
English know-how,
French government,
And American culture.

1965 'O Canada', collected in Al Purdy (ed) *The New Romans* (1968).

Colton, Charles Caleb 1780–1832

British clergyman and writer. He was also a successful sportsman and was known for his gambling, which eventually led to his financial ruin and suicide.

52 Men will wrangle for religion; write for it; fight for it—anything but live for it.

1820 *Lacon*, vol.1, no.25.

53 When you have nothing to say, say nothing.

1820 *Lacon*, vol.1, no.183.

54 Imitation is the sincerest form of flattery.

1820 *Lacon*, vol.1, no.217.

55 Examinations are formidable even to the best prepared, for the greatest fool may ask more than the wisest man can answer.

1820 *Lacon*, vol.1, no.322.

56 If you would be known, and not know, vegetate in a village; if you would know, and not be known, live in a city.
1820 *Lacon*, vol.1, no.334.

Coltrane, John 1926–67

US jazz saxophonist. He was the most influential tenor and soprano saxophonist of the postwar era.

57 The main thing a musician would like to do is to give a picture to the listener of the many wonderful things he knows and senses in the universe.
1966 Quoted in sleeve-note to the re-issue of *Coltrane's Sound* (originally published 1961).

Colum, Padraic 1881–1972

Irish poet, playwright, novelist, biographer, critic and children's writer, a central figure in the Irish Literary Renaissance. Reflecting a peasant background, his work was realistic rather than romantic. His collections include *Wild Earth* (1907).

58 Sunset and silence! A man: around him earth savage, earth broken;
Beside him two horses—a plough!

Earth savage, earth broken, the brutes, the dawn-man there in the sunset,
And the Plough that is twin to the Sword, that is founder of cities!
1907 *Wild Earth*, 'The Plougher'.

59 My young love said to me, 'My brothers won't mind,
And my parents won't slight you for your lack of kind.'
Then she stepped away from me, and this she did say,
'It will not be long, love, till our wedding day.'
1907 *Wild Earth*, 'She Moved through the Fair'.

60 Then the wet, winding roads,
Brown bogs with black water;
And my thoughts on white ships
And the King o' Spain's daughter.
1907 'A Drover'.

61 Oh, to have a little house!
To own the hearth and stool and all!
The heaped-up sods upon the fire,
The pile of turf against the wall!
To have a clock with weights and chains
And pendulum swinging up and down,
A dresser filled with shining delph,
Speckled and white and blue and brown!
c.1907 'An Old Woman of the Roads'.

Columbus, Christopher *Spanish name* ***Cristóbal Colón*** 1451–1506

Genoese explorer, and discoverer of the New World (1492). His *Carta del descubrimiento* (1493) is the first European historical document about America.

62 *Toda la cristiandad debe tomar alegría y hacer grandes fiestas, y dar gracias solemnes a la Santa Trinidad, con muchas oraciones solemnes por el tanto ensalzamiento que habrán, en tornándose tantos pueblos a nuestra Santa Fe, y después por los bienes temporales que no solamente a la España, mas a todos los cristianos tendrán aquí refigerio y ganancia.*
All Christendom ought to feel joyful and make great celebrations and give solemn thanks to the Holy Trinity with many solemn prayers for the great exaltation which it will have, in the turning of so many people to our holy faith, and afterwards for material benefits, since not only Spain but all Christians will hence have refreshment and profit.
1493 *Carta del descubrimiento* (translated as *The Letter in Spanish of Christopher Columbus*, 1889).

Comden, Betty *pseudonym of* ***Elizabeth Cohen*** 1919–

US screenwriter and lyricist, who worked with Adolph Green on a number of musicals. Her scripts include *On the Town* (1949), *Singin' in the Rain* (1952) and *Bells are Ringing* (1960).

63 I can stand anything but failure.
1953 Line delivered by Oscar Levant in *The Band Wagon*.

64 The party's over, it's time to call it a day.
1956 'The Party's Over' (with Adolphe Green, music by Jule Styne).

Commoner, Barry 1917–

US biologist closely associated with issues of ecology, public health and environmental policy.

65 Science is triumphant with far-ranging success, but its triumph is somehow clouded by growing difficulties in providing for the simple necessities of human life on earth.
1966 *Science and Survival*.

66 The gap between brute power and human need continues to grow, as the power fattens on the same faulty technology that intensifies the need.
1972 'The Closing Circle', in *Technology*.

Comnena, Anna 1083–1153

Byzantine princess and historian, daughter of Emperor Alexius I. She retired to a convent to write an account of her father's reign after failing to secure the imperial throne for her husband, Nicephorus Bryennius.

67 A mounted Kelt is irresistible; he would bore his way through the walls of Babylon.
c.1148 Her description of the Frankish knights who passed through Constantinople on the First Crusade, 1097. *The Alexiad of Anna Comnena*, bk.13, ch.8 (translated by E R A Sewter).

Compton-Burnett, Dame Ivy 1892–1969

English novelist. Her novels, which explore the nuances of human relationships, include *Pastors and Masters* (1925), *Brothers and Sisters* (1929), *More Women than Men* (1933) and *Mother and Son* (1955).

68 'Well, of course, people are only human,' said Dudley to his brother, as they walked to the house behind the women. 'But it really does not seem much for them to be.'
1939 *A Family and a Fortune*, ch.2.

69 People don't resent having nothing nearly as much as too little.
1939 *A Family and a Fortune*, ch.4.

70 It will be a beautiful family talk, mean and worried and full of sorrow and spite and excitement. I cannot be asked to miss it in my weak state. I should only fret.
1939 *A Family and a Fortune*, ch.10.

71 As regards plots I find real life no help at all. Real life

seems to have no plots.
1945 *Orion*, no.1,'A Conversation'.

72 And people in life hardly seem definite enough to appear in print. They are not good or bad enough, or clever or stupid enough, or comic or pitiful enough.
1945 *Orion*, no.1,'A Conversation'.

73 We must use words as they are used, or stand aside from life.
1955 *Mother and Son*, ch.9.

74 There is more difference within the sexes than between them.
1955 *Mother and Son*, ch.10.

75 When I die people will say it is the best thing for me. It is because they know it is the worst. They want to avoid the feeling of pity.
1961 *The Mighty and Their Fall*, ch.4.

76 There are different kinds of wrong. The people sinned against are not always the best.
1961 *The Mighty and Their Fall*, ch.7.

77 There's not much to say. I haven't been at all deedy.
1969 When asked about her life. In *The Times*, 30 Aug.

Comte, Auguste Isidore Marie Françoise 1798–1857

French social scientist, mathematician and philosopher of social science, whose work in logical positivism laid the foundations for contemporary social science.

78 To understand a science it is necessary to know its history.
1851–4 *Système de politique positive* (*Positive Philosophy*).

Conant, James Bryant 1893–1978

US educator, President of Harvard University (1933–53).

79 There is only one proved method of assisting the advancement of pure science—that of picking men of genius, backing them heavily, and leaving them to direct themselves.
1945 Letter to the *New York Times*, 13 Aug.

80 It seems as though I were in a lunatic asylum, but I am never sure who is the attendant and who the inmate.
1950 Of Washington. Letter to Bernard Baruch, Feb. Quoted in James G Hershberg *James B Conant* (1993).

81 A Harvard education consists of what you learn at Harvard while you are not studying.
Quoted in *Time*, 29 Sep 1986.

Condon, Richard 1915–96

US writer. He made his reputation with his successful novel of political intrigue, *The Manchurian Candidate* (1959).

82 In Mexico the gods ruled, the priests interpreted and interposed, and the people obeyed. In Spain, the priests ruled, the king interpreted and interposed, and the gods obeyed. A nuance in an ideological difference is a wide chasm.
1961 *A Talent for Loving*, bk.1, ch.6.

83 He was an unzipped fly caught in forever amber.
1967 *The Ecstasy Business*, ch.1.

84 What is art is not likely to be decided for decades or longer after the work has been produced—and then is often redecided—so we must not think badly if we regard literature as entertainment rather than as transcendent enlightenment.
1976 Comment in D L Fitzpatrick (ed) *Contemporary Novelists*.

85 She felt sexual urgings towards Yvonne in the manner that politicians feel an enormous sexual pull towards mirrors.
1978 *Bandicoot*, ch.21.

Confucius *or K'ung Fu-tse, 'The Master K'ung'* 551–479 BC

Chinese philosopher. He was Governor of Chung-tu, Minister of Works and later Minister of Justice. Although his social reform measures were popular, his enemies forced him into exile. His sayings are collected in the *Confucian Analects*, compiled by his pupils after his death.

86 Man has three ways of acting wisely. First, on meditation; that is the noblest. Secondly, on imitation; that is the easiest. Thirdly, on experience; that is the bitterest.
c.479 BC *The Analects*.

87 The people may be made to follow a course of action, but they may not be made to understand it.
c.479 BC *The Analects*.

88 When you meet someone better than yourself, turn your thoughts to becoming his equal.When you meet someone not as good as you are, look within and examine your own self.
c.479 BC *The Analects*.

89 When I have pointed out one corner of a square to anyone and he does not come back with the other three, I will not point it out to him a second time.
c.479 BC *The Analects*.

90 You can rob an army of its commander-in-chief, but you cannot deprive the humblest man of his free will.
c.479 BC *The Analects*.

91 But without the trust of the people, no government can stand.
c.479 BC *The Analects*.

92 He that in his studies wholly applies himself to labour and exercise, and neglects meditation, loses his time, and he that only applies himself to meditation, and neglects labour and exercise, only wanders and loses himself.
Quoted in Colin Jarman *The Guinness Dictionary of Sports Quotations* (1990).

Congreve, William 1670–1729

English dramatist and poet. His first publication was the novel *Incognita* (1692), and he translated Juvenal and wrote original verse. He is best remembered for his witty plays, including *Love for Love* (1695) and *The Way of the World* (1700).

93 I am always of the opinion with the learned, if they speak first.
1692 *Incognita*.

94 In my conscience I believe the baggage loves me, for she never speaks well of me herself, nor suffers any body else to rail at me.
1693 Bellemore to Sharper. *The Old Bachelor*, act 1, sc.3.

95 Man was by Nature Woman's cully made:
We never are, but by ourselves, betrayed.
1693 Lucy to Silvia. *The Old Bachelor*, act 3, sc.1.

96 Bilbo's the word, and slaughter will ensue.
1693 Bluffe to Sir Joseph. *The Old Bachelor*, act 3, sc.7.

97 If this be not love, it is madness, and then it is pardonable.
1693 Heartwell to Sylvia. *The Old Bachelor*, act 3, sc.10.

98 Eternity was in that moment.
1693 Bellmore to Laetitia. *The Old Bachelor*, act 4, sc.7.

99 Now am I slap-dash down in the mouth.
1693 Sir Joseph to Bluffe. *The Old Bachelor*, act 4, sc.9.

1 Thus grief still treads upon the heels of pleasure:
Married in haste, we may repent at leisure.
1693 Sharper to Setter. *The Old Bachelor*, act 5, sc.1.

2 Some by experience find those words mis-placed:
At leisure married, they repent in haste.
1693 Setter to Sharper. *The Old Bachelor*, act 5, sc.1.

3 I could find it in my heart to marry thee, purely to be rid of thee.
1693 Belinda to Bellmore. *The Old Bachelor*, act 5, sc.10.

4 Courtship to marriage, as a very witty prologue to a very dull play.
1693 Bellmore to Belinda. *The Old Bachelor*, act 5, sc.10.

5 It is the business of a comic poet to paint the vices and follies of human kind.
1693 *The Double Dealer*, epistle dedicatory.

6 Retired to their tea and scandal, according to their ancient custom.
1693 Mellefont to Charles. *The Double Dealer*, act 1, sc.1.

7 There is nothing more unbecoming a man of quality than to laugh; Jesu, 'tis such a vulgar expression of the passion!
1693 Lord Froth to Brisk. *The Double Dealer*, act 1, sc.4.

8 Tho' marriage makes man and wife one flesh, it leaves 'em still two fools.
1693 Cynthia to Mellefont. *The Double Dealer*, act 2, sc.3.

9 She lays it on with a trowel.
1693 Brisk to Lord Froth. *The Double Dealer*, act 3, sc.10.

10 See how love and murder will out.
1693 *The Double Dealer*, act 4, sc.6.

11 No mask like open truth to cover lies,
As to go naked is the best disguise.
1693 *The Double Dealer*, act 5, sc.6.

12 Has he not a rogue's face?...a haunting-look to me...has a damned Tyburn-face, without the benefit o' the Clergy.
1695 Of Sir Sampson. *Love for Love*, act 2, sc.7.

13 I came upstairs into the world; for I was born in a cellar.
1695 Jeremy. *Love for Love*, act 2, sc.7.

14 I know that's a secret, for it's whispered every where.
1695 Tattle to Scandal. *Love for Love*, act 3, sc.3.

15 He that first cries out stop thief, is often he that has stolen the treasure.
1695 Scandal to Mrs Foresight. *Love for Love*, act 3, sc.14.

16 Women are like tricks by sleight of hand, which, to admire, we should not understand.
1695 Valentine. *Love for Love*, act 4, sc.21.

17 A branch of one of your antediluvian families, fellows that the flood could not wash away.
1695 Sir Sampson to Angelica. *Love for Love*, act 5, sc.2.

18 To find a young fellow that is neither a wit in his own eye, nor a fool in the eye of the world, is a very hard task.
1695 Sir Sampson to Angelica. *Love for Love*, act 5, sc.2.

19 Aye, 'tis well enough for a servant to be bred at an University. But the education is a little too pedantic for a gentleman.
1695 Tattle to Jeremy. *Love for Love*, act 5, sc.3.

20 Nay, for my part I always despised Mr Tattle of all things; nothing but his being my husband could have made me like him less.
1695 Mrs Frail to Mrs Foresight. *Love for Love*, act 5, sc.11.

21 I confess freely to you, I could never look long upon a Monkey, without very Mortifying Reflections.
1695 Letter to John Dennis, 10 Jul.

22 Music hath charms to soothe a savage breast,
To soften rocks, or bend a knotted oak.
1697 Almeria to Leonora. *The Mourning Bride*, act 1, sc.1.

23 Heaven has no rage, like love to hatred turned,
Nor Hell a fury, like a woman scorned.
1697 Zara. *The Mourning Bride*, act 3, sc.8.

24 Is he then dead?
What, dead at last, quite, quite for ever dead!
1697 Almeria to Leonora. *The Mourning Bride*, act 5, sc.11.

25 They come together like the Coroner's Inquest, to sit upon the murdered reputations of the week.
1700 Fainall to Mirabell. *The Way of the World*, act 1, sc.1.

26 She once used me with that insolence that in revenge I took her to pieces; sifted her, and separated her failings; I studied 'em, and got 'em by rote. The catalogue was so large that I was not without hopes, one day or other, to hate her heartily.
1700 *The Way of the World*, act 1, sc.3.

27 Ay, ay, I have experience: I have a wife, and so forth.
1700 Fainall to Mirabell. *The Way of the World*, act 1, sc.3.

28 FAINALL: 'Tis for the honour of England that all Europe should know that we have blockheads of all ages.
MIRABELL: I wonder there is not an Act of Parliament to save the credit of the nation, and prohibit the exportation of fools.
1700 *The Way of the World*, act 1, sc.5.

29 A wit should no more be sincere than a woman constant; one argues a decay of parts, as t'other of beauty.
1700 *The Way of the World*, act 1, sc.6.

30 What, he speaks unseasonable truths sometimes, because he has not wit enough to invent an evasion.
1700 *The Way of the World*, act 1, sc.6.

31 I always take blushing either for a sign of guilt, or of ill breeding.
1700 Petulant to Mirabell. *The Way of the World*, act 1, sc.9.

32 To pass over youth in dull indifference, to refuse the sweets of life because they once must leave us, is as preposterous as to wish to have been born old, because we one day may be old. For my part, my youth may wear and waste, but it shall never rust in my possession.
1700 *The Way of the World*, act 2, sc.1.

33 Say what you will, 'tis better to be left than never to have been loved.
1700 Mrs Warwood to Mrs Fainall. *The Way of the World*, act 2, sc.1.

34 Beauty is the lover's gift.
1700 Mirabell. *The Way of the World*, act 2, sc.4.

35 Here she comes i' faith full sail, with her fan spread and streamers out, and a shoal of fools for tenders.
1700 Of Mirabell. *The Way of the World*, act 2, sc.5.

36 Nobody knows how to write letters; and yet one has 'em, one does not know why.—They serve one to pin up one's hair.
1700 *The Way of the World*, act 2, sc.5.

37 WITWOUD: Madam, do you pin up your hair with all your letters?
MILLAMANT: Only with those in verse, Mr Witwoud. I never pin up my hair with prose.
1700 *The Way of the World*, act 2, sc.5.

38 To please a fool is some degree of folly.
1700 *The Way of the World*, act 2, sc.6.

39 A fellow that lives in a windmill has not a more whimsical dwelling than the heart of a man that is lodged in a woman.
1700 *The Way of the World*, act 2, sc.7.

40 A little disdain is not amiss; a little scorn is alluring.
1700 Lady Wishfort to Foible. *The Way of the World*, act 3, sc.5.

41 Love's but the frailty of the mind,
When 'tis not with ambition joined;
A sickly flame, which if not fed expires;
And feeding, wastes in self-consuming fires.
1700 *The Way of the World*, act 3, sc.12.

42 Marriage is honourable, as you say; and if so, wherefore should cuckoldom be a discredit, being derived from so honourable a root?
1700 *The Way of the World*, act 3, sc.12.

43 I confess I have deserted the high place I once held of sighing at your feet.
1700 *The Way of the World*, act 3, sc.12.

44 O, nothing is more alluring than a levee from a couch in some confusion.
1700 Lady Wishfort to Foible. *The Way of the World*, act 4, sc.1.

45 Don't let us be familiar or fond, nor kiss before folks, like my Lady Fadler and Sir Francis: nor go to Hyde-Park together the first Sunday in a new chariot, to provoke eyes and whispers, and then never be seen there together again; as if we were proud of one another the first week, and ashamed of one another ever after… Let us be very strange and well-bred: Let us be as strange as if we had been married a great while, and as well-bred as if we were not married at all.
1700 Millamant to Mirabell. *The Way of the World*, act 4, sc.5.

46 These articles subscribed, if I continue to endure you a little longer, I may by degrees dwindle into wife.
1700 Millamant to Mirabell. *The Way of the World*, act 4, sc.5.

47 I hope you do not think me prone to any iteration of nuptials.
1700 Lady Wishfort to Whitwell disguised as Sir Roland. *The Way of the World*, act 4, sc.12.

48 Music alone with sudden charms can bind
The wand'ring sense, and calm the troubled mind.
c.1701 'Hymn to Harmony'.

49 Would I were free from this restraint,
Or else had hopes to win her;
Would she could make of me a saint,
Or I of her a sinner.
'Pious Selinda Goes to Prayers'.

Conklin, Edwin G(rant) 1863–1952

Professor of Embryology at Princeton. He was a specialist in the embryology of marine organisms.

50 Wooden legs are not inherited but wooden heads may be.
Recalled on his death, 21 Nov 1952.

Connally, John Bowden 1917–93

US politician and lawyer. He was Governor of Texas (1963–9).

51 A chess tournament disguised as a circus.
1964 Of US political conventions. In the *National Observer*. Quoted in Edwin A Roberts Jr *Elections 1964* (1964).

52 It's not a sin to be rich anymore—it's a miracle.
1988 In *Time*, 18 Jan.

53 All hat and no cattle.
1989 Responding to George Bush's claim to be a Texan. In the *New York Times*, 14 Feb.

Connally, Tom (Thomas Terry) 1877–1963

US Congressman and lawyer. He was Representative for Texas (1917–29) and a Senator (1929–53). A Democrat, he supported southern business interests and opposed anti-lynching legislation. He was a strong supporter of the UN and NATO.

54 Don't you ever shake that lanky Yankee finger at me.
1963 To Senator Charles Tobey. Reported in *Time*, 8 Nov.

Connell, James 1852–1929

Irish socialist and songwriter.

55 The people's flag is deepest red;
It shrouded oft our martyred dead.
And ere their limbs grew stiff and cold,
Their heart's blood dyed its every fold.
Then raise the scarlet standard high!
Within its shade we'll live or die.
Tho' cowards flinch and traitors sneer,
We'll keep the red flag flying here.
1889 'The Red Flag', official anthem of the Labour Party.

Connery, Sir Sean 1930–

Scottish actor who became an international film star in the role of secret agent James Bond.

56 It is Scotland's rightful heritage that its people should create a modern Parliament… This entire issue is above and beyond any political party.
1997 Speech in Edinburgh. In the *Daily Record*, 8 Sep.

57 We have waited nearly 300 years. My hope is that it will evolve with dignity and integrity and it will truly reflect the new voice of Scotland. My position on Scotland has never changed in 30-odd years. Scotland should be nothing less than an equal of other nations in the world.
1999 On the Scottish Parliament. In the *Daily Telegraph*, 27 Apr.

Connolly, Billy 1942–

Scottish comedian and actor.

58 Marriage is a wonderful invention; but then again so is a bicycle repair kit.
Duncan Campbell *Billy Connolly* (1976).

59 I spent the whole time battering people I liked and singing with my arm round people I loathed.
Talking about his drinking days. Quoted in Pamela Stephenson *Billy* (2001).

60 I decided to stop drinking while it was still my idea.
Quoted in Pamela Stephenson *Billy* (2001).

61 For me, it's about the desire to win. My audience becomes a crowd of wild animals and I have to be the lion-tamer or be eaten.
Quoted in Pamela Stephenson *Billy* (2001).

Connolly, Cyril Vernon 1903–74

English author and journalist. He founded and edited the influential cultural journal *Horizon* (1939–50). His best-known books are *Enemies of Promise* (1938) and *The Unquiet Grave* (1944).

62 Better to write for yourself and have no public, than to write for the public and have no self.
1933 In the *New Statesman*, 25 Feb.

63 Destroy him as you will, the bourgeois always bounces up—execute him, expropriate him, starve him out *en masse*, and he reappears in your children.
1937 In the *Observer*, 7 Mar.

64 A great writer creates a world of his own and his readers are proud to live in it. A lesser writer may entice them in for a moment, but soon he will watch them filing out.
1938 *Enemies of Promise*, ch.1.

65 Literature is the art of writing something that will be read twice; journalism what will be read once.
1938 *Enemies of Promise*, ch.3.

66 As repressed sadists are supposed to become policemen or butchers, so those with an irrational fear of life become publishers.
1938 *Enemies of Promise*, ch.10.

67 I should like to see the custom introduced of readers who are pleased with a book sending the author some small cash token… Not more than a hundred pounds—that would be bad for my character—not less than half a crown—that would do no good to yours.
1938 *Enemies of Promise*, ch.13.

68 Whom the gods wish to destroy they first call promising.
1938 *Enemies of Promise*, ch.13.

69 There is no more sombre enemy of good art than the pram in the hall.
1938 *Enemies of Promise*, ch.14.

70 All charming people have something to conceal, usually their total dependence on the appreciation of others.
1938 *Enemies of Promise*, ch.16.

71 Humorists are not happy men. Like Beachcomber or Saki or Thurber they burn while Rome fiddles.
1938 *Enemies of Promise*, ch.16.

72 A private school has all the faults of a public school without any of its compensations.
1938 *Enemies of Promise*, ch.19.

73 I have called this style the Mandarin style… It is the style of those writers whose tendency is to make their language convey more than they mean or more than they feel, it is the style of most artists and all humbugs.
1938 *Enemies of Promise*, ch.20.

74 Were I to deduce any system from my feelings on leaving Eton, it might be called *The Theory of Permanent Adolescence*.
1938 *Enemies of Promise*, ch.24.

75 The more books we read, the sooner we perceive that the only function of a writer is to produce a masterpiece. No other task is of any consequence.
1944 *The Unquiet Grave*, pt.1.

76 There is no fury like an ex-wife looking for a new lover.
1944 *The Unquiet Grave*, pt.1.

77 In the sex war thoughtlessness is the weapon of the male, vindictiveness of the female.
1944 *The Unquiet Grave*, pt.1.

78 Life is a maze in which we take the wrong turning before we have learnt to walk.
1944 *The Unquiet Grave*, pt.1.

79 Everything is a dangerous drug to me except reality, which is unendurable.
1944 *The Unquiet Grave*, pt.1.

80 The civilization of one epoch becomes the manure of the next.
1944 *The Unquiet Grave*, pt.2.

81 The disasters of the world are due to its inhabitants not being able to grow old simultaneously.
1944 *The Unquiet Grave*, pt.2.

82 Imprisoned in every fat man a thin one is wildly signalling to be let out.
1944 *The Unquiet Grave*, pt.2.

83 The true index of a man's character is the health of his wife.
1944 *The Unquiet Grave*, pt.2.

84 We are all serving a life-sentence in the dungeon of self.
1944 *The Unquiet Grave*, pt.2.

85 Our memories are card-indexes consulted, and then put back in disorder by authorities whom we do not control.
1944 *The Unquiet Grave*, pt.2.

86 It is closing time in the gardens of the West and from now on an artist will be judged only by the resonance of his solitude or the quality of his despair.
1949 *Horizon*, no.120–1, Dec 1949– Jan 1950 (double issue, the final issue of the journal).

87 A romantic interest in our own sex, not necessarily carried as far as physical experiments, was the intellectual fashion.
Of Oxford during his student days. Quoted in Peter Quennell *The Marble Foot* (1977).

Connolly, James 1868–1916

Irish Labour leader and insurgent. He organized the Irish Socialist Republican party and founded *The Workers' Republic*, the first Irish socialist paper. He lectured in the US and organized strikes in Ireland, and was executed for his part in the 1916 Easter rebellion.

88 It is an axiom enforced by all the experience of the ages, that they who rule industrially will rule politically.
1909 *Socialism Made Easy*.

89 Don't be 'practical' in politics. To be practical in that sense means that you have schooled yourself to think along the lines, and in the grooves that those who rob you would desire you to think.
1909 *Socialism Made Easy*.

90 The day has passed for patching up the capitalist system; it must go. And in the work of abolishing it the Catholic and the Protestant, the Catholic and the Jew, the Catholic and the Freethinker, the Catholic and the Buddhist, the Catholic and the Mahometan will co-

operate together... For, as we have said elsewhere, Socialism is neither Protestant nor Catholic, Christian nor Freethinker, Buddhist, Mahometan, nor Jew; it is only HUMAN.
1910 *Labour, Nationality, and Religion.*

91 The worker is the slave of capitalist society, the female worker is the slave of that slave.
1915 *The Re-conquest of Ireland.*

Connor, Sir William Neil *pseudonym* ***Cassandra***
1909–67

English journalist, a columnist with the *Daily Mirror* from 1935 until his death.

92 As I was saying when I was interrupted, it is a powerful hard thing to please all of the people all of the time.
1946 On resuming his Cassandra column in the *Daily Mirror*, Sep, after the end of World War II.

Conrad, Joseph *originally* ***Jozef Teodor Konrad Nalecz Korzeniowski*** 1857–1924

Polish-born British novelist who joined an English merchant ship in 1878, and was naturalized in 1884 as a master mariner. The sea provided the background for much of his work, notably *Heart of Darkness* (1899) and *Lord Jim* (1900).

93 It is only those who do nothing that make no mistakes, I suppose.
1896 *An Outcast of the Islands*, pt.3, ch.2.

94 Any work that aspires, however humbly, to the condition of art should carry its justification in every line.
1897 *The Nigger of the Narcissus*, preface.

95 My task which I am trying to achieve is, by the power of the written word to make you hear, to make you feel—it is, before all, to make you see. That—and no more, and it is everything.
1897 *The Nigger of the Narcissus*, preface.

96 The conquest of the earth, which mostly means the taking it away from those who have a different complexion or slightly flatter noses than ourselves, is not a pretty thing when you look into it too much. What redeems it is an idea only.
1899 *Heart of Darkness*, pt.1 (first published in *Blackwood's Magazine*, collected in *Youth: A Narrative, and Two Other Stories*, 1902).

97 We live, as we dream—alone.
1899 *Heart of Darkness*, pt.1 (first published in *Blackwood's Magazine*, collected in *Youth: A Narrative, and Two Other Stories*, 1902).

98 Exterminate all the brutes!
1899 *Heart of Darkness*, pt.2 (first published in *Blackwood's Magazine*, collected in *Youth: A Narrative, and Two Other Stories*, 1902).

99 He cried in a whisper at some image, at some vision—he cried out twice, a cry that was no more than a breath: 'The horror! The horror!'
1899 Kurtz's final words. *Heart of Darkness*, pt.3 (first published in *Blackwood's Magazine*, collected in *Youth: A Narrative, and Two Other Stories*, 1902).

1 Mistah Kurtz—he dead.
1899 *Heart of Darkness*, pt.3 (first published in *Blackwood's Magazine*, collected in *Youth: A Narrative, and Two Other Stories*, 1902).

2 A man that is born falls into a dream like a man who falls into the sea... The way is to the destructive element submit yourself, and with the exertions of your hands and feet in the water make the deep, deep sea keep you up.
1900 *Lord Jim*, ch.20.

3 You shall judge a man by his foes as well as by his friends.
1900 *Lord Jim*, ch.34.

4 Suddenly a puff of wind, a puff faint and tepid and laden with strange odours of blossoms, of aromatic wood, comes out of the still night—the first sigh of the east on my face.
1902 'Youth'.

5 The mysterious East, perfumed like a flower, silent like death, dark like a grave.
1902 'Youth'.

6 I remember my youth and the feeling that it will never come back any more—the feeling that I could last for ever, outlast the sea, the earth, and all men; the deceitful feeling that lures us on to joys, to perils, to love, to vain effort—to death; the triumphant conviction of strength, the heat of life in the handful of dust, the glow in the heart that with every year grows dim, grows cold, grows small, and expires—and expires, too soon, too soon—before life itself.
1902 'Youth'.

7 Action is consolatory. It is the enemy of thought and the friend of flattering illusions.
1904 *Nostromo*, pt.1, ch.6.

8 Liberty of the imagination should be the most precious possession of a novelist.
1905 'Books'.

9 To be hopeful in an artistic sense it is not necessary to think that the world is good. It is enough to believe that there is no impossibility of it being made so.
1905 'Books'.

10 Of all the inanimate objects, of all men's creations, books are the nearest to us, for they contain our very thoughts, our ambitions, our indignations, our illusions, our fidelity to truth, and our persistent leaning towards error. But most of all they resemble us in their precarious hold on life.
1905 'Books'.

11 The terrorist and the policeman both come from the same basket.
1907 *The Secret Agent*, ch.4.

12 Some kind of moral discovery should be the object of every tale.
1911 *Under Western Eyes*, prologue.

13 Words, as is well known, are the great foes of reality.
1911 *Under Western Eyes*, prologue.

14 The scrupulous and the just, the noble, humane, and devoted natures; the unselfish and the intelligent may begin a movement—but it passes away from them. They are not the leaders of a revolution. They are its victims.
1911 *Under Western Eyes*, pt.2, ch.3.

15 A belief in a supernatural source of evil is not necessary; men alone are quite capable of every wickedness.
1911 *Under Western Eyes*, pt.2, ch.4.

16 All ambitions are lawful except those which climb upwards on the miseries or credulities of mankind.
1912 *Some Reminiscences*, preface.

17 On the contrary, the mere fact of dealing with matters outside the general run of everyday experience laid me under the obligation of a more scrupulous fidelity to the truth of my own sensations. The problem was to make unfamiliar things credible.
1915 *Within the Tides*, preface.

18 Thinking is the great enemy of perfection. The habit of profound reflection, I am compelled to say, is the most pernicious of all the habits formed by civilized man.
1915 *Victory*, author's note.

19 It is not the clear-sighted who rule the world. Great achievements are accomplished in a blessed, warm fog.
1915 *Victory*, author's note.

20 It was amazing to think that in those miles of human habitations there was not probably half a dozen pounds of nails.
1917 Of Bangkok. *The Shadow-Line*.

21 In plucking the fruit of memory one runs the risk of spoiling its bloom.
1920 *The Arrow of Gold*, author's note.

Conran, Shirley Ida *née* *Pearce* 1932–

English designer, fashion editor and author, first wife of the designer and businessman Sir Terence Conran. Her books include *Superwoman* (1975) and *Lace* (1982).

22 Our motto: Life is too short to stuff a mushroom.
1975 *Superwoman*, epigraph.

Conroy, (Donald) Pat(rick) 1945–

US writer. His works include *The Prince of Tides* (1986) and *Beach Music* (1997).

23 It was like walking down the street with the Statue of Liberty.
1995 On walking in Manhattan with the instantly recognizable Barbra Streisand. In *WAMU*, 4 Sep.

Constable, John 1776–1837

English landscape painter. With Turner, one of Britain's most important and best-loved landscape painters.

24 A gentleman's park is my aversion. It is not beauty because it is not nature.
1822 In R B Beckett (ed) *Constable's Correspondence*, Suffolk Records Society (1962–70).

25 In Claude's landscape all is lovely—all amiable—all is amenity and repose; the calm sunshine of the heart.
1836 Lecture, 2 Jun. Quoted in C R Leslie *Memoirs of the Life of John Constable* (1843).

26 When I set down to make a sketch from nature, the first thing I try to do is to forget that I have ever seen a picture.
Quoted in C R Leslie *Memoirs of the Life of John Constable* (1843).

27 There is nothing ugly; *I never saw an ugly thing in my life*: for let the form of an object be what it may—light, shade and perspective will always make it beautiful.
Quoted in C R Leslie *Memoirs of the Life of John Constable* (1843).

28 He seems to paint with tinted steam.
Of Turner. Quoted in *Treasures of the Fitzwilliam Museum* (1982).

Constant (de Rebecque), (Henri) Benjamin 1767–1830

French novelist and politician. He supported the Revolution in Paris (1795) and was banished (1802) for opposing Napoleon. On his return in 1814 he became leader of the liberal opposition. His best-known novel *Adolphe* (1816) is based on his relationship with Mme de Staël.

29 *L'art pour l'art, sans but, car tout but dénature l'art. Mais l'art atteint au but qu'il n'a pas.*
Art for art's sake, with no purpose, for any purpose perverts art. But art achieves a purpose which is not its own.
1804 *Journal intime*, 11 Feb, quoted in the *Revue Internationale*, 10 Jan 1887.

Constantine *full name* ***Flavius Valerius Aurelius Constantinus*** c.274–337 AD

Roman Emperor, who adopted Christianity c.312 AD. He founded a royal residence at Byzantium (Constantinople), an act of great historical importance.

30 *In hoc signo vinces.*
In this sign thou shalt conquer.
AD 312 'Constantine's Vision', quoted in Eusebius *Life of Constantine*.

Cook, Arthur James 1883–1931

Welsh miners' leader, General Secretary of the national union and a key figure in the General Strike of 1926.

31 Not a penny off the pay; not a second on the day.
1926 Miners' strike slogan, coined in a speech, 3 Apr. It is often rendered 'not a minute on the day'.

Cook, Captain James 1728–79

English navigator. He undertook expeditions to the Pacific, the Antarctic and the west coast of North America, charting all these regions. He was killed in Hawaii by local people as he landed to recover a stolen boat.

32 As to a Southern Continent, I do not believe any such thing exists, unless in a high altitude.
1768–71 *Captain Cook's Journal during his First Voyage Round the World made in H. M. Bark 'Endeavour'.*

33 Curse the scientists, and all science into the bargain.
Quoted in J C Beaglehole (ed) *The Voyage of the Resolution* (1961).

Cook, Peter 1937–94

English comedian. He appeared in revue at Cambridge University and went on to write and star in the revue *Beyond the Fringe* (1960).

34 We exchanged many frank words in our respective languages.
1961 Impersonation of Harold Macmillan. *Beyond the Fringe*.

35 I go to the theatre to be entertained. I don't want to see plays about rape, sodomy and drug addiction—I can get all that at home.
Comedy routine. Also used as a cartoon caption in the *Observer*, 8 Jul 1962.

Cook, Robin *originally* ***Robert Finlayson Cook*** 1946–

Scottish Labour politician. In 2001 he became Leader of the House of Commons, a position he resigned in 2003 over the war with Iraq.

36 Chicken masala is now Britain's true national dish, not only because it is the most popular, but because it is a

perfect illustration of the way Britain absorbs and adapts external influences.
2001 Speech to the Social Market Foundation, London, 19 Apr.

37 Iraq probably has no weapons of mass destruction in the commonly understood sense of the term—namely a credible device capable of being delivered against a strategic city target.
2003 Speech to the House of Commons, following his resignation as Leader of the House, 17 Mar.

38 What has come to trouble me most over past weeks is the suspicion that if the hanging chads in Florida had gone the other way and Al Gore had been elected, we would not now be about to commit British troops.
2003 Speech to the House of Commons, following his resignation as Leader of the House, 17 Mar.

Cooke, (Alfred) Alistair 1908–2004

English-born US journalist and broadcaster, best known for his 'Letter from America', first broadcast by the BBC in 1946, which became the world's longest-running radio series with the same presenter. He retired shortly before his death.

39 All Presidents start out pretending to run a crusade, but after a couple of years they find they are running something much less heroic, much more intractable: namely, the Presidency.
1963 In *The Listener*.

40 An episode out of George Orwell rewritten by Charles Dickens.
1979 Of Gerald R Ford's succession to the US presidency on Richard M Nixon's resignation. *The Americans*.

41 Like a christening, a wedding, a graduation ceremony, a holy war, a revolution even…a fireworks display, a gaudy promise of what life ought to be, not life itself.
1979 Of elections. *The Americans*.

42 But after all it's not the winning that matters, is it? Or is it? It's—to coin a word—the amenities that count: the smell of the dandelions, the puff of the pipe, the click of the bat, the rain on the neck, the chill down the spine, the slow, exquisite coming on of sunset and dinner and rheumatism.
Quoted in Helen Exley *Cricket Quotations* (1992).

43 Canned music is like audible wallpaper.
Quoted in David Pickering *Brewer's Twentieth Century Music* (1994).

Coolidge, (John) Calvin 1872–1933

US Republican politician and 30th President (1923–9). A strong supporter of US business interests, he was re-elected in 1924 but refused renomination in 1928.

44 Civilization and profits go hand in hand.
1920 Speech, New York, 27 Nov.

45 There is no right to strike against the public safety by anybody, anywhere, at any time.
1919 Telegram to the President of the American Federation of Labor, while Coolidge was Governor of Massachusetts during the Boston police strike.

46 The chief business of the American people is business.
1925 Speech to the Society of Newspaper Editors, Washington, 17 Jan.

47 Prosperity is only an instrument to be used, not a deity to be worshipped.
1928 Speech, Boston, 11 Jun.

48 Perhaps one of the most important accomplishments of my Administration has been minding my own business.
1929 Press conference, Mar.

49 Patriotism is easy to understand in America. It means looking out for yourself while looking out for your country.
Attributed.

Cooper, Dame Gladys 1888–1971

English actress. She made her stage debut in 1905 and subsequently achieved stardom with her performance in Pinero's *The Second Mrs Tanqueray* (1922).

50 If this is what virus pneumonia does to one, I really don't think I shall bother to have it again.
1971 Last words.

Cooper, James Fenimore 1789–1851

US writer, a prolific novelist and essayist. He is now chiefly remembered for his 5-volume *Leatherstocking Tales*, which includes *The Last of the Mohicans* (1826).

51 The tendency of democracies is, in all things, to mediocrity.
1838 *The American Democrat*, 'On the Disadvantages of Democracy'.

52 Equality of condition is incompatible with civilization, and is found only to exist in those communities that are but slightly removed from the savage state. In practice, it can only mean a common misery.
1838 *The American Democrat*, 'On the Disadvantages of a Monarchy'.

53 Individuality is the aim of political liberty.
1838 *The American Democrat*, 'Individuality'.

54 It is a misfortune that necessity has induced men to accord greater license to this formidable engine, in order to obtain liberty, than can be borne with less important objects in view; for the press, like fire, is an excellent servant, but a terrible master.
1838 *The American Democrat*, 'On the Press'.

Cooper, William *pseudonym of* *Harry Summerfield Hoff* 1910–2002

English novelist. A barbed and witty satirist, he was a forerunner of the 'angry young man' school of the 1950s.

55 I would gladly have thrashed her for it. Unfortunately, thrashing your young woman doesn't make her admire you more as a novelist.
1950 *Scenes from Provincial Life*, pt.3, ch.1.

56 If girls aren't ignorant, they're cultured… You can't avoid suffering.
1950 *Scenes from Provincial Life*, pt.3, ch.2.

57 The trouble about finding a husband for one's mistress, is that no other man seems quite good enough.
1950 *Scenes from Provincial Life*, pt.3, ch.5.

Coover, Robert Lowell 1932–

US novelist, short-story writer and playwright, best known for his experimental stories.

58 The narrative impulse is always with us; we couldn't imagine ourselves through a day without it.
1986 In *Time Out*, 7 May.

Cope, Wendy 1945–

English poet. Her collections include *Making Cocoa for Kingsley Amis* (1986) and *If I Don't Know* (2001).

59 I used to think all poets were Byronic—
Mad, bad and dangerous to know.
And then I met a few.
1986 'Triolet'.
► *See Lamb 486:25.*

60 There are so many kinds of awful men—
One can't avoid them all. She often said
She'd never make the same mistake again:
She always made a new mistake instead.
1986 'Rondeau Redoublé'.

61 Bloody men are like bloody buses—
You wait for about a year
And as soon as one approaches your stop
Two or three others appear.
1992 *Serious Concerns*, 'Bloody Men', stanza 1.

62 My heart has made its mind up
And I'm afraid it's you.
1992 *Serious Concerns*, 'Valentine'.

63 Some socks are loners
They can't live in pairs.
2001 *If I Don't Know*, 'The Sorrow of Socks'.

64 Never trust a journalist.
2001 *If I Don't Know*, 'How to Deal with the Press'.

Copland, Aaron 1900–90

US composer. His early works employed jazz idioms, and he later drew on US folk tradition, as in the ballets *Billy the Kid* (1938) and *Appalachian Spring* (1944). He also composed film scores, operas and symphonies.

65 The whole problem can be stated quite simply by asking, 'Is there a meaning to music?' My answer would be, 'Yes'. And 'Can you state in so many words what the meaning is?' My answer to that would be 'No'.
1939 *What to Listen for in Music*.

66 The difference between Beethoven and Mahler is the difference between watching a great man walk down the street and watching a great actor act the part of a great man walking down the street.
Quoted in the *Wall Street Journal*, 9 Jun 1995.

Coppola, Francis Ford 1939–

US film director, screenwriter and producer. Among his films are *The Godfather* (1972; Part II 1974; Part III, 1990) and his controversial study of the Vietnam War, *Apocalypse Now* (1979).

67 When you start you want to make the greatest film in the world, but when you get into it, you just want to get it done, let it be passable and not embarrassing.
Quoted in Michael Schumacher *Francis Ford Coppola: A Film-Maker's Life* (1999).

Cornford, Frances *née* ***Darwin*** 1886–1960

English poet, the granddaughter of Charles Darwin. She lived most of her life in Cambridge, and her poetry deals with the minute details of emotion.

68 A young Apollo, golden-haired,
Stands dreaming on the verge of strife,
Magnificently unprepared
For the long littleness of life.
1910 Of Rupert Brooke. 'Youth'.

69 O fat white woman whom nobody loves,
Why do you walk through the fields in gloves,
When the grass is soft as the breast of doves
And shivering-sweet to the touch?
Oh why do you walk through the fields in gloves,
Missing so much and so much?
1910 'To a Fat Lady Seen from a Train'.
► *See Chesterton 213:99.*

70 Now we know nothing, nothing is richer now
Because of all he was. O friend we have loved
Must it be thus with you?—and if it must be
How can men bear laboriously to live?
1915 'Rupert Brooke'.

71 I hope to meet my Maker brow to brow
And find my own the higher.
1954 'Epitaph for a Reviewer'.

Cornforth, Sir John Warcup 1917–

Australian organic chemist. Despite being totally deaf from childhood, he pioneered the study of enzyme stereochemistry and was awarded the Nobel prize for chemistry in 1975.

72 In a world where it is so easy to neglect, deny, pervert and suppress the truth, the scientist may find his discipline severe. For him, truth is so seldom the sudden light that shows new order and beauty; more often, truth is the uncharted rock that sinks his ship in the dark.
1975 Nobel prize speech.

Corwin, Thomas 1794–1865

US politician, Governor of Ohio (1840–2), Senator (1845–50) and Secretary of the Treasury (1850–3) under President Fillmore.

73 If I were a Mexican, I would tell you, 'Have you not enough room in your own country to bury your dead men? If you come into mine, we will greet you with bloody hands and hospitable graves.'
1846 Speech to the Senate against the American–Mexican War, 11 Feb.

Cory, William *originally* ***William Johnson*** 1823–92

English academic, translator and poet. He was assistant master at Eton (1845–72), when he wrote the 'Eton Boat Song', but he resigned over controversy about his friendships with pupils. He also tutored Mary Coleridge (1861–1907).

74 They told me, Heraclitus, they told me you were dead,
They brought bitter news to hear, and bitter tears to shed.
I wept as I remembered how often you and I
Had tired the sun with talking and sent him down the sky.
1858 *Ionica, Poems*, 'Heraclitus', his translation of an epigram by Callimachus.

75 A handful of grey ashes, long long ago at rest.
1858 *Ionica, Poems*, 'Heraclitus', his translation of an epigram by Callimachus.

76 You promise heavens free from strife,
Pure truth, and perfect change of will;
But sweet, sweet is this human life,
So sweet, I fain would breathe it still;
Your chilly stars I can forgo,

This warm kind world is all I know.
1858 *Ionica, Poems*, 'Mimnermus in Church'.

77 All beauteous things for which we live
By laws of space and time decay.
But Oh, the very reason why
I clasp them, is because they die.
1858 *Ionica, Poems*, 'Mimnermus in Church'.

78 Jolly boating weather
And a hay-harvest breeze,
Blade on the feather,
Shade off the trees;
Swing, swing together,
With your body between your knees.
1865 'Eton Boat Song'.

Coryate, Thomas c.1577–1617

English traveller and wit. In 1608 he set out on a journey on foot through central Europe, later travelling east as far as India. In 1611 he published *Coryat's Crudities Hastily Gobled Up in Five Moneths' Travells*.

79 Of all the pleasures in the world, travel is (in my opinion) the sweetest and most delightful.
1611 *Coryat's Crudities Hastily Gobled Up in Five Moneths' Travells*.

Costello, Elvis *real name* ***Declan Patrick McManus*** 1954–

English singer-songwriter and composer.

80 It would be like comparing blancmange and mustard gas.
2002 Asked how he would compare Tony Blair and Margaret Thatcher. Quoted on www.independent.co.uk.

81 There is something kind of absurd about people who live in such a comfortable, cushioned, spoiled society tattooing themselves and piercing themselves to make them appear tribal.
2002 In *Interview Magazine*, May.

82 Some music that I don't take to in modern orchestral stuff just seems to be trying to do something with an orchestra that Jimi Hendrix could do so much better with an electric guitar and a fuzzbox. Why create a hideous sound with violas when they were made to sound melodious and agreeable?
2002 In *The Irish Times*, 23 Mar.

83 The songs weren't theirs any more. They were everybody's.
2004 On why the Beatles stopped performing. *Rolling Stone*, 15 Apr.

Cotman, John Sell 1782–1842

English landscape painter and etcher, best known for his work in watercolour.

84 Three quarters of mankind, you know, mind more what is represented than how it is done.
Quoted in William Vaughn *Romantic Art* (1978).

Coubertin, Pierre de, Baron 1863–1937

French educationalist. He revived the Olympic Games at Athens in 1896, in the hope that they would foster national and international understanding through sport.

85 Women have but one task, that of crowning the winner with garlands.
1902 Quoted in Colin Jarman *The Guinness Dictionary of Sports Quotations* (1990).

86 The most important thing in the Olympic games is not winning but taking part—just as the most important thing in life is not the triumph but the struggle. The essential thing in life is not conquering but fighting well.
1908 Speech to Olympic Games officials, London, 24 Jul.

Coué, Émile 1857–1926

French pharmacist, pioneer of 'auto-suggestion'. He opened a free clinic in Nancy in 1910 and 'Couéism' subsequently attracted followers all round the world.

87 *Tous les jours, à tous points de vue, je vais de mieux en mieux.*
Every day, in every way, I am getting better and better.
1915 *De la suggestion et de ses applications*. Maxim recommended by Coué to his patients, to be repeated several times over on rising and on going to bed.

Coupland, Douglas 1961–

Canadian novelist. His *Generation X: Tales for an Accelerated Culture* (1991) was a cult novel defining the angst of the children of the baby boomers.

88 Generation X.
1991 From the title of his satiric novel *Generation X: Tales for an Accelerated Culture*. The phrase refers to young people born in the mid-1960s who are in no hurry to 'find themselves'.

89 MCJOB: A low-pay, low-prestige, low-dignity, no-future job in the service sector. Frequently considered a satisfying career choice for people who have never held one.
1991 *Generation X*, 'The Sun Is Your Enemy'.

90 HISTORICAL OVERDOSING: To live in a period of time when too much seems to happen.
1991 *Generation X*, 'The Sun Is Your Enemy'.

91 HISTORICAL SLUMMING: the act of visiting locations such as diners, smokestack industrial sites, rural villages—locations where time appears to have been frozen many years back—so as to experience relief when one returns back to 'the present'.
1991 *Generation X*, 'Our Parents Had More'.

92 BRAZILIFICATION: The widening gulf between the rich and the poor and the accompanying disappearance of the middle classes.
1991 *Generation X*, 'Our Parents Had More'.

93 CONSENSUS TERRORISM: The process that decides in-office attitudes and behavior.
1991 *Generation X*, 'Quit Recycling the Past'.

94 Marketing is essentially about feeding the poop back to diners fast enough to make them think they're still getting real food.
1991 *Generation X*, 'Quit Your Job'.

95 Shopping is Not Creating.
1991 *Generation X*, chapter heading.

96 Their talk was endless, compulsive, and indulgent, sometimes sounding like the remains of the English language after having been hashed over by nuclear war survivors for a few hundred years.
1991 *Generation X*, 'It Can't Last'.

97 I want to tell them that I envy their upbringings that were so clean, so free of *futurelessness*. And I want to throttle

them for blithely handing over the world to us like so much skid-marked underwear.
1991 Claire speaking of her parents. *Generation X*, 'Eat Your Parents'.

98 BRADYISM: A multisibling sensibility derived from having grown up in large families…symptoms of *Bradyism* include a facility for mind games, emotional withdrawal in situations of overcrowding, and a deeply felt need for a well-defined personal space.
1991 *Generation X*, 'Define Normal'.

99 STRANGELOVE REPRODUCTION: Having children to make up for the fact that one no longer believes in the future.
1991 *Generation X*, 'Define Normal'.

1 PERSONALITY TITHE: A price paid for becoming a couple; previously amusing human beings become boring: *'Thanks for inviting us, but Noreen and I are going to look at flatware catalogs tonight. Afterward we're going to watch the shopping channel.'*
1991 *Generation X*, 'M T V Not Bullets'.

2 NOSTALGIA IS A WEAPON
1991 *Generation X*, 'Welcome Home from Vietnam, Son'.

Cousins, Norman 1915–90

US editor and activist. As director of the *Saturday Review* (1942–71, 1973–7), he broadened its scope and circulation, campaigning on issues such as nuclear disarmament. His works include *Who Speaks for Man?* (1953).

3 The poet reminds men of their uniqueness and it is not necessary to possess the ultimate definition of this uniqueness. Even to speculate is a gain.
1978 In the *Saturday Review*, 15 Apr.

4 President Nixon's motto was, if two wrongs don't make a right, try three.
1979 In the *Daily Telegraph*, 17 Jul.

Cousteau, Jacques Yves 1910–97

French underwater explorer, who helped develop the Aqua-Lung (1943) and later became famous for a series of documentaries about the world's oceans.

5 The sea is the universal sewer.
1971 Testimony before the House Committee on Science and Astronautics, 28 Jan.

Coventry, Thomas, 1st Baron 1578–1640

English judge.

6 The dominion of the sea, as it is an ancient and undoubted right of the crown of England, so it is the best security of the land… The wooden walls are the best walls of this kingdom.
1635 Speech to the Star Chamber, 17 Jun. 'Wooden walls' refers to ships.

Coward, Sir Noël Peirce 1899–1973

English playwright, actor, director, composer and singer. His witty, stylish and sometimes biting plays include *Hay Fever* (1925), *Private Lives* (1930), *Blithe Spirit* (1941) and *Present Laughter* (1943). His films include the Academy Award-winning *In Which We Serve* (1941).

7 Poor Little Rich Girl.
1925 Title of song.

8 There's sand in the porridge and sand in the bed,
And if this is pleasure we'd rather be dead.
1928 'The English Lido' (song).

9 I believe that since my life began
The most I've had is just
A talent to amuse.
Heigho, if love were all!
1929 'If Love Were All'.

10 Very flat, Norfolk.
1930 *Private Lives*, act 1.

11 Extraordinary how potent cheap music is.
1930 *Private Lives*, act 1.

12 Certain women should be struck regularly, like gongs.
1930 *Private Lives*, act 3.

13 Mad dogs and Englishmen
Go out in the midday sun.
1931 'Mad Dogs and Englishmen' (song).

14 In the Philippines, there are lovely screens
To protect you from the glare.
1931 'Mad Dogs and Englishmen' (song).

15 Mad about the boy,
It's pretty funny but I'm mad about the boy.
He has a gay appeal
That makes me feel
There may be something sad about the boy.
1932 'Mad About the Boy' (song).

16 People are wrong when they say the opera isn't what it used to be. It is what it used to be. That's what's wrong with it.
1933 *Design for Living*.

17 Don't put your daughter on the stage, Mrs Worthington,
Don't put your daughter on the stage.
1935 'Mrs Worthington' (song).

18 The stately homes of England,
How beautiful they stand,
To prove the upper classes
Have still the upper hand.
1938 'The Stately Homes of England' (song).

19 Dear Mrs A,
Hooray, hooray,
At last you are deflowered.
On this as every other day
I love you—Noël Coward.
1940 Telegram sent to Gertrude Lawrence the day after her marriage, quoted in Gertrude Lawrence *A Star Danced* (1945).

20 It's discouraging to think how many people are shocked by honesty and how few by deceit.
1941 *Blithe Spirit*.

21 Don't Let's Be Beastly to the Germans.
1943 Song title.

22 Speak clearly, don't bump into people, and if you must have motivation think of your pay packet on Friday.
1962 Speech, Gallery First-Nighters' Club, sharing his advice to young actors. On other occasions he repeated it in the form 'Just say your lines and don't trip over the furniture'.

23 I never realised before that Albert married beneath him.
c.1964 Quoted in Kenneth Tynan *Tynan on Theatre* (1964), alluding to the performance of a particular actress in the role of Queen Victoria.

24 Squash—that's not exercise, it's flagellation.

Quoted in Colin Jarman *The Guinness Dictionary of Sports Quotations* (1990).

25 I love criticism just so long as it's unqualified praise.
Attributed.

26 Two things should have been cut. The second act and that youngster's throat.
After watching a play featuring a 14-year-old child star (sometimes identified as Bonnie Langford). Attributed.

27 He must have been a marvellously good shot.
On hearing that an impresario he disliked had blown his brains out. Attributed.

28 I'm not very keen on Hollywood. I'd rather have a nice cup of cocoa really.
Attributed.

Cowley, Abraham 1618–67

English poet, essayist and Royalist. He served Queen Henrietta Maria in exile during the Civil War, and only returned to England permanently at the Restoration. His works include a lyric collection, *Poetical Blossomes* (1633), and the epic *Davideis* (1656).

29 The world's a scene of changes, and to be
Constant, in Nature were inconstancy.
1647 *The Mistress*, 'Inconstancy'.

30 Such were the numbers which could call
The stones into the Theban wall.
Such miracles are ceased, and now we see
No towns or houses raised by poetry.
1656 *Poems*, 'Ode: Of Wit'.

31 Ye fields of Cambridge, our dear Cambridge, say,
Have ye not seen us walking every day?
Was there a tree about which did not know
The love betwixt us two?
1656 'On the Death of Mr William Harvey'.

32 Life is an incurable disease.
1656 'To Dr Scarborough', stanza 6.

33 Fill all the glasses there, for why
Should every creature drink but I,
Why, man of morals, tell me why?
1656 'Drinking'.

34 God the first garden made, and the first city Cain.
1668 *Essays, in Verse and Prose*, 'The Garden'.

35 This only grant me, that my means may lie
Too low for envy, for contempt too high.
1668 *Essays, in Verse and Prose*, 'Of Myself'.

Cowley, Hannah 1743–1809

English playwright and poet, an early exponent of the comedy of manners. She also wrote long narrative verses (1780–94).

36 But what is woman?—only one of Nature's agreeable blunders.
1779 *Who's the Dupe?*, act 2.

37 Five minutes! Zounds! I have been five minutes too late all my life-time!
1780 *The Belle's Stratagem*, act 1, sc.1.

Cowley, Malcolm 1898–1989

US writer and critic, known for his studies of US expatriate writers in the 1920s and for his works on William Faulkner.

38 A new generation does not appear every 30 years. It appears when writers of the same age join in a common revolt against the fathers and when, in the process of adopting a new life style, they find their own models and spokesmen.
Quoted in the *New York Times*, 29 Mar 1989.

39 I…chopped the manuscript down to size, or sawed it into fireplace lengths.
Quoted in the *New York Times*, 29 Mar 1989.

40 Going back to Hemingway's work after several years is like going back to a brook where you had often fished and finding the woods as deep and cool as they used to be.
Quoted in Pete Hamill *A Drinking Life* (1994).

Cowper, William 1731–1800

English poet, whose work reflects the evangelical revival. Regarded as a precursor of Wordsworth, he wrote *The Task* (1785), a long rural poem, and a collection of moral satires, *Poems* (1782).

41 Damned below Judas; more abhorred than he was.
c.1774 Of himself. 'Hatred and Vengeance, my eternal portion'.

42 O make this heart rejoice or ache;
Decide this doubt for me;
And if it be not broken, break—
And heal it if it be.
1779 *Olney Hymns*, 'The Contrite Heart'.

43 God moves in a mysterious way
His wonders to perform;
He plants his footsteps in the sea,
And rides upon the storm.
1779 *Olney Hymns*, 'Light Shining out of Darkness'.

44 Blind unbelief is sure to err,
And scan his work in vain;
God is his own interpreter,
And he will make it plain.
1779 *Olney Hymns*, 'Light Shining out of Darkness'.

45 Behind a frowning providence
He hides a smiling face.
1779 *Olney Hymns*, 'Light Shining out of Darkness'.

46 Oh! for a closer walk with God,
A calm and heav'nly frame;
A light to shine upon the road
That leads me to the Lamb!
1779 *Olney Hymns*, 'Walking with God'.

47 A tale should be judicious, clear, succinct;
The language plain, and incidents well linked;
Tell not as new what ev'ry body knows,
And new or old, still hasten to a close.
1782 *Poems*, 'Conversation', l.235–8.

48 The pipe with solemn interposing puff,
Makes half a sentence at a time enough;
The dozing sages drop the drowsy strain,
Then pause, and puff—and speak, and pause again.
1782 *Poems*, 'Conversation', l.245–8.

49 His wit invites you by his looks to come,
But when you knock it never is at home.
1782 *Poems* 'Conversation', l.303–4.

50 The discumbered Atlas of the state.
1782 *Poems*, 'Retirement'.

51 He likes the country, but in truth must own,

Most likes it, when he studies it in town.
1782 *Poems*,'Retirement'.

52 Religion Caesar never knew
Thy posterity shall sway,
Where his eagles never flew,
None as invincible as they.
1782 *Poems*,'Boadicea: an Ode'.

53 Rome shall perish—write that word
In the blood that she has spilt.
1782 *Poems*,'Boadicea: an Ode'.

54 I am monarch of all I survey,
My right there is none to dispute;
From the centre all round to the sea,
I am lord of the fowl and the brute.
O Solitude! where are the charms
That sages have seen in thy face?
Better dwell in the midst of alarms,
Than reign in this horrible place.
1782 *Poems*,'Verses Supposed to be Written by Alexander Selkirk, During His Solitary Abode in the Island of Juan Fernandez'.

55 I am out of humanity's reach.
1782 *Poems*,'Verses Supposed to be Written by Alexander Selkirk, During His Solitary Abode in the Island of Juan Fernandez'.

56 When I think of my own native land,
In a moment I seem to be there;
But alas! recollection at hand
Soon hurries me back to despair.
1782 *Poems*,'Verses Supposed to be Written by Alexander Selkirk, During His Solitary Abode in the Island of Juan Fernandez'.

57 Grief is itself a med'cine.
1782 *Poems*,'Charity', l.159.

58 He found it inconvenient to be poor.
1782 *Poems*,'Charity', l.189.

59 Spare the poet for his subject's sake.
1782 *Poems*,'Charity', l.636.

60 The man that hails you Tom or Jack,
And proves by thumps upon your back
How he esteems your merit,
Is such a friend, that one had need
Be very much his friend indeed
To pardon or to bear it.
1782 *Poems*,'Friendship', l.169–74.

61 Remorse, the fatal egg by pleasure laid.
1782 *Poems*,'The Progress of Error', l.239.

62 As creeping ivy clings to wood or stone,
And hides the ruin that it feeds upon,
So sophistry, cleaves close to, and protects
Sin's rotten trunk, concealing its defects.
1782 *Poems*,'The Progress of Error', l.285–8.

63 How much a dunce that has been sent to roam
Excels a dunce that has been kept at home.
1782 *Poems*,'The Progress of Error', l.415–6.

64 Laugh at all you trembled at before.
1782 *Poems*,'The Progress of Error', l.592.

65 Our severest winter, commonly called the spring.
1783 Letter to Rev William Unwin, 8 Jun.

66 There is a mixture of evil in everything we do; indulgence encourages us to encroach, while we exercise the rights of children, we become childish.
1783 Letter to Rev William Unwin, 7 Sep.

67 Thus first necessity invented stools,
Convenience next suggested elbow-chairs,
And luxury the accomplished sofa last.
1785 *The Task*, bk.1,'The Sofa', l.86–8.

68 God made the country, and man made the town.
1785 *The Task*, bk.1,'The Sofa', l.749.

69 At eve
The moonbeam, sliding softly in between
The sleeping leaves, is all the light they wish,
Birds warbling all the music.
1785 *The Task*, bk.1,'The Sofa'.

70 England, with all thy faults I love thee still—
My country!
1785 *The Task*, bk.2,'The Timepiece', l.206–7.

71 There is a pleasure in poetic pains
Which only poets know.
1785 *The Task*, bk.2,'The Timepiece', l.285–6.

72 Variety's the spice of life,
That gives it all its flavour.
1785 *The Task*, bk.2,'The Timepiece', l.606–7.

73 Defend me, therefore, common sense, say I,
From reveries so airy, from the toil
Of dropping buckets into empty wells,
And growing old in drawing nothing up!
1785 *The Task*, bk.3,'The Garden', l.187–90.

74 Detested sport,
That owes its pleasure to another's pain.
1785 Of hunting. *The Task*, bk.3,'The Garden', l.326–7.

75 Studious of laborious ease.
1785 *The Task*, bk.3,'The Garden', l.361.

76 Now stir the fire, and close the shutters fast,
Let fall the curtains, wheel the sofa round,
And, while the bubbling and loud-hissing urn
Throws up a steamy column, and the cups,
That cheer but not inebriate, wait on each,
So let us welcome peaceful evening in.
1785 *The Task*, bk.4,'The Winter Evening', l.34–9.

77 But war's a game, which, were their subjects wise,
Kings should not play at. Nations would do well
To extort their truncheons from the puny hands
Of heroes, whose infirm and baby minds
Are gratified with mischief, and who spoil,
Because men suffer it, their toy the world.
1785 *The Task*, bk.5,'The Winter Morning Walk', l.187–92.

78 Knowledge dwells
In heads replete with thoughts of other men;
Wisdom in minds attentive to their own.
1785 *The Task*, bk.6,'The Winter Walk at Noon', l.89–91.

79 Knowledge is proud that he has learned so much;
Wisdom is humble that he knows no more.
1785 *The Task*, bk.6,'The Winter Walk at Noon', l.96–7.

80 Nature is but a name for an effect,
Whose cause is God.
1785 *The Task*, bk.6,'The Winter Walk at Noon', l.223.

Crabbe, George 1754–1832

English poet and clergyman, whose early career was spent in

poverty until Edmund Burke befriended him. His best-known poem, *The Village* (1783), is a bleak account of rural life.

81 Lo! the poor toper whose untutored sense,
Sees bliss in ale, and can with wine dispense;
Whose head proud fancy never taught to steer,
Beyond the muddy ecstasies of beer.
1775 *Inebriety, a Poem*, pt.1, l.132–5.

82 With awe, around these silent walks I tread;
These are the lasting mansions of the dead.
1781 *The Library* (published 1808), l.105–6.

83 Lo! all in silence, all in order stand,
And mighty folios first, a lordly band:
Then quartos their well-ordered ranks maintain,
And light octavos fill a spacious plain;
See yonder, ranged in more frequented rows,
A humbler band of duodecimos.
1781 *The Library* (published 1808), l.128–33.

84 Fashion, though Folly's child, and guide of fools,
Rules e'en the wisest, and in learning rules.
1781 *The Library* (published 1808), l.167–8.

85 Coldly profane and impiously gay.
1781 *The Library* (published 1808), l.265.

86 Yes, thus the Muses sing of happy swains,
Because the Muses never knew their pains:
They boast their peasants' pipes, but peasants now
Resign their pipes and plod behind the plough.
1783 *The Village*, bk.1, l.21–4.

87 I grant indeed that fields and flocks have charms,
For him that gazes or for him that farms.
1783 *The Village*, bk.1, l.39–40.

88 I paint the cot,
As truth will paint it, and as bards will not.
1783 *The Village*, bk.1, l.53–4.

89 Where Plenty smiles—alas! she smiles for few,
And those who taste not, yet behold her store,
Are as the slaves that dig the golden ore,
The wealth around them makes them doubly poor.
1783 *The Village*, bk.1, l.136–9.

90 The cold charities of man to man.
1783 *The Village*, bk.1, l.245.

91 A potent quack, long versed in human ills,
Who first insults the victim whom he kills;
Whose murd'rous hand a drowsy bench protect,
And whose most tender mercy is neglect.
1783 *The Village*, bk.1, l.282.

92 The murmuring poor, who will not fast in peace.
1785 *The Newspaper*, l.158.

93 A master passion is the love of news.
1785 *The Newspaper*, l.279.

94 Our farmers round, well pleased with constant gain,
Like other farmers, flourish and complain.
1807 *Poems*, 'The Parish Register', pt.1, l.273–4.

95 'What is a church?'—Our honest sexton tells,
''Tis a tall building, with a tower and bells.'
1810 *The Borough*, letter 2, 'The Church', l.11–12.

96 Virtues neglected then, adored become,
And graces slighted, blossom on the tomb.
1810 *The Borough*, letter 2, 'The Church', l.133–4.

97 Ye Lilies male! think (as your tea you sip,
While the Town small-talk flows from lip to lip;
Intrigues half-gathered, conversation-scraps,
Kitchen-cabals, and nursery-mishaps),
If the vast world may not some scene produce,
Some state where your small talents might have use.
1810 *The Borough*, letter 3, 'The Vicar', l.69–74.

98 Habit with him was all the test of truth,
'It must be right: I've done it from my youth.'
1810 *The Borough*, letter 3, 'The Vicar', l.138–9.

99 There anchoring, Peter chose from man to hide,
There hang his head, and view the lazy tide
In its hot slimy channel slowly glide;
Where the small eels that left the deeper way
For the warm shore, within the shallows play;
Where gaping mussels, left upon the mud,
Slope their slow passage to the fallen flood.
1810 *The Borough*, letter 22, 'Peter Grimes', l.185–91.

1 He nursed the feelings these dull scenes produce,
And loved to stop beside the opening sluice;
Where the small stream, confined in narrow bound,
Ran with a dull, unvaried, sad'ning sound;
Where all presented to the eye or ear,
Oppressed the soul! with misery, grief, and fear.
1810 *The Borough*, letter 22, 'Peter Grimes', l.194–9.

2 That all was wrong because not all was right.
1812 *Tales*, 'The Convert', l.313.

3 He tried the luxury of doing good.
1819 *Tales of the Hall*, 'Boys at School', l.139.

4 'The game,' said he, 'is never lost till won.'
1819 *Tales of the Hall*, 'Gretna Green', l.334.

5 The face the index of a feeling mind.
1819 *Tales of the Hall*, 'Lady Barbara', l.124.

6 Secrets with girls, like loaded guns with boys,
Are never valued till they make a noise.
1819 *Tales of the Hall*, 'The Maid's Story', l.84–5.

Craik, Dinah Maria *née Mulock* 1826–87

English novelist, essayist and poet. She published over 20 novels, the best known being *John Halifax, Gentleman* (1858). Although sentimental, her work emphasizes the self-reliance of women.

7 Leonora, Leonora,
How the word rolls—*Leonora*—
Lion-like, in full-mouthed sound,
Marching o'er the metric ground
With a tawny tread sublime;
So your name moves, Leonora,
Down my desert rhyme.
1881 *Collected Poems*, 'Leonora'.

Crane, (Harold) Hart 1899–1932

US poet. He was an alcoholic who led a troubled life which ended in suicide. He has come to be regarded as one of the most important US poets of the 20c.

8 The Cross alone has flown the wave.
But since the Cross sank, much that's warped and cracked
Has followed in its name, has heaped its grave.
1920 'The Mermen', in *The Dial*, no.85, Jul.

9 The bottom of the sea is cruel.
1926 *White Buildings*, 'Voyages', pt.1.

10 And onwards, as bells off San Salvador
Salute the crocus lustres of the stars,
In these poinsettia meadows of her tides.
1926 *White Buildings*, 'Voyages', pt.2.

11 Bequeath us no earthly shore until
Is answered in the vortex of our grave
The seal's wide spindrift gaze toward paradise.
1926 *White Buildings*, 'Voyages', pt.2.

12 Light wrestling there incessantly with light,
Star kissing star through wave on wave unto
Your body rocking!
1926 *White Buildings*, 'Voyages', pt.3.

13 Slow tyranny of moonlight, moonlight loved
And changed.
1926 *White Buildings*, 'Voyages', pt.5.

14 O Sleepless as the river under thee,
Vaulting the sea, the prairies' dreaming sod,
Unto us lowliest sometime sweep, descend
And of the curveship lend a myth to God.
1927 'To Brooklyn Bridge', in *The Dial*, Jun.

15 You who desired so much—in vain to ask—
Yet fed your hunger like an endless task,
Dared dignify the labor, bless the quest—
Achieved that stillness ultimately best,
Being, of all, least sought for: Emily, hear!
1929 'To Emily Dickinson', in *The Nation*, 29 Jun.

16 The last bear, shot drinking in the Dakotas
Loped under wires that span the mountain stream.
Keen instruments, strung to a vast precision
Bind town to town and dream to ticking dream.
1930 *The Bridge*, 'The River'.

17 Hobo-trekkers that forever search
An empire wilderness of freight and rails.
1930 *The Bridge*, 'The River'.

18 Dead echoes! But I knew her body there,
Time like a serpent down her shoulder, dark,
And space, an eaglet's wing, laid on her hair.
1930 *The Bridge*, 'The River'

19 Few evade full measure of their fate.
1930 *The Bridge*, 'The River'.

20 Thin squeaks of radio static,
The captured fume of space foams in our ears.
1930 *The Bridge*, 'Cape Hatteras'.

21 Stars scribble on our eyes the frosty sagas,
The gleaming cantos of unvanquished space.
1930 *The Bridge*, 'Cape Hatteras'.

22 Cowslip and shad-blow, flaked like tethered foam
Around bared teeth of stallions, bloomed that spring
When first I read thy lines, rife as the loam
Of prairies, yet like breakers cliffward leaping!
1930 Of Walt Whitman. *The Bridge*, 'Cape Hatteras'.

23 Our Meistersinger, thou set breath in steel;
And it was thou who on the boldest heel
Stood up and flung the span on even wing
Of that great Bridge, our Myth, whereof I sing.
1930 On Whitman and Brooklyn Bridge. *The Bridge*, 'Cape Hatteras'.

24 Our tongues recant like beaten weather vanes.
1930 *The Bridge*, 'The Tunnel'.

25 The phonographs of hades in the brain
Are tunnels that re-wind themselves, and love
A burnt match skating in a urinal.
1930 *The Bridge*, 'The Tunnel'.

26 The bell-rope that gathers God at dawn
Dispatches me as though I dropped down the knell
Of a spent day.
1932 'The Broken Tower', in the *New Republic*, 8 Jun.

Crane, Stephen 1871–1900

US writer. His reputation rests on *The Red Badge of Courage* (1895), which relates the experience of a soldier in the Civil War. His well-known short stories include *The Open Boat* (1898). He died of tuberculosis in Baden Baden.

27 The Red Badge of Courage.
1895 Title of novel.

28 'It is bitter—bitter,' he answered;
'But I like it
Because it is bitter,
And because it is my heart.'
1895 *The Black Riders*, 'The Heart'. The speaker is a 'naked, bestial' creature which the narrator sees eating its heart in the desert.

29 None of them knew the color of the sky.
1898 *The Open Boat*.

30 A man said to the universe:
'Sir, I exist!'
'However,' replied the universe,
'The fact has not created in me
A sense of obligation.'
1899 *A Man Said to the Universe*.

Cranfield, Ingrid 1945–

Australian-born writer and journalist. Her books on adventurers and travellers include *The Challengers* (1976) and *Skiing down Everest and Other Crazy Adventures* (1983).

31 To Hunt an 'assault' on the mountain merely meant a concerted, military-style operation; whereas to Shipton 'assault' sounded more like a criminal offence.
1978 Of the contrast in approach to the climbing of Mt Everest between Eric Shipton, originally appointed as leader of the 1953 expedition, and John Hunt, who replaced him. In *Expedition*, vol.8, no.4, Jul.

Cranmer, Thomas 1489–1556

English Protestant prelate, Archbishop of Canterbury (1533–53), largely responsible for the Book of Common Prayer (1549, 1552). He was convicted of treason for his part in the plan to divert the succession of the English Crown to Lady Jane Grey, and was burned at the stake.

32 This hath offended! Oh this unworthy hand!
1556 Last words at the stake, referring to the hand which had signed several recantations, later withdrawn.

Crashaw, Richard c.1613–1649

English metaphysical poet. He abandoned Puritanism for Catholicism, but lost his fellowship at Cambridge in 1643 and went to the Continent. His works include *Steps to the Temple* (1646) and *The Delights of the Muses* (1646).

33 *Nympha pudica Deum vidit, et erubuit.*
The conscious water saw its God, and blushed.

1634 Of the water which Jesus turned into wine at Cana.
Epigrammata Sacra, 'Aquae in Vinum Versae' (translated by Dryden).

34 Wellcome, all Wonders in one sight!
Eternity shut in a span.
Summer in Winter, Day in Night.
Heaven in Earth and God in Man.
1646 'Hymn of the Nativity' (published 1652), l.79.

35 I would be married, but I'd have no wife,
I would be married to a single life.
1646 'On Marriage'.

36 Th' have left thee naked, Lord, O that they had!
This garment too I would they had denied.
Thee with thyself they have too richly clad,
Opening the purple wardrobe of thy side.
O never could be found garments too good
For thee to wear, but these, of thine own blood.
1646 'On Our Crucified Lord, Naked and Bloody'.

37 And now where'er he strays
Among the Galilean mountains
Or more unwelcome ways,
He's followed by two faithful fountains;
Two walking baths; two weeping motions;
Portable and compendious oceans.
1646 'Saint Mary Magdalene, or The Weeper'.

38 What heaven-entreated heart is this,
Stands trembling at the gate of bliss,
Holds fast the door, yet dares not venture
Fairly to open it, and enter?
1646 'To the Noblest and Best of Ladies, the Countess of Denbigh'.

39 Say, lingering fair! why comes the birth
Of your brave soul so slowly forth?
1646 'To the Noblest and Best of Ladies, the Countess of Denbigh'.

40 What yet fantastic bands
Keep the free heart from its own hands!
1646 'To the Noblest and Best of Ladies, the Countess of Denbigh'.

41 Yield, then, O yield, that love may win
The fort at last, and let life in.
1646 'To the Noblest and Best of Ladies, the Countess of Denbigh'.

42 In love's field was never found
A nobler weapon than a wound.
'The Flaming Heart Upon the Book and Picture of Saint Teresa', collected in *Carmen Deo Nostro* (published posthumously, 1652).

43 All thy brim-filled bowls of fierce desire
'The Flaming Heart Upon the Book and Picture of Saint Teresa', collected in *Carmen Deo Nostro* (published posthumously, 1652).

Craster, Mrs Edmund d.1874

44 The centipede was happy quite,
Until the toad in fun
Asked him which leg went after which,
Which drove him into such a pitch
He lay distracted in a ditch,
Considering how to run.
Attributed.

Crawford, Joan *originally* *Lucille Fay le Sueur* 1904–77

US film actress. Originally a nightclub dancer, she began in silent films in 1925 and found fame in the 1930s and 1940s.

45 I found that incredible thing, a public.
Quoted in Alexander Walker *Joan Crawford* (1983).

Crichton, Michael 1942–

US writer and film-maker. His many scientific and medical thrillers include *The Andromeda Strain* (1969), *Jurassic Park* (1990) and *Timeline* (1999).

46 Physics was the first of the natural sciences to become fully modern and highly mathematical. Chemistry followed in the wake of physics, but biology, the retarded child, lagged far behind.
1969 *The Andromeda Strain.*

Crick, Francis Harry Compton 1916–2004

English molecular biologist, winner (with James Watson and Maurice Wilkins) of the Nobel prize for physiology or medicine in 1962 for work on the structure of DNA.

47 We have discovered the secret of life!
1953 Announcement, with James Watson, to the patrons of The Eagle public house in Cambridge on solving the structure of DNA.
► *See Watson 890:96.*

48 Almost all aspects of life are engineered at the molecular level, and without understanding molecules we can only have a very sketchy understanding of life itself.
1988 *What Mad Pursuit*, ch.5.

Cripps, Arthur S(hearly) 1869–1952

English clergyman. He was the writer of occasional verse, mainly on rural or religious themes.

49 England has greater counties—
Their peace to hers is small;
Low hills, rich fields, calm rivers,
In Essex seek them all.
Quoted in S P B Mais and Tom Stephenson (eds) *Lovely Britain* (c.1930).

Cripps, Sir (Richard) Stafford 1889–1952

English Labour politician and economist, expelled from the Party for his opposition to appeasement (1939). In 1945 he was readmitted and subsequently became Chancellor of the Exchequer, with a successful austerity policy.

50 There is only a certain sized cake to be divided up, and if a lot of people want a larger slice they can only take it from others who would, in terms of real income, have a smaller one.
1948 Speech, Trades Union Congress, 7 Sep.

Crisp, Quentin 1908–99

English writer. He achieved notoriety with the publication of *The Naked Civil Servant* (1968), an account of his experiences growing up as a flamboyant gay young man in England.

51 Keeping up with the Joneses was a full-time job with my mother and father. It was not until many years later when I lived alone that I realized how much cheaper it was to drag the Joneses down to my level.
1968 *The Naked Civil Servant*, ch.1.

52 As soon as I stepped out of my mother's womb on to dry land, I realized that I had made a mistake…but the trouble with children is that they are not returnable.
1968 *The Naked Civil Servant*, ch.2.

53 This woman did not fly to extremes, she lived there.
1968 *The Naked Civil Servant*, ch.3.

54 I don't hold with abroad and think that foreigners speak English when our backs are turned.
1968 *The Naked Civil Servant*, ch.4.

55 If one is not going to take the necessary precautions to avoid having parents, one must undertake to bring them up.
1968 *The Naked Civil Servant*, ch.5.

56 There was no need to do any housework after all. After the first four years the dirt doesn't get any worse.
1968 *The Naked Civil Servant*, ch.15.

57 Life was a funny thing that happened to me on the way to the grave.
1968 *The Naked Civil Servant*, ch.18.

58 I became one of the stately homos of England.
1968 *The Naked Civil Servant*, ch.24.

59 An autobiography is an obituary in serial form with the last instalment missing
1968 *The Naked Civil Servant*, ch.29.

60 In England, the system is benign and the people are hostile. In America, the people are friendly—and the system is brutal!
1985 In *The Guardian*, 23 Oct.

Critchfield, Richard Patrick 1931–94

US journalist. His books include *The Long Charade: Political Subversion in the Vietnam War* (1968) and *An American Looks at Britain* (1990).

61 What people read most of the time should be as worth mentioning as what they read almost none of the time.
1990 *An American Looks at Britain*

Critchley, Sir Julian Michael Gordon 1930–2000

English Conservative MP, writer and broadcaster, known for his acerbic and witty comments on Westminster life.

62 I was told when a young man that the two occupational hazards of the Palace of Varieties were alcohol and adultery. The hurroosh that follows the intermittent revelation of the sexual goings-on of an unlucky MP has convinced me that the only safe pleasure for a parliamentarian is a bag of boiled sweets.
1982 In *The Listener*, 10 Jun.

63 She has been beastly to the Bank of England, has demanded that the BBC 'set its house in order' and tends to believe the worst of the Foreign and Commonwealth Office. She cannot see an institution without hitting it with her handbag.
1982 Profile of Margaret Thatcher in *The Times*, 21 Jun.

Critias c.460–403 BC

Athenian aristocrat and politician, one of the 30 tyrants who ruled Athens after the Peloponnesian war (404 BC). He was killed in the democratic revolution of 404/3. Only fragments of his poetry and tragedies survive.

64 Is not living at all not better than living badly?
Fragment, quoted in H Diels and W Kranz (eds) *Die Fragmente der Vorsokratiker* (1952), vol.2, 385, no.23.

Croker, John Wilson 1780–1857

Irish politician and essayist, known for his satires on the Irish stage and Dublin society. He became an MP (1807) and helped found the *Quarterly Review* (1809).

65 We are now, as we have always been, decidedly and conscientiously attached to what is called the Tory, and which might with more propriety be called the Conservative party.
1830 *Quarterly Review*, Jan.

Cromer, Evelyn Baring, Earl 1841–1917

English colonial administrator.

66 It is well that Gordon should be under my orders, but a man who habitually consults the prophet Isaiah when he is in difficulty is not apt to obey the orders of anyone.
Of General Charles George Gordon. Quoted in Charles Chevenix Trench *Charley Gordon* (1978).

Crompton, Richmal *originally Richmal Samuel Lamburn* 1890–1969

English writer, a classics teacher until she contracted polio in 1923. Her best-known children's books are those in the 'William' series, beginning with *Just William* (1922).

67 I'll thcream and thcream and thcream until I'm thick.
1925 Violet Elizabeth. *Still— William*, ch.8.

Cromwell, Oliver 1599–1658

English soldier and Puritan statesman. In the Civil War he led his New Model Army to victory at Naseby (1645). After the execution of Charles I, he established a Commonwealth, and later, on dissolving the Rump Parliament (1653) and refusing the crown, a Protectorate.

68 A few honest men are better than numbers.
1643 Letter to Sir William Spring, Sep. Quoted in Thomas Carlyle *Letters and Speeches of Oliver Cromwell* (1845).

69 I had rather have a plain, russet-coated Captain, that knows what he fights for, and loves what he knows, than that which you call a Gentle-man and is nothing else.
1643 Letter to Sir William Spring, Sep. Quoted in Thomas Carlyle *Letters and Speeches of Oliver Cromwell* (1845).

70 The state, in choosing men to serve it, takes no notice of their opinions. If they be willing faithfully to serve it, that satisfies.
1644 Said before the Battle of Marston Moor, 2 Jul.

71 EARL OF MANCHESTER: If we beat the King ninety-nine times, yet he is King still so will his posterity be after him; but if the King beat us once we shall be hanged, and our posterity made slaves.
OLIVER CROMWELL: My Lord, if this be so, why did we take up arms at first? This is against fighting hereafter. If so, let us make peace, be it never so base.
1644 Recorded in *The Calendar of State Papers*, 10 Nov.

72 I beseech you, in the bowels of Christ, think it possible you may be mistaken.
1650 Letter to the General Assembly of the Church of Scotland, 3 Aug.

73 Mr Lely, I desire you would use all your skill to paint my picture truly like me, and not flatter me at all; but remark all these roughnesses, pimples, warts, and everything as you see me, otherwise I will never pay a farthing for it.

1650 Remark to Sir Peter Lely, who was about to paint his portrait. Quoted in H Walpole *Anecdotes of Painting in England*, vol.3 (1763).

74 You have sat too long here for any good you have been doing. Depart, I say, and let us have done with you. In the name of God, go!
1653 On dismissing the Rump Parliament, 20 Apr.

75 Take away that fool's bauble—the Mace.
1653 On dismissing the Rump Parliament, 20 Apr.

76 My desire is to make what haste I can to be gone.
1658 Last words. Quoted in John Morley *Oliver Cromwell* (1900), bk.5, ch.10.

Cronenberg, David 1943–

Canadian sci-fi and horror film director. His films include *The Fly* (1986), *Crash* (1996) and *eXistenZ* (1999).

77 More blood! More blood!
Characteristic on-set declaration. Quoted in Neil Gaiman and Kim Newman *Ghastly Beyond Belief* (1985).

78 I don't have a moral plan. I'm a Canadian.
Quoted in Leslie Halliwell *Halliwell's Filmgoer's and Video Viewer's Companion* (9th edn, 1988).

Cronkite, Walter 1916–

US journalist.

79 And that's the way it is.
Catchphrase, used at the end of the CBS *Evening News* (1962–81).

Cronyn, Hume 1911–2003

Canadian-born actor, writer and director. He was married to Jessica Tandy, with whom he acted many times.

80 The most magical moment in the theater is a silence so complete that you can't even hear people breathe. It means that you've got them.
1990 In *Time*, 2 Apr.

Crosby, Bing *originally* Harry Lillis Crosby 1904–77

US film actor and singer. His many successful films include the *Road to* series with Bob Hope and Dorothy Lamour.

81 That was a great game of golf.
1977 Last words, as he finished play at the 18th hole before suffering a heart attack.

82 He was an average guy who could carry a tune.
Suggesting his own epitaph. Quoted in David Pickering *Brewer's Twentieth Century Music* (1994).

Cross, Douglas

US songwriter.

83 I Left My Heart in San Francisco.
1954 Title of song.

Crossman, Richard Howard Stafford 1907–74

British Labour politician. He chronicled his ministerial career and the workings of government in a series of diaries, begun in 1952, which were published in four volumes (1975–81), despite attempts to suppress them.

84 My Minister's room is like a padded cell, and in certain ways I am like a person who is suddenly certified a lunatic and put safely into this great, vast room, cut off from real life. Of course they don't behave *quite* like nurses, because the Civil Service is profoundly deferential—'Yes, Minister! No, Minister! If you wish it, Minister!'
1964 *The Diaries of a Cabinet Minister*, vol.1 (1975), 22 Oct.

Crowley, (Edward) Aleister 1875–1947

English writer and occultist. He founded his own order and became notorious for rumours of orgies, drugs and the sacrifice of babies in the course of black magic ceremonies.

85 Do what thou wilt shall be the whole of the Law.
1909 *Book of the Law*.

Cruyff, Johan 1947–

Dutch footballer, European Footballer of the Year (1971, 1973, 1974).

86 I am no longer a footballer. I am an industry.
1973 On being transferred from Ajax to Barcelona for a record £922,000. Quoted in Peter Ball and Phil Shaw *The Book of Football Quotations* (1989).

Cruz, Sor Juana Inés de la 1651–95

Mexican intellectual, nun and poet. After she took her vows at the age of 16, attempts were made to stop her writing. Two years after writing her defence, *Respuesta a sor Filotea* (1691), she sold her books and devoted herself to religion.

87 *En perseguirme, Mundo, Qué interesas?*
En qué te ofendo, cuando sólo intento
poner bellezas en mi entendimiento
y no mi entendimiento en las bellezas?
World, in hounding me, what do you gain?
How can it harm you if I choose, astutely,
rather to stock my mind with things of beauty,
than waste its stock on every beauty's claim?
1688 *Poesía, teatro y prosa*, 'Quéjase de la suerte' (translated as 'She Complains about Her Fate', 1985).

88 *Aprendamos a ignorar,*
pensamiento, pues hallamos
que cuanto añado al discurso,
tanto le usurpo a los años.
Thought, let's learn not to know,
since so plainly it appears
that whatever we add to our minds
we take away from our years.
1688 *A Sor Juana Anthology*, 'Acusa la hidropesía de mucha ciencia' (translated as 'She Condemns the Bloatedness of Much Learning', 1985).

89 *Este natural impulso que Dios puso en mí…su Majestad sabe por qué y para qué; y sabe que le he pedido que apague la luz de mi entendimiento dejando sólo lo que baste para guardar su Ley, pues lo demás sobra, (según algunos) en una mujer; y aun hay quien dice que daña.*
This natural impulse which God has implanted in me…only His Majesty knows why and wherefore and His Majesty also knows that I have prayed to Him to extinguish the light of my mind, only leaving sufficient to keep His Law, since any more is overmuch, so some say, in a woman, and there are even those who say it is harmful.
1691 *Poesía, teatro y prosa*, '*Respuesta a sor Filotea*' ('An Answer to Sister Filotea', 1982).

Cuarón, Alfonso 1961–

Mexican film director.

90 You speed up and up then you realise that your scarf has got caught in the machinery and if you don't keep up you're going to be strangled.
2004 On the pace of work involved in directing *Harry Potter and the Prisoner of Azkaban*. Quoted in the *Sunday Herald*, 23 May.

Cullen, Countee 1903–46

Black US poet and novelist, an important figure in the Harlem Renaissance of the 1920s.

91 She even thinks that up in heaven
Her class lies late and snores,
While poor black cherubs rise at seven
To do celestial chores.
1925 *On These I Stand*, 'For a Lady I Know'.

92 What is Africa to me:
Copper sun or scarlet sea,
Jungle star or jungle track,
Strong bronzed men, or regal black
Women from whose loins I sprang
When the birds of Eden sang?
1925 *On These I Stand*, 'Heritage'.

93 One three centuries removed
From the scenes his fathers loved,
Spicy grove, cinnamon tree,
What is Africa to me?
1925 *On These I Stand*, 'Heritage'.

94 So I lie, whose fount of pride,
Dear distress, and joy allied,
Is my somber flesh and skin,
With the dark blood dammed within.
1925 *On These I Stand*, 'Heritage'.

95 Ever at Thy glowing altar
Must my heart grow sick and falter,
Wishing He I served were black.
1925 *On These I Stand*, 'Heritage'.

96 Lord, forgive me if my need
Sometimes shapes a human creed.
1925 *On These I Stand*, 'Heritage'.

cummings, e e *pen name of* *Edward Estlin Cummings* 1894–1962

US writer and painter, best known as an eccentric innovator in lyrical poetry, using idiosyncratic typography. He also wrote a novel, plays and essays.

97 He had no nose, properly speaking, but a large beak of preposterous widthlessness, which gave his whole face the expression of falling gravely downstairs, and quite obliterated the unimportant chin.
1922 *The Enormous Room*, ch.3.

98 Subconsciously every one was, of course, fearful that he himself would go nuts—everyone with the exception of those who had already gone nuts, who were in the wholly pleasant situation of having no fear.
1922 *The Enormous Room*, ch.5.

99 To create is first of all to destroy...there is and can be no such thing as authentic art until the *bons trucs* (whereby we are taught to see and imitate on canvas and in stone and by words this so-called world) are entirely and thoroughly and perfectly annihilated by that vast and painful process of Unthinking which may result in a minute bit of purely personal Feeling. Which minute bit is Art.
1922 *The Enormous Room*, ch.12.

1 The tall, impossibly tall, incomparably tall, city shoulderingly upwards into hard sunlight leaned a little through the octaves of its parallel edges, leaningly strode upwards into firm, hard, snowy sunlight; the noises of America nearingly throbbed with smokes and hurrying dots which are men and which are women and which are things new and curious and hard and strange and vibrant and immense, lifting with a great ondulous stride firmly into immortal sunlight.
1922 *The Enormous Room*, ch.13, closing words.

2 spring
when the world is puddle wonderful
1923 *Tulips and Chimneys*, 'Chanson Innocente'.

3 the Cambridge ladies who live in furnished souls
are unbeautiful and have comfortable minds
1923 *Tulips and Chimneys*, 'Sonnets-Realities', no.1.

4 Buffalo Bill's
defunct
—who used to
—ride a watersmooth-silver
——stallion
and break onetwothreefourfive pigeonsjustlikethat
1923 *Tulips and Chimneys*, 'Portraits', no.8.

5 Humanity i love you because you
are perpetually putting the secret of
life in your pants and forgetting
it's there and sitting down
on it.
1925 *XLI Poems*, no.2, 'La Guerre'.

6 who knows if the moon's
a balloon, coming out of a keen city
in the sky—filled with pretty people?
1925 'Seven Poems, VII'. David Niven used the phrase for his autobiography, *The Moon's a Balloon* (1975).

7 If a poet is anybody, he is somebody to whom things made matter very little—somebody who is obsessed by Making.
1926 *is 5*, foreword.

8 'next to of course god america i
love you land of the pilgrims' and so forth oh
say can you see by the dawn's early my
country 'tis of centuries come and go
and are no more what of it we should worry
in every language even deafanddumb
they sons acclaim you glorious name by gorry
by jingo by gee by gosh by gum
1926 *is 5*, 'Two, III'.

9 why talk of beauty what could be more beautiful than these heroic happy dead
who rushed like lions to the roaring slaughter
they did not stop to think they died instead
then shall the voices of liberty be mute?

He spoke. And drank rapidly a glass of water.
1926 *is 5*, 'Two, III'.

10 America makes prodigious mistakes, America has

colossal faults, but one thing cannot be denied: America is always on the move. She may be going to Hell, of course, but at least she isn't standing still.
1927 'Why I Like America', in *Vanity Fair*, May.

11 nobody, not even the rain, has such small hands
1931 *w*,'somewhere I have never travelled'.

12 unless statistics lie he was
more brave than me: more blond than you
1931 *w*,'i sing of Olaf glad and big'.

13 What about the world, Mr Cummings?
I live in so many: which one do you mean?
1934 Introduction to revised edition of *The Enormous Room*.

14 my father moved through dooms of love
through sames of am through haves of give,
singing each morning out of each night
my father moved through depths of height
1940 *50 poems*,'my father moved through dooms of love'.

15 because my father lived his soul
love is the whole and more than all
1940 *50 poems*,'my father moved through dooms of love'.

16 a politician is an arse upon
which everyone has sat except a man
1944 *1x1*, no.10.

17 pity this busy monster, manunkind,
not. Progress is a comfortable disease.
1944 *1x1*, no.14.

18 We doctors know
a hopeless case if—listen: there's a hell
of a good universe next door; let's go
1944 *1x1*, no.14.

19 anyone lived in a pretty how town
(with up so floating many bells down)
spring summer autumn winter
he sang his didn't he danced his did
1949 *50 poems*, no.29.

20 Knowledge is a polite word for dead but not buried imagination.
1951 'Jottings', in *Wake*, no.10.

21 for whatever we lose (like a you or a me)
it's always ourselves we find in the sea
'maggie and milly and molly and may'.

22 Humane, but not human.
On Ezra Pound. Recalled on Cummings's death, 3 Sep 1962.

23 A draftsman of words.
Self-description. Quoted in the *New York Times*, 30 Oct 1963.

Cunningham, Allan 1784–1842

Scottish poet, friend and acquaintance of James Hogg and Walter Scott.

24 A wet sheet and a flowing sea,
A wind that follows fast,
And fills the white and rustling sail,
And bends the gallant mast
1825 'A Wet Sheet and a Flowing Sea', stanza 1.

25 Wha the deil hae we got for a King,
But a wee, wee German lairdie!
1847 *Poems and Songs*,'The Wee, Wee German Lairdie', stanza 1.

Cunningham, Roseanna 1951–

Scottish advocate and politician. She was an MP (1995–2001) before becoming an MSP in 1999 and Deputy Leader of the Scottish National Party in 2000.

26 Until a woman is free to be as incompetent as the average male then she will never be completely equal.
1995 By-election campaign speech, May.

Cuomo, Mario Matthew 1932–

US lawyer and Democratic politician, Governor of New York (1983–95).

27 We propose it, we massage it, and we often have to ram it.
1988 Of legislation. In the *US News and World Report*, 25 Jan.

28 If there's a plastic surgeon who claims to be responsible for this face, then New York State will decertify him immediately.
1991 On reports that he had undergone plastic surgery. In *Newsweek*, 11 Nov.

29 President Bush…seems to think that the ship [of state] will be saved by imperceptible undercurrents, directed by the invisible hand of some cyclical economic god, that will gradually move the ship so that at the last moment it will miraculously glide past the rocks to safer shores.
1992 Address nominating Bill Clinton as Democratic presidential candidate, 15 Jul.

30 It is as if Homer not only chronicled the siege of Troy, but conducted the siege as well. As if Shakespeare set his play writing aside to lead the English against the Armada.
1992 Tribute to Lincoln's literary and political genius. In the *New York Times*, 18 Nov.

31 Commitment seems to live more in the poetry of our aspirations than in the prose of the realities we have created.
1992 In the *New York Times*, 18 Nov.

32 Ever since the Republican landslide on Nov 8, it's been getting dark outside a little earlier every day. You notice that?
1994 In the *New York Times*, 17 Dec.

33 Dog eat dog produces, inevitably, just one dog.
1994 In the *New York Times*, 31 Dec.

Cupitt, Rev Don 1934–

English radical theologian, Dean of Emmanuel College, Cambridge (1966–91).

34 A belief is made religious, not so much by its content, as rather by the way it is held.
1984 *The Sea of Faith*.

35 It is hardest of all to give up the last slivers and shreds of objectivity, but only by doing so can faith finally free itself from all that is outworn and become as fully voluntary, creative and courageous as it is required to be today.
1984 *The Sea of Faith*.

Curie, Marie *originally* ***Marya Sklodowska*** 1867–1934

Polish-born French chemist, who shared a 1903 Nobel prize with her husband Pierre and with Henri Becquerel for research on radioactivity. In 1911 she again won the Nobel prize for the discovery of radium and polonium.

36 In science, we must be interested in things, not in persons.
Quoted in Eve Curie *Madame Curie* (1937), ch.16 (translated by Vincent Sheean, 1943).

Curnow, (Thomas) Allen Munro 1911–2001

New Zealand poet and critic, whose works focus on his country's past and its quest for national identity.

37 Fluent in all the languages dead or living,
the sun comes up with a word of worlds all spinning
in a world of words.
1979 *An Incorrigible Music*, 'A Balanced Bait in Handy Pellet Form'.

Curran, Charles

US journalist.

38 One of nature's Balkans.
Of his friend and fellow journalist, Rebecca West. Quoted by V S Pritchett in the *New Yorker*, 21 Dec 1987.

39 [She] has several skins fewer than any other human being…a kind of psychological haemophilia, which is one reason why she writes so well, and why she is so vulnerable.
Of his friend and fellow journalist, Rebecca West. Quoted by V S Pritchett in the *New Yorker*, 21 Dec 1987.

Curran, John Philpot 1750–1817

Irish judge and orator, called to the Irish bar in 1775. He entered Parliament in 1783, and although a staunch Protestant strongly opposed the Union.

40 But as in wailing there's nought availing,
And Death unfailing will strike the blow,
Then for that reason, and for a season,
Let us be merry before we go.
?1773 'Let Us Be Merry Before We Go'.

41 The condition upon which God hath given liberty to man is eternal vigilance; which condition if he break, servitude is at once the consequence of his crime, and the punishment of his guilt.
1790 Speech, Dublin, 10 Jul.

42 Like the silver plate on a coffin.
Of Sir Robert Peel's smile. Quoted by Daniel O'Connell in the House of Commons, 26 Feb 1835.

Currie, Edwina 1946–

English Conservative politician and novelist. She was appointed Health Minister (1986–8), and attracted notoriety for her outspoken comments on various health issues.

43 My message to the businessmen of this country when they go abroad on business is that there is one good thing above all they can take with them to stop them catching AIDS—and that is the wife.
1987 Speech as Health Minister, 12 Feb.

44 The strongest possible piece of advice that I could give to any young woman is: Don't screw around and don't smoke.
1988 In the *Observer*, 3 Apr.

45 Most of the egg production in this country, sadly, is now infected with salmonella.
1988 Radio interview as junior Health Minister, 3 Dec, which outraged both the domestic poultry industry and those of her own back-benchers who represented agricultural constituencies, forcing her resignation two weeks later.

Curtis, Charles P

46 Literature is a power line and the motor, mark you, is the reader.
1957 *A Commonplace Book*.

Curtis, Lionel 1872–1955

British writer on international affairs.

47 In private conversation he tries on speeches like a man trying on ties in his bedroom, to see how he would look in them.
1912 Of Winston Churchill. Letter to Nancy Astor.

Curtis, Richard Whalley Anthony 1956–

British writer for film and television, best known for the TV series *Not the Nine O'Clock News* (1979–83) and *Blackadder* (1984–9), and for films including *Four Weddings and a Funeral* (1994), *Notting Hill* (1999) and *Love Actually* (2003).

48 Whatever your script is like, no matter how much stewing and rewriting—if the punters don't want to sleep with the star, you may never be asked to write another one.
1994 Introduction to the published script of *Four Weddings and a Funeral*.

Curtis, Tony *pseudonym of* Bernie Schwartz 1925–

US film actor.

49 Like kissing Hitler.
Of working with Marilyn Monroe on *Some Like It Hot*. Attributed.

Curtiz, Michael *originally* Mihaly Kertesz 1888–1962

Hungarian-born film director.

50 Bring on the empty horses!
1936 Instructions during the filming of *The Charge of the Light Brigade*, subsequently used by David Niven for the title of one of his books. Curtiz's less-than-perfect English was renowned for producing such felicitous phrases.

Curzon (of Kedleston), Lord George Nathaniel 1859–1925

English statesman. As Viceroy of India from 1898 he introduced many social and political reforms and partitioned Bengal. He resigned after a disagreement with Kitchener (1905), but returned to politics as Lord Privy Seal (1915) and Foreign Secretary (1919–24).

51 It is only when you get to see and realize what India is—that she is the strength and the greatness of England—that you feel that every nerve a man may strain, every energy he may put forward, cannot be devoted to a nobler purpose than keeping tight the cords that hold India to ourselves.
1893 Speech at Southport, 15 May.

52 I hesitate to say what the functions of the modern journalist may be, but I imagine that they do not exclude the intelligent anticipation of the facts even before they occur.
1898 House of Commons, 29 Mar.

53 To fight for the right, to abhor the imperfect, the unjust, or the mean, to swerve neither to the right hand nor the left, to care nothing for flattery or applause or odium or abuse—it is so easy to have any of them in India—never to let your enthusiasm be soured or your courage grow dim but to remember that the Almighty has placed your hand on the greatest of his ploughs, in whose furrow the nations of the future are germinating and taking shape, to drive the blade a little forward in your time and to feel that somewhere among those millions you have left, a little justice, or happiness or prosperity, a sense of manliness or moral dignity, a spring of patriotism, a dawn of intellectual enlightenment or a stirring of duty where it did not exist before—that is enough, that is the Englishman's justification in India.

1906 Farewell speech on departing from Bombay as Viceroy of India.

54 I never knew that the lower classes had such white skins.

c.1915 Remark made during a visit of front-line British troops in World War I, after observing some of them bathing in old beer barrels.

55 Gentlemen do not take soup at luncheon.

Attributed. Quoted in E L Woodward *Short Journey* (1942), ch.7.

St Cyprian *full name* ***Thascius Caecilius Cyprianus*** c.200–258 AD

Christian martyr and Father of the Church. Probably born in Carthage, he became a bishop and theologian. He was excommmunicated for his views on baptism and beheaded in Valerian's reign.

56 *Habere non potest Deum patrem qui ecclesiam non habet matrem.*
He cannot have God for his father who has not the church for his mother.

AD 251 *De Ecclesiae Catholicae Unitate*, ch 6.

57 *Salus extra ecclesiam non est.*
There is no salvation outside the church.

AD 256 *Letters*, no.73.

Cyrano de Bergerac, Savinien de 1619–55

French poet and soldier, famous as a duellist. He was a student of Gassendi, who influenced him in the philosophy of free-thinking.

58 *Peut-on être innocent, lorsqu'on aime un coupable?*
Can one be innocent when one loves a guilty person?

1653 *La Mort d'Agrippine*, act 5, sc.5.

59 *Un Philosophe doit juger le vulgaire, et non pas juger comme le vulgaire.*
A philosopher should judge the masses and should not judge like the masses.

1654 *Lettres diverses, Contre les sorciers* (later published as *Voyage dans la lune*).

60 *Non, non, si ce Dieu visible éclaire l'homme, c'est par accident, comme le flambeau du roi éclaire par accident au crocheteur qui passe par la rue.*
No, no, if this manifest God enlightens men, it is purely by accident, just as the king's torch throws its light upon a labourer who passes him in the street.

1656 *L'Autre Monde; ou, Les Estats et empires de la lune* (later published as *Voyage dans la lune*).

d

Daché, Lilly 1904–89

French-born US milliner. Her autobiography, *Talking Through My Hats*, was published in 1946.

61 Glamour is what makes a man ask for your telephone number. But it also is what makes a woman ask for the name of your dressmaker.

1955 'Lilly Daché's Secrets of Lifelong Glamour Book', in *Woman's Home Companion*, vol.82, Jul.

Dafoe, John W 1866–1944

Canadian publisher and editor.

62 A journalist is hardly an authority upon anything—unless perhaps upon the appraisal of the drift of public opinion.

1923 Convocation address at the University of Manitoba, Winnipeg, May. Quoted in Murray Donnelly *Dafoe of the Free Press* (1968).

63 There are only two kinds of government, the scarcely tolerable and the absolutely unbearable.

Characteristic remark, quoted in Murray Donnelly *Dafoe of the Free Press* (1968).

Daily Express

British tabloid newspaper.

64 Britain will not be involved in a European war this year, or next year either.

1938 Headline, 30 Sep. The newspaper used similar phrases frequently, up to 11 Aug 1939, three weeks before the outbreak of World War II.

Daily Mail

British tabloid newspaper.

65 Nobel Prize for British Wife.

1964 Headline announcing that the Nobel prize for chemistry had been awarded to Professor Dorothy Hodgkin.

Daily Mirror

British tabloid newspaper.

66 Whose finger do you want on the trigger?

1951 Headline, 21 Sep, referring to the atom bomb.

Dalai Lama *originally* ***Tenzin Gyatso*** 1935–

Spiritual and temporal leader of Tibet since 1940. He negotiated an autonomy agreement for Tibet with the Chinese in 1951 but went into exile after the suppressed nationalist uprising in 1959. Now living in India, he continues to move for Tibetan independence. He was awarded the Nobel peace prize in 1989.

67 Frankly speaking, it is difficult to trust the Chinese. Once bitten by a snake, you feel suspicious even when you see a piece of rope.

1981 Quoted in the *Observer Colour Magazine*, 5 Apr.

Dalglish, Kenny 1951–

Scottish footballer and manager. As manager of Liverpool, he won the League and Cup double in 1986.

68 The saddest and most beautiful sight I have ever seen.
1989 Of the display of flowers and club scarfs that were piled on Liverpool's Anfield pitch in memory of those who died in the Hillsborough football disaster. Quoted in Peter Ball and Phil Shaw *The Book of Football Quotations* (1989).

Dalí, Salvador 1904–89

Spanish painter, graphic artist and sculptor, the most flamboyant of the Surrealist artists. His work draws on the symbolism of dreams and, later, religion.

69 At the age of six I wanted to be a cook. At seven I wanted to be Napoleon. And my ambition has been growing steadily ever since.
1942 *The Secret Life of Salvador Dalí*, prologue.

70 I do not paint a portrait to look like the subject, rather does the person grow to look like his portrait.
Quoted in Esar *A Treasury of Humorous Quotations* (1951).

71 The first man to compare the cheeks of a young woman to a rose was obviously a poet; the first to repeat it was possibly an idiot.
1968 *Dialogues with Marcel Duchamp*, preface.

72 The famous soft watches are nothing else than the tender, extravagant, solitary, paranoic-critical camembert of time and space.
1969 *Conquest of the Irrational*.

73 Every good painter who aspires to the creation of genuine masterpieces should first of all marry my wife.
Quoted in Saranne Alexandrian *Surrealist Art* (1970).

74 *Le surréalisme, c'est moi.*
I am surrealism.
Quoted in Saranne Alexandrian *Surrealist Art* (1970), ch.5.
► *See Louis XIV 518:93.*

Dallek, Robert 1934–

US historian, Professor at the University of California, Los Angeles.

75 What makes war interesting for Americans is that we don't fight war on our soil, we don't have direct experience of it, so there's an openness about the meanings we give it.
1991 In the *New York Times*, 24 Feb.

Daly, Daniel 1874–1937

US gunnery sergeant in World War I.

76 Come on you sons of bitches! Do you want to live forever?
1918 Attributed, to his troops at Belleau Wood, 4 Jun.
► *See Frederick the Great 335:33.*

Daly, John 1966–

US golfer.

77 I spent $3m on drink and $3m on gambling, but I wasted the rest.
2000 On spending his winnings. Quoted in *The Independent*, 23 Dec.

Daly, Mary 1928–

US feminist theorist and theologian. She advocates a feminist spirituality in *Beyond God the Father* (1973) and *Gyn/Ecology: the Metaethics of Radical Feminism* (1978).

78 Mister-ectomy n.: guaranteed solution to The Contraceptive Problem, tried and true and therefore taboo birth control method, recommended by Gyn/Ecologists, insisted upon by spinsters.
1987 *Webster's First New Intergalactic Wickedary of the English Language* (with Jane Caputi), Word Web 2.

St Peter Damian *or Pietro Damiani* 1007–72

Italian cleric and saint. A swineherd in his youth, he rose to become Bishop of Ostia and a Cardinal. He was active in attempts to reform the clergy in order to correct immorality.

79 *Sanctum Satanum meum.*
My holy Satan.
c.1070 Of Hildebrand, later Pope Gregory VII. Letter to Pope Alexander II and Cardinal Archdeacon Hildebrand.

Damrosch, Walter Johannes 1862–1950

German-born US conductor and composer. Having established a reputation as a conductor of Wagner, he became a champion of works by contemporary composers.

80 If a young man at the age of twenty-three can write a symphony like that, in five years he will be ready to commit murder.
1925 After conducting Aaron Copland's *Symphony for Organ and Orchestra*. Quoted in Machlis *Introduction to Contemporary Music* (1963).

Dana, Charles Anderson 1819–97

US newspaper editor. From 1848 to 1862 he edited the New York *Tribune*. From 1863 to the end of the Civil War he was Assistant-Secretary of War. In 1867 he purchased the New York *Sun*.

81 I have always felt that whatever Divine Providence permitted to occur I was not too proud to report.
1888 *The Art of Newspaper Making*, 'The Modern American Newspaper'.

82 Get the news, get all the news, and nothing but the news.
1888 *The Art of Newspaper Making*, 'The Modern American Newspaper'.

83 The invariable law of the newspaper is to be interesting.
1888 *The Art of Newspaper Making*, 'The Making of a Newspaper Man'.

Danforth, John Claggett 1936–

US lawyer and politician, Senator of Missouri (1976–95).

84 It has locked candidates into ridiculous positions because only ridiculous positions can be compacted into 30-second commercials.
1990 Of television in politics. In the *New York Times*, 18 Mar.

Dangarembga, Tsitsi 1959–

Zimbabwean writer. Her novel *Nervous Conditions* (1988) portrays the effect of white values on black African society, especially women.

85 This business of womanhood is a heavy burden… And these days it is worse, with the poverty of blackness on one side and the weight of womanhood on the other.
1988 *Nervous Conditions*, ch.1.

Dangerfield, George

86 Ireland is one of the few countries—perhaps the last—where the boundaries between politics and art have never been fixed.
1935 *The Strange Death of Liberal England.*

Daniel, Samuel 1562–1619

English poet and dramatist. A private tutor and courtier, he wrote masques, plays and epistles. His poetic works include the sonnet sequence *Delia* (1592) and the epic *Civil Wars Between the Two Houses of Lancaster and York* (1594–1609).

87 I that have loved thee thus before thou fadest,
My faith shall wax, when thou art in thy waning.
The world shall find this miracle in me,
That fire can burn when all the matter's spent.
1592 *Delia*, sonnet 33.

88 Care-charmer Sleep, son of the sable Night,
Brother to Death, in silent darkness born,
Relieve my languish and restore the light;
With dark forgetting of my care return.
And let the day be time enough to mourn
The shipwreck of my ill adventured youth:
Let waking eyes suffice to wail their scorn
Without the torment of the night's untruth.
1592 *Delia*, sonnet 54.

89 O thou whom envy ev'n is force t'admire!
1594 'To the Right Honourable, the Lady Mary, Countess of Pembroke'. Daniel was part of the group of writers who met at Wilton, which also included Jonson and Drayton, and he tutored Pembroke's son.

90 Unless above himself he can
Erect himself, how poor a thing is man!
1594 'To the Lady Margaret, Countess of Cumberland'.

91 Custom that is before all law, Nature that is above all art.
1603 *A Defence of Rhyme.*

92 But years hath done this wrong,
To make me write too much, and live too long.
1605 *Philotas*, 'To the Prince', dedication.

Dante Alighieri *originally* ***Durante*** 1265–1321

Italian poet and scholar, author of *The Divine Comedy* (a poet's journey through hell, purgatory and paradise, begun c.1307). A White Guelf, he was exiled from his native Florence when the Black Guelfs triumphed in 1309. He died in Ravenna.

93 *Nel mezzo del cammin di nostra vita*
mi ritrovai per una selva oscura
ché la diritta via era smarrita.
In the middle of the journey of our life
I found myself in a dark wood
where the straight path was lost.
c.1320 *Divina Commedia*, 'Inferno', canto 1, l.1–3.

94 *Lasciate ogni speranza voi ch'entrate.*
Abandon all hope ye who enter here.
c.1320 Inscription above the gates of Hell. *Divina Commedia*, 'Inferno', canto 3, l.9.

95 *Nessun maggior dolore,*
Che ricordarsi del tempo felice
Nella miseria.
There is no greater pain than to remember a happy time when one is in misery.
c.1320 *Divina Commedia*, 'Inferno', canto 5, l.121–3.

96 *E quindi uscimmo a riveder le stelle.*
Thence we came forth to see the stars again.
c.1320 *Divina Commedia*, 'Inferno', canto 34, l.139.

97 *Lì si vedrà la superbia ch'asseta,*
che fa lo Scotto e l'Inghilese folle,
sì che non può soffrir dentro a sua meta.
There shall you see the pride which causes thirst,
which makes the Scots and the English mad,
so that they cannot remain within their boundaries.
c.1320 *Divina Commedia*, 'Paradiso', canto 1, l.121–3.

98 *E'n la sua voluntade è nostra pace.*
In His will is our peace.
c.1320 *Divina Commedia*, 'Paradiso', canto 3, l.85.

99 *L'amor che move il sole e l'altre stelle.*
The love that moves the sun and the other stars.
c.1320 *Divina Commedia*, 'Paradiso', canto 33, l.145.

Danton, Georges Jacques 1759–94

French revolutionary leader. As Minister of Justice (1792) he voted for the king's death. He tried to moderate the severity of the Revolutionary Tribunal, but lost the leadership to Robespierre and was executed for conspiracy.

1 *De l'audace, et encore de l'audace, et toujours de l'audace!*
Boldness, and again boldness, and always boldness!
1792 Speech to the Legislative Committee of General Defence, 2 Sep.

Darío, Rubén *pseudonym of* ***Félix Rubén García Sarmiento*** 1867–1916

Nicaraguan poet, journalist and diplomat. From 1886 he travelled extensively throughout Latin America and Europe. A key figure of Spanish-American Modernism, he experimented with rhythm, metre and imagery.

2 *Si hay poesía en nuestra América, ella está en las cosas viejas: en Palenke y Uatlán, en el indio legendario y el inca sensual y fino y en el gran Moctezuma de la silla de oro. Lo demás es tuyo, demócrata Walt Whitman.*
If there is poetry in our America, it is in ancient items: in Palenke and Uatlán, in the legendary Indian and in the sensuous and elegant Inca and the great Moctezuma. The rest is yours, democratic Walt Whitman.
1896 *Prosas profanas*, 'Palabras liminares'.

3 *Yo persigo una forma que no encuentra mi estilo,*
botón de pensamiento que busca ser la rosa;
se anuncia con un beso que en mis labios se posa
al abrazo imposible de la Venus de Milo.
I seek a form that my style cannot discover,
a bud of thought that wants to be a rose;
it is heralded by a kiss that is placed on my lips
in the impossible embrace of the Venus de Milo.
1896 *Prosas profanas*, 'Yo persigo una forma...' (translated as 'I seek a form...', 1922).

4 *Dichoso el árbol que es apenas sensitivo,*
y más la piedra dura porque ésa ya no siente,
pues no hay dolor más grande que el dolor de ser vivo,
ni mayor pesadumbre que la vida consciente.
Blessed is the almost insensitive tree,
more blessed is the hard stone that doesn't feel,
for no pain is greater than the pain of being alive,
and no sorrow more intense than conscious life.
1901 *Cantos de vida y esperanza*, 'Lo fatal' ('Fatalism').

Dark, Eleanor *née* **O'Reilly** *pseudonym* **Patricia O'Rane** 1901–85

Australian novelist and poet. Her works include the historical trilogy *The Timeless Land* (1941), *Storm of Time* (1948) and *No Barrier* (1953).

5 Silence ruled this land. Out of silence mystery comes, and magic, and the delicate awareness of unreasoning things.
1941 *The Timeless Land*, pt.1, '1788'.

Darman, Richard G(ordon) 1943–

US government official and businessman, Director of the Office of Management and the Budget in President Bush's Cabinet (1988–93).

6 I am now celebrating the 20th anniversary of the first request for my resignation. I look forward to many more.
Address to the White House press room. Quoted in Brian Kelly *Adventures in Porkland* (1992).

Darnell, Bill c.1940–

Canadian ecologist and activist, one of the original founders of the Greenpeace Foundation in Vancouver, British Columbia.

7 Make it a *green* peace.
1970 Quoted in Robert Hunter *Warriors of the Rainbow* (1979).

Darrow, Clarence Seward 1857–1938

US lawyer. He undertook the defence of John T Scopes (1925) for the teaching of Darwinism in school.

8 I do not consider it an insult but rather a compliment to be called an agnostic. I do not pretend to know where many ignorant men are sure—that is all that agnosticism means.
1925 Speech in defence of John T Scopes, 15 Jul.

Darwin, Charles Robert 1809–82

English naturalist. He joined the HMS *Beagle* scientific survey (1831–6) to South America and Australasia, which led eventually to his theory of evolution and the publication of many scientific works, including *The Origin of Species by Means of Natural Selection* (1859).

9 The naturalist in England, in his walks, enjoys a great advantage over others in frequently meeting with something worthy of attention; here he suffers a pleasant nuisance in not being able to walk a hundred yards without being fairly tied to the spot by some new and wondrous creature.
1832 In Brazil. *Journey of Researches into the Geology and Natural History of the Various Countries Visited during the Voyage of HMS 'Beagle' Round the World* (published 1839).

10 I have called this principle, by which each slight variation, if useful, is preserved, by the term of Natural Selection, in order to mark its relation to man's power of selection.
1859 *The Origin of Species by Means of Natural Selection*, ch.3.

11 From the war of nature, from famine and death, the most exalted object which we are capable of conceiving, namely, the production of the higher animals, directly follows. There is grandeur in this view of life.
1859 *The Origin of Species by Means of Natural Selection*, ch.14.

12 Great is the power of steady misrepresentation—but the history of science shows how, fortunately, this power does not long endure.
1859 *The Origin of Species by Means of Natural Selection*.

13 I have tried lately to read Shakespeare, and found it so intolerably dull that it nauseated me.
1860 *The Life and Letters of Charles Darwin*, vol.1.

14 False facts are highly injurious to the progress of science, for they often long endure; but false views, if supported by some evidence, do little harm, as every one takes a salutary pleasure in proving their falseness.
1871 *The Descent of Man and Selection in Relation to Sex*, ch.13.

15 The chief distinction in the intellectual powers of the two sexes is shewn by man's attaining to a higher eminence in whatever he takes up, than can woman—whether requiring deep thought, reason, or imagination, or merely the use of the senses and hands.
1871 *The Descent of Man and Selection in Relation to Sex*, ch.19.

16 We must however acknowledge, as it seems to me, that man with all his noble qualities...still bears in his bodily frame the indelible stamp of his lowly origin.
1871 *The Descent of Man and Selection in Relation to Sex*, ch.21.

17 I must begin with a good body of facts and not from a principle (in which I always suspect some fallacy) and then as much deduction as you please.
1874 Letter to J Fiske, 8 Dec.

18 A mathematician is a blind man in a dark room looking for a black cat which isn't there.
Quoted in John D Barrow *Pie in the Sky, Counting, Thinking and Being* (1992).

Darwin, Sir Francis 1848–1925

English botanist, son of Charles Darwin. He became a Reader in Botany at Oxford (1888) and produced his father's *Life and Letters* (1887–1903).

19 In science the credit goes to the man who convinces the world, not to the man to whom the idea first occurs.
1914 'Francis Galton', in *Eugenics Review*, vol.6, issue 1, Apr.

Daugherty, Harry Micajah 1860–1941

US politician, manager of Warren G Harding's political career from 1902. He was tried and acquitted (1927) on fraud charges.

20 A group of senators, bleary eyed for lack of sleep, will have to sit down at about two o'clock in the morning around a table in a smoke-filled room in some hotel, and decide the nomination.
1920 On the Republicans' failure to choose a presidential candidate at their convention.

David, Hal 1921–

US lyricist. He frequently worked with Burt Bacharach. His lyrics include *What the World Needs Now Is Love* and *Do You Know the Way to San Jose*.

21 Raindrops Keep Fallin' on My Head.
1969 Title of song. (Music by Burt Bacharach.)

Davidson, John 1857–1909

Scottish poet and writer. He moved to London in 1885, publishing *Fleet Street Eclogues* (1893) and *Ballads and Songs* (1894). He committed suicide by drowning himself at Penzance.

22 The difficultest job a man can do,

is to come it brave and meek with thirty bob a week,
and feel that that's the proper thing for you.
1894 *Ballads and Songs*, 'Thirty Bob a Week', stanza 15.

23 It's naked child against hungry wolf;
it's playing bowls upon a splitting wreck;
it's walking on a string across a gulf
with millstones fore-and-aft about your neck;
but the thing is daily done by many and many a one;
and we fall, face forward, fighting, on the deck.
1894 *Ballads and Songs*, 'Thirty Bob a Week', stanza 16.

24 In anguish we uplift
A new unhallowed song:
The race is to the swift,
The battle to the strong.
1899 'War Song', stanza 1.
► *See Bible 101:85.*

25 And blood in torrents pour
In vain—always in vain,
For war breeds war again.
1899 'War Song', stanza 7.

26 When the pods went pop on the broom, green broom,
And apples began to be golden-skinned,
We harboured a stag in the Priory coomb.
1906 *Holiday and Other Poems*, 'A Runnable Stag', stanza 1.

27 A stag of warrant, a stag, a stag,
A runnable stag, a kingly crop,
Brow, bay and tray and three on top,
A stag, a runnable stag.
1906 *Holiday and Other Poems*, 'A Runnable Stag', stanza 1.

Davie, George Elder 1912–

Scottish philosopher, a pioneer in studies of the Scottish Enlightenment.

28 The Democratic Intellect.
1961 Title of book.

Davies, (Sarah) Emily 1830–1921

English feminist and educational reformer who campaigned vigorously for equal opportunities for women in education.

29 If neither governesses or mothers *know*, how can they teach? So long as education is not provided *for* them, how can it be provided *by* them?
1868 Paper read at the Annual Meeting of the National Association for the Promotion of Social Sciences, published in *Thoughts on Some Questions Relating to Women 1860–1908*.

30 We have persuaded ourselves that Englishmen of the present day are such a nervously excitable race, that the only chance for their descendants is to keep the mothers in a state of coma. The fathers, we think are incurable.
1868 Paper read at the Annual Meeting of the National Association for the Promotion of Social Sciences, published in *Thoughts on Some Questions Relating to Women 1860–1908*.

Davies, Sir John 1569–1626

English poet and civil servant. He held high office in Ireland where he supported severe repressive measures and was nominated Chief Justice (1626). His poems include *Orchestra, or a Poem of Dancing* (1596) and *Hymns to Astrea* (1599).

31 Dancing is a frenzy and a rage.
1596 *Orchestra, or a Poem of Dancing*, stanza 16.

32 This wondrous miracle did Love devise,
For dancing is love's proper exercise.
1596 *Orchestra, or a Poem of Dancing*, stanza 18.

33 Learn then to dance, you that are princes born,
And lawful lords of earthly creatures all;
Imitate them, and thereof take no scorn,
(For this new art to them is natural)
And imitate the stars celestial.
For when pale death your vital twist shall sever,
Your better parts must dance with them forever.
1596 *Orchestra, or a Poem of Dancing*, stanza 60.

34 Skill comes so slow, and life so fast doth fly,
We learn so little and forget so much.
1599 *Nosce Teipsum*, stanza 19.

35 I know my life's a pain and but a span,
I know my sense is mocked in every thing;
And to conclude, I know myself a man,
Which is a proud and yet a wretched thing.
1599 *Nosce Teipsum*, stanza 45.

36 Wedlock, indeed, hath oft compared been
To public feasts where meet a public rout,
Where they that are without would fain go in
And they that are within would fain go out.
1608 'A Contention Betwixt a Wife, a Widow, and a Maid for Precedence', l.193–6.

Davies, Nigel 1960–

English chess player.

37 One very important aspect of actually achieving something is, I believe, the ability to avoid making excuses, in all their guises.
Quoted on www.chessville.com.

Davies, Ray(mond Douglas) 1944–

British songwriter and rock musician, founder of The Kinks (1963). His lyrics are noted for their lightly satirical commentary.

38 One week he's in polka-dots, the next week he's in stripes
'Cos he's a dedicated follower of fashion.
1966 'Dedicated Follower of Fashion'.

Davies, Robertson 1913–95

Canadian novelist, playwright, critic and essayist. After the Deptford trilogy (1970–5) he wrote another trilogy, including *What's Bred in the Bone* (1985), shortlisted for the Booker Prize.

39 There is more to marriage than four bare legs under a blanket.
1957 *Love and Libel*.

40 'Mary, what made you do it?'
She looked him honestly in the face and gave the answer that became famous in Deptford: 'He was very civil, 'Masa. And he wanted it so badly.'
1970 Mrs. Dempster explains to her parson husband why she had sex with a tramp. *Fifth Business*, pt.1, ch.10.

41 I saw corpses, and grew used to their unimportant look, for a dead man without any of the panoply of death is a desperately insignificant object.
1970 Of World War I. *Fifth Business*, pt.2, ch.1.

42 When a man is down on his luck he seems to consume all

he can get of coffee and doughnuts.
1970 *Fifth Business*, pt.4, ch.1.

43 He was killed by the usual cabal: by himself, first of all; by the woman he knew; by the woman he did not know; by the man who granted his inmost wish; and by the inevitable fifth, who was keeper of his conscience and keeper of the stone.
1970 *Fifth Business*, pt.6, ch.8.

44 Canada is not really a place where you are encouraged to have large spiritual adventures.
1972 Interviewed by Peter C Newman, 'The Master's Voice', in *Maclean's*, Sep.

45 The ideal companion in bed is a good book.
Interviewed by Terence M Green, recorded in J Madison Davis (ed) *Conversations with Robertson Davies* (1989).

Davies, Ron(ald) 1946–

Welsh Labour politician, Secretary of State for Wales (1997–8).

46 It was a moment of madness for which I have subsequently paid a very, very heavy price.
1998 Talking about the episode on Clapham common which led to his resignation as Welsh Secretary. Television interview, 30 Oct.

Davies, W(illiam) H(enry) 1871–1940

Welsh poet, who emigrated to the US at the age of 22. He lost a leg there while jumping a train and returned to England, where he lived as a tramp until his poetry found a public. He also wrote novels and autobiographical works.

47 It was the Rainbow gave thee birth,
And left thee all her lovely hues.
1910 'The Kingfisher'.

48 What is this life if, full of care,
We have no time to stand and stare?
1911 'Leisure'.

49 A rainbow and a cuckoo's song
May never come together again;
May never come
This side the tomb.
1914 'A Great Time'.

50 And hear the pleasant cuckoo, loud and long—
The simple bird that thinks two notes a song.
1916 'April's Charms'.

da Vinci, Leonardo

► See Leonardo da Vinci

Davis, Adelle 1904–74

US nutritionist.

51 People in nutrition do get the idea that they are going to live to be 150. And they never do.
1973 Quoted in Daniel Yergin's 'Supernutritionist', *New York Times* magazine, 20 May.

Davis, Bette *originally* *Ruth Elizabeth Davis* 1908–89

US film actress. She made her screen debut in 1931 and in the late 1930s and 1940s starred in a string of romantic melodramas such as *The Old Maid* (1939) and *Now Voyager* (1942).

52 Mother of three; divorcee; American. Twenty years experience as an actress in motion pictures. Mobile still and more affable than rumour would have it. Wants steady employment in Hollywood. (Has had Broadway). References upon request.
1962 Advertisement placed in the Hollywood trade papers.

53 Evil people...you never forget them. And that's the aim of any actress—never to be forgotten.
1966 On her favourite character roles. In the New York State Theater programme, Jun.

54 The best time I ever had with Joan Crawford was when I pushed her down the stairs in *Whatever Happened to Baby Jane?*
Quoted in Doug McClelland *Star Speak* (1987).

55 I have eyes like a bullfrog, a neck like an ostrich and long, limp hair. You just have to be good to survive with that equipment.
Attributed.

56 She's the original good time who was had by all.
On an anonymous starlet. Attributed.

Davis, Jefferson 1808–89

US statesman. He led the Senate's extreme State Rights Party, supported slavery, and was President of the rebel Confederate States during the Civil War (1861–5). Later imprisoned, he was never brought to trial.

57 All we ask is to be let alone.
1861 Inaugural address, 18 Feb.

Davis, Miles Dewey, III 1926–91

US jazz trumpeter and composer. A leading figure in postwar jazz, he also won wide acceptance with rock audiences in the 1970s and 1980s.

58 An artist's first responsibility is to himself.
1961 *Ebony*, Jan.

59 You could be a great musician, an innovative and important artist, but nobody cared if you didn't make the white people who were in control some money.
1989 *Autobiography*, ch.10.

Davis, Sammy, Jnr 1925–90

US jazz musician, actor, dancer and comedian.

60 Being a star has made it possible for me to get insulted in places where the average Negro could never hope to go and get insulted.
1965 *Yes I Can*, pt.3, ch.23.

Davis, Steve 1957–

English snooker player. He won the world championships six times.

61 Billiards is very similar to snooker, except there are only three balls and no one watches it.
1988 Quoted in Colin Jarman *The Guinness Dictionary of Sports Quotations* (1990).

Davis, Stuart 1894–1964

US Cubist painter.

62 An artist who has travelled on a steam train, driven an automobile, or flown in an airplane doesn't feel the same way about form and space as one who has not.
1940 'Is There a Revolution in the Arts?', in *Bulletin of America's Town Meeting of the Air*, vol.5, no.19 (19 Feb).

63 It has been often said, even by proponents of those pictures known in aesthetic slang as Cubist and Abstract, that they have no subject matter. Such a statement is equivalent to saying that life has no subject matter.
1943 'The Cube Root', in *Art News*, vol.41, 1 Feb.

Davis, Thomas Osborne 1814–45

Irish poet and politician, head of the Young Ireland Movement. He cofounded the weekly *Nation* in 1842, and wrote patriotic verses which became anthems of the Sinn Féin movement.

64 'Did they dare, did they dare, to slay Owen Roe O'Neil?'
'Yes, they slew with poison him they feared to meet with steel.'
'May God wither up their hearts! May their blood cease to flow!
May they walk in living death, who poisoned Owen Roe!'
1842 'Lament for the Death of Owen Roe O'Neil'.

65 Sagest in the council was he, kindest in the hall:
Sure we never won a battle—'twas Owen won them all.
Had he lived, had he lived, our dear country had been free;
But he's dead, but he's dead, and 'tis slaves we'll ever be.
1842 'Lament for the Death of Owen Roe O'Neil'.

66 They fought as they revelled, fast, fiery, and true,
And, though victors, they left on the field not a few;
And they who survived fought and drank as of yore,
But the land of their heart's hope they never saw more,
For in far, foreign fields, from Dunkirk to Belgrade
Lie the soldiers and chiefs of the Irish Brigade.
1845 *The Spirit of the Nation*, 'The Battle-Eve of the Brigade'.

67 Our colonel comes from Brian's race,
His wounds are in his breast and face.
1845 *The Spirit of the Nation*, 'Clare's Dragoons'.

68 Viva la the New Brigade!
Viva la the Old One, too!
Viva la, the Rose shall fade,
And the Shamrock shine for ever new!
1845 *The Spirit of the Nation*, 'Clare's Dragoons'.

69 Come in the evening, or come in the morning,
Come when you're looked for, or come without warning.
1846 'The Welcome'.

Davison, Emily Wilding 1872–1913

English militant suffragette, who campaigned fiercely for women's emancipation. She was frequently imprisoned, and died after running in front of the King's horse at the 1913 Derby.

70 As I am a woman and women do not count in the State, I refuse to be counted. Rebellion against tyrants is obedience to God.
1911 Comment on uncompleted Census paper, quoted in Gertrude Colmore *The Life of Emily Wilding Davison* (1913).

Dawkins, Richard 1941–

British ethologist, Professor at Oxford. He has done much to popularize the theories of Charles Darwin, most notably in his work *The Selfish Gene* (1976).

71 There is a better reason for studying zoology than its possible 'usefulness', and the general likeableness of animals. This reason is that we animals are the most complicated and perfectly designed pieces of machinery in the known universe. Put it like that, and it is hard to see why anybody studies anything else!
1976 *The Selfish Gene*, preface.

72 We are survival machines—robot vehicles blindly programmed to preserve the selfish molecules known as genes. This is a truth which still fills me with astonishment.
1976 *The Selfish Gene*, ch.2.

73 It has no vision, no foresight, no sight at all. If it can be said to play the role of watchmaker in nature, it is the *blind* watchmaker.
1986 Of natural selection. *The Blind Watchmaker*, ch.1.
► *See Paley 635:16.*

74 However many ways there may be of being alive, it is certain that there are vastly more ways of being dead.
1986 *The Blind Watchmaker*, ch.1.

Day, Clarence Shepard 1874–1935

US humorist, best known for his writings in the *New Yorker* and for his autobiographical sketches in *Life With Father* (1935).

75 The poets of each generation seldom sing a new song. They turn themes men always have loved, and sing them in the mode of their times.
1921 *The Crow's Nest*, 'Humpty-Dumpty and Adam'.

76 The real world is not easy to live in. It is rough; it is slippery. Without the most clear-eyed adjustments we fall and get crushed. A man must stay sober: not always, but most of the time.
1921 *The Crow's Nest*, 'In His Baby Blue Ship'.

77 I meant to be prompt, but it never occurred to me that I had better try to be early.
1935 *Life With Father*, 'Father teaches me to be prompt'.

78 Imagine the Lord talking French! Aside from a few odd words in Hebrew, I took it for granted that God had never spoken anything but the most dignified English.
1935 *Life With Father*, 'Father interferes'.

79 'If you don't go to other men's funerals,' he told Father stiffly, 'they won't go to yours.'
1935 *Life With Father*, 'Father interferes'.

80 Father declared he was going to buy a new plot in the cemetery, a plot all for himself. 'And I'll buy one on a corner,' he added triumphantly, 'where I can get out.'
1935 *Life With Father*, penultimate paragraph.

Day, Doris *originally* ***Doris Kappelhoff*** 1924–

US singer and film actress, whose sunny personality and girl-next-door image made her a star of 1950s musicals.

81 The really frightening thing about middle age is the knowledge that you'll grow out of it.
Quoted in A E Hotchner *Doris Day* (1978).

Dayan, Moshe 1915–81

Israeli soldier and politician. He left the Labour Party in 1966 to set up the Rafi Party with Ben Gurion. His heavily outnumbered forces were successful in the Six-Day War (1967), and as Foreign Minister he helped secure peace with Egypt (1977).

82 Whenever you accept our views, we shall be in full agreement with you.

Remark to US envoy Cyrus Vance during the Arab–Israeli negotiations, quoted in the *Observer*, 14 Aug 1977.

Day-Lewis, Cecil 1904–72

Irish poet and critic. Professor at Oxford (1951–6) and Harvard (1964–5), he became Poet Laureate in 1968. As well as poetry he wrote criticism, translation and, under the pseudonym Nicholas Blake, detective novels.

83 Tempt me no more; for I
Have known the lightning's hour,
The poet's inward pride,
The certainty of power.
1933 *The Magnetic Mountain*, pt.3, no.24.

84 You that love England, who have an ear for her music,
The slow movement of clouds in benediction,
Clear arias of light thrilling over her uplands,
Over the chords of summer sustained peacefully.
1933 *The Magnetic Mountain*, pt.4, no.32.

85 Do not expect again a phoenix hour,
The triple-towered sky, the dove complaining,
Sudden the rain of gold and heart's first ease
Traced under trees by the eldritch light of sundown.
1935 'From Feathers to Iron'.

86 Now we lament one
Who danced on a plume of words,
Sang with a fountain's panache,
Dazzled like slate roofs in sun
After rain, was flighty as birds
And alone as a mountain ash.
The ribald, inspired urchin
Leaning over the lip
Of his world, as over a rock pool
Or a lucky dip,
Found everything brilliant and virgin.
1953 'In Memory of Dylan Thomas'.

Dean, John 1938–

US lawyer and author. As White House adviser to President Nixon, he was implicated in the Watergate scandal.

87 I am convinced that we are going to make the whole road and put this thing in the funny pages of the history books.
1973 Taped conversation with the President, Feb.

88 We have a cancer within, close to the presidency, that is growing. It is growing daily.
1973 Taped conversation with the President, Mar.

89 Doing time is like climbing a mountain wearing roller skates.
1977 On conviction after the Watergate scandal. In *Newsweek*, 4 Jul.

90 History never exactly repeats itself, but it does some rather good impressions.
Comparing the presidential styles of Richard Nixon and George W Bush. Quoted in *Worse than Watergate* (2004).

de Beauvoir, Simone 1906–86

French philosopher, feminist and writer, who maintained a lifelong association with fellow-existentialist Jean-Paul Sartre. Her *Le Deuxième Sexe* (*The Second Sex*, 1949–50) is a pioneering feminist text.

91 There is a good case for showing that airplanes, machines, the telephone and the radio do not make men of today happier than those of former times.
1948 *Ethics of Ambiguity.*

92 *On ne naît pas femme: on le devient.*
One is not born a woman: one becomes a woman.
1949 *Le Deuxième Sexe* (*The Second Sex*), bk.2, pt.1, ch.1

93 *Ce n'est guère que dans les asiles que les coquettes gardent avec entêtement une foi entière en des regards absents; normalement, elles réclament des témoins.*
Women fond of dress are hardly ever entirely satisfied not to be seen, except among the insane; usually they want witnesses.
1949 *Le Deuxième Sexe* (*The Second Sex*), bk.2, pt.5, ch.18 (translated by H M Parshley, 1952).

94 *La femme…sait que quand on la regarde on ne la distingue pas de son apparence: elle est jugée, respectée, désirée à travers sa toilette.*
Woman…knows that when she is looked at she is not considered apart from her appearance: she is judged, respected, desired, by and through her toilette.
1949 *Le Deuxième Sexe* (*The Second Sex*), bk.2, pt.7, ch.25 (translated by H M Parshley, 1952).

95 *Si l'on vit assez longtemps, on voit que toute victoire se change un jour en défaite.*
If you live long enough, you'll find that every victory turns into a defeat.
1955 *Tous les hommes sont mortels* (*All Men Are Mortal*).

de Bernières, Louis 1954–

English author who achieved international fame with *Captain Corelli's Mandolin* (1994), a love story set on a small island in Greece during World War II.

96 Writing today is like being stood stark naked in Trafalgar Square and being told to get an erection.
2001 On being asked how he was making progress on a successor to *Captain Corelli's Mandolin* (1994), Apr.

de Botton, Alain 1969–

British author, born in Switzerland.

97 How generous was it to offer gifts to people one knew would never accept them?
1994 *The Romantic Movement*, 'Martyrdom'.

98 How Proust Can Change Your Life.
1997 Book title.

Debray, Regis 1941–

French Marxist theorist. He gained international fame through his association with Che Guevara in Latin America.

99 Since the Cuban Revolution and since the invasion of Santo Domingo *a state of emergency* has existed in Latin America. The Marines shoot at anything that moves, regardless of party affiliation.
1967 *Révolution dans la Révolution?*

1 *Vedi Napoli, e poi muori? Oui, mais pour voir Venise, mourez d'abord.*
See Naples and die? Yes, but to see Venice, die first.
1995 *Contre Venise.*

2 *À Naples, personne ne vous demande dans quel hôtel ou chez qui vous êtes descendu: c'est indifférent. À Venise, impossible d'échapper la question: Gritti? Danieli?*

Palazzo du duc de C.? Appartement de M.?
(Consternation si vous répondez: auberge de jeunesse, ou dortoir de l'institut universitaire.)
In Naples, no one asks you which hotel you're in or who you're staying with: it doesn't matter. In Venice, you can't avoid the question: the Gritti? the Danieli? the Duke of C.'s palazzo? M.'s apartment? (Dismay if you reply: the youth hostel, or the university halls of residence.)
1995 *Contre Venise*.

Debussy, Claude Achille 1862–1918

French composer. His writing for piano was described as 'musical Impressionism'. He translated it to the orchestra in *La Mer* (1905), to his opera, *Pelléas et Mélisande*, and to other works.

3 The colour of my soul is iron-grey and sad bats wheel about the steeple of my dreams.
1894 Letter.

4 That old poisoner.
1896 Letter, alluding to Wagner.

5 People don't very much like things that are beautiful—they are so far from their nasty little minds.
1900 Letter.

6 A pink bonbon stuffed with snow.
1903 Of the music of Edvard Grieg. *Gil Blas*.

7 A century of aeroplanes deserves its own music. As there are no precedents, I must create anew.
1913 Quoted in *La Revue S.I.M.*

Decatur, Stephen 1779–1820

US naval officer, who distinguished himself in the war with Tripoli (1801–5) and fought against Britain, capturing the frigate *Macedonian* (1812), but surrendering in 1814.

8 Our country! In her intercourse with foreign nations, may she always be in the right; but our country, right or wrong.
1816 Speech made in Norfolk, Virginia, Apr.
► *See Adams 5:92, Chesterton 211:46.*

Deedes, William Francis Deedes, Baron 1913–

English Conservative politician and journalist. He was an MP (1950–1974), and later pursued a career in journalism, becoming Editor of the *Daily Telegraph* (1974–86).

9 One golden rule for people who want to get on in politics is to keep their traps shut in August.
1999 In *The Mail on Sunday*, 22 Aug.

Deffand, Marquise du 1697–1780

French noblewoman, famous for her wit and beauty. Her salon was frequented by leading figures in Paris literary society, including Voltaire, Montesquieu and D'Alembert.

10 The distance does not matter; it is only the first step that counts.
1763 Commenting on the legend of St Denis, said to have carried his severed head for six miles following his execution. Letter, 7 Jul.

Defoe, Daniel 1660–1731

English writer, best known for his novels *Robinson Crusoe* (1719) and *Moll Flanders* (1722), and for his partly factual *Journal of the Plague Year* (1724). He also wrote a travel book, *A Tour Through the Whole Island of Great Britain* (1724–7).

11 The soul is placed in the body like a rough diamond, and must be polished, or the lustre of it will never appear.
1697 *An Essay upon Projects*, 'Of Academies: An Academy for Women'.

12 The best of men cannot suspend their fate:
The good die early, and the bad die late.
1697 'Character of the Late Dr Annesley'.

13 Wherever God erects a house of prayer,
The Devil always builds a chapel there;
And 'twill be found, upon examination,
The latter hast the largest congregation.
1701 *The True-Born Englishman*, pt.1, l.1–4.

14 From this amphibious ill-born mob began
That vain, ill-natured thing, an Englishman.
1701 *The True-Born Englishman*, pt.1, l.132–3.

15 Your Roman-Saxon-Danish-Norman English.
1701 *The True-Born Englishman*, pt.1, l.139.

16 His lazy, long, lascivious reign.
1701 Of Charles II. *The True-Born Englishman*, pt.1, l.236.

17 Actions receive their tincture from the times,
And as they change are virtues made or crimes.
1703 *A Hymn to the Pillory*, l.29–30.

18 It happened one day, about noon, going towards my boat, I was exceedingly surprised with the print of a man's naked foot on the shore, which was very plain to be seen in the sand. I stood like one thunderstruck, or as if I had seen an apparition.
1719 *Robinson Crusoe*.

19 My man Friday.
1719 *Robinson Crusoe*.

20 Vice came in always at the door of necessity, not at the door of inclination.
1722 *Moll Flanders*.

21 Manchester, one of the greatest, if not really the greatest mere village in England.
1724–7 *A Tour Through the Whole Island of Great Britain*, letter 10.

22 Here is a pleasant situation, and yet nothing pleasant to be seen. Here is a harbour without ships, a port without trade, a fishery without nets, a people without business; and, that which is worse than all, they do not seem to desire business, much less do they understand it.
1724–7 Of Kirkcudbright, Scotland. *A Tour Through the Whole Island of Great Britain*, letter 12.

23 A very fine city; the four principal streets are the fairest for breadth, and the finest built that I have ever seen in one city together... In a word, 'tis the cleanest and beautifullest, and best built city in Britain, London excepted.
1724–7 Of Glasgow. *A Tour Through the Whole Island of Great Britain*, letter 12.

24 Pleasure is a *thief* to business.
1725 *The Complete English Tradesman*, vol.1, ch.9.

25 Things as certain as death and taxes, can be more firmly believed.
1726 *History of the Devil*, bk.2, ch.6.
► *See also Franklin 335:18.*

De Forest, Lee 1873–1961

US inventor, pioneer in the development of wireless telegraphy and radio.

26 While theoretically and technically television may be feasible, commercially and financially I consider it an impossibility, a development of which we need waste little time dreaming.
1926 In the *New York Times*.

Degas, (Hilaire Germain) Edgar 1834–1917

French artist. After a trip to Italy, where he was influenced by Renaissance painters, he returned to Paris and exhibited with the Impressionists (1874–86).

27 Art does not expand, it repeats itself.
1872 Letter to Paul Frölich, 27 Nov.

28 It is essential to do the same subject over again, ten times, a hundred times.
1886 Letter to Bartholomé, 17 Jan.

29 Aren't all beautiful things made by renunciation?
Quoted in P Lafond *Degas* (1918–9).

30 Drawing is not the form; it is the way of seeing the form.
Quoted in P Valéry *Degas, danse, dessin* (1938).

31 Art cannot be made with an intent to please.
Quoted in R H Ives Gammell *The Shop-Talk of Edgar Degas* (1961).

32 It is all very well to copy what you see; it is much better to draw what you see only in memory.
Quoted in R H Ives Gammell *The Shop-Talk of Edgar Degas* (1961).

33 Everybody has talent at twenty-five. The difficult thing is to have it at fifty.
Quoted in R H Ives Gammell *The Shop-Talk of Edgar Degas* (1961).

de Gaulle, Charles 1890–1970

French general. Leader of the Free French during World War II, he became head of the provisional government, and later Prime Minister (1958). As President of the Fifth Republic, he implemented an assertive foreign policy, but in 1969 resigned after the defeat of his referendum proposals for senate and regional reforms.

34 Nothing great will ever be achieved without great men—and men only become great if they are determined to be so.
1934 *Le Fil de l'épée*.

35 *La France a perdu une bataille! Mais la France n'a pas perdu la guerre!*
France has lost a battle! But France has not lost the war!
1940 Proclamation, 18 Jun. Collected in *Discours, messages et déclarations du Général de Gaulle* (1941).

36 *Puisque ceux qui avaient le devoir de manier l'épée de la France l'ont laissée tomber brisée, moi, j'ai ramassé le tronçon du glaive.*
Since those whose duty it was to wield the sword of France have let it fall shattered to the ground, I have taken up the broken blade.
1940 Speech, 13 Jul.

37 The French will only be united under the threat of danger. How else can one govern a country that produces 246 different types of cheese?
1951 Speech. Quoted in *Les Mots du Général* (1962).

38 *Les traités, voyez-vous, sont comme les jeunes filles et comme les roses: ça dure ce que ça dure.*
Treaties are like girls and roses—they last while they last.
1963 Speech at the Elysée Palace, 2 Jul. Quoted in Brian Crozier *De Gaulle the Statesman* (1973).

39 I myself have become a Gaullist only little by little.
1963 In the *Observer*, 29 Dec.

40 I respect only those who resist me, but I cannot tolerate them.
1966 In the *New York Times*, 12 May.

41 Vive le Québec! Vive le Québec libre! Vive le Canada français! Vive la France!
1967 Address to the crowd before Montreal's City Hall, 24 Jul. The slogan 'Québec libre' was identified with the separatist cause.

42 When I want to know what France thinks, I ask myself.
Sons of France.

43 In order to become the master, the politician poses as the servant.
Attributed.

44 Politics is too important to be left to the politicians.
Attributed.

Dekanahwideh fl.c.1450

Native American leader, traditional founder of the Six Nations Confederacy.

45 I, Dekanahwideh, and the Confederated Chiefs, now uproot the tallest pine tree, and into the cavity thereby made we cast all weapons of war… Thus shall the Great Peace be established.
Traditional words from the Six Nations Confederacy (present-day Ontario and the Northeastern United States), one of the world's oldest constitutions, quoted in Paul A W Wallace *The White Roots of Peace* (1946).

Dekker, Thomas c.1570–c.1641

English dramatist. He wrote dramas for both public and private stages, masques, pageants and topical pamphlets, and was imprisoned for debt for three years. He frequently collaborated with other dramatists.

46 Ill is the weather that bringeth no gain.
1600 *The Shoemaker's Holiday*, 'The First Three-men's Song'.

47 Dost thou not know that love respects no blood,
Cares not for difference of birth or state?
1600 *The Shoemaker's Holiday*, act 5, sc.5.

48 Golden slumbers kiss your eyes,
Smiles awake you when you rise;
Sleep, pretty wantons, do not cry,
And I will sing a lullaby,
Rock them, rock them, lullaby.
1603 *The Pleasant Comedy of Patient Grisill*, act 4, sc.2.

49 That great fishpond.
1604 Of the seas. *The Honest Whore*, pt.1, act 1, sc.2.

50 This wench we speak of strays so from her kind,
Nature repents she made her; 'tis a mermaid
Has tolled my son to shipwreck
1611 *The Roaring Girl* (with Thomas Middleton), act 1, sc.2.

51 'Tis the maddest fantasticalest girl. I never knew so much flesh and so much nimbleness put together.
1611 *The Roaring Girl* (with Thomas Middleton), act 2, sc.2.

52 I have no humour to marry; I love to lie o' both sides of the bed myself; and again, o' th' other side.
1611 *The Roaring Girl* (with Thomas Middleton), act 2, sc.2.

53 I have the head now of myself, and am man enough for a woman.
1611 *The Roaring Girl* (with Thomas Middleton), act 2, sc.2.

54 Thou'rt one of those
That thinks each woman thy fond flexible whore.
1611 *The Roaring Girl* (with Thomas Middleton), act 3, sc.1.

de Klerk, F(rederik) W(illem) 1936–

South African politician. He was President of South Africa (1989–94) and in 1993 was jointly awarded the Nobel peace prize with Nelson Mandela.

55 Today we have closed the book on apartheid.
1992 On the endorsement of his government's reform programme following a referendum of white South Africans. In *The Independent*, 19 Mar.

de Kooning, Willem 1904–97

Dutch-born US painter, who emigrated to the US in 1926 and became a leader of Abstract Expressionism, especially in action painting. His works, which focus on the human form, include the controversial series *Woman I–V* (1952–3).

56 Style is a fraud. I always felt the Greeks were hiding behind their columns.
1949 'A Desperate View', lecture given in New York.

57 Flesh was the reason why oil painting was invented.
1980 In *Bulletin*, Pittsburgh International Museum.

Delacroix, (Ferdinand Victor) Eugène 1798–1863

French Romantic painter, whose loose drawing and vivid colour aroused controversy. He continued to experiment with non-classical techniques and the use of colour.

58 What makes men of genius, or rather, what they make, is not new ideas, it is that idea—possessing them—that what has been said has still not been said enough.
1824 *The Journal of Eugène Delacroix* (translated by W Pach, 1948), entry for 15 May.

59 I live in company with a body, a silent companion, exacting and eternal. He it is who notes that individuality which is the seal of the weakness of our race. My soul has wings, but the brutal jailer is strict.
1824 *The Journal of Eugène Delacroix* (translated by W Pach, 1948), entry for 4 Jun.

60 A taste for simplicity cannot endure for long.
1847 *The Journal of Eugène Delacroix* (translated by W Pach, 1948).

61 Painters who are not colourists produce illumination and not painting.
1852 *The Journal of Eugène Delacroix* (translated by W Pach, 1948).

de la Mare, Walter 1873–1956

English poet and novelist. He worked for an oil company until 1908, when he became a full-time writer. His work included volumes of verse, novels, prose fantasy and short stories for both children and adults.

62 Oh, no man knows
Through what wild centuries
Roves back the rose.
1912 'All That's Past'.

63 'Is there anybody there?' said the Traveller,
Knocking on the moonlit door;
And his horse in the silence champed the grasses
Of the forest's ferny floor.
1912 'The Listeners'.

64 'Tell them I came, and no one answered,
That I kept my word,' he said.
1912 'The Listeners'.

65 Aye, they heard his foot upon the stirrup,
And the sound of iron on stone,
And how the silence surged softly backward,
When the plunging hoofs were gone.
1912 'The Listeners'.

66 He is crazed with the spell of far Arabia,
They have stolen his wits away.
1912 'Arabia'.

67 But beauty vanishes; beauty passes;
However rare—rare it be;
And when I crumble, who will remember
This lady of the West Country?
1912 'Epitaph'.

68 Ann, Ann!
Come! quick as you can!
There's a fish that *talks*
In the frying pan.
1913 'Alas, Alack'.

69 Slowly, silently, now the moon
Walks the night in her silver shoon.
1913 'Silver'.

70 A face peered. All the grey night
In chaos of vacancy shone;
Nought but vast Sorrow was there—
The sweet cheat gone.
1918 'The Ghost'.

71 When I lie where shades of darkness
Shall no more assail mine eyes.
1918 'Fare Well'.

72 Look thy last on all things lovely,
Every hour. Let no night
Seal thy sense in deathly slumber
Till to delight
Thou have paid thy utmost blessing.
1918 'Fare Well'.

73 Too late for fruit, too soon for flowers.
Attributed, when asked, while ill, if he would prefer fruit or flowers. Quoted in Clifton Fadiman *The Faber Book of Anecdotes* (1985).

Delaney, Shelagh 1939–

English playwright and screenwriter, whose best-known play, *A Taste of Honey* (produced 1958), was written when she was 17.

74 Women never have young minds. They are born three thousand years old.
1958 *A Taste of Honey*, act 1, sc.2.

DeLillo, Don 1936–

US novelist. His ambitious dissection of modern cultural codes in such novels as *White Noise* (1985), *Libra* (1988) and *Underworld* (1998) have made him an important voice in contemporary fiction.

75 I've come to think of Europe as a hardcover book,

America as the paperback version.
1982 Owen Brademas. *The Names*, ch.1.

76 Tourism is the march of stupidity.
1982 James Axton. *The Names*, ch.3.

77 If I were a writer, how I would enjoy being told the novel is dead. How liberating to work in the margins, outside a central perception. You are the ghoul of literature. Lovely.
1982 Owen Brademas. *The Names*, ch.4.

78 To a writer, madness is a final distillation of self, a final editing down. It's the drowning out of false voices.
1982 Owen Brademas. *The Names*, ch.5.

79 Men with secrets tend to be drawn to each other, not because they want to share what they know but because they need the company of the like-minded, the fellow-afflicted.
1988 Walter Everett, Jr. *Libra*, pt.1,'17 April'.

80 A conspiracy is everything that ordinary life is not. It's the inside game, cold, sure, undistracted, forever closed off to us. We are the flawed ones, the innocents, trying to make some rough sense of the daily jostle. Conspirators have a logic and a daring beyond our reach.
1988 *Libra*, pt.2,'In Dallas'.

81 The dead have come to take the living. The dead in winding sheets, the regimented dead on horseback, the skeleton that plays a hurdy-gurdy.
1998 *Underworld*.

Delius, Frederick 1862–1934

English composer of German-Scandinavian descent. He settled in France in 1890, establishing himself as a prolific and highly original composer. In 1924 he became paralysed and blind, but continued to work with the help of his amanuensis Eric Fenby.

82 It is only that which cannot be expressed otherwise that is worth expressing in music.
1920 'At the Crossroads'.

Deming, W(illiam) Edwards 1900–93

US statistician, inventor of modern quality control.

83 What's the aim of the school of business, for example? They teach students how business is conducted today and how to perpetuate it. Any wonder we're in trouble? They ought to be preparing students for the future, not for the past.
1990 Interview in the *Wall Street Journal*, 4 Jun.

Democritus c.460–c.370 BC

Greek philosopher. Only fragments of his extensive work on ethics have survived.

84 Nothing exists except atoms and empty space; everything else is opinion.
Diogenes Laertius, vol.9.

85 Strength and beauty are the blessings of youth; temperance, however, is the flower of old age.
Fragment quoted in H Diels and W Kranz (eds) *Die Fragmente der Vorsokratiker*, vol.2 (1952), no.294.

Dempsey, (William Harrison) Jack 1895–1983

US boxer. He won the world heavyweight title in 1919 and lost it to Gene Tunney in 1926. He retired in 1940 and became a successful restaurateur.

86 Honey, I forgot to duck.
1926 Attributed, to his wife after he was knocked out by Gene Tunney. US President Ronald Reagan repeated the phrase to his wife when wounded in an attempted assassination, 1981.

87 When you're fighting, you're fighting for one thing—money.
Quoted in Colin Jarman *The Guinness Dictionary of Sports Quotations* (1990).

Deng Xiaoping 1904–97

Chinese political leader who rose to power (1978) after disgrace during the Cultural Revolution. His international esteem suffered after he sanctioned the Tiananmen Square massacre of pro-democracy supporters, Jun 1989.

88 It doesn't matter whether the cat is black or white, as long as it catches mice.
1962 Speech at Communist Youth League conference, Jul.

89 A fundamental contradiction does not exist between socialism and a market economy.
1985 Address to US businessmen organized by *Time* magazine, 18 Dec.

90 Even if they're functioning out of ignorance, they are still participating and must be suppressed. In China, even one million people can be considered a small sum.
1989 Of pro-democracy demonstrators. In *The Times*, 5 Jun.

Denham, Sir John 1615–69

Irish poet and Royalist, who undertook secret missions for Charles I and Charles II during the Civil War and Protectorate, and was knighted in 1661. He is credited with introducing to English verse the couplet form which later dominated 18c poetry.

91 Can knowledge have no bound, but must advance
So far, to make us wish for ignorance?
1642 *Cooper's Hill*, l.145–6.

92 O could I flow like thee, and make thy stream
My great example, as it is my theme!
Though deep, yet clear, though gentle, yet not dull,
Strong without rage, without o'erflowing full.
1642 Of the Thames. *Cooper's Hill*, l.189–92.

93 Such is our pride, our folly, or our fate,
That few, but such as cannot write, translate.
1648 'To Richard Fanshaw'.

94 Old Mother Wit, and Nature gave
Shakespeare and Fletcher all they have;
In Spenser, and in Jonson, Art
Of slower Nature got the start.
1667 'On Mr Abraham Cowley'.

95 Youth, what man's age is like to be doth show;
We may our ends by our beginnings know.
1668 'Of Prudence', l.225–6.

Deniehy, Daniel Henry 1828–65

Australian lawyer, politician, orator and writer, who formed his own famous library.

96 A Bunyip Aristocracy.
1853 Quoted in *The Australian Dictionary of Biography*, vol 4. The bunyip is a mythical, chimerical animal of Australian folklore.

Denis, Maurice 1870–1943

French painter and art theorist, associated with the Nabis group ('prophets' influenced by Gauguin), and Symbolism.

97 Remember that a painting—before it is a battlehorse, a nude woman, or some anecdote—is essentially a flat surface covered with colours assembled in a certain order.
1912 *Théories: 1890–1910.*

Denman, Thomas, 1st Baron 1779–1854

English jurist. A Whig MP (1818–26), he was Attorney-General in Earl Grey's administration (1830–2) and Lord Chief Justice (1832–50).

98 Trial by jury itself, instead of being a security to persons who are accused, will be a delusion, a mockery, and a snare.
1844 Judgement in *O'Connell* v *The Queen*, 4 Sep.

Denning, Alfred Thompson, Lord 1899–1999

English judge. As Master of the Rolls (1962–82) he earned a reputation for his outspoken opinions.

99 A wrong decision can make me very miserable. But I have trust in God. If you have this trust you don't have to worry, as you don't have the sole responsibility.
1982 Speech on his retirement.

Dennis, C(larence Michael) J(ames) 1876–1938

Australian poet and journalist. His poems have been popular for their vernacular humour.

1 Me pal 'e trots 'er up an' does the toff—
'E allus wus a bloke fer showin' off.
'This 'ere's Doreen,' 'e sez. 'This 'ere's the Kid.'
I dips me lid.
1915 *Songs of a Sentimental Bloke*, 'The Intro'. Bill persuades his friend to introduce him to a girl.

Dennis, John 1657–1734

English playwright and critic. He was among the most famous critics of his day, but his own plays met with little success and he was one of the targets of Alexander Pope's satire in *The Dunciad*.

2 Damn them, see how the rascals use me! They will not let my play run, and yet they steal my thunder!
1709 Attributed, when watching a production of *Macbeth* that featured a thunder machine he had designed for use in his own play *Appius and Virginia*, which had been denied a long run. Said to be the origin of the phrase 'to steal one's thunder'.

3 A man who could make so vile a pun would not scruple to pick a pocket.
Of Dennis. In the *Gentleman's Magazine* 1781, editorial note.

Depp, Johnny (John Christopher) 1963–

US actor.

4 If you were waiting for the opportune moment, that was it.
2003 As Captain Jack Sparrow in *Pirates of the Caribbean* (screenplay by Ted Elliott and Terry Rossio).

5 I'm not swimming in the soup bowl. I'm not getting overcooked in that big stew pot.
2004 On why he lives in France rather than in Los Angeles. Quoted in *Scotland on Sunday*, 2 May.

De Quincey, Thomas 1785–1859

English writer. He ran away from school in 1802, lived with a prostitute in London, became an opium addict at Oxford, lived for a time in the Lake District and moved to Edinburgh in 1828.

6 A duller spectacle this earth of ours has not to show than a rainy Sunday in London.
1821 *Confessions of an English Opium Eater* (originally serialized in the *London Magazine*, published 1822).

7 Thou hast the keys of Paradise, oh just, subtle, and mighty opium!
1821 *Confessions of an English Opium Eater* (originally serialized in the *London Magazine*, published 1822).

8 Books, we are told, propose to *instruct* or to *amuse*. Indeed!… The true antithesis to knowledge, in this case, is not *pleasure*, but *power*. All that is literature seeks to communicate power; all that is not literature, to communicate knowledge.
1823 *Letters to a Young Man whose Education has been Neglected*, no.3, in the London Magazine, Jan–Jul.

9 Murder Considered as One of the Fine Arts.
1827 Title of essay, in *Blackwood's Magazine*, Feb.

10 If once a man indulges himself in murder, very soon he comes to think little of robbing; and from robbing he comes next to drinking and sabbath-breaking, and from that to incivility and procrastination.
1839 'On Murder Considered as One of the Fine Arts' (supplementary paper), in *Blackwood's Magazine*, Nov.

Derby, Edward Geoffrey Smith Stanley, 14th Earl of 1799–1869

English statesman and Conservative Prime Minister (1852, 1858–9, 1866–8), formerly a Whig. He entered the Lords in 1844 and headed the Protectionists from 1846, the year he became Party leader.

11 The foreign policy of the noble Earl, Lord Russell, may be summed up in two truly expressive words: meddle and muddle.
1864 Speech in the House of Lords, Feb, referring to the Prime Minister's policy on the American Civil War.

Desai, Anita *née Mazumbar* 1937–

Indian novelist, who writes for children and adults. Her novels *The Clear Light of Day* (1980), *In Custody* (1984) and *Fasting, Feasting* (1999) were all shortlisted for the Booker Prize.

12 Do you know anyone who would—secretly, sincerely, in his innermost self—*really* prefer to return to childhood?
1980 *The Clear Light of Day*, ch.1.

Desbiens, Jean-Paul 1927–

Canadian writer and educator.

13 Education is impossible without love, without loving a few of the great men of the past.
1965 *For Pity's Sake* (translated by Frédéric Côte).

Desbordes-Valmore, Marceline 1786–1859

French poet. She worked in the theatre and published children's stories before turning to poetry. Her poems are written in an open, informal style, often as dialogues.

14 *Par toi tout le bonheur que m'offre l'avenir*
Est dans mon souvenir.

Through you, all the happiness that the future offers
Is in my memory.
1819 *Élegies, Marie et romances*, 'Le Souvenir'.

15 *Ce qu'on donne à l'amour est à jamais perdu.*
What one gives in love is forever lost.
1830 *Poésies*, 'L'Isolement'.

16 *J'ai vécu d'aimer, j'ai donc vécu de larmes.*
I lived to love. I lived, therefore, in tears.
1860 *Poésies posthumes*, 'Rêve intermittent d'une nuit triste'.

Descartes, René 1596–1650

French philosopher and mathematician. He travelled widely before settling in Holland and writing his major works (both popular, in French, and scholarly, in Latin): the *Discours de la méthode* (1637), *Meditationes de prima philosophia* (1641), and *Principia philosophiae* (1644).

17 *La lecture de tous les bons livres est comme une conversation avec les plus honnêtes gens des siècles passés, qui en ont été les auteurs, et même une conversation étudiée en laquelle ils ne nous découvrent que les meilleures de leurs pensées.*
The reading of good books is like a conversation with the best men of past centuries—in fact like a prepared conversation, in which they reveal their best thoughts.
1637 *Discours de la méthode (Discourse on Method)*, 1st discourse (translated by G E M Anscombe and Peter Geach).

18 *Le bon sens est la chose du monde la mieux partagée: car chacun pense en être si bien pourvu, que ceux même qui sont les plus difficiles à contenter en toute autre chose n'ont point coutume d'en désirer plus qu'ils ont. En quoi il n'est pas vraisemblable que tous se trompent; mais plutôt cela témoigne que la puissance de bien juger et distinguer le vrai d'avec le faux, qui est proprement ce qu'on nomme le bon sens ou la raison, est naturellement égale en tous les hommes.*
Good sense is the most fairly distributed thing in the world; for everyone thinks himself so well supplied with it, that even those who are hardest to satisfy in every other way do not usually desire more of it than they already have. In this matter it is not likely that everybody is mistaken; it rather goes to show that the power of judging well and distinguishing truth from falsehood, which is what we properly mean by good sense or reason, is naturally equal in all men.
1637 *Discours de la méthode (Discourse on Method)*, 1st discourse (translated by G E M Anscombe and Peter Geach).

19 *Pour ce qu'alors je désirais vaquer seulement à la recherche de la vérité, je pensai qu'il fallait que je…rejetasse comme absolument faux tout ce en quoi je pourrais imaginer le moindre doute, afin de voir s'il ne resterait point, après cela, quelque chose en ma créance qui fût entièrement indubitable.*
Since my present aim was to give myself up to the pursuit of truth alone, I thought I must…reject as if absolutely false anything as to which I could imagine the least doubt, in order to see if I should not be left at the end believing something that was absolutely indubitable.
1637 *Discours de la méthode (Discourse on Method)*, 4th discourse (translated by G E M Anscombe and Peter Geach).

20 *Je pris garde que, pendant que je voulais ainsi penser que tout était faux, il fallait nécessairement que moi, qui le pensais, fusse quelque chose.*
I noticed that while I was trying to think everything false, it must needs be that I, who was thinking this, was something.
1637 *Discours de la méthode (Discourse on Method)*, 4th discourse (translated by G E M Anscombe and Peter Geach).

21 *Je pense, donc je suis.*
I think, therefore I am.
1637 *Discours de la méthode (Discourse on Method)*, 4th discourse (translated by G E M Anscombe and Peter Geach). Often quoted as 'Cogito, ergo sum', but Descartes wrote the French version before the Latin.

22 *Je pouvais prendre pour règle générale, que les choses que nous concevons fort clairement et fort distinctement sont toutes vraies.*
I could take it as a general rule that whatever we conceive very clearly and very distinctly is true.
1637 *Discours de la méthode (Discourse on Method)*, 4th discourse (translated by G E M Anscombe and Peter Geach).

23 *Animadverti jam ante aliquot annos quam multa, ineunte aetate, falsa pro veris admiserim, et quam dubia sint quaecunque istis postea superextruxi, ac proinde funditus omnia semel in vita esse evertenda, atque a primis fundamentis denno inchoandum, si quid aliquando firmum et mansurum cupiam in scientiis stabilire.*
Some years ago now I observed the multitude of errors that I had accepted as true in my earliest years, and the dubiousness of the whole superstructure I had since then reared on them; and the consequent need of making a clean sweep for once in my life, and beginning again from the very foundations, if I would establish some secure and lasting result in science.
1641 *Meditationes*, 1st meditation (translated by G E M Anscombe and Peter Geach).

24 *Supponam igitur non optimum Deum, fontem veritatis, sed genium aliquum malignum, eundemque summe potentem et callidum, omnem suam industriam in eo posuisse, ut me falleret.*
I will suppose then, not that there is a supremely good God, the source of truth; but that there is an evil spirit, who is supremely powerful and intelligent, and does his utmost to deceive me.
1641 *Meditationes*, 1st meditation (translated by G E M Anscombe and Peter Geach).

25 *Agnoscam fieri non posse ut existam talis naturae qualis sum, nempe ideam Dei in me habens, nisi revera Deus etiam existeret, Deus, inquam, ille idem cujus idea in me est.*
I could not possibly exist with the nature I actually have, that is, one endowed with the idea of God, unless there really is a God; the very God, I mean, of whom I have an idea.
1641 *Meditationes*, 3rd meditation (translated by G E M Anscombe and Peter Geach)

Deschamps, Eustache c.1345–1406

French poet, soldier and courtier.

26 *Rien ne se peut comparer à Paris.*
Nothing can compare to Paris.
c.1370 'Ballade de Paris', refrain.

Deschamps, Yvon 1935–

Canadian entertainer, known for his separatist allegiances.

27 All we want is an independent Quebec within a strong and united Canada.
Quoted by Peter C Newman in *Maclean's*, 13 Nov 1978. This has become the classic formulation of Quebec's national and political aspirations.

Destouches, Philippe *originally* ***Néricault*** 1680–1754

French playwright, a diplomat in England (1717–23). His early comedies are undistinguished, but his masterpiece is *Le Glorieux* (1732, 'The Boaster').

28 *Les absents ont toujours tort.*
The absent are always in the wrong.
1717 *L'Obstacle imprévu*, act 1, sc.6.

Dettori, Frankie (Lanfranco) 1970–

Italian jockey. He was Champion Jockey (1994, 1995) and in 1996 achieved the unparalleled feat of winning all seven races on the card at Ascot.

29 When I'm good, I can be really good—I can do things even I didn't think I could do. I would say my worst is still not so bad, either.
2003 Quoted in *The Times*, 27 Sep.

De Valera, Éamon 1882–1975

Irish statesman, born in the US. He narrowly escaped execution for his part in the 1916 Easter Rebellion, and became leader of Sinn Féin (1917–26). He was Prime Minister (1932–48, 1951–4, 1957–9) and President (1959–73).

30 Why doesn't he use a spoon?
1921 On being told that David Lloyd George had said talking to him was like trying to pick up mercury with a fork.

31 Whenever I wanted to know what the Irish people wanted, I had only to examine my own heart and it told me straight off what the Irish people wanted.
1922 Speech to the Irish Parliament, 6 Jan.

Devlin, Denis 1908–59

Irish poet and diplomat, born in Scotland. His poetry, which assimilates Christian iconography into cosmopolitan settings, was not appreciated until after his death.

32 And sad, Oh sad, that glen with one thin stream
He met his death in; and a farmer told me
There was but one small bird to shoot: it sang
'Better Beast and know your end, and die
Than Man with murderous angels in his head.'
c.1956 'The Tomb of Michael Collins'.

De Voto, Bernard 1897–1955

US historian and writer, known for 'The Easy Chair' in *Harper's Magazine* from 1935. His works include the historical trilogy beginning with *The Year of Decision: 1846* (1943) and he edited Twain's work.

33 The proper union of gin and vermouth is a great and sudden glory; it is one of the happiest marriages on earth, and one of the shortest lived.
1949 In *Harper's Magazine*, Dec.

34 Novelists, whatever else they may be besides, are also children talking to children—in the dark.
1950 *The World of Fiction*.

35 When evening quickens in the street, comes a pause in the day's occupation that is known as the cocktail hour.
1951 *The Hour*.

36 You can no more keep a martini in the refrigerator than you can keep a kiss there.
1951 *The Hour*.

De Vries, Peter 1910–93

US novelist and humorist, best known for *The Tunnel of Love* (1954).

37 It is the final proof of God's omnipotence that he need not exist in order to save us.
1958 *The Mackerel Plaza*, ch.1.

38 Look at it this way: Psychoanalysis is a permanent fad.
1973 *Forever Panting*.

Dewar, Donald Campbell 1937–2000

Scottish Labour politician. He was Secretary of State for Scotland (1997–9) and the first First Minister of the new Scottish Parliament (1999–2000).

39 He could start a party in an empty room—and often did—filling it with good cheer, Gaelic songs, and argument.
1994 Of John Smith, leader of the Labour Party, at his funeral, 19 May.

40 'There shall be a Scottish Parliament.' Through long years, those words were first a hope, then a belief, then a promise. Now they are a reality.
1999 Speech at the official opening of the Scottish Parliament, 1 Jul.

41 We look forward to the time when this moment will be seen as a turning point: the day when democracy was renewed in Scotland, when we revitalized our place in this our United Kingdom.
1999 Speech at the official opening of the Scottish Parliament, 1 Jul.

42 This is about more than our politics and our laws. This is about who we are, how we carry ourselves.
1999 Speech at the official opening of the Scottish Parliament, 1 Jul.

Dewey, John 1859–1952

US philosopher and educator. A leading pragmatist, he developed an influential philosophy of education which stressed learning through experience. His writings include *The Quest for Certainty* (1929) and *The Child and the Curriculum* (1902).

43 When physics, chemistry, biology, medicine, contribute to the detection of concrete human woes and to the development of plans for remedying them and relieving the human estate, they become moral; they become part of the apparatus of moral inquiry or science… When the consciousness of science is fully impregnated with the consciousness of human value, the greatest dualism which now weighs humanity down, the split between the material, the mechanical and the scientific and the moral and ideal will be destroyed.
1920 *Reconstruction in Philosophy*.

44 The function of criticism is the reeducation of perception of works of art… The conception that its business is to appraise, to judge in the legal and moral sense, arrests the perception of those who are

influenced by the criticism that assumes this task.
1934 *Art as Experience*.

De Wolfe, Elsie 1865–1950

English actress, interior decorator and hostess, the wife of the British diplomat Sir Charles Mendl.

45 Beige! Just my color.
On seeing the Acropolis for the first time. Quoted in Nina Campbell and Caroline Seebohm *Elsie de Wolfe: A Decorative Life* (1992), ch.1.

Diaghilev, Sergei 1872–1929

Russian impresario. His Ballets Russes company, formed in 1911, created a sensation throughout Europe and launched the careers of such dancers as Balanchine, Fokine, Nijinsky and Pavlova.

46 *Étonne-moi!*
Astonish me!
1912 Attributed, when Jean Cocteau complained that he was getting insufficient direction when designing the scenario for a new ballet. Quoted in Wallace Fowlie (ed) *Journals of Jean Cocteau* (1956), ch.1.

Diana, Princess of Wales 1961–97

British princess. She married Charles, Prince of Wales, in 1981 and they were divorced in 1996.

47 I'm as thick as a plank.
Remark quoted in *Sunday Today*, 25 Jan 1987.

48 There were three of us in this marriage, so it was a bit crowded.
1995 Of her marriage to Charles, Prince of Wales, and his relationship with Camilla Parker-Bowles. Television interview on BBC1's *Panorama*, 20 Nov.

49 I'd like to be a queen in people's hearts but I don't see myself being Queen of this country.
1995 Television interview on BBC1's *Panorama*, 20 Nov.

Díaz, Jorge 1930–

Chilean dramatist, born in Argentina. He has lived in Spain since 1965. His plays are influenced by the theatre of the absurd and other avant-garde experimental movements.

50 *¡Pero la verdad es que estoy cansada, horriblemente cansada de ser la esposa femenina de ese animal masculino que se rasca, pierde el pelo sistemáticamente y canta tangos pasados de moda!… Quisiera…quisiera engordar, fumar un puro y enviudar de una manera indolora y elegante.*
The truth is, I'm tired, frightfully tired of being the feminine spouse to the masculine animal who scratches himself, systematically loses his hair and sings outdated tangos!… I'd like… I'd like to get fat, to smoke cigars and to become a widow in a painless and elegant fashion.
1961 *El cepillo de dientes* (*The Toothbrush*), act 1.

Diaz, Porfirio 1830–1915

President of Mexico. He supported Juarez in the War of Reform and gained the presidency through rebellion in 1877.

51 Poor Mexico, so far from God and so close to the United States.
1846 Attributed, at the beginning of the American–Mexican War (1846–8).

Dibdin, Charles 1745–1814

English songwriter, who wrote his first operetta (*The Shepherd's Artifice*, performed at Covent Garden 1762) as a boy. He wrote nearly 100 sea songs and 70 dramatic pieces.

52 For a soldier I listed, to grow great in fame,
And be shot at for sixpence a day.
1791 'Charity'.

53 Did you ever hear of Captain Wattle?
He was all for love, and a little for the bottle.
1797 'Captain Wattle and Miss Roe'.

54 Then trust me, there's nothing like drinking
So pleasant this side of the grave;
It keeps the unhappy from thinking,
And makes e'en the valiant more brave.
'Nothing Like Grog'. First published 1803.

55 What argufies pride and ambition?
Soon or late death will take us in tow:
Each bullet has got its commission,
And when our time's come we must go.
'Each Bullet Has Got Its Commission'. First published 1803.

Dick, Philip K(indred) 1928–82

US science-fiction writer. His output was prolific, marked by a strong literary sensibility as well as a powerful, often chilling imagination and humour.

56 Dr Bloodmoney, Or How We Got Along After The Bomb.
1965 Title of novel.

57 I mean, after all; you have to consider that we're only made out of dust. That's admittedly not much to go on and we shouldn't forget that. But even considering, I mean, it's sort of a bad beginning, we're not doing too bad. So I personally have faith that even in this lousy situation we're faced with we can make it. You get me?
1966 *The Three Stigmata of Palmer Eldritch*, closing words.

58 Do Androids Dream Of Electric Sheep?
1968 Title of novel, later the basis for the film *Blade Runner*.

59 Reality is that which, when you stop believing in it, doesn't go away.
1972 Quoted in introduction to *I Hope I Shall Arrive Soon* (1986).

60 Drug misuse is not a disease, it is a decision, like the decision to step out in front of a moving car. You would call that not a disease but an error of judgement.
1977 *A Scanner Darkly*, author's note.

61 The basic tool for the manipulation of reality is the manipulation of words. If you can control the meaning of words, you can control the people who must use the words.
1986 *I Hope I Shall Arrive Soon*, 'How To Build A Universe That Doesn't Fall Apart Two Days Later'.

Dickens, Charles John Huffam 1812–70

English novelist. After a childhood of poverty and hardship, during which his father was sent to a debtors' prison, he became one of England's most popular and prolific novelists, exposing the inhumanities of the 19c with an idiosyncratic blend of wit, satire, sentiment and seriousness and a gallery of memorable characters.

62 Grief never mended no broken bones, and as good people's wery scarce, what I says is, make the most on 'em.
1836–7 *Sketches by Boz*, 'Gin Shops'.

63 We shall never forget the mingled feelings of awe and respect with which we used to gaze on the exterior of Newgate in our schoolboy days…[the doors] looking as if they were made for the express purpose of letting people in, and never letting them out again.
1836–7 *Sketches by Boz*, 'Criminal Courts'.

64 A smattering of everything, and a knowledge of nothing.
1836–7 *Sketches by Boz*, 'Sentiment'.

65 He had used the word in its Pickwickian sense.
1836–7 Of Mr Blotton, a member of the Pickwick Club. *Pickwick Papers*, ch.1.

66 'Heads, heads—take care of your heads!' cried the loquacious stranger, as they came out under the low archway, which in those days formed the entrance to the coachyard. 'Terrible place—dangerous work—five children—mother—tall lady, eating sandwiches —forgot the arch—crash—knock—children look round—mother's head off—sandwich in her hand—no mouth to put it in—head of a family off—shocking, shocking!
1836–7 Jingle. *Pickwick Papers*, ch.2.

67 'I was ruminating,' said Mr Pickwick, 'on the strange mutability of human affairs.' 'Ah! I see—in at the palace door one day, out at the window the next. Philosopher, Sir?' 'An observer of human nature, sir,' said Mr Pickwick.
1836–7 *Pickwick Papers*, ch.2.

68 'Ah! You should keep dogs—fine animals—sagacious creatures—dog of my own once—Pointer—surprising instinct—out shooting one day—entering enclosure—whistled—dog stopped—whistled again—Ponto—no go; stock still—called him—Ponto, Ponto—wouldn't move— dog transfixed—staring at a board—looked up, saw an inscription—"Gamekeeper has orders to shoot all dogs found in this enclosure"— wouldn't pass it—wonderful dog—valuable dog that—very.'
1836–7 Jingle. *Pickwick Papers*, ch.2.

69 Kent, sir—everyone knows Kent—apples, cherries, hops and women.
1836–7 Jingle. *Pickwick Papers*, ch.2.

70 There are very few moments in a man's existence when he experiences so much ludicrous distress, or meets with so little charitable commiseration, as when he is in pursuit of his own hat.
1836–7 *Pickwick Papers*, ch.4.

71 There was a fine gentle wind, and Mr Pickwick's hat rolled sportively before it. The wind puffed, and Mr Pickwick puffed, and the hat rolled over and over as merrily as a lively porpoise in a strong tide.
1836–7 *Pickwick Papers*, ch.4.

72 I wants to make your flesh creep.
1836–7 The Fat Boy. *Pickwick Papers*, ch.8.

73 'It's always best on these occasions to do what the mob do.' 'But suppose there are two mobs?' suggested Mr Snodgrass. 'Shout with the largest,' replied Mr Pickwick.
1836–7 *Pickwick Papers*, ch.13.

74 And a wery good name it is—only one I know, that ain't got a nickname to it.
1836–7 Sam Weller comments on Job Trotter's Christian name. *Pickwick Papers*, ch.16.

75 Tongue; well, that's a wery good thing when it an't a woman's.
1836–7 Sam Weller's father. *Pickwick Papers*, ch.19.

76 Poverty and oysters always seem to go together.
1836–7 Sam Weller. *Pickwick Papers*, ch.22.

77 Dumb as a drum vith a hole in it, sir.
1836–7 Sam Weller. *Pickwick Papers*, ch.25.

78 Our noble society for providing the infant negroes in the West Indies with flannel waistcoats and moral pocket handkerchiefs.
1836–7 Rev Mr Stiggins. *Pickwick Papers*, ch.27.

79 Poetry's unnat'ral; no man ever talked poetry 'cept a beadle on boxin' day, or Warren's blackin', or Rowland's oil, or some o' them low fellows; never you let yourself down to talk poetry, my boy.
1836–7 Sam Weller's father. *Pickwick Papers*, ch.33.

80 It's my opinion, sir, that this meeting is drunk, sir!
1836–7 Rev Mr Stiggins. *Pickwick Papers*, ch.33.

81 'Yes, I have a pair of eyes,' replied Sam, 'and that's just it. If they wos a pair o' patent double million magnifyin' gas microscopes of hextra power, p'raps I might be able to see through a flight o' stairs and a deal door; but bein' only eyes, you see, my wision's limited.'
1836–7 *Pickwick Papers*, ch.34.

82 Miss Bolo rose from the table considerably agitated, and went straight home, in a flood of tears, and a sedan chair.
1836–7 *Pickwick Papers*, ch.35.

83 *We* know, Mr. Weller—we, who are men of the world —that a good uniform must work its way with the women, sooner or later.
1836–7 The Gentleman in Blue. *Pickwick Papers*, ch.37.

84 You're a amiably-disposed young man, sir, I don't think.
1836–7 Sam Weller's father. *Pickwick Papers*, ch.38.

85 It's a regular holiday to them—all porter and skittles.
1836–7 *Pickwick Papers*, ch.41.

86 Anythin' for a quiet life, as the man said wen he took the sitivation at the lighthouse.
1836–7 Sam Weller. *Pickwick Papers*, ch.43.

87 The fact is, that there was considerable difficulty in inducing Oliver to take upon himself the office of respiration—a troublesome practice, but one which custom has rendered necessary to our easy existence; and for some time he lay gasping on a little flock mattress, rather unequally poised between this world and the next: the balance being decidedly in favour of the latter. Now, if during this brief period, Oliver had been surrounded by careful grandmothers, anxious aunts, experienced nurses, and doctors of profound wisdom, he would most inevitably and indubitably have been killed in no time.
1837–9 *Oliver Twist*, ch.1.

88 Please, sir, I want some more.
1837–9 Oliver. *Oliver Twist*, ch.2.

89 It was a nice sickly season just at this time. In commercial phrase, coffins were looking up.
1837–9 *Oliver Twist*, ch.6.

90 What a fine thing capital punishment is! Dead men never repent; dead men never bring awkward stories to light. Ah, it's a fine thing for the trade! Five of 'em strung up in a

row; and none left to play booty, or turn white-livered!
1837–9 Fagin. *Oliver Twist*, ch.9.

91 'Hard,' replied the Dodger. 'As nails,' added Charley Bates.
1837–9 *Oliver Twist*, ch.9.

92 There is a passion for hunting something deeply implanted in the human breast.
1837–9 *Oliver Twist*, ch.10.

93 I'll eat my head.
1837–9 Mr Grimwig. *Oliver Twist*, ch.14.

94 I only know two sorts of boys. Mealy boys, and beef-faced boys.
1837–9 Mr Grimwig. *Oliver Twist*, ch.14.

95 This ain't the shop for justice.
1837–9 The Artful Dodger. *Oliver Twist*, ch.43.

96 'If the law supposes that,' said Mr Bumble…'the law is a ass—a idiot.'
1837–9 *Oliver Twist*, ch.51.

97 The delights—the ten thousand million delights of a pantomime.
1838 *Memoirs of Joseph Grimaldi*, ed Dickens.

98 United Metropolitian Improved Hot Muffin and Crumpet Baking and Punctual Delivery Company.
1838–9 *Nicholas Nickleby*, ch.2.

99 EDUCATION.—At Mr Wackford Squeers's Academy, Dotheboys Hall, at the delightful village of Dotheboys, near Greta Bridge in Yorkshire. Youth are boarded, clothed, booked, furnished with pocket-money, provided with all necessaries, instructed in all languages, living and dead, mathematics, orthography, geometry, astronomy, trigonometry, the use of the globes, algebra, single stick (if required), writing, arithmetic, fortification, and every other branch of classical literature. Terms, twenty guineas per annum. No extras, no vacations, and diet unparalleled.
1838–9 *Nicholas Nickleby*, ch.3.

1 Mr Squeers's appearance was not prepossessing. He had but one eye, and the popular prejudice runs in favour of two.
1838–9 *Nicholas Nickleby*, ch.4.

2 Subdue your appetites, my dears, and you've conquered human nature.
1838–9 *Nicholas Nickleby*, ch.5.

3 There are only two styles of portrait painting, the serious and the smirk.
1838–9 Miss LaCreevy. *Nicholas Nickleby*, ch.10.

4 Oh! They're too beautiful to live, much too beautiful!
1938–9 Mrs Kenwigs, of her four daughters. *Nicholas Nickleby*, ch. 14.

5 Sir, My pa requests me to write to you. The doctors considering it doubtful whether he will ever recuvver the use of his legs which prevents his holding a pen.
1838–9 Fanny Squeers. *Nicholas Nickleby*, ch.15.

6 'What's the water in French, sir?' 'L'eau,' replied Nicholas. 'Ah!' said Mr Lillyvick, shaking his head mournfully, 'I thought as much. Lo, eh? I don't think anything of that language—nothing at all.'
1838–9 *Nicholas Nickleby*, ch.16.

7 'It's very easy to talk,' said Mrs Mantalini. 'Not so easy when one is eating a demnition egg,' replied Mr Mantalini; 'for the yolk runs down the waistcoat, and yolk of egg does not match any waistcoat but a yellow waistcoat, demmit.'
1838–9 *Nicholas Nickleby*, ch.17.

8 Language was not powerful enough to describe the infant phenomenon.
1838–9 *Nicholas Nickleby*, ch.23.

9 'I'm always ill after Shakespeare,' said Mrs Wititterly. 'I scarcely exist the next day; I find the re-action so very great after a tragedy…and Shakespeare is such a delicious creature.'
1838–9 *Nicholas Nickleby*, ch.27.

10 Every baby born into the world is a finer one than the last.
1838–9 *Nicholas Nickleby*, ch.36.

11 Bring in the bottled lightning, a clean tumbler, and a corkscrew.
1838–9 The Gentleman in the Small-Clothes. *Nicholas Nickleby*, ch.49.

12 All is gas and gaiters.
1838–9 The Gentleman in the Small-Clothes. *Nicholas Nickleby*, ch.49.

13 My life is one demd horrid grind!
1838–9 Mr Mantalini. *Nicholas Nickleby*, ch.64.

14 What is the odds so long as the fire of soul is kindled at the taper of conwiviality, and the wing of friendship never moults a feather!
1840–1 Dick Swiveller. *The Old Curiosity Shop*, ch.2.

15 Fan the sinking flame of hilarity with the wing of friendship; and pass the rosy wine.
1840–1 Dick Swiveller. *The Old Curiosity Shop*, ch.7.

16 She's all my fancy painted her, Sir, that's what she is.
1840–1 Dick Swiveller. *The Old Curiosity Shop*, ch.7.

17 Codlin's the friend, not Short.
1840–1 Codlin. *The Old Curiosity Shop*, ch.19.

18 And don't you think you must be a very wicked little child…to be a wax-work child at all?
1840–1 Miss Monflathers to Nell. *The Old Curiosity Shop*, ch.31.

19 'Did you ever taste beer?'
'I had a sip of it once,' said the small servant.
'Here's a state of things!' cried Mr. Swiveller, raising his eyes to the ceiling. 'She *never* tasted it—it can't be tasted in a sip!'
1840–1 *The Old Curiosity Shop*, ch.57.

20 They moved so gently, that their footsteps made no noise; but there were sobs from among the group, and sounds of grief and mourning.
1840–1 The death of little Nell. *The Old Curiosity Shop*, ch.71.

21 Something will come of this. I hope it mayn't be human gore!
1841 Simon Tappertit. *Barnaby Rudge*, ch.4.

22 Polly put the kettle on, we'll all have tea.
1841 Grip, the raven. *Barnaby Rudge*, ch.17.

23 'There are strings,' said Mr Tappertit…'in the human heart that had better not be wibrated.'
1841 Mr Tappertit. *Barnaby Rudge*, ch.22.

24 Oh gracious, why wasn't I born old and ugly?
1841 Miss Miggs. *Barnaby Rudge*, ch.70.

25 Was there ever such a sunny street as this Broadway! The pavement stones are polished with the tread of feet until

they shine again… Heaven save the ladies, how they dress! We have seen more colours in these ten minutes, than we should have seen elsewhere, in as many days. What various parasols! what rainbow silks and satins! what pinking of thin stockings and pinching of thin shoes, and fluttering of ribbons and silk tassels, and display of rich cloaks with gaudy hoods and linings!
1842 *American Notes*.

26 Politics are much discussed, so are banks, so is cotton. Quiet people avoid the question of the Presidency…the great constitutional feature of this institution being, that directly the acrimony of the last election is over, the next one begins.
1842 *American Notes*.

27 'Bah!' said Scrooge, 'Humbug!'
1843 *A Christmas Carol*, stave 1.

28 'You are fettered,' said Scrooge, trembling. 'Tell me why?' 'I wear the chain I forged in life,' replied the Ghost. 'I made it link by link, and yard by yard; I girded it on of my own free will, and of my own free will I wore it.'
1843 *A Christmas Carol*, stave 1.

29 'God bless us every one!' said Tiny Tim, the last of all.
1843 *A Christmas Carol*, stave 3.

30 But however and whenever we part from one another, I am sure we shall none of us forget poor Tiny Tim.
1843 *A Christmas Carol*, stave 4.

31 It *was* a turkey! He could never have stood upon his legs, that bird. He would have snapped 'em off short in a minute, like sticks of sealing-wax.
1843 *A Christmas Carol*, stave 5.

32 The Lord No Zoo.
1843–4 Toby Chuzzlewit. *Martin Chuzzlewit*, ch.1.

33 'The name of those fabulous animals (pagan, I regret to say) who used to sing in the water, has quite escaped me.' Mr George Chuzzlewit suggested 'Swans'. 'No,' said Mr Pecksniff. 'Not swans. Very like swans, too. Thank you.' The nephew…propounded 'Oysters'. 'No,' said Mr Picksniff…'nor oysters. But by no means unlike oysters… Wait! Sirens. Dear me! sirens, of course.'
1843–4 *Martin Chuzzlewit*, ch.4.

34 Any man may be in good spirits and good temper when he's well dressed. There an't much credit in that. If I was very ragged and very jolly, then I should begin to feel I had gained a point, Mr. Pinch.
1843–4 Mark Tapley. *Martin Chuzzlewit*, ch.5.

35 His moral character…was full of promise, but of no performance.
1843–4 Of Mr Pecksniff. *Martin Chuzzlewit*, ch.5.

36 Affection beaming in one eye, and calculation shining out of the other.
1843–4 Of Mrs Todgers. *Martin Chuzzlewit*, ch.8.

37 Let us be moral. Let us contemplate existence.
1843–4 Mr Pecksniff. *Martin Chuzzlewit*, ch.9.

38 Here's the rule for bargains: 'Do other men, for they would do you.' That's the true business precept.
1843–4 Jonas Chuzzlewit. *Martin Chuzzlewit*, ch.11.

39 Buy an annuity cheap, and make your life interesting to yourself and everybody else that watches the speculation.
1843–4 Jonas Chuzzlewit. *Martin Chuzzlewit*, ch.18.

40 'Mrs Harris,' I says, 'leave the bottle on the chimley-piece, and don't ask me to take none, but let me put my lips to it when I am so dispoged.'
1843–4 Mrs Gamp. *Martin Chuzzlewit*, ch.19.

41 Features are an index to the heart.
1843–4 *Martin Chuzzlewit*, ch.24.

42 At the same moment a peculiar fragrance was borne upon the breeze, as if a passing fairy had hiccuped, and had previously been to a wine vaults.
1843–4 On Mrs Gamp's entering a room. *Martin Chuzzlewit*, ch.25.

43 Gamp would certainly have drunk its little shoes right off its feet, as with our precious boy he did, and arterwards send the child a errand to sell his wooden leg for any money it 'ud fetch as matches in the rough, and bring it home in liquor.
1843–4 Mrs Gamp. *Martin Chuzzlewit*, ch.25.

44 She's the sort of woman…one would almost feel disposed to bury for nothing: and do it neatly, too!
1843–4 Mould speaking about Mrs Gamp. *Martin Chuzzlewit*, ch.25.

45 He'd make a lovely corpse.
1843–4 Mrs Gamp speaking of Jonas Chuzzlewit. *Martin Chuzzlewit*, ch.25.

46 We never knows wot's hidden in each other's hearts; and if we had glass winders there, we'd need keep the shutters up, some on us, I do assure you!
1843–4 Mrs Gamp. *Martin Chuzzlewit*, ch.29.

47 A lane was made; and Mrs Hominy…came slowly up it, in a procession of one.
1843–4 *Martin Chuzzlewit*, ch.34.

48 'Mind and matter,' said the lady in the wig, 'glide swift into the vortex of immensity. Howls the sublime, and softly sleeps the calm Ideal, in the whispering chambers of Imagination.'
1843–4 A Transcendental literary lady. *Martin Chuzzlewit*, ch.34.

49 Farewell! Be the proud bride of a ducal coronet, and forget me!… Unalterably, never yours, Augustus.
1843–4 Augustus Moddle. *Martin Chuzzlewit*, ch.54.

50 Oh let us love our occupations,
Bless the squire and his relations,
Live upon our daily rations,
And always know our proper stations.
1844 Lady Bowley. *The Chimes*, second quarter.

51 The earth was made for Dombey and Son to trade in, and the sun and moon were made to give them light. Rivers and seas were formed to float their ships; rainbows gave them promise of fair weather; winds blew for or against their enterprises; stars and planets circled in their orbits, to preserve inviolate a system of which they were the centre.
1846–8 *Dombey and Son*, ch.1.

52 Dombey and Son had often dealt in hides, but never in hearts. They left that fancy ware to boys and girls, and boarding-schools and books.
1846–8 *Dombey and Son*, ch.1.

53 'The sea, Floy, what is it that it keeps on saying?'
She told him that it was only the noise of the rolling waves.
'Yes, yes,' he said. 'But I know that they are always saying something. Always the same thing. What place is over there?'…

She told him there was another country opposite, but he said he didn't mean that; he meant farther away—farther away!
Very often afterwards, in the midst of their talk, he would break off, to try to understand what it was that the waves were always saying; and would rise up in his couch to look towards that invisible region, far away.
1846–8 Of little Paul Dombey. *Dombey and Son*, ch.8.

54 She was dry and sandy with working in the graves of deceased languages. None of your live languages for Miss Blimber. They must be dead—stone dead—and then Miss Blimber dug them up like a Ghoul.
1846–8 *Dombey and Son*, ch.11.

55 As to Mr Feeder, B.A., Doctor Blimber's assistant, he was a kind of human barrel-organ, with a little list of tunes at which he was continually working, over and over again, without any variation.
1846–8 *Dombey and Son*, ch.11.

56 When found, make a note of.
1846–8 Captain Cuttle. *Dombey and Son*, ch.15.

57 Train up a fig-tree in the way it should go, and when you are old sit under the shade of it.
1846–8 Captain Cuttle. *Dombey and Son*, ch.19.

58 The bearings of this observation lays in the application on it.
1846–8 Captain Bunsby. *Dombey and Son*, ch.23.

59 Say, like those wicked Turks, there is no What's-his-name but Thingummy, and What-you-may-call-it is his prophet!
1846–8 Mrs Skewton. *Dombey and Son*, ch.27.

60 If you could see my legs when I take my boots off, you'd form some idea of what unrequited affection is.
1846–8 Mr Toots. *Dombey and Son*, ch.48.

61 I am a lone lorn creetur...and everythink goes contrairy with me.
1849–50 Mrs Gummidge. *David Copperfield*, ch.3.

62 'I feel it more than other people,' said Mrs Gummidge.
1849–50 *David Copperfield*, ch.3.

63 I'd better go into the house, and die and be a riddance!
1849–50 Mrs Gummidge. *David Copperfield*, ch.3.

64 Barkis is willin'.
1849–50 Barkis's proposal of marriage to Peggotty. *David Copperfield*, ch.5.

65 Experientia does it—as papa used to say.
1849–50 Mrs Micawber. *David Copperfield*, ch.11.

66 I never will desert Mr Micawber.
1849–50 Mrs Micawber. *David Copperfield*, ch.12.

67 Annual income twenty pounds, annual expenditure nineteen nineteen six, result happiness. Annual income twenty pounds, annual expenditure twenty pounds ought and six, result misery.
1849–50 Mr Micawber. *David Copperfield*, ch.12.

68 I am well aware that I am the umblest person going... My mother is likewise a very umble person. We live in a numble abode.
1849–50 Uriah Heep. *David Copperfield*, ch.16.

69 We are so very umble.
1849–50 Uriah Heep. *David Copperfield*, ch.17.

70 The mistake was made of putting some of the trouble out of King Charles's head into my head.
1849–50 Mr Dick. *David Copperfield*, ch.17.

71 'Orses and dorgs is some men's fancy. They're wittles and drink to me—lodging, wife, and children—reading, writing and 'rithmetic—snuff, tobacker, and sleep.
1849–50 Man on the Canterbury coach. *David Copperfield*, ch.19.

72 I only ask for information.
1849–50 Rosa Dartle. *David Copperfield*, ch.20.

73 'It was as true,' said Mr Barkis, '...as taxes is. And nothing's truer than them.'
1849–50 *David Copperfield*, ch.21.

74 What a world of gammon and spinnage it is, though, ain't it?
1849–50 Miss Mowcher. *David Copperfield*, ch.22.

75 Accidents will occur in the best-regulated families.
1849–50 Mr Micawber. *David Copperfield*, ch.28.

76 'People can't die, along the coast,' said Mr Peggotty, 'except when the tide's pretty nigh out. They can't be born, unless it's pretty nigh in—not properly born, till flood. He's a going out with the tide.'
1849–50 On the death of Barkis. *David Copperfield*, ch.30.

77 Mrs Crupp had indignantly assured him that there wasn't room to swing a cat there; but, as Mr Dick justly observed to me... 'You know, Trotwood, I don't want to swing a cat. I never do swing a cat. Therefore, what does that signify to me!'
1849–50 *David Copperfield*, ch.35.

78 'No better opening anywhere,' said my aunt, 'for a man who conducts himself well, and is industrious.'
1849–50 Of Mr Micawber's prospects in Australia. *David Copperfield*, ch.52.

79 Fog everywhere. Fog up the river, where it flows among green aits and meadows; fog down the river, where it rolls defiled among the tiers of shipping, and the waterside pollutions of a great (and dirty) city. Fog on the Essex marshes, fog on the Kentish heights. Fog creeping into the cabooses of collier brigs; fog lying out on the yards, and hovering in the rigging of great ships... And hard by Temple Bar, in Lincoln's Inn Hall, at the very heart of the fog, sits the Lord High Chancellor in his High Court of Chancery.
1852–3 *Bleak House*, ch.1.

80 But Jarndyce and Jarndyce still drags its dreary length before the court, perennially hopeless.
1852–3 *Bleak House*, ch.1.

81 The evil of it is, that it is a world wrapped up in too much jeweller's cotton and fine wool, and cannot hear the rushing of the larger worlds, and cannot see them as they circle round the sun. It is a deadened world, and its growth is sometimes unhealthy for want of air.
1852–3 Of the world of fashion. *Bleak House*, ch.2.

82 This is a London particular... A fog, miss.
1852–3 Mr Guppy to Esther. *Bleak House*, ch.3.

83 I expect a judgement. Shortly.
1852–3 Miss Flyte. *Bleak House*, ch.3. The judgement predicted, in the case of *Jarndyce v Jarndyce*, fails to materialize for many decades.

84 The wind's in the east... I am always conscious of an uncomfortable sensation now and then when the wind is blowing in the east.
1852–3 Mr Jarndyce. *Bleak House*, ch.6.

85 It is said that the children of the poor are not brought up, but dragged up.
1852–3 Mr Jarndyce. *Bleak House*, ch.6.

86 I don't feel any vulgar gratitude to you. I almost feel as if *you* ought to be grateful to *me*, for giving you the opportunity of enjoying the luxury of generosity… For anything I can tell, I may have come into the world expressly for the purpose of increasing your stock of happiness.
1852–3 Harold Skimpole. *Bleak House*, ch.6.

87 An oyster of the old school whom nobody can open.
1852–3 Of Mr Tulkinghorn. *Bleak House*, ch.10.

88 He wos wery good to me, he wos!
1852–3 Jo speaking of Nemo. *Bleak House*, ch.11.

89 'For I don't,' says Jo, 'I don't know nothink.'
1852–3 *Bleak House*, ch.16.

90 You are a human boy, my young friend. A human boy. O glorious to be a human boy!…
O running stream of sparkling joy
To be a soaring human boy!
1852–3 Rev Mr Chadband. *Bleak House*, ch.19.

91 Jobling, there *are* chords in the human mind.
1852–3 Mr Guppy. *Bleak House*, ch.20.

92 'It is,' says Chadband, 'the ray of rays, the sun of suns, the moon of moons, the star of stars. It is the light of Terewth.'
1852–3 *Bleak House*, ch.25.

93 'Old girl,' said Mr Bagnet, 'give him my opinion. You know it.'
1852–3 *Bleak House*, ch.27.

94 It is a melancholy truth that even great men have their poor relations.
1852–3 *Bleak House*, ch.28.

95 Never have a mission.
1852–3 Mr Jellyby. *Bleak House*, ch.30.

96 The one great principle of the English law is, to make business for itself. There is no other principle distinctly, certainly, and consistently maintained through all its narrow turnings.
1852–3 *Bleak House*, ch.39.

97 He is not a genuine foreign-grown savage; he is the ordinary home-made article. Dirty, ugly, disagreeable to all the senses, in body a common creature of the common streets, only in soul a Heathen. Homely filth begrimes him, homely parasites devour him, homely sores are in him, homely rags are on him: native ignorance, the growth of English soil and climate, sinks his immortal nature lower than the beasts that perish.
1852–3 Of Jo. *Bleak House*, ch.47.

98 Dead, your Majesty. Dead, my lords and gentlemen. Dead, Right Reverends and Wrong Reverends of every order. Dead, men and women, born with Heavenly compassion in your hearts. And dying thus around us every day.
1852–3 On the death of Jo. *Bleak House*, ch.47.

99 Now, what I want is, Facts. Teach these boys and girls nothing but Facts. Facts alone are wanted in life.
1854 Mr Gradgrind. *Hard Times*, bk.1, ch.1.

1 The speaker, and the schoolmaster, and the third grown person present, all backed a little, and swept with their eyes the inclined plane of little vessels then and there arranged in order, ready to have imperial gallons of facts poured into them until they were full to the brim.
1854 *Hard Times*, bk.1, ch.1.

2 'Girl number twenty unable to define a horse!' said Mr Gradgrind… 'Girl number twenty possessed of no facts, in reference to one of the commonest of animals!'… 'Bitzer' said Thomas Gradgrind. 'Your definition of a horse.'
'Quadruped. Graminivorous. Forty teeth, namely twenty-four grinders, four eye-teeth, and twelve incisive. Sheds coat in the spring; in marshy countries, sheds hoofs, too. Hoofs hard, but requiring to be shod with iron. Age known by marks in mouth.' Thus (and much more) Bitzer.
'Now girl number twenty,' said Mr Gradgrind. 'You know what a horse is.'
1854 *Hard Times*, bk.1, ch.2.

3 It was a town of red brick, or of brick that would have been red if the smoke and ashes had allowed it; but, as matters stood it was a town of unnatural red and black as the painted face of a savage.
1854 Of Coketown. *Hard Times*, bk.1, ch.5.

4 Coketown…ugly citadel, where Nature was as strongly bricked out as killing airs and gases were bricked in.
1854 *Hard Times*, bk.1, ch.10.

5 I see traces of the turtle soup, and venison, and gold spoon in this.
1854 Mr Bounderby. *Hard Times*, bk.1, ch.11.

6 Ah, Rachel, aw a muddle! Fro' first to last, a muddle!
1854 Stephen Blackpool. *Hard Times*, bk.3, ch.6.

7 People mutht be amuthed. They can't be alwayth a learning, nor yet they can't be alwayth a working, they an't made for it.
1854 Mr Sleary. *Hard Times*, bk.3, ch.8.

8 Whatever was required to be done, the Circumlocution Office was beforehand with all the public departments in the art of perceiving—HOW NOT TO DO IT.
1855–7 *Little Dorrit*, bk.1, ch.10.

9 Take a little time—count five-and-twenty, Tattycoram.
1855–7 Mr Meagles. *Little Dorrit*, bk.1, ch.16.

10 In company with several other old ladies of both sexes.
1855–7 *Little Dorrit*, bk.1, ch.17.

11 It was not a bosom to repose upon, but it was a capital bosom to hang jewels upon.
1855–7 Of Mrs Merdle. *Little Dorrit*, bk.1, ch.21.

12 There's milestones on the Dover Road!
1855–7 Mr F's Aunt. *Little Dorrit*, bk.1, ch.23.

13 I revere the memory of Mr F. as an estimable man and most indulgent husband, only necessary to mention Asparagus and it appeared or to hint at any little delicate thing to drink and it came like magic in a pint bottle it was not ecstasy but it was comfort.
1855–7 Flora Finching. *Little Dorrit*, bk.1, ch.24.

14 As to marriage on the part of a man, my dear, Society requires that he should retrieve his fortunes by marriage. Society requires that he should gain by marriage. Society requires that he should found a handsome establishment by marriage. Society does not see, otherwise, what he has to do with marriage.
1855–7 Mrs Merdle. *Little Dorrit*, bk.1, ch.33.

15 Mrs General had no opinions. Her way of forming a mind was to prevent it from forming opinions...Mrs General was not to be told of anything shocking. Accidents, miseries, and offences, were never to be mentioned before her. Passion was to go to sleep in the presence of Mrs General, and blood was to change to milk and water. The little that was left in the world, when all these deductions were made, it was Mrs General's province to varnish.
1855–7 *Little Dorrit*, bk.2, ch.2.

16 Father is rather vulgar, my dear. The word Papa, besides, gives a pretty form to the lips. Papa, potatoes, poultry, prunes, and prism, are all very good words for the lips: especially prunes and prism.
1855–7 Mrs General. *Little Dorrit*, bk.2, ch.5.

17 That it is at least as difficult to stay a moral infection as a physical one; that such a disease will spread with the malignity and rapidity of the Plague; that the contagion, when it has once made head, will spare no pursuit or condition, but will lay hold on people in the soundest health, and become developed in the most unlikely constitutions; is a fact as firmly established by experience as that we human creatures breathe an atmosphere.
1855–7 *Little Dorrit*, bk.2, ch.13.

18 Once a gentleman, and always a gentleman.
1855–7 Rigaud. *Little Dorrit*, bk.2, ch.28.

19 It was the best of times, it was the worst of times, it was the age of wisdom, it was the age of foolishness, it was the epoch of belief, it was the epoch of incredulity, it was the season of Light, it was the season of Darkness, it was the spring of hope, it was the winter of despair, we had everything before us, we had nothing before us, we were all going direct to Heaven, we were all going direct the other way.
1859 *A Tale of Two Cities*, bk.1, ch.1.

20 I pass my whole life, miss, in turning an immense pecuniary Mangle.
1859 Mr Lorry. *A Tale of Two Cities*, bk.1, ch.4.

21 If it was ever intended that I should go across salt water, do you suppose Providence would have cast my lot in an island?
1859 Miss Pross. *A Tale of Two Cities*, bk.1, ch.4.

22 If you must go flopping yourself down, flop in favour of your husband and child, and not in opposition to 'em.
1859 Jerry Cruncher. *A Tale of Two Cities*, bk.2, ch.1.

23 I care for no man on earth, and no man on earth cares for me.
1859 Sydney Carton. *A Tale of Two Cities*, bk.2, ch.4.

24 Although it's a long time on the road, it is on the road and coming. I tell thee it never retreats, and never stops.
1859 Madame Defarge. *A Tale of Two Cities*, bk.2, ch.16.

25 It is a far, far better thing that I do, than I have ever done; it is a far, far better rest that I go to than I have ever known.
1859 Sydney Carton. *A Tale of Two Cities*, bk.3, ch.15.

26 Cleanliness is next to Godliness, and some people do the same by their religion.
1860–1 *Great Expectations*, ch.4.

27 I was always treated as if I had insisted on being born in opposition to the dictates of reason, religion, and morality.
1860–1 Pip. *Great Expectations*, ch.4.

28 Your sister is given to government.
1860–1 Joe Gargery. *Great Expectations*, ch.7.

29 In the little world in which children have their existence, whosoever brings them up, there is nothing so finely perceived and so finely felt, as injustice.
1860–1 *Great Expectations*, ch.8.

30 I had cherished a profound conviction that her bringing me up by hand, gave her no right to bring me up by jerks.
1860–1 *Great Expectations*, ch.8.

31 It is a most miserable thing to feel ashamed of home.
1860–1 *Great Expectations*, ch.14.

32 Probably every new and eagerly expected garment ever put on since clothes came in, fell a trifle short of the wearer's expectation.
1860–1 *Great Expectations*, ch.19.

33 You wouldn't mind being at once introduced to the Aged, would you?
1860–1 Wemmick introduces Pip to his father. *Great Expectations*, ch.25.

34 I loved Estella... I loved her against reason, against promise, against peace, against hope, against happiness, against all discouragement that could be.
1860–1 *Great Expectations*, ch.29.

35 Words cannot state the amount of aggravation and injury wreaked upon me by Trabb's boy, when passing abreast of me, he pulled up his shirt-collar, twined his side-hair, stuck an arm akimbo, and smirked extravagantly by, wriggling his elbows and body, and drawling to his attendants, 'Don't know yah, don't know yah, 'pon my soul don't know yah!'
1860–1 *Great Expectations*, ch.30.

36 'Halloa! Here's a church!... Let's go in!... Here's Miss Skiffins! Let's have a wedding.'
1860–1 *Great Expectations*, ch.55.

37 I listened with hadmiration amounting to haw.
1864–5 Mr Boffin. *Our Mutual Friend*, bk.1, ch.5.

38 A literary man—*with* a wooden leg—and all Print is open to him.
1864–5 Mr Boffin speaking of Silas Wegg. *Our Mutual Friend*, bk.1, ch.5.

39 Mrs Boffin...is a highflyer at Fashion.
1864–5 *Our Mutual Friend*, bk.1, ch.5.

40 'Was you thinking at all of poetry?' Mr Wegg inquired, musing.
'Would it come dearer?' Mr Boffin asked.
'It would come dearer,' Mr Wegg returned. 'For when a person comes to grind off poetry night after night, it is but right he should expect to be paid for its weakening effect on his mind.'
1864–5 *Our Mutual Friend*, bk.1, ch.5.

41 These two ignorant and unpolished people had guided themselves so far on in their journey of life, by a religious sense of duty and desire to do right.
1864–5 Of Mr and Mrs Boffin. *Our Mutual Friend*, bk.1, ch.9.

42 Mr Podsnap was well to do, and stood very high in Mr Podsnap's opinion.
1864–5 *Our Mutual Friend*, bk.1, ch.11.

43 A certain institution in Mr Podsnap's mind which he called 'the young person' may be considered to have been embodied in Miss Podsnap, his daughter...The

question about everything was, would it bring a blush into the cheek of the young person?
1864–5 *Our Mutual Friend*, bk.1, ch.11.

44 'Our Language,' said Mr Podsnap, with a gracious consciousness of being always right, 'is Difficult. Ours is a Copious Language, and Trying to Strangers. I will not Pursue my Question… It merely referred,' Mr Podsnap explained, with a sense of meritorious proprietorship, 'to our Constitution, Sir. We Englishmen are Very Proud of our Constitution, Sir. It Was Bestowed Upon Us By Providence. No Other Country is so Favoured as This Country.'
1864–5 *Our Mutual Friend*, bk.1, ch.11.

45 Mr Podsnap settled that whatever he put behind him he put out of existence… 'I don't want to know about it; I don't choose to discuss it; I don't admit it!'
1864–5 *Our Mutual Friend*, bk.1, ch.11.

46 I think…that it is the best club in London.
1864–5 Mr Twemlow's description of the House of Commons. *Our Mutual Friend*, bk.2, ch.3.

47 Come up and be dead! Come up and be dead!
1864–5 Jenny Wren. *Our Mutual Friend*, bk.2, ch.5.

48 A slap-up gal in a bang-up chariot.
1864–5 The scout's description of Bella. *Our Mutual Friend*, bk.2, ch.8.

49 I want to be something so much worthier than the doll in the doll's house.
1864–5 Bella. *Our Mutual Friend*, bk.4, ch.5.

50 Stranger, pause and ask thyself the question, Canst thou do likewise? If not, with a blush retire.
1870 Mr Sapsea's epitaph for his wife. *Edwin Drood*, ch.4.

Dickinson, Emily Elizabeth 1830–86

US poet who spent her life in seclusion in Massachusetts, writing over 1000 intensely lyrical and personal poems, few of which were published during her lifetime.

51 Success is counted sweetest
By those who ne'er succeed.
c.1859 *Complete Poems*, no.67 (first published 1890).

52 Can I expound the skies?
How still the Riddle lies!
c.1859 *Complete Poems*, no.89 (first published 1890).

53 Surgeons must be very careful
When they take the knife!
Underneath their fine incisions
Stirs the culprit—*Life!*
c.1859 *Complete Poems*, no.108 (first published 1891).

54 To fight aloud, is very brave,
But gallanter, I know,
Who charge within the bosom
The Cavalry of Woe.
c.1859 *Complete Poems*, no.126 (first published 1890).

55 Musicians wrestle everywhere—
All day—among the crowded air
I hear the silver strife—
And—waking—long before the morn—
Such transport breaks upon the town
I think it that 'New Life!'
c.1860 *Complete Poems*, no.157 (first published 1891).

56 'Faith' is a fine invention
When Gentlemen can *see*—
But *Microscopes* are prudent
In an Emergency.
c.1860 *Complete Poems*, no.185 (first published 1891).

57 Inebriate of Air—am I—
And Debauchee of Dew—
Reeling—thro endless summer days—
From inns of Molten Blue—
c.1860 *Complete Poems*, no.214 (first published 1861).

58 'Hope' is the thing with feathers—
That perches in the soul—
And sings the tune without the words—
And never stops—at all—
c.1860 *Complete Poems*, no.254 (first published 1891).

59 Some keep the Sabbath going to Church—
I keep it, staying at Home—
With a Bobolink for a Chorister—
And an Orchard, for a Dome—
c.1860 *Complete Poems*, no.324 (first published 1864).

60 After great pain, a formal feeling comes—
The Nerves sit ceremonious, like Tombs.
c.1862 *Complete Poems*, no.341 (first published 1929).

61 Much Madness is divinest Sense—
To a discerning Eye—
Much Sense—the starkest Madness—
c.1862 *Complete Poems*, no.435 (first published 1890).

62 They shut me up in Prose—
As when a little girl
They put me in the Closet—
Because they liked me 'still'.
c.1862 *Complete Poems*, no.613 (first published 1935).

63 The Brain—is wider than the Sky.
c.1862 *Complete Poems*, no.632 (first published 1896).

64 I cannot live with You—
It would be Life—
And Life is over there—
Behind the Shelf.
c.1862 *Complete Poems*, no.640 (first published 1890).

65 One need not be a Chamber—to be Haunted—
One need not be a House—
The brain has Corridors—surpassing
Material Place—
c.1863 *Complete Poems*, no.670 (first published 1891).

66 Because I could not stop for Death—
He kindly stopped for me—
The carriage held but just Ourselves—
And Immortality.
c.1863 *Complete Poems*, no.712 (first published 1890).

67 Ample make this Bed—
Make this Bed with Awe—
In it wait till Judgement break
Excellent and Fair.
c.1864 *Complete Poems*, no.829 (first published 1891).

68 Of Consciousness, her awful Mate
The soul cannot be rid—
As easy the secreting her
Behind the Eyes of God.
c.1864 *Complete Poems*, no.894 (first published 1945).

69 Faith—is the Pierless Bridge
Supporting what We see

Unto the Scene that We do not.
c.1864 *Complete Poems*, no.915 (first published 1929).

70 Death is a dialogue between
The Spirit and the Dust.
c.1864 *Complete Poems*, no.976 (first published 1890).

71 Tell all the Truth but tell it slant—
Success in Circuit lies
Too bright for our infirm Delight
The Truth's superb surprise.
c.1868 *Complete Poems*, no.1129 (first published 1945).

72 A word is dead
When it is said,
Some say.
I say it just
Begins to live
That day.
?1872 *Complete Poems*, no.1212 (first published 1894).

73 The abdication of Belief
Makes the Behavior small—
Better an ignis fatuus
Than no illume at all.
c.1882 *Complete Poems*, no.1551 (first published 1945).

74 He ate and drank the precious Words,
His Spirit grew robust;
He knew no more that he was poor,
Nor that his frame was Dust.
c.1883 *Complete Poems*, no.1587 (first published 1890).

75 The Pedigree of Honey
Does not concern the Bee—
A Clover, any time, to him,
Is Aristocracy—
c.1884 *Complete Poems*, no.1627 (first published 1890).

76 'Eternity' is there,
We say, as of a station.
Meanwhile, he is so near,
He joins me in my Ramble—
Divides abode with me—
No Friend have I that so persists
As this Eternity.
Complete Poems, no.1684 (first published 1914).

77 Parting is all we know of heaven,
And all we need of hell.
Complete Poems, no.1732 (first published 1896).

78 Rearrange a 'Wife's' affection!
When they dislocate my Brain!
Amputate my freckled Bosom!
Make me bearded like a man!
Complete Poems, no.1737 (first published 1891).

79 The distance that the dead have gone
Does not at first appear—
Their coming back seems possible
For many an ardent year.
Complete Poems, no.1742 (first published 1896).

80 Let us go in; the fog is rising.
Last words, attributed.

Dickinson, John 1732–1808

US revolutionary statesman, leader of conservative opposition to the British. His draft formed the basis of the Articles of Confederation.

81 Then join hand in hand, brave Americans all—
By uniting we stand, by dividing we fall.
1768 'The Liberty Song'.

82 We have counted the cost of this contest, and find nothing so dreadful as voluntary slavery… Our cause is just, our union is perfect.
1775 Declaration of reasons for taking up arms against Britain, 8 Jul, presented to Congress. Quoted in C J Stille *The Life and Times of John Dickinson* (1891), ch.5.

Diderot, Denis 1713–84

French philosopher, novelist, essayist, playwright and critic. A leading figure in the Enlightenment, he is best remembered for his ambitious *Encyclopédie* (1751–72). Other writings include sentimental dramas and theoretical studies of the theatre.

83 *Il ne faut point donner d'esprit à ses personnages; mais savoir les placer dans des circonstances qui leur en donnent.*
You should not give wit to your characters, but know instead how to put them in situations which will make them witty.
1757 *Entretiens sur le fils naturel*, pt.2.

84 *Les passions détruisent plus de préjugés que la philosophie. Et comment le mensonge leur résisterait-il? Elles ébranlent quelquefois la vérité.*
Passions destroy more prejudices than philosophy. And how would lies resist passions? Passions sometimes weaken the truth.
1757 *Entretiens sur le fils naturel*, pt.2.

85 *Les beautés ont, dans les arts, le même fondement que les vérités dans la philosophie. Qu'est-ce que la vérité? La conformité de nos jugements avec les êtres. Qu'est ce que la beauté d'imitation? La conformité de l'image avec la chose.*
Beauty has in art the same foundation as does truth in philosophy. What is the truth? The conformity of our judgements with beings. What is the beauty of imitation? The conformity of the image with the thing.
1757 *Entretiens sur le fils naturel*, pt.3.

86 *Une danse est un poème.*
A dance is a poem.
1757 *Entretiens sur le fils naturel*, pt.3.

87 *Soit donc que vous composiez, soit donc que vous jouiez, ne pensez non plus au spectateur que s'il n'existait pas. Imaginez sur le bord du théâtre, un grand mur qui vous sépare du parterre; jouez comme si la toile ne se levait pas.*
Whether you compose or act, think no more of the spectator than if he did not exist. Imagine at the edge of the stage a large wall which separates you from the orchestra; act as if the curtain never rose.
1758 *Discours sur la poésie dramatique*, introducing the theatrical concept of the 'fourth wall'.

88 *Le génie se sent; mais il ne s'imite point.*
Genius is felt, but it is not imitated.
1758 *Discours sur la poésie dramatique*.

89 *En général, plus un peuple est civilisé, poli, moins ses moeurs sont poétiques; tout s'affaiblit en s'adoucissant.*
In general, the more civilized and refined the people, the less poetic are its morals; everything weakens as it mellows.
1758 *Discours sur la poésie dramatique*.

90 *La poésie veut quelque chose d'énorme, de barbare et de sauvage.*
Poetry needs something on the scale of the grand, the barbarous, the savage.
1758 *Discours sur la poésie dramatique.*

91 *Le public ne sait pas toujours désirer le vrai.*
The public does not always know how to desire the truth.
1758 *Discours sur la poésie dramatique.*

92 *Le rôle d'un auteur est un rôle assez vain; c'est celui d'un homme qui se croit en état de donner des leçons au public. Et le rôle du critique? Il est bien plus vain encore; c'est celui d'un homme qui se croit en état de donner des leçons à celui qui se croit en état d'en donner au public.*
The role of the author is vain enough; it is that of a person who considers himself able to give lessons to the public. And the role of the critic? It is vainer still; it is that of a person who considers himself able to give lessons to he who considers himself able to give them to the public.
1758 *Discours sur la poésie dramatique.*

93 *Ce n'est que par la mémoire que nous sommes un même individu pour les autres et pour nous-mêmes. Il ne me reste peut-être pas, à l'âge que j'ai, une seule molécule du corps que j'apportai en naissant.*
It is only in memory that we are the same person for others and for ourselves. At the age I am now, there is probably not a single molecule of my body that I had when born.
1758 *Discours sur la poésie dramatique.*

94 *Mes pensées sont mes catins.*
My thoughts are my prostitutes.
1761–74 *Le Neveu de Rameau.*

95 *Rien ne dissemble plus de lui que lui-même.*
Nothing resembles him less than himself.
1761–74 *Le Neveu de Rameau.*

96 *Voyez-vous cet oeuf. C'est avec cela qu'on renverse toutes les écoles de théologie, et tous les temples de la terre.*
See this egg. It is with this that all the schools of theology and all the temples of the earth are to be overturned.
1769 *Le Rêve de d'Alembert* (published 1830), pt.1.

97 *Tous les jours on couche avec des femmes qu'on n'aime pas, et l'on ne couche pas avec des femmes qu'on aime.*
Every day we sleep with women we do not love and don't sleep with the women we do love.
c.1773 *Jacques le fataliste et son maître* (published 1796).

98 *L'esprit de l'escalier.*
Staircase wit.
1773–8 That is, the witty reply that comes to mind after leaving the company, while descending the stairs. *Paradoxe sur le comédien* (published 1830).

99 Two qualities essential for the artist: morality and perspective.
1776–81 *Pensées détachées sur la peinture.*

1 One composition is meagre, though it has many figures; another is rich, though it has few.
1776–81 *Pensées détachées sur la peinture.*

2 Paint as they spoke in Sparta.
1776–81 *Pensées détachées sur la peinture.*

3 *L'homme est né pour la société; séparez-le, isolez-le, ses idées se désuniront, son caractère se tournera, mille affections ridicules s'élèveront dans son coeur; des pensées extravagantes germeront dans son esprit, comme les ronces dans une terre sauvage.*
Man is born to live in society: separate him, isolate him, and his ideas disintegrate, his character changes, a thousand ridiculous affectations rise up in his heart; extreme thoughts take hold in his mind, like the brambles in a wild field.
1796 *La Religieuse.*

Didion, Joan 1934–

US writer, a respected essayist on US life and culture. Her works include the novel *A Book of Common Prayer* (1977) and the non-fiction titles *The White Album* (1979) and *Political Fictions* (2001).

4 Innocence ends when one is stripped of the delusion that one likes oneself.
1961 'On Self Respect', collected in *Slouching Towards Bethlehem* (1968).

5 Was there ever in anyone's life span a point free in time, devoid of memory, a night when choice was any more than the sum of all the choices gone before?
1963 *Run River*, ch.4.

6 New York was no mere city. It was instead an infinitely romantic notion, the mysterious nexus of all love and money and power, the shining and perishable dream itself. To think of 'living' there was to reduce the miraculous to the mundane; one does not 'live' at Xanadu.
1967 'Goodbye To All That', collected in *Slouching Towards Bethlehem* (1968).

7 We tell ourselves stories in order to live.
1979 *The White Album*, 'The White Album, 1'.

8 Everything was unmentionable but nothing was unimaginable.
1979 Of Los Angeles in 1968–9. *The White Album*, 'The White Album, 10'.

9 To believe in 'the greater good' is to operate, necessarily, in a certain ethical suspension.
1979 *The White Album*, 'The Woman's Movement'.

Dietz, Howard 1896–1983

US writer and lyricist.

10 That's Entertainment.
1953 Title of song reputedly written by Dietz and Arthur Schwartz for the film *The Band Wagon* in less than an hour.

11 More stars than there are in heaven.
MGM slogan.

Dillard, Annie 1945–

US writer. She is best known for her essay collection *Pilgrim at Tinker Creek* (1974), and has also written poetry and fiction.

12 It was a bitter birthday present from evolution.
1974 Of self-consciousness. *Pilgrim at Tinker Creek*, ch.6.

13 I don't know what it is about fecundity that so appals. I suppose it is the teeming evidence that birth and growth, which we value, are ubiquitous and blind, that life itself is so astonishingly cheap, that nature is as careless as it is bountiful, and that with extravagance goes a crushing waste that will one day include our own cheap lives.
1974 *Pilgrim at Tinker Creek*, ch.10.

14 I think the dying pray at the last not please but thank you as a guest thanks his host at the door.
1974 *Pilgrim at Tinker Creek*, ch.15.

Dillingham, Charles 1868–1934

US theatre producer.

15 I bet you, Ziggie, a hundred bucks that he ain't in here.
1926 Attributed whisper to Florenz Ziegfeld as they acted as pall-bearers at the funeral of escapologist Harry Houdini.

Dillon, Wentworth c.1633–1685

Irish poet and critic.

16 Choose an author as you choose a friend.
1684 *Essay on Translated Verse*, l.96.

17 Immodest words admit of no defence,
For want of decency is want of sense.
1684 *Essay on Translated Verse*, l.113.

DiMaggio, Joe (Joseph Paul) 1914–99

US baseball player. A powerful and elegant centre fielder and hitter, he played for 15 seasons with the New York Yankees, voted Most Valuable Player three times. In 1954 he married (briefly) Marilyn Monroe.

18 There's no skill involved. Just go up there and swing at the ball.
Of baseball. Quoted in Colin Jarman *The Guinness Dictionary of Sports Quotations* (1990).

19 It's no fun being married to an electric light.
Of his marriage to Marilyn Monroe. Quoted in Colin Jarman *The Guinness Dictionary of Sports Quotations* (1990).

Dimbleby, Richard 1913–65

English broadcaster, best known for his commentaries on state occasions. He joined the BBC's news team in 1936, becoming its first war correspondent (1939).

20 The moment of the Queen's crowning is come.
1953 Commentary on the coronation at Westminster Abbey, 2 Jun.

Dinesen, Isak

► *See Blixen, Karen, Baroness*

Diogenes of Sinope c.410–c.320 BC

Greek Cynic philosopher and moralist, student of Antisthenes.

21 Yes...stand out of my sun a little.
His reply when asked by Alexander the Great if he lacked anything. Quoted in Plutarch *Parallel Lives*, 'Alexander'.
► *See Alexander the Great 11:18.*

22 I am looking for an honest man.
His reply when asked why he was wandering the streets of Athens during the day with a lantern.

Dior, Christian 1905–57

French couturier who founded his own Paris house in 1947 and achieved worldwide fame with his 'New Look' in the same year.

23 Women are most fascinating between the ages of thirty-five and forty, after they have won a few races and know how to pace themselves. Since few women ever pass forty, maximum fascination can continue indefinitely.
1955 In *Collier's Magazine*, 10 Jun.

24 In the world today *haute couture* is one of the last repositories of the marvellous, and the *couturiers* the last possessors of the wand of Cinderella's Fairy Godmother.
Dior by Dior (translated by Antonia Fraser, 1957).

Dirksen, Everett McKinley 1896–1969

US Republican politician.

25 The oil can is mightier than the sword.
1964 In *Life*, 5 Jun.

26 I am a man of fixed and unbending principles, the first of which is to be flexible at all times.
Recalled on his death, 7 Sep 1969.

27 A billion here, a billion there. Pretty soon it runs into real money.
Quoted in 'Half a Trillion in Real Money', editorial in the *New York Times*, 2 Dec 1979.

Disch, Thomas M(ichael) 1940–

US writer and critic, best known for his sophisticated, politically conscious science fiction, such as *Camp Concentration* (1968). He has also written several volumes of poetry.

28 Mankind Under The Leash.
1966 Title of novel.

29 A predilection for genre fiction is symptomatic of a kind of arrested development.
1986 In *The Face*, Mar.

30 Science fiction, like Brazil, is where the nuts come from.
1987 In the *Observer*, 23 Aug.
► *See Thomas 852:53.*

Diski, Jenny 1947–

English author and journalist.

31 Statistics are designed to keep you safe.
1997 *Skating to Antarctica*.

32 For the most part, quantum theory has been of little practical value in my life.
1997 *Skating to Antarctica*.

Disney, Walt(er Elias) 1901–66

US artist and film producer. His animated characters such as Mickey Mouse (1928) featured in *Silly Symphonies* (from 1929) and later full-length animated films.

33 Fancy being remembered around the world for the invention of a mouse!
c.1966 Comment to his wife during his last illness. Quoted in Leonard Mosley *Disney's World* (1985).

Disraeli, Benjamin, 1st Earl of Beaconsfield 1804–81

British statesman, first known for his political novels *Coningsby* (1844) and *Sybil* (1845). He became a Tory MP in 1837, Chancellor of the Exchequer (1852, 1858–9 and 1866), and Prime Minister (1868, 1874–80). His second administration (1874–80) was notable both for diplomacy and social reform.

34 Experience is the child of Thought, and Thought is the child of Action. We cannot learn men from books.
1826–7 *Vivian Grey*, bk.5, ch.1.

35 I repeat...that all power is a trust—that we are accountable for its exercise—that, from the people, and for the people, all springs, and all must exist.
1826–7 *Vivian Grey*, bk.6, ch.10.

36 A good eater must be a good man; for a good eater must have a good digestion, and a good digestion depends upon a good conscience.
1831 *The Young Duke*, bk.1, ch.14.

37 'The age of chivalry is past,' said May Dacre. 'Bores have succeeded to dragons.'
1831 *The Young Duke*, bk.2, ch.5.

38 Read no history: nothing but biography, for that is life without theory.
1832 *Contarini Fleming*, pt.1, ch.23.

39 The practice of politics in the East may be defined by one word—dissimulation.
1832 *Contarini Fleming*, pt.5, ch.10.

40 Time is the great physician.
1837 *Henrietta Temple*, bk.6, ch.9.

41 Though I sit down now, the time will come when you will hear me.
1837 On being barracked during his overly ornate maiden speech in the House of Commons, 7 Dec.

42 The Continent will not suffer England to be the workshop of the world.
1838 House of Commons, 15 Mar.

43 No Government can be long secure without a formidable Opposition.
1844 *Coningsby*, bk.2, ch.1.

44 Conservatism discards Prescription, shrinks from Principle, disavows Progress; having rejected all respect for antiquity, it offers no redress for the present, and makes no preparation for the future.
1844 *Coningsby*, bk.2, ch.5.

45 Youth is a blunder; Manhood a struggle; Old Age a regret.
1844 *Coningsby*, bk.3, ch.1.

46 It seems to me a barren thing this Conservatism—an unhappy cross-breed, the mule of politics that engenders nothing.
1844 *Coningsby*, bk.3, ch.5.

47 What Art was to the ancient world, Science is to the modern.
1844 *Coningsby*, bk.4, ch.1.

48 The depository of power is always unpopular.
1844 *Coningsby*, bk.4, ch.13.

49 Man is only truly great when he acts from the passions.
1844 *Coningsby*, bk.4, ch.13.

50 Consider Ireland. Thus you have a starving population, an absentee aristocracy, and an alien Church—and in addition, the weakest executive in the world. That is the Irish Question.
1844 Speech, House of Commons, 16 Feb.

51 I am neither a Whig nor a Tory. My politics are described in one word, and that word is England.
1844 Speech, House of Commons.

52 To do nothing and get something, formed a boy's ideal of a manly career.
1845 *Sybil*, bk.1, ch.5.

53 'Two nations; between whom there is no intercourse and no sympathy; who are as ignorant of each other's habits, thoughts and feelings, as if they were dwellers in different zones, or inhabitants of different planets; who are formed by a different breeding, are fed by a different food, are ordered by different manners, and are not governed by the same laws.' 'You speak of—' said Egremont, hesitatingly. 'THE RICH AND THE POOR.'
1845 *Sybil*, bk.2, ch.5.

54 Little things affect little minds.
1845 *Sybil*, bk.3, ch.2.

55 The Youth of a Nation are the trustees of Posterity.
1845 *Sybil*, bk.6, ch.13

56 The right honourable gentleman caught the Whigs bathing and walked away with their clothes.
1845 House of Commons speech, 28 Feb, attacking Prime Minister Sir Robert Peel for bullying his back-benchers into supporting the Government's action in intercepting the private mail of radical MPs.

57 A Conservative government is an organized hypocrisy.
1845 Speech, House of Commons, 17 Mar.

58 A majority is always the best repartee.
1847 *Tancred*, bk.2, ch.14.

59 London is a modern Babylon.
1847 *Tancred*, bk.5, ch.5.

60 Justice is truth in action.
1851 Speech, House of Commons, 11 Feb.

61 He has to learn that petulance is not sarcasm, and that insolence is not invective.
1852 Of Sir Charles Wood. Speech, House of Commons, 16 Dec.

62 England does not love coalitions.
1852 Speech, House of Commons, 17 Dec.

63 The blue ribbon of the turf.
1852 Of the Derby race. *Life of Lord George Bentinck*, ch.26.

64 If a traveller were informed that such a man was Leader of the House of Commons, he may well begin to comprehend how the Egyptians came to worship an insect.
1852 Of Lord John Russell. Attributed.

65 His temper, naturally morose, has become licentiously peevish. Crossed in his Cabinet, he insults the House of Lords and plagues the most eminent of his colleagues with the crabbed malice of a maundering witch.
1855 Of Lord Aberdeen, whose disagreements with his Whig–Peelite coalition over the Crimean War eventually forced his resignation.

66 Finality is not the language of politics.
1859 Speech, House of Commons, 28 Feb.

67 I hold that the characteristic of the present age is craving credulity.
1864 Speech, Oxford, 25 Nov.

68 Party is organized opinion.
1864 Speech, Oxford, 25 Nov.

69 The question is this: is man an ape or an angel? I am on the side of the angels.
1864 Speech, Oxford, 25 Nov.

70 Assassination has never changed the history of the world.
1865 Speech, House of Commons, 1 May, paying tribute to US President Abraham Lincoln who had been assassinated in Washington, 14 Apr.

71 I have climbed to the top of the greasy pole.
1868 On becoming Prime Minister.

72 The pursuit of science leads only to the insoluble.
1870 *Lothair*, ch.17.

73 A Protestant, if he wants aid or advice on any matter, can only go to his solicitor.
1870 *Lothair*, ch.27.

74 When a man fell into his anecdotage it was a sign for him to retire from the world.
1870 *Lothair*, ch.28.

75 Every woman should marry—and no man.
1870 *Lothair*, ch.30.

76 You know who the critics are? The men who have failed in literature and art.
1870 *Lothair*, ch.35.

77 'My idea of an agreeable person,' said Hugo Bohun, 'is a person who agrees with me.'
1870 *Lothair*, ch.35.

78 Increased means and increased leisure are the two civilizers of man.
1872 Speech at Manchester, 3 Apr.

79 A University should be a place of light, of liberty, and of learning.
1873 Speech, House of Commons, 11 Mar.

80 An author who speaks about his own books is almost as bad as a mother who talks about her own children.
1873 Rectorial address, Glasgow, 19 Nov.

81 Upon the education of the people of this country the fate of this country depends.
1874 Speech, House of Commons, 15 Jun.

82 Posterity will do justice to that unprincipled maniac Gladstone—an extraordinary mixture of envy, vindictiveness, hypocrisy and superstition and with one commanding characteristic. Whether Prime Minister or Leader of the Opposition, whether preaching, praying, speechifying, or scribbling—never a gentleman. He is so vain that he wants to figure in history as the settler of all the great questions; but a parliamentary Constitution is not favourable to such ambitions. Things must be done by parties, not by persons using parties as tools.
c.1874 Letter.

83 I am dead: dead, but in the Elysian fields.
1876 On his elevation to the House of Lords.

84 Gladstone, like Richelieu, cannot write. Nothing can be more unmusical, more involved, or more uncouth than all his scribblement.
1877 Letter, 3 Oct.

85 Lord Salisbury and myself have brought you peace—but a peace, I hope, with honour.
1878 Declaration, 16 Jul, on returning from the Berlin Congress with the guarantees it had produced of continuing peace in Europe.
► *See also Chamberlain 204:63.*

86 A sophistical rhetorician inebriated with the exuberance of his own verbosity.
1878 Of Gladstone. Speech reported in *The Times*, 29 Jul.

87 His Christianity was muscular.
1880 *Endymion*, ch.14.

88 You must dress according to your age, your pursuits, your object in life.
1880 *Endymion*, ch.23.

89 What all men should avoid is the 'shabby genteel'. No man ever gets over it... You had better be in rags.
1880 *Endymion*, ch.23.

90 'Sensible men are all the same religion.' 'And pray what is that?' inquired the prince. 'Sensible men never tell.'
1880 Waldershire. *Endymion*, ch.81.

91 I believe they went out, like all good things, with the Stuarts.
1880 *Endymion*, ch.99.

92 I will not go down to posterity talking bad grammar.
1881 On correcting proofs of his last parliamentary speech, 31 Mar. Quoted in Robert Blake *Disraeli*, ch.32.

93 There are three kinds of lies: lies, damned lies and statistics.
Attributed. Quoted in Mark Twain *Autobiography*, vol.1 (published 1924).

94 Millstones around our neck.
Of the colonies. Quoted in Robert Blake *The Conservative Party from Peel to Churchill* (1970).

95 England is unrivalled for two things—sport and politics.
Quoted in Colin Jarman *The Guinness Dictionary of Sports Quotations* (1990).

Dobson, (Henry) Austin 1840–1921

English poet. He published several volumes of carefully crafted, often humorous verse, and prose studies of famous writers.

96 Time goes, you say? Ah no!
Alas, Time stays, we go.
1877 'Paradox of Time'.

97 Fame is a food that dead men eat,
I have no stomach for such meat.
1906 'Fame is a Fool'.

Dobzhansky, Theodosius G 1900–75

Russian-born US geneticist, Professor at Columbia University and the University of California at Davis.

98 Nature's stern discipline enjoins mutual help at least as often as warfare. The fittest may also be the gentlest.
1962 *Mankind Evolving*.

Docherty, Tommy (Thomas Henderson) 1928–

Scottish footballer and manager. In a tempestuous career he played for Scotland and managed ten clubs, including Manchester United and Queen's Park Rangers, and was briefly manager of Scotland (1971–2).

99 The ideal board of directors should be made up of three men—two dead and the other dying.
1977 Quoted in Colin Jarman *The Guinness Dictionary of Sports Quotations* (1990).

1 Our strikers couldn't score in a brothel.
1985 Of the forwards at Wolverhampton Wanderers. Quoted in Peter Ball and Phil Shaw *The Book of Football Quotations* (1989).

Doctorow, E(dgar) L(awrence) 1931–

US novelist, best known for *Ragtime* (1975) and *Billy Bathgate* (1989).

2 A few professional alienists understood his importance, but to most of the public he appeared as some kind of German sexologist, an exponent of free love who used big words to talk about dirty things. At least a decade would have to pass before Freud would have his revenge and see his ideas begin to destroy sex in America forever.
1975 *Ragtime*, ch.5.

3 There is no longer any such thing as fiction or non-fiction; there's only narrative.
1988 In the *New York Times Book Review*, 27 Jan.

4 Like art and politics, gangsterism is a very important avenue of assimilation into society.
1990 In the *International Herald Tribune*, 1 Oct.

Dodd, Christopher J 1944–

US Democratic politician.

5 Time is the 101st Senator...the ally of the people who want to do nothing.
1994 On the difficulty of passing President Clinton's health programme when legislators were longing for the holidays. In the *New York Times*, 26 Aug.

Dodd, Ken(neth) 1927–

English stand-up comedian, singer and actor.

6 The trouble with Freud is that he never had to play the old Glasgow Empire on a Saturday night after Rangers and Celtic had both lost.
1965 Television interview, discussing Freud's theory of catharsis through laughter, whereby jokes produce a feeling of elation.

Doddridge, Philip 1702–51

English nonconformist minister and hymn-writer.

7 Hark, the glad sound! The Saviour comes,
The Saviour promised long;
Let every heart exult with joy,
And every voice be song!
Hymns, 'Hark, the Glad Sound' (published 1755).

8 O God of Bethel! by whose hand
Thy people still are fed,
Who through this weary pilgrimage
Hast all our fathers led.
Hymns, 'O God of Bethel' (published 1755).

9 Ye servants of the Lord,
Each in his office wait,
Observant of the heavenly word,
And watchful at his gate.
Hymns, 'Ye Servants of the Lord' (published 1755).

10 Father of Peace, and God of love!
We own Thy power to save,
That power by which our Shepherd rose
Victorious o'er the grave.
Hymns, 'Father of Peace' (published 1755).

Dole, Bob (Robert Joseph) 1923–

US Republican politician. Having run unsuccessfully for presidential nomination in 1980 and 1988, he became a presidential candidate in 1996, but lost the election to Bill Clinton.

11 George Meany could run for President, but then why should he step down?
1976 On Meany's status as president of the American Federation of Labor. In the *Wall Street Journal*, 7 Sep.

12 It is inside work with no heavy lifting.
1988 On the vice presidency. ABC TV broadcast, 24 Jul.

13 Contrary to reports that I took the loss badly, I slept like a baby—every two hours I woke up and cried.
1988 On losing the presidential nomination. ABC TV broadcast, 14 Aug.

14 Putting a majority together is like a one-armed man wrapping cranberries.
Quoted in Hedrick Smith *The Power Game* (1988).

15 This President will go down in history as the only President who raised taxes before he took office and cut spending after he left office.
1993 On Bill Clinton's retroactive tax increases and promises of future spending cuts. In the *Los Angeles Times*, 16 Feb.

16 I thought about it a lot and I think every country ought to have a President.
1995 To television host David Letterman on his decision to seek high office. Reported in *Time*, 13 Feb.

17 We really win if we win. But we may even win if we lose.
1995 On the prospect of gaining popularity by reintroducing a balanced budget amendment. In the *New York Times*, 2 Mar.

Dole, Elizabeth Hanford 1936–

US lawyer and Republican politician, former President of the American Red Cross. She is married to Bob Dole.

18 Sometimes I think we're the only two lawyers in Washington who trust each other.
1987 On her marriage to Senator Bob Dole. In *Newsweek*, 3 Aug.

Domínguez Camargo, Hernando 1606–59

Colombian epic poet. A Jesuit, he probably abandoned this calling at the end of his life. His major work, the unfinished *Poema heroyco*, is a long, ambitious narrative in a highly Baroque style.

19 *¡En tantas de la muerte librerías,*
los cuerpos de esos huesos, mal seguro,
estudia, Julio; y en su letra advierte,
que son abecedarios de la muerte!
Julio, in those libraries of death
study the bodies of those bones—an assured evil;
and learn from those characters
that they form the abecedary of death!
1666 *San Ignacio de Loyola, Poema heroyco* ('Heroic Poem of Saint Ignatius of Loyola'), bk.4, canto 6.

Donaghy, Siobhan 1985–

English pop singer, former member of the band the Sugababes.

20 Everyone else gets themselves dressed in the morning so why can't I?
2003 When asked why, unlike other pop stars, she had no stylist. Quoted in the *Sunday Times*, 21 Sep.

Donahue, Phil 1935–

US broadcaster, host of the daytime talk show *Donahue* (1967–96) and credited with inventing the genre. His political talk show was axed after six months in 2003.

21 The breasts, the hallmark of our culture. You cannot sell anything in America without the breasts.
1990 On NBC TV, Aug.

Donald, David Herbert 1920–

US historian and writer, Professor at Harvard (1973–91, emeritus from 1991). His many works include *Charles Sumner and the Coming of the Civil War* (1960, Pulitzer Prize) and *Lincoln* (1995).

22 Their correspondence was something like a duet between a tuba and a piccolo.

1987 On letters of Thomas Wolfe and Aline Bernstein. *Look Homeward: A Life of Thomas Wolfe.*

Donleavy, J(ames) P(atrick) 1926–

US-born Irish writer, best known for his picaresque novel *The Ginger Man* (1955).

23 To marry the Irish is to look for poverty.
1955 *The Ginger Man*, ch.2.

24 But Jesus, when you don't have any money the problem is food. When you have money, it's sex. When you have both it's health, you worry about getting ruptured or something. If everything is simply jake then you're frightened of death.
1955 *The Ginger Man*, ch.5.

25 When I die I want to decompose in a barrel of porter and have it served in all the pubs in Dublin. I wonder would they all know it was me?
1955 *The Ginger Man*, ch.31.

26 I got disappointed in human nature as well and gave it up because I found it too much like my own.
1973 *A Fairy Tale of New York*, ch.18.

27 Writing is turning one's worst moments into money.
1979 In *Playboy*, May.

Donne, John c.1572–1631

English priest and poet. He converted from Catholicism to Anglicanism, becoming Dean of St Paul's.

28 Shall I leave all this constant company,
And follow headlong, wild uncertain thee?
1594–5 *Satires*, no.1.

29 For if one eat my meat, though it be known
The meat was mine, the excrement is his own.
1594–5 *Satires*, no.2.

30 Kind pity chokes my spleen.
1594–5 *Satires*, no.3.

31 On a huge hill,
Cragged, and steep, Truth stands, and he that will
Reach her, about must, and about must go.
1594–5 *Satires*, no.3.

32 Are not your kisses then as filthy, and more,
As a worm sucking an envenomed sore?
Doth not thy fearful hand in felling quake,
As one which gathering flowers, still fears a snake?
Is not your last act harsh, and violent,
As when a plough a stony ground doth rent?
c.1595 *Elegies*, no.8, 'The Comparison'.

33 Filled with her love, may I be rather grown
Mad with much heart than idiot with none.
c.1595 *Elegies*, no.10, 'The Bracelet'.

34 I will not look upon the quickening sun,
But straight her beauty to my sense shall run;
The air shall note her soft, the fire most pure;
Water suggest her clear, and the earth sure;
Time shall not lose our passages.
c.1595 *Elegies*, no.12, 'His Parting from Her'.

35 Come, madam, come, all rest my powers defy,
Until I labour, I in labour lie.
The foe oft-times having the foe in sight,
Is tired with standing though he never fight.
Off with that girdle, like heaven's zone glistering,
But a far fairer world encompassing.
Unpin that spangled breastplate which you wear,
That busy fools may be stopped there.
Unlace yourself, for that harmonious chime
Tells me from you that now 'tis your bed time.
c.1595 *Elegies*, no.19, 'To His Mistress Going to Bed'.

36 License my roving hands, and let them go
Before, behind, between, above, below.
O my America! my new-found-land,
My kingdom, safeliest when with one man manned.
c.1595 *Elegies*, no.19, 'To His Mistress Going to Bed'.

37 I wonder, by my troth, what thou and I
Did, till we loved? were we not weaned till then?
But sucked on country pleasures, childishly?
c.1595–1605 'The Good Morrow', collected in *Songs and Sonnets* (1633).

38 Now thou hast loved me one whole day,
Tomorrow when thou leav'st, what wilt thou say?
c.1595–1605 'Woman's Constancy', collected in *Songs and Sonnets* (1633).

39 Go, and catch a falling star,
Get with child a mandrake root,
Tell me, where all past years are,
Or who cleft the Devil's foot.
c.1595–1605 'Song: Go and catch a falling star', collected in *Songs and Sonnets* (1633).

40 Sweetest love I do not go,
For weariness of thee,
Nor in hope the world can show
A fitter Love for me;
But since that I
Must die at last, 'tis best,
To use myself in jest
Thus by feigned deaths to die.
c.1595–1605 'Song: Sweetest love I do not go', collected in *Songs and Sonnets* (1633).

41 Busy old fool, unruly sun,
Why dost thou thus,
Through windows, and through curtains, call on us?
Must to thy motions lovers' seasons run?
Saucy pedantic wretch, go chide
Late schoolboys, and sour prentices,
Go tell court-huntsmen that the King will ride,
Call country ants to harvest offices;
Love, all alike, no season knows, nor clime,
Nor hours, days, months, which are the rags of time.
c.1595–1605 'The Sun Rising', collected in *Songs and Sonnets* (1633).

42 She's all states, and all princes I,
Nothing else is.
Princes do but play us; compared to this,
All honour's mimic, all wealth alchemy.
c.1595–1605 'The Sun Rising', collected in *Songs and Sonnets* (1633).

43 For God's sake, hold your tongue, and let me love,
Or chide my palsy, or my gout,
My five grey hairs, or ruined fortune flout,
With wealth your state, your mind with arts improve,
Take you a course, get you a place,
Observe his honour, or his grace,
Or the King's real, or his stamped face
Contemplate; what you will, approve,

So you will let me love.
c.1595–1605 'The Canonization', collected in *Songs and Sonnets* (1633).

44 Alas, alas, who's injured by my love?
What merchant's ships have my sighs drowned?
Who says my tears have overflowed his ground?
When did my colds a forward spring remove?
When did the heats which my veins fill
Add one more to the plaguey bill?
Soldiers find wars, and lawyers find out still
Litigious men, which quarrels move,
Though she and I do love.
c.1595–1605 'The Canonization', collected in *Songs and Sonnets* (1633).

45 'Tis the year's midnight, and it is the day's.
c.1595–1605 'Nocturnal upon St Lucy's Day', collected in *Songs and Sonnets* (1633).

46 I sing the progress of a deathless soul.
c.1595–1605 'The Progress of the Soul', stanza 1, collected in *Songs and Sonnets* (1633).

47 Nature's great masterpiece, an Elephant.
c.1595–1605 'The Progress of the Soul', stanza 39, collected in *Songs and Sonnets* (1633).

48 I am two fools, I know,
For loving, and for saying so
In whining poetry.
c.1595–1605 'The Triple Fool', collected in *Songs and Sonnets* (1633).

49 Twice or thrice had I loved thee,
Before I knew thy face or name;
So in a voice, so in a shapeless flame
Angels affect us oft, and worshipped be;
Still when, to where thou wert, I came,
Some lovely glorious nothing did I see.
c.1595–1605 'Air and Angels', collected in *Songs and Sonnets* (1633).

50 He which hath business, and makes love, doth do
Such wrong, as when a married man doth woo.
c.1595–1605 'Break of Day', collected in *Songs and Sonnets* (1633).

51 O more than moon,
Draw not up seas to drown me in thy sphere,
Weep me not dead, in thine arms, but forbear
To teach the sea what it may do too soon.
c.1595–1605 'A Valediction: Of Weeping', collected in *Songs and Sonnets* (1633).

52 Mark but this flea, and mark in this
How little that which thou deny'st me is;
It sucked me first, and now sucks thee,
And in this flea our two bloods mingled be.
c.1595–1605 'The Flea', collected in *Songs and Sonnets* (1633).

53 Come live with me, and be my love,
And we will some new pleasures prove
Of golden sands, and crystal brooks:
With silken lines, and silver hooks.
c.1595–1605 'The Bait', collected in *Songs and Sonnets* (1633).
➤ *See Marlowe 553:17, Raleigh 677:98.*

54 As virtuous men pass mildly away,
And whisper to their souls, to go,
Whilst some of their sad friends do say,
The breath goes now, and some say, no:
So let us melt, and make no noise,
No tear-floods, nor sigh-tempests move;
'Twere profanation of our joys
To tell the laity of our love.
c.1595–1605 'A Valediction: Forbidding Mourning', collected in *Songs and Sonnets* (1633).

55 Our two souls therefore, which are one,
Though I must go, endure not yet
A breach, but an expansion,
Like gold to airy thinness beat.
c.1595–1605 'A Valediction: Forbidding Mourning', collected in *Songs and Sonnets* (1633).

56 Thy firmness makes my circle just,
And makes me end, where I begun.
c.1595–1605 'A Valediction: Forbidding Mourning', collected in *Songs and Sonnets* (1633).

57 Where, like a pillow on a bed,
A pregnant bank swelled up, to rest
The violet's reclining head,
Sat we two, one another's best.
c.1595–1605 'The Ecstasy', collected in *Songs and Sonnets* (1633).

58 Our eye-beams twisted, and did thread
Our eyes, upon one double string.
c.1595–1605 'The Ecstasy', collected in *Songs and Sonnets* (1633).

59 So to engraft our hands, as yet
Was all the means to make us one,
And pictures in our eyes to get
Was all our propagation.

And whilst our souls negotiate there,
We like sepulchral statues lay;
All day, the same our postures were,
And we said nothing all the day.
c.1595–1605 'The Ecstasy', collected in *Songs and Sonnets* (1633).

60 I had rather owner be
Of thee one hour, than all else ever.
c.1595–1605 'A Fever', collected in *Songs and Sonnets* (1633).

61 To what a cumbersome unwieldiness
And burdenous corpulence my love had grown,
But that I did, to make it less,
And keep it in proportion,
Give it a diet, made it feed upon
That which love worst endures, *discretion*.
?1595–1605 'Love's Diet', collected in *Songs and Sonnets* (1633).

62 And seeing the snail, which everywhere doth roam,
Carrying his own house still, still is at home,
Follow (for he is easy paced) this snail,
Be thine own palace, or the world's thy gaol.
1597–8 'To Sir Henry Wotton'.

63 More than kisses, letters mingle souls.
1597–8 'To Sir Henry Wotton'.

64 John Donne, Anne Donne, Un-done.
1602 Letter to his wife from prison. Quoted in Izaak Walton *The Life of Doctor Donne* (1640).

65 Immensity cloistered in thy dear womb.
1609 *La Corona*, 'Nativity'.

66 At the round earth's imagined corners, blow
Your trumpets, angels, and arise, arise

From death, you numberless infinities
Of souls, and to your scattered bodies go.
c.1610–1615 *Holy Sonnets*, no.7.

67 Death be not proud, though some have called thee
Mighty and dreadful, for thou art not so,
For those, whom thou think'st thou dost overthrow,
Die not, poor death, nor yet canst thou kill me.
From rest and sleep, which but thy pictures be,
Much pleasure, then from thee much more must flow,
And soonest our best men with thee do go,
Rest of their bones and soul's delivery.
c.1610–1615 *Holy Sonnets*, no.10.

68 One short sleep past, we wake eternally,
And Death shall be no more: Death, thou shalt die!
c.1610–1615 *Holy Sonnets*, no.10.

69 Oh let me then His strange love still admire.
c.1610–1615 *Holy Sonnets*, no.11.

70 Batter my heart, three-personed God; for You
As yet but knock, breathe, shine, and seek to mend.
c.1610–1615 *Holy Sonnets*, no.14.

71 Take me to You, imprison me, for I,
Except You enthrall me, never shall be free,
Nor ever chaste, except You ravish me.
c.1610–1615 *Holy Sonnets*, no.14.

72 I am a little world made cunningly
Of elements and an angelic sprite.
c.1610–1615 *Holy Sonnets*, no.15.

73 What if this present were the world's last night?
c.1610–1615 *Holy Sonnets*, no.19.

74 And new philosophy calls all in doubt,
The element of fire is quite put out;
The sun is lost, and th'earth, and no man's wit
Can well direct him, where to look for it.
1611 'An Anatomy of the World: The First Anniversary'.

75 If man were anything, he's nothing now.
1611 'An Anatomy of the World: The First Anniversary'.

76 'Tis all in pieces, all coherence gone.
1611 'An Anatomy of the World: The First Anniversary'.

77 She, she is dead; she's dead; when thou know'st this,
Thou know'st how dry a cinder this world is.
1611 'An Anatomy of the World: The First Anniversary'.

78 Verse hath a middle nature: heaven keeps souls,
The grave keeps bodies, verse the fame enrols.
1611 'An Anatomy of the World: The First Anniversary'.

79 It comes equally to us all, and makes us all equal when it comes. The ashes of an oak in the chimney are no epitaph of that oak, to tell me how high or how large that was; it tells me not what flocks it sheltered while it stood, nor what men it hurt when it fell…and when a whirlwind hath blown the dust of the churchyard into the church, and the man sweeps out the dust of the church into the churchyard, who will undertake to sift those dusts again, and to pronounce, This is the Patrician, this the noble flower, and this the yeomanly, this the Plebeian bran.
c.1621 Of death. Sermon, 8 Mar.

80 Since I am coming to that holy room
Where, with Thy choir of saints forevermore,
I shall be made Thy Music, as I come
I tune the instrument here at the door,
And what I must do then, think now before.
c.1623 'Hymn to God My God, in My Sickness'.

81 Wilt thou forgive that sin, where I begun,
Which is my sin, though it was done before?
Wilt thou forgive those sins through which I run
And do them still, though still I do deplore?
When thou hast done, thou hast not done,
For I have more.
c.1623 'Hymn to God the Father'.

82 It is too little to call man a little world; except God, man is a diminutive to nothing.
1624 *Devotions upon Emergent Occasions*, Meditation no.4.

83 But I do nothing upon my self, and yet I am mine own executioner.
1624 *Devotions upon Emergent Occasions*, Meditation no.12.

84 No man is an island, entire of itself; every man is a piece of the continent, a part of the main.
1624 *Devotions upon Emergent Occasions*, Meditation no.17.

85 Any man's death diminishes me, because I am involved in mankind; and therefore never send to know for whom the bell tolls; it tolls for thee.
1624 *Devotions upon Emergent Occasions*, Meditation no.17.

86 My God, my God, thou art a direct God, may I not say a literal God… But thou art also…a figurative, a metaphorical God too.
1624 *Devotions upon Emergent Occasions*, Expostulation 19, 'The Language of God'.

87 The air is not so full of motes, of atoms, as the church is of mercies.
1624 *Sermons*, 'Christmas Day, 1624'.

88 He brought light out of darkness, not out of a lesser light; he can bring thy summer out of winter, though thou have no spring… God comes to thee, not as in the dawning of the day, not as in the bud of the spring, but as the sun at noon to illustrate all shadows, as the sheaves in harvest to fill all penuries. All occasions invite his mercies, and all times are his seasons.
1624 *Sermons*, 'Christmas Day, 1624'.

89 All the four Monarchies, with all their thousands of years, and all the powerful Kings and all the beautiful Queens of this world, were but as a bed of flowers, some gathered at six, some at seven, some at eight, all in one morning, in respect to this day.
1626 On eternity. Sermon, 30 Apr.

90 I throw myself down in my Chamber, and I call in, and invite God, and his Angels thither, and when they are there, I neglect God and his Angels, for the noise of a fly, for the rattling of a coach, for the whining of a door.
1626 Sermon preached at the funeral of Sir William Cockayne, 12 Dec.

91 How imperfect is all our knowledge!
1626 Sermon preached at the funeral of Sir William Cockayne, 12 Dec.

92 Young men mend not their sight by using old men's spectacles.
1626 Sermon preached at the funeral of Sir William Cockayne, 12 Dec.

93 And if there be any addition to knowledge, it is rather a new knowledge than a greater knowledge; rather a singularity in a desire of proposing something that was not known at all before than an improving, an advancing,

a multiplying of former inceptions; and by that means, no knowledge comes to be perfect.
1626 Sermon preached at the funeral of Sir William Cockayne, 12 Dec.

94 He that purchases a manor will think to have an exact survey of the land, but who thinks of taking so exact a survey of his conscience, how that money was got that purchased that manor? We call that a man's means, which he hath; but that is truly his means, what way he came by it.
1626 Sermon preached at the funeral of Sir William Cockayne, 12 Dec.

95 The world is a great volume, and man the index of that book.
1626 'Sermon preached at the Funeral of Sir William Cockayne', 12 Dec.

96 Let man's soul be a sphere, and then, in this,
The intelligence that moves, devotion is.
'Good Friday, 1613. Riding Westward', published 1635.

Donoghue, Denis 1928–

Irish literary critic, Professor at New York University.

97 If there is a distinctive Irish experience, it is one of division, exacerbated by the fact that division in a country so small seems perverse. But the scale doesn't matter.
1986 *We Irish*.

Donoso, José 1924–96

Chilean novelist. After teaching at several universities in Chile and the US, he lived in Europe for 15 years before returning to Chile. *El obsceno pájaro de la noche* (1970), his masterpiece, presents a hallucinatory and grotesque vision of Chilean society.

98 *Los servidores acumulan los privilegios de la miseria…conservan los instrumentos de la venganza porque van acumulando en sus manos ásperas y verrugosas esa otra mitad de sus patrones, la mitad inútil, descartada, lo sucio y lo feo que ellos…les han ido entregando con el insulto de cada enagua gastada que les regalan.*
Servants accumulate the privileges of misery… They save up the instruments of vengeance because their coarse warty hands collect, bit by bit, that other side of their employers—the useless, discarded side, the filth and the sordidness that…they've been putting into their servants' hands with the insult of each shabby skirt they gave them.
1970 *El obsceno pájaro de la noche*, ch.4 (translated as *The Obscene Bird of Night*, 1973).

Doolittle, James Harold 1896–1993

US air force officer. He was the Commanding General, US 8th Air Force, in the ETO (European Theatre of Operations) in 1944.

99 Next to a letter from home, Captain Miller, your organization is the greatest morale builder in the ETO.
1944 Of Glenn Miller's wartime band. Comment on stage after a concert for the troops at Wycombe Abbey, 29 Jul. The words were later attributed to General Eisenhower in the publicity for the film *The Glenn Miller Story* (1954).

Doram-Smith, Sir Reginald Hugh 1899–1977

Irish-born British politician, a former army colonel who became an MP in 1935, Minister of Agriculture and Fisheries (1939–40) and Governor of Burma (1941–6).

1 Let 'Dig for Victory' be the motto of everyone with a garden and of every able-bodied man and woman capable of digging an allotment in their spare time.
1939 Radio broadcast, 3 Oct.

Dorgan, Tad (Thomas Aloysius) 1877–1929

US cartoonist and sportswriter. He was known for his satiric cartoons and colourful use of slang.

2 Yes, We Have No Bananas.
1922 Cartoon caption, later used as the title of a song by Irving Conn and Frank Silver (1923) and as an advertising slogan for Elders and Fyffes, British banana importers.

Dos Passos, John Roderigo 1896–1970

US novelist, playwright, travel writer and poet. He is best known for his novels such as *Manhattan Transfer* (1925) and the massive, formally experimental epic trilogy *U.S.A.* (1930–6).

3 U.S.A. is the slice of a continent. U.S.A. is a group of holding companies, some aggregations of trade unions, a set of laws bound in calf, a radio network, a chain of moving picture theatres, a column of stock quotations rubbed out and written in by a Western Union boy on a black-board, a publiclibrary full of old newspapers and dogeared historybooks with protests scrawled in the margins in pencil. U.S.A. is the world's greatest rivervalley fringed with mountains and hills. U.S.A. is a set of bigmouthed officials with too many bankaccounts. U.S.A. is a lot of men buried in their uniforms in Arlington Cemetery. U.S.A. is the letters at the end of an address when you are away from home. But mostly U.S.A. is the speech of the people
1938 *U.S.A.*, 'U.S.A.' (new prologue to collected trilogy).

4 People don't choose their careers. They are engulfed by them.
1959 In the *New York Times*, 25 Oct.

Dostoevsky, Fyodor Mikhailovich 1821–81

Russian novelist. He was condemned to death in 1849 for his revolutionary connections, but was instead sent to hard labour in Siberia until 1859.

5 The formula 'Two and two is five' is not without its attractions.
1864 *Notes from Underground*.

6 All people seem to be divided into 'ordinary' and 'extraordinary'. The ordinary people must lead a life of strict obedience and have no right to transgress the law because…they are ordinary. Whereas the extraordinary people have the right to commit any crime they like and transgress the law in any way just because they happen to be extraordinary.
1866 *Crime and Punishment*, pt.3, ch.5 (translated by David Magarshak).

7 Power is given only to him who dares to stoop and take it…one must have the courage to dare.
1866 *Crime and Punishment*, pt.5, ch.4 (translated by David Magarshak).

8 If you were to destroy in mankind the belief in immortality, not only love but every living force maintaining the life of the world would at once be dried up.
1879–80 *The Brothers Karamazov*, bk.2, ch.6.

9 If the devil doesn't exist, but man has created him, he has created him in his own image and likeness.
1879–80 *The Brothers Karamazov*, bk.5, ch.4.

10 So long as man remains free he strives for nothing so incessantly and so painfully as to find someone to worship.
1879–80 *The Brothers Karamazov*, bk.5, ch.5.

11 Love all God's creation, the whole of it and every grain of sand in it. Love every leaf, every ray of God's lights. Love the animals, love the plants, love everything. If you love everything, you will perceive the divine mystery in things.
1879–80 *The Brothers Karamazov*, bk.6, ch.3.

Douglas, Lord Alfred Bruce 1870–1945

English poet. He is remembered chiefly for his relationship with Oscar Wilde, which precipitated Wilde's downfall.

12 I am the love that dare not speak its name.
1894 'Two Loves'.

13 All good poetry is forged slowly and patiently, link by link, with sweat and blood and tears.
1919 *Collected Poems*, introduction.

Douglas, Charles 1840–74

New Zealand explorer, who travelled over much uncharted territory in the South Island of New Zealand.

14 I am perfectly aware that the mosquito and sandfly have a purpose in this world, but why don't they attend to it? Their destiny is to keep down microscopic insects…but their sphere of use is when they are in the grub state. Why don't they stick at that and not trouble innocent unoffending prospectors who can't carry a curtain?
1891 Quoted in J Pascoe (ed) *Mr Explorer Douglas* (1957).

15 I believe the reason I escaped, both this time and on other occasions, was the idea of perishing never entered my head. Nothing is so bad as terror for lowering a man's stamina.
1891 Quoted in J Pascoe (ed) *Mr Explorer Douglas* (1957).

Douglas, Gavin c.1474–1522

Scottish poet and, from 1515, Bishop of Dunkeld. His translation of Virgil's *Aeneid* is considered to be one of the greatest achievements of Scots vernacular literature.

16 First I protest, beau schiris, by your leif
Beis weill adivisit my werk or ye reprief;
Consider it warely, read ofter than anis,
Weill, at ane blenk, slee poetry nocht ta'en is.
c.1513 *Eneados*, bk.1, prologue.

17 Riveris ran reid on spate with water broun,
And burnis hurlis all their bankis doun.
c.1513 *Eneados*, bk.7, prologue.

18 And all small fowlys singis on the spray:
Welcum the lord of lycht and lamp of day.
c.1513 *Eneados*, bk.12, prologue.

Douglas, Keith Castellain 1920–44

English poet. Only one volume of his poems was published in his lifetime, and he was killed in action shortly after the D-Day landings in Normandy.

19 Remember me when I am dead
and simplify me when I'm dead.
1941 'Simplify Me When I'm Dead'.

20 For here the lover and killer are mingled
who had one body and one heart.
And death, who had the soldier singled
has done the lover mortal hurt.
1943 'Vergissmeinnicht'.

21 If at times my eyes are lenses
through which the brain explores
constellations of feeling
my ears yielding like swinging doors
admit princes to the corridors
into the mind, do not envy me.
I have a beast on my back.
1944 'Bête Noire'.

22 And all my endeavours are unlucky explorers
come back, abandoning the expedition;
the specimens, the lilies of ambition
still spring in their climate, still unpicked;
but time, time is all I lacked
to find them, as the great collectors before me.
1944 'On a Return from Egypt, 1943–44' (published 1946).

Douglas, (George) Norman 1868–1952

Scottish novelist, travel writer and essayist. His works include *Siren Land* (1911), an account of his travels in Italy, and the novel *South Wind* (1917).

23 Bouillabaisse is only good because cooked by the French, who, if they cared to try, could produce an excellent and nutritious substitute out of cigar stumps and empty matchboxes.
1911 *Siren Land*, 'Rain on the Hills'.

24 Don Francesco was a fisher of men, and of women. He fished *ad maiorem Dei gloriam*, and for the fun of the thing. It was his way of taking exercise.
1917 *South Wind*, ch.2.

25 You can tell the ideals of a nation by its advertisements.
1917 *South Wind*, ch.6.

26 Many a man who thinks to found a home discovers that he has merely opened a tavern for his friends.
1917 *South Wind*, ch.20.

27 It is the drawback of all sea-side places that half the landscape is unavailable for purposes of human locomotion, being covered by useless water.
1921 *Alone*, 'Mentone'.

28 As to abuse—I thrive on it. Abuse, hearty abuse, is a tonic to all save men of indifferent health.
1928 *Some Limericks*.

29 Education is a state-controlled manufactory of echoes.
1929 *How About Europe?*

30 To find a friend one must close one eye. To keep him—two.
1941 *Almanac*.

31 A child of eight is many-sided. By eighteen most of his auspicious angles have been polished away; he is

standardised; transformed, perhaps into the perfect citizen. Your perfect citizen may be a fine fellow, but he is not the perfect man.
1946 *Late Harvest*.

Douglas, William Orville 1898–1980

US lawyer, Associate Justice of the US Supreme Court (1939–80). His consistently liberal decisions were occasionally controversial, such as the stay of execution granted to the Rosenbergs, convicted spies, in 1953.

32 It is procedure that spells much of the difference between rule by law and rule by whim or caprice.
1951 Ruling to strike the Joint Anti-Fascist Refugee Committee and two other organizations from the Attorney General's list of subversive groups until final adjudication, 30 Apr.

33 We are a religious people whose institutions presuppose a Supreme Being.
1952 Ruling to allow the release of public school students for religious instruction, 28 Apr.

34 If the individual is no longer to be sovereign, if the police can pick him up whenever they do not like the cut of his jib…we enter a new regime.
1968 Dissenting opinion in ruling to uphold the police right 'to stop and frisk', 10 Jun.

Douglass, Frederick *originally* ***Frederick Augustus Washington Bailey*** 1817–95

US abolitionist. Born a slave, in 1838 he escaped and changed his name. He lectured on slavery in Great Britain (1845–47) and £150 was collected so that he could purchase his freedom.

35 The white man's happiness cannot be purchased by the black man's misery.
1849 'The Destiny of Colored Americans' in *The North Star*, 16 Nov.

36 To imagine that we shall ever be eradicated is absurd and ridiculous. We can be remodified, changed, and assimilated, but never extinguished.
1849 'The Destiny of Colored Americans' in *The North Star*, 16 Nov.

37 Where justice is denied, where poverty is enforced, where ignorance prevails, and where one class is made to feel that society is an organized conspiracy to oppress, rob, and degrade them, neither persons nor property will be safe.
1886 Speech in Washington DC, commemorating the 24th anniversary of emancipation.

38 No man can point to any law in the U.S. by which slavery was originally established. Men first make slaves and then make laws.
1889 Speech, Bethel Literary and Historical Association, Washington DC, Apr.

Dove, Rita Frances 1952–

US poet. Her poetry collections include *Thomas and Beulah* (1986, Pulitzer Prize), *On the Bus with Rosa Parks* (1999) and *American Smooth* (2004). From 1993 to 1995 she was US Poet Laureate.

39 A good poem is like a bouillon cube. It's concentrated and it nourishes you when you need it.
1989 In *Time*, 18 Oct.

Dowd, Maureen 1952–

US newspaper columnist, winner of the 1999 Pulitzer Prize for distinguished commentary.

40 President Clinton returned today…to the university where he didn't inhale, didn't get drafted, and didn't get a degree.
1994 On President Clinton's visit to Oxford where as a Rhodes Scholar he had tried marijuana, avoided conscription, and left to attend Yale Law School. In the *New York Times*, 9 Jun.

41 Don't write anything down, but save everything that anyone else writes down.
1995 Advice for political survival in Washington. In the *US News and World Report*, 9 Jan.

Dowland, John 1563–1626

English lutenist and songwriter. Having failed, as a Catholic, to win a place at the court of Elizabeth I, he made his name in Europe before returning home. His *First Book of Songes* appeared in 1597 and ran to five editions by 1613.

42 Who loves not music and the heavenly muse,
That man God hates.
1614 Commendatory poem to William Leighton's *Teares or Lamentations of a Sorrowfull Soule*.

Downey, Dr Richard 1881–1953

English prelate, Bishop of Liverpool.

43 If Stalin had learned to play cricket, the world might now be a better place.
1948 Quoted in Colin Jarman *The Guinness Dictionary of Sports Quotations* (1990).

Dowson, Ernest 1867–1900

English poet. A member of the 'decadent' school, he studied at Oxford and became part of the Rhymers' Club. He developed friendships with W B Yeats and Arthur Symons and lived in France, where he died of alcoholism.

44 I have forgot much, Cynara! Gone with the wind,
Flung roses, roses, riotously with the throng,
Dancing, to put thy pale, lost lilies out of mind;
But I was desolate and sick of an old passion,
Yea, all the time, because the dance was long:
I have been faithful to thee, Cynara! in my fashion.
1896 *Verses*, 'Non Sum Qualis Eram Bonae Sub Regno Cynarae'.

45 They are not long, the days of wine and roses:
Out of a misty dream
Our path emerges for a while, then closes
Within a dream.
1896 'Vitae Summa Brevis'.

Doyle, Sir Arthur Conan 1859–1930

Scottish physician and writer. His stories of the brilliant and resourceful detective Sherlock Holmes and his assistant, Dr Watson, are among the most enduringly popular works of crime fiction ever written. He also wrote historical romances and other novels.

46 London, that great cesspool into which all the loungers and idlers of the Empire are irresistibly drained.
1887 *A Study in Scarlet*, ch.1.

47 It is a capital mistake to theorize before one has all the evidence. It biases the judgement.
1887 *A Study in Scarlet*, ch.3.

48 Where there is no imagination there is no horror.
1887 *A Study in Scarlet*, ch.5.

49 It is a mistake to confound strangeness with mystery.
1887 *A Study in Scarlet*, ch.7.

50 Our ideas must be as broad as Nature if they are to interpret Nature.
1887 *A Study in Scarlet*, ch.7.

51 Detection is, or ought to be, an exact science, and should be treated in the same cold and unemotional manner. You have attempted to tinge it with romanticism, which produces much the same effect as if you worked a love-story or an elopement into the fifth proposition of Euclid.
1890 *The Sign of Four*, ch.1.

52 The most winning woman I ever knew was hanged for poisoning three little children for their insurance money.
1890 *The Sign of Four*, ch.2.

53 I never make exceptions. An exception disproves the rule.
1890 *The Sign of Four*, ch.2.

54 How often have I said to you that when you have eliminated the impossible, whatever remains, *however improbable*, must be the truth?
1890 *The Sign of Four*, ch.6.

55 You know my methods. Apply them.
1890 *The Sign of Four*, ch.6.

56 'It is the unofficial force—the Baker Street irregulars.' As he spoke, there came a swift pattering of naked feet upon the stairs, a clatter of high voices, and in rushed a dozen dirty and ragged little street Arabs.
1890 *The Sign of Four*, ch.8.

57 The bow was made in England,
Of true wood, of yew wood,
The wood of English bows.
1891 *The White Company*, 'Song of the Bow'.

58 Singularity is almost invariably a clue. The more featureless and commonplace a crime is, the more difficult it is to bring it home.
1892 *The Adventures of Sherlock Holmes*, 'The Boscombe Valley Mystery'.

59 You know my method. It is founded upon the observance of trifles.
1892 *The Adventures of Sherlock Holmes*, 'The Boscombe Valley Mystery'.

60 It has long been an axiom of mine that the little things are infinitely the most important.
1892 *The Adventures of Sherlock Holmes*, 'A Case of Identity'.

61 Depend upon it, there is nothing so unnatural as the commonplace.
1892 *The Adventures of Sherlock Holmes*, 'A Case of Identity'.

62 The case has, in some respects, been not entirely devoid of interest.
1892 *The Adventures of Sherlock Holmes*, 'A Case of Identity'.

63 It is quite a three-pipe problem, and I beg that you won't speak to me for fifty minutes.
1892 *The Adventures of Sherlock Holmes*, 'The Red-Headed League'.

64 To Sherlock Holmes she is always *the* woman. I have seldom heard him mention her under any other name. In his eyes she eclipses and predominates the whole of her sex.
1892 Of Irene Adler. *The Adventures of Sherlock Holmes*, 'Scandal in Bohemia'.

65 You see, but you do not observe.
1892 *The Adventures of Sherlock Holmes*, 'Scandal in Bohemia'.

66 A man should keep his little brain attic stocked with all the furniture that he is likely to use, and the rest he can put away in the lumber room of his library, where he can get it if he wants it.
1892 *The Adventures of Sherlock Holmes*, 'The Five Orange Pips'.

67 It is my belief, Watson, founded upon my experience, that the lowest and vilest alleys in London do not present a more dreadful record of sin than does the smiling and beautiful countryside.
1892 *The Adventures of Sherlock Holmes*, 'The Copper Beeches'.

68 Crime is common. Logic is rare. Therefore it is upon the logic rather than upon the crime that you should dwell.
1892 *The Adventures of Sherlock Holmes*, 'The Copper Beeches'.

69 A long shot, Watson; a very long shot!
1894 *The Memoirs of Sherlock Holmes*, 'Silver Blaze'.

70 Ex-Professor Moriarty of mathematical celebrity…is the Napoleon of crime, Watson.
1894 *The Memoirs of Sherlock Holmes*, 'The Final Problem'.

71 'Excellent!', I cried.
'Elementary', said he.
1894 *The Memoirs of Sherlock Holmes*, 'The Crooked Man'. The famous phrase 'Elementary, my dear Watson' does not in fact appear in any of the Conan Doyle books. It may have originated with a review of the film *The Return of Sherlock Holmes* in the *New York Times*, 19 Oct 1929.

72 They were the footprints of a gigantic hound!
1902 *The Hound of the Baskervilles*, ch.2.

73 A study of family portraits is enough to convert a man to the doctrine of reincarnation.
1902 *The Hound of the Baskervilles*, ch.13.

74 You mentioned your name as if I should recognise it, but I assure you that, beyond the obvious facts that you are a bachelor, a solicitor, a Freemason, and an asthmatic, I know nothing whatever about you.
1905 *The Return of Sherlock Holmes*, 'The Norwood Builder'.

75 Now, Watson, the fair sex is your department.
1905 *The Return of Sherlock Holmes*, 'The Second Stain'.

76 It is horrible, yet fascinating, this struggle between a set purpose and an utterly exhausted frame.
1908 Of the final moments of the 1908 Olympic marathon, in which the Italian runner Dorando Pietri had to be helped over the finishing line and was thus disqualified. Quoted in Colin Jarman *The Guinness Dictionary of Sports Quotations* (1990).

77 'I am inclined to think—' said I.
'I should do so,' Sherlock Holmes remarked, impatiently.
1915 *The Valley of Fear*, ch.1.

78 Mediocrity knows nothing higher than itself, but talent instantly recognises genius.
1915 *The Valley of Fear*, ch.1.

79 All other men are specialists, but his specialism is omniscience.
1917 *His Last Bow*, 'Bruce-Partington Plans'.

80 Good old Watson! You are the one fixed point in a changing age.
1917 *His Last Bow*, title story.

81 There is but one step from the grotesque to the horrible.
1917 *His Last Bow*, 'Wisteria Lodge'.

82 Matilda Briggs...was a ship which is associated with the giant rat of Sumatra, a story for which the world is not yet prepared.
1927 *The Case-Book of Sherlock Holmes*, 'The Sussex Vampire'.

Doyle, Charles (Mike) 1928–

New Zealand poet, primarily of the city and suburbs. His collections include *A Splinter of Glass* (1956) and *Messages for Herod* (1965). He has lived in Canada since 1968.

83 If only to be born were being invented
Merely, or, better still, to concoct oneself
From an antique alembic, a receipt. How splendid
To take the phial cleanly from its shelf;

Powders and liquids, all one's favourite hues
Making the being one would be, the looker at stars
Or storks on the spires of Denmark, drinker of dews,
Or an eye simply.
'Phials', collected in *Quadrant*, 1964.

Doyle, Roddy 1958–

Irish novelist. His works include the 'Barrytown trilogy'—*The Commitments* (1987), *The Snapper* (1990) and *The Van* (1991)—and the Booker Prize-winning *Paddy Clarke Ha Ha Ha* (1993).

84 The Irish are the niggers of Europe...An' Dubliners are the niggers of Ireland...An' the northside Dubliners are the niggers o' Dublin—Say it loud. I'm black and I'm proud.
1987 *The Commitments*.

85 'A song belongs to no man,' said Joey The Lips. 'The Lord holds copyright on all songs.'
'Me arse,' said Outspan.
1987 *The Commitments*.

86 I said one Hail Mary and four Our Fathers, because I preferred the Our Father to the Hail Mary and it was longer and better.
1993 *Paddy Clarke Ha Ha Ha*.

Drabble, Margaret 1939–

English novelist, critic and editor. Her novels often deal with the experiences and difficulties of educated young women.

87 Sometimes it seems the only accomplishment my education ever bestowed on me was the ability to think in quotations.
1963 *A Summer Birdcage*, ch.1.

88 Perhaps the rare and simple pleasure of being seen for what one is compensates for the misery of being it.
1963 *A Summer Birdcage*, ch.7.

89 What fools middle-class girls are to expect other people to respect the same gods as themselves and E M Forster.
1963 *A Summer Birdcage*, ch.11.

90 Lord knows what incommunicable small terrors infants go through, unknown to all.
1965 *The Millstone*.

91 England's not a bad country... It's just a mean, cold, ugly, divided, tired, clapped-out, post-imperial, post-industrial slag-heap covered in polystyrene hamburger cartons.
1989 *A Natural Curiosity*.

Drake, Sir Francis c.1540–1596

Elizabethan seaman, the first Englishman to circumnavigate the world. In 1585 he sailed on a successful expedition to the Spanish Indies. He commanded the fleet that defended England against the Spanish Armada in 1588.

92 The singeing of the King of Spain's beard.
1587 His description of an expedition to Cadiz, quoted in Francis Bacon *Considerations Touching a War with Spain* (1629).

93 The advantage of time and place in practical actions is half the victory; which being lost is irrecoverable.
1588 Letter to Elizabeth I, 13 Apr.

94 There is plenty of time to win this game, and to thrash the Spaniards too.
1588 Attributed, while finishing a game of bowls at Plymouth Hoe, 20 Jul, before sailing to meet the Armada. Quoted in the *Dictionary of National Biography* (1917–), vol.5, p.1342.

Drapeau, Jean 1916–99

Canadian politician, Mayor of Montreal (1954–57, 1960–86).

95 The Montreal Olympics can no more have a deficit than a man can have a baby.
1973 Comment at press conference, Montreal, 29 Jan. The games went well over budget.

Drayton, Michael 1563–1631

English poet and dramatist. After his first work *The Harmony of the Church* (1591) was condemned by the Church, he turned to pastoral and historical themes. *Polyolbion* (1616–22) is a topographical survey of Britain. Only one play survives, *The First Part of Sir John Oldcastle* (1600).

96 She wore a frock of frolic green.
1593 *Idea, the Shepherd's Garland*, 'The Eighth Eclogue'.

97 So in all humours sportively I range;
My muse is rightly of the English strain,
That cannot long one fashion entertain.
1594 *Ideas Mirrour*, 'To the Reader of These Sonnets'.

98 Dear, why should you command me to my rest,
When now the night doth summon all to sleep?
Methinks this time becometh lovers best;
Night was ordained together friends to keep.
1594 *Ideas Mirrour*, sonnet 37.

99 When Time shall turn those amber locks to grey,
My verse again shall gild and make them gay.
1597 *England's Heroic Epistles*, 'Henry Howard, Earl of Surrey, to the Lady Geraldine'.

1 Fair stood the wind for France
When we our sails advance,
Nor now to prove our chance
Longer will tarry.
1606 *Poems Lyrick and Pastorall*, 'To the Cambro-Britons and Their Harp, His Ballad of Agincourt', describing Henry V's expedition to France, 1415.

2 Upon Saint Crispin's day
Fought was this noble fray,
Which fame did not delay
To England to carry;
Oh, when shall English men
With such acts fill a pen,
Or England breed again
Such a King Harry?

1606 Of the Battle of Agincourt. *Poems Lyrick and Pastorall*, 'To the Cambro-Britons and Their Harp, His Ballad of Agincourt'.

3 But she, good sir,
Did not prefer
You, for that I was ranging;
But for that she
Found faith in me
And she loved to be changing.
1606 *Poems Lyrick and Pastorall*, 'To His Rival'.

4 That shire which we the Heart of England well may call.
1612–22 Of Warwickshire. *Polyolbion*, song 13, l.2.

5 Neat Marlowe, bathed in the Thespian springs,
Had in him those brave translunary things
That the first poets had; his raptures were
All air and fire, which made his verses clear,
For that fine madness still he did retain
Which rightly should possess a poet's brain.
1619 'To My Most Dearly Loved Henry Reynolds, Esquire, of Poets and Poesie'.

6 Since there's no help, come let us kiss and part;
Nay, I have done, you get no more of me,
And I am glad, yea glad with all my heart
That thus so cleanly I myself can free;
Shake hands forever, cancel all our vows,
And when we meet at any time again,
Be it not seen in either of our brows
That we one jot of former love retain.
1619 *Idea*, sonnet 61.

7 The walls of spiders' legs are made,
Well mortised and finely laid;
He was the master of his trade
It curiously builded;
The windows of the eyes of cats,
And for the roof, instead of slats,
Is covered with the skins of bats,
With moonshine that are gilded.
1627 *Nymphidia, the Court of Fairy.*

Drennan, William 1754–1820

Irish patriot and poet.

8 Nor one feeling of vengeance presumed to defile
The cause, or the men, or the Emerald Isle.
1795 *Erin*, stanza 3.

Drexler, Arthur

US art administrator, Director of Architecture and Design at the Metropolitan Museum of Art, New York (1956–87).

9 History is written for the victors and what they leave out is the losers.
1975 In the *New York Review*, 27 Nov.

Driberg, Tom (Thomas Edward Neil), Baron of Bradwell 1905–76

English journalist, broadcaster and politician. On the editorial staff of the *Daily Express* (1928–43), he became an independent (1942) then Labour (1945) MP and was created a life peer in 1975.

10 Sincerity is all that counts is a widespread modern heresy. Think again. Bolsheviks are sincere. Fascists are sincere. Lunatics are sincere. People who believe that the earth is flat are sincere. They can't all be right. Better make certain first that you have something to be sincere about, and with.
1937 In the *Daily Express*.

Drucker, Peter Ferdinand 1909–

Austrian-born US management consultant, Professor of Social Science and Management at Claremont Graduate University, California.

11 Entrepreneurship can be learned, but it can't be taught, so schools are not much good.
1988 Interviewed in 'Adam Smith' *The Roaring '80s* (1988), ch.2.

12 If you ever run into an industry that says it needs better people, sell its shares. There *are* no better people. You have to use ordinary, every-day people and make them capable of doing the work.
1991 In the *Los Angeles Times*, 17 Sep.

Drummond, Thomas 1797–1840

Scottish engineer and statesman, developer of the Drummond Light (limelight). He was appointed Under-Secretary for Ireland in 1835.

13 Property has its duties as well as its rights.
1838 Letter to the Earl of Donoughmore, 22 May.

Dryden, John 1631–1700

English poet, critic and playwright. He was made Poet Laureate in 1668 and his satirical verses such as *Absalom and Achitophel* (1681) were highly regarded. Among his best plays are *Marriage-à-la-Mode* (1672) and *All for Love* (1678); his works were prefaced with critical essays, including the seminal *Essay of Dramatic Poesy* (1668). He became a Catholic in 1685 and on refusing to swear allegiance to William and Mary was deprived of his laureateship.

14 An horrid stillness first invades the ear,
And in that silence we the tempest fear.
1660 *Astraea Redux*, l.7–8.

15 His colours laid so thick on every place,
As only showed the paint, but hid the face.
1660 Epistle 'To my honoured friend Sir Robert Howard', l.75–6.

16 I strongly wish for what I faintly hope:
Like the day-dreams of melancholy men,
I think and think on things impossible,
Yet love to wander in that golden maze.
1664 *The Rival Ladies*, act 3, sc.1.

17 And love's the noblest frailty of the mind.
1665 *The Indian Emperor*, act 2, sc.2.

18 Repentance is the virtue of weak minds.
1665 *The Indian Emperor*, act 3, sc.1.

19 For all the happiness mankind can gain
Is not in pleasure, but in rest from pain.
1665 *The Indian Emperor*, act 4, sc.1.

20 By viewing nature, nature's handmaid art,
Makes mighty things from small beginnings grow:
Thus fishes first to shipping did impart,
Their tail the rudder, and their head the prow.
1667 *Annus Mirabilis*, stanza 155.

21 For secrets are edged tools,
And must be kept from children, and from fools.
1667 *Sir Martin Mar-All*, act 2, sc.2.

22 I am resolved to grow fat and look young till forty, and then slip out of the world with the first wrinkle and the reputation of five-and-twenty.
1668 *The Maiden Queen*, act 3, sc.1.

23 Every age has a kind of universal genius, which inclines those that live in it to some particular studies.
1668 *An Essay of Dramatic Poesy*, 'Shakespeare and Ben Jonson Compared'.

24 A thing well said will be wit in all languages…though it may lose something in the translation.
1668 *An Essay of Dramatic Poesy*, 'The Wit of the Ancients: The Universal'.

25 Shakespeare…was the man who of all modern, and perhaps ancient poets, had the largest and most comprehensive soul. All images of Nature were still present to him, and he drew them, not laboriously, but luckily; when he describes anything, you more than see it, you feel it too. Those who accuse him to have wanted learning, give him the greater commendation: he was naturally learned; he needed not the spectacles of books to read Nature; he looked inwards, and found her there… He is many times flat, insipid; his comic wit degenerating into clenches, his serious swelling into bombast. But he is always great.
1668 *An Essay of Dramatic Poesy*, 'Shakespeare and Ben Jonson Compared'.

26 He invades authors like a monarch; and what would be theft in other poets, is only victory in him.
1668 Of Ben Jonson. *An Essay of Dramatic Poesy*, 'Shakespeare and Ben Jonson Compared'.

27 If by the people you understand the multitude, the *hoi polloi*, 'tis no matter what they think; they are sometimes in the right, sometimes in the wrong: their judgement is a mere lottery.
1668 *An Essay of Dramatic Poesy*, 'Shakespeare and Ben Jonson Compared'.

28 One cannot say he wanted wit, but rather that he was frugal of it.
1668 Of Ben Jonson. *An Essay of Dramatic Poesy*, 'Shakespeare and Ben Jonson Compared'.

29 You seldom find him making love in any of his scenes or endeavouring to move the passions; his genius was too sullen and saturnine to do it gracefully, especially when he knew he came after those who had performed both to such an height.
1668 Of Ben Jonson. *An Essay of Dramatic Poesy*, 'Shakespeare and Ben Jonson Compared'.

30 If I would compare [Jonson] with Shakespeare, I must acknowledge him the more correct poet, but Shakespeare the greater wit.
1668 *An Essay of Dramatic Poesy*, 'Shakespeare and Ben Jonson Compared'.

31 Shakespeare was the Homer, or father of our dramatic poets; Jonson was the Virgil, the pattern of elaborate writing; I admire him, but I love Shakespeare.
1668 *An Essay of Dramatic Poesy*, 'Shakespeare and Ben Jonson Compared'.

32 And he, who servilely creeps after sense,
Is safe, but ne'er will reach an excellence.
1669 *Tyrannic Love*, prologue.

33 All delays are dangerous in war.
1669 *Tyrannic Love*, act 1, sc.1.

34 Pains of love be sweeter far
Than all other pleasures are.
1669 *Tyrannic Love*, act 4, sc.1.

35 I am as free as nature first made man,
Ere the base laws of servitude began,
When wild in woods the noble savage ran.
1670 *The Conquest of Granada*, pt.1, act 1, sc.1.

36 Forgiveness to the injured does belong;
But they ne'er pardon, who have done the wrong.
1670 *The Conquest of Granada*, pt.2, act 1, sc.2.

37 Thou strong seducer, opportunity!
1670 *The Conquest of Granada*, pt.2, act 4, sc.3.

38 I am to be married within these three days; married past redemption.
1672 *Marriage-à-la-Mode*, act 1, sc.1.

39 The very Janus of poets; he wears almost everywhere two faces; and you have scarce begun to admire the one, ere you despise the other.
1672 Of Shakespeare. *Essay on the Dramatic Poetry of the Last Age*.

40 So poetry, which is in Oxford made
An art, in London only is a trade.
1673 'Prologue to the University of Oxon…at the Acting of *The Silent Woman*'.

41 Sure the poet…spewed up a good lump of clotted nonsense at once.
1674 *Notes and Observations on the Empress of Morocco*, 'The First Act'.

42 Death, in itself, is nothing; but we fear,
To be we know not what, we know not where.
1675 *Aureng-Zebe*, act 4, sc.1.

43 None would live past years again,
Yet all hope pleasure in what yet remain;
And, from the dregs of life, think to receive,
What the first sprightly running could not give.
1675 *Aureng-Zebe*, act 4, sc.1.

44 They, who would combat general authority with particular opinion, must first establish themselves a reputation of understanding better than other men.
1677 'The Author's Apology for Heroic Poetry and Heroic Licence', an essay prefacing *State of Innocence*, a libretto based on *Paradise Lost*.

45 Virgil and Horace [were] the severest writers of the severest age.
1677 'The Author's Apology for Heroic Poetry and Heroic Licence', an essay prefacing *State of Innocence*, a libretto based on *Paradise Lost*.

46 A propriety of thoughts and words; or, in other terms, thought and words elegantly adapted to the subject.
1677 Definition of wit. 'The Author's Apology for Heroic Poetry and Heroic Licence', an essay prefacing *State of Innocence*, a libretto based on *Paradise Lost*.

47 All human things are subject to decay,
And, when fate summons, monarchs must obey.
1678 *MacFlecknoe* (published 1682), l.1–2.

48 Shadwell alone, of all my sons, is he
Who stands confirmed in full stupidity.
1678 Richard Flecknoe selects Shadwell as heir to the kingdom of dullness. *MacFlecknoe* (published 1682), l.17–18.

49 The rest to some faint meaning make pretence,
But Shadwell never deviates into sense.
Some beams of wit on other souls may fall,

Strike through and make a lucid interval;
But Shadwell's genuine night admits no ray,
His rising fogs prevail upon the day.
1678 *MacFlecknoe* (published 1682), l.19–24.

50 Thy genius calls thee not to purchase fame
In keen iambics, but mild anagram:
Leave writing plays, and choose for thy command
Some peaceful province in Acrostic Land.
There thou mayest wings display and altars raise,
And torture one poor word ten thousand ways.
1678 *MacFlecknoe* (published 1682), l.203–8.

51 Errors, like straws, upon the surface flow;
He who would search for pearls must dive below.
1678 *All for Love, or The World Well Lost*, prologue.

52 Then he defies the world and bids it pass.
1678 Of Antony. *All for Love, or The World Well Lost*, act 1.

53 Virtue's his path; but sometimes 'tis too narrow
For his vast soul; and then he starts out wide,
And bounds into a vice.
1678 Of Antony. *All for Love, or The World Well Lost*, act 1.

54 Sure there's contagion in the tears of friends.
1678 *All for Love, or The World Well Lost*, act 1.

55 My love's a noble madness.
1678 Cleopatra to Iris. *All for Love, or The World Well Lost*, act 2, sc.1.

56 Give, you gods,
Give to your boy, your Caesar,
The rattle of a globe to play withal,
This gewgaw world, and put him cheaply off:
I'll not be pleased with less than Cleopatra.
1678 Anthony. *All for Love, or The World Well Lost*, act 2, sc.1.

57 Moderate sorrow
Fits vulgar love, and for a vulgar man:
But I have lov'd with such transcendent passion,
I soar'd, at first, quite out of reason's view,
And now am lost above it.
1678 *All for Love, or The World Well Lost*, act 2.

58 O that faint word, *respect*! how I disdain it!
1678 *All for Love, or The World Well Lost*, act 2.

59 My heart's so full of joy,
That I shall do some wild extravagance
Of love in public; and the foolish world,
Which knows not tenderness, will think me mad.
1678 *All for Love, or The World Well Lost*, act 2.

60 We were so clos'd within each other's breasts
The rivets were not found that join'd us first.
That does not reach us yet: we were so mix'd,
As meeting streams, both to ourselves were lost;
We were one mass; we could not give or take,
But from the same; for he was I, I he!
1678 Antony speaking of his friendship with Dollabella. *All for Love, or The World Well Lost*, act 3.

61 What I have left is from my native spring;
I've still a heart that swells, in scorn of fate,
And lifts me to my banks.
1678 *All for Love, or The World Well Lost*, act 3.

62 The worst your malice can,
Is but to say the greatest of mankind
Has been my slave. The next, but far above him
In my esteem, is he whom law calls yours,
But whom his love made mine.
1678 Cleopatra boasts to Octavia of her conquest of Caesar and Antony. *All for Love, or The World Well Lost*, act 3.

63 Men are but children of a larger growth;
Our appetites as apt to change as theirs,
And full as craving too, and full as vain.
1678 Dollabella. *All for Love, or The World Well Lost*, act 4, sc.1.

64 Nature meant me
A wife, a silly, harmless, household dove,
Fond without art, and kind without deceit;
But Fortune, that has made a mistress of me,
Has thrust me out to the wide world, unfurnish'd
Of falsehood to be happy.
1678 Cleopatra. *All for Love, or The World Well Lost*, act 4.

65 Welcome, thou kind deceiver!
Thou best of thieves; who with an easy key,
Dost open life, and, unperceived by us,
Even steal us from ourselves.
1678 Cleopatra speaking of love. *All for Love, or The World Well Lost*, act 5, sc.1.

66 My whole life
Has been a golden dream of love and friendship.
1678 *All for Love, or The World Well Lost*, act 5.

67 All the learn'd are cowards by profession.
1678 *All for Love, or The World Well Lost*, act 5.

68 In pious times, ere priestcraft did begin,
Before polygamy was made a sin.
1681 *Absalom and Achitophel*, pt.1, l.1–2.

69 Then Israel's monarch, after Heaven's own heart,
His vigorous warmth did, variously, impart
To wives and slaves: and, wide as his command,
Scattered his Maker's Image through the land.
1681 *Absalom and Achitophel*, pt.1, l.7–10. An oblique reference to Charles II, who had no legitimate, but many illegitimate, children.

70 Whate'er he did was done with so much ease,
In him alone, 'twas natural to please.
1681 *Absalom and Achitophel*, pt.1, l.27–8.

71 His motions all accompanied with grace;
And paradise was opened in his face.
1681 *Absalom and Achitophel*, pt.1, l.29–30.

72 The Jews, a headstrong, moody, murmuring race.
1681 *Absalom and Achitophel*, pt.1, l.45.

73 But when to sin our biased nature leans,
The careful Devil is still at hand with means;
And providently pimps for ill desires.
1681 *Absalom and Achitophel*, pt.1, l.79–81.

74 Plots, true or false, are necessary things,
To raise up commonwealths and ruin kings.
1681 Alluding to the alleged Popish plot to murder the King, which brought about the Exclusion crisis. *Absalom and Achitophel*, pt.1, l.83–4.

75 Some truth there was, but dashed and brewed with lies,
To please the fools, and puzzle all the wise.
1681 *Absalom and Achitophel*, pt.1, l.114–15.

76 Pleased with the danger, when the waves went high
He sought the storms; but for a calm unfit,
Would steer too nigh the sands to boast his wit.
1681 Alluding to Anthony Ashley Cooper, first Earl of Shaftesbury, leader of the Exclusion forces. *Absalom and Achitophel*, pt.1, l.160–2.

77 Great wits are sure to madness near allied,
And thin partitions do their bands divide.
1681 *Absalom and Achitophel*, pt.1, l.163–4.

78 Why should he, with wealth and honour blest,
Refuse his age the needful hours of rest?
Punish a body which he could not please;
Bankrupt of life, yet prodigal of ease?
And all to leave what with his toil he won
To that unfeathered two-legged thing, a son.
1681 *Absalom and Achitophel*, pt.1, l.165–70.

79 In friendship false, implacable in hate:
Resolved to ruin or to rule the state.
1681 *Absalom and Achitophel*, pt.1, l.173–4.

80 He stood at bold defiance with his prince;
Held up the buckler of the people's cause
Against the crown, and skulked behind the laws.
1681 *Absalom and Achitophel*, pt.1, l.205–7.

81 Politicians neither love nor hate.
1681 *Absalom and Achitophel*, pt.1, l.223.

82 The people's prayer, the glad diviner's theme,
The young men's vision and the old men's dream!
1681 *Absalom and Achitophel*, pt.1, l.238–9.
► *See Bible 106:5.*

83 What cannot praise effect in mighty minds,
When flattery soothes, and when ambition blinds!
1681 *Absalom and Achitophel*, pt.1, l.303–4.

84 Desire of power, on earth a vicious weed,
Yet, sprung from high, is of celestial seed:
In God 'tis glory; and when men aspire,
'Tis but a spark too much of heavenly fire.
1681 *Absalom and Achitophel*, pt.1, l.305–9.

85 All empire is no more than power in trust.
1681 *Absalom and Achitophel*, pt.1, l.411.

86 Better one suffer, than a nation grieve.
1681 *Absalom and Achitophel*, pt.1, l.416.

87 But far more numerous was the herd of such
Who think too little and who talk too much.
1681 *Absalom and Achitophel*, pt.1, l.533–4.

88 A man so various that he seemed to be
Not one, but all mankind's epitome.
Stiff in opinions, always in the wrong;
Was everything by starts, and nothing long:
But, in the course of one revolving moon,
Was chemist, fiddler, statesman, and buffoon.
1681 *Absalom and Achitophel*, pt. 1, l.545–60.

89 In squandering wealth was his peculiar art:
Nothing went unrewarded, but desert.
Beggared by fools, whom still he found too late:
He had his jest, and they had his estate.
1681 *Absalom and Achitophel*, pt.1, l.559–62.

90 Youth, beauty, graceful action seldom fail:
But common interest always will prevail:
And pity never ceases to be shown
To him, who makes the people's wrongs his own.
1681 *Absalom and Achitophel*, pt.1, l.723–6.

91 For who can be secure of private right,
If sovereign sway may be dissolved by might?
Nor is the people's judgement always true:
The most may err as grossly as the few.
1681 *Absalom and Achitophel*, pt.1, l.779–82.

92 Government itself at length must fall
To nature's state, where all have right to all.
1681 *Absalom and Achitophel*, pt.1, l.793–4.

93 The court he practised, not the courtier's art:
Large was his wealth, but larger was his heart.
1681 Of the loyalist James Butler, Duke of Ormond. *Absalom and Achitophel*, pt.1, l.825–6.

94 Swift was the race, but short the time to run.
1681 *Absalom and Achitophel*, pt.1, l.837.

95 Never was patriot yet, but was a fool.
1681 *Absalom and Achitophel*, pt.1, l.968.

96 From plots and treasons Heaven preserve my years,
But save me most from my petitioners.
Unsatiate as the barren womb or grave;
God cannot grant so much as they can crave.
1681 *Absalom and Achitophel*, pt.1, l.985–8.

97 Beware the fury of a patient man.
1681 *Absalom and Achitophel*, pt.1, l.1005.

98 For lawful power is still superior found,
When long driven back, at length it stands the ground.
1681 *Absalom and Achitophel*, pt.1, l.1024–5.

99 Doeg, though without knowing how or why,
Made still a blund'ring kind of melody;
Spurred boldly on, and dashed through thick and thin,
Through sense and nonsense, never out nor in;
Free from all meaning, whether good or bad,
And in one word, heroically mad.
1681 *Absalom and Achitophel*, pt.2, l.412–17.

1 Rhyme is the rock on which thou art to wreck.
1681 *Absalom and Achitophel*, pt.2, l.486.

2 But 'tis the talent of our English nation,
Still to be plotting some new reformation.
1681 *Sophonisba* (2nd edn).

3 There is a pleasure sure,
In being mad, that none but madmen know!
1681 *The Spanish Friar*, act 1, sc.1.

4 And, dying, bless the hand that gave the blow.
1681 *The Spanish Friar*, act 2, sc.2.

5 We loathe our manna, and we long for quails.
1682 *The Medal*, l.131.

6 But treason is not owned when 'tis descried;
Successful crimes alone are justified.
1682 *The Medal*, l.207–8.

7 And this unpolished rugged verse I chose
As fittest for discourse and nearest prose.
1682 *Religio Laici*, l.453–4.

8 Farewell, too little, and too lately known,
Whom I began to think and call my own.
1684 'To the Memory of Mr Oldham'. John Oldham was the author of *Satires upon the Jesuits* (1681).

9 Bold knaves thrive without one grain of sense,
But good men starve for want of impudence.
1684 *Constantine the Great*, epilogue.

10 Mute and magnificent, without a tear.
1685 *Threnodia Augustalis*, stanza 2.

11 Freedom which in no other land will thrive,
Freedom an English subject's sole prerogative.
1685 *Threnodia Augustalis*, stanza 10.

12 Her pencil drew whate'er her soul designed,

And oft the happy draft surpassed the image in her mind.
1686 'To the Pious Memory of the Accomplished Young Lady Mrs Anne Killigrew'.

13 O double sacrilege on things divine,
To rob the relic, and deface the shrine!
1686 'To the Pious Memory of the Accomplished Young Lady Mrs Anne Killigrew'. Killigrew had died of smallpox.

14 And doomed to death, though fated not to die.
1687 *The Hind and the Panther*, pt.1, l.8.

15 For truth has such a face and such a mien
As to be loved needs only to be seen.
1687 *The Hind and the Panther*, pt.1, l.33–4.

16 My thoughtless youth was winged with vain desires,
My manhood, long misled by wandering fires,
Followed false lights; and when their glimpse was gone
My pride struck out new sparkles of her own…
Good life be now my task: my doubts are done;
(What more could fright my faith than Three in One?)
1687 *The Hind and the Panther*, pt.1, l.71–6.

17 Reason to rule, but mercy to forgive:
The first is law, the last prerogative.
1687 *The Hind and the Panther*, pt.1, l.261–2.

18 Either be wholly slaves or wholly free.
1687 *The Hind and the Panther*, pt.2, l.285.

19 Much malice mingled with a little wit
Perhaps may censure this mysterious writ.
1687 *The Hind and the Panther*, pt.3, l.1–2.

20 For present joys are more to flesh and blood
Than a dull prospect of a distant good.
1687 *The Hind and the Panther*, pt.3, l.364–5.

21 By education most have been misled,
So they believe, because they so were bred.
The priest continues what the nurse began,
And thus the child imposes on the man.
1687 *The Hind and the Panther*, pt.3, l.389–92.

22 T'abhor the makers, and their laws approve,
Is to hate traitors and the treason love.
1687 *The Hind and the Panther*, pt.3, l.706–7.

23 For those whom God to ruin has designed,
He fits for fate, and first destroys their mind.
1687 *The Hind and the Panther*, pt.3, l.1093–4.

24 Three poets, in three distant ages born,
Greece, Italy, and England did adorn.
The first in loftiness of thought surpassed,
The next in majesty, in both the last:
The force of Nature could no farther go;
To make a third, she joined the former two.
1688 'Epigram on Milton', engraved on the frontispiece to the 1688 edition of *Paradise Lost*. The three poets are Homer, Virgil and Milton.

25 That fairy kind of writing which depends only upon the force of imagination.
1691 *King Arthur*, dedication.

26 War is the trade of kings.
1691 *King Arthur*, act 2, sc.2.

27 Fairest Isle, all isles excelling,
Seat of pleasures, and of loves;
Venus here will choose her dwelling,
And forsake her Cyprian groves.
1691 *King Arthur*, act 5, 'Song of Venus'.

28 Music, Music for a while
Shall all your cares beguile.
1692 *Oedipus* (with Nathaniel Lee).

29 How easy it is to call rogue and villain, and that wittily! But how hard to make a man appear a fool, a blockhead, or a knave, without using any of those opprobrious terms! To spare the grossness of the names, and to do the thing yet more severely, is to draw a full face, and to make the nose and cheeks stand out, and yet not to employ any depth of shadowing.
1693 *A Discourse Concerning the Original and Progress of Satire*, 'The Art of Satire'.

30 A man may be capable, as Jack Ketch's wife said of his servant, of a plain piece of work, a bare hanging; but to make a malefactor die sweetly was only belonging to her husband.
1693 *A Discourse Concerning the Original and Progress of Satire*, 'The Art of Satire'.

31 Ovid, the soft philosopher of love.
1694 *Love Triumphant*, act 2, sc.1.

32 Thou tyrant, tyrant Jealousy,
Thou tyrant of the mind!
1694 *Love Triumphant*, act 3, sc.1, 'Song of Jealousy'.

33 Happy, happy, happy, pair!
None but the brave,
None but the brave,
None but the brave deserves the fair.
1697 *Alexander's Feast*, l.4–7.

34 With ravished ears
The monarch hears,
Assumes the god,
Affects to nod,
And seems to shake the spheres.
1697 *Alexander's Feast*, l.42–6.

35 Drinking is the soldier's pleasure;
Rich the treasure;
Sweet the pleasure;
Sweet is pleasure after pain.
1697 *Alexander's Feast*, l.57–60.

36 Fallen from his high estate,
And welt'ring in his blood.
Deserted at his utmost need
By those his former bounty fed;
On the bare earth expos'd he lies,
With not a friend to close his eyes.
1697 *Alexander's Feast*, l.78–83.

37 Revolving in his altered soul
The various turns of chance below.
1697 *Alexander's Feast*, l.85–6.

38 War, he sung, is toil and trouble;
Honour but an empty bubble.
Never ending, still beginning,
Fighting still, and still destroying,
If the world be worth thy winning,
Think, oh think, it worth enjoying.
1697 *Alexander's Feast*, l.97–102.

39 Sighed and looked, and sighed again.
1697 *Alexander's Feast*, l.120.

40 Let old Timotheus yield the prize,
Or both divide the crown:
He raised a mortal to the skies;

She drew an angel down.
1697 Of 'Divine Cecilia'. *Alexander's Feast*, l.177–80.

41 We must beat the iron while it is hot, but we may polish it at leisure.
1697 *Aeneis* (his translation of Virgil's *Aeneid*), dedication.

42 Arms, and the man I sing, who, forced by fate,
And haughty Juno's unrelenting hate,
Expelled and exiled, left the Trojan shore.
1697 *Aeneis* (his translation of Virgil's *Aeneid*), bk.1, l.1–3.

43 What judgement I had increases rather than diminishes; and thoughts, such as they are, come crowding in so fast upon me, that my only difficulty is to choose or reject; to run them into verse or give them the other harmony of prose.
1700 *Fables Ancient and Modern*, preface.

44 We can only say that he lived in the infancy of our poetry, and that nothing is brought to perfection at the first.
1700 *Fables Ancient and Modern*, preface, 'In Praise of Chaucer'.

45 [Chaucer] must have been a man of a most wonderful comprehensive nature, because, as it has been truly observed of him, he has taken into the compass of his *Canterbury Tales* the various manners and humours of the whole English nation in his age.
1700 *Fables Ancient and Modern*, preface, 'In Praise of Chaucer'.

46 A perpetual fountain of good sense.
1700 Of Chaucer. *Fables Ancient and Modern*, preface.

47 'Tis sufficient to say, according to the proverb, that here is God's plenty.
1700 Of the *Canterbury Tales*. *Fables Ancient and Modern*, preface, 'In Praise of Chaucer'.

48 One of our great poets is sunk in his reputation, because he could never forgive any conceit which came in his way; but swept like a drag-net, great and small. There was plenty enough, but the dishes were ill-sorted; whole pyramids of sweetmeats, for boys and women; but little of solid meat for men.
1700 Of Abraham Cowley. *Fables Ancient and Modern*, preface.

49 Refined himself to soul, to curb the sense
And made almost a sin of abstinence.
1700 'The Character of a Good Parson', l.10–11.

50 He trudged along unknowing what he sought,
And whistled as he went, for want of thought.
1700 *Cymon and Iphigenia*, l.84–5.

51 She hugged the offender, and forgave the offence.
1700 *Cymon and Iphigenia*, l.367.

52 Of seeming arms to make a short essay,
Then hasten to be drunk, the business of the day.
1700 *Cymon and Iphigenia*, l.407–8.

53 Better to hunt in fields, for health unbought,
Than fee the doctor for a nauseous draught.
The wise, for cure, on exercise depend;
God never made his work, for man to mend.
1700 Epistle, 'To my honoured kinsman John Driden', l.92–5.

54 Even victors are by victories undone.
1700 Epistle, 'To my honoured kinsman John Driden', l.164.

55 But love's a malady without a cure.
1700 *Palamon and Arcite*, bk.2, l.110.

56 Fool, not to know that love endures no tie,
And Jove but laughs at lovers' perjury.
1700 *Palamon and Arcite*, bk.2, l.148–9.

57 And Antony, who lost the world for love.
1700 *Palamon and Arcite*, bk.2, l.607.

58 Repentance is but want of power to sin.
1700 *Palamon and Arcite*, bk.3, l.813.

59 Since every man who lives is born to die,
And none can boast sincere felicity,
With equal mind, what happens, let us bear,
Nor joy nor grieve too much for things beyond our care.
Like pilgrims to th'appointed place we tend;
The world's an inn, and death the journey's end.
1700 *Palamon and Arcite*, bk.3, l.883–8.

60 A virgin-widow, and a mourning bride.
1700 *Palamon and Arcite*, bk.3, l.927.

61 A very merry, dancing, drinking,
Laughing, quaffing, and unthinking time.
1700 *The Secular Masque*, l.39–40.

62 Joy ruled the day, and Love the night.
1700 *The Secular Masque*, l.81.

63 All, all of a piece throughout;
Thy chase had a beast in view;
Thy wars brought nothing about;
Thy lovers were all untrue.
'Tis well an old age is out,
And time to begin a new.
1700 *The Secular Masque*, l.92–7.

Dubin, Al 1891–1945

Swiss-born US lyricist.

64 Come and meet those dancing feet
On the avenue I'm taking you to
Forty-Second Street.
1932 From the title song, *Forty-Second Street*. Music by Harry Warren.

65 You're Getting to be a Habit with Me.
1932 Title of song in *Forty-Second Street*. Music by Harry Warren.

66 We're in the money, we're in the money
We've got a lot of what it takes to get along.
1933 From the song 'We're in the Money' featured in *Gold Diggers of 1933*. Music by Harry Warren.

67 I Only Have Eyes For You.
1934 Title of song from the film *Dames*. Music by Harry Warren.

68 You may not be an angel
Cause angels are so few
But until the day that one comes along
I'll string along with you.
1934 From the song 'I'll String Along With You' in *Twenty Million Sweethearts*. Music by Harry Warren.

69 Come on along and listen to
The Lullaby of Broadway
The hip hooray and bally hoo
The Lullaby of Broadway.
1935 From the song 'Lullaby of Broadway' in *Gold Diggers of 1935*. Music by Harry Warren.

Du Bois, W(illiam) E(dward) B(urghardt) 1868–1963

US writer. He became a leading figure in and spokesman for the black community, and wrote a number of pioneering books on black life and social reform.

70 The problem of the twentieth century is the problem of the colour line.

1900 Address to the Pan-African Conference, London.

71 To be a poor man is hard, but to be a poor race in a land of dollars is the very bottom of hardships.
1903 *The Souls of Black Folk*, ch.1.

72 Herein lies the tragedy of the age: not that men are poor…not that men are wicked…but that men know so little of men.
1903 *The Souls of Black Folk*, ch.12.

73 If there is anybody in this land who thoroughly believes that the meek shall inherit the earth they have not often let their presence be known.
1924 *The Gift of Black Folk*, ch.9.

74 One thing alone I charge you. As you live, believe in life! Always human beings will live and progress to a greater, broader and fuller life. The only possible death is to lose belief in this truth simply because the great end comes slowly, because time is long.
1957 Written 26 Jun, and read as an oration at his funeral.

75 Today I see more clearly than yesterday that back of the problem of race and color, lies a greater problem which both obscures and implements it: and that is the fact that so many civilized persons are willing to live in comfort even if the price of this is poverty, ignorance and disease of the majority of their fellowmen; that to maintain this privilege men have waged war until today war tends to become universal and continuous, and the excuse for this war continues largely to be color and race.
Preface to reprint of *The Souls of Black Folk* (1969).

Du Bos, Jean-Baptiste 1670–1742

French critic, whose work influenced aesthetic theory.

76 *Les larmes d'un inconnu nous émeuvent même avant que nous sachions le sujet qui le fait pleurer.*
The tears of someone we do not know move us even before we know the reason why he weeps.
1719 *Réflexions critiques sur la poésie et la peinture.*

77 *Le sentiment enseigne bien mieux si l'ouvrage touche que toutes les dissertations composées par les critiques.*
Feeling teaches much more than all the writing of critics if the work touches us.
1719 *Réflexions critiques sur la poésie et la peinture.*

Dudek, Louis 1918–2001

Canadian poet, critic, teacher and aphorist, whose works attempt to liberate Candian poetry from its British influences. His early lyric poetry was followed by longer poems such as *En México* (1958).

78 Aphorisms give you more for your time and money than any other literary form. Only the poem comes near to it, but then most good poems either start off from an aphorism or arrive at one… Aphorisms and epigrams are the corner-stones of literary art.
Collected in *Notebooks 1960–1994* (1994).

79 Fame is based on what people say about you, reputation on what they think of you.
Collected in *Notebooks 1960–1994* (1994).

80 If there is a heaven it's no doubt already filled—with horses, chickens, lambs, and other poor creatures. People will simply not get in.
Collected in *Notebooks 1960–1994* (1994).

81 All the ills of mankind spring from belonging to a race, a nation, a city, a group of some kind. The ideal would be to belong to none, and to care for all—but who is capable of that?
Collected in *Notebooks 1960–1994* (1994).

82 Intellectually, most people never wash. They never free their minds of the accumulated rubbish of centuries.
Collected in *Notebooks 1960–1994* (1994).

83 Imagination should be integrated with life, not turned into a separate activity, art, that monopolizes one's whole existence.
Collected in *Notebooks 1960–1994* (1994).

84 Hatred is generalized, but love is for the particular.
Collected in *Notebooks 1960–1994* (1994).

85 The twentieth century had a wonderful capacity for seeing nothing as the sum of everything.
Collected in *Notebooks 1960–1994* (1994).

Duell, Charles H

US government official, Commissioner of the Office of Patents.

86 Everything that can be invented has been invented.
1899 Letter to President William McKinley, suggesting that an Office of Patents was no longer necessary.

Duesenberry, James Stemble 1918–

US economist, Emeritus Professor at Harvard.

87 Economics is all about how people make choices. Sociology is all about why they don't have any choices to make.
1960 In the National Bureau of Economic Research's *Demographic and Economic Change in the Developed World*

Duffield, George 1818–88

US Presbyterian minister and hymnwriter.

88 Stand Up! Stand Up For Jesus!
1858 *The Psalmist*, title of hymn. Duffield's inspiration for the hymn came from the dying words of the evangelist Dudley Atkins Tyng to him: 'Tell them to stand up for Jesus.'

Dugommier, General Jean François Coquille 1736–94

General of the French Republic.

89 *Récompensez, avancez ce jeune homme; car, si l'on était ingrat envers lui, il s'avancerait de lui-même.*
Reward that young man, promote him; for if his services are not recognised, he will promote himself.
1794 Comment to the Minister for War, speaking of the 24-year-old Napoleon Bonaparte, after the siege of Toulon. Quoted in John Julius Norwich *Venice* (1981).

Dulles, John Foster 1888–1959

US Republican politician, Secretary of State from 1953 until his resignation just a week before his death. His vigorous diplomacy led to many personal conferences with statesmen in other countries.

90 You have to take chances for peace, just as you must take chances in war… The ability to get to the verge without getting into the war is the necessary art. If you try to run away from it, if you are scared to go to the brink, you are lost.
1956 Quoted in 'How Dulles Averted War', in *Life* magazine,

16 Jan. His biographer Peter Grose in *Gentleman Spy* (1994) claims Dulles 'never actually used the word '*brinkmanship*', but the label stuck to him as the legacy of a diplomatic strategy that was reckless for the nuclear age'.

91 The Soviets sought not a place in the sun, but the sun itself. Their objective was the world. They would not tolerate compromise on goals, only on tactics.
Comment to his brother Allen. Quoted in Peter Grose *Gentleman Spy* (1994).

Dumas, Alexandre, *père* 1802–70

French novelist and playwright. He began writing plays, but turned to travelogues and historical novels, including *Le Comte de Monte Cristo* (*The Count of Monte Cristo*, 1844–5).

92 *Tous pour un, un pour tous.*
All for one, one for all.
1844 *Les Trois Mousquetaires*, ch.9.

93 *Cherchons la femme.*
Let us look for the woman.
1854–5 *Les Mohicans de Paris.*

Dumas, Alexandre, *fils* 1824–95

French writer, illegitimate son of Dumas père. In addition to his novel *La Dame aux camélias* (1848), he produced many brilliant dramas, essays, letters and speeches, and may have aided George Sand with her work for the stage.

94 The demi-monde does not represent the crowd of courtesans, but the class of declassed women… It is divided from that of honest women by public scandal, and divided from that of the courtesans by money.
1855 On the first performance of his play *La Dame aux camélias*, 20 Mar, the first recorded use of the phrase. Quoted in Joanna Richardson *The Courtesans* (1967), p.227.

95 All generalizations are dangerous, even this one.
Attributed.

du Maurier, Dame Daphne 1907–89

English novelist and short-story writer.

96 Last night I dreamt I went to Manderley again.
1938 *Rebecca*, opening words.

97 Every book is like a purge; at the end of it one is empty…like a dry shell on the beach, waiting for the tide to come in again.
1956 In the *Ladies Home Journal*, Nov.

Dunbar, Paul Laurence 1872–1906

US poet, the son of escaped slaves. He wrote several volumes of poetry in dialect, including *Lyrics of Lowly Life* (1896).

98 We wear the mask that grins and lies,
It hides our cheeks and shades our eyes.
1895 'We Wear the Mask', stanza 1.

99 I know why the caged bird sings!
1895 'Sympathy', stanza 3. This was used by Maya Angelou as the title of her autobiography in 1970.

Dunbar, William c.1460–c.1520

Scottish poet, thought to have graduated from St Andrew's University in 1479. He was a courtier of James IV, and wrote many short poems, remarkable for their range of style and subject.

1 He that may be but sturt or stryfe,
And leif ane lusty plesand lyfe,
And syne with mariege dois him mell,
And bindis him with ane wicket wyfe,
He wirkis sorrow to him sell.
early 16c 'Ane His Awin Ennemy', l.6–10.

2 Now of wemen this I say for me,
Off erthly thingis nane may bettir be;
Thay suld haif wirschep and great honoring
Off men, aboif all uthir erthly thing.
early 16c 'In Prais of Wemen', l. 1–4.

3 Be riche in patience, gif thow in gudis be pure;
Quho levis mirry, he levis michtely:
Without glaidnes availis no tresour.
early 16c 'No Tressour Availis without Glaidnes', l.22–4.

4 Be courtly ay in clething and costly arrayit,
That hurtis yow nought worth a hen; yowr husband pays for all.
early 16c *The Tua Mariit Wemen and the Wedo*, l.268–9.

5 London, thou art of townes *A per se*.
Soveraign of cities, someliest in sight,
Of high renoun, riches, and royaltie;
Of lordis, barons, and many goodly knyght;
Of most delectable lusty ladies bright;
Of famous prelatis in habitis clericall;
Of merchauntis full of sybstaunce and myght;
London, thou art the flour of Cities all.
c.1501 'To the City of London', attributed to 'A Rhymer of Scotland'. Dunbar was a member of the Scots party negotiating the marriage of James IV to Margaret Tudor, and is popularly credited with the verse.

6 I that in heill wes and gladnes
Am trublit now with gret seiknes
And feblit with infermite:
Timor mortis conturbat me.
c.1505 'Lament for the Makaris', stanza 1. The Latin is from the Office for the Dead: 'The fear of death disturbs me'.

7 Sen for the deid remeid is none,
Best is that we for dede dispone
Eftir our deid that lif may we:
Timor mortis conturbat me.
c.1505 'Lament for the Makaris', stanza 25.

8 In to thir dirk and drublie dayis,
Quhone sabill all the hevin arrayis
With mystie vapouris, cluddis and skyis,
Nature all curage me denyis
Off sangis, ballattis, and of playis.
'Meditatioun in Wyntir', stanza 1.

Duncan, Isadora *originally* Angela Duncan 1878–1927

US dancer. She was hailed as one of the most innovative dancers of her day, espousing a free-flowing interpretative style of dance that was quite distinct from conventional ballet.

9 *Adieu, mes amis. Je vais à la gloire!*
Farewell, my friends. I am going to glory!
1927 Last words, shortly before she broke her neck when her long scarf caught in the wheels of her open-topped Bugatti sportscar. Quoted in Mary Desti *Isadora Duncan's End* (1929), ch.25.

Duncan, Robert Edwards *originally* Edward Howard Duncan 1919–88

US poet. He was associated with the Black Mountain Poets

including Charles Olsen and Robert Creeley.

10 Among my friends love is a payment.
It is an old debt for a borrowing foolishly spent.
1946 *Early Poems 1939–46*, 'Among My Friends Love Is a Great Sorrow'.

11 Neither our vices nor our virtues
further the poem.
1960 *The Opening of the Field*, 'Poetry, a Natural Thing'.

12 Noble men in the quiet of morning hear
Indians singing the continent's violent requiem.
1960 *The Opening of the Field*, 'A Poem Beginning with a Line by Pindar'.

13 Desire paces Eternity as if it had bounds, craving death.
The Word climbs upward into its crown.
1964 *Roots and Branches*, 'Structure of Rime X VII'.

14 I would be a falcon and go free.
I tread her wrist and wear the hood,
Talking to myself, and would draw blood.
1968 *Bending the Bow*, 'My Mother Would Be a Falconress'.

15 The great house of our humanity
No longer stands.
1984 *Ground Work: Before the War*, 'Bring It Up from the Dark'.

Dunlop, Ian 1925–

English art historian.

16 The Shock of the New: seven historic exhibitions of modern art.
1972 Title of book.

Dunn, Douglas Eaglesham 1942–

Scottish poet, essayist and anthologizer. A librarian at Hull University, he was encouraged by Philip Larkin. He is one of Scotland's most respected contemporary poets.

17 This masculine invisibility makes gods of them,
A pantheon of boots and overalls.
1969 'Men of Terry Street'.

18 And all their lives, like that, they'll have to rush
Forwards in reverse, always holding their caps.
1979 'Glasgow Schoolboys, Running Backwards'.

19 Snow has begun to fall on the guilty secrets of Europe.
1981 'The Deserter'.

20 Nationalism, and its chum, patriotism, encourage
unedifying hyperbole.
1992 'Language and Liberty', introduction to the *Faber Book of Twentieth Century Scottish Poetry*.

21 What I tell my students is there are three places
where poems must happen and a poem must happen
in these three places simultaneously for it to be a
good poem. It happens between the ears, that's
intelligence; behind the left nipple, heart and
feeling; between the tongue and teeth, the noise it
makes.
1999 Interview in *The Dark Horse*, Autumn.

Dunne, Finley Peter 1867–1936

US humorist, editor of the *Chicago Journal* (1897–1900). His philosopher-bartender Mr Dooley became the exponent of Irish-American topical satire.

22 Glory Be, whin Business gets above sellin' tinpinny nails
in a brown paper cornucopy, 'tis hard to tell it fr'm
murther.
1901 *Mr Dooley's Opinions*, 'On Wall Street'.

23 Even an Englishman was niver improved by bein' blown
up.
'Revolution'. Collected in Louis Filler (ed) *The World of Mr Dooley* (1962).

Dunne, Philip 1908–92

US screenwriter. His films include *Suez* (1938), *How Green Was My Valley* (1941), *Forever Amber* (1947) and *The Robe* (1953).

24 A perfumed parlor snake.
1947 Daniel Gregg's description of Miles Fairley in *The Ghost and Mrs Muir*.

Dunning, John 1731–1820

British lawyer and politician.

25 The influence of the Crown has increased, is increasing,
and ought to be diminished.
1780 Motion passed by the House of Commons.

Duplessis, Maurice 1890–1959

Canadian statesman, Premier of Quebec (1936–9, 1944–59).

26 The bishops eat from my hand.
Characteristic remark, recalled in Conrad Black *Duplessis* (1977).

Durant, William James 1885–1981

US historian and essayist. He wrote a series of popular works culminating in the massive *Story of Civilization* (11 vol, 1935–67), written with his wife.

27 There is nothing in Socialism that a little age or a little
money will not cure.
Attributed.

Dürer, Albrecht 1471–1528

German painter and engraver. He travelled widely (1490–4) and in 1498 published his first major series of woodcuts, illustrations of the Apocalypse. He was employed by Emperor Maximilian I and later Charles V.

28 The art of painting cannot be truly judged save by such as
are themselves good painters; from others verily it is
hidden even as a strange tongue.
c.1512 Quoted in William Martin Conway *Literary Remains of Albrecht Dürer* (1889).

29 He that would be a painter must have a natural turn
thereto. Love and delight are better teachers of the Art of
Painting than compulsion is.
c.1512 *On Painting*. Quoted in William Martin Conway *Literary Remains of Albrecht Dürer* (1889).

Durkheim, Émile 1858–1917

French sociologist, appointed to the first chair of sociology in France in 1913.

30 The economic services that it can render are picayune
compared to the moral effect that it produces, and its
true function is to create in two or more persons a
feeling of solidarity.
1893 Of labour. *The Division of Labor in Society* (translated by George Simpson, 1933).

31 The division of labor does not present individuals to one another, but social functions.
1893 *The Division of Labor in Society* (translated by George Simpson, 1933).

32 Our excessive tolerance of suicide is due to the fact that, since the state of mind from which it springs is a general one, we cannot condemn it without condemning ourselves; we are too saturated with it not partly to excuse it.
1897 *Suicide: a Study in Sociology* (translated by John A Spaulding and George Simpson, 1952).

33 All known religious beliefs, whether simple or complex, present one common characteristic: they presuppose a classification of all things, real and ideal, of which men think, into two classes or opposed groups, generally designated...*profane* and *sacred*.
1912 *The Elementary Forms of the Religious Life* (translated by Joseph Ward Swain, 1965).

34 If the idea of society were extinguished in individual minds and the beliefs, traditions and aspirations of the group were no longer felt and shared by individuals, society would die. We can say of it what we just said of divinity: it is real only in so far as it has a place in the human consciousness, and this place is whatever we may give it.
1912 *The Elementary Forms of the Religious Life* (translated by Joseph Ward Swain, 1965).

Durocher, Leo 1906–91

US baseball manager, noted for his toughness.

35 Nice guys finish last.
1946 When asked if he regretted beating the New York Giants, who had been described as a 'nice bunch of guys'. He later used this as a book title, 1975.

36 Show me a good loser and I'll show you an idiot.
1950 Attributed.

Durranc, Edouard

37 How beautiful the Republic was—under the Empire.
Quoted in Edgar Holt *The Tiger: The Life of Georges Clemenceau 1841–1929* (1976).

Durrell, Lawrence George 1912–90

English novelist, poet, travel writer and playwright, born in India. His best-known works are the novel sequences *The Alexandria Quartet* (1957–60) and *The Avignon Quincunx* (1974–85).

38 I love to feel events overlapping each other, crawling over one another like wet crabs in a basket.
1958 *Balthazar*, pt.1.

39 No one can go on being a rebel too long without turning into an autocrat.
1958 *Balthazar*, pt.2.

40 Poggio's, where people go to watch each other watch each other.
1968 *Tunc*, ch.1.

41 History is the endless repetition of the wrong way of living, and it'll start again tomorrow, if it's moved from here today.
1978 In *The Listener*, 20 Apr.

Dürrenmatt, Friedrich 1921–90

Swiss writer. After several novels he established an international reputation as a playwright with works such as *The Physicists* (1962) and *Play Strindberg* (1969).

42 What was once thought can never be unthought.
1962 *The Physicists*.

Dury, Ian 1942–2000

British rock singer, associated with the punk era of the late 1970s.

43 Sex 'n' drugs 'n' rock 'n' roll.
1977 Title of song.

Duvall, Robert 1931–

US actor.

44 The English have Shakespeare, the Russians have Chekhov, the French Molière but we have the western.
2004 In the *Sunday Times*, 21 Mar.

Dvořák, Antonin 1841–1904

Czech composer and organist. His work, basically classical but with colourful Slavonic motifs, became increasingly popular throughout Europe.

45 I have composed too much.
Letter to Sibelius.

Dworkin, Andrea 1946–

US radical feminist, civil-rights activist and writer, whose work examines the relationship between male power and pornography. In 1983 she made an unsuccessful attempt to define pornography as sexual discrimination under law.

46 A man wants what a woman has—sex. He can steal it (rape), persuade her to give it away (seduction), rent it (prostitution), lease it over the long term (marriage in the United States), or own it outright (marriage in most societies).
1976 In *Ms*, vol.5, no.6, Dec. Collected as 'Phallic Imperialism: why economic recovery will not work for us' in *Letters from a War Zone* (1988).

47 The power of money is a distinctly male power. Money speaks, but it speaks with a male voice. In the hands of women, money stays literal, count it out, it buys what it is worth or less. In the hands of men, money buys women, sex, status, dignity, esteem, recognition, loyalty, all manner of possibility.
1981 *Pornography: Men Possessing Women*.

48 One of the differences between marriage and prostitution is that in marriage you only have to make a deal with one man.
1984 In *The A.B.C.s of Reading*, winter issue. Collected as 'Feminism: An Agenda' *in Letters from a War Zone* (1988).

49 Violation is a synonym for intercourse.
1987 *Intercourse*, 'Occupation/Collaboration'.

Dyer, Sir Edward c.1545–1607

English poet, diplomat and courtier, a friend of Sir Philip Sidney. Only a few of his poems survive.

50 My mind to me a kingdom is;
Such perfect joy therein I find

That it excels all other bliss
That world affords or grows by kind.
Though much I want which most men have,
Yet still my mind forbids to crave.
1588 'In Praise of a Contented Mind'.

51 No princely pomp, no wealthy store,
No force to win the victory,
No wily wit to salve a sore,
No shape to feed each gazing eye;
To none of these I yield as thrall.
For why my mind doth serve for all.
1588 'In Praise of a Contented Mind'.

52 Some weigh their pleasure by their lust,
Their wisdom by their rage of will,
Their treasure is their only trust;
And cloakèd craft their store of skill.
But all the pleasure that I find
Is to maintain a quiet mind.
1588 'In Praise of a Contented Mind'.

53 My wealth is health and perfect ease,
My conscience clear my chief defence;
I neither seek by bribes to please,
Nor by deceit to breed offence.
Thus do I live; thus will I die.
Would all did so well as I!
1588 'In Praise of a Contented Mind'.

Dylan, Bob *pseudonym of* ***Robert Allen Zimmerman*** 1941–

US singer and song-writer. His early acoustic, folk-influenced songs such as 'Blowin' in the Wind' were succeeded in 1965 by rock 'n' roll, with 'Mr Tambourine Man' and 'Like a Rolling Stone'.

54 How many roads must a man walk down
Before you can call him a man?…
The answer, my friend, is blowin' in the wind,
The answer is blowin' in the wind.
1962 'Blowin' in the Wind'.

55 But I can't think for you,
You'll have to decide,
Whether Judas Iscariot
Had God on his side.
1963 'With God on Our Side'.

56 Ah, but I was so much older then,
I'm younger than that now.
1964 'My Back Pages'.

57 The Times They Are A' Changing.
1964 Title of song.

58 The motorcycle black madonna
Two-wheeled gypsy queen.
1965 'Gates of Eden'.

59 Money doesn't talk, it swears.
1965 'It's Alright, Ma (I'm Only Bleeding)'.

60 Hey! Mr Tambourine Man, play a song for me.
I'm not sleepy and there is no place I'm going to.
1965 'Mr Tambourine Man'.

61 Folk music is a bunch of fat people.
Quoted in David Pickering *Brewer's Twentieth Century Music* (1994).

Dyson, Freeman J(ohn) 1923–

English-born US theoretical physicist, a nuclear weapons designer who has subsequently undertaken major work in arms control and disarmament. His works include *Weapons and Hope* (1984) and *The Sun, the Genome, and the Internet* (1999).

62 For insight into human affairs I turn to stories and poems rather than to sociology. This is the result of my upbringing and background. I am not able to make use of the wisdom of the sociologists because I do not speak their language.
1979 *Disturbing the Universe*, ch.1.

63 Science and technology, like all original creations of the human spirit, are unpredictable. If we had a reliable way to label our toys good and bad, it would be easy to regulate technology wisely. But we can rarely see far enough ahead to know which road leads to damnation. Whoever concerns himself with big technology, either to push it forward or to stop it, is gambling in human lives.
1979 *Disturbing the Universe*, ch.1.

Dyson, Will(iam Henry) 1880–1938

Australian-born radical cartoonist of the London *Daily Herald*.

64 Curious! I seem to hear a child weeping.
1919 Cartoon caption in the *Daily Herald*, 17 May. French minister Clemenceau is shown leaving the Palais de Versailles with Woodrow Wilson and Lloyd George after signing the peace treaty with Germany. The 'child' is the generation of 1940.

e

Eagleton, Terry 1943–

English literary critic and Professor of Cultural Theory in the Department of English and American Studies at the University of Manchester.

65 Homosexuality was the badge of the upper class and the sign of a revolt against it; and it is small wonder that someone locked for a lifetime in this impossible contradiction should end up with cirrhosis of the liver.
1993 Review of Sean French's *Patrick Hamilton: a Life* (1993). In the *London Review of Books*, 2 Dec.

66 If there are indeed any iron laws of history, one of them is surely that in any major crisis of the capitalist system, a sector of the liberal middle class will shift to the left, and then shift smartly back again once the crisis has blown over.
1993 In the *London Review of Books*, 2 Dec.

Earhart, Amelia 1897–1937

US aviator. In 1932 she was the first woman to fly solo across the Atlantic and in 1935 she was the first person to fly alone from Hawaii to California.

67 Of course I realized there was a measure of danger. Obviously I faced the possibility of not returning when first I considered going. Once faced and settled there really wasn't any good reason to refer to it.
1928 *20 Hours: 40 Minutes—Our Flight in the Friendship*, ch.5.

Eastwood, Clint 1930–

US actor and director. He achieved fame initially for his roles in westerns, but more recently has directed several well-respected films, including *Unforgiven* (1992) and *Mystic River* (2003).

68 You've got to ask yourself a question. Do I feel lucky. Well do you punk?
1971 As Harry Callahan in *Dirty Harry* (screenplay by Harry Julian Fink, Rita M Fink and Dean Riesner).

69 Nothing wrong with shooting so long as the right people get shot.
1973 As Harry Callahan in *Magnum Force* (screenplay by John Milius and Michael Cimino).

Eban, Abba *originally* ***Aubrey Solomon*** 1915–2002

Israeli diplomat and politician, born in South Africa. He was Israeli UN representative (1948), Ambassador to Washington (1950–9) and Foreign Minister (1966–74), but was unexpectedly defeated in the 1989 general election.

70 History teaches us that men and nations behave wisely once they have exhausted all other alternatives.
1970 Speech, London, 16 Dec.

Ebbinghaus, Hermann 1850–1909

German experimental psychologist. He carried out pioneering research on memory to investigate higher mental processes, and published his findings in *Über das Gedächtnis* (1885).

71 Psychology has a long past, but only a short history.
1885 *Summary of Psychology.*

Eberhart, Richard Ghormley 1904–

US poet and academic.

72 If I could only live at the pitch that is near madness
When everything is as it was in my childhood
Violent, vivid and of infinite possibility.
1947 'If I Could Only Live at the Pitch That Is Near Madness'.

73 You would think the fury of aerial bombardment
Would rouse God to relent; the infinite spaces
Are still silent. He looks on shock-pried faces.
History, even, does not know what is meant.
1951 'The Fury of Aerial Bombardment'.

74 Was man made stupid to see his own stupidity?
Is God by definition indifferent, beyond us all?
Is the eternal truth man's fighting soul
Wherein the Beast ravens in its own avidity?
1951 'The Fury of Aerial Bombardment'.

Eberts, Jake 1941–

Canadian-born film producer. In 1977 he founded Goldcrest Films which made *Chariots of Fire* (1981) and *Local Hero* (1983).

75 My Indecision Is Final.
1990 Title of his book on Goldcrest Films.

Echeverría, Esteban 1805–51

Argentinian poet and fiction writer. An opponent of the dictator Rosas, he was exiled in 1839 and lived in Uruguay until his death. He was the innovator of the Romantic school in Spanish American literature.

76 *A pesar de que la mía es historia, no la empezaré por el arca de Noé y la genealogía de sus ascendientes como acostumbraban hacerlo los antiguos historiadores españoles de América, que deben ser nuestros prototipos.*
I'm going to tell a true story, but I won't start with Noah's Ark and the genealogy of his forefathers, as is usual among the ancient Spanish historians of America, who we consider our prototypes.
1838 *El matadero* (*The Slaughter-House*, 1959).

Eco, Umberto 1932–

Italian novelist and semiotician. He is, perhaps, best known for *The Name of the Rose* (1980), a suspense story set in a medieval monastery.

77 In the United States there's a Puritan ethic and a mythology of success. He who is successful is good. In Latin countries, in Catholic countries, a successful person is a sinner.
1988 In the *International Herald Tribune*, 14 Dec.

78 I enjoyed your article, but I preferred my own.
Speaking to Jeremy Treglown, editor of the *Times Literary Supplement*. Quoted in Derwent May *Critical Times: The History of the Times Literary Supplement* (2001).

The Economist

British journal, founded in 1843.

79 Michael Harrington…was America's leading socialist; a position, one might have thought, that almost epitomized marginality.
1989 *The Economist*, 12 Aug.

80 Corruption is more than a poison afflicting Chinese business life. It *is* Chinese business life.
1994 *The Economist*, 29 Jan.

81 One of the saddest features of the real world is that goods do not spontaneously present themselves for distribution.
1994 *The Economist*, 5 Nov.

82 Why Silvio Berlusconi is unfit to lead Italy.
2001 Front cover headline. In *The Economist*, 28 Apr.

Eddington, Sir Arthur Stanley 1882–1944

English astronomer and physicist, Professor of Astronomy (from 1913) and Director of the Observatory (from 1914) at Cambridge University.

83 Let us draw an arrow arbitrarily. If as we follow the arrow we find more and more of the random element in the world, then the arrow is pointing towards the future; if the random element decreases the arrow points towards the past… I shall use the phrase 'time's arrow' to express this one-way property of time which has no analogue in space.
1928 *The Nature of the Physical World*, ch.4. Martin Amis used the phrase 'Time's Arrow' for the title of his 1991 novel.

84 I ask you to look both ways. For the road to a knowledge of the stars leads through the atom; and important knowledge of the atom has been reached through the stars.
1928 *Stars and Atoms*, lecture 1.

85 I think it is something of the same sort of security we should seek in our relationship with God. The most flawless proof of the existence of God is no substitute for

it; and if we have that relationship, the most convincing disproof is turned aimlessly aside. If I may say it with reverence, the soul and God laugh together over so odd a conclusion.
1929 *Science and the Unseen World.*

86 I believe that there are 15,747,724,136,275,002,577,605, 653,961,181,555,468,044,717,914,527,116,709,366,231, 425,076,185,631,031,296 protons in the universe, and the same number of electrons.
1938 Tarner Lecture.

Eddy, Mary Baker 1821–1910

US founder of the Christian Science Church.

87 Christian Science explains all cause and effect as mental, not physical.
1875 *Science and Health with Key to the Scriptures.*

88 Jesus of Nazareth was the most scientific man that ever trod the globe. He plunged beneath the material surface of things, and found the spiritual cause.
1875 *Science and Health with Key to the Scriptures.*

Eden, Sir (Robert) Anthony, 1st Earl of Avon 1897–1977

Anglo-Irish politician and Conservative Prime Minister (1955–7). He ordered British forces to occupy the Suez Canal Zone (1956), an action which caused widespread condemnation.

89 Everybody is always in favour of general economy and particular expenditure.
1956 In the *Observer*, 17 Jun.

90 We best avoid wars by taking even physical action to stop small ones. Everybody knows that the United Nations is not in a position to do that... We must face the fact that the United Nations is not yet the internal equivalent of our own legal system and rule of law. Police action must be to separate the belligerents and to prevent a resumption of hostilities.
1956 House of Commons, 1 Nov.

91 We are not at war with Egypt. We are in armed conflict.
1956 On the Suez crisis, House of Commons, 4 Nov.

Eden, Lady Clarissa 1920–

Wife of Sir Anthony Eden.

92 During the past few weeks, I felt sometimes that the Suez canal was flowing through my drawing room.
1956 Speech, Nov.

Edgeworth, Maria 1767–1849

Anglo-Irish novelist, whose novels reflect the rhythms of Irish country speech in their wry observation and humour. She is best remembered for *Castle Rackrent* (1800) and *The Absentee* (1812).

93 Possessed, as are all the fair daughters of Eve, of an hereditary propensity, transmitted to them undiminished through succeeding generations, to be 'soon moved with the slightest touch of blame'; very little precept and practice will confirm them in the habit, and instruct them all the maxims, of self-justification.
1795 *Letters for Literary Ladies*, 'An Essay on the Noble Science of Self-Justification'.

94 Man is to be held only by the *slightest* chains; with the idea that he can break them at pleasure, he submits to them in sport.
1795 *Letters for Literary Ladies*, 'Letters of Julia and Caroline', no.1.

95 Sir Patrick died that night—just as the company rose to drink his health with three cheers, he fell down in a sort of fit, and was carried off—they sat it out, and were surprised, on enquiry, in the morning, to find it was all over with poor Sir Patrick.
1800 *Castle Rackrent*, 'An Hibernian Tale'.

96 Sir Patrick Rackrent lived and died a monument of old Irish hospitality.
1800 *Castle Rackrent*, 'An Hibernian Tale'.

97 I've a great fancy to see my funeral before I die.
1800 Sir Cody to Thady. *Castle Rackrent*, 'History of Sir Conolly Rackrent'.

98 Did the Warwickshire militia, who were chiefly artisans, teach the Irish to drink beer, or did they learn from the Irish how to drink whiskey?
1800 *Castle Rackrent*, 'History of Sir Conolly Rackrent'.

99 Come when you're called;
And do as you're bid;
Shut the door after you;
And you'll never be chid.
1804 *The Contrast*, ch.1.

1 What a misfortune it is to be born a woman!... Why seek for knowledge, which can prove only that our wretchedness is irremediable? If a ray of light break in upon us, it is but to make darkness more visible; to show us the new limits, the Gothic structure, the impenetrable barriers of our prison.
1806 *Leonora*, letter I.

2 There need, at all events, be none of this, if people would but live upon their own estates, and kill their own mutton.
1812 Sir Terence O'Fay. *The Absentee*, ch.5.

3 Those enemies to Ireland—those cruel absentees!
1812 Count O'Halloran. *The Absentee*, ch.8.

4 Deeds, not words.
1812 Sir James Brooke's motto. *The Absentee*, ch.9.

5 Let me not, even in my own mind, commit the injustice of taking a speck for the whole.
1812 *The Absentee*, ch.11.

6 Her son saw that the *Londonmania* was now stronger than ever upon her.
1812 *The Absentee*, ch.14.

7 In marrying, a man does not, to be sure, marry his wife's mother; and yet a prudent man, when he begins to think of the daughter, would look sharp at the mother; ay, and back to the grandmother too, and along the whole female line of ancestry.
1812 Count O'Halloran's advice to Lord Colambare. *The Absentee*, ch.15.

Edinburgh, Prince Philip, Duke of 1921–

Consort of Elizabeth II, son of Prince Andrew of Greece and Princess Alice of Battenberg. He entered the Royal Navy in 1939, became a naturalized British subject in 1947, and was created Duke of Edinburgh on the eve of his marriage (20 Nov). In 1956 he began the Duke of Edinburgh Award Scheme to foster the leisure activities of young people.

8 I have very little experience of self-government. In fact, I am one of the most governed people in the world.
1959 In the *New York Times*, 30 Dec.

9 We are suffering a national defeat comparable to any lost military campaign, and what is more, it is self-inflicted... It is about time that we pulled our fingers out... The rest of the world most certainly does not owe us a living.
1961 Speech to British industrialists, London, 17 Oct.

10 There is a widely held and quite erroneously held belief that cricket is just another game.
1975 In *Wisden: Cricketers' Almanack*, 'The Pleasures of Cricket'.

11 The grouse are in no danger at all from people who shoot grouse.
1988 Quoted in *Private Eye*, no.693, 8 Jul.

Edison, Thomas Alva 1847–1931

US inventor, one of the most productive of his time. Among his inventions were the gramophone and the motion picture.

12 The phonograph...is not of any commercial value.
c.1860 Comment to his assistant, Samuel Insull. Edison hoped that his invention would find a place in businesses and offices, rather than in the entertainment world. Quoted in Robert A Conot *A Streak of Luck: The Life and Legend of Thomas Edison* (1979).

13 Genius is one per cent inspiration, ninety-nine per cent perspiration.
c.1903 Quoted in *Harper's Monthly Magazine*, Sep 1932.

Edmeston, John 1721–1867

English architect and hymnwriter.

14 Lead us, Heavenly Father, lead us
O'er the world's tempestuous sea.
1821 *Sacred Lyrics, Set 2*, 'Lead us, Heavenly Father'.

Edward II 1284–1327

King of England (from 1307). His invasion of Scotland resulted in defeat by Robert the Bruce at Bannockburn (1314). He was eventually murdered.

15 Forasmuch as there is great noise in the city caused by hustling over large balls, from which many evils may arise, which God forbid, we command and forbid on behalf of the King, on pain of imprisonment, such game to be used in the city in future.
1314 Royal proclamation, banning football from the streets of London.

Edward III 1312–77

King of England (from 1327). He started hostilities against France in 1337 and assumed the title of King of France in 1340. Victories at Crecy (1346) and Poitiers (1356) led to a large concession of territory by the French. He also invaded Scotland.

16 Also say to them, that they suffre hym this day to wynne his spurres, for if god be pleased, I well this journey be his, and the honoure thereof.
1346 Of his 16-year-old son, Edward the Black Prince. Quoted in the *Chronicle of Froissart* (translated by Sir John Bourchier, Lord Berners, 1523–5), ch.130.

17 *Honi soit qui mal y pense.*
Evil be to him that evil thinks.
c.1348 Motto of the Order of the Garter. Said to have been uttered by Edward when adjusting the Countess of Salisbury's garter, which had slipped down.

Edward VII 1841–1910

King of the UK (from 1901), son of Queen Victoria. In 1863 he married Alexandra of Denmark. His scandalous behaviour as Prince of Wales led to his exclusion from affairs of state, but as King he made several visits to improve international relations.

18 Because a man has a black face and a different religion from ours, there is no reason why he should be treated as a brute.
1875 Letter from India to Lord Granville, 30 Nov.

Edward VIII 1894–1972

King of the UK (1936). He succeeded his father George V in 1936, but abdicated (11 Dec) because of his proposed marriage to divorcee Mrs Wallis Simpson. As Duke of Windsor, he lived in Paris except during his governorship of the Bahamas (1940–5).

19 These works brought all these people here. Something should be done to get them at work again.
1936 Comment while viewing the derelict Dowlais Iron and Steel Works, 18 Nov. It is often rendered 'Something must be done'.

20 I have found it impossible to carry the heavy burden of responsibility, and to discharge my duties as King as I would wish, without the help and support of the woman I love.
1936 Radio broadcast to the nation, 11 Dec, following his abdication to marry Wallis Simpson.

Edwards, Bob (Robert Chambers) 1864–1922

Canadian publisher and writer.

21 One can always tell when one is getting old and serious by the way that holidays seem to interfere with one's work.
1913 In *Eye Opener*, 20 Dec.

Edwards, Oliver 1711–91

English lawyer, an acquaintance of Samuel Johnson.

22 You are a philosopher, Dr Johnson. I have tried too in my time to be a philosopher; but, I don't know how, cheerfulness was always breaking in.
1778 In conversation with Dr Johnson, 17 Apr. Quoted in James Boswell *Life of Samuel Johnson* (1791).

Edwards, Otis C(arl), Jr 1928–

US theologian and educator, ordained into the Episcopal Church in 1954. After serving in several churches as curate and rector, he taught at Nashotah House (1969–74) before being appointed Dean of Seabury-Western Theological Seminary (1974–83).

23 To be loose with grammar is to be loose with the worst woman in the world.
1966 New Testament lecture, Nashotah House, 10 Jan.

Egan, Pierce 1772–1849

English sporting writer. A London journalist, he wrote *Boxiana: or Sketches of Ancient and Modern Pugilism* (1812–13), and is best remembered for *Life in London* (1821), a description of the life of a 'man about town'.

24 Here lies, bowl'd out by Death's unerring ball,
A cricketer renowned, by name John Small;
But though his name was small, yet great was his fame,
For nobly did he play the 'noble game'.
His life was like his innings—long and good;
Full ninety summers had Death withstood,
At length the ninetieth winter came—when (Fate
Not leaving him one solitary mate)
This last of Hambledonians, old John Small,
Gave up his bat and ball—his leather, wax and all.
1832 Epitaph on cricketer John Small. *Pierce Egan's Book of Sports*.

Eggers, Dave 1970–

US magazine editor and novelist.

25 A Heartbreaking Work of Staggering Genius.
2000 Book title.

Ehrlich, Paul Ralph 1932–

US biologist, Professor at Stanford University.

26 The first rule of intelligent tinkering is to save all the parts.
1971 In the *Saturday Review*, 5 Jun.

Ehrlichman, John 1925–99

US government official, Special Counsel to the Nixon White House, implicated in the Watergate scandal.

27 He's the Big Enchilada.
1973 On the possibility of pinning the blame for Watergate on Attorney General John Mitchell. Taped conversation, 27 Mar.

28 I think we ought to let him hang there. Let him twist slowly, slowly in the wind.
1973 Of Patrick Gray, regarding his nomination as Director of the FBI. Taped conversation with John Dean, reported in the *Washington Post*, 27 Jul.

Eichelbaum, Samuel 1894–1969

Argentinian playwright and fiction writer. He began writing in a naturalistic style, but later adopted an emotional realism to show the effect of social environment on the individual.

29 *¡No hay políticos malos! Y buenos, tampoco, ¡qué caray! Los políticos no son ni buenos ni malos. Son hombres de oficio. Como los carpinterios y los albañiles.*
There are no bad politicians! There aren't any good ones either, damn it! Politicians are neither bad nor good. They are professionals, like carpenters or masons.
1940 *Un guapo del 900* ('A Handsome Man from the Nineteen Hundreds'), act 1.

Einstein, Albert 1879–1955

German-born theoretical physicist, who took Swiss (1901) and US (1940) citizenship. His early work on the photoelectric effect pioneered quantum theory and won him the 1921 Nobel prize. He is best known for his special (1905) and general (1916) theories of relativity. After Hitler's rise to power he lectured in the US, and later urged international control of atomic weapons.

30 $E = mc^2$
1905 *Zur Elektrodynamik bewegter Körper* ('The Electrodynamics of Moving Bodies').

31 *Raffiniert ist der Herrgott, aber boshaft ist er nicht.*
God is subtle, but he is not malicious.
1921 Said on a visit to Princeton University, May, and later carved above a fireplace there.

32 *Jedenfalls bin ich überzeugt, dass der nicht würfelt.*
Anyway, I am sure that he [God] does not play dice.
1926 Letter to Max Born, 4 Dec.
► *See Hawking 385:31.*

33 One of the strongest motives that lead people to give their lives to art and science is the urge to flee from everyday life, with its drab and deadly dullness and thus to unshackle the chains of one's own transient desires, which supplant one another in an interminable succession so long as the mind is fixed on the horizon of daily environment.
1933 Prologue to Max Planck *Where is Science Going?* (1933).

34 I think and think for months and years. Ninety-nine times, the conclusion is false. The hundredth time I am right.
1934 *The World as I See It.*

35 It may be possible to set up a nuclear reaction in uranium by which vast amounts of power could be released... This new phenomenon would also lead to the construction of...extremely powerful bombs of a new type.
1939 Letter to President Franklin D Roosevelt.

36 Science without religion is lame, religion without science is blind.
1941 *Science, Philosophy and Religion: A Symposium*, ch.13.

37 The most beautiful emotion we can experience is the mystical. It is the power of all true art and science. He to whom this emotion is a stranger, who can no longer wonder and stand rapt in awe, is as good as dead. To know that what is impenetrable to us really exists, manifesting itself as the highest wisdom and the most radiant beauty, which our dull faculties can comprehend only in their most primitive forms—this knowledge, this feeling, is at the center of true religiousness. In this sense, and in this sense only, I belong to the rank of devoutly religious men.
Quoted in Philipp Frank *Einstein: His Life and Times* (1947), ch.12, section 5.

38 Science can only state what is, not what should be.
1950 *Out of My Later Years.*

39 Perfections of means and confusion of goals seem—in my opinion—to characterize our age.
1950 *Out of My Later Years.*

40 The man of science is a poor philosopher.
1950 *Out of My Later Years.*

41 The whole of science is nothing more than a refinement of everyday thinking.
1950 *Out of My Later Years.*

42 Education is what remains, if one has forgotten everything one learned in school.
1950 *Out of My Later Years.*

43 If *A* is success in life, then *A* equals *x* plus *y* plus *z*. Work is *x*; *y* is play; and *z* is keeping your mouth shut.
1950 In the *Observer*, 15 Jan.

44 The most incomprehensible thing about the world is that it is comprehensible.
1950 In *Life Magazine*.

45 If only I had known, I would have become a watchmaker.
1955 On his part in developing the atom bomb. In the *New Statesman*, 16 Apr.

46 The grand aim of all science is to cover the greatest number of empirical facts by logical deduction from the smallest number of hypotheses or axioms.
1970 Quoted in *Life Magazine*, 9 Jan.

47 As far as the laws of mathematics refer to reality, they are not certain, and as far as they are certain, they do not refer to reality.
Quoted in Fritjof Capra *The Tao of Physics* (1975), ch.2.

48 Everything should be made as simple as possible, but not simpler.
Quoted in *Newsweek*, 16 Apr 1979.

Eisenhower, Dwight D(avid) 1890–1969

US soldier and Republican politician, whose success as Supreme Commander of Allied forces during World War II and later of NATO swept him to victory as 34th US President (1953–61). His main concerns were foreign policy and anti-communism.

49 The eyes of the world are upon you. The hopes and prayers of liberty-loving people everywhere march with you.
1944 Despatch to US forces on D-Day, 6 Jun.

50 Neither a wise man nor a brave man lies down on the tracks of history to wait for the train of the future to run over him.
1952 In *Time*, 6 Oct.

51 I shall go to Korea, to try to end the war.
1952 Presidential campaign pledge, Oct.

52 A soldier's pack is not so heavy a burden as a prisoner's chains.
1953 Inaugural address, 20 Jan.

53 History does not long entrust the care of freedom to the weak or the timid.
1953 Inaugural address, 20 Jan.

54 I just won't get into a pissing contest with that skunk.
1953 Comment to his brother Milton, refusing to publicly contend with Senator Joseph R McCarthy. Quoted in Piers Brandon *Ike* (1986).

55 You have a row of dominoes set up. You knock over the first one, and what will happen to the last is that it will go over very quickly.
1954 Explaining the domino theory in relation to SE Asia, 7 Apr.

56 There can be no law if we were to invoke one code of international conduct for those who oppose us and another for our friends.
1956 Speech on the Suez crisis, 31 Oct.

57 If the United Nations once admits that international disputes can be settled by using force, we will have destroyed the foundation of the organization and our best hope of establishing a world order.
1957 Address to the nation on Israel's invasion of Egypt, 20 Feb.

58 In the councils of government, we must guard against the acquisition of unwarranted influence, whether sought or unsought, by the military-industrial complex. The potential for the disastrous rise of misplaced powers exists and will persist.
1961 Farewell address to the nation, 17 Jan.

59 Now, on Friday noon, I am to become a private citizen. I am proud to do so. I look forward to it.
1961 Concluding his farewell address to the nation, 17 Jan.

60 I want…the $60 GI job and no medals on my chest.
1963 To President Truman, 25 Nov. Quoted in Michael R Beschloss *Eisenhower* (1990).

61 There's one thing to be said about being President—nobody can tell you when to sit down.
1964 Speech.

62 A fine man who, in the middle of a stormy lake, knows nothing of swimming.
His initial impression of President Harry S Truman while he was military chief of staff. Quoted in Michael R Beschloss *Eisenhower* (1990).

63 Just what does he think the Presidency *is*?
On being warned by a doctor to avoid 'irritation, frustration, anxiety, fear, and above all else, anger'. Quoted in Michael R Beschloss *Eisenhower* (1990).

64 This embattled shore, portal of freedom, is forever hallowed by the ideals, the valor and the sacrifices of our fellow countrymen.
Inscription at US cemetery near St-Laurent. Quoted in the *New York Times*, 5 Jun 1994.

Eisenstaedt, Alfred 1898–1995

German-born US photographer and photojournalist, renowned for his candid pictures of both everyday life and historic occasions.

65 The most important thing about photographing people is not clicking the shutter…it is clicking with the subject.
1966 *Witness to Our Time*.

66 I want to be a mouse in a mousehole.
1995 On the unobtrusiveness of the photographer. In NPR broadcast, 24 Aug.

Elgar, Sir Edward 1857–1934

English composer. His *Enigma Variations* (1899) and the oratorio *The Dream of Gerontius* (1900) established his reputation as the leading English composer of his generation. He was Master of the King's Musick from 1924.

67 To my friends pictured within.
1899 Dedication to the *Enigma Variations*.

68 My idea is that there is music in the air, music all around us, the world is full of it and you simply take as much as you require.
Quoted in R J Buckley *Sir Edward Elgar* (1905), ch.4.

Elgin, James Bruce 1811–63

English government official. In 1860 he was in China, enforcing the treaty of Tientsin (1858), and his actions included the burning of the Summer Palace in Beijing.

69 You can scarcely imagine the beauty and magnificence of the buildings we burnt.
1860 Letter, 18 Aug. Quoted in Nigel Cameron *Barbarians and Mandarins* (1989), ch.16.

Eliot, George *pseudonym of* Mary Ann Evans 1819–80

English novelist, renowned for her powers of observation and characterization. Her novels include *Adam Bede* (1859), *The Mill on the Floss* (1860), *Silas Marner* (1861) and her masterpiece, *Middlemarch* (1871–2).

70 Life is too precious to be spent in this weaving and unweaving of false impressions, and it is better to live quietly under some degree of misrepresentation than to attempt to remove it by the uncertain process of letter-writing.
1856 Letter to Mrs Peter Taylor, 8 Jun. Collected in G S Haight (ed) *The George Eliot Letters* (1954), vol.2.

71 In every parting there is an image of death.
1858 *Scenes of Clerical Life*, ch.10.

72 Errors look so very ugly in persons of small means—one feels they are taking quite a liberty in going astray; whereas people of fortune may naturally indulge in a few delinquencies.
1858 *Scenes of Clerical Life*, ch.25.

73 He knew two kinds of Methodists—the ecstatic and the bilious.
1859 *Adam Bede*, ch.2.

74 We are apt to be kinder to the brutes that love us than to the women that love us. Is it because the brutes are dumb?
1859 *Adam Bede*, ch.4.

75 Young souls, in such pleasant delirium as hers, are as unsympathetic as butterflies sipping nectar.
1859 Of Hetty. *Adam Bede*, ch.9.

76 I aspire to give no more than a faithful account of men and things as they have mirrored themselves in my mind.
1859 *Adam Bede*, ch.17.

77 Our deeds determine us, as much as we determine our deeds; and until we know what has been or will be the peculiar combination of outward with inward facts, which constitute a man's critical actions, it will be better not to think ourselves wise about his character.
1859 *Adam Bede*, ch.29.

78 A maggot must be born i' the rotten cheese to like it.
1859 *Adam Bede*, ch.32.

79 There's no pleasure i' living, if you're to be corked up for ivor, and only dribble your mind out by the sly, like a leaky barrel.
1859 Mrs Poyser. *Adam Bede*, ch.32.

80 He was like a cock who thought the sun had risen to hear him crow.
1859 *Adam Bede*, ch.33.

81 Deep, unspeakable suffering may well be called a baptism, a regeneration, the initiation into a new state.
1859 *Adam Bede*, ch.42.

82 We hand folks over to God's mercy, and show none ourselves.
1859 *Adam Bede*, ch.42.

83 The mother's yearning, that completest type of the life in another life which is the essence of real human love, feels the presence of the cherished child even in the debased, degraded man.
1859 *Adam Bede*, ch.43.

84 If art does not enlarge men's sympathies, it does nothing morally.
1859 Letter to Charles Bray, 5 Jul.

85 He would punish everyone who deserved it: why, he wouldn't have minded being punished himself if he deserved it; but, then, he never did deserve it.
1860 Of Tom Tulliver. *The Mill on the Floss*, bk.1. ch.5.

86 Anger and jealousy can no more bear to lose sight of their objects than love.
1860 *The Mill on the Floss*, bk.1, ch.10.

87 The Catholics, bad harvests, and the mysterious fluctuations of trade—three evils mankind had to fear.
1860 *The Mill on the Floss*, bk.1, ch.12.

88 In a mind charged with an eager purpose and an unfinished vindictiveness, there is no room for new feelings.
1860 *The Mill on the Floss*, bk.4, ch.3.

89 Our life is determined for us—and it makes the mind very free when we give up wishing and only think of bearing what is laid upon us and doing what is given us to do.
1860 *The Mill on the Floss*, bk.5, ch.1.

90 The dead level of provincial existence.
1860 *The Mill on the Floss*, bk.5, ch.3.

91 The happiest women, like the happiest nations, have no history.
1860 *The Mill on the Floss*, bk.6, ch.3.

92 I should like to know what is the proper function of women, if it is not to make reasons for husbands to stay at home, and still stronger reasons for bachelors to go out.
1860 *The Mill on the Floss*, bk.6, ch.6.

93 'Character' says Novalis, in one of his questionable aphorisms, 'character is destiny.'
1860 *The Mill on the Floss*, bk.6, ch.6.

94 Half the sorrows of women would be averted if they could repress the speech they know to be useless; nay, the speech they have resolved not to make.
1866 *Felix Holt*, ch.2.

95 There is no private life which has not been determined by a wider public life.
1866 *Felix Holt*, ch.3.

96 An election is coming. Universal peace is declared, and the foxes have a sincere interest in prolonging the lives of the poultry.
1866 *Felix Holt*, ch.5.

97 Speech is often barren; but silence also does not necessarily brood over a full nest. Your still fowl, blinking at you without remark, may all the while be sitting on one addled egg; and when it takes to cackling will have nothing to announce but that addled delusion.
1866 *Felix Holt*, ch.15.

98 A woman can hardly ever choose…she is dependent on what happens to her. She must take meaner things, because only meaner things are within her reach.
1866 *Felix Holt*, ch.27.

99 There's many a one who would be idle if hunger didn't pinch him; but the stomach sets us to work.
1866 *Felix Holt*, ch.30.

1 Women were expected to have weak opinions; but the great safeguard of society and of domestic life was, that opinions were not acted on. Sane people did what their neighbours did, so that if any lunatics were at large, one might know and avoid them.
1871–2 *Middlemarch*, bk.1, ch.1.

2 A woman dictates before marriage in order that she may have an appetite for submission afterwards.
1871–2 *Middlemarch*, bk.1, ch.9.

3 He said he should prefer not to know the sources of the Nile, and that there should be some unknown regions preserved as hunting-grounds for the poetic imagination.
1871–2 *Middlemarch*, bk.1, ch.9.

4 Among all forms of mistake, prophecy is the most gratuitous.
1871–2 *Middlemarch*, bk.1, ch.10.

5 Plain women he regarded as he did the other severe facts of life, to be faced with philosophy and investigated by science.
1871–2 *Middlemarch*, bk.1, ch.11.

6 Any one watching keenly the stealthy convergence of human lots, sees a slow preparation of effects from one life on another, which tells like a calculated irony on the indifference or the frozen stare with which we look at our unintroduced neighbour.
1871–2 *Middlemarch*, bk.1, ch.11.

7 To point out other people's errors was a duty that Mr Bulstrode rarely shrank from.
1871–2 *Middlemarch*, bk.2, ch.13.

8 If we had a keen vision and feeling of all ordinary human life, it would be like hearing the grass grow and the squirrel's heart beat, and we should die of that roar which lies on the other side of silence.
1871–2 *Middlemarch*, bk.2, ch.20.

9 We do not expect people to be deeply moved by what is not unusual. That element of tragedy which lies in the very fact of frequency, has not yet wrought itself into the coarse emotion of mankind.
1871–2 *Middlemarch*, bk.2, ch.20.

10 A woman, let her be as good as she may, has got to put up with the life her husband makes for her.
1871–2 *Middlemarch*, bk.3, ch.25.

11 It is an uneasy lot at best, to be what we call highly taught and yet not to enjoy: to be present at this great spectacle of life and never to be liberated from a small hungry shivering self.
1871–2 *Middlemarch*, bk.3, ch.29.

12 A man is seldom ashamed of feeling that he cannot love a woman so well when he sees a certain greatness in her: nature having intended greatness for men.
1871–2 *Middlemarch*, bk.4, ch.39.

13 Gossip is a sort of smoke that comes from the dirty tobacco-pipes of those who diffuse it: it proves nothing but the bad taste of the smoker.
1876 *Daniel Deronda*, bk.2, ch.13.

14 A difference of taste in jokes is a great strain on the affections.
1876 *Daniel Deronda*, bk.2, ch.15.

15 There is a great deal of unmapped country within us which would have to be taken into account in an explanation of our gusts and storms.
1876 *Daniel Deronda*, bk.3, ch.24.

16 Friendships begin with liking or gratitude—roots that can be pulled up.
1876 *Daniel Deronda*, bk.4, ch.32.

Eliot, T(homas) S(tearns) 1888–1965

US-born English poet, dramatist and critic, whose work enshrined the disillusionment of the post-World War I generation and the advance of modernism. His most significant poetic works are *The Waste Land* (1922) and *Four Quartets* (1935–42). In 1948 he was awarded the Nobel prize for literature.

17 Let us go then, you and I,
When the evening is spread out against the sky
Like a patient etherized upon a table.
1915 'The Love Song of J Alfred Prufrock' (first published in *Poetry* magazine, collected in *Prufrock and Other Observations*, 1917), opening lines.

18 In the room the women come and go
Talking of Michelangelo.
1915 'The Love Song of J Alfred Prufrock' (first published in *Poetry* magazine, collected in *Prufrock and Other Observations*, 1917).

19 Should I, after tea and cakes and ices,
Have the strength to force the moment to its crisis?
1915 'The Love Song of J Alfred Prufrock' (first published in *Poetry* magazine, collected in *Prufrock and Other Observations*, 1917).

20 For I have known them all already, known them all—
Have known the evenings, mornings, afternoons,
I have measured out my life with coffee spoons;
I know the voices dying with a dying fall
Beneath the music from a farther room.
1915 'The Love Song of J Alfred Prufrock' (first published in *Poetry* magazine, collected in *Prufrock and Other Observations*, 1917).

21 I should have been a pair of ragged claws
Scuttling across the floors of silent seas.
1915 'The Love Song of J Alfred Prufrock' (first published in *Poetry* magazine, collected in *Prufrock and Other Observations*, 1917).

22 I am no prophet—and here's no great matter;
I have seen the moment of my greatness flicker,
And I have seen the eternal Footman hold my coat, and snicker,
And in short, I was afraid.
1915 'The Love Song of J Alfred Prufrock' (first published in *Poetry* magazine, collected in *Prufrock and Other Observations*, 1917).

23 No! I am not Prince Hamlet, nor was meant to be;
Am an attendant lord, one that will do
To swell a progress, start a scene or two,
Advise the prince.
1915 'The Love Song of J Alfred Prufrock' (first published in *Poetry* magazine, collected in *Prufrock and Other Observations*, 1917).

24 I grow old...I grow old...
I shall wear the bottoms of my trousers rolled.
1915 'The Love Song of J Alfred Prufrock' (first published in *Poetry* magazine, collected in *Prufrock and Other Observations*, 1917).

25 Do I dare to eat a peach?
1915 'The Love Song of J Alfred Prufrock' (first published in *Poetry* magazine, collected in *Prufrock and Other Observations*, 1917).

26 I have heard the mermaids singing, each to each.
I do not think that they will sing to me.
1915 'The Love Song of J Alfred Prufrock' (first published in *Poetry* magazine, collected in *Prufrock and Other Observations*, 1917).

27 The winter evening settles down
With smell of steaks in passageways
Six o'clock.
The burnt-out ends of smoky days.
1917 *Prufrock and Other Observations*, 'Preludes', pt.1.

28 The morning comes to consciousness
Of faint stale smells of beer
From the sawdust-trampled street.
1917 *Prufrock and Other Observations*, 'Preludes', pt.2.

29 Held in a lunar synthesis,
Whispering lunar incantations
Dissolve the floors of memory
And all its clear relations
Its divisions and precisions.
1917 *Prufrock and Other Observations*, 'Rhapsody on a Windy Night'.

30 Midnight shakes the memory
As a madman shakes a dead geranium.
1917 *Prufrock and Other Observations*, 'Rhapsody on a Windy Night'.

31 Stand on the highest pavement of the stair—
Lean on a garden urn—
Weave, weave the sunlight in your hair.
1917 *Prufrock and Other Observations*, 'La Figlia Che Piange'.

32 Sometimes these cogitations still amaze
The troubled midnight and the noon's repose.
1917 *Prufrock and Other Observations*, 'La Figlia Che Piange'.

33 I am aware of the damp souls of housemaids
Sprouting despondently at area gates.
1917 *Prufrock and Other Observations*, 'Morning at The Window'.

34 Webster was much possessed by death
And saw the skull beneath the skin;
And breastless creatures under ground
Leaned backward with a lipless grin.
1919 'Whispers of Immortality'.

35 Uncorseted, her friendly bust
Gives promise of pneumatic bliss.
1919 'Whispers of Immortality'.

36 Polyphiloprogenitive
The sapient sutlers of the Lord
Drift across the window-panes
In the beginning was the Word.
1919 'Mr Eliot's Sunday Morning Service'.

37 Apeneck Sweeney spreads his knees
Letting his arms hang down to laugh,
The zebra stripes along his jaw
Swelling to maculate giraffe.
1919 'Sweeney among the Nightingales'.

38 And let their liquid siftings fall
To stain the stiff dishonoured shroud.
1919 'Sweeney among the Nightingales'.

39 Here I am, an old man in a dry month,
Being read to by a boy, waiting for rain.
1919 'Gerontion'.

40 Signs are taken for wonders. 'We would see a sign!'
The word within the word, unable to speak a word,
Swaddled with darkness. In the juvescence of the year
Came Christ the tiger.
1919 'Gerontion'.

41 After such knowledge, what forgiveness? Think now
History has many cunning passages, contrived corridors
And issues, deceives with whispering ambitions,
Guides us by vanities.
1919 'Gerontion'.

42 Neither fear nor courage saves us. Unnatural vices
Are fathered by our heroism. Virtues
Are forced upon us by our impudent crimes.
1919 'Gerontion'.

43 Tenants of the house,
Thoughts of a dry brain in a dry season.
1919 'Gerontion'.

44 Where are the eagles and the trumpets?
Buried beneath some snow-deep Alps.
Over buttered scones and crumpets
Weeping, weeping multitudes
Droop in a hundred A.B.C.'s.
1920 'Cooking Egg'.

45 The emotion of art is impersonal.
1920 *The Sacred Wood*, 'Tradition and Individual Talent'.

46 Poetry is not a turning loose of emotion, but an escape from emotion; it is not the expression of personality but an escape from personality.
1920 *The Sacred Wood*, 'Tradition and Individual Talent'.

47 The only way of expressing emotion in the form of art is by finding an 'objective correlative'...such that when the external facts, which must terminate in sensory experience, are given, the emotion is immediately evoked.
1920 *The Sacred Wood*, 'Hamlet and His Problems'.

48 The bad poet dwells partly in a world of objects and partly in a world of words, and he never can get them to fit.
1920 *The Sacred Wood*, 'Swinburne as a Poet'.

49 Immature poets imitate; mature poets steal; bad poets deface what they take, and good poets make it into something better, or at least something different.
1920 *The Sacred Wood*, 'Philip Massinger'.

50 In the seventeenth century a dissociation of sensibility set in from which we have never recovered; and this dissociation, as is natural, was due to the influence of the two most powerful poets of the century, Milton and Dryden.
1921 *Selected Essays* (1932), 'The Metaphysical Poets'.

51 When a poet's mind is perfectly equipped for its work, it is constantly amalgamating disparate experience...in the mind of the poet these experiences are always forming new wholes.
1921 *Selected Essays* (1932), 'The Metaphysical Poets'.

52 April is the cruellest month, breeding
Lilacs out of the dead land, mixing
Memory and desire, stirring
Dull roots with spring rain.
1922 *The Waste Land*, pt.1, 'The Burial of the Dead'.

53 And I will show you something different from either
Your shadow at morning striding behind you
Or your shadow at evening rising to meet you;
I will show you fear in a handful of dust.
1922 *The Waste Land*, pt.1, 'The Burial of the Dead'.

54 Unreal City,
Under the brown fog of a winter dawn,

A crowd flowed over London Bridge, so many,
I had not thought death had undone so many.
1922 *The Waste Land*, pt.1, 'The Burial of the Dead'.

55 'You! hypocrite lecteur!—mon semblable,—mon frère!'
1922 *The Waste Land*, pt.1, 'The Burial of the Dead'.
► *See Baudelaire 64:53.*

56 The Chair she sat in, like a burnished throne,
Glowed on the marble.
1922 *The Waste Land*, pt.2, 'A Game of Chess'.
► *See Shakespeare 764:23.*

57 O O O O that Shakespeherian Rag—
It's so elegant
So intelligent.
1922 *The Waste Land*, pt.2, 'A Game of Chess'.

58 Hurry up please it's time.
1922 *The Waste Land*, pt.2, 'A Game of Chess'.

59 Sweet Thames, run softly till I end my song,
Sweet Thames, run softly, for I speak not loud or long.
But at my back in a cold blast I hear
The rattle of the bones, and chuckle spread from ear
to ear.
1922 *The Waste Land*, pt.3, 'The Fire Sermon'.
► *See Marvell 556:62.*

60 I Tiresias, old man with wrinkled dugs
Perceived the scene, and foretold the rest—
I too awaited the expected guest.
He, the young man carbuncular, arrives,
A small house agent's clerk, with one bold stare,
One of the low on whom assurance sits
As a silk hat on a Bradford millionaire.
1922 *The Waste Land*, pt.3, 'The Fire Sermon'.

61 When lovely woman stoops to folly and
Paces about her room again, alone,
She smoothes her hair with automatic hand,
And puts a record on the gramophone.
1922 *The Waste Land*, pt.3, 'The Fire Sermon'.
► *See Goldsmith 361:47.*

62 A current under sea
Picked his bones in whispers.
1922 *The Waste Land*, pt.4, 'Death by Water'.

63 O you who turn the wheel and look to windward,
Consider Phlebas, who was once handsome and tall
as you.
1922 *The Waste Land*, pt.4, 'Death by Water'.

64 He who was living is now dead
We who were living are now dying
With a little patience.
1922 *The Waste Land*, pt.5, 'What the Thunder Said'.

65 Who is the third who walks always beside you?
When I count, there are only you and I together
But when I look ahead up the white road
There is always another one walking beside you.
1922 *The Waste Land*, pt.5, 'What the Thunder Said'.

66 In this decayed hole among the mountains
In the faint moonlight, the grass is singing
Over the tumbled graves.
1922 *The Waste Land*, pt.5, 'What the Thunder Said'.

67 The awful daring of a moment's surrender
Which an age of prudence can never retract.
1922 *The Waste Land*, pt.5, 'What the Thunder Said'.

68 These fragments I have shored against my ruins.
1922 *The Waste Land*, pt.5, 'What the Thunder Said'.

69 We are the hollow men
We are the stuffed men
Leaning together
Headpiece filled with straw. Alas!
1925 'The Hollow Men'.

70 This is the dead land
This is cactus land
Here the stone images
Are raised, here they receive
The supplication of a dead man's hand
Under the twinkle of a fading star.
1925 'The Hollow Men'.

71 Between the idea
And the reality
Between the motion
And the act
Falls the shadow.
1925 'The Hollow Men'.

72 This is the way the world ends
Not with a bang but a whimper.
1925 'The Hollow Men', closing lines.

73 A cold coming we had of it,
Just the worst time of the year
For a journey, and such a long journey:
The ways deep and the weather sharp,
The very dead of winter.
1927 'The Journey of the Magi'.

74 But set down
This, set down
This: were we led all that way for
Birth or Death? There was a Birth, certainly,
We had evidence and no doubt. I had seen birth and
death
But had thought they were different; this Birth was
Hard and bitter agony for us, like Death, our death.
We returned to our places, these Kingdoms,
But no longer at ease here, in the old dispensation,
With an alien people clutching their gods.
I should be glad of another death.
1927 'The Journey of the Magi'.

75 All great poetry gives the illusion of a view of life.
1927 'Shakespeare and the Stoicism of Seneca'.

76 We know too much and are convinced of too little. Our literature is a substitute for religion, and so is our religion.
1928 'A Dialogue on Dramatic Poetry', collected in *Selected Essays* (1932).

77 Genuine poetry can communicate before it is understood.
1929 *Dante*.

78 Because I do not hope to turn again
Because I do not hope
Because I do not hope to turn.
1930 'Ash Wednesday'.

79 Because these wings are no longer wings to fly
But merely vans to beat the air
The air which is now thoroughly small and dry
Smaller and dryer than the will.
1930 'Ash Wednesday'.

80 Teach us to care and not to care
Teach us to sit still.
1930 'Ash Wednesday'.

81 Lady, three white leopards sat under a juniper-tree
In the cool of the day.
1930 'Ash Wednesday'.

82 Birth, and copulation, and death.
That's all the facts when you come to brass tacks:
Birth, and copulation, and death.
I've been born, and once is enough.
1932 *Sweeney Agonistes*, 'Fragment of an Agon'.

83 Any man has to, needs to, wants to
Once in a lifetime, do a girl in.
1932 *Sweeney Agonistes*, 'Fragment of an Agon'.

84 The people which ceases to care for its literary inheritance becomes barbaric; the people which ceases to produce literature ceases to move in thought and sensibility.
1933 *The Use of Poetry and the Use of Criticism*.

85 Poetry is not a career, but a mug's game.
1933 *The Use of Poetry and the Use of Criticism*.

86 But the essential advantage for a poet...is to be able to see beneath both beauty and ugliness; to see the boredom, and the horror, and the glory.
1933 *The Use of Poetry and the Use of Criticism*.

87 Where is the Life we have lost in living?
Where is the wisdom we have lost in knowledge?
Where is the knowledge we have lost in information?
1934 *The Rock*, pt.1.

88 And the wind shall say: 'Here were decent godless people:
Their only monument the asphalt road
And a thousand lost golf balls.'
1934 *The Rock*, pt.1.

89 What life have you if you have not life together?
There is not life that is not in community,
And no community not lived in praise of God.
1934 Choruses from *The Rock*.

90 A book is not harmless merely because no one is consciously offended by it.
1935 *Religion and Literature*.

91 Those who talk of the Bible as a 'monument of English prose' are merely admiring it as a monument over the grave of Christianity.
1935 *Religion and Literature*.

92 Time present and time past
Are both perhaps present in time future,
And time future contained in time past.
1935 *Four Quartets*, 'Burnt Norton', pt.1.

93 Footfalls echo in the memory
Down the passage which we did not take
Towards the door we never opened
Into the rose-garden. My words echo
Thus, in your mind.
1935 *Four Quartets*, 'Burnt Norton', pt.1.

94 Go, go, go, said the bird: human kind
Cannot bear very much reality.
1935 *Four Quartets*, 'Burnt Norton', pt.1.

95 At the still point of the turning world. Neither flesh nor fleshless;
Neither from nor towards; at the still point, there the dance is,
But neither arrest nor movement.
1935 *Four Quartets*, 'Burnt Norton', pt.2.

96 Time past and time future
Allow but a little consciousness.
1935 *Four Quartets*, 'Burnt Norton', pt.2.

97 Only through time time is conquered.
1935 *Four Quartets*, 'Burnt Norton', pt.2.

98 Time and the bell have buried the day,
The black cloud carries the sun away.
1935 *Four Quartets*, 'Burnt Norton', pt.4.

99 After the kingfisher's wing
Has answered light to light, and is silent, the light is still
At the still point of the turning world.
1935 *Four Quartets*, 'Burnt Norton', pt.5.

1 Or say that the end precedes the beginning,
And the end and the beginning were always there
before the beginning and after the end.
And all is always now.
1935 *Four Quartets*, 'Burnt Norton', pt.5.

2 Words strain,
Crack and sometimes break, under the burden,
Under the tension, slip, slide, perish,
Decay with imprecision, will not stay in place,
Will not stay still.
1935 *Four Quartets*, 'Burnt Norton', pt.5.

3 Yet we have gone on living,
Living and partly living.
1935 *Murder in the Cathedral*, pt.1.

4 The last temptation is the greatest treason:
To do the right deed for the wrong reason.
1935 *Murder in the Cathedral*, pt.1.

5 Clear the air! clean the sky! wash the wind! take the stone from the stone, take the skin from the arm, take the muscle from bone, and wash them.
1935 *Murder in the Cathedral*, pt.2.

6 How unpleasant to meet Mr Eliot!
With his features of clerical cut,
And his brow so grim
And his mouth so prim.
1936 'Five-Finger Exercises'.

7 Success is relative:
It is what we can make of the mess we have made of things.
1939 *The Family Reunion*, pt.2, sc.3.

8 Round and round the circle
Completing the charm
So the knot be unknotted
The cross be uncrossed
The crooked be made straight
And the curse be ended.
1939 *The Family Reunion*, pt.2, sc.3.

9 At first you may think I'm as mad as a hatter
When I tell you a cat must have THREE DIFFERENT NAMES.
1939 *Old Possum's Book of Practical Cats*, 'The Naming of Cats'.

10 When you notice a cat in profound meditation
The reason, I tell you, is always the same:
His mind is engaged in a rapt contemplation
Of the thought, of the thought, of the thought of

his name:
His ineffable effable
Effanineffable
Deep and inscrutable singular name.
1939 *Old Possum's Book of Practical Cats*, 'The Naming of Cats'.

11 Macavity, Macavity, there's no one like Macavity,
There never was a Cat of such deceitfulness and suavity.
He always has an alibi, and one or two to spare:
At whatever time the deed took place—MACAVITY WASN'T THERE!
1939 *Old Possum's Book of Practical Cats*, 'Macavity: The Mystery Cat'.

12 No *vers* is *libre* for the man who wants to do a good job.
1940 Introduction to Ezra Pound *Poems*.

13 In my beginning is my end.
1940 *Four Quartets*, 'East Coker', pt.1.

14 I said to my soul, be still, and wait without hope
For hope would be hope for the wrong thing; wait without love
For love would be love of the wrong thing; there is yet faith
But the faith and the hope and the love are all in the waiting.
Wait without thought, for you are not ready for thought,
So the darkness shall be the light and the stillness the dancing.
1940 *Four Quartets*, 'East Coker', pt.1.

15 A periphrastic study in a worn-out poetical fashion,
Leaving one still with the intolerable wrestle
With words and meanings.
1940 *Four Quartets*, 'East Coker', pt.1.

16 There is, it seems to us,
At best, only a limited value
In the knowledge derived from experience.
1940 *Four Quartets*, 'East Coker', pt.2.

17 Do not let me hear
Of the wisdom of old men, but rather of their folly.
1940 *Four Quartets*, 'East Coker', pt.2.

18 The only wisdom we can hope to acquire
Is the wisdom of humility: humility is endless.
1940 *Four Quartets*, 'East Coker', pt.2.

19 O dark dark dark. They all go into the dark,
The vacant interstellar spaces, the vacant into the vacant.
1940 *Four Quartets*, 'East Coker', pt.3.

20 And what you do not know is the only thing you know
And what you own is what you do not own
And where you are is where you are not.
1940 *Four Quartets*, 'East Coker', pt.3.

21 The wounded surgeon plies the steel
That questions the distempered part;
Beneath the bleeding hands we feel
The sharp compassion of the healer's art
Resolving the enigma of the fever chart.
1940 *Four Quartets*, 'East Coker', pt.4.

22 The dripping blood our only drink,
The bloody flesh our only food:
In spite of which we like to think
That we are sound, substantial flesh and blood—
Again, in spite of that, we call this Friday good.
1940 *Four Quartets*, 'East Coker', pt.4.

23 And so each venture
Is a new beginning, a raid on the inarticulate
With shabby equipment always deteriorating
In the general mess of imprecision of feeling,
Undisciplined squads of emotion.
1940 *Four Quartets*, 'East Coker', pt.5.

24 There is only the fight to recover what has been lost
And found and lost again and again: and now, under conditions
That seem unpropitious. But perhaps neither gain nor loss.
For us, there is only the trying. The rest is not our business.
1940 *Four Quartets*, 'East Coker', pt.5.

25 Home is where one starts from. As we grow older
The world becomes stranger, the pattern more complicated
Of dead and living.
1940 *Four Quartets*, 'East Coker', pt.5.

26 Love is most nearly itself
When here and now cease to matter.
1940 *Four Quartets*, 'East Coker', pt.5.

27 I do not know much about gods; but I think that the river
Is a strong brown god—sullen, untamed and intractable,
1941 *Four Quartets*, 'The Dry Salvages', pt.1.

28 The river is within us, the sea is all about us.
1941 *Four Quartets*, 'The Dry Salvages', pt.1.

29 The tolling bell
Measures time not our time, rung by the unhurried
Ground swell, a time
Older than the time of chronometers.
1941 *Four Quartets*, 'The Dry Salvages', pt.1.

30 We had the experience but missed the meaning,
And approach to the meaning restores the experience
In a different form, beyond any meaning
We can assign to happiness.
1941 *Four Quartets*, 'The Dry Salvages', pt.2.

31 Time the destroyer is time the preserver.
1941 *Four Quartets*, 'The Dry Salvages', pt.2.

32 You cannot face it steadily, but this thing is sure,
That time is no healer: the patient is no longer here.
1941 *Four Quartets*, 'The Dry Salvages', pt.3.

33 And right action is freedom
From past and future also.
1941 *Four Quartets*, 'The Dry Salvages', pt.5.

34 For most of us, there is only the unattended
Moment, the moment in and out of time.
1941 *Four Quartets*, 'The Dry Salvages', pt.5.

35 These are only hints and guesses,
Hints followed by guesses; and the rest
Is prayer, observance, discipline, thought and action.
The hint half guessed, the gift half understood, is
Incarnation.
1941 *Four Quartets*, 'The Dry Salvages', pt.5.

36 Here the impossible union
Of spheres of existence is actual,
Here the past and future
Are conquered, and reconciled.
1941 *Four Quartets*, 'The Dry Salvages', pt.5.

37 Midwinter Spring is its own season

Sempiternal though sodden towards sundown,
Suspended in time, between pole and tropic.
1942 *Four Quartets*, 'Little Gidding', pt.1.

38 And glow more intense than blaze of branch, or brazier,
Stirs the dumb spirit: no wind, but pentecostal fire
In the dark time of the year. Between melting and freezing
The soul's sap quivers.
1942 *Four Quartets*, 'Little Gidding', pt.1.

39 And what you thought you came for
Is only a shell, a husk of meaning
From which the purpose breaks only when it is fulfilled
If at all. Either you had no purpose
Or the purpose is beyond the end you figured
And is altered in fulfilment.
1942 *Four Quartets*, 'Little Gidding', pt.1.

40 And what the dead had no speech for, when living,
They can tell you, being dead: the communication
Of the dead is tongued with fire beyond the language of the living.
1942 *Four Quartets*, 'Little Gidding', pt.1.

41 Dust in the air suspended
Marks the place where a story ended.
1942 *Four Quartets*, 'Little Gidding', pt.2.

42 In the uncertain hour before the morning
Near the ending of interminable night
At the recurrent end of the unending.
1942 *Four Quartets*, 'Little Gidding', pt.2.

43 Since our concern was speech, and speech impelled us
To purify the dialect of the tribe
And urge the mind to aftersight and foresight.
1942 *Four Quartets*, 'Little Gidding', pt.2.

44 From wrong to wrong the exasperated spirit
Proceeds, unless restored by that refining fire
Where you must move in measure, like a dancer.
1942 *Four Quartets*, 'Little Gidding', pt.2.

45 History may be servitude,
History may be freedom.
1942 *Four Quartets*, 'Little Gidding', pt.3.

46 This is the use of memory:
For liberation—not less of love but expanding
Of love beyond desire, and so liberation
From the future as well as the past.
1942 *Four Quartets*, 'Little Gidding', pt.3.

47 The dove descending breaks the air
With flame of incandescent terror
Of which the tongues declare
The one discharge from sin and error.
1942 *Four Quartets*, 'Little Gidding', pt.4.

48 We shall not cease from exploration
And the end of all our exploring
Will be to arrive where we started
And know the place for the first time.
1942 *Four Quartets*, 'Little Gidding', pt.4.

49 What we call the beginning is often the end
And to make an end is to make a beginning.
The end is where we start from.
1942 *Four Quartets*, 'Little Gidding', pt.5.

50 A people without history
Is not redeemed from time, for history is a pattern
Of timeless moments.
1942 *Four Quartets*, 'Little Gidding', pt.5.

51 And all shall be well and
All manner of thing shall be well
When the tongues of flame are in-folded
Into a crowned knot of fire
And the fire and the rose are one.
1942 *Four Quartets*, 'Little Gidding', pt.5.

52 Culture may even be described simply as that which makes life worth living.
1948 *Notes towards a Definition of Culture*, ch.1.

53 You've missed the point completely, Julia:
There *were* no tigers. *That* was the point.
1950 *The Cocktail Party*, act 1, sc.1, opening lines.

54 What is hell?
Hell is oneself,
Hell is alone, the other figures in it
Merely projections. There is nothing to escape from
And nothing to escape to. One is always alone.
1950 *The Cocktail Party*, act 1, sc.3.

Elizabeth I 1533–1603

Queen of England (from 1558), daughter of Henry VIII and Anne Boleyn. Imprisoned by her Catholic half-sister Mary (later Mary I), she ascended the throne as a Protestant ruler on Mary's death. After several conspiracies she had Mary, Queen of Scots executed (1587) and her subsequent persecution of Catholics led Philip of Spain to send an Armada, which was defeated (1588). Elizabeth never married.

55 If I am to disclose to you what I should prefer if I follow the inclination of my nature, it is this: beggar-woman and single, far rather than queen and married!
1563 Attributed reply to an imperial envoy. Quoted in J E Neale *Queen Elizabeth I* (1979).

56 Though I be a woman yet I have as good a courage answerable to my place as ever my father had. I am your anointed queen. I will never be by violence constrained to do anything. I thank God I am indeed endued with such qualities that if I were turned out of the realm in my petticoat I were able to live in any place of Christendom.
1566 Speech to a parliamentary delegation, 5 Nov. Quoted in Christopher Haigh *Elizabeth I* (1988).

57 The doubt of future foes exiles my present joy.
c.1568 'The Doubt of Future Foes'.

58 No foteball player be used or suffered within the City of London and the liberties thereof upon pain of imprisonment.
1572 Royal proclamation, banning football from the streets of London.

59 My care is like my shadow in the sun,
Follows me flying, flies when I pursue it,
Stands and lies by me, doth what I have done.
c.1582 'On Monsieur's Departure'.

60 I know that I have the body of a weak and feeble woman, but I have the heart and stomach of a king—and a king of England too; and think foul scorn that Parma or Spain, or any Prince of Europe, should dare to invade the borders of my realm.
1588 Address at Tilbury on the approach of the Spanish Armada.

61 My lord, we make use of you, not for your bad legs, but for your good head.
c.1590 To her gout-stricken courtier William Cecil. Quoted in F Chamberlain *Sayings of Queen Elizabeth* (1923).

62 To be a King and to wear a crown is a thing more glorious to them that see it than it is pleasant to them that bear it.
1601 Address to parliament. Quoted in G R Elton *Renaissance and Reformation 1300–1648* (2nd edn, 1968), p.134.

63 Little man, little man! The word 'must' is not to be used to princes!
1603 To Robert Cecil when, during her last illness, he told her that she must go to bed. Quoted in Christopher Haigh *Elizabeth I* (1988), p.24.

64 Like strawberry wives, that laid two or three great strawberries at the mouth of their pot, and all the rest were little ones.
Of the Commission of Sales. Quoted in Francis Bacon *Apophthegms New and Old* (1625), no.54.

Elizabeth II 1926–

Queen of the UK and Head of the Commonwealth, daughter of George VI. She was proclaimed Queen on 6 February 1952, and crowned on 2 June 1953. She married Philip, Duke of Edinburgh, in 1947.

65 I think that people will concede that, on this of all days, I should begin my speech with the words, 'My husband and I'.
1972 Speech at a banquet to celebrate her silver wedding anniversary, 20 Nov.

66 Experience shows that great enterprises seldom end with a tidy and satisfactory flourish. Together, we are doing our best to re-establish peace and civil order in the Gulf region, and to help those members of civil and ethnic minorities who continue to suffer through no fault of their own. If we succeed, our military success will have achieved its true objective.
1991 Commenting on the aftermath of the Gulf War in the first address by a British monarch to Congress, 16 May.

67 1992 is not a year I shall look back on with undiluted pleasure. In the words of one of my more sympathetic correspondents, it has turned out to be an *annus horribilis*.
1992 Speech at the Guildhall, 24 Nov.

Elizabeth, Queen, the Queen Mother 1900–2002

Queen Consort of King George VI, mother of Elizabeth II. Until her marriage to the King in 1923, she was Lady Elizabeth Bowes-Lyon.

68 I'm glad we've been bombed. It makes me feel I can look the East End in the face.
1940 Comment to a London policeman, 13 Sep. Quoted in John Wheeler-Bennet *King George VI* (1948), pt.3, ch.6.

Elkin, Stanley Lawrence 1930–95

US novelist and short-story writer. His novels include *Boswell* (1964), *The Magic Kingdom* (1985) and *The MacGuffin* (1991).

69 All books *are* the Book of Job, high moral tests and tasks set in fairy tales, landmined and unforgiving as golf greens, as steeplechase and gameboard and obstacle course.
1991 'The Future of the Novel', in the *New York Times*, 17 Feb.

70 Story is just just deserts...man in the crucible like jack in the box.
1991 'The Future of the Novel', in the *New York Times*, 17 Feb.

Ellerton, John 1826–93

English cleric, hymnologist, hymnwriter and translator.

71 God the Omnipotent! King, who ordainest
Great winds Thy clarions, lightnings Thy sword.
1866 Hymn (with Henry Fothergill Chorley, 1808–72).

72 The day Thou gavest, Lord, is ended,
The darkness falls at Thy behest.
1870 *A Liturgy for Missionary Meetings*, 'The Day Thou Gavest'.

Ellington, Duke (Edward Kennedy) 1899–1974

US composer, bandleader and pianist. He founded his first regular group in New York in 1924 and became a key figure in orchestral jazz. He composed about 2,000 works, including 'Mood Indigo' and 'Sophisticated Lady'.

73 Playing bop is like playing Scrabble with all the vowels missing.
1954 In *Look*, 10 Aug.

74 When it sounds good, it *is* good.
1957 *Such Sweet Thunder*, programme note.

75 Bubber was the first man I heard use the expression, 'it don't mean a thing if it ain't got that swing.' Everything, and I repeat, everything had to swing.
1965 Of trumpeter Bubber Miley. 'The Most Essential Instrument', in *Jazz Journal*, Dec.

76 New music? Hell, there's been no new music since Stravinsky.
1970 Quoted in D Jewell *Duke* (1977).

77 Music is my mistress, and she plays second fiddle to none.
1973 *Music Is My Mistress*.

Elliot, Jean *also known as* ***Jane Elliot*** 1727–1805

Scottish poet and songwriter, whose only surviving work, based on traditional versions, was written as a lament for the Battle of Flodden.

78 I've heard the lilting at our yowe-milking,
Lasses a-lilting before the dawn o' day;
But now they are moaning on ilka green loaning:
'The Flowers of the Forest are a' wede away'.
1769 'The Flowers of the Forest', stanza 1.
► *See Cockburn 224:55.*

Elliott, Charlotte 1789–1871

English religious poet and hymnwriter.

79 Just as I am, without one plea
But that Thy blood was shed for me,
And that Thou bid'st me come to Thee,
O Lamb of God, I come!
1834 *Invalid's Hymn Book*, 'Just As I Am'.

Elliott, Sir Claude Aurelius 1888–1973

English schoolmaster, head and Provost of Eton College.

80 I've often thought I should like to have a set of postcards printed: 'Dear Sir or Madam, Thank you for your communication. Go to hell. Yours sincerely.'
Quoted in the *Times Literary Supplement*, 22 Jan 1988.

Ellis, George 1753–1815

British poet, born in the West Indies. He co-founded the Tory *Anti-Jacobin* (1797) and made important translations of Middle English verse.

81 Snowy, Flowy, Blowy,
Showery, Flowery, Bowery,
Hoppy, Croppy, Droppy,
Breezy, Sneezy, Freezy.
'The Twelve Months'.

Ellis, Havelock 1859–1939

English physician and writer. His seven-volume *Studies in the Psychology of Sex* (1897–1928, rev edn 1936), caused tremendous controversy, and was banned in Great Britain.

82 All civilization has from time to time become a thin crust over a volcano of revolution.
1922 *Little Essays of Love and Virtue*.

83 What we call morals is simply blind obedience to words of command.
1923 *The Dance of Life*.

Ellison, Harlan Jay 1934–

US novelist, essayist, critic and editor. He has written mainly in the genres of science fiction and fantasy, where he has been a radical and outspoken contributor.

84 I Have No Mouth And I Must Scream.
1967 Title of story collection.

85 The reason men are greater than animals isn't because we can dream of the stars…it's because we have something they haven't. Greed.
1970 *The Glass Teat*, introduction.

86 Our childhoods are sowing the wind, our adulthoods are reaping the whirlwind.
1974 *Approaching Oblivion*, introduction.

87 All The Lies That Are My Life.
1989 Title of autobiography

Ellison, Ralph Waldo 1914–94

US novelist, best known for his classic account of black urban existence, *Invisible Man* (1952), his only completed novel. He also wrote essays on music and culture.

88 I am an invisible man. No, I am not a spook like those who haunted Edgar Allen Poe; nor am I one of your Hollywood-movie ectoplasms. I am a man of substance, of flesh and bone, fibre and liquids—and I might even be said to possess a mind. I am invisible, understand, simply because people refuse to see me… When they approach me they see only my surroundings, themselves, or figments of their imagination—indeed, everything and anything except me.
1952 *Invisible Man*, prologue.

89 I was never more hated than when I tried to be honest… On the other hand, I've never been more loved and appreciated than when I tried to 'justify' and affirm someone's mistaken beliefs; or when I've tried to give my friends the incorrect, absurd answers they wished to hear.
1952 *Invisible Man*, epilogue.

90 All novels are about certain minorities: the individual is a minority.
1955 Interview in *Paris Review*, Spring.

91 Part of the problem for the invisible man was that he was invisible to himself, that he didn't grasp his own complexity.
1992 Quoted by Keith Botsford in Ellison's obituary, 18 Apr 1994, in *The Independent*.

Ellwood, David T 1953–

US economist, Professor at John F Kennedy School of Government, Harvard University.

92 The chief source of economic insecurity in America used to be growing old; now it's being born into or raised in a single-parent family.
1991 In the *Washington Post*, 22 Feb.

Eltit, Diamela 1949–

Chilean novelist. Her novels are complex and experimental, but she has found a devoted readership among intellectuals and feminist circles.

93 *Para decirlo de otra manera, no es la herida la que causó el grito, sino exactamente a la inversa; para herirse es preciso el grito, todo lo demás es un pretexto.*
In other words, it was not the wound that caused the scream, but precisely the opposite: to get wounded one needs the scream; the rest is only a pretext.
1983 *Lumpérica*, 1.

Elton, Ben 1959–

English comedian and writer.

94 I did not vote Labour because they've heard of Oasis and nobody is going to vote Tory because William Hague has got a baseball cap.
1998 In *The Radio Times*, 18 Apr.

Elton, Sir Geoffrey Rudolph 1921–94

British historian, Professor at Cambridge University.

95 When I meet a historian who cannot think that there have been great men, great men moreover in politics, I feel myself in the presence of a bad historian; and there are times when I incline to judge all historians by their opinion of Winston Churchill—whether they can see that, no matter how much better the details, often damaging, of man and career become known, he still remains, quite simply, a great man.
1970 *Political History*, ch.2.

Éluard, Paul *pseudonym of* *Eugène Grindel* 1895–1952

French poet, a founder of the Surrealist movement with which he later parted (1938). He was active in political affairs, in the Resistance and the Communist Party.

96 *Le poète est celui qui inspire bien plus que celui qui est inspiré.*
The poet is more the inspirer than the one who is inspired.
1936 *L'Evidence poétique*.

97 *Je suis né pour te connaître*
Pour te nommer
Liberté.
I was born to know you
To give you your name:
Freedom.
1942 *Poésie et vérité*, 'Liberté'.

98 *Adieu tristesse*
Bonjour tristesse.
Farewell sadness
Hello sadness.
1942 *Poésie et vérité*, 'La Vie immédiate'.

Emecheta, Buchi 1944–

Nigerian-born British writer.

99 Sometimes it seemed that matrimony, apart from being a way of getting free sex when men felt like it, was also a legalized way of committing assault and getting away with it.
1972 *In the Ditch.*

1 I am a woman and a woman of Africa. I am a daughter of Nigeria and if she is in shame, I shall stay and mourn with her in shame.
1982 *Destination Biafra.*

Emerson, Ralph Waldo 1803–82

US philosopher and poet, a central figure of the transcendentalist movement. He was a minister in the Unitarian church, but resigned after a controversy over his belief in spiritual independence.

2 By the rude bridge that arched the flood,
Their flag to April's breeze unfurled,
Here once the embattled farmers stood
And fired the shot heard around the world.
1837 'Concord Hymn', opening lines. This poem was sung on 4 Jul 1837 at the dedication of the monument commemorating the battle of 19 Apr 1775.

3 This time, like all times, is a very good one, if we but know what to do with it.
1837 'The American Scholar', lecture at Harvard University.

4 All are needed by each one;
Nothing is fair or good alone.
1839 'Each and All', l.11–12.

5 In every work of genius we recognize our own rejected thoughts: they come back to us with a certain alienated majesty.
1841 *Essays: First Series*, 'Self-Reliance'.

6 Every Stoic was a Stoic; but in Christendom where is the Christian?
1841 *Essays: First Series*, 'Self-Reliance'.

7 Whoso would be a man must be a nonconformist.
1841 *Essays: First Series*, 'Self-Reliance'.

8 A foolish consistency is the hobgoblin of little minds, adored by little statesmen and philosophers and divines. With consistency a great soul has simply nothing to do.
1841 *Essays: First Series*, 'Self-Reliance'.

9 To be great is to be misunderstood.
1841 *Essays: First Series*, 'Self-Reliance'.

10 Nothing can bring you peace but yourself.
1841 *Essays: First Series*, 'Self-Reliance'.

11 The dice of God are always loaded.
1841 *Essays: First Series*, 'Compensation'.

12 There is properly no history; only biography.
1841 *Essays: First Series*, 'History'.

13 All mankind love a lover.
1841 *Essays: First Series*, 'Love'.

14 A friend may well be reckoned the masterpiece of nature.
1841 *Essays: First Series*, 'Friendship'.

15 The only reward of virtue is virtue; the only way to have a friend is to be one.
1841 *Essays: First Series*, 'Friendship'.

16 In skating over thin ice, our safety is in our speed.
1841 *Essays: First Series*, 'Prudence'.

17 People wish to be settled: only as far as they are unsettled is there any hope for them.
1841 *Essays: First Series*, 'Circles'.

18 Nothing great was ever achieved without enthusiasm.
1841 *Essays: First Series*, 'Circles'.

19 Though we travel the world over to find the beautiful, we must carry it with us, or we find it not.
1841 *Essays: First Series*, 'Art'.

20 In sculpture, did ever anybody call the Apollo a fancy piece? Or say of the Laocoön how it might be made different? A masterpiece of art has in the mind a fixed place in the chain of being, as much as a plant or a crystal.
1841 'Thoughts on Art', in *The Dial*, vol.1, no.3, Jan.

21 Have I a lover
Who is noble and free?
I would he were nobler
Than to love me.
1841 'The Sphinx', stanza 12.

22 The reward of a thing well done is to have done it.
1844 'New England Reformers', lecture to the Society, 3 Mar.

23 It is not metres, but a metre-making argument, that makes a poem.
1844 *Essays: Second Series*, 'The Poet'.

24 Let the Stoics say what they please, we do not eat for the good of living, but because the meat is savory and the appetite is keen.
1844 *Essays: Second Series*, 'Nature'.

25 The only gift is a portion of thyself.
1844 *Essays: Second Series*, 'Gifts'.

26 Every man is wanted, and no man is wanted much.
1844 *Essays: Second Series*, 'Nominalist and Realist'.

27 Things are in the saddle,
And ride mankind.
1847 *Poems*, 'Ode', dedicated to W H Channing.

28 Belief consists in affirming the affirmations of the soul; unbelief, in denying them.
1850 *Representative Men*, 'Montaigne; or, The Skeptic'.

29 Is not marriage an open question, when it is alleged, from the beginning of the world, that such as are in the institution wish to get out; and such as are out wish to get in.
1850 *Representative Men*, 'Montaigne; or, The Skeptic'.

30 Keep cool: it will be all one a hundred years hence.
1850 *Representative Men*, 'Montaigne; or, The Skeptic'.

31 I can reason down or deny everything, except this perpetual Belly: feed he must and will, and I cannot make him respectable.
1850 *Representative Men*, 'Montaigne; or, The Skeptic'.

32 The world is upheld by the veracity of good men: they make the earth wholesome.

1850 *Representative Men*, 'Uses of Great Men'.

33 Every hero becomes a bore at last.
1850 *Representative Men*, 'Uses of Great Men'.

34 Perpetual modernness is the measure of merit in every work of art.
1850 *Representative Men*, 'Plato'.

35 Men's actions are too strong for them. Show me a man who has acted, and who has not been the victim and slave of his action.
1850 *Representative Men*, 'Goethe'.

36 The aristocrat is the democrat ripe, and gone to seed.
1850 *Representative Men*, 'Napoleon, the Man of the World'.

37 As long as our civilization is essentially one of property, of fences, of exclusiveness, it will be mocked by delusions. Our riches will leave us sick; there will be bitterness in our laughter; and our wine will burn our mouth.
1850 *Representative Men*, 'Napoleon, the Man of the World'.

38 They have in themselves what they value in their horses, mettle and bottom.
1856 Of Englishmen. *English Traits*, 'Manners'.

39 If the red slayer think he slays,
Or if the slain think he is slain,
They know not well the subtle ways
I keep, and pass, and turn again.
1857 'Brahma'. Collected in *May Day* (1867).
➤ *See Lang 488:90.*

40 A person seldom falls sick, but the bystanders are animated with a faint hope that he will die.
1860 *The Conduct of Life*, 'Considerations by the Way'.

41 Art is a jealous mistress, and if a man have a genius for painting, poetry, music, architecture, or philosophy, he makes a bad husband and an ill provider.
1860 *The Conduct of Life*, 'Wealth'.

42 We are born believing. A man bears beliefs as a tree bears apples.
1860 *The Conduct of Life*, 'Worship'.

43 Immortality will come to such as are fit for it, and he who would be a great soul in future must be a great soul now.
1860 *The Conduct of Life*, 'Worship'.

44 The louder he talked of his honour, the faster we counted our spoons.
1860 *The Conduct of Life*, 'Worship'.

45 The revelation of Thought takes men out of servitude into freedom.
1860 *The Conduct of Life*, 'Fate'.

46 He has not learned the lesson of life who does not every day surmount a fear.
1870 *Society and Solitude*, 'Courage'.

47 Raphael paints wisdom; Handel sings it, Phidias carves it, Shakespeare writes it, Wren builds it, Columbus sails it, Luther preaches it, Washington arms it, Watt mechanizes it.
1870 *Society and Solitude*, 'Art'.

48 Hitch your wagon to a star.
1870 *Society and Solitude*, 'Civilization'.

49 We boil at different degrees.
1870 *Society and Solitude*, 'Eloquence'.

50 Can anybody remember when the times were not hard, and money was not scarce?
1870 *Society and Solitude*, 'Works and Days'.

51 We do not count a man's years, until he has nothing else to count.
1870 *Society and Solitude*, 'Old Age'.

52 America is a country of young men.
1870 *Society and Solitude*, 'Old Age'.

53 A rogue alive to the ludicrous is still convertible. If that sense is lost, his fellow-men can do little for him.
1876 *Letters and Social Aims*, 'The Comic'.

54 Music is the poor man's Parnassus.
1876 *Letters and Social Aims*, 'Poetry and Imagination'.

Emery, Jane c.1918–

US biographer and academic.

55 As thin and neat as a furled umbrella.
1992 On Rose Macaulay. *Rose Macaulay*.

Emin, Tracey 1964–

English artist. She gained widespread public attention with various 'confessional' installation works such as *Everyone I Have Ever Slept With, from 1963 to 1995* (1995), which was later destroyed in a fire.

56 The wheel that squeaks gets the oil.
2001 In the *Observer*, 22 Apr.

57 The majority of the British public have no regard or no respect for what me and my peers do to the point where they actually laugh at a disaster like a fire.
2004 After some of her work (and the work of other contemporary artists) was destroyed in a fire in London. Quoted in *The Scotsman*, 31 May.

58 Just love me.
2004 Words spelled out in a neon light installation she created.

Emmet, Robert 1778–1803

Irish patriot, member of the United Irishmen. In 1803 he plotted an insurrection against the English, and was hanged after returning from the Wicklow Mountains for a last meeting with his sweetheart.

59 I have but one request to make at my departure from this world, it is—the charity of its silence. Let no man write my epitaph; for as no man who knows my motives, dare now vindicate them, let no prejudice or ignorance asperse them. Let them rest in obscurity and peace! Let my memory be left in oblivion, and my tomb remain uninscribed, until other times and other men can do justice to my character. When my country takes her place among the nations of the earth, *then*, and *not till then*, let my epitaph be written.
1803 Speech before being sentenced.

Empson, Sir William 1906–84

English critic and poet. He established his reputation with his first book on textual criticism, *Seven Types of Ambiguity* (1930, revised 1947). An edition of *Collected Poems* was published in 1955.

60 Seven Types of Ambiguity.
1930 Title of book.

61 Slowly the poison the whole blood stream fills.
It is not the effort or the failure tires.

The waste remains, the waste remains and kills.
1935 'Missing Dates'.

62 Ripeness is all; her in her cooling planet
Revere; do not presume to think her wasted.
1935 'To an Old Lady'.

63 But as to risings, I can tell you why.
It is on contradiction that they grow.
It seemed the best thing to be up and go.
Up was the heartening and the strong reply.
The heart of standing is we cannot fly.
1935 'Aubade'.

64 Waiting for the end, boys, waiting for the end.
What is there to be or do?
What's become of me or you?
1940 'Just a Smack at Auden'.

Engels, Friedrich 1820–95

German socialist philosopher, founder of 'scientific socialism'. He first met Karl Marx in Brussels in 1844, collaborated with him on the *Communist Manifesto* (1848), and later edited and translated Marx's writings.

65 [The] English proletariat is becoming more and more bourgeois, so that this most bourgeois of all nations is apparently aiming ultimately at the possession of a bourgeois aristocracy and a bourgeois proletariat *as well as* a bourgeoisie. For a nation which exploits the whole world this is of course to a certain extent justifiable.
1858 Letter to Karl Marx, 7 Oct.

66 *Der Staat wird nicht 'abgeschafft', er stirbt ab.*
The state is not 'abolished'; it withers away.
1878 *Anti-Dühring*, pt.3, ch.2.

67 The British Labour movement is today, and for many years has been, working in a narrow circle of strikes that are looked upon, not as an expedient, and not as a means of propaganda, but as an ultimate aim.
1878 Letter to Eduard Bernstein, 17 Jul.

68 The society that will organize production on the basis of a free and equal association of the producers will put the whole machinery of the state where it will then belong: into the museum of antiquities, by the side of the spinning wheel and the bronze axe.
1884 *The Origin of the Family, Private Property, and the State*.

Engle, Paul Hamilton 1908–91

US poet, novelist and critic, whose writing is formal, elegant and accessible. He ran courses in literature and writing in his native Iowa.

69 Poetry—tries to tell you about a vision in the unvisionary language of farm, city and love.
1956 In *Life*, 28 May.

Ennius, Quintus Ennius c.239–169 BC

Roman poet, probably of Greek extraction. He was a friend of Scipio Africanus the Elder, and he introduced the hexameter into Latin. Only fragments have survived of his work.

70 *Quod est ante pedes nemo spectat, caeli scrutantur plagas.*
No one regards the things before his feet, but views with care the regions of the sky.
Fragment of *Iphigeneia*, quoted in Cicero *De Divinatione*, bk.2 (translated by W A Falconer, 1979).

71 How like us is that ugly brute, the ape!
Quoted in Cicero *De Divinatione*, bk.50 (translated by H Rackham, 1942).

Enright, D(ennis) J(oseph) 1920–2002

English poet, critic and literary journalist. He held posts in universities around the world (1947–60), although his humanistic work rejects academic politics.

72 Metaphysical lederhosen.
On the murky philosophizing and cumbrous symbolism of German novels. Quoted by John Gross in the *New York Times*, 20 Jan 1987.

Ephorus of Cumæ c.400–330 BC

Greek historian.

73 Music was invented to deceive and delude mankind.
History, preface.

Ephron, Nora 1941–

US screenwriter and director.

74 I always say that a successful parent is one who raises a child so that they can pay for their own psychoanalysis.
1995 In *The Guardian*, 26 Jun.

Epstein, Jacob 1880–1959

US-born British sculptor.

75 Why don't they stick to murder and leave art to us?
Attributed. On hearing that his statue, Lazarus, in New College chapel, Oxford, kept Nikita Khrushchev awake at night.

Epstein, Julius J 1909–2000

US screenwriter, twin brother of Philip G Epstein. The two worked as a screenwriting team for many years on films such as *Casablanca* (1942) and *My Foolish Heart* (1949).

76 Of all the gin joints in all the towns in all the world, she walks into mine.
1942 Humphrey Bogart as Rick in *Casablanca* (with Philip G Epstein and Howard Koch).

77 If she can stand it, I can. Play it!
1942 Humphrey Bogart as Rick in *Casablanca* (with Philip G Epstein and Howard Koch). The line is commonly rendered 'Play it again, Sam', a conflation with an earlier line of Ingrid Bergman, 'Play it, Sam. Play *As Time Goes By*.'

78 Here's looking at you, kid.
1942 Humphrey Bogart as Rick in *Casablanca* (with Philip G Epstein and Howard Koch).

79 I'm no good at being noble, but it doesn't take much to see that the problems of three little people don't amount to a hill of beans in this crazy world.
1942 Humphrey Bogart as Rick in *Casablanca* (with Philip G Epstein and Howard Koch).

80 If that plane leaves the ground and you're not with him, you'll regret it. Maybe not today, maybe not tomorrow, but soon and for the rest of your life.
1942 Humphrey Bogart as Rick in *Casablanca* (with Philip G Epstein and Howard Koch).

81 Major Strasser has been shot. Round up the usual suspects.
1942 Claude Rains as Captain Louis Renault in *Casablanca* (with Philip G Epstein and Howard Koch).

82 A woman is beautiful only when she is loved.
1944 *Mr Skeffington* (with Philip Epstein).

83 Honeymoon's over—time to get married.
1972 *Pete 'n Tillie.*

84 When you've reached my age, and your friends are beginning to worry about you, blind dates are a way of life.
1972 *Pete 'n Tillie.*

85 Dear J W, have the bank president finish the script.
Response to a note from Jack Warner which had read 'Railroad presidents get in at nine o'clock, bank presidents get in at nine o'clock, read your contract, you're coming in at nine o'clock.' Quoted in Aljean Harmetz *Round Up the Usual Suspects* (1993).

Erasmus, Desiderius *originally* ***Gerrit Gerritszoon*** 1466–1536

Dutch humanist and scholar, author of the satire *Encomium Moriae* (*Praise of Folly*, 1509) and *Colloquia familiaria* (1519), an audacious treatment of Church abuses. Other works include the first translation of the Greek New Testament.

86 *In regione caecorum rex est luscus.*
In the country of the blind the one-eyed man is king.
c.1500 *Adages*, bk.3, century 4, no.96.

87 Let a king recall that it is better to improve his realm than to increase his territory.
1517 *Querela Pacis.*

Eriksson, Sven Goran 1948–

Swedish football coach, manager of the England football team from 2001.

88 There is more politics in football than in politics.
2004 In *Varsity*, 23 Jan.

Ernst, Max 1891–1976

German-born artist, a founder of the Dada group and later a key figure of Surrealism. He settled in the US in 1941 but returned to France in 1953.

89 The artist is a spectator, indifferent or impassioned, at the birth of his work, and observes the phases of its development.
Quoted in Saranne Alexandrian *Surrealist Art* (1970).

90 Collage is a supersensitive and scrupulously accurate instrument, similar to a seismograph, which is able to record the exact amount of the possibility of human happiness at any period.
Quoted in Saranne Alexandrian *Surrealist Art* (1970).

Ertz, Susan *pseudonym of* ***Mrs Ronald McCrindle*** c.1894–1985

US novelist, born in England. She was the author of a great many popular novels.

91 Someone has somewhere commented on the fact that millions long for immortality who don't know what to do with themselves on a rainy Sunday afternoon.
1943 *Anger in the Sky*, ch.5.

Etherege, Sir George c.1635–1691

English dramatist, who spent most of his life in royal service abroad. Inspired by Molière, he founded the comedy of intrigue in English literature.

92 Like dancers on the ropes poor poets fare,
Most perish young, the rest in danger are.
1676 *The Man of Mode or, Sir Fopling Flutter*, prologue.

93 What a dull, insipid thing is a billet-doux written in cold blood, after the heat of the business is over!
1676 *The Man of Mode or, Sir Fopling Flutter*, act 1, sc.1.

94 Next to the coming to a good understanding with a new mistress, I love a quarrel with an old one.
1676 *The Man of Mode or, Sir Fopling Flutter*, act 1, sc.1.

95 I know he is a devil, but he has something of the angel yet undefaced in him, which makes him so charming and agreeable that I must love him, be he never so wicked.
1676 *The Man of Mode or, Sir Fopling Flutter*, act 2, sc.2.

96 We are not masters of our own affections; our inclinations daily alter: now we love pleasure, and anon we shall dote on business. Human frailty will have it so, and who can help it?
1676 *The Man of Mode or, Sir Fopling Flutter*, act 2, sc.2.

97 When love grows diseased, the best thing we can do is to put it to a violent death. I cannot endure the torture of a lingering and consumptive passion.
1676 *The Man of Mode or, Sir Fopling Flutter*, act 2, sc.2.

98 I must confess I am a fop in my heart; ill customs influence my very senses, and I have been so used to affectation that without the help of the air of the court what is natural cannot touch me.
1688 Letter to Mr Poley, 12 Jan.

Eubank, Chris 1966–

English boxer.

99 All the rudiments of life are to be found ironing trousers.
2003 Quoted in *The Independent*, 29 Dec.

Euclid 4c BC

Greek mathematician, best known for his 13-volume work *The Elements*, dealing with plane and solid geometry and arithmetic.

1 That which was to be proved.
c.300 BC *Elementa*, bk.1, proposition 5. Although originally written in Greek, this phrase is usually quoted in its Latin form, 'Quod erat demonstrandum', sometimes abbreviated to 'QED'.

2 There is no 'royal road' to geometry.
c.300 BC Response to Ptolemy I, when asked if there were an easier way to solve theorems. Quoted in Proclus *Commentary on the First Book of Euclid's Elementa*, prologue.

Eudamidas 4c BC

King of Sparta, the brother of Agis I whom he succeeded in 331/330 BC.

3 The speech is admirable, but the speaker is not to be trusted; for he has never been amid the blare of trumpets.
Of a philosopher who had claimed that philosophers were the only good generals. Quoted in Plutarch *Apophthegmata Laconica*, 220E (translated by F C Babbitt, 1931).

Euripides 480 or 484–406 BC

Greek dramatist. Of more than 80 plays only 18 survive complete. He won the tragic prize only five times, but his plays gained popularity after his death.

4 Regard this day's life as yours, but all else as Fortune's.
Alcestis, l.788–9 (translated by D Kovacs, 1994).

5 I have found nothing stronger than Necessity.
Alcestis, l.965 (translated by D Kovacs, 1994).

6 Nothing else that a wife may suffer, equals this: if she loses her husband, she loses her life.
Andromacha, l.375–6.

7 Women's love is for their men, not for their children.
Electra, l.265.

8 None wise dares hopeless venture.
Helena, l.811 (translated by A S Way, 1959).

9 The life of men is painful.
Hippolytus, l.190.

10 It is necessary for mortals to be worn with toil.
Hippolytus, l.207.

11 Your very silence is your confession.
Clytemnestra to Agamemnon, realizing that he plans to sacrifice their daughter, Iphigenia, to secure favourable winds during the Greek expedition against Troy. *Iphigenia Aulidensis*, l.1142.

12 The meanest life is better than the most glorious death.
Iphigenia Aulidensis, l.1252 (translated by W S Merwin and G E Dimock Jr, 1978).

13 Wrath brings mortal men their gravest hurt.
Medea, l.1080 (translated by D Kovacs, 1994).

14 A change is always nice.
Orestes, l.234 (translated by M L West, 1987).

15 Lucky is the man who has been successful with his children and not got ones who are notorious disasters.
Orestes, l.542–3 (translated by M L West, 1987).

16 And wealth abides not, it is but for a day.
Phoenissae, l.558.

Evans, Bergen 1904–78

US scholar and literary critic, Professor of English at Indiana University.

17 It was said of Metternich that he was so conservative that had *he* been present at the Creation, he would have begged God to have retained Chaos.
1968 Note in his *Dictionary of Quotations*.

Evans, Dame Edith 1888–1976

English actress, best remembered for her starchy Lady Bracknell in Oscar Wilde's *The Importance of Being Earnest* (1939), which she also played on film.

18 People always ask me the most ridiculous questions. They want to know, 'How do you approach a role?' Well, I don't know. I approach it by first saying yes, then getting on with the bloody thing.
Attributed.

Evans, George Essex 1863–1909

Australian poet, born in England. A journalist and literary editor, he is best known for his patriotic ceremonial verse.

19 Not as the songs of other lands
Her song shall be.
'An Australian Symphony', in *Collected Verse* (1920).

Evans, Walker 1903–75

US photographer, chronicler of the harsh life in the rural South during the Great Depression of the 1930s. His photographs appear in James Agee's *Let Us Now Praise Famous Men* (1941).

20 People out of work are not given to talking much about the one thing on their minds. You only sense by indirection, degrees of anger, shades of humiliation and echoes of fear.
Quoted in *Fortune*, 11 Feb 1980.

Evelyn, John 1620–1706

English diarist. His *Diary*, which covers the years 1641–1706, offers an insight into life in post-Restoration England.

21 This knight was indeed a valiant Gent: but not a little given to romance, when he spake of himself.
1651 Diary entry, 6 Sep.

22 I saw *Hamlet Prince of Denmark* played, but now the old plays begin to disgust this refined age.
1661 Diary entry, 26 Nov.

Ewart, Gavin Buchanan 1916–95

Scottish-born poet. His poems are often humorous or scatological in nature, and frequently mimic comic popular forms like the limerick. He published his first book of poems in 1939.

23 Miss Twye was soaping her breasts in the bath
When she heard behind her a meaning laugh
And to her amazement she discovered
A wicked man in the bathroom cupboard.
1939 'Miss Twye'.

24 Sex suppressed will go berserk,
But it keeps us all alive.
It's a wonderful change from wives and work
And it ends at half past five.
1966 'Office Friendships'.

25 Would you rather live in lively London
or where a young penguin lies screaming?
1977 *Where a Young Penguin Lies Screaming*, epigraph.

26 He's very popular among his mates.
I think I'm Auden, he thinks he's Yeats.
1986 'Seamus Heaney'.

27 On the Last Day the wrecks will surface over the sea.
1986 'Resurrection'.

Ewer, William Norman 1885–1976

British writer.

28 How odd
Of God
To choose
The Jews.
1924 In *The Week-End Book*.

Ewing, Winnie 1929–

Scottish Nationalist politician.

29 The Scottish Parliament which adjourned on 25 March in the year 1707 is hereby reconvened.
1999 Speech at the opening of the new Scottish Parliament, 12 May.

30 Time after time, on matters great and small, we are still standing on the sidelines, mutely accepting what is decided elsewhere instead of raising our voices and

making our own choices. Scotland's much vaunted partnership of Jonah and the whale.
Quoted in Michael Russell (ed) *Stop the World: The Autobiography of Winnie Ewing* (2004).

Fackenheim, Emil L 1916–2003

Jewish rabbi and philosopher. He was Professor at the University of Toronto until 1984, when he moved to Jerusalem, where he continued to teach and write.

31 Had every Christian in Hitler's Europe followed the example of the king of Denmark and decided to put on the yellow star, there would be today neither despair in the church nor talk of the death of God.
1968 *Quest for Past and Future.*

Fadiman, Anne 1953–

US writer.

32 Sharing a bed and a future was child's play compared to sharing my copy of *The Complete Poems of W B Yeats.*
1998 On the joys and pain of combining libraries when couples move in together. In *Ex Libris: Confessions of a Common Reader.*

33 If my father were still writing essays, every full-grown 'girl' would probably be transformed into a 'woman'.
1998 On her father, Clifton Fadiman, a renowned man-of-letters. In *Ex Libris: Confessions of a Common Reader.*

Fadiman, Clifton 1904–99

US writer, literary critic and lecturer. He worked as a book reviewer for the *New Yorker.*

34 Liquor is not a necessity. It is a means of momentarily sidestepping necessity.
1955 *Party of One,* 'From My Notebooks'.

35 The mama of dada.
1955 Of Gertrude Stein. *Party of One.*

36 Cheese, milk's leap toward immortality.
1957 *Any Number Can Play,* 'The Cheese Stands Alone'.

37 The police dog of American fiction, except that his hatred is not the result of mere crabbedness but of an eye that sees too deep for comfort.
Of US writer Ring Lardner. Quoted in Scott Meredith *George S Kaufman and His Friends* (1974).

38 Poetry in a bottle.
1985 Of wine. In *Manhattan Inc,* Jul.

Falkland, Lucius Cary, Viscount 1610–43

English statesman and writer, whose house at Tew attracted the brightest intellects of Oxford and London. A Royalist during the Civil War, he was Secretary of State in 1642 and was killed at the first Battle of Newbury.

39 When it is not necessary to change, it is necessary not to change.
1641 Speech, House of Commons, 22 Nov. Collected as 'A Speech concerning Episcopacy' in *Discourses of Infallibility* (1660).

Faludi, Susan 1960–

US journalist and writer. She has written *Backlash: The Undeclared War Against American Women* (1991), a controversial and award-winning study of feminism, and *Stiffed: The Betrayal of Modern Man* (2000).

40 The more women are paid, the less eager they are to marry.
1992 *Backlash* (UK edn), ch.2, 'Man Shortages and Barren Wombs'.

41 Social scientists *could* supply plenty of research to show that one member of the family, at least, is happier and more well adjusted when mum stays home and looks after the children. But that person is dad—a finding of limited use to backlash publicists.
1992 *Backlash* (UK edn), ch.2, 'Man Shortages and Barren Wombs'.

42 A backlash against women's rights is nothing new. Indeed, it's a recurring phenomenon: it returns every time women begin to make some headway towards equality, a seemingly inevitable early frost to the brief flowerings of feminism.
1992 *Backlash* (UK edn), ch.3, 'Backlashes Then and Now'.

Fanon, Frantz Omar 1925–61

French West Indian psychoanalyst and social philosopher, editor of *El Moudjahid* in Tunis and Ambassador to Ghana. He is best remembered for his critiques of colonialism.

43 *Aux colonies, l'infrastructure économique est également une superstructure. La cause est conséquence: on est riche parce que blanc, on est blanc parce que riche.*
In the colonies the economic substructure is also a superstructure. The cause is the consequence; you are rich because you are white, you are white because you are rich.
1961 *Les Damnés de la terre* (*The Wretched of the Earth,* translated by Constance Farrington, 1965), ch.1, 'Concerning Violence'.

44 *Le colonialisme ne se satisfait pas d'enserrer le peuple dans ses mailles, de vider le cerveau colonisé de toute forme et de tout contenu. Par une sorte de perversion de la logique, il s'oriente vers le passé du peuple opprimé, le distort, le défigure, l'anéantit.*
Colonialism is not satisfied merely with holding a people in its grip and emptying the native's brain of all form and content. By a kind of perverted logic, it turns to the past of the oppressed people, and distorts, disfigures and destroys it.
1961 *Les Damnés de la terre* (*The Wretched of the Earth,* translated by Constance Farrington, 1965), ch.4, 'On National Culture'.

45 *Le colonialisme accule le peuple dominé à se poser constamment la question: 'Qui suis-je en réalité?'*
Colonialism forces the people it dominates to ask themselves the question constantly: 'In reality, who am I?'
1961 *Les Damnés de la terre* (*The Wretched of the Earth,* translated by Constance Farrington, 1965), ch.5, 'Colonial War and Mental Disorders'.

Fanthorpe, U(rsula) A(skham) 1929–

English poet.

46 I wasn't good
At growing up. Never learned
The natives' art of life.
1984 'Growing Up'.

Farjeon, Eleanor 1881–1965

English children's writer. Her copious output comprises stories, poems, recountings, fables, saints' lives and prayers, and includes *Nursery Rhymes of London Town* (1916) and 'A Morning Song' (1957).

47 Morning has broken
Like the first morning,
Blackbird has spoken
Like the first bird.
Praise for the singing!
Praise for the morning!
Praise for them springing
Fresh from the Word!
1957 *Children's Bells*, 'A Morning Song'.

48 There's Carol like a rolling car,
And Martin like a flying bird,
And Adam like the Lord's First Word,
And Raymond like the Harvest Moon,
And Peter like a piper's tune,
And Alan like the flowing on
Of water. And there's John, like John.
1958 *Then There Were Three*, 'Boys' Names'.

Farjeon, Herbert 1887–1945

English actor, theatre manager and critic.

49 I've danced with a man, who's danced with a girl, who's danced with the Prince of Wales.
1927 *The Picnic*.

Farquhar, George c.1677–1707

Irish playwright, who turned to soldiering after an early career as an actor. His comic plays include *Love and a Bottle* (1698), *The Recruiting Officer* (1706) and, most famously, *The Beaux' Stratagem* (1707).

50 Poetry's a mere drug, Sir.
1698 *Love and a Bottle*, act 3, sc.2.

51 I hate all that don't love me, and slight all that do.
1699 *The Constant Couple*, act 1, sc.2.

52 Crimes, like virtues, are their own reward.
1702 *The Inconstant*, act 4, sc.2.

53 Hanging and marriage, you know, go by destiny.
1706 *The Recruiting Officer*, act 3, sc.2.

54 Sir, you shall taste my Anno Domini.
1707 *The Beaux' Stratagem*, act 1, sc.1.

55 I have fed purely upon ale; I have eat my ale, drank my ale, and I always sleep upon ale.
1707 *The Beaux' Stratagem*, act 1, sc.1.

56 There is no scandal like rags, nor any crime so shameful as poverty.
1707 *The Beaux' Stratagem*, act 1, sc.1.

57 Since a woman must wear chains, I would have the pleasure of hearing 'em rattle a little.
1707 *The Beaux' Stratagem*, act 2, sc.2.

58 No woman can be a beauty without a fortune.
1707 *The Beaux' Stratagem*, act 2, sc.2.

Farragut, David Glasgow 1801–70

US admiral. He served in the War of 1812 and had minor commands in the American–Mexican War before leading a Union fleet in the Civil War. He was the US navy's first vice-admiral (1864) and admiral (1866).

59 Damn the torpedoes! Full speed ahead.
1864 At the Battle of Mobile Bay, 5 Aug. Quoted in A T Mahan *Great Commanders: Admiral Farragut* (1892), ch.10.

Fassbinder, Rainer Werner 1946–82

German film director, who made over 40 films.

60 I hope to build a house with my films. Some of them are the cellar, some are the walls, and some are the windows. But I hope in time there will be a house.
Quoted in Leslie Halliwell *Halliwell's Filmgoer's Companion* (1993).

Faulkner, William Harrison 1897–1962

US novelist, known for his experiments in literary form and style and for his treatment of social and racial problems in the US South in a series of novels beginning with *Sartoris* (1929). He was awarded the Nobel prize for literature in 1949.

61 *Yes, he thought, between grief and nothing I will take grief.*
1939 Wilborne. *The Wild Palms*, 'Wild Palms', no.5.

62 No man can cause more grief than that one clinging blindly to the vices of his ancestors.
1948 *Intruder in the Dust*, ch.3.

63 He must teach himself that the basest of all things is to be afraid and, teaching himself that, forget it forever, leaving no room in his workshop for anything but the old verities and truths of the heart, the old universal truths lacking which any story is ephemeral and doomed—love and honour and pity and compassion and sacrifice.
1950 Nobel prize acceptance speech.

64 I believe man will not merely endure, he will prevail. He is immortal, not because he, alone among creatures, has an inexhaustible voice but because he has a soul, a spirit capable of compassion and sacrifice and endurance.
1950 Nobel prize acceptance speech.

65 Maybe the only thing worse than having to give gratitude constantly all the time, is having to accept it.
1951 *Requiem for a Nun*, act 2, sc.1.

66 Since his capacity to do is forced into channels of evil through environment and pressures, man is strong before he is moral. The world's anguish is caused by people between twenty and forty.
1956 Interview in *Paris Review*, Spring.

67 An artist is a creature driven by demons.
1956 Interview in *Paris Review*, Spring.

68 The writer's only responsibility is to his art. He will be completely ruthless if he is a good one.
1956 Interview in *Paris Review*, Spring.

69 If a writer has to rob his mother, he will not hesitate; the *Ode on a Grecian Urn* is worth any number of old ladies.
1956 Interview in *Paris Review*, Spring.

70 The aim of every artist is to arrest motion, which is life, by artificial means and hold it fixed so that a hundred years later, when a stranger looks at it, it moves again since it is life.
1956 Interview in *Paris Review*, Spring.

71 All of us failed to match our dreams of perfection. So I rate us on the basis of our splendid failure to do the impossible.
1956 On his generation of writers. Interview in *Paris Review*, Spring.

72 If I were reincarnated, I'd want to come back as a buzzard. Nothing hates him or envies him or wants him or needs him. He is never bothered or in danger, and he can eat anything.
1956 Interview in *Paris Review*, Spring.

73 Success is feminine and like a woman; if you cringe before her she will override you. So the way to treat her is to show her the back of your hand. Then maybe she will do the crawling.
1956 Interview in *Paris Review*, Spring.

74 No man can write who is not first a humanitarian.
1957 In *Time*, 25 Feb.

75 The last sound on the worthless earth will be two human beings trying to launch a homemade spaceship and already quarreling about where they are going next.
1959 Speech to UNESCO Commission, in the *New York Times*, 3 Oct.

76 But a man shouldn't fool with booze until he's fifty; then he's a damn fool if he doesn't.
Quoted in Webb and Wigfall Green *William Faulkner of Oxford* (1965).

Fauré, Gabriel Urbain 1845–1924

French composer. Director of the Conservatoire (1905–20), he is remembered chiefly for his songs and instrumental music, and for his *Requiem* (1887–90).

77 If that was music, I have never understood what music was.
1902 After attending the première of Debussy's *Pelléas et Mélisande*. Quoted in R Orledge *Gabriel Fauré* (1979).

Favre, Jules Claude Gabriel 1809–80

French lawyer and politician. He took part in the July Revolution (1830), becoming a Republican leader and, after the fall of Napoleon III, Foreign Minister. He negotiated the Treaty of Frankfurt (1871).

78 Not an inch of our territory or a stone of our fortresses.
1870 Reply to Bismarck's demands for concessions, 18 Sep, following France's defeat in the Franco-Prussian War. Quoted in A J P Taylor *The Struggle for Mastery in Europe 1848–1918* (1954), p.212.

Fawcett, Percy Harrison 1867–c.1925

English explorer. After military service he made several expeditions to Brazil (1906–25) in search of traces of ancient civilizations, disappearing with his son and a companion in the Mato Grosso region. Their fate is a mystery.

79 There, I believed, lay the greatest secrets of the past yet preserved in our world of today. I had come to the turn of the road; and for better or worse I chose the forest path.
1911 Of South America. Collected in Brian Fawcett (ed) *Exploration Fawcett* (1953).

80 You need have no fear of any failure.
1925 Last words written to his wife. Collected in Brian Fawcett (ed) *Exploration Fawcett* (1953).

Fawkes, Guy 1570–1606

English conspirator. He converted to Catholicism at an early age, and served in the Spanish army in the Netherlands (1593–1604). He was involved in the Gunpowder Plot, and was caught red-handed and hanged.

81 A desperate disease requires a dangerous remedy.
1605 When questioned after his arrest on 5 Nov.

Feibleman, Peter 1930–

US novelist, playwright and literary executor of Lillian Hellmann. His novels include *A Place Without Twilight* (1958) and *The Daughters of Necessity* (1959). With Lillian Hellmann he wrote *Eating Together* (1985).

82 The biggest difference between Lillian as a grown-up and Lillian as a child was that she was taller.
1988 On Lillian Hellman. *Lily*.

Feiffer, Jules 1929–

US cartoonist and writer. His early cartoons in *Village Voice* (1956) were followed by *Little Murders* (a black comedy, 1965), novels and screenplays, including *Carnal Knowledge* (1971). He currently writes and illustrates children's books.

83 I used to think I was poor. Then they told me I wasn't poor, I was needy. They told me it was self-defeating to think of myself as needy, I was deprived. Then they told me underprivileged was overused. I was disadvantaged. I still don't have a dime. But I have a great vocabulary.
1956 Cartoon caption.

84 As a matter of racial pride we want to be called *blacks*. Which has replaced the term *Afro-American*. Which replaced *Negroes*. Which replaced *colored people*. Which replaced *darkies*. Which replaced *blacks*.
Quoted in William Safire *Language Maven Strikes Again* (1990).

Feininger, Lyonel 1871–1956

US Cubist painter, also associated with the German painters of the Blaue Reiter.

85 Each individual work serves as an expression of our most personal state of mind at that particular moment and of the inescapable, imperative need for release by means of an appropriate act of creation: in the rhythm, form, colour and mood of a picture.
1917 Letter to Paul Westheim, quoted in Wolf-Dieter Dube *The Expressionists* (1972).

Fellini, Federico 1920–93

Italian film director. His most famous and controversial work, *La Dolce Vita* (1960, 'The Sweet Life'), was a cynical evocation of modern Roman high life.

86 I always direct the same film. I can't distinguish one from the other.
Quoted in Leslie Halliwell *Halliwell's Filmgoer's Companion* (1993).

Fenton, James 1949–

English satirical poet and critic, formerly a foreign correspondent. He was Professor of Poetry at Oxford (1994–9).

87 It is not what they built. It is what they knocked down.
It is not the houses. It is the spaces between the houses.
It is not the streets that exist. It is the streets that no longer exist.
It is not your memories which haunt you.
It is not what you have written down.
It is what you have forgotten, what you must forget.
What you must go on forgetting all your life.
1981 'A German Requiem'.

88 And I'm afraid, reading this passage now,
That everything I knew has been destroyed
By those whom I admired but never knew;
The laughing soldiers fought to their defeat
And I'm afraid most of my friends are dead.
1982 'In a Notebook'.

89 Oh let us not be condemned for what we are.
It is enough to account for what we do.
1983 'Children in Exile'.

90 English poetry begins whenever we decide to say the modern English language begins, and it extends as far as we decide to say that the English language extends.
2002 *An Introduction to English Poetry.*

Fenwick, Millicent Hammond 1910–93

US politician and diplomat, congresswoman from New Jersey (1975–83). She compiled the *Vogue Book of Etiquette* (1948).

91 The gentle and respectful ways of saying 'To hell with you' are being abandoned.
Recalled on her death, 16 Sep 1993.

Ferber, Edna 1887–1968

US writer. She wrote a number of novels and short stories, and is remembered as the writer of *Show Boat* (1926), which inspired the successful musical.

92 Mother Knows Best.
1923 Title of story.

93 I am not belittling the brave pioneer men but the sunbonnet as well as the sombrero has helped to settle this glorious land of ours.
1929 *Cimarron*, ch.23.

94 America—rather, the United States—seems to me to be the Jew among the nations. It is resourceful, adaptable, maligned, envied, feared, imposed upon. It is warm-hearted, overfriendly; quick-witted, lavish, colorful; given to extravagant speech and gestures; its people are travellers and wanderers by nature, moving, shifting, restless; swarming in Fords, in ocean liners; craving entertainment; volatile.
1939 *A Peculiar Treasure*, ch.1.

95 It was part of the Texas ritual… We know about champagne and caviar but we talk hog and hominy.
1952 *Giant*, ch.2.

96 A woman can look both moral and exciting—if she also looks as if it was quite a struggle.
1954 In *Reader's Digest*, Dec.

97 Science had married the wilderness and was taming the savage shrew.
1958 Of Alaska. *Ice Palace.*

98 Being an old maid is like death by drowning, a really delightful sensation after you cease to struggle.
Quoted in 'Completing the Circle', in R E Drennan *Wit's End* (1973).

99 Dinner parties are for eating, not mating.
Reminder to hostesses who only invite people in pairs. In the *New York Times*, 25 Sep 1984.

Ferdinand I 1503–64

Holy Roman Emperor from 1558, heir to his elder brother, Charles V, whom he joined in battling against Ottoman incursions. He was mainly responsible for the compromise at Augsburg (1555) which ended the religious wars.

1 *Fiat justitia et pereat mundus.*
Let justice be done, though the world may perish.
Motto.
➤ *See Watson 891:1.*

Ferguson, Sir Alex 1941–

Scottish football manager. In 1999 he led Manchester United to the treble (the League Championship, FA Cup and European Championship).

2 Never use sarcasm on players. It doesn't work.
2002 In the *Observer*, 19 May.

Ferguson, Niall 1964–

Scottish historian.

3 It is of course a truth universally acknowledged that large overseas military commitments cannot be sustained without even larger economic resources.
2004 *Colossus: The Rise and Fall of the American Empire.*

4 The United States today is an empire—but a peculiar kind of empire. It is vastly wealthy. It is militarily peerless. It has astonishing cultural reach. Yet by comparison with other empires it often struggles to impose its will beyond its shores.
2004 *Colossus: The Rise and Fall of the American Empire.*

Ferguson, Sir Samuel 1810–86

Irish poet and Celtic scholar, president of the Royal Irish Academy and a key figure in the study of early Irish art. His spirited poetry draws on Irish myth.

5 Wider comprehensions, deeper insights to the dead belong:—
Since for Love thou wakest not, sleeper, yet awake for sake of Song!
c.1864 'The Tain-Quest'.

Fergusson, Robert 1750–74

Scottish poet, much admired by Burns. He wrote primarily of Edinburgh life and died in its lunatic asylum aged 24.

6 For thof ye had as wise a snout on
As Shakespeare or Sir Isaac Newton,
Your judgement fouk wou'd hae a doubt on,
I'll tak my aith,
Till they cou'd see ye wi' a suit on
O' gude Braid Claith.
1772 'Braid Claith', stanza 9.

7 Wanwordy, crazy, dinsome thing,
As e'er was fram'd to jow or ring,
What gar'd them sic in steeple hing
They ken themsel',

But weel wat I they coudna bring
Waur sounds frae hell.
1772 'To the Tron-Kirk Bell', stanza 1.

8 Auld Reikie! wale o' ilka town
That Scotland kens beneath the moon;
Whare couthy chiels at e'ening meet
Their bizzing craigs and mous to weet.
1773 'Auld Reikie, A Poem'.

9 Now gae your wa's—Tho' anes as gude
As ever happit flesh and blude,
Yet part we maun—the case sae hard is,
Amang the writers and the bardies
That lang they'll brook the auld I trow,
Or neibours cry, 'Weel brook the new'.
1773 'To My Auld Breeks'.

Ferlinghetti, Lawrence 1919–

US poet and publisher. A member of the Beat Generation of poets, he founded the important radical bookstore and publishing house, City Lights, in San Francisco.

10 A Coney Island of the Mind.
1958 Title of book.

11 the poet like an acrobat
climbs on rime
to a high wire of his own making.
1958 'A Coney Island of the Mind', section 15.

12 I have a feeling I'm falling
on rare occasions
but most of the time I have my feet on the ground
I can't help it if the ground itself is falling.
1973 'Mock Confessional'.

13 For even bad poetry has relevance
for what it does not say
for what it leaves out.
1988 'Uses of Poetry'.

14 As I get older I perceive
Life has its tail in its mouth.
1988 'Poet as Fisherman'.

Fermat, Pierre de 1601–65

French lawyer, mathematician and founder of number theory. A great deal of his fame stems from Fermat's Last Theorem.

15 To divide a cube into two other cubes, a fourth power or in general any power whatever into two powers of the same denomination above the second is impossible, and I have assuredly found an admirable proof of this, but the margin is too narrow to contain it.
Scribbled note in the margins of his copy of Diophantus's *Arithmetica*. He did not live to provide the promised proof, and the conjecture became famous as Fermat's Last Theorem. In 1993 Andrew Wiles, a British mathematician, claimed to have discovered the proof.

Fermi, Enrico 1901–54

Italian-born US physicist, discoverer of the element neptunium and winner of the 1938 Nobel prize. In 1942 he created the first self-sustaining chain reaction in uranium, which led to the atomic bomb.

16 Whatever Nature has in store for mankind, unpleasant as it may be, men must accept, for ignorance is never better than knowledge.
Quoted in Laura Fermi *Atoms in the Family* (1954).

Fern, Fanny *née Willis* 1811–72

US writer, whose witty sketches were collected in *Fern Leaves from Fanny's Portfolio* (1853). When he made his famous attack on women writers, Nathaniel Hawthorne was careful to exempt her.

17 Well, it is a humiliating reflection, that the straightest road to a man's heart is through his palate.
1854 *Fern Leaves from Fanny's Portfolio, Second Series*, 'Hungry Husbands'. Often quoted as 'The way to a man's heart is through his stomach.'

Fernández, Macedonio 1874–1952

Argentinian philosopher, poet and novelist. He lived a secluded life, reluctant to publish his manuscripts. His philosophical postulates anticipate the work of later writers such as Borges and Bioy Casares.

18 *Todo se ha escrito, todo se ha dicho, todo se ha hecho, oyó Dios que le decían y aún no había creado el mundo, todavía no había nada. También eso ya me lo han dicho, repuso quizá desde la vieja, hendida Nada. Y comenzó.*
Everything has been written, everything has been said, everything has been made: that's what God heard before creating the world, when there was nothing yet. I have also heard that one, he may have answered from the old, split Nothingness. And then he began.
1967 *Museo de la novela de la Eterna* ('The Museum of Eternity's Novel'), 'Prólogo a la eternidad'.

Ferré, Rosario 1943–

Puerto Rican novelist and critic, who has lived and taught in both Puerto Rico and the US.

19 *Dios sólo nos tiene aquí prestados, en este valle de lágrimas no estamos más que de paso. Si llegara algún día a pensar que ha perdido a su hija para el mundo de los hombres, la habrá ganado para el de los ángeles.*
God has us here only on loan, we are transitory in this vale of tears. If you ever come to think that you have lost your daughter to the world of men, think also that you have given her to that of the angels.
1976 *La Bella Durmiente* ('Sleeping Beauty').

Ferrier, Kathleen 1912–53

English contralto. The range and richness of her voice, together with her remarkable technical control, rapidly won her a great reputation until her early death from cancer.

20 Now I'll have eine kleine pause.
1953 Last words. Quoted in Gerald Moore *Am I Too Loud?* (1962).

Feuerbach, Ludwig 1804–72

German philosopher, famous for his interpretation of Christian doctrine in secular terms and for its adaptation by Karl Marx.

21 While Socrates empties the cup of poison with unshaken soul, Christ exclaims, 'If it is possible, let this cup pass from me'. Christ in this respect is the self-confession of human sensibility.
1841 *Das Wesen des Christentums* (translated by MaryAnn Evans (George Eliot) as *The Essence of Christianity*, 1854).

22 The power of miracle is the power of imagination.

1841 *Das Wesen des Christentums* (translated by MaryAnn Evans (George Eliot) as *The Essence of Christianity*, 1854).

23 *Der Mensch ist, was er isst.*
Man is what he eats.
Quoted in Jacob Moleschott *Lehre der Nahrungsmittel: Für das Volk* (1850).

Feynman, Richard P(hillips) 1918–88

US physicist who shared (1965) the Nobel prize in physics for his work on quantum electrodynamics.

24 We have a habit in writing articles published in scientific journals to make the work as finished as possible, to cover up all the tracks, to not worry about the blind alleys or describe how you had the wrong idea first, and so on. So there isn't any place to publish, in a dignified manner, what you actually did in order to do the work.
1966 Nobel lecture.

25 You know how it always is, every new idea, it takes a generation or two until it becomes obvious that there's no real problem. I cannot define the real problem, therefore I suspect there's no real problem, but I'm not sure there's no real problem.
1982 Explaining his feelings on quantum mechanics. In the *International Journal of Theoretical Physics*, vol.21.

26 If I could explain it to the average person, I wouldn't have been worth the Nobel prize.
1985 In *People Magazine*, 22 Jul.

27 For a successful technology, reality must take precedence over public relations, for nature cannot be fooled.
1988 *What Do YOU Care What Other People Think?*

Fiedler, Leslie A(aron) 1917–92

US critic and novelist. His reputation rests on his influential and often controversial books on US 'literary anthropology', of which *Love and Death in the American Novel* (1960) is the best known.

28 Come Back To The Raft Again, Huck Honey!
1955 Title of essay on the repressed homoerotic undercurrent in US writing.

29 To be an American (unlike being English or French or whatever) is precisely to *imagine* a destiny rather than to inherit one; since we have always been, insofar as we are Americans at all, inhabitants of myth rather than history.
1969 'Cross the Border—Close the Gap', in *Playboy*, Dec.

Field, Barron 1786–1846

Australian jurist, born in London. He went to Sydney in 1817 as Judge of the New South Wales Supreme Court and published the first collection of Australian verse, *First Fruits of Australian Poetry* (1819).

30 Kangaroo, Kangaroo!
Thou Spirit of Australia,
That redeems from utter failure,
From perfect desolation,
And warrants the creation
Of this fifth part of the Earth.
1819 *First Fruits of Australian Poetry*, 'The Kangaroo'.

Field, Eugene 1850–95

US writer and theatre critic. A columnist for the *Chicago Morning News*, he achieved a reputation as a humorist and poet with his column 'Sharps and Flats'. He also published several books of children's verse.

31 Mr Creston Clarke played King Lear at the Tabor Grand last night. All through five acts of Shakespeare's tragedy he played the king as though under momentary apprehension that someone else was about to play the ace.
c.1880 Attributed review in the *Denver Post*.

32 Wynken, Blynken, and Nod one night
Sailed off in a wooden shoe—
Sailed on a river of crystal light,
Into a sea of dew.
1889 'Wynken, Blynken, and Nod'.

33 I never lost a little fish. Yes, I am free to say.
It always was the biggest fish I caught that got away.
Attributed.

Field, Frank 1942–

English Labour politician. Director of the Child Poverty Action Group (1969–79) and the Low Pay Unit (1974–80), he became an MP in 1979 and has campaigned strenuously for social justice.

34 The House of Lords is a model of how to care for the elderly.
1981 In the *Observer*, 24 May.

Fielding, Henry 1707–54

English novelist and playwright. After the introduction of the Theatrical Licensing Act in 1737 he turned to fiction, with works such as *The Adventures of Joseph Andrews* (1742), *Tom Jones* (1749) and *Amelia* (1751). He died in Lisbon.

35 Love and scandal are the best sweeteners of tea.
1728 *Love in Several Masques*, act 4, sc.11.

36 Map me no maps, sir, my head is a map, a map of the whole world.
1730 *Rape upon Rape*, act 2, sc.5.

37 Oh! The roast beef of England,
And old England's roast beef!
1731 *Grub Street Opera*, act 3, sc.3.

38 All Nature wears one universal grin.
1731 *Tom Thumb the Great*, act 1, sc.1.

39 I am as sober as a Judge.
1734 *Don Quixote in England*, act 3, sc.14.

40 He in a few minutes ravished this fair creature, or at least would have ravished her, if she had not, by a timely compliance, prevented him.
1743 *Jonathan Wild*, bk.3, ch.7.

41 Thwackum was for doing justice, and leaving mercy to heaven.
1749 *Tom Jones*, bk.3, ch.10.

42 What is commonly called love, namely the desire of satisfying a voracious appetite with a certain quantity of delicate white human flesh.
1749 *Tom Jones*, bk.6, ch.1.

43 His designs were strictly honourable, as the phrase is; that is, to rob a lady of her fortune by way of marriage.
1749 *Tom Jones*, bk.11, ch.4.

44 It hath been often said, that it is not death, but dying, which is terrible.
1751 *Amelia*, bk.3, ch.4.

45 One fool at least in every married couple.
1751 *Amelia*, bk.9, ch.4.

Fields, Dorothy 1905–74

US author and lyricist, daughter of comedian Lew Fields. She wrote the books and lyrics for many Broadway shows and films, often with Jimmy McHugh or Jerome Kern.

46 Grab your coat, and get your hat,
Leave your worry on the doorstep,
Just direct your feet
To the sunny side of the street.
1930 'On the Sunny Side of the Street'.

47 I might as well play bridge with my old maid aunts
I haven't got a chance
This is a fine romance.
1934 'A Fine Romance', song featured in the film *Swing Time* (music by Jerome Kern).

Fields, W C *originally* *William Claude Dukenfield* 1880–1946

US comedian. He wrote and performed in several classic comedies including *The Bank Dick* (1940), *My Little Chickadee* (1940) and *Never Give a Sucker an Even Break* (1940).

48 It ain't a fit night out for man or beast.
1932 *The Fatal Glass of Beer*.

49 Women are like elephants to me. I like to look at them, but I wouldn't want to own one.
1935 *Mississippi*.

50 Egbert, is it true that married people live longer?
No, it just seems longer.
1940 *The Bank Dick*.

51 Never Give a Sucker an Even Break.
1941 Title of film, but an earlier catchphrase of Fields's that may have originated in the 1923 film *Poppy*.

52 I was in love with a beautiful blonde once, dear. She drove me to drink. That's the one thing I'm indebted to her for.
1941 *Never Give a Sucker an Even Break*.

53 Anybody who hates children and dogs can't be all bad.
Attributed.

54 Fish fuck in it.
Attributed, his reason for not drinking water.

Fiennes, Sir Ranulph 1944–

English explorer.

55 To write about hell it helps if you have been there.
2004 *Captain Scott*.

Fierstein, Harvey Forbes 1954–

US playwright and actor. He began as a female impersonator and acts on stage and screen. He has won awards for the semi-autobiographical *Torch Song Trilogy* (produced 1982) and for the book of the Broadway musical *La Cage Aux Folles* (1983).

56 I assume everyone is gay, unless told otherwise.
1994 In *Life*, Jan.

50 Cent *originally* *Curtis Jackson* 1976–

US rapper.

57 Where I grew up if you have two parents you're spoilt.
2003 In the *Sunday Times*, 15 Jun.

Findley, Timothy 1931–2002

Canadian writer and actor. His novels include *The Wars* (1977), *The Piano Man's Daughter* (1995) and *Pilgrim* (1999).

58 He did the thing that no one else would even dare to think of doing. And that to me's as good a definition of a 'hero' as you'll get. Even when the thing that's done is something of which you disapprove.
1977 Juliet D'Orsey. *The Wars*, pt.1, section 3.

59 Dead men are serious.
1977 *The Wars*, pt.1, section 20.

60 Any man whose love of horses is stronger than his fear of being an absurdity is all right with me.
1977 Rodwell. *The Wars*, pt.2, section 8.

Firbank, (Arthur Annesley) Ronald 1886–1926

English novelist. Solitary and somewhat eccentric, he wrote slight but witty and innovative novels. His works include *Valmouth* (1919) and *Prancing Nigger* (1924).

61 There was a pause—just long enough for an angel to pass, flying slowly.
1915 *Vainglory*, ch.6.

62 The world is disgracefully managed, one hardly knows to whom to complain.
1915 *Vainglory*, ch.10.

63 All millionaires love a baked apple.
1915 *Vainglory*, ch.13.

64 She stands, I fear, poor thing, now, for something younger than she looks.
1919 *Valmouth*, ch.1.

65 'I know of no joy,' she airily began, 'greater than a cool white dress after the sweetness of confession.'
1919 *Valmouth*, ch.4.

66 There was really no joy in pouring out one's sins while he sat assiduously picking his nose.
1919 *Valmouth*, ch.6.

67 His Weariness the Prince entered the room in all his tinted orders.
1923 *The Flower Beneath the Foot*, ch.1.

68 'O! help me heaven,' she prayed, 'to be decorative and to do right!'
1923 *The Flower Beneath the Foot*, ch.2.

69 Beneath the strain of expectation even the little iced sugar cakes upon the tea-table looked green with worry.
1923 *The Flower Beneath the Foot*, ch.3.

70 Looking back, I remember the average curate at home as something between a eunuch and a snigger.
1923 *The Flower Beneath the Foot*, ch.4.

71 'Basta!' his master replied with all the brilliant glibness of the Berlitz-school.
1923 *The Flower Beneath the Foot*, ch.5.

72 She looks at other women as if she would inhale them.
1923 *The Flower Beneath the Foot*, ch.5.

73 'I've never travelled,' Dona Consolation blandly confessed, 'but I dare say, dear, you can't judge Egypt by Aïda.'
1926 *Concerning the Eccentricities of Cardinal Pirelli*, ch.9.

Fish, Michael 1944–

English weather forecaster.

74 A woman rang to say she heard there was a hurricane on the way. Well don't worry, there isn't.
1987 Television weather forecast prior to severe gales in southern England, 15 Oct.

Fisher (of Lambeth), Geoffrey Francis Fisher, Baron 1887–1972

English prelate and Archbishop of Canterbury (1945–61). He officiated at the coronation of Elizabeth II in Westminster Abbey (1953).

75 The long and distressing controversy over capital punishment is very unfair to anyone meditating murder.
1957 In the *Sunday Times*, 24 Feb.

Fisher, H(erbert) A(lbert) L(aurens) 1865–1940

English historian. As Education Minister (1916–22) he sponsored the Fisher Act (1918). He wrote on Napoleon, and is best known for his *History of Europe* (1936).

76 Men wiser and more learned than I have discerned in history a plot, a rhythm, a predetermined pattern. Those harmonies are concealed from me. I can see only one emergency following upon another, as wave follows upon wave; only one real fact with respect to which, since it is unique, there can be no generalizations. Only one safe rule for the historian: that he should recognize in the development of human destinies the play of the contingent and the unforeseen.
1936 *History of Europe*, introduction.

77 Purity of race does not exist. Europe is a continent of energetic mongrels.
1936 *History of Europe*, ch.1.

Fisher, M(ary) F(rances) K(ennedy) 1908–92

US cookery writer.

78 Sharing food with another human being is an intimate act that should not be indulged in lightly.
1949 *An Alphabet for Gourmets*, 'A Is for Dining Alone'.

79 In America we eat, collectively, with a glum urge for food to fill us. We are ignorant of flavor. We are as a nation taste-blind.
1976 *The Art of Eating*.

Fiske, John 1842–1901

US historian, tutor and librarian at Harvard. He wrote many popular books on US history, Spencerian philosophy and Darwinism.

80 The element of chance...is expelled. Nobody would now waste his time in theorizing about a fortuitous concourse of atoms. We have so far spelled out the history of creation as to see that all has been done in strict accordance with law. The method has been the method of evolution, and the more we study it the more do we discern in it intelligible coherence.
1900 *Through Nature to God*.

Fitt, Gerry (Gerard) Fitt, Baron 1926–

Northern Ireland politician.

81 The people have spoken and the politicians have had to listen.
1998 In the *Sunday Telegraph*, 24 May.

Fitzgerald, Edward 1809–83

English scholar, poet and translator, a friend of Thackeray, Carlisle and Tennyson. His translation of the *Rubáiyát of Omar Khayyám* was first published anonymously in 1859.

82 Awake! for Morning in the bowl of night
Has flung the stone that puts the stars to flight:
And Lo! the Hunter of the East has caught
The Sultan's turret in a noose of light.
1859 *The Rubáiyát of Omar Khayyám of Naishapur*, stanza 1.

83 Here with a loaf of bread beneath the bough,
A flask of wine, a book of verse—and Thou
Beside me singing in the wilderness—
And wilderness is paradise enow.
1859 *The Rubáiyát of Omar Khayyám of Naishapur*, stanza 12. In the 1879 edn this was changed to 'A Book of Verses underneath the Bough, / A Jug of Wine, a loaf of Bread—and Thou / Beside me singing in the Wilderness— / Oh, Wilderness were Paradise enow!'

84 The moving finger writes; and, having writ,
Moves on: nor all thy piety nor wit
Shall lure it back to cancel half a line,
Nor all thy tears wash out a word of it.
1859 *The Rubáiyát of Omar Khayyám of Naishapur*, stanza 51.

85 Drink! for you know not whence you came, nor why:
Drink! for you know not why you go nor where.
1859 *The Rubáiyát of Omar Khayyám of Naishapur*, stanza 74.

86 And when Thyself with shining foot shall pass
Among the guests star-scattered on the grass,
And in thy joyous errand reach the spot
Where I made one—turn down an empty glass!
1859 *The Rubáiyát of Omar Khayyám of Naishapur*, stanza 75. In the 1879 edition this was changed to 'And when like her, O Saki, you shall pass...'.

Fitzgerald, F(rancis) Scott Key 1896–1940

US novelist who epitomized the Jazz Age in his best-known book, *The Great Gatsby* (1925). He wrote about US expatriates in *Tender is the Night* (1934).

87 At eighteen our convictions are hills from which we look; at forty-five they are caves in which we hide.
1920 'Bernice Bobs Her Hair', in the *Saturday Evening Post*, 1 May.

88 The wise writer, I think, writes for the youth of his own generation, the critics of the next, and the schoolmasters of ever afterward.
1920 Interview in the *New York Tribune*, 7 May.

89 She had once been a Catholic, but discovering that priests were infinitely more attentive when she was in process of losing or regaining faith in Mother Church, she maintained an enchantingly wavering attitude.
1921 Of Beatrice Blaine. *This Side of Paradise*, bk.1, ch.1.

90 If I start to hold somebody's hand they laugh at me, and *let* me, just as if it wasn't part of them. As soon as I get hold of a hand they sort of disconnect it from the rest of them.
1921 *This Side of Paradise*, bk.1, ch.1.

91 The Beautiful and the Damned.
1922 Title of novel.

92 Personality is an unbroken series of successful gestures.
1925 *The Great Gatsby*, ch.1.

93 One of those men who reach such an acute limited excellence at twenty-one that everything afterward savors of anti-climax.
1925 Of Tom Buchanan. *The Great Gatsby*, ch.1.

94 In his blue gardens, men and girls came and went like moths among the whisperings and the champagne and the stars.
1925 *The Great Gatsby*, ch.3.

95 Everyone suspects himself of at least one of the cardinal virtues, and this is mine: I am one of the few honest people that I have ever known.
1925 Nick Carraway, the narrator. *The Great Gatsby*, ch.3.

96 There are only the pursued, the pursuing, the busy, and the tired.
1925 *The Great Gatsby*, ch.4.

97 Reach me a rose, honey, and pour me a last drop into that there crystal glass.
1925 *The Great Gatsby*, ch.4.

98 Her voice is full of money.
1925 *The Great Gatsby*, ch.7.

99 They were careless people, Tom and Daisy—they smashed up things and creatures and then retreated back into their money or their vast carelessness, or whatever it was that kept them together, and let other people clean up the mess they had made.
1925 *The Great Gatsby*, ch.9.

1 And as the moon rose higher the unessential houses began to melt away until gradually I became aware of the old island here that flowered once for Dutch sailors' eyes—a fresh, green breast of the new world... For a transitory enchanted moment man must have held his breath in the presence of this continent, compelled into an aesthetic contemplation he neither understood nor desired, face to face for the last time in history with something commensurate to his capacity for wonder.
1925 *The Great Gatsby*, ch.9.

2 Gatsby believed in the green light, the orgiastic future that year by year recedes before us. It eluded us then, but that's no matter—to-morrow we will run faster, stretch out our arms further... And one fine morning... So we beat on, boats against the current, borne back ceaselessly into the past.
1925 *The Great Gatsby*, ch.9.

3 Let me tell you about the very rich. They are different from you and me.
1926 *All the Sad Young Men*, 'The Rich Boy'. Hemingway published an ironic rejoinder in 'The Snows of Kilimanjaro': 'Yes, they have more money'.
➥ *See Hemingway 394:12.*

4 Though the Jazz Age continued, it became less and less of an affair of youth. The sequel was like a children's party taken over by the elders.
1931 'Echoes of the Jazz Age', *Scribner's Magazine*, Nov.

5 Mostly, we authors repeat ourselves—that's the truth.
1933 'One Hundred False Starts', in the *Saturday Evening Post*, 4 Mar.

6 Tender is the Night.
1934 Title of novel.

7 When people are taken out of their depths they lose their heads, no matter how charming a bluff they may put up.
1934 *Tender is the Night*, bk.3, ch.12.

8 The test of a first-rate intelligence is the ability to hold two opposed ideas in the mind at the same time, and still retain the ability to function.
1936 'The Crack-Up', in *Esquire*, Feb.

9 In a real dark night of the soul, it is always three o'clock in the morning, day after day.
1936 'Handle With Care', in *Esquire*, Mar.

10 Often I think writing is a sheer paring away of oneself leaving always something thinner, barer, more meagre.
1940 Letter, 27 Apr.

11 The faces of most American women over thirty are relief maps of petulant and bewildered unhappiness.
1940 Letter, 5 Oct.

12 It's not a slam at *you* when people are rude—it's a slam at the people they've met before.
1941 *The Last Tycoon*, ch.1.

13 No grand idea was ever born in a conference, but a lot of foolish ideas have died there.
Note Books, E, in Edmund Wilson (ed) *The Crack-Up* (1945).

14 Show me a hero and I will write you a tragedy.
Note Books, E, in Edmund Wilson (ed) *The Crack-Up* (1945).

15 Great art is the contempt of a great man for small art.
Note Books, L, in Edmund Wilson (ed) *The Crack-Up* (1945).

16 When the first-rate author wants an exquisite heroine or a lovely morning, he finds that all the superlatives have been worn shoddy by his inferiors. It should be a rule that bad writers must start with plain heroines and ordinary mornings, and, if they are able, work up to something better.
Note Books, L, in Edmund Wilson (ed) *The Crack-Up* (1945).

Fitzgerald, Penelope Mary 1916–2000

English novelist and biographer. She won the Booker Prize in 1979 for *Offshore*.

17 Patience is passive, resignation is active.
1986 *Innocence*.

18 A human being is old when he has survived long enough to name, with absolute confidence, a year, one of the next thirty, which he won't be there to see.
A House of Air—Selected Writings, 'Last Words' (2003).

19 Twice in your life you know that you are approved of by everyone: when you learn to walk, and when you learn to read.
A House of Air—Selected Writings, 'Schooldays' (2003).

Flanagan, Bud *stage name of* Robert Winthrop 1896–1968

English comedian. He was immensely popular both as one of the Crazy Gang of comedians and in a duo with Chesney Allen.

20 Underneath the Arches,
I dream my dreams away,
Underneath the Arches,
On cobble-stones I lay.
1932 'Underneath the Arches' (song).

21 No dog can go as fast as the money you bet on him.
Quoted in Colin Jarman *The Guinness Dictionary of Sports Quotations* (1990).

Flanders, Michael and Swann, Donald 1922–75, 1923–94

English songwriting team, who made their name with *At the Drop of a Hat* (1956).

22 Mud! Mud! Glorious mud!
Nothing quite like it for cooling the blood.
So follow me, follow,
Down to the hollow,
And there let us wallow
In glorious mud.
1952 'The Hippopotamus'.

23 Eating people is wrong!
1956 'The Reluctant Cannibal'. Malcolm Bradbury took the phrase as the title of his 1959 novel.

24 Ma's out, Pa's out—let's talk rude:
Pee, po, belly, bum, drawers.
c.1956 'P, P, B, B, D'.

25 The English, the English, the English are best!
I wouldn't give tuppence for all of the rest!
1963 'Song of Patriotic Prejudice'.

Flaubert, Anne Justine Caroline 1793–1872

Mother of Gustave Flaubert.

26 Your mania for sentences has dried up your heart.
To her son. Quoted in D J Enright *A Mania for Sentences* (1983), p.101.

Flaubert, Gustave 1821–80

French novelist, master of the realistic novel. He studied law at Paris before turning to writing. His works include *Madame Bovary* (1857) and *Trois contes* (1877). He intended to include a *Dictionnaire des idées reçues* in the second volume of *Bouvard et Pécuchet*.

27 *Je suis autant Chinois que Français.*
I am as much Chinese as French.
1846 Letter to Mme Louise Colet, 8 Aug.

28 *L'Idée seule est éternelle et nécessaire.*
The idea alone is eternal and necessary.
1846 Letter to Mme Louise Colet, 9 Aug.

29 *Il ne faut pas toujours croire que le sentiment soit tout. Dans les arts, il n'est rien sans la forme.*
You must not think that feeling is everything. Art is nothing without form.
1846 Letter to Mme Louise Colet, 12 Aug.

30 *On fait de la critique quand on ne peut pas faire de l'art, de même qu'on se met mouchard quand on ne peut pas être soldat.*
Someone is a critic when he cannot be an artist in the same way that a man becomes an informer when he cannot be a soldier.
1846 Letter to Mme Louise Colet, 22 Oct.

31 *Les oeuvres les plus belles sont celles où il y a le moins de matière; plus l'expression se rapproche de la pensée, plus le mot colle dessus et disparaît, plus c'est beau. Je crois que l'avenir de l'art est dans ces voies.*
The most beautiful works are those that have the least content; the closer the expression is to the thought, the more indistinguishable the word from the content, the more beautiful is the work. I believe that the future of art lies in this direction.
1852 Letter to Mme Louise Colet, 16 Jan.

32 *La courtisane est un mythe. Jamais une femme n'a inventé une débauche.*
The courtesan is a myth. No woman has ever invented any new sensual pleasure.
1852 Letter to Mme Louise Colet, Aug.

33 *L'amour, croyait-elle, devait arriver tout à coup, avec de grands éclats et des fulgurations.*
She believed that love should appear instantaneously, with the brilliance of a lightning storm.
1857 *Madame Bovary*, pt.1, ch.8.

34 *La parole humaine est comme un chaudron fêlé où nous battons des mélodies à faire danser les ours, quand on voudrait attendrir les étoiles.*
Human speech is like a cracked kettle on which we beat out tunes for bears to dance to, when all the time we are longing to move the stars to pity.
1857 *Madame Bovary*, pt.1, ch.12.

35 *Le charme de la nouveauté, peu à peu tombant comme un vêtement, laissait voir à nu l'éternelle monotonie de la passion, qui a toujours les mêmes formes et le même langage.*
The charm of novelty, falling little by little like a robe, revealed the eternal monotony of passion, which has always the same forms and the same language.
1857 *Madame Bovary*, pt.2, ch.12.

36 *Il faut écrire pour soi, avant tout. C'est la seule chance de faire beau.*
It is necessary to write for oneself, above all. It is the only hope of creating something beautiful.
1858 Letter to Mlle Leroyer de Chantepie, 11 Jul.

37 *Un romancier, selon moi, n'a pas le droit de dire son avis sur les choses de ce monde. Il doit, dans sa vocation, imiter Dieu dans la sienne, c'est-à-dire faire et se taire.*
A novelist, in my opinion, does not have the right to give advice on the affairs of the world. He must, in his occupation, imitate God in His; that is to say, create and keep quiet.
1866 Letter to Mlle Bosquet.

38 *Axiome: la haine du bourgeois est le commencement de la vertu.*
Axiom: Hatred of the bourgeois is the beginning of wisdom.
1867 Letter to George Sand, 10 May.

39 *Il tournait dans son désir, comme un prisonnier dans son cachot.*
He was circling in his desire, like a prisoner in his dungeon.
1869 *L'Education sentimentale*, pt.1, ch.5.

40 My kingdom is as wide as the universe and my wants have no limits. I go forward always, freeing spirits and weighing words, without fear, without compassion, without love, without God. I am called science.
1874 *The Temptation of St Antony.*

41 *Antiquité. —en tout ce qui s'y rapporte: Est poncif, embêtant! etc.*
Antiquity. And everything to do with it, clichéd and boring.
Bouvard et Pécuchet avec un choix des scénarios, du Sottisier, L'Album de la Marquise et Le Dictionnaire des idées reçues. (published 1881, translated by Geoffrey Wall, 1994).

42 *Homère. Célèbre par sa façon de rire: rire homérique. N'a jamais existé.*
Homer. Famous for his laugh. 'Homeric laughter'. Never existed.
Bouvard et Pécuchet avec un choix des scénarios, du Sottisier, L'Album de la Marquise et Le Dictionnaire des idées reçues. (published 1881, translated by Geoffrey Wall, 1994).

43 *Latin. Langage naturel de l'homme. Gâte l'écriture. Est seulement utile pour comprendre les inscriptions des fontaines publiques. Il faut se méfier des citations en Latin; elles cachent toujours quelque chose de leste.*
Latin. Man's natural language. Spoils your style. Useful only for reading the inscriptions on public fountains. Beware of quotations in Latin: they always conceal something improper.
Bouvard et Pécuchet avec un choix des scénarios, du Sottisier, L'Album de la Marquise et Le Dictionnaire des idées reçues. (published 1881, translated by Geoffrey Wall, 1994).

Flecker, James Elroy 1884–1915

English poet. He studied Oriental languages and joined the consular service, symptoms of a fascination with the East which is reflected in much of his verse.

44 O friend unseen, unborn, unknown,
Student of our sweet English tongue,
Read out my words at night, alone:
I was a poet, I was young.
1910 'To a Poet a Thousand Years Hence'.

45 We who with songs beguile your pilgrimage
And swear that Beauty lives though lilies die,
We Poets of the proud old lineage
Who sing to find your hearts, we know not why—
What shall we tell you? Tales, marvellous tales
Of ships and stars and isles where good men rest.
1913 'The Golden Journey to Samarkand', epilogue.

46 For lust of knowing what should not be known,
We take the Golden Road to Samarkand.
1913 'The Golden Journey to Samarkand', epilogue.

47 How splendid in the morning glows the lily; with what grace he throws
His supplication to the rose.
1913 'Yasmin'.

48 The dragon-green, the luminous, the dark, the serpent-haunted sea.
1913 'The Gates of Damascus'.

49 For pines are gossip pines the wide world through
And full of runic tales to sigh or sing.
1913 'Brumana'.

50 Half to forget the wandering and pain,
Half to remember days that have gone by,
And dream and dream that I am home again!
1913 'Brumana'.

51 West of these out to seas colder than the Hebrides
I must go
Where the fleet of stars is anchored and the young
Star captains glow.
1913 'The Dying Patriot'.

52 A ship, an isle, a sickle moon—
With few but with how splendid stars
The mirrors of the sea are strewn
Between their silver bars!
1913 'A Ship, an Isle, a Sickle Moon'.

53 I have seen old ships sail like swans asleep.
1915 'The Old Ships'.

Fleming, Ian Lancaster 1908–64

English novelist. He is best known for his creation of the hugely popular secret service agent, James Bond.

54 Live and Let Die.
1954 Title of novel.

55 From Russia with Love.
1957 Title of novel.

56 I would like a medium Vodka dry Martini—with a slice of lemon peel. Shaken and not stirred, please. I would prefer Russian or Polish vodka.
1958 *Dr No*, ch.14.

Fleming, Marjory 1803–11

Scottish child writer, the subject of an essay by Dr John Brown which popularized her image as 'Pet Marjorie' and invented an affectionate relationship with her distant relative Walter Scott.

57 The most Devilish thing is 8 times 8 and 7 times 7 it is what nature itselfe cant endure.
1810 'Journal 2' in F Sidgwick (ed) *The Complete Marjory Fleming* (1934).

58 Many girls have not the advantage I have and I [am] very very glad that satan has not geven me boils and many other Misfortunes.
1810 'Journal 2' in F Sidgwick (ed) *The Complete Marjory Fleming* (1934).

59 To Day I pronunced a word which should never come out of a ladys lips it was that I called John a Impudent Bitch.
1810 'Journal 2' in F Sidgwick (ed) *The Complete Marjory Fleming* (1934).

60 I would rather have a man dog then a women dog because they do not bear like women dogs, it is a hard case it is shoking.
1810 'Journal 2' in F Sidgwick (ed) *The Complete Marjory Fleming* (1934).

61 I hope I will be religious again but as for reganing my charecter I despare for it.
1810 'Journal 2' in F Sidgwick (ed) *The Complete Marjory Fleming* (1934).

62 An annibaptist is a thing I am not a member of:—I am a Pisplikan just now & a Prisbeteren at Kercaldy my native town which thugh dirty is clein in the country.
1811 'Journal 3' in F Sidgwick (ed) *The Complete Marjory Fleming* (1934).

63 Love is a very papithatick thing as well as troublesom & tiresome but O Isabella forbid me to speak about it.
1811 'Journal 3' in F Sidgwick (ed) *The Complete Marjory Fleming* (1934).

Fletcher (of Saltoun), Andrew 1655–1716

Scottish patriot, fierce opponent of Stuart policy and of union with England. After the Union he retired in disgust and devoted himself to agriculture.

64 This will be the issue of that darling Plea, of being one and not two; it will be turned upon the Scots with a Vengeance; and their 45 Scots Members may dance round to all Eternity, in this Trap of their own making.
1706 *State of the Controversy betwixt United and Separate*

Parliaments, a critique of the proposed Union.

65 It is only fit for the slaves who sold it.
1707 Of Scotland, on leaving it after the signing of the Treaty of Union. Quoted in G W T Ormond *Fletcher of Saltoun* (1897).

Fletcher, John 1579–1625

English dramatist, who collaborated with Beaumont until the latter's marriage in 1613, and also with Shakespeare, Jonson, Middleton, Massinger and Rowley, as well as writing on his own. He died of plague.

66 Care-charming Sleep, thou easer of all woes,
Brother to Death.
c.1610–1614 *Valentinian*, act 5, sc.7.

67 Best while you have it use your breath,
There is no drinking after death.
1616 *The Bloody Brother*, act 2, sc.2, song (with Ben Jonson, George Chapman and Philip Massinger).

68 And he that will go to bed sober,
Falls with the leaf still in October.
1616 *The Bloody Brother*, act 2, sc.2, song (with Ben Jonson, George Chapman and Philip Massinger).

69 We are stark naught all, bad's the best of us.
1616 *The Bloody Brother*, act 4, sc.2 (with Ben Jonson, George Chapman and Philip Massinger).

70 We are beasts now, and the beasts are our masters.
c.1621 *The Wild-Goose Chase*, act 1, sc.1.

71 Blush at your faults.
c.1621 *The Wild-Goose Chase*, act 1, sc.1.

72 Give me the plump Venetian, fat, and lusty,
That meets me soft and supple, smiles upon me
As if a cup of full wine leaped to kiss me.
c.1621 *The Wild-Goose Chase*, act 1, sc.2.

73 Health and an able body are two jewels.
c. 1621 *The Wild-Goose Chase*, act 2, sc.1.

74 Nothing is thought rare
Which is not new and follow'd, yet we know
That what was worne some twenty yeare agoe,
Comes into grace againe.
c.1623 *The Noble Gentleman*, prologue.

75 Are you at ease now? Is your heart at rest?
Now you have got a shadow, an umbrella
To keep the scorching world's opinion
From your fair credit.
1624 *Rule a Wife and Have a Wife*, act 3, sc.1.

Florio, John c.1553–1625

English scholar, writer and translator, born of Italian Protestant family in London. His most famous work is his translation of Montaigne's *Essays* (1603); he also published an Italian–English dictionary, *A World of Words* (1598), and two compendiums of Italian proverbs.

76 England is the paradise of women, the purgatory of men, and the hell of horses.
1591 *Second Frutes*, ch.12.

Flynn, Errol 1909–59

Hollywood actor born in Tasmania. He starred in historical swashbucklers such as *Captain Blood* (1935), *The Adventures of Robin Hood* (1938) and *The Sea Hawk* (1940). His off-screen reputation for drinking, drug-taking and womanizing became legendary and eventually affected his career.

77 The public has always expected me to be a playboy and a decent chap never lets his public down.
Quoted in Gary Herman *The Book of Hollywood Quotes* (1979).

78 Inside this Hollywood playboy is a someway decent actor waiting for a chance to prove it. But, since Hollywood will never give me that chance, I drink to obliviate that decent actor.
Quoted in Michael Wilding and Pamela Wilcox *Apple Sauce* (1982).

Fo, Dario 1926–

Italian playwright and actor-manager, whose often controversial plays and revues deal with political themes. His plays include *Accidental Death of an Anarchist* (1970) and *Trumpets and Raspberries* (1984). He was awarded the Nobel prize for literature in 1997.

79 *Non si paga, non si paga.*
We won't pay, we won't pay.
1974 Play title, translated into English in 1981 as *Can't pay? Won't pay!*

Foch, Ferdinand 1851–1929

French marshal, born in Tarbes. He taught at the École de Guerre, and proved himself a great strategist at the Battles of the Marne and Ypres. He commanded the Allied armies in 1918.

80 *Mon centre cède, ma droite recule, situation excellente, j'attaque.*
My centre is giving way, my right is retreating, situation excellent, I am attacking.
1914 Message sent during the first Battle of the Marne, Sep. Quoted in R Recouly *Foch* (1919), ch.6.

81 *Ce n'est pas un traité de paix, c'est un armistice de vingt ans.*
This is not a peace treaty, it is an armistice for twenty years.
1919 At the signing of the Treaty of Versailles. Quoted in Paul Reynaud *Memoires* (1963), vol.2.

Follett, Ken 1949–

Welsh novelist.

82 They are the rent boys of politics.
2000 Of those who give off-the-record briefings against ministers. In the *Observer*, 2 Jul.

83 The polite fiction that the Prime Minister's advisers are responsible is absurd. Control-freak Tony doesn't let Alastair Campbell and Peter Mandelson go around saying anything they like… Peter isn't the Prince of Darkness, though he may be Lady Macbeth.
2000 In the *Observer*, 2 Jul.

Fontenelle, Bernard le Bovier de 1657–1757

French writer, the nephew of Corneille. He introduced mathematics and the natural sciences into the conversation of the salons, and expressed scientific ideas through literature. He was secretary of the Académie des Sciences (1699–1741).

84 *Ah! si l'on ôtait les chimères aux hommes, quel plaisir leur resterait?*
Oh! If man were robbed of his fantasies, what pleasure would be left him?
1683 *Dialogue des morts.*

85 *L'univers…je l'en estime plus depuis que je sais qu'il*

ressemble à une montre; il est surprenant que l'ordre de la nature, tout admirable qu'il est, ne roule que sur des choses si simples.
I have come to esteem the universe more now that I know it resembles a watch; it is surprising that the order of nature, as admirable as it is, only runs on such simple things.
1686 *Entretiens sur la pluralité des mondes.*

86 *Les mouvements les plus naturels, et les plus ordinaires, sont ceux qui se font le moins sentir; cela est vrai jusque dans la morale. Le mouvement de l'amour-propre nous est si naturel que, le plus souvent, nous ne le sentons pas.*
The most natural and ordinary movements are those which are the least felt; this is also true in morals. Pride is so natural to us that, most often, we never feel it.
1686 *Entretiens sur la pluralité des mondes, Premier soir.*

87 *Les vrais philosophes sont comme les éléphants, qui en marchant ne posent jamais le second pied à terre que le premier ne soit bien affermi.*
True philosophers are like elephants, who when walking never place their second foot on the ground until the first is steady.
1686 *Entretiens sur la pluralité des mondes, Sixième soir.*

88 *Un grand obstacle au bonheur, c'est de s'attendre à un trop grand bonheur.*
The greatest obstacle to happiness is the expectation of too great a happiness.
1724 *Du bonheur.*

89 *Leibniz n'était point marié; il y avait pensé à l'âge de cinquante ans; mais la personne qu'il avait en vue voulut avoir le temps de faire ses réflexions. Cela donne à Leibniz le loisir de faire aussi les siennes, et il ne se maria point.*
Leibniz never married; he had considered it at the age of fifty, but the person he had in mind desired time to think about it. This gave Leibniz time to reflect, also, and he didn't marry.
Éloge des académiciens, Leibniz.

Foot, Michael Mackintosh 1913–

English Labour politician. He resigned the leadership of the Labour Party in 1983, after a heavy defeat in the general election. A pacifist and CND supporter, his prolific writings include a two-volume biography of Aneurin Bevan.

90 The only man I knew who could make a curse sound like a caress.
1962 Of Aneurin Bevan. *Aneurin Bevan 1897–1945*, vol.1.

91 The members of our secret service have apparently spent so much time looking under the bed for Communists that they haven't had time to look in the bed.
1963 Attributed comment on the Profumo scandal.

92 A Royal Commission is a broody hen sitting on a china egg.
1964 Speech, House of Commons.

93 Men of power have not time to read; yet men who do not read are unfit for power.
1980 *Debts of Honour.*

Foote, Samuel 1720–77

English actor-manager and playwright. Dubbed the 'English Aristophanes', he excelled in satirical comedy at the Haymarket Theatre, which he managed. He won a limited theatrical patent as compensation when he lost a leg in a practical joke involving the Duke of York. His plays include *The Englishman in Paris* (1753) and *The Minor* (1760).

94 So she went into the garden to cut a cabbage-leaf, to make an apple-pie; and at the same time a great she-bear coming up the street, pops its head into the shop. 'What! no soap?' So he died and she very imprudently married the barber; and there were present the Picninnies, and the Joblillies, and the Garyulies, and the Grand Panjandrum himself, with the little round button at top; and they all fell to playing the game of catch-as-catch-can till the gunpowder ran out of the heels of their boots.
Responding to a challenge from the actor Charles Macklin that there was no speech he could not repeat from memory after just one hearing. Macklin had to acknowledge defeat. Foote's phrases 'no soap' and 'the grand Panjandrum' became widely adopted. Quoted in Maria Edgeworth *Harry and Lucy* (1825), vol.2.

Forbes, (Malcolm Stevenson) 'Steve', Jr 1947–

US publisher. He is President and Chief Executive Officer of Forbes and Editor-in-Chief of *Forbes* magazine and ran for the Republican presidential nomination in 1996 and 2000.

95 People who never get carried away, should be.
1976 In *Town and Country*, Nov.

96 It is unfortunate we can't buy many business executives for what they are worth and sell them for what they think they are worth.
Quoted in David Mahoney *Confessions of a Street-Smart Manager* (1988).

Ford, Anna 1943–

English television news presenter.

97 Let's face it, there are no plain women on television.
1979 In the *Observer*, 23 Sep.

Ford, Ford Madox *originally* *Ford Hermann Hueffer* 1873–1939

English writer and editor. He was associated with the modernist movement, and launched the *English Review* and later the *Transatlantic Review*. His best-known novels are *The Good Soldier* (1915) and the *Parade's End* (1924–8) tetralogy.

98 God knows that the lesson we learn from life is that our very existence in the nature of things is a perpetual harming of somebody else—if only because every mouthful of food that we eat is a mouthful taken from somebody else.
1911 *Ancient Lights*, dedication.

99 I should say that Rossetti was a man without principles at all, who earnestly desired to find salvation along the lines of least resistance.
1911 Of Dante Gabriel Rossetti. *Memories and Impressions.*

1 You cannot be absolutely dumb when you live with a person unless you are an inhabitant of the North of England or the State of Maine.
1915 *The Good Soldier*, pt.3, ch.4.

2 Alas, it does indeed seem a monstrous thing, but after all, what is chaste in Constantinople may have the aspect of

lewdness in Liverpool, and what in Liverpool may pass for virtue in Constantinople is frequently regarded as vice.
1915 Letter to John Lane, 17 Dec.

3 Only two classes of books are of universal appeal. The very best and the very worst.
1924 *Joseph Conrad, a Personal Remembrance*, pt.1.

4 We used to say that a passage of good style began with a fresh, usual word, and continued with fresh, usual words to the end; there was nothing more to it.
1924 *Joseph Conrad, a Personal Remembrance*, pt.3.

5 We agreed that the novel is absolutely the only vehicle for the thought of our day.
1924 *Joseph Conrad, a Personal Remembrance*, pt.3.

6 I have always had the greatest contempt for novels written with a purpose. Fiction should render, not draw morals. But…I sinned against my gods to the extent of saying that I was going—to the level of the light vouchsafed me—to write a work that should have for its purpose the obviating of all future wars.
1934 On *Parade's End*.

Ford, Henry 1863–1947

US automobile engineer and manufacturer. In 1903 he started the Ford Motor Company, pioneering 'assembly line' mass-production techniques for his famous Model T (1908–9), 15 million of which were produced up to 1928.

7 History is more or less bunk. It's tradition.
1916 Interview, *Chicago Tribune*, May.

8 Any color—so long as it's black.
Of the Model T Ford. Quoted in Allan Nevins *Ford* (1957), vol.2.

9 Exercise is bunk. If you are healthy, you don't need it: if you are sick, you shouldn't take it.
Attributed.

Ford, Henry 1917–87

US businessman, grandson of Henry Ford, president of the Ford Motor Co from 1945 and chairman from 1960. He introduced many modernizing measures.

10 My name is on the building.
His habitual justification for having the last word. Recalled on his death, 29 Sep 1987.

Ford, John c.1586–c.1640

English dramatist, who collaborated with Dekker, Fletcher, Rowley and Webster. His works include *The Broken Heart* (1633), *'Tis Pity She's a Whore* (1633) and *Perkin Warbeck* (1634), a historical play.

11 I am…a mushroom
On whom the dew of heaven drops now and then.
1633 *The Broken Heart*, act 1, sc.3.

12 The joys of marriage are the heaven on earth,
Life's paradise, great princess, the soul's quiet,
Sinews of concord, earthly immortality,
Eternity of pleasures; no restoratives
Like to a constant woman.
1633 *The Broken Heart*, act 2, sc.2.

13 He hath shook hands with time.
1633 *The Broken Heart*, act 5, sc.2.

14 Nice philosophy
May tolerate unlikely arguments,
But heaven admits no jest.
1633 *'Tis Pity She's a Whore*, act 1, sc.1.

15 'Tis my destiny
That you must either love, or I must die.
1633 *'Tis Pity She's a Whore*, act 1, sc.2.

16 Busy opinion is an idle fool.
1633 *'Tis Pity She's a Whore*, act 5, sc.3.

17 Why, I hold fate
Clasped in my fist, and could command the course
Of time's eternal motion, hadst thou been
One thought more steady than an ebbing sea.
1633 *'Tis Pity She's a Whore*, act 5, sc.4.

18 Of one so young, so rich in nature's store,
Who could not say, 'tis pity she's a whore?
1633 *'Tis Pity She's a Whore*, act 5, sc.6.

19 Tell us, pray, what devil
This melancholy is, which can transform
Men into monsters.
1638 *The Lady's Trial*, act 3, sc.1.

Ford, Lena Guilbert 1870–1916

English songwriter.

20 Keep the Home-fires burning,
While your hearts are yearning,
Though your lads are far away
They dream of Home.
There's a silver lining
Through the dark clouds shining;
Turn the dark cloud inside out,
Till the boys come Home.
1914 'Till the Boys Come Home', a wartime anthem (music by Ivor Novello).

Ford, Richard 1944–

US writer. He has edited anthologies and written short stories and novels, including *The Sportswriter* (1986) and *Independence Day* (1996, Pulitzer Prize).

21 If there's another thing that sportswriting teaches you, it is that there are no transcendent themes in life. In all cases things are here and they're over, and that has to be enough.
1986 *The Sportswriter*, ch.1.

22 Married life requires shared mystery even when all the facts are known.
1986 *The Sportswriter*, ch.5.

23 Leaving reminds us what we can part with and what we can't, then offers us something new to look forward to, to dream about.
1992 'An Urge for Going', in *Harper's*, Feb.

Foreman, George 1949–

US boxer, world heavyweight champion (1973–4, 1994–5).

24 A boxer never sees the big one that hits him.
Quoted in Colin Jarman *The Guinness Dictionary of Sports Quotations* (1990).

Forgy, Howell Maurice 1908–83

US naval chaplain.

25 Praise the Lord and pass the ammunition.
1941 At Pearl Harbor, 7 Dec. Reported in the *New York Times*,

1 Nov 1942, and used as a song title by Frank Loesser, 1942.
➡ *See Blacker 132:93.*

Formby, George 1904–61

English entertainer. He developed a music-hall act featuring a ukulele and comic songs which translated well to film, and became one of Britain's most popular pre-war stars.

26 When I'm Cleaning Windows.
1936 Title of song (with Harry Gifford and Fred E Cliffe), first featured in the film *Keep Your Seats Please*.

27 It's me Auntie Maggie's home-made remedy
Guaranteed never to fail
Now that's the stuff that will do the trick
It's sold at ev'ry chemist for 'one and a kick'.
1941 'Auntie Maggie's Remedy' (with Eddie Latta), song featured in the film *Turned Out Nice Again*.

Forster, E(dward) M(organ) 1879–1970

English novelist and critic, a member of the Bloomsbury circle. His novels include *Howards End* (1910) and *A Passage to India* (1924). *Maurice* (written 1913–14), on homosexuality, was published posthumously in 1971. He was a prolific essayist and critic.

28 Here is the heart of our island: the Chilterns, the North Downs, the South Downs radiate hence. The fibres of England unite in Wiltshire, and did we condescend to worship her, here should we erect our national shrine.
1907 *The Longest Journey*, ch.13.

29 A Room with a View.
1908 Title of novel.

30 They are our gates to the glorious and the unknown. Through them we pass out into adventure and sunshine, to them, alas! we return.
1910 On railway termini. *Howards End*, ch.2.

31 It will be generally admitted that Beethoven's Fifth Symphony is the most sublime noise that has ever penetrated into the ear of man.
1910 *Howards End*, ch.5.

32 He believed in sudden conversion, a belief which may be right, but which is peculiarly attractive to the half-baked mind.
1910 *Howards End*, ch.6.

33 She felt that those who prepared for all the emergencies of life beforehand may equip themselves at the expense of joy.
1910 *Howards End*, ch.7.

34 The poor cannot always reach those whom they want to love, and they can hardly ever escape from those whom they no longer love.
1910 *Howards End*, ch.7.

35 Personal relations are the important thing for ever and ever, and not this outer life of telegrams and anger.
1910 *Howards End*, ch.19.

36 Only connect! That was the whole of her sermon. Only connect the prose and the passion, and both will be exalted, and human love will be seen at its height. Live in fragments no longer.
1910 *Howards End*, ch.22.

37 Death destroys a man: the idea of death saves him.
1910 *Howards End*, ch.27.

38 There is much to be said for apathy in education.
1913–14 *Maurice* (published 1971), ch.1.

39 Religion is far more acute than science, and if it only added judgement to insight, would be the greatest thing in the world.
1913–14 *Maurice* (published 1971), ch.44.

40 'I don't think I understand people very well. I only know whether I like or dislike them.' 'Then you are an Oriental.'
1924 *A Passage to India*, ch.2.

41 The so-called white races are really pinko-grey.
1924 *A Passage to India*, ch.7.

42 Nothing in India is identifiable, the mere asking of a question causes it to disappear or to merge in something else.
1924 *A Passage to India*, ch.8.

43 The echo began in some indescribable way to undermine her hold on life. Coming at a moment when she chanced to be fatigued, it had managed to murmur, 'Pathos, piety, courage—they exist, but are identical, and so is filth. Everything exists, nothing has value.'
1924 *A Passage to India*, ch.14.

44 Yes—oh dear yes—the novel tells a story.
1927 *Aspects of the Novel*, ch.2.

45 *Ulysses*...is a dogged attempt to cover the universe with mud, an inverted Victorianism, an attempt to make crossness and dirt succeed where sweetness and light failed, a simplification of the human character in the interests of Hell.
1927 Of James Joyce's 1922 novel. *Aspects of the Novel*, ch.6.

46 They go forth into a world...of men who are as various as the sands of the sea; into a world of whose richness and subtlety they have no conception. They go forth into it with well-developed bodies, fairly developed minds, and undeveloped hearts.
1936 On public schoolboys. *Abinger Harvest*, 'Notes on English Character'.

47 It is not that the Englishman can't feel—it is that he is afraid to feel.
1936 *Abinger Harvest*, 'Notes on English Character'.

48 It is frivolous stuff, and how rare, how precious is frivolity! How few writers can prostitute all their powers! They are always implying 'I am capable of higher things.'
1936 *Abinger Harvest*, 'Ronald Firbank'.

49 The historian must have a third quality as well: some conception of how men who are not historians behave. Otherwise he will move in a world of the dead.
1936 *Abinger Harvest*, 'Captain Edward Gibbon'.

50 Works of art, in my opinion, are the only objects in the material universe to possess internal order, and that is why, though I don't believe that only art matters, I do believe in Art for Art's sake.
1951 *Two Cheers for Democracy*, 'Art for Art's Sake'.

51 I do not believe in Belief... Lord I disbelieve—help thou my unbelief.
1951 *Two Cheers for Democracy*, 'What I Believe'.

52 I hate the idea of causes, and if I had to choose between betraying my country and betraying my friend, I hope I should have the guts to betray my country.
1951 *Two Cheers for Democracy*, 'What I Believe'.

53 So two cheers for democracy: one because it admits variety and two because it permits criticism. Two cheers are quite enough: there is no occasion to give three. Only Love the Beloved Republic deserves that.
1951 *Two Cheers for Democracy*, 'What I Believe'. The phrase 'Love the Beloved Republic' is taken from Swinburne's poem 'Hertha'.

54 Think before you speak is criticism's motto; speak before you think creation's.
1951 *Two Cheers for Democracy*, 'Raison d'être of Criticism'.

55 Creative writers are always greater than the causes that they represent.
1951 *Two Cheers for Democracy*, 'Gide and George'.

56 I would suggest that the only books that influence us are those for which we are ready, and which have gone a little farther down our particular path than we have yet got ourselves.
1951 *Two Cheers for Democracy*, 'Books That Influenced Me'.

57 One was left, too, with a gap in Christianity: the canonical gospels do not record that Christ laughed or played. Can a man be perfect if he never laughs or plays? Krishna's jokes may be vapid, but they bridge a gap.
1953 *The Hill of Devi*, 'Gokul Ashtami'.

Foster, Sir George 1847–1931

Canadian politician.

58 These somewhat troublesome days when the great Mother Empire stands splendidly isolated in Europe.
1896 Speech in the House of Commons, 16 Jan. *The Times* reported the speech under the heading of 'Splendid Isolation', 22 Jan.

Foster, Stephen Collins 1826–64

US songwriter. His 125 compositions include 'The Old Folks at Home', 'Camptown Races' and 'Jeannie with the Light Brown Hair', but despite their success, he died in poverty and obscurity.

59 Gwine to run all night,
Gwine to run all day,
I'll bet my money on de bob-tail nag,
Somebody bet on de bay.
1850 'Camptown Races', chorus.

60 Way down upon the Swanee River,
Far, far away,
There's where my heart is turning ever;
There's where the old folks stay.
1851 'The Old Folks at Home'.

61 I dream of Jeannie with the light brown hair,
Floating, like a vapour, on the soft summer air.
1854 'Jeannie with the Light Brown Hair'.

62 Beautiful dreamer, wake unto me,
Starlight and dewdrop are waiting for thee.
1864 'Beautiful Dreamer'.

Foster, Vince(nt W, Jr) 1945–93

US lawyer. Deputy Counsel in the Clinton White House.

63 I was not meant for the spotlight of public life in Washington. Here running people down is considered sport.
1993 Note found after his suicide. Reported in the *New York Times*, 13 Aug.

Foucault, Michel 1926–84

French philosopher and historian of ideas.

64 For the nineteenth century, the initial model of madness would be to believe oneself to be God, while for the preceding centuries it had been to deny God.
1967 *Madness and Civilization*.

Fowles, John Robert 1926–

English novelist. He scored a cult success with *The Magus* (1965, revised 1977), and consolidated his reputation as an ambitious experimental writer with *The French Lieutenant's Woman* (1969, filmed 1981).

65 All perfect republics are a perfect nonsense. The craving to risk death is our last great perversion. We come from night, we go into night. Why live in night?
1965 *The Magus*, ch.19.

66 And if you are wise you will never pity the past for what it did not know, but pity yourself for what it did.
1965 *The Magus*, ch.24.

67 That is the great distinction between the sexes. Men see objects, women see the relationship between objects… It is an extra dimension of feeling which we men are without and one that makes war abhorrent to all real women—and absurd.
1965 *The Magus*, ch.52.

68 In essence the Renaissance was simply the green end of one of civilization's hardest winters.
1969 *The French Lieutenant's Woman*, ch.10.

69 We all write poems; it is simply that poets are the ones who write in words.
1969 *The French Lieutenant's Woman*, ch.19.

70 The more abhorrent a news item the more comforting it was to be the recipient since the fact that it had happened elsewhere proved that it had not happened here, was not happening here, and would therefore never happen here.
1974 *The Ebony Tower*, 'Poor Koko'.

71 Cricket remains for me the game of games, the sanspareil, the great metaphor, the best marriage ever devised of mind and body… For me it remains the Proust of pastimes, the subtlest and most poetic, the most past-and-present; whose beauty can lie equally in days, in a whole, or in one tiny phrase, a blinding split second.
Quick Singles, 'Vain Memories'. Quoted in Helen Exley *Cricket Quotations* (1992).

72 The diary will really try and tell people who you are and what you were. The alternative is writing nothing, or creating a totally lifeless, as it is leafless, garden.
2003 *The Journals: Volume 1*.

73 One degrades oneself sometimes in the effort not to be lonely.
2003 After a late night socializing. In *The Journals: Volume 1*, 24 Dec 1950.

Fox, Charles James 1749–1806

English Liberal statesman. He formed an administration with Lord North in 1783, and on its failure became Pitt's leading parliamentary adversary. He was a strong opponent of the war with France, and an advocate of non-intervention.

74 How much the greatest event it is that ever happened in

the world—and how much the best.
1779 On the fall of the Bastille. Letter to Richard Fitzpatrick, 30 Jul.

75 The worst of a revolution is a restoration.
1785 House of Commons, 10 Dec.

76 I die happy.
1806 Last words. Quoted in Lord John Russell *Life and Times of C J Fox*, vol.3 (1860), ch.9.

Fox, George 1624–91

English itinerant Puritan preacher and writer, who was imprisoned for dissent. He was the founder of Society of Friends (known as 'Quakers').

77 One morning, as I was sitting by the fire, a great cloud came over me, and a temptation beset me, and I sate still… And as I sate still under it and let it alone, a living hope rose in me, and a true voice arose in me which cried: There is a living God who made all things. And immediately the cloud and temptation vanished away, and the life rose over it all, and my heart was glad, and I praised the living God.
1648 *Journal of George Fox*.

78 Walk cheerfully over the world, answering that of God in everyone.
1656 *Journal of George Fox*.

Frame, Janet Paterson *also known as* ***Jean Paterson Frame*** 1924–2004

New Zealand poet and writer. She was misdiagnosed as schizophrenic, and spent eight years in psychiatric hospitals. Her autobiographical trilogy *To the Is-land* (1982), *An Angel at My Table* (1984) and *The Envoy from Mirror City* (1985) was made into an award-winning film by Jane Campion.

79 What use the green river, the gold place, if time and death pinned human in the pocket of my land not rest from taking underground the green all-willowed and white rose and bean flower and morning-mist picnic of song in pepper-pot breast of thrush?
1961 *Owls Do Cry*, pt.1, ch.4.

80 From the first place of liquid darkness, within the second place of air and light, I set down the following record with its mixture of fact and truths and memories of truths and its direction always toward the Third Place, where the starting point is myth.
1982 *To the Is-land*, ch.1, 'In the Second Place'.

81 I was born…with ready-made parents and a sister and brother who had already begun their store of experience, inaccessible to me except through their language and the record, always slightly different, of our mother and father, and as each member of the family was born, each, in a sense with memories on loan, began to supply the individual furnishings of each Was-land, each Is-land, and the hopes and dreams of the Future.
1982 *To the Is-land*, ch.1, 'In the Second Place'.

82 The word *permanent*…had its own kind of revenge on those who misused it, for the Bible said that nothing was permanent and everything came and went.
1982 *To the Is-land*, ch.2, 'Toward the Is-Land'.

France, Anatole *pseudonym of* ***Jacques Anatole François Thibault*** 1844–1924

French novelist, poet and essayist, who won the Nobel prize for literature in 1921. Along with Émile Zola, he championed the cause of Dreyfus.

83 *Le bon critique est celui qui raconte les aventures de son âme au milieu des chefs-d'oeuvres.*
The good critic is one who recognizes the adventures of his own soul in great works of art.
1892 *La Vie littéraire*, préface.

84 *Le livre est l'opium de l'Occident.*
Books are the opium of the West.
1892 *La Vie littéraire*, préface.
► *See Marx 557:94.*

85 *La faim et l'amour sont les deux axes du monde.*
Hunger and love are the two axes of the world.
1892 *La Vie littéraire*, pt.3.

86 *L'histoire est condamnée, par un vice de nature, au mensonge.*
History is condemned, by a defect of nature, to lies.
1892 *La Vie littéraire*, pt.17.

87 *Les vérités découvertes par l'intelligence demeurent stériles.*
Truths discovered by intelligence are sterile.
1892 *La Vie littéraire*, pt.21.

88 *Je tiens à mon imperfection comme à ma raison d'être.*
I hold on to my imperfection as tightly as my reason for being.
1894 *Le Jardin d'Epicure*.

89 *Il y a toujours un moment où la curiosité devient un péché, et le diable s'est toujours mis du côté des savants.*
There is always a moment when curiosity becomes a sin and the devil is always on the side of the learned.
1894 *Le Jardin d'Epicure*.

90 *L'histoire n'est pas une science, c'est un art. On n'y réussit que par l'imagination.*
History is not a science. It is an art. One can succeed in it only through the imagination.
1894 *Le Jardin d'Epicure*.

91 To disarm the strong and arm the weak would be to change the social order which it's my job to preserve. Justice is the means by which established injustices are sanctioned.
1901 *Crainquebille*.

92 *Le poireau, c'est l'asperge du pauvre.*
The leek is the asparagus of the poor.
1906 *Crainquebille*.

93 *La majestueuse égalité des lois, qui interdit au riche comme au pauvre de coucher sous les ponts, de mendier dans les rues et de voler du pain.*
The majestic equality of laws forbids the rich as well as the poor to sleep under bridges, to beg in the streets and to steal bread.
1910 *Le Lys rouge*.

Francis I 1494–1547

King of France (1515–47) after his father-in-law Louis XII. The chief feature of his reign was his military conflict with Emperor Charles V.

94 *De toutes choses ne m'est demeuré que l'honneur et la vie qui est saulve.*
Of all I had, only honour and life have been spared.
1525 Letter to his mother, Louise of Savoy, after his defeat and

capture by Charles V at Pavia, 24 Feb. Collected in *Collection des documents inédits sur l'histoire de France* (1847), vol.1.

95 *Souvent femme varie,*
Mal habil qui s'y fie
Woman is often fickle,
Foolish the man who trusts her.
Couplet scratched by the King on the glass of a window at Chambord. Quoted in Vincent Cronin *Louis XIV* (1964), p.175.

96 But is he a patriot for me?
On being assured of the loyalty of a candidate for high office. The phrase was later used as a title by John Osborne for his 1965 play.

St Francis of Assisi c.1181–1226

Italian monk and saint, founder of the Franciscan order. The son of a wealthy merchant, in 1206 he renounced his patrimony and became a hermit, attracting followers who rejected all forms of property. His works include sermons, ascetic treatises and hymns.

97 *Bene veniat soror mea mors.*
Welcome, my sister Death.
1226 Last words. Quoted in Thomas of Celano *Life of St Francis* (c.1245), bk.2, ch.163.

98 Lord, make me an instrument of Your peace.
Where there is hatred, let me sow love;
Where there is injury, pardon;
Where there is doubt, faith;
Where there is despair, hope;
Where there is darkness, light;
Where there is sadness, joy.

O divine Master, grant that I may not so much seek
To be consoled as to console;
To be understood as to understand;
To be loved as to love.
For it is in giving that we receive;
It is in pardoning that we are pardoned;
And it is in dying that we are born to eternal life.
Attributed prayer, traditionally known as the 'Prayer of St Francis'.

Francis, Dick (Richard Stanley) 1920–

English jockey and writer. In the Grand National of 1956 he was on the point of winning when his horse collapsed. Subsequently he became a writer of popular thrillers with a racing background.

99 I approach chapter one each year with a deeper foreboding than I ever felt facing Becher's.
Quoted in Colin Jarman *The Guinness Dictionary of Sports Quotations* (1990).

Frank, Anne 1929–45

German Jewish diarist, whose diary covers her time in hiding in Amsterdam. She died in Bergen–Belsen concentration camp.

1 It was a terrible time through which I was living. The war raged about us, and nobody knew whether or not he would be alive the next week.
1944 Diary entry, 25 Mar.

2 I want to go on living even after death!
1944 Diary entry, 4 Apr.

3 We all live with the objective of being happy; our lives are all different and yet the same.
1944 Diary entry, 6 Jul.

Frankenthaler, Helen 1928–

US artist, a key figure in the Abstract Expressionism school. Her innovative, colourful works include *The Human Edge* (1967). The Museum of Modern Art in New York presented her retrospective in 1989.

4 A picture that is beautiful, or that comes off, or that works, looks as if it was all made at one stroke.
1972 Quoted in Ian Crofton (ed) *A Dictionary of Art Quotations* (1988).

5 I follow the rules until I go against them all.
1993 On translating her large, lyrical abstracts from paintings to prints. In the *Washington Times*, 16 Apr.

Franklin, Benjamin 1706–90

US statesman, author and scientist, whose popular *Poor Richard's Almanack* first appeared in 1732. He proved that lightning and electricity are identical and suggested that buildings should be protected by lightning conductors. He was involved in the Declaration of Independence (1775), and helped secure British recognition (1783).

6 The body of
Benjamin Franklin, printer,
(Like the cover of an old book,
Its contents worn out,
And stripped of its lettering and gilding)
Lies here, food for worms!
Yet the work itself shall not be lost,
For it will, as he believed, appear once more
In a new
And more beautiful edition,
Corrected and amended
By its Author!
1728 Proposed epitaph for himself.

7 To lengthen thy Life, lessen thy Meals.
1733 *Poor Richard's Almanack*, Jun.

8 He that drinks fast, pays slow.
1733 *Poor Richard's Almanack*, Aug.

9 Necessity never made a good bargain.
1735 *Poor Richard's Almanack*, Apr.

10 Nothing but Money,
Is sweeter than Honey.
1735 *Poor Richard's Almanack*, Jun.

11 Time is money.
1748 *Advice to a Young Tradesman*.

12 Fond Pride of Dress is sure an Empty Curse;
E'er Fancy you consult, consult your Purse.
1751 *Poor Richard Improved*, May.

13 A little neglect may breed mischief…for want of a nail, the shoe was lost; for want of a shoe, the horse was lost; and for want of a horse the rider was lost.
1758 *Poor Richard's Almanack*, preface.

14 Some punishment seems preparing for a people who are so ungratefully abusing the best Constitution and the best king that any nation was ever blessed with.
1768 Speech in London during the Wilkes riots, May.

15 There never was a good war or a bad peace.
1773 Letter, 11 Sep.

16 We must indeed all hang together or, most assuredly, we shall all hang separately.
1776 On signing the Declaration of Independence, 4 Jul.

17 Furnished as all Europe is with Academies of Science, with nice instruments and the spirit of experimentation, the progress of human knowledge will be rapid and discoveries made of which we have at present no conception. I begin to be almost sorry I was born since I cannot have the happiness of knowing what will be known a hundred years hence.
1783 Letter to Sir Joseph Banks, President of the Royal Society, 27 Jul.

18 In this world nothing can be said to be certain, except death and taxes.
1789 Letter to Jean Baptiste Le Roy, 13 Nov.
► *See Defoe 258:25.*

19 What is the use of a new-born child?
Reply when questioned as to the use of a new invention. Quoted in J Parton *Life and Times of Benjamin Franklin* (1864), pt.4, ch.17.

Franklin, (Stella Maria Sarah) Miles *pseudonym Brent of Bin Bin* 1879–1954

Australian novelist, journalist and feminist. After writing *My Brilliant Career* (1901), she moved to the US (1906) then England (1915), returning to Australia in 1927. Other work includes the *Brent of Bin* series (1928), the autobiographical *My Career Goes Bung* (1946) and critical essays.

20 This was life—my life—my career, my brilliant career!
1901 *My Brilliant Career*, ch.5.

21 Grannie remarked that I might have the spirit of an Australian but I had by no means the manners of a lady.
1901 *My Brilliant Career*, ch.19.

22 I am proud that I am an Australian, a daughter of the Southern Cross, a child of the mighty bush. I am thankful I am a peasant, a part of the bone and muscle of my nation, and earn my bread by the sweat of my brow, as man was meant to do. I rejoice I was not born a parasite, one of the blood-suckers who loll on velvet and satin, crushed from the proceeds of human sweat and blood and souls.
1901 *My Brilliant Career*, ch.38.

Franz Josef I 1830–1916

Emperor of Austria (1848) and King of Hungary (1867).

23 Farewell youth!
1848 On signing the document that made him Emperor, following the abdication of Ferdinand. Attributed, quoted in A J P Taylor *From Napoleon to the Second International* (1993).

Franzen, Jonathan 1959–

US novelist. *The Corrections* (2001) won the National Book Award.

24 It's the fate of most Ping-Pong tables in home basements eventually to serve the ends of other, more desperate games.
2001 *The Corrections*.

25 Just as the camera draws a stake through the heart of serious portraiture, television has killed the novel of social reportage.
2002 *How to Be Alone*.

Fraser, Lady Antonia 1932–

English writer, best known for her historical biographies.

26 As with all forms of liberation, of which the liberation of women is only one example, it is easy to suppose in a time of freedom that the darker days of repression can never come again.
1984 *The Weaker Vessel*, epilogue.

Fraser, George MacDonald 1925–

English writer of historical fiction.

27 I have observed, in the course of a dishonest life, that when a rogue is outlining a treacherous plan, he works harder to convince himself than to move his hearers.
1969 *Flashman*.

Fraser, Major Sir Keith Alexander 1867–1935

British politician. After his army career he became MP for Leicestershire (1918–23) and a Justice of the Peace for Ross and Cromarty.

28 I never met anyone in Ireland who understood the Irish question, except one Englishman who had been there only a week.
1919 House of Commons, May.

Fraser, (John) Malcolm 1930–

Australian politician. He became an MP in 1955 and leader of the Liberals in 1975. He formed a caretaker government until becoming Prime Minister. Defeated in the 1983 elections, he retired soon afterwards.

29 Life is not meant to be easy.
1971 The Deakin Lecture, Melbourne, 20 Jul.

Frayne, Trent 1918–

Canadian sportswriter.

30 It is an axiom of sports that the legs go first. For sportswriters, it's the enthusiasm.
1990 *The Tales of an Athletic Supporter*.

Frederick II 1194–1250

Holy Roman Emperor, last of the Hohenstaufen line. His plans to consolidate his power in Italy were frustrated by the Lombard cities and the popes. During the Fifth Crusade in 1228 he took possession of Jerusalem, and crowned himself king there (1229).

31 Our work is to present things that are as they are.
De Ate Venandi cum Avibus.

Frederick II, the Great 1712–86

King of Prussia from 1740. He fought against the Austrians in the War of the Austrian Succession (1740–8) and seized Silesia in 1741. In 1772 he shared in the first partition of Poland. By the time of his death, Prussia had become a world power.

32 Troops always ready to act, my well-filled treasury, and the liveliness of my disposition—these were my reasons for making war on Maria Theresa.
1741 Letter to Voltaire.

33 Rascals, would you live for ever?
1757 Attributed, to hesitant guards at the Battle of Kolin, 18 Jun.
► *See Daly 251:76.*

34 *Chassez les préjugés par la porte, ils rentreront par la fenêtre.*
Drive out prejudices through the door, and they will return through the window.
1771 Letter to Voltaire, 19 Mar.

35 *Vanité des Vanités; Vanité de la géométrie.*
Vanity of vanities! Vanity of mathematics!
1778 Letter to Voltaire, 25 Jan, protesting against the increasing use of mathematical calculation in engineering projects, which he saw as theory triumphing over practical experience.

36 My people and I have come to an agreement that satisfies us both. They are to say what they please, and I am to do what I please.
Attributed.

Freed, Arthur *pseudonym of* ***Arthur Grossman*** 1894–1973

US producer and lyricist. He came to Hollywood in 1929 and worked for MGM, producing many well-known musicals. As a lyricist he frequently worked with composer Nacio Herb Brown.

37 I'll walk down the lane with a happy refrain
And singin' just singin' in the rain.
1929 'Singin' in the Rain' featured in *Hollywood Revue of 1929* and other films, including the famous musical of the same title (music by Nacio Herb Brown).

38 You Are My Lucky Star.
1935 Title of song featured in *Broadway Melody of 1936* (music by Nacio Herb Brown).

Freeman, Bud (Lawrence) 1906–91

US jazz saxophonist. He was a leading figure in the evolution of the Chicago style in the 1920s and 1930s.

39 I think audiences come to hear older musicians like me just to see if we can pick up a horn without falling over.
1989 *Crazeology: The Autobiography of a Chicago Jazzman* (as told to Robert Wolf), ch.9.

Freeman, Edward Augustus 1823–92

English historian, Regius Professor of Modern History at Oxford. Among his prolific output were his *History of Federal Government* (1863) and *History of the Norman Conquest* (1867–76).

40 This would be a grand land if only every Irishman would kill a negro, and be hanged for it.
1881 Of America. Letter to F H Dickinson from New Haven, 4 Dec.

41 Nobody can't do nothing never at all for Ireland—you can't help people against their will; that's what it comes to—let it go, let it go.
1882 Letter to Edith Thompson, 29 Jan.

42 History is past politics, and politics is present history.
1886 *Methods of Historical Study.*

Freeman, John 1880–1929

English poet.

43 In that sharp light the fields did lie
Naked and stone-like; each tree stood
Like a tranced woman, bound and stark,
Far off the wood
With darkness ridged the riven dark.
1916 'Stone Trees'.

44 Than these November skies
Is no sky lovelier. The clouds are deep;
Into their grey the subtle spies
Of colour creep,
Changing their high austerity to delight,
Till ev'n the leaden interfolds are bright.
1916 'November Skies'.

45 It was the lovely moon—she lifted
Slowly her white brow among
Bronze cloud-waves that ebbed and drifted
Faintly, faintlier afar.
1916 'It Was the Lovely Moon'.

Freleng, Friz *born* ***Isadore Freleng*** 1905–95

US cartoon director.

46 That's all folks!
Porky Pig's stammered trademark, sign-off line for Warner Brothers' *Looney Tunes.*

French, Marilyn 1929–

US writer and feminist scholar. She enjoyed a huge success with her bestselling first novel, *The Women's Room* (1977), and has written further novels and feminist studies.

47 'I hate discussions of feminism that end up with who does the dishes,' she said. So do I. But at the end, there are always those damned dishes.
1977 *The Women's Room*, bk.1, ch.21.

48 Whatever they may be in public life, whatever their relations with men, in their relations with women, all men are rapists, and that's all they are. They rape us with their eyes, their laws, and their codes.
1977 *The Women's Room*, bk.5, ch.19.

Freud, Sir Clement 1924–

English writer and broadcaster.

49 If you resolve to give up smoking, drinking and loving, you don't actually live longer; it just seems longer.
1964 In the *Observer*, 27 Dec.

Freud, Sigmund 1856–1939

Austrian neurologist, founder of psychoanalysis. He published his controversial but influential ideas in such works as *The Interpretation of Dreams* (1900), *The Psychopathology of Everyday Life* (1904) and *Ego and Id* (1923).

50 I am actually not at all a man of science… I am by temperament nothing but a conquistador, an adventurer.
1900 Letter to Wilhelm Fliess, Feb.

51 Congratulations and bouquets keep pouring in, as if the role of sexuality had been suddenly recognised by His Majesty, the interpretation of dreams confirmed by the Council of Ministers, and the necessity of the psychoanalytic therapy of hysteria carried by a two-thirds majority in Parliament.
1902 Letter to Wilhelm Fliess, 11 Mar, describing the public enthusiasm in Vienna that greeted his appointment to an associate professorship at the age of 45.

52 The principal task of civilisation, its actual raison d'être, is to defend us against nature.
1903 *Introductory Lectures.*

53 A woman who is very anxious to get children always reads 'storks' for 'stocks'.
1904 *The Psychopathology of Everyday Life.*

54 *Die Anatomie ist das Schicksal.*
Anatomy is destiny.
1924 *Collected Works*, vol.5.

55 At bottom God is nothing more than an exalted father.
1927 *The Future of an Illusion.*

56 The more the fruits of knowledge become accessible to men, the more widespread is the decline of religious belief.
1927 *The Future of an Illusion.*

Friday, Nancy 1937–

US feminist and writer, whose works include *My Secret Garden* (1973), *My Mother, My Self* (1977) and *Women on Top* (1991).

57 If you believe in the maternal instinct and fail at mother love, you fail as a woman. It is a controlling idea that holds us in an iron grip.
1977 *My Mother, My Self*, ch.1.

58 The older I get, the more of my mother I see in myself.
1977 *My Mother, My Self*, ch.1.

Friedan, Betty (Elizabeth) Naomi *née Goldstein* 1921–

US feminist and writer, founder of the National Organization for Women (1966) and author of the seminal feminist text *The Feminine Mystique* (1963).

59 The problem lay buried, unspoken, for many years in the minds of American women. It was a strange stirring, a sense of dissatisfaction, a yearning that women suffered in the middle of the twentieth century in the United States. Each suburban wife struggled with it alone. As she made the beds, shopped for groceries, matched slipcover material, ate peanut butter sandwiches with her children, chauffeured Cub Scouts and Brownies, lay beside her husband at night—she was afraid to ask even of herself the silent question—'Is this all?'
1963 *The Feminine Mystique*, ch.1, 'The Problem that has No Name'.

60 Women, even though they are almost too visible as sex objects in this country, are invisible people.
1969 Speech at First National Conference for Repeal of Abortion Laws, Chicago.

61 Motherhood will only be a joyous and responsible human act when women are free to make, with full conscious choice and full human responsibility, the decisions to become mothers.
1969 Speech at First National Conference for Repeal of Abortion Laws, Chicago.

Friedman, Milton 1912–

US economist. A leading monetarist, his work includes the permanent income theory of consumption, and the role of money in determining events, particularly the US Great Depression. He was awarded the Nobel prize for economics in 1976.

62 Economics as a positive science is a body of tentatively accepted generalizations about economic phenomena that can be used to predict the consequences of changes in circumstances.
1953 'The Methodology of Positive Economics' in *Essays in Positive Economics.*

63 There is no such thing as a free lunch.
1973 Lecture. The phrase is thought to have been coined anonymously, perhaps referring to the 19c US tradition of supplying food in bars to patrons buying drinks.

64 The price that the market sets on the services of our resources is similarly affected by a bewildering mixture of chance and choice. Frank Sinatra's voice was highly valued in twentieth-century United States. Would it have been highly valued in twentieth-century India, if he had happened to be born and to live there?
1981 *Free to Choose* (with Rose Friedman).

65 No major institution in the US has so poor a record of performance over so long a period as the Federal Reserve, yet so high a public reputation.
1988 'The Fed Has No Clothes', in *The Wall Street Journal*, 15 Apr.

Friedrich, Carl J(oachim) 1901–84

German political theorist. He taught at the universities of Harvard and Heidelberg.

66 To be an American is an ideal, while to be a Frenchman is a fact.
1987 In *Time*, 9 Nov.

Friedrich, Caspar David 1774–1840

German painter, who depicted landscape as vast and desolate expanses in which man is a melancholy spectator.

67 Just as the pious man prays without speaking a word and the Almighty hearkens unto him, so the artist with true feelings *paints* and the sensitive man understands and recognizes it.
Quoted in S Hinz *Caspar David Friedrich in Briefen und Bekenntnissen* (1968).

68 The Divine is everywhere, even in a grain of sand, here I have represented it in bull-rushes.
Remark to the German artist Peter Cornelius, quoted in S Hinz *Caspar David Friedrich in Briefen und Bekenntnissen* (1968).

69 Close your bodily eye, so that you may see your picture first with the spiritual eye. Then bring to the light of day that which you have seen in the darkness so that it may react on others from the outside inwards.
Quoted in *Caspar David Friedrich 1774–1840*, Tate Gallery (1972).

70 Despite what even many artists appear to believe, art is not and should not be merely a skill. It should actually be completely and utterly the language of our feelings, our frame of mind; indeed, even of our devotion and our prayers.
Quoted in *Caspar David Friedrich 1774–1840*, Tate Gallery (1972).

71 The artist should not only paint what he sees before him, but also what he sees within him. If, however, he sees nothing within him, then he should also omit to paint that which he sees before him.
Quoted in *Caspar David Friedrich 1774–1840*, Tate Gallery (1972).

72 Every true work of art must express a distinct feeling.
Quoted in William Vaughn *Romantic Art* (1978).

Friel, Brian 1929–

Northern Irish playwright and short-story writer.

73 Two such wonderful phrases—'I understand perfectly'

and 'That is a lie'—a précis of life, aren't they?
1983 *The Communication Cord.*

74 Do you want the whole countryside to be laughing at us?—women of our years?—mature women, *dancing*?
1990 *Dancing at Lughnasa.*

Frisch, Max Rudolph 1911–91

Swiss writer, novelist and playwright. His novels include *I'm Not Stiller* (1954), *Homo Faber* (1957), and *A Wilderness of Mirrors* (1964). His plays include *The Firebugs* (1953) and *Andorra* (1961, translated 1962).

75 *Ich kann nur berichten, was ich weiß.*
I can only report on what I know.
1957 *Homo Faber*, pt.1.

76 *Technik...Kniff, die Welt so einzurichten, dass wir sie nicht erleben müssen.*
Technology...the knack of so arranging the world that we don't have to experience it.
1957 *Homo Faber*, pt.2.

77 *Kein Mensch, wenn er die Welt sieht, die sie ihm hinterlassen, versteht seine Eltern.*
No one understands their parents when we look at the world that they have bequeathed us.
1961 *Andorra*, sc.9.

78 *Ich habe kein Gemüt, sondern Angst.*
I have no comfort, only anxiety.
1961 *Andorra*, sc.9.

79 *Man kann sich seinen Vater nicht wählen.*
A person cannot choose his father.
1961 *Andorra*, 10.

80 *Ich gehe ins Theater ja auch nicht als Voyeur.*
I do not go into the theatre as a voyeur.
1967 *Biographie.*

Frohman, Charles 1860–1915

US theatre manager. Among his many successful productions were several plays by J M Barrie.

81 Why fear death? It's the most beautiful adventure in life.
1915 Last words, paraphrasing a line in J M Barrie's *Peter Pan*, said to the actress Rita Jolivet as the *Lusitania* went down after being torpedoed by a German submarine, 7 May.

Fromm, Erich 1900–80

German-born US psychoanalyst and author, who emigrated in 1934 to the US, where he practised psychoanalysis and lectured at various institutions.

82 The pace of science forces the pace of technique. Theoretical physics forces atomic energy on us; the successful production of the fission bomb forces upon us the manufacture of the hydrogen bomb. We do not choose our problems, we do not choose our products; we are pushed, we are forced—by what? By a system which has no purpose and goal transcending it, and which makes man its appendix.
1955 *The Sane Society.*

Frost, Robert Lee 1874–1963

US poet, whose work is rooted in New England. He established his reputation with *A Boy's World* (1913) and *North of Boston* (1914) and won Pulitzer Prizes in 1924, 1931, 1937 and 1943.

83 Most of the change we think we see in life
Is due to truths being in and out of favour.
1914 *North of Boston*, 'The Black Cottage'.

84 Something there is that doesn't love a wall,
That sends the frozen-ground-swell under it,
And spills the upper boulders in the sun;
And makes gaps even two can pass abreast.
1914 *North of Boston*, 'Mending Wall'.

85 Before I built a wall I'd ask to know
What I was walling in or walling out,
And to whom I was like to give offence.
1914 *North of Boston*, 'Mending Wall'.

86 Part of a moon was falling down the west,
Dragging the whole sky with it to the hills.
1914 *North of Boston*, 'The Death of the Hired Man'.

87 'Home is the place where, when you have to go there,
They have to take you in.'
'I should have called it
Something you somehow haven't to deserve.'
1914 *North of Boston*, 'The Death of the Hired Man'.

88 A sentence is a sound in itself on which sounds called words may be strung.
1914 Letter to John Bartlett, 22 Feb.

89 I shall be telling this with a sigh
Somewhere ages and ages hence:
Two roads diverged in a wood, and I—
I took the one less traveled by,
And that has made all the difference.
1916 'The Road Not Taken'.

90 We love the things we love for what they are.
1916 'Hyla Brook'.

91 The question that he frames in all but words
Is what to make of a diminished thing.
1916 'The Oven Bird'.

92 I'd like to go by climbing a birch tree
And climb black branches up a snow-white trunk
Toward heaven, till the tree could bear no more,
But dipped its top and set me down again.
That would be good both going and coming back.
One could do worse than be a swinger of birches.
1916 'Birches'.

93 They listened at his heart.
Little—less—nothing!—and that ended it.
No more to build on there. And they, since they
Were not the one dead, turned to their affairs.
1916 'Out, Out—'.

94 No wonder poets sometimes have to *seem*
So much more businesslike than businessmen.
Their wares are so much harder to get rid of.
1923 'New Hampshire'.

95 He knew too well for any earthly use
The line where man leaves off and nature starts,
And never overstepped it save in dreams.
1923 'New Hampshire'.

96 Never tell me that not one star of all
That slip from heaven at night and softly fall
Has been picked up with stones to build a wall.
1923 'A Star in a Stoneboat'.

97 Some say the world will end in fire,
Some say in ice.

From what I've tasted of desire
I hold with those who favour fire.
But if I had to perish twice,
I think I know enough of hate
To say that for destruction ice
Is also great
And would suffice.
1923 'Fire and Ice', complete poem.

98 The woods are lovely, dark and deep.
But I have promises to keep,
And miles to go before I sleep,
And miles to go before I sleep.
1923 'Stopping by Woods on a Snowy Evening'.

99 I have been one acquainted with the night.
1928 'Acquainted with the Night'.

1 It is this backward motion toward the source,
Against the stream, that most we see ourselves in.
The tribute of the current to the source.
1928 'West-Running Brook'.

2 The land may vary more;
But wherever the truth may be—
The water comes ashore,
And the people look at the sea.
1928 'Neither Far Out Nor in Deep'.

3 A poet is a person who thinks there is something special about a poet and about his loving one unattainable woman. You'll usually find he takes the physical out on whores. I am defining a romantic poet—and there is no other kind. An unromantic poet is a self-contradiction.
1930 Letter to Louis Untermeyer, 6 Jun.

4 Writing free verse is like playing tennis with the net down.
1935 Address at Milton Academy, Mass, 17 May.

5 What brought the kindred spider to that height,
Then steered the white moth thither in the night?
What but design of darkness to appall?—
If design govern in a thing so small.
1936 'Design'.

6 I never dared be radical when young
For fear it would make me conservative when old.
1936 'Ten Mills, 1. Precaution'.

7 Like a piece of ice on a hot stove the poem must ride on its own melting. A poem may be worked over once it is in being, but may not be worried into being.
1939 'The Figure a Poem Makes', preface to *Collected Poems*.

8 Happiness Makes Up in Height for What It Lacks in Length.
1942 Title of poem.

9 The land was ours before we were the land's.
She was our land more than a hundred years
Before we were her people.
1942 'The Gift Outright'.

10 And were an epitaph to be my story
I'd have a short one ready for my own.
I would have written of me on my stone:
I had a lover's quarrel with the world.
1942 'The Lesson for Today'.

11 We dance round in a ring and suppose,
But the Secret sits in the middle and knows.
1942 'The Secret Sits', complete poem.

12 I have never started a poem yet whose end I knew.
Writing a poem is discovering.
1955 In the *New York Times*, 7 Nov.

13 Forgive, O Lord, my little jokes on Thee
And I'll forgive Thy great big one on me.
1960 'The Preacher', complete poem.

14 Poetry is a way of taking life by the throat.
Quoted in Elizabeth S Sergeant *Robert Frost: The Trial By Existence* (1960).

15 Summoning artists to participate
In the august occasions of the state
Seems something artists ought to celebrate.
1961 'For John F Kennedy: His Inauguration', 20 Jan. Snow-blindness prevented the aged poet from reading beyond the first three lines on the occasion.

16 Courage is in the air in bracing whiffs.
1961 'For John F Kennedy: His Inauguration', 20 Jan.

17 Education is… hanging around until you've caught on.
Recalled on his death, 29 Jan 1963.

18 The mind skating circles around itself as it moves forward.
His definition of style. Recalled on his death, 29 Jan 1963.

19 The right reader of a good poem can tell the moment it strikes him that he has taken an immortal wound—that he will never get over it.
Recalled on his death, 29 Jan 1963.

20 Poetry is what is lost in translation. It is also what is lost in interpretation.
Quoted in Louis Untermeyer *Robert Frost: A Backward Look* (1964).

Froude, James Anthony 1818–94

English writer and historian, who resigned his Oxford fellowship after controversy over his early novels. He wrote a *History of England from the Fall of Wolsey to the Spanish Armada* (12 vols, 1856–69).

21 Wild animals never kill for sport. Man is the only one to whom the torture and death of his fellow-creatures is amusing in itself.
1886 *Oceana*.

Fry, C(harles) B(urgess) 1872–1956

English all-round sportsman, who represented his country in athletics, cricket and soccer. As a cricketer, he played 26 Tests for England, some as captain. After World War II he served as India's delegate to the League of Nations and declined an offer of the throne of Albania.

22 It is a standing insult to sportsmen to have to play under a rule which assumes that players intend to trip, hack and push their opponents, and to behave like cads of the most unscrupulous kidney. The lines marking a penalty area are a disgrace to the playing fields of a public school.
1907 Quoted in Colin Jarman *The Guinness Dictionary of Sports Quotations* (1990).

23 In football it is widely acknowledged that if both sides agree to cheat, cheating is fair.
1911 Quoted in Colin Jarman *The Guinness Dictionary of Sports Quotations* (1990).

24 The game is so full of plot-interest and drama.
Of rugby union. Quoted in E H D Sewell *Rugger: The Man's Game* (1950).

Fry, Christopher *pseudonym of* *Christopher Harris* 1907–

English playwright. His early poetic drama was succeeded by comedies and tragi-comedies such as *A Phoenix Too Frequent* (1946) and *Venus Observed* (1950).

25 The Lady's Not for Burning.
1949 Play title, subsequently reworked by Margaret Thatcher in the form 'The lady's not for turning' at the Conservative Party Conference, 1980.

26 What after all
Is a halo? It's only one more thing to keep clean.
1949 *The Lady's Not for Burning*, act 1.

27 Where in this small-talking world can I find
A longitude with no platitude?
1949 *The Lady's Not for Burning*, act 3.

28 I hope
I've done nothing so monosyllabic as to cheat.
A spade is never so merely a spade as the word
Spade would imply.
1950 *Venus Observed*, act 1.

29 The Dark Is Light Enough.
1954 Title of play.

Fry, Elizabeth 1780–1845

English Quaker prison reformer who devoted her life to prison and asylum reform at home and abroad.

30 Does capital punishment tend to the security of the people? By no means. It hardens the hearts of men, and makes the loss of life appear light to them; and it renders life insecure, inasmuch as the law holds out that property is of greater value than life.
Quoted in Rachel E Cresswell and Katharine Fry *Memoir of the Life of Elizabeth Fry* (1848).

31 Punishment is not for revenge, but to lessen crime and reform the criminal.
Quoted in Rachel E Cresswell and Katharine Fry *Memoir of the Life of Elizabeth Fry* (1848).

Fry, Roger Eliot 1866–1934

English artist and art critic, who championed modern artists such as Cézanne, organizing the first London exhibition of Post-Impressionists in 1910. He devised an aesthetic theory of 'significant form'.

32 The trouble with Moore is that he knows what a work of art is, and is trying to make one.
c.1930 Of Henry Moore. Quoted in Robert Medley *Drawn from the Life: a Memoir* (1983).

33 Art is significant deformity.
Quoted in Virginia Woolf *Roger Fry* (1940), ch.8.

Fry, Stephen 1957–

English actor, writer and broadcaster.

34 Only my tongue, sir.
2004 When asked by a security guard at Heathrow Airport whether he had any sharp objects on him. Quoted in the *Observer*, 6 Jun.

Frye, Northrop 1912–91

Canadian literary critic and Episcopalian priest. His influential *Anatomy of Criticism* (1957) explores the common motifs and myths underlying literature.

35 Literature is a human apocalypse, man's revelation to man, and criticism is not a body of adjudications, but the awareness of that revelation, the last judgment of mankind.
1963 *The Educated Imagination*, 'The Keys of Dreamland'.

36 Literature is conscious mythology: as society develops, its mythical stories become structural principles of story-telling, its mythical concepts, sun-gods and the like, become habits of metaphoric thought. In a fully mature literary tradition the writer enters into a structure of traditional stories and images.
1971 *The Bush Garden*, 'Conclusion'.

37 Where is here?
'Haunted by Lack of Ghosts', in David Staines (ed) *The Canadian Imagination* (1977).

38 Most of my writing consists of an attempt to translate aphorisms into continuous prose.
Quoted in Richard Kostelanetz, 'The Literature Professors' Literature Professor', in *The Michigan Quarterly Review*, Fall 1978.

39 The knowledge that you can have is inexhaustible, and what is inexhaustible is benevolent. The knowledge that you cannot have is of the riddles of birth and death, of our future destiny and the purposes of God. Here there is no knowledge, but illusions that restrict freedom and limit hope. Accept the mystery behind knowledge: It is not darkness but shadow.
1988 Address, Metropolitan United Church, Toronto, 10 Apr, quoted by Alexandra Johnston in *Vic Report*, spring 1991.

40 Even the human heart is slightly left of centre.
Quoted by Paul Wilson in 'Growing Up with Orwell', in *The Idler*, Jul–Aug 1989.

Fuentes, Carlos 1928–

Mexican novelist and playwright, press secretary with the UN and Ambassador to France (1975–7). His works include short stories, and novels such as *Terra nostra* (1975), *The Old Gringo* (1985) and *The Years with Laura Diaz* (1999).

41 *Yo soy un artista. El placer de la carne le resta fuerzas a mi vocación pictórica, prefiero sentir que los jugos de mi sexo fluyen hacia un cuadro, lo irrigan, lo fertilizan, lo realzan; cástrame el goce de la carne, satisfáceme el goce del arte.*
I am an artist. The pleasure of the flesh robs strength from my artistic vocation, I prefer to feel my sexual juices flow toward a painting, wash over it, fertilize it, realize it; the delights of the flesh castrate me, the delights of art satisfy me.
1975 *Terra nostra*, 'El cronista'.

42 What America does best is to understand itself. What it does worst is to understand others.
1986 In *Time*, 16 Jun.

Fulbright, J(ames) William 1905–95

US Democratic politician, lawyer and author. As Chairman of the Senate Committee on Foreign Relations, he became a major critic of the Vietnam War (1964–75).

43 We have the power to do any damn fool thing we want to do, and we seem to do it every 10 minutes.
1952 In *Time*, 4 Feb.

44 In a democracy dissent is an act of faith. Like medicine, the test of its value is not in its taste, but its effects.

1966 Speech to the US Senate, 21 Apr.

45 Fearful and hostile behavior is not rational but neither is it uncommon, either to individuals or to nations, including our own.
1995 On the 'arrogance of power' of US policy on Vietnam. In the *New Yorker*, 6 Mar.

Fulford, Robert 1932–

Canadian cultural commentator.

46 My generation of Canadians grew up believing that, if we were very good or very smart, or both, we would someday *graduate* from Canada.
1970 'Notebook', in *Saturday Night*, Oct.

Fuller, (Sarah) Margaret, Marchioness Ossoli 1810–50

US feminist and literary critic. She edited *Dial* (a transcendentalist journal, 1840–2) and moved to New York (1844) then Italy (1847), where she married Marquis Ossoli and was involved in the Revolution. She was shipwrecked returning to New York.

47 Beware of over-great pleasure in being popular or even beloved.
1840 Letter to her brother, 20 Dec. Collected in Alice Rossi *The Feminist Papers* (1973).

48 As the friend of the negro assumes that one man cannot, by right, hold another in bondage, should the friend of woman assume that man cannot, by right, lay even well-meant restrictions on woman.
1843 'The Great Lawsuit', in *Dial*, vol.4, Jul.

49 It is well known that of every strong woman they say she has a masculine mind.
1843 'The Great Lawsuit', in *Dial*, vol.4, Jul.

Fuller, Peter 1947–90

English art critic, writer and founder of the magazine *Modern Painters*.

50 It is only a mild exaggeration to say that now no one wants Fine Artists, except Fine Artists, and that neither they nor anyone else have the slightest idea what they should be doing, or for whom they should be doing it.
1981 *Beyond the Crisis in Art*.

Fuller, R(ichard) Buckminster 1895–1983

US architect, inventor, engineer and philosopher, whose revolutionary technological designs reflect his personal vision of a better-designed and more efficient future. In 1962 he became Norton Professor of Poetry at Harvard.

51 God, to me, it seems,
is a verb
not a noun
proper or improper.
1940 Poem, published in *No More Secondhand God* (1963).
► *See Hugo 421:83.*

52 I just invent, then wait until man comes around to needing what I've invented.
1964 On his innovative geodesic domes. In *Time*, 10 Jun.

53 Either war is obsolete or men are.
1966 In the *New Yorker*, 8 Jan.

54 I am a passenger on the spaceship, Earth.
1969 *Operating Manual for Spaceship Earth*, ch.1.

55 Now there is one outstandingly important fact regarding Spaceship Earth, and that is that no instruction book came with it.
1969 *Operating Manual for Spaceship Earth*, ch.4.

56 If we do more with less, our response will be adequate to take care of everybody.
1972 In *Playboy*.

Fuller, Roy Broadbent 1912–91

English poet and novelist. His work is marked by careful construction and acute observation.

57 As horrible thoughts,
Loud fluttering aircraft slope above his head
At dusk.
The ridiculous empires break like biscuits.
1942 'The Middle of a War'.

58 The poets get a quizzical ahem.
They reflect time, I am the very ticking.
1944 'A Wry Smile'.

59 Anyone happy in this age and place
Is daft or corrupt. Better to abdicate
From a material and spiritual terrain
Fit only for barbarians.
1954 'Translation'.

Fuller, Thomas 1608–61

English antiquarian and divine. His 11-volume *Church History of Britain* (1655) was attacked as a 'rhapsody'. The unfinished *Great Worthies of England*, a biographical miscellany, was published by his son in 1661.

60 Know most of the rooms of thy native country before thou goest over the threshold thereof.
1642 *The Holy and Profane State*, bk.2, ch.4, 'Of Travelling'.

61 *Mon Mam Cymbry.* That is, Anglesea is the Mother of Wales.
1662 *History of the Worthies of England*, 'Anglesea'. The saying is an old one, meaning that Anglesey's corn is enough to sustain all Wales.

Fuller, Thomas 1654–1734

English physician and writer.

62 Bacchus hath drowned more men than Neptune.
1732 *Gnomologia*, no.830.

63 Borrowed garments never fit well.
1732 *Gnomologia*, no.1008.

64 Eat-well is drink-well's brother.
1732 *Gnomologia*, no.1357.

65 Fine cloth is never out of fashion.
1732 *Gnomologia*, no.1537.

66 God sends meat, and the devil sends cooks.
1732 *Gnomologia*, no.1687.

67 Good clothes open all doors.
1732 *Gnomologia*, no.1705.

68 It is in vain to mislike the current fashion.
1732 *Gnomologia*, no.2968.

69 The present fashion is always handsome.
1732 *Gnomologia*, no.4718.

70 Often drunk, and seldom sober

Falls like the leaves in October.
1732 *Gnomologia*, no.6219.

71 It signifies nothing to play well and lose.
1732 Quoted in Colin Jarman *The Guinness Dictionary of Sports Quotations* (1990).

Furthman, Jules 1888–1966

US screenwriter. His credits include *Shanghai Express* (1932), *Mutiny on the Bounty* (1935), *To Have and Have Not* (1945) and *The Big Sleep* (1946).

72 You know you don't have to act with me, Steve. You don't have to say anything and you don't have to do anything. Not a thing. Oh, maybe just whistle. You know how to whistle, don't you, Steve? You just put your lips together—and blow.
1945 Lauren Bacall as Slim to Humphrey Bogart (Steve) in *To Have and Have Not* (with William Faulkner).

Fuseli, Henry 1741–1825

Swiss-born British painter and art critic. He was a key figure of the Romantic movement.

73 Art, like love, excludes all competition and absorbs the man.
1789 *Aphorisms on Art*, no.3 (published 1831).

74 The superiority of the Greeks seems not so much the result of climate and society, as of the simplicity of their end and the uniformity of their means.
1789 *Aphorisms on Art*, no.148 (published 1831).

75 Art among a religious race produces reliques; among a military one, trophies, among a commercial one, articles of trade.
1789 *Aphorisms on Art*, no.149 (published 1831).

76 The forms of virtue are erect, the forms of pleasure undulate.
1789 *Aphorisms on Art*, no.194 (published 1831).

77 Selection is the invention of the landscape painter.
1789 *Aphorisms on Art*, no.237, (published 1831).

Fyffe, Will 1885–1947

Scottish comedian, singer and actor. He wrote several sketches for Harry Lauder and when they were rejected performed them himself, thereby launching a long and successful career on stage and in film.

78 I belong to Glasgow
Dear old Glasgow town!
But what's the matter with Glasgow?
For it's going round and round.
I'm only a common old working chap,
As anyone can see,
But when I get a couple of drinks on a Saturday,
Glasgow belongs to me.
1921 'I Belong to Glasgow', chorus.

Fyleman, Rose 1877–1957

English children's writer.

79 There are fairies at the bottom of our garden.
1918 *Fairies and Chimneys*, 'The Fairies'.

Gabor, Dennis 1900–79

Hungarian-born British physicist. Gabor studied and worked in Germany but left in 1933 to become professor of electronics at Imperial College, London. He did important work on the electronic microscope and is generally recognized as the main contributor to the discovery of holography.

80 Till now man has been up against Nature: from now on he will be up against his own nature.
1964 *Inventing the Future*.

81 The most important and urgent problems of the technology of today are no longer the satisfactions of the primary needs or of archetypal wishes, but the reparation of the evils and damages wrought by the technology of yesterday.
1970 *Innovations*.

Gabor, Zsa Zsa 1919–

Hungarian-born US actress, sister of Eva Gabor. Her films include *Moulin Rouge* (1953), *Touch of Evil* (1958) and *Arrivederci Baby* (1966).

82 I never hated a man enough to give him diamonds back.
Quoted in the *Observer*, 28 Aug 1957.

83 A girl must marry for love and keep on marrying until she finds it.
Attributed.

Gagarin, Yuri A(lekseyevich) 1934–68

Soviet cosmonaut, the first person to achieve orbital space flight, on 12 Apr 1961.

84 I could have gone on flying through space forever.
1961 In the *New York Times*, 14 Apr.

Gainsborough, Thomas 1727–88

English portrait and landscape painter.

85 I wish you would recollect that Painting and Punctuality mix like Oil and Vinegar, and that Genius and regularity are utter Enemies and must be to the end of time.
1772 Letter to Edward Stratford, 1 May, excusing himself for not yet finishing the portrait of him and his wife.

86 We are all going to heaven, and Vandyke is of the company.
1788 Last words (attributed), quoted in William B Boulton *Thomas Gainsborough* (1905), ch.9.

Gaitskell, Hugh 1906–63

English Labour politician, Leader of the Opposition (1955–63). He opposed Eden's Suez action (1956), and refused to accept a narrow conference vote for unilateral disarmament (1960), surviving the subsequent leadership challenge.

87 Some of us will fight and fight again to save the party we love. We will fight and fight again to bring back sanity and honesty and dignity, so that our party, with its great past,

may retain its glory and its greatness.
1960 Denouncing unilateralists trying to gain control of the party. Labour Party conference speech, Oct.

88 Let us not forget that we can never go farther than we can persuade at least half the people to go.
1061 Labour Party conference speech, Oct.

89 It does mean the end of Britain as an independent European state. It means the end of a thousand years of history.
1962 On Britain joining the European Community. Labour Party conference speech, Oct.

Galbraith, John Kenneth 1908–

Canadian-born US economist and diplomat, Professor at Harvard (1949–75), Ambassador to India (1961–3) and adviser to Presidents Kennedy and Johnson.

90 The charge that an idea is radical, impractical, or long haired is met by showing that a prominent businessman has favored it...an additional tactic in this strategy of defense...is to assert that Winston Churchill once sponsored the particular idea. If one is challenged, a sufficiently careful investigation will show that he did.
1955 *Economics and the Art of Controversy.*

91 Few things are as immutable as the addiction of political groups to the ideas by which they have once won office.
1958 *The Affluent Society.*

92 In the affluent society, no useful distinction can be made between luxuries and necessities.
1958 *The Affluent Society.*

93 It takes a certain brashness to attack the accepted economic legends but none at all to perpetuate them. So they are perpetuated.
1960 *The Liberal Hour.*

94 Politics is not the art of the possible. It consists in choosing between the disastrous and the unpalatable.
1962 Letter to John F Kennedy, 2 Mar.
► *See Butler 176:34.*

95 The line dividing the state from what is called private enterprise, or at least from the highly organized part of it, is a traditional fiction.
1967 *The New Industrial State.*

96 The real accomplishment of modern science and technology consists in taking ordinary men, informing them narrowly and deeply and then, through appropriate organization, arranging to have their knowledge combined with that of other specialized but equally ordinary men. This dispenses with the need for genius. The resulting performance, though less inspiring, is far more predictable.
1967 *The New Industrial State.*

97 There are times in politics when you must be on the right side and lose.
1968 In the *Observer*, 11 Feb.

98 It is the good fortune of the affluent country that the opportunity cost of economic discussion is low and hence it can afford all kinds.
1971 *Economics, Peace, and Laughter.*

99 In a world where for pedagogic and other purposes a very large number of economists is required, an arrangement which discourages many of them from rendering public advice would seem to be well conceived.
1971 *Economics, Peace, and Laughter.*

1 Much discussion of money involves a heavy overlay of priestly incantation.
1975 *Money*, p.4.

2 Much of the world's work, it has been said, is done by men who do not feel quite well. Marx is a case in point.
1977 *The Age of Uncertainty*, ch.3.

3 We have escapist fiction...why not escapist biography?
1980 In the *New York Times*, 27 Jul.

4 Speeches in our culture are the vacuum that fills a vacuum.
1984 Speech at the American University, Washington DC. Quoted in *Time* magazine, 18 Jun.

Galeano, Eduardo 1940–

Uruguayan writer and journalist. His books include *Days and Nights of Love and War* (1978) and the trilogy *Memory of Fire* (1985–8).

5 In the house of words was a table of colors. They offered themselves in great fountains and each poet took the color he needed: lemon yellow or sun yellow, ocean blue or smoke blue, crimson red, blood red, wine red.
1991 *The Book of Embraces.*

Galen *or Claudius Galenus* c.130–c.201AD

Greek physician, imperial physician to Marcus Aurelius, Commodus and Severus. He wrote extensively on medical and philosophical matters, and his theories have been highly influential.

6 Much music marreth men's manners.
Quoted in Roger Ascham *Toxophilus* (1545).

Galilei, Galileo 1564–1642

Italian astronomer, mathematician and physicist, credited with anticipating Newton's laws of motion. He constructed the first astronomical telescope, and controversially argued that the earth revolved around the sun.

7 *Eppur si muove.*
Nevertheless, it moves.
1632 Attributed muttered remark, after being compelled to publicly renounce his arguments against a geocentric universe. This famous quotation is almost certainly an invention.

8 Light held together by moisture.
Attributed, a description of wine.

Gallagher, Noel 1967–

English rock star, founder member of the band Oasis.

9 Some might say they don't believe in heaven
Go and tell it to the man who lives in hell.
1995 'Some Might Say'.

10 I would hope we mean more to people than putting money in a church basket and saying ten Hail Marys on a Sunday. Has God played Knebworth recently?
1997 On the attraction of Oasis. In the *New Musical Express*, 12 Jul.

11 The funny thing is, that mouthing off three years ago about how we were going to be the biggest band in the

world, we actually went and done it. And it was a piece of piss.
1998 Quoted in the *Guinness Rockopedia*.

Gallico, Paul William 1897–1976

US journalist, novelist and short-story writer. His works include *The Snow Goose* (1941) and *The Poseidon Adventure* (1969).

12 College football today is one of the last great strongholds of genuine old-fashioned American hypocrisy.
1938 *Farewell to Sport*.

13 When in Doubt—Wash.
1950 *Jennie*, ch.5, chapter title. Peter, having turned into a cat, is taught the proper etiquette.

14 I have covered boxing, promoted boxing, watched it, thought about it, and after long reflection I cannot find a single thing that is good about it either from the point of view of participant or spectator.
Quoted in Edith Summerskill *The Ignoble Art* (1956).

15 No one can be as calculatedly rude as the British, which amazes Americans, who do not understand studied insult and can only offer abuse as a substitute.
1962 In the *New York Times*, 14 Jan.

Galloway, George 1954–

Scottish Labour politician.

16 I saw 'New Labour' conceived, watched it gestate, witnessed its birth and growth. Now I fervently hope I will be present at its death.
2004 *I'm Not the Only One*.

Galloway, Janice 1956–

Scottish writer. She worked as a teacher, but became a full-time writer after the success of her first novel *The Trick Is to Keep Breathing* (1989), chronicling a mental breakdown. Other works include the short-story collection *Blood* (1991) and the novel *Clara* (2002).

17 The Trick Is to Keep Breathing.
1989 Title of first novel.

18 I write because I hate being told HOW IT IS. I didn't realise that for a long while. I thought it was LIFE I hated: that the unfairnesses that were explained as JUST HOW IT IS were JUST HOW IT IS. BUT HOW IT IS wasn't.
1993 'Objective Truth and the Grinding Machine'. In Brown and Munro (eds) *Writers Writing* (1993).

19 Quiet book-learning in monasteries and ethereal music, sonnets and courtly love—that stuff is all fantasy and veneer… You couldn't afford to let the beauty of the thing seduce you too far or you forgot the truth and the truth was always hard as iron bloody bars.
1994 *Foreign Parts*, ch.7.

Gallup, George Horace 1901–84

US statistician and public opinion expert. He developed the Gallup polls for testing public opinion, which proved their worth by correctly predicting Franklin Roosevelt's 1936 election victory.

20 Polling is merely an instrument for gauging public opinion. When a president or any other leader pays attention to poll results, he is, in effect, paying attention to the views of the people. Any other interpretation is nonsense.
1979 NBC news, 1 Dec.

21 I could prove God statistically.
Attributed.

Galsworthy, John 1867–1933

English novelist and playwright, best known for his series of novels *The Forsyte Saga* (1906–28). His plays, including *Strife* (1909), illustrate his interest in social and ethical issues. He was awarded the Nobel prize in 1932.

22 From all *I* can learn, he's got no business, no income, and no connection worth speaking of; but then, I know nothing—nobody tells me anything.
1906 *The Man of Property*, pt.1, ch.1.

23 When a Forsyte was engaged, married, or born, the Forsytes were present; when a Forsyte died—but no Forsyte had as yet died; they did not die; death being contrary to their principles, they took precautions against it, the instinctive precautions of highly vitalised persons who resent encroachments on their property.
1906 *The Man of Property*, pt.1, ch.1.

24 It is not good enough to spend time and ink in describing the penultimate sensations and physical movements of people getting into a state of rut, we all know them so well.
1914 On D H Lawrence's *Sons and Lovers*, in a letter to Edward Garnett, 13 Apr.

25 He was afflicted by the thought that where Beauty was, nothing ever ran quite straight, which, no doubt, was why so many people looked on it as immoral.
1920 *In Chancery*, pt.1, ch.13.

26 When we began this fight, we had clean hands—are they clean now? What's gentility worth if it can't stand fire?
1920 *The Skin Game*, act 3.

27 Slang is vigorous and apt. Probably most of our vital words were once slang.
1927 *Castles in Spain and Other Screeds*.

Galt, John 1779–1839

Scottish novelist and Canadian pioneer. After a failed business venture in London he travelled in the Levant (1809–11) and later turned to writing.

28 In a word, man in London is not quite so good a creature as he is out of it.
1821 *The Ayrshire Legatees*, ch.7, 'Discoveries and Rebellions', letter 22.

29 From the lone shieling of the misty island
Mountains divide us, and the waste of seas—
Yet still the blood is strong, the heart is Highland,
And we in dreams behold the Hebrides!
Fair these broad meads, these hoary woods are grand;
But we are exiles from our fathers' land.
1829 'Canadian Boat Song', a translation from the Gaelic attributed to Galt, published in *Blackwood's Magazine*, Sep. It has also been attributed to Walter Scott.

Galtieri, Leopoldo Fortunato 1926–2003

Argentinian soldier and politician, President of Argentina (1981–3). In 1982, he ordered the invasion of the disputed

Malvinas (Falkland) Islands; their recovery by Britain led to his downfall.

30 Why are you telling me this? The British won't fight.
1982 Responding to a warning from US Secretary of State Alexander Haig about the consequence of the invasion.

Galton, Sir Francis 1822–1911

English scientist. He travelled widely in Africa and wrote *The Art of Travel* (1855), which became the explorer's standard handbook.

31 There are even times when any assumption of dignity becomes ludicrous, and the traveller must, as Mungo Park once had to do, 'lay down as a rule to make himself as useless and as insignificant as possible, as the only means of recovering his liberty'.
1855 *The Art of Travel.*

Gandhi, Indira Priyad Arshini 1917–84

Indian politician and Prime Minister (1966–77, 1980–4). Although a leader of the developing nations, she failed to suppress sectarian violence at home and was assassinated by Sikh extremists, members of her bodyguard.

32 Even if I die in the service of this nation, I would be proud of it. Every drop of my blood, I am sure, will contribute to the growth of this nation and make it strong and dynamic.
1984 Speech at Orissa, 31 Oct, the day before her assassination.

Gandhi, Mohandas Karamchand *known as* *Mahatma [great soul]* 1869–1948

Indian nationalist leader, who advocated peaceful non-cooperation to achieve independence, but was jailed for conspiracy (1922–4) following his civil disobedience campaign. After independence (1947), his attempts to stop the Hindu–Muslim conflict in Bengal led to his assassination by a Hindu fanatic.

33 I claim that in losing the spinning wheel we lost our left lung. We are, therefore, suffering from galloping consumption. The restoration of the wheel arrests the progress of the…disease.
1921 Speech, 13 Oct.

34 Non-violence is the first article of my faith. It is also the last article of my creed.
1922 Speech at Shahi Bag, 18 Mar.

35 Non-violence is not a garment to be put on and off at will. Its seat is in the heart, and it must be an inseparable part of our very being.
1926 *War or Peace*, 'Young India'.

36 What do I think of Western civilization? I think that it would be a good idea.
Attributed.

Gandhi, Sonia 1946–

Italian-born Indian politician, widow of Rajiv Gandhi and daughter-in-law of Indira Gandhi.

37 There is no question. It is my inner voice, it is my conscience.
2004 On turning down the office of Indian prime minister, 18 May.

Garbo, Greta *pseudonym of* *Greta Lovisa Gustafsson* 1905–90

Swedish-born actress who went to the US in 1925 with director Mauritz Stiller. Her films at MGM during the 1930s include *Queen Christina* (1933), *Anna Karenina* (1936) and *Ninotchka* (1939). She retired in 1941.

38 I want to be alone.
1932 The media have famously attributed these words to Garbo although she always denied she said them. In the film *Grand Hotel* (1932) Grusinskaya (played by Garbo) says 'I want to be left alone'.

39 One day, there's a hand that goes over the face and changes it. You look like an apple that isn't young anymore.
Quoted in *Vanity Fair*, Feb 1994.

García Márquez, Gabriel 1928–

Colombian novelist and journalist, awarded the Nobel prize for literature (1982). His fiction, typically set in the imaginary village of Macondo, tends to magic realism.

40 *No se le había ocurrido pensar hasta entonces que la literatura fuera el mejor juguete que se había inventado para burlarse de la gente.*
It had never occurred to him until then to think that literature was the best plaything that had ever been invented to make fun of people.
1967 *Cien años de soledad* (translated as *One Hundred Years of Solitude*, 1970).

41 The last optimist left in Colombia.
Attributed.

Garcilaso de la Vega, Inca 1539–1616

Peruvian soldier, translator and historian, son of a Spanish father and an Inca princess. He went to Spain in 1560 and became a soldier. His historical compositions draw on both indigenous sources and imagination.

42 *Porque allá los españoles y las otras naciones…como tienen historias divinas y humanas, saben por ellas cuándo empezaron a reinar sus Reyes y los ajenos…todo esto y mucho más saben por sus libros. Empero vosotros, que carecéis de ellos, Qué memoria tenéis de vuestras antiguallas?, Quién fue el primero de nuestros Incas?*
Over there Spaniards and other nations know from their divine and human history when their Kings and other peoples' Kings began their reigns… Their books teach them all of this, and much more. But you, who have no books, what memories do you have of your ancient past? Who was our first Inca?
1609 *Comentarios reales* (*The Royal Commentaries of Peru*, 1688), bk.1, ch.15.

Gardner, Ava *originally* *Lucy Johnson* 1922–90

US film actress. Signed for MGM as a teenager, she achieved fame in *The Killers* (1946) and later *The Barefoot Contessa* (1954) and *Night of the Iguana* (1964). She was married to Mickey Rooney, Artie Shaw and Frank Sinatra.

43 *On the Beach* is a story about the end of the world, and Melbourne sure is the right place to film it.
1959 Alleged comment to Australian journalist Neil Jillett of the Melbourne *Age* at the shooting of a film based on the book by British–Australian novelist Nevil Shute.

44 What I'd really like to say about stardom is that it gave me everything I never wanted.
1990 *Ava: My Story.*

Gardner, John William 1912–77

US public official, Secretary of Health, Education and Welfare (1965–8). In 1970 he founded the citizens' lobby Common Force, which he chaired until his death.

45 We are all faced with a series of great opportunities—brilliantly disguised as insoluble problems.
Quoted in *Reader's Digest*, Mar 1966.

46 We get richer and richer in filthier and filthier communities until we reach a final stage of affluent misery—a crocus on a garbage heap.
1969 In the *New York Times*, 9 Oct.

Garibaldi, Giuseppe 1807–82

Italian patriot, twice forced to flee the country for his revolutionary activities. He returned in 1859 for Italy's war of liberation, leading his thousand 'Red Shirts', conquering Sicily and Naples for the unified kingdom of Italy.

47 England is a great and powerful nation, foremost in human progress, enemy to despotism, the only safe refuge for the exile, friend of the oppressed. If ever England should be so circumstanced as to require the help of any ally, cursed be the Italian who would not step forward with me in her defence.
1854 Letter, 12 Apr.

48 *Soldati, io esco da Roma. Chi vuole continuare la guerra contro lo straniero venga con me. Non posso offrigli né onori né stipendi; gli offro fame, sete, marce forzate, battaglie e morte. Chi ama la Patria me segua.*
Soldiers, I'm getting out of Rome. Anyone who wants to carry on the war against the outsiders, follow me. I can offer you neither honours nor wages, I offer you hunger, thirst, forced marches, battles and death. Anyone who loves his country, follow me.
Quoted in Giuseppe Guerzoni *Garibaldi* (1882), vol.1.

Garland, (Hannibal) Hamlin 1860–1940

US writer. He is remembered chiefly for his stories of Midwest farm life in books including *Main-Travelled Roads* (1891) and *Prairie Folks* (1892), but also wrote novels, essays and memoirs.

49 Like the main-travelled road of life it is traversed by many classes of people, but the poor and the weary predominate.
1891 *Main-Travelled Roads*, 'The Main-Travelled Road of the West'.

50 There is no gilding of setting sun or glamor of poetry to light up the ferocious and endless toil of the farmers' wives.
1899 *Boy Life on the Prairie*, 'Melons and Early Frost'.

Garner, John Nance 1868–1967

US lawyer and politician, Speaker of the House (1931–3) and Vice-President under President Roosevelt (1933–41). He opposed Roosevelt's third-term candidacy and retired in 1941.

51 Worst damnfool mistake I ever made was letting myself be elected Vice-President of the United States. Should have stuck…as Speaker of the House… Gave up the second most important job in Government for eight long years as Roosevelt's spare tire.
1963 In the *Saturday Evening Post*, 2 Nov.

52 The vice-presidency isn't worth a pitcher of warm piss. It doesn't amount to a hill of beans.
Quoted in O C Fisher *Cactus Jack* (1978), ch.11.

Garrick, David 1717–79

English actor and theatre manager. He revolutionized acting with his naturalistic Shakespearean heroes and in 1747 became manager of the Drury Lane theatre, introducing many theatrical reforms.

53 Here lies Nolly Goldsmith, for shortness called Noll,
Who wrote like an angel, but talked like poor Poll.
1773 Of Oliver Goldsmith. 'Impromptu Epitaph'.

54 Are these the choice dishes the Doctor has sent us?
Is this the great poet whose works so content us?
This Goldsmith's fine feast, who has written fine books?
Heaven sends us fine meat, but the Devil sends cooks.
1777 'On Doctor Goldsmith's Characteristical Cookery'.

55 Comedy is a very serious thing.
Attributed, in conversation with the actor Jack Bannister.

Garvey, Marcus 1887–1940

Jamaican activist and advocate of black nationalism. In 1914 he founded the Universal Negro Improvement Association (UNIA). Rejecting integration, he called for a 'back to Africa' movement.

56 We are not engaged in domestic politics, in church building or in social uplift work, but we are engaged in nation building.
1922 Speech to the Principles of the Universal Negro Improvement Association, New York, 25 Nov.

57 There is no humanity before that which starts with yourself.
1923 'African Fundamentalism, a Racial Hierarchy and Empire for Negroes'.

Gaskell, Mrs Elizabeth Cleghorn *née* *Stevenson* 1810–65

English novelist. She is best known for her novels of social realism, including *North and South* (1855), in which she criticized the conditions in English factories, and *Cranford* (1851–3).

58 Their dress is very independent of fashion; as they observe, 'What does it signify how we dress here at Cranford, where everybody knows us?' And if they go from home, their reason is equally cogent, 'What does it signify how we dress here, where nobody knows us?'
1851–3 Of the Cranford ladies. *Cranford*, ch.1.

59 A man…is *so* in the way in the house!
1851–3 *Cranford*, ch.1.

Gass, William H(oward) 1924–

US novelist, literary theorist and philosopher, best known for his experimental story collection *In the Heart of the Heart of the Country* (1968). His massive autobiographical novel, *The Tunnel* (1995), was in progress for more than 20 years.

60 I love metaphor the way some people love junk food.
1977 Interview in *Paris Review*, Summer.

61 One's complete sentences are attempts, as often as not, to complete an incomplete self with words.

1977 Interview in *Paris Review*, Summer.

Gates, Bill (William Henry III) 1955–

US businessman, who founded the Microsoft Corporation with Paul Allen in 1974. In 1980 the company bought an operating system and adapted it for the IBM personal computer; the company is now the world's chief software producer for personal computers.

62 I think business is very simple. Profit. Loss. Take the sales, subtract the costs, you get this big positive number. The math is quite straightforward.
1993 Quoted in the *US News and World Report*, 15 Feb.

63 Technology is just a tool. In terms of getting the kids working together and motivating them, the teacher is the most important.
1997 In the *Independent on Sunday*, 12 Oct.

64 A fundamental new rule for business is that the Internet changes everything.
1999 *Business@the Speed of Thought* (co-written with Collins Hemingway).

65 The Internet is becoming the town square for the global village of tomorrow.
1999 *Business@the Speed of Thought* (co-written with Collins Hemingway).

Gauguin, Paul 1848–1903

French Post-Impressionist painter, printmaker and sculptor.

66 There are noble tones, ordinary ones, tranquil harmonies, consoling ones, others which excite by their vigour.
1885 Letter to Emile Schuffenecker.

67 Some advice: do not paint too much after nature. Art is an abstraction; derive this abstraction from nature while dreaming before it, and think more of the creation which will result than of nature.
1888 Letter to Emile Schuffenecker.

68 You may dream freely when you listen to music as well as when you look at painting. When you read a book you are the slave of the author's mind.
c.1888 *Notes Synthétiques*, quoted in J Rewald *Gauguin* (1938).

Gautier, Théophile 1811–72

French poet, novelist and critic. He propounded the theory of 'art for art's sake', and was honoured by Baudelaire. His many novels include the celebrated *Mademoiselle de Maupin* (1835).

69 *Virginité, mysticisme, mélancolie! Trois mots inconnus, trois maladies nouvelles apportées par le Christ.*
Virginity, mysticism, melancholy! Three unknown words, three new illnesses brought by Christ.
1835 *Mademoiselle de Maupin*.

70 *Hélas! Les femmes n'ont lu que le roman de l'homme et jamais son histoire.*
Alas, women have read only the novel of mankind, not the history.
1835 *Mademoiselle de Maupin*.

71 *L'orgueil sort du coeur le jour où l'amour y entre.*
Pride leaves the heart the moment love enters it.
1835 *Mademoiselle de Maupin*.

72 The religion of money is today the only one which has no unbelievers.
1860s On the France of the Second Republic. Quoted in Joanna Richardson *The Courtesans* (1967), p.2.

Gavarni *real name* Guillaume Sulpice Chevalier 1804–88

French lithographer.

73 *Les Enfants Terribles.*
The Little Terrors.
1842 Title of a series of prints.

Gay, James 1810 91

Canadian poet, the self-styled 'Poet Laureate of Canada'.

74 Hail our Great Queen in her regalia;
One foot in Canada, the other in Australia.
Attributed to Gay by William Arthur Deacon in *The Four Jameses* (1927).

Gay, John 1685–1732

English poet, best known for his extraordinarily popular *The Beggar's Opera* (1728), set to music by Pepusch. In his final years he lived chiefly with his patrons, the Duke and Duchess of Queensberry.

75 Praising all alike, is praising none.
1714 'A Letter to a Lady', l.114.

76 Life is a jest; and all things show it.
I thought so once; but now I know it.
1720 'My Own Epitaph'.

77 A woman's friendship ever ends in love.
1720 *Dione*, act 4, sc.6.

78 And when a lady's in the case,
You know, all other things give place.
1727 *Fables*, 'The Hare and Many Friends', l.41.

79 She who trifles with all
Is less likely to fall
Than she who but trifles with one.
1727 'The Coquet Mother and the Coquet Daughter'.

80 How, like a moth, the simple maid
Still plays around the flame!
1728 *The Beggar's Opera*, act 1, sc.4, air 4.

81 Do you think your mother and I should have lived comfortably so long together, if ever we had been married?
1728 *The Beggar's Opera*, act 1, sc.8.

82 Money, wife, is the true fuller's earth for reputations, there is not a spot or a stain but what it can take out.
1728 *The Beggar's Opera*, act 1, sc.9.

83 The comfortable estate of widowhood, is the only hope that keeps up a wife's spirits.
1728 *The Beggar's Opera*, act 1, sc.10.

84 If with me you'd fondly stray
Over the hills and far away.
1728 *The Beggar's Opera*, act 1, sc.13, air 16.

85 I must have women. There is nothing unbends the mind like them.
1728 *The Beggar's Opera*, act 2, sc.3.

86 To cheat a man is nothing; but the woman must have fine parts indeed who cheats a woman!
1728 *The Beggar's Opera*, act 2, sc.4.

87 How happy I could be with either,
Were t'other dear charmer away!

1728 *The Beggar's Opera*, act 2, sc.13.

88 Music might tame and civilize wild beasts, but 'tis evident it never yet could tame and civilize musicians.
1729 *Polly.*

89 From wine what sudden friendship springs!
1738 *Fables*, 'The Squire and His Cur', l.4.

Gay, Noel *pseudonym of* ***Richard Moxon Armitage*** 1898–1954

British songwriter who wrote for stage and screen. His song 'Leaning on a Lamp-Post' became one of George Formby's greatest successes.

90 I'm leaning on a lamp-post at the corner of the street
In case a certain little lady comes by.
1937 Song sung by George Formby, featured in the film *Feather Your Nest.*

Geddes, Sir Eric Campbell 1875–1937

British politician, a member of the War Cabinet in 1918. He presided over the 'Geddes Axe' committee on national expenditure in 1922.

91 The Germans, if this Government is returned, are going to pay every penny. They are going to be squeezed as a lemon is squeezed—until the pips squeak. My only doubt is not whether we can squeeze hard enough, but whether there is enough juice.
1918 Speech at Cambridge Guildhall, 10 Dec.

Gee, Maggie 1948–

English novelist. She has written a number of highly regarded literary novels.

92 There are people not spoken about, people not written about, people whose name is a way of saying they are not there. *Hibakusha*, atomic victims—the scarred who carry our scars.
1983 Of the victims of the bombing of Hiroshima and Nagasaki. *The Burning Book*, ch.1.

93 The alcohol made the present enough, it held her in its golden hand, where past and future were comprehended, where nothing mattered, nothing was lost, where everything could be known and forgiven, where she herself could be whole at last.
1994 *Lost Children*, ch.35.

Geldof, Bob 1954–

Irish rock musician and philanthropist, founder of the Boomtown Rats (1975–86). He established the pop charity Bandaid in 1984 for African famine relief, and organized simultaneous Live Aid concerts in Philadelphia and London in 1985. He was awarded an honorary KBE in 1986.

94 Most people get into bands for three very simple rock and roll reasons: to get laid, to get fame, and to get rich.
1977 In *Melody Maker*, 27 Aug.

95 Irish Americans are about as Irish as Black Americans are African.
1986 In the *Observer*, 22 Jun.

96 Rock 'n' roll is instant coffee.
Quoted in David Pickering *Brewer's Twentieth Century Music* (1994).

Gellhorn, Martha Ellis 1908–98

US journalist and novelist. She covered numerous wars throughout the world between 1936 and 1985 and also wrote essays and fiction. Her first husband (1940–5) was Ernest Hemingway.

97 I see mysteries and complications wherever I look, and I have never met a steadily logical person.
1959 *The Face of War*, introduction.

98 It would be a bitter cosmic joke if we destroy ourselves due to atrophy of the imagination.
1959 *The Face of War*, introduction.

99 Gradually I came to realize that people will more readily swallow lies than truth, as if the taste of lies was homey, appetizing: a habit.
1959 *The Face of War*, introduction.

1 You define your own horror journey, according to your taste. My definition of what makes a journey wholly or partially horrible is boredom. Add discomfort, fatigue, strain in large amounts to get the purest-quality horror, but the kernel is boredom. I offer that as a universal test of travel; boredom, called by any other name, is why you yearn for the first available transport out. But what bores whom?… The threshold of boredom must be like the threshold of pain, different in all of us.
1979 *Travels with Myself and Another.*

2 We savaged them, though they had never hurt us, and we cannot find it in our hearts, our honor, to give them help—because the government of Vietnam is Communist. And perhaps because they won.
1986 On the Vietnamese. *The Face of War* (rev edn), 'The War in Vietnam— Vietnam Again, 1986'.

Genet, Jean 1910–86

French playwright, author and poet who spent much of his youth in jail. Once his literary talent was discovered, many, including Sartre, came to champion his cause, even dubbing him 'Saint Genet'.

3 *Jean Cocteau me croit un mauvais voleur. C'est parce qu'auprès de lui je suis d'abord un écrivain. Les voleurs me croient un mauvais écrivain.*
Jean Cocteau thinks that I am a poor thief. That's because next to him I am primarily a writer. Thieves think that I am a poor writer.
1949 *Journal du voleur.*

4 *L'artiste n'a pas—ou le poète—pour fonction de trouver la solution pratique des problèmes du mal.*
It is not up to the artist or to the poet to find practical solutions to the problems of evil.
1956 *Le Balcon*, 'Avertissement'.

5 *Prisons, cachots, lieux bénis où le mal est impossible, puisqu'ils sont le carrefour de toute la malédiction du monde. On ne peut pas commettre le mal dans le mal.*
Prison, dungeons, blessed places where evil is impossible because they are the crossroads of all the evil in the world. One cannot commit evil in hell.
1956 *Le Balcon*, 'Deuxième tableau'.

6 *Ce qu'il nous faut, c'est la haine. D'elle naîtront nos idées.*
Hatred is what we need. Ideas are born from hatred.
1958 *Les Nègres*, épigraphe.

7 *Dans les villes actuelles, le seul lieu,—hélas encore vers la périphérie—où un théâtre pourrait être construit, c'est le cimetière.*
In today's cities, the only place—unfortunately on the outskirts—to construct a theatre is a cemetery.
1959 *L'Étrange Mort d'…*

Genghis Khan *originally* ***Temujin*** c.1167–1227

Mongol conqueror. Leader of the Mongols from 1206, he conquered widely throughout Asia, penetrating Persia and Eastern Europe as far as the Dnieper River. His empire was divided between his sons and grandsons on his death.

8 Happiness lies in conquering one's enemies, in driving them in front of oneself, in taking their property, in savouring their despair, in outraging their wives and daughters.
c.1210 Quoted in Witold Rodzinski *The Walled Kingdom: A History of China* (1979).

Geoffrey de Breteuil fl.12c

French ecclesiastic.

9 *Claustrum sine armario quasi castrum sine armamentario. Ipsum armarium nostrum est armamenturium.*
A cloister without a library is like a castle without an armoury. For the library is our armoury.
c.1165 Letter to Peter Mangot.

George I 1660–1727

King of Great Britain and Ireland and Elector of Hanover. He succeeded to the British throne in 1714 on the death of Queen Anne in accordance with the Act of Settlement (1701) and was the first Hanoverian King of Great Britain and Ireland. He never mastered English.

10 I hate all Boets and Bainters.
In John Campbell *Lives of the Chief Justices*, 'Lord Mansfield' (1849).

George II 1683–1760

King of Great Britain and Ireland (1727–60) and Elector of Hanover, last British king to command in the field, at Dettingen, 1743. His reign saw the Jacobite defeat at Culloden (1746), British involvement in India after Plassey (1757) and the onset of the Seven Years War.

11 Oh! he is mad is he? Then I hope he will *bite* some of my other generals.
c.1759 Replying to remarks made about General James Wolfe by the Duke of Newcastle. Quoted in Henry Beckles Wilson *Life and Letters of James Wolfe* (1909), ch.17.

George III 1738–1820

King of Great Britain and Ireland (1760–1820). In the 1770s he was blamed with North for the loss of the American colonies. In 1783 he called Pitt (the Younger) to office, ending the supremacy of the old Whig families. As a result of his supposed insanity (now believed to have been porphyria), his son George was made Regent.

12 I can never suppose this country so far lost to all ideas of self-importance as to be willing to grant America independence; if that could ever be adopted, I shall despair of this country being ever preserved from a state of inferiority, and consequently falling into a very low class among the European states.
1780 Letter to Lord North, 7 Mar.

13 I was the last to consent to the separation, but the separation having been made, and having become inevitable, I have always said that I would be the first to meet the friendship of the United States as an independent power.
1785 Letter to John Adams, first US Ambassador to England, 1 Jun.

George V 1865–1936

King of Great Britain and Northern Ireland (1910–36). He served in the navy and travelled widely in the Empire. His reign saw the Union of South Africa (1910), World War I (1914–18), the Irish Free State Settlement (1922) and the General Strike (1926).

14 I have many times asked myself whether there can be more potent advocates of peace on earth through the years to come than this massed multitude of silent witnesses to the desolation of war.
1922 Message read at the Terlincthun Cemetery, Boulogne, 13 May.

15 Today 23 years ago, dear Grandmama died. I wonder what she would have thought of a Labour government.
1924 Of Queen Victoria. Diary entry, 22 Jan, on having invited Ramsay Macdonald to form the first Labour administration.

16 Bugger Bognor.
1929 or 1936 Reply to a courtier who had remarked 'Cheer up, your Majesty, you will soon be at Bognor again', either during his convalescence or on his deathbed. Quoted in Kenneth Rose *King George V* (1983), ch.9.

17 I will not have another war. If there is another and we are threatened with being brought into it, I will go to Trafalgar Square and wave a red flag myself sooner than allow this country to be brought in.
1935 To David Lloyd George, 10 May.

18 Golf always makes me so damned angry.
Quoted in Colin Jarman *The Guinness Dictionary of Sports Quotations* (1990).

George VI 1895–1952

King of Great Britain and Northern Ireland (1936–52). After ascending the throne (on the abdication of his elder brother, Edward VIII), he remained in bomb-damaged Buckingham Palace during World War II and delivered many broadcasts, mastering a speech impediment.

19 The British Empire has advanced to a new conception of autonomy and freedom, to the idea of a system of British nations, each freely ordering its own individual life, but bound together in unity by allegiance to one Crown, and co-operating in all that concerns the common weal.
1927 Opening, as Duke of York, the first Australian Parliament to assemble in Canberra, 9 May.

20 Abroad is bloody.
Quoted in W H Auden *A Certain World* (1970), 'Royalty'.

George, Chief Dan 1899–1981

Canadian native spokesperson.

21 The heart never knows the colour of the skin.
1974 *My Heart Soars*.

George, Daniel *pseudonym of* ***Daniel George Bunting*** 1890–1967

English author and critic.

22 O Freedom, what liberties are taken in thy name!
1963 *The Perpetual Pessimist.*

George-Brown, George (Alfred) Brown, Baron 1914–85

English Labour politician. He was Vice-Chairman and Deputy Leader of the party (1960–70), and unsuccessfully contested Harold Wilson for party leadership in 1963.

23 Most British statesmen have either drunk too much or womanised too much. I never fell into the second category.
1974 In the *Observer*, Nov.

24 Lovely creature in scarlet, dance with me!
Drunken invitation to a red-robed apostolic delegate. Attributed.

Geracimos, Ann

US journalist and feature writer.

25 Washington is a town where more people probably contemplate writing a book than finish reading one.
1989 In the *Washington Times*, 29 Mar.

Gerald of Wales *also called* ***Giraldus Cambrensis*** c.1146–c.1223

Welsh bishop and historian. He wrote 17 books and planned several others, all in Latin. His best-known works are *The History and Topography of Ireland* (1185) and *Journey through Wales* (1191).

26 Among the smaller islands there is one of fair size that is now called the Isle of Man… There was a great controversy in antiquity concerning the question: to which of the two countries should the island properly belong? Eventually, however, the matter was settled. All agreed that since it allowed poisonous reptiles to live in it, it should belong to Britain.
1185 *The History and Topography of Ireland*, pt.2 (translated by John J O'Meara, 1951).

Gerbert *later* ***Pope Sylvester II*** 940–1003

French divine and scholar, whose chemical, mathematical and philosophical expertise led to claims that he was in league with the devil. In 982 he became Abbot of Bobbio, and was appointed Archbishop of Ravenna in 988. He was elected Pope in 999. He opposed the separatist tendencies of the French Church.

27 *Cum studio bene vivendi semper conjunxi studium bene dicendi.*
I have always combined the study of how to live well with the study of how to speak well.
985 Letter to Ebrard, Abbot of Tours.

28 *An quicquam melius amicas divinitas mortalibus concesserit nescio.*
I do not know if the divinity has provided mortals with anything better than friends.
985 Letter to Abbot Gerald of Aurillac.

29 *Delegimus certum otium studiorum, quam incertum negotium bellorum.*
We have opted for the certain leisure of study, rather than the uncertain business of war.
985 Letter to Monk Raymond.

Gergen, David Richmond 1942–

US government official, an assistant and later adviser to Presidents Nixon, Ford, Reagan and Clinton. He is editor-at-large at *US News & World Report*.

30 About the time you are writing a line that you have written so often that you want to throw up, that is the first time the American people will hear it.
1993 On working as a speech-writer in the Nixon White House. In the *New York Times*, 31 Oct.

31 A naked moment in politics.
1993 On the vulnerability of the President. In the *New York Times*, 31 Oct.

32 We are making politics a spectator sport in which our only duty is to vote somebody into office and then retire to the grandstands.
1993 In *US News & World Report*, 10 May.

Gerhardie, William Alexander 1895–1977

English novelist, born and educated in St Petersburg. His best-known books are the novels *Futility* (1922) and *Polyglots* (1925).

33 She even sighed offensively…as if she meant to charge me with the necessity of doing so.
1922 *Futility*, pt.3, ch.3.

34 There are as many fools at a university as anywhere… But their folly, I admit, has a certain stamp—the stamp of university training, if you like. It is trained folly.
1925 *Polyglots*, ch.7.

35 We are like icebergs in the ocean: one-eighth part consciousness and the rest submerged beneath the surface of articulate apprehension.
1925 *Polyglots*, ch.14.

Gershwin, George 1898–1937

US composer. His early works are Broadway musicals, such as *Lady Be Good* (1924), written with his brother Ira. Other works include *Rhapsody in Blue* (1924, a concert piece in the jazz idiom), *An American in Paris* (1928) and the opera *Porgy and Bess* (1935).

36 Not many composers have ideas. Far more of them know how to use strange instruments which do not require ideas.
1930 'The Composer in the Machine Age'.

37 Jazz is the result of the energy stored up in America.
Quoted in D Morgenstern *Composers on Music* (1958).

Gershwin, Ira *originally* ***Israel Gershowitz*** 1896–1983

US lyricist. He worked exclusively with his brother George Gershwin until George died, and then with other composers including Kurt Weill and Jerome Kern.

38 I got rhythm,
I got music,
I got my man—
Who could ask for anything more.
1930 'I Got Music', featured in the film *Girl Crazy* (music by George Gershwin).

39 Away with the music of Broadway!

Be off with your Irving Berlin!
Oh, I'd give no quarter
to Kern or Cole Porter
and Gershwin keeps pounding on tin.
How can I be civil
when hearing this drivel?
It's only for night-clubbing souses.
Oh, give me the free 'n' easy
waltz that is Viennesey
And go tell the band
if they want a hand
the waltz must be Strauss's!
1936 'By Strauss'.

40 The way you wear your hat,
The way you sip your tea,
The mem'ry of all that—
No, no! They can't take that away from me!
1937 'They Can't Take That Away from Me', song from the film musical *Shall We Dance?* (music by George Gershwin).

41 The way your smile just beams
The way you sing off key
The way you haunt my dreams
No, no! They can't take that away from me!
1937 'They Can't Take That Away from Me', song from the film musical *Shall We Dance?* (music by George Gershwin).

42 You say potato and I say po-tah-to
You say tomato and I say to-mah-to...
Let's call the whole thing off!
1937 'Let's Call the Whole Thing Off', song from the film musical *Shall We Dance?* (music by George Gershwin).

43 A foggy day in London Town
Had me low and had me down.
1937 'A Foggy Day', song from the musical *Damsel in Distress* (music by George Gershwin).

44 Holding hands at midnight
'Neath a starry sky,
Nice work if you can get it,
And you can get it if you try.
1937 'Nice Work If You Can Get It', song from the musical *Damsel in Distress* (music by George Gershwin).

45 In time the Rockies may crumble
Gibraltar may tumble
They're only made of clay,
But our love is here to stay.
1938 'Love Is Here to Stay', sung by Kenny Baker in *The Goldwyn Follies* (music by George Gershwin).

Gervais, Ricky 1961–

English comic writer and performer, whose comedy series *The Office* won two Golden Globes (2004).

46 If you work for Nasa or the Cosa Nostra, I bet it's all the same. Why's his chair bigger than my chair? I've been an assassin longer than him and he gets to sit nearest the water cooler.
2002 In *The Guardian*, 7 Sep.

47 Fact is stranger than fiction. You see people walking down the street that would never be allowed on television. You have to tone it down.
2002 On the Jo Whiley show, BBC Radio 1, 30 Sep.

48 If David Brent is the best thing that I ever come up with, then so be it. What are you supposed to do—time the best thing you do for just before you die?
2003 On his character in the television series *The Office*. Quoted in the *Observer*, 14 Dec.

Getty, Jean Paul 1892–1976

US oil executive, multimillionaire and art collector. He entered the oil business in his early 20s, and merged his father's fortune with his own in 1930. Despite his legendary wealth, he acquired a reputation for miserliness.

49 If you can actually count your money, then you are not really a rich man.
1957 In the *Observer*, 3 Nov.

50 Some people find oil, some don't.
His entire submission when asked by a magazine editor to submit an article entitled 'The Secret of My Success'. Quoted by L M Boyd in the *San Francisco Chronicle*, 2 Mar 1991.

Giacosa, Giuseppe 1847–1906

Italian librettist.

51 *Che gelida manina.*
Your tiny hand is frozen.
1896 Rodolpho to Mimi. *La Bohème* (with Luigi Illica, music by Puccini).

Gibbon, Edward 1737–94

English historian. After a visit to Rome (1764) he embarked on a history of the Roman Empire. He became an MP in 1774, and the first volume of *The Decline and Fall of the Roman Empire* appeared in 1776. Lord Sheffield published his *Miscellaneous Works* (1796), including his autobiography.

52 If a man were called to fix the period in the history of the world during which the condition of the human race was most happy and prosperous, he would, without hesitation, name that which elapsed from the death of Domitian to the accession of Commodus.
1776–88 *The Decline and Fall of the Roman Empire*, ch.3.

53 The principles of a free constitution are irrevocably lost when the legislative power is nominated by the executive.
1776–88 *The Decline and Fall of the Roman Empire*, ch.3.

54 In every age and country, the wiser, or at least the stronger, of the two sexes, has usurped the powers of the state, and confined the other to the cares and pleasures of domestic life.
1776–88 *The Decline and Fall of the Roman Empire*, ch.6.

55 Corruption, the most infallible symptom of constitutional liberty.
1776–88 *The Decline and Fall of the Roman Empire*, ch.21.

56 The Huns...chanted a funeral song to the memory of a hero, glorious in his life, invincible in his death, the father of his people, the scourge of his enemies, and the terror of the world.
1776–88 Description of the funeral of Attila the Hun. *The Decline and Fall of the Roman Empire*, ch.35.

57 The Rhine is not more impassable than the Nile or Euphrates, and the Arabian fleet might have sailed without a naval combat into the mouth of the Thames. Perhaps the interpretation of the Koran would now be taught in the schools of Oxford, and her pupils might demonstrate to a circumcised people the sanctity and truth of the revelation of Mahomet.

1776–88 *The Decline and Fall of the Roman Empire*, ch.52.

58 Persuasion is the resource of the feeble; and the feeble can seldom persuade.
1776–88 *The Decline and Fall of the Roman Empire*, ch.68.

59 All that is human must retrograde if it does not advance.
1776–88 *The Decline and Fall of the Roman Empire*, ch.71.

60 To the University of Oxford I acknowledge no obligation; and she will as cheerfully renounce me for a son, as I am willing to disclaim her for a mother. I spent fourteen months at Magdalen College: they proved the fourteen months the most idle and unprofitable of my whole life.
Memoirs of My Life (published 1796), ch.3.

61 It was here that I suspended my religious inquiries (aged 17).
Memoirs of My Life (published 1796), ch.4.

62 I sighed as a lover, I obeyed as a son.
On his enforced visit to Lausanne, leaving behind Suzanne Curchod. *Memoirs of My Life* (published 1796), ch.4. This passage was inserted (from a draft) by Lord Sheffield.

63 It was at Rome, on the fifteenth of October 1764, as I sat musing amidst the ruins of the Capitol, while the barefooted friars were singing vespers in the temple of Jupiter, that the idea of writing the decline and fall of the City first started to my mind.
Memoirs of My Life (published 1796), ch.6, note. Variations of the lines can be found in the various drafts of Gibbon's autobiography and in the last lines of the *Decline and Fall*: 'It was among the ruins of the Capitol that I first conceived the idea of a work which has amused and exercised near twenty years of my life, and which, however inadequate to my own wishes, I finally deliver to the curiosity and candour of the public' (vol.6, ch.71).

64 My English text is chaste, and all licentious passages are left in the obscurity of a learned language.
Memoirs of My Life (published 1796), ch.8.

Gibbon, Lewis Grassic 1901–35

Scottish novelist.

65 So that was Chris and her reading and schooling, two Chrisses there were that fought for her heart and tormented her. You hated the land and the coarse speak of the folk and learning was brave and fine one day and the next you'd waken with the peewits crying across the hills, deep and deep, crying in the heart of you, and the smell of the earth in your face, almost you'd cry for that, the beauty of it and the sweetness of the Scottish land and skies.
1932 *Sunset Song*.

66 For the cleansing of that horror, if cleanse it they could, I would welcome the English in suzerainty over Scotland till the end of time. I would welcome the end of Braid Scots and Gaelic, our culture, our history, our nationhood under the heels of a Chinese army of occupation if it could cleanse the Glasgow slums, give a surety of food and play—the elementary right of every human being—to those people of the abyss…
1934 *Scottish Scene*, 'Glasgow' (with Hugh MacDiarmid).

Gibbons, Kaye 1960–

US novelist. Her first novel, *Ellen Foster* (1986), was widely acclaimed. Other works include *A Virtuous Woman* (1989) and *Divining Women* (2004).

67 I read about writers' lives with the fascination of one slowing down to get a good look at an automobile accident.
1990 In the *New York Times*, 7 Jan.

Gibbons, Orlando 1583–1625

English composer and organist of Westminster Abbey (from 1623). He wrote little, but some of his anthems, services and madrigals are regarded as masterpieces.

68 The silver swan, who living had no note,
When death approached, unlocked her silent throat;
Leaning her breast against the reedy shore,
Thus sung her first and last, and sung no more:
'Farewell, all joys; Oh death, come close mine eyes;
More geese than swans now live, more fools than wise.'
1612 *The First Set of Madrigals and Motets of Five Parts*, 'The Silver Swan'.

Gibbons, Stella Dorothea 1902–89

English writer. She worked as a journalist, and wrote novels, poetry and short stories. Her reputation rests on her famous parody of rural fiction, *Cold Comfort Farm* (1932).

69 The life of the journalist is poor, nasty, brutish and short. So is his style.
1932 *Cold Comfort Farm*, foreword.

70 And when the spring comes her hour is upon her again. 'Tes the hand of Nature and we women cannot escape it.
1932 Judith Starkadder, of Meriam. *Cold Comfort Farm*, ch.5.

71 Something nasty in the woodshed.
1932 Aunt Ada Doom. *Cold Comfort Farm*, ch.10.

72 He said that, by god, D. H. Lawrence was right when he had said there must be a dumb, dark, dull, bitter belly-tension between a man and a woman, and how else could this be achieved save in the long monotony of marriage?
1932 Mr Mybug, proposing to Rennet. *Cold Comfort Farm*, ch.20.

Gibbs, Wolcott 1902–58

US journalist and critic.

73 Backward ran sentences until reeled the mind.
1936 Parody of *Time* magazine's literary style. 'Time… Fortune… Life… Luce', in the *New Yorker*, 28 Nov.

Gibran, Kahlil 1883–1931

Syrian mystic, author and artist, whose most famous work is *The Prophet* (1923).

74 Your children are not your children.
They are the sons and daughters of Life's longing for itself.
They came through you but not from you
And though they are with you yet they belong not to you.
You may give them your love but not your thoughts,
For they have their own thoughts.
You may house their bodies, but not their souls.
1923 *The Prophet*, 'On Children'.

Gibson, Wilfred Wilson 1878–1962

English poet. He was a prolific writer of both poetry and plays, rooted in the reality of everyday life.

75 But we, how shall we turn to little things

And listen to the birds and winds and streams
Made holy by their dreams,
Nor feel the heart-break in the heart of things?
1918 'Lament'.

Gibson, William Ford 1948–

US science-fiction writer, best known as the author of *Neuromancer* (1984), which spawned the genre of cyberpunk fiction.

76 Cyberspace. A consensual hallucination experienced daily by billions of legitimate operators, in every nation, by children being taught mathematical concepts… A graphical representation of data abstracted from the banks of every computer in the human system. Unthinkable complexity. Lines of light ranged in the non-space of the mind, clusters and constellations of data. Like city lights, receding.
1984 *Neuromancer*. This is the first recorded use of the term 'cyberspace'.

77 Cyberspace is where you are when you're on the telephone.
1994 In the *US News & World Report*, 21 Jun.

Gide, André Paul Guillaume 1869–1951

French writer of fiction, poetry, plays, criticism, biography and translations. His novels focus on the conflict between the spiritual and the physical. He won the Nobel prize for literature in 1947.

78 *Nous avons bâti sur le sable*
Des cathédrales impérissables.
We have built immovable cathedrals
In the sand.
1895 *Paludes*.

79 *Que mon livre t'enseigne à t'intéresser plus à toi qu'à lui-même—puis à tout le reste plus qu'à toi.*
May my book teach you to be more interested in yourself than in it—then, in everyone else more than yourself.
1897 *Les Nourritures terrestres*, pt.1.

80 *La sagesse n'est pas dans la raison, mais dans l'amour.*
Wisdom comes not from reason but from love.
1897 *Les Nourritures terrestres*, pt.1.

81 *Familles! je vous hais! Foyers clos; portes refermées; possessions jalouses du bonheur.*
Families! I hate you! Enclosed hallways, shut doors, jealous possessions of happiness.
1897 *Les Nourritures terrestres*, pt.4.

82 *Chaque instant de notre Vie est essentiellement irremplaçable: sache parfois t'y concentrer uniquement.*
Every instant of Life is essentially irreplaceable: concentrate on it fully from time to time.
1897 *Les Nourritures terrestres*, pt.4.

83 *C'est avec de beaux sentiments qu'on fait de la mauvaise littérature.*
Bad literature is written with beautiful sentiments.
1928 Letter to François Mauriac.

84 *Le bonheur de l'homme n'est pas dans la liberté, mais dans l'acceptation d'un devoir.*
Man's happiness does not come from freedom but in the acceptance of a task.
1932 Journal entry, 8 Feb.

Gielgud, Sir (Arthur) John 1904–2000

English actor and producer. A leading Shakespearean actor, he appeared in many films, notably as Cassius in *Julius Caesar* (1952) and in *Prospero's Books* (1991).

85 When you're my age, you just never risk being ill—because then everyone says: Oh, he's done for.
1988 In the *Sunday Express*, 17 Jul.

86 Daniel Day Lewis has what every actor in Hollywood wants: talent. And what every actor in England wants: looks.
1995 In *The Independent*, 13 May.

87 Being another character is more interesting than being yourself.
Attributed.

Gilbert, Sir Humphrey 1537–83

English navigator and explorer. He took Newfoundland for the crown in 1583, establishing a colony at St John's. He was drowned on the journey home.

88 We are as near to heaven by sea as by land!
1583 Dying words as his frigate *Squirrel* sank in the Atlantic Ocean near the Azores, 5 Aug. Quoted in Richard Hakluyt *Third and Last Volume of the Voyages…of the English Nation* (1600).

Gilbert, Sir W(illiam) S(chwenck) 1836–1911

English parodist and librettist. His humorous verse was collected in 1869 as the *Bab Ballads*. His partnership with Sir Arthur Sullivan, from 1871, produced a succession of light operas, from *Trial by Jury* (1875) to *The Grand Duke* (1896).

89 So I fell in love with a rich attorney's
Elderly, ugly daughter.
1875 *Trial by Jury*.

90 She may very well pass for forty-three
In the dusk with a light behind her!
1875 *Trial by Jury*.

91 I'm called little Buttercup—dear Little Buttercup,
Though I could never tell why.
1878 *HMS Pinafore*, act 1.

92 CAPT: Bad language or abuse,
I never, never use,
Whatever the emergency;
Though 'Bother it' I may
Occasionally say,
I never use a big, big D—
ALL: What, never?
CAPT: No, never!
ALL: What *never*?
CAPT: Well, hardly ever!
ALL: Hardly ever swears a big, big D—
Then give three cheers, and one cheer more,
For the well-bred Captain of the *Pinafore*!
1878 *HMS Pinafore*, act 1.

93 I am the monarch of the sea,
The Ruler of the Queen's Navee,
Whose praise Great Britain loudly chants
And we are his sisters, and his cousins, and his aunts!
1878 *HMS Pinafore*, act 1.

94 When I was a lad I served a term
As office boy to an attorney's firm.
I cleaned the windows and I swept the floor,

And I polished up the handle of the big front door.
I polished up that handle so carefullee
That now I am the Ruler of the Queen's Navee!
1878 *HMS Pinafore*, act 2.

95 In spite of all temptations
To belong to other nations,
He remains an Englishman!
1878 *HMS Pinafore*, act 2.

96 Climbing over rocky mountain,
Skipping rivulet and fountain.
1879 Girls' chorus, *The Pirates of Penzance*, act 1.

97 It is, it is a glorious thing
To be a Pirate King.
1879 Pirate King's song, *The Pirates of Penzance*, act 1.

98 Oh, is there not one maiden here
Whose homely face and bad complexion
Have caused all hopes to disappear
Of ever winning man's affection?
1879 Frederic's song, *The Pirates of Penzance*, act 1.

99 I am the very model of a modern Major-General,
I've information vegetable, animal and mineral,
I know the kings of England, and I quote the fights historical,
From Marathon to Waterloo, in order categorical.
1879 The Major-General's song, *The Pirates of Penzance*, act 1.

1 I can hum a fugue of which I've heard the music's din afore,
And whistle all the airs from that infernal nonsense *Pinafore*.
1879 The Major-General's song, *The Pirates of Penzance*, act 1.

2 Stay, Frederic, stay!
Nay, Mabel, nay!
1879 Mabel and Frederic's duet, *The Pirates of Penzance*, act 2.

3 When a felon's not engaged in his employment
Or maturing his felonious little plans
His capacity for innocent enjoyment
Is just as great as any honest man's—
Ah! When constabulary duty's to be done
A policeman's lot is not a happy one.
1879 Sergeant's song, *The Pirates of Penzance*, act 2.

4 And everyone will say,
As you walk your mystic way,
'If this young man expresses himself in terms too deep for me,
Why, what a very singularly deep young man this deep young man must be!'
1881 Bunthorne's song, *Patience*, act 1.

5 Sing 'Booh to you—
Pooh, pooh to you'—
And that's what I shall say!
1881 Jane and Bunthorne's duet, *Patience*, act 2.

6 A commonplace young man,
A matter-of-fact young man,
A steady and stolid-y, jolly Bank-Holiday
Every-day young man!
1881 Bunthorne and Grosvenor's duet, *Patience*, act 2.

7 A Japanese young man,
A blue and white young man,
Francesca di Rimini, miminy, piminy,
Je-ne-sais-quoi young man.
1881 Bunthorne and Grosvenor's duet, *Patience*, act 2.

8 A Chancery Lane young man,
A Somerset House young man,
A very delectable, highly respectable,
Threepenny-bus young man!
1881 Bunthorne and Grosvenor's duet, *Patience*, act 2.

9 A pallid and thin young man,
A haggard and lank young man,
A greenery-yallery, Grosvenor Gallery,
Foot-in-the-grave young man!
A Sewell & Cross young man,
A Howell & James young man,
A push-ing young par-ti-cle—
'What's the next ar-ti-cle?'—
Wa-ter-loo House young man!
1881 Bunthorne and Grosvenor's duet, *Patience*, act 2.

10 Bow, bow, ye lower middle classes!
Bow, bow, ye tradesmen, bow ye masses!
1882 Chorus, *Iolanthe*, act 1 (first performed 25 Nov, simultaneously in London and New York).

11 The Law is the true embodiment
Of everything that's excellent.
It has no kind of fault or flaw,
And I, my Lords, embody the Law.
1882 *Iolanthe*, act 1.

12 When I went to the Bar as a very young man,
(Said I to myself—said I),
I'll work on a new and original plan,
(Said I to myself—said I).
1882 *Iolanthe*, act 1.

13 I often think it's comical
How Nature always does contrive
That every boy and every gal
That's born into the world alive
Is either a little Liberal
Or else a little Conservative!
1882 Private Willis's song, *Iolanthe*, act 2.

14 The House of Peers, throughout the war,
Did nothing in particular,
And did it very well:
Yet Britain set the world ablaze
In good King George's glorious days!
1882 Lord Mountarat's song, *Iolanthe*, act 2.

15 When you're lying awake with a dismal headache, and repose is taboo'd by anxiety,
I conceive you may use any language you choose to indulge in, without impropriety.
1882 Lord Chancellor's nightmare song, *Iolanthe*, act 2.

16 Expressive glances
Shall be our lances
And pops of Sillery
Our light artillery.
1884 Trio, *Princess Ida*, act 1.

17 I've an irritating chuckle, I've a celebrated sneer,
I've an entertaining snigger, I've a fascinating leer.
To everybody's prejudice I know a thing or two;
I can tell a woman's age in half a minute—and I do.
But although I try to make myself as pleasant as I can,
Yet everybody says I'm such a disagreeable man!
1884 Gama's song, *Princess Ida*, act 1.

18 Oh, doughty sons of Hungary!
May all success

Attend and bless
Your warlike ironmongery!
1884 Chorus, *Princess Ida*, act 3.

19 A wandering minstrel I—
A thing of shreds and patches
Of ballads, songs and snatches
And dreamy lullaby!
1885 Nanki-Poo's song, *The Mikado*, act 1.

20 As in a month you've got to die
If Ko-Ko tells us true,
'Twere empty compliment to cry
'Long life to Nanki-Poo!'
But as one month you have to live
As fellow-citizen,
This toast with three times three we'll give—
'Long life to you—till then!'
1885 Pooh-Bah's solo, *The Mikado*, act 1.

21 As some day it may happen that a victim must be found,
I've got a little list—I've got a little list
Of society offenders who might well be underground,
And who never would be missed— who never would be missed!
There's the pestilential nuisances who write for autographs—
All people who have flabby hands and irritating laughs.
1885 Ko-Ko's song, *The Mikado*, act 1.

22 The idiot who praises, with enthusiastic tone,
All centuries but this, and every country but his own;
And the lady from the provinces, who dresses like a guy,
And who 'doesn't think she dances, but would rather like to try';
And that singular anomaly, the lady novelist—
I don't think she'd be missed— I'm *sure* she'd not be missed!
1885 Ko-Ko's song, *The Mikado*, act 1.

23 Defer, defer,
To the Lord High Executioner!
1885 Chorus, *The Mikado*, act 1.

24 Three little maids from school are we,
Pert as a school-girl well can be
Filled to the brim with girlish glee.
1885 Trio for Yum-yum, Peep-Bo and Pitti Sing, with Chorus of Girls, *The Mikado*, act 1.

25 To sit in solemn silence in a dull, dark dock,
In a pestilential prison, with a life-long lock,
Awaiting the sensation of a short, sharp shock,
From a cheap and chippy chopper on a big black block!
1885 Trio, *The Mikado*, act 1.

26 Here's a how-de-do!
1885 Trio, *The Mikado*, act 2.

27 My object all sublime
I shall achieve in time—
To let the punishment fit the crime.
1885 The Mikado's song, *The Mikado*, act 2.

28 And there he plays extravagant matches
In fitless finger-stalls
On a cloth untrue
With a twisted cue
And elliptical billiard balls.
1885 The doom of the billiard sharp. *The Mikado*, act 2.

29 On a tree by a river a little tom-tit
Sang 'Willow, titwillow, titwillow!'
1885 Ko-Ko's song, *The Mikado*, act 2.

30 This particularly rapid unintelligible patter
Isn't generally heard, and if it is it doesn't matter!
1887 *Ruddigore*, act 2.

31 For I have a song to sing, O!...
It is sung to the moon
By a love-lorn loon,
Who fled from the mocking throng, O!
It's the song of a merryman moping mum,
Whose soul was sad and whose glance was glum
Who sipped no sup and who craved no crumb,
As he sighed for the love of a ladye!
1888 Jack Point's song, *The Yeomen of the Guard*.

32 In enterprise of martial kind,
When there was any fighting,
He led his regiment from behind—
He found it less exciting.
But when away his regiment ran,
His place was at the fore, O
That celebrated,
Cultivated
Underrated
Nobleman,
The Duke of Plaza-Toro!
1889 Duke's song, *The Gondoliers*, act 1.

33 I am a courtier grave and serious
Who is about to kiss your hand:
Try to combine a pose imperious
With a demeanour nobly bland.
1889 *The Gondoliers*, act 2.

34 Take a pair of sparkling eyes.
1889 Marco's song, *The Gondoliers*, act 2.

35 Funny without being vulgar.
1893 Of Sir Henry Beerbohm Tree's performance as Hamlet. Attributed.

36 Do you know how they are going to decide the Shakespeare–Bacon dispute? They are going to dig up Shakespeare and dig up Bacon; they are going to get Tree to recite *Hamlet* to them. And the one who turns in his coffin will be the author of the play.
Letter.

37 My dear chap! Good isn't the word!
To an actor who had just given a very weak performance. Attributed.

Gill, Brendan 1914–97

US writer and critic of film, theatre and architecture. His works include *The Day the Money Stopped* (1957) and *A New York Life: of friends and others* (1990). He received the national Book Award for *The Trouble of One House* (1951).

38 In the later nineteenth century, the tops of skyscrapers often took the shape of domes, surmounted by jaunty gilded lanterns; later came ziggurats, mausoleums, Alexandrian lighthouses, miniature Parthenons. These charming follies contained neither royal corpses nor effigies of gods and goddesses; rather they contained large wooden tanks filled with water.
1982 Quoted in Laura Rosen *Top of the City: New York's hidden rooftop world* (1990), foreword.

39 He stared the assorted meannesses and failed promises

of American life straight in the face, and they stared back.
1990 On Walker Evans's photographs for James Agee's book on the destitute South. *A New York Life.*

40 The big houses sat in self-congratulatory propinquity on their level green lawns…stout matrons seated elbow to elbow, implacably chaperoning a ball.
1990 On a residential boulevard of Rochester, New York. *A New York Life.*

41 A vain attempt to subdue that unsubduable country.
1990 Of Cromwell's settlement of Scots in the north of Ireland. *A New York Life.*

Gill, (Arthur) Eric Rowton 1882–1940

English artist, type designer and writer.

42 That state is a state of Slavery in which a man does what he likes to do in his spare time and in his working time that which is required of him.
1929 *Art-nonsense and Other Essays*, 'Slavery and Freedom'.

43 The artist is not a special kind of man but every man a special kind of artist.
1934 *Art*, introduction.

44 Man cannot live on the human plane, he must be either above or below it.
1940 *Autobiography*, closing words.

45 Science is analytical, descriptive, informative. Man does not live by bread alone, but by science he attempts to do so. Hence the deadliness of all that is purely scientific.
'Art'. Collected in *Essays* (1948).

Gillespie, Dizzy (John Birks) 1917–93

US jazz trumpeter, composer and bandleader. A leading exponent of bebop in the 1940s, he formed several big bands and led an international touring orchestra (1956).

46 It's taken me all my life to learn what not to play.
Quoted in N Hentoff *Jazz Is* (1978).

47 When I first heard Charlie Parker, I said, 'That's how our music should be played.'… After we got it together, yeah, I knew we were making something new. It was magic. Nobody on the planet was playing like that but us.
1991 On bebop. In the *San Francisco Chronicle*, 25 May.

48 Now, our music is universal. It shares the rhythmic content of African music, music of the Western Hemisphere and various lands of the East, and has merged this rhythm with European harmonies, the soul of the slaves, the blues, and the spirituals to create jazz.
1979 *Dizzy– To Be Or Not To Bop* (with Al Fraser), 'Evolutions'.

Gillette, King Camp 1855–1932

US inventor of the safety razor (c.1895), founder of the Gillette Safety Razor Company (1901).

49 To be successful in business, you should produce something cheap, habit-forming, and consumed by use.
Attributed.

Gilligan, Andrew 1968–

English journalist.

50 I have spoken to a British official who was involved in the preparation of the dossier… He said: 'It was transformed in the week before it was published, to make it sexier.'
2003 Referring to the Government's dossier on weapons of mass destruction in Iraq. On BBC Radio 4's *Today* programme, 29 May.

Gilman, Charlotte Anna *pen names* ***Charlotte Perkins Gilman*** *and* ***Charlotte Perkins Stetson*** 1860–1935

US feminist and writer. She lectured on women's and other social issues, and her *Women and Economics* (1898) is regarded as a feminist landmark. Her fiction includes the story 'The Yellow Wall-Paper' (1892), a feminist study of madness.

51 The economic status of women generally depends on that of men generally, and…the economic status of women individually depends upon that of men individually, those men to whom they are related.
1898 *Women and Economics: A Study of the Economic Relation between Men and Women as a Factor in Social Evolution*, ch.1.

52 The labor of women in the house, certainly, enables men to produce more wealth than they otherwise could; and in this way [they] are economic factors in society. But so are horses.
1898 *Women and Economics: A Study of the Economic Relation between Men and Women as a Factor in Social Evolution*, ch.1.

53 Whatever the economic value of the domestic industry of women is, they do not get it. The women who do the most work get the least money, and the women who have the most money do the least work.
1898 *Women and Economics: A Study of the Economic Relation between Men and Women as a Factor in Social Evolution*, ch.1.

54 His dominance is not that of one chosen as best fitted to rule…but it is sovereignty based on the accident of sex.
1898 *Women and Economics: A Study of the Economic Relation between Men and Women as a Factor in Social Evolution*, ch.1.

Gilmore, Dame Mary Jean *née* ***Mary Jean Cameron*** 1865–1962

Australian writer and poet. She sailed to Paraguay in 1893 to help establish the New Australia Movement Utopian community, and when this failed returned to Australia (1902), becoming a journalist. A lifelong supporter of aboriginal rights, in 1936 she was awarded the DBE.

55 I span and Eve span
A thread to bind the heart of man!
1918 *The Passionate Heart and Other Poems*, 'Eve-song'.

56 Lone, lone, and lone I stand,
With none to hear my cry,
As the black feet of the night
Go walking down the sky.
1932 *Under the Wilgas*, 'The Myall in Prison'.

Gilmour of Craiglockhart, Ian Gilmour, Baron 1926–

English Conservative politician, Secretary of State for Defence (1970–4) and Lord Privy Seal (1979–81). He has published several books on politics.

57 It does no harm to throw the occasional man overboard, but it does not do much good if you are steering full speed ahead for the rocks.
1981 In *The Times*, after he was sacked by Margaret Thatcher for publicly criticizing her anti-European stance.

Gingold, Hermione 1897–1987

English actress. A star of intimate revue, she also appeared with success in plays by Noël Coward and in musicals by Stephen Sondheim.

58 I got all the schooling any actress needs. That is, I learned to write enough to sign contracts.
Attributed.

Gingrich, Newt(on Leroy) 1943–

US politician. Originally a history professor, he became representative from Georgia in 1978 and subsequently leader of conservative Republicans in the House. He was Speaker of the House (1995–99).

59 One reason I try to get people to call me Newt is to break down barriers. It's a whole lot easier for someone to say, 'Newt, you've got a spot on your tie,' than it is to say 'Congressman'.
1979 Attributed comment.

Ginsberg, Allen 1926–97

US poet, a key member of the Beat movement with Jack Kerouac and William Burroughs. Despite his anti-establishment views, he was a popular poet and performer. His works include *Kaddish and Other Poems* (1961).

60 A naked lunch is natural to us,
we eat reality sandwiches.
But allegories are so much lettuce.
Don't hide the madness.
1954 'On Burroughs' Work'.

61 The madman bum and angel beat in Time, unknown, yet putting down here what might be left to say in time come after death.
1956 *Howl and Other Poems*, 'Howl, I'.

62 Moloch whose mind is pure machinery! Moloch whose blood is running money! Moloch whose fingers are ten armies! Moloch whose breast is a cannibal dynamo! Moloch whose ear is a smoking tomb!
1956 *Howl and Other Poems*, 'Howl, II'.

63 You were never no locomotive, Sunflower, you were a sunflower!
And you Locomotive, you are a locomotive, forget me not!
1956 *Howl and Other Poems*, 'Sunflower Sutra'.

64 America I've given you all and now I'm nothing.
1956 *Howl and Other Poems*, 'America'.

65 America I'm putting my queer shoulder to the wheel.
1956 *Howl and Other Poems*, 'America'.

66 Democracy! Bah! When I hear that word I reach for my feather Boa!
1960 Journal entry, Oct. Collected in *Journals: Early Fifties Early Sixties*, 'New York City'.

67 and poets should stay out of politics or become monsters
I have become monsterous with politics.
1961 *Kaddish and Other Poems*, 'Death to Van Gogh's Ear!'.

68 A very unique cat...a French Canadian Hinayana Buddhist Beat Catholic savant.
1970 Of Jack Kerouac. *This Fabulous Century 1950–1960*.

69 What if someone gave a war & Nobody came?
Life would ring the bells of Ecstasy and Forever be Itself again.
1973 *The Fall of America*, 'Graffiti 12th Cubicle Men's Room Syracuse Airport'.
► *See Sandburg 713:6.*

70 All this time [San Francisco, from 1955] I realized we were involved as a community with a historical change of consciousness and some kind of cultural revolution... I thought it was really in some respects a contest between further liberation or 1984 authoritarianism, police state; that it was creeping police state or creeping socialism-libertarianism.
1984 Quoted in Gordon Ball (ed) *Allen Ginsberg: Journals Mid-Fifties* (1995), 'Meditations on Record Keeping by Poet, Transcribed by Editor'.

71 Poetry is not an expression of the party line. It's that time of night, lying in bed, thinking what you really think, making the private world public, that's what the poet does.
Quoted in Barry Miles *Ginsberg* (1989), ch.5.

Giovanni, Nikki *in full Yolande Cornelia Giovanni, Jr* 1943–

US poet, a significant voice in the development of black consciousness. Her early work was more radical in tone than subsequent more introspective volumes.

72 Mistakes are a fact of life
It is the response to error that counts.
1968 *Black Judgement*, 'Of Liberation', stanza 16.

73 and I really hope no white person ever has cause to write about me
because they never understand Black love is Black wealth and they'll
probably talk about my hard childhood and never understand that
all the while I was quite happy
1968 *Black Judgement*, 'Nikki–Rosa'.

74 it's a sex object if you're pretty
and no love
or love and no sex if you're fat
1968 *Black Judgement*, 'Woman Poem'.

75 White people really deal more with God and black people with Jesus.
1971 Conversation with James Baldwin, London, 4 Nov. Collected in *A Dialogue* (1973).

76 A white face goes with a white mind. Occasionally a black face goes with a white mind. Very seldom a white face will have a black mind.
1971 Conversation with James Baldwin, London, 4 Nov. Collected in *A Dialogue* (1973).

Gipp, George 1895–1920

US American football player. His success on the field inspired Notre Dame to two unbeaten seasons (1919 and 1920), though his career was cut short by his death from pneumonia.

77 Some time, Rock, when the team's up against it, when things are wrong and the breaks are beating the boys – tell them to go in there with all they've got and win just one for the Gipper.
1920 Last words, to coach Knute Rockne. Rockne told the team about Gipp's request in 1928, when their fortunes were low, and inspired the squad to new efforts. 'Win one for the Gipper' subsequently became a catchphrase throughout US sport.

Giraudoux, (Hippolyte) Jean 1882–1944

French writer, head of propaganda in World War II. He is best known for his poetic plays, including *La Guerre de Troie n'aura pas lieu* (1935, translated as *The Tiger at the Gates*, 1955) and *Pour Lucrèce* (1953, translated as *Duel of Angels*, 1958).

78 *Le plagiat est la base de toutes les littératures, excepté de la première, qui d'ailleurs est inconnue.*
Plagiarism is the base of all literature except the first text which, however, is unknown.
1922 *Siegfried et le Limousin.*

79 *L'humanité est...une entreprise surhumaine.*
Humanity is...a superhuman undertaking.
1933 *Intermezzo*, act 1, sc.6.

80 A golf course is the epitome of all that is purely transitory in the universe, a space not to dwell in, but to get over as quickly as possible.
1933 Quoted in Colin Jarman *The Guinness Dictionary of Sports Quotations* (1990).

81 *Nous savons tous ici que le droit est la plus puissante des écoles de l'imagination. Jamais poète n'a interprété la nature aussi librement qu'un juriste la réalité.*
We all know here that the law is the most powerful of schools for the imagination. No poet ever interpreted nature as freely as a lawyer interprets the truth.
1935 *La Guerre de Troie n'aura pas lieu*, act 2, sc.5.

82 *Il n'est pas très prudent d'avoir des dieux et des légumes trop dorés.*
It is not wise to have either your gods or your vegetables too gilded.
1935 *La Guerre de Troie n'aura pas lieu*, act 2, sc.13.

83 *C'est de là que vient tout le mal: Dieu est un homme.*
All evil comes from this fact: God is a man.
1937 *Sodome et Gomorrhe*, act 1, sc.2.

Girondo, Oliverio 1891–1967

Argentinian poet, who travelled extensively in Europe and Africa and had close contact with the French avant garde. He edited the Ultraist manifesto in the avant-garde magazine *Martín Fierro* (1924).

84 *Cansado,*
sobre todo,
de estar siempre conmigo,
de hallarme cada día,
cuando termina el sueño,
allí, donde me encuentre,
con las mismas narices
y con las mismas piernas.
Tired,
above all,
of being always with myself,
of finding myself everyday,
when the dream comes to an end,
wherever I am,
with the same old nose
and with the same old legs.
1942 *Persuasión de los días*, 'Cansancio' ('Fatigue').

Giscard d'Estaing, Valéry 1926–

French politician, born in Germany. A Resistance worker during World War II, he was Finance Minister (1962–6) before launching the National Federation of Independent Republicans. He was President of France (1974–81) and in 1989 he resigned from the French National Assembly to play, instead, a leading role in the EU.

85 During my seven years in office, I was in love with seventeen million French women... I know this declaration will inspire irony and that English language readers will find it very French.
1988 *Le Pouvoir et la vie.*

Gitlin, Todd

US academic and columnist. He is Professor of Journalism and Sociology at Columbia University. He has written on culture, politics and the media and is also a published poet.

86 There is a misunderstanding by marketers in our culture about what freedom of choice is. In the market, it is equated with multiplying choice. This is a misconception. If you have infinite choice, people are reduced to passivity.
1990 In the *New York Times*, 14 Feb.

Giuliani, Rudy (Rudolph William) 1944–

US lawyer and politician. He was mayor of New York City at the time of the 11 September terrorist attacks on the World Trade Center.

87 Show your confidence. Show you're not afraid. Go to restaurants. Go shopping.
2001 Encouraging the people of New York to resume their normal lives after the terrorist attack of 11 Sep. Press conference, 12 Sep.

88 Our hearts are broken, but they continue to beat, and the spirit of our City has never been stronger.
2001 *One Nation: America Remembers September 11, 2001*, introduction.

Gladstone, W(illiam) E(wart) 1809–98

English Liberal statesman. He entered Parliament as a Conservative (1832), and in 1867 became leader of the Liberal Party. As Prime Minister (1868–74, 1880–5, 1886, 1892–4) he established a system of national education (1870), introduced parliamentary reforms aimed at universal male suffrage and argued for Irish Home Rule.

89 It is upon those who say that it is necessary to exclude forty-nine fiftieths of the working classes [from the vote] to show cause, and I venture to say that every man who is not presumably incapacitated by some consideration of personal unfitness or of political danger, is morally entitled to come within the pale of the Constitution.
1864 House of Commons, 11 May.

90 One cannot fight against the future. Time is on our side.
1866 Speech on the Reform Bill, House of Commons, 27 Apr.

91 Remember the rights of the savage, as we call him. Remember that the happiness of his humble home, remember that the sanctity of life in the hill villages of Afghanistan, among the winter snows, is as inviolable in the eye of Almighty God as can be your own.
1879 Speech at Edinburgh Foresters' Hall, during the Midlothian Campaign, 26 Nov.

92 England's foreign policy should always be inspired by the love of freedom. There should be a sympathy with freedom, a desire to give it scope, founded not upon visionary ideas but upon the long experience of many generations within the shores of this happy isle, that in freedom one lays the firmest foundations both of loyalty and order.
1879 Speech, West Calder, 27 Nov.

93 All the world over, I will back the masses against the classes.
1886 Speech, Liverpool, 28 Jun.

94 We are part of the community of Europe, and we must do our duty as such.
1866 Speech, 10 Apr.

95 What that Sicilian mule was to me, I have been to the Queen.
1894 Memorandum on his relationship with Queen Victoria, 20 Mar.

96 It is not a Life at all. It is a Reticence, in three volumes.
Of J W Cross's *Life of George Eliot*. Quoted in E F Benson *As We Were* (1930), ch.6.

Glasgow, Ellen Anderson Gholson 1874–1945

US novelist. Much of her fiction was set in the South. She won a Pulitzer Prize in 1941 for *In This Our Life*.

97 It was not the matter of the work, but the mind that went into, that counted—and the man who was not content to do small things well would leave great things undone.
1900 *The Voice of the People*, bk.2, ch.4.

98 Women like to sit down with trouble as if it were knitting.
1932 *The Sheltered Life*, pt.3, section 3.

99 No matter how vital experience might be while you lived it, no sooner was it ended and dead than it became as lifeless as the piles of dry dust in a school history book.
1941 *In This Our Life*, pt.3, ch.9.

Gleick, James 1954–

US software designer and science writer. His books include *Faster: The Acceleration of Just About Everything* (1999) and *Isaac Newton* (2003).

1 To some physicists chaos is a science of process rather than state, of becoming rather than being.
1987 *Chaos*.

2 The Internet has taken shape with startlingly little planning... The most universal and indispensable network on the planet somehow burgeoned without so much as a board of directors, never mind a mergers-and-acquisitions department. There is a paradoxical lesson here for strategists. In economic terms, the great corporations are acting like socialist planners, while old-fashioned free-market capitalism blossoms at their feet.
1994 In the *New York Times Magazine*, 1 May.

Glen, Iain 1961–

Scottish actor.

3 I used to have this terrible wish. I didn't mind dying as long as the rest of the world ground to a halt when I did.
2001 In *The Herald*, 8 Jul.

Glennie, Evelyn 1965–

Scottish percussion player. Judged to be a percussionist of outstanding abilities, she is additionally remarkable in her achievements as she experienced a gradual but total loss of hearing in her early teens.

4 If we cannot spare some patience towards a piece of music or art, what hope do we have for showing it to another human being?
2004 In *Scotland on Sunday*, 30 May.

Gloucester, William Henry, 1st Duke of 1743–1805

British nobleman and military officer. He was the son of Frederick Louis, Prince of Wales and Augusta of Saxe-Gotha.

5 Another damned, thick, square book! Always scribble, scribble, scribble! Eh! Mr Gibbon?
1781 Attributed, when presented with the second volume of *The Decline and Fall of the Roman Empire*. These words have also been attributed to George III and the Duke of Cumberland.

Godard, Jean-Luc 1930–

French film critic and director. His first feature *À bout de souffle* (1959) established him as one of the leading members of the 'New Wave'. Other notable films include *Pierrot Le Fou* (1965), *Alphaville* (1965) and *Week-end* (1967).

6 *La photographie, c'est la vérité. Le cinéma: la vérité vingt-quatre fois par seconde.*
Photography is truth. And cinema is truth twenty-four times a second.
1960 *Le Petit Soldat*.

Goebbels, (Paul) Joseph 1897–1945

German Nazi official. In 1926 Hitler appointed him district party leader for Berlin and in 1928 he entered the Reichstag. As Minister for Propaganda from 1933 he was a vociferous and virulent anti-Semite. He killed his family and committed suicide as Berlin fell in 1945.

7 *Ohne Butter werden wir fertig, aber nicht beispielsweise ohne Kanonen. Wenn wir einmal überfallen werden, dann können wir uns nicht mit Butter, sondern nur mit Kanonen verteidigen.*
We can manage without butter but not, for example, without guns. If we are attacked, we can only defend ourselves with guns not butter.
1936 Speech in Berlin, 17 Jan.

8 *Wenn das deutsche Volk die Waffen niederlegte, würden die Sowjets... ganz Ost- und Südosteuropa zuzüglich des größten Teiles des Reiches besetzen. Vor diesem einschließlich der Sowjetunion riesigen Territorium würde sich sofort ein eiserner Vorhang heruntersenken.*
Should the German people lay down their arms, the Soviets... would occupy all eastern and south-eastern Europe together with the greater part of the Reich. Over all this territory, which with the Soviet Union would be of enormous extent, an iron curtain would at once descend.
1945 In *Das Reich*, a Nazi propaganda weekly, quoted in *The Times* and the *Manchester Guardian* on 23 Feb.
► *See also Churchill 217:92.*

Goering, Hermann Wilhelm 1893–1946

German soldier and Nazi leader, commander of the Hitler storm troopers and head of the Gestapo. He was sentenced to death at the Nuremberg Trials, but committed suicide.

9 Our movement took a grip on cowardly Marxism, and from it, extracted the meaning of socialism. It also took from the cowardly, middle-class parties their nationalism. Throwing both into the cauldron of our way of life there emerged, as clear as crystal, the synthesis —German National Socialism.
1933 Speech, Berlin, 9 Apr.

10 Would you rather have butter or guns? ...preparedness

makes us powerful. Butter merely makes us fat.
1936 Speech, Hamburg.
➡ *See Goebbels 359:7.*

11 I hereby commission you to carry out all the preparations with regard to...a total solution of the Jewish question, in those territories of Europe that are under German influence.
1941 Directive to the Nazi High Command, 31 Jul, quoted in William Shirer *The Rise and Fall of the Third Reich* (1962).

Goethe, Johann Wolfgang von 1749–1832

German poet, dramatist and scientist. His early nationalistic, 'Sturm und Drang' dramas were followed by lyric poetry and poetical drama. His masterpiece was *Faust* (1808), on which he worked for most of his life.

12 English plays,
Atrocious in content,
Absurd in form,
Objectionable in action,
Execrable English Theatre!
1749 Attributed.

13 For a woman, she has extraordinary talent. One must look for what she does, not what she fails to do.
1786–8 Of the painter Angelica Kauffman. *Italienische Reise* (published 1816–17, translated by W H Auden and Elizabeth Mayer as *Italian Journey*, 1962).

14 *Wenn es eine Freude ist das Gute zu genießen, so ist es eine größere das Bessere zu empfinden, und in der Kunst ist das Beste gut genug.*
As it is a joy to enjoy what is good, so it is a greater joy to experience what is better, and in art the best is good enough.
1787 *Italienische Reise* 3 Mar (published 1816–17, translated by W H Auden and Elizabeth Mayer as *Italian Journey*, 1962).

15 *Wer nie sein Brot mit Tränen aß,*
Wer nie die kummervollen Nächte,
Auf seinem Bette weinen saß,
Der kennt euch nicht, ihr himmlischen Mächte.
Who never ate his bread in sorrow,
Who never spent the darksome hours
Weeping and watching for the morrow
He knows ye not, ye heavenly powers.
1795–6 *Wilhelm Meisters Lehrjahre* (translated by Carlyle in 1824 as *Wilhelm Meister's Apprenticeship*).

16 *Es irrt der Mensch, so lang er strebt.*
Man will err while yet he strives.
1808 *Faust*, pt.1, 'Prolog im Himmel'.

17 *Grau, teurer Freund, ist alle Theorie.*
Und grün des Lebens goldner Baum.
All theory, dear friend, is grey, but the golden tree of actual life springs ever green.
1808 *Faust*, pt.1, 'Studierzimmer'.

18 *Alles Gescheite ist schon gedacht worden; man muss nur versuchen, es noch einmal zu denken.*
Everything clever has been thought of before. We must try to think it again.
1819 *Sprüche in Prosa, Maximen und Reflexionen*, pt.1.

19 *Der Aberglaube ist die Poesie des Lebens.*
Superstition is the poetry of life.
1819 *Sprüche in Prosa, Maximen und Reflexionen*, pt.3.

20 *Neuere Poeten tun viel Wasser in die Tinte.*
Modern poets mix a lot of water with their ink.
1819 *Sprüche in Prosa, Maximen und Reflexionen*, pt.6.

21 *Das Erste und Letzte, was vom Genie gefordert wird, ist Wahrheitsliebe.*
The first and the last thing demanded of genius is the love of truth.
1819 *Sprüche in Prosa, Maximen und Reflexionen*, pt.6.

22 *Klassisch ist das Gesunde, romantisch das Kranke.*
The classical period was healthy; the romantic diseased.
1819 *Sprüche in Prosa, Maximen und Reflexionen*, pt.7.

23 Lord Byron is only great as a poet; as soon as he reflects he is a child.
1825 Eckermann's *Conversations with Goethe*, 18 Jan.

24 *Ich kenne mich auch nicht und Gott soll mich auch davor behuten.*
I do not know myself, and God forbid that I should.
1829 Eckermann's *Conversations with Goethe*, 10 Apr.

25 *Mehr Licht!*
More light!
1832 Last words.

26 *Ach da ich irrte, hatt' ich viel Gespielen,*
Da ich dich kenne, bin ich fast allein.
Ah! while I erred I had many friends.
Now that I know you, I am alone.
Gedichte, Zuneigung (published 1910).

Goheen, Robert F(rancis) 1919–

US classical scholar and educator, born in India. He joined Princeton University in 1948, and became President there (1957–72). He was Ambassador to India (1977–80).

27 If you feel that you have both feet planted on level ground, then the university has failed you.
1961 Baccalaureate address. Reported in *Time* magazine, 23 Jun.

Golding, Sir William (Gerald) 1911–93

English novelist. He achieved fame with his first novel *Lord of the Flies* (1954), and was awarded the Nobel prize for literature in 1983.

28 Ralph wept for the end of innocence, the darkness of man's heart, and the fall through the air of a true, wise friend called Piggy.
1954 *Lord of the Flies*, ch.12.

29 Sleep is when all the unsorted stuff comes flying out as from a dustbin upset in a high wind.
1956 *Pincher Martin*, ch.6.

30 Philip is a living example of natural selection. He was as fitted to survive in this modern world as a tapeworm in an intestine.
1959 *Free Fall*, ch.2.

31 Eighteen is a good time for suffering. One has all the necessary strength, and no defences.
1967 *The Pyramid*.

32 With lack of sleep and too much understanding I grow a little crazy, I think, like all men at sea who live too close to each other and too close thereby to all that is monstrous under the sun and moon.
1980 *Rites of Passage*, closing words.

33 The theme defeats structuralism, for it is an emotion. The

theme of *Lord of the Flies* is grief, sheer grief, grief, grief, grief.
1982 'Moving Target'.

34 It really means nothing in this country whatsoever—but then being a writer here means nothing either.
1983 On winning the Nobel prize. Quoted in the *Observer*, 31 May.

35 Life should serve up its feast of experience in a series of courses.
1987 *Close Quarters*.

Goldman, William 1931–

US screenwriter, who has written the scripts for films such as *Butch Cassidy and the Sundance Kid* (1969, Academy Award), *All the President's Men* (1976, Academy Award) and *Misery* (1990).

36 Boy, I got vision. The rest of the world wears bifocals.
1969 Anachronistic line delivered by Paul Newman in *Butch Cassidy and the Sundance Kid*.

Goldmark, Peter Carl, Jr 1940–

US government official, President of the Rockefeller Foundation (1988–97) and Director of the Global and Regional Air Program at Environmental Defense (2003–).

37 Welfare is hated by those who administer it; mistrusted by those who pay for it; and held in contempt by those who receive it.
1977 In the *New York Times*, 24 May.

Goldsmith, Oliver 1728–74

Irish novelist, poet, and playwright. After studying medicine and attempting to join the Church, he began a literary career. He is best known for the novel *The Vicar of Wakefield* (1766), the poem *The Deserted Village* (1770) and the play *She Stoops to Conquer* (1773).

38 The doctor found, when she was dead,
Her last disorder mortal.
1759 'Elegy on Mrs Mary Blaize'.

39 Where'er I roam, whatever realms to see,
My heart untravelled fondly turns to thee;
Still to my brother turns with ceaseless pain,
And drags at each remove a lengthening chain.
1764 *The Traveller*, l.7–10.

40 Such is the patriot's boast, where'er we roam,
His first, best country ever is, at home.
1764 *The Traveller*, l.73–4.

41 Laws grind the poor, and rich men rule the law.
1764 *The Traveller*, l.386.

42 How small, of all that human hearts endure,
That part which laws or kings can cause or cure!
1764 *The Traveller*, l.429–30.

43 I was ever of the opinion, that the honest man who married and brought up a large family, did more service than he who continued single and only talked of population.
1766 *The Vicar of Wakefield*, ch.1.

44 Let us draw upon content for the deficiencies of fortune.
1766 *The Vicar of Wakefield*, ch.3.

45 Conscience is a coward, and those faults it has not strength enough to prevent it seldom has justice enough to accuse.
1766 *The Vicar of Wakefield*, ch.13.

46 It seemed to me pretty plain, that they had more of love than of matrimony in them.
1766 *The Vicar of Wakefield*, ch.16.

47 When lovely woman stoops to folly
And finds too late that men betray,
What charm can soothe her melancholy,
What art can wash her guilt away?
1766 *The Vicar of Wakefield*, ch.29.

48 Friendship is a disinterested commerce between equals; love, an abject intercourse between tyrants and slaves.
1768 *The Good-Natured Man*, act 1.

49 Silence is become his mother tongue.
1768 *The Good-Natured Man*, act 2.

50 Sweet Auburn, loveliest village of the plain,
Where health and plenty cheered the labouring swain.
1770 *The Deserted Village*, l.1–2.

51 How often have I paused on every charm,
The sheltered cot, the cultivated farm,
The never-failing brook, the busy mill,
The decent church that topped the neighbouring hill.
1770 *The Deserted Village*, l.9–12.

52 Ill fares the land, to hastening ills a prey
Where wealth accumulates and men decay:
Princes and lords may flourish or may fade;
A breath can make them, as a breath has made;
But a bold peasantry, their country's pride,
When once destroyed, can never be supplied.
1770 *The Deserted Village*, l.51–6.

53 The village preacher's modest mansion rose.
A man he was to all the country dear,
And passing rich with forty pounds a year.
1770 *The Deserted Village*, l.140–2.

54 The village master taught his little school;
A man severe he was and stern to view;
I knew him well, and every truant knew;
Well had the boding tremblers learned to trace
The day's disasters in his morning face;
Full well they laughed, with counterfeited glee,
At all his jokes, for many a joke had he.
1770 *The Deserted Village*, l.196–202.

55 In arguing too, the parson owned his skill,
For e'en though vanquished, he could argue still;
While words of learned length, and thund'ring sound
Amazed the gazing rustics ranged around,
And still they gazed, and still the wonder grew,
That one small head could carry all he knew.
1770 *The Deserted Village*, l.211–16.

56 And, even while fashion's brightest arts decoy,
The heart distrusting asks, if this be joy.
1770 *The Deserted Village*, l.263–4.

57 The rich man's joys increase, the poor's decay,
'Tis yours to judge how wide the limits stand
Between a splendid and a happy land.
1770 *The Deserted Village*, l.266–8.

58 Thus fares the land, by luxury betrayed.
1770 *The Deserted Village*, l.295.

59 In all the silent manliness of grief.
1770 *The Deserted Village*, l.384.

60 I see the rural virtues leave the land.

1770 *The Deserted Village*, l.398.

61 Though very poor, may still be very blest.
1770 *The Deserted Village*, l.426.

62 I love everything that's old: old friends, old times, old manners, old books, old wine.
1773 *She Stoops to Conquer*, act 1, sc.1.

63 Is it one of my well-looking days, child? Am I in face to-day?
1773 *She Stoops to Conquer*, act 1, sc.1.

64 Let school-masters puzzle their brain,
With grammar, and nonsense, and learning;
Good liquor, I stoutly maintain,
Gives genius a better discerning.
1773 *She Stoops to Conquer*, act 1, sc.2.

65 I'll be with you in a squeezing of a lemon.
1773 *She Stoops to Conquer*, act 1, sc.2.

66 It's a damned long, dark, boggy, dirty, dangerous way.
1773 *She Stoops to Conquer*, act 1, sc.2.

67 The first blow is half the battle.
1773 *She Stoops to Conquer*, act 2, sc.1.

68 But there's no love lost between us.
1773 *She Stoops to Conquer*, act 4, sc.1.

69 Our Garrick's a salad; for in him we see
Oil, vinegar, sugar, and saltness agree.
1774 *Retaliation*, l.11–12.

70 Who, too deep for his hearers, still went on refining,
And thought of convincing, while they thought of dining;
Though equal to all things, for all things unfit,
Too nice for a statesman, too proud for a wit.
1774 Of Edmund Burke. *Retaliation*, l.29–32.

71 On the stage he was natural, simple, affecting;
'Twas only that when he was off he was acting.
1774 Of Garrick. *Retaliation*, l.101–2.

72 When they talked of their Raphaels, Correggios, and stuff,
He shifted his trumpet, and only took snuff.
1774 Of Reynolds. *Retaliation*, l.145–6.

Goldwater, Barry M(orris) 1909–98

US politician, Senator from Arizona (1952–64, 1969–87) and leader of the extreme right Republican wing. He was defeated in the 1964 presidential election by Lyndon B Johnson.

73 Extremism in the defence of liberty is no vice, and moderation in the pursuit of justice is no virtue.
1964 Speech to the Republican convention, 16 Jul.

74 In your heart, you know I'm right.
1964 Presidential campaign slogan.

75 He had probably been vaccinated with a phonograph needle.
1979 On the windy presidential candidate Hubert Humphrey. *With No Apologies*.

76 You don't need to be 'straight' to fight and die for your country. You just need to shoot straight.
1993 On homosexuals in the military. In *Life*, Dec.

Goldwyn, Sam(uel) *originally* Schmuel Gelbfisz 1882–1974

Polish-born US film producer. In 1917 he founded Goldwyn Pictures Corporation and in 1925 the Metro-Goldwyn-Mayer Company. His films include *Wuthering Heights* (1939), *The Little Foxes* (1941) and *Guys and Dolls* (1955). He is credited with many artless Goldwynisms, most probably apocryphal.

77 I'll cable Hitler and ask him to shoot around you.
1939 Remark to David Niven, Sep, when Niven left Hollywood to return to England. Quoted in David Niven *Bring on the Empty Horses* (1975).

78 I don't care if it doesn't make a nickel. I just want every man, woman and child in America to see it!
1946 Of *The Best Years of Our Lives*. Quoted in Leslie Halliwell *Halliwell's Filmgoer's and Video Viewer's Companion* (9th edn, 1989).

79 Any man who goes to a psychiatrist should have his head examined.
Quoted in Norman Zierold *Moguls* (1969), ch.3.

80 Please write music like Wagner, only louder.
Note to a composer of a forthcoming film soundtrack. Recalled on his death, 31 Jan 1974.

81 You ought to take the bull between the teeth.
Recalled on his death, 31 Jan 1974.

82 Now why did you name your baby 'John'? Every Tom, Dick and Harry is named 'John'.
Attributed. Quoted in Fred Metcalf (ed) *The Penguin Dictionary of Humorous Quotations* (1986).

83 I seriously object to seeing on the screen what belongs in the bedroom.
Attributed maxim. Quoted in Leslie Halliwell *Halliwell's Filmgoer's and Video Viewer's Companion* (9th edn, 1989).

84 What we want is a story that starts with an earthquake and works its way up to a climax.
Quoted in Leslie Halliwell *Halliwell's Filmgoer's and Video Viewer's Companion* (9th edn, 1989).

85 A verbal contract isn't worth the paper it's written on.
Attributed. Quoted in A Scott Berg *Goldwyn* (1989).

86 I'll give you a definite maybe.
Attributed. Quoted in A Scott Berg *Goldwyn* (1989).

87 Include me out.
Attributed. Quoted in A Scott Berg *Goldwyn* (1989).

88 We are dealing in facts, not realities.
Attributed. Quoted in A Scott Berg *Goldwyn* (1989).

89 You gotta take the sour with the bitter.
Remark allegedly said to Billy Wilder when one of his films flopped. Quoted in A Scott Berg *Goldwyn* (1989).

90 The most important thing in acting is honesty. Once you've learned to fake that, you're in.
Attributed.

91 The only reason so many people showed up at his funeral was because they wanted to make sure he was dead.
Of Louis B Mayer. Attributed.

Gomez, Vernon Louis *known as* 'Lefty' 1908–89

US baseball player, pitcher for the New York Yankees in the 1930s.

92 Tell you what, you keep the salary and pay me the cut.
When asked to take a cut in salary from $20,000 to $7,500 following a poor season. Quoted in Colin Jarman *The Guinness Dictionary of Sports Quotations* (1990).

Goncharov, Ivan Alexandrovich 1812–91

Russian novelist. He led an uneventful life in the civil service and produced *Oblomov* (1857, translated 1915), one of the greatest works of Russian realism.

93 The trouble is that no devastating or redeeming fires have ever burnt in my life… My life began by flickering out.
1859 *Oblomov*, pt.2, ch.4 (translated by David Magarshak).

94 You lost your ability for doing things in childhood… It all began with your inability to put on your socks and ended by your inability to live.
1859 *Oblomov*, pt.4, ch.2 (translated by David Magarshak).

Gonne, Maud 1865–1953

Irish nationalist and actress. She met W B Yeats in the early 1890s and, though Yeats wished to marry her, she ultimately rejected him and married Major John MacBride.

95 Poets should never marry. The world should thank me for not marrying you.
Attributed. Said to W B Yeats.

González Prada, Manuel 1848–1918

Peruvian reformer, journalist and poet. Nationalistic, pro-Indian, anti-Spanish and anti-clerical, he was a virtuoso in the vocabulary of invective, combining intensity of emotion with a pervasive sense of form.

96 *Aunque chillen los pedantes*
y arruguen todos el ceño,
lo declaro yo: Cervantes
suele producirme sueño
Pedants may cry out loud
or frown at me,
but I must say it: Cervantes
usually puts me to sleep.
1937 *Grafitos*, 'Hombres y libros' ('Men and Books')

Gooch, George Peabody 1873–1968

English historian and politician. He wrote several works on political and diplomatic history.

97 We can now look forward with something like confidence to the time when war between civilised nations will be considered as antiquated as a duel.
1911 *History of Our Time 1855–1911.*

Goodall, John 1863–1942

English footballer, captain of Preston North End. He also captained England, winning a total of 14 caps. He subsequently played cricket at county level for Derbyshire.

98 The one passion of my life has been football—the most exhilarating game I know, and the strongest protest against selfishness, without sermonizing, that was ever put before a thoughtful people.
Quoted in Andrew Ward and Anton Rippon *The Derby County Story* (1983).

Gorbachev, Mikhail Sergeyevich 1931–

Russian politician, President of the Supreme Soviet of the USSR (1988–90) and first executive President of the USSR. Despite his historic achievements as the father of *glasnost* (openness of information) and *perestroika* (a radical reform programme), which ended the Cold War, he was forced to resign on 25 Dec 1991. He was awarded the Nobel peace prize in 1990.

99 Some comrades apparently find it hard to understand that democracy is just a slogan.
1987 In the *Observer*, 1 Feb.

1 If the Russian word 'perestroika' has easily entered the international lexicon, it is due to more than just interest in what is going on in the Soviet Union. Now the whole world needs restructuring; that is, progressive development, a fundamental change.
1987 *Perestroika: New Thinking for Our Country and the World.*

2 The Soviet people want full-blooded and unconditional democracy.
1988 Speech, Jul.

3 Life is making us abandon established stereotypes and outdated views; it is making us discard illusions.
1988 Speech, United Nations, 7 Dec.

4 Mitterrand has 100 lovers. One has AIDS, but he doesn't know which one. Bush has 100 bodyguards. One is a terrorist, but he doesn't know which one. Gorbachev has 100 economic advisers. One is smart, but he doesn't know which one.
1990 In the *Sunday Times*, 9 Dec.

Gordon, Adam Lindsay 1833–70

Australian poet, born in the Azores. A series of personal tragedies led to a mental breakdown, and he committed suicide.

5 Question not, but live and labour
Till yon goal be won,
Helping every feeble neighbour,
Seeking help from none;
Life is mostly froth and bubble,
Two things stand like stone:
KINDNESS in another's trouble,
COURAGE in your own.
1866 'Ye Wearie Wayfarer: Hys Ballad. In Eight Fyttes', in *Bell's Life in Victoria*, Nov 1866, collected in *Sea Spray and Smoke Drift* (1867).

6 I would that with sleepy, soft embraces
The sea would fold me—would find me rest
In luminous shades of her secret places,
In depths where her marvels are manifest;
So the earth beneath her should not discover
My hidden couch—nor the heaven above her—
As a strong love shielding a weary lover,
I would have her shield me with shining breast.
'The Swimmer', stanza 5, collected in *Bush Ballads and Galloping Rhymes* (1870).

7 A little season of love and laughter,
Of light and life, and pleasure and pain,
And horror of outer darkness after,
And dust returneth to dust again.
Then the lesser life shall be as the greater,
And the lover of life shall join the hater,
And the one thing cometh sooner or later,
And no one knoweth the loss or gain.
'The Swimmer', stanza 10, collected in *Bush Ballads and Galloping Rhymes* (1870).

Gordon, Mack 1904–59

Polish-born US lyricist.

8 Pardon me boy is that the Chattanooga Choo-choo,

Track twenty nine,
Boy you can give me a shine.
1941 Song 'Chattanooga Choo Choo', featured in *Sun Valley Serenade* (music by Harry Warren).

9 Dinner in the diner
nothing could be finer
than to have your ham'n eggs in Carolina.
1941 Song 'Chattanooga Choo Choo', featured in *Sun Valley Serenade* (music by Harry Warren).

Gordon, Ruth 1896–1985

US actress and playwright, best known for the screenplays she wrote with her husband Garson Kanin, *Adam's Rib* (1949) and *Pat and Mike* (1952). She won an Oscar for her performance in *Rosemary's Baby* (1968).

10 MAX: Say, is it too early for a drink?
POLLY: What's early about it? It's tomorrow in Europe and yesterday in China.
1943 *Over Twenty-One*, act 3.

Gore, Al(bert, Jr) 1948–

US Vice-President under Bill Clinton (1992–2000). In 2000 he ran for President in what turned out to be the closest contest in over 100 years, losing to Republican George W Bush by the narrowest of margins.

11 You get all the French-fries the President can't get to.
1994 On being Vice-President. In the *New York Times*, 8 Apr.

12 It makes no more sense to launch an assault on our civil liberties as the best way to get at terrorists than it did to launch an invasion on Iraq as the best way to get at Osama Bin Laden.
2003 Speech calling for the repeal of the US Patriot Act, 9 Nov.

Gorman, Dave 1971–

English comedian.

13 Fictional comedy tells us that the writer is remarkable. Factual comedy tells us that the world is remarkable. I suppose I prefer to live in a remarkable world.
2004 In *Varsity*, 23 Jan.

Gorostiza, José 1901–73

Mexican poet and diplomat. The most famous member of the avant-garde *Contemporáneos* group, his published poems are few but complex.

14 *¡Oh inteligencia, soledad en llamas,*
que todo lo concibe sin crearlo!
Oh intelligence, flaming solitude,
envisioning all without creating!
1939 *Muerte sin fin*, pt.1 (translated as *Death without End*, 1969).

Gorostiza, Manuel Eduardo de 1789–1851

Mexican dramatist and diplomat. He spent his youth in Spain, returning to Mexico in 1833 where he fought in the US invasion. He was a key figure in Latin American neoclassical theatre.

15 *Yo no digo por eso que el té no sea saludable…cuando duelen las tripas…pero al cabo no pasa de ser agua caliente; sólo podía habernos venido de Inglaterra, que como allí son herejes, ni tendrán vino, ni bueyes cebones.*
I'm not saying that tea is not healthy…when you have a stomach ache…but, all in all, it is only hot water; it could only come from the English, who, being heretics as they are, probably have no wine or good beer.
1833 *Contigo pan y cebolla*, act 1.

Gosse, Sir Edmund 1849–1928

English critic and translator. He wrote biographies of many notable literary figures, and translated the plays of Henrik Ibsen.

16 A sheep in sheep's clothing.
Of Sturge Moore, a poet. Quoted in F Greenslet *Under the Bridge* (1943), ch.10.

17 We were as nearly bored as enthusiasm would permit.
Of a play by Algernon Swinburne. Quoted in C Hassall *Biography of Edward Marsh*.

Gottfried von Strassburg fl.c.1200

German poet. His major work is a version of the Tristan and Isolde legend, *Tristan* (c.1210), but his appraisals of the works of other writers are a striking early example of literary criticism.

18 *Wan swelh wîp tugendet wider ir art,*
diu gerne wider ir art bewart
ir lop, ir êre unde ire lîp,
diu ist niwan mit namen ein wîp
und ist ein man mit muote.
When a woman grows in virtue despite her nature
and gladly preserves the integrity
of her honour, her reputation, and her person,
she is only a woman in name:
in spirit she is a man.
c.1210 *Tristan*, l.17971–3.

Gottlieb, Adolph 1903–74

US painter, one of the leaders of Abstract Expressionism.

19 Certain people always say we should go back to nature. I notice they never say we should go forward to nature. It seems to me they are more concerned that we should go back, than about nature.
1947 In *Tiger's Eye*, vol.1, no.2, Dec, quoted in C Harrison and Paul Wood (eds) *Art in Theory 1900–1990* (1992).

Gould, Glenn 1932–82

Canadian pianist and musical theorist. He performed his last live concert in 1964, thereafter confining himself to recording.

20 The concert is dead.
Quoted in Richard Kostelanetz *Master Minds* (1969).

21 The purpose of art is the lifelong construction of a state of wonder.
Quoted by Lorraine Monk at the Commencement Address, York University, Toronto, 6 Nov 1982.

Gould, Philip 1950–

English political strategist and senior adviser to Tony Blair.

22 The New Labour brand has been badly contaminated. It is the object of constant criticism and, even worse, ridicule.
2000 Internal memo, May, later leaked to the press. In *The Guardian*, 20 Jul.

Gould, Stephen Jay 1941–2002

US palaeontologist, evolutionary biologist and science writer,

Professor at Harvard University (1967–2002).

23 A man does not attain the status of Galileo merely because he is persecuted, he must also be right.
1977 *Ever Since Darwin*.

24 Science must be understood as a social phenomenon, a gutsy, human enterprise, not the work of robots programmed to collect pure information.
1981 *The Mismeasure of Man*.

25 Science is an integral part of culture. It's not this foreign thing, done by an arcane priesthood. It's one of the glories of the human intellectual tradition.
1990 In *The Independent*, 24 Jan.

Gounod, Charles François 1818–93

French composer. His works include operas, masses, hymns and oratorios, and he was popular as a songwriter. He fled to England in the Franco-Prussian War (1870), becoming a commander of the Legion of Honour in 1877.

26 God grant me a failure like that!
1861 Of Wagner's opera *Tannhäuser*, after the disastrous première of its revised version at the *Opéra*, 13 Mar, when it was withdrawn after only three performances. Quoted in Joanna Richardson *La Vie Parisienne* (1971).
➡ *See Mérimée 567:13.*

Gourmont, Rémy de 1858–1915

French writer and critic, leader of the Symbolist movement. He founded the periodical *Le Mercure de France*, and wrote essays, literary criticism and novels.

27 Science is the only truth and it is the great lie. It knows nothing, and people think it knows everything. It is misrepresented. People think that science is electricity, automobilism, and dirigible balloons. It is something very different. It is life devouring itself. It is the sensibility transformed into intelligence. It is the need to know stifling the need to live. It is the genius of knowledge vivisecting the vital genius.
1905 *Promenades philosophiques* (translated by Glen S Burne, 1966).

Gowers, Sir Ernest Arthur 1880–1966

English civil servant, called to the bar in 1906. His *Plain Words* (1948) and *ABC of Plain Words* (1951) are guides for officials in writing clear English. He revised Fowler's *Dictionary of Modern English Usage* (1965).

28 It is not easy nowadays to remember anything so contrary to all appearances as that officials are the servants of the public; and the official must try not to foster the illusion that it is the other way round.
1948 *Plain Words*, ch.3.

29 Sociology is a new science concerning itself not with esoteric matters outside the comprehension of the layman, as the older sciences do, but with the ordinary affairs of ordinary people. This seems to engender in those who write about it a feeling that the lack of any abstruseness in their subject matter demands a compensatory abstruseness in their language.
1965 'Sociologese', in H F Fowler *A Dictionary of Modern English Usage* (2nd rev edn).

Goya, Francisco de 1746–1828

Spanish painter and graphic artist, perhaps best known for his series of etchings *The Disasters of War*.

30 But where do they find these lines in nature? Personally I only see forms that are lit up and forms that are not, planes which advance and planes which recede, relief and depth. My eye never sees outlines or particular features or details. I do not count the hairs in the beard of the man who passes by any more than the buttonholes on his jacket attract my notice. My brush should not see better than I do.
Quoted in Enriqueta Harris *Goya* (1969).

Grace, W(illiam) G(ilbert) 1848–1915

English cricketer and physician. He made his debut in first-class cricket in 1864; by the time he retired in 1908 he had scored 126 first class centuries and 54,896 runs, and taken 2,864 wickets.

31 Let's be getting at them before they get at us.
His reason for always choosing to bat first if his team won the toss. Quoted in Colin Jarman *The Guinness Dictionary of Sports Quotations* (1990).

32 They haven't come to see you umpiring, they have come to see me bat.
On refusing to leave the crease after an umpire gave him out before he had scored, attributed. Other versions of the story have the umpire refusing to call out on the first ball, explaining to the outraged bowler that the crowd had paid not to see him bowl, but to see Grace bat.

Graham, Harry 1874–1936

English writer of light verse. His blackly comic rhymes in *Ruthless Rhymes for Heartless Homes* (1899) and the later *More Ruthless Rhymes* (1930) won widespread popularity.

33 Aunt Jane observed, the second time
She tumbled off a bus,
'The step is short from the Sublime
To the Ridiculous.'
1899 *Ruthless Rhymes for Heartless Homes*, 'Equanimity'.

34 O'er the rugged mountain's brow
Clara threw the twins she nursed,
And remarked, 'I wonder now
Which will reach the bottom first?'
1899 *Ruthless Rhymes for Heartless Homes*, 'Calculating Clara'.

35 Billy, in one of his nice new sashes,
Fell in the fire and was burnt to ashes;
Now, although the room grows chilly,
I haven't the heart to poke poor Billy.
1899 *Ruthless Rhymes for Heartless Homes*, 'Tender-Heartedness'.

36 Weep not for little Léonie
Abducted by a French *Marquis*!
Though loss of honour was a wrench
Just think how it's improved her French.
1930 *More Ruthless Rhymes for Heartless Homes*, 'Compensation'.

Grahame, Kenneth 1859–1932

Scottish children's writer and Secretary of the Bank of England (1898–1908). He wrote essays and country tales but is best remembered for *The Wind in the Willows* (1908).

37 Believe me, my young friend, there is *nothing*—

absolutely nothing—half so much worth doing as simply messing about in boats.
1908 *The Wind in the Willows*, ch.1.

38 The poetry of motion! The *real* way to travel! The *only* way to travel! Here today—in next week tomorrow! Villages skipped, towns and cities jumped—always somebody else's horizon!
1908 Toad rhapsodizes about the motor car. *The Wind in the Willows*, ch.2.

39 The smell of buttered toast simply talked to Toad, and with no uncertain voice; talked of warm kitchens, of breakfasts on bright frosty mornings, of cosy parlour firesides on winter evenings, when one's ramble was over and slippered feet were propped on the fender; of the purring of contented cats, and the twitter of sleepy canaries.
1908 *The Wind in the Willows*, ch.8.

40 The clever men at Oxford
Know all that there is to be knowed.
But they none of them know one half as much
As intelligent Mr Toad.
1908 *The Wind in the Willows*, ch.10.

Gramm, Phil (William Philip) 1942–

US Senator (1985–2002) and economist.

41 If I had to decide today, I would run. But I may come to my senses.
1994 On seeking presidential nomination. In *Time*, 26 Sep.

42 I didn't come to Washington to be loved and I haven't been disappointed.
1995 In NPR broadcast, 24 Feb.

43 Sophia Loren is not a citizen.
1995 On being asked if he would choose a woman as a running mate. In *Newsweek*, 13 Mar.

44 I have the most reliable friend that you can have in American politics—ready money.
1995 On seeking presidential nomination. In the *New York Times*, 23 Apr.

Grand, Sarah *pseudonym of* Frances Elizabeth McFall *née* Clarke 1854–1943

British novelist and feminist, born in Ireland. She was Mayoress of Bath (1923, 1925–9), and is best known for her novels which explore sexual double standards.

45 Both the cow-woman and the scum-woman are well within range of the comprehension of the Bawling Brotherhood, but the new woman is a little above him, and he never thought of looking up to where she has been sitting apart in silent contemplation all these years.
1894 *North American Review*, 'The New Aspect of the Woman Question', Mar.

Grant, Cary *pseudonym of* Archibald Leach 1904–86

English-born US film star. He made his film debut in 1932 and developed a reputation as a suave, debonair performer in sophisticated light comedy. His films include *Bringing up Baby* (1938), *His Girl Friday* (1940), *An Affair to Remember* (1957) and *North by Northwest* (1959).

46 Not only will I not play it, but if Rex Harrison doesn't do it, I won't even go to see it.
c.1963 Response when offered the role of Professor Henry Higgins in the film of *My Fair Lady*. Attributed.

47 Old Cary Grant fine. How you?
His response to a journalist's terse cable to his press agent, 'How old Cary Grant?' Attributed.

Grant, George P 1918–

Canadian philosopher and teacher.

48 We listen to others to discover what we ourselves believe.
Quoted in *CBC Times*, 18 Feb 1959.

Grant, Hugh 1960–

English actor, who became an international star after starring in *Four Weddings and a Funeral* (1994). Subsequent films include *Notting Hill* (1999) and *Bridget Jones's Diary* (2001).

49 I play the sort of character who would sell his grandmother for career advancement, something I've come across a lot with actors.
1994 On his role in *Restoration*. In *Screen International*, 2 Sep.

50 If *Pulp Fiction* had been set in the Sussex countryside—and I'm sure it could have worked—then things might have turned out very differently.
1995 Contrasting *Four Weddings and a Funeral* with a notoriously violent urban US drama. Speech at the British Academy of Film and Television Arts award ceremony, reported in *Screen International*, 28 Apr.

51 I just don't believe in love at first sight any more, even though I've based my whole career on the concept.
Quoted in the *Daily Telegraph*, 1 Jan 2004.

Grant, Sir Robert 1779–1838

English lawyer and politician, Advocate-General and Governor of Bombay.

52 O worship the King, all glorious above;
O gratefully sing his power and his love:
Our Shield and Defender, the Ancient of Days,
Pavilioned in splendour, and girded with praise.
1833 'O worship the King, all glorious above', collected in *Sacred Poems* (1839).

53 O tell of his might, O sing of his grace,
Whose robe is the light, whose canopy space.
His chariots of wrath the deep thunder-clouds form,
And dark is his path on the wings of the storm.
1833 'O worship the King, all glorious above', collected in *Sacred Poems* (1839).

Grant, Ulysses S(impson) 1822–85

US soldier and 18th President (1869–77), Union general in the Civil War, who accepted the Confederate surrender at Appomattox Court House (1865). He presided over the reconstruction of the South, but his administration was marred by scandal and corruption.

54 No terms except unconditional and immediate surrender can be accepted. I propose to move immediately upon your works.
1862 Message to Simon Bolivar Buckner, besieged at Fort Donelson, 16 Feb. Quoted in P C Headley *The Life and Campaigns of General U. S. Grant* (1869), ch.6.

55 I purpose to fight it out on this line, if it takes all summer.
1864 Despatch to Washington from Spottsylvania, 11 May.

Quoted in P C Headley *The Life and Campaigns of General U. S. Grant* (1869), ch.23.

56 I know no method to secure the repeal of bad or obnoxious laws so effective as their stringent execution.
1869 Inaugural address, 4 Mar.

57 I only know two tunes. One of them is 'Yankee Doodle', and the other isn't.
Attributed. Quoted in Derek Watson *Music Quotations* (1991).

Grass, Günter Wilhelm 1927–

German novelist, poet and playwright. Intellectual and experimental in form, theme and language, his books consistently challenge the status quo and question our reading of the past. He was awarded the Nobel prize for literature in 1999.

58 *Ich bin Schriftsteller von Beruf. Ich versuche, gegen die vergehende Zeit anzuschreiben, damit das Vergangene nicht unbekannt bleibt.*
I am a writer by profession. I seek in my writing to hold back time so that the past is not forgotten.
1978 *Denkzettel: Politische Reden und Aufsätze.*

59 *Ich sei nicht nur als Autor, sondern auch als Mann betroffen. Und zwar irgendwie schuldhaft.*
I am moved, not only as an author, but as a person. And feel somehow guilty.
1977 *Der Butt* (translated as *The Flounder*, 1978).

60 We of the long tails! We of the presentient whiskers! We of the perpetually growing teeth! We, the serried footnotes to man, his proliferating commentary. We, indestructible!
1987 *Die Ratten* (translated as *The Rat*, 1987).

Grattan, Henry 1746–1820

Irish statesman. He abandoned law for politics in 1775, leading the fight for independence. Unable to prevent the Act of Union, he sat at Westminster until his death.

61 She hears the ocean protesting against separation, but she hears the sea protesting against union. She follows therefore her physical destination when she protests against the two situations, both equally unnatural—separation and union.
Of Ireland. Quoted in Conor Cruise O'Brien *Parnell and His Party* (1957).

Graves, Robert von Ranke 1895–1985

English writer. He lived abroad for much of his adult life. His works include novels, poems, essays, studies of mythology, criticism, and his autobiography, *Goodbye to All That* (1929).

62 His eyes are quickened so with grief,
He can watch a grass or a leaf
Every instant grow.
1921 'Lost Love'.

63 Love shall come at your command
Yet will not stay.
1923 'Song of Contrariety'.

64 Children are dumb to say how hot the day is,
How hot the scent is of the summer rose.
1927 'The Cool Web'.

65 Goodbye to All That.
1929 Title of autobiography.

66 Take your delight in momentariness,
Walk between dark and dark—a shining space
With the grave's narrowness, though not its peace.
1938 'Sick Love'.

67 In fear begotten, I begot in fear.
Would you have had me cast fear out
So that you should not be?
1938 'Parents to Child'.

68 What, then, was war?
No mere discord of flags
But an infection of the common sky
That sagged ominously upon the earth
Even when the season was the airiest May?
1938 'Recalling War'.

69 To evoke posterity
Is to weep on your own grave,
Ventriloquizing for the unborn.
1938 'To Evoke Posterity'.

70 To bring the dead to life
Is no great magic.
Few are wholly dead:
Blow on a dead man's embers
And a live flame will start.
1938 'To Bring the Dead to Life'.

71 Truth-loving Persians do not dwell upon
The trivial skirmish fought near Marathon.
1945 'The Persian Version'.

72 Stirring suddenly from long hibernation,
I knew myself once more a poet
Guarded by timeless principalities
Against the worm of death.
1945 'Mid-Winter Waking'.

73 To be a poet is a condition rather than a profession.
1946 Response to a questionnaire from the editor of *Horizon*.

74 The function of poetry is religious invocation of the Muse; its use is the experience of mixed exaltation and horror that her presence excites.
1948 *The White Goddess*, foreword.

75 For a woman to have a *liaison* is almost always pardonable, and occasionally, when the lover chosen is sufficiently distinguished, even admirable.
1950 *Occupation: Writer*, 'Lars Porsena'.

76 In love as in sport, the amateur status must be strictly maintained.
1950 *Occupation: Writer*, 'Lars Porsena'.

77 Counting the slow heart beats,
The bleeding to death of time in slow heart beats,
Wakeful they lie.
1951 'Counting the Beats'.

78 Prose books are the show dogs I breed and sell to support my cat.
1958 On writing novels to support his love of writing poetry. In the *New York Times*, 13 Jul.

79 Why have such scores of lovely, gifted girls
Married impossible men?
1958 'A Slice of Wedding Cake'.

80 Julia: how Irishly you sacrifice
Love to pity, pity to ill-humour,
Yourself to love, still haggling at the price.
'Reproach to Julia', collected in *Collected Poems* (1959).

81 Love is a universal migraine
A bright stain on the vision
Blotting out reason.
1961 'Symptoms of Love'.

82 A well-chosen anthology is a complete dispensary of medicine for the more common mental disorders, and may be used as much for prevention as cure.
1962 *On English Poetry*, 'Definitions'.

83 Nine-tenths of English poetic literature is the result either of vulgar careerism, or of a poet trying to keep his hand in. Most poets are dead by their late twenties.
1962 In the *Observer*, 11 Nov.

84 If there's no money in poetry, neither is there poetry in money.
1963 Speech at London School of Economics, 6 Dec.

85 The remarkable thing about Shakespeare is that he is really very good—in spite of all the people who say he is very good.
1964 Attributed.

86 The poet is the unsatisfied child who dares to ask the difficult question which arises from the schoolmaster's answer to his simple question, and then the still more difficult question which arises from that.
Recalled on his death, 7 Dec 1985.

87 Love without hope, as when the young bird-catcher
Swept off his tall hat to the Squire's own daughter,
So let the imprisoned larks escape and fly
Singing about her head, as she rode by.
'Love without Hope'.

Gray, Alasdair James 1934–

Scottish novelist, painter and playwright. His novel *Lanark* (1981) is an inventive semi-fantasy based in Glasgow. He has subsequently written and illustrated several equally unconventional novels.

88 Of course in nature the only ending is death, but death hardly ever happens when people are at their best. That is why we like tragedies. They show men energetically with their wits about them and deserving to do it.
1981 *Lanark*, bk.1, interlude.

89 Art is the only work open to people who can't get along with others and still want to be special.
1981 *Lanark*, bk.3, ch.1.

90 Glasgow, the sort of industrial city where most people live nowadays but nobody imagines living.
1981 *Lanark*, bk.3, ch.11.

Gray, Alexander 1882–1968

Scottish economist, Professor at Aberdeen and Edinburgh Universities.

91 The services of a menial servant, taking him as an example of unproductive labour, 'generally perish in the very instant of their performance'—and forthwith into this galley, along with the menial servant, goes the sovereign, accompanied by all the army, the navy, and the civil service, followed by churchmen, lawyers, buffoons and opera dancers. All these—and it is a hard saying—render services which perish in the very instant of their performance.
1931 *The Development of Economic Doctrine*.

Gray, Thomas 1716–71

English poet. In 1742 he wrote his *Ode on a Distant Prospect of Eton College* (1747) and began the famous *Elegy Written in a Country Churchyard* (1751). He declined the Laureateship (1757), and became Professor of History and Modern Languages at Cambridge (1768).

92 Ye distant spires, ye antique towers,
That crown the wat'ry glade.
1742 *Ode on a Distant Prospect of Eton College* (published 1747), l.1–2.

93 Still as they run they look behind,
They hear a voice in every wind,
And snatch a fearful joy.
1742 *Ode on a Distant Prospect of Eton College* (published 1747), l.38–40.

94 Alas, regardless of their doom,
The little victims play!
No sense have they of ills to come,
Nor care beyond to-day.
1742 *Ode on a Distant Prospect of Eton College* (published 1747), l.51–4.

95 To each his suff'rings, all are men,
Condemned alike to groan;
The tender for another's pain,
Th'unfeeling for his own.

Yet ah! why should they know their fate?
Since sorrow never comes too late,
And happiness too swiftly flies.
Thought would destroy their paradise.
No more; where ignorance is bliss,
'Tis folly to be wise.
1742 *Ode on a Distant Prospect of Eton College* (published 1747), l.91–100.

96 The language of the age is never the language of poetry, except among the French, whose verse, where the thought or image does not support it, differs in nothing from prose.
1742 Letter to Richard West, 8 Apr. Collected in H W Starr (ed) *Correspondence of Thomas Gray* (1971).

97 Demurest of the tabby kind,
The pensive Selima reclined,
Gazed on the lake below.
1747 *Ode on the Death of a Favourite Cat, Drowned in a Tub of Gold Fishes*, l.4–6.

98 The velvet of her paws,
Her coat that with the tortoise vies,
Her ears of jet and emerald eyes,
She saw; and purred applause.
1747 *Ode on the Death of a Favourite Cat, Drowned in a Tub of Gold Fishes*, l.9–12.

99 What female heart can gold despise?
What cat's averse to fish?
1747 *Ode on the Death of a Favourite Cat, Drowned in a Tub of Gold Fishes*, l.23–4.

1 A favourite has no friend!
1747 *Ode on the Death of a Favourite Cat, Drowned in a Tub of Gold Fishes*, l.36.

2 Not all that tempts your wandering eyes
And heedless hearts, is lawful prize;
Nor all that glisters gold.
1747 *Ode on the Death of a Favourite Cat, Drowned in a Tub of

Gold Fishes, l.40–3. Derived from 'All that glitters is not gold', *The Merchant of Venice*, act 2, scene 7.

3 The Attic warbler pours her throat,
Responsive to the cuckoo's note,
The untaught harmony of spring.
1748 *Ode on the Spring*, l.5–7.

4 Where'er the oak's thick branches stretch
A broader browner shade;
Where'er the rude and moss-grown beech
O'er-canopies the glade,
Beside some water's rushy brink
With me the Muse shall sit, and think.
1748 *Ode on the Spring*, l.11–16.

5 How low, how little are the proud,
How indigent the great!
1748 *Ode on the Spring*, l.19–20.

6 The insect youth are on the wing,
Eager to taste the honeyed spring,
And float amid the liquid noon:
Some lightly o'er the current skim,
Some show their gaily-gilded trim
Quick-glancing to the sun.
1748 *Ode on the Spring*, l.25–30.

7 Methinks I hear in accents low
The sportive kind reply:
Poor moralist! and what art thou?
A solitary fly!
1748 *Ode on the Spring*, l.41–4.

8 Shame of the versifying tribe!
Your history whither are you spinning?
Can you do nothing but describe?
1750 *A Long Story*, l.17–20.

9 To celebrate her eyes, her air—
Coarse panegyrics would but tease her.
Melissa is her nom de guerre.
Alas, who would not wish to please her!
1750 *A Long Story*, l.33–6.

10 The curfew tolls the knell of parting day,
The lowing herd wind slowly o'er the lea,
The ploughman homeward plods his weary way,
And leaves the world to darkness and to me.

Now fades the glimmering landscapes on the sight,
And all the air a solemn stillness holds,
Save where the beetle wheels his droning flight,
And drowsy tinklings lull the distant folds.
1751 *Elegy Written in a Country Churchyard*, l.1–8.

11 Save that from yonder ivy-mantled tower
The moping owl does to the moon complain.
1751 *Elegy Written in a Country Churchyard*, l.9–10.

12 Beneath those rugged elms, that yew-tree's shade,
Where heaves the turf in many a mouldering heap,
Each in his narrow cell for ever laid,
The rude forefathers of the hamlet sleep.

The breezy call of incense-breathing Morn,
The swallow twitt'ring from the straw-built shed,
The cock's shrill clarion, or the echoing horn,
No more shall rouse them from their lowly bed.
1751 *Elegy Written in a Country Churchyard*, l.13–20.

13 For them no more the blazing hearth shall burn,
Or busy housewife ply her evening care:
No children run to lisp their sire's return,
Or climb upon his knees the envied kiss to share.
1751 *Elegy Written in a Country Churchyard*, l.21–4.

14 Let not Ambition mock their useful toil,
Their homely joys and destiny obscure;
Nor Grandeur hear, with a disdainful smile,
The short and simple annals of the poor.

The boast of heraldry, the pomp of power,
And all that beauty, all that wealth e'er gave,
Awaits alike th' inevitable hour,
The paths of glory lead but to the grave.
1751 *Elegy Written in a Country Churchyard*, l.29–36.

15 Can storied urn or animated bust
Back to its mansion call the fleeting breath?
Can Honour's voice provoke the silent dust,
Or Flattery soothe the dull cold ear of Death?
1751 *Elegy Written in a Country Churchyard*, l.41–4.

16 But knowledge to their eyes her ample page
Rich with the spoils of time did ne'er unroll;
Chill Penury repressed their noble rage,
And froze the genial current of the soul.
1751 *Elegy Written in a Country Churchyard*, l.49–52.

17 Full many a gem of purest ray serene
The dark unfathomed caves of ocean bear:
Full many a flower is born to blush unseen
And waste its sweetness on the desert air.
1751 *Elegy Written in a Country Churchyard*, l.52–6.

18 Some mute inglorious Milton here may rest,
Some Cromwell guiltless of his country's blood.
1751 *Elegy Written in a Country Churchyard*, l.59–60.

19 Their lot forbad: nor circumscribed alone
Their growing virtues, but their crimes confined;
Forbad to wade through slaughter to a throne,
And shut the gates of mercy on mankind.
1751 *Elegy Written in a Country Churchyard*, l.65–8.

20 Far from the madding crowd's ignoble strife
Their sober wishes never learned to stray;
Along the cool sequestered vale of life
They kept the noiseless tenor of their way.
1751 *Elegy Written in a Country Churchyard*, l.73–6. Thomas Hardy popularized the phrase as the title of his novel *Far From the Madding Crowd* (1874).

21 Their name, their years, spelt by the unlettered muse,
The place of fame and elegy supply:
And many a holy text around she strews,
That teach the rustic moralist to die.
1751 *Elegy Written in a Country Churchyard*, l.81–4.

22 For who to dumb Forgetfulness a prey,
This pleasing anxious being e'er resigned,
Left the warm precincts of the cheerful day,
Nor cast one longing ling'ring look behind?
1751 *Elegy Written in a Country Churchyard*, l.85–8.

23 Mindful of the unhonoured dead.
1751 *Elegy Written in a Country Churchyard*, l.93.

24 Oft have we seen him at the peep of dawn
Brushing with hasty steps the dews away
To meet the sun upon the upland lawn.
1751 *Elegy Written in a Country Churchyard*, l.98–100.

25 Here rest his head upon the lap of earth

A youth to fortune and to fame unknown.
Fair Science frowned not on his humble birth,
And Melancholy marked him for her own.
1751 *Elegy Written in a Country Churchyard*, l.117–20, 'The Epitaph'.

26 No farther seek his merits to disclose,
Or draw his frailties from their dread abode,
(There they alike in trembling hope repose)
The bosom of his Father and his God.
1751 *Elegy Written in a Country Churchyard*, l.125–8, 'The Epitaph'.

27 Ruin seize thee, ruthless King!
Confusion on thy banners wait,
Tho' fanned by Conquest's crimson wing
They mock the air with idle state.
1757 *The Bard. A Pindaric Ode*, l.1–4.

28 To save thy secret soul from nightly fears.
1757 *The Bard. A Pindaric Ode*, l.6.

29 Loose his beard, and hoary hair
Streamed, like a meteor, to the troubled air.
1757 *The Bard. A Pindaric Ode*, l.19–20.

30 Cold is Cadwallon's tongue,
That hushed the stormy main.
1757 *The Bard. A Pindaric Ode*, l.29–30.

31 Dear as the light that visits these sad eyes,
Dear as the ruddy drops that warm my heart,
Ye died amidst your dying country's cries.
1757 *The Bard. A Pindaric Ode*, l.40–2.

32 Weave the warp, and weave the woof,
The winding-sheet of Edward's race.
Give ample room, and verge enough
The characters of hell to trace.
1757 *The Bard. A Pindaric Ode*, l.49–52.

33 Mighty victor, mighty lord,
Low on his funeral couch he lies!
No pitying heart, no eye, afford
A tear to grace his obsequies.
1757 *The Bard. A Pindaric Ode*, l.63–6.

34 Fair laughs the morn and soft the zephyr blows,
While proudly riding o'er the azure realm
In gallant trim the gilded vessel goes;
Youth on the prow, and Pleasure at the helm;
Regardless of the sweeping whirlwind's sway,
That, hushed in grim repose, expects his evening prey.
1757 *The Bard. A Pindaric Ode*, l.71–6.

35 In buskined measures move
Pale Grief and pleasing Pain,
With Horror, tyrant of the throbbing breast.
1757 *The Bard. A Pindaric Ode*, l.128–30.

36 'Be thine despair and sceptred care;
To triumph, and to die, are mine.'
He spoke, and headlong from the mountain's height
Deep in the roaring tide he plunged to endless night.
1757 *The Bard. A Pindaric Ode*, l.141–4.

37 Far from the sun and summer-gale,
In thy green lap was Nature's darling laid.
1757 Of William Shakespeare. *The Progress of Poesy*, l.83–4.

38 Nor second he, that rode sublime
Upon the seraph-wings of ecstasy,
The secrets of th' abyss to spy.
He passed the flaming bounds of place and time:
The living throne, the sapphire-blaze,
Where angels tremble, while they gaze,
He saw; but blasted with excess of light,
Closed his eyes in endless night.
1757 Of Milton. *The Progress of Poesy*, l.95–102.

39 Thoughts, that breathe, and words, that burn.
1757 *The Progress of Poesy*, l.110.

40 Beyond the limits of a vulgar fate,
Beneath the good how far—but far above the great.
1757 *The Progress of Poesy*, l.122–3.

41 It has been usual to catch a mouse or two (for form's sake) in public once a year.
1757 On refusing the Laureateship. Letter to William Mason, 19 Dec.

42 Too poor for a bribe, and too proud to importune,
He had not the method of making a fortune.
1761 'Sketch of His Own Character'.

43 I shall be but a shrimp of an author.
1768 Letter to Horace Walpole, 25 Feb.

44 Any fool may write a most valuable book by chance, if he will only tell us what he heard and saw with veracity.
1768 Letter to Horace Walpole, 25 Feb.

Greeley, Horace 1811–72

US journalist, founding editor of the *New York Tribune*.

45 Go West, young man, and grow up with the country.
1850 *Hints toward Reforms*.

Greenaway, Peter 1942–

English film-maker and painter. His films include *The Cook, the Thief, His Wife and Her Lover* (1989) and *Prospero's Books* (1991).

46 Most cinema is built along 19th-century models. You would hardly think that the cinema had discovered James Joyce sometimes. Most of the cinema we've got is modelled on Dickens and Balzac and Jane Austen.
2004 In *The Guardian*, 10 May.

Greenberg, Clement 1909–94

US art critic.

47 When you don't like something the words come more readily.
1991 Aged 82, on the relative ease of negative criticism over positive. In the *New York Times*, 3 Oct.

48 For every good art critic there may be ten great artists.
1991 In the *New York Times*, 3 Oct.

Greene, (Henry) Graham 1904–91

English writer. His writings included novels (which he divided into 'entertainments' and more serious works), short stories, essays, plays, biography, criticism, travel books and two volumes of autobiography.

49 At one with the One, it didn't mean a thing beside a glass of Guinness on a sunny day.
1938 *Brighton Rock*, pt.1, ch.1.

50 He trailed the clouds of his own glory after him; hell lay about him in his infancy. He was ready for more deaths.
1938 *Brighton Rock*, pt.2, ch.2.
► *See Wordsworth 926:24.*

51 I couldn't eat, just went on drinking coffee, and sweating

it out again. Liquid had no time to be digested; it came through the pores long before it reached the stomach. I lay wet through with sweat for four hours—it was very nearly like happiness.
1939 In Mexico. *The Lawless Roads* (published in the US as *Another Mexico*).

52 There is always one moment in childhood when the door opens and lets the future in.
1940 *The Power and the Glory*, pt.1, ch.1.

53 A virtuous man can almost cease to believe in Hell, but he carried Hell about with him. Sometimes at night he dreamed of it… Evil ran like malaria in his veins.
1940 *The Power and the Glory*, pt.3, ch.1.

54 They had been corrupted by money, and he had been corrupted by sentiment. Sentiment was the more dangerous, because you couldn't name its price.
1948 *The Heart of the Matter*, bk.1, pt.1, ch.2, iii.

55 He felt the loyalty we all feel to unhappiness—the sense that that is where we really belong.
1948 *The Heart of the Matter*, bk.2, pt.2, ch.1, i.

56 His hilarity was like a scream from a crevasse.
1948 *The Heart of the Matter*, bk.3, pt.1, ch.1, i.

57 Of those four winters which I passed in Indo-China opium has left the happiest memory.
1955 *The Quiet American*, introduction.

58 That feeling of exhilaration which a measure of danger brings to the visitor with a return ticket.
1955 *The Quiet American*, introduction.

59 Death was the only absolute value in my world. Lose life and one would lose nothing again for ever… Death was far more certain than God, and with death there would no longer be the daily possibility of love dying.
1955 *The Quiet American*, pt.1, ch.3.

60 Our Man in Havana.
1958 Title of novel.

61 Hail Mary, quite contrary!
1958 *Our Man in Havana*, pt.1, ch.2.

62 Those who marry God…can become domesticated too—it's just as humdrum a marriage as all the others.
1961 *A Burnt-Out Case*, ch.1.

63 Fame is a powerful aphrodisiac.
1964 In the *Radio Times*, 10 Sep.

64 His slang…was always a little out of date, as though he had studied in a dictionary of popular usage, but not in the latest edition.
1966 *The Comedians*, pt.1, ch.1.

65 The man who offers a bribe gives away a little of his own importance; the bribe once accepted, he becomes the inferior, like a man who has just paid for a woman.
1966 *The Comedians*, pt.1, ch.4.

66 We musn't complain too much of being comedians—it's an honourable profession. If only we could be good ones the world might gain at least a sense of style.
1966 *The Comedians*, pt.2, ch.5.

67 An autobiography is only 'a sort of life'—it may contain less errors of fact than a biography, but it is of necessity even more selective: it begins later and it ends prematurely.
1971 *A Sort of Life*, preface.

68 And the motive for recording these scraps of the past? It is much the same motive that has made me a novelist: a desire to reduce a chaos of experience to some sort of order, and a hungry curiosity.
1971 *A Sort of Life*, preface.

69 I put the muzzle of the revolver into my right ear and pulled the trigger… I was out by one. I remember an extraordinary sense of jubilation, as if carnival lights had been switched on in a drab street. My heart knocked in its cage, and life contained an infinite number of possibilities.
1971 Recalling a game of Russian roulette with his brother's revolver in 1923. *A Sort of Life*, ch.6, pt.2.

70 He would certainly have despised Christ for being the son of a carpenter, if the New Testament had not proved in time to be such a howling commercial success.
1980 *Dr Fischer of Geneva*, ch.7.

71 Writing a novel does not become easier with practice.
1980 *Ways of Escape*, ch.5.

72 Writing is a form of therapy; sometimes I wonder how all these people who do not write, compose or paint can manage to escape the madness, the melancholia, the panic fear which is inherent in the human situation.
1980 *Ways of Escape*, ch.9.

73 Perhaps we are all fictions, father, in the minds of God.
1982 *Monsignor Quixote*, pt.1, ch.1.

74 The believer will fight another believer over a shade of difference: the doubter fights only with himself.
1982 *Monsignor Quixote*, pt.1, ch.4.

75 A solitary laugh is often a laugh of superiority.
1982 *Monsignor Quixote*, pt.1, ch.9.

76 The world is not black and white. More like black and grey.
1982 Quoted in 'Sayings of the Year', the *Observer*, Dec.

77 What's the good of a lie if it's seen through? When I tell a lie no-one can tell it from the gospel truth. Sometimes I can't even tell it myself.
1988 The Captain. *The Captain and the Enemy*, pt.1, ch.1.

Greene, Robert 1558–92

English dramatist. His many plays and romances include the prose romance *Pandosto* (1588) and the comedy *Friar Bacon and Friar Bungay* (c.1589). He laid the foundations of English drama.

78 Love taught me that your honour did but jest.
c.1589 *Friar Bacon and Friar Bungay* (published 1594), sc.8.

79 Only your hearts be frolic, for the time
Craves that we taste of naught but jouissance.
c.1589 *Friar Bacon and Friar Bungay* (published 1594), sc.16.

80 For there is an upstart crow, beautified with our feathers, that with his tiger's heart wrapped in a player's hide, supposes he is as well able to bombast out a blank verse as the best of you; and being an absolute *Iohannes fac totum*, is in his own conceit the only Shake-scene in a country.
1592 Of Shakespeare. *The Groatsworth of Wit, Bought with a Million of Repentance. Iohannes fac totum* = 'Jack-of-all-trades'.

Greenspan, Alan 1926–

US financier and economist, chairman of the board of governors of the Federal Reserve System.

81 Since I've become a central banker, I've learned to mumble with great coherence… If I seem unduly clear to you, you must have misunderstood what I said.
1987 Address to Congress, Sep. Quoted by Jonathan Marshall in the *San Francisco Chronicle*, 9 Jun 1995.

82 The buck starts here.
Sign on his desk. Quoted in Bob Woodward *The Agenda* (1994).
► *See Truman 869:45.*

83 The gut-feel of the 55-year old trader is more important than the mathematical elegance of the 25-year old genius.
1995 In the *New York Times*, 6 Mar, shortly after the collapse of Barings in Singapore brought about by a young derivatives trader.

84 I worry incessantly that I might be too clear.
1995 In the *New York Times*, 25 Jun.

85 The free lunch has still to be invented.
2004 On the US budget deficit, 6 May.

Greer, Germaine 1939–

Australian feminist, author and lecturer. Her first book *The Female Eunuch* (1970) challenges male dominance and the misrepresentation of female sexuality, which she attributes to Freud.

86 A full bosom is actually a millstone around a woman's neck.
1970 *The Female Eunuch*, 'Body: Curves'.

87 Freud is the father of psychoanalysis. It had no mother.
1970 *The Female Eunuch*, 'Soul: The Psychological Sell'.

88 If women understand by emancipation the adoption of the masculine role then we are lost indeed.
1970 *The Female Eunuch*, 'Soul: Womanpower'.

89 English children have lost their innocence, for their first lessons have been in the exploitation of their adult slave.
1970 Of the mother's subjugation to her family's demands. *The Female Eunuch*, 'Love: Family'.

90 Many a housewife staring at the back of her husband's newspaper, or listening to his breathing in bed is lonelier than any spinster in a rented room.
1970 *The Female Eunuch*, 'Love: Security'.

91 Libraries are reservoirs of strength, grace and wit, reminders of order, calm and continuity, lakes of mental energy, neither warm nor cold, light nor dark.
1991 In the *New York Times*, 24 Mar.

92 Football is an art more central to our culture than anything the Arts Council deigns to recognize.
1996 In *The Independent*, 28 Jun.

Pope Gregory I *known as 'the Great'* 540–604

Italian divine. He resigned as Praetor of Rome in 575, distributing his wealth to the poor, and entered a monastery. Reluctantly elected Pope in 590, he carried out many reforms. He wrote numerous biblical commentaries and homilies.

93 *Non Angli, sed angeli.*
Not Angles, but angels.
c.580 Reference to Angle slave children seen by Gregory in Rome, which inspired him with the desire to convert Britain to Christianity. Quoted in Bede *Historia Ecclesiastica gentis Anglorum* (c.731), bk.2, ch.1. His exact words according to Bede were 'Nam et angelicam habent faciem, et tales angelorum in caelis decet esse coheredes' ('Since they have the faces of angels, they should be the co-heirs of the angels in heaven').

94 *Scriptura sacra mentis oculis quasi quoddam speculum opponitur, ut interna nostra facies in ipsa videatur.*
Holy scripture is placed before the eyes of our mind like a mirror, so that we may view our inner face therein.
c.582 *Moralia in Job*, bk.2, ch.1, section 1.

Pope Gregory VII *also known as Hildebrand* c.1020–1085

Italian cleric. He was appointed Cardinal by Leo IX and as Pope from 1073 instituted many reforms to the clergy. He asserted the right of the Pope to direct temporal authorities, and conflicted violently with Emperor Henry IV, who appointed an anti-Pope (Clement III) and seized Rome (1084).

95 *Dilexi iustitiam et odi iniquitatem, propterea morior in exilio.*
I have loved righteousness and hated iniquity, and therefore I die in exile.
1085 Last words. Quoted in Christopher Brooke *Europe in the Central Middle Ages 962–1154* (1964), ch.15.

Gregory, Lady Isabella Augusta *née Persse* 1852–1932

Irish playwright. After marrying Sir William Gregory, Governor of Ceylon (1880), she founded with W B Yeats Dublin's Abbey Theatre. Her plays include *Spreading the News* (1904), and she also wrote Irish legends and translated Molière.

96 His eyesight has always been weak, a sort of film over the eyes. A doctor advised him not to read, but he said, 'Then I should be ignorant', and he refused an operation because there was a thousandth chance he might go blind and so remain ignorant.
1924 Of Sean O'Casey. Journal entry, 8 Jun.

Gregory, John Walter 1864–1932

English geologist, geographer and explorer, Professor of Geology at Melbourne University (1900–4), and then at Glasgow. In 1932 he joined an expedition to Peru, where he was drowned on a canoeing trip.

97 The Dead Heart of Australia.
1906 Title of book, dealing with the central deserts of Australia.

Grellet, Stephen 1773–1855

French-born missionary to America.

98 I expect to pass through this world but once. Any good thing, therefore, that I can do, or any kindness that I can show to any fellow-creature, let me do it now…for I shall not pass this way again.
Attributed.

Grenfell, Joyce *née Phipps* 1910–79

English comedienne. She starred in intimate revue in the 1940s and developed a fine line in the art of comic monologues; occasional film appearances included parts in such comedies as *Laughter in Paradise* (1951) and *The Belles of St Trinian's* (1954).

99 George—don't do that.
Catchphrase from one of her comic monologues, also the title of her autobiography, 1977.

1 Stately as a galleon, I sail across the floor,
Doing the Military Two-step, as in the days of yore.
1978 'Stately as a Galleon' (song).

Grenfell, Julian Henry Francis 1888–1915

English poet, killed in action during World War I. He is largely remembered for his patriotic poem 'Into Battle'.

2 And life is colour and warmth and light
And a striving evermore for these;
And he is dead, who will not fight,
And who dies fighting has increase.
1915 'Into Battle', in *The Times*, 27 May.

Grenfell, Sir Wilfred 1865–1940

English medical missionary and writer.

3 The service we render to others is really the rent we pay for our room on this earth.
1938 *A Labrador Logbook*.

Grenville, George 1712–70

English statesman. He became Prime Minister in 1763, and his period of office was marked by the prosecution of John Wilkes and the passing of the American Stamp Act before his resignation in 1765.

4 It is clear that both England and America are now to be governed by the mob.
1765 On the repeal of the Stamp Act, Jul.

Grey of Fallodon, Edward Grey, 1st Viscount 1862–1933

British statesman. He was Liberal MP for Berwick-on-Tweed (1885–1916), and Secretary for Foreign Affairs (1905–16), distinguishing himself in the Balkans peace negotiations (1913) and on the outbreak of World War I in 1914. He was subsequently Ambassador to Washington (1919–20) and Chancellor of Oxford University from 1928.

5 It is the lees left by Bismarck that still foul the cup.
1906 On the duplicity of international diplomacy as practised in the early 20c. Letter to President Roosevelt, Dec. Quoted in G M Trevelyan *Grey of Fallodon* (1937).

6 If there is war, there will be Labour governments in every country—and quite right too.
1914 In conversation with the Italian Ambassador, Jul.

7 The lamps are going out all over Europe. We shall not see them lit again in our lifetime.
1914 Remark made on the eve of World War I, 3 Aug, in his room at the Foreign Office, recounted in *Twenty-Five Years* (1925), vol.2, ch.18.

8 In 1914, Europe had arrived at a point at which every country except Germany was afraid of the present, and Germany was afraid of the future.
1924 House of Lords, 24 Jul.

Greyser, Stephen A

US marketing expert, Professor of Business Administration (Marketing/ Communications) Emeritus at Harvard Business School.

9 The poets of commerce.
1987 Of advertising copywriters. In the *New York Times*, 28 Apr.

Grieg, Edvard Hagerup 1843–1907

Norwegian composer, whose works, much influenced by folk heritage, include orchestral suites, incidental music for Ibsen's *Peer Gynt*, choral music and piano pieces.

10 I am sure my music has a taste of codfish in it.
1903 Speech. Quoted in Ian Crofton and Donald Fraser *A Dictionary of Musical Quotations* (1985).

Griffith, D(avid Lewelyn) W(ark) 1874–1948

US film director. He began as an actor and short-story writer before entering the infant film industry, learning his trade in hundreds of short films. He is best known for *The Birth of a Nation* (1915) and *Intolerance* (1916).

11 Viewed as a drama, the war is somewhat disappointing.
c.1915 Comment on World War I. Quoted in Leslie Halliwell *Halliwell's Filmgoer's Companion* (1984).

12 Out of the cradle, endlessly rocking.
1916 *Intolerance*.

Grillparzer, Franz 1791–1872

Austrian politician, poet and playwright. He was prone to hypochondria and depression.

13 *Es binden Sklavenfesseln nur die Hände,*
Der Sinn, er macht den Freien und den Knecht.
The chains of slavery can only bind the hands.
The mind makes us either free or enslaved.
1818 *Sappho*, act 2, sc.4.

14 *Gold schenkt die Eitelkeit, der rauhe Stolz,*
Die Freundschaft und die Liebe schenken Blumen.
Gold is the gift of vanity and pride,
Friendship and love offer flowers.
1818 *Sappho*, act 2, sc.4.

15 *Ich suchte dich und habe mich gefunden.*
I sought you and I found myself.
1818 *Sappho*, act 5, sc.6.

Grimaldi, Joseph 1779–1837

English comedian, of Italian descent. His Clown figure transformed English pantomime, though his career was virtually over by 1824 as a result of the injuries he suffered in slapstick routines on stage.

16 Here we are again!
c.1800 His customary greeting to the audience on making his entrance as Clown, later adopted as a catchphrase by clowns everywhere.

Grisham, John 1955–

US author, known for his suspenseful courtroom dramas.

17 I cannot write as well as some people; my talent is in coming up with good stories about lawyers. That is what I am good at.
1994 In the *Independent on Sunday*, 5 Jun.

Griswold, Alfred Whitney 1906–63

US educator, President of Yale University (1950–63).

18 A Socrates in every classroom.
1951 On his hopes for the Yale faculty. In *Time*, 11 Jun.

19 Could Hamlet have been written by a committee, or the *Mona Lisa* painted by a club? Could the New Testament have been composed as a conference report?
1957 Baccalaureate address, 9 Jun.

20 Self-respect…comes to us when we are alone, in quiet moments in quiet places when we suddenly realize that, knowing the good, we have done it; knowing the

beautiful, we have served it; knowing the truth, we have spoken it.
1957 Baccalaureate address, 9 Jun.

Gromyko, Andrei Andreyevich 1909–89

Soviet politician, notorious for his austere and humourless demeanour. As Foreign Minister (1957–85) he influenced Soviet relations with the West during the Cold War. President in 1985, he was replaced by Gorbachev.

21 Every night, whisper 'Peace' in your husband's ear.
1984 Said to Nancy Reagan at a White House reception, 28 Sep.

22 This man, Comrades, has a nice smile, but he has iron teeth.
1985 Speech to the Supreme Soviet on proposing Mikhail Gorbachev as the new party leader.

Grossmith, George 1847–1912

English comedian and entertainer. He took leading parts in Gilbert and Sullivan operettas (1877–89) and with his brother, Weedon, wrote *The Diary of a Nobody*, first serialized in *Punch* (published 1892).

23 What's the good of a home if you are never in it?
1892 *The Diary of a Nobody* (with Weedon Grossmith), ch.1.

24 I left the room with silent dignity, but caught my foot in the mat.
1892 *The Diary of a Nobody* (with Weedon Grossmith), ch.7.

Grosvenor, Gilbert M 1875–1966

US geographer and editor, Director then President of the National Geographic Society (1899–1954) and editor of its magazine. He pioneered the use of colour photography, and encouraged conservation and wildlife protection.

25 If you don't know where you are, you're nowhere.
On the NGS's establishment of a $20-million foundation to fight ignorance of geography. Quoted in the *Washington Post*, 14 Jan 1988.

Guare, John 1938–

US dramatist.

26 Everybody on this planet is separated by only six other people. Six degrees of separation. Between us and everybody else on this planet.
1990 *Six Degrees of Separation.*

Guedalla, Philip 1889–1944

English historian and biographer, known for his irreverent wit. His books include *Supers and Supermen* (1920), *Palmerston* (1926), a biography of Wellington, *The Duke* (1931), and *Mr Churchill* (1941).

27 The work of Henry James has always seemed divisible by a simple dynastic arrangement into three reigns: James I, James II, and the Old Pretender.
1920 *Supers and Supermen*, 'Some Critics'.

28 History repeats itself. Historians repeat each other.
1920 *Supers and Supermen*, 'Some Historians'.

29 The Crimean War is one of the bad jokes of history.
1943 *The Two Marshals.*

Guibert of Nogent fl.c.1097

Medieval historian.

30 God has instituted in our time holy wars, so that the order of knights and the crowd running in their wake, who following the example of the ancient pagans have been engaged in slaughtering one another, might find a new way of gaining salvation.
c.1097 *Gesta Dei per Francos*, in *Recueil des historiens de croisades occidentaux*, edited by L'Académie des Inscriptions et Belles-Lettres (1847–95), vol.4, p.124.

Guillén, Nicolás 1902–89

Cuban poet, of mixed African and European descent, a leader of the Afro-Cuban movement. An outspoken member of the Communist Party, he was active in Castro's regime.

31 *Según un yanqui que debe*
ser todo un derrochador,
es Cuba donde mejor
se come siempre y se bebe.
According to a gringo who must
be a true spendthrift,
Cuba is always the best place
to eat and to drink.
1953 *Sátira política*, 'Depende' ('It Depends').

Guimarães Rosa, João 1908–67

Brazilian novelist. He practised medicine, then joined the foreign service. *Grande Sertão* (1956) is derived from the oral tradition of the hinterland of Brazil.

32 *Um está sempre no escuro, só no último derradeiro é que clareiam a sala.*
One is always in the dark, and it is only at the last moment that they turn on the lights in the room.
1956 *Grande Sertão: Verédas* (translated as *The Devil to Pay in the Backlands*, 1963).

Guiraldes, Ricardo 1886–1927

Argentinian poet and novelist, renowned for his masterful blending of the gaucho (cowboy) tale with modernist techniques.

33 *Si sos gaucho en de veras, no has de mudar, porque andequiera que vayas irás con tu alma por delante.*
If you're really a gaucho, you can't change, because wherever you go, you'll go with your soul leading the way.
1926 *Don Segundo Sombra* (translated 1935), ch.26.

Guitry, Sacha 1885–1957

French actor and playwright. Born in Russia, he established himself as a popular light comedian as well as writing a number of screenplays and directing several films.

34 The others were only my wives. But you, my dear, will be my widow.
Attributed reply to his fifth wife, when she expressed jealousy of her predecessors.

Gulbenkian, Nubar Sarkis 1896–1972

British industrialist and philanthropist. He worked with his father in the oil business, advising on Middle East oil negotiations (1926–8, 1948–54), and was honorary counsellor at the Turkish embassy (1966–72).

35 The best number for a dinner party is two—myself and a damn good head waiter.
1965 In the *Daily Telegraph*, 14 Jan.

Gullit, Ruud 1962–

Dutch footballer and manager. He transferred to the Italian club AC Milan for a record £6 million in 1987.

36 If I'd wanted to be an individual, I'd have taken up tennis.
Quoted in Colin Jarman *The Guinness Dictionary of Sports Quotations* (1990).

37 I'm looking forward to seeing some sexy football.
1996 Comment as BBC TV pundit at Euro 96.

Gunn, Jeannie *known as* *Mrs Aeneas Gunn* 1870–1961

Australian writer. In 1901 she married Aeneas James Gunn and went with him to Elsey Station, Northern Territory. When her husband died in 1903 she returned to Melbourne and wrote of her experiences in the outback.

38 There's time enough for everything in the Never-Never.
1908 *We of the Never-Never*, ch.5.

Gunn, Thom(son William) 1929–2004

English poet. He lived in the US from 1954 until his death. He is recognized as one of the major poets of his generation.

39 I saw that lack of love contaminates,
You know I know you know I know you know.
1954 'Carnal Knowledge'.

40 At worst, one is in motion; and at best,
Reaching no absolute, in which to rest,
One is always nearer by not keeping still.
1957 'On the Move'.

Gunther, John 1901–70

US author and journalist. He established his reputation with the best-selling *Inside Europe* (1939), and followed it with a series of *Inside* books.

41 Bright grayness. Both the clothes and hair were neat and gray. The gray-framed spectacles magnified the gray hazel eyes, but there was no grayness in the mind.
Of Harry S Truman. Quoted in David McCullough *Truman* (1992).

Gurney, Dorothy Frances 1858–1932

English poet and hymnwriter.

42 The kiss of the sun for pardon,
The song of the birds for mirth,
One is nearer God's Heart in a garden
Than anywhere else on earth.
1913 'God's Garden'.

Gurney, Ivor 1890–1937

English poet and composer, especially renowned for his war poems.

43 The songs I had are withered
Or vanished clean.
Yet there are bright tracks
Where I have been.
1922 'The Songs I Had'.

44 I paid the prices of life
Standing where Rome immortal heard October's strife,
A war poet whose right of honour cuts falsehood like a knife.
c.1922 'Poem for End'.

Gurney, John Hampden 1802–62

English clergyman and hymnwriter.

45 Ye holy angels bright,
Who wait at God's right hand,
Or through the realms of light
Fly at your Lord's command,
Assist our song,
Or else the theme too high doth seem
For mortal tongue.
1838 'Ye Holy Angels Bright', based on a poem by Richard Baxter (1615–91).

Gustavus II (Adolphus) 1594–1632

King of Sweden (1611), who entered the Thirty Years War by invading Poland in 1621. His armies conquered much of Germany in 1631, and he was killed at the Battle of Lützen, 1632.

46 All the wars that are now afoot in Europe have been fused together, and have become a single war.
1630 Letter to Axel Oxenstierna, referring to the Thirty Years War, 1618–48.

Guston, Philip 1913–80

Canadian-born painter. He moved with his family to California in 1916. His early paintings combine realism with surrealism and his later work is characterized by its cartoon-like style.

47 I go to my studio every day, because one day I may go and the angel will be there. What if I don't go and the angel came?
1991 Quoted by Gail Godwin in the *Washington Post*, 7 Mar.

Guthrie, Woody (Woodrow Wilson) 1912–67

US folk-singer, songwriter and author. His songs draw on traditional country music and blues themes and reflect his social and political concerns.

48 This land is your land, this land is my land,
From California to the New York Island.
From the redwood forest to the Gulf Stream waters
This land was made for you and me.
1956 'This Land is Your Land'.

49 You can't write a good song about a whore-house unless you been in one.
1964 Quoted in *Broadside*.

Guy, Ray 1939–

Canadian columnist.

50 Pity the poor creatures in warmer countries where the seasons never change. Where summer is eternal and they never know the pain of waiting and the joy at last when summer comes.
1976 *That Far Greater Bay*, 'Catching Conners'.

Gwyn, Nell 1650–87

English actress. Originally an orange-seller at Drury Lane, she became a popular performer in comedies; her admirers included Charles II, whose mistress she became in about 1669. She retired from the stage in 1670.

51 Pray, good people, be civil; I am the Protestant whore.
1675 Attributed, when angry crowds pressed round her carriage in the belief that she was Charles II's unpopular Catholic mistress Louise de Kérouaille.

Haas, Ernst Bernard 1921–

Austrian photographer and author. Known for his early black and white photojournalism (particularly his 'Returning Prisoners of War' story in 1949), he was a pioneer of early colour, and his work on colour-blur made his fame. His film assignments include *Moby Dick* (1956), *The Misfits* (1961), *West Side Story* (1961) and *Heaven's Gate* (1980).

52 Beauty pains, and when it pained most, I shot.
1955 In *Life*, 1 Aug. 'The Glow of Paris'.

Habington, William 1605–54

English writer, one of the metaphysical followers of Donne. He published a book of lyrics, *Castara* (1634), a play, *The Queen of Aragon* (1640) and *The History of Edward the Fourth* (1640).

53 O empty boast of flesh.
1634 *Castara*, 'Upon Beauty'.

54 'Cause some make forfeit of their name,
And slave themselves to man's desire;
Shall the sex free
From guilt, damn'd to the bondage be?
1634 *Castara*, 'Against Them Who Lay Unchastity to the Sex of Women'.

Haeckel, Ernst Heinrich 1834–1919

German biologist and philosopher, who popularized Darwinism in the German-speaking world. He became Professor of Comparative Anatomy at the University of Jena.

55 God…a gaseous vertebrate.
1899 *Welträtsel* ('The Riddle of the Universe').

Hagen, Walter 1892–1969

US golfer. The first great professional US golfer, he won the US Open twice and the British Open four times.

56 Give me a man with big hands and big feet and no brains and I'll make a golfer out of him.
Quoted in Michael Hobbs *The Golf Quotation Book* (1992).

Haggai, Thomas 1939–

US businessman.

57 Cast your bread upon the waters, but wait until the tide is coming in to do it.
1988 In *Fortune*, 7 Nov.

Haggard, Sir (Henry) Rider 1856–1925

English novelist. He travelled to Natal and the Transvaal (1875–9) before embarking on a literary life. His first successful novel was *King Solomon's Mines* (1885), followed by *She* (1887) and *Ayesha* (1905), among others.

58 A little while and I will be gone from among you, whither I cannot tell. From nowhere we came, into nowhere we go. What is Life? It is a flash of a firefly in the night. It is a breath of a buffalo in the winter time. It is as the little shadow that runs across the grass and loses itself in the sunset.
1885 Dying words of the African chief Umbopa in *King Solomon's Mines*. John Peter Turner in *The North-West Mounted Police* (1950) credited them to Crowfoot (c.1830–1890), chief of the Blackfoot Indians, who died in his teepee overlooking the Bow River, Alberta, 25 Apr 1890, and this attribution gained popular acceptance.

59 She who must be obeyed.
1887 *She*, ch.6, and passim.

60 What a terrifying reflection it is, by the way, that nearly all our deep love for women who are not our kindred depends—at any rate, in the first instance—upon their personal appearances. If we lost them, and found them again dreadful to look on, though otherwise they were the very same, should we still love them?
1887 *She*, ch.26 'What We Saw', narrator's note.

Hague, William 1961–

English Conservative politician. He was Leader of the Conservative Party from 1997 to 2001.

61 It was inevitable the Titanic was going to set sail, but that doesn't mean it was a good idea to be on it.
1998 In *The Mail on Sunday*, 'Quotes of the Week', 11 Jan.

62 This is a candidate of probity and integrity—I am going to back him to the full.
1999 On Jeffrey Archer as a London mayoral candidate, at the Conservative Party conference, Oct.

63 People work hard and save hard to own a car. They do not want to be told that they cannot drive it by a Deputy Prime Minister whose idea of a park and ride scheme is to park one Jaguar and drive away in another.
1999 Of John Prescott. In the House of Commons, 17 Nov.

Haig, Alexander Meigs, Jr 1924–

US soldier and Republican politician, White House Chief of Staff at the end of Nixon's presidency and Supreme NATO Commander. He was Secretary of State under Reagan (1981–2), and unsuccessfully sought presidential nomination in 1988.

64 As of now, I am in control here in the White House.
1981 Said immediately after the attempted assassination of President Reagan, 30 Mar, in Vice-President George Bush's absence from Washington DC.

65 I take it as a compliment when an agent of the largest and most heinous bully of the century, the Soviet Union, accuses me of being a bully.
1995 On how he was seen as US Secretary of State by former Soviet Ambassador Anatoly Dobrynin. In the *Washington Post*, 27 Oct.

Haig (of Bemersyde), Douglas Haig, 1st Earl 1861–1928

Scottish field marshal. He became Commander of the British Expeditionary Force in 1915. His war of attrition was costly and widely criticized; he led the final successful offensive of World War I in Aug 1918.

66 Every position must be held to the last man: there must be no retirement. With our backs to the wall, and believing in the justice of our cause, each one of us must fight on until the end.
1918 Order to British troops facing the German offensive across

the Somme battlefields, 12 Apr. Quoted in A Duff Cooper *Haig* (1936), vol.2, ch.23.

Haile Selassie *originally* *Prince Ras Tafari Makonnen*
1891–1975

Emperor of Ethiopia (1930–6, 1941–74), leader of the revolution against Lij Yasu (1916). He was exiled after the Italian conquest of Abyssinia (1935–6), and restored after British liberation. Although deposed after the famine of 1973, he is still much revered, notably by Rastafarians.

67 Throughout history it has been the inaction of those who could have acted, the indifference of those who should have known better, the silence of the voice of justice when it mattered most, that has made it possible for evil to triumph.
1963 Address to a special session of the UN General Assembly, 4 Oct, making him the first head of state to address both that organization and the League of Nations.

Hailsham, Quintin (McGarel) Hogg, 2nd Viscount
1907–2001

English Conservative politician. After succeeding to his title (1950), he held a number of senior state posts. In 1963 he renounced his peerage in an unsuccessful bid to become Leader of the Conservative Party. He was later Lord Chancellor.

68 Conservatives do not believe that the political struggle is the most important thing in life… The simplest of them prefer fox-hunting, the wisest religion.
1947 *The Case for Conservatism*, pt.1.

69 A great party ought not to be brought down because of a squalid affair between a woman of easy virtue and a proved liar.
1963 On the Profumo affair, BBC TV, 13 Jun.

70 If the British public falls for this, I say that it will be stark, staring bonkers.
1964 Press conference on the Labour election manifesto, 12 Oct.

71 I've known every prime minister to a greater or lesser extent since Balfour, and most of them have died unhappy.
Attributed.

Halberstam, David 1934–

US journalist and author, staff writer and correspondent for the *New York Times* (1960–7). His books include *The Powers That Be* (1979) and *Firehouse* (2002).

72 He has seen the future and it is hamburgers.
1993 On Ray Kroc's decision to buy and expand the original McDonald's. *The Fifties*.
► *See Steffens 814:6.*

Haldane, J(ohn) B(urdon) S(anderson) 1892–1964

Anglo-Indian biologist. He wrote many popular books on biology and genetics, and was Chairman of the *Daily Worker* (1940–9), but left the Communist Party in 1956.

73 Bad as our urban conditions often are, there is not a slum in the country which has a third of the infantile death-rate of the royal family in the middle ages.
1924 *Daedalus, or Science and the Future*.

74 Now, my own suspicion is that the universe is not only queerer than we suppose, but queerer than we *can* suppose.
1927 *Possible Worlds and Other Essays*, 'Possible Worlds'.

75 You can drop a mouse down a thousand-yard mine shaft; and, on arriving at the bottom, it gets a slight shock and walks away. A rat is killed, a man is broken, a horse splashes.
1927 *Possible Worlds and Other Essays*, 'On Being the Right Size'.

76 I believe that the scientist is trying to expand absolute truth and the artist absolute beauty, so that I find in art and science, and in an attempt to live a good life, all the religion I want.
1931 *Living Philosophies*.

77 My final word, before I'm done,
Is 'Cancer can be rather fun'.
Thanks to the nurses and Nye Bevan
The NHS is quite like heaven
Provided one confronts the tumour
With a sufficient sense of humour.
I know that cancer often kills,
But so do cars and sleeping pills;
And it can hurt one till one sweats,
So can bad teeth and unpaid debts.
1964 'Cancer's a Funny Thing'.

Hale, Nathan 1755–76

American revolutionary soldier. In 1776 he volunteered to penetrate British lines on Long Island and procure intelligence for Washington, but was detected and hanged as a spy.

78 I only regret that I have but one life to lose for my country.
1776 At his execution, 22 Sep.

Hale, Robert Beverly 1901–85

US artist, teacher and curator. He has works in the Whitney, the Metropolitan Museum of Art, New York City, and in many private collections. He was curator at the Metropolitan (1949–85) and lectured at Pennsylvania Academy of Fine Arts (1968–85) and Columbia University. He wrote, edited and translated books on art.

79 New artists must break a hole in the subconscious and go fishing there.
1960 In *Time*, 11 Apr.

Hale, Sarah Josepha *née* *Buell* 1788–1879

US writer. In 1828 she became editor of the *Ladies' Magazine* in Boston. She wrote a novel, *Northwood* (1827), and *Poems for Our Children* (1830).

80 Mary had a little lamb,
Its fleece was white as snow,
And everywhere that Mary went
The lamb was sure to go.
1830 *Poems for Our Children*, 'Mary's Little Lamb'.

Hales, Stephen 1677–1761

English clergyman and physiologist, considered the founder of plant physiology. His investigations are reported in his work *Statickal Essays*, the first of which, *Vegetable Staticks*, was published in 1727.

81 Since we are assured that the all-wise Creator has observed the most exact proportions of number, weight and measure in the make of all things, the most likely way therefore to get any insight into the nature of those parts of the Creation which come within our observation must

in all reason be to number, weigh and measure.
1727 *Vegetable Staticks.*

Haliburton, Thomas Chandler 1796–1865

Canadian lawyer and satirist. In 1835 he began a series of satiric sketches later enlarged as *The Clockmaker; or The Sayings and Doings of Samuel Slick* (1836). *The Old Judge; or Life in a Colony* (1849) combines social history and satire.

82 I was always well mounted. I am fond of a horse, and always piqued myself on having the fastest trotter in the Province. I have made no great progress in the world. I feel doubly, therefore, the pleasure of not being surpassed on the road.
1836 *The Clockmaker* (first series), 'The Trotting Horse'.

83 If a chap seems bent on cheatin' himself, I like to be neighbourly and help him to do it.
1838 *The Clockmaker* (second series), 'A Cure for Smuggling'.

Halifax, Edward Frederick Lindley Wood, 1st Earl of 1881–1959

English Conservative politician, Viceroy of India (1926–31). He was Foreign Secretary (1938–40) under Neville Chamberlain, whose 'appeasement' policy he implemented, and Ambassador to the US (1941–6).

84 I often think how much easier the world would have been to manage if Herr Hitler and Signor Mussolini had been at Oxford.
1937 Speech, York, 4 Nov.

Halifax, George Savile, 1st Marquis of 1633–95

English statesman, created viscount (1668) at the Restoration. Under James II, he was dismissed as President of the Council for opposing the repeal of the Test and Habeas Corpus Acts. He gave allegiance to William of Orange, but joined the Opposition in 1689.

85 Men are not hanged for stealing horses, but that horses may not be stolen.
c.1687 *Political Thoughts and Reflections*, 'Of Punishment'.

86 Anger is never without an argument, but seldom with a good one.
c.1687 *Political Thoughts and Reflections*, 'Of Anger'.

87 Malice is of a low stature, but it hath very long arms.
c.1687 *Political Thoughts and Reflections*, 'Of Malice and Envy'.

88 The best way to suppose what may come, is to remember what is past.
c.1687 *Political Thoughts and Reflections*, 'Miscellaneous Experience'.

89 When the people contend for their liberty, they seldom get anything by their victory but new masters.
c.1687 *Political Thoughts and Reflections*, 'Of Prerogative, Power and Liberty'.

90 Most men's anger about religion is as if two men should quarrel for a lady they neither of them care for.
Collected in *Complete Works* (published 1912).

Hall, Charles 1745–1825

English physician educated in Holland, best known for his socialist work *The Effects of Civilization on the People in European States* (1805). In 1805 he was impoverished by a lawsuit and, refusing aid, later died in prison determined to show that he had been unjustly treated.

91 The effect of trade and commerce with respect to most civilized states is to send out of their countries what the poor, that is, the great mass of mankind, have occasion for, and to bring back, in return, what is consumed almost wholly by a small part of those nations, viz. the rich. Hence it appears that the greater part of manufactures, trade and commerce is highly injurious to the poor as being the chief means of depriving them of the necessaries of life.
1805 *The Effects of Civilization on the People in European States.*

Hall, J(oyce) C(lyde) 1891–1982

US businessman, founder of Hallmark Cards Inc.

92 The art of the masses.
Of illustrated greetings cards. Recalled on his death, quoted in *The Annual Obituary 82* (1983).

Halliwell, Geri 1972–

English pop star, former member of The Spice Girls.

93 The Ginger character was my own invention, of course. It was like putting on a uniform. You don't have to think. You don't have to deal with being a human being.
2002 *Geri—Just For The Record.*

Halsey, W(illiam) F(rederick) *known as* 'Bull' Halsey 1882–1959

US naval officer, commander at the Battle of Leyte Gulf (1944) and others. He received the formal Japanese surrender on his flagship, the USS *Missouri*, on 2 Sep 1945.

94 The Third Fleet's sunken and damaged ships have been salvaged and are retiring at high speed toward the enemy.
1944 Comment, 14 Oct, on hearing claims that the Japanese had virtually annihilated the US fleet. Quoted in E B Potter *Bull Halsey* (1985), ch.17.

Hamer, Robert 1911–63

British film director and screenwriter. He is best known for *It Always Rains on Sunday* (1947), *Kind Hearts and Coronets* (1949, with John Dighton) and *School for Scoundrels* (1960).

95 I shot an arrow in the air. She fell to earth in Berkeley Square.
1949 *Kind Hearts and Coronets* (with John Dighton).

96 Every lunch time I went to see how my inheritance was proceeding. Sometimes the deaths column brought good news. Sometimes the births column brought bad. The advent of twin sons to the Duke was a terrible blow. Fortunately an epidemic of diphtheria restored the status quo almost immediately.
1949 *Kind Hearts and Coronets* (with John Dighton).

97 I always say that my west window has all the exuberance of Chaucer without, happily, any of the concomitant crudities of his period.
1949 *Kind Hearts and Coronets* (with John Dighton).

Hamilton, Alexander c.1755–1804

US statesman, Washington's aide-de-camp in the American Revolution and later a congressman. As Secretary of the Treasury (1789–95) he restored the country's finances, but he was killed in a duel with a rival.

98 A national debt, if it is not excessive, will be to us a national blessing.
1781 Letter to Robert Morris, 30 Apr.

99 To model our political systems upon speculations of lasting tranquillity is to calculate on the weaker springs of the human character.
1787–8 *The Federalist Papers.*

Hamilton, Edith 1867–1963

German-born US classicist, whose popular works include *The Greek Way* (1930).

1 To be able to be caught up into the world of thought—that is educated.
Quoted in the *Saturday Evening Post*, 27 Sep 1958.

Hamilton, (Robert) Ian 1938–2001

English poet. He was editor of *Review* (1962–72) and poetry and fiction editor of the *Times Literary Supplement* (1965–73).

2 If my life were like hers, I'd rather be dead. Come to think of it, if my life were like mine, I'd rather be dead.
Quoted by Al Alvarez in D Harsent (ed) *Another Road at the Pillars: Essays, Poems and Reflections on Ian Hamilton* (1972).

3 Back in the early Sixties, when I first started out, insolvency spelt glamour.
1998 *The Trouble with Money and Other Essays.*

4 Show me an enemy of literature, and I will show him my accounts.
1998 *The Trouble with Money and Other Essays.*

Hammarskjöld, Dag Hjalmar Agne Carl 1905–61

Swedish statesman. As Secretary-General of the United Nations from 1953 he took part in conciliation moves in the Middle East. He was awarded the Nobel peace prize posthumously, after he was killed in an air crash while involved in the Congo crisis.

5 For what has been—thanks!
For what shall be—yes!
1950 *Vägmarken* (translated by L Sjsÿberg and W H Auden as *Markings*, 1964).

6 God does not die on the day when we cease to believe in a personal deity, but we die on the day when our lives cease to be illumined by the steady radiance, renewed daily, of a wonder, the source of which is beyond all reason.
1950 *Vägmarken* (translated by L Sjsÿberg and W H Auden as *Markings*, 1964).

7 Before Thee in humility, with Thee in faith, in Thee in peace.
1955 *Vägmarken* (translated by L Sjsÿberg and W H Auden as *Markings*, 1964).

8 The 'men of the hour', the self-assured who strut among us in the jingling harness of their success and importance, how can you let yourself be irritated by them. Let them enjoy their triumph—on the level to which it belongs.
1956 *Vägmarken* (translated by L Sjsÿberg and W H Auden as *Markings*, 1964).

9 I didn't know Who—or what—put the question, I don't know when it was put. I don't even remember answering. But at some moment I did answer Yes to Someone—or Something—and from that hour I was certain that existence is meaningful and that, therefore, my life, in self-surrender, had a goal.
1961 *Vägmarken* (translated by L Sjsÿberg and W H Auden as *Markings*, 1964).

10 Weep
If you can,
Weep,
But do not complain—
And you must be thankful.
1961 *Vägmarken* (translated by L Sjsÿberg and W H Auden as *Markings*, 1964).

11 Never let success hide its emptiness from you; achievement its nothingness; toil its desolation. Keep alive the incentive to push on further, that pain in the soul that drives us beyond ourselves. Do not look back, and do not dream about the future either. It will neither give you back the past, nor satisfy your other daydreams. Your duty, your reward, your destiny are here and now.
1961 *Vägmarken* (translated by L Sjsÿberg and W H Auden as *Markings*, 1964).

Hammer, Armand 1898–1990

US business executive and art collector.

12 The art world is a jungle echoing to the calls of vicious jealousies and ruthless combat between dealers and collectors; but I have been walking in the jungles of business all my life, and fighting tooth and nail for pictures comes as a form of relaxation to me.
1987 *Hammer, Witness to History*, his autobiography.

13 My Van Gogh is better than *Irises*. I have the whole garden.
On ranking his own Van Gogh, *Hospital at Saint-Rémy*, over the *Irises* that brought £53.9 million at auction. In *Connoisseur*, Jan 1991.

Hammerstein, Oscar, II 1895–1960

US lyricist–librettist. In collaboration with composer Richard Rodgers he wrote such hit musicals as *Oklahoma!* (1943), *South Pacific* (1949) and *The Sound of Music* (1959).

14 Fish got to swim and birds got to fly
I got to love one man till I die
Can't help lovin' dat man of mine.
1927 Song from *Show Boat* (music by Jerome Kern).

15 Ol' Man River.
1927 Title of song from *Show Boat* (music by Jerome Kern).

16 When I grow too old to dream
Your love will live in my heart.
1935 Song from *The Night is Young* (music by Sigmund Romberg).

17 As you walk through the storm,
Hold your head up high,
And don't be afraid of the dark,
At the end of the storm,
Is a golden sky,
And the sweet silver song of the lark,
Walk on through the wind,
Walk on through the rain,
Though your dreams be tossed and blown.
Walk on, walk on,
With hope in your hearts,
And you'll never walk alone,
You'll never walk alone.
1945 *Carousel*, 'You'll Never Walk Alone' (music by Richard Rodgers). The song was subsequently released in a pop version

by Gerry and the Pacemakers in 1963 and adopted as a club song by Liverpool football club.

18 I'm Gonna Wash That Man Right Outa My Hair.
1949 Title of song sung by Mitzi Gaynor in *South Pacific* (music by Richard Rodgers).

19 You've got to be taught to be afraid
Of people whose eyes are oddly made,
Of people whose skin is a different shade.
You've got to be carefully taught.

You've got to be taught before it's too late,
Before you are six or seven or eight,
To hate all the people your relatives hate.
You've got to be carefully taught.
1949 'You've Got to Be Carefully Taught', song from *South Pacific* (music by Richard Rodgers).

20 The hills are alive with the sound of music
With the songs they have sung
For a thousand years.
1959 *The Sound of Music*, title song (music by Richard Rodgers).

Hammett, (Samuel) Dashiell 1894–1961

US crime writer. He joined the Pinkerton Detective Agency as an operator, and later translated his experiences into literature. He suffered from alcohol abuse, which broke his health, and like his partner Lillian Hellman, came into conflict with McCarthy in the anti-Communist trials.

21 He looked rather pleasantly like a blond satan.
1930 Of Sam Spade. *The Maltese Falcon*, 'Spade and Archer'.

22 'I mean that you paid us more than if you'd been telling the truth,' he explained blandly, 'and enough more to make it all right.'
1930 *The Maltese Falcon*, 'The Black Bird'.

23 I distrust a man that says when. If he's got to be careful not to drink too much it's because he's not to be trusted when he does.
1930 *The Maltese Falcon*, 'The Fat Man'.

24 Murder doesn't round out anybody's life except the murdered's and sometimes the murderer's.
1932 *The Thin Man*, ch.31.

Hampton, Christopher 1946–

English playwright and screenwriter. He established his reputation with such plays as *The Philanthropist* (1970). He adapted *Les Liaisons Dangereuses* (1986) from the novel by Laclos and Graham Greene's *The Quiet American* (2002) for screen.

25 Masturbation is the thinking man's television.
1970 *The Philanthropist*.

26 I always divide people into two groups. Those who live by what they know to be a lie, and those who live by what they believe, falsely, to be the truth.
1970 *The Philanthropist*.

27 If I had to give a definition of capitalism, I would say: the process whereby American girls turn into American women.
1974 *Savages*, sc.16.

28 Asking a working writer what he thinks about critics is like asking a lamp-post how it feels about dogs.
Attributed.

Hancock, Lang(ley George) 1909–92

Australian mining industrialist, who discovered iron ore in the Pilbara region with his light aircraft. His various claims, including Rhodes Ridge, made him one of Australia's richest men.

29 The best way to help the poor is not to become one of them.
Quoted in R W Kent (ed) *Money Talks* (1985).

Hand, (Billings) Learned 1872–1961

US jurist, senior judge at the US Court of Appeals for the Second Circuit (1924–51). His legal judgements had enormous influence on the Supreme Court.

30 The spirit of liberty is the spirit which is not too sure that it is right.
1944 Address at 'I Am An American Day' in New York's Central Park, recalled on his death, 18 Aug 1961.

Handel, George Frideric 1685–1759

German-born English composer. He settled in England in 1712, becoming first Director of the Royal Academy of Music (1720). He turned from opera to oratorio in 1739, most notably with *Messiah* (1742). Other works include *Water Music* (1717) and *Music for the Royal Fireworks* (1749).

31 Whether I was in my body or out of my body as I wrote it I know not. God knows.
Of the 'Hallelujah Chorus' in his *Messiah*. Quoted in Romain Rolland *Essays on Music* (1948).

Handy, Charles Brian 1932–

Irish writer and management theorist. His works include *The Making of Managers* (1988) and *The New Alchemists* (1999).

32 Words are the bugles of social change.
1991 *The Age of Unreason*.

Hankey, Katherine 1834–1911

English evangelist and hymnwriter.

33 Tell me the old, old story,
Of unseen things above.
1866 *The Story Wanted*, 'Tell Me the Old, Old Story'.

Hansberry, Lorraine Vivian 1930–65

US playwright. Her semi-autobiographical *A Raisin in the Sun* (1959), the first Broadway play written by a black woman, dealt with the problems facing a black family in a white neighbourhood.

34 Though it be a thrilling and marvelous thing to be merely young and gifted in such times, it is doubly so—doubly dynamic—to be young, gifted and black.
Speech to entrants in the United Negro College Fund writers competition. The phrase was later used as the title of her biography *Young, Gifted and Black* (1969).

Harburg, E(dgar) Y(ip) 1898–1981

US lyricist–librettist, born in New York, who contributed to many Broadway shows. He is best known for the songs in *The Wizard of Oz* (1939).

35 Brother can you spare a dime?
1932 Title of song.

36 Say, it's only a paper moon,

Sailing over a cardboard sea.
1933 'It's Only a Paper Moon' (with Billy Rose, music by Harold Arlen).

37 Lydia the Tattooed Lady.
1939 Title of song featured in the Marx Brothers film *At the Circus* (music by Harold Arlen).

38 Somewhere over the rainbow
Way up high,
There's a land that I heard of
Once in a lullaby.
1939 'Over the Rainbow', sung by Judy Garland in *The Wizard of Oz* (music by Harold Arlen).

Hardie, (James) Keir 1856–1915

Scottish Labour politician, a former miner. He founded and edited the *Labour Leader*, and was Chairman of the Independent Labour Party and of the Labour Party (1906–8), which he helped to found. He was a strong pacifist, and lost his seat opposing the Boer War.

39 From his childhood onward this boy will be surrounded by sycophants and flatterers by the score, and will be taught to believe himself as of a superior creation. A line will be drawn between him and the people whom he is to be called upon some day to reign over. In due course, following the precedent which has already been set, he will be sent on a tour round the world, and probably rumours of a morganatic alliance will follow, and the end of it all will be that the Country will be called upon to pay the bill.
1894 Speech in the House of Commons, 28 Jun, opposing an Address of Congratulation to the Queen being passed in the House of Commons, on the birth of a son (the future Edward VIII) to the Duke and Duchess of York.

40 Can a Man be a Christian on a Pound a Week?
1901 Title of pamphlet.

Hardie, Robert 1904–73

Scottish doctor who, when Singapore fell in 1942, became one of the 61,000 Allied prisoners of war forced by the Japanese to work on the Burma–Siam railway. He kept a secret diary while a prisoner.

41 This is the last day of 1943, a year to be said goodbye to without regret, holding as it did nothing beyond captivity and depression, weary waiting, and above all the sight of immeasurable human misery, suffering and death.
1943 Diary entry, 31 Dec.

Harding, Warren G(amaliel) 1865–1923

US politician and 29th President. A successful journalist, he emerged as a power in the Republican Party, won its nomination and became President (1920–3) when he campaigned against US membership of the League of Nations.

42 America's present need is not heroics but healing; not nostrums but normalcy; not revolution but restoration.
1920 Speech, Boston, Jun.

Hardwicke, Sir Cedric 1893–1964

English actor and director. He made his stage debut in 1912 and appeared in plays by George Bernard Shaw, Emlyn Williams and Shakespeare among others, receiving acclaim on both sides of the Atlantic.

43 I can't act. I have never acted. And I shall never act. What I do is suspend my audience's power of judgement till I've finished.
1945 Attributed.

44 When in doubt, shout—that's the motto.
Attributed, repeating advice that was given to him as a young actor.

Hardy, Godfrey Harold 1877–1947

English mathematician, a professor at Oxford and Cambridge. With Srinivasa Ramanujan, he found an exact formula for the partition function, which expresses the number of ways a number can be written as a sum of smaller numbers.

45 Beauty is the first test: there is no permanent place in the world for ugly mathematics.
1941 *A Mathematician's Apology.*

46 A science is said to be useful if its development tends to accentuate the existing inequities in the distribution of wealth, or more directly promotes the destruction of human life.
1941 *A Mathematician's Apology.*

Hardy, Oliver *originally* Norvell Hardy Jr 1892–1957

US comic actor. He is best known for his partnership with Stan Laurel, and together they produced more than 100 films.

47 Here's another fine mess you've gotten me into.
Of Laurel. Line delivered in *Another Fine Mess* (1930) and other films.

Hardy, Thomas 1840–1928

English novelist and poet. His novels include *The Mayor of Casterbridge* (1886), *Tess of the D'Urbervilles* (1891) and *Jude the Obscure* (1896). His poetry was collected in *Wessex Poems* (1898), and he also wrote a drama, *The Dynasts* (1903–8).

48 Good, but not religious-good.
1872 *Under the Greenwood Tree*, ch.2.

49 That man's silence is wonderful to listen to.
1872 *Under the Greenwood Tree*, ch.14.

50 No man likes to see his emotions the sport of a merry-go-round of skittishness.
1874 *Far from the Madding Crowd*, ch.4.

51 Men thin away to insignificance and oblivion quite as often by not making the most of good spirits when they have them as by lacking good spirits when they are indispensable.
1874 *Far from the Madding Crowd*, ch.22.

52 He was moderately truthful towards men, but to women lied like a Cretan.
1874 Of Sergeant Troy. *Far from the Madding Crowd*, ch.25.

53 It is hard for a woman to define her feelings in language which is chiefly made by men to express theirs.
1874 *Far from the Madding Crowd*, ch.81.

54 Human beings, in their generous endeavour to construct a hypothesis that shall not degrade a First Cause, have always hesitated to conceive a dominant power of a lower moral quality than their own.
1878 *The Return of the Native*, bk.6, ch.1.

55 There was a natural instinct to abjure man as the blot on an otherwise kindly universe.
1886 *The Mayor of Casterbridge*, ch.1.

56 Her bygone simplicity was the art that conceals art.
1886 *The Mayor of Casterbridge*, ch.15.

57 Sex had never before asserted itself in her so strongly, for in former days she had perhaps been too impersonally human to be distinctively feminine.
1886 Of Miss Newson. *The Mayor of Casterbridge*, ch.15.

58 Her occasional pretty and picturesque use of dialect words—those terrible marks of the beast to the truly genteel.
1886 *The Mayor of Casterbridge*, ch.20.

59 It is not by what is, in this life, but by what appears, that you are judged.
1886 *The Mayor of Casterbridge*, ch.25.

60 She whose youth had seemed to teach that happiness was but the occasional episode in a general drama of pain.
1886 *The Mayor of Casterbridge*, ch.45.

61 It was one of those sequestered spots outside the gates of the world.
1887 *The Woodlanders*, ch.1.

62 Why it was that upon this beautiful feminine tissue, sensitive as gossamer, and practically blank as snow as yet, there should have been traced such a coarse pattern as it was doomed to receive; why so often the coarse appropriates the finer thus, the wrong man the woman, the wrong woman the man, many thousand years of analytical philosophy have failed to explain to our sense of order.
1891 *Tess of the D'Urbervilles*, ch.11.

63 'Justice' was done, and the President of the Immortals (in Aeschylean phrase) had ended his sport with Tess.
1891 *Tess of the D'Urbervilles*, ch.59.

64 A novel is an impression, not an argument.
1892 *Tess of the D'Urbervilles*, preface to 5th edn.

65 His face wearing the fixity of a thoughtful child's who has felt the pricks of life somewhat before his time.
1896 *Jude the Obscure*, pt.1, ch.1.

66 What was good for God's birds was bad for God's gardener.
1896 *Jude the Obscure*, pt.1, ch.2.

67 It was better to love a woman than to be a graduate, or a parson; ay, or a pope!
1896 *Jude the Obscure*, pt.1, ch.7.

68 Cruelty is the law pervading all nature and society; and we can't get out of it if we would!
1896 *Jude the Obscure*, pt.5, ch.8.

69 Done because we are too menny.
1896 The note left by Jude's young son, who had hanged his siblings and himself. *Jude the Obscure*, pt.6, ch.2.

70 An aged thrush, frail, gaunt and small,
In blast-beruffled plume,
Had chosen thus to fling his sail
Upon the growing gloom.

So little cause for carollings
Of such ecstatic sound
Was written on terrestrial things
Afar or nigh around,
That I could think there trembled through
His happy good-night air
Some blessed Hope, whereof he knew
And I was unaware.
1902 'The Darkling Thrush'.

71 If way to the Better there be, it exacts a full look at the worst.
1902 'De Profundis'.

72 What we gain by science is, after all, sadness, as the Preacher saith. The more we know of the laws and nature of the Universe the more ghastly a business we perceive it all to be—and the non-necessity of it.
1902 Letter to Edward Clodd, 27 Feb.

73 A local thing called Christianity.
1904 *The Dynasts*, pt.1, act 1, sc.6.

74 War makes rattling good history; but Peace is poor reading.
1904 *The Dynasts*, pt.1, act 2, sc.5.

75 Woman much missed, how you call to me, call to me,
Saying that now you are not as you were
When you had changed from the one who was all to me,
But as at first, when our day was fair.
1914 'The Voice'.

76 This is the weather the cuckoo likes,
And so do I;
When showers betumble the chestnut spikes,
And nestlings fly:
And the little brown nightingale bills his best,
And they sit outside at 'The Travellers' Rest',
And maids come forth sprig-muslin drest,
And citizens dream of the south and west,
And so do I.
1922 *Late Lyrics and Earlier*, 'Weathers'.

77 Well, World, you have kept faith with me,
Kept faith with me;
Upon the whole you have proved to be
Much as you said you were.
1928 *Winter Words*, 'He Never Expected Much'.

Hargreaves, W F 1846–1919

English songwriter. Married to US singer Ella Shields, he wrote such music-hall standards as 'I Must Go Home Tonight'.

78 I acted so tragic the house rose like magic,
The audience yelled, 'You're sublime'.
They made me a present of Mornington Crescent,
They threw it a brick at a time.
'The Night I Appeared as Macbeth' (song).

Harington, Sir John 1561–1612

English courtier and writer, godson of Elizabeth I. He translated Ariosto's *Orlando Furioso* (1591) and published the satiric *The Metamorphosis of Ajax* (1596), which contained the first design of a flushing toilet. His government work in Ireland inspired *A Short View of the State of Ireland* (1605).

79 When I would make a feast
I would my guests should praise it, not the cooks.
1618 *Epigrams*, bk.1, no.5, 'Against Writers That Carp at Other Men's Books'.

80 Treason doth never prosper, what's the reason?
For if it prosper, none dare call it treason.
1618 *Epigrams*, bk.4, no.5.

Harkin, Tom (Thomas) 1939–

US politician, Democratic Senator from Iowa.

81 The Gulf War was like teenage sex. We got in too soon and we got out too soon.
1991 Quoted in the *Independent on Sunday*, 29 Sep.

Harkness, Richard Long 1907–77

US radio and television news commentator. He was also a journalist and government official. As the Washington correspondent for NBC (1943–72) he covered the Roosevelt–Churchill war conferences, as well as UN sessions, NATO and domestic political campaigns.

82 A group of the unwilling, picked from the unfit, to do the unnecessary.
1960 Definition of a committee. In the *New York Herald Tribune*, 15 Jun.

Harlech, William David Ormsby Gore, 5th Baron 1918–85

English Conservative politician and businessman, British Ambassador in Washington (1961–5). On his return he obtained the franchise for Harlech Television (1967). He was President of the British Board of Film Censors at a time of increasing permissiveness.

83 It would indeed be the ultimate tragedy if the history of the human race proved to be nothing more noble than the story of an ape playing with a box of matches on a petrol dump.
1960 In the *Christian Science Monitor*, 25 Oct.

Harlow, Jean *pseudonym of* ***Harlean Carpentier*** 1911–37

US actress, best known for her roles as a fast-talking wisecracking blonde in *Hell's Angels* (1930), *Red Dust* (1932) and *Libelled Lady* (1936). She died young from cerebral oedema.

84 Excuse me while I slip into something more comfortable.
1930 Line delivered in *Hell's Angels* (screenplay by Howard Estabrook and Harry Behn).

Harold II c.1019–1066

Earl of Wessex and King of England (1066). Shipwrecked in Normandy, he swore an oath to support Duke William's claim to the English throne. When he was elected king, William invaded, and Harold was killed at Hastings.

85 He will give him seven feet of English ground, or as much more as he may be taller than other men.
1066 His offer to the invading Norse King Harald Hardrada, quoted in Snorri Sturluson *Heimskringla* (c.1260), 'King Harald's Saga', section 91 (translated by Samuel Laing as *History of the Norse Kings*, 1844).

Harpur, Charles 1813–68

Australian poet. He used traditional, ornate 18c English verse patterns, overlaid with pastoral Australian imagery, in an attempt to create an appropriate colonial style.

86 Stale is their gladness who were never sad.
'Sonnet XIII', collected in C W Salier (ed) *Rosa: Love Sonnets to Mary Doyle* (1949).

Harrington, James 1611–77

English political theorist. Although a republican, he was an attendant of Charles I and was with him at the scaffold. His semi-romance *The Commonwealth of Oceana* (1656) proposed a commonwealth based on property. He was arrested and imprisoned in 1661.

87 No man can be a politician except he first be an historian or a traveller; for except he can see what must be, or what may be, he is no politician.
1656 *The Commonwealth of Oceana.*

Harrington, Michael 1928–89

US political activist and writer. In 1973 he set up the Democratic Socialist Organizing Committee. *The Other America: Poverty in the United States* (1962) is an indictment of poverty in the US.

88 If there is technological advance without social advance, there is, almost automatically, an increase in human misery, in impoverishment.
1962 *The Other America: Poverty in the United States*, ch.1.

89 Clothes make the poor invisible too: America has the best-dressed poverty the world has ever known.
1962 *The Other America: Poverty in the United States*, ch.1.

Harris, Joel Chandler 1848–1908

US author, who worked for the Atlanta *Constitution* (1876–1900). His reputation rests on his Uncle Remus stories, told in dialect. They include *Uncle Remus: His Songs and His Sayings* (1880) and *Nights with Uncle Remus* (1883).

90 Tar-Baby, she stay still, en Brer Fox, he lay low.
1880 *Uncle Remus: His Songs and His Sayings*, 'The Wonderful Tar-Baby Story'.

91 Bred en bawn in a brier-patch!
1880 *Uncle Remus: His Songs and His Sayings*, 'How Mr. Rabbit Was Too Sharp for Mr. Fox'.

92 Licker talks mighty loud w'en it git loose fum de jug.
1880 *Uncle Remus: His Songs and His Sayings*, 'Plantation Proverbs'.

93 Hongry rooster don't cackle w'en he fine a wum.
1880 *Uncle Remus: His Songs and His Sayings*, 'Plantation Proverbs'.

94 Watch out w'en you'er gittin all you want. Fattenin' hogs ain't in luck.
1880 *Uncle Remus: His Songs and His Sayings*, 'Plantation Proverbs'.

95 When folks git ole en strucken wid de palsy, dey mus' speck ter be laff'd at.
1883 *Nights with Uncle Remus*, 'Mr. Man Has Some Meat'.

96 All by my own-alone self.
1883 *Nights with Uncle Remus*, 'Brother Wolf Falls a Victim'.

Harris, Robert 1957–

English writer. He has worked as a news reporter and journalist and has also published novels.

97 The only leaders Labour loves are dead ones.
1996 In the *Sunday Times*, 11 Aug.

Harris, Rolf 1930–

Australian entertainer and artist. He went to London in 1952 to study art, and began working with the BBC children's department. More recently he has been the presenter of the television series *Animal Hospital* (1994–).

98 Tie Me Kangaroo Down, Sport.

1950s Title and chorus of song, passim in BBC children's programme.

Harris, (Theodore) Wilson *pseudonym of* ***Kona Waruk*** 1921–

British novelist, born in Guyana. His best-known work is *The Guyana Quartet* (1960–3).

99 The dark notes rose everywhere, so dark, so sombre, they broke into a fountain—light as the rainbow—sparkling and immaterial as invisible sources and echoes. The savannahs grew lonely as the sea and broke again into a wave and forest. Tall trees with black marching boots and feet were clad in the spurs and sharp wings of a butterfly.
1960 *The Palace of the Peacock*, ch.11.

Harrison, Tony 1937–

English poet. His work has focused on giving voice to working class culture. His best-known work is the inflammatory poem *V* (1985), a denunciation of contemporary British life.

1 Articulation is the tongue-tied's fighting.
1978 'On Not Being Milton'.

2 This pen's all I have of magic wand.
1985 *V.*

3 I have always disliked the idea of an arts ghetto in which poetry is kept on a life-support system.
1989 In the *Observer*, 23 Jul.

Harrison, Wallace K(irkman) 1895–1981

US architect, whose best-known designs include the UN Secretariat building and the Metropolitan Opera House, both in New York. He married into the Rockefeller dynasty.

4 When we started the UN we were not trying to make a monument. We were building a workshop—a workshop for world peace. And we tried to make it the best damn workshop we could.
1952 In *Time*, 22 Sep.

Harrod, Sir Roy 1900–78

English economist, Professor at Oxford (1922–67), noted for his work on international economics and economic growth.

5 The most basic law of economics...that one cannot get something for nothing.
1948 *Towards a Dynamic Economics*.

6 No economy ever stands still.
1963 *The British Economy.*

Hart, Gary *originally* ***Gary Hartpence*** 1936–

US lawyer and Democrat politician. He entered the Senate in 1974, and was narrowly defeated for the presidential nomination by Walter Mondale in 1984. He made a further unsuccessful bid for the presidency in 1988.

7 You can get awful famous in this country in seven days.
1984 Rueful comment after reports of his marital infidelity ended his presidential campaign. In the *New York Times*, 7 Oct.

8 This is one Hart that you will not leave in San Francisco.
1984 Said after his failed bid for the presidential nomination at the Democratic National Convention in San Francisco.

Hart, Ian 1964–

English actor.

9 There's a statistical theory that if you gave a million monkeys typewriters and set them to work, they'd eventually come up with the entire works of Shakespeare. Thanks to the internet, we now know this isn't true.
2001 In the *Sunday Herald*, 30 Dec.

Hart, Lorenz 1895–1943

US songwriter.

10 When love congeals
It soon reveals
The faint aroma of performing seals,
The double-crossing of a pair of heels.
I wish I were in love again!
1937 'I Wish I Were in Love Again' (music by Richard Rodgers), from *Babes in Arms*.

11 I get too hungry for dinner at eight.
I like the theater, but never come late.
I never bother with people I hate.
That's why the lady is a tramp.
1937 'The Lady Is a Tramp' (music by Richard Rodgers), from *Babes in Arms*.

12 I'm wild again
Beguiled again
A simpering, whimpering child again,
Bewitched, bothered and bewildered am I.
1941 'Bewitched' (music by Richard Rodgers), from *Pal Joey.*

Hart, Moss 1904–61

US playwright and author. He won a Pulitzer Prize for *You Can't Take It With You* (1937) and a Perry award for directing his own play *My Fair Lady* (1957). He also wrote *Once in a Lifetime* (1930).

13 A play for me never really takes on an aspect of reality until it has left the dry air of the study and begins to sniff the musty breezes of a bare stage.
1959 *Act One*.

14 The four most dramatic words in the English language: 'Act One, Scene One.'
1959 *Act One*.

Harte, (Francis) Bret 1836–1902

US writer, who wrote sketches of California miners in works such as 'The Luck of Roaring Camp' (1868). Secretary of the US Mint in San Francisco (1864–70), he became US consul at Krefeld (1878–80) and Glasgow (1880–5).

15 I reside at Table Mountain, and my name is Truthful James;
I am not up to small deceit or any sinful games.
1868 'The Society upon the Stanislaus', stanza 1.

16 Which I wish to remark—
And my language is plain—
That for ways that are dark
And for tricks that are vain,
The heathen Chinee is peculiar,
Which the same I would rise to explain.
1870 'Plain Language from Truthful James', stanza 1. The poem became popularly known as 'That Heathen Chinee'.

17 We are ruined by Chinese cheap labour.

1870 'Plain Language from Truthful James', stanza 7.

18 And on that grave where English oak and holly
And laurel wreaths entwine,
Deem it not all a too presumptuous folly,
This spray of Western pine!
1870 On the death of Charles Dickens. 'Dickens in Camp', stanza 10.

19 If, of all words of tongue and pen,
The saddest are, 'It might have been,'

More sad are these we daily see:
'It is, but hadn't ought to be.'
1871 'Mrs. Judge Jenkins'.

Hartley, L(eslie) P(oles) 1895–1972

English writer. His early published works were short stories of a macabre turn. He went on to write successful novels of considerable psychological acuity.

20 The past is a foreign country: they do things differently there.
1953 *The Go-Between*, prologue.

Harvey, P(olly) J(ean) 1969–

English singer and songwriter.

21 There would be more women in the rock scene if they were any good. But there are so few who are.
2004 In *Scotland on Sunday*, 30 May.

Harvey, William 1578–1657

English physician and scientist, who established the foundations of modern medicine. He was the first to demonstrate the function of the heart and the complete circulation of the blood.

22 Nature is nowhere accustomed more openly to display her secret mysteries than in cases where she shows tracings of her workings apart from the beaten paths; nor is there any better way to advance the proper practice of medicine than to give our minds to the discovery of the usual law of nature, by careful investigation of cases of rarer forms of disease.
1657 Letter to John Vlackveld, 24 Apr.

Harvey-Jones, Sir John 1924–

English industrial executive.

23 All in all, if one sought to design a life style which was destructive of the individual, the way that business has structured itself would seem to be almost ideal.
1987 *Making It Happen: Reflections on Leadership.*

Haskell, Molly 1939–

US author and film critic.

24 The propaganda arm of the American Dream machine.
1973 Of Hollywood. *From Reverence to Rape: the treatment of women in the movies.*

Haskins, Minnie Louise 1875–1951

English author and educationist.

25 And I said to the man who stood at the gate of the year: 'Give me a light that I may tread safely into the unknown.' And he replied: 'Go out into the darkness and put your hand into the hand of God. That shall be to you better than light and safer than a known way.'
1908 *Desert*, 'God Knows'. Quoted by King George VI, Christmas address, 25 Dec 1939.

Hattersley, Roy Sydney George Hattersley, Baron 1932–

English Labour politician and writer. He was an MP from 1964 to 1997 and served in the Callaghan government.

26 As a boy I genuinely believed in the man who never ate bacon because its red and white stripes reminded him of Sheffield United—indeed in my blue and white Wednesday heart I applauded and supported his loyalty.
1976 *Goodbye to Yorkshire.*

27 Politicians are entitled to change their minds. But when they adjust their principles some explanation is necessary.
1999 In the *Observer*, 21 Mar.

Haughey, Charles James 1925–

Irish politician and Prime Minister (1979–81, 1982, 1987–92). He became a Fianna Fáil MP (1957), but was dismissed from the Cabinet in 1970 after a quarrel with the Prime Minister, Jack Lynch. His career has been controversial, but he is also responsible for introducing tax exemption for artists.

28 It seems that the historic inability in Britain to comprehend Irish feelings and sensitivities still remains.
1988 In the *Observer*, Feb.

Havel, Václav 1936–

Czech playwright and politician. He was a co founder of Charter '77, President of Czechoslovakia (1989–1992) and first President of the Czech Republic (1993–2003).

29 The worst thing is that we live in a contaminated moral environment. We fell morally ill because we became used to saying something different from what we thought.
1990 Speech, 1 Jan.

Hawes, Hampton 1928–77

US jazz pianist. He was an important (but often undervalued) figure in West Coast jazz.

30 The worst thing that can happen to old good music is that it might become dated for a while, but watch out, in twenty years it will come drifting back like bell-bottoms and W.C. Fields movies.
1974 *Raise Up Off Me* (with Don Asher), ch.22.

Hawking, Stephen William 1942–

English theoretical physicist, theorist of the astronomical bodies known as black holes. He has written several bestselling popular science books including *A Brief History of Time* (1988) and *The Universe in a Nutshell* (2001). From the 1960s he has suffered from a progressive motor neurone disease.

31 God not only plays dice. He also sometimes throws the dice where they cannot be seen.
1975 In *Nature*, vol.257.
➤ *See Einstein 301:32.*

32 If we find the answer to that, it would be the ultimate triumph of human reason—for then we would know the mind of God.
1988 Referring to the question of why we and the universe exist. *A Brief History of Time*, ch.11.

33 What is it that breathes fire into the equations and makes a universe for them to describe... Why does the universe go to all the bother of existing?
1988 *A Brief History of Time*, ch.11.

Hawthorn, Mike 1929–59

English racing driver. Driving for Ferrari, he won the Formula One World Championship in 1958 but then retired from the sport, only to be killed in a road accident a few months later.

34 Motor racing is dangerous; but what is danger? It is dangerous to climb a mountain. It is dangerous to cross main roads. It is dangerous to explore a jungle. One cannot frame regulations to make everything safe.
1959 Shortly before his death. Quoted in Colin Jarman *The Guinness Dictionary of Sports Quotations* (1990).

Hawthorne, Nathaniel 1804–64

US novelist, who worked in the Salem custom house and was Consul at Liverpool (1853–7). Between 1850 and 1852 he lived in Lenox near Herman Melville, where he wrote *The Scarlet Letter* (1850) and *The House of the Seven Gables* (1851).

35 We sometimes congratulate ourselves at the moment of waking from a troubled dream: it may be so the moment after death.
c.1836 *The American Notebooks*, ch.1.

36 The love of posterity is a consequence of the necessity of death. If a man were sure of living forever here, he would not care about his offspring.
1840 *The American Notebooks* (published 1868), ch.3.

37 Bees are sometimes drowned in the honey which they collect—so some writers are lost in their collected learning.
1842 *The American Notebooks* (published 1868), ch.5.

38 Human nature will not flourish, any more than a potato, if it be planted and replanted, for too long a series of generations, in the same worn-out soil.
1850 *The Scarlet Letter*, 'The Custom-House'.

39 The founders of a new colony, whatever Utopia of human virtue and happiness they might originally project, have invariably recognized it among their earliest practical necessities to allot a portion of the virgin soil as a cemetery, and another portion as the site of a prison.
1850 *The Scarlet Letter*, ch.1.

40 Let men tremble to win the hand of woman, unless they win along with it the utmost passion of her heart!
1850 *The Scarlet Letter*, ch.15.

41 No man, for any considerable period, can wear one face to himself, and another to the multitude, without finally getting bewildered as to which may be the true.
1850 *The Scarlet Letter*, ch.20.

42 When a writer calls his work a Romance, it need hardly be observed that he wishes to claim a certain latitude, both as to its fashion and material, which he would not have felt himself entitled to assume had he professed to be writing a Novel.
1851 *The House of the Seven Gables*, preface.

43 Life is made up of marble and mud.
1851 *The House of the Seven Gables*, ch.2.

44 Life, within doors, has few pleasanter prospects than a neatly arranged and well-provisioned breakfast-table.
1851 *The House of the Seven Gables*, ch.7.

45 The world, that grey-bearded and wrinkled profligate, decrepit, without being venerable.
1851 *The House of the Seven Gables*, ch.12.

46 The world owes all its onward impulse to men ill at ease. The happy man inevitably confines himself within ancient limits.
1851 *The House of the Seven Gables*, ch.20.

47 In the depths of every heart, there is a tomb and a dungeon, though the lights, the music, and revelry above may cause us to forget their existence, and the buried ones, or prisoners whom they hide.
1851 *Twice-Told Tales*, 'The Haunted Mind'.

48 The greatest obstacle to being heroic is the doubt whether one may not be going to prove one's self a fool; the truest heroism is to resist the doubt; and the profoundest wisdom, to know when it ought to be resisted and when to be obeyed.
1852 *The Blithedale Romance*, ch.2.

49 America is now wholly given over to a d—d mob of scribbling women.
1855 Quoted in Caroline Ticknor *Hawthorne and His Publisher* (1913).

50 The present is burthened too much with the past.
1856 Entry for 27 Mar at the British Museum, collected in *The English Notebooks* (1870).

51 Nobody has any conscience about adding to the improbabilities of a marvelous tale.
1860 *The Marble Faun*, ch.4.

52 How is it possible to say an unkind or irreverential word of Rome? The city of all time, and of all the world!
1860 *The Marble Faun*, ch.12.

53 Dr Johnson's morality was as English an article as a beefsteak.
1863 *Our Old Home*.

Hay, Ian *pseudonym of* Major-General John Hay Beith 1876–1952

Scottish novelist and dramatist. His light popular novels (eg *Pip*, 1907) were followed by war books, including *The First Hundred Thousand* (1915). His best-known comedies are *Tilly of Bloomsbury* (1919) and *The Housemaster* (1936).

54 What do you mean, funny? Funny peculiar, or funny ha-ha?
1936 *The Housemaster*, act 3.

Hayakawa, S(amuel) I(chiye) 1906–92

Canadian-born US philologist and politician. His semantics works include *Language in Action* (1941, later retitled *Language in Thought and Action*). He was president of San Francisco State College (1968–73) and entered the House as Senator for California (1977–83).

55 In a real sense, people who have read good literature have lived more than people who cannot or will not read.
1941 *Language in Action*.

56 It's ours. We stole it fair and square.
Of the Panama Canal Zone. Attributed.

Haydn, Franz Joseph 1732–1809

Austrian composer. Kapellmeister to the Esterházy family from 1761, he twice visited England and several works were first performed in London. His works include piano music, string quartets, concertos, symphonies, masses and choral works such as the oratorio *The Creation* (1798).

57 But all the world understands my language.
1790 Reply to Mozart, who had advised him against visiting England because he could not speak the language. Quoted in Ian Crofton and Donald Fraser *A Dictionary of Musical Quotations* (1985).

Haydon, Benjamin Robert 1786–1846

English historical painter. He was twice imprisoned for debt, and, after a number of bitter disappointments, shot himself.

58 The French had a more martial air than the English. There seemed to be a species of military instinct in all classes. No young man appeared to have finished his education till after a bloody campaign… They were at this singular period, without the least exaggeration, a century behind us in notions of legal and moral responsibility.
Autobiography (published 1847).

Hayek, Friedrich August von 1899–1992

Austrian-born British political economist and libertarian moral philosopher. Professor at the London School of Economics (1932–50), Chicago (1950–72) and Freiburg (1962–5) and a guru of the New Right, in 1974 he was awarded the Nobel prize for economics with Gunnar Myrdal.

59 The more the state 'plans' the more difficult planning becomes for the individual.
1944 *The Road to Serfdom.*

60 We are only beginning to understand on how subtle a communication system the functioning of an advanced industrial society is based—a communications system which we call the market and which turns out to be a more efficient mechanism for digesting dispersed information than any that man has deliberately designed.
1978 *New Studies in Philosophy, Politics, Economics and the History of Ideas*, 'The Pretence of Knowledge'.

61 [There is] a delusion that macro-economics is both viable and useful (a delusion encouraged by its extensive use of mathematics, which must always impress politicians lacking any mathematical education, and which is really the nearest thing to the practice of magic that occurs among professional economists).
1989 *The Fatal Conceit: The Errors of Socialism*, ch.6.

Hayes, J Milton 1884–1940

British author.

62 There's a one-eyed yellow idol to the north of Khatmandu,
There's a little marble cross below the town,
There's a broken-hearted woman tends the grave of Mad Carew,
And the Yellow God forever gazes down.
1911 *The Green Eye of the Yellow God.*

Hayes, Rutherford B(irchard) 1822–93

US Republican statesman and 19th President (1877–81). Under his presidency, the country recovered commercial prosperity, and his policy included the reform of the civil service and the conciliation of the Southern states.

63 He serves his party best who serves his country best.
1877 Inaugural address, 5 Mar.

Hayward, Thomas Bibb 1924–

US admiral, Chief of Operations in the US Navy (1978–83). He served in both Korea and Vietnam.

64 We are…a one-and-a-half ocean navy with a three-ocean commitment.
1982 Congressional testimony, reported in the *New York Times*, 11 Apr.

Hazlitt, William 1778–1830

English essayist, whose controversial and witty work ranges from theatre and literature to politics and even sports. His various collections of essays include *Table Talk* (1821) and *Spirit of the Age, or Contemporary Portraits* (1825).

65 There is in Kean, an infinite variety of talent, with a certain monotony of genius.
1815 Of the actor Edmund Kean. In *The Examiner*, 10 Dec.

66 Mr Kemble sacrifices too much to decorum. He is chiefly afraid of being contaminated by too close an identity with the character he represents. This is the greatest vice in an actor, who ought never to *bilk* his part.
1816 Of John Philip Kemble's performance as Sir Giles Overreach in Massinger's *A New Way to Pay Old Debts*. In *The Examiner*, 5 May.

67 There is nothing good to be had in the country, or if there is, they will not let you have it.
1817 *The Round Table*, 'Observation on Mr Wordsworth's Poem *The Excursion*'.

68 The art of pleasing consists in being pleased.
1817 *The Round Table*, 'On Manner'.

69 He talked on for ever; and you wished him to talk on for ever.
1818 Of Coleridge. *Lectures on the English Poets*, 'On the Living Poets'.

70 Fashion constantly begins and ends in the two things it abhors most, singularity and vulgarity.
1818 'On Fashion', in the *Scots Magazine*.

71 The love of liberty is the love of others; the love of power is the love of ourselves.
1819 *Political Essays*, 'The Times Newspaper'.

72 Those who make their dress a principal part of themselves, will, in general, become of no more value than their dress.
1819 *Political Essays*, 'On the Clerical Character'.

73 You will hear more good things on the outside of a stagecoach from London to Oxford than if you were to pass a twelvemonth with the undergraduates, or heads of colleges, of that famous university.
1821 *Table Talk*, vol.1, 'The Ignorance of the Learned'.

74 We can scarcely hate any one that we know.
1822 *Table Talk*, vol.2, 'On Criticism'.

75 Give me the clear blue sky over my head, and the green turf beneath my feet, a winding road before me, and a

three hours' march to dinner—and then to thinking! It is hard if I cannot start some game on these lone heaths.
1822 *Table Talk*, vol.2, 'On Going a Journey'.

76 *The Times* is, we suppose, entitled to the character it gives of itself, of being the 'leading journal of Europe', and is perhaps the greatest engine of temporary opinion in the world.
1823 In the *Edinburgh Review*, May.

77 It is a commercial paper, a paper of business, and it is conducted on principles of trade and business. It floats with the tide: it sails with the stream. It has no other principle.
1823 Of *The Times*. In the *Edinburgh Review*, May.

78 It takes up no falling cause; fights no uphill battle; advocates no great principle; holds out a helping hand to no oppressed or obscure individual. It is 'ever strong upon the stronger side'.
1823 Of *The Times*. In the *Edinburgh Review*, May.

79 Paris is a beast of a city to be in—to those who cannot get out of it. Rousseau said well, that all the time he was in it, he was only trying how he should leave it… The continual panic in which the passenger is kept, the alarm and the escape from it, the anger and the laughter at it, must have an effect on the Parisian character, and tend to make it the whiffling, skittish, snappish, volatile, inconsequential, unmeaning thing it is.
1824 *Notes on a Journey through France and Italy* (published 1856).

80 He is a kind of *fourth estate* in the politics of the country.
1825 Of the journalist and reformer William Cobbett. *Spirit of the Age*, 'Mr Cobbett'.

81 Death cancels everything but truth; and strips a man of everything but genius and virtue. It is a sort of natural canonization.
1825 *Spirit of the Age*, 'Lord Byron'.

82 The present is an age of talkers, and not of doers; and the reason is, that the world is growing old. We are so far advanced in the Arts and Sciences, that we live in retrospect, and dote on past achievement.
1825 *Spirit of the Age*, 'Mr Coleridge'.

83 He writes as fast as they can read, and he does not write himself down… His worst is better than any other person's best… His works (taken together) are almost like a new edition of human nature. This is indeed to be an author!
1825 *Spirit of the Age*, 'Sir Walter Scott'.

84 Mr Wordsworth's genius is a pure emanation of the Spirit of the Age. Had he lived in any other period of the world, he would never have been heard of.
1825 *Spirit of the Age*, 'Mr Wordsworth'.

85 The dupe of friendship, and the fool of love; have I not reason to hate and to despise myself? Indeed I do; and chiefly for not having hated and despised the world enough.
1826 *The Plain Speaker*, 'On the Pleasure of Hating'.

86 His sayings are generally like women's letters; all the pith is in the postscript.
1826–7 Of Charles Lamb. *Conversations of James Northcote*.

87 The origin of all science is in the desire to know causes; and the origin of all false science and imposture is in the desire to accept false causes rather than none; or, which is the same thing, in the unwillingness to acknowledge our own ignorance.
1829 In *The Atlas*, 15 Feb.

88 Well, I've had a happy life.
1830 Last words. Quoted in W C Hazlitt *Memoirs of William Hazlitt* (1867).

89 So have I loitered my life away, reading books, looking at pictures, going to plays, hearing, thinking, writing on what pleased me best. I have wanted only one thing to make me happy, but wanting that have wanted everything.
Literary Remains (published 1836), 'My First Acquaintance with Poets'.

90 But of all footmen the lowest class is *literary footmen*.
Sketches and Essays (published 1839), 'Footmen'.

91 A nickname is the heaviest stone that the devil can throw at a man.
Sketches and Essays (published 1839), 'Nicknames'.

92 The greatest offence against virtue is to speak ill of it.
Sketches and Essays (published 1839), 'On Cant and Hypocrisy'.

93 There is an unseemly exposure of mind, as well as of the body.
Sketches and Essays (published 1839), 'On Disagreeable People'.

94 Rules and models destroy genius and art.
Sketches and Essays (published 1839), 'On Taste'.

95 All is without form and void. Someone said of his landscapes that they were pictures of nothing and very like.
Of Turner's painting, quoted in J Lindsay *Turner: The Man and his Art* (1985).

Hazzard, Shirley 1931–

Australian-born US novelist. Her works include short stories, the satirical *People in Glass Houses* (1967) and novels including *The Transit of Venus* (1980) and *The Great Fire* (2003).

96 Nothing…makes a more fanatical official than a Latin. Organization is alien to their natures, but once they get the taste for it they take to it like drink.
1967 *People in Glass Houses*, 'Official Life'.

Head, Bessie 1937–86

South African novelist.

97 Love is mutually feeding each other, not one living on another like a ghoul.
1973 *A Question of Power*.

98 Poverty has a home in Africa—like a quiet second skin. It may be the only place on earth where it is worn with unconscious dignity.
1989 *Tales of Tenderness and Power*.

Healey, Denis Winston Healey, Baron 1917–

English Labour politician, Secretary of State for Defence (1964–70) and Chancellor of the Exchequer (1974–9). Unsuccessful in the Labour leadership contests of 1976 and 1980, he became Deputy Leader (1980–3) and shadow Foreign Secretary (1980–7).

99 That part of his speech was rather like being savaged by a dead sheep.
1978 Responding to a speech by Chancellor of the Exchequer Sir Geoffrey Howe, House of Commons, Jun.

1 For the past few months, [Margaret Thatcher] has been charging around like some bargain-basement Boadicea.
1982 In the *Observer*, 7 Nov.

2 The great She-elephant, the great She-who-must-be-obeyed, the Catherine the Great of Finchley.
1985 Of Margaret Thatcher. Comment when Trade Union recognition was withdrawn for employees working in GCHQ.

Heaney, Seamus Justin 1939–

Irish poet and critic, born in Northern Ireland. He moved to Dublin in 1976, was Professor of Poetry at Oxford (1989–94) and also teaches at Harvard (1981–). His works include *Death of a Naturalist* (1966) and *The Spirit Level* (1997) as well as translations. He won the Nobel prize for literature in 1995.

3 Between my finger and my thumb
The squat pen rests.
I'll dig with it.
1966 *Death of a Naturalist*, 'Digging'.

4 My father worked with a horse-plough,
His shoulders globed like a full sail strung
Between the shafts and the furrow.
1966 *Death of a Naturalist*, 'Follower'.

5 Love, you shall perfect for me this child
Whose small imperfect limits would keep breaking:
Within new limits now, arrange the world
And square the circle: four walls and a ring.
1966 *Death of a Naturalist*, 'Poem: For Marie'.

6 My poor scapegoat,

I almost love you
but would have cast, I know,
the stones of silence.
1975 *North*, 'Punishment'.

7 I hold my lady's head
like a crystal

and ossify myself
by gazing: I am screes
on her escarpments,
a chalk giant

carved upon her downs.
Soon my hands, on the sunken
fosse of her spine
move towards the passes.
1975 *North*, 'Bone Dreams', no.4.

8 He had gone miles away
For he drank like a fish
Nightly, naturally
Swimming towards the lure
Of warm lit-up places.
1979 *Field Work*, 'Casualty'.

9 How culpable was he
That last night when he broke
Our tribe's complicity?
'Now you're supposed to be
An educated man,'
I hear him say. 'Puzzle me
The right answer to that one.'
1979 *Field Work*, 'Casualty'. On a man killed breaking the curfew.

10 Don't be surprised,
If I demur, for, be advised,
My passport's green.
No glass of ours was ever raised
To toast *The Queen*.
1983 'An Open Letter to Blake and Andrew, Editors, Contemporary British Verse, Penguin Books, Middlesex'. Heaney was complaining at his inclusion in the book edited by Blake Morrison and Andrew Motion on the grounds of his Irish nationality.

11 Need I go on? I hate to bite
Hands that led me to the limelight
In the Penguin book, I regret
The awkwardness.
But British, no, the name's not right.
Yours truly, Seamus.
1983 'An Open Letter to Blake and Andrew, Editors, Contemporary British Verse, Penguin Books, Middlesex'. Heaney was complaining at his inclusion in the book edited by Blake Morrison and Andrew Motion on the grounds of his Irish nationality.

12 The riverbed, dried-up, half full of leaves.
Us, listening to a river in the trees.
1987 *The Haw Lantern*, 'For Bernard and Jane McCabe', complete poem.

13 When I landed in the republic of conscience
it was so noiseless when the engines stopped
I could hear a curlew high above the runway.
1987 *The Haw Lantern*, 'From the Republic of Conscience', pt.1, stanza 1.

14 Their embassies, he said, were everywhere
but operated independently
and no ambassador would ever be relieved.
1987 *The Haw Lantern*, 'From the Republic of Conscience', pt.3, stanza 4.

15 She taught me what her uncle once taught her:
How easily the biggest coal block split
If you got the grain and hammer angled right.

The sound of that relaxed alluring blow,
Its co-opted and obliterated echo,
Taught me to hit, taught me to loosen,

Taught me between the hammer and the block
To face the music. Teach me now to listen,
To strike it rich behind the linear black.
1987 *The Haw Lantern*, 'Clearances: In Memoriam M.K.H., 1911–1984'.

16 The Nobel is just another prize; it changes something but it doesn't change your being the way your first writing does.
Quoted in Annalena McAfee (ed) *Lives and Works: Profiles of Leading Novelists, Poets and Playwrights* (2002).

Hearst, William Randolph 1863–1951

US newspaper proprietor. He revolutionized journalism with innovations such as the banner headline, in papers such as the *Chicago Examiner*, *Boston American*, *Cosmopolitan* and *Harper's Bazaar*.

17 You furnish the pictures and I'll furnish the war.
1898 Telegram to the artist Frederic Remington at the beginning of the Spanish–American War in Cuba, Mar. This may be apocryphal, but it inspired a famous line of dialogue in Orson Welles's film *Citizen Kane*.

Heath, Sir Edward Richard George *also called* Ted
1916–

English Conservative politician, chief negotiator for Britain's entry into the European Common Market, and Prime Minister (1970–4). He was replaced as leader by Margaret Thatcher, whose policies he openly criticized.

18 We are the trade union for pensioners and children; the trade union for the disabled and the sick; the trade union for the nation as a whole.
1970 Election campaign speech, 20 Feb.

19 This would, at a stroke, reduce the rise in prices, increase productivity, and reduce unemployment.
1970 Statement on proposed tax cuts and a price freeze by nationalized industries, 16 Jun. These words were contained in a press release, and were never actually spoken by Heath.

20 It is the unpleasant and unacceptable face of capitalism, but one should not suggest that the whole of British industry consists of practices of this kind.
1973 House of Commons, 15 May, referring to the Lonrho tax-avoidance scandal involving 'Tiny' Rowland, owner of Harrods and the London and Rhodesia company.

21 If you want to see the acceptable face of capitalism, go out to an oil rig in the North Sea.
1974 Election campaign speech, 18 Feb.

22 Rejoice! Rejoice! Rejoice!
1990 On hearing of Margaret Thatcher's resignation, Nov.

23 British Conservatives base their entire approach to politics on the rule of law, and rightly so.
1998 *The Course of My Life: My Autobiography.*

24 It was not totally inconceivable that she could have joined me as my wife at No.10.
2000 Of the film star Jayne Mansfield. In the *Sunday Times*, 'Talking Heads', 6 Feb.

25 Ocean racing is like standing under a cold shower tearing up £5 notes.
Quoted in Colin Jarman *The Guinness Dictionary of Sports Quotations* (1990).

Heat-Moon, William Least *originally* William Trogdon
1939–

US writer. He made his name with *Blue Highways: A Journey Into America* (1983), a travelogue of America which, like *Prairyerth* (1991), also explored his Native American heritage.

26 Beware thoughts that come in the night. They aren't turned properly; they come in askew, free of sense and restriction, deriving from the most remote of sources.
1983 *Blue Highways: A Journey Into America*, opening words.

27 There are two kinds of adventurers: those who go truly hoping to find adventure and those who go secretly hoping they won't.
1983 *Blue Highways: A Journey Into America.*

28 To say nothing is out here is incorrect; to say the desert is stingy with everything except space and light, stone and earth is closer to the truth.
1983 *Blue Highways: A Journey Into America.*

29 Motels can be big, but never grand.
1983 *Blue Highways: A Journey Into America.*

30 Whoever the last true cowboy in America turns out to be, he's likely to be an Indian.
1983 *Blue Highways: A Journey Into America.*

Hebbel, Friedrich 1813–63

German dramatist, whose plays typically have a legendary or historical setting, exploring the conflict between the individual and humanity as a whole.

31 *Dies Österreich ist eine kleine Welt,*
In der die große ihre Probe hält.
Austria is a little world in which the big one holds its tryouts.
On the social and political disintegration affecting the Austro-Hungarian Empire in the late 1890s. Quoted in Heinrich Benedikt (ed) *Geschichte der Republik Oesterreich* (1954).

Heber, Reginald 1783–1826

English divine and hymnwriter, Bishop of Calcutta from 1823.

32 Brightest and best of the sons of the morning!
Dawn on our darkness and lend us Thine aid!
1811 In the *Christian Observer*, Nov.

33 By cool Siloam's shady rill
How sweet the lily grows!
1812 In the *Christian Observer*, Apr.

34 From Greenland's icy mountains,
From India's coral strand,
Where Afric's sunny fountains
Roll down their coral strand.
1819 Quoted in the *Christian Observer*, Feb 1823.

35 Holy, Holy, Holy! Lord God Almighty!
Early in the morning our song shall rise to Thee:
Holy, Holy, Holy! merciful and mighty!
God in Three Persons, blessèd Trinity.
1826 'Holy, Holy, Holy!'.

Hecht, Ben 1894–1964

US writer. A journalist in Chicago, he began to write novels, plays and filmscripts. From 1946 he was dedicated to the Zionist cause.

36 The movie-makers are able to put more reality into a picture about the terrors of life at the ocean bottom than into a tale of two Milwaukeeans in love.
1954 In news reports, 13 Jun.

Hedin, Sven Anders 1865–1952

Swedish explorer and geographer, who travelled in unexplored regions of central Asia, where he made the first detailed map (1908). He was outspoken in his political beliefs, including sympathy for Nazi Germany.

37 But the adventure, the conquest of an unknown country, the struggle against the impossible, all have a fascination which draws me with an irresistible force.
1926 *My Life as an Explorer.*

Heffer, Simon 1960–

English journalist and writer.

38 If there is writing on Hadrian's Wall, it reads that the English should leave Scotland to its own devices.
1999 *Nor Shall My Sword: The Reinventing of England.*

39 The more a climate can be created in which neither the English nor the Scots are given cause to resent each other, the better.
1999 *Nor Shall My Sword: The Reinventing of England.*

Hegel, Georg Wilhelm Friedrich 1770–1831

German idealist philosopher. His first major work *Phänomenologie des Geistes* (1807, 'The Phenomenology of the Mind') attacked romantic intuitionism. Other works include *Enzyklopädie der philosophischen Wissenschaften* (1817, 'Encyclopedia of the Philosophical Sciences'), in which he set out his tripartite system of logic, philosophy of nature and of mind.

40 In England, even the poorest of people believe that they have rights; that is very different from what satisfies the poor in other lands.
1821 *The Philosophy of Right.*

41 Experience and history teach...that nations and governments have never learned anything from history, or acted upon any lessons they might have drawn from it.
1830 *Lectures on the Philosophy of World History*, introduction.

42 Political genius consists in identifying oneself with a principle.
Constitution of Germany.

Heidegger, Martin 1889–1976

German philosopher, student of Husserl and Professor of Philosophy at Freiburg. He was an important theoretician of phenomenology. His major work is *Being and Time* (1927).

43 The essence of technology is by no means anything technological.
1949 'The Question Concerning Technology', collected in *Basic Writings* (1977).

44 The mathematical is that evident aspect of things within which we are always already moving and according to which we experience them as things at all, and as such things. The mathematical is this fundamental position we take toward things by which we take up things as already given to us, and as they must and should be given. Therefore, the mathematical is the fundamental presupposition of the knowledge of things.
'Modern Science, Metaphysics and Mathematics', collected in *Basic Writings* (1977).

Heifetz, Jascha 1901–87

US violinist of Russo-Polish birth. A child prodigy, he settled in the US after the Russian Revolution, becoming a citizen in 1924. He first appeared in Britain in 1920.

45 I occasionally play works by contemporary composers and for two reasons. First, to discourage the composer from writing any more, and secondly to remind myself how much I appreciate Beethoven.
1961 In *Life.*

Heine, Heinrich 1797–1856

German poet and critic, who lived most of his life in Paris. An incurable spinal disease left him bedridden from 1848. He became a prominent radical political journalist, writing essays on French and German culture and composing satirical verse.

46 *Alle kräftige Menschen lieben das Leben*
All great, powerful souls love life.
1835 *Idéen, Das Buch Le Grand*, pt.3.

47 *Das Leben ist der Güter höchstes, und das schlimmste Übel ist der Tod.*
Life is the greatest of blessings, and death the worst of evils.
1835 *Idéen, Das Buch Le Grand*, pt.3.

48 *Ich glaube sogar, durch Leidenskämpfe könnten die Tiere zu Menschen werden.*
I believe that by suffering even animals could be made human.
1836 *Französische Zustände.*

49 Nothing is more futile than theorizing about music. No doubt there are laws, mathematically strict laws, but these laws are not music; they are only its conditions... The essence of music is revelation.
1837 *Letters on the French Stage.*

50 *Ich kenn es wohl, dein Missgeschick:*
Verfehltes Leben, verfehlte Liebe!
I know it well, your mishap:
A missed life, a missed love!
1840–4 *Neue Gedichte, Unterwelt*, pt.5.

51 *Dieu me pardonnera. C'est son métier.*
God will forgive me. It is His trade.
1856 Attributed, on his deathbed.

Heinse, Wilhelm 1746–1803

German novelist and art critic, whose work influenced the writers and artists of the Romantic movement.

52 Drawing is only a necessary evil, proportions are easily determined: colour is the goal, the beginning and end of art.
1787 *Ardinghello.*

53 The best subjects for artists, surely, are animals and plants, grasses and trees; these they can represent, but human beings they ought to leave to poets.
1787 *Ardinghello.*

54 Every form is individual, there exists none which is abstract.
Quoted in J J W Heinse *Sämmtliche Werke* (1903–25).

Heisenberg, Werner 1901–76

German physicist, a founder of quantum theory. His 'uncertainty principle' states that it is impossible to determine both the position and momentum of a subatomic particle. He received the 1932 Nobel prize for physics.

55 Natural science does not simply describe and explain nature; it is part of the interplay between nature and ourselves; it describes nature as exposed to our method of questioning.
1959 *Physics and Philosophy.*

56 Unless you stake your life, life will not be won.
1969 *Der Teil und das Ganze*, translated by A J Pomerans as *Physics and Beyond* (1971).

57 An expert is someone who knows some of the worst mistakes that can be made in his subject and who manages to avoid them.
1969 *Der Teil und das Ganze*, translated by A J Pomerans as *Physics and Beyond* (1971).

Heller, Joseph 1923–99

US novelist. He drew on his wartime experience for his black comedy *Catch-22* (1961), which became an international bestseller. Later books include *Something Happened* (1974), *God Knows* (1984) and *Picture This* (1988).

58 He was a self-made man who owed his lack of success to nobody.
1961 Of Colonel Cargill. *Catch-22*, ch.3.

59 He had decided to live forever or die in the attempt, and his only mission each time he went up was to come down alive.
1961 Of Yossarian. *Catch-22*, ch.3.

60 There was only one catch and that was Catch-22, which specified that a concern for one's safety in the face of dangers that were real and immediate was the process of a rational mind. Orr was crazy and could be grounded. All he had to do was ask; and as soon as he did, he would no longer be crazy and would have to fly more missions. Orr would be crazy to fly more missions and sane if he didn't, but if he was sane he had to fly them. If he flew them he was crazy and didn't have to; but if he didn't want to he was sane and had to. Yossarian was moved very deeply by the absolute simplicity of this clause of Catch-22, and let out a respectful whistle.
'That's some catch, that Catch-22,' he observed.
'It's the best there is,' Doc Daneeka agreed.
1961 *Catch-22*, ch.5.

61 'Yossarian? Is that his name? Yossarian? What the hell kind of a name is Yossarian?' Lieutenant Scheisskopf had the facts at his finger tips. 'It's Yossarian's name, sir,' he explained.
1961 *Catch-22*, ch.8.

62 Hungry Joe collected lists of fatal diseases and arranged them in alphabetical order so that he could put his finger without delay on any one he wanted to worry about.
1961 *Catch-22*, ch.17.

63 Frankly, I'd like to see the government get out of the war altogether and leave the whole field to private industry.
1961 Milo Minderbinder. *Catch-22*, ch.24.

64 Success and failure are both difficult to endure. Along with success come drugs, divorce, fornication, bullying, travel, meditation, medication, depression, neurosis and suicide. With failure comes failure.
1975 Interview in *Playboy*, Jun.

65 If Richard Nixon was second-rate, what in the world *is* third-rate?
1979 *Good as Gold*, ch.6.

66 And a man who lay with a beast, said the Lord, would surely die. And if he doesn't lie with a beast, I would have countered, he won't die?
1984 King David. *God Knows*, ch.2.

67 Mankind is resilient: the atrocities that horrified us a week ago become acceptable tomorrow.
1988 *Picture This*, ch.37.

68 I used to joke—and it wasn't much of an exaggeration—that a story I would mail to the *New Yorker* in the morning would be back with its concise, slighting rejection slip in the afternoon mail that same day.
1998 *Now and Then: A Memoir.*

69 There were reviews that were good, a good many that were mixed, and there were reviews that were bad, very bad, almost venomously spiteful, one might be tempted to say (and I am the one that might say it).
1998 Recalling the critical reception to *Catch-22*. In *Now and Then: A Memoir.*

70 Who has?
On being asked why he hadn't written another novel as good as *Catch-22*. Quoted by Peter Guttridge in the postscript of *Now and Then: A Memoir* (1998).

Heller, Walter Wolfgang 1915–87

Chairman of the US Council of Economic Advisers to the President under Kennedy and Johnson (1961–64).

71 An economist is someone who, when he finds something which works in practice, wonders if it will work in theory.
1992 Attributed.

Hellman, Lillian Florence 1907–84

US playwright, whose plays include *The Children's Hour* (1934) and *The Little Foxes* (1939). In 1952 she came before McCarthy's House Un-American Activities Committee. She lived for many years with Dashiell Hammett.

72 That's cynical. [Smiles.] Cynicism is an unpleasant way of saying the truth.
1939 Ben. *The Little Foxes*, act 1.

73 It's an indulgence to sit in a room and discuss your beliefs as if they were a juicy piece of gossip.
1941 Sara. *Watch on the Rhine*, act 2.

74 I do not like subversion or disloyalty in any form and if I had ever seen any I would have considered it my duty to have reported it to the proper authorities. But to hurt innocent people whom I knew many years ago in order to save myself is to me inhuman and indecent and dishonorable.
1952 Letter to John S Wood, 19 May, on being asked to give information for the McCarthy trials. Collected in *US Congress Committee Hearing on Un-American Activities* (1952), pt.8.

75 I cannot and will not cut my conscience to fit this year's fashions, even though I long ago came to the conclusion that I was not a political person and could have no comfortable place in any political group.
1952 Letter to John S Wood, 19 May, on being asked to give information for the McCarthy trials. Collected in *US Congress Committee Hearing on Un-American Activities* (1952), pt.8.

76 That's what you always said, success isn't everything but it makes a man stand straight, and you were right.
1960 Julian. *Toys in the Attic*, act 1.

77 Well, people change and forget to tell each other. Too bad—causes so many mistakes.
1960 Anna. *Toys in the Attic*, act 3.

78 If I had to give young writers advice, I would say don't listen to writers talking about writing or themselves.
1960 In the *New York Times*, 21 Feb.

79 Intellectuals can tell themselves anything, sell themselves any bill of goods, which is why they were so often patsies for the ruling classes in nineteenth-century France and England, or twentieth-century Russia and America.
1967 Journal entry, 30 Apr. Collected in *An Unfinished Woman* (1969), ch.13.

80 It is a mark of many famous people that they cannot part with their brightest hour.
1973 *Pentimento*, 'Theatre'.

81 The English don't raise their voices, Arthur, although they may have other vulgarities.

1973 *Pentimento*,'Arthur W. A. Cowan'.

82 I am suspicious of guilt in myself and in other people: it is usually a way of not thinking, or of announcing one's own fine sensibilities the better to be rid of them.
1976 *Scoundrel Time*.

83 He was getting over a four-day drunk, and I was getting over a 4-year marriage.
1985 On meeting Dashiell Hammett. In the *Christian Science Monitor*, 13 Oct.

Helmholtz, Hermann Ludwig Ferdinand von 1821–94

German scientist and investigator of thermodynamics and electrodynamics. He was Professor of Physics at the University of Berlin.

84 Whoever, in the pursuit of science, seeks after immediate practical utility may rest assured that he seeks in vain.
1862 Lecture at Heidelberg, collected in *Popular Lectures on Scientific Subjects* (1873).

Helmsley, Leona (Mindy) *née Rosenthal* 1920–

US businesswoman. Convicted of tax evasion in 1989, she received a four-year jail sentence, but avoided jail until 1992. She was released in 1994.

85 We don't pay taxes. Only the little people pay taxes.
1989 Remark to a former hotel housekeeper which became a byword of her trial and conviction for tax fraud. Reported in the *New York Times*, 13 Jul.

Héloïse 1101–64

French abbess. At 17 she had a child by her tutor, Peter Abelard. After Abelard was castrated by her family, she entered the convent of Argenteuil, becoming prioress there, and later became abbess at the Paraclete, founded by Abelard.

86 *Et si uxoris nomen sanctius ac validius videtur, dulcius mihi semper exstitit amicæ vocabulum; aut si non indigneris, concubinæ vel scorti.*
If the name of wife seems more blessed or more binding, always sweeter to me will be the word lover, or if I may, concubine or whore.
c.1135 First letter to Peter Abelard.

87 *Non enim quo quisque ditior sive potentior, ideo et melior: fortunae illud est, hoc virtutis.*
To be wealthier or more powerful is not necessarily to be worthier: the former are products of fortune, the latter stems from virtue.
c.1135 First letter to Peter Abelard.

88 *Non enim rei effectus, sed efficientis affectus in crimine est. Nec quæ fiunt, sed quo animo fiunt, æquitus pensat.*
Crime lies not in the deed, but in the doer's intention: it is not what was done, but the spirit in which it was done that justice should consider.
c.1135 First letter to Peter Abelard.

Helpmann, Sir Robert Murray 1909–86

Australian dancer, actor and choreographer. He debuted in Adelaide (1923), studied with Pavlova and in 1931 went to Britain. Star of the new Sadler's Wells Ballet (1933–50), he danced in many films and also acted with the Royal Shakespeare Company. His choreographic work includes *Hamlet* (1942) and *Miracle in the Gorbals* (1944).

89 You see there are portions of the human anatomy which would keep swinging after the music had finished.
c.1968 Disagreeing with the suggestion that there might be a future for nudity in dance. Quoted in Elizabeth Salter *Helpmann* (1978), ch.21. It is sometimes quoted as a comment on the opening night of the musical *Oh, Calcutta!*, as 'The trouble with nude dancing is that not everything stops when the music stops.'

Hemans, Felicia *née Browne* 1793–1835

English poet.

90 The stately homes of England,
How beautiful they stand!
Amid their tall ancestral trees,
O'er all the pleasant land.
1849 'The Homes of England'.
► *See Coward 239:18.*

91 The boy stood on the burning deck
Whence all but he had fled;
The flame that lit the battle's wreck
Shone round him o'er the dead.
1849 'Casabianca'.

Hemingway, Ernest Millar 1899–1961

US novelist, short-story writer and journalist, whose terse prose style was much imitated. He was a legendary figure known for his drinking, big-game hunting, and deep-sea fishing. He won the Nobel prize for literature in 1954. Depressed by his failing powers, he later committed suicide.

92 Switzerland is a small, steep country, much more up and down than sideways, and is all stuck over with large brown hotels built on the cuckoo clock style of architecture.
1922 In the *Toronto Star Weekly*, 4 Mar.

93 A man's got to take a lot of punishment to write a really funny book.
1924 Letter, 6 Dec.

94 God knows people who are paid to have attitudes toward things, professional critics, make me sick: camp-following eunuchs of literature.
1925 Letter to Sherwood Anderson, 23 May.

95 Don't you like to write letters? I do because it's such a swell way to keep from working and yet feel you've done something.
1925 Letter to F Scott Fitzgerald, 1 Jul.

96 Soon I was alone and began cursing the bloody bible because there were no titles in it—although I found the source of practically every good title you ever heard of. But the boys, principally Kipling, had been there before me and swiped all the good ones so I called the book Men Without Women hoping it would have a large sale among the fairies and old Vassar Girls.
1927 Letter to F Scott Fitzgerald, 15 Sep.

97 I did not say anything. I was always embarrassed by the words sacred, glorious and sacrifice and the expression in vain. We had heard them, sometimes standing in the rain almost out of earshot, so that only the shouted words came through, and had read them, on proclamations that were slapped up by billposters over other proclamations, now for a long time, and I had seen nothing sacred, and the things that were glorious had no

glory and the sacrifices were like the stock-yards at Chicago if nothing was done with the meat except to bury it.
1929 Frederic Henry. *A Farewell to Arms*, ch.27.

98 I had the paper but I did not read it because I did not want to read about the war. I was going to forget the war. I had made a separate peace.
1929 Frederic Henry. *A Farewell to Arms*, ch.34.

99 The world breaks everyone and afterwards many are strong at the broken places. But those that will not break it kills. It kills the very good and the very gentle and the very brave impartially. If you are none of these you can be sure it will kill you too but there will be no special hurry.
1929 Frederic Henry. *A Farewell to Arms*, ch.34.

1 I mean grace under pressure.
1929 His definition of 'guts'. Interview with Dorothy Parker in the *New Yorker*, 30 Nov.

2 Hail nothing full of nothing, nothing is with thee.
1932 End of the older waiter's 'nada' prayer. *Winner Take Nothing*, 'A Clean, Well-Lighted Place'.

3 When you have shot one bird flying you have shot all birds flying. They are all different and they fly in different ways but the sensation is the same and the last one is as good as the first.
1932 *Winner Take Nothing*, 'Fathers and Sons'.

4 About morals, I know only that what is moral is what you feel good after and what is immoral is what you feel bad after.
1932 *Death in the Afternoon*, ch.1.

5 Bullfighting is the only art in which the artist is in danger of death and in which the degree of brilliance in the performance is left to the fighter's honor.
1932 *Death in the Afternoon*, ch.9.

6 There is no lonelier man in death, except the suicide, than the man who has lived many years with a good wife and then outlived her. If two people love each other there can be no happy end to it.
1932 *Death in the Afternoon*, ch.11.

7 Madame, all stories, if continued far enough, end in death, and he is no true story-teller who would keep that from you.
1932 *Death in the Afternoon*, ch.11.

8 The great thing is to last and get your work done, and see and hear and understand and write when there is something that you know and not before and not too damn much after.
1932 *Death in the Afternoon*, ch.16.

9 The hardest thing to do is to write straight honest prose on human beings.
1934 'Old Newsman Writes', in *Esquire*, Dec.

10 All modern American literature comes from one book by Mark Twain called *Huckleberry Finn*. American writing comes from that. There was nothing before. There has been nothing good since.
1935 *The Green Hills of Africa*, ch.1.

11 The only time it isn't good for you is when you write or when you fight. You have to do that cold. But it always helps my shooting. Modern life, too, is often a mechanical oppression and liquor is the only mechanical relief.
1935 Of whisky. Letter to Ivan Kashkin, 19 Aug.

12 He remembered poor Julian and his romantic awe of them and how he had started a story once that began, 'The very rich are different from you and me.' And somebody had said to Julian, 'Yes, they have more money.'
1936 'The Snows of Kilimanjaro', in *Esquire*, Aug. In the original version 'Julian' was named as F Scott Fitzgerald, but the pseudonym was used for book publication in *The Fifth Column and Other Stories* (1938).

► *See Fitzgerald 325:3.*

13 'A man…ain't got no hasn't got any can't really isn't any way out… One man alone ain't got…no chance.
1937 Harry Morgan's dying words. *To Have and Have Not*.

14 'Oh,' she said, 'I die each time. Do you not die?'
'No. Almost. But did thee feel the earth move?'
'Yes. As I died. Put thy arm around me, please.'
1940 *For Whom the Bell Tolls*, ch.7.

15 He was just a coward and that was the worst luck any man could have.
1940 *For Whom the Bell Tolls*, ch.30.

16 Cowardice, as distinguished from panic, is almost always simply a lack of ability to suspend the functioning of the imagination.
1942 Introduction to *Men At War*.

17 It wasn't by accident that the Gettysburg address was so short. The laws of prose writing are as immutable as those of flight, of mathematics, of physics.
1945 Letter, 23 Jul.

18 I started out very quiet and I beat Mr Turgenev. Then I trained hard and I beat Mr De Maupassant. I've fought two draws with Stendhal, and I think I had an edge in the last one. But nobody's going to get me in any ring with Mr Tolstoy unless I'm crazy or I keep getting better.
1950 In the *New Yorker*, 13 May.

19 Writing and travel broaden your ass if not your mind and I like to write standing up.
1950 Letter, 9 Jul.

20 All the contact I have had with politics has left me feeling as though I had been drinking out of spittoons.
1950 In the *New York Times*, 17 Sep.

21 A man can be destroyed but not defeated.
1952 *The Old Man and the Sea*.

22 It is because we have had such great writers in the past that a writer is driven out far past where he can go, out to where no one can help him.
1954 Nobel prize acceptance speech, 10 Dec.

23 No classic resembles any previous classic, so do not be discouraged.
1956 Advice to young writers, in *McCall's*, May.

24 Once writing has become your major vice and greatest pleasure only death can stop it.
1958 Interview in the *Paris Review*, Spring.

25 Under the black hat, when I had first seen them, the eyes had been those of an unsuccessful rapist.
1964 Of Percy Wyndham-Lewis. *A Moveable Feast*, ch.12 (published posthumously).

26 I always try to write as good as the best picture that was ever painted.
Quoted in the *Saturday Review*, 9 May 1964.

27 Never confuse movement with action.
Quoted in A E Hotchner *Papa Hemingway* (1966), pt.1, ch.1.

28 Hesitation increases in relation to risk in equal proportion to age.
Quoted in A E Hotchner *Papa Hemingway* (1966), pt.1, ch.3.

29 To be a successful father, there's one absolute rule: when you have a kid, don't look at it for the first two years.
Quoted in A E Hotchner *Papa Hemingway* (1966), pt.2, ch.5.

30 Wearing underwear is as formal as I ever hope I get.
Quoted in A E Hotchner *Papa Hemingway* (1966).

31 My writing is nothing, my boxing is everything.
Quoted in Colin Jarman *The Guinness Dictionary of Sports Quotations* (1990).

Hempstone, Smith 1929–

US journalist, writer and diplomat, Ambassador to Kenya (1989–93). His works include *Africa, Angry Young Giant* (1961) and *Rogue Ambassador: An African Memoir* (1997).

32 If you liked Beirut, you'll love Mogadishu.
1992 To US Marines in Somalia some years after the Corps' losing battle against Kenyan terrorists. Reported in the *Guardian Weekly*, 19 Dec.

33 It will take five years to get Somalia not on its feet but just on its knees.
1992 Reported in the *Guardian Weekly*, 19 Dec.

Henderson, Leon 1895–1986

US economist.

34 Having a little inflation is like being a little pregnant.
Attributed.

Henderson, Sir Nevile Meyrick 1882–1942

English diplomat. He served as Minister to Yugoslavia (1929–35) and as Ambassador to Argentina (1935–7) and to Germany until the outbreak of World War II.

35 When I go to see Herr Hitler I give him the Nazi salute because that is the normal thing. It carries no hint of approval of anything he or his regime may do. And, if I do it, why should you or your team object?
1938 When asked for advice by the England football team in 1938 about giving the Nazi salute before a match in Berlin against Germany. The England team gave the salute, and thereby attracted considerable notoriety at home.

Hendrix, Jimi (James Marshall) 1942–70

US rock guitarist and singer, based in Britain from 1966. Born into poverty, he taught himself guitar and became one of rock music's most innovative and influential instrumentalists before drugs and alcohol caused his death.

36 Purple haze is in my brain
Lately things don't seem the same.
1967 'Purple Haze'.

37 You can't mess with people's heads, that's for sure. But that's what music's all about, messing with people's heads.
Quoted in Nat Shapiro *An Encyclopedia of Quotations about Music* (1978).

Henley, W(illiam) E(rnest) 1849–1903

English poet, playwright, critic and editor. He collaborated with his friend R L Stevenson in four plays. He edited the *Scots Observer* (1889), renaming it *The National Observer*. The best known of his poetry collections is *In Hospital* (1903).

38 In the fell clutch of circumstance,
I have not winced nor cried aloud:
Under the bludgeonings of chance
My head is bloody but unbowed
1888 'Invictus', collected in *In Hospital* (1903).

39 It matters not how strait the gate,
How charged with punishments the scroll,
I am the master of my fate:
I am the captain of my soul.
1888 'Invictus', collected in *In Hospital* (1903).

40 What have I done for you,
England, my England?
1900 'Pro Rege Nostro'.

Henri, Adrian Maurice 1932–2000

English poet, associated with the Mersey poets of the 1960s.

41 Beautiful boys with bright red guitars
In the spaces between the stars.
1967 'Mrs Albion You've Got a Lovely Daughter'.

42 Love is a fanclub with only two fans.
1967 'Love Is…'.

43 I wanted your soft verges
But you gave me the hard shoulder.
1967 'Song of a Beautiful Girl Petrol-pump Attendant'.

Henry II 1133–89

King of England from 1154. He instituted numerous political reforms aimed at diminishing the power of the barons and of the Church.

44 Will no one rid me of this turbulent priest?
1170 Of Thomas à Becket. Quoted in W L Warren *Henry II*, p508. Four of Henry's soldiers took his words to heart and proceeded to Canterbury, where they murdered Becket in the cathedral.

Henry V 1387–1422

King of England from 1413. He won a famous victory against the French at Agincourt in 1415, despite numerical disadvantage.

45 War has three handmaidens ever waiting on her, Fire, Blood, and Famine, and I have chosen the meekest maid of the three.
1418 Comment during the English army's siege of Rouen. Quoted in J R Green *A Short History of the English People*, vol.1 (1915), ch.5, section 6.

Henry VIII 1491–1547

King of England (1509–47). His desire to divorce his first wife, Catherine of Aragon, against papal decree led to ecclesiastical revolution, with Henry as sole head of the Church of England. In all he married six wives. His reign also saw the judicial murder of Sir Thomas More and others who dared to oppose him.

46 We at no time stand so highly in our estate royal as in the time of Parliament, wherein we as head, and you as members, are conjoined and knit together into one body politic, so as whatsoever offence or injury is offered to the meanest member of the House is to be judged as done against our person and the whole

Court of Parliament.
1543 Address to a deputation from the House of Commons, 31 Mar.

Henry, Philip 1631–96

English clergyman.

47 All this, and heaven too!
Quoted in Matthew Henry *Life of Mr Philip Henry* (1698), ch.5.

Henry, Thierry 1977–

French footballer.

48 When you look at other sports, like golf, the players earn a lot more money without running around.
2003 In *The Times*, 31 Dec.

Henryson, Robert c.1425–c.1508

Scottish poet, usually designated 'schoolmaster of Dunfermline', whose surviving poems include *The Testament of Cresseid* (c.1470) and metrical versions of Aesop's fables.

49 For to be yong I wald not, for my wis,
Off all this warld to mak me lord and king:
The more of age, the nerar hevynnis blis.
c.1460 'The Praise of Age', l.5–9.

50 The man that will nocht quhen he may
Sall haif nocht quhen he wald.
c.1460 'Robene and Makeyne', l.91–2.

51 The nuttis schell, thocht it be hard and teuch,
Haldis the kirnell, sueit and delectabill;
Sa lyis thair ane doctrine wyse aneuch
And full of frute vnder ane fenyeit fabill.
c.1470 *Moral Fables*, prologue, l.15–19.

52 Ane bow that is ay bent
Worthis ay unsmart and dullis on the string;
Sa dois the mynd that is ay diligent
In ernistfull thochtis and in studying.
c.1470 *Moral Fables*, prologue, l.21–5.

53 Best thing in eird, I say for me,
Is merry hart with small possessioun.
c.1470 *Moral Fables*, 'The Two Mice', l.387–8.

54 Louers be war and tak gude heid about
Quhome that ye lufe, for quhome ye suffer paine.
I lat yow wit, thair is richt few thairout
Quhome ye may traist to haue trew lufe agane.
c.1470 *The Testament of Cresseid*, l.561–4.

55 Nocht is your fairnes bot ane faiding flour,
Nocht is your famous laud and hie honour
Bot wind inflat in uther mennis eiris.
c.1470 *The Testament of Cresseid*, stanza 65.

Henze, Hans Werner 1926–

German composer. His stage works, often reflecting his socialist commitment, include the operas *Der Junge Lord* (1965) and *The English Cat* (1983). He has also composed orchestral, chamber, vocal and piano music.

56 There is no such thing as an unmusical person.
1969 'Does Music Have to Be Political?'

57 My profession…consists of bringing truths nearer to the point where they explode.
1982 *Music and Politics*.

Hepburn, Katharine 1907–2003

US film and stage actress. She made her professional stage debut in *The Czarina* (1928). Her films included *Bringing up Baby* (1938) and *The African Queen* (1951). *The Lion in Winter* (1968) and *On Golden Pond* (1981) both won her Academy Awards. She was the professional and personal partner of SpencerTracy.

58 The average Hollywood film star's ambition is to be admired by an American, courted by an Italian, married to an Englishman and have a French boyfriend.
1954 In the *Journal American*, 22 Feb.

59 When a man says he likes a woman in a skirt, I tell him to try one.
1994 WETA TV broadcast, Washington, 27 Jun.

60 She gave him sex and he gave her class.
Explaining the success of the Fred Astaire and Ginger Rogers partnership. Attributed.

Hepworth, Dame Barbara 1903–75

English sculptor. She was an important figure in the development of British abstract art.

61 Carving is interrelated masses conveying an emotion: a perfect relationship between the mind and the colour, light and weight which is the stone, made by the hand which feels.
1934 *Unit One*.

62 There is an inside and an outside to every form.
1970 *A Pictorial Autobiography*.

63 My left hand is my thinking hand. The right is only a motor hand.
1970 *A Pictorial Autobiography*.

Heraclitus fl.500 BC

Greek philosopher, born in Ephesus. Only fragments survive of his book 'On Nature', which was written in an aphoristic style.

64 All is flux, nothing is stationary.
c.500 BC Quoted in Aristotle *De caelo*, bk.3, pt.1.18.

65 The path up and down is one and the same.
c.500 BC Quoted in Kirk, Raven and Schofield (eds) *The Presocratic Philosophers* (1957), ch.6.

66 Upon those that step into the same rivers different and different waters flow. They scatter and gather, come together and flow away, approach and depart.
c.500 BC Quoted in Kirk, Raven and Schofield (eds) *The Presocratic Philosophers* (1957), ch.6. Often quoted as 'It is not possible to step into the same river twice', from Plato, *Cratylus* 402a.

67 The world is an ever-living fire.
c.500 BC Quoted in Kirk, Raven and Schofield (eds) *The Presocratic Philosophers* (1957), ch.6.

68 You would not find out the boundaries of the soul, even by travelling along every path: so deep a measure does it have.
c.500 BC Quoted in Kirk, Raven and Schofield (eds) *The Presocratic Philosophers* (1957), ch.6.

69 Education is another sun to the educated.
Fragment quoted in H Diels and W Kranz (eds) *Die Fragmente der Vorsokratiker*, vol.1 (1951), 181, no.134.

70 If you do not expect the unexpected, you will not find it; for it is hard to be sought out, and difficult.
Collected in Charles H Kahn *The Art and Thought of Heraclitus* (1979).

71 The fairest order in the world is a heap of random sweepings.
Collected in Charles H Kahn *The Art and Thought of Heraclitus* (1979).

Herbert, Sir A(lan) P(atrick) 1890–1971

English writer and politician. He was called to the bar but never practised, having established himself as a humorist. His 'Misleading Cases' were accounts of unusual trials, in such collections as *Uncommon Law* (1935). He was an MP (1935–50).

72 Don't tell my mother I'm living in sin,
Don't let the old folks know.
1925 'Don't Tell My Mother I'm Living in Sin'.

73 Don't let's go to the dogs tonight
For mother will be there.
1926 'Don't Let's Go to the Dogs Tonight'.

74 Not huffy, or stuffy, not tiny or tall,
But fluffy, just fluffy, with no brains at all.
1927 Of women. 'I Like Them Fluffy'.

75 Let's find out what everyone is doing
And then stop everyone from doing it.
1930 'Let's Stop Somebody from Doing Something'.

76 As my poor father used to say
In 1863,
Once people start on all this Art
Goodbye, moralitee!
1930 'Lines for a Worthy Person'.

77 Other people's babies—
That's my life!
Mother to dozens,
And nobody's wife.
1930 'Other People's Babies'.

78 Well, fancy giving money to the Government!
Might as well have put it down the drain.
Fancy giving money to the Government!
Nobody will see the stuff again.
1931 'Too Much!'.

79 For Kings and Governments may err
But never Mr Baedeker.
1931 'Mr Baedeker, or Britons Abroad'.

80 Holy Deadlock.
1934 Title of novel.

81 Milord, in that case an Act of God was defined as 'something which no reasonable man could have expected'.
1935 *Uncommon Law*, 'Act of God'.

82 People must not do things for fun. We are not here for fun. There is no reference to fun in any Act of Parliament.
1935 *Uncommon Law*, 'Is it a Free Country?'.

83 The Common Law of England has been laboriously built about a mythical figure—the figure of 'The Reasonable Man'.
1935 *Uncommon Law*, 'The Reasonable Man'.

84 The critical period in matrimony is breakfast-time.
1935 *Uncommon Law*, 'Is Marriage Lawful?'.

85 The Englishman never enjoys himself except for a noble purpose.
1935 *Uncommon Law*, 'Fox-Hunting Fun'.

86 It may be life, but ain't it slow?
1941 'It May be Life'.

87 Nothing is wasted, nothing is in vain:
The seas roll over but the rocks remain.
c.1949 From an operetta, *Tough at the Top*, published in *My Life and Times* (1970), ch.7.

Herbert, George 1593–1633

English metaphysical poet and clergyman. His religious lyrics are collected in *The Temple, Sacred Poems and Private Ejaculations*, published posthumously in 1633.

88 Drink not the third glass, which thou canst not tame,
When once it is within thee.
'The Church-porch', collected in *The Temple, Sacred Poems and Private Ejaculations* (published posthumously, 1633).

89 A broken Altar, Lord, thy servant rears,
Made of a heart, and cemented with tears.
'The Altar', collected in *The Temple, Sacred Poems and Private Ejaculations* (published posthumously, 1633).

90 Avoid, Profaneness; come not here:
Nothing but holy, pure, and clear,
Or that which groaneth to be so,
May at his peril further go.
'Superliminare', collected in *The Temple, Sacred Poems and Private Ejaculations* (published posthumously, 1633).

91 Let all the world in ev'ry corner sing
My God and King.
'Antiphon', collected in *The Temple, Sacred Poems and Private Ejaculations* (published posthumously, 1633).

92 I got me flowers to strew Thy way,
I got me boughs off many a tree;
But Thou wast up by break of day,
And brought'st Thy sweets along with Thee.
'Easter Song', collected in *The Temple, Sacred Poems and Private Ejaculations* (published posthumously, 1633).

93 A servant with this clause
Makes drudgery divine;
Who sweeps a room as for Thy laws
Makes it and th'action fine.
'The Elixir', collected in *The Temple, Sacred Poems and Private Ejaculations* (published posthumously, 1633).

94 Teach me, my God and King,
In all things Thee to see,
And what I do in any thing
To do it as for Thee.
'The Elixir', collected in *The Temple, Sacred Poems and Private Ejaculations* (published posthumously, 1633).

95 Whereas my birth and spirit rather took
The way that takes the town;
Thou didst betray me to a lingering book,
And wrap me in a gown.
'Affliction (1)', collected in *The Temple, Sacred Poems and Private Ejaculations* (published posthumously, 1633).

96 Sorrow was all my soul; I scarce believed,
Till grief did tell me roundly, that I lived.
'Affliction (1)', collected in *The Temple, Sacred Poems and Private Ejaculations* (published posthumously, 1633).

97 I read, and sigh, and wish I were a tree;
For sure then I should grow
To fruit or shade: at least some bird would trust
Her household to me, and I should be just.
'Affliction (1)', collected in *The Temple, Sacred Poems and Private Ejaculations* (published posthumously, 1633).

98 Love bade me welcome: yet my soul drew back;

Guilty of dust and sin.
But quick-ey'd Love, observing me grow slack
From my first entrance in,
Drew nearer to me, sweetly questioning
If I lacked any thing.
'Love', collected in *The Temple, Sacred Poems and Private Ejaculations* (published posthumously, 1633).

99 'You must sit down,' says Love, 'and taste my meat,'
So I did sit and eat.
'Love', collected in *The Temple, Sacred Poems and Private Ejaculations* (published posthumously, 1633).

1 I know the ways of Pleasure, the sweet strains,
The lullings and the relishes of it.
'The Pearl', collected in *The Temple, Sacred Poems and Private Ejaculations* (published posthumously, 1633).

2 King of glory, King of peace
I will love Thee
And that love may never cease,
I will move Thee.
'Praise', collected in *The Temple, Sacred Poems and Private Ejaculations* (published posthumously, 1633).

3 My God, I heard this day,
That none doth build a stately habitation,
But that he means to dwell therein.
What house more stately hath there been,
Or can be, than is Man? to whose creation
All things are in decay.
'Man', collected in *The Temple, Sacred Poems and Private Ejaculations* (published posthumously, 1633).

4 Man is all symmetry,
Full of proportions, one limb to another.
'Man', collected in *The Temple, Sacred Poems and Private Ejaculations* (published posthumously, 1633).

5 O mighty love! Man is one world, and hath
Another to attend him.
'Man', collected in *The Temple, Sacred Poems and Private Ejaculations* (published posthumously, 1633).

6 Who says that fictions only and false hair
Become a verse? Is there in truth no beauty?
Is all good structure in a winding stair?
'Jordan (1)', collected in *The Temple, Sacred Poems and Private Ejaculations* (published posthumously, 1633).

7 I sought out quaint words, and trim invention;
My thoughts began to burnish, sprout, and swell,
Curling with metaphors a plain intention,
Decking the sense, as if it were to sell.
'Jordan (2)', collected in *The Temple, Sacred Poems and Private Ejaculations* (published posthumously, 1633).

8 So did I weave my self into the sense.
'Jordan (2)', collected in *The Temple, Sacred Poems and Private Ejaculations* (published posthumously, 1633).

9 I struck the board, and cried, 'No more.
I will abroad.'
What? shall I ever sigh and pine?
My lines and life are free; free as the road,
Loose as the wind, as large as store.
'The Collar', collected in *The Temple, Sacred Poems and Private Ejaculations* (published posthumously, 1633).

10 Sure there was wine
Before my sighs did dry it; there was corn
Before my tears did drown it.
'The Collar', collected in *The Temple, Sacred Poems and Private Ejaculations* (published posthumously, 1633).

11 My crooked winding ways, wherein I live.
'A Wreath', collected in *The Temple, Sacred Poems and Private Ejaculations* (published posthumously, 1633).

12 The soul in paraphrase.
'Prayer (1)', collected in *The Temple, Sacred Poems and Private Ejaculations* (published posthumously, 1633).

13 O that thou shouldst give dust a tongue
To cry to thee,
And then not hear it crying!
'Denial', collected in *The Temple, Sacred Poems and Private Ejaculations* (published posthumously, 1633).

14 Sweet day, so cool, so calm, so bright,
The bridal of the earth and sky:
The dew shall weep thy fall tonight,
For thou must die.
'Virtue', collected in *The Temple, Sacred Poems and Private Ejaculations* (published posthumously, 1633).

15 Joy, I did lock thee up; but some bad man
Hath let thee out again.
'The Bunch of Grapes', collected in *The Temple, Sacred Poems and Private Ejaculations* (published posthumously, 1633).

16 When God at first made man,
Having a glass of blessings standing by,
'Let us,' said he, 'pour on him all we can:
Let the world's riches, which dispersèd lie,
Contract into a span'.
'The Pulley', collected in *The Temple, Sacred Poems and Private Ejaculations* (published posthumously, 1633).

17 Let him be rich and weary, that at least,
If goodness lead him not, yet weariness
May toss him to My breast.
'The Pulley', collected in *The Temple, Sacred Poems and Private Ejaculations* (published posthumously, 1633).

18 Farewell, sweet phrases, lovely metaphors:
But will ye leave me thus? when ye before
Of stews and brothels only knew the doors,
Then did I wash you with my tears, and more,
Brought you to church well-dressed and clad:
My God must have my best, even all I had.
'The Forerunners', collected in *The Temple, Sacred Poems and Private Ejaculations* (published posthumously, 1633).

19 Throw away thy rod,
Throw away thy wrath:
O my God,
Take the gentle path.
'Discipline', collected in *The Temple, Sacred Poems and Private Ejaculations* (published posthumously, 1633).

20 He that makes a good war makes a good peace.
Outlandish Proverbs (published posthumously, 1640), no.420.

21 Music helps not the toothache.
Jacula Prudentum (published posthumously, 1651). This is probably an older proverb.

22 God's mill grinds slow, but sure.
Jacula Prudentum (published posthumously, 1651).

23 He that will learn to pray, let him go to sea.
Jacula Prudentum (published posthumously, 1651).

Herbert, Xavier 1901–84

Australian writer. His novel *Capricornia* won the Sesquicentennial Literary Prize (1938) and the 1939 Australian Literary Society Gold Medal.

24 Since no normal humble man can help but feel magnificent in a brand-new suit of clothes, it is not surprising that those who don a fresh suit of bright white linen every day should feel magnificent always. Nor is it surprising that a normal humble head should swell beneath a solar topee, since a topee is more a badge of authority than a hat, as is the hat of a soldier.
1938 *Capricornia*, 'Psychological Effect of a Solar Topee'.

Herfindahl, Orris C 1918–72

US economist.

25 Conservation of one resource may entail the sacrifice of another resource which others want to conserve.
1974 *Resource Economics: Selected Writings*, p.6.

Hernández, Felisberto 1902–64

Uruguayan novelist and pianist. He led an obscure life and wrote stories describing banal events with fantastic resolutions. His surrealistic sense of humour paved the way for literary experiments in Latin America and beyond.

26 *Se ha hecho para los vivos y no para los muertos el porqué metafísico y las reflexiones sobre la vida y la muerte, pero no les hace falta aclarar todo el misterio, les hace falta distraerse y soñar en aclararlo.*
Metaphysical questions and reflections on life and death were created for people alive and not for the dead. However, they do not have to solve all mystery; it is enough for them to create some distraction and to dream that they clarify.
1929 *Libro sin tapas*, 'La piedra filosofal' ('The Philosopher's Stone').

Hernández, José 1834–86

Argentinian poet. He had little formal education and was a gaucho (pampas cowboy) in his youth, later becoming a soldier in the civil wars, a newspaper editor and a minor government official.

27 *Yo he conocido cantores*
que era un gusto el escuchar;
mas no quieren opinar
y se divierten cantando;
pero yo canto opinando,
que es mi modo de cantar.
I have known singers
it was a pleasure to listen to;
they amuse themselves singing
and don't care to give opinions;
but I sing giving opinions
and that's my kind of song.
1879 *La vuelta de Martín Fierro*, pt.1 (translated as *Martín Fierro*, 1923).

28 *Hay hombres que de su ciencia*
tienen la cabeza llena;
hay sabios de todas menas,
mas digo, sin ser muy ducho:
es mejor que aprender mucho
el aprender cosas buenas.
There are some men who have their heads
full up with the things they know.
Wise men come in all sizes,
but I don't need so much sense to say
that better than learning a lot of things
is learning things that are good.
1879 *La vuelta de Martín Fierro*, pt.32 (translated as *Martín Fierro*, 1923).

Herodotus c.485 BC–c.425 BC

Greek historian. His *Histories* deal with the wars between the Persians and the Greeks. He is often called 'The Father of History'.

29 In peace, children inter their parents; war violates the order of nature and causes parents to inter their children.
c.440 BC *The Histories of Herodotus*, bk.1, ch.87 (translated by Aubrey de Selincourt).

Herr, Michael 1940–

US journalist and war correspondent. He collaborated on the screenplays of *Apocalypse Now* (1979) and *Full Metal Jacket* (1987).

30 Vietnam was what we had instead of happy childhoods.
1977 *Dispatches*, 'Colleagues', section 3.

31 All the wrong people remember Vietnam. I think all the people who remember it should forget it, and all the people who forgot it should remember it.
1989 In the *Observer*, 15 Jan.

Herrick, Robert 1591–1674

English poet and clergyman, a Royalist who lost his living during the Civil War. His writing, both secular and religious, is collected in *Hesperides* and *Noble Numbers* (both 1648).

32 I write of *Hell*; I sing (and ever shall)
Of *Heaven*, and hope to have it after all.
1648 *Hesperides*, 'The Argument of His Book'.

33 I sing of brooks, of blossoms, birds, and bowers:
Of April, May, of June, and July-flowers.
I sing of May-poles, Hock-carts, wassails, wakes,
Of bride-grooms, brides, and of their bridal-cakes.
1648 *Hesperides*, 'The Argument of His Book'.

34 Is there no way to beget
In my limbs their former heat?
Aeson had (as *Poets* fain)
Baths that made him young again:
Find that *Medicine* (if you can)
For your dry-decrepit man:
Who would but fain his strength renew,
Were it but to pleasure you.
1648 'To His Mistress'.

35 But ah! if empty dreams so please,
Love give me more such nights as these.
1648 'The Vision to *Electra*'.

36 But thou liv'st fearless; and thy face ne'er shows
Fortune when she comes, or goes.
1648 'A Country Life: To His Brother, *M. Tho. Herrick*'.

37 Wealth cannot make a life, but Love.
1648 'A Country Life: To His Brother, *M. Tho. Herrick*'.

38 Soul of my lie, and fame!
Eternal lamp of love! whose radiant flame
Out-glares the Heav'ns *Osiris*; and thy gleams
Out-shine the splendour of his mid-day beams.
1648 'The Welcome to Sack'.

39 'Tis thou, alone, who with thy mystic fan,

Work'st more than Wisdom, Art, or Nature can,
To rouse the sacred madness; and awake
The frost-bound-blood, and spirits; and to make
Them frantic with thy raptures, flashing through
The soul, like lightning, and as active too.
1648 'His Fare-well to Sack'.

40 Let others drink thee freely; and desire
Thee and their lips espous'd; while I admire,
And love thee; but not taste thee. Let my Muse
Fail of thy former helps; and only use
Her inadult'rate strength: what's done by me
Hereafter, shall smell of the lamp, not thee.
1648 'His Fare-well to Sack'.

41 Her legs were such *Diana* shows,
When tuckt up she a hunting goes;
With buskins shortened to descry
The happy dawning of her thigh.
1648 'The Vision'.

42 Get up, get up for shame, the blooming morn
Upon her wings presents the god unshorn.
1648 'Corinna's Going a Maying'.

43 See how *Aurora* throws her fair
Fresh-quilted colours through the air:
Get up, sweet-slug-a-bed, and see
The dew-bespangling herb and tree.
1648 'Corinna's Going a Maying'.

44 So when or you or I are made
A fable, song, or fleeting shade;
All love, all liking, all delight
Lies drowned with us in endless night.
Then while time serves, and we are but decaying;
Come, my *Corinna*, come, let's go a Maying.
1648 'Corinna's Going a Maying'.

45 Gather ye rose-buds while ye may,
Old Time is still a flying:
And this same flower that smiles to day,
Tomorrow will be dying.
1648 'To the Virgins, to Make Much of Time'.

46 Go happy rose, and interwove
With other flowers, bind my love.
Tell her too, she must not be,
Longer flowing, longer free,
That so oft has fetter'd me.
1648 'To the Rose: Song'.

47 Then come on, come on, and yield
A savour like unto a blessed field,
When the bedabbled morn
Washes the golden ears of corn.
1648 'A Nuptial Song, or Epithalamion, on Sir Clipseby Crew and His Lady'.

48 Her eyes, the glow-worm lend thee,
The shooting stars attend thee;
And the elves also,
Whose little eyes glow,
Like the sparks of fire, befriend thee.
1648 'The Night-piece, to Julia', written for his young daughter.

49 When as in silks my *Julia* goes,
Then, then (me thinks) how sweetly flows
That liquefaction of her clothes.
1648 'Upon Julia's Clothes'.

50 A sweet disorder in the dress
Kindles in clothes a wantonness:
A lawn about the shoulders thrown
Into a fine distraction…
A careless shoe-string, in whose tie
I see a wild civility:
Do more bewitch me, than when Art
Is too precise in every part.
1648 'Delight in Disorder'.

51 Where we such clusters had,
As made us nobly wild, not mad;
And yet each verse of thine
Out-did the meat, out-did the frolic wine.
1648 'An Ode for [Ben Jonson]'.

Herriot, James *pseudonym of James Alfred Wight* 1916–95

Scottish-born veterinary surgeon and writer of a series of highly popular novels on the adventures of a country vet.

52 I have long held the notion that if a vet can't catch his patient there's nothing much to worry about.
1976 *Vet in Harness*.

Hersey, John Richard 1914–93

US author, born in China. As Far East correspondent for *Time* magazine, his most famous piece was his eye-witness report in the *New Yorker* (31 Aug 1946) of the bombing of Hiroshima. His novels include *A Bell for Adano* (1944) and *The Walnut Door* (1977).

53 A gifted glassblower of language.
1988 On the British poet and critic I A Richards. In the *New Yorker*, 18 Jul.

Herzen, Alexander Ivanovich 1812–70

Russian political thinker and writer, a revolutionary socialist active in the Paris revolution of 1848. He settled in London (1851), producing propagandist novels and treatises, and smuggling into Russia his journal *Kolokol* (1857–67, 'The Bell').

54 Science, which cuts its way through the muddy pond of daily life without mingling with it, casts its wealth to right and left, but the puny boatmen do not know how to fish for it.
1855 Notebook entry, collected in *Byloe i dumy* (*My Past and Thoughts*), vol.3 (published 1861–7, translated by Constance Garnett, 1924).

55 There are those who prefer to get away *inwardly*, some with the help of a powerful imagination and an ability to abstract themselves from their surroundings…some with the help of opium or alcohol… I prefer shifting my whole body to shifting my brain, and going round the world to letting my head go round.
1861–7 *Byloe i dumy* (*My Past and Thoughts*, translated by Constance Garnett, 1924).

56 There is a certain basis of truth in the fear that the Russian government is beginning to have of communism, for communism is Tsarist autocracy turned upside down.
1861–7 *Byloe i dumy* (*My Past and Thoughts*, translated by Constance Garnett, 1924).

Herzl, Theodor 1860–1904

Hungarian Zionist leader. He graduated in law but wrote essays and plays until the anti-Semitism aroused by the Dreyfus trial (1894) roused him to political action and he convened the First Zionist Congress (1897).

57 Do you know out of what the German Empire arose? Out of dreams, songs, fantasies and black-red-gold ribbons... Bismarck merely shook the tree that fantasies had planted.
Quoted in Carl E Schorske *Fin-de-Siècle Vienna* (1961), p.165.

Herzog, Maurice 1919–

French engineer and mountaineer. He led the French Himalayan Expedition of 1950, which made the first ascent of Annapurna, losing several fingers and toes through frostbite. *Annapurna* was dictated during his subsequent three-year period in hospital.

58 The mountains were there and so was I.
1952 His reason for becoming a mountain climber. Quoted in *Annapurna: Conquest of the First 8000-metre Peak* (1952, translated by Nea Morin and Janet Adam Smith).

59 Annapurna, to which we had gone empty-handed, was a treasure on which we should live the rest of our lives. With this realization we turn the page: a new life begins. There are other Annapurnas in the lives of men.
1952 Quoted in *Annapurna: Conquest of the First 8000-metre Peak* (translated by Nea Morin and Janet Adam Smith).

Heseltine, Michael Ray Dibdin Heseltine, Baron 1933–

British Conservative politician. He was Defence Secretary under Margaret Thatcher, and resigned on the issue of the takeover of Westland Helicopters (1986). Defeated by John Major in the 1990 leadership contest, he became Secretary of State for the Environment (1990–2) and for Trade and Industry (1992–5). He was Deputy Prime Minister from 1995 to 1997 and MP until 2001.

60 It is the only time that I can ever remember the Prime Minister reading out the conclusions of a meeting that did not take place. They were already written before it started.
1986 Of the Cabinet meeting, Jan, on the Westland affair at which he resigned as Defence Minister.

61 I can foresee no circumstance in which I would allow my name to be put forward for the leadership of the Conservative Party.
1990 Said on numerous occasions in the autumn.

62 I am persuaded now that I have a better prospect than Mrs Thatcher of leading the Conservatives to a fourth electoral victory and preventing the ultimate calamity of a Labour government.
1990 On announcing his decision to stand for the leadership, Nov.

63 You can't wield a handbag from an empty chair.
1999 At the launch of 'Britain in Europe', London, 14 Oct.

Hesiod c.8c BC

One of the earliest Greek poets, best known for *Opera et dies* (*Works and Days*), which depicts rural life in archaic Greece, and *Theogony*.

64 Potter is piqued with potter, joiner with joiner, beggar begrudges beggar, and singer singer.
Of a quarrel within a village. *Opera et dies*, 25 (translated by M L West, 1988).

65 The ill design is most ill for the designer.
Opera et dies, 266 (translated by M L West, 1988).

66 Inhibition is no good provider for a needy man, inhibition, which does men great harm and great good, inhibition attaches to poverty, boldness to wealth.
Opera et dies, 317–9 (translated by M L West, 1988).

Hess, Moses 1812–75

German political writer, and an early friend of Marx.

67 Imagine Rousseau, Voltaire, Holbach, Lessing, Heine, and Hegel united in one person—I say united, not lumped together—and you have Dr Marx.
Quoted in A J P Taylor's introduction to the Penguin edition of *The Communist Manifesto* (1967).

Heston, Charlton 1923–

US actor. His major early successes were the Cecil B De Mille films *The Greatest Show on Earth* (1952) and *The Ten Commandments* (1956). He is also remembered for larger-than-life roles in *Ben Hur* (1959, Academy Award) and *El Cid* (1961).

68 I'll give up my gun when you take it from my cold, dead hands.
2000 In his capacity as President of the National Rifle Association, in *The Guardian*, 31 Dec.

Hewart, Gordon Hewart, 1st Viscount 1870–1943

British barrister. He was called to the Bar in 1902 and attended the Paris Peace Conference in 1919 as Attorney General. He was Lord Chief Justice of England (1922–40).

69 Justice should not only be done, but should manifestly and undoubtedly be seen to be done.
1923 Case of *Rex v. Sussex Justices*, 9 Nov.

Hewett, Dorothy Coade *later* Davies *and* Lilley 1923–2002

Australian playwright and poet. Her poetic works include *Windmill Country* (1968) and *Halfway up the Mountain* (2001), and her plays include *The Chapel Perilous* (1971) and *This Old Man Comes Rolling Home* (1976).

70 I had a tremendous world in my head and more than three-quarters of it will be buried with me.
1971 Sally Banner. *The Chapel Perilous*, act 2.

Hewlett, Sylvia Ann

US economist and writer.

71 What we've done in this country in the past few decades is socialize the cost of growing old and privatize the cost of childhood.
1991 In the *Washington Post*, 22 Feb.

Heyerdahl, Thor 1914–2002

Norwegian anthropologist and adventurer, best known for his voyages and journeys, particularly the *Kon-Tiki* and *Ra* expeditions, which reproduced the methods and materials used by early peoples.

72 Just occasionally you find yourself in an odd situation. You get into it by degrees and in the most natural way, but when you are right in the midst of it you are suddenly astonished and ask yourself how in the world it all came about. If, for example, you put to sea on a wooden raft with a parrot and five companions, it is inevitable that sooner or later you will wake up one morning out at sea, perhaps a little better rested than ordinarily, and begin to

think about it.
1948 *The Kon-Tiki Expedition: By Raft across the South Seas* (translated by F H Lyon).

Heyward, Du Bose 1885–1940

US lyricist.

73 Summer time an' the livin' is easy,
Fish are jumpin' an' the cotton is high.
Oh, yo' daddy's rich, and yo' ma is good-lookin',
So hush, little baby, don' yo' cry.
1935 'Summertime' from *Porgy and Bess* (with Ira Gershwin, music by George Gershwin).

74 It ain't necessarily so,
De t'ings dat yo' li'ble
To read in the Bible
It ain't necessarily so.
1935 'It Ain't Necessarily So' from *Porgy and Bess* (with Ira Gershwin, music by George Gershwin).

Heywood, Thomas c.1574–1641

English dramatist, poet and actor. He claimed to have contributed to 220 plays, but much of his work has been lost, including his unpublished 'Lives of All the Poets…'.

75 Content's a kingdom, and I wear that crown.
c.1607 *A Woman Killed with Kindness*, sc.7.

76 That Time could turn up his swift sandy glass,
To untell the days.
c.1607 *A Woman Killed with Kindness*, sc.13.

77 With this kiss I wed thee once again.
c.1607 *A Woman Killed with Kindness*, sc.16.

Hicks, Sir Edward Seymour 1871–1949

English actor-manager and author. A popular light comedian, he appeared in many successful plays written by himself.

78 You will recognize, my boy, the first sign of old age: it is when you go out into the streets of London and realize for the first time how young the policemen look.
Quoted in C R D Pulling *They Were Singing* (1952), ch.7.

Hicks, Sir John Richard 1904–89

English economist, Professor of Political Economy at Manchester (1938–46) and Oxford (1952–65). He laid the foundation of modern welfare economics, and was awarded the Nobel prize for economics in 1972 with Kenneth Arrow.

79 The best of all monopoly profits is a quiet life.
1935 *Econometrica*, 'The Theory of Monopoly'.

80 We ought to define a man's income as the maximum value which he can consume during a week, and still expect to be as well off at the end of the week as he was at the beginning.
1946 *Value and Capital* (2nd edn).

81 Weapons grow rusty if unused, and a Union which never strikes may lose the ability to organise a formidable strike, so that its threats become less effective.
1963 *The Theory of Wages* (2nd edn).

82 There is much of economic theory which is pursued for no better reason than its intellectual attraction; it is a good game.
1979 *Causality in Economics*.

Hickson, William Eward 1803–70

British educator and writer on singing.

83 If at first you don't succeed,
Try, try again.
'Try and Try Again'.

Highfield, Roger

English chemist, science editor of the *Daily Telegraph*.

84 Can Reindeer Fly? The Science of Christmas.
1998 Book title.

85 There is now evidence to suggest that Santa's grotto lies not in icy Lapland, but among Mediterranean olive groves on Gemiler, a tiny island off Turkey.
1998 *Can Reindeer Fly? The Science of Christmas*.

Higley, Brewster d.1911

US songwriter.

86 Oh give me a home where the buffalo roam,
Where the deer and the antelope play,
Where seldom is heard a discouraging word
And the skies are not cloudy all day.
c.1873 'Home on the Range'.

Hill, (Norman) Graham 1929–75

English racing driver. He won the Formula One World Championship in 1962 in a BRM. In 1967 he rejoined Lotus and won the world title for a second time (1968). He retired in 1975 and was killed in an air crash a few months later.

87 It is like balancing an egg on a spoon while shooting the rapids.
On motor racing. Quoted in Colin Jarman *The Guinness Dictionary of Sports Quotations* (1990).

Hill, Joe *originally* ***Joel Hägglund*** 1879–1915

US labour leader and songwriter.

88 You will eat, by and by,
In that glorious land above the sky;
Work and pray, live on hay,
You'll get pie in the sky when you die.
1911 *Songs of the Workers*, 'The Preacher and the Slave'.

Hill, Rowland 1744–1833

English popular preacher. He helped to found the Religious Tract Society and the London Missionary Society, and in 1801 published the popular *Village Dialogues*.

89 I do not see any reason why the devil should have all the good tunes.
Quoted in E W Broome *The Rev. Rowland Hill* (1881), ch.7.

Hillaby, John 1917–96

English writer, naturalist and prodigious walker. He journeyed on foot, usually alone, through Africa, across Europe and across the length of Britain.

90 Walking is a way of being somewhere, rather than striving to arrive.
1964 *Journey to the Jade Sea*.

91 Fortunately for poets and those who like to walk about in the open air, the beauty of landscape is not something that can be reduced easily to basic geology or a few

ready-wrapped phrases about what places are used for. Preference and prejudice creep in.
1968 *Journey through Britain.*

Hillary, Sir Edmund Percival 1919–

New Zealand mountaineer and explorer. He was a member of John Hunt's Everest expedition, and reached the summit with Sherpa Tenzing Norgay on 29 May 1953. He was New Zealand High Commissioner to India (1984–89) and has raised funds to provide hospitals and schools in the Himalayan region.

92 We knocked the bastard off!
1953 On returning from the summit of Everest, Jun. Quoted in his autobiography *Nothing Venture, Nothing Win* (1975), ch.10.

93 Better if he had said something natural like, 'Jesus, here we are.'
1974 Criticizing Neil Armstrong's premeditated words on first stepping onto the moon. Quoted in the *Sunday Times*.
➤ *See Armstrong 30:78.*

Hillebrand, Fred 1893–1963

US musical comedy actor and songwriter. He wrote *Ghosts of Broadway* for television and *Southlands*, an American opera.

94 Home James, and Don't Spare the Horses.
1934 Title of song.

Hillingdon, Lady 1857–1940

95 I am happy now that Charles calls on my bedchamber less frequently than of old. As it is, I now endure but two calls a week and when I hear his steps outside my door I lie down on my bed, close my eyes, open my legs, and think of England.
1912 Journal entry. Quoted in J Gathorne-Hardy *The Rise and Fall of the British Nanny* (1972), ch.3. The phrase is often rendered 'Lie back and think of England'.

Hilton, James 1900–54

English novelist. Several of his books have been filmed, including *Lost Horizon* (1933), *Goodbye, Mr Chips* (1934) and *Random Harvest* (1941).

96 Nothing really wrong with him—only anno domini, but that's the most fatal complaint of all, in the end.
1934 *Goodbye, Mr Chips*, ch.1.

Hindemith, Paul 1895–1963

German composer. His early neo-classical compositions gave way to chromatic works such as *Konzertmusik* (1930–3). His symphony *Mathis der Maler* (1934) was banned by the Nazis and he emigrated to Turkey then Britain, where he continued composing.

97 Tonality is a natural force, like gravity.
1937 *The Craft of Musical Composition.*

98 There are only two things worth aiming for: good music and a clean conscience.
1938 Letter to Willy Strecker.

99 There are only twelve notes. You must treat them carefully.
Quoted in Derek Watson *Music Quotations* (1991).

Hippocrates c.460 BC–c.370 BC

Greek physician, the 'father of medicine', associated with the profession's 'Hippocratic oath'. He practised on Cos. The 'Hippocratic Corpus' is a collection of 72 medical and surgical treatises, but probably not written by him.

1 *Ars longa vita brevis.*
The craft so long [to learn], the life so short.
Quoted in Seneca *De brevitate vitae*, 1. The original was in Greek.

2 Science is the father of knowledge, but opinion breeds ignorance.
The Canon, vol. 4 (translated by John Chadwick).

Hirohito 1901–89

Emperor of Japan during World War II. In 1945 he announced the Japanese surrender in a broadcast to his people and called for their support.

3 We declared war on America and Britain out of Our sincere desire to ensure Japan's self-preservation and the stabilisation of East Asia.
1945 Declaration, 15 Aug. Quoted in Edward Behr *Hirohito* (1989).

4 Endure what is difficult to endure and to suffer what is difficult to suffer.
1945 Declaration, 15 Aug. Quoted in Hugh Cortazzi *The Japanese Achievement* (1990).

5 It was not clear to me that our course was unjustified. Even now I am not sure how historians will allocate the responsibility for the war.
1945 Remark to General Mac Arthur, quoted in Edward Behr *Hirohito* (1989), introduction.

Hirsch, E(ric) D(onald), Jr 1928–

US educational reformer, Professor Emeritus of Education and Humanities at the University of Virginia. His works include *Cultural Literacy: What Every American Needs to Know* (1987) and *The Schools We Need and Why We Don't Have Them* (1996).

6 Cultural literacy is the oxygen of social intercourse.
1987 *Cultural Literacy: What Every American Needs to Know*, introduction.

Hirschfeld, Al 1903–

US artist, theatrical caricaturist for the *New York Times* for over 70 years.

7 I was a sculptor. But that's really drawing—a drawing you fall over in the dark, a three-dimensional drawing.
1988 In the *New York Times*, 21 Jun. 85th birthday interview.

8 The opening-night audience is mostly friends of the cast and backers of the show, and they come to applaud their money.
1988 In the *New York Times*, 21 Jun.

9 Writers who drew, they all seemed to draw the same way. They managed to keep that childlike creativity in their line.
Of Edward Lear and James Thurber. Quoted in Neil A Grauer *Remember Laughter* (1994).

Hirst, Damien 1965–

English painter and installation artist. In 1993 he caused a sensation at the Venice Biennale with his *Mother and Child, Divided*, where a cow and a calf, both sliced in half, expressed the severing of the closest of bonds. He was awarded the 1995 Turner Prize.

10 What I really like is minimum effort for maximum effect.

Like with Picasso's *Bull's Head*—a bike seat and handlebars.
1995 In the *Idler*, 10 Jul.

11 You have to step over the boundaries sometimes just to find out where they are.
2002 Quoted on www.bbc.co.uk, 20 Sep.

12 Sometimes I have nothing to say. I often want to communicate this.
Quoted on www.bbc.co.uk.

Hitchcock, Sir Alfred Joseph 1899–1980

English film director, a master of suspense thrillers. His films include (in Britain) *The Thirty Nine Steps* (1935) and *The Lady Vanishes* (1938), (in Hollywood) *Rebecca* (1940), *Psycho* (1960) and many others.

13 If I made *Cinderella*, the audience would immediately be looking for a body in the coach.
1956 In *Newsweek*, 11 Jun.

14 Television has brought back murder into the home—where it belongs.
1965 In the *Observer*, 19 Dec.

15 The more successful the villain, the more successful the picture.
Quoted in François Truffaut *Hitchcock* (1968).

16 Actors are cattle. Disney probably has the right idea. He draws them and if he doesn't like them he tears them up.
Quoted in Doug McClelland *Star Speak* (1987).

Hitler, Adolf 1889–1945

German dictator, Leader of the Third Reich for 12 years. He was defeated by the Allies in World War II, during which over six million people were killed by the Nazis in concentration camps. He died in a Berlin bunker in 1945.

17 *Die breite Masse eines Volkes…einer großen Lüge leichter zum Opfer fällt als einer kleinen.*
The broad mass of a nation…will more easily fall victim to a big lie than to a small one.
1925 *Mein Kampf* (*My Struggle*, 1939), ch.10.

18 *Wer in Europa die Brandfackel des Krieges erhebt, kann nur das Chaos wünschen.*
Whoever lights the torch of war in Europe can wish for nothing but chaos.
1935 Speech in the Reichstag, Berlin, 21 May.

19 *Ich gehe mit traumwandlerischer Sicherheit den Weg, den mich die Vorsehung gehen heißt.*
I go the way that Providence dictates with the assurance of a sleepwalker.
1936 Speech in Munich, 14 Mar, in Max Domarus (ed) *Hitler: Reden und Proklamationen 1932–1945* (1962), p.606.

20 *Es ist die letzte territoriale Forderung, die ich Europa zu stellen habe, aber es ist die Forderung, von der ich nicht abgehe, und die ich, so Gott will, erfüllen werde.*
It is the last territorial claim which I have to make in Europe, but it is the claim from which I will not recede and which, God-willing, I will make good.
1938 On the Sudetenland. Speech in Berlin, 26 Sep. In Max Domarus (ed) *Hitler: Reden und Proklamationen 1932–1945* (1962), p.927.

21 *In Bezug auf das sudetendeutsche Problem meine Geduld jetzt zu Ende ist!*
With regard to the problem of the Sudeten Germans, my patience is now at an end!
1938 Speech in Berlin, 26 Sep, in Max Domarus (ed) *Hitler: Reden und Proklamationen 1932–1945* (1962), p.932.

Hobbes, Thomas 1588–1679

English political philosopher. He wrote several works on government, and at the exiled English court in Paris wrote his major work, *Leviathan* (1651), combining metaphysics, psychology and political philosophy. In 1652 he returned to England and submitted to Cromwell.

22 Science [is] knowledge of the truth of Propositions and how things are called.
1650 *Human Nature*, ch.6.

23 In Geometry (which is the only science that it hath pleased God hitherto to bestow on mankind) men begin at settling the significations of their words; which…they call Definitions.
1651 *Leviathan*, pt.1, ch.4.

24 Science is the knowledge of consequences and the dependence of one fact upon another.
1651 *Leviathan*, pt.1, ch.5.

25 The value, or worth of a man, is as of all other things, his price; that is to say, so much as would be given for the use of his power.
1651 *Leviathan*, pt.1, ch.10.

26 I put for a general inclination of all mankind, a perpetual and restless desire of power after power, that ceaseth only in death.
1651 *Leviathan*, pt.1, ch.11.

27 Whatsoever therefore is consequent to a time of war, where every man is enemy to every man; the same is consequent to the time wherein men live without other security than what their own strength, and their own invention shall furnish them withall. In such condition, there is no place for industry; because the fruit thereof is uncertain: and consequently no culture of the earth; no navigation, nor use of the commodities that may be imported by sea; no commodious building; no instruments of moving, and removing such things as require much force; no knowledge of the face of the Earth; no account of Time; no Arts; no Letters; no Society; and which is worst of all, continual fear, and danger of violent death; and the life of man, solitary, poor, nasty, brutish, and short.
1651 *Leviathan*, pt.1, ch.13.

28 They that are discontented under monarchy call it tyranny; and they that are displeased with aristocracy call it oligarchy; so also, they which find themselves grieved under a democracy call it anarchy, which signifies the want of government; and yet I think no man believes that want of government is any new kind of government.
1651 *Leviathan*, pt.2, ch.19.

29 A Free Man is he, that in those things, which by his strength and wit he is able to do, is not hindered to do what he has a will to.
1651 *Leviathan*, pt.2, ch.21.

30 The Enemy has been here in the night of our natural ignorance, and sown the tares of spiritual errors.
1651 *Leviathan*, pt.4, ch.44.

Hobhouse, John Cam, 1st Baron Broughton
1786–1869

English statesman. He wrote *Journey through Albania* with Lord Byron (1813), entered Parliament as a radical in 1820, and after succeeding to his baronetcy held several Cabinet posts.

31 It is said to be hard on His Majesty's Ministers to raise objections to this proposition. For my part, I think it no more hard on His Majesty's Opposition to compel them to take this course.
1826 House of Commons, 27 Apr. This is the first recorded use of the term 'His Majesty's Opposition'.

Hobsbawm, Eric (John Ernest) 1917–

English historian, Professor Emeritus at Birkbeck College, London University. He is the author of numerous works of history including *Bandits* (1969) and *The Age of Extremes* (1994).

32 There is not much that even the most socially responsible scientists can do as individuals, or even as a group, about the social consequences of their activities.
1970 In the *New York Review of Books*, 18 Nov.

33 Megalomania is the occupational disease of global victors, unless controlled by fear.
2002 *Interesting Times: A Twentieth-Century Life.*

34 History may judge my politics…readers may judge my books.
2002 *Interesting Times: A Twentieth-Century Life.*

Hobson, John Atkinson 1858–1940

English economist. An unorthodox figure, he believed 'under-consumption' to be the cause of unemployment. His works include an autobiography, *Confessions of an Economic Heretic* (1938).

35 Organised outdoor sports for the old ruling classes.
1902 On militarism and colonialism. *Imperialism.*

Hoby, Sir Edward 1560–1617

English politician.

36 On the 5th November we began our Parliament, to which the King should have come in person but refrained, through a practice but that morning discovered. The plot was to have blown up the King…at one instant to have ruined the whole estate and kingdom of England.
1605 Letter to the British Ambassador to Brussels, describing the Gunpowder Plot, 19 Nov.

Ho Chi Minh *originally* Nguyen That Thanh 1892–1969

Vietnamese political leader, who became President of North Vietnam in 1954. He led his country, first in the independence movement against the French (1946–54) and later in the war against US-backed South Vietnam in the 1960s.

37 Let him who has a rifle use his rifle, let him who has a sword use his sword! And let those who have no sword take up pick-axes and sticks.
1946 Rallying call, Dec. Quoted in J Facouture *Ho Chi-Minh.*

38 It is better to sniff France's dung for a while than eat China's all our lives.
1946 Attributed. Quoted in J Facouture *Ho Chi-Minh.*

Hockney, David 1937–

English painter, photographer, set designer and printmaker.

39 It's a myth that if you're liked by only four people it must be good. It might also be very bad: they might be your mother, your brother, your uncle and your aunt.
1978 *David Hockney.*

40 Art has to move you and design does not, unless it's a good design for a bus.
1988 In *The Guardian*, 26 Oct.

Hodges, Andrew

British mathematician.

41 When the history of science reaches Alan Turing, it hardly feels like history at all.
1987 *Man Masters Nature.*

Hodgson, Ralph 1871–1962

English poet. He published three volumes of Georgian poems, on the themes of nature and England (1907–17). After lecturing in Japan, he settled in the US.

42 Time, you old gipsy man,
Will you not stay,
Put up your caravan
Just for one day?
1917 'Time, You Old Gipsy Man'.

43 I climbed a hill as light fell short,
And rooks came home in scramble sort,
And filled the trees and flapped and fought
And sang themselves to sleep.
1917 'Song of Honour'.

44 I stood upon that silent hill
And stared into the sky until
My eyes were blind with stars and still
I stared into the sky.
1917 'Song of Honour'.

45 When stately ships are twirled and spun
Like whipping tops and help there's none
And mighty ships ten thousand ton
Go down like lumps of lead.
1917 'Song of Honour'.

46 'Twould ring the bells of heaven
The widest peal for years,
If Parson lost his senses
And people came to theirs,
And he and they together
Knelt down with angry prayers
For tamed and shabby tigers
And dancing dogs and bears,
And wretched, blind, pit ponies,
And little hunted hares.
1917 'Bells of Heaven'.

Hoffer, Eric 1902–83

Migratory farm labourer, box factory worker and later longshoreman in San Francisco, who turned to writing social philosophy. His most influential work was *The True Believer* (1951), on mass movements in politics.

47 Where there is the necessary technical skill to move mountains, there is no need for the faith that moves mountains.

1955 *The Passionate State of Mind.*

Hoffman, Abbie 1936–89

US radical activist and writer. In 1968 he helped organize violent anti-Vietnam war demonstrations in Chicago, and was prominent in the 'Chicago Seven' trial in 1969. He was active in public demonstrations until 1986.

48 I always held my flower in a clenched fist.
1980 On his social activism as a 1960s flower child. *Soon to Be a Major Motion Picture.*

Hoffman, Dustin 1937–

US actor. He made his Broadway debut in 1961 and after a modest start achieved fame in the cinema with *The Graduate* (1967). He subsequently won Oscars for *Kramer vs Kramer* (1979) and *Rain Man* (1988).

49 If I'd seen me at a party, I'd never have gone up and met me.
1995 In *Dateline*, NBC TV broadcast, 8 Mar.

Hoffman, Hans 1880–1966

German-born US painter, who emigrated to the US in 1930. His work is characterized by bold, clashing colours.

50 The ability to simplify means to eliminate the unnecessary so that the necessary may speak.
1967 *Search for the Real.*

Hoffmann, Heinrich 1809–94

German physician and children's writer. His character Struwwelpeter is a slovenly, naughty boy who features in a book of cautionary tales written for his four-year-old son. He also wrote poetry, satire and medical works.

51 Augustus was a chubby lad;
Fat, ruddy cheeks Augustus had:
And everybody saw with joy
The plump and hearty, healthy boy.
He ate and drank as he was told,
And never let his soup get cold.
But one day, one cold winter's day,
He screamed out, 'Take the soup away!
O take the nasty soup away!
I won't have any soup today.'
1845 *Struwwelpeter*, 'Augustus'.

52 Look at little Johnny there,
Little Johnny Head-in-Air!
1845 *Struwwelpeter*, 'Johnny Head-in-Air'.

53 The door flew open, in he ran,
The great, long, red-legged scissor-man.
1845 *Struwwelpeter*, 'The Little Suck-a-Thumb'.

Hofstadter, Douglas R(ichard) 1945–

US cognitive scientist and writer, Professor of Cognitive Science and Computer Science at the University of Indiana. His *Gödel, Escher, Bach: An Eternal Golden Braid* (1979, Pulitzer Prize) is a series of ruminations on computers and cognition.

54 Hofstadter's Law: It always takes longer than you expect, even when you take into account Hofstadter's Law.
1979 *Gödel, Escher, Bach: An Eternal Golden Braid.*

Hofstadter, Richard 1916–70

US historian, Professor at Columbia University (1946–70). He applied theories of natural selection and ideology to the study of US capitalism and politics in works such as *The Age of Reform* (1955).

55 The nation seems to slouch onward into its uncertain future like some huge inarticulate beast, too much attainted by wounds and ailments to be robust, but too strong and resourceful to succumb.
Quoted in Hedrick Smith *The Power Game* (1988).

56 It has been our fate as a nation not to have ideologies but to be one.
Quoted in the *New York Times*, 2 Jul 1989.

Hogarth, William 1697–1764

English painter and engraver. He is known for his moral paintings and prints of low life (such as the *Industry and Idleness* series, 1747).

57 Simplicity, without variety, is wholly insipid.
1753 *The Analysis of Beauty.*

Hogg, James 1770–1835

Scottish poet and novelist. The self-taught 'Ettrick Shepherd' divided his time between literary Edinburgh and his native Borders countryside. His best-known work is the psychological novel *The Private Memoirs and Confessions of a Justified Sinner* (1824).

58 Lock the door, Lariston, lion of Liddesdale;
Lock the door, Lariston, Lowther comes on;
The Armstrongs are flying,
The widows are crying,
The Castletown's burning, and Oliver's gone!
c.1810 'Lock the Door, Lariston', stanza 1.

59 'What a wonderful boy he is!' said my mother.
'I'm feared he turn out to be a conceited gowk,' said old Barnet, the minister's man.
1824 *The Private Memoirs and Confessions of a Justified Sinner.*

60 Where the pools are bright and deep,
Where the grey trout lies asleep,
Up the river and o'er the lea,
That's the way for Billy and me.
1831 'A Boy's Song', stanza 1. From *A Poetic Mirror* 1829–31.

Hoggart, Simon David 1946–

English political commentator and broadcaster, political columnist with *Punch* (1979–85) and parliamentary reporter with *The Guardian* (1993–).

61 The nanny seemed to be extinct until 1975, when, like the coelacanth, she suddenly and unexpectedly reappeared in the shape of Margaret Thatcher.
1983 In *Vanity Fair*, Aug.

62 Everything we hear from Buckingham Palace suggests that [the Queen] is surrounded by stupid, blind, stuffy, self-promoting, rivalrous, gin-drinking courtiers, who haven't realised that a modern constitutional Monarch exists no longer by right but by consent and free will.
1997 Following the death of Diana, Princess of Wales. In *The Guardian*, 5 Sep.

63 Peter Mandelson is someone who can skulk in broad daylight.
1998 In *The Guardian*, 10 Jul.

Holiday, Billie 1915–59

US jazz singer. She was one of the most influential singers in jazz, and during the 1940s appeared in several films, although by the end of that decade she was falling victim to drug addiction.

64 Mama may have, papa may have,
But God bless the child that's got his own!
That's got his own.
1941 'God Bless the Child', with Arthur Herzog Jr.

65 People don't understand the sort of fight it takes to record what you want, to record the way you want to record it.
1956 *Lady Sings the Blues*, with William Duffy.

66 You can be up to your boobies in white satin, with gardenias in your hair and no sugar cane for miles, but you can still be working on a plantation.
1956 *Lady Sings the Blues*, with William Duffy.

Holland, Henry Scott 1847–1918

English clergyman and theologian, renowned for his eloquent preaching.

67 Death is nothing at all; it does not count. I have only slipped away into the next room.
1910 Sermon, Whit Sunday.

Hollander, Anne 1930–

US art historian. She explores the connections between fashion and art in *Seeing Through Clothes* (1975) and *Fabric of Vision: Dress and Drapery in Painting* (2002).

68 Dress is a form of visual art, a creation of images with the visible self as its medium.
1975 *Seeing Through Clothes*, ch.5.

Hollinghurst, Alan 1954–

English novelist. His novels include *The Swimming Pool Library* (1988), a highly acclaimed account of gay life; *The Folding Star* (1994); and *The Line of Beauty* (2004).

69 My life was a strange one that summer, the last summer of its kind there was ever to be. I was riding high on sex and self-esteem—it was my time, my *belle époque*—but all the while with a faint flicker of calamity, like flames around a photograph, something seen out of the corner of the eye.
1988 *The Swimming Pool Library*, ch.1.

Holman, James 1786–1857

English naval officer. Although blind from the age of 25 he continued travelling, firstly to the Continent (1819–22), then to the Russian Empire and later to Brazil, South Africa, South Asia, Tasmania, New South Wales and New Zealand.

70 On the summit of the precipice and in the deep green woods emotions as palpable and as true have agitated me as if I were surveying them with the blessing of sight. There was an intelligence in the winds of the hills and in the solemn stillness of the buried foliage that could not be misleading. It entered into my heart and I could have wept, not that I did not see, but that I could not portray all I felt.
1834 *A Voyage round the World*.

Holme (of Cheltenham), Richard Holme, Baron 1936–

British electoral reformer and writer. He represents the Liberal Democrat Party in the House of Lords and was appointed to the Privy Council in 2000.

71 She is the Enid Blyton of economics. Nothing must be allowed to spoil her simple plots.
1980 Of Margaret Thatcher. Speech at the Liberal Party conference, 10 Sep.

Holmes, John Clellon 1926–88

US writer. He is credited with first use of the phrase 'The Beat Generation'. His own novels include *Go* (1952) and *The Horn* (1958).

72 To Walden the saxophone was, at once, his key to the world in which he found himself, and the way by which that world was rendered impotent to brand him either a failure or madman or Negro or saint.
1958 *The Horn*, 'Chorus: Walden'.

73 Jazz music has haunted America for seventy years. It has tempted us out of our lily-white reserve with its black promise of untrammeled joy.
1979 Preface to reprint of *The Horn*.

74 Some books accrete things to themselves like a magnet. The writer risks sterility by subjecting the mysterious power of imagination to the devices of mere comprehension.
1979 Preface to reprint of *The Horn*.

Holmes, Oliver Wendell 1809–94

US physician and writer, who in 1842 discovered that puerperal fever was contagious. His essays in the *Atlantic Monthly* were collected in four volumes, including *The Autocrat of the Breakfast Table* (1857–8) and *The Professor at the Breakfast Table* (1858–9). He also published three novels and several volumes of poetry.

75 Man wants but little drink below,
But wants that little strong.
1848 'A Song of Other Days'.

76 And, when you stick on conversation's burrs,
Don't strew your pathway with those dreadful *urs*.
1848 'A Rhymed Lesson'.

77 They are the brute beasts of the intellectual domain.
1857–8 Of facts. *The Autocrat of the Breakfast Table*, ch.1.

78 A thought is often original, though you have uttered it a hundred times.
1857–8 *The Autocrat of the Breakfast Table*, ch.1.

79 When one has had *all* his conceit taken out of him, when he has lost *all* his illusions, his feathers will soon soak through, and he will fly no more.
1857–8 *The Autocrat of the Breakfast Table*, ch.1.

80 Some of the sharpest men in argument are notoriously unsound in judgment.
1857–8 *The Autocrat of the Breakfast Table*, ch.1.

81 Put not your trust in money, but put your money in trust.
1857–8 *The Autocrat of the Breakfast Table*, ch.2.

82 Build thee more stately mansions, O my soul,
As the swift seasons roll!
Leave thy low-vaulted past!
1857–8 *The Autocrat of the Breakfast Table*, ch.4.

83 Truth is tough. It will not break, like a bubble, at a touch; nay, you may kick it about all day like a football, and it will be round and full at evening.
1857–8 *The Autocrat of the Breakfast Table*, ch.5.

84 Sin has many tools, but a lie is the handle which fits them all.
1857–8 *The Autocrat of the Breakfast Table*, ch.6.

85 Boston State-House is the hub of the solar system. You couldn't pry that out of a Boston man, if you had the tire of all creation straightened out for a crowbar.
1857–8 *The Autocrat of the Breakfast Table*, ch.6.

86 The world's great men have not commonly been great scholars, nor its great scholars great men.
1857–8 *The Autocrat of the Breakfast Table*, ch.6.

87 Talk about those subjects you have had long in your mind, and listen to what others say about subjects you have studied but recently. Knowledge and timber shouldn't be much used till they are seasoned.
1857–8 *The Autocrat of the Breakfast Table*, ch.6.

88 Shabby gentility has nothing so characteristic as its hat.
1857–8 *The Autocrat of the Breakfast Table*, ch.8.

89 Have you heard of the wonderful one-hoss shay
That was built in such a logical way,
It ran a hundred years to a day.
1857–8 *The Autocrat of the Breakfast Table*, ch.11.

90 Nothing is so common-place as to wish to be remarkable.
1857–8 *The Autocrat of the Breakfast Table*, ch.12.

91 Fate tried to conceal him by calling him Smith.
1858 Of Samuel Francis Smith. 'The Boys'.

92 Depart,—be off,—excede,—evade,—erump!
1858 'Aestivation'.

93 We must have a weak spot or two in a character before we can love it much.
1858–9 *The Professor at the Breakfast Table*, ch.3.

94 Apology is only egotism wrong side out.
1858–9 *The Professor at the Breakfast Table*, ch.6.

95 Fashion is only the attempt to realize Art in living forms and social intercourse.
1858–9 *The Professor at the Breakfast Table*, ch.6.

96 A moment's insight is sometimes worth a life's experience.
1857–8 *The Professor at the Breakfast Table*, ch.10.

97 Lord of all being, throned afar,
Thy glory flames from sun and star;
Centre and soul of every sphere,
Yet to each loving heart how near!
1858–9 *The Professor at the Breakfast Table*, 'A Sun-Day Hymn'.

98 It is the province of knowledge to speak, and it is the privilege of wisdom to listen.
1872 *The Poet at the Breakfast Table*, ch.10.

99 To be seventy years young is sometimes far more cheerful and hopeful than to be forty years old.
1879 Letter to Julia Ward Howe, 27 May.

1 The morning cup of coffee has an exhilaration about it which the cheering influence of the afternoon or evening cup of tea cannot be expected to reproduce.
1891 *Over the Teacups*, ch.1.

Holmes, Oliver Wendell, Jr 1841–1935

US lawyer, Professor at Harvard Law School, Justice of the US Supreme Court for 30 years.

2 For the rational study of the law the blackletter man may be the man of the present, but the man of the future is the man of statistics and the master of economics.
1897 'The Path of the Law', in the *Harvard Law Review*, 10:469.

Holroyd, Michael de Courcy Fraser 1935–

English biographer. He is married to the novelist Margaret Drabble.

3 Between history and the novel stands biography, their unwanted offspring, which has brought a great embarrassment to them both.
2002 *Works on Paper: The Craft of Biography & Autobiography*, 'The Case against Biography'.

4 In the historian's view biography is a kind of frogspawn—it takes ten thousand biographies to make one small history.
2002 *Works on Paper: The Craft of Biography & Autobiography*, 'The Case against Biography'.

Holst, Gustav Theodore 1874–1934

British composer, of Swedish origin. Prevented by neuritis in his hand from becoming a concert pianist, he learned the trombone and taught music before establishing himself as a composer.

5 Never compose anything unless the not composing of it becomes a positive nuisance to you.
1921 Letter to W G Whittaker.

Holt, Harold Edward 1908–67

Australian politician. He succeeded Robert Menzies as Prime Minister in 1966 but disappeared while swimming in the sea off Victoria the following year. He was a supporter of US policy in Vietnam.

6 All the way with LBJ.
1966 Speech, Washington DC, Jun.

Holub, Miroslav 1923–98

Czech poet and immunologist.

7 Humankind can generally be divided into hunters and people who cope with consequences.
1990 *The Dimensions of the Present Moment and Other Essays*.

Homans, George C 1910–89

US sociologist, Professor at Harvard University.

8 It is really intolerable that we can say only one thing at a time; for social behavior displays many features at the same time, and so in taking them up one by one we necessarily do outrage to its rich, dark, organic unity.
1961 *Social Behavior: Its Elementary Forms*.

9 The rule of distributive justice is a statement of what ought to be, and what people say ought to be is determined in the long run and with some lag by what they find in fact to be the case.
1974 *Social Behavior: Its Elementary Forms* (rev edn).

Home of the Hirsel, Alec (Alexander Frederick) Douglas-Home, Baron 1903–95

Scottish Conservative statesman. An MP from 1931, he was Chamberlain's secretary during negotiations with Hitler and Mussolini (1937–9). He succeeded as 14th Earl of Home (1951), but after Macmillan's resignation he renounced his peerage and became Prime Minister (1963–4).

10 As far as the fourteenth earl is concerned, I suppose Mr Wilson, when you come to think of it, is the fourteenth Mr Wilson.
1963 Response to Harold Wilson's claim that the democratic process had 'ground to a halt with a fourteenth earl' when Home won the premiership. Reported in the *Daily Telegraph*, 22 Oct.

11 There are two problems in my life. The political ones are insoluble, and the economic ones are incomprehensible.
1964 Speech, Jan.

12 When I read economic documents, I have to have a box of matches and start moving them into position, to illustrate and simplify the points to myself.
1965 *The Making of the Prime Minister.*

13 Fishing is undoubtedly a form of madness but, happily for the once-bitten, there is no cure.
1976 Quoted in Colin Jarman *The Guinness Dictionary of Sports Quotations* (1990).

14 My wife had an uncle who could never walk down the nave of his abbey without wondering whether it would take spin.
In *The Twentieth Century Revisited*, BBC TV programme, 1982.

15 Oh God, if there be cricket in heaven, let there also be rain.
Quoted in Helen Exley *Cricket Quotations* (1992).

Homer 8c BC

Greek epic poet, in antiquity said to have been blind, to whom are attributed the *Iliad* (dealing with episodes in the Trojan War) and the *Odyssey* (dealing with the subsequent wanderings of Odysseus). Scholars now date the poems to the 8c BC, as the culmination of an oral tradition dating back to the Bronze Age.

16 He who battles with the immortals does not live long, nor do his children prattle about his knees when he has returned from battle.
c.700 BC *Iliad*, bk.5, l.407 (translated by Martin Hammond).

17 Like that of leaves is a generation of men.
c.700 BC *Iliad*, bk.6, l.146 (translated by Martin Hammond).

18 Always to be best, and to be distinguished above the rest.
c.700 BC Motto of the hero Glaucus. *Iliad*, bk.6, l.208 (translated by Martin Hammond.

19 Victory switches from man to man.
c.700 BC *Iliad*, bk.6, l.339 (translated by Martin Hammond).

20 One omen is best of all—to fight for your country.
c.700 BC *Iliad*, bk.7, l.243 (translated by Martin Hammond).

21 Tribeless, lawless, homeless is he who loves the horror of civil war.
c.700 BC *Iliad*, bk.9, l.63–4 (translated by Martin Hammond).

22 This is the best portent, to fight in defence of one's country.
c.700 BC *Iliad*, bk.12, l.243 (translated by Martin Hammond).

23 It is no shame for a man to die fighting for his country.
c.700 BC *Iliad*, bk.15, l.496 (translated by Martin Hammond).

24 Tell me, Muse, of the man of many ways, who was driven
far journeys, after he had sacked Troy's sacred citadel.
Many were they whose cities he saw, whose minds he learned of,
many the pains he suffered in his spirit on the wide sea,
struggling for his own life and the homecoming of his companions.
c.700 BC *Odyssey*, bk.1, l.1–5 (translated by Richmond Lattimore).

Homer, Winslow 1836–1910

US painter, known for his watercolours of rural and domestic scenes and especially for his seascapes after 1881.

25 The life that I have chosen gives me my full hours of enjoyment for the balance of my life. The sun will not rise, or set, without my notice, and thanks.
1895 Letter to his brother, Charles, 23 Feb.

26 I regret very much that I have painted a picture that requires any description.
On being asked about the meaning of a painting by a dealer. Quoted by Andrea Bennett in the *New York Times Book Review*, 15 Sep 1991.

Honegger, Arthur 1892–1955

French composer of Swiss descent. One of the group of Parisian composers known as *Les Six*, he established his reputation with the oratorio *King David* (1921). Subsequent works include the dramatic oratorio *Joan of Arc at the Stake* (1936).

27 The modern composer is a madman who persists in manufacturing an article which nobody wants.
1951 *I Am a Composer.*

28 Composing is not a profession. It is a mania — a harmless madness.
1951 *I Am a Composer.*

29 To write music is to raise a ladder without a wall to lean it against. There is no scaffolding: the building under construction is held in balance only by the miracle of a kind of internal logic, an innate sense of proportion.
1951 *I Am a Composer.*

30 The public doesn't want new music: the main thing it demands of a composer is that he be dead.
1951 *I Am a Composer.*

Honorius of Autun fl.1106–35

French ecclesiastic, and the author of numerous philosophical, theological and devotional works.

31 *Universitas in modo citharae sit disposita, in qua diversa genera in modo chordarum sit consonantia.*
The universe is arranged like a cithera, in which different kinds of things sound together harmoniously, just as they do in a chord.
c.1120 *Liber Duodecem Questionum*, ch.2.

32 *Quid confert animae pugna Hectoris, vel disputatio Platonis, aut carmina Maronis, vel neniae Nasonis?*
Of what benefit to the soul are the struggles of Hector, the disputations of Plato, the songs of Virgil, or the dirges of Ovid?
c.1130 *Gemma Animae*, prologue.

Hood, Thomas 1799–1845

English poet and journalist. His collection *Odes and Addresses* (1825) was followed by several volumes of humorous verse and political poems such as 'The Song of the Shirt' (1843).

33 I saw old Autumn in the misty morn
Stand shadowless like Silence, listening
To silence.
1823 'Ode: Autumn'.

34 Ben Battle was a soldier bold,
And used to war's alarms:
But a cannon-ball took off his legs,
So he laid down his arms!
1826 'Faithless Nelly Gray'.

35 For here I leave my second leg,
And the Forty-second Foot!
1826 'Faithless Nelly Gray'.

36 The love that loves a scarlet coat
Should be more uniform.
1826 'Faithless Nelly Gray'.

37 I remember, I remember,
The house where I was born,
The little window where the sun
Came peeping in at morn;
He never came a wink too soon,
Nor brought too long a day,
But now, I often wish the night
Had borne my breath away!
1826 'I Remember'.

38 I remember, I remember,
The fir trees dark and high;
I used to think their slender tops
Were close against the sky:
It was a childish ignorance,
But now 'tis little joy
To know I'm farther off from heav'n
Than when I was a boy.
1826 'I Remember'.

39 She stood breast high amid the corn,
Clasped by the golden light of morn,
Like the sweetheart of the sun,
Who many a glowing kiss had won.
1827 'Ruth'.

40 The sedate, sober, silent, serious, sad-coloured sect.
1839 Of the Quakers. *Comic Annual*, 'The Doves and the Crows'.

41 'Extremes meet', as the whiting said with its tail in its mouth.
1839 *Comic Annual*, 'The Doves and the Crows'.

42 Holland...lies so low they're only saved by being dammed.
1840 *Up the Rhine*, 'Letter from Martha Penny to Rebecca Page'.

43 Home-made dishes that drive one from home.
1841–3 *Miss Kilmansegg and her Precious Leg*, 'Her Misery'.

44 When Eve upon the first of Men
The apple pressed with specious cant,
Oh! what a thousand pities then
That Adam was not Adamant!
1842 'A Reflection'.

45 With fingers weary and worn,
With eyelids heavy and red,
A woman sat, in unwomanly rags
Plying her needle and thread—
Stitch! stitch! stitch!
In poverty, hunger, and dirt.
And still with a voice of dolorous pitch
She sang the 'Song of the Shirt'.
1843 'The Song of the Shirt'.

46 O! men with sisters dear,
O! men with mothers and wives!
It is not linen you're wearing out,
But human creatures' lives!
1843 'The Song of the Shirt'.

47 Oh! God! that bread should be so dear,
And flesh and blood so cheap!
1843 'The Song of the Shirt'.

48 Take her up tenderly,
Lift her with care;
Fashioned so slenderly,
Young, and so fair!
1844 'The Bridge of Sighs'.

49 Mad from life's history,
Glad to death's mystery,
Swift to be hurled—
Anywhere, anywhere,
Out of the world!
1844 'The Bridge of Sighs'.

50 But evil is wrought by want of thought,
As well as want of heart!
1844 'The Lady's Dream'.

51 No sun—no moon!
No morn—no noon
No dawn—no dusk—no proper time of day.
1844 'No'.

52 No warmth, no cheerfulness, no healthful ease,
No comfortable feel in any member—
No shade, no shine, no butterflies, no bees,
No fruits, no flowers, no leaves, no birds,—
November!
1844 'No'.

53 What is a modern poet's fate?
To write his thoughts upon a slate;
The critic spits on what is done,
Gives it a wipe—and all is gone.
'A Joke'. Collected in Hallam Tennyson *Alfred Lord Tennyson* (1897), vol.2, ch.3.

Hooker, Richard 1554–1600

English theologian, writer of an extensive treatise on the basis of Church government, which had a powerful influence on Anglican doctrine.

54 See we not plainly that obedience of creatures unto the law of nature is the stay of the whole world?
1594 *Laws of Ecclesiastical Polity*.

55 Man doth seek a triple perfection: first a sensual, consisting in those things which very life itself requireth either as necessary supplements, or as beauties and ornaments thereof; then an intellectual, consisting in those things which none underneath man is either capable of or acquainted with; lastly a spiritual and divine, consisting in those things whereunto we tend by supernatural means here, but cannot here attain unto them.

1594 *Laws of Ecclesiastical Polity.*

56 They must have hearts very dry and tough, from whom the melody of psalms doth not sometime draw that wherein a mind religiously affected delighteth.

1594 *Laws of Ecclesiastical Polity.*

Hoover, Herbert Clark 1874–1964

US Republican politician. As 31st President (1929–33), his opposition to direct assistance for the unemployed in the recession led to defeat by Roosevelt in 1932. He assisted with various US–European economic relief programmes after World War II.

57 The grass will grow in the streets of a hundred cities, a thousand towns; the weeds will overrun the fields of millions of farms if [tariff protection] is taken away.

1923 Presidential campaign speech, 22 Oct.

58 We are nearer today to the ideal of the abolition of poverty and fear from the lives of men and women than ever before in any land.

1923 Presidential campaign speech, 22 Oct.

59 The American system of rugged individualism.

1928 Speech, New York City, 22 Oct.

60 People moved in hushed and anxious hours while his life lingered on. It was thus I learned that some great man was at the helm of our country.

1951 On President Garfield's assassination, 2 Jul 1881. *The Memoirs of Herbert Hoover*, vol 1.

61 I should have been glad to have humanity forget all about stray alcoholic drinks…but in the present stage of human progress, this vehicle of joy could not be generally suppressed by federal law.

1951 On prohibition. *The Memoirs of Herbert Hoover*, vol.1.

62 All men are equal before a fish.

1951 Quoted in Colin Jarman *The Guinness Dictionary of Sports Quotations* (1990).

63 Democracy is not a polite employer… The only way out of elective office is to get sick or die or get kicked out.

1952 *The Memoirs of Herbert Hoover*, vol.2.

64 The White House…a palace more comfortable than that of most kings.

1952 *The Memoirs of Herbert Hoover*, vol.2.

65 A chameleon on plaid.

On his opponent Franklin D Roosevelt. Quoted in James MacGregor Burns *The Lion and the Fox* (1956).

66 Honour is not the exclusive property of any political party.

1964 In *Christian Science Monitor*, 21 May.

67 Sportsmanship, next to the Church, is the greatest teacher of morals.

Quoted in John Rickards Betts *America's Sporting Heritage: 1850–1950* (1974).

68 Dewey has no inner reserve of knowledge on which to draw for his thinking. A man couldn't wear a moustache like that without having it affect his mind.

Quoted in Richard Norton Smith *An Uncommon Man* (1984).

Hoover, J(ohn) Edgar 1895–1972

US public servant, director of the Federal Bureau of Investigation (1924–72). He remodelled it, making it more efficient, but his vendettas against liberal activists in later years were criticized.

69 We of the FBI are powerless to act in cases of oral–genital intimacy, unless it has in some way obstructed interstate commerce.

Quoted in the *New York Times*, 6 Oct 1980.

70 You are honored by your friends…distinguished by your enemies. I have been very distinguished.

Address to the House Sub-Committee on Appropriations. Quoted in Curt Gentry *J Edgar Hoover* (1991).

Hope, A(lec) D(erwent) 1907–2000

Australian poet and critic. He retired from academic life in 1972 to concentrate on poetry. Works include *The Wandering Isles* (1955), *The Drifting Continent* (1979) and *Orpheus* (1991).

71 Historians spend their lives and lavish ink
Explaining how great commonwealths collapse
From great defects of policy—perhaps
The cause is sometimes simpler than they think.
… Have more states perished, then,
For having shackled the enquiring mind,
Than those who, in their folly not less blind,
Trusted the servile womb to breed free men?

1965 'Advice to Young Ladies', in *Collected Poems 1930–1970* (1972).

72 They call her a young country, but they lie:
She is the last of lands, the emptiest,
A woman beyond her change of life, a breast
Still tender but within the womb is dry.

'Australia', in *Collected Poems 1930–1970* (1972).

Hope, Anthony *pseudonym of* Sir Anthony Hope Hawkins 1863–1933

English novelist. His novel *The Prisoner of Zenda* (1894), a romantic adventure set in fictitious Ruritania, established him as one of the most popular of all Victorian writers.

73 Oh, for an hour of Herod!

1904 On witnessing the first performance of J M Barrie's children's play *Peter Pan*. Quoted in Denis Mackail *Story of JMB* (1941), ch.17. Records exist of something similar having been said by the English actress Dorothea Jordan when watching the child actor William Betty and his imitators in the early 19c.

Hope, Bob *originally* Leslie Townes Hope 1903–2003

English-born US actor and humorist. With Bing Crosby and Dorothy Lamour he appeared in the successful *Road to…* comedies (1940–52). An entertainer of troops in World War II and a noted golfer and humanitarian, he became a show-business institution.

74 If you watch a game, it's fun. If you play it, it's recreation. If you work at it, it's golf.

Quoted in the *Reader's Digest*, Oct 1958.

75 I don't know what people have got against Jimmy Carter. He's done nothing.

1980 Campaign speech for Ronald Reagan, 2 Nov.

76 Fish don't applaud.

1989 When asked why he didn't retire and go fishing, in the *New York Times*, 28 Sep.

Hopkins, Sir Anthony 1937–

Welsh-born US film and stage actor.

77 I always check the last page of the script to see if I'm on it.

I have a bit of an ego, you know.
1997 In the *Toronto Sun*, 24 Sep.

Hopkins, Gerard Manley 1844–89

English poet and Jesuit priest. His work is characterized by religious subjects and the use of natural imagery. His poems include 'The Wreck of the Deutschland' (1876), 'Pied Beauty' (1877) and 'The Windhover' (1877). His poetry was written in secret, only published 30 years after his death.

78 I have desired to go
Where springs not fail,
To fields where flies no sharp and sided hail
And a few lilies blow
And I have asked to be
Where no storms come,
Where the green swell is in the havens dumb,
And out of the swing of the sea.
1864 'Heaven-Haven'.

79 Crystal sincerity hath found no shelter but in a fool's cap.
1864 'Floris in Italy'. Collected in H House and G Storey (eds) *The Journals and Papers of Gerard Manley Hopkins* (1959), p.42.

80 Elected Silence, sing to me
And beat upon my whorled ear,
Pipe me to pastures still and be
The music that I care to hear.
1866 'The Habit of Perfection'.

81 Palate, the hutch of tasty lust,
Desire not to be rinsed with wine:
The can must be so sweet, the crust
So fresh that come in fasts divine!
1866 'The Habit of Perfection'.

82 I did say yes
O at lightning and lashed rod;
Thou heardst me truer than tongue confess
Thy terror, O Christ, O God.
1876 'The Wreck of the Deutschland', pt.1, stanza 2.

83 The world is charged with the grandeur of God.
It will flame out like shining from shook foil…
Generations have trod, have trod, have trod;
And all is seared with trade; bleared, smeared with toil;
And wears man's smudge and shares man's smell: the soil
Is bare now, nor can foot feel, being shod.
1877 'God's Grandeur'.

84 Because the Holy Ghost over the bent
World broods with warm breast and with ah! bright wings.
1877 'God's Grandeur'.

85 Glory be to God for dappled things.
1877 'Pied Beauty'.

86 All things counter, original, spare, strange;
Whatever is fickle, freckled (who knows how?)
With swift, slow; sweet, sour; adazzle, dim;
He fathers-forth whose beauty is past change:
Praise him.
1877 'Pied Beauty'.

87 The glassy peartree leaves and blooms, they brush
The descending blue; that blue is all in a rush
With richness.
1877 'Spring'.

88 Look at the stars! look, look up at the skies!
O look at all the fire-folk sitting in the air!
The bright boroughs, the circle-citadels there!
1877 'The Starlight Night'.

89 I caught this morning morning's minion, kingdom of
Daylight's dauphin, dapple-dawn-drawn Falcon.
1877 'The Windhover'.

90 My heart in hiding
Stirred for a bird,—the achieve of, the mastery of the thing!
1877 'The Windhover'.

91 Towery city and branchy between towers;
Cuckoo-echoing, bell-swarmèd, lark-charmèd, rook-racked, river-rounded.
1879 Of Oxford. 'Duns Scotus's Oxford', published 1918.

92 Ten or twelve, only ten or twelve
Strokes of havoc unselve
The sweet especial scene
Rural scene, a rural scene
Sweet especial rural scene.
1879 'Binsey Poplars'.

93 Margaret, are you grieving
Over Goldengrove unleaving?
1880 'Spring and Fall: to a young child'.

94 Ah! as the heart grows older
It will come to such sights colder
By and by, not spare a sigh
Though worlds of wanwood leafmeal lie;
And yet you *will* weep and know why.
1880 'Spring and Fall: to a young child'.

95 It is the blight man was born for,
It is Margaret you mourn for.
1880 'Spring and Fall: to a young child'.

96 I can scarcely fancy myself to ask a superior to publish a volume of my verse and I own that humanly there is very little likelihood of that ever coming to pass. And to be sure if I chose to look at things on one side and not the other I could of course regret this bitterly. But there is more peace and it is the holier lot to be unknown than to be known.
1881 Letter to Richard Watson Dixon, 29 Oct. Collected in C C Abbott (ed) *The Correspondence of Gerard Manley Hopkins and Richard Watson Dixon* (1935).

97 What would the world be, once bereft
Of wet and wildness? Let them be left,
O let them be left, wildness and wet;
Long live the weeds and the wilderness yet.
1881 'Inversnaid'.

98 Time has three dimensions and one positive pitch or direction. It is therefore not so much like any river or any sea as like the Sea of Galilee, which has the Jordan running through it and giving a current to the whole.
1881 'Creation and Redemption: The Great Sacrifice'. Collected in C Devlin (ed) *The Sermons and Devotional Writings of Gerard Manley Hopkins* (1959), ch.8.

99 God…is so great that all things give him glory if you mean they should.
1882 'The Principle or Foundation', closing words. Collected in G Roberts (ed) *Gerard Manley Hopkins. Selected Prose* (1980).

1 Wild air, world-mothering air,
Nestling me everywhere.
1883 'The Blessed Virgin Compared to the Air We Breathe'.

2 Not, I'll not, carrion comfort, Despair, not feast on thee;

Not untwist—slack they may be—these last strands of man
In me or, most weary, cry *I can no more*. I can;
Can something, hope, wish day come, not choose not to be.
1885 'Carrion Comfort'.

3 That night, that year
Of now done darkness I wretch lay wrestling with (my God!) my God.
1885 'Carrion Comfort'.

4 No worst, there is none. Pitched past pitch of grief,
More pangs will, schooled at forepangs, wilder wring.
Comforter, where, where is your comforting?
1885 'No worst, there is none'.

5 O the mind, mind has mountains; cliffs of fall
Frightful, sheer, no-man-fathomed. Hold them cheap
May who ne'er hung there.
1885 'No worst, there is none'.

6 Here! creep,
Wretch, under a comfort serves in a whirlwind: all
Life death does end and each day dies with sleep.
1885 'No worst, there is none'.

7 The fine pleasure is not to do a thing but to feel that you could… If I could but get on, if I could but produce a work I should not mind its being buried, silenced, and going no further; but it kills me to be time's eunuch and never to beget.
1885 Letter to Robert Bridges, 1 Sep. Collected in C C Abbott (ed) *The Correspondence of Gerard Manley Hopkins and Robert Bridges* (1935).

8 I am all at once what Christ is, since he was what I am, and
This Jack, joke, poor potsherd, patch, matchwood, immortal diamond,
Is immortal diamond.
1888 'That Nature is a Heraclitean Fire'.

9 Thou art indeed just, Lord, if I contend
With thee; but, sir, so what I plead is just.
Why do sinners' ways prosper? and why must
Disappointment all I endeavour end?
1889 'Thou art indeed just, Lord'.

10 Birds build—but not I build; no, but strain,
Time's eunuch, and not breed one work that wakes.
Mine, O thou lord of life, send my roots rain.
1889 'Thou art indeed just, Lord'.

11 The male quality is the creative gift.
Quoted in C C Abbott (ed) *Correspondence of Gerard Manley Hopkins and Richard Watson Dixon* (1935).

12 I always knew in my heart Walt Whitman's mind to be more like my own than any other man's living.
Quoted in Denis Donoghue *England, Their England* (1988).

Hopkins, J Castell 1864–1923

Canadian editor and writer.

13 Canada only needs to be known in order to be great.
1901 *The Story of the Dominion*, preface.

Hopper, Edward 1882–1967

US painter, known for his haunting, atmospheric paintings of empty streets and houses. His works include *Early Sunday Morning* (1930).

14 A nation's art is greatest when it most reflects the character of its people.
Quoted in Anatole Broyard *Aroused by Books* (1974).

15 It's probably a reflection of my own, if I may say, loneliness. I don't know. It could be the whole human condition.
On the mood and content of his paintings. Quoted in the *Washington Post*, 25 Jun 1995.

Hopper, Grace Murray 1906–92

US computer scientist and naval officer, developer of the Cobol computer language.

16 Life was simple before World War II. After that, we had systems.
Quoted in the OCLC Newsletter, no.167, Mar/Apr 1987.

17 We've tended to forget that no computer will ever ask a new question.
Quoted in the OCLC Newsletter, no.167, Mar/Apr 1987.

18 A ship in port is safe but that's not what ships are built for.
1987 Address at Trinity College, Washington. Reported in *Time*, 22 Jun.

Horace *full name* ***Quintus Horatius Flaccus*** 65 BC–8 BC

Roman poet of the Augustan age. His works, which survive in their entirety, include the *Satires* (c.35 BC), *Odes* (c.23–13 BC), *Epistles* (c.19 BC) and the *Ars Poetica* (c.19 BC). His poetry is characterized by an urbane sociability and a love of the country.

19 *Carpe diem.*
Seize the day.
Odes, bk.1, no.11, l.8.

20 *Nunc est bibendum!*
Now is the time to drink!
Odes, bk.1, no.37, l.1.

21 *Eheu fugaces, Postume, Postume,*
labuntur anni.
Oh, my Postumus, Postumus, the fleeting years are slipping by.
Odes, bk.2, no.14, l.1–2.

22 *Odi profanum vulgus et arceo;*
Favete linguis; carmina non prius
Audita Musarum sacerdos
Virginibus puerisque canto.
I despise the uninitiated mob and I warn them off: keep your tongues well-omened; I, priest of the Muses, am singing songs, never heard before, to girls and boys.
Odes, bk.3, no.1, l.1–4 (translated by G Williams).

23 *Dulce et decorum est pro patria mori.*
It is a sweet and seemly thing to die for one's country.
Odes, bk.3, no.2, l.13.
► *See Owen 632:57.*

24 *Exegi monumentum, aere perennius.*
I have completed a memorial more lasting than bronze.
Odes, bk.3, no.30, l.1.

25 *Vixere fortes ante Agamemnona*
Multi; sed omnes illacrimabiles
Urgentur ignotique longa
Nocte, carent quia vate sacro.
Many brave men lived before Agamemnon's time; but

they are all unmourned and unknown, covered by the long night, because they lack their sacred poet.
Odes, bk.4, no.9, l.25–8.

26 *Dulce est desipere in loco.*
Frivolity is sweet, at the right time.
Odes, bk.4, no.12, l.28.

27 *Quo semel est imbuta recens servabit odorem testa diu.*
The first scent you pour in a jar lasts for years.
Epistulae, bk.1, no.2, l.69.

28 *Concordia discors.*
Harmony in discord.
Epistulae, bk.1, no.12, l.7.

29 *Graecia capta ferum victorem cepit et artes*
Intulit agresti Latio.
Captive Greece overcame her savage conqueror and brought the arts into rustic Latium.
Epistulae, bk.2, no.1, l.156–7.

30 *Brevis esse laboro, Obscurus fio.*
I try hard to be succinct, and am merely obscure.
Ars Poetica, l.25–6.

31 *Si vis me flere, dolendum est Primum ipse tibi.*
If you wish me to shed tears you must first feel pain yourself.
Ars Poetica, l.102–3.

32 *Parturiunt montes; nascetur ridiculus mus.*
The mountains are in labour, and there will be born an absurd little mouse.
Ars Poetica, l.139.

33 *Omne tulit punctum, qui miscuit utile dulci.*
The man who has mixed profit with pleasure wins everyone's approval.
Ars Poetica, l.343.

34 *Indignor quandoque bonus dormitat Homerus.*
I am vexed when the worthy Homer nods.
Ars Poetica, l.359.

35 *Est modus in rebus.*
There is a measure in things.
Satirae, bk.1, no.1, l.106.

Horner, Jack 1946–

Curator of Palaeontology, Museum of the Rockies.

36 In the lifetime of one person, we went from figuring out where we came from to figuring out how to get rid of ourselves.
1993 On the 80-year period from Darwin's *Origin of Species* to the first nuclear bomb. In *Time*, 26 Apr.

Hornung, E(rnest) W(illiam) 1866–1921

English novelist. Brother-in-law of Arthur Conan Doyle, he created Raffles the gentleman burglar, hero of *The Amateur Cracksman* (1899), *Mr Justice Raffles* (1909) and many other adventure stories.

37 'Cricket,' said Raffles, 'like everything else, is a good enough sport until you discover a better. As a source of excitement it isn't in it with other things you wot of Bunny, and the involuntary comparison becomes a bore. What's the satisfaction of taking a man's wicket when you want his spoons?'
1899 *The Amateur Cracksman.*

Horsley, Samuel 1733–1806

English prelate, most famous for his theological controversy (1783–9) with Joseph Priestley over the uncreated divinity of Christ. He published several scientific works.

38 In *this* country, my Lords…the individual subject…has nothing to do with the laws but to obey them.
1795 Speech in the House of Lords, 13 Nov.

Hoskins, Bob 1942–

English actor.

39 It's good to talk.
1996 Advertising slogan for British Telecom.

Houllier, Gerard 1947–

French football manager. He was appointed joint manager at Liverpool in 1998, later becoming sole manager (1999–2004).

40 It used to be the rat race. Now it's the sack race.
2004 On being a football manager. In *The Guardian*, 1 Mar.

Housman, A(lfred) E(dward) 1859–1936

English scholar and poet. He was a distinguished classical scholar, and is known primarily for his poetry, particularly *A Shropshire Lad* (1896), an anti-pastoral view of country life which was widely popular after an initially cool reception.

41 Loveliest of trees, the cherry now
Is hung with bloom along the bough,
And stands about the woodland ride
Wearing white for Eastertide.
1896 *A Shropshire Lad*, no.2.

42 Now, of my threescore years and ten,
Twenty will not come again,
And take from seventy springs a score,
It only leaves me fifty more.
1896 *A Shropshire Lad*, no.2.

43 And since to look at things in bloom
Fifty springs are little room,
About the woodlands I will go
To see the cherry hung with snow.
1896 *A Shropshire Lad*, no.2.

44 Clay lies still, but blood's a rover;
Breath's a ware that will not keep.
Up, lad: when the journey's over
There'll be time enough to sleep.
1896 *A Shropshire Lad*, no.4.

45 And naked to the hangman's noose
The morning clocks will ring
A neck God made for other use
Than strangling in a string.
1896 *A Shropshire Lad*, no.9.

46 When I was one-and-twenty
I heard a wise man say,
'Give crowns and pounds and guineas
But not your heart away;
Give pearls away and rubies,
But keep your fancy free.'
But I was one-and-twenty
No use to talk to me.
1896 *A Shropshire Lad*, no.13.

47 Oh, when I was in love with you,

Then I was clean and brave,
And miles around the wonder grew
How well I did behave.
1896 *A Shropshire Lad*, no.18.

48 And now the fancy passes by,
And nothing will remain,
And miles around they'll say that I
Am quite myself again.
1896 *A Shropshire Lad*, no.18.

49 And silence sounds no worse than cheers
After dying has stopped the ears.
1896 *A Shropshire Lad*, no.19.

50 Twice a week the winter through
Here I stood to keep the goal:
Football then was fighting sorrow
For the young man's soul.
1896 *A Shropshire Lad*, no.21.

51 In summertime in Bredon
The bells they sound so clear;
Round both the shires they ring them
In steeples far and near,
A happy noise to hear.
1896 *A Shropshire Lad*, no.21.

52 Here of a Sunday morning
My love and I would lie,
And see the coloured counties,
And hear the larks so high
About us in the sky.
1896 *A Shropshire Lad*, no.21.

53 'Come all to church, good people,'—
Oh, noisy bells, be dumb;
I hear you, I will come.
1896 *A Shropshire Lad*, no.21.

54 The lads in their hundreds to Ludlow come in for the fair,
There's men from the barn and the forge and the mill and the fold,
The lads for the girls and the lads for the liquor are there,
And there with the rest are lads that will never be old.
1896 *A Shropshire Lad*, no.23.

55 On Wenlock Edge the wood's in trouble;
His forest fleece the Wrekin heaves;
The wind it plies the saplings double,
And thick on Severn snow the leaves.
1896 *A Shropshire Lad*, no.31.

56 The gale, it plies the saplings double,
It blows so hard, 'twill soon be gone:
To-day the Roman and his trouble
Are ashes under Uricon.
1896 *A Shropshire Lad*, no.31.

57 From far, from eve and morning
And yon twelve-winded sky,
The stuff of life to knit me
Blew hither: here am I.
1896 *A Shropshire Lad*, no.32.

58 Speak now, and I will answer;
How shall I help you, say;
Ere to the wind's twelve quarters
I take my endless way.
1896 *A Shropshire Lad*, no.32.

59 Into my heart an air that kills
From yon far country blows:
What are those blue remembered hills,
What spires, what farms are those?
1896 *A Shropshire Lad*, no.40.

60 That is the land of lost content,
I see it shining plain,
The happy highways where I went
And cannot come again.
1896 *A Shropshire Lad*, no.40.

61 And bound for the same bourn as I,
On every road I wandered by,
Trod beside me, close and dear,
The beautiful and death-struck year.
1896 *A Shropshire Lad*, no.41.

62 Clunton and Clunbury,
Clungunford and Clun,
Are the quietest places
Under the sun.
1896 *A Shropshire Lad*, no.50, epigraph.

63 With rue my heart is laden
For golden friends I had,
For many a rose-lipt maiden
And many a lightfoot lad.
1896 *A Shropshire Lad*, no.54.

64 By brooks too broad for leaping
The lightfoot boys are laid;
The rose-lipt girls are sleeping
In fields where roses fade.
1896 *A Shropshire Lad*, no.54.

65 Say, for what were hop-yards meant,
Or why was Burton built on Trent?
Oh many a peer of England brews
Livelier liquor than the Muse,
And malt does more than Milton can
To justify God's ways to man.
Ale, man, ale's the stuff to drink
For fellows whom it hurts to think.
1896 *A Shropshire Lad*, no.62.

66 Oh I have been to Ludlow fair
And left my necktie God knows where,
And carried half-way home, or near,
Pints and quarts of Ludlow beer.
1896 *A Shropshire Lad*, no.62.

67 Then the world seemed none so bad,
And I myself a sterling lad;
And down in lovely muck I've lain,
Happy till I woke again.
1896 *A Shropshire Lad*, no.62.

68 I tell the tale that I heard told.
Mithridates, he died old.
1896 *A Shropshire Lad*, no.62.

69 This great College, of this ancient University, has seen some strange sights. It has seen Wordsworth drunk and Porson sober. And here am I, a better poet than Porson, and a better scholar than Wordsworth, betwixt and between.
1911 Speech on taking up the Chair of Latin at Trinity College, Cambridge.

70 Pass me the can, lad; there's an end of May.
1922 *Last Poems*, no.9.

71 May will be fine next year as like as not:
Oh, ay, but then we shall be twenty-four.
1922 *Last Poems*, no.9.

72 We for a certainty are not the first
Have sat in taverns while the tempest hurled
Their hopeful plans to emptiness, and cursed
Whatever brute and blackguard made the world.
1922 *Last Poems*, no.9.

73 The troubles of our proud and angry dust
Are from eternity, and shall not fail.
Bear them we can, and if we can we must.
Shoulder the sky, my lad, and drink your ale.
1922 *Last Poems*, no.9.

74 But men at whiles are sober
And think by fits and starts,
And if they think, they fasten
Their hands upon their hearts.
1922 *Last Poems*, no.10.

75 The laws of God, the laws of man,
He may keep that will and can;
Not I: let God and man decree
Laws for themselves and not for me;
And if my ways are not as theirs
Let them mind their own affairs.
1922 *Last Poems*, no.12.

76 And how am I to face the odds
Of man's bedevilment and God's?
I, a stranger and afraid
In a world I never made.
1922 *Last Poems*, no.12.

77 The candles burn their sockets,
The blinds let through the day,
The young man feels his pockets
And wonders what's to pay.
1922 *Last Poems*, no.21.

78 To think that two and two are four
And neither five nor three
The heart of man has long been sore
And long 'tis like to be.
1922 *Last Poems*, no.35.

79 These, in the day when heaven was falling,
The hour when earth's foundations fled,
Followed their mercenary calling
And took their wages and are dead.
1922 *Last Poems*, no.37, 'Epitaph on an Army of Mercenaries'.

80 Their shoulders held the sky suspended;
They stood, and earth's foundations stay;
What God abandoned, these defended,
And saved the sum of things for pay.
1922 *Last Poems*, no.37, 'Epitaph on an Army of Mercenaries'.

81 For nature, heartless, witless nature,
Will neither care nor know
What stranger's feet may find the meadow
And trespass there and go,
Nor ask amid the dews of morning
If they are mine or no.
1922 *Last Poems*, no.40.

82 Experience has taught me, when I am shaving of a morning, to keep watch over my thoughts, because, if a line of poetry strays into my memory, my skin bristles so that the razor ceases to act.
1933 'The Name and Nature of Poetry', Lecture at Cambridge, 9 May.

83 The seat of this sensation is the pit of the stomach.
1933 'The Name and Nature of Poetry', Lecture at Cambridge, 9 May.

84 The stroke of midnight ceases,
And I lie down alone.
1936 *More Poems*, no.11.

85 Life, to be sure, is nothing much to lose;
But young men think it is, and we were young.
1936 *More Poems*, no.36.

86 Good-night. Ensured release
Imperishable peace,
Have these for yours,
While earth's foundations stand
And sky and sea and land
And heaven endures.
1936 *More Poems*, no.48.

87 That is indeed very good. I shall have to repeat that on the Golden Floor!
1936 Remark made to his doctor after the latter had told him a risqué story on his deathbed.

88 The Grizzly bear is huge and wild;
He has devoured the infant child.
The infant child is not aware
He has been eaten by the bear.
'Infant Innocence', collected *The Oxford Book of Light Verse* (1938).

89 Oh who is that young sinner with the handcuffs on his wrist?
And what has he been after that they groan and shake their fists?
And wherefore is he wearing such a conscience-stricken air?
Oh they're taking him to prison for the colour of his hair.
'Additional Poems', no.18, in *Collected Poems* (1939).

90 'Tis a shame to human nature, such a head of hair as his;
In the good old time 'twas hanging for the colour that it is;
Though hanging isn't bad enough and flaying would be fair
For the nameless and abominable colour of his hair.
'Additional Poems', no.18, in *Collected Poems* (1939).

91 Now hollow fires burn out to black
And lamps are guttering low.
Square your shoulders, lift your pack,
And leave your friends and go.

Oh, never fear, man, nought's to dread
Look not left nor right.
In all the endless road you tread,
There's nothing but the night.
Quoted in Bernard Levin *Hannibal's Footsteps* (1985).

How, William Walsham 1823–97

English churchman and religious writer, the first Bishop of Wakefield.

92 For all the Saints who from their labours rest,
Who Thee by faith before the world confess'd,
Thy name, O Jesu, be for ever blest,
Alleluia!

1864 'For All the Saints', in Earl Nelson *Hymns for Saints' Days*.

93 From earth's wide bounds, from ocean's farthest coast,
Through gates of pearl streams in the countless host,
Singing to Father, Son, and Holy Ghost,
Alleluia!
1864 'For All the Saints', in Earl Nelson *Hymns for Saints' Days*.

Howard, Thomas, Earl of Surrey and 2nd Duke of Norfolk 1443–1524

English nobleman and soldier. He fought for Richard III at Bosworth (1485) and was imprisoned by Henry VII, but regained his estates and led successful campaigns against the Scots, including Flodden (1513).

94 He was my crowned King, and if the Parliamentary authority of England set the crown upon a stock, I will fight for that stock: And as I fought then for him, I will fight for you, when you are established by the said authority.
1485 Explaining before the future Henry VII his reasons for siding with Richard III at Bosworth, 22 Aug. Quoted in William Camden *Remains Concerning Britain* (1605).

Howe (of Aberavon), (Richard Edward) Geoffrey Howe, Baron 1926–

English Conservative politician. In 1989 he became Deputy Prime Minister, Lord President of the Council and Leader of the House of Commons. His resignation from Margaret Thatcher's government in Nov 1990, and his subsequent resignation speech, were instrumental in her downfall.

95 Megaphone diplomacy leads to a dialogue of the deaf.
1985 Quoted in the *Observer*, 29 Sep.

96 How on earth are the Chancellor of the Exchequer and the Governor of the Bank of England...to be taken seriously against that kind of background noise? It is rather like sending your opening batsmen to the crease, only for them to find, the moment the first balls are bowled, that their bats have been broken before the game by the team captain.
1990 Personal statement on his resignation, House of Commons, 13 Nov.

97 If some of my former colleagues are to be believed, I must be the first minister in history to have resigned because he was in full agreement with government policy.
1990 Personal statement on his resignation, House of Commons, 13 Nov.

Howe, Gordie (Gordon) 1928–

Canadian hockey player.

98 All pro athletes are bilingual. They speak English and profanity.
Dismissing Canadian bilingualism. Quoted by George Gamester in the *Toronto Star*, 27 May 1975.

Howe, Joseph 1804–73

Anglo-Canadian journalist and statesman.

99 A wise nation preserves its records, gathers up its muniments, decorates the tombs of its illustrious dead, repairs its great public structures, and fosters national pride and love of country, by perpetual references to the sacrifices and glories of the past.
1871 Address at Framingham, Massachusetts, 31 Aug. Collected in *Poems and Essays* (1874).

Howe, Julia Ward 1819–1910

US feminist and writer, influential in suffragette and Unitarian causes. Her poetry collections include *Passion Flowers* (1854). She made history as the first woman member of the American Academy.

1 Mine eyes have seen the glory of the coming of the Lord:
He is trampling out the vintage where the grapes of wrath are stored.
He hath loosed the fatal lightning of his terrible swift sword:
His truth is marching on.
1862 'Battle Hymn of the Republic'.

Howe, Louis McHenry 1871–1936

US diplomat.

2 You can't adopt politics as a profession and hope to remain honest.
1933 Speech, Columbia University, 17 Jan.

Hoyle, Edmond 1672–1769

English authority on card games. He published manuals on whist, backgammon, brag, quadrille, piquet and chess.

3 When in doubt, win the trick.
A Short Treatise on the Game of Whist (first published 1742, this edn edited by Charles Jones, 1790). This may be an addition by Jones.

Hoyle, Sir Fred 1915–2001

English astronomer and mathematician, one of the first to apply modern physics to cosmology. He was knighted in 1972.

4 To take an almost religious view, this earth is nothing very special. There have probably been millions of earths just like ours each producing a particular intelligent species. That is not to say that they all developed well, that they all achieved some sort of perfection. And if the planner made lots of them and some of them chose to destroy themselves, then we can only suppose that the planner is a hard and practical man.
1974 In the *Daily Mail*.

5 Space isn't remote at all. It's only an hour's drive away if your car could go straight upwards.
1979 Quoted in the *Observer*, 'Sayings of the Week', 9 Sep.

Hubbard, Elbert Green 1856–1915

US writer, editor and printer.

6 Life is just one damned thing after another.
1909 In *The Philistine*, Dec.

7 Little minds are interested in the extraordinary; great minds in the commonplace.
1911 *Thousand and One Epigrams*.

8 One machine can do the work of fifty ordinary men. No machine can do the work of one extraordinary man.
1911 *Thousand and One Epigrams*.

9 Editor: a person employed by a newspaper, whose business it is to separate the wheat from the chaff, and to see that the chaff is printed.
1914 *The Roycroft Dictionary*.

10 College football is a sport that bears the same relation to education that bullfighting does to agriculture.
Quoted in Colin Jarman *The Guinness Dictionary of Sports Quotations* (1990).

Hubble, Edwin Powell 1889–1953

US astronomer. In 1929 he formulated Hubble's law: galaxies recede with speeds directly proportionate to their distance from us, confirming that the universe is expanding. The space telescope launched in 1990 was named in his honour.

11 We measure shadows, and we search among ghostly errors of measurement for landmarks that are scarcely more substantial.
Quoted in Dennis Overbye *Lonely Hearts of the Cosmos* (1991).

Hügel, Friedrich von, Baron 1852–1925

Austrian-born British theologian and Bible critic, son of the Austrian Ambassador in Italy. He settled in England in 1871. His works include *The Mystical Element in Religion* (1908–9) and *The Reality of God* (published 1931).

12 I take these to be the seven great facts and doctrines concerning God—his richness; his double action, natural and supernatural; his perfect freedom; his delightfulness; his otherness; his adorableness and his prevenience.
The Life of Prayer (published 1927).

13 Christianity has taught us to care. Caring is the greatest thing, caring matters most.
Letter to his niece.

Hugh of St Victor c.1096–1141

German divine and scholar, who entered the Augustinian order despite his parents' objections. In 1115 he was sent to the Abbey of St Victor in Paris, where he completed his vows, later becoming master of the school. He composed many treatises on theological, philosophical and devotional subjects.

14 *Delicatus ille est adhuc cui patria dulcis est. Fortis autem jam cui omne solum patria est, perfectus vero cui mundus totus exilium est.*
He whose own homeland is sweet to him is a mere beginner. He to whom every soil is as his native land is strong. But he to whom the whole world is a place of exile has achieved perfection.
c.1127 *Didascalicon*, bk.3, ch.20.

Hughes, Howard Robard 1905–76

US millionaire businessman, film producer and aviator. Known as an eccentric, he left Hollywood in 1932 to design, build and fly aircraft before returning to film production. After 1966 he lived in complete seclusion.

15 That man's ears make him look like a taxi-cab with both doors open.
Of Clark Gable. Quoted in Charles Higham and Joel Greenbert *Celluloid Muse* (1969).

Hughes, (James Mercer) Langston 1902–67

US poet, a leading figure of the Harlem Renaissance, whose poetry and sketches reflect folk culture, jazz, blues and colloquial speech. His works include *Weary Blues* (1926) and the autobiographical *The Big Sea* (1940).

16 I, too, sing America.

I am the darker brother.
They send me to eat in the kitchen
When company comes.
But I laugh
And eat well,
And grow strong.
1925 'I, Too', in *Survey Graphic*, Mar.

17 Tomorrow
I'll sit at the table
When company comes
Nobody'll dare
Say to me,
'Eat in the kitchen'
Then.
1925 'I, Too', in *Survey Graphic*, Mar.

18 Swaying to and fro on his rickety stool
He played that sad raggy tune like a musical fool.
Sweet blues!
1926 'The Weary Blues'.

19 I swear to the Lord,
I still can't see,
Why Democracy means,
Everybody but me.
1943 'The Black Man Speaks'.

20 What happens to a dream deferred?

Does it dry up
like a raisin in the sun?
1951 'Dream Deferred'. Lorraine Hansberry used the phrase for the title of her play *A Raisin in the Sun* (1959).

21 Maybe it just sags
like a heavy load.

Or does it explode?
1951 'Dream Deferred'.

22 You are white—
yet a part of me, as I am a part of you.
That's American.
1951 'Theme for English B'.

23 A wonderful time—the War:
when money rolled in
and blood rolled out.
1951 'Green Memory'.

24 'It's powerful,' he said.
'What?'
'That one drop of Negro blood—because just *one* drop of black blood makes a man coloured. *One* drop—you are a Negro!'
1953 *Simple Takes a Wife*.

Hughes, Richard Arthur Warren 1900–76

English novelist. He is best known for his adventure tale *A High Wind in Jamaica* (1929, entitled *The Innocent Voyage* in the US). Other works include *Hazard: A Sea Story* (1938), *The Fox in the Attic* (1961) and *The Wooden Shepherdess* (1972).

25 Nature is as wasteful of promising young men as she is of fish-spawn. It's not just getting them killed in wars: mere middle age snuffs out ten times more talent than ever wars and sudden death do.

1961 *The Fox in the Attic*, bk.1, ch.18.

26 For a politician rises on the backs of his friends (that's probably all they're good for), but it's through his enemies he'll have to govern afterwards.
1961 *The Fox in the Attic*, bk.2, ch.20.

27 Do your bit to save humanity from lapsing back into barbarity by reading all the novels you can.
1975 Speech at Foyle's Literary Luncheon, London, in honour of his 75th birthday.

Hughes, Robert Studley Forrest 1938–

Australian-born US art critic, writer with *Time* magazine (1970–). His books include *The Fatal Shore* (1987) and *Goya* (2003). He has also written and narrated art documentaries for television including the series *American Visions* (1997).

28 Lentil-soup colors.
1981 Of the paints used by French realists. In *Time*, 13 Apr.

29 The protein of our cultural imagination.
1984 Of the US Museum of Modern Art. In *Time*, 14 May.

30 Close by the Hudson, in MANHATTAN'S TOWN,
The iron palaces of Art glare down
On such as, wandering in the streets below,
Perambulate in glamorous SoHo,
A spot acclaimed by savant and by bard
As forcing chamber of the Avant-Garde.
1984 'The SoHoiad', in the *New York Review of Books*.

31 Popular in our time, unpopular in his. So runs the stereotype of rejected genius.
1985 On a Caravaggio exhibition. In *Time*, 11 Mar.

32 Landscape is to American painting what sex and psychoanalysis are to the American novel.
1985 In *Time*, 30 Dec.

33 [A Gustave Courbet] portrait of a trout...has more death in it than Rubens could get in a whole Crucifixion.
1986 In *Time*, 15 Sep.

34 Its clones have hung on so many suburban walls over the decades that it has become the *Mona Lisa* of the vegetable world.
1987 On Vincent Van Gogh's *Sunflowers*. In *Time*, 13 Apr.

35 The self is now the sacred cow of American culture, self-esteem is sacrosanct, and so we labour to turn arts education into a system in which no one can fail. In the same spirit, tennis could be shorn of its elitist overtones: you just get rid of the net.
1994 *Culture of Complaint: The Fraying of America*.

36 America came up with the idea of therapeutic avant-gardism, and built museums in its name. These temples stood on two pillars. The first was aestheticism... The second was the familiar one of social benefit.
1994 *Culture of Complaint: The Fraying of America*.

37 My idea of a contact sport was chess.
1999 *A Jerk on One End: Reflections of a Mediocre Fisherman*.

Hughes, Ted (Edward James) 1930–98

English poet. His elemental, highly symbolic works include *The Hawk in the Rain* (1957) and *Crow* (1970). Other works include *Birthday Letters* (1998) and books for children. He was Poet Laureate (1984–98).

38 The world rolls under the long thrust of his heel.
Over the cage floor the horizons come.
1957 'The Jaguar'.

39 It took the whole of Creation
To produce my foot, my each feather:
Now I hold Creation in my foot.
1960 'Hawk Roosting'.

40 Nothing has changed since I began.
My eye has permitted no change.
I am going to keep things like this.
1960 'Hawk Roosting'.

41 Pike, three inches long, perfect
Pike in all parts, green tigering the gold.
Killers from the egg: the malevolent aged grin.
1960 'Pike'.

42 The gash in its throat was shocking, but not pathetic.
1960 'View of a Pig'.

43 The deeps are cold:
In that darkness camaraderie does not hold:
Nothing touches but, clutching, devours.
1960 'Relic'.

44 The brassy wood-pigeons
Bubble their colourful voices, and the sun
Rises upon a world well-tried and old.
1967 'Stealing Trout on a May Morning'.

45 No, the serpent did not
Seduce Eve to the apple.
All that's simply
Corruption of the facts.

Adam ate the apple.
Eve ate Adam.
The serpent ate Eve.
This is the dark intestine.

The serpent, meanwhile,
Sleeps his meal off in Paradise—
Smiling to hear
God's querulous calling.
1967 'Theology'.

46 Who owns the whole rainy, stony earth? *Death.*
Who owns all of space? *Death.*
1970 'Examination at the Womb-door'.

47 But who is stronger than death?
Me, evidently.
1970 'Examination at the Womb-door'.

48 And he shivered with the horror of Creation.
1970 'Crow Alights'.

49 But Oedipus he had the luck
For when he hit the ground
He bounced up like a jackinabox
And knocked his Daddy down.
1970 'Song for a Phallus'.

50 And the elephant sings deep in the forest-maze
About a star of deathless and painless peace
But no astronomer can find where it is.
1972 'Crow's Elephant Totem Song'.

51 Black village of gravestones.
1979 'Heptonstall'.

52 Only the rain never tires.
1979 'Heptonstall'.

53 You were the jailer of your murderer—

Which imprisoned you.
And since I was your nurse and your protector
Your sentence was mine too.
1998 In *Birthday Letters*, a collection of poems addressed to Sylvia Plath, his first wife.

Hughes, Thomas 1822–96

English reformer and novelist. Called to the Bar in 1848, a Liberal MP (1865–74) and a county court judge (1882), he is best remembered for his semi-autobiographical classic, *Tom Brown's Schooldays* (1856).

54 Life isn't all beer and skittles—but beer and skittles, or something better of the same sort, must form a good part of every Englishman's education.
1856 *Tom Brown's Schooldays*, pt.1, ch.2.

55 He never wants anything but what's right and fair, only when you come to settle what's right and fair, it's everything that he wants and nothing that you want. And that's his idea of a compromise. Give me the Brown compromise when I'm on his side.
1856 *Tom Brown's Schooldays*, pt.2, ch.2.

56 It's more than a game. It's an institution.
1856 Of cricket. *Tom Brown's Schooldays*, pt.2, ch.7.

Hughes, William Morris 1864–1952

Welsh-born Australian statesman. He emigrated in 1884 and became Minister for External Affairs (1904) in the first Labour government and subsequently Prime Minister (1915–23). He founded the United Australian Party.

57 Mr President, I speak for sixty thousand dead!
1919 Reply to Woodrow Wilson at the Versailles Peace Conference, Jan, referring to the ANZ AC fatalities in World War I. Wilson had asked 'Mr Hughes, I speak for very many millions of people. For whom do you speak?'.

58 Without the Empire we should be tossed like a cork in the cross current of world politics. It is at once our sword and our shield.
1926 Speech, Melbourne.

Hugo, Victor Marie 1802–85

French poet, dramatist and novelist. His great epics are *Notre-Dame de Paris* (1831, *The Hunchback of Notre Dame*) and *Les Misérables* (1862). His writings and theories were enormously influential.

59 *Le beau n'a qu'un type; le laid en a mille.*
Beauty has only one form; ugliness has a thousand.
1827 *Cromwell*, préface.

60 *Les temps primitifs sont lyriques, les temps antiques sont épiques, les temps modernes sont dramatiques.*
The primitive era was lyrical, the classical era was epic and the modern era is dramatic.
1827 *Cromwell*, préface.

61 *Il n'y a ni règles ni modèles; ou plutôt il n'y a d'autres règles que les lois générales de la nature qui planent sur l'art tout entier, et les lois spéciales qui, pour chaque composition, résultent des conditions d'existence propres à chaque sujet.*
There are no rules or models; that is, there are no rules except general laws of nature which hover over art and special laws which apply to specific subjects.
1827 *Cromwell*, préface.

62 *La vérité de l'art ne saurait jamais être…la réalité absolue. L'art ne peut donner la chose même.*
The truth of art should never be…*absolute reality.* Art cannot show the thing itself.
1827 *Cromwell*, préface.

63 *Le but de l'art est presque divin: ressusciter, s'il fait de l'histoire; créer, s'il fait de la poésie.*
The goal of art is almost divine: to resuscitate, if it concerns history; to create, if it concerns poetry.
1827 *Cromwell*, préface.

64 *Le vers est la forme optique de la pensée. Voilà pourquoi il convient surtout à la perspective scénique.*
Verse is the optical form of thought. That is the reason a scenic perspective suits it.
1827 *Cromwell*, préface.

65 *La langue française n'est point fixée et ne se fixera point.*
French is not a *static* language and will never become static.
1827 *Cromwell*, préface.

66 *Sois donc ami sincère ou sincère ennemi,*
Et ne reste pas traître et fidèle à demi.
Be either a sincere friend or a sincere enemy,
And never be half-traitor and half-faithful.
1827 *Cromwell*, act 1, sc.1.

67 *L'Angleterre toujours sera sœur de la France.*
England will always be the sister of France.
1827 *Cromwell*, act 2, sc.2.

68 *Vous me manquez, je suis absente de moi-même.*
I miss you, I am estranged from myself.
1830 *Hernani*, act 1, sc.2.

69 *Nos pères avaient un Paris de pierre, nos fils auront un Paris de plâtre.*
Our fathers had a Paris made of stone; our sons will have a Paris made of plaster.
1831 *Notre-Dame de Paris*, pt.3, ch.2.

70 *Rêver, c'est le bonheur; attendre, c'est la vie.*
To dream is happiness; to wait is life.
1831 *Les Feuilles d'automne*, no.27, 'À mes amis L.B. et S.-B.'.

71 *Au banquet du bonheur bien peu sont conviés.*
Few are invited to the banquet of happiness.
1831 *Les Feuilles d'automne*, no.32, 'Pour les pauvres'.

72 *Mêlez toute votre âme à la création!*
Involve all of your soul in creation!
1831 *Les Feuilles d'automne*, no.38, 'Pan'.

73 *O Virgile! ô poète! ô mon maître divin!*
Oh Virgil! Oh poet! Oh my divine master!
1837 *Les Voix intérieures*, no.7, 'À Virgile'.

74 *Le drame tient de la tragédie par la peinture des passions et de la comédie par la peinture des caractères. Le drame est la troisième grande forme de l'art.*
In drama, tragedy paints the passions and comedy paints characters. Drama is the third great form of art.
1838 *Ruy Blas*, préface.

75 *Je ne veux pas tomber, non, je veux disparaître.*
I do not want to fall; I want to disappear.
1838 *Ruy Blas*, act 1, sc.1.

76 *Visage de traître!*
Quand la bouche dit oui, le regard dit peut-être.
Face of a traitor!
When the mouth says yes, the look says maybe.

1838 *Ruy Blas*, act 1, sc.2.

77 *Sous l'habit d'un valet, les passions d'un roi.*
Beneath the clothing of a manservant, the passions of a king.
1838 *Ruy Blas*, act 1, sc.3.

78 *Les femmes aiment fort à sauver qui les perd.*
Women love to save those who damn them.
1838 *Ruy Blas*, act 1, sc.4.

79 *Dieu s'est fait homme; Soit! Le diable s'est fait femme.*
God made himself a man. So be it! The devil made himself a woman.
1838 *Ruy Blas*, act 2, sc.5.

80 *Tout se fait par intrigue et rien par loyauté.*
Everything is done by intrigue, not by loyalty.
1838 *Ruy Blas*, act 3, sc.2.

81 *Ah! toute nation bénit qui la délie.*
Ah! every nation blesses what undoes it.
1838 *Ruy Blas*, act 3, sc.5.

82 *La popularité? c'est la gloire en gros sous.*
Popularity? It is glory in large coins.
1838 *Ruy Blas*, act 3, sc.5.

83 *Le mot, c'est le Verbe, et le Verbe, c'est Dieu.*
The word is the Verb, and the Verb is God.
1856 *Contemplations*, bk.1, no.8.

84 *Cette cloison qui nous sépare du mystère des choses et que nous appelons la vie.*
Life is a screen which separates us from the mystery of things.
1862 *Les Misérables*, vol.1, bk.1, ch.2.

85 *Ce génie particulier de la femme qui comprend l'homme mieux que l'homme ne se comprend.*
A woman's particular talent is to understand a man better than he understands himself.
1862 *Les Misérables*, vol.1, bk.1, ch.9.

86 *Les livres sont des amis froids et sûrs.*
Books are cold and certain friends.
1862 *Les Misérables*, vol.1, bk.5, ch.3.

87 *Conscience déchirée entraîne vie décousue.*
A torn conscience brings about a disconnected life.
1862 *Les Misérables*, vol.2, bk.1, ch.16.

88 *La symétrie, c'est l'ennui, et l'ennui est le fond même du deuil. Le désespoir bâille.*
Symmetry is boredom and boredom is the foundation of grief. Despair yawns.
1862 *Les Misérables*, vol.2, bk.4, ch.1.

89 *Personne ne garde un secret comme un enfant.*
No one keeps a secret like a child.
1862 *Les Misérables*, vol.2, bk.7, ch.8.

90 *Respirer Paris, cela conserve l'âme.*
To inhale Paris preserves the soul.
1862 *Les Misérables*, vol.3, bk.1, ch.6.

91 *On jugerait bien plus sûrement un homme d'après ce qu'il rêve que d'après ce qu'il pense.*
We would judge a man more certainly according to his dreams than to his thoughts.
1862 *Les Misérables*, vol.3, bk.5, ch.5.

92 *On a voulu, à tort, faire de la bourgeoisie une classe. La bourgeoisie est tout simplement la portion contentée du peuple. Le bourgeois, c'est l'homme qui a maintenant le temps de s'asseoir. Une chaise n'est pas une caste.*
Wrongly, one wanted to make the bourgeoisie a class. The bourgeoisie is simply a contented section of the public. A bourgeois is a man who now has the time to sit down. A chair is not a caste.
1862 *Les Misérables*, vol.4, bk.1, ch.2.

93 *La première égalité, c'est l'équité.*
The first equality is equity.
1862 *Les Misérables*, vol.4, bk.1, ch.4.

94 *Le premier symptôme de l'amour vrai chez un jeune homme, c'est la timidité, chez une jeune fille, c'est la hardiesse.*
The first symptom of true love in a young man is timidity; in a young woman, it is boldness.
1862 *Les Misérables*, vol.4, bk.3, ch.6.

95 *Le dix-neuvième siècle est grand, mais le vingtième sera heureux.*
The nineteenth century is great, but the twentieth will be happy.
1862 *Les Misérables*, vol.5, bk.1, ch.4.

96 *Le suicide, cette mystérieuse voie de fait sur l'inconnu.*
Suicide: that mysterious route towards the unknown.
1862 *Les Misérables*, vol.5, bk.3, ch.10.

97 *Jésus a pleuré, Voltaire a souri; c'est de cette larme divine et de ce sourire humain qu'est faite la douceur de la civilisation actuelle.*
Jesus wept; Voltaire smiled. Of that divine tear and of that human smile the sweetness of present civilization is composed.
1878 Speech on Voltaire's centenary, 30 May.

98 Science says the first word on everything and the last word on nothing.
Attributed.

Huidobro, Vicente 1893–1948

Chilean poet, who wrote in French as well as Spanish. He created the movement known as *creacionismo*, which abandons traditional descriptive poetry.

99 *Que se rompa el andamio de los huesos*
Que se derrumben las vigas del cerebro
Y arrastre el huracán los trozos a la nada al otro lado
En donde el viento azota a Dios
Smash the scaffold of the bones
Pull down the rafters of the brain
Let the hurricane drag the pieces to the nothing on the other side
Where the wind thrashes God
1931 *Altazor o el viaje en paracaídas*, canto 1 (translated as *Altazor, or, A Voyage in a Parachute*, 1988).

Humboldt, Alexander, Baron von 1769–1859

German naturalist and traveller. He travelled through Central and South America (1799–1804), and his observations laid the foundations for the sciences of physical geography and meteorology.

1 In the sphere of natural investigation, as in poetry and painting, the delineation of that which appeals most strongly to the imagination, derives its collective interest from the vivid truthfulness with which the individual features are portrayed.
1845–62 *Kosmos* (translated as *Cosmos*, 1897).

2 The great and solemn spirit that pervades the intellectual

labour (of science) arises from the sublime consciousness of striving toward the infinite, and of grasping all that is revealed to us amid the boundless and inexhaustible fullness of creation, development and being.
1845–62 *Kosmos* (translated as *Cosmos*, 1897).

Hume, David 1711–76

Scottish philosopher and historian. His most important work, the empiricist *A Treatise of Human Nature*, was published anonymously (1739–40). He published a five-volume *History of England* (1754–62) and was secretary to the British Ambassador in Paris (1763–5).

3 Let us fix our attention out of ourselves as much as possible; let us chase our imagination to the heavens, or to the utmost limits of the universe; we never really advance a step beyond ourselves, nor can conceive any kind of existence, but those perceptions, which have appeared in that narrow compass.
1739 *A Treatise of Human Nature*, bk.1, pt.2, section 6.

4 We have no other notion of cause and effect, but that of certain objects, which have been *always conjoined* together, and which in all past instances have been found inseparable.
1739 *A Treatise of Human Nature*, bk.1, pt.3, section 6.

5 For my part, when I enter most intimately into what I call *myself*, I always stumble on some particular perception or other, of heat or cold, light or shade, pain or pleasure. I never can catch *myself* at any time without a perception, and never can observe anything but the perception.
1739 *A Treatise of Human Nature*, bk.1, pt.4, section 6.

6 In all the events of life, we ought still to preserve our scepticism. If we believe that fire warms, or water refreshes, it is only because it costs us too much pains to think otherwise.
1739 *A Treatise of Human Nature*, bk.1, pt.4, section 7.

7 Reason is, and ought only to be the slave of the passions, and can never pretend to any other office than to serve and obey them.
1739 *A Treatise of Human Nature*, bk.2, pt.3, section 3.

8 It is not contrary to reason to prefer the destruction of the whole world to the scratching of my finger.
1739 *A Treatise of Human Nature*, bk.2, pt.3, section 3.

9 It is not, therefore, reason, which is the guide of life, but custom.
1739 *A Treatise of Human Nature*, abstract.

10 Art may make a suit of clothes; But nature must produce a man.
1741–2 *Essays Moral, Political and Literary*, 'The Epicurean'.

11 It cannot reasonably be doubted, but a little miss, dressed in a new gown for a dancing-school ball, receives as complete enjoyment as the greatest orator, who triumphs in the splendour of his eloquence, while he governs the passions and resolutions of a numerous assembly.
1741–2 *Essays Moral, Political and Literary*, 'The Sceptic'.

12 The increase of riches and commerce in any one nation, instead of hurting, commonly promotes the riches and commerce of all its neighbours.
1741–2 *Essays Moral, Political and Literary*, 'Of the Jealousy of Trade'.

13 All the objects of human reason or enquiry may naturally be divided into two kinds, to wit, *Relations of Ideas*, and *Matters of Fact*.
1748 *An Enquiry Concerning Human Understanding*, section 4, pt.1.

14 A wise man proportions his belief to the evidence.
1748 *An Enquiry Concerning Human Understanding*, section 10, pt.1.

15 When we run over libraries, persuaded of these principles, what havoc must we make? If we take in our hand any volume; of divinity or school metaphysics, for instance; let us ask, *Does it contain any abstract reasoning concerning quantity or number?* No. *Does it contain any experimental reasoning concerning matter of fact or existence?* No. Commit it then to the flames: for it can contain nothing but sophistry and illusion.
1748 *An Enquiry Concerning Human Understanding*, section 12, pt.3.

16 Never literary attempt was more unfortunate than my Treatise of Human Nature. It fell *dead-born from the press*, without reaching such distinction, as even to excite a murmur among the zealots.
1777 *My Own Life*, ch.1.

Humphrey, Hubert Horatio 1911–78

US politician. He served as Vice-President under Lyndon B Johnson but failed to win the Democratic candidature in 1968.

17 There are not enough jails, not enough policemen, not enough courts to enforce a law not supported by the people.
1965 Speech, 1 May.

Humphry, Derek 1930–

British journalist and co-founder of the Hemlock Society, which supports euthanasia for the terminally ill.

18 We're not lawbreakers, we're law reformers.
1992 In *Time*, 28 Dec.

Humphrys, John 1943–

Welsh broadcaster, particularly known as a tenacious presenter on BBC Radio 4's *Today* programme (since 1987).

19 It is largely on television and radio that real probing of what politicians are up to has to happen.
2000 *The Devil's Advocate*.

20 It is no good saying we [journalists] must report only what is true because what is true cannot always be proven.
2004 In the *Sunday Times*, 8 Feb.

Hunt, G W 1829–1904

English composer, lyricist and painter.

21 We don't want to fight, but by jingo if we do,
We've got the ships, we've got the men, we've got the money too!
1878 Music-hall song, inspired by Disraeli's speech of 9 Nov 1876 threatening Russia with war if it sent volunteers into Serbia and Montenegro. This is the origin of 'jingoism'.

Hunt, Johnnie B(ryan) 1924–

US businessman of poor origins.

22 I was hungry once and once you're hungry, you're different.
1992 In *Forbes*, 19 Oct.

Hunt, Lamar 1932–

US founder of the Kansas City Chiefs American football club.

23 My definition of utter waste is a coachload of lawyers going over a cliff, with three empty seats.
Quoted in Colin Jarman *The Guinness Dictionary of Sports Quotations* (1990).

Hunt, (James Henry) Leigh 1784–1859

English poet, critic and essayist. With his brother he edited *The Examiner* (1808–21) and popularized Keats and Shelley. His house in Hampstead was a literary meeting place, and he was caricatured by Dickens as Harold Skimpole in *Bleak House*.

24 Never lay yourself open to what is called conviction: you might as well open your waist-coat to receive a knock-down blow.
1808 'Rules for the Conduct of Newspaper Editors', in *The Examiner*, 6 Mar.

25 A playful moderation in politics is just as absurd as a remonstrative whisper to a mob.
1808 'Rules for the Conduct of Newspaper Editors', in *The Examiner*, 6 Mar.

26 She can overpower, astonish, afflict, but she cannot win; her majestic presence and commanding features seem to disregard love, as a trifle to which they cannot descend.
1808 Of Sarah Siddons. *Critical Essays on the Performers of the London Theatres*.

27 The two divinest things this world has got,
A lovely woman in a rural spot!
1816 'The Story of Rimini', canto 3, l.257–8.

28 The laughing queen that caught the world's great hands.
1818 Of Cleopatra. 'The Nile'.

29 Stolen sweets are always sweeter,
Stolen kisses much completer,
Stolen looks are nice in chapels,
Stolen, stolen, be your apples.
1830 'Song of Fairies Robbing an Orchard'.

30 Poetry, in the most comprehensive application of the term, I take to be the flower of any kind of experience, rooted in truth, and issuing forth into beauty.
1832 *The Story of Rimini*, preface to rev edn.

31 The pretension is nothing; the performance everything. A good apple is better than an insipid peach.
1832 *The Story of Rimini*, preface to rev edn.

32 'No love,' quoth he, 'but vanity, sets love a task like that.'
1836 'The Glove and the Lions'.

33 Abou Ben Adhem (may his tribe increase!)
Awoke one night from a deep dream of peace.
1838 'Abou Ben Adhem'.

34 I pray thee then,
Write me as one that loves his fellow-men.
1838 'Abou Ben Adhem'.

35 Jenny kissed me when we met,
Jumping from the chair she sat in;
Time, you thief, who love to get
Sweets into your list, put that in:
Say I'm weary, say I'm sad,
Say that health and wealth have missed me,
Say I'm growing old, but add,
Jenny kissed me.
1838 'Rondeau'.

36 That man must be very much absorbed in reflection, or stupid, or sulky, or unhappy, or a mere hog at his trough, who is not moved to say something when he dines.
1851 *Table-Talk*, 'Table-Talk'.

37 If you are ever at a loss to support a flagging conversation, introduce the subject of eating.
1851 *Table-Talk*, 'Eating'.

Hunt, Sir Rex 1926–

Governor of the Falkland Islands at the time of the Argentine invasion of 1982.

38 It is very uncivilised to invade British territory. You are here illegally.
1982 Attributed remark to an Argentinian general. Quoted in *Life*, Jan 1983.

Hunter, William 1718–83

Scottish anatomist and obstetrician, appointed physician-extraordinary to Queen Charlotte Sophia (1764) and first Professor of Anatomy to the Royal Academy (1768). His Hunterian Museum was bequeathed to Glasgow University.

39 Some physiologists will have it that the stomach is a mill;—others, that it is a fermenting vat;—others again that it is a stew-pan;—but in my view of the matter, it is neither a mill, a fermenting vat, nor a stew-pan—but a *stomach*, gentlemen, a *stomach*.
Quoted in J A Paris *A Treatise on Diet* (1824), epigraph, from a note made by Hunter on one of his lectures.

Hupfeld, Herman 1894–1951

US composer of popular songs, best known for 'Sing Something Simple' and 'As Time Goes By'.

40 You must remember this, a kiss is still a kiss,
A sigh is just a sigh;
The fundamental things apply,
As time goes by.
1931 'As Time Goes By', sung by Dooley Wilson in the film *Casablanca* (1943).

Hussein, ibn Talal 1935–99

King of Jordan (1952–99), four times married. The longest-serving Arab leader, pro-Western in attitude, he moved towards democracy in Jordan.

41 After all the doors were shut, our region is facing a deep abyss after the turning of the Gulf crisis into an imminent catastrophe. We have not left a door that we did not knock on, or a road that we did not take to find a political settlement of this crisis.
1991 On his attempts to intercede for peace in the Gulf War, Jan.

Hussein, Saddam 1937–

Iraqi politician, a key figure in Iraq's 1968 revolution and later President (1979–2003). He engaged in the Iran–Iraq War (1980–8) and in 1990 invaded Kuwait and was repulsed by a coalition of Western and Arab forces. He made further raids on

Iran in 1993, defying UN ceasefire resolutions. He was captured by US forces in Iraq in December 2003.

42 The devil Bush and his treacherous gang, with criminal Zionism, have begun the great showdown, the mother of all battles between good and evil.
1991 Speech in Baghdad, 6 Jan, describing Operation Desert Storm. Quoted in the *Sunday Times*, 27 Jan.

43 There is no other course but the one we have chosen, except the course of humiliation and darkness, after which there will be no bright sign in the sky or brilliant light on earth… All this will make us more patient and steadfast, and better prepared for the battle which God blesses and which good men support. Then there will only be a glorious conclusion, where a brilliant sun will clear the dust of battle, and where the clouds of battles will be dispelled.
1991 Baghdad radio broadcast, 21 Feb.

44 Baghdad is determined to force the Mongols of our age to commit suicide at its gates.
2003 Speech on the anniversary of the Gulf War, 17 Jan.

45 At dawn prayers today on March 20 2003 (17 Muharram 1424), the criminal, reckless little Bush and his aides committed this crime that he was threatening to commit against Iraq and humanity.
2003 Address to the nation of Iraq, broadcast on state television, after a US strike on Baghdad. Quoted in *The Guardian*, 20 Mar.

46 We do not have weapons of mass destruction.
Quoted in George Galloway *I'm Not the Only One* (2004).

47 If they come we are ready. We will fight them on the streets, from the rooftops, from house to house. We will never surrender our independence no matter what happens in any invasion.
Quoted in George Galloway *I'm Not the Only One* (2004).

Huston, John 1906–87

US actor, screenwriter and director, son of Walter Huston. He made his directorial debut with *The Maltese Falcon* (1941). Other successes include *Key Largo* (1948), *The African Queen* (1951), *Moulin Rouge* (1952) and *The Man Who Would Be King* (1975).

48 You're good, you're real good.
1941 Line delivered by Humphrey Bogart in *The Maltese Falcon*.

49 A work of art doesn't dare you to realize it. It germinates and gestates by itself.
1982 Reply to a tribute from the Directors Guild of America. Reported in *Variety*, 26 Apr.

Hutchens, John Kennedy 1905–95

US journalist and editor. He was theatre critic with the *New York Times* (1929–32, 1934–8), editor of the *New York Times Book Review* (1946–8), and was on the editorial board of the Book-of-the-Month Club (1963–88).

50 A writer and nothing else: a man alone in a room with the English language, trying to get human feelings right.
1961 On Stephen Crane. In the *New York Herald Tribune*, 10 Sep.

Hutcheson, Francis 1694–1746

Scottish philosopher, born in Ulster, a Professor of Moral Philosophy at Glasgow (1729–46) and exponent of the theory of moral sense. His ideas were later expanded by David Hume and taken up by the Utilitarians.

51 Wisdom denotes the pursuing of the best ends by the best means.
1725 *An Inquiry into the Original of Our Ideas of Beauty and Virtue*, treatise 1, sect.5.

52 That action is best, which procures the greatest happiness for the greatest numbers.
1725 *An Inquiry into the Original of Our Ideas of Beauty and Virtue*, treatise 2, sect.3. This is the classic exposition of pragmatism.
► *See Bentham 77:65.*

Hutchins, Robert M 1899–1977

US educationalist, Chancellor of the University of Chicago.

53 On the principle laid down by Gilbert and Sullivan that when everybody is somebody, nobody is anybody; if everybody is abnormal, we don't need to worry about anybody.
1951 Farewell address to students at the University of Chicago.

54 Whenever I feel like exercise, I lie down until the feeling passes.
Quoted in Colin Jarman *The Guinness Dictionary of Sports Quotations* (1990).

Huxley, Aldous Leonard 1894–1963

English novelist and essayist. His satirical novels *Crome Yellow* (1921) and *Antic Hay* (1923) established his reputation, and his best-known work is the dystopian novel *Brave New World* (1932). Other works include *Eyeless in Gaza* (1936) and *Time Must Have a Stop* (1944).

55 I can sympathize with people's pains, but not with their pleasures. There is something curiously boring about somebody else's happiness.
1920 *Limbo*, 'Cynthia'.

56 The proper study of mankind is books.
1921 *Crome Yellow*, ch.28.
► *See Pope 660:16.*

57 There are few who would not rather be taken in adultery than in provincialism.
1923 *Antic Hay*, ch.10.

58 Mr Mercaptan went on to preach a brilliant sermon on that melancholy sexual perversion known as continence.
1923 *Antic Hay*, ch.18.

59 Lady Capricorn, he understood, was still keeping open bed.
1923 *Antic Hay*, ch.21.

60 I'm afraid of losing my obscurity. Genuineness only thrives in the dark. Like celery.
1925 *Those Barren Leaves*, pt.1, ch.1.

61 Science has 'explained' nothing: the more we know the more fantastic the world becomes and the profounder the surrounding darkness.
1925 *Views of Holland*.

62 Facts do not cease to exist because they are ignored.
1927 *Proper Studies*, 'Note on Dogma'.

63 Those who believe that they are exclusively in the right are generally those who achieve something.
1927 *Proper Studies*, 'Note on Dogma'.

64 That all men are equal is a proposition to which, at

ordinary times, no sane human being has ever given his assent.
1927 *Proper Studies*, 'The Idea of Equality'.

65 Several excuses are always less convincing than one.
1928 *Point Counter Point*, ch.1.

66 A bad book is as much of a labour to write as a good one; it comes as sincerely from the author's soul.
1928 *Point Counter Point*, ch.13.

67 There is no substitute for talent. Industry and all the virtues are of no avail.
1928 *Point Counter Point*, ch.13.

68 Brought up in an age when ladies apparently rolled along on wheels, Mr Quarles was peculiarly susceptible to calves.
1928 *Point Counter Point*, ch.20.

69 Parodies and caricatures are the most penetrating of criticisms.
1928 *Point Counter Point*, ch.28.

70 Happiness is like coke—something you get as a by-product in the process of making something else.
1928 *Point Counter Point*, ch.30.

71 Too much consistency is as bad for the mind as it is for the body. Consistency is contrary to nature, contrary to life.
1929 *Do What You Will*, 'Wordsworth in the Tropics'.

72 After silence, that which comes nearest to expressing the inexpressible is music.
1931 *Music at Night*.

73 Experience is not what happens to a man; it is what a man does with what happens to him.
1932 *Texts and Pretexts*, introduction.

74 Only man behaves with such gratuitous folly. It is the price he has to pay for being intelligent but not, as yet, quite intelligent enough.
1932 *Texts and Pretexts*, 'Amor Fati'.

75 The escalator from the Social Predestination Room... One circuit of the cellar at ground level, one on the first gallery, half on the second, and on the two hundred and sixty-seventh morning, daylight in the Decanting Room. Independent existence—so called.
1932 *Brave New World*, ch.1.

76 Our Ford...had been the first to reveal the appalling dangers of family life.
1932 *Brave New World*, ch.3.

77 Oh, she's a splendid girl. Wonderfully pneumatic.
1932 *Brave New World*, ch.3.

78 The sexophones wailed like melodious cats under the moon.
1932 *Brave New World*, ch.5.

79 The real pitch lake is simply about two hundred asphalt tennis courts, in very bad condition, set in the midst of some gently undulating green meadows. I am inclined to ask for my money back.
1934 On the Trinidad Pitch Lake. *Beyond the Mexique Bay*.

80 Official dignity tends to increase in inverse ratio to the importance of the country in which the office is held.
1934 *Beyond the Mexique Bay*.

81 'Death,' said Mark Staithes. 'It's the only thing we haven't succeeded in completely vulgarizing.'
1936 *Eyeless in Gaza*, ch.31.

82 The end cannot justify the means, for the simple and obvious reason that the means employed determine the nature of the ends produced.
1937 *Ends and Means*, ch.1.

83 We are living now, not in the delicious intoxication induced by the early successes of science, but in a rather grisly morning-after, when it has become apparent that what triumphant science has done hitherto is to improve the means for achieving unimproved or actually deteriorated ends.
1937 *Ends and Means*, ch.1.

84 So long as men worship the Caesars and Napoleons, Caesars and Napoleons will duly arise and make them miserable.
1937 *Ends and Means*, ch.8.

85 The propagandist's purpose is to make one set of people forget that certain other sets of people are human.
1937 *The Olive Tree*.

86 What is science? Science is angling in the mud—angling for immortality and for anything else that may happen to turn up.
1939 *After Many a Summer Dies the Swan*.

87 The quality of moral behaviour varies in inverse ratio to the number of human beings involved.
1941 *Grey Eminence*, ch.10.

88 There's only one corner of the universe you can be certain of improving, and that's your own self.
1944 *Time Must Have a Stop*.

89 You learn to love by loving—by paying attention and doing what one thereby discovers has to be done.
1944 *Time Must Have a Stop*.

90 Facts are ventriloquist's dummies. Sitting on a wise man's knee they may be made to utter words of wisdom; elsewhere they say nothing, or talk nonsense.
1944 *Time Must Have a Stop*.

91 Most human beings have an infinite capacity for taking things for granted.
1950 'Variations on a Philosopher'.

92 We participate in a tragedy; at a comedy we only look.
1952 *The Devils of Loudun*, ch.11.

93 I was seeing what Adam had seen on the morning of his creation—the miracle, moment by moment, of naked existence.
1954 *The Doors of Perception*.

94 I have spoken so far only of the blissful visionary experience... But visionary experience is not always blissful. It's sometimes terrible. There is hell as well as heaven.
1956 *Heaven and Hell*.

95 'Bed,' as the Italian proverb succinctly puts it, 'is the poor man's opera.'
1956 *Heaven and Hell*.

96 The most distressing thing that can happen to a prophet is to be proved wrong. The next most distressing thing is to be proved right.
1956 'Brave New World Revisited', in *Esquire*.

97 But liberty, as we all know, cannot flourish in a country that is permanently on a war footing, or even a near-war footing. Permanent crisis justifies permanent control of everybody and everything by the agencies of central

government.
1956 'Brave New World Revisited', in *Esquire.*

98 But some of us still believe that, without freedom, human beings cannot become fully human and that freedom is therefore supremely valuable.
1956 'Brave New World Revisited', in *Esquire.*

99 That men do not learn very much from the lessons of history is the most important of all the lessons that history has to teach.
1959 'A Case of Voluntary Ignorance'.

1 Science is the reduction of the bewildering diversity of unique events to manageable uniformity within one of a number of symbol systems, and technology is the art of using these symbol systems so as to control and organize unique events. Scientific observation is always a viewing of things through the refracting medium of a symbol system, and technological praxis is always handling of things in ways that some symbol system has dictated. Education in science and technology is essentially education on the symbol level.
1962 In *Daedalus*, spring issue.

2 Idealism is the noble toga that political gentlemen drape over their will to power.
Quoted in his *New York Herald Tribune* obituary, 24 Nov 1963.

Huxley, Sir Julian Sorell 1887–1975

English biologist and humanist, grandson of T H Huxley. He was the first Director-General of UNESCO, and formulated a pragmatic ethical theory of 'evolutionary humanism'.

3 We all know how the size of sums of money appears to vary in a remarkable way according as they are being paid in or paid out.
1923 *Essays of a Biologist*, ch.5.

4 Operationally, God is beginning to resemble not a ruler but the last fading smile of a cosmic Cheshire cat.
1957 *Religion without Revelation* (rev edn), ch.3.

Huxley, T(homas) H(enry) 1825–95

English biologist, who made significant contributions to palaeontology and comparative anatomy. He famously supported Darwin's controversial theory of evolution by natural selection, and the term 'agnostic' has been attributed to him.

5 The generalizations of science sweep in ever-widening circles, and more aspiring flights, through a limitless creation.
1859 Letter to *The Times*, 26 Dec.

6 Sit down before fact as a little child, be prepared to give up every preconceived notion, follow humbly wherever and to whatsoever abysses Nature leads, or you shall learn nothing.
1860 Letter to Charles Kingsley.

7 Most of my colleagues were *-ists* of one sort or another; and however kind and friendly they might be, I, the man without a rag of a label to cover himself with, could not fail to have some of the uneasy feelings which must have beset the historical fox when, after leaving the trap in which his tail remained, he presented himself to his normally elongated companions. So I took thought, and invented what I conceived to be the appropriate title of 'agnostic'.
1869 *Science and Christian Tradition.*

8 The central propositions [of Descartes]...are these: There is a path that leads to the truth so surely that any one who will follow it must needs reach the goal... And there is one guiding rule by which a man may always find this path...give unqualified assent to no propositions but those the truth of which is so clear and distinct that they cannot be doubted.
1870 *Lay Sermons, Addresses, and Reviews.*

9 The great tragedy of Science—the slaying of a beautiful hypothesis by an ugly fact.
1870 'Biogenesis and Abiogenesis', in the *British Association Annual Report.*

10 Our reverence for the nobility of manhood will not be lessened by the knowledge that man is in substance and in structure, one with the brutes; for he alone possesses the marvellous endowment of intelligible and rational speech whereby...he has slowly accumulated and organized the experience which is almost wholly lost with the cessation of individual life in other animals; so that he now stands raised above it as on a mountain-top, far above the level of his humble fellows, and transfigured from his grosser nature by reflecting, here and there, a ray from the infinite source of truth.
1880 *Man's Place in Nature.*

11 It is the customary fate of new truths to begin as heresies and to end as superstitions.
1880 *Science and Culture and Other Essays*, 'The Coming of Age of the Origin of the Species'.

12 Irrationally held truths may be more harmful than reasoned errors.
1880 *Science and Culture and Other Essays*, 'The Coming of Age of the Origin of the Species'.

13 Science is nothing but trained and organized common sense, differing from the latter only as a veteran may differ from a raw recruit: and its methods differ from those of common sense only as far as the guardsman's cut and thrust differ from the manner in which a savage wields his club.
1893–4 *Collected Essays*, no.4, 'The Method of Zadig'.

14 Some experience of popular lecturing had convinced me that the necessity of making things plain to uninstructed people was one of the very best means of clearing up the obscure corners in one's own mind.
1894 *Man's Place in Nature* (rev edn), preface.

15 Next to being right in this world, the best of all things is to be clearly and definitely wrong. If you go buzzing about between right and wrong, vibrating and fluctuating, you come out nowhere; but if you are absolutely and thoroughly and persistently wrong you must, some of these days, have the extreme good fortune of knocking your head against a fact, and that sets you all straight again.
Attributed.

Huxtable, Ada Louise *née* *Landman* c.1921–

US architectural critic. In her columns for the *New York Times* (1963–82), she denounced new buildings and property speculation which spoiled American cities. Her work helped promote the preservation of historic buildings. She won the first Pulitzer Prize for criticism in 1970.

16 I got a terrible case of the Fountainblues.

1970 On Miami Beach. In the *New York Times*, 15 Oct.

17 America the beautiful,
Let me sing of thee;
Burger King and Dairy Queen
From sea to shining sea.
1971 'Goodbye History, Hello Hamburger', in the *New York Times*, 21 Mar.

18 New York, thy name is irreverence and hyperbole. And grandeur.
1975 In the *New York Times*, 20 Jul.

Hyde, Robin *pseudonym of* ***Iris Guiver Wilkinson*** 1906–39

New Zealand novelist, poet and journalist, born in South Africa. She was one of the few women career journalists of the 1930s. Brief affairs led to the births of two sons; the first, whose name she adopted, was stillborn. Her works include the autobiographical novel *The Godwits Fly* (1938).

19 Something there had been, something delicate, wild and far away. But it was shut out behind the doors of yesterday, lost beyond the hills.
1938 *The Godwits Fly*, ch.3.

20 You were English and not English. It took time to realize that England was far away.
1938 *The Godwits Fly*, ch.3.

21 We live half our lives in England...there can't have been anything quite like this since the Roman colonists settled in Britain: not the hanging on with one hand, and the other hand full of seas.
1938 *The Godwits Fly*, ch.8.

22 Having a lover isn't much to write home about.
1938 *The Godwits Fly*, ch.17.

23 She stands an instant in the sun
Athwart her harsh land's red and green—
Hands of a serf, and warrior eyes
Of some flame-sceptred Irish queen.
... As if she does not care that life
Has reft the jewels from her hair—
But grieves that menial needs and base
Were those that left her palace bare.
1938 *The Godwits Fly*, ch.23. This poem is an adaptation of 'The Farmer's Wife', first published in *The Desolate Star* (1929).

Hyde-White, Wilfred 1903–91

English film actor.

24 The suaveness isn't born of confidence; it's born of fright.
Quoted in his obituary, in the *San Francisco Chronicle*, 7 May 1991.

Hynde, Chrissie 1951–

US singer, member of The Pretenders.

25 I feel displaced when I'm back in America, like a visitor. I feel like if I don't get a cup of tea I'm going to lose my mind.
2003 In the *Daily Telegraph*, 19 Apr.

26 There's the meat eaters and there's us. And that's the way I look at the world.
2003 In *The Independent*, 13 Sep.

Hytner, Nicholas 1956–

English film and theatre director. He has been artistic director at the National Theatre since 2003.

27 The theatre on its own can't and doesn't change society, but plays can define a moment. *The Marriage of Figaro* did seem to predict a revolution, but I doubt it sent anybody onto the streets.
2004 In *Varsity*, 6 Feb.

Iacocca, Lee (Lido Anthony) 1924–

US businessman, president of the Ford Motor Company and later head of Chrysler Corporation (1979–1992).

28 People want economy and they will pay any price to get it.
1974 In the *New York Times*, 13 Oct.

29 Everybody in an organization has to believe their livelihood is based on the quality of the product they deliver.
1988 *Talking Straight*.

30 If you want to continue being leaders in the world, start by getting some of that [Federal] debt off your backs. Debtors can't be leaders. It's the guy holding the IOUs who can call the shots; the other guy is called a hostage.
1992 Quoted in the *New York Times*, 26 May.

Ibarruri Gomez, Dolores *known as* ***La Pasionaria*** 1895–1989

Spanish writer and politician, a founder of the Spanish Communist Party (1920). She urged the fight against the Fascist forces, and left for the USSR when Franco came to power. On returning to Spain in 1977, she was re-elected to the National Assembly.

31 It is better to die on your feet than live on your knees. *No pasarán*!
1936 Speech in Paris, 3 Sep, at the onset of the Spanish Civil War, imploring the people to defend the Republic against the Fascist uprising. 'No pasarán', meaning 'they will not pass' and associated with the World War I Battle of Verdun, was to become the battle-cry of the Republican cause.
► *See Pétain 649:74.*

Ibn Battutah 1304–68

Arab traveller and geographer, who spent 30 years visiting parts of Africa, Asia and southern Europe. He then settled in Fez and wrote the history of his journeys.

32 Never to travel any road a second time.
His guiding principle. *Travels in Asia and Africa 1325–1354* (translated by H A R Gibb, 1929).

Ibsen, Henrik Johan 1828–1906

Norwegian playwright, the founder of modern prose drama. His realistic plays on sensitive social issues revolutionized modern European drama. They include *En dukkehjem* (*A Doll's House*, 1879), *Vildanden* (*The Wild Duck*, 1884) and *Hedda Gabler* (1890).

33 *Flertallet har aldrig retten på sin side. Aldrig, siger jeg! Det er en af disse samfundsløgnere, som en fri, tænkende mand må gøre oprør imod. Hvem er det, som udgør flertallet af beboerne i et land? Er det de kloge folk, eller er det dè dumme? Jeg tænker, vi får vaere enige om, at dumme mennesker er tilstede i en ganske forskrækkelig overvældende majoritet rundt omkring på den hele vide jord.*
The majority never has right on its side. Never, I say! That is one of the social lies that a free, thinking man is bound to rebel against. Who makes up the majority in any given country? Is it the wise men or the fools? I think we must agree that the fools are in a terrible overwhelming majority, all the wide world over.
1882 *En folkefiende* (*An Enemy of the People*), act 4.

34 *En skulde aldrig ha' sine bedste buxer på, nå r en er ude og strider for frihed og sandhed.*
You should never have your best trousers on when you turn out to fight for freedom and truth.
1882 *En folkefiende* (*An Enemy of the People*), act 5.

35 *Luftslotter,—de er så nemme at ty õûnd i, de. Og nemme at bygge også.*
Castles in the air—they are so easy to take refuge in. And so easy to build, too.
1892 *Bygmester Solness* (*The Master Builder*), act 3.

36 On the contrary!
1906 Last words, refuting a nurse's suggestion that he was feeling better.

I Ching c.2000 BC

I Ching (*The Book of Changes*) is reputed to have been composed by a Chinese king and his son under guidance from a Taoist sage. It is a compendium of observations and advice regarding the rise and fall of individuals and their power groups and was later annotated by Confucius.

37 It is unlucky to sound off about happiness.
c.2000 BC *I Ching*, no.16 (translated by Thomas Cleary).

38 Change proves true on the day it is finished.
c.2000 BC *I Ching*, no.49 (translated by Thomas Cleary).

39 Cultured people practise self-examination with trepidation and fear.
c.2000 BC *I Ching*, no.51 (translated by Thomas Cleary).

Ignatieff, Michael 1947–

Canadian author, broadcaster and academic.

40 The medium's gaze is brief, intense, and promiscuous. The shelf life of the moral causes it makes its own is brutally short.
1988 'Is Nothing Sacred? The Ethics of Television', in *Daedalus: Journal of the American Academy of Arts and Sciences*, Fall.

Ignatow, David 1914–97

US poet and academic. He published several volumes of poetry, much of it highly autobiographical in content.

41 Faster and faster it rolled,
with me running after it
bent low, gritting my teeth,
and I found myself doubled over
and rolling down the street
head over heels, one complete somersault
after another like a bagel
and strangely happy with myself.
1968 *Rescue the Dead*, 'The Bagel'.

42 To love is to be a fish.
My boat wallows in the sea.
You who are free,
rescue the dead.
1968 *Rescue the Dead*, 'Rescue the Dead'.

Ihimaera, Witi Tame 1944–

New Zealand writer and diplomat. His novel *Tangi* (1973), about a son's return home to his father's funeral and to his Maori roots, was the first written by a Maori to have been published. Other works include *The Matriarch* (1986), *The Whale Rider* (1987) and *Sky Dancer* (2003).

43 The sunlight falls across the country, lighting up the greenstone years of a boy with his father.
1973 *Tangi*, ch.14.

44 *Titiro ki te rangi tahuri rawa ake, Kahore he whenua e…Kua riro*: We looked up to heaven and before we knew where we were there was no land left…gone.
1986 *The Matriarch*, ch.3.

Illich, Ivan 1926–2002

Austrian-born social critic, former priest and polymath. His works include *Deschooling Society* (1971) and *In the Vineyard of the Text* (1993).

45 Current nationalism is merely the affirmation of the right of colonial elites to repeat history and follow the road travelled by the rich toward the universal consumption of internationally marketed packages, a road which can ultimately lead only to universal pollution and universal frustration.
1970 *Celebration of Awareness*, ch.12.

46 In both rich and poor nations consumption is polarized while expectation is equalized.
1970 *Celebration of Awareness*, ch.12.

47 In a consumer society there are inevitably two kinds of slaves: the prisoners of addiction and the prisoners of envy.
1973 *Tools for Conviviality*, ch.3.

Independent on Sunday

48 Floral fascism and an explosion of almost medieval irrationality.
1997 Editorial reflecting on the response to the death of Diana, Princess of Wales, 9 Nov.

Inge, William Ralph 1860–1954

English prelate and theologian, known as 'The Gloomy Dean' for his pessimistic sermons as Dean of St Paul's (1911–34). His books include *Outspoken Essays* (1919, 1922), *Lay Thoughts of a Dean* (1926, 1931) and more serious theological works.

49 It takes in reality only one to make a quarrel. It is useless for the sheep to pass resolutions in favour of vegetarianism, while the wolf remains of a different opinion.
1919 *Outspoken Essays* (first series), 'Patriotism'.

50 A man may build himself a throne of bayonets, but he cannot sit on it.
1923 *Philosophy of Plotinus*, vol.2, lecture 22.

51 Many people believe that they are attracted by God, or by Nature, when they are only repelled by man.
1931 *More Thoughts of a Lay Dean*, pt.4, ch.1.

52 The enemies of freedom do not argue; they shout and they shoot.
1948 *The End of an Age*, ch.4.

53 The effect of boredom on a large scale in history is underestimated. It is a main cause of revolutions, and would soon bring to an end all the static Utopias and the farmyard civilization of the Fabians.
1948 *The End of an Age*, ch.6.

54 A nation is a society united by a delusion about its ancestry and by a common hatred of its neighbours.
Sagittarius and George.

Ingersoll, Robert 1833–99

US lawyer, orator and freethinker, called 'The Great Agnostic' for his anti-religious views.

55 The hope of science is the perfection of the human race. The hope of theology is the salvation of a few and the damnation of almost everybody.
1867 *The Age of Reason*, Mar.

56 An honest God is the noblest work of man.
1876 *The Gods*, pt.1.
► *See Pope 660:25*.

57 In nature there are neither rewards nor punishments —there are consequences.
1881 *Some Reasons Why*, pt.8, 'The New Testament'.

Ingham, Sir Bernard 1932–

English journalist and businessman, particularly known as Margaret Thatcher's chief press secretary (1979–90).

58 Blood sport is brought to its ultimate refinement in the gossip columns.
1986 Speech, 5 Feb.

Ingram, John Kells 1823–1907

Irish economist and poet, Professor of Oratory then of Greek at Trinity College, Dublin. In 1847 he co-founded the Dublin Statistical Society, attempting in his works to formulate a social rather than purely mathematical science of economics.

59 Who fears to speak of Ninety-Eight?
Who blushes at the name?
When cowards mock the patriot's fate,
Who hangs his head for shame?
He's all a knave or half a slave
Who slights his country thus:
But a *true* man, like you, man,
Will fill your glass with us.
1845 *The Spirit of the Nation*, 'The Memory of the Dead'.

Ingrams, Richard Reid 1937–

English writer, former editor of the satirical magazine *Private Eye*.

60 I have come to regard the law courts not as a cathedral but rather as a casino.
1977 Referring to libel suits against him. Quoted in *The Guardian*, 30 Jul.

Ingres, Jean Auguste Dominique 1780–1867

French painter, leading exponent of the Classical tradition in 19c France. He painted many of his famous nudes while living in Rome (1806–20).

61 Is there anyone among the great men who has not imitated? Nothing is made with nothing.
1821 Quoted in Henri Delaborde *Ingres, sa vie, ses travaux, sa doctrine* (1870).

62 What do these so-called artists mean when they preach the discovery of the 'new'? Is there anything new? Everything has been done, everything has been discovered.
1821 Quoted in Henri Delaborde *Ingres, sa vie, ses travaux, sa doctrine* (1870).

63 Anti-classic art, if it may even be called an art, is merely the art of the idle. It is the doctrine of those who desire to produce without working, to know without learning.
1821 Quoted in Henri Delaborde *Ingres, sa vie, ses travaux, sa doctrine* (1870).

64 Make copies, young man, many copies. You can only become a good artist by copying the masters.
1855 Attributed comment to Degas. Quoted in A Vollard *Souvenirs d'un marchand de tableaux* (1937).

65 They have let the wolf into the sheepfold!
1859 Attributed remark on hearing that Delacroix had been elected to the Academy. Quoted in P Amaury-Duval *L'Atelier d'Ingres* (1878).

66 One must go after the modelling like a fly crawling over a piece of paper.
Attributed aphorism. Quoted in P Valéry *Degas, Danse, Dessin* (1938).

Innis, Harold Adams 1894–1952

Canadian political economist.

67 Canadian nationalism was systematically encouraged and exploited by American capital. Canada moved from colony to nation to colony.
1948 'Great Britain, the United States and Canada', collected in Mary Quayle Innis (ed) *Essays in Canadian Economic History* (1956).

68 Property like incest holds the family together.
Quoted in William Christian (ed) *The Idea File of Harold Adams Innis* (1980).

Pope Innocent III *originally* *Lotario de' Conti di Segni* 1160–1216

Italian prelate and scholar, elected Pope in 1198. He asserted the authority of the papacy over secular princes, and strongly promoted the Fourth Crusade.

69 *Omnis cupidus at avarus contra naturam nititur et molitur. Natura namque pauperem adducit in mundum; natura pauperem reducit a mundo.*
Every covetous and avaricious man struggles and strives against nature. For nature brings him into the world poor, and takes him out of it poor.
1195 *De Miseraria Condicionis Humanae*, bk.2, ch.12.

70 *Gula carum tributem exigit, sed vilissimum reddit, quia quanto sunt delicaciora cibavia, tanto fetidiora sunt stercora.*
Gluttony demands a heavy tribute but gives the basest returns: the more delicate the food, the more reeking

the dung.
1195 *De Miseraria Condicionis Humanae*, bk.2, ch.20.

71 This [Magna Carta] has been forced from the King. It constitutes an insult to the Holy See, a serious weakening of the royal power, a disgrace to the English nation, a danger to all Christendom, since this civil war obstructs the crusade. Therefore…we condemn the charter and forbid the King to keep it, or the barons and their supporters to make him do so, on pain of excommunication.
1215 Papal Bull, 24 Aug.

Inouye, Daniel Ken 1924–

US politician, Democratic senator from Hawaii since 1962. He served on the committees investigating Watergate (1973–4) and (as chairman) the Iran-Contra affair (1987).

72 No times were more dangerous than when our country was born, when revolution was our midwife.
1987 Response to Adm John M Poindexter and Lt Col Oliver L North's contention that their actions were greatly influenced by 'a dangerous world'. In the *New York Times*, 24 Jul.

73 These hearings will be remembered longest not for the facts they elicited, but for the extraordinary and extraordinarily frightening views of government they exposed.
1987 On the Iran-Contra hearings. In the *New York Times*, 24 Jul.

74 A great nation betrayed the principles which have made it great, and thereby became hostage to hostage-takers.
1987 Of the Iran-Contra scandal. In the *New York Times*, 24 Jul.

Ionesco, Eugène 1912–94

French playwright. He pioneered a new style of drama that came to be called the Theatre of the Absurd.

75 *Un fonctionnaire ne plaisante pas.*
A civil servant doesn't make jokes.
1958 *Tueur sans gages*, act 1.

76 *C'est une chose anormale de vivre.*
Living is abnormal.
1959 *Rhinocéros*, act 1.

Irigaray, Luce c.1932–

Belgian-born French feminist literary critic and philosopher who has applied Lacan's psychoanalytic writings to the question of the difference between women's and men's writing.

77 *Il faut renouveler le langage.*
We must re-invent language.
1981 *Corps-à-corps avec la mère.*

Irving, Washington 1783–1859

US essayist. Under the pseudonym 'Geoffrey Crayon' he wrote *The Sketch Book* (1819–20) which included 'Rip Van Winkle' and 'The Legend of Sleepy Hollow'. Several collections are devoted to his European travels, including *Tales of a Traveller* (1824). He was US Ambassador to Spain (1842–6).

78 What is history, in fact, but a kind of Newgate calendar, a register of the crimes and miseries that man has inflicted on his fellow-man?
1809 *A History of New York*, bk.4, ch.1.

79 My native country was full of youthful promise; Europe was rich in the accumulated treasures of age.
1819–20 *The Sketch Book*, 'The Author's Account of Himself'.

80 A tart temper never mellows with age, and a sharp tongue is the only edged tool that grows keener with constant use.
1819–20 *The Sketch Book*, 'Rip Van Winkle'.

81 A woman's whole life is a history of the affections.
1819–20 *The Sketch Book*, 'The Broken Heart'.

82 Whenever a man's friends begin to compliment him about looking young, he may be sure that they think he is growing old.
1822 *Bracebridge Hall*, 'Bachelors'.

83 I am always at a loss to know how much to believe of my own stories.
1824 *Tales of a Traveller*, 'To the Reader'.

84 There is a certain relief in change, even though it be from bad to worse… I have often found in travelling in a stage-coach, that it is often a comfort to shift one's position, and be bruised in a new place.
1824 *Tales of a Traveller*, 'To the Reader'.

85 The almighty dollar, that great object of universal devotion throughout our land.
1855 *Wolfert's Roost*, 'The Creole Village'.

Isaacs, Jorge 1837–95

Colombian novelist. He worked variously as a journalist, businessman, government official and consul to Chile. His much-imitated romantic novel *María* (1867) is notable for its idyllic descriptions of nature.

86 *Las grandes bellezas de la creación no pueden a un tiempo ser vistas y cantadas: es necesario que vuelvan al alma empalidecidas por la memoria infiel.*
The most beautiful things on earth cannot be seen and sung at the same time: they must return to the soul weakened by unfaithful memory.
1867 *María*, ch.2 (translated as *María: A South American Romance*, 1977).

Isaacson, Walter Seff 1952–

US journalist and writer. He has been the managing editor of *Time* magazine (1996–2001) and chairman and chief executive officer of CNN. His books include *Kissinger: A Biography* (1992) and *Benjamin Franklin: An American Life* (2003).

87 He was something between an epitome and a parody.
1992 On Harvard Professor William Elliott, Kissinger's mentor. *Kissinger: A Biography.*

88 No one could shine his shoes, much less fill them.
1992 On President Nixon's self-image at the time of his resignation. *Kissinger: A Biography.*

Isherwood, Christopher William Bradshaw 1904–86

English novelist. He collaborated with Auden in the 1930s. He moved to California in 1939, and became a US citizen in 1946.

89 I am a camera with its shutter open, quite passive, recording, not thinking… Some day, all this will have to be developed, carefully printed, fixed.
1930 'A Berlin Diary', in *Goodbye to Berlin* (1939).

90 Like Shelley and like Baudelaire it may be said of him that he suffered, in his own person, the neurotic ills of an entire generation.
1937 Of T E Lawrence, 'Lawrence of Arabia'. Collected in *Exhumations* (1966).

91 They share the insult of each other's presence.
1962 On characters in his novels. *Down There on a Visit.*

Ishiguro, Kazuo 1954–

British novelist, born in Japan. His first book, *A Pale View of Hills* (1982), was set in Japan, but later works have been English in tone and subject, notably *The Remains of the Day* (1989, Booker Prize).

92 An Artist of the Floating World.
1988 Title of novel.

93 A 'great' butler can only be, surely, one who can point to his years of service and say that he has applied his talents to serving a great gentleman—and through the latter, to serving humanity.
1989 *The Remains of the Day*, 'Day Two—Afternoon'.

94 Perhaps it is indeed time that I began to look at this whole matter of bantering more enthusiastically. After all, when we think about it, it is not such a foolish thing to indulge in—particularly if it is the case that in bantering lies the key to human warmth.
1989 *The Remains of the Day*, 'Day Six—Evening'.

Issigonis, Sir Alec (Alexander Arnold Constantine) 1906–88

Turkish-born British car designer. He came to the English Midlands where he designed some of Britain's most popular and influential cars, including the Morris Minor and the Mini.

95 All creative people hate mathematics. It's the most uncreative subject you can study.
Recalled on his death. Quoted in *The Australian*, 5 Oct 1988.

96 Styling is designing for obsolescence.
Recalled on his death. Quoted in *The Australian*, 5 Oct 1988.

97 A camel is a horse designed by a committee.
Attributed to him in *The Guardian*, 14 Jan 1991.

Ito, Lance Allan 1950–

US jurist, presiding judge at the Los Angeles Superior Court (1989–). His most famous case is the O J Simpson murder trial (1994–5).

98 Rule 1: Be cautious, careful and when in doubt, keep your mouth shut. Rule 2: When tempted to say something, take a deep breath and refer to Rule 1.
1994 In the *New York Times*, 23 Jul.

Ivan IV *known as* Ivan the Terrible 1530–84

Grand Prince of Moscow (1533–84), the first to assume the title of 'tsar' (Latin *Caesar*). In 1564 he began a reign of terror, directed mainly at the aristocracy.

99 To shave the beard is a sin that the blood of all the martyrs cannot cleanse. It is to deface the image of man created by God.
Quoted in David Maland *Europe in the Seventeenth Century* (1968).

Iverson, Allen 1975–

US basketball player.

1 The basket looked like an ocean, and I was just throwing rocks in.
2003 After scoring 55 points for the Philadelphia 76ers against the New Orleans Hornets. Quoted on SI.com, 20 Apr.

Ives, Charles Edward 1874–1954

US composer. His innovative, experimental works were unappreciated for most of his life, but in 1947 he was awarded a Pulitzer Prize for his 3rd symphony (composed 1911).

2 Please don't try to make things nice! All the wrong notes are *right*... I want it that way.
c.1914 Note to the copyist of *The Fourth of July.*

Izzard, Eddie 1962–

British comedian and actor.

3 It's my manifest destiny to wear a skirt in all countries.
2001 Quoted on www.theonionavclub.com, 31 Jan.

4 Drama is a complete meal, vitamins, proteins, carbohydrates. It's a slow burn thing. It's got an arc. Comedy is more like coke.
2004 In *The Guardian*, 17 May.

Jackson, Jesse Louis 1941–

US clergyman and Democratic politician, founder and President of the Rainbow/PUSH (People United to Save Humanity) coalition. In 1984 and 1988 he sought nomination for the presidency, the first black American to be a serious candidate for the office.

5 I cast my bread on the waters long ago. Now it's time for you to send it back to me—toasted, and buttered on both sides.
1984 Addressing black voters, New York, 30 Jan.

6 My constituency is the desperate, the damned, the disinherited, the disrespected, and the despised.
1984 Speech at the Democratic National Convention, San Francisco, 17 Jul.

7 Our flag is red, white and blue, but our nation is a rainbow—red, yellow, brown, black and white—and we are all precious in God's sight... America is not like a blanket—one piece of unbroken cloth, the same color, the same texture, the same size. America is more like a quilt—many patches, many pieces, many colors, many sizes; all woven and held together by a common thread.
1984 Launching his 'rainbow coalition' at the Democratic National Convention, San Francisco, 17 Jul.

8 If I can conceive it and believe it, I can achieve it. It's not my *aptitude* but my *attitude* that will determine my *altitude*—*with a little intestinal fortitude!*
1988 *Ebony*, Aug.

Jackson, Peter 1961–

New Zealand film director, best known for directing the *Lord of the Rings* trilogy (*The Fellowship of the Ring*, 2001; *The Two Towers*, 2002; *The Return of the King*, 2003).

9 I read the book when I was 18 years old and thought 'I can't wait till the movie comes out'. Twenty years later no

one had done it—so I got impatient.
2003 On how he came to direct the *Lord of the Rings*. Quoted in the *Observer*, 30 Nov.

Jackson, Robert Houghwout 1892–1954

US jurist, Associate Justice of the US Supreme Court (1941–54). He took leave to be US Chief Counsel at the Nuremberg war trials (1945–6). His decisions upheld freedom of speech and religion.

10 We are not final because we are infallible, but we are infallible only because we are final.
1953 Ruling to uphold the Supreme Court as the bench of last appeal, 9 Feb.

11 He who must search a haystack for a needle is likely to end up with the attitude that the needle is not worth the search.
1953 Ruling to uphold the Supreme Court as the bench of last appeal, 9 Feb.

Jacobs, Andrew, Jr 1932–

US lawyer and Democratic politician. He retired from Congress in 1997.

12 It's like saying that the patient died but the good news is that he's eating less.
1982 Of the Reagan administration's claim to have reduced inflation. In the *Washington Post*, 6 Jun.

Jacobs, Herman

Pharmaceutical store supplier.

13 It is not the mouse who is the thief, it is the hole that allows the mouse in.
1994 His interpretation of Talmudic principles applied in business. In *Forbes*, 21 Nov.

Jacobs, Joe 1896–1940

US boxing manager. He was manager of boxer Max Schmeling.

14 We wuz robbed!
1932 After Schmeling's unexpected defeat by Jack Sharkey, 21 Jun. Quoted in Peter Heller *In This Corner* (1975). Jack Dempsey in 1927 claimed 'I was robbed of the championship' when he lost to Gene Tunney. The cry was subsequently widely adopted by aggrieved losers.

Jacobs, W(illiam) W(ymark) 1863–1943

English short-story writer. He specialized in colourful yarns about the watermen on the Thames, and macabre stories.

15 'Dealing with a man,' said the night-watchman, 'is as easy as a teetotaller walking along a nice wide pavement; dealing with a woman is like the same teetotaller, after four or five whiskies, trying to get up a step that ain't there.'
1919 *Deep Waters*, 'Husbandry'.

Jagger, Mick and Richards, Keith 1943–, 1943–

English rock musicians, who with Bill Wyman, Charlie Watts and Brian Jones formed The Rolling Stones (1961). Their rebellious image and controversial lifestyles added to the extraordinary success of their music.

16 I can't get no satisfaction
I can't get no girl reaction.
1966 '(I Can't Get No) Satisfaction'.

17 Mother needs something today to calm her down,
And though she's not really ill,
There's a little yellow pill:
She goes running for the shelter
Of a mother's little helper,
And it helps her on her way,
Gets her through her busy day.
1966 'Mother's Little Helper'.

18 Please allow me to introduce myself
I'm a man of wealth and taste.
I've been around for a long, long year
Stole many a man's soul and faith.
And I was around when Jesus Christ
Had his moments of doubt and pain,
Made damn sure that Pilate
Washed his hands and sealed his fate.
Pleased to meet you, hope you guess my name
But what's puzzling you
Is the nature of my game.
1968 'Sympathy for the Devil'.

19 I shouted out, 'Who killed the Kennedys?'
When after all it was you and me.
1968 'Sympathy for the Devil'.

20 It's Only Rock and Roll.
1974 Title of song.

James I 1394–1437

King of Scotland (from 1424). He was imprisoned by the English for 18 years before returning to Scotland to take the throne. His measures to curb the nobles' power led to his murder. *The Kingis Quair* (c.1435), his only surviving work, is thought to have introduced Chaucerian style to Scotland.

21 The bird, the beste, the fisch eke in the see,
They lyve in fredome, euerich in his kynd,
And I, a man, and lakkith libertee!
c.1435 *The Kingis Quair*, stanza 27.

James IV 1473–1513

King of Scotland (from 1488). His marriage to Margaret Tudor, daughter of Henry VII of England, led ultimately to the union of the crowns. He was defeated and killed at Flodden.

22 It is statute and ordained that in na place of the Realme there be used Fute-ball, Golfe, or uther sik unproffitable sportes.
1491 Royal decree.

James V 1512–42

King of Scotland (from 1513). He succeeded to the throne as an infant, amid quarrelling pro-French and pro-English factions. As an adult he ruled with a mixture of good judgement and vindictiveness, strengthening the Crown's power and revenues.

23 Adieu, Farewell, it came with a lass, it will pass with a lass.
1542 Said on his deathbed, 14 Dec, on hearing of the birth of his daughter Mary, referring to the Crown of Scotland passing from the Stewarts. Quoted in Robert Lindsay of Pitscottie (c.1532–1580) *The Historie and Cronicles of Scotland* (published 1728), vol.1.

James, Alice 1848–92

US diarist, sister of Henry and William James. She spent her childhood travelling with her family in Europe. A semi-invalid for much of her life, she lived in England to be near her brother

Henry. Her diary was published posthumously.

24 How heroic to be able to suppress one's vanity to the extent of confessing that the game is too hard.
1889 On suicide. Diary entry, 5 Aug.

25 When will women begin to have the first glimmer that above all other loyalties is the loyalty to Truth, i.e., to yourself, that husband, children, friends and country are as nothing to that.
1889 Diary entry, 19 Nov.

26 How sick one gets of being 'good', how much I should respect myself if I could burst out and make every one wretched for 24 hours.
1889 Diary entry, 11 Dec.

27 I suppose one has a greater sense of intellectual degradation after an interview with a doctor than from any human experience.
1890 Diary entry, 27 Sep.

James, Clive Vivian Leopold 1939–

Australian journalist, writer and broadcaster, famous as a witty and perceptive cultural commentator.

28 A country so precipitously convoluted that the rivers flowing through it look like the silver trails of inebriated slugs.
1978 'Postcard from Japan', in the *Observer* magazine, 4 Jun.

29 She sounded like the book of Revelations read out over a railway station public-address system by a headmistress of a certain age wearing calico knickers.
1979 Of Margaret Thatcher. In the *Observer*.

30 I feared for her as I loved her, and the fear intensified the love.
1997 On the death of Diana, Princess of Wales. In the *New Yorker*, 15 Sep.

31 When you say a man writes badly, you are trying to hurt him. When you say it in words better than his, you have succeeded.
2003 In the *New York Times*, 7 Sep.

James, C(yril) L(ionel) R(obert) 1901–89

Trinidadian writer, lecturer and political activist. Arguing for the freedom of blacks through Marxism and revolution, he was deported from the US and placed under house arrest in Trinidad.

32 Body-line was not an incident, it was not an accident, it was not a temporary aberration. It was the violence and ferocity of our age expressing itself in cricket.
1963 *Beyond the Boundary.*

James, Henry 1843–1916

US-born British novelist, brother of William and Alice James. He took British citizenship in 1915. Many of his novels explore his 'international theme', including *The Ambassadors* (1903) and *The Golden Bowl* (1904). His critical theory is defined in 'The Art of Fiction' (1884).

33 It's a complex fate, being an American, and one of the responsibilities it entails is fighting against a superstitious valuation of Europe.
1872 Letter to Charles Eliot Norton, 4 Feb.

34 It takes a great deal of history to produce a little literature.
1879 *Hawthorne*, ch.1.

35 It is, I think, an indisputable fact that Americans are, as Americans, the most self-conscious people in the world, and the most addicted to the belief that the other nations of the earth are in a conspiracy to under value them.
1879 *Hawthorne*, ch.6.

36 Cats and monkeys—monkeys and cats—all human life is there!
1879 *The Madonna of the Future*, vol.1. The *News of the World* took 'All human life is there' as its slogan from the late 1950s.

37 There are few hours in life more agreeable than the hour dedicated to the ceremony known as afternoon tea.
1881 *The Portrait of a Lady*, ch.1.

38 An Englishman's never so natural as when he's holding his tongue.
1881 Isabel Archer. *The Portrait of a Lady*, ch.10.

39 Money's a horrid thing to follow, but a charming thing to meet.
1881 Gilbert Osmond. *The Portrait of a Lady*, ch.35.

40 Art derives a considerable part of its beneficial exercise from flying in the face of presumptions.
1884 'The Art of Fiction', collected in *Partial Portraits* (1988).

41 The only obligation to which in advance we may hold a novel, without incurring the accusation of being arbitrary, is that it be interesting.
1884 'The Art of Fiction', collected in *Partial Portraits* (1888).

42 Experience is never limited, and it is never complete; it is an immense sensibility, a kind of huge spider-web of the finest silken threads suspended in the chamber of consciousness, and catching every air-borne particle in its tissue.
1884 'The Art of Fiction', collected in *Partial Portraits* (1888).

43 Try to be one of the people on whom nothing is lost!
1884 'The Art of Fiction', collected in *Partial Portraits* (1888).

44 What is character but the determination of incident? What is incident but the illustration of character?
1884 'The Art of Fiction', collected in *Partial Portraits* (1888).

45 The superiority of one man's opinion over another's is never so great as when the opinion is about a woman.
1890 *The Tragic Muse*, ch.9.

46 We work in the dark—we do what we can—we give what we have. Our doubt is in our passion and our passion is our task. The rest is madness.
1893 Dencombe speaking of the artist. 'The Middle Years', in *Scribner's Magazine*, May.

47 The time-honored bread-sauce of the happy ending.
1894–5 *Theatricals, Second Series*, preface.

48 Most English talk is a quadrille in a sentry box.
1899 The Duchess. *The Awkward Age*, bk.5, ch.4.

49 People talk about the conscience, but it seems to me one must just bring it up to a certain point and leave it there. You can let your conscience alone if you're nice to the second housemaid.
1899 Nanda Brookenham. *The Awkward Age*, bk.6, ch.3.

50 Live all you can; it's a mistake not to. It doesn't so much matter what you do in particular, so long as you have your life. If you haven't had that what *have* you had?
1903 Lambert Strether. *The Ambassadors*, bk.5, ch.11.

51 In art economy is always beauty.
1909 Preface for revised New York edn of *The Altar of the Dead* (first published 1895).

52 The terrible *fluidity* of self-revelation.
1909 Preface for revised NewYork edn of *The Ambassadors* (first published 1903).

53 I'm glad you like adverbs—I adore them; they are the only qualifications I really much respect.
1912 Letter to Miss M Bentham Edwards, 5 Jan, quoted in Percy Lubbock (ed) *The Letters of Henry James* (1920).

54 Summer afternoon—summer afternoon; to me those have always been the two most beautiful words in the English language.
Quoted in Edith Wharton *A Backward Glance* (1934), ch.10, section 6.

55 So here it is at last, the distinguished thing!
Quoted in Edith Wharton *A Backward Glance* (1934), ch.14, section 3. According to Wharton, these were James's last words.

56 I hate American simplicity. I glory in the piling up of complications of every sort.
Remark to his niece. Quoted in Leon Edel *The Letters of Henry James* (1953–72), vol.4, introduction.

James (of Holland Park), P(hyllis) D(orothy) James, Baroness 1920–

English writer. She specializes in carefully detailed crime fiction.

57 I thought that writing a detective story would be a wonderful apprenticeship because, whatever people tell you, a crime novel is not easy to write well. As I continued with my craft I became increasingly fascinated by the form and realized that you can use the formula to say something true about men and women and the society in which they live.
1991 'Series Detectives', collected in Brown and Munro (eds) *Writers Writing* (1993).

58 Murder is a unique crime for which we can never make reparation.
1991 'Series Detectives', collected in Brown and Munro (eds) *Writers Writing* (1993).

James, William 1842–1910

US philosopher and psychologist, brother of Henry and Alice James. A 'radical empiricist', he is often considered the founder of pragmatism. *The Principles of Psychology* (1890) places psychology on a physiological basis. Other works include *The Will to Believe* (1897) and *Pragmatism* (1907).

59 Man lives by science as well as bread.
1875 *Vivisection.*

60 Metaphysics means nothing but an unusually obstinate effort to think clearly.
1890 *The Principles of Psychology*, ch.6.

61 But facts are facts, and if we only get enough of them they are sure to combine.
1890 *The Principles of Psychology*, ch.7.

62 The aim of science is always to reduce complexity to simplicity.
1890 *The Principles of Psychology*, ch.9.

63 Consciousness, then, does not appear to itself chopped up in bits. Such words as 'chain' or 'train' do not describe it fitly as it presents itself in the first instance. It is nothing jointed; it flows. A 'river' or a 'stream' are the metaphors by which it is most naturally described. *In talking of it hereafter, let us call it the stream of thought, of consciousness, or of subjective life.*
1890 *The Principles of Psychology*, ch.9. This is the coining of the phrase 'stream of consciousness', later applied to the narrative technique used by Joyce and others.

64 The baby, assailed by eyes, ears, nose, skin, and entrails at once, feels it all as one great blooming, buzzing confusion.
1890 *The Principles of Psychology*, ch.13.

65 As the art of reading (after a certain stage in one's education) is the art of skipping, so the art of being wise is the art of knowing what to overlook.
1890 *The Principles of Psychology*, ch.22.

66 Man is essentially *the* imitative animal. His whole educability and in fact the whole history of civilization depend on this trait, which his strong tendencies to rivalry, jealousy, and acquisitiveness reinforce.
1890 *The Principles of Psychology*, ch.24.

67 If this life be not a real fight, in which something is eternally gained for the universe by success, it is no better than a game of private theatricals from which one may withdraw at will.
1897 *The Will to Believe.*

68 Sobriety diminishes, discriminates, and says no; drunkenness expands, unites, and says yes.
1902 *The Varieties of Religious Experience*, 'Mysticism'.

69 The philosophy which is so important in each of us is not a technical matter; it is our more or less dumb sense of what life honestly and deeply means… it is our individual way of just seeing and feeling the total push and pressure of the cosmos.
1907 *Pragmatism*, lecture 1.

70 Tender-minded and tough-minded.
1907 His terms for two kinds of philosophical temperament. *Pragmatism*, lecture 1.

71 You must bring out of each word its practical cash-value, set it at work within the stream of your experience.
1907 *Pragmatism*, lecture 2.

72 First, you know, a new theory is attacked as absurd; then it is admitted to be true, but obvious and insignificant; finally it is seen to be so important that its adversaries claim that they themselves discovered it.
1907 *Pragmatism*, lecture 6.

73 'The true' to put it very briefly, is only the expedient in the way of our thinking, just as 'the right' is only the expedient in the way of our behaving.
1907 *Pragmatism*, lecture 6.

74 Many persons nowadays seem to think that any conclusion must be very scientific if the arguments in favor of it are derived from twitching of frogs' legs—especially if the frogs are decapitated—and that—on the other hand—any doctrine chiefly vouched for by the feelings of human beings–with heads on their shoulders—must be benighted and superstitious.
1907 *Pragmatism.*

75 Hogamus, higamous
Man is polygamous
Higamus, hogamous
Woman monogamous.
Quoted in the *Oxford Book of Marriage* (1990).

Janeway, Elizabeth Hall 1913–

US author and critic.

76 As long as mixed grills and combination salads are popular, anthologies will undoubtedly continue in favor.
Quoted in Helen Hull (ed) *The Writer's Book* (1950), ch.32.

Janowitz, Tama 1957–

US writer. She has written novels and short stories, and scored a cult success with the story collection *Slaves of New York* (1986).

77 Long after the bomb falls and you and your good deeds are gone, cockroaches will still be here, prowling the streets like armoured cars.
1986 *Slaves of New York*, 'Modern Saint 271'.

78 With publicity comes humiliation.
1992 In the *International Herald Tribune*, 8 Sep.

Jarrell, Randall 1914–65

US poet and critic. A passionate poet and incisive critic, he also wrote one satirical novel, *Pictures from an Institution* (1954), and children's books. He committed suicide.

79 I felt quite funny when Freud died. It was like having a continent disappear.
1939 Letter to Allen Tate, Sep.

80 Six miles from earth, loosed from its dream of life,
I woke to black flak and the nightmare fighters.
When I died they washed me out of the turret with a hose.
1945 'The Death of the Ball Turret Gunner'.

81 A good poet is someone who manages, in a lifetime of standing out in thunderstorms, to be struck by lightning five or six times; a dozen or two dozen times and he is great.
1953 *Poetry and the Age*, 'The Obscurity of the Poet'.

82 President Robbins was so well adjusted to his environment that sometimes you could not tell which was the environment and which was President Robbins.
1954 *Pictures from an Institution*, pt.1, ch.4.

83 To Americans, English manners are far more frightening than none at all.
1954 *Pictures from an Institution*, pt.1, ch.4.

84 She looked at me the way you'd look at a chessman if it made its own move.
1954 *Pictures from an Institution*, pt.2, ch.1.

85 It's better to entertain an idea than to take it home to live with you for the rest of your life.
1954 *Pictures from an Institution*, pt.4, ch.9.

86 You Americans do not rear children, you *incite* them; you give them food and shelter and applause.
1954 *Pictures from an Institution*, pt.4, ch.10.

87 Is an institution always a man's shadow shortened in the sun, the lowest common denominator of everybody in it?
1954 *Pictures from an Institution*, pt.5, ch.9.

88 One of the most obvious facts about grown-ups, to a child, is that they have forgotten what it is like to be a child.
Introduction to Christina Stead *The Man Who Loved Children* (1965).

Jarry, Alfred 1873–1907

French playwright and humorist, best known for the creation of the petty tyrant in *Ubu Roi* (1896), a play first written when he was only 15.

89 *Quant à l'action, elle se passe en Pologne, c'est à dire, nulle part.*
The action takes place in Poland; in other words, nowhere.
1896 *Ubu Roi*, introduction.

90 *Mère Ubu, tu es bien laide aujourd'hui. Est-ce parce que nous avons du monde?*
Mother Ubu, you are very ugly today. Is it because we have company?
1806 *Ubu Roi*, act 1, sc.1.

91 *La mort n'est que pour les médiocres.*
Death is only for the mediocre.
1898 *Gestes et opinions du Docteur Faustroll Pataphysicien*, vol.8, pt.37.

92 *Dieu est le point tangent de zéro et de l'infini.*
God is the tangential point of zero and the infinite.
1898 *Gestes et opinions du Docteur Faustroll Pataphysicien*, vol.8, pt.41.

93 *S'apercevoir que sa mère est vierge.—Les 36 situations dramatiques; trente-septième situation.*
The thirty-seventh dramatic situation out of 36: To become aware that one's mother is a virgin.
1899 *L'Amour absolu*, pt.3, épigraphe.

Jason, David 1940–

English actor, known for a variety of television roles.

94 Why do they call me David 'Del Boy' Jason? You never hear anyone talking about Alec 'Bridge Over the River Kwai' Guinness.
On his ongoing association with his character in *Only Fools and Horses*. Quoted in Stafford Hildred and Tim Ewbank *Arise Sir David Jason* (2003).

Jaurès, (Auguste Marie Joseph) Jean 1859–1914

French socialist leader, writer and orator. He co-founded the socialist paper *L'Humanité* (1904), and was central in the founding of the French Socialist Party. He was assassinated in Paris.

95 There is, then, over the affairs of the army a universal conspiracy of silence, of childlike mysteries, of clannishness, routine and intrigue.
1910 *L'Armée nouvelle.*

Jay, Sir Antony Rupert 1930–

English writer and television producer. He joined the BBC in 1955, editing *Tonight* (1962–3) and co-writing the successful *Yes, Minister* and *Yes, Prime Minister* (1980–8). He was knighted in 1988.

96 From now on you can keep the lot.
Take every single thing you've got,
Your land, your wealth, your men, your dames,
Your dream of independent power,
And dear old Konrad Adenauer,
And stick them up your Eiffel Tower.
1963 On France's rejection of British membership of the Common Market, in *Time*, 8 Feb.

97 The great modern corporations are so similar to independent or semi-independent states of the past that they can only be fully understood in terms of political or constitutional history, and management can only be properly studied as a branch of government.
1967 *Management and Machiavelli.*

98 Efficiency…is measured at the extremities. You do not find the efficiency of an army at headquarters, nor of a firm in head office. It is at the remotest point—the private soldier or humble legionary on the distant frontier, the girl at the counter or the branch-office junior salesman—that the really decisive test of an army or a firm is made. It is there that all the instruction and knowledge of relevant facts and procedural disciplines bear fruit—or wither on the tree.
1967 *Management and Machiavelli.*

99 The bigger the organization, the fewer the jobs worth doing.
1967 *Management and Machiavelli.*

Jay (of Paddington), Margaret Jay, Baroness 1939–

English Labour peer, Leader of the House of Lords (1998–2001).

1 I never aim to be unpredictable.
2000 In the *Observer*, 'They Said What…?', 20 Feb.

Jay, Peter 1937–

English economist, broadcaster and diplomat, Ambassador to the US (1977–9), later economics editor at the BBC (1990–2001).

2 [Prince Charles] is entitled to be as underwhelmed by the prospect of reigning over a fourth-class nation as the rest of us are by the prospect of living in it.
1986 Of Prince Charles. In the *London Illustrated News*, Apr.

Jeffers, (John) Robinson 1887–1962

US poet and dramatist. A number of his works drew on themes from biblical stories and Greek drama. His veneration of nature often went hand in hand with a contempt for the works of humanity.

3 While this America settles in the mould of its vulgarity, heavily
thickening to empire.
1924 *Tamar and Other Poems*, 'Shine, Perishing Republic'.

4 And boys, be in nothing so moderate as in love of man, a clever servant,
insufferable master.
1924 *Tamar and Other Poems*, 'Shine, Perishing Republic'.

5 The poet as well
Builds his monument mockingly;
For man will be blotted out, the blithe earth die, the brave sun
Die blind, his heart blackening:
Yet stones have stood for a thousand years, and pained thoughts found
The honey peace in old poems.
1924 *Tamar and Other Poems*, 'To the Stone-Cutters'.

6 The wing trails like a banner in defeat,
No more to use the sky forever but live with famine
And pain a few days.
1928 *Cawdor*, 'Hurt Hawks'.

7 He is strong and pain is worse to the strong, incapacity is worse.
1928 *Cawdor*, 'Hurt Hawks'.

8 The wild God of the world is sometimes merciful to those
That ask mercy, not often to the arrogant.
You do not know him, you communal people, or you have forgotten him;
Intemperate and savage, the hawk remembers him;
Beautiful and wild, the hawks, and men that are dying, remember him.
1928 *Cawdor*, 'Hurt Hawks'.

9 I'd sooner, except the penalties, kill a man than a hawk.
1928 *Cawdor*, 'Hurt Hawks'.

10 This wild swan of a world is no hunter's game.
Better bullets than yours would miss the white breast,
Better mirrors than yours would crack in the flame.
1935 *Solstice*, 'Love the Wild Swan'.

11 Praise life, it deserves praise, but the praise of life
That forgets the pain is a pebble
Ruttled in dry ground.
1948 *The Double Axe and Other Poems.*

Jefferson, Thomas 1743–1826

US statesman, third President (1801–9). Prominent in the first Continental Congress (1774), he drafted the Declaration of Independence. His administration saw war with Tripoli, the Louisiana Purchase (1803) and the prohibition of the slave trade.

12 We hold these truths to be sacred and undeniable; that all men are created equal and independent; that from that equal creation they derive rights inherent and inalienable, among which are the preservation of life, and liberty, and the pursuit of happiness.
c.1776 Draft of the American Declaration of Independence. Collected in J P Boyd et al *Papers of Thomas Jefferson* (1950), vol.1.

13 Were it left to me to decide whether we should have a government without newspapers, or newspapers without a government, I should not hesitate a moment to prefer the latter.
1787 Letter to Col Edward Carrington, 16 Jan.

14 A little rebellion now and then is a good thing.
1787 Letter to James Madison, 30 Jan.

15 The tree of liberty must be refreshed from time to time with the blood of patriots and tyrants. It is its natural manure.
1787 Letter to W S Smith, 13 Nov.

16 A bill of rights is what the people are entitled to against every government on earth, general or particular, and what no just government should refuse or rest on inference.
1787 Letter to James Madison, 20 Dec.

17 I have seen enough of one war never to wish to see another.
1794 Letter to John Adams, 25 Apr.

18 I am for encouraging the progress of science in all its branches; and not for…awing the human mind by stories of raw-head and bloody bones to a distrust of its own vision and to repose implicitly on that of others.
1799 Letter, 26 Jan.

19 Equal and exact justice to all men…freedom of religion, freedom of the press, freedom of the person under the protection of the habeas corpus; and trial by juries impartially selected—these principles form the bright constellation that has gone before us.
1801 Inaugural address, 4 Mar.

20 When a man assumes a public trust, he should consider himself as public property.
1807 Letter to Baron von Humboldt.

21 Some men look at Constitutions with sanctimonious reverence and deem them like the Ark of the Covenant —too sacred to be touched.
1816 Letter to Samuel Kercheval, 12 Jul.

22 Games played with the ball, and others of that nature, are too violent for the body, and stamp no character on the mind.
Quoted in Colin Jarman *The Guinness Dictionary of Sports Quotations* (1990).

Jeffrey, Lord Francis 1773–1850

Scottish critic, lawyer and judge, founder of the *Edinburgh Review*.

23 This will never do.
1814 Of Wordsworth's *The Excursion* (1814). In the *Edinburgh Review*, Nov.

Jenkins, David Edward 1925–

English churchman, Bishop of Durham (1984–94). He became notorious for his radical and often controversial views.

24 A conjuring trick with bones only proves that it is as clever as a conjuring trick with bones… A resuscitated corpse might be a resuscitated corpse and might be the sign of something, but there is still the question of what it is the symbol of.
1984 Of the Christian doctrine of Christ's physical resurrection. 'Poles Apart', BBC radio broadcast, 4 Oct.

25 Christians are not called to win battles, but to find ways of being in battles.
1988 *Spirituality for Conflict*.

Jenkins (of Hillhead), Roy Harris Jenkins, Baron 1920–2003

Welsh Labour politician and author.

26 I have become increasingly convinced that great men have strong elements of comicality in them.
2001 *Churchill*.

Jensen, Albert D

US soldier, colonel in the air force.

27 We're going faster and lower than anything out there. And we can bomb the knot off a tree.
1987 On the capabilities of the B-1 bomber 10 years after its initial development. In the *New York Times*, 4 Jul.

Jerome, Jerome K(lapka) 1859–1927

English humorous novelist and playwright. He became joint editor of *The Idler* (1892) and started his own weekly, *To-Day*. He is best known for his classic *Three Men in a Boat* (1889).

28 It is impossible to enjoy idling thoroughly unless one has plenty of work to do.
1886 *Idle Thoughts of an Idle Fellow*, 'On Being Idle'.

29 Love is like the measles; we all have to go through it.
1886 *Idle Thoughts of an Idle Fellow*, 'On Being in Love'.

30 We drink one another's healths, and spoil our own.
1886 *Idle Thoughts of an Idle Fellow*, 'On Eating and Drinking'.

31 It is a most extraordinary thing, but I never read a patent medicine advertisement without being impelled to the conclusion that I am suffering from the particular disease therein dealt with in its most virulent form.
1889 *Three Men in a Boat*, ch.1.

32 But there, everything has its drawbacks, as the man said when his mother-in-law died, and they came down upon him for the funeral expenses.
1889 *Three Men in a Boat*, ch.3.

33 I like work: it fascinates me. I can sit and look at it for hours. I love to keep it by me: the idea of getting rid of it nearly breaks my heart.
1889 *Three Men in a Boat*, ch.15.

34 It is always the best policy to speak the truth—unless, of course, you are an exceptionally good liar.
1892 In *The Idler* (edited by Robert Barr and Jerome), Feb.

35 I want a house that has got over all its troubles; I don't want to spend the rest of my life bringing up a young and inexperienced house.
1909 *They and I*, ch.11.

36 I did not know I was a humorist. I have never been sure about it. In the middle ages, I should probably have gone about preaching and got myself burned or hanged.
1926 *My Life and Times*, ch.6.

Jerome, William 1865–1932

US songwriter.

37 Any Old Place I Can Hang My Hat Is Home Sweet Home to Me.
1901 Title of song.

Jerrold, Douglas William 1803–57

English author, dramatist and wit. His works include the play *Black-ey'd Susan* (1829), various comedies and a series of novels. He wrote for *Punch* under the pseudonym 'Q' and edited several magazines.

38 Religion's in the heart, not in the knees.
1830 *The Devil's Ducat*, act 1, sc.2.

39 Earth is here so kind, that just tickle her with a hoe and she laughs with a harvest.
Of Australia. *The Wit and Opinions of Douglas Jerrold* (published 1859), 'A Land of Plenty'.

40 Love's like the measles—all the worse when it comes late in life.
The Wit and Opinions of Douglas Jerrold (published 1859), 'Love'.

41 The best thing I know between France and England is—the sea.
The Wit and Opinions of Douglas Jerrold (published 1859), 'The Anglo-French Alliance'.

42 If an earthquake were to engulf England tomorrow, the English would manage to meet and dine somewhere among the rubbish, just to celebrate the event.
Quoted in Blanchard Jerrold *The Life and Remains of Douglas Jerrold* (1859), ch.14.

43 The only athletic sport I mastered was backgammon.
Quoted in W Jerrold *Douglas Jerrold* (1914), vol.1, ch.1.

Jevons, William Stanley 1835–82

English economist, Professor of Political Economy at University College London (1876–81).

44 Economics, if it is to be a science at all, must be a mathematical science.
1871 *The Theory of Political Economy.*

45 The point of equilibrium will be known by the criterion that an infinitely small amount of commodity exchanged in addition, at the same rate, will bring neither gain nor loss of utility.
1871 *The Theory of Political Economy.*

46 Labour once spent has no influence on the future value of any article; it is gone and lost for ever. In commerce bygones are for ever bygones; and we are always starting clear at each moment, judging the values of things with a view to future utility.
1871 *The Theory of Political Economy.*

47 All classes of society are trade unionists at heart, and differ chiefly in the boldness, ability, and secrecy with which they pursue their respective interests.
1882 *The State in Relation to Labour*, introduction.

48 It is requisite from time to time to remind one generation of the experience which led a former generation to important legislative actions.
1882 *The State in Relation to Labour.*

Jiang Qing *or* *Chiang Ch'ing* 1914–91

Chinese politician, third wife of Mao Zedong. After Mao's death in 1976 she was arrested—as one of the 'gang of four'—and sentenced to death in 1980, later commuted to life imprisonment. She committed suicide.

49 Sex is engaging in the first rounds but what sustains interest in the long run is power.
c.1970 Quoted in Ross Merrill *Mao* (1993), ch.10.

50 Man's contribution to human history is nothing more than a drop of sperm.
1984 In *Newsweek*, 20 Feb.

51 Today the revolution has been stolen by the revisionist clique of Deng.
1991 Remark, May. Quoted in Ross Merrill *Mao* (1993), introduction.

St Joan of Arc 1412–31

French patriot and saint. As a 13-year-old peasant she heard saintly voices bidding her to free Paris from the English, and in 1429 she led troops into Orleans and successfully raised the siege. She was later sold to the English, who burned her as a witch.

52 And as for you, archers, soldiers, gentlemen, and all others who are besieging Orleans, depart in God's name to your own country… I assure you that wherever I find your people in France I shall fight them, and pursue them, and expel them from here, whether they will or not.
1429 Letter to the English at Poitiers, 22 Mar. Quoted in *Les Procès de Jeanne d'Arc* (translated by C Larrington), p.33.

53 *Si je n'y suis, Dieu m'y veuille mettre; et si j'y suis, Dieu m'y veuille tenir.*
If I am not in grace, may God set me there; and if I am, may God keep me there.
1431 Quoted in the record of her trial at Rouen, 24 Feb.

Joel, Billy 1949–

US singer, pianist and songwriter.

54 The piano is a percussion instrument, like a drum. You don't strum a piano. You don't bow a piano. You bang and strike a piano. You beat the shit out of a piano.
2004 *Rolling Stone*, 15 Apr.

Pope John XXIII *originally* *Angelo Giuseppe Roncalli* 1881–1963

Italian prelate, Pope (1958–63). He convened the 21st Ecumenical Council and in 1963 issued the encyclical *Pacem in Terris* ('Peace on Earth'), advocating reconciliation between East and West.

55 In order to imbue civilization with sound principles and enliven it with the spirit of the gospel, it is not enough to be illumined with the gift of faith and enkindled with the desire of forwarding a good cause. For this end it is necessary to take an active part in the various organizations and influence them from within. And since our present age is one of outstanding scientific and technical progress and excellence, one will not be able to enter these organizations and work effectively from within unless he is scientifically competent, technically capable and skilled in the practice of his own profession.
1963 *Pacem in Terris*, 10 Apr.

56 If civil authorities legislate for or allow anything that is contrary to that order and therefore contrary to the will of God, neither the laws made or the authorizations granted can be binding on the consciences of the citizens, since God has more right to be obeyed than man.
1963 *Pacem in Terris*, 10 Apr.

57 The social progress, order, security and peace of each country are necessarily connected with the social progress, order, security and peace of all other countries.
1963 *Pacem in Terris*, 10 Apr.

St John of the Cross *originally* *Juan de Yepes y Álvarez* 1542–91

Spanish Christian mystic, founder of the Order of Discalced Carmelites.

58 God passes through the thicket of the world, and wherever his glance falls he turns all things to beauty.
Cántico espiritual (translated by K Kavanaugh and O Rodriguez as *The Spiritual Canticle*).

John III Sobieski of Poland 1624–96

King of Poland (from 1674), elected after a distinguished military career. He formed the Holy League alliance with Pope Innocent XI and the Holy Roman Emperor, Leopold I, in 1688, campaigning against the Turks.

59 I came, I saw, God conquered.
1683 Message sent to the Pope after the defeat of the Turks at the Battle of Vienna, 12 Sep.
► *See Caesar 184:25, Charles V 207:35.*

Pope John Paul II *originally* ***Karol Jozef Wojtyła*** 1920–

Polish priest and theologian. He became Archbishop and Metropolitan of Cracow in 1964, was elected Cardinal (1967) and then Pope (1978), the first non-Italian pope in 456 years.

60 It is unbecoming for a cardinal to ski badly.
c.1968 Attributed, responding to criticism that it was unbecoming for him, then a cardinal, to be seen skiing.

61 The command 'Thou shalt not kill' must be binding on the conscience of humanity if the terrible tragedy and destiny of Cain is not to be repeated.
1979 Speech at Drogheda, Ireland, 29 Sep.

62 Violence is a lie, for it goes against the truth of our faith, the truth of our humanity… Violence is a crime against humanity, for it destroys the very fabric of society. On my knees I beg you to turn away from the paths of violence.
1979 Speech at Drogheda, Ireland, 29 Sep.

63 Commitment to the poor is based on the Gospel: it does not have to rely on some political manifesto.
1979 Speech at the Third Conference of Latin American Bishops, Puebla.

64 A process of genocide is being carried out before the eyes of the world.
1989 Of the situation in Beirut. In *The Independent*, 16 Aug.

John, Sir Elton Hercules *originally* ***Reginald Kenneth Dwight*** 1947

English pop singer, songwriter and pianist. In a prolific career his albums have included *Tumbleweed Connection* (1970), *Don't Shoot Me I'm Only the Piano Player* (1973), *A Single Man* (1978), *Too Low for Zero* (1983), *Sleeping with the Past* (1989) and *Made in England* (1995).

65 Goodbye England's Rose;
May you ever grow in our hearts.
1997 From 'Candle in the Wind', sung at the funeral of Diana, Princess of Wales, co-written with Bernie Taupin. The song was a reworking of an earlier song to Marilyn Monroe.

66 I'm not a nest-egg person.
2000 On how he manages to spend £2m a month. In *The Guardian*, 31 Dec.

John, Gwen 1876–1939

Welsh painter, sister of Augustus John. From 1904 she worked in Paris as an artist's model, becoming Rodin's mistress. She converted to Roman Catholicism in 1913 and became increasingly reclusive.

67 My religion and my art—they are all my life.
Quoted in K Petersen and J J Wilson *Women Artists* (1979).

Johns, Jasper 1930–

US painter and sculptor, a pioneer of Pop Art in the US. He challenged the relationship between art and reality, painting ordinary objects in a deliberately banal style (eg *Flag*, 1954).

68 Things that are seen but not looked at.
1988 Defining the subject of his art. Quoted by Deborah Solomon in 'The Unflagging Artistry of Jasper Johns', in the *New York Times*, 19 Jun.

Johnson, Ben 1961–

Jamaican-born Canadian sprinter.

69 I have never, ever knowingly taken illegal drugs, and I would never embarrass my family, my friends, my country, and the kids who love me.
1988 Statement at press conference, Toronto, 4 Oct. Johnson tested positive to the use of banned substances, was stripped of his Olympic gold medal, and subsequently admitted using anabolic steroids.

Johnson, Boris 1964–

English journalist and Conservative politician. He has been editor of *The Spectator* since 1999 and MP for Henley since 2001.

70 My chances of being PM are about as good as the chances of finding Elvis on Mars, or my being reincarnated as an olive.
2004 In the *Observer*, 20 Jun.

Johnson, Claudia Alta Taylor *known as* ***Lady Bird*** 1912–

US First Lady (1963–9), the widow of President Lyndon B Johnson. She was active in conservation and improvement programmes. After the presidency she published *A White House Diary* (1970).

71 We had a delicious dinner of too much.
1970 On dining at Manhattan's Plaza Hotel. *A White House Diary*.

72 Somehow that was one of the most poignant sights—that immaculate woman, exquisitely dressed, and caked in blood.
1970 On Jacqueline Kennedy after her husband's assassination. *A White House Diary*.

73 I face the prospect of another campaign like an open-ended stay in a concentration camp.
1970 *A White House Diary*.

74 Mrs Kennedy is going to marry Aristotle Socrates Onassis!… I feel strangely freer! No shadow walks behind me down the halls of the White House.
1970 *A White House Diary*.

75 We were distant. But that suited both of us.
1995 On her relationship with Jacqueline Kennedy Onassis. In the *Washington Post*, 23 Mar.

76 This country needs to be united. And sadly, sadly, he wasn't the man who could do it.
1995 On Lyndon B Johnson's decision not to seek a second term during the Vietnam War. In the *Washington Post*, 23 Mar.

Johnson, Earvin ('Magic') 1959–

US basketball player. He played with the Los Angeles Lakers (1979–91, 1996) and was a member of the gold medal-winning US Olympic basketball team ('Dream Team') in 1992.

77 We've dominated sports and we've dominated entertainment, but our problem has been we've never been able to dominate money. We still don't own our share of business, and it's killing us. It's killing our communities.
2003 On African Americans. Quoted in *Los Angeles Magazine*, Oct.

Johnson, Hiram Warren 1866–1945

US politician. He entered the Senate from California (1917–45) and as a founder of the Progressive Party was Theodore Roosevelt's running mate in his unsuccessful 1912 campaign. He outspokenly opposed the League of Nations.

78 The first casualty when war comes is truth.
1917 Speech, US Senate.

Johnson, Lindley

US scientist, a member of NASA's Near Earth Object Observation Program.

79 It is as likely to happen next week as in a randomly selected week a thousand years from now.
2004 Report to the US Senate on the probability of an object hitting the earth.

Johnson, Lyndon B(aines) *also called LBJ* 1908–73

US politician, 36th President (1963–9). He came to power after Kennedy's assassination, and was returned with a huge majority in 1964. He presided over the Civil Rights Act (1964) and the Voting Rights Act (1965), but the Vietnam War made him unpopular.

80 I am a free man, an American, a United States Senator, and a Democrat, in that order.
1958 *Texas Quarterly*, winter issue.

81 I want to be progressive without getting both feet off the ground at the same time...a progressive who is prudent.
1964 Interview, 16 Mar.

82 You let a bully come into your front yard, and the next day he'll be on your porch.
1964 In *Time*, Apr.

83 We are not about to send American boys 9,000 or 10,000 miles away from home to do what Asian boys ought to be doing for themselves.
1964 On the war in Vietnam. Speech at Akron University, 21 Oct.

84 Better to have him inside the tent pissing out, than outside pissing in.
Of J Edgar Hoover. Quoted in David Halberstam *The Best and the Brightest* (1971), ch.20.

85 I want loyalty. I want him to kiss my ass in Macy's window at high noon and tell me it smells like roses. I want his pecker in my pocket.
Of a potential assistant. Quoted in David Halberstam *The Best and the Brightest* (1971), ch.20.

86 So dumb he can't fart and chew gum at the same time.
Of Gerald Ford. Quoted in Richard Reeves *A Ford, Not a Lincoln*. (1975), ch.2.

87 Let's press the flesh.
Of shaking voters' hands. Quoted in Alistair Cooke *The Americans* (1980).

88 I want every family in America to have a carpet on the floor and a picture on the wall. After bread, you've got to have a picture on the wall.
On visiting Pittsburgh's Polish–Czech area. Quoted in Alistair Cooke *The Americans* (1980).

89 I don't believe I'll ever get credit for anything I do in foreign affairs, no matter how successful it is, because I didn't go to Harvard.
To columnist Hugh Sidey. Quoted in Alistair Cooke *The Americans* (1980).

90 I can teach it round or flat.
When asked by a school board about the shape of the earth. Quoted in Tom Wicker *One of Us* (1991).

Johnson, Michael 1967–

US track athlete. At the 1996 Olympics in Atlanta he won gold medals in both the 200-metre and 400-metre events, the first man ever to do so.

91 Pressure is nothing more than the shadow of great opportunity.
Attributed.

Johnson, Paul 1928–

English author.

92 Hell is being trapped in a night-club with the 'beautiful people' and forced to live in a 'luxury penthouse flat'.
1996 *To Hell With Picasso, and Other Essays*.

93 If we want foxes, to observe and delight in, we must have hunting.
1996 *To Hell With Picasso, and Other Essays*.

Johnson, Pauline 1861–1913

Native Canadian poet and patriot.

94 The Dutch may have their Holland, the Spaniard have his Spain,
The Yankee to the south of us must south of us remain;
For not a man dare lift a hand against the men who brag
That they were born in Canada beneath the British flag.
1903 'Canadian Born', collected in *Flint and Feather* (1912).

Johnson, Philander Chase 1866–1939

US journalist.

95 Cheer up—the worst is yet to come.
1920 In *Everybody's Magazine*, May.

Johnson, Philip Cortelyou 1906–

US architect, best known for his book *The International Style* (1932). His designs include the Lincoln Center (1964) and the American Telephone and Telegraph Headquarters Building (1978) in New York City.

96 American megalomania is largely responsible for the growth of the Skyscraper School.
1931 'The Skyscraper School of Modern Architecture', in *Arts*, X VII (May). Collected in *Writings* (1979).

97 They say a building is good architecture if it works. Of course, this is poppycock. All buildings work... You expect any architect, a graduate of Harvard or not, to be able to put the kitchen in the right place.
1954 'The Seven Crutches of Architecture', informal talk to students, School of Architectural Design, Harvard University, 7 Dec. Published in *Perspecta 3* (1955).

98 It's got to be clear, back in your own mind, that serving the client is one thing and the art of architecture another.
1954 'The Seven Crutches of Architecture', informal talk to students, School of Architectural Design, Harvard University, 7 Dec. Published in *Perspecta 3* (1955).

99 Surely architecture is the organization for pleasure of enclosed space. And what more magnificent enclosure than a town, a *place*, a place where the spirit is cuddled, made serene, made proud, happy, or excited depending on the ceremony, the day, the hour.
1954 'The Seven Crutches of Architecture', informal talk to students, School of Architectural Design, Harvard University, 7 Dec. Published in *Perspecta 3* (1955).

1 You can't learn architecture any more than you can learn a sense of music or of painting. You shouldn't talk about art, you should do it.
1954 'The Seven Crutches of Architecture', informal talk to students, School of Architectural Design, Harvard University,

7 Dec. Published in *Perspecta 3* (1955).

2 The automobile is the greatest catastrophe in the entire history of City architecture.
1955 'The Town and the Automobile or the Pride of Elm Street', published in *Writings* (1979).

3 The delicate operation of separating an American from the four-wheeled part of him has to be performed with tact.
1955 'The Town and the Automobile or the Pride of Elm Street', published in *Writings* (1979).

4 Some of the opera houses in Italy had to be burnt down because people could *neither* see nor hear. They gave up seeing years ago, but they did enjoy the music.
1960 Informal talk, Architectural Association School of Architecture, 28 Nov. Collected in *Writings* (1979).

5 Architecture is the art of how to waste space.
1964 In the *New York Times*, 27 Dec.

6 I'm about four skyscrapers behind.
Excusing himself from a dinner party. Quoted in the *Wall Street Journal*, 20 Jun 1984.

Johnson, Samuel *known as* Dr Johnson 1709–84

English lexicographer, critic, poet and conversationalist, best known for his *A Dictionary of the English Language* (1755) and an edition of Shakespeare (1765). In 1773 he toured Scotland with James Boswell, and wrote *A Journey to the Western Isles of Scotland* (1775). Other works include *Rasselas* (1759) and *Lives of the English Poets* (1779–81).

7 Sir, we are a nest of singing birds.
1730 Of Pembroke College, Oxford. Quoted in James Boswell *The Life of Samuel Johnson* (1791), vol.1.

8 It is incident to physicians, I am afraid, beyond all other men, to mistake subsequence for consequence.
1734 Review of Dr Lucas's *Essay on Waters*, 25 Nov.

9 It is not easy to forbear reflecting with how little reason these men profess themselves the followers of Jesus, who left this great characteristic to his disciples, that they should be known by loving one another, by universal and unbounded charity and benevolence.
1735 Of the Jesuit missionaries in Abyssinia. Johnson's preface to Fr J de Lobo's *Voyage to Abyssinia*.

10 Unmoved though witlings sneer and rivals rail;
Studious to please, yet not ashamed to fail.
c.1737 *Irene*, prologue (first produced 1749).

11 A thousand horrid Prodigies foretold it.
A feeble government, eluded Laws,
A factious Populace, luxurious Nobles,
And all the maladies of stinking states.
c.1737 *Irene*, act 1, sc.1 (first produced 1749).

12 There Poetry shall tune her sacred voice,
And wake from ignorance the Western World.
c.1737 *Irene*, act 4, sc.1 (first produced 1749).

13 For who would leave, unbrib'd, *Hibernia's* Land,
Or change the rocks of *Scotland* for the *Strand*?
1738 *London: a Poem*, l.9–10.

14 By numbers here from shame or censure free,
All crimes are safe, but hated poverty.
This, only this, the rigid law pursues,
This, only this, provokes the snarling muse.
1738 *London: a Poem*, l.158–61.

15 The stage but echoes back the public voice.
The drama's laws the drama's patrons give,
For we, who live to please, must please to live.
1747 Prologue, written for David Garrick on the occasion of the opening of his management of the Theatre Royal, Drury Lane.

16 Let observation with extensive view,
Survey mankind, from China to Peru.
1749 *The Vanity of Human Wishes*, l.1–2.

17 Yet hope not life from grief or danger free,
Nor think the doom of man reversed for thee:
Deign on the passing world to turn thine eyes,
And pause awhile from letters, to be wise;
There mark what ills the scholar's life assail,
Toil, envy, want, the patron and the jail.
1749 *The Vanity of Human Wishes*, l.155–60.

18 Enlarge my life with multitude of days,
In health, in sickness, thus the suppliant prays;
Hides from himself his state, and shuns to know,
That life protracted is protracted woe.
Time hovers o'er, impatient to destroy,
And shuts up all the passages of joy.
1749 *The Vanity of Human Wishes*, l.255–60.

19 Must helpless man, in ignorance sedate,
Roll darkling down the torrent of his fate?
1749 *The Vanity of Human Wishes*, l.345–6.

20 Still raise for good the supplicating voice,
But leave to heaven the measure and the choice.
1749 *The Vanity of Human Wishes*, l.351–2.

21 A man may write at any time, if he will set himself doggedly to it.
1750 Comment, Mar. Quoted in James Boswell *The Life of Samuel Johnson* (1791), vol.1.

22 I'll come no more behind your scenes, David: for the silk stockings and white bosoms of your actresses excite my amorous propensities.
1750 In conversation with the actor-manager David Garrick. Quoted in James Boswell *The Life of Samuel Johnson* (1791), vol.1.

23 There are minds so impatient of inferiority, that their gratitude is a species of revenge, and they return benefits, not because recompense is a pleasure, but because obligation is a pain.
1750–2 In *The Rambler*.

24 No place affords a more striking conviction of the vanity of human hopes, than a public library.
1750–2 In *The Rambler*.

25 Wit, you know, is the unexpected copulation of ideas, the discovery of some occult relation between images in appearance remote from each other.
1750–2 In *The Rambler*.

26 Almost every man wastes part of his life in attempts to display qualities which he does not possess, and to gain applause which he cannot keep.
1750–2 In *The Rambler*.

27 The love of life is necessary to the vigorous prosecution of any undertaking.
1750–2 In *The Rambler*.

28 I have laboured to refine our language to grammatical purity, and to clear it from colloquial barbarisms, licentious idioms, and irregular combinations.
1750–2 In *The Rambler*.

29 A fly, Sir, may sting a stately horse and make him wince;

but one is but an insect, and the other is a horse still.
1754 Of Edwards's criticism of Thomas Warburton. Quoted in James Boswell *The Life of Samuel Johnson* (1791), vol.1.

30 They teach the morals of a whore, and the manners of a dancing master.
1754 Of Lord Chesterfield's letters. Quoted in James Boswell *The Life of Samuel Johnson* (1791), vol.1.

31 This man I thought had been a Lord among wits; but, I find, he is only a wit among Lords.
1754 Of Lord Chesterfield. Quoted in James Boswell *The Life of Samuel Johnson* (1791), vol.1.

32 Ignorance, madam, pure ignorance.
1755 Reply to a lady who had asked why he had defined *pastern* as the 'knee' of a horse. Quoted in James Boswell *The Life of Samuel Johnson* (1791), vol.1.

33 I had done all I could; and no man is well pleased to have his all neglected, be it ever so little.
1755 Letter to Lord Chesterfield, 7 Feb. Quoted in James Boswell *The Life of Samuel Johnson* (1791), vol.1.

34 Is not a Patron, my lord, one who looks with unconcern on a man struggling for life in the water, and, when he has reached ground, encumbers him with help? The notice which you have been pleased to take of my labours, had it been early, had been kind; but it has been delayed till I am indifferent, and cannot enjoy it; till I am solitary, and cannot impart it; till I am known, and do not want it.
1755 Letter to Lord Chesterfield, 7 Feb. Quoted in James Boswell *The Life of Samuel Johnson* (1791), vol.1.

35 There are two things which I am confident I can do very well: one is an introduction to a literary work, stating what it is to contain, and how it should be executed in the most perfect manner; the other is a conclusion, shewing from various causes why the execution has not been equal to what the author promised to himself and to the public.
1755 Quoted in James Boswell *The Life of Samuel Johnson* (1791), vol.1.

36 If a man does not make new acquaintance as he advances through life, he will soon find himself left alone. A man, Sir, should keep his friendship in constant repair.
1755 Quoted in James Boswell *The Life of Samuel Johnson* (1791), vol.1.

37 Change is not made without inconvenience, even from worse to better.
1755 *A Dictionary of the English Language*, preface.

38 It is the fate of those who toil at the lower employments of life…to be exposed to censure, without hope of praise; to be disgraced by miscarriage or punished for neglect… Among these unhappy mortals is the writer of dictionaries… Every other author may aspire to praise; the lexicographer can only hope to escape reproach.
1755 *A Dictionary of the English Language*, preface.

39 I am not yet so lost in lexicography as to forget that words are the daughters of earth, and that things are the sons of heaven. Language is only the instrument of science, and words are but the signs of ideas: I wish, however, that the instrument might be less apt to decay, and that signs might be permanent, like the things which they denote.
1755 *A Dictionary of the English Language*, preface.

40 I have protracted my work till most of those whom I wished to please have sunk into the grave; and success and miscarriage are empty sounds.
1755 *A Dictionary of the English Language*, preface.

41 Every quotation contributes something to the stability or enlargement of the language.
1755 *A Dictionary of the English Language*, preface.

42 But these were the dreams of a poet doomed at last to wake a lexicographer.
1755 *A Dictionary of the English Language*, preface.

43 If the changes we fear be thus irresistible, what remains but to acquiesce with silence, as in the other insurmountable distresses of humanity? It remains that we retard what we cannot repel, that we palliate what we cannot cure.
1755 *A Dictionary of the English Language*, preface.

44 *Dull*. To make dictionaries is dull work.
1755 *A Dictionary of the English Language*.

45 *Excise*. A hateful tax levied upon commodities.
1755 *A Dictionary of the English Language*.

46 *Lexicographer*. A writer of dictionaries, a harmless drudge.
1755 *A Dictionary of the English Language*.

47 *Net*. Anything reticulated or decussated at equal distances, with interstices between the intersections.
1755 *A Dictionary of the English Language*.

48 *Oats*. A grain, which in England is generally given to horses, but in Scotland supports the people.
1755 *A Dictionary of the English Language*.

49 *Patron*. Commonly a wretch who supports with insolence, and is paid with flattery.
1755 *A Dictionary of the English Language*.

50 *Pension*. Pay given to state hireling for treason to his country.
1755 *A Dictionary of the English Language*.

51 The only end of writing is to enable the readers better to enjoy life, or better to endure it.
1757 Reviewing Soame Jenyns *A Free Inquiry into the Nature and Origin of Evil*, in the *Literary Magazine*, Apr–Jul.

52 To us, who are regaled every morning and evening with intelligence, and are supplied from day to day with materials for conversation, it is difficult to conceive how man can subsist without a newspaper.
1758 In *The Idler*, no.7, 27 May.

53 When two Englishmen meet, their first talk is of the weather.
1758 In *The Idler*, no.11, 24 Jun.

54 To these compositions is required neither genius nor knowledge, neither industry nor spriteliness, but contempt of shame, and indifference to truth are absolutely necessary.
1758 Of journalistic reporting. In *The Idler*, no.31, 11 Nov.

55 Among the calamities of War may be justly numbered the diminution of the love of truth, by the falsehoods which interest dictates and credulity encourages.
1758 In *The Idler*, no.31, 11 Nov.

56 Nothing is more hopeless than a scheme of merriment.
1759 In *The Idler*, no.58, 26 May.

57 The Europeans have scarcely visited any coast, but to gratify avarice, and extend corruption; to arrogate dominion without right, and practice cruelty without incentive… But there is reason to hope…that the light of the gospel will at last illuminate the sands of Africa, and

the deserts of America, though its progress cannot but be slow when it is so much obstructed by the lives of Christians.
1759 Introduction to *The World Displayed*.

58 Marriage has many pains, but celibacy has no pleasures.
1759 *Rasselas*, ch.26.

59 No man will be a sailor who has contrivance enough to get himself into jail; for being in a ship is being in a jail, with the chance of being drowned… A man in a jail has more room, better food, and commonly better company.
1759 Remark, 16 Mar. Quoted in James Boswell *The Life of Samuel Johnson* (1791), vol.1.

60 Liberty is, to the lowest rank of every nation, little more than the choice of working or starving.
1760 'The Bravery of the English Common Soldier', in *The British Magazine*, Jan.

61 The notion of liberty amuses the people of England, and helps to keep off the taedium vitae. When a butcher tells you that his heart bleeds for his country he has, in fact, no uneasy feeling.
1763 Remark, 16 May. Quoted in James Boswell *The Life of Samuel Johnson* (1791), vol.1.

62 Yes, Sir, many men, many women, and many children.
1763 Remark, 16 May, on being asked if any man of a modern age could have written *Ossian*. Quoted in James Boswell *The Life of Samuel Johnson* (1791), vol.1.

63 The noblest prospect which a Scotchman ever sees, is the high road that leads him to England!
1763 Remark, 6 Jul. Quoted in James Boswell *The Life of Samuel Johnson* (1791), vol.1.

64 A man ought to read just as inclination leads him; for what he reads as a task will do him little good.
1763 Remark, 14 Jul. Quoted in James Boswell *The Life of Samuel Johnson* (1791), vol.1.

65 But if he does really think that there is no distinction between virtue and vice, why, Sir, when he leaves our houses, let us count our spoons.
1763 Remark, 14 Jul. Quoted in James Boswell *The Life of Samuel Johnson* (1791), vol.1.

66 A man with a good coat upon his back meets with a better reception than he who has a bad one.
1763 Remark, 20 Jul. Quoted in James Boswell *The Life of Samuel Johnson* (1791), vol.1.

67 All the arguments which are brought to represent poverty as no evil, show it to be evidently a great evil. You never find people labouring to convince you that you may live very happily upon a plentiful fortune.
1763 Remark, 20 Jul. Quoted in James Boswell *The Life of Samuel Johnson* (1791), vol.1.

68 Truth, Sir, is a cow, that will yield such people no more milk, and so they are gone to milk the bull.
1763 Of sceptics. Remark, 21 Jul. Quoted in James Boswell *The Life of Samuel Johnson* (1791), vol.1.

69 Young men have more virtue than old men; they have more generous sentiments in every respect.
1763 Remark, 21 Jul. Quoted in James Boswell *The Life of Samuel Johnson* (1791), vol.1.

70 In my early years I read very hard. It is a sad reflection, but a true one, that I knew almost as much at eighteen as I do now.
1763 Remark, 21 Jul. Quoted in James Boswell *The Life of Samuel Johnson* (1791), vol.1.

71 Your levellers wish to level down as far as themselves; but they cannot bear levelling up to themselves.
1763 Remark, 21 Jul. Quoted in James Boswell *The Life of Samuel Johnson* (1791), vol.1.

72 It is burning a farthing candle at Dover, to shew light at Calais.
1763 Summarizing the influence of the plays of Thomas Sheridan upon English literature, 28 Jul. Quoted in James Boswell *The Life of Samuel Johnson* (1791), vol.1.

73 Sir, a woman's preaching is like a dog walking on its hinder legs. It is not done well; but you are surprised to find it done at all.
1763 Remark, 31 Jul. Quoted in James Boswell *The Life of Samuel Johnson* (1791), vol.1.

74 He who does not mind his belly will hardly mind any thing else.
1763 Remark, 5 Aug. Quoted in James Boswell *The Life of Samuel Johnson* (1791), vol.1.

75 'I refute it *thus*.'
1763 Johnson refutes Bishop Berkeley's theory of the non-existence of matter by kicking a large stone, 6 Aug. Quoted in James Boswell *The Life of Samuel Johnson* (1791), vol.1.

76 Nature has given women so much power that the law has very wisely given them little.
1763 Letter to John Taylor, 18 Aug.

77 A very unclubbable man.
1764 Of Sir John Hawkins. Remark quoted in James Boswell *The Life of Samuel Johnson* (1791), vol.1.

78 Nothing can please many, and please long, but just representations of general nature.
1765 *Plays of William Shakespeare*, preface.

79 He that tries to recommend him by select quotations, will succeed like the pedant in Hierocles, who, when he offered his house to sale, carried a brick in his pocket as a specimen.
1765 Of Shakespeare. *Plays of William Shakespeare*, preface.

80 Love is only one of many passions.
1765 *Plays of William Shakespeare*, preface.

81 Notes are often necessary, but they are necessary evils.
1765 *Plays of William Shakespeare*, preface.

82 That all who are happy, are equally happy, is not true. A peasant and a philosopher may be equally satisfied, but not equally happy. Happiness consists in the multiplicity of agreeable consciousness.
1766 Remark, Feb. Quoted in James Boswell *The Life of Samuel Johnson* (1791), vol.2.

83 It is our first duty to serve society, and, after we have done that, we may attend wholly to the salvation of our own souls. A youthful passion for abstracted devotion should not be encouraged.
1766 Remark, Feb. Quoted in James Boswell *The Life of Samuel Johnson* (1791), vol.2.

84 Our tastes greatly alter. The lad does not care for the child's rattle, and the old man does not care for the young man's whore.
1766 Quoted in James Boswell *The Life of Samuel Johnson* (1791), vol.2.

85 It was not for me to bandy civilities with my sovereign.
1767 Remark, Feb. Quoted in James Boswell *The Life of Samuel Johnson* (1791), vol.2.

86 Now, sir, there is the liberty of the press, which you know is a constant topic. Suppose you and I and two hundred

more were restrained from printing our thoughts: what then? What proportion would that restraint upon us bear to the private happiness of the nation?
1768 Remark, May. Quoted in James Boswell *The Life of Samuel Johnson* (1791), vol.2.

87 Sir, if a man has a mind to *prance*, he must study at Christ-Church and All-Souls.
1769 Remark, Autumn. Quoted in James Boswell *The Life of Samuel Johnson* (1791), vol.2.

88 We know our will is free, and there's an end on't.
1769 Remark, 16 Oct. Quoted in James Boswell *The Life of Samuel Johnson* (1791), vol.2.

89 It matters not how a man dies, but how he lives. The act of dying is not of importance, it lasts so short a time.
1769 Remark, 26 Oct. Quoted in James Boswell *The Life of Samuel Johnson* (1791), vol.2.

90 That fellow seems to me to possess but one idea, and that is a wrong one.
1770 Quoted in James Boswell *The Life of Samuel Johnson* (1791), vol.2.

91 The triumph of hope over experience.
1770 On a friend's second marriage shortly after the death of his first, troublesome, wife. Quoted in James Boswell *The Life of Samuel Johnson* (1791), vol.2.

92 I do not care to speak ill of any man behind his back, but I believe the gentleman is an *attorney*.
1770 Quoted in James Boswell *The Life of Samuel Johnson* (1791), vol.2.

93 Every man has a lurking wish to appear considerable in his native place.
1771 Letter to Sir Joshua Reynolds, 17 Jul. Quoted in James Boswell *The Life of Samuel Johnson* (1791), vol.2.

94 I would not give half a guinea to live under one form of government rather than another. It is of no moment to the happiness of an individual.
1772 Remark, 31 Mar. Quoted in James Boswell *The Life of Samuel Johnson* (1791), vol.2.

95 There is more knowledge of the heart in one letter of Richardson's, than in all *Tom Jones*.
1772 Remark, 6 Apr. Quoted in James Boswell *The Life of Samuel Johnson* (1791), vol.2.

96 Grief is a species of idleness.
1773 Letter to Mrs Thrale, whose son had just died, 17 Mar.

97 He has, indeed, done it very well; but it is a foolish thing well done.
1773 Of Oliver Goldsmith, who had responded to Thomas Evans's uncomplimentary open letter with a physical assault, and then published an apology in the *London Chronicle*. Remark, 3 Apr. Collected in James Boswell *The Life of Samuel Johnson* (1791), vol.2.

98 Read over your compositions, and where ever you meet with a passage which you think is particularly fine, strike it out.
1773 Remark, 30 Apr, quoting an old college tutor. Collected in James Boswell *The Life of Samuel Johnson* (1791), vol.2.

99 A lawyer has no business with the justice or injustice of the cause which he undertakes, unless his client asks his opinion, and then he is bound to give it honestly. The justice or unjustice of the cause is to be decided by the judge.
1773 Remark, 15 Aug. Quoted in James Boswell *The Journal of a Tour to the Hebrides* (1785).

1 I inherited a vile melancholy from my father, which has made me mad all my life, at least not sober.
1773 Remark, 16 Sep. Quoted in James Boswell *The Journal of a Tour to the Hebrides* (1785).

2 I am always sorry when any language is lost, because languages are the pedigrees of nations.
1773 Remark, 18 Sep. Quoted in James Boswell *The Journal of a Tour to the Hebrides* (1785).

3 A cucumber should be well sliced, and dressed with pepper and vinegar, and then thrown out, as good for nothing.
1773 Remark, 5 Oct. Quoted in James Boswell *The Journal of a Tour to the Hebrides* (1785).

4 At seventy-seven it is time to be in earnest.
1775 *A Journey to the Western Isles of Scotland*, 'Col'.

5 There are few ways in which a man can be so innocently employed than in getting money.
1775 Remark, 27 Mar. Collected in James Boswell *The Life of Samuel Johnson* (1791), vol.2. This is sometimes rendered 'A man is seldom so innocently occupied as when he is making money.'

6 It is wonderful, when a calculation is made, how little the mind is actually employed in the discharge of any profession.
1775 Remark, 6 Apr. Collected in James Boswell *The Life of Samuel Johnson* (1791), vol.2.

7 The greatest part of a writer's time is spent in reading, in order to write: a man will turn over half a library to make one book.
1775 Remark, 6 Apr. Collected in James Boswell *The Life of Samuel Johnson* (1791), vol.2.

8 Patriotism is the last refuge of a scoundrel.
1775 Remark, 7 Apr. Collected in James Boswell *The Life of Samuel Johnson* (1791), vol.2.

9 Knowledge is of two kinds. We know a subject ourselves, or we know where we can find information upon it.
1775 Remark, 18 Apr. Quoted in James Boswell *The Life of Samuel Johnson* (1791), vol.2.

10 Politics are now nothing more than means of rising in the world.
1775 Remark, 18 Apr. Quoted in James Boswell *The Life of Samuel Johnson* (1791), vol.2.

11 Players, Sir! I look upon them as no better than creatures set upon tables and joint stools to make faces and produce laughter, like dancing dogs.
1775 Letter to James Macpherson.

12 How is it that we hear the loudest yelps for liberty among the drivers of negroes?
1775 *Taxation No Tyranny.*

13 In lapidary inscriptions a man is not upon oath.
1775 Quoted in James Boswell *The Life of Samuel Johnson* (1791), vol.2.

14 There is nothing which has yet been contrived by man, by which so much happiness is produced as by a good tavern or inn.
1776 Remark, 21 Mar. Quoted in James Boswell *The Life of Samuel Johnson* (1791), vol.2.

15 Marriages would in general be as happy, and often more so, if they were all made by the Lord Chancellor, upon a due consideration of characters and circumstances, without the parties having any choice in the matter.
1776 Remark, 22 Mar. Quoted in James Boswell *The Life of Samuel Johnson* (1791), vol.2.

16 I had often wondered why young women should marry, as they have so much more freedom, and so much more attention paid to them while unmarried, than when married.
1776 Remark, 25 Mar. Quoted in James Boswell *The Life of Samuel Johnson* (1791), vol.2.

17 Fine clothes are good only as they supply the want of other means of procuring respect.
1776 Remark, 27 Mar. Quoted in James Boswell *The Life of Samuel Johnson* (1791), vol.2.

18 Consider, Sir, how should you like, though conscious of your innocence, to be tried before a jury for a capital crime, once a week.
1776 Remark, 3 Apr. Quoted in James Boswell *The Life of Samuel Johnson* (1791), vol.3.

19 We would all be idle if we could.
1776 Remark, 3 Apr. Quoted in James Boswell *The Life of Samuel Johnson* (1791), vol.3.

20 No man but a blockhead ever wrote, except for money.
1776 Remark, 5 Apr. Quoted in James Boswell *The Life of Samuel Johnson* (1791), vol.3.

21 It is better that some should be unhappy than that none should be happy, which would be the case in a general state of equality.
1776 Remark, 7 Apr. Quoted in James Boswell *The Life of Samuel Johnson* (1791), vol.3.

22 A man who has not been in Italy, is always conscious of an inferiority, from his not having seen what it is expected a man should see.
1776 Remark, 11 Apr. Quoted in James Boswell *The Life of Samuel Johnson* (1791), vol.3.

23 Every man of any education would rather be called a rascal, than accused of deficiency in the graces.
1776 Remark, May. Quoted in James Boswell *The Life of Samuel Johnson* (1791), vol.3.

24 Sir, you have but two topics, yourself and me. I am sick of both.
1776 Remark, May. Quoted in James Boswell *The Life of Samuel Johnson* (1791), vol.3.

25 If I had no duties, and no reference to futurity, I would spend my life in driving briskly in a post-chaise with a pretty woman.
1777 Remark, 19 Sep. Quoted in James Boswell *The Life of Samuel Johnson* (1791), vol.3.

26 Depend upon it, Sir, when a man knows he is to be hanged in a fortnight, it concentrates his mind wonderfully.
1777 Remark, 19 Sep, alluding to the forthcoming execution of Dr Dodd. Quoted in James Boswell *The Life of Samuel Johnson* (1791), vol.3.

27 When a man is tired of London, he is tired of life; for there is in London all that life can afford.
1777 Remark, 20 Sep. Quoted in James Boswell *The Life of Samuel Johnson* (1791), vol.3.

28 All argument is against it; but all belief is for it.
1778 Remark, 31 Mar, on the existence of ghosts. Quoted in James Boswell *The Life of Samuel Johnson* (1791), vol.3.

29 Seeing Scotland, Madam, is only seeing a worse England.
1778 Remark quoted in a letter to Boswell, 7 Apr. Quoted in James Boswell *The Life of Samuel Johnson* (1791), vol.3.

30 The more contracted that power is, the more easily it is destroyed. A country governed by a despot is an inverted cone.
1778 Remark, 14 Apr. Quoted in James Boswell *The Life of Samuel Johnson* (1791), vol.3.

31 As the Spanish proverb says, 'He, who would bring home the wealth of the Indies, must carry the wealth of the Indies with him.' So it is in travelling; a man must carry knowledge with him, if he would bring home knowledge.
1778 Remark, 17 Apr. Quoted in James Boswell *The Life of Samuel Johnson* (1791), vol.3.

32 Sir, the insolence of wealth will creep out.
1778 Remark, 18 Apr. Quoted in James Boswell *The Life of Samuel Johnson* (1791), vol.3.

33 Wine makes a man better pleased with himself. I do not say that it makes him more pleasing to others.
1778 Remark, 28 Apr. Quoted in James Boswell *The Life of Samuel Johnson* (1791), vol.3.

34 BOSWELL: There is more learning in their [Chinese] language than in any other, from the immense number of their characters.
JOHNSON: It is only more difficult from its rudeness, as there is more labour in hewing down a tree with a stone than with an axe.
1778 Conversation, 8 May. Quoted in James Boswell *The Life of Samuel Johnson* (1791), vol.3.

35 Were it not for imagination, Sir, a man would be as happy in the arms of a chambermaid as of a Duchess.
1778 Remark, 9 May. Quoted in James Boswell *The Life of Samuel Johnson* (1791), vol.3.

36 A man who exposes himself when he is intoxicated, has not the art of getting drunk.
1779 Remark, 24 Apr. Quoted in James Boswell *The Life of Samuel Johnson* (1791), vol.3.

37 Claret is the liquor for boys; port, for men; but he who aspires to be a hero [smiling] must drink brandy.
1779 Remark, 7 Aug. Quoted in James Boswell *The Life of Samuel Johnson* (1791), vol.3.

38 Remember that all tricks are either knavish or childish.
1779 Letter to Boswell, 9 Sep. Quoted in James Boswell *The Life of Samuel Johnson* (1791), vol.3.

39 BOSWELL: Is not the Giant's Causeway worth seeing?
JOHNSON: Worth seeing? Yes, but not worth going to see.
1779 Conversation, 12 Oct. Quoted in James Boswell *The Life of Samuel Johnson* (1791), vol.3.

40 If you are idle, be not solitary; if you are solitary, be not idle.
1779 Letter to Boswell, 27 Oct. Quoted in James Boswell *The Life of Samuel Johnson* (1791), vol.3.

41 Trade could not be managed by those who manage it, if it had much difficulty.
1779 Letter to Hester Thrale, 16 Nov.

42 The true genius is a mind of large general powers, accidentally determined to some particular direction.
1779–81 *Lives of the English Poets*, 'Cowley'.

43 The father of English criticism.
1779–81 Of Dryden. *Lives of the English Poets*, 'Dryden'.

44 To charge all unmerited praise with the guilt of flattery, and to suppose that the encomiast always knows and feels the falsehood of his assertions, is surely to discover great ignorance of human nature and human life. In determinations depending not on rules, but on

experience and comparison, judgement is always to some degree subject to affection. Very near to admiration is the wish to admire.
1779–81 *Lives of the English Poets*, 'Halifax'.

45 It...had the effect, as was ludicrously said, of making Gay *rich*, and Rich *gay*.
1779–81 Of the *Beggar's Opera*, written by Gay and produced by Rich. *Lives of the English Poets*, 'John Gay'.

46 An exotic and irrational entertainment.
1779–81 Of Italian opera. *Lives of the English Poets*, 'Hughes'.

47 I am disappointed by that stroke of death, which has eclipsed the gaiety of nations, and impoverished the public stock of harmless pleasure.
1779–81 His tribute to the recently deceased actor David Garrick. *Lives of the English Poets*, 'Edmund Smith'.

48 Every man has a right to utter what he thinks truth, and every other man has a right to knock him down for it. Martyrdom is the test.
1780 Quoted in James Boswell *The Life of Samuel Johnson* (1791), vol.4.

49 Depend upon it, said he, that if a man talks of his misfortunes there is something in them that is not disagreeable to him; for where there is nothing but pure misery, there never is any recourse to the mention of it.
1780 Quoted in James Boswell *The Life of Samuel Johnson* (1791), vol.4.

50 A wise Tory and a wise Whig, I believe, will agree. Their principles are the same, though their modes of thinking are different.
1781 Written note given to Boswell, May. Quoted in James Boswell *The Life of Samuel Johnson* (1791), vol.4.

51 Classical quotations is the parole of literary men all over the world.
1781 Remark, 8 May. Quoted in James Boswell *The Life of Samuel Johnson* (1791), vol.4.

52 Sir, I have two very cogent reasons for not printing any list of subscribers;—one, that I have lost all the names,—the other, that I have spent all the money.
1781 Remark, May. Quoted in James Boswell *The Life of Samuel Johnson* (1791), vol.4.

53 Why, that is, because, dearest, you're a dunce.
1781 To Lady Corke, who had said that she was affected by Sterne's writings. Quoted in James Boswell *The Life of Samuel Johnson* (1791), vol.4.

54 Always, Sir, set a high value on spontaneous kindness. He whose inclination prompts him to cultivate your friendship of his own accord, will love you more than one whom you have been at pains to attract to you.
1781 Remark, May. Quoted in James Boswell *The Life of Samuel Johnson* (1791), vol.4.

55 I hate a fellow whom pride, or cowardice, or laziness drives into a corner, and who does nothing when he is there but sit and growl; let him come out as I do, and bark.
1782 Remark, 10 Oct, alluding to Jeremiah Markland. Quoted in James Boswell *The Life of Samuel Johnson* (1791), vol.4.

56 Resolve not to be poor; whatever you have, spend less. Poverty is a great enemy to human happiness; it certainly destroys liberty, and it makes some virtues impracticable, and others extremely difficult.
1782 Letter to Boswell, 7 Dec. Quoted in James Boswell *The Life of Samuel Johnson* (1791), vol.4.

57 How few of his friends' houses would a man choose to be at when he is sick.
1783 Quoted in James Boswell *The Life of Samuel Johnson* (1791), vol.4.

58 There is a wicked inclination in most people to suppose an old man decayed in his intellects. If a young or middle-aged man, when leaving a company, does not recollect where he laid his hat, it is nothing; but if the same inattention is discovered in an old man, people will shrug up their shoulders, and say, 'His memory is going.'
1783 Quoted in James Boswell *The Life of Samuel Johnson* (1791), vol.4.

59 Sir, there is no settling the point of precedency between a louse and a flea.
1783 On the relative merits of two minor poets. Quoted in James Boswell *The Life of Samuel Johnson* (1791), vol.4.

60 My dear friend, clear your mind of cant... You may talk in this manner; it is a mode of talking in Society: but don't think foolishly.
1783 Remark, 15 May. Quoted in James Boswell *The Life of Samuel Johnson* (1791), vol.4.

61 It is as bad as bad can be: it is ill-fed, ill-killed, ill-kept, and ill-drest.
1783 Of the roast mutton he was served at an inn, 3 Jun. Quoted in James Boswell *The Life of Samuel Johnson* (1791), vol.4.

62 As I know more of mankind I expect less of them, and am ready now to call a man a good man, upon easier terms than I was formerly.
1783 Remark, Sep. Quoted in James Boswell *The Life of Samuel Johnson* (1791), vol.4.

63 Milton, Madam, was a genius that could cut a Colossus from a rock; but could not carve heads upon cherry-stones.
1784 Remark to Hannah More, 13 Jun, who had commented with surprise that Milton's sonnets failed to compare with his epic *Paradise Lost*. Quoted in James Boswell *The Life of Samuel Johnson* (1791), vol.4.

64 Talking of the Comedy of 'The Rehearsal', he said 'It has not enough wit to keep it sweet.' This was easy;—he therefore caught himself, and pronounced a more rounded sentence; 'It has not vitality enough to preserve it from putrefaction.'
1784 Remark, Jun. Quoted in James Boswell *The Life of Samuel Johnson* (1791), vol.4.

65 Sir, I have found you an argument; but I am not obliged to find you an understanding.
1784 Remark, Jun. Quoted in James Boswell *The Life of Samuel Johnson* (1791), vol.4.

66 No man is a hypocrite in his pleasures.
1784 Remark, Jun. Quoted in James Boswell *The Life of Samuel Johnson* (1791), vol.4.

67 Dictionaries are like watches, the worst is better than none, and the best cannot be expected to go quite true.
1784 Letter to Francesco Sastres, 21 Aug. Quoted in James Boswell *The Life of Samuel Johnson* (1791), vol.4.

68 Sir, I look upon every day to be lost, in which I do not make a new acquaintance.
1784 Remark, Nov. Quoted in James Boswell *The Life of Samuel Johnson* (1791), vol.4.

69 I will be conquered; I will not capitulate.
1784 Of his increasing ill health, Nov. Quoted in James Boswell *The Life of Samuel Johnson* (1791), vol.4.

70 An odd thought strikes me:—we shall receive no letters in the grave.

1784 Remark, Dec. Quoted in James Boswell *The Life of Samuel Johnson* (1791), vol.4.

71 Difficult do you call it, Sir? I wish it were impossible.

Of the playing of a famous violinist. Quoted in G B Hill *Johnsonian Miscellanies*, vol.2 (1784).

72 It is the only sensual pleasure without vice.

1784 Of music. Quoted in Sir John Hawkins *Johnsoniana* (1787).

73 I would rather see the portrait of a dog that I know, than all the allegorical paintings they can show me in the world.

Quoted in Mrs Piozzi *Anecdotes of the Late Samuel Johnson* (1786).

74 Corneille is to Shakespeare…as a clipped hedge is to a forest.

Quoted in Mrs Piozzi *Anecdotes of the Late Samuel Johnson* (1786).

75 It is very strange, and very melancholy, that the paucity of human pleasures should persuade us ever to call hunting one of them.

Quoted in Mrs Piozzi *Anecdotes of the Late Samuel Johnson* (1786).

76 Of all noises I think music the least disagreeable.

Quoted in *The Morning Chronicle*, 1816.

77 Fly fishing may be a very pleasant amusement; but angling or float fishing I can only compare to a stick and a string, with a worm at one end and a fool at the other.

Quoted in Hawker *Instructions to Young Sportsmen* (1859). The attribution is doubtful, and Swift has also been credited with the remark.

78 The use of travelling is to regulate imagination by reality, and instead of thinking how things may be, to see them as they are.

Attributed.

Johnston, Brian 1912–94

English cricket commentator.

79 The bowler's Holding, the batsman's Willey.

1976 Radio commentary, during a Test match between England and the West Indies.

80 Turner looks a bit shaky and unsteady, but I think he's going to bat on—one ball left!

Radio commentary, during an England Test match after batsman Glenn Turner was hit on the box by a cricket ball on the fifth ball of the over.

Johst, Hanns 1890–1978

German dramatist.

81 *Wenn ich Kultur höre…entsichere ich meinen Browning!*
When I hear anyone talk of culture…I take off the safety catch on my Browning!

1933 *Schlageter*, act 1, sc.1. The phrase is often attributed to Hermann Goering, in the form 'Whenever I hear the word culture, I reach for my gun!'.

Jolson, Al *pseudonym of* ***Asa Yoelson*** 1886–1950

Russian-born US actor and singer. He emigrated to the US in 1893 and made his stage debut in *The Children of the Ghetto* (1899). He was the star of the first talking picture *The Jazz Singer* in 1927.

82 You Ain't Heard Nothin' Yet.

1919 Title of a song, allegedly taken from an earlier impromptu remark in a café in which Jolson was performing. It is popularly recognized as a line from *The Jazz Singer* (screenplay by Alfred Cohn), the first major film with sound.

Jonas, George 1935–

Hungarian-born Canadian author and journalist.

83 There are many wrongs in the world, but none that could be righted by the terrorist's program.

1987 *Crocodiles in the Bathtub and Other Perils*.

84 Maybe that's what is crazy: to want to be free. A lot of people wouldn't cross the street for it.

1989 *A Passion Observed: The Story of a Motorcycle Racer*.

Jones, Bobby (Robert Tyre) 1902–71

US golfer. He won the US Open four times, the British Open three times, the US Amateur Championship five times and the British Amateur Championship once. In 1930 he won the 'Grand Slam', and retired from competitive golf.

85 Golf is a game that is played on a five inch course — the distance between your ears.

Quoted in Colin Jarman *The Guinness Dictionary of Sports Quotations* (1990).

Jones, Henry Arthur 1851–1929

English playwright. His early melodramas were followed by more realistic plays and social comedies.

86 O God! Put back Thy universe and give me yesterday.

1907 *The Silver King* (with Henry Herman), act 2, sc.4.

Jones, James 1921–77

US writer. He is best known for his novel set in the run-up to the bombing of Pearl Harbor, *From Here to Eternity* (1951), and its sequel, *The Thin Red Line* (1962).

87 From Here to Eternity.

1951 Title of novel.

88 I therefore solemnly declare to all young men trying to be writers that they do not actually have to become drunkards first.

1959 Interview in the *Paris Review*, Winter.

89 To me politics is like one of those annoying and potentially dangerous, but generally just painful, chronic diseases that you just have to put up with all your life if you happen to have contracted it. Politics is like having diabetes.

1959 Interview in the *Paris Review*, Winter.

90 Conversation is more often likely to be an attempt at deliberate evasion, deliberate confusion, rather than communication. We're all cheats and liars, really.

1959 Interview in the *Paris Review*, Winter.

Jones, John Paul 1747–92

US admiral. He fought the English fleet in the American Revolution, and later became rear-admiral in the Russian navy.

91 Sir, I have not yet begun to fight.

1779 His reply to a request for surrender when his ship was sinking, 23 Sep. He lashed his ship to his enemy's and boarded it, accepting the enemy captain's surrender. Quoted in Anna de Koven *Life and Letters of John Paul Jones* (1913).

Jones, Quincy Delight 1933–

US jazz trumpeter, songwriter and record producer. His many albums include *Body Heat* (1974) and *The Dude* (1981). As Vice-President of Mercury Records he promoted Frank Sinatra and Michael Jackson among others.

92 Jazz has always been a man telling the truth about himself.
Quoted in Alan Kendall *The Tender Tyrant: Nadia Boulanger* (1976).

93 To try to talk to the young people who will run the future—in ten minutes—is a little like trying to put a cantaloupe in a coke bottle.
1995 At Claremont College commencement. Reported in the *New York Times*, 29 May.

Jones, Tom 1940–

Welsh pop singer.

94 My pants are not as tight any more, I don't open my shirt so far and I don't pick up the underwear.
2004 On getting older. Quoted in *Mojo*, May.

Jong, Erica *née* ***Mann*** 1942–

US novelist and poet. She achieved notoriety with her controversial first novel, *Fear of Flying* (1973).

95 Everyone has talent. What is rare is the courage to follow the talent to the dark place where it leads.
1972 'The Artist as Housewife', in *The First Ms. Reader*.

96 If sex and creativity are often seen by dictators as subversive activities, it's because they lead to the knowledge that you own your own body (and with it your own voice), and that's the most revolutionary insight of all.
1972 'The Artist as Housewife', in *The First Ms. Reader*.

97 The zipless fuck is absolutely pure. It is free of ulterior motives. There is no power game. The man is not 'taking' and the woman is not 'giving'. No one is attempting to cuckold a husband or humiliate a wife. No one is trying to prove anything or get anything out of anyone. The zipless fuck is the purest thing there is. And it is rarer than the unicorn. And I have never had one.
1973 *Fear of Flying*, ch.1.

98 Solitude is un-American.
1973 *Fear of Flying*, ch.1.

99 Gossip is the opiate of the oppressed.
1973 *Fear of Flying*, ch.6.

1 Horrible as successful artists often are, there is nothing crueller or more vain than a failed artist.
1973 *Fear of Flying*, ch.9.

2 Jealousy is all the fun you *think* they had.
1977 *How To Save Your Own Life*.

3 Advice is what we ask for when we already know the answer but wish we didn't.
1977 *How To Save Your Own Life*.

4 Friends *love* misery, in fact. Sometimes, especially if we are too lucky or too successful or too pretty, our misery is the only thing that endears us to our friends.
1977 *How To Save Your Own Life*.

5 Every country gets the circus it deserves. Spain gets bullfights. Italy gets the Catholic Church. America gets Hollywood.
1977 *How To Save Your Own Life*.

6 Women are the only exploited group in the world who have been idealized into powerlessness.
1978 In *Time*.

7 Fear of Fifty.
1994 Title of memoir.

Jonson, Ben 1572–1637

English dramatist. Imprisoned for killing a man in a duel, he became a Catholic but later recanted. His plays reject romantic comedy for a more realistic mode and include *Volpone* (1606), *The Silent Woman* (1609) and *The Alchemist* (1610). He was regarded as superior to Shakespeare in his day.

8 Well, I will scourge those apes,
And to these courteous eyes oppose a mirror,
As large as is the stage whereon we act;
Where they shall see the time's deformity
Anatomised in every nerve, and sinew,
With constant courage, and contempt of fear.
1600 *Every Man out of His Humour*, Induction.

9 GENT: He hath been beyond-sea, once, or twice.
CARL: As far as *Paris*, to fetch over a fashion, and come back again.
1600 *Every Man out of His Humour*, act 2, sc.2.

10 Good morning to the day; and next, my gold!
1609 *Volpone*, act 1, sc.1.

11 Yet I glory
More in the cunning purchase of my wealth
Than in the glad possession.
1609 *Volpone*, act 1, sc.1.

12 What should I do,
But cocker up my genius, and live free
To all delights my fortune calls me to?
1609 *Volpone*, act 1, sc.2.

13 Hood an ass with reverend purple,
So you can hide his two ambitious ears,
And he shall pass for a cathedral doctor.
1609 *Volpone*, act 1, sc.3.

14 Give 'em words;
Pour oil into their ears, and send them hence.
1609 *Volpone*, act 1, sc.4.

15 He has no faith in physic. He does think
Most of your doctors are the greater danger,
And worse disease, t'escape.
1609 *Volpone*, act 1, sc.4.

16 'Fore heaven, I wonder at the desperate valour
Of the bold English, that they dare let loose
Their wives to all encounters!
1609 *Volpone*, act 1, sc.5.

17 Calumnies are answered best with silence.
1609 *Volpone*, act 2, sc. 2.

18 Ay, a plague on't,
My conscience fools my wit!
1609 *Volpone*, act 2, sc.7.

19 Success hath made me wanton.
1609 *Volpone*, act 3, sc.1.

20 All my house,
But now, steamed like a bath with her thick breath.
A lawyer could not have been heard; nor scarce

Another woman, such a hail of words
She has let fall.
1609 Of Lady Politic Would-be. *Volpone*, act 3, sc.5.

21 Come, my Celia, let us prove,
While we can, the sports of love,
Time will not be ours for ever,
He, at length, our good will sever;
Spend not then his gifts in vain:
Suns that set may rise again;
But if once we lose this light,
'Tis with us perpetual night.
Why should we defer our joys?
Fame and rumour are but toys.
1609 *Volpone*, 'Song', act 3, sc.7.

22 His soul moves in his fee.
1609 Of the lawyer. *Volpone*, act 4, sc.5.

23 I'd have your tongue, sir, tipped with gold for this.
1609 *Volpone*, act 4, sc.6.

24 A pox of her autumnal face, her pieced beauty!
1609–10 *Epicoene*, act 1, sc.1.

25 Still to be neat, still to be drest,
As you were going to a feast;
Still to be powdered, still perfumed,
Lady, it is to be presumed,
Though art's hid causes are not found,
All is not sweet, all is not sound.

Give me a look, give me a face,
That makes simplicity a grace;
Robes loosely flowing, hair as free:
Such sweet neglect more taketh me,
Than all the adulteries of art;
They strike mine eyes, but not my heart.
1609–10 *Epicoene*, act 1, sc.1.

26 Let me see: all discourses but mine own afflict me; they seem harsh, impertinent, and irksome.
1609–10 *Epicoene*, act 2, sc.1.

27 A man of your head and hair should owe more to that reverend ceremony, and not mount the marriage bed like a town-bull, or a mountain goat; but stay the due season and ascend it then with religion and fear.
1609–10 *Epicoene*, act 3, sc.5.

28 Fortune, that favours fools.
1610 *The Alchemist*, act 1, sc.4.

29 [The play] is like to be a very conceited scurvy one, in plain English.
1614 *Bartholomew Fair*, Induction.

30 WIN LITTLEWIT: Come, indeed, la, you are such a fool, still!
LITTLEWIT: No, but half a one, Win; you are the t'other half: man and wife make one fool, Win.
1614 *Bartholomew Fair*, act 1, sc.1.

31 He is a fellow of a most arrogant and invincible dullness, I assure you.
1614 *Bartholomew Fair*, act 1, sc.1.

32 There is a doing of right out of wrong, if the ways be found.
1614 *Bartholomew Fair*, act 2, sc.2.

33 I see compassion may become a justice, though it be a weakness, I confess, and nearer a vice than a virtue.
1614 *Bartholomew Fair*, act 4, sc.2.

34 There's reason good, that you good laws should make:
Men's manners ne'er were viler, for your sake.
1616 *Epigrams*, 'To the Parliament'.

35 Nor shall our cups make any guilty men:
But, at our parting, we will be, as when
We innocently met. No simple word,
That shall be utter'd at our mirthful board,
Shall make us sad next morning: or affright
The liberty, that we'll enjoy tonight.
1616 *Epigrams*, 'On Inviting a Friend to Supper'.

36 Thou art not, Penshurst, built to envious show
Of touch or marble, nor canst boast a row
Of polished pillars, or a roof of gold;
Thou hast no lantern whereof tales are told,
Or stair, or courts; but standst an ancient pile,
And these grudged at, art reverenced the while.
1616 *The Forest*, 'To Penshurst'.

37 Then hath thy orchard fruit, thy garden flowers,
Fresh as the air, and new as are the hours.
The early cherry, with the later plum,
Fig, grape, and quince, each in his time doth come:
The blushing apricot, and woolly peach
Hang on thy walls, that every child may reach.
1616 *The Forest*, 'To Penshurst'.

38 Freedom doth with degree dispense.
1616 *The Forest*, 'To Sir Robert Wroth'.

39 Nor for my peace will I go far,
As wanderers do, that still do roam,
But make my strengths, such as they are,
Here in my bosom, and at home.
1616 *The Forest*, 'To the World'.

40 Drink to me, only, with thine eyes,
And I will pledge with mine;
Or leave a kiss but in the cup,
And I'll not look for wine.
1616 *The Forest*, 'To Celia'.

41 'Tis grown almost a danger to speak true
Of any good mind, now: There are so few.
1616 *The Forest*, 'Epistle to Katherine, Lady Aubigny'.

42 Rest in soft peace, and, asked, say here doth lie
Ben Jonson his best piece of poetry.
1616 'On My First Son'.

43 Soul of the Age!
The applause, delight, the wonder of our stage!
1623 'To the Memory of My Beloved, the Author, Mr. William Shakespeare, and What He Hath Left Us'.

44 Thou hadst small Latin, and less Greek.
1623 'To the Memory of My Beloved, the Author, Mr. William Shakespeare, and What He Hath Left Us', prefatory dedication to the first folio of Shakespeare's plays.

45 He was not of an age, but for all time!
1623 'To the Memory of My Beloved, the Author, Mr. William Shakespeare, and What He Hath Left Us', prefatory dedication to the first folio of Shakespeare's plays.

46 Sweet Swan of Avon! What a sight it were
To see thee in our waters yet appear,
And make those flights upon the banks of Thames
That so did take Eliza, and our James!
1623 'To the Memory of My Beloved, the Author, Mr. William Shakespeare, and What He Hath Left Us', prefatory dedication to the first folio of Shakespeare's plays.

47 O rare Ben Jonson.
1637 His epitaph in Westminster Abbey. It is thought that the words were inscribed on his gravestone at the order of a certain Sir John Young, possibly in error for 'Orare Ben Jonson' ('Pray for Ben Jonson').

48 For Love's sake, kiss me once again,
I long, and should not beg in vain,
Here's none to spy, or see;
Why do you doubt, or stay?
I'll taste as lightly as the Bee,
That doth but touch his flower, and flies away.
Once more, and (faith) I will be gone:
Can he that loves, ask less than one?
The Underwood, 'A Celebration of Charis', no.7 (published 1640).

49 Minds that are great and free,
Should not on fortune pause,
'Tis crown enough to virtue still, her own applause.
The Underwood, 'An Ode to Himself' (published 1640).

50 Helen, did Homer never see
Thy beauties, yet could write of thee?
The Underwood, 'An Ode' (published 1640).

51 Come, let us here enjoy the shade;
For love in shadow best is made.
Though envy oft his shadow be,
None brooks the sunlight worse than he.
The Underwood, 'A Song' (published 1640).

52 'Tis true, I'm broke! Vows, oaths, and all I had
Of credit lost. And I am now run mad,
Or do upon my self some desperate ill;
This sadness makes no approaches, but to kill.
The Underwood, 'An Elegy', no.40 (published 1640).

53 Wisdom without honesty is mere craft and cozenage. And therefore the reputation for honesty must first be gotten; which cannot be but by living well. A good life is a main argument.
Timber: or Discoveries made upon Men and Matter (published 1640).

54 Poetry in this latter age hath proved but a mean mistress to such as have wholly addicted themselves to her, or given their names up to her family. They who have but saluted her on the by, and now and then tendered their visits, she hath done much for, and advanced in the way of their own professions (both the law and the gospel) beyond all they could have hoped, or done for themselves without her favour.
Timber: or Discoveries made upon Men and Matter (published 1640).

55 I remember that the players have often mentioned it as an honour to Shakespeare that in his writing, whatsoever he penned, he never blotted out a line. My answer hath been, Would he had blotted a thousand: which they thought a malevolent speech…[but] I loved the man and do honour his memory, on this side idolatry, as much as any.
Timber: or Discoveries made upon Men and Matter (published 1640).

56 There was ever more in him to be praised than to be pardoned.
Of Shakespeare. *Timber: or Discoveries made upon Men and Matter* (published 1640).

57 The fear of every man that heard him was, lest he should make an end.
Of Francis Bacon. *Timber: or Discoveries made upon Men and Matter* (published 1640).

58 For a man to write well, there are required three necessaries: to read the best authors, observe the best speakers, and much exercise of his own style.
Timber: or Discoveries made upon Men and Matter (published 1640).

59 Ready writing makes not good writing, but good writing brings on ready writing.
Timber: or Discoveries made upon Men and Matter (published 1640).

60 Custom is the most certain mistress of language, as the public stamp makes the current money.
Timber: or Discoveries made upon Men and Matter (published 1640).

61 Our composition must be more accurate in the beginning and end than in the midst, and in the end more than in the beginning; for through the midst the stream bears us.
Timber: or Discoveries made upon Men and Matter (published 1640).

62 Our style should be as a skein of silk, to be carried and found by the right thread, not ravelled and perplexed; then all is a knot, a heap.
Timber: or Discoveries made upon Men and Matter (published 1640).

Joplin, Janis 1943–70

US rhythm and blues singer.

63 Lord, won't you buy me a Mercedes-Benz,
My friends all drive Porsches,
I must make amends.
1970 'Mercedes-Benz', co-written with Michael McClure and Bob Neuwirth.

Jordan, June 1936–2002

US poet, essayist, political activist and writer for children. Her work was marked by a strong commitment to black consciousness.

64 Body and soul, Black America reveals the extreme questions of contemporary life, questions of freedom and identity: *How can I be who I am?*
1969 'Black Studies: Bringing Back the Person', in the *Evergreen Review*, Oct.

65 We do not deride the fears of prospering white America. A nation of violence and private property has every reason to dread the violated and the deprived.
1969 'Black Studies: Bringing Back the Person', in the *Evergreen Review*, Oct.

66 To rescue our children we will have to let them save us from the power we embody: we will have to trust the very difference that they forever personify.
1978 Keynote address for Child Welfare League of America. Collected as 'Old Stories: New Lives' in *Moving Towards Home* (1989).

67 I am a feminist, and what that means to me is much the same as the meaning of the fact that I am Black: it means that I must undertake to love myself as though my very life depends upon self-love and self-respect.
1978 Address to Black Writers Conference, Howard University. Collected as 'Where Is the Love?' in *Moving Towards Home* (1989).

Jordan, Michael 1963–

US basketball player. He played with the Chicago Bulls (1984–93, 1995–8), set numerous records, and was a member of the US Olympic gold medal-winning basketball teams in 1984 and 1992.

68 Talent wins games, but teamwork wins championships.
Attributed.

Jordan, Neil 1950–

Irish film-maker and writer. His films include *The Crying Game* (1992), *Interview with the Vampire* (1994), *The Butcher Boy* (1997) and *The End of the Affair* (1999).

69 The action movie in the 1980s became like what the silent movie used to be. The same movie could be seen in Los Angeles and Taiwan and Hong Kong and you didn't need subtitles because everybody understands Bruce Willis blowing things up in a torn vest.
2004 In *The Scotsman*, 22 May.

Joseph II 1741–90

Holy Roman Emperor (1756–90), known as 'the revolutionary emperor' for his programme of modernization. He suppressed papal power and in 1781 published an Edict of Toleration for Protestants and Greeks.

70 As I have just come from making my Easter confession on Good Friday and have forgiven all those who trespass against me, I cannot harbour any thoughts of revenge, only contempt for an arrant shit who is bursting with pride, although he is simply being taken for a ride by his women.
1786 Of the senior dignitary of the Holy Roman Empire, the Elector-Archbishop of Mainz. Letter to Trauttmansdorff (his representative at Mainz), 14 Apr. Quoted in T C W Blanning *Joseph II* (1994), p.148.

71 Here lies a prince whose intentions were pure, but who had the misfortune to see all his plans collapse.
Epitaph for himself. Quoted in T C W Blanning *Joseph II* (1994), p.1.

Joseph of Exeter fl.12c

English poet.

72 The youths at cricks did play
Throughout the merry day.
1180 Quoted in Ivor Brown *A Book of England* (1958). This is thought to be the first mention of the game of cricket in English literature.

Josephus, Flavius AD 37–100

Jewish historian and soldier, commander of Galilee. He surrendered to the Romans rather than commit suicide, and later won imperial patronage and lived in Rome. His works include *The Antiquities of the Jews*.

73 Their exercises are unbloody battles, and their battles bloody exercises.
c.75–79 AD Of the Romans. *A History of the Jewish War*, bk.3, ch.5, section 1 (translated by William Whiston).

Jourdan, Louis *originally* Louis Gendre 1921–

French-born actor. He appeared in French films (1940–6), then moved to the US. His many American and European film credits since include *Gigi* (1958), *Can Can* (1960) and *Octopussy* (1983).

74 In New York people don't go to the theater—they go to see hits.
1950 In the *New York Herald Tribune*, 1 Jan.

Jouvet, Louis 1887–1951

French actor and director. Appointed director of the Comédie des Champs-Élysées in 1922, he had a profound impact on the development of French theatre between the wars, making many reforms.

75 The one thing constant in a changing world is the avant-garde.
Attributed.

Jovanovich, William 1920–2001

US publisher. He joined Harcourt Brace Jovanovich Inc in 1947, eventually becoming president and director.

76 The most important single thing in publishing is the English sentence, and the editor who cannot contemplate it again and again with a sense of wonder has not yet gained respect for the complexity of learning.
1964 *Now, Barabbas.*

Jowell, Tessa 1947–

English Labour politician, Secretary of State for Culture, Media and Sport since 2001.

77 In the last Parliament, the House of Commons had more MPs called John than all the women MPs put together.
1999 In the *Independent on Sunday*, 'Quotes', 14 Mar.

Jowett, Benjamin 1817–93

English classical scholar, Professor of Greek at Oxford (1855–93), ordained as an Anglican priest in 1845.

78 One man is as good as another until he has written a book.
Quoted in Evelyn Abbott and Lewis Campbell (eds) *Life and Letters of Benjamin Jowett* (1897), vol.1.

79 Nowhere probably is there more true feeling, and nowhere worse taste, than in a churchyard.
Quoted in Evelyn Abbott and Lewis Campbell (eds) *Letters of Benjamin Jowett* (1899), ch.6.

Joyce, James Augustine Aloysius 1882–1941

Irish writer who lived in exile on the Continent and was plagued for most of his life with deteriorating eyesight. His fiction includes *Dubliners* (1914), *Ulysses* (1922), one of the most influential works of 20c fiction, and *Finnegans Wake* (1939).

80 'O, pa!' he cried. 'Don't beat me, pa! And I'll…I'll say a *Hail Mary* for you… I'll say a *Hail Mary* for you, pa, if you don't beat me.'
1914 *Dubliners*, 'Counterparts'.

81 His soul swooned slowly as he heard the snow falling faintly through the universe and faintly falling, like the descent of their last end, upon all the living and the dead.
1914 *Dubliners*, 'The Dead'.

82 The fellows were practising long shies and bowling lobs and slow twisters. In the soft grey silence he could hear the bump of the balls: and from here and from there through the quiet air the sound of the cricket bats: pick, pack, pock, puck: like drops of water in a fountain falling

softly in the brimming bowl.
1916 *A Portrait of the Artist as a Young Man.*

83 At the door Dante turned round violently and shouted down the room, her cheeks flushed and quivering with rage:
—Devil out of hell! We won! We crushed him to death! Fiend!
The door slammed behind her. Mr Casey, freeing his arms from his holders, suddenly bowed his head on his hands with a sob of pain.
—Poor Parnell! he cried loudly. My dead king!
1916 *A Portrait of the Artist as a Young Man.*

84 The snotgreen sea. The scrotumtightening sea.
1922 *Ulysses.*

85 It is a symbol of Irish art. The cracked looking-glass of a servant.
1922 *Ulysses.*

86 When I makes tea I makes tea, as old mother Grogan said. And when I makes water I makes water…*Begob, ma'am, says Mrs. Cahill, God send you don't make them in the one pot.*
1922 *Ulysses.*

87 History, Stephen said, is a nightmare from which I am trying to awake.
1922 *Ulysses.*

88 Lawn Tennyson, gentleman poet.
1922 *Ulysses.*

89 Come forth, Lazarus! And he came fifth and lost the job.
1922 *Ulysses.*

90 A man of genius makes no mistakes. His errors are volitional and are the portals of discovery.
1922 *Ulysses.*

91 Greater love than this, he said, no man hath that a man lay down his wife for his friend. Go thou and do likewise. Thus, or words to that effect, saith Zarathustra, sometime regius professor of French letters to the university of Oxtail.
1922 *Ulysses.*

92 Mr. Leopold Bloom ate with relish the inner organs of beasts and fowls. He liked thick giblet soup, nutty gizzards, a stuffed roast heart; liver slices fried with crustcrumbs, fried hencod's roes. Most of all he liked grilled mutton kidneys which gave to his palate a fine tang of faintly scented urine.
1922 *Ulysses.*

93 A woman loses a charm with every pin she takes out.
1922 *Ulysses.*

94 Heavenly weather. If life was always like that. Cricket weather. Sit around under sunshades. Over after over. Out. They can't play it here. Still, Captain Buller broke a window in Kildare Street Club with a slog to square leg.
1922 *Ulysses.* Legend has it that W G Grace performed the feat of breaking the Kildare Street Club window while playing at the distant College Park in the 1870s.

95 Her crocus dress she wore, lowcut, belongings on show.
1922 *Ulysses.*

96 yes and how he kissed me under the Moorish wall and I thought well as well him as another and then I asked him with my eyes to ask again yes and then he asked me would I yes to say yes my mountain flower and first I put my arms around him yes and drew him down to me so he could feel my breasts all perfume yes and his heart was going like mad and yes I said yes I will Yes.
1922 *Ulysses*, last words.

97 I read the first 2 pages of the usual sloppy English and [Stuart Gilbert] read me a lyrical bit about nudism in the wood and the end which is a piece of propaganda in favour of something which, outside of D. H. L.'s country at any rates, makes all the propaganda for itself.
1931 On D H Lawrence's *Lady Chatterley's Lover*. Letter to Harriet Weaver, 17 Dec.

98 That ideal reader suffering from an ideal insomnia.
1939 *Finnegans Wake.*

99 Gentes and laitymen, fullstoppers and semicolonials, hybreds and lubberds!
1939 *Finnegans Wake.*

1 All moanday, tearsday, wailsday, thumpsday, frightday, shatterday till the fear of the Law.
1939 *Finnegans Wake.*

Joyce, Nora d.1951

Wife of James Joyce.

2 Well, Jim, I haven't read any of your books but I'll have to someday because they must be good considering how well they sell.
To her husband James Joyce. Recalled on her death, 12 Apr 1951.

Joyce, William *known as* ***Lord Haw Haw*** 1906–46

British traitor. He fled to Germany before World War II, from where he broadcast anti-British propaganda in his upper-class drawl until captured at Flensburg and executed.

3 The Twenty Thousand Thieves.
c.1941 Of the Australian 9th Division troops who were besieged at Tobruk, North Africa. Radio broadcast from Nazi Germany.

Julian of Norwich *known as* ***Lady Julian*** c.1342–1416

English anchoress, who spent much of her life enclosed in a cell attached to the Church of St Julian, Norwich. In 1373 she experienced a series of religious visions which she set down in her *Revelations of Divine Love*.

4 He showed me something small, no bigger than a hazelnut, lying in the palm of my hand, as it seemed to me, and it was as round as a ball. I looked at it with the eye of my understanding, and thought: What can this be? I was amazed that it could last, for I thought that because of its littleness it would suddenly have fallen into nothing. And I was answered in my understanding: It lasts and always will, because God loves it; and thus every thing has being through the love of God.
1373–c.1393 *Revelations of Divine Love*, ch.5.

5 It is true that sin is the cause of all this pain; but all shall be well, and all shall be well, and all manner of things shall be well.
1373–c.1393 *Revelations of Divine Love*, ch.27.

6 Pray inwardly, even though you do not enjoy it. It does good though you feel nothing, even though you think you are doing nothing.
1373–c.1393 *Revelations of Divine Love*, ch.41.

Jumblatt, Walid 1949–

Lebanese politician and hereditary Druze chieftain, who succeeded his father Jumblatt on the latter's assassination in 1977.

7 Here, even the law of the jungle has broken down.
1985 Of the situation in Beirut, in the *Sunday Times*, 29 Dec.

Jung, Carl Gustav 1875–1961

Swiss psychiatrist. After collaborating with Sigmund Freud he published *The Psychology of the Unconscious* (1911–12), departing from Freud's psychosexual emphasis. Subsequently he developed analytical psychology and the concept of the 'collective unconscious'.

8 The pendulum of the mind oscillates between sense and nonsense, not between right and wrong.
1962 *Memories, Dreams and Reflections*.

9 Show me a sane man and I will cure him for you.
Quoted in the *Observer*, 19 Jul 1975.

'Junius' *possibly the pseudonym of* Sir Philip Francis (1740–1818)

The identity of Junius, whose scathing political letters were printed in the *Public Advertiser* between 1769 and 1771 and collected in 1772, has never been established. Sir Philip Francis is a favourite candidate.

10 There is a holy mistaken zeal in politics as well as in religion. By persuading others, we convince ourselves.
1769 *Public Advertiser*, 19 Dec, Letter 35.

11 Let it be impressed upon your minds, let it be instilled into your children, that the liberty of the press is the *Palladium* of all the civil, political, and religious rights of an Englishman.
1772 *Letters*, Dedication to the Authorized Edition.

Just, Ward Swift 1935–

US journalist and writer. He was a correspondent with *Newsweek* (1963–5) and the *Washington Post* (1965–70), before turning full time to fiction with works such as *The American Blues* (1984) and *Echo House* (1997).

12 The place where bulls and foxes dine very well, but lambs end up head down on the hook.
1988 Of Chicago. *Jack Gance*.

Justinian I AD 482–565

Emperor of the East Roman Empire (from 527). His reign saw the restoration of the Roman Empire to its ancient limits and many legal reforms, collected in the *Corpus Juris Civilis*, which had a considerable influence on European law.

13 Justice is the constant and perpetual wish to render to every one his due.
AD 533 *Institutiones*, pt.1.

Juvenal *full name* Decimus Iunius Iuvenalis c.55–c.140 AD

Roman lawyer and satirist. He was banished to Egypt for some years by Domitian for his 16 verse satires (c.100–128 AD), which deal with the corruption and immorality of the times.

14 *Difficile est saturam non scribere.*
It is difficult not to write satire.
Satirae, no.1, l.30.

15 *Quis tulerit Gracchos de seditione querentes?*
Who can bear the Gracchi deploring revolution?
Satirae, no.2, l.24. The brothers Gaius and Tiberius Sempronius Gracchus (2c BC) attempted radical agrarian reforms, and were both killed by political opponents.

16 *Nil habet infelix paupertas durius in se*
Quam quod ridiculos homines facit.
The hardest thing to bear in poverty is the fact that it makes men ridiculous.
Satirae, no.3, l.152–3 (translated by Peter Green).

17 *Sed quis custodiet ipsos custodes?*
But who is to guard the guards themselves?
Satirae, no.6, l.347.

18 *Cantabit vacuus coram latrone viator.*
Travel light and you can sing in the robber's face.
Satirae, no.10, l.22.

19 *Nam qui dabat olim*
imperium, fasces, legiones, omnia, nunc se
continet atque duas tantum res anxius optat,
panem et circenses.
Time was when their plebiscite elected generals, Heads of State, commanders of legions: but now they've pulled in their horns, there's only two things that concern them: bread and games.
Of the people of Rome. *Satirae*, no.10, l.78–81 (translated by Peter Green). 'Panem et circenses' is sometimes translated as 'bread and circuses'

20 *Orandum est ut sit mens sana in corpore sano.*
One should pray to have a sound mind in a sound body.
Satirae, no.10, l.356.

21 *Maxima debetur puero reverentia, si quid turpe paras.*
If you are planning any misdeed, never forget that a child has a first claim on your respect.
Satirae, no.14, l.47 (translated by Peter Green).

Kael, Pauline 1919–2001

US film critic. She was film critic of the *New Yorker* from 1968 to 1991.

22 The words 'Kiss Kiss Bang Bang' which I saw on an Italian movie poster, are perhaps the briefest statement imaginable of the basic appeal of movies.
1968 *Kiss Kiss Bang Bang*.

23 Good movies make you care, make you believe in possibilities again.
1970 *Going Steady*.

Kafka, Franz 1883–1924

Czech novelist and short-story writer who wrote in German. After studying law he worked in Prague at a workers' accident insurance company. He is best known for his bleak studies of the absurdity of the human condition.

24 *Ich glaube, mann sollte überhaupt nur solche Bücher*

lesen, die einen beißen und stechen.
I think we ought to read only the kind of books that wound and stab us.
1904 Letter to Oskar Pollack. Collected in Richard and Clara Winston (eds and trans) *Letters to Friends, Family, and Editors* (1977).

25 *Ist es schwer und kann es ein Außenseiter begreifen, dass man eine Geschichte von ihrem Anfang in sich erlebt, vom fernen Punkt bis zu der heranfahrenden Lokomotive aus Stahl, Kohl und Dampf, sie aber auch jetzt noch nicht verlässt, sondern von ihr gejagt wird und aus eigenem Schwung vor ihr läuft, wohin sie nur stößt und wohin man sie lockt.*
It is so difficult and can an outsider understand that you experience a story within yourself from its beginning, from the distant point up to the approaching locomotive of steel, coal and steam, and you don't abandon it even now, but want to be pursued by it and have time for it, therefore are pursued by it and of your own volition run before it wherever it may thrust and wherever you may lure it.
1911 Diary entry, Aug. Collected in Max Brod (ed) *The Diaries of Franz Kafka, 1910–1913* (1948).

26 *Als Gregor Samsa eines Morgens aus unruhigen Träumen erwachte, fand er sich in seinem Bett zu einem ungeheueren Ungeziefer verwandelt.*
When Gregor Samsa awoke one morning from uneasy dreams he found himself transformed in his bed into a gigantic insect.
1915 *Metamorphosis*, ch.1.

27 *Es ist oft besser, in Ketten als frei zu sein.*
It is often safer to be in chains than to be free.
1925 *Der Prozess* (translated as *The Trial*, 1937).

28 *Ich bin so weit, dass ich Gewissheit gar nicht haben will.*
I have reached the stage where I no longer wish to have certainty.
'Der Bau', collected in Nahum N Glatzer (ed) *The Complete Stories* (1971).

29 *Er lächelte und sagte: 'Von mir willst du den Weg erfahren?' 'Ja,' sagte ich, 'da ich ihn selbst nich finden kann.' 'Gibs auf, gibs auf,' sagte er und wandte sich mit einem großen Schwunge ab, so wie Leute, die mit ihrem Lachen allein sein wollen.*
He smiled and said: 'You asking me the way?' 'Yes,' I said, 'since I cannot find it myself.' 'Give it up! Give it up!' said he, and turned with a sudden jerk, like someone who wants to be alone with his laughter.
'Gibs Auf!', collected in Nahum N Glatzer (ed) *The Complete Stories* (1971).

Kahn, Gus 1886–1941

US lyricist and author. He supplied the lyrics for many classic hit songs of the 1920s and 1930s, among them 'Toot, Toot, Tootsie', 'Carolina in the Morning', 'Yes Sir, That's My Baby', and 'Makin' Whoopee'.

30 There's nothing surer,
The rich get rich and the poor get children.
In the meantime, in between time,
Ain't we got fun.
1921 'Ain't We Got Fun' (with Raymond B Egan).

31 All God's Chillum Got Rhythm.
1937 Title of song.

Kaiko, Takeshi 1930–89

Japanese novelist. His first novel to be translated into English was *Darkness in Summer* (1972).

32 I don't trust anybody who's never eaten bread with the salt of tears.
1963 'The Laughing Stock', in *Five Thousand Runaways* (translated by Cecilia Segawa Seigle).

33 Late one morning, I awoke in the capital of a certain country and found myself—not changed overnight into a large brown beetle, nor feeling exactly on top of the world—merely ready to go home.
1978 'The Crushed Pellet', in *Five Thousand Runaways* (translated by Cecilia Segawa Seigle).

Kames, Henry Home, Lord 1696–1782

Scottish judge, philosopher and agricultural improver, a central figure of the Scottish Enlightenment.

34 Fare ye a' weel, ye bitches!
1782 His alleged words on taking leave of his fellow judges in the Court of Session. He died eight days later. Quoted in Robert Chambers *Traditions of Edinburgh* (1824), 'The Parliament House'.

Kandinsky, Wassily 1866–1944

Russian-born painter and writer on art. He was an important pioneer of abstract art. With Franz Marc he edited the *Blaue Reiter Almanac*.

35 The force that propels the human spirit on the clear way forward and upward is the abstract spirit.
1912 'On the Question of Form', in *Blaue Reiter Almanac*.

36 We should never make a god out of form. We should struggle for form only as long as it serves as a means of expression for the inner sound.
1912 'On the Question of Form', in *Blaue Reiter Almanac*.

37 Every work of art is the child of its time, often it is the mother of our emotions.
1912 *Concerning the Spiritual in Art*.

38 In general, therefore, color is a means of exerting a direct influence upon the soul. Color is the keyboard. The eye is the hammer. The soul is the piano, with its many strings.
Quoted in K C Lindsay and P Vergo (eds and trans) *Kandinsky: Complete Writings on Art* (1982).

Kant, Immanuel 1724–1804

German philosopher, Professor of Logic and Metaphysics at Konigsberg (1770), who developed a theory of knowledge depending on perception and propounded the 'moral argument' for the existence of God. His great work is the *Kritik der reinen Vernunft* (*Critique of Pure Reason*, 1781).

39 *Der Verstand vermag nichts anzuschauen, und die Sinne nichts zu denken. Nur daraus, dass sie sich vereinigen, kann Erkenntnis entspringen.*
The understanding can intuit nothing, the senses can think nothing. Only through their union can knowledge arise.
1781 *Kritik der reinen Vernunft* (*Critique of Pure Reason*), B75 (translated by N Kemp Smith).

40 *Ich habe also demnach keine Erkenntnis von mir, wie ich bin, sondern bloß, wie ich mir selbst erscheine. Das Bewusstsein seiner selbst ist also noch lange nicht eine Erkenntnis seiner selbst.*

I have no *knowledge* of myself as I am but merely as I appear to myself. The consciousness of myself is thus very far from being a knowledge of the self.
1781 *Kritik der reinen Vernunft* (*Critique of Pure Reason*), B158 (translated by N Kemp Smith).

41 *Eben darin Philosophie besteht, seine Grenzen zu kennen.*
It is precisely in knowing its limits that philosophy consists.
1781 *Kritik der reinen Vernunft* (*Critique of Pure Reason*), B755 (translated by N Kemp Smith).

42 *Sapere aude*, have the courage to know: that is the motto of enlightenment.
1783 His reply to a newspaper's challenge to define enlightenment. Quoted in *The Economist*, 16 Mar 1996.

43 *Aus so krummen Holze, als woraus der Mensch gemacht ist, kann nichts ganz Gerades gezimmert werden.*
Out of the crooked timber of humanity, no straight thing can ever be made.
1784 *Idee zu einer allgemeinen Geschichte in weltbürgerlicher Absicht* (*Idea for a General History with a Cosmopolitan Purpose*), prop.6.

44 *Ich solle niemals anders verfahren, als so, dass ich auch wollen könne, meine Maxime solle ein allgemeines Gesetz werden.*
I ought never to act except in such a way *that I can also will that my maxim should become a universal law.*
1785 *Grundlagen zur Metaphysik der Sitten* (*Groundwork to a Metaphysic of Morals*), ch.1 (translated by H J Paton).

45 *Handle so, dass du die Menschheit, sowohl in deiner Person, als in der Person eines jeden andern, jederzeit zugleich als Zweck, niemals bloß als Mittel brauchst.*
Act in such a way that you always treat humanity, whether in your own person or in the person of any other, never simply as a means, but always at the same time as an end.
1785 *Grundlagen zur Metaphysik der Sitten* (*Groundwork to a Metaphysic of Morals*), ch.2 (translated by H J Paton).

46 *Ich musste also das Wissen aufheben, um zum Glauben Platz zu bekommen.*
I have therefore found it necessary to deny *knowledge*, in order to make room for *faith*.
1787 *Kritik der reinen Vernunft* (*Critique of Pure Reason*), preface to 2nd edn (translated by N Kemp Smith).

47 *Zwei Dinge erfüllen das Gemüt mit immer neuer und zunehmender Bewunderung und Ehrfurcht, je öfter und anhaltender sich das Nachdenken damit beschäftigt: der bestirnte Himmel über mir, und das moralische Gesetz in mir.*
Two things fill the mind with ever new and increasing admiration and awe, the oftener and more steadily we reflect on them: *the starry heavens above me and the moral law within.*
1788 *Kritik der praktischen Vernunft* (*Critique of Practical Reason*) (translated by T K Abbott).

Kapitsa, Peter Leonidovich 1894–1984

Soviet physicist who studied in Britain under Ernest Rutherford. Director of the Institute of Physical Problems, he was dismissed by Stalin for refusing to work on an atomic bomb, but was later reinstated.

48 Theory is a good thing but a good experiment lasts forever.
1980 *Experiment, Theory, Practice.*

Karloff, Boris *originally* William Henry Pratt 1887–1969

English-born US film star. He went to Canada and the US aiming at a diplomatic career, but turned to acting, finding fame as the monster in *Frankenstein* (1931) and other horror roles.

49 The monster was indeed the best friend I could ever have.
On his success as Frankenstein's monster. Quoted in *Connoisseur*, Jan 1991.

Karpov, Anatoly 1951–

Russian chess player.

50 Chess is everything—art, science and sport.
Attributed.

Karr, Alphonse 1808–90

French writer and journalist.

51 *Plus ça change, plus c'est la même chose.*
The more things change, the more they stay the same.
1849 *Les Guêpes*, Jan.

Karsh, Yousuf 1908–2002

Turkish-born Canadian portrait photographer.

52 I said, 'Forgive me, sir,' and plucked the cigar out of his mouth. By the time I got back to my camera, he looked so belligerent he could have devoured me. It was at that instant that I took the photograph. The silence was deafening.
1983 Recalling how he snapped the celebrated 'bulldog' photograph of Sir Winston Churchill in the Speaker's Chambers, House of Commons, Ottawa, on 30 Dec 1941. *Karsh: A Fifty-Year Retrospective.*

Kaufman, George S(imon) 1889–1961

US playwright, director and journalist, a member of the Algonquin Round Table circle of literary wits. He collaborated on several successful comedies with Moss Hart, notably *The Man Who Came to Dinner* (1939), and also worked with Edna Ferber and George Gershwin.

53 Am sitting in the last row. Wish you were here.
1932 Telegram sent during a performance of *Of Thee I Sing* to the actor William Gaxton, who was taking various liberties with Kaufman's lines while playing the leading role.

54 Massey won't be satisfied until he's assassinated.
1938 Of Raymond Massey in the title role of *Abe Lincoln in Illinois*. Recalled on Kaufman's death, 2 Jun 1961.

55 Satire is what closes Saturday night.
Quoted in Howard Teichmann *George S Kaufman* (1972).

56 I saw his play under bad conditions. The curtain was up.
Of Alexander Woollcott. Quoted in Scott Meredith *George S Kaufman and His Friends* (1974).

57 Like the Arabs, I fold my tens and silently steal away.
On winning at poker. Quoted in Scott Meredith *George S Kaufman and His Friends* (1974).
► *See Longfellow 516:50.*

58 It's what God would have done if he'd had the money.
On visiting Pocantico Hills, the Rockefeller family's 3,000-acre Hudson River estate. Quoted in Michael Kramer and Sam Roberts *I Never Wanted to Be Vice-President of Anything!* (1976).

59 God finally caught his eye.
Epitaph for a deceased waiter. Quoted in Jon Winokur *The Portable Curmudgeon* (1987).

60 There was scattered laughter in the rear of the theatre, leading to the belief that somebody was telling jokes back there.
Play review.

61 Close the play and keep the store open nights.
Reply when asked by one of his backers, the owner of Bloomingdale's department store, how the première of Kaufman's latest play had gone. Attributed.

62 Over my dead body.
Suggestion for his own epitaph. Attributed.

Kaufman, Gerald 1930–

English Labour politician.

63 We would prefer to see the House run by a philistine with the requisite financial acumen than by the succession of opera and ballet lovers who have brought a great and valuable institution to its knees.
1997 Report of the Commons' Culture, Media and Sport Select Committee on Covent Garden, 3 Dec.

Kaufmann, Christoph 1753–95

Swiss-born German author and critic.

64 *Sturm und Drang.*
Storm and stress.
c.1775 Suggested title for a romantic historical play of F M Klinger, adopted as the defining term for late-18c German drama.

Kaunitz-Rietberg, Wenzel Anton, Prince von 1711–94

Austrian statesman, Ambassador to the French court (1750–2). Appointed Chancellor in 1753, he directed Austrian politics for almost 40 years. Active in the ecclesiastical reforms of Joseph II, he was a liberal patron of arts and sciences.

65 That was very good of him.
1790 Attributed, on hearing that Joseph II had died. Quoted in T C W Blanning *Joseph II* (1994), p.198.

Kavanagh, P(atrick) J(oseph Gregory) 1931–

English poet and novelist. His works include the autobiographical *The Perfect Stranger* (1966) and *A Kind of Journal* (2003), a collection of his *Spectator* columns.

66 Charlie Parker…always filled me with a kind of despair, because he played the way I would have liked to write, and this wasn't possible for me or anyone else. He made poetry seem word-bound.
1966 *The Perfect Stranger*, ch.5.

67 Try not to despise yourself too much—it's only a conceit.
1968 *A Song and Dance*, ch.6.

68 But years ago he had decided never to be afraid of the deafeningly obvious, it is always news to somebody.
1968 *A Song and Dance*, ch.6.

69 Mary lived by wondering what lay round the corner. I lived by knowing there was no corner.
1973 *A Happy Man*, ch.12.

Kazantzakis, Nikos 1883–1957

Greek writer, best known for his novel *Zorba the Greek* (1946, filmed 1964) and the long autobiographical narrative poem, *The Odyssey, a Modern Sequel* (1938).

70 My entire soul is a cry, and all my work is a commentary on that cry.
1965 *Report to Greco.*

Kazin, Alfred 1915–98

US writer, best known for influential books of literary criticism such as *On Native Grounds* (1942) and the autobiographical *A Walker in the City* (1951).

71 In a very real sense, the writer writes in order to teach himself, to understand himself, to satisfy himself; the publishing of his ideas, though it brings gratifications, is a curious anti-climax.
1963 In *Think*, Feb.

72 Only power can get people into a position where they may be noble.
Quoted in M Korda *Power in the Office* (1976).

Keane, Roy 1971–

Irish footballer.

73 They have a few drinks, and maybe the prawn sandwiches, and they don't realise what's going on out on the pitch.
2000 On spectators in the corporate boxes at Manchester United games. In the *Sunday Times*, 31 Dec.

74 I don't give people hell. I tell them the truth and they think it's hell.
2002 On RTE, 28 May.

Keating, Paul John 1944–

Australian Republican politician. He became President of the New South Wales Labor Party (1979–83) and in 1991 was elected Leader of the Australian Labor Party. He was Prime Minister from 1991 to 1996.

75 A banana republic.
1986 On Australia's balance-of-payments crisis and cycle of recession. Radio broadcast, Radio 2GB, Sydney, 14 May.

Keats, John 1795–1821

English Romantic poet. His long mythological poem *Endymion* (1818) was fiercely criticized but *Lamia, Isabella, The Eve of St. Agnes and Other Poems* (1820), containing the romances 'The Eve of St Agnes' and 'Lamia', the epic 'Hyperion' and his major odes, was better received. He died of tuberculosis in Rome.

76 Much have I travell'd in the realms of gold.
1815 'On First Looking into Chapman's Homer', l.1. (Published in *The Examiner* 1816.)

77 Then felt I like some watcher of the skies
When a new planet swims into his ken;
Or like stout Cortez when with eagle eyes
He star'd at the Pacific—and all his men
Look'd at each other with a wild surmise—
Silent, upon a peak in Darien.
1815 'On First Looking into Chapman's Homer', l.9–14. (Published in *The Examiner* 1816.)

78 Sweetly they slept
On the blue fields of heaven, and then there crept
A little noiseless noise among the leaves,
Born of the very sign that silence heaves.
1816 'I Stood Tip-Toe upon a Little Hill', l.9–12.

79 Here are sweet peas, on tiptoe for a flight,
With wings of gentle flush o'er delicate white.
1816 'I Stood Tip-Toe upon a Little Hill', l.57–8.

80 Morality
Weighs heavily on me like unwilling sleep.
1817 'On Seeing the Elgin Marbles'.

81 Yet the sweet converse of an innocent mind,
Whose words are images of thoughts refined,
Is my soul's pleasure; and it sure must be
Almost the highest bliss of human-kind,
When to thy haunts two kindred spirits flee.
1817 'O Solitude! If I Must with Thee Dwell'.

82 Stop and consider! life is but a day;
A fragile dew-drop on its perilous way
From a tree's summit; a poor Indian's sleep
While his boat hastens to the monstrous steep
Of Montmorenci.
1817 'Sleep and Poetry', l.85–9.

83 O for ten years, that I may overwhelm
Myself in poesy, so I may do the deed
That my own soul has to itself decreed.
1817 'Sleep and Poetry', l.96–8.

84 They swayed about upon a rocking horse,
And thought it Pegasus.
1817 'Sleep and Poetry', l.186–7.

85 And they shall be accounted poet kings
Who simply tell the most heart-easing things.
1817 'Sleep and Poetry', l.267–8.

86 It keeps eternal whisperings around
Desolate shores—and with its mighty swell
Gluts twice ten thousand Caverns.
1817 'On the Sea'.

87 I had a dove and the sweet dove died;
And I have thought it died of grieving:
O, what could it grieve for? Its feet were tied,
With a silken thread of my own hands' weaving.
1817 'I had a Dove and the Sweet Dove Died'.

88 A long poem is a test of invention which I take to be the Polar star of poetry, as fancy is the sails, and imagination the rudder.
1817 Letter to Benjamin Bailey, 8 Oct.

89 I am certain of nothing but the holiness of the heart's affections and the truth of the imagination—what the imagination seizes as beauty must be truth—whether it existed before or not.
1817 Letter to Benjamin Bailey, 22 Nov.

90 O for a life of sensations rather than of thoughts!
1817 Letter to Benjamin Bailey, 22 Nov.

91 Negative Capability; that is, when a man is capable of being in uncertainties, mysteries, doubts, without any irritable reaching after fact and reason.
1817 Letter to G and T Keats, 21 Dec.

92 Souls of Poets dead and gone
What Elysium have ye known,
Happy field or mossy cavern,
Choicer than the Mermaid Tavern?
1818 'Lines on the Mermaid Tavern'.

93 When I have fears that I may cease to be
Before my pen has gleaned my teeming brain,
Before high-piled books, in charactery,
Hold like rich garners the full ripened grain.
1818 'When I Have Fears That I May Cease to Be'.

94 When I behold, upon the night's starred face
Huge cloudy symbols of a high romance,
And think that I may never live to trace
Their shadows, with the magic hand of chance;
And when I feel, fair creature of an hour,
That I shall never look upon thee more,
Never have relish in the faery power
Of unreflecting love;—then on the shore
Of the wide world I stand alone, and think
Till love and fame to nothingness so sink.
1818 'When I Have Fears That I May Cease to Be'.

95 If poetry comes not as naturally as leaves to a tree it had better not come at all.
1818 Letter to John Taylor, 27 Feb.

96 Scenery is fine—but human nature is finer.
1818 Letter to Benjamin Bailey, 13 Mar.

97 It is impossible to live in a country which is continually under hatches… Rain! Rain! Rain!
1818 Letter to J H Reynolds, 10 Apr.

98 I think I shall be among the English Poets after my death.
1818 Letter to George and Georgiana Keats, 14 Oct.

99 The imagination of a boy is healthy, and the mature imagination of a man is healthy; but there is a space of life between, in which the soul is in a ferment, the character undecided, the way of life uncertain, the ambition thick-sighted: thence proceeds mawkishness.
1818 *Endymion*, preface.

1 A thing of beauty is a joy for ever:
Its loveliness increases; it will never
Pass into nothingness; but still will keep
A bower quiet for us, and a sleep
Full of sweet dreams, and health, and quiet breathing.
1818 *Endymion*, bk.1, l.1–5.

2 The grandeur of the dooms
We have imagined for the mighty dead.
1818 *Endymion*, bk.1, l.20–1.

3 They always must be with us, or we die.
1818 *Endymion*, bk.1, l.33.

4 Who, of men, can tell
That flowers would bloom, or that green fruit would swell
To melting pulp, that fish would have bright mail,
The earth its dower of river, wood, and vale,
The meadows runnels, runnels pebble-stones,
The seed its harvest, or the lute its tones,
Tones ravishment, or ravishment its sweet,
If human souls did never kiss and greet?
1818 *Endymion*, bk.1, l.835–42.

5 Here is wine,
Alive with sparkles—never, I aver,
Since Ariadne was a vintager,
So cool a purple.
1818 *Endymion*, bk.2, l.441–4.

6 To Sorrow,
I bade good-morrow,
And thought to leave her far away behind;
But cheerly, cheerly,
She loves me dearly;

She is so constant to me, and so kind.
1818 *Endymion*, bk.4, l.173–8.

7 Their smiles,
Wan as primroses gathered at midnight
By chilly fingered spring.
1818 *Endymion*, bk.4, l.969–71.

8 Turn the key deftly in the oiled wards,
And seal the hushed Casket of my Soul.
1819 'To Sleep'.

9 Call the world if you please 'The vale of soul-making'.
1819 Letter to George and Georgiana Keats, 14 Feb.

10 I have met with women whom I really think would like to be married to a poem, and to be given away by a novel.
1819 Letter to Fanny Brawne, 8 Jul.

11 I have two luxuries to brood over in my walks, your loveliness and the hour of my death. O that I could have possession of them both in the same minute.
1819 Letter to Fanny Brawne, 25 Jul.

12 My friends should drink a dozen of Claret on my Tomb.
1819 Letter to Benjamin Bailey, 14 Aug.

13 Give me books, fruit, french wine and fine weather and a little music out of doors, played by somebody I do not know.
1819 Letter to Fanny Keats, 29 Aug.

14 Fanatics have their dreams, wherewith they weave
A paradise for a sect.
1819 'The Fall of Hyperion', l.1–2.
(Published 1856.)

15 'None can usurp this height,' returned that shade,
'But those to whom the miseries of the world
Are misery, and will not let them rest.'
1819 'The Fall of Hyperion', l.147–9.
(Published 1856.)

16 The poet and the dreamer are distinct,
Diverse, sheer opposite, antipodes.
The one pours out a balm upon the world,
The other vexes it.
1819 'The Fall of Hyperion', l.199–202.
(Published 1856.)

17 Oh what can ail thee, knight at arms,
Alone and palely loitering;
The sedge has wither'd from the lake,
And no birds sing.
1820 'La Belle Dame Sans Merci', stanza 1.

18 She found me roots of relish sweet,
And honey wild, and manna dew;
And sure in language strange she said,
'I love thee true.'
1820 'La Belle Dame Sans Merci', stanza 7.

19 I saw pale kings, and princes too,
Pale warriors, death-pale were they all;
Who cry'd—'La belle Dame sans Merci
Hath thee in thrall!'
1820 'La Belle Dame Sans Merci', stanza 10.

20 She was a gordian shape of dazzling hue,
Vermilion-spotted, golden, green, and blue;
Striped like a zebra, freckled like a pard,
Eyed like a peacock, and all crimson barr'd.
1820 *Lamia, Isabella, The Eve of St. Agnes and Other Poems*, 'Lamia', pt.1, l.47–50.

21 Real are the dreams of Gods, and smoothly pass
Their pleasures in a long immortal dream.
1820 *Lamia, Isabella, The Eve of St. Agnes and Other Poems*, 'Lamia', pt.1, l.127–8.

22 Love in a hut, with water and a crust,
Is—Love, forgive us!—cinders, ashes, dust;
Love in a palace is perhaps at last
More grievous torment than a hermit's fast.
1820 *Lamia, Isabella, The Eve of St. Agnes and Other Poems*, 'Lamia', pt.2, l.1–4.

23 That purple-lined palace of sweet sin.
1820 *Lamia, Isabella, The Eve of St. Agnes and Other Poems*, 'Lamia', pt.2, l.31.

24 In pale contented sort of discontent.
1820 *Lamia, Isabella, The Eve of St. Agnes and Other Poems*, 'Lamia', pt.2, l.135.

25 Do not all charms fly
At the mere touch of cold philosophy?
There was an awful rainbow once in heaven:
We know her woof, her texture; she is given
In the dull catalogue of common things.
Philosophy will clip an Angel's wings.
1820 *Lamia, Isabella, The Eve of St. Agnes and Other Poems*, 'Lamia', pt.2, l.229–34.

26 Why were they proud? again we ask aloud,
Why in the name of Glory were they proud?
1820 *Lamia, Isabella, The Eve of St. Agnes and Other Poems*, 'Isabella; or, The Pot of Basil', stanza 16.

27 So the two brothers and their murdered man
Rode past fair Florence.
1820 *Lamia, Isabella, The Eve of St. Agnes and Other Poems*, 'Isabella; or, The Pot of Basil', stanza 27.

28 And she forgot the stars, the moon, and sun,
And she forgot the blue above the trees,
And she forgot the dells where waters run,
And she forgot the chilly autumn breeze;
She had no knowledge when the day was done,
And the new morn she saw not: but in peace
Hung over her sweet Basil evermore,
And moistened it with tears unto the core.
1820 *Lamia, Isabella, The Eve of St. Agnes and Other Poems*, 'Isabella; or, The Pot of Basil', stanza 53.

29 'To steal my Basil-pot away from me.'
1820 *Lamia, Isabella, The Eve of St. Agnes and Other Poems*, 'Isabella; or, The Pot of Basil', stanza 62.

30 St. Agnes' Eve—Ah, bitter chill it was!
The owl, for all his feathers, was a-cold;
The hare limped trembling through the frozen grass,
And silent was the flock in woolly fold.
1820 *Lamia, Isabella, The Eve of St. Agnes and Other Poems*, 'The Eve of St. Agnes', stanza 1.

31 The silver, snarling trumpets 'gan to chide.
1820 *Lamia, Isabella, The Eve of St. Agnes and Other Poems*, 'The Eve of St. Agnes', stanza 4.

32 And soft adorings from their loves receive
Upon the honeyed middle of the night.
1820 *Lamia, Isabella, The Eve of St. Agnes and Other Poems*, 'The Eve of St. Agnes', stanza 6.

33 The music, yearning like a God in pain.
1820 *Lamia, Isabella, The Eve of St. Agnes and Other Poems*, 'The Eve of St. Agnes', stanza 7.

34 Sudden a thought came like a full-blown rose,

Flushing his brow, and in his painted heart
Made purple riot.
1820 *Lamia, Isabella, The Eve of St. Agnes and Other Poems*, 'The Eve of St. Agnes', stanza 16.

35 A poor, weak, palsy-stricken, churchyard thing.
1820 *Lamia, Isabella, The Eve of St. Agnes and Other Poems*, 'The Eve of St. Agnes', stanza 18.

36 A casement high and triple-arched there was,
All garlanded with carven imag'ries
Of fruits, and flowers, and bunches of knot-grass,
And diamonded with panes of quaint device,
Innumerable of stains and splendid dyes,
As are the tiger-moth's deep-damasked wings.
1820 *Lamia, Isabella, The Eve of St. Agnes and Other Poems*, 'The Eve of St. Agnes', stanza 24.

37 Full on this casement shone the wintry moon,
And threw warm gules on Madeleine's fair breast,
As down she knelt for heaven's grace and boon;
Rose-bloom fell on her hands, together prest,
And on her silver cross soft amethyst,
And on her hair a glory like a saint.
She seemed a splendid angel, newly drest,
Save wings, for heaven.
1820 *Lamia, Isabella, The Eve of St. Agnes and Other Poems*, 'The Eve of St. Agnes', stanza 25.

38 By degrees
Her rich attire creeps rustling to her knees.
1820 *Lamia, Isabella, The Eve of St. Agnes and Other Poems*, 'The Eve of St. Agnes', stanza 26.

39 As though a rose should shut, and be a bud again.
1820 *Lamia, Isabella, The Eve of St. Agnes and Other Poems*, 'The Eve of St. Agnes', stanza 27.

40 And still she slept an azure-lidded sleep,
In blanched linen, smooth, and lavendered,
While he from forth the closet brought a heap
Of candied apple, quince, and plum, and gourd;
With jellies soother than the creamy curd,
And lucent syrops, tinct with cinnamon;
Manna and dates, in argosy transferred
From Fez; and spiced dainties, every one,
From silken Samarcand to cedared Lebanon.
1820 *Lamia, Isabella, The Eve of St. Agnes and Other Poems*, 'The Eve of St. Agnes', stanza 30.

41 He played an ancient ditty, long since mute,
In Provence called, 'La belle dame sans mercy'.
1820 *Lamia, Isabella, The Eve of St. Agnes and Other Poems*, 'The Eve of St. Agnes', stanza 33.

42 And the long carpets rose along the gusty floor.
1820 *Lamia, Isabella, The Eve of St. Agnes and Other Poems*, 'The Eve of St. Agnes', stanza 40.

43 And they are gone: aye, ages long ago
These lovers fled away into the storm.
1820 *Lamia, Isabella, The Eve of St. Agnes and Other Poems*, 'The Eve of St. Agnes', stanza 42.

44 Deep in the shady sadness of a vale
Far sunken from the healthy breath of morn,
Far from the fiery noon and eve's one star,
Sat gray-haired Saturn, quiet as a stone,
Still as the silence round about his lair.
1820 *Lamia, Isabella, The Eve of St. Agnes and Other Poems*, 'Hyperion', bk.1, l.1–5.

45 Where the dead leaf fell, there did it rest.
1820 *Lamia, Isabella, The Eve of St. Agnes and Other Poems*, 'Hyperion', bk.1, l.10.

46 But oh! How unlike marble was that face.
1820 *Lamia, Isabella, The Eve of St. Agnes and Other Poems*, 'Hyperion', bk.1, l.34.

47 That large utterance of the early Gods.
1820 *Lamia, Isabella, The Eve of St. Agnes and Other Poems*, 'Hyperion', bk.1, l.51.

48 Season of mists and mellow fruitfulness,
Close bosom-friend of the maturing sun;
Conspiring with him how to load and bless
With fruit the vines that round the thatch-eaves run.
1820 *Lamia, Isabella, The Eve of St. Agnes and Other Poems*, 'To Autumn', stanza 1.

49 Where are the songs of Spring? Ay, where are they?
Think not of them, thou hast thy music too.
1820 *Lamia, Isabella, The Eve of St. Agnes and Other Poems*, 'To Autumn', stanza 3.

50 Thou still unravished bride of quietness,
Thou foster-child of silence and slow time.
1820 *Lamia, Isabella, The Eve of St. Agnes and Other Poems*, 'Ode on a Grecian Urn', stanza 1.

51 What men or Gods are these? What maidens loth?
What mad pursuit? What struggle to escape?
What pipes and timbrels? What wild ecstasy?
1820 *Lamia, Isabella, The Eve of St. Agnes and Other Poems*, 'Ode on a Grecian Urn', stanza 1.

52 Heard melodies are sweet, but those unheard
Are sweeter; therefore, ye soft pipes, play on;
Not to the sensual ear, but, more endeared,
Pipe to the spirit ditties of no tone.
1820 *Lamia, Isabella, The Eve of St. Agnes and Other Poems*, 'Ode on a Grecian Urn', stanza 2.

53 She cannot fade, though thou hast not thy bliss,
For ever wilt thou love, and she be fair!
1820 *Lamia, Isabella, The Eve of St. Agnes and Other Poems*, 'Ode on a Grecian Urn', stanza 2.

54 O Attic shape! Fair attitude!
1820 *Lamia, Isabella, The Eve of St. Agnes and Other Poems*, 'Ode on a Grecian Urn', stanza 5.

55 Thou, silent form, dost tease us out of thought
As doth eternity: Cold Pastoral!
1820 *Lamia, Isabella, The Eve of St. Agnes and Other Poems*, 'Ode on a Grecian Urn', stanza 5.

56 'Beauty is truth, truth beauty,'—that is all
Ye know on earth, and all ye need to know.
1820 *Lamia, Isabella, The Eve of St. Agnes and Other Poems*, 'Ode on a Grecian Urn', stanza 5.

57 My heart aches, and a drowsy numbness pains
My sense, as though of hemlock I had drunk,
Or emptied some dull opiate to the drains
One minute past, and Lethe-wards had sunk:
'Tis not through envy of thy happy lot,
But being too happy in thine happiness
That thou, light-winged Dryad of the trees,
In some melodious plot
Of beechen green, and shadows numberless,
Singest of summer in full-throated ease.
1820 *Lamia, Isabella, The Eve of St. Agnes and Other Poems*, 'Ode to a Nightingale', stanza 1.

58 O, for a draught of vintage! that hath been
Cooled a long age in the deep-delved earth,

Tasting of Flora and the country green,
Dance, and Provençal song, and sunburnt mirth!
O for a beaker full of the warm South,
Full of the true, the blushful Hippocrene,
With beaded bubbles winking at the brim,
And purple-stained mouth;
That I might drink, and leave the world unseen,
And with thee fade away into the forest dim.

1820 *Lamia, Isabella, The Eve of St. Agnes and Other Poems*, 'Ode to a Nightingale', stanza 2.

59 Fade far away, dissolve, and quite forget
What thou among the leaves hast never known,
The weariness, the fever, and the fret
Here, where men sit and hear each other groan;
Where palsy shakes a few, sad, last grey hairs,
Where youth grows pale, and spectre-thin, and dies;
Where but to think is to be full of sorrow
And leaden-eyed despairs.

1820 *Lamia, Isabella, The Eve of St. Agnes and Other Poems*, 'Ode to a Nightingale', stanza 3.

60 Already with thee! tender is the night.

1820 *Lamia, Isabella, The Eve of St. Agnes and Other Poems*, 'Ode to a Nightingale', stanza 4.

61 Fast fading violets covered up in leaves;
And mid-May's eldest child,
The coming musk-rose, full of dewy wine,
The murmurous haunt of flies on summer eves.

1820 *Lamia, Isabella, The Eve of St. Agnes and Other Poems*, 'Ode to a Nightingale', stanza 5.

62 Darkling I listen; and, for many a time
I have been half in love with easeful Death,
Called him soft names in many a musèd rhyme,
To take into the air my quiet breath;
Now more than ever seems it rich to die,
To cease upon the midnight with no pain,
While thou art pouring forth thy soul abroad
In such an ecstasy!

1820 *Lamia, Isabella, The Eve of St. Agnes and Other Poems*, 'Ode to a Nightingale', stanza 6.

63 Thou wast not born for death, immortal Bird!

1820 *Lamia, Isabella, The Eve of St. Agnes and Other Poems*, 'Ode to a Nightingale', stanza 7.

64 Forlorn! the very word is like a bell
To toll me back from thee to my sole self!
Adieu! the fancy cannot cheat so well
As she is famed to do, deceiving elf.

1820 *Lamia, Isabella, The Eve of St. Agnes and Other Poems*, 'Ode to a Nightingale', stanza 8.

65 I know the colour of that blood; it is arterial blood;
I cannot be deceived in that colour; that drop of blood
is my death-warrant—I must die.

1821 On examining a drop of blood that fell from his mouth as he lay dying from tuberculosis. Quoted in John Sutherland *The Oxford Book of Literary Anecdotes* (1975).

66 Here lies one whose name was writ in water.

Epitaph for himself. Quoted in Richard Monckton Milnes *Life, Letters and Literary Remains of John Keats* (1848), vol.2.

Keble, John 1792–1866

English churchman, the father of the Tractarian movement. He was also influential in the Oxford Movement after J H Newman's secession to Rome.

67 New every morning is the love
Our wakening and uprising prove.

1827 *The Christian Year*, 'Morning'.

Keenan, Brian 1950–

Northern Irish teacher and writer. He was kidnapped on 11 April 1986 while working at the American University of Beirut by Iranian terrorists and held hostage for four years.

68 I'm going to visit every country in the world, eat all the food of the world, drink all the drink of the world—and, I hope, make love to every woman in the world. Then I might get a good night's sleep.

1990 Said on his release, BBC TV, 25 Aug.

Keillor, (Gary Edward) Garrison 1942–

US humorous writer and broadcaster. In 1974 he began his live radio show, *A Prairie Home Companion*, telling tales of small-town Minnesota set in fictional Lake Wobegon. His works include *Lake Wobegon Days* (1985) and *Love Me* (2004).

69 Where all the women are strong, all the men are good-looking, and all the children are above average.

from 1974 His description of the fictional mid-Western town Lake Wobegon, used regularly in *A Prairie Home Companion*.

70 Peanut butter has survived everything that has been done to improve it.

1990 In NPR broadcast, 29 Dec.

71 Public radio is a ghetto of good taste.

1991 In National Public Radio broadcast, 9 Feb.

72 March is the month that God designed to show those who don't drink what a hangover is like.

1991 In NPR broadcast, 1 Dec.

73 It's a play that after you've been there for a short while, you wonder how long this is going to take.

1995 Of Edward Albee's *Three Tall Women*. In *New York*, 2 Jan.

74 I look like a tree toad who was changed into a boy but not completely.

2001 *Lake Wobegon Summer 1956*.

Keller, Helen Adams 1880–1968

US writer. She became deaf and blind at 19 months, but educated by Anne Sullivan she learned to speak, graduated in 1904 and became a distinguished lecturer and writer.

75 Everything has its wonders, even darkness and silence, and I learn, whatever state I may be in, therein to be content.

1902 *The Story of My Life*.

76 As the eagle was killed by the arrow winged with its own feather, so the hand of the world is wounded by its own skill.

1912 In the *American Magazine*, Dec.

Kelman, James 1946–

Scottish novelist, whose novels and short stories set in working-class Glasgow are characterized by an uncompromising vernacular style and vocabulary. In 1994 his novel *How late it was, how late* won the Booker Prize.

77 Theoretical webs, dirty webs, fusty webs, old and shrivelling away into nothingness, a fine dust. Who needs that kind of stuff. Far far better getting out into the open air and doing it, actually doing it, something solid

and concrete and unconceptualisable.
1989 *A Disaffection.*

78 Yes, they say, go and write whatever story you want, but don't use whatever language is necessary... By implication those in authority ask the writer to censor and suppress her or his own work. They demand it. If you don't comply then your work isn't produced.
1992 *Some Recent Attacks*, 'The Importance of Glasgow in My Work'.

79 My culture and my language have the right to exist, and no one has the authority to dismiss that.
1994 Speech at the Booker Prize award ceremony, 11 Oct.

80 Ye wake in a corner and stay there hoping yer body will disappear, the thoughts smothering ye; these thoughts; but ye want to remember and face up to things, just something keeps ye from doing it, why can ye no do it; the words filling yer head: then the other words; there's something far far wrong; ye're no a good man, ye're just no a good man.
1994 *How late it was, how late*, opening words.

Kelvin, William Thomson, 1st Baron 1824–1907

Irish-born Scottish physician and mathematician, who developed the temperature scale named after him.

81 At what time does the dissipation of energy begin?
When his wife proposed an afternoon walk. Quoted in A Fleming *Memories of a Scientific Life* (1934).

Kemble, Charles 1775–1854

English actor-manager. A celebrated comic actor, he became manager of Covent Garden in 1822 but subsequently ran into financial difficulties, mitigated in the early 1830s when he presented his daughter Fanny Kemble's stage debut.

82 Sir, I now pay you this exorbitant charge, but I must ask you to explain to Her Majesty that she must not in future look upon me as a source of income.
When reluctantly obliged to pay overdue income tax. Attributed.

Kemble, John Philip 1757–1823

English actor-manager, brother of Sarah Siddons and Charles Kemble. A successful tragic actor, he was manager of the Theatre Royal, Drury Lane and subsequently of Covent Garden, where riots greeted his decision to raise ticket prices.

83 Ladies and gentlemen, unless the play is stopped, the child cannot possibly go on.
Addressing the audience during a performance that was being much disrupted by a child crying. Attributed.

Kempis, St Thomas à c.1380–1471

German monk and author. In 1400 he entered the Augustinian convent of Agnetenberg, near Zwolle, where he was Sub-Prior at the time of his death.

84 *Vere magnus est, qui magnam habet caritatem.*
He is truly great who has great charity.
c.1413 *De Imitatione Christi*, bk.1, ch.4, section 6.

85 *Quam cito transit gloria mundi.*
How quickly the glory of the world passes.
c.1413 *De Imitatione Christi*, bk.1, ch.4, section 6.

86 *Homo proponit, sed Deus disponit.*
Man proposes, but God disposes.
c.1413 *De Imitatione Christi*, bk.1, ch.19, section 2.

87 *Nemo secure præcipit, nisi qui bene obedire didicit.*
Nobody rules safely, but he who has learned well how to obey.
c.1413 *De Imitatione Christi*, bk.1, ch.20, section 2.

88 *Transeunt omnia, et tu cum eis pariter.*
All things perish, and you along with them.
c.1413 *De Imitatione Christi*, bk.2, ch.1, section 4.

89 *Gloria boni hominis, testimonium bonæ conscientiæ.*
The testimony of a good conscience is the good man's glory.
c.1413 *De Imitatione Christi*, bk.2, ch.6, section 1.

90 *In cruce salus, in cruce vita.*
In the cross is salvation, in the cross is life.
c.1413 *De Imitatione Christi*, bk.2, ch.12, section 2.

91 *Si libenter crucem portas, portabit te.*
If you bear your cross willingly, it will bear you.
c.1413 *De Imitatione Christi*, bk.2, ch.12, section 5.

92 *De duobus malis minus est semper eligendum.*
Of two evils the lesser should always be chosen.
c.1413 *De Imitatione Christi*, bk.3, ch.12, section 2.

Ken, Thomas 1637–1711

English churchman and royal chaplain. He became Bishop of Bath and Wells (1685), and was deposed in 1691 when he refused to take the oath of allegiance to William III.

93 Awake my soul, and with the sun
Thy daily stage of duty run.
1709 *Manual of Prayers for the use of the Scholars of Winchester College.*

94 Praise God, from whom all blessings flow,
Praise Him, all creatures here below,
Praise Him above, ye heavenly host,
Praise Father, Son, and Holy Ghost.
1709 *Manual of Prayers for the use of the Scholars of Winchester College.*

Kendall, Henry Clarence 1839–82

Australian poet who worked variously as a civil servant, freelance writer, timber merchant and inspector of forests. His great love of the Australian countryside is evident in his collections *Poems and Songs* (1862), *Leaves from Australian Forests* (1869), and *Songs from the Mountains* (1880).

95 Through breaks of the cedar and sycamore bowers
Struggles the light that is love to the flowers;
And, softer than slumber and sweeter than singing,
The notes of the bell-birds are running and ringing.
The silver-voiced bell-birds, the darlings of daytime!
They sing in September their songs of the May-time.
1869 *Leaves from Australian Forests*, 'Bell-Birds'.

Kennan, George Frost 1904–

US diplomat and historian, adviser to Secretary of State Dean Acheson (1949–52) and US Ambassador in Moscow (1952–53) and Yugoslavia (1961–63). Initially in favour of 'containment' of the USSR, he later called for US disengagement from Europe.

96 The best that an American can look forward to is the lonely pleasure of one who stands at long last on a chilly and inhospitable mountain top where few have been, where few can follow, and where few will consent to believe that he has been.

On negotiating with the Soviets. Quoted in Walter Isaacson and Evan Thomas *The Wise Men* (1986).

97 A guest of one's time and not a member of the household.
Of the feeling of being viewed as a pragmatist. Quoted in Walter Isaacson and Evan Thomas *The Wise Men* (1986).

98 Fig leaves of democratic procedure to hide the nakedness of Stalinist dictatorship.
Of postwar agreements to govern Eastern Europe. Quoted in Walter Isaacson and Evan Thomas *The Wise Men* (1986).

Kennedy, A(lison) L(ouise) 1965–

Scottish novelist. Her short stories and novels have established her as a leading writer of her generation.

99 Night Geometry and the Garscadden Trains.
1990 Title of short story collection.

1 Words just say what you want them to; they don't know any better.
1990 'The Role of Notable Silences in Scottish History'.

2 4. The chosen and male shall go forth unto professions while the chosen and female shall be homely, fecund, docile and slightly artistic.
1993 *Looking for the Possible Dance*, 'The Scottish Method for the Perfection of Children'.

3 7. Joy is fleeting, sinful and the forerunner of despair.
1993 *Looking for the Possible Dance*, 'The Scottish Method for the Perfection of Children'.

4 We all have it in us to be an opium for every conceivable mass.
1995 *So I Am Glad*, ch.1.

5 I am not calm, I am unspontaneous. When something happens to me, I don't know how to feel.
1995 *So I Am Glad*, ch.1.

Kennedy, Edward M(oore) 1932–

US Democratic politician, son of Joseph and brother of John and Robert. His political career was dogged by his involvement in a car accident at Chappaquiddick in 1969, in which a female companion was drowned, and he withdrew as presidential candidate in 1980.

6 I don't mind not being President. I just mind that someone else is.
1986 Speech, Washington, 22 Mar.

7 Sunlight is the best disinfectant.
1990 On sponsoring legislation for the disclosure of graduation rates and crime figures on campuses. In the *New York Times*, 8 Oct.

8 We are the most hated nation in the world as a result of this disastrous policy in the prisons.
2004 Following news coverage of the abuse of Iraqi prisoners by US soldiers, 13 May.

Kennedy, John F(itzgerald) 1917–63

US Democratic politician, 35th President. His *Profiles in Courage* (1956) won the Pulitzer Prize. The first Catholic, and the youngest person, to be elected President (1961–3), he initiated education and civil rights reform and induced the USSR to withdraw its missiles from Cuba (1962). He was assassinated, allegedly by Lee Harvey Oswald, while being driven in an open car through Dallas, Texas.

9 We stand today on the edge of a new frontier. But the new frontier of which I speak is not a set of promises. It is a set of challenges. It sums up not what I intend to offer the American people, but what I intend to ask of them. It appeals to their pride, not their pocketbook—it holds out the promise of more sacrifice instead of more security.
1960 On accepting the Democratic Convention's presidential nomination, 15 Jul.

10 Let us never negotiate out of fear, but let us never fear to negotiate. Together let us explore the stars.
1961 Inaugural address, Washington, 20 Jan.

11 All this will not be finished in the first 100 days, nor will it be finished in the first 1,000 days, nor in the life of this Administration—nor even, perhaps, in our lifetime on this planet. But let us begin.
1961 Inaugural address, Washington, 20 Jan.

12 Let the word go forth from this time and place, to friend and foe alike, that the torch has been passed to a new generation of Americans, born in this century, tempered by war, disciplined by a hard and bitter peace, proud of our ancient heritage, and unwilling to witness or permit the slow undoing of those human rights to which this nation has always been committed, and to which we are committed today at home and around the world. Let every nation know, whether it wishes us well or ill, that we shall pay any price, bear any burden, meet any hardship, support any friend, oppose any foe, to assure the survival and success of liberty.
1961 Inaugural address, Washington, 20 Jan.

13 And so, my fellow Americans, ask not what your country can do for you. Ask what you can do for your country.
1961 Inaugural address, Washington, 20 Jan.

14 I believe that this nation should commit itself to achieving the goal, before this decade is out, of landing a man on the moon and returning him safely to earth.
1961 State of the Union message to Congress, May.

15 Now we have a problem in making our power credible, and Vietnam is the place.
1961 Attributed remark to journalist James Reston, following Kennedy's meeting with Khrushchev, Jun.

16 A form of atomic blackmail.
1961 On the Soviet decision to resume nuclear testing, 31 Aug.

17 The cold reaches of the universe must not become the new area of an even colder war.
1961 Address to the United Nations, 25 Sep.

18 Mankind must put an end to war or war will put an end to mankind.
1961 Address to the United Nations, 25 Sep.

19 Those who make peaceful revolution impossible will make violent revolution inevitable.
1962 Speech to Latin American diplomats, 12 Mar.

20 This is the most extraordinary collection of talent, of human knowledge, that has ever been gathered in the White House—with the possible exception of when Thomas Jefferson dined alone.
1962 Address at a dinner for 49 Nobel laureates, 29 Apr.

21 The cost of freedom is always high, but Americans have always paid it. And one path we shall never choose, and that is the path of surrender, or submission.
1962 Address to the nation, 22 Oct.

22 If you take the wrong course...the President bears the

burden of the responsibility quite rightly. The advisers may move on—to new advice.
1962 Comment to White House Special Counsel Theodore C Sorensen, Dec, after the ill-fated Bay of Pigs invasion of Cuba.

23 His stately ship of life, having weathered the severest storms of a troubled century, is anchored in tranquil waters, proof that courage and faith and zest for freedom are truly indestructible. The record of his triumphant passage will inspire free hearts all over the globe.
1963 On conferring honorary US citizenship on Winston Churchill, 9 Apr.

24 [Winston Churchill] mobilized the English language and sent it into battle.
1963 On conferring honorary US citizenship on Winston Churchill, 9 Apr.

25 Equality of opportunity does not mean equality of responsibility.
1963 Address at Vanderbilt University, 19 May.

26 Man is still the most extraordinary computer of all.
1963 Speech, 21 May.

27 History teaches us that enmities between nations…do not last forever. We must conduct our affairs in such a way that it becomes in the communists' interests to agree on a genuine peace…to let each nation choose its own future, so long as that choice does not interfere with the choices of others. If we cannot now end our differences, at least we can help make the world safe for diversity.
1963 Speech, American University, Washington DC, 10 Jun.

28 The rights of every man are diminished when the rights of one man are threatened.
1963 On sending national guardsmen to ensure peaceful integration at the University of Alabama. Address to the nation, 11 Jun

29 He [John Hoban] believed by incorporating several features of the Dublin style he would make it more home-like for any President of Irish descent. It was a long wait, but I appreciate his efforts.
1963 On the Irish-American architect's design of the White House. Speech to the Irish Parliament reported in the *New York Times*, 19 Jun.

30 Let it not be said of this Atlantic generation that we left ideals and visions to the past, nor purpose and determination to our adversaries. We have come too far, we have sacrificed too much to disdain the future now.
1963 Speech to the West German Parliament, Frankfurt, 25 Jun.

31 There are many people in the world who really don't understand, or say they don't, what is the great issue between the free world and the Communist world. Let them come to Berlin!
1963 Address in Berlin's Rudolf Wilde Platz, 26 Jun, 22 months after the erection of the wall dividing the city.

32 We have never had to put a wall up to keep our people in, to prevent them from leaving us.
1963 Address in Berlin's Rudolf Wilde Platz, 26 Jun, 22 months after the erection of the wall dividing the city.

33 All free men, wherever they may live, are citizens of Berlin, and therefore, as a free man, I take pride in the words, 'Ich bin ein Berliner.' I am a Berliner!
1963 Speech at West Berlin City Hall, Rudolf Wilde Platz, 26 Jun. Unfortunately for Kennedy, his phrase translated into colloquial German as 'I am a doughnut.'

34 For the first time, we have been able to reach an agreement which can limit the dangers of this age.
1963 On the ratification of a treaty to limit nuclear testing, 7 Oct.

35 The highest duty of the writer, the composer, the artist is to remain true to himself… In serving his vision of the truth, the artist best serves his nation.
1963 At the dedication of Amherst College Robert Frost Library, 25 Oct.

36 When power leads man towards arrogance, poetry reminds him of his limitations. When power narrows the area of man's concern, poetry reminds him of the richness and diversity of existence. When power corrupts, poetry cleanses.
1963 At the dedication of Amherst College Robert Frost Library, 25 Oct.

37 I look forward to…a future in which our country will match its military strength with our moral restraint; its wealth with our wisdom; its power with our purpose.
1963 Last major public speech, Amherst College, 26 Oct.

38 The definition of happiness of the Greeks…is full use of your powers along lines of excellence. I find, therefore, the Presidency provides some happiness.
1963 News conference, 31 Oct.

39 We're heading into nut country today.
1963 Spoken to his wife in Fort Worth a few hours before the assassination in Dallas. Quoted in William Manchester *The Death of a President* (1967).

40 We in this country, in this generation, are—by destiny, rather than choice—the watchmen on the walls of the world.
1963 Address prepared for Dallas luncheon on the day he was assassinated, 22 Nov.

41 What your government believes is its own business; what it does in the world is the world's business.
Letter to Nikita Khrushchev. Quoted in Theodore C Sorensen *Kennedy* (1965).

42 The three most overrated things in the world are the state of Texas, the FBI, and hunting trophies.
Quoted in William Manchester *The Death of a President* (1967).

43 You don't fire God.
Expressing reluctance to replace FBI Director J Edgar Hoover. Reported after Kennedy's death in Senate committee findings on US intelligence activities, 1976.

44 You never know what's hit you. A gunshot is the perfect way.
Comment on methods of assassination. Quoted in Peter Collier and David Horowitz *The Kennedys* (1984).

Kennedy, Joseph Patrick 1888–1969

US businessman and diplomat, a supporter of Roosevelt and the 'New Deal'. The grandson of an Irish immigrant, he placed his fortune at the political disposal of his nine children, all of whom except the eldest son, killed in a flying accident, achieved international fame.

45 With the money I spent I could have elected my chauffeur.
Of his contributions to John F Kennedy's presidential campaign. Quoted in Nigel Hamilton *JFK: Reckless Youth* (1992).

46 Don't get mad, get even.
Attributed.

Kennedy, Joseph P(atrick) II 1952–

Former US Democratic congressman (1987–99) and founder of

the Citizens Energy Corporation. He is the son of Joseph Patrick Kennedy.

47 I've had a tough time learning how to act like a Congressman. Today I accidentally spent some of my own money.
1987 In *Newsweek*, 9 Feb.

Kennedy, Nigel 1956–

English violinist.

48 I'd never accept a knighthood because the Queen knows nothing about music, man. How can she say I'm good or bad?
2004 In *The Independent*, 17 Jun.

Kennedy, Robert F(rancis) 1925–68

US politician, son of Joseph. Manager of his brother John's presidential campaign, he became Attorney-General (1961–4) and Senator for New York from 1965. In 1968 he was assassinated after winning the California primary election.

49 Courage is the most important attribute of a lawyer.
1962 Speech at the University of San Francisco Law School, 29 Sep.

50 One fifth of the people are against everything all the time.
1964 In the *Observer*, May.

51 My thanks to you all—and now it's on to Chicago, and let's win there.
1968 Last public remark after winning the Californian primary for the Democratic presidential nomination in Los Angeles, before being assassinated as he left the rally, 4 Jun.

52 It isn't the first step that concerns me, but both sides escalating to the fourth or fifth step—and we don't go to the sixth because there is no one around to do so.
On the possibility of initiating nuclear warfare. *Thirteen Days* (published 1969).

53 Many times...I had heard the military take positions which, if wrong, had the advantage that no one would be around at the end to know.
Recalling discussions on Soviet placement of nuclear missiles in Cuba. *Thirteen Days* (published 1969).

54 Well, we Kennedys, we eat Rockefellers for breakfast.
Quoted in Peter Collier and David Horowitz *The Rockefellers* (1976).

Kennedy, Roger George 1926–

Former director, US National Park Service (1993–97). He has also been a correspondent for NBC and Director, National Museum of American History, Smithsonian Institution. He has written books on architecture, houses and historic America.

55 How do you put a price on the Washington Monument?
1995 On presenting his annual budget to Congress and being asked to produce a price list setting a market value on each of the nation's 368 park units. Reported in the *US News and World Report*, 3 Apr.

Kennedy, William (Joseph) 1928–

US novelist and screenwriter. He won a Pulitzer Prize for *Ironweed* (1983).

56 I don't hold no grudges more'n five years.
1983 Francis Phelan. *Ironweed*.

57 That year an ill wind blew over the city and threatened to destroy flowerpots, family fortunes, reputations, true love, and several types of virtue.
2002 *Roscoe*, opening lines.

Kent, Bruce 1929–

British peace campaigner and former cleric, Chairman (1987–90) and Vice-President (1990–) of the Campaign for Nuclear Disarmament.

58 Preparing for suicide is not a very intelligent means of defence.
1989 Speech.

Kent, Corita *known as 'Sister Corita'* 1918–86

US artist, best remembered for her prints and her 'Love' postage stamp (1985).

59 Women's liberation is the liberation of the feminine in the man and the masculine in the woman.
1974 In the *Los Angeles Times*, 11 Jul.

Kent, Rockwell 1882–1971

US artist and writer, best known for his stark woodcuts, often accompanying his travel writing. His major works include the paintings *Toilers of the Sea* and *Winter* and writings such as *Wilderness* (1921).

60 Sledgehammer sentimentality.
Of his wholesome depiction of contemporary America. Quoted in the *Washington Post*, 6 Jun 1993

Kerouac, Jack (John) 1922–69

US novelist. His fast-moving, stream of consciousness novel *On The Road* (1957) became the quintessential text of the Beat Generation.

61 All of life is a foreign country.
1949 Letter, 24 Jun.

62 But then they danced down the street like dingle-dodies, and I shambled after as I've been doing all my life after people who interest me, because the only people for me are the mad ones, the ones who are mad to live, mad to talk, mad to be saved, desirous of everything at the same time, the ones who never yawn or say a commonplace thing, but burn, burn, burn, like fabulous yellow roman candles exploding like spiders across the stars and in the middle you see the blue centerlight pop and everybody goes 'Awww!'
1957 *On The Road*, pt.1, ch.1.

63 I have nothing to offer anybody except my own confusion.
1957 *On The Road*, pt.2, ch.3.

64 The road is life.
1957 *On The Road*, pt.3, ch.5.

65 John Clellon Holmes...and I were sitting around trying to think up the meaning of the Lost Generation and the subsequent Existentialism and I said, 'You know, this is really a beat generation' and he leapt up and said, 'That's it, that's right!'
1959 Interview in *Playboy*, Jun.

66 Desolation Angels.
1965 Title of novel.

Kerr, Jean *née Collins* 1923–2003

US playwright. Her works include successful Broadway plays and humorous autobiographies. She collaborated with her husband Walter Kerr on several projects, including an adaptation of Werfel's *Song of Bernadette* (1946).

67 Even though a number of people have tried, no one has yet found a way to drink for a living.
1964 *Poor Richard*, act 1.

Kerry, John F 1943–

US politician. Senator for Massachusetts, he ran against President George W Bush in the 2004 presidential election.

68 No young American in uniform should ever be held hostage to America's dependence on oil from the Middle East.
2004 Speech in New Hampshire, 27 Jan.

69 Like father, like son, one term and you're done.
2004 Referring to his contender's chances in the presidential election.

Kesey, Ken Elton 1935–2001

US novelist. He achieved a major success with his novel *One Flew Over the Cuckoo's Nest* (1962), set in a mental hospital, and became a hero of the US counter-culture in the 1960s.

70 One Flew Over the Cuckoo's Nest.
1962 Title of novel, derived from a traditional rhyme.

71 But it's the truth even if it didn't happen.
1962 *One Flew Over The Cuckoo's Nest*, pt.1.

72 I'd rather be a lightning rod than a seismograph.
Quoted in Tom Wolfe *The Electric Kool-Aid Acid Test* (1968), ch.1.

73 We are always acting on what just finished happening. It happened at least 1/30th of a second ago. We think we're in the present, but we aren't. The present we know is only a movie of the past.
Quoted in Tom Wolfe *The Electric Kool-Aid Acid Test* (1968), ch.11.

74 You don't lead by pointing and telling people some place to go. You lead by going to that place and making a case.
1970 Interview in *Esquire*, Jun.

Kethe, William d. c.1608

English divine, army chaplain and hymnwriter. His hymns are characteristically written in metre, like psalms.

75 All people that on earth do dwell,
Sing to the Lord with cheerful voice;
Him serve with fear, His praise forth tell,
Come ye before Him, and rejoice.
1560 *Daye's Psalter*, 'All People That on Earth Do Dwell'.

Key, Francis Scott 1779–1843

US lawyer and poet, best known for his devotional verse and prose. His poem 'The Star-Spangled Banner' was officially adopted as the national anthem of the US in 1931.

76 O say, can you see, by the dawn's early light,
What so proudly we hailed at the twilight's last
gleaming—
Whose broad stripes and bright stars, through the
clouds of the fight,
O'er the ramparts we watched were so gallantly
streaming!
And the rocket's red glare, the bombs bursting in air,
Gave proof through the night that our flag was still there;
O! say, does that star-spangled banner yet wave
O'er the land of the free, and the home of the brave?
1814 'The Star-Spangled Banner', originally published as 'The Defence of Fort M'Henry' in the *Baltimore Patriot*, 20 Sep; it commemorates the bombardment of Fort McHenry, Baltimore, by the British, 13–14 Sep.

Keynes (of Tilton), John Maynard, 1st Baron 1883–1946

English economist. His major works, *A Treatise on Money* (1930) and the revolutionary *General Theory of Employment, Interest and Money* (1936), were inspired by the unemployment crisis. His views influenced Roosevelt's 'New Deal' administration and underpin modern macroeconomics.

77 I work for a government I despise for ends I think criminal.
1917 Letter to Duncan Grant, 15 Dec.

78 Like Odysseus, the President looked wiser when he was seated.
1919 Of Woodrow Wilson. *The Economic Consequences of the Peace*.

79 Lenin was right. There is no subtler, no surer means of overturning the existing basis of society than to debauch the currency. The process engages all the hidden forces of economic law on the side of destruction, and does it in a manner which not one man in a million is able to diagnose.
1919 *The Economic Consequences of the Peace*.

80 England still stands outside Europe. Europe's voiceless tremors do not reach her. Europe is apart, and England is not of her flesh and body.
1919 *The Economic Consequences of the Peace*.

81 The *long run* is a misleading guide to current affairs. *In the long run*, we are all dead. Economists set themselves too easy, too useless a task if in tempestuous seasons they can only tell us that when the storm is long past the ocean is flat again.
1923 *A Tract on Monetary Reform*.

82 If Enterprise is afoot, Wealth accumulates whatever may be happening to Thrift; and if Enterprise is asleep, Wealth decays, whatever Thrift may be doing.
1930 *A Treatise on Money*.

83 A 'sound' banker, alas! is not one who foresees danger and avoids it, but one who, when he is ruined, is ruined in a conventional and orthodox way along with his fellows, so that no one can really blame him.
1931 *Essays in Persuasion*.

84 It is *not* a correct deduction from the Principles of Economics that enlightened self-interest always operates in the public interest... Experience does *not* show that individuals when they make up a social unit are always less clear-sighted than when they act separately.
1931 *Essays in Persuasion*.

85 I agree that our methods of control are unlikely to be sufficiently delicate or sufficiently powerful to maintain continuous full employment. I should be quite content with a reasonable approximation to it, and in practice I should probably relax my expansionist measures a little

before technical full employment had actually been reached.
1936 Letter to E F M Durbin, 30 Apr.

86 It might have been supposed that competition between expert professionals, possessing judgement and knowledge beyond that of the average private investor, would correct the vagaries of the ignorant individual left to himself. It happens, however, that the energies and skills of the professional investor and speculator are mainly occupied elsewhere. For most of these persons are, in fact, largely concerned, not with making superior long-term forecasts of the probable yield on an investment over its whole life, but with foreseeing changes in the conventional bias of valuation a short time ahead of the general public… This battle of wits to anticipate the basis of conventional valuation a few months hence, rather than the prospective yield of an investment over a long term of years, does not even require gulls amongst the public to feed the maws of the professional; it can be played by professionals amongst themselves.
1936 *The General Theory of Employment, Interest, and Money.*

87 Speculators may do no harm as bubbles on a steady stream of enterprise. But the position is serious when enterprise becomes the bubble on a whirlpool of speculation. When the capital development of a country becomes a by-product of the activities of a casino, the job is likely to be ill-done.
1936 *The General Theory of Employment, Interest, and Money.*

88 If the Treasury were to fill old bottles with banknotes, bury them at suitable depths in disused coalmines which are then filled up to the surface with town rubbish, and leave it to private enterprise on well-tried principles of *laissez-faire* to dig the notes up again…there need be no more unemployment and, with the help of the repercussions, the real income of the community, and its capital wealth also, would probably become a good deal greater than it actually is. It would, indeed, be more sensible to build houses and the like; but as there are political and practical difficulties in the way of this, the above would be better than nothing.
1936 *The General Theory of Employment, Interest and Money.*

89 The ideas of economists and political philosophers, both when they are right and when they are wrong, are more powerful than is commonly understood. Indeed the world is ruled by little else. Practical men, who believe themselves to be quite exempt from any intellectual influences, are usually the slaves of some defunct economist. Madmen in authority, who hear voices in the air, are distilling their frenzy from some academic scribbler of a few years back. I am sure the power of vested interests is vastly exaggerated compared with the gradual encroachment of ideas.
1936 *The General Theory of Employment, Interest and Money.*

90 The outstanding faults of the economic society in which we live are its failure to provide for full employment and its arbitrary and inequitable distribution of wealth and incomes.
1936 *The General Theory of Employment, Interest and Money.*

91 We take it as a fundamental psychological rule of any modern community that, when its real income is increased, it will not increase its consumption by an equal absolute amount.
1936 *The General Theory of Employment, Interest, and Money.*

92 Worldly wisdom teaches us that it is better for the reputation to fail conventionally than to succeed unconventionally.
1936 *The General Theory of Employment, Interest and Money.*

93 I believe that there is social and psychological justification for significant inequalities of incomes and wealth, but not for such large disparities as exist today.
1936 *The General Theory of Employment, Interest and Money.*

Khayyám, Omar c.1050–c.1123

Persian poet and scholar. Born in Nishapur, he was summoned to Merv by the sultan, where he reformed the Muslim calendar. A renowned astronomer, he also composed mathematical treatises, and is best remembered for his *Rubáiyát* (c.1100).

94 Know yourself as a snowdrift on the sand
Heaped for two days, or three, then thawed and gone.
c.1100 *Rubáiyát*, stanza 16 (translated by Robert Graves and Omar Ali-Shah, 1972).

95 Never anticipate tomorrow's sorrow;
Live always in this paradisal now.
c.1100 *Rubáiyát*, stanza 21 (translated by Robert Graves and Omar Ali-Shah, 1972).

96 The cheerful bird of youth flutters away—
I hardly noticed how it came or went.
c.1100 *Rubáiyát*, stanza 103 (translated by Robert Graves and Omar Ali-Shah, 1972).

Khomeini, Ayatollah Ruhollah 1900–89

Iranian religious and political leader. Exiled in 1964, he returned to Iran in 1979 after the collapse of the Shah's government and became virtual head of state. He instigated a fundamentalist 'Islamic Revolution'.

97 Music is no different from opium. Music affects the human mind in a way that makes people think of nothing but music and sensual matters… Music is a treason to the country, a treason to our youth, and we should cut out all this music and replace it with something instructive.
1979 Ramadan speech, 23 Jul. Quoted in Lebrecht *Discord* (1982).

Khrushchev, Nikita Sergeyevich 1894–1971

Soviet politician. On the death of Stalin he became First Secretary of the Communist Party (1953–64), and subsequently denounced Stalinism. His period of office was marked by the 1956 Poznan riots, the Hungarian uprising, and the Cuban missile crisis (1962).

98 Those who wait for the USSR to reject Communism must wait until a shrimp learns to whistle.
1955 Speech in Moscow, 17 Sep.

99 Whether you like it not, history is on our side. We will bury you.
1956 Remark to Western diplomats at the Kremlin, 18 Nov. Khrushchev later claimed that he had meant 'We will overtake you [economically]', rather than this more sinister version.

1 Politicians are the same all over. They promise to build a bridge even where there is no river.
1960 Press conference, New York, Oct.

2 When you are skinning your customers, you should leave some skin on to grow so that you can skin them again.
1961 Speech to British industrialists, May.

3 They talk about who won and who lost. Human reason won. Mankind won.
1962 Of the ending of the Cuban missile crisis. In the *Observer*, 11 Nov.

4 We had no use for the teachings of the Gospels: if someone slaps you, just turn the other cheek. We had shown that anyone who slapped us on our cheek would get his head kicked off.
1970 *Khrushchev Remembers*. This biography, published in the West, is of dubious authenticity.

5 What the scientists have in their briefcases is terrifying.
Attributed.

Kidder, Tracy 1945–

US author. He won a Pulitzer Prize for *The Soul of a New Machine* (1981), which was also awarded a National Book Award.

6 The Soul of A New Machine
1981 Book title.

Kierkegaard, Sören Aabye 1813–55

Danish philosopher and religious thinker, who attacked dogmatism and the established Lutheran church and foreshadowed Existentialism.

7 The thing is to find a truth *for me*, to find *the idea for which I can live and die*.
1835 Journal entry (translated by Alexander Dru, 1938).

8 There are many people who reach their conclusions about life like schoolboys; they cheat their master by copying the answer out of a book without having worked out the sum for themselves.
1837 Journal entry (translated by Alexander Dru, 1938).

9 Without risk there is no faith.
1846 *Concluding Unscientific Postscript*, bk.2, pt.2, ch.2 (translated by Swenson and Lowrie).

10 The ethical reality of the individual is the only reality.
1846 *Concluding Unscientific Postscript*, bk.2, pt.2, ch.3 (translated by Swenson and Lowrie).

11 If a man in truth *will* the Good then he must be willing to suffer *for* the Good.
1846 *Purity Of Heart Is To Will One Thing* (translated by D Steere, 1938).

12 It is perfectly true, as philosophers say, that life must be understood backwards. But they forget the other proposition, that it must be lived forwards. And if one thinks over that proposition it becomes more and more evident that life can never really be understood in time simply because at no particular moment can I find the necessary resting-place from which to understand it—backwards.
Journal entry (translated by Alexander Dru, 1938).

13 Father in Heaven, when the thought of Thee wakes in our hearts, let it not awaken like a frightened bird that flies about in dismay, but like a child waking from its sleep with a heavenly smile.
Journal entry (translated by Alexander Dru, 1938).

14 Most people really believe that the Christian commandments (e.g. to love one's neighbour as oneself) are intentionally a little too severe—like putting the clock on half an hour to make sure of not being late in the morning.
Journal entry (translated by Alexander Dru, 1938).

15 The bird on the branch, the lily in the meadow, the stag in the forest, the fish in the sea, the countless joyful creatures sing, God is Love. But beneath all these sopranos, as it were a sustained bass part, is the *De profundis* of the Sacrificed, God is Love.
Journal entry (translated by Alexander Dru, 1938).

Killy, Jean-Claude 1943–

French ski racer. He won the downhill and combined gold medals at the World Championship in Chile in 1966 and a further three gold medals at the Winter Olympics in 1968, after which he turned professional.

16 Skiing is a battle against yourself, always to the frontiers of the impossible. But most of all, it must give you pleasure. It is not an obligation but a joy.
1968 In *Sports Illustrated*, 18 Nov.

Kilmer, Joyce 1886–1918

US poet.

17 I think that I shall never see
A poem lovely as a tree.
1914 'Trees'.

Kilmer, Val 1959–

US actor.

18 On set, you've got 50 people asking if you want a cup of coffee. You throw your shoes in a corner, someone puts them neatly together. It's corrupting.
2004 In the *Observer*, 9 May.

Kilpatrick, James J 1920–

US writer and broadcaster.

19 A whore may be *naked*, but a mistress is *nude*. We are talking class.
1993 *Fine Print: Reflections on the Writing Art*.

Kim Il Sung 1912–94

North Korean soldier and political leader. After proclaiming his country a Republic in 1948 he remained in political control until his death. Within his country he was regarded with awe by the majority of citizens.

20 Everything is decided by a person's thoughts and if he is ideologically motivated, there is nothing he cannot do.
1969 Speech, 20 Apr. Collected in *Selected Works* (1992), vol.1, 'Work with Artists Should be Carried Out in Line with Political Principles'.

Kimball, Donald M

US business executive.

21 There's no place where success comes before work, except in the dictionary.
1986 In *USA Today*, 21 Apr.

Kincaid, Jamaica *originally* ***Elaine Potter Richardson*** 1949–

Antiguan writer; living in the US. Her works include *At the Bottom of the River* (1983), *Annie John* (1985), *Mr Potter* (2002) and a critique of colonialism and tourism, *A Small Place* (1988).

22 There was nothing noble-minded men could not do when they discovered they could slap time on their wrists just like that.
1988 *A Small Place*.

23 A tourist is an ugly human being.
1988 *A Small Place*.

King, Anthony 1934–

Canadian academic and political commentator. Professor of Government at the University of Essex since 1969.

24 It is an asteroid hitting the planet and destroying practically all life on earth.
1997 Attempting to define the scale of Labour's victory in the general election, on BBC1's 'Election Night', 2 May.

King, Billie Jean *née Moffitt* 1943–

US tennis player, who won 20 titles at Wimbledon (1965–80).

25 Ask Nureyev to stop dancing, ask Sinatra to stop singing, then you can ask me to stop playing.
1982 Quoted in Colin Jarman *The Guinness Dictionary of Sports Quotations* (1990).

26 If you're up against a girl with big boobs, bring her to the net and make her hit backhand volleys.
1982 *Billie Jean King*.

King, Carlyle 1907–

Canadian political scientist and socialist.

27 The main business of socialist parties is not to form governments but to change minds.
Attributed, 1940s.

King, Don 1932–

US boxing promoter.

28 Only in America could a Don King happen.
Quoted in Colin Jarman *The Guinness Dictionary of Sports Quotations* (1990). King adopted 'Only in America' as a catchphrase, billing himself as Don 'Only in America' King.

29 This fight is bigger than life itself.
2001 On the heavyweight title bout between Lennox Lewis and Hasim Rahman. In the *Observer*, 30 Dec.

King, Martin Luther Jr 1929–68

US civil rights leader. He advocated passive resistance to segregation and led a boycott (1955–6) against segregated bus lines in Montgomery, Alabama. In 1964 he received both the Kennedy and Nobel peace prizes. He was assassinated by James Earl Ray.

30 He who passively accepts evil is as much involved in it as he who helps to perpetuate it.
1958 *Strides Towards Freedom*.

31 It may be true that the law cannot make a man love me, but it can keep him from lynching me, and I think that's pretty important.
1962 Speech at Cornell College, Mt Vernon, Iowa. Reported in the *Wall Street Journal*, 13 Nov.

32 Injustice anywhere is a threat to justice everywhere.
1963 Letter from Birmingham jail, Alabama, 16 Apr.

33 I have a dream. I have a dream that my four little children will one day live in a nation where they will not be judged by the colour of their skin but by the content of their character.
1963 Washington civil rights rally, 15 Jun.

34 If a man hasn't discovered something he will die for, he isn't fit to live.
1963 Speech in Detroit, 23 Jun.

35 When the architects of our republic wrote the magnificent words of the Constitution and the Declaration of Independence, they were signing a promissory note to which every American was to fall heir... America has defaulted on this promissory note insofar as her citizens of color are concerned.
1963 Speech at the Lincoln Memorial, 28 Aug, during the March on Washington.

36 We have...come to this hallowed spot to remind America of the fierce urgency of now.
1963 Speech at the Lincoln Memorial, 28 Aug, during the March on Washington.

37 Let us not seek to satisfy our thirst for freedom by drinking from the cup of bitterness and hatred...[nor] allow our creative protests to degenerate into physical violence.
1963 Speech at the Lincoln Memorial, 28 Aug, during the March on Washington.

38 You have been the victim of creative suffering.
1963 Speech at the Lincoln Memorial, 28 Aug, during the March on Washington.

39 I have a dream that one day...the sons of former slaves and the sons of former slave owners will be able to sit together at the table of brotherhood.
1963 Speech at the Lincoln Memorial, 28 Aug, during the March on Washington.

40 We have genuflected before the god of science only to find that it has given us the atomic bomb, producing fears and anxieties that science can never mitigate.
1963 *Strength to Love*, ch.13.

41 The church must be reminded that it is not the master or servant of the state, but rather the conscience of the state.
1963 *Strength to Love*.

42 Discrimination is a hellhound that gnaws at negroes in every waking moment of their lives, to remind them that the lie of their inferiority is accepted as truth in the society dominating them.
1967 Speech at the Christian leadership conference, Atlanta, 16 Aug.

43 I've been to the mountain top. I've looked over, and I've seen the promised land. I may not get there with you, but I want you to know tonight that we as a people will get to the promised land. So, I'm happy tonight. Mine eyes have seen the glory of the coming of the Lord.
1968 Speech at Memphis, 3 Apr, the day before he was assassinated.

44 Love is the only force capable of transforming an enemy into a friend.
Attributed, collected in *The Words of Martin Luther King*.

King, Stephen 1947–

US author, known for his highly suspenseful horror novels. His works include *Carrie* (1974), *The Shining* (1976), *Misery* (1988) and *Bag of Bones* (1998).

45 Terror…often arises from a pervasive sense of disestablishment; that things are in the unmaking.
1981 *Danse Macabre*.

46 I believe there is an unseen world all around us.
1993 *Nightmares and Dreamscapes*, introduction.

King, William Lyon Mackenzie 1874–1950

Canadian Liberal politician, Prime Minister 1921–6, 1926–30 and 1935–48. His view that the dominions should be autonomous within the British Empire resulted in the Statute of Westminster (1931).

47 If some countries have too much history, we have too much geography.
1936 Address to the House of Commons, Ottawa, 18 Jun.

Kingsley, Charles 1819–75

English writer. Among his best-known works are the historical novels *Westward Ho!* (1855), and the children's book *The Water Babies* (1863). A Christian Socialist, he also published an immense number of articles on current topics.

48 'Oh Mary, go and call the cattle home,
And call the cattle home,
And call the cattle home,
Across the sands of Dee.'
The western wind was wild and dank with foam,
And all alone went she.
1850 *Alton Locke*, ch.26, 'The Sands of Dee'.

49 Come; and strong within us
Stir the Vikings' blood;
Bracing brain and sinew;
Blow, thou wind of God!
1857 'Ode to the North-East Wind'.

50 Be good, sweet maid, and let who will be clever;
Do noble things, do not dream them, all day long:
And so make life, death, and that vast for-ever
One grand, sweet song.
1858 'A Farewell'.

51 Once upon a time there was a little chimney-sweep, and his name was Tom.
1863 *The Water Babies*, ch.1.

52 The great elm-trees in the gold-green meadows were fast asleep above, and the cows fast asleep beneath them; nay, the few clouds which were about were fast asleep likewise, and so tired that they had lain down on the earth to rest, in long white flakes and bars, among the stems of the elm-trees, and along the tops of the alders by the stream.
1863 *The Water Babies*, ch.1.

53 When all the world is young, lad,
And all the trees are green;
And every goose a swan, lad,
And every lass a queen;
Then hey for boot and horse, lad,
And round the world away:
Young blood must have its course, lad,
And every dog his day.
1863 Song. *The Water Babies*, ch.2.

54 He was as thorough an Englishman as ever coveted his neighbour's goods… [He was] chief professor of Necrobioneopalaeonthydrochthonanthropopithekology.
1863 Professor Ptthmllnsprts. *The Water Babies*, ch.4.

55 The healthiest situation in England, on Easthampstead Plain. Free run of Windsor Forest. *The Times* every morning. A double-barrelled gun and pointers, and leave to shoot three Wellington College boys a week (not more) in case black game was scarce.
1863 The reward for criminal lunacy. *The Water Babies*, ch.4.

56 I am the ugliest fairy in the world, and I shall be till people behave themselves as they ought to do. And then I shall grow as handsome as my sister…Mrs Doasyouwouldbedoneby.
1863 Mrs Bedonebyasyoudid. *The Water Babies*, ch.5.

57 How long would it take a school-inspector of average activity to tumble head over heels from London to York?
1863 *The Water Babies*, ch.8.

58 So Tom went home with Ellie…and he is now a great man of science…and knows everything about everything, except why a hen's egg don't turn into a crocodile, and two or three other little things which no one will know till the coming of the Cocqcigrues. And all this from what he learnt when he was a water-baby, underneath the sea. 'And of course, Tom married Ellie?' My dear child, what a silly notion! Don't you know that no one ever marries in a fairy tale, under the rank of a prince or a princess?
1863 *The Water Babies*, ch.8.

59 We have used the Bible as if it was a constable's handbook—an opium-dose for keeping beasts of burden patient while they are being overloaded.
Letters to the Chartists, no.2.

60 To be discontented with the divine discontent, and to be ashamed with the noble shame, is the very germ and first upgrowth of all virtue.
1874 *Health and Education*.

Kingsley, Mary Henrietta 1862–1900

English writer and traveller. After the death of her invalid parents she travelled to West Africa (1893 and 1895), living among the natives, and wrote accounts of both journeys. She died of enteric fever while serving as a nurse in the second Boer War.

61 A certain sort of friendship soon arose between the Fans and me. We each recognized that we belonged to that same section of the human race with whom it is better to drink than to fight. We knew we would each have killed the other, if sufficient inducement were offered, and so we took a certain amount of care that the inducement should not arise.
1893 *Travels in West Africa* (published 1899).

62 It is at these times that you realise the blessings of a good thick skirt… Save for a good many bruises, here I was with the fulness of my skirt tucked under me, sitting on nine ebony spikes some twelve inches long, in comparative comfort.
1893 *Travels in West Africa* (published 1899).

63 The sooner the Crown Colony system is removed from the sphere of practical politics and put under a glass case in the South Kensington Museum, labelled 'Extinct', the better for everyone.
1899 *West African Studies*.

64 West Africa today is just a quarry of paving stones for Hell, and those stones were cemented in place with

men's blood mixed with wasted gold.
1899 *West African Studies*.

Kington, Miles 1941–

British writer and columnist. He is best known as a humorist, and also writes on jazz.

65 Nobody has ever been able to define jazz satisfactorily. This is probably because anyone who was capable of doing so never really wanted to, knowing how much you would have to leave out of the definition.
1992 *The Jazz Anthology*, ch.1

Kinnock, Neil Gordon 1942–

Welsh Labour politician. In 1983 he succeeded Michael Foot as Party leader, but resigned after the 1992 election defeat. He was Vice-President of the European Commission until 2004, subsequently becoming Chair of the British Council.

66 We cannot remove the evils of capitalism without taking its source of power: ownership.
1975 In *Tribune*.

67 I want to retire at 50. I want to play cricket in the summer and geriatric football in the winter, and sing in the choir.
1980 In *The Times*, 28 Jul.

68 Like Brighton Pier—all right as far as it goes, but inadequate for getting to France.
1981 On Conservative European policy, House of Commons, 2 Feb.

69 It's a pity others had to leave theirs on the ground at Goose Green to prove it.
1983 Reply to a heckler who had said Mrs Thatcher had shown 'guts' in the Falklands Crisis. Quoted in *The Times*, 6 Jun.

70 If Margaret Thatcher wins on Thursday, I warn you not to be ordinary, I warn you not to be young, I warn you not to fall ill, I warn you not to get old.
1983 Speech one day before polling, Jun.

71 I have a lot of sympathy with him. I too was once a young, bald Leader of the Opposition.
1999 On William Hague. In *The Independent*, 3 Oct.

Kinsella, W(illiam) P(atrick) 1935–

Canadian novelist.

72 There was silence in the room. Then a voice, stunning as thunder, clear and common as a train whistle—the voice of a ball-park announcer: 'If you build it, he will come.'
1980 'Shoeless Joe Jackson Comes to Iowa', a short story later expanded into the novel *Shoeless Joe* (1982) and filmed as *Field of Dreams* (1989).

Kipling, (Joseph) Rudyard 1865–1935

English writer, born in Bombay, who lived for several years in India. His verse both celebrated and satirized the British Imperial presence, and won him widespread popularity, while the stories in *The Jungle Book* (1894) are considered classics of their kind. He also wrote novels and a biography, and was awarded the Nobel prize in 1907.

73 The toad beneath the harrow knows
Exactly where each tooth-point goes;
The butterfly upon the road
Preaches contentment to that toad.
1886 'Pagett, MP'.

74 Never praise a sister to a sister, in the hope of your compliments reaching the proper ears.
1888 *Plain Tales from the Hills*, 'False Dawn'.

75 Take my word for it, the silliest woman can manage a clever man; but it takes a very clever woman to manage a fool.
1888 *Plain Tales from the Hills*, 'Three and—an Extra'.

76 Every one is more or less mad on one point.
1888 *Plain Tales from the Hills*, 'On the Strength of a Likeness'.

77 The Man who Would be King.
1888 *Wee Willie Winkie*, title of short story.

78 Being kissed by a man who didn't wax his moustache was—like eating an egg without salt.
1888 *The Story of the Gadsbys*, 'Poor Dear Mamma'.

79 Down to Gehenna or up to the Throne,
He travels fastest who travels alone.
1888 *The Story of the Gadsbys*, 'L'Envoi'. The poem was later renamed 'The Winners' (1912).

80 We're poor little lambs who've lost our way,
Baa! Baa! Baa!
We're little black sheep who've gone astray,
Baa-aa-aa!
Gentlemen-rankers out on the spree,
Damned from here to eternity,
God ha' mercy on such as we,
Baa! Yah! Bah!
1889 'The Gentlemen-Rankers'.

81 Oh, East is East, and West is West, and never the twain shall meet,
Till earth and sky stand presently at God's great Judgement seat;
But there is neither East nor West, Border, nor Breed, nor Birth,
When two strong men stand face to face, tho' they come from the ends of the earth.
1889 'The Ballad of East and West'.

82 A man lives well and happily until he begins to feel unwell. Then he feels worse because the climate allows him no chance of pulling himself together—and then he dies.
1889 Of life in Singapore. *From Sea to Sea*.

83 The Japanese should have no concern with business.
1889 *From Sea to Sea*.

84 Moulmein is situated up the mouth of a river which ought to flow through South America.
1889 *From Sea to Sea*.

85 By the old Moulmein Pagoda, lookin' eastward to the sea,
There's a Burma girl a-settin', and I know she thinks o' me;
For the wind is in the palm trees, an' the temple bells they say:
'Come you back, you British soldier'; come you back to Mandalay!'
1890 'Mandalay'.

86 Come you back to Mandalay,
Where the old Flotilla lay:
Can't you 'ear their paddles chunkin' from Rangoon to Mandalay?
On the road to Mandalay,
Where the flyin'-fishes play,

An' the dawn comes up like thunder outer China 'crost the Bay!
1890 'Mandalay'.

87 An' I seed her first a-smokin' of a whackin' white cheroot,
An' a-wastin' Christian kisses on an 'eathen idol's foot.
1890 'Mandalay'.

88 Ship me somewhere east of Suez, where the best is like the worst,
Where there aren't no Ten Commandments an' a man can raise a thirst.
1890 'Mandalay'.

89 For they're hangin' Danny Deever, you can hear the Dead March play,
The regiment's in 'ollow square—they're hangin' him to-day;
They've taken of his buttons off an' cut his stripes away,
An' they're hangin' Danny Deever in the mornin'.
1890 'Danny Deever'.

90 O it's Tommy this, an' Tommy that, an' 'Tommy, go away';
But it's 'Thank you, Mister Atkins,' when the band begins to play.
1890 'Tommy'.

91 Then it's Tommy this, an' Tommy that, and 'Tommy 'ow's yer soul?'
But it's 'Thin red line of 'eroes' when the drums begin to roll.
1890 'Tommy'.
► *See Russell 706:69.*

92 For it's Tommy this, an' Tommy that, and 'Chuck him out, the brute!'
But it's 'Saviour of 'is country' when the guns begin to shoot.
1890 'Tommy'.

93 When you're wounded and left on Afghanistan's plains
And the women come out to cut up what remains
Just roll to your rifle and blow out your brains
An' go to your Gawd like a soldier.
1890 'The Young British Soldier'.

94 So 'ere's *to* you, Fuzzy-Wuzzy, at your 'ome in the Soudan;
You're a pore benighted 'eathen but a first-class fightin' man;
An' 'ere's *to* you, Fuzzy-Wuzzy, with your 'ayrick 'ead of 'air—
You big black boundin' beggar—for you broke a British square!
1890 'Fuzzy-Wuzzy'.

95 The uniform 'e wore
Was nothin' much before,
An' rather less than 'arf o' that be'ind.
1890 'Gunga Din'.

96 Though I've belted you and flayed you,
By the livin' Gawd that made you,
You're a better man than I am, Gunga Din!
1890 'Gunga Din'.

97 'Ave you 'eard o' the Widow at Windsor
With a hairy gold crown on 'er 'ead?
She 'as ships on the foam—she 'as millions at 'ome,
An' she pays us poor beggars in red.
1890 'The Widow at Windsor'.

98 And the talk slid north, and the talk slid south,
With the sliding puffs from the hookah-mouth.
Four things greater than all things are,—
Women and Horses and Power and War.
1890 'The Ballad of the King's Jest'.

99 Winds of the World, give answer! They are whimpering to and fro—
And what should they know of England who only England know?—
The poor little street-bred people that vapour and fume and brag.
1891 'The English Flag'.

1 If I were damned of body and soul,
I know whose prayers would make me whole,
Mother o' mine, O mother o' mine.
1891 *The Light That Failed*, dedication.

2 There ain't twelve hundred people in the world who understand pictures. The others pretend and don't care.
1891 *The Light That Failed*.

3 When the flush of a new-born sun fell first on Eden's green and gold,
Our father Adam sat under the Tree and scratched with a stick in the mould;
And the first rude sketch that the world had seen was joy to his mighty heart,
Till the Devil whispered behind the leaves, 'It's pretty, but is it Art?'
1892 'The Conundrum of the Workshops'.

4 We know that the tail must wag the dog, for the horse is drawn by the cart;
But the Devil whoops, as he whooped of old: 'It's clever, but is it Art?'
1892 'The Conundrum of the Workshops'.

5 And the end of the fight is a tombstone white, with the name of the late deceased,
And the epitaph drear: 'A fool lies here who tried to hustle the East.'
1892 *The Naulahka*, ch.5.

6 For the sin ye do by two and two ye must pay for one by one!
1892 'Tomlinson'.

7 There be triple ways to take, of the eagle or the snake,
Or the way of a man with a maid;
But the sweetest way to me is a ship's upon the sea
In the heel of the North-East Trade.
1892 'The Long Trail'.

8 There are nine and sixty ways of constructing tribal lays,
And—every—single—one—of—them—is—right!
1892 'In the Neolithic Age'.

9 A man-cub is a man-cub, and he must learn *all* the Law of the Jungle.
1894 *The Jungle Book*, 'Kaa's Hunting'.

10 'We be one blood, thou and I,' Mowgli answered. 'I take my life from thee to-night. My kill shall be thy kill if ever thou art hungry, O Kaa.'
1894 *The Jungle Book*, 'Kaa's Hunting'.

11 Brother, thy tail hangs down behind!
1894 *The Jungle Book*, 'The Road Song of the Bandar-Log'.

12 Now this is the Law of the Jungle—as old and as true as the sky;

And the Wolf that shall keep it may prosper, but the Wolf
that shall break it must die.
1895 *The Second Jungle Book*, 'The Law of the Jungle'.

13 Keep ye the law—be swift in all obedience—
Clear the land of evil, drive the road and bridge the ford.
Make ye sure to each his own
That he reap where he hath sown;
By the peace among our peoples let men know we serve
the Lord!
1896 'A Song of the English'.

14 We have fed our sea for a thousand years
And she calls us, still unfed,
Though there's never a wave of all her waves
But marks our English dead.
1896 'A Song of the Dead'.

15 If blood be the price of admiralty
Lord God, we ha' paid in full!
1896 'A Song of the Dead'.

16 I've taken my fun where I've found it,
An' now I must pay for my fun,
For the more you 'ave known o' the others
The less will you settle for one;
1896 'The Ladies'.

17 For the Colonel's Lady an' Judy O'Grady
Are sisters under their skins!
1896 'The Ladies'.

18 The 'eathen in 'is blindness bows down to wood an'
stone;
'E don't obey no orders unless they is 'is own.
1896 'The 'Eathen'.

19 The 'eathen in 'is blindness must end where 'e began.
But the backbone of the Army is the non-commissioned
man!
1896 'The 'Eathen'.

20 And only the Master shall praise us, and only the Master
shall blame;
And no one shall work for money, and no one shall work
for fame,
But each for the joy of working, and each, in his separate
star,
Shall draw the Thing as he sees It for the God of Things as
They are!
1896 'When Earth's Last Picture is Painted'.

21 The tumult and the shouting dies—
The captains and the kings depart—
Still stands Thine ancient Sacrifice,
An humble and a contrite heart.
Lord God of Hosts, be with us yet,
Lest we forget—lest we forget!
1897 'Recessional'.
► *See Bible 95:31.*

22 If, drunk with sight of power, we loose
Wild tongues that have not Thee in awe—
Such boasting as the Gentiles use,
Or lesser breeds without the Law.
1897 'Recessional'.

23 What the horses o' Kansas think to-day, the horses of America will think tomorrow; an' I tell *you* that when the horses of America rise in their might, the day o' the Oppressor is ended.
1898 *The Day's Work*, 'A Walking Delegate'.

24 Take up the White Man's burden—
Send forth the best ye breed—
Go, bind your sons to exile
To serve your captives' need.
1899 'The White Man's Burden'.

25 Your new-caught, sullen peoples,
Half devil and half child.
1899 'The White Man's Burden'.

26 By all ye will or whisper,
By all ye leave or do,
The silent sullen peoples
Shall weigh your God and you.
1899 'The White Man's Burden'.

27 When you've shouted 'Rule Britannia', when you've sung
'God save the Queen'—
When you've finished killing Kruger with your mouth—
Will you kindly drop a shilling in my little tambourine
For a gentleman in *Kharki* ordered South?
1899 *The Absent-Minded Beggar.*

28 Mr Raymond Martin, beyond question, was born in the gutter, and bred in a Board-School, where they played marbles. He was further (I give the barest handful from great store) a Flopshus Cad, an Outrageous Stinker, a Jelly-bellied Flag-flapper (this was Stalky's contribution), and several other things which it is not seemly to put down.
1899 *Stalky & Co.*

29 Being human, she must have been afraid of something, but one never found out what it was.
c.1900 Of Mary Kingsley (1862–1900), the enterprising English traveller in West Africa. Attributed.

30 Little Friend of all the World.
1901 Kim's nickname. *Kim*, ch.1.

31 Men are as chancy as children in their choice of playthings.
1901 *Kim*, ch.10.

32 One does not own to the possession of money in India.
1901 *Kim*, ch.11.

33 'Noble and generous Cetacean, have you ever tasted Man?' 'No,' said the Whale. 'What is it like?' 'Nice,' said the small 'Stute Fish. 'Nice but nubbly.'
1902 *Just So Stories*, 'How the Whale Got His Throat'.

34 You must not forget the suspenders, Best Beloved.
1902 *Just So Stories*, 'How the Whale Got His Throat'.

35 He had his Mummy's leave to paddle, or else he would never have done it, because he was a man of infinite-resource-and-sagacity.
1902 *Just So Stories*, 'How the Whale Got His Throat'.

36 The camel's hump is an ugly lump
Which well you may see at the Zoo;
But uglier yet is the hump we get
From having too little to do.
1902 *Just So Stories*, 'How the Camel Got His Hump'.

37 The cure for this ill is not to sit still,
Or frowst with a book by the fire;
But to take a large hoe and a shovel also,
And dig till you gently perspire.
1902 *Just So Stories*, 'How the Camel Got His Hump'.

38 Most 'scruciating idle.
1902 *Just So Stories*, 'How the Camel Got His Hump'.

39 'Humph yourself!'
And the Camel humphed himself.
1902 *Just So Stories*, 'How the Camel Got His Hump'.

40 There lived a Parsee from whose hat the rays of the sun were reflected in more-than-oriental splendour.
1902 *Just So Stories*, 'How the Rhinoceros Got His Skin'.

41 But there was one Elephant—a new Elephant—an Elephant's Child—who was full of 'satiable curtiosity, and that means he asked ever so many questions.
1902 *Just So Stories*, 'The Elephant's Child'.

42 The great grey-green, greasy Limpopo River, all set about with fever-trees.
1902 *Just So Stories*, 'The Elephant's Child'.

43 Led go! You are hurtig be!
1902 *Just So Stories*, 'The Elephant's Child'.

44 And I'd like to roll to Rio
Some day before I'm old!
1902 *Just So Stories*, 'The Beginning of the Armadilloes'.

45 'You are making my spots ache,' said Painted Jaguar.
1902 *Just So Stories*, 'The Beginning of the Armadillos'.

46 But the wildest of all the wild animals was the Cat. He walked by himself, and all places were alike to him.
1902 *Just So Stories*, 'The Cat That Walked By Himself'.

47 And he went back through the Wet Wild Woods, waving his wild tail and walking by his wild lone. But he never told anybody.
1902 *Just So Stories*, 'The Cat That Walked By Himself'.

48 He would surprise them out of their jumpsome lives.
1902 *Just So Stories*, 'How the Leopard Got His Spots'.

49 Something lost behind the Ranges.
1903 *The Five Nations*, 'The Explorer'.

50 Who hath desired the Sea?—the sight of salt water unbounded—
The heave and the halt and the hurl and the crash of the comber wind-hounded?
The sleek-barrelled swell before storm, grey, foamless, enormous, and growing
Stark calm on the lap of the Line or the crazy-eyed Hurricane blowing.
1903 'The Sea and the Hills'.

51 And here the sea-fogs lap and cling,
And here, each warning each,
The sheep-bells and the ship-bells ring
Along the hidden beach.
1903 'Sussex'.

52 God gives all men all earth to love,
But since man's heart is small,
Ordains for each one spot shall prove
Belovèd over all.
1903 'Sussex'.

53 Each to his choice, and I rejoice
The lot has fallen to me
In a fair ground—in a fair ground—
Yea, Sussex by the sea!
1903 'Sussex'.
► *See Book of Common Prayer 142:42.*

54 Then ye returned to your trinkets; then ye contented your souls
With the flannelled fools at the wicket or the muddied oafs at the goals.
1903 'The Islanders'.

55 An' it all goes into the laundry
But it never comes out in the wash.
1903 'Stellenbosh'.

56 'Tisn't beauty, so to speak, nor good talk necessarily. It's just It. Some women'll stay in a man's memory if they once walked down a street.
1904 *Traffics and Discoveries*, 'Mrs Bathhurst'.

57 The God who Looks after Small Things had caused the visitor that day to receive two weeks' delayed mails in one.
1904 *Traffics and Discoveries*, 'The Captive'

58 Of all the trees that grow so fair,
Old England to adorn,
Greater are none beneath the Sun,
Than Oak, and Ash, and Thorn.
1906 *Puck of Pook's Hill*, 'Tree Song'.

59 England shall bide till Judgement Tide
By Oak, and Ash, and Thorn.
1906 *Puck of Pook's Hill*, 'Tree Song'.

60 What is a woman that you forsake her,
And the hearth-fire and the home-acre,
To go with the old grey Widow-maker?
1906 *Puck of Pook's Hill*, 'Harp Song of the Dane Women'.

61 If you wake at midnight, and hear a horse's feet,
Don't go drawing back the blind, or looking in the street,
Them that asks no questions isn't told a lie.
Watch the wall, my darling, while the Gentlemen go by!
1906 *Puck of Pook's Hill*, 'Smuggler's Song'.

62 Land of our birth, we pledge to thee
Our love and toil in the years to be;
When we are grown and take our place,
As men and women with our race.
1906 *Puck of Pook's Hill*, 'Children's Song'.

63 Teach us delight in simple things
And mirth that has no bitter springs;
Forgiveness free of evil done,
And love to all men 'neath the sun!
1906 *Puck of Pook's Hill*, 'Children's Song'.

64 But I consort with long-haired things
In velvet collar-rolls,
Who talk about the Aims of Art,
And 'theories' and 'goals',
And moo and coo with women-folk
About their blessed souls.
1909 'In Partibus'.

65 There is sorrow enough in the natural way
From men and women to fill our day;
But when we are certain of sorrow in store,
Why do we always arrange for more?
Brothers and Sisters, I bid you beware
Of giving your heart to a dog to tear.
1909 'The Power of the Dog'.

66 They shut the road through the woods
Seventy years ago.
Weather and rain have undone it again,
And now you would never know
There was once a road through the woods.
1910 *Rewards and Fairies*, 'The Way Through the Woods'.

67 If you can keep your head when all about you

Are losing theirs and blaming it on you;
If you can trust yourself when all men doubt you,
But make allowance for their doubting too;
If you can wait and not be tired by waiting,
Or being lied about, don't deal in lies,
Or being hated, don't give way to hating,
And yet don't look too good, nor talk too wise;
If you can dream—and not make dreams your master;
If you can think—and not make thoughts your aim,
If you can meet with Triumph and Disaster
And treat those two imposters just the same.
1910 *Rewards and Fairies*, 'If—'.

68 If you can talk with crowds and keep your virtue,
Or walk with Kings—nor lose the common touch,
If neither foes nor loving friends can hurt you,
If all men count with you, but none too much;
If you can fill the unforgiving minute
With sixty seconds' worth of distance run,
Yours is the Earth and everything that's in it.
And—which is more—you'll be a Man, my son!
1910 *Rewards and Fairies*, 'If—'.

69 One man in a thousand, Solomon says,
Will stick more close than a brother.
1910 *Rewards and Fairies*, 'The Thousandth Man'

70 It is always a temptation to a rich and lazy nation,
To puff and look important and to say:
'Though we know we should defeat you, we have not the time to meet you,
We will therefore pay you cash to go away.'

And that is called paying the Dane-geld;
But we've proved it again and again,
That if once you have paid him the Dane-geld
You never get rid of the Dane.
1911 'Dane-Geld'.

71 'Oh, where are you going to, all you Big Steamers,
With England's own coal, up and down the salt seas?'
'We are going to fetch you your bread and your butter,
Your beef, pork, and mutton, eggs, apples and cheese.'
1911 'Big Steamers'.

72 Our England is a garden that is full of stately views,
Of borders, beds and shrubberies and lawns and avenues,
With statues on the terraces and peacocks strutting by;
But the Glory of the Garden lies in more than meets the eye.
1911 'The Glory of the Garden'.

73 Our England is a garden, and such gardens are not made
By singing:—'Oh, how beautiful!' and sitting in the shade,
While better men than we go out and start their working lives
At grubbing weeds from gravel paths with broken dinner-knives.
1911 'The Glory of the Garden'.

74 Oh, Adam was a gardener, and God who made him sees
That half a proper gardener's work is done upon his knees,
So when your work is finished, you can wash your hands and pray
For the Glory of the Garden that it may not pass away!
1911 'The Glory of the Garden'.

75 We know the war prepared
On every peaceful home,
We know the hells declared
For such as serve not Rome,
The terror, threats and dread
In market, hearth and field:
We know when all is said
We perish if we yield.
1912 'Ulster'.

76 For all we have and are,
For all our children's fate,
Stand up and take the war.
The Hun is at the gate!
1914 'For All We Have and Are'.

77 There is but one task for all—
For each one life to give.
What stands if freedom fall?
Who dies if England live?
1914 'For All We Have and Are'.

78 It's north you may run to the rime-ringed sun,
Or south to the blind Horn's hate;
Or east all the way into Mississippi Bay,
Or west to the Golden Gate.
1918 *Twenty Poems*, 'The Long Trail'.

79 Pull out, pull out on the Long Trail—the trail that is always new!
1918 *Twenty Poems*, 'The Long Trail'.

80 Their Name Liveth for Evermore.
1919 His suggestion for the text to be carved over the lists of the dead in the Commonwealth war cemeteries after World War I.
► *See Bible 108:67.*

81 If any question why we died,
Tell them, because our fathers lied.
1919 *Rudyard Kipling's Verse*, 'Common Form'.

82 The female of the species is more deadly than the male.
1919 *Rudyard Kipling's Verse*, 'The Female of the Species'.

83 Words are, of course, the most powerful drug used by mankind.
1923 Speech, 14 Feb, collected in *A Book of Words*.

84 As it will be in the future, it was at the birth of Man—
There are only four things certain since Social Progress began:—
That the Dog returns to his Vomit and the Sow returns to her Mire,
And the burnt Fool's bandaged finger goes wabbling back to the Fire.
1927 *Rudyard Kipling's Verse*, 'The Gods of the Copybook Headings'.

85 England's on the anvil—hear the hammers ring—
Clanging from the Severn to the Tyne!
1927 *Rudyard Kipling's Verse*, 'The Anvil'.

Kirkland, (Joseph) Lane 1922–99

US labour leader.

86 My pappy told me never to bet my bladder against a brewery or get into an argument with people who buy ink by the barrel.
Quoted in David Olive *Business Babble* (1993).

Kirkup, James 1923–

English poet. He held academic posts in Japan from the early 1960s, and his work has been greatly influenced by Japanese culture and literature.

87 But the river remains unchanged, sad, refusing rehabilitation.
1962 'No More Hiroshimas'.

Kishen fl.c.1840

Chinese diplomatist.

88 It appears to Your Majesty's slave that we are very deficient in means, and have not the shells and rockets used by the barbarians. We must, therefore, adopt other methods to stop them, which will be easy, as they have opened negotiations.
1841 Report, Mar, to the Chinese Emperor during the 1st Opium War, 1839–42.

Kissinger, Henry Alfred 1923–

US academic and statesman. He was the main US figure in the negotiations to end the Vietnam War (for which he shared the 1973 Nobel peace prize), and Secretary of State (1973–7). His 'shuttle diplomacy', aimed at improving Israeli–Egyptian relations, had much success.

89 It is not often that nations learn from the past—even rarer that they draw the correct conclusions from it. For the lessons of historical experience, as of personal experience, are contingent. They teach the consequences of certain actions, but they cannot force a recognition of comparable situations.
1957 *A World Restored: Castlereagh, Metternich and the Restoration of Peace, 1812–22.*

90 We lost sight of one of the cardinal maxims of guerrilla war: the guerrilla wins if he does not lose. The conventional army loses if it does not win.
1969 On the Vietnam War. In *Foreign Affairs*, Jan.

91 Power is the ultimate aphrodisiac.
1969 Comment at the end of his first year as head of the National Security Council. Quoted in Walter Isaacson *Kissinger* (1992).

92 We are all the President's men, and we must behave accordingly.
1970 On the US invasion of Cambodia, alluding to the nursery rhyme *Humpty Dumpty* ('All the king's men…'). The phrase was used in the title of the book by *Washington Post* reporters Bob Woodward and Carl Bernstein on the Watergate scandal.

93 No foreign policy, no matter how ingenious, has any chance of success if it is born in the minds of a few and carried in the heart of none.
1973 Speech to International Platform Association, 2 Aug.

94 Every civilization that has ever existed has ultimately collapsed.
1974 In the *New York Times*, 13 Oct.

95 History is a tale of efforts that failed…aspirations that weren't realized, or wishes that were fulfilled and then turned out to be different from what one expected.
1974 In the *New York Times*, 13 Oct.

96 There can't be any crisis next week. My schedule is already full.
1977 In *Time*, Jan.

97 High office teaches decision-making, not substance. It consumes intellectual capital; it does not create it. Most high officials leave office with the perceptions and insights with which they entered: they learn how to make decisions, but not what decisions to make.
1979 *The White House Years.*

98 The statesman's duty is to bridge the gap between his nation's experience and his vision.
1982 *Years of Upheaval.*

99 The nice thing about being a celebrity is that when you bore people, they think that it's their fault.
Quoted in *Reader's Digest*, Apr 1985.

1 Whatever must happen ultimately should happen immediately.
1986 Of the Iran–Contra scandal. In *Time*, 8 Oct.

2 Any people who have been persecuted for 2,000 years must be doing something wrong.
Of Israel, after its attack on Egypt. Quoted in Walter Isaacson *Kissinger* (1992).

3 I'd do anything for caviar and probably did.
On his visit to Moscow. Quoted in Walter Isaacson *Kissinger* (1992).

Kitchener of Khartoum and Broome, (Horatio) Herbert, 1st Earl 1850–1916

British field marshal. He served in Palestine, Cyprus and the Sudan, which he regained for the British Empire at Omdurman (1898), and was chief-of-staff and commander-in-chief in the Boer War. In World War I he was Secretary of State for War, but was drowned when HMS *Hampshire* struck a mine.

4 You are ordered abroad as a soldier of the King to help our French comrades against the invasion of a common enemy… In this new experience you may find temptations both in wine and women. You must entirely resist both temptations, and while treating all women with perfect courtesy, you should avoid any intimacy. Do your duty bravely. Fear God. Honour the King.
1914 Message to the soldiers of the British Expeditionary Force, reported in *The Times*, 19 Aug.

5 I don't mind your being killed, but I object to your being taken prisoner.
1914 To the Prince of Wales, later Edward VIII, who had asked to be allowed to the Front, 18 Dec.

Klee, Paul 1874–1940

Swiss painter and graphic artist, one of the most influential teachers of the German Bauhaus.

6 I have now reached the point where I can look over the great art of antiquity and its Renaissance. But, for myself, I cannot find any artistic connection with our own times. And to want to create something outside of one's own age strikes me as suspect.
1901–2 *The Diaries of Paul Klee 1898–1918*, entry 294.

7 The worst state of affairs is when science begins to concern itself with art.
1906 Collected in *The Notebooks of Paul Klee* (published 1957).

8 Color possesses me. I don't have to pursue it. It will possess me always, I know it. That is the meaning of this happy hour: Color and I are one. I am a painter.
1914 *The Diaries of Paul Klee 1898–1918*, entry 926.

9 Art is like Creation: it holds good on the last day as on the first.

1916 *The Diaries of Paul Klee 1898–1918*, entry 1008.

10 *Kunst gibt nicht das Sichtbare wieder, sondern macht sichtbar.*
Art does not reproduce the visible; rather it makes visible.
1920 'Creative Credo', in *Inward Vision* (1958).

Klein, Calvin Richard 1942–

US fashion designer.

11 You have to take things to an extreme and then bring them back to reality.
1988 On the fluctuating length of hemlines. In the *New York Times*, 9 Mar.

Kline, Nancy

12 Withholding information from someone is an act of intellectual imperialism. Not bothering to seek accurate information is an act of intellectual recklessness.
1999 *Time to Think*.

Kneller, Godfrey 1646–1723

German-born painter who spent most of his working life in England, particularly renowned as a portrait painter.

13 Painters of history make the dead live, and do not begin to live themselves till they are dead. I paint the living, and they make me live!
When asked why he preferred portraits to more prestigious history scenes. Quoted in A Cunningham *The Lives of the Most Eminent Painters, Sculptors and Architects* (1829).

Knight, Frank Hyneman 1885–1972

US economist, Professor at the University of Chicago (1927–58) and an opponent of social planning. His most famous works were *Risk, Uncertainty and Profit* (1921) and *The Ethics of Competition* (1923).

14 Costs merely register competing attractions.
1921 *Risk, Uncertainty and Profit*.

15 I have been increasingly moved to wonder whether my job is a job or a racket, whether economists, and particularly economic theorists, may not be in the position that Cicero, citing Cato, ascribed to the augurs of Rome—that they should cover their faces or burst into laughter when they met on the street.
1950 Collected in *Essays on the History and Method of Economics* (1956).

16 Sociology is the science of talk, and there is only one law in sociology. Bad talk drives out good.
Quoted in Paul A Samuelson *The Samuelson Sampler* (1973).

Knox, John c.1513–1572

Scottish Protestant reformer and architect of the Church of Scotland, whose single-minded determination to establish Presbyterianism brought him into conflict with the Catholic Queen Mary.

17 The Monstrous Regiment of Women.
1558 From the title of his pamphlet, *The First Blast of the Trumpet Against the Monstrous Regiment of Women.*

18 To promote a woman to bear rule, superiority, dominion, or empire above any realm, nation, or city, is repugnant to nature, contumely to God, a thing most contrarious to his revealed will and approved ordinance; and, finally, it is the subversion of good order, of all equity and justice.
1558 *First Blast of the Trumpet against the Monstrous Regiment of Women.*

19 If there be not in her, a proud mind, a crafty wit, and an indurate heart against God and his truth, my judgment faileth me.
1561 After his first meeting with Mary, Queen of Scots. *History of the Reformation in Scotland*, vol.2.

20 *Un homme avec Dieu est toujours dans la majorité.*
One man with God is always a majority.
Inscription on the Reformation Monument, Geneva, attributed to Knox.

Knox, Philander Chase 1853–1921

US lawyer and politician. He served as US Attorney General (1901–4) and Secretary of State (1909–13).

21 Oh, Mr President, do not let so great an achievement suffer from any taint of legality.
1903 Quoted in Tom Buckley *Violent Neighbours* (1983), alluding to Theodore Roosevelt's desire to find legal grounds for the seizure of the Panama Canal by the US.

Knox, Ronald Arbuthnot 1888–1957

English writer and Roman Catholic theologian. He wrote many theological works and Bible translations, and also detective novels.

22 There was once a man who said 'God
Must think it exceedingly odd
If he finds that this tree
Continues to be
When there's no-one about in the Quad.'
Attributed. Quoted in Langford Reed *Complete Limerick Book* (1924).
The limericks summarise Bishop George Berkeley's philosophy that everything is dependent at all times on the will of God.
► *See Anonymous 22:51.*

23 It is stupid of modern civilization to have given up believing in the devil, when he is the only explanation of it.
1939 *Let Dons Delight*, ch.8.

24 A loud noise at one end and no sense of responsibility at the other.
His definition of a baby. Attributed.

Knudsen, Semon Emil 1912–98

US automotive executive.

25 Before you tell someone how good you are, you must tell him how bad you used to be.
1959 In *Time* magazine, 25 May.

Koch, Edward I(rving) 1924–

US lawyer and Mayor of New York City (1978–89).

26 You're not a nice guy if you have a gun, even if you are a nice guy.
1980 In *Time*, 3 Mar.

27 Each diploma is a lighted match… Each one of you is a fuse.
1983 Addressing students at NY State University. In the *New York Times*, 10 Jun.

Koestler, Arthur 1905–83

Hungarian-born British writer and journalist. He wrote on science and parapsychology, and is best known for his anti-communist novel *Darkness at Noon* (1940). He and his wife committed suicide after he became terminally ill.

28 The definition of an individual was: a multitude of one million divided by one million.
1940 *Darkness at Noon*, 'The Grammatical Fiction', pt.2.

29 A writer's ambition should be…to trade a hundred contemporary readers for ten readers in ten years' time and for one reader in a hundred years.
1951 In the *New York Times Book Review*, 1 Apr.

30 Space-ships and time machines are no escape from the human condition. Let Othello subject Desdemona to a lie-detector test; his jealousy will still blind him to the evidence. Let Oedipus triumph over gravity; he won't triumph over his fate.
1953 'The Boredom of Fantasy', collected in *The Trail of the Dinosaur* (1955), pt.2.

31 Among all forms of mentation, verbal thinking is the most articulate, the most complex, and the most vulnerable to infectious diseases. It is liable to absorb whispered suggestions, and to incorporate them as hidden persuaders into the code.
1964 *The Act of Creation*.

32 Creativity in science could be described as the act of putting two and two together to make five.
1964 *The Act of Creation*.

33 The most persistent sound that reverberates through men's history is the beating of war drums.
1978 *Janus; A Summing Up*, 'Prologue: The New Calendar', sect.1.

Koffler, Murray 1924–

Canadian pharmacist and philanthropist.

34 Dress British, look Irish, think Yiddish.
His formula for success, quoted in Frank Rasky *Just a Simple Pharmacist: The Story of Murray Koffler, Builder of the Shoppers Drug Mart Empire* (1988).

Koh, Harold Hongju 1954–

US lawyer, Professor of International Law at Yale University.

35 Silence has a sound, and the sound is 'no.'
1991 Testimony to the US Senate Judiciary Committee on the presidential right to enter the Gulf War without congressional approval. Quoted by Senator Joseph R Biden, Jr in NPR broadcast, 10 Jan.

Kohl, Helmut 1930–

German statesman. He was Chancellor from 1982 to 1998.

36 The policy of European integration is in reality a question of war and peace in the 21st century.
1996 Speech, 2 Feb.

Kohlberg, Jerome, Jr 1925–

US investment banker.

37 An ethic is not an ethic, and a value not a value without some sacrifice for it. Something given up, something not gained.
Quoted in Sarah Bartlett *The Money Machine* (1991).

Kollwitz, Käthe 1867–1945

German sculptor and graphic artist. She had two sons, Peter and Hans. Peter was killed at the beginning of World War I, in 1914.

38 As you, the children of my body, have been my tasks, so too are my other works.
1915 Letter to her son Hans, 21 Feb.

39 I have never done any work cold… I have always worked with my blood, so to speak.
1917 Letter to her son Hans, 16 Apr.

The Koran

All quotations are taken from the Arthur J Arberry (1955) translation of The Koran. Line numbers refer to the standard numeration.

40 In the name of God, the Merciful, the Compassionate.
Praise belongs to God, the Lord of all Being,
the All-merciful, the All-compassionate
the Master of the Day of Doom.
Thee only we serve; to Thee alone we pray for succour
Guide us in the straight path,
the path of those whom Thou hast blessed,
not of those against whom Thou art wrathful,
nor of those who are astray.
Sura 1, 1.1–7.

41 We have sent among you, of yourselves, a Messenger, to recite Our signs to you and to purify you, and to teach you the Book and the Wisdom, and to teach you that you knew not. So remember Me, and I will remember you; and be thankful to Me; and be you not ungrateful towards Me.
Sura 2, 1.151–2.

42 O all you who believe, seek you help in patience and prayer; surely God is with the patient.
Sura 2, 1.153.

43 Surely in the creation of the heavens and the earth and the alternation of night and day and the ship that runs in the sea with profit to men, and the water God sends down from heaven therewith reviving the earth after it is dead and His scattering abroad in it all manner of crawling thing, and the turning about of the winds and the clouds compelled between heaven and earth—surely there are signs for a people having understanding.
Sura 2, 1.164.

44 It is not piety that you turn your faces to the East and to the West. True piety is this: to believe in God, and the Last Day, the angels, the Book, and the Prophets, to give of one's substance, however cherished, to kinsmen, and orphans, the needy, the traveller, beggars, and to ransom the slave, to perform the prayer, to pay the alms.
Sura 2, 1.177.

45 And fight in the way of God with those who fight with you, but aggress not: God loves not the aggressors.
Sura 2, 1.190.

46 God charges no soul save to its capacity; standing to account is what it has earned, and against its account what it has merited.
Sura 2, 1.286.

47 And when the angels said: 'Mary, God has chosen thee, and purified thee; He has chosen thee above all women.

Mary be obedient to thy Lord, prostrating and bowing before Him.'
Sura 3, l.42–3

48 You will not attain piety until you expend of what you love.
Sura 3, l.92.

49 It was by some mercy of God that thou wast gentle to them; hadst thou been harsh and hard of heart, they would have scattered from about thee. So pardon them, and pray forgiveness for them, and take counsel with them in the affair; and when thou art resolved, put thy trust in God.
Sura 3, l.159.

50 Every soul shall taste of death; you shall surely be paid in full your wages on the Day of Resurrection. Whosoever is removed from the Fire and admitted to Paradise, shall win the triumph. The present life is but the joy of delusion.
Sura 3, l.185.

51 Surely in the creation of the heavens and earth and in the alternation of night and day there are signs for men possessed of minds who remember God, standing and sitting and on their sides, and reflect upon the creation of the heavens and the earth. 'Our Lord, thou has not created this for vanity!'
Sura 3, l.191.

52 Mankind, fear your Lord, who created you of a single soul, and from it created its mate, and from the pair of them scattered abroad many men and women; and fear God by whom you demand one of another, and the wombs; surely God ever watches over you.
Sura 4, l.1.

53 God commands you to deliver trusts back to their owners.
Sura 4, l.58.

54 How is it with you, that you do not fight in the way of God, and for the men, women, and children who, being abased, say, 'Our Lord, bring us forth from this city whose people are evildoers, and appoint to us a protector from Thee?'
Sura 4, l.75.

55 O believers, be you securers of justice, witnesses for God, even though it be against yourselves, or your parents and kinsmen, whether the man be rich or poor.
Sura 4, l.135

56 We have revealed to thee as We revealed to Noah, and the Prophets after him, and We revealed to Abraham, Ishmael, Isaac, Jacob, and the Tribes, Jesus and Job, Jonah and Aaron and Solomon, and We gave to David Psalms, and Messengers We have already told thee of before, and Messengers We have not told thee of; and unto Moses God spoke directly—Messengers bearing good tidings, and warning, so that mankind might have no argument against God, after the Messengers; God is All-mighty, All-wise.
Sura 4, l.163–4.

57 People of the Book, go not beyond the bounds in your religion, and say not as to God but the truth. The Messiah, Jesus son of Mary, was only the Messenger of God, and His Word that He committed to Mary, and a spirit from Him. So believe in God and His Messengers, and say not, 'Three'. Refrain; better is it for you. God is only One God. Glory be to Him—that He should have a son! To Him belongs all that is in the heavens and the earth; God suffices for a guardian. The Messiah will not disdain to be a servant of God, neither the angels who are near stationed to Him.
Sura 4, l.171–2.

58 O believers, be you securers of justice, witnesses for God. Let not detestation for a people move you not to be equitable.
Sura 5, l.8.

59 No creature is there crawling on the earth, no bird flying with its wings, but they are nations like unto yourselves.
Sura 6, l.38.

60 With Him are the keys of the Unseen; none knows them but He. He knows what is in land and sea; not a leaf falls, but He knows it.
Sura 6, l.59.

61 It is God who splits the grain and the date-stone, brings forth the living from the dead; He brings for the dead too from the living. So that then is God; then how are you perverted? He splits the sky into dawn, and has made the night for a repose, and the sun and moon for a reckoning.
Sura 6, l.96–7.

62 Say: 'As for me, my Lord has guided me to a straight path, a right religion, the creed of Abraham, a man of pure faith; he was no idolater.' Say: 'My prayer, my ritual sacrifice, my living, my dying—all belongs to God, the Lord of all Being.'
Sura 6, l.162.

63 To every nation a term; when their term comes they shall not put it back by a single hour nor put it forward.
Sura 7, l.34.

64 Of the people of Moses there is a nation who guide by the truth, and by it act with justice.
Sura 7, l.159.

65 And when thy Lord took from the Children of Adam, from their loins, their seed, and made them testify touching themselves, 'Am I not your Lord?' They said, 'Yes, we testify'—lest you should say on the Day of Resurrection, 'As for us, we were heedless of this.'
Sura 7, l.172.

66 To God belong the Names Most Beautiful; so call Him by them.
Sura 7, l.180.

67 O believers, fear God, and be with the truthful ones.
Sura 9, l.119.

68 And God summons to the Abode of Peace.
Sura 10, l.26.

69 Surely God wrongs not men anything, but themselves men wrong.
Sura 10, l.45.

70 And the king said: 'I saw in a dream seven fat kine, and seven lean ones devouring them; likewise seven green ears of corn, and seven withered. My counsellors, pronounce to me upon my dream, if you are expounders of dreams.' 'A hotchpotch of nightmares!' they said.
Sura 12, l.43–4.

71 It is He who shows you the lightning, for fear and hope,

and produces the heavy clouds; the thunder proclaims His praise, and the angels, in awe of Him.
Sura 13, 1.13.

72 Hast thou not seen how God has struck a similitude? A good word is as a good tree—its roots are firm, and its branches are in heaven; it gives its produce every season by the leave of its Lord. So God strikes similitudes for men; haply they will remember. And the likeness of a corrupt word is as a corrupt tree—uprooted from the earth, having no stablishment. God confirms those who believe with the firm word, in the present life and in the world to come.
Sura 14, 1.24–7.

73 And when thy Lord said to the angels, 'See, I am creating a mortal of a clay of mud moulded. When I have shaped him, and breathed My spirit in him, fall you down, bowing before him!'
Sura 15, 1.28–9.

74 He created man of a sperm-drop; and behold, he is a manifest adversary.
Sura 16, 1.4.

75 Man prays for evil, as he prays for good; man is ever hasty.
Sura 17, 1.11.

76 Thy Lord has decreed you shall not serve any but Him, and to be good to parents, whether one or both of them attains old age with thee; say not to them 'Fie' neither chide them, but speak unto them words respectful, and lower to them the wing of humbleness out of mercy and say: 'My Lord, have mercy on them, as they raised me up when I was little.'
Sura 17, 1.23–4.

77 They will question thee concerning the Spirit. Say: 'The Spirit is of the bidding of my Lord. You have been given of knowledge nothing except a little.'
Sura 17, 1.85.

78 Say: 'If the sea were ink for the Words of my Lord, the sea would be spent before the Words of my Lord are spent.'
Sura 18, 1.110.

79 Whosoever turns away from My remembrance, his shall be a life of narrowness.
Sura 20, 1.124.

80 God is the Light of the heavens and the earth; the likeness of His Light is as a niche wherein is a lamp (the lamp in a glass, the glass as it were a glittering star) kindled from a Blessed Tree, an olive that is neither of the East nor of the West whose oil wellnigh would shine, even if no fire touched it; Light upon Light; (God guides to His Light whom He will). (And God strikes similitudes for men, and God has knowledge of everything.)
Sura 24, 1.35.

81 Hast thou not seen how that whatsoever is in the heavens and in the earth extols God, and the birds spreading their wings? Each—He knows its prayer and its extolling.
Sura 24, 1.41.

82 And of His signs is that He created for you, of yourselves, spouses, that you might repose in them, and He has set between you love and mercy.
Sura 30, 1.21.

83 And of His signs is the creation of the heavens and the earth and the variety of your tongues and hues.
Sura 30, 1.22.

84 Not a nation there is, but there has passed away in it a warner.
Sura 35, 1.24.

85 And when We bless man, he turns away and withdraws aside; but when evil visits him, he is full of endless prayers.
Sura 41, 1.51.

86 Hast thou seen him who has taken his caprice to be his God?
Sura 45, 1.23.

87 They say: 'There is nothing but our present life; we die, and we live, and nothing but Time destroys us.' Of that they have no knowledge; they merely conjecture.
Sura 45, 1.24.

88 Find not fault with one another, neither revile one another by nicknames.
Sura 49, 1.11.

89 O mankind, We have created you male and female, and appointed you races and tribes, that you may know one another. Surely the noblest among you in the sight of God is the most godfearing of you. God is All-knowing, All-aware.
Sura 49, 1.13.

90 Be not as those who forgot God, and so He caused them to forget their souls.
Sura 59, 1.18.

91 They fulfil their vows, and fear a day whose evil is upon the wing; they give food, for the love of Him, to the needy, the orphan, the captive: 'We feed you only for the Face of God; we desire no recompense from you, no thankfulness.'
Sura 76, 1.7–9.

92 But as for him who feared the Station of his Lord and forbade the soul its caprice, surely Paradise shall be the refuge.
Sura 79, 1.40.

93 When the sun shall be darkened, when the stars shall be thrown down, when the mountains shall be set moving, when the pregnant camels shall be neglected, when the savage beasts shall be mustered, when the seas shall be set boiling, when the souls shall be coupled, when the buried infant shall be asked for what sin she was slain, when the scrolls shall be unrolled, when heaven shall be stripped off, when Hell shall be set blazing, when Paradise shall be brought nigh, then shall a soul know what it has produced.
Sura 81, 1–14.

94 No! I swear by the slinkers, the runners, the sinkers, by the night swarming, by the dawn sighing, truly this is the word of a noble Messenger.
Sura 81, 15–19.

95 By heaven of the returning rain, by earth splitting with verdure, surely it is a decisive word; it is no merriment.
Sura 86, 1.11–14.

96 By the snorting chargers, by the strikers of fire, by the dawn raiders blazing a trail of dust, cleaving there with a host! Surely Man is ungrateful to his Lord.

Sura 100, 1–6.

97 Woe to those that pray and are heedless of their prayers, to those who make display and refuse charity.
Sura 107, 1.4–7.

Korda, Sir Alexander 1893–1956

Hungarian-born British film producer. He worked in Vienna, Berlin and Hollywood before coming to Britain in the early 1930s where he founded London Film Productions and the Denham Studios.

98 One can be unhappy before eating caviar, even after, but at least not *during*.
1979 In *Newsweek*, 26 Nov.

99 Inside every banker, even the governor of the Bank of England, there lies a gambling streak. In me, they recognise one of their own kind.
Quoted in Michael Wilding and Pamela Wilcox *Apple Sauce* (1982).

1 It's not enough to be Hungarian, you must have talent too.
Attributed. The predominance of Eastern European employees at Denham Studios in the 1930s was a topical joke.

Korn, Arthur 1891–1978

German-born architect, planner and teacher.

2 A new glass age has begun, which is equal in beauty to the old one of Gothic windows.
1926 *Glas im Bau und als Gebrauchsgegenstand* (translated as *Glass in Modern Architecture*, 1967).

Korthals, Robert 1933–

Canadian bank president (1981–95).

3 The easiest way to steal from a bank is to own one.
Quoted by Diane Francis in *Controlling Interest: Who Owns Canada?* (1986).

Kosinski, Jerzy Nikodem 1933–91

Polish-born US novelist. His best-known books are *The Painted Bird* (1965) and *Being There* (1971).

4 I rent everything, other than the gift of life itself, which was given to me without any predictable lease, a gift that can be withdrawn at any time.
1991 Interview given three days before his suicide, in the *Weekend Guardian*, 25–6 May.

Kramer, Larry (Lawrence) 1935–

US novelist, playwright and screenwriter. He is best known for his controversial gay novel *Faggots* (1978), and his plays dealing with AIDS, notably *The Normal Heart* (1985).

5 We're all going to go crazy, living this epidemic every minute, while the rest of the world goes on out there, all around us, as if nothing is happening, going on with their own lives and not knowing what it's like, what we're going through. We're living through war, but where they're living it's peacetime, and we're all in the same country.
1985 Ned speaking of gay men with AIDS. *The Normal Heart*, act 2, sc.11.

Krasna, Norman 1909–84

US playwright and screenwriter. He won an Academy Award for *Princess O'Rourke* (1943). Other films include *Bachelor Mother* (1939) and *Indiscreet* (1958).

6 How dare he make love to me and not be a married man?
1958 Line delivered by Ingrid Bergman in *Indiscreet*.

Kraus, Karl 1874–1936

Austrian critic and dramatist, publisher and sole writer of the radical satirical magazine *Die Fackel* ('The Torch', 1899–1936). He wrote the apocalyptic satirical play *The Last Days of Mankind* (1919), and collections of aphorisms.

7 Today's literature: prescriptions written by patients.
Aphorism collected in Heinrich Fischer (ed) *Beim Wort genommen* (1955). Translated by Harry Zohn in *Half-truths and one-and-a-half truths* (1986).

8 Why didn't Eternity have this deformed age aborted ? Its birthmark is the stamp of a newspaper, its medium is printer's ink, and in its veins flows ink.
Aphorism collected in Heinrich Fischer (ed) *Beim Wort genommen* (1955). Translated by Harry Zohn in *Half-truths and one-and-a-half truths* (1986).

9 The making of a journalist: no ideas and the ability to express them.
Aphorism collected in Heinrich Fischer (ed) *Beim Wort genommen* (1955). Translated by Harry Zohn in *Half-truths and one-and-a-half truths* (1986).

10 A historian is often only a journalist facing backwards.
Aphorism collected in Heinrich Fischer (ed) *Beim Wort genommen* (1955). Translated by Harry Zohn in *Half-truths and one-and-a-half truths* (1986).

11 How is the world ruled and led to war? Diplomats lie to journalists and believe these lies when they see them in print.
Aphorism collected in Heinrich Fischer (ed) *Beim Wort genommen* (1955). Translated by Harry Zohn in *Half-truths and one-and-a-half truths* (1986).

12 One ought to acknowledge the significance for mankind of the simultaneous invention of gunpowder and printer's ink.
Aphorism collected in Heinrich Fischer (ed) *Beim Wort genommen* (1955). Translated by Harry Zohn in *Half-truths and one-and-a-half truths* (1986).

Krishnamurti, Jiddu 1895–1986

Indian-born mystic and spiritual teacher. The theosophist Annie Besant in 1925 proclaimed him Messiah and from then on he travelled the world, teaching a way of life free from the conditioning of culture, race or religion.

13 I maintain that truth is a pathless land, and you cannot approach it by any path whatsoever, by any religion, by any sect.
1929 Speech in Holland. Quoted in Terry Lynn Taylor *Messengers of Light*, ch.32.

14 The authority of a belief imposed by religion surely destroys the discovery of reality. One relies on authority because one is afraid to stand alone.
1970 BBC interview, 7 Dec.

Kristol, Irving 1920–

US economist and academic, often considered as the founder of neoconservatism.

15 History does not provide us with any instance of a society that repressed the economic liberties of the

individual while being solicitous of his other liberties.
1978 *Two Cheers for Capitalism*, introduction.

16 The fact of affluence is indisputable… Nevertheless, not many of us *feel* that well off. The instinct for contentment seems to have withered even as our economic condition has radically improved.
1978 *Two Cheers for Capitalism*, ch.1.

17 The elitist attitude is basically suspicious of, and hostile to, the market precisely because the market is so vulgarly democratic—one dollar, one vote.
1978 *Two Cheers for Capitalism*, ch.2.

Kroc, Ray(mond) A 1902–84

US entrepreneur, developer of the McDonald's fast-food chain.

18 Luck is a dividend of sweat. The more you sweat, the luckier you get.
1988 Quoted by Penny Moser 'The McDonald's Mystique', in *Fortune*, 4 Jul.

19 If they were drowning to death, I would put a hose in their mouth.
1988 On competitors. In *Fortune*, 4 Jul.

Kronecker, Leopold 1823–91

German mathematician, who worked in algebraic number theory and the foundations of analysis, and lectured widely. He held that mathematics should be based on whole numbers, rejecting the infinite, irrational and imaginary.

20 God made the integers, man made the rest.
Quoted in F Cajori *A History of Mathematics* (1919).

Kronenberger, Louis 1904–80

US writer, lecturer and critic. His books include novels and autobiographical reminiscences as well as critical works on literature and culture, and biographies.

21 Kings and Desperate Men.
1942 Title of book on 18c England.

22 The trouble with our age is that it is all signpost and no destination.
1954 *Company Manners*, 'The Spirit of The Age'.

Kruger, Paulus 1825–1904

South African soldier and statesman, President of the Transvaal (1883–1902) and head of the provisional government in the first Boer War. During the second Boer War he was forced to flee to Europe, and he died in Switzerland.

23 They have asked me for my trousers, and I have given them; for my coat, and I have given that also; now they want my life, and that I cannot give.
1899 Speech in the Raad, 7 Sep, at the beginning of the second Boer War, 1899–1902.

Krugman, Paul R 1953–

US economist and columnist, Professor of Economics and International Affairs at Princeton University.

24 The trouble with poverty, as an issue, is that it has basically exhausted the patience of the general public.
1992 *The Age of Diminished Expectations*.

25 Given that the deepest problem with the US economy is slow productivity growth, it is difficult to argue for tax increases that might reduce incentives… There seems to be a public consensus that Donald Trump is the price of progress.
1992 *The Age of Diminished Expectations*.

26 The exchange rate is only a statistic, not a symbol of national honor and virility.
1994 Quoted in the *New York Times*, 26 Jun.

Krutch, Joseph Wood 1893–1970

US author, teacher and critic. He is the author of *The Modern Temper* (1929) and *The Measure of Man* (1954).

27 A tragic writer does not have to believe in God, but he must believe in man.
1929 *The Modern Temper*, 'The Tragic Fallacy'.

28 Electronic calculators can solve problems which the man who made them cannot solve; but no government subsidized commission of engineers and physicists could create a worm.
1949 *The Twelve Seasons*, 'February'.

29 The most serious charge which can be brought against New England is not Puritanism but February.
1949 *The Twelve Seasons*, 'February'.

30 Cats seem to go on the principle that it never does any harm to ask for what you want.
1949 *The Twelve Seasons*, 'February'.

Kubrick, Stanley 1928–99

US screenwriter, film producer and director. His films include *Spartacus* (1960), *2001: A Space Odyssey* (1969), the controversial *A Clockwork Orange* (1971) and *Full Metal Jacket* (1987).

31 Gentlemen, you can't fight in here. This is the war room.
1963 *Dr Strangelove: or How I stopped worrying and learned to love the bomb* (with Terry Southern and Peter George).

32 The great nations have always acted like gangsters, and the small nations like prostitutes.
1963 In *The Guardian*.

33 The very meaninglessness of life forces man to create his own meaning. If it can be written or thought, it can be filmed.
Quoted in *Halliwell's Filmgoer's and Video Viewer's Companion* (1999).

Kuhn, Maggie 1905–95

US writer and social reformer, founder of the Gray Panthers.

34 The ultimate indignity is to be given a bedpan by a stranger who calls you by your first name.
1978 In the *Observer*, 20 Aug.

Kuhn, Thomas S(amuel) 1922–96

US historian and philosopher of science. His major work is *The Structure of Scientific Revolutions* (1962), a cornerstone of modern approaches to the philosophy and history of science.

35 Effective research scarcely begins before a scientific community thinks it has acquired firm answers to questions like the following: What are the fundamental entities of which the universe is composed? How do these interact with each other and with the senses? What questions may legitimately be asked about such entities and what techniques employed in seeking solutions?
1962 *The Structure of Scientific Revolutions*.

Kundera, Milan 1929–

Czech-born French novelist.

36 The Unbearable Lightness of Being.
1984 Title of novel.

Küng, Hans 1928–

Swiss Roman Catholic theologian. His questioning of received doctrine aroused controversy, and the Vatican withdrew his authority to teach as a Catholic theologian in 1979. He defended himself in *Why I Am Still A Christian* (1987).

37 A Church which abandons the truth abandons itself.
Die Kirche (translated by Ray and Rosalee Ockenden as *The Church*, 1967).

Kunitz, Stanley Jasspon 1905–

US poet and editor, whose style is at once intellectual and passionate. His poetry collections include *Selected Poems, 1928–1958* (1958, Pulitzer Prize winner) and *Next-to-Last Things: New Poems and Essays* (1985). In 2000 he became the US Poet Laureate.

38 A poem is at once the most primitive and most sophisticated use of language, but my emphasis is on the former.
1985 *Next-to-Last Things*, 'The Wisdom of the Body'.

39 The deepest thing I know is that I am living and dying at once, and my conviction is to report that dialogue.
1987 In the *New York Times*, 11 Mar.

Kuralt, Charles 1934–97

US writer and broadcaster.

40 It takes an earthquake to remind us that we walk on the crust of an unfinished earth.
1994 In *Sunday Morning*, CBS T V, 23 Jan.

Kurosawa, Akira 1910–98

Japanese film director and winner of numerous international awards for his films. Best known in the West for his full-blooded adaptations of Shakespeare.

41 Like a steak spread with butter and topped with good, rich, broiled eels.
1965 His concept of a great film. In *Japan Quarterly*, vol.12.

42 The Japanese see self-assertion as immoral and self-sacrifice as the sensible course to take in life.
1982 *Something like an Autobiography.*

Kushner, Tony 1956–

US playwright, whose highly political plays include the two-part *Angels in America* (1991–2, Pulitzer Prize 1993), on the effects of AIDS in New York.

43 I wanted to attempt something of ambition and size even if that meant I might be accused of straying too close to ambition's ugly twin, pretentiousness.
1993 Of his *Angels in America*, written in two parts. In the *New York Times*, 21 Nov.

Kurz, Mordecai 1934–

US economist, Professor at Stanford University.

44 There is only one truth, and many opinions. Therefore, most people are wrong most of the time.
1985 In *Fortune*, 3 Apr.

Kyd, Thomas 1558–94

English dramatist.

45 In time the savage bull sustains the yoke;
In time all haggard hawks will stoop to lure;
In time small wedges cleave the hardest oak,
In time the flint is pierced with softest shower,
And she in time will fall from her disdain,
And rue the sufferance of your friendly pain.
c.1589 *The Spanish Tragedy*, act 2, sc.1.

46 Where words prevail not, violence prevails;
But gold doth more than either of them both.
c.1589 *The Spanish Tragedy*, act 2, sc.1.

47 Oh eyes, no eyes, but fountains fraught with tears;
Oh life, no life, but lively form of death;
Oh world, no world, but mass of public wrongs.
c.1589 *The Spanish Tragedy*, act 3, sc.2.

48 I'll trust myself, myself shall be my friend.
c.1589 *The Spanish Tragedy*, act 3, sc.2.

49 Thus must we toil in other men's extremes,
That know not how to remedy our own.
c.1589 *The Spanish Tragedy*, act 3, sc.6.

50 For what's a play without a woman in it?
c.1589 *The Spanish Tragedy*, act 4, sc.1.

Labé, Louise 1526–66

A poet of the École Lyonnaise who wrote sonnets, elegies and a prose work, *Débat de Folie et d'Amour* (1555, 'Debate Between Folly and Love').

51 *Quelque rigueur qui loge en votre coeur,*
Amour s'en peut un jour rendre vainqueur.
That little harshness which resides in your heart,
Love will vanquish someday.
1555 *Elégies*, no.1.

52 *Où donc es-tu, ô âme bien-aimée?*
Where are you now, oh soul desired?
1555 *Sonnets*, no.6.

53 *Je vis, je meurs; je me brûle et me noie.*
I live, I die; I am on fire and I drown.
1555 *Sonnets*, no.8.

54 *Ne reprenez, dame, si j'ai aimé,*
Si j'ai senti mille torches ardentes,
Mille travaux, mille douleurs mordantes,
Si, en pleurant, j'ai mon temps consumé.
Do not blame me, madam, if I loved,
If I felt one thousand burning torches,
One thousand labours, or one thousand scathing pains,
If, in crying, I spent all my time.
1555 *Sonnets*, no.24.

Labouchère, Henry Du Pré 1831–1912

English radical journalist and politician. A Liberal MP (1865–8, 1880–1906), in 1876 he founded the investigative journal *Truth*.

55 Nothing has conduced more to shake that decent respect for the living symbol of the state that goes by the name of royalty than the ever-recurring rattle of the money box.
1884 In the *Fortnightly Review*, Feb.

La Bruyère, Jean de 1645–96

French moralist author who tutored Louis de Bourbon, grandson of the Great Condé. His *Caractères de Théophraste* (1688) made his reputation but won him many enemies.

56 *Tout est dit, et l'on vient trop tard depuis plus de sept mille ans qu'il y a des hommes et qui pensent.*
Everything has been said. After seven thousand years of human thought, we have come too late.
1688 *Les Caractères ou les mœurs de ce siècle*, 'Des ouvrages de l'esprit', no.1.

57 *C'est un métier que de faire un livre, comme de faire une pendule; il faut plus que de l'esprit pour être auteur.*
It is as much a trade to write a book as it is to make a watch; it takes more than wit to make an author.
1688 *Les Caractères ou les mœurs de ce siècle*, 'Des ouvrages de l'esprit', no.3.

58 *Une belle femme qui a les qualités d'un honnête homme est ce qu'il y a au monde d'un commerce plus délicieux: l'on trouve en elle tout le mérite des deux sexes.*
A beautiful woman who has the qualities of a gentleman is the most pleasing person in all the world: one finds in her all the merit of both sexes.
1688 *Les Caractères ou les mœurs de ce siècle*, 'Des femmes', no.13.

59 *Les femmes sont extrêmes: elles sont meilleures ou pires que les hommes.*
Women are all in extremes: they are either better or worse than men.
1688 *Les Caractères ou les mœurs de ce siècle*, 'Des femmes', no.53.

60 *Un homme est plus fidèle au secret d'autrui qu'au sien propre; une femme au contraire garde mieux son secret que celui d'autrui.*
A man keeps another person's secret better than his own; a woman, on the contrary, keeps her own secrets better than those of others.
1688 *Les Caractères ou les mœurs de ce siècle*, 'Des femmes', no.58.

61 *Une femme insensible est celle qui n'a pas encore vu celui qu'elle doit aimer.*
A dispassionate woman is one who has yet to see the one she should love.
1688 *Les Caractères ou les mœurs de ce siècle*, 'Des femmes', no.81.

62 *Le temps, qui fortifie les amitiés, affaiblit l'amour.*
Time, which strengthens friendships, weakens love.
1688 *Les Caractères ou les mœurs de ce siècle*, 'Du cœur', no.4.

63 *L'amour et l'amitié s'excluent l'un l'autre.*
Love and friendship exclude one another.
1688 *Les Caractères ou les mœurs de ce siècle*, 'Du cœur', no.7.

64 *L'amour qui naît subitement est le plus long à guérir.*
Love which strikes suddenly takes the longest to cure.
1688 *Les Caractères ou les mœurs de ce siècle*, 'Du cœur', no.12.

65 *Les amours meurent par le dégoût, et l'oubli les enterre.*
Loves die from disgust, and forgetting buries them.
1688 *Les Caractères ou les mœurs de ce siècle*, 'Du cœur', no.32.

66 *Qu'il est difficile d'être content de quelqu'un!*
How difficult it is to be happy with someone!
1688 *Les Caractères ou les mœurs de ce siècle*, 'Du cœur', no.65.

67 *L'esclave n'a qu'un maître; l'ambitieux en a autant qu'il y a des gens utiles à sa fortune.*
A slave has but one master; an ambitious person has as many as he needs to make his fortune.
1688 *Les Caractères ou les mœurs de ce siècle*, 'Du cœur', no.70.

68 *Il fera demain ce qu'il fait aujourd'hui et ce qu'il fit hier; et il meurt ainsi après avoir vécu.*
What he does tomorrow will be what he did today and yesterday; and he shall die after having lived this way.
1688 *Les Caractères ou les mœurs de ce siècle*, 'De la ville', no.12.

69 *La vie est courte et ennuyeuse; elle se passe toute à désirer.*
Life is short and bothersome: all we do is desire what we do not have.
1688 *Les Caractères ou les mœurs de ce siècle*, 'De l'homme', no.19.

70 *Si la vie est misérable, elle est pénible à supporter; si elle est heureuse, il est horrible de la perdre. L'un revient à l'autre.*
If life is miserable, it is difficult to endure; if it is happy, it is horrible to lose. They come to the same thing.
1688 *Les Caractères ou les mœurs de ce siècle*, 'De l'homme', no.33.

71 *A parler humainement, la mort a un bel endroit, qui est de mettre fin à la vieillesse.*
To speak humanely, death has a useful function: It puts an end to old age.
1688 *Les Caractères ou les mœurs de ce siècle*, 'De l'homme', no.45.

72 *Il n'y a pour l'homme que trois événements: naître, vivre et mourir. Il ne se sent pas naître, il souffre à mourir, et il oublie de vivre.*
There are only three great events for a person: to be born, to live and to die. He does not feel his own birth, he suffers upon death and he forgets to live.
1688 *Les Caractères ou les mœurs de ce siècle*, 'De l'homme', no.48.

73 *Les enfants sont hautains, dédaigneux, colères, envieux, curieux, intéressés, paresseux, volages, timides, intempérants, menteurs, dissimulés…ils ne veulent point souffrir de mal, et aiment à en faire: ils sont déjà des hommes.*
Children are haughty, disdainful, angry, envious, curious, interested, lazy, fickle, shy, self-indulgent, liars, deceivers…they do not wish to suffer evil, but like to do evil: they are already adults.
1688 *Les Caractères ou les mœurs de ce siècle*, 'De l'homme', no.50.

74 *Les enfants n'ont ni passé ni avenir, et, ce qui ne nous arrive guère, ils jouissent du présent.*
Children have neither past nor future. They live in the present, something which rarely happens to us.
1688 *Les Caractères ou les mœurs de ce siècle*, 'De l'homme', no.51.

75 *Il y a une espèce de honte d'être heureux à la vue de certaines misères.*
There is a type of shame which comes from being happy at another's distress.
1688 *Les Caractères ou les mœurs de ce siècle*, 'De l'homme', no.82.

76 *La plupart des hommes emploient la meilleure partie de leur vie à rendre l'autre misérable.*
Most people spend the greater part of their lives making others miserable.
1688 *Les Caractères ou les mœurs de ce siècle*, 'De l'homme', no.102.

77 *Le flatteur n'a pas assez bonne opinion de soi ni des autres.*
The flatterer does not have a good opinion of himself or of others.
1688 *Les Caractères ou les mœurs de ce siècle*, 'Des jugements', no.90.

78 *Ceux qui emploient mal leur temps sont les premiers à se plaindre de sa brièveté.*
Those who make poor use of their time are the first to complain of its brevity.
1688 *Les Caractères ou les mœurs de ce siècle*, 'Des jugements', no.101.

79 *L'impossibilité où je suis de prouver que Dieu n'est pas me découvre son existence.*
The impossibility I find myself in to prove that God does not exist proves to me his existence.
1688 *Les Caractères ou les mœurs de ce siècle*, 'Des esprits forts', no.13.

Laclos, Pierre-Ambroise Choderlos de 1741–1803

French artillery officer, best known for his study of human vices and virtues in *Les Liaisons dangereuses* (1782), as well as his advocacy of women's education in *De l'Education des femmes* (1785).

80 *J'ai bien besoin d'avoir cette femme, pour me sauver du ridicule d'en être amoureux.*
I need to possess this woman in order to save myself from the absurdity of being in love with her.
1782 *Les Liaisons dangereuses*, letter 4.

81 *Nos deux passions favorites, la gloire de la défense et le plaisir de la défaite.*
The glory of the resistance and the pleasure of the defeat are our two favourite passions.
1782 *Les Liaisons dangereuses*, letter 10.

82 *Il ne faut se permettre d'excès qu'avec les gens qu'on veut quitter bientôt.*
We should never permit ourselves to behave in excess except with those whom we will leave soon.
1782 *Les Liaisons dangereuses*, letter 10.

83 *En vérité, plus je vis, et plus je suis tenté de croire qu'il n'y a que vous et moi dans le monde, qui valions quelque chose.*
In truth, the more I live, the more I am tempted to believe that only you and I are of any value at all in the world.
1782 *Les Liaisons dangereuses*, letter 100.

84 *J'avoue bien que l'argent ne fait pas le bonheur; mais il faut avouer aussi qu'il le facilite beaucoup.*
I will admit that money does not bring happiness, but it must also be admitted that it facilitates much.
1782 *Les Liaisons dangereuses*, letter 104.

85 *Ce n'est pas assez pour moi de la posséder, je veux qu'elle se livre.*
It's not enough to possess her. I want her to abandon herself.
1782 *Les Liaisons dangereuses*, letter 110.

86 *La haine est toujours plus clairvoyante et plus ingénieuse que l'amitié.*
Hate is always more clairvoyant and ingenious than friendship.
1782 *Les Liaisons dangereuses*, letter 113.

87 *Pour les hommes, l'infidélité n'est pas l'inconstance.*
For men, infidelity is not inconstancy.
1782 *Les Liaisons dangereuses*, letter 134.

88 *On s'ennuie de tout, mon Ange, c'est une loi de la Nature; ce n'est pas ma faute.*
One gets bored of everything, my Angel, it's a law of nature; it's not my fault.
1782 *Les Liaisons dangereuses*, letter 141.

89 *Quand une femme frappe dans le coeur d'une autre, elle manque rarement de trouver l'endroit sensible, et la blessure est incurable.*
When one woman touches another's heart, she rarely has trouble finding the sensitive spot and the wound is incurable.
1782 *Les Liaisons dangereuses*, letter 145.

90 *Apprenez qu'on ne sort de l'esclavage que par une grande révolution.*
Learn that one never escapes slavery except by a great revolution.
1785 *De l'Éducation des femmes*.

Ladd, Alan 1913–64

US film star, best known for *The Blue Dahlia* (1946), *The Great Gatsby* (1949) and *Shane* (1953).

91 A man's gotta do what a man's gotta do.
1953 Line delivered in *Shane* (screenplay by A B Guthrie).

La Fayette, Marie-Madeleine Pioche de La Vergne 1634–93

French novelist. Although married to François Motier, she lived with La Rochefoucauld.

92 *L'amour était toujours mêlé aux affaires et les affaires à l'amour.*
Love has always mixed with politics and politics with love.
1678 *La Princesse de Clèves*.

93 *On persuade aisément une vérité agréable.*
It is easy to persuade one with an agreeable truth.
1678 *La Princesse de Clèves*.

94 *Les passions peuvent me conduire; mais elles ne sauraient m'aveugler.*
Passions can lead me on, but never blind me.
1678 *La Princesse de Clèves*.

95 *La honte est la plus violente de toutes les passions.*
Shame is the most violent of all the passions.
1678 *La Princesse de Clèves*.

La Fontaine, Jean de 1621–95

French poet and moralist. His *Contes et nouvelles en vers* ('Tales and Novels in Verse', 1665) was followed by *Fables choisies mises en vers* ('Selected Fables in Verse', 1668–94).

96 *Je me sers d'animaux pour instruire les hommes.*
I use animals to educate people.
1668 *Fables, à Monseigneur le Dauphin.*

97 *Nous n'écoutons d'instincts que ceux qui sont les nôtres,*
Et ne croyons le mal que quand il est venu.
We only trust our own instincts
And only believe the worst when it comes true.
1668 *Fables*, pt.1, no.8, 'L'hirondelle et les petits oiseaux'.

98 *La raison du plus fort est toujours la meilleure.*
The reason of the strongest is always the best.
1668 *Fables*, pt.1, no.10, 'Le loup et l'agneau'.

99 *Il accusait toujours les miroirs d'être faux.*
He was always blaming mirrors for being untrue.
1668 *Fables*, pt.1, no.11, 'L'homme et son image'.

1 *Plutôt souffrir que mourir,*
C'est la devise des hommes.
It is better to suffer than to die.
That is the motto of mankind.
1668 *Fables*, pt.1, no.16, 'La mort et le bûcheron'.

2 *Je plie, et ne romps pas.*
I bend but do not break.
1668 *Fables*, pt.1, no.22, 'Le chêne et le roseau'. The reed speaks to the oak tree.

3 *Le mensonge et les vers de tout temps sont amis.*
Lies and literature have always been friends.
1668 *Fables*, pt.2, no.1, 'Contre ceux qui ont le goût difficile'.

4 *Patience et longueur de temps*
Font plus que force ni que rage.
Patience and longevity
Are worth more than force and rage.
1668 *Fables*, pt.2, no.11, 'Le lion et le rat'.

5 *C'est double plaisir de tromper le trompeur.*
It's doubly sweet to deceive the deceiver.
1668 *Fables*, pt.2, no.15, 'Le coq et le renard'.

6 *Tout au monde est mêlé d'amertume et de charmes:*
La guerre a ses douceurs, l'hymen a ses alarmes.
Everything in the world is a mixture of the sweet and the sour:
War has its own sweetness and marriage its alarms.
1668 *Fables*, pt.3, no.1, 'Le meunier, son fils et l'âne'.

7 *En toute chose il faut considérer la fin.*
One must consider the end in everything.
1668 *Fables*, pt.3, no.5, 'Le renard et le bouc'.

8 *Amour est un étrange maître.*
Heureux qui peut ne le connaître
Que par récit, lui ni ses coups!
Love is a cruel conqueror.
Happy is he who knows him through stories
And not by his blows!
1668 *Fables*, pt.4, no.1, 'Le lion amoureux'.

9 *Le geai paré des plumes du paon.*
A bluejay in peacock feathers.
1668 *Fables*, pt.4, no.9, 'Le geai paré des plumes du paon'.

10 *Chacun se dit ami; mais fol qui s'y repose:*
Rien n'est plus commun que ce nom,
Rien n'est plus rare que la chose.
Everyone calls himself a friend; foolish is he who believes it:
Nothing is more common than the name friend,
And nothing is more rare than the real thing.
1668 *Fables*, pt.4, no.17, 'Parole de Socrate'.

11 *Ne possédait pas l'or; mais l'or le possédait.*
He never owned his gold; his gold owned him.
1668 *Fables*, pt.4, no.20, 'L'avare qui a perdu son trésor'.

12 *Une ample Comédie à cent actes divers,*
Et dont la scène est l'Univers.
A grand comedy in one hundred different acts,
On the stage of the universe.
1668 *Fables*, pt.5, no.1, 'Le bûcheron et Mercure'.

13 *Un auteur gâte tout quand il veut trop bien faire.*
An author spoils everything when he wants too much to do good.
1668 *Fables*, pt.5, no.1, 'Le bûcheron et Mercure'.

14 *Garde-toi, tant que tu vivras,*
De juger des gens sur la mine.
Beware as long as you live,
Of judging others according to appearance alone.
1668 *Fables*, pt.6, no.5, 'Le cochet, le chat et le souriceau'.

15 *Sur les ailes du Temps la tristesse s'envole.*
Grief is carried off by the wings of time.
1668 *Fables*, pt.6, no.21, 'La jeune veuve'.

16 *Quand l'eau courbe un bâton, ma raison la redresse.*
When water curves a stick, my reason straightens it out.
1668 *Fables*, pt.7, no.18, 'Un animal dans la lune'.

17 *Fortune aveugle suit aveugle hardiesse.*
Blind fortune pursues inconsiderate rashness.
1668 *Fables*, pt.10, no.13, 'Les deux aventuriers et le talisman'.

18 *Tout est mystère dans l'Amour.*
Everything about love is a mystery.
1668 *Fables*, pt.12, no.14, 'L'Amour et la folie'.

19 *Tous chemins vont à Rome.*
All roads lead to Rome.
1668 *Fables*, pt.12, no.29, 'Le juge arbitre, l'hospitalier, et le solitaire'.

Lagerfeld, Karl 1938–

German-born French fashion designer.

20 She never wanted to be sexy, but in those days ambitions were different, and she was the most ambitious of them all.
1993 Of Wallis Simpson, Duchess of Windsor. In the *New York Times*, 19 Sep.

21 Fashion is the image of an age and can tells its story better than a speech.
1994 In the *Daily Telegraph*, 20 Oct.

Lamartine, Alphonse Marie Louis de 1790–1869

French poet and revolutionary politician, a minister in the provisional government after 1848. His best-known work is his first volume of lyrical poems, *Méditations poétiques* (1820). His historical works include the *Histoire de la Révolution de 1848* (1849).

22 *Un seul être vous manque, et tout est dépeuplé.*
One being only is wanting, and your whole world is bereft of people.
1820 *Méditations poétiques*, 'L'Isolement'.

23 France is revolutionary or she is nothing at all. The revolution of 1789 is her political religion.
1847 *Histoire des Girondins.*

24 At its birth, the republic gave voice to three words—Liberty, Equality, Fraternity! If Europe is wise and just, each of those words signifies Peace.
1848 *A Manifesto to the Powers*, 4 Mar.

Lamb, Lady Caroline 1785–1828

English novelist and aristocrat, daughter of the Earl of Bessborough and wife of Prime Minister William Lamb, 2nd Viscount Melbourne, notorious for her nine-month devotion (1812–3) to Lord Byron.

25 Mad, bad, and dangerous to know.
1812 Of Byron. Journal entry, Mar, after meeting the poet at a ball. Quoted in Elizabeth Jenkins *Lady Caroline Lamb* (1932), ch.6.

Lamb, Charles 1775–1834

English essayist and critic. Together with his sister Mary, he wrote *Tales from Shakespeare* (1807), and his *Specimens of English Dramatic Poets* (1808) contributed to a revival of interest in Elizabethan plays. As 'Elia', he contributed essays to the *London Magazine* from 1820.

26 I have something more to do than feel.
1796 Letter to Samuel Taylor Coleridge, 27 Sep, on the death of his mother at his sister Mary's hands. Collected in E W Marrs *Letters of Charles and Mary Lamb*, vol.1 (1975).

27 Cultivate simplicity, Coleridge.
1796 Letter to Samuel Taylor Coleridge, 8 Nov. Collected in E W Marrs *Letters of Charles and Mary Lamb*, vol.1 (1975).

28 The man must have a rare recipe for melancholy, who can be dull in Fleet Street.
1802 Letter to Thomas Manning, 15 Feb. Collected in E W Marrs *Letters of Charles and Mary Lamb*, vol.2 (1975).

29 Nursed amid her noise, her crowds, her beloved smoke—what have I been doing all my life, if I have not lent out my heart with usury to such scenes?
1802 Of London. Letter to Thomas Manning, 15 Feb. Collected in E W Marrs *Letters of Charles and Mary Lamb*, vol.2 (1975).

30 Gone before
To that unknown and silent shore.
1803 'Hester', stanza 7.

31 Nothing puzzles me more than time and space; and yet nothing troubles me less, as I never think about them.
1806 Letter to Thomas Manning, 2 Jan. Collected in E W Marrs (ed) *Letters of Charles and Mary Lamb*, vol.3 (1978).

32 A child's a plaything for an hour.
1809 'Parental Recollections'. This is often attributed to his sister Mary.

33 Anything awful makes me laugh.
1815 Letter to Robert Southey, 9 Aug. Collected in E W Marrs (ed) *Letters of Charles and Mary Lamb*, vol.3 (1978).

34 This very night I am going to leave off tobacco! Surely there must be some other world in which this unconquerable purpose shall be realized.
1815 Letter to Thomas Manning, 26 Dec. Collected in E W Marrs (ed) *Letters of Charles and Mary Lamb*, vol.3 (1978).

35 An Archangel a little damaged.
1816 Of Coleridge. Letter to Wordsworth, 26 Apr. Collected in E W Marrs (ed) *Letters of Charles and Mary Lamb*, vol.3 (1978).

36 The rogue gives you Love Powders, and then a strong horse drench to bring 'em off your stomach that they mayn't hurt you.
1816 Of Coleridge. Letter to Wordsworth, 23 Sep. Collected in E W Marrs (ed) *Letters of Charles and Mary Lamb*, vol.3 (1978).

37 Fanny Kelly's divine plain face.
1818 Letter to Mary Wordsworth, 18 Feb. Collected in H H Harpter (ed) *Letters of Charles Lamb*, vol.4 (1905).

38 Newspapers always excite curiosity. No one ever lays one down without a feeling of disappointment.
1822 In the *London Magazine*, May– Jul. Collected in *Essays of Elia*, 'Detached Thoughts of Books and Reading'.

39 Who first invented work—and tied the free
And holy-day rejoicing spirit down
To the ever-haunting importunity
Of business?
1822 Letter to Bernard Barton, 11 Sep. Collected in H H Harpter (ed) *Letters of Charles Lamb*, vol.4 (1905).

40 I hate a man who swallows it, affecting not to know what he is eating. I suspect his taste in higher matters.
1823 *Essays of Elia*, 'Grace Before Meat'.

41 In everything that relates to science, I am a whole Encyclopedia behind the rest of the world.
1823 *Essays of Elia*, 'The Old and the New Schoolmaster'.

42 I know that a sweet child is the sweetest thing in nature…but the prettier the kind of a thing is, the more desirable it is that it should be pretty of its kind.
1823 *Essays of Elia*, 'A Bachelor's Complaint of the Behaviour of Married People'.

43 If the husband be a man with whom you have lived on a friendly footing before marriage,—if you did not come in on the wife's side,—if you did not sneak into the house in her train, but were an old friend in first habits of intimacy before their courtship was so much as thought on,—look about you… Every long friendship, every old authentic intimacy, must be brought into their office to be new stamped with their currency, as a sovereign Prince calls in the good old money that was coined in some reign before he was born or thought of, to be new marked and minted with the stamp of his authority, before he will let it pass current in the world.
1823 *Essays of Elia*, 'A Bachelor's Complaint of the Behaviour of Married People'.

44 Ceremony is an invention to take off the uneasy feeling which we derive from knowing ourselves to be less the object of love and esteem with a fellow-creature than some other person is. It endeavours to make up, by superior attentions in little points, for that invidious preference which it is forced to deny in the greater.
1823 *Essays of Elia*, 'A Bachelor's Complaint of the Behaviour of Married People'.

45 Sentimentally I am disposed to harmony. But organically I am incapable of a tune.
1823 *Essays of Elia*, 'A Chapter on Ears'.

46 I have no ear.
1823 *Essays of Elia*, 'A Chapter on Ears'.

47 Presents, I often say, endear Absents.
1823 *Essays of Elia*, 'A Dissertation upon Roast Pig'.

48 She unbent her mind afterwards—over a book.
1823 *Essays of Elia*, 'Mrs Battle's Opinions on Whist'.

49 A votary of the desk—a notched and cropt scrivener—one that sucks his substance, as certain sick people are said to do, through a quill.
1823 *Essays of Elia*, 'Oxford in the Vacation'.

50 The uncommunicating muteness of fishes.
1823 *Essays of Elia*, 'A Quakers' Meeting'.

51 The human species, according to the best theory I can form of it, is composed of two distinct races, the men who borrow, and the men who lend.
1823 *Essays of Elia*, 'The Two Races of Men'.

52 Your *borrowers of books*—those mutilators of collections, spoilers of the symmetry of shelves, and creators of odd volumes.
1823 *Essays of Elia*, 'The Two Races of Men'.

53 Not many sounds in life, and I include all urban and rural sounds, exceed in interest a knock at the door.
1823 *Essays of Elia*, 'Valentine's Day'.

54 Credulity is the man's weakness, but the child's strength.
1823 *Essays of Elia*, 'Witches and Other Night-Fears'.

55 How sickness enlarges the dimensions of a man's self to himself.
1823 *Essays of Elia*, 'The Convalescent'.

56 If dirt were trumps, what hands you would hold!
1828 Quoted in Leigh Hunt *Lord Byron and his Contemporaries*, p.299.

57 How sickness enlarges the dimensions of a man's self to himself.
1833 *Last Essays of Elia*, 'The Convalescent'.

58 The drinking man is never less himself than during his sober intervals.
1833 *Last Essays of Elia*, 'Confessions of a Drunkard'.

59 Books think for me.
1833 *Last Essays of Elia*, 'Detached Thoughts on Books and Reading'.

60 Things in book's clothing.
1833 *Last Essays of Elia*, 'Detached Thoughts on Books and Reading'.

61 A poor relation is the most irrelevant thing in nature.
1833 *Last Essays of Elia*, 'Poor Relations'.

62 A pistol let off at the ear; not a feather to tickle the intellect.
1833 Of puns. *Last Essays of Elia*, 'Popular Fallacies', no.9.

63 The greatest pleasure I know, is to do good action by stealth, and to have it found out by accident.
1834 'Table Talk by the late Elia', in *The Athenaeum*, 1834.

64 The last breath I drew in he wished might be through a pipe and exhaled in a pun.
Quoted in W Toynbee *Diaries of William Charles Macready 1833–1851* (1912).

Lamb, Marjorie 1949–

Canadian ecologist.

65 Suppose our ancestors had discovered nuclear power in the middle ages, and had decided to bury their radioactive fuel.
1990 *Two Minutes a Day for a Greener Planet*.

Lambert, Constant 1905–51

English composer, conductor and critic. His first success came with the ballet *Romeo and Juliet*, commissioned by Diaghilev in 1926. Subsequently he worked as conductor for the Camargo Society and for Sadler's Wells Ballet.

66 The Appalling Popularity of Music.
1934 *Music Ho!*, chapter title.

67 There is a definite limit to the length of time a composer can go on writing in one dance rhythm. This limit is obviously reached by Ravel toward the end of *La Valse* and toward the beginning of *Boléro*.
1934 *Music Ho!*

68 To put it vulgarly, the whole trouble with a folk song is that once you have played it through there is nothing much you can do except play it over again and play it rather louder.
1934 *Music Ho!*

Lamming, George Eric 1927–

Barbadian novelist. Winner of the Somerset Maugham Prize for literature for his novel *In the Castle of My Skin* (1953), he has also published *The Emigrants* (1954), *Seasons of Adventure* (1960), and *Natives of My Person* (1972).

69 Histr'y ain't got eyes to see everything.
1953 *In the Castle of My Skin*, ch.6.

70 If you aren't native to a place you have an excellent chance of becoming a gentleman in it.
1953 *In the Castle of My Skin*, ch.14.

Lamport, Allan 1903–

Canadian politician, Mayor of Toronto (1952–42) and a renowned malapropist.

71 If somebody's gonna stab me in the back, I wanna be there.
1990 *Quotations from Chairman Lamport*.

Lancaster, Sir James c.1554–1618

English navigator, soldier and merchant. He visited the East Indies in 1591–4 and in 1595 captured Pernambuco. In 1600–3 he commanded the first fleet of the East India Company to visit the East Indies. He promoted the voyages of Hudson, Baffin and others in search of the Northwest Passage.

72 I cannot tell where you should look for me, if you send out any pinnace to seek me; because I live at the devotion of the wind and seas. And thus fare you well; desiring God to send us a merry meeting in this world, if it be his good will and pleasure.
c.1594 Letter to the East India Company written on the homeward voyage when the two English ships ran into storms off the Cape of Good Hope. Lancaster's ship lost her rudder. Unwilling to risk the other ship, Lancaster ordered her captain to sail straight home, taking the letter with him. *A voyage with three tall ships, the Penelope, admirall, the Marchant Royall, vice-admiral, and the Edward Bonaventure, rear-admiral, to the East Indies... Begun By M. George Raymond, in the yeere 1591, and performed by M. James Lancaster; and written from the mouth of Edmund Barker of Ipswich (his lieutenant in the sayd voyage) by M. Richard Hakluyt.*

Lance, Bert

Former US White House Budget Director.

73 Go out on the front porch of the house, turn the *Washington Post* over with your big toe, and if your name's above the fold, you know you're not going to have a good day.
1993 Of the Bert Lance Toe Test which he devised for his nine months in the Carter administration. In the *Washington Post*, 6 Oct.

Landers, Ann 1918–2002

US newspaper columnist and 'agony aunt', who offered advice and information on topics such as family life, marriage, social issues and health.

74 Women complain about sex more often than men. Their gripes fall into two major categories: (1) Not enough. (2) Too much.
1968 *Truth Is Stranger*…, ch.2.

Landor, Walter Savage 1775–1864

English writer and poet. His *Imaginary Conversations of Literary Men and Statesmen* (1824–9) was celebrated in its day but has lost popularity. Other works include *Hellenics* (1847) and *Dry Sticks Fagoted* (1858).

75 Ah, what avails the sceptred race!
Ah, what the form divine!
1806 'Rose Aylmer'.

76 Clear writers, like clear fountains, do not seem so deep as they are; the turbid look the most profound.
1824 *Imaginary Conversations of Literary Men and Statesmen*, 'Southey and Porson'.

77 Fleas know not whether they are upon the body of a giant or upon one of ordinary size.
1824 *Imaginary Conversations of Literary Men and Statesmen*, 'Southey and Porson'.

78 Past ruined Ilion Helen lives,
Alcestis rises from the shades;
Verse calls them forth; 'tis verse that gives
Immortal youth to mortal maids.
1831 'To Ianthe'.

79 There is delight in singing, tho' none hear
Beside the singer.
1846 'To Robert Browning'.

80 Thee gentle Spenser fondly led;
But me he mostly sent to bed.
1846 'To Wordsworth: Those Who Have Laid the Harp Aside'.

81 There are no fields of amaranth on this side of the grave.
1846 *Imaginary Conversations of Literary Men and Statesmen*, 'Aesop and Rhodope'.

82 Death stands above me, whispering low
I know not what into my ear;
Of his strange language all I know
Is, there is not a word of fear.
1853 'Death stands above me'.

83 I strove with none; for none was worth my strife;
Nature I loved, and, next to Nature, Art.
1853 'Dying Speech of an Old Philosopher'.

84 Ireland never was contented…
Say you so? You are demented.
Ireland was contented when
All could use the sword and pen,
And when Tara rose so high
That her turrets split the sky,
And about her courts were seen
Liveried Angels robed in green,
Wearing, by St. Patrick's bounty,
Emeralds big as half a county.
1853 'Ireland never was contented'.

85 Prose on certain occasions can bear a great deal of poetry: on the other hand, poetry sinks and swoons under a moderate weight of prose.
1853 *Imaginary Conversations of Greeks and Romans*, 'Archdeacon Hare and Walter Landor'.

Landowska, Wanda 1879–1959

Polish pianist, harpsichordist and musical scholar, who founded the École de Musique Ancienne near Paris in 1927, and stimulated a new interest in the harpsichord. She also composed songs and piano and orchestral pieces and wrote on music.

86 You play Bach your way and I'll play him *his* way.
Refusing to adapt her technique to suit another Bach specialist. Quoted in Clifton Fadiman *The Faber Book of Anecdotes* (1985).

Lane, Anthony 1962–

English journalist, film critic at the *New Yorker* since 1993.

87 There is more suspense, more dramatic torque, in one page of [Nathaniel] Hawthorne's heart-racked ruminations on the Christian conscience than in all Demi Moore's woodland gallops and horizontal barn dancing.
On the film adaptation of *The Scarlet Letter*, directed by Roland Joffé. In *Nobody's Perfect: Writings from The New Yorker* (2002).

88 If you are going to spend two hundred million dollars on a movie, this is the way to do it.
Admiring the film *Titanic*. In *Nobody's Perfect: Writings from The New Yorker* (2002).

Lang, Andrew 1844–1912

Scottish man of letters. He specialized in mythology, famously arguing against Max Müller that folktale was the foundation of literary mythology. He also wrote history texts, popular fairy books, studies of literary figures and poetry.

89 Politicians use statistics in the same way that a drunk uses lamp-posts—for support rather than illumination.
1910 Speech. Quoted in Alan L Mackay *The Harvest of a Quiet Eye* (1977).

90 If the wild bowler thinks he bowls
Or if the batsman thinks he's bowled,
They know not, poor misguided souls,
They too shall perish unconsoled.
I am the batsman and the bat,
I am the bowler and the ball,
The umpire, the pavilion cat,
The roller, pitch, and stumps and all.
'Brahma'. Quoted by Alan Richardson in a letter to *The Times*, 18 May, 1963.

➡ *See Emerson 313:39.*

Lang, Fritz 1890–1976

Austrian-born US film director. His many films include *Metropolis* (1926), *You Only Live Once* (1937) and *Beyond a Reasonable Doubt* (1956).

91 Don't forget the western is not only the history of this country, it is what the Saga of the Nibelungen is for the European.
Quoted in Peter Bogdanovich *Fritz Lang in America* (1967).

Langbridge, Frederick 1849–1923

English religious writer.

92 Two men look out through the same bars:

One sees the mud, and one the stars.
1896 *A Cluster of Quiet Thoughts.*

Langland, William c.1332–c.1400

English poet. Little is known of his life but he seems to have been in London in 1362 when he began his only known work, the long poem *Vision of William concerning Piers the Plowman*, the greatest poem of the Middle English Alliterative Revival. It deals with the themes of truth, integrity and social justice. Three versions survive in over 60 manuscipts. It was first printed in 1550.

93 In a somer seson, whan softe was the sonne,
I shoop me into shroudes as I a sheep were,
In habite an heremite unholy of werkes,
Went wide in this world wondres to here.
c.1377 *Piers Plowman* (B text), prologue, l.1–4.
(shoop = got, shroudes = garments)

94 A gloten of wordes.
c.1377 *Piers Plowman* (B text), prologue, l.139.
(gloten = glutton)

95 'Though we hadde ykilled the cat, yat sholde there come another
To cracchen us ans al oure kynde, though we cropen under benches.'
c.1377 The wise mouse advises against belling the cat. *Piers Plowman* (B text), prologue, l.185–6.
(cracchen = scratch, cropen = crept)

96 He was bitelbrowed and baberlipped, with two blered eighen,
And as a letheren purs lolled his chekes.
c.1377 A description of the sin of Envy. *Piers Plowman* (B text), 'Passus 5,' l.188–9. (eighen = eyes, letheren = leather)

97 Al the povere peple tho pescoddes fetten;
Benes and baken apples thei broghte in hir lappe,
Chibolles and chervelles and ripe chiries manye,
And profrede Piers this present to plese with Hunger.
c.1378 A description of the sin of Envy. *Piers Plowman* (B text), 'Passus 6,' l.291–4.
(pescoddes = pea-pod, fetten = fetched, chibolles = spring-onions, chervelles = chervil, plese with Hunger = please hunger with)

98 Ac thorugh his science soothy was nevere no soule ysaved,
Ne broght by hir bokes to blisse ne to joye.
c.1378 *Piers Plowman* (B text), 'Passus 12', l.134–5.
The 'science' and 'books' are those of pagan scholars who developed natural science from empirical observation only.

99 'Counseilleth me, Kynde,' quod I, 'what craft be best to lerne?'
'Lerne to love,' quod kynde, 'and leef alle othere.'
c.1378 *Piers Plowman* (B text), 'Passus 20', l.207–8.

Langner, Lawrence 1890–1962

Co-founder, US Theater Guild.

1 I have no interest in anything but *genius*, so please sit down.
To Tennessee Williams. Recalled in Williams *Memoirs* (1975).

Lanier, Sidney 1842–81

US poet. He fought in the Civil War for the Confederacy. His critical study *The Science of English Verse* (1880) establishes a musical basis for poetry which he tries to exemplify in his verse.

2 Music is Love in search of a word.
1875 *The Symphony.*

Lanyer, Aemilia 1569–1645

English poet. One of the very few professional early female poets, she was unable to secure patronage and published only one work, *Salve Deus Ex Judaeorum* (1611). It has been argued (unconvincingly) that she is the 'dark lady' of Shakespeare's *Sonnets*.

3 Our mother Eve, who tasted of the tree,
Giving to Adam what she held most dear,
Was simply good, and had no power to see.
1611 *Salve Deus Ex Judaeorum*, 'Eve's Apology in Defense of Women'.

4 But surely Adam cannot be excused;
Her fault though great, yet he was most to blame;
What weakness offered, strength might have refused,
Being lord of all, the greater was the shame.
1611 *Salve Deus Ex Judaeorum*, 'Eve's Apology in Defense of Women'.

5 Not Eve, whose fault was only too much love,
Which made her give this present to her dear,
That what she tasted he likewise might prove,
Whereby his knowledge might become more clear;
He never sought her weakness to reprove
With those sharp words which he of God did hear;
Yet men will boast of knowledge, which he took
From Eve's fair hand, as from a learned book.
1611 *Salve Deus Ex Judaeorum*, 'Eve's Apology in Defense of Women'.

6 Then let us have our liberty again,
And challenge to yourselves no sovereignty.
You came not in the world without our pain,
Make that a bar against your cruelty;
Your fault being greater, why should you disdain
Our being your equals, free from tyranny?
1611 *Salve Deus Ex Judaeorum*, 'Eve's Apology in Defense of Women'.

7 Farewell (sweet *Cooke-ham*) where I first obtained
Grace from that grace where perfect grace remained;
And where the muses gave their full consent,
I should have power the virtuous to content;
Where princely palace willed me to indite,
The sacred story of the soul's delight.
1611 *Salve Deus Ex Judaeorum*, 'The Description of Cooke-ham'.
Probably the first 'country-house' poem in English, this work is dedicated to Margaret Russell Clifford, Countess of Cumberland, and her daughter, Anne Clifford, whose family home was Cookham.

8 Never shall my sad eyes again behold
Those pleasures which my thoughts did then unfold.
1611 *Salve Deus Ex Judaeorum*, 'The Description of Cooke-ham'.

Lao-Tzu 6c BC

Chinese philosopher regarded as the inspiration for Taoism. Its major work, the *Tao-te Ching* was compiled some 300 years after his death but is traditionally ascribed to him.

9 Free from desire, you realise the mystery.
Caught in desire, you see only the manifestations.
c.250 BC *Tao-te Ching*, no.1 (translated by Stephen Mitchell, 1988).

10 He who defines himself can't know who he really is.

c.250 BC *Tao-te Ching*, no.24 (translated by Stephen Mitchell, 1988).

11 Even in victory, there is no beauty, and he who calls it beautiful is one who delights in slaughter.
c.250 BC *Tao-te Ching*, no.31. Collected in Lin Yutang (trans and ed) *The Wisdom of China and India* (1942).

12 A victory should be celebrated with the funeral rite.
c.250 BC *Tao-te Ching*, no.31. Collected in Lin Yutang (trans and ed) *The Wisdom of China and India* (1942).

13 When two equally matched armies meet, it is the man of sorrow who wins.
c.250 BC *Tao-te Ching*, no.69. Collected in Lin Yutang (trans and ed) *The Wisdom of China and India* (1942).

Lardner, Dionysus 1793–1859

Irish scientific writer, Professor of Natural Philosophy and Astronomy at University College London (1827). He is best known as the originator and editor of *Lardner's Cabinet Cyclopaedia* (133 vols, 1829–49).

14 Men might as well project a voyage to the Moon as attempt to employ steam navigation against the stormy North Atlantic Ocean.
1838 Speech to the British Association for the Advancement of Science, London.

Lardner, James

US journalist, former staff writer for the *New Yorker*. He is the director and founder of Inequality.org, a non-profit organization.

15 If…Americans do not succeed in engineering an economic revival, we can look forward to being remembered as, of all the nations that have prospered and declined, the one that has done so in the highest state of self-awareness.
1993 'The Declining Middle', in the *New Yorker*, 3 May.

Lardner, Ring(old Wilmer) 1885–1933

US short story writer, novelist and columnist. He is best known for his vernacular, comic, satirical and usually pessimistic short stories.

16 Are you lost daddy I arsked tenderly.
Shut up he explained.
1920 *The Young Immigrunts*, ch.10.

17 I have known what it was like to be hungry, but I always went right to a restaurant.
1927 *The Lardners: My Family Remembered*, ch.1.

18 'Babe' Ruth and Old Jack Dempsey,
Both Sultans of Swat,
One hits where the other people are,
The other where they're not.
Attributed.

Larionov, Mikhail 1881–1964

Russian painter and designer.

19 We declare: the genius of our days to be: trousers, jackets, shoes, tramways, buses, aeroplanes, railways, magnificent ships—what an enchantment—what a great epoch unrivalled in world history.
1913 'Rayonnist Manifesto', quoted in C Gray *The Russian Experiment in Art* (revised edn 1986).

Larkin, Philip Arthur 1922–85

English poet, novelist and essayist. He was librarian at Hull University, and a jazz critic. His meticulously phrased, frequently pessimistic but often tongue-in-cheek poems include 'The Whitsun Weddings' (1964) and 'High Windows' (1974).

20 Always too eager for the future, we
Pick up bad habits of expectancy.
1951 'Next, Please'.

21 What are days for?
Days are where we live.
They come, they wake us
Time and time over.
They are to be happy in:
Where can we live but days?
1953 'Days'.

22 What calls me is that lifted, rough-tongued bell
(Art, if you like) whose individual sound
Insists I too am an individual.
1953 'Reasons for Attendance'.

23 And the case of butterflies so rich it looks
As if all summer settled there and died.
1953 'Autumn'.

24 Nothing, like something, happens anywhere.
1954 'I Remember, I Remember'.

25 On me your voice falls as they say love should,
Like an enormous yes.
1954 'For Sidney Bechet'.

26 Hatless, I take off
My cycle-clips in awkward reverence.
1954 'Church Going'.

27 A serious house on serious earth it is,
In whose blent air all our compulsions meet,
Are recognised, and robed as destinies.
1954 'Church Going'.

28 Why should I let the toad *work*
Squat on my life?
Can't I use my wit as a pitchfork
And drive the brute off?
Six days of the week it soils
With its sickening poison—
Just for paying a few bills!
That's out of proportion.
1954 'Toads'.

29 Marrying left your maiden name disused.
1955 'Maiden Name'.

30 Time has transfigured them into
Untruth. The stone fidelity
They hardly meant has come to be
Their final blazon, and to prove
Our almost-instinct almost true:
What will survive of us is love.
1956 'An Arundel Tomb'.

31 Never such innocence,
Never before or since,
As changed itself to past
Without a word—the men
Leaving the gardens tidy,
The thousands of marriages
Lasting a little while longer:

Never such innocence again.
1960 'MCMXI V'.

32 Get stewed:
Books are a load of crap.
1960 'A Study of Reading Habits'.

33 The widening river's slow presence,
The piled gold clouds, the shining gull-marked mud,
Gathers to the surprise of a large town:
Here domes and statues, spires and cranes cluster
Beside grain-scattered streets, barge-crowded water,
And residents from raw estates.
1961 Of Hull. 'Here'.

34 Give me your arm, old toad;
Help me down Cemetery Road.
1962 'Toads Revisited'.

35 Life is first boredom, then fear.
1963 'Dockery and Son'.

36 I thought of London spread out in the sun,
Its postal districts packed like squares of wheat.
1964 'The Whitsun Weddings'.

37 Sexual intercourse began
In nineteen sixty-three
(Which was rather late for me)—
Between the end of the *Chatterly* ban
And the Beatles' first LP.
1967 'Annus Mirabilis'.

38 They fuck you up, your mum and dad.
They may not mean to, but they do.
They fill you with the faults they had
And add some extra, just for you.
1971 'This Be the Verse'.

39 Man hands on misery to man.
It deepens like a coastal shelf.
Get out as early as you can,
And don't have any kids yourself.
1971 'This Be the Verse'.

40 I should never call myself a book lover, any more than a people lover: it all depends what's inside them.
1972 In the London Antiquarian Book Fair programme.

41 Perhaps being old is having lighted rooms
Inside your head, and people in them, acting.
People you know, yet can't quite name.
1973 'The Old Fools'.

42 You can't put off being young until you retire,
And however you bank your screw, the money you save
Won't in the end buy you more than a shave.
1973 'Money'.

43 And beyond it, the deep blue air, that shows
Nothing, and is nowhere, and is endless.
1974 'High Windows'.

44 That sure extinction that we travel to
And shall be lost in always. Not to be here,
Not to be anywhere,
And soon; nothing more terrible, nothing more true.
1977 'Aubade'.

45 That vast moth-eaten musical brocade
Created to pretend we never die.
1977 Of religion. 'Aubade'.

46 Far too many relied on the classic formula of a beginning, a muddle, and an end.
1978 On judging the Booker Prize entries for 1977, in *New Fiction*, no.15, Jan.

47 Deprivation is for me what daffodils were for Wordsworth.
1983 *Required Writing*.

La Rochefoucauld, François, 6th Duc de 1613–80

French writer. A supporter of the queen, Marie de Médicis, and an opponent of Richelieu, he was entangled in a series of amorous adventures and political intrigues. His *Mémoires*, published secretly in 1662, caused wide offence and were followed by his *Réflexions, ou sentences et maximes morales* (1664).

48 The love of justice in most men is simply the fear of suffering injustice.
1664 *Réflexions, ou sentences et maximes morales*, no.78.

49 *Dans l'adversité de nos meilleurs amis, nous trouvons toujours quelque chose qui ne nous déplaît pas.*
In the misfortune of our best friends, we always find something which is not displeasing to us.
1664 *Réflexions, ou sentences et maximes morales*, no.99.

50 *On n'est jamais si malheureux qu'on croit, ni si heureux qu'on espère.*
One is never as unhappy as one thinks, nor as happy as one hopes.
1664 *Réflexions, ou sentences et maximes morales*, no.128.

51 *Nous avons tous assez de force pour supporter les maux d'autrui.*
We are all strong enough to bear the misfortunes of others.
1678 *Maximes*, no.19.

52 *L'hypocrisie est un hommage que le vice rend à la vertu.*
Hypocrisy is a tribute which vice pays to virtue.
1678 *Maximes*, no.218.

53 *L'absence diminue les médiocres passions, et augmente les grandes, comme le vent éteint les bougies, et allume le feu.*
Absence diminishes commonplace passions, and increases great ones, as wind extinguishes candles and kindles fire.
1678 *Maximes*, no.276.

54 *L'accent du pays où l'on est né demeure dans l'esprit et dans le cœur comme dans le langage.*
The accent of the place in which one was born lingers in the mind and in the heart as it does in one's speech.
1678 *Maximes*, no.342.

Larwood, Harold 1904–95

English cricketer. He became notorious in the 1932–3 tour of Australia, employed by D R Jardine to bowl 'Bodyline', which led to several batsmen being seriously hurt. He retired from Test cricket as a result of the ensuing furore and eventually settled in Australia.

55 A cricket tour in Australia would be a most delightful period in one's life if one was deaf.
1933 *Body-line*.

56 Bodyline was devised to stifle Bradman's batting genius. They said I was a 'killer with the ball', without taking into account that Bradman, with the bat, was the greatest killer of all.
1965 Of the 'Bodyline' controversy. Quoted in Colin Jarman *The*

Guinness Dictionary of Sports Quotations (1990).

57 I darned near bowled him that time.
Attributed. Said to an umpire who had disallowed two previous appeals, on clean bowling a batsman, knocking down the entire wicket.

Lasky, Jesse 1880–1958

US film pioneer. He formed his own production company in 1914 and had his first hit with *The Squaw Man*, going on to produce for Paramount, Fox and Warner.

58 I yearned to trespass on Quality Street.
On his desire to produce better films. Quoted in the *New Yorker*, 21 Mar 1994.

Lassels, Richard c.1603–1668

English classical scholar and priest. As tutor to the young English nobility, he travelled widely in Europe. His *Voyage of Italy* was published posthumously in Paris in 1670, and in London in 1698.

59 Pick out of every country what's best in it.
c.1650 *The Voyage of Italy, or a Compleat Journey through Italy* (published 1670).

60 [Travel] preserves my young nobleman from surfeiting of his parents, and weans him from a dangerous fondness of, his mother. It teacheth him wholesome hardship… Whereas the country gentleman that never travelled, can scarce go to London without making his will, at least without wetting his handkerchief.
c.1650 *The Voyage of Italy, or a Compleat Journey through Italy* (published 1670).

Latimer, Hugh c.1485–1555

English theologian, Bishop of Worcester and Protestant martyr. After Mary I's accession he was tried for heresy and burned at the stake in Oxford.

61 Be of good comfort Master Ridley, and play the man. We shall this day light such a candle by God's grace in England, as (I trust) shall never be put out.
1555 Spoken to Nicholas Ridley, as they waited together to be burned at the stake, 16 Oct. Quoted in Foxe *Acts and Monuments* (1563).

Lauder, Sir Harry (Hugh MacLennan) 1870–1950

Scottish comedian and music-hall entertainer.

62 Will yer stop yer tickling, Jock!
Oh, stop yer tickling, Jock!
Dinna mak' me laugh so hearty, or you'll mak' me choke.
Oh! I wish you'd stop yer nonsense—just look at all the folk.
Will yer stop yer tickling—tickle-ickle-ickle-ing—
Stop yer tickling, Jock!
1904 'Stop Yer Tickling, Jock!', chorus.

63 I love a lassie, a bonnie, bonnie lassie,
She's as pure as the lily in the dell.
She's as sweet as the heather
The bonnie bloomin' heather—
Mary, ma Scotch Bluebell.
1905 'I Love a Lassie', or 'Ma Scotch Bluebell', chorus.

64 Roamin' in the gloamin' on the bonnie banks o' Clyde.
Roamin' in the gloamin' wae my lassie by my side.
When the sun has gone to rest,
That's the time that we love best—
O, it's lovely roamin' in the gloamin'!
1911 'Roamin' in the Gloamin', chorus.

65 Keep right on to the end of the road,
Keep right on to the end.
Tho' the way be long let your heart be strong,
Keep right on round the bend.
Tho' you're tired and weary
Still journey on, till you come to your happy abode,
Where all you love you've been dreaming of
Will be there, at the end of the road.
1924 'The End of the Road', chorus.

Laughlin, J Laurence 1850–1933

US economist, Professor at the University of Chicago.

66 Anything from plumbing to philosophy.
His definition of the scope of sociology. Quoted in Joseph Dorfman *Thorstein Veblen and his America* (1934), p.93.

Laughton, Charles 1899–1962

British actor. His many roles include Henry VIII in *The Private Life of Henry VIII* (1933), Captain Bligh in *Mutiny on the Bounty* (1935) and Quasimodo in *The Hunchback of Notre Dame* (1939).

67 But they can't censor the gleam in my eye.
1934 Of his role of Mr Barrett in *The Barretts of Wimpole Street*.

Lauren, Ralph 1939–

US fashion designer.

68 I don't design clothes, I design dreams.
1986 In the *New York Times*, 19 Apr.

Laurence, Margaret 1926–87

Canadian novelist. Her first works were set in Africa, where she lived for seven years. In London she wrote the five Manawaka novels (1964–74). She has received numerous honours, including the Order of Canada.

69 Privacy is a privilege not granted to the aged or the young.
1964 *The Stone Angel*, ch.1.

70 Even if heaven were real, and measured as Revelation says, so many cubits this way and that, how gimcrack a place it would be, crammed with its pavements of gold, its gates of pearl and topaz, like a gigantic chunk of costume jewelry.
1964 *The Stone Angel*, ch.4.

71 In bygone days, Morag had once believed that nothing could be worse than killing a person. Now she perceived river-slaying as something worse.
1974 *The Diviners*, ch.1.

Laurencin, Marie 1885–1956

French artist, best known for her portraits of women in misty pastel colours. She also illustrated many books with watercolours and lithographs. She exhibited at the Salon des Indépendents in 1907.

72 My ambition is that men should have a voluptuous feeling when they look at the portraits I paint of women. Love interests me more than painting. My pictures are the love stories I tell to myself and which I want to tell others.

Quoted in Gabrielle Buffet 'Marie Laurencin', in *The Arts 3* (1903).

Lautréamont, Comte de *properly* *Isidore Ducasse* 1846–70

French writer, hailed by the Surrealists as one of their forerunners for his psychological poetry. His death at the age of twenty-four remains a mystery.

73 *Il n'était pas menteur, il avouait la vérité et disait qu'il était cruel.*
He was not a liar. He admitted the truth and said that he was cruel.
1868 *Les Chants de Maldoror*, pt.1.

74 *Oui, quel est le plus profond, le plus impénétrable des deux: l'océan ou le cœur humain?*
What is deeper, more impenetrable: the ocean or the human heart?
1868 *Les Chants de Maldoror*, pt.1.

75 *Moi, je n'aime pas les femmes! Ni même les hermaphrodites! Il me faut des êtres qui me ressemblent, sur le front desquels la noblesse humaine soit marquée en caractères plus tranchés et ineffaçables!*
Me, I do not like women! Nor even hermaphrodites! I need beings who resemble me, on whose foreheads nobility is engraved in sharp and unerasable characters.
1868 *Les Chants de Maldoror*, pt.5.

76 *Si vous êtes malheureux, il ne faut pas le dire au lecteur. Gardez cela pour vous.*
If you are miserable, you should not say so to the reader. Keep it for yourself.
1870 *Poésies*, pt.1.

77 *Il faut que la critique attaque la forme, jamais le fond de vos idées, de vos phrases. Arrangez-vous.*
A critic must attack the form, never the foundation of your ideas and phrases. See to it.
1870 *Poésies*, pt.1.

78 *Si la morale de Cléopâtre eût été moins courte, la face du monde aurait changé. Son nez n'en serait pas devenu plus long.*
If Cleopatra's morality had been less short, the face of the world would have been altered. Her nose would not thereby have grown longer.
1870 *Poésies*, pt.2.

79 *La poésie doit être faite par tous. Non par un. Pauvre Hugo!*
Poetry should be composed by everyone. Not by one. Poor Hugo!
1870 *Poésies*, pt.2.

80 *On ne peut juger de la beauté de la vie que par celle de la mort.*
One can only judge the beauty of life through death.
1870 *Poésies*, pt.2.

Laver, James 1899–1975

English poet, writer and art critic, and Keeper at the Victoria and Albert Museum (1922–59). He made a substantial contribution to the history of English costume.

81 The same costume will be
Indecent... 10 years before its time
Shameless... 5 years before its time
Outré (daring)... 1 year before its time
Smart
Dowdy... 1 year after its time
Hideous... 10 years after its time
Ridiculous... 20 years after its time
Amusing... 30 years after its time
Quaint... 50 years after its time
Charming... 70 years after its time
Romantic... 100 years after its time
Beautiful... 150 years after its time.
1937 *Taste and Fashion*, ch.18.

82 A visitor from Mars contemplating a man in a frock coat and top hat and a woman in a crinoline might well have supposed that they belonged to different species.
1969 *The Concise History of Costume and Fashion*, ch.8.

Lavoisier, Antoine Laurent 1743–94

French chemist and physicist, one of the fathers of modern chemistry. He was one of the first to use effective quantitative methods to study chemical reactions.

83 We must trust to nothing but facts. These are presented to us by Nature, and cannot deceive. We ought, in every instance, to submit our reasoning to the test of experiment, and never to search for truth but by the natural road of experiment and observation.
1789 *Traité élémentaire de la chimie* ('Elements of Chemistry', translated by Robert Kerr).

Law, (Andrew) Bonar 1858–1923

Canadian-born British Unionist politician. He was Chancellor of the Exchequer (1916–18) and from 1916 Leader of the House of Commons. He retired in 1921, but returned to serve as Prime Minister (1922–3).

84 I can imagine no length of resistance to which Ulster can go in which I should not be prepared to support them, and in which, in my belief, they would not be supported by the overwhelming majority of the British people.
1912 During the Irish Home Rule crisis, 27 Jul.

Law, William 1686–1761

English divine, whose writings expounded the mysticism of Jakob Boehme.

85 I take it for granted that every Christian that is in health is up early in the morning; for it is much more reasonable to suppose a person up early because he is a Christian than because he is a labourer or a tradesman or a servant or has business that wants him.
1728 *A Serious Call to a Devout and Holy Life*.

86 If, therefore, a man will so live as to show that he feels and believes the most fundamental doctrines of Christianity, he must live above the world.
1728 *A Serious Call to a Devout and Holy Life*.

Lawrence, D(avid) H(erbert) 1885–1930

English novelist, poet and essayist. He was the son of a miner, and much of his fiction reflected his upbringing. His candid treatment of emotion and physical love led to prosecution for obscenity with *The Rainbow* in 1915, and *Lady Chatterley's Lover* in 1928 (and 1961). He lived in Italy and Mexico from 1919.

87 'Be a good animal, true to your instincts,' was his motto.
1911 *The White Peacock*, pt.2, ch.2.

88 Curse the blasted, jelly-boned swines, the slimy, the

belly-wriggling invertebrates, the miserable sodding rotters, the flaming sods, the snivelling, dribbling, dithering, palsied, pulse-less lot that make up England today.
1913 Letter to Edward Garnett, 3 Jul, after the rejection of *Sons and Lovers* by Heinemann.

89 I like to write when I feel spiteful; it's like having a good sneeze.
1913 Letter to Lady Cynthia Asquith, Nov.

90 You mustn't look in my novel for the old stable *ego* of the character.
1914 Letter to Edward Garnett, 5 Jun.

91 People are not fallen angels, they are merely people.
1916 Letter to J Middleton Murry and Katherine Mansfield, 17 Feb.

92 I am only half there when I am ill, and so there is only half a man to suffer. To suffer in one's whole self is so great a violation, that it is not to be endured.
1916 Letter to Catherine Carswell, 16 Apr.

93 Not I, not I, but the wind that blows through me!
A fine wind is blowing the new direction of Time.
1917 'Song of a Man Who Has Come Through'.

94 The glamour
Of childish days is upon me, my manhood is cast
Down in the flood of remembrance, I weep like a child for the past.
1918 'Piano'.

95 Don't you find it a beautiful clean thought, a world empty of people, just uninterrupted grass, and a hare sitting up?
1920 *Women in Love*, ch.11.

96 In China the bat is a symbol of happiness
Not for me!
1921 'Bat'.

97 I like Australia less and less. The hateful newness, the democratic conceit, every man a little pope of perfection.
1922 Letter, 28 May.

98 Morality which is based on ideas, or on an ideal, is an unmitigated evil.
1922 *Fantasia of the Unconscious*, ch.7.

99 Every race which has become self-conscious and idea-bound in the past has perished.
1922 *Fantasia of the Unconscious*, ch.7.

1 Death is the only pure, beautiful conclusion of a great passion.
1922 *Fantasia of the Unconscious*, ch.15.

2 Better passion and death than any more of these 'isms'. No more of the old purpose done up in aspic. Better passion and death.
1922 *Fantasia of the Unconscious*, ch.15.

3 In the *established* sense it is socially nil. Happy-go-lucky, don't-you-bother, we're-in-Australia. But there also seems to be no inside life of any sort: just a long lapse and drift. A rather fascinating indifference, a *physical* indifference to what we call soul or spirit. It's really a weird show.
1922 Of Australia. Letter, collected in A Huxley (ed) *The Letters of D H Lawrence* (1932).

4 I do not want peace nor beauty nor even freedom from pain. I want to fight and to feel new gods in the flesh.
1922 Letter to E H Brewster, 2 Jan.

5 The wonderful Southern night-sky that makes a man feel so lonely, alien: with Orion standing on his head in the west, and his sword-belt upside down, and his Dog-star prancing in mid-heaven, high above him; and with the Southern Cross insignificantly mixed in with the other stars, democratically inconspicuous.
1923 Of night over Sydney. *Kangaroo*, ch.1.

6 What do the facts we know *about* a man amount to? Only two things we can know of him, and this by pure soul-intuition: we can know if he is true to the flame of life and love which is inside his heart, or if he is false to it.
1923 *Kangaroo*, ch.7.

7 The indifference—the fern-dark indifference of this remote golden Australia. Not to care—from the bottom of one's soul not to care.
1923 *Kangaroo*, ch.10.

8 Life makes no absolute statement. It is all Call and Answer.
1923 *Kangaroo*, ch.10.

9 And so, I missed my chance with one of the lords
Of life.
And I have something to expiate;
A pettiness.
1923 'Snake'.

10 Men! The only animal in the world to fear.
1923 'Mountain Lion'.

11 Hanging upside down like rows of disgusting old rags
And grinning in their sleep.
1923 'Bats'.

12 Evil, what is evil?
There is only one evil, to deny life.
1923 'Cypresses'.

13 The dead don't die. They look on and help.
1923 Letter to J Middleton Murry, 2 Feb, on the death of Katherine Mansfield.

14 Never trust the artist. Trust the tale.
1924 *Studies in Classic American Literature*, ch.1.

15 I want to go south, where there is no autumn, where the cold doesn't crouch over one like a snow-leopard waiting to pounce. The heart of the North is dead, and the fingers of cold are corpse fingers.
1924 Letter to J Middleton Murry, 3 Oct.

16 The identifying ourselves with the visual image of ourselves has become an instinct; the habit is already old. The picture of me, the me that is *seen*, is me.
1925 'Art and Morality'.

17 Damn all absolutes. Oh damn, damn, damn all absolutes!
1925 'The Novel'.

18 After the funeral, my father struggled through half a page, and it might as well have been Hottentott. 'And what dun they gi'e thee for that, lad?'
'Fifty pounds, father.' 'Fifty pounds!' He was dumbfounded, and looked at me with shrewd eyes, as if I were a swindler. 'Fifty pounds! An' tha's niver done a day's hard work in thy life.'
1925 Preface to Edward D McDonald (ed) *A Bibliography of D. H. Lawrence*.

19 I'm not sure if a mental relation with a woman doesn't

make it impossible to love her. To know the *mind* of a woman is to end in hating her.
1927 Letter to Dr Trigant Burrow, 3 Aug.

20 You have to have something vicious in you to be a creative writer… God save me from being 'nice'.
1927 Book review, reprinted in *Phoenix*.

21 Ours is essentially a tragic age, so we refuse to take it tragically.
1928 *Lady Chatterley's Lover*, ch.1.

22 John Thomas says goodnight to Lady Jane, a little droopingly, but with a hopeful heart.
1928 *Lady Chatterley's Lover*, ch.19.

23 My God, what a clumsy *olla putrida* James Joyce is! Nothing but old fags and cabbage-stumps of quotations from the Bible and the rest, stewed in the juice of deliberate, journalistic dirty-mindedness.
1928 Letter to Aldous and Maria Huxley, 15 Aug.

24 Sentimentalism is the working off on yourself of feelings you haven't really got.
1928 'John Galsworthy'.

25 I am tired of being told there is no such animal by animals who are merely different.
1929 Letter to J Middleton Murry, 20 May.

26 How beastly the bourgeois is
Especially the male of the species.
1929 'How Beastly the Bourgeois Is'.

27 I never saw a wild thing
Sorry for itself.
1929 'Self-Pity'.

28 When I read Shakespeare I am struck with wonder
That such trivial people should muse and thunder
In such lovely language.
1929 'When I Read Shakespeare'.

29 Pornography is the attempt to insult sex, to do dirt on it.
1929 'Pornography and Obscenity'.

30 Now man cannot live without some vision of himself. But still less can he live with a vision that is not true to his inner experience and inner feeling.
1929 'The Risen Lord'.

31 Now it is autumn and the falling fruit
And the long journey towards oblivion…
Have you built your ship of death, O have you?
1932 'The Ship of Death'.

32 To the Puritan all things are impure, as somebody says.
1932 *Etruscan Places*, 'Cerveteri'.

33 And being a novelist, I consider myself superior to the saint, the scientist, the philosopher, and the poet, who are all great masters of different bits of man alive, but never get the whole hog.
1936 'Why The Novel Matters'.

34 Nothing is more difficult than to determine what a child takes in, and does not take in, of its environment and its teaching. This fact is brought home to me by the hymns which I learned as a child, and never forgot. They mean more to me almost than the finest poetry, and they have for me a more permanent value, somehow or other.
Collected in *Phoenix II: Uncollected, Unpublished and Other Prose Works* (1968).

35 The sense of wonder
that is the sixth sense.
And it is the natural religious sense.
'Hymns in a Man's Life'. Collected in *Pheonix II: Uncollected, Unpublished and Other Prose Works* (1968).

Lawrence, Gertrude 1898–1952

English actress. A star of revue on both sides of the Atlantic, she was highly popular as the lead in Noël Coward's comedies. She died while appearing in the hit Broadway musical *The King and I*.

36 Pardon my long preamble. It's like a chorus girl's tights—it touches everything and covers nothing.
During an after-dinner speech. Attributed.

Lawrence, T(homas) E(dward) *known as* Lawrence of Arabia 1888–1935

Anglo-Irish soldier and writer. In World War I he worked for army intelligence in North Africa (1914–16). Espousing the Arab cause, he led the Arabs in their revolt against the Turks.

37 I loved you, so I drew these tides of men into my hands
—and wrote my will across the sky in stars
To earn you Freedom, the seven pillared worthy house,
—that your eyes might be shining for me
When we came.
1926 *Seven Pillars of Wisdom*, dedication.

38 All men dream, but not equally. Those who dream by night in the dusty recesses of their minds wake in the day to find that it was vanity; but the dreamers of the day are dangerous men, for they may act their dream with open eyes, to make it possible.
1926 *Seven Pillars of Wisdom*, introductory chapter.

39 We were a self-centred army without parade or gesture, devoted to freedom, the second of man's creeds, a purpose so ravenous that it devoured all our strength, a hope so transcendent that our earlier ambitions faded in its glare.
1926 *Seven Pillars of Wisdom*, ch.1.

40 Many men would take the death sentence without a whimper to escape the life-sentence which fate carries in her other hand.
1936 *The Mint*, pt.1, ch.4.

41 A man hates to be moved to folly by a noise.
1936 Of the emotion aroused by the military trumpets. *The Mint*, pt.3, ch.9.

42 The test of nomadism, that most deeply biting of social disciplines.
Introduction to an edition of Charles Montagu Doughty *Travels in Arabia Deserta*.

Lawson, Henry Hertzberg 1867–1922

Australian writer, son of the writer and feminist Louisa Lawson. His writings for the *Bulletin*, 'The Bushman's Bible', have been collected in *Short Stories in Prose and Verse* (1894) and *While the Billy Boils* (1896).

43 And the sun sank again on the grand Australian bush—the nurse and tutor of eccentric minds, the home of the weird, and of much that is different from things in other lands.
1892 'The Bush Undertaker', first published in *The Antipodean*.

44 The departed was a 'Roman', and the majority of the town were otherwise—but unionism is stronger than creed. Drink, however, is stronger than unionism; and, when the hearse presently arrived, more than two-thirds of the funeral were unable to follow.

1893 'The Union Buries its Dead', first published in *Truth*, Apr.

45 Type of a coming nation,
In the land of cattle and sheep,
Worked on Middleton's station,
'Pound a week and his keep.'

'Middleton's Rouseabout', collected in Colin Roderick (ed) *Henry Lawson: Collected Verse* (3 vols, 1967–9).

46 Have you seen the bush by moonlight, from the train, go running by?
Blackened log and stump and sapling, ghostly trees all dead and dry;
Here a patch of glassy water; there a glimpse of mystic sky?
Have you heard the still voice calling—yet so warm, and yet so cold:
'I'm the Mother-Bush that bore you! Come to me when you are old'?

'On the Night Train', collected in Colin Roderick (ed) *Henry Lawson: Collected Verse* (3 vols, 1967–9).

Layamon fl.c.1190

English author and priest who lived at Arley Regis in Worcestershire. He wrote the *Brut*, the first English version of the story of Arthur, largely based on Wace's French *Roman de Brut*.

47 And I will fare to Avalun, to the fairest of all maidens, to Argante the queen, an elf most fair, and she shall make my wounds all sound.

c.1190 *Brut* (translated by Eugene Mason, 1912).

Layton, Irving 1912–

Romanian-born Canadian poet, who came to Montreal as an infant. His 35 books of poetry include *The Black Huntsman* (1951), *The Cold Green Element* (1955) and *A Red Carpet for the Sun* (1959).

48 Death is a name for beauty not in use.

1953 'Composition in Late Spring', collected in *The Collected Poems of Irving Layton* (1971).

49 It amazes me that organs that piss
Can give human beings such perfect bliss.

1969 *The Whole Bloody Bird*, 'Aphs'.

50 Only the tiniest fracton of mankind want freedom. All the rest want someone to tell them they are free.

1969 *The Whole Bloody Bird*.

Lazarus, Emma 1849–87

US poet, a champion of oppressed Jewry. Her poems include *Songs of a Semite* (1882) and *By the Waters of Babylon* (1887). She is best known for her sonnet, 'The New Colossus' which is inscribed on the Statue of Liberty.

51 Give me your tired, your poor,
Your huddled masses yearning to breathe free,
The wretched refuse of your teeming shore,
Send these, the homeless, tempest-tossed, to me:
I lift my lamp beside the golden door.

1883 'The New Colossus', inscribed at the foot of the Statue of Liberty, New York harbour, 1886.

52 Still on Israel's head forlorn
Every nation heaps its scorn.

1886 'The World's Justice'.

Leach, Jim (James Albert Smith) 1942–

US Republican politician.

53 The only thing the Balkans export is history.

1995 WAMU broadcast, Washington, 25 Nov.

Leacock, Stephen Butler 1869–1944

English-born Canadian humorist and economist. Head of Economics at McGill University from 1908, he wrote several books on economics and literary biographies, and is usually remembered for his short stories, essays and parodies, which include *Literary Lapses* (1910), *Nonsense Novels* (1911) and *Winsome Winnie* (1920).

54 There are no handles to a horse, but the 1910 model has a string to each side of its face for turning its head when there is anything you want it to see.

1910 *Literary Lapses*, 'Reflections on Riding'.

55 It takes a good deal of physical courage to ride a horse. This, however, I have. I get it at about forty cents a flask, and take it as required.

1910 *Literary Lapses*, 'Reflections on Riding'.

56 The great man…walks across his century and leaves the marks of his feet all over it, ripping out the dates on his galoshes as he passes.

1910 *Literary Lapses*, 'The Life of John Smith'.

57 I detest life-insurance agents; they always argue that I shall some day die, which is not so.

1910 *Literary Lapses*, 'Insurance Up to Date'.

58 The landlady of a boarding-house is a parallelogram—that is, an oblong angular figure, which cannot be described, but which is equal to anything.

1910 *Literary Lapses*, 'Boarding-House Geometry'.

59 Astronomy teaches the correct use of the sun and the planets.

1910 *Literary Lapses*, 'A Manual of Education'.

60 Electricity is of two kinds, positive and negative. The difference is, I presume, that one comes a little more expensive, but is more durable; the other is a cheaper thing, but the moths get into it.

1910 *Literary Lapses*, 'A Manual of Education'.

61 Get your room full of good air, then shut up the windows and keep it. It will keep for years. Anyway, don't keep using your lungs all the time. Let them rest.

1910 *Literary Lapses*, 'How to Live to Be 200'.

62 Lord Ronald said nothing; he flung himself from the room, flung himself upon his horse and rode madly off in all directions.

1911 *Nonsense Novels*, 'Gertrude the Governess: or, Simple Seventeen'.

63 When you meet Mr. Smith first you think he looks like an over-dressed pirate. Then you begin to think him a character. You wonder at his enormous bulk. Then the utter hopelessness of knowing what Smith is thinking by merely looking at his features gets on your mind and makes the Mona Lisa seem an open book and the ordinary human countenance as superficial as a puddle in the sunlight.

1912 *Sunshine Sketches of a Little Town*, 'The Hostelry of Mr. Smith'.

64 His life was one round of activity which he himself might deplore but was powerless to prevent.

1912 *Sunshine Sketches of a Little Town*, 'The Ministrations of the Rev. Mr. Drone'.

65 The classics are only primitive literature. They belong to the same class as primitive machinery and primitive music and primitive medicine.
1913 *Behind the Beyond*, 'Homer and Humbug'.

66 The parent who could see his boy as he really is, would shake his head and say: 'Willie is no good; I'll sell him.'
1916 *Further Foolishness*, 'The Lot of the Schoolmaster'.

67 A decision of the courts decided that the game of golf may be played on a Sunday, not being a game within the view of the law, but being a form of moral effort.
1923 *Over the Footlights*, 'Why I Refuse to Play Golf'.

68 Advertising may be described as the science of arresting human intelligence long enough to get money from it.
1924 *The Garden of Folly*, 'The Perfect Salesman'.

69 The general idea, of course, in any first-class laundry, is to see that no shirt or collar ever comes back twice.
1926 *Winnowed Wisdom*, ch.6.

70 I am what is called a *professor emeritus*—from the Latin e, 'out', and *meritus*, 'so he ought to be'.
1938 *Here are my Lectures*, ch.14.

71 A sportsman is a man who, every now and then, simply has to go out and kill something. Not that he's cruel. He wouldn't hurt a fly. It's not big enough.
1942 *My Remarkable Uncle*.

72 Presently I shall be introduced as 'this venerable old gentleman' and the axe will fall when they raise me to the degree of 'grand old man'. That means on our continent any one with snow-white hair who has kept out of jail till eighty.
1942 *My Remarkable Uncle*, 'Three Score and Ten'.

73 I have a suspicion it's inevitable, but give me my stick. I'll face it.
1942 On being asked what he thought about death, following a serious throat operation, quoted in John Stevens's introduction to *My Remarkable Uncle* (1965 edn).

Leadbelly *pseudonym of* Huddie William Ledbetter 1889–1949

US blues and folk singer, songwriter and guitarist. He was 'discovered' while serving one of several prison sentences. His recordings include 'Midnight Special' and 'Rock Island Line'.

74 No white man ever had the blues.
Quoted in Joachim Berendt *The Jazz Book* (1984).

Lear, Edward 1812–88

English artist, humorist and traveller, famous for his nonsense verse such as that collected in *A Book of Nonsense* (1846, enlarged 1861, 1863 and 1870), as well as his illustrations and landscapes.

75 There was an Old Man with a beard,
Who said, 'It is just as I feared!—
Two Owls and a Hen,
Four Larks and a Wren,
Have all built their nest in my beard!'
1846 *A Book of Nonsense*.

76 When awful darkness and silence reign
Over the great Gromboolian plain,
Through the long, long wintry nights,
When the angry breakers roar
As they beat on the rocky shore—
When storm-clouds brood on the towering heights
Of the Hills of the Chankly Bore.
1871 *Nonsense Songs, Stories, Botany and Alphabets*, 'The Dong with a Luminous Nose'.

77 And those who watch at that midnight hour
From Hall or Terrace or lofty Tower,
Cry as the wild light passes along,
'The Dong!—the Dong!
The wandering Dong through the forest goes!
The Dong!—the Dong!
The Dong with a Luminous Nose!'
1871 *Nonsense Songs, Stories, Botany and Alphabets*, 'The Dong with a Luminous Nose'.

78 They went to sea in a sieve, they did
In a sieve they went to sea.
1871 *Nonsense Songs, Stories, Botany and Alphabets*, 'The Jumblies'.

79 Far and few, far and few,
Are the lands where the Jumblies live;
Their heads are green, and their hands are blue,
And they went to sea in a Sieve.
1871 *Nonsense Songs, Stories, Botany and Alphabets*, 'The Jumblies'.

80 They called aloud 'Our Sieve ain't big,
But we don't care a button! We don't care a fig!'
1871 *Nonsense Songs, Stories, Botany and Alphabets*, 'The Jumblies'.

81 And they brought an Owl, and a useful Cart,
And a pound of Rice, and a Cranberry Tart,
And a hive of silvery Bees.
And they brought a Pig, and some green Jack-daws,
And a lovely Monkey with lollipop paws, and forty
Bottles of Ring-Bo-Ree,
And no end of Stilton Cheese.
1871 *Nonsense Songs, Stories, Botany and Alphabets*, 'The Jumblies'.

82 Till Mrs Discobbolos said
'Oh! W! X! Y! Z!
It has just come into my head—
Suppose we should happen to fall!!!!
Darling Mr Discobbolos?'
1871 *Nonsense Songs, Stories, Botany and Alphabets*, 'Mr and Mrs Discobbolos'.

83 The Owl and the Pussy-Cat went to sea
In a beautiful pea-green boat.
They took some honey, and plenty of money,
Wrapped up in a five-pound note.
The Owl looked up to the Stars above
And sang to a small guitar,
'Oh lovely Pussy! O Pussy, my love,
What a beautiful Pussy you are'.
1871 *Nonsense Songs, Stories, Botany and Alphabets*, 'The Owl and the Pussy-Cat'.

84 Pussy said to the Owl, 'You elegant Fowl!
How charmingly sweet you sing!
O let us be married! too long we have tarried:
But what shall we do for a ring?'
They sailed away for a year and a day,
To the land where the Bong-tree grows,
And there in a wood a Piggy-wig stood
With a ring at the end of his nose.

1871 *Nonsense Songs, Stories, Botany and Alphabets*, 'The Owl and the Pussy-Cat'.

85 'Dear Pig, are you willing to sell for one shilling
Your ring?' Said the Piggy, 'I will.'

1871 *Nonsense Songs, Stories, Botany and Alphabets*, 'The Owl and the Pussy-Cat'.

86 They dined on mince, and slices of quince,
Which they ate with a runcible spoon;
And hand in hand, on the edge of the sand,
They danced by the light of the moon.

1871 *Nonsense Songs, Stories, Botany and Alphabets*, 'The Owl and the Pussy-Cat'.

87 The Pobble who has no toes
Had once as many as we;
When they said, 'Some day you may lose them all';
He replied—'Fish fiddle de-dee!'
His Aunt Jobiska made him drink
Lavender water tinged with pink,
For she said, 'The world in general knows
There's nothing so good for a Pobble's toes!'

1871 *Nonsense Songs, Stories, Botany and Alphabets*, 'The Pobble Who Has No Toes'.

88 When boats or ships came near him
He tinkledy-binkledy-winkled a bell.

1871 *Nonsense Songs, Stories, Botany and Alphabets*, 'The Pobble Who Has No Toes'.

89 He has gone to fish, for his Aunt Jobiska's
Runcible Cat with crimson whiskers!

1871 *Nonsense Songs, Stories, Botany and Alphabets*, 'The Pobble Who Has No Toes'.

90 'But the longer I live on this Crumpetty Tree
The plainer than ever it seems to me
That very few people come this way
And that life on the whole is far from gay!'
Said the Quangle-Wangle Quee.

1871 *Nonsense Songs, Stories, Botany and Alphabets*, 'The Quangle Wangle's Hat'.

91 And what can we expect if we haven't any dinner,
But to lose our teeth and eyelashes and keep on growing thinner?

1871 *Nonsense Songs, Stories, Botany and Alphabets*, 'The Two Old Bachelors'.

92 Nasticreechia Krorluppia.

1872 *More Nonsense, Pictures, Rhymes, Botany Etc*, 'Nonsense Botany'.

93 There was an old person of Ware,
Who rode on the back of a bear:
When they asked, 'Does it trot?'
He said, 'Certainly not!
He's a Moppsikon Floppsikon bear.'

1872 *More Nonsense, Pictures, Rhymes, Botany Etc*, 'One Hundred Nonsense Pictures and Rhymes'.

94 There was an old man of Thermopylae,
Who never did anything properly;
But they said, 'If you choose
To boil eggs in your shoes,
You shall never remain in Thermopylae.'

1872 *More Nonsense, Pictures, Rhymes, Botany Etc*, 'One Hundred Nonsense Pictures and Rhymes'.

Leary, Timothy Francis 1920–96

US psychologist, Professor at the Universities of California and Harvard, best known for his advocacy of the drug LSD and his association with the counter-cultural movement of the 1960s and 1970s.

95 My advice to people today is as follows: If you take the game of life seriously, if you take your nervous system seriously, if you take your sense organs seriously, if you take the energy process seriously, you must turn on, tune in, and drop out.

1966 Lecture, Jun, collected in *The Politics of Ecstasy* (1968), ch.21.

96 Science is all metaphor.

1980 Interview, 24 Sep, collected in *Contemporary Authors* vol.107.

Lease, Mary Elizabeth Cylens 1853–1933

US reformer, who spoke out for women's suffrage, Irish Home Rule, prohibition and other causes.

97 The farmers of Kansas must raise less corn and more hell.

1890 Speech, Kansas. This phrase became the slogan of the Populist Party.

Leavis, F(rank) R(aymond) 1895–1978

English critic. He taught at Cambridge University, and was a hugely influential figure, although his ideas have now been superseded by new approaches to textual and cultural criticism.

98 Poetry can communicate the actual quality of experience with a subtlety and precision unapproachable by any other means.

1932 *New Bearings in English Poetry*, ch.2.

99 The Sitwells belong to the history of publicity rather than of poetry.

1932 *New Bearings in English Poetry*, ch.2.

1 It is well to start by distinguishing the few really great—the major novelists who count in the same way as the major poets, in the sense that they not only change the possibilities of the art for practitioners and readers, but that they are significant in terms of the human awareness they promote; awareness of the possibilities of life.

1948 *The Great Tradition*, ch.1.

2 The only way to escape misrepresentation is never to commit oneself to any critical judgement that makes an impact—that is, never *say anything*.

1948 *The Great Tradition*, ch.1.

Leavis, Q(ueenie) D(orothy) 1906–81

British literary critic.

3 Really I suppose what I hate myself most on is showing other people where to dig, not having time to do intensive and exclusive digging myself. I am a dowser and not a navvy.

Quoted in the *Times Literary Supplement*, 8 Sep 1989.

Le Bon, Gustave 1841–1931

French psychologist and sociologist, whose works aim to identify national characteristics and thereby racial superiority.

4 Science has promised us truth—an understanding of such relationships as our minds can grasp; it has never promised us either peace or happiness.

1895 *Psychologie des foules*, Introduction.

Lebowitz, Fran(ces Ann) 1951–

US writer. Her work is marked by an aphoristic sensibility and a caustic, world-weary and rather cynical wit.

5 There is no such thing as inner peace. There is only nervousness or death. Any attempt to prove otherwise constitutes unacceptable behaviour.
1978 *Metropolitan Life*, 'Manners'.

6 Nothing succeeds like address.
1978 *Metropolitan Life*, 'The Nail Bank'.

7 Sleep is death without the responsibility.
1978 *Metropolitan Life*, 'Why I Love Sleep'.

8 It is by this painstaking method of careful examination and eventual rejection that we reach a conclusion: life is something to do when you can't get to sleep.
1978 *Metropolitan Life*, 'Mars'.

9 Salad is not a meal. It is a style.
1978 *Metropolitan Life*, 'Food For Thought and Vice Versa'.

10 Perhaps the least cheering statement ever made on the subject of art is that life imitates it.
1978 *Metropolitan Life*, 'Arts'.

11 Original thought is like original sin: both happened before you were born to people you could not possibly have met.
1981 *Social Studies*, 'People'.

12 Great people talk about ideas, average people talk about things, and small people talk about wine.
1981 *Social Studies*, 'People'.

13 The opposite of talking isn't listening. The opposite of talking is waiting.
1981 *Social Studies*, 'People'.

14 There are two modes of transport in Los Angeles: car and ambulance. Visitors who wish to remain inconspicuous are advised to choose the latter.
1981 *Social Studies*, 'Lesson One'.

15 If you're going to America, bring your own food.
1981 *Social Studies*, 'Fran Lebowitz's Travel Hints'.

16 Being offended is the natural consequence of leaving one's home.
1981 *Social Studies*, 'When Smoke Gets In Your Eyes…Shut Them'.

17 War is, undoubtedly, hell, but there is no earthly reason why it has to start so early in the morning.
1981 *Social Studies*, 'War Stories'.

Leboyer, Frédérick 1918–

French gynaecologist and obstetrician, who first drew attention to birth trauma, and has always emphasized the intimate associations between sex, depression and anxiety.

18 Making love is the sovereign remedy for anguish.
1991 *Birth without Violence*.

Le Carré, John *pseudonym of* *David John Moore Cornwell* 1931–

English novelist. He taught at Eton and entered the Foreign Service, resigning in 1964 to become a full-time writer. His works, many of which have been filmed, are set in the dark underworld of international diplomacy and espionage.

19 The Spy who Came in from the Cold.
1963 Title of novel.

20 A committee is an animal with four back legs.
1974 *Tinker, Tailor, Soldier, Spy*, pt.3, ch.34.

21 Sometimes…we have to do a thing in order to find out the reason for it. Sometimes our actions are questions, not answers.
1986 *A Perfect Spy*, ch.1.

22 The only decent diplomat is a deaf Trappist.
1986 *A Perfect Spy*, ch.3.

23 A society that admires its shock troops had better be bloody careful about where it's going.
1986 *A Perfect Spy*, ch.18.

24 Publishers can get their minds halfway round anything.
1989 *The Russia House*, ch.5.

25 One long act of sadism.
1991 On his boyhood at Sherborne School. In *The Times*, 21 Feb.

26 As a maker of fictions, I invent versions of myself, never the real thing, if it exists.
2002 In the *New Yorker*, 18 Feb.

27 How Bush and his junta succeeded in deflecting America's anger from Bin Laden to Saddam Hussein is one of the great public relations conjuring tricks in history.
2003 In *Time*, 27 Jan.

Le Corbusier *pseudonym of* *Charles Édouard Jeanneret* 1887–1965

Swiss architect, co-author of the Purist manifesto. His buildings, which demonstrate the interrelation of machine forms and architectural techniques, include the Cité Universitaire, Paris, and his city planning designs include Buenos Aires (1938). His books have had a worldwide influence.

28 It is a question of building which is at the root of the social unrest of today: architecture or revolution.
1923 *Vers une architecture* (translated as *Towards a New Architecture*, 1927).

29 The day consists of twenty-four hours only. This regulates the size of the house and the rôle it has to fulfil. For the twenty-four hour day is short, and our acts and thoughts are spurred on *by time*. If we were taught to regard the hand of the clock as a beneficent but implacable god, we should order our lives more rationally.
1930 'Twentieth-century living and twentieth-century building'. Collected in Dennis Sharp (ed) *The Rationalists: Theory and Design in the Modern Movement* (1978).

30 Architecture provides the framework for a civilization (housing, work, leisure, circulation); so architecture is also town planning. It is no longer possible to separate architecture and town planning—they are one and the same thing.
1943 'If I had to teach you architecture'. Collected in Dennis Sharp (ed) *The Rationalists: Theory and Design in the Modern Movement* (1978).

Lee, Gypsy Rose *stage-name of* *Rose Louise Hovick* 1914–70

US actress. Her career as a striptease artist in burlesque on Broadway in the 1930s provided the basis for the film *Gypsy* (1959).

31 I know men aren't attracted to me by my mind. They're attracted by what I don't mind.
Attributed.

32 God is love, but get it in writing.
Attributed.

Lee, (Nelle) Harper 1926–

US writer. She wrote only one novel, *To Kill a Mockingbird* (1960, Pulitzer Prize 1961), but it has become a classic of its time.

33 Until I feared I would lose it, I never loved to read. One does not love breathing.
1960 Scout. *To Kill A Mockingbird*, pt.1, ch.2.

34 Shoot all the bluejays you want, if you can hit 'em, but remember it's a sin to kill a mockingbird.
1960 Atticus Finch. *To Kill A Mockingbird*, pt.1, ch.10.

35 The one thing that doesn't abide by majority rule is a person's conscience.
1960 Atticus Finch. *To Kill A Mockingbird*, pt.1, ch.11.

36 Folks don't like to have somebody around knowin' more than they do. It aggravates 'em.
1960 Calpurnia. *To Kill A Mockingbird*, pt.2, ch.12.

37 A court is only as sound as its jury, and a jury is only as sound as the men who make it up.
1960 Atticus Finch. *To Kill A Mockingbird*, pt.2, ch.20.

38 As you grow older, you'll see white men cheat black men every day of your life, but let me tell you something and don't you forget it—whenever a white man does that to a black man, no matter who he is, how rich he is, or how fine a family he comes from, that white man is trash.
1960 Atticus Finch. *To Kill A Mockingbird*, pt.2, ch.23.

Lee, Hsien Loong 1952–

Singaporean politician, son of the former Prime Minister Lee Kuan Yew.

39 In Singapore you don't volunteer to go into politics—you are invited to enter.
1984 Remark. Quoted in Alan Chong *Goh Tok Chong* (1991), ch.4.

Lee, Kuan Yew 1923–

Singaporean politician, the country's first Prime Minister (1959–90), renowned for his authoritarianism and intolerance of political opponents.

40 I have decided that we shall make and build and never give way.
1966 Remark, 27 Dec. Quoted in James Minchin *No Man is an Island* (1986), ch.8.

41 Even from my sick bed, even if you are going to lower me into the grave, and I feel something is wrong, I will get up.
1988 Remark, Aug. Quoted in C M Turnbull *A History of Singapore* (1989).

Lee, Laurie 1914–97

English writer. He fought in the Spanish Civil War, but is best known for *Cider With Rosie* (1959), his evocative account of growing up in an English village between the wars.

42 Such a morning it is when love
leans through geranium windows
and calls with a cockerel's tongue.
1947 'Day of these Days'.

43 I was set down from the carrier's cart at the age of three; and there with a sense of bewilderment and terror my life in the village began.
1959 *Cider With Rosie*, 'First Light'.

44 Effie M. was a monster. Six foot high and as strong as a farm horse. No sooner had she decided that she wanted Uncle Tom than she knocked him off his bicycle and told him.
1959 *Cider With Rosie*, 'The Uncles'.

45 As for me—for me, the grass grew longer, and more sorrowful, and the trees were surfaced like flesh, and girls were no longer to be treated lightly but were creatures of commanding sadness, and all journeys through the valley were now made alone, with passion in every bush, and the motions of wind and cloud and stars were suddenly for myself alone, and voices elected me of all men living and called me to deliver the world, and I groaned from solitude, blushed when I stumbled, loved strangers and bread and butter, and made long trips through the rain on my bicycle, stared wretchedly through lighted windows, grinned wryly to think how little I was known, and lived in a state of raging excitement.
1959 *Cider With Rosie*, 'Last Days'.

Lee, Robert E 1807–70

US Confederate General. He fought in the Mexican War and in Texas. During the Civil War, although he defeated McClellan at Richmond, he surrendered to General Grant at Appomatox, Virginia in 1865.

46 It is well that war is so terrible. We should grow too fond of it.
1862 Attributed, after the Battle of Fredericksburg, Dec.

Lee-Potter, Linda

British journalist.

47 Powerful men often succeed through the help of their wives. Powerful women only succeed in spite of their husbands.
1984 In the *Daily Mail*, 16 May.

Lees-Milne, James 1908–97

English diarist and founding Secretary of the National Trust's Country House Scheme.

48 All creatures give out a smell when aroused, it seems; certainly humans do.
Ancient as the Hills: Diaries, 1973–1974 (1997).

49 Watched [Vladimir] Horowitz playing his first concert in England for over thirty years. His fingers turn up at the ends, like a pig's nose.
Holy Dread: Diaries, 1982–1984 (2001).

Lees-Smith, Hastings Bernard 1878–1941

British politician. He was associated with Ruskin College, Oxford from its foundation in 1899. He was Liberal MP for Northampton (1910–18), and joined the Labour Party in 1919. He was Labour MP for Keighley (1922–23, 1924–31 and 1935–41).

50 Security can only be obtained by a scheme by which the nations of Europe and outside agree together that all will guarantee each, and each will guarantee all. The

purposes of the war will be attained if there is a League of Nations with an absolute and decisive veto upon any mere aggression, and consideration of any legitimate claims that any of the countries engaged in the war may be able to make good.
1916 House of Commons, 21 Oct.

Leeson, Nick 1967

British derivatives trader, who lost over £600 million trading on the Tokyo stockmarket and caused the collapse of Barings Bank.

51 My sincere apologies for the predicament I have left you in.
1995 Part of a faxed letter of resignation.

Léger, Fernand 1881–1946

French painter, a major force in the Cubist movement, although his paintings are more 'tubist' than 'cubist'. He executed murals for the UN building in New York (1952).

52 Modern man lives more and more in a preponderantly geometric order. All human creation mechanical or industrial is dependent upon geometric intentions.
1924 'The Aesthetic of the Machine', in *Bulletin de l'Effort Moderne*.

53 The thing depicted is less stationary, even the object in itself is less discernible than it used to be. A landscape broken into and traversed in a car or an express train loses in descriptive value but gains in synthetic value; the window of the railroad carriage or the windshield of the car, combined with the speed at which you are traveling, have changed the familiar look of things. Modern man registers one hundred times more impressions than did an eighteenth century artist.
Quoted in D Cooper *The Cubist Epoch* (1970).

Le Guin, Ursula *née Kroeber* 1929–

US writer. She is best known for her literate, politically aware works of science fiction, and her children's fantasy novels, notably the *Earthsea* trilogy (1968–72) and its overtly feminist sequel, *Tehanu* (1990).

54 It is a terrible thing, this kindness that human beings do not lose. Terrible because when we are finally naked in the dark and cold, it is all we have.
1969 *The Left Hand of Darkness*, ch.13.

55 To be, the will to power must increase with each fulfilment, making the fulfilment only a step to a further one. The vaster the power gained the vaster the appetite for more.
1971 *The Lathe of Heaven*, ch.9.

56 In so far as one denies what is, one is possessed by what is not, the compulsions, the fantasies, the terrors that flock to fill the void.
1971 *The Lathe of Heaven*, ch.10.

57 The years before and after the menstrual years are vestigial: the only meaningful condition left to women is that of fruitfulness.
1976 'The Space Crone', in *The Co-Evolution Quarterly*, Summer.

58 To me the 'female principle' is, or at least historically has been, basically anarchic. It values order without constraint, rule by custom not by force. It has been the male who enforces order, who constructs power structures, who makes, enforces, and breaks laws.
'Is Gender Necessary?', in Anderson and McIntyre (eds) *Aurora* (1976).

59 The preservation of life seems to be rather a slogan than a genuine goal of the anti-abortion forces; what they want is control. Control over behavior: power over women.
1982 Address to the National Abortion Rights Action League, Jan. Collected as 'The Princess' in *Dancing at the Edge of the World* (1989).

60 Success is the American Dream we can keep dreaming because most people in most places, including thirty million of ourselves, live wide awake in the terrible reality of poverty.
1983 Address at Mills College. Collected as 'A Left-Handed Commencement Address' in *Dancing at the Edge of the World* (1989).

61 We are volcanoes. When we women offer our experience as our truth, as human truth, all the maps change. There are new mountains.
1983 Address at Mills College. Collected as 'A Left-Handed Commencement Address' in *Dancing at the Edge of the World* (1989).

62 The children of the revolution are always ungrateful, and the revolution must be grateful that it is so.
1983 Address to Folger Library Poetry Series, Washington. Collected as 'Reciprocity of Prose and Poetry' in *Dancing at the Edge of the World* (1989).

63 When either the political or the scientific discourse announces itself as the voice of reason, it is playing God, and should be spanked and stood in the corner.
1986 Commencement address at Bryn Mawr College. Collected in *Dancing at the Edge of the World* (1989).

64 My imagination makes me human and makes me a fool; it gives me all the world and exiles me from it.
1990 'Winged Creatures On My Mind', in *Harper's*, Aug.

Lehmann-Haupt, Christopher Charles Herbert 1934–

US literary critic, born in Scotland. He was senior book reviewer on the *New York Times*.

65 One misses the hiss of acid.
1984 On Gore Vidal's biography *Lincoln* (1984). In the *New York Times*, 30 May.

66 We breathe, we think, we conceive of our lives as narratives.
1984 On Peter Brooks *Reading for the Plot* (1984). In the *New York Times*, 11 Jul.

67 The beginning of a plot…is the prompting of desire.
1984 On Peter Brooks *Reading for the Plot* (1984). In the *New York Times*, 11 Jul.

68 Happiest when he is trying to sculpture fog.
1989 On Robert C Christopher. In the *New York Times*, 29 May.

69 Stevenson's convictions were sometimes too complex for the binary political arena to which he devoted his life.
1989 In the *New York Times*, 31 Jul.

70 The only trouble with this book is that its covers are too close together.
1992 On Florence King *With Charity Toward None* (1992). In the *New York Times*, 9 Apr.

Lehrer, Tom (Thomas Andrew) 1928–

US teacher, songwriter and social satirist.

71 In one word he told me the secret of success in mathematics: Plagiarize…only be sure always to call it please 'research'.
1953 'Lobachevski', satirical song.

72 We'll all go together when we go,
Every Hottentot and every Eskimo,
When the air becomes uranious,
We'll all go simultaneous,
Yes, we'll all go together when we go.
1953 'We'll All Go Together When We Go', satirical song.

Leisen, Mitchell 1898–1972

US film director. His films include *Hold Back the Dawn* (1941), *Frenchman's Creek* (1944) and *Kitty* (1945).

73 He was God out there. He wanted it a certain way, that was the MGM style, and that's what you got.
On working for Cedric Gibbons on *Young Man with Ideas* (1952), quoted in David Chierichetti *Hollywood Director* (1972).

Lekota, Mosiuoa 1948–

South African Defence Minister (1999–).

74 When will we cease to be Africans, Coloureds, Indians and Whites and merely South Africans? This is the question we must ask ourselves.
2004 Briefing the South African parliament's portfolio committee on defence, 1 Jun.

LeMay, Curtis Emerson 1906–90

US general and air force chief. After commanding in World War II he became air force Chief of Staff (1961–5) and ran unsuccessfully for Vice-President as George Wallace's running mate, 1968.

75 My solution to the problem would be to tell them that they've got to draw in their horns, or we're going to bomb them into the Stone Age.
Of the North Vietnamese. *Mission with LeMay* (1965).

76 A man should have dinner with his friends, and the commanding general has no friends.
On declining to dine with a group of colonels. Recalled on his death, 1 Oct 1990.

Lemmon, Jack (John Uhler) 1925–2001

US actor. He made his film debut in *It Should Happen to You* (1954), beginning a career as a comic, bittersweet underdog which won him eight Academy Award nominations and two Oscars.

77 I won't quit until I get run over by a truck, a producer or a critic.
1986 In *Newsweek*, 5 May.

78 I would rather play Hamlet with no rehearsal than TV golf.
Quoted in Michael Hobbs *The Golf Quotation Book* (1992).

79 If you think it's hard to meet new people, try picking up the wrong golf ball.
Attributed.

Lemmy 1945–

English heavy metal singer and bass player, member of the band Motörhead.

80 People don't know how to be outrageous any more.
2004 In *The Guardian*, 31 May.

L'Engle, Madeleine *married name* Mrs Hugh Franklin 1918–

US writer, best known for her children's trilogy *A Wrinkle in Time* (1962), *A Wind in the Door* (1973) and *A Swiftly Tilting Planet* (1978). Her many other works include *Troubling the Star* (1994) and the autobiographical *Summer of Great-Grandmother* (1974).

81 Artistic temperament…sometimes seems a battleground for a dark angel of destruction and a bright angel of creativity wrestling.
1982 *A Severed Wasp.*

Lenin, Vladimir Ilyich *originally* Vladimir Ilyich Ulyanov 1870–1924

Russian Marxist revolutionary and politician. After the Feb 1917 revolution he urged the proletariat to seize power, and in Oct 1917 led the Bolshevik Revolution and headed the first Soviet government. After the Civil War (1918–21) he introduced the New Economic Policy, which his critics saw as a retreat from strict socialism.

82 A small, compact core, consisting of reliable, experienced and hardened workers, with responsible agents…connected by all the rules of strict secrecy with the organisations of revolutionists, can, with the wide support of the masses and without an elaborate set of rules, perform all the functions of a trade union.
1902 *What Is to be Done?*

83 One Step Forward, Two Steps Back
1904 Title of book.

84 I greet you as the advance guard of the world proletarian army. The hour is not far off when…the German people will turn their weapons against their capitalist exploiters. The sun of the socialist revolution has already risen.
1917 Speech, Petrograd, 16 Apr.

85 We will now proceed to the building of socialism.
1917 Speech, Oct. Quoted in A J P Taylor *From the Boer War to the Cold War: Essays on Twentieth-Century Europe* (1995), p.192.

86 A good man fallen among Fabians.
Of George Bernard Shaw. Quoted in Arthur Ransome *Six Weeks in Russia in 1919* (1919).

87 Chess is the gymnasium of the mind.
Quoted in Colin Jarman *The Guinness Dictionary of Sports Quotations* (1990).

Lennon, John Winston 1940–80

English rock singer, guitarist and songwriter. A member of The Beatles, he wrote with Paul McCartney many of the hits of the 1960s. He later established himself as a solo artist. He was shot dead by a deranged fan outside his Manhattan apartment.

88 On this next number I want you all to join in. Would those in the cheap seats clap their hands? The rest of you can rattle your jewellery.
1963 Addressing the audience during a Royal Command performance. Quoted in Bill Harry *The Ultimate Beatles Encyclopedia* (1992).

89 We're more popular than Jesus Christ now. I don't know which will go first, rock and roll or Christianity.
1966 In the *Evening Standard*.

90 All we are saying is give peace a chance.
1969 Song (with his wife, Yoko Ono), used widely in protests against the Vietnam War.

91 Imagine there's no heaven,
It's easy if you try,
No hell below us,
Above us only sky,
Imagine all the people
Living for today.
1971 'Imagine'.

92 Women should be obscene and not heard.
Attributed.

Lennon, John Winston and McCartney, Sir (James) Paul 1940–80, 1942–

English songwriters and composers who formed The Beatles in 1960. They gained international fame with their songs and performances. They disbanded in 1970.

93 For I don't care too much for money,
For money can't buy me love.
1964 'Can't Buy Me Love'.

94 It's been a hard day's night,
And I've been working like a dog.
1964 'A Hard Day's Night'.

95 She's got a ticket to ride, but she don't care.
1965 'Ticket to Ride'.

96 Eleanor Rigby picks up the rice in a church where a wedding has been,
Lives in a dream.
Waits at the window, wearing the face that she keeps in a jar by the door,
Who is it for?
All the lonely people, where do they all come from?
1966 'Eleanor Rigby'.

97 Oh I get by with a little help from my friends,
Mm, I get high with a little help from my friends.
1967 'With a Little Help From My Friends'.

98 Will you still need me, will you still feed me,
When I'm sixty four?
1967 'When I'm Sixty Four'.

99 Strawberry fields forever.
1967 Title of song.

1 Back in the USSR.
1968 Title of song.

Lenthall, William 1591–1662

English lawyer and parliamentarian, Speaker of the Long Parliament (1640–53) and Master of the Rolls from 1643. He was again made Speaker in 1654 and 1659, and in 1657 became one of Cromwell's peers.

2 May it please your Majesty, I have neither eye to see nor tongue to speak in this place, but as this House is pleased to direct me, whose servant I am.
1642 To Charles I, on his arrival in the Chamber to arrest five Members, House of Commons, 4 Jan.

Leonard, Elmore John 1925–

US novelist and screenwriter. He has written mainly in the field of crime fiction, where he is widely regarded as the foremost practitioner of his era.

3 The Chekhov of the suburbs.
Of John Cheever. Quoted in *The Annual Obituary 1982* (1983).

4 I try to leave out the parts that people skip.
1985 In *Publisher's Weekly*, 8 Mar.

5 If it sounds like writing, I rewrite it.
1985 In *Newsweek*, 22 Apr.

6 Easy on the Adverbs, Exclamation Points and Especially Hooptedoodle.
2003 Essay title.

Leonard, Sugar Ray 1956–

US boxer.

7 We're all endowed with certain God-given talents. Mine happens to be punching people in the head.
Quoted in Colin Jarman *The Guinness Dictionary of Sports Quotations* (1990).

Leonardo da Vinci 1452–1519

Italian painter, sculptor, architect and engineer, the epitome of the 'Renaissance' man. He entered the service of Cesare Borgia in 1500 as architect and engineer, working alongside Michelangelo, and worked for Louis XII of France in 1506.

8 To devise is the work of the master, to execute the act of the servant.
Treatise on Painting (published 1651, translated by A P McMahon, 1956).

9 I do not find any difference between painting and sculpture except that the sculptor pursues his work with greater physical fatigue than the painter and the painter pursues his with greater mental fatigue.
Treatise on Painting (published 1651, translated by A P McMahon, 1956).

10 Shun those studies in which the work that results dies with the worker.
The Notebooks of Leonardo da Vinci (translated by Edward MacCurdy, 1938), vol.1, pt.1.

11 Painting is poetry which is seen and not heard, and poetry is a painting which is heard but not seen.
Quoted in J P and Irma A Richter *The Literary Works of Leonardo da Vinci* (2 vols, 1939).

12 Force is the same throughout and the whole is in every part of it. Force is a spiritual power, an invisible energy which is imparted by violence from without to all bodies out of their natural balance.
Quoted in Jean-Paul Richter (ed) *The Literary Works of Leonardo da Vinci* (1939).

13 If a man have a tent made in linen of which the apertures have all been stopped up, and it be twelve *braccia* across and twelve in depth, he will be able to throw himself down from any great height without sustaining injury.
Description of a parachute. *Notebooks*. Quoted in Vincent Cronin *The Flowering of the Renaissance* (1969).

14 The air moves like a river and carries the clouds with it; just as running water carries all the things that float upon it.
Notebooks. Quoted in Vincent Cronin *The Flowering of the Renaissance* (1969).

15 He is a poor disciple who does not excel his master.
Quoted in Irma A Richter (ed) *Selections from the Notebooks of Leonardo da Vinci* (1977).

16 A good painter has two chief objects to paint, man and

the intention of his soul; the former is easy, the latter harder, because he has to represent it by the attitudes and movements of the limbs.
Quoted in Irma A Richter (ed) *Selections from the Notebooks of Leonardo da Vinci* (1977).

17 Perspective is the bridle and rudder of painting.
Quoted in Irma A Richter (ed) *Selections from the Notebooks of Leonardo da Vinci* (1977).

18 The span of a man's outspread arms is equal to his height.
Quoted in Irma A Richter (ed) *Selections from the Notebooks of Leonardo da Vinci* (1977).

19 Do not despise my opinion, when I remind you that it should not be hard for you to stop sometimes and look into the stains of walls, or ashes of a fire, or clouds, or mud or like places, in which, if you consider them well, you may find really marvellous ideas.
Quoted in Irma A Richter (ed) *Selections from the Notebooks of Leonardo da Vinci* (1977).

20 Just as a stone flung into the water becomes the centre and cause of many circles, and as sound diffuses itself in circles in the air; so any object, placed in the luminous atmosphere, diffuses itself in circles, and fills the surrounding air with infinite images of itself.
Quoted in Irma A Richter (ed) *Selections from the Notebooks of Leonardo da Vinci* (1977).

21 The painter who draws by practice and judgement of the eye without the use of reason is like a mirror which copies everything placed in front of it without knowledge of the same.
Quoted in Irma A Richter (ed) *Selections from the Notebooks of Leonardo da Vinci* (1977).

Leonidas d.480 BC

King of Sparta, commander of the Greeks when the Persian army of Xerxes invaded mainland Greece. At the narrow pass of Thermopylae he made a heroic stand with 300 Spartans.

22 Come and take them.
Attributed reply when Xerxes summoned him to surrender his weapons at Thermopylae. Quoted in Plutarch, *Apophthegmata Laconica*.

Lerner, Alan Jay 1918–86

US lyricist, screenwriter and producer. He frequently worked in collaboration with Frederick Loewe, and is best known for *Brigadoon* (1955), *Gigi* (1958), *My Fair Lady* (1964) and *Camelot* (1967).

23 Those little eyes so helpless and appealing
One day will flash and send you crashing through the ceiling.
1958 'Thank Heaven for Little Girls', in the musical *Gigi* (music by Frederick Loewe).

24 We met at nine
—We met at eight
I was on time
—No, you were late
Ah yes! I remember it well.
1958 'I Remember it Well', in the musical *Gigi* (music by Frederick Loewe).

25 I've Grown Accustomed To Her Face.
1964 Title of song, in *My Fair Lady* (music by Marcus Loewe).

26 Oozing charm from every pore
He oiled his way around the floor.
1964 'You Did It', from *My Fair Lady* (music by Marcus Loewe).

27 Why can't a woman be more like a man?
Men are so honest, so thoroughly square;
Eternally noble, historically fair;
Who, when you win, will always give your back a pat.
Why can't a woman be like that?
1964 'A Hymn to Him', from *My Fair Lady* (music by Frederick Loewe).

28 Because it saves time.
When Andrew Lloyd Webber asked him 'Why do people take an instant dislike to me?' Quoted by Leah Garchik in the *San Francisco Chronicle*, 27 Nov 1990.

Le Sage, Alain René 1668–1747

French novelist and playwright. He is best remembered for his play *Turcaret* (1709), which satirized the financial world, and the picaresque novel *Gil Blas de Santillane* (1715–35).

29 Justice is such a fine thing that we cannot pay too dearly for it.
1707 *Crispin rival de son maître*, pt.9.

Leslie, David 1601–82

Scottish soldier. He fought at Marston Moor (1644), and defeated Montrose at Philiphaugh (1645). Routed by Cromwell at Dunbar in 1650, he was subsequently imprisoned and held in the Tower until the Restoration. He was made Lord Newark in 1651.

30 How glorious it would be in the eyes of God and men, if we managed to hunt the Catholics from England, follow them to France, and, like the bold King of Sweden, rouse the Protestants in France, plant our religion in Paris by agreement or force, and go from there to Rome to chase the Antichrist and burn the town whence superstition comes.
1643 Said to Lord Hume, Council of Scottish Nobles, Aug.

Lessing, Doris May *née Tayler* 1919–

Rhodesian writer, born in Iran. She has lived much of her adult life in England after being exiled for her opposition to the white Southern Rhodesian government. She was a communist for a time, and later an icon of the women's movement. Her best-known works are the novel sequence *Children of Violence* (1952–69) and *The Golden Notebook* (1962).

31 When old settlers say 'One has to understand the country,' what they mean is, 'You have to get used to our ideas about the native.' They are saying, in effect, 'Learn our ideas, or otherwise get out; we don't want you.'
1950 *The Grass Is Singing*, ch.1.

32 When a white man in Africa by accident looks into the eyes of a native and sees the human being (which it is his chief preoccupation to avoid), his sense of guilt, which he denies, fumes up in resentment and he brings down the whip.
1950 *The Grass Is Singing*, ch.8.

33 I had learned that if one cannot call a country to heel like a dog, neither can one dismiss the past with a smile in an easy gush of feeling, saying: I could not help it, I am also a victim.
1951 *This was the Old Chief's Country*, 'The Old Chief Mshlanga'.

34 For she was suffering that misery peculiar to the young, that they are going to be cheated by circumstances out

of the full life every nerve and instinct is clamouring for.
1952 *Martha Quest*, pt.1, ch.1.

35 She was thinking—for, since she had been formed by literature, she could think in no other way—that all this had been described in Dickens, Tolstoy, Hugo, Dostoevsky, and a dozen others. All that noble and terrific indignation had done nothing, achieved nothing, the shout of anger from the nineteenth century might as well have been silent—for here came the file of prisoners, handcuffed two by two, and on their faces was that same immemorial look of patient, sardonic understanding.
1952 *Martha Quest*, ch.2.

36 In every city there is a group of middle-aged and elderly women who in fact run it. The extent to which they are formally organised is no gauge of their real power. The way in which they respond to danger is that gauge; and from the frankness with which they express their intentions can be measured the extent of the danger.
1954 *A Proper Marriage*, pt.3, ch.1.

37 Martha and Jasmine smiled at each other…the future they dreamed of seemed just around the corner; they could almost touch it. Each saw an ideal town, clean, noble and beautiful, soaring up over the actual town they saw, which consisted in this area of sordid little shops and third-rate cafés.
1958 *A Ripple from the Storm*, pt.1, ch.1.

38 There is only one real sin, and that is to persuade oneself that the second-best is anything but the second-best.
1962 *The Golden Notebook*, 'The Blue Notebook'.

39 It occurred to her that she was going mad… Yet it did not seem to her that she was even slightly mad; but rather that people who were not as obsessed as she was with the inchoate world mirrored in the newspapers were all out of touch with an awful necessity.
1962 *The Golden Notebook*, 'Free Women 5'.

40 But this novel was not a trumpet for Women's Liberation. It described many female emotions of aggression, hostility, resentment. It put them into print. Apparently what many women were thinking, feeling, experiencing came as a great surprise.
1971 *The Golden Notebook*, preface to new edition.

41 Briefing for a Descent into Hell.
1971 Title of novel.

42 It does no harm to repeat, as often as you can, 'Without me the literary industry would not exist'.
1980 In *The Author*, spring.

43 To be in love with a country or a political regime is a tricky business. You get your heart broken even more surely than by being in love with a person.
1992 *African Laughter*, 'Next Time 1988'.

Lessing, Gotthold Ephraim 1729–81

German philosopher and playwright, an important Enlightenment figure, best known for his essay on aesthetics, *Laokoon* (1766).

44 *Wie manches würde in der Theorie unwidersprechlich scheinen, wenn es dem Genie nicht gelungen wäre, das Widerspiel durch die Tat zu erweisen.*
How many things would have appeared incontestable in theory if genius had not proved them wrong in practice.
1766 *Laokoon: an essay upon the limits of painting and poetry*, pt.4.

45 *Ein einziger dankbarer Gedanke gen Himmel ist das vollkommenste Gebet.*
One single grateful thought raised to heaven is the most perfect prayer.
1767 *Minna von Barnhelm*, act 2, sc.7.

46 *Wer richtig räsonniert, erfindet auch; und wer erfinden will, muss räsonnieren können. Nur die glauben, dass sich das eine von dem anderen trennen lasse, die zu keinem von beiden aufgelegt sind.*
The man who can reason properly can invent; and anyone who wants to invent must be able to reason. The only people who think that the one can be separated from the other are those who have no inclination for either.
1769 *Hamburgische Dramaturgie*.

47 *Es ist nicht wahr, dass die kürzeste Linie immer die Gerade ist.*
It is not true that the shortest line is always the straight one.
1780 *Die Erziehung des Menschengeschlechts*.
► *See also Brecht 151:10.*

L'Estrange, Sir Roger 1616–1704

English journalist and pamphleteer. During the Restoration he was Licenser of the Press.

48 Supposing the Press in order, the people in their right wits, and news or no news to be the question, a Public Mercury should not have my Vote, because I think it makes the Multitude too familiar with the actions and counsels of their superiors, too pragmatical and censorious, and gives them not only an itch but a kind of colourable right to be meddling with the government.
1663 *The Intelligencer*, 31 Aug.

Leupold, Jakob 1674–1727

German mechanic, machinery constructor and government mining commissioner, who wrote a large and comprehensive work on the tasks the engineer faced.

49 As in earlier days were our mechanics, such today are our engineers, who may be required not only to tear down a fortress, and then to build it up again, but also to produce all sorts of engines based on mechanical principles, and with equal ease to defend or to annihilate a fortress.
1724 *Theatrum machinarum*.

50 The best machines and to be chosen above all others are those which consist of the fewest parts or which are the simplest, which produce the least friction; which are not too heavily loaded, and where the power can be conveniently applied without any waste.
1724 *Theatrum machinarum*.

Levant, Oscar 1906–72

US composer, pianist, writer, actor and conductor. He played Gershwin's 'Rhapsody in Blue' on its first performance in 1932.

51 It's a right step in the wrong direction.
1935 Attributed remark at the first performance of George

Gershwin's *Porgy and Bess*. He in fact had the deepest respect for Gershwin's music.

52 Chutzpah—that quality which enables a man who has murdered his mother and father to throw himself on the mercy of the court as an orphan.
1968 *The Unimportance of Being Oscar.*

Levenson, Michael

US literary critic, a professor of English at the University of Virginia.

53 Although Brooke never succeeded in becoming the first modern poet, he may deserve to be called the first modern undergraduate, a title of comparable significance.
1987 Of Rupert Brooke. 'Budding Brooke', in the *New Republic*, 31 Aug.

Levenstein, Ros

US copywriter.

54 I'm only here for the beer.
1971 British advertising slogan for Double Diamond beer.

Leverson, Ada 1895–1936

English novelist and journalist, she was friendly with Beerbohm and Wilde, who called her 'the Sphinx'. She wrote six novels.

55 You don't know a woman until you have had a letter from her.
1912 *Tenterhooks*, ch.7.

56 He seemed at ease and to have the look of the last gentleman in Europe.
1930 Of Oscar Wilde. *Letters to the Sphinx*.

Levertov, Denise 1923–97

English-born US poet. She is associated with the Black Mountain group of poets led by Charles Olsen, but has a distinctive voice of her own, reflected in numerous collections.

57 Let's go—much as that dog goes,
intently haphazard.
1958 *Overland to the Islands*, 'Overland to the Islands'.

58 Pergo Park knew me, and Clavering, and Havering-atte-Bower,
Stanford Rivers lost me in osier-beds, Stapleford Abbots
sent me safe home on the dark road after Simeon-quiet evensong,
Wanstead drew me over and over into its basic poetry,
in its serpentine lake I saw bass-viols among the golden dead
leaves,
through its trees the ghost of a great house.
1961 *The Jacob's Ladder*, 'A Map of the Western Part of the County of Essex in England'.

59 The world is
not with us enough.
1964 *O Taste and See*, 'O Taste and See'.
➡ *See Wordsworth 925:4.*

60 Death and pain dominate this world, for though
many are cured, they leave still weak,

still tremulous, still knowing mortality
has whispered to them; have seen in the folding
of white bedspreads according to rule

the starched pleats of a shroud.
1972 *Footprints*, 'The Malice of Innocence'.

Levi, Primo 1919–87

Italian writer and the author of a series of major works of remembrance and analysis of his experiences in Nazi concentration camps in World War II.

61 The future of humanity is uncertain, even in the most prosperous countries, and the quality of life deteriorates; and yet I believe that what is being discovered about the infinitely large and infinitely small is sufficient to absolve this end of the century and millennium. What a very few are acquiring in knowledge of the physical world will perhaps cause this period not to be judged as a pure return of barbarism.
1985 *Other People's Trades*, 'News from the Sky' (translated by Raymond Rosenthal, 1989).

Levin, (Henry) Bernard 1928–2004

English writer, journalist and critic. In 1985 he crossed the Alps on foot, following the path of the Carthaginian general, Hannibal.

62 The musical equivalent of blancmange.
1983 Of the music of Frederick Delius. *Enthusiasms*.

63 I dislike almost all dogs, but Alsatians, I do truly believe, should be prohibited by law in any civilised country… The more I see of dogs, the more I admire men.
1985 *Hannibal's Footsteps*.

64 Baedeker is astonishingly enduring; travellers can use nineteenth-century editions with confidence, providing they take some elementary precautions. Many hotels will long since have disappeared, and the prices will be somewhat different, but if Baedeker says 'On leaving the tunnel, the best view is on the right', it probably still is, unless somebody has shifted the mountain, and his descriptions of scenery and where to go to see it at its best are still valid, as is practically all of his potted history.
1985 *Hannibal's Footsteps*.

Lévis, Duc de 1764–1830

French soldier and writer.

65 *Noblesse oblige.*
Nobility brings obligations.
1812 *Maximes et réflexions*, 'Morale: Maximes et Préceptes', no.73.

Lévi-Strauss, Claude 1908–

French social anthropologist.

66 *La langue est une raison humaine qui a ses raisons, et que l'homme ne connaît pas.*
Language is a form of human reason, and has its reasons which are unknown to man.
1962 *La Pensée sauvage*, ch.9.
➡ *See Pascal 641:23.*

67 The scientific mind does not so much provide the right answers as ask the right questions.
1964 *The Raw and the Cooked* (translated by John and Doreen Weightman 1983).

68 I can't help thinking that science would be more appealing if it had no practical use.
1964 *The Raw and the Cooked* (translated by John and Doreen Weightman 1983).

Lewin, Albert 1895–1968

US screenwriter and director. His films include *The Moon and Sixpence* (1943), *The Picture of Dorian Gray* (1945) and *Pandora and the Flying Dutchman* (1950).

69 The measure of love is what one is willing to give up for it.
1950 *Pandora and the Flying Dutchman.*

Lewis, C(live) S(taples) 1898–1963

English novelist, literary scholar and theological writer. His most widely read works include the children's series *The Chronicles of Narnia* (1950–6), several allegorical science-fiction novels, and the Christian apologetics, *The Screwtape Letters* (1942).

70 Humanity does not pass through phases as a train passes through stations: being alive, it has the privilege of always moving yet never leaving anything behind.
1936 *The Allegory of Love*, ch.1.

71 Out of the Silent Planet.
1938 Title of novel.

72 There is wishful thinking in Hell as well as on earth.
1942 *The Screwtape Letters*, preface.

73 Gratitude looks to the past and love to the present: fear, avarice, lust and ambition look ahead.
1942 *The Screwtape Letters*, no.15.

74 He has a vulgar mind.
1942 Of God. *The Screwtape Letters*, no.22.

75 She's the sort of woman who lives for others—you can always tell the others by their hunted expression.
1942 *The Screwtape Letters*, no.26.

76 Fatigue makes women talk more and men less.
1942 *The Screwtape Letters*, no.30.

77 Courage is not simply one of the virtues but the form of every virtue at the testing point.
Quoted in Cyril Connolly *The Unquiet Grave* (1944), ch.3.

78 I remember summing up what I took to be our destiny, in conversation with my best friend at Chartres, by the formula, 'Term, holidays, term, holidays, till we leave school, and then work, work, work till we die.'
1955 *Surprised by Joy*, ch.4.

79 A sick society must think much about politics, as a sick man must think much about his digestion.
1980 *The Weight of Glory.*

80 All except the best men would rather be called wicked than vulgar.
Quoted in *The Guardian*, 21 Aug 1980.

Lewis, Esther *married name* Clark fl.1747–89

English poet.

81 Are simple women only fit
To dress, to darn, to flower or knit,
To mind the distaff, or the spit?
Why are the needle and the pen
Thought incompatible by men?
1754 'A Mirror for Detractors', l.146–50.

Lewis, Joe E 1902–71

US comedian.

82 I distrust camels and anyone else who can go a week without a drink.
Recalled on his death, 4 Jun 1971.

Lewis, John L(lewellyn) 1880–1969

US labour leader.

83 No tin hat brigade of goose-stepping vigilantes or bibblebabbling mob of blackguarding and corporation-paid scoundrels will prevent the onward march of labor, or divert its purpose to play its natural and rational part in the development of the economic, political, and social life of our nation.
1937 Address, 3 Sep. Recalled on his death 11 Jun 1969.

84 All forms of government fall when it comes up to the question of bread—bread for the family, something to eat. Bread to a man with a family comes first—before his union, before his citizenship, before his church affiliation. Bread!
1963 In the *Saturday Evening Post*, 12 Oct.

Lewis, (Harry) Sinclair 1885–1951

US novelist. His novels satirized the materialism and intolerance of US small town life. He is best known for his novel *Babbitt* (1922), a study of middle-class philistinism. In 1930 he became the first American to receive the Nobel prize for literature.

85 He never put on BVDs without thanking the God of Progress that he didn't wear tight, long, old-fashioned undergarments.
1922 *Babbitt*, ch.1, section 4. BVD is a trademark for a brand of US underwear.

86 His name was George F. Babbitt. He was forty-six years old now, in April, 1920, and he made nothing in particular, neither butter nor shoes nor poetry, but he was nimble in the calling of selling houses for more than people could afford to pay.
1922 *Babbitt*, ch.1.

87 To George F. Babbitt, as to most prosperous citizens of Zenith, his motor car was poetry and tragedy, love and heroism. The office was his pirate ship but the car his perilous excursion ashore.
1922 *Babbitt*, ch.3.

88 In other countries, art and literature are left to a lot of shabby bums living in attics and feeding on booze and spaghetti, but in America the successful writer or picture-painter is indistinguishable from any other decent business man.
1922 *Babbitt*, ch.14.

89 Damn the great executives, the men of measured merriment, damn the men with careful smiles, damn the men that run the shops, oh, damn their measured merriment.
1925 *Arrowsmith*, ch.25.

90 Our American professors like their literature clear and cold and pure and very dead.
1930 Nobel prize address, 12 Dec.

91 Intellectually I know that America is no better than any other country; emotionally I know she is better than

every other country.
1930 Interview in Berlin, 29 Dec.

92 It Can't Happen Here.
1935 Title of novel.

93 A man takes a drink, a drink takes another, and the drink takes the man.
Words to his future wife, Dorothy Thompson. Quoted in Vincent Sheean *Dorothy and Red* (1963).

Lewis, (Percy) Wyndham 1882–1957

English novelist, painter and critic. He co-founded the Vorticist movement with Ezra Pound, and remained an important experimental writer and painter between the wars. He became blind in 1951, but continued to write. His works include *The Apes of God* (1930) and the autobiographical *The Self Condemned* (1954).

94 'Dying for an idea,' again, sounds well enough, but why not let the idea die instead of you?
1926 *The Art of Being Ruled*, pt.1, ch.1.

95 When we say 'science' we can either mean any manipulation of the inventive and organizing power of the human intellect: or we can mean such an extremely different thing as the religion of science, the vulgarized derivative from this pure activity manipulated by a sort of priestcraft into a great religious and political weapon.
1926 *The Art of Being Ruled*.

96 The puritanical potentialities of science have never been forecast. If it evolves a body of organized rites, and is established as a religion, hierarchically organized, things more than anything else will be done in the name of 'decency'. The coarse fumes of tobacco and liquors, the consequent tainting of the breath and staining of white fingers and teeth, which is so offensive to many women, will be the first things attended to.
1926 *The Art of Being Ruled*.

97 The revolutionary simpleton is everywhere.
1927 *Time and Western Man*, pt.1, ch.6.

98 Gertrude Stein's prose song is a cold, black suet-pudding…of fabulously reptilian length.
1927 *Time and Western Man*, pt.1, ch.13.

99 If you must go nowhere, step out.
1928 *The Childermass*, final words.

1 It is to what I have called the Apes of God that I am drawing your attention—those prosperous mountebanks who alternately imitate and mock at and traduce those figures they at once admire and hate.
1930 *The Apes of God*, pt.3.

2 The soul started at the knee-cap and ended at the navel.
1930 *The Apes of God*, pt.12.

3 Give me the *outside* of all things, I am a fanatic for the externality of things.
1937 *Blasting and Bombardiering*, ch.1.

4 Then down came the lid—the day was lost, for art, at Sarajevo. World-politics stepped in, and a war was started which has not ended yet: 'a war to end war'. But it merely ended art. It did not end war.
1937 *Blasting and Bombardiering*, pt.5, 'Toward an Art-Less Society'.

5 'The Art of Being Ruled' might be described from some points of view as an infernal Utopia.
1950 *Rude Assignment*, ch.31.

6 An account…of the decadence occupying the trough between the two world wars introduces us to a moronic inferno of insipidity and decay.
1950 *Rude Assignment*, ch.31.

LeWitt, Sol 1928–

US artist, one of the developers of the branch of Conceptual art referred to as 'Minimalism'.

7 In Conceptual art the idea or concept is the most important aspect of the work…all planning and decisions are made beforehand and the execution is a perfunctory affair. The idea becomes the machine that makes the art.
1967 'Paragraphs on Conceptual Art', in *Artforum*, summer.

8 One usually understands the art of the past by applying the conventions of the present thus misunderstanding the art of the past.
1969 'Sentences on Conceptual Art', in *Art-Language*, vol.1, no.1, May.

Lewontin, Richard Charles 1929–

US evolutionary biologist, geneticist and writer, Professor of Zoology at Harvard.

9 It is characteristic of the design of scientific research that exquisite attention is devoted to methodological problems that can be solved, while the pretense is made that the ones that cannot be solved are really nothing to worry about.
1995 'Sex, Lies, and Social Science', in the *New York Review of Books*, 20 Apr.

10 The social scientist is in a difficult, if not impossible position. On the one hand there is the temptation to see all of society as one's autobiography writ large, surely not the path to general truth. On the other hand, there is the attempt to be general and objective by pretending that one knows nothing about the experience of being human, forcing the investigator to pretend that people usually know and tell the truth about important issues, when we all know from our own lives how impossible that is.
1995 'Sex, Lies, and Social Science', in the *New York Review of Books*, 20 Apr.

Leybourne, George *pseudonym of* Joseph Saunders 1842–84

English singer, entertainer and songwriter, a star of the Victorian music-hall.

11 O, he flies through the air with the greatest of ease,
This daring young man on the flying trapeze.
1868 'The Daring Young Man on the Flying Trapeze'.

Lezama Lima, José 1910–76

Cuban poet, novelist and essayist. His autobiographical novel *Paradiso* (1966) is considered his masterpiece, and he is the key figure of Cuban neo-Baroque literature.

12 *Más que una costumbre, parece como un conjuro para una divinidad que todos desconocemos, que al reunirse varios cubanos…se permanece en un silencio de suspensión, hasta que se oye una voz cualquiera que dice o canta algo, que no tiene relación con la convocatoria para la reunión.*

Rather than custom, it feels more like an invocation to an unknown deity when Cubans get together...they hold a suspenseful silence until any voice is heard saying or singing something that has nothing to do with the purpose of the meeting.
1966 *Paradiso*, ch.3.

Li Po 701–62

Chinese poet, patronized by Emperor Ming Huang until banished from the court. He is said to have drowned after falling intoxicated from a barge, in an attempt to embrace the moon's reflection in the water.

13 Since Life is but a Dream,
Why toil to no avail?
c.750 'A Homily on Ideals in Life, Uttered in Springtime on Rising from a Drunken Slumber', collected in *A Golden Treasury of Chinese Poetry* (translated by John Turner, 1967).

Liberace *pseudonym of* *Wladziu Valentino Liberace* 1919–87

US pianist and entertainer, renowned for his flamboyant lifestyle.

14 What you said hurt me very much. I cried all the way to the bank.
1973 Responding to a hostile critic. *Autobiography.*

Liberman, Alexander 1912–99

Russian-born US artist and editor, artistic director of Vogue (1943–62). His works include *Olympic Iliad* (1984) and *Faith* (1987). He published *The Artist in his Studio* (1960).

15 All art is solitary and the studio is a torture area.
1979 In the *New York Times*, 13 May.

Lichtenberg, Georg Christoph 1742–99

German scientist and philosopher, a lecturer at the University of Göttingen. His philosophical reputation rests on his aphorisms, collected in notebooks throughout his adult life.

16 Every man also has his moral backside which he refrains from showing unless he has to and keeps covered as long as possible with the trousers of decorum.
c.1770 *Aphorisms*, Notebook B (translated by R J Hollingdale, 1990).

17 If an angel were ever to tell us anything of his philosophy I believe many propositions would sound like 2 times 2 equals 13.
c.1770 *Aphorisms*, Notebook B (translated by R J Hollingdale, 1990).

18 When a book and a head collide and a hollow sound is heard, must it always have come from the book?
c.1773–1775 *Aphorisms*, Notebook D (translated by R J Hollingdale, 1990).

19 What they call 'heart' lies much lower than the fourth waistcoat button.
c.1776–1779 *Aphorisms*, Notebook F (translated by R J Hollingdale, 1990).

20 It is almost impossible to bear the torch of truth through a crowd without singeing someone's beard.
c.1779–1783 *Aphorisms*, Notebook G (translated by R J Hollingdale, 1990).

21 To *err* is human also in so far as the animals seldom or never err, or at least only the cleverest of them do so.
c.1779–1783 *Aphorisms*, Notebook G (translated by R J Hollingdale, 1990).

22 Once he has stolen his 100,100 thalers a rogue can walk through the world an honest man.
c.1784–1788 *Aphorisms*, Notebook H (translated by R J Hollingdale, 1990).

23 A golden rule: we must judge men, not by their opinions, but by what their opinions make of them.
c.1791 *Aphorisms*, Notebook J (translated by R J Hollingdale, 1990).

24 Doubt everything at least once, even the proposition that two times two equals four.
c.1796 *Aphorisms*, Notebook K (translated by R J Hollingdale, 1990).

Lichtenstein, Roy 1923–97

US painter, a key figure of Pop Art. He moved from Abstract Expressionism in the 1950s to illustrations from popular magazines and cartoon strips, duplicating the dots of newspaper reproduction in colourful, large-scale works.

25 Paintings are Rorschach ink blots. They are what you want them to be.
1993 In *The Times*, 27 Mar.

Liebermann, Max 1847–1935

German painter and graphic artist. His early works are open air studies and sentimental scenes of humble life, and he later found a more colourful, romantic style, influenced by Impressionism.

26 The art of drawing is the art of omission.
Quoted in Paul Klee *On Modern Art* (1979).

Liebman, David 1946–

US jazz saxophonist, highly regarded as a performer and teacher.

27 A jazz performance centers upon the process of creation. The final objective is not only the finished product, but the path and process taken towards it.
1988 *Self-Portrait of a Jazz-Artist*, ch.3.

Ligne, Charles Joseph, Prince de 1735–1814

Belgian soldier and man of letters, who served in the Seven Year's War (1756–63) and the Russo-Turkish war (1787–93). A skilful diplomat and royal favourite, he also wrote extensively.

28 *Le congrès ne marche pas, il danse.*
The Congress makes no progress; it dances.
1814 On the Congress of Vienna (1814–15). Quoted in Auguste de la Garde-Chambonas *Souvenirs du Congrès de Vienne, 1814–1815* (1820), ch.1.

29 One could forgive the fiend for becoming a torrent, but to become an earthquake was really too much.
1814 Of Napoleon I. Attributed.

Lillie, Beatrice Gladys *stage-name of* *Constance Sylvia Munston, Lady Peel* 1898–1989

Canadian-born actress. A star of light comedy and revue, she married Sir Robert Peel in 1920 and published an autobiography, *Every Other Inch a Lady* (1973).

30 Heard there was a party. Came.
Explaining her presence after staggering to the nearest house, that of film actor John Gilbert, when she was involved

in a car accident in Hollywood. Attributed.

Lillo, George 1693–1739

English dramatist and jeweller, of Dutch extraction. His seven plays were among the first to put middle-class rather than royal characters on the English stage.

31 There's sure no passion in the human soul,
But finds its food in music.
1736 *Fatal Curiosity*, act 1, sc.2.

Lin Yutang 1895–1976

Chinese author and philologist. He lived mainly in the US and was Chancellor of Singapore University (1954–5). He is best known for his novels and essays on Chinese culture and wisdom.

32 All women's dresses, in every age and country, are merely variations on the eternal struggle between the admitted desire to dress and the unadmitted desire to undress.
1945 In the *Ladies Home Journal*.

Lincoln, Abraham 1809–65

US Republican statesman, 16th President (1861–5) and opponent of slavery. In the Civil War he defined the issue in terms of national integrity, not anti-slavery, but proclaimed freedom for all slaves in areas of rebellion. He was shot at Ford's Theatre, Washington, by John Wilkes Booth, an actor, and he died next morning.

33 No man is good enough to govern another man without that other's consent.
1854 Speech, Peoria, 16 Oct.

34 'A house divided against itself cannot stand': I believe that this Government cannot endure permanently half-slave and half-free. I do not expect the Union to be dissolved. I do not expect the house to fall—but I do expect it will cease to be divided. It will become all one thing, or all the other.
1858 Speech, Springfield, 16 Jun.

35 You can fool some of the people some of the time, and some of the people all the time, but you cannot fool all the people all of the time.
1858 Speech, Clinton, 8 Sep.

36 The patent system...added the fuel of *interest* to the *fire* of genius.
1859 Collected in Roy B Basler (ed) *Collected Works* (1953).

37 What is conservatism? Is it not adherence to the old and tried, against the new and untried?
1860 Speech, New York, 27 Feb.

38 Let us have faith that right makes might; and in that faith let us to the end dare to do our duty as we understand it.
1860 Speech, New York, 27 Feb.

39 Four score and seven years ago our fathers brought forth upon this continent a new nation, conceived in liberty and dedicated to the proposition that all men are created equal...we here highly resolve that the dead shall not have died in vain; that this nation, under God, shall have a new birth of freedom; and that government of the people, by the people, and for the people, shall not perish from the earth.
1863 Dedication address, Gettysburg National Cemetery, 19 Nov.

40 The brave men, living and dead, who struggled here, have consecrated [this ground], far above our poor power to add or detract. The world will little note, nor long remember what we say here, but it can never forget what they did here.
1863 Dedication address, Gettysburg National Cemetery, 19 Nov.

41 With malice toward none, with charity for all, with firmness in the right, as God gives us to see the right, let us strive on to finish the work we are in, to bind up the nation's wounds, to care for him who shall have borne the battle, and for his widow and his orphan, to do all which may achieve and cherish a just and and lasting peace among ourselves, and with all nations.
1865 Second inaugural address, 4 Mar, a month before the end of the Civil War.

Lindbergh, Anne Spencer Morrow 1906–2001

US writer, widow of the aviator Charles Augustus Lindbergh. Her works include *North to the Orient*, an account of flights with her husband (1935), and an essay collection, *Earth Shine* (1970).

42 Thoughts die and are buried in the silences between sentences.
1980 Of the conversational style of US Secretary of State John Foster Dulles. *War Within and Without*.

Lindbergh, Charles A(ugustus) 1902–74

US aviator who made the first solo, non-stop transatlantic flight in *The Spirit of St Louis*, landing in Paris on 21 May 1927. He spoke in favour of isolationism at the beginning of World War II, but subsequently flew in combat missions.

43 I have seen the science I worshipped and the aircraft I loved, destroying the civilization I expected them to serve.
1967 In *Time*, 26 May.

Lindsay, John Vliet 1921–2000

US politician, Mayor of New York City (1966–74).

44 You'll make the mummies dance.
To Thomas Hoving, new director of the Metropolitan Museum of Art, who later adopted the phrase as a book title. Quoted in Thomas Hoving *Making the Mummies Dance* (1993).

Lindsay, (Nicholas) Vachel 1879–1931

US poet. He functioned for a time almost as a travelling troubadour across the US, trading his incantatory verses for hospitality. He suffered serious depression in later years, and committed suicide.

45 Booth led boldly with his big brass drum—
(Are you washed in the blood of the Lamb?)
The saints smiled gravely and they said 'He's come.'
1913 *General Booth Enters Into Heaven*, 'General Booth Enters Into Heaven'.

46 Drabs from the alleyways and drug fiends pale—
Minds still passion-ridden, soul-power frail:—
Vermin-eaten saints with moldy breath,
Unwashed legions with the ways of Death—
(Are you washed in the blood of the Lamb?)
1913 *General Booth Enters Into Heaven*, 'General Booth Enters Into Heaven'.

47 Booth died blind and still by faith he trod,

Eyes still dazzled by the ways of God.
1913 *General Booth Enters Into Heaven*, 'General Booth Enters Into Heaven'.

48 Then I saw the Congo, creeping through the black,
Cutting through the forest with a golden track.
1914 *The Congo and Other Poems*, 'The Congo', pt.1.

49 Mumbo-Jumbo is dead in the jungle
1914 *The Congo and Other Poems*, 'The Congo', pt.3.

50 It is portentous, and a thing of state
That here at midnight, in our little town
A mourning figure walks, and will not rest,
Near the old courthouse pacing up and down.
1914 *The Congo and Other Poems*, 'Abraham Lincoln Walks At Midnight'.

51 And who will bring white peace
That he may sleep upon his hill again?
1914 *The Congo and Other Poems*, 'Abraham Lincoln Walks At Midnight'.

52 The flower-fed buffalos of the spring
In the days of long ago,
Ranged where the locomotives sing
And the prairie flowers lie low.
1926 *Going to the Stars*, 'The Flower-Fed Buffaloes'.

53 They gore no more, they bellow no more,
They trundle around the hills no more:—
With the Blackfeet, lying low,
With the Pawnees, lying low,
Lying low.
1926 *Going to the Stars*, 'The Flower-Fed Buffaloes'.

Linklater, Eric Robert 1889–1974

Scottish journalist and writer, born in Wales. While in the US (1928–30) he wrote *Poet's Pub* (1929), the first of a series of satirical novels which include *Juan in America* (1931) and *Private Angelo* (1946). Other works include books for children, such as *The Wind on the Moon* (1944), plays and memoirs.

54 All I've got against it is that it takes you so far from the club house.
1929 Of golf. *Poet's Pub*, ch.3.

55 Authors and uncaptured criminals...are the only people free from routine.
1929 *Poet's Pub*, ch.23.

56 With a heavy step Sir Matthew left the room and spent the morning designing mausoleums for his enemies.
1931 *Juan in America*, prologue.

57 It is notorious that we speak no more than half-truths in our ordinary conversation, and even a soliloquy is likely to be affected by the apprehension that walls have ears.
1931 *Juan in America*, bk.2, pt.4.

58 She looks like a million dollars, but she only knows a hundred and twenty words and she's only got two ideas in her head. The other one's hats.
1931 *Juan in America*, bk.2, pt.5.

59 There won't be any revolution in America... The people are all too clean. They spend all their time changing their shorts and washing themselves. You can't feel fierce and revolutionary in a bathroom.
1931 Isadore. *Juan in America*, bk.5, pt.3.

60 I dislike burdens...and at my back I often hear Time's winged chariot changing gear.
1937 Juan. *Juan in China*, 'End-Piece'.
► See Marvell 556:62.

61 Wanting to know an author because you like his books is like wanting to know a goose because you like pâté.
Quoted by Kenneth Murphy in the *Washington Post*, 27 Nov 1994.

Linnaeus, Carolus 1707–78

Swedish botanist and taxonomist, the founder of modern scientific classification of plants and animals.

62 Nature does not make jumps.
1750 *Philosophia Botanica*, no.77.

63 Minerals grow, plants grow and live, animals grow and live and feel.
'Systema Naturae', collected in E A Hackel *Generelle Morphologie* (1866).

Lippard, Lucy 1937–

US art critic and feminist.

64 The New York Pop artists are often asked whether or not they like their subjects. This, as Dorothy Seckler has noted, is as irrelevant as asking whether Cézanne liked apples, Géricault corpses, or Picasso guitars.
1966 *Pop Art*.

Lippmann, Walter 1899–1974

US journalist, a columnist with the New York *Herald Tribune*, awarded a Pulitzer Prize for international reporting (1962). He also wrote *Public Opinion* (1922) and *The Cold War* (1947).

65 The present crisis of Western democracy is a crisis in journalism.
1920 *Liberty and the News*, 'Journalism and the Higher Law'.

66 There can be no higher law in journalism than to tell the truth and shame the devil.
1920 *Liberty and the News*, 'Journalism and the Higher Law'.
► See Shakespeare 742:17.

67 The news of the day as it reaches the newspaper office is an incredible medley of fact, propaganda, rumor, suspicion, clues, hopes, and fears, and the task of selecting and ordering that news is one of the truly sacred and priestly offices in a democracy. For the newspaper is in all literalness the bible of democracy, the book out of which a people determines its conduct.
1920 *Liberty and the News*, 'What Modern Liberty Means'.

68 Newspapers necessarily and inevitably reflect, and therefore, in greater or lesser measure, intensify, the defective organization of public opinion.
1922 *Public Opinion*, ch.1.

69 Usually it is the stereotyped shape assumed by an event at an obvious place that uncovers the run of the news.
1922 *Public Opinion*, ch.23.

70 The news is not a mirror of social conditions, but the report of an aspect that has obtruded itself.
1922 *Public Opinion*, ch.23.

71 The function of news is to signalize an event, the function of truth is to bring to light the hidden facts, to set them into relation with each other, and make a picture of reality on which men can act. Only at those points, where social conditions take recognizable and measurable shape, do the body of truth and the body of news coincide.
1922 *Public Opinion*, ch.23.

72 Successful politicians…are insecure and intimidated men. They advance politically only as they placate, appease, bribe, seduce, bamboozle, or otherwise manage to manipulate the demanding and threatening elements in their constituencies.
1955 *The Public Philosophy*, ch.2, sect.4.

73 The public interest may be presumed to be what men would choose if they saw clearly, thought rationally, acted disinterestedly and benevolently.
1955 *The Public Philosophy*, ch.4.

Lispector, Clarice 1925–77

Brazilian novelist, born in the Ukraine. Her artistic vision transcends time and place, and her characters (often female) are only incidentally modern or Brazilian.

74 *Dessa civilização só pode sair quem tem como função especial a de sair: a um cientista é dada a licença, a um padre é dada a permissão. Mas não a uma mulher que nem sequer tem as garantias de um título.*
Only he whose special function is departure can depart from that civilization: a scientist is given license, a priest is given permission. But these are not given to a woman who does not even have the guarantee of a title.
1964 *A Paixão Segundo G.H.* (The Passion According to G.H.).

75 *O bom era ter uma inteligência e não entender. Era uma bênção estranha como a de ter loucura sem ser doida. Era um desinteresse manso em relação às coisas ditas do intelecto, uma doçura de estupidez.*
What was good was to have intelligence and yet not understand. It was a strange blessing like experiencing madness without being mad. It was a gentle lack of interest with respect to the so-called things of the intellect, a sweet stupidity.
1969 *Uma Aprendizagem ou O Livro dos Prazeres*, 'Luminescência' (translated as *An Apprenticeship or The Book of Delights*, 1986).

Liszt, Franz 1811–86

Hungarian composer and pianist. An acclaimed technical and lyrical player, his works include symphonic poems, sacred works, masses and vocal and piano works in which he often experimented with new musical forms.

76 *Ich kann warten.*
I can wait.
When it was suggested to him that his music was being neglected. Quoted in F Lamond *Memoirs* (1949).

Littlewood, John Edensor 1885–1977

English mathematician, whose research included the distribution of prime numbers and ballistics (in World War I). Depite a severe nervous affliction, he continued working into old age. He published the popular *Mathematician's Miscellany* (1953).

77 They are not clever school boys or scholarship candidates, but 'Fellows of another college'.
1953 Of the ancient Greeks. *A Mathematician's Miscellany.*

Lively, Penelope (Margaret) 1933–

English writer. She is best known as a novelist, and has also written a memoir of her early childhood in Egypt, children's books, and an introduction to landscape history.

78 One never, of course, knows what people in portraits are thinking.
1982 *Next to Nature, Art*, ch.10.

79 Wars are fought by children—conceived by their mad demonic elders, and fought by boys.
1987 *Moon Tiger*, ch.8.

80 I believe that the experience of childhood is irretrievable. All that remains, for any of us, is a handful of brilliant frozen moments, already dangerously distorted by the wisdoms of maturity.
1994 *Oleander, Jacaranda*, preface.

81 All habits are geared towards the linear, the sequential, but memory refuses such orderliness.
1994 *Oleander, Jacaranda*, ch.3.

82 Literature has a lot to answer for, where concepts of the countryside are concerned.
2001 *A House Unlocked.*

Livingstone, Dr David 1813–73

Scottish missionary, doctor and explorer. He devoted his life to fighting the Portuguese slave trade, and to establishing settlements for missions in central Africa. He also explored widely, discovering Lakes Ngami, Shirwa and Nyasa and exploring the course of the Zaire River.

83 The mere animal pleasure of travelling in a wild unexplored country is also great… The effect of travel on a man whose heart is in the right place is that the mind is made more self-reliant: it becomes more confident of its own resources—there is greater presence of mind… The sweat of one's brow is no longer a curse when one works for God: it proves a tonic to the system, and actually a blessing. No one can truly appreciate the charm of repose unless he has undergone severe exertion.
Collected in H Waller (ed) *The Last Journals of David Livingstone in Central Africa; continued by a narrative of his last moments and sufferings, obtained from his faithful servants, Chuma and Susi* (1874).

Livingstone, Ken 1945–

English Labour politician. He was leader of the Greater London Council from 1981 to 1986, and in 2000 was elected to the newly created post of Mayor of London.

84 The problem is that many MPs never see the London that exists beyond the wine bars and brothels of Westminster.
1987 In *The Times*, 19 Feb.

85 I feel like Galileo going before the Inquisition to explain that the Sun doesn't revolve around the Earth. I hope I have more success.
1999 Before his interview for selection as Labour's nominee for Mayor of London

86 I've met serial killers and professional assassins and nobody scared me as much as Mrs T.
2000 On Margaret Thatcher. In *The Times*, 7 Mar.

87 Every year the international finance system kills more people than the Second World War. But at least Hitler was mad, you know.
2000 In the *Sunday Times*, 'Talking Heads', 16 Apr.

Livy *full name* ***Titus Livius*** 59 BC–AD 17

Roman historian, admitted to the court of Augustus c.29 BC. His

Ab urbe condita libri (History of Rome from its Foundations) consisted of 142 books, of which only parts have survived.

88 *Vae victis!*
Down with the defeated!
Attributed to the Gallic King Brennus, who had captured Rome in 390 BC, bk.5, ch.48.

89 *Dum Romae consulitur, Saguntum expugnatur.*
While they were deliberating in Rome, Saguntum was captured.
Oral tradition deriving from Livy's description of the siege and capture of the Spanish city of Saguntum by the Carthaginians in 219 BC. The Roman senate deliberated endlessly before deciding to take action when it was already too late. Cf. Livy 21.7.1 'Dum ea Romani parant consultantque, iam Saguntum summa vi oppugnabatur'.

Llewellyn, Richard *originally* Richard Doyle Vivian Llewellyn Lloyd 1907–83

Welsh author, who made his name with *How Green was my Valley* (1939), set in a Welsh mining village and later filmed.

90 How Green was my Valley.
1939 Title of book.

Lloyd, Henry Demarest 1847–1903

US journalist, financial writer and editor with the *Chicago Tribune* (1872–85). He crusaded against monopoly, and was a pioneer 'muckraker' journalist.

91 Monopoly is Business at the end of its journey.
1894 *Wealth against Commonwealth*, ch.1.

Lloyd, John 1946–

British journalist and author.

92 There are few hauteurs higher than foreign reporters' disdain for those who have not shared their craft.
2004 *What the Media Are Doing to Our Politics*.

Lloyd, Marie *stage-name of* Matilda Alice Victoria Wood 1870–1922

English singer. Known simply as 'Our Marie', she became a major star of music hall and pantomime, notorious for her suggestive delivery of such songs as 'A Little of What You Fancy Does You Good'.

93 If we didn't laugh at him, we'd cry our eyes out.
c.1891 Of the singer and comedian Dan Leno, who died insane in 1904. Attributed.

Lloyd George (of Dwyfor), David, 1st Earl 1863–1945

British Liberal Prime Minister. Elected MP for Caernarvon in 1890. President of the Board of Trade 1905–8 and Chancellor of the Exchequer 1905–15. Secretary of War in 1916 and coalition Prime Minister in the same year. After the war, his downfall came when he conceded the Irish Free State in 1921.

94 You cannot feed the hungry on statistics.
1904 Speech advocating tariff reform.

95 This is the trusty mastiff that is to watch over our interests, but which runs away at the first snarl of the trade unions. A mastiff? It is the right honourable gentleman's poodle. It fetches and carries for him. It barks for him. It bites anybody that he sets it on.
1908 Speech to the House of Commons, 21 Dec, referring to the obstructive Conservative majority in the House of Lords exploited by the then Tory leader, A J Balfour.

96 There are no credentials. They do not even need a medical certificate. They need not be sound either in body or mind. They only require a certificate of birth—just to prove that they were the first of the litter. You would not choose a spaniel on those principles.
1909 Referring to the House of Lords, Budget speech, Mar.

97 We are placing the burdens on the broadest shoulders. I made up my mind that, in forming the Budget, no cupboard should be barer, no lot should be harder to bear.
1909 Speech on the People's Budget, London, 30 Jul.

98 Four spectres haunt the poor—old age, accident, sickness, and unemployment. We are going to exorcise them. We are going to drive hunger from the hearth. We mean to banish the workhouse from the horizon of every workman in the land.
1910 Speech, Reading, 1 Jan.

99 We have been too comfortable and too indulgent—many, perhaps, too selfish—and the stern hand of fate has scoured us to an elevation where we can see the great everlasting things that matter for a nation; the great peaks we had forgotten, of honour, duty, patriotism, and, clad in glittering white, the great pinnacle of sacrifice pointing like a rugged finger to Heaven. We shall descend into the valleys again, but as long as men and women of this generation last, they will carry in their hearts the image of those great mountain peaks, whose foundations are not shaken, though Europe rock and sway in the convulsions of a great war.
1914 Speech, London, 19 Sep.

1 By the test of our faith the highest standard of civilization is the readiness to sacrifice for others.
1914 Speech in Queen's Hall, London, 21 Sep.

2 It is a great war for the emancipation of Europe from the thraldom of a military caste which has thrown its shadows upon two generations of men, and is now plunging the world into a welter of bloodshed and death.
1914 Speech in Queen's Hall, London, 21 Sep.

3 At eleven o'clock this morning came to an end the cruellest and most terrible war that has ever scourged mankind. I hope we may say that thus, this fateful morning, came to an end all wars.
1918 Speech in the House of Commons, 11 Nov, announcing the armistice.

4 What is our task? To make Britain a fit country for heroes to live in.
1918 Speech at Wolverhampton, Nov, at the end of World War I.

5 Give it because it is right. Give it because it is just. Give it because it is good for Ireland and good for the United Kingdom. Give it because it brings peace and good will, but do not give it because you are bullied by assassins.
1920 Speech on an Irish settlement, Caernarvon, 9 Oct.

6 Every man has a House of Lords in his own head. Fears, prejudices, misconceptions—those are the peers, and they are hereditary.
1927 Speech, Cambridge.

7 It is the old trouble—too late in dealing with Czechoslovakia, too late with Poland, and certainly too late with Finland. It is always too late, or too little, or both. That is the road to disaster.

1940 House of Commons, 13 Mar.

8 A good lord mayor of Birmingham in a lean year.
Of Neville Chamberlain. Quoted in A J P Taylor *From the Boer War to the Cold War: Essays on Twentieth-Century Europe* (1995), p.363

9 A politician is a person with whose politics you don't agree; if you agree with him, he is a statesman.
Attributed.

Lloyd Webber, Julian 1951–

English cellist.

10 Cello players, like other great athletes, must keep their fingers exercised.
2001 In the *Observer*, 30 Dec.

Loach, Ken 1936–

English film-maker. As well as television work, he has directed such films as *Kes* (1969), *Raining Stones* (1993), *Carla's Song* (1997), *My Name is Joe* (1998) and *Bread and Roses* (2000).

11 If the cinema is any kind of force for social change, then it's a force for the bad, because most films are about one guy with a gun solving a problem.
1998 In *Cineaste*, Winter issue.

Lochhead, Liz 1947–

Scottish poet and dramatist.

12 Sexual Etiquette
Sexual Etiquette
How to get more of it
and get more out of what you get.
2003 *The Colours of Black & White: Poems 1984–2000*, 'Sexual Etiquette'.

Locke, John 1632–1704

English philosopher, a formative influence on British Empiricism and on theories of liberal democracy. His most important work is the *Essay Concerning Human Understanding*, published in 1690. His treatises *On Government* (1690) were also influential, inspiring both American and French revolutionaries.

13 Government has no other end but the preservation of property.
1681 *Second Treatise on Civil Government* (published anonymously 1690).

14 Every man has a property in his person. This no body has any right to but himself. The labour of his body, and the work of his hands, we may say, are properly his.
1681 *Second Treatise on Civil Government* (published anonymously 1690).

15 Freedom of men under government is to have a standing rule to live by, common to every one of that society, and made by the legislative power vested in it; a liberty to follow my own will in all things when the rule prescribes not, and not to be subject to the inconstant, uncertain, unknown, arbitrary rule of another man.
1681 *Second Treatise on Civil Government* (published anonymously 1690).

16 It is ambition enough to be employed as an under-labourer in clearing ground a little, and removing some of the rubbish that lies in the way to knowledge.
1690 *Essay Concerning Human Understanding*, 'Epistle to the Reader'.

17 Let us then suppose the mind to be, as we say, white paper, void of all characters, without any ideas; how comes it to be furnished? Whence comes it by that vast store which the busy and boundless fancy of man has painted on it with an almost endless variety? Whence has it all the materials of reason and knowledge? To this I answer, in one word, from *experience*.
1690 *Essay Concerning Human Understanding*, bk.2, pt.1, section 2.

18 These two, I say, viz. external material things, as the objects of SENSATION, and the operations of our own minds within, as the objects of REFLECTION, are to me the only originals from whence all our ideas take their beginnings.
1690 *Essay Concerning Human Understanding*, bk.2, pt.1, section 4.

19 For should the soul of a prince enter and inform the body of a cobbler, as soon as deserted by his own soul, everyone sees he would be the same *person* with the prince, accountable only for the prince's actions; but who would say it was the same *man*?
1690 *Essay Concerning Human Understanding*, bk.2, pt.27, section 15.

20 A sound mind in a sound body is a short but full description of a happy state in this world. He that has those two, has little more to wish for; and he that wants either of them will be little the better for anything else.
1693 *Some Thoughts Concerning Education*, opening words.
➤ *See Juvenal 453:20.*

Lodge, David John 1935–

English novelist, playwright and critic. His best-known novels are set in academic circles, such as *Changing Places* (1975). Other works include *Thinks* (2001) and *Author, Author: A Novel* (2004).

21 Literature is mostly about having sex and not much about having children. Life is the other way round.
1965 *The British Museum is Falling Down*, ch.4.

22 The British, he thought, must be gluttons for satire: even the weather forecast seemed to be some kind of spoof, predicting every possible combination of weather for the next twenty-four hours without actually committing itself to anything specific.
1975 *Changing Places*, ch.2.

23 He understood… Walt Whitman, who laid end to end words never seen in each other's company before outside of a dictionary, and Herman Melville who split the atom of the traditional novel in the effort to make whaling a universal metaphor.
1975 *Changing Places*, ch.5.

24 Conversation is like playing tennis with a ball made of Krazy Putty that keeps coming back over the net in a different shape.
1984 *Small World*, pt.1, ch.1.

25 The world is a global campus, Hilary, you'd better believe it. The American Express card has replaced the library pass.
1984 *Small World*, pt.1, ch.2.

26 I gave up screwing around a long time ago. I came to the conclusion that sex is a sublimation of the work instinct.
1984 *Small World*, pt.1, ch.2.

27 Another law of academic life: *it is impossible to be excessive in flattery of one's peers.*
1984 *Small World*, pt.3, ch.1.

28 As to our universities, I've come to the conclusion that they are élitist where they should be egalitarian, and egalitarian where they should be élitist.
1988 *Nice Work*, pt.5, ch.4.

Lodge, Henry Cabot 1850–1924

US Republican politician and Senator.

29 The businessman dealing with a large political question is really a painful sight. It does seem to me that businessmen, with a few exceptions, are worse when they come to deal with politics than men of any other class.
1902 Letter to Theodore Roosevelt, 20 Oct.

Loengard, John Borg 1934–

US photographer, picture editor of *Life* (1973–87). His works include *Pictures Under Discussion* (1987) and many essays in *Life*.

30 A bit like God confessing he'd never gotten the hang of the thunderstorms.
1987 On Henri Cartier-Bresson's remark that he was only good at casual photography. In *Life*, Dec.

Lofthouse, Nat 1925–

English footballer. A star centre-forward with Bolton Wanderers in the 1950s, he led the team to victory in the 1958 FA Cup final and also scored 30 goals in 33 internationals for England.

31 There was plenty of fellers who would kick your bollocks off. The difference was that at the end they'd shake your hand and help you look for them.
Comparing football in the 1950s with that of later eras. Quoted in Peter Ball and Phil Shaw *The Book of Football Quotations* (1989).

Logau, Friedrich von 1605–55

German writer, author of epigrams.

32 *Gottes Mühlen mahlen langsam, mahlen aber trefflich klein;*
Ob aus Langmut Er sich säumet, bringt mit Schärf' Er alles ein.
Though the mills of God grind slowly, yet they grind exceeding small;
Though with patience He stands waiting, with exactness grinds He all.
1654 *Sinngedichte*, bk.3, pt.2, no.24 (translated as *Retribution* by Henry Wadsworth Longfellow). Logau used an anonymous classical source for the first line.

Lombardi, Vince(nt Thomas) 1913–70

US American football coach.

33 Winning isn't everything; it's the only thing.
Attributed. His exact words were 'Winning isn't everything, but making the effort is'. Some sources attribute the saying to Red Sanders, coach of the University of California team.

34 If you aren't fired with enthusiasm, you'll be fired with enthusiasm.
Attributed.

35 Once you learn to quit, it becomes a habit.
Attributed.

London, Jack (John Griffith) 1876–1916

US writer. His books, such as *The Call of the Wild* (1903) and *White Fang* (1907), reflect his experiences as a sailor, tramp, gold miner in the Klondike and alcoholic. He also wrote a futuristic political novel *The Iron Heel* (1907).

36 The Call of the Wild.
1903 Title of book.

37 In an English ship, they say, it is poor grub, poor pay, and easy work; in an American ship, good grub, good pay, and hard work. And this is applicable to the working populations of both countries.
1903 *The People of the Abyss*, ch.20.

Longden, Robert Paton 1903–40

English classical scholar and historian, writer of limericks on famous figures of Roman history.

38 The Emperor Caligula
's Habits were somewhat irrigula.
When he sat down to lunch
He got drunk at onch.
Quoted and first published in Arnold Silcock *Verse and Worse* (1952), 'Potted Biography'.

39 The Emperor Claudius
Used to keep a baudius.
When he got more criminal
He ran a den on the Viminal.
1952 Quoted and first published in Arnold Silcock, *Verse and Worse* (1952), 'Potted Biography'.

Longfellow, Henry Wadsworth 1807–82

US poet, Professor of Modern Languages and Literature at Harvard for nearly 18 years. His narrative skill made him one of the most popular poets of his day. His best known poems include *Evangeline* (1847), *Hiawatha* (1855) and *Tales of a Wayside Inn* (1863).

40 Music is the universal language of mankind.
1835 *Outre Mer*. Also attributed to Christopher North (1865–1954)

41 Life is real, life is earnest!
And the grave is not its goal;
Dust thou art, to dust returnest,
Was not spoken of the soul.
1838 'A Psalm of Life'. In *Knickerbocker or New York Monthly Magazine*, Sep. Collected in *Voices of the Night* (1839).

42 Art is long, and time is fleeting,
And our hearts, though stout and brave,
Still, like muffled drums, are beating
Funeral marches to the grave.
1838 'A Psalm of Life', stanza 4. In *Knickerbocker or New York Monthly Magazine*, Sep. Collected in *Voices of the Night* (1839).

43 Lives of great men all remind us
We can make our lives sublime,
And departing, leave behind us
Footprints on the sands of time.
1838 'A Psalm of Life', stanza 7. In *Knickerbocker or New York Monthly Magazine*, Sep. Collected in *Voices of the Night* (1839).

44 Under a spreading chestnut-tree
The village smithy stands;
The smith a mighty man is he,
With large and sinewy hands;
And the muscles of his brawny arms

Are strong as iron bands.
1840 'The Village Blacksmith', stanza 1. Collected in *Ballads and other Poems* (1841).

45 His brow is wet with honest sweat,
He earns whate'er he can,
And looks the whole world in the face,
For he owes not any man.
1840 'The Village Blacksmith', stanza 2. Collected in *Ballads and other Poems* (1841).

46 Each morning sees some task begin,
Each evening sees it close;
Something attempted, something done,
Has earned a night's repose.
1840 'The Village Blacksmith', stanza 7. Collected in *Ballads and other Poems* (1841).

47 It was the schooner Hesperus,
That sailed the wintry sea.
1841 *Ballads and other Poems*, 'The wreck of the Hesperus'.

48 The shades of night were falling fast,
As through an Alpine village passed
A youth, who bore, 'mid snow and ice,
A banner with a strange device,
Excelsior!
1841 'Excelsior'.

49 I like that ancient Saxon phrase, which calls,
The burial-ground God's-Acre.
1841 'God's- Acre'.

50 And the night shall be filled with music,
And the cares, that infest the day,
Shall fold up their tents like Arabs,
And as silently steal away.
1844 *The Waif*, 'The Day Is Done', stanza 11.
► *See Kaufman 455:57.*

51 I shot an arrow into the air,
It fell to earth, I knew not where.
1845 'The Arrow and the Song'.

52 This is the forest primeval.
1847 *Evangeline*, prologue.

53 Sorrow and silence are strong, and patient endurance is godlike.
1847 *Evangeline*, pt.2, section 1.

54 Thou, too, sail on, O Ship of State!
Sail on, O UNION, strong and great!
Humanity with all its fears,
With all the hopes of future years,
Is hanging breathless on thy fate!
1849 *The Seaside and Fireside*, 'The Building of the Ship', l.377–81.

55 In the moonlight and the starlight,
Fair Nokomis bore a daughter.
And she called her name Wenonah,
As the first-born of her daughters.
1855 The naming of Hiawatha's mother. *The Song of Hiawatha*, pt.3, 'Hiawatha's Childhood'. The name is now usually spelt Winona.

56 By the shore of Gitche Gumee
By the shining Big-Sea-Water,
Stood the wigwam of Nokomis,
Daughter of the Moon, Nokomis.
Dark behind it rose the forest,
Rose the black and gloomy pine-trees,
Rose the firs with cones upon them;
Bright before it beat the water,
Beat the clear and sunny water,
Beat the shining Big-Sea-Water.
1855 *The Song of Hiawatha*, pt.3, 'Hiawatha's Childhood'.

57 From the waterfall he named her,
Minnehaha, Laughing Water.
1855 *The Song of Hiawatha*, pt.4, 'Hiawatha and Mudjekeewis'.

58 A boy's will is the wind's will,
And the thoughts of youth are long, long thoughts.
1855 'My Lost Youth', in *Putnam's Monthly Magazine*, vol.6, Aug. Collected in *The Courtship of Miles Standish and Other Poems*, 1858. In his diary Longfellow notes that these lines are from an 'old Lapland song'.

59 But ah! what once has been shall be no more!
The groaning earth in travail and in pain
Brings forth its races, but does not restore,
And the dead nations never rise again.
1855 'The Jewish Cemetery at Newport'.

60 A Lady with a Lamp shall stand
In the great history of the land,
A noble type of good,
Heroic womanhood.
1857 Of Florence Nightingale. 'Santa Filomena'.

61 Between the dark and the daylight,
When the night is beginning to lower,
Comes a pause in the day's occupations,
That is known as the Children's Hour.
1863 'The Children's Hour', stanza 1.

62 Listen, my children, and you shall hear
Of the midnight ride of Paul Revere,
On the eighteenth of April in Seventy-five.
1863 *Tales of a Wayside Inn*, pt.1, 'The Landlord's Tale: Paul Revere's Ride'.

63 Our ingress into the world
Was naked and bare;
Our progress through the world
Is trouble and care.
1872 *Tales of a Wayside Inn*, pt.2, 'The Student's Tale: The Cobbler of Hagenau'.

64 Ships that pass in the night, and speak each other in passing,
Only a signal shown and a distant voice in the darkness;
So on the ocean of life, we pass and speak one another,
Only a look and a voice, then darkness again and a silence.
1873 *Tales of a Wayside Inn*, pt.3. 'The Theologian's Tale: Elizabeth'.

65 If you would hit the mark, you must aim a little above it;
Every arrow that flies feels the attraction of earth.
1881 *Elegaic Verse*, stanza 9.

66 The men that women marry,
And why they marry them, will always be
A marvel and a mystery to the world.
1883 *Michael Angelo*, pt.1, sc.5.

67 There was a little girl
Who had a little curl
Right in the middle of her forehead;
And when she was good
She was very, very good,

But when she was bad, she was horrid.
Attributed to Longfellow by Blanch Roosevelt Tucker Macchetta in *The Home Life of Henry W. Longfellow* (1882).

Longworth, Alice Roosevelt 1884–1980

US political hostess, daughter of Theodore Roosevelt, renowned for her wit.

68 If you can't say something good about someone, sit right here by me.
Motto embroidered on a sofa pillow. Quoted in *Time*, 9 Dec 1966.

Lonsdale, Hugh Cecil Lowther, 5th Earl of 1857–1944

English sportsman. As president of the National Sporting Club, he founded and presented the 'Lonsdale belts' for boxing.

69 I have always considered that boxing really combines all the finest and highest inclinations of a man—activity, endurance, science, temper, and, last, but not least, presence of mind.
1915 Foreword in Eugene Corri *Thirty Years a Boxing Referee*.

Loos, Adolf 1870–1933

Austrian architect and design theorist, a major figure of the 'Modern Movement', whose designs reflect his rejection of ornament and an emphasis on elegant functionalism.

70 I have emerged victorious from my thirty years of struggle. I have freed mankind from superfluous ornament.
1930 *Trotzdem 1900–1930*.

71 The evolution of culture is synonymous with the removal of ornament from utilitarian objects.
1931 *Trotzdem 1900–1930*.

Loos, Anita c.1893–1981

US writer, best known for her satirical novel *Gentleman Prefer Blondes* (1925). She also wrote plays, screenplays and memoirs.

72 Gentlemen Prefer Blondes.
1925 Title of novel, and subsequently a film starring Marilyn Monroe and Jane Russell (1953).

73 So this gentleman said a girl with brains ought to do something more with them besides think.
1925 *Gentlemen Prefer Blondes*, ch.1.

74 Gentlemen always seem to remember blondes.
1925 *Gentlemen Prefer Blondes*, ch.1.

75 She said she always believed in the old adage, 'Leave them while you're looking good.'
1925 *Gentlemen Prefer Blondes*, ch.1.

76 You have got to be a Queen to get away with a hat like that.
1925 *Gentlemen Prefer Blondes*, ch.4.

77 Any girl who was a lady would not even think of having such a good time that she did not remember to hang on to her jewelry.
1925 *Gentlemen Prefer Blondes*, ch.4.

78 The Eyefull Tower is devine.
1925 *Gentlemen Prefer Blondes*, ch.4.

79 So I really think that American gentlemen are the best after all, because kissing your hand may make you feel very very good but a diamond and safire bracelet lasts forever.
1925 *Gentlemen Prefer Blondes*, ch.4.

80 Fun is fun but no girl wants to laugh all of the time.
1925 *Gentlemen Prefer Blondes*, ch.4

81 So then Dr Froyd said that all I needed was to cultivate a few inhibitions and get some sleep.
1925 *Gentlemen Prefer Blondes*, ch.5.

82 So then he said that he used to be a member of the choir himself, so who was he to cast the first rock at a girl like I.
1925 *Gentlemen Prefer Blondes*, ch.5.

83 Tallulah never bored anyone, and I consider that humanitarianism of a very high order indeed.
1968 Eulogy at Tallulah Bankhead's funeral. Reported in the *New York Times*, 17 Dec.

84 I'm furious about the Woman's Liberationists. They keep getting up on soap-boxes and proclaiming that women are brighter than men. That's true, but it should be kept very quiet or it ruins the whole racket.
Quoted in the *Observer*, 30 Dec 1973.

Lorca, Federico García 1898–1936

Spanish poet and playwright, assassinated on the order of the Nationalist Civil Governor early in the Civil War. He is best known for his gypsy songs and powerful, elemental tragedies such as *Bodas de Sangre* (1933, translated as *Blood Wedding*, 1947).

85 *Verde que te quiero verde.*
Verde viento. Verdes ramas.
El barco sobre la mar
y el caballo en la montaña.
Green how I love you green.
Green wind. Green boughs.
The ship on the sea
and the horse on the mountain.
1924–7 *Romance sonámbulo*.

86 Spain is the only country where death is the national spectacle.
Quoted in Colin Jarman *The Guinness Dictionary of Sports Quotations* (1990).

Loren, Sophia *pseudonym of* Sofia Scicolone 1934–

Italian actress. Her films include *El Cid* (1961) and *Two Women* (1961), for which she won an Academy Award.

87 Everything you see I owe to spaghetti.
Attributed.

Lorenz, Konrad 1903–89

Austrian zoologist and ethnologist. Lorenz studied the organization of individual animal and group behaviour patterns. He shared the 1973 Nobel prize in physiology or medicine with Karl von Frisch.

88 *Überhaupt ist es für den Forscher ein guter Morgensport, täglich vor dem Frühstück eine Lieblingshypothese einzustampfen—das erhält jung.*
It is a good morning exercise for a research scientist to discard a pet hypothesis every day before breakfast. It keeps him young.
1963 *Das sogenannte Böse* ('The So-Called Evil', translated by Marjorie Latzke as *On Aggression*, 1966), ch.2.

89 Man appears to be the missing link between anthropoid apes and human beings.
1965 In the *New York Times*, 11 Apr.

Louis IX *also called* **St Louis** 1214–70

King of France (1226–70). He led the Seventh Crusade (1248), but was defeated, imprisoned and ransomed. On his return to France (1254) he carried out reforms and encouraged the arts and literature. He began a new Crusade in 1270, but died of plague in Tunis.

90 I would rather have a Scot come from Scotland to govern the people of this kingdom well and justly, than that you should govern them ill in the sight of all the world.
1244 To his son, Louis, at Fontainebleau.

Louis XI 1423–83

King of France (1461–83). By a mixture of force and cunning, he broke the power of the nobility and by 1483 had united most of France under the Crown.

91 I have chased the English out of France more easily than my father ever did, for my father drove them out by force of arms, whereas I have driven them out with venison pies and good wine.
1475 Said after the signing of the Treaty of Picquigny, Sep.

Louis XIV *known as* **the Great** *or* **le Roi Soleil [the Sun King]** 1638–1715

King of France (1643–1715). His aggressive foreign and commercial policies and his attempt to create a Franco–Spanish Bourbon bloc led to the War of the Spanish Succession (1701–13). Although his old age saw military disaster and its financial toll, he was a model of royal absolutism and courtly brilliance.

92 Everyone knows how much trouble your meetings have caused in my State, and how many dangerous results they have had. I have learnt that you intend to continue them. I have come here expressly to forbid you to do this, which I do absolutely.
1655 Address to the Parlement of Paris, 13 Apr.

93 *L'État, c'est moi.*
I am the State.
1655 Address to the Parlement of Paris, 13 Apr. This is probably apocryphal.

94 Every time that I fill a high office, I make one hundred men discontented and one ungrateful.
c.1669 After the disgrace of the Duke of Lauzun. Quoted in Voltaire *Le Siècle de Louis XIV* (1751), ch.26.

95 How could God do this to me after all I have done for him?
1704 On hearing the news of the French defeat at Blenheim, Aug. Quoted in L Norton *Saint-Simon at Versailles* (1958).

96 The function of kings consists primarily of using good sense, which always comes naturally and easily. Our work is sometimes less difficult than our amusements.
Mémoires for the Instruction of the Dauphin.

Louis XVI 1754–93

King of France (1774–93), deposed during the Revolution. He was tried before the National Convention for conspiracy with foreign powers, and executed in Paris.

97 Louis XVI: Is this a revolt?
Duke of Rochefoucauld-Liancourt: No, sir, it's a revolution.
1789 Exchange after the fall of the Bastille, 14 Jul. Quoted in F Dreyfus *La Rochefoucauld-Liancourt* (1903), ch.2, section 3.

Louis XVIII *originally* **Stanislas Xavier** 1755–1824

King of France (from 1795). He fled to Belgium in 1791, proclaiming himself Regent for Louis XVII in 1793 and King in 1795. On the fall of Napoleon, he landed at Calais (1814) and began a severe rule, until Napoleon's return for the Hundred Days (1815). His rule was subsequently more moderate.

98 *L'exactitude est la politesse des rois.*
Punctuality is the politeness of kings.
Quoted in *Souvenirs de J Lafitte* (1844), bk.1, ch.3.

Louis Philippe *known as* **the Citizen King** 1773–1850

King of France (1830–48). Eldest son of the Duc d'Orléans, he renounced his titles and fought in the wars of the Republic, becoming 'Citizen King' after the Revolution of 1830. Demands for electoral reform led to the uprising of 1848 and his forced abdication.

99 Died, has he? Now I wonder what he meant by that.
1838 Said on the death of Talleyrand, his calculating and self-serving adviser, 18 Mar.

1 The entente cordiale.
1843 Speech, 27 Dec. Quoted in Collingham *The July Monarchy* (1988), p.320.

2 What perished in France in 1830 was not respect for a dynasty, but respect for anything.
Of the Revolution which brought him to power. Quoted in A J P Taylor *From Napoleon to the Second International* (1993).

Louis, Joe *pseudonym of* **Joseph Louis Barrow** 1914–81

US boxer. Known as the 'Brown Bomber', he won the world heavyweight title in 1937 and held it for a record 12 years, defending it 25 times. He retired in 1949, attempting two unsuccessful comebacks (1950–1). In all he won 68 of his 71 professional fights.

3 He can run, but he can't hide.
1941 Said during a bout against Billy Conn.

4 Everybody wants to go to heaven, but nobody wants to die.
1965 In *Sports Illustrated*, 'Scorecard', 19 Jul.

5 Every man's got to figure to get beat some time.
Quoted in Colin Jarman *The Guinness Dictionary of Sports Quotations* (1990).

6 I don't like money, actually, but it quiets my nerves.
Quoted in Colin Jarman *The Guinness Dictionary of Sports Quotations* (1990).

7 Why should I? When somebody insulted Caruso, did he sing an aria for him?
When a friend asked why he did not punch a motorist who swore at him following a minor traffic accident. Quoted in Colin Jarman *The Guinness Dictionary of Sports Quotations* (1990).

Love, James *pseudonym of* **James Dance** 1722–74

English actor and writer.

8 Hail Cricket! glorious, manly, British game!
First of all Sports! be first alike in fame!
1744 'Cricket: An Heroic Poem'.

Lovelace, Richard 1618–58

English Cavalier poet. Twice imprisoned (1642 and 1648–49) by the Puritans for his Royalist sympathies, he spent much of his time behind bars writing poetry, which he published in 1649 as the collection *Lucasta*.

9 When I lie tangled in her hair,
And fettered to her eye;
The Gods, that wanton in the air
Know no such liberty.
1649 *Lucasta*, 'To Althea, from Prison'.

10 Stone walls do not a prison make,
Nor iron bars a cage;
Minds innocent and quiet take
That for a hermitage;
If I have freedom in my love,
And in my soul am free;
Angels along that soar above,
Enjoy such liberty.
1649 *Lucasta*, 'To Althea, from Prison'.

11 If to be absent were to be
Away from thee;
Or that when I am gone,
You or I were alone;
Then my *Lucasta* might I crave
Pity from blust'ring wind, or swallowing wave.
1649 *Lucasta*, 'To Lucasta, Going beyond the Seas'.

12 *Amarantha* sweet and fair,
Ah braid no more that shining hair!
As my curious hand or eye,
Hovering round thee let it fly.
1649 *Lucasta*, 'To Amarantha, That She Would Dishevel Her Hair'.

13 Tell me not, Sweet, I am unkind,
That from the nunnery
Of thy chaste breast, and quiet mind,
To war and arms I fly.
1649 *Lucasta*, 'To Lucasta, Going to the Wars'.

14 I could not love thee, Dear, so much,
Loved I not honour more.
1649 *Lucasta*, 'To Lucasta, Going to the Wars'.

15 Thus did they live: Thus did they love,
Repeating only joys above;
And Angels were, but with clothes on,
Which they would put off cheerfully,
To bathe them in the galaxy,
Then gird them with the Heavenly zone.
1649 *Lucasta*, 'Love Made in the First Age'.

16 The asp doth on his feeder feed.
1649 *Lucasta*, 'A Fly Caught in a Cobweb'.

Loveless, George 1805–40

English Methodist preacher, who in 1833 organized the agricultural labourers of Tolpuddle, Dorset, into a trade union. When the men were convicted of taking illegal oaths and transported, a public outcry ensued and they were eventually pardoned.

17 If we have violated any law, it was not done intentionally. We have injured no man's reputation, character, person, or property. We were meeting together to preserve ourselves, our wives, and our children from utter degradation and starvation.
1833 Statement to the Dorchester Assizes, Mar, on behalf of the Tolpuddle martyrs.

Lovell, Sir (Alfred Charles) Bernard 1913–

English astronomer. He was the instigator of the funding, construction and use of the radio telescope at Jodrell Bank.

18 The fate of human civilization will depend on whether the rockets of the future carry the astronomer's telescope or a hydrogen bomb.
1959 *The Individual and the Universe*.

19 A study of history shows that civilizations that abandon the quest for knowledge are doomed to disintegration.
1972 In the *Observer*, 'Sayings of the Week', 14 May.

Lowe, Emily fl.1850s

Englishwoman, who travelled in Norway with her mother.

20 The only use of a gentleman in travelling is to look after the luggage.
1857 *Unprotected Females in Norway*.

Lowell, Amy 1874–1925

US poet. A descendant of James Russell Lowell, she was associated with the Imagist movement, and wrote free verse in a style she named 'unrhymed cadence'. She also wrote prose and criticism.

21 For books are more than books, they are the life
The very heart and core of ages past,
The reason why men lived and worked and died,
The essence and quintessence of their lives.
1912 'The Boston Atheneum'.

22 All books are either dreams or swords,
You can cut, or you can drug, with words.
1914 'Sword Blades and Poppy Seeds'.

23 And the softness of my body will be guarded by embrace
By each button, hook, and lace.
For the man who should loose me is dead,
Fighting with the Duke in Flanders,
In a pattern called a war.
Christ! What are patterns for?
1916 'Patterns'.

24 A man must be sacrificed now and again
To provide for the next generation of men.
1922 'A Critical Fable'.

25 I must be mad, or very tired,
When the curve of a blue bay beyond a railroad track
Is shrill and sweet to me like the sudden springing of a tune,
And the sight of a white church above thin trees in a city square
Amazes my eyes as though it were the Parthenon.
1925 'Meeting House Hill'.

Lowell, James Russell 1819–91

US poet, essayist and diplomat. His popular satiric poems in Yankee dialect were published as *The Biglow Papers* (1848 and 1867). A lecturer at Harvard, he was also editor of the *Atlantic Monthly* and US Minister to Spain (1877–80) and Britain (1880–85).

26 It is mediocrity which makes laws and sets mantraps and spring-guns in the realm of free song, saying thus far shall you go and no further.
1843 'Elizabethan Dramatists, Omitting Shakespeare: John Webster'.

27 Once to every man and nation comes the moment to decide,

In the strife of Truth with Falsehood, for the good or evil side.
1844 'The Present Crisis', in the *Boston Courier*, 11 Dec. Collected in *Poems: Second Series*, 1848. The poem was written in the midst of the controversy over whether Texas should be annexed and slavery extended.

28 They talk about their Pilgrim blood,
Their birthright high and holy!
A mountain-stream that ends in mud
Methinks is melancholy.
1846 'An Interview with Miles Standish', stanza 11.

29 Ez fer war, I call it murder,—
There you hev it plain an' flat;
I don't want to go no furder
Than my Testyment fer that;
God hez sed so plump an' fairly,
It's ez long ez it is broad,
An' you've gut to git up airly
Ef you want to take in God.
1846 'A Letter'. In the *Boston Courier*, 17 Jun. Collected in *The Biglow Papers, First Series* (1848), no.1.

30 'Slavery's a thing thet depends on complexion,
It's God's law thet fetters on black skins don't chafe;
Ef brains wuz to settle it (horrid reflection!)
Wich of our onnable body'd be safe?'
1848 'The Debate in the Sennit', in the *Boston Courier*, 3 May, collected in *The Biglow Papers: First Series* (1848), no. 5.

31 And what is so rare as a day in June?
Then, if ever come perfect days.
1848 'The Vision of Sir Launfal', prelude.

32 There comes Poe, with his raven, like Barnaby Rudge,
Three-fifths of him genius and two-fifths sheer fudge.
1848 'A Fable for Critics'.

33 A reading machine, always wound up and going,
He mastered whatever was not worth knowing.
1848 Of a scholar. 'A Fable for Critics'.

34 Books are the bees which carry the quickening pollen from one to another mind.
1849 'Nationality in Literature', in the *North American Review*, Jul.

35 Every man feels instinctively that all the beautiful sentiments in the world weigh less than a single lovely action.
1867 'Rousseau and the Sentimentalists', in the *North American Review*, Jul.

36 The mind can weave itself warmly in the cocoon of its own thoughts, and dwell a hermit anywhere.
1869 'On a Certain Condescension in Foreigners', in the *Atlantic Monthly*, Jan.

37 Sorrow, the great idealizer.
1876 *Among My Books*, 'Spenser'.

38 There is no good in arguing with the inevitable. The only argument available with an east wind is to put on your overcoat.
1884 'On Democracy', Lowell's inaugural address when he became president of the Birmingham and Midland Institute, 6 Oct.

39 Compromise makes a good umbrella but a poor roof.
1884 'On Democracy', speech in Birmingham, 6 Oct.

40 As life runs on, the road grows strange
With faces new,—and near the end
The milestones into headstones change,
'Neath every one a friend.
1887 'Sixty-Eighth Birthday'.

Lowell, Robert Traill Spence, Jr 1917–77

US poet. His poems are intensely personal and confessional. His public involvement and outspoken comments, especially during the Vietnam War, have made him one of the best known of all contemporary poets.

41 Let there pass
A minute, ten, ten trillion; but the blaze
Is infinite, eternal: this is death.
To die and know it. This is the Black Widow, death.
1950 'Mr Edwards and the Spider'.

42 They died
When time was open-eyed,
Wooden and childish; only bones abide
There, in the nowhere, where their boats were tossed
Sky-high, where mariners had fabled news
of IS, the whited monster.
1950 'The Quaker Graveyard in Nantucket', pt.3.

43 This is the end of the whaleroad and the whale
Who spewed Nantucket bones on the thrashed swell
And stirred the troubled waters to whirlpools
To send the Pequod packing off to hell
1950 'The Quaker Graveyard in Nantucket', pt.4. The Pequod was the ship that sailed after Moby Dick in Melville's novel.

44 The Lord survives the rainbow of his will.
1950 'The Quaker Graveyard in Nantucket', last line.

45 I keep no rank nor station.
Cured, I am frizzled, stale and small.
1956 'Home After Three Months Away'.

46 I myself am hell.
1956 'Skunk Hour'.

47 I often sigh still
for the dark downward and vegetating kingdom
of the fish and reptile.
1964 'For the Union Dead'.

48 William James could almost hear the bronze Negroes breathe.

Their monument sticks like a fishbone
in the city's throat.
1964 'For The Union Dead'.

49 Everywhere,
giant finned cars nose forward like fish;
a savage servility
slides by on grease.
1964 'For the Union Dead'.

50 He is out of bounds now. He rejoices in man's lovely
peculiar power to choose life and die—
when he leads his black soldiers to death,
he cannot bend his back.
1964 'For The Union Dead'. 'He' refers to Colonel Shaw, the white commander of the black regiment commemorated in the monument.

51 The man is killing time—there's nothing else.
1964 'The Drinker'.

52 But I suppose even God was born
too late to trust the old religion—
all those settings out
that never left the ground,

beginning in wisdom, dying in doubt.
1964 'Tenth Muse'.

53 The elect, the elected...they come here bright as dimes,
and die dishevelled and soft.
1964 'July in Washington'.

54 Yours the lawlessness
of something simple that has lost its law.
1964 'Caligula'.

55 O that the spirit could remain
tinged but untarnished by its strain!
1967 'Waking Early Sunday Morning'.

56 Pity the planet, all joy gone
from this sweet volcanic cone
1967 'Waking Early Sunday Morning'.

57 Life is too short to silver over this tarnish.
The gods, employed to haunt and punish husbands,
have no hand for trigger-fine distinctions,
their myopia makes all error mortal.
1968 'New Year's Eve'.

58 My Darling, prickly hedgehog of the heart,
chocolates, cherries, hairshirts, pinks and glass—
when we joined in the sublime blindness of courtship
loving lost all its vice with half its virtue.
1968 'New Year's Eve'.

59 Age is our reconciliation with dullness.
1973 'Last Summer at Milgate'.

60 We feel the machine slipping from our hands
As if someone else were steering;
If we see the light at the end of the tunnel,
It's the light of the oncoming train.
1977 *Day by Day*,'Since 1939'.

61 Those blessed structures, plot and rhyme
why are they no help to me now
I want to make
something imagined, not recalled?
1977 *Day by Day*,'Epilogue'.

62 Pray for the grace of accuracy
Vermeer gave to the sun's illumination
stealing like the tide across a map
to his girl solid with yearning.
1977 *Day by Day*,'Epilogue'.

Lowenthal, Leo 1900–93

German-born US sociologist.

63 We call the heroes of the past heroes of production. We feel entitled to call the present day magazine heroes 'idols of consumption'. Indeed, almost every one of them is directly, or indirectly, related to the sphere of leisure time.
1944 'The Triumph of Mass Idols', collected in *Literature and Mass Culture* (1984).

Lowndes, William 1652–1724

English politician.

64 Take care of the pence, and the pounds will take care of themselves.
Quoted by Lord Chesterfield in a letter to his son, 5 Feb 1750. In an earlier letter, 6 Nov 1747, he refers to the same adage in the form '*for* the pounds'.

Lowry, (Clarence) Malcolm 1909–57

English novelist. He went to sea as a young man and lived in Mexico and Vancouver. He is best known for his novel, *Under the Volcano* (1947), one of the great 20c explorations of alcoholism. He died after choking in his sleep.

65 Nothing in the world was more terrible than an empty bottle! Unless it was an empty glass.
1947 *Under the Volcano*, ch.3.

66 Where are the children I might have had?... Drowned to the accompaniment of the rattling of a thousand douche bags.
1947 *Under the Volcano*, ch.10.

67 How alike are the groans of love to those of the dying.
1947 *Under the Volcano*, ch.12.

68 Dark as the Grave Wherein my Friend is Laid.
Title of novel, published posthumously (1968).

Lucan *full name* ***Marcus Annaeus Lucanus*** AD 39–65

Latin poet, born in Spain, nephew of the philosopher Seneca. A favourite at the court of Nero, he lost imperial favour and in AD 65 joined Piso's conspiracy against Nero, but was betrayed and compelled to commit suicide. His epic poem *Bellum Civile* (or *Pharsalia*) deals with the civil war between Caesar and Pompey.

69 *Victrix causa deis placuit, sed victa Catoni.*
A victorious case pleased the gods, but a lost one Cato.
Pharsalia, bk.1, l.126.

70 *Stat magni nominis umbra.*
There stands the shade of a great name.
Of Pompey. *Pharsalia*, bk.1, l.135.

71 *Coniunx est mihi, sunt nati: dedimus tot pignora fatis.*
I have a wife, I have sons: we have given so many hostages to the fates.
Pharsalia, bk.6, l.661–2.
► *See Bacon 48:86.*

Lucas, E(dward) V(errell) 1868–1938

English essayist and biographer. He was assistant editor of *Punch*, and wrote novels and travel books.

72 I have noticed that people who are late are often so much jollier than the people who have to wait for them.
1926 *365 Days and One More*.

73 Readers of novels are strange folk, upon whose probable or even possible tastes no wise book-maker would ever venture.
1932 *Reading, Writing and Remembering*, ch.1.

74 There can be no defence like elaborate courtesy.
1932 *Reading, Writing and Remembering*, ch.8.

Lucas, F(rank) L(awrence) 1894–1967

English teacher, critic and poet.

75 Unintelligible, the borrowings cheap and the notes useless.
1923 On T S Eliot's *The Waste Land*, in the *New Statesman and Nation*, Nov.

76 The virtues common to good living and good poetry seem to me not so much matters of what used to be called 'virtue' as, above all, of sane vitality.
1936 *The Decline and Fall of the Romantic Ideal*, ch.1.

77 Human temperaments are too diverse; we can never agree how drunk we like our art to be.
1951 *Literature and Psychology*, ch.10.

78 Every author's fairy godmother should provide him not only with a pen but also with a blue pencil.
1955 *Style*, introduction.

Lucas, George 1944–

US film-maker, best known for the series of *Star Wars* and *Indiana Jones* films.

79 May the Force be with you.
1977 Line delivered by Alec Guinness as Obi-Wan Kenobi in *Star Wars*.

80 Art is the retelling of certain themes in a new light, making them accessible to the public of the moment.
1988 In the *New York Times*, 9 Jun.

Luce, Clare Booth 1903–87

US writer, socialite and wit, associate editor of *Vogue* (1930), US Ambassador to Italy (1953–7) and author of several Broadway successes including *Kiss the Boys Goodbye* (1938).

81 Communism is the opiate of the intellectuals, with no cure except as a guillotine might be called a cure for dandruff.
1955 In *Newsweek*, 24 Jan.

Lucretius *full name* Titus Lucretius Carus 98–c.55 BC

Roman poet and philosopher, author of *De Rerum Natura*, a hexameter poem in six books expounding the physical system of Epicurus, in which release from fear, and the mortality of the soul, are central concerns.

82 *Nil posse creari*
De nilo.
Nothing can be created from nothing.
De Rerum Natura, bk.1, line 155–6.

83 *Suave, mari magno turbantibus aequora ventis,*
E terra magnum alterius spectare laborem;
Non quia vexari quemquamst iucunda voluptas,
Sed quibus ipse malis careas quia cernere suave est.
Suave etiam belli certamina magna tueri
Per campos instructa tua sine parte pericli.
Sed nil dulcius est, bene quam munita tenere
Edita doctrina sapientum templa serena,
Despicere unde queas alios passimque videre
Errare atque viam palantis quaerere vitae,
Certare ingenio, contendere nobilitate,
Noctes atque dies niti praestante labore
Ad summas emergere opes rerumque potiri.
What joy it is, when out at sea the stormwinds are lashing the waters, to gaze from the shore at the heavy stress some other man is enduring. Not that anyone's afflictions are in themselves a source of delight; but to realize from what troubles you yourself are free is joy indeed. What joy, again, to watch opposing hosts marshalled on the field of battle when you have yourself no part in their peril! But this is the greatest joy of all: to possess a quiet sanctuary, stoutly fortified by the teaching of the wise, and to gaze down from that elevation on others wandering aimlessly in search of a way of life, pitting their wits one against another, disputing for precedence, struggling night and day with unstinted effort to scale the pinnacles of wealth and power.
De Rerum Natura, bk.2, lines 1–13 (translated by R. E. Latham).

84 *Vitaque mancipio, nulli datur, omnibus usu.*
To none is life given in freehold; to all on lease.
De Rerum Natura, bk.3, line 971 (translated by R. E. Latham).

85 *Ut quod ali cibus est aliis fuat acre venenum.*
What is food to one may be literally poison to others.
De Rerum Natura, bk.4, line 637 (translated by R. E. Latham).

Lugones, Leopoldo 1874–1938

Argentinian poet and critic. As a socialist journalist, he joined the *Modernista* group, later becoming a conservative nationalist and, in 1929, a Fascist.

86 *Si tengo la fortuna*
de que con tu alma mi dolor se integre,
te diré entre melancólico y alegre
las singulares cosas de la luna.
If I am fortunate enough
for your soul to mix with my sorrow,
I will tell you, half with melancholy, half with gladness,
Unique things about the moon.
1909 *Lunario sentimental*, 'Divagación lunar' ('Lunar digression').

Lukács, Georg 1885–1971

Hungarian-born Marxist scholar, philosopher and aesthetician.

87 Nature is a social category.
1923 *History and Class Consciousness*.

Lumière, Auguste Marie Louis Nicolas 1862–1954

French film pioneer, brother of Louis Lumière. The brothers owned a factory in Lyons where photographic products were made. They invented the first successful cine camera and projector and presented their film of workers leaving the Lumière factory in 1895.

88 *Mon frère, en une nuit, avait inventé le cinématographe.*
My brother, in one night, had invented the cinema.
Of the night his brother Louis had a flash of inspiration which resulted in the 'Kinetoscope de projection' patented in 1895.
Quoted in C W Ceram *Archaeology of the Cinema* (1965).

Lurie, Alison 1926–

US novelist and academic. She has written a number of acutely observed novels, often with academic settings, as well as non-fiction and children's literature.

89 That is the worst thing about being a middle-class woman…you have more knowledge of yourself and the world: you are equipped to make choices, but there are none left to make.
1974 *The War Between The Tates*, ch.3.

90 Fashion is free speech, and one of the privileges, if not always one of the pleasures, of a free world.
1981 *The Language of Clothes*.

91 The most desirable mental state for a potential consumer…is a kind of free-floating anxiety and depression, combined with a nice collection of unrealistic goals and desires.
1983 Of advertising. In the *New York Review of Books*, 2 Jun.

Luther, Martin 1483–1546

German theologian. Originally an Augustinian monk, he became the leader of Protestant Reformation in Europe. When he publicly burned the Papal Bull against him he was summoned before the Diet at Worms and banned. His followers later founded the Lutheran Church.

92 *Hier stehe ich. Ich kann nicht anders. Gott helfe mir. Amen.*
Here I stand; I can do no other; God help me; Amen.
1521 Speech in defence of his doctrines at the Diet of Worms, 18 Apr. The Diet subsequently denounced his ideas as heretical.

93 I cannot and will not recant anything, for to go against conscience is neither right nor safe.
1521 Speech in defence of his doctrines at the Diet of Worms, 18 Apr.

94 *Esto peccator et pecca fortiter, sed fortius fide et gaude in Christo.*
Be a sinner and sin boldly, but more boldly believe and rejoice in Christ.
1521 Letter to Melanchthon.

95 *Wenn ich gewusst hätte, dass so viel Teufel auf mich gezielet hätten, als Ziegel auf den Dächern waren zu Worms, wäre ich dennoch eingeritten.*
I would have gone into Worms though there were as many devils as tiles on the roof.
1524 Letter to Frederick, Elector of Saxony, 21 Aug.

96 It is better that all of these peasants should be killed rather than that the sovereigns and magistrates should be destroyed, because the peasants take up the sword without God's authority.
1525 Letter to Nicholas von Ansdorf, 30 May.

97 *Ein' feste Burg ist unser Gott,*
Ein' gute Wehr und Waffen.
A safe stronghold our God is still,
A trusty shield and weapon.
1520 *Ein' feste Burg ist unser Gott* (translated by Thomas Carlyle).

98 *Wo rauff du nu…dein Hertz engest und verlessest, das ist eygentlich dein Gott.*
Whatever your heart clings to and confides in, that is really your God.
1529 *Large Catechism*, 'The First Commandment'.

99 Rough, boisterous, stormy and altogether warlike, I am born to fight against innumerable monsters and devils.
Quoted in Vincent Cronin *The Flowering of the Renaissance* (1969).

1 *Wer nicht liebt Wein, Weib und Gesang,*
Der bleibt ein Narr sein Leben lang.
Who loves not woman, wine and song
Remains a fool his whole life long.
Attributed. This was inscribed in the Luther room at Wartburg, but is probably apocryphal.

Lutyens, Sir Edwin Landseer 1869–1944

English architect. His designs include the Cenotaph, Whitehall and Liverpool Roman Catholic Cathedral.

2 There will never be great architects or great architecture without great patrons.
1915 In *Country Life*, 8 May.

Lydgate, John c.1370–c.1451

English poet and Benedictine monk, who travelled widely in Europe. In 1423 he became Prior of the monastery of Hatfield Broadoak. His many works include *The Siege of Thebes* (1420–2) and *The Fall of Princes* (1431–8).

3 Off our language he was the lodesterre.
1431–8 Of Chaucer. *The Fall of Princes*, prologue, l.252.

4 Lat no man booste of conning nor vertu,
Of tresour, richesse, nor of sapience,
Of worldly support, for all cometh of Jesu.
c.1450 'Lat no man booste', l.1–3.

5 Woord is but wynd; leff woord and tak the dede.
Secrets of Old Philosophers, l.224.

Lyly, John c.1554–1606

English writer and dramatist. He published his prose romance *Euphues, or the Anatomy of Wit* in 1578, and wrote eight plays between 1584 and 1590, including *Endymion, or The Man in the Moon* (1588).

6 Be valiant, but not too venturous. Let thy attire be comely, but not costly.
1578 *Euphues, or the Anatomy of Wit.*

7 What bird so sings, yet so does wail?
O 'tis the ravished nightingale.
Jug, jug, jug, jug, tereu, she cries,
And still her woes at midnight rise.
1584 *Campaspe*, act 5, sc.1.

8 How at heaven's gates she claps her wings,
The morn not waking till she sings.
1584 Of the lark. *Campaspe*, act 5, sc.1.

9 A heat full of coldness, a sweet full of bitterness, a pain full of pleasantness, which maketh thoughts have eyes and hearts ears, bred by desire, nursed by delight, weaned by jealousy, killed by dissembling, buried by ingratitude, and this is love. Fair lady, will you any?
1588 *Gallathea*, act 1, sc.2. The passage gently satirizes the conventions of love sonnets, and is characterized by the yoked opposites called Euphuisms, after Lyly's earlier work, a style later used by the metaphysical poets.

10 If love be a god, why should not lovers be virtuous?
1588 *Gallathea*, act 3, sc.1.

11 Yield, ladies, yield to love, ladies, which lurketh under your eyelids whilst you sleep and playeth with your heartstrings whilst you wake, whose sweetness never breedeth satiety, labour weariness, nor grief bitterness.
1588 *Gallathea*, epilogue.

12 Night hath a thousand eyes.
1600 *The Maydes Metamorphosis*, act 3, sc.1.
► *See Bourdillon 147:28.*

Lynd, Robert 1879–1949

Irish essayist and critic, literary editor of the *Daily News* and a contributor to the *New Statesman* (1913–45). His essay collections include *The Art of Letters* (1920), *The Blue Lion* (1923) and *In Defence of Pink* (1939).

13 It may be that all games are silly. But then, so are humans.
Quoted in Colin Jarman *The Guinness Dictionary of Sports Quotations* (1990).

14 It is almost impossible to remember how tragic a place this world is when one is playing golf.
Attributed.

Lyndon, Neil 1946–

British journalist and writer. His critique of feminism, *No More Sex War: The Failures of Feminism*, was published in 1992.

15 The cardinal tenets of feminism divided my generation, effectively disempowering and disenfranchising its members. It does make me bitterly angry that my generation, which prided itself so complacently on its soul, on its powers of intelligence and analysis, should have fallen so cloddishly for totalitarian simplicities which declared a war of eternal opposition between men and women.
1992 *No More Sex War: The Failures of Feminism.*

Lyte, Henry Francis 1793–1847

Scottish hymn writer, curate of Lower Brixham, Devon, from 1823.

16 Praise, my soul, the King of Heaven;
To his feet thy tribute bring.
Ransomed, healed, restored, forgiven,
Who like me his praise should sing?
1834 'Praise, my Soul, the King of Heaven'.

17 Abide with me; fast falls the eventide;
The darkness deepens; Lord, with me abide;
When other helpers fail and comforts flee,
Help of the helpless, O, abide with me.
1847 *Remains*, 'Abide with Me' (published 1850).

Lyttelton, Humphrey Richard Adeane 1921–

English jazz trumpeter, bandleader and broadcaster. An Old Etonian and former guardsman, he is the *doyen* of the English jazz scene, both as a musician and as a writer and broadcaster.

18 It is this tendency to play with manic enthusiasm on every possible occasion that distinguishes the amateur jazz musician from the professional, often to the public detriment of the latter, who are regarded as snooty and unfriendly.
1984 *Why No Beethoven?*, ch.1.

McAleese, Mary 1951–

Irish politician, elected President of Ireland in 1997.

19 Apart from shamrock, the President should not wear emblems or symbols of any kind.
1997 On why she would not be wearing a poppy at her inauguration on 11 Nov. In *The Guardian*, 13 Apr.

20 The day of the dinosaurs is over. The future belongs to the bridge-builders, not the wreckers.
1998 On the Northern Ireland Assembly. In *The Irish Times*, 27 Jun.

MacArthur, Douglas 1880–1964

US soldier. He commanded troops in the Far East (1941) in World War II, directed the recapture of the SW Pacific (1942–5), formally accepted Japan's surrender, and commanded its occupation (1945–51). He led the UN forces in the Korean War, but was relieved of command when he tried to continue the war against China.

21 I came through and I shall return.
1942 On reaching Australia, having broken through Japanese lines en route from Corregidor, 20 Mar. Reported in the *New York Times*, 21 Mar.

22 There lies the Holy Grail.
1943 Remark, 6 May, one year after the fall of Corregidor to the Japanese, recalled in *A Soldier Speaks*.

23 A great tragedy has ended. A great victory has been won. A new era is upon us… We have had our last chance. If we do not devise some greater and more equitable system, Armageddon will be at our door.
1945 National radio broadcast on the surrender of Japan, 2 Sep.

24 An unsinkable air-craft carrier.
1950 Of Taiwan's military significance for the US. Remark, 27 Aug, recalled in *A Soldier Speaks*.

25 In war, indeed, there can be no substitute for victory.
1951 Address to Congress, 19 Apr. In the *Congressional Record*, vol.97, pt.3, p.4125.

26 The world has turned over many times since I took the oath on the plain at West Point…but I still remember the refrain of one of the most popular ballads of that day which proclaimed most proudly that old soldiers never die; they just fade away.
1951 Address to Congress after being relieved of his duty by President Truman, 19 Apr.

27 I now close my military career and just fade away, an old soldier who tried to do his duty as God gave him the light to see that duty.
1951 Address to Congress after being relieved of his duty by President Truman, 19 Apr.

28 It isn't just dust that is settling in Korea, Senator, it is American blood.
1951 During the Senate inquiry on Mac Arthur's dismissal. Reported in the *New York Times*, 2 May.

29 He'll make a fine president. He was the best clerk who ever served under me.
1952 On Dwight D Eisenhower's election as President. In news summaries, 31 Dec.

30 The chickens are coming home to roost, and you happen to have just moved into the chicken house.
Comment to John F Kennedy on the presidential crisis. Kennedy enjoyed the remark and often quoted it. Quoted in Theodore C Sorensen *Kennedy* (1965).

Macarthur, James 1937–

Actor, only son of Helen Hayes.

31 What a wonderful sight, a full house—my mother would have loved it!
1993 Speaking at the memorial service at New York's Shubert's Theater for his mother, Helen Hayes. Reported in the *New York Times*, 19 Jun.

Macaulay, Dame (Emilie) Rose 1881–1958

English novelist and travel writer whose book, *Pleasure of Ruins* (1953), includes an account of her visit to Cambodia and the ruins of Angkor.

32 You should always believe all you read in newspapers, as

this makes them more interesting.
1925 *A Casual Commentary*,'Problems of a Reader's Life'.

33 My point of view has sadly changed. For now, should all the books in the world be laid before me, my problem would be how many of them I could avoid. Most books are like that.
1925 *A Casual Commentary*,'Problems of a Reader's Life'.

34 Here is one of the points about this planet which should be remembered; into every penetrable corner of it, and into most of the impenetrable corners, the English will penetrate.
1926 *Crewe Train*, pt.1, ch.1.

35 Gentlemen know that fresh air should be kept in its proper place—out of doors—and that, God having given us indoors and out-of-doors, we should not attempt to do away with that distinction.
1926 *Crewe Train*, pt.1, ch.5.

36 All is now desolate, fantastic, and ambushed with ghosts; the archaeologists twitter among them like bats.
1953 Of Angkor Thom. *Pleasure of Ruins*.

37 'Take my camel, dear,' said my aunt Dot, as she climbed down from this animal on her return from High Mass.
1956 *The Towers of Trebizond*, ch.1.

Macaulay (of Rothley), Thomas Babington Macaulay, 1st Baron 1800–59

English essayist and historian, an MP from 1830 and a skilful orator in the Reform Bill debates. He wrote the highly popular *Lays of Ancient Rome* (1842) and contributed to the *Edinburgh Review*, but his major work was the *History of England from the Accession of James II* (1848–61, fifth volume unfinished).

38 Then, beneath the nine-tailed cat
Shall they who use it writhe, sir;
And curates lean, and rectors fat,
Shall dig the ground they tithe, sir.
Down with your Bayleys, and your Bests,
Your Giffords, and your Gurneys;
We'll clear the island of the pests,
Which mortals name attorneys.
1820 'A Radical War Song', stanza 8. The names are those of lawyers and judges who figured in the trial of the Cato Street conspirators.

39 Free trade, one of the greatest blessings which a government can confer on a people, is in almost every country unpopular.
1824 'Essay on Mitford's *History of Greece*', collected in *Works* (published 1906), vol.7, p.688–9.

40 The men of our time are not to be converted or perverted by quartos.
1825 'Milton', in the *Edinburgh Review*, Aug.

41 Perhaps no person can be a poet, or can even enjoy poetry, without a certain unsoundness of mind.
1825 'Milton', in the *Edinburgh Review*, Aug.

42 There is only one cure for the evils which newly acquired freedom produces; and that is freedom... The blaze of truth and liberty may at first dazzle and bewilder nations which have become half blind in the house of bondage. But let them gaze on, and they will soon be able to bear it.
1825 'Milton', in the *Edinburgh Review*, Aug.

43 Many politicians of our time are in the habit of laying it down as a self-evident proposition, that no people ought to be free till they are fit to use their freedom. The maxim is worthy of the fool in the old story, who resolved not to go into the water till he had learnt to swim. If men are to wait for liberty till they become wise and good in slavery, they may indeed wait for ever.
1825 'Milton', in the *Edinburgh Review*, Aug.

44 Every man who has seen the world knows that nothing is so useless as a general maxim.
1827 'Machiavelli', in the *Edinburgh Review*, Mar.

45 It has lately been brought to my knowledge
That the Ministers fully design
To suppress each cathedral and college,
And eject every learned divine.
To assist this detestable scheme
Three nuncios from Rome are come over;
They left Calais on Monday by steam,
And landed to dinner at Dover.
1827 'The Country Clergyman's Trip to Cambridge', stanza 2. A satirical poem against the opposition to Catholic emancipation.

46 Knowledge advances by steps, and not by leaps.
1828 'History' in the *Edinburgh Review*, May.

47 History, at least in its ideal state of perfection, is a compound of poetry and philosophy.
1828 'Hallam's *Constitutional History*' in the *Edinburgh Review*, Sep.

48 We know of no spectacle so ridiculous as the British public in one of its periodical fits of morality.
1828 In the *Edinburgh Review*.

49 The gallery in which the reporters sit has become a fourth estate of the realm.
1828 'Hallam's *Constitutional History*' in the *Edinburgh Review*, Sep.
► *See Hazlitt 388:80.*

50 His writing bears the same relation to poetry which a Turkey carpet bears to a picture.
1830 'Robert Montgomery', in the *Edinburgh Review*, Apr.

51 Mr Robert Montgomery's genius [is] far too free and aspiring to be shackled by the rules of syntax... [His] readers must take such grammar as they can get and be thankful.
1830 'Robert Montgomery', in the *Edinburgh Review*, Apr.

52 From the poetry of Lord Byron they drew a system of ethics, compounded of misanthropy and voluptuousness, a system in which the two great commandments were, to hate your neighbour, and to love your neighbour's wife.
1831 Of the young Byron enthusiasts who emulated and hero-worshipped him. 'Moore's *Life of Lord Byron*', in the *Edinburgh Review*, Jun.

53 Many of the greatest men that ever lived have written biography. Boswell was one of the smallest men that ever lived and he has beaten them all.
1831 'Croker's new edition of *The Life of Samuel Johnson*', in the *Edinburgh Review*, Sep.

54 In the foreground is that strange figure which is as familiar to us as the figures of those among whom we have been brought up, the gigantic body, the huge massy face, seamed with the scars of disease, the brown coat, the black worsted stockings, the grey wig with the scorched foretop, the dirty hands, the nails bitten and

pared to the quick.
1831 Of Dr Samuel Johnson. 'Croker's new edition of *The Life of Samuel Johnson*', in the *Edinburgh Review*, Sep.

55 Dark and terrible beyond any season within my remembrance of political affairs was the day of their flight. Far darker and more terrible will be the day of their return.
1831 On the defeat of the Tory Government, House of Commons, 20 Sep.

56 He [John Hampden] knew that the essence of war is violence, and that moderation in war is imbecility.
1831 'Lord Nugent's *Memorials of Hampden*', in the *Edinburgh Review*, Dec.

57 It is not easy to make a simile go on all fours.
1831 Of the task of the allegorist. 'Robert Southey's edition of Bunyan's *Pilgrims Progress*', in the *Edinburgh Review*, Dec.

58 A broken head in Cold Bath Fields produces a greater sensation among us than three pitched battles in India.
1833 House of Commons, 20 Sep.

59 There was a time when the most powerful of human intellects were deluded by the gibberish of the astrologer and the alchemist… But time advances; facts accumulate; doubts arise… The highest intellects, like the tops of mountains, are the first to catch and to reflect the dawn.
1835 'Sir James Mackintosh's *History of the Revolution in England, in 1688*' in the *Edinburgh Review*, Jul.

60 The history of England is emphatically the history of progress.
1835 'Sir James Mackintosh's *History of the Revolution in England, in 1688*' in the *Edinburgh Review*, Jul.

61 But even Archimedes was not free from the prevailing notion that geometry was degraded by being employed to produce anything useful. It was with difficulty that he was induced to stoop from speculation to practice. He was half ashamed of those inventions which were the wonder of hostile nations, and always spoke of them slightingly as mere amusements, as trifles in which a mathematician might be suffered to relax his mind after intense application to the higher parts of his science.
1837 'Basil Montagu's edition of *The Works of Francis Bacon, Lord Chancellor of England*', in the *Edinburgh Review*, Jul.

62 Lars Porsena of Clusium
By the nine gods he swore
That the great house of Tarquin
Should suffer wrong no more.
1842 *Lays of Ancient Rome*, 'Horatius', stanza 1.

63 Then out spake brave Horatius,
The Captain of the Gate:
'To every man upon this earth
Death cometh soon or late.
And how can man die better
Than facing fearful odds,
For the ashes of his fathers
And the temples of his God?'
1842 *Lays of Ancient Rome*, 'Horatius', stanza 27.

64 'Now who will stand on either hand,
And keep the bridge with me?'
1842 *Lays of Ancient Rome*, 'Horatius', stanza 29.

65 Was none who would be foremost
To lead such dire attack;
But those behind cried 'Forward!'
And those before cried 'Back!'
1842 *Lays of Ancient Rome*, 'Horatius', stanza 50.

66 Alone stood brave Horatius,
But constant still in mind;
Thrice thirty thousand foes before,
And the broad flood behind.
1842 *Lays of Ancient Rome*, 'Horatius', stanza 57.

67 And even the ranks of Tuscany
Could scarce forbear to cheer.
1842 *Lays of Ancient Rome*, 'Horatius', stanza 60.

68 With weeping and with laughter
Still is the story told,
How well Horatius kept the bridge
In the brave days of old.
1842 *Lays of Ancient Rome*, 'Horatius', stanza 70.

69 The rugged miners poured to war from Medip's sunless caves.
1842 'The Armada', in the *Quarterly Magazine*.

70 And broader still became the blaze, and louder still the din,
And fast from every village round the horse came spurring in.
1842 'The Armada', in the *Quarterly Magazine*.

71 We hardly know any instance of the strength and weakness of human nature so striking, and so grotesque, as the character of this haughty, vigilant, resolute, sagacious blue-stocking—half Mithridates and half Trissotin, bearing up against a world in arms, with an ounce of poison in one pocket, and a quire of bad verses in the other.
1843 Of Frederick the Great. *Historical Essays*. 'Frederic the Great', in the *Edinburgh Magazine*, Apr.

72 Forget all feuds, and shed one English tear
O'er English dust. A broken heart lies here.
1845 'A Jacobite's Epitaph', closing lines.

73 I hardly know which is the greater pest to society: a paternal Government; that is to say, a prying meddlesome Government, which intrudes itself into every part of human life and which thinks that it can do everything for everybody better than anyone can do for himself, or a careless, lounging Government, which suffers grievances, such as it could at once remove, to grow and multiply, and which to all complaint and remonstrance has only one answer, 'We must let things take their course, we must let things find their own level.'
1846 House of Commons, 22 May.

74 Persecution produced its natural effect on them. It found them a sect; it made them a faction.
1846 On the Puritans, House of Commons, 22 May.

75 The history of England is emphatically the history of progress.
1846 House of Commons, 22 May.

76 Thus our democracy was, from an early period, the most aristocratic, and our aristocracy the most democratic in the world.
1848 *History of England*, vol.1, ch.1.

77 The Puritan hated bear-baiting, not because it gave pain to the bear, but because it gave pleasure to the spectators.
1849 *History of England*, vol.1, ch.2.

78 The Mountjoy began to move, and soon passed safe through the broken stakes and floating spars. But her brave master was no more. A shot from one of the batteries had struck him; and he died by the most enviable of all deaths, in sight of the city which was his birthplace, which was his home, and which had just been saved by his courage and self-devotion from the most frightful form of destruction.
1849 *History of England*, on the relief of Londonderry, vol.2, ch.12.

McAuliffe, Anthony 1898–1975

US soldier, a general in World War II.

79 Nuts!
1944 Replying to the German demand for surrender at Bastogne, Belgium, 23 Dec. His response was reported in this form in the *New York Times*, 28 Dec; the original may have been more explicit.

MacBeth, George Mann 1932–92

Scottish writer. He is best known as a poet, but also wrote novels and children's books.

80 To leave great themes unfinished is
Perhaps the most satisfying exercise
Of power.
1963 'The Spider's Nest'.

81 No one can read a poem unless he realises that it is a physical object as well as an abstract vehicle for conveying ideas. A poem has a material existence like a piece of music or sculpture or a plate of meat.
1967 Introduction to *Poetry 1900 to 1965*.

82 Heap high the
groaning platter with pink fillets, sucking pig and
thick gammon, celestial chef. Be generous with the
crackling. Let your hand slip with the gravy trough,
dispensing plenty.
1977 'An Ode to English Food'.

MacCaig, Norman Alexander 1910–96

Scottish poet. He was a school-teacher for much of his working life. He was one of Scotland's most distinguished poets.

83 A man's boots with a woman in them
Clatter across the floor.
1960 'Crofter's Kitchen, Evening'.

84 The stone remains, and the cross, to let us know
Their unjust, hard demands, as symbols do.
1960 'Celtic Cross'.

85 A cubic inch of some stars
weighs a hundred tons—Blue tit,
who could measure the power
of your tiny spark of energy?
1980 'Blue Tit on a String of Peanuts'.

McCain, John 1936–

US Republican politician, Senator from Arizona.

86 I will not take the low road to the highest office in the land.
2000 Conceding victory in the South Carolina primary to George W Bush. In *The Guardian*, 24 Feb.

McCann, M(ichael) J(oseph) 1824–1883

Irish teacher, journalist and ballad-writer.

87 Proudly the note of the trumpet is sounding,
Loudly the war-cries arise on the gale,
Fleetly the steed by Loc Suilig is bounding
To join the thick squadrons in Saimear's green vale.
On, every mountaineer,
Strangers to flight and fear:
Rush to the standard of dauntless Red Hugh!
Bonnought and gallowglass,
Throng from each mountain-pass!
On for old Erin—O'Donnell abu!
1845 *The Spirit of the Nation*, 'O'Donnell Abu'.

88 Wildly o'er Desmond the war-wolf is howling,
Fearless the eagle sweeps over the plain,
The fox in the streets of the city is prowling—
All, all who would scare them are banished or slain!
1845 *The Spirit of the Nation*, 'O'Donnell Abu'.

McCarthy, Eugene J(oseph) 1916–

US Democratic politician, Senator from Minnesota (1958–70). An opponent of the Vietnam War, in 1968 he challenged President Johnson for nomination but the bid failed and he left politics to devote himself to teaching and writing.

89 The war in Vietnam…[is] of questionable loyalty and constitutionality…diplomatically indefensible… morally wrong.
1967 Speech to the Conference of Concerned Democrats, 2 Dec, an address noted for crystallizing dissent against the Vietnam War.

90 The message from the administration today is a message of fear—even a message of fear of fear.
1967 Speech to the Conference of Concerned Democrats, 2 Dec.

91 Let us pick up again these lost strands and weave them again into the fabric of America…sort out the music from the sounds and again respond to the trumpet and the steady drum.
1967 Speech to Conference of Concerned Democrats, 2 Dec.

92 Being in politics is like being a football coach. You have to be smart enough to know the game and stupid enough to think it is important.
1991 In the *Los Angeles Times*, 7 Dec.

McCarthy, Joseph R(aymond) 1909–57

US Republican politician and inquisitor. As Chairman of the Permanent Subcommittee on Investigations from 1953, he used hectoring cross-examination and innuendo to arraign many often innocent citizens for communist sympathies.

93 While I cannot take time off to name all the men in the State Department who have been named as members of the Communist Party and members of a spy ring, I have here in my hand a list of 205 that were known to the Secretary of State as being members of the Communist Party, and who nevertheless are still working and shaping the policy of the State Department.
1950 Speech at Wheeling, West Virginia, 9 Feb, which marked the beginning of the McCarthy 'witch hunts' for communists.

94 McCarthyism is Americanism with its sleeves rolled.
1952 Re-election campaign slogan.

McCarthy, Mary Thérèse 1912–89

US writer, critic and social commentator. She is best known for her novel *The Group* (1963).

95 When an American heiress wants to buy a man, she at once crosses the Atlantic. The only really materialistic people I have ever met have been Europeans.
1947 'America the Beautiful', in *Commentary*, Sep.

96 The American character looks always as if it just had a rather bad haircut, which gives it, in our eyes at any rate, a greater humanity than the European, which even among its beggars has an all too professional air.
1947 'America the Beautiful', in *Commentary*, Sep.

97 American life, in large cities, is a perpetual assault on the senses and the nerves; it is out of asceticism, out of unworldliness, precisely, that we bear it.
1947 'America the Beautiful', in *Commentary*, Sep.

98 The happy ending is our national belief.
1947 'America the Beautiful', in *Commentary*, Sep.

99 Liberty, as it is conceived by current opinion, has nothing inherent about it; it is a sort of gift or trust bestowed on the individual by the state pending *good behavior*.
1952 Speech. Collected as 'The Contagion of Ideas', in *On the Contrary* (1961).

1 Every age has a keyhole to which its eye is pasted.
1953 'My Confession'. Collected in *On the Contrary* (1961).

2 In the unreal realms of the canals, as in a Swiftian Lilliput, the real world, with its contrivances, appears as a vast folly.
1956 Of Venice. *Venice Observed*, ch.1.

3 To care for the quarrels of the past, to identify oneself passionately with a cause that became, politically speaking, a losing cause with the birth of the modern world, is to experience a kind of straining against reality, a rebellious nonconformity that, again, is rare in America, where children are instructed in the virtues of the system they live under, as though history had achieved a happy ending in American civics.
1957 Of Catholicism. *Memories of a Catholic Girlhood*, 'To the Reader'.

4 Bureaucracy, the rule of no one, has become the modern form of despotism.
1958 'Vita Activa', in the *New Yorker*, 18 Oct.

5 There are no new truths, but only truths that have not been recognized by those who have perceived them without noticing.
1958 'Vita Activa', in the *New Yorker*, 18 Oct.

6 The labor of keeping house is labor in its most naked state, for labor is toil that never finishes, toil that has to be begun again the moment it is completed, toil that is destroyed and consumed by the life process.
1958 'Vita Activa', in the *New Yorker*, 18 Oct.

7 In violence, we forget who we are.
1961 *On the Contrary*, 'Characters in Fiction'.

8 An interviewer asked me what book I thought best represented the modern American woman. All I could think of to answer was: *Madame Bovary*.
1961 *On the Contrary*, 'Characters in Fiction'.

9 Being abroad makes you conscious of the whole imitative side of human behavior. The ape in man.
1965 *Birds of America*, 'Epistle from Mother Carey's Chicken'.

10 In politics, it seems, retreat is honorable if dictated by military considerations and shameful if even *suggested* for ethical reasons.
1967 *Vietnam*, 'Solutions'.

11 I once said in an interview that every word she writes is a lie, including 'and' and 'the'.
1980 In response to Lillian Hellman's memoir, *Scoundrel Time*, in the *New York Times*, 16 Feb.

McCartney, Sir (James) Paul 1942–

British rock singer, musician and songwriter. With fellow-Beatle John Lennon, he formed the most successful songwriting team of the 1960s.

12 Pop music is the classical music of now.
Quoted in Tony Palmer *All You Need Is Love* (1976).
➡ *See also Lennon 502:89.*

13 You can't reheat a souffle.
Explaining why The Beatles would not be reforming. Quoted in the *Chronicle of the 20th Century* (1977).

McCarty, Maclyn 1911–

US biologist.

14 An alternative device for the recovery of bacteria from large volumes of culture had become available by modification of a machine originally designed as a cream separator.
1985 *The Transforming Principle: Discovering that Genes Are Made of DNA*.

McClellan, George Brinton 1826–85

Union general in the American Civil War, given command of troops in and around Washington after the Battle of Bull Run in 1861. He ran unsuccessfully for election against Abraham Lincoln and resigned from the army in 1864.

15 All quiet along the Potomac.
1862 Attributed.

MacColl, Ewan James Miller 1915–89

English folksinger, composer, collector, author, playwright and socialist, whose work was an important influence on the Scottish and worldwide folk music revivals of the 1950s and 1960s.

16 The first time ever I saw your face
I thought the sun rose in your eyes,
And the moon and the stars were the gifts you gave
To the dark and the empty skies.
1962 'The First Time Ever I Saw Your Face', stanza 1.

McCourt, Frank 1931–

US author known for the bestselling memoir *Angela's Ashes* (1996).

17 Worse than the ordinary miserable childhood is the miserable Irish childhood, and worse yet is the miserable Irish Catholic childhood.
1996 *Angela's Ashes*, ch.1.

McCoy, John B(onnet) 1943–

US banker.

18 I was trying to make it as friendly as you can make an unfriendly offer.

1995 On his unsolicited $5 billion bid in an unsuccessful attempt to acquire the Bank of Boston. In *Fortune*, 21 Aug.

McCrae, John 1872–1915

Canadian soldier, physician, and poet, First Brigade surgeon in the Canadian Field Artillery. His most famous poem, 'In Flanders Fields', was written during the Second Battle of Ypres, Belgium, 3 May 1915.

19 In Flanders fields the poppies blow
Between the crosses, row on row,
That mark our place; and in the sky
The larks, still bravely singing, fly
Scarce heard amid the guns below.
1915 'In Flanders Fields', stanza 1.

McCullers, (Lula) Carson *née* ***Smith*** 1917–67

US writer. Her novels, tragic and often symbolic, have been labelled Southern Gothic. She also wrote a novella, *The Ballad of the Sad Café* (1951) as well as short stories and plays.

20 The Heart Is A Lonely Hunter.
1940 Title of novel.

21 All men are lonely. But sometimes it seems to me that we Americans are the loneliest of all. Our hunger for foreign places and new ways has been with us almost like a national disease.
1940 'Look Homeward, Americans', in *Vogue*, 1 Dec.

22 There's nothing that makes you so aware of the improvisation of human existence as a song unfinished. Or an old address book.
1951 *The Ballad of the Sad Café*, 'The Sojourner'.

23 Nothing is so musical as the sound of pouring bourbon for the first drink on a Sunday morning. Not Bach or Schubert or any of those masters.
1953 *Clock Without Hands.*

McCurry, Michael D

Clinton White House Press Secretary (1995–98).

24 There are people around here who think Hillary Clinton is responsible for the weather.
1995 In the *New York Times*, 7 Jan. New revelations about the First Lady's role in Whitewater land sales and the firing of the presidential travel office had coincided with a heavy Washington snowfall.

MacDiarmid, Hugh *pseudonym of* ***Christopher Murray Grieve*** 1892–1978

Scottish poet, nationalist and communist, the driving-force behind the modern Scottish literary Renaissance. He used complex forms of both Scots and English in his lyrical, philosophical and polemical verse.

25 I myself believe that we have lost this war—in everything but actuality. When I see scores of sheep go to a slaughter-house I do not feel constrained to admire their resignation.
1918 Letter to George Ogilvie, 12 Nov.

26 Earth, thou bonnie broukit bairn!
1925 *Sangschaw*, 'The Bonnie Broukit Bairn'.
Broukit = neglected.

27 But greet, an' in your tears ye'll droun
The haill clanjamfrie.
1925 *Sangschaw*, 'The Bonnie Broukit Bairn'.

28 An' see the deid come loupin' owre
The auld grey wa's.
1925 *Sangschaw*, 'Crowdieknowe', stanza 1.

29 I met ayont the cairney
A lass wi' tousled hair
Singin' till a bairnie
That was nae langer there
1926 *Penny Wheep*, 'Empty Vessel', stanza 1.

30 No' wan in fifty kens a wurd Burns wrote
But misapplied is a'body's property
1926 *A Drunk Man Looks at the Thistle*, l.41–2.

31 I'll hae nae hauf-way hoose, buy aye be whaur
Extremes meet—it's the only way I ken
To dodge the curst conceit o' bein' richt
That damns the vast majority o' men.
1926 *A Drunk Man Looks at the Thistle*, l.141–4.

32 The thistle yet'll unite
Man and the Infinite!
1926 *A Drunk Man Looks at the Thistle*, l.481–2.

33 To be yersel's—and to mak' that worth bein'.
Nae harder job to mortals has been gi'en.
1926 *A Drunk Man Looks at the Thistle*, l.745–6.

34 A'thing that ony man can be's
A mockery o' his soul at last.
1926 *A Drunk Man Looks at the Thistle*, l.1415–7.

35 Be like the thistle, O my soul,
Heedless o' praise and quick to take affront
1926 *A Drunk Man Looks at the Thistle*, l.1709–10.

36 'Let there be Licht,' said God, and there was
A little: but He lacked poo'er
To licht up mair than pairt o' space at aince,
And there is lots o' darkness that's the same
As gin He'd never spoken
1926 *A Drunk Man Looks at the Thistle*, l.2101–5.

37 And Jesus and a nameless ape
Collide and share the selfsame shape
That nocht terrestial can escape?
1926 *A Drunk Man Looks at the Thistle*, l.2476–8.

38 He canna Scotland see wha yet
Canna see the Infinite,
And Scotland in true scale to it.
1926 *A Drunk Man Looks at the Thistle*, l.2527–9.

39 O wha's the bride that cairries the bunch
O' thistles blinterin' white?
Her cuckold bridegroom little dreids
What he sall ken this nicht.
1926 *A Drunk Man Looks at the Thistle.*

40 The number of people who can copulate properly may be few; the number who can write well are infinitely fewer.
1928 Review of D H Lawrence's *Lady Chatterley's Lover* in *The New Age*, 27 Sep. This may very well have been the first published review of Lawrence's novel.

41 Lourd on my hert as winter lies
The state that Scotland's in the day.
Spring to the North has aye come slow
But noo dour winter's like to stay
For guid,
And no' for guid!
1930 *To Circumjack Cencrastus, or The Curly Snake.*

42 Better a'e gowden lyric
Than a social problem solved.
1930 *To Circumjack Cencrastus, or The Curly Snake.*

43 Are my poems spoken in the factories and fields,
In the streets o' the toon?
Gin they're no', then I'm failin' to dae
What I ocht to ha' dune.
1932 *Second Hymn to Lenin.*

44 Scotland is not wholly surrounded by the sea—unfortunately.
1934 *Scottish Scene*, 'The Sea'.

45 We must reconcile ourselves to the stones,
Not the stones to us.
1934 'On a Raised Beach'.

46 The rose of all the world is not for me.
I want for my part
Only the little white rose of Scotland
That smells sharp and sweet—and breaks the heart.
1934 *Stony Limits and other poems*, 'The Little White Rose'.

47 My aim all along has been (in Ezra Pound's term) the most drastic *desuetization* of Scottish life and letters, and, in particular, the de-Tibetanization of the Highlands and Islands, and getting rid of the whole gang of high mucky-mucks, famous fatheads, old wives of both sexes, stuffed shirts, hollow men with headpieces stuffed with straw, bird-wits, lookers-under-beds, trained seals, creeping Jesuses, Scots Wha Ha'evers, village idiots, policemen, leaders of white-mouse factions and noted connoisseurs of bread and butter, glorified gangsters, and what 'Billy' Phelps calls Medlar Novelists (the medlar being a fruit that becomes rotten before it is ripe), Commercial Calvinists, makers of 'noises like a turnip', and all the touts and toadies and lickspittles o the English Ascendancy, and their infernal women-folk, and all their skunkoil skulduggery.
1943 *Lucky Poet*, ch.3, 'The Kind of Poetry I Want'.

48 We do not like the confiding, the intimate, the ingratiating, the hail-fellow-well-met, but prefer the unapproachable, the hard-bitten, the recalcitrant, the sinister, the malignant, the saturnine, the cross-grained and the cankered, and the howling wilderness to the amenities of civilization, the irascible to the affable, the prickly to the smooth. We have no damned fellow-feeling at all.
1952 'The Dour Drinkers of Glasgow', in *The American Mercury*, Mar.

49 So this is what our lives have been given to find,
A language that can serve our purposes,
A marvellous lucidity, a quality of fiery aery light,
Flowing like clear water, flying like a bird
Burning like a sunlit landscape.
1955 'The Task'.

50 My job, as I see it, has never been to lay a tit's egg, but to erupt like a volcano emitting not only flame but a lot of rubbish.
1964 Letter to George Bruce, 1 Jul.

51 Scotland small? Our multiform, infinite Scotland small?
1974 'Direadh'.

McDonald, Alonzo L

US government official and businessman, former chief executive officer of McKinsey & Company and of the Bendix Corporation and staff director at the White House (1979–81).

52 Very few factors help produce economies of scale. Technology may be one, but not people. When it comes to motivating people and using their brainpower, you hit diseconomies of scale early. At that point, bigger isn't better.
1986 'Of Floating Factories and Mating Dinosaurs', in the *Harvard Business Review*, Nov/Dec.

MacDonald, George 1824–1905

Scottish pastor, poet and novelist who wrote fantastical and allegorical works for both adults and children.

53 Here lie I, Martin Elginbrodde:
Hae mercy o' my soul, Lord God;
As I wad do, were I Lord God,
And ye were Martin Elginbrodde.
1863 *David Elginbrod*, bk.1, ch.13.

54 The love of our neighbour is the only door out of the dungeon of self, where we mope and mow, striking sparks, and rubbing phosphorescence out of the walls, and blowing our own breath in our own nostrils, instead of issuing to the fair sunlight of God, the sweet winds of the universe.
1867 *Unspoken Sermons.*

55 Where did you come from, baby dear?
Out of the everywhere into here.
1871 *At the Back of the North Wind*, ch.33, 'Song'.

56 They all were looking for a king
To slay their foes and lift them high:
Thou cam'st, a little baby thing
That made a woman cry.
1883 'That Holy Thing', stanza 1.

57 There is no strength in unbelief. Even the unbelief of what is false is no source of might. It is the truth shining from behind that gives the strength to disbelieve.
The Marquis of Lossie (published 1906).

58 To be trusted is a greater compliment than to be loved.
The Marquis of Lossie (published 1906).

Macdonald, (James) Ramsay 1866–1937

Scottish politician, Prime Minister and Foreign Secretary of the first British Labour government (1924, 1929–31). He met the financial crisis of 1931 by forming a 'National' coalition government, which he led after a general election (1931–5).

59 The League of Nations grows in moral courage. Its frown will soon be more dreaded than a nation's arms, and when that happens, you and I shall have security and peace.
1929 Speech, London, 9 Nov.

60 We hear war called murder. It is not: it is suicide.
1930 Quoted in the *Observer*, 3 May.

MacDonnell, A(rchibald) G(ordon) 1895–1941

Scottish writer who lived most of his life in England, the subject of his best-known satirical novel.

61 England, their England.
1933 Title of novel.
► *See Henley 395:40.*

MacDougall, Ranald 1915–73

US screenwriter whose credits include *The Hasty Heart* (1949), *The Naked Jungle* (1954), *Queen Bee* (1955) and *The Mountain* (1956).

62 Alligators have the right idea, they eat their young.
1945 *Mildred Pierce* (with Catherine Turney).

McElligott, Tom (Thomas James) 1943–

US advertising executive.

63 You're never too bad to win.
1987 In the *Wall Street Journal*, 26 Mar.

McEnroe, John Patrick 1959–

US tennis player. He won four US Open singles titles and three Wimbledon titles. He was known for temperamental behaviour on court.

64 You cannot be serious!
1981 In protest at an umpire's decision at Wimbledon.

65 Being a celebrity is like being raped, and there's absolutely nothing a player can do about it.
Quoted in Colin Jarman *The Guinness Dictionary of Sports Quotations* (1990).

McEwan, Ian Russell 1948–

English writer. He established his reputation with two volumes of short stories before turning to novels. He has also written screenplays.

66 Her eyes, nose, mouth, skin, all might have been designed in committee to meet the barest requirements of feasibility.
1981 *The Comfort of Strangers*, ch.6.

67 Shall there be womanly times? Or shall we die?
1983 Refrain from *Or Shall We Die*, an oratorio.

68 Looking after children is one of the ways of looking after yourself.
1992 *Black Dogs*, preface.

McFadden, Robert D(ennis) 1937–

US journalist and writer. He has worked for the *New York Times* as a senior journalist since 1961, and is the author of two journalism-related books. His numerous press awards have included an Excellence in Journalism award (1994).

69 That rarest of political creatures—a Labor leader who could actually win elections.
1995 Of Harold Wilson. In the *New York Times*, 25 May.

70 He was rotund, provincial, resolutely middle-class, studiously ambiguous and sometimes wavering in his opinions.
1995 Of Harold Wilson. In the *New York Times*, 25 May.

71 In an era of precipitous decline for Britain and its once-global empire, Harold Wilson was a fixture for 30 years, a solid workingman's socialist in a rumpled ready-to-wear suit and his trademark Gannex mackintosh.
1995 Of Harold Wilson. In the *New York Times*, 25 May.

72 The silver-haired, pipe-smoking northerner was a consummate British politician: tenacious, shrewd, manipulative, a blend of homespun tastes, acid wit and pragmatic, often shifting policies…the symbol of an emerging middle-class Briton.
1995 Of Harold Wilson. In the *New York Times*, 25 May.

McFarlane, J A, and Clements, Warren 1944–, 1952–

Canadian journalists.

73 Say *quotes* from the shortstop or the Prime Minister, but *quotations* from the Bible, Browning or Churchill.
1990 *The Globe and Mail Style Book*.

74 The patron saint of journalists, officially named by the church, is St. Francis de Sales. The traditional patron saint of editors is St. John Bosco. (The protector of computer-age journalists may well be St. Anthony of Padua, patron saint of searchers for lost articles.)
1990 *The Globe and Mail Style Book*.

McFarlane, Robert 'Bud' Carl 1937–

US government official. After serving with the Marines, he became National Security adviser to President Reagan (1983–5) and later founder of Global Energy Investors (GEI).

75 He knows so little and accomplishes so much.
Of President Reagan. Quoted in George P Shultz *Turmoil and Triumph* (1993).

MacGill, Patrick 1890–1963

Irish navvy, novelist and poet. Sold into servitude by his farming parents, he escaped to Scotland where he laboured and hawked his verses before coming to literary attention. He emigrated to the US in 1930, where he fell into poverty and developed muscular sclerosis.

76 All the night the frogs go chuckle, all the day the birds are singing
In the pond beside the meadow, by the roadway poplar-lined,
In the field between the trenches are a million blossoms springing
'Twixt the grass of silver bayonets where the lines of battle wind
Where man has manned the trenches for the maiming of his kind.
1917 *Soldier Songs*, 'The Trench'.

McGonagall, William c.1825–1902

Scottish self-styled 'poet and tragedian' from Dundee, most of his work was doggerel. The majority of his poems were originally produced as broadsheets and not collected until after his death.

77 Alas! Lord and Lady Dalhousie are dead, and buried at last,
Which causes many people to feel a little downcast.
1890 *Poetic Gems*, 'The Death of Lord and Lady Dalhousie', stanza 1.

78 Beautiful Railway Bridge of the Silv'ry Tay!
Alas! I am very sorry to say
That ninety lives have been taken away
On the last Sabbath day of 1879,
Which will be remember'd for a very long time.
1890 *Poetic Gems*, 'The Tay Bridge Disaster', stanza 1.

79 Ye lovers of the picturesque, if ye wish to drown your grief,
Take my advice, and visit the ancient town of Crieff;
The climate is bracing, and the walks lovely to see
Besides, ye can ramble over the district, and view the

beautiful scenery.
More Poetic Gems (published 1962), 'Beautiful Crieff', stanza 1.

80 The man that gets drunk is little else than a fool,
And is in the habit, no doubt, of advocating for Home Rule;
But the best Home Rule for him, as far as I can understand,
Is the abolition of strong drink from the land.
Last Poetic Gems (published 1968), 'The Demon Drink', stanza 9.

McGough, Roger 1937–

English poet, playwright and performer, associated with the 1960s Liverpool pop scene. His poetry is characterized by a dry, ironic wit and a feeling for the diction and rhythms of the street. He has also written children's books.

81 Let me die a youngman's death
not a clean and in-between-
the-sheets, holy-water death.
1967 'Let Me Die A Youngman's Death'.

82 Discretion is the better part of Valerie
(though all of her is nice).
1969 'Discretion'.

83 by thus keeping one pace ahead of myself
I need never catch up with the truth.
1973 'unlikely now'.

84 I could never begin a poem: 'When I am dead'
In case it tempted Fate, and Fate gave way.
1982 'When I Am Dead'.

85 Do people who wave at trains
Wave at the driver, or at the train itself?
Or, do people who wave at trains
Wave at the passengers? Those hurtling strangers,
The unidentifiable flying faces?
1982 'Waving At Trains'.

86 This is the mother
who one day chose
to smother the child
with kisses, and blows and blows and blows.
1982 'Kisses and Blows'.

MacGowan, Shane 1957–

English singer, member of The Pogues.

87 They died in their hundreds with no sign to mark where
Save the brass in the pocket of the entrepreneur
By landslide and rockblast they got buried so deep
That in death if not life they'll have peace while they sleep.
1985 'Navigator' (co-written with Jim Finer).

88 You're a bum
You're a punk
You're an old slut on junk
Lying there almost dead on a drip in that bed
You scumbag, you maggot
You cheap lousy faggot
Happy Christmas your arse I pray God it's our last.
1988 'Fairytale of New York' (co-written with Jim Finer).

89 Never mind Dylan and the Dead, this'll be Dylan and the Nearly Dead.
1997 On a gig in which he was to be support act for Bob Dylan. Quoted in *Q Magazine*, Apr.

90 Cram as much pleasure as you can into life, and rail against the pain that you have to suffer as a result.
1997 In *Loaded*, Nov.

91 I don't believe in the Hebrew God, some big hairy bastard with thunderbolts.
1999 In the *Irish Voice*, 9 Jun.

McGovern, George S(tanley) 1922–

US Democratic politician, Senator for South Dakota (1963–81). He made a bid for the presidential nomination in 1968, and unsuccessfully opposed Nixon in the 1972 presidential election. He tried again for the presidential nomination in 1984, but withdrew.

92 To those who charge that liberalism has been tried and found wanting, I answer that the failure is not in the idea but in the course of recent history. The New Deal was ended by World War II. The New Frontier was closed by Berlin and Cuba even before it was opened. And the Great Society lost its greatness in the jungles of Indochina.
1973 Lecture at Oxford University, 21 Jan.

McGregor, Ewan 1971–

Scottish actor.

93 I'm sometimes asked 'Can you lose the accent?' and I say 'No, but I can put on another one'.
2001 In *In Style*, Sep.

McGuigan, Barry 1961–

Irish boxer.

94 There is nothing like wealth for dulling desire.
2003 In *The Independent*, 29 Dec.

Machado de Assis, Joaquim Maria 1839–1908

Brazilian poet and novelist, writer of romantic stories and poems. *Memórias Póstumas de Brás Cubas* (1881) marks the beginning of his mature style, informed by both pessimism and wit.

95 *Cada estação da vida é uma edição, que corrige a anterior, e que será corrigida também, até a edição definitiva, que o editor dá de graça aos vermes.*
Each stage in life is an edition that supersedes the previous one and will also be superseded until the definitive edition: the one that the editor gives to the worms.
1881 *Memórias Póstumas de Brás Cubas*, ch.27 (translated as *Epitaph of a Small Winner*, 1952).

96 *A vida é tão bela que a mesma idéia da morte precisa de vir primeiro a ela, antes de se ver cumprida. Já me vás entendendo; lê agora outro capítulo.*
Life is so beautiful that even the idea of death must be born before it can be realized. You must already understand. Now read another chapter.
1899 *Dom Casmurro*, ch.133.

Machiavelli, Niccolò di Bernardo dei 1469–1527

Italian politician and political theorist. Obliged to withdraw from public life after an accusation of conspiracy (1513), he devoted himself to literature. His masterpiece is the pragmatic manual for statesmen, *Il Principe* ('The Prince', written in 1513, published in 1532).

97 *Gli uomini si debbano o vezzeggiare o spegnere; perché si vendicano delle leggeri offese, delle gravi non possono.*
Men should be either treated generously or destroyed, because they take revenge for slight injuries—for heavy ones they cannot.
1513 *Il Principe*, ch.3 (translated by Alan Gilbert).

98 *Nasce da questo una disputa: s'egli è meglio essere amato che temuto, o è converso. Rispondesi che si vorebbe essere l'uno e l'altro; ma perché egli è difficile accozzarli insieme, è molto più sicuro essere temuto che amato, quando si abbia a mancare dell'uno de'due.*
This leads to a debate: is it better to be loved than feared, or the reverse? The answer is that it is desirable to be both, but because it is difficult to join them together, it is much safer for a prince to be feared than loved, if he is to fail in one of the two.
1513 *Il Principe*, ch.8 (translated by Alan Gilbert).

99 It never or rarely happens that a republic or monarchy is well constituted, or its old institutions entirely reformed, unless it is only done by one individual.
1513–17 *Discourses on First Ten Books of Livy.*

McIlvanney, William Angus 1936–

Scottish writer. He is best known for his Ayrshire novels *Docherty* (1975) and *The Big Man* (1985), and his series of crime novels featuring the Glaswegian detective, Laidlaw. He has also written poetry, essays and short stories.

1 There is a kind of laughter people laugh at public events, as if a joke were a charity auction and they want to be seen to be bidding.
1985 *The Big Man*, ch.1.

2 That would have been a nice place, inside an idea, but it wasn't a place to live. It was necessary to live where the idea and the fact collided.
1985 *The Big Man*, ch.8.

McInerney, Jay 1955–

US author.

3 I'm glad I don't have a book coming out this month.
2001 Comment made by Jay McInerney to Brett Easton Ellis on 11 Sep, when the World Trade Center was destroyed. Ellis replied, 'I was just thinking the same thing'. Quoted in *The Guardian*, 15 Sep.

MacInnes, Colin 1914–79

English writer. He gave a voice to sections of society often ignored. He is best known for his novel *Absolute Beginners* (1959).

4 And I thought, 'My lord, one thing is certain, and that's that they'll make musicals one day about the glamour-studded 1950s.' And I thought, my heaven, one thing is certain too, I'm miserable.
1959 *Absolute Beginners.*

5 Tradition, if not constantly recreated, can be as much a millstone as a mill-wheel.
1961 *England, Half English*, 'England, Half English'.

6 In England, pop art and fine art stand resolutely back to back.
1961 *England, Half English*, 'Pop Songs and Teenagers'.

7 A coloured man can tell, in five seconds dead, whether a white man likes him or not. If the white man *says* he does, he is instantly—and usually quite rightly—mistrusted.
1961 *England, Half English*, 'A Short Guide for Jumbles'.

8 The decorations are like those of the embassy of a nation about to go into voluntary liquidation.
1961 *England, Half English*, 'See You At Mabel's'.

MacInnis, Joseph 1937–

Canadian doctor, environmentalist and undersea explorer.

9 The larger the island of knowledge, the longer the shoreline of wonder.
Quoted by Donald Grant in *The Globe and Mail*, 8 Nov 1986.

Mackay, Alan Lindsay 1926–

British scientist and Fellow of the Royal Society.

10 How can we have any new ideas or fresh outlooks when 90 per cent of all the scientists who have ever lived have still not died?
1969 In *Scientific World*, vol.13.

McKay, Claude *originally* Festus Claudius 1890–1948

Jamaican born US writer. He wrote poetry, novels, autobiography and a study of life in Harlem, and was a key figure in the Harlem Renaissance of the 1920s.

11 If we must die, let it not be like hogs
Hunted and penned in an inglorious spot
While round us bark the mad and hungry dogs,
Making their mock at our accursed lot.
1922 *Harlem Shadows*, 'If We Must Die'.

12 Like men we'll face the murderous cowardly pack,
Pressed to the wall, dying, but fighting back!
1922 *Harlem Shadows*, 'If We Must Die'.

Mackaye, Dorothy Disney 1904–92

US journalist and agony aunt, best known for editing the 'Can This Marriage be Saved?' column for the *Ladies Home Journal* for more than 30 years.

13 'He never listens' is universal in the institution of marriage.
Recalled on her death, 5 Sep 1992.

Macke, August 1887–1914

German painter, one of the founder members of the *Blaue Reiter* group of Expressionist artists.

14 To create forms means: to live. Are not children more creative in drawing directly from the secret of their sensations than the imitator of Greek forms? Are not savages artists who have forms of their own powerful as the form of thunder?
1912 *The Blaue Reiter Almanac.*

Mackellar, (Isobel Marion) Dorothea 1885–1968

Australian popular poet and novelist. Her works include *The Witch Maid* (1914), *Dreamharbour* (1923) and the novel *The Little Blue Devil* (1912). She wrote little after the mid-1920s, but translated widely from various European poets.

15 The love of field and coppice,
Of green and shaded lanes,
Of ordered woods and gardens

Is running in your veins.
Strong love of grey-blue distance
Brown streams and soft, dim skies—I know
but cannot share it,
My love is otherwise.

I love a sunburnt country,
A land of sweeping plains,
Of ragged mountain ranges,
Of droughts and flooding rains.
I love her far horizons,
I love her jewel-sea,
Her beauty and her terror—
The wide brown land for me!

1905 'Core of My Heart', first published in the London *Spectator*. Collected as 'My Country' in *The Closed Door, and Other Verses* (1911).

McKellen, Sir Ian Murray 1939–

English stage and film actor and director.

16 I can't be absolutely certain, 30 years ago when I made the decision to become an actor, but certainly one of the reasons was it was the way to meet other queer men.

Quoted in Blake Green 'A Kingly McKellen as a Fascist in *Richard II*', in the Pink Pages, *San Francisco Chronicle*, 16 Aug 1992.

17 You can always pick out stage actors at the Oscars: they know how to walk.

2002 In the *Observer*, 17 Feb.

MacKenzie, Sir (Edward Montague) Compton 1883–1972

English writer and editor. His best-known books are *Sinister Street* (1913–14) and *Whisky Galore* (1947), which became a famous film.

18 Prostitution. Selling one's body to keep one's soul…one might say of most modern marriages that they were selling one's soul to keep one's body.

1918 *The Adventures of Sylvia Scarlett*, bk.2, ch.5.

19 You are offered a piece of bread and butter that feels like a damp handkerchief and sometimes, when cucumber is added to it, like a wet one.

1927 *Vestal Fire*, bk.1, ch.3.

20 Women do not find it difficult nowadays to behave like men, but they often find it extremely difficult to behave like gentlemen.

1933 *Literature in My Time*, ch.22.

MacKenzie, Lewis W 1940–

Canadian Major-General, retired, United Nations Chief of Staff for peacekeeping in Sarajevo, Bosnia-Herzegovina.

21 Countries that have soldiers in charge seem, more often than not, to be the ones where democracy is but a flickering candle sitting in an open window with a forecast of rain.

1993 Letter about his retirement, in *The Globe and Mail*, 21 Jan.

Mackintosh, Sir James 1765–1832

Scottish writer, philosopher and historian. He studied medicine, but settled in London as a journalist. His *Vindiciae Gallicae* (1791) was a defence of the French Revolution (he later recanted his views, 1815). He spent seven years in Bombay, becoming an MP on his return.

22 Men are never so good or so bad as their opinions.

1830 *Dissertation on the Progress of Ethical Philosophy*, section 6, 'Jeremy Bentham'.

23 Henry VIII perhaps approached as nearly to the ideal standard of perfect wickedness as the infirmities of human nature will allow.

1831 Of Henry's actions in executing Thomas More and Anne Boleyn. *History of England*, vol.2.

MacLaine, Shirley *pseudonym of* *Shirley MacLean Beatty* 1934–

US actress, sister of Warren Beatty. Her films include *The Apartment* (1959), *Irma La Douce* (1963), *Sweet Charity* (1968), *Terms of Endearment* (1983) and *Steel Magnolias* (1989).

24 I've played so many hookers they don't pay me in the regular way any more. They leave it on the dresser.

1989 In *New Woman*, Jul.

McLean, Don 1945–

US singer and songwriter. He enjoyed a series of hits in the early 1970s, among them the classic singles 'American Pie' (1972) and 'Vincent' (1972). He later concentrated on country music.

25 I can't remember if I cried
When I read about his widowed bride.
Something touched me deep inside
The day the music died.

1972 Of the death of Buddy Holly. 'American Pie'.

26 So bye, bye, Miss American Pie,
Drove my Chevy to the levee
But the levee was dry.
Them good old boys was drinkin' whiskey and rye
Singin' 'This'll be the day that I die.'

1972 'American Pie'.

27 And the three men I admired most,
The Father, Son and Holy Ghost,
They caught the last train for the coast
The day the music died.

1972 'American Pie'.

Maclean, Sir Fitzroy Hew 1911–96

English diplomat, soldier and traveller. Sent at his own request to Moscow, he travelled in Central Asia. During World War II he joined the Special Air Service in North Africa and later he was parachuted into Yugoslavia as Churchill's personal representative to contact Tito, then a guerrilla leader.

28 At first sight, landing by plane had seemed an infinitely more normal and agreeable method of entering the country than what Mr Churchill called 'jumping out of a parachute'.

1949 Eastern Approaches.

29 A spirit of contradiction has always, to some extent, guided my behaviour.

1949 Eastern Approaches.

30 It was unhealthy and unsafe, and of no interest whatever. 'But what,' I said, 'about the tigers ?' 'Tigers, perhaps,' he replied pityingly, 'but no culture.'

1949 Of Lenkoran, Azerbaijan, in discussion with an Armenian official. *Eastern Approaches*.

Maclean, John 1879–1923

Scottish Marxist and revolutionary of almost legendary status in Glasgow, appointed Soviet Consul on the Clyde after the Russian Revolution. Ill health accentuated by frequent prison sentences led to his early death.

31 No government is going to take from me my right to speak, my right to protest against wrong, my right to do everything that is for the benefit of mankind. I am not here, then, as the accused; I am here as the accuser of capitalism dripping with blood from head to foot.
1918 Speech at his trial at the High Court, Edinburgh, 9 May, quoted in Nan Milton *John Maclean* (1973), ch.3.

MacLean, Sorley *Gaelic name* Somhairle MacGill-Eain 1911–96

Scottish poet. He wrote in Gaelic, in which language he was the most important late 20th century poet, and prepared his own English translations.

32 *Ma thubhairt ar cainnt gu bheil a' chiall*
co-ionann ris a' ghaol
chan fhior dhi.
If our language has said that reason
is identical with love,
it is not speaking the truth.
1943 'A Chiall's a Ghràidh' ('Reason and Love').

33 *Mairg an t-sùil a chi air fairge*
ian mór marbh na h-albann
Pity the eye that sees on the ocean
the great dead bird of Scotland.
1943 'An t-Eilean', 'The Island'.

34 *Tha tìm, am fiadh, an coille Hallaig.*
Time, the deer, is in the wood of Hallaig.
1970 'Hallaig', epitaph.

35 *Mura tig's ann theànas ni a Hallaig*
a dh' ionnsaigh sàbaid nam marbh,
far a bheil an sluagh a' tathaich,
gach aon ghinealach a dh' fhalbh.
If it does not, I will go down to Hallaig,
to the Sabbath of the dead,
where the people are frequenting,
every single generation gone.
1970 'Hallaig'.

MacLeish, Archibald 1892–1982

US poet, Librarian of Congress (1939–44), Assistant Secretary of State (1944–5) and Professor of Rhetoric at Harvard (1949–62). He won Pulitzer Prizes for *Conquistador* (1932), *Collected Poems 1917–52* (1952) and his verse drama *J.B.* (1958).

36 A Poem should be palpable and mute
As a globed fruit.
1926 'Ars Poetica'.

37 A poem should be wordless
As the flight of birds.
1926 'Ars Poetica'.

38 A poem should not mean
But be.
1926 'Ars Poetica'.

39 We have learned the answers, all the answers:
It is the question that we do not know.
1928 'The Hamlet of A. MacLeish'.

40 If the poem can be improved by its author's explanations, it should never have been published.
1933 Author's note in *Poems*.

41 Keepers of books, keepers of print and paper on the shelves, librarians are keepers also of the records of the human spirit—the records of men's watch upon the world and on themselves.
1941 A Time to Speak, 'Of the Librarian's Profession'.

42 The dissenter is every human being at those moments in his life when he resigns momentarily from the herd and thinks for himself.
1956 'In Praise of Dissent', in the *New York Times*, 16 Dec.

43 Anything can make us look, only art can make us see.
1961 *Poetry and Experience*. 'Riverside'.

44 History, like a badly constructed concert hall, has occasional dead spots where the music can't be heard.
1967 In the *Observer*, 12 Feb.

45 Wildness and silence disappeared from the countryside, sweetness fell from the air, not because anyone wished them to vanish or fall but because throughways had to floor the meadows with cement to carry the automobiles which advancing technology produced.
1968 'The Great American Frustration', in the *Saturday Review*, 9 Jul.

46 To see the earth as we now see it, small and beautiful in that eternal silence where it floats, is to see ourselves as riders on the earth together, brothers on that bright loveliness in the unending night—brothers who *see* now they are truly brothers.
1968 On the first pictures from the moon. In the *New York Times*, 25 Dec.

47 The business of the law is to make sense of the confusion of what we call human life—to reduce it to order but at the same time to give it possibility, scope, even dignity.
1972 'Apologia', in the *Harvard Law Review*, Jun.

48 Poets...are literal-minded men who will squeeze a word till it hurts.
1972 'Apologia', in the *Harvard Law Review*, Jun.

49 We are great as our belief in human liberty—no greater. And our belief in human liberty is only ours when it is larger than ourselves.
1976 'Now Let Us Address The Main Question: Bicentennial of What?', in the *New York Times*, 3 Jul.

50 Poetry is the art of understanding what it is to be alive.
Recalled on his death, 20 Apr 1982.

51 If the art of poetry is...the art of making sense of the chaos of human experience, it's not a bad thing to see a lot of chaos.
On his work in government. Quoted in Scott Donaldson *Archibald MacLeish* (1992).

52 Mr Morgan struck me as a healthy and childish Britisher probably inhabiting the early 19th century.
Of financier J P Morgan. Quoted in Scott Donaldson *Archibald MacLeish* (1992).

MacLennan, Hugh 1927–90

Canadian novelist and essayist.

53 Boy Meets Girl in Winnipeg and Who Cares?
1960 Title of a magazine article in *Scotchman's Return and Other Essays*. It refers to the preference of Canadian editors,

publishers, and readers for romance and drama set in foreign locales.

Macleod, Fiona

➤ *See Sharp, William*

Macleod, Iain Norman 1913–70

English Conservative politician, Chairman of the Conservative Party (1961–3). He refused to serve under Lord Home (having supported R A Butler's leadership claim), and spent two years editing the *Spectator.* He was shadow Chancellor under Heath (1965–70), and briefly Chancellor (1970).

54 The Socialists can scheme their schemes and the Liberals can dream their dreams, but we, at least, have work to do.
1960 Speech at the Conservative Party Conference.

55 We now have the worst of both worlds—not just inflation on the one side or stagnation on the other, but both of them together. We have a sort of stagflation situation.
1965 Speech in the House of Commons, Nov.

McLuhan, (Herbert) Marshall 1911–80

Canadian critic and cultural theorist. He claimed that it is the communication media *per se*, not the information and ideas which they broadcast, that influence society. His books include *The Gutenberg Galaxy* (1962) and *The Medium is the Message* (1969).

56 For tribal man space was the uncontrollable mystery. For technological man it is time that occupies the same role.
1951 *The Mechanical Bride*, 'Magic that Changes Mood'.

57 The medium is the message.
1959 Speech at the University of British Columbia, 30 Jun, following a symposium in Vancouver on the subject of music and the mass media. The phrase was later used as the title of ch.1 in *Understanding Media* (1964), and as a book title (1969).

58 The new electronic independence recreates the world in the image of a global village.
1962 *The Gutenberg Galaxy.*

59 The car has become an article of dress without which we feel uncertain, unclad, and incomplete in the urban compound.
1964 *Understanding Media*, ch.22.

60 Persons grouped around a fire or candle for warmth or light are less able to pursue independent thoughts, or even tasks, than people supplied with electric light. In the same way, the social and educational patterns latent in automation are those of self-employment and artistic autonomy.
1964 *Understanding Media*, ch.33.

61 If the nineteenth century was the age of the editorial chair, ours is the century of the psychiatrist's couch.
1964 *Understanding Media.*

62 Canada is the only country in the world that knows how to live without an identity.
1967 'Canada: A Borderline Case', CBC radio broadcast, 29 May.

63 Life. Consider the alternative.
1968 *War and Peace in the Global Village.*

64 Television brought the brutality of war into the comfort of the living room. Vietnam was lost in the living rooms of America, not on the battlefields of Vietnam.
1975 Quoted in the *Montreal Gazette*, May.

65 Gutenburg made everybody a reader. Xerox makes everybody a publisher.
1977 In the *Guardian Weekly*, 12 Jun.

Macmillan, Sir (Maurice) Harold, 1st Earl of Stockton 1894–1986

English Conservative politician. He succeeded Eden as Prime Minister (1957), and was re-elected in 1959. He resigned through ill health in 1963.

66 We have not overthrown the divine right of kings to fall down for the divine right of experts.
1950 Speech, Strasbourg, 16 Aug.

67 I thought that the best thing to do was to settle up these little local difficulties, and then turn to the wider vision of the Commonwealth.
1956 On departing for a Commonwealth conference, after sacking several members of his Cabinet in his Night of the Long Knives, Jan.

68 Forever poised between a cliché and an indiscretion.
1956 On the role of a Foreign Secretary, in *Newsweek*, Apr.

69 Let us be frank about it. Most of our people have never had it so good. Go around the country, go to the industrial towns, go to the farms, and you will see a state of prosperity such as we have never had in my lifetime—nor indeed ever in the history of this country.
1957 Speech, Bedford, 20 Jul. This is the original form of the oft-misquoted 'You never had it so good'.

70 At home, you always have to be a politician. When you are abroad, you almost feel yourself to be a statesman.
1958 Speech during the first visit of a British Prime Minister to Australia, 17 Feb.

71 The most striking of all the impressions that I have formed since I left London a month ago is of the strength of African national consciousness. In different places it may take different forms, but it is happening everywhere. The wind of change is blowing through this continent. Whether we like it or not, the growth of national consciousness is a political fact.
1960 Speech to the South African Parliament, 3 Feb.

72 Are we so sure that with 15 representatives…in NATO, acting under the unanimity rule, the deterrent would continue to deter? There may be one finger on the trigger, but there will be 15 fingers on the safety catch.
1960 House of Commons, 30 May.

73 I was determined that no British government should be brought down by the action of two tarts.
1963 On the Profumo scandal, referring specifically to Christine Keeler and Mandy Rice-Davies, Jul.

74 I have never found, in a long experience of politics, that criticism is ever inhibited by ignorance.
1963 In the *Wall Street Journal*, 13 Aug.

75 A man who trusts nobody is apt to be the kind of man whom nobody trusts.
1963 In the *New York Herald Tribune*, 17 Dec.

76 Tradition does not mean that the living are dead; it means that the dead are living.
1963 In the *Manchester Guardian*, 18 Dec.

77 There are three bodies no sensible man directly challenges: the Roman Catholic Church, the Brigade of Guards, and the National Union of Mineworkers.

1981 In the *Observer*, 22 Feb.

78 There is a growing division in our comparatively prosperous society between the South and the North and Midlands, which are ailing, that cannot be allowed to continue. There is a general sense of tension. The old English way might be to quarrel and have battles, but they were friendly. I can only describe as wicked the hatred that has been introduced, and which is to be found among different types of people today. Not merely an intellectual but a moral effort is required to get rid of it.

1984 Maiden speech as the Earl of Stockton (60 years after first entering the House of Commons), House of Lords, 13 Nov.

79 First of all the Georgian Silver goes, and then all that nice furniture that used to be in the salon. Then the Canalettos go.

1985 Speech at a private dinner of the Tory Reform Group, 8 Nov, in a reference to privatization and the selling of profitable state-owned enterprises.

80 Margaret Thatcher is a brilliant tyrant surrounded by mediocrities.

1986 In *Newsweek*, 12 Oct.

81 A man who was alleged to have the rigidity of a poker without its occasional warmth.

Of Charles de Gaulle, whose nickname was 'Ramrod'. Quoted by Henry Fairlie in the *New Republic*, 20 Mar 1989.

82 If people want a sense of purpose, they should get it from their archbishop, they should certainly not get it from their politicians.

Quoted in *The Life of Politics*.

83 You've reached the stage where you must decide whether you're going to be a good writer or a good public servant. You can't be both.

Attributed comment to Michael O'Donovan (real name of the writer Frank O'Connor).

McMurtry, Larry Jeff 1936–

US novelist. Several of his novels have been filmed successfully, but his most significant work is the epic fusion of generic western and historical novel in *Lonesome Dove* (1985).

84 The Last Picture Show.

1966 Title of novel, subsequently filmed.

85 Terms of Endearment.

1975 Title of novel, subsequently filmed.

86 'We'll be the Indians, if we last another twenty years,' Augustus said. 'The way this place is settling up it'll be nothing but churches and dry-goods stores before you know it. Next thing you know they'll have to round up us old rowdies and stick us on a reservation to keep us from scaring the ladies.'

1985 *Lonesome Dove*, ch.42

87 The cowboys had lived for months under the great bowl of the sky, and yet the Montana skies seemed deeper than the skies of Texas or Nebraska. Their depth and blueness robbed even the sun of its harsh force—it seemed smaller, in the vastness, and the whole sky no longer turned white at noon as it had in the lower plains. Always, somewhere to the north, there was a swath of blueness, with white cloads floating in it like petals in a pond.

1985 *Lonesome Dove*, ch.93.

88 Self-parody is the first portent of age.

1989 *Some Can Whistle*, pt.1, ch.14.

89 But the sorrowing are nomads, on a plain with few landmarks and no boundaries; sorrow's horizons are vague and its demands are few.

1989 *Some Can Whistle*, pt.4, ch.9.

McNamara, Robert Strange 1916–

US Democratic politician and businessman, Secretary of Defense in the Kennedy administration (1961) during the Vietnam War. He resigned to become President of the World Bank (1968–81), and later emerged as a critic of the nuclear arms race and of the Vietnam conflict, expressing regret for his role in the latter.

90 I don't object to it being called 'McNamara's war'... It is a very important war and I am pleased to be identified with it and do whatever I can to win it.

1964 On the Vietnam War. In the *New York Times*, 25 Apr.

91 A test case of US capacity to help a nation meet a Communist 'war of liberation'.

1964 Of the Vietnam War. Quoted in N Sheehan *The Pentagon Papers*.

92 Neither conscience nor sanity itself suggests that the United States is, or should or could be the global gendarme.

1966 Speech to US newspaper editors. Reported in the *New York Times*, 19 May.

93 I wondered if I'd ever see another Saturday night.

On the threat of nuclear war from Russian warheads in Cuba, Oct 1962. Quoted in Elie Abel *Missile Crisis* (1966).

94 One cannot fashion a credible deterrent out of an incredible action.

1968 On nuclear weapons. *The Essence of Security*.

95 We had a two-track approach, one political and the other military, and the military was designed to move us along the political track.

On the Vietnam War in late 1967. Quoted in Deborah Shapley *Promise and Power* (1993).

96 We tend to justify our actions and in a sense we color history to achieve that objective.

Quoted in Robert Siegel (ed) *The NPR Interviews* (1994).

97 Although we sought to do the right thing and believed we were doing the right thing—in my judgement, hindsight proves us wrong.

1995 *In Retrospect: The tragedy and lessons of Vietnam* (with Brian Van de Mark).

MacNeice, (Frederick) Louis 1907–63

Irish poet born in Belfast. He was closely associated with the British left-wing poets of the 1930s, especially W H Auden with whom he wrote *Letters from Iceland* (1937). He also wrote radio drama, including *The Dark Tower* (broadcast 1946, published 1947). His *Collected Poems* was published in 1966.

98 Something of glass about her, of dead water,
Chills and holds us,
Far more fatal than painted flesh or the lodestone of live hair
This despair of crystal brilliance.

1935 *Poems*, 'Circe'.

99 World is crazier and more of it than we think,
Incorrigibly plural.

1935 *Poems*, 'Snow'.

1 The little sardine men crammed in a monster toy
Who tilt their aggregate beast against our crumbling Troy.
1935 *Poems*, 'Turf-stacks'.

2 It's no go the merrygoround, it's no go the rickshaw,
All we want is a limousine and a ticket for the peepshow.
Their knickers are made of crêpe-de-chine, their shoes are made of python,
Their halls are lined with tiger rugs and their walls with the heads of bison.
1937 'Bagpipe Music', stanza 1.

3 It's no go my honey love, it's no go my poppet;
Work your hands from day to day, the winds will blow the profit.
The glass is falling hour by hour, the glass will fall for ever,
But if you break the bloody glass, you won't hold up the weather.
1937 'Bagpipe Music', stanza 10.

4 And the gods are absent and the men are still—
Noli me tangere, my soul is forfeit.

Some are now happy in the hive of home,
Thigh over thigh and a light in the night nursery,
And some are hungry under the starry dome
And some sit turning handles.
1938 *Autumn Journal*, part 2.

5 Spider, spider, spin
Your register and let me sleep a little,
Not now in order to end but to begin
The task begun so often.
1938 *Autumn Journal*, part 2.

6 All of London littered with remembered kisses.
1938 *Autumn Journal*, part 4.

7 Tonight we sleep
On the banks of Rubicon—the die is cast;
There will be time to audit
The accounts later, there will be sunlight later
And the equation will come out at last.
1938 *Autumn Journal*, part 24.

8 Time was away and somewhere else.
1939 'Meeting Point'. Collected in *Collected Poems 1925–1948* (1949).

9 In my childhood trees were green
And there was plenty to be seen.

Come back early or never come.
1941 *Plant and Phantom*, 'Autobiography', l.1–3.

10 The dark was talking to the dead;
The lamp was dark beside my bed.
1941 *Plant and Phantom*, 'Autobiography', l.13–14.

11 The best people never land, sir.
1946 Steward to Roland. *The Dark Tower* (published 1947).

12 For the last blossom is the first blossom
And the first blossom is the best blossom
And when from Eden we take our way
The morning after is the first day.
'Apple Blossom', in *Collected Poems*, 1966.

13 His father gave him a box of truisms
Shaped like a coffin, then his father died;
The truisms remained on the mantelpiece.
'The Truisms', in *Collected Poems*, 1966.

McNeil, Robert

14 Mein Banff.
Suggested title for a biography of Alex Salmond, leader of the Scottish Nationalist Party and MP for Banff and Buchan.

MacQueen, Robert, Lord Braxfield 1722–99

Scottish judge who presided over many famous trials in Edinburgh. Notorious for his harsh sentencing and cruel humour, he was known as the 'hanging judge', and was the original for R L Stevenson's Lord Hermiston in *Weir of Hermiston*.

15 Muckle he made o' that; he was hanget.
1794 Riposte at the trial of a political reformer, when the defendant remarked that all great men had been reformers, 'even our Saviour himself'. Quoted in Lord Cockburn *Memorials of his Time* (1856), ch.2.

16 Ye're a verra clever chiel', man, but ye wad be nane the waur o'a hanging.
Quoted in John G Lockhart *Memoirs of the Life of Sir Walter Scott, Bart.* (1837–8), ch.48.

17 Let them bring me prisoners, and I'll find them law.
Quoted in Lord Cockburn *Memorials of his Time* (1856), ch.2.

MacRéamoinn, Sean Seamas Criostoir 1921–

Irish broadcaster and journalist.

18 I am becoming like the Irish Census, broken down by Age, Sex, and Religion.
1991 Chairing a lecture on Parnell, Merriman Summer School.

Madan, Geoffrey 1895–1947

English aphorist.

19 Conservative ideal of freedom and progress: everyone to have an unfettered opportunity of remaining exactly where they are.
Collected in *Geoffrey Madan's Notebooks* (published 1981).

Madison, James 1751–1836

US politician and 4th President (1809–17), co-author of the *Federalist Papers* (1787–8). Originator of the Virginia Plan, his compromise measure on the status of slaves ensured adoption of the Constitution in slave states. He presided over the 1812 war with Britain.

20 The diversity in the faculties of men, from which the rights of property originate, is not less an insuperable obstacle to a uniformity of interests. The protection of those faculties is the first object of government.
1787 *The Federalist*, Nov.

21 What is government itself but the greatest of all reflections on human nature? If men were angels, no government would be necessary. If angels were to govern men, neither external nor internal controls on government would be necessary.
1788 *The Federalist*, Jan.

Madonna *full name Madonna Louise Veronica Ciccone* 1958–

US pop singer and actress.

22 We are living in a material world

And I am a material girl.
1985 'Material Girl'.

23 Many people see Eva Perón as either a saint or as the incarnation of Satan. That means I can definitely identify with her.
1996 On playing Eva Perón in the film *Evita*. Quoted in *Newsweek*, 5 Feb.

24 If I had known I would be so universally misunderstood, maybe I wouldn't have been so rebellious and outspoken.
Quoted in the *Guinness Rockopedia* (1998).

Maeterlinck, Maurice 1862–1949

Belgian playwright and poet. The success enjoyed by his play *Pelléas et Mélisande* (1892) established him as the leading playwright of the Symbolist movement. He was awarded a Nobel prize in 1911.

25 *L'Oiseau bleu.*
The Blue Bird.
1908 Title of play.

Magidson, Herb 1906–86

US songwriter.

26 Music, Maestro, Please.
1938 Title of song.

Magna Carta

The Great Charter obtained from King John in 1215, the basis of English political and personal liberty.

27 *Nullius liber homo capiatur, vel imprisonetur, aut dissaisiatur, aut utlagetur, aut exuletur, aut aliquo modo destruator, nec super eum ibimus, nec super eum mittemus, nisi per legale judicium parium suorum vel per legem terrae.*
No free man shall be taken or imprisoned or dispossessed, or outlawed or exiled, or in any way destroyed, nor will we go upon him, nor will we send against him except by the lawful judgement of his peers or by the law of the land.
1215 Clause 39.

28 *Nulli vendemus, nulli negabimus aut differemus, rectum aut justitiam.*
To no man will we sell, or deny, or delay, right or justice.
1215 Clause 40.

Mahathir, Mohamad 1925–

Malaysian politician and the country's longest serving Prime Minister, holding office from 1981 to 2003.

29 I'm brash and abrasive but that's because I've noticed when people are nice and polite they never get anywhere.
c.1990 Quoted in the *Eastern Express*, 24 Apr 1995.

30 If you can't be famous, at least you can be notorious.
c.1994 Quoted in the *Eastern Express*, 24 Apr 1995.

Mahler, Gustav 1860–1911

Austrian composer, conductor and artistic director at the Vienna State Opera (1897). He resigned after 10 years to conduct the New York Philharmonic (1908–11). He is best known for the song-symphony *Das Lied von der Erde* ('The Song of the Earth').

31 A symphony must be like the world, it must embrace everything.
1907 In conversation with Sibelius. Quoted in Ian Crofton and Donald Fraser *A Dictionary of Musical Quotations* (1985).

32 *Endlich fortissimo!*
Fortissimo at last!
1907 On seeing the Niagara Falls. Quoted in Charles Osborne *The Dictionary of Composers* (1977).

33 He is young and perhaps he is right. Maybe my ear is not sensitive enough.
Of Schoenberg's music. Quoted in Lebrecht *Discord* (1982).

Mahony, Francis Sylvester *pseudonym* Father Prout 1804–66

Irish priest and humorous writer. He became a Jesuit priest but was expelled after a late-night frolic. After a spell as a priest in Italy, he turned to journalism in London.

34 And cymbals glorious
Swinging uproarious
In the gorgeous turrets
Of Notre Dame.
'The Bells of Shandon'.

35 O the bells of Shandon
Sound far more grand on
The pleasant waters
Of the River Lee.
'The Bells of Shandon'.

Mailer, Norman Kingsley 1923–

US novelist and journalist. An inveterate polemicist and high-profile public figure, he is arguably the most controversial figure in post-war US letters.

36 The Naked and the Dead.
1948 Title of novel.

37 Hip is the sophistication of the wise primitive in a giant jungle.
1957 In *Dissent*, Summer.

38 Each day a few more lies eat into the seed with which we are born, little institutional lies from the print of newspapers, the shock waves of television, and the sentimental cheats of the movie screen.
1959 *Advertisements for Myself*, 'First Advertisement for Myself'.

39 America is a hurricane, and the only people who do not hear the sound are those fortunate if incredibly stupid and smug White Protestants who live in the center, in the serene eye of the big wind.
1959 *Advertisements for Myself*, 'Advertisement for "Games and Ends"'.

40 There is probably no sensitive heterosexual alive who is not preoccupied with his latent homosexuality.
1959 *Advertisements for Myself*, 'The Homosexual Villain'.

41 The final purpose of art is to intensify, even, if necessary, to exacerbate, the moral consciousness of people.
1959 'Hip, Hell, and The Navigator', in *Western Review*, no.23, Winter.

42 Every moment of one's existence one is growing into more or retreating into less. One is always living a little more or dying a little bit.
1959 'Hip, Hell, and The Navigator', in *Western Review*, no. 23, Winter.

43 Once a newspaper touches a story, the facts are lost

forever, even to the protagonists.
1960 In *Esquire*, Jun.

44 A modern democracy is a tyranny whose borders are undefined; one discovers how far one can go only by traveling in a straight line until one is stopped.
1963 *The Presidential Papers*, preface.

45 In America few people will trust you unless you are irreverent.
1963 *The Presidential Papers*, preface.

46 Ultimately a hero is a man who would argue with the gods, and so awakens devils to contest his vision.
1963 *The Presidential Papers*, preface.

47 In America all too few blows are struck into flesh. We kill the spirit here, we are experts at that. We use psychic bullets and kill each other cell by cell.
1963 *The Presidential Papers*, 'Fourth Presidential Paper'.

48 A high church for the true mediocre.
1963 Of the FBI. *The Presidential Papers*, 'Sixth Presidential Paper'.

49 Writing books is the closest men ever come to childbearing.
1965 'Mr Mailer Interviews Himself', in the *New York Times Book Review*, 17 Sep.

50 The sense of a long last night over civilization is back again.
1966 *Cannibals and Christians*, 'Introducing Our Argument'.

51 Sentimentality is the emotional promiscuity of those who have no sentiment.
1966 *Cannibals and Christians*, 'My Hope For America'.

52 There is one expanding horror in American life. It is that our long odyssey toward liberty, democracy and freedom-for-all may be achieved in such a way that utopia remains forever closed, and we live in freedom and hell, debased of style, not individual from one another, void of courage, our fear rationalized away.
1966 *Cannibals and Christians*, 'My Hope For America'.

53 What characterizes a member of a minority group is that he is forced to see himself as both exceptional and insignificant, marvelous and awful, good and evil.
1966 *Cannibals and Christians*, 'A Speech At Berkeley on Vietnam Day'.

54 The surest way not to be remembered is to talk about the way you want to be.
1968 Interview in *Playboy*, Aug.

55 New York is one of the capitals of the world and Los Angeles is a constellation of plastic. San Francisco is a lady, Boston has become Urban Renewal, Philadelphia and Baltimore and Washington blink like dull diamonds in the smog of Eastern Megalopolis, and New Orleans is unremarkable past the French Quarter. Detroit is a one-trade town, Pittsburgh has lost its golden triangle. St Louis has become the golden arch of the corporation, and nights in Kansas City close early. The oil depletion allowance makes Houston and Dallas naught but checkerboards for this sort of game. But Chicago is a great American city. Perhaps it is the last of the great American cities.
1969 *Miami and the Siege of Chicago*, 'The Siege of Chicago'.

56 The horror of the Twentieth Century was the size of each event, and the paucity of its reverberation.
1970 *Of A Fire On The Moon*, pt.1, ch.2.

57 The difference between writing a book and being on television is the difference between conceiving a child and having a baby made in a test tube.
1971 'The Siege of Mailer: Hero to Historian', in *Village Voice*, 21 Jan.

58 So we think of Marilyn who was every man's love affair with America, Marilyn Monroe who was blonde and beautiful and had a sweet little rinky-dink of a voice and all the cleanliness of all the clean American backyards.
1973 *Marilyn*.

59 No physical activity is so vain as boxing. A man gets into the ring to attract admiration. In no sport, therefore, can you be more humiliated.
1976 *The Fight*.

60 The true religion of America has always been America.
1984 Interview in *Time Out*, 27 Sep–3 Oct.

61 All the security around the American President is just to make sure the man who shoots him gets caught.
1990 In the *Sunday Telegraph*, 4 Mar.

62 When a novel comes, it's a grace. Something in the cosmos has forgiven you long enough so that you can start.
1991 In *The Guardian*, 5 Oct.

63 Writing a best-seller with conscious intent to do so is, after all, a state of mind that is not without comparison to the act of marrying for money only to discover that the absence of love is more onerous that anticipated.
2003 *The Spooky Art: Some Thoughts on Writing*.

64 Movies are more likely than literature to reach deep feelings in people.
2003 *The Spooky Art: Some Thoughts on Writing*.

Maillart, Ella Kini 1903–97

Swiss explorer, writer, actress and athlete. She captained the Swiss women's hockey team and represented Switzerland in skiing and sailing. In 1932 she travelled alone to Russian Turkestan and in 1934 to northeastern China.

65 No. Cost what it may I am determined to go East. The nomad's life enthralls me. Its restlessness pursues me: it is as much part of me as of the sailor. All parts and none are home to me, and all arriving only a new setting forth.
1934 *Des Monts Célestes aux Sables Rouges* (translated by John Rodder as *Turkestan Solo: One Woman's Expedition from the Tien Shan to the Kizil Kum*).

66 Wherever I go, it is always the secret life of such simple, straightforward races that I seek, people whom a fair face is sufficient to content. Only by returning to their way of life, can we ever hope to find a way out of the bogs in which we vainly stumble.
1934 *Des Monts Célestes aux Sables Rouges* (translated by John Rodder as *Turkestan Solo: One Woman's Expedition from the Tien Shan to the Kizil Kum*).

67 So far I like India.
1935 On crossing the Mintaka Pass at the extreme border of China. Quoted in Peter Fleming *News from Tartary* (1936).

Maimonides *properly* *Moses ben Maimon* 1135–1204

Spanish-born Jewish philosopher, rabbi and physician, one of the greatest Hebrew scholars. His philosophical work *Guide to the Perplexed* (1190) attempts to reconcile Greek philosophy and Judaism.

68 There is one [disease] which is widespread, and from which men rarely escape. This disease varies in degree in different men… I refer to this: that every person thinks his mind…more clever and more learned than it is… I have found that this disease has attacked many an intelligent person… They…express themselves [not only] upon the science with which they are familiar, but upon other sciences about which they know nothing… If met with applause…so does the disease itself become aggravated.
Aphorisms. Quoted in *Bulletin of the History of Medicine*, vol.3, p.555 (1935).

Maintenon, Françoise d'Aubigné, Marquise de *known as* ***Madame de Maintenon*** 1635–1719

Second wife of Louis XIV of France. Impoverished widow of the crippled poet Paul Scarron, in 1669 she became governess to Louis' sons. After the queen's death (1683) he married her secretly. She retired to her educational foundation at St-Cyr after his death.

69 You must make use of people according to their abilities, and realize that absolutely no one is perfect.
1679 Letter to Count d'Aubigné, 25 Sep.

Major, John 1943–

English Conservative politician and Prime Minister (1990–7). He rose quickly under Margaret Thatcher to become Chancellor of the Exchequer on Lawson's resignation (1989). After Thatcher's downfall he became Prime Minister, and his government was re-elected in 1992.

70 I hope…to build a society of opportunity. By opportunity, I mean an open society—a society in which what people fulfil will depend upon their talent, their application, and their good fortune. What people achieve should depend particularly on those things, and I hope increasingly in the future that that will be the case.
1990 Address on entering No.10 Downing Street for the first time as Prime Minister, 27 Nov.

71 I think that we had better start again, somewhere else.
1991 Attributed remark during a Cabinet meeting when the Cabinet Room was rocked by an IRA mortar attack on No.10 Downing Street, 7 Feb.

72 Only in Britain could it be thought a defect to be 'too clever by half'. The probability is that too many people are too stupid by three-quarters.
1991 Quoted in the *Observer*, 7 Jul.

73 When the final curtain comes down, it's time to get off the stage.
1997 Outside 10 Downing Street on 2 May, leaving office as Prime Minister and announcing that he would resign as Party Leader. In *The Guardian*, 3 May.

74 So right. OK. We lost.
1997 On election night. In *The Guardian*, 3 May.

75 Margaret has been at her happiest confronting political dragons: I chose consensus.
1999 On the difference between his approach to politics and that of Margaret Thatcher. In *The Autobiography*.

Makin, Bathsua b. c.1600

English poet and educator. She was appointed tutor to Princess Elizabeth in the 1640s, a post usually held by a man.

76 A Learned Woman is thought to be a Comet, that bodes Mischief, when ever it appears.
1673 *An Essay to Revive the Antient Education of Gentlewomen In Religion, Manners, Art and Tongues, With An Answer to the Objections against this Way of Education.*

Makwetu, Clarence 1931–

South African politician, president of the radical Pan-Africanist Congress (1990–7). Initially opposed to negotiation, he agreed to talks with other parties in the early 1990s.

77 We are determined to confront the oppressor with one voice.
1991 Addressing the first formal joint meeting for 30 years of the PAC and the rival African National Congress, 15 Apr.

Malamud, Bernard 1914–86

US Jewish writer. Novels including *The Assistant* (1957), *The Fixer* (1966), *Dublin's Lives* (1979) and *God's Grace* (1982) established his reputation as one of the finest novelists of the post-war period.

78 Levin wanted friendship and got friendliness; he wanted steak and they offered spam.
1961 *A New Life*, pt.6.

79 'Mourning is a hard business,' Cesare said. 'If people knew there'd be less death.'
1963 *Idiot's First*, 'Life Is Better Than Death'.

80 There comes a time in a man's life when to get where he has to go—if there are no doors or windows he walks through a wall.
1973 *Rembrandt's Hat*, 'The Man in the Drawer'.

81 I think I said 'All men are Jews except they don't know it.' I doubt I expected anyone to take the statement literally. But I think it's an understandable statement and a metaphoric way of indicating how history, sooner or later, treats all men.
'An Interview', in L and J Fields (eds) *Bernard Malamud* (1975).

82 Comedy, I imagine, is harder to do consistently than tragedy, but I like it spiced in the wine of sadness.
1975 Interview in *Paris Review*, Spring.

83 I love metaphor. It provides two loaves where there seems to be one. Sometimes it throws in a load of fish.
1975 Interview in *Paris Review*, Spring.

84 The past exudes legend: one can't make pure clay of time's mud. There is no life that can be recaptured wholly; as it was. Which is to say that all biography is ultimately fiction.
1979 *Dubin's Lives*.

Malcolm X *originally* ***Malcolm Little*** 1925–65

US black nationalist leader. Converted to the Black Muslims while in prison, on his release he assumed a new name and promoted the sect. He later founded his own organization, for Afro-American Unity, and in the resulting factional feuding was assassinated.

85 If you're born in America with a black skin, you're born in prison.
1963 Interview, Jun.

86 It has always been my belief that I, too, will die by violence. I have done all that I can to be prepared.
1965 *The Autobiography of Malcolm X*.

87 We didn't land on Plymouth Rock. It landed on us.
Quoted in *Life*, Fall issue 1990.

Malevich, Kasimir 1878–1935

Russian painter and designer. A pioneer of abstract art.

88 Only when the habit of one's consciousness to see in paintings bits of nature, madonnas and shameless nudes has disappeared, shall we see a pure-painting composition.
1915 Manifesto, quoted in C Gray *The Russian Experiment in Art* (rev edn 1986).

Mallarmé, Stéphane 1842–98

French poet, a leading writer in the Symbolist movement.

89 *Il n'y a que la Beauté—et elle n'a qu'une expression parfaite, la Poésie.*
There is only beauty—and it has only one perfect expression, poetry.
1867 Letter to Cazalis.

90 *Le vierge, le vivace et le bel aujourd'hui.*
The virgin, the vibrant and the beautiful today.
1881 *Plusieurs Sonnets*, no.1.

91 *La Poésie est l'expression, par le langage humain ramenée à son rythme essentiel, du sens mystérieux des aspects de l'existence; elle doue ainsi d'authenticité notre séjour et constitue la seule tâche spirituelle.*
Poetry is an expression, through human language restored to its essential rhythm, of the mysteriousness of existence; it endows our life with authenticity and constitutes our only spiritual task.
1884 Letter to M. Léo d'Orfer, 27 Jun.

92 *La chair est triste, hélas! et j'ai lu tous les livres.*
The flesh is sad, alas! and I've read all the books.
1887 'Brise marine', in *Poésies, Du Parnasse Contemporain* (1893).

93 *Dire au peintre qu'il faut prendre la nature comme elle est, vaut de dire au virtuose qu'il peut s'asseoir sur le piano.*
Telling a painter that he must take nature as it is is like telling a virtuoso that he can sit on the piano.
1888 *Le 'ten o'clock' de M. Whistler.*

94 *Nuit blanche de glaçons et de neige cruelle!*
White night of icicles and bitter snow!
1893 *Poésies, Hérodiade*, 'La Nourrice'.

95 *Donner un sens plus pur aux mots de la tribu.*
Bestow a purer sense on the language of the horde.
1893 *Poésies, Hommages et Tombeaux*, 'Le Tombeau d'Edgar Poe' (translated by Henry Weinfield, 1994).

96 *Tel qu'en Lui-même enfin l'éternité le change.*
As for Himself at last eternity changes him.
1893 *Poésies, Hommages et Tombeaux*, 'Le Tombeau d'Edgar Poe' (translated by Henry Weinfield, 1994).

97 *Un coup de dés n'abolira jamais le hasard.*
A throw of the dice will never abolish chance.
1914 Title of poem, in *Cosmopolis*, May.

Mallet-Stevens, Robert 1886–1945

French architect.

98 Architecture is an art which is basically geometrical. The cube is the basis of architecture because the right angle is necessary—the steps of a staircase consist of vertical and horizontal planes and the corners of rooms are nearly always right angles. We need right angles.
1924 'Architecture and Geometry', in *Bulletin de la Vie Moderne*, Paris.

Mallory, George Leigh 1886–1924

English mountaineer. He disappeared while attempting to climb Everest.

99 Because it's there.
1923 When asked 'Why do you want to climb Mount Everest?'. Quoted in the *New York Times*, 18 Mar.

Malory, Sir Thomas d.1471

English writer. His masterpiece, the *Morte d'Arthur*, a cycle of Arthurian legends, influenced Tennyson and other. It was completed c.1470 and a version was printed by Caxton in 1485.

1 The third sister, Morgan le Fey, was put to scole in a nonnery, and ther she lerned so moche that she was a grete clerke of nygromancye.
c.1470 *Morte d'Arthur*, bk.1, ch.2.

2 So the child was delyverd unto Merlyn, and so he bare it forth unto syre Ector and made an holy man to crysten hym and named hym Arthur.
c.1470 *Morte d'Arthur*, bk.1, ch.2.

3 'WHOSO PULLETH OUTE THIS SWERD OF THIS STONE AND ANVYLD IS RIGHTWYS KYNGE BORNE OF ALL ENGLOND'
c.1470 *Morte d'Arthur*, bk.1, ch.4. Inscription on the sword. Arthur was able to remove the sword with ease, and thus became king.

4 And there had Arthure the firste syght of queene Gwenyvere, the kyngis doghter of the londe of Camylarde, and ever afftir he loved hir.
c.1470 *Morte d'Arthur*, bk.1, ch.18.

5 'That is the Ladye of the Lake,' seyde Merlion. 'There ys a grete roche, and therein ys as fayre a paleyce as ony on erthe, and rychely besayne. And thys damesel woll come to you anone, and than speke ye fayre to hir, that she may gyff you that swerde.'
c.1470 To Arthur. *Morte d'Arthur*, bk.1, ch.25.

6 And so kyng Lodgreaunce delyverd hys doughtir Gwenyver unto Merlion, and the Table Rounde.
c.1470 *Morte d'Arthur*, bk.3, ch.1.

7 'What tydynges at Camelot?' seyde that on knyght. 'By my hede, there have I been and aspied the courte of kynge Arthure, and there ys such a felyshyp that they may never be brokyn, and well-nyghe all the world holdith with Arthure, for there ys the floure of chevalry.'
c.1470 *Morte d'Arthur*, bk.3, ch.14.

8 And so at that tyme sir Launcelot had the grettyste name of ony knyght of the worlde, and moste he was honoured of hyghe and lowe.
c.1470 *Morte d'Arthur*, bk.6, ch.18.

9 'But one thyng begyled us, that we myght nat se the Holy Grayle hit was so preciously coverde. Wherefore I woll make here a vow that to-morne, withoute longer abydynge, I shall laboure in the queste of the Sankgreall.'
c.1470 Sir Gawain. *Morte d'Arthur*, bk.13, ch.7.

10 And thus hit passes on frome Candylmas untyll Ester, that the moneth of May was com, whan every lusty harte begynnith to blossom and to burgyne. For, lyke as trees and erbys burgenyth and florysshyth in May, lyke wyse every lusty harte that is ony maner of lover spryngith, burgenyth, buddyth, and florysshyth in lusty dedis.

c.1470 *Morte d'Arthur*, bk.18, ch.25.

11 And there he bounde the gyrdyll aboute the hyltis, and threw the swerde as farre into the watir as he myght. And there cam an arme and an honde above the watir, and toke hit and cleyght hit, and shoke hit thryse and braundysshed, and than vanysshed with the swerde into the watir.
c.1470 *Morte d'Arthur*, bk.21, ch.5.

12 Yet som men say in many partys of Inglonde that kynge Arthur ys nat dede…and men say that he shall com agayne, and he shall win the Holy Crosse. Yet I woll nat say that hit shall be so, but rather I wolde sey: here in thys there ys wrytten uppon the tumbe thys: HIC IACET ARTHURUS, REX QUONDAM REXQUE FUTURUS. [Here lies Arthur, the once and future king].
c.1470 *Morte d'Arthur*, bk.21, ch.7.

13 Herein may be seen noble chyvalrye, curtosye, humanyté, frendlynesse, hardynesse, love, frendshyp, cowardyse, murdre, hate, vertue, and synne.
c.1485 *Morte d'Arthur*, Caxton's preface.

Malouf, David 1934

Australian novelist and librettist, of Lebanese and English extraction. His works include *An Imaginary Life* (1978), *Remembering Babylon* (1993) and *Dream Stuff* (2000).

14 'Do not shoot,' it shouted. 'I am a B-b-british object!'
1993 *Remembering Babylon*, ch.1.

Malthus, Thomas Robert 1766–1834

English economist. His anonymous *Essay on the Principle of Population* (1798) argued that population tends to increase faster than the means of subsistence, and that efforts should be made to cut the birth rate. He also wrote *Principles of Political Economy* (1820).

15 Population, when unchecked, increases in geometrical ratio. Subsistence only increases in arithmetical ratio.
1798 *An Essay on the Principle of Population*.

16 All the immediate checks to population—seem to be resolvable into moral restraint, vice and misery.
1798 *An Essay on the Principle of Population*.

17 The perpetual struggle for room and food.
1798 *An Essay on the Principle of Population*

18 A man who is born into a world already possessed, if he cannot get subsistence from his parents on whom he has a just demand, and if the society do not want his labour, has no claim of *right* to the smallest portion of food, and, in fact, has no business to be where he is.
1803 *An Essay on the Principle of Population* (revised edn).

19 The employment of the poor in roads and public works, and a tendency among landlords and persons of property to build, to improve and beautify their grounds, and to employ workmen and menial servants, are the means most within our power and most directly calculated to remedy the evils arising from disturbance in the balance of produce and consumption.
1820 *Principles of Political Economy*.

Mamet, David Alan 1947–

US dramatist, screenwriter and director. His demotic language and hard-hitting social observation have made him a significant voice in modern US theatre. He has translated works by Chekhov and written various screenplays. He has also directed films and published essay collections.

20 Sexual Perversity in Chicago.
1976 Title of play.

21 We respond to a drama to that extent to which it corresponds to our dream life.
1986 *Writing in Restaurants*, 'A National Dream-Life'.

22 We live in oppressive times. We have, as a nation, become our own thought police; but instead of calling the process by which we limit our expression of dissent and wonder 'censorship', we call it 'concern for commercial viability'.
1986 *Writing in Restaurants*, 'Radio Drama'.

23 Policemen so cherish their status as keepers of the peace and protectors of the public that they have occasionally been known to beat to death those citizens or groups who question that status.
1986 *Writing in Restaurants*, 'Some Thoughts On Writing In Restaurants'.

24 In a world we find terrifying, we ratify that which doesn't threaten us.
1986 *Writing in Restaurants*, 'Notes For a Catalogue for Raymond Saunders'.

25 We recipients of the boon of liberty have always been ready, when faced with discomfort, to discard any and all first principles of liberty, and, further, to indict those who do not freely join with us in happily arrogating those principles.
1986 *Writing in Restaurants*, 'First Principles'.

26 The product of the artist has become less important than the *fact* of the artist. We wish to absorb this person. We wish to devour someone who has experienced the tragic. In our society this person is much more important than anything he might create.
1986 *Writing in Restaurants*, 'Exuvial Magic: An Essay Concerning Magic'.

27 The absence of the urge to create is decadence.
1986 *Writing in Restaurants*, 'Decadence'.

28 Our semantic chickens have come home to roost… We have come to accept all sorts of semantic inversions, just as George Orwell told us we would.
1986 *Writing in Restaurants*, 'Semantic Chickens'.

29 We live in a world ruined by Reason.
1986 *Writing in Restaurants*, 'Oscars'.

30 We Americans have always considered Hollywood, at best, a sinkhole of depraved venality. And, of course, it is. It is not a Protective Monastery of Aesthetic Truth.
1986 *Writing in Restaurants*, 'A Playwright in Hollywood'.

31 There is such a thing as luck. There is such a thing as a *run of luck*. This is an instructive insight I have gained from poker—that all things have a rhythm, even the most seemingly inanimate of statistics.
1986 *Writing in Restaurants*, 'Things I Have Learned Playing Poker On The Hill'.

32 The poker player learns that sometimes both science and common sense are wrong; that the bumblebee *can* fly; that, perhaps, one should never trust an expert; that there are more things in heaven and earth than are dreamt of by those with an academic bent.
1986 *Writing in Restaurants*, 'Things I Have Learned Playing Poker On The Hill'.

33 All plays are about decay... That is why the theater has always been essential to human psychic equilibrium.
1986 *Writing in Restaurants*, 'Decay: Some Thoughts for Actors'.

34 The problems of the world, AIDS, cancer, nuclear war, pollution, are, finally, no more solvable than the problems of a tree which has borne fruit: the apples are overripe and they are falling—what can be done?... What can be done about the problems which beset our life? *Nothing* can be done, and nothing needs to be done. Something *is* being done—the organism is preparing to rest.
1986 *Writing in Restaurants*, 'Decay: Some Thoughts for Actors'.

35 The Film Industry is the American Monarchy: it is strict entailed succession and Horatio Alger in one. Except for the money manipulators and speculators on the top, it is a society built on work, achievement, and fealty to those in power.
1986 *Writing in Restaurants*, 'Observations of a Backstage Wife'.

36 Life in the movie business is like the beginning of a new love affair: it's full of surprises and you are constantly getting fucked.
1988 Charlie. *Speed The Plough*, sc.1.

37 A good film script should be able to do completely without dialogue.
1988 In *The Independent*, 11 Nov.

38 Film is the least realistic of art forms.
1989 In *The Guardian*, 16 Feb.

39 All of us write plays in our heads all the time...before we're going to visit our girl friend, before we're going to talk to a boss—we rehearse.
Quoted in Susan Stamberg *Talk* (1993).

Manchester, William Raymond 1922–

US novelist, foreign correspondent and contemporary historian, born in Attleboro, Massachusetts. His chief work is *The Death of a President* (1967), a landmark account written at the behest of the Kennedys.

40 A leader cut from whipcord.
1967 Of Governor John B Connally Jr. *The Death of a President*.

41 Johnson approached a strongly fortified position by outflanking it, or burrowing under it, or surprising the defenders from the rear, or raining down obstacles upon them from the sky, or starving them into submission... Rarely, and then only reluctantly, would he proceed directly from A to B, to him the shortest distance between two points was a tunnel.
1967 Of Lyndon B Johnson. *The Death of a President*.

42 His critics called him a wheeler-dealer. They overlooked the subtlety of Johnsonian strategy, his use of wheels within wheels.
1967 Of Lyndon B Johnson. *The Death of a President*.

43 Actors who have tried to play Churchill and MacArthur have failed abysmally because each of those men was a great actor playing himself.
1983 In *Book of the Month Club News*, Jun.

44 He resolved to lead Britain and her fading empire in one last great struggle...to arm the nation, not only with weapons but also with the mace of honor, creating in every English breast a soul beneath the ribs of death.
1988 Of Winston Churchill. *The Last Lion*.

45 It would be inaccurate to say that Churchill and I conversed. Like Gladstone speaking to Victoria, he addressed me as though I were a one-man House of Commons.
1988 *The Last Lion*.

Mandela, Nelson Rolihlahla 1918–

African Nationalist leader, sentenced to life imprisonment in 1964. A potent symbol of black resistance, he was released in Feb 1990, and elected President (1991) of the ANC. In 1993 he was jointly awarded the Nobel peace prize with F W de Klerk, and in 1994 became South Africa's first black President. His term ended in 1999.

46 During my lifetime I have dedicated my life to this struggle of the African people. I have fought against white domination, and I have fought against black domination. I have cherished the ideals of a democratic and free society in which all persons live together in harmony with equal opportunities. It is an ideal which I hope to live for, and to see realized. But My Lord, if needs be, it is an ideal for which I am prepared to die.
1964 Speech in court, 20 Apr, when charged under the Suppression of Communism Act and facing the death penalty.

47 We are not a political party. We have not changed at all. On the contrary, the ANC is a Government in waiting.
1991 Interviewed for BBC T V, Feb.

48 My fellow South Africans, today we are entering a new era for our country and its people. Today we celebrate not the victory of a party, but a victory for all the people of South Africa.
1994 Speech after his election to the presidency, Cape Town, 9 May.

49 No one is born hating another person because of the colour of his skin, or his background, or his religion. People must learn to hate, and if they can learn to hate, they can be taught to love, for love comes more naturally to the human heart than its opposite.
1994 *Long Walk to Freedom*.

50 One of the things I learnt when I was negotiating was that until I changed myself I could not change others.
2000 In the *Sunday Times*, 16 Apr.

Mandela, (Nomzano) Winnie 1934–

South African civil rights activist, who joined her husband Nelson Mandela in his work with the ANC and on release from prison became controversially involved in the militant politics of the townships. She was divorced by her husband in 1996.

51 With that stick of matches, with our necklaces, we shall liberate this country.
1986 Speech in the black townships, reported in *The Guardian*, 15 Apr. The 'necklaces' were home-made bombs, car tyres filled with petrol.

Mandelson, Peter 1953–

English Labour politician, he has twice resigned from government posts and in 2004 was appointed European Commissioner.

52 Few politicians are good at taking the high ground and throwing themselves off it.
1996 Of Tony Blair and the revision of Clause Four. In the *New Yorker*, 5 Feb.

53 You'll say that I'm in charge of a Mickey Mouse project.
1998 Declining to be photographed holding a balloon at Disney World, while in charge of the ill-fated Millennium Dome project. In the *Daily Telegraph*, 5 Jan.

Mandeville, Bernard 1670–1733

Dutch-born English satirist. After obtaining an MD degree from Leiden in 1691 he practised as a physician in London. He was widely denounced for encouraging immorality through his principle 'private vices are public benefits'.

54 The root of Evil, Avarice
That damn'd ill-natur'd, baneful Vice,
Was Slave to Prodigality,
That noble Sin; whilst Luxury
Employed a Million of the Poor,
And odious Pride a Million more;
Envy itself, and Vanity,
Were Ministers of Industry;
Their darling Folly, Fickleness,
In Diet, Furniture and Dress
That strange ridic'lous Vice, was made
That very Wheel that turned the Trade.
1723 *The Fable of the Bees, or, Private Vices, Publick Benefits* (2nd edn.).

Manguel, Alberto 1948–

Argentinian-born Canadian writer.

55 The world that is a book is devoured by a reader who is a letter in the world's text; thus a circular metaphor is created for the endlessness of reading; We are what we read.
1996 *A History of Reading*.

Manilow, Barry 1946–

US singer and songwriter.

56 I think my music is like anchovies—some people love it, some people get nauseous.
2003 In *Readers Digest*, Mar.

Mankiewicz, Herman 1897–1953

US journalist, screenwriter and film producer. He initially worked in newspapers as a foreign correspondent in Berlin and as a drama editor in New York, moving to Hollywood in 1926 where he worked on his screenplays. He is best remembered for his Academy Award-winning film *Citizen Kane* (1941), although Orson Welles originally claimed this script as his own work. He is the elder brother of the film director Joseph Mankiewicz.

57 Old age…it's the only disease you don't look forward to being cured of.
1941 *Citizen Kane* (with Orson Welles).

58 Rosebud.
1941 Kane's last word, the opening word of the film, and constantly referred to throughout. *Citizen Kane* (with Orson Welles).

59 Don't believe everything you hear on the radio.
1941 *Citizen Kane* (with Orson Welles).

60 There are millions to be grabbed out here and your only competition is idiots. Don't let this get around.
Cable to Ben Hecht in the early days of Hollywood. Quoted in the *New York Times*, 8 Jan 1993.

Mankiewicz, Joseph 1909–93

US director, producer and writer, brother of Herman. He won an Oscar for the script of *A Letter for Three Wives* (1949) and an Oscar for the direction and script of *All About Eve* (1950).

61 Fasten your seat belts, it's going to be a bumpy night!
1950 Bette Davis as Margo Channing in *All About Eve*.

62 We are a breed apart from the rest of humanity, we theatre folk. We are the original displaced personalities, concentrated gatherings of neurotics, egomaniacs, emotional misfits and precocious children.
1950 George Sanders as Addison De Witt in *All About Eve*.

Mann, Thomas 1875–1955

German novelist and short story writer who left Germany during World War II and settled in California. He received the Nobel prize for literature in 1929.

63 *Wahrscheinlich sind sie der interessanteste Reiz und Stoff unseres Nachdenkens und unserer Tätigkeit.*
Probably they are the most interesting stimulus and object of our meditation and our activity
1924 Of illnesses. *Der Zauberberg* (*The Magic Mountain*), vol.1.

64 *Bier, Tabak und Musik. Da haben wir Ihr Vaterland!*
Beer, tobacco, and music. There we have the Fatherland!
1924 *Der Zauberberg* (*The Magic Mountain*), vol.1.

65 *Leben ist, dass im Wechsel der Materie die Form erhalten bleibt.*
Life is that the form is maintained through the change of substance.
1924 *Der Zauberberg* (*The Magic Mountain*), vol.1.

66 *Dass nicht alles auf einmal da ist, bleibt als Bedingung des Lebens und der Erzählung zu achten, und man wird sich doch wohl gegen die gottgegebenen Formen menschlicher Erkenntnis nich auflehnen wollen*
Let us not forget the condition of life as narration: that we can never see the whole picture at once—unless we propose to throw overboard all the God-conditioned forms of human knowledge.
1924 *Der Zauberberg* (*The Magic Mountain*), vol.2.

67 *Zum Leben gibt es zwei Wege: Der eine ist der gewöhnliche, direkte und brave. Der andere ist schlimm, er führt über den Tod, und das ist der geniale Weg!*
There are two paths in life: one is the regular one, direct, honest. The other is bad, it leads through death—that is the way of genius!
1924 *Der Zauberberg* (*The Magic Mountain*), vol.2.

68 *Und wenn man sich für das Leben interessiert, so interessiert man sich namentlich für den Tod.*
If a person concerns himself with life, he also concerns himself with death.
1924 *Der Zauberberg* (*The Magic Mountain*), vol.2.

69 *Die Zeit hat in Wirklichkeit keine Einschnitte, es gibt kein Gewitter oder Drommetengetön beim Beginn eines neuen Monats oder Jahres, und selbst bei dem eines neuen Säkulums sind es nur wir Menschen, die schießen und läuten.*
Time has no divisions to mark its passage, there is never a thunderstorm or blare of trumpets to announce the beginning of a new month or year. Even when a new century begins it is only we mortals who ring bells and

fire off pistols.
1924 *Der Zauberberg* (*The Magic Mountain*), ch.4, section 4 (translated by H T Lowe-Porter).

70 *Unser Sterben ist mehr eine Angelegenheit der Weiterlebenden als unserer selbst.*
A man's dying is more the survivors' affair than his own.
1924 *Der Zauberberg* (*The Magic Mountain*), ch.6, section 8 (translated by H T Lowe-Porter).

71 *Die Zeit ist das Element der Erzählung, wie sie das Element des Lebens ist,—unlösbar damit verbunden, wie mit den Körpern im Raum. Sie ist auch das Element der Musik, als welche die Zeit misst und gliedert, sie kurzweilig und kostbar auf einmal macht.*
For time is the medium of narration, as it is the medium of life. Both are inextricably bound up with it, as are bodies in space. Similarly, time is the medium of music; music divides, measures, articulates time, and can shorten it, yet enhance its value, both at once.
1924 *Der Zauberberg* (*The Magic Mountain*), ch.7, section 1 (translated by H T Lowe-Porter).

72 *Liebe zu sich selbst ist immer der Anfang eines romanhaften Lebens.*
Self-love is always the beginning of a novelistic affair.
1933 *Joseph und seine Brüder* ('Joseph and his Brothers').

73 *Man kann sehr wohl in einer Geschichte sein, ohne sie zu verstehen.*
A person can be fully involved in a story without understanding it.
1933 *Joseph und seine Brüder* ('Joseph and his Brothers').

74 *Denn dem Menschen ist am Wiedererkennen gelegen; er möchte das Alte im Neuen wiederfinden und das Typische im Individuellen.*
For man always searches for recognition: he would like to find the old in the new and the ordinary in the individual.
1936 *Freud und die Zukunft*.

75 *Ist die Liebe das Beste im Leben, so ist in der Liebe das Beste der Kuss.*
If love is the best thing in life, then the best part of love is the kiss.
1939 *Lotte im Weimar*.

76 *Das Seelische [ist] immer das Primäre und eigentlich Motivierende; die politische Aktion ist zweiter Ordnung, Reflex, Ausdruck, Instrument.*
The mental state is always the primary and ultimately the motivating state. Political action is of second rank, reflex, expression, instrument.
1947 *Doktor Faustus*.

Mann, Thomas Edward 1944–

US political scientist. He is Senior Fellow in Governance Studies at the Brookings Institution and is the author and co-editor of many books on American political science and congressional election studies, such as *Renewing Congress* (1992) and *Vital Statistics on Congress* (2002).

77 He's a great ex-president. It's a shame he couldn't have gone directly to the ex-presidency.
1994 Of Jimmy Carter and his successful visit to Korea. In *Newsweek*, 27 Jun.

Mannheim, Karl 1893–1947

Hungarian-born German sociologist, who taught at the University of Heidelberg until expelled by Hitler and later at the LSE, known for his contributions to the sociology of knowledge.

78 Even the categories in which experiences are subsumed, collected, and ordered vary according to the social position of the observer.
1936 *Ideology and Utopia*.

Manning, Henry Edward 1808–92

English Roman Catholic prelate. He succeeded as Archbishop of Westminster in 1865 and became a cardinal in 1875. Noted for his support for the temperance and benevolent movements, he was also a keen cricketer and captained the Harrow Eleven team.

79 That bat that you were kind enough to send,
Seems (for as yet I have not tried it) good:
And if there's anything on earth can mend
My wretched play, it is that piece of wood.
1826 Verse sent to Charles Wordsworth, nephew of the poet William Wordsworth, after the latter sent him the present of a cricket bat.

80 To put labour and wages first and human or domestic life second is to invert the order of God and of nature.
1889 On the London dock strike.

Mansfield, Katherine *pseudonym of Kathleen Mansfield Beauchamp* 1881–1923

New Zealand writer. She moved to London to pursue a literary career and married John Middleton Murry. She died prematurely of tuberculosis. She is best known for her finely crafted short stories, in collections such as *Bliss and Other Stories* (1920). Her *Journal* was published in 1927.

81 Talk of our enlightened days and our emancipated country—pure nonsense! We are firmly held with the self-fashioned chains of slavery. Yes, now I see that they *are* self-fashioned, and must be self-removed.
1908 Journal entry, May.

82 The trouble with women like me is—they can't keep their nerves out of the job in hand… I walk about with a mind full of ghosts of saucepans and primus stoves and 'Will there be enough to go round?' I loathe myself, today. I detest this woman who 'superintends' you and rushes about, slamming doors and slopping water—all untidy with her blouse out and her nails grimed.
1913 Letter to John Middleton Murry, summer.

83 Why haven't I got a real 'home'—a real life—why haven't I got a Chinese nurse with green trousers and two babies who rush at me and clasp my knees? I'm not a girl—I'm a woman. I *want* things…all this love and joy that fights for outlet—and all this life drying up, like milk in an old breast.
1915 Letter to John Middleton Murry, 23 Mar.

84 I want for one moment to make our undiscovered country leap into the eyes of the Old World. It must be mysterious, as though floating. It must take the breath. It must be 'one of those islands…'.
1916 Journal entry, 22 Jan.

85 E M Forster never gets any further than warming the teapot. He's a rare fine hand at that. Feel this teapot. Is it not beautifully warm? Yes, but there ain't going to be no tea. And I can never be perfectly certain whether Helen

was got with child by Leonard Bast or by his fatal forgotten umbrella. All things considered, I think it must have been the umbrella.
1917 Journal entry, May.

86 Her underlip protruded a little; she had a way of sucking it in that somebody else had told her was awfully fascinating.
1920 *Bliss and Other Stories*, 'Prelude'.

87 True to oneself! Which self? Which of my many...hundreds of selves?... There are moments when I feel I am nothing but the small clerk of some hotel without a proprietor, who has all his work cut out to enter the names and hand the keys to the wilful guests.
1920 Journal entry, Apr.

88 I believe that people are like portmanteaux—packed with certain things, started going, thrown about, tossed away, dumped down, lost and found, half emptied suddenly, or squeezed fatter than ever, until finally the Ultimate Porter swings them on to the Ultimate Train and away they rattle.
1920 *Bliss and Other Stories*, 'Je Ne Parle Pas Français'.

89 Is it not possible that the rage for confession, autobiography, especially for memories of earliest childhood, is explained by our persistent yet mysterious belief in a self which is continuous and permanent; which, untouched by all we acquire and all we shed, pushes a green spear through the dead leaves and through the mould, thrusts a scaled bud through years of darkness until, one day, the light discovers it and shakes the flower free and—we are alive—we are flowering for our moment upon the earth? This is the moment which after all, we live for—the moment of direct feeling when we are most ourselves and least personal.
1920 Journal entry, Apr.

90 If there was one thing he hated more than another it was the way she had of waking him in the morning... It was her way of establishing her grievance for the day.
1920 *Bliss and Other Stories*, 'Mr Reginald Peacock's Day'.

91 The aloe seemed to ride...like a ship with the oars lifted. Bright moonlight hung upon the lifted oars like water, and on the green wave glittered the dew.
1920 *Bliss and Other Stories*, 'Prelude'.

92 He stands, smiling encouragement, like a clumsy dentist.
1922 *The Garden Party and Other Stories*, 'Bank Holiday'.

93 She couldn't possibly go back to the gentleman's flat; she had no right to cry in strangers' houses.
1922 *The Garden Party and Other Stories*, 'The Life of Ma Parker'.

94 What would father say when he found out? For he was bound to find out sooner or later. He always did. 'Buried. You two girls had me *buried*!' She heard his stick thumping. Oh, what would they say? What possible excuse could they make? It sounded such an appallingly heartless thing to do. Such a wicked advantage to take of a person because he happened to be helpless at the moment.
1922 *The Garden Party and Other Stories*, 'The Daughters of the Late Colonel'.

95 Whenever I prepare for a journey I prepare as though for death. Should I never return, all is in order. This is what life has taught me.
1922 Journal entry, 29 Jan.

96 The longer I live the more I turn to New Zealand. I thank God I was born in New Zealand. A young country is a real heritage, though it takes one time to recognize it. But New Zealand is in my very bones. What I wouldn't give to have a look at it!
1922 Letter to her father, Sir Harold Beauchamp, 18 Mar.

97 Looking back, I imagine I was always writing. Twaddle it was, too. But better far write twaddle or anything, anything, than nothing at all.
1922 Journal entry.

Mansfield, Michael Joseph 1903–2001

US Democratic senator and ambassador. A professor of history and political science (1933–42), he became a congressional member (1943–53) and Senator for Montana (1953–77). As US Ambassador to Japan (1977–89) in Tokyo, he represented the US on several trips to China.

98 A half-creature of the Senate and a half-creature of the executive.
1969 On the role of the Vice-President as the Senate's presiding officer. In *Time*, 14 Nov.

Mansfield, William Murray, 1st Earl 1705–93

English judge and MP. He was chief-justice of the king's Bench (1756) and a member of the Cabinet. His rulings developed the law of maritime contracts, insurance and bills, and influenced international law.

99 We must not regard political consequences, however formidable they may be. If rebellion was the certain consequence, we are bound to say, 'Justitia fiat, ruat coelum' (Let Justice be done, though the skies may fall).'
1768 Judgement against the sentence imposed on John Wilkes for publishing the anti-ministerial political newspaper *North Briton*, 28 Apr.
► *See Ferdinand I 320:1.*

1 Every man who comes to England is entitled to the protection of the English law, whatever oppression he may heretofore have suffered, and whatever may be the colour of his skin, whether it is black or whether it is white.
1772 Judgement on the Somersett slavery case, May.

Mao Zedong *or* *Mao Tse-tung* 1893–1976

Chinese military and political leader who became the first Chairman (1949) of the People's Republic. After the failure of the 1958–60 'Great Leap Forward' economic programme, his hold on power was weakened but he regained control by launching the 1966–9 'Cultural Revolution'.

2 But just think how good communism is! The state won't bother us anymore.
1919 Attributed remark. Quoted in Ross Terrill *Mao: A Biography* (1980), ch.4.

3 A revolution is not a dinner party.
1927 *The Little Red Book*, section 2.

4 A single spark can start a forest fire. Our forces, although small at present, will grow rapidly.
1930 Letter, 5 Jan.

5 If you want to know the taste of a pear, you must taste the pear by eating it for yourself. If you want to know the theory and methods of revolution, you must take part in

revolution. All genuine knowledge originates in direct experience.
1937 Address to the Anti-Japanese Military and Political College, Jul.

6 Politics is war without bloodshed; war is politics with bloodshed.
1938 'On Protracted War', speech, May.

7 Every Communist must grasp the truth that political power grows out of the barrel of a gun.
1938 'Problems of War and Strategy', speech, 6 Nov.

8 China has stood up.
1949 Proclaiming the establishment of the People's Republic of China, 1 Oct.

9 When a man reaches old age, he will die and the same is true of a party.
1950 Collected in *Selected Works* (1975), vol.4.

10 If the worst came to the worst and half of mankind died, the other half would remain while imperialism would be razed to the ground and the whole world could become socialist.
1954 Quoted in the *Peking Review*, 9 Jun 1963.

11 All the so-called powerful reactionaries are paper tigers, for they are cut off from their people. Was not Hitler a paper tiger, and was he not overthrown? US imperialism has not yet been overthrown, and it has atomic bombs—but I believe that it too will be overthrown. It, too, is a paper tiger.
1957 Speech to Communist International Congress, Moscow, Nov.

12 Letting a hundred flowers blossom and a hundred schools of thought contend is the policy for promoting the progress of the arts and the sciences and a flourishing culture in our land.
1957 Speech, Peking, 27 Feb.

13 The east wind prevails over the west wind.
1957 Spoken at an international conference of Communist leaders in Moscow. Quoted in Ross Terrill *Mao: A Biography* (1980), ch.14.

14 People of the world, unite and defeat the US aggressors and all their running dogs.
1958 Speech, Jul.

15 I have seen Lenin's manuscripts, which are filled with changes. He too made mistakes.
1959 Quoted in Ross Terrill *Mao: A Biography* (1980), ch.15.

16 Water too pure breeds no fish.
Quoted in Han Suyin *Wind in the Tower* (1974).

17 The more books one reads, the more stupid one becomes.
1976 Quoted in Ross Terrill *Mao: A Biography* (1980), ch.22.

Map, Walter c.1140–c.1209

Welsh poet and ecclesiast, author of *De Nugis Curialium* (c.1181) and possibly new versions of the Arthurian Romances.

18 *Dura est manus cirurgi, sed sanans.*
The hand of the surgeon is hard, but healing.
c.1181 *De Nugis Curialium*, Distinction 4, ch.4.

19 *Numquam enim audiendi quod aliquis monachus super puerum incubuisset, quin statim post ipsum surrexisset puer.*
I have heard before of a monk throwing himself on a boy, but the boy always rose again afterwards.
c.1181 On hearing of an unsuccessful attempt by Saint Bernard of Clairvaux to revive a dead boy by throwing himself on the body and praying. *De Nugis Curialium*, Distinction 4, ch.5.

20 *Hoc solum deliqui, quod uiuo.*
My only fault is that I am alive.
c.1181 On the refusal of many of his contemporaries to believe that his *Dissuasio Valerii ad Rufinum* could have been composed by a modern writer. *De Nugis Curialium*, Distinction 4, ch.5.

Maradona, Diego 1960–

Argentinian footballer.

21 It was the hand of God.
1986 To reporters after Argentina's World Cup defeat of England in which he scored a goal with his hand, 22 Jun.

Maraniss, David 1949–

US journalist and author. As a journalist for the *Washington Post* (of which he later became an associate editor) he received the Pulitzer Prize for national reporting in 1993, and has written a biography of President Bill Clinton.

22 It is…classic Bill Clinton, sincere and deceptive at the same time, requiring a careful reading between the lines.
1995 On President Clinton's letter as a graduate student, 3 Dec 1969, to arrange RO TC enlistment to avoid being drafted for the Vietnam War, a position that was to haunt his future campaigning. *First in His Class.*

23 Natural politicians are skilled actors, recreating reality, adjusting and ad-libbing, synthesizing the scenes, saying the same thing over and over again and making it seem that they are saying it for the first time.
1995 Of Bill Clinton. *First in His Class.*

24 At 34, he fit the ironic description of the quintessential Rhodes Scholar: someone with a great future behind him.
1995 Of Bill Clinton, the youngest defeated state governor in US history. *First in His Class.*

25 He is a congenital campaigner.
1995 Predicting that Bill Clinton would always be a candidate for office or an advocate. CNBC broadcast, 7 Mar.

Marc, Franz 1880–1916

German painter, founder member of the Munich-based Blaue Reiter (Blue Rider) group. Most of his paintings were of animals (eg *Blue Horses*, 1911) portrayed in forceful colours. He was killed at Verdun during World War I.

26 Today art is moving in a direction of which our fathers would never even have dreamed. We stand before the new pictures as in a dream and we hear the apocalyptic horsemen in the air.
1912 Subscription prospectus of the *Blaue Reiter Almanac*, Jan.

27 Art will liberate itself from the needs and desires of men. No longer will we paint a forest or a horse as we like or as they appear to us, but as they really are.
1914–15 *Aphorisms.*

28 Traditions are lovely things—to create traditions, that is, not to live off them.
1914–15 *Aphorisms.*

29 Who is able to paint the existence of a dog as Picasso paints the existence of a cubic shape?

Quoted in *Briefe, Aufzeichnungen und Aphorismen* (2 vols, 1920), translated by Chipp in his *Theories of Modern Art* (1968).

Marceau, Marcel 1923–

French mime artist. Celebrated for his performances in the role of the white-faced Bip, he is the foremost exponent of the mime theatre of Charles Dullin and Jean-Louis Barrault.

30 Life is a cycle, and mime is particularly suitable for showing fluidity, transformation, metamorphosis.
Words can keep people apart; mime can be a bridge between them.
Attributed.

Marcos, Ferdinand Edralin 1917–89

Filipino politician, elected President in 1965 and again in 1969. His years of office became increasingly notorious for widespread corruption but US backing helped keep him in power. He declared martial law in 1972 but was overthrown in 1986 by a popular 'People's Power' campaign.

31 It is easier to run a revolution than a government.
1977 In *Time*, 6 Jun.

32 Some people say the president is incapable of enforcing the law. Let them say that once more and I will set the tanks on them.
1986 Quoted in 'The Snap Revolution', in James Fenton *All the Wrong Places*.

33 History isn't through with me yet.
1986 Remark, quoted in Sterling Seagrave *The Marcos Dynasty*.

Marcos, Imelda Romualdez 1927–

Wife of President Ferdinand Marcos of the Philippines, with whom she fled in 1986. She later faced charges of theft and corruption.

34 Some are smarter than others.
c.1985 Her reply to a question about the great wealth she had accumulated. Quoted in Sterling Seagrave *The Marcos Dynasty*.

35 The real index of this country is the smiles of the people, not the economic index.
c.1985 Quoted in Sterling Seagrave *The Marcos Dynasty*.

Marcus Aurelius *full name* *Marcus Aelius Aurelius Antoninus* AD 121–180

Roman emperor and philosopher. His spiritual reflections, the *Meditations*, are considered a classic work of Stoicism.

36 Nothing is so conducive to greatness of mind as the ability to examine systematically and honestly everything that meets us in life.
Meditations, vol.3, pt.2 (translated by Charles Reginald Haines, 1901).

Marguerite d'Angoulême 1492–1549

Queen of Navarre and sister of François I. She was a patron of the arts, and wrote poetry.

37 *Je n'ai plus ni père, ni mère,*
Ni sœur, ni frère
Sinon Dieu seul auquel j'espère.
I no longer have a father, nor a mother,
Nor a sister, nor a brother.
I only have God to trust in.
1547 *Cantique spirituel*.

38 *Plus j'ai d'amour plus j'ai de fâcherie.*
The more I love, the more I quarrel.
1547 *Dizains*.

39 *Depuis qu'Ève fit pécher Adam, toutes les femmes ont pris possession de tourmenter, tuer et damner les hommes.*
Ever since Eve made Adam sin, women have taken it upon themselves to torment, kill and damn men.
1558 *Heptaméron*, pt.1.

40 *Seulement les sots sont punis, et non les vicieux.*
Only the foolish are punished, never the truly vicious.
1558 *Heptaméron*, pt.13.

41 *Un malheureux cherche l'autre.*
One unhappy person seeks out another.
1558 *Heptaméron*, pt.21.

42 *Le scandale est souvent pire que le péché.*
The scandal is often worse than the sin itself.
1558 *Heptaméron*, pt.25.

43 *Votre plaisir gît déshonorer les femmes, et votre honneur tuer les hommes en guerre; qui sont deux points formellement contraires à la loi de Dieu.*
Your pleasure lies in dishonouring women and your honour lies in killing men at war; two acts which stand in contradiction to the law of God.
1558 *Heptaméron*, pt.26.

44 *Mariage est un état de si longue durée qu'il ne doit être commencé légèrement, ni sans l'opinion de nos meilleurs amis et parents.*
Marriage is a state of such long duration that it should not begin lightly, nor without the opinion of our best friends and parents.
1558 *Heptaméron*, pt.40.

45 *L'amour n'est pas un feu que l'on tient dans la main.*
Love is not a flame that one holds in the hand.
1558 *Heptaméron*, pt.47.

46 *À force de jurer, on engendre quelque doute à la vérité.*
When forced to swear an oath, one can encounter doubt about the truth.
1558 *Heptaméron*, pt.61.

Marhabal fl.216 BC

Carthaginian soldier, a cavalry commander under Hannibal at the Battle of Cannae (216 BC).

47 You know how to gain a victory, Hannibal: you know not how to use one.
216 BC Comment to Hannibal after victory at Cannae. Quoted in Livy *Ab urbe condita*, bk.22.

Mariátegui, José Carlos 1895–1930

Peruvian political leader and essayist, who applied Marxist principles to Peruvian problems, while acknowledging the value of religion and myth to the indigenous peoples.

48 *Mientras en Norteamérica la colonización depositó los gérmenes de un espíritu y una economía que se plasmaban entonces en Europa y a los cuales pertenecía el porvenir, a la América española trajo los efectos y los métodos de un espíritu y una economía que declinaban ya y a los cuales no pertenecía sino el pasado.*
Whereas in North America colonization planted the seeds of the spirit and economy then growing in Europe

and representing the future, the Spaniard brought to America the effects and methods of an already declining spirit and economy that belonged to the past.
1928 *Siete ensayos de interpretación de la realidad peruana*, 'El problema de la tierra' (translated as *Seven Interpretive Essays on Peruvian Reality*, 1971).

Marie de France fl.1160–70

French poet, author of *Lais* and *Fables*. Born in Normandy, she spent most of her life in England. Her *Lais* in particular were of great influence on French literature.

49 *Qui Deus a duné esciënce*
e de parler bone eloquence,
ne s'en deit taisir ne celer,
ainz se deit voluntiers mustrer.
Whoever God has given knowledge
and eloquence in speaking,
should not be silent or secretive,
but should willingly show it.
c.1170 *Lais*, prologue, l.1–4.

50 *Ki qu'en plurt ne ki qu'en chant,*
le dreit estuet aler avant.
Whether it makes one cry or sing,
justice must be carried out.
c.1170 *Lanval*, l.437–8.

51 *Mult est fole, ki hume creit.*
She is a fool, who trusts a man.
c.1170 *Eliduc*, l.1084.

Marinetti, Emilio Filippo Tomasso 1876–1944

Italian dramatist, novelist and poet. He published his influential manifesto for Futurism in *Figaro* in 1909, and became a Fascist in 1919. His writings glorify war, the machine age and dynamism, disparaging all traditional forms of art.

52 We sing the love of danger. Courage, rashness, and rebellion are the elements of our poetry. Hitherto literature has tended to exalt thoughtful immobility, ecstasy, and sleep, whereas we are for aggressive movement, febrile insomnia, mortal leaps, and blows with the fist. We proclaim that the world is richer for a new beauty of speed, and our praise is for the man at the wheel. There is no beauty now save in struggle, no masterpiece can be anything but aggressive, and hence we glorify war, militarism and patriotism.
1909 *Manifesto of Futurism.* Quoted in Denis Mack Smith *Italy: A Modern History* (1959), p.270.

53 We affirm that the world's magnificence has been enriched by a new beauty: the beauty of speed. A racing car whose hood is adorned with great pipes, like serpents of explosive breath—a roaring car that seems to ride on grapeshot is more beautiful than the *Victory of Samothrace*.
1909 *Manifesto of Futurism.*

54 It is from Italy that we launch through the world this violently upsetting incendiary manifesto of ours. With it, today, we establish *Futurism*, because we want to free this land from its smelly gangrene of professors, archaeologists, *ciceroni* and antiquarians. For too long has Italy been a dealer in second-hand clothes. We mean to free her from the numberless museums that cover her like so many graveyards.
1909 *Manifesto of Futurism.*

Marion, Frances *originally Frances Marion Owens* 1888–1973

US screenwriter and novelist. She wrote prolifically for the silent screen before working as a war correspondent, and subsequently translated her skills to talking pictures. She later turned to novel writing.

55 Gimme visky… ginger ale on the side. And don't be stingy baby.
1931 Opening lines delivered by Greta Garbo in *Anna Christie*.

56 I read somewhere that machinery is going to take the place of every profession.
Oh my dear that's something you'll never have to worry about.
1933 Dialogue between Jean Harlow and Marie Dressler in *Dinner At Eight* (with Herman Mankiewicz).

Maritain, Jacques 1882–1973

French philosopher and critic. He converted from Protestantism to Catholicism (1906) and gained renown for his interpretations of St Thomas Aquinas. He based his own philosophy on Aristotle and Aquinas.

57 Poetry proceeds from the totality of man, sense, imagination, intellect, love, desire, instinct, blood and spirit together.
Quoted in Robert Fitzgerald (ed) *Enlarging the Change* (1985).

58 The poet knows himself only on the condition that things resound in him, and that in him, at a single awakening, they and he come forth together out of sleep.
Quoted in Robert Fitzgerald (ed) *Enlarging the Change* (1985).

Marivaux, Pierre Carlet de Chamblain de 1688–1763

French author best known for his comedies in which language, more than characters, dictates the action.

59 *Un mari porte un masque avec le monde, et une grimace avec sa femme.*
A husband wears a mask in the world and a smirk with his wife.
1730 *Le jeu de l'amour et du hasard*, act 1, sc.2.

60 *Dans ce monde, il faut être un peu trop bon pour l'être assez.*
In this world, one must be a little too good in order to be good enough.
1730 *Le jeu de l'amour et du hasard*, act 1, sc.2.

61 *Les bienfaits des hommes sont accompagnés d'une maladresse si humiliante pour les personnes qui les reçoivent!*
The generosity of men is accompanied by such a humiliating embarrassment for those who benefit from it.
1731 *La vie de Marianne*, ch.1.

62 *C'est presque toujours le péché qui prêche la vertu dans nos chaires.*
It's almost always sin which preaches virtue in our pulpits.
1731 *La vie de Marianne*, ch.4.

63 *Qu'est-ce qu'une charité qui n'a point de pudeur avec le misérable, et qui, avant de le soulager, commence par écraser son amour-propre.*
What is that charity worth which does not spare the wretched person's feelings, which instead, before

providing comfort, begins by wiping out his self-esteem.
1731 *La vie de Marianne*, ch.14.

64 *L'âme se raffine à mesure qu'elle se gâte.*
The soul refines itself in proportion to how it spoils itself.
1735 *Le paysan parvenu*, ch.4.

Markham, Dewey 'Pigmeat' 1906–81

US songwriter and comedy writer.

65 Here comes the judge.
1968 Song title, co-written with Dick Alen, Bob Astor and Sarah Harvey. Often quoted as a vaudeville catchphrase, 'Here come de judge'.

Marks, Leo 1920–2001

British writer. He acted as adviser on the film *Carve Her Name With Pride* (1958), partly based on his own wartime work in cryptography. He also wrote the script of *Peeping Tom* (1960).

66 The life that I have is all that I have
and the life that I have is yours
The love that I have of the life that I have
Is yours and yours and yours
1958 Poem recited by Virginia McKenna as Violette Szabo in *Carve Her Name With Pride*.

Marlborough, John Churchill, 1st Duke of 1650–1722

English general. He helped quell Monmouth's rebellion at Sedgemoor, but deserted to William of Orange in 1688. Under Queen Anne he was appointed supreme commander of British forces in the War of the Spanish Succession, rewarded for his success with a dukedom.

67 I have not time to say any more, but to beg you will give my duty to the Queen, and let her know her army has had a glorious victory. Monsieur Tallard and two other generals are in my coach, and I am following the rest.
1704 Note written on a tavern bill to his wife, Sarah, 13 Aug, after the Battle of Blenheim.

Marley, Bob (Robert Nesta) 1945–81

Jamaican singer, guitarist, and composer of reggae music. His hits include 'No woman, no cry', 'I Shot the Sheriff', and 'Exodus'. Among his albums were *Catch a Fire* (1972), *Rastaman Vibration* (1976) and *Uprising* (1980).

68 Get up, stand up
Stand up for your rights
Get up, stand up
Don't give up the fight.
1973 'Get Up, Stand Up'.

69 Don't just move to the music, listen to what I'm saying.
Quoted in Johnson and Pines *Reggae* (1982).

Marlowe, Christopher 1564–93

English poet and playwright. It is thought that he was a spy for the English in the Netherlands, and that he was killed in a tavern brawl. His many dramatic works include *Doctor Faustus* (1592), and his poems include the unfinished *Hero and Leander* and lyrics such as 'The Passionate Shepherd to his Love'.

70 From jigging veins of rhyming mother-wits,
And such conceits as clownage keeps in pay,
We'll lead you to the stately tents of war.
1587 *Tamburlaine the Great* (published 1590), pt.1, prologue.

71 Come, lady, let not this appall your thoughts.
1587 *Tamburlaine the Great* (published 1590), pt.1, act 1, sc.2.

72 Tamburlaine!—
A Scythian shepherd so embellishèd
With nature's pride and richest furniture!
His looks do menace heaven and dare the gods.
His fiery eyes are fixed upon the earth.
1587 *Tamburlaine the Great* (published 1590), pt.1, act 1, sc.2.

73 Accurst be he that first invented war.
1587 *Tamburlaine the Great* (published 1590), pt.1, act 2, sc.4.

74 A god is not so glorious as a king.
I think the pleasure they enjoy in Heaven,
Cannot compare with kingly joys in earth.
To wear a crown enchased with pearl and gold,
Whose virtues carry with it life and death;
To ask and have, command and be obeyed;
When looks breed love, with looks to gain the prize,
Such power attractive shines in princes' eyes!
1587 *Tamburlaine the Great* (published 1590), pt.1, act 2, sc.5.

75 Nature that framed us of four elements,
Warring within our breasts for regiment,
Doth teach us all to have aspiring minds:
Our souls, whose faculties can comprehend
The wondrous architecture of the world,
And measure every wandering planet's course,
Still climbing after knowledge infinite,
And always moving as the restless spheres,
Wills us to wear ourselves, and never rest,
Until we reach the ripest fruit of all,
That perfect bliss and sole felicity,
The sweet fruition of an earthly crown.
1587 *Tamburlaine the Great* (published 1590), pt.1, act 2, sc.7.

76 Virtue is the fount whence honour springs.
1587 *Tamburlaine the Great* (published 1590), pt.1, act 4, sc.4.

77 What is beauty, saith my sufferings, then?
If all the pens that ever poets held
Had fed the feeling of their masters' thoughts,
And every sweetness that inspired their hearts,
Their minds, and muses on admirèd themes;
If all the heavenly quintessence they still
From their immortal flowers of poesy,
Wherein, as in a mirror, we perceive
The highest reaches of a human wit;
If these had made one poem's period,
And all combined in beauty's worthiness,
Yet should there hover in their restless heads
One thought, one grace, one wonder, at the least,
Which into words no virtue can digest.
1587 *Tamburlaine the Great* (published 1590), pt.1, act 5, sc.1.

78 And every warrior that is rapt with love
Of fame, of valour, and of victory,
Must needs have beauty beat on his conceits:
I thus conceiving and subduing both,
That which hath stopped the tempest of the gods,
Even from the fiery-spangled veil of heaven,
To feel the lovely warmth of shepherds' flames,
And march in cottages of strowèd weeds,
Shall give the world to note, for all my birth,
That virtue solely is the sum of glory,
And fashions men with true nobility.
1587 *Tamburlaine the Great* (published 1590), pt.1, act 5, sc.1.

79 Helen, whose beauty summoned Greece to arms,

And drew a thousand ships to Tenedos.
1587 *Tamburlaine the Great* (published 1590), pt.2, l.3055–6.

80 More childish valorous than manly wise.
1587 *Tamburlaine the Great* (published 1590), pt.2, l.3690.

81 Holla, ye pampered Jades of Asia;
What, can ye draw but twenty miles a day?
1587 *Tamburlaine the Great* (published 1590), pt.2, l.3980–1.

82 I count religion but a childish toy,
And hold there is no sin but ignorance.
c.1589 *The Jew of Malta* (published 1633), 'Prologue to the Stage, At the Cock-pit'.

83 Might first made kings, and laws were then most sure
When…they were writ in blood.
c.1589 *The Jew of Malta* (published 1633), 'Prologue'.

84 Thus methinks should men of judgement frame
Their means of traffic from the vulgar trade,
And as their wealth increaseth, so enclose
Infinite riches in a little room.
c.1589 *The Jew of Malta* (published 1633), act 1, sc.1.

85 The sad presaging raven, that tolls
The sick man's passport in her hollow beak,
And in the shadow of the silent night
Doth shake contagion from her sable wings.
c.1589 *The Jew of Malta* (published 1633), act 2, sc.1.

86 As for myself, I walk abroad o'nights
And kill sick people groaning under walls:
Sometimes I go about and poison wells.
c.1589 *The Jew of Malta* (published 1633), act 2, sc.3.

87 Barnardine: Thou hast committed—
Barabas: Fornication—but that was in another country; and besides, the wench is dead.
c.1589 *The Jew of Malta* (published 1633), act 4, sc.1.

88 'My father is deceased. Come, Gaveston,
And share the kingdom with thy dearest friend.'
Ah, words that make me surfeit with delight!
What greater bliss can hap to Gaveston
Than live and be the favourite of a king?
Sweet prince, I come; these, these thy amorous lines
Might have enforced me to have swum from France,
And, like Leander, gasped upon the sand,
So thou would'st smile, and take me in thy arms.
c.1591 Gaveston is reading a letter from King Edward. *Edward II* (published 1594), act 1, sc.1.

89 My men, like satyrs grazing on the lawns,
Shall with their goat feet dance an antic hay.
c.1591 *Edward II* (published 1594), act 1, sc.1.

90 The griefs of private men are soon allayed,
But not of kings.
c.1591 *Edward II* (published 1594), act 5, sc.1.

91 But what are kings, when regiment is gone,
But perfect shadows in a sunshine day?
c.1591 *Edward II* (published 1594), act 5, sc.1.

92 He hath a body able to endure
More than we can inflict: and therefore now
Let us assail his mind another while.
c.1591 *Edward II* (published 1594), act 5, sc.4.

93 Sweet Analytics, 'tis thou has ravished me!
c.1592 *Doctor Faustus* (published 1604), act 1, sc.1.

94 I'll have them fly to India for gold,
Ransack the ocean for orient pearl.
c.1592 *Doctor Faustus* (published 1604), act 1, sc.1.

95 Is, to dispute well, logic's chiefest end?
Affords this art no greater miracle?
c.1592 *Doctor Faustus* (published 1604), act 1, sc.1.

96 Oh, what a world of profit and delight,
Of power, of honour, and omnipotence,
Is promised to the studious artisan!
c.1592 *Doctor Faustus* (published 1604), act 1, sc.1.

97 All things that move between the quiet poles
Shall be at my command: emperors and kings
Are but obeyed in their several provinces,
Nor can they raise the wind, or rend the clouds;
But his dominion that exceeds in this
Stretcheth as far as doth the mind of man;
A sound magician is a demi-god.
c.1592 *Doctor Faustus* (published 1604), act 1, sc.1.

98 How am I glutted with conceit of this!
Shall I make spirits fetch me what I please,
Resolve me of all ambiguities,
Perform what desperate enterprise I will?
I'll have them fly to India for gold,
Ransack the ocean for orient pearl,
And search all corners of the new found world
For pleasant fruits and princely delicates.
c.1592 *Doctor Faustus* (published 1604), act 1, sc.1.

99 Why, this is hell, nor am I out of it:
Thinkst thou that I who saw the face of God,
And tasted the eternal joys of heaven,
Am not tormented with ten thousand hells
In being deprived of everlasting bliss!
c.1592 *Doctor Faustus* (published 1604), act 1, sc.3.

1 Hell hath no limits, nor is circumscribed
In one self place; but where we are is hell,
And where hell is, there must we ever be:
And, to be short, when all the world dissolves,
And every creature shall be purified,
All places shall be hell that is not heaven.
c.1592 *Doctor Faustus* (published 1604), act 2, sc.1.

2 But think'st thou heaven is such a glorious thing?
I tell thee, Faustus, it is not half so fair
As thou, or any man that breathes on earth.
c.1592 *Doctor Faustus* (published 1604), act 2, sc.2.

3 Have I not made blind Homer sing to me?
c.1592 *Doctor Faustus* (published 1604), act 2, sc.2.

4 O gentle Faustus, leave this damnèd art,
This magic, that will charm thy soul to hell.
c.1592 *Doctor Faustus* (published 1604), act 5, sc.1.

5 Was this the face that launched a thousand ships,
And burnt the topless towers of Ilium?
Sweet Helen, make me immortal with a kiss!
Her lips suck forth my soul: see, where it flies!
Come Helen, come give me my soul again.
Here will I dwell, for heaven be in these lips,
And all is dross that is not Helena.
c.1592 *Doctor Faustus* (published 1604), act 5, sc.1.

6 Now hast thou but one bare hour to live,
And then thou must be damned perpetually!
Stand still, you ever-moving spheres of heaven,
That time may cease, and midnight never come.
Fair nature's eye, rise, rise, again, and make
Perpetual day; or let this hour be but

A year, a month, a week, a natural day,
That Faustus may repent and save his soul!
O lente, lente currite, noctis equi:
The stars move still, time runs, the clock will strike,
The devil will come, and Faustus must be damned.
Oh, I'll leap up to my God!—Who pulls me down?—
See, see, where Christ's blood streams in the firmament!
One drop would save my soul, half a drop, ah, my Christ.
c.1592 *Doctor Faustus* (published 1604), act 5, sc.2.

7 You stars that reigned at my nativity,
Whose influence hath allotted death and hell,
Now draw up Faustus like a foggy mist,
Into the entrails of yon labouring cloud,
That when you vomit forth into the air,
My limbs may issue from your smoky mouths,
So that my soul may but ascend to heaven.
c.1592 *Doctor Faustus* (published 1604), act 5, sc.2.

8 Ah, Pythagoras' metempsychosis, were that time,
This soul should fly from me, and I be changed
Unto some brutish beast.
c.1592 *Doctor Faustus* (published 1604), act 5, sc.2.

9 Cut is the branch that might have grown full straight,
And burnèd is Apollo's laurel bough,
That sometime grew within this learned man.
c.1592 *Doctor Faustus* (published 1604), epilogue.

10 Where Venus in her naked glory strove
To please the careless and disdainful eyes
Of proud Adonis.
1593 *Hero and Leander* (published 1598), pt.1, l.12–14.

11 So lovely fair was Hero, Venus' nun,
As Nature wept, thinking she was undone.
1593 *Hero and Leander* (published 1598), pt.1, l.45–6.

12 His body was as straight as Circe's wand;
Jove might have sipped out nectar from his hand.
1593 *Hero and Leander* (published 1598), pt.1, l.61–2.

13 It lies not in our power to love, or hate,
For will in us is overruled by fate.
When two are stripped, lo ere the course begin
We wish that one should lose, the other win;
And one especially do we affect
Of two gold ingots, like in each respect.
The reason no man knows, let it suffice,
What we behold is censured by our eyes.
Where both deliberate, the love is slight;
Who ever loved, that loved not at first sight?
1593 *Hero and Leander* (published 1598), pt.1, l.167–76.

14 Virginity, albeit some highly prize it,
Compared with marriage, had you tried them both,
Differs as much as wine and water doth.
1593 *Hero and Leander* (published 1598), pt.1, l.268–9.

15 And as she wept, her tears to pearl he turned,
And wound them on his arm, and for her mourned.
1593 The mourner is Cupid. *Hero and Leander* (published 1598), pt.1, l.375–6.

16 And to this day is every scholar poor;
Gross gold from them runs headlong to the boor.
1593 *Hero and Leander* (published 1598), pt.1, l.477–8.

17 Come live with me and be my love,
And we will all the pleasures prove
That valleys, groves, hills, and fields,
Woods, or steepy mountain yields.

And we will sit upon the rocks,
Seeing shepherds feed their flocks,
By shallow rivers to whose falls
Melodious birds sing madrigals.

And I will make thee beds of roses
And a thousand fragrant posies,
A cap of flowers, and a kirtle
Embroidered all with leaves of myrtle.
'The Passionate Shepherd to His Love' (published 1599).
► *See Raleigh 677:98.*

Marples, Morris

English writer and traveller.

18 The soul of a journey is liberty, perfect liberty to think, feel, do just as one pleases. We go on a journey chiefly to be free of all impediments and of all inconveniences; to leave ourselves behind, much more to get rid of others. It is because I want a little breathing space to muse on different matters…that I absent myself from the town for a while.
Quoted in John Hillaby *Journey through Britain* (1968).

Marquand, John P(hillips) 1893–1960

US novelist. He began as a writer of popular stories for magazines, and later turned to realist novels in the manner of Sinclair Lewis.

19 His father watched him across the gulf of years and pathos which always must divide a father from his son.
1937 *The Late George Apley*, ch.10.

Marqués, René 1919–79

Puerto Rican playwright, short story writer and nationalist. Most of his plays and essays are concerned with the problem of national identity in relation to language, literature and the prevailing social conditions of Puerto Rico.

20 *Hombre, tienes un hijo, un hijo que te hicieron creer podría inmortalizarte llevando el germen de ti mismo por siglos de generaciones… Tu carne, Hombre, carne deleznable, carne podrida que no puede soportar el peso de tu inmortalidad. No, no hay nada de ti mismo en esa carne. ¡Tu hijo no te hará inmortal!'*
Man, you have a son, a son who they made you believe would make you immortal by carrying your seed through centuries of generations… Your flesh, O man, your despicable and rotten flesh that cannot bear the sight of your immortality. No: there's nothing of yourself in that flesh. Your son won't make you immortal!'
1948 *El hombre y sus sueños* ('Man and His Dreams'), act 2.

Marquis, Don(ald Robert Perry) 1878–1937

US novelist, playwright and poet. He worked as a journalist and wrote serious work, but is remembered for his comic poems, notably in the *archy and mehitabel* series, the tales of a cockroach who can't reach the upper-case keys of the typewriter, and an alley cat.

21 but wotthehell wotthehell
oh i should worry and fret
death and I will coquette

there s a dance in the old dame yet
toujours gai toujours gai.
1927 *archy and mehitabel*, 'the song of mehitabel'.

22 live so that you
can stick out your tongue
at the insurance.
1927 *archy and mehitabel*, 'certain maxims of archy'.

23 procrastination is the
art of keeping
up with yesterday.
1927 *archy and mehitabel*, 'certain maxims of archy'.

24 millionaires and
bums taste
about alike to me.
1927 *archy and mehitabel*, 'certain maxims of archy'.

25 an optimist is a guy
that has never had
much experience.
1927 *archy and mehitabel*, 'certain maxims of archy'.

26 coarse
jocosity
catches the crowd
shakespeare
and i
are often
low browed
1927 *archy and mehitabel*, 'archy confesses'.

27 persian pussy from over the sea
demure and lazy and smug and fat
none of your ribbons and bells for me
ours is the zest of the alley cat
1927 *archy and mehitabel*, 'mehitabels extensive past'.

28 but wotthehell archy wotthehell
jamais triste archy jamais triste
that is my motto.
1927 *archy and mehitabel*, 'mehitabel sees paris'.

29 honesty is a good
thing but
it is not profitable to
its possessor
unless it is
kept under control.
1933 *archys life of mehitabel*, 'archygrams'.

30 did you ever
notice that when
a politician
does get an idea
he usually
gets it all wrong.
1933 *archys life of mehitabel*, 'archygrams'.

31 now and then
there is a person born
who is so unlucky
that he runs into accidents
which started to happen
to somebody else.
1933 *archys life of mehitabel*, 'archy says'.

32 boss there is always
a comforting thought
in time of trouble when
it is not our trouble
1935 *archy does his part*, 'comforting thoughts'.

33 Writing a book of poetry is like dropping a rose petal down the Grand Canyon and waiting for the echo.
Quoted in E Anthony *O Rare Don Marquis* (1962), ch.6.

34 The art of newspaper paragraphing is to stroke a platitude until it purrs like an epigram.
Quoted in E Anthony *O Rare Don Marquis* (1962), ch.11.

35 By the time a bartender knows what drink a man will have before he orders, there is little else about him worth knowing.
Quoted in E Anthony *O Rare Don Marquis* (1962), ch.11.

36 Bores bore each other, too; but it never seems to teach them anything.
Quoted in E Anthony *O Rare Don Marquis* (1962), ch.11.

37 A demagogue is a person with whom we disagree as to which gang should mismanage the country.
Quoted in E Anthony *O Rare Don Marquis* (1962), ch.11.

38 Fishing is a delusion entirely surrounded by liars in old clothes.
Attributed.

Marshall, George C(atlett) 1880–1959

US soldier and statesman. He directed the US army throughout the war as chief of staff (1939–45), and as Secretary of State (1947–9) he originated the Marshall Aid plan for the post-war reconstruction of Europe. He was awarded the Nobel peace prize in 1953.

39 Our policy is directed not against any country or doctrine, but against hunger, poverty, desperation and chaos. The purpose shall be the revival of a working economy in the world so as to permit the emergence of political and social conditions in which free institutions can exist.
1947 Speech at Harvard, 5 Jun, announcing the European Recovery Plan (ERA) that became known as the Marshall Plan.

40 We want you to feel unhampered tactically and strategically to proceed north of the 38th parallel.
1950 Telegram to General Douglas Mac Arthur during the Korean War, Sep, later used by Mac Arthur as justification for continuing operations after the Chinese had made their presence known. Quoted in David S McLellan *Dean Acheson: The State Department Years* (1976).

Marshall, Thurgood 1908–93

US jurist and civil rights advocate. He worked with the National Association for the Advancement of Colored People and the Court of Appeals (1961–5). Solicitor General (1965–7), he became the first black Justice of the US Supreme Court (1967–91).

41 If the United States is indeed the great melting pot, the negro either didn't get in the pot or he didn't get melted down.
1987 In the *New York Times*, 9 Sep.

Martel, Yann 1963–

Canadian author. His novel *Life of Pi* (2002) was awarded the Booker Prize.

42 If we, citizens, do not support our artists, then we sacrifice our imagination on the altar of crude reality and we end up believing in nothing and having worthless dreams.
2002 *Life of Pi*.

43 In the literature can be found legions of examples of animals that could escape but did not, or did and returned.
2002 *Life of Pi.*

Martí, José 1853–95

Cuban national hero. A journalist, editor and poet, he was a key figure in Cuba's struggle for independence. Exiled for his revolutionary activities, he travelled in Europe and the Americas. He died fighting at Boca de Dos Ríos.

44 *¡Robaron los conquistadores una página al Universo! Aquellos eran los pueblos que llamaban a la Vía Láctea 'el camino de las almas'; para quienes el Universo estaba lleno del Grande Espíritu, en cuyo seno se encerraba toda luz.*
The conquistadores stole a page from the Universe! Those were the good people who called the Milky Way 'the souls' path'; for them the Universe was full of the Great Spirit, within which all light was contained.
1884 *Obra literaria*, 'El hombre antiguo de América y sus artes primitivas' ('Ancient Man in America and his Primitive Arts')

45 *Yo soy un hombre sincero*
De donde crece la palma,
Y antes de morirme quiero
Echar mis versos del alma.
I am a sincere man
from where the palm tree grows;
and before I die I want
to loose my verses from my heart.
1891 *Versos sencillos* ('Simple Verses'), no.1.

Martial *full name* ***Marcus Valerius Martialis*** c. 40–104 AD

Latin poet, born in Spain. He went to Rome and became an associate of Lucan and the younger Seneca, who were also Spanish. Martial's most important work is the twelve books of *Epigrams*, each a concise expression of one idea or theme.

46 *Non est, crede mihi, sapientis dicere 'Vivam':*
Sera nimis vita est crastina: vive hodie.
Believe me, wise men do not say 'I shall live on.'
Tomorrow's life's too late; live today.
Epigrams, bk.1, no.15.

47 *Non amo te, Sabidi, nec possum dicere quare:*
Hoc tantum possum dicere, non amo te.
I do not love you, Sabidius, and I can't tell you why; all I can say is this, I don't love you.
Epigrams, bk.1, no.32.

48 *Laudant illa sed ista legunt.*
They praise those works, but read these.
Epigrams, bk.4, no.49, l.9–10.

49 *Bonosque*
Soles effugere atque abire sentit,
Qui nobis pereunt et imputantur.
Each of us feels the good days speed and depart, and they're lost to us and counted against us.
Epigrams, bk.5, no.20, l.11–13.

50 *Non est vivere, sed valere vita est.*
Life is not just to be alive, but to be well.
Epigrams, bk.6, no.70.

51 *Difficilis facilis, iucundus acerbus es idem:*
Nec tecum possum vivere nec sine te.
Difficult or easy, pleasant or bitter, you are the same:
I cannot live with you—or without you.
Epigrams, bk.12, no.46.

52 *Rus in urbe.*
Country in the town.
Epigrams, bk.12, no.57, l.21.

Martin, Sir George 1926–

English record producer, particularly known for his association with The Beatles.

53 If you were poor fifty years ago, it meant you didn't have enough to eat. If you're poor now, it means you only have one car.
2003 In *Esquire*, Jan.

Marvell, Andrew 1621–78

English poet. Educated at Cambridge, he held various government posts. His poems cover a variety of genres and classical forms, but he also published anonymously political and satirical prose works.

54 The inglorious arts of peace.
1650 'An Horatian Ode upon Cromwell's Return from Ireland'

55 He nothing common did or mean
Upon that memorable scene:
But with his keener eye
The axe's edge did try.
1650 Of Charles I. 'An Horatian Ode upon Cromwell's Return from Ireland'.

56 How fit he is to sway
That can so well obey.
1650 'An Horatian Ode upon Cromwell's Return from Ireland'.

57 See how the Orient dew,
Shed from the bosom of the morn
Into the blowing roses,
Yet careless of its mansion new;
For the clear region where 'twas born
Round in its self encloses:
And in its little globes extent,
Frames as it can its native element.
c.1650–1652 'On a Drop of Dew' (published 1681).

58 There is not such another in
The world, to offer for their sin.
c.1650–1652 'The Nymph Complaining for the Death of her Fawn' (published 1681).

59 Had it lived long, it would have been
Lilies without, roses within.
c.1650–1652 'The Nymph Complaining for the Death of her Fawn' (published 1681)

60 I have a garden of my own,
But so with roses overgrown,
And lilies, that you would it guess
To be a little wilderness.
c.1650–1652 'The Nymph Complaining for the Death of her Fawn' (published 1681).

61 Had we but world enough, and time,
This coyness Lady were no crime.
We would sit down, and think which way
To walk, and pass our long love's day.
Thou by the Indian Ganges' side
Shouldst rubies find: I by the tide
Of Humber would complain. I would
Love you ten years before the flood.

c.1650–1652 'To His Coy Mistress' (published 1681).

62 My vegetable love should grow
Vaster than empires, and more slow,
An hundred years should go to praise
Thine eyes, and on thy forehead gaze.
Two hundred to adore each breast:
But thirty thousand to the rest.
An age at least to every part,
And the last age should show your heart.
For Lady you deserve this state;
Nor would I love at lower rate.
But at my back I always hear
Time's winged chariot hurrying near:
And yonder all before us lie
Deserts of vast eternity.
c.1650–1652 'To His Coy Mistress' (published 1681).

63 Then worms shall try
That long preserved virginity:
And your quaint honour turn to dust;
And into ashes all my lust.
The grave's a fine and private place,
But none I think do there embrace.
c.1650–1652 'To His Coy Mistress' (published 1681).

64 Now let us sport us while we may;
And now, like amorous birds of prey,
Rather at once our time devour,
Than languish in his slow-chapped power.
c.1650–1652 'To His Coy Mistress' (published 1681).

65 Let us roll all our strength, and all
Our sweetness, up into one ball:
And tear our pleasures with rough strife,
Through the iron gates of life.
Thus, though we cannot make our sun
Stand still, yet we will make him run.
c.1650–1652 'To His Coy Mistress' (published 1681), closing lines.

66 My love is of a birth as rare
As 'tis for object strange and high:
It was begotten by Despair
Upon Impossibility.

Magnanimous Despair alone
Could show me so divine a thing,
Where feeble Hope could ne'er have flown
But vainly flapped its tinsel wing.
c.1650–1652 'The Definition of Love' (published 1681).

67 As lines so loves oblique may well
Themselves in every angle greet
But ours so truly parallel,
Though infinite can never meet.

Therefore the love which doth us bind,
But fate so enviously debars,
Is the conjunction of the mind,
And opposition of the stars.
c.1650–1652 'The Definition of Love' (published 1681).

68 Ye living lamps, by whose dear light
The nightingale does sit so late,
And studying all the summer night,
Her matchless songs does meditate.
c.1650–1652 'The Mower to the Glo-Worms' (published 1681).

69 And now, when I have summed up all my store,
Thinking (so I myself deceive)
So rich a chaplet thence to weave
As never yet the King of Glory wore,
Alas! I find the serpent old,
That, twining in his speckled breast,
About the flowers disguised does fold
With wreaths of fame and interest.
c.1650–1652 'The Coronet' (published 1681).

70 My mind was once the true survey
Of all these meadows fresh and gay;
And in the greenness of the grass
Did see its hopes as in a glass.
c.1650–1652 'The Mower's Song' (published 1681).

71 How vainly men themselves amaze
To win the palm, the oak, or bays;
And their uncessant labours see
Crown'd from some single herb or tree.
Whose short and narrow verged shade
Does prudently their toils upbraid;
While all flow'rs and all trees do close
To weave the garlands of repose.
c.1650–1652 'The Garden' (published 1681).

72 Fair quiet, have I found thee here,
And Innocence thy Sister dear!
Mistaken long, I sought you then
In busy companies of men.
c.1650–1652 'The Garden' (published 1681).

73 Society is all but rude,
To this delicious solitude.
c.1650–1652 'The Garden' (published 1681).

74 What wondrous life is this I lead!
Ripe apples drop about my head;
The luscious clusters of the vine
Upon my mouth do crush their wine;
The nectarine, and curious peach,
Into my hands themselves do reach;
Stumbling on melons, as I pass,
Ensnared with flowers, I fall on grass.
c.1650–1652 'The Garden' (published 1681), stanza 5.

75 Annihilating all that's made
To a green thought in a green shade.
c.1650–1652 'The Garden' (published 1681), stanza 6.

76 Such was that happy garden-state,
While man there walked without a mate.
c.1650–1652 'The Garden' (published 1681), stanza 8.

77 'Twas beyond a mortal's share
To wander solitary there:
Two paradises 'twere in one
To live in paradise alone.
c.1650–1652 'The Garden' (published 1681), stanza 8.

78 No creature loves an empty space;
Their bodies measure out their place.
c.1650–1652 'Upon Appleton House, to My Lord Fairfax' (published 1681), stanza 2.

79 'Tis not, what once it was, the world;
But a rude heap together hurl'd.
c.1650–1652 'Upon Appleton House, to My Lord Fairfax' (published 1681), stanza 96.

80 Oh thou, that dear and happy isle
The garden of the world ere while,

Thou paradise of four seas,
Which heaven planted us to please,
But, to exclude the world, did guard
With watery if not flaming sword;
What luckless apple did we taste,
To make us mortal, and thee waste?
c.1650–1652 'Upon Appleton House, to My Lord Fairfax' (published 1681), stanza 41.

81 What should we do but sing the praise
That led us through the watery maze,
Unto an isle so long unknown,
And yet far kinder than our own?
c.1653 'Bermudas' (published 1681).

Marvell, Holt *originally* ***Eric Maschwitz*** 1901–69

English songwriter.

82 These Foolish Things Remind Me of You.
1935 Title of song.

Marx, Chico *originally* ***Leonard Marx*** 1891–1961

US film comedian, one of the Marx Brothers, best known as the piano player.

83 I wasn't kissing her, I was just whispering in her mouth.
Explanation to his wife, on being discovered in a compromising position with a chorus girl. Quoted in Groucho Marx and Richard J Anobile *Marx Brothers Scrapbook* (1973), ch.24.

Marx, Groucho *originally* ***Julius Henry Marx*** 1895–1977

US film comedian, one of the Marx Brothers. He appeared in many films including *Animal Crackers* (1930), *Monkey Business* (1931), *Horse Feathers* (1932) and *Duck Soup* (1933).

84 What's a thousand dollars? Mere chicken feed. A poultry matter.
1929 Line delivered in *The Cocoanuts* (screenplay by George Kaufman and Morrie Ryskind).

85 One morning I shot an elephant in my pyjamas. How he got into my pyjamas I don't know.
1930 Line delivered in *Animal Crackers* (screenplay by George Kaufman and Morrie Ryskind).

86 You go Uruguay and I'll go mine.
1930 Line delivered in *Animal Crackers* (screenplay by George Kaufman and Morrie Ryskind).

87 I could dance with you till the cows come home. On second thoughts I'll dance with the cows and you come home.
1933 Line delivered in *Duck Soup* (screenplay by Bert Kalmar, Harry Ruby and Arthur Sheekman).

88 There ain't no Sanity Claus.
1935 Line delivered in *A Night at the Opera* (screenplay by George Kaufman and Morrie Ryskind).

89 Either he's dead or my watch has stopped.
1937 Line delivered in *A Day at the Races* (screenplay by George Seaton, Robert Pirosh and George Oppenheimer).

90 Marry me and I'll never look at another horse.
1937 Line delivered in *A Day at the Races* (screenplay by George Seaton, Robert Pirosh and George Oppenheimer).

91 Please accept my resignation. I don't want to belong to any club that will accept me as a member.
1959 Recalled in his autobiography, *Groucho and Me* (1959), ch.26.

92 When's the game itself going to begin?
While watching a game of cricket at Lord's. Quoted in Colin Jarman *The Guinness Dictionary of Sports Quotations* (1990).

Marx, Harpo *originally* ***Adolf Marx*** 1893–1961

US film comedian, one of the Marx Brothers. His role within the team was that of dumb clown and harp maestro. He published an autobiography in 1961.

93 No worse than a bad cold.
His winning suggestion when a critic set up a competition for readers' reviews of the long-running play *Abie's Irish Rose* by Anne Nichols. Attributed.

Marx, Karl Heinrich 1818–83

German-born political and economic theorist who began his career as a journalist in 1843. With his lifelong literary collaborator Friedrich Engels he wrote *The Communist Manifesto* (1848), and settled in London the next year, where he began his unfinished *Das Kapital* (vol.1, 1867, the rest posthumously).

94 Religion is the sigh of the oppressed creature, the feelings of a heartless world, and the spirit of conditions that are unspiritual. It is the opium of the people.
1843–4 *A Contribution to the Critique of Hegel's Philosophy of Right.*

95 The worker becomes poorer the more wealth he produces and the more his production increases in power and extent. The worker becomes an ever cheaper commodity the more good he creates. The *devaluation* of the human world increases in direct relation with the *increase in value* of the world of things. Labour does not only create goods; it also produces itself and the worker *as a commodity*, and indeed in the same proportion as it produces goods.
1844 Collected in T B Bottomore (trans and ed) *Early Writings* (1964), p.121.

96 Political economy thus does not recognize the unoccupied worker, the working man so far as he is outside this work relationship. Swindlers, thieves, beggars, the unemployed, the starving, poverty-stricken and criminal working man, are figures which do not exist for political economy, but only for other eyes; for doctors, judges, grave-diggers, beadles, etc. They are ghostly figures outside the domain of political economy.
1844 Collected in T B Bottomore (trans and ed) *Early Writings* (1964), p.137–9.

97 The *division of labour* is nothing but the *alienated* establishment of human activity.
1844 Collected in T B Bottomore (trans and ed) *Early Writings* (1964), p.181.

98 The philosophers have only interpreted the world in various ways; the point is to change it.
1845 *Theses on Feuerbach*, no.11.

99 In communist society, where nobody has one exclusive sphere of activity but each can become accomplished in any branch he wishes, society regulates the general production and thus makes it possible for me to do one thing today and another tomorrow, to hunt in the morning, fish in the afternoon, rear cattle in the evening or criticize after dinner, just as I desire, without ever becoming hunter, fisherman, shepherd or critic.
1845 *The German Ideology* (with Friedrich Engels).

1 Assume a particular state of development in the

productive facilities of man and you will get a particular form of commerce and consumption. Assume particular stages of development in production, commerce and consumption and you will have a corresponding social constitution, a corresponding organisation of the family, of orders or of classes, in a word, a corresponding civil society. Assume a particular civil society and you will get particular political conditions which are only the official expression of civil society.
1846 Letter to P V Annenkov, 26 Dec.

2 The history of all hitherto existing society is the history of class struggles.
1848 *The Communist Manifesto* (with Friedrich Engels, translated by Samuel Moore, 1888), opening sentence.

3 The theory of the Communists may be summed up in the single sentence: Abolition of private property.
1848 *The Communist Manifesto* (with Friedrich Engels, translated by Samuel Moore, 1888).

4 A spectre is haunting Europe—the spectre of communism. All the powers of old Europe have entered into a holy alliance to exorcise this spectre; Pope and Tsar, Metternich and Guizot, French Radicals and German police spies.
1848 *The Communist Manifesto* (with Friedrich Engels, translated by Samuel Moore, 1888).

5 Let the ruling classes tremble at a communist revolution. The proletarians have nothing to lose but their chains. they have a world to win. Working men of all countries, unite!
1848 *The Communist Manifesto* (with Friedrich Engels, translated by Samuel Moore, 1888), closing words. This translation was approved by Engels, but the phrase is also known as 'Workers of the world, unite'. The literal translation of the German is 'Proletarians of all lands, unite.'

6 If capital is growing rapidly, wages may rise; the profit of capital rises incomparably more rapidly. The material position of the worker has improved, but at the cost of his social position. The social gulf that divides him from the capitalist has widened.
1849 'Wage Labour and Capital', collected in Robert C Tucker (ed) *The Marx–Engels Reader* (2nd edn, 1972), p.211.

7 Hegel says somewhere that all great events and personalities in the world reappear in one fashion or another. He forgot to add: the first time as tragedy, the second as farce.
1852 *The Eighteenth Brumaire of Louis Bonaparte*, section 1.

8 All our inventions have endowed material forces with intellectual life and degraded human life into material force.
1856 Speech, 14 Apr.

9 Society does not consist of individuals; it expresses the sum of connections and relationships in which individuals find themselves.
1857–8 *The Grundrisse* (translated by David McLellan, 1971), p.77.

10 The product of mental labour—science—always stands far below its value, because the labour-time necessary to reproduce it has no relation at all to the labour-time required for its original production.
1862 *Theory of Surplus Value.*

11 The production of surplus-value, or the extraction of surplus labour, is the specific end and aim, the sum and substance, of capitalist production.
1867 *Das Kapital.*

12 The instruments of labour, when they assume the form of machinery, acquire a kind of material existence which involves the replacement of human forces by the forces of Nature, and of rule-of-thumb methods by the purposeful application of natural science.
1867 *Das Kapital.*

13 In manufacture and in handicrafts, the worker uses a tool; in the factory, he serves a machine.
1867 *Das Kapital.*

14 Only in a higher phase of communist society...can the narrow horizon of bourgeois right be crossed in its entirety, and society inscribe on its banners, 'From each according to his ability, to each according to his needs!'
1875 Critique of the Gotha Programme, May.
► *See Bakunin 53:25.*

15 All I know is that I am not a Marxist.
Recalled by Friedrich Engels in letter to Conrad Schmidt, 3 Aug 1890.

16 What I did that was new was to prove that the existence of classes is only bound up with particular, historical phases in the development of production; that the class struggle necessarily leads to the dictatorship of the proletariat; and that dictatorship itself only constitutes the transition to the abolition of all classes and to a classless society.
In Karl Marx and Friedrich Engels *Correspondence* (1934).

Mary of Teck *formerly* ***Princess Victoria Mary Augusta Louise Olga Pauline Claudine Agnes*** *known as* ***Princess May*** 1867–1953

Queen-Consort of George V of Britain (married 1893). She helped mould her husband into a 'people's king' and throughout her son's reign was involved in women's war work and philanthropy.

17 God grant that we may not have a European war thrust upon us, and for such a stupid reason too, no I don't mean stupid, but to have to go to war on account of tiresome Serbia beggars belief.
1914 Letter to her aunt Princess Augusta, Grand-Duchess of Mecklenburg-Strelitz, 28 Jul.

Mary, Queen of Scots 1542–87

Queen of Scotland, the daughter of James V. A Catholic, she succeeded to the throne at the age of one week but was forced to sign an act of abdication in favour of her son James VI in 1567. She fled to England and was imprisoned by Elizabeth I for 20 years before being executed.

18 *En ma fin git mon commencement.*
In my end is my beginning.
Embroidered motto, quoted in Antonia Fraser *Mary Queen of Scots* (1969), ch.21, 'My Norfolk'.

Mary Tudor *also known as* ***Mary I*** 1516–58

Queen of England and Ireland (from 1553). On Edward VI's death she ousted Lady Jane Grey with popular support and repealed anti-Catholic legislation. Public anger at her persecutions of Protestants and her unpopular marriage, and the loss of Calais to the French, broke her down.

19 When I am dead and opened, you shall find 'Calais' lying in my heart.
Quoted in Holinshed *Chronicles* (1808), vol.4.

Masaryk, Tomás Garrigue 1850–1937

Czechoslovak statesman. An ardent Slovak, while in exile during World War I he organized the Czech independence movement. As the first President of Czechoslovakia (1918–35), he was re-elected on three occasions.

20 Our whole history inclines us towards the democratic powers. Our renaissance is a logical link between us and the democracies of the west.
1918 Inaugural address, 23 Dec.

Masefield, John Edward 1878–1967

English poet and novelist. He served his apprenticeship in the merchant navy, before ill-health forced him to concentrate on writing about the sea rather than sailing it. He became Poet Laureate in 1930.

21 I must down to the seas again, to the lonely sea and the sky,
And all I ask is a tall ship and a star to steer her by,
And the wheel's kick and the wind's song and the white sail's shaking,
And a grey mist on the sea's face and a grey dawn breaking.
1902 'Sea Fever'.

22 I must down to the seas again, for the call of the running tide
Is a wild call and a clear call that may not be denied.
1902 'Sea Fever'.

23 I must down to the seas again, to the vagrant gypsy life,
To the gull's way and the whale's way where the wind's like a whetted knife;
And all I ask is a merry yarn from a laughing fellow-rover,
And quiet sleep and a sweet dream when the long trick's over.
1902 'Sea Fever'.

24 It's a warm wind, the west wind, full of bird's cries;
I never hear the west wind but tears are in my eyes.
1902 'West Wind'.

25 It is good to be out on the road, and going one knows not where.
1902 'Tewkesbury Road'.

26 Quinquireme of Nineveh from distant Ophir
Rowing home to haven in sunny Palestine,
With a cargo of ivory,
And apes and peacocks,
Sandalwood, cedarwood, and sweet white wine.
1903 'Cargoes'.

27 Dirty British coaster with a salt-caked smoke-stack,
Butting through the Channel in the mad March days.
1903 'Cargoes'.

28 I have seen dawn and sunset on moors and windy hills
Coming in solemn beauty like slow old tunes of Spain.
1903 'Beauty'.

29 Oh some are fond of Spanish wine, and some are fond of French,
And some'll swallow tay and stuff fit only for a wench.
1903 'Captain Stratton's Fancy'.

30 Most roads lead men homewards,
My road leads me forth.
1903 'Roadways'.

31 My road leads me seawards
To the white dipping sails.
1903 'Roadways'.

32 Death opens unknown doors. It is most grand to die.
1910 *Pompey the Great*, act 2.

33 In the dark room where I began
My mother's life made me a man.
Through all the months of human birth
Her beauty fed my common earth.
I cannot see, nor breathe, nor stir,
But through the death of some of her.
1910 'C.L.M.'.

34 Out into the street I ran uproarious
The devil dancing in me glorious.
1911 'The Everlasting Mercy'.

35 And he who gives a child a treat
Makes joy-bells ring in Heaven's street,
And he who gives a child a home
Builds palaces in Kingdom come,
And she who gives a baby birth
Brings Saviour Christ again to Earth.
1911 'The Everlasting Mercy'.

36 In this life he laughs longest who laughs last.
1912 *The Widow in Bye Street*, ch.4.

37 The days that make us happy make us wise.
1914 'Biography'.

38 Life's battle is a conquest for the strong;
The meaning shows in the defeated thing.
1914 'The Wanderer'.

39 I have seen flowers come in stony places
And kind things done by men with ugly faces,
And the gold cup won by the worst horse at the races,
So I trust, too.
1914 'An Epilogue'.

40 And all the way that wild high crying,
To cold his blood with the thought of dying.
1919 *Reynard the Fox*, pt.2, stanza 49.

41 People who leave their own time out of their work cannot be surprised if their time fails to find them interesting.
1925 'With the Living Voice'.

Massinger, Philip 1583–1640

English dramatist. He attended Oxford, but left to join Henslowe's company. He collaborated with Thomas Dekker, Ben Jonson and George Chapman, and particularly John Fletcher, with whom he is buried. His works include *A New Way to Pay Old Debts* (1633).

42 He that would govern others, first should be
The master of himself.
1623 *The Bondman*, act 1, sc.3.

43 Soar not too high to fall; but stoop to rise.
1623 *The Duke of Milan*, act 1, sc.2.

44 Oh that thou hadst like others been all words,
And no performance.
1624 *The Parliament of Love*, act 4, sc.2.

45 Pleasures of worse natures

Are gladly entertained, and they that shun us
Practice in private sports the stews would blush at.
1626 Of the theatre. *The Roman Actor*, act 1, sc.1.

46 Nay, droop not, fellows; innocence should be bold.
1626 *The Roman Actor*, act 1, sc.1.

47 They are only safe
That know to soothe the prince's appetite
And serve his lusts.
1626 *The Roman Actor*, act 1, sc.1.

48 O master doctor, he is past recovery;
A lethargy hath seized him.
1626 *The Roman Actor*, act 2, sc.1.

49 How strangely hopes delude men.
1626 *The Roman Actor*, act 5, sc.2.

50 Greatness, with private men
Esteem'd a blessing, is to me a curse;
And we, whom, for our high births, they conclude
The happy freemen, are the only slaves.
Happy the golden mean!
1627 *The Great Duke of Florence*, act 1, sc.1.

51 Virgin me no virgins!
I must have you lose that name, or you lose me.
1633 *A New Way to Pay Old Debts*, act 3, sc.2.

Masters, Edgar Lee 1869–1950

US poet. Although he wrote a number of books of both poetry and prose, he is chiefly remembered for the satirical free verse epitaphs on real and imaginary occupants of a midwestern cemetery in *Spoon River Anthology* (1915).

52 Where are Elmer, Herman, Bert, Tom and Charley,
The weak of will, the strong of arm, the clown, the boozer, the fighter?
All, all, are sleeping on the hill.
1915 *Spoon River Anthology*, 'The Hill'.

53 Why, a moral truth is a hollow tooth
Which must be propped with gold.
1915 *Spoon River Anthology*, 'Sersmith the Dentist'.

54 Your eight-page paper—behind which you huddle,
Bawling through the megaphone of big type:
'This is I, the giant.'
1915 *Spoon River Anthology*, 'Editor Whedon'.

Matak, Sirik c.1930–1975

Cambodian politician and business leader who joined with Lol Nol to overthrow Sihanouk in 1970. Prime Minister of the US-backed Khmer Republic (1970–5), he was executed by the Khmer Rouge after refusing to leave with the US Ambassador.

55 But mark it well, if I shall die here on the spot and in my country that I love, it is too bad because we are all born and must die one day. I have only committed this mistake of believing in you, the Americans.
1975 Letter to John Dean, US Ambassador to Cambodia (1974–5), Apr.

Mathew, Sir James Charles 1830–1908

Irish judge. He was appointed judge (1881–1901) and Lord Justice of Appeal (1901–6).

56 In England, justice is open to all—like the Ritz Hotel.
Quoted in R E Megarry *Miscellany-at-Law* (1955). Sometimes attributed to Lord Darling.

Mathews, Harry Burchell 1930–

US writer and translator. His fiction is marked by a rich vein of lexical experiment and unconventional fantasy. He also translates and has written original literary works in French.

57 Translation is the paradigm, the exemplar of all writing… It is translation that demonstrates most vividly the yearning for transformation that underlies every act involving speech, that supremely human gift.
1980 *Country Cooking and Other Stories*, 'The Dialect of the Tribe'.

58 Syntax and vocabulary are overwhelming constraints—the rules that run us. Language is using *us* to talk—we think we're using the language, but language is doing the thinking, we're its slavish agents.
1988 Interview in *City Limits*, 26 May.

Mathias, Charles McCurdy, Jr 1922–

US lawyer and Republican politician. He was a Congressman (1961–69), then Senator from Maryland (1969–87).

59 Most of us are honest all the time, and all of us are honest most of the time.
1967 Of congressional ethics. In *Time*, 31 Mar.

Mathison, Melissa 1949–

US screenwriter, best known for *E.T.—the Extraterrestrial* (1982).

60 E.T. phone home.
1982 *E.T.—the Extraterrestrial*.

61 How do you explain school to a higher intelligence?
1982 *E.T.—the Extraterrestrial*.

Matisse, Henri Émile Benoît 1869–1954

French painter, sculptor, designer and graphic artist, from 1904 leader of the Fauves. His paintings typically display bold use of colour organized within a rhythmic two-dimensional design.

62 Expression, for me, does not reside in passions glowing in a human face or manifested by violent movement. The entire arrangement of my picture is expressive: the place occupied by the figures, the empty spaces around them, the proportions, everything has its share.
1908 'Notes d'un peintre', in *La Grande Revue*.

63 What I dream of is an art of balance, of purity and serenity…a soothing, calming influence on the mind, rather like a good armchair which provides relaxation from physical fatigue.
1908 'Notes d'un peintre', in *La Grande Revue*.

64 If drawing belongs to the realm of the Spirit and colour to that of the Senses, you must draw first, to cultivate the Spirit and to be able to lead colour through the paths of the Spirit.
1948 Letter to Henry Clifford, quoted in Jack D Flam *Matisse on Art* (1973).

Matlovich, Leonard 1943–88

US soldier, the first active-duty soldier openly to acknowledge his homosexuality.

65 A Gay Vietnam Veteran—They gave me a medal for killing two men, and a discharge for loving one.
Tombstone inscription. Quoted in the *Washington Post*, 22 Apr 1988.

Matos, Gregório de c.1623–1696

Brazilian poet and epigrammatist, born into the slave-owning gentry. His scandalous private life brought him into conflict with the clergy, government and respectable society, but his frankness and rebellious spirit made him a cultural hero.

66 *De dois ff se compõe*
Esta cidade a meu ver:
Um furtar, outro foder.
Of two f's,
as I see it,
is this city composed:
one fraud, the other fornication.
'Define a suà cidade' ('He defines his city'), collected in *Crônica do viver bahiano* (published 1882).

Matthews, Christopher J

US journalist. Former political aide and speechwriter for President Carter. He has written several books, including *Kennedy Nixon: The Rivalry that Shaped Postwar America* (1996).

67 Hang a lantern on your problem.
1987 Advice to political candidates to expose their personal frailties before they can be discovered by the media. In the *New York Times*, 10 Jul.

68 The key is to be a porcupine—have a reputation for being difficult.
Advice for success in the political world. Quoted in Hedrick Smith *The Power Game* (1988).

Matthews, Sir Stanley 1915–2000

English footballer. He was acclaimed the finest winger of his generation and won a total of 54 caps before his eventual retirement in 1955.

69 I played 33 years and never got cautioned. I like that.
1995 Television interview, on his 80th birthday.

Matthiessen, Peter 1927–

US writer, naturalist and explorer. His novels include *Far Tortuga* (1975) and *Killing Mister Watson* (1990). He also writes non-fiction and he won a National Book Award in 1978 for his account of a mystical journey through Tibet, *The Snow Leopard*.

70 At Play In The Fields Of The Lord.
1965 Title of novel.

71 For some time I watch the coming of the night... Above is the glistening galaxy of childhood, now hidden in the Western world by air pollution and the glare of artificial light; for my children's children, the power, peace and healing of the night will be obliterated.
1978 Of the night sky in Nepal. *The Snow Leopard*, 'Northward, October 18'.

Mature, Victor 1915–99

US actor whose credits include *Samson and Delilah* (1949), *Androcles and the Lion* (1952) and *The Robe* (1953).

72 Actually, I am a golfer. That is my real occupation. I never was an actor; ask anybody, particularly the critics.
Attributed.

Maugham, W(illiam) Somerset 1874–1965

British writer, born in Paris of Irish descent. He served as a secret agent in World War II, and travelled widely in south-east Asia. His works include the autobiographical novel *Of Human Bondage* (1915) and his satirical masterpiece, *Cakes and Ale* (1930).

73 At a dinner party one should eat wisely but not too well, and talk well but not too wisely.
1896 *A Writer's Notebook* (published 1949).

74 Impropriety is the soul of wit.
1919 *The Moon and Sixpence*.

75 I hate people who play bridge as though they were at a funeral and knew their feet were getting wet.
1921 Quoted in Colin Jarman *The Guinness Dictionary of Sports Quotations* (1990).

76 Hypocrisy is the most difficult and nerve-racking vice that any man can pursue; it needs an unceasing vigilance and a rare detachment of spirit. It cannot, like adultery or gluttony, be practised at spare moments; it is a whole-time job.
1930 *Cakes and Ale*, ch.1.

77 There is no silence in the East.
1930 *The Gentleman in the Parlour*.

78 Mandalay has its name; the falling cadence of the lovely word has gathered about itself the chiaroscuro of romance.
1930 *The Gentleman in the Parlour*.

79 The Chinese are the aristocracy of the East.
1930 *The Gentleman in the Parlour*.

80 They are like a face full of character that intrigues and excites you, but that on closer acquaintance you discover is merely the mask of a vulgar soul. Such is Tourane.
1930 Of Tourane, now Da Nang, Vietnam. *The Gentleman in the Parlour*.

81 Observing these people I am no longer surprised that there is such a scarcity of domestic servants at home.
1960 Said in an uncharacteristically loud voice after being refused entry to the premier British expatriate club in Singapore. Quoted in Robert Calder *Willie* (1989).

Maupassant, Guy de 1850–93

French writer, best known for his captivating short stories which explored a wide range of characters and, often, the supernatural world.

82 *L'histoire, cette vieille dame exaltée et menteuse.*
History, this old, honoured and lying woman.
1876 *Sur l'eau*.

83 *Le talent provient de l'originalité, qui est une manière spéciale de penser, de voir, de comprendre et de juger.*
Talent comes from originality which is a special manner of thinking, of seeing, of understanding and of judging.
1888 *Pierre et Jean*, préface.

84 *Raconter tout serait impossible.*
To tell all would be impossible.
1888 *Pierre et Jean*, préface.

85 *Les grands artistes sont ceux qui imposent à l'humanité leur illusion particulière.*
Great artists impose their particular illusion on humanity.
1888 *Pierre et Jean*, préface.

86 *La moindre chose contient un peu d'inconnu. Trouvons-le.*
The least thing contains something mysterious. Find it.
1888 *Pierre et Jean*, préface.

87 *On finirait par devenir fou, ou par mourir, si on ne pouvait pas pleurer.*
We would end by becoming crazy or by dying, if we could not cry.
1889 *Fort comme la mort*, bk.2, ch.1.

Maxton, James 1885–1946

Socialist politician, born in Glasgow, elected as a Labour MP in 1922. One of the group of 'Red Clydesiders', he was a brilliant and colourful orator rather than a skilful political tactician.

88 In the interests of economy they condemned hundreds of children to death and I call it murder.
1923 Speech against the withdrawal of child benefits, including the supply of milk, in Scotland. In *Hansard*, 27 Jun.

89 All I say is, if you cannot ride two horses you have no right in the circus.
1931 On the Scottish Independent Labour Party's proposed disaffiliation from the Labour Party. In the *Daily Herald*, 12 Jan.

May, Elaine *originally* ***Elaine Berlin*** 1932–

US actress, director and screenwriter. She wrote screenplays for *A New Leaf* (1971) and *Primary Colours* (1998).

90 All I am or was is rich, and that's all I ever wanted to be.
1971 Line delivered by Walter Matthau in *A New Leaf*.

Mayakovsky, Vladimir 1894–1930

Russian Futurist poet, a supporter of the Bolsheviks in the 1917 Revolution. His works include plays, poems and satirical plays. He committed suicide in Moscow.

91 I'll be irreproachably tender;
not a man, but—a cloud in trousers!
1915 'The Cloud in Trousers' (translated by Samuel Charteris).

92 We do not need art museums to worship dead works, we need living factories of the soul—in the streets, in the trams, in the factories, in studios, and in the workers' houses.
1918 Quoted in *Futurismo e Futurismi* (1986).

93 To us love says humming that the heart's stalled motor has begun working again.
1928 'Letter from Paris to Comrade Kostorov on the Nature of Love' (translated by Samuel Charteris).

Maybeck, Bernard Ralph 1862–1957

US architect, renowned for his eclectic combinations of styles and materials. His works include the Palace of Fine Arts, San Francisco (1915) and Clyde, a town in California (1917).

94 Let the thing fall down in peace.
On the crumbling remains of his Corinthian classic Palace of Fine Arts, designed for San Francisco's 1915 Panama–Pacific Exposition. Recalled in the *New York Times*, 9 May 1965.

Mayer, Louis B(urt) *originally* ***Eliezer Mayer*** 1885–1957

Russian-born US film mogul. A co-founder of Metro Films in 1915, he joined with Sam Goldwyn to form Metro-Goldwyn-Mayer (MGM) in 1924. He received an honorary Academy Award in 1950.

95 We are the only company whose assets all walk out the gates at night.
Quoted in Leslie Halliwell *The Filmgoer's Book of Quotes* (1973).

Mayhew, Alex

Professor of Political Science, Georgetown University.

96 The future of America is based on one generation sacrificing for the next.
Quoted by David Maraniss in CNBC broadcast, 7 Mar 1995. The phrase was popularized by Mayhew's former student, Bill Clinton.

Mayo, Charles Horace 1865–1939

US surgeon. An authority on the treatment of goitre, he co-founded the Mayo Clinic with his brother in 1905 within what is now St Mary's Hospital, Rochester.

97 The definition of a specialist as one who 'knows more and more about less and less' is good and true.
1939 In *Modern Hospital*, Sep.

Mazarin, Jules, Cardinal 1602–61

Neapolitan statesman. He entered Louis XIII's service in 1639, and succeeded Richelieu as Chief Minister (1642), becoming the lover of Anne of Austria. His domestic policy was problematic, but he negotiated the Peace of Westphalia (1648) and the Treaty of the Pyrenees (1659).

98 The French are nice people. I allow them to sing and to write, and they allow me to do whatever I like.
Attributed by the Duchess of Orléans in a letter dated 25 Oct 1715.

Mazzini, Giuseppe 1805–72

Italian patriot, a leader of the Risorgimento and founder of the revolutionary Young Italy Association. His underground journal, *La Giovine Italia*, fomented revolt throughout Europe.

99 Insurrection—by means of guerrilla bands—is the true method of warfare for all nations desirous of emancipating themselves from a foreign yoke.
1833 *General Instructions for the Members of Young Italy*, section 4.

1 I had thought to evoke the soul of Italy but all I find before me is its corpse.
Attributed. Quoted in Denis Mack Smith *Italy: A Modern History* (1959).

2 A nation is the universality of citizens speaking the same tongue.
In *La Giovine Italia* ('Young Italy').

Mead, Margaret 1901–78

US anthropologist. After expeditions to Samoa and New Guinea she wrote books on her experiences, arguing that personality characteristics are shaped by conditioning rather than heredity.

3 The greatest invention since the novel.
1974 Of television. Comment, 31 Dec.

Meat Loaf 1947–

US rock singer.

4 I don't have a rock voice. I have to force it. I am like an opera singer.
2003 In the *Observer*, 7 Dec.

Medawar, Sir Peter Brian 1915–87

British zoologist and immunologist, born in Rio de Janeiro.

Professor of Anatomy at University College London, he pioneered experiments in immunological toleration and skin and organ grafting, winning a Nobel prize with Sir Macfarlane Burnet in 1960.

5 I cannot give any scientist of any age better advice than this: the intensity of a conviction that a hypothesis is true has no bearing over whether it is true or not.
1979 *Advice to a Young Scientist.*

6 A scientist soon discovers that he has become a member of the cast of 'them' in the context 'what mischief are they up to now?'
1979 *Advice to a Young Scientist.*

7 Good scientists often possess old-fashioned virtues of the kind school teachers have always professed to despair of ever inculcating in us. These are: a sanguine temperament that expects to solve a problem; power of application and the kind of fortitude that keeps scientists erect in the face of much that might otherwise cast them down; and above all, persistence, a refusal bordering upon obstinacy to give in and admit defeat.
1984 *The Limits of Science.*

Meijer, Frederik 1919–

US retail executive and Chairman Emeritus of Meijer Inc.

8 I am more poor than you think.
On trying to secure a low profile. Quoted in *Forbes*, 19 Oct 1992.

Meilhac, Henri 1831–97

French playwright. From 1855 he produced a long series of light comedies, often in conjunction with Ludovic Halévy, with whom he also wrote the librettos for Offenbach's operettas and Bizet's *Carmen.*

9 *L'amour est un oiseau rebelle*
Que nul ne peut apprivoiser.
Love's a bird that will live in freedom
That no man ever learned to tame.
1875 The *Habañera. Carmen*, act 1.

10 *La fleur que tu m'avais jetée*
Here is the flower that you threw me
1875 *Carmen*, act 2, 'Flower Song' (Don José).

11 *Toreador, en garde!*
1875 *Carmen*, act 2, 'Couplets' (Escamillo).

Meir, Golda 1898–1978

Israeli politician. She was elected Prime Minister in 1969, but her efforts for peace in the Middle East were halted by the fourth Arab–Israeli War (1973) and she resigned in 1974.

12 Those that perished in Hitler's gas chambers were the last Jews to die without standing up to defend themselves.
1967 Speech in New York, 11 Jun.

13 Women's Liberation is just a lot of foolishness. It's the men who are discriminated against. They can't bear children. And no-one's likely to do anything about that.
1972 In *Newsweek*, 23 Oct.

Melba, Dame Nellie *real name* ***Helen Mitchell*** 1861–1931

Australian soprano, who took her stage name from her native Melbourne. Notorious for her many 'farewell' performances, her earthy Australian character contrasted oddly with the graces she adopted in her stage persona.

14 What are you going to sing? All I can say is—sing 'em muck! It's all they can understand!
c.1907 Advice to Dame Clara Butt on her first tour of Australia. Quoted in Winifred Ponder *Clara Butt: Her Life-Story* (1928).

15 If you wish to understand me at all (and to write an autobiography is only to open a window into one's heart) you must understand first and foremost, that I am an Australian… I shall always come back to rest in the shadow of the blue mountains, in the heart of this vast, deserted continent which gave me birth.
1925 *Melodies and Memories*, ch.1.

16 The first rule in opera is the first rule in life: see to everything yourself.
1925 *Melodies and Memories.*

17 If I'd been a housemaid I'd have been the best in Australia—I couldn't help it. It's got to be perfection for me.
Said to the conductor Fritz Hart. Quoted in John Thompson *On Lips of Living Men* (1962).

Melbourne, William Lamb, 2nd Viscount 1779–1848

English statesman, Chief Secretary for Ireland (1827–8), Home Secretary (1830–4), and Whig Prime Minister (1834, 1835–41), a confidante of the young Queen Victoria. Defeated in the election of 1841, he resigned and thereafter took little part in public affairs.

18 I wish that I was as cocksure of anything as Tom Macaulay is of everything.
1889 Attributed by Earl Cowper.

Melchett, Peter Robert Henry Mond, Baron 1948–

English Labour peer, executive director of Greenpeace UK (1989–2000).

19 The menu could not guarantee GM-free food but I ate vegetarian shepherd's pie.
1999 After spending two days in prison for leading a raid to destroy GM crops. In the *Sunday Times*, 'Talking Heads', 1 Aug.

Mellor, D H 1938–

British Emeritus Professor of Philosophy at Cambridge University. He has written several books on philosophy.

20 Appeals to rationality are mostly bluff. There is no good theory of what it is nor of how to recognize it.
1983 'Objective Decision Making', in *Social Theory and Practice*, Summer–Fall.

Melly, George 1926–

English jazz singer.

21 Jazz is an impure art. There's a great deal of romantic nostalgia involved.
1965 *Owning Up*, ch.2.

Melville, Andrew 1545–c.1622

Scottish religious and educational reformer, consolidating the Presbyterianism of the reformed Church of Scotland, and a fierce critic of royal authority where it impinged on that of the Kirk. In 1596 he headed a deputation to 'remonstrate' with James VI.

22 God's silly vassal.
1596 Said of (and to) King James VI, as reported in his nephew James Melville's *Diary*: 'Mr Andrew bore him down and uttered the commission as from the mighty God, calling him but "God's silly vassal".'

Melville, Herman 1819–91

US novelist. Between 1839 and 1844 he spent time at sea, working as a cabin-boy and on whaling ships. His experiences gave him material for many of his best-known books, including *Typee* (1846) and his masterpiece, *Moby Dick* (1851).

23 We may have civilized bodies and yet barbarous souls.
1849 *Redburn*, ch.58.

24 Toil is man's allotment; toil of brain, or toil of hands, or a grief that's more than either, the grief and sin of idleness.
1849 *Mardi*, ch.63.

25 Call me Ishmael.
1851 *Moby Dick*, ch.1, opening words.

26 Better sleep with a sober cannibal than a drunken Christian.
1851 *Moby Dick*, ch.3.

27 Faith, like a jackal, feeds among the tombs, and even from these dead doubts she gathers her most vital hope.
1851 *Moby Dick*, ch.7.

28 A whale ship was my Yale College and my Harvard.
1851 *Moby Dick*, ch.24.

29 Old age is always wakeful; as if, the longer linked with life, the less man has to do with aught that looks like death.
1851 *Moby Dick*, ch.29.

30 All visible objects, man, are but as pasteboard masks. But in each event—in the living act, the undoubted deed—there, some unknown but still reasoning thing puts forth the mouldings of its features from behind the unreasoning mask. If man will strike, strike through the mask!
1851 Captain Ahab. *Moby Dick*, ch.36.

31 Though in many of its aspects this visible world seems formed in love, the invisible spheres were formed in fright.
1851 *Moby Dick*, ch.42.

32 It was the whiteness of the whale that above all things appalled me…for all these accumulated associations, with whatever is sweet, and honourable, and sublime, there yet lurks an elusive something in the innermost idea of this hue, which strikes more of a panic to the soul than that redness which affrights in blood.
1851 Ishmael. *Moby Dick*, ch.42.

33 It may seem strange that of all men sailors should be tinkering at their last wills and testaments, but there are no people in the world more fond of that diversion.
1851 *Moby Dick*, ch.49.

34 There is a wisdom that is woe; but there is a woe that is madness.
1851 *Moby Dick*, ch.96.

35 To produce a mighty book, you must choose a mighty theme. No great and enduring volume can ever be written on the flea, though many there be who have tried it.
1851 *Moby Dick*, ch.104.

36 For whatever is truly wonderous and fearful in man, never yet was put into words or books.
1851 *Moby Dick*, ch.110.

37 Come; let us squeeze hands all round; nay, let us all squeeze ourselves into each other; let us squeeze ourselves universally into the very milk and sperm of kindness.
1851 Ishmael. *Moby Dick*, ch.114.

38 Warmest climes but nurse the cruellest fangs: the tiger of Bengal crouches in spiced groves of ceaseless verdure.
1851 *Moby Dick*, ch.119.

39 Oh God! that man should be a thing for immortal souls to sieve through!
1851 Captain Ahab. *Moby Dick*, ch.125.

40 Let me look into a human eye; it is better than to gaze into sea or sky; better than to gaze upon God.
1851 Captain Ahab. *Moby Dick*, ch.132.

41 Guinea-coast slavery of solitary command!
1851 Captain Ahab. *Moby Dick*, ch.132.

42 He says NO! in thunder; but the Devil himself cannot make him say *yes*. For all men who say *yes*, lie; and all men who say *no*,—why, they are in the happy condition of judicious, unencumbered travellers in Europe; they cross the frontiers into Eternity with nothing but a carpet bag.
1851 Of Nathaniel Hawthorne.

43 The calm, the coolness, the silent grass-growing mood in which a man *ought* always to compose,—that, I fear, can seldom be mine. Dollars damn me; and the malicious Devil is forever grinning in upon me, holding the door ajar… What I feel most moved to write, that is banned,—it will not pay. So the product is a final hash, and all my books are botches.
1851 Letter to Nathaniel Hawthorne, Jun.

44 Why, ever since Adam, who has got to the meaning of this great allegory—the world? Then we pygmies must be content to have our paper allegories but ill comprehended.
1851 Letter to Nathaniel Hawthorne, Nov.

45 Nothing so aggravates an earnest person as a passive resistance.
1853 'Bartleby the Scrivener', in *Putnam's Monthly Magazine*, Nov–Dec.

46 If some books are deemed most baneful and their sale forbid, how, then, with deadlier facts, not dreams of doting men? Those whom books will hurt will not be proof against events. Events, not books, should be forbid.
1854 'The Encantadas, Sketch Eighth', in *Putnam's Monthly Magazine*, May.

47 Who in the rainbow can draw the line where the violet tint ends and the orange tint begins? Distinctly we see the difference of the colors, but where exactly does the one first blendingly enter into the other? So with sanity and insanity.
1891 *Billy Budd, Foretopman* (first published 1924), ch.21.

48 There is nothing nameable but that some men will, or undertake to, do it for pay.
1891 *Billy Budd, Foretopman* (first published 1924), ch.21.

Menander c.343–291 BC

Greek comic poet, born in Athens. He wrote more than 100

comedies, most of which are lost. Various fragments and one complete play (*Dyscolus*) have been rediscovered in recent times.

49 He whom the gods love dies young.
Dis Exapaton, fragment 4.

50 The man who runs away will fight again.
Fragment quoted in Aulus Gellius *Noctes Atticae*, 17.21.31 (translated by J C Rolfe, 1967).

Mencius *properly* ***Meng-tzu*** c.371–c.289 BC

Chinese philosopher and sage. He helped to develop and popularize Confucian ideas and founded a school to promote their study. His sayings were recorded by his pupils after his death, and included proposals for social and political reform.

51 If the king loves music, there is little wrong in the land.
3c BC *Discourses*.

Mencken, H(enry) L(ouis) 1880–1956

US journalist and critic. He wrote much literary and political criticism as editor of *The Smart Set* (1914–23) and co-founder and editor of the *American Mercury* (1924 33), and various essays were collected in *Prejudices* (6 vols, 1919–27). Other publications included autobiographical writings and *The American Language* (1919).

52 Democracy is the theory that the common people know what they want, and deserve to get it good and hard.
1916 *Little Book in C Major.*

53 Conscience: the inner voice which warns us that someone may be looking.
1916 *Little Book in C Major.*

54 I can't remember a single masculine figure created by a woman who is not, at bottom, a booby.
1918 *In Defence of Women*, ch.1, pt.1.

55 All successful newspapers are ceaselessly querulous and bellicose.
1919 *Prejudices*, 1st series, ch.13.

56 If, after I depart this vale, you ever remember me and have thought to please my ghost, forgive some sinner and wink your eye at some homely girl.
1921 In *The Smart Set*, Dec.

57 Poetry is a comforting piece of fiction set to more or less lascivious music.
1922 *Prejudices*, 3rd series, ch.7.

58 Faith may be defined briefly as an illogical belief in the occurrence of the improbable.
1922 *Prejudices*, 3rd series, ch.14.

59 The man who boasts that he habitually tells the truth is simply a man with no respect for it. It is not a thing to be thrown about loosely, like small change; it is something to be cherished and hoarded, and disbursed only when absolutely necessary.
1922 *Prejudices*, 3rd series, ch.14.

60 [Jeremy] Bentham held no post at the mercy of bankers and tripe sellers; he was a man of independent means, a lawyer and politician and a heretic in general practice. It is impossible to imagine such a man occupying a chair at Harvard or Princeton. He had a hand in too many pies; he was too rebellious and contumacious; he had too little respect for authority, either academic or worldly. Moreover, his mind was too wide for a professor; he could never remain safely in a groove; the whole field of social organization invited his inquiries and experiments.
1922 'The Dismal Science', in *The Smart Set*, Jun.

61 Hygiene is the corruption of medicine by morality.
1922 *Prejudices*.

62 The opera…is to music what a bawdy house is to a cathedral.
1925 Letter to Isaac Goldberg.

63 No one in this world, so far as I know—and I have searched the record for years, and employed agents to help me—has ever lost money by underestimating the intelligence of the great masses of the plain people.
1926 'Notes on Journalism' in the *Chicago Sunday Tribune*, 19 Sep. The phrase is commonly quoted as 'No one ever went broke underestimating the intelligence of the American people.'

64 The saddest life is that of a political aspirant under democracy. His failure is ignominious and his success is disgraceful.
1929 In the *Baltimore Evening Sun*, 9 Dec.

65 Here, indeed, was his one peculiar Fach, his one really notable talent. He slept more than any other President, whether by day or night. Nero fiddled, but Coolidge only snored.
1933 Of Calvin Coolidge. In the *American Mercury*, Apr.

66 Roosevelt will probably go down into American history as a great hero. It is one of our Heavenly Father's characteristic jokes upon the American people, and in the usual bad taste.
1944 Journal entry. Collected in *The Diary of H. L. Mencken* (published 1990).

67 I've made it a rule never to drink by daylight and never to refuse a drink after dark.
1945 In the *New York Post*, 18 Sep.

68 When women kiss it always reminds one of prize fighters shaking hands.
1949 *Chrestomathy*, ch.30.

69 Love is the delusion that one woman differs from another.
1949 *Chrestomathy*, ch.30.

70 Men have a much better time of it than women. For one thing, they marry later. For another thing, they die earlier.
1949 *Chrestomathy*, ch.30

71 Puritanism. The haunting fear that someone, somewhere, may be happy.
1949 Chrestomathy, ch.30.

72 He is a man who sits in the outer office of the White House hoping to hear the President sneeze.
Of the Vice-President. Recalled on his death, 29 Jan 1956.

73 Science, at bottom, is really anti-intellectual. It always distrusts pure reason, and demands the production of objective fact.
'Minority Report'. Collected in *Notebooks* (1956).

74 Some people read too much: the bibliobuli…who are constantly drunk on books, as other men are drunk on whiskey or religion. They wander through the most diverting and stimulating of worlds in a haze, seeing nothing and hearing nothing.
'Minority Report'. Collected in *Notebooks* (1956).

75 We must respect the other fellow's religion, but only in the sense and to the extent that we respect his theory that his wife is beautiful and his children smart.
'Minority Report'. Collected in *Notebooks* (1956).

76 Men always try to make virtues of their weaknesses. Fear of death and fear of life become piety.
'Minority Report'. Collected in *Notebooks* (1956).

77 It is now quite lawful for a Catholic woman to avoid pregnancy by a resort to mathematics, though she is still forbidden to resort to physics and chemistry.
'Minority Report'. Collected in *Notebooks* (1956).

78 The capacity of human beings to bore one another seems to be vastly greater than that of any other animals. Some of their most esteemed inventions have no other apparent purpose, for example, the dinner party of more than two, the epic poem, and the science of metaphysics.
'Minority Report'. Collected in *Notebooks* (1956).

79 Men are the only animals who devote themselves assiduously to making one another unhappy. It is, I suppose, one of their godlike qualities.
'Minority Report'. Collected in *Notebooks* (1956).

80 War will never cease until babies begin to come into the world with larger cerebrums and smaller adrenal glands.
'Minority Report'. Collected in *Notebooks* (1956).

81 Whenever one comes to close grips with so-called idealism, as in war time, one is shocked by its rascality.
'Minority Report'. Collected in *Notebooks* (1956).

82 I hate all sports as rabidly as a person who likes sports hates common sense.
Quoted in Fred Metcalfe *The Penguin Dictionary of Modern Humorous Quotations* (1986).

83 The greatest of all the contributions of the American way of life to the salvation of humanity.
Of the cocktail. Quoted by William Grimes in 'The American Cocktail', *Americana*, Dec 1992.

84 The varnishers and veneerers have been busily converting Abe into a plaster saint...to pump all his human weaknesses out of him, and so leave him a mere moral apparition, a sort of amalgam of John Wesley and the Holy Ghost.
Of popular perceptions of Abraham Lincoln. Quoted in Fred Hobson *Mencken: A Life* (1994).

85 His whole carcass seemed to be made of iron. There was no give in him—no bounce, no softness. He sailed through American history like a steel ship loaded with monoliths made of granite.
Of President Grover Cleveland. Quoted in Fred Hobson *Mencken: A Life* (1994).

86 A third-rate political wheel-horse, with the face of a moving-picture actor, the intelligence of a respectable agricultural implement dealer, and the imagination of a lodge joiner...a benign blank—a decent, harmless, laborious, hollow-headed mediocrity.
Of President Warren G Harding. Quoted in Fred Hobson *Mencken: A Life* (1994).

87 His English reminds me of tattered washing on the line...of stale bean-soup, of college yells, of dogs barking idiotically through endless nights. It is so bad that a sort of grandeur creeps into it.
Of President Warren G Harding. Quoted in Fred Hobson *Mencken: A Life* (1994).

88 He was, on his plane, as insufferable as a Methodist on his.
Of Oscar Wilde. Introduction to a new edition of Wilde *A House of Pomegranates*.

Menzies, Sir Robert Gordon 1894–1978

Australian statesman, Prime Minister (1939–41), Leader of the Opposition (1943–9) and thereafter Premier of the coalition government. He headed the Five Nations Committee which sought a settlement with Nasser on the question of Suez (1956).

89 What Great Britain calls the Far East is to us the near north.
1939 Quoted in the *Sydney Morning Herald*, 27 Apr. Menzies was one of the first Australian statesmen to recognize the importance to his country of Asia.

90 If I were the Archangel Gabriel, madam, I'm afraid you would not be in my constituency.
Attributed reply to a woman who had heckled him with the words 'I wouldn't vote for you if you were the Archangel Gabriel.' Quoted in Ray Robinson *The Wit of Robert Menzies* (1966).

Mercer, David 1928–80

English playwright. Such plays as *A Climate of Fear* (1962) and *In Two Minds* (1967) explored his fascination with mental health, psychiatry and his struggle to reconcile a belief in socialism with the repression revealed during his stays in Eastern Europe. Other writings included the films *Morgan* (1965) and *Providence* (1977) and several plays for television.

91 A Suitable Case for Treatment.
1962 Play title.

Mercer, Johnny 1909–76

US songwriter. His songs include 'Accentuate the Positive', 'Black Magic', 'In the Cool Cool of the Evening' and 'Something's Gotta Give'.

92 Hooray for Hollywood.
1937 Title of song which first appeared in the film *Hollywood Hotel*, performed by Johnny Davis and Frances Langford.

Meredith, George 1828–1909

English novelist and poet. He married the daughter of Thomas Love Peacock but she left him for the painter Henry Wallis, for whose *Death of Chatterton* Meredith was the model. His volumes of poetry include *Modern Love* (1862) and *Poems and Lyrics of the Joy of the Earth* (1883). His novels include *The Ordeal of Richard Feverel* (1859), *Evan Harrington* (1860) and *The Egoist* (1879).

93 Lovely are the curves of the white owl sweeping
Wavy in the dusk lit by one large star.
Lone on the fir-branch, his rattle-note unvaried,
Brooding o'er the gloom, spins the brown eve-jar.
1851 *Poems*, 'Love in the Valley', stanza 5. The poem was revised and republished in 1878.

94 Happy happy time, when the white star hovers
Low over dim fields fresh with blooming dew,
Near the face of dawn, that draws athwart the darkness,
Threading it with colour, like yewberries the yew.
1851 *Poems*, 'Love in the Valley', stanza 7. The poem was revised and republished in 1878.

95 I expect that Woman will be the last thing civilized by Man.
1859 *The Ordeal of Richard Feverel*, ch.1.

96 Away with systems! Away with a corrupt world! Let us breathe the air of the Enchanted island. Golden lie the meadows; golden run the streams; red gold is on the pine-stems. The sun's coming down to earth, and walks the fields and the waters. The sun is coming down to earth, and the fields and the waters shout to him golden shouts.
1859 *The Ordeal of Richard Feverel*, ch.19.

97 Kissing don't last: cookery do!
1859 *The Ordeal of Richard Feverel*, ch.28.

98 Speech is the small change of silence.
1859 *The Ordeal of Richard Feverel*, ch.34.

99 It became known that death had taken Mr Melchisedec Harrington, and struck one off the list of living tailors.
1860 *Evan Harrington*, ch.1.

1 He fainted on his vengefulness, and strove
To ape the magnanimity of love.
1862 *Modern Love*, 2.

2 O have a care of natures that are mute!
1862 *Modern Love*, 35.

3 Much benevolence of the passive order may be traced to a disinclination to inflict pain upon oneself.
1866 *Vittoria*, ch.24.

4 A dainty rogue in porcelain.
1879 *The Egoist*, ch.5

5 Cynicism is intellectual dandyism.
1879 *The Egoist*, ch.7.

6 'But do care a bit for flattery, my lady,' said De Craye. ''Tis the finest of the Arts; we might call it moral sculpture. Adepts in it can cut their friends to any shape they like.'
1879 De Craye to Lady Busshe. *The Egoist*, ch.36.

7 Enter these enchanted woods,
You who dare.
1883 *Poems and Lyrics of the Joy of Earth*, 'The Woods of Westermain'.

8 Soaring through wider zones that pricked his scars
With memory of the old revolt from Awe,
He reached the middle height, and at the stars,
Which are the brain of heaven, he looked, and sank.
Around the ancient track marched, rank on rank,
The army of unalterable law.
1883 *Poems and Lyrics of the Joy of Earth*, 'Lucifer in Starlight'.

9 For singing till his heaven fills
'Tis love of earth that he instils,
And ever winging up and up,
Our valley is his golden cup,
And he the wine which overflows.
1883 *Poems and Lyrics of the Joy of Earth*, 'The Lark Ascending'.

10 'Tis Ireland gives England her soldiers, her generals too.
1885 *Diana of the Crossways*, ch.2.

11 Affairs of the world he could treat competently; he had a head for high politics and the management of men; the feminine half of the world was a confusion and a vexation to his intelligence, characterless; and one woman at last appearing decipherable, he fancied it must be owing to her possession of character, a thing prized the more in women because of his latent doubt of its existence.
1885 Percy Dacier's opinion of Diana. *Diana of the Crossways*, ch.28.

12 A wind sways in the pines,
And below
Not a breath of wild air;
Still as the mosses that glow
On the flooring and over the lines
Of the roots here and there.
The pine tree drops its dead;
They are quiet, as under the sea.
Overhead, overhead
Rushes life in a race,
As the clouds the clouds chase;
And we go,
And we drop like the fruits of the tree,
Even we,
Even so.
1888 *A Reading of Earth*, 'Dirge in the Woods'.

Mérimée, Prosper 1803–70

French novelist, Inspector-General of Historical Remains in France (1833) and a Senator (1853). He wrote many short stories and novels, including *Colomba* (1841) and *Carmen* (1847), as well as archaeological and historical dissertations and travel stories.

13 A colossal bore… I feel I could write something like it tomorrow, if my cat inspired me by walking over the piano.
1861 Of Wagner's opera *Tannhäuser*, after the disastrous première of its revised version at the Paris Opéra, 13 Mar. Quoted in Joanna Richardson *La Vie Parisienne* (1971), p.262.

► *See Gounod 365:26.*

Merman, Ethel *stage-name of Ethel Agnes Zimmermann* 1909–84

US singer and actress. Nicknamed 'The Golden Foghorn' because of her powerful singing voice, she established her reputation in cabaret and subsequently starred in such musicals as *Annie Get Your Gun* (1946) and *Hello, Dolly!* (1970).

14 She's OK, if you like talent.
1958 Of Mary Martin. In *Theater Arts*, Sep.

15 Can you imagine the name Zimmermann in bright lights? It would burn you to death!
Explaining why she took a stage-name. Attributed.

Merrifield, D(udley) Bruce 1921–

US former government official and Professor Emeritus of the Wharton Business School. He was Assistant Secretary of Commerce in the Reagan administration.

16 Innovate, automate—or evaporate!
1987 Address at London's Guildhall to Britain's senior industrialists and bankers. Reported in *The Times*, 19 Feb.

Merrill, James Ingram 1926–95

US poet, the 'ouija poet', whose interest in the occult led him to use a ouija board to communicate with the spirit world. The experience is recorded in an epic poem, *The Changing Light at Sandover* (1982, rev 1992). His collections include *Nights and Days* (1966) and *Divine Comedies* (1976, Pulitzer Prize), and he also wrote plays and novels.

17 Here one is in Later Life, and it's perfectly pleasant really, not for a moment that garden of cactus and sour grapes I'd always assumed it *must* be.
1972 Letter to a friend at age 46.

18 What one wants in this world isn't so much to 'live' as to... *be* lived, to be used by life for its own purposes.
Quoted in the *New Yorker*, 27 Mar 1995.

Merrin, Edward H

Antiquities dealer.

19 The price was quite reasonable. It just happened to be a lot of money.
1989 In the *New York Times*, 16 Jul. On paying $2.09 million for a nine-inch, 5,000-year-old Greek head.

Merton, Paul 1957–

English comedian.

20 They say the closer you sit to the stage, the better chance you have of winning. Angus Deayton is sitting in Row G—at the Theatre Royal, Drury Lane.
2003 At the BAFTA television awards night at the London Palladium—assessing his fellow TV presenter's chances, 13 Apr.

21 I don't consider myself a fashion victim. I consider fashion a victim of me.
2003 In the *Daily Telegraph*, 21 Apr.

Merton, Robert King 1910–2003

US sociologist, Columbia University (1941–2003). He was awarded the National Medal of Science in 1994.

22 The self-fulfilling prophecy is, in the beginning, a *false* definition of the situation evoking a new behavior which makes the originally false conception come *true*. The specious validity of the self-fulfilling prophecy perpetuates a reign of error.
1948 'The Self-Fulfilling Prophecy', in *Social Theory and Social Structure* (rev. edn, 1968), p.477. This is the first use of the phrase 'self-fulfilling prophecy'.

23 It would be a curious reading of the history of thought to suggest that the absence of disagreement testifies to a developing discipline.
1961 Defending internal disputes among sociologists. 'Now the Case *for* Sociology', in the *New York Times Magazine*, 16 Jul.

24 The sociologists of knowledge have been among those raising high the banner which reads: 'We don't know if what we say is true, but it is at least significant.' The sociologists and psychologists engaged in the study of public opinion and mass communications are most often found in the opposed camp of the empiricists... 'We don't know that what we say is particularly significant, but it is at least true.'
1968 *Social Theory and Social Structure* (rev. edn), pt.3, introduction.

Merwin, W(illiam) S(tanley) 1927–

US poet. His poetry includes *A Mask for Janus* (1952), *The Carrier of Ladders* (1970, Pulitzer Prize), *Opening the Hand* (1983) and *The River Sound* (1999). He is also a translator, notably of *The Cid* (1959).

25 The thing that makes poetry different from all of the other arts...[is] you're using language, which is what you use for everything else—telling lies and selling socks, advertising, and conducting law. Whereas we don't write little concerts or paint little pictures.
1994 On receiving the $100,000 Tanning Prize for Poetry. In the *Washington Post*, 30 Sep.

Metternich, Prince Clemens Lothar Wenzel 1773–1859

Austrian statesman, Foreign Minister from 1809. He was a powerful influence for conservatism in Europe, contributing to the tension that produced the upheavals of 1848 and popular rebellions in many countries.

26 When Paris sneezes, Europe catches cold.
1830 Letter, 26 Jan.

27 Italy is a geographical expression.
1847 Letter, 6 Aug.

28 I have been a rock of order.
1859 Attributed, shortly before his death. Quoted in Andrew Milne *Metternich* (1975).

29 Error has never approached my spirit.
Said to Guizot on the steps of the British Museum. Quoted in A J P Taylor *From the Boer War to the Cold War: Essays on Twentieth-Century Europe* (1995).

Meyer, Karl Ernest 1928–

US journalist and author, formerly of the *Washington Post* and the *New York Times*.

30 Whatever his private behavior, the man and his work existed in different realms. Mencken's defects were commonplace; his virtues were not. So wonderfully uninhibited was his style that even a single sentence in a routine article proclaimed its begetter.
1994 Of H L Mencken. In the *New York Times Book Review*, 8 May.

Michael, George *originally* *Georgios Kyriacos Panayiotou* 1963–

English pop singer and songwriter.

31 I have never felt any ethnic connection between the Greeks and me other than how hairy I am.
2004 In *Scotland on Sunday*, 14 Mar.

Michelangelo *full name* *Michelangelo Buonarroti* 1475–1564

Italian painter, sculptor, architect, draughtsman and poet. Born near Florence, he is one of the most important figures of the Italian Renaissance.

32 I've finished that chapel I was painting. The Pope is quite satisfied.
1512 Letter written to his father after 18 months of painting the vault of the Sistine Chapel, quoted in Robert J Clements (ed) *Michelangelo: A Self-Portrait* (1968).

33 Nothing the greatest artist can conceive
That every marble block doth not confine
Within itself; and only its design
The hand that follows intellect can achieve.
c.1538 Quoted in Robert J Clements (ed) *Michelangelo: A Self-Portrait* (1968).

34 Your Lordship sends to tell me that I should paint and have no doubts. I answer that painting is done with the brain, not the hands.
1542 Letter written to a Cardinal, Oct, collected in Creighton Gilbert (ed and trans) *Complete Poems and Selected Letters of Michelangelo* (1963).

35 I have only too much of a wife in this art of mine, who has always kept me in tribulation, and my children shall be the works I leave, which, even if they are naught, will live a while.

In response to a priest and friend who had said it was a pity he had not married and had children to whom he could leave his works. Attributed in Giorgio Vasari *Lives of the Artists* (1568).

36 They are so beautiful that they would grace the entrance to Paradise.

Of Ghiberti's doors for the Florence Baptistery. Quoted in Giorgio Vasari *Lives of the Artists* (1568).

37 In my opinion painting should be considered excellent in proportion as it approaches the effect of relief, while relief should be considered bad in proportion as it approaches the effect of painting.

Quoted in Robert J Clements (ed) *Michelangelo. A Self-Portrait* (1968).

Middleton, Thomas c.1570–1627

English dramatist, who collaborated with Dekker, Webster, Rowley, Massinger, Beaumont and Fletcher and probably Shakespeare. His works include *A Mad World, My Masters* (1608), *Women Beware Women* (1620–7) and *A Chaste Maid in Cheapside* (published 1630). He also wrote pageants and masques for the city of London.

38 But you are dull, nothing comes nimbly from you; you dance like a plumber's daughter and deserve two thousand pound in lead to your marriage, and not in goldsmith's ware.

1613 *A Chaste Maid in Cheapside* (published 1630), act 1, sc.1.

39 Lie soft, sleep hard, drink wine, and eat good cheer.

1613 *A Chaste Maid in Cheapside* (published 1630), act 1, sc.1.

40 Nay, good sir, be not so violent; with speed
I cannot render satisfaction
Unto the dear companion of my soul,
Virginity, whom I thus long have lived with,
And part with it so rude and suddenly.
Can such friends divide, never to meet again,
Without a solemn farewell?

1622 *The Changeling* (with William Rowley), act 1, sc.1.

41 Our eyes are sentinels unto our judgements
And should give certain judgement what they see;
But they are rash sometimes and tell us wonders
Of common things, which when our judgements find,
They can then check the eyes and call them blind.

1622 *The Changeling* (with William Rowley), act 1, sc.1.

42 Now I know
She had rather wear my pelt tanned in a pair
Of dancing pumps.

1622 *The Changeling* (with William Rowley), act 1, sc.1.

43 There's scarce a thing but is both loved and loathed.

1622 *The Changeling* (with William Rowley), act 1, sc.1.

44 I shall run mad with joy.

1622 *The Changeling* (with William Rowley), act 2, sc.2.

45 I'm up to the chin in heaven.

1622 *The Changeling* (with William Rowley), act 2, sc.2.

46 Paper blushes not.

1622 *The Changeling* (with William Rowley), act 3, sc.4.

47 Y'are the deed's creature.

1622 *The Changeling* (with William Rowley), act 3, sc.4.

48 Beneath the stars, upon yon meteor
Ever hung my fate, 'mongst things corruptible;
I ne'er could pluck it from him. My loathing
Was prophet to the rest, but ne'er believed.

1622 *The Changeling* (with William Rowley), act 5, sc.3.

Midler, Bette 1945–

US comedienne, singer and actress, whose bawdy nightclub act led to a successful career on Broadway and then in films.

49 There comes a time when you have to let your clothes go out in the world and try to make it on their own.

1987 On relinquishing the mermaid costume she wore in the 1970s film *Clams on the Half Shell*. In *People*, 31 Aug.

Mies van der Rohe, Ludwig 1886–1969

German born US architect and furniture designer, a pioneer of glass skyscrapers. He was director of the Bauhaus in Dessau (1930–3) and emigrated to the US in 1937.

50 Architecture is the will of the age conceived in spatial terms.

1922 *De Stijl*, vol.6.

Mikes, George 1912–87

Hungarian-born writer who wrote humorous books about his experience of being a foreigner in England.

51 On the Continent people have good food; in England people have good table manners.

1946 *How to Be an Alien*.

52 Many continentals think life is a game, the English think cricket is a game.

1946 *How to be an Alien*.

Milestone, Lewis *pseudonym of* *Levis Milstein* 1895–1980

US film director, best known for *All Quiet on the Western Front* (1930), which won an Academy Award.

53 I've got your happy ending. We'll let the Germans win the war.

c 1929 Response when asked to provide an upbeat ending for *All Quiet on the Western Front*.

Milius, John 1944–

US screenwriter and director. His writing credits include *The Life and Times of Judge Roy Bean* (1973), *Magnum Force* (1973), *Apolcalyse Now* (co-writer, 1979) and *The Wind and the Lion* (1975) which he also directed.

54 I know the law since I have spent my entire life in its flagrant disregard.

1972 *The Life and Times of Judge Roy Bean*.

Mill, James 1773–1836

Scottish philosopher, historian and economist. He was a friend of Jeremy Bentham and an enthusiastic proponent of Utilitarianism.

55 The government and the people are under a moral necessity of acting together; a free press compels them to bend to one another.

1811 In the *Edinburgh Review*, May–Aug.

Mill, John Stuart 1806–73

English empiricist philosopher, MP (1863–8) and reformer, a supporter of women's suffrage (*Subjection of Women*, 1869) and liberalism. His works include *System of Logic* (1843), *Principles of Political Economy* (1848), *On Liberty* (1859) and *Utilitarianism* (1863).

56 Unlike the Laws of Production, those of Distribution are partly of human institution, since the manner in which wealth is distributed in any given society, depends on the statutes or usages therein obtaining.
1848 *Principles of Political Economy, with Some Applications to Social Philosophy.*

57 A stationary condition of capital and population implies no stationary state of human improvement. There could be as much scope as ever for all kinds of mental culture, and moral and social progress.
1848 *Principles of Political Economy, with Some Applications to Social Philosophy.*

58 Happily, there is nothing in the laws of value which remains for the present or any future writer to clear up; the theory of the subject is complete.
1848 *Principles of Political Economy, with Some Applications to Social Philosophy.*

59 I am not charmed with the ideal of life held out by those who think that the normal state of human beings is that of struggling to get on. I know not why it should be a matter of congratulation that persons who are already richer than any one needs to be, should have doubled their means of consuming things which give little or no pleasure except as representative of wealth.
1848 *Principles of Political Economy, with Some Applications to Social Philosophy.*

60 The average condition of the people improving or deteriorating, depends upon whether population is advancing faster than improvement, or improvement than population.
1848 *Principles of Political Economy, with Some Applications to Social Philosophy.*

61 That the whole or any part of the education of the people should be in State hands, I go so far as anyone in deprecating… A general State education is a mere contrivance for molding people to be exactly like one another.
1856 *Utilitarianism, Liberty and Representative Government.*

62 The only purpose for which power can be rightfully exercised over any member of a civilized community, against his will, is to prevent harm to others.
1859 *On Liberty.*

63 A party of order or stability, and a party of progress or reform, are both necessary elements of a healthy state of political life.
1859 *On Liberty.*

64 Everyone who receives the protection of society owes a return for the benefit, and the fact of living in a society renders it indispensable that each should be bound to observe a certain line of conduct towards the rest. That conduct consists…in each person bearing his share of the labours and sacrifices incurred for defending the society or its members from injury and molestation.
1859 *On Liberty.*

65 If all mankind minus one were of one opinion, and only one person were of the contrary opinion, mankind would no more be justified in silencing that one person than he, if he had the power, would be justified in silencing mankind.
1859 *On Liberty.*

66 If the roads, the railways, the banks, the insurance offices, the great joint-stock companies, the universities, and the public charities, were all of them branches of government; if, in addition, the municipal corporations and local boards, with all that now devolves on them, became departments of the central administration; if the employees of all these different enterprises were appointed and paid by the government, and looked to the government for every rise in life; not all the freedom of the press and popular constitution of the legislature would make this or any other country free otherwise than in name.
1859 *On Liberty.*

67 The Conservatives, as being by the law of their existence the stupidest party.
1861 *Considerations on Representative Government*, ch.7, note.

68 The worth of the State, in the long run, is the worth of the individuals composing it.
1861 *Considerations on Representative Government.*

69 It is better to be a human being dissatisfied than a pig satisfied; better to be Socrates dissatisfied than a fool satisfied.
1863 *Utilitarianism*, ch.2.

70 The creed which accepts as the foundation of morals, Utility, or the Greatest Happiness Principle, holds that actions are right in proportion as they tend to promote happiness, wrong as they tend to produce the reverse of happiness.
1863 *Utilitarianism*, ch.2.

71 The sole evidence it is possible to produce that anything is desirable, is that people do actually desire it.
1863 *Utilitarianism*, ch.4.

72 If the universe had a beginning, its beginning, by the very condition of the cases, was supernatural; the laws of Nature cannot account for their own origin.
1865 *Auguste Comte and Positivism.*

73 It is always easy to find fault with a classification. There are a hundred ways of arranging any set of objects, and something may almost always be said against the best, and in favour of the worst of them. But the merits of a classification depend on the purposes to which it is instrumental.
1865 *Auguste Comte and Positivism.*

74 I never was a boy, never played at cricket; it is better to let Nature take her course.
1867 *Autobiography.*

75 It may be asserted without scruple, that no other class of dependants have had their character so entirely distorted from its natural proportions by their relations with their masters.
1869 *The Subjection of Women*, ch.1.

76 With equality of experience and of general faculties, a woman usually sees much more than a man of what is immediately before her.
1869 *The Subjection of Women*, ch.3.

77 Women cannot be expected to devote themselves to the emancipation of women, until men in considerable number are prepared to join with them in the undertaking.
1869 *The Subjection of Women*, ch.3.

78 Marriage is the only actual bondage known to our law. There remain no legal slaves, except the mistress of every house.
1869 *The Subjection of Women*, ch.4.

79 The self-worship of the monarch, or of the feudal superior, is matched by the self-worship of the male.
1869 *The Subjection of Women*, ch.4.

Millay, Edna St Vincent 1892–1950

US poet. Despite her contemporary subject matter, she was a formalist and her poems show a strong technical skill. Her collections include *The Harp-Weaver* (1923), which won a Pulitzer Prize.

80 World, world, I cannot get thee close enough!
Long have I known a glory in it all,
But never knew like this;
Here such a pattern is
As stretcheth me apart. Lord, I do fear
Thou'st made the world too beautiful this year:
My soul is all but out of me—let fall
No burning leaf; prithee, let no bird call.
1917 *God's World.*

81 My candle burns at both ends;
It will not last the night;
But ah, my foes, and oh, my friends—
It gives a lovely light.
1920 *A Few Figs From Thistles*, 'First Fig'.

82 Safe upon solid rock the ugly houses stand:
Come and see my shining palace built upon the sand.
1920 *A Few Figs From Thistles*, 'Second Fig'.

83 Death devours all lovely things;
Lesbia with her sparrow
Shares the darkness—presently
Every bed is narrow.
1921 *Second April*, 'Passer Mortuus Est'.

84 After all, my erstwhile dear,
My no longer cherished,
Need we say it was not love,
Now that love is perished?
1921 *Second April*, 'Passer Mortuus Est'.

85 What lips my lips have kissed, and where, and why,
I have forgotten, and what arms have lain
Under my head till morning; but the rain
Is full of ghosts tonight, that tap and sigh
Upon the glass and listen for reply
1923 *Harp-Weaver and Other Poems*, 'Sonnet 19: What lips my lips have kissed'.

86 Thus in the winter stands the lonely tree,
Nor knows what birds have vanished one by one,
Yet knows its boughs more silent than before
1923 *Harp-Weaver and Other Poems*, 'Sonnet 19: What lips my lips have kissed'.

87 I only know that summer sang in me
A little while, that in me sings no more.
1923 *Harp-Weaver and Other Poems*, 'Sonnet 19: What lips my lips have kissed'.

88 Euclid alone
Has looked on Beauty bare. Fortunate they
Who, though once only and then but far away,
Have heard her massive sandal set on stone.
1923 *Harp-Weaver and Other Poems*, 'Sonnet 22: Euclid alone has looked on Beauty bare'.

89 Down, down, down into the darkness of the grave
Gently they go, the beautiful, the tender, the kind;
Quietly they go, the intelligent, the witty, the brave.
I know. But I do not approve. And I am not resigned.
1928 *The Buck in the Snow*, 'Dirge Without Music'.

90 It's not true that life is one damn thing after another—it's one damn thing over and over.
1930 Letter to Arthur Davison Ficke, 24 Oct.

91 Love is not all; it is not meat nor drink.
1931 *Fatal Interview*, title of poem.

92 Childhood is not from birth to a certain age and at a certain age
The child is grown, and puts away childish things.
Childhood is the kingdom where nobody dies.
Nobody that matters, that is.
1934 *Wine From These Grapes*, 'Childhood is the Kingdom where Nobody dies'.

Miller, Arthur 1915–

US playwright. *Death of a Salesman* (1949) won a Pulitzer Prize and established him as a leading contemporary playwright, dealing with the realities of family life. Subsequent plays have included *After the Fall* (1964), thought to have been inspired by his unhappy marriage to Marilyn Monroe.

93 A small man can be just as exhausted as a great man.
1949 Linda. *Death of a Salesman*, act 1.

94 Willie was a salesman. And for a salesman, there is no rock bottom to life… He's a man way out there in the blue, riding on a smile and a shoeshine. And when they start not smiling back—that's an earthquake.
1949 Charley. *Death of a Salesman*, 'Requiem'

95 A salesman is got to dream, boy. It comes with the territory.
1949 Charley. *Death of a Salesman*, 'Requiem'.

96 They believed, in short, that they held in their steady hands the candle that would light the world. We have inherited this belief, and it has helped and hurt us.
1953 Of the settlers in Salem in 1692. *The Crucible*, act 1.

97 Spare me! You forget nothin' and forgive nothin'. Learn charity, woman. I have gone tiptoe in this house all seven month since she is gone. I have not moved from there to there without I think to please you, and still an everlasting funeral marches around your heart.
1953 Proctor to Elizabeth. *The Crucible*, act 2.

98 Theology, sir, is a fortress; no crack in a fortress may be accounted small.
1953 Hale. *The Crucible*, act 2.

99 Oh, no, the machine, the machine is necessary. A man comes into a great hotel and says, I am a messenger. Who is this man? He disappears walking, there is no noise, nothing. Maybe he will never come back, maybe he will never deliver the message. But a man who rides up on a great machine, this man is responsible, this man exists. He will be given messages.
1955 Rodolpho. *A View From the Bridge*, act 1.

1 A genuine invention in the realm of ideas must first emerge as an abstruse and even partial concept… At first blush a new idea appears to be very close to insanity because to be new it must reverse important basic beliefs and assumptions which, in turn, have been

institutionalized and are administered by one or another kind of priesthood with a vested interest in an old idea.
1958 *The Collected Plays*, 'Introduction, II'.

2 A good newspaper, I suppose, is a nation talking to itself.
1961 In the *Observer*, 26 Nov.

3 How few the days are that hold the mind in place; like a tapestry hanging on four or five hooks. Especially the day you stop becoming; the day you merely are. I suppose it's when the principles dissolve, and instead of the general gray of what ought to be you begin to see what is... The word 'Now' is like a bomb through the window, and it ticks.
1964 Quentin. *After the Fall*, act 1.

4 A suicide kills two people, Maggie. That's what it's for.
1964 Quentin. *After the Fall*, act 2.

5 Part of knowing who we are is knowing we are not someone else. And Jew is only the name we give to that stranger, the agony we cannot feel, the death we look at like a cold abstraction. Each man has his Jew; it is the other.
1964 Leduc. *Incident at Vichy*, act 1.

6 The concentration camp is the final expression of human separateness and its ultimate consequence. It is organized abandonment.
1966 Interview in the *Paris Review*, Summer.

7 Success, instead of giving freedom of choice, becomes a way of life.
1966 Interview in the *Paris Review*, Summer.

8 [Plays that would] cut through time like a knife through a layer cake or a road through a mountain revealing its geologic layers.
1987 Describing the plays he always wished to write. *Timebends: A Life*.

9 Without alienation, there can be no politics.
1988 In *Marxism Today*, Jan.

10 I'm the end of the line; absurd and appalling as it may seem, serious New York theater has died in my lifetime.
1989 In *The Times*, 11 Jan.

11 Maybe all one can do is hope to end up with the right regrets.
1991 Tom. *The Ride Down Mount Morgan*, act 1.

12 Witch-hunts are always spooked by women's horrifying sexuality awakened by the superstud Devil.
1998 On President Clinton's relationship with Monica Lewinsky. In the *New York Times*, 15 Oct.

13 Mr Clinton, according to Toni Morrison, the Nobel prize-winning novelist, is our first black President, the first to come from the broken home, the alcoholic mother, the under-the-bridge shadows of our ranking system.
1998 In the *New York Times*, 15 Oct.

Miller, Henry Valentine 1891–1980

US novelist. An exile in Paris in the 1930s, he later returned to live in California. His novels, notorious for sexual explicitness, include *Tropic of Cancer* (1934) and *Tropic of Capricorn* (1939), both at one time banned in the US.

14 The wallpaper with which the men of science have covered the world of reality is falling to tatters.
1934 *The Tropic of Cancer*.

15 This is not a book in the ordinary sense of the word. No, this is a prolonged insult, a gob of spit in the face of Art, a kick in the pants to God, Man, Destiny, Time, Love, Beauty... what you will. I am going to sing for you, a little off-key perhaps, but I will sing.
1934 *Tropic of Cancer*.

16 Chaos is the score upon which reality is written.
1934 *Tropic of Cancer*.

17 Every man with a bellyful of the classics is an enemy of the human race.
1934 *Tropic of Cancer*.

18 We live in the mind, in ideas, in fragments.
1936 *Black Spring*, 'The Fourteenth Ward'.

19 There are passages of Ulysses which can be read only in the toilet—if one wants to extract the full flavour of their content.
1936 *Black Spring*, 'A Saturday Afternoon'.

20 The world is the mirror of myself dying.
1936 Black Spring, 'Third or Fourth Day of Spring'.

21 I see America as a black curse upon the world. I see a long night settling in and that mushroom which has poisoned the world withering at the roots.
1936 *Black Spring*, 'Third or Fourth Day of Spring'.

22 What does it matter how one comes by the truth so long as one pounces upon it and lives by it.
1939 *Tropic of Capricorn*.

23 The artist does not tinker with the universe; he recreates it out of his own experience and understanding of life.
1939 *The Cosmological Eye*, 'An Open Letter to Surrealists Everywhere'.

24 Example moves the world more than doctrine.
1939 *The Cosmological Eye*, 'An Open Letter to Surrealists Everywhere'.

25 Life has no other discipline to impose, if we would but realize it, than to accept life unquestioningly... Every moment is a golden one for him who has the vision to recognize it as such.
1940 *The World of Sex*.

26 Morally, spiritually, we are fettered. What have we achieved in mowing down mountain ranges, harnessing the energy of mighty rivers, or moving whole populations about like chess pieces, if we ourselves remain the same restless, miserable, frustrated creatures we were before. To call such activity progress is utter delusion.
1940 *The World of Sex*.

27 Until we do lose ourselves there is no hope of finding ourselves.
1940 *The World of Sex*.

28 All that matters is that the miraculous becomes the norm.
1940 *The World of Sex*.

29 Though I've never read a line of Homer I believe the Greek of today is essentially unchanged. If anything he is more Greek than he ever was.
1941 *The Colossus of Maroussi*, pt.1.

30 If men cease to believe that they will one day become gods then they will surely become worms.
1941 *The Colossus of Maroussi*, pt.3.

31 To live without killing is a thought which could electrify the world, if men were only capable of staying awake long enough to let the idea soak in.

1944 *Sunday After The War*, 'Reunion in Brooklyn'.

32 No man would set a word down on paper if he had the courage to live out what he believed in.
1945 *Sexus*, ch.1.

33 The world has *not* to be put in order: the world *is* order incarnate. It is for us to put ourselves in unison with this order.
1945 *Sexus*, ch.9.

34 The great joy of the artist is to become aware of a higher order of things, to recognize by the compulsive and spontaneous manipulation of his own impulses the resemblance between human creation and what is called 'divine' creation.
1945 *Sexus*, ch.9.

35 Imagination is the voice of daring. If there is anything Godlike about God it is that. He dared to imagine everything.
1945 *Sexus*, ch.14.

36 Nowhere have I encountered such a dull, monotonous fabric of life as here in America. Here boredom reaches its peak.
1945 *The Air-Conditioned Nightmare*, preface.

37 Man has demonstrated that he is master of everything—except his own nature.
1945 *The Air-Conditioned Nightmare*, 'With Edgar Varèse in the Gobi Desert'.

38 The world goes on because a few men in every generation believe in it utterly, accept it unquestioningly, underwrite it with their lives.
1945 *The Air-Conditioned Nightmare*, 'With Edgar Varèse in the Gobi Desert'.

39 Back of every creation, supporting it like an arch, is faith. Enthusiasm is nothing: it comes and goes. But if one *believes*, then miracles occur.
1945 *The Air-Conditioned Nightmare*, 'With Edgar Varèse in the Gobi Desert'.

40 The study of crime begins with the knowledge of oneself. All that you despise, all that you loathe, all that you reject, all that you condemn and seek to convert by punishment springs from you.
1945 *The Air-Conditioned Nightmare*, 'The Soul of Anaesthesia'.

41 Art is only a means to life, to the life more abundant. It is not in itself the life more abundant… In becoming an end it defeats itself.
1947 *The Wisdom of the Heart*, 'Reflections on Writing'.

42 I have always looked upon decay as being just as wonderful an expression of life as growth.
1947 *The Wisdom of the Heart*, 'Reflections on Writing'.

43 It is the creative nature of man which has refused to let him lapse back into that unconscious unity with life which characterizes the animal world from which he made his escape.
1947 *The Wisdom of the Heart*, 'Creative Death'.

44 The poem is the dream made flesh, in a two-fold sense: as work of art, and as life, which is a work of art.
1947 *The Wisdom of the Heart*, 'Creative Death'.

45 All growth is a leap in the dark, a spontaneous unpremeditated act without benefit of experience.
1947 *The Wisdom of the Heart*, 'The Absolute Collective'.

46 Life, as it is called, is for most of us one long postponement.
1947 *The Wisdom of the Heart*, 'The Enormous Womb'.

47 It is the American vice, the democratic disease which expresses its tyranny by reducing everything unique to the level of the herd.
1947 On democracy. *The Wisdom of the Heart*, 'Raimu'.

48 History is the myth, the true myth, of man's fall made manifest in time.
1949 *Plexus*, ch.12.

49 In this age, which believes that there is a short cut to everything, the greatest lesson to be learned is that the most difficult way is, in the long run, the easiest.
1951 *The Books in My Life*, preface.

50 Every genuine boy is a rebel and an anarch.
1951 *The Books in My Life*, ch.4.

51 Words divested of their magic are but dead hieroglyphs.
1951 *The Books in My Life*, ch.7.

52 If we are always arriving and departing, it is also true that we are eternally anchored. One's destination is never a place but rather a new way of looking at things.
1957 *Big Sur and the Oranges of Hieronymous Bosch*, 'The Oranges of the Millennium'.

53 We resist only what is inevitable.
1957 *Big Sur and the Oranges of Hieronymous Bosch*, 'Paradise Lost'.

54 Obscenity is a cleansing process, whereas pornography only adds to the murk.
1962 Interview in the *Paris Review*, Summer.

55 The word 'civilization' to my mind is coupled with death. When I use the word, I see civilization as a crippling, thwarting thing, a stultifying thing… Civilization is the arteriosclerosis of culture.
1962 Interview in the *Paris Review*, Summer.

56 The moment you praise a book too highly you waken a resistance in your listener.
1957 *The Books in My Life*.

57 One has to be a lowbrow, a bit of a murderer, to be a politician; ready and willing to see people sacrificed, slaughtered, for the sake of an idea—whether a good one or a bad one.
In Malcolm Crowley (ed) *Writers at Work* (1958).

Miller, Jonathan Wolfe 1934–

British stage and opera director and writer, trained as a doctor.

58 In fact, I'm not really a *Jew*. Just Jew-*ish*. Not the whole hog you know.
1960 *Beyond the Fringe*, 'Real Class'.

59 The human species is, to some extent, the result of mistakes which arrested our development and prevented us from assuming the somewhat unglamorous form of our primitive ancestors.
1977 *The Body in Question*.

60 I wasn't driven into medicine by a social conscience but by rampant curiosity.
1983 In the *Observer*, 5 Feb.

Miller, William 1810–72

Scottish poet, born in Glasgow, known as the 'Laureate of the Nursery' for his children's rhymes, of which only 'Willie Winkie' is now remembered.

61 Wee Willie Winkie rins through the toun,
Up stairs and doun stairs in his nicht-gown,
Tirling at the window, crying at the lock,
'Are the weans in their bed, for it's now ten o'clock?'
1841 'Willie Winkie', stanza 1.

Millett, Kate (Katherine) *née Murray* 1934–

US feminist critic, activist and sculptor. Her PhD thesis was published as *Sexual Politics* (1970). Other works include the autobiographical *Flying* (1974), *The Loony Bin Trip* (1991) and *Mother Millett* (2001).

62 Patriarchy's chief institution is the family. It is both a mirror of and a connection with the larger society; a patriarchal unit within a patriarchal whole.
1970 *Sexual Politics*, ch.2, 'Theory of Sexual Politics'.

63 Aren't women prudes if they don't and prostitutes if they do?
1975 Speech at the Women Writers' Conference, Los Angeles, 22 Mar.

Milligan, Spike 1918–2002

Irish humorist.

64 Money couldn't buy friends but you got a better class of enemy.
1963 *Puckoon*, ch.6.

65 I am not going to thank anybody—because I did it all myself.
1994 Acceptance speech after being awarded the British Comedy Award for Lifetime Achievement.

66 Dúirt mé leat go raibh mé breoite.
2002 Gaelic inscription on his gravestone at Winchelsea, East Sussex. English translation: I told you I was ill.

Millman, Dan 1946–

US writer, who was world trampoline champion before meeting a remarkable gas station attendant called Socrates. He now writes self-help books and runs courses helping athletes and others make the most of their potential.

67 There are no ordinary moments.
1980 *The Way of the Peaceful Warrior*.

Mills, C(harles) Wright 1916–62

US sociologist, a professor at Columbia University.

68 No social study that does not come back to the problems of biography, of history and of their intersections within a society has completed its intellectual journey.
1959 *The Sociological Imagination*, ch.1.

69 In so far as the family as an institution turns women into darling little slaves and men into their chief providers and unweaned dependents, the problem of a satisfactory marriage remains incapable of purely private solution.
1959 *The Sociological Imagination*, ch.1.

70 If everything is caused by innumerable 'factors,' then we had best be very careful in any practical actions we undertake. We must deal with many details, and so it is advisable to proceed to reform this little piece and see what happens, before we reform that little piece too.
1959 *The Sociological Imagination*, ch.4.

Mills, Irving 1884–1985

US jazz manager, music publisher and lyricist.

71 It don't mean a thing
If it ain't got that swing.
1932 Song (music by Duke Ellington).

Mills, Sir John Lewis Ernest Watts 1908–

English actor, known for his stiff-upper-lip heroes in such films as *In Which We Serve* (1942), *Scott of the Antarctic* (1948) and *The Colditz Story* (1954). He won an Academy Award for his role in *Ryan's Daughter* (1970).

72 I played the young Earl of Dudley and was beheaded in the third reel—not, in my opinion, a moment too soon.
1980 Of his role in the 1936 film *Tudor Rose*. *Up in the Clouds, Gentlemen Please*.

Milne, A(lan) A(lexander) 1882–1956

English writer. He was an editor at *Punch* and wrote comedies and light essays. His works for children, which he began writing for his son Christopher Robin, are *When We Were Very Young* (1924), *Winnie-the-Pooh* (1926), *Now We Are Six* (1927) and *The House at Pooh Corner* (1928).

73 It is impossible to win gracefully at chess. No man has yet said 'Mate!' in a voice which failed to sound to his opponent bitter, boastful and malicious.
1919 *Not That It Matters*.

74 They're changing guard at Buckingham Palace—
Christopher Robin went down with Alice.
Alice is marrying one of the guard.
'A soldier's life is terribly hard,'
Says Alice.
1924 *When We Were Very Young*, 'Buckingham Palace'.

75 Little Boy kneels at the foot of the bed,
Droops on the little hands, little gold head;
Hush! Hush! Whisper who dares!
Christopher Robin is saying his prayers.
1924 *When We Were Very Young*, 'Vespers'.

76 The King said
'Butter, eh?'
And bounced out of bed.
1924 *When We Were Very Young*, 'The King's Breakfast'.

77 I have just been thinking, and I have come to a very important decision. *These are the wrong sort of bees*.
1926 *Winnie-the-Pooh*, ch.1.

78 Would you read a Sustaining Book, such as would help and comfort a Wedged Bear in Great Tightness?
1926 Pooh, stuck in the entrance to Rabbit's house after eating too much honey. *Winnie-the-Pooh*, ch.2.

79 I am a Bear of Very Little Brain, and long words Bother me.
1926 *Winnie-the-Pooh*, ch.4.

80 'Help, help!' cried Piglet, 'a Heffalump, a Horrible Heffalump!' and he scampered off as hard as he could, still crying out, 'Help, help, a Herrible Hoffalump! Hoff, Hoff, a Hellible Horralump! Holl, Holl, a Hoffable Hellerump!'
1926 *Winnie-the-Pooh*, ch.5.

81 'I ought to say,' explained Pooh as they walked down to the shore of the island, 'that it isn't just an ordinary sort of boat. Sometimes it's a Boat, and sometimes it's more of

an Accident. It all depends.'
'Depends on what?'
'On whether I'm on the top of it or underneath it.'
1926 *Winnie-the-Pooh*, ch.9.

82 The more it
SNOWS-tiddely-pom,
The more it
GOES-tiddely-pom
The more it
GOES-tiddely-pom
On
Snowing.
1928 *The House at Pooh Corner*, ch.1.

83 'It's snowing still,' said Eeyore gloomily.
'So it is.'
'*And* freezing.'
'Is it?'
'Yes,' said Eeyore. 'However,' he said, brightening up a little, 'we haven't had an earthquake lately.'
1928 *The House at Pooh Corner*, ch.1.

84 But whatever his weight in pounds, shillings, and ounces,
He always seems bigger because of the bounces.
1928 Pooh's song about Tigger. *The House at Pooh Corner*, ch.2.

85 I could spend a happy morning
Seeing Roo,
I could spend a happy morning
Being Pooh,
For it doesn't seem to matter,
If I don't get any fatter
(And I don't get any fatter),
What I do.
1928 *The House at Pooh Corner*, ch 4

86 Then he dropped two in at once, and leant over the bridge to see which of them would come out first; and one of them did; but as they were both the same size, he didn't know if it was the one which he wanted to win, or the other one. So the next time he dropped one big one and one little one, and the big one came out first, which was what he had said it would do, and the little one came out last, which was what he had said it would do, so he had won twice… And that was the beginning of the game called Poohsticks.
1928 *The House at Pooh Corner*, ch.6.

87 But what care I? It's the game that calls me—
Simply to be on the field of play;
How can it matter what fate befalls me,
With ten good fellows and one good day!
Quoted in Helen Exley *Cricket Quotations* (1992).

88 Golf is so popular simply because it is the best game in the world at which to be bad.
Attributed.

Milner, Alfred, 1st Viscount Milner 1854–1925

English statesman. He held a succession of top administrative posts, including High Commissioner for South Africa during the Boer Wars, Secretary for War (1918–19) and Colonial Secretary (1921). He recommended virtual independence for Egypt.

89 If we believe a thing to be bad, and if we have a right to prevent it, it is our duty to try to prevent it and damn the consequences.
1909 On the blocking by the Conservative majority in the House of Lords of the Liberal Government's budget. Speech at Glasgow, Nov.

Milosevic, Slobodan 1941–

Serbian politician. He became Presdient of Serbia in 1988. In 1996 he was re-elected amidst furious accusations of electoral rigging and from 1998 onwards oversaw Serb military incursions into the province of Kosovo. This led to NATO air strikes and the establishment of a NATO-led peacekeeping force in the province, forcing a Serb withdrawal. He was defeated at the polls in 2000 by opposition candidate Vojislav Kostunica. He was subsequently indicted for crimes against humanity by the International Criminal Tribunal in the Hague and arrested in 2001 to face trial.

90 Kosovo is not a part of Serbia. It is the very heart of Serbia.
Quoted in Dusko Doder and Louise Branson *Milosevic: Portrait of a Tyrant* (1999).

91 I'm the Ayatollah Khomeini of Serbia. The Serbs will follow me no matter what!
Quoted in Dusko Doder and Louise Branson *Milosevic: Portrait of a Tyrant* (1999).

Milton, John 1608–74

English poet and controversial pamphleteerist, official apologist for the Commonwealth. Blind from 1652, he devoted himself to poetry after the Restoration. His best-known work is the religious epic *Paradise Lost* (1667), followed by *Paradise Regained* and *Samson Agonistes* (both 1671).

92 This is the month, and this the happy morn
Wherein the son of Heaven's eternal King,
Of wedded maid and virgin mother born,
Our great redemption from above did bring.
1629 'On the Morning of Christ's Nativity', 'The Hymn', stanza 1.

93 It was the winter wild
While the Heaven born child
All meanly wrapped in the rude manger lies;
Nature in awe to him
Had doffed her gaudy trim
With her great Master so to sympathize;
It was no season then for her
To wanton with the sun, her lusty paramour.
1629 'On the Morning of Christ's Nativity', 'The Hymn', stanza 3.

94 But peaceful was the night
Wherein the Prince of Light
His reign of peace upon the earth began:
The winds, with wonder whist,
Smoothly the waters kissed,
Whispering new joys to the mild oceàn,
Who now hath quite forgot to rave,
While birds of calm sit brooding on the charmèd wave.
1629 'On the Morning of Christ's Nativity', 'The Hymn', stanza 3.

95 The stars with deep amaze
Stand fixed in steadfast gaze.
1629 'On the Morning of Christ's Nativity', 'The Hymn', stanza 6.

96 Nature that heard such sound
Beneath the hollow round
Of Cynthia's seat, the airy region thrilling,
Now was almost won
To think her part was done,
And that her reign had here its last fulfilling;
She knew such harmony alone

Could hold all heaven and earth in happier uniòn.
1629 'On the Morning of Christ's Nativity', 'The Hymn', stanza 10.

97 Ring out, ye crystal spheres,
Once bless our human ears
(If ye have power to touch our senses so),
And let your silver chime
Move in melodious time,
And let the bass of Heaven's deep organ blow;
And with your ninefold harmony
Make up full consort to th'angelic symphony.
1629 'On the Morning of Christ's Nativity', 'The Hymn', stanza 13.

98 For if such holy song
Enwrap our fancy long,
Time will run back, and fetch the age of gold,
And speckled vanity
Will sicken soon and die.
1629 'On the Morning of Christ's Nativity', 'The Hymn', stanza 14.

99 The oracles are dumb;
No voice or hideous hum
Runs through the archèd roof in words deceiving.
1629 'On the Morning of Christ's Nativity', 'The Hymn', stanza 19.

1 But see! the Virgin blessed
Hath laid her Babe to rest.
Time is our tedious song should here have ending.
1629 'On the Morning of Christ's Nativity', 'The Hymn', stanza 27.

2 What needs my Shakespeare for his honoured bones
The labour of an age in pilèd stones,
Or that his hallowed relics should be hid
Under a star-y-pointing pyramid?
Dear son of memory, great heir of fame,
What need'st thou such weak witness of thy name?
Thou in our wonder and astonishment
Hast built thyself a livelong monument.
1630 'On Shakespeare'.

3 And so sepùlchered in such pomp dost lie,
That kings for such a tomb would wish to die.
1630 'On Shakespeare'.

4 Hence loathèd Melancholy,
Of Cerberus and blackest midnight born,
In Stygian cave forlorn
'Mongst horrid shapes, and shrieks, and sights unholy,
Find out some uncouth cell,
Where brooding Darkness spreads his jealous wings,
And the night-raven sings.
c.1631 *L'Allegro*, opening lines.

5 The frolic wind that breathes the spring,
Zephyr with Aurora playing,
As he met her once a-Maying,
There on beds of violets blue,
And fresh-blown roses washed in dew,
Filled her with a daughter fair,
So buxom, blithe, and debonair.
c.1631 *L'Allegro*, l.18–24. The 'daughter fair' is Euphrosyne, or Mirth, one of the Three Graces.

6 Come, and trip it as ye go
On the light fantastic toe.
c.1631 *L'Allegro*, l.33–4.

7 While the cock with lively din
Scatters the rear of darkness thin,
And to the stack or the barn door,
Stoutly struts his dames before.
c.1631 *L'Allegro*, l.49–52.

8 Straight mine eye hath caught new pleasures
Whilst the landscape round it measures,
Russet lawns and fallows grey,
Where the nibbling flocks do stray,
Mountains on whose barren breast
The labouring clouds do often rest;
Meadows trim with daisies pied,
Shallow brooks, and rivers wide.
c.1631 *L'Allegro*, l.69–76.

9 Then to the spicy nut-brown ale.
c.1631 *L'Allegro*, l.100.

10 Towered cities pleased us then,
And the busy hum of men,
Where throngs of knights and barons bold
In weeds of peace high triumphs hold,
With store of ladies, whose bright eyes
Rain influence, and judge the prize
Of wit or arms, while both contend
To win her grace, whom all commend.
c.1631 *L'Allegro*, l.117–24.

11 Such sights as youthful poets dream
On summer eves by haunted stream.
c.1631 *L'Allegro*, l.129–30.

12 Hence vain deluding Joys,
The brood of Folly without father bred,
How little you bestead,
Or fill the fixèd mind with all your toys;
Dwell in some idle brain,
And fancies fond with gaudy shapes possess,
As thick and numberless
As the gay motes that people the sunbeams.
c.1631 *Il Penseroso*, opening lines.

13 But hail thou Goddess sage and holy,
Hail, divinest Melancholy,
Whose saintly visage is too bright
To hit the sense of human sight,
And therefore to our weaker view
O'erlaid with black, staid Wisdom's hue.
c.1631 *Il Penseroso*, l.11–16.

14 There held in holy passion still,
Forget thyself to marble.
c.1631 *Il Penseroso*, l.37–8.

15 Sweet bird that shunn'st the noise of folly,
Most musical, most melancholy!
c.1631 Of the nightingale. *Il Penseroso*, l.61–2.

16 And missing thee, I walk unseen
On the dry smooth-shaven green,
To behold the wandering moon,
Riding near her highest noon,
Like one that had been led astray
Through the heaven's wide pathless way;
And oft as if her head she bowed,
Stooping through a fleecy cloud.
c.1631 *Il Penseroso*, l.65–72.

17 Where glowing embers through the room
Teach light to counterfeit a gloom,
Far from all resort of mirth.
Save the cricket on the hearth.
c.1631 *Il Penseroso*, l.79–82.

18 Or bid the soul of Orpheus sing

Such notes as, warbled to the string,
Drew iron tears down Pluto's cheek,
And made Hell grant what Love did seek.
c.1631 *Il Penseroso*, l.105–8.

19 Where more is meant than meets the ear.
c.1631 *Il Penseroso*, l.120.

20 Till civil-suited Morn appear,
Not tricked and frounced as she was wont
With the Attic boy to hunt,
But kerchiefed in a comely cloud.
c.1631 *Il Penseroso*, l.122–5.

21 There in close covert by some brook,
Where no profaner eye may look,
Hide me from day's garish eye,
While the bee with honied thigh,
That at her flowery work doth sing,
And the waters murmuring
And such consort as they keep,
Entice the dewy-feathered Sleep.
c.1631 *Il Penseroso*, l.139–46.

22 But let my due feet never fail
To walk the studious cloister's pale,
And love the high embowèd roof,
With antic pillars massy proof,
And storied windows richly dight
Casting a dim religious light.
c.1631 *Il Penseroso*, l.155–60.

23 And may at last my weary age
Find out the peaceful hermitage,
The hairy gown and mossy cell,
Where I may sit and rightly spell
Of every star that heaven doth shew,
And every herb that sips the dew,
Till old experience to attain
To something like prophetic strain.
c.1631 *Il Penseroso*, l.167–74.

24 Such sweet compulsion doth in music lie.
1633 *Arcades*.

25 Before the starry threshold of Jove's court
My mansion is, where those immortal shapes
Of bright aerial spirits live inspher'd
In regions mild of calm and serene air,
Above the smoke and stir of this dim spot,
Which men call earth.
1634 *Comus, A Mask*, opening lines.

26 All other parts remaining as they were,
And they, so perfect in their misery,
Not once perceive their foul disfigurement,
But boast themselves more comely than before
And all their friends, and native home forget
To roll with pleasure in a sensual sty.
1634 Of Odysseus's men changed to beasts by Circe. *Comus, A Mask*, l.72–7.

27 The star that bids the shepherd fold,
Now the top of heav'n doth hold,
And the gilded car of day,
His glowing axle doth allay
In the steep Atlantic stream.
1634 *Comus, A Mask*, l.93–7.

28 What hath night to do with sleep?
1634 *Comus, A Mask*, l.122.

29 Come, knit hands, and beat the ground,
In a light fantastic round.
1634 *Comus, A Mask*, l.143–4.

30 Thus I hurl
My dazzling spells into the spongy air.
1634 *Comus, A Mask*, l.153–4.

31 A thousand fantasies
Begin to throng into my memory
Of calling shapes, and beckoning shadows dire,
And airy tongues, that syllable men's names
On sands, and shores, and desert wildernesses.
1634 *Comus, A Mask*, l.204–8.

32 These thoughts may startle well, but not astound
The virtuous mind, that ever walks attended
By a strong siding champion conscience.
1634 *Comus, A Mask*, l.209–11.

33 Sweet Echo, sweetest nymph, that liv'st unseen
Within thy airy shell
By slow meander's margent green,
And in the violet-embroidered vale.
1634 *Comus, A Mask*, l.230–3.

34 How sweetly did they float upon the wings
Of silence, through the empty-vaulted night
At every fall smoothing the raven down
Of darkness till it smil'd.
1634 *Comus, A Mask*, l.248–51.

35 Virtue could see to do what Virtue would
By her own radiant light, though sun and moon
Were in the flat sea sunk. And Wisdom's self
Oft seeks to sweet retired solitude,
Where with her best nurse contemplation
She plumes her feathers, and lets grow her wings
That in the various bustle of resort
Were all too ruffl'd, and sometimes impair'd.
He that has light within his own clear breast
May sit i' the centre, and enjoy bright day,
But he that hides a dark soul, and foul thoughts
Benighted walks under the midday sun;
Himself is his own dungeon.
1634 *Comus, A Mask*, l.372–83.

36 Yet where an equal poise of hope and fear
Does arbitrate the event, my nature is
That I incline to hope, rather than fear,
And gladly banish squint suspicion.
1634 *Comus, A Mask*, l.410–13.

37 Of dire chimeras and enchanted isle
And rifted rocks whose entrance leads to Hell,——
For such there be, but unbelief is blind.
1634 *Comus, A Mask*, l.515–17.

38 A pleasing fit of melancholy.
1634 *Comus, A Mask*, l.545.

39 And filled the air with barbarous dissonance.
1634 *Comus, A Mask*, l.550.

40 I was all ear,
And took in strains that might create a soul.
Under the ribs of Death.
1634 *Comus, A Mask*, l.560–2.

41 Thou canst not touch the freedom of my mind
With all thy charms, although this corporal rind
Thou hast immanacl'd, while heav'n sees good.
1634 *Comus, A Mask*, l.663–5.

42 The unexempt condition
By which all mortal frailty must subsist,
Refreshment after toil, ease after pain.
1634 *Comus, A Mask*, l.684–6.

43 But now my task is smoothly done,
I can fly, or I can run
Quickly to the green earth's end,
Where the bow'd welkin slow doth bend,
And from thence can soar as soon
To the corners of the Moon.
1634 *Comus, A Mask*, l.1011–16.

44 Mortals that would follow me,
Love virtue, she alone is free,
She can teach ye how to climb
Higher than the sphery chime;
Or if virtue feeble were,
Heav'n itself would stoop to her.
1634 *Comus, A Mask*, l.1017–22.

45 Yet once more, O ye laurels, and once more
Ye myrtles brown, with ivy never-sere
I come to pluck your berries harsh and crude,
And with forc'd fingers rude,
Shatter your leaves before the mellowing year.
Bitter constraint, and sad occasion dear,
Compels me to disturb your season due
For Lycidas is dead, dead ere his prime
Young Lycidas, and hath not left his peer.
1637 *Lycidas*, opening lines.

46 For we were nursed upon the self-same hill,
Fed the same flock; by fountain, shade, and rill.
1637 *Lycidas*, l.23–4.

47 But O the heavy change, now thou art gone,
Now thou art gone, and never must return!
Thee shepherd, thee the woods, and desert caves,
With wild thyme and the gadding vine o'ergrown,
And all their echoes mourn.
1637 *Lycidas*, l.37–41.

48 Where were ye Nymphs when the remorseless deep
Clos'd o'er the head of your lov'd Lycidas?
1637 *Lycidas*, l.50–1.

49 Alas! What boots it with uncessant care
To tend the homely slighted Shepherd's trade,
And strictly meditate the thankless muse;
Were it not better done as others use,
To sport with Amaryllis in the shade,
Or with the tangles of Neaera's hair?
Fame is the spur that the clear spirit doth raise
(That last infirmity of noble mind)
To scorn delights, and live laborious days;
But the fair guerdon when we hope to find,
And think to burst out into sudden blaze,
Comes the blind Fury with th' abhorred shears,
And slits the thin-spun life.
1637 *Lycidas*, l.64–76.

50 Fame is no plant that grows on mortal soil.
1637 *Lycidas*, l.78.

51 Blind mouths! that scarce themselves know how to hold
A sheep-hook.
1637 *Lycidas*, l.119–20.

52 They are sped;
And when they list, their lean and flashy songs
Grate on their scrannel Pipes of wretched straw,
The hungry sheep look up, and are not fed,
But swollen with wind, and the rank mist they draw,
Rot inwardly, and foul contagion spread,
Besides what the grim wolf with privy paw
Daily devours apace, and nothing said,
But that two-handed engine at the door,
Stands ready to smite once, and smite no more.
1637 *Lycidas*, l.122–31.

53 Ye valleys low where the mild whispers use,
Of shades and wanton winds, and gushing brooks,
On whose fresh lap the swart star sparely looks,
Throw hither all your quaint enameled eyes,
That on the green turf such the honeyed showers,
And purple all the ground with vernal flowers.
1637 *Lycidas*, l.136–41.

54 Bring the rathe primrose that forsaken dies,
The tufted crow-toe, and pale gessamine,
The white pink, and the pansy freaked with jet,
The glowing violet,
The musk-rose, and the well attir'd woodbine,
With cowslips wan that hang the pensive head,
And every flower that sad embroidery wears:
Bid amaranthus all his beauty shed,
And daffadillies fill their cups with tears,
To strew the laureate hearse where Lycid lies.
1637 *Lycidas*, l.142–51. rathe = early.

55 For to interpose a little ease,
Let our frail thoughts dally with false surmise.
1637 *Lycidas*, l.152–3.

56 Look homeward Angel, now, and melt with ruth.
1637 *Lycidas*, l.163. The phrase was used by Thomas Clayton Wolfe for his 1929 novel, *Look Homeward Angel*.

57 Weep no more, woeful shepherds, weep no more,
For Lycidas your sorrow is not dead,
Sunk though he be beneath the watery floor,
So sinks the day-star in the ocean bed,
And yet anon repairs his drooping head,
And tricks his beams, and with new spangled ore,
Flames in the forehead of the morning sky:
So Lycidas sunk low, but mounted high,
Through the dear might of Him that walked the waves.
1637 *Lycidas*, l.165–73.

58 There entertain him all the saints above,
In solemn troops, and sweet societies
That sing, and singing in their glory move,
And wipe the tears for ever from his eyes.
1637 *Lycidas*, l.178–81.

59 At last he rose, and twitched his mantle blue:
Tomorrow to fresh woods, and pastures new.
1637 *Lycidas*, l.192–3.

60 This manner of writing wherein knowing myself inferior to myself… I have the use, as I may account it, but of my left hand.
1642 Of his use of prose. *The Reason of Church Government*, bk.2, introduction, 'Plans and Projects'.

61 Beholding the bright countenance of truth in the quiet and still air of delightful studies.
1642 *The Reason of Church Government*, bk.2, introduction, 'Plans and Projects'.

62 As good almost kill a man as kill a good book: who kills a

man kills a reasonable creature, God's image; but he who destroys a good book, kills reason itself, kills the image of God, as it were in the eye.
1644 *Areopagitica: a speech for the liberty of unlicensed printing.*

63 Promiscuous reading is necessary to the constituting of human nature. The attempt to keep out evil doctrine by licensing is like the exploit of that gallant man who thought to keep out the crows by shutting the park gate.
1644 *Areopagitica: a speech for the liberty of unlicensed printing.*

64 A good book is the precious life-blood of a master spirit, embalmed and treasured up on purpose to a life beyond life.
1644 *Areopagitica: a speech for the liberty of unlicensed printing.*

65 It was from out the rind of one apple tasted, that the knowledge of good and evil, as two twins cleaving together, leaped forth into the world.
1644 *Areopagitica: a speech for the liberty of unlicensed printing.*

66 Where there is much to learn, there of necessity will be much arguing, much writing, many opinions; for opinion in good men is but knowledge in the making.
1644 *Areopagitica: a speech for the liberty of unlicensed printing.*

67 As therefore the state of man now is, what wisdom can there be to choose, what continence to forbear, without the knowledge of good and evil?
1644 *Areopagitica: a speech for the liberty of unlicensed printing.*

68 Give me the liberty to know, to utter, and to argue freely according to conscience, above all liberties.
1644 *Areopagitica: a speech for the liberty of unlicensed printing.*

69 And though all the winds of doctrine were let loose to play upon the earth, so Truth be in the field, we do injuriously by licensing and prohibiting to misdoubt her strength. Let her and Falsehood grapple; who ever knew Truth put to the worse in a free and open encounter?
1644 *Areopagitica: a speech for the liberty of unlicensed printing.*

70 I cannot praise a fugitive and cloistered virtue, unexercised and unbreathed, that never sallies out and sees her adversary, but slinks out of the race where that immortal garland is to be run for, not without dust and heat. Assuredly we bring not innocence into the world, we bring impurity much rather; that which purifies us is trial, and trial is by what is contrary.
1644 *Areopagitica: a speech for the liberty of unlicensed printing.*

71 For who knows not that Truth is strong next to the Almighty? She needs no policies, nor stratagems, nor licensings to make her victorious.
1644 *Areopagitica: a speech for the liberty of unlicensed printing.*

72 That virtue therefore which is but a youngling in the contemplation of evil, and knows not the utmost that vice promises to her followers, and rejects it, is but a blank virtue, not a pure; her whiteness is but an excremental whiteness.
1644 *Areopagitica: a speech for the liberty of unlicensed printing.*

73 Since therefore the knowledge and survey of vice is in this world so necessary to the constituting of human virtue, and the scanning of error to the confirmation of truth, how can we more safely, and with less danger, scout into the regions of sin and falsity than by reading all manner of tractates and hearing all manner of reason? And this is the benefit which may be had of books promiscuously read.
1644 *Areopagitica: a speech for the liberty of unlicensed printing.*

74 When God gave [Adam] reason, he gave him freedom to choose, for reason is but choosing; he had been else a mere artificial Adam.
1644 *Areopagitica: a speech for the liberty of unlicensed printing.*

75 Wherefore did he [God] create passions within us, pleasures round about us, but that these rightly tempered are the very ingredients of virtue?
1644 *Areopagitica: a speech for the liberty of unlicensed printing.*

76 They are not skilful considerers of human things, who imagine to remove sin by removing the matter of sin.
1644 *Areopagitica: a speech for the liberty of unlicensed printing.*

77 We ourselves esteem not of that obedience, or love, or gift, which is of force: God therefore let him free, set before him a provoking object, ever almost in his eyes; herein consisted his merit, herein the right of his reward, the praise of his abstinence.
1644 *Areopagitica: a speech for the liberty of unlicensed printing.*

78 Though ye take from a covetous man all his treasure, he has yet one jewel left: ye cannot bereave him of his covetousness.
1644 *Areopagitica: a speech for the liberty of unlicensed printing.*

79 Truth indeed came once into the world with her divine Master, and was a perfect shape most glorious to look on: but…a wicked race of deceivers…took the virgin Truth, hewed her lovely form into a thousand pieces, and scattered them to the four winds. From that time ever since, the sad friends of Truth, such as durst appear, imitating the careful search that Isis made for the mangled body of Osiris, went up and down gathering up limb by limb, still as they could find them. We have not yet found them all…nor ever shall do, till her Master's second coming; he shall bring together every joint and member, and shall mould them into an immortal feature of loveliness and perfection.
1644 *Areopagitica: a speech for the liberty of unlicensed printing.*

80 Lords and Commons of England, consider what nation it is whereof ye are, and whereof ye are the governors: a nation not slow and dull, but of a quick, ingenious, and piercing spirit, acute to invent, subtle and sinewy to discourse, not beneath the reach of any point the highest that human capacity can soar to.
1644 *Areopagitica: a speech for the liberty of unlicensed printing.*

81 God is decreeing to begin some new and great period in his Church, even to the reforming of Reformation itself. What does he then but reveal Himself to his servants, and as his manner is, first to his Englishmen?
1644 *Areopagitica: a speech for the liberty of unlicensed printing.*

82 Methinks I see in my mind a noble and puissant nation rousing herself like a strong man after sleep, and shaking her invincible locks: methinks I see her as an eagle mewing her mighty youth, and kindling her undazzled eyes at the full midday beam; purging and unscaling her long-abused sight at the fountain itself of heavenly radiance; while the whole noise of timorous birds, with those also that love the twilight, flutter about, amazed at what she means.
1644 *Areopagitica: a speech for the liberty of unlicensed printing.*

83 I did but prompt the age to quit their clogs
By the known rules of ancient liberty,
When strait a barbarous noise environs me
Of owls and cuckoos, asses, apes and dogs.

c.1646 'On the Detraction Which Follow'd Upon My Writing Certain Treatises'.

84 None can love freedom heartily, but good men; the rest love not freedom, but licence.
1648–9 *The Tenure of Kings and Magistrates*.

85 No man who knows aught, can be so stupid to deny that all men naturally were born free.
1648–9 *The Tenure of Kings and Magistrates*.

86 The power of kings and magistrates is nothing else but what is only derivative; transformed and committed to them in trust from the people to the common good of them all, in whom the power yet remains fundamentally, and cannot be taken from them without a violation of their natural birthright.
1648–9 *The Tenure of Kings and Magistrates*.

87 Yet much remains
To conquer still; peace hath her victories
No less renowned then war, new foes arise
Threatening to bind our souls with secular chains:
Help us to save free conscience from the paw
Of hireling wolves whose gospel is their maw.
1652 'To the Lord General Cromwell'.

88 When I consider how my light is spent,
E're half my days, in this dark world and wide,
And that one talent which is death to hide,
Lodg'd with me useless, though my soul more bent
To serve therewith my Maker, and present
My true account, least he returning chide,
Doth God exact day-labour, light denied,
I fondly ask; But patience to prevent
That murmur, soon replies, God doth not need
Either man's work or his own gifts, who best
Bear his mild yoke, they serve him best, his state
Is kingly. Thousands at his bidding speed
And post o'er land and ocean without rest:
They also serve who only stand and wait.
c.1652 *Sonnets*, no.16, 'When I Consider'.

89 Methought I saw my late espoused Saint
Brought to me like Alcestis from the grave,
c.1658 *Sonnets*, no.19, 'Methought I Saw'.

90 But O as to embrace me she enclin'd
I wak'd, she fled, and day brought back my night.
c.1658 *Sonnets*, no.19, 'Methought I Saw'.

91 Of man's first disobedience, and the fruit
Of that forbidden tree, whose mortal taste
Brought death into the world, and all our woe,
With loss of Eden, till one greater Man
Restore us, and regain the blissful seat.
1665 *Paradise Lost* (published 1667), bk.1, opening lines.

92 Things unattempted yet in prose or rhyme.
1665 *Paradise Lost* (published 1667), bk.1, l.15.

93 And chiefly thou O spirit, that does prefer
Before all temples th'upright heart and pure,
Instruct me, for thou know'st; thou from the first
Wast present, and with mighty wings outspread
Dove-like sat'st brooding on the vast abyss
And mad'st it pregnant: what in me is dark
Illumine, what is low raise and support;
That to the highth of this great argument
I may assert Eternal Providence,
And justify the ways of God to men.
1665 *Paradise Lost* (published 1667), bk.1, l.16–25.

94 Who first seduced them to that foul revolt?
1665 *Paradise Lost* (published 1667), bk.1, l.33.

95 Him the Almighty Power
Hurled headlong flaming from th' ethereal sky
With hideous ruin and combustion down
To bottomless perdition, there to dwell
In adamantine chains and penal fire.
1665 *Paradise Lost* (published 1667), bk.1, l.44–8.

96 Now the thought
Both of lost happiness and lasting pain
Torments him.
1665 Of Satan. *Paradise Lost* (published 1667), bk.1, l.54–6.

97 A dungeon horrible, on all sides round
As one great furnace flamed; yet from those flames
No light, but rather darkness visible
Served only to discover sights of woe,
Regions of sorrow, doleful shades, where peace
And rest can never dwell, hope never comes
That comes to all.
1665 Of Hell. *Paradise Lost* (published 1667), bk.1, l.61–7.

98 O how fall'n! how changed
From him, who in the happy realms of light
Clothed with transcendent brightness didst outshine
Myriads though bright.
1665 Of Satan. *Paradise Lost* (published 1667), bk.1, l.84–7.

99 United thoughts and counsels, equal hope
And hazard in the glorious enterprise.
1665 *Paradise Lost* (published 1667), bk.1, l.88–9.

1 What though the field be lost?
All is not lost; the unconquerable will,
And study of revenge, immortal hate,
And courage never to submit or yield.
1665 Satan addressing the fallen angels. *Paradise Lost* (published 1667), bk.1, l.105–8.

2 Vaunting aloud, but racked with deep despair.
1665 *Paradise Lost* (published 1667), bk.1, l.126.

3 To be weak is miserable
Doing or suffering, but of this be sure,
To do aught good never will be our task,
But ever to do ill our sole delight.
1665 *Paradise Lost* (published 1667), bk.1, l.157–60.

4 If then his providence
Out of our evil seek to bring forth good,
Our labour must be to pervert that end,
And out of good still to find means of evil.
1665 *Paradise Lost* (published 1667), bk.1, l.162–5.

5 What reinforcement we may gain from hope;
If not, what resolution from despair.
1665 *Paradise Lost* (published 1667), bk.1, l.190–1.

6 Forthwith upright he rears from off the pool
His mighty stature; on each hand the flames
Driv'n backward slope their pointing spires, and rolled
In billows, leave i' th' midst a horrid vale.
1665 Of Satan. *Paradise Lost* (published 1667), bk.1, l.221.

7 The mind is its own place, and in itself
Can make a heav'n of hell, a hell of heav'n.
1665 *Paradise Lost* (published 1667), bk.1, l.254–5.

8 Better to reign in hell, than serve in heav'n.
1665 Satan. *Paradise Lost* (published 1667), bk.1, l.263.

9 For Spirits when they please
Can either sex assume, or both; so soft
And uncompounded is their essence pure,
Not tied or manacled with joint or limb,
Nor founded on the brittle strength of bones,
Like cumbrous flesh; but in what shape they choose
Dilated or condensed, bright or obscure,
Can execute their airy purposes,
And works of love or enmity fulfil.
1665 *Paradise Lost* (published 1667), bk.1, l.423–31.

10 And when night
Darkens the streets, then wander forth the sons
Of Belial, flown with insolence and wine.
1665 *Paradise Lost* (published 1667), bk.1, l.500–2.

11 With high words, that bore
Semblance of worth, not substance, gently raised
Their fainting courage, and dispelled their fears.
1665 *Paradise Lost* (published 1667), bk.1, l.528–30.

12 A shout that tore hell's concave, and beyond
Frighted the reign of Chaos and old Night.
1665 *Paradise Lost* (published 1667), bk.1, l.542–3.

13 For who can yet believe, though after loss,
That all these puissant legions, whose exile
Hath emptied heav'n, shall fail to reascend
Self-raised, and repossess their native seat?
1665 *Paradise Lost* (published 1667), bk.1, l.631–4.

14 Who overcomes
By force, hath overcome but half his foe.
1665 *Paradise Lost* (published 1667), bk.1, l.648–9.

15 War then, war
Open or understood must be resolved.
1665 Satan. *Paradise Lost* (published 1667), bk.1, l.661–2.

16 Let none admire
That riches grow in hell; that soil may best
Deserve the precious bane.
1665 *Paradise Lost* (published 1667), bk.1, l.690–2.

17 Pandemonium, the high capital
Of Satan and his peers.
1665 *Paradise Lost* (published 1667), bk.1, l.756–7.

18 Satan exalted sat, by merit raised
To that bad eminence; and from despair
Thus high uplifted beyond hope.
1665 *Paradise Lost* (published 1667), bk.2, l.5–7.

19 Where there is then no good
For which to strive, no strife can grow up there
From faction; for none sure will claim in hell
Precédence, none, whose portion is so small
Of present pain, that with ambitious mind
Will covet more.
1665 Satan. *Paradise Lost* (published 1667), bk.2, l.30–5.

20 His trust was with the eternal to be deemed
Equal in strength, and rather than be less
Cared not to be at all; with that care lost
Went all his fear.
1665 Of Moloch. *Paradise Lost* (published 1667), bk.2, l.46–9.

21 He seemed
For dignity composed and high exploit:
But all was false and hollow; though his tongue
Dropped manna, and could make the worse appear
The better reason.
1665 Of Belial. *Paradise Lost* (published 1667), bk.2, l.110–14.

22 To be no more; sad cure; for who would lose,
Though full of pain, this intellectual being,
Those thoughts that wander through eternity,
To perish rather, swallowed up and lost
In the wide womb of uncreated night,
Devoid of sense and motion?
1665 Belial. *Paradise Lost* (published 1667), bk.2, l.146–51.

23 Thus Belial with words clothed in reason's garb
Counselled ignoble ease, and peaceful sloth,
Not peace.
1665 *Paradise Lost* (published 1667), bk.2, l.226–8.

24 Our torments also may in length of time
Become our elements, these piercing fires
As soft as now severe, our temper changed
Into their temper.
1665 Mammon. *Paradise Lost* (published 1667), bk.2, l.274–7.

25 There is a place
(If ancient and prophetic fame in heav'n
Err not) another world, the happy seat
Of some new race called Man.
1665 Beelzebub. *Paradise Lost* (published 1667), bk.2, l.345–8.

26 This would surpass
Common revenge.
1665 Beelzebub speaking of the plan to tempt Man away from God. *Paradise Lost* (published 1667), bk.2, l.370–1.

27 When his darling sons
Hurled headlong to partake with us, shall curse
Their frail original, and faded bliss,
Faded so soon.
1665 Beelzebub. *Paradise Lost* (published 1667), bk.2, l.373–6.

28 Who shall tempt with wand'ring feet
The dark unbottomed infinite abyss
And through the palpable obscure find out
His uncouth way, or spread his aery flight
Upborne with indefatigable wings
Over the vast abrupt, ere he arrive
The happy isle.
1665 Beelzebub. *Paradise Lost* (published 1667), bk.2, l.404–10.

29 Long is the way
And hard, that out of hell leads up to light.
1665 *Paradise Lost* (published 1667), bk.2, l.432–3.

30 O shame to men! Devil with devil damned
Firm concord holds, men only disagree
Of creatures rational.
1665 *Paradise Lost* (published 1667), bk.2, l.496–8.

31 Meanwhile the Adversary of God and man,
Satan with thoughts inflamed of highest design,
Puts on swift wings, and towards the gates of hell
Explores his solitary flight.
1665 *Paradise Lost* (published 1667), bk.2, l.629–32.

32 Chaos umpire sits,
And by decision more embroils the fray
By which he reigns; next him high arbiter
Chance governs all.
1665 *Paradise Lost* (published 1667), bk.2, l.681–4.

33 Whence and what art thou, execrable shape?
1665 *Paradise Lost* (published 1667), bk.2, l.681.

34 A race of upstart creatures.
1665 Satan speaks to his daughter, Sin, of Man. *Paradise Lost* (published 1667), bk.2, l.834.

35 And fast by hanging in a golden chain

This pendent world.
1665 *Paradise Lost* (published 1667), bk.2, l.1051–2.

36 Hail holy Light, offspring of Heav'n first-born.
Bright effluence of bright essence increate.
1665 *Paradise Lost* (published 1667), bk.3, l.5–6.

37 Thee I revisit safe,
And feel thy sovran vital lamp; but thou
Revisit'st not these eyes, that roll in vain
To find thy piercing ray, and find no dawn;
So thick a drop serene hath quenched their orbs,
Or dim suffusion veiled.
1665 Of his blindness. *Paradise Lost* (published 1667), bk.3, l.22–7.

38 Thus with the year
Seasons return, but not to me returns
Day, or the sweet approach of ev'n or morn,
Or sight of vernal bloom, or summer's rose,
Or flocks, or herds, of human face divine;
But cloud instead, and ever-during dark
Surrounds me, from the cheerful ways of men
Cut off, and for the book of knowledge fair
Presented with a universal blank
Of nature's works to me expunged and razed,
And wisdom at one entrance quite shut out.
1665 *Paradise Lost* (published 1667), bk.3, l.40–50.

39 Our two first parents, yet the only two
Of mankind, in the happy garden placed,
Reaping immortal fruits of joy and love,
Uninterrupted joy, unrivalled love
In blissful solitude.
1665 *Paradise Lost* (published 1667), bk.3, l.65–9.

40 So bent he seems
On desperate revenge, that shall redound
Upon his own rebellious head.
1665 Of Satan. *Paradise Lost* (published 1667), bk.3, l.84–6.

41 Whose fault?
Whose but his own? Ingrate, he had of me
All he could have; I made him just and right,
Sufficient to have stood, though free to fall.
1665 God speaking of Satan. *Paradise Lost* (published 1667), bk.3, l.96–9.

42 Freely they stood who stood, and fell who fell.
1665 *Paradise Lost* (published 1667), bk.3, l.102.

43 I formed them free, and free they must remain,
Till they enthrall themselves
1665 *Paradise Lost* (published 1667), bk.3, l.124–5.

44 And I will place within them as a guide
My umpire conscience, whom if they will hear
Light after light well used they shall attain,
And to the end persisting, safe arrive.
1665 *Paradise Lost* (published 1667), bk.3, l.194–7.

45 Die he or justice must.
1665 *Paradise Lost* (published 1667), bk.3, l.210.

46 Behold me then, me for him, life for life
I offer, on me let thine anger fall;
Account me man; I for his sake will leave
Thy bosom, and this glory next to thee
Freely put off, and for him lastly die
Well pleased, on me let Death wreck all his rage.
1665 Christ speaking to God. *Paradise Lost* (published 1667), bk.3, l.236–241.

47 O thou
My sole complacence!
1665 God speaking to Christ. *Paradise Lost* (published 1667), bk.3, l.275–6.

48 So on this windy sea of land, the Fiend
Walked up and down alone bent on his prey.
1665 *Paradise Lost* (published 1667), bk.3, l.440–1.

49 Into a limbo large and broad, since called
The Paradise of Fools, to few unknown.
1665 *Paradise Lost* (published 1667), bk.3, l.495–6.

50 The pure marble air.
1665 *Paradise Lost* (published 1667), bk.3, l.564.

51 For neither man nor angel can discern
Hypocrisy, the only evil that walks
Invisible, except to God alone,
By his permissive will, through heav'n and earth.
1665 *Paradise Lost* (published 1667), bk.3, l.681–4.

52 Horror and doubt distract
His troubled thoughts, and from the bottom stir
The hell within him, for within him hell
He brings, and round about him, nor from hell
One step no more than from himself can fly.
1665 Of Satan. *Paradise Lost* (published 1667), bk.4, l.18–22.

53 Now conscience wakes despair
That slumbered, wakes the bitter memory
Of what he was, what is, and what must be
Worse; of worse deeds worse sufferings must ensue.
1665 Of Satan. *Paradise Lost* (published 1667), bk.4, l.23–6.

54 A grateful mind
By owing owes not, but still pays, at once
Indebted and discharged; what burden then?
1665 *Paradise Lost* (published 1667), bk.4, l.55–7.

55 Which way I fly is hell; myself am hell;
And in the lowest deep a lower deep
Still threat'ning to devour me opens wide,
To which the hell I suffer seems a heav'n.
1665 Satan. *Paradise Lost* (published 1667), bk.4, l.75–8.

56 The lower still I fall, only supreme
In misery; such joy ambition finds.
1665 Satan. *Paradise Lost* (published 1667), bk.4, l.91–2.

57 For never can true reconcilement grow
Where wounds of deadly hate have pierced so deep.
1665 Satan. *Paradise Lost* (published 1667), bk.4, l.98–9.

58 So clomb this first grand thief into God's fold:
So since into his church lewd hirelings climb.
Thence up he flew, and on the Tree of Life,
The middle tree and highest there that grew,
Sat like a cormorant.
1665 Of Satan. *Paradise Lost* (published 1667), bk.4, l.192–6.

59 Out of the fertile ground he caused to grow
All trees of noblest kind for sight, smell, taste;
And all amid them stood the Tree of Life,
High eminent, blooming ambrosial fruit
Of vegetable gold; and next to life
Our death the Tree of Knowledge grew fast by,
Knowledge of good bought dear by knowing ill.
1665 *Paradise Lost* (published 1667), bk.4, l.218–24.

60 Flowers of all hue, and without thorn the rose.
1665 *Paradise Lost* (published 1667), bk.4, l.256.

61 Two of far nobler shape erect and tall,

God-like erect, with native honor clad
In naked majesty seemed lords of all.
1665 Of Adam and Eve. *Paradise Lost* (published 1667), bk.4, l.288–90.

62 Though both
Not equal, as their sex not equal seemed;
For contemplation he and valour formed,
For softness she and sweet attractive grace,
He for God only, she for God in him.
1665 Of Adam and Eve. *Paradise Lost* (published 1667), bk.4, l.295–9.

63 Yielded with coy submission, modest pride,
And sweet reluctant amorous delay.
1665 Of Eve. *Paradise Lost* (published 1667), bk.4, l.310–11.

64 Ah gentle pair, ye little think how nigh
Your change approaches, when all these delights
Will vanish and deliver ye to woe,
More woe, the more your taste is now of joy.
1665 *Paradise Lost* (published 1667), bk.4, l.366–9.

65 Sole partner and sole part of all these joys.
1665 Adam to Eve. *Paradise Lost* (published 1667), bk.4, l.411.

66 These two
Emparadised in one another's arms
The happier Eden, shall enjoy their fill
Of bliss on bliss.
1665 Of Adam and Eve. *Paradise Lost* (published 1667), bk.4, l.505–8.

67 Man hath his daily work of body or mind
Appointed, which declares his dignity,
And the regard of Heav'n on all his ways.
1665 Adam to Eve. *Paradise Lost* (published 1667), bk.4, l.618–20.

68 God is thy law, thou mine: to know no more
Is woman's happiest knowledge and her praise.
With thee conversing I forget all time.
1665 Eve to Adam. *Paradise Lost* (published 1667), bk.4, l.637–9.

69 Millions of spiritual creatures walk the earth
Unseen, both when we wake, and when we sleep.
1665 *Paradise Lost* (published 1667), bk.4, l.677–8.

70 Iris all hues, roses, and jessamine
Reared high their flourished heads between, and wrought
Mosaic; underfoot the violet,
Crocus, and hyacinth with rich inlay
Broidered the ground, more coloured than with stone
Of costliest emblem: other creature here
Beast, bird, insect, or worm durst enter none;
Such was their awe of man.
1665 *Paradise Lost* (published 1667), bk.4, l.698–705.

71 Nor turned I ween
Adam from his fair spouse, nor Eve the rites
Mysterious of connubial love refused:
Whatever hypocrites austerely talk
Of purity and place and innocence,
Defaming as impure what God declares
Pure, and commands to some, leaves free to all.
1665 *Paradise Lost* (published 1667), bk.4, l.741–7.

72 Hail, wedded love, mysterious law, true source
Of human offspring, sole propriety
In Paradise of all things common else.
1665 *Paradise Lost* (published 1667), bk.4, l.750–2.

73 Him there they found
Squat like a toad, close at the ear of Eve.
1665 *Paradise Lost* (published 1667), bk.4, l.799–800.

74 When I am thy captive talk of chains,
Proud limitary cherub.
1665 *Paradise Lost* (published 1667), bk.4, l.970–1.

75 But wherefore thou alone? Wherefore with thee
Came not all hell broke loose?
1665 *Paradise Lost* (published 1667), bk.4, l.917–18.

76 My fairest, my espoused, my latest found,
Heav'n's last best gift, my ever new delight.
1665 Adam to Eve. *Paradise Lost* (published 1667), bk.5, l.18–19.

77 Best image of myself and dearer half.
1665 Adam to Eve. *Paradise Lost* (published 1667), bk.5, l.95.

78 Nor jealousy
Was understood, the injured lover's hell.
1665 *Paradise Lost* (published 1667), bk.5, l.449–50.

79 In contemplation of created things
By steps we may ascend to God.
1665 Adam to Raphael. *Paradise Lost* (published 1667), bk.5, l.511–12.

80 God made thee perfect, not immutable.
1665 Raphael to Adam. *Paradise Lost* (published 1667), bk.5, l.524.

81 Hear all ye angels, progeny of light,
Thrones, dominations, princedoms, virtues, powers.
1665 *Paradise Lost* (published 1667), bk.5, l.600–1.

82 All seemed well pleased, all seemed, but were not all.
1665 *Paradise Lost* (published 1667), bk.5, l.616.

83 Servant of God, well done, well hast thou fought
The better fight.
1665 God to his faithful angels. *Paradise Lost* (published 1667), bk.6, l.29–30.

84 Proud, art thou met?
1665 Abdiel to Satan. *Paradise Lost* (published 1667), bk.6, l.131.

85 This is servitude,
To serve th' unwise, or him who hath rebelled
Against his worthier, as thine now serve thee,
Thyself not free, but to thyself enthralled.
1665 Abdiel to Satan. *Paradise Lost* (published 1667), bk.6, l.178–81.

86 But pain is perfect misery, the worst
Of evils, and excessive, overturns
All patience.
1665 *Paradise Lost* (published 1667), bk.6, l.461–3.

87 On war and mutual slaughter bent.
1665 Of Mankind. *Paradise Lost* (published 1667), bk.6, l.506.

88 Headlong themselves they threw
Down from the verge of heaven, eternal wrath
Burnt after them to the bottomless pit.
1665 Pursued to the wall of Heaven by the Messiah, Satan and his rebelling angels fall to their punishment as the wall opens. *Paradise Lost* (published 1667), bk.6, l.864–6.

89 Standing on earth, not rapt above the pole,
More safe I sing with mortal voice, unchanged
To hoarse or mute, though fall'n on evil days,
On evil days though fallen, and evil tongues.
1665 *Paradise Lost* (published 1667), bk.7, l.23–6.

90 But knowledge is as food, and needs no less
Her temperance over appetite, to know

In measure what the mind may well contain,
Oppresses else with surfeit, and soon turns
Wisdom to folly, as nourishment to wind.
1665 *Paradise Lost* (published 1667), bk.7, l.126–30.

91 Necessity and chance
Approach not me, and what I will is fate.
1665 God. *Paradise Lost* (published 1667), bk.7, l.172–3.

92 He took the golden compasses, prepared
In God's eternal store, to circumscribe
This universe, and all created things:
One foot he centred, and the other turned
Round through the vast profundity obscure,
And said, 'Thus far extend, thus far thy bounds
This be thy just circumference, O world.'
1665 *Paradise Lost* (published 1667), bk.7, l.225–31.

93 And the earth self-balanced on her centre hung.
1665 *Paradise Lost* (published 1667), bk.7, l.242.

94 The great creator from his work returned
Magnificent, his six days' work, a world.
1665 *Paradise Lost* (published 1667), bk.7, l.567–8.

95 Witness this new-made world, another heav'n
From heaven gate not far, founded in view
On the clear hyaline, the glassy sea;
Of amplitude almost immense, with stars
Numerous, and every star perhaps a world
Of destined habitation.
1665 *Paradise Lost* (published 1667), bk.7, l.617–22.

96 O when meet now
Such pairs, in love and mutual honour joined?
1665 *Paradise Lost* (published 1667), bk.8, l.57–8.

97 He his fabric of the heavens
Hath left to their disputes, perhaps to move
His laughter at their quaint opinions wide
Hereafter, when they come to model heaven
And calculate the stars, how they will wield
The mighty frame, how build, unbuild, contrive
To save appearances, how gird the sphere
With centric and eccentric scribbled o'er,
Cycle and epicycle, orb in orb.
1665 *Paradise Lost* (published 1667), bk.8, l.76–84.

98 Heaven is for thee too high
To know what passes there; be lowly wise:
Think only what concerns thee and thy being.
Dream not of other worlds, what creatures there
Live, in what state, condition, or degree,
Contented that thus far hath been revealed
Not of earth only but of highest heav'n.
1665 Raphael to Adam. *Paradise Lost* (published 1667), bk.8, l.172–8.

99 For man to tell how human life began
Is hard; for who himself beginning knew?
1665 Adam to Raphael. *Paradise Lost* (published 1667), bk.8, l.250–1.

1 In solitude
What happiness, who can enjoy alone,
Or all enjoying, what contentment find?
1665 Adam. *Paradise Lost* (published 1667), bk.8, l.364–6.

2 Among unequals what society
Can sort, what harmony or true delight?
1665 Adam. *Paradise Lost* (published 1667), bk.8, l.383–4.

3 Yet when I approach
Her loveliness, so absolute she seems
And in herself complete, so well to know
Her own, that what she wills to do or say,
Seems wisest, virtuousest, discreetest, best.
1665 Adam speaking of Eve. *Paradise Lost* (published 1667), bk.8, l.546–50.

4 All higher knowledge in her presence falls
Degraded, wisdom in discourse with her
Loses discount'nanced, and like folly shows.
1665 Adam speaking of Eve. *Paradise Lost* (published 1667), bk.8, l.551–3.

5 Love refines
The thoughts, and heart enlarges, hath his seat
In reason, and is judicious, is the scale
By which to heav'nly love thou may'st ascend,
Not sunk in carnal pleasure, for which cause
Among the beasts no mate for thee was found.
1665 Raphael to Adam. *Paradise Lost* (published 1667), bk.8, l.589–94.

6 My celestial patroness, who deigns
Her nightly visitation unimplored,
And dictates to me slumbering, or inspires
Easy my unpremeditated verse:
Since first this subject for heroic song
Pleased me long choosing, and beginning late.
1665 *Paradise Lost* (published 1667), bk.9, l.21–6.

7 And the more I see
Pleasures about me, so much more I feel
Torment within me.
1665 Satan. *Paradise Lost* (published 1667), bk.9, l.119–21.

8 This man of clay, son of despite.
1665 Satan speaking of Adam. *Paradise Lost* (published 1667), bk.9, l.176.

9 For nothing lovelier can be found
In woman, than to study household good,
And good works in her husband to promote.
1665 Adam to Eve. *Paradise Lost* (published 1667), bk.9, l.232–4.

10 For solitude sometimes is best society,
And short retirement urges sweet return.
1665 *Paradise Lost* (published 1667), bk.9, l.249–50.

11 That space the Evil One abstracted stood
From his own evil, and for the time remained
Stupidly good, of enmity disarmed,
Of guile, of hate, of envy, of revenge.
1665 Satan gazes upon Eve. *Paradise Lost* (published 1667), bk.9, l.463–6.

12 She fair, divinely fair, fit love for gods.
1665 Satan speaking of Eve. *Paradise Lost* (published 1667), bk.9, l.489.

13 Her rash hand in evil hour
Forth reaching to the fruit, she plucked, she ate:
Earth felt the wound, and nature from her seat
Sighing through all her works gave signs of woe,
That all was lost.
1665 *Paradise Lost* (published 1667), bk.9, l.781–5.

14 O fairest of creation, last and best
Of all God's works, creature in whom excelled
Whatever can to sight or thought be formed,
Holy, divine, good, amiable, or sweet!
How art thou lost, how on a sudden lost,
Defaced, deflow'red, and now to death devote?

1665 Adam to Eve. *Paradise Lost* (published 1667), bk.9, l.896–91.

15 Flesh of flesh,
Bone of my bone thou art, and from thy state
Mine never shall be parted, bliss or woe.
1665 Adam to Eve. *Paradise Lost* (published 1667), bk.9, l.914–16.

16 What thou art is mine;
Our state cannot be severed, we are one,
One flesh; to lose thee were to lose my self.
1665 Adam to Eve. *Paradise Lost* (published 1667), bk.9, l.957–9.

17 Linked in love so dear,
To undergo with me one guilt, one crime,
If any be, of tasting this fair fruit.
1665 Eve to Adam. *Paradise Lost* (published 1667), bk.9, l.970–2.

18 As with new wine intoxicated both
They swim in mirth, and fancy that they feel
Divinity within them breeding wings
Wherewith to scorn the earth.
1665 *Paradise Lost* (published 1667), bk.9, l.1007–10.

19 Thus they in mutual accusation spent
The fruitless hours, but neither self-condemning,
And of their vain contést appeared no end.
1665 *Paradise Lost* (published 1667), bk.9, l.1187–9.

20 Yet I shall temper so
Justice with mercy.
1665 *Paradise Lost* (published 1667), bk.10, l.77–8.

21 Love was not in their looks, either to God
Or to each other.
1665 *Paradise Lost* (published 1667), bk.10, l.111–12.

22 Adorned
She was indeed, and lovely to attract
Thy love, not thy subjection.
1665 Christ speaking to Adam of Eve. *Paradise Lost* (published 1667), bk.10, l.151–3.

23 Now possess,
As lords, a spacious world, to our native heaven
Little inferior, by my adventure hard
With peril great achieved.
1665 Satan, returning triumphantly from Earth to Hell after tempting Eve. *Paradise Lost* (published 1667), bk.10, l.466–9.

24 He hears
On all sides, from innumerable tongues
A dismal universal hiss, the sound
Of public scorn.
1665 Satan and the rebel angels are turned to snakes. *Paradise Lost* (published 1667), bk.10, l.506–9.

25 O fleeting joys
Of Paradise, dear bought with lasting woes!
1665 Adam's lament. *Paradise Lost* (published 1667), bk.10, l.741–2.

26 But say
That death be not one stroke, as I supposed,
Bereaving sense, but endless misery
From this day onward, which I feel begun
Both in me, and without me, and so last
To perpetuity; ay me, that fear
Comes thund'ring back with dreadful revolution
On my defenceless head; both Death and I
Am found eternal, and incorporate both,
Nor I on my part single, in me all
Posterity stands cursed: fair patrimony
That I must leave ye, sons; O were I able
To waste it all myself, and leave ye none!
1665 Adam muses on death. *Paradise Lost* (published 1667), bk.10, l.808–20.

27 O why did God,
Creator wise, that peopled highest heav'n
With Spirits masculine, create at last
This novelty on earth, this fair defect
Of nature, and not fill the world at once
With men as angels without feminine,
Or find some other way to generate
Mankind?
1665 Adam speaking of Eve. *Paradise Lost* (published 1667), bk.10, l.888–95.

28 Let us seek Death, or he not found, supply
With our own hands his office on ourselves;
Why stand we longer shivering under fears,
That show no end but death, and have the power,
Of many ways to die the shortest choosing,
Destruction with destruction to destroy.
1665 Eve. *Paradise Lost* (published 1667), bk.10, l.1001–6.

29 So send them forth, though sorrowing, yet in peace.
1665 God speaking to Michael of Adam and Eve. *Paradise Lost* (published 1667), bk.11, l.117.

30 Moping melancholy
And moon-struck madness.
Michael shows Adam a vision of what will happen before the Flood. *Paradise Lost* (published 1667), bk.11, l.485–6.

31 So may'st thou live, till like ripe fruit thou drop
Into thy mother's lap, or be with ease
Gathered, not harshly plucked, for death mature:
This is old age; but then thou must outlive
Thy youth, thy strength, thy beauty, which will change
To withered weak and grey.
1665 Michael to Adam. *Paradise Lost* (published 1667), bk.11, l.535–40.

32 Nor love thy life, nor hate; but what thou liv'st
Live well, how long or short permit to heaven.
1665 *Paradise Lost* (published 1667), bk.11, l.553–4.

33 Now I see
Peace to corrupt no less than war to waste.
1665 *Paradise Lost* (published 1667), bk.11, l.783–4.

34 O goodness infinite, goodness immense!
That all this good of evil shall produce,
And evil turn to good; more wonderful
Than that which by creation first brought forth
Light out of darkness!
1665 Adam to Michael. *Paradise Lost* (published 1667), bk.12, l.470–4.

35 This having learnt, thou hast attained the sum
Of wisdom; hope no higher, though all the stars
Thou knew'st by name, and all th'ethereal powers,
All secrets of the deep, all nature's works,
Or works of God in heav'n, air, earth, or sea,
And all the riches of this world enjoy'dst,
And all the rule, one empire; only add
Deeds to thy knowledge answerable, add faith,
Add virtue, patience, temperance, add love,
By name to come called charity, the soul
Of all the rest: then wilt thou not be loath
To leave this Paradise, but shalt possess

A paradise within thee, happier far.
1665 Michael to Adam. *Paradise Lost* (published 1667), bk.12, l.575–87.

36 Let us descend now therefore from this top
Of speculation.
1665 *Paradise Lost* (published 1667), bk.12, l.588–9.

37 Some natural tears they dropped, but wiped them soon;
The world was all before them, where to choose
Their place of rest, and Providence their guide:
They hand in hand with wand'ring steps and slow,
Through Eden took their solitary way.
1665 *Paradise Lost* (published 1667), bk.12, l.645–9.

38 For what can I increase
Or multiply, but curses on my head?
1665 Adam's lament. *Paradise Lost* (published 1667), bk.10, l.731–2.

39 Skill'd to retire, and in retiring draw
Hearts after them tangled in amorous nets.
1671 *Paradise Regained*, bk.2, l.161–2.

40 The childhood shows the man,
As morning shows the day. Be famous then
By wisdom; as thy empire must extend,
So let extend thy mind o'er all the world.
1671 *Paradise Regained*, bk.4, l.220–3.

41 The first and wisest of them all professed
To know this only, that he nothing knew.
1671 Of Socrates. *Paradise Regained*, bk.4, l.293–4.

42 Athens, the eye of Greece, mother of arts
And eloquence, native to famous wits
1671 *Paradise Regained*, bk.4, l.240–1.

43 Who reads
Incessantly, and to his reading brings not
A spirit and judgement equal or superior
(And what he brings, what needs he elsewhere seek?)
Uncertain and unsettled still remains,
Deep-versed in books and shallow in himself.
1671 *Paradise Regained*, bk.4, l.322–7.

44 But here I feel amends,
The breath of Heav'n fresh-blowing, pure and sweet,
With day-spring born; here leave me to respire.
1671 *Samson Agonistes*, l.9–11.

45 Ask for this great deliverer now, and find him
Eyeless in Gaza at the mill with slaves.
1671 *Samson Agonistes*, l.40–1.

46 O impotence of mind, in body strong!
But what is strength without a double share
Of wisdom, vast, unwieldy, burdensome,
Proudly secure, yet liable to fall
By weakest subtleties, not made to rule,
But to subserve where wisdom bears command.
1671 *Samson Agonistes*, l.52–7.

47 O loss of sight, of thee I most complain!
Blind among enemies, O worse than chains,
Dungeon, or beggary, or decrepit age!
Light the prime work of God to me is extinct,
And all her various objects of delight
Annull'd, which might in part my grief have eas'd,
Inferior to the vilest now become
Of man or worm; the vilest here excel me,
They creep, yet see, I dark in light expos'd
To daily fraud, contempt, abuse and wrong,
Within doors, or without, still as a fool,
In power of others, never in my own;
Scarce half I seem to live, dead more than half.
1671 *Samson Agonistes*, l.67–79.

48 If it be true
That light is in the soul,
She all in every part; why was the sight
To such a tender ball as th' eye confin'd?
1671 *Samson Agonistes*, l.91–4.

49 To live a life half dead, a living death.
1671 *Samson Agonistes*, l.100.

50 Thou art become (O worst imprisonment!)
The Dungeon of thy self.
1671 *Samson Agonistes*, l.155–6.

51 Salve to thy sores, apt words have power to suage
The tumours of a troubl'd mind,
And are as Balm to fester'd wounds.
1671 *Samson Agonistes*, l.184–6.

52 Just are the ways of God,
And justifiable to men;
Unless there be who think not God at all.
1671 *Samson Agonistes*, l.293–5.

53 So much I feel my genial spirits droop,
My hopes all flat, nature within me seems
In her functions weary of herself.
1671 *Samson Agonistes*, l.594–6.

54 My race of glory run, and race of shame,
And I shall shortly be with them that rest.
1671 *Samson Agonistes*, l.597–8.

55 God of our Fathers, what is man!
That thou towards him with hand so various,
Or might I say contrarious,
Temperst thy providence through his short course,
Not evenly, as thou rul'st
The angelic orders and inferior creatures mute,
Irrational and brute.
1671 *Samson Agonistes*, l.667–73.

56 That grounded maxim
So rife and celebrated in the mouths
Of wisest men; that to the public good
Private respects must yield.
1671 *Samson Agonistes*, l.865–8.

57 In argument with men a woman ever
Goes by the worse, whatever be her cause.
1671 *Samson Agonistes*, l.903–4.

58 At distance I forgive thee, go with that.
1671 *Samson Agonistes*, l.954.

59 Yet beauty, though injurious, hath strange power,
After offence returning, to regain
Love once possessed.
1671 *Samson Agonistes*, l.1003–5.

60 Love-quarrels oft in pleasing concord end.
1671 *Samson Agonistes*, l.1008.

61 Lords are lordliest in their wine.
1671 *Samson Agonistes*, l.1418.

62 Evil news rides post, while good news baits.
1671 *Samson Agonistes*, l.1538.

63 Death to life is crown or shame.
1671 *Samson Agonistes*, l.1579.

64 Not willingly, but tangl'd in the fold

Of dire necessity.
1671 *Samson Agonistes*, l.1665–6.

65 Nothing is here for tears, nothing to wail
Or knock the breast, no weakness, no contempt,
Dispraise, or blame, nothing but well and fair,
And what may quiet us in a death so noble.
1671 Of Samson's heroic death. *Samson Agonistes*, l.1721–4.

66 All is best, though we oft doubt,
What the unsearchable dispose
Of highest wisdom brings about,
And ever best found in the close.
1671 *Samson Agonistes*, l.1745–8.

67 Calm of mind, all passion spent.
1671 *Samson Agonistes*, l.1758.

Min, Anchee 1957–

Chinese writer who left China for America in 1984. Her autobiography *Red Azalea* (1993) is named after Madame Mao's propaganda film in which Min was an actress.

68 My parents lived like—as the neighbours described them— a pair of chopsticks, always in harmony.
1993 *Red Azalea*.

69 The Chairman looked dissatisfied lying on his death bed.
1993 Of Mao Zedong. *Red Azalea*.

Mingus, Charles 1922–79

US composer and bass player. He was one of the great idiosyncratic geniuses of modern jazz, and his musical legacy is only now being fully absorbed.

70 Today musicians listen to see who makes the most money on a style, and then they set to copying him. And they don't copy the ones that are beautiful, creative and good.
1977 Interview in Enstice and Rubin *Jazz Spoken Here* (1992).

Minot, Laurence d. c.1352

English poet.

71 War yit with the Skottes, for thai er ful of gile.
early to mid 14c 'Skottes out of Berwik', l.6.

Minow, Newton Norman 1926–

US lawyer, author and communications executive. Named Chair of the Federal Communications Commission (1961–3) by President Kennedy, he was noted for his controversial criticism of television broadcasting standards in the US. Since 1987 he has been director of the Annenberg Washington Program in Communications Policy Studies of Northwestern University in Washington.

72 When television is good, nothing is better. When it's bad, nothing is worse.
1961 Speech to the National Association of Broadcasters. Reported in the *New York Times*, 10 May.

73 You will observe a vast wasteland.
1961 Speech to the National Association of Broadcasters, inviting them to watch a full day of television. Reported in the *New York Times*, 10 May.

Minsky, Marvin Lee 1927–

US computer scientist and artificial intelligence researcher.

74 Logic doesn't apply to the real world.
1981 In Douglas R Hofstadter and Daniel C Dennett (eds) *The Mind's I: fantasies and reflections on self and soul.*

Mirabeau, Honoré Gabriel Riqueti, Comte de 1749–91

French revolutionary politician. After the publication of his *Essai sur le despotisme*, he was sentenced to death, but only served three years in prison. He espoused the Revolution, and died soon after he was elected President of the Assembly in 1791.

75 War is the national industry of Prussia.
1788 Attributed to Mirabeau by Albert Sorel (1842–1906), suggested by Mirabeau's introduction to *De la monarchie prussienne sous Frédéric le Grand*.

76 We will only leave our places by the force of the bayonet!
1789 Speech at the *Séance Royale*. Quoted in Webster *The French Revolution* (1919), p.50.

77 To administer is to govern; to govern is to reign. That is the problem.
1790 Memorandum, 3 Jul.

Miró, Joán 1893–1983

Spanish painter, graphic artist and designer.

78 I will break their guitar.
Of the Cubists and their reliance upon the still-life. Attributed in Saranne Alexandrian *Surrealist Art* (1970).

Mishan, E J 1917–

British economist.

79 If frequent teabreaks and other manifestations of disguised leisure are regarded as goods—and economics suggests that they be so regarded—their inclusion in any index of output per capita might go some way to enhance Britain's comparative performance.
Quoted in Alex Rubner *Three Sacred Cows of Economics* (1970), p.47.

Mishima, Yukio *pseudonym of* ***Hiraoka Kimitake*** 1925–70

Japanese writer of novels, plays and short stories. A keen advocate of the chivalrous ideals of Imperial Japan, he committed suicide by performing *seppuku* after a token effort at rallying his country to the right-wing nationalist traditions of pre-war Japan.

80 Teachers—a bunch of men all armed with the same information.
Acts of Worship, 'Cigarette' (translated by John Bester, 1989).

81 Held in the custody of childhood is a locked chest; the adolescent, by one means or another, tries to open it. the chest is opened: inside, there is nothing.
Acts of Worship, 'Cigarette' (translated by John Bester, 1989).

82 He'd been mistaken in thinking that if he killed himself the sordid bourgeois world would perish with him.
Acts of Worship, 'Raisin Bread' (translated by John Bester, 1989).

83 As he saw it, there was only one choice—to be strong and upright, or to commit suicide.
Acts of Worship, 'Sword' (translated by John Bester, 1989).

84 Human beings...they go on being born and dying, dying and being born. It's kind of boring, isn't it?
Acts of Worship, 'Sword' (translated by John Bester, 1989).

Mitchel, John 1815–75

Irish patriot. After starting the *United Irishman* (1848) he was tried for 'treason-felony' and transported, but in 1853 he escaped from Van Diemen's Land (Tasmania) to the USA. He returned to Ireland in 1874, and was elected to parliament but declared ineligible.

85 Surely, it is in youth man is most thoroughly depraved.
Hell lies about us in our infancy. The youthful innocency sung by aged poets (who forget their first childhood) is nothing but ignorance of evil. As the child comes to know evil, he loves it.
1849 In the *Jail Journal*, 13 Apr.

Mitchell, Adrian 1932–

English writer. His poetry is populist and political in nature. He has also written novels, plays, and works for children.

86 Most people ignore most poetry because most poetry ignores most people.
1964 *Poems*, introduction.

87 The man who believes in giraffes would swallow anything.
1971 'Loose Leaf Poem'.

88 Poetry is an extra hand. It can caress or tickle. It can clench and fight.
1972 'Poetry Lives', in the *Sunday Times*, 13 Feb.

Mitchell, Austin 1934–

English Labour politician.

89 Welcome to Britain's New Political Order. No passion… No Right. No Left. Just multi-hued blancmange.
1999 In the *Observer*, 'Sayings of the Week', 11 Apr.

Mitchell, Joni (Roberta Joan) *née Anderson* 1943–

Canadian singer and songwriter. Her highly original and personal compositions made her a central figure in the folk movement of the 1960s. Her albums include *Ladies of the Canyon* (1970) and *Blue* (1971).

90 Woke up, it was a Chelsea morning, and the first thing that I knew
There was milk and toast and honey and a bowl of oranges, too.
And the sun poured in like butterscotch and stuck to all my senses.
1967 'Chelsea Morning'.

91 Don't it always seem to go
That you don't know what you've got
Till it's gone.
They paved paradise
And put up a parking lot.
1970 'Big Yellow Taxi'.

Mitchell, Margaret 1900–49

US writer. She worked as a journalist with the Atlanta *Constitution*. Her only novel, *Gone with the Wind* (written 1926–36, published 1936, Pulitzer Prize), rapidly became a bestseller and was made into a celebrated film in 1939.

92 I'm tired of everlastingly being unnatural and never doing anything I want to do…and I'm tired of pretending I don't know anything, so men can tell me things and feel important while they're doing it.
1936 Scarlett O'Hara. *Gone with the Wind*, ch.5.

93 Land is the only thing in the world worth working for, worth fighting for, worth dying for, because it's the only thing that lasts. It will come to you, this love of the land.
1939 *Gone with the Wind*.

94 Young misses whut eats heavy mos' gener'ly doan never ketch husbands.
1936 Mammy. *Gone with the Wind*, ch.5.

95 Until you've lost your reputation, you never realize what a burden it was or what freedom really is.
1936 Rhett Butler. *Gone with the Wind*, ch.9.

96 I'm going to live through this, and when it's over, I'm never going to be hungry again. No, nor any of my folks. If I have to steal or kill—as God is my witness, I'm never going to be hungry again.
1936 Scarlett O'Hara. *Gone with the Wind*, ch.25.

97 Fighting is like champagne. It goes to the heads of cowards as quickly as of heroes. Any fool can be brave on a battlefield when it's be brave or else be killed.
1936 Ashley Wilkes. *Gone with the Wind*, ch.31.

98 Southerners can never resist a losing cause.
1936 Rhett Butler. *Gone with the Wind*, ch.34.

99 Death and taxes and childbirth! There's never any convenient time for any of them!
1936 Scarlett O'Hara. *Gone with the Wind*, ch.38.

1 What is broken is broken, and I'd rather remember it as it was at its best than mend it and see broken places as long as I lived… I wish I could care what you do or where you go, but I can't. My dear, I don't give a damn.
1936 Rhett Butler's parting speech to Scarlett O'Hara. *Gone with the Wind*, ch.63; the more famous version of the final line from the film script by Sidney Howard (1939, spoken by Clark Gable) ran 'Frankly, my dear, I don't give a damn'.

2 Tomorrow, I'll think of some other way to get him back. After all, tomorrow is another day.
1936 Scarlett O'Hara's final words. *Gone with the Wind*, ch.63.

Mitchell, Warren 1926–

English actor.

3 You don't retire in this business. You just notice that the phone has not rung for ten years.
2000 In *The Guardian*, 31 Dec.

Mitford, Mary Russell 1787–1855

English novelist and dramatist, best known for her sketches of country manners, scenery and character that were collected as *Our Village* (1824–32). Other publications include *Recollections of a Literary Life* (1852).

4 To think of playing cricket for hard cash! Money and gentility would ruin any pastime under the sun.
1823 Letter to R B Haydon, 24 Aug.

5 Who would think that a little bit of leather, and two pieces of wood, had such a delightful and delighting power!
1824–32 *Our Village*.

Mitford, Nancy Freeman 1904–73

English writer. A daughter of the aristocracy, she achieved a considerable reputation for her witty novels.

6 Like all the very young we took it for granted that making

love is child's play.
1945 *The Pursuit of Love*, ch.3.

7 Aunt Sadie…so much disliked hearing about health that people often took her for a Christian Scientist, which, indeed, she might have become had she not disliked hearing about religion even more.
1945 *The Pursuit of Love*, ch.4.

8 I have only ever read one book in my life, and that is *White Fang*. It's so frightfully good I've never bothered to read another.
1945 *The Pursuit of Love*, ch.9.

9 Abroad is unutterably bloody and foreigners are fiends.
1945 Uncle Matthew. *The Pursuit of Love*, ch.15.

10 'Always be civil to the girls, you never know who they may marry' is an aphorism which has saved many an English spinster from being treated like an Indian widow.
1949 *Love in a Cold Climate*, pt.1, ch.2.

11 'Twenty three and a quarter minutes past,' Uncle Matthew was saying furiously, 'in precisely six and three-quarter minutes the damned fella will be late.'
1949 *Love in a Cold Climate*, pt.1, ch.13.

12 When the loo paper gets thicker and the writing paper thinner, it's always a bad sign, at home.
1949 *Love in a Cold Climate*, pt.2, ch.2.

13 An aristocracy in a republic is like a chicken whose head has been cut off: it may run about in a lively way, but in fact it is dead.
1956 *Noblesse Oblige*.

Mitsuharu, Kaneko 1895–1975

Japanese poet, noted for his unconventionality. He spent a number of years in Belgium and France and wrote a poem, 'Awa' ('Foam'), about Japanese atrocities in China.

14 The sky snivels green snot.
There is war.
c.1938 *Shijin* (Poet), 'Awa' (translated by A R Davies, 1988).

Mizner, Wilson 1876–1933

US dramatist and wit.

15 Be nice to people on your way up because you'll meet them on your way down.
Quoted in A Johnston *The Legendary Mizners* (1953).

16 Working for Warner Brothers was like fucking a porcupine—it's a hundred pricks against one.
Quoted in David Niven *Bring on the Empty Horses* (1975).

17 A trip through a sewer in a glass-bottomed boat.
1979 Of life in Hollywood. Quoted in Gary Herman *The Book of Hollywood Quotes* (1979).

Mo Yan *pseudonym of* ***Guan Moye*** 1956–

Chinese writer and the winner of nearly all the prestigious literary awards in China. He has written a number of novels. *Red Sorghum* (1993), his fourth novel, is set principally during the 1930s when Japanese forces occupied the country.

18 Words spoken on the road are heard by snakes in the grass.
1993 *Red Sorghum* (translated by Howard Goldblatt).

Mo, Timothy 1950–

British novelist. He was born in Hong Kong, and achieved prominence with *Sour Sweet*, set in the Chinese community in London.

19 The Chens had been living in the UK for four years, which was long enough to have lost their place in the society from which they had emigrated but not long enough to feel comfortable in the new.
1982 *Sour Sweet*, opening words.

20 It's all honourable enough in its way, but it creates societies which simply cannot sustain any kind of democratic structure. It always leads to totalitarian and corrupt tyrannies… There's no tradition of moral individual courage in Chinese culture.
1982 Of Chinese tradition. In *The Fiction Magazine*, vol.1, no.4.

21 The assaying of tea is an art and not a science. It is the man, and not his instruments, which is the most important. There can be no substitute for my experience and intuited knowledge.
1986 *An Insular Possession*, ch.4.

22 I see you belong to the category, old friend, which will have things in the round, which does love an end, causes, the balance sheet drawn and equalled. But, my dear Gid, the world is not like that—it *is* untidy, there are no reasons, the final sum never balances.
1986 *An Insular Possession*, ch.44.

23 There's no such thing as a hero—only ordinary people asked extraordinary things in terrible circumstances —and delivering.
1991 *The Redundancy of Courage*, ch.30.

Modersohn-Becker, Paula *née* ***Becker*** 1876–1907

German painter, a member of the Worpswede artists' colony near Bremen and an early Expressionist. In her later works naturalism gives way to simple forms and strong lyrical colour. She died soon after the birth of her first child.

24 In art one is usually totally alone with oneself.
1906 Diary entry, Paris, 18 Nov, quoted in Gillian Perry *Paula Modersohn-Becker* (1979).

Mola, Emilio 1887–1937

Spanish general, a nationalist leader during the Spanish Civil War.

25 *La quinta columna.*
The fifth column.
1936 Speech, Oct. Of the rebel sympathizers within Madrid who would help the four columns of nationalist rebels besieging it. Quoted in Hugh Thomas *The Spanish Civil War* (1961), ch.4, p.317.

Molière, Jean Baptiste Poquelin 1622–73

French actor and playwright who formed a theatrical company in 1643 and toured the provinces until 1658. He gained the patronage of the Duc d'Orléans and later of Louis XIV.

26 *On ne meurt qu'une fois, et c'est pour si longtemps!*
We only die once; and it's for such a long time!
1656 *Le dépit amoureux*, act 5, sc.3.

27 *Hors de Paris, il n'y a point de salut pour les honnêtes gens.*
Outside of Paris, there is no salvation for gentlemen.
1659 *Les précieuses ridicules*, sc.9.

28 *Les verrous et les grilles*
Ne font pas la vertu des femmes ni des filles.

Bolts and bars will not keep wives and daughters chaste.
1661 *L'École des maris*, act 1, sc.2.

29 *Le siècle s'encanaille furieusement.*
Our times have become vulgar.
1663 *La critique de l'École des femmes*, sc.6.

30 *Je voudrais bien savoir si la grande*
règle de toutes les règles n'est pas de plaire.
I shouldn't be surprised if the greatest
rule of all weren't to give pleasure.
1663 *La critique de l'École des femmes*, sc.6.

31 *Le Ciel défend, de vrai, certains contentements;*
Mais on trouve avec lui des accommodements.
True, heaven forbids us certain pleasures;
But we always find a way to arrange things.
1664 *Le Tartuffe*, act 4, sc.5.

32 *Le scandale du monde est ce qui fait l'offense,*
Et ce n'est pas pécher que pécher en silence.
A scandal is that which gives offence to the world.
To sin in private is not to sin at all.
1664 *Le Tartuffe*, act 4, sc.5.

33 *Qui vit sans tabac n'est pas digne de vivre.*
Anyone who lives without tobacco is not worthy of living.
1665 *Dom Juan*, act 1, sc.1.

34 *La naissance n'est rien où la vertu n'est pas.*
Birth counts for little when virtue is lacking.
1665 *Dom Juan*, act 4, sc.4.

35 *L'ami du genre humain n'est point du tout mon fait.*
I have no use at all for the friend of mankind.
1666 *Le misanthrope*, act 1, sc.1.

36 *J'aime mieux un vice commode*
Qu'une fatigante vertu.
I prefer easygoing vice to tiresome virtue.
1668 *Amphitryon*, act 1, sc.4.

37 *Quand il y a à manger pour huit, il y en a bien pour dix.*
When there is enough food for eight, there is enough for ten.
1668 *L'Avare*, act 3, sc.1.

38 *Il faut manger pour vivre, et non pas vivre pour manger.*
One should eat to live, not live to eat.
1668 *L'Avare*, act 3, sc.1.

39 *Ils commencent ici par faire pendre un*
homme, et puis ils lui font son procès.
Here they hang a men first, and try
him afterwards.
1669 In Paris. *Monsieur de Pourceaugnac*, act 3, sc.2.

40 *Par ma foi! il y a plus de quarante ans*
que je dis de la prose sans que j'en susse rien!
Good heavens! I've been speaking prose for
forty years without knowing it!
1670 *Le bourgeois gentilhomme*, act 2, sc.4.

41 *La grammaire qui sait régenter jusqu'aux rois.*
Even kings must bow to grammar.
1672 *Les femmes savantes*, act 2, sc.6.

42 *Je vis de bonne soupe, et non de beau langage.*
It's good food and not fine words that keeps me alive.
1672 *Les femmes savantes*, act 2, sc.7.

43 *Un sot savant est sot plus qu'un sot ignorant.*
A learned fool is more foolish than an ignorant fool.
1672 *Les femmes savantes*, act 4, sc.3.

44 *Presque tous les hommes meurent de leurs remèdes, et*
non de leurs maladies.
Almost all men die from their medicines and not from
their illnesses.
1673 *Le malade imaginaire*, act 3, sc.3.

45 We reason with one another; he prescribes the
remedies; I omit to take them and I recover.
On his relationship with his doctor, Mauvillan, in the presence of Louis XI V. Quoted in Vincent Cronin *Louis XI V* (1964), p.291.

Moltke, Helmuth von, Count 1800–91

Prussian general. Chief of the General Staff of the Prussian army 1858—88. He presided over successful wars with Denmark (1863–4), Austria (1866) and France (1870–1).

46 Everlasting peace is a dream, and not even a pleasant one; and war is a necessary part of God's arrangement with the world... Without war the world would deteriorate into materialism.
1880 Letter to Dr J K Bluntschi, 11 Dec, collected in *Helmuth von Moltke as a Correspondent* (1893).

47 What our sword has won in half a year, our sword must guard for half a century.
1891 *The Franco-Prussian War of 1870–71.*

Mondale, Walter F(rederick) 1928–

US Democratic politician and lawyer. He served under President Carter as Vice-President (1977–81), and was the Democratic nominee for President in 1984, when he lost to Ronald Reagan. He was US Ambassador to Japan (1993–6).

48 I don't want to spend the next two years in Holiday Inns.
1976 On withdrawing from the presidential campaign.

49 In our system, at about 11.30pm on election night, they just push you off the edge of the cliff—and that's it. You might scream on the way down, but you're going to hit the bottom, and you're not going to be in office.
1984 On losing to Ronald Reagan in the presidential elections, in the *New York Times*, 4 Mar.

Mondrian, Piet 1872–1944

Dutch painter, one of the most important artists in the development of abstract painting.

50 I hate everything approaching temperamental inspiration, 'sacred fire' and all those attributes of genius which serve only as cloaks for untidy minds.
Quoted in F Elgar *Mondrian* (1968).

51 Why should art continue to follow nature when every other field has left nature behind?
Quoted in F Elgar *Mondrian* (1968).

52 The unconscious in us warns us that in art we have to follow one particular path. And if we follow it, it is not the sign of an unconscious act. On the contrary, it shows that there is in our ordinary consciousness a greater awareness of our unconsciousness.
Quoted in F Elgar *Mondrian* (1968).

Monet, Claude 1840–1926

French Impressionist painter. One of the creators of Impressionism, it was his *Impression: soleil levant* (1872) that gave the movement its name. He spent the last years of his life as a recluse in Giverny.

53 When you go out to paint, try to forget what objects you have before you—a tree, a house, a field, or whatever. Merely think, here is a little square of blue, here an oblong of pink, here a streak of yellow, and paint it just as it looks to you, the exact colour and shape, until it gives your own naive impression of the scene before you.
Attributed, in reminiscences written in 1927 by the young American artist Lilla Cabot Perry.

54 It was as if a veil had been torn suddenly away; I had understood, I had grasped what painting could be.
After painting with the artist Boudin in the open air. Quoted in J Isaacson *Claude Monet* (1978).

Monod, Jacques 1910–76

French biologist and author. He proposed (1961) the concepts of messenger RNA. He shared the 1965 Nobel prize in physiology or medicine.

55 There are living systems; there is no 'living matter'.
1967 Lecture, College of France.

56 The scientific attitude implies... the postulate of objectivity—that is to say, the fundamental postulate that there is no plan; that there is no intention in the universe.
1970 *Le Hasard et la Necéssité*.

Monro, Harold Edward 1879–1932

English poet. He founded the influential *Poetry Review* in 1912. A *Collected Poems* appeared in 1933.

57 When the tea is brought at five o'clock,
And all the neat curtains are drawn with care,
The little black cat with bright green eyes
Is suddenly purring there.
1914 'Milk for the Cat'.

58 The white saucer like some full moon descends
At last from the clouds of the table above.
1914 'Milk for the Cat'.

Monroe, Marilyn *pseudonym of* ***Norma Jean Baker*** 1926–62

US film actress. Her sex appeal was exploited in films such as *How to Marry a Millionaire* and *Gentlemen Prefer Blondes* (both 1953), but she went on to light comedy (eg *Some Like It Hot*, 1959) and more serious roles such as *The Misfits* (1961), written by her third husband, Arthur Miller. Her suicide made her an icon, and a symbol of Hollywood's ruthlessness.

59 He's not a director, he's a dictator.
c.1959 On Billy Wilder, the director of *Some Like It Hot*, attributed.

60 He's the only person I know who's in worse shape than I am.
1961 On Montgomery Clift, her co-star in *The Misfits*.

Montagu, (Alexander) Victor Edward Paulet 1906–95

Conservative politician, private secretary to Stanley Baldwin (1932–4) and chairman of the Tory Reform Committee (1943–4). He succeeded as 10th Earl of Sandwich in 1962 but disclaimed his peerage for life the next year. His publications include *The Conservative Dilemma* (1970).

61 Lord Hailsham said the other day that the machinery of Government was creaking. My Lords, it is not even moving sufficiently to emit a noise of any kind.
1963 House of Lords, 20 Apr, shortly before disclaiming his peerage.

Montagu, Ashley *originally* ***Israel Ehrenberg*** 1905–99

English-born US anthropologist, author of a number of scholarly and popular works. He has been closely associated with the view that cultural phenomena are not the result of genetics.

62 As the god of contemporary man's idolatry, science is a two-handed engine, and as such science is too important a human activity to leave to the scientists.
1964 Book review in the *New York Times*, 26 Apr.

Montagu, Lady Mary Wortley *née* ***Pierrepoint*** 1689–1762

English writer and socialite. She accompanied her ambassador husband to Constantinople (1716–18), writing there many entertaining letters. She introduced smallpox inoculation into England, and settled in Italy with her husband in 1739.

63 'Tis certain we have but very imperfect accounts of the manners and religion of these people; this part of the world being seldom visited, but by merchants, who mind little but their own affairs; or travellers, who make too short a stay to be able to report anything exactly of their own knowledge.
c.1716 Of Turkey. Collected in Lord Wharncliffe (ed) *The Letters and Works of Lady Mary Wortley Montagu* (1837).

64 Thus you see, Sir, that these people are not so unpolished as we represent them. 'Tis true, their magnificence is of a different taste from ours, and perhaps of a better. I am almost of opinion, they have a right notion of life. They consume it in music, gardens, wine, and delicate eating, while we are tormenting our brains with some scheme of politics, or studying some science to which we can never attain, or, if we do, cannot persuade other people to set that value upon it we do ourselves... We die or grow old before we can reap the fruit of our labours. Considering what short-lived weak animals men are, is there any study so beneficial as the study of present pleasure?
c.1716 Collected in Lord Wharncliffe (ed) *The Letters and Works of Lady Mary Wortley Montagu* (1837).

65 I was here convinced of the truth of a reflection I had often made, that if it was the fashion to go naked, the face would be hardly observed.
c.1716 In a Turkish bath in Sofia. Collected in Lord Wharncliffe (ed) *The Letters and Works of Lady Mary Wortley Montagu* (1837).

66 If your daughters are inclined to love reading, do not check their inclination by hindering them of the diverting part of it. It is as necessary for the amusement of women as the reputation of men; but teach them not to expect any applause from it... Ignorance is as much the fountain of vice as idleness, and indeed generally produces it. People that do not read or work for a livelihood have many hours they know not how to employ, especially women, who commonly fall into vapours or something worse.
1750 Letter, Jan. Collected in R Halsband (ed) *Selected Letters of Lady Mary Wortley Montagu* (1970).

67 Their whole business abroad (as far as I can perceive) being to buy new clothes, in which they shine in some obscure coffee-house, where they are sure of meeting only one-another… I look upon them as the greatest blockheads.

1763 On those making the Grand Tour. Quoted in Eric Newby (ed) *A Book of Travellers' Tales* (1985).

Montague, C(harles) E(dward) 1867–1928

English novelist and essayist of Irish parentage. He wrote various novels, a collection of essays and many articles for the *Manchester Guardian* (1890–1925).

68 War hath no fury like a non-combatant.

1922 *Disenchantment*, ch.16.

► *See Congreve 231:23.*

69 I was born below par to the extent of two whiskies.

1923 'Fiery Particles'.

70 The Swiss are inspired hotel-keepers. Some centuries since, when the stranger strayed into one of their valleys, their simple forefathers would kill him and share out the little money he might have about him. Now they know better. They keep him alive and writing cheques.

1926 *The Right Place*.

Montaigne, Michel Eyquem de 1533–92

French essayist. He was a city counsellor of Bordeaux and later its Mayor. From 1571 he lived the life of a country gentleman and started composing his *Essais* (1580), a classic of French literature.

71 *Certes, c'est un sujet merveilleusement vain, divers et ondoyant, que l'homme.*

Man (in good earnest) is a marvellous vain, fickle, and unstable subject.

1580 *Essais*, bk.1, ch.1 (translated by Charles Cotton).

72 *Il faut estre tousjours boté et prest à partir.*

We should always be booted and spurred, and ready to go.

1580 *Essais*, bk.1, ch.20 (translated by Charles Cotton).

73 *Que la mort me trouve plantant mes choux, mais nonchalant d'elle, et encore plus de mon jardin imparfait.*

I would like death to come to me while I am planting cabbages, caring little for death and even less for the imperfection of my garden.

1580 *Essais*, bk.1, ch.20 (translated by Charles Cotton).

74 *Si on me presse de dire pourquoy je l'aymois, je sens que cela ne se peut exprimer, qu'en respondant: 'Parce que c'estoit luy; par ce que c'estoit moy.'*

If a man should importune me to give a reason why I loved him, I find it could no otherwise be expressed, than by making answer: because it was he, because it was I.

1580 *Essais*, bk.1, ch.28 (translated by Charles Cotton).

75 *Or la fin, ce crois-je, en est tout'une, d'en vivre plus à loisir et à son aise.*

Now the end, I take it, is all one, to live at more leisure and at one's ease.

1580 *Essais*, bk.1, ch.39 (translated by Charles Cotton).

76 *Il se faut reserver une arriere boutique toute nostre, toute franche, en laquelle nous establissons nostre vraye liberté et principale retraite et solitude.*

We must reserve a backshop, wholly our own and entirely free, wherein to settle our true liberty, our principle solitude and retreat.

1580 *Essais*, bk.1, ch.39 (translated by Charles Cotton).

77 *La plus grande chose du monde, c'est de sçavoir estre à soy.*

The greatest thing in the world is for a man to know that he is his own.

1580 *Essais*, bk.1, ch.39 (translated by Charles Cotton).

78 *La gloire et le repos sont choses qui ne peuvent loger en mesme giste.*

Fame and tranquillity are two things that can't live under the same roof.

1580 *Essais*, bk.1, ch.39 (translated by Charles Cotton).

79 *Mon mestier et mon art, c'est vivre.*

My trade and art is to live.

1580 *Essais*, bk.2, ch.6 (translated by Charles Cotton).

80 *Quand je me jouë à ma chatte, qui sçait si elle passe son temps de moy plus que je ne fay d'elle?*

When I play with my cat, who knows whether I do not make her more sport than she makes me?

1580 *Essais*, bk.2, ch.12 (translated by Charles Cotton).

81 *L'homme est bien insensé. Il ne sçauroit forger un ciron, et forge des Dieux à douzaines.*

Man is quite insane. He wouldn't know how to make a maggot, and he makes Gods by the dozen.

1580 *Essais*, bk.2, ch.12 (translated by Charles Cotton).

82 *Nous veillons dormants, et veillants dormons.*

We wake sleeping, and sleep waking.

1580 *Essais*, bk.2, ch.12 (translated by Charles Cotton).

83 *Il n'y a point de fin en nos inquisitions. Nostre fin est en l'autre monde.*

There is no end to our researches; our end is in the other world.

1588 *Essays*, bk.3, ch.13 (translated by Donald M Frame).

84 *Nous sommes par tout vent.*

We are all wind throughout.

1588 *Essais*, bk.3, ch.13 (translated by Charles Cotton).

85 *Nostre grand et glorieux chef-d'œuvre, c'est vivre à propos.*

The great and glorious masterpiece of man is to know how to live to purpose.

1588 *Essais*, bk.3, ch.13 (translated by Charles Cotton).

Montcalm, Marquis de 1712–59

French Governor of Quebec, who unsuccessfully defended the city against General Wolfe's English troops in the Battle of the Plains of Abraham, 13 Sep 1759.

86 I am happy that I shall not live to see the surrender of Quebec.

1759 Spoken to his aides, 13 Sep. He died the following day. Quoted in Francis Parkman *Montcalm and Wolfe* (1884).

Monterroso, Augusto 1921–2003

Guatemalan writer who lived in exile in Mexico from 1944. His works are mainly collections of short stories in which paradox and a whimsical sense of humour are prominent.

87 *La Historia no se detiene nunca. Día y noche su marcha es incesante. Querer detenerla sería como querer detener la Geografía.*

History never stops. It progresses ceaselessly day and night. Trying to stop it is like trying to stop Geography.

1978 *Lo demás es silencio* ('The Rest is Silence'), 'Aforismos, dichos, etc'.

Montesquieu, Charles Louis de Secondat, Baron de la Brède et de 1689–1755

French philosopher and jurist, who turned from law to scientific research and literary work. His study of legal and social issues *De l'Esprit des lois* (1748, 'The Spirit of Laws') was very influential in 18c Europe.

88 *Si l'on vient à savoir mon nom, dès ce moment je me tais. Je connais une femme qui marche assez bien, mais qui boite dès qu'on la regarde.*
Once someone wants to know my name, I become quiet. I know a woman who walks rather well, but who limps once she sees someone watching her.
1721 *Lettres persanes*, introduction.

89 *Il n'y a jamais eu de royaume où il y ait eu tant de guerres civiles que dans celui du Christ.*
No kingdom has ever been so divided by civil wars as that of Christ.
1721 *Lettres persanes*, no.29.

90 *Il faut pleurer les hommes à leur naissance, et non pas à leur mort.*
A person should be mourned at his birth, not at his death.
1721 *Lettres persanes*, no.40.

91 *Si les triangles faisaient un dieu, ils lui donneraient trois côtés.*
If triangles had made a god, it would have three sides.
1721 *Lettres persanes*, no.59.

92 *Le droit des gens est naturellement fondé sur ce principe: que les diverses nations doivent se faire, dans la paix, le plus de bien, et, dans la guerre, le moins de mal qu'il est possible, sans nuire à leurs véritables intérêts.*
Law is naturally founded on this principle: that different nations should do, in peace and as far as best as they can in war, the least harm as possible, without harming their true interests.
1748 *De l'esprit des lois*, vol.1, ch.3.

93 *Le gouvernement est comme toutes les choses du monde; pour le conserver, il faut l'aimer.*
Government is like everything else in the world; to conserve it, we must love it.
1748 *De l'esprit des lois*, vol.4, ch.5.

94 *L'amour de la démocratie est celui de l'égalité.*
Love of democracy is love of equality.
1748 *De l'esprit des lois*, vol.5, ch.3.

95 *Les républiques finissent par le luxe; les monarchies, par la pauvreté.*
Republics end by wealth; monarchies end by poverty.
1748 *De l'esprit des lois*, vol.7, ch.4.

96 *La liberté est le droit de faire tout ce que les lois permettent.*
Freedom is the right to do anything the laws permit.
1748 *De l'esprit des lois*, vol.11, ch.3.

97 *Il en est de la luxure comme de l'avarice: elle augmente sa soif par l'acquisition des trésors.*
The same rule applies for lust, as for avarice: it increases its thirst by the acquisition of wealth.
1748 *De l'esprit des lois*, vol.16, ch.6.

98 *Le divorce a ordinairement une grande utilité politique; et quant à l'utilité civile, il est établi pour le mari et pour la femme, et n'est pas toujours favorable aux enfants.*
Divorce generally has a great political use; as for its civil use, it is established for the husband and wife and is not always favourable to the children.
1748 *De l'esprit des lois*, vol.16, ch.15.

99 *Les lois inutiles affaiblissent les lois nécessaires.*
Useless laws weaken the necessary ones.
1748 *De l'esprit des lois*, vol.29, ch.16.

Montgomery of Alamein, Bernard Law, 1st Viscount 1887–1976

British field marshal. He led the 8th Army in World War II, defeating Rommel at El Alamein (1942), and was Commander-in-Chief of Allied ground forces for the invasion of Normandy (1944), Chief of the Imperial General Staff (1946–8) and Supreme Commander of Nato forces in Europe (1951–8).

1 Rule 1, on page 1 of the book of war is: 'Do not march on Moscow'...[Rule 2] is: 'Do not go fighting with your land armies in China.'
1962 Speech in the House of Lords, 30 May.

Montgomery, L(ucy) M(aud) 1874–1942

Canadian novelist. Her first book was the phenomenally successful *Anne of Green Gables* (1908), the story of an orphan girl adopted in error for a boy by an elderly brother and sister. She followed it with several sequels.

2 The point of good writing is knowing when to stop.
1917 *Anne's House of Dreams*, ch.24.

Montrose, James Graham, 1st Marquis of 1612–50

Scottish soldier and poet, who, after first supporting the National Covenant in 1638, fought a brilliant campaign for Charles I during the Civil War from 1644 to 1645. Captured in 1650 after an abortive attempt to win Scotland for Charles II, he was hanged in Edinburgh.

3 My dear and only love, I pray
That little world of thee
Be governed by no other sway
Than purest monarchy.
c.1642 'My Dear and Only Love', stanza 1.

4 He either fears his fate too much,
Or his deserts are small,
That dares not put it to the touch,
To gain or lose it all.
c.1642 'My Dear and Only Love', stanza 2.

5 Let them bestow on every airth a limb,
Then open all my veins that I may swim
To thee, my Maker, in that crimson lake;
Then place my parboiled head upon a stake,
Scatter my ashes, strew them in the air—
Lord! since thou knowest where all these atoms are,
I'm hopeful thou'lt recover once my dust,
And confident thou'lt raise me with the just.
1650 'Lines Composed on the Eve of his Execution'.

Moodie, Susanna *née* *Strickland* 1803–85

English-born Canadian writer of fiction, non-fiction, poetry and letters. She reluctantly emigrated to Canada with her husband in 1832 and wrote for many magazines but is best remembered for *Roughing it in the Bush* (1852) and *Life in the*

Clearing, versus the Bush (1853).

6 Dear husband! I take shame to myself that my purpose was less firm, that my heart lingered so far behind yours in preparing for this great epoch in our lives; that like Lot's wife, I still turned and looked back, and clung with all my strength to the land I was leaving. It was not the hardships of an emigrant's life I dreaded. I could bear mere physical privations philosophically enough; it was the loss of society in which I had moved, the want of congenial minds, of persons engaged in congenial pursuits, that made me so reluctant to respond to my husband's call.
1852 *Roughing It in the Bush; or, A Life in Canada*, vol.1, ch.11, 'The Charivari'.

7 Speaking of the coldness of one particular day, a genuine brother Jonathan remarked, with charming simplicity, that it was thirty degrees below zero that morning, and it would have been much colder if the thermometer had been longer.
1852 'Brother Jonathan' refers to a typical Yankee. *Roughing It in the Bush; or, A Life in Canada*, vol.2, ch.9, 'The Fire'.

8 If these sketches should prove the means of deterring one family from sinking their property, and shipwrecking all their hopes, by going to reside in the backwoods of Canada, I shall consider myself amply repaid for revealing the secrets of the prison-house, and feel that I have not toiled and suffered in the wilderness in vain.
1852 *Roughing It in the Bush; or, A Life in Canada*, vol.2, ch.14, 'Adieu to the Woods'.

9 In most instances, emigration is a matter of necessity, not of choice.
1854 *Roughing It in the Bush; or, A Life in Canada*, introduction to the 3rd edition.

10 Will they ever forgive me for writing *Roughing It*? They know that it was the truth, but have I not been a mark for every vulgar editor of a village journal, throughout the length and breadth of the land to hurl a stone at, and point out as the enemy to Canada.
1856 Letter to her publisher, Richard Bentley, 19 Aug.

Moody, William Vaughn 1869–1910

US poet and playwright. He taught at the University of Chicago. His best-known prose play, *The Sabine Woman* (1906), was highly successful and focuses on the contrast between a puritanical woman and a free-thinking man. It was retitled *The Great Divide* (1909).

11 A man's a fool to look at things too near:
They look back, and begin to cut up queer.
1901 'The Menagerie'.

Moore, Brian 1921–99

Northern Irish-born writer, who emigrated to Canada in 1948, and also lived in California and New York. His first novel, *The Lonely Passion of Judith Hearne* (1955), was filmed in 1989. Later works include *Black Robe* (1985, filmed 1991), *Lies of Silence* (1990) and *The Statement* (1995).

12 He bathes daily in a running tap of words.
1987 Of a military colonel's desk work. *The Color of Blood*.

Moore, Charles W(illard) 1925–93

US architect, Professor of Architecture at UCLA, California (1975–85). His writings include *The Place of Houses* (1974) and *The Poetics of Gardens* (1988).

13 You bind the goods and trappings of your life together with your dreams to make a place that is uniquely your own.
1974 *The Place of Houses*, introduction.

Moore, Clement 1779–1863

US writer and poet.

14 'Twas the night before Christmas, when all through the house
Not a creature was stirring, not even a mouse.
1822 *The Night Before Christmas*.

15 The stockings were hung by the chimney with care,
In hopes that St. Nicholas soon would be there;
The children were nestled all snug in their beds,
While visions of sugarplums danced in their heads.
1822 *The Night Before Christmas*.

16 The moon on the breast of the new-fallen snow,
Gave the lustre of midday to objects below,
When, what to my wondering eyes should appear,
But a miniature sleigh, and eight tiny reindeer.
1822 *The Night Before Christmas*.

17 More rapid than eagles his coursers they came,
And he whistled, and shouted, and called them by name;
'Now, *Dasher!* Now, *Dancer!* Now, *Prancer* and *Vixen!*
On, *Comet!* On, *Cupid!* On, *Donder* and *Blitzen!*
To the top of the porch! To the top of the wall!
Now dash away! Dash away! Dash away all!'
1822 *The Night Before Christmas*.

18 He was dressed all in fur, from his head to his foot,
And his clothes were all tarnished with ashes and soot;
A bundle of toys he had flung on his back,
And he looked like a pedlar just opening his pack.
1822 *The Night Before Christmas*.

19 He sprang to his sleigh, to his team gave a whistle,
And away they all flew like the down of a thistle.
But I heard him exclaim, ere he drove out of sight,
'Happy Christmas to all. And to all a good night.'
1822 *The Night Before Christmas*.

Moore, G(eorge) E(dward) 1873–1958

English Empiricist philosopher. He studied and taught at Cambridge, where he was Professor of Mental Philosophy and Logic (1925–39). His most famous and influential work was *Principia Ethica* (1903).

20 'Good', then, if we mean by it that quality which we assert to belong to a thing, when we say that the thing is good, is incapable of any definition, in the most important sense of the word.
1903 *Principia Ethica*, ch.1.

21 By far the most valuable things, which we know or can imagine, are certain states of consciousness, which may be roughly described as the pleasures of human intercourse and the enjoyment of beautiful objects.
1903 *Principia Ethica*, ch.6.

Moore, George 1852–1933

Irish novelist, poet and playwright. A co-founder of the Irish Literary Theatre with W B Yeats, he collaborated with Yeats on such poetic dramas as *The Bending of the Bough* (1900) and *Diarmuid and Grania* (1901).

22 A year passed; a year of art and dissipation—one part art, two parts dissipation. We mounted and descended at pleasure the rounds of society's ladder.
1870 *Confessions of a Young Man* (published 1888).

23 Acting is therefore the lowest of the arts, if it be an art at all.
1891 *Impressions and Opinions*, 'Mummer-Worship'.

Moore, Henry Spencer 1898–1986

English sculptor and graphic artist. He travelled widely in Europe and was an official war artist (1940–2). His sculptures, mainly semi-abstract figures and groups, are influenced by landscape forms and primitive art.

24 Sculpture in stone should look honestly like stone… to make it look like flesh and blood, hair and dimples is coming down to the level of the stage conjuror.
1930 In the *Architectural Association Journal*.

Moore, Jo

British political adviser.

25 It's now a very good day to get out anything we want to bury.
2001 E-mail sent on 11 Sep, after hijacked planes destroyed the World Trade Center in New York.

Moore, John 1729–1802

Scottish physician and writer. He travelled with Douglas, Duke of Hamilton (1772–8), writing accounts of these journeys, then settled in London. His novel *Zeluco* (1789) was the inspiration for Byron's *Childe Harold*.

26 There is no manner of doubt that a town surrounded by water is a very fine sight, but a town surrounded by land is much finer. Can there be any comparison in point of beauty, between the dull monotony of a watery surface, and the delightful variety of gardens, meadows, hills and woods?
c.1780 *A View of Society and Manners in Italy.*

Moore, Lorrie 1957–

US writer. Her writings include short stories and novels, such as *Who Will Run the Frog Hospital?* (1994) and *Birds of America* (1998).

27 Literature… is lonely and waited for, brilliant and pure and frightened, a marriage of birds, a conversation of the blind.
1988 In the *New York Times*, 10 Jul.

Moore, Marianne Craig 1887–1972

US poet, whose crisp language, wit and idiosyncratic style established her as a leading literary figure. Her works include *Observations* (1924, rev 1925), *Collected Poems* (1951, Pulitzer Prize) and *Complete Poems* (1967, rev 1981).

28 It comes to this: of whatever sort it is,
it must be 'lit with piercing glances into the life of things';
it must acknowledge the spiritual forces which have
made it.
1921 *Poems*, 'When I Buy Pictures'.

29 I, too, dislike it: there are things that are important
beyond all this fiddle.
Reading it, however, with a perfect contempt for it, one
discovers in
it, after all, a place for the genuine.
1921 *Poems*, 'Poetry'.

30 If 'compression is the first grace of style,'
you have it.
1924 *Observations*, 'To A Snail'.

31 My father used to say,
'Superior people never make long visits,
have to be shown Longfellow's grave
or the glass flowers at Harvard.'
1924 *Observations*, 'Silence'.

32 Nor was he insincere in saying, 'Make my house
your inn.'
Inns are not residencies.
1924 *Observations*, 'Silence'.

33 You are menaced by the goodness of your mechanics.
1937 To fellow-poet Elizabeth Bishop. Quoted in David Kalstone *Becoming a Poet* (1989), p.57.

34 A place as kind as it is green,
the greenest place I've never seen.
Every name is a tune.
1941 *What Are Years*, 'Spencer's Ireland'.

35 I do not write for money or fame… One writes because one has a burning desire to objectify what it is indispensible to one's happiness to express.
1956 Ewing Lecture, University of California, 3 Oct.

36 Omissions are not accidents.
1956 Ewing Lecture, University of California, 3 Oct.

37 O to be a dragon,
a symbol of the power of Heaven—of silkworm
size or immense; at times invisible.
Felicitous phenomenon!
1959 *O To Be A Dragon*, 'O To Be A Dragon'.

38 A connoisseur of tame excitement.
1960 Self-description, in *Vogue*, 1 Aug.

39 Any writer overwhelmingly honest about pleasing himself is almost sure to please others.
1963 In *Vogue*, 15 Aug.

40 I am governed by the pull of the sentence as the pull of a fabric is governed by gravity.
Quoted in Louis Untermeyer 'Five Famous Poetesses', in *Ladies' Home Journal*, May 1964.

41 Subjects choose me… I lie in wait like a leopard on a branch-strained metaphor.
Quoted in Louis Untermeyer 'Five Famous Poetesses', in *Ladies' Home Journal*, May 1964.

42 Omissions are not accidents.
1967 Epigraph to *Complete Poems*.

43 To cite passages is to pull one quill from a porcupine.
Quoted in Patricia C Willis (ed) *The Complete Prose of Marianne Moore* (1986).

Moore, Michael 1954–

US film-maker and writer.

44 The things I believe in, I believe strongly enough in them and I think I'm right. When I'm wrong, then I change my mind and I'm right again.
2002 In a question and answer session at the National Film Theatre, London, 11 Nov.

45 We live in a time when we have fictitious election results that elect a fictitious president, a time where we have a man sending us to war for fictitious reasons. We are against this war, Mr Bush. Shame on you, Mr Bush. Shame on you.
2003 At the 76th Academy Awards, where he was awarded an Oscar for Best Documentary Director.

Moore, Sir Patrick 1923–

English astronomer, author and broadcaster. He began his popular television series, *The Sky at Night*, in 1957, and it has continued since that time.

46 The Moon is a splendid object in our skies, and we naturally tend to think of it as important.
1976 *Guide to the Moon.*

Moore, Thomas 1780–1852

Irish poet, songwriter and biographer. He wrote a number of patriotic songs and poems as well as lives of Sheridan, Byron (a close friend) and others. He also wrote satirical pieces and novels, including *The Fudge Family in Paris* (1818). He is remembered for *Lallah Rookh* (1817), a series of oriental tales in verse, and for the popular songs 'The Harp that once through Tara's Halls', 'The Minstrel-boy', and 'Tis the Last Rose of Summer'.

47 There is not in the wide world a valley so sweet
As that vale in whose bosom the bright waters meet;
Oh! the last rays of feeling and life must depart
Ere the bloom of that valley shall fade from my heart.
1807 *Irish Melodies*, 'The Meeting of the Waters'.

48 Let Erin remember the days of Old,
Ere her faithless sons betrayed her;
When Malachi wore the collar of gold
Which he won from her proud invader;
When her kings, with standards of green unfurled,
Led the Red-Branch Knights to danger;
Ere the emerald gem of the western world
Was set in the crown of a stranger.
1807 *Irish Melodies*, 'Let Erin Remember'.

49 The Minstrel-boy to the war is gone,
In the ranks of death you'll find him;
His father's sword he has girded on,
And his wild harp slung behind him.
1807 *Irish Melodies*, 'The Minstrel-boy'.

50 'Tis the last rose of summer
Left blooming alone;
All her lovely companions
Are faded and gone.
1807 *Irish Melodies*, '' Tis the Last Rose of Summer'.

51 The harp that once through Tara's halls
The soul of music shed,
Now hangs as mute on Tara's walls
As if that soul were fled.
1807 *Irish Melodies*, 'The Harp that once through Tara's Halls'.

52 No, there's nothing half so sweet in life
As love's young dream.
1807 *Irish Melodies*, 'Love's Young Dream'.

53 Oh! ever thus, from childhood's hour,
I've seen my fondest hopes decay;
I never loved a tree or flower,
But 'twas the first to fade away.
I never nursed a dear gazelle,
To glad me with its soft black eye,
But when it came to know me well,
And love me, it was sure to die!
1817 *Lallah Rookh*, 'The Fire Worshippers'.

54 Yet, who can help loving the land that has taught us
Six hundred and eighty-five ways to dress eggs?
1818 *The Fudge Family in Paris*, letter 8.

Moorhouse, Geoffrey 1931–

English writer and traveller. He attempted to cross the Sahara from Mauretania to the Nile, but in March 1973, having travelled 2,000 miles (3,200km), 300 miles (480km) on foot after the last of his camels died, he reached Tamanrasset and gave up.

55 There was nothing but pain in the desert, for human beings and animals alike. Life was pain. Only in death was there relief.
1974 *The Fearful Void.*

Moran, Richard John McMoran Wilson, 2nd Baron 1924–

British diplomat and soldier. He filled a succession of diplomatic posts, including High Commissioner in Canada (1981–4). As John Wilson he wrote a Whitbread Award-winning biography of Sir Henry Campbell-Bannerman (1973).

56 Courage is a moral quality; it is not a chance gift of nature, like an aptitude for games. It is a cold choice between two alternatives; the fixed resolve not to quit, an act of renunciation that must be made not once but many times by the power of the will.
1945 *The Anatomy of Courage.*

More, Sir Thomas 1478–1534

English statesman, scholar and writer. Educated at Oxford in the new humanism, he was appointed Lord Chancellor by Henry VIII. He refused to take the oath of supremacy and was executed. His most famous work is *Utopia* (1516; translated into English 1556); other works include *History of King Richard III* (1513) and meditations in prison.

57 In the first place, most princes apply themselves to the arts of war, in which I have neither ability nor interest, instead of to the good arts of peace. They are generally more set on acquiring new kingdoms by hook or by crook than on governing well those that they already have.
1516 *Utopia* (English translation 1556), bk.1.

58 It is only natural, of course, that each man should think his own opinions best: the old crow loves his fledglings, and the ape his cubs.
1516 *Utopia* (English translation 1556), bk.1.

59 Such proud, obstinate, ridiculous judgements I have encountered many times, and once even in England.
1516 *Utopia* (English translation 1556), bk.1.

60 Severe and terrible punishments are enacted against theft, when it would be much better to enable every man to earn his own living, instead of being driven to the awful necessity of stealing and then dying for it.
1516 *Utopia* (English translation 1556), bk.1.

61 The law of Moses is harsh and severe, as for an enslaved and stubborn people, but it punishes theft with a fine,

not death. Let us not think that in his new law of mercy, where he treats us with the tenderness of a father, God has given us greater license to be cruel to one another.
1516 *Utopia* (English translation 1556), bk.1.

62 A king who wants to maintain an army can never have too much gold.
1516 *Utopia* (English translation 1556), bk.1.

63 A king has no dignity when he exercises authority over beggars, only when he rules over prosperous and happy subjects.
1516 *Utopia* (English translation 1556), bk.1.

64 The only real thing they accomplish that I can see is to make men feel a little more secure in their consciences about doing evil.
1516 Of preachers. *Utopia* (English translation 1556), bk.1.

65 Hardly any of the women, who are a full half of the population, work; or if they do, then as a rule their husbands lie snoring in bed.
1516 *Utopia* (English translation 1556), bk.2.

66 For where money is the standard of everything, many vain, superfluous trades are bound to be carried on simply to satisfy luxury and licentiousness.
1516 *Utopia* (English translation 1556), bk.2.

67 The chief aim of their constitution is that, whenever public needs permit, all citizens should be free, so far as possible, to withdraw their time and energy from the service of the body, and devote themselves to the freedom and culture of the mind. For that, they think, is the real happiness of life.
1516 *Utopia* (English translation 1556), bk.2.

68 They find pearls by the seashore, diamonds and rubies in certain cliffs, but never go out of set purpose to look for them. If they happen to find some, they polish them, and give them to the children who, when they are small, feel proud and pleased with such gaudy decorations. But after, when they grow a bit older, and notice that only babies like such toys, they lay them aside. Their parents don't have to say anything, they simply put these trifles away out of a shamefaced sense that they're no longer suitable, just as our children when they grow up put away their rattles, marbles and dolls.
1516 *Utopia* (English translation 1556), bk.2.

69 Thus they say that nature herself prescribes for us a joyous life, in other words, pleasure, as the goal of our actions; and living according to her prescriptions is to be defined as virtue.
1516 *Utopia* (English translation 1556), bk.2.

70 Two evils—greed and faction—are the destruction of all justice.
1516 *Utopia* (English translation 1556), bk.2.

71 Is not this house as nigh heaven as my own?
c.1534 Of the Tower of London. Attributed in William Roper *Life of Sir Thomas More* (ed E V Hitchcock, 1935).

72 I pray you, master Lieutenant, see me safe up, and my coming down let me shift for myself.
1535 On mounting the scaffold. Attributed in William Roper *Life of Sir Thomas More* (ed E V Hitchcock, 1935).

73 This hath not offended the king.
1535 Said on the scaffold as he drew his beard to one side. Attributed in William Roper *Life of Sir Thomas More* (ed E V Hitchcock, 1935).

Morell, Thomas 1703–84

English poet and librettist.

74 See, the conquering hero comes!
Sound the trumpets, beat the drums!
1747 *Judas Maccabeus*, 'A Chorus of Youths'.

Morey, Larry

US lyricist who frequently worked with Frank Churchill. Best known for contributing to *Snow White and the Seven Dwarfs* (1937) and *Bambi* (1941).

75 Heigh ho, heigh ho
It's off to work we go.
1937 First lines of the song 'Heigh-Ho' from the film *Snow White and the Seven Dwarfs*. Music by Frank Churchill.

76 Whistle While You Work.
1937 Title of song from the film *Snow White and the Seven Dwarfs*. Music by Frank Churchill.

Morgan, Edwin George 1920–

Scottish poet and critic, Professor Emeritus of English at Glasgow University. One of the most important Scottish writers, he is a skilled translator as well as an original poet.

77 Many things are unspoken
In the life of a man, and with a place
there is an unspoken love also
in undercurrents, drifting, waiting its time.
1968 'The Second Life'.

78 And later, wondering farmers as they passed would hear
beyond the lighted window in the autumn evening
two handsome yellow-bosomed basset-hounds
howling to a melodious basset-horn
1968 'An Addition to the Family'.

79 Deplore what is to be deplored,
and then find out the rest.
1968 'King Billy'.

80 The man lies late since he has lost his job,
smokes on one elbow, letting his coughs fall
thinly into an air too poor to rob.
1973 'Glasgow Sonnets, I'.

81 No deliverer ever rose
from these stone tombs to get the hell they made
unmade.
1973 'Glasgow Sonnets, II'.

Morgan, Elaine 1920–

British science writer, journalist and playwright. She worked on the award-winning television screening of Vera Brittain's *Testament of Youth* (1980). Her controversial book *The Descent of Woman* (1972), which explores the origins of mankind, with special reference to women's evolution, was followed by *The Aquatic Ape* (1982).

82 It takes two to make a woman into a sex object.
1972 *The Descent of Woman*, ch.11.

Moritz, Karl Philipp 1756–93

German writer, an early Romantic. After travelling in England and Italy he wrote *Reisen eines Deutschen in England* (1783) and *Reisen eines Deutschen in Italien* (1792–3). His autobiographical novel *Anton Reise* (1785–90) influenced Goethe.

83 When you see how in this happy country the lowest and poorest member of society takes an interest in all public affairs; when you see how high and low, rich and poor, are all willing to declare their feelings and convictions; when you see how a carter, a common sailor, a beggar is still a man, nay, even more, an Englishman—then, believe me, you find yourself very differently affected from the experience you feel when staring at our soldiers drilling in Berlin.
1782 Letter to a friend after observing a London by-election.

Morley, Christopher Darlington 1890–1957

US writer and poet, founder and editor (1924–41) of the *Saturday Review*. His many novels include *Parnassus on Wheels* (1917).

84 Life is a foreign language: all men mispronounce it.
1925 *Thunder on the Left*, ch.14.

85 Dancing is a wonderful training for girls, it's the first way you learn to guess what a man is going to do before he does it.
1939 *Kitty Foyle*, ch.11.

86 When you sell a man a book, you don't sell him 12 ounces of paper and ink and glue—you sell him a whole new life.
Recalled on his death, 28 Mar 1957.

Morley, Robert 1908–92

English actor. A popular comic actor, he also made many film and television appearances, including *Beat the Devil* (1953), *Oscar Wilde* (1960) and *Who is Killing the Great Chefs of Europe?* (1978).

87 The French are a logical people, which is one reason the English dislike them so intensely. The other is that they own France, a country which we have always judged to be much too good for them.
1974 *A Musing Morley*, 'France and the French'.

88 It is a great help for a man to be in love with himself. For an actor, it is absolutely essential.
1979 In *Playboy*.

89 I started off in films as a king—a French king, admittedly, but nevertheless a king in *Marie Antoinette*—and stayed in that sort of income bracket.
Quoted in *The Best of Robert Morley* (1981).

90 Anyone who works is a fool. I don't work: I merely inflict myself on the public.
Attributed.

Morris, Desmond John 1928–

British ethologist and writer. His interest in primate behaviour led to his best-known work, the popular *The Naked Ape* (1967).

91 The Human Zoo.
1969 Title of book.

92 Clearly, then, the city is not a concrete jungle, it is a human zoo.
1969 *The Human Zoo*, introduction.

Morris, Jan *formerly* James Morris 1926–

English reporter and writer. As James Morris he wrote books and essays on travel. He accompanied the 1953 first ascent of Everest, covering it for *The Times*. As Jan Morris she has written a moving account of her sex change *Conundrum* (1974), the *Pax Britannica* trilogy (1968–78) and other novels. She was made a CBE in 1999.

93 Venice will linger in your mind…and wherever you go in life you will feel somewhere over your shoulder, a pink, castellated, shimmering presence, the domes and riggings and crooked pinnacles of the Serenissima. There's romance for you! There's the lust and dark wine of Venice! No wonder George Eliot's husband fell into the Grand Canal.
1960 *Venice*.

94 The genius of Canada remains essentially a deflationary genius.
1976 'On the Confederation Special,' in *Travels*.

95 If I was an aspirant litterateur, I was also an aspirant anarchist. I have disliked Authority always, though sometimes seduced by its resplendence.
2003 *A Writer's World: Travels 1950–2000*, prologue.

Morris, John 1895–1980

English writer, traveller and academic. He travelled in Asia and Africa, and took part in two Everest expeditions. He taught at Keio University in Japan (1938–42) and later became Head of the Far Eastern Service then Controller of the Third Programme at the BBC (1952–8).

96 The Japanese…have a saying that there are two kinds of fool: those who have never climbed Mount Fuji, and those who have climbed it more than once.
1943 *Traveller from Tokyo*.

Morris, Sir Lewis 1833–1907

Engish versifier.

97 We hold a vaster Empire than has been.
'Song of Empire', written to celebrate Queen Victoria's Jubilee, 20 Jun. The words were printed on Canada's first commemorative postage stamp, 1898.

Morris, William 1834–96

English craftsman and poet, associated with the Pre-Raphaelite Brotherhood, a major figure in the Arts and Crafts Movement. He joined the Social Democratic Federation in 1883, and organized the Socialist League. In 1890 he set up the private Kelmscott Press.

98 The Socialist papers…came out full to the throat of well-printed matter…admirable and straightforward expositions of the doctrines and practice of Socialism, free from haste and spite and hard words…with a kind of May-day freshness amidst the worry and terror of the moment.
1890 *News from Nowhere*.

99 Between complete socialism and communism there is no difference whatever in my mind. Communism is in fact the completion of socialism; when that ceases to be militant and becomes triumphant, it will be communism.
1893 Addressing Hammersmith Socialist Society.

Morris, Wright Marion 1910–98

US writer. He wrote novels, short stories, memoirs and critical essays. He was an accomplished photographer, and published several books marrying text with photographs.

1 A Bill of Rites, A Bill of Wrongs, A Bill of Goods.
1968 Title of essay collection.

Morrison, R F

2 Just a wee deoch-an-doris,
Just a wee yin, that's a'.
Just a wee deoch-an-doris,
Afore we gang awa'.
There's a wee wifie waitin'
In a wee but-an-ben;
If ye can say 'It's a braw bricht moonlicht nicht',
Ye're a' richt, ye ken.
1911 'Just a Wee Deoch-an-Doris', chorus. The song was popularized by Sir Harry Lauder.

Morrison, Toni Chloe Anthony *née* ***Wofford*** 1931–

US novelist. Her novels have reflected black American experience and consciousness through a sophisticated literary sensibility. She was awarded the Nobel prize for literature in 1993.

3 We have to acknowledge that the thing we call 'literature' is more pluralistic now, just as society ought to be. The melting pot never worked.
1981 In *Newsweek*, 30 Mar.

4 How soon country people forget. When they fall in love with a city it is forever, and it is like forever… There, in a city, they are not so much new as themselves: their stronger, riskier selves.
1991 *Jazz*, ch.2.

5 In this country American means white. Everybody else has to hyphenate.
1992 In *The Guardian*, 29 Jan.

6 Slavery broke the world in half, it broke it in every way. It broke Europe. It made them into something else, it made them slave masters, it made them crazy. You can't do that for hundreds of years and it not take a toll. They had to dehumanize, not just the slaves but themselves.
Quoted in Paul Gilroy *Small Acts* (1993), 'Living memory: a meeting with Toni Morrison'.

7 I have always wanted to develop a way of writing that was irrevocably black. I don't have the resources of a musician but I thought that if it was truly black literature, it would not be black because I was, it would not even be black because of its subject matter. It would be something intrinsic, indigenous, something in the way it was put together—the sentences, the structure, texture and tone—so that anyone who read it would realize.
Quoted in Paul Gilroy *Small Acts* (1993), 'Living memory: a meeting with Toni Morrison'.

Morrissey *full name* ***Steven Patrick Morrissey*** 1959–

English singer and songwriter, former member of The Smiths.

8 Heaven Knows I'm Miserable Now.
1984 Song title.

9 No—he lives next door to me.
2002 When asked whether it was true that he lived next door to Johnny Depp. In the *Observer*, 15 Sep.

10 My best friend is myself… It's a lifelong relationship and divorce will never come into it.
2002 In the *Observer*, 15 Sep.

Morse, Samuel F(inley) B(reese) 1791–1872

US inventor and painter, who demonstrated (1844) the practicability of an electrical telegraph device to Congress. He had earlier trained as an artist.

11 Alas! My dear sir, the very name of *pictures* produces a sadness of heart I cannot describe. Painting has been a smiling mistress to many, but she has been a cruel jilt to me.
1849 Letter to his friend the writer James Fenimore Cooper, 20 Nov.

Mortimer, Sir John Clifford 1923–

English playwright, novelist and barrister. Called to the bar in 1948, he took part in several celebrated civil cases before achieving wider fame as a writer, notably as creator of the fictitious barrister Horace Rumpole. His other publications include volumes of autobiography, novels such as *Paradise Postponed* (1985) and *Summer's Lease* (1988) and several plays.

12 No brilliance is needed in the law. Nothing but common sense, and relatively clean finger nails.
1971 *A Voyage Round My Father*, act 1.

13 The law seems like a sort of maze through which a client must be led to safety, a collection of reefs, rocks, and underwater hazards through which he or she must be piloted.
1982 *Clinging to the Wreckage*, ch.7.

14 They do you a decent death in the hunting field.
1985 *Paradise Postponed*, ch.18.

15 The shelf life of the modern hardback writer is somewhere between the milk and the yoghurt.
1987 In the *Observer*, 28 Jun.

16 Life itself is a mystery which defies solution.
1990 In the *Sunday Times*, 1 Apr.

17 But plots come from—God knows where. They can't be summoned at will. They come reluctantly, unexpectedly, stealthily, when you have given up hope of them ever paying you a visit.
1993 'A Plot at Last', in Brown and Munro (eds) *Writers Writing* (1993).

Mortimer, (Charles) Raymond Bell 1895–1980

English literary and art critic.

18 People don't learn to enjoy pictures because they seldom look at them; and they seldom look at pictures because they have never learnt to enjoy them.
1976 *Try Anything Once*.

Morton, Jelly Roll (Ferdinand) 1890–1941

US jazz pianist. He was an important pioneer of the New Orleans jazz style, but was much given to making extravagant claims about his role in it.

19 It is evidently known, beyond contradiction, that New Orleans is the cradle of *jazz*, and I, myself, happened to be the creator in the year 1902… *Jazz* music is a style, not compositions; any kind of music may be played in *jazz*, if one has the knowledge.
1938 In *Downbeat*, Aug.

Morton, J(ohn Cameron Andrieu) B(ingham Michael) *pseudonym* ***Beachcomber*** 1893–1979

English writer. He wrote many books of humour, fantasy, satire and history, but is chiefly remembered for his humorous columns in the *Daily Express*, under the nom de plume 'Beachcomber'.

20 One disadvantage of being a hog is that at any moment some blundering fool may try to make a silk purse out of your wife's ear.
1931 *By the Way.*

21 Hush, hush!
Nobody cares!
Christopher Robin
Has
Fallen
Down
Stairs.
1931 *By the Way.*

22 The Doctor is said also to have invented an extraordinary weapon which will make war less brutal. It is described as a very powerful liquid which rots braces at a distance of a mile.
1936 'Bracerot'.

Morton, Rogers Clark Ballard 1914–1979

US former Republican politician. He was president of a flour manufacturing company and representative for Maryland in the 88th–92nd Congresses. He was Secretary of the Interior (1971–5) and a counsellor to the President on economic and domestic matters (1976–7).

23 I have no intention of rearranging the furniture on the deck of the Titanic.
1976 On declining to rescue President Ford's disastrous election campaign.

Morton, Thomas c.1764–1838

English playwright. He is usually remembered for his comedy *Speed the Plough* (1798).

24 What will Mrs Grundy say? What will Mrs Grundy think?
1798 *Speed the Plough.*

Moses, Anna Mary Robertson *known as 'Grandma Moses'* 1860–1961

US painter. The wife of a farmer in New York state, with no art training, she did not begin painting until in her 70s. Her primitive paintings are colourful, simple scenes of everyday rural life.

25 Paintin's not important. What's important is keepin' busy.
1954 In news summaries, 2 Jan.

Moses, Ed 1955–

US track athlete. He was unbeaten in any 400-metre hurdle race from August 1977 to June 1987, and was Olympic champion in 1976 and 1984 and four times world record holder.

26 There are three universal languages: love, music and sports.
2004 In the *Boston Herald*, 12 May.

Mosk, Stanley 1912–2001

US lawyer and Justice of State Supreme Court. He practised law in Los Angeles until 1939 and was Attorney General of California 1959–64. He was a Justice of the Supreme Court of California from 1964 until his death.

27 Little old ladies in tennis shoes.
Characterizing older, activist women. Quoted in William Safire *Safire's Political Dictionary* (1975).

Moss, Gary

US marketing coach, a former vice-president of marketing communications, Campbell Soup Co.

28 You can teach an elephant to dance, but the likelihood of its stepping on your toes is very high.
1993 On the decline of the advertising agencies' monopoly in marketing. In *Forbes*, 15 Mar.

Moss, Sir Stirling 1929–

English racing driver. Although he never won the World Championship, he became one of the most celebrated of all drivers, winning numerous Grand Prix races driving for a variety of teams. He retired in 1962 after a serious crash.

29 It is necessary to relax your muscles when you can. Relaxing your brain is fatal.
1955 In *Newsweek*, 16 May.

30 There are two things no man will admit he can't do well—drive and make love.
Quoted in Colin Jarman *The Guinness Dictionary of Sports Quotations* (1990).

Motherwell, Robert 1915–91

US painter and writer, an exponent of Abstract Realism. His works typically consist of large, amorphous blocks of strong colour, such as his most famous series, *Elegies to the Spanish Republic* (1975).

31 One of the most striking of abstract art's appearance is her nakedness, an art stripped bare.
1951 Paper given at a symposium, 5 Feb, at the Museum of Modern Art, New York, published in *What Abstract Art Means to Me: Bulletin of the Museum of Modern Art* (Spring 1951).

32 Every intelligent painter carries the whole culture of modern painting in his head...everything he paints is both an homage and a critique.
1977 In the *Los Angeles Times*, 31 Jul.

33 All my life I've been working on the work—every canvas a sentence or paragraph of it. Each picture is only an approximation of what I want.
Recalled on his death, 16 Jul 1991.

Motion, Andrew 1952–

English poet and biographer, Poet Laureate from 1999.

34 Earth's axle creeks; the year jolts on; the trees
begin to slip their brittle leaves, their flakes of rust;
and darkness takes the edge off daylight, not
because it wants to—never that. Because it must.
1997 'Mythology', written for the funeral of Diana, Princess of Wales. Published in *Public Property* (2002).

35 O Jonny the power of your boot
And the accurate heart-stopping route
Of your goal as it ghosts
Through Australian posts
Is a triumph we gladly salute.
2004 'A Song for Jonny', written to commemorate England winning the rugby World Cup and the player Jonny Wilkinson.

Motson, John 1946–

English football commentator.

36 It's Arsenal 0 Everton 1 and the longer it stays like that the more you've got to fancy Everton.
Quoted in *Motson's National Obsession* (2004).

37 Nearly all the Brazilian supporters are wearing yellow shirts— it's a fabulous kaleidoscope of colour.
Quoted in *Motson's National Obsession* (2004).

38 For those of you watching in black and white, Spurs are in the all-yellow strip.
Quoted in *Motson's National Obsession* (2004).

Mountbatten of Burma, Louis Francis Albert Victor Nicholas, 1st Earl 1900–79

English admiral and statesman, chief of Combined Operations Command (1942) in World War II. As Supreme Commander, SE Asia, he received the Japanese surrender at Singapore, and in 1947 became last Viceroy of India. He returned to the Admiralty as First Sea Lord (1954) and Chief of the Defence Staff (1959). He retired in 1965 and in 1979 was assassinated by Irish Republican terrorists.

39 As a military man who has given half a century of active service, I say in all sincerity that the nuclear arms race has no military purpose. Wars cannot be fought with nuclear weapons; their existence only adds to our perils because of the illusions that they have generated. The world now stands on the brink of the final abyss. Let us all resolve to take all possible practicable steps to ensure that we do not, through our own folly, go over the edge.
1979 Speech at the Council of Europe in Strasbourg, 11 May.

Mowlam, Mo (Marjorie) 1949–

English Labour politician. She was Secretary of State for Northern Ireland from 1997 to 1999.

40 Ian Paisley said he pitied my husband having to put up with 'the sinner', which is what he often called me.
2000 In the *Sunday Times*, 16 Apr.

Moynihan, Daniel Patrick 1927–2003

US sociologist and diplomat, adviser to Presidents Kennedy, Johnson, Nixon and Ford. He was Ambassador to India (1973–5), US representative to the UN (1975–6), and subsequently a Senator (1976–2001). His writings include *Beyond the Melting Pot* (with Nathan Glazer, 1963).

41 We've come full circle but the best remains the heart of the city, the greatest center of the greatest city, our Acropolis, where our Christmas tree is lighted.
1991 On New York's Rockefeller Centre. In the *New York Times*, 15 Mar.

42 Things become complicated if there are enough people to complexify them.
1991 Of the 19,000-member congressional back-up staff. In the *New York Times*, 12 Nov.

43 They live off secrecy…[it] keep the mistakes secret.
1993 Of government intelligence agencies. *President Kennedy.*

44 The Lord looks after drunks and Americans.
1995 Of the avoidance of casualties in the Haitian intervention. In the *US News and World Report*, 9 Jan.

Mozart, (Johann Chrysostom) Wolfgang Amadeus 1756–91

Austrian composer. An infant prodigy, who suffered throughout his life from poverty and overwork, his many compositions include symphonies, concertos, string quintets, string quartets, numerous piano and violin sonatas, choral works and operas such as *The Marriage of Figaro* (1786), *Don Giovanni* (1787), *Così fan tutte* (1790) and *The Magic Flute* (1791).

45 It is much easier to play a thing quickly than to play it slowly.
1778 Letter.

46 Melody is the very essence of music. When I think of a good melodist I think of a fine race horse. A contrapuntist is only a post-horse.
1786 Letter to Michael Kelly.

Mugabe, Robert Gabriel 1924–

Zimbabwean politician. He co-founded ZANU (Zimbabwe African National Union, 1963), and on Zimbabwe's independence in 1980 became first Prime Minister (1980–7) and subsequently President (1987–).

47 Cricket? It civilises people and creates good gentlemen. I want everyone to play cricket in Zimbabwe. I want ours to be a nation of gentlemen.
Quoted in Helen Exley *Cricket Quotations* (1992).

Muggeridge, Malcolm 1903–90

English journalist. He was Editor of *Punch* from 1953 to 1957, and appeared frequently on television as reporter and interviewer. In his later years he became a Roman Catholic.

48 The orgasm has replaced the cross as the focus of longing and the image of fulfilment.
1966 *Tread Softly for You Tread on My Jokes.*

49 The media have, indeed, provided the Devil with perhaps the greatest opportunity accorded him since Adam and Eve were turned out of the Garden of Eden.
1970 *Christ and the Media*, introduction.

50 Future historians will surely see us as having created in the media a Frankenstein monster whom no one knows how to control or direct, and marvel that we should have so meekly subjected ourselves to its destructive and often malign influence.
1976 *Christ and the Media*, 'Lecture 1'.

51 It's very nearly impossible to tell the truth in television.
1976 *Christ and the Media*, 'Questions following the 3rd lecture'.

Muir, Edwin 1887–1959

Scottish writer and translator. He is best known as a poet, but also wrote literary and cultural criticism, and an autobiography.

52 The curse of Scottish literature is the lack of a whole language, which finally means the lack of a whole mind.
1936 *Scott and Scotland*, introduction.

53 The hills and towers
Stood otherwise than they should stand,
And without fear the lawless roads
Ran wrong throughout the land.
1937 *Journeys and Places*, 'Hölderlin's Journey', stanza 11.

54 There is a road that turning always
Cuts off the country of Again.

Archers stand there on every side
And as it runs time's deer is slain,
And lies where it has lain.
1937 'The Road'.

55 All through that summer at ease we lay,
And daily from the turret wall
We watched the mowers in the hay
And the enemy half a mile away.
They seemed no threat to us at all.
1946 *The Voyage*, 'The Castle', stanza 1.

56 It was not meant for human eyes,
That combat on the shabby patch
Of clods and trampled earth that lies
Somewhere beneath the sodden skies
For eye of toad or adder to catch.
1949 *The Labyrinth*, 'The Combat'.

57 Oh these deceits are strong almost as life.
Last night I dreamt I was in the labyrinth,
And woke far on. I did not know the place.
1949 *The Labyrinth*, 'The Labyrinth'.

58 We have seen
Good men made evil wrangling with the evil,
Straight minds grown crooked fighting crooked minds.
Our peace betrayed us; we betrayed our peace.
Look at it well. This was the good town once.
1949 *The Labyrinth*, 'The Good Town'.

59 Kindness and courage can repair time's faults,
And serving him breeds patience and courtesy
In us, light sojourners and passing subjects.
1949 *The Labyrinth*, 'The Good Town'.

60 The life of every man is an endlessly repeated performance of the life of man.
1954 *An Autobiography*, ch.1.

61 Since then they have pulled our ploughs and borne our loads.
But that free servitude still can pierce our hearts.
Our life is changed; their coming our beginning.
1956 *One Foot in Eden*, 'The Horses'.

62 Barely a twelvemonth after
The seven days war that put the world to sleep,
Late in the evening the strange horses came.
1956 *One Foot in Eden*, 'The Horses'.

63 One foot in Eden still, I stand
And look across the other land.
The world's great day is growing late,
Yet strange these fields that we have planted
So long with crops of love and hate.
1956 *One Foot in Eden*, 'One Foot in Eden'.

Muir, John 1838–1914

Scottish naturalist. He emigrated with his family to America as a boy, and became a champion of wilderness areas and the establishment of National Parks in the US. He is regarded as the father of the environmental movement.

64 The tendency nowadays to wander in wildernesses is delightful to see. Thousands of tired, nerve-shaken, over-civilized people are beginning to find out that going to the mountains is going home; that wildness is a necessity; and that mountain parks and reservations are useful not only as fountains of timber and irrigating rivers, but as fountains of life.
1901 *Our National Parks*, ch.1, 'The Wild Parks and Forest Reservations of the West'.

65 When we contemplate the whole globe as one great dewdrop, striped and dotted with continents and islands, flying through space with other stars all singing and shining together as one, the whole universe appears as an infinite storm of beauty.
Travels in Alaska, ch.1, 'The Puget Sound and British Columbia' (published 1915).

66 I have precious little sympathy for the selfish propriety of civilized man, and if a war of races should occur between the wild beasts and Lord Man, I would be tempted to sympathise with the bears.
A Thousand-Mile Walk to the Gulf, ch.5, 'Through Florida Swamps and Forests' (published 1916).

Muir, Willa (Wilhelmina) Johnstone *née* *Anderson* *also known as* *Agnes Neill Scott* 1890–1970

Scottish poet, novelist and translator, wife of the poet Edwin Muir whose unconventional religious beliefs forced her resignation from a teaching position in 1915. Her published works include many translations, several novels and a book of poetry.

67 Apparently the average man sees woman alternately as an inferior being and as an angel.
1925 *Women: An Inquiry*, pt.1, published as Hogarth Essay no.10 in *The Hogarth Essays* (Second Series, 1926).

68 A man can be a parent without knowing it: a woman cannot.
1925 *Women: An Inquiry*, pt.1, published as Hogarth Essay no.10 in *The Hogarth Essays* (Second Series, 1926).

Mullan, Peter 1960–

Scottish actor and director.

69 Worst script I've ever read.
2003 On *Braveheart*. In *The Herald*, 1 Feb.

70 There's no such thing as an actor giving positive criticism to a director. The minute you say 'Don't you think it would look nicer…', that director's going to hate your guts. Particularly if it's a good idea.
2003 In a question and answer session at the National Film Theatre, London, 4 Nov.

71 Nine out of ten delinquents are frustrated actors.
2003 In a question and answer session at the National Film Theatre, London, 4 Nov.

Muller, Herbert Joseph 1905–80

US writer.

72 Few have probably ever heard of Fra Luca Pacioli, the inventor of double-entry bookkeeping; but he has probably had much more influence on human life than has Dante or Michelangelo.
1957 *Uses of the Past*, ch.8.

Mulroney, (Martin) Brian 1939–

Canadian Conservative politician, Prime Minister (1984–93). His radical reforms included the Meech Lake Accords (which aimed at settling disputes between the provinces and the centre, but which later collapsed) and a free-trade agreement with the US.

73 In politics, madame, you need two things: friends, but

above all an enemy.
1990 Remark made to a journalist following the by-election victory of Liberal leader Jean Chrétien, 10 Dec, quoted two days later by Graham Fraser in *The Globe and Mail.*

Mumford, Lewis 1895–1990

US sociologist and author. A literary critic and journal editor, he began to write on architecture and urbanization in such works as *The Story of Utopias* (1922) and *The City in History* (1961), stressing the dehumanizing effects of technology.

74 Every generation revolts against its fathers and makes friends with its grandfathers.
1931 *The Brown Decades*, p.3.

75 However far modern science and technics have fallen short of their inherent possibilities, they have taught mankind at least one lesson: Nothing is impossible.
1934 *Technics and Civilization.*

76 The Fujiyama of Architecture…at once a lofty mountain and a national shrine.
1953 Of Frank Lloyd Wright. 'A Phoenix Too Infrequent', in the *New Yorker*, 28 Nov.

77 Our national flower is the concrete cloverleaf.
Collected in *Quote Magazine*, 8 Oct 1961.

78 The life-efficiency and adaptability of the computer must be questioned. Its judicious use depends upon the availability of its human employers quite literally to keep their own heads, not merely to scrutinize the programming but to reserve for themselves the right of ultimate decision. No automatic system can be intelligently run by automatons—or by people who dare not assert human intuition, human autonomy, human purpose.
1970 *The Myth of the Machine.*

79 As full of flavor as hickory smoke.
1994 Of geotechnic expert Benton MacKaye. In *Harvard University Magazine*, Jul.

Munch, Edvard 1863–1944

Norwegian painter and graphic artist.

80 One evening, I was walking along a path, the city was on one side and the fjord below. I felt tired and ill. I stopped and looked out over the fjord—the sun was setting, and the clouds turning blood red. I sensed a scream passing through nature; it seemed to me that I heard the scream. I painted this picture, painted the clouds as actual blood. The colour shrieked. This became The Scream.
1889 *Diary.*

Münch, Richard Friedrich 1945–

German sociologist, professor at the University of Bamberg.

81 Social life is mutual negotiation and society, social order, relies on this mutual negotiation between individuals; this represents both creed and particular reality in American society. In no other society is this creed and the corresponding reality as prominent as the United States.
1986 'The American Creed in Sociological Theory', in *Sociological Theory*, vol.4, issue 43.

Mundy, Peter c.1596–1667

English trader and seafarer. He was sent to France at the age of 12 to learn French. At 15 he went to sea and travelled continually thereafter. His journal was edited by the Hakluyt Society.

82 We all three got up on our elephant which brought us hither. For my own part I found [it] very uneasy riding, being badly seated and not accustomed (he had such a shuffling, jogging justling pace), sitting hindermost on the ridge of his monstrous massy chine bones, and nothing at all under me (nor they neither) that I wished myself on foot and would have let myself fall off but that it was somewhat too high. In fine, we alighted off from his back into the upper galleries of the house and saved the labour going upstairs.
c.1620 On riding on an elephant. *Travels* (pubished c.1650).

83 So that finding myself at present in or about one hundred and twenty degrees off east longitude from England, it bred in me a desire to proceed on the same easterly course till I had ended where I began, and so to have once made one circle round the globe of the earth, which would have been a voyage of voyages.
c.1640 Objections were raised and Mundy was unable to fulfil this aim. *Travels* (published c.1650).

Munro, Alice *née* Laidlaw 1931–

Canadian short-story writer; her first collection of short stories *Dance of the Happy Shades* (1968) won the Governor-General's Award, as did *Lives of Girls and Women* (1971).

84 Boys' hate was dangerous, it was keen and bright, a miraculous birthright, like Arthur's sword snatched out of the stone.
1971 *Lives of Girls and Women*, 'Changes and Ceremonies'.

85 I thought of my mother, who would publicly campaign for birth control but would never even think she needed to talk to me, so firmly was she convinced that sex was something no woman—no *intelligent* woman would ever submit to unless she had to.
1971 *Lives of Girls and Women*, 'Baptizing'.

86 She had reached an age where she thought she could not stand to know any more…she pushed any discovery aside with embarassment.
1978 *Lives of Girls and Women*, 'Royal Beatings'.

87 Country manners. Even if somebody phones up to tell you your house is burning down, they ask first how you are.
1987 *The Progress of Love*, 'The Progress of Love'.

88 Hatred is always a sin, my mother told me. Remember that. One drop of hatred in your soul will spread and discolor everything like a drop of black ink in white milk. I was struck by that and meant to try it, but knew I shouldn't waste the milk.
1987 *The Progress of Love*, 'The Progress of Love'.

89 People live within winter in a way outsiders do not understand. They are watchful, provident, fatigued, exhilarated.
1987 *The Progress of Love*, 'Fits'.

90 Do such moments really mean, as they seem to, that we have a life of happiness with which we only occasionally, knowingly, intersect? Do they shed such light before and after that all that has happened in our lives—or that we've made to happen—can be dismissed?
1987 *The Progress of Love*, 'The Moon in the Orange Street Skating Rink'.

Münster, Count Georg 1794–1868

Hanoverian diplomat.

91 An intelligent Russian once remarked to me, 'Every country has its own Constitution. Ours is absolutism moderated by assassination.'
Political Sketches of the State of Europe 1814–1867

Murdoch, Dame (Jean) Iris 1919–99

Irish novelist and philosopher, of Anglo-Irish descent. Her novels, exploring human relationships with subtlety and humour, include *The Sea, The Sea* (1978) and *The Philosopher's Pupil* (1983).

92 All our failures are ultimately failures in love.
1958 *The Bell.*

93 Love is the extremely difficult realisation that something other than oneself is real. Love, and so art and morals, is the discovery of reality.
1959 'The Sublime and the Good'.

94 What can one do with the past?
Forgive it. Let it enter into you in peace.
1968 *The Nice and the Good.*

95 He was a sociologist; he had gotten into an intellectual muddle early on in life and never managed to get out.
1983 *The Philosopher's Pupil*, 'The Events in Our Town'.

Murdoch, (Keith) Rupert 1931–

Australian-born US newspaper publisher. He expanded his publishing empire first in Australia, then in Britain, buying the *News of the World* in 1969, *The Times* and the *Sunday Times* in 1981. He moved into the US market in 1976 and created a successful television network, the Fox Network. He became a US citizen in 1985.

96 I did not come all this way not to interfere.
c.1969 Quoted in S Somerfield *Banner Headlines* (1979). Somerfield was editor of the *News of the World* and complained that Murdoch, who had recently bought the paper, was interfering with his editorial role.

97 I have heard cynics who say he's a very political old monk shuffling around in Gucci shoes.
1999 On the Dalai Lama. In the *Daily Telegraph*, 7 Sep.

Murkowski, Frank H 1933–

US Governor of Alaska (2002–). Former Vice-Chair, US Senate Select Committee on Intelligence.

98 Low morale and high indigestion.
1991 Of the mood of the Senate confirming CIA Director Robert M Gates. In the *New York Times*, 12 Nov.

Murphy, Dervla 1931–

Irish writer and traveller. In 1963 she cycled to India, where she worked with Tibetan children.

99 On my tenth birthday a bicycle and an atlas coincided as presents and a few days later I decided to cycle to India.
1965 *Full Tilt: Ireland to India with a Bicycle.*

1 It is on occasions such as these that I thank God for my sanguine temperament, which refuses to allow me to believe in disaster until it is finally manifest.
1965 *Full Tilt: Ireland to India with a Bicycle.*

2 Each human spirit is immortal—for time cannot destroy whatever element within us reverences the glory of a dawn in the mountains.
1968 *In Ethiopia with a Mule.*

3 Never before had I embarked on a journey that required courage.
1978 On embarking on travels and research into the problems of Northern Ireland. *A Place Apart.*

Murphy, Ian

Architect, lecturer at the University of Westminster.

4 The technology of decentralization can be the saviour or assassin of contemporary and future society. The role of architects may be uncertain, but the role of architecture is not. In order to look forward society may sometimes have to look back. This it should do in order to learn from previous mistakes and oversights and to preclude similar eventualities in the future. This does not imply historical dependency, as some would assert. The symbiosis of architecture and technology should prevail, engendered by honesty and integrity. The task will not be easy.
1993 'The impact of the environment: the shock of the new', in Ben Farmer and Hentie Louw (eds) *Companion to Contemporary Architectural Thought* (1993).

Murphy, Tom (Thomas) S 1925–

US media company executive, president (1964–72) and chair (1966–96) of ABC Inc.

5 If you hire mediocre people, they will hire mediocre people.
1991 In *Fortune*, 6 May.

Murray, Les(lie Allan) 1938–

Australian poet and writer whose exuberant verse reflects both his farming background and his preoccupation with language. His collections include *The Ilex Tree* (1965), *The Weatherboard Cathedral* (1969), *Subhuman Redneck Poems* (1996) and *Conscious and Verbal* (1999).

6 The houses there wear verandahs out of shyness.
1986 *Selected Poems*, 'Driving Through Sawmill Towns'.

7 If the cardinal points of costume
are Robes, Tato, Rig and Scunge,
where are shorts in this compass?

They are the never Robes
as other bareleg outfits have been:
the toga, the kilt, the lava-lava,
the Mahatma's cotton dhoti;

archbishops and field marshals
at their ceremonies never wear shorts.
The very word
means underpants in North America.
1986 *Selected Poems*, 'The Dream of Wearing Shorts Forever'.

8 A for adrenalin, the original A-bomb, fuel
and punishment of aspiration, the Enlightenment's
air-burst
Back when God made me, I had no script. It was better.
For all the death, we also die unrehearsed.
In *Collected Poems* (1998).

Murray, Mike (Michael) c.1956–

US computer executive and philanthropist. Vice-President of Human Resources and Administration at Microsoft until 1999.

9 If Microsoft were a car it would have a large gas pedal and a small but workable brake. It would not have a rear-view mirror.
1994 In *Newsweek*, 11 Jul.

Murrow, Edward (Edgar) R(oscoe) 1908–65

US journalist and broadcaster. As CBS correspondent from Britain from 1937, he conveyed wartime spirit to the US. He became a producer of current affairs television programmes after the war, and his questioning of Joseph McCarthy contributed to the Senator's fall from grace.

10 He mobilized the English language and sent it into battle to steady his fellow countrymen and hearten those Europeans upon whom the long dark night of tyranny had descended.
1954 Of Churchill. Broadcast, 30 Nov, quoted in *In Search of Light* (1967).

11 The people you have seen have the strength to harvest your fruit and vegetables. They do not have the strength to influence legislation. Maybe you do.
1960 *Harvest of Shame*, CBS TV documentary on migrant labour, 25 Nov, concluding words.

12 The politician is trained in the art of inexactitude. His words tend to be blunt or rounded, because if they have a cutting edge they may later return to wound him.
Attributed.

Muschamp, Herbert

Architecture critic for the *New York Times*.

13 Red-and-gold disease...an itch, the theater a place to scratch it...a yearning for the wider world.
1995 In the *New York Times*, 30 Jul. The phrase 'red-and-gold disease' was coined by Lincoln Kirstein's mother when her son began haunting theatres.

Musgrove, F(rank)

English educationalist.

14 It is the business of education to eliminate the influence of parents on the life-chances of the young.
1966 *The Family, Education and Society.*

Mussolini, Benito *also called* *Il Duce [the Leader]* 1883–1945

Italian politician and Prime Minister (1922). By 1925 he had established himself as dictator. His declaration of war on Britain and France exposed Italy's military unpreparedness, and was followed by a series of defeats; his popularity waned, and he was overthrown and arrested (Jul 1943). Rescued by German paratroopers to head the puppet Italian Social Republic, in 1945 he was captured by the Italian Resistance and shot.

15 I could have transformed this grey assembly hall into an armed camp of Blackshirts, a bivouac for corpses. I could have nailed up the doors of Parliament.
1922 Inaugural speech to the Lower House as Prime Minister, 16 Nov.

16 If I advance, follow me. If I retreat, kill me. If I die, avenge me.
1926 Said to senior officials after an attempt on his life, 6 Apr.

17 Better one day as a lion than a hundred years as a sheep.
c.1930 Quoted in Denis Mack-Smith *Mussolini's Roman Empire* (1976), p.47.

18 War alone can carry to the maximum tension all human energies and imprint with the seal of nobility those people who have the courage to confront it; every other test is a mere substitute.
c.1930 Quoted in Denis Mack-Smith *Mussolini's Roman Empire* (1976), p.47.

19 Words are beautiful things, but muskets and machine guns are even more beautiful.
c.1932 Quoted in Denis Mack-Smith *Mussolini's Roman Empire* (1976).

20 A nation, to remain healthy, should make war every twenty-five years.
1934 Quoted in Denis Mack-Smith *Mussolini's Roman Empire* (1976), p.63.

21 War is to man as maternity to women.
1934 Speech, May. Quoted in Denis Mack-Smith *Mussolini's Roman Empire* (1976), p.54.

22 When the war in Spain is over I shall have to find something else: the Italian character has to be formed through fighting.
1936 Quoted in Thomas *The Spanish Civil War*, p.226.

23 Fascism accepts the individual only insofar as his interests coincide with the state's.
Quoted in the *Enciclopedia Italiana*.

Myers, Mike 1963–

US actor.

24 Party on, dude!
1992 As Wayne Campbell in *Wayne's World*.

25 Yeah, baby!
1997 As Austin Powers in *Austin Powers—International Man of Mystery*.

Myrdal, (Karl) Gunnar 1898–1987

Swedish economist. Professor of Economics, Stockholm University (1933–9, 1961–5). A prominent member of the 'Stockholm School' of macroeconomics of the 1930s. Swedish Minister for Trade and Commerce (1945–7) and Executive Secretary of the UN Economic Commerce (1947–57). In 1974 he was jointly awarded the Nobel prize for economics with Friedrich Hayek. His wife Alva was awarded the Nobel prize for peace in 1982 with Alfonso Garcia Robles.

26 Quantities defined in terms of measurements made at the end of the period in question are referred to as ex *post*; quantities defined in terms of action planned at the beginning of the period in question are referred to as ex *ante*.
1939 *Monetary Equilibrium.*

Nabokov, Vladimir 1899–1977

Russian-born US writer. He left Russia in 1917 and began writing in English in the 1940s. His most widely known novel is *Lolita* (1955). His work is multi-layered and highly literary.

27 There are aphorisms that, like airplanes, stay up only while they are in motion.
1937 *The Gift*, ch.1.

28 Poor Knight! he really had two periods, the first—a dull man writing broken English, the second—a broken man writing dull English.
1941 *The Real Life of Sebastian Knight*, ch.1.

29 The cradle rocks above an abyss, and common sense tells us that our existence is but a brief crack of light between two eternities of darkness.
1951 *Conclusive Evidence* (revised as *Speak, Memory*, 1966), ch.1.

30 Lolita, light of my life, fire of my loins. My sin, my soul. Lo-lee-ta: the tip of the tongue taking a trip of three steps down the palate to tap, at three, on the teeth. Lo. Lee. Ta.
1955 Humbert Humbert. *Lolita*, pt.1, ch.1.

31 You can always count on a murderer for a fancy prose style.
1955 Humbert Humbert. *Lolita*, ch.1.

32 The tiny madman in his padded cell.
1955 Humbert Humbert's description of an embryo. *Lolita*, ch.11.

33 Like so many ageing college people, Pnin had long ceased to notice the existence of students on campus.
1957 *Pnin*, ch.3, section 6.

34 As to the rest, I am no more guilty of imitating 'real life' than 'real life' is responsible for plagiarizing me.
1958 *Nabokov's Dozen*, bibliographical note.

35 Life is a great surprise. I do not see why death should not be an even greater one.
1962 *Pale Fire*.

36 Human life is but a series of footnotes to a vast, obscure unfinished masterpiece.
1962 *Pale Fire*, 'Commentary'.

37 Solitude is the playfield of Satan.
1962 *Pale Fire*, 'Commentary'.

38 I know more than I can express in words, and the little I can express would not have been expressed, had I not known more.
1964 Interview in *Playboy*, Jan.

39 A novelist is, like all mortals, more fully at home on the surface of the present than in the ooze of the past.
1964 Interview in *Playboy*, Jan.

40 A work of art has no importance whatever to society. It is only important to the individual, and only the individual reader is important to me.
1964 Interview in *Playboy*, Jan.

41 Style and structure are the essence of a book; great ideas are hogwash.
1967 Interview in the *Paris Review*, Summer.

42 Derivative writers seem versatile because they imitate many others, past and present. Artistic originality has only itself to copy.
1967 Interview in the *Paris Review*, Summer.

43 Satire is a lesson, parody is a game.
1967 Interview in *Wisconsin Studies in Contemporary Literature*, Spring.

44 Those Eggheads are terrible Philistines. A real good head is not oval but round.
1967 Interview in *Wisconsin Studies in Contemporary Literature*, Spring.

45 A good laugh is the best pesticide.
1968 Interview on BBC television. Reported in *The Listener*, 10 Oct.

46 I think like a genius, I write like a distinguished author, and I speak like a child.
1973 *Strong Opinions*, foreword.

47 Her exotic daydreams do not prevent her from being small-town bourgeois at heart, clinging to conventional ideas or committing this or that conventional violation of the conventional, adultery being a most conventional way to rise above the conventional.
'Madame Bovary'. Collected in *Lectures on Literature* (published 1980).

48 My answer to your question 'Does the writer have a social responsibility?' is NO. You owe me ten cents, sir.
Letter to an editor who had offered him $200 for 2,000 words. Quoted by Eleanor Blau in the *New York Times*, 24 Aug 1989.

Naipaul, Sir V(idiadhar) S(urajprasad) 1932–

Trinidadian writer. His works include *The Mystic Masseur* (1957, John Llewelyn Rhys Memorial Prize), *Miguel Street* (1959, Somerset Maugham Award), *A House for Mr. Biswas* (1961), *A Bend in the River* (1979, Booker Prize) and the autobiographical *Finding the Centre* (1984). He was awarded the Nobel prize for literature in 2001.

49 Worse, to have lived without even attempting to lay claim to one's portion of the earth; to have lived and died as one had been born, unnecessary and unaccommodated.
1961 *A House for Mr. Biswas*, prologue.

50 All that I know of our history and the history of the Indian Ocean I have got from books written by Europeans… Without Europeans, I feel, all our past would have been washed away, like the scuff marks of fishermen on the beach.
1979 *A Bend in the River*, ch.1, 'The Second Rebellion'.

51 I do not regard the knighthood as a social accomplishment.
1993 Quoted in 'Kingdom of Naipaul' by Zoë Heller in the *Independent on Sunday Review*, 28 Mar.

52 Take it on the chin and move on.
Attributed comment to Paul Theroux after their friendship ended. In *Sir Vidia's Shadow: A Friendship Across Five Continents by Paul Theroux* (1998).

Nairne, Caroline, Lady 1766–1845

Scottish songwriter, who collected traditional airs and wrote lyrics to them, often on Jacobite themes.

53 The laird o' Cockpen, he's proud an' he's great,
His mind is ta'en up wi' things o' the State.
'The Laird o' Cockpen', stanza 1.

54 I'm wearin' awa', John
Like snaw-wreaths in thaw, John,
I'm wearin' awa'
To the land o' the leal.
'The Land o' the Leal', stanza 1.

55 Bonnie Charlie's now awa,
Safely owre the friendly main;
Mony a heart will break in twa,
Should he ne'er come back again.

Will ye no come back again?
Will ye no come back again?
Better lo'ed ye canna be,
Will ye no come back again?
'Will Ye No Come Back Again?', stanza 1 and chorus.

Namath, Joe Willie (Joseph William) 1943–

US football player. Known as 'Broadway Joe', he was an outstanding quarterback with Alabama University and, from 1965, the New York Jets. In 1969 he led the Jets to unexpected victory in the Superbowl.

56 When you win, nothing hurts.
Quoted in Colin Jarman *The Guinness Dictionary of Sports Quotations* (1990).

Napier, Sir Charles James 1782–1853

Scottish soldier, born in London. He served in Ireland, Portugal, against the US and in 1841 was sent to India, where he broke the power of the amirs at the Battle of Meeanee and became Governor of Sind.

57 *Peccavi.*
I have sinned [Sind].
1843 Attributed encoded message, 24 Mar, sent after the Battle of Hyderabad and the capture of Sind.

Napoleon I 1769–1821

French general and Emperor. Born in Corsica, he rose to prominence during the French Revolution, and was appointed to command the army of Italy in 1796. Campaigns in Egypt and Austria followed, and his successes allowed him to lead a coup against the government and become dictator. Although he was exiled to Elba by the Allies in 1814, he returned in 1815, when he was finally defeated at Waterloo and exiled to St Helena.

58 *Soldats, songez que, du haut de ces pyramides, quarante siècles vous contemplent.*
Soldiers, think that, from the summit of these pyramids, forty centuries look down upon you.
1798 Speech to the Army of Egypt, before the Battle of the Pyramids, 21 Jul. Quoted in Gaspard Gourgaud *Mémoires* (1823), vol.2, 'Egypte, Bataille des Pyramides'.

59 China? There lies a sleeping giant. Let him sleep! For when he wakes he will move the world.
c.1800 Attributed.

60 Wisdom and policy dictate that we must do as destiny demands and keep peace with the irresistible march of events.
1808 Said to Alexander I of Russia, 2 Feb.

61 In war, three-quarters turns on moral considerations; the balance of actual forces counts only for the remaining quarter.
1808 Comment, 27 Apr. Quoted in *Observations sur les affaires de l'Espagne, Saint Cloud*, in *Correspondance de Napoleon Ier* (1858–69), vol.17.

62 France has more need of me than I have of France.
1813 Speech to Corps Législatif, Paris, 31 Dec.

63 How beautifully the English fight! But they must give way.
1815 Attributed, at the Battle of Waterloo, 18 Jun.

64 The English conquered us; but they are far from being our equals.
1815 Letter to Gaspar Gourgaud from St Helena, after the Battle of Waterloo.

65 An army marches on its stomach.
1816 Attributed. Probably condensed from a long passage dated 14 Nov in E A de Las Cases *Le Mémoriale de Sainte-Hélène* (1823), vol.4.

66 In war, as in love, we must come into contact before we can triumph.
Quoted in A G De Liancourt (ed) *Maximes de Napoleon* (1842).

67 William behaved like a bashful girl, who is afraid of her lover's bad reputation and therefore avoids being alone with him.
Of William I of Prussia, who invited other German Princes to attend a meeting with Napoleon at Baden-Baden in June originally intended to be a private discussion on the possibility of a joint alliance with Russia. Quoted in A J P Taylor *Struggle for Mastery in Europe 1848–1918* (1954), p.121.

68 England is a nation of shopkeepers.
Attributed while in exile on St Helena.

69 Power is my mistress. I have worked too hard in conquering her to allow anyone to take her from me, or even to covet her.
The Journal of Roederer.

70 Prussia was hatched from a cannon-ball.
Attributed.

Napoleon III *until 1852* Louis-Napoleon *in full* Charles Louis Napoleon Bonaparte 1808–73

President of the Second French Republic (1848–52) and Emperor of the French (1852–70). He encouraged economic expansion and modernization, and presided over the Crimean conflict (1854–6) and the ill-starred intervention in Mexico (1861–7). After defeat by Prussia in 1870, the remainder of his life was spent in exile in England.

71 For too long, society has resembled a pyramid that has been turned upside down and made to rest on its summit. I have replaced it on its base.
1852 Speech to the Legislative Assembly, 29 Mar.

72 We must not seek to fashion events, but let them happen of their own accord.
1865 In conversation with Bismarck, Biarritz, 4 Oct.

73 When a man of my name is in power, he must do great things.
Quoted in A J P Taylor *From Napoleon to the Second International* (1993).

Narogin, Mudrooroo *formerly* Colin Jackson 1938–

Australian writer and poet, who has piloted Aboriginal literature courses at several Australian universities. His works include *Dr. Wooreddy's Prescription for Enduring the Ending of the World* (1983), the song cycle *Dalwurra: The Black Bittern* (1988), the anthology *Writing from the Fringe* (1990) and *The Promised Land* (2000).

74 The Aboriginal writer is a Janus-type figure with one face turned to the past and the other to the future while existing in a postmodern, multicultural Australia in which he or she must fight for cultural space.
1990 *Writing from the Fringe*, ch.1, 'Writing from the Fringe'.

Nash, (Frederic) Ogden 1902–71

US light versifier. His popular verse was published frequently in the *New Yorker* and helped establish its sophisticated tone. His collections include *Hard Lines* (1931) and *Boy is a Boy* (1960).

75 The cow is of the bovine ilk;
One end is moo, the other, milk.
1931 *Free Wheeling*, 'The Cow'.

76 The song of canaries
Never varies,
And when they're moulting
They're pretty revolting.
1931 *Free Wheeling*, 'The Canary'.

77 A bit of talcum
Is always walcum.
1931 *Free Wheeling*, 'The Baby'.

78 One would be in less danger
From the wiles of a stranger
If one's own kin and kith
Were more fun to be with.
1931 *Hard Lines*, 'Family Court'.

79 A girl whose cheeks are covered with paint
Has an advantage with me over one whose ain't.
1931 *Hard Lines*, 'Biological Reflection'.

80 Candy
Is dandy
But liquor
Is quicker.
1931 *Hard Lines*, 'Reflections on Ice-Breaking'.

81 The turtle lives 'twixt plated decks
Which practically conceal its sex.
I think it clever of the turtle
In such a fix to be so fertile.
1931 *Hard Lines*, 'Autres Bêtes, Autres Moeurs'.

82 It's better to be dead, or even perfectly well, than to suffer from the wrong affliction. The man who owns up to arthritis in a beri-beri year is as lonely as a woman in a last month's dress.
1933 'How's Your Sacro-iliac?', in the *Saturday Evening Post*, 14 Oct.

83 Any kiddie in school can love like a fool,
But hating, my boy, is an art.
1933 *Happy Days*, 'Plea for Less Malice Toward None'.

84 I think that I shall never see
A billboard lovely as a tree.
Perhaps, unless the billboards fall,
I'll never see a tree at all.
1933 *Happy Days*, 'Song of the Open Road'.
► *See Kilmer 467:17.*

85 Children aren't happy with nothing to ignore
And that's what parents were created for.
1933 *Happy Days*, 'The Parent'.

86 Home is heaven and orgies are vile,
But you *need* an orgy, once in a while.
1935 *The Primrose Path*, 'Home, 9944/100% Sweet Home'.

87 The camel has a single hump;
The dromedary, two;
Or else the other way around,
I'm never sure. Are you?
1936 *The Bad Parents' Garden of Verse*, 'The Camel'.

88 Let us pause to consider the English,
Who when they pause to consider themselves they get all reticently thrilled and tinglish,
Because every Englishman is convinced of one thing, viz.:
That to be an Englishman is to belong to the most exclusive club there is.
1938 *I'm a Stranger Here Myself*, 'England Expects'.

89 There was a young belle of old Natchez
Whose garments were always in patchez.
When comment arose
On the state of her clothes,
She drawled, When Ah itchez, Ah scratchez.
1938 *I'm a Stranger Here Myself*, 'Requiem'.

90 The trouble with a kitten is
THAT
Eventually it becomes a
CAT.
1940 *The Face Is Familiar*, 'The Kitten'.

91 One day he missed his loving bride.
She had, the guide informed him later,
Been eaten by an alligator.
Professor Twist could not but smile.
'You mean,' he said, 'a crocodile.'
1940 *The Face Is Familiar*, 'The Purist'.

92 Oh, what a tangled web do parents weave
When they think that their children are naïve.
1940 *The Face Is Familiar*, 'Baby, What Makes the Sky Blue'.

93 This infant whose middle
Is diapered still
Will want to marry
My daughter Jill.

Oh sweet be his slumber and moist his middle!
My dreams, I fear, are infanticiddle.
1940 *The Face Is Familiar*, 'Song to be Sung by the Father of Infant Female Children'.

94 Sure, deck your lower limbs in pants;
Yours are the limbs, my sweeting.
You look divine as you advance—
Have you seen yourself retreating?
1940 *The Face Is Familiar*, 'What's The Use'.

95 Life is not having been told that the man has just waxed the floor.
1942 *Good Intentions*, 'You and Me and P. B. Shelley'.

96 Beneath this slab
John Brown is stowed.
He watched the ads,
And not the road.
1942 *Good Intentions*, 'Lather As You Go'.

97 I have a bone to pick with Fate.
Come here and tell me, girlie,
Do you think my mind is maturing late,

Or simply rotted early?
1942 *Good Intentions*, 'Lines On Facing Forty'.

98 I test my bath before I sit,
And I'm always moved to wonderment
That what chills the finger not a bit
Is so frigid upon the fundament.
1942 *Good Intentions*, 'Samson Agonistes'.

99 Women would rather be right than be reasonable.
1942 *Good Intentions*, 'Frailty, Thy Name is a Misnomer'.

1 Parsley
Is gharsely.
1942 *Good Intentions*, 'Further Reflections on Parsley'.

2 God in His wisdom made the fly
And then forgot to tell us why.
1942 *Good Intentions*, 'The Fly'.

3 One thing that literature would be greatly the better for
Would be a more restricted employment by authors of simile and metaphor.
1945 *Many Long Years Ago*, 'Very Like A Whale'.

4 He tells you when you've got on too much lipstick,
And helps you with your girdle when your hips stick.
1949 *Versus*, 'The Perfect Husband'.

5 All winter long,
I am one for whom the bell is tolling;
I can arouse no interest in basketball,
Indoor fly casting or bowling;
The sports pages are strictly no soap!
And until the cry Play Ball! I simply mope.
1957 Quoted in Colin Jarman *The Guinness Dictionary of Sports Quotations* (1990).

6 It is a fact that a lady wants to be dressed exactly like everybody else but she gets pretty upset if she sees anybody else dressed exactly like her.
1964 *Marriage Lines*, 'Thoughts Thought on an Avenue'.

7 My verse represents a handle I can grasp in order not to yield to the centrifugal forces which are trying to throw me off the world.
Recalled on his death, 9 May 1971.

8 Basketball, a game which won't be fit for people until they set the basket umbilicus-high and return the giraffes to the zoo.
Quoted in Colin Jarman *The Guinness Dictionary of Sports Quotations* (1990).

9 I eat my peas with honey;
I've done it all my life.
They do taste kinda funny,
but it keeps 'em on the knife.
Attributed.

Nashe, Thomas 1567–1601

English dramatist and satirist. His play *The Isle of Dogs* (1597, now lost) was so scathing on the subject of state abuses that it was suppressed, the theatre closed down and he himself thrown into Fleet prison. *The Unfortunate Traveller* (1594) is a picaresque tale, one of the earliest of its kind.

10 'New herrings, new!' we must cry, every time we make ourselves public, or else we shall be christened with a hundred new titles of idiotism.
1592 *Pierce Penniless, His Supplication to the Devil*, 'An Invective Against Enemies of Poetry'.

11 Poetry is the honey of all flowers, the quintessence of all sciences, the marrow of wit, and the very phrase of angels.
1592 *Pierce Penniless, His Supplication to the Devil*, 'An Invective Against Enemies of Poetry'.

12 If I be evil intreated, or sent away with a flea in mine ear, let him look that I will rail on him soundly; nor for an hour or a day, whiles the injury is fresh in my memory; but in some elaborate polished poem, which I will leave to the world when I am dead, to be a living image to all ages of his beggarly parsimony and ignoble illiberality.
1592 *Pierce Penniless, His Supplication to the Devil*, 'An Invective Against Enemies of Poetry'.

13 I will confer with thee somewhat gravely, although thou beest a goosecap and hast no judgement.
1592 *Strange News of the Intercepting Certain Letters*.

14 Immortal Spenser, no frailty hath thy fame but the imputation of this idiot's friendship!
1592 *Strange News of the Intercepting Certain Letters*.

15 Spring, the sweet spring, is the year's pleasant king,
Then blooms each thing, then maids dance in a ring,
Cold doth not sting, the pretty birds do sing:
Cuckoo, jug-jug, pu-we, to-witta-woo!
1592 *Summer's Last Will and Testament*, 'Song'.

16 Fair summer droops, droop men and beasts therefore:
So fair a summer look for never more.
All good things vanish, less than in a day,
Peace, plenty, pleasure, suddenly decay.
Go not yet away, bright soul of the sad year;
The earth is hell when thou leav'st to appear.
1592 *Summer's Last Will and Testament*, 'Song'.

17 From winter, plague and pestilence, good lord, deliver us!
1592 *Summer's Last Will and Testament*.

18 Beauty is but a flower
Which wrinkles will devour;
Brightness falls from the air;
Queens have died young and fair;
Dust hath closèd Helen's eye.
I am sick, I must die.
Lord, have mercy on us!
1592 'A Litany in Time of Plague'.

19 He that is a traveller must have the back of an ass to bear all, a tongue like the tail of a dog to flatter all, the mouth of a hog to eat all what is set before him, the ear of a merchant to hear all and say nothing; and if this be not the highest step of thraldom, there is no liberty or freedom.
1594 *The Unfortunate Traveller, or the Life of Jack Wilton*.

Nathan, George Jean 1882–1958

US theatre critic. He was co-editor of *The Smart Set* (1914–24) and founded the *American Mercury* with H L Mencken in 1924. Among the emerging playwrights to whom he gave support was Eugene O'Neill.

20 The most loyal and faithful woman indulges her imagination in a hypothetical liaison whenever she dons a new street frock for the first time.
1921 *The Theatre, the Drama, the Girls*, 'Woman'.

21 The test of a real comedian is whether you laugh at him before he opens his mouth.
Quoted in *American Mercury*, Sep 1929.

22 I always said that I'd like Barrymore's acting till the cows came home. Well, ladies and gentlemen, last

night the cows came home.
1939 Review of John Barrymore's performance in *My Dear Children*.

23 Impersonal criticism...is like an impersonal fist fight or an impersonal marriage, and as successful.
Quoted in Charles Angoff (ed) *The World of George Jean Nathan* (1952).

24 The dramatic critic who is without prejudice is on the plane with the general who does not believe in taking human life.
Attributed.

Nation, Carry Amelia *née* Moore 1846–1911

US temperance agitator. She went on saloon-smashing expeditions with a hatchet and was frequently imprisoned for breach of the peace.

25 A woman is stripped of everything by them [saloons]. Her husband is torn from her; she is robbed of her sons, her home, her food, and her virtue; and then they strip her clothes off and hang her up bare in these dens of robbery and murder. Truly does the saloon make a woman bare of all things!
c.1893 Quoted in Carleton Beals *Cyclone Carry* (1962), ch.14.

Naughton, Bill 1910–92

Irish novelist and screenwriter. His screen credits include *Alfie* (1966), *The Family Way* (1966) and *Spring and Port Wine* (1970).

26 It seems to me if they ain't got you one way they got you another. So what's the answer? That's what I keep asking myself. What's it all about? Know what I mean?
1966 Line delivered by Michael Caine in *Alfie*.

Neale, J(ames) M(ason) 1818–66

English clergyman and hymn writer.

27 All glory, laud and honour
To Thee, Redeemer, King,
To whom the lips of children
Made sweet hosannas ring.
1851 'All Glory, Laud and Honour'.

28 Jerusalem the golden,
With milk and honey blessed,
Beneath thy contemplation
Sink heart and voice oppressed.
I know not, O I know not
What joys await us there,
What radiancy of glory,
What light beyond compare.
1858 'Jerusalem the Golden', translated from the original Latin of St Bernard of Cluny.

Nehru, Jawaharlal 1889–1964

Indian statesman, President of the Indian National Congress (1929) and India's first Prime Minister (1947–64). Neutral in the Cold War, he embarked on industrialization, reorganized the states linguistically and ended the dispute with Pakistan over Kashmir peacefully.

29 Stalin...that great lover of peace, a man of giant stature who moulded, as few other men have done, the destinies of his age... The occasion is not merely the passing away of a great figure but perhaps the ending of an historic era.
1953 Tribute, Indian Parliament, 9 Mar.

Neilson, John Shaw 1872–1942

Australian poet. His first work was published in the *Bulletin* and first collected in *Heart of Spring* (1919), followed by *Ballad and Lyrical Poems* (1923) and *New Poems* (1927). *Collected Poems* (1934) was followed by posthumous collections.

30 The young girl stood beside me. I
Saw not what her young eyes could see:
—A light, she said, not of the sky
Lives somewhere in the Orange Tree.
1923 *Ballad and Lyrical Poems*, 'The Orange Tree', stanza 1.

31 Here is the ecstasy
Of sun-fed wine and song:
Drink! it is melody
Under a kurrajong.
'Under a Kurrajong', stanza 1, in R H Croll (ed) *Collected Poems of John Shaw Neilson* (1934).

Nelson, Horatio, Viscount Nelson 1758–1805

English admiral. In 1794 he commanded at Bastia and Calvi, where he lost the sight of his right eye, and at Santa Cruz in 1796, where he lost his right arm. In 1798 he destroyed Napoleon's fleet in Aboukir Bay, and subsequently began an affair with Emma, Lady Hamilton. In 1805 he defeated the combined French and Spanish fleet at Trafalgar, but was mortally wounded.

32 A fleet of British ships of war are the best negotiators in Europe.
1801 Letter to Lady Hamilton, Mar, before the Battle of Copenhagen.

33 You know, Foley, I have only one eye—I have a right to be blind sometimes... I really do not see the signal.
1801 Said to Captain Foley during the Battle of Copenhagen, 2 Apr. Nelson disregarded the order of his superior, Admiral Hyde-Parker, to break off action and went on to win the engagement.

34 I wish to say Nelson confides that every man will do his duty.
1805 Instructions to the flag officer on HMS *Victory*, 21 Oct. The signal was amended to begin, 'England expects...'.

35 Kiss me, Hardy.
1805 Attributed, as he lay dying in the cockpit of the *Victory* during the Battle of Trafalgar, 21 Oct.

36 Thank God, I have done my duty.
1805 Last words at the Battle of Trafalgar, quoted in Robert Southey *Life of Nelson* (1813), ch.9.

Nemerov, Howard 1920–91

US poet, novelist and playwright. He was US Poet Laureate from 1988 to 1990, and won a National Book Award for his *Collected Poems* in 1977.

37 Children, to be illustrious is sad.
1958 *Mirrors and Windows*, 'The Statues in the Public Gardens'.

38 Till I, high in the tower of my time
Among familiar ruins, began to cry
For accident, sickness, justice, war and crime,
Because all died, because I had to die.
The snow fell, the trees stood, the promise kept,
And a child I slept.
1960 *New Poems*, 'The View from an Attic Window'.

39 For a Jewish Puritan of the middle class, the novel is serious, the novel is work, the novel is conscientious application—why, the novel is practically the retail business all over again.
1965 *Journal of the Fictive Life*, 'Reflexions of the Novelist Felix Ledger'.

40 I've never read a political poem that's accomplished anything. Poetry makes things happen, but rarely what the poet wants.
1988 In the *International Herald Tribune*, 14 Oct.
► See Auden 40:2.

Nero AD 37–68

Roman Emperor (AD 54–68). He was adopted by his stepfather Claudius and declared Emperor on Claudius's death. Ancient authors depict him as a debauched tyrant, and accuse him of starting the great fire of Rome in AD 64 (he blamed the Christians). A coup in AD 68 brought Galba to the throne, and Nero committed suicide.

41 *Qualis artifex pereo!*
Dead! And so great an artist!
Attributed words on the point of taking his life. Quoted in Suetonius *Nero*, 49.1 (translated by Robert Graves, 1957).

Neruda, Pablo *pseudonym of* ***Neftalí Ricardo Reyes Basoalto*** 1904–73

Chilean poet, essayist and diplomat, who travelled widely as a diplomat. His poetic themes range from subjective love to socially committed epic poems influenced by a communist ideology. He was awarded a Nobel prize in 1971.

42 *Sucede que me canso de mis pies y mis uñas*
y mi pelo y mi sombra.
Sucede que me canso de ser hombre.
I happen to be tired of my feet and my nails
and my hair and my shadow.
I happen to be tired of being a man.
1935 *Residencia en la tierra*, 'Walking Around' (translated as *Residence on Earth*, 1946).

43 *A nosotros nos enseñaron a respetar la iglesia,*
a no toser, a no escupir en el atrio,
a no lavar la ropa en el altar
y no es así: la vida rompe las religiones.
We were taught respect for the church,
no hawking and spitting on porticos,
don't soak your socks on the altar—
but things are different: life smashes religions.
1973 *La rosa separada*, 'Los hombres' (translated as *The Separate Rose*, 'The Men', 1985).

Nerval, Gérard de *pseudonym of* ***Gérard Labrunie*** 1808–55

French poet, novelist and author of critical essays, he was admired later by the Surrealists for his fantastic short tales.

44 *Philosophie! dont la lumière, comme celle des enfers de Milton, ne sert qu'à rendre les ténèbres visibles.*
Philosophy! In whose light, like that in Milton's hell, only serves to make the shadows visible.
1852 *Fragments*, 'Paradoxe et vérité'.

45 *Il n'y a qu'un seul vice dont on ne voie personne se vanter, c'est l'ingratitude.*
There is only one vice of which no one boasts—ingratitude.
1852 *Fragments*, 'Paradoxe et vérité'.

46 *La vie d'un poète est celle de tous.*
The life of the poet is the life of everyone.
1855 *Petits Châteaux de Bohême*, 'À un ami'.

Nervo, Amado *pseudonym of* ***Juan Crisóstomo Ruiz de Nervo*** 1870–1919

Mexican poet and diplomat. He abandoned the priesthood in 1888 to work as a journalist. He studied Buddhist philosophy in depth, and his introspective poetry is characterized by deep religious feeling and simple form.

47 *No te juzgues incompleto porque no responden a tus ternuras; el amor lleva en sí su propia plenitud.*
Siempre que haya un hueco en tu vida, llénalo de amor.
Don't judge yourself incomplete when your tenderness gets no response; love carries within itself its own plenitude.
Whenever there is a void in your life, fill it with love.
1918 *Plenitud*, 'Llénalo de amor' (translated as 'Fill It with love', 1928).

Nevelson, Louise 1900–88

Russian-born US sculptor. Her work incorporates pieces of wood, found objects, cast metal, and other materials, creating great mysterious walls or boxes of complex, abstract forms. Her autobiography, *Dawns and Dusks*, was published in 1976.

48 There's no denying that Caruso came with a voice...that Beethoven came with music in his soul, Picasso was drawing like an angel in the crib. You're born with it.
1976 *Dawns and Dusks*.

Neville, Katherine 1945–

US novelist.

49 'In Scotland,' Tavish muttered, picking up my bags, 'the *women* do the hod carrying while we blokes retire to the nearest pub—to deliberate upon the role of labour in society.'
1992 *A Calculated Risk*.

New York Times

First published 1851 as the *New-York Daily Times*.

50 Who owns history? The public servants who make it, or the people who hire them and to whom they are accountable?
1983 'Who Owns History?', editorial, 19 Nov.

51 Armed with a notebook, ingratiating grin and fine intelligence, he grew to be a most discerning witness of America's most distinctive rite, not just the election but the making of our presidents.
1986 Of journalist Theodore H White. 'Teddy White, the Maker of Epics', editorial, 17 May.

52 The best way to read [a poem] is off the top of your head, and out of the corner of your eye.
1987 *Noted With Pleasure*, in the *New York Times*, 16 Mar.

53 For Palestinians, PLO is a homeland of the mind.
1988 Editorial, 20 Mar.

54 Empty luggage may be easier to carry, but it's still empty.
1988 Of Michael S Dukakis's presidential campaign. 'The Painless Platform', editorial, 20 Jul.

55 Millions drew up before the international hearth of television.

1991 On international media coverage of the Allied deadline for Iraq's withdrawal from Kuwait. 'With Our Own Eyes', editorial, 24 Feb.

56 Lightning rods have had it better than Nancy Reagan.
1991 On the publication of Kitty Kelley's unauthorized biography *Nancy Reagan*. 'Scratching at the Teflon', editorial, 10 Apr.

57 Who is quickest on the drawl?
1992 On claims to Texas by both George Bush and rival presidential aspirant Ross Perot. Editorial, 9 Jun.

58 When it comes to the final judgements on political conduct, history is not merciful. It is just.
1994 'Justice and Mercy in Arkansas', editorial, 17 Dec.

Newman, Arnold 1918–

US photographer.

59 We don't take our pictures with cameras. We take them with our hearts, and we take them with our minds.
1992 In *Sunday Morning*, CBS TV, 2 Aug.

Newman, James R 1907–66

US mathematician and mathematical historian. He was the compiler of the magnum opus *The World of Mathematics* (1956).

60 There are two ways to teach mathematics. One is to take real pains toward creating understanding—visual aids, that sort of thing. The other is the old British style of teaching until you're blue in the face.
1956 Quoted in the *New York Times*, 30 Sep.

Newman, John Henry 1801–90

English theologian, active in Oxford in the Tractarian movement of the Church of England. He converted to the Roman Catholic faith in 1845 and was appointed Cardinal by Pope Leo XIII in 1879.

61 It is as absurd to argue men, as to torture them, into believing.
1831 'The Usurpations of Reason', collected in *Oxford University Sermons* (1843).

62 Lead, kindly Light, amid the encircling gloom,
Lead thou me on;
The night is dark, and I am far from home,
Lead thou me on.
Keep Thou my feet; I do not ask to see
The distant scene; one step enough for me.
1833 'Lead, kindly Light'.

63 May He support us all the day long, till the shades lengthen, and the evening comes, and the busy world is hushed, and the fever of life is over, and our work is done! Then in His mercy may He give us a safe lodging, and a holy rest, and peace at the last.
1834 'Wisdom and Innocence', collected in *Sermons Bearing on Subjects of the Day*.

64 *We can believe what we choose*. We are answerable for what we choose to believe.
1848 Letter to Mrs William Froude, 27 Jun.

65 It is very difficult to get up resentment towards persons whom one has never seen.
1864 *Apologia pro Vita Sua*, 'Mr Kingsley's Method of Disputation'.

66 Praise to the Holiest in the height,
And in the depth be praise;
In all His words most wonderful,
Most sure in all His ways.
1865 *The Dream of Gerontius*. In *The Month* (published in book form in 1866).

Newman, Peter C 1929–

Austrian-born Canadian author and political columnist.

67 And what I've learned is not to believe in magical leaders any more; that character and compassion are more important than ideology; and that even if it's absurd to think you can change things, it's even more absurd to think that it's foolish and unimportant to try.
1973 *Home Country: People, Places, and Power Politics*.

68 The rich don't have children; they have heirs.
1982 *The Establishment Man: A Portrait of Power*.

Newton, Sir Isaac 1642–1727

English mathematician and physicist, considered the greatest scientist of modern time. Newton was Professor of Mathematics (1669–1701) at Cambridge. Between 1664 and 1666 he discovered the law of gravitation, and began to develop differential calculus.

69 *Corpus omne perseverare in statu suo quiescendi vel movendi uniformiter in directum, nisi quatenus illud a viribus impressis cogitur statum suum mutare.*
Every body continues in its state of rest, or of uniform motion in a right line, unless it is compelled to change that state by forces impressed thereon.
1687 First Law of Motion. *Philosophiae Naturalis Principia Mathematica* (translated by Andrew Motte, 1729).

70 *Mutationem motus proportionalem esse vi motrici impressae et fieri secundum lineam rectam qua vis illa imprimitur.*
The alteration of motion is ever proportional to the motive force impressed; and is made in the direction of the right line in which that force is impressed.
1687 Second Law of Motion. *Philosophiae Naturalis Principia Mathematica* (translated by Andrew Motte, 1729).

71 We are to admit no more causes of natural things than such as are both true and sufficient to explain their appearances… Nature is pleased with simplicity, and affects not the pomp of the superfluous causes.
1687 Newton's First Rule of Reasoning in Philosophy. *Philosophiae Naturalis Principia Mathematica* (translated by Andrew Motte, 1729).

72 *Actioni contrarium semper et aequalem esse reactionem: sive corporum duorum actiones in se mutuo semper esse aequales et in partes contrarias dirigi.*
To every action there is always opposed an equal reaction: or, the mutual actions of two bodies upon each other are always equal, and directed to contrary parts.
1687 Third Law of Motion. *Philosophiae Naturalis Principia Mathematica* (translated by Andrew Motte, 1729).

73 Geometry is that part of universal mechanics which accurately proposes and demonstrates the art of measuring.
1687 *Philosophiae Naturalis Principia Mathematica* (translated by Andrew Motte, 1729).

74 I know not what I may appear to the world, but to myself I seem to have been only like a boy playing on the sea shore, and diverting myself in now and then finding a

smoother pebble or a prettier shell than ordinary, whilst the great ocean of truth lay all undiscovered before me.
Quoted in D Brewster (ed) *Memoirs of Newton* (1855), vol.2, ch.27.

75 In the absence of any other proof, the thumb alone would convince me of God's existence.
Attributed.

Newton, John 1725–1807

English divine and writer, who converted to Christianity in 1748 and became Curate of Olney, Buckinghamshire, in 1764.

76 Amazing grace! How sweet the sound
That saved a wretch like me!
I once was lost, but now am found,
Was blind, but now I see.
1779 *Olney Hymns*, 'Amazing Grace'.

77 Glorious things of thee are spoken,
Zion, city of our God!
1779 *Olney Hymns*, 'Glorious things of thee are spoken'.

78 How sweet the name of Jesus sounds
In a believer's ear!
1779 *Olney Hymns*, 'How sweet the name of Jesus sounds'.

Ngũugĩ wa Thiong'o *originally* James Nguũgĩ 1938–

Kenyan writer. His early works were written in English, but he now chooses to write solely in his native Gikuyu. Works include *Weep Not Child* (1964), *The River Between* (1965), *A Grain of Wheat* (1967) and *Matigari* (1987).

79 Today, children, I am going to tell you about the history of Mr. Blackman in three sentences. In the beginning he had the land and the mind and the soul together. On the second day, they took the body away to barter it for silver coins. On the third day, seeing that he was still fighting back, they brought priests and educators to bind his mind and soul so that these foreigners could more easily take his land and produce.
1977 *Petals of Blood*, ch.8.

80 He who produces should be able to control that which he produces.
1990 Quoted in Carol Sicherman *Ngũũgõũ wa Thiong'o: The Making of a Rebel*, pt.1, ch.2, 'Nguũgõũ on Nguũgõũ' (by Nguũgõũ himself).

Nguyen, Xuan Oanh 1921–2003

Vietnamese economist who rose to become South Vietnam's acting Prime Minister briefly in 1964. After the country was reunited in 1975 he remained in limbo for ten years before his ideas for economic change were accepted. He is now regarded as the unofficial architect of Vietnam's economic reforms.

81 There is no such thing as communism versus capitalism. There are only degrees of communism and degrees of capitalism.
1995 In the *Eastern Express*, 17 May.

82 Patriotism in Vietnam took the communist road because it was the only one available. It had the appeal of a dream, a dream of social justice.
1995 In the *Eastern Express*, 17 May.

Nicholas I 1796–1855

Tsar of Russia (from 1825). During his reign, wars with Persia and Turkey increased Russia's territory. He died during the Crimean War, when Russia's attempts to absorb Turkey were resisted by Britain and France.

83 Russia has two generals in whom she can confide—Janvier and Février.
1855 Referring to the severe Russian winter climate. Quoted in *Punch*, 10 Mar.

Nicholas II 1868–1919

Last Emperor of Russia (1894–1917), whose reign was marked by alliance with France (1894), *entente* with Britain, disastrous war with Japan (1904–5) and the establishment of the Duma (1906). He fought against the Central Powers in 1915. Forced to abdicate at the Revolution, he was shot with his family by the Red Guards.

84 There are senseless dreams of the participation of local government representatives in the affairs of internal administration. I shall maintain the principle of autocracy just as firmly and unflinchingly as it was upheld by my own, ever to be remembered dead father.
1896 Declaration, 17 Jan.

Nichols, Grace 1950–

Guyanese poet, novelist and journalist, married to the poet John Agard; her publications include *Trust You, Wriggly!* (1981) and *The Poet Cat* (2000) for children, and the poetry sequences *i is a long memoried woman* (1983) (Commonwealth Poetry Prize) and *The Fat Black Woman's Poems* (1984).

85 I have crossed an ocean
I have lost my tongue
from the root of the old one
a new one has sprung
1983 *i is a long memoried woman*, epilogue.

86 IT'S BETTER TO DIE IN THE FLESH OF HOPE
THAN TO LIVE IN THE SLIMNESS OF DESPAIR.
1984 *The Fat Black Woman's Poems*, 'The Fat Black Woman's Motto on Her Bedroom Door'.

Nichols, Mike *originally* Michael Peschowsky 1931–

American stage and film director. He collected Tony Awards for the plays *Barefoot in the Park* (1963), *The Odd Couple* (1965) and *Plaza Suite* (1968). More recently he directed *Death and the Maiden* (New York, 1992) and the television adaptation of *Angels in America* (2003). His many films include *The Graduate* (1967, Academy Award), *Catch-22* (1969), *Silkwood* (1983), *Working Girl* (1988), *Postcards From The Edge* (1990) and *The Birdcage* (1995).

87 Style is beginning something in the manner which will make it necessary for things that happen later to happen.
1991 In *Film Comment*, May.

Nicholson, Bill 1919–2004

English footballer and manager. He played with Tottenham Hotspur, and as manager of the club achieved the double of the FA Cup and the League Championship (1961). He won two more FA Cup titles (1962 and 1967), the European Cup Winners' Cup (1963), two more League Championships (1971 and 1973) and the UEFA Cup (1972).

88 I prefer players not to be too good or clever at other things. It means they concentrate on football.
1973 Quoted in Peter Ball and Phil Shaw *The Book of Football Quotations* (1989).

Nicholson, Jack 1937–

US film actor. An office boy at MGM, he made his film debut in *Cry Baby Killer* (1958) and survived a decade of low-budget exploitation films before *Easy Rider* (1969) established his reputation. He has received twelve Academy Award nominations, winning three Oscars.

89 She's like a delicate fawn, crossed with a Buick.
1984 Of actress Jessica Lange. In *Vanity Fair*, Oct.

Nicholson, Vivian 1936–

English housewife. In 1961 her husband Keith won £152,000 on the football pools, but the couple subsequently had difficulty coping with their fortune. Keith died in a car crash and Viv spent the money in just four years and turned to religion after several failed marriages and alcohol and drug abuse.

90 I want to spend, and spend, and spend!
1961 Quoted in the *Daily Herald*, 28 Sep, when asked what her plans were on winning the pools. The words 'Spend, spend, spend!' were later used as the title of her autobiography and for a biographical television play by Jack Rosenthal in 1977.

Nicias c.470–413 BC

Athenian statesman and soldier, who negotiated a short-lived peace with Sparta (421 BC). He was a commander in the disastrous naval expedition against Sicily in 418 BC, and following a siege of Syracuse was captured and put to death.

91 For it is men that make a city, and not its walls, nor its ships empty of men.
413 BC Speech to the defeated Athenian army. Quoted in Thucydides 7.77.

Nicklaus, Jack William *known as* *'the Golden Bear'* 1940–

US golfer. He won the US Open Championship in 1962, the first of 20 major tournaments. He went into semi-retirement in 1986 and is now in demand as a golf course designer.

92 Golf is not and never has been a fair game.
Quoted in Colin Jarman *The Guinness Dictionary of Sports Quotations* (1990).

93 I think I fail a bit less than everyone else.
Quoted in Michael Hobbs *The Golf Quotation Book* (1992).

Nicolle, Charles Jules Henri 1866–1936

French physician and microbiologist, Director of the Pasteur Institute in Tunis, Tunisia and Professor of Bacteriology at the Collège de France. He was awarded a Nobel prize in 1928 for demonstrating the transmission of typhus by lice.

94 All method is imperfect. Error is all around it, and at the least opportunity invades it… But what can we do? There is no other way.
1932 *Biologie de l'Invention.*

Nicolson, Sir Harold 1886–1968

English diplomat, author and critic, born in Tehran. A distinguished diplomat (1909–29), he turned to journalism and was a National Liberal MP (1935–45). He wrote works of literary criticism and literary and historical biography.

95 My first impression is of a slightly bearded spinster: my second is of Willie King made up like Philip II: my third of some thin little bird, peeking, crooked, reserved, violent and timid.
1931 On meeting James Joyce. Diary entry, 30 Jul.

96 I feel pretty glum and devote myself to reviewing. There is Joyce's *Finnegans Wake*. I try very hard indeed to understand that book but fail completely. It is almost impossible to decipher, and when one or two lines of understanding emerge like telegraph poles above a flood, they are at once countered by other poles going in the opposite direction.
1939 Diary entry, 29 Apr.

Niebuhr, Reinhold 1892–1971

US theologian, Professor at the Union Theological Seminary, New York.

97 All men who live with any degree of serenity live by some assurance of grace.
1934 *Reflections on the End of Our Era.*

98 Perhaps the most sublime insights of the Jewish prophets and the Christian gospel is the knowledge that since perfection is love, the apprehension of perfection is at once the means of seeing one's imperfections and the consoling assurance of grace which makes this realization bearable. This ultimate paradox of high religion is not an invention of theologians or priests. It is constantly validated by the most searching experiences of life.
1934 *Reflections on the End of an Era.*

99 The pretensions of final truth are always partly an effort to obscure a darkly felt consciousness of the limits of human knowledge.
1941 *The Nature and Destiny of Man*, vol.1.

1 God, give us grace to accept with serenity the things that cannot be changed, courage to change the things that should be changed, and the wisdom to distinguish the one from the other.
In Richard Wightman Fox *Reinhold Neibuhr* (1985), ch.12. Attributed to Neibuhr, but more probably 18c German.

Nielsen, Carl August 1865–1931

Danish composer, who experimented with polytonality and developed a characteristic contrapuntal style.

2 Music is life, and, like it, inextinguishable.
1916 Symphony No. 4, motto.

Niemöller, Martin 1892–1984

German submarine commander, pastor and theologian, leader of Christian opposition to Nazism.

3 When Hitler attacked the Jews I was not a Jew, therefore, I was not concerned. And when Hitler attacked the Catholics, I was not a Catholic, and therefore, I was not concerned. And when Hitler attacked the unions and the industrialists, I was not a member of the unions and I was not concerned. Then, Hitler attacked me and the Protestant church—and there was nobody left to be concerned.
1944 *Children of Light and Darkness*, foreword.

Nietzsche, Friedrich Wilhelm 1844–1900

German philosopher, scholar and writer. Professor of Classical Philology at the University of Basel (1868–78), he resigned in ill health. From 1872 he produced a stream of brilliant, unclassifiable works, rejecting Christianity for a new, heroic morality. In 1889 he had a complete mental and physical breakdown, from which he never recovered. His reputation suffered when his ideas were adopted in a distorted form by the Nazis, but he is now regarded as a major influence on 20c thought.

4 *Überzeugungen sind gefährlichere Feinde der Wahrheit als Lügen.*
Convictions are more dangerous enemies of truth than lies.
1878 *Menschliches, Allzumenschliches* (*Human, All Too Human*), section 483 (translated by R J Hollingdale).

5 The press, the machine, the railway, the telegraph are premises whose thousand-year conclusion no one has yet dared to draw.
1880 *The Wanderer and His Shadow*, aphorism 278.

6 *Gott ist tot: aber so wie die Art der Menschen ist, wird es vielleicht noch Jahrtausende lang Höhlen geben, in denen man seinen Schatten zeigt.—Und wir—wir müssen auch noch seinen Schatten besiegen!*
God is dead; but given the way of men, there may still be caves for thousands of years in which his shadow will be shown.—And we—we still have to vanquish his shadow, too.
1882 *Die fröhliche Wissenschaft* (*The Gay Science*), section 108 (translated by W Kaufmann). This is the first occurrence of the famous phrase, which appears elsewhere in Nietzsche's work.

7 *Moralität ist Herden-Instinkt im Einzelnen.*
Morality is herd instinct in the individual.
1882 *Die fröhliche Wissenschaft* (*The Gay Science*), section 116 (translated by W Kaufmann).

8 *Und, alles in allem und großem: ich will irgendwann einmal nur noch ein Jasagender sein!*
And all in all and on the whole: some day I wish to be only a Yes-sayer.
1882 *Die fröhliche Wissenschaft* (*The Gay Science*), section 276 (translated by W Kaufmann).

9 *Glaubt es mir!—das Geheimnis, um die größte Fruchtbarkeit und den großten Genuss vom Dasein einzuernten, heißt: gefährlich leben!*
For believe me: the secret for harvesting from existence the greatest fruitfulness and the greatest enjoyment is—*to live dangerously*.
1882 *Die fröhliche Wissenschaft* (*The Gay Science*), section 283 (translated by W Kaufmann).

10 *Eins ist not.—Seinem Charakter 'Stil geben'.*
One thing is needful.—To 'give style' to one's character.
1882 *Die fröhliche Wissenschaft* (*The Gay Science*), section 290 (translated by W Kaufmann).

11 *Ich lehre euch den Übermenschen. Der Mensch ist Etwas, das überwunden werden soll.*
I teach you the Superman. Man is something that should be surpassed.
1883–92 *Also sprach Zarathustra* (*Thus Spake Zarathustra*), prologue, section 3 (translated by R J Hollingdale).

12 *Der Mensch ist ein Seil, geknüpft zwischen Tier und Übermensch,—ein Seil über einem Abgrunde.*
Man is a rope, fastened between animal and Superman—a rope over an abyss.
1883–92 *Also sprach Zarathustra* (*Thus Spake Zarathustra*), prologue, section 4 (translated by R J Hollingdale).

13 *Was groß ist am Menschen, das ist, dass er eine Brücke und kein Zweck ist.*
What is great in man is that he is a bridge and not a goal.
1883–92 *Also sprach Zarathustra* (*Thus Spake Zarathustra*), prologue, section 4 (translated by R J Hollingdale).

14 *Ich sage euch: man muss noch Chaos in sich haben, um einem tanzenden Stern gebären zu können.*
I tell you: one must have chaos in one, to give birth to a dancing star.
1883–92 *Also sprach Zarathustra* (*Thus Spake Zarathustra*), prologue, section 5 (translated by R J Hollingdale).

15 *Du gehst zu Frauen? Vergiss die Peitsche nicht!*
You are going to women? Do not forget the whip!
1883–92 *Also sprach Zarathustra* (*Thus Spake Zarathustra*), bk.1 (translated by R J Hollingdale).

16 Distrust all in whom the impulse to punish is powerful.
1883–92 *Also sprach Zarathustra* (*Thus Spake Zarathustra*) (translated by R J Hollingdale).

17 *Gesetzt, wir wollen Wahrheit: warum nicht lieber Unwahrheit? Und Ungewissheit? Selbst Unwissenheit?*
Granted we want truth: why not rather untruth? And uncertainty? Even ignorance?
1886 *Jenseits von Gut und Böse* (*Beyond Good and Evil*), section 1 (translated by R J Hollingdale).

18 *Allmählich hat sich mir herausgestellt, was jede große Philosophie bisher war: nämlich das Selbstbekenntnis ihres Urhebers und eine Art ungewollter und unvermerkter mémoires.*
It has gradually become clear to me what every great philosophy has hitherto been: a confession on the part of its author and a kind of involuntary and unconscious memoir.
1886 *Jenseits von Gut und Böse* (*Beyond Good and Evil*), section 6 (translated by R J Hollingdale).

19 *Sie schafft immer die Welt nach ihrem Bilde, sie kann nicht anders; Philosophie ist dieser tyrannische Treib selbst, der geistigste Wille zur Macht, zur 'Schaffung der Welt'.*
It [philosophy] always creates the world in its own image, it cannot do otherwise; philosophy is this tyrannical drive itself, the most spiritual will to power, to 'creation of the world'.
1886 *Jenseits von Gut und Böse* (*Beyond Good and Evil*), section 9 (translated by R J Hollingdale).

20 *Alles, was tief ist, liebt die Maske.*
Everything profound loves the mask.
1886 *Jenseits von Gut und Böse* (*Beyond Good and Evil*), section 40 (translated by R J Hollingdale).

21 The thought of suicide is a great source of comfort across many a bad night.
1886 *Jenseits von Gut und Böse* (*Beyond Good and Evil*), section 157 (translated by R J Hollingdale).

22 *Das moralische Urteilen und Verurteilen ist die Lieblings-Rache der Geistig-Beschränkten an denen, die es weniger sind.*
Moral judgement and condemnation is the favourite form of revenge of the spiritually limited on those who are less so.
1886 *Jenseits von Gut und Böse* (*Beyond Good and Evil*), section 219 (translated by R J Hollingdale).

23 *Durch schlechte Köchinnen—durch den vollkommenen Mangel an Vernunft in der Küche ist die Entwicklung des Menschen am längsten aufgehalten, am schlimmsten beeinträchtigt worden.*

Through bad female cooks—through the entire lack of reason in the kitchen—the development of mankind has been longest retarded and most interfered with.
1886 *Jenseits von Gut und Böse* (*Beyond Good and Evil*), section 234 (translated by Helen Zimmern, 1907).

24 *Herren-Moral und Sklaven-Moral.*
Master morality and slave morality.
1886 *Jenseits von Gut und Böse* (*Beyond Good and Evil*), section 260 (translated by R J Hollingdale).

25 Oh, how much is today hidden by science! Oh, how much it is expected to hide!
1887 *The Genealogy of Morals*, essay 3, 'What Do Ascetic Ideals Mean?'

26 *Hat je sich ein Weib, das sich gut bekleidet wusste, erkältet?*
Has a woman who knew she was well dressed ever caught a cold?
1889 *Die Götzen-Dämmerung* (*Twilight of the Idols*), 'Maxims and Arrows', no.25 (translated by R J Hollingdale).

27 Without music, life would be a mistake.
1889 *Die Götzen-Dämmerung* (*Twilight of the Idols*, translated by R J Hollingdale)

28 *Das, worin man die nationalen Unterschiede findet, ist viel mehr, als man bis jetzt eingesehen hat, nur der Unterschied verschiedener Kulturstufen und zum geringsten Teile etwas Bleibendes (und auch dies nicht in einem strengen Sinne).*
National differences consist, far more than has hitherto been observed, only in the differences of various grades of culture, and are only to a very small extent permanent (and not even that in a strict sense).
Nachgelassene Fragmente.

Nightingale, Benedict 1939–

British author and theatre critic. He has written for *The Times* since 1990.

29 He handles symbolism rather like an Olympic weight lifter, raising it with agonizing care, brandishing it with a tiny grunt of triumph, then dropping it with a terrible clang.
1984 Of playwright William Inge. In the *New York Times*, 28 Jul.

Nightingale, Florence 1820–1910

English nurse and hospital reformer during the Crimean War. She subsequently formed an institution for the training of nurses in London.

30 Why have women Passion, intellect, moral activity—these three—and a place in society where no one of the three can be exercised?
1852 'Cassandra' pt.1, part of an unpublished work *Suggestions for Thought to Searchers after Religious Truth* (revised and privately printed 1859). Published as an appendix in Ray Strachey *The Cause: A Short History of the Women's Movement in Great Britain* (1928).

31 Give us back our suffering, we cry to Heaven in our hearts—suffering rather than indifferentism; for out of nothing comes nothing... Better have pain than paralysis!
1852 'Cassandra' pt.1, part of an unpublished work *Suggestions for Thought to Searchers after Religious Truth* (revised and privately printed 1859). Published as an appendix in Ray Strachey *The Cause: A Short History of the Women's Movement in Great Britain* (1928).

32 Look at the poor lives we lead. It is a wonder that we are so good as we are, not that we are so bad.
1852 'Cassandra' pt.2, part of an unpublished work *Suggestions for Thought to Searchers after Religious Truth* (revised and privately printed 1859). Published as an appendix in Ray Strachey *The Cause: A Short History of the Women's Movement in Great Britain* (1928).

33 Marriage is the only chance (and it is but a chance) offered to women for escape from this death...and how eagerly and how ignorantly it is embraced.
1852 'Cassandra' pt.3, part of an unpublished work *Suggestions for Thought to Searchers after Religious Truth* (revised and privately printed 1859). Published as an appendix in Ray Strachey *The Cause: A Short History of the Women's Movement in Great Britain* (1928).

34 The next Christ will perhaps be a female Christ.
1852 'Cassandra' pt.4, part of an unpublished work *Suggestions for Thought to Searchers after Religious Truth* (revised and privately printed 1859). Published as an appendix in Ray Strachey *The Cause: A Short History of the Women's Movement in Great Britain* (1928).

35 No *man*, not even a doctor, ever gives any other definition of what a nurse should be than this—'devoted and obedient'. This definition would do just as well for a porter. It might even do for a horse. It would not do for a policeman.
1859 *Notes on Nursing.*

Nimitz, Admiral Chester (William) 1885–1966

US naval officer. He was Commander-in-Chief of the Pacific Fleet (1941–5), contributing significantly to the defeat of Japan. As fleet admiral he signed the Japanese surrender documents in Tokyo Bay (1945). He was chief of naval operations (1945–7).

36 A ship is always referred to as 'she' because it costs so much to keep her in paint and powder.
1959 In the *New York Times*, 24 May.

Nin, Anaïs 1903–77

US writer, born in Paris to parents of Spanish–Cuban descent. Her works explored sexuality and feminism with a frankness unusual in her era.

37 I stopped loving my father a long time ago. What remained was the slavery to a pattern.
1944 *Under a Glass Bell*, 'Birth'.

Nisbet, Robert 1913–96

US sociologist.

38 Countless works in the social sciences reveal the inability of their authors to bear in mind the crucial difference between what may properly be called the *logic of discovery* and the *logic of demonstration*. The second is properly subject to rules and prescriptions; the first isn't.
1976 *Sociology as an Art Form*, introduction.

39 With all allowance made for Marx's erudition and his historic impact upon the social sciences, especially sociology, it is as an art united with prophecy, virtually religious prophecy, that Marxism survives.
1976 *Sociology as an Art Form*, ch.5.

Niven, David *originally* ***James David Graham Nevins*** 1910–83

English actor. Signed by Samuel Goldwyn, he developed into a polished light comedian in films such as *The Charge of the Light Brigade* (1936), *The Dawn Patrol* (1938) and *Bachelor Mother* (1939). He won an Academy Award for *Separate Tables* (1958).

40 He passed rapidly through his marriages to Virginia Cherrill, Barbara Hutton and Betsy Drake and filled in the lonely gaps between them by falling in and out of love with most of his leading ladies, which, as his output of films was prodigious, underlined the excellence of his physical condition.

1975 Of Cary Grant. *Bring on the Empty Horses*.

Nixon, Pat 1912–93

Wife of President Richard M Nixon. She financed herself through college and taught typing until she married Nixon in 1940. She bore two daughters and was known for her gracious hospitality during her years in the White House. She was unswervingly loyal to her husband during and after his resignation in 1974.

41 The hearings are just like a snake about to devour people.

1973 On Watergate. Letter to a friend, quoted in Julie Nixon Eisenhower *Pat Nixon* (1986).

42 Dick, I don't know how you get up in the morning!

To her husband, who later wrote that he replied 'I do it to confound my enemies'. Quoted in Julie Nixon Eisenhower *Pat Nixon* (1986).

Nixon, Richard M(ilhous) 1913–94

US Republican politician and 37th President (1969–74). He resigned under threat of impeachment after the implication of leading members of his government in the Watergate affair. As President, he sought to end the Vietnam War and had diplomatic success with China and the USSR.

43 I don't believe that I ought to quit because I am not a quitter.

1952 National TV broadcast after allegations that he was financing his vice-presidential candidacy from a secret fund, Sep.

44 Tonight—to you, the great silent majority of my fellow Americans—I ask for your support.

1969 Appeal to the nation, 3 Nov, for support in the Vietnam War.

45 This is not an invasion of Vietnam.

1970 Television address to the nation announcing the invasion of Cambodia, 30 Apr.

46 I don't give a shit what happens. I want you all to stonewall…plead the Fifth Amendment, cover-up, or anything else. If that will save it, save the plan.

1973 From the White House tapes relating to the Watergate scandal, recorded Mar.

47 There will be no whitewash in the White House.

1973 Statement on the Watergate affair, 17 Apr.

48 In giving you these tapes, blemishes and all, I am placing my trust in the basic fairness of the American people.

1974 National address, 30 May, on relinquishing the Watergate tapes after the House Judiciary Committee warned him that refusal 'might constitute a ground for impeachment'.

49 Well, I screwed it up real good, didn't I?

1974 Comment to Chief of Staff Alexander M Haig and Press Secretary Ronald L Zeigler, 3 Aug, on beginning work on his resignation address. Recalled in *RN: The Memoirs of Richard Nixon* (1978).

50 When the president does it, that means that it is not illegal… But I brought myself down. I gave them a sword and they stuck it in and twisted it with relish. And I guess that if I had been in their position, I'd have done the same thing.

1977 Interviewed by David Frost, May.

51 American people don't believe anything until they see it on television.

1994 In *Newsweek*, 2 May. He estimated that 80% of US citizens get their news from television.

Noble, Richard 1946–

English car racer. He established a new land-speed record of 1,019.467kmph (633.468mph) in 1983 in the specially built *Thrust 2*.

52 We did it for Britain and for the hell of it.

1983 After setting a new world land-speed record. Quoted in the *Sunday Times*, 'The Week in Words', 9 Oct.

Nofziger, Lyn (Franklin)

Press secretary and later Chief of the White House Office of Political Affairs in the Reagan administration.

53 Cashing in. That's what we all do. It's called experience.

1988 In *This Week*, 31 Jul.

Nolan, Sir Sidney Robert 1917–92

Australian painter. He made his name with a series of *Ned Kelly* paintings (begun 1946), followed by an 'explorer' series.

54 I wanted to know the true nature of the 'otherness' I had been born into. It was not a European thing. I wanted to paint the great purity and implacability of the landscape. I wanted a visual form of the 'otherness' of the thing not seen.

1971 Quoted in E Lynn *Sidney Nolan—Australia* (1979).

Noonan, Peggy 1950–

US writer. She was speechwriter for President Reagan (1984–9) and has since been a columnist for *Newsweek*, the *New York Times* and *Time* and contributing editor to the *Wall Street Journal*. She has written several books.

55 The battle for the mind of Ronald Reagan was like the trench warfare of World War I. Never have so many fought so hard for such barren terrain.

1990 *What I Saw at the Revolution*.

56 A speech is poetry: cadence, rhythm, imagery, sweep…and reminds us that words, like children, have the power to make dance the dullest beanbag of a heart.

1990 *What I Saw at the Revolution*.

Noonuccal, Oodgeroo *formerly* ***Kath Walker*** *née* ***Kathleen Jean Mary Ruska*** 1920–93

Australian poet and Aboriginal rights activist. Her works include *We Are Going* (1964), the first book by an Aboriginal writer to be published in English. She returned an MBE awarded to her in 1970, in protest at planned Australian bicentennial celebrations.

57 Do you know, Mr Menzies, that where I come from you

could be gaoled for supplying alcohol to an Aborigine?
1962 Remark to the then Prime Minister of Australia, Robert Menzies, when he offered her and other Aboriginal delegates a drink after a meeting. Quoted in Kathie Cochrane *Oodgeroo* (1994), pt.1, 'Protest'.

58 What can I tell you, son of mine?
I could tell you of heartbreak, hatred blind,
I could tell of crimes that shame mankind,
Of brutal wrong and deeds malign,
Of rape and murder, son of mine;
But I'll tell instead of brave and fine
When lives of black and white entwine,
And men in brotherhood combine—
This would I tell you, son of mine.
1964 *We Are Going*, 'Son of Mine'.

59 No more boomerang
No more spear;
Now all civilized—
Colour-bar and beer.
1970 *My People*, 'No More Boomerang'.

Norden, Denis 1922–

English broadcaster and humorist.

60 It's a funny kind of month, October. For the really keen cricket fan it's when you realise that your wife left you in May.
Quoted in *She* magazine, 1977.

Norman, Barry 1933–

English journalist and broadcaster. He made his name as an influential film critic through the television series that began with *Film '73* (1973–81, 1983–98).

61 The worst films were always bad but now they are bad in a more cynical way. They pander to an audience of 12–24 year olds, mostly male and mostly governed by raging testosterone. Dialogue is kept to a minimum because it holds up the action. Ditto characterisation and the building of it. As for wit, let's not bother with wit.
2002 *And Why Not?*.

Norman, Greg 1955–

Australian golfer. He won the Open championships in 1986 and 1993. The only player of modern times to have competed in a grand slam of playoffs, unfortunately he lost them all.

62 In the tournament of life, which is the biggest major, I have one of the best records ever.
2003 In *Golf Magazine*, Jul.

Norman, Major Mike

British marine. He was commanding officer of the 68 Royal marines who comprised the Falklands garrison at the time of the Argentinian invasion.

63 We've never surrendered before. It's not part of our training.
1982 Comment, Apr. Quoted in The Sunday Times Insight Team *The Falklands War* (1982), p.7.

Norris, Frank Benjamin Franklin 1870–1902

US novelist. He worked for the San Francisco *Chronicle* and while reporting became involved in the Jameson raid in South Africa. He was influenced by Zola and was one of the first US naturalist writers. His novels include *McTeague* (1899) and *The Pit* (1903).

64 The kind of a man that *men* like—not women—is the kind of man that makes the best husband.
1903 *The Pit*, ch.2.

65 Here, of all her cities, throbbed the true life—the true power and spirit of America; gigantic, crude with the crudity of youth, disdaining rivalry; sane and healthy and vigorous; brutal in its ambition, arrogant in the new-found knowledge of its giant strength, prodigal of its wealth, infinite in its desires.
1903 Of Chicago. *The Pit*, ch.2.

North, Christopher *pseudonym of* John Wilson
1785–1854

Scottish critic and essayist, Professor of Moral Philosophy at Edinburgh University (1820–51), and regular contributor to *Blackwood's Magazine* under the pseudonym 'Christopher North'.

66 His Majesty's dominions, on which the sun never sets.
1829 'Noctes Ambrosianae', no.42, in *Blackwood's Magazine*, Apr.

67 Laws were made to be broken.
1830 'Noctes Ambrosianae', no.49, in *Blackwood's Magazine*, May.

68 It may be divided into three parts; in one you cannot hear, in another you cannot see, and in the third you can neither see nor hear. I remember once sitting alone in the third division—and never before or since have I had such a profound feeling of the power of solitude.
1832 Of the Theatre Royal, Glasgow. 'Noctes Ambrosianae', no.64, in *Blackwood's Magazine*, Nov.

69 Such accidents will happen in the best-regulated families.
1834 'Noctes Ambrosianae', no.67, in *Blackwood's Magazine*, Aug.

North, Oliver 1943–

US soldier, later columnist and broadcaster. He was a National Security official involved in the 1986 Iran–Contra scandal (the supporting of anti-government Contra rebels in Nicaragua with the proceeds of secret arms sales to Iran). Despite appeals to patriotism, he was convicted on three of twelve charges, which were later dropped on appeal.

70 I don't think there's another person in America that wants to tell this story as much as I do.
1986 Invoking the Fifth Amendment at the House Committee investigating arms sales to Iran, 10 Dec.

71 I thought using the Ayatollah's money to support the Nicaraguan resistance...was a neat idea.
1987 Testimony at the House Committee investigating arms sales to Iran, 8 Jul.

Novak, Michael 1933–

US critic, writer and philosopher.

72 Baseball is a Lockean game, a kind of contract theory in ritual form, a set of atomic individuals who assent to patterns of limited co-operation in their mutual interest.
1976 *The Joys of Sport*, pt.1.

Novalis *pseudonym of* Friedrich von Hardenberg
1772–1801

German poet, a leading early Romantic. The early death of the woman he loved left a lasting impression on him, and he wrote the prose lyrics of *Hymnen an die Nicht* (1800) in her memory. He died of tuberculosis.

73 *Der Tod ist das romantisierende Prinzip unsers Lebens. Der Tod ist—das Leben. Durch den Tod wird das Leben verstärkt.*
Death is the romantic principle of Life. Death is—life. Through death life is intensified.
1802 *Schriften, II, Fragmente.*

74 *Ein Charakter ist ein vollkommen gebildeter Willen.*
A character is a perfectly cultivated will.
1802 *Schriften, II, Fragmente.*

75 *Jeder Engländer ist eine Insel.*
Every Englishman is an island.
1802 *Schriften, II, Fragmente.*

76 *Mensch werden ist eine Kunst.*
To become human is art.
1802 *Schriften, II, Fragmente.*

Noyes, Alfred 1880–1958

English writer. He was best known for his florid poems, and especially his sea poems, but also wrote literary essays, plays and memoirs.

77 Go down to Kew in lilac-time (it isn't far from London!)
And you shall wander hand in hand with love in summer's wonderland.
1904 'The Barrel-Organ'.

78 The wind was a torrent of darkness among the gusty trees,
The moon was a ghostly galleon tossed upon cloudy seas,
The road was a ribbon of moonlight over the purple moor,
And the highwayman came riding—
Riding—riding—
The highwayman came riding, up to the old inn-door.
1907 'The Highwayman'.

79 Watch for me by moonlight;
I'll come to thee by moonlight, though hell should bar the way.
1907 'The Highwayman'.

Nozick, Robert 1938–2002

US philosopher, Professor at Harvard University.

80 The socialist society would have to forbid capitalist acts between consenting adults.
1974 *Anarchy, State, and Utopia*, p.163.

Nugent, Ted 1949–

US rock guitarist. His albums include *Free For All* (1976), *Cat Scratch Fever* (1977) and *Take No Prisoners* (2003).

81 If it's too loud, you're too old.
Quoted in David Pickering *Brewer's Twentieth-Century Music* (1994).

Nunn, Sir Trevor 1940–

English stage director. He was artistic director of the Royal Shakespeare Company (1968–86) and of the National Theatre (1997–2003).

82 The National [Theatre] is an organisation that benefits directly from taxpayers' money. I know of no edict that says that only those taxpayers with degrees in English literature pay for this place.
2001 In the *New Statesman*, 22 Oct.

Nuttgens, Patrick 1930–2004

British architect and educationalist. Director of Leeds Polytechnic (1969–86), his works include *The Landscape of Ideas* (1972) and *Understanding Modern Architecture* (1988).

83 In the final analysis, all architecture reveals the application of human ingenuity to the satisfaction of human needs. And among these needs are not only shelter, warmth and accommodation, but also the needs, felt at every moment in every part of the world in endlessly different ways, for something more profound, evocative and universal, for beauty, for permanence, for immortality.
1993 'The Nature of Architecture', in Ben Farmer and Hentie Louw (eds) *Companion to Contemporary Architectural Thought* (1993).

Nye, Joseph S, Jr 1937–

Professor of International Relations and Dean of the Kennedy School, Harvard. Formerly Assistant Secretary of Defense for International Security Affairs and Chair of the National Intelligence Council.

84 Not their style to say no. But when you listen… you don't hear yes.
1994 On asking for Saudi Arabia's help with the $500-million cost of US troop buildup in the Gulf. In the *New York Times*, 4 Nov.

Oakeshott, Michael Joseph 1901–90

English philosopher and political theorist, Professor of Political Science at the London School of Economics (1951–69). His key philosophical work was *Experience and its Modes* (1933), a broadly idealistic view which he developed in economic theory.

85 The politics of our society are a conversation in which past, present and future each has a voice; and though one or other of them may on occasion properly prevail none permanently dominates, and on this account we are free.
1962 *Rationalism in Politics.*

86 We consider ourselves to be free because no one in our society is allowed unlimited power—no leader, faction, party or 'class', no majority, no government, church, corporation, trade, or professional association or trade union. The secret of its freedom is that it is composed of a multitude of organisations in the constitution of the best of which is reproduced that diffusion of power

which is characteristic of the whole.
1962 *Rationalism in Politics*.

87 It is difficult to think of any circumstances where learning may be said to be impossible.
Quoted in R S Peters (ed) *The Concept of Education* (1966), ch.10, 'Learning and Teaching'.

88 Every human being is born an heir to an inheritance to which he can succeed only in a process of learning.
Quoted in R S Peters (ed) *The Concept of Education* (1966), ch.10, 'Learning and Teaching'.

Oakley, Charles Edward 1832–65

English clergyman and hymn writer.

89 Hills of the North, rejoice:
Rivers and mountain-spring,
Hark to the advent voice!
Valley and lowland, sing!
Though absent long, your Lord is nigh,
He judgement brings, and victory.
1870 Hymn.

Oates, Joyce Carol 1938–

US writer. She is best known as a novelist, but has also published several volumes of poetry, and essays, critical writings and journalism.

90 The worst cynicism: a belief in luck.
1970 *Do What You Will*, pt.2, ch.15.

91 Nothing is accidental in the universe—this is one of my Laws of Physics—except the entire universe itself, which is Pure Accident, pure divinity.
1970 *Do What You Will*, 'The Summing-Up: Meredith Dawe'.

92 Women Whose Lives Are Food, Men Whose Lives Are Money.
1978 Title of poetry collection.

93 I used to think getting old was about vanity—but actually it's about losing people you love.
1989 In *The Guardian*, 18 Aug.

94 Because It Is Bitter, And Because It Is My Heart.
1990 Title of novel.

95 For what *is* passes so swiftly and irrevocably into what *was*, no human claim can be of the least significance.
1994 *What I Lived For*, prologue, pt.1.

96 And Corky'd protested, You mean it isn't enough to be *right*?—they have to *like* me, too?
1994 *What I Lived For*, pt.1.

Oates, Lawrence Edward Grace 1880–1912

English explorer, one of the members of Captain Scott's ill-fated Antarctic expedition that set out for the South Pole in 1910.

97 I am just going outside and may be some time.
1912 Last words, Mar.
► *See Scott 722:82.*

O'Brien, (Donal) Conor (Dermod David Donat) Cruise 1917–

Irish historian, diplomat, critic and politician. He wrote *To Katanga and Back* (1962), an autobiographical narrative of the Congo crisis. He has also been a newspaper editor and written numerous books of biography, politics and history.

98 Irishness is not primarily a question of birth or blood or language: it is the condition of being involved in the Irish situation, and usually of being mauled by it. On that definition Swift is more Irish than Goldsmith or Sheridan, although by the usual tests they are Irish and he is pure English.
1959 Reviewing *The Oxford Book of Irish Verse* in the *New Statesman*, 17 Jan (written under the pseudonym Donat O'Donnell).

99 Of history and its consequences it may be said: 'Those who can, gloat; those who can't, brood.' Englishmen are born gloaters; Irishmen born brooders. There are, it is true, brooders who take to gloating, and they did much to build the Empire. Yet the brooder-gloater, such as the Irishman turned Englishman, is not, as a human type, altogether a success. He is a little too much on his guard, like an excessively assimilated Jew, or a son of Harlem who has decided to 'pass'. The past of the Irishman, the Jew, the Negro, is, psychologically, too explosive to be buried.
1962 *To Katanga and Back: a UN case history.*

1 In any case you Papists have no right to complain! If you won't have contraception how can you control the population without the assistance of Herod? You ought to be grateful.
1970 *King Herod Explains.*

2 We dislike the IRA, most of us, and fear it. We are a peaceful and democratic people. But our history, our idealistic pretensions and our fatal ambivalence have stuck us with an ideology that is warlike and anti-democratic, and calls increasingly for further human sacrifice.
1985 In the *New York Review of Books*, 29 Apr.

3 The United Nations cannot do anything, and never could. It is not an animate entity or agent. It is a place, a stage, a forum and a shrine…a place to which powerful people can repair when they are fearful about the course on which their own rhetoric seems to be propelling them.
1985 In *New Republic*, 4 Nov.

O'Brien, Edna 1932–

Irish novelist, short-story writer and playwright. Her works include *The Country Girls* (1960), *The Lonely Girl* (1962), *Girls in Their Married Bliss* (1964), *House of Splendid Isolation* (1994) and *Wild Decembers* (1999).

4 Ordinary life bypassed me, but I also bypassed it. It couldn't have been any other way. Conventional life and conventional people are not for me.
In Annalena Mc Afee (ed) *Lives and Works: Profiles of Leading Novelists, Poets and Playwrights* (2002).

O'Brien, Flann *pseudonym of* Brian O'Nolan *also known as* Myles na Gopaleen 1911–66

Irish writer who worked in the Irish Civil Service until 1953. In 1940 he began writing for *The Irish Times* under the pseudonym of Myles na Gopaleen and developed a reputation for being an eccentric and idiosyncratic columnist. He is best known for his novel, *At Swim-Two-Birds* (1939).

5 When things go wrong and will not come right,
Though you do the best you can,
When life looks black as the hour of night—

A PINT OF PLAIN IS YOUR ONLY MAN.
1939 *At Swim-Two-Birds*, ch.1, 'The Workman's Friend' (as Flann O'Brien).

6 There was a frightful, appalling row.
As a matter of fact the Pope told us all to go to hell. He threatened to silence Father Fahrt.
1961 *The Hard Life*.

7 And now the curse has come upon us, because I have personally met in the streets of Ireland persons who are clearly out of Synge's plays. They talk and dress like that, and damn the drink they'll swally but the mug of porter in the long nights after Samhain.
1968 *The Best of Myles*.

O'Brien, John J

Washington correspondent, Philadelphia *Inquirer*.

8 The only candidate who can whistle Dixie while humming the *Battle Hymn of the Republic*.
1976 Of President Johnson. Quoted in Harold Brayman (ed) *The President Speaks Off the Record* (1976).

O'Brien, (Angela Maxine) Margaret 1937–

US child actress, best known for her performance in *Meet Me in St Louis* (1944).

9 When I cry, shall I let the tears run all the way down my face or shall I stop them halfway down?
1944 Attributed remark to director Henry Koster when making *Music for Millions* (1944). Quoted by Larry Adler in *It Ain't Necessarily So* (1984).

O'Brien, Virginia

Manhattan office worker.

10 Crouch, swivel, tug, pull and plop.
1987 Advice on how to seat oneself at a picnic while wearing a mini-skirt. In the *New York Times*, 17 Jul.

O'Brien, William 1852–1928

Irish journalist and politician, born a Catholic but educated at a Protestant college. He founded the Land League journal *United Ireland* (1881) and became a Nationalist MP (1883–95, 1900–18).

11 What are we learning French or the piano for, I would like to know, if it is not to be sold to a man some day... We have to cringe, and manoeuvre, and grimace for a husband—a husband who may be deaf or have a hump if he is rich—a husband that may attack you in *delirium tremens* to-day if he makes a devout act of contrition for it to-morrow.
1890 *When We Were Boys*.

Ó Bruadair, Dáibhídh c.1625–1698

Irish-Gaelic poet, who recorded the destruction of his culture. His patrons were exiled by wars and proscription, and he became a farm labourer.

12 I will sing no more songs: the pride of my country I sang
Through forty long years of good rhyme, without any avail;
And no one cared even as much as the half of a hang
For the song or the singer, so here is an end of the tale.
Adapted from the Irish by James Stephens.

O'Casey, Sean 1884–1964

Irish playwright. His early plays, including *Juno and the Paycock* (1924), deal with Dublin working-class life and were written for the Abbey Theatre. His later, more experimental, plays include *Cockadoodle Dandy* (1949).

13 Th' whole worl's in a state o' chassis!
1924 Boyle speaking. *Juno and the Paycock*, act 1.

14 JUNO: Sacred Heart o' Jesus, take away our hearts o' stone, and give us hearts o' flesh! Take away this murdherin' hate, an' give us Thine own eternal love!
1924 *Juno and the Paycock*, act 3.

15 She dhresses herself to keep him with her, but it's no use—afther a month or two, th' wondher of a woman wears off.
1926 *The Plough and the Stars*, act 1.

16 There's no reason to bring religion into it. I think we ought to have as great a regard for religion as we can, so as to keep it out of as many things as possible.
1926 *The Plough and the Stars*, act 1.

17 English literature's performing flea.
Of P G Wodehouse. In P G Wodehouse *Performing Flea* (1953).

Occam, William of c.1285–c.1349

English philosopher, theologian and political writer. He was perhaps the most influential of later medieval philosophers

18 *Entia non sunt multiplicanda praeter necessitatem.*
No more things should be presumed than is necessary.
This principle of intellectual economy, known as Occam's Razor, is not found in this form in his writings. Similar expressions can be found, eg *Pluralitas non est ponenda sine necessitate* ('Plurality should not be posited unnecessarily'), in *Scriptum in Librum Primum Sententiarum*.

O'Connell, Daniel *known as* the Liberator 1775–1847

Irish Catholic political leader, able to take his Commons seat only after Catholic Emancipation (1829). He fought against tithes and in 1840 founded the Repeal Association, agitating to end the union with Britain. In 1844 he was imprisoned on a charge of sedition, and his influence subsequently waned.

19 Let us never tolerate the slightest inroad on the discipline of our holy Church. Let us never consent that she should be made the hireling of the Ministry. Our forefathers would have died—nay, perished in hopeless slavery—rather than consent to such degradation.
1814 Speech, Dublin, 23 Feb.

20 Not for all the universe contains would I, in the struggle for what I conceive to be my country's cause, consent to the effusion of a single drop of human blood, except my own.
1843 Speech, 18 Feb.

21 While I have a tongue I'll abuse you, you most inimitable periphery. Look at her, boys! there she stands—a convicted perpendicular in petticoats! There's contamination in her circumference, and she trembles with guilt down to the extremities of her corollaries. Ah! you're found out, you rectilineal antecedent, and equiangular old hag! 'Tis with you the devil will fly away, you porter-swiping similitude of the bisection of a vortex!
Winning thrust in a vituperation contest with Dublin's champion virago, Biddy Moriarty, reported by Daniel Owen-Madden in *Revelations of Ireland* (1877).

O'Connor, Edwin 1918–68

US novelist, originally a radio announcer and producer, best known for his novel *The Last Hurrah* (1956). *The Edge of Sadness* (1961) won a Pulitzer Prize.

22 The Last Hurrah.
1956 Title of novel, based on the career of politician James M Curley.

O'Connor, (Mary) Flannery 1925–64

US novelist and short-story writer. Her fiction, set in the Deep South, reflects a mordant sense of humour. Her works include two novels and two volumes of short stories.

23 I preach there are all kinds of truth, your truth and somebody else's. But behind all of them there is only one truth and that is that there's no truth.
1952 Hazel Motes. *Wise Blood*, ch.10.

24 While the South is hardly Christ-centred, it is most certainly Christ-haunted.
1960 'Some Aspects of the Grotesque in Southern Fiction'. Paper read at Wesleyan College, Fall.

25 There was a time when the average reader read a novel simply for the moral he could get out of it, and however naïve that may have been, it was a good deal less naïve than some of the limited objectives he has now.
1960 'Some Aspects of the Grotesque in Southern Fiction'. Paper read at Wesleyan College, Fall.

26 It's like building a nest. First she thinks about it, then she begins to gather the materials, then she begins to put it together.
On her mother's two-month process of making a fruit cake. Quoted in Sally Fitzgerald (ed) *The Habit of Being* (1979).

O'Connor, Frank *pseudonym of* Michael O'Donovan 1903–66

Irish writer, a member of the IRA in his teens and imprisoned after the War of Independence. His ideal medium was the short story, but he also wrote plays and literary criticism.

27 Every time I leave the old man I feel like a thousand dollars.
1948 Of Yeats. Quoted in Richard Ellmann *Yeats: the Man and the Masks* (1948).

O'Connor, Cardinal John Joseph 1920–2000

Catholic Archbishop of New York.

28 It is increasingly rare for many of us…to believe that people can be poor, but honest, poor but deserving of respect. Poverty is no longer blamed on anyone but the poor themselves. Contempt for the poor has become a virtue.
1994 In *Catholic New York*, quoted in the *New York Times*, 24 Nov.

Odets, Clifford 1906–63

US playwright and actor, an important figure in the US theatre of the 1930s.

29 Go out and fight so life shouldn't be printed on dollar bills.
1935 Jacob. *Awake and Sing*, act 1.

30 Music is the great cheer-up in the language of all countries.
1937 Mr Bonaparte. *Golden Boy*, act 1, sc.2.

O'Donnell, Kenneth P(hillip) 1924–77

Special Assistant to President Kennedy.

31 Mr President, the president is dead.
1963 To Lyndon B Johnson after the assassination of John F Kennedy, 22 Nov.

Oerter, Al(fred) 1936–

US athlete and discus-thrower. He won an unsurpassed four gold medals for the discus, at Melbourne (1956), Rome (1960), Tokyo (1964) and Mexico (1968).

32 I never had technique.
1978 In the *New York Times*, 16 May.

O'Faolain, Sean 1900–91

Irish writer and educator. He began writing in and translating from Gaelic. A successful novel, *A Nest of Simple Folk* (1933), was followed by biographies of Irish figures.

33 If we turn to early Irish literature, as we naturally may, to see what sort of people the Irish were in the infancy of the race, we find ourselves wandering in delighted bewilderment through a darkness shot with lightning and purple flame.
1947 *The Irish*.

34 He was like a man who takes a machine-gun to a shooting gallery. Everybody falls flat on his face, the proprietor at once takes to the hills, and when you cautiously peep up, you find that he has wrecked the place but got three perfect bull's-eyes.
On Frank O'Connor (pseudonym of Michael O'Donovan), attributed.

O'Flaherty, Liam 1897–1984

Irish Republican writer. He went to London in 1922 to become a writer, finding fame with his novel *The Informer* (1926). In addition to other novels, he wrote three volumes of autobiography (1930–4).

35 When the parish priest rebuked him for his celibacy, saying it would lead him into debauchery and sin, he said that a man who had to be muzzled by a wife as a protection against debauchery was not worthy of the joy of innocence. After that people began to treat him with priestly respect.
'The Mermaid'.

Ogden, Frank *also known as* 'Dr Tomorrow' 1920–

Canadian futurist.

36 Although I am a futurist today, if I don't change tomorrow, I will be a historian.
1994 *Ogdenisms: The Frank Ogden Quote Book*.

37 As the planet globalizes, groups tribalize.
1994 *Ogdenisms: The Frank Ogden Quote Book*.

38 Holidays are the greatest learning experience unknown to man.
1994 *Ogdenisms: The Frank Ogden Quote Book*.

39 Technology breaks the laws and makes the laws.
1994 *Ogdenisms: The Frank Ogden Quote Book*.

40 My idea of long-range planning is lunch.
1994 *Ogdenisms: The Frank Ogden Quote Book*.

Ogilvy, David 1911–99

British-born US advertising executive, founder of Ogilvy and Mather.

41 It is the professional duty of the advertising agent to conceal his artifice. When Aeschines spoke, they said, 'How well he speaks', but when Demosthenes spoke, they said 'Let us march against Philip.'
1963 *Confessions of an Advertising Man*, ch.5.

42 The consumer isn't a moron. She's your wife.
1963 *Confessions of an Advertising Man*, ch.5.

Ogilvy, James, 1st Earl of Seafield 1644–1730

Scottish advocate, MP and political manager. He was one of the Scottish commissioners appointed to negotiate the Union of Parliaments.

43 There's ane end of ane auld sang.
1707 On signing the Treaty of Union between Scotland and England. Quoted in George Lockhart of Carnwath *Memoir of the Affairs of Scotland* (1714), vol.1.

O'Hagan, John *pseudonym* **Sliabh Cuilinn** 1822–90

Irish lawyer and poet.

44 My native heath is brown beneath,
My native waters blue;
But crimson red o'er both shall spread,
Ere I am false to you,
Dear land!
Ere I am false to you.
1845 'Dear Land' in *The Spirit of the Nation*.

O'Hanlon, Redmond 1947–

English naturalist, critic and traveller. With James Fenton, he made an expedition into the heart of Borneo in 1983 and wrote entertainingly about the land and its people.

45 The Iban, when they decide that something is really funny, and know that they are going to laugh for a long time, lie down first.
Dana, Leon and Inghai lay down.
1984 *Into the Heart of Borneo*.

O'Hara, Frank 1926–66

US poet and art critic. He published several volumes of poetry, which were closely linked to the New York environment in which he moved.

46 and I am sweating a lot by now and thinking of
leaning on the john door in the 5 SPOT
while she whispered a song along the keyboard
to Mal Waldron and everyone and I stopped
breathing
1964 Of Billie Holiday. *Lunch Poems*, 'The Day Lady Died'.

O'Hara, John Henry 1905–70

US novelist and short-story writer. His best-known works, several of which were successfully filmed, included *Appointment in Samarra* (1934), *Butterfield 8* (1935) and *Pal Joey* (1940).

47 George Gershwin died last week. I don't have to believe it if I don't want to.
1937 Quoted in Ian Crofton and Donald Fraser *A Dictionary of Musical Quotations* (1985).

48 But whats the use of being old if you cant be dumb?
1940 *Pal Joey*, ch.1.

49 I am making a little trip to N.Y. in the near future and we will have a little talk and you can explain your positon, altho the way I feel now if I saw you now your positon would be horizontle.
1940 *Pal Joey*, ch.2.

50 Illinois is a state of suspended animation and the people live in hibernation from Oct. to whenever it ever gets warmer.
1940 *Pal Joey*, ch.9.

O Henry *pseudonym of* **William Sydney Porter** 1862–1910

US writer. He is best known for his comic short stories.

51 Life is made up of sobs, sniffles, and smiles, with sniffles predominating.
1906 *The Four Million*, 'The Gift of the Magi'.

52 If men knew how women pass the time when they are alone, they'd never marry.
1906 *The Four Million*, 'Memoirs of a Yellow Dog'.

53 It was beautiful and simple as all truly great swindles are.
1908 *The Gentle Grafter*, 'The Octopus Marooned'.

54 Whenever he saw a dollar in another man's hands he took it as a personal grudge if he couldn't take it any other way.
1908 *The Gentle Grafter*, 'The Octopus Marooned'.

55 If ever there was an aviary overstocked with jays it is that Yaptown-on-the-Hudson, called New York.
1908 *The Gentle Grafter*, 'A Tempered Wind'.

56 A story with a moral appended is like the bite of a mosquito. It bores you, and then injects a stinging drop to irritate your conscience.
1910 *Strictly Business*, 'The Gold That Glittered'.

57 Turn up the lights; I don't want to go home in the dark.
Last words. Quoted in Charles Alphonso Smith *O. Henry* (1916), ch.9. The words are taken from the popular song by Harry Williams 'I'm afraid to come home in the dark' (1907).

58 A burglar who respects his art always takes his time before taking anything else.
Sixes and Sevens, 'Makes The Whole World Kin' (1911).

O'Keeffe, Georgia 1887–1986

US painter, a pioneer of abstract art (eg *Blue and Green Music*, 1919). She later moved towards a more figurative style, painting close-ups of parts of flowers and plants. Her works include *Black Iris* (New York, 1949).

59 Nobody sees a flower—really—it is so small—we haven't time—and to see takes time like to have a friend takes time… So I said to myself—I'll paint what I see—what the flower is to me, but I'll paint it big and they will be surprised into taking time to look at it—I will make even busy New Yorkers take time to see what I see of flowers.
Quoted in Goodrich and Bry *Georgia O'Keeffe* (1970).

60 The men liked to put me down as the best woman painter. I think I'm one of the best painters.
Quoted in W Chadwick *Women, Art and Society* (1990).

Okri, Ben 1959–

Nigerian writer, winner of the 1987 Commonwealth Prize for Africa for *Incidents at the Shrine* (1986) and the 1991 Booker Prize for *The Famished Road*. Other works include *Songs of Enchantment* (1993), *Dangerous Love* (1996) and *In Arcadia* (2002).

61 We feared the heartlessness of human beings, all of whom are born blind, few of whom ever learn to see.
1991 *The Famished Road*, ch.1.

Oldenburg, Claes Thure 1929–

Swedish-born US sculptor. From 1958 he was one of the pioneers of Pop Art. His works include giant hamburgers and other foodstuffs, the *Giant Clothespin* in Philadelphia (1975) and projects in Cologne, Eindhoven, Milan and London.

62 I am for an art that helps old ladies across the street… I am for Kool-art, 7-UP art, Pepsi-art, Sunshine art, 39 cents art, 15 cents art, Vatronol art, Dro-bomb art, Vam art, Menthol art, L & M art, Ex-lax art, Venida art, Heaven Hill art, Pamryl art, San-o-med art, Rx art, 9.99 art, Now art, New art, How art, Fire sale art, Last Chance art, Only art, Diamond art, Tomorrow art, Franks art, Ducks art, Meat-o-rama art.
1961 Written for an exhibition in New York, 1961, quoted in Arts Council of Great Britain *Oldenburg* (1970).

Oldman, Gary 1958–

English actor.

63 The industry has changed. Two years ago I could tell a company I've got Russell Crowe and that would get the film made. Now they'd ask 'And who's the girl?' Just one famous face isn't enough any more.
2004 In *Scotland on Sunday*, 30 May.

Oliphant, Margaret *née* *Wilson* 1828–97

Scottish novelist, essayist and critic. Widowed and debt-ridden at an early age with a large extended family dependent upon her, she was a prolific writer and maintained a long association with *Blackwood's Magazine* and *The Cornhill* as well as completing over 100 novels.

64 A woman who cannot be a governess or a novel-writer must fall back on that poor little needle, the primitive and original handicraft of femininity.
1858 'The Condition of Women', in *Blackwood's Magazine*, vol.83, Feb.

Oliver, Mary 1935–

US poet. Her work includes *American Primitive* (1983, Pulitzer Prize), *New and Selected Poems* (1992, National Book Award) and *The Leaf and the Cloud* (2000).

65 Poetry happens because of life. Poetry happens because of language. And poetry happens because of other poets.
1992 In the *New York Times*, 20 Nov.

Olivier, Laurence Kerr, Baron 1907–89

English actor, producer and director. A great Shakespearean actor, he also produced, directed and played in films of *Henry V* (1944), *Hamlet* (1948) and *Richard III* (1955). He campaigned for the foundation of the National Theatre.

66 Make up your mind dearheart. Do you want to be a great actor or a household word?
c.1962 Comment to Richard Burton while filming *Cleopatra*. Burton replied 'Both'.

67 Acting is a masochistic form of exhibitionism. It is not quite the occupation of an adult.
1978 Quoted in *Time*, 3 Jul.

68 I'm not so artistic that I despise profit.
Attributed.

69 It looks like rows and rows of empty seats.
On being shown the view of the jungle enjoyed from Noël Coward's house on a Jamaican hillside. Attributed.

70 Shakespeare—the nearest thing in incarnation to the eye of God.
Quoted in *Kenneth Harris Talking To*…, 'Sir Laurence Olivier'.

71 What is the main problem of the actor? It is to keep the audience awake, and not let them go to sleep, then wake up and go home feeling they've wasted their money.
Attributed.

Ollivier, Émile 1825–1913

French politician, charged by Napoleon III to form a constitutional ministry. He rushed into war with Germany, was overthrown on 9 Aug 1870, and withdrew to Italy. He wrote numerous works, including *L'Empire libéral* (16 vols, 1894–1912), a defence of his policy.

72 One is never weaker than when one appears to have everybody's support.
1870 Letters.

Olsen, Tillie 1913–

US writer and feminist. She wrote proletarian fiction in the 1930s. In the 1960s she emerged as an advocate of feminism, and her work attracted wide attention for the first time. Her later work includes *Tell Me a Riddle* (1960).

73 Vinegar he poured on me all his life; I am well marinated; how can I be honey now?
1960 *Tell Me a Riddle*, section 1.

Olson, Charles 1910–70

US poet and literary theorist. He taught at Black Mountain College, North Carolina, where his ideas were influential on such poets as Robert Creeley and Robert Duncan. As a poet, he is best known for the sequence *The Maximus Poems* (1953).

74 I take SPACE to be the central fact to man born in America… I spell it large because it comes large here. Large and without mercy.
1947 *Call Me Ishmael*, section 1.

75 But that which matters, that which insists, that which will last,
that! o my people, where shall you find it, how, where, where shall you
listen
when all is become billboards, when, all, even silence, is spray-gunned?
1953 *The Maximus Poems*, 'I, Maximus of Gloucester, To You, 3'.

76 one loves only form,
and form only comes
into existence when
the thing is born.
1953 *The Maximus Poems*, 'I, Maximus of Gloucester, To You, 4'.

Olson, Elder James 1909–92

US poet and critic. In both his formal, cerebral poetry and criticism he adhered to the neo-Aristotelian principles espoused at the University of Chicago, where he taught.

77 We shall never know all about art or the values of art until all art is at an end; meanwhile artists will continue to instruct us.
Quoted in Elmer Borklund (ed) *Contemporary Literary Critics* (1977).

Onassis, Jacqueline Lee Kennedy *née Bouvier* 1929–94

Wife of President John F Kennedy. She supervised the restoration of the White House and wielded a powerful and widespread influence on fashion. After her husband's assassination she returned to private life, and in 1968 she married Aristotle Onassis, the Greek shipping magnate.

78 Put your brilliant mind to work for…dresses for public appearances…that I would wear if Jack were President of France.
1960 Letter to Oleg Cassini, 13 Dec. Quoted in Oleg Cassini *In My Fashion* (1987).

79 I felt like a moth hanging on the window pane.
1961 On her first night in the White House, in *Newsweek*, 1 Jan.

80 Lincoln's bedroom! And you see that great bed, it looks like a cathedral.
1961 On her first night in the White House, in *Newsweek*, 1 Jan.

81 You worked together for the finest things in the finest years… Later on when a series of disastrous Presidents and Prime Ministers…will have botched up everything—people will say 'Do you remember those days—how perfect they were?' The days of you and Jack.
1964 To Harold Macmillan, 31 Jan.

82 I cast only one vote—for Jack. It is a rare thing to be able to vote for one's husband for President and I didn't want to dilute it by voting for anyone else
On the 1960 elections. Quoted in Arthur M Schlesinger Jr *A Thousand Days* (1965).

83 There'll never be another Camelot again.
On Frederick Lowe's lyrics from Alan Jay Lerner's *Camelot*, a title that became synonymous with the Kennedy administration—'Don't let it be forgot, that once there was a spot, for one brief shining moment that was known as Camelot.' Quoted in Theodore H White *In Search of History* (1978).

84 Uncle Cornpone and his Little Porkchop.
On the Johnsons. Quoted in *Newsweek*, 30 May 1994.

Ondaatje, (Philip) Michael 1943–

Sri Lankan-born Canadian poet and novelist. His poetry includes *Rat Jelly* (1973) and *Secular Love* (1987); other works include novels such as *Running in the Family* (1982), *The English Patient* (1992, Booker Prize) and *Anil's Ghost* (2000).

85 There was always, he thought, this pleasure ahead of him, an ace of joy up his sleeve so he could say you can do anything to me, take everything away, put me in prison, but I will know [her] when we are old.
1987 *In the Skin of a Lion*, 'Remorse'.

O'Neal, Shaquille 1972–

US basketball player. As centre for Orlando in 1995, he was the NBA leading scorer with 2,315 points from 79 games. He played for Orlando Magic from 1992 to 1996, when he joined the Los Angeles Lakers.

86 Nietzsche was so intelligent and advanced. And that's how I am. I'm the black, basketball-playing Nietzsche.
2003 On himself, having previously likened himself to Aristotle. In *Book*, Mar/Apr.

O'Neill, Eugene Gladstone 1888–1953

US playwright. His play *Beyond the Horizon* (1920) won a Pulitzer Prize, and he established his reputation with such serious-minded plays as *Mourning Becomes Electra* (1931), *The Iceman Cometh* (1946) and *Long Day's Journey into Night* (1956). He was awarded a Nobel prize in 1936.

87 The action of the play takes place on an island in the West Indies as not yet self-determined by White Mariners. The form of native government is, for the time being, an Empire.
1920 *The Emperor Jones*, scene direction.

88 For de little stealin' dey gits you in jail soon or late. For de big stealin' dey makes you Emperor and puts you in de Hall o' Fame when you croaks.
1921 Jones. *The Emperor Jones*, sc.1.

89 Life is for each man a solitary cell whose walls are mirrors.
1927 Lazarus. *Lazarus Laughed*, act 2, sc.1.

90 When men make gods, there is no God!
1927 Lazarus. *Lazarus Laughed*, act 2, sc.2.

91 Man's loneliness is but his fear of life!
1927 Lazarus. *Lazarus Laughed*, act 3, sc.2.

92 The old—like children—talk to themselves, for they have reached that hopeless wisdom of experience which knows that though one were to cry it in the streets to multitudes, or whisper it in the kiss to one's beloved, the only ears that can ever hear one's secrets are one's own!
1927 Tiberius. *Lazarus Laughed*, act 4, sc.1.

93 Life is perhaps most wisely regarded as a bad dream between two awakenings, and every day is a life in miniature.
1928 Chu-Yin. *Marco Millions*, act 2, sc.2.

94 The devil!…what beastly things our memories insist on cherishing!
1928 Marsden. *Strange Interlude*, pt.1, act 2.

95 Strange interlude! Yes, our lives are merely strange dark interludes in the electrical display of God the Father!
1928 Nina. *Strange Interlude*, pt.2, act 9.

96 Mourning Becomes Electra.
1931 Title of play.

97 The sea hates a coward!
1931 Bryant. *Mourning Becomes Electra*, pt.2, act 4.

98 EDMUND: (*sits down opposite his father—contemptuously*). Yes, facts don't mean a thing, do they? What you want to believe, that's the only truth! (*Derisively.*) Shakespeare was an Irish Catholic, for example.
TYRONE: (*stubbornly*). So he was. The proof is in his plays.
1939–41 *Long Day's Journey Into Night*, act 4 (published 1956).

99 Where do you get your taste in authors—That damned library of yours! (*He indicates the small bookcase at rear.*) Voltaire, Rousseau, Schopenhauer, Nietzsche, Ibsen! Atheists, fools, and madmen! And your poets! This Dowson, and this Baudelaire, and Swinburne and

Oscar Wilde, and Whitman and Poe! Whoremongers and degenerates! Pah! When I've three good sets of Shakespeare there (*he nods at the large bookcase*) you could read.

1939–41 Tyrone. *Long Day's Journey Into Night*, act 4 (published 1956).

1 A Long Day's Journey Into Night.

1939–41 Title of play (published 1956).

2 The Iceman Cometh.

1946 Title of play.

3 Little subconscious mind, say I each night, bring home the bacon.

Quoted in Kenneth Tynan *Tynan Right and Left* (1988). Tynan added the question, 'But how much of the bacon can we nowadays stomach?'

O'Neill, Martin 1952–

Northern Irish footballer and football manager.

4 I never try to make a right decision. I make a decision and then try to make it right.

2002 In *The Independent*, 20 Dec.

O'Neill, Molly

US writer, food columnist and restaurant critic.

5 Out of the kitchen, to stew is to fret, to worry, to agitate. In the kitchen, however, to stew is to have great expectations.

1994 In the *New York Times*, 30 Jan.

O'Neill, Thomas P *known as 'Tip'* 1912–94

US Congressman and Speaker of the House of Representatives.

6 Take advantage of the good cigars. You don't get much else in that job.

1977 Advice to Vice-President Walter P Mondale. Quoted in *Time*, 4 Jun 1984.

7 Ronald Reagan…wasn't without leadership ability, but he lacked most of the management skills that a President needs. But let me give him his due: he would have made a hell of a king.

1987 *Man of the House*.

8 You can teach an old dog new tricks—if the old dog wants to learn.

1989 On working with President Reagan. In NPR broadcast, 2 Jan.

9 Herbert Hoover with a smile, a cheerleader for selfishness.

On President Reagan. Recalled on O'Neill's death in the *New York Times*, 7 Jan 1994.

10 Keep your left hand high.

Recommending the boxer's defensive posture to President Carter. Recalled on O'Neill's death in the *New York Times*, 7 Jan 1994.

11 The Democratic Party has succeeded so well that many of its members are now Republicans.

Quoted in WAMU radio broadcast, Washington, 29 Mar 1995.

Onetti, Juan Carlos 1909–94

Uruguayan novelist. He moved to Buenos Aires in 1943 and later to Madrid, where he spent his final years. In many of his novels he sets the action in the mythical city of Santa María.

12 *Es asombroso ver en qué se puede convertir la revolución rusa a través del cerebro de un comerciante yanqui; basta ver las fotos de las revistas norteamericanas, nada más que las fotos porque no sé leerlas, para comprender que no hay pueblo más imbécil que ése sobre la tierra; no puede haberlo porque también la capacidad de estupidez es limitada en la raza humana.*

It's astonishing to see what the Russian Revolution can become thanks to the brain of a Yankee entrepreneur; you only have to see the photos in North American magazines, only the photos because I can't read them, to realize they're the most stupid people on earth; that's quite possible because even the human race has a limited potential for idiocy.

1939 *El pozo* (translated as *The Pit*, 1991).

Oppenheimer, J(ulius) Robert 1904–67

US physicist, lecturer at the University of California and the California Institute of Technology and from 1947 director of the Institute for Advanced Study at Princeton. He was director (1942–5) of the laboratory at Los Alamos, New Mexico, that designed and built the first atomic bomb.

13 When you see something that is technically sweet, you go ahead and do it and you argue about what to do about it only after you have had your technical success. That is the way it was with the atomic bomb.

1954 'In the Matter of J. Robert Oppenheimer', USAEC transcript of hearing before Personnel Security Board.

14 I remembered the line from the Hindu scripture, the *Bhagavad Gita*… 'I am become death, the destroyer of worlds.'

On the detonation of the first atomic bomb, 16 Jul 1945. Quoted in Len Giovanitti and Fred Freed *The Decision to Drop the Bomb* (1965).

15 Science has, as its whole purpose, the rendering of the physical world understandable and beautiful. Without this you have only tables and statistics.

1966 In *Look* magazine.

16 Science is not everything, but science is very beautiful.

1966 In *Look* magazine.

17 No man should escape our universities without knowing how little he knows.

1967 In *Partisan Review*, Summer issue.

18 The theory of our modern technic shows that nothing is as practical as the theory.

1977 In *Reflex*, Jul.

19 Those two scorpions in a bottle.

On the US and USSR in the early 1950s. Quoted in Anthony Cave Brown *Treason in the Blood* (1994).

O'Rahilly, Egan *Gaelic name* ***Aodhagán Ó Rathaille*** 1670–1726

Gaelic poet. Little is known of his life except that he lived and died in great poverty and was buried at Muckross Abbey. His *Vision* is regarded as one of the finest poems in Irish Gaelic.

20 For the future I cease, Death approaches with little delay,
Since the dragons of Laune and Lane and Lee are
destroyed;
I'll follow the heroes far from the light of day,
The princes my ancestors followed before Christ died.

c.1729 Closing lines of his last known poem, translated

from the Irish by Owen Dudley Edwards.

21 That my old bitter heart was pierced in this black doom,
That foreign devils have made our land a tomb,
That the sun that was Munster's glory has gone down
Has made me a beggar before you, Valentine Brown.
'Valentine Brown', translated from the Irish by Michael O'Donovan (pseudonym Frank O'Connor).

O'Rourke, P(atrick) J(ake) 1947–

US writer and editor. He has written books and articles on government, politics, social mores and travel.

22 The best thing about the violence in Northern Ireland is that it's all so ancient and honorable… The Irish are in the same terrific position as the Shiites in Lebanon, the peasants in El Salvador, the blacks in America, the Jews in Palestine, the Palestinians in Israel (and everybody everywhere, if you read your history)—enough barbarism has been visited on the Irish to excuse all barbarities by the Irish barbarians.
1988 *Holidays in Hell.*

23 Communism doesn't really starve or execute that many people. Mostly it just bores them to death.
1988 *Holidays in Hell.*

24 Republicans are the party that says government doesn't work, and then they get elected and prove it.
1991 *Parliament of Whores.*

25 Sometimes it's hard to remember that bourgeois property is the real revolutionary force these days. All over the world we're bringing down dictatorships—or at least forcing them to go condo.
1992 *Give War a Chance.*

26 For reasons of high aesthetic principle, I do not write on a computer.
2003 In *Writers on Writing, Volume II: More Collected Essays from the New York Times.*

Orozco, José Clemente 1883–1949

Mexican painter, one of the three foremost artists in the revival of monumental fresco painting.

27 The highest, the most logical, the purest and strongest form of painting is the mural… It is, too, the most disinterested form, for it cannot be made a matter of private gain; it cannot be hidden away for the benefit of a certain privileged few. It is for the people. It is for ALL.
1929 *Creative Art.*

Ortega y Gasset, José 1883–1955

Spanish essayist and philosopher, Professor of Metaphysics at Madrid. He gained international fame with *The Revolt of the Masses* (1929), which argued in favour of an intellectual governing elite.

28 The man who discovers a new scientific truth has previously had to smash to atoms almost everything he had learnt, and arrives at the new truth with hands blood stained from the slaughter of a thousand platitudes.
1930 *The Revolt of the Masses.*

Orton, Joe *originally* John Kingsley 1933–67

English dramatist, known for his blackly comic, outrageous farces such as *Entertaining Mr Sloane* (1964). He was murdered by his lover, Kenneth Halliwell, who then committed suicide.

29 I'd the upbringing a nun would envy… Until I was fifteen I was more familiar with Africa than my own body.
1964 *Entertaining Mr Sloane*, act 1.

30 Every luxury was lavished on you — atheism, breast-feeding, circumcision.
1966 *Loot*, act 1.

31 Reading isn't an occupation we encourage among police officers. We try to keep the paperwork down to a minimum.
1966 *Loot*, act 2.

Orwell, George *pseudonym of* Eric Arthur Blair 1903–50

English novelist, essayist and journalist. He fought in the Spanish Civil War and during World War II worked for the BBC. He developed his own brand of socialism in *The Road to Wigan Pier* (1937) and other essays, but is best known for his satire of totalitarian ideology in *Animal Farm* (1945), and the prophetic novel, *Nineteen Eighty-Four* (1949).

32 While the journalist exists merely as the publicity agent of big business, a large circulation, got by fair means or foul, is a newspaper's one and only aim.
1928 In *G.K.'s Weekly*, 29 Dec.

33 He was an embittered atheist (the sort of atheist who does not so much disbelieve in God as personally dislike Him), and took a sort of pleasure in thinking that human affairs would never improve.
1933 *Down and Out in Paris and London*, ch.30.

34 Keep the Aspidistra Flying.
1936 Title of novel.

35 In the early morning the mill girls clumping down the cobbled street, all in clogs, making a curiously formidable sound, like an army hurrying into battle. I suppose this is the typical sound of Lancashire.
1936 Diary entry, 18 Feb. He used this as material for his book *The Road to Wigan Pier* (1937).

36 It is only because miners sweat their guts out that superior persons can remain superior.
1937 *The Road to Wigan Pier*, ch.2.

37 A thousand influences constantly press a working man into a *passive* role. He does not act, he is acted upon.
1937 *The Road to Wigan Pier*, ch.3.

38 A person of bourgeois origin goes through life with some expectation of getting what he wants, within reasonable limits. Hence the fact that in times of stress 'educated' people tend to come to the front.
1937 *The Road to Wigan Pier*, ch.3.

39 I sometimes think the price of liberty is not so much eternal vigilance as eternal dirt.
1937 *The Road to Wigan Pier*, ch.4.

40 In a Lancashire cotton-town you could probably go for months on end without once hearing an 'educated' accent, whereas there can hardly be a town in the South of England where you could throw a brick without hitting the niece of a bishop.
1937 *The Road to Wigan Pier*, ch.7.

41 As with the Christian religion, the worst advertisement for Socialism is its adherents.
1937 *The Road to Wigan Pier*, ch.11.

42 To the ordinary working man, the sort you would meet in any pub on Saturday night, Socialism does not mean

much more than better wages and shorter hours and nobody bossing you about.
1937 *The Road to Wigan Pier*, ch.11.

43 The underlying motive of many Socialists is, I believe, a hypertrophied sense of order…what they desire, basically, is to reduce the world to something resembling a chessboard.
1937 *The Road to Wigan Pier*, ch.11.

44 The high-water mark, so to speak, of Socialist literature is W.H. Auden, a sort of gutless Kipling.
1937 *The Road to Wigan Pier*, ch.11.

45 Cease to use your hands, and you have lopped off a huge chunk of your consciousness.
1937 *The Road to Wigan Pier*, ch.12.

46 It is usual to speak of the Fascist objective as the 'beehive state', which does a grave injustice to bees. A world of rabbits ruled by stoats would be nearer the mark.
1937 *The Road to Wigan Pier*, ch.12.

47 We of the sinking middle class…have nothing to lose but our aitches.
1937 *The Road to Wigan Pier*, ch.13.

48 The era of free speech is closing down. The freedom of the press in Britain was always something of a fake, because in the last resort, money controls opinion; still, so long as the legal right to say what you like exists, there are always loopholes for an unorthodox writer.
1938 In the *New Leader*, 24 Jun.

49 Roughly speaking it was the sensation of being *at the centre* of an explosion… I fancy you would feel much the same if you were struck by lightning. I knew immediately that I was hit, but because of that seeming bang and flash, I thought it was a rifle nearby that had gone off accidentally and shot me.
1938 Of his wounding during the Spanish Civil War. *Homage to Catalonia*, ch.12.

50 When you have had a glimpse of such a disaster as this…the result is not necessarily disillusionment and cynicism. Curiously enough, the whole experience has left me with not less but more belief in the decency of human beings.
1938 *Homage to Catalonia*, ch.14.

51 Down here it was still the England I had known in my childhood:…all sleeping the deep, deep sleep of England, from which I sometimes fear that we shall never wake till we are jerked out of it by the roar of bombs.
1938 *Homage to Catalonia*, ch.14.

52 I'm fat, but I'm thin inside. Has it ever struck you that there's a thin man inside every fat man, just as they say there's a statue inside every block of stone?
1939 *Coming Up For Air*, pt.1, ch.3.
► *See Connolly 233:82.*

53 Before the war, and especially before the Boer War, it was summer all the year round.
1939 *Coming Up For Air*, pt.2, ch.1.

54 If the war didn't happen to kill you it was bound to start you thinking. After that unspeakable idiotic mess you couldn't go on regarding society as something eternal and unquestionable, like a pyramid. You knew it was just a balls-up.
1939 *Coming Up For Air*, pt.2, ch.8.

55 Most revolutionaries are potential Tories, because they imagine that everything can be put right by altering the *shape* of society; once that change is effected, as it sometimes is, they see no need for any other.
1939 'Charles Dickens', collected in *Inside the Whale* (1940).

56 The novel is practically a Protestant form of art; it is the product of the free mind, of the autonomous individual.
1940 *Inside the Whale*, 'Inside The Whale'.

57 Contrary to popular belief, the past was not more eventful than the present. If it seems so it is because when you look backward things that happened years apart are telescoped together, and because very few of your memories come to you genuinely virgin.
1940 *Inside the Whale*, 'My Country Right or Left'.

58 As I write, highly civilized human beings are flying overhead, trying to kill me.
1941 *The Lion and the Unicorn: Socialism and the English Genius*, pt.1, 'England Your England'.

59 England is not the jewelled isle of Shakespeare's much-quoted passage, nor is it the inferno depicted by Dr Goebbels. More than either it resembles a family, a rather stuffy Victorian family, with not many black sheep in it but with all its cupboards bursting with skeletons.
1941 *The Lion and the Unicorn: Socialism and the English Genius*, pt.3, 'Shopkeeper at War'.

60 A family with the wrong members in control—that, perhaps, is as near as one can come to describing England in a phrase.
1941 *The Lion and the Unicorn: Socialism and the English Genius*, pt.3, 'The English Revolution'.

61 Probably the battle of Waterloo *was* won on the playing-fields of Eton, but the opening battles of all subsequent wars have been lost there. One of the dominant facts in English life during the past three-quarters of a century has been the decay of ability in the ruling class.
1941 *The Lion and the Unicorn: Socialism and the English Genius*, pt.4.

62 The great enemy of clear language is insincerity. When there is a gap between one's real and one's declared aims, one turns instinctively to long words and exhausted idioms—like cuttlefish squirting out ink.
1941 *The Lion and the Unicorn: Socialism and the English Genius*.

63 I believe that the BBC, in spite of the stupidity of its foreign propaganda and the unbearable voices of its announcers, is very truthful. It is generally regarded here as more reliable than the press.
1941 In the *Partisan Review*, 15 Apr. Reprinted in *Collected Essays, Journalism and Letters*, vol.2.

64 All propaganda is lies, even when one is telling the truth.
1942 Diary entry, 14 Mar.

65 Whatever is funny is subversive, every joke is ultimately a custard pie… A dirty joke is not, of course, a serious attack upon morality, but it is a sort of mental rebellion, a momentary wish that things were otherwise.
1942 'The Art of Donald McGill'.

66 On the whole, human beings want to be good, but not too good, and not all the time.
1942 'The Art of Donald McGill'.

67 Reminds me of nothing so much as a recently-dead fish before it has had time to stiffen.
1942 Of Clement Attlee. Diary entry, 19 May.

68 Any daily journalist will tell you that one of the most important secrets of his trade is the trick of making it appear that there is news when there is no news.
1944 In the *Tribune*, 21 Apr.

69 To blame someone like Northcliffe for making money in the quickest way is like blaming a skunk for stinking.
1944 In the *Tribune*, 21 Apr.

70 Cricket is a game full of forlorn hopes and sudden dramatic changes of fortune and its rules are so ill-defined that their interpretation is partly an ethical business.
1944 *Raffles and Miss Blandish.*

71 If liberty means anything at all, it means the right to tell people what they do not want to hear.
1945 Written for a rejected preface to *Animal Farm.*

72 Man is the only creature that consumes without producing.
1945 *Animal Farm*, ch.1.

73 Four legs good, two legs bad.
1945 *Animal Farm*, ch.3.

74 Napoleon had commanded that once a week there should be held something called a Spontaneous Demonstration.
1945 *Animal Farm*, ch.9.

75 All animals are equal but some animals are more equal than others.
1945 *Animal Farm*, ch.10.

76 The creatures outside looked from pig to man, and from man to pig, and from pig to man again; but already it was impossible to say which was which.
1945 *Animal Farm*, ch.10.

77 No modern Irish writer, even of the stature of Yeats or Joyce, is completely free from traces of nationalism.
1945 'Notes on Nationalism'.

78 In broadcasting your audience is conjectural, but it is an audience of *one*.
1945 'Poetry and the Microphone'.

79 Poetry on the air sounds like the Muses in striped trousers.
1945 'Poetry and the Microphone'.

80 To walk through the ruined cities of Germany is to feel actual doubt about the continuity of civilization.
1945 In the *Observer*, 8 Apr.

81 The books one reads in childhood, and perhaps most of all the bad and good bad books, create in one's mind a sort of false map of the world, a series of fabulous countries into which one can retreat at odd moments throughout the rest of life, and which in some cases can even survive a visit to the real countries which they are supposed to represent.
1946 'Riding Down from Bangor'.

82 Prolonged, indiscriminate reviewing of books involves constantly inventing reactions towards books about which one has no spontaneous feelings whatever.
1946 'Confessions of A Book Reviewer'.

83 The atom bombs are piling up in the factories, the police are prowling through the cities, the lies are streaming from the loudspeakers, but the earth is still going round the sun, and neither the dictators nor the bureaucrats, deeply as they disapprove of the process, are able to prevent it.
1946 'Some Thoughts on the Common Toad'.

84 To see what is in front of one's nose needs a constant struggle.
1946 'In Front of Your Nose'.

85 Good prose is like a window pane.
1946 'Why I Write'.

86 All writers are vain, selfish and lazy, and at the very bottom of their motives lies a mystery.
1946 'Why I Write'.

87 In our time, political speech and writing are largely the defence of the indefensible.
1946 'Politics and the English Language', collected in *Shooting an Elephant* (1950).

88 The inflated style is itself a kind of euphemism.
1946 'Politics and the English Language', collected in *Shooting an Elephant* (1950).

89 The great enemy of clear language is insincerity.
1946 'Politics and the English Language', collected in *Shooting an Elephant* (1950)

90 In prose, the worst thing one can do with words is surrender to them.
1946 'Politics and the English Language', collected in *Shooting an Elephant* (1950).

91 Political language…is designed to make lies sound truthful and murder respectable, and to give an appearance of solidity to pure wind.
1946 'Politics and the English Language', collected in *Shooting an Elephant* (1950).

92 The Catholic and the Communist are alike in assuming that an opponent cannot be both honest and intelligent.
1946 'The Prevention of Literature', in *Polemic*, Jan.

93 The controversy over freedom of speech and of the press is at the bottom a controversy over the desirability, or otherwise, of telling lies. What is really at issue is the right to report events truthfully, or as truthfully as is consistent with the ignorance, bias and self-deception from which every observer necessarily suffers.
1946 'The Prevention of Literature', in *Polemic*, Jan.

94 The friends of totalitarianism in this country tend to argue that since absolute truth is not attainable, a big lie is no worse than a little lie.
1946 'The Prevention of Literature', in *Polemic*, Jan.

95 Literature is doomed if liberty of thought perishes.
1946 'The Prevention of Literature', in *Polemic*, Jan.

96 The quickest way of ending a war is to lose it.
1946 'Second Thoughts on James Burnham', in *Polemic*, May.

97 It was a bright cold day in April, and the clocks were striking thirteen.
1949 *Nineteen Eighty-Four*, pt.1, ch.1.

98 On each landing, opposite the lift shaft, the poster with the enormous face gazed from the wall. It was one of those pictures which are so contrived that the eyes follow you about when you move. BIG BROTHER IS WATCHING YOU, the caption beneath it ran.
1949 *Nineteen Eighty-Four*, pt.1, ch.1.

99 War is peace. Freedom is slavery. Ignorance is strength.
1949 *Nineteen Eighty-Four*, pt.1, ch.1.

1 'Who controls the past,' ran the Party slogan, 'controls the future: who controls the present controls the past.'
1949 *Nineteen Eighty-Four*, pt.1, ch.3.

2 Freedom is the freedom to say that two plus two make four. If that is granted, all else follows.
1949 *Nineteen Eighty-Four*, pt.1, ch.7.

3 *Doublethink* means the power of holding two contradictory beliefs in one's mind simultaneously, and accepting both of them.
1949 *Nineteen Eighty-Four*, pt.2, ch.9.

4 If you want a picture of the future, imagine a boot stamping on a human face—for ever.
1949 *Nineteen Eighty-Four*, pt.3, ch.3.

5 Power is not a means, it is an end. One does not establish a dictatorship in order to safeguard a revolution; one makes the revolution in order to establish the dictatorship.
1949 *Nineteen Eighty-Four*, pt.3, ch.3.

6 Saints should always be judged guilty until they are proved innocent.
1949 'Reflections on Gandhi', collected in *Shooting an Elephant* (1950).

7 At 50, everyone has the face he deserves.
1949 Notebook entry, 17 Apr.

8 Serious sport has nothing to do with fair play. It is bound up with hatred, jealousy, boastfulness, disregard of all rules and sadistic pleasure in witnessing violence: in other words it is war minus the shooting... there are quite enough real causes of trouble already, and we need not add to them by encouraging young men to kick each other on the shins amid the roars of infuriated spectators.
1950 'The Sporting Spirit'.

9 One ought to be able to hold in one's head simultaneously the two facts that Dali is a good draughtsman and a disgusting human being. The one does not invalidate or, in a sense, affect the other.
Quoted in Michael Shelden *Orwell* (1991).

Osborne, Dorothy 1627–95

Wife of Sir William Temple, English diplomat and essay writer.

10 All letters, methinks, should be free and easy as one's discourse, not studied as an oration, nor made up of hard words like a charm.
1653 Letter to William Temple.

Osborne, John 1929–94

English playwright and actor. The success of *Look Back in Anger* (1956), with its anti-hero Jimmy Porter, marked a new departure in postwar English drama and identified the author as the most famous of the 'angry young men' of the 1950s. Later works included *The Entertainer* (1957), *Luther* (1961), *Inadmissible Evidence* (1964) and *A Patriot for Me* (1969).

11 She's so clumsy. I watch for her to do the same things every night. The way she jumps on the bed, as if she were stamping on someone's face, and draws the curtains back with a great clatter, in that casually destructive way of hers. It's like someone launching a battleship. Have you ever noticed how noisy women are? Have you? The way they kick the floor about, simply walking over it? Or have you watched them sitting at their dressing tables, dropping their weapons and banging down their bits of boxes and brushes and lipsticks?
1956 *Look Back in Anger.*

12 Don't clap too hard—it's a very old building.
1957 *The Entertainer*, 7.

13 There will be a quick rash of hairy American filth, but it shouldn't threaten the existence of decent, serious British filth.
1967 On the opening of the US musical *Hair*, in *Time* magazine.

Osler, Sir William 1849–1919

Canadian physician.

14 The greater the ignorance the greater the dogmatism.
1902 Quoted in *Montreal Medical Journal*, Sep.

15 The desire to take medicine is perhaps the greatest feature which distinguishes man from animals.
Quoted in H Cushing *Life of Sir William Osler* (1925), vol.1, ch.14.

16 One of the first duties of the physician is to educate the masses not to take medicine.
Collected in W B Bean (ed) *Sir William Osler: Aphorisms from His Bedside Teachings and Writings* (1950).

17 Failure to examine the throat is a glaring sin of omission, especially in children. One finger in the throat and one in the rectum makes a good diagnostician.
Collected in W B Bean (ed) *Sir William Osler: Aphorisms from His Bedside Teachings and Writings* (1950).

18 To talk of diseases is a sort of *Arabian Nights* entertainment.
Quoted in Oliver Sacks *The Man Who Mistook his Wife for a Hat*, epigraph (1985).

Otis, James 1725–83

American politician and patriot. As Advocate General he refused to assist royal revenue officers to search individual's homes and resigned to fight for popular rights. In 1769 he was beaten by revenue officers and received a head wound from which he never really recovered.

19 Taxation without representation is tyranny.
c.1761 His defence, which became a rallying call of the American Revolution.

O'Toole, Peter 1932–

Irish actor. His performance in *Lawrence of Arabia* (1962) made him an international film star, and he has since played a wide variety of roles.

20 I'm one of the younger oldies. I'm in the prime of senility.
2000 In *The Guardian*, 31 Dec.

Otway, Thomas 1652–85

English dramatist. Educated at Oxford. His first play was the tragedy *Alcibiades* (1675); in it his alleged lover, Elizabeth Barry, made her debut. His most famous play is *Venice Preserved, or a Plot Discovered* (1682).

21 Ere man's corruptions made him wretched, he
Was born most noble that was born most free;
Each of himself was lord; and unconfin'd
Obey'd the dictates of his godlike mind.
1676 *Don Carlos*, act 2.

22 You wags that judge by rote, and damn by rule.
1677 *Titus and Berenice*, prologue.

23 And for an apple damn'd mankind.
1680 *The Orphan*, act 3.

24 I may boldly speak

In right, though proud oppression will not hear me!
1682 *Venice Preserved, or a Plot Discovered*, act 1, sc.1.

25 May the hard hand of a vexatious need
Oppress and grind you; till at last you find
The curse of disobedience all your portion.
1682 *Venice Preserved, or a Plot Discovered*, act 1, sc.1.

26 Home I would go
But that my doors are hateful to my eyes,
Fill'd and damm'd up with gaping creditors,
Watchful as fowlers when their game will spring.
1682 *Venice Preserved, or a Plot Discovered*, act 1, sc.1.

27 I'm thinking…how that damn'd starving quality
Call'd honesty, got footing in the world.
1682 *Venice Preserved, or a Plot Discovered*, act 1, sc.1.

28 Honesty was a cheat invented first
To bind the hands of bold deserving rogues,
That fools and cowards might sit safe in power,
And lord it uncontroll'd above their betters.
1682 *Venice Preserved, or a Plot Discovered*, act 1, sc.1.

29 'Tis a ragged virtue.
1682 *Venice Preserved, or a Plot Discovered*, act 1, sc.1.

30 If love be treasure, we'll be wondrous rich.
1682 *Venice Preserved, or a Plot Discovered*, act 1, sc.1.

31 Is the world
Reform'd since our last meeting?
1682 *Venice Preserved, or a Plot Discovered*, act 1, sc.1.

32 No praying, it spoils Business.
1682 *Venice Preserved, or a Plot Discovered*, act 2, sc.1.

33 Give but an Englishman his whore and ease,
Beef and a sea-coal fire, he's yours forever.
1682 *Venice Preserved, or a Plot Discovered*, act 2, sc.3.

34 The poor sleep little.
1682 *Venice Preserved, or a Plot Discovered*, act 2, sc.3.

35 No, this vile world and I have long been jangling,
And cannot part on better terms than now,
When only men like thee are fit to live in't.
1682 *Venice Preserved, or a Plot Discovered*, act 4, sc.2.

Oud, J(acobus) J(ohannes) P(ieter) 1890–1963

Dutch architect, a pioneer of the modern architectural style based on simplified forms and pure planes.

36 If I was not optimistic, I would not be an architect.
Quoted in the *New York Times*, 4 Dec 1994.

Overbury, Sir Thomas 1581–1613

English poet and courtier.

37 He disdains all things above his reach, and preferreth all countries before his own.
1632 'An Affected Traveller', collected in *Miscellaneous Works*.

Overton, Robert fl.1642–68

English soldier. He fought for Parliament in the English Civil War and was made governor of Hull. He was imprisoned in 1656 for two years after he fought under Cromwell in Scotland and was suspected of planning an insurrection against the government. When Cromwell fell, Overton was released, but the doubts about him remained and his further support for a republic led to imprisonment for almost the rest of his life. The date and place of his death are unknown.

38 Whatever our forefathers were, or whatever they did or suffered, or were enforced to yield unto, we are the men of the present age, and ought to be absolutely free from all kinds of exorbitancies, molestations, or arbitrary power.
1646 Remonstrance to the House of Commons

Ovid *full name* ***Publius Ovidius Naso*** 43 BC–AD 17

Roman poet, who trained for law but turned to poetry. His many works include the *Ars Amatoria*, the *Metamorphoses* and the *Fasti*. He was banished by Augustus in AD 8 to Tomi on the Black Sea, where he wrote the *Tristia*.

39 *Procul omen abesto!*
Far away be that fate!
Amores, bk.1, no.14, l.41.

40 *Iuppiter ex alto periuria ridet amantum.*
Jupiter from above laughs at lovers' perjuries.
Ars Amatoria, bk.1, l.633.

41 *Iam seges est ubi Troia fuit.*
Now there are cornfields where Troy once was.
Heroides, no.1, l.53.

42 *Chaos, rudis indigestaque moles.*
Chaos, a rough unordered mass.
Metamorphoses, bk.1, l.7.

43 *Medio tutissimus ibis.*
You will go most safely by the middle way.
Daedalus speaking to his son, Icarus. *Metamorphoses*, bk.2, l.137 (translated by Peter Green).

44 *Inopem me copia fecit.*
Plenty has made me poor.
Metamorphoses, bk.3, l.466.

45 *Video meliora, proboque;*
Deteriora sequor.
I see the better things, and approve; I follow the worse.
Metamorphoses, bk.7, l.20–1 (translated by Peter Green).

46 *Tempus edax rerum.*
Time the devourer of everything.
Metamorphoses, bk.15, l.234 (translated by Peter Green).

47 *Nec species sua cuique manet, rerumque novatrix*
ex aliis alias reddit natura figuras.
nec perit in toto quidquam, mihi credite, mundo,
sed variat faciemque novat, nascique vocatur
incipere esse aliud, quam quod fuit ante, morique,
desinere illud idem. cum sint huc forsitan illa,
haec translata illuc, summa tamen omnia constant.
No species remains constant: that great renovator of matter
Nature, endlessly fashions new forms from old: there's nothing
in the whole universe that perishes, believe me; rather
it renews and varies its substance. What we describe as birth
is no more than incipient change from a prior state, while dying
is merely to quit it. Though the parts may be transported
hither and thither, the sum of all matter is constant.
Metamorphoses, bk.15, l.252–8 (translated by Peter Green).

48 *Donec eris felix, multos numerabis amicos*
Tempora si fuerint nubila, solus eris.
So long as you are fortunate, you will count many

friends; if your life should become clouded, you will be alone.
Tristia, bk.1, no.9, l.5–6.

Owen, David Anthony Llewellyn Owen, Baron 1938–

English politician, one of the 'Gang of Four' who formed the Social Democratic Party (SDP) in 1981, becoming its leader in 1983. He resigned in 1987 rather than merge with the Liberal party, and led a minority, reconstituted SDP, dissolved in 1990. From 1992 to 1995 he was co-chairman (initially with Cyrus R Vance) of the international peace conference on the former Yugoslavia.

49 We are fed up with fudging and nudging, with mush and slush.
1980 Speech to Labour's national conference shortly before leaving the party to found the Social Democratic Party, Oct.

Owen, Robert 1771–1858

Welsh social reformer and philanthropist.

50 All the world is queer save thee and me, and even thou art a little queer.
Attributed. Said to his partner W Allen when they ended their business relationship.

Owen, Wilfred 1893–1918

English poet. Injured in the trenches in 1917, he met Siegfried Sassoon while recuperating in Edinburgh. He died in the last week of the war, and most of his poems were published posthumously. Their vivid and unsentimental realism is a powerful indictment of war, and they were memorably used by Benjamin Britten in his *War Requiem*, first performed in Coventry Cathedral (1962).

51 What passing-bells for these who die as cattle?
Only the monstrous anger of the guns.
Only the stuttering rifles' rapid rattle
Can patter out their hasty orisons.
1917 'Anthem for Doomed Youth'.

52 The pallor of girls' brows shall be their pall;
Their flowers the tenderness of patient minds,
And each slow dusk a drawing-down of blinds.
1917 'Anthem for Doomed Youth'.

53 Red lips are not so red
As the stained stones kissed by the English dead.
1917 'Greater Love'.

54 This book is not about heroes. English poetry is not yet fit to speak of them.
1918 *Poems* (published 1920), preface.

55 Above all, this book is not concerned with Poetry. The subject of it is War, and the pity of War. The Poetry is in the pity.
1918 *Poems* (published 1920), preface.

56 All the poet can do today is to warn.
That is why the true Poet must be truthful.
1918 *Poems* (published 1920), preface.

57 If you could hear, at every jolt, the blood
Come gargling from the froth-corrupted lungs,
Bitter as the cud
Of vile, incurable sores on innocent tongues,—
My friend, you would not tell with such high zest
To children ardent for some desperate glory
The old Lie: Dulce et decorum est
Pro patria mori.
1918 'Dulce et Decorum Est', collected in *Poems* (published 1920).
► *See Horace 413:23.*

58 It seemed that out of battle I escaped
Down some profound dull tunnel, long since scooped
Through granites which titanic wars had groined.
1918 'Strange Meeting', collected in *Poems* (published 1920).

59 And by his smile, I knew that sullen hall,
By his dead smile I knew we stood in Hell.
1918 'Strange Meeting', collected in *Poems* (published 1920).

60 'Strange friend,' I said, 'here is no cause to mourn.'
'None,' said the other, 'save the undone years,
The hopelessness. Whatever hope is yours
Was my life also; I went hunting wild
After the wildest beauty in the world.'
1918 'Strange Meeting', collected in *Poems* (published 1920).

61 I am the enemy you killed, my friend.
1918 'Strange Meeting', collected in *Poems* (published 1920).

62 Move him into the sun—
Gently its touch awoke him once,
At home, whispering of fields unsown.
1918 'Futility', collected in *Poems* (published 1920).

63 If anything might rouse him now
The kind old sun will know.
1918 'Futility', collected in *Poems* (published 1920).

64 Was it for this the clay grew tall?
—O what made fatuous sunbeams toil
To break earth's sleep at all?
1918 'Futility', collected in *Poems* (published 1920).

65 So secretly, like wrongs hushed-up, they went.
1918 'The Send-Off', collected in *Poems* (published 1920).

66 Whatever mourns when many leave these shores:
Whatever shares
The eternal reciprocity of tears.
1918 'Insensibility', collected in *Poems* (published 1920).

Owens, Jesse James Cleveland 1913–80

US athlete. The greatest sprinter of his generation, he won four gold medals at the Berlin Olympics in 1936, embarrassing the Nazi hosts, who had hoped to demonstrate the supremacy of Aryan athletes.

67 I let my feet spend as little time on the ground as possible. From the air, fast down, and from the ground, fast up.
Quoted in Colin Jarman *The Guinness Dictionary of Sports Quotations* (1990).

Ozick, Cynthia 1928–

US writer. She claimed to have begun her first novel, *Trust* (1966), an American writer and finished it six and a half years later a Jewish one. Other works include the short stories *The Shawl* (1989) and the novel *The Puttermesser Papers* (1997).

68 Yiddish is a household tongue, and God, like other members of the family, is sweetly informal in it.
1989 *Metaphor and Memory.*

Pacheco, José Emilio 1939–

Mexican poet, novelist, critic and translator. His poetry expresses his metaphysical concerns in brilliant images. The novel *Morirás lejos* (1967) documents the purges of Jews throughout history.

69 *Porque todo es irreal en este cuento. Nada sucedió como se indica. Hechos y sitios se deformaron por el empeño de tocar la verdad mediante una ficción, una mentira. Todo irreal, nada sucedió como aquí se refiere. Pero fue un pobre intento de contribuir a que el gran crimen nunca se repita.*
For everything in this story is unreal. Nothing happened the way it was suggested. Facts and places were distorted by that persistent desire to touch the truth by means of fiction, a lie. All of it is unreal; nothing happened the way it is told here. It was a poor attempt to help ensure that the great crime is never repeated.
1967 *Morirás lejos* (translated as *You Will Die in a Distant Land*, 1991).

Packard, David 1912–96

US businessman.

70 Flexitime is the essence of respect for and trust in people.
1995 *The HP Way.*

Packard, Vance 1914–96

US writer and journalist.

71 The Hidden Persuaders.
1957 Title of a book on advertising.

Packer, Herbert Leslie 1925–72

US Professor of Law, Stanford University (1959–72). He was admitted to the New York Bar in 1950, and later the Supreme Court. He practised law in Washington before teaching at Stanford.

72 Crime is a socio-political artifact, not a natural phenomenon. We can have as much or as little crime as we please, depending on what we choose to count as criminal.
1968 *The Limits of Criminal Sanction*, p.364.

Packer, Kerry 1937–

Australian media executive.

73 If a British guy saw someone at the wheel of a Rolls-Royce, he'd say 'come the revolution and we'll take that away from you, mate', where the American would say 'one day I'll have one of those, when I have worked hard enough'. It's unfortunate we Australians inherited the British mentality.
1977 In *The Guardian*, 1 Sep.

Packwood, Bob 1932–

US Republican Senator and lawyer. He was Senator for Oregon from 1969 until his resignation in 1995.

74 I am accused of kissing women…perhaps overeagerly kissing women. And that is the charge, not drugging, not robbing, kissing!
1995 Replying to charges of sexual misconduct, lobbying, and editing diaries subpoenaed by the Senate Ethics Committee. In the *New York Times*, 7 Sep.

75 More than Francis of Assisi…less than Wilt Chamberlain.
1995 Estimating the amount of controversial activity documented in his diaries. In the *New York Times*, 9 Sep.

Paderewski, Ignace Jan 1860–1941

Polish pianist, composer and statesman, director of the Warsaw Conservatory (from 1909). In 1919 he became premier of Poland. He retired from politics to return to his music, but in 1940 was elected President by Poland's provisional parliament in Paris.

76 If I don't practise for one day, I know it; if I don't practise for two days, the critics know it; if I don't practise for three days, the audience knows it.
Quoted in Nat Shapiro *An Encyclopedia of Quotations about Music* (1978).

Page, Geraldine 1924–87

US actress. She made her name with the lead role in Tennessee Williams's *Summer and Smoke* (1954).

77 Name me one character in literature or drama who can't be described as neurotic… We wouldn't want to know the people we get to see on the stage. How would you like to have Medea for dinner? Or Macbeth slurping your soup? Or Oedipus with his bloody, blinded eyes dripping all over your tablecloth?
Attributed.

Pagels, Heinz R(udolf) 1939–88

US theoretical physicist and social activist, the author of several works describing the complexities of modern physics for the public.

78 A good simulation, be it a religious myth or scientific theory, gives us a sense of mastery over experience. To represent something symbolically, as we do when we speak or write, is somehow to capture it, thus making it one's own. But with this appropriation comes the realization that we have denied the immediacy of reality and that in creating a substitute we have but spun another thread in the web of our grand illusion.
1988 *The Dreams of Reason.*

79 Science provides a vision of reality seen from the perspective of reason, a perspective that sees the vast order of the universe, living and non-living matter, as a material system governed by rules that can be known by the human mind. It is a powerful vision, formal and austere but strangely silent about many of the questions that deeply concern us. Science shows us what exists but not what to do about it.
1988 *The Dreams of Reason.*

Paglia, Camille 1947–

US writer, Professor of Humanities at the University of the Arts, Philadelphia. Her works include *Sexual Personae* (1990) and *Vamps and Tramps* (1994).

80 The historical repugnance to woman has a rational basis: disgust is reason's proper response to the grossness of procreative nature.
1990 *Sexual Personae: Art and Decadence from Nefertiti to Emily Dickinson*, ch.1, 'Sex and Violence, or Nature and Art'.

81 No woman has to prove herself a woman in the grim way a man has to prove himself a man. He must perform, or the show does not go on. Social convention is irrelevant. A flop is a flop.
1990 *Sexual Personae: Art and Decadence from Nefertiti to Emily Dickinson*, ch.1, 'Sex and Violence, or Nature and Art'.

82 Feminism has become a catch-all vegetable drawer where bunches of clingy sob sisters can store their moldy neuroses.
1992 'The Return of Carry Nation: Catharine Mackinnon and Andrea Dworkin', in *Playboy*, Oct. Collected in *Vamps and Tramps* (1994).

83 I like Hillary because she's kind of a bitch.
1993 In the *Sunday Times* magazine, 18 Apr. Collected as 'Kind of a Bitch: Why I Like Hillary Clinton' in *Vamps and Tramps* (1994).

Pagnol, Marcel 1895–1974

French dramatist and film director, best known for his popular trilogy about Marseilles, *Marius* (1929), *Fanny* (1931) and *César* (1936).

84 *Les coupables, il vaut mieux les choisir que les chercher.*
It's better to choose the culprits than to seek them out.
1928 *Topaze*, act 1.

85 *L'honneur, c'est comme les allumettes: ça ne sert qu'une fois.*
Honour is like a match, you can use it only once.
1929 *Marius*, act 4, sc.5.

86 One has to look out for engineers—they begin with sewing machines and end up with the atomic bomb.
1949 *Critique des critiques*, ch.3.

Paige, Satchel (Leroy Robert) 1906–82

US baseball player. One of the first blacks to play in the major leagues, he was a celebrated pitcher with the Cleveland Indians and the St Louis Browns.

87 1. Avoid fried meats which angry up the blood.
2. If your stomach disputes you, lie down and pacify it with cool thoughts.
3. Keep the juices flowing by jangling around gently as you move.
4. Go very light on vices such as carrying on in society. The social ramble ain't restful.
5. Avoid running at all times.
6. Don't look back. Something may be gaining on you.
1976 'Six Rules for a Happy Life', which he had inscribed on business cards, offered to fans seeking his autograph.

Paine, Thomas 1737–1809

English radical political writer. His *Common Sense* (1776) argued for complete American independence, and *The Rights of Man* (1791–2) supported the French Revolution. Arraigned for treason, he fled to Paris, and wrote *The Age of Reason* (1794) in favour of deism.

88 These are the times that try men's souls. The summer soldier and the sunshine patriot will, in this crisis, shrink from the service of his country; but he that stands it *now*, deserves the love and thanks of man and woman.
1776 *The Crisis*, introduction, Dec.

89 Not all the treasures of the world, so far as I believe, could have induced me to support an offensive war, for I think it murder; but if a thief breaks into my house, burns and destroys my property, and kills or threatens to kill me or those that are in it, and to '*bind me in all cases whatsoever*' to his absolute will, am I to suffer it?
1776 *The Crisis*, introduction, Dec.

90 Government, even in its best state, is but a necessary evil; in its worst state, an intolerable one. Government, like dress, is the badge of lost innocence; the palaces of kings are built upon the bowers of paradise.
1776 *Common Sense*, ch.1.

91 As to religion, I hold it to be the indispensable duty of government to protect all conscientious professors thereof, and I know of no other business which government hath to do therewith.
1776 *Common Sense*, ch.4.

92 Man is not the enemy of Man, but through the medium of a false system of government.
1791–2 *The Rights of Man.*

93 To establish any mode to abolish war, however advantageous it might be to nations, would be to take from such Government the most lucrative of its branches.
1791–2 *The Rights of Man.*

94 Persecution is not an original feature of *any* religion; but it is always the strongly marked feature of all law-religions, or religions established by law.
1791–2 *The Rights of Man.*

95 My country is the world, and my religion is to do good.
1791–2 *The Rights of Man.*

96 The final event to himself has been, that as he rose like a rocket, he fell like the stick.
1792 Of Edmund Burke. *Letters to the Addressers on the late Proclamation.*

97 It is a fraud of the Christian system to call the sciences human invention; it is only the application of them that is human. Every science has for its basis a system of principles as fixed and unalterable as those by which the universe is regulated and governed. Man cannot make principles, he can only discover them.
1794 *The Age of Reason*, pt.1.

98 It is necessary to the happiness of man that he be mentally faithful to himself. Infidelity does not consist in believing, or in disbelieving, it consists in professing to believe what one does not believe.
1794 *The Age of Reason*, pt.1.

99 One step above the sublime, makes the ridiculous; and one step above the ridiculous, makes the sublime again.
1795 *The Age of Reason*, pt.2.

Paisley, Bob 1919–96

English football manager. He succeeded Bill Shankly as manager of Liverpool in 1974 and led the team through a golden era of League success.

1 Yes, we've had bad times at Anfield; one year we came second.
Quoted in Peter Ball and Phil Shaw *The Book of Football Quotations* (1989).

Paisley, Ian 1926–

Northern Irish clergyman and politician, founder of the Free Presbyterian Church of Ulster. A vociferous opponent of Irish unification, he is the object of fanatical devotion from Ulster loyalists.

2 I would rather be British than just.
1971 In the *Sunday Times*, 12 Dec.

3 I will walk on no grave of Ulster's honoured dead to do a deal with the IRA or the British government.
1997 Speech at the annual conference of the Democratic Unionist Party. In *The Irish Times*, 'This Week They Said', 6 Dec.

4 The mother of all treachery.
1998 On the Good Friday agreement. In *The Times*, 16 Apr.

5 She has become a parrot.
1998 On the perceived readiness of the Queen to repeat the views of her Prime Minister. In the *Daily Telegraph*, 27 May.

Palacký, František 1798–1876

Czech historian and politician in Prague, and the founder of historiography in Bohemia. He served in the first Austrian Reichstag and campaigned for the formation of a separate Czech nation.

6 If the Austrian Empire did not exist, it would have to be created in the interest of Europe and of humanity.
Quoted in A J P Taylor *From Napoleon to the Second International* (1993), p.160.

Palafox, José de c.1776–1847

Spanish general in the Peninsular War, who defended Saragossa with an improvised garrison of civilians. Despite breaching the city wall, the French were unable to capture the city.

7 *Guerra a cuchillo.*
War to the knife.
1808 His reply to the French suggestion that he surrender during the siege of Saragossa, 4 Aug. The phrase was inscribed on survivors' medals.

Paley, Grace *née* Goodside 1922–

US writer and political activist. She is best known as a writer of short stories, often set in a Jewish milieu in New York, but she has also published poetry and collections of essays.

8 The Little Disturbances of Man.
1959 Title of story collection.

9 Enormous Changes at the Last Minute.
1974 Title of story collection.

10 Literature, fiction, poetry, whatever, makes justice in the world. That's why it almost always has to be on the side of the underdog.
1974 In *Ms* magazine.

11 All that is really necessary for survival of the fittest, it seems, is an interest in life, good, bad, or peculiar.
1976 In D L Fitzpatrick (ed) *Contemporary Novelists*.

12 No metaphor reinvents the job of the nurture of children except to muddy or mock.
1992 *Begin Again: New and Collected Poems*, 'Stanzas: Old Age and the Conventions of Retirement Have Driven My Friends from the Work They Love'.

13 Poets!
Madness is a gift
god-given
(though not to me).
1992 *Begin Again: New and Collected Poems*, 'On the Bank Street Pier'.

14 It is the responsibility of society to let the poet be a poet
It is the responsibility of the poet to be a woman.
1992 *Begin Again: New and Collected Poems*, 'Responsibility'.

15 It is the responsibility of the poet to be lazy to hang out and prophesy.
1992 *Begin Again: New and Collected Poems*, 'Responsibility'.

Paley, William 1743–1805

English theologian, Archdeacon of Carlisle (1782) and Sub-Dean of Lincoln (1795). His most popular work was *Natural Theology, or Evidences of the Existence and Attributes of the Deity* (1802).

16 Suppose I had found a *watch* upon the ground, and it should be enquired how the watch happened to be in that place... The inference, we think, is inevitable; that the watch must have had a maker, that there must have existed, at some time and at some place or other, an artificer or artificers, who formed it for the purpose which we find it actually to answer; who comprehended its construction, and designed its use.
1802 *Natural Theology*, ch.1.

Palmer, Arnold 1929–

US golfer. Between 1958 and 1964 he won the US Masters four times, the British Open twice and the US Open once. He was twice captain of the US Ryder Cup team.

17 Winning isn't everything, but wanting to is.
Quoted in Colin Jarman *The Guinness Dictionary of Sports Quotations* (1990).

18 If Tiger Woods slamming his club into the ground is the biggest worry we have, our sport is in pretty good shape.
2000 Quoted in *Golf Digest*, Jan.

Palmerston, Henry John Temple, 3rd Viscount 1784–1865

English politician, Foreign Secretary (1830–41, 1846–51) and Prime Minister (1855–8, 1859–65). His abrasive, bullying approach to foreign affairs and propensity for brinkmanship made him unpopular with his colleagues and the public.

19 Half the wrong conclusions at which mankind arrive are reached by the abuse of metaphors, and by mistaking general resemblance or imaginary similarity for real identity.
1839 Letter to Henry Bulwer, 1 Sep.

20 Diplomats and protocols are very good things, but there are no better peace-keepers than well-appointed three-deckers.
c.1840 Quoted in Denis Judd *Palmerston* (1975). A three-decker is a warship.

21 We said to the Chinese, 'You have behaved very ill; we have had to teach you better manners; it has cost us something to do it, but we will send our bill in, and you must pay our charges.' That was done, and they have

certainly profited by the lesson. They have become free traders too.

1847 On the Opium Wars of 1839–42. Election speech at Tiverton, Devon.

22 We have no eternal allies, and we have no perpetual enemies. Our interests are eternal, and it is our duty to follow them.

1848 Speech, House of Commons, 1 Mar.

23 Large republics seem to be essentially and inherently aggressive.

1848 Letter to the British Ambassador to Paris, 5 Mar.

24 I therefore fearlessly challenge the verdict which this house...is to give on the question now brought before it...whether, as the Roman, in days of old, held himself free from indignity, when he could say *Civis Romanus sum*; so also a British subject, in whatever land he may be, shall feel confident that the watchful eye and the strong arm of England will protect him against injustice and wrong.

1850 From his four-and-a-half hour Don Pacifico speech, Jun. Don Pacifico was a Portuguese Jew resident in Athens, born in Gibraltar and therefore a British subject. In support of his claims for compensation from the Greek government for damage done to his property by a mob, Palmerston sent the British fleet to blockade Piraeus and brought the two countries to the brink of war.

25 You may call it coalition, you may call it the accidental and fortuitous concurrence of atoms...but when gentlemen are in the habit of finding themselves in the same Lobby, it is not unnatural to suppose that they may, under certain circumstances, be ready to unite themselves together for the purpose of forming an Administration and becoming responsible for the opinions that they severally entertain.

1858 Speech on the rumoured Palmerston–Disraeli coalition, 5 Mar.

26 England is one of the greatest powers of the world. No event or series of events bearing on the balance of power, or on probabilities of peace or war, can be matters of indifference to her, and her right to have and to express opinions on matters thus bearing on her interests is unquestionable.

1859 Letter to Queen Victoria, 23 Aug.

Panama, Norman and Frank, Melvin 1914–2003, 1917–88

US screenwriters, who worked together on films such as *The Road to Utopia* (1945), *The Court Jester* (1955) and *Li'l Abner* (1959).

27 The pellet with the poison's in the chalice from the palace
The flagon with the dragon has the brew that is true.

1955 Lines delivered by Danny Kaye in *The Court Jester*.

Pangkor, Treaty of

The British signed a treaty (1874) with a claimant to the Perak Sultanate on the island of Pangkor, off the west coast of what is now peninsular Malaysia, and thereby formalized their economic and political interest in the region. It led to British control over the whole of the peninsula for the following 83 years.

28 A British officer to be called Resident who shall be accredited to his Court and whose advice must be asked and acted upon on all questions other than those touching Malay religion and custom.

1874 Treaty, Nov.

Pankhurst, Christabel 1880–1958

English suffragette and religious writer. Co-founder with her mother Emmeline Pankhurst of the Women's Social and Political Union (1903), she studied law (LLB 1906) and applied to join Lincoln's Inn, but was rejected, as a woman.

29 How long you women have been trying for the vote. For my part, I mean to get it.

c.1890 Childhood remark, quoted by her mother, Emmeline Pankhurst, in *My Own Story* (1914), ch.2.

Pankhurst, Emmeline *née* *Goulden* 1858–1928

English suffragette, organizer of the Women's Social and Political Union. A militant campaigner, she was frequently imprisoned and undertook hunger strikes. During World War I she turned her attention to the industrial mobilization of women.

30 Women never took a single step forward without being pushed back first of all by their opponents.

1912 Speech, 14 Jan, during a tour of Canada.

31 There is something that Governments care for far more than human life, and that is the security of property. So it is through property that we shall strike the enemy... Be militant each in your own way... I incite this meeting to rebellion.

1912 Speech, Royal Albert Hall, 17 Oct.

32 Women had always fought for men, and for their children. Now they were ready to fight for their own human rights.

1914 *My Own Story*, ch.3.

33 What is the use of fighting for the vote if we do not have a country to vote in? With that patriotism that has nerved women to endure torture in prison for the national good, we ardently desire that our country shall be victorious.

1914 Declaring a truce on suffragette activities for the duration of World War I, 10 Aug.

34 There are women today who never thought to envy men their manhood, but who would, at least for this purpose, be glad to be men.

1914 Speech appealing for the right to fight, 30 Nov, at a meeting organized by the Women's Social and Political Union, in the Kingsway Hall, London.

Parens, Erik

US academic. He is Associate for Philosophical Studies at the Hastings Center, a bioethics research institute.

35 On Why Talking about Behavioral Genetics Is Important and Difficult.

2004 Subtitle of the Hastings Center Report 'Genetic Differences and Human Identities'.

Pareto, Vilfredo 1848–1923

French-born Swiss economist and sociologist.

36 All governments use force and all assert that they are founded on reason. In fact, whether universal suffrage prevails or not, it is always an oligarchy that governs, finding ways to give to 'the will of the people' the

expression which the few desire.
Quoted in Arthur Livingstone (ed) *The Mind and Society* (1935).

Parfitt, Harold Robert 1921–

US soldier. He served in Vietnam and advanced through the army grades to reach Major-General in 1971. He was decorated many times. He became governor of the Panama Canal Zone in 1975.

37 There will be no more tomorrows, only yesterdays, for the Canal Zone.
1979 On relinquishing authority as last governor of the Panama Canal Zone. Quoted in *Time*, 15 Oct.

Park, Mungo 1771–1806

Scottish explorer. He explored the Niger in 1796, then returned to Scotland and worked as a doctor, publishing *Travels in the Interior Districts of Africa* (1799), before leaving in 1805 for Africa again, sending back journals and letters.

38 I think it not unlikely but I shall be in England before you receive this—You may be sure that I feel happy at turning my face towards home. We this morning have done with all intercourse with the natives; and the sails are now hoisting for our departure for the coast.
1805 Last letter to his wife before leaving Sansanding on the River Niger. Collected in *Journal of a Mission to the Interior of Africa in the Year 1805* (published 1815). Park and his party reportedly drowned in the river when they were ambushed and their boat sank.

Parker, Charlie *known as 'Bird'* 1920–55

US saxophonist, bandleader and composer, architect of the bebop style. Despite addiction to heroin and alcohol and recurring mental illness, he led jazz groups until his death. His works include 'Now's the Time' and 'Ornithology'.

39 It's just music. It's trying to play clean and looking for the pretty notes.
1949 On bebop. Quoted in Gary Giddins *Celebrating Bird* (1987), ch.1.

40 There is no boundary line to art. Music is your own experience, your thoughts, your wisdom. If you don't live it, it won't come out of your horn.
1950 Quoted in Ross Russell *Bird Lives!* (1972), pt.4, ch.22.

Parker, Dorothy *née Rothschild* 1893–1967

US writer and humorist, a central figure of the legendary Algonquin Hotel Round Table. She was an influential book and drama critic, contributing incisive and caustic reviews to the *New Yorker*. Her works include *Enough Rope* (1926) and *Here Lies* (1939).

41 Brevity is the soul of lingerie, as the Petticoat said to the Chemise.
1916 Caption for *Vogue*. Quoted in J Keats *You Might as Well Live* (1970).

42 Excuse My Dust.
1925 Suggested epitaph for herself. Quoted in Alexander Woollcott *While Rome Burns* (1934), 'Our Mrs Parker'. She also suggested 'This is on me' for her tombstone.

43 Lady, lady, should you meet
One whose ways are all discreet,
One who murmurs that his wife
Is the lodestar of his life,
One who keeps assuring you
That he never was untrue,
Never loved another one...
Lady, lady, better run!
1926 *Enough Rope*, 'Social Note'.

44 Where's the man could ease a heart
Like a satin gown?
1926 *Enough Rope*, 'The Satin Dress', stanza 1.

45 The affair between Margot Asquith and Margot Asquith will live as one of the prettiest love stories in all literature.
1927 Book review in the *New Yorker*, 22 Oct.

46 If, with the literate, I am
Impelled to try an epigram,
I never seek to take the credit;
We all assume that Oscar said it.
1928 *Sunset Gun*, 'Oscar Wilde'.

47 And it is that word 'hummy', my darlings, that marks the first place in 'The House at Pooh Corner' at which Tonstant Weader fwowed up.
1928 Book review in the *New Yorker*, 20 Oct.

48 More glutton than artist...he commences to chew up the scenery.
1930 Play review, alluding to an unidentified actor. This is said to have been the origin of the phrase 'chew up the scenery', used to describe an actor who is 'hamming it up'.

49 Now that you've got me right down to it, the only thing I didn't like about *The Barretts of Wimpole Street* was the play.
1931 Play review in the *New Yorker*.

50 *House Beautiful* is play lousy.
1933 Review in the *New Yorker*. Quoted in P Hartnoll *Plays and Players* (1984).

51 How did they know?
1933 Attributed response on hearing of the death of President Calvin Coolidge.

52 Katharine Hepburn runs the gamut of the emotions from A to B.
1933 Remark during the interval of *The Lake* on its Broadway première. Quoted in G Carey *Katharine Hepburn* (1983), ch.6.

53 That woman speaks eighteen languages, and can't say No in any of them.
Quoted in Alexander Woollcott *While Rome Burns* (1934), 'Our Mrs Parker'.

54 And there was that wholesale libel on a Yale prom. If all the girls attending it were laid end to end, Mrs Parker said, she wouldn't be at all surprised.
Quoted in Alexander Woollcott *While Rome Burns* (1934), 'Our Mrs Parker'.

55 Good work, Mary. We all knew you had it in you.
On the arrival of a baby. Quoted in Alexander Woollcott *While Rome Burns* (1934), 'Our Mrs Parker'.

56 Whose love is given over-well
Shall look on Helen's face in hell
Whilst they whose love is thin and wise
Shall see John Knox in Paradise.
1937 *Not So Deep as A Well*, 'Partial Comfort'.

57 Why is it no one ever sent me yet
One perfect limousine, do you suppose?
Ah no, it's always just my luck to get
One perfect rose.
1937 *Not So Deep as A Well*, 'One Perfect Rose'.

58 Four be the things I'd been better without:

Love, curiosity, freckles, and doubt.
1937 *Not So Deep as A Well*, 'Inventory'.

59 By the time you say you're his,
Shivering and sighing
And he vows his passion is
Infinite, undying—
Lady, make a note of this:
One of you is lying.
1937 *Not So Deep as A Well*, 'Unfortunate Coincidence'.

60 Oh, life is a glorious cycle of song,
A medley of extemporanea;
And love is a thing that can never go wrong;
And I am Marie of Roumania.
1937 *Not So Deep as A Well*, 'Comment'.

61 Drink and dance and laugh and lie,
Love, the reeling midnight through,
For tomorrow we shall die!
(But, alas, we never do).
1937 *Not So Deep as A Well*, 'The Flaw in Paganism'.
► *See Bible 121:16.*

62 He lies below, correct in cypress wood,
And entertains the most exclusive worms.
1937 *Not So Deep as A Well*, 'Tombstones in the Starlight'.

63 Men seldom make passes
At girls who wear glasses.
1937 *Not So Deep as A Well*, 'News Item'.

64 Scratch a lover, and find a foe.
1937 *Not So Deep as A Well*, 'Ballade of a Great Weariness'.

65 Razors pain you
Rivers are damp;
Acids stain you;
And drugs cause cramp.
Guns aren't lawful;
Nooses give;
Gas smells awful;
You might as well live.
1937 *Not So Deep as A Well*, 'Résumé'.

66 Sorrow is tranquillity remembered in emotion.
1939 *Here Lies*, 'Sentiment'.
► *See Wordsworth 925:10.*

67 And I'll stay off Verlaine, too; he was always chasing Rimbauds.
1939 *Here Lies*, 'The Little Hours'.

68 You can always tell that the crash is coming when I start getting tender about Our Dumb Friends. Three highballs and I think I'm St Francis of Assisi.
1939 *Here Lies*, 'Just a Little One'.

69 There's a hell of a distance between wise-cracking and wit. Wit has truth in it; wise-cracking is simply callisthenics with words.
1956 In the *Paris Review*, Summer.

70 All those writers who write about their childhood! Gentle God, if I wrote about mine you wouldn't sit in the same room with me.
1956 In the *Paris Review*, Summer.

71 It serves me right for putting all my eggs in one bastard.
On her abortion. Quoted in J Keats *You Might as Well Live* (1970).

72 You can lead a horticulture, but you can't make her think.
Response to a challenge to use 'horticulture' in a sentence. Quoted in J Keats *You Might as Well Live* (1970).

73 One more drink and I'd have been under the host.
Quoted in H Teichmann *George S Kaufman* (1972).

74 That should assure us of at least forty-five minutes of undisturbed privacy.
Attributed, after pressing the button marked 'nurse' when her secretary came to visit her in hospital. Quoted in Clifton Fadiman *The Faber Book of Anecdotes* (1985).

75 Three be the things I shall never attain:
Envy, content, and sufficient champagne.
Quoted in Marion Meade *Dorothy Parker* (1988).

76 All writers are either 29 or Thomas Hardy.
On being asked Hemingway's age. Quoted in Marion Meade *Dorothy Parker* (1988).

77 As American as a sawed-off shotgun.
Of Dashiell Hammett. Quoted in Marion Meade *Dorothy Parker* (1988).

78 Upon my honour, I saw a Madonna
Standing in a niche
Above the door of the private whore
Of the world's worst son of a bitch.
Jotted into the visitor's book of William Randolph Hearst's house at San Simeon after she had seen a Della Robbia Madonna over the entrance to Marion Davies's bedroom. Quoted in R Hughes *Culture of Complaint* (1994).

Parker, Hubert Lister 1900–72

English judge. He served as Lord Chief Justice of England.

79 A judge is not supposed to know anything about the facts of life until they have been presented in evidence and explained to him at least three times.
1961 Quoted in the *Observer*, 12 Mar.

Parker, John 1729–75

Commander of the Lexington militia company in the opening engagement of the American Revolution.

80 Stand your ground. Don't fire unless fired upon, but if they mean to have a war, let it begin here!
1775 Attributed command before the Battle of Lexington, 19 Apr.

Parker, Ross and Charles, Hugh 1914–74, 1907–95

British songwriters.

81 There'll always be an England
While there's a country lane,
Wherever there's a cottage small
Beside a field of grain.
1939 Song.

Parker, Stewart 1941–88

Northern Irish playwright. A lecturer at Cornell University, he turned to full-time writing for the stage, TV and radio. His best-known plays are *Spokesong* (1976) and *Pentecost* (1987).

82 The Kamikaze Ground Staff Re-union Dinner.
1979 Title of play.

Parkes, Sir Henry 1815–96

English-born Australian statesman, who emigrated to New South Wales in 1839. A member of the colonial parliament in 1854, he held various offices, from 1872 was repeatedly Prime Minister, and was identified with free trade.

83 Why should not the name of an Australian be equal to

that of a Briton…to that of a citizen of the proudest country under the sun? Make yourselves a united people, appear before the world as one, and the dream of going 'home' will die away.
1880 Speech to the Australian Federation Conference, Feb.

Parkinson, C(yril) Northcote 1909–93

English political scientist and Professor of History, best remembered for his seriocomic tilt at bureaucratic malpractices, *Parkinson's Law: the Pursuit of Progress* (1958).

84 Work expands so as to fill the time available for its completion.
1958 *Parkinson's Law: the Pursuit of Progress*, ch.1.

85 Time spent on any item of the agenda will be in inverse proportion to the sum involved.
1958 *Parkinson's Law: the Pursuit of Progress*, ch.3.

86 Men enter local politics solely as a result of being unhappily married.
1958 *Parkinson's Law: the Pursuit of Progress*, ch.10.

87 Expenditure rises to meet income.
1960 *The Law and the Profits*, ch.1.

Parkinson, Norman *originally* ***Ronald William Parkinson Smith*** 1913–90

English magazine photographer.

88 A photographer without a magazine behind him is like a farmer without fields.
1984 In the *New Yorker*, 10 Dec.

89 The camera can be the most deadly weapon since the assassin's bullet. Or it can be the lotion of the heart.
1984 In the *New Yorker*, 10 Dec.

Parks, Rosa Lee *née* ***McCauley*** 1913–

US civil rights protester.

90 All I was doing was trying to get home from work.
On refusing to give up her seat to a white man in Montgomery, Alabama, which led to the 1955 Montgomery bus boycott and in turn to a Supreme Court ruling that bus segregation was unconstitutional, and fuelled the civil rights movement. Quoted in *Time*, 15 Dec 1975.

Parnell, Charles Stewart 1846–91

Irish politician, elected President of the Irish National Land League (1878). In 1886 he allied with the Liberals in support of Gladstone's Home Rule bill, but was forced to retire as leader of the Irish Nationalists in 1890 in disgrace when cited as co-respondent in a divorce case.

91 When a man takes a farm from which another has been evicted, you must show him on the roadside when you meet him; you must show him in the streets of the town; you must show him in the fair and the market place; and even in the house of worship, by leaving him severely alone—by putting him into a moral Coventry, by isolating him from his kind as if he were a leper of old. You must show him your detestation of the crimes that he has committed.
1880 Speech that established the practice of boycotting, Ennis, 19 Sep.

92 And it is a good sign that this masquerading knight-errant, this pretended champion of the rights of every other nation except those of the Irish nation, should be obliged to throw off the mask today, and to stand revealed as the man who by his own utterances is prepared to carry fire and sword into your homesteads unless you humbly abase yourselves before him, and before the landlords of the country.
1881 Speech successfully inciting Gladstone to arrest him, 9 Oct.

93 No man has a right to fix the boundary of the march of a nation. No man has a right to say to his country, 'Thus far thou shalt go and no further.'
1885 Speech, Cork, 21 Jan.

Parra, Nicanor 1914–

Chilean physicist, poet and lecturer. He addresses common problems in a clear and dirct language, with black humour and a highly ironic vision.

94 *Padre nuestro que estás en el cielo*
Lleno de toda clase de problemas
Con el ceño fruncido
Como si fueras un hombre vulgar y corriente
No pienses más en nosotros.
Our Father who art in Heaven
Full of all kinds of problems
Ceaselessly frowning
As if you were a simple man:
Stop thinking about us.
1969 *Obra gruesa*, 'Padre nuestro' ('Our Father').

Parr-Davies, Harry 1914–55

Welsh songwriter, best known for the songs he wrote for Gracie Fields. His credits include 'Sing As We Go' (1934), 'Queen of Hearts' (1936) and 'Shipyard Sally' (1939).

95 Wish me luck, as you wave me goodbye—
Cheerio, here I go, on my way.
1939 Sung by Gracie Fields in *Shipyard Sally*.

Parris, Matthew 1949–

British author, journalist and broadcaster, former Conservative MP (1979–86).

96 Wilde's captors were the police. But his persecutors were to be found on the letters page of the *Daily Telegraph*.
1993 In *The Times*, 7 Apr.

97 Being an MP feeds your vanity and starves your self-respect.
1994 In *The Times*, 9 Feb.

98 Bring on the fruitcakes, we want a fruitcake for an unlovable seat.
1997 On the day before the Kensington and Chelsea Conservatives chose Alan Clark as their parliamentary candidate. In the *Daily Mail*, 26 Jan.

Parry, Sir Charles Hubert Hastings 1848–1918

English composer. Director of the Royal College of Music from 1895, he composed the oratorios *Judith* (1888), *Job* (1892) and *King Saul* (1894); an opera, symphonies, quartets and cantatas. He also wrote various books on music.

99 Look out for this man's music; he has something to say and knows how to say it.
1899 After the première of Elgar's *Enigma Variations*. Quoted in Ian Crofton and Donald Fraser *A Dictionary of Musical Quotations* (1985).

Parsons, Talcott 1902–79

US sociologist and social theorist. A member of the faculty of Harvard University (1927–74), his chief works include *The Social System* (1951) and *Sociological Theory and Modern Society* (1967).

1 Science is intimately integrated with the whole social structure and cultural tradition. They mutually support one another—only in certain types of society can science flourish, and conversely without a continuous and healthy development and application of science such a society cannot function properly.
1951 *The Social System*, ch.8.

Parton, Dolly 1946–

US country singer, songwriter and actress.

2 Some people say that less is more. But I think more is more.
Attributed.

3 You'd be surprised how much it costs to look this cheap.
Attributed.

Parvin, Landon 1948–

US speechwriter. He was formerly speechwriter to President Reagan. He runs his own speechwriting and communications consultancy.

4 What you do is take the truth and just skew it a bit.
1991 On creating political wit for the Washington press's annual Gridiron dinners. In the *New York Times*, 29 Mar.

Pascal, Blaise 1623–62

French philosopher, mathematician and physicist, whose inventions included a calculating machine, barometer, hydraulic press and syringe, and who pioneered probability theory. An ascetic Christian and member of the Jansenist movement, he wrote much spiritual literature. Notes found after his death were published as *Pensées* in 1670.

5 *Il y a deux sortes d'esprits, l'un géométrique, et l'autre que l'on peut appeler de finesse. Le premier a des vues lentes, dures et inflexibles; mais le dernier a une souplesse de pensée.*
There are two kinds of mind, one mathematical, the other what one might call the intuitive. The first takes a slow, firm, inflexible view, but the latter has flexibility of thought.
c.1653 *Discours sur les passions de l'amour* (*Discourse on the Passions of Love*). This is usually attributed to Pascal.

6 *Dans une grande âme tout est grand.*
In a great soul everything is great.
c.1653 *Discours sur les passions de l'amour* (*Discourse on the Passions of Love*). This is usually attributed to Pascal.

7 *Quelque étendue d'esprit que l'on ait, l'on n'est capable que d'une grande passion.*
However vast a man's spirit, he is only capable of one great passion.
c.1653 *Discours sur les passions de l'amour* (*Discourse on the Passions of Love*). This is usually attributed to Pascal.

8 *La netteté de l'esprit cause aussi la netteté de la passion; c'est pourquoi un esprit grand et net aime avec ardeur, et il voit distinctement ce qu'il aime.*
Clarity of mind results in clarity of passion; that is why a great mind loves ardently and sees distinctly what it loves.
c.1653 *Discours sur les passions de l'amour* (*Discourse on the Passions of Love*). This is usually attributed to Pascal.

9 *L'on a beau se cacher à soi-même, l'on aime toujours.*
We vainly conceal from ourselves the fact that we are always in love.
c.1653 *Discours sur les passions de l'amour* (*Discourse on the Passions of Love*). This is usually attributed to Pascal.

10 *La vraie éloquence se moque de l'éloquence, la vraie morale se moque de la morale.*
True eloquence has no time for eloquence, true morality has no time for morality.
c.1654–1662 *Pensées*, no.4 (translated by A Krailsheimer).

11 *La dernière chose qu'on trouve en faisant un ouvrage, est de savoir celle qu'il faut mettre la première.*
The last thing one discovers in composing a work is what to put first.
c.1654–1662 *Pensées*, no.19 (translated by A Krailsheimer).

12 *Quand on voit le style naturel, on est tout étonné et ravi, car on s'attendait de voir un auteur, et on trouve un homme.*
When we see a natural style we are quite amazed and delighted, because we expected to see an author and find a man.
c.1654–1662 *Pensées*, no.29 (translated by A Krailsheimer).

13 *L'homme n'est qu'un sujet plein d'erreur, naturelle et ineffaçable sans la grâce.*
Man is nothing but a subject full of natural error that cannot be eradicated except through grace.
c.1654–1662 *Pensées*, no.83 (translated by A Krailsheimer).

14 *Condition de l'homme: inconstance, ennui, inquiétude.*
Man's condition. Inconstancy, boredom, anxiety.
c.1654–1662 *Pensées*, no.127 (translated by A Krailsheimer).

15 *Notre nature est dans le mouvement; le repos entier est la mort.*
Our nature consists in movement; absolute rest is death.
c.1654–1662 *Pensées*, no.129 (translated by A Krailsheimer).

16 *Tout le malheur des hommes vient d'une seule chose, qui est de ne savoir pas demeurer en repos, dans une chambre.*
The sole cause of man's unhappiness is that he does not know how to stay quietly in his room.
c.1654–1662 *Pensées*, no.139 (translated by A Krailsheimer).

17 *Le nez de Cléopâtre: s'il eût été plus court, toute la face de la terre aurait changé.*
Cleopatra's nose: if it had been shorter the whole face of the earth would have been different.
c.1654–1662 *Pensées*, no.162 (translated by A Krailsheimer).

18 *Le silence éternel de ces espaces infinis m'effraie.*
The eternal silence of these infinite spaces fills me with dread.
c.1654–1662 *Pensées*, no.206 (translated by A Krailsheimer).

19 *Combien de royaumes nous ignorent!*
How many kingdoms know nothing of us!
c.1654–1662 *Pensées*, no.207 (translated by A Krailsheimer).

20 *Le dernier acte est sanglant, quelque belle que soit la comédie en tout le reste; on jette enfin de la terre sur la tête, et en voilà pour jamais.*
The last act is bloody, however fine the rest of the play. They throw earth over your head and it is finished forever.
c.1654–1662 *Pensées*, no.210 (translated by A Krailsheimer).

21 *Pesons le gain et la perte, en prenant croix que Dieu est. Estimons ces deux cas: si vous gagnez, vous gagnez tout; si vous perdez, vous ne perdez rien. Gagez donc qu'il est, sans hésiter.*
Let us weigh up the gain and loss involved in calling heads that God exists. Let us assess the two cases: if you win you win everything, if you lose you lose nothing. Do not hesitate then; wager that he does exist.
c.1654–1662 *Pensées*, no.233 (translated by A Krailsheimer).

22 *Tout notre raisonnement se réduit à céder au sentiment.*
All our reasoning comes down to surrendering to feeling.
c.1654–1662 *Pensées*, no.274 (translated by A Krailsheimer).

23 *Le cœur a ses raisons, que la raison ne connaît point.*
The heart has its reasons of which reason knows nothing.
c.1654–1662 *Pensées*, no.277 (translated by A Krailsheimer).

24 *L'homme n'est qu'un roseau, le plus faible de la nature; mais c'est un roseau pensant.*
Man is only a reed, the weakest in nature, but he is a thinking reed.
c.1654–1662 *Pensées*, no.347 (translated by A Krailsheimer).

25 *Le moi est haïssable.*
The self is hateful.
c.1654–1662 *Pensées*, no.455 (translated by A Krailsheimer).

26 *À mesure qu'on a plus d'esprit, on trouve qu'il y a plus d'hommes originaux. Les gens du commun ne trouvent pas de différence entre les hommes.*
The more intelligent one is, the greater the differences one finds among men. Ordinary persons do not perceive differences among men.
c.1654–1662 *Pensées*, pt.1, no.7.

27 *Éloquence qui persuade par douceur, non par empire, en tyran, non en roi.*
Eloquence should persuade gently, not by force or like a tyrant or king.
c.1654–1662 *Pensées*, pt.1, no.15.

28 *Qu'est-ce que l'homme dans la nature? Un néant à l'égard de l'infini, un tout à l'égard du néant, un milieu entre rien et tout.*
What is man in nature? Nothing in comparison to the infinite, all in comparison to nothing, a mean between nothing and everything.
c.1654–1662 *Pensées*, pt.2, no.72.

29 *La chose la plus importante à toute la vie est le choix du métier: le hasard en dispose.*
The most important thing in life is to choose a profession: chance arranges for that.
c.1654–1662 *Pensées*, pt.2, no.97.

30 Knowledge of physical science will not console me for ignorance of morality in time of affliction, but knowledge of morality will always console me for ignorance of physical science.
c.1654–1662 *Pensées*, no.23.

31 *L'homme n'est ni ange ni bête, et le malheur veut que qui veut faire l'ange fait la bête.*
Man is neither angel nor beast. Unfortunately, he who wants to act the angel often acts the beast.
c.1654–1662 *Pensées*, pt.6, no.358.

32 *En un mot, l'homme connaît qu'il est misérable: il est donc misérable, puisqu'il l'est; mais il est bien grand, puisqu'il le connaît.*
In one word, man knows that he is miserable and therefore he is miserable because he knows it; but he is also worthy, because he knows his condition.
c.1654–1662 *Pensées*, pt.6, no.416.

33 *Il n'y a que deux sortes d'hommes: les uns justes, qui se croient pécheurs; les autres pécheurs, qui se croient justes.*
There are only two types of people: the virtuous who believe themselves to be sinners and the sinners who believe themselves to be virtuous.
c.1654–1662 *Pensées*, pt.7, no.534.

34 *Il est non seulement impossible, mais inutile de connaître Dieu sans Jésus-Christ.*
It is not only impossible, but also useless to recognize God without Jesus.
c.1654–1662 *Pensées*, pt.7, no.549.

35 *Je ne crois que les histoires dont les témoins se feraient égorger.*
I only believe in histories told by witnesses who would have had their throats slit.
c.1654–1662 *Pensées*, pt.9, no.593.

36 *Le silence est la plus grande persécution: jamais les saints ne se sont tus.*
Silence is the greatest of all persecutions: no saint was ever silent.
c.1654–1662 *Pensées*, pt.14, no.920.

37 *Console-toi, tu ne me chercherais pas si tu ne m'avais trouvé.*
Comfort yourself. You would not seek me if you had not found me.
c.1654–1662 *Pensées*, pt.7, no.553 (translated by L Braunschvicg, 1909).

38 *Je n'ai fait plus longue que parce que je n'ai pas eu le loisir de la faire plus courte.*
I have made this letter longer than usual, only because I have not had the time to make it shorter.
1657 *Lettres provinciales*, letter 16.

39 FEU. *Dieu d'Abraham, Dieu d'Isaac, Dieu de Jacob, non des philosophes et savants. Certitude. Certitude. Sentiment. Joie. Paix.*
FIRE. God of Abraham, God of Isaac, God of Jacob, not of the philosophers and scholars. Certainty. Certainty. Feeling. Joy. Peace.
c.1662 Note found after his death on a parchment stitched to his coat.

Passell, Peter

US financial journalist, editor of the Milken Institute Review.

40 Six percent unemployment only looks good from the vantage point of the other 94 percent.
1994 In the *New York Times*, 31 Mar.

Pasternak, Boris 1890–1960

Russian poet and novelist. He was awarded a Nobel prize for literature in 1958, but refused it.

41 Yet the order of the acts is planned
And the end of the way inescapable.
I am alone; all drowns in the Pharisees' hypocrisy.
1958 *Doctor Zhivago*.

42 The whole wide world is a cathedral;
I stand inside, the air is calm,
And from afar at times there reaches
My ear the echo of a psalm.
1958 *When It Clears Up* (translated by Lydia Pasternak Slater).

Pasteur, Louis 1822–95

French chemist, the father of modern bacteriology. He promoted inoculation as a means of preventing diseases, and in 1888 he founded the Institut Pasteur and served as its first director.

43 *Dans les champs de l'observation le hasard ne favorise que les esprits préparés.*
Where observation is concerned, chance favours only the prepared mind.
1854 Speech at the inauguration of the Faculty of Science, University of Lille, 7 Dec.

44 Science proceeds by successive answers to questions more and more subtle, coming nearer and nearer to the very essence of phenomena.
c.1856 *Études sur la bière*, ch.6 (translated by René Dubois).

45 *Il n'existe pas de sciences appliquées, mais seulement des applications de la science.*
There are no such things as applied sciences, only applications of science.
1872 Speech, Lyons, 11 Sep.

46 I am imbued with two deep impressions; the first, that science knows no country; the second, which seems to contradict the first, although it is really a direct consequence of it...that science is the highest personification of the nation. Science knows no country because knowledge belongs to humanity, and is the torch which illuminates the world. Science is the highest personification of the nation because that nation will remain the first which carries the furthest the works of thought and intelligence.
1876 Toast at the banquet of the International Congress of Sericulture (translated by René Dubois).

47 Outside their laboratories, the physician and chemist are soldiers without arms on the field of battle.
Some Reflections on Science in France, pt.1.

Patchen, Kenneth 1911–72

US author, playwright and poet. His many verse collections, illustrated by him, include *Before the Brave* (1936) and *Hallelujah Anyway* (1967), and his novels include *Memoirs of a Shy Pornographer* (1945).

48 For greatness is only the drayhorse that coaxes
The built cart out; and where we go is reason.
But genius is an enormous littleness, a trickling
Of heart that covers alike the hare and the hunter.
1939 *First Will and Testament*, 'The Character of Love Seen as a Search for the Lost'.

49 Dogs with broken legs are shot; men with broken souls write through the night.
1941 *The Journal of Albion Moonlight*.

50 God must have loved the People in Power, for he made them so very like their own image of him.
Quoted by Adrian Mitchell in *The Guardian*, 1 Feb 1972.

Pater, Walter 1839–94

English critic and essayist, whose highly polished prose style was very influential. He wrote many essays on Renaissance art, and won a wider audience with a romance, *Marius the Epicurean* (1885).

51 She is older than the rocks among which she sits; like the vampire, she has been dead many times, and learned the secrets of the grave.
1873 Of the *Mona Lisa*. 'Leonardo da Vinci' in *Studies in the History of the Renaissance*.

52 All art constantly aspires towards the condition of music.
1873 'The School of Giorgione' in *Studies in the History of the Renaissance*.

53 Of such wisdom, the poetic passion, the desire of beauty, the love of art for its own sake, has most. For art comes to you proposing frankly to give nothing but the highest quality to your moments as they pass, and simply for those moments' sake.
1873 'Conclusion' in *Studies in the History of the Renaissance*.

Paterson, Banjo (Andrew Barton) 1864–1941

Australian poet and journalist. He worked on a station near Yass and later practised as a solicitor, contributing to the satirical weekly *Bulletin* as 'The Banjo'. His first collection of bush ballads, *The Man from Snowy River* (1895), gained him massive popularity.

54 Oh there once was a swagman camped in the billabongs,
Under the shade of a Coolibah tree;
And he sang as he looked at the old billy boiling,
'Who'll come a-waltzing Matilda with me.'

Who'll come a-waltzing Matilda, my darling,
Who'll come a-waltzing Matilda with me.
Waltzing Matilda and leading a water-bag,
Who'll come a-waltzing Matilda with me.
1885 'Waltzing Matilda', in the *Bulletin*, Apr.

55 I had written him a letter which I had, for want of better Knowledge, sent to where I met him, down the Lachlan, years ago.
He was shearing when I knew him, so I sent the letter to him,
Just 'on spec', addressed as follows: 'Clancy, of the Overflow'.
And an answer came directed in a writing unexpected,
(And I think the same was written with a thumbnail dipped in tar)
'Twas his shearing mate who wrote it, and verbatim I will quote it:
'Clancy's gone to Queensland droving, and we don't know where he are.'
1895 'Clancy of the Overflow', first published in the *Bulletin*, collected in *The Man from Snowy River and Other Verses* (1895).

56 In all museums throughout the world one may see plaster casts of footprints of weird animals, footprints preserved for posterity, not because the animals were particularly good of their sort, but because they had the luck to walk on the lava while it was cooling. There is just a faint hope that something of the same sort may happen to us.
Of Henry Lawson and himself writing in a new land. Quoted in Rosamund Campbell and Philippa Harvie *A Literary Heritage: 'Banjo' Paterson* (1988), introduction.

Patmore, Coventry Kersey Dighton 1823–96

English poet. He was associated with the Pre-Raphaelite brotherhood. His best work, *The Angel in the House* (4 vols. 1854–63), was a poetic treatment of married love which delighted a generation devoid of cynicism to whom he and his first wife, Emily, epitomized Victorian values.

57 Oh, wasteful woman, she who may
On her sweet self set her own price,
Knowing man cannot choose but pay,
How has she cheapened paradise:
How given for naught her priceless gift,
How spoiled the bread and spilled the wine,
Which, spent with due, respective thrift,
Had made brutes men, and men divine.
1854 *The Angel in the House*, bk.1, *The Betrothal*, canto 3, prelude 3, 'Unthrift'.

58 Love wakes men, once a lifetime each:
They lift their heavy lids, and look;
And, lo, what one sweet page can teach,
They read with joy, then shut the book.
1854 *The Angel in the House*, bk.1, *The Betrothal*, canto 8, prelude 2, 'The Revelation'.

59 'I saw you take his kiss!' ''Tis true.'
'O modesty!' ''Twas strictly kept:
He thought me asleep—at least, I knew
He thought I thought he thought I slept.'
1854 *The Angel in the House*, bk.2, *The Espousal*, canto 8, prelude 3, 'The Kiss'.

60 A woman is a foreign land.
1854 *The Angel in the House*, bk.2, *The Espousal*, canto 9, prelude 2, 'The Foreign Land'.

61 It was not like your great and gracious ways!
Do you, that have naught other to lament,
Never, my love, repent.
1877 *To the Unknown Eros*, bk.1, no.8, 'Departure'.

62 With all my will, but much against my heart,
We two now part.
1877 *To the Unknown Eros*, bk.1, no.16, 'A Farewell'.

63 'O say,
Shall we no voluntary bars
Set to our drift? I, Sister of the Stars,
And Thou, my glorious, course-compelling Day!'
1877 *To the Unknown Eros*, bk.2, no.2, 'The Contract'.

64 No writer, sacred or profane, ever uses the words 'he' or 'him' of the soul. It is always 'she' or 'her'; so universal is the intuitive knowledge that the soul, with regard to God who is her life, is feminine.
1896 *The Rod, the Root, and the Flower*, 'Aurea Dicta', no.21.

65 Those who know God know that it is a quite a mistake to suppose that there are only five senses.
1896 *The Rod, the Root, and the Flower*, 'Aurea Dicta', no.142.

66 May I know by love and speak by silence.
1896 *The Rod, the Root, and the Flower*, 'Aphorisms and Extracts'.

67 He that but once too nearly hears
The music of forfended spheres
Is thenceforth lonely, and for all
His days as one who treads the Wall
Of China, and, on this hand, sees
Cities and their civilities
And, on the other, lions.
1863 *The Victories of Love*, bk.1.

68 Some dish more sharply spiced than this
Milk-soup men call domestic bliss.
Olympus (published 1906).

Paton, Alan 1903–88

South African writer and educator. President of the South African Liberal Party (1953–60), he is best remembered for his novel *Cry, the Beloved Country* (1948), on racial divisions in South Africa.

69 Cry, the Beloved Country.
1948 Title of book.

70 No second Johannesburg is needed upon the earth. One is enough.
1948 *Cry, the Beloved Country*, bk.2, section 6.

St Patrick 5c AD

Bishop and Apostle of Ireland.

71 Christ for my guardianship today: against poison, against burning, against drowning, against wounding, that there may come to me a multitude of rewards;
Christ with me,
Christ before me,
Christ behind me,
Christ in me,
Christ over me,
Christ to right of me,
Christ to left of me,
Christ in lying down,
Christ in sitting,
Christ in rising up,
Christ in the heart of every person who may think of me,
Christ in the mouth of every person who may speak of me,
Christ in every eye, which may look on me!
Christ in every ear, which may hear me!
St Patrick's Breastplate, traditionally attributed to the saint.

Patrick, John *pseudonym of* John Patrick Goggan 1905–95

US playwright and screenwriter. He received the Pulitzer Prize for the play *The Teahouse of the August Moon* (1953) and his screenplays include *Three Coins in the Fountain* (1954) and *Love is a Many Splendoured Thing* (1955).

72 Punctuality is the vice of virtuous women.
1954 Line delivered by Clifton Webb in *Three Coins in the Fountain*.

Patton, George Smith *known as* Old Blood and Guts 1885–1945

US soldier, a daring and flamboyant commander in World War II. He led numerous expeditions, including the 3rd Army invasion of France, and was killed in a road accident in Germany soon after being appointed general.

73 The object of war is not to die for your country. The object of war is to make damn sure the other sonofabitch dies for *his*.
Attributed.

Paul, Leslie 1905–85

Irish writer and poet.

74 Angry Young Man.
1951 Title of book. Later associated with John Osborne.

Pauli, Wolfgang 1900–58

Austrian–Swiss theoretical physicist and Nobel prize winner (1945).

75 I don't mind your thinking slowly: I mind your publishing faster than you think.
Attributed.

Pauling, Linus Carl 1901–94

US chemist. He was Professor at the California Institute of Technology and won the Nobel prize for chemistry in 1954. He was awarded the Nobel peace prize in 1962.

76 Science is a search for truth—it is not a game in which one tries to best his opponent, to do harm to others.
1958 *No More War.*

Pavarotti, Luciano 1935–

Italian tenor.

77 If I could live my life over again there is one thing I would change. I would want to be able to eat less.
1997 In *The Times*, 8 Dec.

78 Horse riding is a perfect comparison with singing. You must know where the double fences are.
2002 In *The Guardian*, 7 Jan.

Pavlov, I(van) P(etrovich) 1849–1936

Russian physiologist and experimental psychologist, famed for his work on the physiology of the digestive system. He received the 1904 Nobel prize for physiology or medicine.

79 Learn the ABC of science before you try to ascend to its summit.
1936 *Bequest to the Academic Youth of Soviet Russia.*

Pavlov, Valentin Sergeyevich 1937–2003

Russian politician. He was Prime Minister from January 1991 until August of that year, when he was arrested as an accomplice in the failed coup d'état against Mikhail Gorbachev. He was granted amnesty by parliament in 1994.

80 Privatization must come after the liberalization of prices… How on earth can you privatize or denationalize anything if you have no means of assessing the value of assets before offering them on the market?
1991 Interview, *The Independent*, 18 Apr.

81 Civil war is impossible in the Soviet Union.
1991 Interview, *The Independent*, 18 Apr.

82 It is no use making revolutionary cavalry charges against the problems that we are facing.
1991 On Boris Yeltsin's proposals for economic republican autonomy. Interview, *The Independent*, 18 Apr.

Pavlova, Anna 1882–1931

Russian ballerina.

83 Although one may fail to find happiness in theatrical life, one never wishes to give it up after having once tasted its fruits. To enter the School of the Imperial Ballet is to enter a convent whence frivolity is banned, and where merciless discipline reigns.
Quoted in A H Franks (ed) *Pavlova: A Biography*, 'Pages of My Life' (1956).

Paxman, Jeremy 1950–

English journalist and broadcaster. He is perhaps best known as the presenter of such current affairs programmes as *Panorama* (1979–85), and *Newsnight* (1989–).

84 Did you threaten to overrule him?
1997 Question asked 14 times of Conservative politician Michael Howard, relating to the sacking of a prison governor by the director of the Prison Service, Derek Lewis. On BBC's *Newsnight*.

85 Once upon a time the English knew who they were.
1998 *The English: A Portrait of a People.*

86 Scots are Jocks, Welshmen Taffies, and Irishmen Paddies or Micks but…it is noticeable there is no similar designation for the English.
1998 *The English: A Portrait of a People.*

87 The more you look back into English history, the more you are forced to the conclusion that alongside civility and the deeply held convictions about individual rights, the English have a natural taste for disorder.
1998 *The English: A Portrait of a People.*

Paz, Octavio 1914–98

Mexican poet, writer and diplomat. He sided with the Republican cause during the Spanish Civil War. In Paris, he was strongly influenced by the Surrealist movement. He was awarded a Nobel prize in 1990.

88 *Amar es combatir, es abrir puertas,*
dejar de ser fantasma con un número
a perpetua cadena condenado
por un amo sin rostro.
To love is to battle, to open doors,
to cease to be a ghost with a number
forever in chains, forever condemned
by a faceless master.
1949 *Libertad bajo palabra*, 'Piedra de sol' (translated as 'The Sun Stone', 1963).

89 *Sin duda la cercanía de la muerte y la fraternidad de las armas producen, en todos los tiempos y en todos los países, una atmósfera propicia a lo extraordinario, a todo aquello que sobrepasa la condición humana y rompe el círculo de soledad que rodea a cada hombre.*
No doubt the nearness of death and the brotherhood of men-at-wars, at whatever time and in whatever country, always produce an atmosphere favorable to the extraordinary, to all that rises above the human condition and breaks the circle of solitude that surrounds each one of us.
1950 *El laberinto de la soledad*, pt.1 (translated as *The Labyrinth of Solitude*, 1961).

90 Technology is not an image of the world but a way of operating on reality. The nihilism of technology lies not only in the fact that it is the most perfect expression of the will to power…but also in the fact that it lacks meaning.
1967 *Alternating Current.*

Peace Pilgrim *real name* Mildred Norman c.1908–1981

US writer and mystic. From 1952 to 1981 she walked through North America, carrying only the bare minimum of necessities and teaching wherever she went; her intention was to stop walking only when there was total peace in the world.

91 I never give out my zodiac sign. Do you honestly think I can be pushed around by a planet? Good heavens, your divine nature is always free.
Quoted in Susan Hayward and Malcolm Cohen *The Bag of Jewels* (1988).

Peacock, Thomas Love 1785–1866

English novelist. He entered the service of the East India Company (1819–56) after producing three satirical romances, attacking common prejudices and affectations, and produced further works along similar lines.

92 Marriage may often be a stormy lake, but celibacy is almost always a muddy horsepond.
1817 *Melincourt*, ch.7.

93 Laughter is pleasant, but the exertion is too much for me.
1818 *Nightmare Abbey*, ch.5.

94 Sir, I have quarrelled with my wife; and a man who has quarrelled with his wife is absolved from all duty to his country.
1818 *Nightmare Abbey*, ch.11.

95 The mountain sheep are sweeter,
But the valley sheep are fatter;
We therefore deemed it meeter
To carry off the latter.
We made an expedition;
We met a host, and quelled it;
We forced a strong position,
And killed the men who held it.
1829 *The Misfortunes of Elphin*, 'The War-Song of Dinas Vawr'.

96 But though first love's impassioned blindness
Has passed away in colder light,
I still have thought of you with kindness,
And shall do, till our last goodnight.
The ever-rolling silent hours
Will bring a time we shall not know,
When our young days of gathering flowers
Will be an hundred years ago.
1860 'Love and Age'.

Pearson, Karl 1857–1936

English mathematician and Professor of Mathematics and Eugenics at University College London. Pearson is generally considered one of the founders of modern statistical theory.

97 When every fact, every present or past phenomenon of [the] universe, every phase of present or past life therein, has been examined, classified, and coordinated with the rest, then the mission of science will be completed. What is this but saying that the task of science can never end till man ceases to be, till history is no longer made, and development itself ceases?
1892 *The Grammar of Science*, pt.1, ch.5.

Pearson, Lester Bowles 1897–1972

Canadian politician, president of the UN General Assembly (1952–3). He won the Nobel peace prize (1957). Opposition leader from 1958, he was Prime Minister 1963–8.

98 The grim fact, however, is that we prepare for war like precocious giants and for peace like retarded pygmies.
1957 Acceptance speech on receiving the Nobel peace prize, 11 Dec.

99 Politics is the skilled use of blunt objects.
Quoted in Canadian Broadcasting Corporation tribute on his death, 1972.

Peary, Robert Edwin 1856–1920

US admiral and explorer. He made eight Arctic voyages by the Greenland coast. In 1906 he reached latitude 87° 6 mins N and on 6 Apr 1909 was the first to reach the North Pole.

1 I have got the North Pole out of my system after twenty-three years of effort, hard work, disappointments, hardships, privations, more or less suffering, and some risks… The work is the finish, the cap and climax of nearly four hundred years of effort, loss of life, and expenditure of fortunes by the civilized nations of the world, and it has been accomplished in a way that is thoroughly American. I am content.
1909 Diary entry, Apr. Quoted in *The North Pole* (published 1910).

2 In a march of only a few hours, I had passed from the western to the eastern hemisphere and had verified my position at the summit of the world. It was hard to realise that on the first miles of the brief march we had been travelling due north, while on the last few miles of the same march we had been travelling due south, although we had all the time been travelling precisely in the same direction.
1909 Description of crossing and then passing the Pole. *The North Pole* (published 1910).

Peck, M(organ) Scott 1936–

US writer and psychiatrist, author of the seminal self-help work *The Road Less Traveled* (1978). Later works, combining Christian teaching with psychiatric principles, include *The Different Drum* (1987).

3 Once we truly know that life is difficult—once we understand and accept it—then life is no longer difficult. Because once it is accepted, it no longer matters.
1978 *The Road Less Traveled*, ch.1.

4 The evil in this world is committed by the spiritual fat cats who think that they are without sin because they are unwilling to suffer the discomfort of significant self-examination.
1985 *What Return Can I Make?*

5 What being a Christian means, at the very least, is that whenever there is a decision to be made, which may be several times a day, an alternative should not be discarded simply because it is sacrificial.
1985 *What Return Can I Make?*

6 Simply seek happiness, and you are not likely to find it. Seek to create and love without regard to your happiness, and you will likely be happy much of the time.
1987 *The Different Drum*.

7 The healthy life is hardly one marked by an absence of crises. In fact, an individual's psychological health is distinguished by how early he or she can meet crisis.
1987 *The Different Drum*.

Peel, Sir Robert 1788–1850

English Tory statesman, Secretary for Ireland (1812–18), known as 'Orange Peel' for his strong anti-Catholic spirit. As Home Secretary (1822–7, 1828–30), he carried through the Catholic Emancipation Act (1829) and reorganized the London police force (the 'Peelers' or 'Bobbies'). As Prime Minister (1834–5, 1841–6), his decision to repeal the Corn Laws (1846) split his party, and precipitated his resignation, though he remained in Parliament as leader of the 'Peelites'.

8 If the spirit of the Reform Bill implies merely a careful review of institutions, civil and ecclesiastical, undertaken in a friendly temper, combining with the firm maintenance of established rights the correction of private abuses and the redress of real grievances, I can for myself and my colleagues undertake to act in such a spirit and with such intentions.
1834 *The Tamworth Manifesto.*

9 During my tenure of power, my earnest wish has been to impress the people of this country with a belief that the legislature was animated by a sincere desire to frame its legislation upon the principles of equity and justice… Deprive me of power tomorrow, but you can never deprive me of the consciousness that I have exercised the powers committed to me from no corrupt or interested motives, from no desire to gratify ambition, or to attain any personal object.
1846 On the repeal of the Corn Laws, House of Commons, 15 May.

10 It asks more steadiness, self-control, ay, and manly courage, than any other exercise. You must take as well as give—eye to eye, toe to toe, and arm to arm.
Of boxing. Quoted in John Boyle O'Reilly *Ethics of Boxing and Manly Sport* (1888).

Peele, George c.1556–1596

English dramatist and poet.

11 Fair and fair, and twice so fair,
As fair as any may be;
The fairest shepherd on our green,
A love for any lady.
1584 *The Arraignment of Paris*, act 1, sc.5.

12 What thing is love for (well I wot) love is a thing.
It is a prick, it is a sting,
It is a pretty, pretty thing;
It is a fire, it is a coal
Whose flame creeps in at every hole.
c.1591 *The Hunting of Cupid.*

Pei, I(eoh) M(ing) 1917–

Chinese-born US architect. He emigrated to the US in 1935 and was naturalized in 1954. A controversial and adventurous designer, his works include Mile High Center, Denver and the glass pyramid at the Louvre, Paris.

13 Let's do it right. This is for the ages.
1978 Quoted by J Carter Brown, Director, National Gallery of Art, Washington, in the *Washington Post*, 27 Aug 1995. On his design for the gallery's East Building which was soaring to an unbudgeted cost of $94.4m.

14 *Comment respecter la tradition, et innover en même temps? Quel pari difficile!*
How to respect tradition and to innovate at the same time? What a difficult challenge!
1989 *Les Grands desseins du Louvre* (with E J Biasini).

15 *L'architecture est le miroir même de la vie. Il n'est que de jeter les yeux sur des édifices pour sentir la présence du passé, l'esprit d'un lieu; ils sont le reflet de la société.*
Architecture is the very mirror of life. You only have to cast your eyes on buildings to feel the presence of the past, the spirit of a place; they are the reflection of society.
1989 *Les Grands desseins du Louvre* (with E J Biasini).

Pelé *pseudonym of* Edson Arantes do Nascimento 1940–

Brazilian footballer. He won World Cup medals with Brazil (1958 and 1970) and scored over 1,000 goals in first-class football.

16 A penalty is a cowardly way to score.
Quoted in Peter Ball and Phil Shaw *The Book of Football Quotations* (1989).

17 I was born for soccer, just as Beethoven was born for music.
Quoted in Colin Jarman *The Guinness Dictionary of Sports Quotations* (1990).

18 Football is like a religion to me. I worship the ball, and I treat it like a god. Too many players think of a football as something to kick. They should be taught to caress it and to treat it like a precious gem.
Quoted in David Pickering *The Cassell Soccer Companion* (1994).

Penecuik, Dr Alex 1652–1722

Scottish poet.

19 To curle on the ice, does greatly please,
Being a manly Scottish exercise;
It clears the Brains, stirs up the Native Heat,
And gives a gallant appetite for Meat.
1715 Quoted in Colin Jarman *The Guinness Dictionary of Sports Quotations* (1990).

Penfield, Wilder Graves 1891–1976

US-born Canadian neurosurgeon, who worked mainly at Montreal's Allan Memorial Institute, where he was first director (1934–60). He famously worked on the exposed brains of living human subjects, and on retirement turned to writing fiction and biography.

20 In all our studies of the brain, no mechanism has been discovered that can force the mind to think, or the individual to believe, anything. The mind continues free. That is a statement I have long considered. I have made every effort to disprove it, without success.
1970 *Second Thoughts: Science, the Arts, and the Spirit.*

Peniakoff, Vladimir 1897–1951

Belgian-born soldier and writer.

21 A message came on the wireless for me. It said: 'SPREAD ALARM AND DESPONDENCY'. So the time had come, I thought, Eighth Army was taking the offensive. The date was, I think, May 18th, 1942.
1950 *Popski's Private Army.*

Penn, William 1644–1718

English Quaker, imprisoned for his beliefs. In 1681, in settlement of Charles II's debt to his father, he was granted land in America, and founded the colony of Pennsylvania as a refuge for persecuted Quakers.

22 This day my country was confirmed to me under the great seal of England, with large powers and privileges, by the name of *Pennsylvania*; a name the king would give it in honor of my father.
1681 Letter to Robert Turner, 14 Mar.

23 Inquire often, but judge rarely, and thou wilt not often be mistaken.
1693 *Some Fruits of Solitude.*

People's Daily

The official daily newspaper of the Communist Party of China. Speaking for the Chinese government, in 1979 a series of articles denounced the Democracy Wall Movement. Changan Road in Beijing had been a centre for posters and news-sheets demanding democratic rights.

24 The imperialists brought the Chinese people cannons rather than flowers, death instead of 'human rights'… How can they be in a position to instruct us on 'civil rights'?
1979 *People's Daily*, 22 Mar.

Pepys, Samuel 1633–1703

English civil servant and diarist. He rose in the naval service to become Secretary to the Admiralty, 1672. His diary, covering the years 1660 to 1669, is an important historical and social document.

25 Boys do now cry 'Kiss my Parliament!' instead of 'Kiss my arse!' so great and general a contempt is the Rump come to among all men, good and bad.
1660 Diary entry, 7 Feb. The Rump Parliament was that which persisted after the fall of Richard Cromwell, and before the restoration of Charles II.

26 And so to bed.
1660 Diary entry, 20 Apr and passim.

27 A silk suit, which cost me much money, and I pray God to make me able to pay for it.
1660 Diary entry, 1 Jul.

28 I went out to Charing Cross to see Major-General Harrison hanged, drawn and quartered—which was done there—he looking as cheerfully as any man could do in that condition… Thus it was my chance to see the King beheaded at Whitehall and to see the first blood shed in revenge for the blood of the King at Charing Cross.
1660 Diary entry, 13 Oct.

29 A good honest and painful sermon.
1661 Diary entry, 17 Mar.

30 But methought it lessened my esteem of a king, that he should not be able to command the rain.
1662 Diary entry, 19 Jul.

31 I see it is impossible for the King to have things done as cheap as other men.
1662 Diary entry, 21 Jul.

32 To the King's Theatre, where we saw *Midsummer Night's Dream*, which I had never seen before, nor shall ever again, for it is the most insipid, ridiculous play that ever I ever saw in my life.
1662 Diary entry, 29 Sep.

33 But Lord! to see the absurd nature of Englishmen, that cannot forbear laughing and jeering at everything that looks strange.
1662 Diary entry, 27 Nov.

34 Then over the park (where I first in my life, it being a great frost, did see people sliding with their skates, which is a very pretty art).
1662 Diary entry, 1 Dec.

35 My wife, who, poor wretch, is troubled with her lonely life.
1662 Diary entry, 19 Dec.

36 After dinner to the Duke's house, and there saw *Twelfth Night* acted well, though it be but a silly play.
1663 Diary entry, 6 Jan.

37 Most of their discourse was about hunting, in a dialect I understand very little.
1663 Diary entry, 22 Nov.

38 To the Tennis Court, and there saw the King play at tennis and others; but to see how the King's play was extolled, without any cause at all, was a loathsome sight.
1664 Diary entry, 4 Jan.

39 Up, and by coach to Sir Ph. Warwickes, the street being full of footballs, it being a great frost.
1665 Diary entry, 3 Jan. Frost restricted the amount of horse traffic in the streets of London, making football a possibility.

40 This day, much against my will, I did in Drury Lane see two or three houses marked with a red cross upon the doors, and 'Lord have mercy upon us' writ there—which was a sad sight to me, being the first of that kind that to my remembrance I ever saw.
1665 Diary entry, 7 Jun. The houses were afflicted with bubonic plague, which lasted in London until the summer of 1666.

41 Up, all of us, and to Billiards.
1665 Diary entry, 17 Jul.

42 The people die so, that now it seems they are fain to carry the dead to be buried by daylight, the nights not sufficing to do it in. And my Lord Mayor commands people to be within at 9 at night, all (as they say) that the sick may have liberty to go abroad for ayre.
1665 Diary entry, 12 Aug.

43 And it is a wonder what will be the fashion after the plague is done as to periwigs, for nobody will dare to buy any haire for fear of the infection—that it had been cut off the heads of people dead of the plague.
1665 Diary entry, 3 Sep.

44 Strange to say what delight we married people have to see these poor fools decoyed into our condition.
1665 Diary entry, 25 Dec.

45 Music and women I cannot but give way to, whatever my business is.
1666 Diary entry, 9 Mar.

46 Poor people staying in their houses as long as till the very fire touched them, and then running into boats or clambering from one pair of stair by the waterside to another. And among other things, the poor pigeons I perceive were loath to leave their houses, but hovered about the windows and balconies till they were some of them burned, their wings, and fell down.
1666 Diary entry, 2 Sep. The Great Fire of London continued for four days, destroying four-fifths of the total area of the city.

47 A most horrid malicious bloody flame… It made me weep to see it.
1666 Observing the Great Fire of London. Diary entry, 2 Sep.

48 Hardly one lighter or boat in three that had the goods of a house in, but there was a pair of virginalls in it.
1666 Describing the chaos on the Thames as people attempted to rescue their possessions from the flames. Diary entry, 2 Sep.

49 But it is pretty to see what money will do.
1668 Diary entry, 21 Mar.

Percy, Walker 1916–90

US novelist. His best-known work of fiction is *The Moviegoer* (1961), but he wrote several novels, and volumes of collected essays and non-fiction.

50 As Einstein once said, ordinary life in an ordinary day in the modern world is a dreary business. I mean *dreary*. People will do anything just to escape this dreariness.
1977 Interview in *Esquire*, Dec.

51 Unlike God the artist does not start with nothing and make something of it. He starts with himself as nothing and makes something of the nothing with the things at hand.
1977 Interview in *Esquire*, Dec.

Perdue, Franklin P

US businessman, former chief executive of Perdue Farms Inc.

52 I hate pudgy poultry.
1987 In the *New Yorker*, 6 Jul.

Perelman, S(ydney) J(oseph) 1904–79

US humorist. He was a scriptwriter, and later one of the circle of wits who wrote for the *New Yorker*. He published a number of books.

53 I have Bright's disease and he has mine, sobbed the panting palooka.
1929 In *Judge*, 16 Nov. A palooka is US slang for a clumsy person, especially in sports.

54 Crazy Like a Fox.
1944 Title of book.

55 A feeling of emulsion swept over me.
1944 *Crazy Like a Fox*, 'The Love Decoy'.

56 He bit his lip in a manner which immediately awakened my maternal sympathy, and I helped him bite it.
1944 *Crazy Like a Fox*, 'The Love Decoy'.

57 I guess I'm just an old mad scientist at bottom. Give me an underground laboratory, half a dozen atomsmashers, and a beautiful girl in a diaphanous veil waiting to be turned into a chimpanzee, and I care not who writes the nation's laws.
1944 *Crazy Like a Fox*, 'Captain Future, Block That Kick'.

58 She had the rippling muscles of a panther, the solidity of a water buffalo, and the lazy insolence of a shoe salesman.
1944 *Crazy Like a Fox*, 'Kitchen Bouquet'.

59 For years I have let dentists ride roughshod over my teeth; I have been sawed, hacked, chopped, whittled, bewitched, bewildered, tattooed, and signed on again; but this is cuspid's last stand.
1944 *Crazy Like a Fox*, 'Nothing But the Tooth'.

60 You've got a sharp tongue in your head, Mr Essick. Look out it doesn't cut your throat.
1961 *The Rising Gorge*, 'All Out...'.

61 English life, while very pleasant, is rather bland. I expected kindness and gentility and I found it, but there is such a thing as too much couth.
1971 In the *Observer*, 24 Sep.

62 The dogs had eaten the upholstery of a Packard convertible that afternoon, and were consequently somewhat subdued.
1981 *The Last Laugh*, 'The Last Laugh'.

Peres, Shimon 1923–

Israeli statesman. In 1994 he shared the Nobel peace prize with Yasser Arafat and Yitzhak Rabin.

63 Television has made dictatorship impossible, but democracy unbearable.
1995 In the *Financial Times*, 31 Jan.

Pericles c.490–429 BC

Athenian statesman, who initiated democratic reforms and a great building programme (including the Parthenon). His famous *epitaphios* (Funerary Oration on the death of the first year of the Peloponnesian War) was reported by Thucydides. He died of the plague which struck Athens in 430 BC.

64 Famous men have the whole earth as their memorial.
Quoted in Thucydides *History of the Peloponnesian War*, 2.43 (translated by R Warner, 1961).

65 Your great glory is not to be inferior to what you have been given by nature, and the greatest glory of a woman is to be least talked about by men, whether they are praising or criticizing you.
Address to women in the Funerary Oration. Quoted in Thucydides *History of the Peloponnesian War*, 2.45.2 (translated by R Warner, 1961).

Perkins, Carl 1932–98

US songwriter and composer. A key figure of early rock 'n' roll, his guitar playing combined blues and country music.

66 Don't you step on my blue suede shoes.
1956 'Blue Suede Shoes'.

Perkins, Frances 1882–1965

US social reformer and politician. Educated at Mount Holyoke College, Massachusetts, she was the first woman to hold Cabinet rank in the US. She was appointed US Secretary of Labor (1933–45) in President Franklin D Roosevelt's Cabinet.

67 No one had any measure of its progress; no one had any plan for stopping it. Everyone tried to get out of its way.
On the depression of the 1930s which inspired her to set up the Social Security system. Recalled on her death, 14 May 1965.

Perry, Grayson 1960–

English potter who won the Turner Prize in 2003.

68 It's about time a transvestite potter won the Turner Prize.
2003 In his acceptance speech, referring to his habit of dressing as his alter ego, Claire.

Persius *properly* Aulus Persius Flaccus AD 34–62

Roman satirist and Stoic. Only one book of satires has survived.

69 *Quis leget haec?*
Who'll read that sort of thing?
Satirae, no.1, 1.2 (translated by W S Merwin, 1961).

Perth, James, 4th Earl of 1648–1716

Scottish Justice-General (1682) and Chancellor (1684). He was imprisoned in Stirling Castle (1688–96), after the fall of James II and VII, but then joined the exiled court of the King at St Germain, where he remained for the rest of his life. He was created Duke of Perth and Knight of the Garter.

70 I have been here a fortnight and I think I shall be here fifteen or twenty days longer, although I do not very

much like the place, for this puddling in a tub continually is no charm to me.
On Venice. Collected in *Letters to his sister the Countess of Erroll, and other members of his family.*

Pessoa, Fernando António Nogueira 1888–1935

Portuguese poet, an important figure in the Modernist movement.

71 *Sê plural como o universo!*
Be plural, like the universe!
Páginas Íntimas e de Auto-interpretação.

72 *Estrangeiro aqui como em toda a parte.*
I'm a stranger here, as I am everywhere.
1926 *Lisbon Revisited.*

73 *Não sou nada.*
Nunca serei nada.
Não posso querer ser nada.
À parte isso, tenho em mim todos os sonhos do mundo.
I am not nothing.
I will never be nothing.
I cannot ever want to be nothing.
Apart from that, I have in me all the dreams of the world.
1928 *Tabacaria* ('The Tobacconist's').

Pétain, (Henri) Philippe 1856–1951

French soldier and politician. In World War I his defence of Verdun (1916) made him a national hero, and he became Commander-in-Chief (1917) and Marshal of France (1918). When France collapsed in 1940, he negotiated the armistice with Germany and Italy, became chief of state, and collaborated with Germany in an attempt to keep France out of the war. He is regarded by some as a patriot, by others as a traitor.

74 They shall not pass.
This phrase came to symbolize the stubborn defence of Verdun against Ludendorf's siege, which cost 300,000 German and 400,000 French troops.
► *See Ibarruri Gomez 427:31.*

75 I was with you in the days of glory. At the head of the Government, I shall remain with you during the days of darkness. Stay by my side.
1940 Radio broadcast announcing his intention to seek an armistice, 20 Jun.

Peter, Laurence J 1919–90

Canadian academic and writer, professor at the University of South California.

76 In a hierarchy every employee tends to rise to his level of incompetence; the cream rises until it sours.
1969 *The Peter Principle*, ch.1 (with Raymond Hull).

77 Bureaucracy defends the status quo long past the time when the quo has lost its status.
1978 In the *San Francisco Chronicle*, 29 Jan.

Peters, Richard Stanley 1919–

English educationalist, Professor of the Philosophy of Education at the University of London Institute of Education (1962–82). He has written widely on education.

78 What matters is not what any individual thinks, but what is true. A teacher who does not equip his pupils with the rudimentary tools to discover this is substituting indoctrination for teaching.
1966 *Ethics and Education.*

Petersen, Henry Edward 1921–

US Assistant Attorney General for Prosecutions. He went from clerk to chief of the organized crime and racketeering section of the FBI, Washington (1948–69).

79 What you have just said, Mr President, speaks very well of you as a man. It does not speak well of you as a president.
1973 On President Nixon's remark that he would need proof of the guilt of aides John Ehrichman and H R Hadelman on the Watergate break-in and cover-up before he could fire them. Quoted in Richard M Nixon *RN: The Memoirs of Richard Nixon* (1978).

Petersen, Wolfgang 1941–

German film director.

80 It has been condensed and moved around a bit. And we left out the gods.
2004 On how he adapted Homer to make the film *Troy*. Quoted in *The Scotsman*, 14 May.

Petrarch (Francesco Petrarca) 1304–74

Italian poet and classical scholar, responsible for the discovery of several works, including Cicero's letters and two of his orations, and a portion of Quintilian's *De Oratio*. In 1341 he was crowned Poet Laureate in Rome. Most famous for the lyrics of his *Canzionere*, he also composed prose treatises, historical works, and letters.

81 *Continue morimur, ego dum hec scribo, tu dum leges, alii dum audient dumque non audient, ego quoque dum hec leges moriar, tu moreris dum hec scribo, ambo morimur, omnes morimur, semper morimur.*
We are dying continuously: I while I write this, you while you read it, others while they hear or do not hear it. I will be dying as you read this, you will be dying as I write it. We are both dying, we are all dying, we are always dying.
c.1360 Letter to Philippe de Cabassoles.

Petronius Arbiter d. AD 66

Roman satirical writer, usually thought to be the Gaius Petronius whom Tacitus calls the 'arbiter elegantiae' at the court of Nero. His *Satyricon* wittily depicts the licentious life of the moneyed class of freedmen in southern Italy.

82 *Abiit ad plures.*
He has gone to the majority.
(ie He has died.) *Satyricon*, 42.

83 *Qualis dominus talis est servus.*
Like master like man.
Satyricon, 58.

Petty, Sir William 1623–87

English physician and pioneer economist. From humble beginnings he rose to become Professor of Anatomy at Oxford and of Music at Gresham's College, London. As Physician-General to Cromwell's army he acquired an immense fortune, and he was a founder of the Royal Society of London.

84 If a man bring to London an ounce of Silver out of the Earth in Peru in the same time that he can produce a

bushel of Corn, then one is the natural price of the other.
1662 *Treatise of Taxes.*

85 Labour is the Father and active principle of Wealth, as lands are the Mother.
1662 *Treatise of Taxes.*

86 Instead of using only comparative Words and intellectual Arguments, I have taken the course...to express myself in Terms of Number, Weight, or Measure; to use only Arguments of Sense, and to consider only such Causes, as have visible Foundations in Nature.
1690 *Political Arithmetick.*

Phelps, Edward John 1822–1900

US lawyer and diplomat.

87 The man who makes no mistakes does not usually make anything.
1889 In a speech given in London.

Philby, Kim 1912–88

British double-agent.

88 To betray, you must first belong.
1967 In the *Sunday Times*, 17 Dec.

Philip II 1527–98

King of Spain (1556–98), Naples and Sicily (1554–98) and Portugal (1580–98). He married Mary I in 1554, becoming joint sovereign of England until her death in 1558. A secular champion of the Counter-Reformation, he had more success against Turks than Protestant Dutch and English.

89 England's chief defence depends upon the navy being always ready to defend the realm against invasion.
c.1555 Submission to the Privy Council while King-Consort of England.

Philips, Ambrose c.1675–1749

English poet.

90 The flowers anew, returning seasons bring;
But beauty faded has no second spring.
1708 *The First Pastoral*, 'Lobbin'.

Philips, Katherine *née Fowler* 1632–64

English poet. Her reputation was greater during her brief life, when she was known as 'the Matchless Orinda', than after her death, but she proved a significant model to later female poets. Her poems were surreptitiously printed in 1664 and issued in 1667.

91 Thus our twin souls in one shall grow,
And teach the world new love,
Redeem the age and sex, and show
A flame fate dares not move:
And courting death to be our friend,
Our lives, together too, shall end.
1664 'To Mrs. M. A. at Parting'.

92 I did but see him, and he disappeared,
I did but touch the rosebud, and it fell;
A sorrow unforeseen and scarcely feared,
So ill can mortals their afflictions spell.
'On the Death of My First and Dearest Child, Hector Philips'. (Issued 1667).

Phillips, Arthur Angell 1900–85

Australian academic and literary critic. He wrote for the Melbourne literary journal *Meanjin* and much of his critical writing was collected as *Responses* (1971).

93 Cultural Cringe.
1950 On Australia's reliance on British cultural values. In *Meanjin.*

Phillips, Edward O 1931–

Canadian novelist.

94 To grow older is to realize the universe is Copernican, not Ptolemaic, and that self and the loved one do not form the epicentre of the solar system.
1990 *Sunday Best.*

Phillips, Wendell 1811–84

US abolitionist, born in Boston, Massachusetts. Called to the Bar in 1834, by 1837 he was chief orator of the anti-slavery party, associated with William Lloyd Garrison.

95 Some doubt the courage of the Negro. Go to Haiti and stand on those fifty thousand graves of the best soldiers France ever had, and ask them what they think of the Negro's sword.
1861 Address on Toussaint l'Ouverture, referring to the War of Haitian Independence, 1804.

Picasso, Pablo Ruiz y 1881–1973

Spanish painter, graphic artist, sculptor and ceramicist. The melancholy studies of his early 'blue period' (1902–4) gave way to a life-affirming 'pink period' (1904–6). In later works he moved towards Cubism, along with Georges Braque.

96 There is no abstract art. You must always start with something. Afterward you can remove all traces of reality.
1935 In an interview with Christian Zervos, editor of *Cahiers d'Art*, translated by Alfred H Barr Jr in his *Picasso: Fifty Years of His Art* (1946).

97 Art is not the application of a canon of beauty but what the instinct and the brain can conceive beyond any canon. When we love a woman we don't start measuring her limbs.
1935 In an interview with Christian Zervos, editor of *Cahiers d'Art*, translated by Alfred H Barr Jr in his *Picasso: Fifty Years of His Art* (1946).

98 No, painting is not done to decorate apartments. It is an instrument of war for attack and defense against the enemy.
1945 Responding to claims that his Communism was a mere caprice. Quoted in Alfred H Barr Jr *Picasso: Fifty Years of His Art* (1946).

99 I paint objects as I think them, not as I see them.
Quoted in John Golding *Cubism* (1959).

1 God is really only another artist. He invented the giraffe, the elephant, and the cat. He has no real style. He just goes on trying other things.
Quoted in F Gilot and C Lake *Life with Picasso* (1964), pt.1.

2 We all know that art is not truth. Art is a lie that makes us realize truth.
Quoted in Dore Ashton *Picasso on Art* (1972).

Pickens, T(homas) Boone, Jr 1928–

US oilman and hydrocarbon investor, a geologist with Phillips

Petroleum Co (1951–5) then founder and chair of Mesa Petroleum Co until 1996.

3 Work eight hours and sleep eight hours and make sure they are not the same.
1992 In NPR broadcast, 28 May.

Pickford, Mary *originally Gladys Mary Smith* 1893–1979

US actress, born in Canada. Known as 'America's sweetheart', she played innocent heroines in a series of silent films (1909–29), and made her sound debut in 1929.

4 Adding sound to movies would be like putting lipstick on the Venus de Milo.
Recalled on her death, 29 May 1979.

Pierce, C(harles) S(aunders) 1839–1914

US philosopher.

5 It is the man of science, eager to have his every opinion regenerated, his every idea rationalized, by drinking at the fountain of fact, and devoting all the energies of his life to the cult of truth, not as he understands it, but as he does not yet understand it, that ought properly to be called a philosopher.
Selected Writings, 'Lessons on the History of Science'.

Piercy, Marge 1936–

US novelist and poet. Novels including *Woman on the Edge of Time* (1975) trace the emerging feminist consciousness of the post-1960s generation. Later works include the novel *Three Women* (1999) and the volume of poetry *Colors Passing Through Us* (2003).

6 Burning dinner is not incompetence but war.
1983 *Stone, Paper, Knife*, 'What's that smell in the kitchen?'

7 Your anger was a climate I inhabited
like a desert in a dry frigid weather
of high thin air and ivory sun,
sand dunes the wind lifted into stinging
clouds that blinded and choked me
where the only ice was in the blood.
1983 *Stone, Paper, Knife*, 'The Weight'.

8 On this twelfth day of my diet
I would rather die satiated
than slim.
1983 *Stone, Paper, Knife*, 'On Mental Corsets'.

9 Art is a game only if you play at it,
a mirror that reflects from the inside out.
1983 *Stone, Paper, Knife*, 'Stone, Paper, Knife'.

10 Hope sleeps in our bones like a bear
waiting for spring to rise and walk.
1983 *Stone, Paper, Knife*, 'Stone, Paper, Knife'.

Piero della Francesca c.1420–1492

Italian Renaissance painter.

11 Painting is nothing but a representation of surfaces and solids foreshortened or enlarged, and put on the plane of the picture in accordance with the fashion in which the real objects seen by the eye appear on this plane.
c.1480–1490 *De Prospectiva Pingendi*.

Piggott, Lester Keith 1935–

English jockey. He became champion jockey 11 times, from 1948, and totalled 30 Classic winners, including nine Derbies.

12 People ask me why I ride with my bottom in the air. Well, I've got to put it somewhere.
Quoted in Colin Jarman *The Guinness Dictionary of Sports Quotations* (1990).

13 When I won the Derby on Never Say Die I went home and cut the lawn. I haven't cut the lawn since.
2004 In the *Observer*, 30 May.

Piglia, Ricardo 1941–

Argentinian novelist and critic.

14 *Sencillamente se me ocurre que la parodia se ha desplazado y hoy invade los gestos, las acciones. Donde antes había acontecimientos, experiencias, pasiones, hoy quedan sólo parodias. Eso trataba a veces de decirle a Marcelo en mis cartas: que la parodia ha sustituido por completo a la historia.*
It's simply that I believe that parody has been displaced and that it now invades all gestures and actions. Where there used to be events, experiences, passions, now there are nothing but parodies. This is what I tried to tell Marcelo so many times in my letters: that parody had completely replaced history.
1980 *Respiración artificial*, pt.2, ch.4 (translated as *Artificial Respiration*, 1994).

Pigou, Arthur Cecil 1877–1959

English economist, a professor at Cambridge (1908–43).

15 If a man marries his housekeeper or his cook, the national dividend is diminished.
1920 *Economics of Welfare*.

Pilger, John 1939–

Australian journalist, writer and film-maker highly regarded for his investigative work in Vietnam and Cambodia. His documentary films include *Year Zero—The Silent Death of Cambodia* (1979), *Death of a Nation* (1994), about the slaughter in East Timor, and *Breaking the Silence: Truth and Lies in the War on Terror* (2003).

16 I used to see Vietnam as a war rather than a country.
1978 *Do you remember Vietnam?*

17 What Nixon and Kissinger began, Pol Pot completed.
Collected in *Distant Voices* (1992).

Pindar c.522–440 BC

Greek lyric poet, born near Thebes in Boeotia.

18 Seek not, my soul, immortal life, but make the most of the resources that are within your reach.
Pythia, 3.109.

Pinochet Ugarte, Augusto 1915–

Chilean soldier and dictator. He led the coup that overthrew the government of Salvador Allende (1973) and in 1980 enacted a constitution giving himself an eight-year presidential term (1981–9); he retained his military command until 1998, the year he was arrested in the UK at the request of Spain. General Pinochet was ruled unfit to face extradition, and in 2000 returned to Chile where attempts have been made to remove his immunity from prosecution.

19 I am not a dictator. It's just that I have a grumpy face.
Attributed.

Pinter, Harold 1930–

English playwright, director and actor. Such early plays as *The Birthday Party* (1958) were dismissed as obscure, but after *The Caretaker* (1960) his work underwent a reappraisal and he was acknowledged as one of the most interesting playwrights of his generation. Subsequent works for the stage have included *The Homecoming* (1965) and *Celebration* (1999). He has also written numerous filmscripts, including *The Servant* (1963) and *The French Lieutenant's Woman* (1981).

20 If only I could get down to Sidcup! I've been waiting for the weather to break. He's got my papers, this man I left them with, it's got it all down there, I could prove everything.
1960 *The Caretaker*, act 1.

21 The weasel under the cocktail cabinet.
1962 His reply when asked what his plays were about. Quoted in J Russell Taylor *Anger and After*.

22 I no longer feel banished from myself.
1995 On completing his first full-length play in 17 years. In *Newsweek*, 18 Sep.

Pirandello, Luigi 1867–1936

Italian playwright, novelist and short-story writer. His play *Right You Are (If You Think You Are)* (1917) was followed by such innovative works as *Six Characters in Search of an Author* (1921), *Enrico IV* (1922) and *Tonight We Improvise* (1929). He was awarded a Nobel prize in 1934.

23 Six Characters in Search of an Author.
1921 Title of play (translated 1922).

24 Drama is action, sir, action and not confounded philosophy.
1921 *Six Characters in Search of an Author* (translated 1922).

Pirsig, Robert M(aynard) 1928–

US writer. His most noted book is *Zen and the Art of Motorcycle Maintenance* (1974), a rumination on life and technology after a cross-country motorcycle trip.

25 The Buddha, the Godhead, resides quite as comfortably in the circuits of a digital computer or the gears of a cycle transmission as he does at the top of a mountain or in the petals of a flower.
1974 *Zen and the Art of Motorcycle Maintenance*, pt.1, ch.1.

26 When people are fanatically dedicated to political or religious faiths or any other kind of dogmas or goals, it's always because these dogmas or goals are in doubt.
1974 *Zen and the Art of Motorcycle Maintenance*, pt.2, ch.3.

27 Mental reflection is so much more interesting than TV it's a shame more people don't switch over to it. They probably think what they hear is unimportant but it never is.
1974 *Zen and the Art of Motorcycle Maintenance*, pt.3, ch.17.

28 One thing about pioneers that you don't hear mentioned is that they are invariably, by their nature, mess-makers.
1974 *Zen and the Art of Motorcycle Maintenance*, pt.3, ch.21.

29 One geometry can not be more true than another; it can only be more *convenient*. Geometry is not true, it is advantageous.
1974 *Zen and the Art of Motorcycle Maintenance*, pt.3, ch.22.

30 Traditional scientific method has always been at the very *best*, 20-20 hindsight. It's good for seeing where you've been. It's good for testing the truth of what you think you know, but it can't tell you where you *ought* to go.
1974 *Zen and the Art of Motorcycle Maintenance*, pt.3, ch.24.

31 That's the classical mind at work, runs fine inside but looks dingy on the surface.
1974 *Zen and the Art of Motorcycle Maintenance*, pt.3, ch.26.

Pissarro, Camille 1830–1903

French Impressionist artist. Most of his works were painted in or around Paris.

32 But as I see it, the most corrupt art is the sentimental—the art of orange blossoms which make pale women swoon.
1883 Letter to his son Lucien.

33 Watercolour is not especially difficult, but I must warn you to steer clear of those pretty English watercolourists, so skilful and alas so weak, and so often too truthful.
1883 Letter to his son Lucien, Jul.

34 Draw more and more often—remember Degas.
1883 Letter to his son Lucien, Oct.

35 Observe that it is a grave error to believe that all mediums of art are not closely tied to their time.
1898 Letter to his son Lucien.

Pitt, William, 1st Earl of Chatham *known as* ***the Elder*** 1708–78

English statesman and orator. In 1756 he became Secretary of State, virtual Prime Minister. Forced to resign in 1757 by George II, he was recalled by public demand but resigned again in 1761 when his Cabinet refused to declare war on Spain. He formed a new ministry in 1766, but resigned in ill health (1768).

36 The atrocious crime of being a young man, which [Walpole] has, with such spirit and decency, charged upon me, I shall neither attempt to palliate nor deny; but content myself with wishing that I may be one of those whose follies cease with their youth, and not of those who continue ignorant in spite of their age and experience.
1741 Speech to the House of Commons, 6 Mar.

37 It is now apparent that this great, this powerful, this formidable kingdom is considered only as a province of a despicable electorate.
1742 Speech to the House of Commons, 10 Dec.

38 I know that I can save this country and that no one else can.
1756 In conversation with one of his private secretaries, Nov.

39 I was called by my sovereign and by the voice of the people to assist the State when others had abdicated the service of it. That being so, no one can be surprised that I will go on no longer, since my advice is not taken. Being responsible, I will direct—and will be responsible for nothing that I do not direct.
1761 On informing Cabinet of his resignation, 3 Oct.

40 I rejoice that America has resisted. Three millions of people, so dead to all the feelings of liberty, as voluntarily to submit to be slaves, would have been fit instruments to make slaves of the rest.

1766 Speech to the House of Commons, 14 Jan.

41 Where laws end, tyranny begins.
1770 Speech to the House of Lords, 2 Mar.

42 The spirit that now resists your taxation in America is...the same spirit that established the great fundamental, essential maxim of your liberties—that no subject of England shall be taxed but by his own consent. The glorious spirit of Whiggism animates three million in America, who prefer poverty with liberty to gilded chains and sordid affluence; and who will die in defence of their rights as men, as free men.
1775 Speech to the House of Lords, 20 Jan.

43 You cannot conquer America.
1777 Speech to the House of Lords, 18 Nov.

44 If I were an American, as I am an Englishman, while a foreign troop was landed in my country, I never would lay down my arms—never—never—never!
1777 Speech to the House of Lords, 18 Nov.

Pitt, William *known as* ***the Younger*** 1759–1806

English statesman and Prime Minister (1783–1801, 1804–6), son of William Pitt, the Elder. Elected MP in 1781, he became Chancellor in 1782 and Britain's youngest-ever Prime Minister in 1783. He resigned over the King's opposition to the union with Ireland in 1801 but returned in 1804 to lead a coalition of European powers against Napoleon.

45 I am sure that the immediate abolition of the slave trade is the first, the principal, the most indispensable act of policy, of duty and of justice the legislature of this country has to take, if it is indeed their wish to secure those important objects... For we continue to this hour a barbarous traffic in slaves, we continue it even yet, in spite of all our great and undeniable pretensions as civilisation.
1792 Speech to the House of Commons, 2 Apr. The House did not abolish slavery until 1806.

46 We must recollect...what it is we have at stake, what it is we have to contend for. It is for our property, it is for our liberty, it is for our independence, nay for our existence as a nation; it is for our character, it is for our very name as Englishmen, it is for everything dear and valuable to man on this side of the grave.
1803 Speech, 22 Jul, on the breaking of the Peace of Amiens and the resumption of the war with Napoleon. Quoted in *Speeches of the Rt. Hon. William Pitt* (1806), vol.4.

47 Amid the wreck and the misery of nations it is our just exaltation that we have continued superior to all that ambition or despotism could effect; and our still higher exaltation ought to be that we provide not only for our own safety but hold out a prospect for nations now bending under the yoke of tyranny of what the exertions of a free people can effect.
1804 Speech to the House of Commons, 25 Apr.

48 Roll up that map; it will not be wanted these ten years.
1805 Of a map of Europe. Remark on hearing of Napoleon's victory at Austerlitz, Dec. Quoted in Earl Stanhope *Life of the Rt. Hon. William Pitt*, vol.4 (1862), ch.43.

49 England has saved herself by her exertions, and will, as I trust, save Europe by her example.
1805 Replying to a toast in which he had been described as the saviour of his country in the wars with France. Quoted in R Coupland *War Speeches of William Pitt* (1915).

50 I think that I could eat one of Bellamy's veal pies.
1806 Attributed last words, 23 Jan.

Pittacus of Mytilene 650–570 BC

Greek ruler, one of the Seven Wise Men of Greece.

51 Know thine opportunity.
Attributed. Quoted in *Chambers Biographical Dictionary* (5th edn, 1990).

Pius II *real name* ***Enea Silvio de Piccolomini*** 1405–64

Italian-born churchman, Pope from 1458. After entering the service of Emperor Frederick II he took orders, becoming Bishop of Trieste and, on returning to Italy (1456), Cardinal then Pope. He tried unsuccessfully to organize a crusade against the Turks.

52 Of the two lights of Christendom, one has been extinguished.
1453 Attributed, on hearing of the fall of Constantinople to the Turks, 29 May.

53 Glorious deeds are not embraced by democracies, least of all by merchants, who, being by their nature intent on profit, loathe those splendid things that cannot be achieved without expense.
1584 *Commentaries*. Quoted in J H Plumb (ed) *The Horizon Book of the Renaissance* (1961, new edn by Penguin, 1982).

54 Nothing gives the Scots more pleasure than to hear the English abused.
1584 *Commentaries*. Quoted in J H Plumb (ed) *The Horizon Book of the Renaissance* (1961, new edn by Penguin, 1982).

Pius XII *real name* ***Eugenio Pacelli*** 1876–1958

Italian-born churchman, Pope from 1939.

55 Sport, rightly conceived, is an occupation carried out by the whole man. It renders the body a more perfect instrument of the soul and at the same time makes the soul itself a finer instrument of the whole man in seeking for Truth and in transmitting it to others. In this way it helps a man to reach that End to which all other ends are subordinate, the service and the greater glory of his Creator.
1945 Speech to the Central School of Sports of the USA, 29 Jul.

Pizzaro, Eddie

US stonecarver.

56 We're not all perfect, but we can do something perfect.
1990 On his work at New York's Cathedral of St John the Divine. Quoted in the *New York Times*, 14 Jul.

Planck, Max Karl Ernst 1858–1947

German physicist. He hypothesized that atoms emit and absorb energy only in discrete bundles called quanta and laid the foundations for quantum theory, the basis of contemporary theorizing in physics. He received the 1918 Nobel prize in physics for his work on radiation.

57 Science cannot exist without some small portion of metaphysics.
1931 *The Universe in the Light of Modern Physics*, ch.7.

58 Scientific discovery and scientific knowledge have been achieved only by those who have gone in pursuit of them without any practical purpose whatsoever in view.
1932 *Where is Science Going?* pt.4 (translated by James Murphy).

59 Science cannot solve the ultimate mystery of nature. And that is because, in the last analysis, we ourselves are part of nature and therefore part of the mystery that we are trying to solve.
1932 *Where is Science Going?* pt.4 (translated by James Murphy).

60 A new scientific truth does not triumph by convincing its opponents and making them see the light, but rather because its opponents eventually die, and a new generation grows up that is familiar with it.
A Scientific Autobiography and Other Papers (translated by Frank Gaynor, published 1949).

Plante, Jacques 1929–86

Canadian hockey player, a leading goalkeeper.

61 How would you like a job where, every time you make a mistake, a big red light goes on and 18,000 people boo?
Attributed. Quoted in John Robert Colombo (ed) *Colombo's All-Time Great Canadian Quotations* (1994).

Plath, Sylvia 1932–63

US poet who settled in England after her marriage to Ted Hughes. Her poetry and her only novel, *The Bell Jar* (1963), are deeply introspective. She committed suicide, and much of her work was published posthumously.

62 I am afraid of getting married. Spare me from cooking three meals a day—spare me from the relentless cage of routine and rote.
1949 Diary entry, 13 Nov. Collected in Aurelia Schober Plath (ed) *Letters Home by Sylvia Plath*, 'Diary Supplement' (1949).

63 I could never be a complete scholar or a complete housewife or a complete writer: I must combine a little of all, and thereby be imperfect in all.
1956 Letter to her mother, Aurelia Schober Plath, 25 Feb. Collected in Aurelia Schober Plath (ed) *Letters Home by Sylvia Plath* (1949).

64 Apparently, the most difficult feat for a Cambridge male is to accept a woman not merely as feeling, not merely as thinking, but as managing a complex, vital interweaving of both.
1956 Written while a student at Cambridge University, in *Isis*, 6 May.

65 Love set you going like a fat gold watch.
The midwife slapped your footsoles, and your bald cry
Took its place among the elements.
1961 'Morning Song', published posthumously by Ted Hughes (*Ariel*, 1965).

66 A sort of walking miracle, my skin
Bright as a Nazi lampshade.
1962 'Lady Lazarus', published posthumously by Ted Hughes (*Ariel*, 1965).

67 Dying,
Is an art, like everything else.
I do it exceptionally well.
1962 'Lady Lazarus', published posthumously by Ted Hughes (*Ariel*, 1965).

68 Out of the ash
I rise with my red hair
And I eat men like air.
1962 'Lady Lazarus', published posthumously by Ted Hughes (*Ariel*, 1965).

69 Not God but a swastika
So black no sky could squeak through.
Every woman adores a Fascist,
The boot in the face, the brute
Brute heart of a brute like you.
1962 'Daddy', published posthumously by Ted Hughes (*Ariel*, 1965).

70 Daddy, daddy, you bastard, I'm through.
1962 'Daddy', published posthumously by Ted Hughes (*Ariel*, 1965).

71 Winter is for women—
The woman still at her knitting,
At the cradle of Spanish walnut,
Her body a bulb in the cold and too dumb to think.
1962 'Wintering', published posthumously by Ted Hughes (*Ariel*, 1965).

72 I saw my life branching out before me like the green fig-tree in the story.
From the tip of every branch, like a fat purple fig, a wonderful future beckoned and winked. One fig was a husband and a happy home and children, and another fig was a famous poet…I saw myself sitting in the crotch of this fig-tree, starving to death, just because I couldn't make up my mind which of the figs I would choose. I wanted each and every one of them, but choosing one meant losing all the rest, and, as I sat there, unable to decide, the figs began to wrinkle and go black, and, one by one, they plopped to the ground at my feet.
1963 *The Bell Jar*, ch.7.

73 If neurotic is wanting two mutually exclusive things at one and the same time, then I'm neurotic as hell. I'll be flying back and forth between one mutually exclusive thing and another for the rest of my days.
1963 *The Bell Jar*, ch.8.

Platini, Michel 1955–

French footballer. He scored a record 41 goals in 72 games for France (winning the European championship in 1984). He retired as a player in 1987 and was France's manager from then until 1992.

74 What Zidane does with a ball Maradona could do with an orange.
2000 In *The Independent*, 23 Dec.

Plato c.428–c.348 BC

Greek philosopher, a pupil of Socrates and the teacher of Aristotle. He wrote in the form of dialogues, often with Socrates as a leading character. Some 30 philosophical dialogues and some letters (not all considered genuine) have survived.

75 Let no one ignorant of mathematics enter here.
c.380 BC Inscription over the door of the Academy at Athens.

76 The wisest of you men is he who has realized, like Socrates, that in respect of wisdom he is really worthless.
Apology, 23b (translated by H Tredennick).

77 Socrates is guilty of corrupting the minds of the young, and of believing in deities of his own invention instead of the gods recognized by the state.
The formal indictment in Socrates' trial, quoted in the *Apology*, 24b (translated by H Tredennick).

78 For I spend all my time going about trying to persuade you, young and old, to make your first and chief concern

not for your bodies nor for your possessions, but for the highest welfare of your souls, proclaiming as I go, Wealth does not bring goodness, but goodness brings wealth and every other blessing, both to the individual and to the state.
Apology, 30b (translated by H Tredennick).

79 The unexamined life is not worth living.
Apology, 38a (translated by H Tredennick).

80 Now it is time that we were going, I to die and you to live, but which of us has the happier prospect is unknown to anyone but God.
Apology, 42a (translated by H Tredennick).

81 It is not living, but living well, which we ought to consider most important.
Crito, 48b (translated by H North Fowler, 1923).

82 Your country is more precious and more to be revered and is holier and in higher esteem among the gods and among men of understanding than your mother and your father and all your ancestors.
Crito, 51a–b (translated by H North Fowler, 1923).

83 Men of sound sense have Law for their god, but men without sense Pleasure.
Epistulae, 8. 354e (translated by R G Bury, 1925).

84 To do wrong is the greatest of evils.
Gorgias, 469b (translated by W D Woodhead). There is a similar remark in the *Crito*, 49b.

85 Much more wretched than lack of health in the body, it is to dwell with a soul that is not healthy, but corrupt.
Gorgias, 479b (translated by W R M Lamb, 1967).

86 No one can escape his destiny.
Gorgias, 512e (translated by W R M Lamb, 1967).

87 All the gold upon the earth and all the gold beneath it, does not compensate for lack of virtue.
Leges, 728a (translated by Trevor J Saunders, 1970).

88 Every unjust man is unjust against his will.
Leges, 731c (translated by Trevor J Saunders, 1970).

89 Is virtue something that can be taught?
Meno, 70a (translated by W K C Guthrie).

90 If we are ever to have pure knowledge of anything, we must get rid of the body and contemplate things by themselves with the soul by itself.
Phaedo, 66d (translated by H Tredennick).

91 One should die in silence.
Phaedo, 117e (translated by D Gallop, 1993).

92 Crito, we ought to offer a cock to Asclepius. See to it, and don't forget.
Phaedo, 118a (translated by H Tredennick).

93 For myself I am fairly certain that no wise man believes anyone sins willingly or willingly perpetrates any evil or base act.
Protagoras, 345e (translated by W K C Guthrie).

94 We must now examine whether just people also live better and are happier than unjust ones. I think it's clear already that this is so, but we must look into it further, since the argument concerns no ordinary topic, but the way we ought to live.
Republic, bk.1, 352d (translated by G M A Grube, revised by C D C Reeve).

95 Justice is superior to injustice.
Republic, bk.1, 367b (translated by P Shorey, 1953).

96 The most important stage of any enterprise is the beginning.
Republic, bk.2, 377b (translated by R Waterfield, 1993).

97 Justice is doing one's work and not meddling with what isn't one's own.
Republic, bk.4, 433a (translated by G M A Grube, revised by C D C Reeve).

98 Until philosophers rule as kings or those who are now called kings and leading men genuinely and adequately philosophize, that is, until political power and philosophy entirely coincide...cities will have no rest from evils, nor, I think, will the human race.
Republic, bk.5, 473c (translated by G M A Grube, revised by C D C Reeve).

99 Every soul pursues the good and does whatever it does for its sake.
Republic, bk.6, 505e (translated by G M A Grube, revised by C D C Reeve).

1 The power to learn is present in everyone's soul, and the instrument with which each learns is like an eye that cannot be turned around from darkness to light without turning the whole body.
Republic, bk.7, 518c (translated by G M A Grube, revised by C D C Reeve).

2 If the study of all these sciences which we have enumerated, should ever bring us to their mutual association and relationship, and teach us the nature of the ties which bind them together, I believe that the diligent treatment of them will forward the objects which we have in view, and that the labor, which otherwise would be fruitless, will be well bestowed.
Republic, bk 7, 531d (translated by G M A Grube, revised by C D C Reeve).

3 Extreme freedom can't be expected to lead to anything but a change to extreme slavery, whether for a private individual or for a city.
Republic, bk.8, 564a (translated by G M A Grube, revised by C D C Reeve).

4 God is a geometrician.
Quoted in Plutarch *Symposium*.

Plautus, Titus Maccius c.250–184 BC

Roman comic poet, who worked as a trader and craftsman before writing plays in middle life. He became the most important Latin adapter of the Greek New Comedy, which dealt with social life to the exclusion of politics. Only 21 of his comedies have survived.

5 *Lupus est homo homini, non homo, quom qualis sit non novit.*
A man is a wolf, and not a man, to another man, for as long as he doesn't know what he is like.
Asinaria, 495. The phrase is often rendered 'Homo homini lupus' ('Man is a wolf to another man').

Pliny *full name* Gaius Plinius Secundus *known as* the Elder AD 23–79

Roman statesman, scholar and writer. His only surviving work is his universal encyclopedia, *Historia Naturalis* (37 vols, AD 77). He was killed while observing the eruption of Vesuvius.

6 *Vulgoque veritas iam attributa vino est.*
And truth has come to be proverbially credited to wine.
AD 77 *Historia Naturalis*, bk.14, section 28 (translated by H

Rackham). The phrase is often rendered as 'in vino veritas'.

7 *Addito salis grano.*
With the addition of a pinch of salt.
AD 77 *Historia Naturalis*, bk.23, section 8. This is probably a version of a more ancient proverb, commonly rendered 'cum grano salis'.

Plomer, William 1903–73

South African-born British writer.

8 Out of that bungled, unwise war
An alp of unforgiveness grew.
1960 'The Boer War'.

9 On a sofa upholstered in panther skin
Mona did researches in original sin.
1960 'Mews Flat Mona'.

Plout, David

10 Deathbed utterances, like suicide notes, are a powerful coinage, stamped by an awareness that words can outlive us.
1990 In the *Wall Street Journal*, 26 Sep, reviewing J M Coetzee *Age of Iron* (1990).

Plutarch c.46–c.120 AD

Greek historian, biographer and philosopher. His extant writings include the essays in *Opera Moralia*, and the biographical *Bioi paralleloi* (*Parallel Lives*, translated into English by Thomas North in 1759), a major source for Shakespeare.

11 He who cheats with an oath acknowledges that he is afraid of his enemy, but that he thinks little of God.
Parallel Lives, 'Lysander', ch.8.

12 Though others before him had triumphed three times, Pompeius, by having gained his first triumph over Libya, his second over Europe, and this the last over Asia, seemed in a manner to have brought the whole world into his three triumphs.
Referring to Pompey's victories against the Marian party in Africa, in Spain, and against Mithridates in Asia Minor (c.62 BC).
Parallel Lives, 'Pompeius', ch.45.

Pobedonostsev, Constantin Petrovich 1827–1907

Russian jurist, tutor to Alexander III and Nicholas II. Initially a liberal, he became an uncompromising champion of autocracy and the supremacy of the Russian Orthodox Church, strongly opposed to westernization.

13 Parliaments are the great lie of our time.
Moskovskii Shornik.

Po Chü-I 772–846

Chinese poet and civil servant who rose to become the Governor of a number of different cities in China.

14 But now that age comes
A moment of joy is harder and harder to get.
812 'The Chrysanthemums in the Eastern Garden' (in *Chinese Poems*, translated by Arthur Waley, 1946).

15 Deeper and deeper, one's love of old friends;
Fewer and fewer, one's dealings with young men.
835 *Old Age*.

Poe, Edgar Allan 1809–49

US poet and short-story writer, a pioneer of the modern detective story, whose poetry emphasizes the beauty of melancholy. He is best known for stories such as 'The Tell-Tale Heart' (1843) and his poem 'The Raven' (1845).

16 I know not how it was—but, with the first glimpse of the building, a sense of insufferable gloom pervaded my spirit… There was an iciness, a sinking, a sickening of the heart—an unredeemed dreariness of thought which no goading of the imagination could torture into aught of the sublime.
1839 'The Fall of the House of Usher', in the *Gentleman's Magazine*, Sep.

17 As the strong man exults in his physical ability, delighting in such exercises as call his muscles into action, so glories the analyst in that moral activity which *disentangles*.
1841 Of detective work. 'The Murders in the Rue Morgue', in the *Gentleman's Magazine*, Apr.

18 It will be found, in fact, that the ingenious are always fanciful, and the *truly* imaginative never otherwise than analytic.
1841 'The Murders in the Rue Morgue', in the *Gentleman's Magazine*, Apr.

19 And now was acknowledged the presence of the Red Death. He had come like a thief in the night. And one by one dropped the revellers in the blood-bedecked halls of their revel, and died each in the despairing posture of his fall.
1842 'The Masque of the Red Death', in the *Gentleman's Magazine*, May.

20 There is something in the unselfish and self-sacrificing love of a brute, which goes directly to the heart of him who has had frequent occasion to test the paltry friendship and gossamer fidelity of mere *Man*.
1843 'The Black Cat', in the *United States Saturday Post*, 19 Aug.

21 I have no faith in human perfectibility… Man is now only more active—not more happy—nor more wise, than he was 6,000 years ago.
1844 Letter to James Russell Lowell, 2 Jul.

22 On desperate seas long wont to roam,
Thy hyacinth hair, thy classic face,
Thy Naiad airs have brought me home
To the glory that was Greece,
And the grandeur that was Rome.
1845 'To Helen', stanza 2.

23 Yes, Heaven is thine; but this
Is a world of sweets and sours;
Our flowers are merely—flowers.
1845 'Israfel', stanza 7.

24 'Take thy beak from out my heart, and take thy form from off my door!'
Quoth the raven, 'Nevermore.'
1845 'The Raven', stanza 17. In *American Review*, Feb 1845.

25 The death…of a beautiful woman is, unquestionably, the most poetical topic in the world.
1846 'The Philosophy of Composition', in *Graham's Magazine*, Apr.

26 Mournful and Never-ending Remembrance.
1846 Of the significance of the bird in his poem 'The Raven'. 'The Philosophy of Composition', in *Graham's Magazine*, Apr.

27 To be *thoroughly* conversant with a Man's heart is to take our final lesson in the iron-clasped volume of despair.

1849 'Marginalia', in the *Southern Literary Messenger*, Jun.

28 The nose of a mob is its imagination. By this, at any time, it can be quietly led.
1849 'Marginalia', in the *Southern Literary Messenger*, Jul.

29 To vilify a great man is the readiest way in which a little man can himself attain greatness.
1849 *Marginalia 1844–49*.

30 Thank Heaven! the crisis—
The danger is past,
And the lingering illness
Is over at last—
And the fever called 'Living'
Is conquered at last.
1850 'For Annie'.

Poelzig, Hans 1869–1936

German Expressionist architect, Professor of Architecture at Breslau Academy of Arts (1900) and later director.

31 We cannot do without the past in solving the architectural problems of our own day.
1906 *Das Deutsche Kunstgewerbe 1906*.

Poincaré, (Jules) Henri 1854–1912

French mathematician and physicist. In his research in the theory of functions he contributed greatly to the field of mathematical physics.

32 If we ought not to fear mortal truth, still less should we dread scientific truth. In the first place it can not conflict with ethics… But if science is feared, it is above all because it can give no happiness… Man, then, can not be happy through science but today he can much less be happy without it.
1904 *The Value of Science*.

33 Science is facts. Just as houses are made of stones, so science is made of facts. But a pile of stones is not a house and a collection of facts is not necessarily a science.
1905 *Science and Hypothesis*, ch.9.

34 The scientist does not study nature because it is useful to do so. He studies it because he takes pleasure in it, and he takes pleasure in it because it is beautiful.
1909 *Science and Method*, vol.1, ch.1 (translated by Francis Maitland).

Poindexter, John Marlan 1936–

US naval officer and statesman, chief of naval operations in the 1970s. He became Reagan's National Security Adviser in 1985. He resigned (Nov 1986) after implication in the Irangate scandal, and was later convicted. His sentence was overturned by the Federal appeals court in 1991. He was head of the Pentagon's controversial Information Awareness Office until 2003.

35 I made a very deliberate decision not to ask the President, so that I could insulate him from the decision and provide some future deniability for him if it ever leaked out.
1987 On his action in diverting funds from arms sales at Iran–Contra hearings, 15 Jul.

Polanski, Roman 1933–

French–Polish film director, scriptwriter and actor, known for such films as *Rosemary's Baby* (1968).

36 The best films are the best because of no one but the director.
Quoted in Leslie Halliwell *Halliwell's Filmgoer's Book of Quotes* (1973).

Pollock, (Paul) Jackson 1912–56

US artist, best known for his technique of pouring or dripping paint on the canvas. A leader of 'action painting' and the Abstract Expressionist movement, his works include the enormous *One* and the monochrome *Echo and Blue Poles*.

37 On the floor I am more at ease, I feel nearer, more a part of the painting, since this way I can walk around it, work from the four sides and literally be 'in' the painting.
1947 Quoted in Italo Tomassoni *Pollock* (1968).

38 Abstract painting is abstract. It confronts you.
Quoted in Francis V O'Connor *Jackson Pollock* (1967).

Polo, Marco c.1254–1324

Venetian trader and traveller. In 1271–5 he accompanied his father and uncle to China and stayed on for 16 years, becoming the envoy of Kublai Khan. He returned to Venice in 1295 and, imprisoned by the Genoese, used his time to dictate his memoirs.

39 Now it came to pass…that the Tartars made them a King whose name was Chinghis Kaan [Genghis Khan]. He was a man of great worth, and of great ability, and valour. And as soon as the news that he had been chosen King was spread abroad through those countries, all the Tartars in the world came to him and owned him for their Lord.
c.1310 Quoted in Col. Henry Yule (ed and trans) *The Book of Ser Marco Polo, the Venetian, Concerning the Kingdoms and Marvels of the East* (1871), 2 vols

40 I have not told even the half of the things that I have seen.
c.1320 On being accused of exaggeration in his accounts of China. Quoted in R H Poole and P Finch (eds) *Newnes Pictorial Knowledge* (1950), vol.2.

Pol Pot *real name* Saloth Sar 1925–98

Cambodian political and military leader whose Khmer Rouge army took over Cambodia in 1975. Prime Minister of Kampuchea (1976–8), he presided over the deaths of over a million people, by starvation or murder, before Vietnam liberated the country in Dec 1978.

41 We will burn the old grass and the new will grow.
c.1975 Quoted in John Pilger *Distant Voices* (1992), section 5.

42 If our people can build Angkor Wat they can do anything.
1979 Quoted by Dennis Bloodworth in the *Observer*, 20 Jan 1980.

Pol-Roger, Christian

US vintner.

43 Champagne! In victory, one deserves it; in defeat, one needs it.
1988 'Champagne, a Magnum Opus', in the *New York Times*, 31 Dec.

Pomfret, John 1667–1702

English clergyman and poet.

44 We live and learn, but not the wiser grow.
1700 'Reason'.

Pompadour, Madame de *full name* ***Jeanne Antoinette Poisson, Marquise de Pompadour*** 1721–64

French mistress of Louis XV. Installed at Versailles (1745), she assumed control of public affairs and swayed state policy, appointing her favourites. She was a lavish patron of the arts and literature.

45 The Duke takes a town in the same light-hearted way as he seduces a woman.
1756 Of Cardinal Duc de Richelieu, following his capture of the reputedly impregnable Fort St Phillip, Minorca, by taking his men up a cliff face to surprise the defenders. Quoted in Nancy Mitford *Madame de Pompadour* (1954), p.201.

46 *Après nous le déluge.*
After us the deluge.
1757 Quoted in Madame de Hausset *Mémoires* (1824).

Pompéia, Raul d'Avila 1863–95

Brazilian novelist, best known for *O Atenéu* (1888), the story of life in an oppressive boarding school. Unable to cope any longer with his emotional problems, he committed suicide at the age of 32.

47 *O tédio é a grande enfermidade da escola, o tédio corruptor que tanto se pode gerar da monotonia do trabalho como da ociosidade.*
Tedium is the worst disease in schools, the corrupting tedium that comes equally from monotony, work or leisure.
1888 *O Atenéu* ('The Atheneum'), ch.7.

Pompidou, Georges 1911–74

Second President (1969–74) of the Fifth French Republic. He served in the Resistance during World War II, and was a member of Charles de Gaulle's staff (1944–6) before taking control of the provisional government.

48 There are three roads to ruin—women, gambling and technicians. The most pleasant is women, the quickest is with gambling, but the surest is with technicians.
1968 In the *Sunday Telegraph*.

Pop, Iggy 1947–

US rock singer and songwriter.

49 What seems to pass for guitar more and more now is some wimp with a fuzz box. Somewhere around Hendrix, the line was crossed. Hendrix had both: he had the hands and he had the fuzz box. Now all they have is the fuzz box.
2004 In *Rolling Stone*, 15 Apr.

Pope, Alexander 1688–1744

English poet and essayist, crippled at 12 by a tubercular infection of the spine. His work, distinguished by its technical brilliance and skilful satire, includes *The Rape of the Lock* (1712, enlarged 1714), *The Dunciad* (1728, revised 1742) and *An Essay on Man* (1732–4).

50 Where'er you walk, cool gales shall fan the glade,
Trees where you sit, shall crowd into a shade:
Where'er you tread, the blushing flowers shall rise,
And all things flourish where you turn your eyes.
1709 *Pastorals*, 'Summer', l.73–6.

51 Some are bewildered in the maze of schools,
And some made coxcombs Nature meant but fools.
1711 *An Essay on Criticism*, l.26–7.

52 Some have at first for wits, then poets passed,
Turned critics next, and proved plain fools at last.
1711 *An Essay on Criticism*, l.36–7.

53 First follow Nature, and your judgement frame
By her just standard, which is still the same:
Unerring Nature, still divinely bright,
One clear, unchanged, and universal light,
Life, force and beauty must to all impart,
At once the source and end and test of art.
1711 *An Essay on Criticism*, l.68–73.

54 A little learning is a dangerous thing;
Drink deep, or taste not the Pierian spring:
There shallow draughts intoxicate the brain,
And drinking largely sobers us again.
1711 *An Essay on Criticism*, l.215–8.

55 Poets like painters, thus unskilled to trace
The naked nature and the living grace,
With gold and jewels cover ev'ry part,
And hide with ornaments their want of art.
True wit is Nature to advantage dressed,
What oft was thought, but ne'er so well expressed.
1711 *An Essay on Criticism*, l.293–8.

56 Expression is the dress of thought.
1711 *An Essay on Criticism*, l.318.

57 In Words, as Fashions, the same rule will hold;
Alike Fantastic, if too New, or Old;
Be not the *first* by whom the New are try'd,
Nor the *last* to lay the Old aside.
1711 *An Essay on Criticism*, l.333–6.

58 As some to church repair,
Not for the doctrine, but the music there.
1711 *An Essay on Criticism*, l.342–3.

59 True ease in writing comes from art, not chance,
As those move easiest who have learned to dance.
'Tis not enough no harshness gives offence,
The sound must seem an echo to the sense.
1711 *An Essay on Criticism*, l.362–5.

60 To err is human; to forgive, divine.
1711 *An Essay on Criticism*, l.525.

61 All seems infected that th'infected spy,
As all looks yellow to the jaundiced eye.
1711 *An Essay on Criticism*, l.558–9.

62 The bookful blockhead, ignorantly read,
With loads of learned lumbers in his head.
1711 *An Essay on Criticism*, l.612–3.

63 For fools rush in where angels fear to tread.
1711 *An Essay on Criticism*, l.625.

64 What dire offence from am'rous causes springs,
What mighty contests rise from trivial things.
1714 *The Rape of the Lock*, canto 1, l.1–2.

65 Now lap-dogs give themselves the rousing shake,
And sleepless lovers, just at twelve, awake.
1714 *The Rape of the Lock*, canto 1, l.15–16.

66 They shift the moving Toyshop of their heart.
1714 *The Rape of the Lock*, canto 1, l.100.

67 Bright as the sun, her eyes the gazers strike,
And, like the sun, they shine on all alike.
1714 *The Rape of the Lock*, canto 2, l.13–14.

68 If to her share some female errors fall,

Look on her face, and you'll forget 'em all.
1714 *The Rape of the Lock*, canto 2, l.17–18.

69 Belinda smiled, and all the world was gay.
1714 *The Rape of the Lock*, canto 2, l.52.

70 Whether the nymph shall break Diana's law,
Or some frail china jar receive a flaw,
Or stain her honour, or her new brocade,
Forget her pray'rs, or miss a masquerade.
1714 *The Rape of the Lock*, canto 2, l.105–8.

71 Here thou, great Anna! whom three realms obey,
Dost sometimes counsel take—and sometimes tea.
1714 *The Rape of the Lock*, canto 3, l.7–8.

72 At ev'ry word a reputation dies.
1714 *The Rape of the Lock*, canto 3, l.16.

73 The hungry judges soon the sentence sign,
And wretches hang that jury-men may dine.
1714 *The Rape of the Lock*, canto 3, l.21–2.

74 Let spades be trumps! she said, and trumps they were.
1714 *The Rape of the Lock*, canto 3, l.46.

75 Not louder shrieks to pitying heav'n are cast,
When husbands or when lapdogs breathe their last.
1714 *The Rape of the Lock*, canto 3, l.157–8.

76 Sir Plume, of amber snuff-box justly vain,
And the nice conduct of a clouded cane.
1714 *The Rape of the Lock*, canto 4, l.123–4.

77 Beauties in vain their pretty eyes may roll;
Charms strike the sight, but merit wins the soul.
1714 *The Rape of the Lock*, canto 5, l.33–4.

78 Happy the man, whose wish and care
A few paternal acres bound,
Content to breathe his native air,
In his own ground.
1717 'Ode on Solitude'.

79 Is there no bright reversion in the sky,
For those who greatly think or bravely die?
1717 *Elegy to the Memory of an Unfortunate Lady*, l.9–10.

80 On all the line a sudden vengeance waits,
And frequent hearses shall besiege your gates.
1717 *Elegy to the Memory of an Unfortunate Lady*, l.37–8.

81 By foreign hands thy dying eyes were closed,
By foreign hands thy decent limbs composed,
By foreign hands thy humble grave adorned,
By strangers honoured, and by strangers mourned.
1717 *Elegy to the Memory of an Unfortunate Lady*, l.51–4.

82 Oh happy state! when souls each other draw,
When love is liberty, and nature, law:
All then is full, possessing, and possessed,
No craving void left aching in the breast.
1717 'Eloisa to Abelard'.

83 No, make me mistress to the man I love;
If there be yet another name more free,
More fond than mistress, make me that to thee!
1717 'Eloisa to Abelard'.

84 Of all affliction taught a lover yet,
'Tis sure the hardest science to forget!
How shall I lose the sin, yet keep the sense,
And love th'offender, yet detest th'offence?
How the dear object from the crime remove,
Or how distinguish penitence from love?
1717 'Eloisa to Abelard'.

85 How happy is the blameless Vestal's lot!
The world forgetting, by the world forgot.
1717 'Eloisa to Abelard'.

86 And wine can of their wits the wise beguile,
Make the sage frolic, and the serious smile.
1726 *Odyssey*, bk.14, l.520–1.

87 Welcome the coming, speed the parting guest.
1726 *Odyssey*, bk. 15, l.83.

88 To endeavour to work upon the vulgar with fine sense, is like attempting to hew blocks with a razor.
1727 *Miscellanies*, 'Thoughts on Various Subjects', vol.2.

89 A man should never be ashamed to own he has been in the wrong, which is but saying, in other words, that he is wiser to-day than he was yesterday.
1727 *Miscellanies*, 'Thoughts on Various Subjects', vol.2.

90 It is with narrow-souled people as with narrow-necked bottles: the less they have in them, the more noise they make in pouring it out.
1727 *Miscellanies*, 'Thoughts on Various Subjects', vol.2.

91 When men grow virtuous in their old age, they only make a sacrifice to God of the devil's leavings.
1727 *Miscellanies*, 'Thoughts on Various Subjects', vol.2.

92 The most primitive men are the most credulous.
1727 *Miscellanies*, 'Thoughts on Various Subjects', vol.2.

93 Consult the genius of the place in all.
1731 *Epistles to Several Persons*, 'To Lord Burlington', l.57.

94 Still follow sense, of ev'ry art the soul,
Parts answering parts shall slide into a whole.
1731 *Epistles to Several Persons*, 'To Lord Burlington', l.65–6.

95 No pleasing Intricacies intervene,
No artful wildness to perplex the scene;
Grove nods at grove, each a mirror of the other.
The suff'ring eye inverted Nature sees,
Trees cut to Statues, Statues thick as trees,
With here a Fountain, never to be play'd,
And there a Summer-house, that knows no shade;
Here Amphitrite sails thro' myrtle bow'rs
There Gladiators fight, or die, in flow'rs
Un-water'd see the drooping sea-horse mourn,
And swallows roost in Nilus' dusty Urn.
1731 *Epistles to Several Persons*, 'To Lord Burlington', l.115–25.

96 To rest, the cushion and soft Dean invite,
Who never mentions Hell to ears polite.
1731 *Epistles to Several Persons*, 'To Lord Burlington', l.149–50.

97 Another age shall see the golden ear
Imbrown the slope, and nod on the parterre,
Deep harvests bury all his pride has planned,
And laughing Ceres re-assume the land.
1731 *Epistles to Several Persons*, 'To Lord Burlington', l.173–6.

98 'Tis use alone that sanctifies expense,
And splendour borrows all her rays from sense.
1731 *Epistles to Several Persons*, 'To Lord Burlington', l.179–80.

99 How often are we to die before we go quite off this stage? In every friend we lose a part of ourselves, and the best part.
1732 Letter to Swift, 5 Dec.

1 Who shall decide, when doctors disagree,
And soundest casuists doubt, like you and me?
1733 *Epistles to Several Persons*, 'To Lord Bathurst', l.1–2.

2 But thousands die, without or this or that,

Die, and endow a college, or a cat.
1733 *Epistles to Several Persons*, 'To Lord Bathurst', l.95–6.

3 The ruling passion be it what it will,
The ruling passion conquers reason still.
1733 *Epistles to Several Persons*, 'To Lord Bathurst', l.155–6.

4 Who sees pale Mammon pine amidst his store,
Sees but a backward steward for the poor;
This year a reservoir, to keep and spare,
The next a fountain, spouting through his heir,
In lavish streams to quench a country's thirst,
And men and dogs shall drink him 'till they burst.
1733 *Epistles to Several Persons*, 'To Lord Bathurst', l.173–8.

5 In the worst inn's worst room, with mat half-hung,
The floors of plaister, and the walls of dung,
On once a flock-bed, but repaired with straw,
With tape-tied curtains, never meant to draw,
The George and Garter dangling from that bed
Where tawdry yellow strove with dirty red,
Great Villiers lies.
1733 *Epistles to Several Persons*, 'To Lord Bathurst', l.229–35.

6 Awake, my St. John! leave all meaner things
To low ambition, and the pride of kings.
Let us (since Life can little more supply
Than just to look about us and to die)
Expatiate free o'er all this scene of man;
A mighty maze! but not without a plan.
1733 *An Essay on Man*, epistle 1, l.1–6.

7 Eye Nature's walks, shoot Folly as it flies,
And catch the Manners living as they rise.
Laugh where we must, be candid where we can;
But vindicate the ways of God to man.
1733 *An Essay on Man*, epistle 1, l.13–16.
➡ *See Milton 580:93.*

8 Observe how system into system runs,
What other planets circle other suns.
1733 *An Essay on Man*, epistle 1, l.25–6.

9 Who sees with equal eye, as God of all,
A hero perish, or a sparrow fall,
Atoms or systems into ruin hurled,
And now a bubble burst, and now a world.
1733 *An Essay on Man*, epistle 1, l.87–90.

10 Hope springs eternal in the human breast:
Man never Is, but always To be blest.
1733 *An Essay on Man*, epistle 1, l.95–6.

11 Lo! the poor Indian, whose untutored mind
Sees God in clouds, or hears him in the wind;
His soul proud Science never taught to stray
Far as the solar walk, or milky way;
Yet simple Nature to his hope has giv'n,
Behind the cloud-topped hill, an humbler heav'n.
1733 *An Essay on Man*, epistle 1, l.99–104.

12 Pride still is aiming at the blest abodes,
Men would be angels, angels would be gods.
1733 *An Essay on Man*, epistle 1, l.125–6.

13 The spider's touch, how exquisitely fine!
Feels at each thread, and lives along the line.
1733 *An Essay on Man*, epistle 1, l.217–8.

14 All are but parts of one stupendous whole,
Whose body, Nature is, and God the soul.
1733 *An Essay on Man*, epistle 1, l.267–8.

15 All nature is but art, unknown to thee;
All chance, direction, which thou canst not see;
All discord, harmony, not understood;
All partial evil, universal good:
And, spite of Pride, in erring Reason's spite,
One truth is clear, 'Whatever Is, is RIGHT'
1733 *An Essay on Man*, epistle 1, l.289–94.

16 Know then thyself, presume not God to scan;
The proper study of mankind is man.
Placed on this isthmus of a middle state,
A being darkly wise, and rudely great:
With too much knowledge for the sceptic side,
With too much weakness for the stoic's pride,
He hangs between; in doubt to act or rest,
In doubt to deem himself a god, or beast;
In doubt his mind or body to prefer,
Born but to die, and reas'ning but to err;
Alike in ignorance, his reason such,
Whether he thinks too little, or too much.
1733 *An Essay on Man*, epistle 2, l.1–12.

17 Created half to rise, and half to fall;
Great lord of all things, yet a prey to all;
Sole judge of truth, in endless error hurled;
The glory, jest, and riddle of the world!
1733 *An Essay on Man*, epistle 2, l.15–18.

18 Vice is a monster of so frightful mien,
As, to be hated, needs but to be seen;
Yet seen too oft, familiar with her face,
We first endure, then pity, then embrace.
1733 *An Essay on Man*, epistle 2, l.217–19.

19 The learn'd is happy nature to explore,
The fool is happy that he knows no more.
1733 *An Essay on Man*, epistle 2, l.263–4.

20 For forms of government let fools contest;
Whate'er is best administered is best.
1733 *An Essay on Man*, epistle 3, l.303–4.

21 In faith and hope the world will disagree,
But all mankind's concern is charity.
1733 *An Essay on Man*, epistle 3, l.307–8.

22 Thus God and nature linked the gen'ral frame,
And bade self-love and social be the same.
1733 *An Essay on Man*, epistle 3, l.317–18.

23 Oh Happiness! our being's end and aim!
Good, pleasure, ease, content! whate'er thy name:
That something still which prompts th' eternal sigh,
For which we bear to live, or dare to die.
1734 *An Essay on Man*, epistle 4, l.1–4.

24 Order is Heaven's first law.
1733 *An Essay on Man*, epistle to 4, l.49.

25 A wit's a feather, and a chief a rod;
An honest man's the noblest work of God.
1734 *An Essay on Man*, epistle 4, l.247–8.

26 If parts allure thee, think how Bacon shined,
The wisest, brightest, meanest of mankind:
Or ravished with the whistling of a name,
See Cromwell, damned to everlasting fame!
1734 *An Essay on Man*, epistle 4, l.281–4.

27 Slave to no sect, who takes no private road,
But looks thro' Nature, up to Nature's God.
1734 *An Essay on Man*, epistle 4, l.331–2.

28 All our knowledge is, ourselves to know.
1734 *An Essay on Man*, epistle 4, l.398.

29 Alas! in truth the man but changed his mind,
Perhaps was sick, in love, or had not dined.
1734 *Epistles to Several Persons*, 'To Lord Cobham', l.127–8.

30 'Tis from high life high characters are drawn;
A saint in crape is twice a saint in lawn.
1734 *Epistles to Several Persons*, 'To Lord Cobham', l.134–6.

31 Search then the Ruling Passion: There, alone,
The wild are constant and the cunning known;
The fool consistent, and the false sincere;
Priests, princes, women, no dissemblers here.
This clue once found, unravels all the rest.
1734 *Epistles to Several Persons*, 'To Lord Cobham', l.174–8.

32 Odious! in woollen! 'twould a saint provoke!
1734 *Epistles to Several Persons*, 'To Lord Cobham', l.246.

33 Shut, shut the door, good John! fatigued I said,
Tie up the knocker; say I'm sick, I'm dead.
The Dog-star rages!
1735 'An Epistle to Dr Arbuthnot', l.1–3.

34 You think this cruel? take it for a rule,
No creature smarts so little as a fool.
Let peals of laughter, Codrus! round thee break,
Thou unconcerned canst hear the mighty crack.
Pit, box, and gallery in convulsions hurled,
Thou stand'st unshook amidst a bursting world.
1735 'An Epistle to Dr Arbuthnot', l.83–8.

35 Destroy his fib, or sophistry; in vain,
The creature's at his dirty work again.
1735 'An Epistle to Dr Arbuthnot', l.91–2.

36 Pretty! in amber to observe the forms
Of hairs, or straws, or dirt, or grubs, or worms!
The things, we know are neither rich nor rare,
But wonder how the Devil they got there.
1735 'An Epistle to Dr Arbuthnot', l.169–72.

37 And he, whose fustian's so sublimely bad,
It is not poetry, but prose run mad.
1735 'An Epistle to Dr Arbuthnot', l.187–8.

38 Damn with faint praise, assent with civil leer,
And without sneering, teach the rest to sneer;
Willing to wound, and yet afraid to strike,
Just hint a fault, and hesitate dislike.
1735 Of Addison. 'An Epistle to Dr Arbuthnot', l.201–4.

39 But still the great have kindness in reserve,
He helped to bury whom he helped to starve.
1735 Of a patron. 'An Epistle to Dr Arbuthnot', l.247–8.

40 Let Sporus tremble—'What? that thing of silk,
Sporus, that mere white curd of ass's milk?
Satire or sense, alas! can Sporus feel?
Who breaks a butterfly upon a wheel?
1735 Of Lord Hervey. 'An Epistle to Dr Arbuthnot', l.305–8.

41 And he himself one vile antithesis.
1735 Of Lord Hervey. 'An Epistle to Dr Arbuthnot', l.325.

42 Unlearn'd, he knew no schoolman's subtle art,
No language, but the language of the heart.
1735 Of Pope's father. 'An Epistle to Dr Arbuthnot', l.398–9.

43 Most women have no characters at all.
1735 *Epistles to Several Persons*, 'To a Lady', l.2.

44 A very heathen in the carnal part,
Yet still a sad, good Christian at her heart.
1735 *Epistles to Several Persons*, 'To a Lady', l.67–8.

45 Chaste to her husband, frank to all beside,
A teeming mistress, but a barren bride.
1735 *Epistles to Several Persons*, 'To a Lady', l.71–2.

46 'With every pleasing, every prudent part,
Say, what can Cloe want?'—She wants a heart.
1735 *Epistles to Several Persons*, 'To a Lady', l.159–60.

47 Virtue she finds too painful an endeavour,
Content to dwell in decencies for ever.
1735 *Epistles to Several Persons*, 'To a Lady', l.163–4.

48 In men, we various ruling passions find,
In women, two almost divide the kind;
Those, only fixed, they first or last obey
The love of pleasure, and the love of sway.
1735 *Epistles to Several Persons*, 'To a Lady', l.207–10.

49 Men, some to business, some to pleasure take,
But every woman is at heart a rake:
Men, some to quiet, some to public strife;
But every lady would be Queen for life.
1735 *Epistles to Several Persons*, 'To a Lady', l.215–8.

50 Still round and round the ghosts of Beauty glide,
And haunt the places where their honour died.
See how the world its veterans rewards!
A youth of frolics, an old age of cards.
1735 *Epistles to Several Persons*, 'To a Lady', l.241–4.

51 Woman's at best a contradiction still.
1735 *Epistles to Several Persons*, 'To a Lady', l.270.

52 Who now reads Cowley? if he pleases yet,
His moral pleases, not his pointed wit.
1737 *Imitations of Horace*, bk.2, epistle 1, l.75–6.

53 The people's voice is odd,
It is, and it is not, the voice of God.
1737 *Imitations of Horace*, bk.2, epistle 1, l.89–90.

54 But those who cannot write, and those who can,
All rhyme, and scrawl, and scribble, to a man.
1737 *Imitations of Horace*, bk.2, epistle 1, l.187–8.

55 Ev'n copious Dryden, wanted, or forgot,
The last and greatest art, the art to blot.
1737 *Imitations of Horace*, bk.2, epistle 1, l.280–1.

56 There still remains, to mortify a wit,
The many-headed monster of the pit.
1737 *Imitations of Horace*, bk.2, epistle 1, l.304–5.

57 The more you drink, the more you crave.
1737 *Imitations of Horace*, bk.2, espistle 2, l.212.

58 Not to go back, is somewhat to advance,
And men must walk at least before they dance.
1738 *Imitations of Horace*, bk.1, epistle 1, l.53–4.

59 Not to admire, is all the art I know,
To make men happy, and to keep them so.
1738 *Imitations of Horace*, bk.1, epistle 6, l.1–2.

60 The worst of madmen is a saint run mad.
1738 *Imitations of Horace*, bk.1, epistle 6, l.27.

61 Ask you what provocation I have had?
The strong antipathy of good to bad.
1738 *Imitations of Horace*, epilogue to the satires, dialogue 2, l.197–8.

62 Yes, I am proud; I must be proud to see
Men not afraid of God, afraid of me.
1738 *Imitations of Horace*, epilogue to the satires, dialogue 2, l.208–9.

63 Teach me to feel another's woe;
To hide the fault I see;
That mercy I to others show,
That mercy show to me.
1738 *The Universal Prayer.*

64 Books and the Man I sing, the first who brings
The Smithfield Muses to the Ear of Kings.
Say great Patricians! (since your selves inspire
These wond'rous works; so Jove and Fate require)
Say from what cause, in vain decry'd and curst,
Still Dunce the second reigns like Dunce the first?
1742 *The Dunciad*, bk.1, l.1–6.

65 Poetic Justice, with her lifted scale,
Where, in nice balance, truth with gold she weighs,
And solid pudding against empty praise.
1742 *The Dunciad*, bk.1, l.52–4.

66 Here gay Description Aegypt glads with showers;
Or gives to Zembla fruits, to Barca flowers;
Glitt'ring with ice here hoary hills are seen,
There painted vallies of eternal green.
1742 *The Dunciad*, bk.1, l.71–4.

67 While pensive poets painful vigils keep,
Sleepless themselves, to give their readers sleep.
1742 *The Dunciad*, bk.1, l.93–4.

68 In each she marks her image full exprest,
But chief, in Tibbald's monster-breeding breast;
Sees Gods with Daemons in strange league ingage,
And earth, and heav'n, and hell her battles wage.
1742 *The Dunciad*, bk.1, l.105–8.

69 Or where the pictures for the page atone,
And Quarles is saved by beauties not his own.
1742 *The Dunciad*, bk.1, l.139–40.

70 A brain of feathers, and a heart of lead.
1742 *The Dunciad*, bk.2, l.44.

71 How little, mark! that portion of the ball,
Where, faint at best, the beams of science fall.
1742 *The Dunciad*, bk.3, l.83–4.

72 None need a guide, by sure attraction led,
And strong impulsive gravity of head.
1742 *The Dunciad*, bk.4, l.75–6.

73 A wit with dunces, and a dunce with wits.
1742 *The Dunciad*, bk.4, l.90.

74 Leave not a foot of verse, a foot of stone,
A Page, a Grave, that they can call their own;
But spread, my sons, your glory thin or thick,
On passive paper, or on solid brick.
1742 *The Dunciad*, bk.4, l.127–30.

75 Whate'er the talents, or howe'er designed,
We hang one jingling padlock on the mind.
1742 *The Dunciad*, bk.4, l.161–2.

76 The Right Divine of Kings to govern wrong.
1742 *The Dunciad*, bk.4, l.187.

77 How parts relate to parts, or they to whole,
The body's harmony, the beaming soul.
1742 *The Dunciad*, bk.4, l.235–6.

78 Isles of fragrance, lily-silver'd values.
1742 *The Dunciad*, bk.4, l.303.

79 Love-whispering woods, and lute-resounding waves.
1742 *The Dunciad*, bk.4, l.306.

80 —She marked thee there,
Stretched on the rack of a too easy chair,
And heard thy everlasting yawn confess
The pains and penalties of idleness.
1742 *The Dunciad*, bk.4, l.341–4.

81 O! would the Sons of Men once think their Eyes
And Reason giv'n them but to study Flies?
See Nature in some partial narrow shape,
And let the Author of the Whole escape.
1742 *The Dunciad*, bk.4, l.453–6.

82 Religion blushing veils her sacred fires,
And unawares Morality expires.
1742 *The Dunciad*, bk.4, l.649–50.

83 Lo! thy dread empire, Chaos! is restored;
Light dies before thy uncreating word:
Thy hand, great Anarch! lets the curtain fall;
And universal darkness buries all.
1742 *The Dunciad*, bk.4, l.653–6.

84 I am his Highness' dog at Kew;
Pray, tell me sir, whose dog are you?
'Epigram Engraved on the Collar of a Dog which I gave to His Royal Highness'.

85 Here am I, dying of a hundred good symptoms.
1744 His response to reassurance from his doctors that his health was showing signs of improvement. Quoted in Joseph Spence *Anecdotes by and about Alexander Pope* (1820).

Popova, Lyubov Sergeyevna 1889–1924

Russian painter and theatre and textile designer.

86 Texture is the content of painterly surfaces.
Quoted in W Chadwick *Women, Art and Society* (1990).

Popper, Sir Karl Raimund 1902–94

Anglo-Austrian philosopher, professor (1949–69) at the London School of Economics. He expounded his political theory in *The Open Society and Its Enemies* (1945), and his philosophy of science in *The Logic of Scientific Discovery* (1934).

87 It must be possible for an empirical system to be refuted by experience.
1934 *The Logic of Scientific Discovery.*

88 Every scientific statement must remain *tentative for ever.*
1934 *The Logic of Scientific Discovery.*

89 In order that a new theory should constitute a discovery or step forward it should conflict with its predecessor …it should contradict its predecessor; it should overthrow it. In this sense, progress in science—or at least striking progress—is always revolutionary.
1934 *The Logic of Scientific Discovery.*

90 It is not his possession of knowledge, of irrefutable truth, that makes the man of science, but his persistent and recklessly critical quest for truth.
1934 *The Logic of Scientific Discovery.*

91 We may become the makers of our fate when we have ceased to pose as its prophets.
1945 *The Open Society and Its Enemies*, introduction.

92 There is no history of mankind, there are only many histories of all kinds of aspects of human life. And one of these is the history of political power. This is elevated into the history of the world.
1945 *The Open Society and Its Enemies*, vol.2, ch.25.

93 The belief that we can start with pure observations

alone, without anything in the nature of a theory, is absurd.
1953 *Conjectures and Refutations* (published 1963), ch.1.

94 Observation is always selective. It needs a chosen object, a definite task, an interest, a point of view, a problem.
1953 *Conjectures and Refutations* (published 1963), ch.1.

95 There is at least one philosophical problem in which all thinking men are interested. It is the problem of cosmology: *the problem of understanding the world—including ourselves, and our knowledge, as part of the world*. All science is cosmology, I believe, and for me the interest of philosophy, no less than that of science, lies solely in the contributions which it has made to it.
1959 *The Logic of Scientific Discovery* (1934), preface to 1959 edition.

96 In so far as a scientific statement speaks about reality, it must be falsifiable: and in so far as it is not falsifiable, it does not speak about reality.
1959 *The Logic of Scientific Discovery* (1934), appendix to 1959 edition.

97 What we should do, I suggest, is to give up the idea of ultimate sources of knowledge, and admit that all knowledge is human; that it is mixed with our errors, our prejudices, our dreams, and our hopes; that all we can do is to grope for truth even though it be beyond our reach.
1960 *Conjectures and Refutations* (published 1963), introduction.

98 The history of science, like the history of all human ideas, is a history of irresponsible dreams, of obstinacy, and of error. But science is one of the very few human activities—perhaps the only one—in which errors are systematically criticized and fairly often, in time, corrected. This is why we can say that, in science, we often learn from our mistakes, and why we can speak clearly and sensibly about making progress there.
1960 *Conjectures and Refutations* (published 1963), ch.10.

99 Science starts only with problems.
1960 *Conjectures and Refutations* (published 1963), ch.10.

1 For this, indeed, is the true source of our ignorance—the fact that our knowledge can only be finite, while our ignorance must necessarily be infinite.
1960 Lecture to the British Academy, 20 Jan.

2 Science may be described as the art of systematic over-simplification.
1982 Quoted in the *Observer*, 1 Aug.

Porter, Cole 1891–1964

US composer. He studied law at Harvard before turning to music, composing and writing lyrics for a string of successful stage and screen musicals including *Kiss Me Kate* (1948, filmed 1953), *High Society* (1956) and *Can-Can* (1953, filmed 1960).

3 I get no kick from champagne;
Mere alcohol doesn't thrill me at all.
So tell me why should it be true
That I get a kick out of you?
1934 'I Get a Kick Out of You', from the show *Anything Goes*.

4 In olden days a glimpse of stocking
Was looked on as something shocking.
But now, God knows,
Anything goes.
1934 'Anything Goes', from the show *Anything Goes*.

5 I'm a worthless check, a total wreck, a flop
But if baby I'm the bottom, you're the top.
1936 'You're the Top', from the show *Anything Goes*.

6 You're the top
You're the Louvr' Museum
You're a melody from a symphony by Strauss.
1936 'You're the Top', from the show *Anything Goes*.

7 My sole inspiration is a telephone call from a director.
1955 Interview, 8 Feb.

8 Who wants to be a millionaire?
And go to ev'ry swell affair?
1956 'Who Wants to Be a Millionaire', from the show *High Society*.

Porter, Katherine Anne 1890–1980

US novelist and short-story writer. Her works include the novella *Pale Horse, Pale Rider* (1939) and the long allegorical novel *The Ship of Fools* (1962).

9 Most people won't realize that writing is a craft. You have to take your apprenticeship in it like anything else.
1962 In the *Saturday Review*, 31 Mar.

10 The real sin against life is to abuse and destroy beauty, even one's own—even more, one's own, for that has been put in our care and we are responsible for its well-being.
1962 *Ship of Fools*, pt.3.

11 The pimple on the face of American literature.
On Truman Capote. Quoted in Gerald Clarke *Capote* (1988).

12 Oh, poor Pearl Buck! She has no more bounce than a boiled potato.
Quoted from the journals of Glenway Westcott, in Robert Phelps and Jerry Rosco (eds) *Continuous Lessons* (1990).

Porteus, Beilby 1731–1808

English prelate and poet.

13 One murder made a villain
Millions a hero.
1759 'Death'.

14 War its thousands slays, Peace its ten thousands.
1759 'Death'.

15 Teach him how to live,
And, oh! still harder lesson! how to die.
1759 'Death'.

Portillo, Michael 1953–

English Conservative politician. He was regarded as a potential future leader, but lost his seat in the 1997 general election. Victory in a 1999 by-election led to his return to the Commons.

16 A truly terrible night for the Conservatives.
1997 After losing Enfield South to Labour in the general election, 2 May. Quoted in Brian Cathcart *Were You Still Up for Portillo?*.

Pott, Frances 1832–1909

English cleric and translator.

17 The strife is o'er, the battle done;
Now is the Victor's triumph won;

O let the song of praise be sung;
Alleluia!
1861 Hymn, translated from the original Latin 'Finita iam sunt praelia'.

Potter, Beatrix 1866–1943

English author and illustrator of books for children, whose characters have become classics of children's literature.

18 Don't go into Mr McGregor's garden: your father had an accident there, he was put into a pie by Mr McGregor.
1902 *The Tale of Peter Rabbit.*

19 In the time of swords and periwigs and full-skirted coats with flowered lappets—when gentlemen wore ruffles, and gold-laced waistcoats of paduasoy and taffeta—there lived a tailor in Gloucester.
1903 *The Tailor of Gloucester.*

Potter, Henry Codman 1835–1908

US religious leader. For 15 years he was rector of Grace Church, New York City. He was elected Bishop Co-Adjutor of New York in 1883 and Bishop in 1887. He was known for his diplomacy and was outspoken on corruption.

20 If there be no nobility of descent in a nation, it is all the more indispensable that there should be nobility of ascent; a character in them that bear rule, so fine and high and pure, that as men come within the circle of its influence, they involuntarily pay homage to that which is the one pre-eminent distinction—the royalty of virtue.
1889 Washington centennial address, 30 Apr.

Potter, Stephen 1900–69

English humorous writer.

21 How to be one up—how to make the other man feel that something has gone wrong, however slightly.
1950 *Lifemanship.*

22 Each of us can, by ploy or gambit, most naturally gain the advantage.
1950 *Lifemanship.*

Pound, Ezra Loomis 1885–1972

US poet, a key figure in the Modernist movement, whose chief work was the massive poetic cycle *The Cantos* (collected 1970). He spent much of his life in Italy, and was committed to an asylum for a time after World War II, during which he espoused Fascist sympathies.

23 Bah! I have sung women in three cities,
But it is all the same;
And I will sing of the sun.
1908 *Personae*, 'Cino'.

24 No good poetry is written in a manner twenty years old, for to write in such a manner shows conclusively that the writer thinks from books, convention and cliché; and not from life.
1912 'Prolegomena', in *The Poetry Review*, Feb.

25 All great art is born of the metropolis.
1913 Letter to Harriet Monroe, 7 Nov.

26 Poetry must be *as well written as prose.*
1915 Letter to Harriet Monroe, Jan.

27 Winter is icummen in,
Lhude sing Goddamm,
Raineth drop and staineth slop,
And how the wind doth ramm!
Sing: Goddamm.
1916 *Lustra*, 'Ancient Music'.
► *See Anonymous 19:83.*

28 The apparition of these faces in the crowd;
Petals on a wet, black bough.
1916 *Lustra*, 'In a Station of the Metro'.

29 She is dying piece-meal
of a sort of emotional anaemia.
And round about there is a rabble
of the filthy, sturdy, unkillable infants
of the very poor.
1916 *Lustra*, 'The Garden'.

30 I make a pact with you, Walt Whitman—
I have detested you long enough.
I come to you as a grown child
Who has had a pig-headed father
I am old enough not to make friends.
1916 *Lustra*, 'A Pact'.

31 Poetry must be read as music and not as oratory.
1917 'Vers Libre and Arnold Dolmetsch', in *The Egoist*, Jul.

32 A chryselephantine poem of immeasurable length which will occupy me for the next four decades unless it becomes a bore.
1917 On beginning the poetic series *The Cantos*, which remained unfinished on his death.

33 A man of genius has a right to any mode of expression.
1918 Letter to J B Yeats, 4 Feb.

34 Of all those young women
Not one has enquired the cause of the world
Nor the modus of lunar eclipses
Nor whether there be any patch left of us
After we cross the infernal ripples.
1919 *Quia Pauper Amavi*, 'Homage to Sextus Propertius'.

35 For three years, out of key with his time,
He strove to resuscitate the dead art
Of poetry; to maintain 'the sublime'
In the old sense. Wrong from the start—

No, hardly, but seeing he had been born
In a half savage country, out of date.
1920 *Hugh Selwyn Mauberley*, pt.1.

36 His true Penelope was Flaubert,
He fished by obstinate isles;
Observed the elegance of Circe's hair
Rather than the mottoes on sundials.
1920 *Hugh Selwyn Mauberley*, pt.1.

37 Better mendacities
Than the classics in paraphrase!
1920 *Hugh Selwyn Mauberley*, pt.2.

38 Christ follows Dionysus
Phallic and ambrosial
Made way for macerations;
Caliban casts out Ariel.
1920 *Hugh Selwyn Mauberley*, pt.3.

39 Died some, *pro patria*,
non 'dulce' non 'et decor'…
walked eye-deep in hell
believing in old men's lies, then unbelieving
came home, home to a lie,

home to many deceits
home to old lies and new infamy;
usury age-old and age-thick
and liars in public places.
1920 *Hugh Selwyn Mauberley*, pt.4.

40 There died a myriad,
And of the best, among them,
For an old bitch gone in the teeth,
For a botched civilization.
1920 *Hugh Selwyn Mauberley*, pt.5.

41 And no one knows, at first sight, a masterpiece.
And give up verse, my boy.
There's nothing in it.
1920 *Hugh Selwyn Mauberley*, 'MR NIXON'.

42 I never mentioned a man but with the view
Of selling my own works.
The tip's a good one, as for literature
It gives no man a sinecure.
1920 *Hugh Selwyn Mauberley*, 'MR NIXON'.

43 The haven from sophistications and contentions
Leaks through its thatch;
He offers succulent cooking;
The door has a creaking latch.
1920 *Hugh Selwyn Mauberley*, pt.10.

44 The curse of me and my nation is that we always think things can be bettered by immediate action of some sort, *any* sort rather than no sort.
1920 Letter to James Joyce, 7–8 Jun.

45 And then went down to the ship,
Set keel to breakers, forth on the godly sea.
1925 *Draft of XVI Cantos*, no.1.

46 And even I can remember
A day when the historians left blanks in their writings,
I mean for things they didn't know.
1930 *Draft of XXX Cantos*, no.13.

47 Great literature is simply language charged with meaning to the utmost possible degree.
1931 *How To Read*, pt.2.

48 Any general statement is like a cheque drawn on a bank. Its value depends on what is there to meet it.
1934 *The ABC of Reading*, ch.1.

49 One of the pleasures of middle age is to *find out* that one WAS right, and that one was much righter than one knew at say 17 or 23.
1934 *The ABC of Reading*, ch.1.

50 Literature is news that STAYS news.
1934 *The ABC of Reading*, ch.2.

51 Real education must ultimately be limited to one who INSISTS on knowing, the rest is mere sheep-herding.
1934 *The ABC of Reading*, ch.8.

52 The author's conviction on this day of New Year is that music begins to atrophy when it departs too far from the dance; that poetry begins to atrophy when it gets too far from music . . .
1934 *The ABC of Reading*, 'Warning'.

53 To the beat of the measure
From star-up to the half-dark
From half-dark to half-dark
Unceasing the measure.
1934 *Eleven New Cantos*, no.34.

54 People find ideas a bore because they do not distinguish between live ones and stuffed ones on a shelf.
1938 *Guide to Kulcher*, pt.1, section 1, ch.5.

55 Man is an over-complicated organism. If he is doomed to extinction he will die out for want of simplicity.
1938 *Guide to Kulcher*, pt.3, section 5, ch.19.

56 Civilization itself is a certain sane balance of values.
1938 *Guide to Kulcher*, pt.3, section 5, ch.20.

57 Adolf Hitler was a Jeanne d'Arc, a saint. He was a martyr. Like many martyrs, he held extreme views.
1945 In the *Philadelphia Record* and *Chicago Sun*, 9 May.

58 What thou lovest well remains,
The rest is dross
What thou lov'st well shall not be reft from thee
What thou lov'st well is thy true heritage.
1948 *The Pisan Cantos*, no.81.

59 The ant's a centaur in his dragon world.
Pull down thy vanity, it is not man
Made courage, or made order, or made grace.
1948 *The Pisan Cantos*, no.81.

60 Learn of the green world what can be thy place
In scaled invention or true artistry,
Pull down thy vanity,
Paquin pull down!
The green casque has outdone your elegance.
1948 *The Pisan Cantos*, no.81.

61 Thou art a beaten dog beneath the hail,
A swollen magpie in a fitful sun,
Half black half white
Nor knowst'ou wing from tail
Pull down thy vanity.
1948 *The Pisan Cantos*, no.81.

62 Tching prayed on the mountain and wrote MAKE IT NEW
on his bath tub.
Day by day make it new
cut underbrush,
pile the logs
keep it growing.
1954 *The Cantos*, no.53.

63 Artists are the antennae of the race, but the bullet-headed many will never learn to trust their great artists.
1954 *Literary Essays*, 'Henry James'.

64 How did it go in the madhouse? Rather badly. But what other place could one live in America?
1958 On his release after 13 years in St Elizabeth's Hospital, Washington DC. Recalled on his death, 1 Nov 1972.

65 The worst mistake I made was that stupid, suburban prejudice of anti-Semitism.
1968 Remark to Allen Ginsberg, 7 Jun. Quoted in H Carpenter *A Serious Character* (1988), pt.5.

66 Art very possibly *ought* to be the supreme achievement, the 'accomplished', but there is the other satisfactory effect—that of a man hurling himself at an indomitable chaos and yanking and hauling as much of it as possible into some sort of order (or beauty) aware of it both as chaos and as potential.
Quoted in H Kenner (ed) *The Pound Era* (1973).

67 A dirty book worth reading.
Of Henry Miller *Tropic of Cancer* (1934). Recalled on Miller's death, 7 Jun 1980.

68 All America is an insane asylum.

Quoted in Patricia C Willis (ed) *The Complete Poems of Marianne Moore* (1986).

69 Some poems have form as a tree has form and some as water poured into a vase.
Quoted in Patricia C Willis (ed) *The Complete Poems of Marianne Moore* (1986).

70 The great writer is always the plodder.
Quoted in Patricia C Willis (ed) *The Complete Poems of Marianne Moore* (1986).

71 The true poet is most easily distinguished from the false when he trusts himself to the simplest expression and writes without adjectives.
Quoted in Patricia C Willis (ed) *The Complete Poems of Marianne Moore* (1986).

72 Use no word that under stress of emotion you could not actually say.
Quoted in Patricia C Willis (ed) *The Complete Poems of Marianne Moore* (1986).

73 Great poets seldom make bricks without straw. They pile up all the excellences they can beg, borrow, or steal from their predecessors and contemporaries and then set their own inimitable light atop the mountain.
Quoted in Patricia C Willis (ed) *The Complete Poems of Marianne Moore* (1986).

Pound, (Nathan) Roscoe 1870–1964

US jurist, Professor of Law at Harvard University.

74 Wealth, in a commercial age, is made up largely of promises.
1922 *An Introduction to the Philosophy of Law*, ch.6.

Poussin, Nicolas 1594–1665

French painter who spent most of his working life in Rome. The Classical tradition in French painting developed from his work.

75 The grand manner consists of four elements: subject or theme, concept, structure, and style. The first requirement, fundamental to all the others, is that the subject and the narrative be grandiose, such as battles, heroic actions, and religious themes.
Quoted in Giovanni Pietro Bellori *Lives of the Modern Painters* (1672).

Powell, Anthony Dymoke 1905–2000

English novelist. His major work is the sequence of twelve novels chronicling 20c English upper-middle-class life, collectively known as *A Dance to the Music of Time* (1951–75).

76 All the same, you know parents—especially step-parents—are sometimes a disappointment to their children. They don't fulfil the promise of their early years.
1952 *A Buyer's Market*, ch.2.

77 There is a strong disposition in youth, from which some individuals never escape, to suppose that everyone else is having a more enjoyable time than we are ourselves.
1952 *A Buyer's Market*, ch.4.

78 He fell in love with himself at first sight and it is a passion to which he has always remained faithful. Self-love seems so often unrequited.
1955 *The Acceptance World*, ch.1.

79 Dinner at the Huntercombes possessed 'only two dramatic features—the wine was a farce and the food a tragedy.'
1955 *The Acceptance World*, ch.4.

80 All men are brothers, but, thank God, they aren't all brothers-in-law.
1957 *At Lady Molly's*, ch.4.

81 Books Do Furnish a Room.
1971 Title of novel.

82 Growing old is like being increasingly penalised for a crime you haven't committed.
1973 *Temporary Kings*, ch.1.

83 People think that because a novel's invented, it isn't true. Exactly the reverse is the case.
1975 *Hearing Secret Harmonies*, ch.3.

84 One of the worst things about life is not how nasty the nasty people are. You know that already. It is how nasty the nice people can be.
1975 *Hearing Secret Harmonies*, ch.7.

85 In this country it is rare for anyone, let alone a publisher, to take writers seriously.
1979 In the *Daily Telegraph*, 8 Feb.

86 If you don't spend every morning of your life writing, it's awfully difficult to know what to do otherwise.
1984 In the *Observer*, 3 Apr.

Powell, Colin Luther 1937–

US army general. He fought in Vietnam, and became National Security Adviser to President Reagan (1987–9). He was appointed chairman of the Joint Chiefs of Staff (1989–93), and controlled US strategy during the Gulf War. In 2001 he was appointed Secretary of State by President George W Bush.

87 We have decapitated him from the dictatorship.
1988 On evicting from office Panama's General Manuel Noriega. Quoted in the *Washington Post*, 21 Dec.

88 The American people do not want their young dying for $1.50 a gallon oil.
1990 Urging caution against interfering with Iraq's invasion of oil-rich Kuwait in a White House meeting 2 Aug. Quoted in the *New York Times*, 23 Oct 1994.

89 First we're going to cut it off, and then we're going to kill it.
1991 On the opposition to Operation Desert Storm. In the *US News and World Report*, 4 Feb.

90 I remember the front door. I remember the auditorium. I remember the feeling that you can't make it. But you can.
1991 On revisiting the South Bronx high school from which he graduated in 1954. In the *New York Times*, 16 Apr.

91 I sleep like a baby too—every two hours I wake up screaming.
2003 On being reminded that George W Bush claims to sleep like a baby. In the *New Yorker*, 10 Feb.

Powell, (John) Enoch 1912–98

English Conservative and Ulster Unionist politician. Professor of Greek at Sydney University (1937–9), he was elected MP in 1950. Minister of Health (1960–3), he was dismissed from the shadow Cabinet in 1968 for his attitude to immigration. He was returned as an Ulster Unionist in 1974, but lost his seat in 1987. His books include *A Nation Not Afraid* (1965).

92 History is littered with the wars which everybody knew would never happen.
1967 Speech to Conservative Party conference, 19 Oct.

93 As I look ahead, I am filled with much foreboding. Like the Roman, I seem to see 'the River Tiber foaming with much blood'.
1968 Speech at Birmingham on racial tension in Britain, Apr.

94 I was born a Tory, am a Tory, and shall die a Tory. I never yet heard that it was any part of the faith of a Tory to take the institutions and liberties, the laws and customs that his country has evolved over the centuries, and merge them with those of eight other nations into a new-made artificial state—and what is more, to do so without the willing approbation and consent of the nation.
1974 Speech against Britain's entry into the Common Market, Shipley, 25 Feb.

95 All political lives, unless they are cut off in mid-stream at a happy juncture, end in failure, because that is the nature of politics and of human affairs.
1977 *Joseph Chamberlain.*

Powell, Michael 1905–90

English film-maker. He made various 'quota quickies' in the 1930s and then began a partnership with Emeric Pressburger. Known as 'the Archers', they collaborated on such films as *The Life and Death of Colonel Blimp* (1943), *Black Narcissus* (1947) and *The Red Shoes* (1948).

96 What do they know of England, who only the West End know?
1950 Attributed comment in defence of *Gone to Earth.*
► *See Kipling 471:99.*

Powys, John Cowper 1872–1963

English novelist and essayist.

97 It is that cricket field that, in all the sharp and bitter moments of life as they come to me now, gives me a sense of wholesome proportion. 'At least I am not playing cricket!'
Quoted in Helen Exley *Cricket Quotations* (1992).

Prather, Hugh

US minister, counsellor and writer.

98 If the ocean was pure mind and I was a wave, I would be in terror if I tried to distinguish myself from the water that produced me. What is a wave without water, and what is a mind without God?
1982 *The Quiet Answer.*

99 Forgive and be happy. That is the ancient secret…the only wisdom ever to be attained.
1982 *The Quiet Answer.*

Pratt, Edwin John 1882–1964

Canadian poet. Born in Newfoundland, he obtained a PhD in divinity from the University of Toronto and became Professor of English there in 1919. He is best known for his documentary poetry, including *The Titanic* (1935), *Brébeuf and His Brethren* (1940) and *Towards the Last Spike* (1952).

1 It was the same world then as now—the same,
Except for little differences of speed
And power, and means to treat myopia
To show an axe-blade infinitely sharp
Splitting things infinitely small.
1952 *Towards the Last Spike.* The poet is speaking of the building of the Canadian National Railway, from coast to coast.

Prescott, John 1938–

English Labour politician, Deputy Prime Minister since 1997.

2 People like me were branded, pigeon-holed, a ceiling put on our ambitions.
1996 Speech at Oxford, 13 Jun. Quoted in *The Guardian*, 14 Jun.

3 Tony will go on and on and on.
2004 On Prime Minister Tony Blair. On BBC Radio 4's *Today* programme.

Presley, Elvis Aaron 1935–77

US singer and actor.

4 You ain't nothin' but a hound dog
cryin' all the time.
You ain't nothin' but a hound dog
cryin' all the time.
Well, you ain't never caught a rabbit
and you ain't no friend of mine.
1956 'Hound Dog' (written by Jerry Leiber and Mike Stoller).

5 Well since my baby left me
I found a new place to dwell
It's down at the end of lonely street
At Heartbreak Hotel.
1956 'Heartbreak Hotel' (with Mae Boren Axton and Tommy Durden).

6 I learned very early in life that: 'Without a song, the day would never end; without a song, a man ain't got no friend; without a song the road would never bend—without a song'. So I keep on singing. Goodnight. Thank you.
1971 Acceptance speech, Ten Outstanding Men of the Year Awards, 16 Jan.

7 I don't know anything about music—In my line you don't have to.
Quoted in David Pickering *Brewer's Twentieth Century Music* (1994).

Preston, James E 1933–

US businessman. He joined Avon Products in 1964 as a management trainee, becoming Chief Executive Officer (1988–98) and Chairman (1989–98).

8 A bad reputation is like a hangover. It takes a while to get rid of, and it makes everything else hurt.
1992 In *Fortune*, 10 Feb.

Previn, André (George) 1929–

German-born US conductor and composer. A US citizen from 1943, he conducted major orchestras around the world from 1967. His own compositions include musicals, film scores and orchestral works.

9 The basic difference between classical music and jazz is that in the former music is always greater than its performance—whereas the way jazz is performed is always more important than what is being played.
1967 Quoted in *The Times.*

Prévost, Abbé Antoine-François 1697–1763

French novelist, educated in the Jesuit tradition. He enlisted in the army before eventually deciding on a religious life after an unhappy love affair.

10 *Il ne reste donc que l'exemple qui puisse servir de règle à*

quantité de personnes dans l'exercice de la vertu.
Most people can learn only by example to be virtuous.
1731 *Histoire du chevalier Des Grieux et de Manon Lescaut*, Avis de l'auteur.

11 *Crois-tu qu'on puisse être bien tendre lorsqu'on manque de pain?*
Do you believe that a person can be truly affectionate when he is starving?
1731 *Histoire du chevalier Des Grieux et de Manon Lescaut*, ch.1.

12 *Il faut compter ses richesses par les moyens qu'on a de satisfaire ses désirs.*
We must count our riches by the means we have to satisfy our desires.
1731 *Histoire du chevalier Des Grieux et de Manon Lescaut*, ch.2.

Prial, Frank J

US writer and wine columnist for the *New York Times*.

13 Macaulay, Gibbon, Tolstoy, Francis Parkman and other immortals…never said anything in two pages that might possibly sound better in 10.
Quoted in the *New York Times*, 31 Mar 1990.

Price, Raymond

Nixon White House speechwriter.

14 The response is to the image, not to the man, since 99 percent of the voters have no contact with the man.
1967 Memo, 28 Nov. Quoted in the *New York Times*, 31 Oct 1993.

15 It's not what's *there* that counts, it's what's projected —and…it's not what *he* projects but rather what the voter receives… It's not the man we have to change, but rather the *received* impression.
1967 Memo, 28 Nov. Quoted in the *New York Times*, 31 Oct 1993.

Prichard, Katharine Susannah *married name* Throssell 1883–1969

Australian journalist, novelist and political activist. Western Australia is the background for her later novels including *Coonardoo* (1929).

16 Coonardoo they called it, the dark well, or the well in the shadows.
1929 *Coonardoo*, ch.1.

Priestley, J(ohn) B(oynton) 1894–1984

English writer, whose works include the novel *The Good Companions* (1929) and plays such as *Dangerous Corner* (1932). He achieved national renown as deliverer of radio 'postscripts' during World War II.

17 To say that these men paid their shillings to watch twenty-two hirelings kick a ball is merely to say that a violin is wood and catgut, that *Hamlet* is so much paper and ink. For a shilling the Bruddersford United AFC offered you Conflict and Art.
1929 *The Good Companions*, bk.1, ch.1.

18 The earth is nobler than the world we have put upon it.
1939 *Johnson Over Jordan*, act 3.

19 This little steamer, like all her brave and battered sisters, is immortal. She'll go sailing proudly down the years in the epic of Dunkirk. And our great-great-grand-children, when they learn how we began this war by snatching glory out of defeat, and then swept on to victory, may also learn how the little holiday steamers made an excursion to hell and came back glorious.
1940 Radio broadcast, 5 Jun, quoted in *The Listener*, 13 Jun.

20 An Inspector Calls.
1947 Title of play.

21 The trouble is that we drink too much tea. I see in this the slow revenge of the Orient, which has diverted the Yellow River down our throats.
1949 In the *Observer*, 15 May.

22 Sometimes you might think that the machines we worship make all the chief appointments, promoting the human beings who seem closest to them.
1957 *Thoughts in the Wilderness*.

23 *Finnegans Wake* took him seventeen years to write, a length of time that suggests an elaborate hobby rather than a passionate desire to create something.
1960 Of James Joyce. *Literature and Western Man*.

24 He was a black Irish type, with centuries of rebelliousness behind him, and I decided to chance it.
1961 *Saturn Over the Water*.

25 I can't help feeling wary when I hear anything said about the masses. First you take their faces from 'em by calling 'em the masses and then you accuse 'em of not having any faces.
1961 *Saturn Over the Water*, ch.2.

26 It is hard to tell where the MCC ends and the Church of England begins.
1962 In the *New Statesman*, 20 Jul.

27 Some time ago, in an interview that turned towards the Theatre, I suggested that 'Pubic hair is not an adequate substitute for wit'. My point now is that depending upon shock tactics is easy, whereas writing a good play is difficult.
1974 *Outcries and Asides*, 'Danger of Shock Tactics'.

28 England is not ruined because sinewy brown men from a distant colony sometimes hit a ball further and oftener than our men do.
Quoted in Colin Jarman *The Guinness Dictionary of Sports Quotations* (1990).

Prince *in full* Prince Roger Nelson 1958–

US pop singer and composer. His works include the album *1999* (1982), and the film and album *Purple Rain* (1984).

29 Maybe at one time they could get Little Richard for a new car and a bucket of chicken. We don't roll like that no more.
2004 In *Rolling Stone*, 27 May.

Prior, Matthew 1664–1721

English poet and diplomat. His verse includes *The Hind and the Panther Transvers'd to the Story of the Country Mouse and the City Mouse* (with Charles Montagu, 1687, a satire on Dryden). He is remembered for his many witty, epigrammatic occasional verses.

30 They never taste who always drink;
They always talk who never think.
1697 'Upon this Passage in Scaligerana'.

31 Nobles and heralds, by your leave,
Here lies what once was Matthew Prior,
The son of Adam and of Eve,

Can Stuart or Nassaw go higher?
1702 'Epitaph'. In a later version 'Stuart' was changed to 'Bourbon'.

32 Be to her virtues very kind;
Be to her faults a little blind;
Let all her ways be unconfined,
And clap your padlock—on her mind.
1705 'An English Padlock'.

33 And of the pangs of absence to remove
By letters, soft interpreters of love.
1708 'Henry and Emma'.

34 But of good household features her person was made,
Nor by faction cry'd up nor of censure afraid,
And her beauty was rather for use than parade.
1708 'Jinny the Just' (first printed 1907). The title was given by A R Waller.

35 Cured yesterday of my disease,
I died last night of my physician.
1714 'The Remedy Worse than the Disease'.

36 Venus, take my votive glass;
Since I am not what I was,
What from this day I shall be
Venus never let me see.
1718 'The Lady Who Offered Her Looking-Glass to Venus'.

37 No, no; for my virginity,
When I lose that, says Rose, I'll die:
Behind the elms last night, cried Dick,
Rose, were you not extremely sick?
1718 'A True Maid'.

38 They walked and eat, good folks: What then?
Why then they walked and eat again:
They soundly slept the night away:
They did just nothing all the day.
1718 'An Epitaph', l.9–12.

39 Their beer was strong; their wine was port;
Their meal was large; their grace was short.
They gave the poor the remnant meat,
Just when it grew not fit to eat.
1718 'An Epitaph', l.29–32.

40 On his death bed poor Lubin lies:
His spouse is in despair.
With frequent sobs and mutual cries
They both express their care.

A different cause, says parson Sly,
The same effect may give:
Poor Lubin fears, that he shall die:
His wife, that he may live.
1718 'A Reasonable Affliction'.

41 What I speak, my fair Chloe, and what I write shows
The difference there is betwixt Nature and Art:
I court others in verse: but I love thee in prose:
And they have my whimsies, but thou hast my heart.
1718 'A Better Answer', stanza 4.

42 So when I am wearied with wandering all day;
To thee my delight in the evening I come:
No matter what beauties I saw in my way:
They were but my visits; but thou art my home.
1718 'A Better Answer', stanza 6.

43 And 'twould be a cruel thing,
When her black eyes have raised desire,
Should she not her bucket bring
And kindly help to quench the fire.
'Chloe Beauty Has and Wit'. (Date unknown. In *Matthew Prior: Literary Works*, edited by H B Wright and M K Spears, 2 vols, 1959.)

44 Rise not till noon, if life be but a dream,
As Greek and Roman poets have exprest:
Add good example to so grave a theme,
For he who sleeps the longest lives the best.
'Epigram'. (Date unknown. In *Matthew Prior: Literary Works*, edited by H B Wright and M K Spears, 2 vols, 1959.)

Pritchett, Sir V(ictor) S(awdon) 1900–97

English writer. He wrote novels and works of literary criticism and biography, but is best known for his short stories.

45 The principle of procrastinated rape is said to be the ruling one in all of the great best-sellers.
1946 *The Living Novel*, 'Clarissa'.

46 A touch of science, even bogus science, gives an edge to the superstitious tale.
1946 *The Living Novel*, 'An Irish Ghost'.

47 The detective novel is…the classic example of a specialized form of art removed from contact with the life it pretends to build on.
1951 In the *New Statesman*, 16 Jun.

48 He watched his restless hands, surprised they had remembered to come with him.
1951 *Mr Beluncle*, ch.15.

49 If evil does not exist, what is going to happen to literature?
1951 *Mr Beluncle*, ch.23.

50 Dickens was not the first or the last novelist to find virtue more difficult to portray than the wish for it.
1953 'Oliver Twist', collected in *Books in General* (1981).

51 It is well known that, when two or three authors meet, they at once start talking about money—like everyone else.
1978 In *The Author*, Spring.

52 What Chekhov saw in our failure to communicate was something positive and precious: the private silence in which we live, and which enables us to endure our own solitude.
1979 *The Myth Makers*, 'Chekhov'.

53 It is the role of the poet to look at what is happening in the world and to know that quite other things are happening.
1979 *The Myth Makers*, 'Pasternak'.

54 The poet is a master of the quotidian, of conveying a whole history in two or three lines that point to an exact past drama and intensify a future one.
1979 *The Myth Makers*, 'Borges'.

55 A short story is always a disclosure.
1981 *The Oxford Book of Short Stories* (edited by Pritchett), introduction.

56 'The firm'—a proud Victorian word. It evokes the lost sense of Victorian regard for the pride of people in their daily trade.
'Betjeman', in the *New Yorker*, 24 Jun.

Private Eye

British satirical magazine, founded 1962.

57 Kill An Argie—Win A Metro!
1982 Front page headline during the Falklands War, parodying the jingoism of tabloid coverage of the conflict.

Proctor, Adelaide Ann *pseudonym of* Mary Berwick
1825–64

English poet. She won renown with her *Legends and Lyrics* (1858–60), and her poem 'The Lost Chord' was set to music by Sir Arthur Sullivan.

58 Seated one day at the organ,
I was weary and ill at ease,
And my fingers wandered idly
Over the noisy keys;
I know not what I was playing,
Or what I was dreaming then,
But I struck one chord of music,
Like the sound of a great Amen.
1858 'The Lost Chord'.

Profumo, John Dennis 1915–

English Conservative politician, Secretary of State for War in 1960. He resigned in 1963 during the 'Profumo Affair', admitting that he had deceived the House over the nature of his relationship with Christine Keeler, who was at the time also involved with a Russian diplomat. He turned to charitable service, and was awarded the CBE in 1975.

59 There was no impropriety whatsoever in my acquaintanceship with Miss Keeler… I shall not hesitate to issue writs for libel and slander if scandalous allegations are made or repeated outside the House.
1963 House of Commons, Mar.

Prokofiev, Sergei Sergeyevich 1891–1953

Russian composer, who lived in exile in the West (1918–36). His works include the *Classical Symphony* (1917), the opera *The Love for Three Oranges* (1919), the ballets *The Prodigal Son* (1928) and *Romeo and Juliet* (1936), *Peter and the Wolf* (1936) and the opera *War and Peace* (1943).

60 Bach on the wrong notes.
Of the music of Stravinsky. Quoted in V Seroff *Sergei Prokofiev* (1968).

Propertius, Sextus 1C BC

Roman poet.

61 *Navita de ventis, de tauris narrat arator,*
Enumerat miles vulnera, pastor oves.
The sailor tells stories of the winds, the ploughman of bulls; the soldier lists his wounds, the shepherd his sheep.
Elegies, bk.2, no.1, l.43–4.

62 *Cedite Romani scriptores, cedite Grai!*
Nescioquid maius nascitur Iliade.
Make way, Roman writers, make way, Greeks! Something greater than the *Iliad* is born.
Of Virgil's *Aeneid*. *Elegies*, bk.2, no.34, l.65–6.

Protagoras c.490–c.420 BC

Greek Sophist and teacher, the first and most famous of the Sophists who, for a fee, offered professional training in public life and other skills. His works survive only as fragments in other writers (notably Plato).

63 Man is the measure of all things, of the existence of the things that are, and the non-existence of the things that are not.
Fragment quoted in Plato *Theaetetus*, 152a (translated by H North Fowler, 1977).

64 He said that there is no art without practice, and no practice without art.
Fragment quoted in H Diels and W Kranz (eds) *Die Fragmente der Vorsokratiker*, vol.2 (1952), 268, no.10.

65 Concerning the gods I am not in a position to know either that they are or that they are not, or what they are like in appearance; for there are many things that are preventing knowledge, the obscurity of the matter and the brevity of human life.
Quoted in G B Kerferd *The Sophistic Movement* (1981), ch.13.

Proudhon, Pierre Joseph 1809–65

French socialist and political theorist, the founder of French radicalism. His works include the great *Système des contradictions économiques* (1846, *System of Economic Contradictions*). Imprisoned for three years in 1849 and again in 1858, he spent the time writing further works arguing for liberty, equality and justice.

66 *La propriété, c'est le vol.*
Property is theft.
1840 *Qu'est-ce que la propriété?*.

67 Universal suffrage is counter-revolution.
On Europe after the 1848 revolution. Quoted in A J P Taylor *From Napoleon to the Second International* (1993).

Proulx, Annie 1935–

US author whose works include *The Shipping News* (1993), which won a number of awards including the Pulitzer Prize (1994).

68 If you get the landscape right, the characters will step out of it, and they'll be in the right place.
1993 *Time*, 29 Nov.

69 At thirty-six, bereft, brimming with grief and thwarted love, Quoyle steered away to Newfoundland, the rock that had generated his ancestors, a place he had never been nor thought to go.
1993 *The Shipping News*, ch.1.

Proust, Marcel 1871–1922

French novelist who withdrew (c.1905) from society because of asthma, the death of his parents and disillusionment with the world. He introduced psychological analysis into fiction, notably in his 13-volume novel sequence *À la recherche du temps perdu* (1913–27).

70 *Il vaut mieux rêver sa vie que la vivre, encore que la vivre ce soit encore la rêver.*
It's better to dream your life than to live it, and even though you live it, you will still dream it.
1896 *Les Plaisirs et les jours*.

71 *Le bonheur est dans l'amour un état anormal.*
In love, happiness is abnormal.
1919 *À la recherche du temps perdu*, 'À l'ombre des jeunes filles en fleurs'.

72 *Nous sommes tous obligés, pour rendre la réalité supportable, d'entretenir en nous quelques petites folies.*
We must all indulge in a few follies if we are to make reality bearable.

1919 *À la recherche du temps perdu*, 'À l'ombre des jeunes filles en fleurs'.

73 *L'adolescence est le seul temps où l'on ait appris quelque chose.*
Adolescence is the only time when we can learn something.
1919 *À la recherche du temps perdu*, 'À l'ombre des jeunes filles en fleurs'.

74 *On devient moral dès qu'on est malheureux.*
We become moral once we are miserable.
1919 *À la recherche du temps perdu*, 'À l'ombre des jeunes filles en fleurs'.

75 *On ne reçoit pas la sagesse, il faut la découvrir soi-même, après un trajet que personne ne peut faire pour nous, ne peut nous épargner.*
We do not receive wisdom. We must discover it ourselves after experiences which no one else can have for us and from which no one else can spare us.
1919 *À la recherche du temps perdu*, 'À l'ombre des jeunes filles en fleurs'.

76 *Il n'y avait pas d'anormaux quand l'homosexualité était la norme.*
There was nothing abnormal about it when homosexuality was the norm.
1921 *À la recherche du temps perdu*, 'Sodome et Gomorrhe'.

77 *La médecine a fait quelques petits progrès dans ses connaissances depuis Molière, mais aucun dans son vocabulaire.*
Medicine has made a few, small advances in knowledge since Molière, but none in its vocabulary.
1921 *À la recherche du temps perdu*, 'Sodome et Gomorrhe'.

78 Neurosis has an absolute genius for malingering. There is no illness which it cannot counterfeit perfectly.
1922 *Sodom and Gomorrah.*

79 *L'amour, c'est l'espace et le temps rendus sensibles au cœur.*
Love is space and time made tender to the heart.
1923 *À la recherche du temps perdu*, 'La Prisonnière'.

80 *La possession de ce qu'on aime est une joie plus grande encore que l'amour.*
Possessing what one loves is an even greater joy than love itself.
1923 *À la recherche du temps perdu*, 'La Prisonnière'.

81 *On a dit que la beauté est une promesse de bonheur. Inversement, la possibilité du plaisir peut être un commencement de beauté.*
It has been said that beauty is a guarantee of happiness. Conversely, the possibility of pleasure can be the beginning of beauty.
1923 *À la recherche du temps perdu*, 'La Prisonnière'.

82 *L'adultère introduit l'esprit dans la lettre que bien souvent le mariage eût laissée morte.*
Adultery breathes new life into marriages which have been left for dead.
1923 *À la recherche du temps perdu*, 'La Prisonnière'.

83 *L'idée qu'on mourra est plus cruelle que mourir, mais moins que l'idée qu'un autre est mort.*
The idea of dying is worse than dying itself, but less cruel than the idea that another has died.
1923 *À la recherche du temps perdu*, 'La Prisonnière'.

84 [Music] a pederast might hum when raping a choirboy.
Of Fauré's *Romances sans paroles*. Quoted in *Musical Quarterly*, 1924.

85 *Laissons les jolies femmes aux hommes sans imagination.*
Leave the pretty women for the men without imagination.
1925 *À la recherche du temps perdu*, 'Albertine disparue'.

86 *Le mensonge est essentiel à l'humanité. Il y joue peut-être un aussi grand rôle que la recherche du plaisir, et d'ailleurs est commandé par cette recherche.*
Lies are essential to humanity. They play perhaps as great a role as the pursuit of pleasure, and are indeed controlled by this pursuit.
1925 *À la recherche du temps perdu*, 'Albertine disparue'.

87 *Si notre vie est vagabonde, notre mémoire est sédentaire.*
Even though our lives wander, our memories remain in one place.
1927 *À la recherche du temps perdu*, 'Le Temps retrouvé'.

88 *Le temps qui change les êtres ne modifie pas l'image que nous avons gardée d'eux.*
Although time changes people, it cannot change the image we have already made of them.
1927 *À la recherche du temps perdu*, 'Le Temps retrouvé'.

89 *Le bonheur est salutaire pour les corps, mais c'est le chagrin qui développe les forces de l'esprit.*
Happiness is healthy for the body, but it is sorrow which enhances the forces of the mind.
1927 *À la recherche du temps perdu*, 'Le Temps retrouvé'.

90 *Le style, pour l'écrivain aussi bien que pour le peintre, est une question non de technique mais de vision.*
For the writer as well as for the painter, style is not a question of technique, but of vision.
1927 *À la recherche du temps perdu*, 'Le Temps retrouvé'.

91 *Pour écrire ce livre essentiel, le seul livre vrai, un grand écrivain n'a pas, dans le sens courant, à l'inventer puisqu'il existe déjà en chacun de nous, mais à le traduire.*
To write the essential book, the only true book, a great writer does not need to invent because the book already exists inside each one of us and merely needs translation.
1927 *À la recherche du temps perdu*, 'Le Temps retrouvé'.

92 *En réalité, chaque lecteur est, quand il lit, le propre lecteur de soi-même. L'ouvrage de l'écrivain n'est qu'une espèce d'instrument optique qu'il offre au lecteur afin de lui permettre de discerner ce que, sans ce livre, il n'eût peut-être pas vu en soi-même.*
In reality, each reader reads only what is already within himself. The book is only a kind of optical instrument which the writer offers to the reader to enable him to discover in himself what he could not have found but for the aid of the book.
1927 *À la recherche du temps perdu*, 'Le Temps retrouvé'.

Prout, Father

► *See Mahony, Francis Sylvester*

Prynne, William 1600–69

English Puritan. An opponent of the theatre, he was imprisoned for publishing *Histrio Mastix: The Players' Scourge, or Actors' Tragedie* (1633), with its criticism of Charles I's queen Henrietta

Maria. His ears were cut off as a punishment in 1634 and he was imprisoned again in 1650 for refusing to pay taxes.

93 Stage-plays…are sinfull, heathenish, lewd, ungodly Spectacles and most pernicious Corruptions, condemned in all ages as intolerable Mischiefes to Churches, to Republickes, to the manners, mindes and soules of men. And that the Profession of Play-poets, of Stage-players; together with the penning, acting and frequenting of Stage-plays are unlawfull, infamous and misbeseeming Christians.
1633 *Histrio Mastix: The Players' Scourge, or Actors' Tragedie.*

Pryor, Richard 1940–

US comedian.

94 Two things people throughout history have had in common are hatred and humour. I am proud that I have been able to use humour to lessen people's hatred.
2004 In *The Scotsman*, 5 Jun.

Publilius Syrus 1c BC

Writer of Latin mimes.

95 *Formosa facies muta commendatio est.*
A beautiful face is a dumb commendation.
Sententiae.

96 *Inopi beneficium bis dat qui dat celeriter.*
He who gives quickly gives the poor man twice as much.
Sententiae.

Puccini, Giacomo Antonio Domenico Michele Secondo Maria 1858–1924

Italian composer, best known for his operas *La Bohème* (1896), *Tosca* (1900) and *Madama Butterfly* (1900). His last opera, *Turandot*, was unfinished.

97 Who sent you to me—God?
To Caruso, who was auditioning for him. Quoted in Derek Watson *Music Quotations* (1991).

Puckett, B Earl

US businessman, President of Allied Stores Corp.

98 It is our job to make women unhappy with what they have.
Recalled on his death, in *Newsweek*, 23 Feb 1976.

Pudney, John Sleigh 1909–77

British poet, journalist and novelist. He is best known for his poem 'For Johnny' (1941) and his novel *The Net* (1952).

99 Do not despair
For Johnny Head-in-Air
He sleeps as sound
As Johnny Underground.
1941 'For Johnny', spoken by Sir Michael Redgrave at the end of the film *The Way to the Stars* (1945).

Puig, Manuel 1932–90

Argentinian novelist. He studied cinema in Rome and spent several years in New York. His novels, which often exploit society's popular icons, include *El beso de la mujer araña* (1976), adapted for stage, screen and Broadway musical.

1 *Porque, sí, fuera de la celda están nuestros opresores, pero adentro no. Aquí nadie oprime a nadie. Lo único que hay, de perturbador, para mi mente…cansada, o condicionada o deformada…es que alguien me quiere tratar bien, sin pedir nada a cambio.*
Because, well, outside of this cell we may have our oppressors, yes, but not inside. Here no one oppresses the other. The only thing that seems to disturb me…because I'm exhausted, or conditioned, or perverted…is that someone wants to be nice to me, without asking anything back for it.
1976 *El beso de la mujer araña*, ch.11 (translated as *Kiss of the Spider Woman*, 1978).

Pulitzer, Joseph 1847–1911

Hungarian-born US newspaper proprietor. He emigrated to the US in 1864, became a reporter and began to acquire and revitalize old newspapers, notably the New York *World*. He established the annual Pulitzer prizes.

2 I want to talk to a nation, not to a select committee.
1909 In *Pearson's Magazine*, Mar.

3 We are a democracy, and there is only one way to get a democracy on its feet in the matter of its individual, its social, its municipal, its State, its National conduct, and that is by keeping the public informed about what is going on. There is not a crime, there is not a dodge, there is not a trick, there is not a swindle, there is not a vice which does not live by secrecy. Get these things out in the open, describe them, attack them, ridicule them in the press, and sooner or later public opinion will sweep them away.
c.1910 Quoted in Alleyne Ireland *An Adventure with a Genius*, ch.4.

4 What a newspaper needs in its news, in its headlines, and on its editorial page is terseness, humor, descriptive power, satire, originality, good literary style, clever condensation and accuracy, accuracy, accuracy.
c.1910 Quoted in Alleyne Ireland *An Adventure with a Genius*, ch.4.

Punch

British humorous weekly periodical, founded 1841.

5 Advice to persons about to marry—don't.
1845

6 You pays your money and you takes your choice.
1846

7 Let us be a nation of shopkeepers as much as we please, but there is no necessity that we should become a nation of advertisers.
1848 Quoted in David Ogilvy *Confessions of an Advertising Man* (1963), ch.2.
► *See Smith 798:50.*

8 Never do today what you can put off till tomorrow.
1849

9 Nothink for nothink 'ere, and precious little for sixpence.
1869

10 Sure, the next train has gone ten minutes ago.
1871

11 Go directly—see what she's doing, and tell her she mustn't.
1872

12 There was one poor tiger that hadn't *got* a Christian.
1875

13 I am not hungry; but thank goodness, I am greedy.
1878

14 Nearly all our best men are dead! Carlyle, Tennyson, Browning, George Eliot!—I'm not feeling very well myself.
1891

15 Botticelli isn't a wine, you Juggins! Botticelli's a *cheese!*
1891

16 Sometimes I sits and thinks, and then again I just sits.
1906

Purdy, Al 1918–2000

Canadian poet. Born in rural Ontario, he settled there again after some years away. He published nearly 30 volumes of poetry, including *The Cariboo Horses* (1965), *The Stone Bird* (1981) and *To Paris Never Again: New Poems* (1997).

17 Uneasily the leaves fall at this season,
forgetting what to do or where to go;
the red amnesiacs of autumn
drifting thru the graveyard forest.

What they have forgotten they have forgotten:
what they meant to do instead of fall
is not in earth or time recoverable—
the fossils of intention, the shapes of rot.
1962 *Poems for All the Annettes*, 'Pause' (revised 1968).

18 This is the country of defeat.
1965 *The Cariboo Horses*, 'The Country North of Belleville' (revised 1972).

19 They had their being once
and left a place to stand on.
1968 *Poems for All the Annettes*, 'Roblin Mills' (revised 1972).

Pushkin, Aleksandr Sergeyevich 1799–1837

Russian poet and writer. He is best known for the novel in verse *Eugene Onegin* (1833) and the tragic drama *Boris Godunov* (1825). He also wrote ballads and prose pieces. He was killed in a duel with his brother-in-law.

20 Moscow…what surge that sound can start
In every Russian's inmost heart!
1833 *Eugene Onegin*, ch.7, stanza 36 (translated by Adrian Room, 1995).

Putnam, Israel 1718–90

American general in the American Revolution.

21 Men, you are all marksmen—don't one of you fire until you see the white of their eyes.
1775 Order before the Battle of Bunker Hill. Quoted in R Frothingham *History of the Siege of Boston* (1873), ch.5.

Pu Yi 1906–67

Chinese puppet emperor. He was proclaimed Emperor at the age of two, but after the Chinese Revolution (1911) he was given a pension and a summer palace. He eventually became a private citizen. The story of his life was made into a film, *The Last Emperor*, in 1988.

22 For the past 40 years I had never folded my own quilt, made my own bed, or poured out my own washing. I had never even washed my own feet or tied my shoes.
1964 *From Emperor to Citizen: The Autobiography of Aisin-Gioro Pu Yi* (translated by W J F Jenner).

Puzo, Mario 1920–99

US novelist. His breakthrough as a writer came with his novel about the Mafia, *The Godfather* (1969). It became a bestseller and the basis of a trilogy of films directed by Francis Ford Coppola.

23 I'll make him an offer he can't refuse.
1969 *The Godfather*, bk.1, ch.1.

24 A lawyer with a briefcase can steal more than a hundred men with guns.
1969 *The Godfather*, bk.1, ch.1.

25 Like many businessmen of genius he learned that free competition was wasteful, monopoly efficient. And so he simply set about achieving that efficient monopoly.
1969 *The Godfather*, bk.3, ch.14.

26 Show me a gambler and I'll show you a loser, show me a hero, and I'll show you a corpse.
1978 *Fools Die*, ch.2.

27 Our own death wish is our only real tragedy.
1978 *Fools Die*, ch.55.

28 No, I never heard nothing about it, but when they name any disease after two guys, it's got to be terrible!
On Guillain-Barré syndrome. Quoted in Heller and Vogel *No Laughing Matter* (1986).

Pyke, Magnus 1908–92

British scientist and broadcaster.

29 Once a man or woman begins to take a serious interest in the way the universe works—that is to say in science —there is no telling what may turn up.
1976 *Butter Side Up*.

Pyrrhus of Epirus 319 272 BC

Greek king, renowned for his wars against the Romans. From 281 BC he fought Rome on behalf of the Tarentines and won battles in 280 BC and 279 BC, but with very high casualties (hence the expression a 'Pyrrhic victory'). He was killed in a street fight in Argos during a war with the Macedonians.

30 One more such victory, and we are lost!
279 BC After defeating the Romans at Asculum. Quoted in Plutarch *Regum et imperatorum apophthegmata*, 184c.

Pythagoras 6C BC

Greek philosopher and mathematician. He founded a school in Crotona but was persecuted there and settled in Lucania. He taught an abstemious way of life and a doctrine of transmigration, but is best remembered for his mathematical work.

31 There is geometry in the humming of the strings. There is music in the spacings of the spheres.
Quoted in Aristotle *Metaphysics*.

Q

Qaboos, Bin Said 1940–

Sultan of Oman. On the deposition of his father in 1970 he became Oman's ruler. He is also Prime Minister and Minister of Foreign Affairs, Defence and Finance.

32 Don't wait for schools to be built. Teach the children under the nearest tree.
1995 Quoted by Rosalind Miles in 'An Oxonian in Oman', in *Oxford Today*, vol.7, no.2, Hilary Issue, 1995.

Qian, Zhang

33 They gave us our rice bowl and we don't want it broken.
1993 On the need to avoid offending the government that permitted broadcasts by Shanghai's Radio Orient. In the *New York Times*, 26 Apr.

Quant, Mary 1934–

English fashion designer. She opened a small boutique, Bazaar, in Chelsea in 1955. In the 1960s she became one of the best-known designers of the 'swinging Britain' era when the simplicity of her designs, especially the mini-skirt, and the originality of her colours attracted international attention.

34 A fashionable woman wears clothes; the clothes don't wear her.
1966 *Quant by Quant*.

35 Fashion should be a game.
1966 *Quant by Quant*.

36 A woman is as young as her knee.
Attributed.

Quarles, Francis 1592–1644

English religious poet. His best-known works are *Emblems* (1635), a series of symbolic pictures with verse commentary, and a book of aphorisms, *Enchyridion* (1640).

37 My soul; sit thou a patient looker-on;
Judge not the play before the play is done:
Her plot hath many changes, every day
Speaks a new scene; the last act crowns the play.
1630 *Epigram, Respice Finem*.

Quayle, Dan (James Danforth) 1947–

US politician. He became a member of Congress (1977–81) and the Senate (1981–8) and served as Vice-President under George Bush (1988–92).

38 It doesn't help…when primetime TV has a character…bearing a child alone…just another lifestyle choice.
1992 Criticism of Murphy Brown, played by Candice Bergen. In the *Washington Post*, 21 May. The comment set off a great controversy about single mothers and freedom of choice.
► *See Bentsen 78:84*.

Quennell, Sir Peter Courtney 1905–93

English biographer, Professor of English at Tokyo (1930). He wrote travel books, verse and novels, but is best known for his biographies of literary figures.

39 Every occupation, unless it employs the whole mind and satisfies the human creative instinct, is to some extent absurd; and about the advertising business what I chiefly disliked was not so much the work I did as its general atmosphere of unreality. We dealt in fairy-gold—in fugitive dreams and illusions.
1977 *The Marble Foot: an Autobiography, 1905–1938*, p.227.

Quiller-Couch, Sir Arthur Thomas *known as 'Q'* 1863–1944

English writer and critic. His prominence as a critic dates from 1900, when he edited the *Oxford Book of English Verse*. He also wrote novels, short stories, children's books and poetry.

40 He that loves but half of Earth
Loves but half enough for me.
1896 'The Comrade'.

41 Not as we wanted it,
But as God granted it.
1896 'To Bearers'.

42 O the Harbour of Fowey
Is a beautiful spot,
And it's there I enjowey
To sail in a yot;
Or to race in a yacht
Round a mark or a buoy—
Such a beautiful spacht
Is the Harbour of Fuoy!
1899 *A Fowey Garland*, 'The Harbour of Fowey'.

43 The best is the best, though a hundred judges have declared it so.
1900 *The Oxford Book of English Verse*, preface.

44 Our fathers have, in process of centuries, provided this realm, its colonies and wide dependencies, with a speech as malleable and pliant as Attic, dignified as Latin, masculine, yet free of Teutonic guttural, capable of being precise as French, dulcet as Italian, sonorous as Spanish, and captaining all these excellences to its service.
1900 *The Oxford Book of English Verse*, preface.

45 Literature is not an abstract science, to which exact definitions can be applied. It is an Art rather, the success of which depends on personal persuasiveness, on the author's skill to give as on ours to receive.
1913 Inaugural lecture as Professor of English at Cambridge University.

46 Gilbert had a baddish streak or two in him; and one in particular which was not only baddish but so thoroughly caddish that no critic can ignore or, in my view, extenuate it. The man, to summarize, was essentially cruel, and delighted in cruelty.
1929 Of W S Gilbert. *Studies in Literature*, 3rd series, 'Lecture on W.S. Gilbert', no.4.

47 There was an old man of St Omer
Who objected, 'This town's a misnomer;
You've no right to translate
And beatificate
A simple digamma in Homer.'
1941 'A Limerick', in *Chanticlere*, Michaelmas Term.

48 Swinburne is just emptiness to me as he gets older, and the more maddening as he goes on exploiting a heavenly

gift. I wish he had just shut up, like Coleridge, and left us surmising wonders.
Quoted in A L Rowse *Quiller-Couch: a Portrait of 'Q'* (1988).

Quin, James 1693–1766

English actor. A performer in the tradition of heroic tragedy, whose most acclaimed roles included Falstaff, he outlived the popularity of the bombastic declamatory style of which he was the master but steadfastly refused to change with the times. He was also noted for his fiery temper.

49 If the young fellow is right, I and the rest of the players have been all wrong.
c.1741 Of David Garrick and his revolutionary, more naturalistic acting style. Attributed.

Quindlen, Anna 1953

US journalist and author. She worked as a reporter for the *New York Times* (1977–81) and is now a syndicated columnist. She won the Pulitzer Prize for Commentary in 1992 and was named Woman of the Year for 1991 by *Glamour* magazine.

50 The purse is the mirror of the soul.
1987 In the *New York Times*, 16 Dec.

Quine, Willard Van Orman 1908–2000

US philosopher and logician, Professor of Philosophy at Harvard (1948 78). He wrote many works on logic and language, including *Two Dogmas of Empiricism* (1951), *Word and Object* (1960) and *From Stimulus to Science* (1995).

51 To define an expression is, paradoxically speaking, to explain how to get along without it. To define is to eliminate.
1987 *Quiddities*, 'Definition'.

52 We can applaud the state lottery as a public subsidy of intelligence, for it yields public income that is calculated to lighten the tax burden of us prudent abstainers at the expense of the benighted masses of wishful thinkers.
1987 *Quiddities*, 'Gambling'

Quinet, Edgar 1803–75

French writer and politician.

53 *La famille des Bourbons est un poignard que l'étranger en 1814 a laissé dans le cœur de la France: changez le manche comme il vous plaira, dorez la lame si vous voulez, le poignard reste poignard.*
The Bourbon family is a dagger which the foreigner left in the heart of France in 1814: change the haft if you please, gild the blade if you will, the dagger remains a dagger.
1877 *Œuvres*, vol.3, p.267.

Quinn, Jane Bryant 1939–

US journalist, broadcaster and financial pundit. Her works include *Everyone's Money Book* (1979) and *Making the Most of Your Money* (1991).

54 Half of them don't know what's going to happen tomorrow and the other half don't know they don't know.
1994 Of stock market players. On CNN TV, 4 Apr.

Quintilian *properly* Marcus Fabius Quintilianus c.35–c.100 AD

Roman rhetorician born in Spain. He studied oratory at Rome and settled there as an advocate and teacher of rhetoric. His pupils included Pliny the Younger. His reputation rests on his *Institutio Oratoria* ('Education of an Orator').

55 *Mendaces memorem esse oportere.*
Liars need to have good memories.
Institutio Oratoria, 4.2.91 (translated by H E Butler, 1968).

56 *Scribitur ad narrandum, non ad probandum.*
It is written for the purpose of narrative, not of proof.
Of history. *Institutio Oratoria*, 10.1.31 (translated by H E Butler, 1968).

Quiroga, Horacio 1878–1937

Uruguayan short-story writer, who spent most of his life in the Argentinian province of Misiones, where most of his stories, generally dealing with morbid themes, are set. He committed suicide in a charity hospital.

57 *Se comprende muy bien que el advenimiento del cinematógrafo haya sido para mí el comienzo de un nueva era, por la cual cuento las noches sucesivas en que he salido mareado y pálido del cine, porque he dejado mi corazón…en la pantalla que impregnó por tres cuartos de hora el encanto de Brownie Vernon.*
It is easy to understand that, for me, cinema was the beginning of a new era which marked my nights, one after the other, as I left the theatre, dizzy and pale after leaving my heart on the screen…on that screen that for forty-five minutes was impregnated by Brownie Vernon's charm.
1921 *Anaconda*, 'Miss Dorothy Phillips, mi esposa' ('Miss Dorothy Phillips, My Wife').

Raban, Jonathan 1942–

English writer. He has written novels and literary criticism, but is best known for his travel books. He now lives in the US.

58 The Falklands held a mirror up to our own islands, and it reflected, in brilliantly sharp focus, all our injured belittlement, our sense of being beleaguered, neglected and misunderstood.
1986 *Coasting*, ch.3.

59 If we live inside a bad joke, it is up to us to learn, at best and worst, to tell it well.
1986 *Coasting*, ch.6.

60 Good travel books are novels at heart.
Recalled by Christopher Lehmann-Haupt in the *New York Times*, 26 Jan 1987, reviewing Raban's novel *Coasting* (1986).

61 The mythical America…—that marvellous, heroic, sentimental land—was an object of faith. It challenged you to make the believer's leap over the rude facts at your feet.
1990 *Hunting Mister Heartbreak*, ch.2.

Rabelais, François c.1494–c.1553

French humanist and satirist, who began his career as a

Franciscan monk. He studied Greek and Latin as well as medicine, law and philology, and wrote two novels under the pseudonym Alcofribas Nasier.

62 *Science sans conscience n'est que ruine de l'âme.*
Science without conscience is the soul's perdition.
1532 *Pantagruel*, bk.2, ch.8.

63 *Il avait soixante et trois manières d'en trouver toujours à son besoin, dont la plus honorable et la plus commune était par façon de larcin furtivement fait.*
He had sixty-three ways to find the money when he needed it, the most honourable and most ordinary of which was to steal secretively.
1532 *Pantagruel*, bk.2, ch.16.

64 *Mieux est de ris que de larmes écrire*
Pour ce que rire est le propre de l'homme.
It is better to write of laughter than of tears
For laughter is the basis of humankind.
1534 *Gargantua*, Aux lecteurs.

65 *L'odeur du vin, ô combien plus est friand, riant, priant, plus céleste et délicieux que d'huile!*
The odour of wine, oh how much sweeter, more cheerful, pleasing, heavenly and delicious it is than oil!
1534 *Gargantua*, Prologue de l'auteur.

66 *Rompre l'os et sucer la substantifique moelle.*
Break the bone and suck out the very substance.
1534 *Gargantua*, Prologue de l'auteur.

67 *L'appétit vient en mangeant.*
Appetite comes with eating.
1534 *Gargantua*, bk.1, ch.5.

68 *Du cheval donné toujours regardait en la gueule.*
Always look a gift horse in the mouth.
1534 *Gargantua*, bk.1, ch.11.

69 *Lever matin n'est point bonheur;*
Boire matin est le meilleur.
Getting up in the morning does not make you happy;
Drinking in the morning is the best.
1534 *Gargantua*, bk.1, ch.22.

70 *Nature n'endure mutations soudaines sans grande violence.*
Nature does not endure sudden changes without great violence.
1534 *Gargantua*, bk.1, ch.23.

71 *Thésauriser est fait de vilain.*
To hoard is a villainous act.
1534 *Gargantua*, bk.1, ch.33.

72 *Jamais je ne m'assujettis aux heures: les heures sont faites pour l'homme, et non l'homme pour les heures.*
I never subject myself to hours: hours are made for men; men are not made for hours.
1534 *Gargantua*, bk.1, ch.41.

73 *En leur règle n'était que cette clause:* FAIS CE QUE VOUDRAS.
In their laws there was but this one clause: DO WHAT YOU WISH.
1534 *Gargantua*, bk.1, ch.57.

74 *Un fol enseigne bien un sage.*
A fool has a lot to teach a wise man.
1546 *Tiers Livre*, pt.37.

75 *O que trois et quatre fois heureux sont ceux qui plantent choux!*
Oh, those who plant cabbages are three and four times happier than the rest of us!
1548 *Quart Livre*, pt.18.

76 *Pantagruélisme…est certaine gaieté d'esprit confite en mépris des choses fortuites.*
Pantagruelism is a certain liveliness of mind made in contempt of chance happenings.
1552 *Quart Livre*, Prologue de l'auteur.

77 *Ignorance est mère de tous les maux.*
Ignorance is the mother of all evils.
1564 *Cinquième Livre*, pt.7.

78 Abandon yourself to Nature's truths, and let nothing in this world be unknown to you.
Quoted in J H Plumb (ed) *The Horizon Book of the Renaissance* (1961).

Rabi, Isidor Isaac 1898–1988

US physicist, born in Austria. He taught physics at Columbia from 1929 and served as an adviser to the US Atomic Energy Commission. Rabi won the 1944 Nobel prize in physics for his discovery and measurement of the radio-frequency spectra of atomic nuclei.

79 It is only in science, I find, that we can get outside ourselves. It's realistic, and to a great degree verifiable, and it has this tremendous stage on which it plays. I have the same feeling—to a certain degree—about some religious expressions…but only to a certain degree. For me, the proper study of mankind is science, which also means that the proper study of mankind is man.
Quoted in Jeremy Bernstein *Experiencing Science* (1978).

Rabin, Yitzhak 1922–95

Israeli soldier and statesman. He was awarded the Nobel peace prize jointly with Shimon Peres and Yasser Arafat in 1994.

80 We say to you today in a loud and a clear voice: enough of blood and tears. Enough.
1993 To the Palestinians. Speech in Washington, 13 Sep.

Rachmaninov, Sergei Vasilevich 1873–1943

Russian composer and pianist, who settled in the US in 1918, best known for his piano music. His style epitomizes the lush romanticism of the later 19c, still apparent in his last major composition, *Rhapsody on a Theme of Paganini* (1934).

81 My dear hands. Farewell, my poor hands.
On being told that he was dying of cancer. Quoted in H Schonberg *The Great Pianists* (1964).

Racine, Jean 1639–99

French court dramatist who studied at Port Royal and went on to write many of his dramatic works for performance there.

82 *Ah! je l'ai trop aimé pour ne le point haïr!*
Oh! I loved him too much not to hate him now!
1667 *Andromaque*, act 2, sc.1.

83 *Les témoins sont fort chers, et n'en a pas qui veut.*
Witnesses are expensive and not everyone can afford them.
1668 *Les Plaideurs*, act 3, sc.3.

84 *J'aimais jusqu'à ses pleurs que je faisais couler.*
I loved even the tears which I made her cry.
1669 *Britannicus*, act 2, sc.2.

85 *J'embrasse mon rival, mais c'est pour l'étouffer.*
If I embrace my rival, it is to strangle him.
1669 *Britannicus*, act 4, sc.3.

86 *Ainsi que la vertu, le crime a ses degrés.*
Crime, like virtue, has its degrees.
1677 *Phèdre*, act 4, sc.2.

87 *Pensez-vous être saint et juste impunément?*
You think you can be holy and righteous with impunity?
1691 *Athalie*, act 1, sc.1.

Radisson, Pierre-Esprit 1636–1710

French traveller, explorer of New France (Canada).

88 We were Caesars, there being nobody to contradict us.
Attributed boast of the *coureur de bois* in the Canadian North West. Quoted in Arthur T Adams (ed) *The Explorations of Pierre-Esprit Radisson* (1961).

Rado, James 1939–

US composer and librettist.

89 This is the dawning of the age of Aquarius.
1968 *Hair*, 'Aquarius' (music by Galt MacDermot).

Rae, John 1931–

English writer.

90 War is, after all, the universal perversion.
1960 *The Custard Boys*, ch.13.

Rahner, Karl 1904–84

German Jesuit priest, who taught at Innsbruck and Munich and who was widely recognized as a leading Roman Catholic theologian.

91 But there is yet another form of this hidden heresy, and, paradoxically, it can affect those who are proudest of their long-standing and unimpeachable orthodoxy; heresy in the form of indifference.
1963 'Natur und Gnade' in *Fragen der Theologie Heute* (translated by Dinah Wharton as *Nature and Grace*, 1963).

Rainborowe, Thomas 1598–1648

English soldier.

92 The poorest He that is in England hath a life to live as well as the greatest He, and therefore, truly Sirs, I think that every man that is to live under a Government ought first, by his own consent, to put himself under that Government.
1647 Said to Cromwell during the Army Debates, Putney, 29 Oct.

Raine, Craig Anthony 1944–

English poet and critic. His collections include *A Martian Sends a Postcard Home* (1979) and *Collected Poems 1978–1999* (1999).

93 We live in the great indoors:
the vacuum cleaner grazes
over the carpet, lowing,
its udder a swollen wobble.
1978 'An Inquiry into Two Inches of Ivory'.
➤ *See Austen 43:88.*

94 Caxtons are mechanical birds with many wings
and some are treasured for their markings.
1979 'A Martian Sends a Postcard Home'.

95 But time is tied to the wrist
or kept in a box, ticking with impatience.
1979 'A Martian Sends a Postcard Home'.

96 The mind is a museum
to be looted at night.
1984 'The Grey Boy'.

Raine, Kathleen Jessie 1908–2003

English poet and critic. Her poetry reflects a mystical, visionary appreciation of nature, and she was a sympathetic critic of symbolists such as Blake, Hopkins and Yeats.

97 Nowadays harmony comes almost as a shock.
Letter to Arthur Bliss.

Raleigh, Sir Walter 1552–1618

English courtier, navigator and poet. His writings include lyric poems, *The Discovery of Guyana* (1596) and an unfinished *History of the World* (1614). Implicated in a plot to overthrow Queen Elizabeth, his death sentence was suspended until 1618, when he was beheaded.

98 If all the world and love were young,
And truth in every shepherd's tongue
These pretty pleasures might me move
To live with thee and be thy love.
c.1592 'The Nymph's Reply to the Shepherd', a response to Marlowe's 'The Passionate Shepherd to His Love', attributed to Raleigh.
➤ *See Marlowe 553:17.*

99 Give me my scallop shell of quiet,
My staff of faith to walk upon,
My scrip of joy, immortal diet,
My bottle of salvation,
My gown of glory, hope's true gage,
And thus I'll take my pilgrimage
1604 *The Passionate Man's Pilgrimage.*

1 What is our life? a play of passion;
Our mirth the music of division;
Our mothers' wombs the tiring-houses be
Where we are dressed for this short comedy.
Heaven the judicious sharp spectator is,
That sits and marks still who doth act amiss;
Our graves that hide us from the searching sun
Are like drawn curtains when the play is done.
Thus march we, playing, to our latest rest,
Only we die in earnest—that's no jest.
1612 'On the Life of Man'.

2 I shall never be persuaded that God hath shut up all light of learning within the lantern of Aristotle's brain.
1614 *The History of the World.*

3 Even such is Time, which takes in trust
Our youth, our joys, and all we have,
And pays us but with age and dust,
Who in the dark and silent grave
When we have wandered all our ways
Shuts up the story of our days,
And from which earth, and grave, and dust
The Lord shall raise me up, I trust.
1618 'The Author's Epitaph, Made by Himself'. Poem written the night before his death.

Rambert, Dame Marie 1888–1982

Polish-born British ballet dancer and teacher.

4 One is often asked whether his jump was really as high as it is always described. To that I answer: 'I don't know how far from the ground it was, but I know it was near the stars.' Who would watch the floor when he danced?
1960 On Vaslav Nijinsky. *Quicksilver.*

Ramón y Cajal, Santiago 1852–1934

Spanish physician and histologist. He made use of the specialized histological staining techniques of Camillo Golgi, and the two men shared the 1906 Nobel prize for physiology or medicine.

5 In my systematic explorations through the realms of microscopic anatomy, there came the turn of the nervous system, that masterpiece of life.
1937 *Recollections of My Life.*

Ramos, Graciliano 1892–1953

Brazilian novelist. In 1936 he was arrested and imprisoned, and on his release settled in Rio de Janeiro. His work explores the lives of characters shaped by the rural misery of north-east Brazil.

6 *Sempre que os homens sabidos lhe diziam palavras difíceis, ele saía logrado. Sobressaltava-se escutando-as. Evidentemente só serviam para encobrir ladroeiras. Mas eram bonitas.*
Whenever men with book learning used big words in dealing with him, he came out the loser. It startled him just to hear those words. Obviously they were just a cover for robbery. But they sounded nice.
1938 *Vidas secas* (translated as *Barren Lives*, 1965), 'Contas'.

Ramsey, Sir Alf(red) 1922–99

English footballer and manager. A player with Southampton and Tottenham Hotspur, he managed Ipswich Town in the early 1960s and went on to manage the England side that won the World Cup in 1966.

7 I feel like jumping over the moon.
1962 Quoted in Nigel Rees *Dictionary of Popular Phrases* (1990). This is one of the earliest records of the phrase 'over the moon' being used in the context of football.

8 Listen to them moan, but those people will be going mad if we beat West Germany by a goal in the World Cup Final.
1966 Of press criticism after England lost against West Germany in February, several months before England won the World Cup. Quoted in Bryon Butler *The Official History of the Football Association* (1986).

9 You've beaten them once. Now go out and bloody beat them again.
1966 Addressing his players when the World Cup final went into extra time.

Rand, Ayn 1905–82

Russian-born US novelist, screenwriter and ardent propagandist for her philosophy of self-interest against the altruistic tendencies of the welfare state. Her novels include *The Fountainhead* (1943) and *Atlas Shrugged* (1957).

10 The entire history of science is a progression of exploded fallacies, not of achievements.
1957 *Atlas Shrugged.*

Randall, Clarence Beldan 1891–1967

US businessman, Chief Executive Officer of Inland Steel. He wrote several books on business.

11 Every man who has lived his life to the full, should, by the time his senior years are reached, have established a reserve inventory of unfinished thinking.
1963 *Sixty-Five Plus.*

12 The leader must know, must know that he knows and must be able to make it abundantly clear to those about him that he knows.
1964 *Making Good in Management.*

Randall, Dudley 1914–2000

US poet and librarian. He established the Broadside Press, which prints the work of black US poets, including his own books.

13 Musing on roses and revolutions,
I saw night close down on the earth like a great dark
wing.
1968 *Cities Burning*, 'Roses and Revolutions'.

14 I saw dawn upon them like the sun a vision
of a time when all men walk proudly through the earth
and the bombs and missiles lie at the bottom of the
ocean
like the bones of dinosaurs buried under the shale of
eras.
1968 *Cities Burning*, 'Roses and Revolutions'.

15 Then washed in the brightness of this vision,
I saw how in its radiance would grow and be nourished
and suddenly
burst into terrible and splendid bloom
the blood-red flower of revolution.
1968 *Cities Burning*, 'Roses and Revolutions'.

Ranjitsinhji, Prince 1872–1933

Indian nobleman and England cricketer. A star batsman with Sussex and England, he succeeded as Jam Sahib of Nawanagar in 1906 (Maharaja in 1918), and did much to modernize and improve conditions in his home state.

16 He turned the old one-stringed instrument into a many-chorded lyre… W.G. discovered batting; he turned its many narrow straight channels into one great winding river.
1897 Of W G Grace. *The Jubilee Book of Cricket.*

17 Find out where the ball is, get there; hit it.
Explaining his tactics as a batsman. Quoted in Colin Jarman *The Guinness Dictionary of Sports Quotations* (1990).

Rankin, Ian 1960–

Scottish author, known for his detective novels featuring Inspector Rebus.

18 It was one of those cool, crepuscular days that could have belonged to any of at least three Scottish seasons, a sky like slate roofing and a wind that Rebus's father would have called 'snell'.
2001 *The Falls.*

Rankin, Jeanette 1880–1973

US pacifist and politician, the first woman in Congress. She voted against US entry into both World Wars and demonstrated against the war in Vietnam.

19 As a woman I can't go to war, and I refuse to send anyone else.
Quoted in Hannah Josephson *Lady in Congress* (1974).

20 You can no more win a war than you can win an earthquake.
Quoted in Hannah Josephson *Lady in Congress* (1974).

Ransom, John Crowe 1888–1974

US poet and critic. He was an influential figure in the rise of the New Criticism movement in the US, and an important Southern poet.

21 Here lies a lady of beauty and high degree.
Of chills and fever she died, of fever and chills,
The delight of her husband, her aunts, an infant of three,
And of medicos marvelling sweetly on her ills.
1924 *Chills and Fever*, 'Here Lies a Lady'.

22 The little cousin is dead, by foul subtraction,
A green bough from Virginia's aged tree.
1924 *Chills and Fever*, 'Dead Boy'.

23 Tawny are the leaves turned but they still hold,
And it is harvest; what shall this land produce?
A meagre hill of kernels, a runnel of juice;
Declension looks from our land, it is old.
Therefore let us assemble, dry, gray, spare,
And mild as yellow air.
1924 *Chills and Fever*, 'Antique Harvesters'.

24 The curse of hell upon the sleek upstart
That got the Captain finally on his back
And took the red red vitals of his heart
And made the kites to whet their beaks clack clack.
1924 *Chills and Fever*, 'Captain Carpenter'.

25 Two evils, monstrous either one apart,
Possessed me, and were long and loath at going:
A cry of Absence, Absence, in the heart,
And in the wood the furious winter blowing.
1924 *Chills and Fever*, 'Winter Remembered'.

26 And if no Lethe flows beneath your casement,
And when ten years have not brought full effacement,
Philosophy was wrong, and you may meet.
1924 *Grace after Meat*, 'Parting at Dawn'.

27 Old Hodge stays not his hand, but whips to kennel
The renegade. God's peace betide the souls
Of the pure in heart. But in the box that fennel
Grows around, are two red eyes that stare like coals.
1927 *Two Gentlemen in Bonds*, 'Dog'.

28 God have mercy on the sinner
Who must write with no dinner,
No gravy and no grub,
No pewter and no pub,
No belly and no bowels,
Only consonants and vowels.
1955 *Poems and Essays*, 'Survey of Literature'.

Raphael, Frederic 1931–

British novelist and screenwriter.

29 City of perspiring dreams.
1976 Of Cambridge. *The Glittering Prizes*, ch.3.

Rapoport, Anatol 1911–

Russian-born Canadian mathematician, social philosopher and peace advocate.

30 Cooperate on move one; thereafter, do whatever the other player did the previous move.
The two commands for his computer program, Tit for Tat, designed at the University of Toronto. It outperformed all other programs at an international computer tournament in 1979, and it continues to excel in tournaments. The program initiates reciprocal cooperation yet responds in kind to provocation.

Rattigan, Sir Terence 1911–77

English playwright.

31 When you're between any sort of devil and the deep blue sea, the deep blue sea sometimes looks very inviting.
1952 *The Deep Blue Sea*.

32 You can be in the Horseguards and still be common, dear.
1954 *Separate Tables*.

Rauschenberg, Robert 1925–

US artist, whose paintings and collages incorporate images and objects from everyday life. *Gloria* (1956) is a typical example of his 'combines', or collages.

33 I don't like masterpieces having one-night stands in collectors' homes between auctions.
1989 On quick-turnover profits on his work. In the *New York Times*, 10 May.

34 Most artists try to break your heart, or they accidentally break their own hearts. But I find the quietness in the ordinary much more satisfying.
2004 In the *New York Times*, 15 Feb.

35 They block the view.
2004 When asked what he had against mountains. In the *New York Times*, 15 Feb.

Ravel, (Joseph) Maurice 1875–1937

French composer. A pupil of Fauré, his innovative early compositions include *Schéhérazade* and the *Pavane pour une infante défunte* (both 1899). Other notable works include the ballet *Daphnis et Chloé* (1912), and *Boléro* (1928).

36 I've still so much music in my head. I have said nothing. I have so much more to say.
1937 Spoken on his deathbed. Quoted in Jourdan-Morhange *Ravel et nous* (1945).

37 A piece for orchestra without music.
Of his *Boléro*. Quoted in R Nichols *Ravel* (1977).

Ravitch, Diane Silvers 1938–

US historian, writer and Research Professor of Education at New York University. She was a member of the US Department of Education from 1991 to 1993.

38 The person who knows 'how' will always have a job. The person who knows 'why' will always be his boss.
1985 Speech at Reed College commencement. Reported in *Time*, 17 Jun.

Rawnsley, Andrew 1962–

English author, broadcaster and journalist.

39 The Millennium Dome was intended to be New Labour's Xanadu and Tony Blair its Kubla Khan.
2000 *Servants of the People: The Inside Story of New Labour.*

Ray, Dixy Lee 1914–94

US politician and administrator.

40 The general public has long been divided into two parts: those who think that science can do anything, and those who are afraid that it will.
1973 In *New Scientist*, 5 Jul.

Ray, James Earl 1928–98

US assassin of Martin Luther King. He was imprisoned in 1960 for armed robbery but escaped in 1967 and shot King. He was apprehended in London and sentenced in Memphis to 99 years.

41 I was in Tennessee 24 hours and got 99 years.
1988 On beginning the 20th year of his prison sentence for the assassination of Martin Luther King. In *Life*, March.

Rayburn, Sam(uel Taliaferro) 1882–1961

US politician. A Democrat, he represented Texas (1913–61) and was Speaker of the House for a record 17 terms between 1940 and 1961. He was a supporter of Roosevelt's New Deal.

42 I like to make running water walk.
Quoted in Valton J Young *The Speaker's Agent* (1956).

43 These…society women never serve chilli.
His reason for not attending parties. Quoted in David Brinkley *Washington Goes to War* (1988).

44 Go along and get along.
On politics as a process of accommodation, recalled by former Speaker Gerald R Ford in the *Washington Times*, 24 May 1995.

Read, Sir Herbert Edward 1893–1968

English poet and art critic. Editor of the *Burlington Magazine* (1933–9) and Professor of Fine Art at Edinburgh (1931–3), he wrote works on art criticism and *Naked Warriors* (1919), a poetry collection inspired by his war experiences.

45 I saw him stab
And stab again
A well-killed Boche.
1919 *Naked Warriors*, 'The Scene of War, 4. The Happy Warrior'.

46 This is the happy warrior,
This is he.
1919 *Naked Warriors*, 'The Scene of War, 4. The Happy Warrior'.

47 It is defiant—the desperate act of men too profoundly convinced of the rottenness of our civilization to want to save a shred of its respectability.
1936 Catalogue of the International Surrealist Exhibition, New Burlington Galleries, London, Jun/Jul, introduction.

48 But one thing we learned: there is no glory in the deed
Until the soldier wears a badge of tarnished braid.
1948 'To a Conscript of 1940'.

49 It will be a gay world. There will be lights everywhere except in the minds of men, and the fall of the last civilization will not be heard above the din.
1964 Quoted in Hoggart and Johnston, *An Idea of Europe* (1987), 'Pyramids and Planes'.

Reade, Charles 1814–84

English novelist and playwright.

50 Take courage, my friend, the devil is dead!
1861 *The Cloister and the Hearth.*

Reagan, Nancy 1923–

US actress and First Lady, second wife of US President Ronald Reagan.

51 If the President has a bully pulpit, then the First Lady has a white glove pulpit…more refined, restricted, ceremonial, but it's a pulpit all the same.
1988 In the *New York Times*, 10 Mar.

52 I'm more aware if somebody is trying to end-run him…it just never occurs to him.
1988 On protecting her husband. In *Time*, 28 Nov.

53 For eight years I was sleeping with the President, and if that doesn't give you special access, I don't know what does!
1989 *My Turn* (with William Novack).

Reagan, Ronald Wilson 1911–2004

US Republican politician, 40th President (1981–9), a radio sports announcer and film star. A Democrat turned Republican, he won nomination in 1980, defeating Carter to become President. He introduced economic reform, took a strong anti-communist stand and introduced the Strategic Defence Initiative ('Star Wars'). In 1981 he was wounded in an assassination attempt. Re-elected in 1984, he achieved a major arms-reduction accord with Gorbachev. His reputation was tarnished by the Iran–Contra affair.

54 To sit back hoping that some day, some way, someone will make things right is to go on feeding the crocodile, hoping that he will eat you last—but eat you he will.
1974 CBS News, 7 Nov.

55 Recession is when your neighbour loses his job. Depression is when you lose yours.
1980 Election campaign speech, Jersey City, 1 Sep.
➤ *See Truman 868:38.*

56 I can tell a lot about a fellow's character by the way that he eats jelly beans.
1981 In the *Daily Mail*, Jan.

57 Honey, I forgot to duck.
1981 Said to his wife, Nancy, after being shot by John R Hinckley, Jr, 30 Mar.
➤ *See Dempsey 261:86.*

58 Who's minding the store?
1981 After he was shot by John R Hinckley, Jr, 30 Mar.

59 This is not the end of anything. This is the beginning of everything.
1984 On his re-election. In *Time*, Nov.

60 We are not going to tolerate these attacks from outlaw states, run by the strangest collection of misfits, looney tunes and squalid criminals since the advent of the Third Reich.
1985 Speech after terrorist attacks by Shi'ite Muslims, Jul.

61 We must say something but not much because I'm being held out to dry.
1986 Comment at a meeting with National Security Council advisers, 10 Nov. Quoted by Theodore Draper *A Very Thin Line* (1991).

62 We make history and changing it is within our power.
1987 On welcoming Soviet premier Mikhail S Gorbachev to the White House, 8 Dec.

63 We don't know where that money came from and we don't know who had it and we don't know where it went.
1988 Of the Iran–Contra funding. In the *New York Times*, 17 Mar.

64 I paid for this microphone.
1988 To a New Hampshire moderator who tried to keep President Reagan from speaking on behalf of other candidates. Reported in *Congressional Quarterly*, 23 May.

65 There is our little bungalow down there.
1989 On viewing the White House from a helicopter the day he left office. Quoted in the *Washington Post*, 22 Apr 1991.

66 Washington is a sieve…it was virtually impossible to find out who was doing the leaking and shut them up.
1990 Deposition on the Iran–Contra arms sales. In the *New York Times*, 23 Feb.

67 Politics is just like show business…a hell of an opening, you coast for a while, you have a hell of a closing.
1995 In the *New York Times*, 23 Apr.

68 When men fail to drive toward a goal or purpose, but only drift, the drift is always towards barbarism.
Quoted in Edmund Morris *Dutch: A Memoir of Ronald Reagan* (1999).

Reardon, Ray 1932–

Welsh snooker player. He was world champion in 1970, 1973, 1976 and 1978.

69 I cannot remember anyone ever asking 'Who came second?' Can you?
Quoted in Colin Jarman *The Guinness Dictionary of Sports Quotations* (1990).

70 If I had to make the choice between staying married and playing snooker, snooker would win.
Quoted in Colin Jarman *The Guinness Dictionary of Sports Quotations* (1990).

Red Cloud *original name* Mahpiua Luta 1822–1909

Oglala Sioux chief who led the Indian war against the Americans.

71 You have heard the sound of the white soldier's axe on the Little Piney. His presence here is…an insult to the spirits of our ancestors. Are we to give up their sacred graves to be ploughed for corn? Dakotas, I am for war.
1866 Speech before war council at Fort Laramie, Wyoming.

Redmond, John Edward 1856–1918

Irish politician. A champion of Home Rule, he was Chairman of the Nationalist Party in 1900. He declined a seat in Asquith's coalition ministry (1915), but supported World War I, deplored the Irish rebellion, and opposed Sinn Féin.

72 The government may tomorrow withdraw every one of their troops from Ireland. Ireland will be defended by her armed sons from foreign invasion, and for that purpose the armed Catholics in the south will be only too glad to join arms with the armed Protestant Ulsterman. Is it too much to hope that out of this situation a result may spring that will be good not merely for the Empire but for the future welfare and integrity of the Irish nation?
1914 Speech, House of Commons, 3 Aug.

Redon, Odilon 1840–1916

French Symbolist painter and graphic artist, also well known for his work in pastel.

73 What distinguishes the artist from the dilettante? Only the pain that the artist feels. The dilettante looks only for pleasure in art.
c.1871 Journal entry, quoted in *Portfolio*, no.8, Spring 1964 (translated by Richard Howard).

74 All my originality consists…in giving life in human fashion to beings which are impossible according to the laws of possibility.
Quoted in Edward Lucie-Smith *Symbolist Art* (1972).

75 I am repelled by those who voice the word 'nature', without having any trace of it in their hearts.
Quoted in Edward Lucie-Smith *Symbolist Art* (1972).

Redtenbacher, Ferdinand 1818–83

German engineer, Professor of Mechanical Engineering and author on the construction of machinery.

76 Thanks to his bodily form and thanks to his mind, [man] is a universal machine, capable of an infinite diversity of movement.
1840 *Resultate fur den Maschinenbau* (published 1848).

Reed, Henry 1914–86

English poet and dramatist. He is best known for his war poems and for his radio plays, notably *The Private Life of Hilda Tablet* (1954). 'Chard Whitlow' (1946) is a parody of T S Eliot's 'Burnt Norton'.

77 Today we have naming of parts. Yesterday,
We had daily cleaning. And tomorrow morning,
We shall have what to do after firing. But today,
Today we have naming of parts. Japonica
Glistens like coral in all of the neighbouring gardens
And today we have naming of parts.
1946 *Lessons of the War*, pt.1, 'Naming of Parts'.

78 We can slide it
Rapidly backwards and forwards: we call this
Easing the spring. And rapidly backwards and forwards
The early bees are assaulting and fumbling the flowers:
They call it easing the Spring.
1946 *Lessons of the War*, pt.1, 'Naming of Parts'.

79 There may be dead ground in between; and I may not have got
The knack of judging a distance; I will only venture
A guess that perhaps between me and the apparent lovers,
(Who, incidentally, appear by now to have finished,)
At seven o'clock from the houses, is roughly a distance
Of about one year and a half.
1946 *Lessons of the War*, pt.2, 'Judging Distances'.

80 As we get older we do not get any younger.
Seasons return, and today I am fifty-five,
And this time last year I was fifty-four,
And this time next year I shall be sixty-two.
1946 'Chard Whitlow (Mr Eliot's Sunday Evening Postscript)', a parody of T S Eliot's style.

81 It is, we believe,
Idle to hope that the simple stirrup-pump
Can extinguish hell.
1946 'Chard Whitlow (Mr Eliot's Sunday Evening Postscript)'.

82 Modest? My word, no… He was an all-the-lights-on man.
1953 *A Very Great Man Indeed*, radio play.

83 And the sooner the tea's out of the way, the sooner we can get out the gin, eh?
1954 *The Private Life of Hilda Tablet*, radio play.

84 In a civil war, a general must know—and I'm afraid it's a thing rather of instinct than of practice—he must know exactly when to move over to the other side.
1959 *Not a Drum Was Heard: The War Memoirs of General Gland*, unpublished radio play.

Reed, Ishmael Scott 1938–

US novelist, poet and publisher. He founded the experimental literary magazine *East Village Other* in New York. His works include the novels *The Free-Lance Pallbearers* (1967) and *Mumbo Jumbo* (1972).

85 When State Magic fails unofficial magic becomes stronger.
1968 *Yellow Back Radio Broke Down*, 'II. The Loop Garou Kid Comes Back Mad'.

86 Hoo-doo, which in America flowered in New Orleans, was an unorganized religion without ego-games or death worship.
1968 *Yellow Back Radio Broke Down*, 'V. A Jigsaw of a Last Minute Rescue'.

Reed, John 1887–1920

US writer and journalist. He is best known as a war correspondent in Mexico and Europe, and for his reports from Russia in the wake of the revolution.

87 Ten Days That Shook the World.
1919 Title of book.

88 In the relations of a weak Government and a rebellious people there comes a time when every act of the authorities exasperates the masses, and every refusal to act excites their contempt.
1919 *Ten Days That Shook the World*, ch.3.

Rees-Mogg, William Rees-Mogg, Baron 1928–

English journalist. He joined the *Financial Times* (1952) and the *Sunday Times* (1960), becoming deputy editor (1964). He was editor of *The Times* (1967–81) and headed the Broadcasting Standards Council (1988–93).

89 Information, free from interest or prejudice, free from the vanity of the writer or the influence of a Government, is as necessary to the human mind as pure air and water to the human body.
1970 *Christian Science Monitor*, 22 Sep.

Reeve, Christopher 1952–2004

US actor, best known for his role as the superhero in *Superman* (1978) and subsequent films. Paralysed in a horse-riding accident, he became a spokesperson for medical research into treatments and cures for spinal injuries.

90 Every scientist should remove the word 'impossible' from their lexicon.
2004 In the *Observer*, 15 Feb.

Regan, Donald Thomas 1918–2003

US financier, writer and lecturer. He was chair of Merrill Lynch & Co Inc (1973–81), secretary to the US Treasury Department (1981–85) and White House Chief of Staff (1985–87) for President Reagan. Following the Tower Commission Report on the Iran–Contra affair, he was forced to resign.

91 The buck doesn't even *pause* here.
1987 Of his job. In the *New York Times*, 31 Jul.
► See *Truman 869:45*.

92 I thought I was Chief of Staff to the President, not to his wife.
1988 On submitting his resignation. *For the Record*.

93 Mistaken in its assumptions, defective in its evidence and wrong in its conclusions.
1988 Of the congressional report faulting him on lack of direction and public disclosure of Iran–Contra arms sales. *For the Record*.

Reger, Max 1873–1916

German composer. He was Director of Music (1907) and professor (1908) at Leipzig University. His work includes organ music, piano concertos, choral works and songs.

94 *Ich sitze in dem kleinsten Zimmer in meinem Hause. Ich habe Ihre Kritik vor mir. Im nächsten Augenblick wird sie hinter mir sein.*
I am sitting in the smallest room of my house. I have your review before me. In a moment it will be behind me.
1906 Written in response to an unfavourable review by Rudolf Louis. Quoted in Nicolas Slonimsky *Lexicon of Musical Invective* (2nd edn, 1969), p.139.

Reid, Alastair 1926–

Scottish-born poet, essayist and translator of Spanish and Latin American literature. After serving in the Navy in World War II, he became a professional itinerant, his only permanent address the *New Yorker*. His witty poetry collections include *Weathering* (1978).

95 The point is the seeing—the grace
beyond recognition, the ways
of the bird rising, unnamed, unknown,
beyond the range of language, beyond its noun.
Eyes open on growing, flying, happening,
and go on opening. Manifold, the world
dawns on unrecognizing, realizing eyes.
Amazement is the thing.
Not love, but the astonishment of loving.
1978 *Weathering*, 'Growing, Flying, Happening'.

Reid, Thomas Mayne 1818–83

Irish writer of boys' stories. After work as a journalist and soldier in the Mexican War of 1847, he won a wide readership with a string of adventure tales, which included such titles as *The Rifle Rangers* (1850), *War Trail* (1857) and *Boy Tar* (1859).

96 Praise the sports of the land
And water, each one—
The bath by the beach, or the yacht on the sea—
But of all the sweet pleasures
Known under the sun;
A good game of Croquet's the sweetest to me.
1863 Quoted in Colin Jarman *The Guinness Dictionary of Sports Quotations* (1990).

Remarque, Erich Maria 1898–1970

German-born US novelist, who served in World War I. His novels were banned by the Nazis in 1933, and he emigrated to the US in 1939.

97 *Im Westen nichts Neues.*
All Quiet on the Western Front.
1929 Title of novel.

Renan, (Joseph) Ernest 1823–92

French philologist and historian, whose studies led him to abandon traditional faith. His works include *Histoire général des langues sémitiques* (1854), *Études d'histoire religieuse* (1856) and the controversial *Vie de Jésus* (1863), the first of a series on the history of Christianity.

98 War is a condition of progress; the whip-cut that prevents a country from going to sleep and forces satisfied mediocrity to shake off its apathy.
1871 *La Reforme intellectuelle et morale.*

Reno, Janet 1938–

US politician and lawyer. She was State Attorney in Florida (1978–93) and subsequently US Attorney-General in the Clinton administration (1993–2001).

99 I'm just an awkward old maid with a very great affection for men.
1993 Denying rumours that she was a lesbian. In the *Washington Times*, 22 Feb.

1 Nothing can make me madder than lawyers who don't care about others.
1993 Address to the American Bar Association. In the *New York Times*, 9 Aug.

2 Vengeance is a personal reaction. But not one that government can indulge in.
1994 Opposing the death penalty. In the *New York Times*, 15 May.

3 I made the decision long ago that to be afraid would be to diminish my life.
1995 Interview in NPR broadcast, 18 Jul.

Renoir, Jean 1894–1979

French film director, son of Pierre Auguste Renoir. His *La Grande Illusion* (1937) and *La Bête humaine* (1939) are among the masterpieces of the cinema.

4 A director makes only one film in his life. Then he breaks it into pieces and makes it again.
Quoted in Leslie Halliwell *Halliwell's Filmgoer's Companion* (1993).

5 Goodbye Mr Zanuck. It certainly has been a pleasure working for 16th Century Fox.
On leaving Hollywood. Attributed.

Renoir, Pierre Auguste 1841–1919

French Impressionist painter, born in Limoges. He exhibited with the Impressionists, and his *Moulin de la Galette* (1876) with sunlight filtering through leaves epitomizes his colourful, happy art. His visit to Italy in 1880 was followed by a series of *Bathers* (1884–7) in a more cold and classical style. He then returned to reds, orange and gold to portray nudes in sunlight, a style which he continued to develop until his death. His works include *The Umbrellas* (c.1883) and *The Judgement of Paris* (c.1914).

6 There is something in painting which cannot be explained, and that something is essential. You come to nature with your theories, and nature knocks them all flat.
c.1915 Quoted in Ambroise Vollard *Renoir, an Intimate Record* (1930).

7 I have a horror of the word 'flesh', which has become so shopworn. Why not 'meat' while they're about it? What I like is skin, a young girl's skin that is pink and shows that she has a good circulation.
Quoted in Jean Renoir *Renoir, My Father* (translated by R and D Weaver, 1962).

8 The only reward one should offer an artist is to buy his work.
From Renoir's notebook, quoted in L Nochlin *Impressionism and Post-Impressionism 1874–1904* (1966).

9 It is impossible to repeat in one period what was done in another. The point of view is not the same, any more than are the tools, the ideals, the needs, or the painters' techniques.
From Renoir's notebook, quoted in L Nochlin *Impressionism and Post-Impressionism 1874–1904* (1966).

10 They were madmen, but they had in them that little flame which never dies.
On the Communards. Quoted in A J P Taylor *From Napoleon to the Second International* (1993).

11 Why shouldn't art be pretty? There are enough unpleasant things in the world.
Quoted in Ian Chilvers and Harold Osborne (eds) *The Oxford Dictionary of Art* (1994).

Repplier, Agnes 1858–1950

US writer and social critic.

12 Science may carry us to Mars, but it will leave the Earth peopled as ever by the inept.
1936 *In Pursuit of Laughter.*

Reston, James B(arrett) 1909–95

Scottish born US journalist and author. He enjoyed a distinguished career with the *New York Times* and his national news reporting in World War II was recognized in a Pulitzer Prize (1945) and in his promotion to Chief of the Washington Bureau (1953–1964). He won a second Pulitzer Prize in 1957. He was vice-president of the *New York Times* (1969–74) and internationally respected for his political analysis.

13 Smarter than most of his colleagues in the Truman cabinet, but not smart enough to hide it.
1991 Of Secretary of State Dean Acheson. *Deadline.*

14 A little shorter than the Washington monument, erect, elegant, dogmatic, and ironically witty.
1991 Of Secretary of State Dean Acheson. *Deadline*

15 He could strut sitting down.
1991 Of Senator Arthur Vandenberg. *Deadline.*

16 They were always…getting more credit than they deserved, more sorrow than they could bear, climbing into jobs before they were ready and failing just when they were succeeding.
1991 Of John F, Robert F and Edward M Kennedy. *Deadline.*

17 He not only knew a lot about foreign affairs, he *was* a foreign affair.
1991 Of former Secretary of State Henry A Kissinger. *Deadline.*

18 The American people…were like him: cheerful, optimistic, patriotic, inconsistent, and casually inattentive.
1991 Of President Ronald Reagan. *Deadline.*

Revlon, Charles Haskell 1906–75

US cosmetics salesman, founder with his brother Joseph and chemist Charles Lachman of Revlon Inc (1932). His success was due to initiatives such as giving exotic names to colours and also to intimidation and attacks on competitors.

19 I don't meet competition. I crush it.
1958 In *Time*, 16 Jun.

20 In the factory, we make cosmetics; in the store we sell hope.
Quoted in Andrew P Tobias *Fire and Ice* (1976), ch.8.

Reyes, Alfonso 1889–1959

Mexican poet, novelist, essayist, critic, educator and diplomat. His classical background and humanistic approach lend his writings a distinctive elegance.

21 *El orbe hispano nunca se vino abajo, ni siquiera a la caída del imperio español, sino que se ha multiplicado en numerosas facetas de ensanches todavía insospechados… No somos pueblos en estado de candor, que se deslumbren fácilmente con los instrumentos externos de que se acompaña la cultura, sino pueblos que heredan una vieja civilización y exigen la excelencia misma de la cultura.*
The Hispanic world never crumbled, not even after the Spanish Empire fell, but instead has multiplied itself in broad ways that are still largely unknown… Our people are not naive and are not blinded by the external tools that go together with culture; we are rather the inheritors of an old civilization, and we demand the excellence proper to culture itself.
1941 *Páginas escogidas*, 'Valor de la literatura hispanoamericana' (translated as 'The Value of Hispanic American Literature').

Reynolds, Sir Joshua 1723–92

English painter, writer on art and the first President of the Royal Academy. He is one of the most important figures in the history of English painting.

22 A mere copier of nature never produces anything great.
1770 *Discourses on Art*, no.3, 14 Dec.

Rhodes, Cecil John 1853–1902

South African statesman. He entered the Cape House of Assembly, where he secured the charter for the British South Africa Company (1889), whose territory was later named Rhodesia. Prime Minister of Cape Colony (1890–6), he resigned after the Jameson raid (when the Boers defeated Dr Jameson's attempt to reach Johannesburg). During the Boer War of 1899–1902 he organized the defences of Kimberley.

23 Remember that you are an Englishman, and have consequently won first prize in the lottery of life.
Quoted in Peter Ustinov *Dear Me* (1977). This has also been attributed to Lord Milner.

Rhys, Jean *pseudonym of* Ellen Gwendolen Rees Williams 1894–1979

British novelist, born in the West Indies, of Welsh and Creole descent. Of her novels and short stories *Wide Sargasso Sea* (1966), redefining Charlotte Brontë's first Mrs Rochester, is the best known.

24 The perpetual hunger to be beautiful and that thirst to be loved which is the real curse of Eve.
1927 *The Left Bank*, 'Illusion'.

25 I wanted to be black. I always wanted to be black… Being black is warm and gay, being white is cold and sad.
1934 *Voyage in the Dark*, ch.1.

26 It's funny when you feel as if you don't want anything more in your life except to sleep, or else to lie without moving. That's when you can hear time sliding past you, like water running.
1934 *Voyage in the Dark*, ch.2.

27 Cold—cold as truth, cold as life. No, nothing can be as cold as life.
1934 *Voyage in the Dark*, ch.3.

28 The feeling of Sunday is the same everywhere, heavy, melancholy, standing still. Like when they say 'As it was in the beginning, is now, and ever shall be, world without end'.
1934 *Voyage in the Dark*, ch.4, pt.1.

29 We will watch the sun set again—many times, and perhaps we'll see the Emerald Drop, the green flash that brings good fortune.
1966 *Wide Sargasso Sea*, pt.2.

30 There is no looking-glass here and I don't know what I am like now. I remember watching myself brush my hair and how my eyes looked back at me. The girl I saw was myself and yet not quite myself. Long ago when I was a child and very lonely I tried to kiss her. But the glass was between us—hard, cold and misted over with my breath. Now they have taken everything away. What am I doing in this place and who am I?
1966 The consciousness of Antoinette Mason/Bertha Rochester at a point of intersection with the text of *Jane Eyre*. *Wide Sargasso Sea*, pt.3.

Ricardo, David 1772–1823

English political economist. He set up in business as a young man, and in 1817 produced his chief work, *Principles of Political Economy and Taxation*. In 1819 he became an MP, and was influential in the free-trade movement.

31 It is not to be understood that the natural price of labour, estimated even in food and necessaries, is absolutely fixed and constant. It varies at different times in the same country and very materially differs in different countries. It essentially depends on the habits and customs of the people.
1817 *Principles of Political Economy and Taxation*.

32 In every case, agricultural as well as manufacturing profits are lowered by a rise in the price of raw produce, if it be accompanied by a rise of wages. The natural tendency of profits is to fall; for in the progress of society and wealth, the additional quantity of food required is obtained by the sacrifice of more and more labour.
1817 *Principles of Political Economy and Taxation*.

33 Like all other contracts, wages should be left to the fair and free competition of the market, and should never be controlled by the interference of the legislature.
1817 *Principles of Political Economy and Taxation*.

34 Possessing utility, commodities derive their exchangeable value from two sources: from their scarcity and from the labour required to obtain them. By far the greatest part of those goods which are the

objects of desire, are procured by labour.
1817 *Principles of Political Economy and Taxation.*

35 The interest of the landlord is always opposed to the interests of every other class in the community.
1817 *Principles of Political Economy and Taxation.*

36 The natural price of labour is that price which is necessary to enable the labourers, one with another, to subsist and to perpetuate their race, without either increase or diminution.
1817 *Principles of Political Economy and Taxation.*

Rice, Grantland 1880–1954

US sportswriter and poet. He is remembered for his colourful reporting style and popular verse.

37 For when the One Great Scorer comes
To write against your name,
He marks—not that you won or lost—
But how you played the game.
1941 *Only the Brave*, 'Alumnus Football'.

38 All wars are planned by old men
In council rooms apart.
1955 *The Final Answer*, 'The Two Sides of War'.

39 Play ball! Means something more than runs
Or pitches thudding into gloves!
Remember through the summer suns
This is the game your country loves.
Quoted in Colin Jarman *The Guinness Dictionary of Sports Quotations* (1990)

Rice-Davies, Mandy 1944–

Welsh model and show girl.

40 He would, wouldn't he?
1963 On hearing that during the trial of Stephen Ward, Lord Astor had denied her allegations of orgies at his house parties at Cliveden, 29 Jun.

Rich, Adrienne Cecile 1929–

US poet. She is one of the most prominent feminist poets of her generation. Her best-known work includes *Diving into the Wreck* (1973).

41 Weather abroad
And weather in the heart alike come on
Regardless of prediction.
1951 *A Change of World*, 'Storm Warnings'.

42 Love only what you do,
And not what you have done.
1955 *The Diamond Cutters and Other Poems*, 'The Diamond Cutters'.

43 Your mind now, moldering like wedding-cake,
heavy with useless experience, rich
with suspicion, rumour, fantasy,
crumbling to pieces under the knife-edge
of mere fact. In the prime of your life.
1963 *Snapshots of a Daughter-in-Law*, 'Snapshots of a Daughter-in-Law, 1'.

44 Only
a fact could be so dreamlike.
1966 *Necessities of Life*, 'Like This Together'.

45 Only where there is language is there world.
1969 *Leaflets*, 'The Demon Lover'.

46 All wars are useless to the dead.
1969 *Leaflets*, 'Implosions'.

47 I am an instrument in the shape
of a woman trying to translate pulsations
into images for the relief of the body
and the reconstruction of the mind.
1971 *The Will to Change*, 'Planetarium'.

48 It's exhilarating to be alive in a time of awakening consciousness; it can also be confusing, disorienting, and painful.
1971 Talk delivered to Forum on 'The Woman Writer in the Twentieth Century'. Collected as 'When We Dead Awaken: Writing as Re-Vision', in *College English*, Oct 1972.

49 the thing I came for:
the wreck and not the story of the wreck
the thing itself and not the myth.
1973 *Diving into the Wreck*, 'Diving into the Wreck'.

50 When did we begin to dress ourselves?
1973 *Diving into the Wreck*, 'Blood-Sister'.

51 Any woman's death diminishes me.
1974 *Poems: Selected and New*, 'From an Old House in America, 16'.
► See Donne 281:85.

52 Without contemplating last and late
the true nature of poetry. The drive
to connect. The dream of a common language.
1978 *The Dream of a Common Language*, 'Origins and History of Consciousness'.

53 Since we're not young, weeks have to do time for years of missing each other. Yet only this odd warp in time tells me we're not young.
1978 *The Dream of a Common Language*, 'Twenty-One Love Poems, III'.

54 Anger and tenderness: my selves.
And now I can believe they breathe in me
as angels, not polarities.
1981 *A Wild Patience Has Taken Me This Far*, 'Integrity'.

55 I refuse to become a seeker for cures.
Everything that has ever
helped me has come through what already
lay stored in me.
1986 *Your Native Land, Your Life*, 'Sources, II'.

56 This is the day of atonement; but do my people forgive me?
If a cloud knew loneliness and fear, I would be that cloud.
1986 *Your Native Land, Your Life*, 'Yom Kippur, 1984'.

57 Experience is always larger than language.
1991 Interview in the *American Poetry Review*, Jan–Feb.

Richard I *known as 'the Lionheart'* 1157–99

King of England (from 1189). He led the Crusaders in 1190 and after concluding a peace sailed for home (1191), but was captured by Leopold, Duke of Austria and handed over to Emperor Henry VI. Ransomed in 1194, he went to France where he warred against Philip II until he was killed in the siege of Chalus.

58 *Si inuenissem emptorum, Londoniam uendidissem.*
If I could have found a buyer I would have sold London itself.
1190 Of his fundraising for the Crusade to Palestine. Quoted in Richard of Devizes *Chronicle of Richard of Devizes of the Time of King Richard I* (c.1192).

Richard of Devizes fl.c.1190

English Benedictine monk and chronicler.

59 *Si nolueris habitare cum turpidis, non habitatis Londonie.*
If you do not want to live among wicked people, do not live in London.
c.1192 *Chronicle of Richard of Devizes of the Time of King Richard I.*

Richards, Ann 1933–

US Democratic politician. State Treasurer of Texas from 1982 to 1990, she then became Governor of Texas (1991–5).

60 You can put lipstick on a hog, and it's still a pig.
1992 On Republicans' attempts to enhance their candidates. In *Sunday Morning*, CBS TV broadcast, 25 Oct.

Richards, Sir Gordon 1904–86

English jockey. In 34 seasons (1921–54) he was champion jockey 26 times, and rode 4,870 winners. In 1953 he won his first Derby, on Pinza, and also received a knighthood.

61 Mother always told me my day was coming, but I never realized I'd end up being the shortest knight of the year.
1953 Quoted in Colin Jarman *The Guinness Dictionary of Sports Quotations* (1990).

Richards, I(vor) A(rmstrong) 1893–1979

English scholar and literary critic. He was the initiator of the influential 'New Criticism' school of textual criticism at Cambridge University in the 1920s.

62 To be forced by desire into any unwarrantable belief is a calamity.
1924 *Principles of Literary Criticism.*

63 Poetry…is capable of saving us; it is a perfectly possible means of overcoming chaos.
1926 *Science and Poetry*, ch. 7.

Richardson, Henry Handel *pen-name of* *Ethel Florence Lindesay Robertson* *née* *Richardson* 1870–1946

Australian novelist, who settled in England in 1904. Her first novel was *Maurice Guest* (1908) but she made her name with a trilogy set in Australia, *The Fortunes of Richard Mahoney* (1917–29). She was nominated for the Nobel prize in 1932.

64 You're blessed with a woman's brain: vague, slippery, inexact, interested only in the personal aspect of a thing.
1910 *The Getting of Wisdom*, ch.9.

Richardson, Tony (Cecil Antonio) 1928–91

British film and stage director. He made a number of highly acclaimed films at the beginning of the 1960s including *The Entertainer* (1960), *A Taste of Honey* (1961) and *Tom Jones* (1963), which won an Academy Award.

65 People in this country haven't got the cinema in their blood—the real creative talent has been drained off into theatre.
1961 On Britain. Quoted in the *Monthly Film Bulletin*, Apr 1993.

Richelieu, Armand Jean du Plessis, Duc de *known as* *Cardinal Richelieu* 1585–1642

French statesman. A protégé of the regent Marie de Médicis, he became Minister of State (1624), and as Chief Minister to Louis XIV (1624–42) was effective ruler of France. He succeeded in destroying Huguenot power, securing universal obedience to the Bourbon monarchy, checking Habsburg power and enhancing France's international prestige, but his ruthless severity, his intrigues and his high taxes earned him the hatred of many.

66 Not least among the qualities in a great King is a capacity to permit his Ministers to serve him.
1688 *Testament Politique.*

67 Secrecy is the first essential in the affairs of State.
1688 *Testament Politique.*

68 When people are too comfortable, it is not possible to restrain them within the bounds of their duty… They may be compared to mules who, being accustomed to burdens, are spoilt by rest rather than labour.
1688 *Testament Politique.*

69 Wounds inflicted by the sword heal more easily than those inflicted by the tongue.
1688 *Testament Politique.*

Richler, Mordecai 1931–2001

Canadian novelist, journalist and essayist. His greatest works, including *The Apprenticeship of Duddy Kravitz* (1959), *St Urbain's Horseman* (1971) and *Joshua Then and Now* (1980), are darkly comic novels about the working-class Jewish community in Montreal in which he grew up.

70 Thousands of miles of wheat, indifference, and self-apology.
1971 Of Canada. *St Urbain's Horseman*, ch.1.

71 Tomorrow country then, tomorrow country now.
1971 Of Canada. *St Urbain's Horseman*, ch.1.

72 Even in Paris, I remained a Canadian. I puffed hashish, but I didn't inhale.
1971 *St Urbain's Horseman*, ch.2. The last phrase was later popularized by Bill Clinton, responding to claims that he had taken drugs as a student.

73 The Canadian kid who wants to grow up to be Prime Minister isn't thinking big, he is setting a limit to his ambitions rather early.
Quoted in *Time* (Canadian edition), 31 May 1971.

Rickword, Edgell 1898–1982

English poet and critic. His early work was influenced by Sassoon. He edited *Left Review* in the 1930s.

74 The oldest griefs of summer seem less sad
than drone of mowers on suburban lawns
and girls' thin laughter, to the ears that hear
the soft rain falling of the failing stars.
1921 'Regret for the Passing of the Entire Scheme of Things'.

75 My soul's a trampled duelling ground where Sade,
the gallant marquis, fences for his life
against the invulnerable retrograde
Masoch, his shade, more constant than a wife.
1928 'Chronique Scandaleuse'.

76 Why stir the wasps that rim Fame's luscious pot?
Love costs us nothing, satire costs a lot!
1931 'The Contemporary Muse'.

Ridge, W(illiam) Pett 1857–1930

English novelist. He was a prolific writer, publishing over 60 books in total.

77 He took her up in his arms in the way of a bachelor who has had amateur experience of the carrying of nieces.
1902 *Lost Property*, pt.1, ch.8.

78 Ballard admitted he was no hand at giving descriptions; the man was apparently a gentleman and the woman—well, not exactly a lady, although she had a very fine flow of language.
1905 *Mrs Galer's Business*, ch.6.

79 Gertie recommended her to adopt the habit of not magnifying grievances; if you wanted to view trouble, you could take opera-glasses, but you should be careful to hold them the wrong way round.
1912 *Love at Paddington Green*, ch.4.

80 'How did you think I managed at dinner, Clarence?'
'Capitally!'
'I had a knife and two forks left at the end,' she said regretfully.
1912 *Love at Paddington Green*, ch.6.

Riding, Laura *née* *Reichenthal* 1901–91

US poet and fiction writer. She was first published by Leonard and Virginia Woolf's Hogarth Press, and is more admired as a poet than for her polemical prose writings.

81 Art, whose honesty must work through artifice, cannot avoid cheating truth.
1975 *Selected Poems: In Five Sets*, preface.

Rifkind, Simon Hirsch 1901–95

US judge. He was a partner in his legal firm and an adviser to General Eisenhower on Jewish matters in the American occupied zone (1945).

82 Impartiality is an acquired taste, like olives. You have to be habituated to it.
1979 In *Time*, 20 Aug.

Rilke, Rainer Maria 1875–1926

German poet who travelled widely and lived throughout Europe.

83 *Ach, aber mit Versen ist so wenig getan, wenn man sie früh schreibt. Man sollte warten damit und Sinn und Süßigkeit sammeln ein ganzes Leben lang und ein langes womöglich, und dann, ganz zum Schluss, vielleicht könnte man dann zehn Zeilen schreiben, die gut sind.*
Ah, poems amount to so little when you write them too early in your life.You ought to wait and gather sense and sweetness for a whole lifetime, and a long one if possible, and then, at the very end, you might perhaps be able to write ten good lines.
1910 *Die Aufzeichnungen des Malte Laurids Brigge* (translated by Stephen Mitchell in *The Selected Poetry of Rainer Maria Rilke*, 1989).

84 *Ich habe um meine Kindheit gebeten, und sie ist wiedergekommen, und ich fühle, dass sie immer noch so schwer ist wie damals, und dass es nichts genützt hat, älter zu werden.*
I prayed to rediscover my childhood, and it has come back, and I feel that it is just as difficult as it used to be, and that growing older has served no purpose at all.
1910 *Die Aufzeichnungen des Malte Laurids Brigge* (translated by Stephen Mitchell in *The Selected Poetry of Rainer Maria Rilke*, 1989).

85 *Und das Totsein ist mühsam*
und voller Nachholn, dass man allmählich ein wenig
Ewigkeit spürt.
And being dead is hard work
and full of retrieval before one can gradually feel
a trace of eternity.
1923 *Duinieser Elegien*, no.1 (translated by Stephen Mitchell in *The Selected Poetry of Rainer Maria Rilke*, 1989).

86 *Siehe, wir lieben nicht, wie die Blumen, aus einem*
einzigen Jahr; uns steigt, wo wir lieben,
unvordenklicher Saft in die Arme.
No, we don't accomplish our love in a single year
as the flowers do; an immemorial sap
flows up through our arms when we love.
1923 *Duinieser Elegien*, no.3 (translated by Stephen Mitchell in *The Selected Poetry of Rainer Maria Rilke*, 1989).

87 *Wer zeigt ein Kind, so wie es steht? Wer stellt*
es ins Gestirn und gibt das Maß des Abstands
ihm in die Hand?
Who shows a child as he really is? Who sets him
in his constellation and puts the measuring-rod
of distance in his hand?
1923 *Duinieser Elegien*, no.4 (translated by Stephen Mitchell in *The Selected Poetry of Rainer Maria Rilke*, 1989).

Rimbaud, (Jean Nicolas) Arthur 1854–91

French poet who wrote his entire work before the age of 20. His relationship with poet Paul Verlaine was notorious. He eventually became an arms trader in Abyssinia.

88 *Et j'ai vu quelquefois ce que l'homme a cru voir.*
I've sometimes seen what other men have only dreamed of seeing.
1871 *Poésies*, 'Le Bateau ivre'.

89 *Je regrette l'Europe aux anciens parapets!*
I long for Europe of the ancient parapets!
1871 *Poésies*, 'Le Bateau ivre'.

90 *Ô mes petites amoureuses,*
Que je vous hais!
Oh my little mistresses,
How I hate you!
1871 *Poésies*, 'Mes petites amoureuses'.

91 *On n'est pas sérieux, quand on a dix-sept ans.*
When you are seventeen, you are not serious.
1871 *Poésies*, 'Roman', no.1.

92 *Le poète est vraiment voleur de feu.*
The poet is the true fire-stealer.
1871 Letter to Paul Demeny, 15 May.

93 *La Poésie ne rythmera plus l'action; elle sera en avant.*
Poetry will no longer keep step with the action; it will be *ahead of it*.
1871 Letter to Paul Demeny, 15 May.

94 *Elle est retrouvée.*
Quoi?—L'Éternité.
C'est la mer allée
Avec le soleil.
It has been recovered.
What?—Eternity.
It is the sea escaping
With the sun.
1872 *Derniers vers, Fêtes de la patience*, 'L'Éternité'.

95 *J'ai fait la magique étude*

Du Bonheur, que nul n'élude.
I studied the magic lore of Happiness
Which no one can escape.
1872 *Derniers vers, Fêtes de la faim*, 'Ô saisons, ô châteaux!'.

96 *Un soir, j'ai assis la Beauté sur mes genoux.—Et je l'ai trouvée amère.—Et je l'ai injuriée.*
One evening, I sat Beauty on my knees.—And I found her bitter.—And I hurt her.
1873 *Une saison en enfer*, 'Jadis, si je me souviens bien'.

97 *Je me crois en enfer, donc j'y suis.*
I believe myself to be in hell; therefore I am.
1873 *Une saison en enfer*, 'Mauvais sang'.

98 *Le Bonheur était ma fatalité, mon remords, mon ver: ma vie serait toujours trop immense pour être dévouée à la force et à la beauté.*
Happiness was my fate, my remorse, my worm: my life would always be too large to be dedicated to force and to beauty.
1873 *Une saison en enfer, Délires*, no.2, 'Alchimie du verbe'.

Rimsky-Korsakov, Nikolai Andreievich 1844–1908

Russian composer. He established his reputation with three great orchestral masterpieces (1887–8), *Capriccio Espagnol, Easter Festival* and *Scheherazade*. He then turned to opera, producing *The Snow Maiden* (1882), *Legend of Tsar Saltan* (1900), *The Invisible City of Kitesh* (1906) and *The Golden Cockerel* (1906).

99 I have already heard it. I had better not go: I will start to get accustomed to it and finally like it.
Of the music of Debussy, when invited to a concert where it was to be performed. Quoted in Igor Stravinsky *Chronicles of My Life* (1936).

Riva, Maria 1924–

Daughter and biographer of Marlene Dietrich.

1 They filled our hall like a monogrammed Stonehenge.
1992 Of the six closet-size wardrobe trunks used by her mother. *Marlene Dietrich*.

Rivera, Diego 1886–1957

Mexican painter, one of the three foremost artists in the revival of monumental fresco painting.

2 The subject is to the painter what the rails are to a locomotive. He cannot do without it.
1929 *Creative Art*.

Rivera, José Eustasio 1889–1928

Colombian lawyer, poet and novelist. A journey through the Amazon jungle with a commission to settle the boundary dispute between Colombia and Venezuela inspired him to write the magnificently descriptive novel *La vorágine* (1924).

3 *Antes que me hubiera apasionado por mujer alguna, jugué mi corazón al azar y me lo ganó la violencia.*
Before I felt passion for any woman, I gambled my heart and lost it to violence.
1924 *La vorágine*, pt.1 (translated as *The Vortex*, 1935).

Rivers, Joan *pseudonym of* Joan Alexandra Molinsky 1933–

US comedienne and writer. An acid-tongued stand-up comedienne in the 1960s, she went on to host television shows, as well as directing and appearing in films, recording an album and publishing books.

4 I'm Jewish. I don't work out. If God had wanted us to bend over he'd've put diamonds on the floor.
Quoted in Colin Jarman *The Guinness Dictionary of Sports Quotations* (1990).

Robb, Charles S(pittal) 1939–

US lawyer, Senator for Virginia (1989–2001).

5 The threat to morale comes not from the orientation of a few, but from the closed minds of the many.
1993 On gays in the military. In the *New York Times*, 5 Feb.

Robbe-Grillet, Alain 1922–

French novelist, scriptwriter and film director, whose repetitive style blurs the standard narrative distinctions in writing.

6 *On n'échappe pas à son sort.*
One cannot escape destiny.
1953 *Les Gommes*.

7 *Deux mètres—ou un peu plus—séparent donc l'homme de la femme.*
Two metres, or a little more, separates a man from a woman.
1955 *Le Voyeur*.

8 *Le lecteur, lui non plus, ne voit pas les choses du dehors. Il est dans le labyrinthe aussi.*
The reader [as well as the main character] does not view the work from outside. He too is in the labyrinth.
1959 *Dans le labyrinthe*.

9 *Et une fois de plus je m'avançais le long de ces mêmes couloirs, marchant depuis des jours, depuis des mois, depuis des années, à votre rencontre.*
And one more time, I advanced along these same hallways, walking for *days*, for *months*, for *years*, to meet you.
1961 *L'Année dernière à Marienbad*.

10 *Car loin de le [le lecteur] négliger, l'auteur aujourd'hui proclame l'absolu besoin qu'il a de son concours actif, conscient, créateur. Ce qu'il lui demande, ce n'est plus de recevoir tout fait un monde achevé, plein, clos sur lui-même, c'est au contraire de participer à une création, d'inventer à son tour l'œuvre—et le monde—et d'apprendre ainsi à inventer sa propre vie.*
Far from neglecting him [the reader], the author today proclaims the absolute necessity of the reader's active, conscious and creative assistance. What he demands of the reader is no longer to receive a ready-made world, complete, full, closed in upon itself. On the contrary, the reader is asked to participate in the creation, to invent for himself a work—and the world—and to understand thus how to invent his own life.
1963 *Pour un nouveau roman*.

11 *L'amour est un jeu, la poésie est un jeu, la vie doit devenir un jeu (c'est le seul espoir de nos luttes politiques) et 'la révolution elle-même est un jeu', comme disaient les plus conscients des révolutionnaires de mai.*
Love is a game, poetry is a game, life should become a game (it's the only hope for our political struggles) and 'the revolution itself is a game', as the most aware of the May revolutionaries said.
1970 *Projet pour une révolution à New York*.

12 *Première approximation: j'écris pour détruire, en les décrivant avec précision, des monstres nocturnes qui menacent d'envahir ma vie éveillée.*
First general point: I write to destroy, by describing exactly the nocturnal monsters that threaten to invade my waking life.
1984 *Le Miroir qui revient.*

Robbins, Colonel

US Red Cross representative at Petrograd.

13 A four-kind son-of-a-bitch, but the greatest Jew since Jesus Christ.
Of Leon Trotsky. Quoted by A J P Taylor in the *New Statesman and Nation*, 20 Feb 1954.

Robbins, Lionel Charles, Baron Robbins of Clare Market 1898–1984

English economist, Professor at the London School of Economics and later chairman of the *Financial Times*.

14 Economics is the science which studies human behaviour as a relationship between scarce resources and ends which have alternative uses… It does not attempt to pick out certain *kinds* of behaviour, but focuses attention on a particular *aspect* of behaviour, the form imposed by the influence of scarcity.
1932 *An Essay on the Nature and Significance of Economic Science*, p.16–17.

Robbins, Tim 1958–

US actor and director, whose acting credits include *Jacob's Ladder* (1990), *The Player* (1992) and *The Shawshank Redemption* (1994).

15 As we applaud the hard-edged realism of the opening battle scene of *Saving Private Ryan*, we cringe at the thought of seeing the same on the nightly news. We are told it would be pornographic.
2003 Speech to the National Press Club, Washington DC, 15 Apr.

16 I had been unaware that baseball was a Republican sport.
2003 In a letter to Dale Petroskey, president of the National Baseball Hall of Fame, after his appearance there was cancelled when he criticized President George W Bush, Apr.

Robert of Clari fl.c.1216

Pickard knight.

17 When they were on that sea and had spread their sails and had their banners set high on the poops of the ships and their ensigns, it seemed indeed as if the sea were all a-tremble and all on fire with the ships they were sailing and the great joy they were making.
1203 Describing the Venetian fleet setting out. *The Conquest of Constantinople* (translated by E H McNeal, 1936), p.42–3.

Roberts, Sir Charles George Douglas 1860–1943

Canadian poet, naturalist, novelist and short-story writer. His first book of poems, *Orion, and Other Poems* (1880), inspired the group later known as 'The Confederation Poets'. In 1892 he published his first animal story, of which there would eventually be about 20 collected volumes. Roberts also translated French–Canadian literature into English.

18 This is the voice of high midsummer's heat.
The rasping vibrant clamour soars and shrills
O'er all the meadowy range of shadeless hills,
As if a host of giant cicadae beat
The cymbals of their wings with tireless feet,
Or brazen grasshoppers with triumphing note
From the long swath proclaimed the fate that smote
The clover and timothy-tops and meadowsweet.
1893 'The Mowing'.

19 When Winter scourged the meadow and the hill
And in the withered leafage worked his will,
Then water shrank, and shuddered, and stood still,—
Then built himself a magic house of glass,
Irised with memories of flowers and grass,
Wherein to sit and watch the fury pass.
1898 'Ice'.

20 And I turned and fled, like a soul pursued,
From the white, inviolate solitude.
1901 'The Skater'.

Robertson (of Port Ellen), George Islay Macneill Robertson, Baron 1946–

Scottish Labour politician, Secretary-General of NATO since 1999.

21 Serbs out, Nato in, refugees back.
1999 Summing up the Nato objective in Kosovo, 7 Jun.

Robeson, Paul 1898–1976

US singer, actor and civil rights activist.

22 My father was a slave, and my people died to build this country, and I am going to stay here and have a piece of it, just like you.
1956 Statement to the House of Representatives Committee on Un-American Activities.

Robin, Leo 1899–1985

US lyricist best known for his collaboration with composer Ralph Rainger between 1932 and 1942. After Rainger's death he wrote with various other composers.

23 Thanks for the Memory.
1937 Title of song, which became Bob Hope's signature tune. Music by Ralph Rainger.

Robinson, (Edward) Austin George 1897–1993

English economist, professor at Cambridge University.

24 All industrial efficiency consists in trying to do with eight men what we have hitherto been doing with ten men. It consists in creating unemployment.
1931 *The Structure of Competitive Industry.*

Robinson, Casey 1903–79

US screenwriter. His credits include *Captain Blood* (1935), *Now, Voyager* (1942) and *The Snows of Kilimanjaro* (1952).

25 Don't let's ask for the moon. We have the stars.
1942 Line delivered by Bette Davis to Paul Henreid in *Now, Voyager.*

26 Where's the rest of me?
1942 Line delivered by Ronald Reagan on discovering his legs have been amputated in *King's Row.*

Robinson, Edward G *pseudonym of* ***Emanuel Goldenberg*** 1893–1973

Hungarian-born US actor, whose portrayal of a vicious gangster in *Little Caesar* (1930) brought him stardom. Other films include *The Whole Town's Talking* (1935), *Double Indemnity* (1944) and *Key Largo* (1948).

27 Mother of Mercy, is this the end of Rico?
1930 Line delivered by him in *Little Caesar* (screenplay by Francis Faragoh and Robert E Lee).

Robinson, Edwin Arlington 1869–1935

US poet. He created a fictional New England village, Tilbury Town, in which his best poetry is set. He won three Pulitzer Prizes (1922, 1925 and 1928).

28 In fine, we thought that he was everything
To make us wish that we were in his place.

So on we worked, and waited for the light,
And went without meat, and cursed the bread;
And Richard Cory, one calm summer night,
Went home and put a bullet through his head.
1897 *The Children of the Night*, 'Richard Cory'.

29 Friends
To borrow my books and set wet glasses on them.
1902 *Captain Craig*, 'Captain Craig', pt.2.

30 Miniver Cheevy, child of scorn,
Grew lean while he assailed the seasons;
He wept that he was ever born,
And he had reasons.
1910 *The Town down the River*, 'Miniver Cheevy'.

31 Miniver loved the Medici,
Albeit he had never seen one;
He would have sinned incessantly
Could he have been one.
1910 *The Town down the River*, 'Miniver Cheevy'.

32 Miniver Cheevy, born too late,
Scratched his head and kept on thinking;
Miniver coughed, and called it fate,
And kept on drinking.
1910 *The Town down the River*, 'Miniver Cheevy'.

33 The world is…a kind of kindergarten, where millions of bewildered infants are trying to spell God with the wrong blocks.
1917 *Literature in the Making*.

34 I shall have more to say when I am dead.
1920 *The Three Taverns*, 'John Brown'.

35 Below him, in the town among the trees,
Where friends of other days had honored him,
A phantom salutation of the dead
Rang thinly till old Eben's eyes were dim.
1921 *Avon's Harvest*, 'Mr Flood's Party'.

36 The Man Who Died Twice.
1924 Title of book.

37 Joy shivers in the corner where she knits
And Conscience always has the rocking-chair,
Cheerful as when she tortured into fits
The first cat that was ever killed by Care.
1925 *Dionysus in Doubt*, 'New England'.

Robinson, Joan Violet *née* ***Maurice*** 1903–83

English economist, a leader of the Cambridge school which developed macroeconomic theories of growth and distribution based on the work of Keynes. Her works include *The Economics of Imperfect Competition* (1933) and *Economic Heresies* (1971).

38 The typical entrepreneur is no longer the bold and tireless man of Marshall, or the sly and rapacious Moneybags of Marx, but a mass of inert shareholders, indistinguishable from *rentiers*, who employ salaried managers to run their concerns.
1947 *An Essay on Marxian Economics*.

39 The purpose of studying economics is not to acquire a set of ready-made answers to economic questions, but to learn how to avoid being deceived by economists.
1955 Quoted in *Contributions to Modern Economics* (1978), p.75.

40 It is impossible to understand the economic system in which we are living if we try to interpret it as a rational scheme. It has to be understood as an awkward phase in a continuing process of historical development.
1966 *Economics: an Awkward Corner*.

41 Hitler had already found out how to cure unemployment before Keynes had finished explaining why it occurred.
1971 Collected in *Contributions to Modern Economics* (1978), p.10.

Robinson, John Arthur Thomas 1919–83

English churchman and radical theologian, Bishop of Woolwich, latterly Dean of Clare College, Cambridge.

42 Jesus never claims to be God, personally, yet he always claims to bring God, completely.
1963 *Honest to God*.

Robinson, Mary 1944–

Irish Labour politician, President (1990–7) and UN High Commissioner for Human Rights (1997–2002).

43 Instead of rocking the cradle, they rocked the system.
1990 Paying tribute to Irish women, in her victory speech. Quoted in *The Times*, 10 Nov.

Robson, Sir Bobby 1933–

English footballer and football manager. He has been manager of Ipswich Town (1969–82), England (1982–90) and Newcastle United (1999–2004).

44 I'd have given my right arm to be a pianist.
2000 On what he would have done if he were not a football manager. In *The Times*, 26 Dec.

Roche, Sir Boyle 1743–1807

Irish politician. He joined the British army and fought in the war in America. On returning to Ireland he entered parliament in 1776 and remained an MP until the Act of Union (1800). He opposed Catholic emancipation and supported the Union. He was granted a pension for his constant support of the government.

45 Mr Speaker, I think the noble young man has no business to make any apology. He is a gentleman, and none such should be asked to make an *apology*, because no *gentleman* could *mean* to *give offence*.
c.1796 Debate on motion to expel Lord Edward Fitzgerald from Irish House of Commons, quoted in Sir Jonah Barrington

Personal Sketches and Recollections of his own Times (1827).

46 Sir, there is no Levitical degrees between nations, and on this occasion I can see neither sin nor shame in *marrying our own sister.*

c.1800 Debate on the Act of Union between Great Britain and Ireland, Irish House of Commons, quoted in Sir Jonah Barrington *Personal Sketches and Recollections of his own Times* (1827).

47 What, Mr Speaker! and so we are to beggar ourselves for fear of vexing posterity! Now, I would ask the honourable gentleman, and *still more* honourable House, why should we put ourselves out of our way to do anything for *posterity*; for what has *posterity* done for *us*?

Debate in Irish House of Commons, quoted in Sir Jonah Barrington *Personal Sketches and Recollections of his own Times* (1827).

► *See Addison 7:40.*

48 The best way to *avoid* danger is to *meet it plump.*

Quoted in Sir Jonah Barrington *Personal Sketches and Recollections of his own Times* (1827).

Rochester, John Wilmot, 2nd Earl of 1647–80

English courtier and lyric poet. He is noted for his entertaining letters, for satires, including 'A Satyr Against Mankind' (1674), and for his verses and songs, many of which are sexually frank or defamatory.

49 I hold you six to four I love you with all my heart, if I would bet with other people I'm sure I could get ten to one.

c.1667 Letter from Newmarket to his wife. In *The Letters of John Wilmot, Earl of Rochester*, edited by Jeremy Treglown (1980).

50 Naked she lay, clasped in my longing arms,
I filled with love, and she all over charms,
Both equally inspired with eager fire,
Melting through kindness, flaming in desire;
With arms, legs, lips, close clinging to embrace.

c.1672 'The Imperfect Enjoyment', l.1–6 (published 1680).

51 'Is there no more?'
She cries. 'All this to love, and rapture's due,
Must we not pay a debt to pleasure too?'

c.1672 'The Imperfect Enjoyment', l.22–4 (published 1680).

52 Restless, he rolls about from whore to whore,
A merry Monarch, scandalous and poor.

1673 Of Charles II. 'I' th' Isle of Britain', l.14–15. The poem resulted in a brief period of exile for Rochester.

53 Great Negative, how vainly would the wise
Enquire, define, distinguish, teach, devise,
Didst thou not stand to point their blind
Philosophies.

c.1673 'Upon Nothing', stanza 10 (published 1679).

54 French truth, Dutch prowess, British policy,
Hibernian learning, Scotch civility,
Spaniards' dispatch, Danes' wit, are mainly seen in thee.

c.1673 'Upon Nothing', stanza 16 (published 1679).

55 Were I (who to my loss already am
One of those strange prodigious creatures, Man)
A spirit, free to choose for my own share
What case of flesh and blood I'd choose to wear,
I'd be a dog, a monkey, or a bear.

1674 'A Satyr Against Mankind', l.1–5 (published 1679).

56 Reason, an ignis fatuus in the mind,
Which leaving light of nature, sense behind,
Pathless and dangerous wandering ways it takes,
Through error's fenny bogs and thorny brakes;
Whilst the misguided follower climbs, with pain,
Mountains of whimsy heaped in his own brain.

1674 'A Satyr Against Mankind', l.12–17 (published 1679).

57 Then old age and experience, hand in hand,
Lead him to death, and make him understand,
After a search so painful and so long,
That all his life he has been in the wrong.
Huddled in dirt, the reasoning engine lies,
Who was so proud, so witty, and so wise.

1674 'A Satyr Against Mankind', l.25–30 (published 1679).

58 Birds feed on birds, beasts on each other prey,
But savage man alone does man betray.

1674 'A Satyr Against Mankind', l.129–30 (published 1679).

59 That cordial drop heaven in our cup has thrown
To make the nauseous draught of life go down.

c.1674 Of love. 'A Letter from Artemisia in the Town to Chloe in the Country', l.44–5 (published 1679).

60 What vain, unnecessary things are men,
How well we do without 'em!

c.1674–1675 'Fragment of a Satire on Men', l.1–2 (published in full 1953).

61 Dear Madam, You are stark mad, and therefore the fitter for me to love; and that is the reason I think I can never leave to be Your humble servant.

c.1675 Letter to his mistress, the actress Elizabeth Barry. In *The Letters of John Wilmot, Earl of Rochester*, edited by Jeremy Treglown (1980).

62 To pick out the wildest and most fantastical odd man alive, and to place your kindness there, is an act so brave and daring as will show the greatness of your spirit and distinguish you in love, as you are in all things else, from womankind.

c.1675 Letter to his mistress, the actress Elizabeth Barry. In *The Letters of John Wilmot, Earl of Rochester*, edited by Jeremy Treglown (1980).

63 They who would be great in our little government seem as ridiculous to me as schoolboys who…climb a crab-tree, venturing their necks for fruit which solid pigs would disdain if they were not starving.

c.1676 Letter to Henry Savile. In *The Letters of John Wilmot, Earl of Rochester*, edited by Jeremy Treglown (1980).

64 He is a rarity which I cannot but be fond of, as one would be of a hog that could fiddle, or a singing owl.

c.1676 Of Dryden. Letter to Henry Savile. In *The Letters of John Wilmot, Earl of Rochester*, edited by Jeremy Treglown (1980).

65 Son of a whore, God damn you! can you tell
A Peerless Peer the readiest way to Hell?

c.1676 'To the Post-Boy', l.1–2 (published 1926). The postboy's answer is 'The readiest way, my lord, is by Rochester'.

66 My most neglected wife, till you are a much respected widow, I find you will scarce be a contented woman, and to say no more than the plain truth, I do endeavour so fairly to do you that last good service.

c.1677 Letter to his wife, 20 Nov. In *The Letters of John Wilmot, Earl of Rochester*, edited by Jeremy Treglown (1980).

67 There can be no danger in sweetness and youth
Where love is secured by good nature and truth,
On her beauty I'll gaze, and of pleasure complain,
While every kind look adds a link to my chain.

'The Submission', l.13–16 (published 1680).

68 Farewell Woman, I Intend,
Henceforth, every night to sit,
With my lewd well natured friend,
Drinking, to engender wit.
'Love a Woman!', l.9–12 (published 1680).

69 Since 'tis nature's law to change,
Constancy alone is strange.
'A Dialogue between Strephon and Daphne', l.31–2 (published 1691).

70 An age in her embraces passed,
Would seem a winter's day;
Where life and light, with envious haste,
Are torn and snatched away.

But, oh how slowly minutes roll,
When absent from her eyes
That feed my love, which is my soul,
It languishes and dies.
'The Mistress', l.1–8 (published 1691).

71 Ancient Person, for whom I
All the flattering youth defy;
Long be it ere thou grow old,
Aching, shaking, crazy, cold;
But still continue as thou art,
Ancient person of my heart.
'A Song of a Young Lady to Her Ancient Lover', stanza 1 (published 1691).

72 God bless our good and gracious King
Whose promise none relies on,
Who never said a foolish thing
Nor ever did a wise one.
Of Charles II (published 1707). The verse was later changed to an epitaph ('Here lies a great and mighty king…').

Rockefeller, David 1915–

US banker and philanthropist, born into the wealthy Rockefeller dynasty, Chairman and Chief Executive Officer of the Chase Manhattan Bank (1969–81).

73 One thing this family does not need to do is make itself resented by thousands more people.
Explaining his reluctance to join the management of the Chase Manhattan Bank. Quoted in Peter Collier and David Horowitz *The Rockefellers* (1976).

74 I was born into wealth and there was nothing I could do about it. It was there like food or air.
1990 In *Merchants and Masterpieces*, WETA TV broadcast, 31 Dec.

Rockefeller, John D(avison) 1839–1937

US industrialist and philanthropist. In 1875 he founded with his brother William the Standard Oil Company, securing control of US oil trade. After 1897 he devoted himself to philanthropy, and in 1913 established the Rockefeller Foundation 'to promote the wellbeing of mankind'.

75 The growth of a large business is merely a survival of the fittest… The American Beauty rose can be produced in the splendor and fragrance which bring cheer to its beholder only by sacrificing the early buds which grow up around it.
Quoted in W J Ghent *Our Benevolent Feudalism* (1902).

Rockefeller, John D(avison), Jr 1874–1960

US business and oil magnate. He took over his father's business empire in 1911 and continued the Rockefeller philanthropic tradition. He founded the Rockefeller Center, New York (1931, completed 1939).

76 The secretaries here have an advantage I never had. They can prove to themselves their commercial worth.
1950 Speech to the New York Chamber of Commerce, 6 Apr. Quoted in Peter Collier and David Horowitz *The Rockefellers* (1976).

77 The rendering of useful service is the common duty of mankind, and…only in the purifying fire of sacrifice is the dross of selfishness consumed and the greatness of the human soul set free.
Credo engraved in Rockefeller Center Plaza, New York.

Rockefeller, John D(avison), III 1906–78

US businessman and art collector, Governor of West Virginia.

78 If my name were John D Smith IV I wouldn't have been elected to anything.
1970 On becoming West Virginia's Secretary of State (before moving on to be Governor). In the *New York Times*, 4 Oct.

79 It's like orchestrating a symphony of unhappiness.
1971 On the necessity of compromise in health-care financing. In the *Washington Post*, 1 Jul.

Rockefeller, Laurance S 1910–2004

US businessman, son of John D Rockefeller, Jr. He has been involved with a variety of conservation and environmental organizations.

80 Lyndon gave me that instead of the Hawaii air route.
Of the Medal of Freedom which he received from President Johnson after Eastern Airlines failed to receive permission to fly a coveted route. Quoted in Peter Collier and David Horowitz *The Rockefellers* (1978).

Rockefeller, Nelson A(ldrich) 1908–79

US Republican politician. Director of the Rockefeller Center (1931–58), he became Governor of New York State (1958–73) and Vice-President (1974–7) under Ford, after failing to win the presidential nomination.

81 If there is anything more satisfying than dedicating a new building, it is dedicating eight new buildings.
1970 On Albany's Government Mall. In the *New York Times*, 13 Mar.

82 When you think of what I had, what else was there to aspire to?
Of his lifelong ambition to be US President. Quoted in Michael Kramer and Sam Roberts *I Never Wanted to be Vice President of Anything* (1976).

Rockefeller, Winthrop 1912–73

US businessman and politician, son of John D Rockefeller Jr, who ran a farm in Arkansas on experimental principles. He served as Republican Governor of Arkansas (1967–70).

83 In them one can see the spontaneous—and often aesthetic—expression of a people reflected, not in a gilt-framed drawing room mirror, but in an honest glass held up to the face of a nation.
1962 On an exhibition of American folk art at the US Embassy, London. In news summaries, 31 Jan.

84 In the springtime of America's cultural life, its itinerant folk artists took to the road to record the life and times of a people. Perhaps never again will we have an artistic record created in such direct and unassuming terms.
1962 On an exhibition of American folk art at the US Embassy, London. In news summaries, 31 Jan.

Rockne, Knute Kenneth 1888–1931

Norwegian-born US football coach. Coach for the University of Notre Dame team after World War I, he dominated US college football until his death in an air crash.

85 When the going gets tough, the tough get going.
His catchphrase, later adopted by John F Kennedy.

Rockwell, Norman 1894–1978

US popular illustrator, best known for his *Saturday Evening Post* covers. His style is typically anecdotal, idealized scenes of everyday American small-town life.

86 If the public dislikes one of my *Post* covers, I can't help disliking it myself.
Quoted in the *New York Times*, 28 Sep 1986.

Rodchenko, Alexander 1891–1956

Russian artist who was a leader of the Russian Constructivist painters before he took up photography in 1922 and became active in the field of typography and photographic journalism.

87 Tell me, frankly, what ought to remain of Lenin:
an art bronze,
oil portraits,
etchings,
watercolours,
his secretary's diary, his friends' memoirs—
or
a file of photographs taken of him at work and rest,
archives of his books, writing pads, notebooks,
shorthand reports, films, phonograph records?
I don't think there's any choice.
Art has no place in modern life… Every cultured modern
man must wage war against art, as against opium.

Photograph and be photographed!
Quoted in Robert Hughes *The Shock of the New* (1980).

Roddenberry, Gene 1921–91

US scriptwriter, producer and director. A former air force pilot, he made his name as the creator of the popular *Star Trek* television series.

88 Space—the final frontier.
1966 Introductory voiceover to *Star Trek*.

89 To boldly go where no man has gone before.
1966 The mission of the starship *Enterprise*. Introductory voiceover to *Star Trek*.

90 Beam us up, Mr Scott.
1966 *Star Trek*, 'Gamesters of Triskelion'. The phrase is often misquoted as 'Beam me up, Scotty'.

Roddick, Anita 1942–

English retail entrepreneur, founder (in 1976) of the Body Shop.

91 I think that business practices would improve immeasurably if they were guided by 'feminine' principles—qualities like love and care and intuition.
1991 *Body and Soul.*

Rodgers, Richard and Hart, Lorenz 1902–79; 1896–1943

US composer and songwriter partnership. They wrote a series of popular musicals including *Pal Joey* (1940).

92 Sigmund Freud has often stated
Dreams and drives are all related.
Zip, I am such a scholar!
1940 'Zip', in *Pal Joey.*

Rodgers, T J

US businessman. He is founder, president and chief executive officer of Cypress Semiconductor Corporation.

93 Most entrepreneurs who have the guts to take on a big challenge are a lot like Babe Ruth—they set records for both home runs and strike outs.
1993 Letter about Steven Jobs of Next in the *San Francisco Chronicle*, 6 Dec.

Rodó, José Enrique 1872–1917

Uruguayan essayist and philosopher, a leading stylist and thinker of the Modernist group. His most famous work, *Ariel*, admonishes the youth of South America to cultivate spiritual (Ariel) rather than material (Caliban) values.

94 *La visión de una América deslatinizada por propia voluntad, sin la extorsión de la conquista, y regenerada luego a imagen y semejanza del arquetipo del Norte, flota ya sobre los sueños de muchos sinceros interesados por nuestro porvenir… Tenemos nuestra nordomanía. Es necesario oponerle los límites que la razón y el sentimiento señalan.*
The vision of an America de-Latinized of its own will, without threat of conquest, and reconstituted in the image and likeness of the North, now looms in the nightmares of many who are genuinely concerned about our future… We have our *USA-mania*. It must be limited by the boundaries our reason and sentiment jointly dictate.
1900 *Ariel* (translated 1922), pt.5.

Rodriguez, Richard 1944–

US writer and journalist.

95 The genius of American culture and its integrity comes from fidelity to the light. Plain as day, we say. Happy as the day is long. Early to bed, early to rise. American virtues are daylight virtues: honesty, integrity, plain speech. We say yes when we mean yes and no when we mean no, and all else comes from the evil one. America presumes innocence and even the right to happiness.
1990 *Frontiers*, 'Night and Day'.

96 In the modern city, it takes on the status of a cathedral, our Chartres, our Notre Dame, our marble museum of the soul.
1995 On San Francisco's new Museum of Modern Art. In the *MacNeil-Lehrer Report*, 27 Feb.

Rodriguez, Sue 1950–94

Canadian campaigner for euthanasia, who suffered from ALS (amyotrophic lateral sclerosis, or Lou Gehrig's disease, a progressive and terminal illness).

97 I want to ask you gentlemen, if I cannot give consent to my own death, then whose body is this? Who owns my life?

1992 Videotaped presentation to the Justice Committee of the House of Commons, Ottawa, Nov. Reported by Deborah Wilson in *The Globe and Mail*, 5 Dec. The Supreme Court of Canada denied Rodriguez's request for a physician-assisted death.

Roethke, Theodore 1908–63

US poet. Professor of English at the University of Washington from 1948, he won a Pulitzer Prize for his collection *The Waking* (1953).

98 I have known the inexorable sadness of pencils,
Neat in their boxes, dolor of pad and paper-weight,
All the misery of manila folders and mucilage,
Desolation in immaculate public places.

1948 *The Lost Son*, 'Dolor'.

99 And I have seen dust from the walls of institutions,
Finer than flour, alive, more dangerous than silica,
Sift, almost invisible, through long afternoons of tedium.

1948 *The Lost Son*, 'Dolor'.

1 To know that light falls and fills, often without our knowing,
As an opaque vase fills to the brim from quick pouring,
Fills and trembles at the edge yet does not flow over,
Still holding and feeding the stem of the contained flower.

1948 *The Lost Son*, 'The Shape of Fire'.

2 And what a congress of stinks!—
Roots ripe as old bait,
Pulpy stems, rank, silo-rich,
Leaf-mold, manure, lime, piled against slippery planks.
Nothing would give up life:
Even the dirt kept breathing a small breath.

1948 *The Lost Son*, 'Root Cellar'.

3 I wake to sleep, and take my waking slow.
I feel my fate in what I cannot fear.
I learn by going where I have to go.

1953 *The Waking*, 'The Waking'.

4 Over this damp grave I speak the words of my love;
I, with no rights in this matter,
Neither father nor lover.

1953 Poem addressed to a dead student. *The Waking*, 'Elegy for Jane'.

5 Of her choice virtues only gods should speak,
Or English poets who grew up on Greek
(I'd have them sing in chorus, cheek to cheek).

1958 *Words for the Wind*, 'I Knew a Woman'.

6 What's freedom for? To know eternity.
I swear she cast a shadow white as stone.
But who would count eternity in days?
These old bones live to learn her wanton ways:
(I measure time by how a body sways).

1958 *Words for the Wind*, 'I Knew a Woman'.

7 In a dark time the eye begins to see.

1963 *Sequence, Sometimes Metaphysical*, 'In a Dark Time'.

8 The self persists like a dying star,
In sleep, afraid.

1964 *The Far Field*, 'Meditation at Oyster River'.

Rogers, Carl Ransom 1902–87

US psychologist and pioneer of client-centred counselling. His *Client-Centred Therapy* (1951) and *On Becoming a Person* (1961) emphasized the value of genuine empathy with the patient.

9 Unconditional positive regard.

c.1950 The slogan of the Rogerian counselling movement.

Rogers, Richard George Rogers, Baron 1933–

English architect, concerned with advancing technology in architecture and pushing the limits of design. His works include the Beaubourg or Pompidou Centre, Paris (1971–9, with Renzo Piano), Lloyds Building, London (1979–85), the Millennium Dome (1999) and the National Assembly for Wales (1999).

10 'Form follows profit' is the aesthetic principle of our times. Thus, design skill is measured today by the architect's ability to build the largest possible enclosure for the smallest investment in the quickest time.

1990 22nd annual Walter Neurath lecture. Collected in *Architecture: a Modern View*.

11 Architects cannot work in a vacuum; unlike other artists they are totally dependent on a site, a brief and finance.

1990 22nd annual Walter Neurath lecture. Collected in *Architecture: a Modern View*.

12 The problem is not style but quality, not aesthetics but ethics.

1990 22nd annual Walter Neurath lecture. Collected in *Architecture: a Modern View*.

Rogers, Will 1879–1935

US actor, rancher and humorist. Best known for his ready wisecracks, he had a syndicated column, and wrote a number of books, including a posthumously compiled *Autobiography*.

13 Will you please tell me what you do with all the vice presidents a bank has?... The United States is the biggest business institution in the world and they only have one vice president and nobody has ever found anything for him to do.

1922 Speech, International Bankers' Association.

14 Well, all I know is what I read in the papers.

1923 In the *New York Times*, 30 Sep.

15 You know everybody is ignorant, only on different subjects.

1924 In the *New York Times*, 31 Aug.

16 The more you read and observe about this Politics thing, you got to admit that each party is worse than the other. The one that's out always looks the best.

1924 *The Illiterate Digest*, 'Breaking into the Writing Game'.

17 Everything is funny as long as it is happening to Somebody Else.

1924 *The Illiterate Digest*, 'Warning to Jokers: Lay Off the Prince'.

18 The Income Tax return has made more Liars out of the American people than Golf has. Even when you make one out on the level, you don't know when it's through if you are a Crook or a Martyr.

1924 *The Illiterate Digest*, 'Helping the Girls with Their Income Taxes'.

19 I bet you if I had met him and had a chat with him, I would have found him a very interesting and human fellow, for I never yet met a man that I didn't like.

1926 On Trotsky. In the *Saturday Evening Post*, 6 Nov.

20 Communism is like prohibition, it's a good idea but it won't work.
1927 Syndicated column, Nov. Collected in *The Weekly Articles*, vol. 3 (1981).

21 You can't say civilization don't advance, however, for in every war they kill you in a new way.
1929 In the *New York Times*, 23 Dec.

22 Half our life is spent trying to find something to do with the time we have rushed through life trying to save.
1930 In the *New York Times*, 29 Apr.

23 The United States is the only country ever to go to the poorhouse in an automobile.
c.1930 Attributed.

24 I was born because it was a habit in those days, people didn't know anything else.
The Autobiography of Will Rogers (published 1949), ch.1.

25 There is only one thing that can kill the Movies, and that is education.
The Autobiography of Will Rogers (published 1949), ch.6.

26 When a man goes in for politics over here, he has no time to labour, and any man that labours has no time to fool with politics. Over there, politics is an obligation; over here it's a business.
On Britain electing a Labour government. *The Autobiography of Will Rogers* (published 1949), ch.14.

27 It's great to be great but it's greater to be human.
The Autobiography of Will Rogers (published 1949), ch.15.

28 Being a hero is about the shortest-lived profession on earth.
Quoted in 'A Rogers Thesaurus' in *The Saturday Review*, 25 Aug 1962. Another form of the quote appeared in a syndicated newspaper article, 15 Feb 1925: 'Heroing is one of the shortest-lived professions there is'.

29 I don't make jokes—I just watch the government and report the facts.
Quoted in 'A Rogers Thesaurus' in *The Saturday Review*, 25 Aug 1962.

30 I guess there is nothing that will get your mind off everything like golf. I have never been depressed enough to take up the game but they say you get so sore at yourself you forget to hate your enemies.
Quoted in Michael Hobbs *The Golf Quotation Book* (1992).

Rogers, William Pierce 1913–2001

US lawyer and government official. As Deputy Attorney General (1953–7) he supported the 1957 Civil Rights Act, becoming Attorney General (1957–61). As Secretary of State (1969–73) he brought about a Middle East ceasefire.

31 Making foreign policy is like pornographic movies…more fun doing it than watching it.
1982 On becoming Under-Secretary of State for Economic Affairs, 7 Jun.

Rolleston, Humphrey 1862–1944

English physician.

32 Medicine is a noble profession but a damn bad business.
1944 Quoted in *Who Said What When* (1988).

Rollins, Sonny (Theodore Walter) 1930–

US jazz saxophonist. He is a leading figure in the development of jazz in the post-bebop era.

33 America is deeply rooted in Negro culture: its colloquialisms, its humour, its music. How ironic that the Negro, who more than any other people can claim America's culture as his own, is being persecuted and repressed, that the Negro, who has exemplified the humanities in his very existence, is being rewarded with inhumanity.
1958 Statement on sleeve of *Freedom Suite*.

Romani, Felice 1788–1865

Italian librettist, poet, essayist and critic. He provided libretti for more than 100 composers, striking a balance between Classicism and Romanticism. He is best known for his collaborations with Donizetti and Bellini.

34 *Casta Diva.*
Chaste goddess.
1831 Norma's aria. *Norma*, act 1 (music by Bellini, published 1832).

35 *Una furtiva lagrima.*
A furtive tear.
1832 Nemorino's aria. *L'Elisir d'Amore*, act 2 (music by Donizetti).

Romney, George W 1907–95

US politician. He was Governor of Michigan (1963–9) and member of the Nixon administration (1969–73).

36 I didn't say I didn't say it. I said I didn't say I said it. I want to make that very clear.
1967 Clarifying his policy. In the *National Review*, 12 Dec.

Roosevelt, (Anna) Eleanor 1884–1962

US humanitarian and diplomat, wife and adviser of Franklin D Roosevelt. After his death she was US delegate to the UN (1945–53, 1961), chair of the Human Rights Commission (1946–51) and US representative to the General Assembly (1946–52).

37 You always admire what you don't really understand.
1956 In *Meet the Press*, NBC TV broadcast, 16 Sep.

38 She can talk beautifully about democracy but doesn't know how to live democracy.
Of Madame Chiang Kai-shek. Recalled on Mrs Roosevelt's death, 7 Nov 1962.

39 Where, after all, do human rights begin? They begin in small places, close to home—so close and so small that they cannot be seen on any map of the world.
1965 Quoted in the *New York Times*, 26 Dec.

40 A woman is like a tea bag; when she is in hot water she just gets stronger.
Quoted by Hillary Rodham Clinton in the *Wall Street Journal*, 30 Sep 1994.

Roosevelt, Franklin D(elano) 1882–1945

US Democratic statesman, 32nd President (1933–45) despite being stricken with polio in 1921. He introduced a 'New Deal' for national recovery (1933), and was re-elected three times. He entered World War II after Pearl Harbor (1941), meeting Churchill and Stalin at Teheran (1943) and Yalta (1945), but died just before the German surrender.

41 I pledge you, I pledge myself, to a New Deal for the American people.
1932 Speech accepting the Democratic Convention's

presidential nomination, Chicago, 2 Jul.

42 In the field of world policy, I would dedicate this nation to the policy of the good neighbour.
1933 Inaugural address, 4 Mar.

43 Let me assert my belief that the only thing that we have to fear is fear itself—nameless, unreasoning, unjustified terror that paralyses needed efforts to convert retreat into advance.
1933 Inaugural address, 4 Mar.

44 Better the occasional faults of a Government that lives in a spirit of charity than the consistent omissions of a Government frozen in the ice of its own indifference.
1936 Renomination acceptance speech, Philadelphia, 27 Jun.

45 I have seen war... I hate war.
1936 Speech at Chantauqua, New York, 14 Aug.

46 When peace has been broken anywhere, the peace of all countries is in danger.
1939 Radio broadcast, 3 Sep.

47 A conservative is a man with two perfectly good legs who has never learned to walk forwards. A reactionary is a somnambulist walking backwards. A radical is a man with both feet planted firmly in the air.
1939 Radio broadcast, Oct.

48 I have said this before, but I shall say it again and again and again: Your boys are not going to be sent into any foreign wars.
1940 Speech in Boston, 30 Oct.

49 We have the men—the skill—the wealth—and above all, the will... We must be the great arsenal of democracy.
1940 'Fireside chat' radio broadcast, 29 Dec.

50 In the future days, which we seek to make secure, we look forward to a world founded upon four essential freedoms. The first is freedom of speech and expression, everywhere in the world. The second is the freedom of every person to worship God in his own way, everywhere in the world. The third is freedom from want... The fourth is freedom from fear.
1941 Third inaugural address, 6 Jan.

51 Yesterday, December 7, 1941—a date which will live in infamy—the United States of America was suddenly and deliberately attacked by naval and air forces of the Empire of Japan.
1941 Address to Congress, 8 Dec, following the Japanese attack on Pearl Harbor.

Roosevelt, Theodore 1858–1919

US Republican statesman and 26th President (1901–9). Elected Vice-President in 1900, he became President on McKinley's assassination and was re-elected in 1904. His expansionist policies included a strong navy, the regulation of trusts and monopolies, and his 'Square Deal' policy for social reform.

52 There is a homely adage that runs, 'Speak softly and carry a big stick, and you will go far.' If the American nation will speak softly and yet build, and keep at a pitch of the highest training, the Monroe Doctrine will go far.
1901 Vice-presidential speech, Sep.

53 In the western hemisphere, the adherence of the United States to the Monroe Doctrine may force the United States, however reluctantly, in flagrant cases of wrongdoing or impotence, to the exercise of an international police power.
1904 Message to Congress, 6 Dec.

54 The men with the muck-rakes are often indispensable to the well-being of society, but only if they know when to stop raking the muck.
1906 House of Representatives, 14 Apr.

55 I stand for the square deal...not merely for fair play under the present rules of the game, but for having those rules changed, so as to work for a more substantial equality of opportunity and of reward for equally good service.
1910 Speech, Osawatomie, 31 Aug.

56 Do not hit at all if it can be avoided, but never hit softly.
1913 *Theodore Roosevelt: an Autobiography.*

57 Practical efficiency is common, and lofty idealism is not uncommon; it is the combination that is necessary, and that combination is rare.
1913 *Theodore Roosevelt: an Autobiography.*

58 There is no reason why people should not call themselves Cubists, or Octagonists, or Parallelopipedonists, or Knights of the Isosceles Triangle, or Brothers of the Cosine, if they so desire; as expressing anything serious and permanent, one term is as fatuous as another.
1913 His opinion on the *International Exhibition of Modern Art* in New York, popularly known as *The Armoury Show.* 'A Layman's Views of an Art Exhibition', in *The Outlook* (9 Mar).

59 We are fighting in the quarrel of civilization against barbarism, of liberty against tyranny. Germany has become a menace to the whole world. She is the most dangerous enemy of liberty now existing.
1917 Speech at Oyster Bay, Long Island, Apr.

60 We have room in this country but for one flag, the Stars and Stripes. We have room for but one loyalty, loyalty to the United States. We have room for but one language, the English language.
1919 Message to the American Defense Society two days before his death, 3 Jan.

Rosebery, Archibald Philip Primrose, 5th Earl of 1847–1929

English statesman, Foreign Secretary (1886, 1892–4) under Gladstone, whom he succeeded as Prime Minister for a brief period in 1894 before the Liberals lost the election of 1895. He was noted for his racehorse stables, and as a biographer of British statesmen.

61 It is beginning to be hinted that we are a nation of amateurs.
1900 Rectorial address, Glasgow University, 16 Nov.

62 For the present at any rate, I must proceed alone. I must plough my own furrow alone—but before I get to the end of that furrow, it is possible that I may not find myself alone.
1901 On breaking from the Liberal Party, Jul.

Rosenberg, Harold 1906–78

US critic of the modern movement in painting and literature.

63 At a certain moment the canvas began to appear to one American painter after another as an arena in which to act—rather than as a space in which to reproduce,

re-design, analyze or 'express' an object, actual or imagined. What was to go on the canvas was not a picture but an event.
1952 'The American Action Painters', in *Art News*, no.51, Dec.

64 A painting that is an act is inseparable from the biography of the artist.
1952 'The American Action Painters', in *Art News*, no.51, Dec.

65 Everyone knows that the label Modern Art no longer has any relation to the words that compose it. To be Modern Art a work need not be either modern nor art; it need not even be a work. A three-thousand-year-old mask from the South Pacific qualifies as Modern and a piece of wood found on a beach becomes Art.
1952 'The American Action Painters', in *Art News*, no.51, Dec.

66 As we have seen Modern Art does not have to be actually new; it only has to be new to somebody—to the last lady who found out about the driftwood.
1952 'The American Action Painters', in *Art News*, no.51, Dec.

Rosenberg, Isaac 1890–1918

English poet and artist. He published two volumes of poems before being killed in action in France. A third appeared posthumously, and his *Collected Works* (1937, rev edn 1973) revived his reputation.

67 The darkness crumbles away—
It is the same old druid Time as ever.
1916 'Break of Day in the Trenches'.

68 Droll rat, they would shoot you if they knew
Your cosmopolitan sympathies.
1916 'And God Knows What Antipathies'.

69 Earth has waited for them,
All the time of their growth
Fretting for their decay:
Now she has them at last.
1917 'Dead Man's Dump'.

70 Death could drop from the dark
As easily as song.
1917 'Returning, We Hear the Larks'.

Rosenblum, Robert 1927–

US art historian. His works include *Cubism and Twentieth Century Art* (1960) and *Andy Warhol: Portrait of the 70s* (1981).

71 She transformed junkyards of secular carpentry into almost sacred altarpieces.
1988 On sculptor Louise Nevelson. In *Time*, 26 Dec.

Ross, Edward Alsworth 1866–1951

US sociologist, Professor at the University of Wisconsin.

72 A society...which is riven by a dozen oppositions along lines running in every direction, may actually be in less danger of being torn with violence or falling to pieces than one split along just one line. For each new cleavage contributes to narrow the cross clefts, so that one might say that society is *sewn together* by its internal conflicts.
1920 *The Principles of Sociology*.

Rossetti, Christina Georgina 1830–94

English poet and sister of Dante Gabriel Rossetti. She helped found with her brother the Pre-Raphaelite Brotherhood. A devout Christian, her poetry has a melancholic and religiously intense quality.

73 Because the birthday of my life
Is come, my love is come to me.
1862 *Goblin Market and Other Poems*, 'A Birthday'.

74 Come to me in the silence of the night;
Come in the speaking silence of a dream;
Come with soft rounded cheeks and eyes as bright
As sunlight on a stream;
Come back in tears,
O memory, hope, love of finished years.
1862 *Goblin Market and Other Poems*, 'Echo'.

75 For there is no friend like a sister
In calm or stormy weather;
To cheer one on the tedious way,
To fetch one if one goes astray,
To lift one if one totters down,
To strengthen whilst one stands.
1862 *Goblin Market and Other Poems*, 'Goblin Market'.

76 The hope I dreamed of was a dream,
Was but a dream; and now I wake,
Exceeding comfortless, and worn, and old,
For a dream's sake.
1862 *Goblin Market and Other Poems*, 'Mirage'.

77 Oh roses for the flush of youth,
And laurel for the perfect prime;
But pluck an ivy branch for me
Grown old before my time.
1862 *Goblin Market and Other Poems*, 'Oh Roses for the Flush of Youth'.

78 Remember me when I am gone away,
Gone far away into the silent land.
1862 *Goblin Market and Other Poems*, 'Remember'.

79 Better by far you should forget and smile
Than that you should remember and be sad.
1862 *Goblin Market and Other Poems*, 'Remember'.

80 O Earth, lie heavily upon her eyes;
Seal her sweet eyes weary of watching, Earth.
1862 *Goblin Market and Other Poems*, 'Rest'.

81 Silence more musical than any song.
1862 *Goblin Market and Other Poems*, 'Rest'.

82 Does the road wind up-hill all the way?
Yes, to the very end.
Will the day's journey take the whole long day?
From morn to night, my friend.
1862 *Goblin Market and Other Poems*, 'Up-Hill'.

83 When I am dead, my dearest,
Sing no sad songs for me;
Plant thou no roses at my head,
Nor shady cypress tree:
Be the green grass above me
With showers and dewdrops wet;
And if thou wilt, remember,
And if thou wilt, forget.
1862 *Goblin Market and Other Poems*, 'When I Am dead'.

84 In the bleak mid-winter
Frosty wind made moan,
Earth stood hard as iron,
Water like a stone;
Snow had fallen, snow on snow,
Snow on snow,

In the bleak mid-winter,
Long ago.
1875 'Mid-Winter'.

85 Love came down at Christmas,
Love all lovely, Love Divine;
Love was born at Christmas,
Star and angels gave the sign.
1893 *Verses*, 'Love Came Down at Christmas'.

Rossetti, Dante Gabriel 1828–82

English painter and poet, who with his sister Christina Rossetti, Millais and Holman Hunt, founded the Pre-Raphaelite Brotherhood. His poetic works include *Poems* (1870) and *Ballads and Sonnets* (1881).

86 The blessed damozel leaned out
From the gold bar of Heaven;
Her eyes were deeper than the depth
Of waters stilled at even;
She had three lilies in her hand,
And the stars in her hair were seven.
1870 *Poems*, 'The Blessed Damozel', stanza 1.

87 Her hair that lay along her back
Was yellow like ripe corn.
1870 *Poems*, 'The Blessed Damozel', stanza 2.

88 As low as where this earth
Spins like a fretful midge.
1870 *Poems*, 'The Blessed Damozel', stanza 6.

89 And the souls mounting up to God
Went by her like thin flames.
1870 *Poems*, 'The Blessed Damozel', stanza 7.

90 'We two,' she said, 'will seek the groves
Where the lady Mary is,
With her five handmaidens, whose names
Are five sweet symphonies,
Cecily, Gertrude, Magdalen,
Margaret and Rosalys.'
1870 *Poems*, 'The Blessed Damozel', stanza 18.

91 I have been here before,
But when or how I cannot tell:
I know the grass beyond the door,
The sweet keen smell,
The sighing sound, the lights around the shore.
1870 *Poems*, 'Sudden Light'.

92 A sonnet is a moment's monument,—
Memorial from the Soul's eternity
To one dead deathless hour.
1881 *The House of Life*, introduction.

93 'Tis visible silence, still as the hour-glass.
1881 *The House of Life*, 'Silent Noon', pt.1.

94 Deep in the sun-searched growths the dragon-fly
Hangs like a blue thread loosened from the sky:—
So this winged hour is dropt to us from above.
Oh! clasp we to our hearts, for deathless dower,
This close-companioned inarticulate hour
When twofold silence was the song of love.
1881 *The House of Life*, 'Silent Noon', pt.1.

95 Lo! as that youth's eyes burned at thine, so went
Thy spell through him, and left his straight neck bent
And round his heart one strangling golden hair.
1881 *The House of Life*, 'Body's Beauty', pt.2.

96 They die not,—for their life was death,—but cease;
And round their narrow lips the mould falls close.
1881 *The House of Life*, 'The Choice', pt.1.

97 I do not see them here; but after death
God knows I know the faces I shall see,
Each one a murdered self, with low last breath.
'I am thyself,—what hast thou done to me?'
'And I—and I—thyself,' (lo! each one saith,)
'And thou thyself to all eternity!'
1881 *The House of Life*, 'Lost Days', pt.2.

98 Give honour unto Luke Evangelist;
For he it was (the aged legends say)
Who first taught Art to fold her hands and pray.
1881 *The House of Life*, 'Old and New Art', pt.2.

99 When vain desire at last and vain regret
Go hand in hand to death, and all is vain,
What shall assuage the unforgotten pain
And teach the unforgetful to forget?
1881 *The House of Life*, 'The One Hope', pt.2.

1 Look in my face; my name is Might-have-been;
I am also called No-more, Too-late, Farewell.
1881 *The House of Life*, 'A Superscription', pt.2.

2 Sleepless with cold commemorative eyes.
1881 *The House of Life*, 'A Superscription', pt.2.

3 Unto the man of yearning thought
And aspiration, to do nought
Is in itself almost an act.
1881 *Ballads and Sonnets*, 'Soothsay', stanza 10.

Rossini, Gioacchino Antonio 1792–1868

Italian composer. His early operas including *La Scala de seta* (1812) and *L'Italiana in Algeri* (1813) were followed by his masterpiece, *Il Barbiere de Seviglia* (1816). His later works, mostly written in Paris, include *La Gazza Ladra* (1817), *Semiramide* (1823) and *Guillaume Tell* (1829).

4 I was born for *opera buffa*, as well Thou knowest. Little skill, a little heart, and that is all. So be Thou blessed and admit me to Paradise.
1863 Manuscript inscription on the score of his 'Petite Messe Solennelle'.

5 Monsieur Wagner has good moments, but awful quarters of an hour!
1867 Quoted in Emile Naumann *Italienische Tondichter* (1883).

Rosso, Medardo 1858–1928

Italian sculptor. Sometimes known as the 'Impressionist' sculptor, he was a major influence on the Italian Futurists.

6 When I make a portrait, I cannot limit it to the lines of the head, for that head belongs to a body, it exists in a setting which influences it, it is part of a totality that I cannot suppress. The impression you produce upon me is not the same if I catch sight of you alone in a garden or if I see you in the midst of a group of other people, in a living room or on the street.
Quoted in Edmond Claris *De l'impressionisme en sculpture*, 'Medardo Rosso' (1902).

7 One does not walk around a statue any more than one walks around a painting, because one does not walk around a figure to receive an impression from it. Nothing is material in space.

Quoted in Edmond Claris *De l'impressionisme en sculpture*, 'Medardo Rosso' (1902).

Rostand, Jean 1894–1977

French biologist and writer.

8 A body of work such as Pasteur's is inconceivable in our time: no man would be given a chance to create a whole science. Nowadays a path is scarcely opened up when the crowd begins to pour in.
1939 'Pensées d'un Biologiste', collected in *The Substance of Man* (translated by Irma Brandeis, 1962).

9 Nothing leads the scientist so astray as a premature truth.
1939 'Pensées d'un Biologiste', collected in *The Substance of Man* (translated by Irma Brandeis, 1962).

Rosten, Leo Calvin 1908–97

US writer, humorist and anthologist. He is best known for his humorous compendium *The Joys of Yiddish* (1968), but has also written novels and stage plays (some as Leonard Ross).

10 The only thing I can say about W C Fields, whom I have admired since the day he advanced upon Baby LeRoy with an ice pick, is this: any man who hates dogs and babies can't be all bad.
1939 Speech at a Hollywood dinner in honour of W C Fields, 16 Feb.

11 The only reason for being a professional writer is that you just can't help it.
In D L Kirkpatrick (ed) *Contemporary Novelists* (1976).

Roth, Guenther 1931–

German-born US sociologist, Professor of Sociology at Columbia University.

12 My draft-dodging father proved that in the struggle for survival the fittest are most likely to get killed off.
'Partisanship and Scholarship', collected in Bennett Berger (ed) *Authors of Their Own Lives* (1990).

Roth, Henry 1906–95

US novelist. His novel of Jewish life in New York, *Call It Sleep* (1934), was rediscovered on its paperback publication in 1962. Apart from the shorter writings collected in *Shifting Landscape* (1987), he did not publish another until the first part of a massive six-book project, *Mercy of a Rude Stream* (1994).

13 The mind shuttles and reminds: we go this way only once; and shuttles again and rejoins: once is enough.
1960 'The Dun Dakotas', in *Commentary*, 30 Aug.

14 Detach the writer from the milieu where he has experienced his greatest sense of belonging, and you have created a discontinuity within his personality, a short circuit in his identity. The result is his originality, his creativity comes to an end. He becomes the one-book novelist or the one-trilogy writer.
1987 'The Eternal Plebeian and Other Matters', in *Shifting Landscape*.

Roth, Philip Milton 1933–

US novelist. His *succès de scandale*, *Portnoy's Complaint* (1969), was followed by a series of highly literary novels featuring his fictional alter ego, Nathan Zuckerman, all dealing with questions of Jewish identity.

15 Since I was a little girl I always wanted to be Very Decent to People. Other little girls wanted to be nurses and pianists. They were less dissembling.
1962 *Letting Go*, pt.1, ch.1.

16 It's the little questions from women about tappets that finally push men over the edge.
1962 *Letting Go*, pt.1, ch.1.

17 It's a family joke that when I was a tiny child I turned from the window out of which I was watching a snowstorm, and hopefully asked, 'Momma, do we believe in winter?'
1969 *Portnoy's Complaint*, 'The Most Unforgettable Character I've Ever Met'.

18 A Jewish man with parents alive is a fifteen-year-old boy, and will remain a fifteen-year-old boy until *they die*!
1969 *Portnoy's Complaint*, 'Cunt Crazy'.

19 Doctor, doctor, what do you say, LET'S PUT THE ID BACK IN YID!
1969 *Portnoy's Complaint*, 'Cunt Crazy'.

20 Know that famous proverb? When the prick stands up, the brains get buried in the ground!
1969 *Portnoy's Complaint*, 'Cunt Crazy'.

21 My Life as a Man.
1974 Title of novel.

22 Satire is moral outrage transformed into comic art.
1975 *Reading Myself and Others*, 'On *Our Gang*'.

23 The road to hell is paved with works-in-progress.
1979 In the *New York Times Book Review*, 15 Jul.

24 In America everything goes and nothing matters, while in Europe nothing goes and everything matters.
1983 Interview in *Time*, Nov.

25 In Israel it's enough to live—you don't have to do anything else and you go to bed exhausted. Have you ever noticed that Jews shout? Even one ear is more than you need.
1987 *The Counterlife*, ch.2.

26 What makes you a normal Jew, Nathan, is how you are riveted by Jewish abnormality.
1987 *The Counterlife*, ch.2.

27 Is an intelligent human being likely to be much more than a large-scale manufacturer of misunderstanding?
1987 *The Counterlife*, ch.5.

28 For me, as for most novelists, every genuine imaginative event begins down there, with the facts, with the specific, and not with the philosophical, the ideological, or the abstract.
1988 *The Facts: A Novelist's Autobiography*, 'Dear Zuckerman'.

29 In our lore, the Jewish family was an inviolate haven against every form of menace, from personal isolation to gentile hostility. Regardless of internal friction and strife, it was assumed to be an indissoluble consolidation… Family indivisibility, the first commandment.
1988 *The Facts: A Novelist's Autobiography*, 'Dear Zuckerman'.

30 I write fiction and I'm told it's autobiography, I write autobiography and I'm told it's fiction, so since I'm so dim and they're so smart, let *them* decide what it is or it isn't.
1990 Of critics. *Deception*, 'Philip'.

31 It was the summer when a president's penis was on everyone's mind, and life, in all its shameless impurity,

once again confounded America.
2001 *The Human Stain.*

32 I want to make it clear that it wasn't impotence that led me in to a reclusive existence.
2001 *The Human Stain.*

Roth, William V, Jr 1921–

US senator. A member of Congress for Delaware (1967–71), he became a Senator (1971–) and a member of the finance government affairs committee.

33 If only trimmed, it inevitably creeps back…thicker and more deeply rooted than before.
1995 Of bureaucracy, compared to crab grass. In the *Washington Times*, 19 May.

Rothko, Mark *originally* Marcus Rothkovitch 1903–70

Latvian-born painter, who emigrated to the US as a child. A largely self-taught artist, he moved from Surrealism to a distinctively meditative form of Abstract Expressionism, filling large canvases with blocks of pure colour.

34 I am not interested in relationships of color or form or anything else… I am interested only in expressing the basic human emotions—tragedy, ecstasy, doom, and so on—and the fact that lots of people break down and cry when confronted with my pictures shows that I *communicate* with those basic human emotions. The people who weep before my pictures are having the same religious experience I had when I painted them. And if you, as you say, are moved only by their color relationships, then you miss the point!
Quoted in R Rosenblum *Modern Painting and the Northern Romantic Tradition* (1975).

Rothwell, Talbot 1916–74

British screenwriter who wrote for film and television, best known for his contribution to many of the *Carry On*… films.

35 Infamy! Infamy! They've all got it in for me!
1964 Line delivered by Kenneth Williams as Julius Caesar in *Carry On Cleo.*

36 The eunuchs are on strike. They are complaining about loss of assets.
1964 *Carry On Cleo.*

Rotten, Johnny *stage name of* John Lydon 1956–

English punk singer, member of The Sex Pistols.

37 Ever get the feeling you've been cheated?
1978 Having walked offstage at the Winterland Ballroom during The Sex Pistols tour of the US, 14 Jan.

Rouault, Georges Henri 1871–1958

French painter and engraver. Apprenticed to a stained-glass designer in his youth, he retained the characteristic glowing colour outlined in black in his later work. He joined the Fauves c.1904. His works include the large religious engravings *Miserere* and *Guerre*.

38 Decorative art does not exist—only art, intimate, heroic, or epic.
1937 *La Renaissance.*

Rous, Sir Stanley 1895–1986

English football administrator. A former player and referee, he became Secretary of the Football Association in 1934 and President of FIFA in 1961. His codification of the rules of football into 17 laws is still followed today.

39 If this can be termed the century of the common man, then soccer, of all sports, is surely his game… In a world haunted by the hydrogen and napalm bomb, the football field is a place where sanity and hope are still left unmolested.
1952 Quoted in Bryon Butler *The Official History of the Football Association* (1986).

Rousseau, Jean Jacques 1712–78

French political philosopher, educationalist and writer. The father of French Romanticism, he wrote in many different genres. He is best known for his novel *Julie, ou la Nouvelle Héloïse* (1761), his autobiography, his posthumously published *Confessions*, and for *Du contrat social* (*The Social Contract*, 1762).

40 *Le premier qui, ayant enclos un terrain, s'avisa de dire: 'Ceci est à moi' et trouva des gens assez simples pour le croire, fut le vrai fondateur de la société civile.*
The first person who fenced in a piece of land, ventured to say: 'This is mine,' and found others simple enough to believe him, was the true founder of civil society.
1755 *Discours sur l'origine et les fondements de l'inégalité parmi les hommes*, ch.1.

41 *L'homme est né libre, et partout il est dans les fers.*
Man is born free, yet everywhere he is in chains.
1762 *Du contrat social* (*The Social Contract*), bk.1, ch.1 (translated by M Cranston).

42 *La force a fait les premiers esclaves, leur lâcheté les a perpétués.*
Force made the first slaves; their cowardice perpetuated slavery.
1762 *Du contrat social* (*The Social Contract*), bk.1, ch.2 (translated by M Cranston).

43 *Si l'on recherche en quoi consiste précisément le plus grand bien de tous, qui doit être le fin de tout système de législation, on trouvera qu'il se réduit à ces deux objets principaux, la liberté et l'égalité.*
If we enquire wherein lies precisely the greatest good of all, which ought to be the goal of every system of law, we shall find that it comes down to two main objects, *freedom* and *equality.*
1762 *Du contrat social* (*The Social Contract*), bk.2, ch.11 (translated by M Cranston).

44 *L'éducation de l'homme commence à sa naissance; avant de parler, avant que d'entendre, il s'instruit déjà.*
A man's education begins when he is born; before speaking, before understanding, he is already teaching himself.
1762 *Émile ou de l'éducation*, pt.1.

45 *J'aime mieux être homme à paradoxes qu'homme à préjugés.*
I would rather be a man of paradoxes than of prejudices.
1762 *Émile ou de l'éducation*, pt.2.

46 *C'est dans le cœur de l'homme qu'est la vie du spectacle de la nature; pour le voir, il faut le sentir.*
The spectacle of nature is in the heart of a man; to see it, he must feel it.
1762 *Émile ou de l'éducation*, pt.3.

47 *L'homme dit ce qu'il sait, la femme dit ce qui plaît.*

A man says what he knows, a woman says what pleases.
1762 *Émile ou de l'éducation*, pt.5.

48 War, then, is not a relationship between man and man, but between State and State, in which private persons are only enemies accidentally.
Quoted in A J P Taylor *From the Boer War to the Cold War: Essays on Twentieth-Century Europe* (1995), 'War and Peace', p.15.

Rowbotham, Sheila 1943–

English social historian and feminist. Together with Segel and Wainwright, she wrote the controversial *Beyond the Fragments: Feminism and the Making of Socialism* (1979). She has also written *Women, Resistance and Revolution* (1972) and *Women Resist Globalization: Mobilizing for Livelihood and Rights* (2001).

49 There is no 'beginning' of feminism in the sense that there is no beginning to defiance in women.
1972 *Women, Resistance and Revolution*, ch.1.

Rowland, Helen 1876–1950

US journalist, writer and humorist.

50 When you see what some girls marry, you realize how they must hate to work for a living.
1909 *Reflections of a Bachelor Girl.*

51 Never trust a husband too far, or a bachelor too near.
1915 *The Rubaiyat of a Bachelor.*

52 A husband is what is left of the lover after the nerve has been extracted.
1922 *A Guide to Men.*

53 The follies which a man regrets most in his life are those which he didn't commit when he had the opportunity.
1922 *A Guide to Men.*

Rowling, J K 1965–

English author whose first children's book, *Harry Potter and the Philosopher's Stone* (1997, published in the US as *Harry Potter and the Sorcerer's Stone*, 1998), set in the Hogwarts School of Witchcraft and Wizardry, was an immediate success, and was followed by equally successful sequels.

54 Before we begin our banquet, I would like to say a few words. And here they are: Nitwit! Blubber! Oddment! Tweak!
1997 *Harry Potter and the Philosopher's Stone* (published in the US as *Harry Potter and the Sorcerer's Stone*, 1998), ch.7.

55 Harry Potter was a highly unusual boy in many ways. For one thing, he hated the summer holidays more than any other time of year. For another, he really wanted to do his homework, but was forced to do it in secret, in the dead of night. And he also happened to be a wizard.
1999 *Harry Potter and the Prisoner of Azkaban*, opening lines.

Roy, Arundhati 1960–

Indian author and environmental activist. Her first novel, *The God of Small Things* (1997), won the Booker Prize.

56 The whole of contemporary history, the World Wars, the War of Dreams, the Man on the Moon, science, literature, philosophy, the pursuit of knowledge—was no more than a blink of the Earth Woman's eye.
1997 *The God of Small Things.*

Roy, Gabrielle 1909–83

Canadian novelist and memoirist.

57 Every writer must eventually write his Ninth Symphony or give in to despair.
1973 Letter, 1 Aug, quoted in Joan Hind-Smith *Three Voices* (1975).

Royden, (Agnes) Maude 1876–1956

English social worker and preacher who took a religious and moral approach to women's suffrage.

58 The Church of England should no longer be satisfied to represent only the Conservative Party at prayer.
1917 Address to the Life and Liberty Movement, London, 16 Jul.

Rubenstein, Helena 1870–1965

Polish cosmetics businesswoman. She developed and sold the first tinted foundation and face powder when she moved to New York In World War I and pioneered the use of silk in cosmetics. She used methods of mass production and marketing to attract customers who were intimidated by the cosmetics of her biggest rival—Elizabeth Arden.

59 Some women won't buy anything unless they can pay a lot.
1965 In *Time*, 9 Apr.

Ruckelshaus, William D(oyle) 1932–

US government administrator, lawyer and businessman. He served Indiana in the House of Representatives (1967–9) as majority leader and was administrator of the new Environmental Protection Agency, Washington (1970–3, 1983–5).

60 Everybody wants you to pick it up, and nobody wants you to put it down.
1988 Articulating 'the First Law of Garbage'. In *Fortune*, 21 Nov.

Rudofsky, Bernard 1905–88

Austrian-born architect, engineer and critic. He studied in Vienna, but worked in New York.

61 For it seems that long before the first enterprising man bent some twigs into a leaky roof, many animals were already accomplished builders.
1964 *Architecture without Architects.*

62 There is much to learn from architecture before it became an expert's art.
1964 *Architecture without Architects.*

Ruether, Rosemary Radford 1936–

US theologian, leading Roman Catholic exponent of feminist and liberation theology.

63 Indeed, if one can say that Christ comes to the oppressed and the oppressed especially hear him, then it is women within these marginal groups who are often seen both as the oppressed of the oppressed and also as those particularly receptive to the gospel.
1981 *To Change the World: Christology and Cultural Criticism.*

Ruiz, Juan c.1290–c.1350

Spanish poet, arch-priest of Hita. He was a vagabond for several years before entering the Church. In 1337 he was imprisoned for 13 years by the Archbishop of Toledo, Don Gil de Ardonoz.

64 *El amor siempre fabla mentiroso.*
Love is always a liar.
c.1330 *Libro de Buen Amor*, stanza 161.

65 *Por las verdades se pierden los amigos,*
e per las non dezir se fazen desamigos.
Telling the truth loses you friends;
not telling it gains you enemies.
c.1330 *Libro de Buen Amor*, stanza 165.

Rulfo, Juan 1918–86

Mexican writer. He grew up in the rural countryside that provides the setting for his two masterpieces, the short story collection *El llano en llamas* (1953) and the novel *Pedro Páramo* (1955). Although his writing output is slim, it has been enormously influential.

66 *Sólo yo entiendo lo lejos que está el cielo de nosotros; pero conozco cómo acortar las veredas. Todo consiste en morir, Dios mediante, cuando uno quiera y no cuando Él lo disponga. O, si tú quieres, forzarlo a disponer antes de tiempo.*
I know how far away Heaven is, all right, but I know the shortcuts. You just die, God willing, when you want to, not when He arranges it. Or if you want you can make Him arrange it earlier.
1955 *Pedro Páramo* (translated 1959).

Rumsfeld, Donald 1932–

US politician. He was US ambassador to NATO (1973–4), White House Chief of Staff (1974–5) and Secretary of Defense (1975–7), and in 2001 was appointed Secretary of Defense for a second time by George W Bush.

67 You're thinking of Europe as Germany and France. I don't. I think that's old Europe.
2003 Responding to questions about European hostility to military intervention in Iraq, 22 Jan.

68 They seem to be a country that disagrees with a lot of other countries.
2003 Discussing the French standpoint on Iraq. In *Time*, 17 Feb.

69 Answering the question as to whether we are winning—that is a very difficult one.
2004 Television interview, 27 Jun.

70 We don't seek empires. We're not imperialistic.
Quoted in Niall Ferguson *Colossus: The Rise and Fall of the American Empire* (2004).

Runcie, Robert Alexander Kennedy Runcie, Baron 1921–2000

English Anglican prelate and Archbishop of Canterbury (1980–91). His career was marked by a papal visit to Canterbury, controversies over homosexuality and women in the Church, the Falklands War, and his envoy Terry Waite's captivity in Beirut (1987–91).

71 Royalty puts a human face on the operations of government.
1980 Sermon at a service to mark the Queen Mother's 80th birthday, St Paul's Cathedral, 15 Jul.

72 Those who dare to interpret God's will must never claim Him as an asset for one nation or group rather than another. War springs from the love and loyalty that should be offered to God being applied to some God substitute—one of the most dangerous being nationalism.
1982 Sermon at Thanksgiving Service after the Falklands War, St Paul's Cathedral, 26 Jul.

Runciman, Sir Steven 1903–2000

English historian of the Crusades. His works include *The Fall of Constantinople, 1453* (1965) and *Byzantine Style and Civilization* (1975).

73 The triumphs of the Crusades were the triumphs of faith. But faith without wisdom is a dangerous thing.
1954 *A History of the Crusades*, vol.3.

Runge, Philipp Otto 1777–1810

German painter and draughtsman, a member of the German Romantic movement.

74 Art of all periods teaches us that humanity changes, and that a period, once past, never returns.
1802 Letter, Feb. Quoted in L Eitner *Neoclassicism and Romanticism 1750–1850* (1964).

75 But could we not reach the point of highest perfection in a new kind of art, in this art of landscape, and perhaps reach a higher beauty than existed before?
1802 Letter, quoted in L Eitner *Neoclassicism and Romanticism 1750–1850* (1964).

76 Colour is the ultimate in art. It is still and will always remain a mystery to us, we can only apprehend it intuitively in flowers.
1802 Letter, quoted in L Eitner *Neoclassicism and Romanticism 1750–1850* (1964).

77 We must become children again if we wish to achieve the best.
1802 Letter, quoted in R Rosenblum *Modern Painting and the Northern Romantic Tradition* (1975).

Runyon, (Alfred) Damon 1884–1946

US journalist, sportswriter and humorist. He is remembered for the colourful argot of his New York stories, which have been gathered in several collections, and provided the basis of the musical *Guys and Dolls* (1931).

78 'My boy,' he says, 'always try to rub up against money, for if you rub up against money long enough, some of it may rub off on you.'
1931 *Guys and Dolls*, 'A Very Honourable Guy'.

79 'You are snatching a hard guy when you snatch Bookie Bob. A very hard guy, indeed. In fact,' I say, 'I hear the softest thing about him is his front teeth.'
1933 *Blue Plate Special*, 'Snatching of Bookie Bob'.

80 Any time you see him he is generally by himself because being by himself is not apt to cost him anything.
1933 *Blue Plate Special*, 'Little Miss Marker'.

81 The best thing to do right now is to throw a feed into her as the chances are that her stomach thinks her throat is cut.
1933 *Blue Plate Special*, 'Little Miss Marker'.

82 'In fact,' Sam the Gonoph says, 'I long ago come to the conclusion that all life is 6 to 5 against.'
1935 *Money from Home*, 'A Nice Price'.

83 I do not approve of guys using false pretences on dolls, except, of course, when nothing else will do.
1935 *Money from Home*, 'It Comes Up Mud'.

84 He is without strict doubt a Hoorah Henry, and he is

generally figured as nothing but a lob as far as doing anything useful in this world is concerned.
1935 *Money from Home*, 'Tight Shoes'.

85 I always claim the mission workers came out too early to catch any sinners on this part of Broadway. At such an hour the sinners are still in bed resting up from their sinning of the night before, so they will be in good shape for more sinning a little later on.
1944 *Runyon à la Carte*, 'The Idyll of Miss Sarah Brown'.

86 You can keep the things of bronze and stone and give me one man to remember me just once a year.
1946 Last words.

Rushdie, (Ahmed) Salman 1947–

British novelist, born in Bombay. His works include *Midnight's Children* (1981, Booker Prize), *The Moor's Last Sigh* (1995) and *Fury* (2001). His novel *The Satanic Verses* (1988) provoked Iran's Ayatollah Khomeini to issue a fatwa against him (1989) forcing Rushdie to live in hiding for several years.

87 Most of what matters in your life takes place in your absence.
1981 *Midnight's Children*, 'Alpha and Omega', bk.2.

88 A poet's work… To name the unnamable, to point at frauds, to take sides, start arguments, shape the world and stop it from going to sleep.
1988 *The Satanic Verses*, pt.2.

89 To burn a book is not to destroy it. One minute of darkness will not make us blind.
1989 Book review in the *Weekend Guardian*, 14–15 Oct.

90 No story comes from nowhere; new stories are born from old—it is the new combinations that make them new.
1990 *Haroun and the Sea of Stories*.

91 Books have to teach their readers how to read them.
1995 Quoted in the *Observer Review*, 16 Apr.

92 We are the lethal voyeurs.
1997 Reflecting on the death of Diana, Princess of Wales.

93 I know of very few great film-makers who might have been good novelists—Satyajit Ray, Ingmar Bergman, Woody Allen, Jean Renoir, and that's about it.
2002 *Step Across This Line: Collected Non-Fiction 1992–2002*.

94 [Charlton] Heston thinks America should arm its teachers; he seems to believe that schools would be safer if staff had the power to gun down children in their charge.
2002 *Step Across This Line: Collected Non-Fiction 1992–2002*.

95 I knew a man whose thing it was to wreck the toilets in office buildings and write a slogan on the ruined walls: 'If the cistern cannot be changed it must be destroyed.' I'm beginning to understand how he felt.
2002 *Step Across This Line: Collected Non-Fiction 1992–2002*.

Rushworth, John c.1612–1690

English historian, whose *Historical Collections of Private Passages of State* (8 vols, 1659–1701) cover the period 1618–48. Clerk-assistant to the House of Commons in the Long Parliament (1640), and a parliamentary secretary, in 1684 he was imprisoned for debt.

96 His Majesty entered the House, and as he passed up towards the Chair, he cast his eye on the right hand near the Bar of the House where Mr Pym used to sit; but His Majesty, not seeing him there (knowing him well) went up to the Chair and said, 'By your leave, Mr Speaker, I must borrow your chair a little.'
1642 His account of the attempt made by Charles I to arrest five Members of Parliament on 4 Jan.

Rusk, (David) Dean 1909–94

US politician. As Secretary of State under Kennedy and Johnson (1961–9), he played a major role in the Cuban Missile Crisis of 1962.

97 We were eyeball to eyeball and the other fellow just blinked.
1962 Recalling his words on the retreat of Soviet ships during the Cuban Missile Crisis. In the *Saturday Evening Post*, 8 Dec.

98 Communications today puts a special emphasis on what happens next, for an able, sophisticated and competitive press knows that what happens today is no longer news—it is what is going to happen tomorrow that is the object of interest and concern.
1963 At *Time*'s 40th anniversary dinner, 17 May.

99 We looked into the mouth of the cannon, the Russians flinched.
Of the Cuban Missile Crisis. Quoted in Robert F Kennedy *Thirteen Days* (1969).

Ruskin, John 1819–1900

English author, the major art critic and social philosopher of his day, champion of Turner and the pre-Raphaelites and an opponent of Utilitarianism. His most famous works are *Modern Painters* (1843–60) and *Seven Lamps of Architecture* (1849).

1 I believe the right question to ask, respecting all ornament, is simply this: Was it done with enjoyment—was the carver happy while he was about it?
1849 *Seven Lamps of Architecture*, 'The Lamp of Life', sect.24.

2 Better the rudest work that tells a story or records a fact, than the richest without meaning.
1849 *Seven Lamps of Architecture*, 'The Lamp of Memory', sect.7.

3 When we build, let us think that we build for ever.
1849 *Seven Lamps of Architecture*, 'The Lamp of Memory', sect.10.

4 Remember that the most beautiful things in the world are the most useless; peacocks and lilies for instance.
1851–3 *The Stones of Venice*, vol.i, ch.2.

5 But for me, the Alps and their people were alike beautiful in their snow, and their humanity; and I wanted, neither for them nor myself, sight of any thrones in heaven but the rocks, or of any spirits in heaven but the clouds.
1851–3 *The Stones of Venice*, vol.i, ch.2.

6 The purest and most thoughtful minds are those which love colour the most.
1851–3 *The Stones of Venice*, vol.ii, ch.5.

7 All things are literally better, lovelier, more beloved for the imperfections which have been divinely appointed.
1851–3 *The Stones of Venice*, vol.ii, ch.6.

8 No person who is not a great sculptor or painter can be an architect. If he is not a sculptor or painter, he can only be a *builder*.
1854 *Lectures on Architecture and Painting*.

9 What is poetry?… The suggestion, by the imagination, of noble grounds for the noble emotions.

1856 *Modern Painters*, vol.3, pt.4, ch.1.

10 All violent feelings…produce in us a falseness in all our impressions of external things, which I would generally characterize as the 'Pathetic Fallacy'.
1856 *Modern Painters*, vol.3, pt.4, ch.12.

11 Mountains are the beginning and the end of all natural scenery.
1856 *Modern Painters*, vol.4, pt.5, ch.20.

12 Fine art is that in which the hand, the head, and the heart of man go together.
1859 *The Two Paths*, lecture 2.

13 Not only is there but one way of *doing* things rightly, but there is only one way of *seeing* them, and that is, seeing the whole of them.
1859 *The Two Paths*, lecture 2.

14 Nobody cares much at heart about Titian; only there is a strange undercurrent of everlasting murmur about his name, which means the deep consent of all great men that he is greater than they.
1859 *The Two Paths*, lecture 2.

15 It ought to be quite as natural and straightforward a matter for a labourer to take his pension from his parish, because he has deserved well of his parish, as for a man in higher rank to take his pension from his country, because he has deserved well of his country.
1862 *Unto this Last*, preface.

16 The force of the guinea you have in your pocket depends wholly on the default of a guinea in your neighbour's pocket. If he did not want it, it would be of no use to you.
1862 *Unto this Last*, essay 2.

17 Political economy (the economy of a State, or of citizens) consists simply in the production, preservation, and distribution, at fittest time and place, of useful or pleasurable things.
1862 *Unto this Last*, essay 2.

18 Soldiers of the ploughshare as well as soldiers of the sword.
1862 *Unto this Last*, essay 3.

19 Government and co-operation are in all things the laws of life; anarchy and competition the laws of death.
1862 *Unto this Last*, essay 3.

20 Whereas it has long been known and declared that the poor have no right to the property of the rich, I wish it also to be known and declared that the rich have no right to the property of the poor.
1862 *Unto this Last*, essay 3.

21 There is no wealth but life.
1862 *Unto this Last*, essay 4.

22 All books are divided into two classes, the books of the hour, and the books of all time.
1865 *Sesame and Lilies*, 'Of Kings' Treasures'.

23 Be sure that you go to the author to get at his meaning, not to find yours.
1865 *Sesame and Lilies*, 'Of Kings' Treasures'.

24 Which of us…is to do the hard and dirty work for the rest—and for what pay? Who is to do the pleasant and clean work, and for what pay?
1865 *Sesame and Lilies*, 'Of Kings' Treasures'.

25 You hear of me, among others, as a respectable architectural man-milliner; and you send for me, that I may tell you the leading fashion.
1866 *The Crown of Wild Olive*, 'Traffic', lecture 2.

26 Labour without joy is base. Labour without sorrow is base. Sorrow without labour is base. Joy without labour is base.
1867 *Time and Tide*, letter 5.

27 Your honesty is *not* to be based either on religion or policy. Both your religion and policy must be based on *it*.
1867 *Time and Tide*, letter 8.

28 The first duty of a state is to see that every child born therein shall be well housed, clothed, fed and educated, till it attain years of discretion.
1867 *Time and Tide*, letter 13.

29 Life without industry is guilt, and industry without art is brutality.
1870 *Lectures on Art*, 'The Relation of Art to Morals', lecture 3, section 95.

30 Engraving then, is, in brief terms, the Art of Scratch.
1870–85 *Ariadne Florentina*, lecture 1.

31 Thackeray settled like a meat-fly on whatever one had got for dinner, and made one sick of it.
1873 *Fors Clavigera* (published 1871–84), letter no.31, 1 Jul.

32 English artists are usually entirely ruined by residence in Italy.
1873 *Modern Painters*, vol.1, pt.1, 'Of General Principles'.

33 The greatest thing a human soul ever does in this world is to *see* something, and tell what it *saw* in a plain way. Hundreds of people can talk for one who can think, but thousands can think for one who can see. To see clearly is poetry, prophecy, and religion, all in one.
1873 *Modern Painters*, vol.3, pt.4, ch.16.

34 I have seen, and heard, much of Cockney impudence before now; but never expected to hear a coxcomb ask two hundred guineas for flinging a pot of paint in the public's face.
1877 On Whistler's *Nocturne in Black and Gold. Fors Clavigera* (published 1871–84), letter no.79, 18 Jun.

35 Men don't and can't live by exchanging articles, but by producing them. They don't live by trade, but by work. Give up that foolish and vain title of Trades Unions; and take that of Labourers' Unions.
1880 Open letter to English Trades Unions, 29 Sep.

36 Beethoven always sounds to me like the upsetting of a bag of nails, with here and there an also dropped hammer.
1881 Letter.

37 Of all the affected, sapless, soulless, beginningless, endless, topless, bottomless, topsiturviest, scrannel-pipiest, tongs and boniest doggerel of sounds I ever endured the deadliest of, that eternity of nothing was the deadliest.
1882 Of Wagner's *Die Meistersinger*. Letter to Mrs Burne-Jones, 30 Jun.

38 There was a rocky valley between Buxton and Bakewell…divine as the vale of Tempe; you might have seen the gods there morning and evening—Apollo and the sweet Muses of the Light… You enterprised a railroad…you blasted its rocks away… And, now, every fool in Buxton can be at Bakewell in half-an-hour, and every fool in Bakewell at Buxton.
1886–8 *Praeterita*, vol.3, pt.4, 'Joanna's Cave', note.

Russell, Bertrand Arthur William Russell, 3rd Earl
1872–1970

English philosopher and mathematician, a controversial public figure ('an enemy of religion and morality') who produced a stream of popular and provocative works on social, moral and religious issues. After 1949 he championed nuclear disarmament, and engaged in correspondence with several world leaders. He won the Nobel prize for literature in 1950.

39 Mathematics possesses not only truth, but supreme beauty—a beauty cold and austere, like that of sculpture.
1903 *The Principles of Mathematics.*

40 Philosophy, if it cannot *answer* so many questions as we could wish, has at least the power of *asking* questions which increase the interest of the world, and show the strangeness and wonder lying just below the surface even in the commonest things of daily life.
1912 *The Problems of Philosophy,* ch.1.

41 The essential characteristic of philosophy, which makes it a study distinct from science, is *criticism*. It examines critically the principles employed in science and in daily life; it searches out any inconsistencies there may be in these principles, and it only accepts them when, as the result of a critical inquiry, there is no reason for rejecting them.
1912 *The Problems of Philosophy,* ch.14.

42 Philosophy is to be studied, not for the sake of any definite answers to its questions, since no definite answers can, as a rule, be known to be true, but rather for the sake of the questions themselves; because these questions enlarge our conception of what is possible, enrich our intellectual imagination, and diminish the dogmatic assurance which closes the mind against speculation; but above all because, through the greatness of the universe which philosophy contemplates, the mind also is rendered great, and becomes capable of that union with the universe which constitutes its highest good.
1912 *The Problems of Philosophy,* ch.14.

43 Every proposition which we can understand must be composed wholly of constituents with which we are acquainted.
1917 *A Free Man's Worship,* 'Knowledge by Acquaintance and Knowledge by Description'.

44 The true spirit of delight, the exaltation, the sense of being more than man, which is the touchstone of the highest excellence, is to be found in mathematics as surely as in poetry.
1917 *Mysticism and Logic.*

45 The typical Westerner wishes to be the cause of as many changes as possible in his environment; the typical Chinese wishes to enjoy as much and as delicately as possible.
1922 *The Problems of China.*

46 In science men have discovered an activity of the very highest value in which they are no longer, as in art, dependent for progress upon the appearance of continually greater genius, for in science the successors stand upon the shoulders of their predecessors; where one man of supreme genius has invented a method, a thousand lesser men can apply it.
1923 *A Free Man's Worship and Other Essays.*

47 Machines are worshipped because they are beautiful, and valued because they confer power; they are hated because they are hideous, and loathed because they impose slavery.
1928 *Sceptical Essays.*

48 The scientific attitude of mind involves a sweeping away of all other desires in the interest of the desire to know.
1930 Interview in the *New Statesman,* 24 May.

49 It is, of course, clear that a country with a large foreign population must endeavour, through its schools, to assimilate the children of immigrants... It is, however, unfortunate that a large part of this process should be effected by means of a somewhat blatant nationalism.
1935 *In Praise of Idleness,* 'Modern Homogeneity'.

50 No rules, however wise, are a substitute for affection and tact.
1935 *In Praise of Idleness,* 'Education and Discipline'.

51 I think modern educational theorists are inclined to attach too much importance to the negative virtue of not interfering with children, and too little to the positive merit of enjoying their company.
1935 *In Praise of Idleness,* 'Education and Discipline'.

52 Two men who differ as to the ends of life cannot hope to agree about education.
1935 *In Praise of Idleness,* 'Education and Discipline'.

53 Can a society in which thought and technique are scientific persist for a long period, as, for example, ancient Egypt persisted, or does it necessarily contain within itself forces which must bring either decay or explosion?
1949 'Can a Scientific Community Be Stable?', Lloyd Roberts lecture to the Royal Society of Medicine, 29 Nov.

54 There is only one constant preoccupation: I have throughout been anxious to discover how much we can be said to know and with what degree of certainty or doubtfulness.
1959 *My Philosophical Development,* ch.1.

55 I do not think it possible to get anywhere if we start from scepticism. We must start from a broad acceptance of whatever seems to be knowledge and is not rejected for some specific reason.
1959 *My Philosophical Development,* ch.16.

56 Ever since I was engaged on *Principia Mathematica*, I have had a certain method of which at first I was scarcely conscious, but which has gradually become more explicit in my thinking. The method consists in an attempt to build a bridge between the world of sense and the world of science.
1959 *My Philosophical Development,* ch.16.

57 This idea of weapons of mass extermination is utterly horrible, and is something that no one with a spark of humanity can tolerate. I will not pretend to obey a Government that is organizing a mass massacre of mankind.
1961 Speech urging civil disobedience in support of nuclear disarmament, Birmingham, 15 Apr.

58 Obscenity is what happens to shock some elderly and ignorant magistrate.
1961 Quoted in *Look* magazine.

59 I've got a one-dimensional mind.
Quoted in R Crawshay-Williams *Russell Remembered* (1970), ch.2.

Russell, Dora 1894–1986

English feminist and pacifist, second wife of Bertrand Russell. In her many works she advocated sexual freedom and birth control.

60 We want better reasons for having children than not knowing how to prevent them.
1925 *Hypatia: or Women and Knowledge*, ch.4.

Russell, George William *pseudonym Æ* 1867–1935

Irish poet, painter, writer and economist. He met Yeats in Dublin and turned from his art studies to theosophy. His first book *Homeward: Songs by the Way* (1894) established his role in the Irish literary renaissance. He edited the *Irish Homestead* (1906–23) and subsequently the *Irish Statesman* (1923–30).

61 As Michael read the Gaelic scroll
It seemed the story of the soul;
And those who wrought, lest there should fail
From earth the legend of the Gael,
Seemed warriors of Eternal Mind
Still holding in a world gone blind,
From which belief and hope had gone,
The lovely magic of its dawn.
1922 *The Interpreters*, 'Michael'.

62 In ancient shadows and twilights
Where childhood had strayed,
The world's great sorrows were born
And its heroes were made.
In the lost boyhood of Judas,
Christ was betrayed.
1930 *Enchantment and Other Poems*, 'Germinal'.

63 No blazoned banner we unfold—
One charge alone we give to youth,
Against the sceptred myth to hold,
The golden heresy of truth.
'On Behalf of Some Irishmen not Followers of Tradition'.

Russell, John Russell, 1st Earl 1792–1878

English Whig politician, proposer of the first Reform Bill (1832) and Prime Minister (1846–52, 1865–6).

64 If peace cannot be maintained with honour, it is no longer peace.
1853 Speech, Greenock, 19 Sep.
► *See Cecil 202:26, Chamberlain 204:63, Disraeli 277:85.*

Russell, John 1919–

English-born US art critic. He was art critic for the *Sunday Times* (1949–74) and the *New York Times* (1974–2001). His many books include *The Meanings of Modern Art* (1981) and *Matisse: Father and Son* (1999).

65 It was not in Dalí's nature to play Gilbert to someone else's Sullivan.
1989 On Salvador Dalí's death. In the *New York Times*, 24 Jan.

66 When Dalí hallucinated…the whole world hallucinated with him.
1989 On Salvador Dalí's death. In the *New York Times*, 24 Jan.

Russell, Mary Annette Russell, Countess *née Beauchamp pseudonym Elizabeth* 1866–1941

New Zealand-born writer, cousin of Katherine Mansfield. She came to Britain in 1871 and in 1891 married Count Von Arnim and moved to Germany, where she wrote her best-known novel, *Elizabeth and her German Garden* (1898). After his death in 1910 she married Francis, 2nd Earl Russell, brother of Bertrand (1916, separated 1919). In later life she spent much time in the US, where she enjoyed considerable popularity.

67 Far from being half a woman, a widow is the only complete example of her sex. In fact, the finished article.
1936 *All the Dogs of My Life*, pt.2, dog 9, 'Coco'.

Russell, Rosalind 1911–76

US actress. A graduate, she started her acting career in summer stock. After a contract with MGM, she formed the production company Independent Artists with her husband in 1947 and appeared in 51 films. She starred in the Broadway shows *Wonderful Town* (1953) and *Auntie Mame* (1956).

68 Flops are a part of life's menu, and I've never been a girl to miss out on any of the courses.
1957 In the *New York Herald Tribune*, 11 Apr.

Russell, Sir William Howard 1820–1907

Irish-born British war correspondent. He joined *The Times* in 1843, and wrote despatches from the Crimean War (1854–5) which swayed British public opinion against the conflict. He subsequently wrote from the Indian Mutiny (1858), the American Civil War (1861) and the Austro-Prussian War (1866).

69 They dashed on towards that thin red line tipped with steel.
1877 Of the Russians charging the British at the Battle of Balaclava, 14 Nov 1854. *The British Expedition to the Crimea*.

Russell, Willy (William) 1947–

English playwright, best known for *Educating Rita* (1979) and *Shirley Valentine* (1986).

70 Of course I'm drunk—you don't really expect me to teach this stuff when I'm sober.
1979 *Educating Rita*.

Rutherford, Ernest, Baron Rutherford of Nelson 1871–1937

New Zealand-born English physicist, who taught at McGill, Montreal and the University of Manchester (1907–19). In 1919 he became director of the Cavendish Laboratory, Cambridge. Rutherford researched radiation and received the 1908 Nobel prize in chemistry.

71 All science is either physics or stamp collecting.
Quoted in J B Birks *Rutherford at Manchester* (1962).

72 We haven't got the money, so we've got to think.
Quoted in *Bulletin of the Institute of Physics*, vol.13, 1962.

Ryan, Desmond 1893–1964

Irish journalist. He fought at the GPO in the 1916 Rising and became a journalist on his release from internment. His books include *The Man Called Pearse* (1919), *The Phoenix Flame* (1937) and *The Rising* (1949).

73 The triumph of failure.
1949 Of the Irish uprising of 1916. *The Rising*, closing words.

Rybczynski, Witold Marian 1943–

Scottish-born Canadian architect and writer, professor at the University of Pennsylvania. His works include *Home: A Short History of an Idea* (1986) and *The Look of Architecture* (2001).

74 The most beautiful house in the world is the one that you build for yourself.
Quoted by Pamela Young in *Maclean's*, 19 Jun 1989.

75 It is truly a place for self-presentation—of oneself, to oneself. A fitting sign of the self-absorbed 1980s.
1992 On the increasing luxuriousness of bathrooms. *Looking Around*.

Ryder, Albert Pinkham 1847–1917

US painter, whose works are characterized by dreamlike figures and landscapes, evoking a romantic, lonely mood, such as *Toilers of the Sea*. His experimental technique of loading paint on the canvas caused many works to deteriorate. He became misanthropic in later life.

76 The artist needs but a roof, a crust of bread, and his easel, and all the rest God gives him in abundance. He must live to paint and not paint to live.
Quoted in Sherman *Albert Pinkham Ryder* (1920).

77 The artist should fear to become the slave of detail. He should strive to express his thought and not the surface of it. What avails a storm cloud accurate in form and colour if the storm is not therein?
Quoted in Goodrich *Albert Pinkham Ryder* (1959).

Ryle, Gilbert 1900–76

English philosopher and Professor of Philosophy at Oxford. His most famous work was *The Concept of Mind* (1949) in which he denounced Cartesian ideas of mind.

78 The dogma of the Ghost in the Machine.
1949 *The Concept of Mind*.

79 The sorts of things that I can find out about myself are the same as the sorts of things that I can find out about other people and the methods of finding them out are much the same.
1949 *The Concept of Mind*.

80 As every teacher, like every drill-sergeant or animal trainer, knows in his practice, teaching and training have virtually not yet begun, so long as the pupil is too young, too stupid, too scared or too sulky to respond—and to respond is not just to yield. Where there is a modicum of alacrity, interest or anyhow docility in the pupil, where he tries, however faintheartedly, to get things right rather than awkward, where, even, he registers even a slight contempt for the poor performances of others, of chagrin at his own, pleasure at his own successes and envy of those of others, then he is, in however slight a degree, co-operating and so self-moving.
Quoted in R S Peters (ed) *The Concept of Education* (1966), ch.7.

S

Saarinen, Aline Bernstein *née* *Louchelm* 1914–72

US art critic. In 1955 she married the architect Eero Saarinen, who was one of the leaders of a trend in experimentation in American architecture in the 1950s.

81 He meant to gather for America an undreamed-of collection of art so great and complete that a trip to Europe would be superfluous.
1991 On the philanthropist and collector John Pierpont Morgan. In *Antiques*, Oct.

Sábato, Ernesto 1911–

Argentinian novelist, journalist and essayist. Trained in physics, he increasingly devoted himself to literature. *El túnel* (1948) is a typical existential novel that confronts the problem of the condition of human life.

82 *Había un solo túnel, oscuro y solitario: el mío, el túnel en que había transcurrido mi infancia, mi juventud, toda mi vida... Y entonces, mientras yo avanzaba siempre por mi pasadizo, ella vivía afuera su vida normal, la vida agitada que llevan esas gentes que viven afuera.*
There was only one tunnel, dark and solitary: *mine*, the tunnel in which I had spent my childhood, my youth, my entire life... And then, while I kept moving through my passageway, she lived her normal life outside, the exciting life of people who live outside.
1948 *El túnel*, ch.36 (translated as *The Outsider*, 1950).

Sachar, Abram Leon 1899–1993

US educator, president of Brandeis University, Massachusetts (1948–68), chancellor there (1968–82, emeritus from 1982). His works include *A History of the Jews* (1929) and *The Redemption of the Unwanted* (1983).

83 A university where, at last, the Jews are hosts, and not guests as we have always been before.
1956 Of Brandeis University, on its 10th anniversary. Speech, 19 Nov.

Sacks, Jonathan 1948–

English rabbi, Chief Rabbi of Great Britain since 1991.

84 Religious law is like the grammar of language. Any language is governed by such rules; otherwise it ceases to be a language. But within them, you can say many different sentences and write many different books.
1994 In *The Independent*, 30 Jun.

85 After the destruction of the Second Temple Jews lived by an ancient and fundamental insight, that God does not live in buildings but in the human heart.
1995 *Community of Faith*.

Sacks, Oliver Wolf 1933–

English-born US neurologist and writer.

86 The Man Who Mistook His Wife for a Hat.
1985 Title of book.

Sackville-West, Vita (Victoria Mary) 1892–1962

English novelist. The daughter of the 3rd Baron Sackville, she married the diplomat Harold Nicolson. She wrote novels, poetry and memoirs, and a regular gardening column for the *Observer*.

87 Forget not bees in winter, though they sleep,
For winter's big with summer in her womb.
1926 *The Land*, 'Spring'.

88 All craftsmen share a knowledge.
They have held
Reality down fluttering to a bench.
1926 *The Land*, 'Summer'.

89 The country habit has me by the heart,
For he's bewitched for ever who has seen,
Not with his eyes but with his vision, Spring
Flow down the woods and stipple leaves with sun.
1926 *The Land*, 'Winter'.

90 The greater cats with golden eyes
Stare out between the bars.
Deserts are there, and different skies,
And night with different stars.
1929 'The Greater Cats with Golden Eyes'.

91 I have come to the conclusion, after many years of sometimes sad experience, that you cannot come to any conclusion at all.
1953 'In Your Garden Again'.

Sadat, Anwar el- 1918–81

Egyptian soldier and politician, jointly awarded the Nobel peace prize with Menachem Begin in 1978.

92 Peace is much more precious than a piece of land.
1978 *In Search of Identity*.

Sade, Donatien Alphonse François, Marquis de 1740–1814

French libertine who expressed his critique of society and the Enlightenment through his controversial behaviour. He spent most of his adult life in the prisons of Vincennes, was released during the Revolution, and eventually died in confinement.

93 *La cruauté, bien loin d'être un vice, est le premier sentiment qu'imprime en nous la nature; l'enfant brise son hochet, mord le téton de sa nourrice, étrangle son oiseau, bien avant que d'avoir l'âge de raison.*
Far from being a vice, cruelty is the primary feeling that nature imprints in us. The infant breaks its rattle, bites its nurse's nipple, and strangles a bird, well before reaching the age of reason.
1795 *La Philosophie dans le boudoir*.

94 *Quand l'athéisme voudra des martyrs, qu'il le dise et mon sang est tout prêt.*
When atheism wants martyrs, let it say so and my blood will be ready.
1797 *La Nouvelle Justine*.

Safer, Morley 1931–

Canadian-born journalist and broadcaster, who moved to the US in 1964. His distinguished career includes work for Reuters, London (1955), the BBC (1961) and CBS, as Vietnam correspondent (1964–71) and as co-host of *60 Minutes* news (1970–). He has seven Emmy and several Peabody awards.

95 BBC Radio is a never-never land of broadcasting, a safe haven from commercial considerations, a honey pot for every scholar and every hare-brained nut to stick a finger into.
1985 In *60 Minutes*, CBS TV broadcast, 15 Sep.

Safire, William 1929–

US journalist and author. A correspondent for radio and TV, he ran his own public relations company before President Nixon made him a special assistant (1969–73). A Pulitzer Prize winner for distinguished commentary (1978), he is a columnist for the *New York Times* (1973–).

96 The new, old, and constantly changing language of politics is a lexicon of conflict and drama...ridicule and reproach...pleading and persuasion.
1968 *Safire's Political Dictionary*, introduction.

97 Color and bite permeate a language designed to rally many men, to destroy some, and to change the minds of others.
1968 *Safire's Political Dictionary*, introduction.

98 Cover your ass—the bureaucrat's method of protecting his posterior from posterity.
1968 *Safire's Political Dictionary*, introduction.

99 A man who lies, thinking it is the truth, is an honest man, and a man who tells the truth, believing it to be a lie, is a liar.
1975 *After the Fall*, referring to Watergate and the resignation of Richard M Nixon.

1 President Reagan is a rhetorical roundheels, as befits a politician seeking empathy with his audience.
1990 *Language Maven Strikes Again*.

2 The remarkable legion of the unremarked, whose individual opinions are not colorful or different enough to make news, but whose collective opinion, when crystallized, can make history.
1993 Of the so-called 'silent majority'. *Safire's New Political Dictionary*.

3 I was egregiously wrong.
1995 Of serving as a speech-writer for President Nixon. In *USA Today*, 30 Aug.

Sagan, Carl Edward 1934–96

US astronomer and popularizer of science. He has advised NASA on interplanetary probes, was president of the Planetary Society (1979–96) and was a strong proponent of SETI, the search for extraterrestrial intelligence.

4 There is a lurking fear that some things are not meant 'to be known', that some inquiries are too dangerous for human beings to make.
1979 *Broca's Brain*.

5 Science is a way of thinking much more than it is a body of knowledge.
1979 'Can We Know the Universe? Reflections on a Grain of Salt'.

6 Sceptical scrutiny is the means, in both science and religion, by which deep thoughts can be winnowed from deep nonsense.
1980 Interview in *The Times*, 20 Oct.

Sagan, Françoise 1935–

French novelist.

7 Art must take reality by surprise.
1958 *Writers at Work*.

8 To jealousy, nothing is more frightful than laughter.
1965 *La Chamade*, ch.9.

Sage, Lorna 1943–2001

British literary critic and author.

9 The night I finished *Dracula* was a lot more exciting than Saturday night at the Regal.
2000 *Bad Blood*.

Saifoutdinov, Anvar

10 Life is not easy. I paint the memory of happiness.
Quoted by M S Mason in *Christian Science Monitor*, 19 Nov 1992.

Saint-Exupéry, Antoine de 1900–44

French author and aviator. A commercial and wartime pilot, his works include *Vol de nuit* (1931) and the children's fable *Le Petit Prince* (1943). He was declared missing after a flight to North Africa in 1944.

11 *Il n'y a pas de fatalité extérieure. Mais il y a une fatalité intérieure.*
There is no exterior fatality, only an interior one.
1931 *Vol de nuit*.

12 *L'expérience nous montre qu'aimer ce n'est point nous regarder l'un l'autre mais regarder ensemble dans la même direction.*
Life has taught us that love does not consist in gazing at each other but in looking together in the same direction.
1939 *Terre des hommes*.

13 *Quand une femme me paraît belle, je n'ai rien à en dire. Je la vois sourire, tout simplement. Les intellectuels démontent le visage, pour l'expliquer par les morceaux, mais ils ne voient plus le sourire.*
When I find a woman attractive, I have nothing at all to say. I simply watch her smile. Intellectuals take apart her face in order to explain it bit by bit, but they no longer see the smile.
1942 *Pilote de guerre*.

14 *Je combattrai pour l'Homme. Contre ses ennemis. Mais aussi contre moi-même.*
I shall fight for mankind. Against his enemies. But also against myself.
1942 *Pilote de guerre*.

15 *Les grandes personnes ne comprennent jamais rien toutes seules, et c'est fatigant, pour les enfants, de toujours et toujours leur donner des explications.*
Adults never understand anything for themselves, and it is tiresome for children to be always and forever explaining things to them.
1943 *Le Petit Prince*.

16 *On est un peu seul dans le désert.*
—On est seul aussi chez les hommes.
One is a little bit alone in the desert.
One is also alone among others.
1943 *Le Petit Prince*.

17 *On ne voit bien qu'avec le cœur. L'essentiel est invisible pour les yeux.*
Only with the heart can a person see rightly; what is essential is invisible to the eye.
1943 *Le Petit Prince*.

18 *Un sourire est souvent l'essentiel. On est payé par un sourire. On est récompensé par un sourire. On est animé par un sourire. Et la qualité d'un sourire peut faire que l'on meure.*
A smile is often the key thing. One is paid with a smile. One is rewarded with a smile. One is brightened by a smile. And the quality of a smile can make one die.
1943 *Lettre à un otage*.

19 *La vie crée l'ordre, mais l'ordre ne crée pas la vie.*
Life creates order, but order does not create life.
1943 *Lettre à un otage*.

20 *Je suis triste pour ma génération qui est vide de toute substance humaine.*
I am sad for my generation which is empty of all human substance.
1944 *Lettre au general*, no.10. Published 10 Apr 1948 in *Le Figaro littéraire*.

21 *J'aime l'homme délivré par sa religion et vivifié par les dieux que je fonde en lui.*
I admire the person freed from his religion and inspired by the gods inside of himself.
Citadelle (published 1948).

22 *L'homme, c'est ce qui est, non point ce qui s'exprime.*
Man is who he is, not how he expresses himself.
Citadelle (published 1948).

23 *Car l'homme, je te le dis, cherche sa propre destinée et non pas son bonheur.*
Because man, I tell you, is looking for his own destiny, not his own happiness.
Citadelle (published 1948).

24 *Prendre conscience, disait ailleurs mon père, c'est d'abord acquérir un style.*
To become conscious, as my father said, one must first acquire a style.
Citadelle (published 1948).

25 *Quiconque craint la contradiction et demeure logique tue en lui la vie.*
Whoever fears contradiction and remains logical kills life within himself.
Carnets (published 1953).

26 *La vérité, pour l'homme, c'est ce qui fait de lui un homme.*
Truth, for a human, is what makes him or her a human being.
Un Sens à la vie (unedited texts collected by Claude Reynal, published 1956).

Saint Laurent, Louis 1882–1973

Canadian politician, Prime Minister (1948–57). He was fluently bilingual, having a French father and an English mother.

27 I didn't know at first that there were two languages in Canada. I just thought that there was one way to speak to my father and another to talk to my mother.
Attributed. Quoted in Dale C Thomson *Louis St. Laurent* (1967).

28 Socialists are Liberals in a hurry.
Attributed. Quoted in Dale C Thomson *Louis St. Laurent* (1967).

Saint-Saëns, (Charles) Camille 1835–1921

French composer, music critic, pianist and organist. Founder of the Société Nationale de Musique in 1871, he composed widely and prolifically.

29 There are two kinds: one takes the music too fast, and the other too slow. There is no third!
Of conductors. Quoted in Sir Thomas Beecham *A Mingled Chime* (1944).

Saki *pseudonym of* Hector Hugh Munro 1870–1916

British novelist and short-story writer. His short stories are humorous, macabre, and filled with eccentric wit. He was a gifted satirist of the Edwardian world. His collections include *Reginald* (1904) and *The Chronicles of Clovis* (1911). He was killed in World War I.

30 I always say beauty is only sin deep.
1904 *Reginald*, 'Reginald's Choir Treat'.

31 People can say what they like about the decay of Christianity; the religious system that produced green Chartreuse can never really die.
1904 *Reginald*, 'Reginald on Christmas Presents'.

32 Her frocks are built in Paris, but she wears them with a strong English accent.
1904 *Reginald*, 'Reginald on Worries'.

33 The young have aspirations that never come to pass, the old have reminiscences of what never happened.
1904 *Reginald*, 'Reginald at the Carlton'.

34 There may have been disillusionments in the lives of the medieval saints, but they would scarcely have been better pleased if they could have foreseen that their names would be associated nowadays chiefly with racehorses and the cheaper clarets.
1904 *Reginald*, 'Reginald at the Carlton'.

35 The cook was a good cook, as cooks go; and as good cooks go, she went.
1904 *Reginald*, 'Reginald on Besetting Sins'.

36 But, good gracious, you've got to educate him first. You can't expect a boy to be vicious till he's been to a good school.
1910 *Reginald in Russia*, 'The Baker's Dozen'.

37 'Is your maid called Florence?' 'Her name is Florinda.' 'What an extraordinary name to give a maid!' 'I did not give it to her; she arrived in my service already christened'. 'What I mean is,' said Mrs Riversedge, 'that when I get maids with unsuitable names I call them Jane; they soon get used to it.' 'An excellent plan,' said the aunt of Clovis coldly; 'unfortunately I have got used to being called Jane myself. It happens to be my name.'
1911 *The Chronicles of Clovis*, 'The Secret Sin of Septimus Brope'.

38 The censorious said that she slept in a hammock and understood Yeats's poems, but her family denied both stories.
1911 *The Chronicles of Clovis*, 'The Jesting of Arlington Stringham'.

39 The people of Crete unfortunately make more history than they can consume locally.
1911 *The Chronicles of Clovis*, 'The Jesting of Arlington Stringham'.

40 You needn't tell me that a man who doesn't love oysters and asparagus and good wines has got a soul, or a stomach either. He's simply got the instinct for being unhappy highly developed.
1911 *The Chronicles of Clovis*, 'The Match-Maker'.

41 His socks compelled one's attention without losing one's respect.
1911 *The Chronicles of Clovis*, 'Ministers of Grace'.

42 There's nothing in Christianity or Buddhism that quite matches the sympathetic unselfishness of an oyster.
1911 *The Chronicles of Clovis*, 'The Match-Maker'.

43 All decent people live beyond their incomes nowadays, and those who aren't respectable live beyond other peoples'. A few gifted individuals manage to do both.
1911 *The Chronicles of Clovis*, 'The Match-Maker'.

44 One of the great advantages of Ireland as a place of residence is that a large number of excellent people never go there.
1914 Ludovic. *The Watched Pot, or The Mistress of Briony.*

45 'But why should you want to shield him?' cried Egbert; 'the man is a common murderer.'
'A common murderer, possibly, but a very uncommon cook.'
1914 *Beasts and Super-Beasts*, 'The Blind Spot'.

46 'Waldo is one of those people who would be enormously improved by death,' said Clovis.
1914 *Beasts and Super-Beasts*, 'The Feast of Nemesis'.

47 'I believe I take precedence,' he said coldly; 'you are merely the Club Bore: I am the Club Liar.'
1914 *Beasts and Super-Beasts*, 'A Defensive Diamond'.

48 I should be the last person to say anything against temptation, naturally, but we have a proverb down here 'in baiting a mouse-trap with cheese, always leave room for the mouse'.
The Square Egg, 'The Infernal Parliament' (published 1924).

49 A little inaccuracy sometimes saves tons of explanation.
The Square Egg, 'Clovis on the Alleged Romance of Business' (published 1924).

Sala, George Augustus Henry 1828–95

English journalist, book illustrator and novelist, born in London of Italian ancestry. He was in the US during the Civil War, in Italy with Garibaldi, in France in 1870–71, in Russia in 1876 and in Australia in 1885.

50 The foaminess of the Falls, together with the tinge of tawny yellow in the troubled waters, only reminded me of so much unattainable soda and sherry, and made me feel thirstier than ever.
1865 On seeing Niagara Falls for the first time. *My Diary in America in the Midst of War.*

Salinger, J(erome) D(avid) 1919–

US novelist. His novel *The Catcher in the Rye* (1951) is one of the most widely read novels of the era. He has published little since, and lives as a recluse in New Hampshire.

51 If you really want to hear about it, the first thing you'll probably want to know is where I was born, and what my lousy childhood was like, and how my parents were occupied and all before they had me, and all that David Copperfield kind of crap, but I don't feel like going into it.
1951 *The Catcher in the Rye*, ch.1.

52 What really knocks me out is a book that, when you're all

done reading it, you wish the author that wrote it was a terrific friend of yours and you could call him up on the phone whenever you felt like it.
1951 *The Catcher in the Rye*, ch.3.

53 Sex is something I really don't understand too hot. You never know *where* the hell you are. I keep making up these sex rules for myself, and then I break them right away.
1951 *The Catcher in the Rye*, ch.9.

54 That's the thing about girls. Every time they do something pretty, even if they're not much to look at, or even if they're sort of stupid, you fall half in love with them, and then you never know *where* you are.
1951 *The Catcher in the Rye*, ch.10.

55 He looked like the kind of guy that wouldn't talk to you much unless he wanted something off you. He had a lousy personality.
1951 *The Catcher in the Rye*, ch.11.

56 The thing is it's really hard to be room-mates with people if your suitcases are much better than theirs—if yours are really good and theirs aren't. You think if they're intelligent and all, the other person, and have a good sense of humour, that they don't give a damn whose suitcases are better, but they do.
1951 *The Catcher in the Rye*, ch.15.

57 The trouble with me is, I always have to read that stuff by myself. If an actor reads it out, I hardly listen. I keep worrying about whether he's going to do something phoney every minute.
1951 Of Hamlet. *The Catcher in the Rye*, ch.16.

58 Take most people, they're crazy about cars… I'd rather have a goddam horse. A horse is at least *human*, for God's sake.
1951 *The Catcher in the Rye*, ch.17.

59 The trouble with girls is, if they like a boy, no matter how big a bastard he is, they'll say he has an inferiority complex, and if they don't like him, no matter how nice a guy he is, or how big an inferiority complex he has, they'll say he's conceited. Even smart girls do it.
1951 *The Catcher in the Rye*, ch.18.

60 Sally said I was a sacrilegious atheist. I probably am. The thing that Jesus *really* would've liked would be the guy that plays the kettle drums in the orchestra.
1951 *The Catcher in the Rye*, ch.18.

61 Anyway, I keep picturing all these little kids playing some game in this big field of rye and all. Thousands of little kids, and nobody's around—nobody big, I mean—except me. And I'm standing on the edge of some crazy cliff. What I have to do, I have to catch everybody if they start to go over the cliff—I mean if they're running and they don't look where they're going I have to come out from somewhere and catch them. That's all I'd do all day. I'd just be the catcher in the rye and all. I know it's crazy, but that's the only thing I'd really like to be.
1951 *The Catcher in the Rye*, ch.22.

62 Never tell anyone anything. If you do you start missing everyone.
1951 *The Catcher in the Rye*, last words.

63 For Esmé—with Love and Squalor.
1953 Title of story.

64 Poetry, surely, is a crisis, perhaps the only actionable one we can call our own.
1959 'Seymour: An Introduction'.

65 A confessional passage has probably never been written that didn't stink a little bit of the writer's pride in having given up his pride.
1959 'Seymour: An Introduction'.

66 One of the reasons that I quit going to the theatre when I was about twenty was that I resented like hell filing out of the theatre because some playwright was forever slamming down his silly curtain.
1959 'Seymour: An Introduction'.

Salisbury, Robert Arthur Talbot Gascoyne Cecil, 3rd Marquis of 1830–1903

English Conservative statesman. He succeeded Disraeli as Leader of the Opposition, and was subsequently Prime Minister (1885–6, 1886–92, 1895–1902), as well as holding other posts. He was head of government during the Boer War (1889–1902).

67 Horny-handed sons of toil.
1873 In the *Quarterly Review*, Oct.

68 No lesson seems to be so deeply inculcated by the experience of life as that you should never trust experts. If you believe the doctors, nothing is wholesome: if you believe the theologians, nothing is innocent: if you believe the soldiers, nothing is safe. They all require to have their strong wine diluted by a very large admixture of insipid common sense.
1877 Letter to Lord Lytton, 15 Jun. Quoted in Lady Gwendolen Cecil *Life of Robert, Marquis of Salisbury* (1921–32), vol.2, ch.4.

69 We are part of the community of Europe and we must do our duty as such.
1888 Speech at Caernarvon, 10 Apr. In *The Times*, 11 Apr.

70 By office boys for office boys.
Of the *Daily Mail*. The phrase recalls Thackeray's Pendennis who started a newspaper 'by gentlemen for gentlemen'. Quoted in S J Taylor *The Great Outsiders: Northcliffe, Rothermere and the Daily Mail* (1966), ch.2.

Sallust *in full* *Gaius Sallustius Crispus* 86–34 BC

Roman historian and politician. As Governor of Numidia he enriched himself enormously. He wrote *Bellum Catilinae*, *Bellum Iugurthinum* and *Historiarum libri quinque*, of which only fragments survive.

71 *Alieni appetens, sui profusus.*
Greedy for the belongings of others, extravagant with his own.
Bellum Catilinae, 5.

72 *Esse quam videri bonus malebat.*
He preferred to be good, rather than seem good.
Of Cato. *Bellum Catilinae*, 54.

73 *Punica fide.*
With Punic faith.
Used ironically (meaning treacherously) of the Numidian Bocchus, a double agent between Iugurtha and Sulla. *Bellum Iugurthinum*, 108.3.

Salter, Sir (James) Arthur, 1st Baron Salter 1881–1975

English economist and international civil servant.

74 The normal economic system works itself.

Quoted in Ronald H Coase *Essays on Economics and Economists* (1994), p.6.

Salvianus c.400–c.470 AD

Christian writer from Gaul. His surviving works include nine epistles, *Ad Ecclesiam* and the unfinished *De Gubernatione Dei*. He urged that all estates be bequeathed to the poor, and denounced inherited wealth.

75 *Quot curiales, tot tyranni.*
As many councillors, so many tyrants.
De Gubernatione Dei, 5.18.27.

Sampson, Anthony (Terrell Seward) 1926–

English journalist and writer. His most influential book was *The Anatomy of Britain* (1962), which was followed by other titles on the same theme. He was a staff member of the *Observer* (1955–66).

76 In America journalism is apt to be regarded as an extension of history: in Britain, as an extension of conversation.
1965 *The Anatomy of Britain Today*, ch.9.

Samuel, Herbert Louis, 1st Viscount Samuel 1870–1963

English Liberal statesman and philosophical writer, Home Secretary (1916, 1931–2) and High Commissioner for Palestine (1920–5). His philosophical works include *Practical Ethics* (1935), *Belief and Action* (1937) and *In Search of Reality* (1957).

77 The House of Lords must be the only institution in the world that is kept efficient by the persistent absenteeism of its members.
1948 In *American News Review*, 5 Feb.

78 Hansard is history's ear, already listening.
1949 House of Lords, Dec.

Samuelson, Paul Anthony 1915–

US economist and journalist, professor at Massachusetts Institute of Technology (1940–85). His works include *Foundations of Economic Analysis* (1947) and the classic *Economics* (1948). He won the Nobel prize for economics in 1970.

79 The consumer, so it is said, is the king…each is a voter who uses his money as votes to get the things done that he wants done.
1948 *Economics*.

80 Commentators quote economic studies alleging that market downturns predicted four out of the last five recessions. That is an understatement. Wall Street indexes predicted nine out of the last five recessions!
1966 Quoted in *The Samuelson Sampler* (1973).

Samuelson, Sir Sydney 1925–

British film commissioner. He started in the film industry in 1939 and worked as a cinema projectionist, editor and cameraman. He founded Samuelson Film Service and in 1991 was appointed the first British Film Commissioner.

81 We welcome all enquiries about the UK climate—after all, we have more weather available in this country than anywhere else.
1994 *Check Book*.

Sand, George *pseudonym of* Amandine Aurore Lucille Dupin, Baronne Dudevant 1804–76

French novelist, the illegitimate daughter of Marshal de Saxe, known for her scandalous bohemian lifestyle and her liaisons with Musset and Chopin, and later with prominent politicians.

82 *L'amour, heurtant son front aveugle à tous les obstacles de la civilisation.*
Love, knocking its blind forehead against all of civilization's obstacles.
1832 *Indiana*, preface.

83 *En France particulièrement, les mots ont plus d'empire que les idées.*
In France particularly, words reign over ideas.
1832 *Indiana*, pt.1, ch.2.

84 *L'homme qui a un peu usé ses émotions est plus pressé de plaire que d'aimer.*
The person who has used his emotions even a little is more anxious to please than to love.
1832 *Indiana*, pt.1, ch.5.

85 *La société ne doit rien exiger de celui qui n'attend rien d'elle.*
Society should not ask anything of the person who expects nothing from society.
1832 *Indiana*, conclusion.

86 *Nous ne pouvons arracher une seule page de notre vie, mais nous pouvons jeter le livre au feu.*
We cannot tear out a single page from our life, but we can throw the entire book in the fire.
1832 *Mauprat*.

87 *Nulle créature humaine ne peut commander à l'amour.*
No human being can give orders to love.
1833 *Jacques*.

88 *Le vrai est trop simple, il faut y arriver toujours par le compliqué.*
Truth is too simple; it must always be arrived at in a complicated manner.
1867 Letter to Armand Barbès, May.

89 *L'art pour l'art est un vain mot. L'art pour le vrai, l'art pour le beau et le bon, voilà la religion que je cherche.*
Art for art's sake is an empty phrase. Art for the sake of the true, art for the sake of the good and the beautiful, that is the faith I search for.
1872 Letter to Alexandre Saint-Jean.

Sandburg, Carl 1878–1967

US poet, originally a journalist in Chicago. His volumes of poetry, celebrating US life in free verse, include *Chicago Poems* (1916) and *Good Morning, America* (1928). He also published a collection of folk-songs, *The American Songbag* (1927), and a *Life of Abraham Lincoln* (6 vols, 1926–39, Pulitzer Prize). He was awarded another Pulitzer Prize for his *Complete Poems* (1950).

90 The ache to utter and see in word
The silhouette of a brooding soul.
1904 Describing the poet's motivation. *In Reckless Ecstasy*.

91 Hog Butcher for the World,
Tool Maker, Stacker of Wheat,
Player with Railroads and the Nation's Freight Handler;
Stormy, husky, brawling,
City of the Big Shoulders.
1916 *Chicago Poems*, 'Chicago'.

92 The fog comes
on little cat feet.

It sits looking
over harbor and city
on silent haunches
and then moves on.
1916 *Chicago Poems*, 'Fog'.

93 (All the coaches shall be scrap and rust and all the men and women
laughing in the diners and sleepers shall pass to ashes.)
I ask a man in the smoker where he is going and he answers: 'Omaha'.
1916 *Chicago Poems*, 'Limited'.

94 I tell you the past is a bucket of ashes.
1918 *Cornhuskers*, 'Prairie'.

95 When Abraham Lincoln was shovelled into the tombs,
he forgot the copperheads and the assassin…
in the dust, in the cool tombs.
1918 *Cornhuskers*, 'Cool Tombs'.

96 Pile the bodies high at Austerlitz and Waterloo.
Shovel them under and let me work—
I am the grass; I cover all.
1918 *Cornhuskers*, 'Grass'.

97 Why is there always a secret singing
When a lawyer cashes in?
Why does a hearse horse snicker
Hauling a lawyer away?
1920 *Smoke and Steel*, 'The Lawyers Know Too Much'.

98 Look how you use proud words,
When you let proud words go, it is not easy to call them back,
They wear long boots, hard boots; they walk off proud; they can't hear you calling
look out how you use proud words.
1922 *Slabs of the Sunburnt West*, 'Primer Lesson'.

99 Poetry is the opening and closing of a door, leaving those who look through to guess about what is seen during a moment.
1923 'Poetry Considered', in the *Atlantic Monthly*, Mar.

1 Poetry is the achievement of the synthesis of hyacinths and biscuits.
1923 'Poetry Considered', in the *Atlantic Monthly*, Mar.

2 The people will live on.
The learning and blundering will live on.
They will be tricked and sold and again sold
And go back to the nourishing earth for rootholds.
1936 *The People, Yes*.

3 I never made a mistake in grammar but once
in my life and as soon as I done it I seen it.
1936 *The People, Yes*.

4 'Would you just as soon get off the earth?'
holding ourselves aloof in pride of distinction
saying to ourselves this costs us nothing
as though hate has no cost
as though hate ever grew anything worth growing.
1936 On 'the red men'. *The People, Yes*.

5 or we may hold them in respect and affection
as fellow creepers on a commodious planet
saying, 'Yes you too you too are people'.
1936 On 'the red men'. *The People, Yes*.

6 Sometime they'll give a war and nobody will come.
1936 *The People, Yes*

7 The people know what the land knows.
1936 *The People, Yes*.

8 I am still studying verbs and the mystery of how they connect nouns. I am more suspicious of adjectives than at any other time in all my born days.
c.1940 On receiving nearly a dozen honorary doctorates for his biography of Lincoln. Quoted in *The Complete Poems of Carl Sandburg* (1986), 'Notes for a Preface'.

9 A baby is God's opinion that life should go on.
1948 *Remembrance Rock*, ch.2.

10 Slang is a language that rolls up its sleeves, spits on its hands and goes to work.
1959 In the *New York Times*, 13 Feb.

11 In these times you have to be an optimist to open your eyes when you wake in the morning.
1960 In the *New York Post*, 9 Sep.

12 The simple dignity of a child drinking a bowl of milk embodies the fascination of an ancient rite.
Quoted in *Personalia, the Complete Poems of Carl Sandburg* (1970).

13 In the spacious highways of books major or minor, each poet is allowed the stride that will get him where he wants to go if, God help him, he can hit that stride and keep it.
Quoted in *The Complete Poems of Carl Sandburg* (1986), 'Notes for a Preface'.

14 The more rhyme there is in poetry the more danger of its tricking the writer into something other than the urge in the beginning.
Quoted in *The Complete Poems of Carl Sandburg* (1986), 'Notes for a Preface'.

15 There is a formal poetry perfect only in form…the number of syllables, the designated and required stresses of accent, the rhymes if wanted—they come off with the skill of a solved crossword puzzle.
Quoted in *The Complete Poems of Carl Sandburg* (1986), 'Notes for a Preface'.

Sanders, George 1906–72

British actor who became renowned for playing cads and sophisticated villains. Among his many roles, his parts in *Rebecca* (1940), *The Moon and Sixpence* (1942), *The Picture of Dorian Gray* (1944), *All About Eve* (1950) and *A Shot in the Dark* (1964) were particularly notable.

16 Dear World, I am leaving because I am bored. I feel I have lived long enough. I am leaving you with your worries in this sweet cesspool. Good luck.
1972 His suicide note.

Sandys, George 1578–1644

English translator and traveller, youngest son of the Archbishop of York. He published a verse translation of Ovid's *Metamorphoses*, written while treasurer to the colony in Virginia. He also wrote poetic versions of the *Psalms* (1636) and the *Song of Solomon* (1641).

17 Men ignorant of letters, studious for their bellies, and ignominiously lazy.
1610 On the monks of Patmos. *Relation of a Journey Begun An. Dom. 1610*.

Santayana, George *originally Jorge Augustín Nicolás Ruiz de Santayana* 1863–1952

Spanish–US philosopher, poet and novelist, Professor of Philosophy at Harvard (1907–12). His writing career began as a poet with *Sonnets and Other Verses* (1894), but he later became known as a philosopher and stylist, in such works as *The Life of Reason* (5 vols, 1905–6), *Realms of Being* (4 vols, 1927–40), and his novel *The Last Puritan* (1935). He moved to Europe in 1912, stayed at Oxford during World War I, then settled in Rome.

18 Fashion is something barbarous, for it produces innovation without reason and imitation without benefit.
1905–6 *The Life of Reason*, 'Reason in Religion'.

19 Those who cannot remember the past are condemned to repeat it.
1905–6 *The Life of Reason*.

20 For an idea ever to be fashionable is ominous, since it must afterwards be always old-fashioned.
1913 *Winds of Doctrine*, 'Modernism and Christianity'.

21 Philosophy to him was rather like a maze in which he happened to find himself wandering, and what he was looking for was the way out.
1920 Of William James. *Character and Opinion in the United States*.

22 The empiricist...thinks he believes only what he sees, but he is much better at believing than at seeing.
1955 *Scepticism and Animal Faith*.

23 Art is dedicated echo.
Quoted in John Gassner and Sidney Thomas (eds) *The Nature of Art* (1964).

24 Nothing is so poor and melancholy as an art that is interested in itself and not in its subject.
Quoted in John Gassner and Sidney Thomas (eds) *The Nature of Art* (1964).

25 A building without ornamentation is like a heaven without stars.
Quoted in the *Christian Science Monitor*, 14 Dec 1990.

26 Pure poetry is pure experiment...memorable nonsense.
Quoted in Helen Gardner (ed) *The New Oxford Book of English Verse* (1991).

Sappho 7c BC

Greek lyric poetess, born on Lesbos. Most of her surviving poems are from papyrus fragments discovered in recent times.

27 He looks to me to be in heaven, that man who sits across from you and listens near you to your soft speaking, your laughing lovely: that, I vow, makes the heart leap in my breast; for watching you a moment, speech fails me, my tongue is paralysed, at once a light fire runs beneath my skin, my eyes are blinded, and my ears drumming, the sweat pours down me, and I shake all over, sallower than grass: I feel as if I'm not far off dying.
D L Page (ed) *Lyrica Graeca Selecta* (1968), no.199 (translated by M L West).

28 Just as the sweet-apple reddens on the high branch, high on the highest, and the apple-pickers missed it, or rather did not miss it out, but could not reach it.
Of a girl before her marriage. D L Page (ed) *Lyrica Graeca Selecta* (1968), no.224.

Sarduy, Severo 1937–93

Cuban novelist and essayist. He left his country for Paris in 1960. A practitioner and a theoretician of so-called neo-Baroque, he used in his novels a variety of experimental techniques, satire, parody and a carnivalistic approach.

29 *¡Ah sí, ponerse a escribir otra vez, qué vomitivo! ¡Como si todo esto sirviera para algo, como si todo esto fuera a entrar en alguna cabezota, a entretener a alguno de los lectores babosos, ovillados en sus poltronas, frente al sopón soporífero de cada día!*
Ah yes, going back to writing, how disgusting! As if all this had some purpose, as if all this would penetrate some thick skull, amuse some drivelling reader curled up in his armchair before the soporific stew of every day!
1967 *De donde son los cantantes* (translated as *From Cuba with a Song*, 1972), 'La Dolores Rondón'.

Sargent, John Singer 1856–1925

US painter.

30 Every time I paint a portrait I lose a friend.
Attributed.

Sargent, Sir (Harold) Malcolm Watts 1895–1967

English conductor. Originally trained as an organist, he was conductor of the Royal Choral Society from 1928, was in charge of the Liverpool Philharmonic Orchestra (1942–48) and led the BBC Symphony Orchestra (1950–57).

31 Just a little more reverence, please, and not so much astonishment.
Attributed, admonishing a choir singing Handel's 'For Unto Us a Child is Born'.

Sarnoff, David 1891–1971

Russian-born US radio and television pioneer. He began with the Marconi Wireless Co, covering the Titanic disaster (1912), and became president (1930) and chairman of the board (1947) of the Radio Corporation of America, a key figure in the development of television.

32 Seldom is it given to one generation to have such an opportunity to rise again, but now before you is that opportunity in television—a larger, richer, broader opportunity than ever existed in radio.
c.1948 Speech to NBC station affiliates. Recalled on his death, 12 Dec 1971.

33 Competition brings out the best in products and the worst in people.
Attributed.

Saroyan, William 1908–81

US playwright and novelist. He was awarded the Pulitzer Prize in 1939 for his best-known play, *The Time of Your Life*.

34 The Daring Young Man on the Flying Trapeze.
1934 Title of story collection.

35 The events of life have never fallen into the form of the short story or the form of the poem, or into any other form. Your own consciousness is the only form you need.
1934 *The Daring Young Man on the Flying Trapeze*, 'A Cold Day'.

36 Now what?
1981 Last words.

Sarraute, Nathalie 1902–99

French novelist and literary critic.

37 *Le mot 'psychologie' est un de ceux qu'aucun auteur d'aujourd'hui ne peut entendre prononcer à son sujet sans baisser les yeux et rougir.*
The word 'psychology' is one that no author today can hear said about her work without lowering her eyes and blushing.
1956 *L'Ère du soupçon.*

38 *Vous savez qu'on doit se sentir heureux. Tous les vrais écrivains ont éprouvé ce sentiment. Quand on ne l'éprouve pas, je suis obligé de vous en avertir, c'est mauvais signe.*
You know that one should feel happy. All the true writers have experienced this feeling. When one does not experience it, I am obliged to tell you that it is a bad sign.
1968 *Entre la vie et la mort.*

39 *Chacun peut éprouver en soi ce double mouvement: désir de s'intégrer à la société, besoin de se réaliser par soi-même en dehors d'elle.*
We all have this double impulse within ourselves: the desire to integrate into society, and the need to fulfil ourselves outside of it, through our own efforts.
La Quinzaine littéraire, 50.

Sarton, George A 1884–1956

US academic and historian of science.

40 Definition—Science is systematized positive knowledge, what has been taken as such in different ages and in different places. Theorem—The acquisition and systematization of positive knowledge are the only human activities which are truly cumulative and progressive. Corollary—The history of science is the only history which can illustrate the progress of mankind. In fact, progress has no definite and unquestionable meaning in other fields than the field of science.
1957 *The Study of the History of Science.*

Sarton, May 1912–95

US poet and novelist. Her poetry collections include *Inner Landscape* (1939), *The Land of Silence* (1953) and *The Silence Now* (1988), and she wrote other works such as *Mrs Stevens Hears the Mermaids Singing* (1965).

41 The poet must be free to love or hate as the spirit moves him, free to change, free to be a chameleon, free to be an *enfant terrible.* He must above all never worry about his effect on other people. Power requires that one do just that all the time. Power requires that the inner person never be unmasked. No, we poets have to go naked. And since this is so, it is better that we stay private people; a naked public person would be rather ridiculous, what?
1965 Hilary Stevens. *Mrs Stevens Hears the Mermaids Singing,* pt.2.

42 I write poems, have always written them, to transcend the painfully personal and reach the universal.
Quoted in *Encore: A Journal of the 80th Year* (1993).

43 When you're a poet, you're a poet first. When it comes, it's like an angel.
Quoted by Mel Gussow in her obituary, in the *New York Times,* 18 Jul 1995.

Sartre, Jean-Paul 1905–80

French existentialist philosopher and writer, a prominent intellectual and friend of Simone de Beauvoir. His works include the trilogy *Les Chemins de la liberté* (1945–9, *The Roads to Freedom*) and many plays. His philosophy is presented in *L'Être et le néant* (1943, *Being and Nothingness*). In 1964 he published his autobiography *Les Mots* (*Words*), and was awarded (but declined) the Nobel prize for literature.

44 *Trois heures, c'est toujours trop tard ou trop tôt pour tout ce qu'on veut faire.*
Three o'clock is always either too late or too early for anything one might want to do.
1938 *La Nausée,* 'Vendredi'.

45 *L'homme est une passion inutile.*
Man is a useless passion.
1943 *L'Être et le néant (Being and Nothingness,* 1957) pt.4, ch.2, section 3 (translated by Hazel Barnes).

46 *L'Enfer, c'est les Autres.*
Hell is other people.
1945 *Huis clos.*

47 *Est-ce qu'au fond, ce qui fait peur, dans la doctrine que je vais essayer de vous exposer, ce n'est pas le fait qu'elle laisse une possibilité de choix à l'homme?*
For at bottom, what is alarming in the doctrine that I am about to try to explain to you is—is it not?—that it confronts man with a possibility of choice.
1946 *L'Existentialisme est un humanisme* (*Existentialism and Humanism,* 1948) (translated by Philip Mairet).

48 *Ce qu'ils ont en commun, c'est simplement le fait qu'ils estiment que l'existence précède l'essence, ou, si vous voulez, qu'il faut partir de la subjectivité.*
What [existentialists] have in common is simply the fact that they believe that *existence* comes before *essence*—or, if you will, that we must begin from the subjective.
1946 *L'Existentialisme est un humanisme* (*Existentialism and Humanism,* 1948) (translated by Philip Mairet).

49 *Qu'est-ce que signifie que l'existence précède l'essence? Cela signifie que l'homme existe d'abord, se rencontre, surgit dans le monde, et qu'il se définit après.*
What do we mean by saying that existence precedes essence? We mean that man first of all exists, encounters himself, surges up in the world—and defines himself afterwards.
1946 *L'Existentialisme est un humanisme* (*Existentialism and Humanism,* 1948) (translated by Philip Mairet).

50 *L'homme n'est rien d'autre que ce qu'il se fait. Tel est le premier principe de l'existentialisme.*
Man is nothing else but that which he makes of himself. That is the first principle of existentialism.
1946 *L'Existentialisme est un humanisme* (*Existentialism and Humanism,* 1948) (translated by Philip Mairet).

51 *L'homme est condamné à être libre.*
Man is condemned to be free.
1946 *L'Existentialisme est un humanisme* (*Existentialism and Humanism,* 1948) (translated by Philip Mairet).

52 *Un homme n'est rien d'autre qu'une série d'entreprises.*
A man is no other than a series of undertakings.
1946 *L'Existentialisme est un humanisme* (*Existentialism and Humanism,* 1948) (translated by Philip Mairet).

53 *Il n'y a pas d'autre univers qu'un univers humain, l'univers de la subjectivité humaine.*

There is no other universe except the human universe, the universe of human subjectivity.
1946 *L'Existentialisme est un humanisme* (*Existentialism and Humanism*, 1948) (translated by Philip Mairet).

54 *Vous êtes libre, choisissez, c'est-à-dire, inventez. Aucune morale générale ne peut vous indiquer ce qu'il y a à faire.*
You are free, therefore choose—that is to say, invent. No rule of general morality can show you what you ought to do.
1946 *L'Existentialisme est un humanisme* (*Existentialism and Humanism*, 1948) (translated by Philip Mairet).

55 The status of 'native' is a nervous condition introduced and maintained by the settler among colonized people *with their consent*.
1961 Preface to Franz Fanon *Les Damnês de la terre* (*The Wretched of the Earth*, 1967, translated by Constance Farrington). Tsitsi Dangarembga uses this sentence to supply both epigraph and title of her 1988 novel *Nervous Conditions*.

Sassoon, Siegfried Louvain 1886–1967

English poet and novelist. He established his reputation as a war poet while serving in World War I. He wrote a semi-autobiographical trilogy, *The Memoirs of George Sherston* (1928–36), and several volumes of actual memoirs.

56 I am making this statement as an act of wilful defiance of military authority, because I believe that the War is being deliberately prolonged by those who have the power to end it.
1917 'A Soldier's Declaration'. Statement sent to his commanding officer which was read out in the House of Commons and printed in *The Times*.

57 I'd like to see a Tank come down the stalls,
Lurching to rag-time tunes, or 'Home sweet Home',—
And there'd be no more jokes in Music-halls
To mock the riddled corpses round Bapaume.
1917 'Blighters'.

58 How right it seemed that he should reach the span
Of comfortable years allowed to man!
Splendid to eat and sleep and choose a wife,
Safe with his wound, a citizen of life.
He hobbled blithely through the garden gate,
And thought: 'Thank God they had to amputate!'
1917 'The One-Legged Man'.

59 We'd gained our first objective hours before
While dawn broke like a face with blinking eyes,
Pallid, unshaved and thirsty, blind with smoke.
1918 'Counter-Attack'.

60 Soldiers are citizens of death's grey land,
—Drawing no dividend from time's to-morrows.
In the great hour of destiny they stand,
—Each with his feuds, and jealousies, and sorrows.
Soldiers are sworn to action; they must win
—Some flaming, fatal climax with their lives.
Soldiers are dreamers; when the guns begin
—They think of firelit homes, clean beds and wives.
1918 'Dreamers'.

61 If I were fierce and bald and short of breath
I'd live with scarlet Majors at the Base,
And speed glum heroes up the line to death.
1918 'Base Details'.

62 And when war is done and youth stone dead
I'd toddle safely home and die—in bed.
1918 'Base Details'.

63 'Good-morning; good-morning!' the General said
When we met him last week on our way to the line.
Now the soldiers he smiled at are most of 'em dead,
And we're cursing his staff for incompetent swine.
'He's a cheery old card,' grunted Harry to Jack
As they slogged up to Arras with rifle and pack.

But he did for them both by his plan of attack.
1918 'The General'.

64 Does it matter?—losing your sight?...
There's such splendid work for the blind;
And people will always be kind
As you sit on the terrace remembering
And turning your face to the light.
1918 'Does It Matter'.

65 From you, Beethoven, Bach, Mozart,
The substance of my dreams took fire.
You built cathedrals in my heart,
And lit my pinnacled desire.
1918 'Dead Musicians'.

66 You have no part with lads who fought
And laughed and suffered at my side.
Your fugues and symphonies have brought
No memory of my friends who died.
1918 'Dead Musicians'.

67 Why do you lie with your legs ungainly huddled,
And one arm bent across your sullen cold
Exhausted face?
1918 'The Dug-Out'.

68 You are too young to fall asleep for ever;
And when you sleep you remind me of the dead.
1918 'The Dug-Out'.

69 Everyone suddenly burst out singing;
And I was filled with such delight
As prisoned birds must find in freedom,
1919 'Everyone Sang'.

70 But the past is just the same,—and
War's a bloody game.
1919 'Aftermath'.

71 When all is said and done, leading a good life is more important than keeping a good diary.
1923 Diary entry, 8 Jul.

72 In me the tiger sniffs the rose.
1928 *The Heart's Journey*, pt.7, 'In me, past, present, future meet'.

73 And what is time but shadows that were cast
By these storm-sculptured stones while centuries fled?
The stones remain; their stillness can outlast
The skies of history hurrying overhead.
1928 *The Heart's Journey*, pt.9, 'What is Stonehenge? It is the roofless past'.

74 *Alone*... The word is life endured and known.
It is the stillness where our spirits walk
And all but inmost faith is overthrown.
1928 *The Heart's Journey*, pt.11, '"When I'm alone"—the words tripped off his tongue'.

75 They have spoken lightly of my deathless friends,
(Lamps for my gloom, hands guiding where I stumble,)
Quoting, for shallow conversational ends,

What Shelley shrilled, what Blake once wildly muttered…
How can they use such names and be not humble?
1928 *The Heart's Journey*, pt.15, 'Grandeur of Ghosts'.

76 Who will remember, passing through this Gate,
The unheroic Dead who fed the guns?
Who shall absolve the foulness of their fate,—
Those doomed, conscripted, unvictorious ones?
1928 *The Heart's Journey*, pt.21, 'On Passing the New Menin Gate'.

77 Here Vaughan lies dead, whose name flows on for ever
Through pastures of the spirit washed with dew
And starlit with eternities unknown.
1928 *The Heart's Journey*, pt.23, 'At the Grave of Henry Vaughan'.

78 The skull that housed white angels and had vision
Of daybreak through the gateways of the mind.
1928 *The Heart's Journey*, pt.23, 'At the Grave of Henry Vaughan'.

79 A man may be born a poet, but he has to make himself an artist as well.
1939 *On Poetry*.

Satie, Erik Alfred Leslie 1866–1925

French composer. A pupil of Vincent d'Indy and Albert Roussel, he wrote ballets, lyric dramas and numerous whimsical pieces in which he rebelled against Wagnerism and orthodoxy in general. His music had some influence on Debussy, Ravel and others.

80 Before I compose a piece, I walk round it several times, accompanied by myself.
Quoted in *Bulletin des éditions musicales* (1913).

81 To be played with both hands in the pocket.
Instruction on one of his piano compositions. Quoted in Oscar Levant *The Unimportance of Being Oscar* (1968).

82 It is not enough to refuse the Legion d'Honneur. One should never have deserved it.
Of Maurice Ravel, who had declined the honour. Quoted by Alister Kershaw in *The Australian*, 1991.

Sayers, Dorothy L(eigh) 1893–1957

English detective-story writer. Her hero, Lord Peter Wimsey, is one of the most popular of the great detectives, and her books are distinguished by realistically created settings as well as stylish wit. She also wrote plays and poems.

83 I admit it is more fun to punt than to be punted, and that a desire to have all the fun is nine-tenths of the law of chivalry.
1935 *Gaudy Night*, ch.14.

84 I can't see that she could have found anything nastier to say if she'd thought it out with both hands for a fortnight.
1937 'Prothalamion'.

85 Plain lies are dangerous.
1937 'The Psychology of Advertising', in *The Spectator*, 19 Nov.

86 Those who prefer their English sloppy have only themselves to thank if the advertisement writer uses his mastery of vocabulary and syntax to mislead their weak minds.
1937 'The Psychology of Advertising', in *The Spectator*, 19 Nov.

87 The moral of all this…is that we have the kind of advertising we deserve.
1937 'The Psychology of Advertising', in *The Spectator*, 19 Nov.

88 As I grow older and older,
And totter towards the tomb,
I find that I care less and less
Who goes to bed with whom.
'That's Why I Never Read Modern Novels', collected in Janet Hitchman *Such a Strange Lady* (1975), ch.12.

Scargill, Arthur 1938–

English trade union leader, president of the National Union of Mineworkers (1981–2002). A powerful orator, his strong defence of miners and his socialist politics led to conflict with government, particularly in the miners' strike of 1984–5. He started a new socialist party in 1996.

89 My father still reads the dictionary every day. He says that your life depends on your power to master words.
1982 In the *Sunday Times*, 10 Jan.

90 I speak of that most dangerous duo—President Ray Gun and the plutonium blonde, Margaret Thatcher.
1984 Quoted in *Time*, 3 Dec.

91 I wouldn't vote for Ken Livingstone if he were running for mayor of Toytown.
2000 In *The Guardian*, 3 May.

Scève, Maurice c.1510–c.1564

French poet of the École Lyonnaise. His most famous collection of poems, *Délie, objet de plus haute vertu* (1544), is a meditation on love.

92 *Car loi d'Amour est de l'un captiver,*
L'autre donner d'heureuse liberté.
The law of love is to captivate one,
And to give another joyous freedom.
1544 *Délie*, no.40.

93 *En toi je vis, où que tu sois absente,*
En moi je meurs, où que je sois présent.
Tant loin sois-tu, toujours tu es présente;
Pour près que sois, encore suis-je absent.
I live in you, wherever you are, when you are absent;
I die in myself wherever I am.
No matter how far away you are, you are always present;
And no matter how near you are, I am always absent.
1544 *Délie*, no.144.

94 *Tu es le Corps, Dame, et je suis ton ombre.*
You are the body, lady, and I am your shadow.
1544 *Délie*, no.376.

Schacht, Hjalmar Horace Greely 1877–1970

German financier. As president of the Reichsbank (1923) he ended inflation, and recalled by the Nazis from resignation in 1933, he restored the German trade balance by unorthodox methods. Dismissed after disagreement with Hitler, he was later acquitted at Nuremberg of crimes against humanity.

95 I wouldn't believe that Hitler was dead, even if he told me himself.
1945 Attributed remark, 8 May.

Schaw, Janet b.c.1730

Scottish traveller. She was distantly related to Sir Walter Scott and was well educated, but little is known of her other than what is told in her *Journal of a Lady of Quality*, an account of her travels in the West Indies in 1774–6.

96 At last America is in my view; a dreary waste of white barren sand, and melancholy, nodding pines. In the course of many miles, no cheerful cottage has blest my eyes. All seems dreary, savage and desert; and was it for this such sums of money, such streams of British blood have been lavished away? Oh, thou dear land, how dearly hast thou purchased this habitation for bears and wolves. Dearly has it been purchased, and at a price far dearer still it will be kept. My heart dies within me, while I view it.

c.1776 On her first sight of the country around Cape Fear. *Journal of a Lady of Quality; Being the Narrative of a Journey from Scotland to the West Indies, North Carolina, and Portugal, in the years 1774 to 1776.*

Scheckter, Jody 1950–

South African Formula One driver.

97 Fewer girls, more technology.
1997 On how Formula One had changed since he won the world championship in 1979. In *The Times*, 29 Dec.

Schiaparelli, Elsa 1890–1973

Italian fashion designer who opened one of the first couture boutiques in Paris in 1935. She was known for introducing the colour 'shocking pink' into the fashion world.

98 So fashion is born by small facts, trends, or even politics, never by trying to make little pleats and furbelows, by trinkets, by clothes easy to copy, or by the shortening or lengthening of a skirt.
1954 *A Shocking Life*, ch.9.

99 A good cook is like a sorceress who dispenses happiness.
1954 *A Shocking Life*, ch.21.

Schiller, Friedrich 1759–1805

German poet and playwright who was briefly a surgeon before turning his attention to writing and travelling.

1 *In seinen Göttern malt sich der Mensch.*
Humankind is reflected in its gods.
1789 *Was heißt und zu welchem Ende studiert man Universalgeschichte?*

2 *Alle anderen Dinge müssen; der Mensch ist das Wesen, welches will.*
All other things must; man is the being who wills.
1794 *Über das Erhabene.*

3 *Man kann den Menschen nicht verwehren,*
Zu denken, was sie wollen.
One cannot prevent people from thinking what they please.
1800 *Maria Stuart*, act 1, sc.8.

4 *Was man scheint,*
Hat jedermann zum Richter; was man ist, hat keine.
What we appear to be is subject to the judgement
Of all mankind, and what we truly are, of no one.
1800 *Maria Stuart*, act 2, sc.5.

5 *Was man nicht aufgibt, hat man nie verloren.*
What is not abandoned is never completely lost.
1800 *Maria Stuart*, act 2, sc.5.

6 *Das Leben ist*
Nur ein Moment, der Tod ist auch nur einer.
Life is but a moment. Death is but a moment, too.
1800 *Maria Stuart*, act 3, sc.6.

7 *Den stolzen Sieger stürzt sein eignes Glück.*
The victor is often vanquished by his own success.
1801 *Die Jungfrau von Orléans*, act 1, sc.5.

8 *Mehr als das Leben lieb' ich meine Freiheit.*
More than life, I cherish freedom.
1801 *Die Jungfrau von Orléans*, act 2, sc.2.

9 *Mitt der Dummheit kämpfen Götter selbst vergebens.*
Even the gods themselves struggle in vain against stupidity.
1801 *Die Jungfrau von Orléans*, act 3, sc.6.

Schlesinger, Arthur Meier 1888–1965

US historian. His works include *New Viewpoints in American History* (1922) and a *History of American Life* (13 vols, 1928–43).

10 The military struggle may frankly be regarded for what it actually was, namely a war for independence, an armed attempt to impose the views of the revolutionists on the British government and large sections of the colonial population at whatever cost to freedom of opinion or the sanctity of life and property.
1919 'The American Revolution Reconsidered', in *Political Science Quarterly*, Mar.

Schlesinger, Arthur M(eier), Jr 1917–

US historian and special assistant to President Kennedy (1961–3). His works include the Pulitzer prize-winning *The Age of Jackson* (1945) and *A Thousand Days: John F Kennedy in the White House* (1965). He became president of the American Institute of Arts and Letters (1981).

11 He read partly for information, partly for comparison, partly for insight, partly for the sheer joy of felicitous statement. He delighted particularly in quotations which distilled the essence of an argument.
1965 Of John F Kennedy. *A Thousand Days*.

12 Ceremony, circus, farce, melodrama, tragedy…nothing else offers all at once the whirl, the excitement, the gaiety, the intrigue and the anguish.
1965 On national political conventions. *A Thousand Days*.

13 At the time it is all a confusion; in retrospect…all a blur.
1965 On national political conventions. *A Thousand Days*.

14 The things people had once held against her… unconventional beauty…un-American elegance, the taste for French clothes and French food—were suddenly no longer liabilities but assets.
1965 On Jacqueline Kennedy's post-election image. *A Thousand Days*.

15 Television has spread the habit of instant reaction and has stimulated the hope of instant results.
1970 In *Newsweek*, 6 Jul.

Schlesinger, James 1932–

16 The notion of a defence that will protect American cities is one that will not be achieved, but it is that goal that supplies the political magic in the President's vision.
1987 Senate Foreign Relations Committee, 6 Feb.

Schmitt, Wolfgang Rudolph 1944–

German-born US businessman. He joined houseware manufacturers Rubbermaid Inc in 1966, becoming president in 1991.

17 Innovation most of the time is simply taking A, B, C and D, which already exist, and putting them together in a form called E.
1994 In *Fortune*, 14 Nov.

Schnabel, Artur 1882–1951

Austrian pianist and composer. He studied under Leschetizsky and made his debut at the age of eight. Subsequently he toured throughout Europe and the US, where he settled in 1939. He was an authoritative player of a small range of German classics—notably Beethoven, Mozart and Schubert.

18 The notes I handle no better than many pianists. But the pauses between the notes—ah, that is where the art resides.
1958 In the *Chicago Daily News*, 11 Jun.

19 Applause is a receipt, not a bill.
Explaining why he did not play encores. Quoted in I Kolodin *The Musical Life* (1958).

20 I know two kinds of audience only—one coughing and one not coughing.
1961 *My Life and Music.*

21 I don't think there was ever a piece of music that changed a man's decision on how to vote.
1961 *My Life and Music.*

22 When a piece gets difficult make faces.
Quoted in Oscar Levant *The Unimportance of Being Oscar* (1968).

23 The sonatas of Mozart are unique; they are too easy for children, and too difficult for artists.
Quoted in Nat Shapiro *An Encyclopedia of Quotations about Music* (1978).

Schoenbaum, Thomas J

Professor of Political Science, University of Georgia.

24 [He] made himself the rock against which crashed the successive waves of dissent.
1988 Of Secretary of State Dean Rusk during the Vietnam War. *Waging Peace and War.*

Schoenberg, Arnold Franz Walter 1874–1951

Austrian composer, conductor and teacher. A self-taught pioneer of atonality, his works include the tone poem *Pelleas und Melisande* (1903), the song cycle *Pierrot Lunaire* (1912), operas, chamber music and other choral and orchestral pieces. He lived in the US from 1933.

25 Harmony! Harmony!
1951 Attributed last words.

26 My music is not modern, it is merely badly played.
Quoted in C Rosen *Schoenberg* (1976).

27 If it is art it is not for all, and if it is for all it is not art.
Quoted in Ian Crofton and Donald Fraser *A Dictionary of Musical Quotations* (1985).

Schopenhauer, Arthur 1788–1860

German philosopher, whose work is often characterized as a systematic philosophical pessimism. His major work was *Die Welt als Wille und Vorstellung* (*The World as Will and Representation*), published in 1819. A second enlarged edition followed in 1844.

28 *Alle Befriedigung, oder was man gemeinhin Glück nennt, ist eigentlich und wesentlich immer nur negativ und durchaus nie positiv.*
All satisfaction, or what is commonly called happiness, is really and essentially always *negative* only, and never positive.
1819 *Die Welt als Wille und Vorstellung* (*The World as Will and Representation*), vol.1, bk.4, ch.58 (translated by E F J Payne).

29 *Wir tappen im Labyrinth unsers Lebenswandels und im Dunkel unserer Forschungen umher: helle Augenblicke erleuchten dabei wie Blitze unsern Weg.*
We grope about in the labyrinth of our life and in the obscurity of our investigations; bright moments illuminate our path like flashes of lightning.
1844 *Die Welt als Wille und Vorstellung* (*The World as Will and Representation*), vol.2, ch.15 (translated by E F J Payne).

30 *Das Ganze der Erfahrung gleicht einer Geheimschrift und die Philosophie der Entzifferung derselben.*
The whole of experience is like a cryptograph, and philosophy is like the deciphering of it.
1844 *Die Welt als Wille und Vorstellung* (*The World as Will and Representation*), vol.2, ch.17 (translated by E F J Payne).

31 *Ist es an und für sich absurd, das Nichtsein für ein Übel zu halten; da jedes Übel wie jedes Gut das Dasein zur Voraussetzung hat, ja sogar das Bewusstsein.*
It is in and by itself absurd to regard non-existence as an evil; for every evil, like every good, presupposes existence, indeed even consciousness.
1844 *Die Welt als Wille und Vorstellung* (*The World as Will and Representation*), vol.2, ch.41 (translated by E F J Payne).

32 *Unsterblichkeit der Individualität verlangen heißt eigentlich einen Irrtum ins Unendliche perpetuieren wollen. Denn im Grunde ist doch jede Individualität nur ein spezieller Irrtum, Fehltritt, etwas, das besser nicht wäre, ja wovon uns zurückzubringen der eigentliche Zweck des Lebens ist.*
To desire immortality for the individual is really the same as wanting to perpetuate an error for ever; for at bottom every individuality is really only a special error, a false step, something that it would be better should not be, in fact something from which it is the real purpose of life to bring us back.
1844 *Die Welt als Wille und Vorstellung* (*The World as Will and Representation*), vol.2, ch.41 (translated by E F J Payne).

33 *Alle Verliebtheit [...] wurzelt allein im Geschlechtstriebe.*
All amorousness [...] is rooted in the sexual impulse alone.
1844 *Die Welt als Wille und Vorstellung* (*The World as Will and Representation*), vol.2, ch.44 (translated by E F J Payne).

34 *Was man auch sagen mag, der glücklichste Augenblick des Glücklichen ist doch der seines Einschlafens wie der unglücklichste des Unglücklichen der seines Erwachens.*
Whatever we may say, the happiest moment of the happy man is that of his falling asleep, just as the unhappiest moment of the unhappy man is that of his awakening.
1844 *Die Welt als Wille und Vorstellung* (*The World as Will and Representation*), vol.2, ch.46 (translated by E F J Payne).

35 *Es gibt nur einen Irrtum, und es ist der, dass wir dasind, um glücklich zu sein.*
There is only one inborn error, and that is the notion that we exist in order to be happy.
1844 *Die Welt als Wille und Vorstellung* (*The World as Will and Representation*), vol.2, ch.49 (translated by E F J Payne).

36 *Die Szenen unsers Lebens gleichen den Bildern in großer Mosaik, welche in der Nähe keine Wirkung tun, sondern von denen man fern stehn muss, um sie schön zu finden.*
The scenes of our life resemble pictures in rough mosaic; they are ineffective from close up, and have to be viewed from a distance if they are to seem beautiful.
1851 *Parerga und Paralipomena*, ch.11 (translated by R J Hollingdale).

37 *Jede Trennung gibt einen Vorgeschmack des Todes—und jedes Wiedersehen einen Vorgeschmack der Auferstehung.*
Every parting is a foretaste of death, and every reunion a foretaste of resurrection.
1851 *Parerga und Paralipomena*, ch.26 (translated by R J Hollingdale).

Schreiner, Olive Emily Albertina *pseudonym Ralph Iron* 1855–1920

South African feminist, novelist and polemicist. Educated at home against a strict religious background, she is best known for her semi-autobiographical novel, *The Story of an African Farm* (1883), which rejects the spiritual aridity of colonial life and loveless marriage.

38 This pretty ring... I will give it to the first man who tells me he would like to be a woman. It is delightful to be a woman; but every man thanks the Lord devoutly that he isn't one.
1883 *The Story of an African Farm*, ch.17,'Lyndall'.

39 We are cursed, Waldo, born cursed from the time our mothers bring us into the world till the shrouds are put on us.
1883 Lyndall. *The Story of an African Farm*, ch.17,'Lyndall'.

40 We sit...and look out at the boys in their happy play...we kneel still with one little cheek wistfully pressed against the pane...and we go and stand before the glass. We see the complexion we were not to spoil, and the white frock... Then the curse begins to act upon us. It finishes its work when we are grown women, who no more look out wistfully at a more healthy life; we are contented. We fit our sphere as a Chinese woman's foot fits her shoe, exactly, as though God made both—and yet he knows nothing of either.
1883 Lyndall. *The Story of an African Farm*, ch.17,'Lyndall'.

41 Men are like the earth and we are the moon; we turn always one side to them, and they think there is no other, because they don't see it—but there is.
1883 Lyndall. *The Story of an African Farm*, ch.17,'Lyndall'.

42 Give us labour and the training which fits for labour! We demand this, not for ourselves alone, but for the race.
1911 *Women and Labour*, ch.1.

43 With each generation the entire race passes through the body of its womanhood as through a mould, reappearing with the indelible marks of that mould upon it, that as the *os cervix* of woman, through which the head of the human infant passes at birth, forms a ring, determining for ever the size at birth of the human head...so exactly the intellectual capacity, the physical vigour, the emotional depth of woman, forms also an untranscendable circle, circumscribing with each successive generation the limits of expansion of the human race.
1911 *Women and Labour*, ch.3.

Schroeder, Patricia Scott 1940–

US Congresswoman and lawyer. She practised law in Denver and then became a faculty member of the University of Colorado (1969–72), before being elected to Congress (1972–96).

44 I was cooking breakfast this morning for my kids and I thought, 'He's just like Teflon. Nothing sticks to him.'
1984 Of President Ronald Reagan. In the *Boston Globe*, 24 Oct.

45 Washington is awash in post-war testosterone.
1991 On her decision not to seek presidential nomination in the wake of victory in the Gulf War. In the *New York Times*, 30 Jun.

Schulberg, Budd Wilson 1914–

US novelist and scritpwriter. He is best known for his screenplay for the film *On the Waterfront* (1954).

46 What Makes Sammy Run?
1941 Title of novel.

47 You don't understand. I could have had class. I could have been a contender. I could have been somebody—instead of a bum, which is what I am, let's face it.
1954 Lines spoken by Marlon Brando. *On the Waterfront*.

Schultz, Howard 1952–

US businessman.

48 Retail is detail.
1994 On building Starbucks, the largest US coffee-bar chain and mail-order business. In the *New York Times*, 14 Dec.

Schulz, Charles Monroe 1922–2000

US cartoonist. He created the syndicated comic strip *Peanuts* (1950), internationally loved for its characters of Charlie Brown, Snoopy, Lucy, Linus, Schroeder, Peppermint Patty, Pigpen, Marcie and the bird Woodstock.

49 Jogging is very beneficial. It's very good for your legs and your feet. It's also very good for the ground. It makes it feel needed.
Quoted in Colin Jarman *The Guinness Dictionary of Sports Quotations* (1990).

Schumacher, E(rnst) F(riedrich) 1911–77

British economist and public servant, member of the Control Commission in Germany (1946–50) and economist of the National Coal Board (1950–70).

50 Small Is Beautiful: a Study of Economics as if People Mattered.
1973 Title of book.

51 I have no doubt that it is possible to give a new direction to technological development, a direction that shall lead it back to the real needs of man, and that also means: to the actual size of man. Man is small, and, therefore, small is beautiful. To go for giantism is to go for self-destruction.
1973 *Small Is Beautiful*.

Schumacher, Michael 1969–

German Formula One driver, winner of the world championship in 1994 and 1995, and 2000–4.

52 To control 800 horse power relying just on arm muscles and foot sensitivity can turn out to be a dangerous exercise.
2003 In the *Observer*, 2 Mar.

Schumpeter, Joseph Alois 1883–1950

Austrian-born US economist, who emigrated to the US in 1932 and later became professor at Harvard. He emphasized the importance of the entrepreneur in the business cycle and traced the economic history of capitalism.

53 When I was a young man, I wanted to be three things: I wanted to be the world's greatest horseman, the world's greatest economist, and the world's greatest lover. Unfortunately I never became the world's greatest horseman.
1940s Attributed, Harvard oral tradition.

54 The cold metal of economic theory is in Marx's pages immersed in such a wealth of steaming phrases as to acquire a temperature not naturally its own.
1942 *Capitalism, Socialism, and Democracy*, p.21.

55 Can capitalism survive? No, I do not think it can.
1942 *Capitalism, Socialism, and Democracy*, p.61.

56 Queen Elizabeth owned silk stockings. The capitalist achievement does not typically consist in providing more silk stockings for queens but in bringing them within the reach of factory girls in return for steadily decreasing amount of effort.
1942 *Capitalism, Socialism, and Democracy*, p.67.

57 The question that is so clearly in many potential parents' minds: 'Why should we stunt our ambitions and impoverish our lives in order to be insulted and looked down upon in our old age?'
1942 *Capitalism, Socialism, and Democracy*, ch.14.

58 Bureaucracy is not an obstacle to democracy but an inevitable complement to it.
1942 *Capitalism, Socialism, and Democracy*, ch.18.

Schwartz, Eugene M

US art collector, known for amassing one of the nation's leading collections of contemporary art and giving it away with almost as much zeal.

59 Collecting is the only socially commendable form of greed.
1995 In the *New York Times*, 7 Sep.

Schwartz, Sanford

US writer.

60 Dalí's importance for the Surrealists at that time, and for art historians now, is that he found a way to put Freud on canvas.
1994 In the *New Republic*, 17 Oct.

Schwarzenegger, Arnold 1947–

Austrian-born US actor and politician. He began as a body builder, winning the Mr Universe title, and became a Hollywood star in adventure films such as *The Terminator* (1984) and *True Lies* (1994). He was elected Republican Governor of California in 2003.

61 Posing is a performing art.
Quoted in *The Guardian*, 1975.

62 I'll be back.
1984 *The Terminator*.

63 Hasta la vista, baby.
1991 *Terminator 2: Judgment Day*.

64 I am humbled, I am honoured and I am moved beyond words to be your governor.
2003 On being sworn in as Governor of California, 17 Nov.

Schwarzkopf, H Norman 1934–

US army general. He served in the Vietnam War and as deputy commander in Grenada (1983), and in 1991 commanded allied troops in the Gulf War. He retired the following year.

65 We are not going after Saddam Hussein. If I can eliminate his ability to communicate with his forces, I would be entirely satisfied with that result.
1991 Press briefing on the start of the Gulf War, 15 Jan.

66 I don't consider myself dovish and I certainly don't consider myself hawkish. Maybe I would describe myself as owlish—that is wise enough to understand that you want to do everything possible to avoid war.
1991 In the *New York Times*, 28 Jan.

67 I asked you to be the thunder and lightning of Desert Storm. You were all of that and more.
1991 Message to US units on the cease-fire that ended the Gulf War.

68 Seven months ago I could give a single command and 541,000 people would immediately obey it. Today I can't get a plumber to come to my house.
1991 In *Newsweek*, 11 Nov.

Schweikart, Russell 1935–

US astronaut.

69 The most beautiful sight in orbit…is a urine dump at sunset, because as the stuff comes out and as it hits the exit nozzle it instantly flashes into ten million little ice crystals which go out almost in a hemisphere… It's really a spectacular sight.
1981 *The Next Whole Earth Catalog*.

Schweitzer, Albert 1875–1965

German medical missionary, theologian, musician and philosopher. In 1896 he vowed to live for science and art until he was 30, and then devote his life to serving humanity. He became principal of a theological college (1903) and wrote *Von Reimarus zu Wrede* (1906, *The Quest for the Historical Jesus*) and major works on St Paul. Despite his international reputation in music and theology, he turned to medicine in 1905, and with his wife set up a hospital in French Equatorial Africa. He was awarded the Nobel peace prize in 1952.

70 He comes to us as One unknown, without a name, as of old, by the lakeside, He came to those who knew Him not. He speaks to us the same word: 'Follow thou me!' and sets us to the tasks which He has to fulfil for our time. He commands. And to those who obey Him, whether they be wise or simple, He will reveal Himself in the toils, the conflicts, the sufferings which they shall pass through in His fellowship, and, as an ineffable mystery, they shall learn in their own experience who He is.
1906 *Von Reimarus zu Wrede* (translated by W Montgomery as *The Quest for the Historical Jesus*, 1910).

71 An optimist is a person who sees a green light everywhere, while the pessimist sees only the red stop-light. The truly wise person is colour-blind.
1965 Quoted in CBS News tribute, 14 Jan.

Scorsese, Martin 1942–

US film director. With films such as *Taxi Driver* (1976) and *Raging Bull* (1980), he established himself as one of the foremost directors of his generation.

72 I always tell the younger film-makers and students: Do it like the painters used to… Study the old masters. Enrich your palette. Expand the canvas. There's always so much more to learn.
1997 *Scorsese: A Personal Journey Through American Movies*.

73 Cinema is a matter of what's in the frame and what's out.
1997 *Scorsese: A Personal Journey Through American Movies*.

Scott, C(harles) P(restwich) 1846–1932

English newspaper editor and Liberal MP (1895–1906). At the age of 26 he became editor of the *Manchester Guardian*, and made it a serious liberal rival of *The Times* by a highly independent and often controversial editorial policy and high literary standards.

74 The newspaper is of necessity something of a monopoly, and its first duty is to shun the temptations of a monopoly. Its primary office is the gathering of News. At the peril of its soul it must see that the supply is not tainted. Neither in what it gives, nor in what it does not give, nor in the mode of presentation, must the unclouded face of Truth suffer wrong. Comment is free, but facts are sacred.
1921 Of the newspaper industry. In the *Manchester Guardian*, special centenary issue, 6 May.

75 One of the virtues, perhaps almost the chief virtue, of a newspaper is its independence. Whatever its position or character, at least it should have a soul of its own.
1921 In the *Manchester Guardian*, special centenary issue, 6 May.

Scott, Duncan Campell 1862–1947

Canadian poet. One of the 'Confederation Poets', he also wrote short stories, biographies and a play.

76 How strange the stars have grown;
The presage of extinction glows on their crests
And they are beautied with impermanence.
1916 'The Height of Land'.

Scott, F(rancis) R(eginald) 1899–1985

Canadian poet. A lawyer, professor and politician (a founder of the Canadian social democratic party, the Co-operative Commonwealth Federation), he established several important literary reviews. His collected poems were published in 1981.

77 I have sat by night beside a cold lake
And touched things smoother than moonlight on still water,
But the moon on this cloud sea is not human,
And here is no shore, no intimacy,
Only the start of space, the road to suns.
1945 'Trans Canada'.

78 Hidden in wonder and snow, or sudden with summer,
This land stares at the sun in a huge silence
Endlessly repeating something we cannot hear.
Inarticulate, arctic,
Not written on by history, empty as paper,
It leans away from the world with songs in its lakes
Older than love, and lost in the miles.
1954 Of Canada. 'Laurentian Shield'.

79 Newspapers are born free and everywhere are in chains.
1973 Aphorism, collected in John Robert Colombo (ed) *Colombo's Canadian Quotations* (1974).
► *See Rousseau 700:41.*

Scott, Robert Falcon 1868–1912

English Antarctic explorer. In 1900–4 he commanded the National Antarctic Expedition to the Ross Sea. On his second expedition he reached the South Pole (Jan 1912), only to discover that Amundsen had beaten him by a month. He and his party died on the way back; their bodies and diaries were found by a search party eight months later.

80 Great God! This is an awful place and terrible enough for us to have laboured to it without the reward of priority.
1912 Journal entry, 18 Jan. *Scott's Last Expedition: The Personal Journals of Captain R F Scott, CVO, RN, on His Journey to the South Pole* (published 1923).

81 Had we lived, I should have had a tale to tell of the hardihood, endurance, and courage of my companions which would have stirred the heart of every Englishman. These rough notes and our dead bodies must tell the tale.
1912 Message to the public. Quoted in *The Times*, 11 Feb 1913.

82 It seems a pity but I do not think I can write more. For God's sake look after our people.
1912 Last entry in journal, 29 Mar. In *Scott's Last Expedition: The Personal Journals of Captain R F Scott, CVO, RN, on His Journey to the South Pole* (published 1923).

Scott, Rose 1847–1925

Australian feminist.

83 Life is too short to waste on the admiration of one man.
Her habitual response to offers of marriage. Quoted in Jennifer Uglow (ed) *The Macmillan Dictionary of Women's Biography* (2nd edn, 1989).

Scott, Sir Walter 1771–1832

Scottish novelist and poet. He studied law and became an advocate and later a sheriff, but achieved worldwide fame as a writer of epic poetry and as the author of the *Waverley Novels*, promoting a fundamentally romantic image of history and in particular of Scotland's past.

84 The way was long, the wind was cold,
The Minstrel was infirm and old;
His withered cheek, and tresses grey,
Seemed to have known a better day;
The harp, his sole remaining joy,
Was carried by an orphan boy,
The last of all the Bards was he,
Who sung of Border chivalry.
1805 *The Lay of the Last Minstrel*, introduction.

85 He poured, to lord and lady gay,
The unpremeditated lay.
1805 *The Lay of the Last Minstrel*, introduction.

86 And said I that my limbs were old,
And said I that my blood was cold,
And that my kindly fire was fled,
And my poor withered heart was dead,
And that I might not sing of Love?
1805 *The Lay of the Last Minstrel*, canto 1, stanza 1.

87 If thou would'st view fair Melrose aright,
Go visit it by the pale moonlight.
1805 *The Lay of the Last Minstrel*, canto 2, stanza 1.

88 The woodland brook he bounding crossed,
And laughed, and shouted, 'Lost! lost! lost!'
1805 *The Lay of the Last Minstrel*, canto 3, stanza 13.

89 The Harper smiled, well pleased; for ne'er
Was flattery lost on poet's ear:
A simple race! they waste their toil
For the vain tribute of a smile.
1805 *The Lay of the Last Minstrel*, canto 4, conclusion.

90 Call it not vain:—they do not err
Who say, that when the Poet dies,
Mute Nature mourns her worshipper,
And celebrates his obsequies.
1805 *The Lay of the Last Minstrel*, canto 5, stanza 1.

91 Breathes there the man, with soul so dead,
Who never to himself hath said,
This is my own, my native land!
Whose heart hath ne'er within him burned,
As home his footsteps he hath turned
From wandering on a foreign strand!
1805 *The Lay of the Last Minstrel*, canto 6, stanza 1.

92 O Caledonia! stern and wild,
Meet nurse for a poetic child!
Land of brown heath and shaggy wood,
Land of the mountain and the flood,
Land of my sires! what mortal hand
Can e'er untie the filial band
That knits me to thy rugged strand!
1805 *The Lay of the Last Minstrel*, canto 6, stanza 2.

93 November's sky is chill and drear,
November's leaf is red and sear.
1808 *Marmion*, canto 1, introduction.

94 And come he slow, or come he fast,
It is but Death who comes at last.
1808 *Marmion*, canto 2, stanza 30.

95 Still is thy name in high account,
And still thy verse has charms,
Sir David Lindesay of the Mount,
Lord Lion King-at-arms!
1808 *Marmion*, canto 4, stanza 7.

96 O, young Lochinvar is come out of the west,
Through all the wide Border his steed was the best;
And save his good broadsword he weapon had none,
He rode all unarmed, and he rode all alone.
So faithful in love, and so dauntless in war,
There never was knight like the young Lochinvar.
1808 *Marmion*, canto 5, stanza 12, 'Lochinvar'.

97 Heap on more wood!—the wind is chill;
But let it whistle as it will,
We'll keep our Christmas merry still.
1808 *Marmion*, canto 6, introduction.

98 And dar'st thou then
To beard the lion in his den,
The Douglas in his hall?
1808 *Marmion*, canto 6, stanza 14.

99 Oh what a tangled web we weave,
When first we practise to deceive!
1808 *Marmion*, canto 6, stanza 17.

1 O Woman! in our hours of ease,
Uncertain, coy, and hard to please,
And variable as the shade
By the light quivering aspen made;
When pain and anguish wring the brow,
A ministering angel thou!
1808 *Marmion*, canto 6, stanza 30.

2 The stubborn spearmen still made good
Their dark impenetrable wood,
Each stepping where his comrade stood
The instant that he fell.
1808 *Marmion*, canto 6, stanza 34.

3 Still from the sire the son shall hear
Of the stern strife, and carnage drear,
Of Flodden's fatal field,
Where shivered was fair Scotland's spear,
And broken was her shield!
1808 *Marmion*, canto 6, stanza 34.

4 The stag at eve had drunk his fill,
Where danced the moon on Monan's rill.
1810 *The Lady of the Lake*, canto 1, stanza 1.

5 Hail to the Chief who in honour advances!
Honoured and bless'd be the evergreen Pine!
1810 *The Lady of the Lake*, canto 2, stanza 19, 'Boat Song'.

6 Time rolls his ceaseless course.
1810 *The Lady of the Lake*, canto 3, stanza 1.

7 He is gone on the mountain,
He is lost to the forest,
Like a summer-dried fountain,
When our need was the sorest.
1810 *The Lady of the Lake*, canto 3, stanza 16, 'Coronach'.

8 Like the dew on the mountain,
Like the foam on the river,
Like the bubble on the fountain,
Thou art gone, and for ever!
1810 *The Lady of the Lake*, canto 3, stanza 16, 'Coronach'.

9 Merry it is in the good greenwood,
When the mavis and merle are singing,
When the deer sweeps by, and the hounds are in cry,
And the hunter's horn is ringing.
1810 *The Lady of the Lake*, canto 4, stanza 12, 'Alice Brand'.

10 O, Brignal banks are wild and fair,
And Greta woods are green
And you may gather garlands there
Would grace a summer queen.
1813 *Rokeby*, canto 3, stanza 16.

11 A weary lot is thine, fair maid,
A weary lot is thine!
To pull the thorn thy brow to braid,
And press the rue for wine!
1813 *Rokeby*, canto 3, stanza 28, 'Song'.

12 Look back, and smile at perils past!
1813 *The Bridal of Triermain*, introduction.

13 He that steals a cow from a poor widow, or a stirk from a cottar, is a thief; he that lifts a drove from a Sassenach laird, is a gentleman-drover. And, besides, to take a tree from the forest, a salmon from the river, a deer from the hill, or a cow from a Lowland strath, is what no Highlander need ever think shame upon.
1814 Evan Dhu Maccombich to Edward Waverley. *Waverley*, ch.18.

14 I am heartily glad you continued to like Waverley to the end—the hero is a sneaking piece of imbecility and if he had married Flora she would have set him up upon the

chimney-piece as Count Boralaski's wife used to do with him.
1814 Letter to John Morritt, 28 Jul. Joseph Borowlaski was a Polish dwarf known as 'The Little Count' who left France at the Revolution and exhibited himself at fairs throughout Britain.

15 Then strip lads, and to it, though sharp be the weather,
And if, by mischance, you should happen to fall,
There are worse things in life than a tumble on the heather
And life is itself a game of football.
1815 On a match between the Scottish teams Ettrick and Selkirk, published in the *Edinburgh Journal*.

16 But ruffian stern, and soldier good,
The noble and the slave,
From various cause the same wild road,
On the same bloody morning, trode,
To that dark inn—the Grave!
1815 *The Lord of the Isles*, canto 6, stanza 26.

17 Pro-di-gi-ous!
1815 Dominie Sampson. *Guy Mannering*, ch.8.

18 'That sounds like nonsense, my dear.'
'Maybe so, my dear; but it may be very good law for all that.'
1815 Mrs and Mr Bertram in conversation. *Guy Mannering*, ch.9.

19 Gin by pailfuls, wine in rivers,
Dash the window-glass to shivers!
For three wild lads were we, brave boys,
And three wild lads were we;
Thou on the land, and I on the sand,
And Jack on the gallows-tree!
1815 *Guy Mannering*, ch.34.

20 The frolicsome company had begun to practise the ancient and now forgotten pastime of *High Jinks*.
1815 *Guy Mannering*, ch.36.

21 'Why weep ye by the tide, ladie?
Why weep ye by the tide?
I'll wed ye to my youngest son,
And ye sall be his bride:
And ye sall be his bride, ladie,
Sae comely to be seen'—
But aye she loot the tears down fa'
For Jock of Hazeldean.
1816 'Jock of Hazeldean', stanza 1.

22 'A chain of gold ye sall not lack,
Nor braid to bind your hair;
Nor mettled hound, nor managed hawk,
Nor palfrey fresh and fair.'
1816 'Jock of Hazeldean', stanza 3.

23 They sought her baith by bower and ha';
The ladie was not seen!
She's o'er the Border and awa'
Wi' Jock of Hazeldean.
1816 'Jock of Hazeldean', stanza 4.

24 Prætorian here, prætorian there, I mind the bigging o't.
1816 Edie Ochiltree to Jonathan Oldbuck. *The Antiquary*, ch.4.

25 It's no fish ye're buying—it's men's lives.
1816 Maggie Mucklebackit to Oldbuck. *The Antiquary*, ch.11.

26 It's weel wi' you gentles, that can sit in the house wi' handkerchers at your een when ye lose a friend; but the like o' us maun to our wark again, if our hearts were beating as hard as my hammer.
1816 Saunders Mucklebackit to Oldbuck. *The Antiquary*, ch.34.

27 He that is without name, without friends, without coin, without country, is still at least a man; and he that has all these is no more.
1817 Rob Roy to Francis Osbaldistone. *Rob Roy*, ch.21.

28 Come fill up my cup, come fill up my cann,
Come saddle my horses, and call up my man;
Come open your gates, and let me gae free,
I daurna stay langer in Bonny Dundee!
1817 *Rob Roy*, ch.23.

29 If your honour disna ken when ye hae a gude servant, I ken when I hae a gude master, and the deil be in my feet gin I leave ye.
1817 Andrew Fairservice to Francis Osbaldistone. *Rob Roy*, ch. 24.

30 It's ill taking the breeks aff a Hielandman.
1817 Andrew Fairservice to Bailie Nicol Jarvie. *Rob Roy*, ch.27.

31 There's a gude time coming.
1817 Rob Roy to the Duke. *Rob Roy*, ch.32.

32 Speak out, sir, and do not Maister or Campbell me—my foot is on my native heath, and my name is MacGregor!
1817 Rob Roy to Francis Osbaldistone. *Rob Roy*, ch.34.

33 Ye ken weel eneugh that women and gear are at the bottom of a' the mischief in this warld.
1817 Rob Roy to Francis Osbaldistone. *Rob Roy*, ch.35.

34 The hour's come, but not the man.
1818 *The Heart of Midlothian*, ch.4, motto.

35 'I dinna ken muckle about the law,' answered Mrs Howden; 'but I ken, when we had a king, and a chancellor, and parliament-men o' our ain, we could aye peeble them wi' stanes when they werena gude bairns—But naebody's nails can reach the length o' Lunnon.'
1818 *The Heart of Midlothian*, ch.4.

36 Jock, when ye hae naething else to do, ye may be aye sticking in a tree; it will be growing, Jock, when ye're sleeping.
1818 The Laird of Dumbiedikes to his son. *The Heart of Midlothian*, ch.8.

37 Never mind my grace, lassie; just speak out a plain tale, and show you have a Scotch tongue in your head.
1818 The Duke of Argyle to Jeanie Deans. *The Heart of Midlothian*, ch.35.

38 Dinna be chappit back or cast down wi' the first rough answer.
1818 Jeanie Deans to the Duke of Argyle. *The Heart of Midlothian*, ch.35.

39 Proud Maisie is in the wood,
Walking so early;
Sweet Robin sits on the bush,
Singing so rarely.
1818 *The Heart of Midlothian*, ch.40 (Madge Wildfire's song).

40 Look not thou on beauty's charming,—
Sit thou still when kings are arming.—
Taste not when the wine-cup glistens,—
Speak not when the people listens,—
Stop thine ear against the singer,—
From the red gold keep thy finger,—
Vacant heart, and hand, and eye,—
Easy live and quiet die.
1819 *The Bride of Lammermoor*, ch.3 (Lucy Ashton's song).

41 But no one shall find me rowing against the stream. I care not who knows it—I write for the general amusement.
1822 *The Fortunes of Nigel*, introductory epistle.

42 For a con-si-de-ra-tion.
1822 Trapbois. *The Fortunes of Nigel*, ch.22.

43 O Geordie, Jingling Geordie, it was grand to hear Baby Charles laying down the guilt of dissimulation and Steemie lecturing on the turpitude of incontinence.
1822 *The Fortunes of Nigel*, ch.31.

44 Carle, now the King's come!
Carle, now the King's come!
Thou shalt dance, and I will sing,
Carle, now the King's come!
1822 'Carle, Now the King's Come', written in celebration of George IV's visit to Edinburgh.

45 Ah! County Guy, the hour is nigh,
The sun has left the lea,
The orange flower perfumes the bower,
The breeze is on the sea.
1823 *Quentin Durward*, ch.4.

46 Fair, fat, and forty.
1823 *St Ronan's Well*, ch.7.

47 It's ill speaking between a fou man and a fasting.
1824 *Redgauntlet*, letter 11, 'Wandering Willie's Tale'.

48 The ae half of the warld thinks the tither daft.
1824 Peter Peebles to Justice Foxley. *Redgauntlet*, ch.7.

49 'Then, gentlemen,' said Redgauntlet, clasping his hands together as the words burst from him, 'the cause is lost for ever!'
1824 *Redgauntlet*, ch.23.

50 Widowed wife, and married maid,
Betrothed, betrayer, and betrayed!
1825 *The Betrothal*, ch.15.

51 Came through cold roads to as cold news.
1826 *Journal*, 16 Jan, referring to the financial collapse of his publisher, Constable, which led directly to Scott's own bankruptcy.

52 We had better remain in union with England, even at the risk of becoming a subordinate species of Northumberland, as far as national consequence is concerned, than remedy ourselves by even hinting the possibility of a rupture. But there is no harm in wishing Scotland to have just so much ill-nature, according to her own proverb, as may keep her good-nature from being abused.
1826 *Letters of Malachi Malagrowther on the Proposed Change of Currency*, letter 1.

53 If I can but get the sulky Scottish spirit set up, the devil won't turn them.
1826 *Journal*, 25 Feb.

54 The Big Bow-wow strain I can do myself like any now going; but the exquisite touch, which renders ordinary commonplace things and characters interesting, from the truth of description and the sentiment, is denied to me.
1826 On Jane Austen. *Journal*, 14 Mar.

55 But if you *unscotch* us you will find us damned mischievous Englishmen.
1826 Letter to J W Croker, 19 Mar.

56 I would like to be there, were it but to see how the cat jumps. One knows nothing of the world, if you are absent from it so long as I have been.
1826 *Journal*, 7 Oct, expressing frustration and wonder at the machinations of London bureaucracy which prevented him accessing government papers for his *Life of Napoleon*.

57 Long life to thy fame and peace to thy soul, Rob Burns! When I want to express a sentiment which I feel strongly, I find the phrase in Shakespeare—or thee. The blockheads talk of my being like Shakespeare—not fit to tie his brogues.
1826 *Journal*, 11 Dec.

58 To the Lords of convention 'twas Claver'se who spoke,
'Ere the King's crown shall fall there are crowns to be broke;
So let each Cavalier who loves honour and me,
Come follow the bonnet of Bonny Dundee.'
1830 *The Doom of Devorgoil*, act 2, sc.2, 'Bonny Dundee', stanza 1.

59 No repose for Sir Walter but in the grave. Friends, don't let me expose myself—get me to bed—that's the only place.
1832 Quoted in John G Lockhart *Memoirs of the Life of Sir Walter Scott, Bart.* (1837–8). Scott had fallen asleep in his bath-chair while trying to write a few words.

60 Be a good man—be virtuous—be religious—be a good man. Nothing else will give you any comfort when you come to lie here.
1832 Last words, addressed to Lockhart, quoted in John G Lockhart *Memoirs of the Life of Sir Walter Scott, Bart.* (1837–8). Scott concluded by saying 'God bless you all.'

Scottish Metrical Psalms

61 The Lord's my shepherd, I'll not want.
He makes me down to lie
In pastures green: he leadeth me
the quiet waters by.
My soul he doth restore again:
and me to walk doth make
Within the paths of righteousness,
ev'n for his own name's sake.

Yea, though I walk in death's dark vale,
yet will I fear no ill:
For thou art with me; and thy rod
and staff me comfort still.
1650 Translation of Psalm 23:1–4.

62 God is our refuge and our strength,
in straits a present aid;
Therefore, although the earth remove,
we will not be afraid.
1650 Psalm 46:1–2.

63 How lovely is thy dwelling-place
O Lord of hosts, to me!
The tabernacles of thy grace
how pleasant, Lord, they be!
1650 Psalm 84:1.

64 All people that on earth do dwell,
Sing to the Lord with cheerful voice.
Him serve with mirth, his praise forth tell,
Come ye before him and rejoice.
Know that the Lord is God indeed;
Without our aid he did us make:

We are his folk, he doth us feed,
And for his sheep he doth us take.
1650 Psalm 100:1–3.

65 I to the hills will lift mine eyes,
from whence doth come mine aid.
My safety cometh from the Lord,
Who heav'n and earth hath made.
1650 Psalm 121:1–2.

Scribner, Charles, Jr 1921–95

US publisher, chairman of Charles Scribner's Sons (1977–8) and Scribner Book Companies from 1978. His autobiography is *In the Company of Writers: Life in Publishing* (1991).

66 Nowadays a sales conference resembles a Passion play: everybody is invited to participate and marvel at the drama.
1991 *In the Company of Writers: A Life in Publishing*.

Seaborg, Glenn 1912–99

US atomic scientist. His principal work was with Enrico Fermi's team, which achieved the first chain reaction in uranium-235 in 1942. He shared the 1951 Nobel prize for chemistry.

67 People must understand that science is inherently neither a potential for good nor for evil. It is a potential to be harnessed by man to do his bidding.
1964 Interview, 29 Sep.

Seacole, Mary c.1805–1884

Jamaican nurse and adventurer.

68 I wonder if the people of other countries are as fond of carrying with them everywhere their home habits as the English. I think not.
1857 *Wonderful Adventures of Mrs Seacole in Many Lands*.

Seaton, George *pseudonym of* George Stenius 1911–79

US screenwriter and director. He won Academy Awards for both *Miracle on 34th Street* (1947) and *The Country Girl* (1954).

69 For those who believe in God no explanation is necessary. For those who do not believe in God no explanation is possible.
1943 Prologue to *The Song of Bernadette*.

Seeger, Alan 1888–1916

US poet. He settled in Paris, and enlisted in the French Foreign Legion when World War I broke out. He was killed at the Battle of the Somme.

70 I have a rendezvous with Death
At some disputed barricade,
When Spring comes round with rustling shade
And apple blossoms fill the air.
I have a rendezvous with Death
When Spring brings back blue days and fair.
1916 'I Have a Rendezvous with Death', in the *North American Review*, Oct.

Seeger, Pete 1919–

US folk singer and songwriter.

71 Where have all the flowers gone?
1961 Title of song.

Seeley, Sir John Robert 1834–95

English historian, Professor of Modern History at Cambridge (1869). His *Ecce Homo* (1865), a popular life of Christ, caused much controversy. Other works include the authoritative *Life and Times of Stein* (1874), *Natural Religion* (1882) and *The Expansion of England* (1883).

72 We [the English] seem to have conquered and peopled half the world in a fit of absence of mind.
1883 *The Expansion of England*.

Segal, Erich 1937–

US novelist. He is known for the popular success of *Love Story*, which was both a bestselling novel and a major film.

73 Love means not ever having to say you're sorry.
1970 *Love Story*, ch.13.

Segovia, Andrés 1893–1987

Spanish guitarist. Influenced by the Spanish nationalist composers, he evolved a revolutionary guitar technique permitting the performance of a wide range of music, and many composers wrote works for him.

74 Electric guitars are an abomination, whoever heard of an electric violin? An electric cello? Or for that matter an electric singer?
Quoted in Rick Friedman *The Beatles: Words without Music* (1968).

Seibel, Cathy

Assistant US Attorney.

75 Just because you're rich doesn't mean you're not cheap.
1989 On the prosecution of hotel owner Leona Helmsley. In the *New York Times*, 24 Aug.

Seinfeld, Jerry 1954–

US comedian.

76 Everybody lies about sex. People lie during sex. If it weren't for lies, there'd be no sex.
1998 In the *New York Times*, 18 Dec.

Selden, John 1584–1654

English jurist, historian and antiquary. A member of the Long Parliament in 1640, he withdrew from politics after the execution of Charles I, of which he disapproved. His many writings on constitutional matters included *Titles of Honour* (1614), *Analecton Britannicon* (1615) and *History of Tithes* (1618). The most notable of his many tracts and treatises was the posthumous *Table Talk* (published 1689).

77 Every law is a contract between the king and the people and therefore to be kept.
Table Talk (published 1689).

78 Ignorance of the law excuses no man; not that all men know the law, but because 'tis an excuse every man will plead, and no man can tell how to confute him.
Table Talk (published 1689).

79 Those that govern most make least noise.
Table Talk (published 1689).

Self, Will 1961–

English novelist, columnist and critic. He was a cartoonist with the *New Statesman*, but turned to writing fiction. He was awarded the Geoffrey Faber Memorial Award in 1992.

80 No one ever complains if a great artist says that he was driven to create a masterpiece by a hunger for recognition and money. But a scientist? Well, he is meant to be disinterested, pure, his ambition merely to descry the cement of the universe. He isn't meant to use it to start laying his own patio.
1991 *The Quantity Theory of Insanity and Five Supporting Propositions*, 'The Quantity Theory of Insanity'.

81 I think in retrospect that all those 'alternative' modes of living were little more than exercises in arrested development.
1991 *The Quantity Theory of Insanity and Five Supporting Propositions*, 'The Quantity Theory of Insanity'.

82 I make no apology for preoccupying myself with architecture, television, conceptual art, restaurants and Jane Asher's cakes.
2001 *Feeding Frenzy.*

Sellar, W(alter) C(arruthers) and Yeatman, R(obert) J(ulian) 1898–1951, 1897–1968

British humorous writers.

83 [Gladstone] spent his declining years trying to guess the answer to the Irish Question. Unfortunately, whenever he was getting warm, the Irish secretly changed the question.
1930 *1066 and All That.*

84 The National Debt is a very Good Thing, and it would be dangerous to pay it off for fear of Political Economy.
1930 *1066 and All That.*

Sellers, Peter 1925–80

English actor and comedian. He came to prominence in the *Goon Show* on radio, but is perhaps best remembered as the incompetent French detective Inspector Clouseau in a series of films that began with *The Pink Panther* (1963).

85 If you ask me to play myself, I will not know what to do. I do not know who or what I am.
Attributed.

Selye, Hans 1907–83

Austrian-born Canadian endocrinologist, founder of Montreal's Institute of Experimental Medicine.

86 Stress is the state manifested by a specific syndrome which consists of all the nonspecifically inducted changes within a biologic system.
1956 *The Stress of Life.*

Selznick, David O(liver) 1902–65

US cinema mogul. He founded his own company in 1936, producing the screen adaptation of *Gone with the Wind* in 1939. Other successes include *Rebecca* (1940), *Duel in the Sun* (1946) and *A Farewell to Arms* (1957).

87 This is the story of the unconquerable fortress—the American home.
1944 *Since You Went Away*, opening line.

88 If they will only do their job…that is all that they are being overpaid for.
Of his stars, while filming *The Garden of Allah*. Quoted in Maria Riva *Marlene Dietrich* (1992).

Seneca *full name* Lucius Annaeus Seneca *called* the Younger c.4 BC–65 AD

Roman Stoic philosopher, statesman and tragedian, son of the orator Seneca the Elder. He tutored Nero and for a time enjoyed considerable political influence, but he lost favour and was forced to commit suicide. His works include the *Epistulae morales ad Lucilium*, the *Apocolocyntosis divi Claudii* (literally 'The Pumpkinification of the Divine Claudius'), and several tragedies.

89 *Utrumque enim vitium est, et omnibus credere et nulli.*
It is equally unsound to trust everyone and to trust no one.
Epistulae, 3.4

90 *Longum iter est per praecepta, breve et efficax per exempla.*
The way is long if one follows precepts, but short and helpful, if one follows patterns.
Epistulae, 6.5 (translated by R M Gummere).

91 *Homines dum docent discunt.*
Men learn while they teach.
Epistulae 7.8 (translated by R M Gummere).

92 *Vitae, non scholae discimus.*
It is for life, not for school that we learn.
Oral tradition based on Seneca's conclusion of a letter to Lucilius which says the opposite: 'Non vitae, sed scholae discimus', *Epistulae*, 106.12.

93 *Qui timide rogat, docet negare.*
Who makes timid requests, invites denial.
Phaedra, 593–4 (translated by F J Miller).

Senghor, Léopold Sédar 1906–2001

Senegalese poet who explored the theme of black African culture.

94 *J'ai choisi mon peuple noir peinant, mon peuple paysan, toute la race paysanne, par le monde.*
I chose my black people struggling, my country people, all country people, in the world.
1945 *Chants d'ombre*, 'Que m'accompagnent kára et balafong, 3'.

95 *Seul le rythme provoque le court-circuit poétique et transmue le cuivre en or, la parole en verbe.*
Only rhythm brings about a poetic short-circuit and transforms the copper into gold, the words into life.
1956 *Éthiopiques*, postface.

96 *Au contraire de l'Européen classique, le Négro-Africain ne se distingue pas de l'objet, il ne le tient pas à distance, il ne le regarde pas, il ne l'analyse pas… Il le touche, il le palpe, il le sent.*
Unlike the classical European, the Black-African does not distinguish himself from an object. He does not hold it at a distance, he does not look at it, he does not examine it… He touches it, he fingers it, he *feels* it.
1960 Au Congrès de l'Union nationale de la Jeunesse du Mali, Dakar.

97 *Danser, c'est découvrir et recréer, surtout lorsque la danse est danse d'amour. C'est, en tout cas, le meilleur mode de connaissance.*
To dance is to discover and to recreate, above all when the dance is the dance of love. It is the best mode of knowledge.
1960 Au Congrès de l'Union nationale de la Jeunesse du Mali, Dakar.

Senior, Nassau William 1790–1864

English economist. He stressed the importance of the last hour's work in the cotton factories and opposed the trade unions. His works include *On the Cost of Obtaining Money* (1830), *An Outline of the Science of Political Economy* (1836) and *Value of Money* (1840).

98 This barbarous feeling of nationality…has become the curse of Europe.
1850 *Diary*, 20 May.

Senna, Ayrton 1960–94

Brazilian Formula One driver. World champion in 1988, 1990, and 1991, he died after crashing during the San Marino Grand Prix.

99 To survive in grand prix racing, you need to be afraid. Fear is an important feeling. It helps you to race longer and live longer.
1994 In *The Times*, 3 May.
➤ *See Berger 79:93.*

Service, Robert William 1874–1958

English-born poet. He emigrated to Canada, and became famous for his popular ballads of life in the Canadian wilderness, which earned him the nickname 'The Canadian Kipling'. He also wrote several novels.

1 This is the law of the Yukon, that only the Strong shall thrive;
That surely the Weak shall perish, and only the Fit survive.
1907 *Songs of a Sourdough*, 'The Law of the Yukon'.

2 A promise made is a debt unpaid, and the trail has its own stern code.
1907 *Songs of a Sourdough*, 'The Cremation of Sam McGhee'.

3 Back of the bar, in a solo game, sat dangerous Dan McGrew,
And watching his luck was his light-o'-love, the lady that's known as Lou.
1907 *Songs of a Sourdough*, 'The Shooting of Dan McGrew'.

4 Ah! The clock is always slow;
It is later than you think.
1921 *Ballads of a Bohemian*, 'It Is Later Than You Think'.

5 When we, the Workers, all demand: What are WE fighting for?
Then we'll end that stupid crime, that devil's madness—War.
1921 *Ballads of a Bohemian*, 'Michael'.

Seuss, Dr *pseudonym of* ***Theodor Seuss Geisel*** 1904–91

US children's author and illustrator, remembered for his 'Beginner Books', intended to help teach reading, starting with *The Cat in the Hat* (1957).

6 We looked!
Then we saw him step in on the mat!
We looked!
And we saw him!
The Cat in the Hat!
1957 *The Cat in the Hat*.

7 You will see something new.
Two things. And I call them
Thing One and Thing Two.
1957 *The Cat in the Hat*.

8 Do you like green eggs and ham?
1960 *Green Eggs and Ham*.

Sévigné, Marie de Rabutin-Chantal, Marquise de 1626–96

French writer famed for her letters which recounted daily life at court and in her family. They were collected by her daughter and published in 1725.

9 *La grande amitié n'est jamais tranquille.*
Great friendship is never peaceful.
1671 Letter to Mme de Grignan, 16 Sep.

10 *Le temps vole et m'emporte malgré moi; j'ai beau vouloir le retenir, c'est lui qui m'entraîne; et cette pensée me fait grande peur: vous devinez à peu près pourquoi.*
Time flies and takes me with it despite my efforts; I'd like to hold it back, but it keeps dragging me along and this thought frightens me greatly: you can perhaps guess why.
1691 Letter to the Comte de Bussy-Rabutin, 12 Jul.

Sexton, Anne *née* ***Harvey*** 1928–74

US poet, lecturer, and writer of children's books. Her works include *To Bedlam and Part Way Back* (1962), *All My Pretty Ones* (1962), *Live or Die* (1966), for which she won a Pulitzer Prize (1967), and *The Death Notebooks* (1974). She committed suicide.

11 Go child, who is my sin and nothing more.
1962 *To Bedlam and Part Way Back*, 'Unknown Child in the Maternity Ward'.

12 Now I fold you down, my drunkard, my navigator,
my first lost keeper, to love or look at later.
1962 On photographs of her dead father. *All My Pretty Ones*, 'All My Pretty Ones'.

13 Whether you are pretty or not, I outlive you,
bend down my strange face to yours and forgive you.
1962 *All My Pretty Ones*, 'All My Pretty Ones'.

14 In a dream you are never eighty.
1962 *All My Pretty Ones*, 'Old'.

15 But suicides have a special language.
Like carpenters they want to know *which tools*.
They never ask *why build*.
1964 'Wanting To Die', dated 3 Feb. Collected in *Live or Die* (1966).

16 I was tired of being a woman,
tired of the spoons and the pots,
tired of my mouth and my breasts
tired of the cosmetics and the silks…
I was tired of the gender of things.
1966 *Live or Die*, 'Consorting with Angels'.

17 The sea is mother-death and she is a mighty female, the one who wins, the one who sucks us all up.
1971 Journal entry, 19 Nov, in *The Poet's Story*, 'A Small Journal'.

18 It doesn't matter who my father was; it matters who I remember he was.
1972 Journal entry, 1 Jan, in *The Poet's Story*, 'A Small Journal'.

19 The Awful Rowing Toward God.
1975 Title of book.

20 God owns heaven
but He craves the earth.
1975 *The Awful Rowing Toward God*, 'The Earth'.

Shaffer, Peter 1926–

English dramatist. His best-known plays include *Equus* (1973) and *Amadeus* (1979).

21 All my wife has ever taken from the Mediterranean—
from that whole vast intuitive culture—are four bottles
of Chianti to make into lamps.
1973 *Equus*, act 1, sc.18.

22 We keep saying old people are square. Then when they
aren't—we don't like it!
1973 *Equus*, act 2, sc.31.

Shakespeare, William 1564–1616

English poet, playwright and actor. He lived in Stratford-upon-Avon, the home of his wife and children, and in London, where he worked in the theatre, becoming England's greatest playwright. His influence on literature and language throughout the world has been immense. The dates of composition of many of the plays are uncertain. Line numbers conform to *The Oxford Shakespeare* (Oxford University Press, 1988).

23 Home-keeping youth have ever homely wits.
1590–1 Valentine. *The Two Gentlemen of Verona*, act 1, sc.1, l.2.

24 He was more than over-shoes in love.
1590–1 Proteus, of Lysander. *The Two Gentlemen of Verona*, act 1, sc.1, l.24.

25 I have no other but a woman's reason:
I think him so because I think him so.
1590–1 Lucetta, explaining her preference for Proteus. *The Two Gentlemen of Verona*, act 1, sc.2, l.23–4.

26 O, how this spring of love resembleth
The uncertain glory of an April day,
Which now shows all the beauty of the sun,
And by and by a cloud takes all away.
1590–1 Proteus. *The Two Gentlemen of Verona*, act 1, sc.3, l.84–7.

27 I was in love with my bed.
1590–1 Speed. *The Two Gentlemen of Verona*, act 2, sc.1, l.76.

28 What, gone without a word?
Ay, so true love should do. It cannot speak,
For truth hath better deeds than words to grace it.
1590–1 Proteus. *The Two Gentlemen of Verona*, act 2, sc.2, l.16–18.

29 A fine volley of words, gentlemen, and quickly shot off.
1590–1 Silvia to Thurio and Valentine. *The Two Gentlemen of Verona*, act 2, sc.4, l.32.

30 When I was sick, you gave me bitter pills,
And I must minister the like to you.
1590–1 Proteus to Valentine. *The Two Gentlemen of Verona*, act 2, sc.4, l.147–8.

31 For love, thou know'st, is full of jealousy.
1590–1 Valentine. *The Two Gentlemen of Verona*, act 2, sc.4, l.175.

32 As one nail by strength drives out another,
So the remembrance of my former love
Is by a newer object quite forgotten.
1590–1 Proteus. *The Two Gentlemen of Verona*, act 2, sc.4, l.191–3.

33 Didst thou but know the inly touch of love
Thou wouldst as soon go kindle fire with snow
As seek to quench the fire of love with words.
1590–1 Julia to Lucetta. *The Two Gentlemen of Verona*, act 2, sc.7, l.18–20.

34 Win her with gifts if she respects not words.
Dumb jewels often in their silent kind
More than quick words do move a woman's mind.
1590–1 Valentine to Duke. *The Two Gentlemen of Verona*, act 3, sc.1, l.89–91.

35 Love is like a child
That longs for everything that he can come by.
1590–1 Duke to Valentine. *The Two Gentlemen of Verona*, act 3, sc.1, l.124–5.

36 Except I be by Silvia in the night
There is no music in the nightingale.
Unless I look on Silvia in the day
There is no day for me to look upon.
1590–1 Valentine. *The Two Gentlemen of Verona*, act 3, sc.1, l.178–81.

37 Slander Valentine
With falsehood, cowardice, and poor descent,
Three things that women highly hold in hate.
1590–1 Proteus to Duke. *The Two Gentlemen of Verona*, act 3, sc.2, l.31–3.

38 You must lay lime to tangle her desires
By wailful sonnets.
1590–1 Proteus to Thurio. *The Two Gentlemen of Verona*, act 3, sc.2, l.68–9.

39 Who is Silvia? What is she,
That all our swains commend her?
1590–1 Song. *The Two Gentlemen of Verona*, act 4, sc.2, l.38–9.

40 How use doth breed a habit in a man!
1590–1 Valentine. *The Two Gentlemen of Verona*, act 5, sc.4, l.1.

41 O heaven, were man
But constant, he were perfect!
1590–1 Proteus. *The Two Gentlemen of Verona*, act 5, sc.4, l.109–10.

42 My thoughts are whirlèd like a potter's wheel;
I know not where I am, nor what I do.
1592 Talbot. *Henry VI Part One*, act 1, sc.7, l.19–20.

43 I have heard it said, 'Unbidden guests
Are often welcomest when they are gone'.
1592 Bedford. *Henry VI Part One*, act 2, sc.2, l.55–6

44 Faith, I have been a truant in the law,
And never yet could frame my will to it,
And therefore frame the law unto my will.
1592 Suffolk. *Henry VI Part One*, act 2, sc.4, l.7–9.

45 We will bestow you in some better place,
Fitter for sickness and for crazy age.
1592 Talbot to Bedford. *Henry VI Part One*, act 3, sc.5, l.47–8.

46 I owe him little duty and less love.
1592 Somerset, of York. *Henry VI Part One*, act 4, sc.4, l.34.

47 Beauty's princely majesty is such,
Confounds the tongue, and makes the senses rough.
1592 Suffolk. *Henry VI Part One*, act 5, sc.5, l.26–7.

48 She's beautiful, and therefore to be wooed;
She is a woman, therefore to be won.
1592 Suffolk, of Margaret. *Henry VI Part One*, act 5, sc.5, l.34–5.

49 To be a queen in bondage is more vile
Than is a slave in base servility,
For princes should be free.
1592 Margaret. *Henry VI Part One*, act 5, sc.5, l.68–70.

50 Marriage is a matter of more worth
Than to be dealt in by attorneyship.
1592 Suffolk. *Henry VI Part One*, act 5, sc.7, l.55–6.

51 O Lord that lends me life,

Lend me a heart replete with thankfulness.
1592 Henry of Queen Margaret. *Henry VI Part Two*, act 1, sc.1, l.19–20.

52 All his mind is bent to holiness,
To number Ave-Maries on his beads.
1592 Queen Margaret of Henry. *Henry VI Part Two*, act 1, sc.3, l.58–9.

53 Could I come near your beauty with my nails,
I'd set my ten commandments in your face.
1592 Duchess to Queen Margaret. *Henry VI Part Two*, act 1, sc.3, l.144–5.

54 How irksome is this music to my heart!
When such strings jar, what hope of harmony?
1592 Henry. *Henry VI Part Two*, act 2, sc.1, l.59–60.

55 God shall be my hope,
My stay, my guide, and lantern to my feet.
1592 Henry. *Henry VI Part Two*, act 2, sc.3, l.24–5.

56 Smooth runs the water where the brook is deep,
And in his simple show he harbours treason.
1592 Suffolk to Henry. *Henry VI Part Two*, act 3, sc.1, l.53–4.

57 The fox barks not when he would steal the lamb.
1592 Suffolk. *Henry VI Part Two*, act 3, sc.1, l.55.

58 The commons, like an angry hive of bees
That want their leader, scatter up and down
And care not who they sting.
1592 Warwick to Henry. *Henry VI Part Two*, act 3, sc.2, l.125–7.

59 What stronger breastplate than a heart untainted?
Thrice is he armed that hath his quarrel just;
And he but naked, though locked up in steel,
Whose conscience with injustice is corrupted.
1592 Henry. *Henry VI Part Two*, act 3, sc.2, l.232–5.

60 Forbear to judge, for we are sinners all.
1592 Henry. *Henry VI Part Two*, act 3, sc.3, l.31.

61 The gaudy, babbling, and remorseful day
Is crept into the bosom of the sea.
1592 Captain. *Henry VI Part Two*, act 4, sc.1, l.1–2.

62 I say it was never merry world in England since gentlemen came up.
1592 Second rebel. *Henry VI Part Two*, act 4, sc.2, l.9–10.

63 There shall be in England seven halfpenny loaves sold for a penny, the three-hooped pot shall have ten hoops, and I will make it felony to drink small beer.
1592 Cade. *Henry VI Part Two*, act 4, sc.2, l.67–9.

64 The first thing we do let's kill all the lawyers.
1592 The Butcher. *Henry VI Part Two*, act 4, sc.2, l.78.

65 And Adam was a gardener.
1592 Cade. *Henry VI Part Two*, act 4, sc.2, l.133.

66 Thou hast most traitorously corrupted the youth of the realm in erecting a grammar school; and, whereas before, our forefathers had no other books but the score and the tally, thou hast caused printing to be used and, contrary to the King his crown and dignity, thou hast built a paper-mill. It will be proved to thy face that thou hast men about thee that usually talk of a noun and a verb and such abominable words as no Christian ear can endure to hear.
1592 Cade. *Henry VI Part Two*, act 4, sc.7, l.30–8.

67 Ignorance is the curse of God,
Knowledge the wing wherewith we fly to heaven.
1592 Saye. *Henry VI Part Two*, act 4, sc.7, l.72–3.

68 It is great sin to swear unto a sin,
But greater sin to keep a sinful oath.
1592 Salisbury to Henry. *Henry VI Part Two*, act 5, sc.1, l.180–1.

69 Farewell, faint-hearted and degenerate king,
In whose cold blood no spark of honour bides.
1592 Westmorland to Henry. *Henry VI Part Three*, act 1, sc.1, l.184–5.

70 O tiger's heart wrapped in a woman's hide!
1592 York to Margaret. *Henry VI Part Three*, act 1, sc.4, l.138.

71 Women are soft, mild, pitiful and flexible—
Thou stern, obdurate, flinty, rough, remorseless.
1592 York to Margaret. *Henry VI Part Three*, act 1, sc.4, l.142–3.

72 Many strokes, though with a little axe,
Hews down and fells the hardest-timbered oak.
1592 Messenger to Richard telling of his father York's death. *Henry VI Part Three*, act 2, sc.1, l.54–5.

73 To weep is to make less the depth of grief;
Tears, then, for babes—blows and revenge for me!
1592 Richard. *Henry VI Part Three*, act 2, sc.1, l.85–6.

74 This battle fares like to the morning's war,
When dying clouds contend with growing light,
What time the shepherd, blowing of his nails,
Can neither call it perfect day nor night.
1592 Henry. *Henry VI Part Three*, act 2, sc.5, l.1–4.

75 O God! Methinks it were a happy life
To be no better than a homely swain.
To sit upon a hill, as I do now;
To carve out dials quaintly, point by point.
1592 Henry. *Henry VI Part Three*, act 2, sc.5, l.21–4.

76 Thereby to see the minutes how they run:
How many makes the hour full complete,
How many hours brings about the day,
How many days will finish up the year,
How many years a mortal man may live.
1592 Henry. *Henry VI Part Three*, act 2, sc.5, l.25–9.

77 Gives not the hawthorn bush a sweeter shade
To shepherds looking on their seely sheep
Than doth a rich embroidered canopy
To kings that fear their subjects' treachery?
1592 Henry. *Henry VI Part Three*, act 2, sc.5, l.42–5.

78 The common people swarm like summer flies,
1592 Clifford. *Henry VI Part Three*, act 2, sc.6, l.8.

79 I know I am too mean to be your queen,
And yet too good to be your concubine.
1592 Lady Gray to Edward. *Henry VI Part Three*, act 3, sc.2, l.97–8.

80 Hasty marriage seldom proveth well.
1592 Richard of Gloucester. *Henry VI Part Three*, act 4, sc.1, l.18.

81 What fates impose, that men must needs abide.
It boots not to resist both wind and tide.
1592 Edward. *Henry VI Part Three*, act 4, sc.4, l.31–2.

82 Fearless minds climb soonest unto crowns.
1592 Richard of Gloucester. *Henry VI Part Three*, act 4, sc.8, l.62.

83 My pity hath been balm to heal their wounds.
1592 Henry. *Henry VI Part Three*, act 4, sc.10, l.9.

84 Lo now my glory smeared in dust and blood.
My parks, my walks, my manors that I had,
Even now forsake me, and of all my lands
Is nothing left me but my body's length.
1592 Warwick wounded and dying. *Henry VI Part Three*, act 5, sc.2, l.23–6.

85 Why, courage, then—what cannot be avoided
'Twere childish weakness to lament or fear.
1592 Margaret. *Henry VI Part Three*, act 5, sc.4, l.37–8.

86 Down, down to hell; and say I sent thee thither!
1592 Richard of Gloucester to Henry. *Henry VI Part Three*, act 5, sc.6, l.67.

87 Since the heavens have shaped my body so,
Let hell make crooked my mind to answer it.
I had no father, I am like no father;
I have no brother, I am like no brother;
And this word, 'love', which greybeards call divine,
Be resident in men like one another
And not in me—I am myself alone.
1592 Richard of Gloucester. *Henry VI Part Three*, act 5, sc.6, l.78–84.

88 Wilt thou draw near the nature of the gods?
Draw near them then in being merciful.
1592 Tamora to Titus. *Titus Andronicus*, act 1, sc.1, l.117–18.

89 Give me a staff of honour for mine age,
But not a sceptre to control the world.
1592 Titus. *Titus Andronicus*, act 1, sc.1, l.198–9.

90 Vengeance is in my heart, death in my hand,
Blood and revenge are hammering in my head.
1592 Aaron to Tamora. *Titus Andronicus*, act 2, sc.3, l.38–9.

91 Dost thou not perceive
That Rome is but a wilderness of tigers?
1592 Titus to Lucius. *Titus Andronicus*, act 3, sc.1, l.52–3.

92 To weep with them that weep doth ease some deal,
But sorrow flouted at is double death.
1592 Marcus. *Titus Andronicus*, act 3, sc.1, l.243–4.

93 My heart, all mad with misery,
Beats in the hollow prison of my flesh.
1592 Titus. *Titus Andronicus*, act 3, sc.2, l.9–10.

94 I'll to thy closet and go read with thee
Sad stories chancèd in the times of old.
1592 Titus to Lavinia. *Titus Andronicus*, act 3, sc.2, l.81–2.

95 I have heard my grandsire say full oft
Extremity of griefs would make men mad.
1592 Young Lucius. *Titus Andronicus*, act 4, sc.1, l.18–19.

96 The eagle suffers little birds to sing,
And is not careful what they mean thereby,
Knowing that with the shadow of his wings
He can at pleasure stint their melody.
1592 Tamora to Saturninus. *Titus Andronicus*, act 4, sc.4, l.83–6.

97 If one good deed in all my life I did
I do repent it from my very soul.
1592 Aaron. *Titus Andronicus*, act 5, sc.3, l.188–9.

98 Now is the winter of our discontent
Made glorious summer by this son of York.
1592–3 Richard. *Richard III*, act 1, sc.1, l.1–2.

99 Grim-visaged war hath smoothed his wrinkled front,
And now—instead of mounting barbèd steeds
To fright the souls of fearful adversaries—
He capers nimbly in a lady's chamber
To the lascivious pleasing of a lute.
But I, that am not shaped for sportive tricks
Nor made to court an amorous looking-glass.
1592–3 Richard. *Richard III*, act 1, sc.1, l.9–15.

1 Cheated of feature by dissembling nature,
Deformed, unfinished, sent before my time
Into this breathing world scarce half made up.
1592–3 Richard. *Richard III*, act 1, sc.1, l.19–21.

2 I in this weak piping time of peace
Have no delight to pass away the time,
Unless to spy my shadow in the sun
And descant on mine own deformity.
1592–3 Richard. *Richard III*, act 1, sc.1, l.24–7.

3 Teach not thy lip such scorn, for it was made
For kissing, lady, not for such contempt.
1592–3 Richard to Lady Anne. *Richard III*, act 1, sc.2, l.159–60.

4 Was ever woman in this humour wooed?
Was ever woman in this humour won?
1592–3 Richard. *Richard III*, act 1, sc.2, l.215–16.

5 Were you snarling all before I came,
Ready to catch each other by the throat,
And turn you all your hatred now on me?
1592–3 Margaret. *Richard III*, act 1, sc.3, l.185–7.

6 They that stand high have many blasts to shake them,
And if they fall they dash themselves to pieces.
1592–3 Margaret. *Richard III*, act 1, sc.3, l.257–8.

7 And thus I clothe my naked villainy
With odd old ends, stol'n forth of Holy Writ,
And seem a saint when most I play the devil.
1592–3 Richard. *Richard III*, act 1, sc.3, l.334–6.

8 O Lord! Methought what pain it was to drown,
What dreadful noise of waters in my ears,
What sights of ugly death within my eyes.
Methoughts I saw a thousand fearful wrecks,
Ten thousand men that fishes gnawed upon,
Wedges of gold, great ouches, heaps of pearl,
Inestimable stones, unvalued jewels,
All scattered in the bottom of the sea.
1592–3 Clarence, shortly before he is murdered. *Richard III*, act 1, sc.4, l.21–8.

9 Woe to that land that's governed by a child.
1592–3 Third Citizen. *Richard III*, act 2, sc.3, l.11.

10 So wise so young, they say, do never live long.
1592–3 Richard, aside. *Richard III*, act 3, sc.1, l.79.

11 Talk'st thou to me of 'ifs'? Thou art a traitor.—
Off with his head.
1592–3 Richard. *Richard III*, act 3, sc.4, l.75–6.

12 I am not in the giving vein today.
1592–3 Richard. *Richard III*, act 4, sc.2, l.119.

13 Thou cam'st on earth to make the earth my hell.
1592–3 Duchess of York to Richard. *Richard III*, act 4, sc.4, l.167.

14 True hope is swift, and flies with swallows' wings.
1592–3 Henry, Earl of Richmond. *Richard III*, act 5, sc.2, l.23.

15 The King's name is a tower of strength.
1592–3 Richard. *Richard III*, act 5, sc.3, l.12.

16 Give me another horse! Bind up my wounds!
Have mercy, Jesu!—Soft, I did but dream.
O coward conscience, how dost thou afflict me?
1592–3 Richard. *Richard III*, act 5, sc.5, l.131–3.

17 Richard loves Richard; that is, I am I.
1592–3 Richard. *Richard III*, act 5, sc.5, l.137.

18 My conscience hath a thousand several tongues,
And every tongue brings in a several tale,
And every tale condemns me for a villain.
1592–3 Richard. *Richard III*, act 5, sc.5, l.147–9.

19 There is no creature loves me,

And if I die no soul will pity me.
Nay, wherefore should they?—Since that I myself
Find in myself no pity to myself.
1592–3 Richard. *Richard III*, act 5, sc.5, l.154–7.

20 Methought the souls of all that I had murdered
Came to my tent, and every one did threat
Tomorrow's vengeance on the head of Richard.
1592–3 Richard on the eve of the Battle of Bosworth. *Richard III*, act 5, sc.5, l.158–60.

21 Conscience is but a word that cowards use,
Devised at first to keep the strong in awe.
Our strong arms be our conscience; swords, our law.
March on, join bravely! Let us to't, pell mell—
If not to heaven, then hand in hand to hell.
1592–3 Richard. *Richard III*, act 5, sc.6, l.39–43.

22 A thousand hearts are great within my bosom.
Advance our standards! Set upon the foes!
Our ancient word of courage, fair Saint George,
Inspire us with the spleen of fiery dragons.
Upon them! Victory sits on our helms!
1592–3 Richard. *Richard III*, act 5, sc.6, l.77–81.

23 A horse! A horse! My kingdom for a horse!
1592–3 Richard. *Richard III*, act 5, sc.7, l.7.

24 Slave, I have set my life upon a cast,
And I will stand the hazard of the die.
1592–3 Richard. *Richard III*, act 5, sc.7, l.9–10.

25 Frame your mind to mirth and merriment,
Which bars a thousand harms, and lengthens life.
1593 Messenger to Sly. *The Taming of the Shrew*, Induction 2, l.131–2.

26 Think'st thou, Hortensio, though her father be very rich, any man is so very a fool to be married to hell?
1593 Gremio. *The Taming of the Shrew*, act 1, sc.1, l.122–4.

27 There's small choice in rotten apples.
1593 Hortensio to Gremio. *The Taming of the Shrew*, act 1, sc.1, l.133–4.

28 I come to wive it wealthily in Padua;
If wealthily, then happily in Padua.
1593 Petruccio to Hortensio. *The Taming of the Shrew*, act 1, sc.2, l.74–5.

29 O this learning, what a thing it is!
1593 Gremio. *The Taming of the Shrew*, act 1, sc.2, l.157.

30 She is your treasure, she must have a husband.
I must dance barefoot on her wedding day,
And for your love to her lead apes in hell.
1593 Katherine. *The Taming of the Shrew*, act 2, sc.1, l.32–4.

31 I am rough, and woo not like a babe.
1593 Petruccio. *The Taming of the Shrew*, act 2, sc.1, l.137.

32 Good morrow, Kate, for that's your name, I hear.
1593 Petruccio. *The Taming of the Shrew*, act 2, sc.1, l.182.

33 You are called plain Kate,
And bonny Kate, and sometimes Kate the curst,
But Kate, the prettiest Kate in Christendom,
Kate of Kate Hall, my super-dainty Kate.
1593 Petruccio. *The Taming of the Shrew*, act 2, sc.1, l.185–8.

34 Your father hath consented
That you shall be my wife, your dowry 'greed on,
And will you, nill you, I will marry you.
1593 Petruccio to Kate. *The Taming of the Shrew*, act 2, sc.1, l.263–5.

35 We will have rings, and things, and fine array;
And kiss me, Kate. We will be married o' Sunday.
1593 Petruccio. *The Taming of the Shrew*, act 2, sc.1, l.319–20.

36 Preposterous ass, that never read so far
To know the cause why music was ordained!
Was it not to refresh the mind of man
After his studies or his usual pain?
1593 Lucentio to Hortensio. *The Taming of the Shrew*, act 3, sc.1, l.9–12.

37 Old fashions please me best. I am not so nice
To change true rules for odd inventions.
1593 Bianca to Hortensio. *The Taming of the Shrew*, act 3, sc.1, l.78–9.

38 Go, girl. I cannot blame thee now to weep.
For such an injury would vex a very saint.
1593 Baptista. *The Taming of the Shrew*, act 3, sc.2, l.27–8.

39 To me she's married, not unto my clothes.
1593 Petruccio. *The Taming of the Shrew*, act 3, sc.2, l.117.

40 He took the bride about the neck
And kissed her lips with such a clamorous smack
That at the parting all the church did echo.
1593 Gremio, of Petruccio. *The Taming of the Shrew*, act 3, sc.3, l.50–2.

41 This is a way to kill a wife with kindness.
1593 Petruccio. *The Taming of the Shrew*, act 4, sc.1, l.194.

42 How say you to a fat tripe finely broiled?
1593 Grumio to Katherine. *The Taming of the Shrew*, act 4, sc.3, l.20.

43 What, is the jay more precious than the lark
Because his feathers are more beautiful?
Or is the adder better than the eel
Because his painted skin contents the eye?
1593 Petruccio to Kate. *The Taming of the Shrew*, act 4, sc.3, l.173–6.

44 Your plainness and your shortness please me well.
1593 Baptista to Pedant. *The Taming of the Shrew*, act 4, sc.4, l.38.

45 Then God be blessed, it is the blessèd sun,
But sun it is not when you say it is not,
And the moon changes even as your mind.
What you will have it named, even that it is,
And so it shall be still for Katherine.
1593 Katherine. *The Taming of the Shrew*, act 4, sc.6, l.19–23.

46 Thy husband is thy lord, thy life, thy keeper,
Thy head, thy sovereign.
1593 Katherine. *The Taming of the Shrew*, act 5, sc.2, l.151–2.

47 I am ashamed that women are so simple
To offer war where they should kneel for peace.
1593 Katherine. *The Taming of the Shrew*, act 5, sc.2, l.166–7.

48 Come on, and kiss me, Kate.
1593 Katherine. *The Taming of the Shrew*, act 5, sc.2, l.185.

49 Hunting he loved, but love he laughed to scorn.
1593 *Venus and Adonis*, stanza 1, l.4.

50 Make use of time; let not advantage slip.
Beauty within itself should not be wasted.
Fair flowers that are not gathered in their prime
Rot, and consume themselves in little time.
1593 *Venus and Adonis*, stanza 22, l.129–32.

51 Bid me discourse, I will enchant thine ear.
1593 *Venus and Adonis*, stanza 25, l.145.

52 Love is a spirit all compact of fire,

Not gross to sink, but light, and will aspire.
1593 *Venus and Adonis*, stanza 25, l.149–50.

53 Affection is a coal that must be cooled;
Else, suffered, it will set the heart on fire.
1593 *Venus and Adonis*, stanza 65, l.387–8.

54 Dismiss your vows, your feignèd tears, your flatt'ry;
For where a heart is hard they make no batt'ry.
1593 *Venus and Adonis*, stanza 71, l.425–6.

55 Melodious discord, heavenly tune harsh sounding,
Ear's deep-sweet music, and heart's deep-sore wounding.
1593 *Venus and Adonis*, stanza 72, l.431–2.

56 Love comforteth, like sunshine after rain.
1593 *Venus and Adonis*, stanza 134, l.799.

57 Their copious stories, oftentimes begun,
End without audience, and are never done.
1593 *Venus and Adonis*, stanza 141, l.845–6.

58 I to the world am like a drop of water
That in the ocean seeks another drop.
1594 Antipholus of Syracuse. *The Comedy of Errors*, act 1, sc.2, l.35–6.

59 They say this town is full of cozenage,
As nimble jugglers that deceive the eye,
Dark-working sorcerers that change the mind,
Soul-killing witches that deform the body.
1594 Antipholus of Syracuse. *The Comedy of Errors*, act 1, sc.2, l.97–100.

60 Am I so round with you as you with me,
That like a football you do spurn me thus?
You spurn me hence, and he will spurn me hither.
If I last in this service, you must case me in leather.
1594 Dromio of Ephesus. *The Comedy of Errors*, act 2, sc.1, l.81–4.

61 They brought one Pinch, a hungry lean-faced villain,
A mere anatomy, a mountebank,
A threadbare juggler, and a fortune-teller,
A needy, hollow-eyed, sharp-looking wretch,
A living dead man.
1594 Antipholus of Ephesus. *The Comedy of Errors*, act 5, sc.1, l.238–42.

62 Respect and reason wait on wrinkled age!
1594 *The Rape of Lucrece*, stanza 39, l.275.

63 Thy beauty hath ensnared thee to this night.
1594 *The Rape of Lucrece*, stanza 70, l.485.

64 To show the beldame daughters of her daughter,
To make the child a man, the man a child,
To slay the tiger that doth live by slaughter,
To tame the unicorn and lion wild,
To mock the subtle in themselves beguiled,
To cheer the ploughman with increasing crops,
And waste huge stones with little water drops.
1594 *The Rape of Lucrece*, stanza 137, l.953–9.

65 Like an unpractised swimmer plunging still,
With too much labour drowns for want of skill.
1594 *The Rape of Lucrece*, stanza 157, l.1098–9.

66 It cannot be, I find,
But such a face should bear a wicked mind.
1594 *The Rape of Lucrece*, stanza 220, l.1539–40.

67 Let fame, that all hunt after in their lives,
Live registered upon our brazen tombs,
And then grace us in the disgrace of death
When, spite of cormorant devouring time,
Th'endeavour of this present breath may buy
That honour which shall bate his scythe's keen edge
And make us heirs of all eternity.
1594–5 King. *Love's Labour's Lost*, act 1, sc.1, l.1–7.

68 Study is like the heavens' glorious sun,
That will not be deep searched with saucy looks.
1594–5 Biron. *Love's Labour's Lost*, act 1, sc.1, l.84–5.

69 Small have continual plodders ever won,
Save base authority from others' books.
1594–5 Biron to King. *Love's Labour's Lost*, act 1, sc.1, l.86–7.

70 How well he's read, to reason against reading!
1594–5 King. *Love's Labour's Lost*, act 1, sc.1, l.94.

71 At Christmas I no more desire a rose
Than wish a snow in May's new-fangled shows.
1594–5 Biron. *Love's Labour's Lost*, act 1, sc.1, l.105–6.

72 Necessity will make us all forsworn.
1594–5 Biron. *Love's Labour's Lost*, act 1, sc.1, l.147.

73 A man in all the world's new fashion planted,
That hath a mint of phrases in his brain.
One who the music of his own vain tongue
Doth ravish like enchanting harmony.
1594–5 King, of Armado. *Love's Labour's Lost*, act 1, sc.1, l.162–5.

74 A child of our grandmother Eve, a female, or, for thy more sweet understanding, a woman.
1594–5 Armado's letter. *Love's Labour's Lost*, act 1, sc.1, l.255.

75 Assist me, some extemporal god of rhyme, for I am sure I shall turn sonnet. Devise wit, write pen, for I am for whole volumes, in folio.
1594–5 Armado. *Love's Labour's Lost*, act 1, sc.2, l.174–6.

76 This wimpled, whining, purblind, wayward boy,
This Signor Junior, giant dwarf, Dan Cupid,
Regent of love-rhymes, lord of folded arms,
Th'anointed sovereign of sighs and groans,
Liege of all loiterers and malcontents,
Dread prince of plackets, king of codpieces,
Sole imperator and great general
Of trotting paritors—O my little heart!
1594–5 Biron. *Love's Labour's Lost*, act 3, sc.1, l.174–81.

77 A giving hand, though foul, shall have fair praise.
1594–5 Princess. *Love's Labour's Lost*, act 4, sc.1, l.23.

78 O thou monster ignorance, how deformed dost thou look!
1594–5 Holofernes, to Dull. *Love's Labour's Lost*, act 4, sc.2, l.23.

79 He hath never fed of the dainties that are bred in a book.
He hath not eat paper, as it were, he hath not drunk ink.
1594–5 Nathaniel, of Dull. *Love's Labour's Lost*, act 4, sc.2, l.24–5.

80 The elegancy, facility, and golden cadence of poesy.
1594–5 Holofernes. *Love's Labour's Lost*, act 4, sc.2, l.123.

81 By heaven, I do love; and it hath taught me to rhyme, and to be melancholy.
1594–5 Biron. *Love's Labour's Lost*, act 4, sc.3, l.11.

82 What fool is not so wise
To lose an oath to win a paradise?
1594–5 Longueville. *Love's Labour's Lost*, act 4, sc.3, l.69–70.

83 Love's feeling is more soft and sensible
Than are the tender horns of cockled snails.
1594–5 Biron. *Love's Labour's Lost*, act 4, sc.3, l.313–14.

84 And when love speaks, the voice of all the gods
Make heaven drowsy with the harmony.

1594–5 Biron. *Love's Labour's Lost*, act 4, sc.3, l.320–1.

85 Never durst poet touch a pen to write
Until his ink were tempered with love's sighs.
1594–5 Biron. *Love's Labour's Lost*, act 4, sc.3, l.322–3.

86 From women's eyes this doctrine I derive.
They sparkle still the right Promethean fire.
They are the books, the arts, the academes
That show, contain, and nourish all the world,
Else none at all in aught proves excellent.
1594–5 Biron. *Love's Labour's Lost*, act 4, sc.3, l.326–30.

87 He draweth out the thread of his verbosity finer than the staple of his argument.
1594–5 Holofernes, of Armado. *Love's Labour's Lost*, act 5, sc.1, l.16.

88 O, they have lived long in the alms-basket of words.
I marvel thy master hath not eaten thee for a word,
for thou art not so long by the head as
honorificabilitudinitatibus. Thou art easier swallowed
than a flapdragon.
1594–5 Costard. *Love's Labour's Lost*, act 5, sc.1, l.38–42.

89 A light heart lives long.
1594–5 Catherine. *Love's Labour's Lost*, act 5, sc.2, l.18.

90 There's no such sport as sport by sport o'erthrown.
1594–5 Princess. *Love's Labour's Lost*, act 5, sc.2, l.152.

91 Taffeta phrases, silken terms precise,
Three-piled hyperboles, spruce affectation,
Figures pedantical—these summer flies
Have blown me full of maggot ostentation.
1594–5 Biron. *Love's Labour's Lost*, act 5, sc.2, l.406–10.

92 Mirth cannot move a soul in agony.
1594–5 Biron. *Love's Labour's Lost*, act 5, sc.2, l.843.

93 A jest's prosperity lies in the ear
Of him that hears it, never in the tongue
Of him that makes it.
1594–5 Rosaline. *Love's Labour's Lost*, act 5, sc.2, l.847–9.

94 When icicles hang by the wall,
And Dick the shepherd blows his nail,
And Tom bears logs into the hall,
And milk comes frozen home in pail;
When blood is nipped, and ways be foul,
Then nightly sings the staring owl:
Tu-whit, tu-whoo!—a merry note,
While greasy Joan doth keel the pot.
1594–5 Winter's song. *Love's Labour's Lost*, act 5, sc.2, l.897–904.

95 When all aloud the wind doth blow,
And coughing drowns the parson's saw,
And birds sit brooding in the snow,
And Marian's nose looks red and raw;
When roasted crabs hiss in the bowl.
1594–5 Winter's song. *Love's Labour's Lost*, act 5, sc.2, l.905–9.

96 Our doctors say this is no time to bleed.
1595 Richard. *Richard II*, act 1, sc.1, l.157.

97 I am disgraced, impeached, and baffled here,
Pierced to the soul with slander's venomed spear.
1595 Mowbray to Richard. *Richard II*, act 1, sc.1, l.170–1.

98 Lions make leopards tame.
1595 Richard. *Richard II*, act 1, sc.1, l.174.

99 The purest treasure mortal times afford
Is spotless reputation; that away,
Men are but gilded loam, or painted clay.
A jewel in a ten-times barred-up chest
Is a bold spirit in a loyal breast.
Mine honour is my life. Both grow in one.
Take honour from me, and my life is done.
1595 Mowbray to Richard. *Richard II*, act 1, sc.1, l.177–83.

1 As gentle and as jocund as to jest
Go I to fight. Truth hath a quiet breast.
1595 Mowbray. *Richard II*, act 1, sc.3, l.95–6.

2 This must my comfort be:
That sun that warms you here shall shine on me.
1595 Bolingbroke to Richard. *Richard II*, act 1, sc.3, l.138–9.

3 How long a time lies in one little word!
Four lagging winters and four wanton springs
End in a word: such is the breath of kings.
1595 Bolingbroke. *Richard II*, act 1, sc.3, l.206–8.

4 O, who can hold a fire in his hand
By thinking on the frosty Caucasus,
Or cloy the hungry edge of appetite
By bare imagination of a feast,
Or wallow naked in December snow
By thinking on fantastic summer's heat?
1595 Bolingbroke. *Richard II*, act 1, sc.3, l.257–62.

5 Methinks I am a prophet new-inspired,
And thus, expiring, do foretell of him.
His rash, fierce blaze of riot cannot last,
For violent fires soon burn out themselves.
1595 John of Gaunt, to Richard. *Richard II*, act 2, sc.1, l.31–4.

6 Small showers last long, but sudden storms are short.
1595 John of Gaunt. *Richard II*, act 2, sc.1, l.35.

7 With eager feeding food doth choke the feeder.
1595 John of Gaunt. *Richard II*, act 2, sc.1, l.37.

8 This royal throne of kings, this sceptred isle,
This earth of majesty, this seat of Mars,
This other Eden, demi-paradise,
This fortress built by nature for herself
Against infection and the hand of war,
This happy breed of men, this little world,
This precious stone set in the silver sea,
Which serves it in the office of a wall,
Or as a moat defensive to a house
Against the envy of less happier lands;
This blessèd plot, this earth, this realm, this England.
1595 John of Gaunt. *Richard II*, act 2, sc.1, l.40–50.

9 England that was wont to conquer others
Hath made a shameful conquest of itself.
1595 John of Gaunt. *Richard II*, act 2, sc.1, l.65–6.

10 Each substance of a grief hath twenty shadows,
Which shows like grief itself.
1595 Bushy. *Richard II*, act 2, sc.2, l.14–15.

11 Comfort's in heaven, and we are on the earth,
Where nothing lives but crosses, cares, and griefs.
1595 York. *Richard II*, act 2, sc.2, l.78–9.

12 Hope to joy is little less in joy
Than hope enjoyed.
1595 Northumberland. *Richard II*, act 2, sc.3, l.15–16.

13 I count myself in nothing else so happy
As in a soul rememb'ring my good friends.
1595 Bolingboke. *Richard II*, act 2, sc.3, l.46–7.

14 Things past redress are now with me past care.
1595 York. *Richard II*, act 2, sc.3, l.170.

15 Not all the water in the rough rude sea
Can wash the balm from an anointed king.
1595 Richard. *Richard II*, act 3, sc.2, l.50–1.

16 O, call back yesterday, bid time return,
And thou shalt have twelve thousand fighting men.
Today, today, unhappy day too late.
1595 Salisbury. *Richard II*, act 3, sc.2, l.65–7.

17 Time hath set a blot upon my pride.
1595 Richard. *Richard II*, act 3, sc.2, l.77.

18 Cry woe, destruction, ruin, loss, decay;
The worst is death, and death will have his day.
1595 Richard. *Richard II*, act 3, sc.2, l.98–9.

19 And nothing can we call our own but death,
And that small model of the barren earth
Which serves as paste and cover to our bones.
1595 Richard. *Richard II*, act 3, sc.2, l.148–50.

20 For God's sake, let us sit upon the ground,
And tell sad stories of the death of kings—
How some have been deposed, some slain in war,
Some haunted by the ghosts they have deposed,
Some poisoned by their wives, some sleeping killed,
All murdered. For within the hollow crown
That rounds the mortal temples of a king
Keeps Death his court; and there the antic sits,
Scoffing his state and grinning at his pomp,
Allowing him a breath, a little scene,
To monarchize, be feared, and kill with looks,
Infusing him with self and vain conceit,
As if this flesh which walls about our life
Were brass impregnable; and humoured thus,
Comes at the last, and with a little pin
Bores through his castle wall; and farewell, king.
1595 Richard. *Richard II*, act 3, sc.2, l.151–166.

21 O, that I were as great
As is my grief, or lesser than my name,
Or that I could forget what I have been,
Or not remember what I must be now!
1595 Richard. *Richard II*, act 3, sc.3, l.135–8.

22 What must the King do now? Must he submit?
The King shall do it. Must he be deposed?
The King shall be contented. Must he lose
The name of King? A God's name, let it go.
I'll give my jewels for a set of beads,
My gorgeous palace for a hermitage,
My gay apparel for an almsman's gown,
My figured goblets for a dish of wood,
My sceptre for a palmer's walking staff,
My subjects for a pair of carvèd saints,
And my large kingdom for a little grave.
1595 Richard. *Richard II*, act 3, sc.3, l.142–52.

23 Alack, why am I sent for to a king
Before I have shook off the regal thoughts
Wherewith I reigned? I hardly yet have learned
To insinuate, flatter, bow, and bend my knee.
Give sorrow leave awhile to tutor me
To this submission. Yet I well remember
The favours of these men. Were they not mine?
Did they not sometime cry, 'All hail!' to me?
So Judas did to Christ. But He in twelve
Found the truth in all but one; I, in twelve thousand,
none.
God save the King! Will no man say 'Amen'?
Am I both the priest and clerk? Well then, Amen.
1595 Richard. *Richard II*, act 4, sc.1, l.153–164.

24 You may my glories and my state depose,
But not my griefs; still am I king of those.
1595 Richard. *Richard II*, act 4, sc.1, l.182–3.

25 Mine eyes are full of tears; I cannot see.
And yet salt water blinds them not so much
But they can see a sort of traitors here.
Nay, if I turn mine eyes upon myself
I find myself a traitor with the rest.
1595 Richard. *Richard II*, act 4, sc.1, l.234–8.

26 I am sworn brother, sweet,
To grim necessity, and he and I
Will keep a league till death.
1595 Richard. *Richard II*, act 5, sc.1, l.20–1.

27 The love of wicked friends converts to fear;
That fear to hate.
1595 Richard. *Richard II*, act 5, sc.1, l.66–7.

28 Had not God, for some strong purpose steeled
The hearts of men, they must perforce have melted.
1595 York. *Richard II*, act 5, sc.2, l.34–5.

29 Say 'Pardon', king. Let pity teach thee how.
The word is short, but not so short as sweet;
No word like 'Pardon' for kings' mouths so meet.
1595 Duchess of York. *Richard II*, act 5, sc.3, l.115–16.

30 Thoughts tending to ambition, they do plot
Unlikely wonders: how these vain weak nails
May tear a passage through the flinty ribs
Of this hard world.
1595 Richard. *Richard II*, act 5, sc.5, l.18–21.

31 How sour sweet music is
When time is broke and no proportion kept.
So is it in the music of men's lives.
1595 Richard. *Richard II*, act 5, sc.5, l.42–4.

32 Mount, mount, my soul; thy seat is up on high,
Whilst my gross flesh sinks downward, here to die.
1595 Richard. *Richard II*, act 5, sc.5, l.111–12.

33 From forth the fatal loins of these two foes
A pair of star-crossed lovers take their life.
1595 Chorus. *Romeo and Juliet*, Prologue, l.5–6.

34 Alas that love, so gentle in his view,
Should be so tyrannous and rough in proof.
1595 Benvolio to Romeo. *Romeo and Juliet*, act 1, sc.1, l.166–7.

35 'Tis not hard, I think,
For men so old as we to keep the peace.
1595 Capulet. *Romeo and Juliet*, act 1, sc.2, l.2–3.

36 Such comfort as do lusty young men feel
When well-apparell'd April on the heel
Of limping winter treads.
1595 Capulet. *Romeo and Juliet*, act 1, sc.2, l.24–6.

37 Is love a tender thing? It is too rough,
Too rude, too boist'rous, and it pricks like thorn.
1595 Romeo. *Romeo and Juliet*, act 1, sc.4, l.25–6.

38 She is the fairies' midwife, and she comes
In shape no bigger than an agate stone
On the forefinger of an alderman,
Drawn with a team of little atomi
Athwart men's noses as they lie asleep.
1595 Mercutio. *Romeo and Juliet*, act 1, sc.4, l.55–9.

39 Her chariot is an empty hazelnut
Made by the joiner squirrel or old grub,
Time out o' mind the fairies' coachmakers.
And in this state she gallops night by night
Through lovers' brains, and then they dream of love.
1595 Mercutio. *Romeo and Juliet*, act 1, sc.4, l.68–72.

40 I talk of dreams,
Which are the children of an idle brain,
Begot of nothing but vain fantasy.
1595 Mercutio. *Romeo and Juliet*, act 1, sc.4, l.96–8.

41 You and I are past our dancing days.
1595 Capulet to his cousin. *Romeo and Juliet*, act 1, sc.5, l.31.

42 O, she doth teach the torches to burn bright!
It seems she hangs upon the cheek of night
As a rich jewel in an Ethiope's ear—
Beauty too rich for use, for earth too dear.
1595 Romeo of Juliet. *Romeo and Juliet*, act 1, sc.5, l.43–6.

43 Did my heart love till now? Forswear it, sight,
For I ne'er saw true beauty till this night.
1595 Mercutio. *Romeo and Juliet*, act 1, sc.5, l.51–2.

44 My only love sprung from my only hate!
Too early seen unknown, and known too late!
1595 Juliet. *Romeo and Juliet*, act 1, sc.5, l.137–8.

45 He jests at scars that never felt a wound.
But soft, what light through yonder window breaks?
It is the east, and Juliet is the sun.
1595 Romeo. *Romeo and Juliet*, act 2, sc.1, l.43–5.

46 O, speak again, bright angel; for thou art
As glorious to this night, being o'er my head,
As is a wingèd messenger of heaven.
1595 Romeo of Juliet. *Romeo and Juliet*, act 2, sc.1, l.68–70.

47 O Romeo, Romeo, wherefore art thou Romeo?
Deny thy father and refuse thy name,
Or if thou will not, be but sworn my love,
And I'll no longer be a Capulet.
1595 Juliet. *Romeo and Juliet*, act 2, sc.1, l.75–8.

48 What's in a name? That which we call a rose
By any other word would smell as sweet.
1595 Juliet. *Romeo and Juliet*, act 2, sc.1, l.85–6.

49 Call me but love and I'll be new baptized.
Henceforth I never will be Romeo.
1595 Romeo. *Romeo and Juliet*, act 2, sc.1, l.93–4.

50 If thou think'st I am too quickly won,
I'll frown and be perverse and say thee nay,
So thou wilt woo.
1595 Juliet. *Romeo and Juliet*, act 2, sc.1, l.137–9.

51 O swear not by the moon, th'inconstant moon
That monthly changes in her circled orb,
Lest that thy love prove likewise variable.
1595 Juliet. *Romeo and Juliet*, act 2, sc.1, l.151–3.

52 My bounty is as boundless as the sea,
My love as deep. The more I give to thee
The more I have, for both are infinite.
1595 Juliet. *Romeo and Juliet*, act 2, sc.1, l.175–7.

53 Parting is such sweet sorrow
That I shall say good-night till it be morrow.
1595 Juliet. *Romeo and Juliet*, act 2, sc.1, l.229–30.

54 Sleep dwell upon thine eyes, peace in thy breast.
1595 Romeo. *Romeo and Juliet*, act 2, sc.1, l.231.

55 O mickle is the powerful grace that lies
In plants, herbs, stones, and their true qualities,
For nought so vile that on the earth doth live
But to the earth some special good doth give.
1595 Friar Laurence. *Romeo and Juliet*, act 2, sc.2, l.15–18.

56 Virtue itself turns vice, being misapplied,
And vice sometime's by action dignified.
1595 Friar Laurence. *Romeo and Juliet*, act 2, sc.2, l.21–2.

57 Care keeps his watch in every old man's eye.
1595 Friar Laurence to Romeo. *Romeo and Juliet*, act 2, sc.2, l.35.

58 Wisely and slow. They stumble that run fast.
1595 Friar Laurence to Romeo. *Romeo and Juliet*, act 2, sc.2, l.94.

59 A gentleman, Nurse, that loves to hear himself talk, and will speak more in a minute than he will stand to in a month.
1595 Romeo. *Romeo and Juliet*, act 2, sc.3, l.138–9.

60 These violent delights have violent ends.
1595 Friar Laurence. *Romeo and Juliet*, act 2, sc.5, l.9.

61 Thy head is as full of quarrels as an egg is full of meat.
1595 Mercutio to Benvolio. *Romeo and Juliet*, act 3, sc.1, l.20.

62 A plague o' both your houses.
They have made worms' meat of me.
1595 Mercutio, dying stabbed by Tybalt. *Romeo and Juliet*, act 3, sc.1, l.106–7.

63 Come, civil night,
Thou sober-suited matron all in black.
1595 Juliet. *Romeo and Juliet*, act 3, sc.2, l.10–11.

64 So tedious is this day
As is the night before some festival
To an impatient child that hath new robes
And may not wear them.
1595 Juliet. *Romeo and Juliet*, act 3, sc.2, l.28–31.

65 Steal immortal blessing from her lips.
1595 Romeo. *Romeo and Juliet*, act 3, sc.3, l.37.

66 Hang up philosophy!
Unless philosophy can make a Juliet.
1595 Romeo. *Romeo and Juliet*, act 3, sc.3, l.57–8.

67 A joy past joy calls out on me.
1595 Romeo. *Romeo and Juliet*, act 3, sc.3, l.172.

68 It was the nightingale, and not the lark,
That pierced the fear-full hollow of thine ear.
Nightly she sings on yon pom'granate tree.
1595 Juliet to Romeo. *Romeo and Juliet*, act 3, sc.5, l.2–4.

69 Night's candles are burnt out, and jocund day
Stands tiptoe on the misty mountaintops.
I must be gone and live, or stay and die.
1595 Romeo to Juliet. *Romeo and Juliet*, act 3, sc.5, l.9–11.

70 O, fortune, fortune, all men call thee fickle.
1595 Juliet. *Romeo and Juliet*, act 3, sc.5, l.60.

71 Mistress minion, you,
Thank me no thankings, nor proud me no prouds,
But fettle your fine joints 'gainst Thursday next
To go with Paris to Saint Peter's Church,
Or I will drag thee on a hurdle thither.
Out, you green-sickness carrion! Out, you baggage,
You tallow-face!
1595 Capulet, to Juliet, ordering her marriage to Paris. *Romeo and Juliet*, act 3, sc.5, l.151–7.

72 Is there no pity sitting in the clouds,
That sees into the bottom of my grief?
1595 Juliet. *Romeo and Juliet*, act 3, sc.5, l.196–7.

73 I think it best you married with the County.
O, he's a lovely gentleman!
Romeo's a dishclout to him.
1595 Nurse to Juliet. *Romeo and Juliet*, act 3, sc.5, l.217–19.

74 'Tis an ill cook that cannot lick his own fingers.
1595 Servingman to Capulet. *Romeo and Juliet*, act 4, sc.2, l.6.

75 I have a faint cold fear thrills through my veins
That almost freezes up the heat of life.
1595 Juliet. *Romeo and Juliet*, act 4, sc.3, l.15–16.

76 Out, alas, she's cold.
Her blood is settled, and her joints are stiff.
Life and these lips have long been separated.
Death lies on her like an untimely frost
Upon the sweetest flower of all the field.
1595 Capulet, of Juliet, as she feigns death. *Romeo and Juliet*, act 4, sc.4, l.52–6.

77 She's not well married that lives married long,
But she's best married that dies married young.
1595 Friar Laurence. *Romeo and Juliet*, act 4, sc.4, l.104–5.

78 I dreamt my lady came and found me dead—
Strange dream, that gives a dead man leave to think!—
And breathed such life with kisses in my lips
That I revived and was an emperor.
1595 Romeo. *Romeo and Juliet*, act 5, sc.1, l.6–9.

79 Art thou so bare and full of wretchedness,
And fear'st to die? Famine is in thy cheeks,
Need and oppression starveth in thy eyes,
Contempt and beggary hangs upon thy back.
The world is not thy friend, nor the world's law.
1595 Romeo to Apothecary. *Romeo and Juliet*, act 5, sc.1, l.68–72.

80 Give me thy hand,
One writ with me in sour misfortune's book.
1595 Romeo to Paris, whom he has just killed. *Romeo and Juliet*, act 5, sc.3, l.81–2.

81 Here, here will I remain
With worms that are thy chambermaids. O, here
Will I set up my everlasting rest,
And shake the yoke of inauspicious stars
From this world-wearied flesh.
1595 Romeo. *Romeo and Juliet*, act 5, sc.3, l.108–12.

82 Never was a story of more woe
Than this of Juliet and her Romeo.
1595 Prince. *Romeo and Juliet*, act 5, sc.3, l.308–9.

83 To you your father should be as a god.
1595 Theseus to Hermia. *A Midsummer Night's Dream*, act 1, sc.1, l.47.

84 The course of true love never did run smooth.
1595 Lysander to Hermia. *A Midsummer Night's Dream*, act 1, sc.1, l.134.

85 Your eyes are lodestars, and your tongue's sweet air
More tuneable than lark to shepherd's ear
When wheat is green, when hawthorn buds appear.
1595 Helena. *A Midsummer Night's Dream*, act 1, sc.1, l.183–5.

86 Love looks not with the eyes, but with the mind,
And therefore is winged Cupid painted blind.
1595 Helena. *A Midsummer Night's Dream*, act 1, sc.1, l.234–5.

87 Marry, our play is The Most Lamentable Comedy and Most Cruel Death of Pyramus and Thisbe.
1595 Quince. *A Midsummer Night's Dream*, act 1, sc.2, l.11–12.

88 That will ask some tears in the true performing of it. If I do it, let the audience look to their eyes. I will move stones.
1595 Bottom. *A Midsummer Night's Dream*, act 1, sc.2, l.21–3.

89 Nay, faith, let not me play a woman. I have a beard coming.
1595 Flute, on his reluctance to act the role of Thisbe. *A Midsummer Night's Dream*, act 1, sc.2, l.43–4.

90 SNUG: Have you the lion's part written? Pray you, if it be, give it me; for I am slow of study.
QUINCE: You may do it extempore, for it is nothing but roaring.
BOTTOM: Let me play the lion too. I will roar that I will do any man's heart good to hear me. I will roar that I will make the Duke say 'Let him roar again; let him roar again'.
1595 *A Midsummer Night's Dream*, act 1, sc.2, l.62–69.

91 I will roar you as gently as any sucking dove. I will roar you an 'twere any nightingale.
1595 Bottom. *A Midsummer Night's Dream*, act 1, sc.2, l.77–8.

92 Over hill, over dale,
Thorough bush, thorough brier,
Over park, over pale,
Thorough flood, thorough fire:
I do wander everywhere
Swifter than the moon's sphere,
And I serve the Fairy Queen
To dew her orbs upon the green.
The cowslips tall her pensioners be.
In their gold coats spots you see;
Those be rubies, fairy favours;
In those freckles live their savours.
I must go seek some dewdrops here,
And hang a pearl in every cowslip's ear.
1595 Fairy. *A Midsummer Night's Dream*, act 2, sc.1, l.2–15.

93 Ill met by moonlight, proud Titania
1595 Oberon. *A Midsummer Night's Dream*, act 2, sc.1, l.60.

94 Yet marked I where the bolt of Cupid fell.
It fell upon a little western flower—
Before, milk-white; now, purple with love's wound—
And maidens call it love-in-idleness.
1595 Oberon. *A Midsummer Night's Dream*, act 2, sc.1, l.165–8.

95 I'll put a girdle round about the earth
In forty minutes.
1595 Robin Goodfellow. *A Midsummer Night's Dream*, act 2, sc.1, l.175–6.

96 We cannot fight for love as men may do;
We should be woo'd, and were not made to woo.
1595 Helena. *A Midsummer Night's Dream*, act 2, sc.1, l.241–2.

97 I know a bank where the wild thyme blows,
Where oxlips and the nodding violet grows,
Quite overcanopied with luscious woodbine,
With sweet musk-roses, and with eglantine.
1595 Oberon. *A Midsummer Night's Dream*, act 2, sc.1, l.249–52.

98 You spotted snakes with double tongue,
Thorny hedgehogs, be not seen;
Newts and blindworms, do no wrong;
Come not near our Fairy Queen.
1595 First Fairy. *A Midsummer Night's Dream*, act 2, sc.2, l.9–12.

99 A surfeit of the sweetest things
The deepest loathing to the stomach brings.
1595 Lysander. *A Midsummer Night's Dream*, act 2, sc.2, l.143–4.

1 A lion among ladies is a most dreadful thing.
1595 Bottom. *A Midsummer Night's Dream*, act 3, sc.1, l.28.

2 FLUTE: (as Thisbe)
Most radiant Pyramus, most lily-white of hue,
Of colour like the red rose on triumphant brier;
Most bristly juvenile, and eke most lovely Jew,
As true as truest horse that yet would never tire:
I'll meet thee, Pyramus, at Ninny's tomb.
QUINCE: Ninus' tomb, man!
1595 *A Midsummer Night's Dream*, act 3, sc.1, l.87–92.

3 What angel wakes me from my flow'ry bed?
1595 Titania, of Bottom. *A Midsummer Night's Dream*, act 3, sc.1, l.122.

4 I pray thee, gentle mortal, sing again.
Mine ear is much enamoured of thy note;
So is mine eye enthrallèd to thy shape;
And thy fair virtue's force perforce doth move me
On the first view to say, to swear, I love thee.
1595 Titania. *A Midsummer Night's Dream*, act 3, sc.1, l.130–4.

5 I go, I go—look how I go,
Swifter than arrow from the Tartar's bow.
1595 Robin Goodfellow to Oberon. *A Midsummer Night's Dream*, act 3, sc.2, l.100–1.

6 Lord, what fools these mortals be!
1595 Robin Goodfellow. *A Midsummer Night's Dream*, act 3, sc.2, l.115.

7 Sleep, that sometimes shuts up sorrow's eye,
Steal me a while from mine own company.
1595 Helena. *A Midsummer Night's Dream*, act 3, sc.3, l.23–4.

8 I must to the barber's, monsieur, for methinks I am marvellous hairy about the face; and I am such a tender ass, if my hair do but tickle me I must scratch.
1595 Bottom. *A Midsummer Night's Dream*, act 4, sc.1, l.23–6.

9 Methinks I have a great desire to a bottle of hay. Good hay, sweet hay, hath no fellow.
1595 Bottom. *A Midsummer Night's Dream*, act 4, sc.1, l.32–3.

10 My Oberon, what visions have I seen!
Methought I was enamoured of an ass.
1595 Titania. *A Midsummer Night's Dream*, act 4, sc.1, l.75–6.

11 I have had a dream past the wit of man to say what dream it was.
1595 Bottom. *A Midsummer Night's Dream*, act 4, sc.1, l.202–3.

12 Lovers and madmen have such seething brains,
Such shaping fantasies, that apprehend
More than cool reason ever comprehends.
1595 Theseus. *A Midsummer Night's Dream*, act 5, sc.1, l.4–6.

13 The lunatic, the lover, and the poet
Are of imagination all compact.
One sees more devils than vast hell can hold:
That is the madman. The lover, all as frantic,
Sees Helen's beauty in a brow of Egypt.
The poet's eye, in a fine frenzy rolling,
Doth glance from heaven to earth, from earth to heaven,
And as imagination bodies forth
The forms of things unknown, the poet's pen
Turns them to shapes, and gives to airy nothing
A local habitation and a name.
Such tricks hath strong imagination
That if it would but apprehend some joy
It comprehends some bringer of that joy;
Or in the night, imagining some fear,
How easy is a bush supposed a bear!
1595 Theseus. *A Midsummer Night's Dream*, act 5, sc.1, l.7–22.

14 [LYSANDER] (reads)
'A tedious 'brief' scene of young Pyramus
And his love Thisbe: very tragical mirth.'
THESEUS:
'Merry' *and* 'tragical'? 'Tedious' *and* 'brief'?—
That is, hot ice and wondrous strange black snow.
1595 *A Midsummer Night's Dream*, act 5, sc.1, l.56–9.

15 A play there is, my lord, some ten words long,
Which is as brief as I have known a play;
But by ten words, my lord, it is too long.
1595 [Egeus]. *A Midsummer Night's Dream*, act 5, sc.1, l.61–3.

16 Anon comes Pyramus, sweet youth and tall,
And finds his trusty Thisbe's mantle slain;
Whereat with blade—with bloody, blameful blade—
He bravely broached his boiling bloody breast;
And Thisbe, tarrying in mulberry shade,
His dagger drew and died.
1595 Quince's prologue to Pyramus and Thisbe. *A Midsummer Night's Dream*, act 5, sc.1, l.143–8.

17 O dainty duck, O dear!
Thy mantle good,
What, stained with blood?
Approach, ye furies fell.
O fates, come, come,
Cut the thread and thrum,
Quail, crush, conclude, and quell.
1595 Bottom (as Pyramus). *A Midsummer Night's Dream*, act 5, sc.1, l.276–82.

18 His eyes were green as leeks.
1595 Flute (as Thisbe). *A Midsummer Night's Dream*, act 5, sc.1, l.330.

19 If we shadows have offended,
Think but this, and all is mended:
That you have but slumbered here,
While these visions did appear.
1595 Robin Goodfellow. *A Midsummer Night's Dream*, act 5, sc.2, l.1–4.

20 By how much unexpected, by so much
We must awake endeavour for defence,
For courage mounteth with occasion.
1596 Duke of Austria. *King John*, act 2, sc.1, l.80–2.

21 Well, whiles I am a beggar I will rail,
And say there is no sin but to be rich,
And being rich, my virtue then shall be
To say there is no vice but beggary.
Since kings break faith upon commodity,
Gain, be my lord, for I will worship thee.
1596 Bastard. *King John*, act 2, sc.1, l.594–9.

22 I will instruct my sorrows to be proud,
For grief is proud and makes his owner stoop.
1596 Constance. *King John*, act 2, sc.2, l.68–9.

23 My grief's so great
That no supporter but the huge firm earth
Can hold it up. Here I and sorrows sit.
1596 Constance. *King John*, act 2, sc.2, l.71–3.

24 Bell, book, and candle shall not drive me back
When gold and silver becks me to come on.
1596 Bastard. *King John*, act 3, sc.3, l.12–13.

25 Grief fills the room up of my absent child,
Lies in his bed, walks up and down with me.

1596 Constance. *King John*, act 3, sc.4, l.93–4.

26 Life is as tedious as a twice-told tale
Vexing the dull ear of a drowsy man.
1596 Louis the Dauphin. *King John*, act 3, sc.4, l.108–9.

27 When Fortune means to men most good,
She looks upon them with a threat'ning eye.
1596 Pandolf. *King John*, act 3, sc.4, l.119–20.

28 He that stands upon a slipp'ry place
Makes nice of no vile hold to stay him up.
1596 Pandolf. *King John*, act 3, sc.4, l.137–8.

29 Strong reasons make strange actions.
1596 Louis the Dauphin. *King John*, act 3, sc.4, l.182.

30 To gild refinèd gold, to paint the lily,
To throw a perfume on the violet,
To smooth the ice, or add another hue
Unto the rainbow, or with taper-light
To seek the beauteous eye of heaven to garnish,
Is wasteful and ridiculous excess.
1596 Salisbury. *King John*, act 4, sc.2, l.11–16.

31 The rich advantage of good exercise?
1596 Pembroke. *King John*, act 4, sc.2, l.60.

32 Think you I bear the shears of destiny?
Have I commandment on the pulse of life?
1596 John. *King John*, act 4, sc.2, l.91–2.

33 Entreat the north
To make his bleak winds kiss my parchèd lips,
And comfort me with cold. I do not ask you much;
I beg cold comfort.
1596 John to Prince Henry. *King John*, act 5, sc.7, l.39–42.

34 This England never did, nor never shall,
Lie at the proud foot of a conqueror.
1596 Bastard. *King John*, act 5, sc.7, l.112–3.

35 Now, by two-headed Janus,
Nature hath framed strange fellows in her time:
Some that will evermore peep through their eyes
And laugh like parrots at a bagpiper.
1596–7 Solanio. *The Merchant of Venice*, act 1, sc.1, l.50–3.

36 I hold the world but as the world, Graziano;
A stage where every man must play a part,
And mine a sad one.
1596–7 Antonio. *The Merchant of Venice*, act 1, sc.1, l.77–9.

37 Let me play the fool.
With mirth and laughter let old wrinkles come.
1596–7 Graziano to Antonio. *The Merchant of Venice*, act 1, sc.1, l.79–80.

38 O my Antonio, I do know of these
That therefore only are reputed wise
For saying nothing.
1596–7 Graziano. *The Merchant of Venice*, act 1, sc.1, l.95–7.

39 Fish not with this melancholy bait
For this fool gudgeon, this opinion.
1596–7 Graziano. *The Merchant of Venice*, act 1, sc.1, l.101–2.

40 For silence is only commendable
In a neat's tongue dried and a maid not vendible.
1596–7 Graziano. *The Merchant of Venice*, act 1, sc.1, l.111–2.

41 Graziano speaks an infinite deal of nothing, more than any man in all Venice. His reasons are as two grains of wheat hid in two bushels of chaff: you shall seek all day ere you find them, and when you have them they are not worth the search.
1596–7 Bassanio to Antonio. *The Merchant of Venice*, act 1, sc.1, l.114–18.

42 They are as sick that surfeit with too much as they that starve with nothing.
1596–7 Nerissa. *The Merchant of Venice*, act 1, sc.2, l.5–6.

43 I can easier teach twenty what were good to be done than to be one of the twenty to follow mine own teaching.
1596–7 Portia. *The Merchant of Venice*, act 1, sc.2, l.15–17.

44 The brain may devise laws for the blood, but a hot temper leaps o'er a cold decree.
1596–7 Portia. *The Merchant of Venice*, act 1, sc.2, l.17–18.

45 He doth nothing but talk of his horse.
1596–7 Portia. *The Merchant of Venice*, act 1, sc.2, l.39–40.

46 I fear he will prove the weeping philosopher when he grows old, being so full of unmannerly sadness in his youth.
1596–7 Portia, of her suitor the County Palatine. *The Merchant of Venice*, act 1, sc.2, l.47–9.

47 God made him, and therefore let him pass for a man.
1596–7 Portia, of her suitor M. le Bon. *The Merchant of Venice*, act 1, sc.2, l.54–5.

48 I will do anything, Nerissa, ere I will be married to a sponge.
1596–7 Portia. *The Merchant of Venice*, act 1, sc.2, l.95–6.

49 There is not one among them but I dote on his very absence, and I pray God grant them a fair departure.
1596–7 Portia, of the suitors. *The Merchant of Venice*, act 1, sc.2, l.106–8.

50 Yes, to smell pork, to eat of the habitation which your prophet the Nazarite conjured the devil into! I will buy with you, sell with you, talk with you, walk with you, and so following, but I will not eat with you, drink with you, nor pray with you.
1596–7 Shylock, invited to dine with Bassanio. *The Merchant of Venice*, act 1, sc.3, l.31–5.

51 How like a fawning publican he looks.
I hate him for he is a Christian.
1596–7 Shylock, of Antonio. *The Merchant of Venice*, act 1, sc.3, l.39–40.

52 The devil can cite Scripture for his purpose.
An evil soul producing holy witness
Is like a villain with a smiling cheek,
A goodly apple rotten at the heart.
O, what a goodly outside falsehood hath!
1596–7 Antonio. *The Merchant of Venice*, act 1, sc.3, l.97–101.

53 Signor Antonio, many a time and oft
In the Rialto you have rated me
About my moneys and my usances.
Still have I borne it with a patient shrug,
For suff'rance is the badge of all our tribe.
1596–7 Shylock. *The Merchant of Venice*, act 1, sc.3, l.105–109.

54 If thou wilt lend this money, lend it not
As to thy friends; for when did friendship take
A breed for barren metal of his friend?
1596–7 Antonio to Shylock. *The Merchant of Venice*, act 1, sc.3, l.130–3.

55 I like not fair terms and a villain's mind.
1596–7 Bassanio. *The Merchant of Venice*, act 1, sc.3, l.178.

56 It is a wise father that knows his own child.
1596–7 Lancelot. *The Merchant of Venice*, act 2, sc.2, l.72–3.

57 I'll take my leave of the Jew in the twinkling.
1596–7 Lancelot to Gobbo. *The Merchant of Venice*, act 2, sc.2, l.161–2.

58 Alack, what heinous sin is it in me
To be ashamed to be my father's child!
But though I am a daughter to his blood,
I am not to his manners.
1596–7 Jessica. *The Merchant of Venice*, act 2, sc.3, l.16–19.

59 Then it was not for nothing that my nose fell a-bleeding on Black Monday.
1596–7 Lancelot. *The Merchant of Venice*, act 2, sc.5, l.23–5.

60 There is some ill a-brewing towards my rest,
For I did dream of money-bags tonight.
1596–7 Shylock. *The Merchant of Venice*, act 2, sc.5, l.17–18.

61 But love is blind, and lovers cannot see
The pretty follies that themselves commit.
1596–7 Jessica. *The Merchant of Venice*, act 2, sc.6, l.36.

62 I will not choose what many men desire,
Because I will not jump with common spirits
And rank me with the barbarous multitudes.
1596–7 Aragon. *The Merchant of Venice*, act 2, sc.9, l.30–2.

63 O, that estates, degrees, and offices
Were not derived corruptly, and that clear honour
Were purchased by the merit of the wearer!
1596–7 Aragon. *The Merchant of Venice*, act 2, sc.9, l.40–2.

64 The ancient saying is no heresy;
Hanging and wiving goes by destiny.
1596–7 Nerissa. *The Merchant of Venice*, act 2, sc.9, l.81–2.

65 A day in April never came so sweet,
To show how costly summer was at hand.
1596–7 Messenger, of Bassanio's arrival. *The Merchant of Venice*, act 2, sc.9, l.92.

66 The bird was fledged; and then it is the complexion of them all to leave the dam.
1596–7 Solanio, of Jessica. *The Merchant of Venice*, act 3, sc.1, l.27.

67 Let him look to his bond.
1596–7 Shylock, of Antonio. *The Merchant of Venice*, act 3, sc.1, l.45–6.

68 Hath not a Jew eyes? Hath not a Jew hands, organs, dimensions, senses, affections, passions; fed with the same food, hurt with the same weapons, subject to the same diseases, healed by the same means, warmed and cooled by the same winter and summer as a Christian is? If you prick us do we not bleed? If you tickle us do we not laugh? If you poison us do we not die? And if you wrong us shall we not revenge? If we are like you in the rest, we will resemble you in that.
1596–7 Shylock. *The Merchant of Venice*, act 3, sc.1, l.54–63.

69 Let music sound while he doth make his choice.
Then if he lose he makes a swanlike end,
Fading in music.
1596–7 Portia to Bassanio. *The Merchant of Venice*, act 3, sc.2, l.43–5.

70 There is no vice so simple but assumes
Some mark of virtue on his outward parts.
1596–7 Bassiano, aside. *The Merchant of Venice*, act 3, sc.2, l.81–2.

71 Look on beauty
And you shall see 'tis purchased by the weight,
Which therein works a miracle in nature,
Making them lightest that wear most of it.
1596–7 Bassanio, aside. *The Merchant of Venice*, act 3, sc.2, l.88–91.

72 Thou gaudy gold,
Hard food for Midas, I will none of thee.
1596–7 Bassiano, aloud. *The Merchant of Venice*, act 3, sc.2, l.101–2.

73 An unlessoned girl, unschooled, unpractisèd,
Happy in this, she is not yet so old
But she may learn.
1596–7 Portia, of herself. *The Merchant of Venice*, act 3, sc.2, l.159–61.

74 Madam, you have bereft me of all words.
Only my blood speaks to you in my veins.
1596–7 Bassanio to Portia. *The Merchant of Venice*, act 3, sc.2, l.175–6.

75 Here are a few of the unpleasant'st words
That ever blotted paper.
1596–7 Bassanio, reading of Antonio's misfortunes. *The Merchant of Venice*, act 3, sc.2, l.249–50.

76 Let it serve for table-talk.
Then, howsome'er thou speak'st, 'mong other things
I shall digest it.
1596–7 Lorenzo. *The Merchant of Venice*, act 3, sc.5, l.83–5.

77 Some men there are love not a gaping pig,
Some that are mad if they behold a cat,
And others when the bagpipe sings i'th' nose
Cannot contain their urine.
1596–7 Shylock. *The Merchant of Venice*, act 4, sc.1, l.46–49.

78 We turned o'er many books together.
1596–7 Bellario's letter of recommendation for Portia (as Balthasar). *The Merchant of Venice*, act 4, sc.1, l.154–5.

79 The quality of mercy is not strained.
It droppeth as the gentle rain from heaven
Upon the place beneath. It is twice blest:
It blesseth him that gives, and him that takes.
1596–7 Portia. *The Merchant of Venice*, act 4, sc.1, l.181–4.

80 It is enthronèd in the hearts of kings;
It is an attribute to God himself,
And earthly power doth then show likest God's
When mercy seasons justice.
1596–7 Portia. *The Merchant of Venice*, act 4, sc.1, l.190–4.

81 A Daniel come to judgement, yea, a Daniel!
O wise young judge, how I do honour thee!
1596–7 Shylock, of the disguised Portia. *The Merchant of Venice*, act 4, sc.1, l.220–1.

82 Antonio, I am married to a wife
Which is as dear to me as life itself,
But life itself, my wife, and all the world
Are not with me esteemed above thy life.
I would lose all, ay, sacrifice them all
Here to this devil, to deliver you.
1596–7 Bassanio. *The Merchant of Venice*, act 4, sc.1, l.279–84.

83 Take thou thy pound of flesh.
1596–7 Portia to Shylock. *The Merchant of Venice*, act 4, sc.1, l.305.

84 Nay, take my life and all, pardon not that.
You take my house when you do take the prop
That doth sustain my house; you take my life
When do you take the means whereby I live.
1596–7 Shylock to the Duke. *The Merchant of Venice*, act 4, sc.1, l.371–4.

85 How sweet the moonlight sleeps upon this bank!

Here will we sit, and let the sounds of music
Creep in our ears.
1596–7 Lorenzo to Jessica. *The Merchant of Venice*, act 5, sc.1, l.54–6.

86 Look how the floor of heaven
Is thick inlaid with patens of bright gold.
There's not the smallest orb which thou behold'st
But in his motion like an angel sings.
1596–7 Lorenzo to Jessica. *The Merchant of Venice*, act 5, sc.1, l.58–61.

87 I am never merry when I hear sweet music.
1596–7 Jessica. *The Merchant of Venice*, act 5, sc.1, l.69.

88 The man that hath no music in himself,
Nor is not moved with concord of sweet sounds,
Is fit for treasons, stratagems, and spoils.
1596–7 Lorenzo. *The Merchant of Venice*, act 5, sc.1, l.83–5.

89 How far that little candle throws his beams—
So shines a good deed in a naughty world.
1596–7 Portia. *The Merchant of Venice*, act 5, sc.1, l.90–1.

90 A substitute shines brightly as a king
Until a king be by.
1596–7 Portia. *The Merchant of Venice*, act 5, sc.1, l.94–5.

91 The crow doth sing as sweetly as the lark
When neither is attended.
1596–7 Portia. *The Merchant of Venice*, act 5, sc.1, l.102–3.

92 A light wife doth make a heavy husband.
1596–7 Portia. *The Merchant of Venice*, act 5, sc.1, l.130.

93 O, that it could be proved
That some night-tripping fairy had exchanged
In cradle clothes our children where they lay.
1596–7 King Henry of his son, Harry, and Northumberland's son, Hotspur. *Henry IV Part One*, act 1, sc.1, l.85–7.

94 What a devil hast thou to do with the time of the day? Unless hours were cups of sack, and minutes capons, and clocks the tongues of bawds, and dials the signs of leaping-houses, and the blessed sun himself a fair hot wench in flame-coloured taffeta, I see no reason why thou shouldst be so superfluous to demand the time of the day.
1596–7 Prince Harry to Falstaff. *Henry IV Part One*, act 1, sc.2, l.6–12.

95 How now, how now, mad wag? What, in thy quips and thy quiddities? What a plague have I to do with a buff jerkin?
1596–7 Falstaff to Prince Harry. *Henry IV Part One*, act 1, sc.2, l.44–6.

96 I would to God thou and I knew where a commodity of good names were to be bought.
1596–7 Falstaff. *Henry IV Part One*, act 1, sc.2, l.82–3.

97 'Tis my vocation, Hal. 'Tis no sin for a man to labour in his vocation.
1596–7 Falstaff, of stealing. *Henry IV Part One*, act 1, sc.2, l.104–5.

98 What says Monsieur Remorse? What says Sir John, sack-and-sugar Jack? How agrees the devil and thee about thy soul, that thou soldest him on Good Friday last, for a cup of Madeira and a cold capon's leg?
1596–7 Poins to Falstaff. *Henry IV Part One*, act 1, sc.2, l.111–15.

99 He was never yet a breaker of proverbs: he will give the devil his due.
1596–7 Prince Harry. *Henry IV Part One*, act 1, sc.2, l.117–8.

1 He made me mad
To see him shine so brisk, and smell so sweet,
And talk so like a waiting gentlewoman
Of guns, and drums, and wounds, God save the mark!
And telling me the sovereign'st thing on earth
Was parmacity for an inward bruise,
And that it was great pity, so it was,
This villainous saltpetre should be digged
Out of the bowels of the harmless earth,
Which many a good tall fellow had destroyed
So cowardly, and but for these vile guns
He would himself have been a soldier.
1596–7 Hotspur. *Henry IV Part One*, act 1, sc.3, l.52–63.

2 To put down Richard, that sweet lovely rose,
And plant this thorn, this canker, Bolingbroke?
1596–7 Hotspur. *Henry IV Part One*, act 1, sc.3, l.173–4.

3 If he fall in, good night, or sink or swim.
1596–7 Hotspur. *Henry IV Part One*, act 1, sc.3, l.192.

4 —O, the blood more stirs
To rouse a lion than to start a hare!
1596–7 Hotspur. *Henry IV Part One*, act 1, sc.3, l.195–6

5 By heaven, methinks it were an easy leap
To pluck bright honour from the pale-faced moon,
Or dive into the bottom of the deep,
Where fathom-line could never touch the ground,
And pluck up drownèd honour by the locks.
1596–7 Hotspur. *Henry IV Part One*, act 1, sc.3, l.199–203.

6 I am joined with no foot-landrakers, no longstaff sixpenny strikers, none of these mad mustachio purple-hued maltworms, but with nobility and tranquillity, burgomasters and great 'oyez'-ers; such as can hold in, such as will strike sooner than speak, and speak sooner than drink, and drink sooner than pray.
1596–7 Gadshill. *Henry IV Part One*, act 2, sc.1, l.73–8.

7 I am bewitched with the rogue's company. If the rascal have not given me medicines to make me love him, I'll be hanged.
1596–7 Falstaff, of Prince Harry. *Henry IV Part One*, act 2, sc.2, l.17–20.

8 A plague upon't when thieves cannot be true one to another.
1596–7 Falstaff. *Henry IV Part One*, act 2, sc.2, l.27–8.

9 Hang thyself in thine own heir-apparent garters!
1596–7 Falstaff to Prince Harry. *Henry IV Part One*, act 2, sc.2, l.43.

10 Out of this nettle danger we pluck this flower safety.
1596–7 Hotspur. *Henry IV Part One*, act 2, sc.4, l.9–10.

11 Constant you are,
But yet a woman; and for secrecy
No lady closer, for I well believe
Thou wilt not utter what thou dost not know.
1596–7 Hotspur to Kate. *Henry IV Part One*, act 2, sc.4, l.105–8.

12 I am not yet of Percy's mind, the Hotspur of the North—he that kills me some six or seven dozen of Scots at a breakfast, washes his hands, and says to his wife, 'Fie upon this quiet life! I want work.'
1596–7 Prince Harry. *Henry IV Part One*, act 2, sc.5, l.102–6.

13 There lives not three good men unhanged in England, and one of them is fat and grows old.
1596–7 Falstaff, of himself. *Henry IV Part One*, act 2, sc.5, l.130–1.

14 Give you a reason on compulsion? If reasons were as

plentiful as blackberries, I would give no man a reason upon compulsion.
1596–7 Falstaff. *Henry IV Part One*, act 2, sc.5, l.242–4.

15 PRINCE HARRY: This sanguine coward, this bed-presser, this horse-backbreaker, this huge hill of flesh—
SIR JOHN: 'Sblood, you starveling, you elf-skin, you dried neat's tongue, you bull's pizzle, you stock-fish—O, for breath to utter what is like thee!—you tailor's yard, you sheath, you bow-case, you vile standing tuck.
1596–7 *Henry IV Part One*, act 2, sc.5, l.245–52.

16 SIR JOHN: Sweet Jack Oldcastle, kind Jack Oldcastle, true Jack Oldcastle, valiant Jack Oldcastle, and therefore more valiant being, as he is, old Jack Oldcastle
Banish not him thy Harry's company,
Banish not him thy Harry's company.
Banish plump Jack, and banish all the world.
PRINCE HARRY: I do; I will.
1596–7 Falstaff. *Henry IV Part One*, act 2, sc.5, l.480–6.

17 I can teach thee, coz, to shame the devil,
By telling truth: 'Tell truth, and shame the devil'.
1596–7 Hotspur to Glyndwr. *Henry IV Part One*, act 3, sc.1, l.55–6.

18 Mincing poetry.
'Tis like the forced gait of a shuffling nag.
1596–7 Hotspur. *Henry IV Part One*, act 3, sc.1, l.130–1.

19 I understand thy kisses, and thou mine,
And that's a feeling disputation.
1596–7 Mortimer to his wife. *Henry IV Part One*, act 3, sc.1, l.200–1.

20 Now I perceive the devil understands Welsh;
And 'tis no marvel, he is so humorous.
1596–7 Hotspur. *Henry IV Part One*, act 3, sc.1, l.226–7.

21 Swear me, Kate, like a lady as thou art,
A good mouth-filling oath.
1596–7 Hotspur. *Henry IV Part One*, act 3, sc.1, l.249–50.

22 Do thou amend thy face, and I'll amend my life.
1596–7 Falstaff to Bardolph. *Henry IV Part One*, act 3, sc.3, l.23.

23 Thou knowest in the state of innocency Adam fell, and what should poor Jack Oldcastle do in the days of villainy? Thou seest I have more flesh than another man, and therefore more frailty.
1596–7 Falstaff. *Henry IV Part One*, act 3, sc.3, l.165–7.

24 I am as vigilant as a cat to steal cream.
1596–7 Falstaff. *Henry IV Part One*, act 4, sc.2, l.58–9.

25 Rebellion lay in his way, and he found it.
1596–7 Falstaff, of Worcester. *Henry IV Part One*, act 5, sc.1, l.28.

26 I would 'twere bed-time, Hal, and all well.
1596–7 Falstaff. *Henry IV Part One*, act 5, sc.1, l.125.

27 Honour pricks me on. Yea, but how if honour prick me off when I come on? How then?
1596–7 Falstaff. *Henry IV Part One*, act 5, sc.1, l.129–131.

28 What is honour? A word.
1596–7 Flastaff. *Henry IV Part One*, act 5, sc.1, l.133–4.

29 Who hath it [honour]? He that died o' Wednesday.
1596–7 Falstaff. *Henry IV Part One*, act 5, sc.1, l.135–6.

30 Treason is but trusted like the fox,
Who, ne'er so tame, so cherished and locked up,
Will have a wild trick of his ancestors.
1596–7 Worcester. *Henry IV Part One*, act 5, sc.2, l.9–11.

31 O gentlemen, the time of life is short.
To spend that shortness basely were too long
If life did ride upon a dial's point,
Still ending at the arrival of an hour.
1596–7 Hotspur. *Henry IV Part One*, act 5, sc.2, l.81–4.

32 Sound all the lofty instruments of war,
And by that music let us all embrace,
For, heaven to earth, some of us never shall
A second time do such a courtesy.
1596–7 Hotspur. *Henry IV Part One*, act 5, sc.2, l.97–100.

33 I am as hot as molten lead, and as heavy too.
1596–7 Falstaff. *Henry IV Part One*, act 5, sc.3, l.33–4.

34 Time, that takes survey of all the world,
Must have a stop.
1596–7 Hotspur. *Henry IV Part One*, act 5, sc.4, l.81–2.

35 Fare thee well, great heart.
Ill-weaved ambition, how much art thou shrunk!
When that this body did contain a spirit,
A kingdom for it was too small a bound,
But now two paces of the vilest earth
Is room enough.
1596–7 Prince Harry, of Hotspur. *Henry IV Part One*, act 5, sc.4, l.86–91.

36 The better part of valour is discretion, in the which better part I have saved my life.
1596–7 Falstaff. *Henry IV Part One*, act 5, sc.4, l.118–20.

37 In poison there is physic; and these news,
Having been well, that would have made me sick,
Being sick, have in some measure made me well.
1597–8 Northumberland. *Henry IV Part Two*, act 1, sc.1, l.137–9.

38 I am not only witty in myself, but the cause that wit is in other men.
1597–8 Falstaff. *Henry IV Part Two*, act 1, sc.2, l.9–10.

39 Your lordship, though not clean past your youth, hath yet some smack of age in you, some relish of the saltness of time.
1597–8 Falstaff, of the Lord Justice. *Henry IV Part Two*, act 1, sc.2, l.98–9.

40 I am as poor as Job, my lord, but not so patient.
1597–8 Falstaff. *Henry IV Part Two*, act 1, sc.2, l.128.

41 If it be a hot day and I brandish anything but my bottle, would I might never spit white again.
1597–8 Falstaff. *Henry IV Part Two*, act 1, sc.2, l.211–13.

42 It was alway yet the trick of our English nation, if they have a good thing, to make it too common.
1597–8 Falstaff. *Henry IV Part Two*, act 1, sc.2, l.215–17.

43 I can get no remedy against this consumption of the purse. Borrowing only lingers and lingers it out, but the disease is incurable.
1597–8 Falstaff. *Henry IV Part Two*, act 1, sc.2, l.237–9.

44 [He] lined himself with hope,
Eating the air on promise of supply.
1597–8 Lord Bardolph, of Hotspur. *Henry IV Part Two*, act 1, sc.3, l.27–8.

45 Away, you scullion, you rampallion, you fustilarian! I'll tickle your catastrophe!
1597–8 Page to Mistress Quickly. *Henry IV Part Two*, act 2, sc.1, l.61–2.

46 He hath eaten me out of house and home.
1597–8 Mistress Quickly, of Falstaff. *Henry IV Part Two*, act 2, sc.1, l.75–6.

47 Thus we play the fools with the time, and the spirits of

the wise sit in the clouds and mock us.
1597–8 Prince Harry. *Henry IV Part Two*, act 2, sc.2, l.133–5.

48 He was indeed the glass
Wherein the noble youth did dress themselves.
1597–8 Lady Percy, of Hotspur. *Henry IV Part Two*, act 2, sc.3, l.21–2.

49 Shall pack-horses
And hollow pampered jades of Asia,
Which cannot go but thirty mile a day,
Compare with Caesars and with cannibals,
And Trojan Greeks?
Nay, rather damn them with King Cerberus,
And let the welkin roar.
1597–8 Pistol. *Henry IV Part Two*, act 2, sc.4, l.160–6.

50 Thou whoreson little tidy Bartholomew boar-pig, when wilt thou leave fighting o'days, and foining o'nights, and begin to patch up thine old body for heaven?
1597–8 Doll Tearsheet, of Falstaff. *Henry IV Part Two*, act 2, sc.4, l.232–5.

51 Is it not strange that desire should so many years outlive performance?
1597–8 Poins. *Henry IV Part Two*, act 2, sc.4, l.262–3.

52 O sleep, O gentle sleep,
Nature's soft nurse, how have I frighted thee,
That thou no more wilt weigh my eyelids down.
1597–8 King Henry. *Henry IV Part Two*, act 3, sc.1, l.5–7.

53 Canst thou, O partial sleep, give thy repose
To the wet sea-boy in an hour so rude,
And in the calmest and most stillest night,
With all appliances and means to boot,
Deny it to a king? Then happy low, lie down.
Uneasy lies the head that wears a crown.
1597–8 King Henry. *Henry IV Part Two*, act 3, sc.1, l.25–31.

54 Death, as the Psalmist saith, is certain to all: all shall die.
How a good yoke of bullocks at Stamford fair?
1597–8 Shallow. *Henry IV Part Two*, act 3, sc.2, l.35–6.

55 We have heard the chimes at midnight, Master Shallow.
1597–8 Falstaff. *Henry IV Part Two*, act 3, sc.2, l.211.

56 A man can die but once. We owe God a death.
1597–8 Feeble. *Henry IV Part Two*, act 3, sc.2, l.233–4.

57 Lord, Lord, how subject we old men are to this vice of lying!
1597–8 Falstaff. *Henry IV Part Two*, act 3, sc.2, l.298–9.

58 When a was naked, he was for all the world like a forked radish, with a head fantastically carved upon it with a knife.
1597–8 Falstaff, of Shallow. *Henry IV Part Two*, act 3, sc.2, l.305–7.

59 An iron man,
Cheering a rout of rebels with your drum,
Turning the word to sword, and life to death.
1597–8 Prince John. *Henry IV Part Two*, act 4, sc.1, l.234–6.

60 Sudden sorrow
Serves to say thus: some good thing comes tomorrow.
1597–8 Westmorland. *Henry IV Part Two*, act 4, sc.1, l.309–10.

61 A peace is of the nature of a conquest,
For then both parties nobly are subdued,
And neither party loser.
1597–8 Archbishop of York. *Henry IV Part Two*, act 4, sc.1, l.315–17.

62 He saw me, and yielded, that I may justly say, with the hook-nosed fellow of Rome, 'I came, saw, and overcame'.
1597–8 Falstaff. *Henry IV Part Two*, act 4, sc.2, l.39–41.

63 A man cannot make him laugh. But that's no marvel; he drinks no wine.
1597–8 Falstaff. *Henry IV Part Two*, act 4, sc.2, l.85–6.

64 Will fortune never come with both hands full,
But write her fair words still in foulest letters?
1597–8 Henry, receiving good news when ill. *Henry IV Part Two*, act 4, sc.3, l.103–4.

65 How quickly nature falls into revolt
When gold becomes her object!
1597–8 King Henry, of his son Harry. *Henry IV Part Two*, act 4, sc.3, l.195–6.

66 Revel the night, rob, murder, and commit
The oldest sins the newest kind of ways?
1597–8 King Henry to Harry. *Henry IV Part Two*, act 4, sc.3, l.254–5.

67 I know thee not, old man. Fall to thy prayers.
How ill white hairs becomes a fool and jester!
1597–8 The newly-crowned King Harry, rejecting Falstaff. *Henry IV Part Two*, act 5, sc.5, l.47–8.

68 Here will be an old abusing of God's patience and the King's English.
1597–8 Mistress Quickly. *The Merry Wives of Windsor*, act 1, sc.4, l.4–5.

69 His worst fault is that he is given to prayer; he is something peevish that way.
1597–8 Mistress Quickly. *The Merry Wives of Windsor*, act 1, sc.4, l.11–12.

70 Why, then the world's mine oyster, which I with sword will open.
1597–8 Pistol. *The Merry Wives of Windsor*, act 2, sc.2, l.4–5.

71 Think'st thou I'll endanger my soul gratis?
1597–8 Falstaff. *The Merry Wives of Windsor*, act 2, sc.2, l.16–17.

72 If money go before, all ways do lie open.
1597–8 Ford (as Brooke). *The Merry Wives of Windsor*, act 2, sc.2, l.164–5.

73 Money is a good soldier, sir, and will go on.
1597–8 Falstaff. *The Merry Wives of Windsor*, act 2, sc.2, l.166.

74 There is money. Spend it, spend it; spend more.
1597–8 Ford (as Brooke). *The Merry Wives of Windsor*, act 2, sc.2, l.223–4.

75 I cannot tell what the dickens his name is.
1597–8 Mistress Page. *The Merry Wives of Windsor*, act 3, sc.2, l.16.

76 He capers, he dances, he has eyes of youth; he writes verses, he speaks holiday, he smells April and May. He will carry't, he will carry't; 'tis in his buttons he will carry't.
1597–8 Host, of Master Feuton. *The Merry Wives of Windsor*, act 3, sc.2, l.61–4.

77 O, what a world of vile ill-favoured faults
Looks handsome in three hundred pounds a year!
1597–8 Anne. *The Merry Wives of Windsor*, act 3, sc.4, l.31–2.

78 A woman would run through fire and water for such a kind heart.
1597–8 Mistress Quickly. *The Merry Wives of Windsor*, act 3, sc.4, l.101–2.

79 Have I lived to be carried in a basket like a barrow of butcher's offal, and to be thrown in the Thames? Well, if I be served such another trick, I'll have my brains ta'en out

and buttered, and give them to a dog for a New Year's gift. 'Sblood, the rogues slighted me into the river with as little remorse as they would have drowned a blind bitch's puppies, fifteen i'th' litter! And you may know by my size that I have a kind of alacrity in sinking.
1597–8 Falstaff. *The Merry Wives of Windsor*, act 3, sc.5, l.4–12.

80 They say there is divinity in odd numbers, either in nativity, chance, or death.
1597–8 Falstaff. *The Merry Wives of Windsor*, act 5, sc.1, l.3–4.

81 Let the sky rain potatoes, let it thunder to the tune of 'Greensleeves'.
1597–8 Falstaff. *The Merry Wives of Windsor*, act 5, sc.5, l.17–18.

82 A victory is twice itself when the achiever brings home full numbers.
1598 Leonato. *Much Ado About Nothing*, act 1, sc.1, l.8–9.

83 How much better is it to weep at joy than to joy at weeping!
1598 Leonato. *Much Ado About Nothing*, act 1, sc.1, l.27–8.

84 He wears his faith but as the fashion of his hat, it ever changes with the next block.
1598 Beatrice, of Benedick. *Much Ado About Nothing*, act 1, sc.1, l.71–3.

85 He is sooner caught than the pestilence.
1598 Beatrice, of Claudio. *Much Ado About Nothing*, act 1, sc.1, l.82.

86 I wonder that you will still be talking, Signor Benedick. Nobody marks you.
1598 Beatrice. *Much Ado About Nothing*, act 1, sc.1, l.110–11.

87 What, my dear Lady Disdain! Are you yet living?
1598 Benedick to Beatrice. *Much Ado About Nothing*, act 1, sc.1, l.112–13.

88 I had rather hear my dog bark at a crow than a man swear he loves me.
1598 Beatrice. *Much Ado About Nothing*, act 1, sc.1, l.125–6.

89 Were she other than she is she were unhandsome, and being no other but as she is, I do not like her.
1598 Benedick, of Hero. *Much Ado About Nothing*, act 1, sc.1, l.166–7.

90 If he send me no husband, for the which blessing I am at him upon my knees every morning and evening. Lord, I could not endure a husband with a beard on his face. I had rather lie in the woollen.
1598 Beatrice. *Much Ado About Nothing*, act 2, sc.1, l.24–7.

91 He shows me where the bachelors sit, and there live we as merry as the day is long.
1598 Beatrice, of St Peter. *Much Ado About Nothing*, act 2, sc.1, l.42–4.

92 I have a good eye, uncle. I can see a church by daylight.
1598 Beatrice to Leonato. *Much Ado About Nothing*, act 2, sc.1, l.74–5.

93 Beauty is a witch
Against whose charms faith melteth into blood.
1598 Claudio. *Much Ado About Nothing*, act 2, sc.1, l.169–70.

94 She speaks poniards, and every word stabs. If her breath were as terrible as her terminations, there were no living near her, she would infect to the North Star.
1598 Benedick, of Beatrice. *Much Ado About Nothing*, act 2, sc.1, l.231–4.

95 Will your grace command me any service to the world's end? I will go on the slightest errand now to the Antipodes that you can devise to send me on. I will fetch you a tooth-picker now from the furthest inch of Asia, bring you the length of Prester John's foot, fetch you a hair off the Great Cham's beard, do you any embassage to the pigmies, rather than hold three words' conference with this harpy.
1598 Benedick, of Beatrice. *Much Ado About Nothing*, act 2, sc.1, l.246–53.

96 O God, sir, here's a dish I love not. I cannot endure my Lady Tongue.
1598 Benedick, of Beatrice. *Much Ado About Nothing*, act 2, sc.1, l.256–7.

97 Silence is the perfectest herald of joy. I were but little happy if I could say how much.
1598 Claudio. *Much Ado About Nothing*, act 2, sc.1, l.287–8.

98 Your silence most offends me, and to be merry best becomes you; for out o' question, you were born in a merry hour.
1598 Don Pedro to Beatrice. *Much Ado About Nothing*, act 2, sc.1, l.310–12.

99 But then there was a star danced, and under that was I born.
1598 Beatrice. *Much Ado About Nothing*, act 2, sc.1, l.313–14.

1 There's little of the melancholy element in her, my lord. She is never sad but when she sleeps, and not ever sad then; for I have heard my daughter say she hath often dreamt of unhappiness and waked herself with laughing.
1598 Leonato, of Beatrice. *Much Ado About Nothing*, act 2, sc.1, l.321–5.

2 If they were but a week married they would talk themselves mad.
1598 Leonato, of Beatrice and Benedick. *Much Ado About Nothing*, act 2, sc.1, l.330–1.

3 Time goes on crutches till love have all his rites.
1598 Claudio. *Much Ado About Nothing*, act 2, sc.1, l.334–5.

4 He was wont to speak plain and to the purpose, like an honest man and a soldier, and now is he turned orthography. His words are a very fantastical banquet, just so many strange dishes.
1598 Benedick, of Claudio. *Much Ado About Nothing*, act 2, sc.3, l.18–21.

5 Is it not strange that sheep's guts should hale souls out of men's bodies?
1598 Benedick. *Much Ado About Nothing*, act 2, sc.3, l.57–9.

6 Sigh no more, ladies, sigh no more.
Men were deceivers ever,
One foot in sea, and one on shore,
To one thing constant never.
1598 Balthasar's song. *Much Ado About Nothing*, act 2, sc.3, l.61–4.

7 He doth indeed show some sparks that are like wit.
1598 Don Pedro, of Benedick. *Much Ado About Nothing*, act 2, sc.3, l.178–9.

8 I will be horribly in love with her.
1598 Benedick, of Beatrice, having been tricked into thinking she secretly loves him. *Much Ado About Nothing*, act 2, sc.3, l.222–3.

9 Look where Beatrice like a lapwing runs
Close by the ground to hear our conference.
1598 Hero to Ursula. *Much Ado About Nothing*, act 3, sc.1, l.24–5.

10 From the crown of his head to the sole of his foot he is all mirth.
1598 Don Pedro, of Benedick. *Much Ado About Nothing*, act 3, sc.2, l.7–9.

11 He hath twice or thrice cut Cupid's bow-string, and the little hangman dare not shoot at him. He hath a heart as sound as a bell, and his tongue is the clapper, for what his heart thinks his tongue speaks.
1598 Don Pedro, of Benedick. *Much Ado About Nothing*, act 3, sc.2, l.9–13.

12 Everyone can master a grief but he that has it.
1598 Benedick. *Much Ado About Nothing*, act 3, sc.2, l.26–7.

13 The barber's man hath been seen with him, and the old ornament of his cheek hath already stuffed tennis balls.
1598 Claudio, of Benedick. *Much Ado About Nothing*, act 3, sc.2, l.41–3.

14 Seest thou not, I say, what a deformed thief this fashion is, how giddily a turns about all the hot-bloods between fourteen and five-and-thirty...?
1598 Borachio to Conrad. *Much Ado About Nothing*, act 3, sc.3, l.126–9.

15 The fashion wears out more apparel than the man.
1598 Conrad to Borachio. *Much Ado About Nothing*, act 3, sc.3, l.134–5.

16 Comparisons are odorous.
1598 Dogberry to Verges. *Much Ado About Nothing*, act 3, sc.5, l.15.

17 As they say, when the age is in, the wit is out.
1598 Dogberry. *Much Ado About Nothing*, act 3, sc.5, l.32–3.

18 Well, God's a good man. An two men ride of a horse, one must ride behind.
1598 Dogberry to Verges. *Much Ado About Nothing*, act 3, sc.5, l.35–6.

19 O, what authority and show of truth
Can cunning sin cover itself withal!
1598 Claudio, of Hero. *Much Ado About Nothing*, act 4, sc.1, l.35–6.

20 'Tis all men's office to speak patience
To those that wring under the load of sorrow.
1598 Leonato. *Much Ado About Nothing*, act 5, sc.1, l.27–8.

21 There was never yet philosopher
That could endure the toothache patiently.
1598 Leonato. *Much Ado About Nothing*, act 5, sc.1, l.35–6.

22 Though care killed a cat, thou hast mettle enough in thee to kill care.
1598 Claudio, of Benedick. *Much Ado About Nothing*, act 5, sc.1, l.133–4.

23 Marry, sir, they have committed false report, moreover they have spoken untruths, secondarily they are slanders, sixth and lastly they have belied a lady, thirdly they have verified unjust things, and to conclude, they are lying knaves!
1598 Dogberry to Don Pedro. *Much Ado About Nothing*, act 5, sc.1, l.208–12.

24 I can find out no rhyme to 'lady' but 'baby', an innocent rhyme; for 'scorn' 'horn', a hard rhyme; for 'school' 'fool', a babbling rhyme. Very ominous endings. No, I was not born under a rhyming planet, nor I cannot woo in festival terms.
1598 Benedick. *Much Ado About Nothing*, act 5, sc.2, l.35–9.

25 If a man do not erect in this age his own tomb ere he dies, he shall live no longer in monument than the bell rings and the widow weeps.
1598 Benedick. *Much Ado About Nothing*, act 5, sc.2, l.69–72.

26 Good morrow, Benedick. Why, what's the matter
That you have such a February face,
So full of frost, of storm and cloudiness?
1598 Don Pedro. *Much Ado About Nothing*, act 5, sc.4, l.40–2.

27 Let's have a dance ere we are married, that we may lighten our own hearts and our wives' heels.
1598 Benedick. *Much Ado About Nothing*, act 5, sc.4, l.116–18.

28 Prince, thou art sad, get thee a wife, get thee a wife.
1598 Benedick to Don Pedro. *Much Ado About Nothing*, act 5, sc.4, l.121–2.

29 O for a muse of fire, that would ascend
The brightest heaven of invention.
1598–9 Chorus. *Henry V*, prologue to act 1, l.1–2.

30 When we have matched our rackets to these balls,
We will in France, by God's grace, play a set
Shall strike his father's crown into the hazard.
1598–9 King Harry, on the gift of tennis balls from the Dauphin. *Henry V*, act 1, sc.2, l.261–3.

31 'Tis ever common
That men are merriest when they are from home.
1598–9 King Harry. *Henry V*, act 1, sc.2, l.271–2.

32 Now all the youth of England are on fire,
And silken dalliance in the wardrobe lies.
1598–9 Chorus. *Henry V*, prologue to act 2, l.1–2.

33 O England! model to thy inward greatness,
Like little body with a mighty heart,
What might'st thou do, that honour would thee do,
Were all thy children kind and natural.
1598–9 Chorus. *Henry V*, prologue to act 2, l.16–19.

34 Though Patience be a tired mare, yet she will plod.
1598–9 Nim. *Henry V*, act 2, sc.1, l.22–3.

35 Treason and murder ever kept together,
As two yoke-devils sworn to either's purpose.
1598–9 King Harry. *Henry V*, act 2, sc.2, l.102–3.

36 I saw him fumble with the sheets, and play with flowers, and smile upon his finger's end.
1598–9 Hostess, describing Falstaff's death. *Henry V*, act 2, sc.3, l.13–15.

37 NIM: They say he cried out of sack.
HOSTESS: Ay, that a did.
BARDOLPH: And of women.
HOSTESS: Nay, that a did not.
BOY: Yes, that a did, and said they were devils incarnate.
HOSTESS: A could never abide carnation, 'twas a colour he never liked.
1598–9 Of Falstaff's death. *Henry V*, act 2, sc.3, l.26–32.

38 Look to my chattels and my movables.
Let senses rule. The word is 'Pitch and pay'.
Trust none, for oaths are straws, men's faiths are wafer-cakes,
And Holdfast is the only dog, my duck.
1598–9 Pistol to Nim. *Henry V*, act 2, sc.3, l.45–8.

39 Let us do it with no show of fear,
No, with no more than if we heard that England
Were busied with a Whitsun morris dance.
For, my good liege, she is so idly kinged,
Her sceptre so fantastically borne
By a vain, giddy, shallow, humorous youth,
That fear attends her not
1598–9 Dauphin, to King Charles. *Henry V*, act 2, sc.4, l.23–9.

40 In cases of defence 'tis best to weigh
The enemy more mighty than he seems.

1598–9 Dauphin. *Henry V*, act 2, sc.4, l.43–4.

41 Self-love, my liege, is not so vile a sin
As self-neglecting.
1598–9 Dauphin, to King Charles. *Henry V*, act 2, sc.4, l.73–4.

42 Once more unto the breach, dear friends, once more,
Or close the wall up with our English dead.
In peace there's nothing so becomes a man
As modest stillness and humility.
But when the blast of war blows in our ears,
Then imitate the action of the tiger.
Stiffen the sinews, conjure up the blood,
Disguise fair nature with hard-favoured rage.
1598–9 King Harry rallying his men at the siege of Harfleur. *Henry V*, act 3, sc.1, l.1–8.

43 I see you stand like greyhounds in the slips,
Straining upon the start. The game's afoot.
1598–9 King Harry rallying his men at the siege of Harfleur. *Henry V*, act 3, sc.1, l.31–2.

44 Cry, 'God for Harry! England and Saint George!'
1598–9 King Harry rallying his men at the siege of Harfleur. *Henry V*, act 3, sc.1, l.34.

45 FLUELLEN: Captain Macmorris, I think, look you, under your correction, there is not many of your nation—
MACMORRIS: Of my nation? What ish my nation? Ish a villain and a bastard and a knave and a rascal? What ish my nation? Who talks of my nation?
1598–9 *Henry V*, act 3, sc.3, l.64–8.

46 From camp to camp through the foul womb of night
The hum of either army stilly sounds.
1598–9 Chorus. *Henry V*, prologue to act 4, l.4–5.

47 A little touch of Harry in the night.
1598–9 Chorus. *Henry V*, prologue to act 4, l.47.

48 There is some soul of goodness in things evil,
Would men observingly distil it out.
1598–9 King Harry. *Henry V*, act 4, sc.1, l.4–5.

49 The King's a bawcock and a heart-of-gold,
A lad of life, an imp of fame,
Of parents good, of fist most valiant.
I kiss his dirty shoe, and from my heartstring
I love the lovely bully.
1598–9 Pistol to King Harry, disguised. *Henry V*, act 4, sc.1, l.45–9.

50 Every subject's duty is the King's, but every subject's soul is his own.
1598–9 King Harry. *Henry V*, act 4, sc.1, l.175–6.

51 Be friends, you English fools, be friends. We have French quarrels enough, if you could tell how to reckon.
1598–9 Bates. *Henry V*, act 4, sc.1, l.220–1.

52 Upon the King.
'Let us, our lives, our souls, our debts, our care-full wives,
Our children, and our sins, lay on the King.'
1598–9 King Harry. *Henry V*, act 4, sc.1, l.227–9.

53 O God of battles, steel my soldiers' hearts.
1598–9 King Harry, before Agincourt. *Henry V*, act 4, sc.1, l.286.

54 O that we now had here
But one ten thousand of those men in England
That do no work today.
1598–9 Warwick, before Agincourt. *Henry V*, act 4, sc.3, l.16–18.

55 If it be a sin to covet honour
I am the most offending soul alive.
1598–9 King Harry. *Henry V*, act 4, sc.3, l.28–9.

56 He which hath no stomach to this fight,
Let him depart.
1598–9 King Harry, before Agincourt. *Henry V*, act 4, sc.3, l.35.

57 He that shall see this day and live t'old age,
Will yearly on the vigil feast his neighbours
And say, 'Tomorrow is Saint Crispian.'
1598–9 King Harry, before Agincourt. *Henry V*, act 4, sc.3, l.44–6.

58 Then will he strip his sleeve and show his scars
And say, 'These wounds I had on Crispin's day.'
Old men forget; yet all shall be forgot,
But he'll remember.
1598–9 King Harry, before Agincourt. *Henry V*, act 4, sc.3, l.47–50.

59 Then shall our names,
Familiar in his mouth as household words...
Be in their flowing cups freshly remembered.
1598–9 King Harry, before Agincourt. *Henry V*, act 4, sc.3, l.51–5.

60 This story shall the good man teach his son,
And Crispin Crispian shall ne'er go by
From this day to the ending of the world
But we in it shall be rememberèd,
We few, we happy few, we band of brothers.
1598–9 King Harry, before Agincourt. *Henry V*, act 4, sc.3, l.56–60.

61 He today that sheds his blood with me
Shall be my brother; be he ne'er so vile.
1598–9 King Harry, before Agincourt. *Henry V*, act 4, sc.3, l.61–2.

62 And gentlemen in England now abed
Shall think themselves accursed they were not here,
And hold their manhoods cheap whiles any speaks
That fought with us upon Saint Crispin's day.
1598–9 King Harry, before Agincourt. *Henry V*, act 4, sc.3, l.64–7.

63 Let life be short, else shame will be too long.
1598–9 Bourbon, returning to the battle. *Henry V*, act 4, sc.5, l.19.

64 There is occasions and causes why and wherefore in all things.
1598–9 Fluellen. *Henry V*, act 5, sc.1, l.3–4.

65 Not for Cadwallader and all his goats.
1598–9 Pistol, refusing to eat leeks. *Henry V*, act 5, sc.1, l.27.

66 An angel is like you, Kate, and you are like an angel.
1598–9 King Harry, wooing Catherine. *Henry V*, act 5, sc.2, l.109–10.

67 Thou wouldst find me such a plain king that thou wouldst think I had sold my farm to buy my crown.
1598–9 King Harry, wooing Catherine. *Henry V*, act 5, sc.2, l.125–7.

68 You have witchcraft in your lips, Kate. There is more eloquence in a sugar touch of them than in the tongues of the French Council.
1598–9 King Harry, wooing Catherine. *Henry V*, act 5, sc.2, l.274–6.

69 God, the best maker of all marriages,
Combine your hearts in one, your realms in one.
1598–9 Queen Isabel, on the marriage of King Harry and Catherine. *Henry V*, act 5, sc.2, l.354–5.

70 Hence, home, you idle creatures, get you home!
1599 Flavius. *Julius Caesar*, act 1, sc.1, l.1.

71 You blocks, you stones, you worse than senseless things!
O, you hard hearts, you cruel men of Rome,
Knew you not Pompey?
1599 Murellus, to the citizens of Rome. *Julius Caesar*, act 1, sc.1, l.34–7.

72 Beware the ides of March.
1599 Soothsayer to Caesar. *Julius Caesar*, act 1, sc.2, l.19.

73 Poor Brutus, with himself at war,
Forgets the shows of love to other men.
1599 Brutus. *Julius Caesar*, act 1, sc.2, l.48–9.

74 Set honour in one eye and death i' the other,
And I will look on both indifferently.
1599 Brutus. *Julius Caesar*, act 1, sc.2, l.88–9.

75 I cannot tell what you and other men
Think of this life; but for my single self,
I had as lief not be, as live to be
In awe of such a thing as I myself.
I was born free as Caesar, so were you.
1599 Cassius to Brutus. *Julius Caesar*, act 1, sc.2, l.95–9.

76 He doth bestride the narrow world
Like a Colossus, and we petty men
Walk under his huge legs, and peep about
To find ourselves dishonourable graves.
Men at sometime were masters of their fates.
The fault, dear Brutus, is not in our stars,
But in ourselves, that we are underlings.
1599 Cassius, of Caesar. *Julius Caesar*, act 1, sc.2, l.136–42.

77 Brutus and Caesar: what should be in that 'Caesar'?
Why should that name be sounded more than
yours?
Write them together: yours is as fair a name.
Sound them: it doth become the mouth as well.
Weigh them: it is as heavy. Conjure with 'em:
'Brutus' will start a spirit as soon as 'Caesar'.
1599 Cassius to Brutus. *Julius Caesar*, act 1, sc.2, l.143–8.

78 Upon what meat doth this our Caesar feed
That he is grown so great?
1599 Cassius to Brutus. *Julius Caesar*, act 1, sc.2, l.150–1

79 Let me have men about me that are fat;
Sleek-headed men, and such as sleep o'nights;
Yond Cassius has a lean and hungry look;
He thinks too much: such men are dangerous.
1599 Caesar. *Julius Caesar*, act 1, sc.2, l.193–6.

80 Seldom he smiles, and smiles in such a sort
As if he mocked himself.
1599 Caesar, of Cassius. *Julius Caesar*, act 1, sc.2, l.206–7.

81 Cassius from bondage will deliver Cassius.
Therein, ye gods, you make the weak most strong;
Therein, ye gods, you tyrants do defeat.
Nor stony tower, nor walls of beaten brass,
Nor airless dungeon, nor strong links of iron,
Can be retentive to the strength of spirit;
But life, being weary of these worldly bars,
Never lacks power to dismiss itself.
1599 Cassius. *Julius Caesar*, act 1, sc.3, l.89–96.

82 It is the bright day that brings forth the adder,
And that craves wary walking.
1599 Brutus. *Julius Caesar*, act 2, sc.1, l.14–15.

83 Between the acting of a dreadful thing
And the first motion, all the interim is
Like a phantasma or a hideous dream.
1599 Brutus. *Julius Caesar*, act 2, sc.1, l.63–5.

84 Let's carve him as a dish fit for the gods,
Not hew him as a carcass fit for hounds.
1599 Brutus, of Caesar. *Julius Caesar*, act 2, sc.1, l.173–4.

85 Am I your self
But as it were in sort or limitation?
To keep with you at meals, comfort your bed,
And talk to you sometimes? Dwell I but in the suburbs
Of your good pleasure? If it be no more,
Portia is Brutus' harlot, not his wife.
1599 Portia. *Julius Caesar*, act 2, sc.1, l.281–6.

86 You are my true and honourable wife,
As dear to me as are the ruddy drops
That visit my sad heart.
1599 Brutus to Portia. *Julius Caesar*, act 2, sc.1, l.287–9.

87 When beggars die there are no comets seen;
The heavens themselves blaze forth the death of
princes.
1599 Calpurnia. *Julius Caesar*, act 2, sc.2, l.30–1.

88 Cowards die many times before their deaths;
The valiant never taste of death but once.
1599 Caesar. *Julius Caesar*, act 2, sc.2, l.32–3.

89 Of all the wonders that I yet have heard,
It seems to me most strange that men should fear,
Seeing that death, a necessary end,
Will come when it will come.
1599 Caesar. *Julius Caesar*, act 2, sc.2, l.34–7.

90 Danger knows full well
That Caesar is more dangerous than he.
1599 Caesar. *Julius Caesar*, act 2, sc.2, l.44–5.

91 The cause is in my will; I will not come.
1599 Caesar. *Julius Caesar*, act 2, sc.2, l.71.

92 Ay me! How weak a thing
The heart of woman is!
1599 Portia. *Julius Caesar*, act 2, sc.4, l.41–2.

93 I could be well moved if I were as you.
If I could pray to move, prayers would move me.
But I am constant as the Northern star,
Of whose true fixed and resting quality
There is no fellow in the firmament.
The skies are painted with unnumbered sparks;
They are all fire, and every one doth shine;
But there's but one in all doth hold his place.
So in the world: 'tis furnished well with men,
And men are flesh and blood, and apprehensive;
Yet in the number I do know but one
That unassailable holds on his rank,
Unshaked of motion; and that I am he
Let me a little show it even in this—
That I was constant Cimber should be banished,
And constant do remain to keep him so.
1599 Caesar. *Julius Caesar*, act 3, sc.1, l.58–73.

94 Et tu, Brutè?—Then fall Caesar.
1599 *Julius Caesar*, act 3, sc.1, l.76.

95 Ambition's debt is paid.
1599 Brutus, after he has killed Caesar. *Julius Caesar*, act 3, sc.1, l.82.

96 Fates, we will know your pleasures.
That we shall die, we know; 'tis but the time
And drawing days out that men stand upon.
1599 Brutus. *Julius Caesar*, act 3, sc.1, l.99–101.

97 He that cuts off twenty years of life
Cuts off so many years of fearing death.
1599 Casca. *Julius Caesar*, act 3, sc.1, l.102–3.

98 How many ages hence
Shall this our lofty scene be acted over,
In states unborn and accents yet unknown!
1599 Cassius, of the murder of Caesar. *Julius Caesar*, act 3, sc.1, l.112–14.

99 O mighty Caesar! Dost thou lie so low?
Are all thy conquests, glories, triumphs, spoils,
Shrunk to this little measure?
1599 Antony. *Julius Caesar*, act 3, sc.1, l.149–51.

1 O pardon me, thou bleeding piece of earth,
That I am meek and gentle with these butchers.
1599 Antony. *Julius Caesar*, act 3, sc.1, l.257–8.

2 Caesar's spirit, ranging for revenge,
With Ate by his side come hot from hell,
Shall in these confines with a monarch's voice
Cry 'havoc!', and let slip the dogs of war,
That this foul deed shall smell above the earth
With carrion men, groaning for burial.
1599 Antony. *Julius Caesar*, act 3, sc.1, l.273–8.

3 This is my answer: not that I loved Caesar less, but that I loved Rome more.
1599 Brutus, explaining his reasons for killing Caesar. *Julius Caesar*, act 3, sc.2, l.20–1.

4 As Caesar loved me, I weep for him. As he was fortunate, I rejoice at it. As he was valiant, I honour him. But as he was ambitious, I slew him.
1599 Brutus. *Julius Caesar*, act 3, sc.2, l.24–7.

5 Friends, Romans, countrymen, lend me your ears.
I come to bury Caesar, not to praise him.
The evil that men do lives after them;
The good is oft interrèd with their bones.
So let it be with Caesar. The noble Brutus
Hath told you Caesar was ambitious.
If it were so, it was a grievous fault,
And grievously hath Caesar answered it.
Here, under leave of Brutus and the rest—
For Brutus is an honourable man,
So are they all, all honourable men—
Come I to speak in Caesar's funeral.
He was my friend, faithful and just to me.
1599 Antony. *Julius Caesar*, act 3, sc.2, l.74–86.

6 When that the poor have cried, Caesar hath wept.
Ambition should be made of sterner stuff.
1599 Antony. *Julius Caesar*, act 3, sc.2, l.92–3.

7 O judgement! thou art fled to brutish beasts,
And men have lost their reason!
1599 Antony. *Julius Caesar*, act 3, sc.2, l.105–6.

8 Bear with me.
My heart is in the coffin there with Caesar,
And I must pause till it come back to me.
1599 Antony. *Julius Caesar*, act 3, sc.2, l.106–8.

9 But yesterday the word of Caesar might
Have stood against the world. Now lies he there,
And none so poor to do him reverence.
1599 Antony. *Julius Caesar*, act 3, sc.2, l.119–21.

10 If you have tears, prepare to shed them now.
1599 Antony. *Julius Caesar*, act 3, sc.2, l.167.

11 This was the most unkindest cut of all.
For when the noble Caesar saw him stab,
Ingratitude, more strong than traitors' arms,
Quite vanquished him.
1599 Antony of Brutus. *Julius Caesar*, act 3, sc.2, l.181–4.

12 O now you weep, and I perceive you feel
The dint of pity. These are gracious drops.
1599 Antony to the crowd. *Julius Caesar*, act 3, sc.2, l.191–2.

13 I am no orator as Brutus is,
But, as you know me all, a plain blunt man.
1599 Antony. *Julius Caesar*, act 3, sc.2, l.212–13.

14 Fortune is merry,
And in this mood will give us anything.
1599 Antony. *Julius Caesar*, act 3, sc.2, l.259–60.

15 Good reasons must of force give place to better.
1599 Brutus. *Julius Caesar*, act 4, sc.2, l.255.

16 There is a tide in the affairs of men
Which, taken at the flood, leads on to fortune;
Omitted, all the voyage of their life
Is bound in shallows and in miseries.
1599 Brutus. *Julius Caesar*, act 4, sc.2, l.270–3.

17 We'll along ourselves, and meet them at Philippi.
1599 Cassius. *Julius Caesar*, act 4, sc.2, l.277.

18 I should not urge thy duty past thy might.
1599 Brutus to Lucius. *Julius Caesar*, act 4, sc.2, l.312.

19 Good words are better than bad strokes.
1599 Brutus to Octavius. *Julius Caesar*, act 5, sc.1, l.29.

20 Blow wind, swell billow, and swim bark.
The storm is up, and all is on the hazard.
1599 Cassius, at Philippi. *Julius Caesar*, act 5, sc.1, l.67–8.

21 Since the affairs of men rest still incertain,
Let's reason with the worst that may befall.
1599 Cassius to Brutus. *Julius Caesar*, act 5, sc.1, l.95–6.

22 O that a man might know
The end of this day's business ere it come!
But it sufficeth that the day will end,
And then the end is known.
1599 Brutus. *Julius Caesar*, act 5, sc.1, l.123–6.

23 I prithee, Strato, stay thou by thy lord.
Thou art a fellow of a good respect.
Thy life hath had some smatch of honour in it.
Hold then my sword, and turn away thy face
While I do run upon it.
1599 Brutus, killing himself. *Julius Caesar*, act 5, sc.5, l.44–8.

24 Caesar, now be still,
I killed not thee with half so good a will.
1599 Brutus, killing himself. *Julius Caesar*, act 5, sc. 5, l.50–1.

25 This was the noblest Roman of them all.
All the conspirators save only he
Did that they did in envy of great Caesar.
He only in a general honest thought
And common good to all made one of them.
His life was gentle, and the elements
So mixed in him that nature might stand up
And say to all the world 'This was a man'.
1599 Antony, of Brutus. *Julius Caesar*, act 5, sc.5, l.67–74.

26 Let us sit and mock the good housewife Fortune from her wheel, that her gifts may henceforth be bestowed equally.
1599–1600 Celia to Rosalind. *As You Like It*, act 1, sc.2, l.30–2.

27 Where is this young gallant that is so desirous to lie with his mother earth?
1599–1600 Charles to Orlando. *As You Like It*, act 1, sc.2, l.188–9.

28 My pride fell with my fortunes.

1599–1600 Rosalind. *As You Like It*, act 1, sc.2, l.241.

29 Fare you well.
Hereafter, in a better world than this,
I shall desire more love and knowledge of you.
1599–1600 Le Beau to Orlando. *As You Like It*, act 1, sc.2, l.273–4.

30 Thy words are too precious to be cast away upon curs.
Throw some of them at me.
1599–1600 Celia to Rosalind. *As You Like It*, act 1, sc.3, l.4–6.

31 Thou art thy father's daughter—there's enough.
1599–1600 Duke Frederick to Rosalind, explaining why he does not trust her. *As You Like It*, act 1, sc.3, l.57.

32 What danger will it be to us,
Maids as we are, to travel forth so far!
Beauty provoketh thieves sooner than gold.
1599–1600 Rosalind to Celia. *As You Like It*, act 1, sc.3, l.107–9.

33 Sweet are the uses of adversity
Which, like the toad, ugly and venomous,
Wears yet a precious jewel in his head.
1599–1600 Duke Senior. *As You Like It*, act 2, sc.1, l.12–14.

34 And this our life, exempt from public haunt,
Finds tongues in trees, books in the running brooks,
Sermons in stones, and good in everything.
1599–1600 Duke Senior. *As You Like It*, act 2, sc.1, l.15–17.

35 Sweep on, you fat and greasy citizens.
1599–1600 First Lord, quoting Jaques. *As You Like It*, act 2, sc.1, l.55.

36 I love to cope him in these sullen fits,
For then he's full of matter.
1599–1600 Duke Senior, of Jaques. *As You Like It*, act 2, sc.1, l.67–8.

37 Unregarded age in corners thrown.
1599–1600 Adam. *As You Like It*, act 2, sc.3, l.43.

38 He that doth the ravens feed,
Yea providently caters for the sparrow,
Be comfort to my age.
1599–1600 Adam to Orlando. *As You Like It*, act 2, sc.3, l.44–6.

39 Though I look old, yet I am strong and lusty,
For in my youth I never did apply
Hot and rebellious liquors in my blood,
Nor did not with unbashful forehead woo
The means of weakness and debility.
Therefore my age is as a lusty winter.
1599–1600 Adam to Orlando. *As You Like It*, act 2, sc.3, l.48–53.

40 Thou art not for the fashion of these times,
Where none will sweat but for promotion.
1599–1600 Orlando, of Adam. *As You Like It*, act 2, sc.3, l.60–1.

41 I think you have no money in your purse.
1599–1600 Touchstone to Celia. *As You Like It*, act 2, sc.4, l.12.

42 Now I am in Ardenne; the more fool I. When I was at home I was in a better place; but travellers must be content.
1599–1600 Touchstone. *As You Like It*, act 2, sc.4, l.14–15.

43 Under the greenwood tree
Who loves to lie with me,
And turn his merry note
Unto the sweet bird's throat.
1599–1600 Amiens's song. *As You Like It*, act 2, sc.5, l.1–4.

44 I can suck melancholy out of a song as a weasel sucks eggs.
1599–1600 Jaques. *As You Like It*, act 2, sc.5, l.11–12.

45 I'll go sleep if I can. If I cannot, I'll rail against all the firstborn of Egypt.
1599–1600 Jaques. *As You Like It*, act 2, sc.5, l.57–8.

46 A fool, a fool, I met a fool i'th' forest,
A motley fool—a miserable world!—
As I do live by food, I met a fool,
Who laid him down and basked him in the sun,
And railed on Lady Fortune in good terms,
In good set terms, and yet a motley fool.
1599–1600 Jaques. *As You Like It*, act 2, sc.7, l.12–17.

47 'Thus we may see', quoth he, 'how the world wags.
'Tis but an hour ago since it was nine,
And after one hour more 'twill be eleven.
And so from hour to hour we ripe and ripe,
And then from hour to hour we rot and rot;
And thereby hangs a tale.'
1599–1600 Jaques, quoting Touchstone. *As You Like It*, act 2, sc.7, l.23–8.

48 All the world's a stage,
And all the men and women merely players.
They have their exits and their entrances,
And one man in his time plays many parts.
1599–1600 Jaques. *As You Like It*, act 2, sc.7, l.139–42.

49 The whining schoolboy with his satchel
And shining morning face.
1599–1600 Jaques. *As You Like It*, act 2, sc.7, l.145–6.

50 Jealous in honour, sudden, and quick in quarrel,
Seeking the bubble reputation
Even in the cannon's mouth.
1599–1600 Jaques, of the soldier. *As You Like It*, act 2, sc.7, l.151–3.

51 Second childishness and mere oblivion,
Sans teeth, sans eyes, sans taste, sans everything.
1599–1600 Jaques, of old age. *As You Like It*, act 2, sc.7, l.165–6.

52 Blow, blow, thou winter wind,
Thou art not so unkind
As man's ingratitude.
1599–1600 Amiens singing. *As You Like It*, act 2, sc.7, l.175–7.

53 Most friendship is feigning, most loving, mere folly.
1599–1600 Amiens. *As You Like It*, act 2, sc.7, l.182.

54 These trees shall be my books
And in their barks my thoughts I'll character.
1599–1600 Orlando. *As You Like It*, act 3, sc.2, l.5–6.

55 Run, run, Orlando; carve on every tree
The fair, the chaste, and unexpressive she.
1599–1600 Orlando. *As You Like It*, act 3, sc.2, l.9–10.

56 Hast any philosophy in thee, shepherd?
1599–1600 Touchstone to Corin. *As You Like It*, act 3, sc.2, l.21–2.

57 I earn that I eat, get that I wear; owe no man hate, envy no man's happiness.
1599–1600 Corin. *As You Like It*, act 3, sc.2, l.71–2.

58 This is the very false gallop of verses.
1599–1600 Touchstone, of Orlando's poem. *As You Like It*, act 3, sc.2, l.111.

59 I was never so berhymed since Pythagoras' time that I was an Irish rat, which I can hardly remember.
1599–1600 Rosalind. *As You Like It*, act 3, sc.2, l.172–4.

60 O wonderful, wonderful, and most wonderful-wonderful, and yet again wonderful, and after that out of all whooping!

1599–1600 Celia, on the arrival of Orlando. *As You Like It*, act 3, sc.2, l.187–9.

61 Do you not know that I am a woman? When I think, I must speak.
1599–1600 Rosalind to Celia. *As You Like It*, act 3, sc.2, l.244–5.

62 I do desire we may be better strangers.
1599–1600 Orlando to Jaques. *As You Like It*, act 3, sc.2, l.253.

63 Time travels in divers paces with divers persons.
1599–1600 Rosalind. *As You Like It*, act 3, sc.2, l.301–2.

64 Love is merely a madness, and, I tell you, deserves as well a dark house and a whip as madmen do.
1599–1600 Rosalind to Orlando. *As You Like It*, act 3, sc.2, l.386–8.

65 I would the gods had made thee poetical.
1599–1600 Touchstone to Audrey. *As You Like It*, act 3, sc.3, l.12–13.

66 The truest poetry is the most feigning.
1599–1600 Touchstone to Audrey. *As You Like It*, act 3, sc.3, l.16–17.

67 Honesty coupled to beauty is to have honey a sauce to sugar.
1599–1600 Touchstone to Audrey. *As You Like It*, act 3, sc.3, l.26–7.

68 His kissing is as full of sanctity as the touch of holy bread.
1599–1600 Rosalind. *As You Like It*, act 3, sc.4, l.12–13.

69 Mistress, know yourself; down on your knees
And thank heaven, fasting, for a good man's love.
1599–1600 Rosalind, in disguise, to Phoebe. *As You Like It*, act 3, sc.5, l.58–9.

70 I pray you do not fall in love with me,
For I am falser than vows made in wine.
Besides, I like you not.
1599–1600 Rosalind, in disguise, to Phoebe. *As You Like It*, act 3, sc.5, l.73–5.

71 Dead shepherd, now I find thy saw of might:
'Who ever loved that loved not at first sight?'
1599–1600 Phoebe, in love with Rosalind (disguised as a young man). *As You Like It*, act 3, sc.5, l.82–3.

72 It is a melancholy of mine own, compounded of many simples, extracted from many objects, and indeed the sundry contemplation of my travels.
1599–1600 Jaques. *As You Like It*, act 4, sc.1, l.15–17.

73 A traveller! By my faith, you have great reason to be sad. I fear you have sold your own lands to see other men's.
1599–1600 Rosalind to Jaques. *As You Like It*, act 4, sc.1, l.20–2.

74 I had rather have a fool to make me merry than experience to make me sad—and to travel for it too!
1599–1600 Rosalind to Jaques. *As You Like It*, act 4, sc.1, l.25–7.

75 JAQUES: Nay then, God b'wi'you an you talk in blank verse.
ROSALIND: Farewell, Monsieur Traveller. Look you lisp, and wear strange suits; disable all the benefits of your own country; be out of love with your nativity, and almost chide God for making you that countenance you are, or I will scarce think you have swam in a gondola.
1599–1600 *As You Like It*, act 4, sc.1, l.29–36.

76 Come, woo me, woo me, for now I am in a holiday humour, and like enough to consent.
1599–1600 Rosalind, in disguise, to Orlando. *As You Like It*, act 4, sc.1, l.64–5.

77 Men have died from time to time, and worms have eaten them, but not for love.
1599–1600 Rosalind, in disguise, to Orlando. *As You Like It*, act 4, sc.1, l.99–101.

78 Can one desire too much of a good thing?
1599–1600 Rosalind, in disguise, to Orlando. *As You Like It*, act 4, sc.1, l.115–16.

79 Men are April when they woo, December when they wed. Maids are May when they are maids, but the sky changes when they are wives.
1599–1600 Rosalind, in disguise, to Orlando. *As You Like It*, act 4, sc.1, l.139–41.

80 Make the doors upon a woman's wit, and it will out at the casement. Shut that, and 'twill out at the key-hole. Stop that, 'twill fly with the smoke out at the chimney.
1599–1600 Rosalind, in disguise, to Orlando. *As You Like It*, act 4, sc.1, l.153–4.

81 'Tis no matter how it be in tune, so it make noise enough.
1599–1600 Jaques. *As You Like It*, act 4, sc.2, l.8–9.

82 The horn, the horn, the lusty horn
Is not a thing to laugh to scorn.
1599–1600 Lords, singing. *As You Like It*, act 4, sc.2, l.18–19.

83 I do now remember a saying: 'The fool doth think he is wise, but the wise man knows himself to be a fool.'
1599–1600 Touchstone to William. *As You Like It*, act 5, sc.1, l.29–31.

84 To wit, I kill thee, make thee away, translate thy life into death, thy liberty into bondage. I will deal in poison with thee, or in bastinado, or in steel. I will bandy with thee in faction, I will o'errun thee with policy. I will kill thee a hundred and fifty ways. Therefore tremble, and depart.
1599–1600 Touchstone. *As You Like It*, act 5, sc.1, l.51–6.

85 [They] no sooner looked but they loved; no sooner loved but they sighed; no sooner sighed but they asked one another the reason; no sooner knew the reason but they sought the remedy.
1599–1600 Rosalind, of Celia and Oliver. *As You Like It*, act 5, sc.2, l.32–5.

86 How bitter a thing it is to look into happiness through another man's eyes.
1599–1600 Orlando. *As You Like It*, act 5, sc.2, l.41–2.

87 I can live no longer by thinking.
1599–1600 Orlando. *As You Like It*, act 5, sc.2, l.48.

88 It was a lover and his lass,
With a hey, and a ho, and a hey-nonny-no,
That o'er the green cornfield did pass
In spring-time, the only pretty ring-time,
When birds do sing, hey ding-a-ding ding,
Sweet lovers love the spring.
1599–1600 Pages' song. *As You Like It*, act 5, sc.3, l.15–20.

89 A poor virgin, sir, an ill-favoured thing, sir, but mine own.
1599–1600 Touchstone, of Audrey. *As You Like It*, act 5, sc.4, l.57–8.

90 I durst go no further than the Lie Circumstantial, nor he durst not give me the Lie Direct; and so we measured swords, and parted.
1599–1600 Touchstone. *As You Like It*, act 5, sc.4, l.83–5.

91 O sir, we quarrel in print, by the book, as you have books for good manners. I will name you the degrees. The first, the Retort Courteous; the second, the Quip Modest; the third, the Reply Churlish; the fourth, the Reproof Valiant; the fifth, the Countercheck Quarrelsome; the sixth, the

Lie with Circumstance; the seventh, the Lie Direct.
1599–1600 Touchstone. *As You Like It*, act 5, sc.4, l.88–94.

92 Your 'if' is the only peacemaker; much virtue in 'if'.
1599–1600 Touchstone. *As You Like It*, act 5, sc.4, l.100–1.

93 He uses his folly like a stalking-horse, and under the presentation of that he shoots his wit.
1599–1600 Duke Senior, of Touchstone. *As You Like It*, act 5, sc.4, l.104–5.

94 If it be true that good wine needs no bush,
'tis true that a good play needs no epilogue.
1599–1600 Rosalind. *As You Like It*, epilogue.

95 For this relief much thanks. 'Tis bitter cold,
And I am sick at heart.
1600–1 Francisco. *Hamlet*, act 1, sc.1, l.6–7.

96 Thus twice before, and just at this dead hour,
With martial stalk hath he gone by our watch.
1600–1 Marcellus, of the ghost of Hamlet's father. *Hamlet*, act 1, sc.1, l.64–5.

97 And then it started like a guilty thing
Upon a fearful summons.
1600–1 Horatio, of the ghost. *Hamlet*, act 1, sc.1, l.129–30.

98 The head is not more native to the heart,
The hand more instrumental to the mouth,
Than is the throne of Denmark to thy father.
1600–1 Claudius to Laertes. *Hamlet*, act 1, sc.2, l.47–9.

99 A little more than kin and less than kind.
1600–1 Hamlet, of Claudius. *Hamlet*, act 1, sc.2, l.65.

1 I am too much i' th' sun.
1600–1 Hamlet. *Hamlet*, act 1, sc.2, l.67.

2 Good Hamlet, cast thy nightly colour off,
And let thine eye look like a friend on Denmark.
Do not for ever with thy vailèd lids
Seek for thy noble father in the dust.
1600–1 Gertrude. *Hamlet*, act 1, sc.2, l.68–71.

3 Seems, madam? Nay, it *is*. I know not 'seems'.
1600–1 Hamlet to Gertrude. *Hamlet*, act 1,sc.2, l.76.

4 But I have that within which passeth show—
These but the trappings and the suits of woe.
1600–1 Hamlet to Gertrude. *Hamlet*, act 1, sc.2, l.85–6.

5 O that this too too solid flesh would melt,
Thaw, and resolve itself into a dew,
Or that the Everlasting had not fixed
His canon 'gainst self-slaughter!
1600–1 Hamlet. *Hamlet*, act 1, sc.2, l.129–32.

6 How weary, stale, flat, and unprofitable
Seem to me all the uses of this world!
1600–1 Hamlet. *Hamlet*, act 1, sc.2, l.133–4.

7 So loving to my mother
That he might not beteem the winds of heaven
Visit her face too roughly!
1600–1 Hamlet, of his father. *Hamlet*, act 1, sc.2, l.140–3.

8 Frailty, thy name is woman.
1600–1 Hamlet, of Gertrude. *Hamlet*, act 1, sc.2, l.146.

9 We'll teach you to drink deep ere you depart.
1600–1 Hamlet to Horatio. *Hamlet*, act 1, sc.2, l.174.

10 Thrift, thrift, Horatio. The funeral baked meats
Did coldly furnish forth the marriage tables.
1600–1 Hamlet to Horatio, on the reason for his mother's swift marriage to Claudius. *Hamlet*, act 1, sc.2, l.179–80.

11 A was a man. Take him for all in all,
I shall not look upon his like again.
1600–1 Hamlet, of his father. *Hamlet*, act 1, sc.2, l.186–7.

12 A countenance more
In sorrow than in anger.
1600–1 Horatio, of Hamlet's father's ghost. *Hamlet*, act 1, sc.2, l.228–9.

13 I doubt some foul play. Would the night were come.
Till then, sit still, my soul. Foul deeds will rise,
Though all the earth o'erwhelm them, to men's eyes.
1600–1 Hamlet. *Hamlet*, act 1, sc.2, l.255–7.

14 And keep within the rear of your affection,
Out of the shot and danger of desire.
1600–1 Laertes to Ophelia. *Hamlet*, act 1, sc.3, l.34–5.

15 The chariest maid is prodigal enough
If she unmask her beauty to the moon.
1600–1 Laertes to Ophelia. *Hamlet*, act 1, sc.3, l.36–7.

16 Do not, as some ungracious pastors do,
Show me the steep and thorny way to heaven,
Whilst, like a puffed and reckless libertine
Himself the primrose path of dalliance treads.
1600–1 Ophelia to Laertes. *Hamlet*, act 1, sc.3, l.47–50.

17 The friends thou hast, and their adoption tried,
Grapple them to thy soul with hoops of steel.
1600–1 Polonius to Laertes. *Hamlet*, act 1, sc.3, l.62–3.

18 Beware
Of entrance to a quarrel, but being in,
Bear't that th' opposèd may beware of thee.
1600–1 Polonius to Laertes. *Hamlet*, act 1, sc.3, l.65–7.

19 Give every man thine ear but few thy voice.
Take each man's censure, but reserve thy judgement.
1600–1 Polonius to Laertes. *Hamlet*, act 1, sc.3, l.68–9.

20 Costly thy habit as thy purse can buy,
But not expressed in fancy; rich not gaudy;
For the apparel oft proclaims the man.
1600–1 Polonius to Laertes. *Hamlet*, act 1, sc.3, l.70–2.

21 Neither a borrower nor a lender be.
1600–1 Polonius to Laertes. *Hamlet*, act 1, sc.3, l.75.

22 This above all—to thine own self be true,
And it must follow, as the night the day,
Thou canst not then be false to any man.
1600–1 Polonius to Laertes. *Hamlet*, act 1, sc.3, l.78–80.

23 Ay, springes to catch woodcocks. I do know
When the blood burns how prodigal the soul
Lends the tongue vows.
1600–1 Polonius. *Hamlet*, act 1, sc.3, l.115–7.

24 And to my mind, though I am native here
And to the manner born, it is a custom
More honoured in the breach than the observance.
1600–1 Hamlet. *Hamlet*, act 1, sc.4, l.16–18.

25 Be thou a spirit of health or goblin damned,
Bring with thee airs from heaven or blasts from hell,
Be thy intents wicked or charitable,
Thou com'st in such a questionable shape
That I will speak to thee.
1600–1 Hamlet to the ghost. *Hamlet*, act 1, sc.4, l.21–5.

26 I do not set my life at a pin's fee,
And for my soul, what can it do to that,
Being a thing immortal as itself?
1600–1 Hamlet. *Hamlet*, act 1, sc.4, l.46–8.

27 Something is rotten in the state of Denmark.

1600–1 Marcellus. *Hamlet*, act 1, sc.4, l.67.

28 I could a tale unfold whose lightest word
Would harrow up thy soul, freeze thy young blood,
Make thy two eyes like stars start from their spheres,
Thy knotty and combinèd locks to part,
And each particular hair to stand on end
Like quills upon the fretful porcupine.
1600–1 Ghost to Hamlet. *Hamlet*, act 1, sc.5, l.15–20.

29 Murder most foul, as in the best it is,
But this most foul, strange, and unnatural.
1600–1 Ghost to Hamlet. *Hamlet*, act 1, sc.5, l.27–8.

30 O my prophetic soul! Mine uncle?
1600–1 Hamlet to the ghost. *Hamlet*, act 1, sc.5, l.41.

31 [My] love was of that dignity
That it went hand-in-hand even with the vow
I made to her in marriage.
1600–1 Ghost, of Gertrude. *Hamlet*, act 1, sc.5, l.48–50.

32 In the porches of mine ears.
1600–1 Ghost. *Hamlet*, act 1, sc.5, l.63.

33 Let not the royal bed of Denmark be
A couch for luxury and damnèd incest.
1600–1 Ghost to Hamlet. *Hamlet*, act 1, sc.5, l.82–4.

34 O all you host of heaven! O earth! What else?
And shall I couple hell? O fie! Hold, hold, my heart,
And you, my sinews, grow not instant old,
But bear me stiffly up. Remember thee?
Ay, thou poor ghost, while memory holds a seat
In this distracted globe.
1600–1 Hamlet. *Hamlet*, act 1, sc.5, l.92–7.

35 My tables—meet it is I set it down
That one may smile and smile and be a villain.
1600–1 Hamlet. *Hamlet*, act 1, sc.5, l.108–9.

36 There's ne'er a villain dwelling in all Denmark
But he's an arrant knave.
1600–1 Hamlet. *Hamlet*, act 1, sc.5, l.127–8.

37 Well said, old mole. Canst work i'th' earth so fast?
1600–1 Hamlet. *Hamlet*, act 1, sc.5, l.164.

38 There are more things in heaven and earth, Horatio,
Than are dreamt of in our philosophy.
1600–1 Hamlet. *Hamlet*, act 1, sc.5, l.168–9.

39 The time is out of joint. O cursèd spite
That ever I was born to set it right!
1600–1 Hamlet. *Hamlet*, act 1, sc.5, l.189–90.

40 Lord Hamlet, with his doublet all unbraced,
No hat upon his head, his stockings fouled,
Ungartered, and down-gyvèd to his ankle.
1600–1 Ophelia. *Hamlet*, act 2, sc.1, l.79–81.

41 This is the very ecstasy of love,
Whose violent property fordoes itself
And leads the will to desperate undertakings.
1600–1 Polonius, of Hamlet. *Hamlet*, act 2, sc.1, l.103–5.

42 Brevity is the soul of wit.
1600–1 Polonius. *Hamlet*, act 2, sc.2, l.91.

43 More matter with less art.
1600–1 Gertrude to Polonius, urging him to speak more plainly. *Hamlet*, act 2, sc.2, l.96.

44 'To the celestial and my soul's idol, the most beautified Ophelia'—that's an ill phrase, a vile phrase, 'beautified' is a vile phrase.
1600–1 Polonius to Gertrude, quoting Hamlet's letter to Ophelia. *Hamlet*, act 2, sc.2, l.110–12.

45 Doubt thou the stars are fire,
Doubt that the sun doth move,
Doubt truth to be a liar,
But never doubt I love.
1600–1 Polonius to Gertrude, quoting Hamlet's letter to Ophelia. *Hamlet*, act 2, sc.2, l.116–19.

46 If circumstances lead me I will find
Where truth is hid, though it were hid indeed
Within the centre.
1600–1 Polonius, of Hamlet's madness. *Hamlet*, act 2, sc.2, l.159–61.

47 To be honest, as this world goes, is to be one man picked out of ten thousand.
1600–1 Hamlet to Polonius. *Hamlet*, act 2, sc.2, l.180–1.

48 POLONIUS: What do you read, my lord?
HAMLET: Words, words, words.
1600–1 *Hamlet*, act 2, sc.2, l.193–5.

49 Though this be madness, yet there is method in't.
1600–1 Polonius (aside), of Hamlet. *Hamlet*, act 2, sc.2, l.207–8.

50 POLONIUS: My lord, I will take my leave of you.
HAMLET: You cannot, sir, take from me anything that I will more willingly part withal—except my life, my life, my life.
1600–1 *Hamlet*, act 2, sc.2, l.215–19.

51 [We are] happy in that we are not over-happy,
On Fortune's cap we are not the very button.
1600–1 Guildenstern to Hamlet. *Hamlet*, act 2, sc.2, l.230–1.

52 HAMLET: What's the news?
ROSENCRANTZ: None, my lord, but that the world's grown honest.
HAMLET: Then is doomsday near.
1600–1 *Hamlet*, act 2, sc.2, l.238–41.

53 There is nothing either good or bad, but thinking makes it so.
1600–1 Hamlet. *Hamlet*, act 2, sc.2, l.251–2.

54 I could be bounded in a nutshell and count myself a king of infinite space, were it not that I have bad dreams.
1600–1 Hamlet. *Hamlet*, act 2, sc.2, l.256–8.

55 I hold ambition of so airy and light a quality that it is but a shadow's shadow.
1600–1 Rosencrantz. *Hamlet*, act 2, sc.2, l.263–4.

56 I have of late—but wherefore I know not—lost all my mirth, forgone all custom of exercise; and indeed it goes so heavily with my disposition that this goodly frame, the earth, seems to me a sterile promontory. This most excellent canopy the air, look you, this brave o'erhanging, this majestical roof fretted with golden fire—why, it appears no other thing to me than a foul and pestilent congregation of vapours.
1600–1 Hamlet. *Hamlet*, act 2, sc.2, l.296–304.

57 What a piece of work is a man! How noble in reason, how infinite in faculty, in form and moving how express and admirable, in action how like an angel, in apprehension how like a god—the beauty of the world, the paragon of animals! And yet to me what is this quintessence of dust?
1600–1 Hamlet. *Hamlet*, act 2, sc.2, l.305–10.

58 Man delights not me—no, nor woman neither.
1600–1 Hamlet. *Hamlet*, act 2, sc.2, l.310–11.

59 If you delight not in man what lenten entertainment the players shall receive from you.
1600–1 Rosencrantz. *Hamlet*, act 2, sc.2, l.317–19.

60 There is something in this more than natural, if philosophy could find it out.
1600–1 Hamlet. *Hamlet*, act 2, sc.2, l.367–9.

61 I am but mad north-north-west; when the wind is southerly, I know a hawk from a handsaw.
1600–1 Hamlet to Guildenstern. *Hamlet*, act 2, sc.2, l.380–1.

62 The best actors in the world, either for tragedy, comedy, history, pastoral, pastoral-comical, historical-pastoral, tragical-historical, tragical-comical-historical-pastoral, scene individable, or poem unlimited.
1600–1 Polonius. *Hamlet*, act 2, sc.2, l.398–401.

63 Thy face is valanced since I saw thee last. Com'st thou to beard me in Denmark?
1600–1 Hamlet to one of the players. *Hamlet*, act 2, sc.2, l.426–7.

64 The play, I remember, pleased not the million. 'Twas caviare to the general.
1600–1 Hamlet to one of the players. *Hamlet*, act 2, sc.2, l.438–40.

65 Will you see the players well bestowed? Do ye hear? —let them be well used, for they are the abstracts and brief chronicles of the time.
1600–1 Hamlet to Polonius. *Hamlet*, act 2, sc.2, l.524–7.

66 Use every man after his desert, and who should scape whipping?
1600–1 Hamlet to Polonius. *Hamlet*, act 2, sc.2, l.532–3.

67 O, what a rogue and peasant slave am I!
Is it not monstrous that this player here,
But in a fiction, in a dream of passion,
Could force his soul so to his whole conceit
That from her working all his visage wanned,
Tears in his eyes, distraction in 's aspect,
A broken voice, and his whole function suiting
With forms to his conceit? And all for nothing.
For Hecuba!
What's Hecuba to him, or he to Hecuba,
That he should weep for her?
1600–1 Hamlet. *Hamlet*, act 2, sc.2, l.552–62.

68 But I am pigeon-livered and lack gall
To make oppression bitter
1600–1 Hamlet. *Hamlet*, act 2, sc.2, l.579–80.

69 Why, what an ass am I? Ay, sure, this is most brave,
That I, the son of the dear murderèd,
Prompted to my revenge by heaven and hell,
Must, like a whore, unpack my heart with words.
1600–1 Hamlet. *Hamlet*, act 2, sc.2, l.585–8.

70 Murder, though it have no tongue, will speak
With most miraculous organ.
1600–1 Hamlet. *Hamlet*, act 2, sc.2, l.595–6.

71 The spirit I have seen
May be the devil, and the devil hath power
T'assume a pleasing shape.
1600–1 Hamlet. *Hamlet*, act 2, sc.2, l.600–2.

72 The play's the thing
Wherein I'll catch the conscience of the King.
1600–1 Hamlet. *Hamlet*, act 2, sc.2, l.606–7.

73 The harlot's cheek, beautied with plast'ring art,
Is not more ugly to the thing that helps it
Than is my deed to my most painted word.
1600–1 Claudius. *Hamlet*, act 3, sc.1, l.53–5.

74 To be, or not to be; that is the question:
Whether 'tis nobler in the mind to suffer
The slings and arrows of outrageous fortune,
Or to take arms against a sea of troubles,
And, by opposing, end them. To die, to sleep—
No more, and by a sleep to say we end
The heartache and the thousand natural shocks
That flesh is heir to—'tis a consummation
Devoutly to be wished. To die, to sleep.
To sleep, perchance to dream. Ay, there's the rub,
For in that sleep of death what dreams may come
When we have shuffled off this mortal coil
Must give us pause. There's the respect
That makes calamity of so long life,
For who would bear the whips and scorns of time,
Th'oppressor's wrong, the proud man's contumely,
The pangs of disprized love, the law's delay,
The insolence of office, and the spurns
That patient merit of th'unworthy takes,
When he himself might his quietus make
With a bare bodkin? Who would these fardels bear,
To grunt and sweat under a weary life,
But that the dread of something after death,
The undiscovered country from whose bourn
No traveller returns, puzzles the will,
And makes us rather bear those ills we have
Than fly to others that we know not of?
Thus conscience does make cowards of us all,
And thus the native hue of resolution
Is sicklied o'er with the pale cast of thought,
And enterprises of great pith and moment
With this regard their currents turn awry,
And lose the name of action.
1600–1 Hamlet. *Hamlet*, act 3, sc.1, l.58–90.

75 To the noble mind
Rich gifts wax poor when givers prove unkind.
1600–1 Ophelia to Hamlet. *Hamlet*, act 3, sc.1, l.102–4.

76 The power of beauty will sooner transform honesty from what it is to a bawd than the force of honesty can translate beauty into his likeness.
1600–1 Hamlet to Ophelia. *Hamlet*, act 3, sc.1, l.113–15.

77 Get thee to a nunnery. Why wouldst thou be a breeder of sinners?
1600–1 Hamlet to Ophelia. *Hamlet*, act 3, sc.1, l.123–4.

78 I am very proud, revengeful, ambitious, with more offences at my beck than I have thoughts to put them in, imagination to give them shape, or time to act them in.
1600–1 Hamlet. *Hamlet*, act 3, sc.1, l.126–9.

79 What should such fellows as I do crawling between heaven and earth?
1600–1 Hamlet. *Hamlet*, act 3, sc.1, l.129–31.

80 Let the doors be shut upon him, that he may play the fool nowhere but in's own house.
1600–1 Hamlet, of Polonius. *Hamlet*, act 3, sc.1, l.134–5.

81 God has given you one face, and you make yourselves another.
1600–1 Hamlet, of women. *Hamlet*, act 3, sc.1, l.145–7.

82 I say we will have no more marriages; those that are married already—all but one—shall live. The rest shall

keep as they are.
1600–1 Hamlet to Ophelia. *Hamlet*, act 3, sc.1, l.150–2.

83 O what a noble mind is here o'erthrown!
1600–1 Ophelia, of Hamlet. *Hamlet*, act 3, sc.1, l.153.

84 Madness in great ones must not unwatched go.
1600–1 Claudius, of Hamlet. *Hamlet*, act 3, sc.1, l.191.

85 Speak the speech, I pray you, as I pronounced it to you —trippingly on the tongue; but if you mouth it, as many of your players do, I had as lief the town-crier had spoke my lines.
1600–1 Hamlet to the players. *Hamlet*, act 3, sc.2, l.1–4.

86 Hold as 'twere the mirror up to nature, to show virtue her own feature, scorn her own image.
1600–1 Hamlet to the players. *Hamlet*, act 3, sc.2, l.22–3.

87 Let those that play your clowns speak no more than is set down for them.
1600–1 Hamlet to the players. *Hamlet*, act 3, sc.2, l.38–9.

88 A man that Fortune's buffets and rewards
Hath ta'en with equal thanks.
1600–1 Hamlet, of Horatio. *Hamlet*, act 3, sc.2, l.65–6.

89 Give me that man
That is not passion's slave, and I will wear him
In my heart's core.
1600–1 Hamlet. *Hamlet*, act 3, sc.2, l.69–71.

90 OPHELIA: 'Tis brief, my lord.
HAMLET: As woman's love.
1600–1 *Hamlet*, act 3, sc.2, l.146–7.

91 Our wills and fates do so contrary run
That our devices still are overthrown.
1600–1 Player King. *Hamlet*, act 3, sc.2, l.202–3.

92 The lady protests too much, methinks.
1600–1 Gertrude to Hamlet, of the Player Queen. *Hamlet*, act 3, sc.2, l.219.

93 No, no, they do but jest, poison in jest.
1600–1 Hamlet, of the play. *Hamlet*, act 3, sc.2, l.224.

94 KING CLAUDIUS: What do you call the play?
HAMLET: *The Mousetrap*.
1600–1 *Hamlet*, act 3, sc.2, l.225–6.

95 Let the galled jade wince, our withers are unwrung
1600–1 Hamlet, of the play. *Hamlet*, act 3, sc.2, l.231.

96 'Sblood, do you think I am easier to be played on than a pipe?
1600–1 Hamlet to Guildenstern. *Hamlet*, act 3, sc.2, l.357–8.

97 'Tis now the very witching time of night,
When churchyards yawn and hell itself breathes out
Contagion to this world.
1600–1 Hamlet. *Hamlet*, act 3, sc.2, l.377–9.

98 I will speak daggers to her, but use none;
My tongue and soul in this be hypocrites.
1600–1 Hamlet, of Gertrude. *Hamlet*, act 3, sc.2, l.385–6.

99 O, my offence is rank! It smells to heaven.
1600–1 Claudius. *Hamlet*, act 3, sc.3, l.36.

1 Try what repentance can. What can it not?
Yet what can it when one cannot repent?
1600–1 Claudius. *Hamlet*, act 3, sc.3, l.65–6.

2 O limèd soul that, struggling to be free,
Art more engaged! Help, angels! make assay.
1600–1 Claudius. *Hamlet*, act 3, sc.3, l.68–9.

3 My words fly up, my thoughts remain below.
Words without thoughts never to heaven go.
1600–1 Claudius. *Hamlet*, act 3, sc.3, l.97–8.

4 You shall not budge.
You go not till I set you up a glass
Where you may see the inmost part of you.
1600–1 Hamlet to Gertrude. *Hamlet*, act 3, sc.4, l.18–20.

5 How now, a rat? Dead for a ducat, dead.
1600–1 Hamlet, hearing Polonius behind the arras. *Hamlet*, act 3, sc.4, l.23.

6 A bloody deed—almost as bad, good-mother,
As kill a king and marry with his brother.
1600–1 Hamlet. *Hamlet*, act 3, sc.4, l.27–8.

7 Thou wretched, rash, intruding fool, farewell.
I took thee for thy better.
1600–1 Hamlet to Polonius, whom Hamlet has just stabbed. *Hamlet*, act 3, sc.4, l.29–31.

8 You cannot call it love, for at your age
The heyday in the blood is tame.
1600–1 Hamlet to Gertrude. *Hamlet*, act 3, sc.4, l.67–8.

9 To flaming youth let virtue be as wax
And melt in her own fire.
1600–1 Hamlet to Gertrude. *Hamlet*, act 3, sc.4, l.74–5.

10 Nay, but to live
In the rank sweat of an enseamèd bed,
Stewed in corruption, honeying and making love
Over the nasty sty.
1600–1 Hamlet to Gertrude. *Hamlet*, act 3, sc.4, l.81–4.

11 Confess yourself to heaven;
Repent what's past, avoid what is to come.
1600–1 Hamlet to Gertrude. *Hamlet*, act 3, sc.4, l.140–1.

12 In the fatness of these pursy times
Virtue itself of vice must pardon beg.
1600–1 Hamlet to Gertrude. *Hamlet*, act 3, sc.4, l.144–5.

13 Assume a virtue if you have it not.
1600–1 Hamlet to Gertrude. *Hamlet*, act 3, sc.4, l.151.

14 I'll lug the guts into the neighbour room.
1600–1 Hamlet, of Polonius, whom he has killed. *Hamlet*, act 3, sc.4, l.186.

15 A man may fish with the worm that hath eat of a king, and eat of the fish that hath fed of that worm.
1600–1 Hamlet to Claudius. *Hamlet*, act 4, sc.3, l.27–8.

16 He is dead and gone, lady,
He is dead and gone.
At his head a grass-green turf,
At his heels a stone.
1600–1 Ophelia, singing. *Hamlet*, act 4, sc.5, l.29–32.

17 We know what we are, but know not what we may be.
1600–1 Ophelia. *Hamlet*, act 4, sc.5, l.42–3.

18 Good night, ladies, good night, sweet ladies, good night, good night.
1600–1 Ophelia. *Hamlet*, act 4, sc.5, l.71–2.

19 When sorrows come they come not single spies,
But in battalions.
1600–1 Claudius to Gertrude. *Hamlet*, act 4, sc.5, l.76–7.

20 The people muddied,
Thick and unwholesome in their thoughts and whispers.
1600–1 Claudius to Gertrude. *Hamlet*, act 4, sc.5, l.78–9.

21 There's such divinity doth hedge a king
That treason can but peep to what it would.
1600–1 Claudius to Gertrude. *Hamlet*, act 4, sc.5, l.122–3.

22 O, how the wheel becomes it!
1600–1 Ophelia. *Hamlet*, act 4, sc.5, l.172.

23 There's rosemary, that's for remembrance. Pray, love, remember. And there is pansies; that's for thoughts.
1600–1 Ophelia. *Hamlet*, act 4, sc.5, l.175–7.

24 Where th'offence is, let the great axe fall.
1600–1 Claudius. *Hamlet*, act 4, sc.5, l.216.

25 There is a willow grows aslant a brook
That shows his hoar leaves in the glassy stream.
Therewith fantastic garlands did she make
Of crow-flowers, nettles, daisies, and long purples,
That liberal shepherds give a grosser name,
But our cold maids do dead men's fingers call them.
1600–1 Gertrude, describing the scene of Ophelia's death. *Hamlet*, act 4, sc.7, l.138–42.

26 Her garments, heavy with their drink,
Pulled the poor wretch from her melodious lay
To muddy death.
1600–1 Gertrude, describing how Ophelia drowned. *Hamlet*, act 4, sc.7, l.153–5.

27 Too much of water hast thou, poor Ophelia,
And therefore I forbid my tears.
1600–1 Laertes. *Hamlet*, act 4, sc.7, l.158–9.

28 There is no ancient gentlemen but gardeners, ditchers, and gravemakers; they hold up Adam's profession.
1600–1 First Clown. *Hamlet*, act 5, sc.1, l.29–31.

29 This might be the pate of a politician which this ass o'er-offices, one that would circumvent God, might it not?
1600–1 Hamlet to Horatio. *Hamlet*, act 5, sc.1, l.77–9.

30 HAMLET: Ay, marry, why was he [Hamlet] sent into England?
FIRST CLOWN: Why, because a was mad. A shall recover his wits there, or if a do not, 'tis no great matter there.
HAMLET: Why?
FIRST CLOWN: 'Twill not be seen in him there. There the men are as mad as he.
1600–1 *Hamlet*, act 5, sc.1, l.146–152.

31 Alas, poor Yorick. I knew him, Horatio — a fellow of infinite jest, of most excellent fancy. He hath borne me on his back a thousand times; and now, how abhorred my imagination is! My gorge rises at it.
1600–1 Hamlet, of Yorick's skull. *Hamlet*, act 5, sc.1, l.180–4.

32 HAMLET: Dost thou think Alexander looked o' this fashion i'th' earth?
HORATIO: E'en so.
HAMLET: And smelt so? Pah!
1600–1 *Hamlet*, act 5, sc.1, l.193–6.

33 Imperial Caesar, dead and turned to clay,
Might stop a hole to keep the wind away.
1600–1 Hamlet. *Hamlet*, act 5, sc.1, l.208–9.

34 Hold off the earth a while,
Till I have caught her once more in mine arms.
1600–1 Laertes, of Ophelia, at her burial. *Hamlet*, act 5, sc.1, l.245–6.

35 For though I am not splenative and rash,
Yet have I something in me dangerous,
Which let thy wiseness fear.
1600–1 Hamlet to Laertes. *Hamlet*, act 5, sc.1, l.258–9.

36 Let Hercules himself do what he may,
The cat will mew, and dog will have his day.
1600–1 Hamlet to Laertes. *Hamlet*, act 5, sc.1, l.288–9.

37 There's a divinity that shapes our ends,
Rough-hew them how we will.
1600–1 Hamlet to Horatio. *Hamlet*, act 5, sc.2, l.10–11.

38 The bravery of his grief did put me
Into a tow'ring passion.
1600–1 Hamlet, of Laertes. *Hamlet*, act 5, sc.2, l.80–1.

39 A hit, a very palpable hit.
1600–1 Osric. *Hamlet*, act 5, sc.2, l.232.

40 I am more an antique Roman than a Dane.
Here's yet some liquor left.
1600–1 Horatio, intending to drink from the poisoned chalice. *Hamlet*, act 5, sc.2, l.294–5.

41 Absent thee from felicity a while,
And in this harsh world draw thy breath in pain
To tell my story.
1600–1 Hamlet to Horatio. *Hamlet*, act 5, sc.2, l.299–301.

42 O, I die, Horatio!
The potent poison quite o'ercrows my spirit.
1600–1 Hamlet. *Hamlet*, act 5, sc.2, l.304–5.

43 The rest is silence.
1600–1 Hamlet's last words. *Hamlet*, act 5, sc.2, l.310.

44 Good night, sweet prince,
And flights of angels sing thee to thy rest.
1600–1 Horatio. *Hamlet*, act 5, sc.2, l.312–13.

45 If music be the food of love, play on,
Give me excess of it that, surfeiting,
The appetite may sicken and so die.
That strain again, it had a dying fall.
O, it came o'er my ear like the sweet sound
That breathes upon a bank of violets,
Stealing and giving odour. Enough, no more,
'Tis not so sweet now as it was before.
1601 Orsino. *Twelfth Night*, act 1, sc.1, l.1–8.

46 O spirit of love, how quick and fresh art thou
That, notwithstanding thy capacity
Receiveth as the sea, naught enters there,
Of what validity and pitch so e'er,
But falls into abatement and low price
Even in a minute! So full of shapes is fancy
That it alone is high fantastical.
1601 Orsino. *Twelfth Night*, act 1, sc.1, l.9–15.

47 O, when mine eyes did see Olivia first
Methought she purged the air of pestilence;
That instant was I turned into a hart,
And my desires, like fell and cruel hounds,
E'er since pursue me.
1601 Orsino. *Twelfth Night*, act 1, sc.1, l.18–22.

48 He plays o'th' viol-de-gamboys, and speaks three or four languages word for word without book, and hath all the good gifts of nature.
1601 Sir Toby, of Sir Andrew. *Twelfth Night*, act 1, sc.3, l.23–6.

49 He's a great quarreller, and but that he hath the gift of a coward to allay the gust he hath in quarrelling, 'tis thought among the prudent he would quickly have the gift of a grave.
1601 Maria, of Sir Andrew. *Twelfth Night*, act 1, sc.3, l.28–31.

50 I'll drink to her as long as there is a passage in my throat and drink in Illyria.
1601 Sir Toby. *Twelfth Night*, act 1, sc.3, l.36–8.

51 I am a great eater of beef, and I believe that does harm to my wit.
1601 Sir Andrew. *Twelfth Night*, act 1, sc.3, l.83–4.

52 I have unclasped
To thee the book even of my secret soul.
1601 Orsino to Viola, disguised as Cesario. *Twelfth Night*, act 1, sc.4, l.13–14.

53 Many a good hanging prevents a bad marriage.
1601 Orsino. *Twelfth Night*, act 1, sc.5, l.18.

54 'Better a witty fool than a foolish wit.'
1601 Feste. *Twelfth Night*, act 1, sc.5, l.32–3.

55 Virtue that transgresses is but patched with sin.
1601 Feste. *Twelfth Night*, act 1, sc.5, l.44–5.

56 (*He belches*) A plague o' these pickle herring!
1601 Sir Toby. *Twelfth Night*, act 1, sc.5, l.116–17.

57 I would be loath to cast away my speech, for besides that it is excellently well penned, I have taken great pains to con it.
1601 Viola, in disguise, to Olivia. *Twelfth Night*, act 1, sc.5, l.165–7.

58 O sir, I will not be so hard-hearted. I will give out divers schedules of my beauty. It shall be inventoried and every particle and utensil labelled to my will, as *item*, two lips, indifferent red; *item*, two grey eyes, with lids to them; *item*, one neck, one chin, and so forth. Were you sent hither to praise me?
1601 Olivia to Viola (disguised as a young man). *Twelfth Night*, act 1, sc.5, l.233–8.

59 Make me a willow cabin at your gate
And call upon my soul within the house,
Write loyal cantons of contemnèd love,
And sing them loud even in the dead of night;
Halloo your name to the reverberate hills,
And make the babbling gossip of the air
Cry out 'Olivia!' O, you should not rest
Between the elements of air and earth
But you should pity me.
1601 Viola, describing how she would woo Olivia, were she in love with her. *Twelfth Night*, act 1, sc.5, l.258–65.

60 O mistress mine, where are you roaming?
O stay and hear, your true love's coming,
That can sing both high and low.
Trip no further, pretty sweeting.
Journeys end in lovers meeting,
Every wise man's son doth know.
1601 Feste's song. *Twelfth Night*, act 2, sc.3, l.38–43.

61 What is love? 'Tis not hereafter,
Present mirth hath present laughter.
What's to come is still unsure.
In delay there lies no plenty,
Then come kiss me, sweet and twenty.
Youth's a stuff will not endure.
1601 Feste's song. *Twelfth Night*, act 2, sc.3, l.46–51.

62 Is there no respect of place, persons, nor time in you?
1601 Malvolio to Feste, Sir Andrew and Sir Toby. *Twelfth Night*, act 2, sc.3, l.88–9.

63 Dost thou think because thou art virtuous there shall be no more cakes and ale?
1601 Sir Toby to Feste. *Twelfth Night*, act 2, sc.3, l.110–11.

64 Let still the woman take
An elder than herself. So wears she to him;
So sways she level in her husband's heart.
1601 Orsino. *Twelfth Night*, act 2, sc.4, l.28–30.

65 Then let thy love be younger than thyself,
Or thy affection cannot hold the bent;
For women are as roses, whose fair flower
Being once displayed, doth fall that very hour.
1601 Orsino. *Twelfth Night*, act 2, sc.4, l.35–8.

66 Now the melancholy god protect thee, and the tailor make thy doublet of changeable taffeta, for thy mind is a very opal.
1601 Feste to Orsino. *Twelfth Night*, act 2, sc.4, l.72–4.

67 My father had a daughter loved a man
As it might be, perhaps, were I a woman
I should your lordship.
1601 Viola, in disguise, to Orsino. *Twelfth Night*, act 2, sc.4, l.107–9.

68 She never told her love,
But let concealment, like a worm i' th' bud,
Feed on her damask cheek.
1601 Viola, in disguise, to Orsino. *Twelfth Night*, act 2, sc.4, l.110–12.

69 With a green and yellow melancholy
She sat like patience on a monument,
Smiling at grief.
1601 Viola, in disguise, to Orsino. *Twelfth Night*, act 2, sc.4, l.113–15.

70 By my life, this is my lady's hand. These be her very c's, her u's, and her t's, and thus makes she her great P's. It is in contempt of question her hand.
1601 Malvolio. *Twelfth Night*, act 2, sc.5, l.84–7.

71 Be not afraid of greatness. Some are born great, some achieve greatness, and some have greatness thrust upon 'em.
1601 Malvolio. *Twelfth Night*, act 2, sc.5, l.139–41.

72 He will come to her in yellow stockings, and 'tis a colour she abhors, and cross-gartered, a fashion she detests.
1601 Maria, of Malvolio. *Twelfth Night*, act 2, sc.5, l.192–4.

73 Fools are as like husbands as pilchards are to herrings—the husband's the bigger.
1601 Feste to Viola. *Twelfth Night*, act 3, sc.1, l.32–4.

74 Now Jove in his next commodity of hair send thee a beard.
1601 Feste to Viola. *Twelfth Night*, act 3, sc.1, l.43–4.

75 Most excellent accomplished lady, the heavens rain odours on you.
1601 Viola to Olivia. *Twelfth Night*, act 3, sc.1, l.83–4.

76 O world, how apt the poor are to be proud!
1601 Olivia. *Twelfth Night*, act 3, sc.1, l.126.

77 Then westward ho!
1601 Viola. *Twelfth Night*, act 3, sc.1, l.133.

78 O, what a deal of scorn looks beautiful
In the contempt and anger of his lip!
1601 Olivia, of Viola (as Cesario). *Twelfth Night*, act 3, sc.1, l.143–4.

79 Love sought is good, but given unsought, is better.
1601 Olivia. *Twelfth Night*, act 3, sc.1, l.154.

80 You are now sailed into the north of my lady's opinion, where you will hang like an icicle on a Dutchman's beard unless you do redeem it by some laudable attempt either of valour or policy.
1601 Fabian, of Sir Toby. *Twelfth Night*, act 3, sc.2, l.24–8.

81 There is no love-broker in the world can more prevail in man's commendation with woman than report of valour.
1601 Sir Toby to Sir Andrew. *Twelfth Night*, act 3, sc.2, l.34–6.

82 For Andrew, if he were opened and you find so much blood in his liver as will clog the foot of a flea, I'll eat the rest of th'anatomy.
1601 Sir Toby. *Twelfth Night*, act 3, sc.2, l.58–60.

83 Why, this is very midsummer madness.
1601 Olivia, of Malvolio. *Twelfth Night*, act 3, sc.4, l.54.

84 If this were played upon a stage now, I could condemn it as an improbable fiction.
1601 Fabian. *Twelfth Night*, act 3, sc.4, l.125–6.

85 Still you keep o' th' windy side of the law.
1601 Fabian. *Twelfth Night*, act 3, sc.4, l.162.

86 A terrible oath, with a swaggering accent sharply twanged off, gives manhood more approbation than ever proof itself would have earned him.
1601 Sir Toby to Sir Andrew. *Twelfth Night*, act 3, sc.4, l.176–8.

87 I am sure no man hath any quarrel to me. My remembrance is very free and clear from any image of offence done to any man.
1601 Viola (as Cesario) to Sir Toby. *Twelfth Night*, act 3, sc.4, l.221–3.

88 In nature there's no blemish but the mind.
None can be called deformed but the unkind.
1601 Antonio. *Twelfth Night*, act 3, sc.4, l.359–60.

89 There is no darkness but ignorance.
1601 Feste to Malvolio. *Twelfth Night*, act 4, sc.2, l.43–4.

90 Thus the whirligig of time brings in his revenges.
1601 Feste. *Twelfth Night*, act 5, sc.1, l.373.

91 I'll be revenged on the whole pack of you.
1601 Malvolio. *Twelfth Night*, act 5, sc.1, l.374.

92 When that I was and a little tiny boy,
With hey, ho, the wind and the rain,
A foolish thing was but a toy,
For the rain it raineth every day.
1601 Feste. *Twelfth Night*, act 5, sc.1, l.385–8.

93 Then everything includes itself in power,
Power into will, will into appetite;
And appetite, an universal wolf.
1602 Ulysses. *Troilus and Cressida*, act 1, sc.3, l.119–21.

94 The general's disdained
By him one step below; he, by the next;
That next, by him beneath. So every step,
Exampled by the first pace that is sick
Of his superior, grows to an envious fever
Of pale and bloodless emulation.
1602 Ulysses. *Troilus and Cressida*, act 1, sc.3, l.129–134.

95 The nature of the sickness found, Ulysses,
What is the remedy?
1602 Agamemnon. *Troilus and Cressida*, act 1, sc.3, l.140–1.

96 In such indices, although small pricks
To their subsequent volumes, there is seen
The baby figure of the giant mass
Of things to come at large.
1602 Nestor. *Troilus and Cressida*, act 1, sc.3, l.337–40.

97 The common curse of mankind, folly and ignorance, be thine.
1602 Thersites. *Troilus and Cressida*, act 2, sc.3, l.26–7.

98 He that is proud eats up himself. Pride is his own glass, his own trumpet, his own chronicle.
1602 Agamemnon. *Troilus and Cressida*, act 2, sc.3, l.153–5.

99 To make a sweet lady sad is a sour offence.
1602 Helen to Pandarus. *Troilus and Cressida*, act 3, sc.1, l.71.

1 I am giddy. Expectation whirls me round.
Th'imaginary relish is so sweet
That it enchants my sense.
1602 Troilus, on the prospect of an assignation with Cressida. *Troilus and Cressida*, act 3, sc.2, l.16–18.

2 Words pay no debts.
1602 Pandarus to Troilus. *Troilus and Cressida*, act 3, sc.2, l.54.

3 This is the monstruosity in love, lady—that the will is infinite and the execution confined; that the desire is boundless and the act a slave to limit.
1602 Troilus to Cressida. *Troilus and Cressida*, act 3, sc.2, l.77–80.

4 Some men creep in skittish Fortune's hall
Whiles others play the idiots in her eyes.
1602 Ulysses. *Troilus and Cressida*, act 3, sc.3, l.129–30.

5 Time hath, my lord,
A wallet at his back, wherein he puts
Alms for oblivion.
1602 Ulysses to Achilles. *Troilus and Cressida*, act 3, sc.3, l.139–41.

6 Perseverance, dear my lord,
Keeps honour bright. To have done is to hang
Quite out of fashion, like a rusty mail
In monumental mock'ry.
1602 Ulysses. *Troilus and Cressida*, act 3, sc.3, l.144–7.

7 One touch of nature makes the whole world kin.
1602 Ulysses to Achilles. *Troilus and Cressida*, act 3, sc.3, l.169.

8 I see my reputation is at stake.
My fame is shrewdly gored.
1602 Achilles. *Troilus and Cressida*, act 3, sc.3, l.220–1.

9 The busy day,
Waked by the lark, hath roused the ribald crows,
And dreaming night will hide our joys no longer.
1602 Troilus to Cressida. *Troilus and Cressida*, act 4, sc.2, l.10–11.

10 The kiss you take is better than you give.
1602 Cressida to Menelaus. *Troilus and Cressida*, act 4, sc.6, l.39.

11 With too much blood and too little brain these two may run mad.
1602 Thersites, of Achilles and Patroclus. *Troilus and Cressida*, act 5, sc.1, l.45–7.

12 Lechery, lechery, still wars and lechery! Nothing else holds fashion.
1602 Thersites. *Troilus and Cressida*, act 5, sc.2, l.197–8.

13 Words, words, mere words, no matter from the heart.
1602 Troilus, on his letter from Cressida. *Troilus and Cressida*, act 5, sc.3, l.111.

14 Scare Troy out of itself. But march away.
1602 Troilus. *Troilus and Cressida*, act 5, sc.11, l.21

15 Heaven doth with us as we with torches do,
Not light them for themselves.
1603 Duke. *Measure for Measure*, act 1, sc.1, l.32–3.

16 I had as lief have the foppery of freedom as the morality of imprisonment.
1603 Lucio to Claudio. *Measure for Measure*, act 1, sc.2, l.125–6.

17 Our doubts are traitors,
And makes us lose the good we oft might win,
By fearing to attempt.

1603 Lucio to Isabella. *Measure for Measure*, act 1, sc.4, l.77–9.

18 We must not make a scarecrow of the law,
Setting it up to fear the birds of prey,
And let it keep one shape till custom make it
Their perch, and not their terror.
1603 Angelo. *Measure for Measure*, act 2, sc.1, l.1–4.

19 'Tis one thing to be tempted, Escalus,
Another thing to fall.
1603 Angelo. *Measure for Measure*, act 2, sc.1, l.17–18.

20 I not deny
The jury passing on the prisoner's life
May in the sworn twelve have a thief or two
Guiltier than him they try.
1603 Angelo. *Measure for Measure*, act 2, sc.1, l.18–21.

21 The jewel that we find, we stoop and take't
Because we see it, but what we do not see
We tread upon.
1603 Angelo. *Measure for Measure*, act 2, sc.1, l.24–26.

22 Some rise by sin, and some by virtue fall.
1603 Escalus. *Measure for Measure*, act 2, sc.1, l.38.

23 The law hath not been dead, though it hath slept.
1603 Angelo to Isabella. *Measure for Measure*, act 2, sc.2, l.92.

24 ISABELLA: Yet show some pity,
ANGELO: I show it most of all when I show justice,
For then I pity those I do not know.
1603 *Measure for Measure*, act 2, sc.2, l.101–3.

25 O, it is excellent
To have a giant's strength, but it is tyrannous
To use it like a giant.
1603 Isabella to Angelo. *Measure for Measure*, act 2, sc.2, l.109–11.

26 But man, proud man,
Dressed in a little brief authority,
Most ignorant of what he's most assured,
His glassy essence, like an angry ape
Plays such fantastic tricks before high heaven
As makes the angels weep.
1603 Isabella to Angelo. *Measure for Measure*, act 2, sc.2, l.120–5.

27 Great men may jest with saints; 'tis wit in them,
But in the less, foul profanation.
1603 Isabella to Angelo. *Measure for Measure*, act 2, sc.2, l.130–1.

28 Thieves for their robbery have authority,
When judges steal themselves.
1603 Angelo. *Measure for Measure*, act 2, sc.2, l.181–2.

29 When men were fond, I smiled, and wondered how.
1603 Angelo. *Measure for Measure*, act 2, sc.2, l.191–2.

30 When I would pray and think, I think and pray
To several subjects; heaven hath my empty words,
Whilst my invention, hearing not my tongue,
Anchors on Isabel.
1603 Angelo. *Measure for Measure*, act 2, sc.4, l.1–4.

31 The miserable have no other medicine
But only hope.
1603 Claudio to the Duke. *Measure for Measure*, act 3, sc.1, l.2–3.

32 Reason thus with life
If I do lose thee, I do lose a thing
That none but fools would keep.
1603 Duke to Claudio. *Measure for Measure*, act 3, sc.1, l.6–8.

33 If thou art rich, thou'rt poor,
For like an ass whose back with ingots bows,
Thou bear'st thy heavy riches but a journey,
And death unloads thee.
1603 Duke to Claudio. *Measure for Measure*, act 3, sc.1, l.25–8.

34 The sense of death is most in apprehension,
And the poor beetle that we tread upon
In corporal sufferance finds a pang as great
As when a giant dies.
1603 Isabella to Claudio. *Measure for Measure*, act 3, sc.1, l.76–9.

35 If I must die,
I will encounter darkness as a bride,
And hug it in mine arms.
1603 Claudio to Isabella. *Measure for Measure*, act 3, sc.1, l.81–3.

36 Sure it is no sin,
Or of the deadly seven it is the least.
1603 Claudio to Isabella, of fornication. *Measure for Measure*, act 3, sc.1, l.109–10.

37 Ay, but to die, and go we know not where;
To lie in cold obstruction, and to rot.
1603 Claudio. *Measure for Measure*, act 3, sc.1, l.118–19.

38 The weariest and most loathèd worldly life
That age, ache, penury, and imprisonment
Can lay on nature is a paradise
To what we fear of death.
1603 Claudio to Isabella. *Measure for Measure*, act 3, sc.1, l.129–32.

39 Virtue is bold, and goodness never fearful.
1603 Duke to Isabella. *Measure for Measure*, act 3, sc.1, l.210.

40 Take, O take thy lips away
That so sweetly were forsworn.
1603 Boy, singing. *Measure for Measure*, act 4, sc.1, l.1–2.

41 Music oft hath such a charm
To make bad good, and good provoke to harm.
1603 Duke. *Measure for Measure*, act 4, sc.1, l.14–15.

42 You weigh equally; a feather will turn the scale.
1603 Provost to Abhorson. *Measure for Measure*, act 4, sc.2, l.28–29.

43 Every true man's apparel fits your thief.
1603 Abhorson. *Measure for Measure*, act 4, sc.2, l.41.

44 Drunk many times a day, if not many days entirely drunk.
1603 Provost, of Barnardine. *Measure for Measure*, act 4, sc.2, l.151–2.

45 Death's a great disguiser.
1603 Duke to Provost. *Measure for Measure*, act 4, sc.2, l.175.

46 If she be mad, as I believe no other,
Her madness hath the oddest frame of sense.
1603 Duke to Isabella. *Measure for Measure*, act 5, sc.1, l.60–1.

47 Haste still pays haste, and leisure answers leisure;
Like doth quit like, and measure still for measure.
1603 Duke. *Measure for Measure*, act 5, sc.1, 407–8.

48 They say best men are moulded out of faults,
And, for the most, become much more the better
For being a little bad. So may my husband.
1603 Mariana, of Angelo. *Measure for Measure*, act 5, sc.1, l.436–8.

49 In following him I follow myself.
1603–4 Iago, of Othello. *Othello*, act 1, sc.1, l.58.

50 For when my outward action doth demonstrate
The native act and figure of my heart
In compliment extern, 'tis not long after
But I will wear my heart upon my sleeve

For daws to peck at. I am not what I am.
1603–4 Iago. *Othello*, act 1, sc.1, l.60–5.

51 Though he in a fertile climate dwell,
Plague him with flies.
1603–4 Iago, of Brabanzio. *Othello*, act 1, sc.1, l.70–1.

52 Even now, now, very now, an old black ram
Is tupping your white ewe.
1603–4 Iago to Brabanzio. *Othello*, act 1, sc.1, l.88–89.

53 I am one, sir, that comes to tell you your daughter and the Moor are now making the beast with the two backs.
1603–4 Iago to Brabanzio. *Othello*, act 1, sc.1, l.117–9.

54 Though in the trade of war I have slain men,
Yet do I hold it very stuff o'th' conscience
To do no contrived murder. I lack iniquity,
Sometime, to do me service. Nine or ten times
I had thought to've yerked him here, under the ribs.
1603–4 Iago. *Othello*, act 1, sc.2, l.1–5.

55 But that I love the gentle Desdemona
I would not my unhousèd free condition
Put into circumscription and confine
For the seas' worth.
1603–4 Othello. *Othello*, act 1, sc.2, l.25–8.

56 Whether a maid so tender, fair, and happy,
So opposite to marriage that she shunned
The wealthy curlèd darlings of our nation,
Would ever have, t'incur a general mock,
Run from her guardage to the sooty bosom
Of such a thing as thou.
1603–4 Brabanzio to Othello. *Othello*, act 1, sc.2, l.67–72.

57 My particular grief
Is of so floodgate and o'erbearing nature
That it engluts and swallows other sorrows,
And it is still itself.
1603–4 Brabanzio, learning of Desdemona's marriage. *Othello*, act 1, sc.3, l.55–8.

58 For nature so preposterously to err,
Being not deficient, blind, or lame of sense,
Sans witchcraft could not.
1603–4 Brabanzio, of Desdemona's marriage. *Othello*, act 1, sc.3, l.62–4.

59 Rude am I in my speech,
And little blessed with the soft phrase of peace.
1603–4 Othello. *Othello*, act 1, sc.3, l.81–2.

60 A maiden never bold,
Of spirit so still and quiet that her motion
Blushed at herself—and she in spite of nature,
Of years, of country, credit, everything,
To fall in love with what she feared to look on!
It is a judgement maimed and most imperfect
That will confess perfection so could err
Against all rules of nature.
1603–4 Brabanzio of Desdemona. *Othello*, act 1, sc.3, l.94–100.

61 The Anthropophagi, and men whose heads
Do grow beneath their shoulders.
1603–4 Othello. *Othello*, act 1, sc.3, l.143–4.

62 She gave me for my pains a world of kisses.
She swore in faith 'twas strange, 'twas passing strange,
'Twas pitiful, 'twas wondrous pitiful.
She wished she had not heard it, yet she wished
That heaven had made her such a man.
1603–4 Othello, of his courtship of Desdemona. *Othello*, act 1, sc.3, l.158–162.

63 She loved me for the dangers I had passed,
And I loved her that she did pity them.
1603–4 Othello, of Desdemona. *Othello*, act 1, sc.3, l.166–7.

64 My noble father,
I do perceive here a divided duty.
1603–4 Desdemona. *Othello*, act 1, sc.3, l.179–80.

65 For your sake, jewel,
I am glad at soul I have no other child,
For thy escape would teach me tyranny,
To hang clogs on 'em.
1603–4 Brabanzio to Desdemona. *Othello*, act 1, sc.3, l.194–7.

66 When remedies are past, the griefs are ended
By seeing the worst which late on hopes depended.
To mourn a mischief that is past and gone
Is the next way to draw new mischief on.
1603–4 Duke to Brabanzio. *Othello*, act 1, sc.3, l.201–4.

67 The robbed that smiles steals something from the thief;
He robs himself that spends a bootless grief.
1603–4 Duke. *Othello*, act 1, sc.3, l.207–8.

68 But words are words. I never yet did hear
That the bruised heart was piercèd through the ear.
1603–4 Brabanzio. *Othello*, act 1, sc.3, l.217–8.

69 I never found man that knew how to love himself. Ere I would say I would drown myself for the love of a guinea-hen, I would change my humanity with a baboon.
1603–4 Iago to Roderigo. *Othello*, act 1, sc.3, l.313–6.

70 Virtue? A fig! 'Tis in ourselves that we are thus or thus. Our bodies are our gardens, to the which our wills are gardeners.
1603–4 Iago to Roderigo. *Othello*, act 1, sc.3, l.319–21.

71 Make all the money thou canst. If sanctimony and a frail vow betwixt an erring barbarian and a super-subtle Venetian be not too hard for my wits and all the tribes of hell, thou shalt enjoy her.
1603–4 Iago to Roderigo. *Othello*, act 1, sc.3, l.352–6.

72 The Moor is of a free and open nature,
That thinks men honest that but seem to be so,
And will as tenderly be led by th' nose
As asses are.
I ha't. It is ingendered. Hell and night
Must bring this monstrous birth to the world's light.
1603–4 Iago. *Othello*, act 1, sc.3, l.391–6.

73 You are pictures out of doors,
Bells in your parlours; wildcats in your kitchens,
Saints in your injuries; devils being offended,
Players in your housewifery, and hussies in your beds.
1603–4 Iago of women. *Othello*, act 2, sc.1, l.112–15.

74 With as little web as this will I ensnare as great a fly as Cassio.
1603–4 Iago (aside). *Othello*, act 2, sc.1, l.171–2.

75 If it were now to die
'Twere now to be most happy, for I fear
My soul hath her content so absolute
That not another comfort like to this
Succeeds in unknown fate.
1603–4 Othello to Desdemona. *Othello*, act 2, sc.1, l.190–4.

76 The heavens forbid
But that our loves and comforts should increase

Even as our days do grow.
1603–4 Desdemona to Othello. *Othello*, act 2, sc.1, l.194–6.

77 [I'll] make the Moor thank me, love me, and reward me
For making him egregiously an ass.
1603–4 Iago. *Othello*, act 2, sc.1, l.307–8.

78 Reputation, reputation, reputation! O—I ha' lost my reputation, I ha' lost the immortal part of myself, and what remains is bestial.
1603–4 Cassio to Iago. *Othello*, act 2, sc.3, l.256–8.

79 Reputation is an idle and most false imposition, oft got without merit and lost without deserving.
1603–4 Iago to Cassio. *Othello*, act 2, sc.3, l.262–4.

80 O God, that men should put an enemy in their mouths to steal away their brains!
1603–4 Cassio, of wine. *Othello*, act 2, sc.3, l.283–5.

81 So will I turn her virtue into pitch,
And out of her own goodness make the net
That shall enmesh them all.
1603–4 Iago. *Othello*, act 2, sc.3, l.351–3.

82 How poor are they that ha' not patience!
What wound did ever heal but by degrees?
1603–4 Iago to Roderigo. *Othello*, act 2, sc.3, l.360–1.

83 Excellent wretch! Perdition catch my soul
But I do love thee, and when I love thee not,
Chaos is come again.
1603–4 Othello, of Desdemona. *Othello*, act 3, sc.3, l.91–3.

84 I know thou'rt full of love and honesty,
And weigh'st thy words before thou giv'st them breath.
1603–4 Othello to Iago. *Othello*, act 3, sc.3, l.123–4.

85 Good name in man and woman, dear my lord,
Is the immediate jewel of their souls.
Who steals my purse steals trash; 'tis something, nothing;
'Twas mine, 'tis his, and has been slave to thousands.
But he that filches from me my good name
Robs me of that which not enriches him
And makes me poor indeed.
1603–4 Iago to Othello. *Othello*, act 3, sc.3, l.160–6.

86 O, beware, my lord, of jealousy,
It is the green-eyed monster which doth mock
The meat it feeds on.
1603–4 Iago to Othello. *Othello*, act 3, sc.3, l.169–71.

87 Poor and content is rich, and rich enough,
But riches fineless is as poor as winter
To him that ever fears he shall be poor.
1603–4 Iago to Othello. *Othello*, act 3, sc.3, l.176–8.

88 I humbly do beseech you of your pardon
For too much loving you.
1603–4 Iago to Othello. *Othello*, act 3, sc.3, l.216–7.

89 If I do prove her haggard,
Though that her jesses were my dear heart-strings
I'd whistle her off and let her down the wind
To prey at fortune.
1603–4 Othello. *Othello*, act 3, sc.3, l.264–7.

90 If she be false, O then heaven mocks itself!
I'll not believe't.
1603–4 Othello, of Desdemona. *Othello*, act 3, sc.3, l.282–3.

91 Trifles light as air
Are to the jealous confirmations strong
As proofs of holy writ.
1603–4 Iago. *Othello*, act 3, sc.3, l.326–8.

92 Not poppy nor mandragora
Nor all the drowsy syrups of the world
Shall ever medicine thee to that sweet sleep
Which thou owedst yesterday.
1603–4 Iago, of Othello. *Othello*, act 3, sc.3, l.334–7.

93 He that is robbed, not wanting what is stol'n,
Let him not know't and he's not robbed at all.
1603–4 Othello to Iago. *Othello*, act 3, sc.3, l.347–8.

94 I had been happy if the general camp,
Pioneers and all, had tasted her sweet body,
So I had nothing known. O, now for ever
Farewell the tranquil mind, farewell content,
Farewell the plumèd troops and the big wars
That makes ambition virtue! O, farwell,
Farewell the neighing steed and the shrill trump,
The spirit-stirring drum, th'ear-piercing fife,
The royal banner, and all quality,
Pride, pomp, and circumstance of glorious war!
And O, you mortal engines whose rude throats
Th'immortal Jove's dread clamours counterfeit,
Farewell! Othello's occupation's gone.
1603–4 Othello. *Othello*, act 3, sc.3, l.350–62.

95 But this denoted a foregone conclusion.
1603–4 Othello. *Othello*, act 3, sc.3, l.433.

96 My bloody thoughts with violent pace
Shall ne'er look back, ne'er ebb to humble love,
Till that a capable and wide revenge
Swallow them up.
1603–4 Othello to Iago. *Othello*, act 3, sc.3, l.460–3.

97 Jealous souls will not be answered so.
They are not ever jealous for the cause,
But jealous for they're jealous. It is a monster
Begot upon itself, born on itself.
1603–4 Emilia to Desdemona. *Othello*, act 3, sc.4, l.156–9.

98 But yet the pity of it, Iago. O, Iago, the pity of it, Iago!
1603–4 Othello. *Othello*, act 4, sc.1, l.191–2.

99 Do it not with poison. Strangle her in her bed.
1603–4 Iago to Othello. *Othello*, act 4, sc.1, l.202–3.

1 Is this the noble Moor whom our full senate
Call all-in-all sufficient? Is this the nature
Whom passion could not shake, whose solid virtue
The shot of accident nor dart of chance
Could neither graze nor pierce?
1603–4 Lodovico. *Othello*, act 4, sc.1, l.266–70.

2 O thou weed,
Who art so lovely fair, and smell'st so sweet,
That the sense aches at thee—would thou hadst ne'er been born!
1603–4 Othello, of Desdemona. *Othello*, act 4, sc.2, l.69–72.

3 I cry you mercy then.
I took you for that cunning whore of Venice
That married with Othello.
1603–4 Othello to Desdemona. *Othello*, act 4, sc.2, l.93–4.

4 I will be hanged, if some eternal villain,
Some busy and insinuating rogue,
Some cogging, cozening slave, to get some office,
Have not devised this slander.
1603–4 Emilia. *Othello*, act 4, sc.2, l.134–7.

5 Mine eyes do itch. Doth that bode weeping?
1603–4 Desdemona to Emilia. *Othello*, act 4, sc.3, l.56–7.

6 Let husbands know
Their wives have sense like them. They see, and smell,
And have their palates both for sweet and sour,
As husbands have.
1603–4 Emilia to Desdemona. *Othello*, act 4, sc.3, l.92–5.

7 It is the cause, it is the cause, my soul.
Let me not name it to you, you chaste stars.
It is the cause. Yet I'll not shed her blood,
Nor scar that whiter skin of hers than snow,
And smooth as monumental alabaster.
Yet she must die, else she'll betray more men.
Put out the light, and then put out the light.
1603–4 Othello. *Othello*, act 5, sc.2, l.1–7.

8 When I have plucked thy rose
I cannot give it vital growth again.
It needs must wither. I'll smell thee on the tree.
1603–4 Othello. *Othello*, act 5, sc.2, l.13–15.

9 Had all his hairs been lives, my great revenge
Had stomach for 'em all.
1603–4 Othello, of Cassio. *Othello*, act 5, sc.2, l.81–2.

10 Kill me tomorrow; let me live tonight.
1603–4 Desdemona to Othello. *Othello*, act 5, sc.2, l.87.

11 It is the very error of the moon,
She comes more nearer earth than she was wont,
And makes men mad.
1603–4 Othello. *Othello*, act 5, sc.2, l.118–20.

12 Not Cassio killed? Then murder's out of tune,
And sweet revenge grows harsh.
1603–4 Othello. *Othello*, act 5, sc.2, l.124–5.

13 She's like a liar gone to burning hell.
'Twas I that killed her.
1603–4 Othello. *Othello*, act 5, sc.2, l.138–9.

14 May his pernicious soul
Rot half a grain a day.
1603–4 Emilia, of Iago. *Othello*, act 5, sc.2, l.162–3.

15 Thou hast not half that power to do me harm
As I have to be hurt. O gull, O dolt,
As ignorant as dirt!
1603–4 Emilia to Othello. *Othello*, act 5, sc.2, l.169–71.

16 Here is my journey's end, here is my butt
And very sea-mark of my utmost sail.
1603–4 Othello. *Othello*, act 5, sc.2, l.274–5.

17 O ill-starred wench,
Pale as thy smock! When we shall meet at count
This look of thine will hurl my soul from heaven,
And fiends will snatch at it.
1603–4 Othello, of Desdemona. *Othello*, act 5, sc.2, l.279–2.

18 Demand me nothing. What you know, you know.
From this time forth I never will speak word.
1603–4 Iago to Othello. *Othello*, act 5, sc.2, l.309–10.

19 I pray you, in your letters,
When you shall these unlucky deeds relate,
Speak of me as I am. Nothing extenuate,
Nor set down aught in malice. Then must you speak
Of one that loved not wisely but too well,
Of one not easily jealous but, being wrought,
Perplexed in the extreme; of one whose hand,
Like the base Indian, threw a pearl away
Richer than all his tribe; of one whose subdued eyes,
Albeit unusèd to the melting mood,
Drops tears as fast as the Arabian trees
Their medicinable gum. Set you down this,
And say besides that in Aleppo once,
Where a malignant and a turbaned Turk
Beat a Venetian and traduced the state,
I took by th' throat the circumcisèd dog
And smote him thus.
1603–4 Othello's speech as he stabs himself. *Othello*, act 5, sc.2, l.349–65.

20 I kiss thee ere I killed thee. No way but this:
Killing myself, to die upon a kiss.
1603–4 Othello. *Othello*, act 5, sc.2, l.368–9.

21 Be checked for silence,
But never taxed for speech.
1604–5 Countess to Bertram. *All's Well That Ends Well*, act 1, sc.1, l.64–5.

22 'Twere all one
That I should love a bright particular star
And think to wed it, he is so above me.
1604–5 Helen, of Bertram. *All's Well That Ends Well*, act 1, sc.1, l.84–6.

23 The hind that would be mated by the lion
Must die for love.
1604–5 Helen, of Bertram. *All's Well That Ends Well*, act 1, sc.1, l.90–1.

24 Virginity is peevish, proud, idle, made of self-love —which is the most inhibited sin in the canon. Keep it not.
1604–5 Paroles to Helen. *All's Well That Ends Well*, act 1, sc.1, l.141–3.

25 Get thee a good husband, and use him as he uses thee.
1604–5 Paroles to Helen. *All's Well That Ends Well*, act 1, sc.1, l.209–10.

26 Our remedies oft in ourselves do lie
Which we ascribe to heaven.
1604–5 Helen. *All's Well That Ends Well*, act 1, sc.1, l.212.

27 Though honesty be no puritan, yet it will do no hurt.
1604–5 Lavatch. *All's Well That Ends Well*, act 1, sc.3, l.91–2.

28 He and his physicians
Are of a mind: he, that they cannot help him;
They, that they cannot help.
1604–5 Countess, of the King. *All's Well That Ends Well*, act 1, sc.3, l.235–7.

29 They say miracles are past, and we have our philosophical persons to make modern and familiar things supernatural and causeless. Hence it is that we make trifles of terrors, ensconcing ourselves into seeming knowledge when we should submit ourselves to an unknown fear.
1604–5 Lafeu. *All's Well That Ends Well*, act 2, sc.3, l.1–6.

30 Why, these balls bound, there's noise in it. 'Tis hard:
A young man married is a man that's marred.
1604–5 Paroles. *All's Well That Ends Well*, act 2, sc.3, l.294–5.

31 The soul of this man is his clothes.
1604–5 Lafeu. *All's Well That Ends Well*, act 2, sc.5, l.43.

32 No legacy is so rich as honesty.
1604–5 Mariana to Diana. *All's Well That Ends Well*, act 3, sc.5, l.12–13.

33 'Tis not the many oaths that make the truth,

But the plain single vow that is vowèd true.
1604–5 Diana. *All's Well That Ends Well*, act 4, sc.2, l.22–3.

34 My chastity's the jewel of our house,
Bequeathèd down from many ancestors,
Which were the greatest obloquy i' th' world
In me to lose.
1604–5 Diana. *All's Well That Ends Well*, act 4, sc.2, l.47–50.

35 A heaven on earth I have won by wooing thee.
1604–5 Bertram to Diana. *All's Well That Ends Well*, act 4, sc.2, l.67.

36 The web of our life is of mingled yarn, good and ill together.
1604–5 First Lord Dumaine. *All's Well That Ends Well*, act 4, sc.3, l.74–5.

37 Drunkenness is his best virtue, for he will be swine-drunk, and in his sleep he does little harm, save to his bedclothes.
1604–5 Paroles, of the Duke. *All's Well That Ends Well*, act 4, sc.3, l.257–9.

38 'Twas a good lady, 'twas a good lady. We may pick a thousand salads ere we light on such another herb.
1604–5 Lafeu, of Helen. *All's Well That Ends Well*, act 4, sc.5, l.13–15.

39 I am for the house with the narrow gate, which I take to be too little for pomp to enter. Some that humble themselves may, but the many will be too chill and tender, and they'll be for the flow'ry way that leads to the broad gate and the great fire.
1604–5 Lavatch to Lafeu. *All's Well That Ends Well*, act 4, sc.5, l.50–5.

40 Praising what is lost
Makes the remembrance dear.
1604–5 King. *All's Well That Ends Well*, act 5, sc.3, l.19–20.

41 Th'inaudible and noiseless foot of time.
1604–5 King. *All's Well That Ends Well*, act 5, sc.3, l.42.

42 I wonder men dare trust themselves with men.
1605 Apemantus. *Timon of Athens*, act 1, sc.2, l.42.

43 Grant I may never prove so fond
To trust man on his oath or bond.
1605 Apemantus' grace. *Timon of Athens*, act 1, sc.2, l.63–4.

44 Men shut their doors against a setting sun.
1605 Apemantus. *Timon of Athens*, act 1, sc.2, l.141.

45 Every man has his fault, and honesty is his.
1605 Lucullus, of Timon. *Timon of Athens*, act 3, sc.1, l.27–8.

46 Men must learn now with pity to dispense,
For policy sits above conscience.
1605 First Stranger. *Timon of Athens*, act 3, sc.2, l.87–8.

47 Nothing emboldens sin so much as mercy.
1605 First Senator. *Timon of Athens*, act 3, sc.6, l.3.

48 This yellow slave
Will knit and break religions, bless th'accursed.
1605 Timon, of gold. *Timon of Athens*, act 4, sc.3, l.34–5.

49 Thanks I must you con
That you are thieves professed, that you work not
In holier shapes; for there is boundless theft
In limited professions.
1605 Timon to thieves. *Timon of Athens*, act 4, sc.3, l.426–30.

50 Trust not the physician;
His antidotes are poison, and he slays
More than you rob.
1605 Timon to thieves. *Timon of Athens*, act 4, sc.3, l.433–5.

51 Rich men deal gifts,
Expecting in return twenty for one?
1605 Timon to Flavius. *Timon of Athens*, act 4, sc.3, l.510–11.

52 I cannot heave
My heart into my mouth. I love your majesty
According to my bond, nor more nor less.
1605–6 Cordelia to Lear. *King Lear*, act 1, sc.1, l.91–3.

53 Thy youngest daughter does not love thee least,
Nor are those empty-hearted whose low sounds
Reverb no hollowness.
1605–6 Kent to Lear. *King Lear*, act 1, sc.1, l.152–4.

54 If for I want that glib and oily art
To speak and purpose not—since what I well intend,
I'll do't before I speak—that you make known
It is no vicious blot, murder, or foulness,
No unchaste action or dishonoured step
That hath deprived me of your grace and favour,
But even the want of that for which I am richer—
A still-soliciting eye, and such a tongue
That I am glad I have not, though not to have it
Hath lost me in your liking.
1605–6 Cordelia to Lear. *King Lear*, act 1, sc.1, l.224–33.

55 Time shall unfold what pleated cunning hides.
1605–6 Cordelia. *King Lear*, act 1, sc.1, l.280.

56 Fine word, 'legitimate'.
Well, my legitimate, if this letter speed
And my invention thrive, Edmond the base
Shall to th' legitimate. I grow, I prosper.
Now gods, stand up for bastards!
1605–6 Edmond. *King Lear*, act 1, sc.2, l.18–22.

57 We make guilty of our disasters the sun, the moon, and stars, as if we were villains on necessity, fools by heavenly compulsion, knaves, thieves, and treachers by spherical predominance, drunkards, liars, and adulterers by an enforced obedience of planetary influence, and all that we are evil in by a divine thrusting on. An admirable evasion of whore-master man, to lay his goatish disposition on the charge of a star!
1605–6 Edmond. *King Lear*, act 1, sc.2, l.118–26.

58 You base football player.
1605–6 Kent to Oswald. *King Lear*, act 1, sc.4, l.84–5.

59 Have more than thou showest,
Speak less than thou knowest,
Lend less than thou owest.
1605–6 Fool to Kent. *King Lear*, act 1, sc.4, l.117–19.

60 The hedge-sparrow fed the cuckoo so long
That it's had it head bit off by it young.
1605–6 Fool, singing to Lear. *King Lear*, act 1, sc.4, l.198–9.

61 As you are old and reverend, should be wise.
1605–6 Goneril to Lear. *King Lear*, act 1, sc.4. l.218.

62 Ingratitude, thou marble-hearted fiend,
More hideous when thou show'st thee in a child
Than the sea-monster.
1605–6 Lear. *King Lear*, act 1, sc.4, l.237–9.

63 How sharper than a serpent's tooth it is
To have a thankless child.
1605–6 Lear. *King Lear*, act 1, sc.4, l.268–9.

64 O, let me not be mad, not mad, sweet heaven!
Keep me in temper. I would not be mad!
1605–6 Lear. *King Lear*, act 1, sc.5, l.45–6.

65 Thou whoreson Z, thou unnecessary letter.
1605–6 Kent. *King Lear*, act 2, sc.2, l.63.

66 I have seen better faces in my time
Than stands on any shoulder that I see
Before me at this instant.
1605–6 Kent. *King Lear*, act 2, sc.2, l.91–3.

67 A good man's fortune may grow out at heels.
1605–6 Kent. *King Lear*, act 2, sc.2, l.148.

68 All the stored vengeances of heaven fall
On her ingrateful top!
1605–6 Lear to Regan. *King Lear*, act 2, sc.2, l.334–5.

69 Return to her, and fifty men dismissed?
No, rather I abjure all roofs, and choose
To be a comrade with the wolf and owl,
To wage against the enmity o'th' air,
Necessity's sharp pinch!
1605–6 Lear, of Goneril. *King Lear*, act 2, sc.2, l.380–4.

70 Touch me with noble anger,
And let not women's weapons, water-drops,
Stain my man's cheeks. No, you unnatural hags,
I will have such revenges on you both
That all the world shall—I will do such things—
What they are, yet I know not; but they shall be
The terrors of the earth. You think I'll weep.
No, I'll not weep. I have full cause of weeping,
But this heart shall break into a hundred thousand flaws
Or ere I'll weep.—O Fool, I shall go mad!
1605–6 Lear. *King Lear*, act 2, sc.2, l.450–9.

71 Blow, winds, and crack your cheeks! Rage, blow,
You cataracts and hurricanoes, spout
Till you have drenched our steeples, drowned the cocks!
1605–6 Lear. *King Lear*, act 3, sc.2, l.1–3.

72 Thou all-shaking thunder,
Strike flat the thick rotundity o' th' world.
1605–6 Lear. *King Lear*, act 3, sc.2, l.6–7.

73 There was never yet fair woman, but she made mouths in a glass.
1605–6 Fool. *King Lear*, act 3, sc.2, l.35–6.

74 I am a man
More sinned against than sinning.
1605–6 Lear to Kent. *King Lear*, act 3, sc.2, l.59–60.

75 How dost, my boy? Art cold?
I am cold myself.—Where is this straw, my fellow?
The art of our necessities is strange,
And can make vile things precious.
1605–6 Lear to Fool. *King Lear*, act 3, sc.2, l.68–71.

76 He that has and a little tiny wit,
With heigh-ho, the wind and the rain,
Must make content with his fortunes fit,
Though the rain it raineth every day.
1605–6 Fool. *King Lear*, act 3, sc.2, l.74–7.

77 O, that way madness lies.
1605–6 Lear. *King Lear*, act 3, sc.4, l.21.

78 Poor naked wretches, wheresoe'er you are,
That bide the pelting of this pitiless storm,
How shall your houseless heads and unfed sides,
Your looped and windowed raggedness, defend you
From seasons such as these?
1605–6 Lear. *King Lear*, act 3, sc.4, l.28–32.

79 Child Roland to the dark tower came,
His word was still 'Fie, fo, and fum;
I smell the blood of a British man.'
1605–6 Edgar. *King Lear*, act 3, sc.4, l.170–2.

80 Let them anatomize Regan; see what breeds about her heart. Is there any cause in nature that makes these hard-hearts?
1605–6 Lear. *King Lear*, act 3, sc.6, l.34–6.

81 Out, vile jelly!
Where is thy lustre now?
1605–6 Cornwall, pulling out Gloucester's other eye. *King Lear*, act 3, sc.7, l.81–2.

82 Turn out that eyeless villain. Throw this slave
Upon the dunghill.
1605–6 Cornwall to his servants. *King Lear*, act 3, sc.7, l.94–5.

83 The worst is not
So long as we can say 'This is the worst'.
1605–6 Edgar. *King Lear*, act 4, sc.1, 27–8.

84 As flies to wanton boys are we to th' gods;
They kill us for their sport.
1605–6 Gloucester. *King Lear*, act 4, sc.1, l.37–8.

85 GONERIL: I have been worth the whistling.
ALBANY: O Goneril,
You are not worth the dust which the rude wind
Blows in your face.
1605–6 *King Lear*, act 4, sc.2, l.29–32.

86 Alack, 'tis he! Why, he was met even now,
As mad as the vexed sea, singing aloud,
Crowned with rank fumitor and furrow-weeds,
With burdocks, hemlock, nettles, cuckoo-flowers,
Darnel, and all the idle weeds that grow
In our sustaining corn.
1605–6 Cordelia, of Lear. *King Lear*, act 4, sc.3, l.1–6.

87 GLOUCESTER: The trick of that voice I do well remember.
Is't not the King?
LEAR: Ay, every inch a king.
1605–6 *King Lear*, act 4, sc.5, l.106–7.

88 When I do stare, see how the subject quakes!
I pardon that man's life. What was thy cause?
Adultery? Thou shalt not die. Die for adultery!
No, the wren goes to't, and the small gilded fly
Does lecher in my sight. Let copulation thrive.
1605–6 Lear. *King Lear*, act 4, sc.5, l.108–12.

89 Down from the waist
They're centaurs, though women all above.
But to the girdle do the gods inherit;
Beneath is all the fiend's. There's hell, there's darkness,
there is the sulphurous pit, burning, scalding stench,
consumption. Fie, fie, fie; pah, pah! Give me an ounce of
civet, good apothecary, sweeten my imagination.
1605–6 Lear. *King Lear*, act 4, sc.5, l.121–7.

90 O ruined piece of nature! This great world
Shall so wear out to naught. Dost thou know me?
1605–6 Gloucester to Lear. *King Lear*, act 4, sc.5, l.130–1.

91 Hark in thine ear. Change places, and handy-dandy, which is the justice, which is the thief?
1605–6 Lear. *King Lear*, act 4, sc.5, l.148–50.

92 A dog's obeyed in office.
Thou rascal beadle, hold thy bloody hand.
Why dost thou lash that whore? Strip thy own back.
Thou hotly lusts to use her in that kind

For which thou whip'st her.
1605–6 Lear. *King Lear*, act 4, sc.5, l.154–9.

93 Get thee glass eyes,
And, like a scurvy politician, seem
To see the things thou dost not.
1605–6 Lear. *King Lear*, act 4, sc.5, l.166–8.

94 When we are born, we cry that we are come
To this great stage of fools.
1605–6 Lear to Gloucester. *King Lear*, act 4, sc.5, l.178–9.

95 I know thee well—a serviceable villain.
1605–6 Edgar, of Oswald. *King Lear*, act 4, sc.5, l.250.

96 Mine enemy's dog though he had bit me, should have stood
That night against my fire.
1605–6 Cordelia. *King Lear*, act 4, sc.6, l.30–1.

97 You do me wrong to take me out o'th' grave.
Thou art a soul in bliss, but I am bound
Upon a wheel of fire, that mine own tears
Do scald like molten lead.
1605–6 Lear to Cordelia. *King Lear*, act 4, sc.6, l.38–41.

98 Pray do not mock.
I am a very foolish, fond old man,
Fourscore and upward,
Not an hour more nor less; and to deal plainly,
I fear I am not in my perfect mind.
1605–6 Lear to Cordelia. *King Lear*, act 4, sc.6, l.52–6.

99 Men must endure
Their going hence even as their coming hither.
Ripeness is all.
1605–6 Edgar. *King Lear*, act 5, sc.2, l.9–11.

1 [We'll] take upon's the mystery of things
As if we were God's spies.
1605–6 Lear to Cordelia. *King Lear*, act 5, sc.3, l.16–17.

2 The gods are just, and of our pleasant vices
Make instruments to plague us.
1605–6 Edgar to Edmond. *King Lear*, act 5, sc.3, l.161–2.

3 The wheel is come full circle. I am here.
1605–6 Edmond to Edgar. *King Lear*, act 5, sc.3, l.165.

4 His flawed heart—
Alack, too weak the conflict to support—
'Twixt two extremes of passion, joy and grief,
Burst smilingly.
1605–6 Edgar, of Gloucester. *King Lear*, act 5, sc.3, l.188–91.

5 Howl, howl, howl, howl! O, you are men of stones.
Had I your tongues and eyes, I'd use them so
That heaven's vault should crack.
1605–6 Lear, grief-stricken at the death of Cordelia. *King Lear*, act 5, sc.3, l.232–4.

6 Her voice was ever soft,
Gentle, and low, an excellent thing in woman.
1605–6 Lear, of Cordelia. *King Lear*, act 5, sc.3, l.247–8.

7 Why should you a dog, a horse, a rat have life,
And thou no breath at all? Thou'lt come no more.
Never, never, never, never, never.
Pray you, undo this button.
1605–6 Edgar. *King Lear*, act 5, sc.3, l.282–5.

8 The weight of this sad time we must obey,
Speak what we feel, not what we ought to say.
The oldest hath borne most. We that are young
Shall never see so much, nor live so long.
1605–6 Edgar. *King Lear*, act 5, sc.3, l.299–302.

9 His captain's heart,
Which in the scuffles of great fights hath burst
The buckles on his breast.
1606 Philo, of Antony. *Antony and Cleopatra*, act 1, sc.1, l.6–8.

10 The triple pillar of the world transformed
Into a strumpet's fool. Behold and see.
1606 Philo, of Antony. *Antony and Cleopatra*, act 1, sc.1, l.12–13.

11 There's beggary in the love that can be reckoned.
1606 Antony to Cleopatra. *Antony and Cleopatra*, act 1, sc.1, l.15.

12 Let Rome in Tiber melt, and the wide arch
Of the ranged empire fall.
1606 Antony to Cleopatra. *Antony and Cleopatra*, act 1, sc.1, l.35–6.

13 In nature's infinite book of secrecy
A little I can read.
1606 Soothsayer. *Antony and Cleopatra*, act 1, sc.2, l.9–10.

14 I love long life better than figs.
1606 Charmian. *Antony and Cleopatra*, act 1, sc.2, l.28.

15 The tears live in an onion that should water this sorrow.
1606 Enobarbus, of the death of Fulvia. *Antony and Cleopatra*, act 1, sc.2, l.161–2.

16 In time we hate that which we often fear.
1606 Charmian. *Antony and Cleopatra*, act 1, sc.3, l.12.

17 Eternity was in our lips and eyes,
Bliss in our brow's bent; none our parts so poor
But was a race of heaven.
1606 Cleopatra to Antony. *Antony and Cleopatra*, act 1, sc.3, l.35–7.

18 The strong necessity of time commands
Our services a while, but my full heart
Remains in use with you.
1606 Antony to Cleopatra. *Antony and Cleopatra*, act 1, sc.3, l.42–4.

19 Age from folly could not give me freedom.
1606 Cleopatra. *Antony and Cleopatra*, act 1, sc.3, l.57.

20 Sir, you and I must part; but that's not it.
Sir, you and I have loved; but there's not it;
That you know well. Something it is I would—
O, my oblivion is a very Antony,
And I am all forgotten.
1606 Cleopatra to Antony. *Antony and Cleopatra*, act 1, sc.3, l.88–92.

21 Now I feed myself
With most delicious poison.
1606 Cleopatra, thinking of Antony. *Antony and Cleopatra*, act 1, sc.5, l.26–7.

22 My salad days,
When I was green in judgement.
1606 Cleopatra. *Antony and Cleopatra*, act 1, sc.5, l.72–3.

23 The barge she sat in, like a burnished throne
Burned on the water. The poop was beaten gold;
Purple the sails, and so perfumèd that
The winds were love-sick with them. The oars were silver,
Which to the tune of flutes kept stroke, and made
The water which they beat to follow faster,
As amorous of their strokes. For her own person,
It beggared all description.
1606 Enobarbus, of Cleopatra. *Antony and Cleopatra*, act 2, sc.2, l.198–205.

24 Antony,
Enthroned i'th' market-place, did sit alone,
Whistling to th'air, which but for vacancy
Had gone to gaze on Cleopatra too,
And made a gap in nature.
1606 Enobarbus. *Antony and Cleopatra*, act 2, sc.2, l.221–5.

25 I saw her once
Hop forty paces through the public street,
And having lost her breath, she spoke and panted,
That she did make defect perfection.
1606 Enobarbus, of Cleopatra. *Antony and Cleopatra*, act 2, sc.2, l.235–8.

26 Age cannot wither her, nor custom stale
Her infinite variety.
1606 Enobarbus, of Cleopatra. *Antony and Cleopatra*, act 2, sc.2, l.241–2.

27 If thou dost play with him at any game
Thou art sure to lose; and of that natural luck
He beats thee 'gainst the odds.
1606 Soothsayer. *Antony and Cleopatra*, act 2, sc.3, l.23–5.

28 Give me some music—music, moody food
Of us that trade in love.
1606 Cleopatra. *Antony and Cleopatra*, act 2, sc.5, l.1–2.

29 Let it alone. Let's to billiards.
1606 Cleopatra. *Antony and Cleopatra*, act 2, sc.5, l.3.

30 I laughed him out of patience, and that night
I laughed him into patience, and next morn,
Ere the ninth hour, I drunk him to his bed.
1606 Cleopatra, of Antony. *Antony and Cleopatra*, act 2, sc.5, l.19–21.

31 There is gold, and here
My bluest veins to kiss—a hand that kings
Have lipped, and trembled kissing.
1606 Cleopatra to a messenger bringing news of Antony. *Antony and Cleopatra*, act 2, sc.5, l.28–30.

32 I will praise any man that will praise me.
1606 Enobarbus. *Antony and Cleopatra*, act 2, sc.6, l.90.

33 If I lose mine honour,
I lose myself.
1606 Antony to Octavia. *Antony and Cleopatra*, act 3, sc.4, l.22–3.

34 We have kissed away
Kingdoms and provinces.
1606 Scarus. *Antony and Cleopatra*, act 3, sc.10, l.7–8.

35 I have offended reputation;
A most unnoble swerving.
1606 Antony. *Antony and Cleopatra*, act 3, sc.11, l.48–9.

36 Thou knew'st too well
My heart was to thy rudder tied by th' strings,
And thou should'st tow me after.
1606 Antony. *Antony and Cleopatra*, act 3, sc.11, l.56–8.

37 Fortune knows
We scorn her most when most she offers blows.
1606 Antony. *Antony and Cleopatra*, act 3, sc.11, l.74–5.

38 He wears the rose
Of youth upon him.
1606 Antony, of Caesar. *Antony and Cleopatra*, act 3, sc.13, l.19–20.

39 I dare him therefore
To lay his gay caparisons apart
And answer me declined, sword against sword,
Ourselves alone.
1606 Antony's message to Caesar. *Antony and Cleopatra*, act 3, sc.13, l.24–7.

40 Let's have one other gaudy night. Call to me
All my sad captains. Fill our bowls once more.
Let's mock the midnight bell.
1606 Antony. *Antony and Cleopatra*, act 3, sc.13, l.185–7.

41 Never anger
Made good guard for itself.
1606 Maecenas. *Antony and Cleopatra*, act 4, sc.1, l.9–10.

42 To business that we love we rise betime,
And go to't with delight.
1606 Antony. *Antony and Cleopatra*, act 4, sc.4, l.20–1.

43 O sovereign mistress of true melancholy,
The poisonous damp of night disponge upon me,
That life, a very rebel to my will,
May hang no longer on me.
1606 Enobarbus. *Antony and Cleopatra*, act 4, sc.10, l.11–14.

44 There is left us
Ourselves to end ourselves.
1606 Antony to Eros. *Antony and Cleopatra*, act 4, sc.15, l.21–2.

45 All strange and terrible events are welcome,
But comforts we despise.
1606 Cleopatra. *Antony and Cleopatra*, act 4, sc.16, l.3–4.

46 Is it sin
To rush into the secret house of death
Ere death dare come to us?
1606 Cleopatra. *Antony and Cleopatra*, act 4, sc.16, l.82–4.

47 But I will be
A bridegroom in my death, and run into't
As to a lover's bed.
1606 Antony. *Antony and Cleopatra*, act 4, sc.15, l.99–101.

48 Let him that loves me strike me dead.
1606 Antony. *Antony and Cleopatra*, act 4, sc.15, l.108.

49 So it should be,
That none but Antony should conquer Antony.
1606 Cleopatra. *Antony and Cleopatra*, act 4, sc.16, l.16–17.

50 Of many thousand kisses the poor last
I lay upon thy lips.
1606 Antony to Cleopatra. *Antony and Cleopatra*, act 4, sc.16, l.21–2.

51 Shall I abide
In this dull world, which in thy absence is
No better than a sty?
1606 Cleopatra to Antony. *Antony and Cleopatra*, act 4, sc.16, l.62–4.

52 There is nothing left remarkable
Beneath the visiting moon.
1606 Cleopatra, of the death of Antony. *Antony and Cleopatra*, act 4, sc.16, l.69–70.

53 What's brave, what's noble,
Let's do it after the high Roman fashion,
And make death proud to take us.
1606 Cleopatra. *Antony and Cleopatra*, act 4, sc.16, l.88–90.

54 It is great
To do that thing that ends all other deeds.
1606 Cleopatra. *Antony and Cleopatra*, act 5, sc.2, l.4–5.

55 I dreamt there was an Emperor Antony,
O, such another sleep, that I might see

But such another man!
1606 Cleopatra. *Antony and Cleopatra*, act 5, sc.2, l.75–7.

56 His legs bestrid the ocean; his reared arm
Crested the world.
1606 Cleopatra, of Antony. *Antony and Cleopatra*, act 5, sc.2, l.81–2.

57 The bright day is done,
And we are for the dark.
1606 Iras. *Antony and Cleopatra*, act 5, sc.2, l.189–90.

58 Hast thou the pretty worm
Of Nilus there, that kills and pains not?
1606 Cleopatra. *Antony and Cleopatra*, act 5, sc.2, l.238–9.

59 His biting is immortal; those that do die of it do seldom or ever recover.
1606 Clown. *Antony and Cleopatra*, act 5, sc.2, l.241–3.

60 Give me my robe. Put on my crown. I have
Immortal longings in me.
1606 Cleopatra. *Antony and Cleopatra*, act 5, sc.2, l.275–6.

61 Husband, I come.
Now to that name my courage prove my title.
1606 Cleopatra. *Antony and Cleopatra*, act 5, sc.2, l.282–3.

62 If thou and nature can so gently part,
The stroke of death is as a lover's pinch,
Which hurts and is desired. Dost thou lie still?
If thus thou vanishest, thou tell'st the world
It is not worth leave-taking.
1606 Cleopatra. *Antony and Cleopatra*, act 5, sc.2, l.289–93.

63 A lass unparalleled. Downy windows, close,
And golden Phoebus never be beheld
Of eyes again so royal.
1606 Charmian. *Antony and Cleopatra*, act 5, sc.2, l.310–12.

64 When shall we three meet again?
In thunder, lightning, or in rain?
1606 First Witch. *Macbeth*, act 1, sc.1, l.1–2.

65 Fair is foul, and foul is fair,
Hover through the fog and filthy air.
1606 Witches. *Macbeth*, act 1, sc.1, l.10–11.

66 Fortune on his damnèd quarry smiling
Showed like a rebel's whore.
1606 Captain. *Macbeth*, act 1, sc.2, l.14–15.

67 A sailor's wife had chestnuts in her lap,
And munched, and munched, and munched. 'Give me,'
quoth I.
'Aroint thee, witch,' the rump-fed runnion cries.
Her husband's to Aleppo gone, master o'th' Tiger.
But in a sieve I'll thither sail,
And like a rat without a tail
I'll do, I'll do, and I'll do.
1606 First Witch. *Macbeth*, act 1, sc.3, l.3–9.

68 I'll drain him dry as hay.
Sleep shall neither night nor day
Hang upon his penthouse lid.
He shall live a man forbid.
Weary sennights nine times nine
Shall he dwindle, peak, and pine.
Though his barque cannot be lost,
Yet it shall be tempest-tossed.
1606 First Witch. *Macbeth*, act 1, sc.3, l.17–23.

69 The weird sisters hand in hand,
Posters of the sea and land,
Thus do go about, about.
1606 Witches. *Macbeth*, act 1, sc.3, l.30–2.

70 So foul and fair a day I have not seen.
1606 Macbeth. *Macbeth*, act 1, sc.3, l.36.

71 Live you, or are you aught
That man may question? You seem to understand me
By each at once her choppy finger laying
Upon her skinny lips. You should be women,
And yet your beards forbid me to interpret
That you are so.
1606 Banquo. *Macbeth*, act 1, sc.3, l.40–4.

72 If you can look into the seeds of time
And say which grain will grow and which will not,
Speak then to me.
1606 Banquo to the witches. *Macbeth*, act 1, sc.3, l.56–9.

73 To be king
Stands not within the prospect of belief.
1606 Macbeth to the witches. *Macbeth*, act 1, sc.3, l.71–2.

74 The earth hath bubbles, as the water has,
And these are of them.
1606 Banquo, of the witches. *Macbeth*, act 1, sc.3, l.77–8.

75 What, can the devil speak true?
1606 Banquo, hearing that the first of the witches' predictions has come true. *Macbeth*, act 1, sc.3, l.105.

76 The Thane of Cawdor lives. Why do you dress me
In borrowed robes?
1606 Macbeth. *Macbeth*, act 1, sc.3, l.106–7.

77 Come what come may,
Time and the hour runs through the roughest day.
1606 Macbeth. *Macbeth*, act 1, sc.3, l.145–6.

78 Nothing in his life
Became him like the leaving of it. He died
As one that had been studied in his death
To throw away the dearest thing he owed
As 'twere a careless trifle.
1606 Malcolm, of Cawdor. *Macbeth*, act 1, sc.4, l.7–11.

79 There's no art
To find the mind's construction in the face.
He was a gentleman on whom I built
An absolute trust.
1606 King Duncan, of Cawdor. *Macbeth*, act 1, sc.4, l.11–14.

80 Yet do I fear thy nature;
It is too full o'th' milk of human kindness
To catch the nearest way.
1606 Lady Macbeth, of Macbeth. *Macbeth*, act 1, sc.5, l.15–17.

81 Thou wouldst be great,
Art not without ambition, but without
The illness should attend it.
1606 Lady Macbeth, of Macbeth. *Macbeth*, act 1, sc.5, l.17–19.

82 Come, you spirits
That tend on mortal thoughts, unsex me here,
And fill me from the crown to the toe top-full
Of direst cruelty.
1606 Lady Macbeth. *Macbeth*, act 1, sc.5, l.39–42.

83 Your face, my thane, is as a book where men
May read strange matters.
1606 Lady Macbeth to Macbeth. *Macbeth*, act 1, sc.5, l.61–2.

84 Bear welcome in your eye,
Your hand, your tongue; look like the innocent flower,
But be the serpent under't.

1606 Lady Macbeth to Macbeth. *Macbeth*, act 1, sc.5, l.63–5.

85 KING DUNCAN: This castle hath a pleasant seat. The air
Nimbly and sweetly recommends itself
Unto our gentle senses.
BANQUO: This guest of summer,
The temple-haunting marlet, does approve
By his loved mansionry that the heavens' breath
Smells wooingly here. No jutty, frieze,
Buttress, nor coign of vantage but this bird
Hath made his pendant bed and procreant cradle;
Where they most breed and haunt I have observed
The air is delicate.
1606 *Macbeth*, act 1, sc.6, l.1–10.

86 If it were done when 'tis done, then 'twere well
It were done quickly. If th'assassination
Could trammel up the consequence, and catch
With his surcease success: that but this blow
Might be the be-all and the end-all, here,
But here upon this bank and shoal of time,
We'd jump the life to come. But in these cases
We still have judgement here, that we but teach
Bloody instructions which, being taught, return
To plague th'inventor.
1606 Macbeth, on the prospect of murdering Duncan. *Macbeth*, act 1, sc.7, l.1–10.

87 Besides, this Duncan
Hath borne his faculties so meek, hath been
So clear in his great office, that his virtues
Will plead like angels, trumpet-tongued against
The deep damnation of his taking-off,
And pity, like a naked new-born babe,
Striding the blast, or heaven's cherubin, horsed
Upon the sightless couriers of the air,
Shall blow the horrid deed in every eye
That tears shall drown the wind. I have no spur
To prick the sides of my intent, but only
Vaulting ambition which o'erleaps itself
And falls on th'other.
1606 Macbeth. *Macbeth*, act 1, sc.7, l.16–29.

88 Wouldst thou have that
Which thou esteem'st the ornament of life,
And live a coward in thine own esteem,
Letting 'I dare not' wait upon 'I would',
Like the poor cat i'th' adage?
1606 Lady Macbeth to Macbeth. *Macbeth*, act 1, sc.7, l.41–45.

89 I dare do all that may become a man;
Who dares do more is none.
1606 Macbeth to Lady Macbeth. *Macbeth*, act 1, sc.7, l.46–7.

90 Screw your courage to the sticking-place
And we'll not fail.
1606 Lady Macbeth to Macbeth. *Macbeth*, act 1, sc.7, l.60–1.

91 Bring forth men-children only,
For thy undaunted mettle should compose
Nothing but males.
1606 Macbeth to Lady Macbeth. *Macbeth*, act 1, sc.7, l.72–4.

92 Away, and mock the time with fairest show.
False face must hide what the false heart doth know.
1606 Macbeth. *Macbeth*, act 1, sc.7, l.81–2.

93 There's husbandry in heaven,
Their candles are all out.
1606 Banquo. *Macbeth*, act 2, sc.1, l.4–5.

94 Is this a dagger which I see before me,
The handle toward my hand? Come, let me clutch thee.
I have thee not, and yet I see thee still.
1606 Macbeth. *Macbeth*, act 2, sc.1, l.33–5.

95 Mine eyes are made the fool o'th' other senses,
Or else worth all the rest.
1606 Macbeth. *Macbeth*, act 2, sc.1, l.44–5.

96 Whiles I threat, he lives.
Words to the heat of deeds too cold breath gives.
I go, and it is done. The bell invites me.
Hear it not, Duncan; for it is a knell
That summons thee to heaven or to hell.
1606 Macbeth, steeling himself to murder Duncan. *Macbeth*, act 2, sc.1, l.60–4.

97 That which hath made them drunk hath made me bold.
What hath quenched them hath given me fire.
1606 Lady Macbeth. *Macbeth*, act 2, sc.2, l.1–2.

98 Th'attempt and not the deed
Confounds us.
1606 Lady Macbeth. *Macbeth*, act 2, sc.2, l.10–11.

99 I laid their daggers ready;
He could not miss 'em. Had he not resembled
My father as he slept, I had done't.
1606 Lady Macbeth, of Duncan. *Macbeth*, act 2, sc.2, l.11–13.

1 I had most need of blessing, and 'Amen'
Stuck in my throat.
1606 Macbeth. *Macbeth*, act 2, sc.2, l.30–1.

2 Methought I heard a voice cry 'Sleep no more,
Macbeth does murder sleep'—the innocent sleep,
Sleep that knits up the ravelled sleave of care.
1606 Macbeth. *Macbeth*, act 2, sc.2, l.33–5.

3 Still it cried 'Sleep no more' to all the house,
'Glamis hath murdered sleep, and therefore Cawdor
Shall sleep no more, Macbeth shall sleep no more.'
1606 Macbeth. *Macbeth*, act 2, sc.2, l.39–41.

4 Infirm of purpose!
Give me the daggers. The sleeping and the dead
Are but as pictures. 'Tis the eye of childhood
That fears a painted devil.
1606 Lady Macbeth. *Macbeth*, act 2, sc.2, l.50–4.

5 Will all great Neptune's ocean wash this blood
Clean from my hand? No, this my hand will rather
The multitudinous seas incarnadine,
Making the green one red.
1606 Macbeth. *Macbeth*, act 2, sc.2, l.58–61.

6 A little water clears us of this deed.
1606 Lady Macbeth. *Macbeth*, act 2, sc.2, l.65.

7 But this place is too cold for hell. I'll devil-porter it no further. I had thought to have let in some of all professions that go the primrose way to th'everlasting bonfire.
1606 Porter. *Macbeth*, act 2, sc.3, l.15–18.

8 The labour we delight in physics pain.
1606 Macbeth. *Macbeth*, act 2, sc.3, l.49.

9 Confusion now hath made his masterpiece.
Most sacreligious murder hath broke ope
The Lord's anointed temple and stole thence
The life o'th' building.
1606 Macduff, announcing Duncan's murder. *Macbeth*, act 2, sc.3, l.65–8.

10 There's daggers in men's smiles.
1606 Donalbain. *Macbeth*, act 2, sc.3, l.139.

11 Go not my horse the better,
I must become a borrower of the night
For dark hour or twain.
1606 Banquo. *Macbeth*, act 3, sc.1, l.26–8.

12 I could
With barefaced power sweep him from my sight.
1606 Macbeth, of Banquo. *Macbeth*, act 3, sc.1, l.119–20.

13 Things without all remedy
Should be without regard. What's done is done.
1606 Lady Macbeth. *Macbeth*, act 3, sc.2, l.13–14.

14 Duncan is in his grave.
After life's fitful fever he sleeps well.
Treason has done his worst.
1606 Macbeth. *Macbeth*, act 3, sc.2, l.24–5.

15 Come, seeling night,
Scarf up the tender eye of pitiful day.
1606 Macbeth. *Macbeth*, act 3, sc.2, l.47–8.

16 Light thickens, and the crow
Makes wing to th' rooky wood.
Good things of day begin to droop and drowse,
Whiles night's black agents to their preys do rouse.
1606 Macbeth. *Macbeth*, act 3, sc.2, l.51–4.

17 Thou canst not say I did it. Never shake
Thy gory locks at me.
1606 Macbeth to Banquo's ghost. *Macbeth*, act 3, sc.4, l.49–50.

18 You make me strange
Even to the disposition that I owe,
When now I think you can behold such sights
And keep the natural ruby of your cheeks,
When mine is blanched with fear.
1606 Macbeth to Lady Macbeth. *Macbeth*, act 3, sc.4, l.111–15.

19 I am in blood
Stepped in so far that, should I wade no more,
Returning were as tedious as go o'er.
1606 Macbeth. *Macbeth*, act 3, sc.4, l.135–7.

20 Double, double, toil and trouble,
Fire burn, and cauldron bubble.
1606 Witches. *Macbeth*, act 4, sc.1, l.10–11.

21 By the pricking of my thumbs,
Something wicked this way comes.
1606 Second witch. *Macbeth*, act 4, sc.1, l.61–2.

22 MACBETH: How now, you secret, black, and midnight hags,
What is't you do?
WITCHES: A deed without a name.
1606 *Macbeth*, act 4, sc.1, l.63–5.

23 Be bloody, bold, and resolute. Laugh to scorn
The power of man, for none of woman born
Shall harm Macbeth.
1606 Second apparition to Macbeth. *Macbeth*, act 4, sc.1, l.95–7.

24 Macbeth shall never vanquished be until
Great Birnam Wood to high Dunsinane Hill
Shall come against him.
1606 Third Apparition. *Macbeth*, act 4, sc.1, l.108–10.

25 No boasting like a fool;
This deed I'll do before this purpose cool.
1606 Macbeth, intending to murder Macduff's family. *Macbeth*, act 4, sc.1, l.169–70.

26 Our fears do make us traitors.
1606 Lady Macduff. *Macbeth*, act 4, sc.2, l.4.

27 He loves us not,
He wants the natural touch.
1606 Lady Macduff, of Macduff. *Macbeth*, act 4, sc.2, l.8–9.

28 Each new morn
New widows howl, new orphans cry, new sorrows
Strike heaven on the face.
1606 Macduff. *Macbeth*, act 4, sc.3, l.4–6.

29 MACDUFF: Stands Scotland where it did?
ROSS: Alas, poor country,
Almost afraid to know itself.
1606 *Macbeth*, act 4, sc.3, l.165–6.

30 MACDUFF: He has no children. All my pretty ones?
Did you say all? O hell-kite! All?
What, all my pretty chickens and their dam
At one fell swoop?
MALCOLM: Dispute it like a man.
MACDUFF: I shall do so,
But I must also feel it as a man.
I cannot but remember such things were
That were most precious to me. Did heaven look on
And would not take their part?
1606 Macduff, of his murdered wife and children. *Macbeth*, act 4, sc.3, l.217–26.

31 The night is long that never finds the day.
1606 Malcolm. *Macbeth*, act 4, sc.3, l.242.

32 It is an accustomed action with her, to seem thus washing her hands. I have known her continue in this a quarter of an hour.
1606 Gentlewoman, of Lady Macbeth. *Macbeth*, act 5, sc.1, l.27–9.

33 Out, damned spot; out, I say. One, two,—why, then 'tis time to do't. Hell is murky. Fie, my lord, fie, a soldier and afeard? What need we fear who knows it when none can call our power to account? Yet who would have thought the old man to have had so much blood in him?
1606 Lady Macbeth, sleepwalking, of the murdered Duncan. *Macbeth*, act 5, sc.1, l.33–8.

34 The Thane of Fife had a wife. Where is she now? What, will these hands ne'er be clean?
1606 Lady Macbeth. *Macbeth*, act 5, sc.1, l.40–1.

35 Now does he feel
His secret murders sticking on his hands.
Now minutely revolts upbraid his faith-breach.
Those he commands move only in command,
Nothing in love. Now does he feel his title
Hang loose about him, like a giant's robe
Upon a dwarfish thief.
1606 Angus, of Macbeth. *Macbeth*, act 5, sc.2, l.16–22.

36 The devil damn thee black, thou cream-faced loon!
1606 Macbeth to his servant. *Macbeth*, act 5, sc.3, l.11.

37 I have lived long enough. My way of life
Is fall'n into the sere, the yellow leaf,
And that which should accompany old age,
As honour, love, obedience, troops of friends,
I must not look to have.
1606 Macbeth. *Macbeth*, act 5, sc.3, l.24–8.

38 Canst thou not minister to a mind diseased,
Pluck from the memory a rooted sorrow,
Raze out the written troubles of the brain,

And with some sweet oblivious antidote
Cleanse the fraught bosom?
1606 Macbeth to the doctor, of Lady Macbeth. *Macbeth*, act 5, sc.3, l.42–5.

39 Throw physic to the dogs; I'll none of it.
1606 Macbeth. *Macbeth*, act 5, sc.3, l.49.

40 What rhubarb, cyme, or what purgative drug
Would scour these English hence?
1606 Macbeth to the doctor. *Macbeth*, act 5, sc.3, l.57–8.

41 I have supped full with horrors.
Direness, familiar to my slaughterhouse thoughts,
Cannot once start me.
1606 Macbeth. *Macbeth*, act 5, sc.5, l.13–14.

42 She should have died hereafter.
There would have been a time for such a word.
Tomorrow, and tomorrow, and tomorrow
Creeps in this petty pace from day to day
To the last syllable of recorded time,
And all our yesterdays have lighted fools
The way to dusty death. Out, out, brief candle.
Life's but a walking shadow, a poor player
That struts and frets his hour upon the stage,
And then is heard no more. It is a tale
Told by an idiot, full of sound and fury,
Signifying nothing.
1606 Macbeth, hearing of Lady Macbeth's death. *Macbeth*, act 5, sc.5, l.16–27.

43 They have tied me to a stake. I cannot fly,
But bear-like I must fight the course.
1606 Macbeth. *Macbeth*, act 5, sc.7, l.1–2.

44 YOUNG SIWARD: What is thy name?
MACBETH: Thou'lt be afraid to hear it.
YOUNG SIWARD: No, though thou call'st thyself a hotter name
Than any in hell.
MACBETH: My name's Macbeth.
1606 *Macbeth*, act 5, sc.7, l.5–8.

45 Macduff was from his mother's womb
Untimely ripped.
1606 Macduff. *Macbeth*, act 5, sc.10, l.15–16.

46 Lay on, Macduff,
And damned be him that first cries 'Hold, enough!'
1606 Macbeth. *Macbeth*, act 5, sc.10, l.33–4.

47 Your cause of sorrow
Must not be measured by his worth, for then
It hath no end.
1606 Ross to Siward. *Macbeth*, act 5, sc.11, l.10–12.

48 Kings are earth's gods; in vice their law's their will,
And if Jove stray, who dares say Jove doth ill?
1607 Pericles. *Pericles*, sc.1, l.146–7.

49 They do abuse the King that flatter him,
For flatt'ry is the bellows blows up sin.
1607 Helicanus. *Pericles*, sc.2, l.43–4.

50 'Tis time to fear when tyrants seems to kiss.
1607 Pericles. *Pericles*, sc.2, l.84.

51 We'll mingle our bloods together in the earth
From whence we had our being and our birth.
1607 Helicanus to Pericles. *Pericles*, sc.2, l.118–9.

52 I'll take thy word for faith, not ask thine oath;
Who shuns not to break one will sure crack both.
1607 Pericles to Helicanus. *Pericles*, sc.2, l.125–6.

53 Shall we rest us here
And, by relating tales of others' griefs,
See if 'twill teach us to forget our own?
1607 Cleon to Dioniza. *Pericles*, sc.4, l.1–3.

54 One sorrow never comes but brings an heir
That may succeed as his inheritor.
1607 Cleon. *Pericles*, sc.4, l.62–3.

55 He's a very dog to the commonalty.
1608 Fourth citizen. *Coriolanus*, act 1, sc.1, l.27.

56 What's the matter, you dissentious rogues,
That, rubbing the poor itch of your opinion,
Make yourselves scabs?
1608 Martius. *Coriolanus*, act 1, sc.1, l.162–4.

57 They threw their caps
As they would hang them on the horns o'th' moon.
1608 Martius. *Coriolanus*, act 1, sc.1, l.210–11.

58 Nature teaches beasts to know their friends.
1608 Sicinius. *Coriolanus*, act 2, sc.1, l.6.

59 [I am] one that loves a cup of hot wine with not a drop of allaying Tiber in't.
1608 Menenius. *Coriolanus*, act 2, sc.1, l.47–8.

60 What I think, I utter, and spend my malice in my breath.
1608 Menenius. *Coriolanus*, act 2, sc.1, l.52–3.

61 That's a brave fellow, but he's vengeance proud and loves not the common people.
1608 First Officer, of Coriolanus. *Coriolanus*, act 2, sc.2, l.5–6.

62 He seeks their hate with greater devotion than they can render it him.
1608 First Officer, of Coriolanus. *Coriolanus*, act 2, sc.2, l.18–19.

63 Ingratitude is monstrous, and for the multitude to be ingrateful were to make a monster of the multitude.
1608 Third Citizen. *Coriolanus*, act 2, sc.3, l.9–10.

64 'Shall remain'?
Hear you this Triton of the minnows? Mark you
His absolute 'shall'?
1608 Coriolanus. *Coriolanus*, act 3, sc.1, l.91–3.

65 On both sides more respect.
1608 Menenius. *Coriolanus*, act 3, sc.1, l.183.

66 You common cry of curs, whose breath I hate
As reek o'th' rotten fens, whose loves I prize
As the dead carcasses of unburied men
That do corrupt my air: I banish you.
1608 Coriolanus to the citizens. *Coriolanus*, act 3, sc.3, l.124–7.

67 Now we have shown our power,
Let us seem humbler after it is done.
1608 Brutus. *Coriolanus*, act 4, sc.2, l.3–4.

68 Anger's my meat, I sup upon myself,
And so shall starve with feeding.
1608 Volumnia. *Coriolanus*, act 4, sc.2, l.53–4.

69 He'll shake your Rome about your ears.
1608 Cominius. *Coriolanus*, act 4, sc.6, l.103.

70 Like a dull actor now
I have forgot my part, and I am out
Even to a full disgrace.
1608 Coriolanus. *Coriolanus*, act 5, sc.3, l.40–2.

71 O, a kiss
Long as my exile, sweet as my revenge!
1608 Coriolanus to Virgilia. *Coriolanus*, act 5, sc.3, l.44–5.

72 O mother, mother!
What have you done? Behold, the heavens do ope,
The gods look down, and this unnatural scene
Thay laugh at.
1608 Coriolanus. *Coriolanus*, act 5, sc.3, l.183–6.

73 Cut me to pieces, Volsces. Men and lads,
Stain all your edges on me. 'Boy'! False hound,
If you have writ your annals true, 'tis there
That, like an eagle in a dove-cot, I
Fluttered your Volscians in Corioles.
Alone I did it. 'Boy'!
1608 Coriolanus. *Coriolanus*, act 5, sc.6, l.112–7.

74 We were, fair Queen,
Two lads that thought there was no more behind
But such a day tomorrow as today,
And to be boy eternal.
1609 Polixenes to Hermione. *The Winter's Tale*, act 1, sc.2, l.63–6.

75 One good deed dying tongueless
Slaughters a thousand waiting upon that.
1609 Hermione. *The Winter's Tale*, act 1, sc.2, l.94–5.

76 He makes a July's day as short as December.
1609 Polixenes, of Mamillius. *The Winter's Tale*, act 1, sc.2, l.170.

77 Should all despair
That have revolted wives, the tenth of mankind
Would hang themselves.
1609 Leontes. *The Winter's Tale*, act 1, sc.2, l.199–201.

78 I saw his heart in's face.
1609 Polixenes, of Leontes. *The Winter's Tale*, act 1, sc.2, l.447.

79 A sad tale's best for winter.
1609 Mamillius. *The Winter's Tale*, act 2, sc.1, l.27.

80 It is an heretic that makes the fire,
Not she which burns in't.
1609 Paulina. *The Winter's Tale*, act 2, sc.3, l.115–6.

81 *Exit, pursued by a bear.*
1609 Stage Direction. *The Winter's Tale*, act 3, sc.3, l.57.

82 A snapper-up of unconsidered trifles.
1609 Autolycus, of himself. *The Winter's Tale*, act 4, sc.3, l.25–6.

83 Jog on, jog on, the footpath way,
And merrily hent the stile-a.
A merry heart goes all the day,
Your sad tires in a mile-a.
1609 Autolycus, singing. *The Winter's Tale*, act 4, sc.3, l.123–6.

84 Let's be red with mirth.
1609 Florizel. *The Winter's Tale*, act 4, sc.4, l.54.

85 Blasts of January
Would blow you through and through.
1609 Perdita, of Camillo. *The Winter's Tale*, act 4, sc.4, l.111–12.

86 Daffodils,
That come before the swallow dares, and take
The winds of March with beauty.
1609 Perdita. *The Winter's Tale*, act 4, sc.4, l.118–20.

87 When you speak, sweet,
I'd have you do it ever; when you sing,
I'd have you buy and sell so, so give alms,
Pray so; and for the ord'ring your affairs,
To sing them too. When you do dance, I wish you
A wave o'th' sea, that you might ever do
Nothing but that, move still, still so,
And own no other function. Each your doing,
So singular in each particular,
Crowns what you are doing in the present deeds,
That all your acts are queens.
1609 Florizel to Perdita. *The Winter's Tale*, act 4, sc.4, l.136–46.

88 Good sooth, she is
The queen of curds and cream.
1609 Camillo, of Perdita. *The Winter's Tale*, act 4, sc.4, l.160–1.

89 Garlic to mend her kissing with!
1609 Dorcas, of Mopsa. *The Winter's Tale*, act 4, sc.4, l.162–3.

90 He says he loves my daughter:
I think, so too, for never gazed the moon
Upon the water as he'll stand and read,
As 'twere, my daughter's eyes.
1609 Old Shepherd. *The Winter's Tale*, act 4, sc.4, l.172–5.

91 He has the prettiest love songs for maids, so without bawdry, which is strange, with such delicate burdens of dildos and fadings, 'Jump her, and thump her'; and where some stretch-mouthed rascal would, as it were, mean mischief and break a foul gap into the matter, he makes the maid to answer, 'Whoop, do me no harm, good man!'
1609 Servant. *The Winter's Tale*, act 4, sc.4, l.193–200.

92 Lawn as white as driven snow.
1609 Autolycus. *The Winter's Tale*, act 4, sc.4, l.219.

93 If I were not in love with Mopsa thou shouldst take no money of me, but being enthralled as I am, it will also be the bondage of certain ribbons and gloves.
1609 Clown to Autolycus (in disguise). *The Winter's Tale*, act 4, sc.4, l.231–3.

94 I love a ballad in print, alife, for then we are sure they are true.
1609 Mopsa to Autolycus (in disguise). *The Winter's Tale*, act 4, sc.4, l.258–9.

95 Though I am not naturally honest, I am so sometimes by chance.
1609 Autolycus. *The Winter's Tale*, act 4, sc.4, l.712–13.

96 Stars, stars,
And all eyes else, dead coals!
1609 Leontes. *The Winter's Tale*, act 5, sc.1, l.67–8.

97 Women will love her that she is a woman
More worth than any man; men, that she is
The rarest of all women.
1609 Servant, of Perdita. *The Winter's Tale*, act 5, sc.1, l.110–12

98 My lord, your sorrow was too sore laid on,
Which sixteen winters cannot blow away,
So many summers dry. Scarce any joy
Did ever so long live.
1609 Camillo to Leontes. *The Winter's Tale*, act 5, sc.3, l.49–52.

99 O, she's warm!
If this be magic, let it be an art
Lawful as eating.
1609 Leontes, of the now animated statue of Hermione. *The Winter's Tale*, act 5, sc.3, l.109–11.

1 Thou art thy mother's glass, and she in thee
Calls back the lovely April of her prime.
1609 *Sonnets*, sonnet 3.

2 Music to hear, why hear'st thou music sadly?
Sweets with sweets war not, joy delights in joy.
Why lov'st thou that which thou receiv'st not gladly?
1609 *Sonnets*, sonnet 8.

3 For thou art so possessed with murd'rous hate

That 'gainst thyself thou stick'st not to conspire.
1609 *Sonnets*, sonnet 10.

4 If I could write the beauty of your eyes
And in fresh numbers number all your graces,
The age to come would say 'This poet lies;
Such heavenly touches ne'er touched earthly faces.'
1609 *Sonnets*, sonnet 17.

5 Shall I compare thee to a summer's day?
Thou art more lovely and more temperate.
Rough winds do shake the darling buds of May,
And summer's lease hath all too short a date.
Sometime too hot the eye of heaven shines,
And often is his gold complexion dimmed,
And every fair from fair sometime declines,
By chance or nature's changing course untrimmed;
But thy eternal summer shall not fade
Nor lose possession of that fair thou ow'st,
Nor shall death brag thou wander'st in his shade
When in eternal lines to time thou grow'st.
So long as men can breathe or eyes can see,
So long lives this, and this gives life to thee.
1609 *Sonnets*, sonnet 18.

6 Yet do thy worst, old time; despite thy wrong
My love shall in my verse ever live young.
1609 *Sonnets*, sonnet 19.

7 A woman's face with nature's own hand painted
Hast thou, the master-mistress of my passion.
1609 *Sonnets*, sonnet 20.

8 My glass shall not persuade me I am old
So long as youth and thou are of one date;
But when in thee time's furrows I behold,
Then look I death my days should expiate.
1609 *Sonnets*, sonnet 22.

9 Presume not on thy heart when mine is slain:
Thou gav'st me thine not to give back again.
1609 *Sonnets*, sonnet 22.

10 O let my books be then the eloquence
And dumb presagers of my speaking breast,
Who plead for love, and look for recompense
More than that tongue that more hath more expressed.
O learn to read what silent love hath writ;
To hear with eyes belongs to love's fine wit.
1609 *Sonnets*, sonnet 23.

11 Now see what good turns eyes for eyes have done:
Mine eyes have drawn thy shape, and thine for me
Are windows to my breast, wherethrough the sun
Delights to peep, to gaze therein on thee.
Yet eyes this cunning want to grace their art:
They draw but what they see, know not the heart.
1609 *Sonnets*, sonnet 24.

12 The painful warrior famousèd for might,
After a thousand victories once foiled
Is from the book of honour razèd quite,
And all the rest forgot for which he toiled.
1609 *Sonnets*, sonnet 25.

13 Weary with toil I haste me to my bed,
The dear repose for limbs with travel tired;
But then begins a journey in my head
To work my mind when body's work's expired.
1609 *Sonnets*, sonnet 27.

14 When, in disgrace with fortune and men's eyes,
I all alone beweep my outcast state,
And trouble deaf heaven with my bootless cries,
And look upon myself and curse my fate,
Wishing me like to one more rich hope,
Featured like him, like him with friends possessed,
Desiring this man's art and that man's scope,
With what I most enjoy contented least:
Yet in these thoughts myself almost despising,
Haply I think on thee, and then my state,
Like to the lark at break of day arising
From sullen earth, sings hymns at heaven's gate;
For thy sweet love remembered such wealth brings
That then I scorn to change my state with kings'.
1609 *Sonnets*, sonnet 29.

15 When to the sessions of sweet silent thought
I summon up remembrance of things past,
I sigh the lack of many a thing I sought,
And with old woes new wail my dear time's waste.
Then can I drown an eye unused to flow
For precious friends hid in death's dateless night,
And weep afresh love's long-since-cancelled woe,
And moan th'expense of many a vanished sight.
Then can I grieve at grievances foregone,
And heavily from woe to woe tell o'er
The sad account of fore-bemoanèd moan,
Which I new pay as if not paid before.
But if the while I think on thee, dear friend,
All losses are restored, and sorrows end.
1609 *Sonnets*, sonnet 30.

16 Full many a glorious morning have I seen
Flatter the mountain tops with sovereign eye,
Kissing with golden face the meadows green.
1609 *Sonnets*, sonnet 33.

17 As a decrepit father takes delight
To see his active child do deeds of youth,
So I, made lame by fortune's dearest spite,
Take all my comfort of thy worth and truth.
1609 *Sonnets*, sonnet 37.

18 All days are nights to see till I see thee,
And nights bright days when dreams do show thee me.
1609 *Sonnets*, sonnet 43.

19 O how much more doth beauty beauteous seem
By that sweet ornament which truth doth give!
1609 *Sonnets*, sonnet 54.

20 The rose looks fair, but fairer we it deem
For that sweet odour which doth in it live.
1609 *Sonnets*, sonnet 54.

21 Not marble nor the gilded monuments
Of princes shall outlive this powerful rhyme,
But you shall shine more bright in these contents
Than unswept stone besmeared with sluttish time.
1609 *Sonnets*, sonnet 55.

22 So, till the judgement that yourself arise,
You live in this, and dwell in lovers' eyes.
1609 *Sonnets*, sonnet 55.

23 Being your slave, what should I do but tend
Upon the hours and times of your desire?
I have no precious time at all to spend,
Nor services to do, till you require;
Nor dare I chide the world-without-end hour
Whilst I, my sovereign, watch the clock for you,

Nor think the bitterness of absence sour
When you have bid your servant once adieu.
Nor dare I question with my jealous thought
Where you may be, or your affairs suppose,
But like a sad slave stay and think of naught
Save, where you are, how happy you make those.
So true a fool is love that in your will,
Though you do anything, he thinks no ill.
1609 *Sonnets*, sonnet 57.

24 Like as the waves make towards the pebbled shore,
So do our minutes hasten to their end.
1609 *Sonnets*, sonnet 60.

25 Since brass, nor stone, nor earth, nor boundless sea,
But sad mortality o'ersways their power,
How with this rage shall beauty hold a plea,
Whose action is no stronger than a flower?
O how shall summer's honey breath hold out
Against the wrackful siege of battering days
When rocks impregnable are not so stout,
Nor gates of steel so strong, but time decays?
O fearful meditation! where, alack,
Shall time's best jewel from time's chest lie hid,
Or what strong hand can hold his swift foot back,
Or who his spoil of beauty can forbid?
O none, unless this miracle have might:
That is black ink my love may still shine bright.
1609 *Sonnets*, sonnet 65.

26 Right perfection wrongfully disgraced.
1609 *Sonnets*, sonnet 66.

27 Simple truth miscalled simplicity.
1609 *Sonnets*, sonnet 66.

28 They look into the beauty of thy mind,
And that in guess they measure by thy deeds.
1609 *Sonnets*, sonnet 69.

29 No longer mourn for me when I am dead
Than you shall hear the surly sullen bell
Give warning to the world that I am fled
From this vile world with vilest worms to dwell.
Nay, if you read this line, remember not
The hand that writ it; for I love you so
That I in your sweet thoughts would be forgot
If thinking on me then should make you woe.
O, if, I say, you look upon this verse
When I perhaps compounded am with clay,
Do not so much as my poor name rehearse,
But let your love even with my life decay,
Lest the wise world should look into your moan
And mock you with me after I am gone.
1609 *Sonnets*, sonnet 71.

30 That time of year thou mayst in me behold
When yellow leaves, or none, or few, do hang
Upon those boughs which shake against the cold,
Bare ruined choirs where late the sweet birds sang.
In me thou seest the twilight of such day
As after sunset fadeth in the west,
Which by and by black night doth take away,
Death's second self. that seals up all in rest.
1609 *Sonnets*, sonnet 73.

31 O know, sweet love, I always write of you,
And you and love are still my argument.
1609 *Sonnets*, sonnet 76.

32 For as the sun is daily new and old,
So is my love, still telling what is told.
1609 *Sonnets*, sonnet 76.

33 Thy glass will show thee how thy beauties wear,
Thy dial how thy precious minutes waste,
The vacant leaves thy mind's imprint will bear,
And of this book this learning mayst thou taste:
The wrinkles which thy glass will truly show
Of mouthèd graves will give thee memory;
Thou by thy dial's shady stealth mayst know
Time's thievish progress to eternity.
1609 *Sonnets*, sonnet 77.

34 Who is it that says most which can say more
Than this rich praise: that you alone are you.
1609 *Sonnets*, sonnet 84.

35 Farewell—thou art too dear for my possessing,
And like enough thou know'st thy estimate.
The charter of thy worth gives thee releasing;
My bonds in thee are all determinate.
For how do I hold thee but by thy granting,
And for that riches where is my deserving?
The cause of this fair gift in me is wanting,
And so my patent back again is swerving.
Thyself thou gav'st, thy own worth then not knowing,
Or me to whom thou gav'st it else mistaking;
So thy great gift, upon misprision growing,
Comes home again, on better judgement making.
Thus have I had thee as a dream doth flatter:
In sleep a king, but waking no such matter.
1609 *Sonnets*, sonnet 87.

36 So shall I live supposing thou art true
Like a deceived husband; so love's face
May still seem love to me, though altered new.
1609 *Sonnets*, sonnet 93.

37 They that have power to hurt and will do none,
That do not do the thing they most do show,
Who moving others are themselves as stone,
Unmovèd, cold, and to temptation slow—
They rightly do inherit heaven's graces,
And husband nature's riches from expense;
They are the lords and owners of their faces,
Others but stewards of their excellence.
1609 *Sonnets*, sonnet 94.

38 For sweetest things turn sourest by their deeds:
Lilies that fester smell far worse than weeds.
1609 *Sonnets*, sonnet 94.

39 How like a winter hath my absence been
From thee, the pleasure of the fleeting year!
What freezings have I felt, what dark days seen.
What old December's bareness everywhere.
1609 *Sonnets*, sonnet 97.

40 From you have I been absent in the spring
When proud-pied April, dressed in all his trim,
Hath put a spirit of youth in everything.
1609 *Sonnets*, sonnet 98.

41 Nor did I wonder at the lily's white,
Nor praise the deep vermilion in the rose.
1609 *Sonnets*, sonnet 98.

42 To me, fair friend, you never can be old;
For as you were when first your eye I eyed,

Such seems your beauty still.
1609 *Sonnets*, sonnet 104.

43 Kind is my love today, tomorrow kind,
Still constant in a wondrous excellence.
1609 *Sonnets*, sonnet 105.

44 Not mine own fears nor the prophetic soul
Of the wide world dreaming on things to come
Can yet the lease of my true love control,
Supposed as forfeit to a confined doom.
1609 *Sonnets*, sonnet 107.

45 What's in the brain that ink may character
Which hath not figured to thee my true spirit?
What's new to speak, what now to register,
That may express my love or thy dear merit?
Nothing, sweet boy; but yet like prayers divine
I must each day say o'er the very same,
Counting no old thing old, thou mine, I thine,
Even as when first I hallowed thy fair name.
1609 *Sonnets*, sonnet 108.

46 O never say that I was false of heart,
Though absence seemed my flame to qualify.
1609 *Sonnets*, sonnet 109.

47 Then give me welcome, next my heaven the best,
Even to thy pure and most loving breast.
1609 *Sonnets*, sonnet 110.

48 Let me not to the marriage of true minds
Admit impediments. Love is not love
Which alters when it alteration finds,
Or bends with the remover to remove.
O no, it is an ever fixèd mark
That looks on tempests and is never shaken;
It is the star to every wand'ring barque,
Whose worth's unknown although his height be
taken.
Love's not time's fool, though rosy lips and cheeks
Within his bending sickle's compass come;
Love alters not with his brief hours and weeks,
But bears it out even to the edge of doom.
If this be error and upon me proved,
I never writ, nor no man ever loved.
1609 *Sonnets*, sonnet 116.

49 What potions have I drunk of siren tears
Distilled from limbecks foul as hell within,
Applying fears to hopes and hopes to fears,
Still losing when I saw myself to win!
1609 *Sonnets*, sonnet 119.

50 For if you were by my unkindness shaken,
As I by yours, you've passed a hell of time.
1609 *Sonnets*, sonnet 120.

51 My mistress' eyes are nothing like the sun;
Coral is far more red than her lips' red.
If snow be white, why then her breasts are dun;
If hairs be wires, black wires grow on her head.
I have seen roses damasked, red and white,
But no such roses see I in her cheeks;
And in some perfumes is there more delight
Than the breath that from my mistress reeks.
I love to hear her speak, yet well I know
That music hath a far more pleasing sound.
I grant I never saw a goddess go:
My mistress when she walks treads on the ground.
And yet, by heaven, I think my love as rare
As any she belied with false compare.
1609 *Sonnets*, sonnet 130.

52 Whoever hath her wish, thou hast thy Will,
And Will to boot, and Will in overplus.
1609 *Sonnets*, sonnet 135.

53 So thou, being rich in Will, add to thy Will
One will of mine to make thy large Will more.
Let no unkind no fair beseechers kill;
Think all but one, and me in that one Will.
1609 *Sonnets*, sonnet 135.

54 When my love swears that she is made of truth
I do believe her though I know she lies.
1609 *Sonnets*, sonnet 138.

55 Two loves I have, of comfort and despair,
Which like two spirits do suggest me still.
The better angel is a man right fair,
The worser spirit a woman coloured ill.
1609 *Sonnets*, sonnet 144.

56 My love is as a fever, longing still
For that which longer nurseth the disease,
Feeding on that which doth preserve the ill,
Th'uncertain sickly appetite to please.
My reason, the physician to my love,
Angry that his prescriptions are not kept,
Hath left me, and I desperate now approve
Desire is death, which physic did except.
Past cure I am, now reason is past care,
And frantic mad with evermore unrest.
My thoughts and my discourse as madmen's are,
At random from the truth vainly expressed;
For I have sworn thee fair, and thought thee bright,
Who art as black as hell, as dark as night.
1609 *Sonnets*, sonnet 147.

57 Was there ever man had such luck? When I kissed the jack upon an upcast to be hit away! I had a hundred pound on't, and then a whoreson jackanapes must take me up for swearing.
1610 Cloten. *Cymbeline*, act 2, sc.1, l.1–4.

58 When a gentleman is disposed to swear it is not for any standers-by to curtail his oaths.
1610 Cloten. *Cymbeline*, act 2, sc.1, l.10–11.

59 On her left breast
A mole, cinque-spotted, like the crimson drops
I'th' bottom of a cowslip.
1610 Giacomo, of Innogen. *Cymbeline*, act 2, sc.2, l.37–9.

60 I am advised to give her music o' mornings; they say it will penetrate.
1610 Cloten, of Innogen. *Cymbeline*, act 2, sc.3, l.11–12.

61 Hark, hark, the lark at heaven gate sings,
And Phoebus gins arise.
1610 Musician, singing. *Cymbeline*, act 2, sc.3, l.19–20.

62 Is there no way for men to be, but women
Must be half-workers? We are bastards all.
1610 Posthumus. *Cymbeline*, act 2, sc.5, l.1–2.

63 I thought her
As chaste as unsunned snow.
1610 Posthumus, of Innogen. *Cymbeline*, act 2, sc.5, l.12–13.

64 I am stale, a garment out of fashion.
1610 Innogen. *Cymbeline*, act 3, sc.4, l.51.

65 Against self-slaughter
There is a prohibition so divine
That cravens my weak hand.
1610 Innogen. *Cymbeline*, act 3, sc.4, l.76–8.

66 Thus may poor fools
Believe false teachers.
1610 Innogen. *Cymbeline*, act 3, sc.4, l.84–5.

67 Though those that are betrayed
Do feel the treason sharply, yet the traitor
Stands in worse case of woe.
1610 Innogen. *Cymbeline*, act 3, sc.4, l.85–7.

68 Hath Britain all the sun that shines? Day, night,
Are they not but in Britain? I'th' world's volume
Our Britain seems as of it but not in't,
In a great pool a swan's nest.
1610 Innogen to Pisanio. *Cymbeline*, act 3, sc.4, l.137–40.

69 Thou art all the comfort
The gods will diet me with.
1610 Innogen to Pisanio. *Cymbeline*, act 3, sc.4, l.180–1.

70 Weariness
Can snore upon the flint when resty sloth
Finds the down pillow hard.
1610 Belarius. *Cymbeline*, act 3, sc.6, l.33–5.

71 By Jupiter, an angel—or, if not,
An earthly paragon.
1610 Belarius, of Innogen in disguise. *Cymbeline*, act 3, sc.6, l.42–3.

72 All gold and silver rather turn to dirt.
1610 Arviragus. *Cymbeline*, act 3, sc.6, l.52.

73 Society is no comfort
To one not sociable.
1610 Innogen. *Cymbeline*, act 4, sc.2, l.12–13.

74 Fear no more the heat o'th' sun,
Nor the furious winter's rages.
Thou thy worldly task hast done,
Home art gone and ta'en thy wages.
Golden lads and girls all must,
As chimney-sweepers, come to dust.
1610 Guiderius. *Cymbeline*, act 4, sc.2, l.259–64.

75 By medicine life may be prolonged, yet death
Will seize the doctor too.
1610 Cymbeline. *Cymbeline*, act 5, sc.6, l.29–30.

76 The power that I have on you is to spare you.
1610 Posthumus to Giacomo. *Cymbeline*, act 5, sc.6, l.419.

77 What seest thou else
In the dark backward and abyss of time?
1611 Prospero to Miranda. *The Tempest*, act 1, sc.2, l.49–50.

78 I find my zenith doth depend upon
A most auspicious star, whose influence
If now I court not, but omit, my fortunes
Will ever after droop.
1611 Prospero to Miranda. *The Tempest*, act 1, sc.2, l.182–5.

79 Thou art inclined to sleep; 'tis a good dullness,
And give it way. I know thou canst not choose.
1611 Prospero to Miranda. *The Tempest*, act 1, sc.2, l.186–7.

80 You taught me language, and my profit on't
Is I know how to curse.
1611 Caliban to Miranda. *The Tempest*, act 1, sc.2, l.365–6.

81 Come unto these yellow sands,
And then take hands.
1611 Ariel, singing. *The Tempest*, act 1, sc.2, l.377–8.

82 This music crept by me upon the waters,
Allaying both their fury and my passion
With its sweet air.
1611 Ferdinand. *The Tempest*, act 1, sc.2, l.394–6.

83 Full fathom five thy father lies.
Of his bones are coral made.
1611 Ariel. *The Tempest*, act 1, sc.2, l.399–400.

84 Nothing of him that doth fade
But doth suffer a sea-change
Into something rich and strange.
1611 Ariel. *The Tempest*, act 1, sc.2, l.402–4.

85 He receives comfort like cold porridge.
1611 Sebastian, of Alonso. *The Tempest*, act 2, sc.1, l.11.

86 Look, he's winding up the watch of his wit.
By and by it will strike.
1611 Sebastian, of Gonzalo. *The Tempest*, act 2, sc.1, l.13–14.

87 Misery acquaints a man with strange bedfellows.
1611 Trinculo, of Caliban. *The Tempest*, act 2, sc.2, l.39.

88 'Ban, 'ban, Cacaliban
Has a new master.—Get a new man!
1611 Caliban. *The Tempest*, act 2, sc.2, l.183–4.

89 FERDINAND: I do beseech you,
Chiefly that I might set it in my prayers,
What is your name?
MIRANDA: Miranda. O my father,
I have broke your hest to say so!
FERDINAND: Admired Miranda!
Indeed the top of admiration, worth
What's dearest to the world.
1611 *The Tempest*, act 3, sc.1, l.36–9.
Shakespeare invented the name Miranda, taking it from the Latin word meaning 'worthy to be admired'.

90 Remember
First to possess his books, for without them
He's but a sot as I am, nor hath not
One spirit to command–they all do hate him
As rootedly as I. Burn but his books.
1611 Caliban, of Prospero. *The Tempest*, act 3, sc.2, l.92–6.

91 He that dies pays all debts.
1611 Stefano. *The Tempest*, act 3, sc.2, l.134.

92 The isle is full of noises,
Sound, and sweet airs, that give delight and hurt not.
1611 Caliban. *The Tempest*, act 3, sc.2, l.138–9.

93 Thou shalt find that she will outstrip all praise,
And make it halt behind her.
1611 Prospero, of Miranda. *The Tempest*, act 4, sc.1, l.10–11.

94 The cloud-capped towers, the gorgeous palaces,
The solemn temples, the great globe itself,
Yea, all which it inherit, shall dissolve;
And, like this insubstantial pageant faded,
Leave not a rack behind.
1611 Prospero. *The Tempest*, act 4, sc.1, l.152–6.

95 We are such stuff
As dreams are made on, and our little life
Is rounded with a sleep.
1611 Prospero. *The Tempest*, act 4, sc.1, l.156–8.

96 They were red-hot with drinking;
So full of valour that they smote the air
For breathing in their faces.
1611 Ariel. *The Tempest*, act 4, sc.1, l.171–3.

97 This rough magic
I here abjure.
1611 Prospero. *The Tempest*, act 5, sc.1, l.50–1.

98 I'll break my staff,
Bury it certain fathoms in the earth,
And deeper than did ever plummet sound
I'll drown my book.
1611 Prospero. *The Tempest*, act 5, sc.1, l.54–7.

99 Where the bee sucks, there suck I:
In a cowslip's bell I lie;
There I couch when owls do cry.
On the bat's back I do fly
After summer merrily.
Merrily, merrily shall I live now
Under the blossom that hangs on the bough.
1611 Ariel's song. *The Tempest*, act 5, sc.1, l.88–94.

1 How beauteous mankind is! O brave new world
That hath such people in't!
1611 Miranda. *The Tempest*, act 5, sc.1, l.186–7.

2 What a thrice-double ass
Was I to take this drunkard for a god,
And worship this dull fool!
1611 Caliban. *The Tempest*, act 5, sc.1, l.299–301.

3 Now my charms are all o'erthrown,
And what strength I have's mine own.
1611 Prospero. *The Tempest*, epilogue, l.1–2.

4 Heat not a furnace for your foe so hot
That it do singe yourself.
1613 Norfolk. *Henry VIII*, act 1, sc.1, l.140–1.

5 Travelled gallants
That fill the court with quarrels, talk, and tailors.
1613 Lovell. *Henry VIII*, act 1, sc.3, l.19–20.

6 Good company, good wine, good welcome
Can make good people.
1613 Guildford. *Henry VIII*, act 1, sc.4, l.6–7.

7 Two women placed together makes cold weather.
1613 Lord Chamberlain. *Henry VIII*, act 1, sc.4, l.22.

8 If I chance to talk a little wild, forgive me.
I had it from my father.
1613 Sands. *Henry VIII*, act 1, sc.4, l.26–7.

9 Those you make friends
And give your hearts to, when they once perceive
The least rub in your fortunes, fall away
Like water from ye.
1613 Buckingham. *Henry VIII*, act 2, sc.1, l.128–31.

10 I would not be a queen
For all the world.
1613 Anne Boleyn. *Henry VIII*, act 2, sc.3, l.45–6.

11 You have many enemies that know not
Why they are so, but, like to village curs,
Bark when their fellows do.
1613 Henry to Wolsey. *Henry VIII*, act 2, sc.4, l.155–7.

12 Orpheus with his lute made trees,
And the mountain tops that freeze,
Bow themselves when he did sing.
1613 Gentlewoman, singing. *Henry VIII*, act 3, sc.1, l.3–5.

13 Everything that heard him play,
Even the billows of the sea,
Hung their heads, and then lay by.
In sweet music is such art,
Killing care and grief of heart
Fall asleep, or hearing, die.
1613 Gentlewoman, singing. *Henry VIII*, act 3, sc.1, l.9–14.

14 Methought
I stood not in the smile of heaven.
1613 Henry. *Henry VIII*, act 2, sc.4, l.183–4.

15 In sweet music is such art,
Killing care and grief of heart
Fall asleep, or hearing die.
1613 Gentlewoman. *Henry VIII*, act 3, sc.1, l.13–15.

16 Yet I know her for
A spleeny Lutheran, and not wholesome to
Our cause.
1613 Cardinal Wolsey, of Anne Boleyn. *Henry VIII*, act 3, sc.2, l.99–101.

17 Nature does require
Her times of preservation.
1613 Wolsey to Henry. *Henry VIII*, act 3, sc.2, l.147–8.

18 I have touched the highest point of all my greatness,
And from that full meridian of my glory
I haste now to my setting.
1613 Wolsey. *Henry VIII*, act 3, sc.2, l.224–6.

19 I feel within me
A peace above all earthly dignities,
A still and quiet conscience.
1613 Wolsey. *Henry VIII*, act 3, sc.2, l.379–81.

20 This is the state of man. He puts forth
The tender leaves of hopes; tomorrow blossoms,
And bears his blushing honours thick upon him;
The third day comes a frost, a killing frost,
And when he thinks, good easy man, full surely
His greatness is a-ripening, nips his root,
And then he falls, as I do.
1613 Wolsey. *Henry VIII*, act 3, sc.2, l.352–8.

21 Had I but served my God with half the zeal
I served my King, He would not in mine age
Have left me naked to mine enemies.
1613 Wolsey. *Henry VIII*, act 3, sc.2, l.456–8.

22 Still in thy right hand carry gentle peace
To silence envious tongues.
1613 Wolsey. *Henry VIII*, act 3, sc.2, l.446–7.

23 An old man broken with the storms of state
Is come to lay his weary bones among ye.
Give him a little earth, for charity.
1613 Griffith, recalling Wolsey. *Henry VIII*, act 4, sc.2, l.21–3.

24 Men's evil manners live in brass, their virtues
We write in water.
1613 Griffith. *Henry VIII*, act 4, sc.2, l.45–6.

25 That comfort comes too late,
'Tis like a pardon after execution.
1613 Katherine. *Henry VIII*, act 4, sc.2, l.121–2.

26 Good grows with her.
In her days every man shall eat in safety
Under his own vine what he plants, and sing
The merry songs of peace to all his neighbours.
1613 Cranmer, of Elizabeth. *Henry VIII*, act 5, sc.4, l.32–5.

Shange, Ntozake *originally* Paulette Williams 1948–

Black US writer, who adopted a Zulu name for political reasons. She has written mainly for the stage, often adopting a multimedia approach combining poetry, dance and music.

27 For coloured girls who have considered suicide / when the rainbow is enuf.
1975 Title of 'choreo-poem'.

Shankly, Bill (William) 1913–81

Scottish footballer and manager. A player with Preston North End and Scotland, he established a reputation as one of the finest managers of his generation through his management of Liverpool in the 1960s and was widely known for his grim determination and biting wit.

28 Some people think football is a matter of life and death. I don't like that attitude. I can assure them it is much more serious than that.
Quoted in the *Sunday Times*, 4 Oct 1981.

29 I don't drop players, I make changes.
Quoted in Peter Ball and Phil Shaw *The Book of Football Quotations* (1990).

30 If Everton were playing down at the bottom of my garden, I'd draw the curtains.
Quoted in Colin Jarman *The Guinness Dictionary of Sports Quotations* (1990).

31 If you're in the penalty area and aren't sure what to do with the ball, just stick it in the net, and we'll discuss your options afterwards.
Quoted in Colin Jarman *The Guinness Dictionary of Sports Quotations* (1990).

32 Of course I didn't take my wife to see Rochdale as an anniversary present. It was her birthday. Would I have got married during the football season? And anyway it wasn't Rochdale, it was Rochdale reserves.
Quoted in Peter Ball and Phil Shaw *The Book of Football Quotations* (1990).

33 This town has two great teams—Liverpool and Liverpool reserves.
Deliberately ignoring rival team Everton. Quoted in Colin Jarman *The Guiness Dictionary of Sports Quotations* (1990).

34 We murdered them 0–0.
Quoted in Colin Jarman *The Guiness Dictionary of Sports Quotations* (1990).

35 Me having no education, I had to use my brains.
Quoted in David Pickering *The Cassell Soccer Companion* (1994)

Shapin, Steven 1955–

US sociologist

36 The very power of science to hold knowledge as collective knowledge is founded upon a degree and a quality of trust which are arguably unparalleled elsewhere in our culture… Scientists know so much about the natural world by knowing so much about whom they can trust.
1994 *A Social History of Truth*.

Sharansky, Natan Anatoly Borisovich 1948–

Ukrainian-born Soviet dissident, human rights activist and politician. He was imprisoned (1977–86) by the Soviet government. As a Jew, he applied for emigration rights to Israel in 1975, but was harassed by the KGB and discharged from his job. He was arrested in 1977 and accused of treason and espionage. On his release from prison he was allowed to go to Israel, where he became a politician.

37 All the resources of a superpower cannot isolate a man who hears the voice of freedom; a voice that I heard from the very chamber of my soul.
1986 Speech, New York, 11 May, shortly after his release following nine years in a Soviet labour colony.

Sharp, William *pseudonym* ***Fiona Macleod*** 1855–1905

Scottish writer and traveller. He published poetry and literary criticism, but he is best known as the author of a series of neo-Celtic romantic tales written under the pseudonym he systematically refused to acknowledge.

38 My heart is a lonely hunter that hunts on a lonely hill.
1896 'The Lonely Hunter', stanza 6. Carson McCullers adapted the phrase as the title of a 1940 novel, *The Heart Is a Lonely Hunter*.

Sharpe, Tom (Thomas Ridley) 1928–

English novelist. His early works were plays written in South Africa. He returned to England in 1961, and became known for the vigorous satire of his comic novels.

39 The South African police would leave no stone unturned to see that nothing disturbed the even terror of their lives.
1973 *Indecent Exposure*, ch.1.

40 Skullion had little use for contraceptives at the best of times. Unnatural, he called them, and placed them in the lower social category of things along with elastic-sided boots and made-up bow ties. Not the sort of attire for a gentleman.
1974 *Porterhouse Blue*, ch.9.

41 And besides, Mrs Forthby in the flesh was a different kettle of fish to Mrs Forthby in his fantasies. In the latter she had a multitude of perverse inclinations, which corresponded exactly with his own unfortunate requirements, while possessing a discretion that would have done credit to a Trappist nun. In the flesh she was disappointingly different.
1975 *Blott on the Landscape*, ch.3.

42 In the lotus position at her yoga class she managed to exude energy, and her attempts at Transcendental Meditation had been likened to a pressure-cooker on simmer.
1976 *Wilt*, ch.1.

43 God, in his view, had created a perfect world if the book of Genesis was to be believed and it had been going downhill ever since.
1976 *Wilt*, ch.17.

44 All you had to do was tell people what they wanted to hear and they would believe you no matter how implausible your story might be.
1976 *Wilt*, ch.18.

45 The Rev St John Froude put the phone down thoughtfully. The notion that he was sharing the house with a disembodied and recently murdered woman was not one that he had wanted to put to his caller. His reputation for eccentricity was already sufficiently widespread without adding to it.
1976 *Wilt*, ch.19.

46 If any writer thinks the world is full of middle-class people of nice sensibilities, then he is out of his mind.
1985 In the *Observer*, 3 Feb.

Shaw, George Bernard 1856–1950

Anglo-Irish dramatist and socialist. He moved to London in 1876 and in 1882 joined the Fabian Society. He wrote over 40 plays including *Arms and the Man* (1894, published 1898), *Candida* (1895), *Man and Superman* (1903), *Pygmalion* (1913), *Saint Joan* (1923, published 1924) and *The Apple Cart* (1929). He was also a lifelong advocate of vegetarianism, and a passionate supporter of spelling reform. In 1935 he was awarded the Nobel prize for literature.

47 Money is indeed the most important thing in the world: and all sound and successful personal and national morality should have this fact for its basis.
1880 *The Irrational Knot*, preface.

48 Reminiscences make one feel so deliciously aged and sad.
1880 *The Irrational Knot*, ch.14.

49 A man who has no office to go to—I don't care who he is—is a trial of which you can have no conception.
1880 *The Irrational Knot*, ch.18.

50 'Do you know what a pessimist is?'
'A man who thinks everybody is as nasty as himself, and hates them for it.'
1887 *An Unsocial Socialist*, ch.5.

51 Don't ask me for promises until I know what I am promising.
1894 Catherine to Raina. *Arms and the Man*, act 1.

52 You can always tell an old soldier by the inside of his holsters and cartridge boxes. The young ones carry pistols and cartridges; the old ones, grub.
1894 The Man to Raina. *Arms and the Man*, act 1.

53 Oh, you are a very poor soldier—a chocolate cream soldier!
1894 Raina to The Man. *Arms and the Man*, act 1.

54 You're not a man, you're a machine.
1894 Sergius to Bluntschli. *Arms and the Man*, act 3.

55 We have no more right to consume happiness without producing it than to consume wealth without producing it.
1895 Morell to Lexy. *Candida*, act 1.

56 Do you think that the things people make fools of themselves about are any less real and true than the things they behave sensibly about? They are more true: they are the only things that are true.
1895 Marchbanks to Morell. *Candida*, act 1.

57 It is easy—terribly easy—to shake a man's faith in himself. To take advantage of that to break a man's spirit is devil's work.
1895 Morell to Marchbanks. *Candida*, act 1.

58 Wicked people means people who have no love: therefore they have no shame. They have the power to ask for love because they don't need it: they have the power to offer it because they have none to give. But we, who have love, and long to mingle it with the love of others: we cannot utter a word. You find that, don't you?
1895 Marchbanks to Proserpine. *Candida*, act 2.

59 I'm only a beer teetotaller, not a champagne teetotaller.
1895 Proserpine. *Candida*, act 3.

60 I no longer desire happiness: life is nobler than that.
1895 Marchbanks. *Candida*, act 3.

61 We're from Madeira, but perfectly respectable, so far.
1896 Philip Clandon to Valentine. *You Never Can Tell*, act 1.

62 We don't bother much about dress and manners in England, because, as a nation, we don't dress well and we've no manners.
1896 Valentine to Dolly and Philip Clandon. *You Never Can Tell*, act 1.

63 The great advantage of a hotel is that it's a refuge from home life.
1896 Waiter. *You Never Can Tell*, act 2.

64 Well, sir, you never can tell. That's a principle in life with me, sir, if you'll excuse my having such a thing, sir.
1896 Waiter to Fergus Crampton. *You Never Can Tell*, act 2.

65 There is nothing so bad or so good that you will not find Englishmen doing it; but you will never find an Englishman in the wrong. He does everything on principle. He fights you on patriotic principles; he robs you on business principles; he enslaves you on imperial principles; he bullies you on manly principles; he supports his king on loyal principles and cuts off his head on republican principles.
1897 *The Man of Destiny.*

66 The worst sin towards our fellow creatures is not to hate them, but to be indifferent to them: that's the essence of inhumanity.
1897 Pastor Anderson to Judith Anderson. *The Devil's Disciple*, act 2.

67 Martyrdom...the only way in which a man can become famous without ability.
1897 *The Devil's Disciple*, act 3.

68 I never expect a soldier to think, sir.
1897 Richard Dudgeon to Major Swindon. *The Devil's Disciple*, act 3.

69 'I can't believe it! What will History say?'
'History, sir, will tell lies as usual.'
1897 Major Swindon and Gen Burgoyne. *The Devil's Disciple*, act 3.

70 Your friend the British soldier can stand up to anything except the British War Office.
1897 Gen Burgoyne to Major Swindon. *The Devil's Disciple*, act 3.

71 Brains are not everything.
1898 Rev Samuel Gardner. *Mrs Warren's Profession*, act 1.

72 If there is anything I hate in a woman, it's want of character.
1898 Mrs Warren. *Mrs Warren's Profession*, act 2.

73 The only way for a woman to provide for herself decently is for her to be good to some man that can afford to be good to her.
1898 Mrs Warren to Vivie Warren. *Mrs Warren's Profession*, act 2.

74 There are no secrets better kept than the secrets everybody guesses.
1898 Sir George Crofts. *Mrs Warren's Profession*, act 3.

75 'Damn you!'
'You need not. I feel among the damned already.'
1898 Sir George Crofts and Vivie Warren. *Mrs Warren's Profession*, act 3.

76 Miss Warren is a great devotee of the Gospel of Getting On.
1898 Praed. *Mrs Warren's Profession*, act 4.

77 He is a barbarian, and thinks that the customs of his tribe

and island are the laws of nature.
1899 Of the Briton. Caesar to Theodotus. *Caesar and Cleopatra*, act 2.

78 When a stupid man is doing something he is ashamed of, he always declares that it is his duty.
1899 Apollodorus. *Caesar and Cleopatra*, act 3.

79 A man of great common sense and good taste, meaning thereby a man without originality or moral courage.
1899 Of Caesar. *Caesar and Cleopatra*, notes.

80 But a lifetime of happiness! No man alive could bear it: it would be hell on earth.
1903 John Tanner. *Man and Superman*, act 1.

81 I am proud of your contempt for my character and opinions, sir.
1903 Roebuck Ramsden to John Tanner. *Man and Superman*, act 1.

82 The more things a man is ashamed of, the more respectable he is.
1903 John Tanner. *Man and Superman*, act 1.

83 Vitality in a woman is a blind fury of creation.
1903 John Tanner to Octavius Robinson. *Man and Superman*, act 1.

84 Of all human struggles there is none so treacherous and remorseless as the struggle between the artist man and the mother woman.
1903 John Tanner. *Man and Superman*, act 1.

85 A sensitive boy's humiliations may be very good fun for ordinary thick-skinned grown-ups; but to the boy himself they are so acute, so ignominious, that he cannot confess them—cannot but deny them passionately.
1903 John Tanner. *Man and Superman*, act 1.

86 There is no love sincerer than the love of food.
1903 John Tanner to Octavius Robinson. *Man and Superman*, act 1.

87 That damnable woman's trick of heaping obligations on a man, of placing yourself so entirely and helplessly at his mercy that at last he dare not take a step without running to you for leave. I know a poor wretch whose one desire in life is to run away from his wife. She prevents him by threatening to throw herself in front of the engine of the train he leaves her in. That is what all women do. If we try to go where you do not want us to go there is no law to prevent us; but when we take the first step your breasts are under our foot as it descends: your bodies are under our wheels as we start. No woman shall ever enslave me in that way.
1903 John Tanner to Ann Whitefield. *Man and Superman*, act 1.

88 You think that you are Ann's suitor; that you are the pursuer and she the pursued… Fool: it is you who are pursued, the marked down quarry, the destined prey.
1903 John Tanner to Octavius Robinson. *Man and Superman*, act 2.

89 'I am a brigand: I live by robbing the rich.'
'I am a gentleman: I live by robbing the poor.'
1903 Mendoza and John Tanner. *Man and Superman*, act 3.

90 Hell is full of musical amateurs: music is the brandy of the damned.
1903 Don Juan to the Devil. *Man and Superman*, act 3.

91 Englishmen never will be slaves: they are free to do whatever the Government and public allow them to do.
1903 The Devil to Ann Whitefield. *Man and Superman*, act 3.

92 An Englishman thinks he is moral when he is only uncomfortable.
1903 The Devil. *Man and Superman*, act 3.

93 In the arts of life man invents nothing; but in the arts of death he outdoes Nature herself, and produces by chemistry and machinery all the slaughter of plague, pestilence and famine.
1903 The Devil to Don Juan. *Man and Superman*, act 3.

94 In the arts of peace Man is a bungler.
1903 The Devil to Don Juan. *Man and Superman*, act 3.

95 As an old soldier I admit the cowardice: it's as universal as sea sickness, and matters just as little.
1903 The Statue. *Man and Superman*, act 3.

96 Sexually, Woman is Nature's contrivance for perpetuating its highest achievement.
1903 Don Juan to Ana. *Man and Superman*, act 3.

97 When the military man approaches, the world locks up its spoons and packs off its womankind.
1903 Don Juan. *Man and Superman*, act 3.

98 What is virtue but the Trade Unionism of the married?
1903 Don Juan to Ann Whitefield. *Man and Superman*, act 3.

99 Marriage is the most licentious of human institutions.
1903 Don Juan. *Man and Superman*, act 3.

1 Those who talk most about the blessings of marriage and the constancy of its vows are the very people who declare that if the claim were broken and the prisoners were left free to choose, the whole social fabric would fly asunder. You can't have the argument both ways. If the prisoner is happy, why lock him in? If he is not, why pretend that he is?
1903 Don Juan to Ann Whitefield. *Man and Superman*, act 3.

2 Beauty is all very well at first sight; but who ever looks at it when it has been in the house three days?
1903 Ann Whitefield. *Man and Superman*, act 4.

3 Revolutions have never lightened the burden of tyranny: they have only shifted it to another shoulder.
1903 *Man and Superman*, 'The Revolutionist's Handbook and Pocket Companion, by John Tanner', foreword.

4 The art of government is the organization of idolatry.
1903 *Man and Superman*, 'Maxims for Revolutionists: Idolatry'.

5 Democracy substitutes election by the incompetent many for appointment by the corrupt few.
1903 *Man and Superman*, 'Maxims for Revolutionists: Democracy'.

6 Liberty means responsibility. That is why most men dread it.
1903 *Man and Superman*, 'Maxims for Revolutionists: Liberty and Equality'.

7 He who can, does. He who cannot, teaches.
1903 *Man and Superman*, 'Maxims for Revolutionists: Education'.

8 Marriage is popular because it combines the maximum of temptation with the maximum of opportunity.
1903 *Man and Superman*, 'Maxims for Revolutionists: Marriage'.

9 Titles distinguish the mediocre, embarrass the superior, and are disgraced by the inferior.
1903 *Man and Superman*, 'Maxims for Revolutionists: Titles'.

10 When domestic servants are treated as human beings it is not worth while to keep them.
1903 *Man and Superman*, 'Maxims for Revolutionists: Servants'.

11 If you strike a child take care that you strike it in anger,

even at the risk of maiming it for life. A blow in cold blood neither can nor should be forgiven.
1903 *Man and Superman*, 'Maxims for Revolutionists: How to Beat Children'.

12 Beware of the man whose God is in the skies.
1903 *Man and Superman*, 'Maxims for Revolutionists: Religion'.

13 The most intolerable pain is produced by prolonging the keenest pleasure.
1903 *Man and Superman*, 'Maxims for Revolutionists: Beauty and Happiness'.

14 Economy is the art of making the most of life.
1903 *Man and Superman*, 'Maxims for Revolutionists: Virtues and Vices'.

15 Self-denial is not a virtue: it is only the effect of prudence on rascality.
1903 *Man and Superman*, 'Maxims for Revolutionists: Virtues and Vices'.

16 A moderately honest man with a moderately faithful wife, moderate drinkers both, in a moderately healthy house: that is the true middle-class unit
1903 *Man and Superman*, 'Maxims for Revolutionists: Moderation'.

17 The reasonable man adapts himself to the world: the unreasonable one persists in trying to adapt the world to himself. Therefore all progress depends on the unreasonable man.
1903 *Man and Superman*, 'Maxims for Revolutionists: Reason'.

18 The man who listens to Reason is lost: Reason enslaves all whose minds are not strong enough to master her.
1903 *Man and Superman*, 'Maxims for Revolutionists: Reason'.

19 Decency is Indecency's conspiracy of silence.
1903 *Man and Superman*, 'Maxims for Revolutionists: Decency'.

20 Life levels all men: death reveals the eminent.
1903 *Man and Superman*, 'Maxims for Revolutionists: Fame'.

21 Home is the girl's prison and the woman's workhouse.
1903 *Man and Superman*, 'Maxims for Revolutionists: Women in the Home'.

22 Every man over forty is a scoundrel.
1903 *Man and Superman*, 'Maxims for Revolutionists: Stray Sayings'.

23 Youth, which is forgiven everything, forgives itself nothing: age, which forgives itself everything, is forgiven nothing.
1903 *Man and Superman*, 'Maxims for Revolutionists: Stray Sayings'.

24 Take care to get what you like or you will be forced to like what you get.
1903 *Man and Superman*, 'Maxims for Revolutionists: Stray Sayings'.

25 Beware of the man who does not return your blow: he neither forgives you nor allows you to forgive yourself.
1903 *Man and Superman*, 'Maxims for Revolutionists: Stray Sayings'.

26 Self-sacrifice enables us to sacrifice other people without blushing.
1903 *Man and Superman*, 'Maxims for Revolutionists: Self-Sacrifice'.

27 Do not do unto others as you would they should do to you. Their tastes may not be the same.
1903 *Man and Superman*, 'Maxims for Revolutionists: The Golden Rule'.

28 The golden rule is that there are no golden rules.
1903 *Man and Superman*, 'Maxims for Revolutionists: The Golden Rule'.

29 When a man wants to murder a tiger he calls it sport; when a tiger wants to murder him he calls it ferocity.
1903 *Man and Superman*, 'Maxims for Revolutionists: Crime and Punishment'.

30 An Irishman's imagination never lets him alone, never convinces him, never satisfies him; but it makes him that he can't face reality nor deal with it nor handle it nor conquer it: he can only sneer at them that do, and be 'agreeable to strangers', like a good-for-nothing woman on the streets.
1904 Larry Doyle to Tom Broadbent. *John Bull's Other Island*, act 1.

31 An Irishman's heart is nothing but his imagination.
1904 Larry Doyle to Tom Broadbent. *John Bull's Other Island*, act 1.

32 The poor silly-clever Irishman takes off his hat to God's Englishman.
1904 Larry Doyle. *John Bull's Other Island*, act 1.

33 My way of joking is to tell the truth. It's the funniest joke in the world.
1904 Peter Keegan to Nora Reilly. *John Bull's Other Island*, act 2.

34 I am sincere; and my intentions are perfectly honourable. I think you will accept the fact that I'm an Englishman as a guarantee that I am not a man to act hastily or romantically.
1904 Tom Broadbent to Nora Reilly. *John Bull's Other Island*, act 2.

35 You just keep your air on and listen to me. You Awrish people are too well off: thet's wots the matter with you.
1904 Hodson to Matthew Haffigan. *John Bull's Other Island*, act 3.

36 There are only two qualities in the world: efficiency and inefficiency, and only two sorts of people: the efficient and the inefficient.
1904 Tom Broadbent. *John Bull's Other Island*, act 4.

37 In my dreams is a country where the State is the Church and the Church the people: three in one and one in three. It is a commonwealth in which work is play and play is life: three in one and one in three. It is a temple in which the priest is the worshipper and the worshipper the worshipped: three in one and one in three. It is a godhead in which all life is human and all humanity divine: three in one and one in three. It is, in short, the dream of a madman.
1904 Of Heaven, Keegan speaking. *John Bull's Other Island*, act 4.

38 The greatest of evils and the worst of crimes is poverty…our first duty—a duty to which every other consideration should be sacrificed—is not to be poor.
1905 *Major Barbara*, preface.

39 Nobody can say a word against Greek: it stamps a man at once as an educated gentleman.
1905 Lady Britomart Undershaft to Stephen. *Major Barbara*, act 1.

40 I am a Millionaire. That is my religion.
1905 Undershaft to Barbara Undershaft. *Major Barbara*, act 2.

41 I can't talk religion to a man with bodily hunger in his eyes.
1905 Barbara Undershaft. *Major Barbara*, act 2.

42 Alcohol is a very necessary article… It makes life bearable to millions of people who could not endure their existence if they were quite sober. It enables Parliament to do things at eleven at night that no sane person would do at eleven in the morning.
1905 Undershaft to Barbara Undershaft. *Major Barbara*, act 2.

43 It's nao good: you cawnt get rahnd me nah. Aw downt blieve in it; and Awve seen tody that Aw was rawt. Sao long, aol soupkitchener! Ta, ta, Mijor Earl's Grendorter! Wot prawce selvytion nah? Snobby Prawce! Ha! ha!
1905 Bill Walker to Barbara Undershaft. *Major Barbara*, act 2.

44 He knows nothing; and he thinks he knows everything. That points clearly to a political career.
1905 Undershaft speaking of Stephen. *Major Barbara*, act 3.

45 Like all young men, you greatly exaggerate the difference between one young woman and another.
1905 Undershaft about Adolphus Cusins. *Major Barbara*, act 3.

46 Fashions, after all, are only induced epidemics.
1906 *The Doctor's Dilemma*, 'Preface on Doctors: Fashions and Epidemics'.

47 Science becomes dangerous only when it imagines that it has reached its goal.
1906 *The Doctor's Dilemma*, preface, 'The Latest Theories'.

48 There is at bottom only one genuinely scientific treatment for all diseases, and that is to stimulate the phagocytes.
1906 BB (Sir Ralph Bloomfield Bonington). *The Doctor's Dilemma*, act 1.

49 All professions are conspiracies against the laity.
1906 Sir Patrick Cullen. *The Doctor's Dilemma*, act 1.

50 A man's behaviour may be quite harmless and even beneficial, when he is morally behaving like a scoundrel. And he may do great harm when he is morally acting on the highest principles.
1906 BB. *The Doctor's Dilemma*, act 3.

51 The criminal law is no use to decent people.
1906 Sir Patrick. *The Doctor's Dilemma*, act 3.

52 There's almost as many different sorts of marriage as there's different sorts of people. There's the young things that marry for love, not knowing what they're doing, and the old things that marry for money and comfort and companionship. There's the people that marry for children. There's the people that don't intend to have children and that aren't fit to have them. There's the people that marry because they're so much run after by the other sex that they have to put a stop to it somehow. There's the people that want to try a new experience, and the people that want to have done with experiences.
1908 Bill Collins. *Getting Married*.

53 Home life as we understand it is no more natural to us than a cage is natural to a cockatoo.
1908 *Getting Married*, preface, 'Hearth and Home'.

54 The one point on which all women are in furious secret rebellion against the existing law is the saddling of the right to a child with the obligation to become the servant of a man.
1908 *Getting Married*, preface, 'The Right to Motherhood'.

55 Physically there is nothing to distinguish human society from the farmyard except that children are more troublesome and costly than chickens and calves, and that men and women are not so completely enslaved as farm stock.
1908 *Getting Married*, preface, 'The Personal Sentimental Basis of Monogamy'.

56 You see, family life is all the life she knows: she's like a bird born in a cage, that would die if you let it loose in the woods.
1908 Bill Collins about his wife. *Getting Married*.

57 A man is like a phonograph with half-a-dozen records. You soon get tired of them all; and yet you have to sit at table whilst he reels them off to every new visitor. In the end you have to be content with his common humanity.
1908 The Bishop of Chelsea. *Getting Married*.

58 I am a snob, not only in fact, but on principle.
1908 St John Hotchkiss. *Getting Married*.

59 Optimistic lies have such immense therapeutic value that a doctor who cannot tell them convincingly has mistaken his profession.
1910 *Misalliance*, preface.

60 Anybody on for a game of tennis?
1910 *Misalliance*. This may be the origin of 'Anyone for tennis?', as used in archetypal theatrical drawing-room comedies.

61 The English have no respect for their language, and will not teach their children to speak it. They spell it so abominably that no man can teach himself what it sounds like. It is impossible for an Englishman to open his mouth without making some other Englishman hate or despise him.
1913 *Pygmalion*, Preface.

62 He's a gentleman: look at his boots.
1913 Bystander. *Pygmalion*, act 1.

63 I don't want to talk grammar, I want to talk like a lady.
1913 Eliza Doolittle. *Pygmalion*, act 2.

64 Have you ever met a man of good character where women are concerned?
1913 Higgins to Pickering. *Pygmalion*, act 2.

65 'Have you no morals, man?'
'Can't afford them, Governor.'
1913 Col Pickering and Alfred Doolittle. *Pygmalion*, act 2.

66 I'm one of the undeserving poor… up agen middle-class morality all the time… What is middle-class morality? Just an excuse for never giving me anything.
1913 Alfred Doolittle. *Pygmalion*, act 2.

67 Gin was mother's milk to her.
1913 Eliza, speaking of her Aunt. *Pygmalion*, act 3.

68 Walk! Not bloody likely. I am going in a taxi.
1913 Eliza to Freddy. *Pygmalion*, act 3.

69 The secret of being miserable is to have leisure to bother about whether you are happy or not. The cure for it is occupation.
1914 *Parents and Children*.

70 A perpetual holiday is a good working definition of hell.
1914 *Parents and Children*.

71 I am a woman of the world, Hector; and I can assure you that if you will only take the trouble always to do the perfectly correct thing, and to say the perfectly correct thing, you can do just what you like.

1919 Lady Utterword to Hector Hushabye. *Heartbreak House*, act 1.

72 It's prudent to gain the whole world and lose your own soul. But don't forget that your soul sticks to you if you stick to it; but the world has a way of slipping through your fingers.
1919 Captain Shotover. *Heartbreak House*, act 2.

73 There are only two classes in good society in England: the equestrian classes and the neurotic classes.
1919 Lady Utterword. *Heartbreak House*, act 3.

74 Go anywhere in England where there are natural, wholesome, contented, and really nice English people; and what do you always find? That the stables are the real centre of the household.
1919 Lady Utterword. *Heartbreak House*, act 3.

75 This souls' prison we call England.
1919 Hector Hushabye. *Heartbreak House*, act 3.

76 The captain is in his bunk, drinking bottled ditch-water; and the crew is gambling in the forecastle. She will strike and sink and split. Do you think the laws of God will be suspended in favour of England because you were born in it?
1919 Captain Shotover. *Heartbreak House*, act 3.

77 Everyone can see that the people who hunt are the right people and the people who don't are the wrong ones.
1919 Lady Usherword to Mrs Hushabye. *Heartbreak House*, act 3.

78 All great truths begin as blasphemies.
1919 *Annajanska*.

79 I enjoy convalescence. It is the part that makes illness worth while.
1921 *Back to Methuselah*.

80 Silence is the most perfect expression of scorn
1921 *Back to Methuselah*.

81 If ever I utter an oath again may my soul be blasted to eternal damnation!
1923 Captain La Hire. *Saint Joan*, sc.2.

82 No Englishman is ever fairly beaten.
1923 The Chaplain. *Saint Joan*, sc.4.

83 How can what an Englishman believes be heresy? It is a contradiction in terms.
1923 The Chaplain to Peter Cauchon. *Saint Joan*, sc.4.

84 Some men are born kings; and some are born statesmen. The two are seldom the same.
1923 Peter Cauchon. *Saint Joan*, sc.4.

85 Must then a Christ perish in torment in every age to save those that have no imagination?
1923 *Saint Joan*, epilogue.

86 Idiots are always in favour of inequality of income (their only chance of eminence), and the really great in favour of equality.
1928 *The Intelligent Woman's Guide to Socialism and Capitalism*.

87 Many men would hardly miss their heads, there is so little in them.
1929 King Magnus. *The Apple Cart*, act 1.

88 One man that has a mind and knows it can always beat ten men who haven't and don't.
1929 Joe Proteus. *The Apple Cart*, act 1.

89 As interesting as a wall can be.
c.1930 Asked what he thought of the Great Wall after his flight over China. Quoted in Hesketh Pearson *Bernard Shaw: His Life and Personality* (1961).

90 The fact is, there are no rules and there never were any rules, and there never will be any rules of musical composition except rules of thumb; and thumbs vary in length, like ears.
1931 *Music in London, 1890–1894*.

91 [The Red Flag] is the funeral march of a fried eel.
Quoted by Winston Churchill in *Great Contemporaries* (1937).

92 A perpendicular expression of a horizontal desire.
Of dancing. Quoted in the *New Statesman*, 23 Mar 1962.

93 That's the difference between us. You talk of art Mr Goldwyn, I think of money.
To Samuel Goldwyn. Quoted in David Niven *Bring on the Empty Horses* (1975).

94 Baseball has the great advantage over cricket of being sooner ended. It combines the best features of that primitive form of cricket known as Tip-and-Run with those of lawn tennis, Puss-in-the-corner and Handel's Messiah.
Quoted in Colin Jarman *The Guinness Dictionary of Sports Quotations* (1990).

95 No sportsman wants to kill a fox or the pheasant as I want to kill him when I see him doing it.
Quoted in Colin Jarman *The Guinness Dictionary of Sports Quotations* (1990).

96 There is no reason why the infield should not try to put the batter off his stride at the critical moment, by neatly-timed disparagements of his wife's fidelity and his mother's respectability.
Alluding to baseball. Quoted in Colin Jarman *The Guinness Dictionary of Sports Quotations* (1990).

97 Who is this 'Babe' Ruth? And what does she do?
Of the legendary baseball star 'Babe' Ruth. Quoted in Colin Jarman *The Guinness Dictionary of Sports Quotations* (1990).

98 England and America are two countries divided by a common language.
Attributed.

99 If all the economists in the world were laid end to end, they would not reach a conclusion.
Attributed.

1 To begin with, I was born with an unreasonably large stock of relations, who have increased and multiplied ever since. My aunts and uncles were legion, and my cousins as the sands of the sea without number. Consequently, even a low death-rate meant, in the course of mere natural decay, a tolerably steady supply of funerals for a by no means affectionate but exceedingly clannish family to go to. Add to this that the town we lived in, being divided in religious opinion, buried its dead in two great cemeteries, each of which was held by the opposite faction to be the ante-chamber of perdition, and by its own patrons to be the gate of paradise.
'Music in London'.

2 You see things, and you say, 'Why?' But I dream things that never were; and I say 'Why not?'
The Serpent

3 [Lord Rosebery] was a man who never missed an occasion to let slip an opportunity.
Quoted by Winston Churchill in *Great Contemporaries* (1937).

Shawcross, Sir Hartley William, Baron Shawcross 1902–2003

English jurist, Attorney General (1945–51) and President of the Board of Trade (1951). He established his reputation as chief British prosecutor at the Nuremberg Trials (1945–6), and as prosecutor in the Fuchs atom spy case (1950). He was made a life peer in 1959.

4 We are the masters at the moment, and not only at the moment, but for a very long time to come.
1946 Alluding to Labour's victory in the general election, House of Commons, 2 Apr.

5 The so-called new morality is too often the old immorality condoned.
1963 In the *Observer*, 17 Jul.

Shawcross, William 1946–

English journalist whose book *Sideshow* (1979) detailed US involvement in Cambodia up to 1975.

6 Cambodia was not a mistake; it was a crime. The world is diminished by the experience.
1979 *Sideshow*, afterword.

Sheehy-Skeffington, Francis 1878–1916

Irish pacifist and feminist.

7 A crank is a small engine that causes revolutions.
On being described as a crank, quoted by his son Owen.

Sheen, Fulton John 1895–1979

US Roman Catholic prelate, who argued strenuously against Communism and birth control.

8 Our Lord... said that if men withheld their praise of him, 'the very stones would cry out', which they did as, later, they burst into Gothic cathedrals.
1962 *These Are the Sacraments*.

Shelley, Mary Godwin 1797–1851

English novelist, who married Percy Bysshe Shelley (1816). Her most famous work is *Frankenstein* (1818), written when she was only 19. After her husband's death she wrote *Valperga* (1823), *The Last Man* (1826), *Perkin Warbeck* (1830), *Lodore* (1835) and *Falkner* (1837) and edited her husband's works.

9 You seek for knowledge and wisdom as I once did; and I ardently hope that the gratification of your wishes may not be a serpent to sting you, as mine has been.
1818 *Frankenstein*, letter 4.

10 I was their plaything and their idol, and something better—their child.
1818 Frankenstein, speaking of his parents. *Frankenstein*, ch.1.

11 So much has been done, exclaimed the soul of Frankenstein—more, far more, will I achieve; treading the steps already marked, I will pioneer a new way, explore unknown powers, and unfold to the world the deepest mysteries of creation.
1818 *Frankenstein*, ch.3.

12 All men hate the wretched; how, then, must I be hated, who am miserable beyond all living things! Yet you, my creator, detest and spurn me, thy creature, to whom thou art bound by ties only dissoluble by the annihilation of one of us.
1818 Frankenstein's monster. *Frankenstein*, ch.10.

13 Everywhere I see bliss, from which I alone am irrevocably excluded.
1818 Frankenstein's monster. *Frankenstein*, ch.10.

Shelley, Percy Bysshe 1792–1822

English lyric poet, who eloped with and later married Mary Godwin. He was a leading light of the Romantic movement and a lifelong atheist. His early poems include *Queen Mab* (1813). He later wrote tragedies such as *The Cenci* (1818), lyrical poems such as 'Ode to the West Wind' (1819) and lyric dramas such as *Prometheus Unbound* (1820).

14 The discussion of any subject is a right that you have brought into the world with your heart and tongue. Resign your heart's blood before you part with this inestimable privilege of man.
1812 *An Address to the Irish People*.

15 Titles are tinsel, power a corrupter, glory a bubble, and excessive wealth a libel on its possessor.
1812 *Declaration of Rights*, article 27.

16 That sweet bondage which is freedom's self.
1813 *Queen Mab*, canto 9.

17 There is no disease, bodily or mental, which adoption of vegetable diet and pure water has not infallibly mitigated, wherever the experiment has been fairly tried.
1813 'A Vindication of Natural Diet'.

18 Mont Blanc yet gleams on high: the power is there,
The still and solemn power of many sights
And many sounds, and much of life and death.
In the long glare of day, the snows descend
Upon that Mountain; none beholds them there,
Nor when the flakes burn in the sinking sun,
Or the sunbeams dart through them.
1816 'Mont Blanc'.

19 The awful shadow of some unseen Power
Floats though unseen among us,—visiting
This various world with as inconstant wing
As summer winds that creep from flower to flower.
1816 'Hymn to Intellectual Beauty'.

20 While yet a boy I sought for ghosts, and sped
Through many a listening chamber, cave and ruin,
And starlight wood, with fearful steps pursuing
Hopes of high talks with the departed dead.
1816 'Hymn to Intellectual Beauty'.

21 The day becomes more solemn and serene
When noon is past—there is a harmony
In autumn, and a lustre in its sky,
Which through the summer is not heard or seen,
As if it could not be, as if it had not been!
1816 'Hymn to Intellectual Beauty'.

22 Nought may endure but Mutability.
1816 'Mutability'.

23 In honoured poverty thy voice did weave
Songs concentrate to truth and liberty,—
Deserting these, thou leavest me to grieve,
Thus having been, that thou shouldst cease to be.
1816 'To Wordsworth'.

24 I love all waste
And solitary places; where we taste
The pleasure of believing what we see
Is boundless, as we wish our souls to be.
1818 'Julian and Maddalo', l.14–16.

25 Thou Paradise of exiles, Italy!
1818 'Julian and Maddalo', l.57.

26 Me—who am as a nerve o'er which do creep
The else unfelt oppressions of this earth.
1818 'Julian and Maddalo', l.449–50.

27 Most wretched men
Are cradled into poetry by wrong:
They learn in suffering what they teach in song.
1818 'Julian and Maddalo', l.544–7.

28 Beneath is spread like a green sea
The waveless plain of Lombardy,
Bounded by the vaporous air,
Islanded by cities fair;
Underneath Day's azure eyes,
Ocean's nursling, Venice lies,—
A peopled labyrinth of walls,
Amphitrite's destined halls.
1818 'Lines written amongst the Euganean Hills', l.90–7.

29 Sun-girt city, thou hast been
Ocean's child, and then his queen;
Now is come a darker day,
And thou soon must be his prey.
1818 'Lines written amongst the Euganean Hills', l.115–18.

30 The City's voice itself is soft like Solitude's.
1818 'Stanzas Written in Dejection, near Naples'.

31 I see the waves upon the shore,
Like light dissolved in star-showers, thrown.
1818 'Stanzas Written in Dejection, near Naples'.

32 Alas! I have nor hope nor health,
Nor peace within nor calm around,
Nor that content surpassing wealth
The sage in meditation found.
1818 'Stanzas Written in Dejection, near Naples'.

33 With hue like that when some great painter dips
His pencil in the gloom of earthquake and eclipse.
1818 'The Revolt of Islam'.

34 An old, mad, blind, despised, and dying king.
1819 'England in 1819' (published in 1839).

35 His big tears, for he wept well,
Turned to mill-stones as they fell.
And the little children, who
Round his feet played to and fro,
Thinking every tear a gem,
Had their brains knocked out by them.
1819 Of Fraud (ie, Lord Eldon). 'The Mask of Anarchy'.

36 I met Murder on the way—
He had a mask like Castlereagh.
1819 'The Mask of Anarchy', alluding to English foreign secretary Viscount Castlereagh, who was held responsible for the Peterloo Massacre in 1819.

37 On his brow this mark I saw—
'I AM GOD, AND KING, AND LAW!'
1819 'The Mask of Anarchy'.

38 Rise like Lions after slumber
In unvanquishable number—
Shake your chains to earth like dew
Which in sleep has fallen on you—
Ye are many—they are few.
1819 'The Mask of Anarchy'.

39 I wield the flail of the lashing hail,
And whiten the green plains under,
And then again I dissolve it in rain,
And laugh as I pass in thunder.
1819 'The Cloud'.

40 That orbèd maiden, with white fire laden,
Whom mortals call the Moon.
1819 'The Cloud'.

41 I am the daughter of Earth and Water,
And the nursling of the Sky;
I pass through the pores of the ocean and shores;
I change, but I cannot die,
For after the rain when with never a stain
The pavilion of Heaven is bare,
And the winds and sunbeams with their convex gleams
Build up the blue dome of air,
I silently laugh at my own cenotaph,
And out of the caverns of rain,
Like a child from the womb, like a ghost from the tomb,
I arise and unbuild it again.
1819 'The Cloud'.

42 The fountains mingle with the river,
And the rivers with the ocean;
The winds of heaven mix for ever
With a sweet emotion;
Nothing in the world is single;
All things, by a law divine,
In one spirit meet and mingle.
Why not I with thine?
1819 'Love and Philosophy'.

43 O wild West Wind, thou breath of Autumn's being,
Thou, from whose unseen presence the leaves dead
Are driven, like ghosts from an enchanter fleeing.
1819 'Ode to the West Wind', l.1–3.

44 Wild Spirit, which art moving everywhere;
Destroyer and preserver; hear, oh, hear!
1819 'Ode to the West Wind', l.13–4.

45 Thou who didst waken from his summer dreams
The blue Mediterranean, where he lay,
Lulled by the coil of his crystalline streams

Beside a pumice isle in Baiae's bay,
And saw in sleep old palaces and towers
Quivering within the wave's intenser day,

All overgrown with azure moss and flowers
So sweet, the sense faints picturing them.
1819 'Ode to the West Wind', l.29–36.

46 Oh, lift me as a wave, a leaf, a cloud!
I fall upon the thorns of life! I bleed!
1819 'Ode to the West Wind', l.53–4.

47 Make me thy lyre, even as the forest is:
What if my leaves are falling like its own!
The tumult of thy mighty harmonies
Will take from both a deep, autumnal tone,
Sweet though in sadness.
1819 'Ode to the West Wind', l.57–61.

48 And, by the incarnation of this verse,
Scatter, as from an unextinguished hearth
Ashes and sparks, my words among mankind!
Be through my lips to unawakened earth

The trumpet of a prophecy! O, Wind,
If Winter comes, can Spring be far behind?
1819 'Ode to the West Wind', l.65–70.

49 I met a traveller from an antique land
Who said: Two vast and trunkless legs of stone
Stand in the desert.
1819 'Ozymandias'.

50 'My name is Ozymandias, king of kings:
Look on my works, ye Mighty, and despair!'
Nothing beside remains. Round the decay
Of that colossal wreck, boundless and bare
The lone and level sands stretch far away.
1819 'Ozymandias'.

51 Hell is a city much like London—
A populous and smoky city.
1819 'Peter Bell the Third' pt.3, stanza 1.

52 But from the first 'twas Peter's drift
To be a kind of moral eunuch,
He touched the hem of Nature's shift,
Felt faint—and never dared uplift
The closest, all-concealing tunic.
1819 'Peter Bell the Third', pt.4, stanza 11.

53 Men of England, wherefore plough
For the lords who lay you low?
1819 'Song to the Men of England'.

54 Hail to thee, blithe Spirit!
Bird thou never wert,
That from Heaven, or near it,
Pourest thy full heart
In profuse strains of unpremeditated art.
1820 'To a Skylark', stanza 1.

55 Higher still and higher
From the earth thou springest
Like a cloud of fire;
The blue deep thou wingest
And singing still dost soar, and soaring ever singest.
1820 'To a Skylark', stanza 2.

56 In the golden lightning
Of the sunken sun
O'er which clouds are brightening,
Thou dost float and run
Like an unbodied joy whose race is just begun.
1820 'To a Skylark', stanza 3.

57 Keen as are the arrows
Of that silver sphere,
Whose intense lamp narrows
In the white dawn clear
Until we hardly see, we feel that it is there.
1820 'To a Skylark', stanza 5.

58 Like a Poet hidden
In the light of thought,
Singing hymns unbidden,
Till the world is wrought
To sympathy with hopes and fears it heeded not.
1820 'To a Skylark', stanza 8.

59 What objects are the fountains
Of thy happy strain?
What fields, or waves, or mountains?
What shapes of sky or plain?
What love of thine own kind? What ignorance of pain?
1820 'To a Skylark', stanza 15.

60 With thy clear keen joyance
Languor cannot be:
Shadow of annoyance
Never came near thee:
Thou lovest—but ne'er knew love's sad satiety.
1820 'To a Skylark', stanza 16.

61 We look before and after,
And pine for what is not:
Our sincerest laughter
With some pain is fraught:
Our sweetest songs are those that tell of saddest thought.
1820 'To a Skylark', stanza 18.

62 Better than all measures
Of delightful sound,
Better than all treasures
That in books are found,
Thy skill to poet were, thou scorner of the ground!
1820 'To a Skylark', stanza 21.

63 Teach me half the gladness
That thy brain must know,
Such harmonious madness
From my lips would flow
The world should listen then—as I am listening now.
1820 'To a Skylark', stanza 21.

64 Chameleons feed on light and air:
Poet's food is love and game.
1820 'An Exhortation'.

65 London, that great sea, whose ebb and flow
At once is deaf and loud, and on the shore
Vomits its wrecks, and still howls on for more.
1820 'Letter to Maria Gisborne', l.193–5.

66 You will see Coleridge—he who sits obscure
In the exceeding lustre and the pure
Intense irradiation of a mind,
Which, through its own internal lighting blind,
Flags wearily through darkness and despair—
A cloud-encircled meteor of the air,
A hooded eagle among blinking owls—
You will see Hunt—one of those happy souls
Which are the salt of the earth, and without whom
This world would smell like what it is—a tomb.
1820 'Letter to Maria Gisborne' l.202–11.

67 Have you not heard
When a man marries, dies, or turns Hindoo,
His best friends hear no more of him?
1820 'Letter to Maria Gisborne' l.235–7.

68 His fine wit
Makes such a wound, the knife is lost in it.
1820 Of Thomas Love Peacock. 'Letter to Maria Gisborne', l.240–1.

69 Ere Babylon was dust,
The Magus Zoroaster, my dead child,
Met his own image walking in the garden,
That apparition, sole of men, he saw.
1820 *Prometheus Unbound*, act 1, l.191–4.

70 Cruel he looks, but calm and strong,
Like one who does, not suffers wrong.
1820 *Prometheus Unbound*, act 1, l.238–9.

71 It doth repent me: words are quick and vain:
Grief for a while is blind, and so was mine.

I wish no living thing to suffer pain.
1820 *Prometheus Unbound*, act 1, l.303–5.

72 Kingly conclaves stern and cold,
Where blood with guilt is bought and sold.
1820 *Prometheus Unbound* act 1, l.530–1.

73 The good want power, but to weep barren tears.
The powerful goodness want: worse need for them.
The wise want love; and those who love want wisdom.
1820 *Prometheus Unbound* act 1, l.625–7.

74 Peace is in the grave.
The grave hides all things beautiful and good:
I am a God and cannot find it there.
1820 *Prometheus Unbound* act 1, l.638–40.

75 The dust of creeds outworn.
1820 *Prometheus Unbound* act 1, l.697.

76 On a poet's lips I slept
Dreaming like a love-adept
In the sound his breathing kept.
1820 *Prometheus Unbound*, act 1, l.737–9.

77 To be
Omnipotent but friendless is to reign.
1820 *Prometheus Unbound*, act 2, sc.4, l.47–8.

78 He gave man speech, and speech created thought,
Which is the measure of the universe.
1820 *Prometheus Unbound*, act 2, sc.4, l.72–3.

79 Fate, Time, Occasion, Chance, and Change? To these
All things are subject but eternal love.
1820 *Prometheus Unbound*, act 2, sc.4, l.119–20.

80 My soul is an enchanted boat,
Which, like a sleeping swan, doth float
Upon the silver waves of thy sweet singing.
1820 *Prometheus Unbound*, act 2, sc.5, l.72–4.

81 The loathsome mask has fallen, the man remains
Sceptreless, free, uncircumscribed, but man
Equal, unclassed, tribeless, and nationless,
Exempt from awe, worship, degree, the king
Over himself; just, gentle, wise: but man
Passionless?—no, yet free from guilt or pain,
Which were, for his will made or suffered them,
Nor yet exempt, though ruling them like slaves,
From chance, and death, and mutability,
The clogs of that which else might oversoar
The loftiest star of unascended heaven,
Pinnacled dim in the intense inane.
1820 *Prometheus Unbound*, act 3, sc.4, l.193–204.

82 A traveller from the cradle to the grave
Through the dim night of this immortal day.
1820 *Prometheus Unbound*, act 4, l.551–2.

83 To suffer woes which Hope thinks infinite;
To forgive wrongs darker than death or night;
To defy Power, which seems omnipotent:
To love, and bear; to hope till Hope creates
From its own wreck the thing it contemplates;
Neither to change, nor falter, nor repent;
This, like thy glory, Titan, is to be
Good, great and joyous, beautiful and free;
This is alone Life, Joy, Empire and Victory.
1820 *Prometheus Unbound*, act 4, l.570–8.

84 A Sensitive Plant in a garden grew.
1820 'The Sensitive Plant', pt.1, l.1.

85 And the rose like a nymph to the bath addressed,
Which unveiled the depth of her glowing breast,
Till, fold after fold, to the fainting air
The soul of her beauty and love lay bare.
1820 'The Sensitive Plant', pt.1, l.29–32.

86 And the jessamine faint, and the sweet tuberose,
The sweetest flower for scent that blows.
1820 'The Sensitive Plant', pt.1, l.37–8.

87 A lovely lady, garmented in light
From her own beauty.
1820 'The Witch of Atlas', stanza 5.

88 For she was beautiful—her beauty made
The bright world dim, and everything beside
Seemed like the fleeting image of a shade.
1820 'The Witch of Atlas', stanza 12.

89 The cemetery is an open space among the ruins, covered in winter with violets and daisies. It might make one in love with death, to think that one should be buried in so sweet a place.
1821 *Adonais*, preface.

90 I weep for Adonais—he is dead!
O, weep for Adonais! though our tears
Thaw not the frost which binds so dear a head!
1821 *Adonais*, stanza 1.

91 He died,
Who was the Sire of an immortal strain,
Blind, old and lonely.
1821 *Adonais*, stanza 4.

92 To that high Capital, where kingly Death
Keeps his pale court in beauty and decay,
He came.
1821 *Adonais*, stanza 7.

93 The quick Dreams,
The passion-winged Ministers of thought
1821 *Adonais*, stanza 9.

94 Lost Angel of a ruined Paradise!
She knew not 'twas her own; as with no stain
She faded, like a cloud which had outwept its rain.
1821 *Adonais*, stanza 10.

95 Ah, woe is me! Winter is come and gone,
But grief returns with the revolving year.
1821 *Adonais*, stanza 18.

96 From the great morning of the world when first
God dawned on Chaos.
1821 *Adonais*, stanza 19.

97 Alas! that all we loved of him should be,
But for our grief, as if it had not been,
And grief itself be mortal!
1821 *Adonais*, stanza 21.

98 Whence are we, and why are we? Of what scene
The actors or spectators?
1821 *Adonais*, stanza 21.

99 A pard-like Spirit, beautiful and swift—
A love in desolation masked;—a Power
Girt round with weakness;—it can scarce uplift
The weight of the superincumbent hour;
It is a dying lamp, a falling shower,
A breaking billow;—even whilst we speak
Is it not broken?
1821 *Adonais*, stanza 32.

1 Our Adonais has drunk poison—oh!
What deaf and viperous murderer could crown
Life's early cup with such a draught of woe?
1821 *Adonais*, stanza 36.

2 He wakes or sleeps with the enduring dead;
Thou canst not soar where he is sitting now—
Dust to the dust! but the pure spirit shall flow
Back to the burning fountain whence it came,
A portion of the Eternal.
1821 *Adonais*, stanza 38.

3 He hath awakened from the dream of life—
'Tis we, who lost in stormy visions, keep
With phantoms an unprofitable strife,
And in mad trance, strike with our spirit's knife
Invulnerable nothings.
1821 *Adonais*, stanza 39.

4 He has out-soared the shadow of our night;
Envy and calumny and hate and pain,
And that unrest which men miscall delight,
Can touch him not and torture not again;
From the contagion of the world's slow stain
He is secure, and now can never mourn
A heart grown cold, a head grown grey in vain.
1821 *Adonais*, stanza 40.

5 He lives, he wakes,—'tis Death is dead, not he.
1821 *Adonais*, stanza 41.

6 He is a portion of the loveliness
Which once he made more lovely.
1821 *Adonais*, stanza 43.

7 The One remains, the many change and pass;
Heaven's light forever shines, Earth's shadows fly:
Life, like a dome of many-coloured glass,
Stains the white radiance of Eternity,
Until Death tramples it to fragments.
1821 *Adonais*, stanza 52.

8 I never was attached to that great sect,
Whose doctrine is that each one should select
Out of the crowd a mistress or a friend,
And all the rest, though fair and wise, commend
To cold oblivion.
1821 'Epipsychidion', l.149–53.

9 The beaten road
Which those poor slaves with weary footsteps tread,
Who travel to their home among the dead
By the broad highway of the world, and so
With one chained friend, perhaps a jealous foe,
The dreariest and the longest journey go.
1821 'Epipsychidion', l.154–9.

10 True Love in this differs from gold and clay,
That to divide is not to take away.
1821 'Epipsychidion', l.160–1.

11 An isle under Ionian skies
Beautiful as a wreck of Paradise.
1821 'Epipsychidion', l.422–3.

12 I pant, I sink, I tremble, I expire!
1821 'Epipsychidion', l.591.

13 The vanity of translation; it were as wise to cast a violet into a crucible that you might discover the formal principle of its colour and odour, as seek to transfuse from one language to another the creations of a poet. The plant must spring again from its seed, or it will bear no flower.
1821 *A Defence of Poetry.*

14 The great instrument of moral good is the imagination; and poetry administers to the effect by acting on the cause.
1821 *A Defence of Poetry.*

15 A single word even may be a spark of inextinguishable thought.
1821 *A Defence of Poetry.*

16 Poetry is a record of the best and happiest moments of the happiest and best minds.
1821 *A Defence of Poetry.*

17 Poets are the hierophants of an unapprehended inspiration; the mirrors of the gigantic shadows which futurity casts upon the present; the words which express what they understand not; the trumpets which sing to battle, and feel not what they inspire; the influence which is moved not, but moves. Poets are the unacknowledged legislators of the world.
1821 *A Defence of Poetry.*

18 Death will come when thou art dead,
Soon, too soon—
Sleep will come when thou art fled;
Of neither would I ask the boon
I ask of thee, belovèd Night—
Swift be thine approaching flight,
Come soon, soon!
1821 'To Night'.

19 Life may change, but it may fly not,
Hope may vanish, but can die not;
Truth be veiled, but still it burneth;
Love repulsed,—but it returneth!
1822 'Hellas', l.34–7.

20 Let there be light! Said Liberty,
And like sunrise from the sea,
Athens arose!
1822 'Hellas', l.682–4.

21 The world's great age begins anew,
The golden years return,
The earth doth like a snake renew
Her winter weeds outworn;
Heaven smiles, and faiths and empires gleam,
Like wrecks of a dissolving dream.
1822 'Hellas', l.1060–5.

22 O cease! must hate and death return,
Cease! must men kill and die?
Cease! drain not to its dregs the urn
Of bitter prophecy.
The world is weary of the past,
Oh, might it die or rest at last!
1822 'Hellas', l.1096–101.

23 I dreamed that, as I wandered by the way,
Bare Winter suddenly was changed to Spring,
And gentle odours led my steps astray,
Mixed with a sound of water's murmuring
Along a shelving bank of turf, which lay
Under a copse, and hardly dared to fling
Its green arms round the bosom of the stream,
But kissed it and then fled, as thou mightst in dream.
1822 'The Question', stanza 1.

24 Daisies, those pearled Arcturi of the earth,
The constellated flower that never sets.
1822 'The Question', stanza 2.

25 And in the warm hedge grew lush eglantine,
Green cowbind and the moonlight-coloured may.
1822 'The Question', stanza 3.

26 Less oft peace in Shelley's mind,
Than calm in waters seen.
1822 'To Jane: The Recollection'.

27 Music when soft voices die,
Vibrates in the memory—
Odours, when sweet violets sicken,
Live within the sense they quicken.
'To—: Music when soft voices die' (published 1824).

28 I pursued a maiden and clasped a reed:
Gods and men, we are all deluded thus!
It breaks in our bosom and then we bleed.
'Hymn of Pan' (published 1824).

29 Swiftly walk o'er the western wave,
Spirit of Night!
Out of the misty eastern cave,
Where, all the long and lone daylight,
Thou wovest dreams of joy and fear,
Which make thee terrible and dear,
Swift be thy flight!
'To Night' (published 1824).

30 Art thou pale for weariness
Of climbing heaven, and gazing on the earth,
Wandering companionless
Among the stars that have a different birth,—
And ever-changing, like a joyless eye
That finds no object worth its constancy?
'To the Moon' (published 1824).

31 And like a dying lady, lean and pale,
Who totters forth, wrapped in a gauzy veil.
'The Waning Moon' (published 1824).

Sheridan, Philip Henry 1831–88

American Union cavalry commander in the Civil War and the American-Indian wars.

32 The only good Indian is a dead Indian.
1869 Attributed comment at Fort Cobb, Jan.

33 We took away their country and their means of support, broke up their mode of living, their habits of life, introduced disease and decay among them and it was for this and against this they made war. Could anyone expect less?
c.1870 Quoted in Thomas C Leonard *Above the Battle* (1978).

Sheridan, Richard Brinsley 1751–1816

Irish dramatist. His major plays, *The Rivals*, *The Duenna*, and *The Critic*, were produced between 1775 and 1779. He became an MP and in 1782 under-secretary for foreign affairs, a renowned orator. He lost his seat in 1812.

34 Promise to forget this fellow—to illiterate him, I say, quite from your memory.
1775 Mrs Malaprop to Lydia. *The Rivals*, act 1, sc.2.

35 What business have you, miss, with preference and aversion?... You ought to know, that as both always wear off, 'tis safest in matrimony to begin with a little aversion.
1775 Mrs Malaprop to Lydia. *The Rivals*, act 1, sc.2.

36 Madam, a circulating library in a town is as an evergreen tree of diabolical knowledge!... Depend upon it, Mrs Malaprop, that they who are so fond of handling the leaves, will long for the fruit at last.
1775 Sir Anthony Absolute. *The Rivals*, act 1, sc.2.

37 I'll make my old clothes know who's master. I shall straightaway cashier the hunting-frock, and render my leather breeches incapable. My hair has been in training some time.
1775 Bob Acres. *The Rivals*, act 2, sc.1.

38 Though one eye may be very agreeable, yet as the prejudice has always run in favour of two, I would not wish to affect a singularity in that article.
1775 Jack Absolute. *The Rivals*, act 3, sc.1.

39 He is the very pine-apple of politeness.
1775 Mrs Malaprop of Jack Absolute. *The Rivals*, act 3, sc.3.

40 Sure, if I reprehend anything in this world it is the use of my oracular tongue, and a nice derangement of epitaphs.
1775 Mrs Malaprop. *The Rivals*, act 3, sc.3.

41 She's as headstrong as an allegory on the banks of the Nile.
1775 Mrs Malaprop of Lydia Languish. *The Rivals*, act 3, sc.3.

42 That's too civil by half.
1775 Bob Acres to Sir Lucius O' Trigger. *The Rivals*, act 3, sc.4.

43 Pray, sir, be easy; the quarrel is a very pretty quarrel as it stands; we should only spoil it by trying to explain it.
1775 Sir Lucius O'Trigger to Jack Absolute. *The Rivals*, act 4, sc.3.

44 [To] have an unmannerly fat clerk ask the consent of every butcher in the parish to join John Absolute and Lydia Languish, spinster. Oh that I should live to hear myself called spinster!
1775 Lydia Languish, who had hoped for a romantic elopement. *The Rivals*, act 5, sc.1.

45 Oh, poor Dolly! I never shall see her like again; such an arm for a bandage—veins that seemed to invite the lancet.
1775 Dr Rosy. *St Patrick's Day*, act 1, sc.1.

46 A bumper of good liquor,
Will end a contest quicker
Than justice, judge or vicar.
1775 *The Duenna*, act 2, sc.3.

47 Conscience has no more to do with gallantry than it has with politics.
1775 Isaac to Don Antonio. *The Duenna*, act 2, sc.4.

48 BERINTHIA: Your lordship, I suppose, is fond of music?
LORD FOP: Oh, passionately, on Tuesdays and Saturdays.
1777 *A Trip to Scarborough*, act 2, sc.1.

49 Ah, Amanda, it's a delicious thing to be a young widow!
1777 *A Trip to Scarborough*, act 2, sc.1.

50 Alas! the devil's sooner raised than laid.
So strong, so swift, the monster there's no gagging:
Cut Scandal's head off, still the tongue is wagging.
1777 *The School for Scandal*, prologue.

51 I think you will like them, when you shall see them on a beautiful quarto page, where a neat rivulet of text shall meander through a meadow of margin.
1777 Sir Benjamin Backbite, of his love elegies to Maria. *The School for Scandal*, act 1, sc.1.

52 I'm called away by particular business. But I leave my character behind me.
1777 Sir Peter Teazle, leaving a gathering of gossips. *The School for Scandal*, act 2, sc.2.

53 I hate to see prudence clinging to the green suckers of youth; 'tis like ivy round a sapling, and spoils the growth of the tree.
1777 Sir Oliver Surface. *The School for Scandal*, act 2, sc.3.

54 Here's to the maiden of bashful fifteen;
Here's to the widow of fifty;
Here's to the flaunting extravagant quean;
And here's to the housewife that's thrifty.
Chorus. Let the toast pass,
Drink to the lass—
I'll warrant she'll prove an excuse for a glass!
1777 Song. *The School for Scandal*, act 3, sc.3.

55 Wine does but draw forth a man's natural qualities.
1777 Charles Surface. *The School for Scandal*, act 3, sc.3.

56 When a scandalous story is believed against one, there is certainly no comfort like the conscience of having deserved it.
1777 Joseph Surface. *The School for Scandal*, act 4, sc.3.

57 There needs no small degree of address to gain the reputation of benevolence without incurring the expense.
1777 Joseph Surface. *The School for Scandal*, act 5, sc. 1.

58 The *newspapers! Sir, they are the most villainous—licentious—abominable—infernal—Not that I ever read them—No—I make it a rule never to look into a newspaper.*
1779 *The Critic*, act 1, sc.1.

59 If there is anything to one's praise, it is a foolish vanity to be gratified at it; and, if it is abuse—why one is always sure to hear of it from one damned good-natured friend or other!
1779 Sir Fretful Plagiary, of newspaper criticism. *The Critic*, act 1, sc.1.

60 Mr Dangle, here are two very civil gentlemen trying to make themselves understood, and I don't know which is the interpreter.
1779 Mrs Dangle. *The Critic*, act 1, sc.2.

61 Puffing is of various sorts; the principal are, the puff direct, the puff preliminary, the puff collateral, the puff collusive, and the puff oblique, or puff by implication.
1779 Mr Puff. *The Critic*, act 1, sc.2.

62 The number of those who undergo the fatigue of judging for themselves is very small indeed.
1779 Mr Puff. *The Critic*, act 1, sc.2.

63 The puff collusive is the newest of any; for it acts in the disguise of determined hostility. It is much used by bold booksellers and enterprising poets.
1779 Mr Puff. *The Critic*, act 1, sc.2.

64 No scandal about Queen Elizabeth, I hope?
1779 Mr Sneer, of Mr Puff's tragedy 'The Spanish Armada'. *The Critic*, act 2, sc.1.

65 I open with a clock striking, to beget an awful attention in the audience: it also marks the time, which is four o'clock in the morning, and saves a description of the rising sun, and a great deal about gilding the eastern hemisphere.
1779 Mr Puff, of his tragedy 'The Spanish Armada'. *The Critic*, act 2, sc.2.

66 BEEFEATER: [a character in Mr Puff's play within a play, 'The Spanish Armanda'] Perdition catch my soul but I do love thee.
SNEER: Haven't I heard that line before?
PUFF: No, I fancy not.—Where pray?
DANGLE: Yes, I think there is something like it in *Othello*.
PUFF: Gad! now you put me in mind on't, I believe there is—but that's of no consequence; all that can be said is, that two people happened to hit upon the same thought—and Shakespeare made use of it first, that's all.
1779 *The Critic*, act 3, sc.1.

67 When a heroine goes mad, she always goes into white satin.
1779 Mr Puff. *The Critic*, act 3, sc.1.

68 An oyster may be crossed in love!
1779 Tilburnia's 'mad' speech from 'The Spanish Armada'. *The Critic*, act 3, sc.1.

69 Give me the liberty of the Press, and I will give the Minister a venal House of Peers, I will give him a corrupt and servile House of Commons...armed with the liberty of the Press, I will go forth to meet him undismayed.
1810 Speech, House of Commons.

Sherman, Richard M and Robert B 1928–, 1925–

US song-writing brothers, who wrote songs for Disney films from 1959 and also complete scores for musicals. Among their best-known films are *Mary Poppins* (1964) and *Chitty Chitty Bang Bang* (1968).

70 Supercalifragilisticexpialidocious.
1964 Title of song from *Mary Poppins*.

71 Protocoligorically Correct.
1976 Title of song from *The Slipper and the Rose*.

Sherman, William Tecumseh 1820–91

US general. He was Union commander during the American Civil War, when he captured Atlanta in 1864 and divided Confederate forces by his 'march to the sea', hastening the surrender of the South.

72 There is many a boy here today who looks on war as all glory, but, boys, it is all hell.
1880 Speech at Columbus, Ohio, 11 Aug. Quoted in Lloyd Lewis Sherman *Fighting Prophet* (1932).

Sherriff, R(obert) C(edric) 1896–1975

British playwright, novelist and screenwriter. He achieved an international reputation with his first play *Journey's End* (1929). He also wrote screenplays for films such as *The Invisible Man* (1933), *Goodbye Mr Chips* (1939) and *The Odd Man Out* (1947).

73 Even the moon is frightened of me, frightened to death! The whole world is frightened to death!
1933 Line delivered by Claude Rains in *The Invisible Man* (with Philip Wylie).

Shevardnadze, Eduard Ambrosievich 1928–

Georgian-born Soviet politician. In 1978 he was inducted into the Politburo and was appointed Foreign Minister in 1985. He rapidly overhauled the Soviet foreign policy machine for a new era of détente. In 1992 he returned to Georgia, where he became Chairman of the Supreme Council and Head of State (1992–95) then President (1995–).

74 Democrats are fleeing in all directions. Reformers are going into hiding. A dictatorship is beginning, and no one knows what shape it will take or who will come to power.

1990 On the increasing disarray in the USSR caused by failing Soviet reforms, rivalry between the Gorbachev and Yeltsin factions and unrest in the Baltic states, in the *Sunday Times*, 23 Dec.

Shinwell, Emanuel Shinwell, Baron 1884–1986

English Labour politician. A 'street-corner' socialist in Glasgow, he became Secretary of State for War (1947) and Minister of Defence (1950–1). Known for his belligerence, he mellowed into a backbench 'elder statesman'. He wrote several autobiographical works.

75 We know that you, the organized workers of the country, are our friends... As for the rest, they do not matter a tinker's curse.

1947 Trade union conference, 7 May.

Shipton, Eric Earle 1908–77

British mountaineer, explorer and writer. The foremost mountain explorer of his generation, he facilitated the successful ascent of Everest in 1953. He wrote seven books, including an autobiography, *That Untravelled World* (1969).

76 I have never been able to decide whether, in mountain exploration, it is the prospect of tackling an unsolved problem, or the performance of the task itself, or the retrospective enjoyment of successful effort, which affords the greatest amount of pleasure.

1936 *Nanda Devi*.

77 Whatever may have been my enthusiasm or impatience to be up and doing on the night before, the hour for getting up always finds me with no other ambition in the world than to be permitted to lie where I am and sleep, sleep, sleep. Not so Tilman. I have never met anyone with such a complete disregard for the sublime comforts of the early morning bed. However monstrously early we might decide, the night before, to get up, he was about at least half an hour before the time. He was generally very good about it, and used to sit placidly smoking his pipe over the fire.

1936 On climbing with H W (Bill) Tilman. *Nanda Devi*.

78 We were now actually in the inner sanctuary of the Nanda Devi Basin, and at each step I experienced that subtle thrill which anyone of imagination must feel when treading hitherto unexplored country... My most blissful dream as a child was to be in some such valley, free to wander where I liked, and discover for myself some hitherto unrevealed glory of Nature. Now the reality was no less wonderful than that half-forgotten dream; and of how many childish fancies can that be said, in this age of disillusionment ?

1936 *Nanda Devi*.

Shirley, James 1596–1666

English dramatist. Educated at Oxford and Cambridge, he took holy orders but renounced them upon conversion to Catholicism. He died in the Great Fire of London. He wrote plays and masques, including the comedies *Hyde Park* (1634) and *The Lady of Pleasure* (1635), the tragedy *The Cardinal* (1641), and the masque *The Contention of Ajax and Ulysses* (1659).

79 How little room
Do we take up in death, that, living know
No bounds?

1626 *The Wedding*, act 4, sc.4.

80 'Tis no shame for men
Of his high birth to love a wench; his honour
May privilege more sins. Next to a woman,
He loves a running-horse.

1634 *Hyde Park*, act 1, sc.1.

81 RIDER: ...we can be but
What we are.
VENTURE: A pair of credulous fools.

1634 *Hyde Park*, act 1, sc.1.

82 I presume you're mortal, and may err.

1635 *The Lady of Pleasure*, act 2, sc.2.

83 The glories of our blood and state
Are shadows, not substantial things;
There is no armour against fate;
Death lays his icy hand on kings:
Scepter and crown
Must tumble down,
And in the dust be equal made
With the poor crooked scythe and spade.

1659 *The Contention of Ajax and Ulysses*, act 1, sc.3.

Shultz, George P(ratt) 1920–

US Former Secretary of State. A Professor of Chicago University's graduate business school (1957–68), he was US Secretary of Labor (1969–70), then assistant to President Nixon (1972–4). He was Secretary of State to President Reagan (1982–89). A fellow of the Hoover Institution, Stanford University (1989–) he is a distinguished author and was awarded the Seoul Peace Prize (1992).

84 He made a combative apology.

1987 On the ability of Elliott Abrams, Assistant Secretary for Inter-American Affairs, to acknowledge a sensitive question without giving a definite reply. In the *New York Times*, 25 Jul.

85 Gardening...is one of the most underrated aspects of diplomacy.

1993 On the need to meet people 'on their own turf'. *Turmoil and Triumph*.

86 Washington is a resigning town. Nothing else holds the special excitement of a rumored resignation.

1993 *Turmoil and Triumph*.

87 The way to keep weeds from overwhelming you is to deal with them constantly and in their early stages.

1993 *Turmoil and Triumph*.

88 The Soviet game is chess...ours is poker. We will have to play a creative mixture of both games.

1993 Comment to President Reagan. Recalled in *Turmoil and Triumph*.

89 Better to use force when you *should* rather than when you *must*.

1993 On Soviet alarm at the prospect of US science 'turned on' and venturing into the realm of space defence. *Turmoil and Triumph*.

90 Agreement reached by the negotiators...usually starts to collapse in the hands of those who implement it, no matter how carefully cleared at the top.

1993 On negotiating the release of Russian political prisoners. *Turmoil and Triumph*.

91 The decision makers face each other. No safety screen stands between the issues and the highest authorities.
1993 Of summit meetings, particularly that between the US and the Soviets at Reykjavik, Iceland, 9–12 Oct 1986. *Turmoil and Triumph.*

92 A 'staffocracy' has been created.
1993 On the National Security Council. *Turmoil and Triumph.*

93 You can't figure him out like a fact, because to Reagan the main fact was a vision… He came from the heartland of the country, where people could be down-to-earth yet feel that the sky is the limit—not ashamed of, or cynical about, the American dream.
1993 Of Ronald Reagan. *Turmoil and Triumph.*

Shute, Nevil *originally* ***Nevil Shute Norway*** 1899–1960

English writer. An aeronautical engineer, he began to write novels in 1926 and after World War II emigrated to Australia, the setting for most of his later books, notably *A Town Like Alice* (1949) and *On the Beach* (1957).

94 A Town Like Alice
1949 Title of book.

Sidgwick, Henry 1838–1900

British economist, Professor at Cambridge.

95 We cannot not say how much wealth there is in a country till we know how it is shared among its inhabitants.
1883 *Principles of Political Economy.*

Sidmouth, Henry Addington, 1st Viscount 1757–1844

English statesman and Tory Prime Minister (1801–4) after the resignation of William Pitt the Younger. As Home Secretary (1812–21) he had to deal with the Luddite riots and the 'Peterloo Massacre' in Manchester (1819).

96 I hate liberality. Nine times out of ten it is cowardice—and the tenth time, lack of principle.
Attributed.

Sidney, Algernon 1622–83

English Whig politician. He fought for the Parliamentary army in the English Civil War and in 1645 entered Parliament, but he resented Cromwell's assumption of power, and retired to Penshurst (1653–9). In exile after the Restoration, in 1677 he was pardoned and returned, but was implicated in the Rye House Plot (1683) and beheaded.

97 Liars ought to have good memories.
Discourses Concerning Government (published 1689).

Sidney, Sir Philip 1554–86

English poet and patron. Educated at Oxford, he travelled widely; in 1585 he was made Governor of Flushing. He died after being wounded in the battle of Zutphen. His sonnet sequence *Astrophel and Stella* (published 1591) was an early example of the genre in English, as was his prose romance *The Arcadia* (*The Old Arcadia*, as it is called, was not published during Sidney's lifetime; a revised version, *The New Arcadia*, was first published in 1590); his *Defence of Poetry* (published 1595) was the first English essay on literary criticism.

98 I readily admit that I am often more serious than I should be at my age or in my present circumstances, yet I know from experience that I am never less given to melancholy than when I am keenly applying the feeble powers of my mind to some arduous and difficult matter.
1574 Letter to Hubert Languet, 4 Feb.

99 O wretched state of man in self-division!
1581 *The Old Arcadia*, 'First Eclogues'.

1 She was stricken with most obstinate love to a young man.
1581 *The Old Arcadia*, 'First Eclogues'.

2 What allurements she used indifferently were long to tell.
1581 *The Old Arcadia*, 'Second Eclogues'.

3 What be the fruits of speaking art? What grows by the words?
1581 *The Old Arcadia*, 'Second Eclogues'.

4 My true love hath my heart and I have his,
By just exchange one for the other giv'n;
I hold his dear, and mine he cannot miss,
There never was a better bargain driv'n.
1581 *The Old Arcadia*, 'Third Eclogues'.

5 O sweet, on a wretch wilt thou be revenged?
Shall such high planets tend to the loss of a worm?
1581 *The Old Arcadia*, 'Fourth Eclogues'.

6 A lamentable tune is the sweetest music to a woeful mind.
1590 *Arcadia*, pt.2.

7 Loving in truth, and vain in verse my love to show,
That she (dear she) might take some pleasure of my pain,
Pleasure might cause her read, reading might make her know;
Knowledge might pity win, and pity grace obtain.
1591 *Astrophel and Stella*, sonnet 1.

8 But words came halting forth, wanting Invention's stay;
Invention, Nature's child, fled step-dame Study's blows…
Biting my truant pen, beating myself for spite,
'Fool,' said my muse to me; 'look in thy heart, and write.'
1591 *Astrophel and Stella*, sonnet 1.

9 Your rhubarb words.
1591 *Astrophel and Stella*, sonnet 14.

10 Come sleep, O sleep, the certain knot of peace,
The baiting place of wit, the balm of woe,
The poor man's wealth, the prisoner's release,
The indifferent judge between the high and low.
1591 *Astrophel and Stella*, sonnet 39.

11 That sweet enemy, France.
1591 *Astrophel and Stella*, sonnet 41.

12 Hope, art thou true, or dost thou flatter me?
1591 *Astrophel and Stella*, sonnet 67.

13 Oh heav'nly fool, thy most kiss-worthy face
Anger invests with such a lovely grace
That Anger's self I needs must kiss again.
1591 *Astrophel and Stella*, sonnet 73.

14 I am no pick-purse of another's wit.
1591 *Astrophel and Stella*, sonnet 74.

15 Stella, think not that I by verse seek fame;
Who seek, who hope, who love, who live, but thee:
Thine eyes my pride, thy lips my history;
If thou praise not, all other praise is shame.
1591 *Astrophel and Stella*, sonnet 90.

16 I have just cause to make a pitiful defence of poor poetry, which from almost the highest estimation of learning is

fallen to be the laughing stock of children.
1595 *The Defence of Poetry.*

17 And truly, even Plato, whosoever well considereth shall find that in the body of his work, though the inside and strength were philosophy, the skin as it were and beauty depended most on poetry.
1595 *The Defence of Poetry.*

18 [Nature's] world is brazen, the poets only deliver a golden.
1595 *The Defence of Poetry.*

19 Poetry therefore, is an art of imitation... A speaking picture, with this end: to teach and delight.
1595 *The Defence of Poetry.*

20 With a tale forsooth he cometh unto you, with a tale which holdeth children from play, and old men from the chimney corner.
1595 Of the poet. *The Defence of Poetry.*

21 Comedy is an imitation of the common errors of our life, which he representeth in the most ridiculous and scornful sort that may be, so as it is impossible that any beholder can be content to be such a one.
1595 *The Defence of Poetry.*

22 I...am admitted into the company of paper-blurrers.
1595 *The Defence of Poetry.*

23 [This] much curse I must send you, in the behalf of all poets, that while you live, you live in love, and never get favour for lacking skill of a sonnet, and, when you die, your memory die from the earth for want of an epigraph.
1595 *The Defence of Poetry.*

Siegel, Jerome 1914–92

US writer, co-creator of Superman.

24 I'm lying in bed counting sheep when all of a sudden it hits me...a character like Samson, Hercules and all the strong men I heard tell of rolled into one. Only more so.
Recalling the inspiration behind Superman, created 1938. Quoted in *Time*, 14 Mar 1988.

25 Faster than a speeding bullet! More powerful than a locomotive! Able to leap tall buildings in a single bound!
Introduction for the Superman radio serial. Quoted in *Time*, 14 Mar 1988.

Sièyes, Emmanuel Joseph, Comte *also called* Abbé Sièyes 1748–1836

French cleric and political theorist. His pamphlet, *Qu'est-ce que le tiers-état?* ('What is the Third Estate?', 1789) was very popular with the bourgeoisie. He helped organize the revolution of 18th Brumaire (in which Napoleon overthrew the Directory, 1799). Exiled at the Restoration (1815), he returned after the July Revolution (1830).

26 Who will dare deny that the Third Estate contains within itself all that is needed to constitute a nation?... What would the Third Estate be without the privileged classes? It would be a whole in itself, and a prosperous one. Nothing can be done without it, and everything would be done far better without the others.
1789 *Qu'est-ce que le tiers-état?*

Sigismund 1368–1437

Holy Roman Emperor from 1433. He became King of Hungary in 1387 and as Emperor presided over the Council of Constance, which ended the Great Schism (1414–18).

27 Only do always in health what you have often promised to do when you are sick.
His advice for a happy life, quoted in Clifton Fadiman *Faber Book of Anecdotes* (1985).

Sigourney, Lydia Howard *née* Huntley 1791–1865

American poet. Her pious, sentimental poetry made her the most popular woman poet of her generation. She was an important campaigner in the cause of higher education for women. Her collections include *Moral Pieces in Prose and Verse* (1815)

28 Ye say, they all have passed away,
That noble race and brave,
That their light canoes have vanished
From off the crested wave;
That 'mid the forests where they roamed
There rings no hunter's shout;
But their name is on your waters,
Ye may not wash it out.
1848 *Select Poems*, 'Indian Names'.

Sihanouk, Prince Norodom 1922–

Cambodian politician who as Prime Minister tried but failed to keep his country out of the Vietnam War. He was deposed in 1970 by a military coup but returned in 1993 and was elected king. He attacked the intensive US bombing of his country.

29 What is the difference between burning and gassing people in ovens and doing it to a whole nation out in the open?
1973 Of the US bombing of Cambodia. *My War with the CIA* (with W Burchett).

30 The humble people of Cambodia are the most wonderful in the world. Their great misfortune is that they always have terrible leaders who make them suffer. I am not sure I was much better myself, but perhaps I was the least bad.
1978 In an interview with William Shawcross, author of *Sideshow* (1979)

Sikorski, Gerry 1948–

US politician.

31 Like a toothless terrier on Valium.
1987 On the workings of the Office of Government Ethics. In the *New York Times*, 8 Jul.

Sikorsky, Igor Ivan 1889–1972

Russian-born US aeronautical engineer. He built and flew the first four-engined aeroplane (1913), then founded the Sikorsky Aero Engineering Corporation in the USA (1923). He built several flying boats, and in 1939 produced the first successful helicopter.

32 The work of the individual still remains the spark that moves mankind ahead, even more than teamwork.
Quoted in his *New York Times* obituary, 27 Oct 1972.

Sillitoe, Alan 1928–

English novelist. Several of his novels set in the north of England have been adapted as successful films, notably *Saturday Night and Sunday Morning* (1960).

33 The Loneliness of the Long Distance Runner.
1962 Title of book.

Silva, José Asunción 1865–96

Colombian poet whose life was marked by financial reverses, the death of loved ones, and the loss of his manuscripts in a shipwreck. His poetry is characteristically melancholy, and after only ten years of writing he committed suicide.

34 *Y si evitas la sífilis, siguiendo*
la sabia profilaxia,
al llegar los cuarenta irás sintiendo
un principio de ataxia.
And if you manage to avoid syphilis
by following a wise course of prophylaxis,
when you turn forty you will feel
the beginnings of ataxia.

1908 *Gotas amargas*, 'Filosofías' ('Philosophies').

Silvers, Phil *originally* ***Philip Silver*** 1912–85

US comic actor. His success in films and on Broadway led to the *Phil Silvers Show* (1955–9) on television, where he introduced the character of Sergeant Bilko. He won three Emmy awards during his career, and a Tony Award for his performance in *A Funny Thing Happened on the Way to the Forum* (1972).

35 Be funny on a golf course? Do I kid my best friend's mother about her heart condition?

Quoted in Michael Hobbs *The Golf Quotation Book* (1992).

Simon, Caroline K(lein) d.1993

Judge, NY State Court of Claims.

36 Look like a girl, act like a lady, think like a man and work like a dog.

Comment the year after her candidacy for Postmaster General was barred by federal officials who claimed the job was unsuited to a woman. Recalled on her death, in the *New York Times*, 30 Jul 1993.

Simon, Herbert A 1916–2001

US psychologist and economist; awarded a Nobel prize in economics (1978).

37 It is a fatal defect of current principles of administration that, like proverbs, they occur in pairs. For almost every principle one can find an equally plausible and acceptable contradictory principle. Although the two principles of the pair will lead to exactly opposite recommendations, there is nothing in the theory to indicate which is the appropriate one to apply.

1945 *Administrative Behavior.*

Simon (of Stackpole Elidor), John Allsebrook Simon, 1st Viscount 1873–1954

English Liberal politician and lawyer. Attorney-General (1913–15) and Home Secretary (1915–16), he resigned from the Cabinet over conscription. Deserting the Liberals to form the Liberal National Party, he supported Ramsay MacDonald's coalition governments and became Foreign Secretary (1931–5), Home Secretary (1935–7), Chancellor of the Exchequer (1937–40) and Lord Chancellor (1940–5).

38 If Joan of Arc had been born in Austria and worn a moustache, she might have conveyed much the same impression.

1935 Letter to George V, referring to his first meeting with Adolf Hitler, 27 Mar.

Simon, (Marvin) Neil 1927–

US playwright. His plays and musicals include *Barefoot in the Park* (1963), *The Odd Couple* (1965) and the semi-autobiographical trilogy *Brighton Beach Memoirs* (1983), *Biloxi Blues* (1984) and *Broadway Bound* (1986). More recent works include *Lost in Yonkers* (1991), which won him a Pulitzer Prize and a Tony Award, and *London Suite* (1995).

39 I've already had medical attention—a dog licked me when I was on the ground.

1982 *Only When I Laugh.*

40 I would have been disappointed if I hung up my pen without ever getting one…[and] now I hope to get one every 30 years like clockwork.

1991 On receiving the Pulitzer Prize for *Lost in Yonkers*. In the *Washington Post*, 10 Apr.

Simone, Nina *pseudonym of* ***Eunice Waymon*** 1933–2003

US singer and pianist. She was a gifted classical pianist as a teenager, but her career was blocked by the racial prejudice of the time, and she went on to become a cult figure in jazz, gospel and soul music.

41 It wasn't a matter of becoming interested in music; music is a gift and a burden I've had since I can remember who I was. I was born into music. The decision was how to make the best use of it.

Quoted in Art Taylor *Notes and Tones* (1977), 'Nina Simone'.

Simonides of Ceos c.556–468 BC

Greek lyric poet. His poetry survives only in fragments, but he is known to have written epitaphs for Greeks who fell in the Persian Wars, and in 489 BC he beat Aeschylus in a competition for the best elegy on those who fell at Marathon.

42 Go, stranger, and tell the Spartans that here we lie, obedient to their commands.

c.480 BC Epitaph for the Spartan army dead after the Battle of Thermopylae. Quoted in Herodotus *Histories*, bk.7, ch.228.

43 Man's strength is but little, and futile his concerns.

Lyrica Graeca Selecta, (ed. D L Page), no.354.

Simons, Henry C 1899–1946

US economist, Professor at the University of Chicago.

44 Monopoly power must be abused. It has no use save abuse.

1944 *Economic Policy for a Free Society*, p.129.

Simple, Peter *pseudonym of* ***Michael Wharton*** 1913–

45 Rentacrowd Ltd—the enterprising firm that supplies crowds for all occasions, and has done so much to keep progressive causes in the public eye.

1962 In the *Daily Telegraph.*

Simpson, Alan (Kooi) 1931–

US Senator and lawyer. He was a member of Wyoming's House of Representatives (1964–77) and acted as a majority whip (1973–5) and floor leader (1975–7). He became a member of the US Senate for Wyoming in 1978.

46 Like giving dry birth to a porcupine.

1989 On the passage of immigration reform bill. In the *Washingtonian*, Mar.

47 I come from a state where gun control is just how

steady you hold your weapon.
1991 In *Fortune*, 30 Dec.

Simpson, Kirke L 1881–1972

US journalist. He was awarded a Pulitzer Prize in 1921 for his article on the Unknown Soldier.

48 Chosen by a group of men in a smoke-filled room.
Of Warren G Harding, presidential candidate. Recalled on Simpson's death in the *New York Times*, 17 Jun 1972. The 'smoke-filled room' became a common phrase in presidential nomination.

Simpson, O J (Orenthal James) 1947–

US former professional football player, actor and sports commentator. He joined the Buffalo Bills professionally in 1969, and retired in 1979 to become an actor and broadcaster. He was charged with the murders of his estranged wife Nicole and Ronald Goodman, but was acquitted in 1995.

49 Absolutely 100 per cent not guilty.
1994 Plea on arraignment for the murder of his estranged wife. Reported in the *New York Times*, 23 Jul. Simpson was later found not guilty.

Simpson, Tom 1938–67

English cyclist. In 1962 he became the first Briton ever to wear the leader's yellow jersey in the Tour de France. He died from heart failure during the Tour de France.

50 Put me back on my bike.
1967 Last words.

Sinatra, Frank (Francis Albert) 1915–98

US singer and actor. He began with the Tommy Dorsey orchestra (1940–2), and starred on radio and in films (eg *Anchors Aweigh*, 1945). His recordings (1956–65) include *Songs For Swinging Lovers*, *Come Fly With Me*, and *That's Life*. His highly publicized and controversial personal life included four marriages (amongst them, to Ava Gardner and Mia Farrow).

51 My greatest teacher was not a vocal coach, not the work
of other singers, but the way Tommy Dorsey breathed
and phrased on the trombone.
Foreword to George T Simon *The Big Bands* (1967).

Singer, Isaac Bashevis 1904–91

US Yiddish writer of novels and short stories. Awarded the Nobel prize for literature (1978).

52 Children…have no use for psychology.
1978 Speech on receiving his Nobel prize.

Singh, Vijay 1963–

Fijian golfer whose wins include the US Masters in 2000 and US Open in 2004.

53 Golf is to Fiji what cricket is to America.
2000 In *The Independent*, 23 Dec.

Sisco, Joseph John 1919–

US diplomat and businessman. He set up his own management consultancy, and also acted as a consultant and adviser to the UN.

54 Welcome to shuttle diplomacy!
1995 Comment to reporters Marvin Kalb and Ted Koppel on Henry A Kissinger's first trip to the Middle East after the Yom Kippur War. Reported in the *New York Times*, 29 Oct.

Sisson, C(harles) H(erbert) 1914–2003

English poet and critic. One of the leading poets of the period, he also wrote novels and an autobiography.

55 Here lies a civil servant. He was civil
To everyone, and servant to the devil.
1961 'Civil Servant'.

Sitting Bull *real name* ***Tatanka Iyotake*** 1834–90

Chief of the Dakota Sioux, who led the defeat of Custer at Little Big Horn, 1876. He later featured in Buffalo Bill Cody's Wild West Show, 1885, but was killed evading arrest during the 'ghost dance' uprising of 1890.

56 When I was a boy the Sioux owned the world; the sun rose and set on their land; they sent ten thousand men to battle. Where are the warriors today? Who slew them? Where are our lands? Who owns them?… What law have I broken? Is it wrong for me to love my own? Is it wicked for me because my skin is red? Because I am a Sioux; because I was born where my father lived; because I would die for my country?
c.1866 Quoted in T C McLuhan *Touch the Earth* (1973).

Sitwell, Dame Edith Louisa 1887–1964

English poet and essayist, sister of Osbert and Sacheverell Sitwell. Her poems were designed to shock her audiences and revitalize English poetry. Her numerous prose works reflect her interest in English history. Her books include *Façade* (1923, set to music by Walton), *English Eccentrics* (1933), and *Fanfare of Elizabeth* (1946).

57 Lady Venus on the settee of the horsehair sea!
1923 *Façade*, 'Hornpipe'.

58 This minx, of course,
Is as sharp as any lynx and blacker—deeper than the drinks and quite as
Hot as any hottentot, without remorse!
1923 *Façade*, 'Hornpipe'.

59 An admiral red, whose only notion,
(A butterfly poised on a pigtailed ocean)
Is of the peruked sea whose swell
Breaks on the flowerless rocks of Hell.
1923 *Façade*, 'En Famille'.

60 The Admiral said, 'You could never call—
I assure you it would not do at all!
She gets down from the table without saying 'please',
Forgets her prayers and to cross her T's,
In short, her scandalous reputation
Has shocked the whole of the Hellish nation'.
1923 *Façade*, 'En Famille'.

61 Those trains will run over their tails, if they can,
Snorting and sporting like porpoises. Flee
The burly, the whirligig wheels of the train,
As round as the world and as large again.
1923 *Façade*, 'Mariner Man'.

62 The light is braying like an ass.
1923 *Façade*, 'Long Steel Grass'.

63 Through gilded trellises
Of the heat, spangles
Pelt down through the tangles
Of bell-flowers.

1923 *Façade*, 'Through Gilded Trellises'.

64 But a word stung him like a mosquito...
For what they hear, they repeat!
1923 *Façade*, 'Tango-Pasodoble'.

65 In a room of the palace
Black Mrs Behemoth
Gave way to wrath
And the wildest malice.
1923 *Façade*, 'Black Mrs Behemoth'.

66 Where the satyrs are chattering, nymphs with their flattering
Glimpse of the forest enhance
All the beauty of marrow and cucumber narrow
And Ceres will join in the dance.
1923 *Façade*, 'Tarantella'.

67 That hobnailed goblin, the bob-tailed Hob,
said, 'It is time I began to rob'.
1923 *Façade*, 'Country Dance'.

68 And shade is on the brightest wing,
And dust forbids the birds to sing.
1923 *Façade*, 'Popular Song'.

69 Came the great Popinjay
Smelling his nosegay:
In cage like grots
The birds sing gavottes.
1923 *Façade*, 'Came the Great Popinjay'.

70 Jane, Jane,
Tall as a crane,
The morning light creaks down again.
1923 *Façade*, 'Aubade'.

71 The fire was furry as a bear.
1923 *Façade*, 'Dark Song'.

72 Daisy and Lily,
Lazy and silly,
Walk by the shore of the wan grass sea,—
Talking once more 'neath a swan-bosomed tree.
1923 *Façade* 'Valse'.

73 Still falls the Rain—
Dark as the world of man, black as our loss—
Blind as the nineteen hundred and forty nails
Upon the cross.
1942 'The Raids, 1940. Night and Dawn'.

74 The Englishwoman's clothes, too, have improved out of all knowledge...no longer are our hats, as in Victorian days, a kind of Pageant of Empire, whereon the products of all the colonies battle for precedence.
1942 *English Women*.

75 I have often wished I had time to cultivate modesty... But I am too busy thinking about myself.
1950 In the *Observer*, 30 Apr.

76 I enjoyed talking to her, but thought *nothing* of her writing. I considered her 'a beautiful little knitter'.
1955 Of Virginia Woolf. Letter to Geoffrey Singleton, 11 Jul.

77 Mr Lewis's pictures appeared, as a very great painter said to me, to have been painted by a mailed fist in a cotton glove.
1965 On Wyndham Lewis. *Taken Care Of*, ch.11.

78 I wish the Government would put a tax on pianos for the incompetent.
Collected in *Letters, 1916–1964* (1970).

Sitwell, Sir (Francis) Osbert 1892–1969

English writer. He was the brother of Edith and Sacheverell Sitwell, and a friend of Eliot, Pound and Wyndham Lewis, whose radical aesthetic he shared.

79 The British Bourgeosie
Is not born
And does not die,
But, if it is ill,
It has a frightened look in its eyes.
1921 *At the House of Mrs Kinfoot*.

80 But what is Dust,
Save Time's most lethal weapon,
Her faithful ally and our sneaking foe?
1927 'Mrs Southern's Enemy'.

81 *Educated: during the holidays from Eton.*
1929 From his entry in *Who's Who*.

82 Now the nimble fingers are no more nimble,
And the silver thimble lies cold and tarnished black.
1931 'Mrs Mew's Windowbox'.

83 But he was never, well,
What I call
A Sportsman:
For forty days
He went out into the desert
—And never shot anything.
1931 Of Jesus Christ. 'Old Fashioned Sportsmen'.

84 The artist, like the idiot or clown, sits on the edge of the world, and a push may send him over it.
1946 *The Scarlet Tree*, bk.4, ch.2.

85 A word is the carving and colouring of a thought, and gives it permanence.
1949 *Laughter in the Next Room*, ch.7.

86 In reality, killing time
Is only the name for another of the multifarious ways
By which Time kills us.
1958 'Milordo Inglese'.

87 Hunting the author, painter and musician is a traditional and popular sport. In this country poet-baiting at an early stage assumed the place of bull-baiting.
1963 'What It Feels Like to be an Author'.

Sixtus V *originally* ***Felice Peretti*** 1521–90

Franciscan preacher and a professor of theology, created cardinal in 1570. Elected Pope in 1585, because of his presumed feebleness, he implemented vigorous moral, legal and financial reforms.

88 Just see how well she governs! She is only a woman, only the mistress of half an island, and yet she makes herself feared by Spain, by France, by the Empire, by all!
1588 Of Elizabeth I. Quoted in L von Pastor *The History of the Popes* (edited by Kerr R F, 1932), vol.22, p.34.

Skelton, John c.1460–1529

English poet. Educated at Oxford and Cambridge, he was tutor to Prince Henry (later Henry VIII). He began his poetic career with translations and elegies, but turned to writing satirical vernacular poetry, including *Colin Clout* (1521) and *Why Come Ye Not to Court?* (1521), both of which were attacks on Cardinal Wolsey.

89 The sovereign'st thing that any man may have

Is little to say, and much to hear and see.
1499 *The Bouge of Court*, l. 211.

90 With Mannerly Margery milk and ale.
1523 'Mannerly Margery Milk and Ale'.

91 Far may be sought
Erst that ye can find
So courteous, so kind,
As Merry Margaret,
This midsummer flower,
Gentle as falcon
Or hawk of the tower.
1523 *The Garland of Laurel*, 'To Mistress Margaret Hussey'.

92 With lullay, lullay, like a child,
Thou sleepest too long, thou art beguiled.
1527 'Lullay, Lullay, Like a Child'.

93 What dreamest thou, drunkard, drowsy pate?
Thy lust and liking is from thee gone.
Thou blinkard blowboll, thou wakest too late.
1527 'Lullay, Lullay, Like a Child'.

Skelton, (Archibald) Noel 1880–1935

Scottish-born politician and lawyer. He was MP for Perth (1922–3 and 1924–31) and Parliamentary Under-Secretary in the Scottish Office (1931–5).

94 To state as clearly as may be what means lie ready to develop a property-owning democracy, to bring the industrial and economic status of the wage-earner abreast of his political and educational status, to make democracy stable and four-square.
1923 In *The Spectator*, 19 May.

Skelton, Red (Richard) 1913–97

US comedian. A star of radio and television, he also made a few films in the 1940s, among them *Whistling in the Dark* (1941) and *DuBarry Was a Lady* (1943).

95 Exercise? I get it on the golf course. When I see my friends collapse, I run for the paramedics.
Attributed.

Skelton, Robin 1925–97

English-born Canadian poet and aphorist.

96 When someone says, 'It is good business', you may be sure it is bad morality.
1991 *A Devious Dictionary.*

97 Some part of us still believes that men should kill.
1991 *A Devious Dictionary.*

98 Death is the only mystery we all solve.
1991 *A Devious Dictionary.*

99 Never believe what you cannot doubt.
1991 *A Devious Dictionary.*

1 Headlines pass; breadlines continue.
1991 *A Devious Dictionary.*

2 Anything said off the cuff has usually been written on it first.
1991 *A Devious Dictionary.*

3 It requires less skill to love than to be loved.
1991 *A Devious Dictionary.*

4 When one hears of progress one should ask for whom.
1991 *A Devious Dictionary.*

5 Procrustes was an editor.
1991 *A Devious Dictionary.*

6 Kneel to nobody; bow to everyone.
1991 *A Devious Dictionary.*

7 Those who have the habit of revelation lose the habit of thought.
1991 *A Devious Dictionary.*

8 More dreams are destroyed in bed than are ever found there.
1991 *A Devious Dictionary.*

Skinner, B(urrhus) F(rederic) 1904–90

US psychologist and social philosopher, developer and exponent of behaviourism, which views human behaviour and learning as physiological responses. His works include *Walden Two* (1961) and *The Technology of Teaching* (1968).

9 Education is what survives when what has been learnt has been forgotten.
1964 In *New Scientist*, 21 May.

10 The real problem is not whether machines think but whether men do.
1969 *Contingencies of Reinforcement*, ch.9.

Skinner, Cornelia Otis 1902–79

US actress, singer and writer.

11 It's as though some poor devil were to set out for a large dinner party with the knowledge that the following morning he would be hearing exactly what each of the other guests thought of him.
1959 Of opening night reviews. *The Ape In Me.*

12 There are compensations for growing older. One is the realization that to be sporting isn't at all necessary. It is a great relief to reach this stage of wisdom.
Attributed.

Skinner, John 1721–1807

Jacobite songwriter and Episcopalian minister in Aberdeenshire, whose 'Tullochgorum' was described by Robert Burns as 'the best Scotch song ever Scotland saw'.

13 Come, gie's a sang, Montgomery cry'd,
And lay your disputes a'aside;
What signifies't for folks to chide
For what's been done before them?
Let Whig and Tory a'agree,
Whig and Tory, Whig and Tory,
Whig and Tory a'agree
To drop their whigmigmorum;
Let Whig and Tory a'agree
To spend this night wi' mirth and glee,
And cheerfu' sing, alang wi' me,
The Reel o' Tullochgorum.
'Tullochgorum', stanza 1.

Skirving, Adam 1719–1803

Scottish composer of Jacobite songs.

14 Hey, Johnnie Cope, are ye wauking yet?
Or are your drums a-beating yet?
If ye were wauking I wad wait
To gang to the coals i' the morning.
1745 'Johnnie Cope', chorus (commemorating the Battle of

Prestonpans and General Cope's flight to Newcastle).

Slessor, Kenneth Adolf 1901–71

Australian poet and journalist. In 1924 he published *Thief of the Moon* and in 1926 *Earth-Visitors*. *Darlinghurst Nights and Morning Glories* (1933) celebrates 'The Cross', the bohemian district of Sydney where he lived for most of his life. His verse was collected in *One Hundred Poems: 1919–1939* (1944, reissued as *Poems*, 1957), and his prose in *Bread and Wine* (1970).

15 Time that is moved by little fidget wheels
Is not my Time, the flood that does not flow.
Between the double and the single bell
Of a ship's hour, between a round of bells
From the dark warship riding there below,
I have lived many lives, and this one life
Of Joe, long dead, who lives between five bells.

1939 *Five Bells*, title poem. The poem was written as an elegy for Joe Lynch, a friend who fell overboard from a Sydney ferry.

Slezak, Leo 1873–1946

Czech tenor. Tall and commanding, he was internationally famous as an interpreter of the heroes of Wagnerian opera.

16 *Wann geht der nächste Schwan?*
What time's the next swan?

1900 When the swan-boat failed to arrive to take him off in Wagner's *Lohengrin*. Quoted in Hugh Vickers *Great Operatic Disasters* (1979).

Sloan, John French 1871–1951

US painter of the Ashcan school, painting everyday subjects, particularly street life in New York City. His works include *Sunday, Women Drying Their Hair* (1912) and *Backyards, Greenwich Village* (1914).

17 Facility is a dangerous thing. Where there is too much technical ease the brain stops criticising. Don't let the hand fall into a smart way of putting the mind to sleep.

1939 *Gist of Art*.

18 Artists are the only people in the world who really live. The others have to hope for heaven.

Recalled on his death, 7 Sep 1951, and quoted in the *Smithsonian*, Apr 1988.

Slovo, Gillian 1952–

South African writer.

19 In most families it is the children who leave home. In mine it was the parents.

1997 Both her parents, Joe Slovo and Ruth First, were anti-apartheid activists. In *Every Secret Thing*.

Small, Albion W 1854–1926

US sociologist; first head of the first department of sociology in the US, at the University of Chicago.

20 Sociology was born of the modern ardor to improve society.

1894 *An Introduction to the Study of Society* (with George E Vincent, 1894).

21 The social problem of the twentieth century is whether civilized nations can restore themselves to sanity after their nineteenth-century aberrations of individualism and capitalism.

1914 'A Vision of Social Efficiency', in the *American Journal of Sociology*, Jan.

Smart, Christopher 1722–71

English poet. He made a precarious living as a writer, helped by Dr Johnson and others, but suffered from bouts of insanity. His poetry includes *The Hilliad* (1753, a satire on doctors modelled on *The Dunciad*) and the structurally complex *A Song To David* (1763). During one of his confinements in a private madhouse he wrote the extraordinary and highly allusive *Jubliate Agno* (1758–63, first published as *Rejoice in the Lamb* 1939, edited by W F Stead).

22 Night, with all her negro train,
Took possession of the plain;
In an hearse she rode reclined,
Drawn by screech-owls slow and blind:
Close to her, with printless feet,
Crept Stillness, in a winding sheet.

1748 'A Night-Piece; or, Modern Philosophy', stanza 2. In the *London Magazine*, no.14, Dec. Collected in *Poems on Several Occasions* (1752).

23 Let Eli rejoice with Leucon—he is an honest fellow, which is a rarity.
For I have seen the White Raven and Thomas Hall of Willingham and am myself a greater curiosity than both.
Let Jemuel rejoice with Charadrius, who is from the HEIGHT and the sight of him is good for the jaundice.
For I look up to heaven which is my prospect to escape envy by surmounting it.

1758–63 *Jubilate Agno*, fragment B, stanzas 25–6 (first published 1939). Both the white raven and Thomas Hall, a giant of four feet at the age of three, were curiosities exhibited in the 1740s.

24 For every word has its marrow in the English tongue for order and for delight.
For the dissyllables such as able table &c are the fiddle rhymes.
For all dissyllables and some trissyllables are fiddle rhymes.
For the relations of words are in pairs first.
For the relations of words are sometimes in oppositions.
For the relations of words are according to their distances from the pair.

1758–63 *Jubilate Agno*, fragment B, l.595–600. (First published 1939.)

25 For I will consider my cat Jeoffry.
For he is the servant of the Living God duly and daily serving him.
For at the first glance of the glory of God in the East he worships in his way.

1758–63 Of his cat Jeoffry. *Jubilate Agno*, fragment B, l.695–7. (First published 1939.)

26 For he counteracts the powers of darkness by his electrical skin and glaring eyes.
For he counteracts the Devil, who is death, by brisking about the life.
For in his morning orisons he loves the sun and the sun loves him.
For he is of the tribe of Tiger.

1758–63 Of his cat Jeoffry. *Jubilate Agno*, fragment B, l.719–22. (First published 1939.)

27 For ADORATION seasons change,
And order, truth, and beauty range,
Adjust, attract, and fill:

The grass the polyanthus cheques;
And polished porphyry reflects,
By the descending rill.
1763 *A Song to David*, stanza 52.

28 Strong is the lion—like a coal
His eye-ball—like a bastion's mole
His chest against the foes:
Strong, the gier-eagle on his sail,
Strong against tide, th'enormous whale
Emerges as he goes.
1763 *A Song to David*, stanza 76.

29 Beauteous the fleet before the gale;
Beauteous the multitudes in mail,
Rank'd arms and crested heads:
Beauteous the garden's umbrage mild,
Walk, water, meditated wild,
And all the bloomy beds.
1763 *A Song to David*, stanza 78.

30 Glorious the northern lights astream;
Glorious the song, when God's the theme;
Glorious the thunder's roar:
Glorious hosanna from the den;
Glorious the catholic amen;
Glorious the martyr's gore.
1763 *A Song to David*, stanza 85.

31 Lo, thro' her works gay nature grieves
How brief she is and frail,
As ever o'er the falling leaves
Autumnal winds prevail.
Yet still the philosophic mind
Consolatory food can find,
And hope her anchorage maintain:
We never are deserted quite;
'Tis by succession of delight
That love supports his reign.
1764 *Ode to the Earl of Northumberland, with Some Other Pieces*, 'On a Bed of Guernsey Lilies: written in September 1763', stanza 2.

Smiles, Samuel 1812–1904

Scottish writer and social reformer who settled as a surgeon in Leeds, and published works encouraging self-improvement such as *Self-Help* (1859), *Character* (1871), *Thrift* (1875) and *Duty* (1880).

32 The spirit of self-help is the root of all genuine growth in the individual.
1859 *Self-Help*, ch.1.

33 The shortest way to do many things is to do only one thing at once.
1859 *Self-Help*, ch.9.

34 The healthy spirit of self-help created among working people would, more than any other measure, serve to raise them as a class; and this, not by pulling down others, but by levelling them up to a higher and still advancing standard of religion, intelligence, and virtue.
1859 *Self-Help*, ch.10.

35 We often discover what *will* do, by finding out what will not do; and probably he who never made a mistake never made a discovery.
1859 *Self-Help*, ch.11.

Smith, A J M 1902–80

Canadian-born US poet and anthologist.

36 McLuhan put a telescope to his ear;
What a lovely smell, he said, we have here.
1967 *Poems*, 'The Taste of Space'. When McLuhan first heard this couplet, his response was 'Synaesthesia!'

Smith, Adam 1723–90

Scottish economist and philosopher. His *Inquiry into the Nature and Causes of the Wealth of Nations* (1776), the first major work of political economy, examined in detail the consequences of economic freedom—division of labour, the function of markets and the international implications of a *laissez-faire* economy. He was Professor of Moral Philosophy at the University of Glasgow.

37 In ease of body, peace of mind, all the different ranks of life are nearly upon a level and the beggar who suns himself by the side of the highway, possesses that security which kings are fighting for.
1759 *The Theory of Moral Sentiments*.

38 The greatest improvement in the productive powers of labour, and the greater part of the skill, dexterity and judgement with which it is any where directed, as applied, seem to have been the effects of the division of labour.
1776 *An Inquiry into the Nature and Causes of the Wealth of Nations*, bk.1, ch.1.

39 It is not from the benevolence of the butcher, the brewer, or the baker, that we expect our dinner, but from their regard to their own interest.
1776 *An Inquiry into the Nature and Causes of the Wealth of Nations*, bk.1, ch.2.

40 The difference between the most dissimilar characters, between a philosopher and a common street porter, seems to arise not so much from nature, as from habit, custom and education
1776 *An Inquiry into the Nature and Causes of the Wealth of Nations*, bk.1, ch.2.

41 The word VALUE, it is to be observed, has two different meanings, and sometimes the utility of some particular object, and sometimes the power of purchasing other goods which the possession of that object conveys. This one may be called 'value in use'; the other, 'value in exchange'. The things which have the greatest value in use have frequently little or no value in exchange; and on the contrary, those which have the greatest value in exchange have frequently little or no value in use. Nothing is more useful than water: but it will purchase scarce any thing; scarce any thing can be had in exchange for it. A diamond, on the contrary, has scarce any value in use; but a very great quantity of other goods may frequently be had in exchange for it.
1776 *An Inquiry into the Nature and Causes of the Wealth of Nations*, bk.1, ch.4.

42 The real price of everything, what everything really costs to the man who wants to acquire it, is the toil and trouble of acquiring it. Labour was the first price, the original purchase money that was paid for all things.
1776 *An Inquiry into the Nature and Causes of the Wealth of Nations*, bk.1, ch.5.

43 The common wages of labour depends every where

upon the contract usually made between those two parties whose interests are by no means the same…Masters are always and every where in a sort of tacit, but constant and uniform combination, not to raise the wages of labour above their actual rate.
1776 *An Inquiry into the Nature and Causes of the Wealth of Nations*, bk.1, ch.8.

44 People of the same trade seldom meet together, even for merriment and diversion, but the conversation ends in a conspiracy against the public, or in some contrivance to raise prices.
1776 *An Inquiry into the Nature and Causes of the Wealth of Nations*, bk.1, ch.10, pt.2.

45 The rate of profit does not, like rent and wages, rise with the prosperity, and fall with the declension, of the society. On the contrary, it is naturally low in rich, and high in poor countries, and it is always highest in the countries which are going fastest to ruin.
1776 *An Inquiry into the Nature and Causes of the Wealth of Nations*, bk.1, ch.11, conclusion.

46 Capitals are increased by parsimony, and diminished by prodigality and misconduct. By what a frugal man annually saves he not only affords maintenance to an additional number of productive hands…but…he establishes as it were a perpetual fund for the maintenance of an equal number in all times to come.
1776 *An Inquiry into the Nature and Causes of the Wealth of Nations*, bk.2, ch.3.

47 The principle which prompts to save is the desire of bettering our condition—a desire which…comes with us from the womb and never leaves us till we go into the grave.
1776 *An Inquiry into the Nature and Causes of the Wealth of Nations*, bk.2, ch.3.

48 It is the maxim of every prudent master of a family never to attempt to make at home what it will cost him more to make than to buy. The taylor does not attempt to make his own shoe… All of them find it for their interest to employ their whole industry in a way in which they have some advantage over their neighbours and to purchase with a part of its produce…whatever else they have occasion for… What is prudence in the conduct of every private family, can scarce be folly in that of a great kingdom… Would it be a reasonable law to prohibit the importation of all foreign wines, merely to encourage the making of claret and burgundy in Scotland?
1776 *An Inquiry into the Nature and Causes of the Wealth of Nations*, bk.4, ch.2.

49 Every individual…intends only his own gain, and he is in this as in many other cases led by an invisible hand to promote an end which was no part of his intention… By pursuing his own interest he frequently promotes that of the society more effectually than when he really intends to promote it. I have never known much good done by those who affected to trade for the publick good.
1776 *An Inquiry into the Nature and Causes of the Wealth of Nations*, bk.4, ch.3.

50 To found a great Empire for the sole purpose of raising up a people of customers, may at first sight appear a project fit only for a nation of shopkeepers. It is, however, a project altogether unfit for a nation of shopkeepers; but extremely fit for a nation that is governed by shopkeepers.
1776 *An Inquiry into the Nature and Causes of the Wealth of Nations*, bk.4, ch.7, pt.3.
➤ *See Napoleon 607:68, Punch 672:7, Stoppard 825:66.*

51 Consumption is the sole end and purpose of all production.
1776 *An Inquiry into the Nature and Causes of the Wealth of Nations*, bk.4, ch.8.

52 The man whose life is spent in performing a few simple operations of which the effects too are, perhaps, always the same or very nearly the same, has no occasion to exert his understanding, or to exercise his invention. He generally becomes as stupid and ignorant as it is possible for a human creature to become.
1776 *An Inquiry into the Nature and Causes of the Wealth of Nations*, bk.5, ch.1, pt.3, article 2.

53 Science is the great antidote to the poison of enthusiasm and superstition.
1776 *An Inquiry into the Nature and Causes of the Wealth of Nations*, bk.5, ch.1, pt.3, article 3.

54 There is no art which one government sooner learns of another than that of draining money from the pockets of the people.
1776 *An Inquiry into the Nature and Causes of the Wealth of Nations*, bk.5, ch.2.

Smith, Al(fred) Emmanuel 1873–1944

US Democrat politician, who rose from newsboy to be Governor of New York State (1919–20, 1923–8). He was defeated as Democratic candidate for the Presidency in 1928.

55 Nobody shoots Santa Claus.
1936 Denouncing criticisms of the US aid programme.

56 No matter how thin you slice it, it's still baloney.
1936 Election campaign speech, October.

Smith, Alexander McCall 1949–

Scottish Professor of Medical Law and author of numerous works of fiction and non-fiction.

57 The No.1 Ladies' Detective Agency.
1998 Novel title.

Smith, Arthur 1954–

English comedian and broadcaster.

58 On paper, England are a good cricket team. The trouble is they play on grass.
Attributed.

Smith, Sir Cyril 1928–

English Liberal politician, who founded a spring manufacturing company before his election to Parliament in 1972. A popular MP, of unusually large physical dimensions, he was knighted in 1988.

59 If the fence is strong enough, I'll sit on it.
1974 In the *Observer*, 15 Sep.

Smith, Dodie 1896–1990

English playwright, novelist and theatre producer, whose works include the highly popular children's book *The Hundred and One Dalmatians* (1956).

60 The family—that dear octopus from whose tentacles we never quite escape.
1938 *Dear Octopus*.

Smith, Godfrey 1926–

English writer and columnist. He was Associate Editor of the *Sunday Times* from 1972 to 1991 and has written novels and books about English social life and customs. He has also compiled anthologies.

61 A scoop of pure honey set in a green bowl.
1984 Of Bath. *The English Companion*.

62 Try as one may to stress the cultural and historical role of the place…it still conveys one overwhelmingly powerful image to your average Englishman: the dirty weekend.
1984 Of Brighton. *The English Companion*.

Smith, Iain Crichton *Gaelic name* *Blain Mac A'Ghobhainn* 1928–98

Scottish poet and novelist, who wrote in both English and Gaelic. His novels include *Consider the Lilies* (1968). His *Collected Poems* were published in 1992.

63 Here they have no time for the fine graces
of poetry, unless it freely grows
in deep compulsion, like water in the well,
woven into the texture of the soil
in a strong pattern.
1955 'Poem of Lewis'.

64 And she, being old, fed from a mashed plate
as an old mare might droop across a fence
to the dull pastures of her ignorance.
Her husband held her upright while he prayed

to God who is all-forgiving to send down
some angel somewhere who might land perhaps
in his foreign wings among the gradual crops.
She munched, half dead, blindly searching the spoon
1961 *Thistles and Roses*, 'Old Woman', stanzas 1–2.

65 This is the land God gave to Andy Stewart—we have our inheritance.
There shall be no ardour, there shall be indifference.
There shall not be excellence, there shall be the average.
We shall be the intrepid hunters of golf balls.
1969 'The White Air of March'.

66 I tremble in this factory of books.
What love he must have lost to write so much.
1985 After seeing an exhibit of Sir Walter Scott's manuscripts. 'At the Scott Exhibition, Edinburgh Festival', collected in *Selected Poems* (1985).

Smith, Iain Duncan 1954–

English Conservative politician, leader of the Conservative Party from 2001 to 2003.

67 The quiet man is here to stay, and he's turning up the volume!
2003 At the Conservative Party Conference, Oct.

Smith, Ian Douglas 1919–

Zimbabwean (Rhodesian) politician, a founder of the pro-independence Rhodesian Front. Prime Minister from 1964, he unilaterally declared independence in 1965. Britain applied sanctions, and in 1979 majority rule was granted. He was suspended from government (1987) for South African links.

68 We have the happiest Africans in the world.
1971 In the *Observer*, 28 Nov.

69 Let me say it again, I don't believe in black majority rule ever in Rhodesia. Not in a thousand years.
1976 Radio broadcast, 20 Mar.

Smith, John 1938–94

Scottish politician. He was called to the Bar in 1967, and made a QC in 1983. He became MP for Lanarkshire North in 1970, and for Monklands East in 1983. He served as a cabinet minister under Harold Wilson and James Callaghan, and in the shadow cabinet (1972–92). He succeeded Neil Kinnock as leader of the Labour Party in 1992.

70 The settled will of the Scottish people.
1994 Of the creation of a Scottish parliament, in a speech at the Scottish Labour Conference, 11 Mar.

71 We will do our best to reward your faith in us, but please give us the opportunity to serve our country, that is all we ask.
1994 Address to a European Gala Dinner, 11 May. They were his final public words; he died the next morning of a heart attack.

Smith, Logan Pearsall 1865–1946

US-born British writer, who took British nationality in 1913. He is best known for his polished essays and aphorisms, gathered in books such as *Afterthoughts* (1931); he also wrote criticism and short stories.

72 The denunciation of the young is a necessary part of the hygiene of older people, and greatly assists the circulation of their blood.
1931 *Afterthoughts*, 'Age and Death'.

73 There are two things to aim at in life: first, to get what you want; and, after that, to enjoy it. Only the wisest of mankind achieve the second.
1931 *Afterthoughts*, 'Life and Human Nature'.

74 How awful to reflect that what people say of us is true!
1931 *Afterthoughts*, 'Life and Human Nature'.

75 There are few sorrows, however poignant, in which a good income is of no avail.
1931 *Afterthoughts*, 'Life and Human Nature'.

76 An improper mind is a perpetual feast.
1931 *Afterthoughts*, 'Life and Human Nature'.

77 There is more felicity on the far side of baldness than young men can possibly imagine.
1931 *Afterthoughts*, 'Age and Death'.

78 What music is more enchanting than the voices of young people, when you can't hear what they say?
1931 *Afterthoughts*, 'Age and Death'.

79 Most people sell their souls, and live with a good conscience on the proceeds.
1931 *Afterthoughts*, 'Other People'.

80 A friend who loved perfection would be the perfect friend, did not that love shut his door on me.
1931 *Afterthoughts*, 'Other People'.

81 All Reformers, however strict their social conscience, live in houses just as big as they can pay for.
1931 *Afterthoughts*, 'Other People'.

82 When they come downstairs from their Ivory Towers,

Idealists are very apt to walk straight into the gutter.
1931 *Afterthoughts*, 'Other People'.

83 Married women are kept women, and they are beginning to find it out.
1931 *Afterthoughts*, 'Other People'.

84 A best-seller is the gilded tomb of a mediocre talent.
1931 *Afterthoughts*, 'Art and Letters'.

85 People say that life is the thing, but I prefer reading.
1931 *Afterthoughts*, 'Myself'.

86 Thank heavens, the sun has gone in, and I don't have to go out and enjoy it.
1931 *Afterthoughts*, 'Myself'.

87 What I like in a good author is not what he says, but what he whispers.
1933 *All Trivia*, 'Afterthoughts'.

Smith, Margaret Chase 1897–1995

US Senator. Elected to the US Senate in 1948, she served four terms and continued to be politically active afterwards. She supported the draft for women, was a teacher and a syndicated columnist. She held 95 honorary degrees from various universities and colleges.

88 The greatest deliberative body in the world...has too often been debased to the level of a forum of hate and character assassination sheltered by the shield of congressional immunity.
1950 'Declaration of Conscience' address to the Senate, 1 Jun, denouncing accusations by Senator Joseph R McCarthy.

Smith, Patti 1946–

US singer, songwriter, poet and political activist.

89 Everybody's got to reclaim these things—poetry, rock'n'roll, political activism—and it's got to be done over and over again. It's like eating: you can't say, 'Oh, I ate yesterday'. You have to eat again.
2004 In *Rolling Stone* , 27 May.

Smith, Red 1905–82

US sportswriter.

90 It was an ideal day for football—too cold for the spectators and too cold for the players.
1963 Reporting on a match between the Chicago Bears and the New York Giants.

Smith, Samuel Francis 1808–95

US clergyman and poet.

91 My country, 'tis of thee,
Sweet land of liberty,
Of thee I sing:
Land where my fathers died,
Land of the pilgrims' pride,
From every mountain-side
Let the freedom ring.
1831 'America'.

Smith, Stevie (Florence Margaret) 1902–71

English poet and novelist. She lived most of her life with her aunt in a London suburb, and much of her work reflected that setting. Loneliness is a persistent theme, but she was also adept at dealing wittily with serious matters.

92 If you cannot have your dear husband for a comfort and a delight, for a breadwinner and a crosspatch, for a sofa, chair or a hot-water bottle, one can use him as a Cross to be Borne.
1936 *Novel On Yellow Paper.*

93 A Good Time was Had By All.
1937 Title of poetry collection.

94 This Englishwoman is so refined
She has no bosom and no behind.
1937 *A Good Time was Had By All*, 'This Englishwoman'.

95 Here is all straight and narrow as a tomb
Oh shut me not within a little room.
1950 *Harold's Leap*, 'The Commuted Sentence'.

96 Let all the little poets be gathered together in classes
And let prizes be given to them by the Prize Asses.
1950 *Harold's Leap*, 'To School!'

97 Oh, no, no, no, it was too cold always
(Still the dead one lay moaning)
I was much too far out all my life
And not waving but drowning.
1957 *Not Waving but Drowning*, 'Not Waving but Drowning'.

98 People who are always praising the past
And especially the times of faith as best
Ought to go and live in the Middle Ages
And be burnt at the stake as witches and sages.
1957 *Not Waving but Drowning*, 'The Past'.

99 Shall I tell you the signs of a New Age coming?
It is a sound of drubbing and sobbing
Of people crying, We are old, we are old
And the sun is going down and becoming cold.
1957 *Not Waving but Drowning*, 'The New Age'.

1 Why does my Muse only speak when she is unhappy?
She does not, I only listen when I am unhappy
When I am happy I live and despise writing
For my Muse this cannot but be dispiriting.
1962 *Selected Poems*, 'My Muse'.

2 I long for the Person from Porlock
To bring my thoughts to an end.
I am growing impatient to see him
I think of him as a friend.
1962 *Selected Poems*, 'Thoughts About the Person from Porlock' (a reference to the 'person from Porlock' mentioned in Coleridge's preliminary note to 'Kubla Khan').

3 Private Means is dead
God rest his soul, officers and fellow-rankers said.
1962 *Selected Poems*, 'Private Means is Dead'.

4 'This night shall thy soul be required of thee.'
My soul is never required of *me*
It always has to be somebody else of course.
Will my soul be required of me tonight perhaps?
1972 *Scorpion*, 'Scorpion'.
➡ *See Bible 115:42.*

5 Scorpion so wishes to be gone.
1972 *Scorpion*, 'Scorpion'.

6 Oh I am a cat that likes to
Gallop about doing good.
1972 *Scorpion*, 'The Galloping Cat'.

Smith, Rev Sydney 1771–1845

English journalist, clergymen and preacher and lecturer on moral philosophy, also one of the founders of the *Edinburgh*

Review. He wrote letters and pamphlets in favour of Catholic emancipation, the ballot, the abolition of prison abuses and other causes, and is best known as a conversationalist and wit.

7 The moment that the very name of Ireland is mentioned, the English seem to bid adieu to common feeling, common prudence, and common sense, and to act with the barbarity of tyrants and the fatuity of idiots.
1807–8 *Peter Plymley's Letters.*

8 I look upon Switzerland as an inferior sort of Scotland.
1815 Letter to Lord Holland, [August]. In *The Letters of Sydney Smith* edited by Nowell C Smith (1953), vol. 1.

9 What two ideas are more inseparable than Beer and Britannia.
1823 In the *Edinburgh Review*, quoted in H Pearson *The Smith of Smiths* (1934), ch.11.

10 Alas, alas, how easily a priest begets children and with what difficulty he provides for them; a priest I mean who is extravagant enough to keep a conscience; a point wherein our profession commits (I must say) little excess.
1825 Letter to Lord Holland, 14 Jul. In *The Letters of Sydney Smith* edited by Nowell C Smith (1953), vol. 1.

11 He who drinks a tumbler of London Water has literally in his stomach more animated beings than there are men, Women and Children on the face of the globe.
1834 Letter to Lady Grey, 19 Nov.

12 No furniture so charming as books.
Quoted in Lady Holland *Memoir* (1855), vol 1, ch. 9.

13 Take short views, hope for the best, and trust in God.
Quoted in Lady Holland *Memoir* (1855), vol 1, ch. 6.

14 That knuckle-end of England—that land of Calvin, oat-cakes and sulphur.
Quoted in Lady Holland *Memoir* (1855), vol 1, ch. 2.

15 I heard him [Jeffrey] speak disrespectfully of the Equator!
Quoted in Lady Holland *Memoir* (1855), vol 1, ch.2.

16 As the French say, there are three sexes—men, women, and clergymen.
Quoted in Lady Holland *Memoir* (1855), vol.1, ch.9.

17 He is like a book in breeches.
Of Lord Macaulay. Quoted in Lady Holland *Memoir* (1855), vol.1, ch.11.

18 He has occasional flashes of silence that make his conversation perfectly delightful.
Of Lord Macaulay. Quoted in Lady Holland *Memoir* (1855), vol.1. ch.11.

19 My definition of marriage... It resembles a pair of shears, so joined that they cannot be separated; often moving in opposite directions, yet always punishing anyone who comes between them.
Quoted in Lady Holland *Memoir* (1855), vol.1, ch.11.

20 Let onion atoms lurk within the bowl,
And, half-suspected, animate the whole.
'Receipt for a Salad', quoted in Lady Holland *Memoir* (1855), vol.1, ch.11.

21 Serenely full, the epicure would say,
'Fate cannot harm me, I have dined today.'
'Receipt for a Salad', concluding lines, quoted in Lady Holland *Memoir*, (1855), vol.1, ch.11.

22 My idea of heaven is, eating *paté de foie gras* to the sound of trumpets.
Quoted in H Pearson *The Smith of Smiths*, (1934), ch.10.

23 What a pity it is we have no amusements in England but vice and religion!
Quoted in H Pearson *The Smith of Smiths*, (1934), ch.10.

24 I am just going to pray for you at St Paul's, but with no very lively hope of success.
Quoted in H Pearson *The Smith of Smiths*, (1934), ch.10.

Smith, Sydney Goodsir 1915–75

New Zealand-born Scottish poet and critic, who played an important part in the 20c revival of poetry in the Scots language. His first volume, *Skail Wind* (1941), was followed by several others. He also edited works on Scottish literature.

25 This rortic wretched city
Sair come down frae its auld hiechts
—The hauf o't smug, complacent,
Lost til all pride of race or spirit,
The tither wild and rouch as ever
In its secret hairt
But lost alsweill, the smeddum tane,
The man o'independent mind has cap in hand the day
—Sits on its craggy spine
And drees the wind and rain
That nourished all its genius
—Weary wi centuries
This empty capital snorts like a great beast
Caged in its sleep, dreaming of freedom.
1954 Of Edinburgh. 'Kynd Kittock's Land' (Kynd Kittock is a character in the poetry of the 16c Scottish poet William Dunbar.) rortie=splendid, smeddum=spirit, drees=endures.

Smith, Walter Chalmers 1824–1908

Scottish clergyman and poet.

26 Immortal, invisible, God only wise,
In light inaccessible hid from our eyes,
Most blessèd, most glorious, the Ancient of Days,
Almighty, victorious, Thy great name we praise.
1867 'Immortal, Invisible', hymn.

Smollett, Tobias George 1721–71

Scottish novelist. He wrote a history of England and from 1753 edited the *Critical Review*, which led to his being imprisoned for libel in 1760. His unfavourable account of his travels in France and Italy, which he was ordered to visit for the sake of his health, earned him Sterne's designation as 'Smelfungus'. His novel *Humphrey Clinker* (1771) remains popular.

27 I think for my part one half of the nation is mad—and the other not very sound.
1762 *The Adventures of Sir Launcelot Greaves*, ch.6.

28 They have no education, no taste for reading, no housewifery, nor, indeed, any earthly occupation but that of dressing their hair, and adorning their bodies. They hate walking, and would never go abroad, if they were not stimulated by the vanity of being seen... Nothing can be more parsimonious than the economy of these people. They live upon soup and bouille, fish and salad.
1766 Of the nobility of Boulogne. *Travels through France and Italy.*

29 The capital is become an overgrown monster; which, like a dropsical head, will in time leave the body and extremities without nourishment and support.
1771 Of London. Letter from Matthew Bramble, 29 May, *Humphrey Clinker*, vol.1.

30 I am pent up in frowzy lodgings, where there is not room enough to swing a cat.
1771 Letter from Matthew Bramble, 8 Jun, *Humphrey Clinker*, vol.1.

Smuts, Jan Christian 1870–1950

South African general and statesman, Prime Minister (1919–24). A significant figure at Versailles, he was instrumental in the founding of the League of Nations. As Minister of Justice under Hertzog, his coalition with the Nationalists in 1934 produced the United Party, and he became Premier again (1939–48).

31 Perhaps it is God's will to lead the people of South Africa through defeat and humiliation to a better future and a brighter day.
1902 Speech at the Vereeniging peace talks, 31 May.

32 What was everybody's business in the end proved to be nobody's business. Each one looked to the other to take the lead, and the aggressors got away with it.
1943 Explaining the failure of the League of Nations to the Empire Parliamentary Association, London, 25 Nov.

Snagge, John 1904–96

English radio commentator.

33 I can't tell who's leading—it's either Oxford or Cambridge.
1949 Radio commentary on the Boat Race, when the engine of Snagge's launch broke down. Quoted in C Dodd *Oxford and Cambridge Boat Race* (1983), ch.14.

Snow, Carmel 1887–1961

Irish-born US journalist. She was fashion editor (1932–35) and then editor-in-chief (1935–57) of *Harper's Bazaar*.

34 Elegance is good taste *plus* a dash of daring.
1962 *The World of Carmel Snow.*

Snow, C(harles) P(ercy), 1st Baron 1905–80

English novelist and physicist. His works include a cycle of novels portraying English life from 1920, including *Strangers and Brothers* (1940), *The Masters* (1951), *The New Men* (1954) and *Corridors of Power* (1964). In his controversial *Two Cultures* (Rede lecture, 1959) he discussed the need for closer contact of science and literature.

35 Drinking the best tea in the world in an empty cricket ground—that, I think, is the final pleasure left to man.
1932 Quoted in Colin Jarman *The Guinness Dictionary of Sports Quotations* (1990).

36 The official world, the corridors of power, the dilemmas of conscience and egotism—she disliked them all.
1956 *Homecomings*, ch.22. This phrase was later used as the title of his 1964 novel, *Corridors of Power.*

37 A good many times I have been present at gatherings of people who...are thought highly educated and who have...been expressing their incredulity at the illiteracy of scientists. Once or twice I have been provoked and have asked the company how many of them could describe the Second Law of Thermodynamics. The response was cold: it was also negative.
1959 *The Two Cultures*, Rede Lecture, ch.1.

38 I believe the intellectual life of the whole of western society is increasingly being split into two polar groups... Literary intellectuals at one pole—at the other scientists, and as the most representative, the physical scientists. Between the two a gulf of mutual incomprehension.
1959 *The Two Cultures*, Rede Lecture.

39 'I grant you that he's not two-faced,' I said. 'But what's the use of that when the one face he has got is so peculiarly unpleasant?'
1960 *The Affair*, ch.4.

40 Technology...is a queer thing. It brings you great gifts with one hand, and it stabs you in the back with the other.
1971 In the *New York Times*, 15 Mar.

41 There have been many crimes committed in the name of duty and obedience—many more than in the name of dissent.
1971 'Testimony of Four Peers', in *Esquire*, Dec.

42 Writers are much more esteemed in Russia, they play a much larger part in society than they do in the West. The advantage of not being free is that people listen to you.
1971 Interview on Radio Moscow.

43 In not much over a generation, physicists have changed our world.
1981 *The Physicists* (published posthumously).

44 There are no secrets in science.
1981 *The Physicists* (published posthumously).

Snow, Clyde Collins 1928–

Forensic anthropologist.

45 The ground is like a beautiful woman. If you treat her gently, she'll tell you all her secrets.
1991 On exploring the massacre of thousands of Mayan Indians in Guatemala in the early 1980s. In the *Washington Post*, 18 Dec.

Snowden, Philip Snowden, 1st Viscount 1864–1937

English Labour statesman, crippled in a cycling accident. A socialist MP from 1906, he opposed conscription and as Chancellor of the Exchequer from 1924 aggravated the financial crises. A free trader, he resigned in 1932, and wrote an *Autobiography* (1934).

46 The Labour Party's election programme...is the most fantastic and impracticable programme ever put before the electors. This is not socialism. It is bolshevism run mad.
1931 Radio broadcast, 17 Oct.

Snyder, Gary Sherman 1930–

US poet. The 'Japhy Ryder' of Kerouac's *The Dharma Bums*, his writings reflect an almost sacramental vision of man's relationship to his natural environment.

47 I cannot remember things I once read
A few friends, but they are in cities.
Drinking cold snow-water from a tin cup
Looking down for miles
Through high still air.
1959 *Riprap*, 'Mid-August at Sourdough Mountain Lookout'.

48 A clear, attentive mind
Has no meaning but that
Which sees is truly seen.
1959 *Riprap*, 'Piute Creek'.

49 In ten thousand years the Sierras
Will be dry and dead, home of the scorpion.
Ice-scratched slabs and bent trees.
No paradise, no fall,
Only the weathering land
The wheeling sky,
Man, with his Satan
Scouring the chaos of the mind.
Oh Hell!
1959 *Riprap*, 'Milton By Firelight (Piute Creek, August 1955)'.

50 After weeks of watching the roof leak
I fixed it tonight
by moving a single board.
1968 *The Back Country*, 'Hitch Haiku'.

51 Down for a new radio, to Ross Lake, and back up. Three days walking. Strange how unmoved this place leaves one;
neither articulate or worshipful; rather the pressing need to look
within and adjust the mechanism of perception.
1969 *Earth House Hold*, 'Lookout's Journal, Crater Shan 28 July'.

52 Beware of anything that promises freedom or enlightenment—traps for eager and clever fools—a dog has a keener nose—every creature in a cave can justify himself. Three-fourths of philosophy and literature is the talk of people trying to convince themselves that they really like the cage they were tricked into entering.
1969 *Earth House Hold*, 'Japan First Time Around, 24: X'.

53 I recalled when I worked in the woods
and the bars of Madras, Oregon.
That short-haired joy and roughness—
America   your stupidity.
I could almost love you again.
1974 *Turtle Island*, 'I Went Into The Maverick Bar'.

Socrates 469–399 BC

Greek philosopher. Our knowledge of his life and teaching derives mainly from the work of his pupil Plato, in dialogues including the *Republic*, and the *Apology*, *Crito* and *Phaedo*, which describe Socrates' trial for 'corrupting the young' and his death by drinking hemlock.

54 I am so far like the midwife that I cannot myself give birth to wisdom, and the common reproach is true, that, though I question others, I can myself bring nothing to light because there is no wisdom in me.
Quoted in Plato *Theaetetus*, 150c (translated by F M Cornford).

55 This sense of wonder is the mark of the philosopher. Philosophy indeed has no other origin.
Quoted in Plato *Theaetetus*, 150c (translated by F M Cornford).

56 How many things I can do without!
On viewing goods for sale. Quoted in Diogenes Laertius *Vitae Philosophorum*, 2.25 (translated by R D Hicks, 1950).

57 The unexamined life is not worth living.
Quoted in Plato *Apology*, 38a.

58 There is only one good, knowledge, and only one evil, ignorance.
Quoted in Diogenes Laertius *Vitae Philosophorum*, 2.31 (translated by R D Hicks, 1950).

Solon c.640–c.559 BC

Athenian lawgiver and poet. Archon in 594 BC (or 591 BC), he reformed the constitution, abolishing debt-slavery and admitting a fourth class to the Assembly. After 10 years of voluntary exile he returned to Athens in 580 BC

59 As I grow older, I constantly learn more.
Quoted in Bergk (ed) *Poetae Lyrici Graeci*, 'Solon', no.18.

Solow, Robert M 1924–

US economist, winner of the Nobel prize (1987).

60 Thinking precisely and systematically about something as complex and irregular as a modern economy is very difficult, maybe impossible.
1984 In the *New York Times Book Review*, 30 Dec.

61 Merely to adopt the more powerful assumption is no more than to assume the more powerful conclusion.
1994 In the *Journal of Economic Perspectives*, 8:53.

Solzhenitsyn, Aleksandr Isayevich 1918–

Russian writer, a labour camp prisoner (1945–53). His *One Day in the Life of Ivan Denisovich* (1962) was widely acclaimed, but his subsequent denunciation of Soviet censorship led to the banning of his novels *Cancer Ward* (1968) and *The First Circle* (1968). He was awarded the Nobel prize for literature in 1970 (received 1974). After *The Gulag Archipelago* (3 vols, 1973–6), an account of the Stalinist terror, he was exiled (1974). His citizenship was restored in 1990, and the treason charges against him dropped in 1991. In 1994 he returned to Russia.

62 You only have power over people so long as you do not take everything away from them. But when you have robbed man of everything, he is no longer in your pocket—he is free.
1968 *The First Circle*.

63 In our country the lie has become not just a moral category but a pillar of the State.
1974 Quoted in the *Observer*, 29 Dec.

64 For us in Russia, communism is a dead dog, while, for many people in the West, it is still a living lion.
1979 In the *Listener*, 15 Feb.

Somerville, Edith (Anna Oenone) and Martin, Violet Florence *née* *Ross* *who wrote under the pseudonym Martin Ross* 1858–1949; 1862–1915

Irish cousins who first met in 1886. They formed a lasting successful literary partnership and are both known for a series of novels that makes fun of the Irish.

65 'May the divil choke ye!' says he, pleasant enough, but I knew by the blush he had he was vexed.
1898 *Some Experiences of an Irish R.M.*, 'Lisheen Races, Second-Hand'.

66 'I call it a criminal thing in any one's great-great-grandfather to rear up a preposterous troop of sons and plant them all out in his own country', Lady Knox said to me with apparent irrelevance. 'I detest collaterals. Blood may be thicker than water, but it is also a great deal nastier.'
1898 *Some Experiences of an Irish R.M.*, 'Philippa's Fox-Hunt'.

67 Every known class of refusal was successfully exhibited. One horse endeavoured to climb the rails into the Grand Stand; another, having stopped dead at the critical point, swung round, and returned in consternation to the starting-point, with his rider hanging like a locket around his neck. Another, dowered with a sense of humour

unusual among horses, stepped delicately over the furze-bushes, and, amidst rounds of applause, walked through the lime with a stoic calm.
1908 *Further Experiences of an Irish R.M.*, 'A Royal Command'.

Somoza, (García) Anastasio 1925–80

Nicaraguan dictator, educated in the US. As Chief of the National Guard he established himself in supreme power in the early 1930s, and retained it until assassinated, when the rule passed to his sons.

68 You won the elections. But I won the count.
1977 In *The Guardian*, 17 Jun.

Sontag, Susan 1933–

US writer and critic. Although she emerged first as an experimental fiction writer her main impact has been as a critic.Her essays in leading journals were expanded into books including *On Photography* (1976) and *Illness As Metaphor* (1978). Later publications include the novels *The Volcano Lover* (1992) and *In America* (2000), and a play, *Alice in Bed* (1993).

69 Ambition if it feeds at all, does so on the ambition of others.
1963 *The Benefactor*, ch.1.

70 Interpretation is the revenge of the intellect upon art.
1964 In *The Evergreen Review*, Dec.

71 Perversity is the muse of modern literature.
1966 *Against Interpretation*, 'Camus' Notebooks'.

72 What pornography is really about, ultimately, isn't sex but death.
1967 In *Partisan Review*, Spring.

73 The white race *is* the cancer of human history, it is the white race, and it alone—its ideologies and inventions—which eradicates autonomous civilizations wherever it spreads, which has upset the ecological balance of the planet, which now threatens the very existence of life itself.
1967 In *Partisan Review*, Winter.

74 The camera makes everyone a tourist in other people's reality, and eventually in one's own.
1974 In the *New York Review of Books*, 18 Apr. Later published in book form as *On Photography* (1976).

75 When we're afraid we shoot. But when we're nostalgic we take pictures.
1974 In the *New York Review of Books*, 18 Apr.

76 The most interesting ideas are heresies.
1975 Interview in *Salmagundi*, Fall–Winter.

77 Illness is the night-side of life, a more onerous citizenship. Everyone who is born holds dual citizenship, in the kingdom of the well and in the kingdom of the sick. Although we all prefer to use only the good passport, sooner or later each of us is obliged, at least for a spell, to identify ourselves as citizens of that other place.
1978 In the *New York Review of Books*, 26 Jan.

78 It seems the very model of all the catastrophes privileged populations feel await them.
1989 Of AIDS. *AIDS and Its Metaphors*, ch.8.

79 I envy paranoids; they actually feel people are paying attention to them.
1992 In *Time Out*, 19 Aug.

80 In the matter of courage (a morally neutral virtue): whatever may be said of the perpetrators of Tuesday's slaughter, they were not cowards.
2001 Reflecting on the 11 Sep terrorist attacks in New York. In the *New Yorker*, 24 Sep.

Sophocles c.496–405 BC

Athenian playwright. He wrote well over 100 plays, of which seven tragedies have survived, including *Oedipus Tyrannus*.

81 Woman, silence makes a woman beautiful.
Ajax, 293 (translated by H Lloyd-Jones, 1994).

82 Hope has often caused the love of gain to ruin men.
Antigone, 222 (translated by H Lloyd-Jones, 1994).

83 Many things are formidable, and none more formidable than man.
Antigone, 332–3 (translated by H Lloyd-Jones, 1994).

84 One must obey the man whom the city sets up in power in small things and in justice and in its opposite.
Creon speaking. *Antigone*, 666–7 (translated by H Lloyd-Jones, 1994).

85 You see how when rivers are swollen in winter those trees that yield to the flood retain their branches, but those that offer resistance perish, trunk and all.
Haemon speaking. *Antigone*, 712–14 (translated by H Lloyd-Jones, 1994).

86 Love invincible in battle.
Antigone, 781–90 (translated by H Lloyd-Jones, 1994).

87 Remember there is no success without hard work.
Electra, 945 (translated by H Lloyd-Jones, 1994).

88 When I do not understand, I like to say nothing.
Oedipus Tyrannus, 569 (translated by H Lloyd-Jones, 1994).

89 It is best to live anyhow, as one may; do not be afraid of marriage with your mother! Many have lain with their mothers in dreams too. It is he to whom such things are nothing who puts up with life best.
Jocasta to Oedipus, her son and husband, before they both discover the truth of the prophecy. *Oedipus Tyrannus*, 979–83 (translated by H Lloyd-Jones, 1994).

Sorley, Charles Hamilton 1895–1915

Scottish poet, killed in action during World War I.

90 When you see millions of the mouthless dead
Across your dreams in pale battalions go,
Say not soft things as other men have said,
That you'll remember. For you need not so.
Give them not praise. For, deaf, how should they know
It is not curses heaped on each gashed head?
Marlborough and Other Poems, 'A Sonnet' (published 1916).

Soule, John Babsone Lane 1815–91

91 Go West, young man, go West!
Terre Haute Express.

Sousa, John Philip 1854–1932

US composer and bandmaster. He became conductor of the United States Marine Band in 1880 and formed his own band, which built up an international reputation, 12 years later. As well as more than a hundred popular marches, he composed 10 comic operas.

92 Jazz will endure just as long as people hear it

through their feet instead of their brains.
c.1920 Attributed.

Soutar, William 1898–1943

Scottish poet and diarist, who was confined to bed for the last 13 years of his life with a form of spondylitis. His poems in Scots for adults and children were praised by Hugh MacDiarmid and others.

93 O luely, luely cam she in
And luely she lat doun:
I kent her be her caller lips
And her breists sae sma' an' roun'.

A' thru the nicht we spak nae word
Nor sinder'd bane frae bane:
A' thru the nicht I heard her hert
Gang soundin' wi' my ain.
1932 'The Tryst', stanzas 1–2.

94 Sae luely, luely, cam she in
Sae luely was she gaen
And wi' her a' my simmer days
Like they had never been.
1932 'The Tryst', stanza 4.

Southey, Robert 1774–1843

English poet and writer and friend of Wordsworth. His epics include *Thalaba* (1801) and *Madoc* (1805). His shorter poems are 'The Battle of Blenheim' and 'The Inchcape Rock'. He also wrote a *Life of Nelson* (1813), and became Poet Laureate in 1813.

95 She has made me in love with a cold climate, and frost and snow, with a northern moonlight.
1797 On Mary Wollstonecraft. Letter to his brother Thomas Southey, 28 Apr.

96 You are old, Father William, the young man cried,
The few locks which are left you are grey;
You are hale, Father William, a hearty old man,
Now tell me the reason, I pray.
1799 'The Old Man's Comforts'.
► *See Carroll 194:67.*

97 In the days of my youth I remembered my God!
And He hath not forgotten my age.
1799 'The Old Man's Comforts'.

98 It was a summer evening,
Old Kasper's work was done,
And he before his cottage door
Was sitting in the sun,
And by him sported on the green
His little grandchild Wilhelmine.
1800 'The Battle of Blenheim'.

99 Now tell us all about the war,
And what they fought each other for.
1800 'The Battle of Blenheim'.

1 'And everybody praised the Duke,
Who this great fight did win.'
'But what good came of it at last?'
Quoth little Peterkin.
'Why that I cannot tell,' said he,
'But 'twas a famous victory.'
1800 'The Battle of Blenheim'.

2 Blue, darkly, deeply, beautifully blue.
1805 *Madoc*, 'Lincoya', pt.1, canto 5, l.102.

3 We wage no war with women nor with priests.
1805 *Madoc*, 'The Excommunication', pt.1, canto 15, l.65.

4 Curses are like young chickens, they always come home to roost.
1810 *The Curse of Kehama*, motto.

5 Thou has been called, O Sleep! the friend of Woe,
But 'tis the happy who have called thee so.
1810 *The Curse of Kehama*, canto 15, stanza 12.

6 Your true lover of literature is never fastidious.
1812 *The Doctor*, ch.12.

7 Show me a man who cares no more for one place than another, and I will show you in that same person one who loves nothing but himself. Beware of those who are homeless by choice.
1812 *The Doctor*, ch.34.

8 Live as long as you may, the first twenty years are the longest half of your life.
1812 *The Doctor*, ch.130.

9 The death of Nelson was felt in England as something more than a public calamity; men started at the intelligence, and turned pale, as if they had heard of the loss of a dear friend.
1813 *The Life of Nelson*, ch.9.

10 My name is Death: the last best friend am I.
1816 'The Lay of the Laureate', stanza 87.

11 The arts babblative and scribblative.
1829 *Colloquies on the Progress and Prospects of Society*, no.10, pt.2.

12 The march of intellect.
1829 *Colloquies on the Progress and Prospects of Society*, no.14.

Soyinka, Wole *pseudonym of* Akinwande Oluwole Soyinka 1934–

Nigerian dramatist, poet and novelist. He was held as a political prisoner for two years (1967–9). His writing is concerned with the tension between old and new in modern Africa, and includes his first novel, *The Interpreters* (1964), the poetic collection *A Shuttle in the Crypt* (1972), the mostly prose 'prison notes', *The Man Died* (1973) and the play *The Beatification of Area Boy* (1995). He was awarded the Nobel prize for literature in 1986.

13 But the skin of progress
Masks, unknown, the spotted wolf of sameness.
1959 *The Lion and the Jewel* (published 1962), 'Night'.

14 Americans expect to be loved.
1964 *The Interpreters*.

Spacey, Kevin 1959–

US actor. His film appearances include *Glengarry Glen Ross* (1992), *The Usual Suspects* (1995), *LA Confidential* (1997), *American Beauty* (1999) and *The Shipping News* (2001).

15 The less you know about me the easier it is to convince you that I'm the character on screen.
2004 In *The Scotsman*, 20 Apr.

Spark, Dame Muriel Sarah *née* Camberg 1918–

Scottish novelist, poet, playwright and writer of short stories. Her many works include biographical studies on Mary Wollstonecraft Shelley (1951) and Emily Brontë (1953) and her best-known novel, *The Prime of Miss Jean Brodie* (1961). She converted to Catholicism in 1954 and lives in Italy.

16 The one certain way for a woman to hold a man is to leave him for religion.
1957 *The Comforters*, ch.1.

17 Parents learn a lot from their children about coping with life.
1957 *The Comforters*, ch.6.

18 Selwyn MacGregor, the nicest boy who ever committed the sin of whisky.
1958 *The Go-Away Bird*, 'A Sad Tale's Best for Winter'.

19 She doesn't have anything to do with youth clubs. There are classes within classes in Peckham.
1960 *The Ballad of Peckham Rye*, ch.3.

20 A short neck denotes a good mind… You see, the messages go quicker to the brain because they've shorter to go.
1960 *The Ballad of Peckham Rye*, ch.7.

21 I am putting old heads on your young shoulders…all my pupils are the crème de la crème.
1961 *The Prime of Miss Jean Brodie*, ch.1.

22 One's prime is elusive. You little girls, when you grow up, must be on the alert to recognise your prime at whatever time of your life it may occur. You must live it to the full.
1961 *The Prime of Miss Jean Brodie*, ch.1.

23 Give me a girl at an impressionable age, and she is mine for life.
1961 *The Prime of Miss Jean Brodie*, ch.1.

24 'Whoever has opened the window has opened it too wide,' said Miss Brodie. 'Six inches is perfectly adequate. More is vulgar.'
1961 *The Prime of Miss Jean Brodie*, ch.3.

25 All the nice people were poor; at least, that was a general axiom, the best of the rich being poor in spirit.
1963 *The Girls of Slender Means*, ch.1.

26 A nice girl should only fall in love once in her life.
1963 *The Girls of Slender Means*, ch.2.

27 Every communist has a fascist frown, every fascist a communist smile.
1963 *The Girls of Slender Means*.

28 Well, it's about everything in particular, isn't it?
1988 Of Proust. *A Far Cry from Kensington*, ch.6.

29 Beware of men bearing flowers.
Her personal motto, quoted by John Cornwell in the *Sunday Times*, 15 May 1994.

30 Writing a novel you have to be quite aware that what you are writing is not all true. Such a character did not cross the road at such a time; this is not true.
In John Tusa *On Creativity: Interviews Explaining the Process* (2003).

31 I believe I have liberated the novel in many ways, showing how anything whatsoever can be narrated, including sheer damn cheek. I think I have opened doors and windows in the mind, and challenged fears—especially the most inhibiting fears about what a novel should be.
2004 In the *Sunday Herald*, 22 Feb.

32 The dedication of an artist involves willing oblivion to everybody else while the art is being practised, and for the hours ambiguous to it.
2004 *The Finishing School*.

33 Most marriages, where both or one is an artist, are rickety.—Most marriages of this kind comprise one failed artist.
2004 *The Finishing School*.

Sparshott, Francis 1926–

Canadian philosopher and professor.

34 For every philosopher, in every age, the first question must be: Just what is philosophy?
1972 *Looking for Philosophy*, 'Speculation and Reflection'.

Speke, John Hanning 1827–64

English explorer. In 1854, with Richard Burton, he searched for the equatorial lakes of Africa. While travelling alone he discovered Victoria Nyanza, source of the Nile, and in 1860 tracked the Nile flowing out of it. His findings were controversial, and on the day he was to meet with Burton to discuss them he was killed by a shot from his own rifle.

35 The expedition had now performed its functions. I saw that old father Nile without any doubt rises in the Victoria Nyanza, and as I had foretold, that lake is the great source of the holy river which cradled the first expounder of our religious belief.
1863 *Journal of the Discovery of the Source of the Nile*.

36 As fattening is the first duty of fashionable female life, it must be duly enforced by the rod if necessary. I got up a bit of flirtation with missy, and induced her to rise and shake hands with me. Her face was lovely, but her body was as round as a ball.
1863 In Karagwe, west of Lake Victoria, among the Galla people. *Journal of the Discovery of the Source of the Nile*.

Spencer, Charles, Earl 1964–

English writer and broadcaster.

37 I pledge that we, your blood family, will do all we can to continue the imaginative way in which you were steering these two exceptional young men [the princes, William and Harry] so that their souls are not simply immersed by duty and tradition, but can sing openly as you planned.
1997 Oration at the funeral of his sister, Diana, Princess of Wales, 6 Sep.

Spencer, Herbert 1820–1903

English philosopher. He expounded his evolutionary theories in *Principles of Psychology* (1855), and was a leading advocate of 'Social Darwinism'. Other works included *Social Statics* (1851), *System of Synthetic Philosophy* (1862–93) and an *Autobiography* (1904).

38 No one can be perfectly free until all are free; no one can be perfectly moral till all are moral; no one can be perfectly happy till all are happy.
1851 *Social Statics*, pt.4, ch.30, section 16.

39 Science is organized knowledge.
1861 *Education*, ch. 2.

40 The preservation of health is a *duty*. Few seem conscious that there is such a thing as physical morality.
1861 *Education*, ch.4.

41 It cannot but happen…that those will survive whose functions happen to be most nearly in equilibrium with the modified aggregate of external forces… This survival of the fittest implies multiplication of the fittest.
1865 *Principles of Biology*, pt.3, ch.12, sect.164.

42 How often misused words generate misleading thoughts.
1879 *Principles of Ethics*, bk.1, pt.2, ch.8, sect.152.

43 The liberty that the citizen enjoys is to be measured not by the governmental machinery that he lives under, whether representative or otherwise, but by the paucity of restraints that it imposes upon him.
1884 *The Man Versus the State.*

44 The Republican form of government is the highest form of government; but because of this, it requires the highest type of human nature—a type nowhere at present existing.
'The Americans', collected in *Essays* (1891).

45 It was remarked to me by the late Mr Charles Roupell…that to play billiards well was a sign of an ill-spent youth.
Quoted in Duncan *Life and Letters of Spencer*, ch.20. Robert Louis Stevenson has also been credited with this observation.

Spender, Sir Stephen Harold 1909–95

English poet and critic. A liberal idealist, he served in the Spanish Civil War, and was a fireman in London during the Blitz. He co-edited *Horizon* (with Cyril Connolly) and later *Encounter*, and published several volumes of poetry and criticism, as well as journals and memoirs.

46 I think continually of those who were truly great.
1933 'I Think Continually of Those'.

47 The names of those who in their lives fought for life,
Who wore at their hearts the fire's centre.
Born of the sun they travelled a short while towards the sun,
And left the vivid air signed with their honour.
1933 'I Think Continually of Those'.

48 What I had not foreseen
Was the gradual day
Weakening the will
Leaking the brightness away
1933 'What I Expected, Was'.

49 For I had expected always
Some brightness to hold in trust,
Some final innocence
To save from dust
1933 'What I Expected, Was'.

50 They lounge at corners of the street
And greet friends with a shrug of shoulder
And turn their pockets out,
The cynical gestures of the poor.
1933 'Moving Through the Silent Crowd'.

51 Never being, but always at the edge of Being.
1933 'Never Being'.

52 My parents kept me from children who were rough
Who threw words like stones and who wore torn clothes
1933 'My Parents Kept Me from Children Who Were Rough'.

53 Who live under the shadow of war,
What can I do that matters?
1933 'Who Live Under the Shadow'.

54 After the first powerful plain manifesto
The black statement of pistons, without more fuss,
But gliding like a queen, she leaves the station.
1933 'The Express'.

55 Pylons, those pillars
Bare like nude, giant girls that have no secret.
1933 'Pylons'.

56 Different living is not living in different places
But creating in the mind a map.
1933 'Different Living'.

57 Consider: only one bullet in ten thousand kills a man.
Ask: was so much expenditure justified
On the death of one so young and so silly
Stretched under the olive trees, Oh, world, Oh, death?
1939 'Regum Ultimo Ratio'.

58 Their collected
Hearts wound up with love, like little watch springs.
1939 'The Past Values'.

59 The light in the window seemed perpetual
Where you stayed in the high room for me
1942 'The Room Above The Square'.

60 The poet shares with other artists the faculty of seeing things as though for the first time.
1942 *Life and the Poet.*

61 Poetry cannot take sides except with life.
1942 *Life and the Poet.*

62 My uncle was famous for his balanced point of view. At the time of which I am writing (when he was nearly seventy) it had become so balanced, that the act of balancing seemed rather automatic. One had only to offer him an opinion for him to balance it with a counter-opinion of exactly the same weight, as a grocer puts a pound weight against a pound of sugar.
1951 *World within World*, p.77.

63 My brothers and sister and I were brought up in an atmosphere which I would describe as 'Puritan decadence'. Puritanism names the behaviour which is condemned; Puritan decadence regards the name itself as indecent, and pretends that the object behind that name does not exist until it is named.
1951 *World within World*, p.314–15.

64 People sometimes divide others into those you laugh at and those you laugh with. The young Auden was someone you could laugh-at-with.
1973 Address at Auden's Memorial Service, Oxford, 27 Oct.

65 But reading is not idleness…it is the passive, receptive side of civilization without which the active and creative world would be meaningless. It is the immortal spirit of the dead realised within the bodies of the living. It is sacramental.
1980 Journal entry, 4 Jan.

66 We were obsessed by the feeling that this was the supreme cause of our time. The cause of poets and of writers. The cause of freedom. And that unless the cause of anti-Fascism was won, unless Fascism was defeated, we would be unable to exist as writers.
1982 Speaking on the ITV series *The Spanish Civil War*, no.3, 'Battleground for idealists'.

Spenser, Edmund c.1552–1599

English poet. Educated at Cambridge, he held positions in government, including secretary to the lord deputy in Ireland during a period of rebellion, for most of his life, although he died in poverty. His epic Protestant romance, *The Faerie Queen*, was published in two instalments, Books I–III (1590) and Books

IV–VI (1596). Other works include *The Shepherd's Calendar* (1579), *Colin Clout's Come Home Again* (1595), *Amoretti* and *Epithalamion* (1595), and *Four Hymns* (1596).

67 Go little book, thy self present,
As child whose parent is unkent:
To him that is the president
Of noblesse and of chivalry,
And if that Envy bark at thee,
As sure it will, for succour flee.
1579 *The Shepherd's Calendar*, 'To His Book'.

68 Bring hither the pink and purple columbine,
With gillyflowers:
Bring coronation, and sops in wine,
Worn of paramours.
Strew me the ground with daffadowndillies,
And cowslips, and kingcups, and loved lilies.
1579 *The Shepherd's Calendar*, 'April', l.136–41.

69 And he that strives to touch the stars,
Oft stumbles at a straw.
1579 *The Shepherd's Calendar*, 'July', l.99–100.

70 Uncouth unkist, said the old famous poet Chaucer.
1579 *The Shepherd's Calendar*, 'Letter to Gabriel Harvey'.

71 So now they have made our English tongue a gallimaufry or hodgepodge of all other speeches.
1579 *The Shepherd's Calendar*, 'Letter to Gabriel Harvey'.

72 A gentle knight was pricking on the plain.
1590 *The Faerie Queen*, bk.1, canto 1, stanza 1.

73 The sailing pine, the cedar proud and tall,
The vine-prop elm, the poplar never dry,
The builder oak, sole king of forests all,
The aspen good for staves, the cypress funeral.

The laurel, meed of mighty conquerors
And poets sage, the fir that weepeth still,
The willow worn of forlorn paramours,
The ewe obedient to the benders will,
The birch for shafts, the sallow for the mill,
The myrrh sweet bleeding in the bitter wound,
The warlike beech, the ash for nothing ill,
The fruitful olive, and the platan round,
The carver holme, the maple seldom inward sound.
1590 *The Faerie Queen*, bk.1, canto 1, stanzas 8–9.
plantan=plane tree; holme=holly.

74 Oft fire is without smoke.
1590 *The Faerie Queen*, bk.1, canto 1, stanza 12.

75 A stately palace built of squarèd brick,
Which cunningly was without mortar laid,
Whose walls were high, but nothing strong, nor thick,
And golden foil all over them displayed,
That purest sky with brightness they dismayed.
1590 Of the palace of pride. *The Faerie Queen*, bk.1, canto 4, stanza 4.

76 And by his side rode loathsome Gluttony,
Deformèd creature, on a filthy swine.
1590 *The Faerie Queen*, bk.1, canto 4, stanza 21.

77 Fretting grief the enemy of life.
1590 *The Faerie Queen*, bk.1, canto 4, stanza 35.

78 But who can turn the stream of destiny,
Or break the chain of strong necessity?
1590 Night argues against the necessity of faith. *The Faerie Queen*, bk.1, canto 5, stanza 25.

79 What worlds delight, or joy of living speech
Can heart, so plunged in sea of sorrows deep,
And heapèd with so huge misfortunes, reach?
The careful cold beginneth for to creep,
And in my heart his iron arrow steep,
Soon as I think upon my bitter bale.
1590 *The Faerie Queen*, bk.1, canto 7, stanza 39.

80 Still as he fled, his eye was backward cast,
As if his fear still followed him behind.
1590 *The Faerie Queen*, bk.1, canto 9, stanza 21.

81 Sleep after toil, port after stormy seas,
Ease after war, death after life does greatly please.
1590 *The Faerie Queen*, bk.1, canto 9, stanza 40.

82 Where justice grows, there grows eke greater grace.
1590 *The Faerie Queen*, bk.1, canto 9, stanza 53

83 His iron coat all overgrown with rust,
Was underneath envelopèd with gold,
Whose glistering gloss darkened with filthy dust,
Well yet appearèd, to have been of old
A work of rich entail, and curious mold,
Woven with antics and wild imagery.
1590 Of Mammon. *The Faerie Queen*, bk.2, canto 7, stanza 4.

84 And all for love, and nothing for reward.
1590 *The Faerie Queen*, bk.2, canto 8 stanza 2.

85 Of all God's works, which do this world adorn,
There is no one more fair and excellent,
Then is mans body both for power and form,
Whiles it is kept in sober government.
1590 *The Faerie Queen*, bk.2, canto 9, stanza 1.

86 So passeth, in the passing of a day,
Of mortal life the leaf, the bud, the flower,
No more doth flourish after first decay,
That erst was sought to deck both bed and bower,
Of many a lady, and many a paramour:
Gather therefore the rose, whilst yet is prime,
For soon comes age, that will her pride deflower:
Gather the rose of love, whilst yet is time,
Whilst loving thou mayst lovèd be with equal crime.
1590 *The Faerie Queen*, bk.2, canto 12, stanza 75.

87 Nought so of love this looser dame did skill,
But as a coal to kindle fleshly flame,
Giving the bridle to her wanton will,
And treading underfoot her honest name.
1590 Of Malecasta. *The Faerie Queen*, bk.3, canto 1, stanza 50.

88 But as it falleth, in the gentlest hearts
Imperious love hath highest set his throne,
And tyrannizeth in the bitter smarts
Of them, that to him buxom are and prone.
1590 *The Faerie Queen*, bk.3, canto 2, stanza 23.
buxom = 'yielding'.

89 Most sacred fire, that burnest mightily
In living breasts, ykindled first above,
Amongst th'eternal spheres and lamping sky,
And thence poured into men, which men call Love.
1590 *The Faerie Queen*, bk.3, canto 3, stanza 1.

90 Where is the antique glory now become,
What whilom wont in women to appear?
Where be the brave achievements doen by some?
Where be the battles, where the shield and spear,
And all the conquests, which them high did rear,
That matter made for famous poet's verse,

And boastful men so oft abashed to hear?
Bene they all dead, and laid in doleful hearse?
Or doen they only sleep, and shall again reverse?
1590 *The Faerie Queen*, bk.3, canto 4, stanza 1.

91 But ah, who can deceive his destiny,
Or ween by warning to avoid his fate?
1590 *The Faerie Queen*, bk.3, canto 4, stanza 27.

92 There is continual spring, and harvest there
Continual, both meeting at one time:
For both the boughs do laughing blossoms bear,
And with fresh colours deck the wanton prime,
And eke attonce the heavy trees they climb,
Which seem to labour under their fruits load:
The whiles the joyous birds make their pastime
Amongst the shady leaves, their sweet above,
And their true loves without suspicion tell abroad.
1590 Of the Garden of Adonis. *The Faerie Queen*, bk.3, canto 6, stanza 42.

93 Yet never can he die, but dying lives,
And doth himself with sorrow new sustain,
That death and life attonce unto him gives,
And painful pleasure turns to pleasing pain.
1590 *The Faerie Queen*, bk.3, canto 10, stanza 60.

94 And as she looked about, she did behold,
How over that same door was likewise writ,
Be bold, be bold, and everywhere Be bold…
At last she spied at that room's upper end
Another iron door, on which was writ
Be not too bold.
1590 *The Faerie Queen*, bk.3, canto 11, stanza 54.

95 Of such deep learning little had he need,
Ne yet of Latin, ne of Greek that breed
Doubts 'mongst divines, and difference of texts,
From when arise diversity of sects,
And hateful heresies.
1591 *Prosopopoia*, l.385–9.

96 Most glorious Lord of Life! that, on this day,
Didst make Thy triumph over death and sin;
And having harrowed hell, didst bring away
Captivity thence captive, us to win:
1595 *Amoretti*, sonnet 68.

97 But when I plead, she bids me play my part,
And when I weep, she says tears are but water:
And when I sigh, she says I know the art,
And when I wail, she turns herself to laughter.
1595 *Amoretti*, sonnet 18.

98 The merry cuckoo, messenger of Spring,
His trumpet shrill hath thrice already sounded.
1595 *Amoretti*, sonnet 19.

99 Most glorious Lord of Life! that, on this day,
Didst make Thy triumph over death and sin;
And having harrowed hell, didst bring away
Captivity thence captive, us to win:
1595 *Amoretti*, sonnet 68.

1 One day I wrote her name upon the strand,
But came the waves and washèd it away;
Again I wrote it with a second hand,
But came the tide, and made my pains his prey.
'Vain man,' said she, 'that doest in vain assay
A mortal thing so to immortalise,
For I my self shall like to this decay,
And eke my name be wipèd out likewise.'
'Not so,' quod I, 'let baser things devise
To die in dust, but you shall live by fame:
My verse your virtues rare shall eternise,
And in the heavens write your glorious name.
Where when as death shall all the world subdue,
Our love shall live, and later life renew.'
1595 *Amoretti*, sonnet 75.

2 In youth, before I waxèd old,
The blind boy, Venus' baby,
For want of cunning made me bold,
In bitter hive to grope for honey.
1595 *Amoretti*, 'Anacreontics', no.1.

3 Open the temple gates unto my love,
Open them wide that she may enter in.
1595 *Epithalamion*, section 12.

4 Pour out the wine without restraint or stay,
Pour not by cups, but by the belly full,
Pour out to all that will,
And sprinkle all the posts and walls with wine,
That they may sweat, and drunken be withal.
1595 *Epithalamion*, section 14.

5 Ah when will this long weary day have end,
And lend me leave to come unto my love?
How slowly do the hours their numbers spend!
How slowly does sad Time his feathers move!
1595 *Epithalamion*, section 16.

6 Dan Chaucer, well of English undefiled,
On Fame's eternal beadroll worthy to be filed.
1596 *The Faerie Queen*, bk.4, canto 2, stanza 32.

7 O sacred hunger of ambitious minds.
1596 *The Faerie Queen*, bk.5, canto 12, stanza 1.

8 A monster, which the Blatant beast men call,
A dreadful fiend of gods and men ydrad.
1596 *The Faerie Queen*, bk.5, canto 12, stanza 37.

9 Me seems the world is run quite out of square,
And being once amiss grows daily worse and worse.
1596 *The Faerie Queen*, bk.5, proem, stanza 1.

10 For that which all men then did virtue call,
Is now called vice; and that which vice was hight,
Is now hight virtue, and so used of all:
Right now is wrong, and wrong that was is right,
1596 *The Faerie Queen*, bk.5, proem, stanza 4.

11 Yet is that glass so gay, that it can blind
The wisest sight, to think gold that is brass.
1596 Of the mirror of fashion. *The Faerie Queen*, bk.6, proem, stanza 5.

12 The gentle mind by gentle deeds is known.
For a man by nothing is so well bewrayed,
As by his manners.
1596 *The Faerie Queen*, bk.6, canto 3, stanza 1.

13 Sweet Thames, run softly, till I end my song.
1596 *Prothalamion*, l.1.

14 What man that sees the ever-whirling wheel
Of Change, the which all mortal things doth sway,
But that thereby doth find, and plainly feel,
How mutability in them doth play
Her cruel sports, to many men's decay?
1609 *The Faerie Queen*, 'Mutability', canto 6, stanza 1.

15 First, sturdy March with brows full sternly bent,

And armèd strongly, rode upon a ram,
The same which over Hellespontus swam:
Yet in his hand a spade he also hent,
And in a bag all sorts of seeds ysame,
Which on the earth he strowèd as he went,
And filled her womb with fruitful hope of nourishment.
1609 *The Faerie Queen*,'Mutability', canto 7, stanza 32.
hent = grasped; ysame = together.

16 Jolly June, arrayed
All in green leaves, as he a Player were.
1609 *The Faerie Queen*,'Mutability', canto 7, stanza 35.

17 Next was November, he full gross and fat,
As fed with lard, and that right well might seem;
For, he had been a fatting hogs of late.
1609 *The Faerie Queen*,'Mutability', canto 7, stanza 40.

18 I was promised on a time,
To have reason for my rhyme;
From that time unto this season,
I received nor rhyme nor reason.
'Lines on his Pension.' Attributed.

Spielberg, Steven 1947–

US film-maker. His many films include *Jaws* (1975), *Close Encounters of the Third Kind* (1977), *The Color Purple* (1985), *Schindler's List* (1993), *Men in Black* (1997) and *Saving Private Ryan* (1998).

19 I hope we're such a communal society that we'll always insist on sharing an adventure in the dark with strangers, no matter what the platform hardware. That's my wish and dream—that we never give up the communal experience. It started a long time ago with cave paintings and I hope it doesn't go away.
2002 On whether cinema has a future. Quoted on www.filmmonthly.com, 12 Dec.

20 Technology can be our best friend, and technology can also be the biggest party pooper of our lives. It interrupts our own story, interrupts our ability to have a thought or a daydream, to imagine something wonderful because we're too busy bridging the walk from the cafeteria back to the office on the cell phone.
2002 In *Wired*, Jun.

Spillane, Mickey *properly* ***Frank Morrison Spillane*** 1918–

US popular novelist. He wrote for pulp magazines to pay for his education, and produced his first novel *I, the Jury* in 1947. His private detective character Mike Hammer inspired many films and a television series.

21 There are more salted peanuts consumed than caviar.
Defending his low-brow fiction. Quoted in Neil J Jones (ed) *A Book of Days for the Literary Year* (1984).

Spinoza, Baruch *also known as* ***Benedict de Spinoza*** 1632–77

Dutch philosopher, of Jewish descent. The *Tractatus Theologico-Politicus* was published in 1670, and the more famous *Ethics* in 1677. His pantheistic monism led to accusations of atheism but was influential in the development of metaphysics.

22 *Sedulo curavi, humanas actiones non ridere, non lugare, neque detestari, sed intelligere.*
I have striven not to laugh at human actions, not to weep at them, nor to hate them, but to understand them.
1670 *Tractatus Theologico-Politicus*, bk.1, pt.4.

23 *Quicquid est, in Deo est, et nihil sine Deo esse necque concipi potest.*
Whatever is, is in God, and nothing can exist or be conceived without God.
1677 *Ethics*, bk.1, prop.15.

24 *In rerum natura nullum datur contingens; sed omnia ex necessitate divinae naturae determinata sunt ad certo modo existandum et operandum.*
In the nature of things nothing contingent is granted, but all things are determined by the necessity of divine nature for existing and working in a certain way.
1677 *Ethics*, bk.1, prop.29.

25 *Nempe falluntur homines, quod se liberos esse putant; quae opinio in hoc solo consistit, quod suarum actionum sint conscii, et ignari causarum, a quibus determinantur. Haec ergo est eorum libertatis idea, quod suarum actionum nullam cognoscant causam.*
Men are mistaken in thinking themselves free; and this opinion consists of this alone, that they are conscious of their actions and ignorant of the causes by which they are determined. This, therefore, is their idea of liberty, that they should know no cause of their actions.
1677 *Ethics*, bk.2, prop.35, note.

26 *Veritas norma sua est.*
Truth is its own standard.
1677 *Ethics*, bk.2, prop.43, note.

27 *De natura Rationis est, res sub quadam aeternitatis specie percipere.*
It is the nature of reason to perceive things under a certain species of eternity.
1677 *Ethics*, bk.2, prop.44, corollary 2.

28 *Unaquaeque res, quantum in se est, in suo esse perseverare conatur.*
Everything in so far as it is in itself endeavours to persist in its own being.
1677 *Ethics*, bk.3, prop.6.

29 *Nihil nos conari, velle, appetere, neque cupere, quia id bonum esse judicamus; sed contra, nos propterea aliquid bonum esse judicare, quia id conamur, volumus, appetimus, atque cupimus.*
We endeavour, wish, desire, or long for nothing because we deem it good; but on the other hand, we deem a thing good because we endeavour, wish for, desire, or long for it.
1677 *Ethics*, bk.3, prop.9, note.

30 *Nempe Amor nihil aliud est, quam Laeititia concomitante idea causae externae; et Odium nihil aliud est, quam Tristitia concomitante idea causae externae.*
Love is nothing else than pleasure accompanied by the idea of an external cause; and hate pain accompanied by the idea of an external cause.
1677 *Ethics*, bk.3, prop.13, note.

31 *Ex virtute absoluto agere nihil aliud in nobis est, quam ex ductu Rationis agere, vivere, suum esse conservare (haec tria idem significant) ex fundamento proprium utile quaerendi.*
To act absolutely according to virtue is nothing else in us than to act under the guidance of reason, to live so, and to preserve one's being (these three have the same

meaning) on the basis of seeking what is useful to oneself.
1677 *Ethics*, bk.4, prop.24.

32 *Summum Mentis bonum est Dei cognitio, et summa Mentis virtus Deum cognoscere.*
The greatest good of the mind is the knowledge of God, and the greatest virtue of the mind is to know God.
1677 *Ethics*, bk.4, prop.28.

33 *Homo liber de nulla re minus quam de morte cogitat; et ejus sapienta non mortis, sed vitae meditatio est.*
A free man thinks of nothing less than of death, and his wisdom is a meditation not of death but of life.
1677 *Ethics*, bk.4, prop.67.

34 *In vita itaque apprime utile est, intellectum seu Rationem, quantum possumus, perficere, et in hoc uno summa hominis felicitas seu beatitudo consistit; quippe beatitudo nihil aliud est, quam ipsa animi acquiescentia quae ex Dei intuitiva cognitione oritur.*
It is therefore extrememly useful in life to perfect as much as we can the intellect or reason, and of this alone does the greatest happiness or blessedness of man exist: for blessedness is nothing else than satisfaction of mind which arises from the intuitive knowledge of God.
1677 *Ethics*, bk.4, appendix.

35 *Ex tertio cognitionis genere oritur necessario Amor Dei intellectualis.*
From the third kind of knowledge [intuition] arises necessarily the intellectual love of God.
1677 *Ethics*, bk.5, prop.32, corollary.

36 *Per Deum intelligo ens absolute infinitum, hoc est, substantiam constantem infinitis attributis, quorum unumquodque aeternam et infinitam essentiam exprimit.*
By God I mean a being absolutely infinite—that is, a substance consisting in infinite attributes, of which each expresses eternal and infinite essentiality.
1677 *Ethics*.

Spock, Dr Benjamin McLane 1903–98

US paediatrician. His *Common Sense Book of Baby and Child Care* (1946) sold over 30 million copies, transforming childcare. He gave up psychiatry to devote himself to pacifism, and ran for the presidency in 1972.

37 You know more than you think you do.
1946 *The Common Sense Book of Baby and Child Care*, opening words.

38 To win in Vietnam, we will have to exterminate a nation.
1968 *Dr Spock on Vietnam*, ch.7.

Spring-Rice, Sir Cecil Arthur 1858–1918

English diplomat.

39 I vow to thee, my country—all earthly things above—
Entire and whole and perfect, the service of my love.
1918 *I Vow To Thee, My Country.*

Springsteen, Bruce 1949–

US rock singer and guitarist. His albums include *Born To Run* (1975) and *Born In The USA* (1984).

40 We gotta get out while we're young
'Cause tramps like us, baby, we were born to run.
1975 'Born to Run'.

Spurgeon, Charles Haddon 1834–92

English Baptist preacher, famous for his eloquent sermons. A strong Calvinist, he left the Evangelical Alliance (1864) and Baptist Union (1887) over doctrinal differences and a concern for orthodoxy.

41 If you want truth to go round the world you must hire an express train to pull it; but if you want a lie to go round the world, it will fly: it is as light as a feather, and a breath will carry it. It is well said in the old proverb, 'a lie will go round the world while truth is pulling its boots on'.
Collected in *Gems from Spurgeon* (1859).

Squire, Sir J(ohn) C(ollings) 1884–1958

English poet and editor. He was an influential anti-modernist figure in the 1920s, with a gift for amusing parody.

42 It did not last: the Devil howling 'Ho!
Let Einstein be!' restored the status quo.
1926 'In Continuation of Pope on Newton'.

43 But I'm not so think as you drunk I am.
1931 'Ballade of Soporific Absorption'.

Staël, Germaine Necker, Baronne de 1766–1817

French author of important critical, political and philosophical essays as well as novels and plays seen as precursors of Romanticism. She was an opponent of Napoleon.

44 *L'amour est l'histoire de la vie des femmes, c'est un épisode dans celle des hommes.*
Love is the story of a woman's life, but only an episode in the life of a man.
1796 *De l'influence des passions sur le bonheur des individus et des nations.*

45 *La force de l'esprit ne se développe toute entière qu'en attaquant la puissance.*
The mind fully develops its faculties when it attacks power.
1800 *De la littérature considereree dans ses rapports avec les institutions sociales.*

46 *En cherchant la gloire, j'ai toujours espéré qu'elle me ferait aimer.*
I have pursued fame always in the hope of winning her love.
1807 *Corinne ou de l'Italie.*

47 *Quand une fois on a tourné l'enthousiasme en ridicule, on a tout défait, excepté l'argent et le pouvoir.*
Once we have made enthusiasm ridiculous, there is nothing left but money and power.
1807 *Corinne ou de l'Italie.*

48 *Les païens ont divinisé la vie, et les chrétiens ont divinisé la mort.*
Pagans deified life and Christians deified death.
1807 *Corinne ou de l'Italie.*

49 *On dirait que l'âme des justes donne, comme les fleurs, plus de parfums vers le soir.*
It seems that the soul of the just gives off, like flowers, a stronger scent towards evening.
1807 *Corinne ou de l'Italie.*

50 *On cesse de s'aimer si quelqu'un ne nous aime.*
We stop loving ourselves when no one loves us.
1810 *De l'Allemagne.*

51 *La première condition pour écrire, c'est une manière de sentir vive et forte.*
The primary requirement for a writer is to feel keenly and strongly.
1810 *De l'Allemagne.*

52 *En France, on étudie les hommes; en Allemagne, les livres.*
In France, they study men; in Germany, books.
1810 *De l'Allemagne.*

53 *La poésie est le langage naturel de tous les cultes.*
Poetry is the natural language of all religions.
1810 *De l'Allemagne.*

54 *Le sentiment de l'infini est le véritable attribut de l'âme.*
To feel the infinite is the true attribute of the soul.
1810 *De l'Allemagne.*

Stalin, Joseph *originally* ***Iosif Vissarionovich Dzhugashvili*** 1879–1953

Soviet leader. Appointed General Secretary to the Communist Party Central Committee (1922), enabling him to take power after Lenin's death in 1924. His collectivization was responsible for millions of deaths, as were his political purges (1934–38). Although he signed a non-aggression pact with Hitler (1939), he declared war, joining the Allies, when Hitler threatened the Soviet Union in 1941.

55 In the name of the Constitution, Cromwell took up arms, executed the king, dissolved Parliament, imprisoned some, and beheaded others.
1934 In conversation with H G Wells, Moscow.

56 To attempt to export revolution is nonsense.
1936 Said to Roy Howard, US newspaper proprietor, 1 Mar.

57 History shows that there are no invincible armies.
1941 Radio broadcast, 3 Jul, announcing the declaration of war against Germany, three weeks before Hitler invaded.

58 Communism fits Germany as a saddle fits a cow.
1944 In conversation with the Polish politician, Stanislaw Mikolajcik, Aug.

Stallone, Sylvester 1946–

US actor and film director, best known for his roles in action films such as *Rocky* (1976) and *Rambo* (1985) and their sequels.

59 Playing polo is like trying to play golf during an earthquake.
1990 Quoted in Colin Jarman *The Guinness Dictionary of Sports Quotations* (1990).

Stamp, Sir Josiah Charles, Baron Stamp of Shortlands 1880–1941

British economist and statistician, who published early estimates of the British national income.

60 The first argument that is brought against every new proposal departing from conventional lines is nearly always that it is impracticable.
1921 *Fundamental Principles of Taxation*, p.95.

Stanley, Sir Henry Morton *originally* ***John Rowlands*** 1841–1904

Welsh-born US explorer and journalist. He fought on both sides in the American Civil War and then, as a journalist, was commissioned by the *New York Herald* to lead an expedition in search of Dr David Livingstone, who was rumoured to have died while exploring rivers in Central Africa. On one of the three subsequent expeditions he travelled the length of the Congo.

61 I would have run to him, only I was a coward in the presence of such a mob—would have embraced him, only, he being an Englishman, I did not know how he would receive me; so I did what cowardice and false pride suggested was the best thing—walked deliberately to him, took off my hat, and said:
'Dr Livingstone, I presume?'
'Yes,' said he, with a kind smile, lifting his cap slightly.
I replace my hat on my head, and he puts on his cap, and we both grasp hands, and I then say aloud:
'I thank God, Doctor, I have been permitted to see you.'
He answered, 'I feel thankful that I am here to welcome you.'
1872 *How I Found Livingstone in Central Africa.*

Stanton, Elizabeth *née* ***Cady*** 1815–1902

US reformer and suffragette; organizer of the first Women's Rights Convention, Seneca Falls, US (1848). She is remembered chiefly as co-author of *The History of Woman Suffrage* (1881–6) and she also wrote *The Women's Bible* (1895).

62 We hold these truths to be self-evident: that all men and women are created equal; that they are endowed by their Creator with certain inalienable rights; that among these are life, liberty, and the pursuit of happiness.
1848 'Declaration of Sentiments', Seneca Falls Women's Rights Convention, 19–20 Jul. This is modelled on the American Declaration of Independence of 4 Jul 1776.

63 Quite as many false ideas prevail as to woman's true position in the home as to her status elsewhere. Womanhood is the great fact in her life; wifehood and motherhood are but incidental relations.
1881 *The History of Woman Suffrage 1848–61*, vol.1, introduction.

64 Men are the Brahmin, women the Pariahs, under our existing civilization.
1881 *The History of Woman Suffrage 1848–61*, vol.1, ch.1, 'Preceding Causes'.

65 Although woman has performed much of the labor of the world, her industry and economy have been the very means of increasing her degradation.
1881 *The History of Woman Suffrage 1848–61*, vol.1, ch.1, 'Preceding Causes'.

66 As to woman's subjection...it is important to note that equal dominion is given to woman over every living thing, but not one word is said giving man dominion over woman.
1895 *The Woman's Bible*, pt.1, ch.1, 'Comments on Genesis'.

67 The Old Testament makes woman a mere after-thought in creation; the author of evil; cursed in her maternity; a subject in marriage; and all female life, animal and human, unclean.
1898 *The Woman's Bible*, pt.2, preface.

68 'Self-development is a higher duty than self-sacrifice', should be a woman's motto henceforward.
1898 *The Woman's Bible*, pt.2, 'Comments on Mark'.

Stanwyck, Barbara *originally* ***Ruby Stevens*** 1907–90

American film, television and radio actress. She was a dancer in the Ziegfeld Follies at the age of 13 and went on to play gutsy, pioneering women in westerns such as *Annie Oakley* (1935), as well as sultry femmes fatales in films noirs, including *Double*

Indemnity (1944). She became a successful radio star in the 1960s.

69 To eat, to survive and to have a good coat.
1987 Her three goals in life, recalled on receiving the American Film Institute Life Achievement Award. Reported in the *New York Times*, 11 Apr.

Stapledon, Olaf 1886–1950

English writer and social philosopher. He used science fiction as a means of embodying his social theories.

70 That strange blend of the commercial traveller, the missionary, and the barbarian conqueror, which was the American abroad.
1930 *Last and First Men*, ch.3.

Stark, Dame Freya Madeleine 1893–1993

English writer and traveller, born in Paris. She studied Arabic and made her first journey to the Middle East in 1928, after which she travelled extensively in Europe, the Middle East and Asia, writing over 30 books.

71 The great and almost only comfort about being a woman is that one can always pretend to be more stupid than one is and no one is surprised.
1934 *The Valley of the Assassins*.

72 I came to the conclusion that some more ascetic reason than mere enjoyment should be found if one wishes to travel in peace: to do things for fun smacks of levity, immorality almost, in our utilitarian world. And though personally I think the world is wrong, and I know in my heart of hearts that it is a most excellent reason to do things merely because one likes the doing of them, I would advise all those who wish to see unwrinkled brows in passport offices to start out ready labelled as entomologists, anthropologists, or whatever other - ology they think suitable and propitious.
1936 *The Valleys of the Assassins and other Persian Travels*.

73 The true call of the desert, of the mountains, or the sea, is their silence—free of the networks of dead speech.
1948 *Perseus in the Wind*.

74 This is the prospect from the watershed, and when the traveller reaches it, it is a good thing to take an hour's leisure and look out on the visible portions of the journey, since never in one's life can one see the same view twice.
1948 *Perseus in the Wind*.

75 The *inscrutability* of the East is, indeed, I believe a myth... The ordinary inhabitant is incomprehensible merely to people who never trouble to have anything much to do with them.
1963 *The Journey's Echo*.

Stark, John 1728–1822

American revolutionary commander. He saw service in the French and Indian war (1754–9), and at Bunker Hill (1775) and Bennington (1777) during the American Revolution.

76 We beat them today or Molly Stark's a widow.
1777 Speech before the Battle of Bennington, 16 Aug. Quoted in *Cyclopaedia of American Biography*, vol.5.

Starr, Roger

77 A busy man who can keep up a daily journal resembles a person preparing for bed with the shades up... When such a man publishes parts of his journal, the reader must conclude he always knew the lights were on.
1989 On George F Kennan *Sketches From a Life* (1989). In the *Washington Post*, 8 May.

Steacie, E W 1900–62

Canadian government official, President of the National Research Council of Canada (1952).

78 The academic atmosphere, produced mainly by the humanities, is the only atmosphere in which pure science can flourish.
1956 Collected in J D Babbitt (ed) *Science in Canada: Selections from the Speeches of E. W. Steacie* (1965).

79 An efficient organization is one in which the accounting department knows the exact cost of every useless administrative procedure which they themselves have initiated.
Quoted by J D Babbitt in his introduction to Steacie's *Science in Canada* (published posthumously, 1965).

Stead, William Thomas 1849–1912

English journalist and reformer. Editor of the *Pall Mall Gazette* (1883–90). He drowned in the *Titanic* disaster.

80 The Press is at once the eye and the ear and the tongue of the people. It is the visible speech, if not the voice, of the democracy. It is the phonograph of the world.
1886 'Government by Journalism', in the *Contemporary Review*, May. Collected in *A Journalist on Journalism* (1892).

81 He may be more potent than any other man. The damnable iteration day after day of earnest conviction wears like the dropping of the water upon the stone.
1886 Of the journalist. 'Government by journalism', in the *Contemporary Review*, May. Collected in *A Journalist on Journalism* (1892).

82 An editor is the uncrowned king of an educated democracy.
1886 'Government by Journalism', in the *Contemporary Review*, May. Collected in *A Journalist on Journalism* (1892).

83 The duty of a journalist is the duty of a watchman.
1886 'Government by Journalism', in the *Contemporary Review*, May. Collected in *A Journalist on Journalism* (1892).

84 It is the great inspector, with a myriad eyes, who never sleeps, and whose daily reports are submitted, not to a functionary or department, but to the whole people.
1886 Of a newspaper. 'Government by Journalism', in the *Contemporary Review*, May. Collected in *A Journalist on Journalism* (1892).

85 What a marvellous opportunity for attacking the devil!
Letter of appointment to the *Northern Echo*, quoted by Harold Evans in his preface to Ray Boston *The Essential Fleet Street* (1990).

Steel, David Martin Scott Steel, Baron 1938–

Scottish Liberal politician. He sponsored a controversial bill to reform abortion laws (1966–7), and was active in the anti-apartheid movement. The last Liberal leader (1976–88), he led the Liberals into an Alliance with the Social Democrats (1981) and later negotiated their merger. From 1999 to 2003 he was the Presiding Officer of the Scottish Parliament.

86 I have the good fortune to be the first Liberal for over half a century who is able to say to you at the end of our

annual Assembly, go back to your constituencies and prepare for government.
1981 Speech at party conference, 18 Sep.

87 [Margaret Thatcher] has turned the British bulldog into a Reagan poodle.
1986 In *Time*, 28 Apr.

88 I trust that the Duke of Edinburgh will not disagree that this ancient capital whose name he bears, with its legal and ecclesiastical headquarters and its worldwide reputation for quality education and financial management has nonetheless until now seemed like a body with its heart missing.
1999 At the opening of the Scottish Parliament, 12 May.

Steele, Sir Richard 1672–1729

Irish essayist, dramatist and politician. His plays include *The Funeral* (1701). He founded the *Tatler* (1709–11), a periodical published three times a week, on which he was joined by Joseph Addison. Together they founded the *Spectator*, a daily which ran from 1711 to 1712 under their joint editorship.

89 Dear Prue,
If a servant I sent last night got to Hampton-court, you received 29 walnuts and a letter from me. I inclose the Gazette; and am, with all my soul,
Your passionate lover, and faithful husband,
RICH. STEELE
1708 Letter, 20 Sep (published 1787).

90 I am, dear Prue, a little in drink, but at all times your faithful husband,
RICH. STEELE
1708 Letter, 27 Sep (published 1787).

91 It is to be noted that when any part of this paper appears dull there is a design in it.
1709 In the *Tatler*, no.38, 7 Jul.

92 To love her is a liberal education.
1709 Of Lady Elizabeth Hastings *Tatler*, no.49, 2 Aug.

93 Every man is the maker of his own fortune
1709 In the *Tatler*, no.52, 9 Aug.

94 It gave me a great notion of the credit of our present government and administration, to find people press as eagerly to pay money as they would to receive it; and, at the same time, a due respect for that body of men who have found out so pleasing an expedient for carrying on the common cause, that they have turned a tax into a diversion.
1710 On the first state lottery of 1710. In the *Tatler*, no.124, 24 Jan.

95 Reading is to the mind what exercise is to the body.
1710 In the *Tatler*, no.147, 18 Mar. Also attributed to Addison.

96 Let your precept be, Be Easy.
1710 In the *Tatler*, no.196, 11 Jul.

97 I was undone by my Auxiliary; when I had once called him in, I could not subsist without Dependance on him.
1711 Of Addison's contribution to the *Tatler*. Preface to vol.4 of the collected edition.

98 I have heard Will Honeycomb say, A Woman seldom Writes her Mind but in her Postscript.
1711 In the *Spectator*, no.79, 30 May.

99 We were in some little time fixed in our seats, and sat with that dislike which people not too good-natured usually conceive of each other at first sight.
1711 Embarking on a coach journey. In the *Spectator*, no.132, 1 Aug.

1 I am confident that no boy, who will not be allured to letters without blows, will ever be brought to anything with them.
1711 On flogging in schools. In the *Spectator*, no.157, 30 Aug.

2 Those grave fellows are my aversion who sift everything with the utmost nicety, and find the malignity of a lie in a piece of humour, pushed a little beyond exact truth.
1713 In the *Guardian*, no.42, 29 Apr.

Stefansson, Vilhjalmur 1879–1962

Canadian Arctic explorer and author.

3 There are two kinds of Arctic problems, the imaginary and the real. Of the two, the imaginary are the most real.
1945 *The Arctic in Fact and Fable*.

4 What is the difference between unethical and ethical advertising? Unethical advertising uses falsehoods to deceive the public; ethical advertising uses truth to deceive the public.
Discovery (published 1964).

5 A land may be said to be discovered the first time a European, presumably an Englishman, sets foot on it.
Discovery (published 1964).

Steffens, (Joseph) Lincoln 1866–1936

US journalist. While editor of *McClure's Magazine* (1902–6), his revision of an article on city corruption led to a series published as *The Shame of the Cities* (1904), a key work in urban reform. His *Struggle for Self-Government* (1906) analysed corruption and reform at state level.

6 I have seen the future and it works.
1919 On his visit to post-Revolutionary Russia, in *Autobiography* (2 vols, 1931).
► *See Toynbee 864:30.*

Stegner, Wallace Earle 1909–93

US novelist. Professor of English at Stanford University.

7 A political animal can be defined as a body that will go on circulating a petition even with its heart cut out.
1954 *Beyond the Hundredth Meridian*.

8 If you're going to get old, you might as well get as old as you can get.
1989 On his 80th birthday. Reported in the *San Francisco Chronicle*, 6 Mar.

Steichen, Edward Jean 1879–1973

Belgian-born US photographer, credited with developing photography as an art form. He also pioneered aerial and naval photography during World Wars I and II.

9 Photography was conceived as a mirror of the universal elements and emotions of the everydayness of life—as a mirror of the essential oneness of mankind throughout the world.
Quoted in *Dialogue*, May 1989.

Stein, Gertrude 1874–1946

US writer, influential in the development of Modernism. She settled in Paris in 1903, where with her friend Alice B Toklas she dominated expatriate life. Her less experimental works include *The Autobiography of Alice B. Toklas* (1933) and *Everybody's Autobiography* (1937).

10 You are so afraid of losing your moral sense that you are not willing to take it through anything more dangerous than a mud-puddle.
1903 'Q.E.D.', bk.1. Collected in *Fernhurst, Q.E.D., and Other Early Writings* (1971).

11 Rose is a rose is a rose is a rose, is a rose.
1914 *Tender Buttons*, 'Sacred Emily'.

12 You are all a lost generation.
Quoted as epigraph in Ernest Hemingway *The Sun Also Rises* (1926).

13 He had added to his stories a little story of meditations and in these he said that The Enormous Room was the greatest book he had ever read. It was then that Gertrude Stein said, Hemingway, remarks are not literature.
1933 *The Autobiography of Alice B. Toklas*, ch.7.

14 Pigeons on the grass alas.
1934 *Four Saints in Three Acts*, act 3, sc.2.

15 Disillusionment in living is the finding out nobody agrees with you . . . Complete disillusionment is when you realise that no one can for they can't change.
1934 *The Making of Americans*, ch.5.

16 In the United States there is more space where nobody is than where anybody is. That is what makes America what it is.
1936 *The Geographical History of America*.

17 Native always means people who belong somewhere else, because they had once belonged somewhere. That shows that the white race does not really think they belong anywhere because they think of everybody else as native.
1937 *Everybody's Autobiography*, ch.1.

18 Anything scares me, anything scares anyone but really after all considering how dangerous everything is nothing is really very frightening.
1937 *Everybody's Autobiography*, ch.2.

19 It takes a lot of time to be a genius, you have to sit around so much doing nothing, really doing nothing.
1937 *Everybody's Autobiography*, ch.2.

20 What was the use of my having come from Oakland it was not natural to have come from there yes write about it if I like or anything if I like but not there, there is no there there.
1937 *Everybody's Autobiography*, ch.4.

21 Two things are always the same the dance and war.
1937 *Everybody's Autobiography*, ch.5.

22 Everybody gets so much information all day long that they lose their common sense.
1959 'Reflection on the Atomic Bomb', collected in Robert A Goodwin (ed) *Readings in World Politics* (1959).

23 Nature is commonplace. Imitation is more interesting.
Quoted in Sir Charles Spencer Chaplin *My Autobiography* (1964).

24 You should only read what is truly good or what is frankly bad.
Quoted in Ernest Hemingway *A Moveable Feast* (1964), ch.3.

25 Anyone who marries three girls from St Louis hasn't learned much.
Of Ernest Hemingway. Quoted in R Mellow *Charmed Circle* (1974), ch.16.

26 Just before she died she asked, 'What is the answer?' No answer came. She laughed and said, 'In that case what is the question?' Then she died.
Last words, as quoted in D Sutherland *Gertrude Stein* (1951), ch.6.

27 She said he was a village explainer, excellent if you were a village, but if you were not, not.
Of Ezra Pound. Quoted in J Hobhouse *Everyone Who Was Anybody* (1975), ch.6.

Stein, Herbert 1916–99

US economist, member of the Council of Economic Advisers under Nixon, Ford and Reagan.

28 *Consumer*: A person who is capable of choosing a president but incapable of choosing a bicycle without help from a government agency.
1979 *Washington Bedtime Stories*.

29 Whatever may be the distribution of uncertainty among economists, the public only gets to hear from those who have certain opinions.
1979 *Washington Bedtime Stories*.

30 A few weeks ago I had a revelation and told my secretary that I could give him a synthesis of forty-six years of living with economic policy. It is: 'Economic policy is random with respect to the performance of the American economy, but, thank God, there isn't much of it.'
1979 *Washington Bedtime Stories*.

Steinbeck, John Ernest 1902–68

US novelist. His works include *Of Mice and Men* (1937), *The Grapes of Wrath* (1939) and *East of Eden* (1952). He received the Nobel prize for literature in 1962.

31 Man, unlike any other thing organic or inorganic in the universe, grows beyond his work, walks up the stairs of his concepts, emerges ahead of his accomplishments.
1939 *The Grapes of Wrath*, ch.14.

32 I know this . . . a man got to do what he got to do.
1939 *The Grapes of Wrath*, ch.18.

33 Okie use' ta mean you was from Oklahoma. Now it means you're a dirty son-of-a-bitch. Okie means you're scum. Don' mean nothing itself, it's the way they say it.
1939 *The Grapes of Wrath*, ch.18.

34 Well, maybe like Casy says, a fellow ain't got a soul of his own, but on'y a piece of a big one—an then— . . . Then it don' matter. Then I'll be all aroun' in the dark. I'll be everywhere—wherever you look. Wherever they's a fight so hungry people can eat, I'll be there. Wherever they's a cop beatin' up a guy, I'll be there. If Casy knowed, why, I'll be in the way guys yell when they're mad an'—I'll be in the way kids laugh when they're hungry an' they know supper's ready. An' when our folks eat the stuff they raise an' live in the houses they build—why, I'll be there. See?
1939 *The Grapes of Wrath*, ch.28.

35 All Americans believe that they are born fishermen. For a man to admit a distaste for fishing would be like denouncing mother-love or hating moonlight.
1954 Quoted in Colin Jarman *The Guinness Dictionary of Sports Quotations* (1990).

36 Unless the bastards have the courage to give you unqualified praise, I say ignore them.

1958 Of critics. Quoted in J K Galbraith *The Affluent Society* (1977), introduction.

37 I pulled to the side of the street and got out my book of road maps. But to find where you are going, you must know where you are, and I didn't.
1962 *Travels With Charley In Search of America*.

38 A journey is like a marriage. The certain way to be wrong is to think you control it.
1962 *Travels With Charley In Search of America*, pt.1.

39 It is the nature of a man as he grows older, a small bridge in time, to protest against change, particularly change for the better.
1962 *Travels With Charley In Search of America*, pt.2.

40 The profession of book writing makes horse racing seem like a solid, stable business.
1962 In *Newsweek*, 24 Dec.

41 A good writer always works at the impossible.
Recalled on his death, 20 Dec 1968.

Steinem, Gloria 1934–

US feminist and writer. She emerged as a leading figure in the women's movement in the 1960s, and as a campaigner against the Vietnam War and racism. She co-founded the Women's Action Alliance (1970) and *Ms* magazine (1971).

42 A woman needs a man like a fish needs a bicycle.
c.1970 Attributed, in various forms.

43 This is what forty looks like. We've been lying so long who would know?
c.1974 Response when complimented by a reporter on not looking forty years old, quoted by Lisa Jardine in 'Still Angry After All These Years', in the *Sunday Times*, 15 May 1994.

44 What would happen if...men could menstruate and women could not? Clearly, menstruation would become an enviable, boast-worthy, masculine event: Men would brag about how long and how much. Young boys would talk about it as the envied beginning of manhood... Generals, right-wing politicians, and religious fundamentalists would cite ...*'mens*-truation' as proof that only men could serve God and country in combat... If men could menstruate, the power justifications would go on and on. If we let them.
1978 'If Men could Menstruate', collected in *Outrageous Acts and Everyday Rebellions* (1983).

45 I've finally figured out why soap operas are, and logically should be, so popular with generations of housebound women. *They are the only place in our culture where grown-up men take seriously all the things that grown-up women have to deal with all day long.*
1980 'Night Thoughts of a Media Watcher', collected in *Outrageous Acts and Everyday Rebellions* (1983).

Steiner, George 1929–

French-born US literary critic and scholar.

46 Where God's presence is no longer a tenable proposition and where his absence is no longer a felt, indeed overwhelming weight, certain dimensions of thought and creativity are no longer attainable.
1989 *Real Presences*.

Steinmetz, Charles Proteus 1865–1923

German-born US electrical engineer and inventor, whose most notable work was the development of alternating current.

47 In the realm of science, all attempts to find any evidence of supernatural beings, of metaphysical concepts, as God, immortality, infinity, etc have thus far failed, and if we are honest, we must confess that in science there exists no God, no immortality, no soul or mind, as distinct from the body.
1941 In the *American Freeman*, Jul.

Steloff, Frances 1887–1989

US bookseller. She worked at Loeser's Department Store, New York City, then at Bretanos where she ran the drama department (1917–19). She founded Gotham Book Mart, New York City, in 1920.

48 Wise men fish here.
Sign for Gotham Book Mart. Quoted in the *New York Times*, 30 Dec 1987.

Stendhal *pseudonym of* Henri Beyle 1783–1842

French writer who lived many years in Italy, he wrote novels and treatises on literature. He held a modernist concept of Romanticism and was opposed to those who sought literary models from the past.

49 *L'esprit et le génie perdent vingt-cinq pour cent de leur valeur, en débarquant en Angleterre.*
The mind and genius lose twenty-five percent of their value on entry into England.
1830 *Le Rouge et le noir*, bk.2, ch.7.

50 *La politique au milieu des intérêts d'imagination, c'est un coup de pistolet au milieu d'un concert.*
Politics mixed with the imagination is like a shot fired in the middle of a concert.
1830 *Le Rouge et le noir*, bk.2, ch.22.

51 *Grand Dieu! Pourquoi suis-je moi?*
Great God! Why am I me?
1830 *Le Rouge et le noir*, bk.2, ch.28.

52 *Le pire des malheurs en prison, pensa-t-il, c'est de ne pouvoir fermer sa porte.*
The worst of prison life, he thought, was not being able to close his door.
1830 *Le Rouge et le noir*, bk.2, ch.44.

53 *Les gens qu'on honore ne sont que des fripons qui ont eu le bonheur de n'être pas pris en flagrant délit.*
Respected people are only rascals who have had the good fortune not to be caught in the act.
1830 *Le Rouge et le noir*, bk.2, ch.44.

Stengel, Casey (Charles Dillon) 1890–1975

US baseball player and manager. An outfielder with the Brooklyn Dodgers and other teams, he became manager of the New York Yankees (1949–62), leading them to seven World Series victories, and of the New York Mets (1962–5).

54 The secret of managing a ball club is to keep the five guys who hate you away from the five who are undecided.
Quoted in Colin Jarman *The Guinness Dictionary of Sports Quotations* (1990).

55 There's three things you can do in a baseball game—you can win, you can lose, or it can rain.
Quoted in Colin Jarman *The Guinness Dictionary of Sports Quotations* (1990).

56 Without losers, where would the winners be?
Quoted in Colin Jarman *The Guinness Dictionary of Sports Quotations* (1990).

57 Not bad. Most people my age are dead. You could look it up.
Attributed, when asked how he was. 'You could look it up' was one of his catchphrases.

Stephen, J(ames) K(enneth) 1859–92

English lawyer and journalist, a cousin of Virginia Woolf. He began a weekly paper, *The Reflector* in 1888 and was a successful parodist and light versifier.

58 Two voices are there: one is of the deep;
It learns the storm-clouds thundrous melody,
Now roars, now murmurs with the changing sea,
Now bird-like pipes, now closes soft in sleep:
And one is of an old half-witted sheep
Which bleats articulate monotony,
And indicates that two and one are three,
That grass is green, lakes damp, and mountains stoop
And, Wordsworth, both are thine.
1896 *Lapsus Calami*, 'A Sonnet'.

59 Will there never come a season
Which shall rid us of the curse
Of a prose which knows no reason
And an unmelodious verse...
When there stands a muzzled stripling,
Mute, beside a muzzled bore:
When the Rudyards cease from kipling
And the Haggards Ride no more.
'To R K'.

Stephenson, Bette 1924–

Former President of the Canadian Medical Association and Ontario Minister of Health.

60 Men are very fragile creatures. Their psyches are so closely tied to their epididymis.
1975 Interviewed by Christina McCall Newman in *The Globe and Mail*, 12 Jul. The epididymis is the tube carrying sperm out from the testicle.

Sterling, Bruce 1954–

US science fiction writer.

61 Unfortunately, computers are...stupid. Unlike human beings, computers possess the truly profound stupidity of the inanimate.
1992 *The Hacker Crackdown: law and disorder on the electronic frontier.*

62 It's a truism in technological development that no silver lining comes without its cloud.
1993 Opening statement to the House Subcommittee on Telecommunications and Finance, Washington DC, 29 Apr.

63 Cyberspace is the funhouse mirror of our own society.
1993 National Academy of Sciences Convocation on Technology and Education, Washington DC, 10 May.

Sterling, Rod

64 Every writer is a frustrated actor who recites his lines in the hidden auditorium of his skull.
1957 In *Vogue*, 1 Apr.

Stern, Robert A(rthur) M(orton) 1939–

US architect and writer, author of *New Directions in American Architecture* (1969, revised 1977) and *The House that Bob Built* (1991).

65 The dialogue between client and architect is about as intimate as any conversation you can have because, when you're talking about building a house, you're talking about dreams.
1985 'The Trend-Setting Traditionalism of Architecture', in the *New York Times*, 13 Jan.

66 Our greatest responsibility is not to be pencils of the past.
1985 'The Trend-Setting Traditionalism of Architecture', in the *New York Times*, 13 Jan.

Sterne, Laurence 1713–68

Irish novelist. He extended the scope of the novel with his major work *Tristram Shandy* (1759–67). As his health failed, he spent much of his time in France and Italy and published *A Sentimental Journey through France and Italy* in 1768.

67 I wish either my father or my mother, or indeed both of them, as they were in duty both equally bound to it, had minded what they were about when they begot me.
1759–67 *Tristram Shandy*, bk.1, ch.1.

68 'Pray, my dear,' quoth my mother, 'have you not forgot to wind up the clock?'—'Good G—?' cried my father, making an exclamation, but taking care to moderate his voice at the same time,—'Did ever woman, since the creation of the world, interrupt a man with such a silly question?'
1759–67 *Tristram Shandy*, bk.1, ch.6.

69 As we jog on, either laugh with me, or at me, or in short do anything,—only keep your temper.
1759–67 Tristram to reader. *Tristram Shandy*, bk.1, ch.6.

70 Have not the wisest of men in all ages, not excepting Solomon himself,—have they not had their Hobby-Horses...and so long as a man rides his Hobby-Horse peaceably and quietly along the King's highway, and neither compels you or me to get up behind him,—pray, Sir, what have either you or I to do with it?
1759–67 *Tristram Shandy*, bk.1, ch.7.

71 He was in a few hours of giving his enemies the slip for ever.
1759–67 Of Eugenis. *Tristram Shandy*, bk.1, ch.12.

72 'Tis known by the name of perseverance in a good cause,—and of obstinacy in a bad one.
1759–67 Toby. *Tristram Shandy*, bk.1, ch.17.

73 What is the character of a family to an hypothesis? my father would reply.
1759–67 *Tristram Shandy*, bk.1, ch.21.

74 My uncle Toby would never offer to answer this by any other kind of argument, than that of whistling half a dozen bars of Lillabullero.
1759–67 *Tristram Shandy*, bk.1, ch.21.

75 Digressions, incontestably, are the sunshine;—they are the life, the soul of reading;—take them out of this book for instance,—you might as well take the book along with them.
1759–67 *Tristram Shandy*, bk.1, ch.22.

76 I should have no objection to this method, but that I think

it must smell too strong of the lamp.
1759–67 Toby. *Tristram Shandy*, bk.1, ch.23.

77 Writing, when properly managed (as you may be sure I think mine is) is but a different name for conversation.
1759–67 *Tristram Shandy*, bk.2, ch.11.

78 'I'll not hurt thee,' says my uncle Toby, rising from his chair, and going across the room, with the fly in his hand, 'I'll not hurt a hair of thy head:—Go,' says he, lifting up the sash, and opening his hand as he spoke, to let it escape;—'go, poor devil, get thee gone, why should I hurt thee?—This world surely is wide enough to hold both thee and me.'
1759–67 *Tristram Shandy*, bk.2, ch.12.

79 Whenever a man talks loudly against religion,—always suspect that it is not his reason, but his passions which have got the better of his creed.
1759–67 Trim. *Tristram Shandy*, bk.2, ch.17.

80 It is the nature of an hypothesis, when once a man has conceived it, that it assimilates everything to itself, as proper nourishment; and, from the first moment of your begetting it, it generally grows the stronger by every thing you see, hear, read, or understand.
1759–67 *Tristram Shandy*, bk.2, ch.19.

81 'Our armies swore terribly in Flanders,' cried my uncle Toby,—'but nothing to this.'
1759–67 *Tristram Shandy*, bk.3, ch.11.

82 The corregiescity of Corregio.
1759–67 *Tristram Shandy*, bk.3, ch.12.

83 Of all the cants which are canted in this canting world,—though the cant of hypocrites may be the worst,—the cant of criticism is the most tormenting.
1759–67 *Tristram Shandy*, bk.3, ch.12.

84 Is this a fit time, said my father to himself, to talk of Pensions and Grenadiers?
1759–67 *Tristram Shandy*, bk.4, ch.5.

85 True *Shandeism*, think what you will against it, opens the heart and lungs, and like all those affections which partake of its nature, it forces the blood and other vital fluids of the body to run freely through its channels, and makes the wheel of life run long and cheerfully round.
1759–67 *Tristram Shandy*, bk.4, ch.32.

86 'There is no terror, brother Toby, in its looks, but what it borrows from groans and convulsions—and the blowing of noses, and the wiping away of tears with the bottoms of curtains, in a dying man's room—Strip it of these, what is it?'—'Tis better in battle than in bed,' said my uncle Toby.
1759–67 Of death. *Tristram Shandy*, bk.5, ch.3.

87 There is a North-west passage to the intellectual World.
1759–67 *Tristram Shandy*, bk.5, ch.42.

88 To say a man is fallen in love,—or that he is deeply in love,—or up to the ears in love,—and sometimes even over head and ears in it,—carries an idiomatical kind of implication, that love is a thing below a man:—this is recurring again to Plato's opinion, which, with all his divinityship,—I hold to be damnable and heretical:—and so much for that. Let love therefore be what it will,—my uncle Toby fell into it.
1759–67 *Tristram Shandy*, bk.6, ch.37.

89 My brother Toby, quoth she, is going to be married to Mrs Wadman. Then he will never, quoth my father, lie *diagonally* in his bed again as long as he lives.
1759–67 *Tristram Shandy*, bk.6, ch.39.

90 Now hang it! quoth I, as I look'd towards the French coast—a man should know something of his own country too, before he goes abroad.
1759–67 Tristram. *Tristram Shandy*, bk.7, ch.2.

91 And who are you? Said he.—Don't puzzle me, said I.
1759–67 Tristram to the commissary. *Tristram Shandy*, bk.7, ch.33.

92 'A soldier,' cried my uncle Toby, interrupting the corporal, 'is no more exempt from saying a foolish thing, Trim, than a man of letters.'—'But not so often, an' please your honour,' replied the corporal.
1759–67 *Tristram Shandy*, bk.8, ch.19.

93 Everything presses on—whilst thou art twisting that lock,—see! It grows grey; and every time I kiss thy hand to bid adieu, and every absence which follows it, are preludes to that eternal separation which we are shortly to make.
1759–67 Tristram to Jenny. *Tristram Shandy*, bk.9, ch.8.

94 '—d!' said my mother, 'what is all this story about?'—'A Cock and a Bull,' said Yorick.
1759–67 *Tristram Shandy*, bk.9, ch.33.

95 A man cannot dress, but his ideas get cloath'd at the same time.
1759–67 *Tristram Shandy*, bk.9, ch.13.

96 This sad vicissitude of things.
1767 *Sermons*, 'The Character of Shimei', no.16.

97 They order, said I, this matter better in France.
1768 *A Sentimental Journey*, opening words.

98 As an Englishman does not travel to see Englishmen, I retired to my room.
1768 *A Sentimental Journey*, 'Preface. In the Desobligeant'.

99 I pity the man who can travel from Dan to Beersheba, and cry, 'tis all barren.
1768 *A Sentimental Journey*, 'In the Street. Calais'.

1 I had had an affair with the moon, in which there was neither sin nor shame.
1768 *A Sentimental Journey*, 'The Monk, Calais'.

2 If ever I do a mean action, it must be in some interval betwixt one passion and another.
1768 *A Sentimental Journey*, 'Montriul'.

3 Vive l'amour! Et vive la bagatelle!
1768 *A Sentimental Journey*, 'The Latter'.

4 Hail, ye small sweet courtesies of life.
1768 *A Sentimental Journey*, 'The Pulse, Paris'.

5 There are worse occupations in this world than feeling a woman's pulse.
1768 *A Sentimental Journey*, 'The Pulse, Paris'.

6 God tempers the wind, said Maria, to the shorn lamb.
1768 *A Sentimental Journey*, 'Maria'. This is an allusion to an old French proverb.

7 Dear sensibility! Source inexhausted of all that's precious in our joys, or costly in our sorrows!
1768 *A Sentimental Journey*, 'The Bourbonnois'.

Steuart (later Denham), Sir James 1712–80

Scottish advocate and economist. A fervent Jacobite who was a member of the Council of Prince Charles Edward Stuart in 1745 and subsequently in exile until 1763, travelling extensively on the Continent and studying political economy. His *Principles of Political Oeconomy* (1767) was soon eclipsed by the *Wealth of Nations* of Adam Smith.

8 To preserve a trading state from decline, the greatest care must be taken, to support a perfect balance between the hands employed in work and the demand for their labour.
1767 *Inquiry into the Principles of Political Oeconomy.*

9 It is the business of a statesman to judge of the expediency of different schemes of economy, and by degrees to model the minds of his subjects so as to induce them from the allurement of private interest to concur in the execution of his plan.
1767 *Inquiry into the Principles of Political Oeconomy*

Stevens, Brooks 1911–95

US industrial designer.

10 Our whole economy is based on planned obsolescence… We make good products, we induce people to buy them, and then the next year we deliberately introduce something that will make these products old-fashioned, out of date, obsolete.
Quoted in Vance Packard *The Waste Makers* (1960), ch.6. This is thought to be the first use of the phrase 'planned obsolescence'.

Stevens, Roger Lacey 1910–98

US theatrical producer. He worked as a real estate broker (1934–60) but was increasingly involved as a producer in over 200 theatrical productions. He was Chair of the National Council on the Arts (1965–9), and a member of the President's Committee on Arts and Humanities.

11 Whenever I think, I make a mistake.
1955 In 'How Businessmen Make Decisions', *Fortune*, Aug

Stevens, Wallace 1879–1955

US poet. He began as a journalist and lawyer, then joined an insurance company. *Harmonium*, his first collection of philosophical verse, appeared in 1923. Further works include *The Man with the Blue Guitar* (1937) and *Collected Poems* (1954, winner of a Pulitzer Prize).

12 I placed a jar in Tennessee,
And round it was, upon a hill.
It made the slovenly wilderness
Surround that hill.
1923 *Harmonium*, 'Anecdote of the Jar'.

13 Poetry is the supreme fiction, madame.
Take the moral law and make a nave of it
And from the nave build haunted heaven.
1923 *Harmonium*, 'A High-Toned Old Christian Woman'.

14 Call the roller of big cigars,
The muscular one, and bid him whip
In kitchen cups of concupiscent curds.
1923 *Harmonium*, 'The Emperor of Ice-Cream'.

15 The only emperor is the emperor of ice-cream.
1923 *Harmonium*, 'The Emperor of Ice-Cream'.

16 I shall whisper
Heavenly labials in a world of gutterals.
It will undo him.
1923 *Harmonium*, 'The Plot Against the Giant'.

17 Complacencies of the peignoir, and late
Coffee and oranges in a sunny chair,
And the green freedom of a cockatoo
Upon a rug mingle to dissipate
The holy hush of ancient sacrifice.
1923 *Harmonium*, 'Sunday Morning', pt.1.

18 What is divinity if it can come
Only in silent shadows and in dreams?
1923 *Harmonium*, 'Sunday Morning', pt.2.

19 And, in the isolation of the sky,
At evening, casual flocks of pigeons make
Ambiguous undulations as they sink,
Downward to darkness, on extended wings.
1923 *Harmonium*, 'Sunday Morning', pt.8.

20 Chieftain Iffucan of Azcan in caftan
Of tan with henna hackles, halt!
1923 *Harmonium*, 'Bantams in Pine-Woods'.

21 Just as my fingers on these keys
Make music, so the self-same sounds
On my spirit make a music, too.

Music is feeling, then, not a sound;
And thus it is that what I feel,
Here in this room, desiring you,

Thinking of your blue-shadowed silk,
Is music.
1923 *Harmonium*, 'Peter Quince at the Clavier', pt.1.

22 I do not know which to prefer,
The beauty of inflections
Or the beauty of innuendoes,
The blackbird whistling
Or just after.
1923 *Harmonium*, 'Thirteen Ways of Looking At A Blackbird', pt.5.

23 I know noble accents
And lucid, inescapable rhythms;
But I know, too,
That the blackbird is involved
In what I know.
1923 *Harmonium*, 'Thirteen Ways of Looking At A Blackbird', pt.8.

24 What counted was the mythology of self,
Blotched out beyond unblotching.
1923 *Harmonium*, 'The Comedian as the Letter C', pt.1.

25 Like a dull scholar, I behold, in love,
An ancient aspect touching a new mind.
It comes, it blooms, it bears its fruit and dies.
This trivial trope reveals a way of truth.
Our bloom is gone. We are the fruit thereof.
1923 *Harmonium*, 'Le Monocle de Mon Oncle', pt.8.

26 Only, here and there, an old sailor,
Drunk and asleep in his boots,
Catches tigers
In red weather.
1923 *Harmonium*, 'Disillusionment of Ten O'Clock'.

27 It was her voice that made
The sky acutest at its vanishing.
She measured to the hour its solitude.
She was the single artificer of the world
In which she sang.
1935 *Ideas of Order*, 'The Idea of Order at Key West'.

28 They said, 'You have a blue guitar,
You do not play things as they are.'

The man replied, 'Things as they are
Are changed upon a blue guitar.'
1937 *The Man with the Blue Guitar and Other Poems*, title poem.

29 It has to be living, to learn the speech of the place,
It has to face the man of the time.
1942 *Parts of a World*, 'Of Modern Poetry'.

30 The first idea was not our own.
1942 *Notes Toward A Supreme Fiction*, 'It Must Be Abstract'.

31 There was a muddy centre before we breathed
There was a myth before the myth began,
Venerable and articulate and complete.
1942 *Notes Toward A Supreme Fiction*, 'It Must Be Abstract'.

32 They will get it straight one day at the Sorbonne.
We shall return at twilight from the lecture
Pleased that the irrational is rational.
1942 *Notes Toward A Supreme Fiction*, 'It Must Give Pleasure'.

33 Not evocations but last choirs, last sounds,
With nothing else compounded, carried full,
Pure rhetoric of a language without words.
1947 *Transport to Summer*, 'Credences of Summer'.

34 Sentimentality is a failure of feeling.
1957 *Opus Posthumous*, Aphorisms, 'Adagia'.

35 Poetry is a means of redemption.
1957 *Opus Posthumous*, Aphorisms, 'Adagia'.

36 Literature is based not on life but on propositions about life, of which this is one.
1957 *Opus Posthumous*, Aphorisms, 'Adagia'.

37 Poetry must resist the intelligence almost successfully.
1957 *Opus Posthumous*, Aphorisms, 'Adagia'.

38 All poetry is experimental poetry.
1957 *Opus Posthumous*, Aphorisms, 'Adagia'.

39 Ethics are no more a part of poetry than they are of painting.
1957 *Opus Posthumous*, Aphorisms, 'Adagia'.

40 The poet makes silk dresses out of worms.
1957 *Opus Posthumous*, Aphorisms, 'Adagia'.

41 After one has abandoned a belief in God, poetry is the essence which takes its place as life's redemption.
1957 *Opus Posthumous*, Aphorisms, 'Adagia'.

42 Authors are actors, books are theatres.
1957 *Opus Posthumous*, Aphorisms, 'Adagia'.

43 The poet represents the mind in the act of defending us against itself.
1957 *Opus Posthumous*, Aphorisms, 'Adagia'.

44 Poetry is a rich, full-blooded whistle, cracked ice crunching in pails, the night that numbers the leaf, the duet of two nightingales, the sweet pea, that has run wild, Creation's tears in shoulder blades.
Quoted in *Life*, 13 Jun 1960.

45 Money is a kind of poetry.
Quoted in *Harper's*, Oct 1985.

46 Words of the world are the life of the world.
Quoted in Brendan Gill *A New York Life* (1990).

47 Poetry is the supreme fiction, madame.
Quoted in Helen Gardner (ed) *The New Oxford Book of English Verse* (1991).

Stevenson, Adlai E(wing) 1900–65

US Democratic politician, Governor of Illinois (1948). He helped to found the United Nations (1946), stood twice against Eisenhower as presidential candidate (1952, 1956), and was the US Delegate to the UN (1961–5).

48 A lie is an abomination unto the Lord, and a very present help when in trouble.
1951 Speech, Washington, Jan.

49 It is often easier to fight for principles than to live up to them.
1952 Speech, New York, 27 Aug.

50 If Republicans will stop telling lies about the United States, we will stop telling the truth about them.
1952 Speech at Bakersfield, California. Quoted in *Time*, 10 Sep.

51 Looking back, I am content. Win or lose I have told you the truth as I see it. I have said what I meant and meant what I said.
1952 Concluding his campaign. Reported in *Time*, 10 Sep.

52 Man has wrested from nature the power to make the world a desert or to make the deserts bloom. There is no evil in the atom—only in men's souls.
1952 Speech, Connecticut, 18 Sep.

53 When political ammunition runs low, inevitably the rusty artillery of abuse is wheeled into action.
1952 Speech, New York, 22 Sep.

54 My definition of a free society is a society in which it is safe to be unpopular.
1952 Speech, Detroit, Oct.

55 Eggheads of the world unite; you have nothing to lose but your yolks.
1952 Presidential election campaign speech.

56 Via ovum cranium difficilis est. The way of the egghead is hard.
1954 Reply to charges that he was too intellectual. Lecture at Harvard, 17 Mar.

57 Shouting is not a substitute for thinking and reason is not the subversion but the salvation of freedom.
1954 Lecture at Harvard, 17 Mar.

58 Technology, while adding daily to our physical ease, throws daily another loop of fine wire around our souls. It contributes hugely to our mobility, which we must not confuse with freedom. The extensions of our senses, which we find so fascinating, are not adding to the discrimination of our minds, since we need increasingly to take the reading of a needle on a dial to discover whether we think something is good or bad, or right or wrong.
1955 'My Faith in Democratic Capitalism', in *Fortune*, Oct.

59 You will find that the truth is often unpopular and the contest between agreeable fancy and disagreeable fact is unequal. For, in the vernacular, we Americans are suckers for good news.
1958 Speech, Michigan, 8 Jun.

60 Freedom is not an ideal; it is not even a protection, if it means nothing more than the freedom to stagnate.
1960 *Putting First Things First.*

61 We have confused the free with the free and easy.
1960 *Putting First Things First.*

62 The Republican Party needs to be dragged kicking and screaming into the 20th century.
Quoted in Kenneth Tynan *Curtains* (1961).

63 It will be helpful in our mutual objective to allow every

man in America to look his neighbour in the face and see a man—not a colour.
1964 In the *New York Times*, 22 Jun.

64 He who slings mud generally loses ground.
Recalled on his death, 14 Jul 1965.

65 You can't teach an underdog new tricks.
On presidential hopeful Estes Kefauver's replay of his anti-bossism theme. Quoted in *Newsweek*, 1 Nov 1971.

66 The best politics is good government.
Quoted by New York Governor Mario Cuomo in the *New York Times*, 26 Aug 1990.

67 A politician is a statesman who approaches every question with an open mouth.
Attributed.

68 He is the kind of politician who would cut down a redwood tree and then mount the stump to make a speech for conservation.
On Richard M Nixon. Attributed.

69 In America, any boy may become president. I suppose that's just one of the risks that he takes.
Attributed.

Stevenson, Robert Louis 1850–94

Scottish author. He wrote travel sketches, essays, short stories, serials and romantic thrillers, including *Treasure Island* (1883), *The Strange Case of Dr Jekyll and Mr Hyde* (1886) and *Kidnapped* (1886). In his early years he toured Belgium and northern France by canoe and the Cévennes by donkey, described in *Travels with a Donkey in the Cévennes* (1879). He struggled for many years against tuberculosis and spent the last five years of his life living on his estate in Samoa.

70 For will anyone dare to tell me that business is more entertaining than fooling among boats? He must have never seen a boat, or never seen an office, who says so. And for certain the one is a great deal better for the health.
1878 *An Inland Voyage*, 'The Royal Sport Nautique'.

71 Respectability is a very good thing in its way, but it does not rise superior to all considerations. I would not for a moment venture to hint that it was a matter of taste; but I think I will go as far as this: that if a position is admittedly unkind, uncomfortable, unnecessary, and superfluously useless, although it were as respectable as the Church of England, the sooner a man is out of it, the better for himself, and all concerned.
1878 *An Inland Voyage*, 'At Maubeuge'.

72 The gauger walked with willing foot,
And aye the gauger played the flute;
And what should Master Gauger play
But *Over the hills and far away*?
1878 'A Song of the Road', stanza 1 (dated 'Forest of Montargis, 1878'), collected in *Underwoods* (1887), bk.1, no.2.

73 If a man knows he will sooner or later be robbed upon a journey, he will have a bottle of the best in every inn, and look upon all his extravagances as so much gained upon the thieves.
1878 *An Inland Voyage*, 'The Oise in Flood'.

74 The most patient people grow weary at last with being continually wetted with rain; except, of course, in the Scottish Highlands, where there are not enough fine intervals to point the difference.
1878 *An Inland Voyage*, 'Down the Oise: to Compiègne'.

75 For my part, I travel not to go anywhere, but to go. I travel for travel's sake. The great affair is to move.
1879 *Travels with a Donkey*, 'Cheylard and Luc'.

76 I opened a tin of Bologna sausage and broke a cake of chocolate, and that was all I had to eat. It may sound offensive, but I ate them together, bite by bite, by way of bread and meat. All I had to wash down this revolting mixture was neat brandy; a revolting beverage in itself. But I was rare and hungry; ate well, and smoked one of the best cigarettes in my experience. Then I put a stone in my straw hat, pulled the flap of my fur cap over my neck and eyes, put my revolver ready to hand, and snuggled well down among the sheepskins.
1879 *Travels with a Donkey.*

77 I own I like definite form in what my eyes are to rest upon; and if landscapes were sold, like the sheets of characters of my boyhood, one penny plain and twopence coloured, I should go the length of twopence every day of my life.
1879 *Travels with a Donkey*, 'Father Apollinaris'.

78 To live out of doors with the woman a man loves is of all lives the most complete and free.
1879 *Travels with a Donkey*, 'A Night Among the Pines'.

79 The fact is, we are much more afraid of life than our ancestors, and cannot find it in our hearts either to marry or not to marry. Marriage is terrifying, but so is a cold and forlorn old age.
1881 *Virginibus Puerisque*, 'Virginibus Puerisque', pt.1.

80 In marriage, a man becomes slack and selfish, and undergoes a fatty degeneration of his moral being.
1881 *Virginibus Puerisque*, 'Virginibus Puerisque', pt.1.

81 I see women marry indiscriminately with staring burgesses and ferret-faced, white-eyed boys, and men dwell in contentment with noisy scullions, or taking into their lives acidulous vestals.
1881 *Virginibus Puerisque*, 'Virginibus Puerisque', pt.1.

82 And you have only to look these happy couples in the face, to see they have never been in love, or in hate, or in any other high passion all their days.
1881 *Virginibus Puerisque*, 'Virginibus Puerisque', pt.1.

83 Even if we take marriage at its lowest, even if we regard it as no more than a sort of friendship recognised by the police.
1881 *Virginibus Puerisque*, 'Virginibus Puerisque', pt.1.

84 Lastly (and this is, perhaps, the golden rule) no woman should marry a teetotaller, or a man who does not smoke.
1881 *Virginibus Puerisque*, 'Virginibus Puerisque', pt.1.

85 Marriage is a step so grave and decisive that it attracts light-headed, variable men by its very awfulness.
1881 *Virginibus Puerisque*, 'Virginibus Puerisque', pt.1.

86 Marriage is like life in this—that it is a field of battle, and not a bed of roses.
1881 *Virginibus Puerisque*, 'Virginibus Puerisque', pt.1.

87 Times are changed with him who marries; there are no more by-path meadows, where you may innocently linger, but the road lies long and straight and dusty to the grave. Idleness, which is often becoming and even wise in the bachelor, begins to wear a different aspect when

you have a wife to support.
1881 *Virginibus Puerisque*, 'Virginibus Puerisque', pt.2.

88 To marry is to domesticate the Recording Angel. Once you are married, there is nothing left for you, not even suicide, but to be good.
1881 *Virginibus Puerisque*, 'Virginibus Puerisque', pt.2.

89 Man is a creature who lives not upon bread alone, but principally by catchwords.
1881 *Virginibus Puerisque*, 'Virginibus Puerisque', pt.2.

90 The cruellest lies are often told in silence.
1881 *Virginibus Puerisque*, 'Truth of Intercourse'.

91 Most of our pocket wisdom is conceived for the use of mediocre people, to discourage them from ambitious attempts, and generally console them in their mediocrity.
1881 *Virginibus Puerisque*, 'Crabbed Age and Youth'.

92 Old and young, we are all on our last cruise.
1881 *Virginibus Puerisque*, 'Crabbed Age and Youth'.

93 It is better to be a fool than to be dead.
1881 *Virginibus Puerisque*, 'Crabbed Age and Youth'.

94 For God's sake give me the young man who has brains enough to make a fool of himself!
1881 *Virginibus Puerisque*, 'Crabbed Age and Youth'.

95 To travel hopefully is a better thing than to arrive, and the true success is to labour.
1881 *Virginibus Puerisque*, 'El Dorado'.

96 Books are good enough in their own way, but they are a mighty bloodless substitute for life.
1881 *Virginibus Puerisque*, 'An Apology for Idlers'.

97 Extreme *busyness*, whether at school or college, kirk or market, is a symptom of a deficient vitality; and a faculty for idleness implies a catholic appetite and a strong sense of personal identity.
1881 *Virginibus Puerisque*, 'An Apology for Idlers'.

98 There is no duty we so much underrate as the duty of being happy.
1881 *Virginibus Puerisque*, 'An Apology for Idlers'.

99 We live the time that a match flickers; we pop the cork of a ginger-beer bottle, and the earthquake swallows us on the instant. Is it not odd, is it not incongruous, is it not, in the highest sense of human speech, incredible, that we should think so highly of the ginger-beer, and regard so little the devouring earthquake?
1881 *Virginibus Puerisque*, 'Aes Triplex'.

1 Think of the heroism of Johnson, think of that superb indifference to mortal limitation that set him upon his dictionary, and carried him through triumphantly until the end! Who, if he were wisely considerate of things at large, would ever embark upon any work much more considerable than a halfpenny post-card? Who would project a serial novel, after Thackeray and Dickens had each fallen in mid-course? Who would find heart enough to begin to live, if he dallied with the consideration of death?
1881 *Virginibus Puerisque*, 'Aes Triplex'.

2 Even if the doctor does not give you a year, even if he hesitates about a month, make one brave push and see what can be accomplished in a week.
1881 *Virginibus Puerisque*, 'Aes Triplex'.

3 Though we are mighty fine fellows nowadays, we cannot write like Hazlitt.
1881 *Virginibus Puerisque*, 'Walking Tours'.

4 We are in such haste to be doing, to be writing, to be gathering gear, to make our voice audible a moment in the derisive silence of eternity, that we forget that one thing, of which these are but the parts—namely, to live.
1881 *Virginibus Puerisque*, 'Walking Tours'.

5 It seems he had no design except to appear respectable, and here he keeps a private book to prove that he was not.
1882 Of Samuel Pepys and his *Diary. Familiar Studies of Men and Books*.

6 Politics is perhaps the only profession for which no preparation is thought necessary.
1882 *Familiar Studies of Men and Books*, 'Yoshida-Torajiro'.

7 Fifteen men on a dead man's chest—
Yo-ho-ho, and a bottle of rum!
Drink and the devil had done for the rest—
Yo-ho-ho, and a bottle of rum!
1883 *Treasure Island*, ch.1, 'The Old Sea-Dog at the 'Admiral Benbow''.

8 Pieces of eight!
1883 *Treasure Island*, ch.10, 'The Voyage'.

9 You mightn't happen to have a piece of cheese about you, now? No? Well, many's the long night I've dreamed of cheese—toasted, mostly—and woke up again, and here I were.
1883 Ben Gunn to Jim Hawkins. *Treasure Island*, ch.15, 'The Man of the Island'.

10 Under the wide and starry sky,
Dig the grave and let me lie.
Glad did I live and gladly die,
And I laid me down with a will.

This be the verse you grave for me:
Here he lies where he longed to be,
Home is the sailor, home from sea,
And the hunter home from the hill.
1884 'Requiem' (dated 'Hyères, May 1884'), collected in *Underwoods* (1887), bk.1, no.21.

11 In winter I get up at night
And dress by yellow candle-light.
In summer, quite the other way,
I have to go to bed by day.

I have to go to bed and see
The birds still hopping on the tree,
Or hear the grown-up people's feet
Still going past me in the street.
1885 *A Child's Garden of Verses*, no.1, 'Bed in Summer', stanzas 1–2.

12 A child should always say what's true,
And speak when he is spoken to,
And behave mannerly at table:
At least as far as he is able.
1885 *A Child's Garden of Verses*, no.5, 'Whole Duty of Children'.

13 Whenever the moon and stars are set,
Whenever the wind is high,
All night long in the dark and wet,
A man goes riding by.
Late in the night when the fires are out,
Why does he gallop and gallop about?
1885 *A Child's Garden of Verses*, no.9, 'Windy Nights', stanza 1.

14 When I am grown to man's estate
I shall be very proud and great,
And tell the other girls and boys
Not to meddle with my toys.
1885 *A Child's Garden of Verses*, no.12, 'Looking Forward'.

15 Whenever Auntie moves around,
Her dresses make a curious sound;
They trail behind her up the floor,
And trundle after through the door.
1885 *A Child's Garden of Verses*, no.15, 'Auntie's Skirts'.

16 When I was sick and lay a-bed,
I had two pillows at my head,
And all my toys beside me lay
To keep me happy all the day.
1885 *A Child's Garden of Verses*, no.16, 'The Land of Counterpane', stanza 1.

17 I have a little shadow that goes in and out with me,
And what can be the use of him is more than I can see.
1885 *A Child's Garden of Verses*, no.18, 'My Shadow', stanza 1.

18 The world is so full of a number of things,
I'm sure we should all be as happy as kings.
1885 *A Child's Garden of Verses*, no.24, 'Happy Thought'.

19 Children, you are very little,
And your bones are very brittle;
If you would grow great and stately,
You must try to walk sedately.
1885 *A Child's Garden of Verses*, no.27, 'Good and Bad Children', stanza 1.

20 My tea is nearly ready and the sun has left the sky;
It's time to take the window to see Leerie going by;
For every night at tea-time and before you take your seat,
With lantern and with ladder he comes posting up the street.
1885 *A Child's Garden of Verses*, no.30, 'The Lamplighter', stanza 1.

21 Must we to bed indeed? Well then,
Let us arise and go like men,
And face with an undaunted tread
The long black passage up to bed.
1885 *A Child's Garden of Verses*, XLI, 'North-West Passage', pt.1, 'Good Night', stanza 3.

22 In the Land of Nod at last.
1885 *A Child's Garden of Verses*, XLI, 'North-West Passage', pt.3, 'In Port', stanza 3.

23 Am I no a bonny fighter?
1886 Alan Breck to David Balfour. *Kidnapped*, ch.10.

24 Even though his tongue acquire the Southern knack, he will still have a strong Scots accent of the mind.
1887 *Memories and Portraits*, ch.1, 'The Foreigner at Home'.

25 I have thus played the sedulous ape to Hazlitt, to Lamb, to Wordsworth, to Sir Thomas Browne, to Defoe, to Hawthorne, to Montaigne, to Baudelaire and to Obermann.
1887 *Memories and Portraits*, ch.4, 'A College Magazine'

26 Every one lives by selling something, whatever be his right to it.
1888 'Beggars', originally published in *Scribner's Magazine*.

27 Here lies one who meant well, tried a little, failed much:—surely that may be his epitaph, of which he need not be ashamed.
1892 *Across the Plains*, 'A Christmas Sermon', pt.4.

28 The bright face of danger.
1892 *Across the Plains*, 'The Lantern-Bearers', pt.4.

29 Life is not all Beer and Skittles. The inherent tragedy of things works itself out from white to black and blacker, and the poor things of a day look ruefully on. Does it shake my cast-iron faith? I cannot say it does. I believe in an ultimate decency of things: ay, and if I woke in hell, should still believe it!
1893 Letter to Sidney Colvin, 23 Aug.

30 Give to me the life I love,
Let the lave go by me,
Give the jolly heaven above
And the byway nigh me.
Bed in the bush with the stars to see,
Bread I dip in the river—
There's the life for a man like me,
There's the life for ever.
1894 *Songs of Travel* (published 1896), no.1, 'The Vagabond', stanza 1.

31 Wealth I ask not, hope nor love,
Nor a friend to know me.
All I ask, the heaven above,
And the road below me.
1894 *Songs of Travel* (published 1896), no.1, 'The Vagabond', stanza 4.

32 I will make you brooches and toys for your delight
Of bird-song at morning and star-shine at night.
I will make a palace fit for you and me
Of green days in forests and blue days at sea.
I will make my kitchen, and you shall keep your room,
Where white flows the river and bright blows the broom,
And you shall wash your linen and keep your body white
In rainfall at morning and dewfall at night.
1894 *Songs of Travel* (published 1896), no.11, stanza 1.

33 In the highlands, in the country places,
Where the old plain men have rosy faces,
And the young fair maidens
Quiet eyes.
1894 *Songs of Travel* (published 1896), no.16.

34 Trusty, dusky, vivid, true,
With eyes of gold and bramble-dew,
Steel-true and blade-straight,
The great artificer
Made my mate.
1894 *Songs of Travel* (published 1896), 'My Wife'.

35 Blows the wind to-day, and the sun and the rain are flying,
Blows the wind on the moors to-day and now,
Where about the graves of the martyrs the whaups are crying,
My heart remembers how!
1894 *Songs of Travel* (published 1896), no.45, 'To S.R. Crockett (in reply to a dedication)', stanza 1.

36 Be it granted to me to behold you again in dying,
Hills of home! and to hear again the call;
Hear about the graves of the martyrs the peeweets crying,
And hear no more at all.
1894 *Songs of Travel* (published 1896), no.45, 'To S.R. Crockett (in reply to a dedication)', stanza 3.

37 And all that I could think of, in the darkness and the cold,

Was just that I was leaving home and my folks were growing old.
1894 'Christmas at Sea', stanza 11.

38 I saw rain falling and the rainbow drawn
On Lammermuir. Hearkening I heard again
In my precipitous city beaten bells
Winnow the keen sea wind. And here afar,
Intent on my own race and place, I wrote.
1894 *Weir of Hermiston* (published 1896), Dedication 'To My Wife'.

39 It seemed unprovoked, a wilful convulsion of brute nature…
1894 *Weir of Hermiston* (published 1896), ch.9, 'At the Weaver's Stone'. These are the last words of the unfinished novel, dictated by Stevenson on the morning of his death from a blood-clot on the brain.

40 The *bourgeoisie's* weapon is starvation. If as a writer or artist you run counter to their narrow notions they simply and silently withdraw your means of subsistence. I sometimes wonder how many people of talent are executed in this way every year.
Quoted by Lloyd Osbourne in 'The Death of Stevenson', preface to Tusitala edition of *Weir of Hermiston* (published 1924).

41 The saddest object in civilization, and to my mind the greatest confession of its failure, is the man who can work, who wants work, and who is not allowed to work.
Quoted by Lloyd Osbourne in 'The Death of Stevenson', preface to Tusitala edition of *Weir of Hermiston* (published 1924).

Stewart, John Innes Mackintosh 1906–94

Scots-born academic, author and critic, Chair of Literature at Adelaide University (1935–45). His sequence of novels on life at Oxford, *A Staircase in Surrey*, began in 1974 with *The Gaudy*. As 'Michael Innes' he wrote erudite detective novels.

42 I am most grateful to the CLF [Commonwealth Literary Fund] for providing the funds to give these lectures in Australian literature, but unfortunately they have neglected to provide any literature. I will lecture therefore on D H Lawrence's 'Kangaroo'.
1940 Quoted in the *London Magazine*, Nov 1985.

43 On the platform stood a policeman of normal proportions, and instead of a revolver and a truncheon he carried a copy of *Ben Hur* translated into Irish, which he was evidently studying for an examination important to his professional advancement. Mr Thewless realised that the imperial might of Great Britain lay behind him and that in front was the philosophic republic of Mr de Valera.
1949 *The Journeying Boy.*

44 'In about half a mile you cross the river by an Irish bridge—'
'Whatever is that?'
'It's just a bridge, but built under the water instead of over it.'
'Extremely sensible.'
1969 *A Family Affair.*

Stigler, George Joseph 1911–91

US economist, University of Chicago; awarded a Nobel prize (1982).

45 The branch of economics dealing with how to enrich a new nation ('economic development' was the title) was actually forbidden by the courts, on the grounds that no university could pay for the damage its teachers did.
1973 'The History of Truth in Teaching', in *The Intellectual and the Marketplace* (1984).

Still, Bayrd 1906–92

US historian and archivist.

46 The tombstone of capitalism…with windows.
1956 Of the Rockefeller Center. *Mirror for Gotham.*

Stilwell, General Joseph 1883–1946

US general, commander in the Far East during World War II, who led the successful attack against the Japanese in Myanmar (1943–4). His acerbic manner earned him the nickname of 'Vinegar Joe'.

47 This little book contains none of your damn business.
Note on flyleaf of 1906 diary. Quoted in Barbara Tuchman *General Stilwell and the American Experience in China* (1970).

Stinchcombe, Arthur S 1933–

US sociologist, University of Chicago.

48 The question of how to apply social theory to historical materials, as it is usually posed, is ridiculous. One does not apply theory to history; rather one uses history to develop theory.
1978 *Theoretical Methods in Social History*, p.1.

Sting *originally* ***Gordon Matthew Sumner*** 1951–

English singer-songwriter and actor, also known as a campaigner to save Brazilian rainforests.

49 If I were a Brazilian without land or money or the means to feed my children, I would be burning the rainforest too.
1989 In the *International Herald Tribune*, 14 Apr.

Stipe, Michael 1960–

US singer and songwriter, member of the band REM.

50 Everybody hurts sometimes
Everybody cries
1992 'Everybody Hurts' (co-written by members of REM).

51 We don't get groupies. We get teenagers who want to read us their poetry.
1994 In *Q*, 1 Sep.

52 There is always something of the writer in the work but I don't think Melville had to be swallowed by a whale to write a great novel. If I had lived the lives of all the characters of the songs I've written, that would truly be an extraordinary story.
2001 In the *Daily Telegraph*, 20 Oct.

Stockwood, (Arthur) Mervyn 1913–95

English cleric. As Bishop of Southwark (1959–80) he was renowned for his liberal writings on the uniformity of faith and the communality of belief.

53 A psychiatrist is a man who goes to the Folies-Bergère and looks at the audience.
1961 In the *Observer*, 15 Oct.

Stoker, Bram 1847–1912

Irish writer best remembered for the classic vampire story *Dracula* (1897).

54 The mouth, so far as I could see it under the heavy moustache, was fixed and rather cruel-looking, with peculiarly sharp white teeth; these protuded over the lips, whose remarkable ruddiness showed astonishing vitality in a man of his years.
1897 Describing Count Dracula. *Dracula*, ch.2.

Stokowski, Leopold *pseudonym of* ***Antoni Stanislaw Boleslawowich*** 1882–1977

US conductor of Polish origin. He built up an international reputation as conductor of the Philadelphia Symphony Orchestra (1912–36), the New York Philharmonic (1946–50) and the Houston Symphony Orchestra (1955–60). He also worked in films and founded the American Symphony Orchestra in New York in 1962.

55 Musicians paint their pictures on silence—we provide the music, and you provide the silence.
Addressing an audience at Carnegie Hall. Quoted in Derek Watson *Music Quotations* (1991).

Stone, Robert Anthony 1937–

US novelist and screenwriter. His best-known book is the novel *Dog Soldiers* (1974).

56 People are getting to be a disgrace to the planet.
1982 *A Flag for Sunrise*, ch.6.

Stone, Samuel John 1839–1900

English cleric and hymnwriter

57 The Church's one foundation
Is Jesus Christ, her Lord;
She is his new creation
By water and the word;
From heaven he came and sought her
To be his holy bride,
With his own blood he bought her.
And for her life he died.
1866 *Lyra fidelium*.

Stopes, Marie 1880–1958

British birth-control pioneer and palaeobotanist.

58 An impersonal and scientific knowledge of the structure of our bodies is the surest safeguard against prurient curiosity and lascivious gloating.
1918 *Married Love*, ch.5.

59 Each coming together of a man and wife, even if they have been mated for many years, should be a fresh adventure; each winning should necessitate a fresh wooing.
1918 *Married Love*, ch.10.

Stoppard, Sir Tom *originally* ***Tom Straussler*** 1937–

Czech-born British dramatist. After writing for radio, he made his name with *Rosencrantz and Guildenstern are Dead* (1967) at the Edinburgh Festival. Other plays include the philosophical satire *Jumpers* (1972), *Travesties* (1974) and *Arcadia* (1993). He shared an Academy Award with Marc Norman for the screenplay of *Shakespeare in Love* (1998).

60 The House of Lords, an illusion to which I have never been able to subscribe—responsibility without power, the prerogative of the eunuch throughout the ages.
1966 *Lord Malquist and Mr Moon*, pt.6.
► *See Baldwin 54:46.*

61 To sum up: your father, whom you love, dies, you are his heir, you come back to find that hardly was the corpse cold before his younger brother popped on to his throne and into his sheets, thereby offending both legal and natural practice. Now why exactly are you behaving in this extraordinary manner.
1967 To Hamlet. *Rosencrantz and Guildenstern are Dead*, act 1.

62 Sometimes I dream of revolution, a bloody *coup d'état* by the second rank—troupes of actors slaughtered by their understudies, magicians sawn in half by indefatigably smiling glamour girls, cricket teams wiped out by marauding bands of twelfth men.
1968 *The Real Inspector Hound*.

63 It's not the voting that's democracy; it's the counting.
1972 *Jumpers*.

64 War is capitalism with the gloves off.
1974 *Travesties*.

65 I learned three things in Zurich during the war… Firstly you're either a revolutionary or you're not, and if you're not you might as well be an artist as anything else. Secondly, if you can't be an artist, you might as well be a revolutionary… I forget the third thing.
1974 *Travesties*, final lines.

66 Maybe Napoleon was wrong when he said we were a nation of shopkeepers… Today England looked like a nation of goalkeepers.
1977 *Professional Foul*.
► *See Napoleon 607:68.*

67 Ambushing the audience is what theatre is all about.
1984 In *Newsweek*, 16 Jan.

68 I don't think I can be expected to take seriously a game which takes less than three days to reach its conclusion.
1984 Of baseball. In *The Guardian*, 24 Dec.

69 We're better at predicting events at the edge of the galaxy or inside the nucleus of an atom than whether it'll rain on auntie's garden party three Sundays from now.
1993 *Arcadia*.

Storr, Robert 1949–

US art administrator, curator of painting and sculpture at the Museum of Modern Art. His writings include *Philip Guston* (1986).

70 It's a letting go of distances.
1995 On the necessity of establishing an intimacy and trust between artist and sitter. In the *New York Times*, 1 Jan.

Stowe, Harriet (Elizabeth) *née* ***Beecher*** 1811–96

US novelist. Her novel *Uncle Tom's Cabin* (1852) was written in anger after the passage of the Fugitive Slave Law. She caused a furore with *Lady Byron Vindicated* (1870) in which she accused Byron of having an incestuous relationship with his sister.

71 What makes saintliness in my view, as distinguished from ordinary goodness, is a certain quality of magnanimity and greatness of soul that brings life within the circle of the heroic.

1846 'The Cathedral', in the *Atlantic Monthly*, Dec.

72 So long as the law considers all these human beings, with beating hearts and living affections, only as so many *things* belonging to the master—so long as the failure, or misfortune, or imprudence, or death of the kindest owner, may cause them any day to exchange a life of kind protection and indulgence for one of hopeless misery and toil—so long is it impossible to make anything beautiful or desirable in the best-regulated administration of slavery.
1852 *Uncle Tom's Cabin*, ch.1.

73 I've got just as much conscience as any man in business can afford to keep,—just a little, you know, to swear by, as 't were.
1852 *Uncle Tom's Cabin*, ch.1.

74 'Do you know who made you?'
'Nobody, as I knows on,' said the child... I 'spect I grow'd. Don't think nobody never made me.'
1852 *Uncle Tom's Cabin*, ch.20. The child is Topsy.

75 Whipping and abuse are like laudanum; you have to double the dose as the sensibilities decline.
1852 *Uncle Tom's Cabin*, ch.20.

76 The longest day must have its close,—the gloomiest night will wear on to a morning. An eternal, inexorable lapse of moments is ever hurrying the day of the evil to an eternal night, and the night of the just to an eternal day.
1852 *Uncle Tom's Cabin*, ch.40.

77 The bitterest tears shed over graves are for words left unsaid and deeds left undone.
1865 *Little Foxes*, ch.3.

78 The obstinancy of cleverness and reason is nothing to the obstinancy of folly and inanity.
1865 *Little Foxes*, ch.4.

Strachey, (Evelyn) John 1901–63

British writer and political leader.

79 If socialists lose sight of the central importance of social ownership of the means of production, they will cease, in a very real sense, to be socialists at all: they will subside into the role of well-intentioned, amiable, rootless, drifting social reformers.
1956 *Contemporary Capitalism*.

Strachey, (Giles) Lytton 1880–1932

English writer. He is best known for his biographies, especially *Eminent Victorians* (1918), which challenged established concepts of the Victorian age.

80 The history of the Victorian age will never be written: we know too much about it. For ignorance is the first requisite of the historian—ignorance, which simplifies and clarifies, which selects and omits, with a placid perfection unattainable by the highest art.
1918 *Eminent Victorians*, preface.

81 The time was out of joint, and he was only too delighted to have been born to set it right.
1918 Of Hurrell Froude. *Eminent Victorians*, 'Cardinal Manning'.

82 'Before she came,' said a soldier, 'there was cussin' and swearin', but after that it was 'oly as a church.' The most cherished privilege of the fighting man was abandoned for the sake of Miss Nightingale.
1918 *Eminent Victorians*, 'Florence Nightingale'.

83 Yet her conception of God was certainly not orthodox. She felt towards Him as she might have felt towards a glorified sanitary engineer; and in some of her speculations she seems hardly to distinguish between the Deity and the Drains.
1918 *Eminent Victorians*, 'Florence Nightingale'.

84 His legs, perhaps, were shorter than they should have been.
1918 *Eminent Victorians*, 'Dr Arnold'.

85 Johnson's aesthetic judgements are almost invariably subtle, or solid, or bold; they have always some good quality to recommend them—except one: they are never right.
1922 On Samuel Johnson. *Books and Characters*, 'Lives of the Poets'.

86 Asked by the chairman the usual question: 'I understand, Mr Strachey, that you have a conscientious objection to war?' he replied (in his curious falsetto voice), 'Oh no, not at all, only to *this* war.' Better than this was his reply to the chairman's other stock question, which had previously never failed to embarrass the claimant. 'Tell me, Mr Strachey, what would you do if you saw a German soldier trying to violate your sister?' With an air of noble virtue: 'I would try to get between them.'
On his appearance before a military tribunal, in Robert Graves *Goodbye To All That* (1929), ch.23.

87 If this is dying, then I don't think much of it.
1932 Last words, attributed.

Strafford, Thomas Wentworth, 1st Earl of 1593–1641

English statesman. As Lord Deputy of Ireland from 1632 he imposed firm rule, and in 1639 became the King's principal adviser. After failing to suppress the rebellion in Scotland (1639–40), he was impeached by the Long Parliament and executed despite a famous defence.

88 Divide not between Protestant and Papist. Divide not nationally, betwixt English and Irish. The King makes no distinction betwixt you.
1634 To the Irish Parliament, 15 Jul.

89 I would desire that every man would lay his hand on his heart, and consider seriously whether the beginnings of the people's happiness should be written in letters of blood.
1641 At his execution on Tower Hill, 12 May.

Stravinsky, Igor Fedorovich 1882–1971

Russian composer, who achieved fame with his ballet *The Firebird* (1910). Other ballets include *Petrushka* (1911) and the innovative *Rite of Spring* (1913). Among his significant later works are *The Soldier's Tale* (1918), *Orpheus* (1948, using the 12-tone system), *Oedipus Rex* (1927) and the opera *The Rake's Progress* (1951). He lived in France from 1934 and finally settled in the US (1945).

90 My music is best understood by children and animals.
1961 In the *Observer*, 8 Oct.

91 The most perfect of Swiss clockmakers.
Of Ravel. Quoted in R Nichols *Ravel* (1977).

Streeton, Sir Arthur Ernest 1867–1943

Australian landscape painter, one of the founders of the

influential Heidelberg School and a contributor to the *9x5 Impression Exhibition* (1889), Australia's first Impressionist exhibition. He was official war artist in France in World War I.

92 Nature's scheme of colour in Australia is gold and blue.
Quoted in William Moore *The Story of Australian Art* (1934), vol. 1.

Streisand, Barbra 1942–

US actress, director and bestselling singer.

93 We elected a President, not a Pope.
1998 Referring to Bill Clinton. To journalists at the White House, 5 Feb.

Strindberg, August 1849–1912

Swedish dramatist and novelist, regarded as Sweden's greatest modern writer.

94 Family!... the home of all social evil, a charitable institution for comfortable women, an anchorage for house-fathers, and a hell for children.
1886 *The Son of a Servant*.

Strong, L(eonard) A(lfred) G(eorge) 1896–1958

English novelist and poet.

95 Have I a wife? Bedam I have! But we was badly mated.
I hit her a great clout one night And now we're separated.
And mornin's going to me work I meets her on the quay:
'Good mornin' to you, ma'am!' says I, 'To hell with ye!'
says she.
1921 *Dublin Days*, 'The Brewer's Man'.

Stuart, Francis 1902–2000

Australian-born Irish novelist and poet. He was interned by the Free State government as an Irish republican (1922–3), and by the Germans during World War II after he taught at Berlin University. He later lived and wrote in Paris, London and Ireland.

96 Those are old patterns, faded and bleached in the glare of the pressing present moments in the story.
'Jacob: An Episode from a Theme Based upon the Biblical Story of Jacob, Laban and Two Daughters'.

Stuart, John McDouall 1815–66

Scottish-born explorer, who emigrated to Australia aged 25. He led six expeditions from Adelaide (1858–62), becoming in 1860 the first European to reach the centre of the continent and in 1862 the first to cross Australia from south to north. His health was wrecked by his adventures.

97 To-day I find from my observations of the sun...that I am now camped in the centre of Australia. I have marked a tree and planted the British flag there. There is a high mount about two miles and a half to the north-north-east. I wish it had been in the centre; but on it to-morrow I will raise a cone of stones, and plant the flag there, and name it 'Central Mount Stuart'.
1860 Journal entry, 22 Apr. On reaching the centre of Australia, at Small Gum Creek. Collected in W. Hardman (ed) *Journals of John McDou'all Stuart during the Years 1858, 1859, 1860, 1861 and 1862*.

98 If this country is settled, it will be one of the finest Colonies under the Crown, suitable for the growth of any and everything.
1862 On reaching the sea at the Gulf of Carpentaria. Journal entry, Jul.

Stuart, Mary *known as* *Mary, Queen of Scots* 1542–87

Daughter of James V of Scotland, she married the Dauphin of France in 1558. During her stormy rule, she attempted to support Roman Catholicism in Reformation Scotland, was deposed and fled to England, eventually being imprisoned and executed for treason against her cousin, Queen Elizabeth I of England.

99 *O Domine Deus! speravi in Te;*
O care mi Jesu! nunc libera me;
In dura catena, in misera poena,
Desidero Te,
Languendo, gemendo, et genu flectendo
Adoro, imploro, ut liberes me!
O Lord my God, I hope in thee;
My dear Lord Jesus, set me free;
In chains, in pains
On bended knee
I adore thee, implore thee
To set me free.
1587 Poem composed just before her execution (translated by E Milner-White and G W Briggs, 1941).

Stubbes, Philip 1543–93

English Puritan pamphleteer. His *Anatomie of Abuses in the Realme of England* (1583) was a vehement denunciation of the luxury of the times.

1 Lord, remove these exercises from the Sabbath. Any exercise which withdraweth from godliness either upon the Sabbath or on any other day, is wicked and to be forbidden.
1583 *Anatomie of Abuses in the Realme of England*.

2 For as concerning football playing, I protest unto you it may be rather called a friendly kind of fight than a play or recreation, a bloody or murmuring practice than a fellowly sport or pastime.
1583 *Anatomie of Abuses in the Realme of England*.

3 Football causeth fighting, brawling, contention, quarrel-picking, murder, homicide, and a great effusion of blood, as daily experiences teaches.
1583 *Anatomie of Abuses in the Realme of England*.

Studdert Kennedy, G(eoffrey) A(nketell) *known as* *'Woodbine Willie'* 1883–1929

Army chaplain, theologian and poet of World War I.

4 Waste of Blood, and waste of Tears,
Waste of youth's most precious years,
Waste of ways the saints have trod,
Waste of Glory, waste of God,
War!
1919 *More Rough Rhymes of a Padre*, 'Waste'.

5 When Jesus came to Birmingham they simply passed
Him by,
They never hurt a hair of him, they only let Him die.
For men had grown more tender and they would not give
Him pain,
They only just passed down the street, and left Him in the
rain.
1921 *Peace Rhymes of a Padre*, 'Indifference'.

Su Wu fl.c.100 BC

Chinese general whose poem *To his Wife* expresses his dismay at their forced parting when he was called to battle.

6 With all your might enjoy the spring flowers,
But do not forget the time of our love and pride
c.100 BC *To his Wife* (translated by Arthur Waley).

Suckling, Sir John 1609–41

English poet and playwright. His father was Secretary of State, and he served as ambassador, but upon his inheritance devoted himself to extravagance and court life. Works include the plays *Aglaura* (1638) and *The Goblins* (by 1641), the mock-ballad *The Wits* (1637) and shorter lyrics. By 1641 he had fled to France, where Aubrey says he committed suicide.

7 Why so pale and wan, fond lover?
Prithee, why so pale?
Will, when looking well can't move her,
Looking ill prevail?
1637 *Aglaura*, act 4, sc.1, 'Song'.

8 'Tis love in love that makes the sport.
c.1638 Sonnet no.2.

9 'Tis not the meat; but 'tis the appetite
Makes eating a delight.
c.1638 Sonnet no.2.

10 Women enjoyed (whatsoe'er before they've been)
Are like romances read, or sights once seen:
Fruition's dull, and spoils the play much more
Than if one read or knew the plot before;
'Tis expectation makes a blessing dear;
It were not heaven, if we knew what it were.
1646 'Against Fruition'.

11 The maid (and thereby hangs a tale)
For such a maid no Whitson-ale
Could ever yet produce:
No grape that's kindly ripe, could be
So round, so plump, so soft as she,
Nor half so full of juice.
1646 'Ballad: Upon a Wedding'.

12 Love is the fart
Of every heart:
It pains a man when 'tis kept close,
And others doth offend, when 'tis let loose.
1646 'Love's Offence'.

13 Out upon it! I have loved
Three whole days together;
And am like to love three more,
If it prove fair weather.
1656 'Out Upon It!'

Sullivan, Andrew 1963–

English journalist and writer, based in the US.

14 From the moment she danced with John Travolta, she became an honorary American.
1997 On Diana, Princess of Wales. In the *Sunday Times*, 7 Sep.

Sullivan, Anne 1866–1936

US educator, best known as the teacher of Helen Keller, whom she taught using the manual alphabet and touch-teaching.

15 Language grows out of life, out of its needs and experiences.
1894 Speech to the American Association to Promote the Teaching of Speech to the Deaf, Jul.

16 *Language* and *knowledge* are indissolubly connected; they are interdependent. Good work in language presupposes and depends on a real knowledge of things.
1894 Speech to the American Association to Promote the Teaching of Speech to the Deaf, Jul.

Sullivan, Timothy Daniel 1827–1914

17 High upon the gallows tree
Swung the noble-hearted three
By the vengeful tyrant stricken in their bloom;
But they met him face to face
With the courage of their race,
And they went with souls undaunted to their doom.
'God save Ireland!' said the heroes;
'God save Ireland', say they all:
Whether on the scaffold high
Or the battlefield we die,
Oh, what matter when for Erin dear we fall.
1867 'God Save Ireland'.

Sumner, William Graham 1840–1910

US sociologist, formerly an Episcopal rector, Professor of Political and Social Science at Yale University. He was a disciple of Herbert Spencer, and a strong believer in laissez-faire and free economy.

18 It would be hard to find a single instance of a direct assault by positive effort upon poverty, vice, and misery which has not either failed or, if it has not failed directly and entirely, has not entailed other evils greater than the one which it removed.
1881 'Sociology', collected in *War and Other Essays* (1911).

19 The law of the survival of the fittest was not made by man and cannot be abrogated by man. We can only by interfering with it, produce the survival of the unfittest.
1881 'Sociology', collected in *War and Other Essays* (1911).

20 Society needs first of all to be free from meddlers—that is, to be let alone.
Attributed.

The Sun

British tabloid newspaper.

21 GOTCHA!
1982 Headline, 4 May, reporting the sinking of the Argentinian battleship *General Belgrano* by the British nuclear submarine *HMS Conqueror*. It was withdrawn after the first edition.

22 UP YOURS DELORS
1990 Headline, 1 Nov, supporting Margaret Thatcher's speech in defiance of European Commission president Jacques Delors' wish for Britain to adopt the Ecu.

23 IT'S THE SUN WOT WON IT
1992 Headline, 11 Apr, after the general election victory by the Conservatives.

Sun Tzu c.500–c.320 BC

Name used by the Chinese authors of the *Art of War*. The core text was probably written by one person, perhaps a feudal warrior, but the exact date is unknown. It includes many commentaries by later Chinese philosophers.

24 The art of war is of vital importance to the state.
c.500–320 BC *The Art of War*, ch.1, 'Laying Plans', section 1 (translated by James Clavell, 1981).

25 All warfare is based on deception.
c.500–320 BC *The Art of War*, ch.1, 'Laying Plans', section 18 (translated by James Clavell, 1981).

26 There is no instance of a country having benefitted from prolonged warfare.
c.500–320 BC *The Art of War*, ch.2, 'Waging War', section 6 (translated by James Clavell, 1981).

27 Know the enemy and know yourself; in a hundred battles, you will never be defeated.
c.500 BC *Art of War*, ch.3 (translated by Yuan Shibang, 1987).

28 A victorious general is able to make his soldiers fight with the effect of pent-up waters which, suddenly released, plunge into a bottomless abyss.
c.500 BC *Art of War*, ch.4 (translated by Yuan Shibang, 1987).

29 The business of a general is to kick away the ladder behind soldiers when they have climbed up a height.
c.500 BC *Art of War*, ch.10 (translated by Yuan Shibang, 1987).

30 The general who advances without coveting fame and retreats without fearing disgrace, whose only thought is to protect the country and do good service to his sovereign, is the jewel of the kingdom.
c.500–320 BC *The Art of War*, ch.10, 'Terrain', section 24 (translated by James Clavell, 1981).

31 There is no place where espionage is not possible.
c.500 BC *Art of War*, ch.13 (translated by Yuan Shibang, 1987).

Sun Yat-Sen *or* *Sun Yixian* 1867–1925

Chinese non-Communist revolutionary, regarded as the father of the Chinese Republic. Founder and early leader of China's Nationalist Party, he founded the Society for the Revival of China, but was kidnapped by the Chinese legation in London. After his release he organized risings in South China. The assassination of his follower, Sung Chiao-Jen, led to civil war (1913), and he set up a separate government at Guangzhou (Canton).

32 Modern European culture is nothing but a culture of natural sciences.
1924 Speech, Nov, calling for a union of Japan and China to liberate Asia from European influence. Quoted in John Wu *Sun Yat-Sen: The Man and His Ideas* (1971).

33 The foundation of the government of a nation must be built upon the rights of the people, but the administration must be entrusted to experts. We must not look upon those experts as stately and grand presidents and ministers, but simply as our chauffeurs, guards at the gate, cooks, physicians, carpenters, or tailors.
1927 *The Three Principles of the People.*

Surrey, Henry Howard, Earl of c.1517–1547

English poet; of royal blood, he served Henry VIII at court and in France. In the turmoil over the succession, he became the target of the rival Seymour family, and was arrested and executed on trumped-up charges. He, with Wyatt, introduced the sonnet to England. *Tottel's Miscellany* (1557) contained forty of his poems.

34 Love, that doth reign and live within my thought,
And built his seat within my captive breast,
Clad in the arms wherein with me he fought,
Oft in my face he doth his banner rest.
1557 'Love, that doth reign'.

35 Alas! so all things now do hold their peace,
Heaven and earth disturbed in no thing…
Calm is the sea, the waves work less and less;
So am not I whom love, alas, doth wring,
Bringing before my face the great increase
Of my desires, whereat I weep and sing,
In joy and woe, as in a doubtful ease.
For my sweet thoughts sometime do pleasure bring,
But by and by the cause of my disease
Gives me a pang that inwardly doth sting,
When that I think what grief it is again
To live and lack the thing should rid my pain.
1557 'Alas! so all things now do hold their peace'.

36 Wyatt resteth here, that quick could never rest;
Whose heavenly gifts increased by disdain,
And virtue sank the deeper in his breast;
Such profit he of envy could obtain.
1557 'Wyatt resteth here'.

37 So cruel prison how could betide, alas,
As proud Windsor? Where I in lust and joy
With a king's son my childish years did pass
In greater feast than Priam's sons of Troy.
1557 'So cruel prison'.

38 London, hast thou accused me
Of breach of laws, the root of strife?
Within whose breast did boil to see,
So fervent hot, thy dissolute life,
That even the hate of sins that grow
Within thy wicked walls so rife,
For to break forth did convert so
That terror could it not repress.
1557 'London, hast thou accused me'.

39 O happy dames, that may embrace
The fruit of your delight,
Help to bewail the woeful case
And eke the heavy plight
Of me, that wonted to rejoice
The fortune of my pleasant choice.
Good ladies, help to fill my mourning voice.
1557 'O happy dames'.

40 Set me whereas the sun doth parch the green,
Or where his beams may not dissolve the ice,
In temperate heat, where he is felt and seen,
With proud people, in presence sad and wise;
Set me in base, or yet in high degree,
In the long night, or in the shortest day,
In clear weather, or where mists thickest be,
In lusty youth, or when my hairs be grey…
Yours will I be, and with that only thought
Comfort myself when that my hap is nought.
'Set me whereas the sun doth parch the green'.

Surtees, Robert Smith 1803–64

English journalist and novelist. Founder of the *New Sporting Magazine* in 1831, he introduced the popular Cockney character John Jorrocks. Later works include *Jorrocks' Jaunts and Jollities* (1838) and *Hillingdon Hall* (1845).

41 The horse loves the hound, and I loves both.
Quoted in Colin Jarman *The Guinness Dictionary of Sports Quotations* (1990).

42 There is no secret so close as that between a rider and his horse.
Attributed.

Sutherland, Arthur Jr 1902–73

US lawyer, Professor of Law at Harvard University.

43 One can scarcely imagine a speaker at a meeting of a county medical society discussing the possible elimination of some disease by public health measures, and then qualifying his observations by the statement that many practitioners make a living out of treating the disease in question; and that unless the physicians are vigilant to prevent the adoption of such measures, this source of business will be taken from them. Yet speakers at bar association meetings are frequently heard to make similar observations about the effect of proposed reforms.
1938 'A New Society and an Old Calling,' in the *Cornell Law Quarterly.*

Swanson, Gloria *originally* *Gloria May Josephine Svensson* 1897–1983

US film actress. She rose from an extra in silent films in 1915 to leading roles as a chic sophisticate in the front line of the battle of the sexes, under the direction of Cecil B de Mille in the 1920s.

44 Arriving Monday… Arrange ovation.
Transatlantic cable to Adolf Zukor. Quoted in the *New Yorker*, 21 Mar 1994.

Sweetenham, Bill 1950–

Australian swimming coach.

45 The Romans conquered the world not because they held committees but because they killed the opposition. That's where I'm coming from.
2003 In *The Independent*, 29 Dec.

Sweezy, Paul Malor 1910–2004

Independent US Marxist economist, founder of the *Monthly Review* (1949).

46 Capitalism only works well when it has a strong opposition, because that forces it to be more egalitarian than it wants to be.
1992 Interview in *The Progressive*, May.

Swettenham, Sir Frank Athelstane 1850–1946

English colonial administrator, serving as the British Resident in Selangor and Perak before being appointed the Resident General in the Federated Malay States (1896–1901)

47 The Malay Peninsula, with the climate of a perpetual Turkish bath.
1906 *British Malaya*.

Swift, Graham 1949–

English writer. He has written several novels including *Waterland* (1983), which was shortlisted for the Booker Prize, and *Last Orders*, which won the Booker Prize in 1996.

48 Life is one-tenth Here and Now, nine-tenths a history lesson. For most of the time the Here and Now is neither now nor here.
1983 *Waterland*, ch.8.

49 People die when curiosity goes. People have to find out, people have to know. How can there be any true revolution till we know what we're made of?
1983 *Waterland*, ch.27.

Swift, Jonathan 1667–1745

Anglo-Irish poet, novelist, essayist, pamphleteer and letter writer. Born in Ireland, he became a satirist in London but returned to Dublin to become Dean of St Patrick's. His works, characterized by biting wit, include *Gulliver's Travels* (1726), a satire on religious dissension, *A Tale of a Tub* (1704), *A Modest Proposal* (1729) and *Drapier's Letters* (1724), in which he campaigned for Irish liberty.

50 Th' artillery of words.
1692 'My Lady's Lamentation'.

51 Philosophy! the lumber of the schools.
1692 'Ode to Dr William Sancroft'.

52 Satire is a sort of glass, wherein beholders do generally discover everybody's face but their own.
1704 *The Battle of the Books*, preface.

53 Instead of dirt and poison we have rather chosen to fill our hives with honey and wax; thus furnishing mankind with the two noblest of things, which are sweetness and light.
1704 *The Battle of the Books.*

54 Books, like men their authors, have no more than one way of coming into the world, but there are ten thousand to go out of it, and return no more.
1704 *A Tale of a Tub*, 'Epistle Dedicatory'.

55 Satire, being levelled at all, is never resented for an offence by any.
1704 *A Tale of a Tub*, 'Author's Preface'.

56 What though his head be empty, provided his commonplace book be full.
1704 *A Tale of a Tub*, 'Digression in praise of digression', ch.7.

57 Last week I saw a woman flayed, and you will hardly believe, how much it altered her person for the worse.
1704 *A Tale of a Tub*, ch.9.

58 Laws are like cobwebs, which may catch small flies, but let wasps and hornets break through.
1709 *A Critical Essay upon the Faculties of the Mind.*

59 There is nothing in this world constant, but inconstancy.
1709 *A Critical Essay upon the Faculties of the Mind.*

60 Surely mortal man is a broomstick!
1710 *A Meditation upon a Broomstick*.

61 We are so fond of one another, because our ailments are the same.
1711 *Journal to Stella*, 1 Feb.

62 Will she pass in a crowd? Will she make a figure in a country church?
1711 *Journal to Stella*, 9 Feb.

63 I love good creditable acquaintance; I love to be the worst of the company.
1711 *Journal to Stella*, 17 May.

64 He was a fiddler, and consequently a rogue.
1711 *Journal to Stella*, 25 July.

65 He showed me his bill of fare to tempt me to dine with him; poh, said I, I value not your bill of fare, give me your bill of company.
1711 *Journal to Stella*, 2 Sep.

66 We have just enough religion to make us hate, but not enough to make us love one another.
1711 *Thoughts on Various Subjects*.

67 When a true genius appears in the world, you may know

him by this sign, that the dunces are all in confederacy against him.
1711 *Thoughts on Various Subjects.*

68 What they do in heaven we are ignorant of: what they do *not* we are told expressly, that they neither marry, nor are given in marriage.
1711 *Thoughts on Various Subjects.*

69 The stoical scheme of supplying our wants, by lopping off our desires, is like cutting off our feet when we want shoes.
1711 *Thoughts on Various Subjects.*

70 The reason why so few marriages are happy, is, because young ladies spend their time in making nets, not in making cages.
1711 *Thoughts on Various Subjects.*

71 We were to do more business after dinner, but after dinner is after dinner—an old saying and a true, 'much drinking, little thinking'.
1712 *Journal to Stella*, 26 Feb.

72 Proper words in proper places, make the true definition of style.
1720 *Letter to a Young Gentleman lately entered into Holy Orders.*

73 Indeed the arguments on both sides were invincible; for in reason, all government without the consent of the governed is the very definition of slavery; but in fact eleven men well armed will certainly subdue one single man in his shirt.
1724 *Fourth letter to…Ireland*, written under the pseudonym of 'M B Drapier'.

74 I have heard of a man who had a mind to sell his house, and therefore carried a piece of brick in his pocket, which he shewed as a pattern to encourage purchasers.
1724 *Drapier's Letters*, no.2.

75 In Church your grandsire cut his throat;
To do the job too long he tarried,
He should have had my hearty vote,
To cut his throat before he married.
1724 'Verses on the Upright Judge'.

76 'Libertas et natale solum':
Fine words! I wonder where you stole 'em.
1724 'Whitshed's motto on his Coach'.

77 He is taller by almost the breadth of my nail than any of his court, which alone is enough to strike an awe into the beholders.
1726 Of the Emperor. *Gulliver's Travels*, 'A Voyage to Lilliput', ch.2.

78 It is alleged indeed, that the high heels are most agreeable to our ancient constitution: but however this be, his Majesty hath determined to make use of only low heels in the administration of the government.
1726 *Gulliver's Travels*, 'A Voyage to Lilliput', ch.4.

79 I cannot but conclude the bulk of your natives to be the most pernicious race of little odious vermin that nature ever suffered to crawl upon the surface of the earth.
1726 *Gulliver's Travels*, 'A Voyage to Brobdingnag', ch.6.

80 And he gave it for his opinion, that whoever could make two ears of corn or two blades of grass to grow upon a spot of ground where only one grew before, would deserve better of mankind, and do more essential service to his country than the whole race of politicians put together.
1726 *Gulliver's Travels*, 'A Voyage to Brobdingnag', ch.7.

81 He had been eight years upon a project for extracting sun-beams out of cucumbers, which were to be put into vials hermetically sealed, and let out to warm the air in raw inclement summers.
1726 *Gulliver's Travels*, 'A Voyage to Laputa, etc.' ch.5.

82 These unhappy people were proposing schemes for persuading monarchs to choose favourites upon the score of their wisdom, capacity and virtue; of teaching ministers to consult the public good; of rewarding merit, great abilities and eminent services; of instructing princes to know their true interest by placing it on the same foundation with that of their people: of choosing for employment persons qualified to exercise them; with many other wild impossible chimeras, that never entered before into the heart of man to conceive, and confirmed in me the old observation, that there is nothing so extravagant and irrational which some philosophers have not maintained for truth.
1726 *Gulliver's Travels*, 'A Voyage to Laputa, etc.' ch.6.

83 He replied that I must needs be mistaken, or that I *said the thing which was not*. (For they have no word in their language to express lying or falsehood.)
1726 *Gulliver's Travels*, 'A Voyage to the Houyhnhnms', ch.3.

84 I told him…that we ate when we were not hungry, and drank without the provocation of thirst.
1726 *Gulliver's Travels*, 'A Voyage to the Houyhnhnms', ch.6.

85 Few are qualified to shine in company; but it is in most men's power to be agreeable.
1727 *Thoughts on Various Subjects* (enlarged edn).

86 Every man desires to live long; but no man would be old.
1727 *Thoughts on Various Subjects* (enlarged edn).

87 A nice man is a man of nasty ideas.
1727 *Thoughts on Various Subjects* (enlarged edn).

88 Old men and comets have been reverenced for the same reason; their long beards, and pretences to foretell events.
1727 *Thoughts on Various Subjects* (enlarged edn).

89 How haughtily he lifts his nose,
To tell what every schoolboy knows.
1727 'The Journal', l.81–2.

90 Walls have tongues, and hedges ears.
1727 'A Pastoral Dialogue between Richmond Lodge and Marble Hill', l.8.

91 Hail fellow, well met,
All dirty and wet:
Find out, if you can,
Who's master, who's man.
1728 'My Lady's Lamentation', l.171.

92 These *Mothers*, instead of being able to work for their honest livelihood, are forced to beg Sustenance for their *helpless Infants*; who, as they grow up either turn *Thieves* for want of Work; or leave their dear native country, to fight for the *Pretender* in Spain; or sell themselves to the *Barbadoes*.
1729 *A Modest Proposal for Preventing the Children of Ireland from being a Burden to their Parents or Country.*

93 I have been assured by a very knowing American of my Acquaintance in London; that a young healthy Child, well nursed, is, at a Year old, a most delicious, nourishing, and wholesome Food; whether Stewed, Roasted, Baked, or Boiled; and, I make no doubt, that it will equally serve

in a Fricassee, or a Ragout.
1729 *A Modest Proposal for Preventing the Children of Ireland from being a Burden to their Parents or Country.*

94 A Child will make two Dishes at an Entertainment for Friends; and when the Family dines alone, the fore or hind Quarter will make a reasonable Dish; and seasoned with a little Pepper or Salt, will be very good Boiled on the fourth Day, especially in Winter.
1729 *A Modest Proposal for Preventing the Children of Ireland from being a Burden to their Parents or Country.*

95 Say, Britain, could you ever boast,—
Three poets in an age at most?
Our chilling climate hardly bears
A sprig of bays in fifty years.
1733 'On Poetry', l.5–8.

96 Then, rising with Aurora's light,
The Muse invoked, sit down to write;
Blot out, correct, insert, refine,
Enlarge, diminish, interline.
1733 'On Poetry', l.85–8.

97 As learned commentators view
In Homer than Homer knew.
1733 'On Poetry', l.103–4.

98 So geographers, in Afric-maps,
With savage-pictures fill their gaps;
And o'er unhabitable downs
Place elephants for want of towns.
1733 'On Poetry', l.177–80.

99 He gives direction to the town,
To cry it up, or run it down.
1733 'On Poetry', l.269–70.

1 Hobbes clearly proves, that every creature
Lives in a state of war by nature.
1733 'On Poetry', l.319–20.

2 So, naturalists observe, a flea
Hath smaller fleas on him prey;
And these have smaller fleas to bite 'em,
And so proceed *ad infinitum*.
Thus every poet, in his kind,
Is bit by him that comes behind.
1733 'On Poetry', l.337–42.

3 I mean, you lie—under a mistake.
1738 *Polite Conversation*, dialogue 1.

4 I think she was cut out for a Gentlewoman, but she was spoiled in the making. She wears her clothes as if they were thrown on with a pitchfork; and, for the fashion, I believe they were made in the days of Queen Bess.
1738 *Polite Conversation*, dialogue 1.

5 The more careless, the more modish.
1738 *Polite Conversation*, dialogue 1.

6 I won't quarrel with my Bread and Butter.
1738 *Polite Conversation*, dialogue 1.

7 He was a bold Man that first ate an Oyster.
1738 *Polite Conversation*, dialogue 2.

8 Faith, that's as well said, as if I had said it myself.
1738 *Polite Conversation*, dialogue 2.

9 I always love to begin a journey on Sundays, because I shall have the prayers of the church, to preserve all that travel by land, or by water.
1738 *Polite Conversation*, dialogue 2.

10 Lord, I wonder what fool it was that first invented kissing!
1738 *Polite Conversation*, dialogue 2.

11 Promises and pie-crust are made to be broken.
1738 *Polite Conversation.*

12 Be she barren, be she old,
Be she slut, or be she scold,
Eat my oysters, and lie near her,
She'll be fruitful, never fear her.
1746 'Verses Made for the Women Who Cry Oysters'.

13 I never saw, heard, nor read, that the clergy were beloved in any nation where Christianity was the religion of the country. Nothing can render them popular, but some degree of persecution.
1765 *Thoughts on Religion.*

14 I must complain the cards are ill shuffled till I have a good hand.
Quoted in Colin Jarman *The Guinness Dictionary of Sports Quotations* (1990).

Swinburne, Algernon Charles 1837–1909

English playwright and poet. He made his name with *Poems and Ballads* (1866). Later works include *A Song of Italy* (1867), *Erechtus* (1876) and *Tristam of Lyonesse* (1882).

15 Swallow, my sister, O sister swallow,
How can thine heart be full of the spring?
A thousand summers are over and dead.
What hast thou found in the spring to follow?
What hast thou found in thine heart to sing?
What wilt thou do when the summer is shed?
1864 'Itylus'.

16 Till life and death remember,
Till thou remember and I forget.
1864 'Itylus'.

17 Maiden, and mistress of the months and stars
Now folded in the flowerless fields of heaven.
1865 *Atlanta in Calydon*, l.1

18 When the hounds of spring are on winter's traces,
The mother of months in meadow or plain
Fills the shadows and windy places
With lisp of leaves and ripple of rain;
And the brown bright nightingale amorous
Is half assured for Itylus,
For the Thracian ships and the foreign faces,
The tongueless vigil and all the pain.
1865 *Atlanta in Calydon*, chorus, 'When the hounds of spring'.

19 For winter's rains and ruins are over,
And all the season of snows and sins;
The days dividing lover and lover,
The light that loses, the night that wins;
And time remembered is grief forgotten,
And frosts are slain and flowers begotten,
And in green underwood and cover
Blossom by blossom the spring begins.
1865 *Atlanta in Calydon*, chorus, 'When the hounds of spring'.

20 And soft as lips that laugh and hide
The laughing leaves of the tree divide,
And screen from seeing and leave in sight
The god pursuing, the maiden hid.
1865 *Atlanta in Calydon*, chorus 'When the hounds of spring'.

21 Before the beginning of years
There came to the making of man

Time with a gift of tears,
Grief with a glass that ran.
1865 *Atlanta in Calydon*, chorus, 'Before the beginning of years'.

22 Strength without hands to smite,
Love that endures for a breath;
Night, the shadow of light,
And Life, the shadow of death.
1865 *Atlanta in Calydon*, chorus, 'Before the beginning of years'.

23 For words divide and rend;
But silence is most noble till the end.
1865 *Atlanta in Calydon*, chorus, 'Who hath given man speech'.

24 Ah, yet would God this flesh of mine might be
Where air might wash and long leaves cover me;
Where tides of grass break into foam of flowers,
Or where the wind's feet shine along the sea.
1866 'Laus Veneris'.

25 Superflux of pain.
1866 *Poems and Ballads*, 'Anactoria'

26 We shift and bedeck and bedrape us,
Thou art noble and nude and antique.
1866 *Poems and Ballads*, 'Dolores', stanza 7.

27 Change in a trice
The lilies and languors of virtue
For the raptures and roses of vice.
1866 *Poems and Ballads*, 'Dolores', stanza 9.

28 O splendid and sterile Dolores,
Our Lady of Pain.
1866 *Poems and Ballads*, 'Dolores', stanza 9.

29 Ah beautiful passionate body
That never has ached with a heart!
1866 *Poems and Ballads*, 'Dolores', stanza 11.

30 For the crown of our life as it closes
Is darkness, the fruit thereof dust;
No thorns go as deep as a rose's,
And love is more cruel than lust.
Time turns the old days to derision,
Our loves into corpses or wives;
And marriage and death and division
Make barren our lives.
1866 *Poems and Ballads*, 'Dolores', stanza 20.

31 I shall remember while the light lives yet
And in the night time I shall not forget.
1866 *Poems and Ballads*, 'Erotion'.

32 Pale, beyond porch and portal,
Crowned with calm leaves, she stands
Who gathers all things mortal
With cold immortal hands.
1866 *Poems and Ballads*, 'The Garden of Proserpine'.

33 Here, where the world is quiet,
Here, where all trouble seems
Dead winds' and spent waves' riot
In doubtful dreams of dreams.
1866 *Poems and Ballads*, 'The Garden of Proserpine'.

34 Yea, is not even Apollo, with hair and harpstring of gold,
A bitter God to follow, a beautiful God to behold?
1866 *Poems and Ballads*, 'Hymn to Proserpine'.

35 Thou hast conquered, O pale Galilean; the world has grown grey from Thy breath;
We have drunken of things Lethean, and fed on the fullness of death.
1866 *Poems and Ballads*, 'Hymn to Proserpine'.

36 Though these that were Gods are dead, and thou being dead art God,
Though before thee the throned Cytherean be fallen, and hidden her head,
Yet thy kingdom shall pass, Galilean, thy dead shall go down to thee dead.
1866 *Poems and Ballads*, 'Hymn to Proserpine'.

37 I remember the way we parted,
The day and the way we met;
You hoped we were both broken-hearted,
And knew we should both forget.
1866 *Poems and Ballads*, 'An Interlude'.

38 And the best and the worst of this is
That neither is most to blame
If you have forgotten my kisses
And I have forgotten your name.
1866 *Poems and Ballads*, 'An Interlude'.

39 If love were what the rose is,
And I were like the leaf,
Our lives would grow together
In sad or singing weather,
Blown fields or flowered closes,
Green pleasure or grey grief.
1866 *Poems and Ballads*, 'A Match'.

40 I will go back to the great sweet mother,
Mother and lover of men, the sea.
I will go down to her, I and no other,
Close with her, kiss her and mix her with me.
1866 *Poems and Ballads*, 'The Triumph of Time'.

41 I shall sleep, and move with the moving ships,
Change as the winds change, veer in the tide.
1866 *Poems and Ballads*, 'The Triumph of Time'.

42 There lived a singer in France of old
By the tideless dolorous midland sea.
In a land of sand and ruin and gold
There shone one woman, and none but she.
1866 *Poems and Ballads*, 'The Triumph of Time'.

43 O slain and spent and sacrificed
People, the grey-grown speechless Christ.
1871 *Songs before Sunrise*, 'Before a Crucifix'.

44 But God, if a God there be, is the substance of men which is man.
1871 *Songs before Sunrise*, 'Hymn of Man'.

45 Glory to Man in the highest! for Man is the master of things.
1871 *Songs before Sunrise*, 'Hymn of Man'.

46 There was a poor poet named Clough,
Whom his friends all united to puff,
But the public, though dull,
Had not such a skull
As belonged to believers in Clough.
1875 *Essays and Studies*, 'Matthew Arnold'.

47 For a day and a night Love sang to us, played with us,
Folded us round from the dark and the light;
And our hearts were fulfilled with the music he made with us,
Made with our hands and our lips while he stayed with us,
Stayed in mid passage his pinions from flight
For a day and a night.

1878 *Poems and Ballads* (2nd edn), 'At Parting'.

48 The deep division of prodigious breasts,
The solemn slope of mighty limbs asleep.
1878 *Poems and Ballads* (2nd edn), 'Ave Atque Vale', stanza 6.

49 Sleep; and if life was bitter to thee, pardon,
If sweet, give thanks; thou hast no more to live;
And to give thanks is good, and to forgive.
1878 *Poems and Ballads* (2nd edn), 'Ave Atque Vale', stanza 17.

50 Villon, our sad bad glad mad brother's name.
1878 *Poems and Ballads* (2nd edn), 'Ballad of François Villon'.

51 In a coign of the cliff between lowland and highland,
At the sea-down's edge between windward and lee,
Walled round with rocks as an inland island,
The ghost of a garden fronts the sea.
1878 *Poems and Ballads* (2nd edn), 'A Forsaken Garden'.

52 As a god self-slain on his own strange altar,
Death lies dead.
1878 *Poems and Ballads* (2nd edn), 'A Forsaken Garden'.

53 Fiddle, we know, is diddle: and diddle, we take it, is dee.
1880 *The Heptalogia*, 'The Higher Pantheism in a Nutshell'.

Symington, Stuart 1901–88

US Senator. In 1939 he became President and Chairman of the Emerson Electric Manufacturing Company. He was the first Secretary of the Air Force (1945–48) and was elected Senator for Missouri in 1952.

54 I found out that he was a bachelor, as was his father before him.
1960 On hiring a speechwriter. Address to Washington's Gridiron Club, 12 Mar, quoted in Harold Brayman *The President Speaks-off-the-Record* (1976).

Synge, John Millington 1871–1909

Irish dramatist. On the advice of W B Yeats he travelled to the Aran Islands and there found materials for his plays which include *Riders to the Sea* (1904) and his masterpiece, *The Playboy of the Western World* (1907), which caused riots when it was first staged in Dublin.

55 No man at all can be living for ever, and we must be satisfied.
1904 *Riders to the Sea*.

56 They're all gone now, and there isn't anything more the sea can do to me.
1904 Maurya speaking. *Riders to the Sea*.

57 Well, if the worst comes in the end of all, it'll be great game to see if there's none to pity him but a widow woman, the like of me, has buried her children and destroyed her man.
1907 Widow Quin. *The Playboy of the Western World*, act 2.

58 Drink a health to the wonders of the western world, the pirates, preachers, poteen-makers, with the jobbing jockies; parching peelers, and the juries fill their stomachs selling judgments of the English law.
1907 *The Playboy of the Western World*, act 2.

59 I'll say, a strange man is a marvel, with his mighty talk; but what's a squabble in your back-yard, and the blow of a loy, have taught me that there's a great gap between a gallous story and a dirty deed.
1907 Pegeen Mike. *The Playboy of the Western World*, act 3.

60 Oh my grief, I've lost him surely. I've lost the only Playboy of the Western World.
1907 Pegeen Mike. *The Playboy of the Western World*, act 3, closing words.

Szasz, Thomas Stephen 1920–

Hungarian-born US psychiatrist. His books argue that disease is physical, hence mental illness is a myth, that the individual should be allowed complete freedom within the law, and all psychiatric therapy should be contractual.

61 Formerly, when religion was strong and science weak, men mistook magic for medicine, now, when science is strong and religion weak, men mistake medicine for magic.
1974 *The Second Sin*.

62 Men are rewarded and punished not for what they do, but rather for how their acts are defined. This is why men are more interested in better justifying themselves than in better behaving themselves.
1974 *The Second Sin*.

63 Psychiatrists classify a person as neurotic if he suffers from his problems in living, and a psychotic if he makes others suffer.
1974 *The Second Sin*.

Szent-Györgyi, Albert von Nagyrapolt 1893–1986

Hungarian-born US biochemist, authority on the processes of biological combustion. He was educated at the universities of Budapest and Cambridge. In 1947, he migrated to the US to join the Marine Biological Laboratories, Massachusetts. He was awarded the 1937 Nobel prize in physiology or medicine.

64 Discovery consists of seeing what everybody has seen and thinking what nobody has thought.
Quoted in Irving Good (ed) *The Scientist Speculates* (1962).

65 Knowledge is a sacred cow, and my problem will be how we can milk her while keeping clear of her horns.
1964 In *Science*, vol.146.

Szilard, Leo 1898–1964

Hungarian-born US nuclear physicist, who contributed to the development of controlled nuclear fission. He left the University of Berlin with the advent of Hitler, jointing Columbia University in 1938. He urged Albert Einstein to write to President Roosevelt warning of the possible military use of atomic energy by the Nazis.

66 We turned the switch, saw the flashes, watched for ten minutes, then switched everything off and went home. That night I knew the world was headed for sorrow.
1939 After an early experiment at Columbia University which proved the possibility of splitting the atom. Quoted in James B Simpson *Simpson's Contemporary Quotations* (1988).

67 Don't lie if you don't have to.
1972 In *Science*, vol.176, p.966.

Taaffe, Eduard Franz Josef, Graf von 1833–95

Austrian statesman, Minister of the Interior (1867) and Chief Minister (1869–70, 1879–93).

68 As a Minister, it is my policy to keep all the nationalities within the Habsburg monarchy in a balanced state of well-modulated dissatisfaction.
1881 Letters.

Tacitus, Cornelius *full name* ***Publius or Gaius Cornelius Tacitus*** AD 55–c.120

Roman historian and orator, who lived under Domitian, Nerva, Trajan and Hadrian. He wrote a biography of his father-in-law Agricola. His major historical works are the *Historiae* (Histories), of which only the first four books survive whole, and the *Annales* (Annals), of which only eight books survive.

69 *Solitudinem faciunt pacem appellant.*
They make a wilderness and they call it peace.
Speech of the British chieftain Calgacus, before the battle of Mons Graupius, referring to the Romans. *Agricola*, ch.30.

70 *Proprium humani ingenii est odisse quem laeseris.*
It is part of human nature to hate a man you have hurt.
Agricola, ch.42.

71 *Perdomita Britannia et statim omissa.*
Britain was conquered and immediately lost.
Referring to Agricola's conquest of Britain, and the loss of much of it under Domitian. *Histories*, bk.1, ch.2.

72 *Deos fortioribus adesse.*
The gods support those who are stronger.
Histories, bk.4, ch.17.

73 *Miseram pacem vel bello bene mutari.*
Even war is preferable to a shameful peace.
Annals, bk.3, ch.44.

74 *Auctor nominis eius Christus, Tiberio imperitante, per procuratorem Pontium Pilatum, supplicio affectus erat.*
Christ, the leader of the sect, had been put to death by the procurator Pontius Pilate in the reign of Tiberius.
Annals, bk.15, ch.44.

75 *Elegantiae arbiter.*
The arbiter of taste.
Of Petronius. *Annals*, bk.16, ch.18.

Taft, Robert A(lphonso) 1889–1953

US politician. Son of US President William Howard Taft, he entered the Senate in 1932 and was a prominent isolationist. He co-sponsored the Taft-Hartley Act (1947), which acted against the 'closed shop' power of trade unions. He failed three times (1940, 1948, 1952) to gain the Republican nomination for the US presidency.

76 Lending arms is like lending chewing gum. You don't get it back.
On the lend-lease agreement. Quoted in David Brinkley *Washington Goes to War* (1988).

Taft, William Howard 1857–1930

US Republican politician and 27th US President. Secretary of War (1904–8) and provisional governor of Cuba (1906), he became President in 1909 and remained in the post until 1913, when he was defeated by Woodrow Wilson. Subsequently he became US Chief Justice (1921).

77 There are a great many people who are in favor of conservation no matter what it means.
Quoted in J W Milliman *Land Economics* (1962).

78 Golf is in the interest of good health and good manners. It promotes self-restraint and affords a chance to play the man and act the gentleman.
Quoted in Michael Hobbs *The Golf Quotation Book* (1992).

Takuboku, Ishikawa 1886–1902

Japanese poet whose first book of poems, *Akogare* (Longing), was published in 1905. Five years later, a second collection, *Ichiaku no Suna* (A Handful of Dust), broke new ground by writing about aspects of everyday life.

79 There are some lives duller
Than dusty glass
1910 *Ichiaku no Suna* (translated by Sakanishi Shio).

80 Like a stone
That rolls down a hill,
I have come to this day.
1910 *Ichiaku no Suna* (translated by Sakanishi Shio)

Talbot, Godfrey Walker 1908–2000

English broadcaster and writer. He was the BBC's war correspondent in World War II and their court correspondent from 1948 to 1969. He wrote articles on the Royal Family and an autobiography, *Ten Seconds from Now* (1973).

81 A man who, until he made the journey from London, thought that woad began at Watford.
1973 *Ten Seconds from Now*, ch.3. An early reference to the 'north of Watford' concept, in which Watford is regarded as the limit of 'civilization' northwards from London.

Talese, Gay 1932–

US writer and journalist. His works include *New York: A Serendipiter's Journey* (1961), *Fame and Obscurity* (1970) and *Unto the Sons* (1992).

82 New glass skyscrapers stand shoulder to shoulder, reflecting one another narcissistically.
1965 In the *New York Times*, 23 Jun.

Talleyrand-Périgord, Charles-Maurice de, Prince of Benevento 1754–1838

French statesman, President of the Assembly (1790). He lived in exile until the fall of Robespierre. As Foreign Minister under the Directory (1797–1807) he helped consolidate Napoleon's position, but alarmed by his ambitions resigned in 1807 to become leader of the anti-Napoleonic faction. Foreign Minister under Louis XVIII, he represented France at the Congress of Vienna (1814–15). He was Louis Philippe's chief adviser at the July Revolution, and Ambassador to England (1830–4).

83 *Ils n'ont rien appris, ni rien oublié.*
They have learned nothing, and forgotten nothing.
Attributed.

84 *Voilà le commencement de la fin.*

This is the beginning of the end.
Attributed.

85 The allies are too frightened to fight each other, too stupid too agree.
1814 Congress of Vienna, Nov.

Tally, Ted 1952–

US screenwriter, best known for *The Silence of the Lambs* (1991) for which he won an Academy Award for Best Adapted Screenplay.

86 A census taker once tried to test me, I ate his liver with some fava beans and a nice Chianti.
1991 Anthony Hopkins as Dr Hannibal Lecter ('Hannibal the Cannibal') in *The Silence of the Lambs*.

87 I do wish we could chat longer but I'm having an old friend for dinner.
1991 Anthony Hopkins as Dr Hannibal Lecter ('Hannibal the Cannibal') in *The Silence of the Lambs*.

Talma, François-Joseph 1763–1826

French actor-manager. He established his reputation as a powerful tragedian in the central role of Chénier's *Charles IX* in 1789, which caused a sensation; subsequently he formed his own company and staged admired productions of Corneille, Shakespeare and others. As head of the French national theatre under Napoleon he introduced various important reforms.

88 *Voltaire! Comme Voltaire, toujours comme Voltaire.*
Voltaire! Like Voltaire, always like Voltaire.
1826 Last words.

Tanaka, Kakuei 1918–93

Japanese politician who rose through the ranks of the Liberal Democratic party to become Prime Minister. Arrested in 1976 for bribery, he resigned the premiership, although he remained influential.

89 The politics of numbers.
1983 Describing democracy, in an interview with the *Nihon Keizai Shimbun*, 25 Jan.

90 Why should not a large shareholder sometimes name the president?
1983 Responding to criticism that candidates for the premiership must win his approval. Quoted in the *Financial Times*, 11 Oct.

Tannahill, Robert 1774–1810

Scottish poet and songwriter, born in Paisley, the son of a weaver.

91 The sun has gane down o'er the lofty Benlomond,
And left the red clouds to preside o'er the scene,
While lanely I stray, in the calm simmer gloamin',
To muse on sweet Jessie, the flower o' Dunblane.
How sweet is the brier wi' its saft faulding blossom,
And sweet is the birk, wi' its mantle o' green;
Yet sweeter, and fairer, and dear to this bosom,
Is lovely young Jessie, the flower o' Dunblane.
1807 'Jessie, the Flower o' Dunblane', stanza 1.

T'ao Ch'ien AD 372–427

Chinese poet about whom little is known.

92 I beg you listen to this advice—
When you get wine, be sure to drink it.
c.400 AD Collected in *Substance, Shadow and Spirit*, translated by Arthur Waley.

Tarantino, Quentin 1963–

US director and screenwriter, known for the brutality and violent escapism of his films. One of his many scripts was made into his debut film as director, *Reservoir Dogs* (1993). In 1994 his second film, *Pulp Fiction*, won the Palme d'Or at the Cannes Film Festival. Later films include *Jackie Brown* (1997).

93 Violence in real life is terrible; violence in movies can be cool. It's just another colour to work with.
1994 In the *Observer*, 'Sayings of the Week', 16 Oct.

94 Violence is fun, man.
2004 In *The Times*, 17 May.

Tarkington, (Newton) Booth 1869–1946

US novelist, best known for his Penrod books, *Penrod* (1914) and *Seventeen* (1916). His novel *The Magnificent Ambersons* (1918) won the Pulitzer Prize and was made into a successful film by Orson Welles.

95 There are two things that will be believed of any man whatsoever, and one of them is that he has taken to drink.
1914 *Penrod*, ch.10.

96 The Magnificent Ambersons.
1918 Title of novel.

97 An ideal wife is any woman who has an ideal husband.
1924 *Looking Forward And Others*, 'The Hopeful Pessimist'.

Tarrant, Chris 1946–

English radio and television presenter.

98 Is that your final answer?
Catchphrase on the television show *Who Wants To Be A Millionaire?*.

Tartt, Donna 1963–

US author. She achieved widespread succes with her first novel, *The Secret History* (1992). Her second novel, *The Little Friend* (2002), appeared a decade later.

99 The snow in the mountains was melting and Bunny had been dead for several weeks before we came to understand the gravity of our situation.
1992 *The Secret History*.

1 I'd love to write a book a year, but I don't think I'd have any fans.
2002 In the *Sunday Times*, 2 Jun.

2 Birds—birds, everywhere, great black cawing explosions of them, like radioactive fall-out, like shrapnel.
2002 *The Little Friend*.

Tate, (John Orley) Allen 1899–1979

US poet, critic and biographer. He was the editor of the influential *Sewanee Review* (1944–7). His own poetry was strongly influenced by T S Eliot.

3 Row upon row with strict impunity
The headstones yield their names to the element.
1948 *Poems 1922–1947*, 'Ode to the Confederate Dead'.

4 Autumn is desolation in the plot
Of a thousand acres, where these memories grow
From the inexhaustible bodies that are not
Dead, but feed the grass, row after rich row.
1948 *Poems 1922–1947*, 'Ode to the Confederate Dead'.

5 The brute curiosity of an angel's stare
Turn you like them to stone.
1948 *Poems 1922–1947*, 'Ode to the Confederate Dead'.

6 I've heard the wolves scuffle, and said: So this
Is man; so—what better conclusion is there—
The day will not follow night, and the heart
Of man has a little dignity, but less patience
Than a wolf's, and a duller sense that cannot
Smell its own mortality.
1948 *Poems 1922–1947*, 'The Wolves'.

Tate, Greg

US writer and music critic.

7 Commodity fetishism is the true God of this nation.
1992 In *Vibe*, reported in *USA Today*, 14 Sep.

Tawney, R(ichard) H(enry) 1880–1962

British economic historian, active in the Workers' Educational Association at Rochdale, Lancashire, and its President (1928–44). He was Professor of Economic History at London (1931–49) and wrote a number of studies in English economic history.

8 The instinct of mankind warns it against accepting at their face value spiritual demands that cannot satisfy themselves by practical achievements. The road along which the organized workers, like any other class, must climb to power starts from the provision of a more effective economic service than their masters, as their grip upon industry becomes increasingly vacillating and uncertain, are able to supply.
1926 *The Acquisitive Society*.

9 As long as men are men, a poor society cannot be too poor to find a right order of life; nor a rich society too rich to have need to seek it.
1926 *The Acquisitive Society*.

Taylor, A(lan) J(ohn) P(ercivale) 1906–90

English historian, whose major work was *The Struggle for Mastery in Europe 1848–1918* (1954). His controversial revisionist *Origins of the Second World War* (1961) argued against a grand design. Other works include *English History 1914–1945* (1965), *The Trouble Makers* (1957), on critics of British foreign policy, and *A Personal History* (1983).

10 Crimea: The War That Would Not Boil.
1952 *Rumours of Wars*, ch.6, chapter title.

11 Human blunders usually do more to shape history than human wickedness.
1961 *The Origins of the Second World War*.

12 The First World War had begun—imposed on the statesmen of Europe by railway timetables. It was an unexpected climax to the railway age.
1963 *The First World War*, ch.1.

13 Like most of those who study history, Napoleon learned from the mistakes of the past how to make new ones.
1963 BBC radio broadcast, 6 Jun.

14 History gets thicker and thicker as it approaches recent times.
1965 *English History 1914–1945*.

Taylor, Dwight 1902–86

US screenwriter. Best known for his screenplays for two of the Fred Astaire/Ginger Rogers musicals *Top Hat* (1935) and *Follow the Fleet* (1936).

15 Are you sure you didn't forget yourself in the park?
Positive. If I ever forget myself with that girl I'd remember it.
1935 Dialogue between Edward Everett Horton and Fred Astaire in *Top Hat* (with Allan Scott).

Taylor, Elizabeth Rosemond 1932–

English-born US film actress. She graduated from child star to screen goddess in films such as *A Place in the Sun* (1951), *Raintree County* (1957), *Butterfield 8* (1960), *Cleopatra* (1962) and *Who's Afraid of Virginia Woolf?* (1966). She has had seven husbands, most famously Richard Burton, whom she married twice.

16 It will be fun to be the first Jewish Queen of Egypt.
c.1962 On taking the title role in *Cleopatra*. Attributed.

17 If someone was stupid enough to offer me a million dollars to make a picture—I was certainly not dumb enough to turn it down.
Quoted in David Niven *The Moon's a Balloon* (1975).

18 Success is a great deodorant.
1977 ABC TV broadcast, 6 Apr.

19 You help them get elected, and then the Senate becomes the wife, the mistress. That was one lady I couldn't begin to fight. She was too tough.
1987 After her marriage to Senator John Warner. In *Cosmopolitan*, Sep.

20 Some of my best leading men have been horses and dogs.
Attributed.

Taylor, Graham 1944–

English football manager. Manager of Aston Villa and other sides, he succeeded Bobby Robson as manager of England in 1990 but resigned three years later after England failed to qualify for the 1994 World Cup.

21 Agents do nothing for the good of football. I'd like to see them lined up against a wall and machine-gunned …some accountants and solicitors with them.
1983 Quoted in Peter Ball and Phil Shaw *The Book of Football Quotations* (1989).

22 Do I not like that!
1993 During England defeat to Norway, recorded in television documentary.

Taylor, Jeremy 1613–67

English divine, whose sermons and devotional writings are masterpieces and considered to be of sacred eloquence.

23 Faith gives new light to the soul, but it does not put our eyes out; and what God hath given us in our nature could never be intended as a snare to Religion, or engage us to believe a lie.
1660 *The Worthy Communicant*.

Taylor, John Vincent

24 The Holy Spirit is the invisible third party who stands between me and the other, making us mutually aware.
1972 *The Go-Between God.*

25 [God's] changelessness means that he cannot cease to be what he is, but it does not preclude his doing some new thing to express what he is.
1992 *The Christlike God.*

Taylor, Maxwell Davenport 1901–87

US soldier, air commander in World War II and superintendent of West Point (1945–9). After commanding in Korea and the Far East, he was appointed army chief of staff (1955–9) but resigned when his proposals for army reorganization were disregarded. He was instrumental in securing US support for the war in Vietnam.

26 They didn't know how it ran, where you put in the gas, where you put in the oil, where you turn the throttle.
On the Kennedy White House and the botched invasion of Cuba's Bay of Pigs. Quoted in Ralph G Martin *A Hero for Our Time* (1983).

Teal, Clare

English jazz singer.

27 Jazz is a small word for a vast sound.
2002 In *The Guardian*, 29 Dec.

Tebbit, Norman (Beresford) Tebbit, Baron 1931–

English Conservative politician, Employment Secretary (1981–3) and Secretary for Trade and Industry (1983–5). In 1984 he and his wife were injured by an IRA bomb in Brighton. In 1985 he became Chairman of the Party, but after 1987 he returned to the backbenches until his retirement in 1992.

28 He didn't riot. He got on his bike and looked for work, and he kept looking till he found it.
1981 Speaking of his father after criticism of high unemployment under the Conservative Government, party conference, 15 Oct.

29 The cricket test—which side do they cheer for?
1990 On the loyalties of immigrants in Britain. In the *Los Angeles Times*, Apr.

Te Kanawa, Dame Kiri 1944–

New Zealand soprano.

30 When men reach about the age of 50 they tend to digress and don't want to do anything. You can't inspire them to do anything—they almost go to sleep in their bodies.
2001 In *The Mail on Sunday*, 25 Nov.

Teller, Edward 1908–2003

Hungarian-born US physicist, called the father of the hydrogen bomb. He was born in Budapest, and educated in Germany. In 1941 he became a US citizen and joined the US atomic bomb development project known as the Manhattan Project.

31 If there ever was a misnomer, it is 'exact science'. Science has always been full of mistakes; they require a genius to correct them. Of course, we do not see our own mistakes.
1991 *Conversations on the Dark Secrets of Physics.*

Temple, William 1881–1944

English prelate. Headmaster of Repton School (1910–14), he became a bishop in 1921, Archbishop of York in 1919, and succeeded as Archbishop of Canterbury in 1942. He was an outspoken advocate of social reform.

32 Personally, I have always looked upon cricket as organized loafing.
c.1914 Address to parents of pupils at Repton School, Derbyshire.

33 Christianity is the most materialist of all great religions.
1939 *Readings in St John's Gospel*, vol.1.

34 I believe in the Church, one Holy Catholic and Apostolic Church; and nowhere does it exist.
Attributed.

Templeton, Charles 1915–2001

Canadian media personality and author.

35 You are born with two things: existence and opportunity, and these are the raw materials out of which you can make a successful life.
1989 *Succeeding.*

Tennyson, Alfred, 1st Baron *also called* Alfred, Lord Tennyson 1809–92

English lyric poet, a master of rhythm, mood and imagery. He became Poet Laureate in 1850. Among the finest poems are *Morte d'Arthur* (1842), the elegiac *In Memoriam* (1850) and *The Idylls of the King* (1859).

36 Below the thunders of the upper deep;
Far, far beneath in the abysmal sea,
His ancient, dreamless, uninvaded sleep
The Kraken sleepeth.
1830 *Poems, Chiefly Lyrical*, 'The Kraken', l.1–4.

37 There hath he lain for ages and will lie
Battening upon huge seaworms in his sleep
Until the latter fire shall heat the deep.
1830 *Poems, Chiefly Lyrical*, 'The Kraken', l.11–13.

38 Vex not thou the poet's mind
With thy shallow wit:
Vex not thou the poet's mind;
For thou canst not fathom it.
1830 *Poems, Chiefly Lyrical*, 'The Poet's Mind', l.1–4.

39 Airy, fairy Lilian.
1830 *Poems*, 'Lilian', l.1.

40 A daughter of the gods, divinely tall,
And most divinely fair.
1832 *Poems*, 'A Dream of Fair Women', l.87–8.

41 O Love, O fire! once he drew
With one long kiss my whole soul through
My lips, as sunlight drinketh dew.
1832 *Poems*, 'Fatima', stanza 3.

42 On either side the river lie
Long fields of barley and of rye,
That clothe the wold and meet the sky;
And through the field the road runs by
To many-towered Camelot.
1832 *Poems*, 'The Lady of Shalott' (revised 1842), pt.1, l.1–5.

43 Willows whiten, aspens quiver,
Little breezes dusk and shiver.
1832 *Poems*, 'The Lady of Shalott' (revised 1842), pt.1, l.10–11.

44 Four grey walls, and four grey towers,
Overlook a space of flowers,
And the silent isle imbowers
The Lady of Shalott.
1832 *Poems*, 'The Lady of Shalott' (revised 1842), pt.1, l.15–18.

45 Only reapers, reaping early
In among the bearded barley,
Hear a song that echoes cheerly
From the river winding clearly,
Down to towered Camelot.
1832 *Poems*, 'The Lady of Shalott' (revised 1842), pt.1, l.28–32.

46 And moving through a mirror clear
That hangs before her all the year,
Shadows of the world appear.
1832 *Poems*, 'The Lady of Shalott' (revised 1842), pt.2, l.46–8.

47 Or when the moon was overhead,
Came two young lovers lately wed;
'I am half sick of shadows,' said
The Lady of Shalott.
1832 *Poems*, 'The Lady of Shalott' (revised 1842), pt.2, l.69–72.

48 A bow-shot from her bower-eaves,
He rode between the barley-sheaves,
The sun came dazzling through the leaves,
And flamed upon the brazen greaves
Of bold Sir Lancelot.
A red-cross knight forever kneeled
To a lady in his shield,
That sparkled on the yellow field,
Beside remote Shalott.
1832 *Poems*, 'The Lady of Shalott' (revised 1842), pt.3, l.73–81.

49 All in the blue unclouded weather
Thick-jewelled shone the saddle leather,
The helmet and the helmet-feather
Burned like one burning flame together,
As he rode down to Camelot.
1832 *Poems*, 'The Lady of Shalott' (revised 1842), pt.3, l.91–5.

50 She left the web, she left the loom,
She made three paces through the room,
She saw the water-lily bloom,
She saw the helmet and the plume,
She looked down to Camelot.
Out flew the web and floated wide;
The mirror cracked from side to side;
'The curse is come upon me', cried
The Lady of Shalott.
1832 *Poems*, 'The Lady of Shalott' (revised 1842), pt.3, l.109–17.

51 Down she came and found a boat
Beneath a willow left afloat,
And round about the prow she wrote
The Lady of Shalott.
1832 *Poems*, 'The Lady of Shalott' (revised 1842), pt.4, l.123–6.

52 But Lancelot mused a little space;
He said, 'She has a lovely face;
God in his mercy lend her grace,
The Lady of Shalott.'
1832 *Poems*, 'The Lady of Shalott' (revised 1842), pt.4, l.168–71.

53 'Courage!' he said, and pointed toward the land,
'This mounting wave will roll us shoreward soon.'
In the afternoon they came unto a land
In which it seemèd always afternoon.
All round the coast the languid air did swoon,
Breathing like one that hath a weary dream.
1832 *Poems*, 'The Lotos–Eaters', l.1–6.

54 There is sweet music here that softer falls
Than petals from blown roses on the grass,
Or night dews on still waters between walls
Of shadowy granite, in a gleaming pass;
Music that gentlier on the spirit lies,
Than tired eyelids upon tired eyes.
1832 *Poems*, 'The Lotos–Eaters', Choric Song, stanza 1, l.46–51.

55 There is no joy but calm!
1832 *Poems*, 'The Lotos–Eaters', Choric Song, stanza 2, l.68.

56 Death is the end of life; ah, why
Should life all labour be?
1832 *Poems* 'The Lotos–Eaters', Choric Song, stanza 4, l.86–87.

57 Live and lie reclined
On the hills like Gods together, careless of mankind.
For they lie beside their nectar, and the bolts are hurled
Far below them in the valleys, and the clouds are lightly curled
Round their golden houses, girdled with the gleaming world.
1832 *Poems*, 'The Lotos–Eaters', Choric Song, stanza 8, l.154–8.

58 Surely, surely, slumber is more sweet than toil, the shore
Than labour in the deep mid-ocean, wind and wave and oar;
Oh rest ye, brother mariners, we will not wander more.
1832 *Poems*, 'The Lotos–Easters', Choric Song, stanza 8, l.171–3.

59 I built my soul a lordly pleasure-house,
Wherein at ease for aye to dwell.
1832 *Poems*, 'The Palace of Art', stanza 1, l.1–2.

60 And 'while the world runs round and round,' I said,
'Reign thou apart, a quiet king,
Still as, while Saturn whirls, his steadfast shade
Sleeps on his luminous ring.'
1832 *Poems*, 'The Palace of Art', stanza 4, l.13–16.

61 An English home—grey twilight poured
On dewy pasture, dewy trees,
Softer than sleep—all things in order stored,
A haunt of ancient Peace.
1832 *Poems*, 'The Palace of Art', stanza 22, l.85–8.

62 It little profits that an idle king
By this still hearth, among these barren crags,
Matched with an agèd wife, I mete and dole
Unequal laws unto a savage race,
That hoard, and sleep, and feed, and know not me.
1833 *Poems*, 'Ulysses' (published 1842), l.1–5.

63 I cannot rest from travel: I will drink
Life to the lees: all times I have enjoyed
Greatly, have suffered greatly, both with those
That loved me, and alone; on shore, and when
Through scudding drifts the rainy Hyades
Vext the dim sea: I am become a name;
For always roaming with a hungry heart
Much have I seen and known; cities of men
And manners, climates, council, governments,
Myself not least, but honoured of them all;
And drunk delight of battle with my peers,
Far on the ringing plains of windy Troy.
I am part of all that I have met;
Yet all experience is an arch wherethrough
Gleams that untravelled world, whose margin fades

For ever and for ever when I move.
How dull it is to pause, to make an end,
To rust unburnished, not to shine in use!
As though to breathe were life.
1833 *Poems*, 'Ulysses' (published 1842), l.6–24.

64 This grey spirit yearning in desire
To follow knowledge like a sinking star,
Beyond the utmost bound of human thought.
1833 *Poems*, 'Ulysses' (published 1842), l.30–2.

65 This is my son, mine own Telemachus.
1833 *Poems*, 'Ulysses' (published 1842), l.33.

66 There lies the port; the vessel, puffs her sail:
There gloom the dark broad seas. My mariners,
Souls that have toiled, and wrought, and thought with me—
That ever with a frolic welcome took
The thunder and the sunshine, and opposed
Free hearts, free foreheads—you and I are old:
Old age hath yet his honour and his toil;
Death closes all: but something ere the end,
Some work of noble note, may yet be done,
Not unbecoming men that strove with gods.
The lights begin to twinkle from the rocks:
The long day wanes: the slow moon climbs: the deep
Moans round with many voices. Come, my friends,
'Tis not too late to seek a newer world.
Push off, and sitting well in order smite
The sounding furrows: for my purpose holds
To sail beyond the sunset, and the baths
Of all the western stars, until I die.
It may be that the gulfs will wash us down:
It may be we shall touch the Happy Isles,
And see the great Achilles, whom we knew.
Though much is taken, much abides: and though
We are not now that strength which in old days
Moved earth and hearth: that which we are, we are:
One equal temper of heroic hearts,
Made weak by time and fate, but strong in will
To strive, to seek, to find, and not to yield.
1833 *Poems*, 'Ulysses' (published 1842), l.44–70.

67 Break, break, break,
On thy cold grey stones, O Sea!
And I would that my tongue could utter
The thoughts that arise in me.
1842 *Poems*, 'Break, Break, Break', stanza 1.

68 And the stately ships go on
To their haven under the hill;
But O for the touch of a vanished hand,
And the sound of a voice that is still!
1842 *Poems*, 'Break, Break, Break', stanza 3.

69 'Tis not your work, but Love's. Love, unperceived,
A more ideal Artist he than all,
Came, drew your pencil from you, made those eyes
Darker than the darkest pansies, and that hair
More black than ashbuds in the front of March.
1842 *Poems*, 'The Gardener's Daughter', l.24–8.

70 A sight to make an old man young.
1842 *Poems*, 'The Gardener's Daughter', l.140.

71 Then she rode forth, clothed on with chastity.
1842 *Poems*, 'Godiva', l.53.

72 With twelve great shocks of sound, the shameless noon
Was clashed and hammered from a hundred towers.
1842 *Poems*, 'Godiva', l.74–5.

73 At me you smiled, but unbeguiled
I saw the snare, and I retired:
The daughter of a hundred Earls,
You are not one to be desired.
1842 *Poems*, 'Lady Clara Vere de Vere', stanza 1, l.5–8.

74 From yon blue heavens above us bent
The gardener Adam and his wife
Smile at the claims of long descent.
Howe'er it be, it seems to me,
'Tis only noble to be good.
Kind hearts are more than coronets,
And simple faith than Norman blood.
1842 *Poems*, 'Lady Clara Vere de Vere', stanza 7, l.50–6.

75 In the Spring a fuller crimson comes upon the robin's breast;
In the Spring the wanton lapwing gets himself another crest
In the Spring a livelier iris changes on the burnished dove;
In the Spring a young man's fancy lightly turns to thoughts of love.
1842 *Poems*, 'Locksley Hall', l.17–20.

76 And our spirits rushed together at the touching of the lips.
1842 *Poems*, 'Locksley Hall', l.38.

77 He will hold thee, when his passion shall have spent its novel force,
Something better than his dog, a little dearer than his horse.
1842 *Poems*, 'Locksley Hall', l.49–50.

78 This is truth the poet sings,
That a sorrow's crown of sorrow is remembering happier things.
1842 *Poems*, 'Locksley Hall' l.75–6.

79 Like a dog, he hunts in dreams.
1842 *Poems*, 'Locksley Hall', l.79.

80 But the jingling of the guinea helps the hurt that Honour feels.
1842 *Poems*, 'Locksley Hall', l.105.

81 Men, my brothers, men the workers, ever reaping something new:
That which they have done but earnest of the things that they shall do:

For I dipped into the future, far as human eye could see,
Saw the vision of the world, and all the wonder that would be;

Saw the heaven fill with commerce, argosies of magic sails,
Pilots of the purple twilight, dropping down with costly bales;

Heard the heavens fill with shouting, and there rained a ghastly dew
From the nations' airy navies grappling in the central blue;

Far along the world-wide whisper of the south-wind rushing warm,

With the standards of the peoples plunging through the thunder-storm;

Till the war-drum throbbed no longer, and the battle-flags were furled
In the Parliament of man, the Federation of the world.
1842 *Poems*, 'Locksley Hall', l.117–28.

82 Science moves, but slowly slowly, creeping on from point to point.
1842 *Poems*, 'Locksley Hall', l.134.

83 Yet I doubt not through the ages one increasing purpose runs,
And the thoughts of men are widened with the process of the suns.
1842 *Poems*, 'Locksley Hall', l.137–8.

84 Knowledge comes, but wisdom lingers, and I linger on the shore,
And the individual withers, and the world is more and more.
1842 *Poems*, 'Locksley Hall', l.141–2.

85 I will take some savage woman, she shall rear my dusky race.
1842 *Poems*, 'Locksley Hall', l.168.

86 I the heir of all the ages, in the foremost files of time.
1842 *Poems*, 'Locksley Hall', l.178.

87 Forward, forward let us range,
Let the great world spin for ever down the ringing grooves of change.
1842 *Poems*, 'Locksley Hall', l.181–2.

88 Better fifty years of Europe than a cycle of Cathay.
1842 *Poems*,' Locksley Hall', l.184.

89 This truth within thy mind rehearse,
That in a boundless universe
Is boundless better, boundless worse.
1842 *Poems*, 'The Two Voices', stanza 9, l.25–7.

90 No life that breathes with human breath
Has ever truly longed for death.
1842 *Poems*, 'The Two Voices', stanza 132, l.395–6.

91 Fill the cup, and fill the can:
Have a rouse before the morn:
Every moment dies a man,
Every moment one is born.
1842 *Poems*, 'The Vision of Sin', pt.4, stanza 9, l.95–8.

92 I grow in worth, and wit, and sense,
Unboding critic-pen,
Or that eternal want of pence,
Which vexes public men.
1842 *Poems*, 'Will Waterproof's Lyrical Monologue', stanza 6, l.41–4.

93 A land of settled government,
A land of just and old renown,
Where Freedom slowly broadens down
From precedent to precedent.
1842 *Poems*, 'You ask me, why, though ill at ease', stanza 3, l.9–12.

94 But we grow old, Ah! when shall all men's good
Be each man's rule, and universal peace
Lie like a shaft of light across the land,
And like a lane of beams athwart the sea,
Through all the circle of the golden year.
1846 'The Golden Year', l.47–51.

95 With prudes for proctors, dowagers for deans,
And sweet girl-graduates in their golden hair.
1847 *The Princess*, 'Prologue', l.141–2.

96 A classic lecture, rich in sentiment,
With scraps of thundrous Epic lilted out
By violet-hooded Doctors, elegies
And quoted odes, and jewels five-words-long,
That on the stretched forefinger of all Time
Sparkle for ever.
1847 *The Princess*, pt.2, l.352–7.

97 Man is the hunter; woman is his game:
The sleek and shining creatures of the chase,
We hunt them for the beauty of their skins;
They love us for it, and we ride them down.
1847 *The Princess*, pt.5, l.147–50.

98 The woman is so hard
Upon the woman.
1847 *The Princess*, pt.6, l.205–6.

99 No little lily-handed baronet he,
A great broad-shouldered genial Englishman,
A lord of fat prize-oxen and of sheep,
A raiser of huge melons and of pine,
A patron of some thirty charities,
A pamphleteer on guano and on grain.
1847 *The Princess*, 'Conclusion', l.84–9.

1 And blessings on the falling out
That all the more endears,
When we fall out with those we love
And kiss again with tears!
1850 *The Princess*, pt.2, added song, l.6–9.

2 Sweet and low, sweet and low,
Wind of the western sea,
Low, low, breathe and blow,
Wind of the western sea!
Over the rolling waters go,
Come from the dying moon, and blow,
Blow him again to me;
While my little one, while my pretty one, sleeps.

Sleep and rest, sleep and rest,
Father will come to thee soon;
Rest, rest, on mother's breast,
Father will come to thee soon;
Father will come to his babe in the nest,
Silver sails all out of the west
Under the silver moon:
Sleep, my little one, sleep, my pretty one, sleep.
1850 *The Princess*, pt.3, added song, stanzas 1–2.

3 The splendour falls on castle walls
And snowy summits old in story:
The long light shakes across the lakes,
And the wild cataract leaps in glory.
Blow, bugle, blow, set the wild echoes flying,
Blow, bugle; answer, echoes, dying, dying, dying.
1850 *The Princess*, pt.4, added song, stanza 1.

4 O hark, O hear! how thin and clear
And thinner, clearer, farther going!
O sweet and far from cliff and scar
The horns of Elfland faintly blowing!
Blow, let us hear the purple glens replying:

Blow, bugle; answer, echoes, dying, dying, dying.
1850 *The Princess*, pt.4, added song, stanza 2.

5 O love, they die in yon rich sky,
They faint on hill or field or river:
Our echoes roll from soul to soul,
And grow for ever and for ever.
1850 *The Princess*, pt.4, added song, stanza 3.

6 Tears, idle tears, I know not what they mean,
Tears from the depth of some divine despair
Rise in the heart, and gather to the eyes,
In looking on the happy autumn-fields,
And thinking of the days that are no more.
1850 *The Princess*, pt.4, added song, stanza 1.

7 So sad, so fresh, the days that are no more.
1850 *The Princess*, pt.4, added song, stanza 2.

8 Ah, sad and strange as in dark summer dawns
The earliest pipe of half-awakened birds
To dying ears, when unto dying eyes
The casement slowly grows a glimmering square;
So sad, so strange, the days that are no more.

Dear as remembered kisses after death,
And sweet as those by hopeless fancy feigned
On lips that are for others; deep as love,
Deep as first love, and wild with all regret;
O Death in Life, the days that are no more.
1850 *The Princess*, pt.4, added song, stanzas 3–4.

9 O Swallow, Swallow, flying, flying South,
Fly to her, and fall upon her gilded eaves,
And tell her, tell her, what I tell to thee.
O tell her, Swallow, thou that knowest each,
That bright and fierce and fickle is the South,
And dark and true and tender is the North.
1850 *The Princess*, pt.4, added song, stanzas 1–2.

10 O tell her, Swallow that thy brood is flown:
Say to her, I do but wanton in the South,
But in the North long since my nest is made.
1850 *The Princess*, pt.4, added song, stanza 6.

11 Home they brought her warrior dead.
She nor swooned, nor uttered cry:
All her maidens, watching said,
'She must weep or she will die.'
1850 *The Princess*, pt.6, added song, stanza 1.

12 Rose a nurse of ninety years,
Set his child upon her knee–
Like summer tempest came her tears–
'Sweet my child, I live for thee.'
1850 *The Princess*, pt.6, added song, stanza 4.

13 Ask me no more: what answer should I give?
I love not hollow cheek or faded eye:
Yet, O my friend, I will not have thee die!
Ask me no more, lest I should bid thee live.
1850 *The Princess*, pt.7, added song, stanza 2.

14 Now sleeps the crimson petal, now the white;
Nor waves the cypress in the palace walk;
Nor winks the gold fin in the porphyry font:
The fire-fly wakens: waken thou, with me.

Now droops the milk-white peacock like a ghost,
And like a ghost she glimmers on to me.
Now lies the Earth all Danaë to the stars,
And all thy heart lies open unto me.

Now slides the silent meteor on, and leaves
A shining furrow, as thy thoughts in me.

Now folds the lily all her sweetness up,
And slips into the bosom of the lake:
So fold thyself, my dearest, thou, and slip
Into my bosom and be lost in me.
1850 *The Princess*, pt.7, added song, complete.

15 Come down, O maid, from yonder mountain height:
What pleasure lives in height?
1850 *The Princess*, pt.7, added song, l.1–2.

16 For love is of the valley, come thou down
And find him; by the happy threshold, he,
Or hand in hand with Plenty in the maize,
Or red with spirited purple of the vats,
Or foxlike in the vine; nor cares to walk
With Death and Morning on the silver horns.
1850 *The Princess*, pt.7, added song, l.184–9.

17 Sweet is every sound,
Sweeter thy voice, but every sound is sweet;
Myriads of rivulets hurrying through the lawn,
The moan of doves in immemorial elms,
With murmuring of innumerable bees.
1850 *The Princess*, pt.7, added song, l.203–7.

18 Come not, when I am dead,
To drop thy foolish tears upon my grave,
To trample round my fallen head,
And vex the unhappy dust thou wouldst not save.
There let the wind sweep and the plover cry;
But thou, go by.

Child, if it were thine error or thy crime
I care no longer, being all unblest;
Wed whom thou wilt, but I am sick of Time,
And I desire to rest.
Pass on, weak heart, and leave me where I lie:
Go by, go by.
1850 'Come not, when I am dead', complete poem.

19 Strong Son of God, immortal Love,
Whom we, that have not seen thy face,
By faith, and faith alone, embrace,
Believing where we cannot prove.
1850 *In Memoriam A.H.H.*, prologue, l.1–4.

20 Thou madest man, he knows not why,
He thinks he was not made to die;
And thou hast made him: thou art just.
1850 *In Memoriam A.H.H.*, prologue, l.10–12.

21 Our little systems have their day;
They have their day and cease to be;
They are but broken lights of thee,
And thou, O Lord, art more than they.
1850 *In Memoriam A.H.H.*, prologue, l.17–20.

22 Let knowledge grow from more to more,
But more of reverence in us dwell;
That mind and soul, according well,
May make one music as before.
1850 *In Memoriam A.H.H.*, prologue, l.25–8.

23 I sometimes hold it half a sin
To put in words the grief I feel;

For words, like Nature, half reveal
And half conceal the Soul within.

But, for the unquiet heart and brain,
A use in measured language lies;
The sad mechanic exercise,
Like dull narcotics, numbing pain.
1850 *In Memoriam A.H.H.*, canto 5, l.1–8.

24 And common is the commonplace,
And vacant chaff well meant for grain.
1850 *In Memoriam A.H.H.*, canto 6, l.3–4.

25 Never morning wore
To evening, but some heart did break.
1850 *In Memoriam A.H.H.*, canto 6, l.7–8.

26 His heavy-shotted hammock-shroud
Drops in his vast and wandering grave.
1850 *In Memoriam A.H.H.*, canto 6, l.15–16.

27 Dark house, by which once more I stand
Here in the long unlovely street,
Doors, where my heart was used to beat
So quickly, waiting for a hand.
1850 *In Memoriam A.H.H.*, canto 7, l.1–4.

28 And ghastly through the drizzling rain
On the bald street breaks the blank day.
1850 *In Memoriam A.H.H.*, canto 7, l.11–12.

29 The last red leaf is whirled away,
The rooks are blown about the skies.
1850 *In Memoriam A.H.H.*, canto 15, l.3–4.

30 There twice a day the Severn fills;
The salt sea-water passes by,
And hushes half the babbling Wye,
And makes a silence in the hills.
1850 *In Memoriam A.H.H.*, canto 19, l.5–8.

31 The Shadow cloaked from head to foot,
Who keeps the keys of all the creeds.
1850 *In Memoriam A.H.H.*, canto 23, l.4–5.

32 And Thought leapt out to wed with Thought
Ere Thought could wed itself with Speech.
1850 *In Memoriam A.H.H.*, canto 23, l.15–16.

33 I envy not in any moods
The captive void of noble rage,
The linnet born within the cage,
That never knew the summer woods.
1850 *In Memoriam A.H.H.*, canto 27, l.1–4.

34 I hold it true, whate'er befall;
I feel it, when I sorrow most;
'Tis better to have loved and lost
Than never to have loved at all.
1850 *In Memoriam A.H.H.*, canto 27, l.13–16.

35 A solemn gladness even crowned
The purple brows of Olivet.
1850 *In Memoriam A.H.H.*, canto 31, l.11–12.

36 Who trusted God was love indeed
And love Creation's final law—
Though Nature, red in tooth and claw
With ravine, shrieked against his creed.
1850 *In Memoriam A.H.H.*, canto 31.

37 Her eyes are homes of silent prayer.
1850 *In Memoriam A.H.H.*, canto 32, l.1.

38 Short swallow-flights of song, that dip
Their wings in tears, and skim away.
1850 *In Memoriam A.H.H.*, canto 48, l.15–16.

39 Be near me when my light is low,
When the blood creeps, and the nerves prick
And tingle; and the heart is sick,
And all the wheels of Being slow.

Be near me when the sensuous frame
Is racked with pains that conquer trust;
And Time, a maniac scattering dust,
And Life, a Fury slinging flame.
1850 *In Memoriam A.H.H.*, canto 50, l.1–8.

40 Oh yet we trust that somehow good
Will be the final goal of ill.
1850 *In Memoriam A.H.H.*, canto 54, l.1–2.

41 That nothing walks with aimless feet;
That not one life shall be destroyed,
Or cast as rubbish to the void,
When God hath made the pile complete.
1850 *In Memoriam A.H.H.*, canto 54, l.5–8.

42 Behold, we know not anything;
I can but trust that good shall fall
At last—far off—at last, to all,
And every winter change to spring.

So runs my dream: but what am I?
An infant crying in the night:
An infant crying for the light:
And with no language but a cry.
1850 *In Memoriam A.H.H.*, canto 54, l.13–20.

43 So careful of the type she seems,
So careless of the single life.
1850 Of Nature. *In Memoriam A.H.H.*, canto 55, l.7–8.

44 The great world's altar-stairs
That slope through darkness up to God.
1850 *In Memoriam A.H.H.*, canto 55, l.15–16.

45 Man, her last work, who seemed so fair,
Such splendid purpose in his eyes,
Who rolled the psalm to wintry skies,
Who built him fanes of fruitless prayer,
Who trusted God was love indeed
And love Creation's final law—
Though Nature, red in tooth and claw
With ravine, shrieked against his creed.
1850 *In Memoriam A.H.H.*, canto 56, l.9–16.

46 Peace; come away: the song of woe
Is after all an earthly song:
Peace; come away: we do him wrong
To sing so wildly: let us go.
1850 *In Memoriam A.H.H.*, canto 57, l.1–4.

47 O Sorrow, wilt thou live with me
No casual mistress, but a wife.
1850 *In Memoriam A.H.H.*, canto 59, l.1–2.

48 Dost thou look back on what hath been,
As some divinely gifted man,
Whose life in low estate began
And on a simple village green;

Who breaks his birth's invidious bar,
And grasps the skirts of happy chance,
And breasts the blows of circumstance,

And grapples with his evil star.
1850 *In Memoriam A.H.H.*, canto 64, l.1–8.

49 So many worlds, so much to do,
So little done, such things to be.
1850 *In Memoriam A.H.H.*, canto 73, l.1–2.

50 Death has made
His darkness beautiful with thee.
1850 *In Memoriam A.H.H.*, canto 74, l.11–12.

51 And round thee with the breeze of song
To stir a little dust of praise.
1850 *In Memoriam A.H.H.*, canto 75, l.11–12.

52 O last regret, regret can die!
1850 *In Memoriam A.H.H.*, canto 78, l.17.

53 Laburnums, dropping-wells of fire.
1850 *In Memoriam A.H.H.*, canto 83, l.12.

54 God's finger touched him, and he slept.
1850 *In Memoriam A.H.H.*, canto 85, l.20.

55 He brought an eye for all he saw;
He mixed in all our simple sports;
They pleased him, fresh from brawling courts
And dusty purlieus of the law.
1850 *In Memoriam A.H.H.*, canto 89, l.9–12.

56 You tell me, doubt is Devil-born.
1850 *In Memoriam A.H.H.*, canto 96, l.4.

57 There lives more faith in honest doubt,
Believe me, than in half the creeds.
1850 *In Memoriam A.H.H.*, canto 96, l.11–12.

58 Their meetings made December June,
Their every parting was to die.
1850 *In Memoriam A.H.H.*, canto 97, l.11–12.

59 He seems so near and yet so far.
1850 *In Memoriam A.H.H.*, canto 97, l.23.

60 Ring out, wild bells, to the wild sky,
The flying cloud, the frosty light:
The year is dying in the night;
Ring out, wild bells, and let him die.

Ring out the old, ring in the new,
Ring, happy bells, across the snow:
The year is going, let him go;
Ring out the false, ring in the true.
1850 *In Memoriam A.H.H.*, canto 106, l.1–8.

61 Ring out the want, the care, the sin,
The faithless coldness of the times;
Ring out, ring out my mournful rhymes,
But ring the fuller minstrel in.

Ring out false pride in place and blood,
The civic slander and the spite;
Ring in the love of truth and right,
Ring in the common love of good.

Ring out old shapes of foul disease;
Ring out the narrowing lust of gold;
Ring out the thousand wars of old,
Ring in the thousand years of peace.

Ring in the valiant man and free,
The larger heart, the kindlier hand;
Ring out the darkness of the land;
Ring in the Christ that is to be.
1850 *In Memoriam A.H.H.*, canto 106, l.17–32.

62 Not the schoolboy heat,
The blind hysterics of the Celt.
1850 *In Memoriam A.H.H.*, canto 109, l.15–16.

63 Now fades the last streak of snow,
Now burgeons every maze of quick
About the flowering squares, and thick
By ashen roots the violets blow.
1850 *In Memoriam A.H.H.*, canto 115, l.1–4.

64 And drowned in yonder living blue
The lark become a sightless song.
1850 *In Memoriam A.H.H.*, canto 115, l.7–8.

65 There, where the long street roars, hath been
The stillness of the central sea.
1850 *In Memoriam A.H.H.*, canto 123, l.3–4.

66 And thou art worthy; full of power;
As gentle; liberal-minded, great,
Consistent; wearing all that weight
Of learning lightly like a flower.
1850 *In Memoriam A.H.H.*, epilogue, l.37–40.

67 One God, one law, one element,
And one far-off divine event,
To which the whole creation moves.
1850 *In Memoriam A.H.H.*, epilogue, l.142–4.

68 He clasps the crag with crooked hands;
Close to the sun in lonely lands,
Ringed with the azure world, he stands.

The wrinkled sea beneath him crawls;
He watches from his mountain walls,
And like a thunderbolt he falls.
1851 'The Eagle', complete poem.

69 Gigantic daughter of the West,
We drink to thee across the flood,
We know thee most, we love thee best,
For art thou not of British blood?
1852 'Hands all Round', stanza 4, l.37–40.

70 The last great Englishman is low.
1852 'Ode on the Death of the Duke of Wellington', stanza 3, l.18.

71 O good grey head which all men knew!
1852 'Ode on the Death of the Duke of Wellington', stanza 4, l.35.

72 O fall'n at length that tower of strength
Which stood four-square to all the winds that blew!
1852 'Ode on the Death of the Duke of Wellington', stanza 4, l.38–9.

73 That world-earthquake, Waterloo!
1852 'Ode on the Death of the Duke of Wellington', stanza 6, l.133.

74 Who never sold the truth to serve the hour,
Nor paltered with Eternal God of power.
1852 'Ode on the Death of the Duke of Wellington', stanza 7, l.179–80.

75 Half a league, half a league,
Half a league onward,
All in the valley of Death
Rode the six hundred.
1854 'The Charge of the Light Brigade', l.1–4.

76 'Forward, the Light Brigade!'
Was there a man dismayed?
Not though the soldier knew

Some one had blundered:
Their's not to make reply,
Their's not to reason why,
Their's but to do and die:
Into the valley of Death
Rode the six hundred.

Cannon to right of them,
Cannon to left of them,
Cannon in front of them
Volleyed and thundered.
1854 'The Charge of the Light Brigade', l.9–21.

77 Into the jaws of Death,
Into the mouth of Hell
Rode the six hundred.
1854 'The Charge of the Light Brigade', l.24–6.

78 Faultily faultless, icily regular, splendidly null,
Dead perfection, no more.
1855 *Maud*, pt.1, sect.2, l.82–3.

79 The passionate heart of the poet is whirled into folly and vice.
1855 *Maud*, pt.1, sect.4, stanza 7, l.139.

80 And most of all would I flee from the cruel madness of love,
The honey of poison-flowers and all the measureless ill.
1855 *Maud*, pt.1, sect.4, stanza 10, l.156–7.

81 That jewelled mass of millinery,
That oiled and curled Assyrian Bull.
1855 *Maud*, pt.1, sect.6, stanza 6, l.232–3.

82 She came to the village church,
And sat by a pillar alone;
An angel watching an urn
Wept over her, carved in stone.
1855 *Maud*, pt.1, sect.8, l.301–4.

83 I heard no longer
The snowy-banded, dilettante,
Delicate-handed priest intone.
1855 *Maud*, pt.1, sect.8, l.309–11.

84 Ah God, for a man with heart, head, hand,
Like some of the simple great ones gone
For ever and ever by,
One still strong man in a blatant land,
Whatever they call him, what care I,
Aristocrat, democrat, autocrat—one
Who can rule and dare not lie.
1855 *Maud*, pt.1, sect.10, stanza 5, l.389–95.

85 And ah for a man to arise in me
That the man I am may cease to be!.
1855 *Maud*, pt.1, sect.10, stanza 6, l.396–7.

86 I kissed her slender hand,
She took the kiss sedately;
Maud is not seventeen,
But she is tall and stately.
1855 *Maud*, pt.1, sect.12, stanza 4, l.424–7.

87 Gorgonised me from head to foot
With a stony British stare.
1855 *Maud*, pt.1, sect.13, stanza 2, l.464–5.

88 A livelier emerald twinkles in the grass,
A purer sapphire melts into the sea.
1855 *Maud*, pt.1, sect.18, stanza 6, l.649–50.

89 Come into the garden, Maud,
For the black bat, night, has flown,
Come into the garden, Maud,
I am here at the gate alone;
And the woodbine spices are wafted abroad,
And the musk of the rose is blown.

For a breeze of morning moves,
And the planet of Love is on high,
Beginning to faint in the light that she loves
On a bed of daffodil sky.
1855 *Maud*, pt.1, sect.22, stanza 1, l.850–9.

90 All night has the casement jessamine stirred
To the dancers dancing in tune;
Till a silence fell with the waking bird,
And a hush with the setting moon.
1855 *Maud*, pt.1, sect.22, stanza 3, l.864–7.

91 Queen rose of the rosebud garden of girls.
1855 *Maud*, pt.1, sect.22, stanza 9, l.902.

92 There has fallen a splendid tear
From the passion-flower at the gate.
She is coming, my dove, my dear;
She is coming, my life, my fate;
The red rose cries, 'She is near, she is near;'
And the white rose weeps, 'She is late;'
The larkspur listens, 'I hear, I hear;'
And the lily whispers, 'I wait.'

She is coming, my own, my sweet;
Were it ever so airy a tread,
My heart would hear her and beat,
Were it earth in an earthy bed;
My dust would hear her and beat;
Had I lain for a century dead;
Would start and tremble under her feet,
And blossom in purple and red.
1855 *Maud*, pt.1, sect.22, stanzas 10–11, l. 908–23.

93 O that 'twere possible
After long grief and pain
To find the arms of my true love
Round me once again!
1855 *Maud*, pt.2, sect.4, stanza 1, l.141–4.

94 Dead, long dead,
Long dead!
And my heart is a handful of dust,
And the wheels go over my head.
1855 *Maud*, pt.2, sect.5, stanza 1, l.239–42.

95 But the churchmen fain would kill their church,
As the churches have killed their Christ.
1855 *Maud*, pt.2, sect.5, stanza 2, l.266–7.

96 O me, why have they not buried me deep enough?
Is it kind to have made me a grave so rough,
Me, that was never a quiet sleeper?
1855 *Maud*, pt.2, sect. 5, stanza 11, l.334–6.

97 My life has crept so long on a broken wing
Through cells of madness, haunts of horror and fear,
That I come to be grateful at last for a little thing.
1855 *Maud*, pt.3, sect.6, stanza 1, l.1–3.

98 When the face of night is fair on the dewy downs,
And the shining daffodil dies.
1855 *Maud*, pt.3, sect.6, stanza 1, l.5–6.

99 And now by the side of the Black and the Baltic deep,
And deathful-grinning mouths of the fortress, flames
The blood-red blossom of war with a heart of fire.
1855 *Maud*, pt.3, sect.6, stanza 4, l.51–3.

1 It is better to fight for the good, than to rail at the ill;
I have felt with my native land, I am one with my kind,
I embrace the purpose of God, and the doom assigned.
1855 *Maud*, pt.3, sect.6, stanza 5, l.57–9.

2 I come from haunts of coot and hern,
I make a sudden sally
And sparkle out among the fern,
To bicker down a valley.
1855 'The Brook', l.23–6.

3 For men may come and men may go,
But I go on for ever.
1855 'The Brook', l.33–4.

4 That a lie which is all a lie may be met and fought with outright,
But a lie which is part a truth is a harder matter to fight.
1859 'The Grandmother', stanza 8, l.31–2.

5 Wearing the white flower of a blameless life,
Before a thousand peering littlenesses,
In that fierce light which beats upon a throne,
And blackens every blot.
1859 *Idylls of the King*, dedication, l.24–7.

6 For man is man and master of his fate.
1859 *Idylls of the King*, 'The Marriage of Geraint', l.355.

7 Our hoard is little, but our hearts are great.
1859 *Idylls of the King*, 'The Marriage of Geraint', l.374.

8 They take the rustic murmur of their bourg
For the great wave that echoes round the world.
1859 *Idylls of the King*, 'The Marriage of Geraint', l.419–20.

9 It is little rift within the lute,
That by and by will make the music mute,
And ever widening slowly silence all.
1859 *Idylls of the King*, 'Merlin and Vivien', l.388–90.

10 And trust me not at all or all in all.
1859 *Idylls of the King*, 'Merlin and Vivien', l.396.

11 Man dreams of fame while woman wakes to love.
1859 *Idylls of the King*, 'Merlin and Vivien', l.458.

12 With this for motto, 'Rather use than fame'.
1859 *Idylls of the King*, 'Merlin and Vivien', l.478.

13 Where blind and naked Ignorance
Delivers brawling judgements, unashamed,
On all things all day long.
1859 *Idylls of the King*, 'Merlin and Vivien', l.662–4.

14 But every page having an ample marge,
And every marge enclosing in the midst
A square of text that looks a little blot.
1859 *Idylls of the King*, 'Merlin and Vivien', l.667–9.

15 Elaine the fair, Elaine the loveable,
Elaine the lily maid of Astolat.
1859 *Idylls of the King*, 'Lancelot and Elaine'.

16 He is all fault who hath no fault at all:
For who loves me must have a touch of earth.
1859 *Idylls of the King*, 'Lancelot and Elaine', l.132–3.

17 In me there dwells
No greatness, save it be some far-off touch
Of greatness to know well I am not great.
1859 *Idylls of the King*, 'Lancelot and Elaine', l.447–9.

18 I know not if I know what true love is,
But if I know, then, if I love not him,
I know there is none other I can love.
1859 *Idylls of the King*, 'Lancelot and Elaine', l.672–4.

19 The shackles of an old love straitened him,
His honour rooted in dishonour stood,
And faith unfaithful kept him falsely true.
1859 *Idylls of the King*, 'Lancelot and Elaine', l.870–2.

20 —Never yet
Was noble man but made ignoble talk.
He makes no friend who never made a foe.
1859 *Idylls of the King*, 'Lancelot and Elaine', l.1081–2.

21 To reverence the King, as if he were
Their conscience, and their conscience as their King,
To break the heathen and uphold the Christ,
To ride abroad redressing human wrongs,
To speak no slander, no, nor listen to it,
To honour his own words as if his God's.
1859 *Idylls of the King*, 'Guinevere', l.465–70.

22 To love one maiden only, cleave to her,
And worship her by years of noble deeds,
Until they won her; for indeed I knew
Of no more subtle master under heaven
Than is the maiden passion for a maid,
Not only to keep down the base in man,
But teach high thought, and aimable words
And courtliness, and the desire of fame,
And love of truth, and all that makes man.
1859 *Idylls of the King*, 'Guinevere', l.472–80.

23 I thought I could not breathe in that fine air
That pure severity of perfect light—
I yearned for warmth and colour which I found
In Lancelot.
1859 *Idylls of the King*, 'Guinevere', l.640–3.

24 It was my duty to have loved the highest;
It surely was my profit had I known:
It would have been my pleasure had I seen.
We needs must love the highest when we see it,
Not Lancelot, nor another.
1859 *Idylls of the King*, 'Guinevere', l.652–6.

25 The woods decay, the woods decay and fall,
The vapours weep their burthen to the ground,
Man comes and tills the field and lies beneath,
And after many a summer dies the swan.
Me only cruel immortality
Consumes: I wither slowly in thine arms,
Here at the quiet limit of the world.
1860 'Tithonus' (revised 1864), l.1–7.

26 Why wilt thou ever scare me with thy tears,
And make me tremble lest a saying learnt,
In days far-off, on that dark earth, be true?
'The gods themselves cannot recall their gifts.'
1860 'Tithonus' (revised 1864), l.46–9.

27 Of happy men that have the power to die,
And grassy barrows of the happier dead.
1860 'Tithonus' (revised 1864), l.70–1.

28 O mighty-mouthed inventor of harmonies,
O skilled to sing of Time or Eternity,
God-gifted organ-voice of England,
Milton, a name to resound for ages.
1863 'Milton: Alcaics', l.1–4.

29 All that bowery loneliness,
The brooks of Eden mazily murmuring.
1863 'Milton: Alcaics', l.9–10.

30 O you chorus of indolent reviewers.
1863 'Milton: Hendecasyllabics', l.1.

31 And when they buried him the little port
Had seldom seen a costlier funeral.
1864 'Enoch Arden', closing words.

32 The voice of the dead was a living voice to me.
1864 'In the Valley of Cauteretz', l.10.

33 I saw the flaring atom-streams
And torrents of her myriad universe,
Ruining along the illimitable inane
Fly on to clash together again, and make
Another and another frame of things
For ever.
1868 'Lucretius', l.38–40.

34 Nor at all can tell
Whether I mean this day to end myself,
Or lend an ear to Plato where he says,
That men like soldiers may not quit the post
Allotted by the Gods.
1868 'Lucretius', l.145–9.

35 Passionless bride, divine Tranquillity,
Yearned after by the wisest of the wise,
Who fail to find thee, being as thou art
Without one pleasure and without one pain.
1868 'Lucretius', l.265–8.

36 Speak to Him thou for He hears, and Spirit with Spirit can meet—
Closer is He than breathing, and nearer than hands and feet.
1869 'The Higher Pantheism', l.11–12.

37 Man's word is God in man.
1869 *Idylls of the King*, 'The Coming of Arthur', l.132.

38 Clothed in white samite, mystic, wonderful.
1869 *Idylls of the King*, 'The Coming of Arthur', l.284.

39 Rain, rain, and sun! a rainbow in the sky!
A young man will be wiser by and by;
An old man's wit may wander ere he die.
1869 *Idylls of the King*, 'The Coming of Arthur', l.402–4.

40 From the great deep to the great deep he goes.
1869 *Idylls of the King*, 'The Coming of Arthur', l.410.

41 Blow trumpet, for the world is white with May.
1869 *Idylls of the King*, 'The Coming of Arthur', l.481.

42 For good ye are and bad, and like to coins,
Some true, some light, but every one of you
Stamped with the image of the King.
1869 *Idylls of the King*, 'The Holy Grail', l.25–7.

43 I will be deafer than the blue-eyed cat,
And thrice as blind as any noonday owl,
To holy virgins in their ecstasies.
1869 *Idylls of the King*, 'The Holy Grail', l.862–4.

44 I found Him in the shining of the stars,
I marked Him in the flowering of His fields,
But in His ways with men I find Him not.
1869 *Idylls of the King*, 'The Passing of Arthur', l.9–11.

45 So all day long the noise of battle rolled
Among the mountains by the winter sea.
1869 *Idylls of the King*, 'The Passing of Arthur', l.170–1.

46 On one side lay the Ocean, and on one
Lay a great water, and the moon was full.
1869 *Idylls of the King*, 'The Passing of Arthur', l.179–80.

47 Authority forgets a dying king.
1869 *Idylls of the King*, 'The Passing of Arthur', l.289.

48 Clothed with his breath, and looking, as he walked,
Larger than human on the frozen hills.
He heard the deep behind him, and a cry
Before.
1869 *Idylls of the King*, 'The Passing of Arthur', l.350–3.

49 And the days darken round me, and the years,
Among new men, strange faces, other minds.
1869 *Idylls of the King*, 'The Passing of Arthur', l.405–6.

50 The old order changeth, yielding place to new,
And God fulfils himself in many ways,
Lest one good custom should corrupt the world.
1869 *Idylls of the King*, 'The Passing of Arthur', l.408–10.

51 If thou shouldst never see my face again,
Pray for my soul. More things are wrought by prayer
Than this world dreams of. Wherefore, let thy voice
Rise like a fountain for me night and day.
For what are men better than sheep or goats
That nourish a blind life within the brain,
If, knowing God, they lift not hands of prayer
Both for themselves and those who call them friend?
For so the whole round earth is every way
Bound by gold chains about the feet of God.
1869 *Idylls of the King*, 'The Passing of Arthur', l.414–23.

52 I am going a long way
With these thou se'st—if indeed I go
(For all my mind is clouded with a doubt)—
To the island valley of Avilion;
Where falls not hail, or rain, or any snow,
Nor ever wind blows loudly; but it lies
Deep-meadowed, happy, fair with orchard lawns
And bowery hollows crowed with summer sea,
Where I will heal me of my grievous wound.
1869 *Idylls of the King*, 'The Passing of Arthur', l.424–32.

53 Like some full-breasted swan
That, fluting a wild carol ere her death,
Ruffles her pure cold plume, and takes the flood
With swarthy webs.
1869 *Idylls of the King*, 'The Passing of Arthur', l.434–7.

54 But I knaw'd a Quaäker feller as often 'as towd ma this:
'Doänt thou marry for munny, but goä wheer munny is!'
1869 'Northern Farmer. New Style', stanza 5.

55 Taäke my word for it, Sammy, the poor in a loomp is bad.
1869 'Northern Farmer. New Style', stanza 12.

56 The dirty nurse, Experience, in her kind
Hath fouled me.
1871 *Idylls of the King*, 'The Last Tournment', l.317–18.

57 The greater man, the greater courtesy.
1871 *Idylls of the King*, 'The Last Tournment', l.628.

58 Live pure, speak true, right wrong, follow the King—
Else, wherefore born?
1872 *Idylls of the King*, 'Gareth and Lynette', l.117–18.

59 The city is built
To music, therefore never built at all,
And therefore built for ever.
1872 *Idylls of the King*, 'Gareth and Lynette', l.272–4.

60 At Flores in the Azores Sir Richard Grenville lay,
And a pinnace, like a fluttered bird, came flying from far away:
'Spanish ships of war at sea! We have sighted fifty-three!'
Then sware Lord Thomas Howard: "Fore God I am no coward;
But I cannot meet them here, for my ships are out of gear,
And the half my men are sick. I must fly, but follow quick.
We are six ships of the line; can we fight with fifty-three?'

Then spake Sir Richard Grenville: 'I know you are no coward;
You fly them for a moment to fight with them again.
But I've ninety men and more that are lying sick ashore.
I should count myself the coward if I left them, my Lord Howard,
To these Inquisition dogs and the devildoms of Spain.'

So Lord Howard passed away with five ships of war that day,
Till he melted like a cloud in the silent summer heaven.
1878 'The Revenge', stanzas 1–3, l.1–14.

61 And Sir Richard said again: 'We be all good English men.
Let us bang these dogs of Seville, the children of the devil,
For I never turned my back upon Don or devil yet.'
1878 'The Revenge', stanza 4, l.29–31.

62 And the sun went down, and the stars came out far over the summer sea,
But never a moment ceased the fight of the one and the fifty-three.
1878 'The Revenge', stanza 9, l.56–7.

63 'Sink me the ship, Master Gunner—sink her, split her in twain!
Fall into the hands of God, not into the hands of Spain!'

And the gunner said 'Ay, ay,' but the seamen made reply:
'We have children we have wives,
And the Lord hath spared our lives.'
1878 'The Revenge', stanzas 11–12, l.89–93.

64 And they praised him to his face with their courtly foreign grace;
But he rose upon their decks, and he cried:
'I have fought for Queen and Faith like a valiant man and true;
I have only done my duty as a man is bound to do:
With a joyful spirit I Sir Richard Grenville die!'
And he fell upon their decks, and he died.
1878 'The Revenge', stanza 13, l.99–104.

65 And little Revenge herself went down by the island crags
To be lost evermore in the main.
1878 'The Revenge', stanza 14, l.118–19.

66 That man's the true Conservative
Who lops the mouldered branch away.
1882 'Hands All Round', l.7–8.

67 Pray God our greatness may not fail
Through craven fears of being great.
1882 'Hands All Round', l.31–2.

68 For nothing worthy proving can be proven,
Nor yet disproven: wherefore thou be wise,
Cleave ever to the sunnier side of doubt.
1885 'The Ancient Sage', l.66–8.

69 France had shown a light to all men, preached a Gospel, all men's good;
Celtic Demos rose a Demon, shriek'd and slaked the light with blood.
1886 'Locksley Hall Sixty Years After', l.89–90.

70 Twilight and evening bell,
And after that the dark!
And may there be no sadness of farewell,
When I embark;

For though from out our bourne of Time and Place
The flood may bear me far,
I hope to see my Pilot face to face
When I have crossed the bar.
1889 'Crossing the Bar', l.9–16. This was Tennyson's last poem.

71 The mellow lin-lan-lone of evening bells.
1889 'Far-Far-Away', l.5.

72 Launch your vessel,
And crowd your canvas,
And, ere it vanishes
Over the margin,
After it, follow it,
Follow The Gleam.
1889 'Merlin and The Gleam', stanza 9, l.126–31.

73 What is it all but a trouble of ants in the gleam of a million million of suns?
1889 'Vastness', stanza 2, l.4.

74 A louse in the locks of literature.
Of Churton Collins. Quoted in Evan Charteris *Life and Letters of Sir Edmund Gosse* (1931), ch.14.

Tenzing Norgay *known as* ***Sherpa Tenzing*** 1914–86

Nepalese mountaineer. He took part in several Himalayan expeditions before accompanying Edmund Hillary to the summit of Everest in 1953. Subsequently he became head of the Institute of Mountaineering in Darjeeling and President of the Sherpa Association.

75 We done the bugger!
1953 On reaching the summit of Everest, 29 May.

Terence *full name* ***Publius Terentius Afer*** 185–159 BC

Roman comic dramatist. A freed slave, he enjoyed his first success with *Andria* ('The Andrian Girl', 166 BC). His six surviving comedies are Greek in origin and scene, and four are directly based on Menander. Many of his conventions were later used by European dramatists.

76 *Homo sum: nihil humani a me alienum puto.*
I am a man, I regard nothing that is human alien to me.
163 BC *Heauton timorumenos*, 77.

77 *Fortis fortuna adiuvat.*
Fortune favours the brave.
161 BC *Phormio*, 203.

78 *Nil est dictu facilius.*
Nothing is easier to say.
161 BC *Phormio*, 300.

79 *Quot homines tot sententiae: suo quoique mos.*
There are as many opinions as there are people: each has his own view.
161 BC *Phormio*, 454.

Terentianus Maurus 2/3C BC

Latin grammarian from north Africa. He is remembered for his didactic poem *De litteris syllabis et metris.*

80 *Pro captu lectoris habent sua fata libelli.*
Depending on the reception of the reader, books have their own fate.
De litteris syllabis et metris, 1286. The phrase is often incorrectly attributed to Horace.

Terry, Quinlan 1937–

English architect.

81 An architect is only really a glorified tailor and if people want a suit—as long as they don't ask for three sleeves or something—it's do-able.
2004 In the *Observer*, 7 Mar.

Tertullian *full name Quintus Septimius Florens Tertullianus* c.160–c.220 AD

Christian theologian, a lawyer in Rome until he converted in c.196 AD, an opponent of worldliness in the Church and leader of the Montanist sect (c.207 AD). His most famous work is *Apologeticus* (c. 197 AD), an impassioned defence of Christianity against pagan charges of immorality, economic worthlessness and political subversion.

82 *Plures efficimus quoties metimur a vobis, semen est sanguis Christianorum.*
As often as we are mown down by you, the more we grow in numbers; the blood of the Christians is the seed.
Apologeticus, ch.50, section 13. The phrase is often quoted as 'The blood of the martyrs is the seed of the church.'

83 *Certum est quia impossibile est.*
It is certain because it is impossible.
De Carne Christi, ch.5. The phrase is commonly rendered 'It is so extraordinary that it must be true.'

Tessimond, A(rthur) S(eymour) J(ohn) 1902–62

84 Cats, no less liquid than their shadows,
Offer no angles to the wind.
They slip, diminished, neat, through loopholes
Less than themselves.
'Cats', pt.2.

Thackeray, William Makepeace 1811–63

English novelist. He earned his living from journalism, working for *Punch* from 1842–54. He provided a complex view of the changing nature of English society with its mingling of rich parvenus and decadent upper class. His best-known novels include *Vanity Fair* (1847–8) and *Henry Esmond* (1852).

85 'A chilli,' said Rebecca, gasping, 'Oh, yes!' She thought a chilli was something cool, as its name imported, and was served with some. 'How fresh and green they look,' she said, and put one into her mouth. It was hotter than the curry; flesh and blood could bear it no longer. She laid down her fork. 'Water, for Heaven's sake, water!' she cried.
1847–8 *Vanity Fair*, ch.3

86 A woman with fair opportunities and without a positive hump, may marry whom she likes.
1847–8 Rebecca Sharp. *Vanity Fair*, ch.4.

87 Whenever he met a great man he grovelled before him, and my-lorded him as only a free-born Briton can do.
1847–8 Of Old Osbourne. *Vanity Fair*, ch.13.

88 If a man's character is to be abused, say what you will, there's nobody like a relation to do the business.
1847–8 Miss Crawley. *Vanity Fair*, ch.19.

89 Them's my sentiments!
1847–8 Fred Bullock. *Vanity Fair*, ch.21.

90 Darkness came down on the field and city: and Amelia was praying for George, who was lying on his face, dead, with a bullet through his heart.
1847–8 *Vanity Fair*, ch.32.

91 Nothing like blood, sir, in hosses, dawgs, and men.
1847–8 James Crawley. *Vanity Fair*, ch.35.

92 How to Live Well on Nothing a Year.
1847–8 *Vanity Fair*, ch.36, title of chapter.

93 I think I could be a good woman if I had five thousand a year.
1847–8 *Vanity Fair*, ch.36.

94 Ah! Vanitas Vanitatum! Which of us is happy in this world? Which of us has his desire? or, having it, is satisfied?—Come, children, let us shut up the box and the puppets, for our play is played out.
1847–8 Concluding words. *Vanity Fair*, ch.67.

95 He who meanly admires mean things is a Snob.
1848 *The Book of Snobs*, ch.2.

96 Yes, I am a fatal man, Madame Fribsbi. To inspire hopeless passion is my destiny.
1848–50 Mirobolant. *Pendennis*, ch.23.

97 Remember, it is as easy to marry a rich woman as a poor woman.
1848–50 *Pendennis*, ch.28.

98 The Pall Mall Gazette is written by gentlemen for gentlemen.
1848–50 *Pendennis*, ch.32.

99 For a slashing article, sir, there's nobody like the Capting.
1848–50 Mr Bungay. *Pendennis*, ch.32.

1 'Tis not the dying for a faith that's so hard, Master Harry—every man of every nation has done that—'tis the living up to it that is difficult.
1852 *The History of Henry Esmond*, bk.1, ch.6.

2 'Tis strange what a man may do, and a woman yet think him an angel.
1852 *The History of Henry Esmond*, bk.1, ch.7.

3 What money is better bestowed than that of a school-boy's tip?
1853–5 *The Newcomes*, vol.1, ch.16.

4 He lifted up his head a little, and quickly said, 'Adsum!' and fell back... He, whose heart was as that of a little child, had answered to his name, and stood in the presence of The Master.
1853–5 *The Newcomes*, vol.1, ch.80.

5 Werther had a love for Charlotte
Such as words could never utter;
Would you know how first he met her?
She was cutting bread and butter.
1855 'Sorrows of Werther'.

6 Business first; pleasure afterwards
1855 *The Rose and the Ring*, ch.1.

Tharp, Twyla 1941–

US dancer and choreographer.

7 The notion of doing something impossibly new usually turns out to be an illusion.
1995 In *The Independent*, 8 Dec.

Thatcher, Margaret Hilda Thatcher, Baroness 1925–

English Conservative politician and Prime Minister (1979–90). A research chemist, she entered Parliament (1959) and was Minister of Education (1970–4), becoming party leader in 1975. As premier she instituted privatization of nationalized industries and utilities. She resigned (Nov 1990) after a leadership challenge following controversy over economic union with Europe.

8 No woman in my time will be Prime Minister or Chancellor of the Exchequer or Foreign Secretary—not the top jobs. Anyway, I would not want to be Prime Minister; you have to give yourself 100 per cent.
1969 On her appointment as a junior Education Minister, in the *Sunday Telegraph*, 26 Oct.

9 I owe nothing to Women's Lib.
1974 Quoted in the *Observer*, 1 Dec.

10 In politics, if you want anything said, ask a man. If you want anything done, ask a woman.
1975 *People*, 15 Sep.

11 Let our children grow tall, and some taller than others if they have it in them to do so.
1975 Speech, Oct.

12 I stand before you tonight in my green chiffon evening gown, my face softly made up, my fair hair gently waved…the Iron Lady of the Western World? Me? A Cold War warrior? Well, yes—if that is how they wish to interpret my defence of values and freedoms fundamental to our way of life.
1976 Speech, Dorking. Alluding to the title bestowed upon her by the Soviet defence journal, in *Red Star*, 31 Jan.

13 We want a society in which we are free to make choices, to make mistakes, to be generous and compassionate. That is what we mean by a moral society—not a society in which the State is responsible for everything, and no one is responsible for the State.
1977 Speech, Zurich University, 14 Mar.

14 Let us make this country safe to work in. Let us make this a country safe to walk in. Let us make it a country safe to grow up in. Let us make it a country safe to grow old in.
1979 General election party broadcast, 30 Apr.

15 Unless we change our ways and our direction, our greatness as a nation will soon be a footnote in the history books, a distant memory of an offshore island, lost in the mist of time like Camelot, remembered kindly for its noble past.
1979 General election campaign speech, Bolton, 2 May.

16 Where there is discord, may we bring harmony. Where there is error, may we bring truth. Where there is doubt, may we bring faith. Where there is despair, may we bring hope.
1979 Said on entering No.10 Downing Street for the first time as Prime Minister; 4 May. A misquotation of St Francis of Assisi.
► *See St Francis 334:98.*

17 Any woman who understands the problems of running a home will be nearer to understanding the problems of running a country.
1979 Interviewed by the *Observer* four days after becoming Britain's first woman Prime Minister, 8 May.

18 Pennies don't fall from heaven. They have to be earned here on earth.
1979 Quoted in the *Observer*, 'Sayings of the Week', 18 Nov.
► *See Burke 169:53.*

19 There is no easy popularity, in that I believe that people accept that there is no alternative.
1980 On her Government's stringent economic policies. Speech at the Conservative Women's Conference, 21 May.

20 To those who wait with bated breath for that favourite media catchphrase, the U-turn, I have only this to say. You turn if you want to. The lady's not for turning.
1980 Address to the Conservative Party Conference.
► *See Fry 340:25.*

21 It is exciting to have a real crisis on your hands, when you have spent half your political life dealing with humdrum issues like the environment.
1982 Of the Falklands conflict. Speech to the Scottish Conservative Party Conference, 14 May.

22 This is the day that I was meant not to see.
1984 On attending church the Sunday after she had narrowly escaped being killed in the IRA bomb explosion at the Grand Hotel, Brighton, Oct.

23 I like Mr Gorbachev. We can do business together.
1984 Said on her first meeting with him, before he became premier, 17 Dec.

24 Democracies must try to find ways to starve the terrorist and the hijackers of the oxygen of publicity on which they depend.
1985 Speech to the American Bar Association meeting in London, referring in particular to increasing British press coverage of IRA terrorist activities, 15 Jul.

25 I always cheer up immensely if an attack is particularly wounding because…it means that they have not a single political argument left.
1986 In the *Daily Telegraph*, 21 Mar.

26 If you want to cut your own throat, don't come to me for a bandage.
1986 Comment to Robert Mugabe, Prime Minister of Zimbabwe, when he pressed for sanctions against South Africa. Quoted in *Time*, 7 Jul.

27 To wear your heart on your sleeve isn't a very good plan. You should wear it inside, where it functions best.
1987 Interview, ABC TV, 18 Mar.

28 There is no such thing as society. There are individual men and women, and there are families.
1987 In *Woman's Own*, 31 Oct.

29 I don't mind how much my Ministers talk—as long as they do what I say.
1987 In *The Times*.

30 If one leads a country such as Britain—a strong country that has taken a lead in world affairs in good times and bad, that is always reliable, then you must have a touch of iron about you.
1987 In *The Times*.

31 We have become a grandmother.
1989 *The Times*, 4 Mar.

32 I seem to smell the stench of appeasement in the air.

1990 Describing the western attitude to the Gulf crisis. In *The Independent*, 31 Oct.

33 After three general election victories, leading the only party with clear policies, resolutely carried out, I intend to continue.
1990 On Michael Heseltine's challenge for the leadership of the Conservative Party, in the *Sunday Times*, 18 Nov.

34 I shall fight. I will fight on.
1990 To reporters, on learning that she had not won the necessary majority to secure her re-election as party leader, two days before announcing her decision to step down, 21 Nov.

35 There is no way in which one can buck the market.
1990 Speech to the Commons on 10 Mar, before the Budget, complaining about what she called 'excessive' intervention in the exchange markets which would lead to inflation.

36 If you are guided by opinion polls, you are not practising leadership—you are practising followship.
1991 US TV interview, 5 Mar.

37 Marxism is at the root of debunking journalism.
Quoted in John Birt *The Harder Path* (2002).

38 Is he one of us?
Attributed comment on considering a candidate for office in her new Government.

Theophilus c.10c

Greek writer and courtier. His *Diversarum Artium Schedula* was the most important art book of the Middle Ages, describing the methods of ecclesiastical art of his time.

39 All arts are taught by degrees. The first process in art of the painter is the composition of colours. Let your mind be afterwards applied to the study of the mixtures.
An Essay Upon Various Arts (translated by Robert Hendrie, 1847), bk.1, preface.

Theophrastus c.372–286 BC

Greek philosopher. A student of Aristotle, he succeeded him as head of the Lyceum from 322. Most of his prolific output is lost; among the writings that survive is a volume of *Characters*, containing 30 sketches of different moral types, which has been widely translated and imitated.

40 The sound of the flute will cure epilepsy and sciatic gout.
Quoted in David Pickering *Brewer's Twentieth-Century Music* (1994).

Theresa (of Calcutta), Mother *originally* *Agnes Gonxha Bojaxhiu* 1910–97

Roman Catholic nun, born in Yugoslavia. She went to India in 1928 and in 1948 left a convent school to work in the slums. She founded the Missionaries of Charity sisterhood (1950) and a House for the Dying (1952), and in 1957 began work with lepers and in disaster areas of the world. She was awarded the Pope John XXIII Peace Prize in 1971, and the Nobel peace prize in 1979.

41 The biggest disease today is not leprosy or tuberculosis, but rather the feeling of being unwanted.
Quoted in the *Observer*, 3 Oct 1971.

42 To keep a lamp burning, we have to keep putting oil in it.
1975 In *Time*, 29 Dec.

43 There should be less talk; a preaching point is not a meeting point. What do you do then? Take a broom and clean someone's house. That says enough.
1975 *A Gift for God*, 'Carriers of Christ's Love'.

44 We need to find God, and he cannot be found in noise and restlessness. God is the friend of silence. See how nature—trees, flowers, grass—grows in silence; see the stars, the moon and the sun, how they move in silence… We need silence to be able to touch souls.
1975 *A Gift for God*, 'Willing Slaves to the Will of God'.

Theroux, Paul Edward 1941–

US novelist and travel writer. His best-known novel is *The Mosquito Coast* (1982), but he is particularly regarded for his travel writings, notably those concerned with epic rail journeys.

45 Extensive travelling induces a feeling of encapsulation, and travel, so broadening at first, contracts the mind.
1975 *The Great Railway Bazaar*, ch.21.

46 Nothing happens in Burma, but then nothing is expected to happen.
1975 *The Great Railway Bazaar*, ch.23.

47 I went to Vietnam to take the train; people have done stranger things in that country.
1975 *The Great Railway Bazaar*, ch.24.

48 The Japanese have perfected good manners and made them indistinguishable from rudeness.
1975 *The Great Railway Bazaar*, ch.28.

49 Like a lower form of life, like the cross-eyed planarian or squashed amoeba, the sort of creature that can't die even when it is cut to pieces.
1975 Of Laos. *The Great Railway Bazaar*.

50 In Turkey it was always 1952, in Malaysia 1937; Afghanistan was 1910 and Bolivia 1949. It is twenty years ago in the Soviet Union, ten in Norway, five in France. It is always last year in Australia and next week in Japan.
1983 *The Kingdom By The Sea*, ch.1.

Thesiger, Sir Wilfred Patrick 1910–2003

English explorer. He twice crossed the Empty Quarter (Rub'al Khali) between 1946 and 1949 and wrote sensitively about the Bedu and their changing way of life.

51 For me, exploration was a personal venture. I did not go to the Arabian desert to collect plants nor to make a map; such things were incidental. At heart I knew that to write or even to talk of my travels was to tarnish the achievement. I went there to find peace in the hardship of desert travel and the company of desert people. I set myself a goal on these journeys, and, although the goal itself was unimportant, its attainment had to be worth every effort and sacrifice.
1959 *Arabian Sands*.

Thiers, (Louis) Adolphe 1797–1877

French statesman, twice Prime Minister (1836, 1839). He supported Napoleon in 1848, but was banished in the *coup d'état* of 1851 and re-entered the Chamber in 1863 as a critic. After the collapse of the Second Empire he suppressed the Paris Commune and became first President of the Third Republic (1871–3). Defeated by monarchists, he resigned in 1873. He wrote *L'histoire du consulat et de l'empire* ('History of the Consulate and the Empire', 20 vols, 1845–62).

52 The Republic will be conservative, or it will be nothing.
1872 Presidential address to the French National Assembly, Nov.

Thomas, (Walter) Brandon 1857–1914

English playwright, actor and songwriter. He is usually remembered for his classic farce, *Charley's Aunt* (1892).

53 Where the nuts come from.
1892 Of Brazil. *Charley's Aunt*.

Thomas, D(onald) M(itchell) 1935–

English writer. He made his initial reputation as a poet, but became better known as the author of the novel *The White Hotel* (1981).

54 Freud becomes one of the dramatis personae, in fact, as discoverer of the great and beautiful modern myth of psychoanalysis. By myth, I mean a poetic, dramatic expression of a hidden truth; and in placing this emphasis, I do not intend to put into question the scientific validity of psychoanalysis.
1981 *The White Hotel*, author's note.

55 She was cut off from the past and therefore did not live in the present. But suddenly, as she stood close against a pine tree and breathed in its sharp, bitter scent, a clear space opened to her childhood, as though a wind had sprung from the sea, clearing a mist. It was not a memory from the past, it was the past itself, as alive, as real; and she knew that she and the child of forty years ago were the same person.
1981 *The White Hotel*, ch.4.

56 The soul of man is a far country, which cannot be approached or explored. Most of the dead were poor and illiterate. But every single one of them had dreamed dreams, seen visions and had amazing experiences, even the babes in arms (perhaps especially the babes in arms).
1981 *The White Hotel*, ch.5.

Thomas, Dylan Marlais 1914–53

Welsh poet. The son of a schoolmaster, he worked as a journalist for a time. He also wrote short stories and novels, and later turned to drama, notably the celebrated radio play *Under Milk Wood* (published 1954). His tempestuous lifestyle culminated in his death from alcohol abuse on a lecture tour of the US.

57 The force that through the green fuse drives the flower
Drives my green age; that blasts the roots of trees
Is my destroyer.
And I am dumb to tell the crooked rose
My youth is bent by the same wintry fever.
1934 'The Force That Through the Green Fuse Drives the Flower'.

58 Light breaks where no sun shines;
Where no sea runs, the waters of the heart
Push in their tides.
1934 'Light Breaks Where No Sun Shines'.

59 Man be my metaphor.
1934 'If I Were Tickled by The Rub of Love'.

60 I am getting more obscure day by day.
1934 Letter to Pamela Hansford Johnson, 9 May.

61 Though they go mad they shall be sane
Though they sink through the sea they shall rise again;
Though lovers be lost love shall not;
And death shall have no dominion.
1936 'And Death Shall Have No Dominion'.

62 The hand that signed the paper felled a city;
Five sovereign fingers taxed the breath,
Doubled the globe of dead and halved a country;
These five kings did a king to death.
1936 'The Hand That Signed the Paper Felled a City'.

63 The hand that signed the treaty bred a fever,
And famine grew, and locusts came;
Great is the hand that holds dominion over
Man by a scribbled name.
1936 'The Hand That Signed the Paper Felled a City'.

64 What is the metre of the dictionary?
1936 'Altarwise by Owl-light'.

65 Shall gods be said to thump the clouds
When clouds are cursed by thunder?
1936 'Shall Gods be Said to Thump the Clouds'.

66 I hold a beast, an angel and a madman within me, and my enquiry is as to their working, and my problem is their subjugation and victory, downthrow and upheaval, and my effort is their self expression.
1938 Letter to Henry Treece.

67 Her fist of a face died clenched on a round pain;
And sculptured Ann is seventy years of stone.
1939 'After the Funeral'.

68 I don't think it does any harm to the artist to be lonely as an artist.
1939 Letter to Pennar Davies.

69 Portrait of the Artist as a Young Dog.
1940 Title of book.

70 And the wild boys innocent as strawberries.
1946 'The Hunchback in the Park'.

71 Now as I was young and easy under the apple boughs
About the lilting house and happy as the grass was green.
1946 'Fern Hill'.

72 Oh as I was young and easy in the mercy of his means,
Time held me green and dying
Though I sang in my chains like the sea.
1946 'Fern Hill'.

73 After the first death, there is no other.
1946 'A Refusal to Mourn the Death, By Fire, of a Child in London'.

74 It was my thirtieth year to heaven
Woke to my hearing from harbour and neighbour wood
And the mussel pooled and the heron
Priested shore.
1946 'Poem in October'.

75 Pale rain over the dwindling harbour
And over the sea wet church the size of a snail
With its horns through mist and the castle
Brown as owls.
1946 'Poem in October'.

76 And I rose
In rainy autumn
And walked abroad in the shower of all my days.
1946 'Poem in October'.

77 I hear John Arlott's voice every weekend, describing cricket matches. He sounds like Uncle Tom Cobleigh reading Neville Cardus to the Indians.
1947 Letter to Margaret Taylor, 11 Jul.

78 The joy and function of poetry is, and was, the celebration of man, which is also the celebration of God.
1951 Letter to a student.

79 If you want a definition of poetry, say: 'Poetry is what makes me laugh or cry or yawn, what makes my toenails twinkle, what makes me want to do this or that or nothing' and let it go at that.
1951 Letter to a student.

80 I fell in love—that is the only expression I can think of—at once, and am still at the mercy of words, though sometimes now, knowing a little of their behaviour very well, I think I can influence them slightly and have even learned to beat them now and gain, which they appear to enjoy.
1951 Letter to a student.

81 Do not go gentle into that good night,
Old age should burn and rave at close of day;
Rage, rage against the dying of the light.
1952 'Do Not Go Gentle Into That Good Night'.

82 These poems, with all their crudities, doubts, and confusions, are written for the love of Man, and in praise of God, and I'd be a damn' fool if they weren't.
1952 *Collected Poems*, author's note.

83 The land of my fathers. My fathers can have it.
1953 Of Wales. In *Adam*, Dec.

84 I've had eighteen straight whiskies. I think that's the record.
1953 Attributed, supposedly said before lapsing into his final coma.

85 To begin at the beginning: It is spring, moonless night in the small town, starless and bible-black, the cobblestreets silent and the hunched, courters'-and-rabbits' wood limping invisible down to the sloeblack, slow, black, crowblack, fishingboat-bobbing sea.
1954 *Under Milk Wood*, opening words

86 Oh I'm a martyr to music.
1954 *Under Milk Wood.*

87 The boys are dreaming wicked or of the bucking ranches of the night and the jolly-rogered sea.
1954 *Under Milk Wood.*

88 And before you let the sun in, mind it wipes its shoes.
1954 *Under Milk Wood.*

89 Alone until she dies, Bessie Bighead, hired help, born in the workhouse, smelling of the cowshed, snores bass and gruff on a couch of straw in a loft in Salt Lake Farm and picks a posy of daisies in Sunday Meadow to put on the grave of Gomer Owen who kissed her once by the pig-sty when she wasn't looking and never kissed her again although she was looking all the time.
1954 *Under Milk Wood.*

90 Straightfaced in his cunning sleep he pulls the legs of his dreams.
1954 *Under Milk Wood.*

91 Nothing grows in our garden, only washing. And babies. And where's their fathers live, my love? Over the hills and far away.
1954 *Under Milk Wood.*

92 You're thinking, you're no better than you should be, Polly, and that's good enough for me. Oh, isn't life a terrible thing, thank God?
1954 *Under Milk Wood.*

93 Hullo, Polly, my love, can you hear the dumb goose-hiss of the wives as they huddle and peck or flounce at a waddle away? Who cuddled you when? Which of their gandering hubbies moaned in Milk Wood for your naughty mothering arms and body like a wardrobe, love?
1954 *Under Milk Wood.*

94 The sun hums down through the cotton flowers of her dress into the bell of her heart and buzzes in the honey there and couches and kisses, lazy-loving and boozed, in her red-berried breast.
1954 *Under Milk Wood.*

95 Alone in the hissing laboratory of his wishes, Mr Pugh minces among bad vats and jeroboams, tiptoes through spinneys of murdering herbs, agony dancing in his crucibles, and mixes especially for Mrs Pugh a venomous porridge unknown to toxicologists which will scald and viper through her until her ears fall off like figs, her toes grow big and black as balloons, and steam comes screaming out of her navel.
1954 *Under Milk Wood.*

96 You just wait. I'll sin until I blow up!
1954 *Under Milk Wood.*

97 Too many of the artists of Wales spend too much time talking about the position of the artists of Wales. There is only one position for an artist anywhere: and that is, upright.
1954 *Quite Early One Morning*, 'Wales and the Artist'.

98 The best poem is that whose worked-upon unmagical passages come closest, in texture and intensity, to those moments of magical accident.
1954 *Quite Early One Morning*, 'On Poetry'.

99 A good poem is a contribution to reality. The world is never the same once a good poem has been added to it.
1954 *Quite Early One Morning*, 'On Poetry'.

1 One Christmas was much like another... I can never remember whether it snowed for six days and six nights when I was twelve or whether it snowed for twelve days and twelve nights when I was six.
1954 *A Child's Christmas in Wales.*

2 Years and years ago, when I was a boy, when there were wolves in Wales, and birds the colour of red-flannel petticoats whisked past the harp-shaped hills, when we sang and wallowed all night and day in caves that smelt like Sunday afternoons in damp front farmhouse parlours, and we chased, with the jawbones of deacons, the English and the bears, before the motor car, before the wheel, before the duchess-faced horse, when we rode the daft and happy hills bareback, it snowed and it snowed.
1954 *A Child's Christmas in Wales.*

Thomas, (Philip) Edward 1878–1917

English nature writer and poet. His poetry was all written during World War I, in which he was killed in action at Arras. Very few poems were published in his lifetime, but posthumous collections established his reputation as a great nature poet.

3 A merely great intellect can produce great prose, but not poetry, not one line.
1908 Letter to Gordon Bottomley, 26 Feb.

4 When Gods were young
This wind was old.
1914 'The Mountain Chapel'.

5 The Past is a strange land, most strange.
1915 'Parting'.

6 Yes; I remember Adlestrop—
The name, because one afternoon
Of heat the express-train drew up there
Unwontedly. It was late June.
1915 'Adlestrop'.

7 And for that minute a blackbird sang
Close by, and round him, mistier,
Farther and farther, all the birds
Of Oxfordshire and Gloucestershire.
1915 'Adlestrop'.

8 The men, the music piercing that solitude
And silence, told me truths I had not dreamed,
And have forgotten since their beauty passed.
1915 'Tears'.

9 The last light has gone out of the world, except
This moonlight lying on the grass like frost
Beyond the brink of the tall elm's shadow.
1915 'Liberty'.

10 This is no case of petty right or wrong
That politicians or philosophers
Can judge. I hate not Germans, nor grow hot
With love of Englishmen, to please newspapers.
1915 'This Is No Case of Petty Right Or Wrong'.

11 The dark-lit stream has drowned the Future and the Past.
1915 'The Bridge'.

12 The new moon hangs like an ivory bugle
In the naked frosty blue.
1915 'The Penny Whistle'.

13 It is a fine world and I wish I knew how to make £200 a year in it.
1915 Letter to Gordon Bottomley, 16 Jun.

14 The past is the only dead thing that smells sweet,
The only sweet thing that is not also fleet.
1916 'Early One Morning'.

15 For the life in them he loved most living things,
But a tree chiefly.
1916 'Bob's Lane'.

16 That girl's clear eyes utterly concealed all
Except that there was something to reveal.
1916 'That Girl's Clear Eyes'.

17 I have come to the borders of sleep,
The unfathomable deep
Forest, where all must lose
Their way, however straight
Or winding, soon or late;
They cannot choose.
1916 'Lights Out'.

18 As well as any bloom upon a flower
I like the dust on the nettles, never lost
Except to prove the sweetness of a shower.
1916 'Tall Nettles'.

19 Now all the roads lead to France
And heavy is the tread
Of the living: but the dead
Returning lightly dance.
1916 'Roads'.

20 Out in the dark over the snow
The fallow fawns invisible go
With the fallow doe;
And the winds blow
Fast as the stars are slow.
1916 'Out in the Dark'.

21 The sorrow of true love is a great sorrow
And true love parting blackens a bright morrow.
1917 'Last Poem'.

Thomas, Sir George 1881–1972

English badminton administrator, founder and first president of the International Badminton Federation.

22 The art of badminton is to deceive.
Quoted in *The Guinness Book of Badminton* (1983).

Thomas, John Parnell 1895–1970

US congressman. He was an insurance broker before entering Congress (1937–49). He served as Chairman of the Committee on Un-American Activities.

23 Are you now, or have you ever been, a member of the Communist Party?
1947–57 Stock question to those called before the House of Representatives Committee on Un-American Activities.

Thomas, Michael M 1936–

US novelist.

24 Bankers' genes were Wall St. genes, especially in the big cities. If the banks were conservative just now [1955], it was because bankers still awoke in the middle of the night, trembling and sweaty with thoughts of the Crash. But in time a new generation would take over: ambitious, overcompetitive young men to whom 1929 would be merely a date on a page; such men would sever the roots of memory as if with an ax, not realizing that those tendrils were also the rudder cables.
1987 *The Ropespinner Conspiracy.*

Thomas, R(onald) S(tuart) 1913–2000

Welsh poet and priest. His poetry characteristically deals with the themes of nature, religion and his love of Wales.

25 We were a people taut for war; the hills
Were no harder, the thin grass
Clothed them more warmly than the coarse
Shirts our small bones.
1952 'Welsh History'.

26 An impotent people,
Sick with inbreeding.
Worrying the carcase of an old song.
1952 'Welsh Landscape'.

27 We will listen to the wind's text
Blown through the roof, or the thrush's song
In the thick bush that proved him wrong,
Wrong from the start, for nature's truth
Is primary and her changing seasons
Correct out of a vaster reason
The vague errors of the flesh.
1953 'The Minister'.

28 For the first twenty years you are still growing,
Bodily that is; as a poet, of course,
You are not born yet. It's the next ten
You cut your teeth on to emerge smirking

For your brash courtship of the muse.
1963 'To A Young Poet'.

29 Prompt me, God,
But not yet. When I speak
Though it be you who speak
Through me, something is lost.
The meaning is the waiting.
1968 'Kneeling'.

30 The poem in the rock and
The poem in the mind
Are not one.
It was in dying
I tried to make them so.
1972 'The Epitaph'.

31 Among the forests
Of metal the one human
Sound was the lament of
The poets for deciduous language.
1972 'Postscript'.

32 Life is not hurrying
on to a receding future, nor hankering after
an imagined past. It is the turning
aside like Moses to the miracle
of the lit bush, to a brightness
that seemed as transitory as your youth
once, but is the eternity that awaits you.
1976 *Laboratories of the Spirit*, 'The Bright Field'.

33 We are beginning to see
now it is matter is the scaffolding
of spirit; that the poet emerges
from morphemes and phonemes; that
as form in sculpture is the prisoner
of the hard rock, so in everyday life
it is the plain facts and natural happenings
that conceal God and reveal him to us
little by little under the mind's tooling.
1978 *Frequencies*, 'Emerging'.

Thompson, E P 1924–93

British historian.

34 This going into Europe will not turn out to be the thrilling mutual exchange supposed. It is more like nine middle-aged couples with failing marriages meeting in a darkened bedroom in a Brussels hotel for a group grope.
1975 On Britain's entry into the EEC, in the *Sunday Times*, 27 Apr.

Thompson, Francis 1859–1907

English poet. His poems, mainly religious in theme and collected in such publications as *Poems* (1893) and *Sister Songs* (1895), include the well-known 'The Hound of Heaven'.

35 The fairest things have fleetest end,
Their scent survives their close:
But the rose's scent is bitterness
To him that loved the rose.
'Daisy' (published 1890).

36 I fled Him, down the nights and down the days;
I fled Him, down the arches of the years;
I fled Him, down the labyrinthine ways
Of my own mind; and in the midst of tears
I hid from Him, and under running laughter.
1893 *Poems*, 'The Hound of Heaven'.

37 I said to Dawn: Be sudden—to Eve: Be soon.
1893 *Poems*, 'The Hound of Heaven'.

38 O world invisible, we view thee,
O world intangible, we touch thee,
O world unknowable, we know thee,
Inapprehensible, we clutch thee!
1897 'In No Strange Land'.

39 It is little I repair to the matches of the Southron folk,
Though my own red roses there may blow;
It is little I repair to the matches of the Southron folk,
Though the red roses crest the caps, I know.
For the field is full of shades as I near the shadowy coast,
And a ghostly batsman plays to the bowling of a ghost,
And I look through my tears on a soundless-clapping
host
As the run-stealers flicker to and fro,
To and fro:—
O my Hornby and my Barlow long ago!
1907 'At Lord's', poem dedicated to friends to explain why he could not attend a match at Lord's at their invitation for fear of the sadness it would cause him, remembering the long-dead friends who had played there (for Lancashire) back in 1878.

40 There is no expeditious road
To pack and label men for God,
And save them by the barrel-load,
Some may perchance, with strange surprise,
Have blundered into Paradise.
1913 'A Judgment in Heaven', epilogue.

41 Wake! for the Ruddy Ball has taken flight
That scatters the slow Wicket of the Night;
And the swift Batsman of the Dawn has driven
Against the Star-spiked Rails a fiery smite.
'Wake! for the Ruddy Ball has Taken Flight', parody of Edward Fitzgerald, quoted in J C Squire *Apes and Parrots* (1929).
► *See Fitzgerald 324:82*

Thompson, Hunter S(tockton) 1939–

US writer, inventor of a semi-fictionalized participatory journalism he dubbed 'gonzo'. His work for *Rolling Stone* magazine made him a cult figure. He sometimes writes as 'Raoul Duke'.

42 Weird heroes and mould-breaking champions exist as living proof to those who need it that the tyranny of 'the rat race' is not yet final.
1969 'Those Daring Young Men In Their Flying Machines... Ain't What They Used To Be!', in *Pageant*, Sep.

43 History is hard to know...but...it seems entirely reasonable to think that every now and then the energy of a whole generation comes to a head in a long fine flash, for reasons that nobody really understands at the time—and which never explain, in retrospect, what actually happened.
1971 *Fear and Loathing in Las Vegas*, ch.8.

44 Absolute truth is a very rare and dangerous commodity in the context of professional journalism.
1973 'Fear and Loathing at the Superbowl', in *Rolling Stone*, 15 Feb.

45 In a nation ruled by swine, all pigs are upwardly-mobile—and the rest of us are fucked until we can put our acts together: not necessarily to win, but mainly to keep from losing completely. We owe that to ourselves and our crippled self-image as something better than a

nation of panicked sheep.
1979 *The Great Shark Hunt*, 'Jacket Copy for *Fear and Loathing in Las Vegas*'.

46 Going to trial with a lawyer who considers your whole life-style a Crime in Progress is not a happy prospect.
1990 Letter to *The Champion*, a legal journal, Jul.

Thompson, James R 1936–

US lawyer and politician, Republican governor of Illinois (1977–91).

47 It is not so much who you elect, it's who you throw out.
1981 On the campaign to clean up government. In the *Chicago Tribune*, 26 Jul.

Thompson, Robert 1914–97

Canadian politician, leader of the Social Credit Party of Canada (1961–7) and renowned malapropist.

48 The Americans are our best friends, whether we like it or not.
Oft-quoted remark recalled by Peter C Newman in *Home Country* (1973).

Thompson, Tommy

Canadian public official, Parks Commissioner, Metropolitan Toronto.

49 Please Walk on the Grass
1960 Message on a sign erected in Toronto's Edwards Gardens, which attracted national and then international attention for its 'hands-on' approach to public parks.

Thomson, David 1914–88

Scottish writer. His often autobiographical books include *Woodbrook* and *Nairn in Darkness and Light*.

50 The vice of meanness, condemned in every other country, is in Scotland translated into a virtue called 'thrift'.
1987 *Nairn in Darkness and Light*.

51 Even stroking a cat may be regarded by strict Presbyterians as a carnal sin.
1987 *Nairn in Darkness and Light*.

Thomson, James 1700–48

Scottish poet. He studied for the ministry but moved to London to become a writer. His chief works were *The Castle of Indolence* (1748) and *The Seasons*, an early nature poem extensively revised between 1730 and 1746.

52 When Britain first, at heaven's command,
Arose from out the azure main,
This was the charter of the land,
And guardian angels sung this strain:
'Rule, Britannia, rule the waves;
Britons never will be slaves.'
1740 *Alfred: a Masque*, act 2, sc.5.

53 Delightful task! to rear the tender thought,
To teach the young idea how to shoot.
1746 *The Seasons*, 'Spring', l.1152–3.

54 An elegant sufficiency, content,
Retirement, rural quiet, friendship, books,
Ease and alternate labour, useful life,
Progressive virtue, and approving Heaven!
1746 *The Seasons*, 'Spring', l.1161–4.

55 Or sighed and looked unutterable things.
1746 *The Seasons*, 'Summer', l.188.

56 Poor is the triumph o'er the timid hare!
1746 *The Seasons*, 'Autumn', l.401.

57 Welcome, kindred glooms!
Congenial horrors, hail!
1746 *The Seasons*, 'Winter', l.5–6.

58 There studious let me sit,
And hold high converse with the mighty dead.
1746 *The Seasons*, 'Winter', l.431–2.

59 A little round, fat, oily man of God,
Was one I chiefly marked among the fry:
He had a roguish twinkle in his eye.
1748 *The Castle of Indolence*, canto 1, stanza 69.

Thomson, James *pseudonym 'BV', Bysshe Vanolis* 1834–82

Scottish poet born in Port Glasgow. He trained as an army schoolmaster but was dismissed from army service in 1862 for alcoholism. He worked in London as a poet, journalist and critic, and published his greatest work *The City of Dreadful Night* in 1874.

60 As we rush, as we rush in the train,
The trees and the houses go wheeling back,
But the starry heavens above that plain
Come flying on our track.
1863–5 'Sunday at Hampstead', stanza 10.

61 The City is of Night, but not of Sleep;
There sweet Sleep is not for the weary brain;
The pitiless hours like years and ages creep,
A night seems termless hell.
1874 *The City of Dreadful Night*, pt.1.

62 The City is of Night; perchance of Death,
But certainly of Night.
1874 *The City of Dreadful Night*, pt.1.

63 As I came through the desert thus it was,
As I came through the desert: All was black,
In heaven no single star, on earth no track;
A brooding hush without a stir or note;
The air so thick it clotted in my throat.
1874 *The City of Dreadful Night*, pt.4.

64 Yet I strode on austere;
No hope could have no fear.
1874 *The City of Dreadful Night*, pt.4.

Thomson, Roy Herbert, 1st Baron Thomson of Fleet 1894–1976

Canadian-born British newspaper and television magnate. After setting up his first radio station in 1931 and buying many Canadian and US newspapers, he settled in Edinburgh on acquiring *The Scotsman* (1952), and bought the Kemsley newspapers (1959) and *The Times* (1966).

65 A TV licence is a licence to print money.
1957 On being awarded the licence to operate Scottish Television Ltd, 19 Jun. Recalled in his memoirs *After I Was Sixty* (1975).

Thomson, Virgil 1896–1989

US composer and critic. His work, notable for its simplicity of style, includes the operas *Four Saints in Three Acts* (1934) and *The Mother of Us All* (1947) in addition to symphonies, ballets, choral, chamber and film music. He was music critic of the *New York Herald* (1940–54).

66 A libretto that should never have been accepted on a subject that should never have been chosen by a man who should never have attempted it.
1935 Of Gershwin's *Porgy and Bess. Modern Music.*

67 The way to write American music is simple. All you have to do is be an American and then write any kind of music you wish.
Quoted in Machlis *Introduction to Contemporary Music* (1963).

Thoreau, Henry David 1817–62

US essayist and poet, known as 'the hermit of Walden'. In 1839 he began his nature studies, and lived as a hermit (1845–7). His works include *Walden, or Life in the Woods* (1854) and his nature observations, beginning with *Early Spring in Massachusetts* (1881). His essay *Civil Disobedience* (1849) was provoked by his opposition to the Mexican war.

68 We seem but to linger in manhood to tell the dreams of our childhood, and they vanish out of memory ere we learn the language.
1841 Journal entry, 19 Feb.

69 Being is the great explainer.
1841 Journal entry, 26 Feb.

70 Men reverence one another, not yet God.
1849 *A Week on the Concord and Merrimack Rivers*, 'Sunday'.

71 Under a government which imprisons any unjustly, the true place for a just man is also a prison.
1849 *Civil Disobedience.*

72 Read the best books first, or you may not have a chance to read them at all.
1849 *A Week on the Concord and Merrimack Rivers*, 'Sunday'.

73 The lawyer's truth is not Truth, but consistency or a consistent expediency.
1849 *Civil Disobedience.*

74 It takes two to speak the truth,—one to speak, and another to hear.
1849 *A Week on the Concord and Merrimack Rivers*, 'Wednesday'.

75 A truly good book is something as wildly natural and primitive, mysterious and marvelous, ambrosial and fertile, as a fungus or a lichen.
1850 Journal entry, 16 Nov. In Bradford Torrey and F H Allen (eds) *The Journals of Henry David Thoreau* (1906).

76 Some circumstantial evidence is very strong, as when you find a trout in the milk.
1850 Journal entry, 11 Nov.

77 How many a man has dated a new era in his life from the reading of a book!… The at present unutterable things we may find somewhere uttered.
1854 *Walden, or Life in the Woods*, 'Reading'.

78 If we knew all the laws of Nature, we should need only one fact, or the description of one actual phenomenon, to infer all the particular results at that point. Now we know only a few laws, and our result is vitiated, not, of course, by any confusion or irregularity in Nature, but by our ignorance of essential elements in the calculation. Our notions of law and harmony are commonly confined to those instances which we detect; but the harmony which results from a far greater number of seemingly conflicting, but really concurring, laws, which we have not detected, is still more wonderful. The particular laws are as our points of view, as, to the traveler, a mountain outline varies with every step, and it has an infinite number of profiles, though absolutely but one form. Even when cleft or bored through it is not comprehended in its entireness.
1854 *Walden, or Life in the Woods*, 'The Pond in Winter'.

79 Every man is the builder of a temple, called his body, to the god he worships, after a style purely his own, nor can he get off by hammering marble instead. We are all sculptors and painters, and our material is our own flesh and blood and bones.
1854 *Walden, or Life in the Woods*, 'Higher Laws'.

80 It is a part of the destiny of the human race, in its gradual improvement, to leave off eating animals, as surely as the savage tribes have left off eating each other when they come in contact with the more civilized.
1854 *Walden, or Life in the Woods*, 'Higher Laws'.

81 We can never have enough of nature. . . . We need to witness our own limits transgressed, and some life pasturing freely where we never wander.
1854 *Walden, or Life in the Woods*, 'Spring'.

82 There is no odor so bad as that which arises from goodness tainted.
1854 *Walden, or Life in the Woods*, 'Economy'.

83 The mass of men lead lives of quiet desperation.
1854 *Walden, or Life in the Woods*, 'Economy'.

84 Our inventions are wont to be pretty toys, which distract our attention from serious things. They are but improved means to an unimproved end.
1854 *Walden, or Life in the Woods*, 'Economy'.

85 Men have become the tools of their tools.
1854 *Walden, or Life in the Woods*, 'Economy'.

86 I have yet to hear the first syllable of valuable or even earnest advice from my seniors.
1854 *Walden, or, Life in the Woods*, 'Economy'.

87 As for Doing-good, that is one of the professions which are full.
1854 *Walden, or Life in the Woods*, 'Economy'.

88 I say, beware of all enterprises that require new clothes, and not rather a new wearer of clothes.
1854 *Walden, or Life in the Woods*, 'Economy'.

89 Every generation laughs at the old fashions, but follows religiously the new.
1854 *Walden, or Life in the Woods*, 'Economy'.

90 As long as possible live free and uncommitted. It makes but little difference whether you are committed to a farm or the county jail.
1854 *Walden, or Life in the Woods*, 'Where I Lived, and What I Lived For'.

91 I went to the woods because I wished to live deliberately, to front only the essential facts of life, and see if I could not learn what it had to teach, and not, when I came to die, discover that I had not lived.
1854 *Walden, or Life in the Woods*, 'Where I Lived, and What I Lived For'.

92 Our life is frittered away by detail.
1854 *Walden, or Life in the Woods*, 'Where I Lived, and What I Lived For'.

93 We do not ride on the railroad; it rides upon us.

1854 *Walden, or Life in the Woods*, 'Where I Lived and What I Lived For'.

94 Will you be a reader, a student merely, or a seer? Read your fate, see what is before you, and walk on into futurity.
1854 *Walden, or Life in the Woods*, 'Sounds'.

95 I never found the companion that was so companionable as solitude.
1854 *Walden, or Life in the Woods*, 'Solitude'.

96 I was determined to know beans.
1854 *Walden, or Life in the Woods*, 'The Bean-Field'.

97 If a man does not keep pace with his companions, perhaps it is because he hears a different drummer.
1854 *Walden, or Life in the Woods*, 'Conclusion'.

98 Why level downward to our dullest perception always, and praise that as common sense?
1854 *Walden, or Life in the Woods*, 'Conclusion'.

99 As for style of writing—if one has anything to say, it drops from him simply and directly, as a stone falls to the ground.
1857 Letter to Daniel Ricketson, 18 Aug.

1 I fear that I have not got much to say about Canada, not having seen much; what I got by going to Canada was a cold.
1866 *A Yankee in Canada*.

2 A gun gives you the body, not the bird.
Quoted in Colin Jarman *The Guinness Dictionary of Sports Quotations* (1990).

Thorndike, Dame (Agnes) Sybil 1882–1976

English actress. She made her stage debut in 1904 and went on to distinguish herself in both modern and classical tragedies. Her most famous roles included Medea, George Bernard Shaw's St Joan and Shakespeare's Volumnia. She was married to the actor and director Sir Lewis Casson.

3 You're never too old to play Saint Joan; you're only too young.
Quoted in *Julie Harris Talks to Young Actors* (1971).

Thorne, James 1815–81

English antiquary. He contributed topographical articles to many publications and spent many years researching material for his *Handbook to the Environs of London* (1876), in which he combines factual knowledge with entertaining passages on places and personalities of local interest.

4 An unenviable reputation for dirt and ill odours.
1876 Of Brentford, Middlesex, now in Greater London. *Handbook to the Environs of London*.

5 A town of narrow streets, old houses, shops curiously low, with little in it to interest any one.
1876 Of Hatfield, Hertfordshire. *Handbook to the Environs of London*.

6 A waste of modern tenements, mean, monotonous, and wearisome.
1876 On Penge, Surrey, now in Greater London. *Handbook to the Environs of London*.

7 A populous railway town of hideous brick shops and habitations.
1876 Of Redhill, Surrey. *Handbook to the Environs of London*.

8 Twickenham is one of those happy places which is not burdened with a history.
1876 *Handbook to the Environs of London*.

Thorneycroft, Lord (George Edward) Peter 1909–94

English politician. He entered the House of Commons in 1938, and was President of the Board of Trade (1951–7). Appointed Chancellor of the Exchequer in 1957, he resigned a year later, in disagreement with the government's financial policy, and lost his seat in 1966. He was created a life peer in 1967, and was Chairman of the Conservative Party (1975–81).

9 The choice in politics isn't usually between black and white. It is between two horrible shades of grey.
1979 In the *Sunday Telegraph*, 11 Feb.

10 Some men go through life absolutely miserable because, despite the most enormous achievements, they just didn't do one thing—like the architect who didn't build St Paul's. I didn't quite build St Paul's, but I stood on more mountain tops than possibly I deserved.
1979 In the *Sunday Telegraph*, 11 Feb.

Thornton, Sir Henry 1871–1933

Canadian pioneer of public broadcasting.

11 It is essential that broadcasting be surrounded with such safeguards as will prevent the air becoming what might be described as an atmospheric billboard.
1926 Address to the Advertising Clubs of the World, Philadelphia, 21 Jun. Quoted in E Austin Weir *The Struggle for National Broadcasting in Canada* (1965).

Thorpe, (John) Jeremy 1929–

English politician. Leader of the Liberal Party from 1967, he resigned in 1976 following allegations concerning a previous homosexual relationship with a Mr Norman Scott and was later acquitted of charges of conspiracy and incitement to murder Mr Scott.

12 Greater love hath no man than this, that he lay down his friends for his life.
1962 On Harold Macmillan's sacking of several Cabinet members, House of Commons.

13 Looking around the House, one realizes that we are all minorities now.
1974 On the absence of a clear party majority, House of Commons, 6 Mar.
► *See Shawcross 782:4.*

Thrasymachus 5c BC

Greek sophist and rhetorician from Chalcedon in Bithynia, he figures in Plato's *Republic* defending the proposition that might is right.

14 Morality is nothing other than the advantage of the stronger party.
Quoted in Plato *Republic*, 338b (translated by Robin Waterfield, 1993).

Thubron, Colin Gerald Dryden 1939–

English travel writer, novelist and film-maker.

15 Around me, around them [the dissidents], the total, all-eclipsing Soviet world, which renders any other world powerless and far away, had become profoundly, morally hostile.
1983 *Among the Russians* (published in the US as *Where the Nights are Longest*).

Thucydides c.460–c.400 BC

Athenian politician and historian. As a naval commander in the Peloponnesian war he failed to relieve the Amphipolis in 424, and was exiled from Athens. He began a *History of the Peloponnesian War*, but died before its completion.

16 *Ktema es aei.*
A possession intended to last for ever.
Of his *History of the Peloponnesian War*, 1.22.4.

Thurber, James Grover 1894–1961

US humorist and cartoonist. In 1927 he was appointed managing editor of the *New Yorker* where he published many sketches and cartoons. Collections of his work include *Men Women and Dogs* (1943). His best-known short story is *The Secret Life of Walter Mitty* (1939) which was later filmed (1946).

17 It takes that *je ne sais quoi* which we call sophistication for a woman to be magnificent in a drawing-room when her faculties have departed but she herself has not yet gone home.
1930 In the *New Yorker*, 2 Aug.

18 All right, have it your own way—you heard a seal bark!
1932 Cartoon caption, in the *New Yorker*, 30 Jan.

19 That's my first wife up there and this is the *present* Mrs Harris.
1933 Cartoon caption, in the *New Yorker*, 16 Mar.

20 I myself have accomplished nothing of excellence except a remarkable and, to some of my friends, unaccountable expertness in hitting empty ginger ale bottles with small rocks at a distance of thirty paces.
1933 *My Life and Hard Times*, preface.

21 They lead, as a matter of fact, an existence of jumpiness and apprehension. They sit on the edge of the chair of Literature. In the house of Life they have the feeling that they have never taken off their overcoats.
1933 On humorists. *My Life and Hard Times*, preface.

22 I suppose that the high-water mark of my youth in Columbus, Ohio, was the night the bed fell on my father.
1933 *My Life and Hard Times*, ch.1.

23 Her own mother lived the latter years of her life in the horrible suspicion that electricity was dripping invisibly all over the house.
1933 *My Life and Hard Times*, ch.2.

24 The war between men and women.
1934 Title of series of cartoons in the *New Yorker*, 20 Jan–28 Apr.

25 The Middle-Aged Man on the Flying Trapeze.
1935 Title of book.

26 It's a naïve domestic Burgundy without any breeding, but I think you'll be amused by its presumption.
1937 Cartoon caption, in the *New Yorker*, 27 Mar.

27 Well, if I called the wrong number, why did you answer the phone?
1937 Cartoon caption, in the *New Yorker*, 5 Jun.

28 There is no safety in numbers, or in anything else.
1939 'The Fairly Intelligent Fly', in the *New Yorker*, 4 Feb.

29 Early to rise and early to bed makes a male healthy and wealthy and dead.
1939 'The Shrike and the Chipmunks', in the *New Yorker*, 18 Feb.

30 It's our *own* story *exactly*! He bold as a hawk, she soft as the dawn.
1939 Cartoon caption, in the *New Yorker*, 28 Feb.

31 Then, with that faint fleeting smile playing about his lips, he faced the firing squad; erect and motionless, proud and disdainful, Walter Mitty, the undefeated, inscrutable to the last.
1939 'The Secret Life of Walter Mitty', in the *New Yorker*, 18 Mar.

32 You might as well fall flat on your face as lean over too far backward.
1939 'The Bear Who Let It Alone', in the *New Yorker*, 29 Apr.

33 You can fool too many of the people too much of the time.
1939 'The Owl Who Was God', in the *New Yorker*, 29 Apr.
► *See Lincoln 510:35.*

34 Art—the one achievement of Man which has made the long trip from all fours seem well advised.
1939 In *Forum and Century* magazine, Jun.

35 It is better to have loafed and lost than never to have loafed at all.
1940 *Fables for Our Time*, 'The Courtship of Arthur and Al'.

36 No oyster ever profited from its pearl.
1940 *Fables for Our Time*, 'The Philosopher and the Oyster'.

37 My World—And Welcome To It.
1942 Title of book.

38 If he knew where he was going, it is not apparent from this distance. He fell down a great deal during this period, because of a trick he had of walking into himself.
1945 Of his young self. *The Thurber Carnival*, preface.

39 I suppose that even the most pleasurable of imaginable occupations, that of batting baseballs through the windows of the RCA Building, would pall a little as the days ran on.
1945 *The Thurber Carnival*, 'Memoirs of a Drudge'.

40 He who hesitates is sometimes saved.
1945 *The Thurber Carnival*, 'The Glass in the Field'.

41 She developed a persistent troubled frown which gave her the expression of someone who is trying to repair a watch with his gloves on.
1948 *The Beast In Me and Other Animals*, 'Look Homeward, Jeannie'.

42 'We all have flaws,' he said, 'and mine is being wicked.'
1950 *The 13 Clocks*, ch.8.

43 'For God, for Country and for Yale', the outstanding single anti-climax in the English language.
1951 In *Time*, 11 Jun.

44 The theater is the primary evidence of a nation's culture.
1952 In the *New York Times*, 27 Jul.

45 Try to imagine a famous witty saying that is not immediately clear.
1954 Letter to Malcolm Cowley, 11 Mar.

46 With sixty staring me in the face, I have developed inflammation of the sentence structure and definite hardening of the paragraphs.
1955 In the *New York Post*, 30 Jun.

47 Seeing is deceiving. It's eating that's believing.
1956 *Further Fables for Our Time*.

48 'I think this calls for a drink' has long been one of our national slogans.
1957 *Alarms and Diversions*, 'Merry Christmas'.

49 'Poe,' I said, 'was perhaps the first great nonstop literary drinker of the American nineteenth century. He made the indulgences of Coleridge and De Quincey seem like a bit of mischief in the kitchen with the cooking sherry.

1957 *Alarms and Diversions*, 'The Moribundant Life, or, Grow Old Along with Whom?'.

50 I was seized by the stern hand of Compulsion, that dark, unseasonable Urge that impels women to clean house in the middle of the night.
1957 *Alarms and Diversions*, 'There's A Time For Flags'.

51 The laughter of man is more terrible than his tears, and takes more forms—hollow, heartless, mirthless, maniacal.
1958 In the *New York Times Magazine*, 7 Dec.

52 The power that created the poodle, the platypus and people has an integrated sense of both comedy and tragedy.
1959 Letter to Frances Glennon, Jun.

53 'Humour,' he said, 'is emotional chaos remembered in tranquillity.'
1960 In the *New York Post*, 29 Feb.
➡ *See Wordsworth 925:10.*

54 Ours is a precarious language, as every writer knows, in which the merest shadow line often separates affirmation from negation, sense from nonsense, and one sex from another.
1961 Of English. *Lanterns and Lances*, 'Such a Phrase as Drifts Through Dreams'.

55 Writers of comedy have outlook, whereas writers of tragedy have, according to them, insight.
1961 *Lanterns and Lances*, 'The Case for Comedy'.

56 The only rules comedy can tolerate are those of taste, and the only limitations those of libel.
1961 *Lanterns and Lances*, 'The Duchess and the Bugs'.

57 God bless… God damn!
1961 Last words.

58 I have the reputation of having read all of Henry James, which would argue a misspent youth *and* middle age.
Recalled on his death, 2 Nov 1961.

59 Word has somehow got around that the split infinitive is always wrong. That is of a piece with the outworn notion that it is always wrong to strike a lady.
Recalled on his death, 2 Nov 1961.

60 Unless [artists] can remember what it was to be a little boy, they are only half complete as artist and as man.
Quoted in Helen Thurber and Edward Weeks (eds) *Selected Letters of James Thurber* (1981).

61 Laughter need not be cut out of anything, since it improves everything.
Quoted in Helen Thurber and Edward Weeks (eds) *Selected Letters of James Thurber* (1981).

62 There is something about a poet which leads us to believe that he died, in many cases, as long as 20 years before his birth.
Quoted in Helen Thurber and Edward Weeks (eds) *Selected Letters of James Thurber* (1981).

63 Some American writers who have known each other for years have never met in the daytime or when both were sober.
Quoted in Neil T Jones (ed) *A Book of Days for the Literary Year* (1984).

64 It had only one fault. It was kind of lousy.
Of a play he had recently seen. Attributed.

Thurow, Lester C(arl) 1938–

US economist, professor at Massachusetts Institute of Technology.

65 America no longer lives behind its great wall. Economically, Genghis Khan has arrived.
1992 *Head to Head.*

Tilden, Bill (William Tatem II) 1893–1953

US tennis player. One of the greatest players of his time, he was Wimbledon singles champion three times (1920, 1921, 1930) and doubles champion (1927). He was also six times US singles champion and four times doubles champion in the 1920s.

66 Never change a winning game: always change a losing one.
Quoted in Colin Jarman *The Guinness Dictionary of Sports Quotations* (1990).

Tillich, Paul Johannes 1886–1965

German pastor, theologian and philosopher. Dismissed from his professorship by Nazis in 1933, he left to teach in the US. His theories blend philosophical and psychoanalytical elements with the theological.

67 Neurosis is the way of avoiding non-being by avoiding being.
1952 *The Courage to Be.*

68 Faith comprises both itself and doubt of itself.
1955 *Biblical Religion and the Search for Ultimate Reality.*

69 Faith is the state of being ultimately concerned.
1957 *Dynamics of Faith.*

70 I had the honor to be the first non-Jewish professor dismissed from a German university.
Recalled on his death, 22 Oct 1965.

Tilman, Bill (Harold William) 1898–1977

English mountaineer, explorer and sailor. He went to Kenya as a planter and there met Eric Shipton, with whom he made many notable explorations and climbs. After serving in World War II he took up sailing in remote areas such as Patagonia, the Arctic and the Antarctic. He disappeared on a voyage to the South Shetland Islands in 1977.

71 We live and learn, and big mountains are stern teachers.
1949 *Two Mountains and a River.*

Time

US news periodical.

72 The old man puffed into sight like a venerable battlewagon pressing up over the horizon. First a smudge of smoke, then the long cigar, then the familiar, stoop-shouldered hulk that a generation has come to know as the silhouette of greatness.
1952 Of Winston Churchill disembarking from the *Queen Mary*. 14 Jan.

73 The mighty US suddenly seemed as impotent as a beached whale.
1968 On the fall of 28 of South Vietnam's 44 provincial capitals. 15 Feb.

74 His career was a text book example of the rise of a patrician in the snug embrace of the American establishment.
1971 Of Dean Acheson. 25 Oct.

75 The rescuers had to rescue themselves.
1980 On the ill-fated helicopter attempt to free the hostages held in Iran. 5 May.

The Times

British newspaper, founded as the *Daily Universal Register* on 1 Jan 1785. It changed its name to *The Times* on 1 Jan 1788.

76 Of all journals, and of all writers, those will obtain the largest measure of public support who have told the truth most constantly and most fearlessly.
1852 Leading article, 6 Feb.

77 The first duty of the press is to obtain the earliest and most correct intelligence of the events of the time, and by disclosing them, to make them the common property of the nation.
1852 Leading article, 6 Feb.

Tintoretto *real name* ***Jacopo Robusti*** 1518–94

Venetian painter.

78 In judging paintings, you should consider whether the first impression pleases the eye and whether the artist has followed the rules; as for the rest, everyone makes some mistakes.
Quoted in Carlo Ridolfi *Life of Tintoretto* (1642).

Tobin, James 1918–2002

US economist, winner of the Nobel prize in economics (1981) and a professor at Yale University.

79 Why do so many talented economic theorists believe and teach elegant fantasies so obviously refutable by plainly evident facts?
1992 'An Old Keynesian Counterattacks', in the *Eastern Economic Journal*, Fall issue.

Tocqueville, Alexis Charles Henri Clérel de 1805–59

French historian and politician, Minister of Foreign Affairs for a few months in 1849. His major works are *De la Démocratie en Amérique* (1835–40, *Democracy in America*) and *L'Ancien Régime et la Révolution* (1856, *The Old Regime and the Revolution*).

80 Why, as civilization spreads, do outstanding men become fewer? Why, when attainments are the lot of all, do great intellectual talents become rarer? Why, when there are no longer lower classes, are there no longer upper classes? Why, when knowledge of how to rule reaches the masses, is there a lack of great abilities in the direction of society? America clearly poses these questions. But who can answer them?
1831 Translated by George Lawrence. Quoted in J P Mayer (ed) *Journey to America* (1960).

81 From this foul drain the greatest stream of human industry flows out to fertilize the whole world. From this filthy sewer pure gold flows. Here humanity attains its most complete development and its most brutish, here civilization works its miracles and civilized man is turned almost into a savage.
1835 Of Manchester. Journal entry, 2 Jul. *Journeys to England and Ireland* (translated by George Lawrence and J P Mayer, 1958).

82 *En matière de presse, il n'y a donc réellement pas de milieu entre la servitude et la licence. Pour recueillir les biens inestimables qu'assure la liberté de la presse, il faut savoir se soumettre aux maux inévitables qu'elle fait naître.*
As for the press, there is no middle way between servitude and extreme licence. In order to enjoy the invaluable benefits ensured by freedom of the press, it is necessary to submit to the inevitable evils that it engenders.
1835–40 *De la Démocratie en Amérique* (*Democracy in America*), vol.1, pt.2, ch.3.

83 *C'est un axiome de la science politique aux États-Unis, que le seul moyen de neutraliser les effets des journaux est d'en multiplier le nombre.*
It is an axiom of politics in the United States, that the only means of neutralising the effects of newspapers is to increase their number.
1835–40 *De la Démocratie en Amérique* (*Democracy in America*), vol.1, pt.2, ch.3.

84 *La presse exerce encore un immense pouvoir en Amérique. Elle fait circuler la vie politique dans toutes les portions de ce vaste territoire. C'est elle dont l'œil toujours ouvert met sans cesse à nu les secrets ressorts de la politique, et force les hommes publics à venir tour à tour comparaître devant le tribunal de l'opinion. C'est elle qui rallie les intérêts autour de certaines doctrines et formule le symbole des partis; c'est par elle que ceux-ci se parlent sans se voir, s'entendent sans être mis en contact.*
The press has enormous power in America. It is the press that circulates political life through all parts of this vast territory. Its eye is always open, and making known the secret springs of politics, thus forcing public men to appear before the tribunal of public opinion. It is the press which rallies the interests of the community round certain principles and forms the creed of different parties. Through the press these parties can speak to each other without seeing each other, can listen without meeting.
1835–40 *De la Démocratie en Amérique* (*Democracy in America*), vol.1, pt.2, ch.3.

85 *Le journal représente l'association; l'on peut dire qu'il parle à chacun de ses lecteurs au nom de tous les autres, et il les entraîne d'autant plus aisément qu'ils sont individuellement plus faibles. L'empire des journaux doit donc croître à mesure que les hommes s'égalisent.*
A newspaper represents an association; one might say that it addresses each of its readers in the name of all the others, and influences them in proportion to their individual weakness. The power of newspapers should therefore increase as men become more equal.
1835–40 *De la Démocratie en Amérique* (*Democracy in America*), vol.2, pt.2, ch.6.

86 *Il n'y a qu'un journal qui puisse venir déposer au même moment dans mille esprits la même pensée.*
Only a newspaper can place at the same time in a thousand minds the same thought.
1835–40 *De la Démocratie en Amérique* (*Democracy in America*), vol.2, pt.2, ch.6.

87 *Un journal est un conseiller qu'on n'a pas besoin d'aller chercher, mais qui se présente de lui-même et qui vous parle tous les jours et brièvement de l'affaire commune, sans vous déranger de vos affaires particulières.*
A newspaper is an adviser whom one does not need to

seek out, but one who comes of his own accord and speaks to you every day, briefly, of public affairs, without disturbing you from your own.
1835–40 *De la Démocratie en Amérique* (*Democracy in America*), vol.2, pt.2, ch.6.

88 *Ce serait diminuer leur importance que de croire qu'ils ne servent qu'à garantir la liberté; ils maintiennent la civilisation.*
It would diminish the importance [of newspapers] to believe that they only serve to guarantee freedom; they maintain civilization.
1835–40 *De la Démocratie en Amérique* (*Democracy in America*), vol.2, pt.2, ch.6.

Todd, Mike 1907–58

89 No gals, no gags, no chance.
1943 On attending rehearsals for *Oklahoma!* Quoted in the *US News and World Report*, 12 Apr 1993, on the 50th anniversary of the musical that ran six years, won a Pulitzer Prize, and was to have 750 revivals in 1993.

Todd, Ron(ald) 1927–

English trade union leader, a member of the Transport and General Workers' Union. He became General-Secretary in 1985, with strong left-wing support.

90 You don't have power if you surrender all your principles—you have office.
1988 Speech, London, Jun.

Toffler, Alvin 1928–

US writer and journalist, one of the most successful trend-spotters of the age. Toffler coined the phrase 'future shock' and convinced a sizable number of the reading public and policy administrators that what ailed them was the fact that everything was changing so fast.

91 'Future shock'...the shattering stress and disorientation that we induce in individuals by subjecting them to too much change in too short a time.
1970 *Future Shock*.

92 That great, growing engine of change—technology.
1970 *Future Shock*.

93 Technology feeds on itself. Technology makes more technology possible.
1970 *Future Shock*.

Tojo, Hideki 1885–1948

Japanese soldier who rose to become Minister of War (1940–1) and from 1941 premier and dictator of Japan. He was sentenced to death in 1948.

94 This is farewell.
I shall wait beneath the moss
Until the flowers are fragrant
In this island country of Japan.
1948 His final statement before execution, 23 Dec. Quoted in R J C Butow *Tojo and the Coming War* (1961).

Tolkien, J(ohn) R(onald) R(euel) 1892–1973

English writer and philologist. He was born in South Africa, educated in England, and he taught at Oxford. He wrote scholarly books, but is famous for his hugely popular fantasy novels *The Hobbit* (1937) and *The Lord of the Rings* trilogy (1954–6).

95 In a hole in the ground there lived a hobbit. Not a nasty, dirty, wet hole, filled with the ends of worms and an oozy smell, nor yet a dry, bare, sandy hole with nothing in it to sit down on or to eat: it was a hobbit-hole, and that means comfort.
1937 *The Hobbit*, ch.1.

96 My political opinions lean more and more to anarchy (philosophically understood, meaning abolition of control not whiskered men with bombs)... The most improper job of any man is bossing other men.
1943 Letter to Christopher Tolkien, 29 Apr.

97 There is only one bright spot and that is the growing habit of disgruntled men of dynamiting factories and power stations. I hope that, encouraged now as patriotism, it may remain a habit! But it won't do any good, if it is not universal.
1943 Letter to Christopher Tolkien, 29 Apr.

98 One Ring to rule them all, One Ring to find them,
One Ring to bring them all and in the darkness bind them.
In the Land of Mordor where the Shadows lie.
1954 *The Fellowship of the Ring*, epigraph and passim.

99 But I cordially dislike allegory in all its manifestations, and always have done so since I grew old and wary enough to detect its presence. I much prefer history, true or feigned, with its varied applicability to the thought and experience of readers.
1954 *The Fellowship of the Ring*, foreword.

1 Hobbits are an unobtrusive but very ancient people, more numerous formerly than they are today; for they love peace and quiet and good tilled earth: a well-ordered and well-farmed countryside was their favourite haunt... Even in ancient days they were, as a rule, shy of 'the Big Folk', as they call us, and now they avoid us with dismay and are becoming hard to find.
1954 *The Fellowship of the Ring*, prologue.

2 Do not meddle in the affairs of Wizards, for they are subtle and quick to anger.
1954 Gandalf. *The Fellowship of the Ring*, bk.1, ch.3.

3 Where iss it, where iss it: my Precious, my Precious? It's ours, it is, and we wants it.
1955 Gollum. *The Two Towers*, ch.1.

Tolstoy, Leo Nikolayevich 1828–1910

Russian novelist, social philosopher, social critic and sometime mystic. His best-known works are *War and Peace* (1868–9) and *Anna Karenina* (1875–7).

4 Our body is a machine for living. It is organized for that, it is its nature. Let life go on in it unhindered and let it defend itself, it will do more than if you paralyse it by encumbering it with remedies.
1869 *War and Peace*, bk.10, ch.29.

5 All happy families resemble each other; each unhappy family is unhappy in its own way.
1874 *Anna Karenina*, opening words.

6 I sit on a man's back, choking him and making him carry me, and yet assure myself and others that I am very sorry for him and wish to ease his lot by all possible means—except by getting off his back.
1886 *What Then Must We Do?*, ch.16 (translated by Maude).

7 What is called science today consists of a haphazard heap of information, united by nothing, often utterly unnecessary, and not only failing to present one unquestionable truth, but as often as not containing the grossest errors today put forward as truths, and tomorrow overthrown.
1898 *What is Art?* (translated by V Tchertkoff).

8 I am convinced that the history of so-called scientific work in our famous centers of European civilization will, in a couple of hundred years, represent an inexhaustible source of laughter and sorrow for future generations. The learned men of the small western part of our European continent lived for several centuries under the illusion that the eternal blessed life was the West's future. They were interested in the problem of when and where this blessed life would come. But they never thought of how they were going to make their life better.
1898 *What is Art?* (translated by V Tchertkoff).

Tomé Pires c.1480–1525

Portuguese scholar and diplomat who came to Malacca in 1512, shortly after his country's conquest of the region. Portuguese control of new sea routes meant that valuable spices no longer needed to travel via Venice to reach Europe.

9 Whoever is Lord of Malacca has his hand on the throat of Venice.
1512–15 *The Suma Oriental of Tomé Pires* (translated by Armando Cortasao, 1944).

Tomlinson, (Alfred) Charles 1927–

English poet and critic. Emeritus Professor of English, University of Bristol. His publications include *Poems* (1964) and *The Flood* (1981).

10 Everything we see
Teaches the time that we are living in.
1984 'Poem for My Father'.

Tomlinson, H(enry) M(ajor) 1873–1958

English writer. He wrote novels, travel books, memoirs and a biography of Norman Douglas.

11 I will never believe again that the sea was ever loved by anyone whose life was married to it.
1912 *The Sea and the Jungle*, ch.1.

Toole, John Kennedy 1937–69

US novelist. He published nothing in his lifetime, and committed suicide. His novel *A Confederacy of Dunces* was published to great acclaim in 1980, and *The Neon Bible* in 1989.

12 Her logic was a combination of half-truths and clichés, her worldview a compound of misconceptions deriving from a history of our nation as written from the perspective of a subway tunnel.
A Confederacy of Dunces (published 1980), ch.5, pt.3.

13 The human desire for food and sex is relatively equal. If there are armed rapes why should there not be armed hot dog thefts?
A Confederacy of Dunces (published 1980), ch.7, pt.1.

14 You can always tell employees of the government by the total vacancy which occupies the space where most other people have faces.
A Confederacy of Dunces (published 1980), ch.9, pt.1.

Toplady, Augustus Montague 1740–78

English clergyman and hymn writer.

15 Rock of Ages, cleft for me,
Let me hide myself in Thee,
Let the water and the blood,
From thy riven side which flowed,
Be of sin the double cure,
Cleanse me from its guilt and power.
1776 Hymn.

Torrance, Sam 1953–

Scottish golfer, captain of the successful European Ryder Cup team in 2002.

16 I just led them to the water and they drank copiously.
2002 On his victorious European Ryder Cup team. In *The Times*, 28 Dec.

Toscanini, Arturo 1867–1957

Italian conductor. He made his debut at La Scala in 1898 and remained there until 1908, returning between 1920 and 1929. He conducted many major orchestras, and created the National Broadcasting Orchestra of America (1937–53). He had a reputation as a tyrannical perfectionist.

17 God tells me how he wants this music played—and you get in his way.
1930 Berating players in his orchestra. Quoted in Howard Tubman *Etude*.

18 After I die I am coming back to earth as the doorkeeper of a bordello. And I won't let a one of you in.
To an uncooperative orchestra. Quoted in Norman Lebrecht *Discord* (1982).

Towne, Robert 1936–

US screenwriter. His credits include *The Tomb of Ligeia* (1964), *Chinatown* (1974), *Greystoke: the Legend of Tarzan* (1984), *Mission: Impossible* (1996) and *Mission: Impossible II* (2000).

19 Why are you doing it? What can you buy that you can't already afford?
The future, Mr Gittes, the future.
1974 *Chinatown*.

20 Forget it, Jake, it's Chinatown.
1974 *Chinatown*, closing line.

Townsend, Sue 1945–

English writer. She has written novels and plays, but is best known for her 'Adrian Mole' books.

21 The Secret Diary of Adrian Mole Aged 13¾.
1982 Title of book.

22 I have decided to be a poet. My father said there isn't a suitable career structure for poets and no pensions and other boring things, but I am quite decided.
1982 *The Secret Diary of Adrian Mole Aged 13¾*, 'Monday, May 25th'.

23 I think it's essential for comic writers to have a hate figure, a despot, a regime to react against, and I think Thatcher was perfect for me, I loathed everything she stood for.
2002 In the *Observer*, 24 Mar.

Townshend, Pete 1945–

British rock musician.

24 Hope I die before I get old.
1900 'My Generation'.

Toynbee, Arnold 1852–83

English economic historian and social reformer, best known as the author of *The Industrial Revolution in England* (1884). Toynbee Hall, Whitechapel was founded in his memory in 1885.

25 The Industrial Revolution.
1880–1 Title of Oxford lectures, published posthumously in 1884. The phrase passed into common usage.

Toynbee, Arnold Joseph 1889–1975

English historian, nephew of Arnold Toynbee. His greatest work is *A Study of History*, published in 10 volumes (1934–54).

26 No annihilation without representation.
1947 Advocating greater British representation at the United Nations.
► *See Otis 630:19.*

27 America is a large, friendly dog in a very small room. Every time it wags its tail, it knocks over a chair.
1949 Letter, 26 Oct.

28 Civilisation is a movement and not a condition; a voyage and not a harbour.
Quoted in *Reader's Digest*, Oct 1958.

29 Angkor is perhaps the greatest of Man's essays in rectangular architecture that has yet been brought to life.
1958 *East to West*.

Toynbee, (Theodore) Philip 1916–81

English novelist and journalist, son of the historian Arnold Joseph Toynbee. An experimental writer, his semi-autobiographical Pantaloon sequence is particularly innovative.

30 I have seen the future and it does not work.
1974 Of the USA. In the *Observer*, 27 Jan.
► *See Steffens 814:6.*

31 He was the type of man who was always trying to live beyond his moral means.
1975 Of J Middleton Murry. In the *Observer*, 12 Jan.

32 The basic command of religion is not 'do this!' or 'do not do that!' but simply 'look!'
1978 Journal entry, 15 Feb. Collected in *Part of a Journey* (1981).

33 The primary duty of a serious biographer is to illuminate his subject's life work, not to play the spy in his bedroom.
1979 Book review in the *Observer*, 18 Mar.

Toynbee, Polly 1946–

English journalist, columnist at *The Guardian* (1977–88, 1998–).

34 I hate to join the chortling ranks of [Millennium] Dome rubbishers in the right-wing press…but, alas, I have to admit the Dome is a lemon.
2000 In *The Guardian*, 5 Jan.

Traherne, Thomas c.1636–1674

English poet and mystic. Educated at Oxford, he took holy orders and in 1667 became Chaplain to the Lord Keeper of the Great Seal. He wrote religious prose, including *Roman Forgeries* (1673), *Christian Ethics* (1675) and *Centuries of Religious Meditations* (published 1908); his poetry was not published until 1903.

35 In unexperienc'd Infancy
Many a sweet mistake doth lie.
'Shadows in the Water' (published 1903).

36 Some unknown joys there be
Laid up in store for me.
'Shadows in the Water' (published 1903).

37 Sleep is cousin-german unto death:
Sleep and death differ, no more, than a carcass
And a skeleton.
'A Serious and a Curious Night-Meditation' (published 1903).

38 A Stranger here
Strange things doth meet, strange glories see;
Strange Treasures lodg'd in this fair world appear,
Strange all, and New to me,
But that they mine should be, who nothing was,
That Strangest is of all, yet brought to pass.
The Salutation (published 1903).

39 You never enjoy the world aright, till the sea itself floweth in your veins, till you are clothed with the heavens, and crowned with the stars: and perceive yourself to be the sole heir of the whole world.
Centuries of Meditations, 'First Century', section 29 (published 1908).

Travers, Ben 1886–1980

English dramatist and screenwriter.

40 The really great batsmen fall into two categories. One comes to the wicket saying to the bowlers 'I am going to slaughter you'. The other comes to the wicket saying 'You can't get me out'.
1981 *94 Declared Cricket Reminiscences*.

Travers, P(amela) L(yndon) 1906–96

British writer. She worked as a journalist, actress and dancer, and for the British Ministry of Information in the US during World War II. *Mary Poppins* was published in 1934; subsequent titles include *Mary Poppins Comes Back* (1935), *Mary Poppins Opens the Door* (1943) and *Mary Poppins in the Park* (1952).

41 'Now,' she said, 'spit-spot into bed.'
1934 *Mary Poppins*, ch.1.

42 From the [empty] carpet-bag she took out seven flannel night-gowns, four cotton ones, a pair of boots, a set of dominoes, two bathing-caps and a postcard album. Last of all came a folding camp-bedstead with blankets and eiderdown complete.
1934 *Mary Poppins*, ch.1.

43 Mary Poppins looked down at her feet and rubbed the toe of one shoe along the pavement two or three times. Then she smiled at the shoe in such a way that the shoe knew quite well that the smile wasn't meant for it.
1934 *Mary Poppins*, ch.2.

44 'Don't you know,' she said pityingly, 'that everybody's got a Fairyland of their own?'
1934 *Mary Poppins*, ch.2.

45 If I laugh on that particular day I become so filled with Laughing Gas that I simply can't keep on the ground. Even if I smile it happens. The first funny thought, and I'm up like a balloon. And until I can think of something serious I can't get down again.
1934 Mr Wigg, Mary Poppins's uncle. The 'particular day' is when his birthday falls on a Friday. *Mary Poppins*, ch.3.

46 Oh, my Gracious, Glorious, Galumphing Goodness!
1934 Mr Wigg. *Mary Poppins*, ch.3.

47 The Red Cow was very respectable, she always behaved like a perfect lady and she knew What was What. To her a thing was either black or white—there was no question of it being grey or perhaps pink. People were good or they were bad—there was nothing in between. Dandelions were either sweet or sour—there were never any moderately nice ones.
1934 *Mary Poppins*, ch.5.

48 He could smell her crackling white apron and the faint flavour of toast that always hung about her so deliciously.
1934 Michael's impressions of Mary Poppins. *Mary Poppins*, ch.6.

49 Feed the Birds, Tuppence a Bag! Feed the Birds, Tuppence a Bag!
1934 *Mary Poppins*, ch.7.

50 Trouble trouble and it will trouble you!
1934 Mary Poppins. *Mary Poppins*, ch.12.

Tree, Sir Herbert (Draper) Beerbohm 1852–1917

English actor-manager. He played a wide range of roles, of which the most successful included Svengali in George du Maurier's *Trilby*, Higgins in George Bernard Shaw's *Pygmalion* and Charles Dickens's Fagin. He assumed the management of the Comedy Theatre in London in 1887 and then spent a prosperous 10 years as manager of the Haymarket before opening Her Majesty's in 1897. He was also the founder of the Royal Academy of Dramatic Art (1904).

51 Ladies, just a little more virginity, if you don't mind.
To actresses playing the roles of ladies-in-waiting. Quoted in Alexander Woollcott *Shouts and Murmurs* (1923), 'Capoulo Criticism'.

52 He is an old bore. Even the grave yawns for him.
Of Israel Zangill. Quoted in Hesketh Pearson *Beerbohm* (1956).

53 It is difficult to live up to one's poster… When I pass my name in large letters I blush, but at the same time instinctively raise my hat.
Quoted in Hesketh Pearson *Beerbohm* (1956).

54 The national sport of England is obstacle-racing. People fill their rooms with useless and cumbersome furniture, and spend the rest of their lives trying to dodge it.
Quoted in Hesketh Pearson *Beerbohm* (1956).

Treitschke, Georg Friedrich 1776–1842

German librettist and translator best known for revising the libretto for the final version (1814) of Beethoven's opera *Fidelio* from earlier versions by Stefan von Breuning (1806) and Joseph Sonnleithner (1805).

55 *Abscheulicher!*
Perfidious wretch!
1814 Leonora's recitative and aria. *Fidelio*, act 1.

56 *O welche Lust!*
Oh what delight!
1814 The prisoners' chorus. *Fidelio*, act 1.

Trevelyan, George Macaulay 1876–1962

English historian. After serving in World War I, he became Professor of Modern History at Cambridge (1927–40). A pioneer social historian, he wrote *English Social History* (1944) —a companion volume to his *History of England* (1926).

57 Disinterested intellectual curiosity is the life-blood of real civilisation.
1944 *English Social History.*

58 Village cricket spread fast through the land. In those days, before it became scientific, cricket was the best game in the world to watch—each ball a potential crisis.
Quoted in Helen Exley *Cricket Quotations* (1992).

Trevelyan, John 1904–85

British executive. He was secretary of the British Board of Film Censors between 1958 and 1970.

59 Censors are paid to have dirty minds.
1970 Attributed.

Trevino, Lee Buck 1939–

US golfer. He won his first US Open in 1968 and in 1971 established a record by winning three Open titles (the US, Canadian and British) in the same year, retaining his British title the following year.

60 I'm not saying my golf game went bad, but if I grew tomatoes they'd come up sliced.
Quoted in *Scholastic Coach*, 'Coaches' Corner', Dec 1982.

61 If my IQ had been two points lower, I'd have been a plant somewhere.
Quoted in Colin Jarman *The Guinness Dictionary of Sports Quotations* (1990).

62 I'm hitting the driver so good, I gotta dial the operator for long distance after I hit it.
Attributed.

Trevor-Roper, Hugh Redwald, Baron Dacre of Glanton 1914–2003

English historian, known for his vivid reconstruction of *The Last Days of Hitler* (1947). He was Professor at Oxford (1957–80) and Master of Peterhouse, Cambridge (1980–7).

63 Any society, so long as it is, or feels itself to be, a working society, tends to invest in itself: a military society tends to become more military, a bureaucratic society more bureaucratic, a commercial society more commercial, as the status and profits of war or office or commerce are enhanced by success, and institutions are framed to forward it. Therefore, when such a society is hit by a general crisis, it finds itself partly paralyzed by the structural weight of increased social investment. The dominant military or official or commercial classes cannot easily change their orientation: and their social dominance, and the institutions through which it is exercised, prevent other classes from securing power or changing policy.
1965 *The Rise of Christian Europe.*

Trillin, Calvin Marshall 1935–

US journalist and author.

64 A shelf life somewhere between butter and yoghurt.
1987 On the plethora of new book titles. In the *New York Times*, 14 Jun.

65 Math was my worst subject because I could never persuade the teacher that my answers were meant ironically.
1990 In the *New York Times*, 7 Oct.

Trilling, Lionel 1905–75

US literary critic whose works, such as *The Liberal Imagination* (1950) and *Beyond Culture* (1965), gained him a reputation for scholarly and astute social comment. He also wrote a novel, *The Middle of the Journey* (1947).

66 Literature is the human activity that takes the fullest and most precise account of variousness, possibility, complexity, and difficulty.
1950 *The Liberal Imagination*, preface.

67 We are all ill: but even a universal sickness implies an idea of health.
1950 *The Liberal Imagination*, 'Art and Neurosis'.

68 We who are liberal and progressive know that the poor are our equals in every sense except that of being equal to us.
1950 *The Liberal Imagination*, 'Princess Casamassima'.

69 It would seem that Americans have a kind of resistance to looking closely at society.
1950 *The Liberal Imagination*, 'Manners, Morals and the Novel'.

70 The poet... may be used as a barometer, but let us not forget that he is also part of the weather.
1950 *The Liberal Imagination*.

71 The function of literature through all its mutations, has been to make us aware of the particularity of selves, and the high authority of the self in its quarrel with its society and its culture. Literature is in that sense subversive.
1965 *Beyond Culture*, introduction.

Trinder, Tommy 1909–89

English comedian and actor, whose famous catchphrase was 'You lucky people'.

72 Overpaid, overfed, oversexed, and over here.
Of US troops stationed in Britain during World War II. This phrase is associated with Trinder, but was probably not his invention.

Trollope, Anthony 1815–82

English novelist. He is best known for his two novel sequences, the Barchester novels and the 'Palliser' novels, both of which chronicle the life of a region and are distinguished by their slow pace and quiet comedy. His novels include *Barchester Towers* (1857) and *Can You Forgive Her?* (1864).

73 The tenth Muse, who now governs the periodical press.
1855 *The Warden*, ch.14.

74 She was rich in apparel, but not bedizened with finery... She well knew the great architectural secret of decorating her constructions, and never descended to construct a decoration.
1857 Of Mrs Stanhope. *Barchester Towers*, ch.9.

75 There is no road to wealth so easy and respectable as that of matrimony.
1858 *Doctor Thorne*, ch.16.

76 Let no man boast himself that he has got through the perils of winter till at least the seventh of May.
1858 *Doctor Thorne*, ch.47.

77 Those who have courage to love should have courage to suffer.
1859 *The Bertrams*, ch.27.

78 For the most of us, if we do not talk of ourselves, or at any rate of the individual circles of which we are the centres, we can talk of nothing. I cannot hold with those who wish to put down the insignificant chatter of the world.
1861 *Framley Parsonage*, ch.10.

79 We cannot bring ourselves to believe it possible that a foreigner should in any respect be wiser than ourselves. If any such point out to us our follies, we at once claim those follies as the special evidence of our wisdom.
1862 Stavely. *Orley Farm*, ch.18.

80 It is because we put up with bad things that hotel-keepers continue to give them to us.
1862 Stavely. *Orley Farm*, ch.18.

81 As for conceit, what man will do any good who is not conceited? Nobody holds a good opinion of a man who has a low opinion of himself.
1862 *Orley Farm*, ch.22.

82 Mr Palliser was one of those politicians in possessing whom England has perhaps more reason to be proud than of any other of her resources, and who, as a body, give to her that exquisite combination of conservatism and progress which is her present strength and best security for the future.
1864 *Can You Forgive Her?*, ch.24.

83 To think of one's absent love is very sweet; but it becomes monotonous... I doubt whether any girl would be satisfied with her lover's mind if she knew the whole of it.
1864 *The Small House at Allington*, ch.4.

84 Why is it that girls so constantly do this, so frequently ask men who have loved them to be present at their marriages with other men? There is no triumph in it. It is done in sheer kindness and affection. They intend to offer something which shall soften and not aggravate the sorrow that they have caused... I fully appreciate the intention, but in honest truth, I doubt the eligibility of the proffered entertainment.
1864 John Eames. *The Small House at Allington*, ch.9.

85 It may almost be a question whether such wisdom as many of us have in our mature years has not come from the dying out of the power of temptation, rather than as the results of thought and resolution.
1864 *The Small House at Allington*, ch.14.

86 Never think that you're not good enough yourself. A man should never think that. My belief is that in life people will take you much at your own reckoning.
1864 Lord De Guest to Johnny. *The Small House at Allington*, ch.32.

87 With many women I doubt whether there be any more effectual way of touching their hearts than ill-using them and then confessing it. If you wish to get the sweetest fragrance from the herb at your feet, tread on it and bruise it.
1865 *Miss Mackenzie*, ch.10.

88 It was manifest to me that there was something in the Roman Catholic religion which made the priests very dear to the people; for I doubt whether in any village in England, had such an accident happened to the rector, all the people would have roused themselves at midnight to wreak their vengeance on the assailant.
1866 *Argosy*, 'Father Giles of Ballymoy', May.

89 How I did respect you when you dared to speak the truth to me! Men don't know women, or they would be harder to them.
1867 *The Claverings*, ch.15.

90 She understood how much louder a cock can crow in its own farmyard then elsewhere.
1867 *The Last Chronicle of Barset*, ch.17.

91 It's dogged as does it. It ain't thinking about it.
1867 *The Last Chronicle of Barset*, ch.61, 'Giles Hoggett'.

92 They who do not understand that a man may be brought to hope that which of all things is the most grievous to him, have not observed with sufficient closeness the perversity of the human mind.
1869 Of Trevelyan's paranoia about his wife's fidelity. *He Knew He Was Right*, ch.38.

93 A faineant government is not the worst government that England can have. It has been the great fault of our politicians that they have all wanted to do something.
1869 *Phineas Finn*, ch.13.

94 Mr Turnball had predicted evil consequences…and was now doing the best in his power to bring about the verification of his own prophecies.
1869 *Phineas Finn*, ch.25.

95 Perhaps there is no position more perilous to a man's honesty than that…of knowing himself to be quite loved by a girl whom he almost loves himself.
1869 *Phineas Finn*, ch.50.

96 She knew how to allure by denying, and to make the gift rich by delaying it.
1869 *Phineas Finn*, ch.57.

97 We cannot have heroes to dine with us. There are none. And were those heroes to be had, we should not like them…the persons whom you cannot care for in a novel, because they are so bad, are the very same that you so dearly love in your life, because they are so good.
1873 Of Frank Greystock. *The Eustace Diamonds*, ch.35.

98 What man thinks of changing himself so as to suit his wife? And yet men expect that women shall put on altogether new characters when they are married, and girls think that they can do so.
1874 Lady Chiltern to Mr Maule. *Phineas Redux*, ch.3.

99 It is the necessary nature of a political in this country to avoid, as long as it can be avoided, the consideration of any question which involves a great change… The best carriage horses are those which can most steadily hold back against the coach as it trundles down the hill.
1874 *Phineas Redux*, ch.4.

1 Is it not singular how some men continue to obtain the reputation of popular authorship without adding a word to the literature of their country worthy of note?… To puff and to get one's self puffed have become different branches of a new profession.
1875 *The Way We Live Now*, ch.1.

2 Love is like any other luxury. You have no right to it unless you can afford it.
1875 *The Way We Live Now*, ch.84.

3 Equality would be a heaven, if we could attain it.
1876 Prime Minister to Phineas. *The Prime Minister*, ch.68.

4 I hold that gentleman to be the best dressed whose dress no one observes.
1879 *Thackeray*, ch.9.

5 A man's mind will very generally refuse to make itself up until it be driven and compelled by emergency.
1881 Houston. *Ayala's Angel*, ch.41.

6 He must have known me had he seen me as he was wont to see me, for he was in the habit of flogging me constantly. Perhaps he did not recognize me by my face.
1883 *Autobiography*, ch.1.

7 She was neither clear-sighted nor accurate; and in her attempts to describe morals, manners, and even facts, was unable to avoid the pitfalls of exaggeration.
1883 Of his mother, Frances Trollope, author of *The Domestic Manners of the Americans*. *Autobiography*, ch.2.

8 Take away from English authors their copyrights, and you would very soon take away from England her authors.
1883 *Autobiography*, ch.6.

9 It is admitted that a novel can hardly be made interesting or successful without love… It is necessary because the passion is one which interests or has interested all. Everyone feels it, has felt it, or expects to feel it.
1883 *Autobiography*, ch.12.

10 Three hours a day will produce as much as a man ought to write.
1883 *Autobiography*, ch.15.

11 I think that Plantagenet Palliser, Duke of Omnium, is a perfect gentleman. If he be not, then I am unable to describe a gentleman.
1883 *Autobiography*, ch.20.

Trollope, Joanna 1943–

English writer. She is best known for her novels set in rural English communities, but also writes historical fiction and, under the name Caroline Harvey, romances.

12 Contentment and fulfilment don't make for very good fiction.
1994 In *The Times*, 25 Jun.

Trotsky, Leon *originally Lev Davidovich Bronstein* 1879–1940

Russian Jewish revolutionary, born in Ukraine. Already a noted revolutionary, he played a major role in the October Revolution (1917), and created the Red Army. After Lenin's death (1924) his influence began to decline and under Stalin he was expelled from the Soviet Union (1929) and sentenced to death (1937). He was assassinated in Mexico by one of Stalin's agents.

13 You have played out your role. Go where you belong: to the dustheap of history.
1917 To the Mensheviks, at the first Congress of Soviets following the October Revolution. Quoted in A J P Taylor *From the Boer War to the Cold War: Essays on Twentieth-Century Europe* (1995), p.271.

14 A cossack's whip wrapped in the parchment of a constitution.
1905 On the October Manifesto, a package of limited constitutional reforms conceded by the Tzarist government following the strikes and civil unrest of early October 1905. Quoted in Lionel Kochan *Russia in Revolution* (1967).

15 The Soviet Republic needs an army that will be able to fight and conquer.
1918 Speech to the Moscow Soviet of Workers', Soldiers' and Peasants' Deputies, 19 Mar.

16 It was the supreme expression of the mediocrity of the apparatus that Stalin himself rose to his position.
1930 *My Life*, p.501.

17 Civilization has made the peasantry its pack animal. The

bourgeoisie in the long run only changed the form of the pack.
1934 *History of the Russian Revolution* (translated by Max Eastman, 1934), vol.3, pt.3.

18 Old age is the most unexpected of all things that happens to a man.
1935 *Diary in Exile.*

19 In a country that is economically backward, the proletariat can take power earlier than in countries where capitalism is advanced.
1931 *The Permanent Revolution.*

20 Marxism is, above all, a method of analysis.
1931 *The Permanent Revolution.*

21 The end may justify the means, as long as there is something that justifies the end.
Attributed.

Trudeau, Pierre Elliott 1919–2000

Canadian politician. As Minister of Justice and Attorney-General (1967) he opposed the separation of Quebec from Canada. He became Liberal Prime Minister (1968–79, 1980–4), urging independence from US influence and home economic control. He proposed a new constitution for complete Canadian independence, secured Apr 1982.

22 The state has no place in the bedrooms of the nation.
1967 Of the liberalization of the Criminal Code. Interview in Ottawa, 22 Dec. The remark is based on similar words written by the journalist Martin O'Malley in an unsigned editorial in the *Globe and Mail*, 12 Dec 1967.

23 Living next to you is like sleeping with an elephant. No matter how friendly and even-tempered the beast, one is affected by every twitch and grunt.
1969 Of the US. Speech, National Press Club, Washington DC, 25 Mar. Quoted in Lawrence Martin *The Presidents and the Prime Ministers* (1982).

24 Fuddle-duddle.
1971 Neologism coined by Trudeau when accused of uttering a 'four-letter word' in the House of Commons, Ottawa, 16 Feb. 'No, it was fuddle-duddle,' replied Trudeau. The reply led an opposition Member of Parliament to observe, 'Mr. Trudeau wants to be obscene but not heard.'

Trueman, Fred (Frederick Sewards) 1931–

English cricketer, a notoriously fast bowler. He played for Yorkshire (1949–68) and made 67 Test appearances for England (1952–65). He took a record 307 Test wickets.

25 If there is any game in the world that attracts the half-baked theorist more than cricket I have yet to hear of it.
1964 *Freddie Trueman's Book of Cricket.*

26 The difference between a fast bowler and a good fast bowler is not extra muscle but extra brains.
1964 *Freddie Trueman's Book of Cricket.*

27 We didn't have metaphors in my day. We didn't beat about the bush.
1996 Quoted in the *Sunday Times*, 22 Dec.

Truman, Harry S 1884–1972

US Democratic statesman, 33rd President (1945–53), responsible for the first atom bombing on Japan, the postwar loan to Britain, the establishment of NATO (1949) and the sending of US troops to South Korea (1950). He gave military and economic aid to countries threatened by communist interference, and introduced a 'Fair Deal' of economic reform at home.

28 When I first came to Washington, for the first six months I wondered how the hell I ever got here. For the next six months, I wondered how the hell the rest of them ever got here.
1940 Speech, Apr.

29 Every segment of our population, and every individual, has a right to expect from his Government a Fair Deal.
1945 Speech to Congress, 6 Sep.

30 If you think somebody is telling a big lie about you, the only way to answer is with the whole truth.
1950 On Senator Joseph R McCarthy. Quoted in John Hersey *Aspects of the Presidency* (1980).

31 The only thing you have to worry about is bad luck. I never had bad luck.
1950 After an assassination attempt, 1 Nov.

32 If you can't stand the heat you better get out of the kitchen.
1952 Address to the Aero Club of Washington, 27 Dec, quoting a colleague from his days as a county judge.

33 Why, this fellow doesn't know any more about politics than a pig on Sunday.
1952 Of presidential hopeful Eisenhower. Quoted in Richard M Nixon *RN: Memoirs of Richard Nixon* (1978).

34 In 1945 we did much more than draft an international agreement among 50 nations. We set down on paper the only principles that will enable civilized human life to continue to survive on this globe.
1955 On the 10th anniversary of the United Nations, 24 Jun.

35 Party platforms are contracts with the people.
1956 *Memoirs: Years of Trial and Hope*.

36 I never give them hell. I just tell the truth and they think it is hell.
1956 Interview, in *Look*, 3 Apr.

37 A politician is a man who understands government, and it takes a politician to run a Government. A statesman is a politician who has been dead 10 or 15 years.
1958 New York World Telegram, 12 Apr.

38 It's a recession when your neighbour loses his job; it's a depression when you lose yours.
1958 In the *Observer*, 13 Apr.
► *See Reagan 680:55.*

39 Too many…pass judgement on wartime decisions in the luxury of a peacetime environment.
1963 Reply to a Boston University official who had criticized Truman's use of the atomic bomb. Truman Library archives, 23 Sep.

40 The President hears a hundred voices telling him that he is the greatest man in the world. He must listen carefully indeed to hear the one voice that tells him he is not.
1964 In *This Week*, 5 Apr.

41 Being criticized…he never did get it through his head that that's what politics is all about.
Of President Eisenhower. Quoted in Merle Miller (ed) *Plain Speaking* (1974).

42 Can't somebody bring me a one-handed economist?
Recalled on the death of his economic adviser Edwin Nourse, 9 Apr 1974. Nourse had been fond of saying 'on one hand…but on the other'.

43 I told him to fire away. He did and it is dynamite.
On asking Joseph Stalin for the Soviet agenda at the Potsdam Conference. Quoted in the *New York Times*, 2 Jun 1980.

44 Being president is like riding a tiger…keep on riding or be swallowed.
Quoted in the *New York Times*, 28 Dec 1984.

45 The buck stops here.
Motto displayed on a sign on his desk. Quoted in William Safire *Safire's New Political Dictionary* (1993).

46 I don't much care for your law, but, by golly, this bourbon is good.
To US Supreme Court Justice William O Douglas. Attributed.

Trump, Donald 1946–

US businessman, renowned for his flamboyant and initially successful dealings in real estate. His best-known developments include Trump Tower, New York City, and Trump Castle, Trump Plaza and the Taj Mahal casino in Atlantic City.

47 I like thinking big. If you're going to be thinking anyway, you might as well think big.
1989 In *Time*, 16 Jan.

48 A gambler is someone who plays slot machines. I prefer to own slot machines.
1990 On the opening of his Atlanta City Taj Mahal casino. In *Time*, 9 Apr.

49 See that gold Cadillac down the street? That's the color I want those handrails. Gold. Cadillac Gold. Not yellow like a daisy.
Of the handrails in Manhattan's Trump Tower. Quoted by Paul Trachtman in the *Smithsonian*, Mar 1995, reviewing Alexander Theroux *The Primary Colors*.

Truss, Lynne

English writer and broadcaster.

50 The Zero Tolerance Approach to Punctuation.
2003 Subtitle of *Eats, Shoots & Leaves*.

Truth, Sojourner *née* *Isabella* c.1797–1883

American abolitionist. Born a slave, she gained her freedom and later became an ardent evangelist. In 1843 she changed her name to Sojourner Truth and campaigned against slavery and for woman suffrage.

51 Well, chilern, whar dar is so much racket dar must be something out o' kilter. I tink dat 'twixt de niggers of de Souf and de women at de Norf all a talkin' 'bout rights, de white men will be in a fix pretty soon.
1851 Women's Rights Convention, Akron, Ohio. Quoted in *Narrative of Sojourner Truth* (1875), pt.2, 'Book of Life'.

52 Look at me! Look at my arm!… I have plowed, and planted, and gathered into barns, and no man could head me—and ar'n't I a woman? I could work as much and eat as much as a man (when I could get it), and bear de lash as well—and ar'n't I a woman? I have borne thirteen chilern and seen 'em mos' all sold off into slavery, and when I cried out with a mother's grief, none but Jesus heard—and ar'n't I a woman?
1851 Women's Rights Convention, Akron, Ohio. Quoted in *Narrative of Sojourner Truth* (1875), pt.2, 'Book of Life'.

Ts'ao Sung c.830–910

Chinese poet from Anhui about whom very little is known. He was in his seventies before finally passing a set of literary examinations.

53 I charge thee, sir, not to talk of high honours,
A single general achieves fame on the rotting bones of ten thousand.
c.879 'Written in the year Chi hai (879)', collected in *A Book of Chinese Verse* (translated by N L Smith and R H Kotewall).

Tsongas, Paul Efthemios 1941–97

US politician, Senator from Massachusetts and a candidate for Democratic presidential nomination.

54 We are becoming an economic colony. America is up for sale. One percent of Japan's manufacturing base is foreign-owned; 2 per cent of Germany's is; 3 per cent of France's. Ours is 18 per cent and growing rapidly.
1992 Quoted in the *Los Angeles Times*, 17 Mar.

55 You cannot be pro-jobs and anti-government at the same time. You cannot love employees and despise employers. You cannot redistribute wealth that you never created. No goose, no golden egg.
1992 Quoted in the *Los Angeles Times*, 19 Feb.

Tu Fu 712–70

Chinese poet who never achieved a settled existence and is known to have spent a large part of his life travelling in a state of hardship.

56 Sundered by peaks unscalable,
Tomorrow shall we strangers be.
c.750 'Visiting an Old Friend', collected in *A Golden Treasury of Chinese Poetry* (translated by John Turner, 1967).

Tuchman, Barbara W(ertheim) 1912–89

US historian, best known for *The Guns of August* (1962, Pulitzer Prize), tracing the origins of World War I, and *Stilwell and the American Experience in China* (1970, Pulitzer Prize). Other works include *A Distant Mirror* (1978).

57 Dead battles, like dead generals, hold the military mind in their dead grip.
1962 *The Guns of August*, ch.2.

58 No more distressing moment can ever face a British Government than that which requires it to come to a hard and fast and specific decision.
1962 *The Guns of August*, ch.9.

59 Reasonable orders are easy enough to obey; it is capricious, bureaucratic or plain idiotic demands that form the habit of discipline.
1970 *Stilwell and the American Experience in China*, pt.1, ch.1.

60 Most people are relieved to find a superior on whose judgment they can rest. That, indeed, is the difference between most people and Generals.
1972 Address at US Army War College, Apr. Collected in *Practising History* (1981).

61 To a historian libraries are food, shelter, and even muse.
1981 *Practising History*, 'The Houses of Research'.

Tucker, Sophie *pseudonym of* *Sophia Abuza* 1884–1966

US jazz singer, born in Russia. A legendary star of cabaret and vaudeville in the 1920s, she included among her biggest hits such songs as 'Some of These Days' (1926) and 'My Yiddische Momma' (1928). She led her own band in the 1930s and made several appearances on Broadway and in musical films.

62 I've been rich and I've been poor. Believe me, honey, rich is better.
1945 *Some of These Days*.

63 The Last of the Red-Hot Mamas.
Title of song, adopted by Tucker as her nickname.

Turgenev, Ivan 1818–83

Russian novelist. His best-known work is the novel *Fathers and Sons* (1862).

64 Nature is not a temple, but a workshop, and man's the workman in it.
1862 *Fathers and Sons* (translated by Rosemary Edmonds), ch.9.

65 I share no one's ideas. I have my own.
1862 *Fathers and Sons* (translated by Rosemary Edmonds), ch.13.

66 Whatever a man prays for, he prays for a miracle. Every prayer reduces itself to this: Great God, grant that twice two be not four.
1881 *Poems in Prose*, 'Prayer'.

Turner, Bruce 1922–93

British jazz saxophonist. He played in the Humphrey Lyttelton Band for many years, as well as leading his own groups.

67 Jazz musicians are not demigods. They are warm, vulnerable human beings with a desperate need to go on paying the rent.
1984 *Hot Air, Cool Music*, ch.10.

Turner, Joseph Mallard William 1775–1851

English painter, one of Britian's most important 19c artists.

68 This is the end of Art. I am glad I have had my day.
Attributed, on first seeing a daguerrotype. Quoted in J G Links *Canaletto and his Patrons* (1977).

Tutu, Desmond Mpilo 1931–

Black South African prelate, the first black Bishop of Johannesburg (1984) and Archbishop of Cape Town (1986). A fierce critic of apartheid, advocating international sanctions, he also condemned the use of violence, seeking instead a negotiated solution. He was awarded the Nobel peace prize in 1984.

69 Be nice to whites. They need you to rediscover their humanity.
1984 In the *New York Times*, 19 Oct.

70 I am not interested in picking up crumbs of compassion thrown from the table of someone who considers himself to be my master. I want the full menu of rights.
1985 NBC News, 9 Jan.

71 We don't want apartheid liberalized. We want it dismantled. You can't improve something that is intrinsically evil.
1985 Speech, Mar.

72 I have struggled against tyranny. I didn't do that in order to substitute one tyranny with another.
1998 In *The Irish Times*, 'This Week They Said', 31 Oct.

Twain, Mark *pseudonym of* Samuel Langhorne Clemens 1835–1910

US writer. He worked as a steamboat pilot and took his pen-name from a term used for measuring the depth of the Mississippi. His novel *Huckleberry Finn* (1884) is a classic. His work ranges from the lightly comic *The Innocents Abroad* (1869) to the darkly pessimistic *What is Man?* (1906).

73 No woman can look as well out of the fashion as in it.
1867 Letter, 16 Apr, quoted in Franklin Walker and G Ezra Dane (eds) *Mark Twain's Travels with Mr. Brown* (1940), letter 14.

74 I must have a prodigious quantity of mind; it takes me as much as a week to make it up.
1869 *The Innocents Abroad*, ch.7.

75 They spell it Vinci and pronounce it Vinchy; foreigners always spell better than they pronounce.
1869 *The Innocents Abroad*, ch.19.

76 The French are polite, but it is often mere ceremonious politeness. A Russian imbues his polite things with a heartiness that compels belief in their sincerity.
1869 *The Innocents Abroad*.

77 Lump the whole thing! Say that the Creator made Italy from designs by Michael Angelo!
1869 *The Innocents Abroad*.

78 Travel is fatal to prejudice.
1869 *The Innocents Abroad*, conclusion.

79 Soap and education are not as sudden as a massacre, but they are more deadly in the long run.
1872 *A Curious Dream*, 'Facts Concerning the Recent Resignation'.

80 Nothing helps scenery like ham and eggs.
1872 *Roughing It*, ch.17.

81 Well-a-well, man that is born of woman is of few days and full of trouble, as the Scripture says.
1876 Aunt Polly. *The Adventures of Tom Sawyer*, ch.1.

82 I reckon you're a kind of singed cat, as the saying is—better'n you look.
1876 Aunt Polly to Tom. *The Adventures of Tom Sawyer*, ch.1.

83 He was not the Model Boy of the village. He knew the model boy very well though—and loathed him.
1876 *The Adventures of Tom Sawyer*, ch.1.

84 Tom turned in without the added vexation of prayers.
1876 *The Adventures of Tom Sawyer*, ch.3.

85 He held curls to be effeminate, and his own filled his life with bitterness.
1876 *The Adventures of Tom Sawyer*, ch.4.

86 Often, the less there is to justify a traditional custom, the harder it is to get rid of it.
1876 *The Adventures of Tom Sawyer*, ch.5.

87 Church ain't shucks to a circus.
1876 *The Adventures of Tom Sawyer*, ch.7.

88 So they inwardly resolved that so long as they remained in the business, their piracies should not again be sullied with the crime of stealing.
1876 *The Adventures of Tom Sawyer*, ch.13.

89 There comes a time in every rightly constructed boy's life when he has a raging desire to go somewhere and dig for hidden treasure.
1876 *The Adventures of Tom Sawyer*, ch.25.

90 The cross of the Legion of Honour has been conferred upon me. However, few escape that distinction.
1880 *A Tramp Abroad*, ch.8.

91 An Irishman is lined with copper, and the beer corrodes it.

But whiskey polishes the copper and is the saving of him.
1883 *Life on the Mississippi*, ch.23.

92 In the South, the war is what AD is elsewhere: they date from it.
1883 Of the American Civil War. *Life on the Mississippi*, ch.45.

93 Persons attempting to find a motive in this narrative will be prosecuted; persons attempting to find a moral in it will be banished; persons attempting to find a plot in it will be shot.
1884 *The Adventures of Huckleberry Finn*, 'Notice'.

94 She allowed she would sivilize me.
1884 *The Adventures of Huckleberry Finn*, ch.1.

95 If you are with the quality, or at a funeral, or trying to go to sleep when you ain't sleepy…why you itch all over in upward of a thousand places.
1884 *The Adventures of Huckleberry Finn*, ch.2.

96 You think you're a good deal of a big bug, *don't* you.
1884 Huck's Pap to Huck. *The Adventures of Huckleberry Finn*, ch.5.

97 [He] reckoned a body could reform the old man with a shotgun, maybe, but he didn't know no other way.
1884 Judge Thatcher's opinion of Pap. *The Adventures of Huckleberry Finn*, ch.5.

98 Pap warn't in a good humor—so he was his natural self.
1884 *The Adventures of Huckleberry Finn*, ch.6.

99 A body would 'a thought he was Adam—he was just all mud.
1884 *The Adventures of Huckleberry Finn*, ch.6.

1 After supper Pap took the jug, and said he had enough whisky there for two drunks and one delirium tremens.
1884 *The Adventures of Huckleberry Finn*, ch.6.

2 How slow and still the time did drag along.
1884 *The Adventures of Huckleberry Finn*, ch.6.

3 I's rich now, come to look at it. I owns myself, en I's wuth eight hund'd dollars.
1884 Jim. *The Adventures of Huckleberry Finn*, ch.8.

4 But it warn't no time to be sentimentering.
1884 *The Adventures of Huckleberry Finn*, ch.13.

5 It was fifteen minutes before I could work myself up to go and humble myself to a nigger—but I done it, and I warn't ever sorry for it afterwards, neither. I didn't do him no more mean tricks, and I wouldn' done that one if I'd a knowed it would make him feel that way.
1884 Huck, of Jim. *The Adventures of Huckleberry Finn*, ch.15.

6 Jim said it made him all over trembly and feverish to be so close to freedom.
1884 *The Adventures of Huckleberry Finn*, ch.16.

7 To be, or not to be; that is the bare bodkin
That makes calamity of so long life;
For who would fardels bear, till Birnam Wood do come
to Dunsinane,
But that the fear of something after death
Murders the innocent sleep,
Great nature's second course,
And makes us rather sling the arrows of outrageous
fortune
Than fly to others that we know not of.
There's the respect must give us pause:
Wake Duncan with thy knocking! I would thou couldst;
For who would bear the whips and scorns of time,
The oppressor's wrong, the proud man's contumely,
The law's delay, and the quietus which his pangs might
take,
In the dead waste and middle of the night, when
Churchyards yawn
In customary suits of solemn black,
But that the undiscovered country from whose bourne
no traveler returns,
Breathes forth contagion on the world,
And thus the native hue of resolution, like the poor cat i'
the adage,
Is sicklied o'er with care,
And all the clouds that lowered o'er our housetops,
With this regard their currents turn awry,
And lose the name of action.
'Tis a consummation devoutly to be wished.
But soft you, the fair Ophelia:
Ope not thy ponderous and marble jaws,
But get thee to a nunnery—go!
1884 The Duke's version of Hamlet's soliloquy, combining elements of other speeches by Hamlet and pieces of *Macbeth*. *The Adventures of Huckleberry Finn*, ch.21.
➥ *See Shakespeare 753:74.*

8 All kings is mostly rapscallions.
1884 *The Adventures of Huckleberry Finn*, ch.22.

9 Hain't we got all the fools in town on our side? And ain't that a big enough majority in any town?
1884 *The Adventures of Huckleberry Finn*, ch.26.

10 It don't make no difference whether you do right or wrong, a person's conscience ain't got no sense, and just goes for him *anyway*. If I had a yaller dog that didn't know no more than a person's conscience does I would poison him. It takes up more room than all the rest of a person's insides, and yet ain't no good, nohow. Tom Sawyer he says the same.
1884 *The Adventures of Huckleberry Finn*, ch.33.

11 But that's always the way; it don't make no difference whether you do right or wrong, a person's conscience ain't got no sense, and just goes for him *anyway*.
1884 Huck. *The Adventures of Huckleberry Finn*, ch.33.

12 But I reckon I got to light out for the territory ahead of the rest, because Aunt Sally she's going to adopt me and sivilize me, and I can't stand it. I been there before.
1884 Huck. *The Adventures of Huckleberry Finn*, closing words.

13 The boy's mouth is a trifle more Irishy than is necessary.
1884 Letter to his publishers.

14 An experienced, industrious, ambitious, and often quite picturesque liar.
1885 'The Private History of a Campaign That Failed'.

15 Many a small thing has been made large by the right kind of advertising.
1889 *A Connecticut Yankee in King Arthur's Court*, ch.22.

16 The master minds of all nations, in all ages, have sprung in affluent multitude from the mass of the nation, and from the mass of the nation only—not from its privileged classes.
1889 *A Connecticut Yankee in King Arthur's Court*, ch.25.

17 If you pick up a starving dog and make him prosperous, he will not bite you. This is the principal difference between a dog and a man.
1894 *Pudd'nhead Wilson*, ch.16.

18 Few things are harder to put up with than the annoyance of a good example.
1894 *Pudd'nhead Wilson*, ch.19.

19 Familiarity breeds contempt—and children.
c.1894 Quoted in Albert Bigelow Paine (ed) *Mark Twain's Notebook* (1935).

20 What marriage is to morality, a properly conducted licensed liquor traffic is to sobriety.
1895 Quoted in Albert Bigelow Paine (ed) *Mark Twain's Notebook* (1935), ch.23.

21 When in doubt, tell the truth.
1897 *Following the Equator*, ch.2.

22 I admire him, I frankly confess it; and when his time is come I shall buy a piece of the rope for a keepsake.
1897 Of Cecil Rhodes. *Following the Equator*, ch.2.

23 Man is the Only Animal that Blushes. Or needs to.
1897 *Following the Equator*, ch.27.

24 When people do not respect us we are sharply offended; yet deep down in his private heart no man much respects himself.
1897 *Following the Equator*, ch.29.

25 The man with a new idea is a crank until the idea succeeds.
1897 *Following the Equator*, ch.32.

26 There are several good protections against temptation but the surest is cowardice.
1897 *Following the Equator*, ch.36.

27 It takes your enemy and your friend, working together, to hurt you to the heart; the one to slander you and the other to get the news to you.
1897 *Following the Equator*, ch.45.

28 Human nature is the same everywhere; it deifies success, it has nothing but scorn for defeat.
1897 *Joan of Arc*, bk.1, ch.8.

29 Education consists mainly in what we have unlearned.
c.1897 Quoted in Albert Bigelow Paine (ed) *Mark Twain's Notebook* (1935).

30 There are many scapegoats for our blunders, but the most popular one is Providence.
c.1897 Quoted in Albert Bigelow Paine (ed) *Mark Twain's Notebook* (1935).

31 The report of my death was an exaggeration.
1897 In the *New York Journal*, 2 Jun. This was the substance of Twain's cable to the Associated Press in response to the news item that he had died.

32 I am a democrat only on principle, not by instinct—nobody is *that*. Doubtless some people *say* they are, but this world is grievously given to lying.
1898 *Notebook*, ch.31, Feb–Mar.

33 A classic...something that everybody wants to have read and nobody wants to read.
1900 Speech on 'The Disappearance of Literature' at the Nineteenth Century Club, 20 Nov. Quoted in Albert Bigelow Paine (ed) *Mark Twain's Speeches* (1910).

34 Always do right. This will gratify some people, and astonish the rest.
1901 Speech, Brooklyn, 16 Feb.

35 The man who is a pessimist before 48 knows too much; if he is an optimist after it, he knows too little.
1902 Notebook, ch.33, Dec.
► *See also Willkie 914:67.*

36 Of the delights of this world man cares most for sexual intercourse. He will go any length for it—risk fortune, character, reputation, life itself.
c.1906 Quoted in Albert Bigelow Paine (ed) *Mark Twain's Notebook* (1935).

37 Scientists have odious manners, except when you prop up their theory; then you can borrow money off them.
The Bee (published 1917).

38 I have been told that Wagner's music is better than it sounds.
Autobiography (published in 1924).

39 I have never taken any exercise, except sleeping and resting, and I never intend to take any. Exercise is loathsome.
Quoted in Colin Jarman *The Guinness Dictionary of Sports Quotations* (1990).

40 Golf is a good walk spoiled.
Attributed.

41 I don't know anything that mars good literature so completely as too much truth.
'The Savage Club Dinner'. Quoted in Albert Bigelow Paine (ed) *Mark Twain's Speeches* (1923).

42 A habit cannot be tossed out of the window, it must be coaxed down the stairs one step at a time.
Attributed.

Tynan, Kenneth 1927–80

English theatre critic. Writing for the *Observer* and for the *New Yorker*, he argued strongly for the foundation of the National Theatre and lent his support to many talented radical playwrights. He was also the moving force behind the stylish erotic revue *Oh, Calcutta!* (1969).

43 There was a heated division of opinion in the lobbies during the interval but a small conservative majority took the view that it might be as well to remain in the theatre.
1953 Reviewing the play *The Glorious Days*.

44 A good many inconveniences attend play-going in any large city, but the greatest of them is usually the play itself.
1957 In the *New York Herald Tribune*.

45 A novel is a static thing that one moves through; a play is a dynamic thing that moves past one.
1961 *Curtains*.

46 Forty years ago he was Slightly in *Peter Pan*, and you might say that he has been wholly in *Peter Pan* ever since.
1961 Of Noël Coward. *Curtains*.

47 A critic is a man who knows the way but can't drive the car.
1966 In the *New York Times Magazine*, 9 Jan.

48 A good drama critic is one who perceives what is happening in the theatre of his time. A great drama critic also perceives what is *not* happening.
1967 *Tynan Right and Left*, foreword.

49 I doubt if I could love anyone who did not wish to see *Look Back in Anger*.
1956 In the *Observer*, 13 May.

50 A useful word previously unknown to me: 'ergophobia',

meaning 'fear or hatred of work'. At last I can define myself in one word.
The Diaries of Kenneth Tynan (2001), entry for 26 Oct 1975.

51 Dichotomy = operation performed on lesbians to make them normal.
The Diaries of Kenneth Tynan (2001), entry for 11 Oct 1977.

Tyson, Don(ald) John 1930–

US businessman, chairman and chief executive officer of Tyson Foods Inc, Arkansas.

52 If you can take $20,000 in one-hundred-dollar bills and walk up on a windy hill and tear them up and watch them blow away, and it doesn't bother you, then you should go into the commodities market.
1994 In the *New Yorker*, 30 May.

Tyson, Mike 1966–

US boxer.

53 Everybody in America is so money-hungry. It's like a rat race and even when you win you're still a freaking rat.
2000 In *The Times*, Dec 26.

54 I'm not Mother Teresa. I'm not Charles Manson either.
2002 In *The Independent*, 20 Dec.

55 My main objective is to be professional, but to kill him.
2002 On Lennox Lewis. In *The Independent*, 20 Dec.

Tzara, Tristan *pseudonym of* *Samy Rosenstock* 1896–1963

Romanian-born poet, essayist and editor in Paris, a leader of the Dadaist movement.

56 *La mort serait un beau long voyage et les vacances illimitées de la chair des structures et des os.*
Death should be a long, beautiful voyage and limitless vacations of the flesh.
1923 *De nos oiseaux*, 'La mort de Guillaume Apollinaire'.

57 *Dada ne signifie rien.*
Dada means nothing.
1921 *Sept manifestes Dada*, 'Manifeste Dada 1918'.

58 *Liberté:* DADA DADA DADA, *hurlement de couleurs crispées, entrelacements des contraires et de toutes les contradictions, des grotesques, des inconséquences:* LA VIE.
Freedom: DADA DADA DADA, a howl of unnerving colours, intertwinings of contrarities and contradictions, of the grotesque, of inconsistencies: LIFE.
1924 *Sept manifestes Dada*, 'Manifeste Dada 1918'.

59 All pictorial or plastic art is useless; art should be a monster which casts servile minds into terror.
Quoted in Saranne Alexandrian *Surrealist Art* (1970).

60 Dada began not as an art form but as a disgust.
Quoted in Saranne Alexandrian *Surrealist Art* (1970).

Uccello, Paolo 1397–1475

Florentine painter. One of the first Italian painters of the Renaissance to explore the use of perspective.

61 O what a lovely thing this perspective is!
Attributed in Giorgio Vasari *Lives of the Artists* (1568, translated by George Bull, 1965).

Umaseo, Tadao c.1950–

Japanese intellectual who has written about and commented on his country's social and political traditions.

62 In terms of communication, Japan is like the black hole of the universe. It receives signals but does not emit them.
Quoted in David Halberstam *The Reckoning* (1986).

Unamuno, Miguel de 1864–1936

Spanish fatalist philosopher and writer. Rector at the University of Salamanca, he first supported and then denounced Franco and subsequently died at the hands of the Fascists.

63 *La vida es duda, y la fe sin la duda es solo muerte.*
Life is doubt, and faith without doubt is nothing but death.
1907 *Poesias*, 'Salmo II'.

64 It is not usually our ideas that make us optimistic or pessimistic, but it is our optimism or pessimism of physiological or pathological origin that makes our ideas.
1913 *The Tragic Sense of Life*.

65 Science is a cemetery of dead ideas.
1913 *The Tragic Sense of Life* (translated by P Smith, 1953).

66 True science teaches, above all, to doubt and to be ignorant.
1913 *The Tragic Sense of Life* (translated by P Smith, 1953).

67 Science robs men of wisdom and usually converts them into phantom beings loaded up with facts.
Collected in *Essays and Soliloquies* (translated by J E Crawford Flitch, 1925).

Unesco Constitution

An organization founded (in 1946) to promote collaboration among nations through education, science and culture.

68 Since wars begin in the minds of men, it is in the minds of men that the defences of peace must be constructed.
1945 Signed 16 Nov. The Unesco Constitution came into force 4 Nov 1946.

United Nations Charter

Drafted during World War II by the US, UK and USSR. Key figures included John Foster Dulles, Ralph Bunche and Field Marshal Jan Smuts.

69 We the Peoples of the United Nations, determined to save succeeding generations from the scourge of war, which twice in our lifetime has brought untold sorrow to

mankind, and to reaffirm faith in fundamental human rights, in the dignity and worth of the human person, in the equal rights of men and women and of nations large and small, and to establish conditions under which justice and respect for the obligations arising from treaties and other sources of international law can be maintained, and to promote social progress and better standards of life in larger freedom, and for these ends, to practice tolerance and live together in peace with one another as good neighbours, and to unite our strength to maintain international peace and security, and to ensure by the acceptance of principles and the institution of methods, that armed force shall not be used, save in the common interest, and to employ international machinery for the promotion of the economic and social advancement of all peoples, have resolved to combine our efforts to accomplish these aims.
1945 26 Jun.

Unseld, Siegfried 1924–2002

German publisher, head of Suhrkamp Verlag (Frankfurt).

70 One of the signs of Napoleon's greatness—according to a sociologist who recently wrote to our publishing house—is that he once had a publisher shot.
1978 *The Author and his Publisher* (translated by H and H Hannum, 1980), p.1.

Untermeyer, Louis 1885–1977

US writer and editor, best known as the editor of anthologies such as *Modern American Poetry* (1919), which introduced some important new voices, and *Treasury of Great Poems* (1955).

71 Every poet knows the pun is Pierian, that it springs from the same soil as the Muse...a matching and shifting of vowels and consonants, an adroit assonance sometimes derided as jackassonance.
1965 *Bygones*.

Updike, John Hoyer 1932–

US novelist, poet and critic. He is best known for his novels, notably the 'Rabbit' series, but has also written poetry, short stories, criticism and *Self-Consciousness* (1989), a volume of memoirs.

72 Everybody who tells you how to act has whisky on their breath.
1960 *Rabbit, Run*.

73 The difficulty with humorists is that they will mix what they believe with what they don't; whichever seems likelier to win an effect.
1960 *Rabbit, Run*.

74 Many-maned scud-thumper, tub
of male whales, maker of worn wood, shrub-
ruster, sky-mocker, rave!
portly pusher of waves, wind-slave.
1960 *Telephone Poles and Other Poems*, 'Winter Ocean'.

75 School is where you go between when your parents can't take you and industry can't take you.
1963 *The Centaur*, ch.4.

76 One out of three hundred and twelve Americans is a bore, for instance, and a healthy male adult bore consumes each year one and a half times his own weight in other people's patience.
1965 *Assorted Prose*, 'Confessions of a Wild Bore'.

77 The first breath of adultery is the freest; after it, constraints aping marriage develop.
1968 *Couples*, ch.2.

78 Sex is like money; only too much is enough.
1968 *Couples*, ch.5.

79 Facts are generally overesteemed. For most practical purposes, a thing is what men think it is. When they judged the earth flat, it was flat. As long as men thought slavery tolerable, it was tolerable. We live down here among shadows, shadows among shadows.
1974 Buchanan. *Buchanan Dying*, act 1.

80 To be President of the United States, sir, is to act as advocate for the blind, venomous, and ungrateful client; still, one must make the best of the case, for the purposes of Providence.
1974 Polk. *Buchanan Dying*, act 2.

81 In general the churches...bore for me the same relation to God that billboards did to Coca-Cola: they promoted thirst without quenching it.
1975 *A Month of Sundays*, ch.2.

82 Americans have been conditioned to respect newness, whatever it costs them.
1975 *A Month of Sundays*, ch.18.

83 One of the last...of the great narrating English virgins.
Of Mildred Lathbury, protagonist of Barbara Pym's *Excellent Women* (1978). Attributed.

84 America is a vast conspiracy to make you happy.
1980 *Problems*, 'How to Love America and Leave It at the Same Time'.

85 Writing criticism is to writing fiction and poetry as hugging the shore is to sailing in the open sea.
1984 *Hugging The Shore*, foreword.

86 Why does one never hear of government funding for the preservation and encouragement of comic strips, girlie magazines and TV soap operas? Because these genres still hold the audience they were created to amuse and instruct.
1985 In the *New York Review of Books*, 18 Jul.

87 There's a crystallization that goes on in a poem which the young man can bring off, but which the middle-aged man can't.
1986 In the *New York Times*, 24 Mar.

88 How circumstantial reality is! Facts are like individual letters, with their spikes and loops and thorns, that make up words: eventually they hurt our eyes, and we long to take a bath, to rake the lawn, to look at the sea.
1989 *Self-Consciousness*, I. 'A Soft Spring Night in Shillington'.

89 A writer's self-consciousness, for which he is much scorned, is really a mode of interestedness, that inevitably turns outward.
1989 *Self-Consciousness*, I. 'A Soft Spring Night in Shillington'.

90 The essential self is innocent, and when it tastes its own innocence knows that it lives forever.
1989 *Self-Consciousness*, I. 'A Soft Spring Night in Shillington'.

91 The throat: how strange, that there is not more erotic emphasis upon it. For here, through this compound pulsing pillar, our life makes its leap into spirit, and in the other direction gulps down what it needs of the material world.

1989 *Self-Consciousness*, III. 'Getting The Words Out'.

92 The great temple of fiction has no well-marked front portal; most devotees arrive through a side door, and not dressed for worship.
1989 *Self-Consciousness*, III. 'Getting The Words Out'.

93 In fact we do not try to picture the afterlife, nor is it our selves in our nervous tics and optical flecks that we wish to perpetuate; it is the self as the window on the world that we can't bear to think of shutting.
1989 *Self-Consciousness*, VI. 'On Being A Self Forever'.

94 Not only are selves conditional but they die. Each day, we wake slightly altered, and the person we were yesterday is dead.
1989 *Self-Consciousness*, VI. 'On Being A Self Forever'.

95 So writing is my sole remaining vice. It is an addiction, an illusory release, a presumptuous taming of reality, a way of expressing lightly the unbearable.
1989 *Self-Consciousness*, VI. 'On Being A Self Forever'.

96 Now that I am sixty, I see why the idea of elder wisdom has passed from currency.
1992 In the *New Yorker*, Nov.

97 [There is] an undercurrent of emotion bred of the deep acquaintance that can take a landscape and its inhabitants to be a vocabulary, a set of wordless symbols effortlessly shared.
1995 On the artist Edward Hopper. In the *Washington Post*, 25 Jun.

98 The United States, democratic and various though it is, is not an easy country for a fiction-writer to enter: the slot between the fantastic and the drab seems too narrow.
1995 *Rabbit Angstrom: The Four Novels*, introduction.

99 Clarence's mind was like a many-legged, wingless insect that had long and tediously been struggling to climb up the walls of a slick-walled porcelain basin; and now a sudden impatient wash of water swept it down the drain.
1996 *In the Beauty of the Lilies*.

1 But when has happiness ever been the subject of fiction? The pursuit of it is just that—a pursuit.
2003 *The Early Stories: 1953–1975*, foreword.

Urey, Harold Clayton 1893–1981

US chemist and discoverer of deuterium, or heavy hydrogen. He taught at the Universities of Montana, John Hopkins, Columbia, Chicago and Oxford, and was awarded the 1934 Nobel prize in chemistry.

2 I thought it might have a practical use in something like neon signs.
c.1934 Recalling his 1932 discovery of heavy water which proved critical to the development of the atomic bomb.

Ustinov, Sir Peter Alexander 1921–2004

English actor, playwright and director, of Russian descent. He appeared in a wide range of European works, including both comedies and tragedies, and also enjoyed success in plays of his own, among them *The Love of Four Colonels* (1951), *Romanoff and Juliet* (1956) and *Beethoven's Tenth* (1983). His talent as a witty raconteur and his many film appearances also contributed to his international reputation.

3 Critics search for ages for the wrong word, which, to give them credit, they eventually find.
1952 BBC radio broadcast, Feb.

4 A diplomat these days is nothing but a head waiter who's allowed to sit down occasionally.
1956 *Romanoff and Juliet*.

5 Would it have helped Ben Hur if Christ had not been crucified?
1962 Comment when the financiers of his *Billy Budd* expressed their preference for a happy ending. Recalled in his autobiography *Dear Me* (1977).

6 Thanks to the movies, gunfire has always sounded unreal to me, even when being fired at.
1977 *Dear Me*.

7 There is always something engagingly lunatic about Ralph, a Quixotic quality, although his windmills are ditches and his faithful nag a powerful motor-cycle.
1977 Of Sir Ralph Richardson. *Dear Me*.

8 Toronto is a kind of New York operated by the Swiss.
Quoted by John Bentley Mays in the *Globe and Mail*, 1 Aug 1987.

9 I was relieved to hear that your welcome was not excessive.
To the audience, opening a one-man show at the Curran Theater. Quoted in the *San Francisco Chronicle*, 25 Apr 1991.

Uttley, Alison 1884–1976

English writer. She is remembered for her books for children, notably the 'Little Grey Rabbit' series (1929 onwards).

10 For a long time we dreamed of a real leather ball, and at last my brother had one for his birthday. The feel of the leather, the stitching round it, the faint gold letters stamped upon it, the touch of the seam, the smell of it, all affected me so deeply that I still have that ache of beauty when I hold a cricket ball.
1948 *Carts and Candlesticks*.

V

Vachell, Horace Annesley 1861–1955

British writer.

11 In nature there are no rewards or punishments; there are only consequences.
1906 *The Face of Clay*.

Valenzuela, Luisa 1940–

Argentinian fiction writer.

12 *Siendo el esperar sentada la forma más muerta de la espera muerta, siendo el esperar la forma menos estimulante de muerte.*
To wait, seated in a chair, is the deadest form of dead anticipation, and waiting the most uninspired form of death.
1982 *Cambio de armas*, 'Ceremonias de rechazo' (translated as *Other Weapons*, 'Rituals of Rejection', 1985).

Valéry, Paul 1871–1945

French poet, writer and critic, considered one of the great

modern philosophical writers in French verse. He wrote widely on philosophical issues and on the metaphysics of life.

13 *Un poème n'est jamais achevé—c'est toujours un accident qui le termine, c'est-à-dire qui le donne au public.*
A poem is never finished; it is always an accident that puts a stop to it, that gives it to the public.
1930 *Littérature.*

14 *Il faut n'appeler Science que l'ensemble des recettes qui réussissent toujours.—Tout le reste est littérature.*
Science means simply the aggregate of all the recipes that are always successful. All the rest is literature.
1932 *Moralités.*

15 *Dieu créa l'homme, et ne le trouvant pas assez seul, il lui donne une compagne pour lui faire mieux sentir sa solitude.*
God created man and, finding him not sufficiently alone, gave him a companion to make him feel his solitude more keenly.
1941 *Tel Quel 1*, 'Moralités'.

16 *La politique est l'art d'empêcher les gens de se mêler de ce qui les regarde.*
Politics is the art of preventing people from taking part in affairs which concern them.
1943 *Tel Quel 2*, 'Rhumbs'.

Valle y Caviedes, Juan del c.1652–?1695

Peruvian poet born in a small town in Andalusia, Spain. He lived most of his life in Lima. Little is known of his life. His collection *Diente del Parnaso* (1689) is an earthy satire of the medical profession.

17 *Y así, enfermos, ojo alerta,*
y a ningún médico admitan;
mueran de gorra, sin dar
un real a la medicina.
Be careful then, patients,
and don't accept any doctor;
die for free and do not give
a single coin to medicine.
1689 *Diente del Parnaso* ('Parnassus' Tooth'), 'Prólogo al que leyere este tratado'.

Vallejo, César Abraham 1892–1938

Peruvian poet. A first-hand witness to poverty and the injustices done to the indigenous peoples, after the publication of his collection *Trilce* (1922), he left Peru (1923) and spent the rest of his life in France and Spain living in precarious circumstances and without publishing a single poem. He also wrote novels and non-fiction.

18 *Yo nací un día*
que Dios estuvo enfermo.
I was born on a day
God was sick.
1918 *Los heraldos negros* (translated as *The Black Heralds*, 1990), 'Espergesia'.

19 *Absurdo, sólo tú eres puro.*
Absurdo, este exceso sólo ante ti se
suda de dorado placer.
Absurdity, only you are pure.
Absurdity, only before you
is this excess sweated out of golden pleasure.
1922 *Trilce* (translated 1973), no.73.

20 *Me moriré en París con aguacero,*
un día del cual tengo ya el recuerdo.
Me moriré en París—y no me corro—
tal vez un jueves, como es hoy, de otoño.
I will die in Paris with a sudden shower,
a day I can already remember.
I will die in Paris—and I don't budge—
maybe a Thursday, like today is, in autumn.
1939 *Poemas humanos*, 'Piedra negra sobre una piedra blanca' (translated as 'Black Stone on a White Stone', 1968).

Vance, Paul and Pockriss, Lee

US songwriters who have composed many popular songs, including 'Catch a Falling Star' which was made popular by Perry Como.

21 Itsy Bitsy Teenie Weenie Yellow Polkadot Bikini.
1960 Title of song.

van den Berghe, Pierre L 1933–

US sociologist, Emeritus Professor at the University of Washington.

22 I suffer the anthropological malady diagnosed by Lévi-Strauss in *Tristes tropiques*: I find it much more difficult to suspend value judgments about the society in which I normally reside than I do abroad. It takes physical and cultural distance to gain moral detachment and political noncommitment. Relativism implies a solid measure of indifference.
'From the Popocatepetl to the Limpopo', collected in Bennett Berger (ed) *Authors of their Own Lives* (1990).

23 Sociology seems to have missed every intellectually promising boat in the last half century.
'From the Popocatepetl to the Limpopo', collected in Bennett Berger (ed) *Authors of their Own Lives* (1990).

Vanderbilt, Amy 1908–74

US hostess and writer, an authority on social etiquette.

24 Breakfast is the one meal at which it is perfectly good manners to read the paper.
1954 *Amy Vanderbilt's Complete Book of Etiquette*.

van der Post, Sir Laurens 1906–96

South African soldier, explorer, writer and philosopher.

25 Human beings are perhaps never more frightened than when they are convinced beyond doubt that they are right.
1958 *Lost World of the Kalahari*.

van de Wetering, Janwillem 1931–

Dutch murder-mystery writer.

26 The desire to make money is a symptom of all sorts of emotional disturbances—greed is only one of them.
1988 *The Maine Massacre*.

Van Druten, John William 1901–57

US playwright of Dutch extraction, who was born in London. His mainly light comic plays include *Old Acquaintance* (1940), *Bell, Book and Candle* (1950) and *I Am a Camera* (1951), a stage adaptation of Isherwood's Berlin stories.

27 If I were a woman I'd wear coffee as a perfume.
Quoted in *Think*, Feb 1963.

van Gogh, Vincent 1853–90

Dutch Post-Impressionist painter. He was an evangelistic preacher in Le Borinage (1878–80) and after studying in Paris he settled in Arles (1888), where the light and colour transformed his art. He became increasingly mentally disturbed, and finally shot himself.

28 There is no blue without yellow and without orange.
1888 Letter to Émile Bernard, Jun.

29 I have a terrible lucidity at moments when nature is so beautiful. I am not conscious of myself any more, and the pictures come to me as if in a dream.
1888 Letter to his brother Theo, c.27 Sep.

30 It is no more easy to make a good picture than it is to find a diamond or a pearl. It means trouble and you risk your life for it.
1888 From a letter to his brother Theo, early Oct.

31 I cannot help it that my paintings do not sell. The time will come when people will see that they are worth more than the price of the paint.
1888 Letter to his brother Theo, 24 Oct.

Van Hooijdonk, Pierre 1969–

Dutch footballer.

32 £7,000 a week would be fine for the homeless. But not for me.
1997 Rejecting a new wage deal at Celtic Football Club. Quoted in the *Observer*, 6 Jun 2004.

Van Horne, Harriet 1920–

US journalist.

33 Cooking is like love. It should be entered into with abandon or not at all.
1956 *Vogue*, Oct.

34 After nightfall, I wouldn't leave a burning building without an escort.
1969 On muggings in Manhattan. In the *Washington Post*, 26 Feb.

Varèse, Edgar 1883–1965

US composer of Italo-French parentage. He settled in New York in 1919 and founded the New Symphony Orchestra to further the cause of modern music. In 1921 he founded the international Composers' Guild, which has become the leading organ of progressive musicians. His work is almost entirely orchestral, examples including the largely abstract *Hyperprism* (1923) and *Ionisation* (1931).

35 There is no avant-garde: only some people a bit behind.
Attributed.

Vargas Llosa, Mario 1936–

Peruvian writer, who spent his early life in Bolivia and moved to Paris in 1959, living in several European cities. He was a defeated candidate for the Peruvian presidency (1990), having declined an offer of the premiership in 1984, and remains active and often controversial in literary and political matters.

36 *Por qué esos personajes que se servían de la literatura como adorno o pretexto iban a ser más escritores que Pedro Camacho, quien sólo vivía para escribir? Porque ellos habían leído (o, al menos, sabían que deberían haber leído) a Proust, a Faulker, a Joyce, y Pedro Camacho era poco más que un analfabeto?*
Why should those persons who used literature as an ornament or pretext have any more right to be considered real writers than Pedro Camacho, who lived *only* to write? Because they had read (or at least knew that they should have read) Proust, Faulkner, Joyce, while Pedro Camacho was very nearly illiterate?
1977 *La tía Julia y el escribidor* (translated as *Aunt Julia and the Scriptwriter*, 1982), ch.11.

Vasari, Giorgio 1511–74

Italian painter, architect and author of the first biography of the Italian Renaissance artists.

37 According to Pliny, painting was brought to Egypt by Gyges of Lydia; for he says that Gyges once saw his own shadow cast by the light of a fire and instantly drew his own outline on the wall with a piece of charcoal.
1568 *Lives of the Artists* (translated by George Bull, 1965).

38 [Michelangelo] Buonarotti commended it [Titian's painting] highly, saying that his colouring and his style pleased him very much but that it was a shame that in Venice they did not learn to draw well from the beginning.
1568 *Lives of the Artists* (translated by George Bull, 1965).

Vasconcelos, José 1882–1959

Mexican educator, politician, essayist and philosopher, Minister of Education (1920–4). His political activism led to exile on several occasions. His works call for the incorporation of native culture into Mexican life to transcend the limitations of Western culture.

39 *La America Latina debe lo que es al europeo blanco y no va a renegar de él…Sin embargo, aceptamos los ideales superiores del blanco, pero no su arrogancia.*
Latin America owes its being to the European, and should not deny it…but, while accepting the white man's superior ideals, we do not accept his arrogance.
1925 *La raza cósmica* (translated as *The Cosmic Race*, 1979), pt.1, ch.2.

Vaughan Williams, Ralph 1872–1958

British composer. He established his reputation with the choral *Sea Symphony* (1910) and promoted the English folksong movement. His works include *Fantasia on a Theme of Tallis* (1909), for strings, the *Pastoral Symphony* (1922), the opera *The Pilgrim's Progress* (1948–9) and many choral works.

40 Misbegotten abortions.
1930 Of critics. Letter to Holst.

41 I don't know whether I like it, but it's what I meant.
Of his Fourth Symphony. Quoted in Ian Crofton and Donald Fraser *A Dictionary of Musical Quotations* (1985).

42 It takes perhaps a thousand poor musicians to produce one virtuoso.
1954 In *The New York Times*, 5 Dec.

Vaughan, Henry 1622–95

Welsh religious poet. Educated at Oxford, he later practised as a physician. His verse publications include *Silex Scintillans* (1650, enlarged 1655) and *Olor Iscansus* (1651); prose meditations include *The Mount of Olives* (1652) and *Flores Solitudinis* (1652).

43 The skin and shell of things
Though fair
are not
Thy wish nor prayer
but got
My meer despair
of wings.
1650 *Silex Scintillans*, 'The Search'.

44 Happy those early days when I
Shined in my Angel-infancy.
Before I understood this place
Appointed for my second race,
Or taught my soul to fancy aught
But a white, celestial thought;
When yet I had not walked above
A mile or two from my first love,
And looking back (at that short space)
Could see a glimpse of His bright face.
When on some gilded cloud or flower
My gazing soul would dwell an hour
And in those weaker glories spy
Some shadows of eternity.
1650 *Silex Scintillans*, 'The Retreat'.

45 Before I taught my tongue to wound
My conscience with a sinful sound,
Or had the black art to dispense
A several sin to every sense,
But felt through all this fleshly dress
Bright shoots of everlastingness.
1650 *Silex Scintillans*, 'The Retreat'.

46 Some men a forward motion love,
But I by backward steps would move,
And when this dust falls to the urn
In that state I came, return.
1650 *Silex Scintillans*, 'The Retreat'.

47 My soul, there is a country
Far beyond the stars,
Where stands a wingèd sentry
All skilful in the wars;
1650 *Silex Scintillans*, 'Peace'.

48 King of comforts, King of life,
Thou hast cheered me,
And when fears and doubts were rife,
Thou hast cleared me.

Not a hook in all my breast
But thou fill'st it,
Not a thought in all my rest
But thou kill'st it.

Wherefore with my utmost strength
I will praise thee,
And as thou giv'st line, and length,
I will raise thee.
1650 *Silex Scintillans*, 'Praise'.

49 I saw Eternity the other night
Like a great ring of pure and endless light,
All calm, as it was bright,
And round beneath it, Time in hours, days, years
Driven by the spheres
Like a vast shadow moved.
1650 *Silex Scintillans*, 'The World'.

50 Man is the shuttle, to whose winding quest
And passage through these looms
God ordered motion, but ordained no rest.
1650 *Silex Scintillans*, 'Man'.

51 They are all gone into the world of light,
And I alone sit lingering here;
Their very memory is fair and bright,
And my sad thoughts doth clear.
1650 *Silex Scintillans*, 'They Are All Gone'.

52 I played with fire, did counsel spurn,
Made life my common stake;
But never thought that fire would burn,
O that a soul could ache.
1650 *Silex Scintillans*, 'The Garland'.

Vaz de Caminha, Pero late 15c–early 16c

Portuguese historian, who came to the New World only eight years after Columbus. His account avoids the prevalent hyperbole, striving instead to give a realistic picture of the native peoples.

53 *Esta gente é boa e de boa simplicidade. E imprimir-se-á ligeiramente neles cualquer cunho, que les quiserem dar. E logo lhes, Nosso Senhor, deu bons corpos e bons rostos, como a bons homens, e Ele que nos por aqui trouxe, creio que não foi sem causa. E portanto, Vossa Alteza, pois tanto deseja acrescentar na santa fé católica, deve entender em sua salvação.*
These people are good and simple. You can stamp on them any design that you wish to give them. And Our Lord gave them good bodies and good faces, and I think that it was his plan that we arrive here. Therefore, Your Majesty, since you wish so much to increase Catholic faith, you must provide for their salvation.
Carta (published 1817).

Veblen, Thorstein 1857–1929

US economist and social critic. He attacked commercial values in his best-known work, *Theory of the Leisure Class* (1899). He was instrumental in breaking the hold of neo-classical economic theory and became a leader in the institutional school of economics.

54 The corset is… a mutilation, undergone for the purpose of lowering the subject's vitality and rendering her permanently and obviously unfit for work.
1899 *Theory of the Leisure Class.*

55 When seen in the perspective of half-a-dozen years or more, the best of our fashions strike us as grotesque, if not unsightly.
1899 *Theory of the Leisure Class.*

56 Conspicuous consumption of valuable goods is a means of reputability to the gentleman of leisure.
1899 *Theory of the Leisure Class.*

Vega Carpio, Lope Félix de 1562–1635

Spanish playwright and poet. His prolific output included some 1,800 plays, of which around 600 survive. He served with the Spanish Armada in 1588 and was ordained as a priest in 1614, though he continued to enjoy numerous love affairs.

57 All right, then, I'll say it: Dante makes me sick.
1635 Last words.

Vegetius *full name* ***Flavius Vegetius Renatus***
fl.c.385–400 AD

Roman military writer under Theodosius I, the Great. After AD 375 he produced the *Epitoma Rei Militaris*, mainly extracted from other authors, which was a supreme authority on warfare during the Middle Ages.

58 *Qui desiderat pacem, praeparat bellum.*
Let him who desires peace prepare for war.
c.380 AD *Epitoma Rei Militaris*, no.3, prologue. This became familiar in the Middle Ages as *Si vis pacem para bellum* (If you want peace, prepare for war).

Venables, Terry 1943–

English footballer and manager. He was dismissed as manager of Tottenham Hotspur in 1993, but appointed manager of England a year later. He resigned after the 1996 European championships.

59 I had mixed feelings—like watching your mother-in-law drive over a cliff in your car.
1992 Of Paul Gascoigne's move from Tottenham Hotspur to the Italian club Lazio. Quoted in David Pickering *The Cassell Soccer Companion* (1994).

60 Never's a hard call, isn't it? Never-ish.
2000 On whether he would ever manage England again. In *The Times*, 26 Dec.

61 If you can't stand the heat in the dressing room, get out of the kitchen.
Attributed.
► *Truman 868:32.*

Venturi, Robert Charles 1925–

US architect, renowned for his eclectic and sometimes humorous designs, a key figure of the postmodernist school.

62 [It is] drawing a moustache on a madonna.
1977 On designing an addition to Oberlin College's 1917 Allen Memorial Art Museum. In the *New York Times*, 30 Jan.

Vergniaud, Pierre Victurnien 1753–93

French revolutionary politician, leader of the Girondists. When the Girondists clashed with the Montagnards, who wished to retain dictatorial power, he and his party were arrested and guillotined.

63 *Il a été permis de craindre que la Révolution, comme Saturne, dévorât successivement tous ses enfants.*
There is reason to fear that the Revolution may, like Saturn, devour each of her children one by one.
1793 Spoken at his trial, Oct.

Verlaine, Paul 1844–96

French poet who befriended and promoted the poetry of Arthur Rimbaud with whom he had a volatile relationship.

64 *Les sanglots longs*
Des violons
De l'automne
Blessent mon cœur
D'une langueur
Monotone.
Slow sobs
Of the violins
Of autumn
Wound my heart
With a monotonous languor.
1866 *Poèmes saturniens, Paysages tristes, V*: 'Chansons d'Automne'.

65 *Un vaste et tendre*
Apaisement
Semble descendre
Du firmament . . .
C'est l'heure exquise.
A vast and tender
Calm
Seems to descend
From the heavens . . .
This is the exquisite hour.
1866 *Poèmes saturniens*, 'La Bonne Chanson, no.6'.

66 *Il pleure dans mon cœur*
Comme il pleut sur la ville.
The tears fall in my heart
As the rain over the town.
1874 *Romances sans paroles*, 'Ariettes oubliées, no.3'.

67 *Voici des fruits, des fleurs, des feuilles et des branches*
Et puis voici mon cœur qui ne bat que pour vous.
Here are fruits, flowers, leaves and branches
And here also is my heart which beats only for you.
1874 *Romances sans paroles*, 'Aquarelles, Green'.

68 *Pas la Couleur, rien que la Nuance!*
No colour, only nuance!
1884 *Jadis et naguère*, 'Art poétique'.

69 *Prends l'éloquence et tords-lui son cou!*
Take eloquence and break its neck!
1884 *Jadis et naguère*, 'Art poétique'.

70 *Que ton vers soit la bonne aventure*
Éparse au vent crispé du matin
Qui va fleurant la menthe et le thym.
Et tout le reste est littérature.
May your verse be a glorious adventure
Strewn by the crisp morning air
Which helps the mint and the thyme grow.
Everything else is mere literature.
1884 *Jadis et naguère*, 'Art poétique'.

Verne, Jules 1828–1905

French novelist. His best-known works include *A Journey to the Centre of the Earth* (1864), *Twenty Thousand Leagues Under the Sea* (1869) and *Around the World in Eighty Days* (1873).

71 An Englishman does not joke about such an important matter as a bet.
1873 *Around the World in Eighty Days.*

Vespasian *full name* ***Titus Flavius Vespasianus*** AD 9–79

Roman Emperor, commander of the legions in the East when Nero was deposed. He was proclaimed emperor by his troops in Alexandria, and after defeating his rival Vitellius (AD 69) reached Rome and restored order. He began an ambitious building programme, including the Colosseum, and extended and consolidated the Empire.

72 *Pecunia non olet.*
Money does not smell.
Attributed. His son Titus had objected to a tax on the contents of

the city's urinals (used by fullers). Vespasian held a coin to Titus's nose, asking him whether it smelled. When Titus said no he replied 'Atqui e lotio est' ('And yet, it comes from urine'). Quoted in Suetonius *Vespasian*, 23.

73 *Vae, puto deus fio.*
Dear me, I must be turning into a god.
AD 79 Attributed last words. Quoted in Suetonius *Vespasian*, 23 (translated by Robert Graves, 1967).

Vettriano, Jack 1953–

Scottish artist whose works have proved particularly popular as prints and posters.

74 Rather the poster on the student's wall than the original unseen on a shelf in a big gallery storeroom.
2004 In *The Times*, 13 Mar.

Vian, Boris 1920–59

French novelist associated with the Surrealist movement.

75 *Les gens ne changent pas. Ce sont les choses qui changent.*
People do not change. Things change.
1947 *L'Écume des jours.*

76 *Les masses ont tort et les individus toujours raison.*
The masses are wrong; individuals are always right.
1947 *L'Écume des jours.*

77 *Mais enfin, bande de critiques, les livres que vous ne comprenez pas ne vaudraient-ils pas au moins que vous les signaliez?*
For heaven's sake, gang of critics, don't the books which you do not understand at least deserve recognition?
1948 In *La Seine*, 19 Apr.

78 *Rien n'est plus parfait, plus achevé qu'un cadavre.*
Nothing is more perfect, more complete than a corpse.
1950 *L'Herbe rouge.*

79 *Savoir qu'il existe des passions et ne pas le ressentir, c'est affreux.*
To know that there are passions and to not feel any, that is horrible.
1950 *L'Herbe rouge.*

80 *Les femmes et les hommes ne vivent pas sur le même plan.*
Women and men do not live according to the same design.
1953 *L'Arrache-cœur.*

81 *Un poète*
C'est un être unique
À des tas d'exemplaires
Qui ne pense qu'en vers
Et n'écrit qu'en musique
Sur des sujets divers
Des rouges ou des verts
Mais toujours magnifiques.
A poet
Is a unique being
From an exemplary multitude
Who only thinks in verse
And only writes in music
On diverse subjects
Reds and greens
But always magnificently.
1962 *Je voudrais pas crever.*

Vicious, Sid *pseudonym of* ***John Simon Ritchie*** 1957–79

British rock bassist. He played with the notorious punk rock group The Sex Pistols in the 1970s, and died of a drug overdose while awaiting trial for the murder of his girlfriend, Nancy Spungen, in the US.

82 You just pick a chord, go twang, and you've got music.
1976 In *The Sun.*

Victoria *in full* ***Alexandrina Victoria*** 1819–1901

Queen of Great Britain (1837–1901). She married Prince Albert of Saxe-Coburg and Gotha (1840), and bore him nine children. After his death (1861) she neglected her duties, but her recognition as Empress of India (1876) and the celebratory Golden (1887) and Diamond (1897) Jubilees restored her prestige. She had strong preferences for certain Prime Ministers (eg Melbourne and Disraeli) over others (notably Peel and Gladstone).

83 This mad, wicked folly of 'Women's Rights' with all its attendant horrors, on which her poor sex is bent, forgetting every sense of womanly feeling and propriety. Lady Amberley ought to get a good whipping.
1870 Letter to Sir Theodore Martin, 29 Mar. The feminist Lady Amberley was Bertrand Russell's mother.

84 Oh, if the Queen were a man, she would like to go and give those Russians, whose word one cannot believe, such a beating! We shall never be friends again till we have it out.
1878 Letter to Lord Beaconsfield, 10 Jan.

85 Please understand that there is no one depressed in this house. We are not interested in the possibilities of defeat; they do not exist.
1899 On the 2nd Boer War. Comment to the Prime Minister, Arthur Balfour, Dec. Quoted in Lady Gwendolen Cecil *Life of Robert, Marquis of Salisbury* (1931), vol.3, ch.6.

86 A strange, horrible business, but I suppose good enough for Shakespeare's day.
Attributed comment after watching a performance of *King Lear.*

87 He speaks to Me as if I were a public meeting.
Of Gladstone. Attributed in G W E Russell *Collections and Recollections.*

88 We are not amused.
Attributed.

Vidal, Gore *originally* ***Eugene Luther Vidal, Jr*** 1925–

US writer and polemicist. He ran for congress in 1960 and spent some time as a TV commentator. His novels include the satirical comedies *Myra Breckenridge* (1968) and *Duluth* (1983), and the historical trilogy *Burr* (1974), *1876* (1976) and *Lincoln* (1984). He published his memoirs, *Palimpsest*, in 1995.

89 A talent for drama is not a talent for writing, but is an ability to articulate human relationships.
1956 In the *New York Times*, 17 Jun.

90 I'm all for bringing back the birch. But only between consenting adults.
1966 Interview on *The Frost Programme.*

91 It is the spirit of the age to believe that any fact, no matter how suspect, is superior to any imaginative exercise, no matter how true.
1967 'French Letters: Theories of the New Novel', in *Encounter*, Dec.

92 Astronauts! Rotarians in space!
1968 *Myra Breckenridge.*

93 There is something about a bureaucrat that does not like a poem.
1968 *Sex, Death and Money*, preface.
► *See Frost 338:84.*

94 People who obtain power do so because it delights them for its own sake and for no other reason.
1970 In *Esquire*, Sep.

95 From primeval ooze to the stars, we killed anything that stood in our way, including each other.
1970 On the human race. In *Esquire*, Sep.

96 Whenever a friend succeeds, a little something in me dies.
1973 In the *Sunday Times Magazine*, 16 Sep.

97 It is not enough to succeed. Others must fail.
Quoted in G Irvine *Antipanegyric for Tom Driberg* (1976).

98 A triumph of the embalmer's art.
1981 Of Ronald Reagan. Quoted in the *Observer*, 26 Apr.

99 But to ignore the absence of evidence is the basis of true faith.
1981 'Pink Triangle and Yellow Star', in the *Nation*, 14 Nov.

1 For certain people, after fifty, litigation takes the place of sex.
1981 Quoted in the *Evening Standard*.

2 Democracy is supposed to give you the feeling of choice, like Painkiller X and Painkiller Y. But they're both just aspirin.
1982 Interview in the *Observer*, 7 Feb.

3 It's a country evenly divided between conservatives and reactionaries.
1984 Of the US. In the *Observer*, 16 Sep.

4 American men do not read novels because they feel guilty when they read books which do not have facts in them.
1984 In *Saturday Review*, 18 Jun.

5 The century that began with a golden age in all the arts (or at least the golden twilight of one) is ending not so much without art as without the idea of art.
Introduction to Logan Pearsall Smith *All Trivia* (1984).

6 Fifty per cent of them won't vote and the other half doesn't read newspapers. I hope it's the same.
1991 In *Emmy*, May.

7 When it comes to getting things wrong, the English are born masters.
1991 'Reflections on Glory Reflected and Otherwise', in the *Threepenny Review*, Spring.

8 Meanwhile, let us give Clinton his due. Lincoln to one side, he does better funerals than any American president in an increasingly murderous history.
1997 *Virgin Islands: Essays 1992–1997.*

9 We are, said President Clinton, the one indispensable—or was it indisposable?—nation.
1997 *Virgin Islands: Essays 1992–1997.*

10 There are as many good writers as ever there were. The problem is that there are so few good readers.
2003 Quoted in *Writers on Writing, Volume II: More Collected Essays from the New York Times*.

Vidor, King Wallis 1894–1982

US film director, born in Galveston, Texas. In Hollywood from 1915, he worked as a writer and extra before moving into directing. His many films include *The Big Parade* (1925), *The Crowd* (1928), *Our Daily Bread* (1934) and *The Fountainhead* (1949).

11 The crowd laughs with you always but it will cry with you for only a day.
1929 *The Crowd* (with John V A Weaver and Harry Behn).

Vieira, Antônio 1608–97

Jesuit missionary, orator, diplomat and writer, condemned by the Inquisition and briefly imprisoned. His sermons, letters and state papers are a valuable index to the climate of opinion in 17c Brazil and Portugal.

12 *Que coisa é a formosura, senão uma caveira bem vestida, a que a menor enfermidade tira a cor, e antes de a morte a despir de todo, os anos lhe vão mortificando a graça daquela exterior e aparente superfície, de tal sorte, que, se os olhos pudessem penetrar o interior dela, o não poderiam ver sem horror?*
What is beauty, but a well-dressed skull that loses colour with the slightest illness, and, before death robs it of everything, the grace of its external and apparent surface is mortified by the years in such a way that, if eyes could penetrate within beauty, they could watch it only full of horror?
c.1666 *Sermões*, 'Sermão do demónio mudo' ('Sermon of the Silent Devil').

Villon, François b.1431

French poet, member of the criminal organization 'The Brotherhood of the Cocquille'. Several times sentenced to death for various crimes, he was repeatedly pardoned. In 1463 he received his final death sentence, but this was commuted to banishment.

13 *Mais où sont les neiges d'antan?*
But where are last year's snows?
1461 'Ballade des Dames du Temps Jadis', refrain.

St Vincent of Lérins *known as* Vincentius Lerinensis d.c.450 AD

A native of Gaul, and monk on the island of Lerna (Lérins).

14 *Quod ubique, quod semper, quod ab omnibus creditum est.*
What is everywhere, what is always, what is by all people believed.
Commonitorium Primum, section 2 (translated by Heurtley, 1895).

Viner, Jacob 1892–1970

US economist, a professor at the University of Chicago and Princeton University.

15 The classical economists were not wholly free from error, for they were only mortals, even if of a superior species.
1930 *The Long View and the Short.*

Virgil *full name* Publius Vergilius Maro 70–19 BC

Roman poet, under the patronage of Maecenas and Augustus. He published the *Eclogues*, a collection of pastorals, in 37 BC, and the *Georgics* (a didactic poem on husbandry in four books) in 30 BC. The *Aeneid*, a national epic based on the legendary founder of the Roman nation, was published posthumously.

16 *Arma virumque cano, Troiae qui primus ab oris*
Italiam fato profugus Laviniaque venit
Litora.
This is a tale of arms and of a man. Fated to be an exile, he was the first to sail from the land of Troy and reach Italy, at its Lavinian shore.
Aeneid, opening lines (translated by W F Jackson Knight).

17 *Non ignara mali, miseris succurrere disco.*
No stranger to trouble myself, I am learning to help those who are in distress.
Dido, queen of Carthage. *Aeneid*, bk.1, l.630.

18 *Conticuere omnes intentique ora tenebant*
Inde toro pater Aeneas sic orsus ab alto.
They fell silent, every one, and each face was turned intently towards him. From high on the dais Aeneas, Troy's Chieftain, began to speak.
Aeneid, bk.2, l.1–2 (translated by W F Jackson Knight).

19 *Quidquid id est, timeo Danaos et dona ferentis.*
Whatever it may be, I fear the Greeks, even when bearing gifts.
Spoken by Laocoon, a Trojan prince and priest of Apollo, warning the city against the wooden horse left by the Greeks. *Aeneid*, bk.2, l.49.

20 *Una salus victis nullam sperare salutem.*
Nothing can save the conquered but the knowledge that they cannot now be saved.
Aeneid, bk.2, l.354 (translated by W F Jackson Knight).

21 *Dis aliter visum.*
The gods thought otherwise.
Aeneid, bk.2, l.428.

22 *Fama, malum qua non aliud velocius ullum.*
Rumour is of all pests the swiftest.
Aeneid, bk.4, l.174 (translated by W F Jackson Knight).

23 *Quis fallere possit amantem?*
Who can deceive a lover?
Aeneid, bk.4, l.296.

24 *Varium et mutabile semper*
femina.
Women were ever things of many changing moods.
Aeneid, bk.4, l.569–70 (translated by W F Jackson Knight).

25 *Audentis Fortuna iuvat!*
Fortune helps those who dare.
Aeneid, bk.10, l.284. The phrase is often rendered as 'Fortune favours the brave'.

26 *Experto credite.*
Believe one who has experienced it.
Aeneid, bk.11, l.283.

27 *Latet anguis in herba.*
A snake lurks in the grass.
Eclogues, 3.93.

28 *Sicelides Musae, paulo maiora canamus.*
Non omnis arbusta iuvant humilesque myricae.
Sicilian Muses, let us sing a somewhat loftier strain. Not all do orchards please and the lowly tamarisks.
Eclogues, 4.1–2 (translated by H Rushton Fairclough).

29 *Non omnia possumus omnes.*
We cannot all do everything.
Eclogues, 8.63 (translated by H Rushton Fairclough).

30 *Omnia vincit amor.*
Love conquers all things.
Eclogues, 10.69.

31 *Labor omnia vicit*
improbus et duris urgens in rebus egestas.
Toil conquered the world, unrelenting toil, and want that pinches when life is hard.
Georgics, 1.145–6 (translated by H Rushton Fairclough).

32 *Felix qui potuit rerum cognoscere causas.*
Blessed is he who has been able to win knowledge of the causes of things.
Georgics, 2.490 (translated by H Rushton Fairclough).

33 *Mantua me genuit, Calabri rapuere, tenet nunc*
Parthenope; cecini pascua rura duces.
Mantua brought me life, Calabria death; now Naples holds me: I sang of flocks and farms and heroes.
19 BC Epitaph on his tomb near Naples, supposedly dictated on his deathbed. Quoted in Donatus *Vita Vergilii*, 'Life of Virgil'.

Vitruvius *full name* ***Marcus Vitruvius Pollio*** c.70 BC–25 BC

Roman architect and engineer whose ten books on architecture, *De Architectura*, are the oldest surviving work on the subject.

34 Neither talent without instruction, nor instruction without talent can produce the perfect craftsman.
c.25 BC *On Architecture.*

Vlaminck, Maurice de 1876–1958

French painter, graphic artist and writer.

35 Good painting is like good cooking: it can be tasted, but not explained.
Attributed.

Voltaire *pseudonym of* ***François Marie Arouet*** 1694–1778

French philosopher. He was imprisoned for lampooning the Duc d'Orleans, 1717–18, and later went into exile in England, 1726–9. He returned to France, but moved to Berlin in 1750 to the court of Frederick the Great. His works include *Œdipe* (1718), *Candide* (1759) and the *Dictionnaire philosophique* (1764).

36 *Le superflu, chose très nécessaire.*
The superfluous, a very necessary thing.
1736 *Le Mondain.*

37 *Dans ce pays-ci il est bon de tuer de temps en temps un amiral pour encourager les autres.*
In this country it is considered a good thing to kill an admiral from time to time, to encourage the others.
1759 Of England. Reference to the execution of Admiral Byng following his failure to engage the French at Menorca, 1757. *Candide*, ch.23.

38 *Tout est pour le mieux dans le meilleur des mondes possibles.*
All is for the best in the best of all possible worlds.
1759 *Candide*, ch.30.

39 *Cela est bien dit, répondit Candide, mais il faut cultiver notre jardin.*
'Well said', Candide replied, 'but we must cultivate our own garden.'
1759 Candide, ch.30.

40 I am the best-tempered man there ever was, yet I have killed three men, and two of them were priests!
1759 *Candide*, ch.15.

41 You know that these two nations have been at war over a few acres of snow near Canada, and that they are

spending on this fine struggle more than Canada itself is worth.
1759 Of the French and English struggle in Quebec. *Candide*, ch.23.

42 Men will always be mad, and those who think they can cure them are the maddest of all.
1762 Letter.

43 *La superstition met le monde entier en flammes; la philosophie les éteint.*
Superstition sets the whole world in flames; philosophy puts out the fire.
1764 *Dictionnaire philosophique*, 'Superstition'.

44 *En effet, l'histoire n'est que le tableau des crimes et des malheurs.*
In fact, history is nothing but a tableau of crimes and misfortunes.
1767 *L'Ingénu*, ch.10.

45 *Ce corps qui s'appelait et qui s'appelle encore le saint empire romain n'était en aucune manière ni saint, ni romain, ni empire.*
This state which was called and is still called the Holy Roman Empire, was not in any way holy, or Roman or an Empire.
1769 *Essai sur Les Moeurs et l'Ésprit des Nations.*

46 *La foi consiste à croire ce que la raison ne croit pas… Il ne suffit pas qu'une chose soit possible pour la croire.*
Faith consists in believing what reason cannot…In order to believe something, it is not enough that it should be possible.
1770 *Questions sur l'Encyclopédie.*

47 *Le mieux est l'ennemi du bien.*
The best is the enemy of the good.
1772 *Contes*, 'La Bégueule', 1.2. He is quoting an Italian proverb, *Il meglio è l'inimico del bene.*

48 This enormous dunghill.
1776 Of the works of William Shakespeare. Letter to d'Argental, 19 Jul.

49 *On doit des égards aux vivants; on ne doit aux morts que la vérité.*
We should be considerate to the living; to the dead we owe only the truth.
'Première Lettre sur Œdipe'. In *Œuvres*, vol.1 (published 1785).

50 *Dieu n'est pas pour les gros bataillons, mais pour ceux qui tirent le mieux.*
God is on the side not of the big battalions, but of the best shots.
In *Voltaire's Notebooks*, edited by Th. Besterman (1952).

51 *Il faut, dans le gouvernement, des bergers et des bouchers.*
Governments need both shepherds and butchers.
In *Voltaire's Notebooks*, edited by Th. Besterman (1952).

52 One goes to see a tragedy to be moved, to the opera one goes either for want of any other interest or to facilitate digestion.
Quoted in J Wechsberg *The Opera* (1972).

53 *Si Dieu n'existait pas, il faudrait l'inventer.*
If God did not exist, it would be necessary to invent him.
Epîtres, 'À l'Auteur du Livre des Trois Imposteurs'.

54 The art of medicine consists of amusing the patient while Nature cures the disease.
Attributed.

55 I disapprove of what you say, but I will defend to the death your right to say it.
Attributed.

Vonnegut, Kurt, Jr 1922–

US novelist. *Player Piano* (1952) was his first novel and there were another three before *Slaughterhouse-Five* (1969), the central event of which is the destruction of Dresden during World War II, an event witnessed by the author as a prisoner-of-war.

56 The British had no way of knowing it, but the candles and the soap were made from the fat of rendered Jews and Gypsies and fairies and communists, and other enemies of the state. So it goes.
1969 *Slaughterhouse Five*, ch.5.

57 Their only English-speaking guard told them to memorize their simple address, in case they got lost in the city. Their address was this: 'Schlachthof-fünf'. *Schlachthof* meant *slaughterhouse*. *Fünf* was good old *five*.
1969 *Slaughterhouse-Five*, ch.6.

Vorster, John *originally* ***Balthazar Johannes Vorster*** 1915–83

South African Nationalist politician, an extreme Afrikaner. As Prime Minister (1966–78) he maintained a policy of apartheid and protected white interests. In 1978 he became President, but resigned over a financial scandal.

58 As far as criticism is concerned, we don't resent that unless it is absolutely biased—as it is in most cases.
1969 In the *Observer*, 9 Nov.

Vreeland, Diana *originally* ***Diana Dalziel*** 1906?–1989

US journalist, editor of *Vogue*. Born in Paris, she married Thomas Vreeland in 1924 in New York and joined Vogue as editor-in-chief in 1962. She transformed the high-fashion magazine into a society journal. She also acted as consultant to the costume institute at the Metropolitan Museum of Art.

59 A little bad taste is like a splash of paprika. We all need a splash of bad taste—it's hearty, it's healthy, it's physical.
1984 *D.V.* (her autobiography, edited by George Plimpton and Christopher Hemphill).

60 The biggest thing since the atom bomb.
1990 On the bikini. In her obituary in the *New York Times*, 1 Apr.

61 People who eat white bread have no dreams.
Quoted in Annette Tapert and Diana Edkins *The Power of Style* (1994).

Vukovich, Bill 1918–55

US motor-racing driver. He won the Indianapolis 500 in 1953 and 1954 but was killed in the race while in the lead the following year.

62 There's no secret. You just press the accelerator to the floor and steer left.
1954 Of his tactics in the Indianapolis 500. Quoted in Colin Jarman *The Guinness Dictionary of Sports Quotations* (1990).

Waddington, Miriam 1917–2004

Canadian poet and critic. Of Russian-Jewish origin, she was a social worker in Montreal and taught at York University, Toronto. Her works include poetry such as *The Glass Trumpet* (1966), *The Price of Gold* (1976) and *The Visitants* (1981), and short stories and essays.

63 Keep bees and
grow asparagus,
watch the tides
and listen to the
wind instead of
the politicians
make up your own
stories and believe
them if you want to
live the good life.
1972 *Driving Home: Poems New and Selected*, 'Advice to the Young'.

Wagner, Otto 1841–1918

Austrian architect and teacher, considered the founder of the modern movement.

64 The whole basis of the views of architecture prevailing today must be displaced by the recognition that the only possible point of departure for our artistic creation is modern life.
1895 *Modern Architecture* (1895), preface.

Wagner, Robert Ferdinand, Jr 1944–93

US former deputy mayor of New York City.

65 When in danger, ponder. When in trouble, delegate. And when in doubt, mumble.
1991 In the *New York Times*, 17 Feb.

Wain, John Barrington 1925–94

English writer. He is known primarily as a critic and novelist, but he also wrote poetry, plays and a biography of Samuel Johnson.

66 Poetry is to prose as dancing is to walking.
1976 BBC radio broadcast, 13 Jan.

Waite, Terry (Terence Hardy) 1939–

English religious adviser, envoy of Archbishop of Canterbury Robert Runcie from 1980. On 20 Jan 1987, while making inquiries in Beirut about European hostages, he was kidnapped. Following worldwide efforts to secure his release and that of his fellow hostages, 1,763 days later he was freed.

67 Politics come from man. Mercy, compassion, and justice come from God.
1985 In the *Observer*, 13 Jan.

68 Freeing hostages is like putting up a stage set—which you do with the captors, agreeing on each piece as you slowly put it together. Then you leave an exit through which both the captor and the captive can walk with sincerity and dignity.
1986 Interviewed on ABC news, 3 Nov.

Waits, Tom 1949–

US singer, songwriter, musician and actor. His albums include *Heartattack and Vine* (1980), *Swordfishtrombones* (1983) and *Mule Variations* (1999).

69 There's a lot of intelligence in the hands. When you pick up a shovel, the hands know what to do. The same thing's true of sitting at the piano.
1999 In the *Dallas Observer*, 6 May.

Walcott, Derek Alton 1930–

West Indian poet and dramatist. He founded the Trinidad Theatre Workshop in 1959 and is Visiting Professor of English at Boston University. His poetry includes *In A Green Night* (1962), *Castaway* (1965), *The Gulf* (1969) and *Collected Poems* (1986). He was awarded the Nobel prize for literature in 1992.

70 I who have cursed
The drunken officer of British rule, how choose
Between this Africa and the English tongue I love?
Betray them both, or give back what they give?
How can I face such slaughter and be cool?
How can I turn from Africa and live?
1962 *In a Green Night*, 'A Far Cry from Africa'.

71 I'm just a red nigger who love the sea,
I had a sound colonial education,
I have Dutch, nigger, and English in me,
and either I'm nobody or I'm a nation.
1980 *The Star-Apple Kingdom*, 'The Schooner *Flight*', pt.1.

72 Who knows
who his grandfather is, much less his name?
1980 *The Star-Apple Kingdom*, 'The Schooner *Flight*', pt.5.

73 But we live like our names and you would have
to be colonial to know the difference,
to know the pain of history words contain.
1980 *The Star-Apple Kingdom*, 'The Schooner *Flight*', pt.6.

74 I see these islands and I feel to bawl,
'area of darkness' with V.S. Nightfall.
1982 *The Fortunate Traveller*, 'The Spoiler's Return'.

75 The English language is nobody's special property. It is the property of the imagination: it is the property of the language itself.
Interviewed in George Plimpton (ed) *Writers at Work* (8th series, 1988).

76 every 'I'
is a fiction finally.
1990 *Omeros*, bk.1, ch.5, section 2.

77 Time is the metre, memory the only plot.
1990 *Omeros*, bk.2, ch.24, section 2.

78 'We were the colour of shadows when we came down
with tinkling leg-irons to join the chains of the sea,
for the silver coins multiplying on the sold horizon.'
1990 *Omeros*, bk.3, ch.28, section 1.

79 The worst crime is to leave a man's hands empty.
Men are born makers, with that primal simplicity
in every maker since Adam.
1990 *Omeros*, bk.3, ch.28, section 2.

80 Art is History's nostalgia, it prefers a thatched
roof to a concrete factory, and the huge church
above a bleached village.
1990 *Omeros*, bk.6, ch.45, section 2.

81 Poetry…is perfection's sweat but most seen as fresh as
the raindrops on a statue's brow.
1992 In the *New York Times*, 8 Dec.

82 The fate of poetry is to fall in love with the world, in spite of History.
1992 In the *New York Times*, 8 Dec.

83 The process of poetry is one of excavation and of self-discovery.
1992 In the *New York Times*, 8 Dec.

84 V S Nightfall.
Nickname for V S Naipaul. Attributed to Derek Walcott by Paul Theroux, in *Sir Vidia's Shadow: A Friendship Across Five Continents* (1998).

Wald, George 1906–97

US biochemist and member of the faculty at Harvard University. He shared the 1967 Nobel prize in physiology or medicine and became known widely for his view opposing the War in Vietnam.

85 We are the products of editing, rather than of authorship.
1975 'The Origin of Optical Activity', in *Annals of the New York Academy of Sciences*, vol.69.

Wald, Jerry 1911–62

US writer and producer. His films include *Mildred Pierce* (1945), *Johnny Belinda* (1948) and *The Glass Menagerie* (1950).

86 He used to be a big shot.
1939 The words of Panama Smith (Gladys George) as Eddie Bartlett (James Cagney) dies on the steps of the church in *The Roaring Twenties*. With Richard Macauley and Robert Rossen.

Waldron, Hicks

Chair, Boardroom Consultants Inc.

87 People do what you pay them to do, not what you ask them to do.
1991 In the *Wall Street Journal*, 17 Apr.

Walesa, Lech 1943–

Polish trade unionist, politician and President. A former shipyard worker, he became leader of the independent trade union, Solidarity, which openly challenged the government's policies, and was imprisoned under martial law (1981). Released in 1982, he was awarded the Nobel peace prize in 1983. He was President from 1990 to 1995.

88 He who once became aware of the power of Solidarity and who breathed the air of freedom will not be crushed.
1983 Nobel peace prize lecture, read on his behalf, 11 Dec.

89 The English are all right. They're quiet, they're slow, they count things carefully, they hesitate—and I'm switching to their track.
1991 In *The Times*, 17 Apr, on the eve of his state visit to London.

90 The Soviet Union remains a superpower in the military and nuclear sense—only its economy is in difficulty. People want me to lead the troops out or to chuck them over the border, but I have neither the strength nor the will to do it.
1991 In *The Times*, 17 Apr.

Waley, Arthur David 1889–1966

English poet and Sinologist. He was a distinguished translator of Chinese and Japanese literature.

91 It is not difficult to censor foreign news.
What is difficult today is to censor one's own
thoughts,—
To sit by and see the blind man
On the sightless horse, riding into the bottomless abyss.
1940 'Censorship'.

Walken, Christopher 1943–

US actor. His numerous films include *The Deer Hunter* (1978), *A View to a Kill* (1985), *True Romance* (1993) and *Sleepy Hollow* (1999).

92 I'm better off not socialising. I make a better impression if I'm not around.
2004 In *The Scotsman*, 12 Jun.

Walker, Alice Malsenior 1944–

US writer. She has written poetry and non fiction, and established her reputation with her novels, notably *The Color Purple* (1983, filmed 1985).

93 The gift of loneliness is sometimes a radical vision of society or one's people that has not previously been taken into account.
1973 Interview in J O'Brien (ed) *Interviews with Black Writers*.

94 It is healthier, in any case, to write for the adults one's children will become than for the children one's 'mature' critics often are.
1976 'A Writer Because of, Not in Spite of, Her Children', in *Ms.*, Jan.

95 Writing saved me from the sin and inconvenience of violence.
1979 '*One* Child of One's Own', in *Ms.*, Aug.

96 The good news may be that Nature is phasing out the white man, but the bad news is that's who She thinks we all are.
1982 'Nuclear Madness: What You Can Do', in *Black Scholar*, Spring.

97 Anybody can observe the Sabbath, but making it holy surely takes the rest of the week.
1983 *In Search of Our Mothers' Gardens*, 'To the Editors of *Ms.* Magazine'.

98 The trouble with our people is as soon as they got out of slavery they didn't want to give the white man nothing else. But the fact is, you got to give 'em something. Either your money, your land, your woman or your ass.
1985 Pa. *The Color Purple*.

99 She say, Celie, tell the truth, have you ever found God in church? I never did. I just found a bunch of folks hoping for him to show. Any God I ever felt in church I brought in with me. And I think all the other folks did too. They come to church to *share* God, not find God.
1985 Shug. *The Color Purple*.

1 There are those who believe Black people possess the secret of joy and that it is this which will sustain them through any spiritual or moral or physical devastation.
1992 *Possessing the Secret of Joy*, epigraph.

Wall Street Journal

Leading US financial newspaper.

2 God is registered to vote for Hollywood as a Republican. However, Jesus Christ is a Democrat from Santa Monica.
1995 'God Lives in Hollywood', editorial on California's voter registration lists, 12 Jul.

Wall, Mervyn 1908–97

Irish writer.

3 The Bishop gave vent to a long-drawn sigh. 'Did it ever occur to you to wonder why God created women?' he asked. 'It's the one thing that tempts me at times to doubt His infinite goodness and wisdom.'
1946 *The Unfortunate Fursey.*

4 The odour of sanctity was clearly discernible from his breath and person.
1946 *The Unfortunate Fursey.*

5 'Did you ever hear the like?' said the Devil, and a hard note crept into his voice. 'If there's one thing I can't stand', he said, 'it's superstition.'
1946 *The Unfortunate Fursey.*

Wallace, George Corley 1919–98

US Democratic lawyer and politician, opponent of the civil rights movement and Governor of Alabama (1963–7, 1971–4, 1975–8 and 1983–7). A presidential bid ended with an assassination attempt, on 15 May 1972, which left him paralyzed.

6 Segregation now, segregation tomorrow, and segregation for ever.
1963 Inaugural speech as Governor of Alabama, 19 Feb.

7 I've climbed my last political mountain.
1972 On retiring after being crippled in an assassination attempt. Quoted in the *New York Times*, 3 Apr 1986.

8 A great deal has been lost and a great deal gained…may your message be heard…your lessons never be forgotten.
1995 Reversing the 'segregation for ever' stance of 1963. In news reports, 11 Mar.

Wallace, Henry Agard 1888–1965

US agriculturist and statesman, editor of *Wallace's Farmer* (1933–40) until nominated Vice-President to Roosevelt. Chairman of the Board of Economic Welfare (1941–5) and Secretary of Commerce (1945–6), he stood unsuccessfully as President in 1948.

9 The century on which we are entering, the century that will come out of this war, can be and must be the century of the common man.
1942 Speech, New York, 8 May.

Wallace, William Ross 1819–81

US poet. Only a few of his poems, mostly militant patriotic songs, have survived as anthology works. He practised as a lawyer in New York from 1841 until his death and was a contributor to Harper's magazine. Stimulated by the American Civil War, he wrote *Sword of Bunker Hill* (1861) and *The Liberty Bell* (1862).

10 The hand that rocks the cradle
Is the hand that rules the world.
c.1865 *John o' London's Treasure Trove.*

Wallach, Eli 1915–

US actor. A star of both stage and screen, he appeared in such films as *The Moonspinners* (1964), *The Tiger Makes Out* (1967) and *The Sentinel* (1977). On the stage he has won particular acclaim in plays by Tennessee Williams and others.

11 There's something about a crowd like that that brings a lump to my wallet.
1964 Observing the crowds that were gathering at the box office to see the highly successful Broadway show *Luv.* Attributed.

Waller, Edmund 1606–87

English poet and politician. Educated at Cambridge, he went on to be an MP; his involvement in a plot against Parliament during the Civil War led to his banishment in 1643. His collected poems were published in 1645.

12 Go, lovely rose,
Tell her that wastes her time and me,
That now she knows,
When I resemble her to thee,
How sweet and fair she seems to be.
1645 'Go, lovely rose'.

13 Small is the worth
Of beauty from the light retir'd;
Bid her come forth,
Suffer her self to be desir'd,
And not blush to be admir'd.
1645 'Go, lovely rose'.

14 Phillis, why shou'd we delay
Pleasures shorter than the day?
1645 'To Phillis'.

15 Since thou wouldst needs, bewitched with some ill charms,
Be buried in those monumental arms:
As we can wish, is, may that earth lie light
Upon thy tender limbs, and so good night.
1645 'To One Married to an Old Man'.

16 Poets may boast (as safely-vain)
Their work shall with the world remain:
Both bound together, live, or die,
The verses and the prophecy.

But who can hope his lines shou'd long
Last, in a daily changing tongue?
While they are new, envy prevails,
And as that dies, our language fails.
1645 'Of English Verse'.

17 We write in sand, our language grows,
And like our tide ours overflows.
1645 'Of English Verse'.

18 Verse thus design'd has no ill fate,
If it arrive but at the date
Of fading beauty, if it prove
But as long-liv'd as present love.
1645 'Of English Verse'.

Waller, Fats (Thomas Wright) 1904–43

US jazz pianist, composer and entertainer. A professional musician at 15, he began his recording career in 1922. Among the jazz standards he wrote were 'Ain't Misbehavin'' and 'Honeysuckle Rose'.

19 Madam, if you don't know by now, don't mess with it!
When asked what jazz was. Quoted in Marshall Stearns *The Story of Jazz* (1956).
► *See Armstrong 30:75.*

Wallis, Hal 1898–1986

US producer. He worked in Hollywood for many years and then became an independent producer.

20 Louis, I think this is the beginning of a beautiful friendship.
1942 Closing words of *Casablanca*, one of his contributions to a script largely written by the Epstein twins and Howard Koch.

Walpole, Horace, 4th Earl of Orford 1717–97

English writer and politician. Architectural pursuits, correspondence, writing, visits to Paris, his house, Strawberry Hill, and the establishment of a private press were the main occupations of his life. He exchanged more than 1600 letters with Mme du Deffand between 1769 and 1797 and corresponded also with Sir Horace Mann and the Countess of Upper Ossory.

21 We were eight days in coming hither from Lyons; the four last in crossing the Alps. Such uncouth rocks, and such uncomely inhabitants!
1739 Letter to Richard West. Collected in P Cunningham (ed) *The Letters of Horace Walpole, Fourth Earl of Orford* (1857–9).

22 I am very glad that I see Rome while it yet exists; before a great number of years are elapsed, I question whether it will be worth seeing. Between the ignorance and poverty of the present Romans, every thing is neglected and falling to decay.
1740 Letter. Collected in P Cunningham (ed) *The Letters of Horace Walpole, Fourth Earl of Orford* (1857–9).

23 It is a little plaything-house that I got out of Mrs Chevenix's shop, and it is the prettiest bauble you ever saw. It is set in enamelled meadows with filigree hedges…barges as solemn as Barons of the Exchequer move under my window… Thank God! the Thames is between me and the Duchess of Queensberry.
1747 Of Strawberry Hill, the first 'Gothic' cottage, a showplace in its day. Letter to Henry Seymour Conway, 8 Jun. In W S Lewis (ed) *Selected Letters of Horace Walpole* (1973). Mrs Chevenix kept a well-known toy-shop.

24 Every drop of ink in my pen ran cold.
1752 Letter to George Montague, 30 Jul. In *The Correspondence of Horace Walpole* (Yale edition, 1937–8).

25 One of the greatest geniuses that ever existed, Shakespeare, undoubtedly wanted taste.
1764 Letter to Christopher Wren, 9 Aug. In *The Correspondence of Horace Walpole* (Yale edition, 1937–8).

26 It is charming to totter into vogue.
1765 Letter to George Selwyn, 2 Dec. In *The Correspondence of Horace Walpole* (Yale edition, 1937–8).

27 Wondrously clean, but as evidently an actor as Garrick.
1766 Of the Methodist preacher John Wesley. Letter to John Chute, 10 Oct. In William Hadley (ed) *The Letters of Horace Walpole* (1926).

28 It was easier to conquer it than to know what to do with it.
1772 Of the Orient. Letter to Sir Horace Mann, 27 Mar. In *The Correspondence of Horace Walpole* (Yale edition, 1937–8).

29 The way to ensure summer in England is to have it framed and glazed in a comfortable room.
1774 Letter to William Cole, 28 May. In *The Correspondence of Horace Walpole* (Yale edition, 1937–8).

30 By the waters of Babylon we sit down and weep, when we think of thee, O America!
1775 Letter to William Mason, 12 Jun. In *The Correspondence of Horace Walpole* (Yale edition, 1937–8).

31 The world is a comedy to those that think, a tragedy to those that feel.
1776 Letter to Lady Ossory, 11 Dec. In W S Lewis (ed) *Selected Letters of Horace Walpole* (1973).

32 Your daughters, I hope, will be married to Americans, and not in this dirty, despicable little island.
1777 Letter to Lady Ossory, 11 Dec. In W S Lewis (ed) *Selected Letters of Horace Walpole* (1973).

33 When will the world know that peace and propagation are the two most delightful things in it?
1778 Letter to Sir Horace Mann, 7 Jul. In *The Correspondence of Horace Walpole* (Yale edition, 1937–8).

34 It is the story of a mountebank and his zany.
1785 Of Boswell's account of his *Tour of the Hebrides* with Dr Johnson. Letter to Henry Conway, 6 Oct. In *The Correspondence of Horace Walpole* (Yale edition, 1937–8).

35 All the sensible Tories that I ever knew were either Jacobites or became Whigs; those that remained Tories remained fools.
Memoirs of the Reign of King George III (published 1845).

36 Virtue knows to a farthing what it has lost by not being vice.
Quoted in L Kronenberger *The Extraordinary Mr Wilkes* (1973).

37 A fertile pedant.
Of Margaret Cavendish, Duchess of Newcastle. Quoted in Nicholas T Parsons *The Joy of Bad Verse* (1988).

Walpole, Sir Robert, 1st Earl of Orford 1676–1745

English statesman and leading minister of George I and II. Elected as a Whig MP in 1701, he became Secretary for War (1708), Treasurer of the Navy (1710) and Chancellor of the Exchequer (1715). Recognized as England's first Prime Minister from 1721, he resigned in 1742, when a war he had opposed broke out.

38 Madam, there are fifty thousand men slain this year in Europe, and not one an Englishman.
1734 To Queen Caroline, on avoiding British participation in the War of the Polish Succession. Quoted in John Hervey *Memoirs 1734–43* (1848), vol.1.

39 They may ring their bells now; before long they will be wringing their hands.
1739 Remark on hearing church bells celebrating the declaration of war against Spain, 19 Oct.

40 I have lived long enough in the world to know that the safety of a Minister lies in his having the approbation of this House. Former Ministers neglected that and therefore they fell; I have always made it my first study to obtain it, and therefore I hope to stand.
1739 Speech, House of Commons, 21 Nov.

41 Patriots spring up like mushrooms. I could raise 50 of them within the four and twenty hours. I have raised many of them in one night. It is but refusing to gratify an immeasurable or insolent demand, and up starts a patriot.
1741 Speech, House of Commons, 13 Feb.

42 All those men have their price.
Quoted in William Coxe *Memoirs of Sir Robert Walpole* (1798).

Walters, Julie 1950–

English actress. On television she has appeared in both comedy and drama, and her films include *Educating Rita* (1983) and *Billy Elliot* (2000).

43 There's something great about going through the menopause and being in your 50s. You trade in that youthful thing, where everything is brand new. You swap it hopefully for some kind of wisdom; all the stuff you've learned. And I think HRT and plastic surgery kind of stopped that.
2003 In *The Guardian*, 1 Sep.

Walther Von der Vogelweide c.1170–1230

German poet. One of the most celebrated poets of his time, he found particular favour at the Austrian court, and was awarded a small estate by Emperor Frederick II.

44 *Jâ leider desn mac nicht gesîn,*
Das guot und wertlich êre
Und gotes hulde mêre
Zesamene in ein herze komen.
It is sadly impossible
For wealth and a good name,
along with God's favour,
to be united in one heart.
c.1195 'Ich sass ûf eime steine', l.16–19.

Walton, Izaak 1593–1683

English writer. He is remembered for *The Compleat Angler* (1653), which discusses the business of fishing and is interspersed with scraps of dialogue, moral reflections, quaint old verses, songs and sayings, and idyllic glimpses of country life.

45 But God, who is able to prevail, wrestled with him, as the Angel did with Jacob, and marked him; marked him for his own.
1653 Of Donne. *Life of John Donne.*

46 Angling may be said to be so like mathematics, that it can never be fully learnt.
1653 *The Compleat Angler*, 'Epistle to the Reader'.

47 I shall stay [the reader] no longer than to wish him a rainy day to read this…discourse; and that if he be an honest angler, the east wind may never blow when he goes a-fishing.
1653 *The Compleat Angler*, 'Epistle to the Reader'.

48 Angling is somewhat like poetry, men are to be born so: I mean with inclination to it.
1653 *The Compleat Angler*, pt.1, ch.1.

49 Sir Henry Wotton…was also a most dear lover, and a frequent practiser of the art of angling; of which he would say, 'it was an employment for his idle time…a rest to his mind, a cheerer of his spirits, a diverter of sadness, a calmer of unquiet thoughts, a moderator of passions, a procurer of contentedness; and that it begat habits of peace and patience in those that professed and practised it.'
1653 *The Compleat Angler*, pt.1, ch.1.

50 An excellent angler, and now with God.
1653 Of Sir George Hastings, *The Compleat Angler*, pt.1, ch.4.

51 She and I both love all anglers, they be such honest, civil quiet men.
1653 The milkwoman. *The Compleat Angler*, pt.1, ch.4.

52 No life, my honest scholar, no life so happy and so pleasant as the life of a well-governed angler; for when the lawyer is swallowed up with business, and the statesman is preventing or contriving plots, then we sit on cowslip-banks, hear the birds sing, and possess ourselves in as much quietness as these silver streams, which we now see glide so quietly by us.
1653 *The Compleat Angler*, pt.1, ch.5.

53 He would often say, Religion does not banish mirth, but only moderates and sets rules to it.
1670 Of George Herbert. *Life of George Herbert*.

Walton, Sir William Turner 1902–83

British composer. His works include *Façade* (1923), designed to accompany verses by Edith Sitwell, the *Sinfonia Concertante* (1927), the biblical cantata *Belshazzar's Feast* (1931), the opera *Troilus and Cressida* (1954) and much incidental music for films.

54 I seriously advise all sensitive composers to die at the age of thirty-seven. I know I've gone through the first halcyon period, and am just about ripe for my critical damnation.
1939 Letter.

Wang Xizhe 1956–

Chinese dissident, released from prison in 1993 after 12 years for his role in the Democracy Wall Movement.

55 You may keep me under surveillance until the year 2000, but will you even be able to hold on to power until then?
1995 Quoted in the *Eastern Express*, 10 May.

Ward, Artemus *pseudonym of* Charles Farrar Browne 1834–67

US humorist. In 1857 he began to publish letters from 'Artemus Ward' in the Cleveland *Plain Dealer*. His backwoods humour was an immediate success, and Lincoln interrupted a Cabinet meeting to read from him. In 1866 he moved to England where he worked for *Punch* and became a popular lecturer.

56 Traters…are a unfortunate class of people. If they wasn't they wouldn't be traters. They conspire to bust up a country—they fail, and they're traters. They bust her, and they become statesmen and heroes.
1867 *Artemus Ward in London and Other Papers*, 'The Tower of London'.

57 Let us all be happy, and live within our means, even if we have to borrow the money to do it with.
1867 *Artemus Ward in London, and Other Papers*, 'Science and Natural History'.

58 I am happiest when I am idle.
I could live for months without performing any kind of labour, and at the expiration of that time I should feel fresh and vigorous enough to go right on in the same way for numerous more months.
1867 *Artemus Ward in London, and Other Papers*, 'Pyrotechny', 3.

59 Why care for grammar as long as we are good?
1867 *Artemus Ward in London, and Other Papers*, 'Pyrotechny', 5.

60 He [Brigham Young] is dreadfully married. He's the most married man I ever saw in my life.
1869 *Artemus Ward's Lecture*, 'Brigham Young's Palace'.

61 'Why is this thus? What is the reason of this thusness?'
1869 *Artemus Ward's Lecture*, 'Heber C. Kimball's Harem'

Warhol, Andy 1928–87

US graphic artist, painter and film-maker. He was one of the most controversial figures in American Pop Art.

62 If you want to know all about Andy Warhol, just look at the surface of my paintings and films and me, there I am. There's nothing behind it!
1967 Quoted in Gretchen Berg 'Andy: My True Story', in the *LA Free Press*, 17 Mar.

63 In the future everybody will be world famous for fifteen minutes.
Quoted in Andy Warhol, Kasper König, Pontus Hultén and Olle Granath (eds) *Andy Warhol* (1968).

64 The Pop artists did images that anybody walking down Broadway could recognize in a split second—comics, picnic tables, men's trousers, celebrities, shower curtains, refrigerators, Coke bottles—all the great modern things that the Abstract Expressionists tried so hard not to notice at all.
Quoted in Andy Warhol and Pat Hackett *POPism: The Warhol '60s* (1980).

65 When you think about it, department stores are kind of like museums.
1985 *America*.

Warner, Marina Sarah 1946–

British writer and literary and social critic. Her works include *Alone of All Her Sex* (1976) and *From the Beast to the Blonde* (1994), and novels such as *Indigo* (1992). In 1994 she delivered the Reith Lectures, later published as *Managing Monsters* (1994).

66 Although Mary cannot be a model for the New Woman, a goddess is better than no goddess at all, for the sombre-suited masculine world of the Protestant religion is altogether too much like a gentlemen's club to which the ladies are only admitted on special days.
1976 *Alone of All Her Sex: the Myth and Cult of the Virgin Mary*, epilogue.

Warner, Sir Pelham Plum 1873–1963

English cricketer, born in Trinidad. He played for Middlesex and captained England on tours of Australia and South Africa. He was secretary (1939–45) and president (1950) of the MCC and was knighted in 1937.

67 Cricket is the greatest game that the wit of man has yet devised.
Quoted in Colin Jarman *The Guinness Dictionary of Sports Quotations* (1990).

Warren, Earl 1891–1974

US politician and judge. As chief justice of the US Supreme Court (1943–53) he was a liberalizing influence, ending segregation in schools and protecting accused persons from police abuses. He headed the Commission into the assassination of John F Kennedy (1963–4).

68 We conclude that in the field of public education the doctrine of 'separate but equal' has no place.
1954 Ruling to declare segregated schools unconstitutional, 17 May.

69 The freedom to marry has long been recognized as one of the vital personal rights essential to the orderly pursuit of happiness by free men.
1957 2 Jun. Unanimous ruling against a Virginian law forbidding intermarriage of blacks and whites.

70 I always turn to the sports section first. The sports page records people's accomplishments; the front page has nothing but man's failures.
1968 In *Sports Illustrated*, 'Scorecard', 22 Jul.

Warren, Harry *pseudonym of* ***Salvatore Guaragno*** 1893–1981

US songwriter, born in Brooklyn. During the 1930s, he collaborated with Al Dubin on several Busby Berkeley movies. During the war years he worked with Mark Gordon for Fox and then also for MGM.

71 Walk two Oscars behind me.
1975 Comment to Harold Arlen on winning a second Oscar for *On the Atchison, Topeka and the Santa Fe*. Quoted in Tony Thomas *Harry Warren*.

Warren, Robert Penn 1905–89

US writer, Professor of English at Louisiana, Minnesota and Yale. He established an international reputation with his novel *All the King's Men* (1943, filmed 1949), and wrote several other novels, short stories and volumes of poetry.

72 The poem…is a little myth of man's capacity of making life meaningful. And in the end, the poem is not a thing we see—it is, rather, a light by which we may see—and what we see is life.
1958 In the *Saturday Review*, 22 Mar.

73 The urge to write poetry is like having an itch. When the itch becomes annoying enough, you scratch it.
1969 In the *New York Times*, 16 Dec.

74 How do poems grow? They grow out of your life.
1985 In the *New York Times*, 12 May.

75 What is a poem but a hazardous attempt at self-understanding? It is the deepest part of autobiography.
1985 In the *New York Times*, 12 May.

76 I don't expect you'll hear me writing any poems to the greater glory of Ronald and Nancy Reagan.
1986 On being appointed the first US Poet Laureate. In the *Washington Post*, 27 Feb.

77 He woke me from the torpor of the accustomed.
On familiar scenes more fully realized through Walker Evans's realistic photographs. Quoted in Belinda Rathbone *Walker Evans* (1995).

Washington, Booker Taliaferro 1856–1915

African-American educationalist, born a slave in Virginia. He became principal of the Tuskegee Institute in Alabama in 1881 and was a moderate in the negro movement. His autobiography, *Up from Slavery*, was published in 1901.

78 No race can prosper until it learns that there is as much dignity in tilling a field as in writing a poem. It is at the bottom of life we must begin, and not at the top.
1895 'The Atlanta Exposition Address', in *Up from Slavery* (1901), ch.14.

79 In all things that are purely social we can be as separate as the fingers, yet one as the hand in all things essential to mutual progress.

1895 'The Atlanta Exposition Address,' in *Up from Slavery* (1901), ch.14.

Washington, George 1732–99

American soldier and statesman, first President. As commander of American forces in the War of Independence he displayed great powers of leadership, suffering defeats at Brandywine and Germantown, but holding his army together through the winter of 1777–8 at Valley Forge. After the alliance with France (1778), he forced the surrender of Cornwallis (1781) then retired to Mount Vernon, and sought strong constitutional government. In 1787 he presided over the Constitutional Convention and became President, eventually joining the Federalist Party, and retired in 1797.

80 Father, I cannot tell a lie. I did it with my little hatchet.
In childhood, on admitting to vandalizing a cherry tree, attributed by Mason Locke Weems (Parson Weems) in his *Life and Memorable Actions of George Washington* (5th edn, c.1810). Weems claimed to have heard the tale from an elderly lady, a distant relation of Washington's, 20 years earlier.

81 When we assumed the soldier, we did not lay aside the citizen.
1775 Address to the New York legislature, 26 Jun.

82 I can answer for but three things: a firm belief in the justice of our cause, close attention in the prosecution of it, and the strictest integrity.
1775 On being elected Commander of the Unionist Army, 19 Jun.

83 The time is now near at hand which must probably determine whether Americans are to be freemen or slaves… The fate of unborn millions will now depend, under God, on the courage and conduct of this army. Our cruel and unrelenting enemy leaves us only the choice of brave resistance or abject submission. We have, therefore, to resolve to conquer or die.
1776 General orders, 2 Jul. Quoted in J C Fitzpatrick (ed) *Writings of George Washington* (1932), vol.5.

84 An old-fashioned Virginia fox hunt, gentlemen.
1777 Comment on the skirmish at Princeton, 3 Jan. Attributed.

85 The preservation of the sacred fire of liberty, and the destiny of the republican model of government, are justly considered as deeply, perhaps as finally staked, on the experiment entrusted to the hands of the American people.
1789 Inaugural address, 30 Apr.

86 To be prepared for war is one of the most effective means of preserving peace.
1790 First Annual Address, 8 Jan.

87 It is our true policy to steer clear of permanent alliance with any portion of the foreign world.
1796 Farewell address to the union, 17 Sep.

Washington Post

US newspaper.

88 The Closest of Strangers.
1994 Headline, 9 Jan, on the sharing of Nobel peace prize by South Africa's F W de Klerk and Nelson Mandela.

Washington Times

US newspaper.

89 Cool is Hot.
1988 Headline, 9 May, on Massachusetts Governor Michael Dukakis's low-key campaign for Democratic presidential nomination.

90 There's no crime like the present.
1995 In the week in which three persons jumped the White House fence, 25 May.

Waterhouse, Keith Spencer 1929–

English novelist, dramatist, humorist and journalist. His whimsical novel *Billy Liar* (1959) was adapted for the stage the next year and filmed in 1963, and he continued writing mordantly humorous novels, such as *Jubb* (1963) and *Office Life* (1978). Later works include *Unsweet Charity* (1992), a novel, and two volumes of autobiography, *City Lights* (1994) and *Streets Ahead* (1995).

91 Lying in bed, I abandoned the facts again and was back in Ambrosia.
1959 *Billy Liar*, opening sentence.

92 I cannot bring myself to vote for a woman who has been voice-trained to speak to me as though my dog has just died.
1978 On Margaret Thatcher, attributed.

93 The 50s face was angry, the 60s face was well-fed, the 70s face was foxy. Perhaps it was the right expression: there was a lot to be wary about.
1979 In the *Observer Magazine*, 30 Dec.

94 Why should it take three times longer to elect a Mayor for London as it does to set up an entire Scottish Parliament?
1999 In the *Observer*, 'They Said What…?', 24 Oct.

Waterman, Pete 1947–

English pop record producer, one of the founder members of Stock Aitken and Waterman (1984–93).

95 I wish there was a formula. I'd be billionaire instead of a millionaire.
2003 On making hit records. In *Varsity*, 28 Nov.

Watson, James D(ewey) 1928–

US biochemist who with Francis Crick helped to determine the structure of the nucleic acid known as DNA. Crick, Maurice Wilkins and Watson shared the 1962 Nobel prize in physiology or medicine. Watson wrote *The Double Helix* (1968), the story of the discovery of the structure of DNA.

96 We wish to suggest a structure for the salt of deoxyribose nucleic acid (DNA).
1953 First sentence of the paper describing the structure of DNA, with Francis Crick. *Nature*, 25 Apr.

97 [Science] seldom proceeds in the straightforward logical manner imagined by outsiders. Instead, its steps forward…are often very human events in which personalities and cultural traditions play major roles.
1968 *The Double Helix*.

Watson, Thomas John 1874–1956

US businessman and computing pioneer, president of IBM.

98 I think there is a world market for about five computers.
1943 Quoted in Christopher Cerf and Victor Navasky *The Experts Speak* (1984).

Watson, Thomas John, Jr 1914–93

US businessman, president (1952–61), chairman (1961–71) and chairman of the executive board (1972–9) at IBM. He also served as Ambassador to the USSR (1979–81).

99 Solve it quickly, solve it right or wrong.
1977 His advice on dealing with problems. In *Fortune*.

Watson, William c.1559–1603

English Catholic conspirator and secular priest.

1 *Fiat justitia et ruant coeli.*
Let justice be done, though the heavens may fall.
1602 *A Decacordon of Ten Quodlibeticall Questions Concerning Religion and State.* This was an influential reworking of Ferdinand I's motto.
► *See Ferdinand I 320:1.*

Watt, James 1736–1819

Scottish inventor and mechanical engineer, best remembered for his refinements to the steam engine.

2 That vessel in which the powers of steam are to be employed to work the engine, which is called the Cylinder in common fire engines, and which I call the Steam Vessel, must, during the whole time the engine is at work, be kept as hot as the steam that enters it; first, by enclosing it in a case of wood, or any other materials that transmit heat slowly; secondly, by surrounding it with steam or other heated bodies; and thirdly, by suffering neither water nor any other substance colder than steam to enter and touch it during that time.
1769 Specification of patent, 5 Jan, for a new method of lessening the consumption of steam and fuel in fire engines.

Watts, Isaac 1674–1748

English independent preacher and hymn writer.

3 When I survey the wondrous cross
On which the prince of glory died,
My richest gain I count but loss,
And pour contempt on all my pride.
1707 *Hymns and Spiritual Songs*, 'Crucifixion to the World, by the Cross of Christ'.

4 Jesus shall reign where'er the sun
Does his successive journeys run;
His kingdom stretch from shore to shore,
Till moons shall wax and wane no more.
1719 *The Psalms of David Imitated*, Psalm 72.

5 Our God, our help in ages past
Our hope for years to come,
Our shelter from the stormy blast
And our eternal home.
1719 *The Psalms of David Imitated*, Psalm 90 (in 1738 John Wesley substituted 'O God' for 'Our God').

Waugh, Auberon Alexander 1939–2001

English writer and editor, the eldest son of Evelyn Waugh. He was a journalist and novelist, and the editor of the *Literary Review*.

6 I will endeavour to put the word sex in capital letters on the cover of every issue of the *Literary Review* under my editorship, regardless of its actual contents… My purpose is simply to embolden booksellers.
1986 In the *Daily Telegraph*, 9 May.

7 It was inevitable that as soon as we had enjoyed a few days of reasonable summer weather, the country would suffer an acute water shortage. It can rain for 100 days, but if the sun shines on the 101st there will be hosepipe restrictions on the 102nd.
1997 *Way of the World: The Forgotten Years: 1995–6.*

8 Those who argue that the free supply of heroin to elderly addicts in Denmark would help to cut the crime rate—nine out of 10 burglaries are thought to be drug-related—ignore an important question. How many Copenhagen burglaries are committed by the elderly?
1997 *Way of the World: The Forgotten Years: 1995–6.*

Waugh, Evelyn Arthur St John 1903–66

English novelist. He enjoyed great success with his first novel, *Decline and Fall* (1928), the first of a series of barbed satirical novels which included *Vile Bodies* (1930) and *Scoop* (1938). Preoccupied with the decline of English civilization, his works include *Brideshead Revisited* (1945) and the *Sword of Honour* trilogy (1952–61). A supreme stylist, and considered one of the great comic novelists, he also wrote travel books and biographies.

9 I expect you'll be becoming a schoolmaster, sir. That's what most of the gentlemen does, sir, that gets sent down for indecent behaviour.
1928 *Decline and Fall*, Prelude.

10 'We class schools, you see, into four grades: Leading School, First-rate School, Good School, and School. Frankly,' said Mr Levy, 'School is pretty bad.'
1928 *Decline and Fall*, pt.1, ch.1.

11 That's the public-school system all over. They may kick you out but they never let you down.
1928 *Decline and Fall*, pt.1, ch.3.

12 You can't get into the soup in Ireland, do what you like.
1928 *Decline and Fall*, pt.1, ch.3.

13 Meanwhile, you will write an essay on 'self-indulgence'. There will be a prize of half a crown for the longest essay, irrespective of any possible merit.
1928 *Decline and Fall*, pt.1, ch.5.

14 For generations the British bourgeoisie have spoken of themselves as gentlemen, and by that they have meant, among other things, a self-respecting scorn of irregular perquisites. It is the quality that distinguishes the gentleman from both the artist and the aristocrat.
1928 *Decline and Fall*, pt.1, ch.6.

15 There aren't many left like him nowadays, what with education and whisky the price it is.
1928 *Decline and Fall*, pt.1, ch.7.

16 'I often think,' he continued, 'that we can trace almost all the disasters of English history to the influence of Wales!'
1928 *Decline and Fall*, pt.1, ch.8.

17 I have noticed again and again since I have been in the Church that lay interest in ecclesiastical matters is often a prelude to insanity.
1928 *Decline and Fall*, pt.1, ch.8.

18 I have often observed in women of her type a tendency to regard all athletics as inferior forms of fox-hunting.
1928 *Decline and Fall*, pt.1, ch.10.

19 I'm one of the blind alleys off the main road of procreation.
1928 *Decline and Fall*, pt.1, ch.12.

20 I haven't been to sleep for over a year. That's why I go to bed early. One needs more rest if one doesn't sleep.
1928 *Decline and Fall*, pt.2, ch.3.

21 There is a species of person called a 'Modern Churchman' who draws the full salary of a beneficed clergyman and need not commit himself to any religious belief.
1928 *Decline and Fall*, pt.2, ch.4.

22 Instead of this absurd division into sexes, they ought to class people as static and dynamic.
1928 *Decline and Fall*, pt.2, ch.7.

23 I came to the conclusion many years ago that almost all crime is due to the repressed desire for aesthetic expression.
1928 *Decline and Fall*, pt.3, ch.1.

24 Anyone who has been to an English public school will always feel comparatively at home in prison. It is the people brought up in the gay intimacy of the slums, Paul learned, who find prison so soul-destroying.
1928 *Decline and Fall*, pt.3, ch.4.

25 Creative Endeavour lost her wings, Mrs Ape.
1930 *Vile Bodies*, ch.1.

26 Particularly against books the Home Secretary is. If we can't stamp out literature in the country, we can at least stop it being brought in from outside.
1930 *Vile Bodies*, ch.2.

27 When the war broke out she took down the signed photograph of the Kaiser and, with some solemnity, hung it in the men-servants' lavatory; it was her one combative action.
1930 *Vile Bodies*, ch.3.

28 All this fuss about sleeping together. For physical pleasure I'd sooner go to my dentist any day.
1930 *Vile Bodies*, ch.6.

29 'The Beast stands for strong mutually antagonistic governments everywhere,' he said. 'Self-sufficiency at home, self-assertion abroad.'
1938 *Scoop*, bk.1, ch.1.

30 Mr Salter's side of the conversation was limited to expressions of assent. When Lord Copper was right, he said, 'Definitely, Lord Copper'; when he was wrong, 'Up to a point.'
1938 *Scoop*, bk.1, ch.1.

31 'He's supposed to have a particularly high-class style: "Feather footed through the plashy fen passes the questing vole"...would that be it?' 'Yes,' said the Managing Editor. 'That must be good style.'
1938 *Scoop*, bk.1, ch.1.

32 News is what a chap who doesn't care much about anything wants to read. And it's only news until he's read it. After that it's dead.
1938 *Scoop*, bk.1, ch.5.

33 'I will not stand for being called a woman in my own house,' she said.
1938 *Scoop*, bk.2, ch.1.

34 Other nations use 'force'; we Britons alone use 'might'.
1938 *Scoop*, bk.2, ch.5.

35 Lady Peabury was in the morning room reading a novel; early training gave a guilty spice to this recreation, for she had been brought up to believe that to read a novel before luncheon was one of the gravest sins it was possible for a gentlewoman to commit.
1939 'An Englishman's Home'.

36 Like German opera, too long and too loud.
1941 Of warfare. Attributed.

37 I do not think I shall ever forget the sight of Etna at sunset... Nothing I have ever seen in Art or Nature was quite so revolting.
1946 *Labels*.

38 The historic destiny of the Irish is being fulfilled on the other side of the Atlantic, where they have settled in their millions, bringing with them all their ancient grudges and the melancholy of the bogs, but also their hard, ancient wisdom. They alone of the newcomers are never for a moment taken in by the multifarious frauds of modernity. They have been changed from peasants and soldiers into townsmen. They have learned some of the superficial habits of 'good citizenship', but at heart they remain the same adroit and joyless race that broke the hearts of all who ever tried to help them.
1947 'The American Epoch in the Catholic Church'.

39 You never find an Englishman among the under-dogs—except in England, of course.
1948 *The Loved One*, ch.1.

40 In the dying world I come from, quotation is a national vice. No one would think of making an after-dinner speech without the help of poetry. It used to be classics, now it's lyric verse.
1948 *The Loved One*, ch.9.

41 Words should be an intense pleasure, just as leather should be to a shoemaker.
1950 In the *New York Times*, 19 Nov.

42 Most writers in the course of their careers become thick-skinned and learn to accept vituperation, which in any other profession would be unimaginably offensive, as a healthy counterpoise to unintelligent praise.
1952 In the *New York Times Magazine*, 30 Nov.

43 He sat at the cocktail bar... It wore the air of a fashion magazine, once stiff and shiny, which too many people had handled.
1955 *Officers and Gentlemen*, bk.1, ch.8.

44 Enclosing every thin man, there's a fat man demanding elbow room.
1955 *Officers and Gentlemen*, interlude.
► *See Connolly 233:82, Orwell 628:52.*

45 He did not, even in his extremity, quite abandon his faith in the magic of official forms. In bumf lay salvation.
1955 *Officers and Gentlemen*, bk.2, ch.5.

46 We are all American at puberty; we die French.
1961 Diary note, 18 Jul.

47 Most of the world's troubles seem to come from people who are too busy. If only politicians and scientists were lazier, how much happier we should all be.
1962 *Seven Deadly Sins*.

48 Punctuality is the virtue of the bored.
1962 Diary note, 26 Mar.

49 Manners are especially the need of the plain. The pretty can get away with anything.

1962 In the *Observer*, 15 Apr.

50 One can write, think and pray exclusively of others; dreams are all egocentric.
1962 Diary entry, 5 Oct.

51 One forgets words as one forgets names. One's vocabulary needs constant fertilizing or it will die.
1962 Diary entry, 25 Dec.

52 All fictional characters are flat.
1963 'The Art of Fiction XXX: Evelyn Waugh', in *The Paris Review*, no.8, Summer/Fall.

53 No writer before the middle of the 19th century wrote about the working classes other than as grotesques or as pastoral decorations. Then when they were given the vote certain writers started to suck up to them.
1963 'The Art of Fiction XXX: Evelyn Waugh', in *The Paris Review*, no.8, Summer/Fall.

54 Only when one has lost all curiosity has one reached the age to write an autobiography.
1964 *A Little Learning*, opening words.

55 With a thorough knowledge of the Bible, Shakespeare and Wisden, you cannot go far wrong.
1964 *A Little Learning.*

56 Randolph Churchill went into hospital...to have a lung removed. It was announced that the trouble was not 'malignant'. Seeing Ed Stanley in White's, on my way to Rome, I remarked that it was a typical triumph of modern science to find the only part of Randolph that was not malignant and remove it.
1964 Diary note, Mar.

57 To watch him fumbling with our rich and delicate English language is like seeing a Sèvres vase in the hands of a chimpanzee.
Of Sir Stephen Spender. Quoted by Eric Pace in Spender's obituary in the *New York Times*, 18 Jul 1995.

Wavell, Archibald Percival, Ist Earl 1883–1950

British field-marshal. He held the Middle East Command from 1939 and was Viceroy of India 1943–7. His *Generals and Generalship* (1941) served as a combat handbook to his most formidable opponent, Erwin Rommel.

58 For sheer courage and endurance, physical and mental, the two men stand together as examples of what toughness the body will find, if the spirit within it is tough; and as very worthy representatives of our national capacity for individual enterprise, which it is hoped even the modern craze for regulating every detail of our lives will never stifle.
1948 Of F Spencer Chapman and T E Lawrence. Quoted in foreword to F Spencer Chapman *The Jungle is Neutral* (1950).

59 The story of Colonel Chapman's adventures is typical of the British way of war, and therefore begins with a complete lack of preparation.
1948 Quoted in foreword to F Spencer Chapman *The Jungle is Neutral* (1950).

Waxman, Howard

Editor of the *Ice Cream Reporter.*

60 The relation between the human tongue, the human psyche and butterfat is not very complex. The first two love the third.
1992 In *Newsweek*, 30 Nov.

Weatherill, (Bruce) Bernard Weatherill, Baron 1920–

English politician, chair of the Ways and Means Committee (1979–1983) and Speaker of the House of Commons (1987–1992). He oversaw with enthusiasm the televising of parliamentary proceedings.

61 Mine is one of the jobs that, if you want it, you will never get it—and if you're seen to want it you will certainly never get it.
1991 In *The House Magazine*, Jan.

Webb, (Martha) Beatrice *née Potter* 1858–1943

English social reformer, social historian, and economist. She wrote many studies with her husband, Sidney Webb.

62 His sensuality has all drifted into sexual vanity, delight for being the candle to the moths, with a dash of intellectual curiosity to give flavour to his tickled vanity... His incompleteness as a thinker, his shallow and vulgar view of many human relationships—the lack of a sterner kind of humour which would show him the dreariness of his farce and the total absence of proportion and inadequateness in some of his ideas—all these defects came largely from the flippant and worthless self-complacency brought about by the worship of rather second-rate women.
1897 Of George Bernard Shaw. Diary entry, 8 May.

63 All along the line, physically, mentally, morally, alcohol is a weakening and deadening force, and it is worth a great deal to save women and girls from its influence.
1917 *Health of Working Girls*, ch.10.

Webb, Phyllis 1927–

Canadian poet, university teacher and broadcaster. Her poetry includes *The Sea is Also a Garden* (1962), *Naked Poems* (1965) and *Wilson's Bowl* (1980); she has also published a collection of her essays.

64 Some people swim lakes, others climb flagpoles,
some join monasteries, but we, my friends,
who have considered suicide take our daily walk
with death and are not lonely.
In the end it brings more honesty and care
than all the democratic parliaments of tricks.
1956 *Even Your Right Eye*, 'To Friends Who Have Also Considered Suicide'.

Webb, Sidney James 1859–1947

English social reformer, historian and economist. A lawyer and Fabian, he wrote many powerful tracts and in 1892 married fellow socialist Beatrice Potter. They wrote a classic *History of Trade Unionism* (1894) and *English Local Government* (1906–29, 9 vols), and began the *New Statesman* (1913). He became President of the Board of Trade (1924), Dominions and Colonial Secretary (1929–30) and Colonial Secretary (1930–1).

65 No philosopher now looks for anything but the gradual evolution of the new order from the old... History shows us no example of the sudden substitutions of Utopian and revolutionary romance.
1889 *Fabian Essays.*

66 How anyone can fear that the British electorate, whatever mistakes it can make or may condone, can ever go too far or too fast is incomprehensible... The Labour Party, when in due course it comes to be entrusted with

power, will naturally not want to do everything at once. Once we face the necessity of putting our principles into execution from one end of the kingdom to the other, the inevitability of gradualness cannot fail to be appreciated.
1923 Labour Party Conference, 26 Jun.

Weber, Max 1864–1920

German sociologist and economist.

67 In Baxter's view, the care of external goods should only lie on the shoulders of the 'saint like a light cloak, which can be thrown aside at any moment.' But fate decreed that the cloak should become an iron cage.
1904–5 *The Protestant Ethic and the Spirit of Capitalism* (translated by Talcott Parsons, 1930), ch.5. Richard Baxter (1615–91) was an eminent Puritan, chaplain of Cromwell's army.

68 The impulse to acquisition, pursuit of gain, of money, of the greatest possible amount of money, has in itself nothing to do with capitalism. This impulse exists among waiters, physicians, coachmen, artists, prostitutes, dishonest officials, soldiers, nobles, crusaders, gamblers, and beggars. One may say that it has been common to all sorts and conditions of men at all times and in all cultures of the earth, wherever the objective possibility of it is or has been given.
1904–5 *The Protestant Ethic and the Spirit of Capitalism* (translated by Talcott Parsons, 1930).

69 Capital accounting in its formally most rational shape…presupposes *the battle of man with man.*
1922 Collected in Guenther Roth and Claus Wittich (eds) *Economy and Society* (1978), ch.1.

70 However many people may complain about the 'red tape', it would be sheer illusion to think for a moment that continuous administrative work can be carried out in any field except by means of officials working in offices… The choice is only that between bureaucracy and dilettantism in the field of administration.
1922 Collected in Guenther Roth and Claus Wittich (eds) *Economy and Society* (1978), ch.3.

Webster, Daniel 1782–1852

US lawyer and statesman, one of the greatest of US orators. As Secretary of State (1840–3) he negotiated the Webster–Ashburton treaty with Great Britain. A supporter of free trade, nationality and established institutions, he was unwilling to break the Union to abolish slavery.

71 [Alexander Hamilton] smote the rock of the national resources, and abundant streams of revenue gushed forth. He touched the dead corpse of the public credit, and it sprang upon its feet.
1831 Speech, New York, 10

72 There is always room at the top.
On being advised against joining the overcrowded legal profession, attributed.

Webster, John c.1580–c.1625

English dramatist. He collaborated with Dekker, Drayton, Marston and others. He is best known for two great tragedies, *The White Devil* (1612) and *The Duchess of Malfi* (1623).

73 Fortune's a right whore:
If she give aught, she deals it in small parcels,
That she may take away all at one swoop.
1612 *The White Devil*, act 1, sc.1.

74 All the damnable degrees
Of drinking have you staggered through.
1612 *The White Devil*, act 1, sc.1.

75 Perfumes, the more they are chafed, the more they render
Their pleasing scents; and so affliction
Expresseth virtue fully.
1612 *The White Devil*, act 1, sc.1.

76 Oh, they are politic: they know our desire is increased by the difficulty of enjoying, whereas satiety is a blunt, weary, and drowsy passion.
1612 Of women. *The White Devil*, act 1, sc.1.

77 See, the curse of children!
In life they keep us frequently in tears,
And in the cold grave leave us in pale fears.
1612 *The White Devil*, act 1, sc.2.

78 'Tis just like a summer birdcage in a garden; the birds that are without despair to get in, and the birds that are within despair, and are in a consumption, for fear they shall never get out.
1612 *The White Devil*, act 1, sc.2.

79 Lust carries her sharp whip
At her own girdle.
1612 *The White Devil*, act 2, sc.1.

80 See, a good habit makes a child a man,
Whereas a bad one makes a man a beast.
1612 *The White Devil*, act 2, sc.1.

81 A mere tale of a tub, my words are idle.
1612 *The White Devil*, act 2, sc.1.

82 Only the deep sense of some deathless shame.
1612 *The White Devil*, act 2, sc.1.

83 Find me but guilty, sever head from body,
We'll part good friends.
1612 *The White Devil*, act 3, sc.2.

84 For your names
Of whores and murderers, they proceed from you,
As if a man should spit against the wind;
The filth returns in's face.
1612 *The White Devil*, act 3, sc.2.

85 Sum up my faults, I pray, and you shall find,
That beauty, and gay clothes, a merry heart,
And a good stomach to a feast, are all,
All the poor crimes that you can charge me with.
1612 *The White Devil*, act 3, sc.2.

86 VITTORIA: A rape! a rape!
MONTICELSO: How!
VITTORIA: Yes, you have ravished justice,
Forced her to do your pleasure.
1612 *The White Devil*, act 3, sc.2.

87 Woman to man
Is either a God or a wolfe.
1612 *The White Devil*, act 4, sc.2.

88 For your gifts,
I'll return them all; and I do wish
That I could make you full executor
To all my sins.
1612 *The White Devil*, act 4, sc.2.

89 He could not have invented his own ruin,
Had he despaired, with more propriety.
1612 *The White Devil*, act 5, sc.1.

90 They that sleep with dogs shall rise with fleas.
1612 *The White Devil*, act 5, sc.1.

91 O, the rare tricks of a Machiavellian!
He doth not come, like a gross plodding slave,
And buffet you to death; no, my quaint knave,
He tickles you to death, makes you die laughing.
1612 *The White Devil*, act 5, sc.3.

92 Call for the robin-red-breast and the wren,
Since o'er shady groves they hover,
And with leaves and flowers do cover
The friendless bodies of unburied men.
1612 *The White Devil*, act 5, sc.4.

93 I have heard grief named the eldest child of sin.
1612 *The White Devil*, act 5, sc.4.

94 Are you grown an atheist? Will you turn your body,
Which is the goodly palace of the soul,
To the soul's slaughter-house? Oh, the cursèd devil,
Which doth present us with all other sins
Thrice-candied o'er.
1612 *The White Devil*, act 5, sc.6.

95 Oh, yes, thy sins
Do run before thee to fetch fire from hell,
To light thee thither.
1612 *The White Devil*, act 5, sc.6.

96 I myself have heard a very good jest, and have scorned to seem to have so silly a wit as to understand it.
1623 *The Duchess of Malfi*, act 1, sc.1.

97 Then the law to him
Is like a foul black cobweb to a spider;
He makes it his dwelling, and a prison
To entangle those shall feed him.
1623 *The Duchess of Malfi*, act 1, sc.1.

98 DUCHESS: Diamonds are of most precious value
They say, that have passed through most jewellers' hands.
FERDINAND: Whores, by that rule, are precious.
1623 *The Duchess of Malfi*, act 1, sc.1.

99 Wisdom begins at the end.
1623 *The Duchess of Malfi*, act 1, sc.1.

1 DUCHESS: What do you think of marriage?
ANTONIO: I take't, as those that deny purgatory,
It locally contains or heaven, or hell;
There's no third place in't.
1623 *The Duchess of Malfi*, act 1, sc.2.

2 Ambition, madam, is a great man's madness,
That is not kept in chains, and close-pent rooms,
But in fair lightsome lodgings, and is girt
With the wild noise of prattling visitants,
Which makes it lunatic beyond all cure.
1623 *The Duchess of Malfi*, act 1, sc.1.

3 I have long served virtue,
And never ta'en wages of her.
1623 *The Duchess of Malfi*, act 1, sc.1.

4 The misery of us, that are born great,
We are forced to woo because none dare woo us.
1623 *The Duchess of Malfi*, act 1, sc.1.

5 I hope in time 'twill grow into a custom
That noblemen shall come with cap and knee
To purchase a night's lodging of their wives.
1623 *The Duchess of Malfi*, act 3, sc.2.

6 I would sooner swim to the Bermudas on
Two politicians' rotten bladders, tied
Together with an intelligencer's heartstring,
Than depend on so changeable a prince's favour.
1623 *The Duchess of Malfi*, act 3, sc.2.

7 A politician is the devil's quilted anvil,
He fashions all sins on him, and the blows
Are never heard.
1623 *The Duchess of Malfi*, act 3, sc.2.

8 Love mixed with fear is sweetness.
1623 *The Duchess of Malfi*, act 3, sc.2.

9 That curious engine, your white hand.
1623 *The Duchess of Malfi*, act 3, sc.2.

10 Why should only I...
Be cased up, like a holy relic? I have youth
And a little beauty.
1623 *The Duchess of Malfi*, act 3, sc.2.

11 You have shook hands with Reputation
And made him invisible.
1623 *The Duchess of Malfi*, act 3, sc.2.

12 Her melancholy seems to be fortified
With a strange disdain.
1623 *The Duchess of Malfi*, act 4, sc.1.

13 Other sins only speak; murder shrieks out.
1623 *The Duchess of Malfi*, act 4, sc.2.

14 What's this flesh? A little crudded milk, fantastical puff-paste.
1623 *The Duchess of Malfi*, act 4, sc.2. crudded = curdled.

15 What would it pleasure me, to have my throat cut
With diamonds? Or to be smothered
With cassia? Or to be shot to death, with pearls?
1623 *The Duchess of Malfi*, act 4, sc.2.

16 O, that it were possible,
We might but hold some two days' conference
With the dead!
1623 *The Duchess of Malfi*, act 4, sc.2.

17 I am Duchess of Malfi still.
1623 *The Duchess of Malfi*, act 4, sc.2.

18 I know death hath ten thousand several doors
For men to take their exits.
1623 *The Duchess of Malfi*, act 4, sc.2.

19 FERDINAND: Cover her face; mine eyes dazzle: she died young.
BOSOLA: I think not so; her infelicity
Seemed to have years too many.
1623 *The Duchess of Malfi*, act 4, sc.2.

20 Physicians are like kings,—they brook no contradiction.
1623 *The Duchess of Malfi*, act 5, sc.2.

21 We are merely the stars' tennis-balls, struck and bandied
Which way please them.
1623 *The Duchess of Malfi*, act 5, sc.4.

Webster, Margaret 1905–72

US actress and director.

22 You must not wear your heart on your sleeve for daws to pick at.
c.1940 To Tennessee Williams on the out-of-town closing of his first professionally produced play *Battle of Angels*. Recalled by Williams in the *New York Times*, 17 Mar 1957.
➤ *See Shakespeare 758:50.*

Wei Jingsheng 1950–

Chinese dissident, considered one of the fathers of the Chinese dissident movement, released in 1993 after serving a 14-year jail sentence for his role in the Democracy Wall Movement. He was arrested again in April 1994 and was released in 1997.

23 No leader deserves the unconditional confidence of his people.
1979 Part of a statement appearing on Democracy Wall under the pseudonym 'Voice of Today'. Quoted in Uli Franz *Deng Xiaoping* (1988).

Weighell, Sidney 1922–2002

British trade union leader. He was General Secretary of the National Union of Railwaymen (1975–83) and a member of the Trades Union General Council (1975–83). He joined the LNER in 1938 and became a full-time union official in 1954.

24 If you…believe in the philosophy of the pig trough—that those with the biggest snouts should get the largest share—I reject it.
1978 Labour Party Conference, 10 Apr.

25 I don't see how we can talk with Mrs Thatcher… I will say to the lads, 'Come on, get your snouts in the trough.'
1979 Speech, London, 10 Apr.

Weil, Simone 1909–43

French philosophical writer and mystic, who undertook manual labour to experience working-class life and served as a Republican in the Spanish Civil War (1936). A mystic Catholic who distrusted organized religion, she worked for the Free French in London, and starved herself to death in sympathy with the victims of war. Her works include *La Pesanteur et la Grâce* (*Gravity and Grace*, 1947) and *Attente de Dieu* (*Waiting for God*, 1950).

26 To us, men of the West, a very strange thing happened at the turn of the century; without noticing it, we lost science, or at least the thing that had been called by that name for the last four centuries. What we now have in place of it is something different, radically different, and we don't know what it is. Nobody knows what it is.
1941 *On Science, Necessity and the Love of God*, 'Classical Science and After' (translated by Richard Rees, 1968).

27 Science is voiceless; it is the scientists who talk.
1941 *On Science, Necessity and the Love of God* (translated by Richard Rees, 1968).

28 The future is made of the same stuff as the present.
1941 *On Science, Necessity, and the Love of God* (translated by Richard Rees, 1968).

29 *Tous les péchés sont des tentatives pour combler des vides.*
All sins are attempts to fill voids.
La Pesanteur et la Grâce (published 1947).

30 The beauty of the world is almost the only way by which we can allow God to penetrate us…the beauty of the world is the commonest, easiest and most natural way of approach.
Attente de Dieu (translated as *Waiting for God*, 1951).

31 Bourgeois society is infected by monomania: the monomania of accounting. For it, the only thing that has value is what can be counted in francs and centimes. It never hesitates to sacrifice human life to figures which look well on paper, such as national budgets or industrial balance sheets.
La condition ouvrière, 'La rationalisation' (published 1951).

32 One might lay down as a postulate: All conceptions of God which are incompatible with the movement of pure charity are false.
Letter to a Priest (translated by A F Wills, published 1954).

33 The word 'revolution' is a word for which you kill, for which you die, for which you send the labouring masses to their deaths; but which does not contain any content.
Oppression and Liberty (translated by A F Wills and J Petrie, published 1958).

Weinberger, Caspar Willard 1917–

American politician. A former lawyer, he was state finance director of California when Ronald Reagan was Governor (1968–9), served in the administrations of Presidents Nixon and Ford, then became Secretary of Defense under President Reagan (1981–87).

34 Wishful thinking is equally as effective for arms control as it is for birth control.
1986 In *USA Today*, 6 Oct.

Weizsäcker, Richard Freiherr, Baron von 1920–

German politician. A member of the conservative Christian Democratic Union, he served as CDU Deputy Chairman (1972–9) and Mayor of West Berlin (1981–4) until being elected President of the Federal Republic of Germany (1984, re-elected 1989). In 1990 he signed the treaty that reunited East and West Germany. He served as President of Germany from 1990 to 1994.

35 There were many ways of not burdening one's conscience, of shunning responsibility, looking away, keeping silent. When the unspeakable truth of the Holocaust became known at the end of the war, all too many of us claimed that they had not known anything about it, or even suspected anything… Whoever refuses to remember the inhumanity is prone to new risks of infection… Seeking to forget makes exile all the longer; the secret of redemption lies in remembrance.
1985 On the 40th anniversary of the end of World War II, in the *New York Times*, 12 May.

Weldon, Fay *originally* ***Franklin Birkinshaw*** 1931–

English writer, an advertising copywriter before turning to novels and screenplays. She is best known for her fiction, which deal with recurring themes, including the nature of women's sexuality and experience in a patriarchal world. Her works include *Female Friends* (1974), *The Life and Loves of a She-Devil* (1983), *The Cloning of Joanna May* (1989) and *The Bulgari Connection* (2001).

36 Go to work on an egg.
1957 Advertising slogan for the British Egg Marketing Board.

37 The Life and Loves of a She-Devil.
1983 Title of novel.

38 It will do us no harm to retool our imaginations. AIDS is a major revolution in how writers write… Our heroes and heroines will have to change. The only thing AIDS is good for is fiction. Writers will have to think differently.
1987 In *The Guardian*, 7 Mar.

39 Pride comes before a fall; a sense of sisterhood with sad experience.
1987 *The Heart of the Country*, 'Chomp, Chomp, Grittle-Grax, Gone!'

40 Christianity is really a man's religion: there's not much in it for women except docility, obedience, who-sweeps-the-room-as-for-thy-cause, downcast eyes and death in childbirth. For the men it's better: all power and money and fine robes, the burning of the heretics—fun, fun, fun!—and the Inquisition fulminating from the pulpit.
1987 *The Heart of the Country*, 'Love Your Enemy'.

41 To journey is better than to arrive—or so say those who have already arrived.
1987 *The Heart of the Country*, 'Doing It All Wrong'.

42 It's full time work being on social security. They really make you earn your living.
1987 *The Heart of the Country*, 'Driven Mad'.

43 Men are so romantic, don't you think? They look for a perfect partner when what they should be looking for is perfect love.
1987 In the *Sunday Times*, 6 Sep.

44 I didn't set out to be a feminist writer. I just look at the sheep out of the window and watch their behaviour.
1989 In the *Observer*, 30 Apr.

45 I think if you had ever written a book you were absolutely pleased with, you'd never write another. The same probably goes for having children.
1991 In *The Guardian*, 28 Nov.

46 Nature's only interest is in having you procreate, then it throws you away.
1992 In *The Guardian*, 15 Jan.

Welland, Colin 1934–

British actor and writer. Best known for his screenplays for *Yanks* (1979, with Walter Bernstein) and *Chariots of Fire* (1981), for the second of which he won an Academy Award.

47 The British are coming.
1982 At the Academy Award ceremony in Los Angeles, 29 Mar.

Welles, (George) Orson 1915–85

US director and actor. He is best known for his radio production of H G Wells's *The War of the Worlds* (1938), and for the films *Citizen Kane* (1941), a masterpiece of cinema technique, and his adaptation of Booth Tarkington's *The Magnificent Ambersons* (1942).

48 In Italy for thirty years under the Borgias they had warfare, terror, murder, bloodshed—they produced Michelangelo, Leonardo da Vinci and the Renaissance. In Switzerland they had brotherly love, five hundred years of democracy and peace, and what did they produce? The cuckoo clock.
1949 Harry Lime's speech to Holly Martins as he leaves the great wheel, *The Third Man*. This phrase was added to the script by Welles who played Harry Lime.

49 A film is never really good unless the camera is an eye in the head of a poet.
1958 'Un ruban de rêves' in *L'Express*, 5 Jun. Reprinted in English in *International Film Annual*, no.2.

50 A typewriter needs only paper; a camera uses film, requires subsidiary equipment by the truckload and several hundreds of technicians. That is always the central fact about the filmmaker as opposed to any other artist: he can never afford his own tools.
1958 Letter in the *New Statesman*.

51 I started at the top and worked down.
Attributed.

52 Every actor in his heart believes everything bad that's printed about him.
Attributed.

Wellington, Arthur Wellesley, 1st Duke of 1769–1852

British soldier and statesman. He was made a duke after his defeat of French forces in the Peninsular War, and took command of British forces again after Napoleon's escape from Elba in 1815. After victory at Waterloo, he went into politics, becoming Prime Minister in 1828. His dispatches and other papers were published in three series (1834–80).

53 As Lord Chesterfield said of the generals of his day, 'I only hope that when the enemy reads the list of their names, he trembles as I do'.
1810 Letter, 29 Aug, during the Peninsular War. Collected in *Supplementary Despatches* (1860).

54 We have in the service the scum of the earth as common soldiers.
1813 Comment 21 Jun, before the Battle of Vitoria. Quoted in Elizabeth Longford *Wellington: The Years of the Sword*, p.321.

55 Hard pounding this, gentlemen, let's see who will pound longest.
1815 At the Battle of Waterloo, 18 Jun. Quoted in Sir Walter Scott *Paul's Letters* (1816), letter 8.

56 Up guards and at them!
1815 Attributed shout at the Battle of Waterloo, 18 Jun.

57 It has been a damned serious business—Blucher and I have lost 30,000 men. It has been a damned nice thing—the nearest run thing you ever saw in your life... By God! I don't think it would have done if I had not been there!
1815 Comment to Thomas Creevey at Brussels, 19 Jun, the day after the Battle of Waterloo. Quoted in Sir Thomas Creevey *The Creevey Papers* (edited by Sir H Maxwell, 1904), p.142.

58 Napoleon did not manoeuvre at all. He just moved forward in the old style, in columns, and was driven off in the old style.
1815 Letter to Sir William Beresford, 2 Jul.

59 Next to a battle lost, the greatest misery is a battle gained.
1815 Of the Battle of Waterloo. Comment to Lady Shelley, Jul. Quoted in Richard Edgecumbe (ed) *The Diary of Frances, Lady Shelley* (1912), vol.1, ch.9, p.102.

60 The history of a battle is not unlike the history of a ball. Some individuals may recollect all the little events of which the great result is the battle won or lost; but no individual can recollect the order in which, or the exact moment at which, they occurred, which makes all the difference.
1815 Of the Battle of Waterloo. Letter, 8 Aug.

61 Beginning reform is beginning revolution.
1830 Attributed remark, 7 Nov.

62 I used to say of him that his presence on the field made the difference of 40,000 men.
1831 Of Napoleon. Comment, 2 Nov. Quoted in Philip Henry Stanhope *Notes of Conversations with the Duke of Wellington* (1888).

63 Our course in the House of Lords ought to be very firm and uncompromising but moderate…an example of what has since been called the politics of the extreme centre.
1832 Conduct of Opposition speech, Dec.

64 There is no such thing as a little war for a great nation.
1838 House of Lords, 16 Jan.

65 All the business of war, and indeed all the business of life, is to endeavour to find out what you don't know by what you do; that's what I call 'guessing what was at the other side of the hill'.
Quoted in John Wilson Croker *The Croker Papers* (edited by Bernard Pool, 1885), vol.3, ch.28.

66 Don't quote Latin; say what you have to say, and then sit down.
Advice to a new member of Parliament.

67 The Battle of Waterloo was won on the playing fields of Eton.
Attributed, and probably apocryphal. Quoted in Count Charles de Montalembert *De l'Avenir politique de l'Angleterre* (1856), ch.10: 'C'est ici qu'a été gagné la bataille de Waterloo'.

68 There is no mistake; there has been no mistake, and there shall be no mistake.
Quoted in William Fraser *Words on Wellington* (1889).

69 Publish and be damned.
To the publisher of the *Memoirs* of the courtesan Hariette Wilson, attempting blackmail. Attributed.

70 If you believe that, you'll believe anything.
Attributed.

Wells, H(erbert) G(eorge) 1866–1946

English writer and Fabian, best known for his scientific fantasies *The Time Machine* (1895) and *The War of the Worlds* (1898). He also wrote popular comic novels, notably *Kipps* (1905) and *The History of Mr Polly* (1910), and socio-political works on science and world peace (*The Outline of History*, 1920 and *The Work, Wealth and Happiness of Mankind*, 1931).

71 He was a practical electrician but fond of whisky, a heavy, red-haired brute with irregular teeth. He doubted the existence of the Deity but accepted Carnot's cycle, and he had read Shakespeare and found him weak in chemistry.
1894 'The Lord of the Dynamos'.

72 Bah! the thing is not a nose at all, but a bit of primordial chaos clapped on to my face.
1895 *Select Conversations with an Uncle*, 'The Man with a Nose'.

73 Yet, across the gulf of space, minds that are to our minds as ours are to the beasts that perish, intellects vast and cool and unsympathetic, regarded this earth with envious eyes, and slowly and surely drew their plans against us.
1898 *The War of the Worlds*, bk.1, ch.1.

74 At times I suffer from the strangest sense of detachment from myself and the world about me; I seem to watch it all from the outside, from somewhere inconceivably remote, out of time, out of space, out of the stress and tragedy of it all.
1898 *The War of the Worlds*, bk.1, ch.7.

75 The Social Contract is nothing more or less than a vast conspiracy of human beings to lie to and humbug themselves and one another for the general Good. Lies are the mortar that bind the savage individual man into the social masonry.
1900 *Love and Mrs Lewisham*, ch.23.

76 Notice the smug suppressions of his face. In his mouth are Lies in the shape of false teeth.
1900 *Love and Mrs Lewisham*, ch.23.

77 In the country of the blind, the one-eyed man is king.
1904 'The Country of the Blind', collected in *The Country of the Blind and Other Stories* (1911).

78 Of course we can Learn even from Novels, Nace Novels that is, but it isn't the same thing as serious reading.
1905 *Kipps*, bk.2, ch.2.

79 He found that a fork in his inexperienced hand was an instrument of chase rather than capture.
1905 *Kipps*, bk.2, ch.7.

80 'I expect,' he said, 'I was thinking jest what a Rum Go everything is.'
1905 *Kipps*, bk.3, ch.3.

81 'You're a Christian?' 'Church of England,' said Mr Polly. 'Mm,' said the employer, a little checked. 'For good all round business work, I should have preferred a Baptist.'
1909 *The History of Mr Polly*, ch.3, pt.2.

82 Arson, after all, is an artificial crime… A large number of houses deserve to be burnt.
1909 *The History of Mr Polly*, ch.10, pt.1.

83 Once they heard someone call for 'Snooks'. 'I always thought that name was invented by novelists,' said Miss Winchelsea. 'Fancy! Snooks. I wonder which is Mr. Snooks?' Finally they picked out a stout and resolute little man in a large check suit. 'If he isn't Snooks, he ought to be,' said Miss Winchelsea.
1913 *Tales of Life and Adventure*, 'Miss Winchelsea's Heart'.

84 The War that will End War.
1914 Title of book.

85 Moral indignation is jealousy with a halo.
1914 *The Wife of Sir Isaac Harman*, ch.9.

86 The uglier a man's legs are, the better he plays golf. It's almost a law.
1915 *Bealby*.

87 He had the face of a saint, but he had rendered this generally acceptable by growing side-whiskers.
1915 'The Story of The Last Trump'.

88 Cynicism is humour in ill-health.
1915 'The Story of The Last Trump'.

89 Human history becomes more and more a race between education and catastrophe.
1920 *The Outline of History*, vol.2, ch.41.

90 Now it is on the whole more convenient to keep history and theology apart.
1922 *A Short History of the World*, ch.37.

91 I am reported to be 'pessimistic' about broadcasting… [The] truth is that I have anticipated its complete disappearance—confident that the unfortunate people, who must now subdue themselves to 'listening-in', will soon find a better pastime for their leisure.
1928 *The Way the World is Going*.

92 In England we have come to rely upon a comfortable time-lag of fifty years or a century intervening between the perception that something ought to be done and a serious attempt to do it.

1931 *The Work, Wealth and Happiness of Mankind*, ch.2.

93 The Shape of Things to Come.
1933 Title of book.

94 If his thinking has been sound, then this world is at the end of its tether. The end of everything we call life is close at hand and cannot be evaded.
1945 *Mind at the End of Its Tether*, ch.1.

Welsh, Irvine 1958–

Scottish writer. He scored a major critical success with his first novel, *Trainspotting* (1993, filmed 1995).

95 I grew up in what was not so much a family as a genetic disaster.
1995 *Marabou Stork Nightmares*, ch.2.

96 A symbol of all that's perfectly hideous about Scotland
1996 On the poet Hugh MacDiarmid. In *Scotland on Sunday*, 28 Jan.

97 There's fuck-all to say about my books other than what's written in them.
Quoted in Annalena McAfee *Lives and Works: Profiles of Leading Novelists, Poets and Playwrights* (2002).

Welty, Eudora 1909–2001

US novelist and short-story writer. She wrote five novels, set in her native Mississippi, and several collections of short stories, issued as *Collected Stories* (1981).

98 I have been told, both in approval and accusation, that I seem to love all my characters. What I do in writing of any character is to try to enter into the mind, heart and skin of a human being who is not myself. Whether this happens to be a man or a woman, old or young, with skin black or white, the primary challenge lies in making the jump itself. It is the act of a writer's imagination that I set most high.
1981 *The Collected Stories of Eudora Welty*, preface.

99 It had been startling and disappointing to me to find out that story books had been written by *people*, that books were not natural wonders, coming up themselves like green grass.
1984 *One Writer's Beginnings*, I.'Listening'.

1 The events in our lives happen in a sequence in time, but in their significance to ourselves they find their own order, a timetable not necessarily—perhaps not possibly—chronological... It is the continuous thread of revelation.
1984 *One Writer's Beginnings*, II.'Learning to See'.

2 A sheltered life can be a daring life as well. For all serious daring starts from within.
1984 *One Writer's Beginnings*, III.'Finding a Voice'.

Wenger, Arsène 1949–

French footballer and football manager. He has been manager of Arsenal since 1996.

3 A football team is like a beautiful woman. When you do not tell her so, she forgets she is beautiful.
2002 In *The Times*, 28 Dec.

Wentworth, Peter 1530–96

English parliamentarian. He was a prominent Puritan in the reign of Elizabeth I, to whom he presented challenges on the issues of religion and royal succession. He supported the liberties of parliament against encroachments by Elizabeth I. His speech to Parliament in 1576 was examined by the Star Chamber and he was sent to the Tower of London for it. He was imprisoned twice more, and it is thought he never regained his freedom the second time.

4 In this House, which is termed a place of free speech, there is nothing so necessary for the preservation of the Prince and State as free speech; and without it, it is a scorn and a mockery to call it a Parliament House, for in truth it is none but a very school of flattery and dissimulation, and so fit a place to serve the devil and his angels in, and not to glorify God and benefit the Commonwealth.
1576 House of Commons, 8 Feb.

Wentworth, William Charles 1790–1872

Statesman and explorer, born aboard a convict ship on which his mother was being transported for theft. One of the first to explore successfully beyond the Blue Mountains, he established the first Australian newspaper and was one of the founders of Sydney University. His *Australasia* (1823) was the first book of verse by a native-born Australian.

5 Illustrious Cook, Columbus of our shore,
To whom was left this unknown world t'explore,
Its untraced bounds on faithful chart to mark,
And leave a light where all before was dark.
1823 *Australasia*.

Werefkin, Marianne 1860–1938

Russian-born painter who emigrated to Germany just before 1900. She was a founding member of the Blaue Reiter group in Munich.

6 Art is not made only one way, art is a point of view... Rembrandt in our days would be Rembrandt again, because the work of the master is his self. But in order to be Rembrandt in our days he would have used new ways that would give a new culture.
1902 *Lettres à un Inconnu* (1901–05). Translated by Mara R Witzling (ed) in *Voicing Our Visions: Writings by Women Artists* (1992).

7 There is no history of art—there is the history of artists.
1905 *Lettres à un Inconnu* (1901–05). Translated by Mara R Witzling (ed) in *Voicing Our Visions: Writings by Women Artists* (1992).

Wesker, Arnold 1932–

English playwright.

8 And then I saw the menu... It said 'Chips with everything'. Chips with every damn thing. You breed babies and you eat chips with everything.
1962 *Chips with Everything* act 1, sc.2

Wesley, Charles 1707–88

English Methodist hymn writer and preacher, brother of John Wesley.

9 Long my imprisoned spirit lay
Fast bound in sin and nature's night;
Thine eye diffused a quickening ray—
I woke, the dungeon flamed with light,
My chains fell off, my heart was free,

I rose, went forth, and followed thee.
1738 Hymn. 'And Can it Be'.

10 Hark! how all the welkin rings,
Glory to the King of kings.
Peace on earth and mercy mild,
God and sinners reconciled.
1739 'Hymn for Christmas'. In *Hymns and Sacred Poems*. The first two lines were changed to 'Hark! the herald-angels sing/ Glory to the new born king' in Whitfield's *Hymns for Social Worship* (1753).

11 Jesu, lover of my soul,
Let me to thy bosom fly,
While the nearer waters roll,
While the tempest still is high;
Hide me, O my Saviour, hide,
Till the storm of life is past;
Safe into the haven guide,
O receive my soul at last.
1740 'In Temptation', collected in *Hymns and Sacred Poems*.

12 Gentle Jesus, meek and mild,
Look upon a little child;
Pity my simplicity,
Suffer me to come to thee.
1742 'Gentle Jesus', collected in *Hymns and Sacred Poems*.

13 Rejoice, the Lord is King!
Your Lord and King adore;
Mortals, give thanks and sing,
And triumph evermore:
Lift up your heart, lift up your voice;
Rejoice, again, I say rejoice.
1746 'Rejoice, the Lord is King'. In *Hymns for our Lord's Resurrection*.

14 Love divine, all loves excelling,
Joy of heav'n, to earth come down,
Fix in us thy humble dwelling,
All thy faithful mercies crown.
Jesu, thou art all compassion,
Pure unbounded love thou art;
Visit us with thy salvation,
Enter every trembling heart.
1747 'Love Divine', collected in *Hymns for those that seek…Redemption*.

15 Forth in thy name, O Lord, I go,
My daily labour to pursue,
Thee, only thee, resolved to know,
In all I think or speak or do.
1749 'Forth in Thy Name', collected in *Hymns and Sacred Poems*.

16 Lo! He comes with clouds descending,
Once for favoured sinners slain;
Thousand thousand Saints attending
Swell the triumph of His train.
1758 'Lo! He Comes'. In *Hymns of Intercession for all Mankind*.

Wesley, John 1703–91

English evangelist, preacher and writer. Although he himself remained loyal to the Church of England, he is recognized as the principal founder of Methodism. He published his *Rules* for the Methodist Societies in 1743.

17 I felt my heart strangely warmed. I felt I did trust in Christ, Christ alone for salvation; and an assurance was given me that he had taken away *my* sins, even *mine*, and saved *me* from the law of sin and death.
1738 Journal entry, 24 May.

18 Thou hidden love of God, whose height,
Whose depth unfathomed no man knows,
I see from far thy beauteous light,
Only I sigh for thy repose.
1738 *A Collection of Psalms and Hymns*, 'Divine Love'.

19 I look upon all the world as my parish.
1739 Journal entry, 11 Jun.

20 Do all the good you can
By all the means you can
In all the ways you can
In all the places you can
To all the people you can
As long as ever you can.
1743 'Rules of Conduct'.

21 Lord, let me not live to be useless!
1763 Journal entry, 22 Dec.

22 Sure a more consummate coxcomb never saw the sun! How amazingly full of himself! Whatever he speaks, he pronounces as an oracle.
1770 Of Rousseau. Journal entry, 3 Feb.

23 I have none of the infirmities of old age, and have lost several I had in my youth. The grand cause is, the good pleasure of God, who does whatever pleases him. The chief means are: 1. My constantly rising at four, for about fifty years. 2. My generally preaching at five in the morning; one of the most healthy exercises in the world. 3. My never travelling less, by sea or land, than four thousand five hundred miles in a year.
1774 Journal entry, 28 Jun.

24 I spent two hours with that great man, Dr Johnson, who is sinking into the grave by a gentle decay.
1783 Journal entry, 18 Dec.

25 The best of all is, God is with us!
1791 Quoted in *John Wesley's Journal*, edited by Robert Backhouse (1993), p.256.

26 Beware you be not swallowed up in books! An ounce of love is worth a pound of knowledge.
Quoted in R Southey *Life of Wesley* (1820), ch.16.

West, Benjamin 1738–1820

US painter who spent most of his working life in England.

27 Always remember, sir, that light and shadow never stand still.
Advice to the young John Constable, attributed in C R Leslie *Memoirs of the Life of John Constable* (1845).

West, Mae 1893–1980

US vaudeville and film actress born in Brooklyn, New York. She wrote many of the plays she starred in, including *Sex* (1929) and *Diamond Lil* (1928) later filmed as *She Done Him Wrong* (1933). Other films included *I'm No Angel* (1933) and *My Little Chickadee* (1940).

28 'Goodness what beautiful diamonds!'
'Goodness had nothing to do with it.'
1932 *Night After Night* (screenplay by Vincent Lawrence).

29 Why don't you come up sometime, see me?
1933 As Lou in *She Done Him Wrong*. The line is popularly rendered 'Come up and see me sometime.'

30 When I'm good I'm very very good, but when I'm bad I'm better.
1933 *I'm No Angel.*

31 Beulah, peel me a grape.
1933 *I'm No Angel.*

32 A man has one hundred dollars and you leave him with two dollars, that's subtraction.
1940 Line spoken in *My Little Chickadee.*

33 Lieutenant, is that your sword, or are you just glad to see me?
1944 Ad-libbed when her stage lover in *Catherine Was Great* became entangled with his sword scabbard as he attempted to embrace her. Attributed.

34 Catherine had three hundred lovers. I did the best I could do in a couple of hours.
1944 Curtain speech at the end of her play *Catherine Was Great.* Attributed.

35 I've been in Who's Who and I know what's what, but it's the first time I ever made the dictionary.
Reputedly said on learning that a life jacket was to be named after her.

36 It isn't what I do, but how I do it.
It isn't what I say, but how I say it—
And how I look when I do and say it.
Attributed.

West, Nathanael *pseudonym of* ***Nathan Wallenstein Weinstein*** 1903–40

US novelist, who lived for two years in Paris. After he wrote his most famous novel *Miss Lonelyhearts*, he spent his last five years writing scripts for a Hollywood film studio, which provided the material for a final masterpiece, *The Day of the Locust* (1939, filmed 1975).

37 Prayers for the condemned man will be offered on an adding machine. Numbers constitute the only universal language.
1933 *Miss Lonelyhearts.*

West, Dame Rebecca *formerly* ***Cecily Isabel Fairfield*** 1892–1983

Anglo-Irish novelist, journalist, biographer and critic. She trained for the stage but her involvement with the suffragettes led her into journalism, and her studies arising out of the Nuremberg war trials include *The Meaning of Treason* (1947) and *A Train of Powder* (1955). She bore a son to H G Wells during an affair which lasted 10 years.

38 Women know the damnation of charity because the habit of civilisation has always been to throw them cheap alms rather than give them good wages.
1912 'The Personal Service Association: Work for Idle Hands to Do', in *The Clarion*, 13 Dec.

39 Antifeminists, from Chesterton down to Dr Lionel Tayler, want women to specialise in virtue. While men are rolling round the world having murderous and otherwise sinful adventures of an enjoyable nature, in commerce, exploration or art, women are to stay at home earning the promotion of the human race to a better world.
1912 'The Personal Service Association: Work for Idle Hands to Do', in *The Clarion*, 13 Dec.

40 I saw in my own education some of the things which eat the power out of women.
1913 'Training in Truculence: The Working Women's College', in *The Clarion*, 14 Feb.

41 We have asked men for votes, they have given us advice. At present they are also giving us abuse.
1913 'The Sex War: Disjointed Thoughts on Men', in *The Clarion*, 18 Apr.

42 I have horrible nightmares of Sir Almwroth Wright's limp sentences wandering through the arid desert of his mind looking for dropped punctuation marks.
1913 'Lynch Law: The Tragedy of Ignorance', in *The Clarion*, 17 Oct. Almwroth Wright was one of the most vocal opponents of women's suffrage.

43 Who is there in that lot one would want as a father, except perhaps Mrs Thatcher? That choice would be irregular but safe.
1982 Of British Prime Ministers. *1900*, introduction.

44 There is, of course, no reason for the existence of the male sex except that one sometimes needs help with moving the piano.
Attributed.

Wharton, Edith Newbold *née* ***Jones*** 1861–1937

US novelist. She wrote more than 50 books in all, but is best known for her sophisticated novels of manners, which include *The House of Mirth* (1905) and *The Age of Innocence* (1920).

45 I despair of the Republic!... What a horror it is for a whole nation to be developing without a sense of beauty, and eating bananas for breakfast.
1904 On the US. Letter to Sara Norton, 19 Aug.

46 If I were shabby no one would have me: a woman is asked out as much for her clothes as for herself.
1905 *The House of Mirth*, bk.1, ch.1.

47 She was like a disembodied spirit who took up a great deal of room.
1905 *The House of Mirth*, bk.1, ch.2.

48 Of course, being fatally poor and dingy, it was wise of Gerty to have taken up philanthropy and symphony concerts.
1905 *The House of Mirth*, bk.1, ch.8.

49 Miss Farish, who was accustomed, in the way of happiness, to such scant light as shone through the cracks of other people's lives.
1905 *The House of Mirth*, bk.1, ch.14.

50 She keeps on being Queenly in her own room, with the door shut.
1905 *The House of Mirth*, bk.2, ch.1.

51 Paying for what she doesn't get rankles so dreadfully with Louisa; I can't make her see that it's one of the preliminary steps to getting what you haven't paid for.
1905 *The House of Mirth*, bk.2, ch.2.

52 Almost everyone in the neighbourhood had 'troubles', frankly localized and specified; but only the chosen had 'complications'. To have them was in itself a distinction, though it was also, in most cases, a death warrant. People struggled on for years with 'troubles', but they almost always succumbed to 'complications'.
1911 *Ethan Frome*, ch.7.

53 Mrs Ballinger is one of the ladies who pursue Culture in bands, as though it were dangerous to meet it alone.
1916 *Xingu and Other Stories*, 'Xingu'.

54 An unalterable and unquestioned law of the musical world required that the German text of French operas sung by Swedish artists should be translated into Italian for the clearer understanding of English speaking audiences.
1920 *The Age of Innocence*, bk.1, ch.1.

55 What can you expect of a girl who was allowed to wear black satin at her coming-out ball?
1920 *The Age of Innocence*, bk.1, ch.5.

56 Blessed are the pure in heart for they have so much more to talk about.
1932 In *John O'London's Weekly*, 10 Apr.

57 There is no such thing as old age, there is only sorrow.
1934 *A Backward Glance*, 'A First Word'.

Whately, Richard 1787–1863

English scholar and prelate, Archbishop of Dublin (1831), writer of treatises on logic and rhetoric. A founder of the Broad Church party, he supported Catholic emancipation and rejected sectarianism, but his caustic wit and outspokenness made him unpopular.

58 Preach not because you have to say something, but because you have something to say.
1854 *Apophthegms*.

59 Happiness is no laughing matter.
1854 *Apophthegms*.

Whistler, James (Abbott) McNeill 1834–1903

US artist, who moved to Paris and later London, where he was controversially received. He is best known for his 'nocturnes', including *Old Battersea Bridge* (1872–5, Tate, London), and the portrait of his mother (*The Artist's Mother*, 1871–2, Louvre, Paris).

60 I am not arguing with you—I am telling you.
1890 *The Gentle Art of Making Enemies*.

61 A picture is finished when all trace of the means used to bring about the end has disappeared.
1890 *The Gentle Art of Making Enemies*.

62 A life passed among pictures makes not a painter—else the policeman in the National Gallery might assert himself.
1890 *The Gentle Art of Making Enemies*.

63 To say to the painter, that Nature is to be taken as she is, is to say to the player, that he may sit on the piano.
1890 *The Gentle Art of Making Enemies*.

64 The imitator is a poor kind of creature. If the man who paints only the tree, or a flower, or other surface he sees before him were an artist, the king of artists would be the photographer.
1890 *The Gentle Art of Making Enemies*.

65 Art should be independent of all clap-trap—should stand alone, and appeal to the artistic sense of eye or ear, without confounding this with emotions entirely foreign to it, as devotion, pity, love, patriotism and the like. All these have no kind of concern with it; and that is why I insist on calling my works 'arrangements' and 'harmonies'.
1890 *The Gentle Art of Making Enemies*.

66 Poor lawyers, like poor paintings, are dear at any price.
On the cost and quality of some of the lawyers he had hired. Quoted in Arthur Jerome Eddy *Recollections and Impressions of J.A.M. Whistler* (1903).

Whitbread, Samuel 1758–1815

English radical Whig politician, founder of the famous brewing firm. The intimate friend of Fox, under Pitt he was Leader of the Opposition, and in 1805 headed the attack on the treasurer of the navy, Viscount Melville.

67 The nation suspects that the regular ministerial majorities in Parliament are bought, and that the Crown has made a purchase of the House with the money of the people. Hence the ready, tame and servile compliance to every royal verdict issued by Lord North… It is almost universally believed that this debt has been contracted in corrupting the representatives of the people.
1777 House of Commons, 16 Apr.

68 In a political point of view, nothing can possibly afford greater stability to a popular Government than the education of the people.
1807 House of Commons, 19 Feb.

White, Andrew Dickson 1832–1918

US educationalist. President of Cornell University.

69 I will not permit thirty men to travel four hundred miles to agitate a bag of wind.
On refusing permission for a team from Cornell University to visit Michigan to play a game of American football. Quoted in D Wallechinsky *The People's Almanac* (1975).

White, Edmund 1940–

US writer. His sensitive assessments of gay life have appeared in novels including *A Boy's Own Story* (1982) and *The Beautiful Room Is Empty* (1988), as well as in his essays.

70 In fact, they are the classic scapegoats. Our old fears about our sissiness, still with us though masked by the new macho fascism, are now located, isolated, quarantined through our persecution of the transvestite.
1980 *States of Desire: Travels in Gay America*, ch.2.

71 Those who believe machismo reeks of violence alone choose to forget it once stood for honor as well.
1980 *States of Desire: Travels in Gay America*, ch.5.

72 The AIDS epidemic has rolled back a big rotting log and revealed all the squirming life underneath it, since it involves, all at once, the main themes of our existence: sex, death, power, money, love, hate, disease and panic. No American phenomenon has been so compelling since the Vietnam War.
1986 'Afterword—AIDS: An American Epidemic', added to later editions of *States of Desire: Travels in Gay America*.

73 Paris is a city where even the most outrageous story of incest and murder is greeted with a verbal shrug: 'Mais c'est normal!'
2001 In *The Flâneur*.

White, E(lwyn) B(rooks) 1899–1985

US essayist, children's novelist, poet and parodist. He was closely associated with the rise and development of the *New Yorker* magazine.

74 MOTHER: It's broccoli, dear.
CHILD: I say it's spinach, and I say the hell with it.
1928 Cartoon caption, in the *New Yorker*, 8 Dec.

75 All poets who, when reading from their own works, experience a choked feeling, are major. For that matter,

all poets who read from their own works are major, whether they choke or not.
1939 *Quo Vadimus?*, 'How To Tell A Major Poet From A Minor Poet'.

76 It is easier for a man to be loyal to his club than to his planet; the by-laws are shorter, and he is personally acquainted with the other members.
1942 *One Man's Meat*, 'One Man's Meat'.

77 The duty of a democracy is to know then what it knows now.
1942 *One Man's Meat*, 'One Man's Meat'.

78 A poet's pleasure is to withhold a little of his meaning, to intensify by mystification. He unzips the veil from beauty, but does not remove it.
1942 *One Man's Meat*, 'Poetry'.

79 Democracy is the recurrent suspicion that more than half the people are right more than half the time.
1944 In the *New Yorker*, 3 Jul.

80 You can see in pantomime the puppets fumbling with their slips of paper…see them pick up their phone…see the noiseless, ceaseless capital of memoranda, in touch with Calcutta, in touch with Reykjavik, and always fooling with something.
1949 On office windows at twilight. *Here Is New York*.

81 I'm less than two months old and I'm tired of living.
1952 Wilbur the pig. *Charlotte's Web*, ch.3.

82 I can surely fool a man. People are not as smart as bugs.
1952 Charlotte. *Charlotte's Web*, ch.10.

83 It was the best place to be, thought Wilbur, this warm delicious cellar, with the garrulous geese, the changing seasons, the heat of the sun, the passage of swallows, the nearness of rats, the sameness of sheep, the love of spiders, the smell of manure, and the glory of everything.
1952 *Charlotte's Web*, ch.22.

84 It is not often that someone comes along who is a true friend and a good writer. Charlotte was both.
1952 *Charlotte's Web*, ch.22.

85 The time not to become a father is eighteen years before a war.
1954 *The Second Tree from the Corner*, 'The Second Tree from the Corner'.

86 Thurber did not write the way a surgeon operates, he wrote the way a child skips rope, the way a mouse waltzes.
1961 In the *New Yorker*, 11 Nov. Tribute to James Thurber.

87 A man who publishes his letters becomes a nudist—nothing shields him from the world's gaze except his bare skin.
1975 Letter to Corona Macheiner, 11 Jun.

88 She would write 8 or 10 words, then draw her gun and shoot them down.
1979 On his wife and fellow editor Katharine S White. *Onward and Upward in the Garden*.

89 Commuter—one who spends his life
In riding to and from his wife;
A man who shaves and takes a train,
And then rides back to shave again.
1982 *Poems and Sketches*, 'The Commuter'.

White, George Malcolm 1920–

US architect, designer of the Capitol, Washington.

90 The fact that you don't buy a teenager new clothes doesn't mean he isn't going to grow.
1987 On the need for a fourth Senate office building. In *Connoisseur*, Apr.

White, Patrick Victor Martindale 1912–90

Australian novelist, born in London, who went to Australia as an infant and settled there after World War II. He received the Nobel prize for literature in 1973, and numerous other awards, particularly for *Voss* (1957).

91 She would imprison the child in her house by the force of love.
1955 *The Tree of Man*, ch.7.

92 So that in the end there were the trees. The boy walking through them with his head drooping as he increased in stature. Putting out shoots of green thought. So that, in the end, there was no end.
1955 *The Tree of Man*, ch.26.

93 The mystery of life is not solved by success, which is an end in itself, but in failure, in perpetual struggle, in becoming.
1957 *Voss*, ch.10.

94 Perhaps true knowledge only comes of death by torture in the country of the mind.
1957 *Voss*, ch.16.

95 There is nothing like a rain of bombs to start one trying to assess one's own achievement.
1958 Essay on his literary career, in *Australian Letters*, 'The Prodigal Son', vol.1, no.3, Apr.

96 In all directions stretched the Great Australian Emptiness, in which the mind is the least of possessions…and the march of material ugliness does not raise a quiver from the average nerves.
It was the exaltation of the 'average' that made me panic most.
1958 Essay on his literary career, in *Australian Letters*, 'The Prodigal Son', vol.1, no.3, Apr.

97 Above all I was determined to prove that the Australian novel is not necessarily the dreary, dun-coloured offspring of journalistic realism.
1958 Essay on his literary career, in *Australian Letters*, 'The Prodigal Son', vol.1, no.3, Apr.

White, Theodore H(arold) 1915–86

US journalist and political commentator. His *The Making of the President, 1960* (1961), with its characteristic reportage style, won a Pulitzer Prize in 1962.

98 Chafing in action when his nature yearned to act, conscious of indignities real and imagined, Johnson went through three years of slow burn.
Of Lyndon B Johnson as John F Kennedy's Vice President. Quoted in Arthur M Schlesinger, Jr *A Thousand Days* (1965).

99 The best time to listen to a politician is when he is on a street corner, in the rain, late at night, when he's exhausted. Then he doesn't lie.
1969 In the *New York Times*, 5 Jan.

1 He was almost a force of nature, like a slumbering volcano, wreathed in clouds, occasionally emitting smoke which soothsayers attempted to interpret.
1969 Of Nelson Rockefeller. *The Making of the President, 1968*.

2 The epitaph on the Kennedy administration became

Camelot—a magic moment in American history, when gallant men danced with beautiful women, when great deeds were done, when artists, writers and poets met at the White House and the barbarians beyond the walls were held back.
1978 *In Search of History.*

3 Eisenhower has…a magic in American politics that is peculiarly his: he makes people happy.
Of Dwight D Eisenhower's appearances during Richard M Nixon's 1960 presidential campaign. Quoted in Michael R Beschloss *Eisenhower* (1990).

White, Thomas 1550–1624

English Puritan.

4 The cause of plagues is sin, if you look to it well; and the cause of sin are plays; therefore the cause of plagues are plays.
Attributed.

Whitehead, Alfred North 1861–1947

English mathematician and philosopher. He taught at Imperial College London and later at Harvard University. With his former pupil Bertrand Russell he wrote *Principia Mathematica* (1910–13).

5 It is a safe rule to apply that, when a mathematical or philosophical author writes with a misty profundity, he is talking nonsense.
1911 *Introduction to Mathematics.*

6 Knowledge does not keep any better than fish.
1916 'The Aims of Education; a plea for reform', address as president of the Mathematical Association.

7 Familiar things happen, and mankind does not bother about them. It requires a very unusual mind to undertake the analysis of the obvious.
1925 *Science and the Modern World.*

8 Religion is something which stands beyond, behind, and within the passing flux of immediate things; something which is real, and yet waiting to be realized; something which is a remote possibility, and yet the greatest of present facts; something that gives meaning to all that passes, and yet eludes apprehension; something whose possession is the final good, and yet is beyond all reach; something which is the ultimate ideal, and the hopeless quest.
1925 *Science and the Modern World.*

9 The worship of God is not a rule of safety—it is an adventure of the spirit, a flight after the unattainable. The death of religion comes with the repression of the high hope of adventure.
1925 *Science and the Modern World.*

10 Mathematics is thought moving in the sphere of complete abstraction from any particular instance of what it is talking about.
1925 *Science And the Modern World.*

11 Religion is what a man does with his solitariness.
1926 *Religion in the Making.*

12 The safest general characterization of the European philosophical tradition is that it consists of a series of footnotes to Plato.
1929 *Process and Reality*, pt.2, ch.1, section 1.

13 The power of Christianity lies in its revelation in act, of that which Plato divined in theory.
1938 *Adventures of Ideas.*

14 The essence of Christianity is the appeal to the life of Christ as a revelation of the nature of God and of his agency in the world. The record is fragmentary, inconsistent and uncertain… But there can be no doubt as to the elements in the record that have evoked the best in human nature. The Mother, the Child and the bare manger: the lowly man, homeless and self-forgetful, with his message of peace, love and sympathy: the suffering, the agony, the tender words as life ebbed, the final despair: and the whole with the authority of supreme victory.
1938 *Adventures of Ideas.*

15 What is morality in any given time or place? It is what the majority then and there happen to like, and immorality is what they dislike.
1941 Conversation, 30 Aug. Collected in *Dialogues* (1954).

Whitehead, Hal

Canadian marine biologist.

16 'Scientific whaling' is like the prostitution of the profession: using the name of science for a totally bogus purpose.
2004 *New Scientist*, May.

Whitehorn, Katharine 1926–

English journalist.

17 Hats divide generally into three classes: offensive hats, defensive hats, and shrapnel.
1963 *Shouts and Murmurs.*

Whitelaw, William Stephen Ian, 1st Viscount 1918–99

Scottish Conservative politician, Leader of the House of Commons (1970–2), Secretary of State for Northern Ireland (1972–3) and Employment (1973–4) and Home Secretary (1979–83). Loyal to Heath and then Thatcher, he led the House of Lords until 1988.

18 I do not intend to prejudge the past.
1973 On arriving in Ulster for the first time as Secretary of State for Northern Ireland, 2 Dec.

19 He is going round the country stirring up apathy.
1974 Of Harold Wilson during the general election campaign. Attributed.

20 A short, sharp shock.
1979 At the Conservative Party Conference, 10 Oct, on the need for more effective treatment of young offenders.
► *See Gilbert 355:25.*

Whiteman, Paul 1891–1967

US bandleader. A pioneer of 'sweet style' jazz in the 1920s, he recruited such talents as trumpeter Bix Beiderbecke. He developed Gershwin's 'symphonic jazz' experiments, commissioning *Rhapsody in Blue* in 1924.

21 Jazz came to America three hundred years ago in chains.
1926 *Jazz.*

Whiteread, Rachel 1963–

English sculptor. In 1993 she came to prominence when she made a cast of an entire disused house in East London. She won the 1993 Turner Prize.

22 When I visited concentration camps, I was more interested in how people responded to the camps than in the actual places. I watched kids picnicking on the ovens and other people stricken with grief.
2001 From an interview on www.guggenheim.org, 18 Apr.

Whiting, George 1884–1943

US songwriter.

23 When You're All Dressed Up and Have No Place To Go.
1912 Title of song (music by Newton Harding).

Whitlam, (Edward) Gough 1916–

Australian politician, leader of the Labor Party from 1967 and Prime Minister (1972–5). He resigned in 1978 to move into academia. His works include *The Italian Inspiration in English Literature* (1980).

24 The importance of an historical event lies not in what happened but in what later generations believe to have happened.
1973 Speech at Ballarat, Victoria, 3 Dec.

25 I do not mind the Liberals, still less do I mind the Country party, calling me a bastard. In some circumstances, I am only doing my job if they do. But I hope that you will not publicly call me a bastard, as some bastards in the Caucus have.
1974 Speech to the Australian Labor Party, 9 Jun.

26 We may say 'God Save the Queen', because nothing will save the Governor-General… Maintain your rage and your enthusiasm for the election now to be held and until polling day.
1975 On the Governor-General Sir John Kerr's action in dissolving the Australian Parliament, 11 Nov. Whitlam lost the subsequent election.

Whitman, Christine Todd 1947–

US Republican politician, Governor of New Jersey (1994–2001), she is a former freeholder in Somerset County, New Jersey and a former president of the State Board of Public Utilities.

27 The states are the laboratories of democracy.
1995 In the *New York Times*, 29 Jan.

Whitman, Walt(er) 1819–91

US poet. He was editor of the *Brooklyn Eagle* and worked as a nurse during the Civil War. His poetry reflected his mystical faith in democracy and was attacked for indecency because it addressed many taboo subjects. It is collected in *Leaves of Grass* (1855–92).

28 The Americans of all nations at any time upon the earth have probably the fullest poetical nature. The United States themselves are essentially the greatest poem.
1855 *Leaves of Grass*, preface.

29 As soon as histories are properly told there is no more need of romances.
1855 *Leaves of Grass*, preface.

30 I celebrate myself, and sing myself,
And what I assume you shall assume,
For every atom belonging to me as good belongs to you.
1855 *Leaves of Grass*, 'Song of Myself', section 1.

31 All goes onward and outward, nothing collapses,
And to die is different from what any one supposed, and luckier.
1855 *Leaves of Grass*, 'Song of Myself', section 6.

32 I believe a leaf of grass is no less than the journey-work of the stars.
1855 *Leaves of Grass*, 'Song of Myself', section 31.

33 I think I could turn, and live with animals, they are so placid and self-contain'd.
1855 *Leaves of Grass*, 'Song of Myself', section 32.

34 I have said that the soul is not more than the body,
And I have said that the body is not more than the soul,
And nothing, not God, is greater to one than one's self is.
1855 *Leaves of Grass*, 'Song of Myself', section 48.

35 Do I contradict myself?
Very well then I contradict myself,
(I am large, I contain multitudes.)
1855 *Leaves of Grass*, 'Song of Myself', section 51.

36 I too am not a bit tamed, I too am untranslatable,
I sound my barbaric yawp over the roofs of the world.
1855 *Leaves of Grass*, 'Song of Myself', section 52.

37 How beggarly appear arguments before a defiant deed!
1855 Leaves of Grass, 'Broad-Axe Song', later 'Song of the Broad-Axe' (from 1867).

38 If anything is sacred the human body is sacred.
1855 *Leaves of Grass*, 'Children of Adam', 'I Sing the Body Electric', section 8.

39 I do not think seventy years is the time of a man or woman,
Nor that seventy millions of years is the time of a man or woman,
Nor that years will ever stop the existence of me, or any one else.
1855 *Leaves of Grass*, 'Autumn Rivulets', 'Who Learns My Lesson Complete?'

40 Henceforth I whimper no more, postpone no more, need nothing,
Done with indoor complaints, libraries, querulous criticisms,
Strong and content I travel the open road.
1856 *Leaves of Grass*, 'Song of the Open Road', section 1.

41 What can ever be more stately and admirable to me than mast-hemm'd Manhattan?
1856 *Leaves of Grass*, 'Crossing Brooklyn Ferry', section 8.

42 He or she is greatest who contributes the greatest original practical example.
1856 *Leaves of Grass*, 'By Blue Ontario's Shores', section 13.

43 And I will show that nothing can happen more beautiful than death.
1860 *Leaves of Grass*, 'Proto-Leaf', later renamed 'Starting From Paumanok' (from 1867).

44 I hear it was charged against me that I sought to destroy institutions,
But really I am neither for nor against institutions.
1860 *Leaves of Grass*, 'Calamus', 'I Hear It Was Charged Against Me'.

45 Camarado, this is no book,
Who touches this touches a man.
1860 *Leaves of Grass*, 'Songs of Parting', 'So Long!'

46 O Captain! my Captain! our fearful trip is done,
The ship has weather'd every rack, the prize we sought is won,

The port is near, the bells I hear, the people all exulting.
1865 *Leaves of Grass*, 'Memories of President Lincoln', 'O Captain! My Captain!'

47 When lilacs last in the dooryard bloom'd,
And the great star early droop'd in the western sky in the night,
I mourn'd, and yet shall mourn with ever-returning spring.
1865–66 *Leaves of Grass*, 'Memories of President Lincoln', 'When Lilacs Last in the Dooryard Bloom'd', section 1.

48 Come lovely and soothing death,
Undulate round the world, serenely arriving, arriving,
In the day, in the night, to all, to each,
Sooner or later delicate death.
1865–66 *Leaves of Grass*, 'Memories of President Lincoln', 'When Lilacs Last in the Dooryard Bloom'd', section 14.

49 The Past—the dark unfathom'd retrospect!
The teeming gulf—the sleepers and the shadows!
The past! the infinite greatness of the past!
For what is the present after all but a growth out of the past?
1871 *Passage to India*, opening verse.

50 Political democracy, as it exists and practically works in America, with all its threatening evils, supplies a training-school for making first-class men. It is life's gymnasium, not of good only, but of all.
1871 *Democratic Vistas.*

51 In this broad earth of ours,
Amid the measureless grossness and the slag,
Enclosed and safe within its central heart,
Nestles the seed perfection.
1874 *Leaves of Grass*, 'Birds of Passage', 'Song of the Universal', section 1.

52 After you have exhausted what there is in business, politics, conviviality, love, and so on—and found that none of these finally satisfy, or permanently wear—what remains? Nature remains.
1876–77 *Speciman Days*, 'New Themes Entered Upon'.

53 Youth, large, lusty, loving—youth full of grace, force, fascination,
Do you know that Old Age may come after you with equal grace, force, fascination?
1881 *Leaves of Grass*, 'Youth, Day, Old Age and Night', stanza 1.

54 Have you not learn'd great lessons from those who reject you,
and brace themselves against you? or who treat you with
contempt, or dispute the passage with you?
1888 Leaves of Grass, 'Sands at Seventy', 'Stronger Lessons'.

55 No one will get at my verses who insists upon viewing them as a literary performance.
1888 'A Backward Glance O'er Travel'd Roads'.

Whittier, John Greenleaf 1807–92

US poet and abolitionist. A Quaker, he devoted himself to the cause of emancipation. His ballads and sentimental poems, such as 'Barbara Freitchie', which was included in *In War Time* (1864), were extremely popular in their day. His best work is the nostalgic narrative poem, *Snow-Bound* (1866).

56 When the care-wearied man seeks his mother once more,
And the worn matron smiles where the girl smiled before,
What moistens the lip and what brightens the eye?
What calls back the past, like the rich Pumpkin pie?
1844 'The Pumpkin,' stanza 3.

57 When faith is lost, when honor dies,
The man is dead!
1850 'Ichabod', stanza 8.

58 Beneath her torn hat glowed the wealth
Of simple beauty and rustic health.
1854 'Maud Muller', l.3–4.

59 For of all sad words of tongue or pen,
The saddest are these: 'It might have been!'
1854 'Maud Muller', l.105–6.

60 The age is dull and mean. Men creep,
Not walk.
1855 'Lines, Inscribed to Friends Under Arrest for Treason Against the Slave Power', stanza 1.

61 Up from the meadows rich with corn,
Clear in the cool September morn.
1863 'Barbara Frietchie', opening lines.

62 'Shoot, if you must this old grey head,
But spare your country's flag,' she said.
1863 'Barbara Frietchie', l.35–36.

63 Dear Lord and Father of mankind,
Forgive our foolish ways!
Re-clothe us in our rightful mind,
In purer lives thy service find,
In deeper reverence praise
1872 'The Brewing of Soma'.

Whitton, Charlotte 1896–1975

Canadian politician, Mayor of Ottawa (1951–6, 1960–4), the first woman to serve as mayor of a Canadian city.

64 Whatever women do they must do twice as well as men to be thought half so good…luckily, it's not difficult.
1963 In *Canada Month*, Jun.

Whymper, Edward 1840–1911

English wood-engraver and mountaineer. In 1860–9 he conquered several hitherto unscaled peaks of the Alps, including the Matterhorn. He later published several books based on his travels in the Alps and elsewhere.

65 Do nothing in haste, look well to each step, and from the beginning think what may be the end.
1871 *Scrambles Amongst the Alps.*

Widdecombe, Anne 1947–

English Conservative politician and novelist.

66 He has something of the night in him.
1997 Of fellow Conservative Michael Howard. In the *Sunday Times*, (electronic edition) 11 May.

Wiener, Norbert 1894–1964

US academic, who studied mathematics with Bertrand Russell and taught at MIT. His work contributed to the development of the understanding of information systems. He coined the word *cybernetics* to describe the science of feedback control in systems.

67 The automatic machine, whatever we think of any

feelings it may or may not have, is the precise economic equivalent of the slave.
1949 *The Human Use of Human Beings.*

68 The new industrial revolution is a two-edged sword. It may be used for the benefit of humanity, assuming that humanity survives long enough to reach a period in which such a benefit is possible. If, however, we proceed along the clear and obvious lines of our traditional behavior, and follow our traditional worship of progress and the fifth freedom—the freedom to exploit—it is practically certain that we shall have to face a decade or more of ruin and despair.
1949 *The Human Use of Human Beings.*

69 Scientific discovery consists in the interpretation for our own convenience of a system of existence which has been made with no eye to our convenience at all.
1949 *The Human Use of Human Beings.*

Wilberforce, Samuel 1805–73

English prelate, Canon of Winchester, later Dean of Westminster and Bishop of Oxford.

70 If I were a cassowary
On the plains of Timbuctoo,
I would eat a missionary,
Cassock, band, and hymn-book too.
Attributed.

Wilbur, Richard 1921–

US poet. He taught at Harvard and Wesleyan Universities, and wrote a significant body of poems. He also contributed lyrics to Leonard Bernstein's opera, *Candide* (1957).

71 We milk the cow of the world, and as we do
We whisper in her ear, 'You are not true.'
1950 *Ceremony and Other Poems*, 'Epistemology'.

72 Forgive the hero, you who would have died
Gladly with all you knew; he rode that tide
To Ararat; all men are Noah's sons.
1950 *Ceremony and Other Poems*, 'Still, Citizen Sparrow'.

73 Outside the open window
The morning air is all awash with angels.
1956 *Things of This World*, 'Love Calls Us to the Things of This World'.

74 The soul shrinks
From all that it is about to remember,
From the punctual rape of every blessèd day
1956 *Things of This World*, 'Love Calls Us to the Things of This World'.

75 Columbus and his men, they say,
Conveyed the virus hither
Whereby my features rot away
And vital powers wither;
Yet had they not traversed the seas
And come infected back,
Why, think of all the luxuries
That modern life would lack.
1957 'Pangloss's Song', from *Candide*.

76 It is not tricks of sense
But the time's fright within me which distracts
Least fancies into violence
1969 *Walking to Sleep*, 'On the Marginal Way'.

77 All night, this headland
Lunges into the rumpling
Capework of the wind.
1976 *The Mind Reader*, 'Sleepless at Crown Point'.

78 Writing is…waiting for the word that may not be there until next Tuesday.
1987 In the *Los Angeles Times*, 13 Oct.

79 Most women know that sex is good for headaches.
1987 Quoted in the *Observer*, 1 Nov.

Wilcox, Ella Wheeler 1850–1919

US poet who wrote over 30 volumes of sentimental verse. Her temperance poems were collected in *Drops of Water* (1872). *Poems of Passion* (1883) was attacked for its immorality.

80 Laugh, and the world laughs with you;
Weep, and you weep alone;
For the sad old earth must borrow its mirth,
It has trouble enough of its own.
1883 *Poems of Passion*, 'Solitude'.

Wilde, Jane Francesca *née Elgee* 1826–96

Irish Poet and folklorist, mother of Oscar Wilde. She was an ardent nationalist and contributed verse and prose to the *Nation* under the pen name 'Speranza'.

81 'Tis midnight, falls the lamp light dull and sickly
On a pale and anxious crowd,
Through the court, and round the judges thronging thickly,
With prayers they dare not speak aloud—
Two youths, two noble youths, stand prisoners at the bar—
You can see them through the gloom—
In the pride of life and manhood's beauty, there they are
Awaiting their death-doom.
'The Brothers'.

82 Weary men, what reap ye?—Golden corn for the stranger.
What sow ye?—Human corpses that wait for the avenger.
Fainting forms, hunger stricken, what see ye in the offing?
Stately ships to bear our food away, amid the stranger's scoffing.
There's a proud array of soldiers—what do they round your door?
They guard our master's granaries from the thin hands of the poor.
Pale mothers, wherefore weeping? Would to God that we were dead—
Our children swoon before us, and we cannot give them bread.
'The Famine Year'.

Wilde, Oscar Fingal O'Flahertie Wills 1854–1900

Anglo-Irish poet and dramatist, renowned for his wit and flamboyant lifestyle. His works include *The Picture of Dorian Gray* (1891), *Lady Windermere's Fan* (1892), *An Ideal Husband* (1895), *The Importance of Being Earnest* (1895) and *The Ballad of Reading Gaol* (1898). He was ruined by a trial arising from his homosexual relationships.

83 To make a good salad is to be a brilliant diplomatist—the problem is entirely the same in both cases. To know

exactly how much oil one must put with one's vinegar.
1880 *Vera, or The Nihilists*, act 2.

84 I have nothing to declare except my genius.
1882 On passing through US customs on a lecture tour. Quoted in F Harris, *Oscar Wilde* (1918), p.75.

85 Over the piano was printed a notice: 'Please do not shoot the pianist. He is doing his best.'
1883 *Impressions of America: Leadville*.

86 What captivity was to the Jews, exile has been to the Irish: America and American influence have educated them. Their first practical leader is an Irish-American.
1889 Of Charles Stewart Parnell. 'The Two Chiefs of Dunboy: or, an Irish Romance of the Last Century' in *Pall Mall Gazette*, 13 Apr.

87 Books of poetry by young writers are usually promissory notes that are never met. Now and then, however, one comes across a volume that is so far above the average that one can hardly resist the fascinating temptation of recklessly prophesying a fine future for its author. Such a book Mr Yeats's *Wanderings of Oisin* certainly is. Here we find nobility of treatment and nobility of subject-matter, delicacy of poetic instinct and richness of imaginative resource.
1889 In the *Pall Mall Gazette*, 12 Jul.

88 Newspapers have degenerated. They may now be absolutely relied upon.
1889 'The Decay of Lying', first published in the *Nineteenth Century Review*.

89 Art never expresses anything but itself.
1889 'The Decay of Lying', first published in the *Nineteenth Century Review*.

90 After playing Chopin, I feel as if I had been weeping over sins that I had never committed.
1891 *Intentions*, 'The Critic as Artist'.

91 Every great man nowadays has his disciples, and it is always Judas who writes the biography.
1891 *Intentions*, 'The Critic as Artist'.

92 Meredith is a prose Browning, and so is Browning.
1891 *Intentions*, 'The Critic as Artist'.

93 The one duty we owe to history is to rewrite it.
1891 *Intentions*, 'The Critic as Artist'.

94 It is through Art, and through Art only, that we can realise our perfection; through Art, and through Art only, that we can shield ourselves from the sordid perils of actual existence.
1891 *Intentions*, 'The Critic as Artist'.

95 All art is immoral.
1891 *Intentions*, 'The Critic as Artist'.

96 A little sincerity is a dangerous thing, and a great deal of it is absolutely fatal.
1891 *Intentions*, 'The Critic as Artist'.

97 Modern journalism justifies its own existence by the great Darwinian principle of the survival of the vulgarest.
1891 *Intentions*, 'The Critic as Artist'.

98 All that I desire to point out is the general principle that Life imitates Art far more than Art imitates Life.
1891 *Intentions*, 'The Decay of Lying'.

99 There is no such thing as a moral or an immoral book. Books are well written, or badly written.
1891 *The Picture of Dorian Gray*, preface.

1 The nineteenth century dislike of Realism is the rage of Caliban seeing his own face in the glass.
1891 *The Picture of Dorian Gray*, preface.

2 The moral life of man forms part of the subject matter of the artist, but the morality of art consists in the perfect use of an imperfect medium.
1891 *The Picture of Dorian Gray*, preface.

3 There is only one thing in the world worse than being talked about, and that is not being talked about.
1891 *The Picture of Dorian Gray*, ch.1.

4 A man cannot be too careful in the choice of his enemies.
1891 *The Picture of Dorian Gray*, ch.1.

5 I like Wagner's music better than anybody's. It is so loud that one can talk the whole time without other people hearing what one says.
1891 *The Picture of Dorian Gray*, ch.4.

6 If one hears bad music, it is one's duty to drown it by one's conversation.
1891 *The Picture of Dorian Gray*, ch.4.

7 A cigarette is the perfect type of a perfect pleasure. It is exquisite, and it leaves one unsatisfied. What more can one want?
1891 *The Picture of Dorian Gray*, ch.6.

8 It is better to be beautiful than to be good. But…it is better to be good than to be ugly.
1891 *The Picture of Dorian Gray*, ch.17.

9 Anybody can be good in the country.
1891 *The Picture of Dorian Gray*, ch.19.

10 Murder is always a mistake… One should never do anything that one cannot talk about after dinner.
1891 *The Picture of Dorian Gray*, ch.19.

11 As for the virtuous poor, one can pity them, of course, but one cannot possibly admire them.
1891 'The Soul of Man under Socialism'.

12 Democracy means simply the bludgeoning of the people by the people for the people.
1891 'The Soul of Man under Socialism'.

13 I can resist everything except temptation.
1892 Lord Darlington. *Lady Windermere's Fan*, act 1.

14 Many a woman has a past, but I am told that she has at least a dozen, and that they all fit.
1892 Said by Duchess of Berwick. *Lady Windermere's Fan*, act 1.

15 Do you know, Mr Hopper, dear Agatha and I are so much interested in Australia. It must be so pretty with all the dear little kangaroos flying about. Agatha has found it on the map. What a curious shape it is! Just like a large packing case.
1892 Duchess of Berwick to Mr Hopper. *Lady Windermere's Fan*, act 2.

16 We are all in the gutter, but some of us are looking at the stars.
1892 Said by Lord Darlington. *Lady Windermere's Fan*, act 3.

17 There is nothing in the whole world so unbecoming to a woman as a Nonconformist conscience.
1892 Cecil Graham. *Lady Windermere's Fan*, act 3.

18 A man who knows the price of everything and the value of nothing.
1892 Lord Darlington's definition of a cynic. *Lady Winderemere's Fan*, act 3.

19 Experience is the name everyone gives to their mistakes.

1892 Dumby. *Lady Windermere's Fan*, act 3.

20 The play was a great success, but the audience was a disaster.
1892 Attributed comment after the poor reception of *Lady Windermere's Fan.*

21 LORD ILLINGWORTH: The Book of Life begins with a man and a woman in a garden.
MRS ALLONBY: It ends with Revelations.
1893 *A Woman of No Importance*, act 1.

22 The English country gentleman galloping after a fox–the unspeakable in full pursuit of the uneatable.
1893 Lord Illingworth. *A Woman of No Importance*, act 1.

23 MRS ALLONBY: They say, Lady Hunstanton, that when good Americans die they go to Paris.
LADY HUNSTANTON: Indeed? And when bad Americans die, where do they go to?
LORD ILLINGWORTH: Oh, they go to America.
1893 *A Woman of No Importance*, act 1.

24 The youth of America is their oldest tradition. It has been going on now for three hundred years.
1893 Lord Illingworth. *A Woman of No Importance*, act 1.

25 One should never trust a woman who tells one her real age. A woman who would tell one that, would tell one anything.
1893 Lord Illingworth. *A Woman of No Importance*, act 1.

26 Children begin by loving their parents; after a time they judge them; rarely, if ever, do they forgive them.
1893 Lord Illingworth. *A Woman of No Importance*, act 2.

27 After a good dinner one can forgive anybody, even one's own relations.
1893 Lady Caroline. *A Woman of No Importance*, act 2.

28 GERALD: I suppose society is wonderfully delightful!
LORD ILLINGWORTH: To be in it is merely a bore. But to be out of it is simply a tragedy.
1893 *A Woman of No Importance*, act 3.

29 No woman should have a memory. Memory in a woman is the beginning of dowdiness.
1893 Lord Illingworth. *A Woman of No Importance*, act 3.

30 You should study the Peerage, Gerald... It is the best thing in fiction the English have ever done.
1893 Lord Illingworth. *A Woman of No Importance*, act 3.

31 A man who can dominate a London dinner-table can dominate the world.
1893 Lord Illingworth. *A Woman of No Importance*, act 3.

32 I'm afraid I play no outdoor games at all, except dominoes. I have sometimes played dominoes outside a French café.
1895 Quoted by Gelett Burgess in 'A Talk with Mr Oscar Wilde' in *The Sketch*, 9 Jan.

33 JACK: I think Jack, for instance, a charming name.
GWENDOLEN: Jack?... No, there is very little music in the name Jack, if any at all, indeed. It does not thrill. It produces absolutely no vibrations... I have known several Jacks, and they all, without exception, were more than usually plain. Besides, Jack is a notorious domesticity for John! And I pity any woman who is married to a man called John. She would probably never be allowed to know the entrancing pleasure of a single moment's solitude. The only really safe name is Ernest.
1895 *The Importance of Being Earnest*, act 1.

34 Really, if the lower orders don't set us a good example, what on earth is the use of them?
1895 Algernon. *The Importance of Being Earnest*, act 1.

35 It is very vulgar to talk like a dentist when one isn't a dentist. It produces a false impression.
1895 Jack. *The Importance of Being Earnest*, act 1.

36 The truth is rarely pure, and never simple.
1895 Algernon. *The Importance of Being Earnest*, act 1.

37 In married life three is company and two none.
1895 Algernon. *The Importance of Being Earnest*, act 1.

38 Ignorance is like a delicate exotic fruit; touch it and the bloom is gone. The whole theory of modern education is radically unsound. Fortunately, in England, at any rate, education produces no effect whatsoever.
1895 Lady Bracknell. *The Importance of Being Earnest*, act 1.

39 To lose one parent, Mr Worthing, may be regarded as a misfortune; to lose both looks like carelessness.
1895 Lady Bracknell. *The Importance of Being Earnest*, act 1.

40 All women become like their mothers. That is their tragedy. No man does. That's his.
1895 Algernon. *The Importance of Being Earnest*, act 1, also in *A Woman of No Importance* (1893), act 2.

41 The good ended happily, and the bad unhappily. That is what fiction means.
1895 Miss Prism. *The Importance of Being Earnest*, act 2.

42 The chapter on the fall of the Rupee you may omit. It is somewhat too sensational.
1895 Miss Prism. *The Importance of Being Earnest*, act 2.

43 I hope you have not been leading a double life, pretending to be wicked and being really good all the time. That would be hypocrisy.
1895 Said by Cecily. *The Importance of Being Earnest*, act 2.

44 Charity, dear Miss Prism, charity! None of us are perfect. I myself am peculiarly susceptible to draughts.
1895 Dr Chasuble. *The Importance of Being Earnest*, act 2.

45 CECILY: When I see a spade I call it a spade.
GWENDOLEN: I am glad to say that I have never seen a spade.
1895 *The Importance of Being Earnest*, act 3.

46 Thirty-five is a very attractive age. London society is full of women of the very highest birth who have, of their own free choice, remained thirty-five for years.
1895 Lady Bracknell. *The Importance of Being Earnest*, act 3.

47 She wore far too much rouge last night, and not quite enough clothes. That is always a sign of despair in a woman.
1895 Lord Goring. *An Ideal Husband*, act 2.

48 Nothing is so dangerous as being too modern. One is apt to grow old-fashioned quite suddenly.
1895 Lord Markby. *An Ideal Husband*, act 2.

49 Fashion is what one wears oneself. What is unfashionable is what other people wear.
1895 Lord Goring. *An Ideal Husband*, act 3.

50 If one could only teach the English how to talk, and the Irish how to listen, society here would be quite civilised.
1895 Mrs Cheveley speaking. *An Ideal Husband*, act 3.

51 If this is the way Queen Victoria treats her prisoners she doesn't deserve to have any.
1895 On being obliged to stand in the rain as he awaited transport to take him to prison. Attributed.

52 He did not wear his scarlet coat,
For blood and wine are red,
And blood and wine were on his hands
When they found him with the dead.
1898 *The Ballad of Reading Gaol*, pt.1, stanza 1.

53 I never saw a man who looked
With such a wistful eye
Upon that little tent of blue
Which prisoners call the sky.
1898 *The Ballad of Reading Gaol*, pt.1, stanza 3.

54 Yet each man kills the thing he loves,
By each let this be heard,
Some do it with a bitter look,
Some with a flattering word.
The coward does it with a kiss,
The brave man with a sword!
1898 *The Ballad of Reading Gaol*, pt.1, stanza 7.

55 The Governer was strong upon
The Regulation Act:
The Doctor said that Death was but
A scientific fact:
And twice a day the Chaplain called,
And left a little tract.
1898 *The Ballad of Reading Gaol*, pt.3, stanza 3.

56 Something was dead in each of us,
And what was dead was Hope.
1898 *The Ballad of Reading Gaol*, pt.3, stanza 31.

57 And the wild regrets, and the bloody sweats,
None knew so well as I:
For he who lives more lives than one
More deaths than one must die.
1898 *The Ballad of Reading Gaol*, pt.3, stanza 37.

58 I know not whether Laws be right,
Or whether Laws be wrong;
All that we know who lie in gaol
Is that the wall is strong;
And that each day is like a year,
A year whose days are long.
1898 *The Ballad of Reading Gaol*, pt.5, stanza 1.

59 How else but through a broken heart
May Lord Christ enter in?
1898 *The Ballad of Reading Gaol*, pt.5, stanza 14.

60 I am dying, as I have lived, beyond my means.
1900 Accepting a glass of champagne shortly before his death. Attributed.

61 Either that wallpaper goes or I do.
1900 As he lay dying in a Paris hotel bedroom. Attributed.

62 Football is all very well as a game for rough girls, but it is hardly suitable for delicate boys.
Quoted in Alvin Redman *The Epigrams of Oscar Wilde* (1952).

63 The only possible form of exercise is to talk, not to walk.
Quoted in Alvin Redman *The Epigrams of Oscar Wilde* (1952).

64 Mr Bernard Shaw has no enemies, but is intensely disliked by all his friends.
Quoted in W B Yeats *Autobiographies* (1955).

65 It requires one to assume such indecent postures.
His reason for not playing cricket. Quoted in *Bloomsbury Thematic Dictionary of Quotations* (1988)

66 Work is the curse of the drinking classes.
Attributed.

67 Henry James wrote fiction as if it were a painful duty.
Attributed.

68 The three women I have admired most are Queen Victoria, Sarah Bernhardt and Lillie Langtry. I would have married any one of them with pleasure.
Attributed.

Wilder, Billy (Samuel) 1906–2002

Austrian-born writer and director who moved to Hollywood in 1934. He won Academy Awards for *The Lost Weekend* (1945), *Sunset Boulevard* (1950) and *The Apartment* (1960). Other successes include *Double Indemnity* (1944), *The Seven Year Itch* (1955) and *Some Like It Hot* (1959).

69 Johnny, keep it out of focus. I want to win the foreign picture award.
1950 Remark to cameraman John Seitz during the making of *Sunset Boulevard*.

70 Making a picture with Marilyn Monroe was like going to the dentist. It was hell at the time, but after it was all over it was wonderful.
Quoted in Doug McClelland *Star Speak* (1987).

71 No one ever leaves a star.
1950 *Sunset Boulevard*.

72 Fasten your cigarettes.
1972 *Avanti* (with I A L Diamond).

73 I don't object to foreigners speaking a foreign language; I just wish they'd all speak the same foreign language.
1972 *Avanti* (with I A L Diamond).

74 Hindsight is always twenty-twenty.
Attributed.

Wilder, Thornton Niven 1897–1975

US playwright and novelist. His most successful plays included *Our Town* (1938) and *The Skin of Our Teeth* (1942), while his other writings included the novel *The Bridge of San Luis Rey* (1927). His play *The Matchmaker* (1954) provided the basis for the hit musical *Hello, Dolly!*

75 From what human ill does not dawn seem to be an alleviation.
1927 *The Bridge of San Luis Rey*, ch.3.

76 Most everybody in the world climbs into their graves married.
1938 *Our Town*, act 2.

77 Marriage is a bribe to make a housekeeper think she's a householder.
1939 *The Merchant of Yonkers*, act 1.

78 The fights are the best part of married life. The rest is merely so-so.
1939 *The Merchant of Yonkers*, act 2.

79 My advice to you is not to inquire why or whither, but just enjoy your ice-cream while it's on your plate,—that's my philosophy.
1942 *The Skin of Our Teeth*, act 1.

80 When you're at war you think about a better life; when you're at peace you think about a more comfortable one.
1942 *The Skin of Our Teeth*, act 1.

81 We'll trot down to the movies and see how girls with wax faces live.
1942 *The Skin of Our Teeth*, act 3.

82 I've never forgotten for long at a time that living is a struggle. I know that every good and excellent thing in the world stands moment by moment on the razor-edge of danger and must be fought for—whether it's a field, or a home, or a country.
1942 *The Skin of Our Teeth*, act 3.

83 Literature is the orchestration of platitudes.
1953 In *Time*, 12 Jan.

84 A living is made, Mr Kemper, by selling something that everybody needs at least once a year. Yes, sir! And a million is made by producing something that everybody needs every day. You artists produce something that nobody needs at any time.
1954 *The Matchmaker*, act 1.

85 Ninety-nine percent of the people in the world are fools, and the rest of us are in great danger of contagion.
1954 *The Matchmaker*, act 1.

86 Never support two weaknesses at the same time. It's your combination sinners—your lecherous liars and your miserly drunkards—who dishonour the vices and bring them into bad repute.
1954 *The Matchmaker*, act 3.

87 But there comes a time in everybody's life when he must decide whether he'll live among human beings or not—a fool among fools or a fool alone.
1954 *The Matchmaker*, act 4.

88 I am not interested in the ephemeral—such subjects as the adulteries of dentists. I am interested in those things that repeat and repeat in the lives of the millions.
1961 In the *New York Times*, 6 Mar.

89 The less seen, the more heard. The eye is the enemy of the ear in real drama.
1961 In the *New York Times*, 6 Nov.

90 The process of learning is accompanied by alternations of pain and brief quickenings that resemble pain.
1967 *The Eighth Day*.

Wilding, Michael 1912–79

English actor. He is usually remembered for his performances in such films as *Piccadilly Incident* (1946) and *Spring in Park Lane* (1948).

91 You can pick out actors by the glazed look that comes into their eyes when the conversation wanders away from themselves.
Attributed.

Wilhelm II, Kaiser 1859–1941

Kaiser and King of Prussia 1888–1918. Dismissed Bismarck in 1890, beginning a long period of personal rule. Although his bellicosity contributed to the origins of World War I, he became a figurehead during the course of it. He abdicated at the end of the war and settled in the Netherlands.

92 We have…fought for our place in the sun and have won it. It will be my business to see that we retain this place in the sun unchallenged.
1901 Speech in Hamburg, 18 Jun. Quoted in *The Times*, 20 Jun.

93 You will be home before the leaves have fallen from the trees.
1914 Address to German troops leaving for the Front, Aug.

94 We draw the sword with a clean conscience and with clean hands.
1914 Address from the throne, Berlin, 4 Aug.

95 The machine is running away with him as it ran away with me.
1939 Of Adolf Hitler at the start of World War II, said to Sir Robert Bruce-Lockhart, 27 Aug.

Wilkinson, Anne 1910–61

Canadian poet. One of the founders of the important literary magazine, *The Tamarack Review*, she published poetry (*Counterpoint to Sleep*, 1951, and *The Hangman Ties the Holly*, 1955), a family history (*Lions in the Way*, 1956) and a children's book. Her collected poems were published in 1968.

96 Fabulous the insects
Stud the air
Or walk on running water,
Klee-drawn saints
And bright as angels are.
1955 *The Hangman Ties the Holly*, 'In June and Gentle Oven'.

97 Our hearts, unrisen, yield a heavy bread.
1955 *The Hangman Ties the Holly*, 'Topsoil to the Wind'.

Wilkinson, Jonny 1979–

English rugby player, member of the successful England Rugby World Cup team (2003).

98 The first game I ever played I scored a goal from the halfway line. Didn't have a clue what I was doing. Ball just came to me, so I whacked it.
2002 On his childhood attempts to play football. Quoted in *The Guardian*, 28 Jan.

99 I play with the fear of letting people down. That's what motivates me.
2004 Quoted on www.bbc.co.uk.

Will, George

1 What the federal government does basically is borrow money from people and mail it to people.
1993 Of entitlement programs. ABC TV broadcast, 19 Sep.

William of Poitiers 11c.

French chronicler of the life of William the Conqueror.

2 A strange manner of battle, where one side works by constant motion and ceaseless charges, while the other can but endure passively as it stands fixed to the sod. The Norman arrow and sword worked on: in the English ranks the only movement was the dropping of the dead: the living stood motionless.
c.1071 Of the Battle of Hastings, 14 Oct 1066. *Gesta Guillelmi ducis Normannorum et regis Anglorum* (edited by R Foreville, 1952).

William of Wykeham 1324–1404

Bishop of Winchester and Chancellor of England.

3 Manners makyth man.
Proverb common from the 14th century and said to be Wykeham's motto.

William III *also called* William of Orange 1650–1702

Dutch-born King of Great Britain (1689–1702), and Stadholder of the United Provinces (1672–1702). Husband of Mary, daughter of James II, he was invited by Protestant elements to assume the throne in the Glorious Revolution of 1688.

4 People in Parliament occupy themselves with private animosities and petty quarrels, and think little of the national interest. It is impossible to credit the serene indifference with which they consider events outside their own country.
1699 Letter, Jan.

5 The eyes of all England are on this Parliament. If you do in good earnest wish to see England hold the balance of Europe and to be indeed at the head of the Protestant interest, it will appear by your right improving the present opportunity.
1701 At the State Opening of Parliament, Dec.

6 Every bullet has its billet.
Quoted by John Wesley, journal entry, 6 Jun 1765.

Williams, (Hiram) Hank 1923–53

US country singer, the 'Father of Country Music'. His hits include 'Lovesick Blues', 'Hey, Good Lookin'', 'Jambalaya' and 'Your Cheatin' Heart'. His death was the result of alcoholism and drug abuse.

7 You got to have smelt a lot of mule manure before you can sing like a hillbilly.
Quoted in *Rolling Stone*, 1969.

Williams, Harry Abbott 1919–

English cleric and scholar, a member of the Anglican Community of the Resurrection. In his theological writings he combines theology with insights from psychology.

8 The prelude to resurrection as we experience it in this life is always powerlessness. We cannot raise ourselves by our own bootstrings.
1972 *The True Resurrection*.

Williams, Raymond 1921–88

Welsh critic and novelist. He is best known for his works mixing socio-cultural and literary criticism, including *The Long Revolution* (1966) and *The Country and the City* (1973).

9 The human crisis is always a crisis of understanding: what we genuinely understand we can do.
1958 *Culture and Society*, ch.3.

10 When art communicates, a human experience is actively offered and actively received. Below this activity threshold there can be no art.
1966 *The Long Revolution*, pt.1, ch.1.

Williams, Robin 1952–

US comedian and film actor. He starred in the TV series *Mork and Mindy* (1970s) and in such films as *The World According to Garp* (1982), *Good Morning, Vietnam* (1987), *Dead Poets Society* (1989), *The Fisher King* (1991), *Mrs Doubtfire* (1993), *The Birdcage* (1995) and *Good Will Hunting* (1997).

11 I thought lacrosse was what you find in la church.
1982 Interview in *Playboy*.

12 Cricket is baseball on valium.
Quoted in Colin Jarman *The Guinness Dictionary of Sports Quotations* (1990).

Williams, Shirley Vivien Teresa Brittain Williams, Baroness 1930–

English politician, a Labour MP from 1964. She lost her seat in 1979, co-founded the Social Democratic Party in 1981 and became its first elected MP. She lost her seat in 1983 but remained as SDP President (1982–8), and supported the merger with the Liberal Party in 1988. A professor at Harvard University, she remains active in British politics.

13 The British Civil Service…is a beautifully designed and effective braking mechanism.
1980 Speech at the Royal Institute of Public Administration, 11 Feb.

Williams, Tennessee Thomas Lanier 1911–83

US playwright. He won recognition as a leading contemporary writer with his play *The Glass Menagerie* (1945), which was followed by such intense, atmospheric and often brutal dramas as *A Streetcar Named Desire* (1947), *The Rose Tattoo* (1951), *Cat On A Hot Tin Roof* (1955), *Suddenly Last Summer* (1958) and *The Night of the Iguana* (1962).

14 In memory everything seems to happen to music.
1945 Tom. *The Glass Menagerie*, sc.1.

15 I didn't go to the moon, I went much further—for time is the longest distance between two places.
1945 Tom. *The Glass Menagerie*, sc.7.

16 I can't stand a naked light bulb, any more than I can a rude remark or a vulgar action.
1947 Blanche. *A Streetcar Named Desire*, sc.3

17 I have always depended on the kindness of strangers.
1947 Blanche. *A Streetcar Named Desire*, sc.11.

18 The only thing worse than a liar is a liar that's also a hypocrite!
1951 Rosa. *The Rose Tattoo*, act 3.

19 It is a terrible thing for an old woman to outlive her dogs.
1953 *Camino Real*, prologue.

20 Caged birds accept each other but flight is what they long for.
1953 Marguerite. *Camino Real*, block 7.

21 Bohemia has no banner. It survives by discretion.
1953 Marguerite. *Camino Real*, block 7.

22 We have to distrust each other. It's our only defence against betrayal.
1953 Marguerite. *Camino Real*, block 10.

23 We're all of us guinea pigs in the laboratory of God. Humanity is just a work in progress.
1953 The Gipsy. *Camino Real*, block 12.

24 Some mystery should be left in the revelation of character in a play, just as a great deal of mystery is always left in the revelation of character in life, even in one's own character to himself.
1955 *Cat on a Hot Tin Roof*, stage direction.

25 What is the victory of a cat on a hot tin roof?—I wish I knew… Just staying on it, I guess, for as long as she can.
1955 Maggie. *Cat on a Hot Tin Roof*, act 1.

26 You can be young without money but you can't be old without it.
1955 Maggie. *Cat on a Hot Tin Roof*, act 1.

27 A drinking man's someone who wants to forget he isn't still young an' believing.
1955 *Cat on a Hot Tin Roof*, act 2.

28 BRICK: Well, they say nature hates a vacuum, Big Daddy.
BIG DADDY: That's what they say, but sometimes I think that a vacuum is a hell of a lot better than some of the stuff that nature replaces it with.
1955 *Cat on a Hot Tin Roof*, act 2.

29 Mendacity is a system that we live in. Liquor is one way out an' death's the other.
1955 Brick. *Cat on a Hot Tin Roof*, act 2.

30 At the age of 14 I discovered writing as an escape from…being called a sissy by the neighborhood kids, and Miss Nancy by my father.
1957 In the *New York Times*, 17 Mar.

31 The world is a funny paper read backwards. And that way it isn't so funny.
1957 In the *Observer*, 7 Apr.

32 Don't look forward to the day you stop suffering, because when it comes you'll *know* you're dead.
1958 In the *Observer*, 26 Jan.

33 We're all of us sentenced to solitary confinement inside our own skins, for life!
1958 Val. *Orpheus Descending*, act 2, sc.1.

34 It haunts me, the passage of time. I think time is a merciless thing. I think life is a process of burning oneself out and time is the fire that burns you. But I think the spirit of man is a good adversary.
1958 In the *New York Post*, 30 Apr.

35 He was meddling too much in my private life.
1961 Explaining why he had dispensed with the services of his psychoanalyst. Attributed.

36 All cruel people describe themselves as paragons of frankness!
1963 Mrs Goforth. *The Milk Train Doesn't Stop Here Anymore*, sc.1.

37 Life is all memory except for the one present moment that goes by you so quick you hardly catch it going.
1963 Mrs Goforth. *The Milk Train Doesn't Stop Here Anymore*, sc.3

38 We all live in a house on fire, no fire department to call; no way out, just the upstairs window to look out of while the fire burns the house down with us trapped, locked in it.
1963 Chris. *The Milk Train Doesn't Stop Here Anymore*, sc.6.

Williams, Venus 1980–

US tennis player. Her first Grand Slam singles victory came in 2000 when she won the Wimbledon title. As well as other singles titles, she has won numerous doubles titles with her sister Serena.

39 I guess there's always going to be jobs that pay more than others, and I suppose I have one of those.
2002 In the *Observer*, 9 Jun.

Williams, William Carlos 1883–1963

US poet, a paediatrician as well as a writer. His poetry and objectivist aesthetic made him a major Modernist figure. He also wrote novels, stories, plays, literary and cultural essays and memoirs.

40 I will teach you my townspeople
how to perform a funeral
for you have it over a troop
of artists—
unless one should scour the world—
you have the ground sense necessary.
1917 *Al Que Quiere!*, 'Tract'.

41 Covertly the hands of a great clock
go round and round! Were they to
move quickly and at once the whole
secret would be out and the shuffling
of all ants be done forever.
1921 *Sour Grapes*, 'Overture to a Dance of Locomotives'.

42 Lifeless in appearance, sluggish
dazed spring approaches—

They enter the new world naked,
cold, uncertain of all
save that they enter.
1923 *Spring and All*, 'Spring and All'.

43 One by one the objects are defined—
It quickens: clarity, outline of leaf

But now the stark dignity of
entrance—Still, the profound change
has come upon them: rooted, they
grip down and begin to awaken.
1923 *Spring and All*, 'Spring and All'.

44 so much depends
upon

a red wheel
barrow

glazed with rain
water

beside the white
chickens.
1923 *Spring and All*, 'The Red Wheelbarrow'.

45 —through metaphor to reconcile
the people and the stones.
1944 *The Wedge*, 'A Sort of Song'.

46 Is it any better in Heaven, my friend Ford,
Than you found it in Provence?
1944 *The Wedge*, 'To Ford Madox Ford in Heaven'.

47 To make a start,
out of particulars
and make them general, rolling
up the sum, by defective means—
Sniffing the trees, just another dog
among a lot of dogs. What
else is there? And to do?
1946 *Paterson*, bk.1, preface.

48 For the beginning is assuredly
the end—since we know nothing, pure
and simple, beyond
our own complexities.
1946 *Paterson*, bk.1, preface.

49 Minds like beds always made up
(more stony than a shore)
unwilling or unable.
1946 *Paterson*, bk.1, preface.

50 Say it, no ideas but in things.
1946 *Paterson*, bk.1, 'The Delineaments of the Giants', 1.

51 Divorce is
the sign of knowledge in our time.
1946 *Paterson*, bk.1, 'The Delineaments of the Giants', 2.

52 Without invention nothing is well-spaced.
1948 *Paterson*, bk.2, 'Sunday in the Park', 1.

53 Unless there is
a new mind there cannot be a new
line, the old will go on
repeating itself with recurring
deadliness:
1948 *Paterson*, bk.2, 'Sunday in the Park',1.

54 Beyond the gap where the river
plunges into the narrow gorge, unseen

—and the imagination soars, as a voice
beckons, a thundrous voice, endless
—as sleep: the voice
that has ineluctably called them—
that unmoving roar!
1948 *Paterson*, bk.2, 'Sunday in the Park', 1.

55 For what we cannot accomplish, what
is denied to love,
what we have lost in the anticipation—
a descent follows,
endless and indestructible.
1948 *Paterson*, bk.2, 'Sunday in the Park', 1.

56 For there is a wind or a ghost of wind
in all books echoing the life
there, a high wind that fills the tubes
of the ear until we think we hear a wind,
actual.
1949 *Paterson*, bk.3, 'The Library'.

57 and there grows in the mind
a scent, it may be, of locust blossoms
whose perfume is itself a wind moving
to lead the mind away.
1949 *Paterson*, bk.3, 'The Library'.

58 It isn't what he says that counts as a work of art, it's what he makes with such intensity of perception that it lives with an intrinsic movement of its very own to verify the authenticity.
Of the poet. Quoted by Richard Eberhart in the *New York Times*, 17 Dec 1950.

59 I have never been one to write by rule, not even by my own rules.
1954 Letter to Richard Eberhart, 23 May.

60 Love is that common tone
shall raise his fiery head
and sound his note.
1954 *The Desert Music*, 'The Orchestra'.

61 All writing is a disease. You can't stop it.
Quoted in *Newsweek*, 7 Jan 1957.

62 Nothing whips my blood like verse.
Quoted in John Thirlwall (ed) *The Selected Letters of William Carlos Williams* (1957).

63 Though he is approaching death he is possessed by many poems.
1958 *Paterson*, bk.5.

64 Anything is good material for poetry. Anything.
1958 *Paterson*, bk.5.

Williamson, Roy 1937–90

Scottish folksinger and musician, a partner in the Corries with Ronnie Browne from 1961, and composer of 'Flower of Scotland', adopted by many as an unofficial Scottish national anthem.

65 O flower of Scotland, when will we see your like again,
That fought and died for your wee bit hill and glen
And stood against him, proud Edward's army,
And sent him homeward tae think again.
1968 'Flower of Scotland', stanza 1.

Willis, Bruce 1955–

US actor. He has appeared in a number of action-man roles in such films as *Die Hard* (1988) and its sequels, as well as taking character parts.

66 Frankly, reviews are mostly for people who still read. Like most of the written word, it is going the way of the dinosaur.
1997 In *Time*, 19 May.

Willkie, Wendell Lewis 1892–1944

US politician, Republican candidate for the presidency (1940).

67 Any man who is not something of a Socialist before he is forty has no heart. Any man who is still a Socialist after he is forty has no head.
Quoted in Richard Norton Smith *Thomas E. Dewey and his Times* (1982), p.294.
► *See Twain 872:35.*

Wilmer, Val(erie) 1941–

English writer and photographer. Her books on jazz include *Jazz People* (1970), *As Serious As Your Life* (1977) and the autobiographical *Mama Said There'd Be Days Like This* (1989).

68 A rather bitter British musician once remarked sourly to a friend of mine: 'Oh, all *she* knows about music she learned in bed with musicians.' To that, I can only add, what better place to learn?
1989 *Mama Said There'd Be Days Like This*, ch.3.

Wilson, A(ndrew) N(orman) 1950–

English writer. He has written novels, criticism, journalism and biography, including the controversial *Jesus* (1992).

69 It had never occurred to Giles that there was something perfectly sensible about wanting to hold onto innocence. He had always gone in for the idea that since we only pass this way once, *experience* counts for everything.
1982 *Wise Virgins*, ch.6.

70 Religion is the tragedy of mankind… But I do know, from the inside as well as from personal observation, that religion appeals to something deep and irrational and strong within us, and that is what makes it so dangerous.
1991 *Against Religion*, no.19.

71 I should prefer to have a politician who regularly went to a massage parlour than one who promised a laptop computer for every teacher.
1999 In the *Observer*, 21 Mar.

Wilson, Sir Angus Frank Johnstone 1931–91

English writer. He wrote literary criticism, short stories and a play, but was best known for his novels including *Anglo-Saxon*

Attitudes (1956) and *The Old Men in the Zoo* (1961).

72 'God knows how you Protestants can be expected to have any sense of direction,' she said. 'It's different with us, I haven't been to mass for years, I've got every mortal sin on my conscience, but I know when I'm doing wrong. I'm still a Catholic, it's there, nothing can take it away from me.' 'Of course, duckie,' said Jeremy…'once a Catholic always a Catholic.'
1949 *The Wrong Set*, 'Significant Experience'.

73 She was more than ever proud of the position of the bungalow, so almost in the country.
1957 'A Flat Country Christmas'.

74 All fiction is for me a kind of magic and trickery—a confidence trick, trying to make people believe something is true that isn't.
1957 In *The Paris Review*, no.17.

75 The impulse to write a novel comes from a momentary unified vision of life.
1963 *The Wild Garden*.

76 I have no concern for the common man except that he should not be so common.
1967 *No Laughing Matter*.

77 My theme is always *humanistic*. Life today is junglelike…it is complex, it is inhuman in its materialism.
1972 Letter to David Farrer, his publisher, Jul. Quoted in Margaret Drabble *Angus Wilson—A Biography* (1995).

78 All are deceptions, substitutes for the hard job of using reason and industry and intuition and compassion to solve even a little bit of the muddle with humaneness and awe for the natural world and the complexity of human beings.
1972 Letter to David Farrer, his publisher, Jul. Quoted in Margaret Drabble *Angus Wilson—A Biography* (1995).

79 People are able to live with only half a heart, to live without real compassion, because they are able to use words that are only forms.
1972 Interview in *Iowa Review*, no.3, Fall.

80 The novelist must be his own most harsh critic and also his own most loving admirer—and about both he must say nothing.
1976 Author's comment in D L Kirkpatrick (ed) *Contemporary Novelists*.

Wilson, Charles *called 'Engine Charlie'* 1890–1961

President of General Motors and Secretary of Defense. He was nicknamed 'Engine Charlie' to distinguish him from 'Electric Charlie' Wilson, president of General Electric.

81 For years I thought what was good for our country was good for General Motors, and vice versa. The difference did not exist. Our company is too big. It goes with the welfare of the country.
1953 Statement to US Senate, Committee on Armed Services, Jan.

Wilson, David Gordon

English-born US mechanical engineer and bicycling enthusiast.

82 You must invent because you enjoy it.
2004 On making his first recumbent bicycle in 1955.

Wilson, Edmund 1895–1972

US literary critic, social commentator, and novelist. Although his own fiction, plays and poems are now little read, he was an influential critic with a wide-ranging perspective on art, history and society.

83 In a sense, one can never read the book that the author originally wrote, and one can never read the same book twice.
1938 *The Triple Thinkers*, introduction.

84 Of all the great Victorian writers, he was probably the most antagonistic to the Victorian age itself.
1941 Of Dickens. *The Wound and the Bow*, 'Dickens: The Two Scrooges'.

Wilson, Edward O(sborne) 1929–

US biologist, Professor of Entomology at Harvard University. His works include *Insect Societies* (1971), *Sociobiology: The New Synthesis* (1975) and *Biophilia* (1984).

85 It came by a lightning flash like knowledge from the gods.
1975 On the 1953 discovery of the DNA molecule. *Sociobiology*.

86 Important science is not just any similarity glimpsed for the first time. It offers analogies that map the gateways to unexplored terrain.
1984 *Biophilia*.

87 To a considerable degree science consists in originating the maximum amount of information with the minimum expenditure of energy.
1984 *Biophilia*.

Wilson, Ernest 1876–1930

English plant hunter.

88 Smoke That Thunders.
1927 Book title, referring to Victoria Falls.

Wilson of Rievaulx, (James) Harold Wilson, Baron 1916–95

English Labour politician and Prime Minister (1964–70, 1974–6). A renowned debater, his economic plans were hampered by a balance of payments crisis. He faced too the problems of Rhodesian independence, opposition to Britain's proposed entry into the Common Market, and conflict within the Party. After a third general election victory, he resigned in 1976.

89 The school that I went to in the north was a school where more than half the children in my class never had any boots or shoes to their feet. They wore clogs, because they lasted longer than shoes of comparable price.
1948 Speech, Birmingham, 28 Jul.
► *See Bulmer-Thomas 166:55.*

90 All the little gnomes in Zurich and other finance centres.
1956 Speech, House of Commons, 12 Nov.

91 Every time that Mr Macmillan comes back from abroad, Mr Butler goes to the airport and grips him warmly by the throat.
1957 Attributed.

92 We are redefining and restating our socialism in terms of the scientific revolution… The Britain that will be forged in the white heat of this revolution will be no place for restrictive practices or outdated methods on either side of industry.

1963 Labour Party Conference, 1 Oct. His phrase has since been memorably rendered as 'the white heat of the technological revolution'.

93 The Labour Party is a moral crusade, or it is nothing.
1964 Scottish Labour Party conference, 5 Sep.

94 A week is a long time in politics.
1964 Comment to lobby correspondents, Oct. As such meetings are off the record, there is no exact source for this famous phrase.

95 Given a fair wind, we will negotiate our way into the Common Market, head held high, not crawl in... Negotiations? Yes. Unconditional acceptance of whatever terms we are offered? No.
1966 Speech, Bristol, 20 Mar.

96 In a recent interview, I was asked what, above all, I associated with socialism in this modern age. I answered that if there was one word I would use to identify modern socialism, it was 'Science'.
1967 Speech, 17 Jun.

97 From now on the pound abroad is worth 14 per cent or so less in terms of other currencies. That does not mean, of course, that the pound here in Britain—in your pocket or purse, or in your bank—has been devalued.
1967 National broadcast, 19 Nov. The speech gave rise to the well-known phrase, 'the pound in your pocket'.

98 We are creating a Britain of which we can be proud, and the world knows it. The world's tourists are coming here in their millions...because the new Britain is exciting. Yes, Britain with a Labour Government is an exciting place.
1969 Speech, Labour Party Conference, 30 Sep.

99 One man's wage rise is another man's price increase.
1970 In the *Observer*, 11 Jan.

1 Have you ever noticed how we only win the World Cup under a Labour government?
1971 Quoted in Peter Ball and Phil Shaw *The Book of Football Quotations* (1989).

2 The greatest asset that a head of state can have is the ability to get a good night's sleep.
1975 BBC Radio 4 broadcast, 16 Apr.

3 The party must protect itself against the activities of small groups of inflexible political persuasion...having in common only their arrogant dogmatism... I have no wish to lead a party of political zombies.
1975 Labour Party Conference, 30 Sep.

4 The main essentials of a successful Prime Minister are sleep and a sense of history.
1976 *The Governance of Britain*.

5 A constant effort to keep a party together, without sacrificing either principle or the essentials of basic strategy, is the very stuff of political leadership. Macmillan was canonized for it.
1979 *Final Term: The Labour Government 1974–76*.

Wilson, Michael 1937–

Canadian Minister of Finance in the 1980s.

6 No matter how we define the term, Canada has an acute shortage of rich people.
1985 Giving one reason why taxing the wealthy would not ensure the continuation of Canada's social programs, at the Canadian Economics Association, Montreal, 30 May.

Wilson, (Thomas) Woodrow 1856–1924

US statesman and 28th President (1913–21). He was twice elected Democratic President. His administration was chiefly remembered for Prohibition, woman's suffrage, US entry into World War I, and his championing of the League of Nations. He was awarded the Nobel peace prize (1919).

7 The feelings with which we face this new age of right and opportunity sweep across our heartstrings like some air out of God's own presence, where justice and mercy are reconciled, and the judge and the brother are one.
1913 Inaugural address, 4 Mar.

8 Human rights, national integrity, and opportunity as against material interests...are the issues that we now must face. I take this occasion to say that the United States will never again seek one additional foot of territory by conquest.
1913 Speech, Alabama, 27 Oct.

9 The people of the United States are drawn from many nations, and chiefly from the nations now at war. Some will wish one nation, others another, to succeed in this monumental struggle. I venture to speak a solemn word of warning. The United States must be neutral in fact as well as in name during these days that are to try men's souls. We must be impartial in thought as well as in action.
1914 Message to the Senate, 19 Aug.

10 There is such a thing as a man being too proud to fight; there is such a thing as a nation being so right that it does not need to convince others by force that it is right.
1915 Speech in Philadelphia, 10 May.

11 We are constantly thinking of the great war...which saved the Union...but it was a war which did a great deal more than that. It created in this country what had never existed before—a national consciousness.
1915 Memorial Day Address at Arlington National Cemetery, Virginia, 31 May.

12 America cannot be an ostrich, with its head in the sand.
1916 Speech, New Mexico, 1 Feb.

13 Nations should with one accord adopt the doctrine of President Monroe as the doctrine of the world; that every people should be left free to determine its own policy, its own way of development, unhindered, unthreatened, unafraid—the little along with the great and powerful. Those are American principles, American policies. We could stand for no others. They are also the principles of mankind, and must prevail.
1917 Speech to the Senate, 22 Jan.

14 Armed neutrality is ineffectual enough at best.
1917 Speech before a joint session of Congress, 2 Apr, to request a declaration that a state of war exists between Germany and the US.

15 The world must be made safe for democracy. Its peace must be planted on the tested foundations of political liberty.
1917 Speech before a joint session of Congress, 2 Apr, to request a declaration that a state of war exists between Germany and the US.

16 It is not an army that we must train for war; it is a nation.
1917 Speech, Washington, 12 May.

17 In this war, we demand nothing that is peculiar to ourselves; only that the world be made fit and safe to live

in. The programme of the world's peace, therefore, is our programme.
1918 The 'Fourteen Points' speech to Congress, 8 Jan.

18 People and provinces must not be bartered about from sovereign to sovereign as if they were chattels, or pawns in a game. Self-determination is not a mere phrase. It is an imperative principle, which statesmen will henceforth ignore at their peril.
1918 Address to Congress, 11 Feb.

19 People call me an idealist. That is how I know that I am an American. America is the only idealistic nation in the world.
1919 Speech, Sioux Falls, 8 Sep.

Wimperis, Arthur 1874–1953

British screenwriter. He provided the screenplays for such movies as *The Private Life of Henry VIII* (1932) and *Mrs Miniver* (1942).

20 My dear fellow, a unique evening! I wouldn't have left a turn unstoned.
After watching a vaudeville show. Quoted in E Short *Fifty Years of Vaudeville* (1946).

Winchell, Walter 1897–1972

US theatre critic and actor. His publications included *Broadway Thro' a Keyhole* (1933).

21 A newspaperman, whose sweetheart ran away with an actor.
Defining a drama critic. Attributed.

Winfrey, Oprah 1954–

US actress, talk-show host and businesswoman. She was the first woman to own and produce her own talk show and the first African-American to own a large television studio.

22 I am a product of every other black woman before me who has done or said anything worthwhile. Recognizing that I am part of history is what allows me to soar.
Quoted in Brian Lanker *I Dream a World: Portraits of Black Women Who Changed America* (1989).

Winkworth, Catherine 1827–78

English hymn writer and translator.

23 Now thank we all our God,
With heart and hands and voices,
Who wondrous things hath done,
In whom his world rejoices;
Who from our mother's arms
Hath blessed us on our way
With countless gifts of love,
And still is ours to-day.
1858 *Lyra Germanica* (translated from the original German of Martin Rinkart 'Nun danket alle Gott', c.1636).

Winner, Langdon

US academic and social critic with an interest in issues relating to technology and society.

24 The map of the world shows no country called Technopolis, yet in many ways we are already its citizens.
1986 *The Whale and the Reactor.*

Winner, Michael 1935–

British director. Credits include *Chato's Land* (1972), *Death Wish* (1974) and *The Wicked Lady* (1983).

25 Who says that actors are cattle? Show me a cow who can earn a million dollars a film.
Quoted by David Lewin in *Cinema Today*, 1 Jul 1970.

26 Keeping awake for ten weeks at a stretch.
1970 When asked what is the hardest part of directing. John Player Lecture, London, Sep.

27 A writer of talent needs only a typewriter and paper, a painter only needs brushes, canvas and paint, but I need a million dollars or more to be in business. That's a hell of a business to be in.
1974 In the *Observer Magazine*, 7 Jul.

28 I don't go to restaurants, I go to tables.
2004 In the *Observer*, 25 Jan.

29 A team effort is a lot of people doing what I say.
Attributed.

Winterson, Jeanette 1959

English novelist. Her autobiographical first novel, *Oranges Are Not the Only Fruit* (1985), described her upbringing as an Evangelical Pentecostalist and her subsequent realization of her homosexuality. Subsequent novels include *Sexing the Cherry* (1989), *Written on the Body* (1992), *Art and Lies* (1994) and *The.PowerBook* (2000).

30 I asked why he was a priest and he said that if you have to work for anybody an absentee boss is best.
1987 *The Passion*, ch.1.

31 Adults talk about being happy because largely they are not.
1987 *The Passion*, ch.1.

32 I call him Jordan and it will do. He has no other name before or after. What was there to call him, fished as he was from the stinking Thames? A child can't be called Thames, no and not Nile either, for all his likeness to Moses. But I wanted to give him a river name, a name not bound to anything, just as the waters aren't bound to anything.
1989 *Sexing the Cherry.*

33 I have met a great many people on their way towards God and I wonder why they have chosen to look for him rather than themselves.
1989 *Sexing the Cherry.*

34 I don't hate men, I just wish they'd try harder. They all want to be heroes and all we want is for them to stay at home and help with the housework and the kids. That's not the kind of heroism they enjoy.
1989 *Sexing the Cherry.*

35 When I was born, my father wanted to drown me, but my mother persuaded him to let me live in disguise, to see if I could bring any wealth to the household.
2000 *The.PowerBook.*

36 In this life you have to be your own hero.
2000 *The.PowerBook.*

Wisdom, Norman 1915–

English comedian, born in London. He made his stage debut in 1946 and his first film appearance in *Trouble in Store* (1953). This was followed by a string of successes including *Man of the Moment* (1955), *Just My Luck* (1958) and *Follow a Star* (1959).

37 They don't seem to realize that I have grown up and can get laughs without falling downstairs.
1991 Quoted in Richard Dacre *Trouble in Store: Norman Wisdom, a Career in Comedy* (1991).

Witte, Sergei Yulevich 1849–1915

Russian politician. As Minister of Finance (1892) he encouraged capitalism and industrialization, making Russia a leading industrial power. He became first Prime Minister (1905–6) in the Revolution of 1905, but was unable to satisfy either conservatives or liberals.

38 The world is in flames today for a cause that interests Russia first and foremost; a cause that is essentially the cause of the Slavs, and which is of no concern to France or to England.
1914 Said to the French Ambassador, 10 Sep.

Wittgenstein, Ludwig Josef Johann 1889–1951

Austrian-born British philosopher who became one of the most influential and charismatic figures in British philosophy in this century. He was Professor of Philosophy at Cambridge (1939–47), and published only one book in his lifetime, the *Tractatus Logico-Philosophicus* (1921). Of his many posthumous publications, by far the most important is the *Philosophical Investigations* (1953).

39 *Was sich überhaupt sagen lässt, lässt sich klar sagen; und wovon man nicht reden kann, darüber muss man schweigen.*
What can be said at all can be said clearly; and whereof one cannot speak thereof one must be silent.
1921 *Tractatus Logico-Philosophicus*, preface (translated by Frank Ramsey).

40 *Die Welt ist alles, was der Fall ist.*
The world is all that is the case.
1921 *Tractatus Logico-Philosophicus*, prop.1 (translated by Pears and McGuinness).

41 *Die Welt ist die Gesamtheit der Tatsachen, nicht der Dinge.*
The world is the totality of facts, not of things.
1921 *Tractatus Logico-Philosophicus*, prop.1.1 (translated by Pears and McGuinness).

42 *Der Tod ist kein Ereignis des Lebens. Den Tod erlebt man nicht.*
Death is not an event in life: we do not live to experience death.
1921 *Tractatus Logico-Philosophicus*, prop 6.4311 (translated by Pears and McGuinness).

43 *Die Probleme werden gelöst, nicht durch Beibringen neuer Erfahrung, sondern durch Zusammenstellung des längst Bekannten. Die Philosophie ist ein Kampf gegen die Verhexung unseres Verstandes durch die Mittel unserer Sprache.*
The problems are solved, not by giving new information, but by arranging what we have always known.
Philosophy is a battle against the bewitchment of our intelligence by means of language.
1945 *Philosophische Untersuchungen* (*Philosophical Investigations*), section 109 (translated by G E M Anscombe).

44 *Ein philosophisches Problem hat die Form: 'Ich kenne mich nicht aus'.*
A philosophical problem has the form: 'I don't know my way about'.
1945 *Philosophische Untersuchungen* (*Philosophical Investigations*), section 123 (translated by G E M Anscombe).

45 *Der Philosoph behandelt eine Frage wie eine Krankheit.*
The philosopher's treatment of a question is like the treatment of an illness.
1945 *Philosophische Untersuchungen* (*Philosophical Investigations*), section 255 (translated by G E M Anscombe).

46 *Was ist dein Ziel in der Philosophie?—'Der Fliege den Ausweg aus dem Fliegenglas zeigen'.*
What is your aim in philosophy?—To show the fly the way out of the fly-bottle.
1945 *Philosophische Untersuchungen* (*Philosophical Investigations*), section 309 (translated by G E M Anscombe).

47 *Ein 'innerer Vorgang' bedarf äußerer Kriterien.*
An 'inner process' stands in need of outward criteria.
1945 *Philosophische Untersuchungen* (*Philosophical Investigations*), section 580 (translated by G E M Anscombe).

48 *Wenn ein Löwe sprechen könnte, wir könnten ihn nicht verstehen.*
If a lion could talk, we could not understand him.
1945 *Philosophische Untersuchungen* (*Philosophical Investigations*), pt.2, section 11 (translated by G E M Anscombe).

Wittig, Monique 1935–2003

French feminist novelist who questioned traditional gender stereotypes in her writing.

49 *L'expérience…d'une femme écrivain est complètement schizophrénique. Il faut toujours faire coupure entre les deux: d'une part, employer un langage qui n'est pas le nôtre…et la lutte qu'on mène sur un autre plan, qui tend à casser tout ça, à essayer de faire à travers et dans le langage autre chose.*
The experience…of the woman writer is completely schizophrenic. One is always torn between two approaches: on the one hand, to use a language that is not ours…and on the other, the battle one fights to break all this up, in order to do something else through and in language.
Quoted in Jean-François Josselin 'Lettre à Sapho' in *Le Nouvel Observateur* (1973).

Wodehouse, Sir P(elham) G(renville) *also known as Plum* 1881–1975

Anglo-American writer, renowned for his humorous stories of the English country aristocracy. He lived in the US after World War II, taking citizenship in 1955, but never shed his quintessential Englishness.

50 An English peer of the right sort can be bored nearer to the point where mortification sets in, without showing it, than anyone else in the world.
1915 *Something Fresh*, ch.3.

51 She fitted into my biggest arm-chair as if it had been built round her by someone who knew they were wearing arm-chairs tight about the hips that season.
1919 *My Man Jeeves*, 'Jeeves and the Unbidden Guest'.

52 What with excellent browsing and sluicing and cheery conversation and what-not, the afternoon passed quite happily.
1919 *My Man Jeeves*, 'Jeeves and the Unbidden Guest'.

53 'What ho!' I said.
'What ho!' said Motty.
'What ho! What ho!'
'What ho! What ho! What ho!'
After that it seemed rather difficult to go on with the conversation.
1919 *My Man Jeeves*, 'Jeeves and the Unbidden Guest'.

54 In this matter of shimmering into rooms the chappie is rummy to a degree… He moves from point to point with as little uproar as a jellyfish.
1919 *My Man Jeeves*, 'Jeeves and the Hard-Boiled Egg'.

55 Chumps always make the best husbands. When you marry, Sally, grab a chump. Tap his forehead first, and if it rings solid, don't hesitate. All the unhappy marriages come from the husbands having brains. What good are brains to a man? They only unsettle him.
1920 *The Adventures of Sally*, ch.10.

56 I turned to Aunt Agatha, whose demeanour was now rather like that of one who, picking daisies on the railway, has just caught the down express in the small of the back.
1923 *The Inimitable Jeeves*, ch.4.

57 Jeeves coughed one soft, low, gentle cough like a sheep with a blade of grass stuck in its throat.
1923 *The Inimitable Jeeves*, ch.13.

58 As a rule, you see, I'm not lugged into Family Rows. On the occasions when Aunt is calling to Aunt like mastodons bellowing across the primeval swamps…the clan has a tendency to ignore me. It's one of the advantages I get from being a bachelor—and, according to my nearest and dearest, practically a half-witted bachelor at that.
1923 *The Inimitable Jeeves*, ch.16.

59 It was my Uncle George who discovered that alcohol was a food well in advance of medical thought.
1923 *The Inimitable Jeeves*, ch.16.

60 'Alf Todd,' said Ukridge, soaring to an impressive burst of imagery, 'has about as much chance as a one-armed blind man in a dark room trying to shove a pound of melted butter into a wild cat's left ear with a red-hot needle.'
1924 *Ukridge*, ch.5.

61 Honoria…is one of those robust, dynamic girls with the muscles of a welter-weight and a laugh like a squadron of cavalry charging over a tin bridge.
1925 *Carry On, Jeeves*, 'The Rummy Affair of Old Biffy'.

62 He looked haggard and careworn, like a Borgia who has suddenly remembered that he has forgotten to shove the cyanide in the consommé, and the dinner-gong due any moment.
1925 *Carry On, Jeeves*, 'Clustering Around Young Bingo'.

63 To my daughter Leonora without whose never-failing sympathy and encouragement this book would have been finished in half the time.
1926 *The Heart of a Goof*, dedication.

64 The Right Hon was a tubby little chap who looked as if he had been poured into his clothes and had forgotten to say 'When!'
1930 *Very Good, Jeeves*, 'Jeeves and the Impending Doom'.

65 I have at last come to a momentous decision. I am going to give up my press-clippings agency. I find that even a favourable notice makes me feel sick nowadays, while an unfavourable one, even from a small provincial newspaper, puts me off my work for days.
1934 Letter to Denis Mackail, 15 Oct.

66 Into the face of the young man…had crept a look of furtive shame, the shifty, hangdog look which announces that an Englishman is about to talk French.
1935 *The Luck of the Bodkins*, ch.1.

67 It is never difficult to distinguish between a Scotsman with a grievance and a ray of sunshine.
1935 *Blandings Castle and Elsewhere*, 'The Custody of the Pumpkin'.

68 I can't do with any more education. I was full up years ago.
1938 *The Code of the Woosters*, ch.1.

69 He spoke with a certain what-is-it in his voice, and I could see that, if not actually disgruntled, he was far from being gruntled.
1938 *The Code of the Woosters*, ch.1.

70 Slice him where you like, a hellhound is always a hellhound.
1938 *The Code of the Woosters*, ch.1.

71 Roderick Spode? Big chap with a small moustache and the sort of eye that can open an oyster at sixty paces?
1938 *The Code of the Woosters*, ch.2.

72 He felt like a man who, chasing rainbows, has had one of them suddenly turn and bite him in the leg.
1940 *Eggs, Beans and Crumpets*, 'Anselm Gets His Chance'.

73 My war history has been a simple one. I have just sat in my chair and written all the time.
1946 Letter to Ira Gershwin, 24 Jan.

74 Ice formed on the butler's upper slopes.
1952 *Pigs Have Wings*, ch.5.

75 Has anyone ever seen a dramatic critic in the daytime? Of course not. They come out after dark, up to no good.
1955 In the *New York Mirror*, 27 May.

76 There'll always be an England, but who wants an England full of morons reading the *Express*?
1959 Letter to Denis Mackail, 22 Apr.

Wogan, Terry 1938–

Irish broadcaster and writer.

77 People confuse longevity with merit. Look at Cliff Richard.
2004 In the *Observer*, 28 Mar.

78 Ah, to be able to recognise when the tide is going out, when to get off the beach.
2004 On deciding when to retire. In the *Observer*, 28 Mar.

Wolf, Naomi 1962–

US writer; she was a Rhodes Scholar in 1986. *The Beauty Myth* (1990) and *Fire with Fire* (1993) examine the relationship between patriarchal power and female beauty.

79 The more legal and material hindrances women have broken through, the more strictly and heavily and cruelly images of female beauty have come to weigh upon them.
1990 *The Beauty Myth*, ch.1, 'The Beauty Myth'.

80 'Beauty' is a currency like the gold standard. Like any

economy it is determined by politics, and in the modern age in the West it is the last, best belief system that keeps male domination intact.
1990 *The Beauty Myth*, ch.1, 'The Beauty Myth'.

81 When women breached the power structure in the 1980s…two economies finally merged. Beauty was no longer just a symbolic form of currency: it literally *became* money.
1990 *The Beauty Myth*, ch.2 'Work'.

Wolfe, James 1727–59

English general. He fought against the Jacobites at Culloden and was sent to Canada in 1756. Promoted to general after his prominence in the capture of Louisberg, he commanded the British force which took Quebec.

82 Gentlemen, I would rather have written those lines than take Quebec tomorrow.
1759 To his troops, 12 Sep, after reciting Thomas Gray's 'Elegy, Written in a Country Churchyard' the evening before storming the ramparts of Quebec and dying a hero's death on the Plains of Abraham the following day. Quoted in Francis Parkman *Montcalm and Wolfe* (1884).

83 Now God be praised, I will die in peace.
1759 Last words, on hearing of the defeat of the French at Quebec. Quoted in J Knox *Historical Journal of the Campaigns in North America* (1909), ch.17.

Wolfe, Thomas Clayton 1900–38

US novelist. Unsuccessful in drama, he wrote a series of sprawling, uneven but often powerful novels, two of which were published posthumously.

84 Most of the time we think we're sick, it's all in the mind.
1929 *Look Homeward, Angel*, pt.1, ch.1.

85 'Where they got you stationed now, Luke?'… 'At the p-p-p-present time in Norfolk at the Navy base,' Luke answered, 'm-m-making the world safe for hypocrisy.'
1929 *Look Homeward, Angel*, pt.3, ch.36.

86 My efforts to cut out 50,000 words may sometimes result in my adding 75,000.
1929 Letter to his editor, Maxwell Perkins.

87 If a man has a talent and cannot use it, he has failed. If he has a talent and uses only half of it, he has partly failed. If he has a talent and learns somehow to use the whole of it, he has gloriously succeeded, and won a satisfaction and a triumph few men ever know.
The Web and the Rock (published 1939), ch.29.

88 It was a cruel city, but it was a lovely one, a savage city, yet it had such tenderness, a bitter, harsh, and violent catacomb of stone and steel and tunnelled rock, slashed savagely with light, and roaring, fighting a constant ceaseless warfare of men and machinery; and yet it was so sweetly and so delicately pulsed, as full of warmth, of passion, and of love, as it was full of hate.
1939 *The Web and the Rock* (published 1939), ch.30.

89 You Can't Go Home Again.
Title of novel (published 1940).

Wolfe, Tom (Thomas Kennerley) 1931–

US journalist and novelist. He was a leading proponent of the New Journalism, with a propensity for a racy style and attention-grabbing titles. His book on the astronauts, *The Right Stuff* (1979), was filmed, as was his novel *The Bonfire of the Vanities* (1987).

90 The Electric Kool-Aid Acid Test
1968 Title of book.

91 Radical chic invariably favors radicals who seem primitive, exotic and romantic.
1970 *Radical Chic*.

92 Not 'Seeing is Believing', you ninny, but 'Believing is Seeing'. For modern art has become completely literary: the paintings and other works exist only to illustrate the text.
1975 *The Painted Word*, ch.1.

93 The idea was to prove at every foot of the way up…that you were one of the elected and anointed ones who had the right stuff and could move higher and higher and even—ultimately, God willing, one day—that you might be able to join that special few at the very top, that elite who had the capacity to bring tears to men's eyes, the very Brotherhood of the Right Stuff itself.
1979 *The Right Stuff*.

94 A cult is a religion with no political power.
1980 *In Our Time*, ch.2.

95 From Bauhaus to Our House.
1981 Title of book.

96 Today educated people look upon traditional religious ties—Catholic, Episcopal, Presbyterian, Methodist, Baptist, Jewish—as matters of social pedigree. It is only art that they look upon religiously.
1984 'The Worship of Art: Notes on the New God', in *Harper's*, Oct.

97 Yes, the labour movement was truly religious, like Judaism itself. It was one of those things you believed in for all mankind and didn't care about for a second in your own life.
1987 *The Bonfire of the Vanities*, ch.8.

98 A liberal is a conservative who has been arrested.
1987 *The Bonfire of the Vanities*, ch.24.

99 Pornography was the great vice of the Seventies; plutography—the graphic depiction of the acts of the rich—is the great vice of the Eighties.
1988 In the *Sunday Times Magazine*, 10 Jan.

1 The Versailles of American corporate culture.
1992 Of Manhattan's Four Seasons restaurant, in the *New York Times*, 14 Nov.

2 In the year 2000, a Tolstoy or a Flaubert wouldn't have stood a chance in the United States.
2000 *Hooking Up*.

Wollstonecraft, Mary *also known as* ***Mrs Godwin*** 1759–97

Anglo-Irish feminist and writer. Her *Vindication of the Rights of Man* (1790) was followed by *Vindication of the Rights of Woman* (1792), advocating gender equality. After bearing an illegitimate daughter to Captain Gilbert Imlay (1794) she married political writer William Godwin (1797) but died on the birth of their daughter, Mary Wollstonecraft Shelley.

3 I now speak of the sex in general. Many individuals have more sense than their male relatives; and…some women govern their husbands without degrading

themselves, because intellect will always govern.
1792 *A Vindication of the Rights of Woman*, introduction.

4 Men, in general, seem to employ their reason to justify prejudices, which they have imbibed, they can scarcely trace how, rather than root them out.
1792 *A Vindication of the Rights of Woman*, pt.1, ch.1.

5 Men, indeed, appear to me to act in a very unphilosophical manner when they try to secure the good conduct of women by attempting to keep them always in a state of childhood.
1792 *A Vindication of the Rights of Woman*, pt.1, ch.2.

6 Strengthen the female mind by enlarging it, and there will be an end to blind obedience; but as blind obedience is ever sought for by power, tyrants and sensualists are in the right when they endeavour to keep women in the dark, because the former only want slaves, and the latter a play-thing.
1792 *A Vindication of the Rights of Woman*, pt.1, ch.2.

7 Gentleness, docility, and a spaniel-like affection are, on this ground, consistently recommended as the cardinal virtues of the sex; and, disregarding the arbitrary economy of nature, one writer has declared that it is masculine for a woman to be melancholy. She was created to be the toy of man, his rattle, and it must jingle in his ears, whenever, dismissing reason, he chooses to be amused.
1792 *A Vindication of the Rights of Woman*, pt.1, ch.2.

8 Liberty is the mother of virtue, and if women be, by their very constitution, slaves, and not allowed to breathe the sharp invigorating air of freedom, they must ever languish like exotics, and be reckoned beautiful flaws in nature.
1792 *A Vindication of the Rights of Woman*, pt.1, ch.2.

9 The *divine right* of husbands, like the divine right of kings, may it is to be hoped, in this enlightened age, be contested without danger.
1792 *A Vindication of the Rights of Woman*, pt.1, ch.3.

10 A king is always a king—and a woman always a woman; his authority and her sex, ever stand between them and rational converse.
1792 *A Vindication of the Rights of Woman*, pt.1, ch.4.

11 I do not wish them to have power over men; but over themselves.
1792 Of women. *A Vindication of the Rights of Woman*, pt.1, ch.4.

12 Necessity never makes prostitution the business of men's lives; though numberless are the women who are thus rendered systematically vicious.
1792 *A Vindication of the Rights of Woman*, pt.1, ch.4.

13 Let woman share the rights and she will emulate the virtues of man, for she must grow more perfect when emancipated.
1792 *A Vindication of the Rights of Woman*, pt.1, ch.13.

Wolpert, Lewis 1929–

British developmental biologist.

14 The physics of motion provides one of the clearest examples of the counter-intuitive and unexpected nature of science.
1992 *The Unnatural Nature of Science.*

Wolstenholme, Kenneth 1920–2002

English football commentator. He broadcast for the BBC from 1948 to 1971, covering 22 FA Cup finals and five World Cups.

15 There are people on the pitch…they think it's all over…it is now!
1966 Radio commentary on the last goal of the World Cup final, in which England beat West Germany at Wembley.

Wood, Victoria 1953–

English playwright, lyricist and comedienne. Her comic plays include *Talent* (1979) and *Happy Since I Met You* (1981), and her television work is collected in *Mens Sana in Thingummy Doodah* (1991).

16 Jogging is for people who aren't intelligent enough to watch Breakfast TV.
1989 *Victoria Wood*, television series. Published in *Mens Sana in Thingummy Doodah* (1991).

17 LILL: My massage was marvellous. I feel really relaxed. And my masseur, Harold—
VICTORIA: You can't have a masseur called Harold. It's like having a member of the Royal Family called Ena.
1989 *Victoria Wood*, television series. Published in *Mens Sana in Thingummy Doodah* (1991).

Woodcock, George 1912–95

Canadian writer, poet, social critic and biographer. He also wrote several travel books. He has been described as a philosophical anarchist.

18 Well-founded fear, which takes one through the valley of the shadow of death without abandoning one there, is what makes the worst of worse journeys; the situation is made all the more intense when the fear is somehow mingled with delight.
'My Worst Journeys', collected in Keath Fraser (ed) *Worst Journeys: The Picador Book of Travel* (1991).

Woodman, Marion 1928–

Canadian therapist and author.

19 To strive for perfection is to kill love because perfection does not recognize humanity.
1982 *Addition to Perfection: The Still Unravished Bride.*

Woodroofe, Thomas 1899–1978

British naval officer.

20 The whole fleet's lit up. When I say 'lit up', I mean by fairy lamps.
1937 BBC radio commentary of the Spithead review, 20 May, Britain's first live outside broadcast. 'Lit up' was a common euphemism for 'drunk'.

Woods, Donald 1933–2001

South African editor and Black civil rights campaigner.

21 When I left South Africa, I arrogantly predicted that within seven years, apartheid would be gone. It has taken a bit longer than that.
1991 BBC TV broadcast, Feb.

Woods, Tiger 1975–

US golfer. He has won numerous events, including the US

Masters (1997, 2001, 2002), the British Open (2000) and the US Open (2000, 2002).

22 Growing up, I came up with this name: I'm a Cablinasian.
1997 Explaining his dissatisfaction with the term 'African-American' to describe his own Caucasian, African-American, Native American, Chinese and Thai ancestry. In an interview with Oprah Winfrey, 21 Apr.

23 My dad once told me: no matter what anyone says or writes, really, none of those people have to hit your four-foot putt. You have to go do it yourself.
2001 *QuotableTiger.*

Woodsworth, James Shaver 1874–1942

Canadian politician, socialist and pacifist. An MP from 1921, in 1932 he founded the Co-operative Commonwealth Federation, serving as its chairman and parliamentary leader.

24 I take my place with the children.
1939 Casting the sole dissenting voice to ratify Canada's entry into World War II, in the House of Commons, Ottawa, 9 Sep.

Wooldridge, Adrian 1959–

English journalist with *The Economist* (London).

25 America has mitigated poverty by massively increasing pauperism.
1995 'Damned Statistics', in the *Wall Street Journal*, 27 Jul.

Woolf, (Adeline) Virginia *née Stephen* 1882–1941

English novelist, critic and essayist. Daughter of Sir Leslie Stephen and sister of Vanessa Bell, she married Leonard Woolf and in 1917 they formed the Hogarth Press. Her experimental novels include *Mrs. Dalloway* (1925) and *To the Lighthouse* (1927). *A Room of One's Own* (1929) is a feminist classic. She committed suicide by drowning.

26 Life…is a luminous halo, a semi-transparent envelope surrounding us from the beginning of consciousness to the end.
1919 'Modern Fiction'.

27 Each had his past shut in him like the leaves of a book known to him by heart; and his friends could only read the title.
1922 *Jacob's Room*, ch.5.

28 It's not catastrophes, murders, deaths, diseases, that age and kill us; it's the way people look and laugh, and run up the steps of omnibuses.
1922 *Jacob's Room*, ch.6.

29 Never did I read such tosh.
1922 On James Joyce's *Ulysses*. Letter to Lytton Strachey, 24 Apr.

30 I believe that all novels…deal with character, and that it is to express character—not to preach doctrines, sing songs, or celebrate the glories of the British Empire, that the form of the novel, so clumsy, verbose, and undramatic, so rich, elastic, and alive, has been evolved.
1924 'Mr Bennett and Mrs Brown'.

31 Life itself, every moment of it, every drop of it, here, this instant, now, in the sun, in Regent's Park, was enough. Too much, indeed.
1925 *Mrs Dalloway.*

32 It is vain and foolish to talk of knowing Greek.
1925 *The Common Reader*, 'On Not Knowing Greek'.

33 The interest in life does not lie in what people do, nor even in their relations to each other, but largely in the power to communicate with a third party, antagonistic, enigmatic, yet perhaps persuadable, which one may call life in general.
1925 *The Common Reader*, 'On Not Knowing Greek'.

34 For the self-centred and self-limited writers have a power denied the more catholic and broad-minded… Nothing issues from their minds which has not been marked with their own impress.
1925 *The Common Reader*, 'Jane Eyre and Wuthering Heights'.

35 A good essay must have this permanent quality about it; it must draw its curtain round us, but it must be a curtain that shuts us in not out.
1925 *The Common Reader*, 'The Modern Essay'.

36 We are nauseated by the sight of trivial personalities decomposing in the eternity of print.
1925 *The Common Reader*, 'The Modern Essay'.

37 *Middlemarch*, the magnificent book which with all its imperfections is one of the few English novels for grown up people.
1925 *The Common Reader*, 'George Eliot'.

38 London is enchanting. I step out upon a tawny coloured magic carpet, it seems, and get carried into beauty without raising a finger… People pop in and out, lightly, divertingly like rabbits; and I look down Southampton Row, wet as a seal's back or red and yellow with sunshine, and watch the omnibuses going and coming and hear the old crazy organs. One of these days I will write about London, and how it takes up the private life and carries it on, without any effort.
1926 Diary entry, 26 May.

39 So that is marriage, Lily thought, a man and a woman looking at a girl throwing a ball.
1927 *To the Lighthouse*, pt.1, ch.13.

40 She faded…became more inconspicuous than ever, in her little grey dress.
1927 *To the Lighthouse*, pt.1, ch.17.

41 One cannot think well, love well, sleep well, if one has not dined well.
1929 *A Room of One's Own*, ch.1.

42 A woman must have money and a room of her own if she is to write fiction.
1929 *A Room of One's Own*, ch.1.

43 Women have served all these centuries as looking-glasses possessing the magic and delicious power of reflecting the figure of man at twice its natural size.
1929 *A Room of One's Own*, ch.2.

44 I would venture to guess that Anon, who wrote so many poems without signing them, was often a woman.
1929 *A Room of One's Own*, ch.3.

45 Literature is strewn with the wreckage of men who have minded beyond reason the opinion of others.
1929 *A Room of One's Own*, ch.3.

46 It is obvious that the values of women differ very often from the values which have been made by the other sex… Yet it is the masculine values that prevail.
1929 *A Room of One's Own*, ch.4.

47 We think back through our mothers if we are women.
1929 *A Room of One's Own*, ch.4.

48 For there is a spot the size of a shilling at the back of the

head which one can never see for oneself. It is one of the good offices that sex can discharge for sex—to describe that spot.
1929 *A Room of One's Own*, ch.5.

49 For all the dinners are cooked; the plates and cups washed; the children sent to school and gone out into the world. Nothing remains of it all. All has vanished. No biography or history has a word to say about it.
1929 *A Room of One's Own*, ch.5.

50 I am not trying to tell a story. Yet perhaps it might be done in that way. A mind thinking. They might be islands of light—islands in the stream that I am trying to convey; life itself going on.
1929 Diary entry, 28 May.

51 Killing the Angel in the House was part of the occupation of a woman writer.
1931 'Professions for Women', lecture to the National Society for Women's Service, 21 Jan. Woolf's solution was to throw the inkpot at the Angel (the embodiment of stereotyped Victorian femininity) whenever she appeared.

52 Things have dropped from me. I have outlived certain desires; I have lost friends, some by death—Percival—others through sheer inability to cross the street.
1931 *The Waves*.

53 Yes, always keep the Classics at hand to prevent flop.
1937 Diary entry, 23 Jun.

54 Somewhere, everywhere, now hidden, now apparent in whatever is written down, is the form of a human being. If we seek to know him, are we idly occupied?
The Captain's Death Bed, 'Reading' (published 1950).

55 The poet gives us his essence, but prose takes the mould of the body and mind entire.
The Captain's Death Bed, 'Reading' (published 1950).

Woollcott, Alexander Humphreys 1887–1943

US critic, writer, actor and broadcaster. He became theatre critic for the *New York Times* in 1914 and subsequently became one of the celebrated Algonquin Round Table of wits and literary figures. Noted for his biting humour, he was the inspiration for Kaufman and Hart's play *The Man Who Came to Dinner*.

56 She is so odd a blend of Little Nell and Lady Macbeth. It is not so much the familiar phenomenon of a hand of steel in a velvet glove as a lacy sleeve with a bottle of vitriol concealed in its folds.
1934 Of Dorothy Parker. *While Rome Burns*, 'Our Mrs Parker'.

57 I have no need of your God-damned sympathy. I only wish to be entertained by some of your grosser reminiscences.
1942 Letter to Rex O'Malley. Quoted in Samuel Adams *Alexander Woollcott* (1945), ch.34.

58 A broker is a man who takes your fortune and runs it into a shoestring.
Quoted in Samuel Adams *Alexander Woollcott* (1945), ch.15.

59 Harold Ross…had a contempt for anything he didn't understand, which was practically everything.
Quoted in James Thurber *The Years With Ross* (1959), ch.15.

60 All the things I really like to do are either illegal, immoral or fattening.
Quoted in R Drennan *Wit's End* (1968).

61 The play left a taste of lukewarm parsnip juice.
Play review. Quoted in H Techmann *Smart Alex* (1976).

62 My doctor forbids me to play, unless I win.
Of croquet. Quoted in Colin Jarman *The Guinness Dictionary of Sports Quotations* (1990).

63 It is no game for the soft of sinew and the gentle of spirit. The higher and dirtier croquet-player can use the guile of a cobra and the inhumanity of a boa constrictor.
Quoted in Colin Jarman *The Guinness Dictionary of Sports Quotations* (1990).

64 Always a godfather, never a god!
On serving as godfather at a christening celebration for the 19th time. Attributed.

65 Just what God would do if he had the money.
On being shown round Moss Hart's splendid country retreat. Attributed.

66 The scenery was beautiful, but the actors got in front of it.
Play review.

Wordsworth, William 1770–1850

English poet. At first given to agnosticism and a revolutionary passion for social justice, he then turned to exploring the lives of humble people living in contact with nature. He succeeded Robert Southey as Poet Laureate in 1843.

67 Now, in this blank of things, a harmony,
Home-felt, and home-created, comes to heal
That grief for which the senses still supply
Fresh food.
1786 'Calm is all nature as a resting wheel', l.7–10. Published in the *Morning Post*, 13 Feb. 1802.

68 In this universe,
Where the least things control the greatest, where
The faintest breath that breathes can move a world.
1795–6 Oswald. *The Borderers*, act 3, l.1562–4 (published 1842).

69 These beauteous forms,
Through a long absence, have not been to me
As is a landscape to a blind man's eye:
But oft, in lonely rooms, and 'mid the din
Of towns and cities, I have owed to them,
In hours of weariness, sensations sweet,
Felt in the blood, and felt along the heart.
1798 'Lines composed a few miles above Tintern Abbey, on revisiting the banks of the Wye', l.22–8.

70 That best portion of a good man's life,
His little, nameless, unremembered, acts
Of kindness and of love.
1798 'Lines composed a few miles above Tintern Abbey, on revisiting the banks of the Wye', l.33–5.

71 For I have learned
To look on nature, not as in the hour
Of thoughtless youth; but hearing often-times
The still, sad music of humanity,
Nor harsh nor grating, though of ample power
To chasten and subdue. And I have felt
A presence that disturbs me with the joy
Of elevated thoughts; a sense sublime
Of something far more deeply interfused,
Whose dwelling is the light of setting suns,
And the round ocean and the living air,
And the blue sky, and in the mind of man.
1798 'Lines composed a few miles above Tintern Abbey, on

revisiting the banks of the Wye', l.88–99.

72 Therefore am I still
A lover of the meadows and the woods,
And mountains; and of all that we behold
From this green earth; of all the mighty world
Of eye, and ear,—both what they half create
And what perceive.
1798 'Lines composed a few miles above Tintern Abbey, on revisiting the banks of the Wye', l.102–6.

73 Away we go—and what care we
For treasons, tumults, and for wars?
We are as calm in our delight
As is the crescent moon so bright
Among the scattered stars.
1798 'Peter Bell', prologue, stanza 5 (published 1819).

74 Books! 'tis a dull and endless strife:
Come, hear the woodland linnet
How sweet his music! on my life
There's more of wisdom in it.
1798 'The Tables Turned', stanza 3.

75 One impulse from a vernal wood
May teach you more of man,
Of moral evil and of good,
Than all the sages can.

Sweet is the lore which Nature brings;
Our meddling intellect
Mis-shapes the beauteous forms of things:—
We murder to dissect.

Enough of science and of art;
Close up those barren leaves;
Come forth and bring with you a heart
That watches and receives.
1798 'The Tables Turned', stanzas 6–8.

76 I heard a thousand blended notes,
While in a grove I sate reclined,
In that sweet mood when pleasant thoughts
Bring sad thoughts to the mind.
1798 'Lines Written in Early Spring', stanza 1.

77 To her fair works did Nature link
The human soul that through me ran;
And much it grieved my heart to think
What man has made of man.
1798 'Lines Written in Early Spring', stanza 2.

78 She dwelt among the untrodden ways
Beside the springs of Dove,
A maid whom there were none to praise
And very few to love:

A violet by a mossy stone
Half hidden from the eye!
—Fair as a star, when only one
Is shining in the sky.

She lived unknown, and few could know
When Lucy ceased to be;
But she is in her grave, and, oh,
The difference to me!
1799 'She dwelt among the untrodden ways', complete poem (published 1800).

79 Three years she grew in sun and shower,
The Nature said, 'A lovelier flower
On earth was never sown;
This Child I to myself will take;
She shall be mine, and I will make
A Lady of my own.'
1799 'Three Years she grew in sun and shower', stanza 1 (published 1800).

80 A slumber did my spirit seal;
I had no human fears:
She seemed a thing that could not feel
The touch of earthly years.

No motion has she now, no force;
She neither hears nor sees;
Rolled round in earth's diurnal course
With rocks, and stones and trees.
1799 'A slumber did my spirit seal', complete poem (published 1800).

81 Physician art thou?—one, all eyes,
Philosopher!—a fingering slave,
One that would peep and botanize
Upon his mother's grave?
1799 'A Poet's Epitaph', stanza 5 (published 1800).

82 One to whose smooth-rubbed soul can cling
Nor form, nor feeling, great or small;
A reasoning, self-sufficing thing,
An intellectual All-in-all!
1799 'A Poet's Epitaph', stanza 8 (published 1800).

83 Shut close the door; press down the latch;
Sleep in thy intellectual crust;
Nor lose ten tickings of thy watch
Near this unprofitable dust.
1799 'A Poet's Epitaph', stanza 9 (published 1800).

84 In common truths that round us lie
Some random truths he can impart,—
The harvest of a quiet eye
That broods and sleeps on his own heart.
1799 'A Poet's Epitaph', stanza 13 (published 1800).

85 Wisdom and Spirit of the universe!
Thou soul, that art the eternity of thought,
And giv'st to forms and images a breath
And everlasting motion.
1799 'Influence of Natural Objects', l.1–4 (published in *The Friend* 28 Dec 1809).

86 Leaving the tumultuous throng,
To cut across the reflex of a star;
Image that, flying still before me, gleamed
Upon the glassy plain.
1799 'Influence of Natural Objects', l.49–52 (published in *The Friend* 28 Dec 1809).

87 When we had given our bodies to the wind,
And all the shadowy banks on either side
Came sweeping through the darkness, spinning still
The rapid line of motion, then at once
Have I, reclining back upon my heels,
Stopped short; yet still the solitary cliffs
Wheeled by me—even as if the earth had rolled
With visible motion her diurnal round!
1799 'Influence of Natural Objects', l.53–60 (published in *The Friend* 28 Dec 1809).

88 Oh there is blessing in this gentle breeze,
A visitant that while it fans my cheek

Doth seem half conscious of the joy it brings
From the green fields, and from yon azure sky.
Whate'er its mission, the soft breeze can come
To none more grateful than to me; escaped
From the vast city, where I long had pined
A discontented sojourner: now free,
Free as a bird to settle where I will.
1799–1805 *The Prelude*, bk.1, l.1–9 (published 1850).

89 I, methought, while the sweet breath of heaven
Was blowing on my body, felt within
A correspondent breeze, that gently moved
With quickening virtue, but is now become
A tempest, a redundant energy,
Vexing its own creation.
1799–1805 *The Prelude*, bk.1, l.33–8 (published 1850).

90 Either still I find
Some imperfection in the chosen theme,
Or see of absolute accomplishment
Much wanting, so much wanting, in myself,
That I recoil and droop, and seek repose
In listlessness from vain perplexity,
Unprofitably travelling towards the grave.
1799–1805 *The Prelude*, bk.1, l.261–7 (published 1850).

91 Fair seed-time had my soul, and I grew up
Fostered alike by beauty and by fear.
1799–1805 *The Prelude*, bk.1, l.301–2 (published 1850).

92 Dust as we are, the immortal spirit grows
Like harmony in music; there is a dark
Inscrutable workmanship that reconciles
Discordant elements, makes them cling together
In one society.
1799–1805 *The Prelude*, bk.1, l.340–4 (published 1850).

93 Then, the calm
And dead still water lay upon my mind
Even with a weight of pleasure, and the sky,
Never before so beautiful, sank down
Into my heart, and held me like a dream.
1799–1805 *The Prelude*, bk.2, l.70–4 (published 1850).

94 I was taught to feel, perhaps too much,
The self-sufficing power of Solitude.
1799–1805 *The Prelude*, bk.2, l.76–7 (published 1850).

95 Science appears but what in truth she is,
Not as our glory and our absolute boast,
But as a succedaneum, and a prop
To our infirmity.
1799–1805 *The Prelude*, bk.2, l.212–15 (published 1850).

96 That false secondary power
By which we multiply distinctions, then
Deem that our puny boundaries are things
That we perceive, and not that we have made.
1799–1805 *The Prelude*, bk.2, l.216–19 (published 1850).

97 A babe, by intercourse of touch
I held mute dialogues with my Mother's heart.
1799–1805 *The Prelude*, bk.2, l.267–8 (published 1850).

98 From my pillow, looking forth by light
Of moon or favouring stars, I could behold
The antechapel where the statue stood
Of Newton with his prism and silent face,
The marble index of a mind for ever
Voyaging through strange seas of Thought alone.
1799–1805 *The Prelude*, bk.3, l.58–63 (published 1850).

99 There's not a man
That lives who hath not known his god-like hours.
1799–1805 *The Prelude*, bk.3, l.190–1 (published 1850).

1 Visionary power
Attends the motions of the viewless winds,
Embodied in the mystery of words.
1799–1805 *The Prelude*, bk.5, l.595–7 (published 1850).

2 Even forms and substances are circumfused
By that transparent veil with light divine,
And, through the turnings intricate of verse,
Present themselves as objects recognised,
In flashes, and with glory not their own.
1799–1805 *The Prelude*, bk.5, l.601–5 (published 1850).

3 An open place it was, and overlooked,
From high, the sullen water far beneath,
On which a dull red image of the moon
Lay bedded, changing oftentimes its form
Like an uneasy snake.
1799–1805 *The Prelude*, bk.6, l.703–7 (published 1850).

4 In the very world, which is the world
Of all of us,—the place where, in the end,
We find our happiness, or not at all!
1799–1805 *The Prelude*, bk.11, l.142–4 (published 1850).

5 I shook the habit off
Entirely and for ever, and again
In Nature's presence stood, as now I stand,
A sensitive being, a *creative* soul.
1799–1805 *The Prelude*, bk.12, l.204–7 (published 1850).

6 A balance, an ennobling interchange
Of action from without and from within;
The excellence, pure function, and best power
Both of the object seen, and eye that sees.
1799–1805 *The Prelude*, bk.13, l.375–8 (published 1850).

7 The thought of death sits easy on the man
Who has been born and dies among the mountains.
c.1800 The Priest. 'The Brothers', l.182–3.

8 The moving accident is not my trade;
To freeze the blood I have no ready arts:
'Tis my delight, alone in summer shade,
To pipe a simple song for thinking hearts.
1800 'Hart-Leap Well', part 2, l.97–100.

9 I travelled among unknown men
In lands beyond the sea;
Nor England! did I know till then
What love I bore to thee.
1801 'I Travelled Among Unknown Men', stanza 1 (published 1807).

10 Poetry is the spontaneous overflow of powerful feelings: it takes its origin from emotion recollected in tranquillity.
1802 Preface to *Lyrical Ballads* (2nd ed. 1802; *Lyrical Ballads* first published 1798, preface added 1800, enlarged 1802).

11 Milton! thou shouldst be living at this hour:
England hath need of thee: she is a fen
Of stagnant waters: altar, sword and pen,
Fireside, the heroic wealth of hall and bower,
Have forfeited their ancient English dower
Of inward happiness. We are selfish men;
Oh! raise us up, return to us again;
And give us manners, virtue, freedom, power.
Thy soul was like a star, and dwelt apart;

Thou hadst a voice whose sound was like the sea:
Pure as the naked heavens, majestic, free,
So didst thou travel on life's common way,
In cheerful godliness; and yet thy heart
The lowliest duties on herself did lay.

1802 'Milton! thou shouldst be living at this hour', complete poem (published 1807).

12 Thrice welcome, darling of the Spring
Even yet thou are to me
No bird, but an invisible thing,
A voice, a mystery.

1802 'To the Cuckoo', stanza 4 (published 1807).

13 It is a beauteous evening, calm and free,
The holy time is quiet as a nun
Breathless with adoration; the broad sun
Is sinking down in its tranquillity;
The gentleness of heaven broods o'er the sea:
Listen! the mighty being is awake,
And doth with his eternal motion make
A sound like thunder—everlastingly.

1802 'It is a beauteous evening calm and free', l.1–8 (published 1807).

14 With little here to do or see
Of things that in the great world be,
Sweet Daisy! oft I talk to thee
For thou art worthy,
Thou unassuming commonplace
Of Nature, with that homely face,
And yet with something of a grace
Which love makes for thee!

1802 'To the Daisy', stanza 1 (published 1807).

15 My heart leaps up when I behold
A rainbow in the sky:
So was it when my life began;
So is it now I am a man;
So be it when I shall grow old,
Or let me die!
The Child is father of the Man;
And I could wish my days to be
Bound each to each by natural piety.

1802 'My heart leaps up when I behold', complete poem (published 1807).

16 My whole life have I lived in pleasant thought,
As if life's business were a summer mood;
As if all needful things would come unsought
To genial faith, still rich in genial good.

1802 'Resolution and Independence', stanza 6 (published 1807).

17 I thought of Chatterton, the marvellous boy,
The sleepless soul that perished in his pride.
Of him who walked in glory and in joy
Following his plough along the mountainside:
By our own spirits are we deified.
We poets in our youth begin in gladness;
But thereof comes in the end despondency and
madness.

1802 Of the poet Thomas Chatterton, who committed suicide at the age of 17. 'Resolution and Independence', stanza 7 (published 1807).

18 The fear that kills;
And hope that is unwilling to be fed.

1802 'Resolution and Independence', stanza 17 (published 1807).

19 Earth hath not anything to show more fair:
Dull would he be of soul who could pass by
A sight so touching in its majesty:
This City now doth like a garment wear
The beauty of the morning; silent, bare,
Ships, towers, domes, theatres, and to the sky;
All bright and glittering in the smokeless air.
Never did sun more beautifully steep
In his first splendour, valley, rock, or hill;
Ne'er saw I, never felt, a calm so deep!
The river glideth at his own sweet will;
Dear God! the very houses seem asleep;
And all that mighty heart is lying still!

1802 Of London. 'Composed upon Westminster Bridge', complete poem. (Published 1807).

20 Once did she hold the gorgeous East in fee,
And was the safeguard of the West: the worth
Of Venice did not fall below her birth,
Venice, the eldest child of Liberty.

1802 Of Venice. 'On the Extinction of the Venetian Republic', l.1–4 (published 1807).

21 There was a time when meadow, grove, and stream,
The earth, and every common sight,
To me did seem
Apparelled in celestial light,
The glory and the freshness of a dream.
It is not now as it hath been of yore;—
Turn whereso'er I may,
By night or day,
The things which I have seen I now can see no more.

c.1802–1803 'Ode. Intimations of Immortality from Recollections of Early Childhood', stanza 1 (published 1807).

22 Thou Child of Joy,
Shout round me, let me hear thy shouts.

c.1802–1803 'Ode. Intimations of Immortality from Recollections of Early Childhood', stanza 3 (published 1807).

23 But there's a tree, of many, one,
A single field which I have looked upon,
Both of them speak of something that is gone:
The pansy at my feet
Doth the same tale repeat:
Whither is fled the visionary gleam?
Where is it now, the glory and the dream?

c.1802–1803 'Ode. Intimations of Immortality from Recollections of Early Childhood', stanza 4 (published 1807).

24 Our birth is but a sleep and a forgetting:
The soul that rises with us, our life's star,
Hath had elsewhere its setting,
And cometh from afar:
Not in entire forgetfulness
And not in utter nakedness,
But trailing clouds of glory do we come
From God, who is our home:
Heaven lies about us in our infancy!
Shades of the prison-house begin to close
Upon the growing boy,
But he beholds the light, and whence it flows,
He sees it in his joy;
The youth, who daily farther from the east
Must travel, still is nature's priest,
And by the vision splendid
Is on his way attended;

At length the man perceives it die away,
And fade into the light of common day.
c.1802–1803 'Ode. Intimations of Immortality from Recollections of Early Childhood', stanza 5 (published 1807).

25 O joy! that in our embers
Is something that doth live,
That nature yet remembers
What was so fugitive!
c.1802–1803 'Ode. Intimations of Immortality from Recollections of Early Childhood', stanza 9 (published 1807).

26 Those obstinate questionings
Of sense and outward things,
Fallings from us, vanishings;
Blank misgivings of a creature
Moving about in worlds not realised,
High instincts before which our mortal nature
Did tremble like a guilty thing surprised.
c.1802–1803 'Ode. Intimations of Immortality from Recollections of Early Childhood', stanza 9 (published 1807).

27 Our noisy years seem moments in the being
Of the eternal silence: truths that wake,
To perish never:
Which neither listlessness, nor mad endeavour,
Nor man nor boy,
Nor all that is at enmity with joy,
Can utterly abolish or destroy!
Hence in a season of calm weather,
Though inland far we be,
Our souls have sight of that immortal sea
Which brought us hither,
Can in a moment travel thither,
And see the children sport upon the shore,
And hear the mighty waters rolling evermore.
c.1802–1803 'Ode. Intimations of Immortality from Recollections of Early Childhood', stanza 9 (published 1807).

28 Though nothing can bring back the hour
Of splendour in the grass, of glory in the flower;
We will grieve not.
c.1802–1803 'Ode. Intimations of Immortality from Recollections of Early Childhood', stanza 10 (published 1807).

29 Thanks to the human heart by which we live,
Thanks to its tenderness, its joys, and fears,
To me the meanest flower that blows can give
Thoughts that do often lie too deep for tears.
c.1802–1803 'Ode. Intimations of Immortality from Recollections of Early Childhood', stanza 11 (published 1807).

30 Let beeves and home-bred kine partake
The sweets of Burn-mill meadow;
The swan on still St Mary's Lake
Float double, swan and shadow!
We will not see them; will not go,
To-day, nor yet to-morrow;
Enough if in our hearts we know
There's such a place as Yarrow.

Be Yarrow stream unseen, unknown;
It must, or we shall rue it:
We have a vision of our own,
Ah! why should we undo it?
The treasured dreams of times long past,
We'll keep them, winsome Marrow!
For when we're there, although 'tis fair,
'Twill be another Yarrow!
1803 'Yarrow Unvisited', stanzas 6–7 (published 1807).

31 For thou wert still the poor man's stay,
The poor man's heart, the poor man's hand;
And all the oppressed, who wanted strength,
Had thine at their command.
1803 'Rob Roy's Grave', l. 109–12 (published 1807).

32 Thy friends are exultations, agonies,
And love, and man's unconquerable mind.
1803 'To Toussaint L'Ouverture', l.13–14 (published in the *Morning Post* 2 Feb).

33 What, you are stepping westward?
1803–5 'Stepping Westward', l.1 (published 1807).

34 Behold her, single in the field,
Yon solitary Highland Lass!
Reaping and singing by herself;
Stop here, or gently pass!
1803–5 'The Solitary Reaper', l.1–4 (published 1807).

35 She was a Phantom of delight
When first she gleamed upon my sight;
A lovely apparition sent
To be a moment's ornament.
1804 'She was a Phantom of delight', l.1–4 (published 1807).

36 And now I see with eye serene
The very pulse of the machine;
A being breathing thoughtful breath,
A traveller between life and death;
The reason firm, the temperate will,
Endurance, foresight, strength, and skill;
A perfect woman, nobly planned,
To warn, to comfort, and command.
1804 'She was a Phantom of delight', l.21–8 (published 1807).

37 Chains tie us down by land and sea;
And wishes, vain as mine, may be
All that is left to comfort thee.
1804 'The Affliction of Margaret', stanza 8 (published 1807).

38 My apprehensions come in crowds;
I dread the rustling of the grass;
The very shadows of the clouds
Have power to shake me as they pass.
1804 'The Affliction of Margaret', stanza 10 (published 1807).

39 Oh! pleasant exercise of hope and joy!
For mighty were the auxiliars which then stood
Upon our side, we who were strong in love!
Bliss it was in that dawn to be alive,
But to be young was very heaven!
1804 'The French Revolution as it appeared to enthusiasts at its commencement', l.1–5 (published in *The Friend*, 26 Oct. 1809).

40 I wandered lonely as a cloud
That floats on high o'er vales and hills,
When all at once I saw a crowd,
A host, of golden daffodils;
Beside the lake, beneath the trees,
Fluttering and dancing in the breeze.
1804 'I wandered lonely as a cloud', stanza 1 (published 1807).

41 Continuous as the stars that shine
And twinkle on the milky way
They stretched in never-ending line
Along the margin of a bay:
Ten thousand saw I at a glance,
Tossing their heads in sprightly dance.

1804 'I wandered lonely as a cloud', stanza 2 (published 1807).

42 The waves beside them danced; but they
Out-did the sparkling waves in glee:
A poet could not but be gay,
In such a jocund company:
I gazed—and gazed—but little thought
What wealth the show to me had brought.
1804 'I wandered lonely as a cloud', stanza 3 (published 1807).

43 For oft, when on my couch I lie
In vacant or in pensive mood,
They flash upon that inward eye
Which is the bliss of solitude;
And then my heart wih pleasure fills,
And dances with the daffodils.
1804 'I wandered lonely as a cloud', stanza 4 (published 1807).

44 If mine had been the painter's hand,
To express what then I saw; and add the gleam,
The light that never was, on sea or land,
The consecration, and the poet's dream.
1805 'Elegiac Stanzas: suggested by a picture of Peele Castle in a storm', stanza 4 (published 1807).

45 Not for a moment could I now behold
A smiling sea, and be what I have been.
1805 'Elegiac Stanzas: suggested by a picture of Peele Castle in a storm', stanza 10 (published 1807).

46 The world is too much with us; late and soon,
Getting and spending we lay waste our powers:
Little we see in nature that is ours;
We have given our hearts away, a sordid boon!
The sea that bares her bosom to the moon;
The winds that will be howling at all hours,
And are up-gathered now like sleeping flowers;
For this, for everything, we are out of tune;
It moves us not.—Great God! I'd rather be
A pagan suckled in a creed outworn;
So might I, standing on this pleasant lea,
Have glimpses that would make me less forlorn;
Have sight of Proteus rising from the sea;
Or hear old Triton blow his wreathèd horn.
1806 'The world is too much with us; late and soon', complete poem (published 1807).

47 Two voices are there; one is of the sea,
One of the mountains; each a mighty voice:
In both from age to age thou didst rejoice,
They were thy chosen music, Liberty!
1807 'Thought of a Briton on the Subjugation of Switzerland', l.1–4.

48 These people in the senseless hurry of their idle lives do not *read* books, they merely snatch a glance at them that they may talk about them. And even if this were not so, never forget what I believe was observed by Coleridge, that every great and original writer, in proportion as he is great or original, must himself create the taste by which he is to be relished.
1807 Letter to Lady Beaumont, 21 May, on his *Poems in Two Volumes* (1807). In *The Letters of William Wordsworth* edited by Alan G Hill (1984).

49 Surprised by joy—impatient as the wind
I turned to share the transport—Oh! with whom
But thee, deep buried in the silent tomb,
That spot which no vicissitude can find?
c.1812 'Surprised by joy—impatient as the wind', l.1–4 (published 1815). The poet's second daughter, Catherine, who died in June 1812, is the 'thee' referred to in the poem.

50 On Man, on Nature, and on Human Life,
Musing in solitude, I oft perceive
Fair trains of images before me rise,
Accompanied by feelings of delight
Pure, or with no unpleasing sadness mixed.
1814 'The Excursion', preface, l.1–5.

51 Not Chaos, not
The darkest pit of lowest Erebus
Nor aught of blinder vacancy, scooped out
By help of dreams—can breed such fear and awe
As fall upon us often when we look
Into our Minds, into the Mind of Man—
My haunt, and the main region of my song.
1814 'The Excursion', preface, l.35–41.

52 What soul was his, when, from the naked top
Of some bold headland, he beheld the sun
Rise up, and bathe the world in light!
He looked—
Ocean and earth, the solid frame of earth
And ocean's liquid mass, in gladness lay
Beneath him:—Far and wide the clouds were touched,
And in their silent faces he could read
Unutterable love.
1814 'The Excursion', bk.1, l.198–205.

53 This dull product of a scoffer's pen.
1814 Of Voltaire's novel *Candide*. 'The Excursion', bk.2, l.484.

54 Compassed round by pleasure, sighed
For independent happiness; craving peace,
The central feeling of all happiness,
Not as a refuge from distress or pain,
A breathing-time, vacation, or a truce,
But for its absolute self.
1814 'The Excursion', bk.3, l.380–5.

55 Society became my glittering bride,
And airy hopes my children.
1814 'The Excursion', bk.3, l.735–6.

56 'To every Form of being is assigned,'
Thus calmly spake the venerable Sage,
'An *active* Principle:—howe'er removed
From sense and observation, it subsists
In all things, in all natures.'
1814 'The Excursion', bk.9, l.1–5.

57 For all the startled scaly tribes that slink
Into his coverts, and each fearless link
Of dancing insects forged upon his breast.
1820 *The River Duddon*, no.28, 'Journey Renewed', l.6–8.

58 Still glides the stream, and shall for ever glide;
The Form remains, the function never dies;
While we, the brave, the mighty, and the wise,
We Men, who in our morn of youth defied
The elements, must vanish;—be it so!
1820 *The River Duddon*, no.34, 'After-Thought', l.5–9.

59 Enough, if something from our hands have power
To live, and act, and serve the future hour;
And if, as toward the silent tomb we go,
Through love, through hope, and faith's transcendent dower,
We feel that we are greater than we know.
1820 *The River Duddon*, no.34, 'After-Thought', l.10–14.

60 Ethereal minstrel! pilgrim of the sky!
Dost thou despise the earth where cares abound?
Or, while the wings aspire, are heart and eye
Both with thy nest upon the dewy ground?
1825 'To a Skylark', l.1–4 (published 1827).

61 Type of the wise who soar, but never roam;
True to the kindred points of Heaven and Home!
1825 'To a Skylark', l.11–12 (published 1827).

62 But who is innocent? By grace divine,
Not otherwise, O Nature! we are thine.
1834 'Evening Voluntaries', no.4, l.16–17 (published 1835).

63 Even so for me a vision sanctified
The sway of death; long ere my eyes had seen
Thy countenance—the still rapture of thy mien—
When thou, dear Sister! wert become death's bride:
No trace of pain or languor could abide
That change—age on thy brow was smoothed—thy cold
Wan cheek at once was privileged to unfold
A loveliness to living youth denied.
Oh! if within me hope should e'er decline,
The lamp of faith, lost Friend! too faintly burn;
The may that heaven-revealing smile of thine,
The bright assurance, visibly return:
And let my spirit in that power divine
Rejoice, as, through that power, it ceased to mourn.
1836 'November 1836', complete poem (published 1837).

64 The softest breeze to fairest flowers gives birth:
Think not that Prudence dwells in dark abodes,
She scans the future with the eye of gods.
1837 'At Bologna, In Remembrance of the Late Insurrections: Continued', l.12–14 (published 1842).

65 Before us lay a painful road,
And guidance have I sought in duteous love
From Wisdom's heavenly Father. Hence hath flowed
Patience, with trust that, whatsoe'er the way
Each takes in this high matter, all may move
Cheered with the prospect of a brighter day.
1839–40 *Sonnets upon the Punishment of Death*, no.14, 'Apology', l.9–14 (published in the *Quarterly Review* 1841).

66 With what nice care equivalents are given,
How just, how bountiful, the hand of Heaven.
1840 'Poor Robin', l.35–6 (published 1842).

67 That to this mountain-daisy's self were known
The beauty of its star-shaped shadow, thrown
On the smooth surface of this naked stone!
1844 'So fair so sweet', stanza 2 (published 1845).

68 21st May—a glorious day for beauty. I wish you could see how lovely our country is at this fine season.
1846 Letter to William Boxall, 21 May.

Worley, Helen

69 Dance, little words, on the end of your string. I can make you do most anything I want to. I can hide anywhere and watch you say the things I would never dare.
1982 *The Soul Survivor*, 'Puppetry and Poetry'.

Wotton, Sir Henry 1568–1639

English traveller, diplomat, scholar and poet. A trusted ambassador of James I and VI, he served in Venice and Germany. His tracts and letters were collected as *Reliquiae Wottonianae* (1651).

70 An ambassador is an honest man sent to lie abroad for the good of his country.
Quoted in Izaak Walton's *Life* (1651).

Wragg, Ted (Edward) Conrad 1938–

English educator, a Professor of Education at the University of Exeter.

71 Nobody loves a bad teacher.
1986 *Education: an Action Guide for Parents*.

Wright, Sir Almroth Edward 1861–1947

English bacteriologist and Professor of Experimental Pathology, known for his work on parasitic diseases. A vocal opponent of the suffragettes, he wrote *The Unexpurgated Case against Woman Suffrage* (1913).

72 The recruiting field for the militant suffragists is the million of our excess female population—that million which had better long ago have gone out to mate with its complement of men beyond the sea.
1912 Letter to *The Times*, 28 Mar.

73 The primordial argument against giving woman the vote is that that vote would not represent physical force.
1913 *The Unexpurgated Case against Woman Suffrage*, pt.2.

74 The woman voter would be pernicious to the State not only because she could not back her vote by physical force, but also by reason of her intellectual defects.
1913 *The Unexpurgated Case against Woman Suffrage*, pt.2.

75 Practically every man feels that there is in woman…an element of unreason which, when you come upon it, summarily puts an end to purely intellectual intercourse.
1913 *The Unexpurgated Case against Woman Suffrage*, pt.5

Wright, Betsey

Aide to President Clinton.

76 Bimbo eruptions.
1994 On an explosion of charges of sexual harassment against President Clinton. In the *Washington Post*, 30 May.

Wright, Frank Lloyd 1867–1959

US architect, known for his original and controversial designs exploiting modern technology and cubist spatial concepts. His works include the Imperial Hotel, Tokyo (1916–20) and the Guggenheim Museum of Art, New York (1959).

77 Architecture is man's great sense of himself embodied in a world of his own making. It may rise as high in quality only as its source because great art is great life.
1930 In Frederick Gutheim (ed) *Frank Lloyd Wright on Architecture: selected writings (1894–1940)*.

78 I know we can't have a great architecture while it is only for the landlord.
1932 In Frederick Gutheim (ed) *Frank Lloyd Wright on Architecture: selected writings (1894–1940)*.

79 The physician can bury his mistakes, but the architect can only advise his client to plant vines.
1953 In the *New York Times*, 4 Oct.

Wright, James C, Jr 1922–

US Congressman, former speaker of the US House of Representatives.

80 The boiling, churning caldron of America.
1987 On the House of Representatives. In *Life*.

81 I know how that pancake feels when you pour the syrup all over it.
1991 Of his official portrait, unveiled two years after he was forced to resign. In the *International Herald Tribune*, 12 Jul.

Wright, Judith Arundell *also known as* ***Judith Wright McKinney*** 1915–2000

Australian poet and conservationist, whose awards include the Robert Frost Memorial Prize (1976). Selected works have been published in *A Human Pattern* (1990).

82 The easy Eden-dreamtime then
in a country of birds and trees
made me your shadow-sister, child,
dark girl I couldn't play with.
1990 *A Human Pattern*, 'Two Dreamtimes', stanza 14. The poem is dedicated to Kath Walker (now Oodgeroo Noonuccal).

83 I am born of the conquerors,
you of the persecuted.
Raped by rum and an alien law,
progress and economics,

are you and I and a once-loved land
peopled by tribes and trees;
doomed traders and stock-exchanges,
bought by faceless strangers.
1990 *A Human Pattern*, 'Two Dreamtimes', stanzas 17–18. The poem is dedicated to Kath Walker (now Oodgeroo Noonuccal).

Wright, Kenyon 1932–99

Scottish Methodist minister, General Secretary of the Scottish Council of Churches since 1981, and Executive of the Scottish Constitutional Convention (1989–99).

84 What if that other single voice we know so well responds by saying, 'We say no, and we are the State'? Well, we say yes—and we are the people.
1989 Calling for a Scottish Parliament. Speech at the inaugural meeting of the Scottish Constitutional Convention, 30 Mar. The 'single voice' is that of Prime Minister Margaret Thatcher.

Wright, Orville and Wright, Wilbur 1871–1948, 1867–1912

Born in Dayton, Ohio, early mechanics and tinkerers, and eventually self-taught aviation engineers.

85 SUCCESS FOUR FLIGHTS THURSDAY MORNING ALL AGAINST TWENTY-ONE MILE WIND STARTED FROM LEVEL WITH ENGINE POWER ALONE AVERAGE SPEED THROUGH AIR THIRTY-ONE MILES LONGEST 59 SECONDS INFORM PRESS HOME CHRISTMAS.
1903 Telegram from the brothers at Kitty Hawk, North Carolina to their father, 17 Dec.

Wriston, Walter Bigelow 1919–

US banker. He joined Citibank in 1946 and worked his way up to chairman (1970–84).

86 Our banking system grew by accident; and wherever something happens by accident, it becomes a religion.
1975 In *Business Week*, 20 Jan.

87 When you retire…you go from who's who to who's that.
1985 In the *New York Times*, 21 Apr.

88 If you put a floor under wages and a ceiling over prices, a free man cannot long stand erect.
1986 *Risk and Other Four-Letters Words*.

89 The Doomsayers have always had their uses, since they trigger the coping mechanism that often prevents the events they forecast.
1986 *Risk and Other Four-Letter Words*.

90 Our current tendency to take our economic blood pressure every few minutes…obfuscates thought on many problems.
1986 *Risk and Other Four-Letter Words*.

91 Banking is a branch of the information business.
1986 *Risk and Other Four-Letters Words*.

92 It is a maxim of cryptology that what one man can devise, another can unravel. This principle keeps armies of tax lawyers and accountants employed, but adds nothing to our national productivity.
1986 *Risk and Other Four-Letters Words*.

93 Rising prices or wages do not cause inflation; they only report it. They represent an essential form of economic speech, since money is just another form of information.
1986 *Risk and Other Four-Letter Words*.

94 Every line in the government's budget has its own constituency.
1986 *Risk and Other Four-Letter Words*.

95 It's a Texas wrestling match with a new team against you every night.
1993 On life as a chief executive officer. In the *New York Times*, 25 Apr.

Wu-ti 157–87 BC

Chinese emperor of the Han dynasty who became its sixth ruler at the age of 16. The Han dynasty saw the Chinese expanding their political power westwards into Central Asia.

96 Autumn wind rises; white clouds fly.
Grass and trees wither; geese go south.
c.127 BC 'The Autumn Wind' (translated by Arthur Waley). The poem is a lament on leaving his mistress behind while he travelled on official business.

Wyatt, Sir Thomas (the Elder) 1503–42

English courtier and poet under Henry VIII. Twice imprisoned on capital offences—on charges of adultery with Anne Boleyn and for treason—he was twice released. Many of his poems were published in *Tottel's Miscellany* (1557). He is credited with introducing the sonnet form to English; many of his are translations from Petrarch.

97 In lusty leas at liberty I walk.
1536 'Mine Own John Poins'.

98 But here I am in Kent and Christendom,
Among the Muses, where I read and rhyme.
1536 'Mine Own John Poins'.

99 Farewell, Love, and all thy laws forever,
Thy baited hooks shall tangle me no more.
1557 'Farewell, Love'.

1 And graven with diamonds in letters plain
There is written, her fair neck round about:
Noli me tangere, for Caesar's I am,
And wild for to hold, though I seem tame.
1557 'Whoso List to Hunt'. The subject of the poem is thought to be Anne Boleyn.
► *See Bible 118:23*.

2 My lute, awake! Perform the last
Labour that thou and I shall waste,
And end that I have now begun;
For when this song is sung and past,
My lute, be still, for I have done.
1557 'My Lute, Awake!'

3 They flee from me, that sometime did me seek,
With naked foot, stalking in my chamber.
I have seen them gentle, tame, and meek,
That now are wild, and do not remember
That sometime they put themselves in danger
To take bread at my hand; and now they range,
Busily seeking with a continual change.
1557 'They Flee from Me'.

4 But all is turned, through my gentleness,
Into a strange fashion of forsaking.
1557 'They Flee from Me'.

Wycherley, William c.1640–1716

English dramatist. Educated at Oxford and Middle Temple. Although a successful playwright who garnered attention and support from both Charles II and James II, his fortunes were unsteady. Plays include *The Gentleman Dancing-Master* (1672), *Love in a Wood* (1671), *The Country Wife* (1675) and *The Plain Dealer* (1677), the last two of which were based on plays by Molière.

5 Fy! madam, do you think me so ill bred as to love a husband?
1671 *Love in a Wood*, act 3, sc.4.

6 A good name is seldom got by giving it one's self.
1675 *The Country Wife*, act 1, sc.1.

7 A mistress should be like a little country retreat near the town, not to dwell in constantly, but only for a night and away.
1675 *The Country Wife*, act 1, sc.1.

8 Your virtue is your greatest affectation.
1675 *The Country Wife*, act 1, sc.1.

9 Women serve but to keep men from better company.
1675 *The Country Wife*, act 1, sc.1.

10 Mistresses are like books. If you pore upon them too much, they doze you, and make you unfit for company; but if used discreetly, you are the fitter for conversation by 'em.
1675 *The Country Wife*, act 1, sc.1.

11 'Tis as hard to be a good fellow, a good friend, and a lover of women, as 'tis to be a good fellow, a good friend, and a lover of money.
1675 *The Country Wife*, act 1, sc.1.

12 Wine gives you liberty, love takes it away.
1675 *The Country Wife*, act 1, sc.1.

13 For my part, I will have only those glorious manly pleasures of being very drunk and very slovenly.
1675 *The Country Wife*, act 1, sc.1.

14 Wit is more necessary than beauty; and I think no young woman ugly that has it, and no handsome woman agreeable without it.
1675 *The Country Wife*, act 1, sc.1.

15 He's a fool that marries; but he's a greater that does not marry a fool.
1675 *The Country Wife*, act 1, sc.1.

16 Poetry in love is no more to be avoided than jealousy.
1675 *The Country Wife*, act 3, sc.2.

17 I love to be envied, and would not marry a wife that I alone could love; loving alone is as dull as eating alone.
1675 *The Country Wife*, act 3, sc.2.

Wycliffe, John c.1330–1384

English religious reformer. His many popular vernacular tracts attacked Church hierarchy, priestly powers, and the doctrine of transubstantiation, and he issued the first English translation of the Bible. Although condemned, his teaching was influential in its insistence on inward religion instead of formalism. His followers were derisively known as 'Lollards'.

18 Christ during His life upon earth was of all men the poorest, casting from Him all worldly authority. I deduce from these premises…that the Pope should surrender all temporal authority to the civil power and advise his clergy to do the same.
1384 Dismissing an order to appear before the Papal Court.

Wyeth, Andrew Newell 1917–

US painter, known for his meticulous depictions of the Pennsylvanian and Maine countryside. His most famous work is *Christina's World* (1948).

19 I get excited by the shape of a person's nose, the tone of their eyes, or the way their back looks when they're turned away from me. That's my reason for painting.
1991 In *National Geographic*, Jul.

Wylie, Betty Jane 1931–

Canadian dramatist and writer.

20 First deal with your own tears; tomorrow do something about acid rain.
1986 *Successfully Single*.

21 There are all kinds of ways of being unfaithful, not the worst of them with your body.
1988 *All in the Family: A Survival Guide for Living and Loving in a Changing World*.

22 Listening is one of the lesser-known skills that mistresses offer.
1988 *All in the Family: A Survival Guide for Living and Loving in a Changing World*.

23 There is a line between sexuality and promiscuity, and the line is closer to celibacy than not.
1988 *All in the Family: A Survival Guide for Living and Loving in a Changing World*.

24 Poverty isn't being broke; poverty is never having enough.
1989 *Everywoman's Money Book* (with Lynne MacFarlane).

Wyman, Jane *originally* ***Sarah Jane Fulks*** 1914–

First wife of Ronald Reagan and best known as a film actress, she married Reagan (her second husband) in 1940 and divorced in 1948. She won an Academy Award for *Johnny Belinda* (1948).

25 Ask him what time it is and he'll tell you how the watch was made.
Of Ronald Reagan. Quoted in Jack Finney *From Time to Time* (1995).

Xenophon c.435–c.354 BC

Athenian historian and soldier.

26 *Thalatta! Thalatta!*
The sea! The sea!
Anabasis bk. 4, 24. Shouted by the Greek soldiers from the Expedition of Cyrus in 401 BC when they reached the sea after months inland.

Yarborough, Ralph 1903–96

US liberal politician and Governor of Texas (1957–71).

27 It is the only case on record of a man swimming toward a sinking ship.
1973 On former Texas Governor John B Connally's switch from Democratic to the Republican party in his bid for the presidential nomination. Quoted in the *Washington Post*, 18 Jan 1988.

Yeats, Georgie *née* *Hyde-Lees* 1892–1968

Wife of Irish poet W B Yeats. Her attempts at automatic writing on their honeymoon in 1917 profoundly influenced Yeats' subsequent writing.

28 After your death people will write of your love affairs, but I shall say nothing, because I will remember how proud you were.
Quoted in Richard Ellman *A Long the Riverrun: Selected Essays* (1988), p.253.

Yeats, W(illiam) B(utler) 1865–1939

Irish poet. He was a prolific writer influenced by Irish mythology and by his close relationships with a number of women, eventually evolving his own system of symbolism which underlies much of his work. He also edited many books, including the controversial *Oxford Book of Modern Verse* (1936), and served as a Senator of the Irish Free State (1922–9).

29 Down by the salley gardens my love and I did meet;
She passed the salley gardens with little snow-white feet.
She bid me take love easy, as the leaves grow on the tree;
But I, being young and foolish, with her would not agree.

In a field by the river my love and I did stand,
And on my leaning shoulder she laid her snow-white hand.
She bid me take life easy, as the grass grows on the weirs;
But I was young and foolish, and now am full of tears.
1888 'Down by the Salley Gardens', complete poem. Collected in *Crossways*.

30 I will arise and go now, and go to Innisfree,
And a small cabin build there, of clay and wattles made:
Nine bean-rows will I have there, a hive for the honey-bee,
And live alone in the bee-loud glade.

And I shall have some peace there, for peace comes dropping slow,
Dropping from the veils of the morning to where the cricket sings;
There midnight's all a-glimmer, and noon a purple glow,
And evening full of the linnet's wings.
1888 'The Lake Isle of Innisfree', stanzas 1–2. Collected in *The Rose* (1893).

31 O Oisin, mount by me and ride
To shores by the wash of the tremulous tide,
Where men have heaped no burial-mounds,
And the days pass by like a wayward tune.
1889 'The Wanderings of Oisin', l.80–3.

32 The brawling of a sparrow in the eaves,
The brilliant moon and all the milky sky,
And all that famous harmony of leaves,
Has blotted out man's image and his cry.
1891 'The Sorrow of Love', stanza 1. Collected in *The Rose* (1893).

33 When you are old and grey and full of sleep,
And nodding by the fire, take down this book,
And slowly read, and dream of the soft look
Your eyes had once, and of their shadows deep;

How many loved your moments of glad grace,
And loved your beauty with love false or true,
But one man loved the pilgrim soul in you,
And loved the sorrows of your changing face;

And bending down beside the glowing bars,
Murmur, a little sadly how Love fled
And paced among the mountains overhead
And hid his face amid a crowd of stars.
1891 'When You Are Old', complete poem. Collected in *The Rose* (1893).

34 Rose of all Roses, Rose of all the World!
The tall thought-woven sails, that flap unfurled
Above the tide of hours, trouble the air,
And God's bell buoyed to be the water's care.
1891 'The Rose of Battle', l.1–4. Collected in *The Rose* (1893).

35 Out-worn heart, in a time out-worn,
Come clear of the nets of wrong and right;
Laugh, heart, again in the grey twilight,
Sigh, heart, again in the dew of the morn.
1893 'Into the Twilight', stanza 1. Collected in *The Wind Among the Reeds* (1899).

36 And walk among long dappled grass,
And pluck till time and times are done
The silver apples of the moon,
The golden apples of the sun.
1897 'The Song of Wandering Aengus', l.21–4. Collected in *The Wind Among the Reeds* (1899).

37 Half close your eyelids, loosen your hair,
And dream about the great and their pride;

They have spoken against you everywhere,
But weigh this song with the great and their pride;
I made it out of a mouthful of air,
Their children's children shall say they have lied.

1898 'He Thinks of Those who have Spoken Evil of His Beloved', complete poem. Collected in *The Wind Among the Reeds* (1899).

38 Had I the heavens' embroidered cloths,
Enwrought with golden and silver light,
The blue and the dim and the dark cloths
Of night and light and the half-light,
I would spread the cloths under your feet:
But I, being poor, have only my dreams;
I have spread my dreams under your feet;
Tread softly because you tread on my dreams.

1899 'He Wishes for the Cloths of Heaven', complete poem. Collected in *The Wind Among the Reeds* (1899).

39 You have disgraced yourselves again. You are rocking the cradle of a new masterpiece.

1907 Addressing the rioting audience at Dublin's Abbey Theatre at the première of J M Synge's *The Playboy of the Western World*.

40 What could have made her peaceful with a mind
That nobleness made simple as a fire,
With beauty like a tightened bow, a kind
That is not natural in an age like this,
Being high and solitary and most stern?
Why, what could she have done, being what she is?
Was there another Troy for her to burn?

1908 'No Second Troy', l.6–12. Collected in *The Green Helmet and Other Poems* (1910).

41 You say, as I have often given tongue
In praise of what another's said or sung,
'Twere politic to do the like by these;
But was there ever dog that praised his fleas?

1909 'To a Poet, who would have me Praise certain Bad Poets, Imitators of His and Mine', complete poem. Collected in *The Green Helmet and Other Poems* (1910).

42 I have made my song a coat
Covered with embroideries
Out of old mythologies
From heel to throat;
But the fools caught it,
Wore it in the world's eyes
As though they'd wrought it.
Song, let them take it,
For there's more enterprise
In walking naked.

1912 'A Coat', complete poem. Collected in *Responsibilities* (1914).

43 Romantic Ireland's dead and gone,
It's with O'Leary in the grave.

1913 'September 1913', refrain. Collected in *Responsibilities* (1914).

44 I have met them at close of day
Coming with vivid faces
From counter or desk among grey
Eighteenth-century houses.

1916 'Easter, 1916', l.1–4. Collected in *Michael Robartes and the Dancer* (1921).

45 The horse that comes from the road,
The rider, the birds that range
From cloud to tumbling cloud,
Minute by minute they change;
A shadow of cloud on the stream
Changes minute by minute;
A horse-hoof slides on the brim,
And a horse plashes within it;
The long-legged moor-hens dive,
And hens to moor-cocks call;
Minute by minute they live:
The stone's in the midst of all.

1916 'Easter 1916', l.45–56. Collected in *Michael Robartes and the Dancer* (1921).

46 Too long a sacrifice
Can make a stone of the heart.

1916 'Easter 1916', l.57–8. Collected in *Michael Robartes and the Dancer* (1921).

47 There's nothing but our own red blood
Can make a right Rose Tree.

1917 'The Rose Tree', stanza 3. Collected in *Michael Robartes and the Dancer* (1921).

48 I know that I shall meet my fate
Somewhere among the clouds above;
Those that I fight I do not hate,
Those that I guard I do not love.

1918 'An Irish Airman Foresees his Death', l.1–4. Collected in *The Wild Swans at Coole* (1919).

49 Very nice, but if I had rehearsed you it would have been much better.

1919 Of Lady Gregory's title role performance in his *Kathleen Ni Houlihan*. Recorded in Lady Gregory's journal, entry for 19 Mar.

50 Turning and turning in the widening gyre
The falcon cannot hear the falconer;
Things fall apart; the centre cannot hold;
Mere anarchy is loosed upon the world,
The blood-dimmed tide is loosed, and everywhere
The ceremony of innocence is drowned;
The best lack all conviction, while the worst
Are full of passionate intensity.

1919 'The Second Coming', l.1–8. Collected in *Michael Robartes and the Dancer* (1921).

► *See Achebe 2:18.*

51 And what rough beast, its hour come round at last,
Slouches towards Bethlehem to be born?

1919 'The Second Coming', l.21–2. Collected in *Michael Robartes and the Dancer* (1921).

52 An aged man is but a paltry thing,
A tattered coat upon a stick, unless
Soul clap its hands and sing, and louder sing
For every tatter in its mortal dress.

1926 'Sailing to Byzantium', stanza 8. Collected in *The Tower* (1928).

53 O chestnut tree, great-rooted blossomer,
Are you the leaf, the blossom, or the bole?
O body swayed to music, O brightening glance,
How can we know the dancer from the dance?

1927 'Among School Children', stanza 8. collected in *The Tower* (1928).

54 Never to have lived is best, ancient writers say;
Never to have drawn the breath of life, never to have looked into the eye of day;
The second best's a gay goodnight and quickly turn away.

1927 'From Oedipus at Colonnus', stanza 4. Collected in *The Tower* (1928).

55 The innocent and the beautiful
Have no enemy but time.
1927 'In Memory of Eva Gore-Booth and Con Markiewicz', l.24–5. Collected in *The Winding Stair and Other Poems* (1933).

56 If I make the lashes dark
And the eyes more bright
And the lips more scarlet,
Or ask if all be right
From mirror after mirror,
No Vanity's displayed:
I'm looking for the face I had
Before the world was made.
1928 'A Woman Young and Old', part 2 'Before the World was Made', stanza 1. Collected in *The Winding Stair and Other Poems* (1933).

57 A starlit or a moonlit dome disdains
All that man is,
All mere complexities
The fury and the mire of human veins.
1930 'Byzantium', stanza 1. Collected in *The Winding Stair and Other Poems* (1933).

58 Marbles of the dancing floor
Break bitter furies of complexity,
Those images that yet
Fresh images beget,
That dolphin-torn, that gong-tormented sea.
1930 'Byzantium', stanza 5. Collected in *The Winding Stair and Other Poems* (1933).

59 Only God, my dear,
Could love you for yourself alone
And not your yellow hair.
1930 'For Anne Gregory', l.16–18. Collected in *The Winding Stair and Other Poems* (1933).

60 Grant me an old man's frenzy.
Myself I must remake
Till I am Timon and Lear
Or that William Blake
Who beat upon the wall
Till Truth obeyed his call.
1936 'An Acre of Grass', stanza 3. Collected in *New Poems* (1938).

61 John Bull has gone to India
And all must pay him heed
For histories are there to prove
That none of another breed
Has had a like inheritance,
Or sucked such milk as he,
And there's no luck about a house
If it lacks honesty.
The ghost of Roger Casement
Is beating on the door.
1936 'The Ghost of Roger Casement', stanza 3. Collected in *New Poems* (1938).

62 Now that my ladder's gone,
I must lie down where all the ladders start,
In the foul rag-and-bone shop of the heart.
1937–8 'The Circus Animals' Desertion', part 3, l.6–8. Collected in *Last Poems* (1939).

63 Our master Caesar is in the tent
Where the maps are spread,
His eyes fixed upon nothing,
A hand under his head.
Like a long-legged fly upon the stream
His mind moves upon silence.
1938 'Long-Legged Fly', l.5–10. Collected in *Last Poems* (1939).

64 When Pearse summoned Cuchulain to his side,
What stalked through the Post Office? What intellect,
What calculation, number, measurement, replied?
We Irish, born into that ancient sect
But thrown upon this filthy modern tide
And by its formless spawning fury wrecked,
Climb to our proper dark, that we may trace
The lineaments of a plummet-measured face.
1938 'The Statues', stanza 4. Collected in *Last Poems* (1939).

65 Swear by what the sages spoke
Round the Mareotic Lake
That the Witch of Atlas knew,
Spoke and set the cocks a-crow.
1938 'Under Ben Bulben', stanza 1. Collected in *Last Poems* (1939).

66 Under bare Ben Bulben's head
In Drumcliffe churchyard Yeats is laid,
An ancestor was rector there
Long years ago; a church stands near,
By the road an ancient Cross.
No marble, no conventional phrase,
On limestone quarried near the spot
By his command these words are cut:
Cast a cold eye
On life, on death.
Horseman, pass by!
1938 'Under Ben Bulben', stanza 6. Collected in *Last Poems* (1939). The last three lines were used as his epitaph.

67 Propinquity had brought
Imagination to that pitch where it casts out
All that is not itself. I had grown wild
And wandered murmuring everywhere, 'My child, my child.'
1939 'A Bronze Head', l.18–21. Collected in *Last Poems* (1939).

68 OLD MAN: Do not let him touch you! It is not true
That drunken men cannot beget,
And if he touch he must beget
And you must bear his murderer.
Deaf! Both deaf!
1939 *Purgatory.*

Yellen, Jack 1892–1991

US lyricist.

69 Happy Days are Here Again.
1930 Title of song. It became linked with US Democrat campaigns.

Yeltsin, Boris 1931–

President of Russia. He graduated as a construction engineer in 1955 and entered work for the Communist Party. Called to Moscow in 1985 by Gorbachev, he was sacked in 1987 and against Gorbachev's wishes became Chairman of the Russian Parliament. He was elected President in 1991. His programme for a rapid transition to a market economy, support for other republics to be treated equally, and for multiparty democracy, helped him survive the following politically tumultuous years, but his policies have caused much domestic criticism. He resigned in 1999 and was replaced by Vladimir Putin.

70 The West has not lived through totalitarianism, with a

single ideology for 70 years. We are escaping from the burden of the past, and only after we have done that will we be ready to integrate with Europe—and Europe needs Russia.
1991 Addressing socialist MPs in Strasbourg, 15 Apr.

71 I ask you to forgive me for not fulfilling some hopes of those people who believed that we would be able to jump from the totalitarian past into a bright, rich and civilized future in one go.
2000 On his retirement. In the *Observer*, 2 Jan.

Yevtushenko, Yevegeny Aleksandrovich 1933–

Russian poet. He emerged as a poet representing the young post-Stalin generation with such works as *The Third Snow* (1955), *Chausée Eutuziastov* (1956) and *The Promise* (1957). Later works have included *Babi Yar* (1962), concerning anti-Semitism in Russia, *Love Poems* (1977), *Ivan the Terrible and Ivan the Fool* (1979) and the novel *Berries* (1981).

72 I love sport because I love life, and sport is one of the basic joys of life.
1966 In *Sports Illustrated*, 19 Dec.

Yokoi, Shoichi 1915–97

Japanese corporal who emerged from the jungles of Guam in 1972 after hiding for 28 years. He was obeying his commanding officer's 1944 order to evade capture by the enemy.

73 I am deeply ashamed at my failure to serve His Majesty.
1972 Announcement to journalists at Tokyo airport, 2 Feb. Quoted in Edward Behr *Hirohito*, epilogue.

York, Sarah, Duchess of 1959–

English Duchess and children's author, ex-wife of Prince Andrew, Duke of York.

74 Women leave the Royal Family in only one mode—with their heads cleaved from the shoulders.
1997 *My Story*.

Yost, Elwy 1925–

Canadian television personality.

75 If you work very hard, and give life everything you've got, you may not quite make it.
1990 Comment, 17 Jan.

Young, Arthur 1741–1820

British agriculturalist and writer.

76 Give a man the secure possession of a bleak rock, and he will turn it into a garden; give him a nine years' lease on a garden, and he will convert it into a desert.... The magic of PROPERTY turns sand to gold.
1787 Journal entries, 30 Jul and 7 Nov, published in *Travels in France and Italy* (1794).

Young, Brigham 1801–77

US Mormon leader.

77 This is the place!
1847 On first seeing Great Salt Lake Valley, Utah, 24 Jul.

Young, Douglas 1913–73

Scottish poet, scholar and nationalist. He was jailed for refusing to serve in the British Army in 1941. After the war he taught classics at universities in Scotland, Canada and the US.

78 The Minister said it wald dee,
the cypress-buss I plantit.
But the buss grew til a tree,
naething dauntit.

It's growan, stark and heich,
derk and straucht and sinister,
kirkyairdielike and dreich.
But whaur's the Minister?
1943 *Auntran Blads*, 'Last Lauch'.

Young, Edward 1683–1765

English poet, tragedian and cleric, best known for his satires, *The Love of Fame, the Universal Passion* (1725–8) and the remarkable *Complaint, or Night Thoughts on Life, Death and Immortality* (1742–5), written on the death of his wife.

79 Some, for *renown*, on scraps of learning doat,
And think they grow immortal as they *quote*.
1725 *The Love of Fame, the Universal Passion* 'Satire 1'.

Yourcenar, Marguerite *pseudonym of* Marguerite de Crayencour 1903–87

French novelist. Born into aristocracy, she spent her childhood travelling in Europe and in 1937 left for the US, taking dual US–French nationality. She is best known for her historical novel *Mémoires d'Hadrien* (Memoirs of Hadrian, 1951), and for being the first woman elected to the Académie Française.

80 *Un homme qui lit, ou qui pense, ou qui calcule, appartient à l'espèce et non au sexe; dans ses meilleurs moments, il échappe même à l'humain.*
A person who reads or thinks or calculates, belongs to a kind and not to a gender; in his or her best moments, he or she escapes being human.
1951 *Mémoires d'Hadrien*.

81 *Les trois quarts de nos exercices intellectuels ne sont plus que broderies sur le vide.*
Three quarters of our intellectual performances are no more than decorations over a void.
1951 *Mémoires d'Hadrien*.

82 *Tout bonheur est un chef-d'œuvre: la moindre erreur le fausse, la moindre hésitation l'altère, la moindre lourdeur le dépare, la moindre sottise l'abêtit.*
Happiness is always a work of art: the least fault distorts it, the least hesitation changes it, a little dullness spoils it, the smallest foolish act makes it idiotic.
1951 *Mémoires d'Hadrien*.

83 *Entre le rôle de sauveur et celui de complice du bourreau, j'aperçois tout au plus l'incommode emploi de victime.*
Between the role of saviour and that of butcher's accomplice, all I see left for you is the unsavoury role of victim.
1963 *Qui n'a pas son Minotaure?*, pt.3.

84 *Que le Dieu qui nous tue nous vienne en aide!*
God who kills us, come to our rescue!
1963 *Qui n'a pas son Minotaure?*, pt.3.

85 ARIANE: *Tu n'es que la réponse la plus courte qu'on puisse faire aux questions des hommes.*
DIEU: *En sais-tu de meilleur?*

ARIANE: *Oui. Le mot rien est aussi court que le mot Dieu.*
ARIADNE: You are only the shortest possible answer to all the questions of men.
GOD (BACCHUS): Do you know a better one?
ARIADNE: Yes, the word no is just as short as the word God.
1963 *Qui n'a pas son Minotaure?*, pt.9.

86 Out of the debris of a statue thoroughly shattered a new art work is born: a naked foot unforgettably resting on a stone; a candid hand; a bent knee which contains all the speed of the foot race; a torso which has no face to prevent us from loving it.
Quoted in the *New York Times*, 10 May 1992.

Yüan Mei 1716–98

Chinese poet who was a magistrate for six years before retiring to live off his writings. Unorthodox and hedonistic, he also championed women poets.

87 If I can rejoice for a moment,
Death at an early age would still be a long life.
c.746 Collected in *A Book of Chinese Verse* (translated by N L Smith and R H Kotewall).

Z

Zangwill, Israel 1864–1926

English writer and leading Zionist, known for his novels on Jewish themes including *Children of the Ghetto* (1892) and *Ghetto Tragedies* (1894). Other works include the early collections of witty tales *The Bachelors' Club* (1891) and *The Old Maids' Club* (1892), and the plays *The Melting Pot* (1908) and *We Moderns* (1925).

88 America is God's Crucible, the great Melting Pot where all the races of Europe are melting and re-forming… God is making the American.
1908 *The Melting Pot.*

Zatopek, Emil 1922–2000

Czech athlete and middle-distance runner. He won the gold medal for the 10,000 metres at the 1948 Olympics in London and subsequently broke 13 world records as well as gold medals in the 10,000 metres and 5,000 metres events at the Helsinki Olympics in 1952.

89 An athlete cannot run with money in his pockets. He must run with hope in his heart and dreams in his head.
Quoted by Christopher Brasher in the *Observer*, 12 Sep 1982.

90 You can't climb up to the second floor without a ladder. When you set your aim too high and don't fulfil it, then your enthusiasm turns to bitterness. Try for a goal that's reasonable, and then gradually raise it. That's the only way to get to the top.
Quoted in Colin Jarman *The Guinness Dictionary of Sports Quotations* (1990).

Zeldin, Theodore

Historian and writer

91 Brilliant lecturers shouldn't be wasted in lecture rooms: they should appear on TV. We need black market universities, in which people just help each other, and which don't leave out the poor.
1995 Quoted in Christina Hardyment 'Zeldin and the art of human relationships', in *Oxford Today*, vol.7, no.2, Hilary Issue.

Zel'dovich, Yakov 1914–87

Russian astrophysicist.

92 Without publicity there is no prosperity.
Quoted by Tony Rothman in *Bostonia*, summer 1993, p.58.

Zhang, Jie 1937–

Chinese writer whose first short story appeared in 1978 and whose writing often sets romantic themes in the contemporary Chinese world of rapid modernization.

93 When we reach communism, will there still be cases of marriage without love?
1979 'Love Must Not Be Forgotten', in *Seven Contemporary Women Writers* (1982).

94 To live single is not such a fearful disaster. I believe it may be a sign of a step forward in culture, education and the quality of life.
1979 'Love Must Not Be Forgotten', in *Seven Contemporary Women Writers* (1982).

Zhao, Zhenkai *pen name Beo Dao* 1949–

Chinese writer who has written poetry and fiction and was associated with China's Democracy Movement. He is currently living in Norway. The use of pen names dates back to the Cultural Revolution when secrecy was often essential.

95 They say the ice age ended years ago.
Why are there icicles everywhere?
c.1989 'Answer', collected in Donald Finkel *A Splintered Mirror* (1991).

96 Freedom is only the distance
between the hunter and his prey.
c.1989 'Answer', collected in Donald Finkel *A Splintered Mirror* (1991).

Zhivkov, Todor 1911–98

Bulgarian statesman, part of the Communist coup d'état of 1944. Prime Minister from 1962 and Chairman of the Council of State from 1971, he was effectively President of the Republic. Conservative and unquestioningly loyal to the USSR, he was ousted in 1989 and expelled from the Party, charged with nepotism, corruption and abuse of power.

97 If I had to do it over again, I would not even be a communist. And if Lenin were alive today, he would say the same thing.
1990 In the *Sunday Times*, 9 Dec.

Zhou Enlai *or Chou En-Lai* 1898–1975

Chinese Communist Party leader, Prime Minister of the People's Republic from its creation in 1949 until his death. Under Mao Zedong he became the Party's chief negotiator and diplomat, and vastly increased China's international influence. In the Cultural Revolution (1966–76), he worked to preserve national unity.

98 For us, it is all right if the talks succeed; and it is all right if they fail.
1971 On President Nixon's visit, 5 Oct.

Zia Ul-Haq, Mohammed 1924–88

Pakistani soldier and politician. He led the military coup against Zulfikar Ali Bhutto (1977), becoming President a year later. He introduced a new policy of Islamization and freer-market economic programme, finally lifting martial law in 1985. He was killed in an aircrash.

99 Cricket can be a bridge and a glue... Cricket for peace is my mission.
Quoted in Helen Exley *Cricket Quotations* (1992).

Zidane, Zinedine 1972–

French footballer, Fifa World Player of the Year in 1998, 2000 and 2003.

1 Every day I think about where I come from and I am still proud to be who I am: first, a Kabyle from La Castellane, then an Algerian from Marseille, and then a Frenchman.
2004 Explaining his identity—his father was a Berber from the Kabylie region of Algeria and Zidane grew up in the Marseille suburb of La Castellane. In the *Observer*, 4 Apr.

Zoeller, Fuzzy 1951–

US golfer, his wins include the US Masters (1979) and the US Open (1984).

2 Even on the mornings when I creak out of bed, I still get pumped up about hitting that silly little white ball.
2001 In *Golf World*, 13 Apr.

Zola, Émile 1840–1902

French novelist, a pioneer of naturalism. His novels include *Thérèse Raquin* (1867) and the great series called *Les Rougon-Macquart*, which depicts all aspects of society under the Second Empire. After impeaching the military authorities over the Dreyfus case, Zola was sentenced to imprisonment (1898), but escaped for a year to England, and was welcomed back as a hero. He died in Paris, accidentally suffocated by charcoal fumes.

3 *J'accuse.*
I accuse.
1898 Title of open letter to the President of France regarding the Dreyfus case.

4 A dead reign...a strange epoch of folly and shame.
On the France of the Second Empire. Quoted in Joanna Richardson *La Vie Parisienne* (1971), p.276.

Zolotow, Maurice

5 There is no more offensive act of theatrical rudeness than coming late to a performance.
1958 In *Theater Arts*, Feb.

Zuckerman, Solly Zuckerman, Baron 1904–84

South African-born English scientist, zoologist and educator, the author of several studies of primate behavior.

6 Science creates the future without knowing what the future will be. If scientists knew tomorrow's discovery they would make it.
1964 In the *Daily Mirror*.

Zwerin, Mike 1930–

US writer and musician. He plays trombone, and has written extensively on jazz.

7 Jazz musicians have some outlaw in them somewhere if they are serious about this music... There is no valid motivation for it other than love—outlaw motivation in a profit-motivated society.
1985 *La Tristesse de Saint Louis: Swing Under the Nazis*, ch.4.

INDEX

A

school history b. GLAS 359:99
seal the b. BIBLE 106:1
seldom peruses a b. ADDI 6:9
sell a man a b. MORL 598:86
sour misfortune's b. SHAK 737:80
take down this b. YEATS 932:33
take them out of this b. STER 817:75
tastes no wise b.-maker LUCAS 521:73
The B. of Life WILDE 909:21
then shut the b. PATM 643:58
Things in b.'s clothing LAMB 487:60
This b. is not about heroes OWEN 632:54
this b. is not concerned with Poetry OWEN 632:55
this is no b. WHIT 905:45
This little b. contains STIL 824:47
throw the entire b. in the fire SAND 712:86
To produce a mighty b. MELV 564:35
to write a really funny b. HEMI 393:93
To write the essential b. PROU 671:91
truly good b. THOR 857:75
understand that b. but fail NICO 614:96
until he has written a b. JOWE 451:78
when you read a b. GAUG 347:68
Who is worthy to open the b. BIBLE 126:56
word for word without b. SHAK 755:48
Would you read a Sustaining B. MILNE 574:78
write a b. a year TARTT 836:1
writing a b. GERA 350:25
Writing a b. of poetry MARQ 554:33
book-case red mahogany b.-c. BETJ 83:82
Bookie snatch B. Bob RUNY 702:79
book-keeping double-entry b.-k. MULL 602:72
book-learning b.-l. in monasteries GALL 344:19
books All b. are the Book of Job ELKIN 310:69
all my b. are botches MELV 564:43
all the b. you can export CHIS 213:16
archives of his b. RODC 693:87
are the b., the arts SHAK 734:86
author because you like his b. LINK 511:61
author who speaks about his own b. DISR 277:80
base authority from others' b. SHAK 733:69
Before high-piled b. KEATS 457:93
be not swallowed up in b.! WESL 900:26
bibliobuli…who are…drunk on b. MENC 565:74
B. and the man I sing POPE 662:64
B. are a load of crap LARK 491:32
B. are cold and certain HUGO 421:86
b. are divided RUSK 704:22
b. are either dreams LOWE 519:22
B. are good enough STEV 822:96
b. are more than b. LOWE 519:21
b. are theatres STEV 820:42
B. are the bees LOWE 520:34
b.…are the nearest to us CONR 234:10
B. are the opium FRAN 333:84
B. are written by martyr-men CARL 193:30
b., convention and cliché POUND 664:24
B. do furnish a room POWE 666:81
B. echoing the life WILL 914:56
B. from Boots BETJ 83:85
B. have had their day BENN 77:58
b. have their own fate TERE 849:80
B. have to teach RUSH 703:91
b.…how many of them I could avoid MACA 525:33
b. in the running brooks SHAK 749:34
B., like men SWIFT 830:54
B. make sense of life BARN 60:70
B. must follow sciences BACON 50:66
B. of poetry…promissory notes WILDE 908:87
b. one reads in childhood ORWE 629:81
b. promiscuously read MILT 579:73
B.…propose to instruct DE 262:8
b. teach them GARC 345:42
b. that have a lot of dreck BART 62:10
b. that influence us FORS 332:56
b. that wound KAFKA 453:24
B. think for me LAMB 487:59
B.! 'tis a dull…strife WORD 924:74
b. to blisse ne to joye LANG 489:98
b. were read BELL 73:66
b. which do not have facts VIDAL 881:4
b. which you do not understand VIAN 880:77
b. written by Europeans NAIP 606:50
borrowers of b. LAMB 487:52
British…taste for bad b. BRAD 148:61
cannot learn men from b. DISR 275:34
Deep-versed in b. MILT 586:43
everybody could write b. BAIN 52:7
factory of b. SMITH 799:66
First to possess his b. SHAK 774:90
forefathers had no other b. SHAK 730:66
Forsake thy b., and mateless play BRON 155:91
Friends To borrow my b. ROBI 690:29
fuck-all to say about my b. WELSH 899:97
Give me b., fruit, french wine KEATS 458:13
God has written all the b. BUTL 178:78
Good travel b. RABAN 675:60
haven't read any of your b. JOYCE 452:2
If my b. had been any worse CHAN 204:79
In b. lies the soul of the whole Past CARL 193:34
indiscriminate reviewing of b. ORWE 629:82
in Germany, b. STAEL 812:52
I've read all the b. MALL 542:92
Keepers of b. MACL 535:41
let my b. be…eloquence SHAK 771:10
luminous plectrum of b. BELLI 72:42
Mistresses are like b. WYCH 931:10
more b. one reads MAO 548:17
more b. we read CONN 233:75
never yet was put into words or b. MELV 564:36
of making many b. there is no end BIBLE 101:93
old b. GOLD 362:62
people…do not read b. WORD 928:48
pictures of obscene b.! ARLT 30:66
reading of good b. DESC 263:17
Read the best b. first THOR 857:72
so charming as b. SMITH 801:12
Some b. accrete things HOLM 407:74
some b. are deemed most baneful MELV 564:46
Some b. are lies BURNS 170:67
Some b. are to be tasted BACON 50:53
Some b. are undeservedly forgotten AUDEN 41:18
spacious highways of b. SAND 713:13
spectacles of b. DRYD 288:25
story b.…written by people WELTY 899:99
study of mankind is b. HUXL 424:56
trees shall be my b. SHAK 749:54
true University…is a collection of b. CARL 193:35
turned o'er many b. SHAK 740:78
two classes of b. FORD 330:3
who has written fine b. GARR 346:54
worse crimes than burning b. BROD 154:58
Writing b. is the closest men MAIL 540:49
booksellers bold b. SHER 788:63
embolden b. WAUGH 891:6
boomerang b. No more spear NOON 618:59
boon for heaven's grace and b. KEATS 459:37
Of neither would I ask the b. SHEL 786:18
recipients of the b. of liberty MAMET 543:25
sordid b.! WORD 928:46
boot b. in the face, the brute PLATH 654:69
imagine a b. stamping ORWE 630:4
power of your b. MOTI 600:35
Then hey for b. and horse KING 469:53
booted always be b. and spurred MONT 592:72
Booth B. died blind LIND 510:47
B. led boldly LIND 510:45
bootless spends a b. grief SHAK 759:67
boots a pair of b. TRAV 864:42
asleep in his b. STEV 819:26
before the truth has got its b. on CALL 185:40
children…never had any b. WILS 915:89
elastic-sided b. SHAR 776:40
It b. not to resist SHAK 730:81
look at his b. SHAW 780:62
pantheon of b. and overalls DUNN 295:17
truth is pulling its b. on SPUR 811:41
wear long b., hard b. SAND 713:98
went to school without any b. BULM 166:55
when I take my b. off DICK 269:60
bootstrings raise ourselves by our own b. WILL 912:8
booty none left to play b. DICK 266:90
booze B., of course, and then curtains AMIS 14:94
feeding on b. and spaghetti LEWIS 507:88
man shouldn't fool with b. FAUL 319:76
boozer clown, the b., the fighter? MAST 560:52
boozes tell a man who b. BURT 174:65
bop Playing b. is like playing Scrabble ELLI 310:73
Boralaski as Count B.'s wife SCOTT 723:14
bordello doorkeeper of a b. TOSC 863:18
border across the b. to get a drink ANON 22:49
chuck them over the b. WALE 885:90
Night Mail crossing the b. AUDEN 39:81
o'er the B. and awa' SCOTT 724:23
sung of B. chivalry SCOTT 722:84
Through all the wide B. SCOTT 723:96
borders b., beds and shrubberies KIPL 474:72
invade the b. of my realm ELIZ 309:60
no walls, no b. ATWO 38:50
tyranny whose b. are undefined MAIL 540:44
bore A colossal b. MERI 567:13
beside a muzzled b. STEP 817:59
complaints are a b. ACHE 2:36
Every hero becomes a b. EMER 313:33
healthy male adult b. UPDI 874:76
If your husband is a b. BELL 73:80
in it is merely a b. WILDE 909:28
is an old b. TREE 865:52
merely the Club B. SAKI 710:47
People find ideas a b. POUND 665:54
unless it becomes a b. POUND 664:32
bored better that aged diplomats be b. AUST 44:4
b. nearer to…mortification WODE 918:50
I am heavy b. BERR 82:63
leaving because I am b. SAND 713:16
nearly b. GOSSE 364:17
Never to be b. BALL 55:63
People do not read to be b. BEAV 67:27
Punctuality…virtue of the b. WAUGH 892:48
so b. with it all CHUR 218:12
boredom b. and pain of it BUEC 165:44
b., and the horror ELIOT 307:86
b. makes you old CAST 199:74
effect of b. on a large scale INGE 429:53
Here b. reaches its peak MILL 573:36
Inconstancy, b., anxiety PASC 640:14
Life is first b. LARK 491:35
not waiting for them to die of b. BLAN 136:89
Symmetry is b. HUGO 421:88
what makes a journey…horrible is b. GELL 348:1
bores B. and Bored BYRON 182:96
B. bore each other MARQ 554:36
B. have succeeded to dragons DISR 276:37
Borgia B. who has suddenly WODE 919:62
Borgias dining with the B. tonight BEER 70:88
thirty years under the B. WELL 897:48
boring Antiquity…clichéd and b. FLAU 326:41
Life…is b. BERR 82:62
previously amusing…become b. COUP 239:1
something curiously b. HUXL 424:55
work is less b. than amusement BAUD 65:80
born all b. and must die MATAK 560:55
as a poet…not b. yet THOM 854:28
as if I had insisted on being b. DICK 271:27
as natural…to be b. BACON 47:75
as soon as we were b. BIBLE 107:34
because you were b. in it? SHAW 781:76
bird b. in a cage SHAW 780:56
blight man was b. for HOPK 412:95
b.…among the mountains WORD 925:7
b. and dying, dying MISH 587:84
b., And he had reasons ROBI 690:30
b. below par to the extent MONT 592:69
B. but to die POPE 660:16
b. free as Caesar SHAK 747:75
b. in a merry hour SHAK 744:98
b. in Canada JOHN 440:94
b. in the minds of a few KISS 475:93
b. into music SIMO 792:41
b. into the world alive GILB 354:13
B. of the sun SPEN 807:47
b. of woman TWAIN 870:81
b. out of due time BIBLE 121:12
b. to know you ELUA 311:97
b. to run SPRI 811:40
b. to set it right STRA 826:81
b.…when wits were fresh and clear ARNO 32:22
b. where my father lived SITT 793:56
b. with an unreasonably large stock SHAW 781:1
b.…with ready-made parents FRAME 333:81
b. with two things TEMP 838:35
Bred en b. in a brier-patch HARR 383:91
British Bourgeosie Is not b. SITW 794:79
can't be b., unless it's…in DICK 269:76
Else, wherefore b.? TENN 847:58
engaged, married, or b. GALS 344:23
Every moment one is b. TENN 841:91
Except a man be b. again BIBLE 117:79
fashion is b. by small facts SCHI 718:98
If…b. were being invented DOYLE 286:83
if he had happened to be b.…there FRIE 337:64

D

E

F

H

all who are h. JOHN 443:82
Anyone h. in this age FULL 341:59
bread-sauce of the h. ending JAMES 433:47
conspiracy to make you h. UPDI 874:84
die h. FOX 333:76
difficult…to be h. with someone! LABR 483:66
duty of being h. STEV 822:98
Eisenhower…makes people h. WHITE 904:3
exist in order to be h. SCHO 719:35
Forgive and be h. PRAT 667:99
Getting up…does not make you h. RABE 676:69
happiest moment of the h. man SCHO 719:34
h. as the grass was green THOM 852:71
H. Days are Here Again YELL 934:69
h. families resemble each other TOLS 862:5
H., h., h., pair! DRYD 291:33
h.…is not a characteristic CHAN 205:3
H. is the country AGATE 8:67
H. is the man BIBLE 99:12
H. is the man BIBLE 127:90
H. is the man BIBLE 98:93
H. is the man that findeth wisdom BIBLE 99:12
h. land GOLD 361:57
H.…like Ulysses BELL 72:39
h. man inevitably confines HAWT 386:46
h. much of the time PECK 645:6
H. those early days VAUG 878:44
h. through science POIN 657:32
H. till I woke again HOUS 415:67
h. time when one is in misery DANTE 252:95
h.…we are not over-h. SHAK 752:51
h. who have called thee so SOUT 805:5
have been very h. ATTL 38:43
How h. I could be GAY 347:87
human race was most h. GIBB 351:52
if life is…h. LABR 483:70
If the prisoner is h. SHAW 778:1
If you are as h. BUCH 164:31
in nothing else so h. SHAK 734:13
I've had a h. life HAZL 388:88
I were but little h. SHAK 744:97
keep me h. all the day STEV 823:16
Let us all be h. WARD 888:57
look these h. couples STEV 821:82
make men h. POPE 661:59
Marriages would…be as h. JOHN 444:15
no h. end to it HEMI 394:6
none should be h. JOHN 445:21
no one can be perfectly h. SPEN 806:30
nor as h. as one hopes LARO 491:50
not a h. one GILB 354:3
not a h. prospect THOM 856:46
now to be most h. SHAK 759:75
one of those h. places THOR 858:8
one of those h. souls SHEL 784:66
one should feel h. SARR 715:38
only one thing to make me h. HAZL 388:89
prevent me being h. ANOU 26:95
remote from the h.. AUDEN 40:11
shame…from being h. LABR 484:75
so few h. marriages ASTE 36:25
so few marriages are h. SWIFT 831:70
so h. as to sigh for BEAU 67:7
So, I'm h. tonight KING 468:43
someone, somewhere, may be h. MENC 565:71
strangely h. with myself IGNA 428:41
think themselves h. BACON 48:3
This is the h. warrior READ 680:46
thy h. strain? SHEL 784:59
too h. in thine happiness KEATS 459:57
twentieth will be h. HUGO 421:95
unfurnish'd Of falsehood to be h. DRYD 289:64
Was he h.? AUDEN 40:96
When I am h. I live SMITH 800:1
whether you are h. or not SHAW 780:69
Which of us is h. THAC 849:94
wretched…once to have been h. BOET 138:29
Happy Isles touch the H. I. TENN 840:66
harbour a voyage and not a h. TOYN 864:28
h. and neighbour wood THOM 852:74
h. without ships DEFOE 258:22
looking over h. and city SAND 713:92
O the H. of Fowey QUIL 674:42
rain over the dwindling h. THOM 852:75
hard game is too h. JAMES 433:24
gave me the h. shoulder HENRI 395:43
h. and practical man HOYLE 417:4
h. on His Majesty's Opposition HOBH 405:31
'H.,' replied the Dodger DICK 267:91
h. rhyme SHAK 745:24
h. to be room-mates SALI 711:56
h. to be sought out HERA 396:70
no success without h. work SOPH 804:87
powerful h. thing CONN 234:92
read very h. JOHN 443:70
The woman is so h. TENN 841:98
when the times were not h. EMER 313:50
where a heart is h. SHAK 733:54
hardcover Europe…a h. book DELI 260:75
harden H. not your heart BIBLE 97:58
harder they would be h. to them TROL 866:89
hardest h. thing to bear JUVE 453:16
h. thing to do HEMI 394:9
hardhearted more cruel and h. BACON 48:90
hard-hearts nature…makes these h.-h. SHAK 763:80
hardship experience nothing but h. BELL 72:41
meet any h. KENN 462:12
teacheth him wholesome h. LASS 492:60
hardships disappointments, h. PEARY 645:1
h. of an emigrant's life MOOD 594:6
very bottom of h. DU 293:71
Hardy either 29 or Thomas H. PARK 638:76
Kiss me, H. NELS 610:35
hare covers…the h. and the hunter PATC 642:48
grass, and a h. sitting up? LAWR 494:95
h. limped trembling KEATS 458:30
o'er the timid h.! THOM 856:56
start a h.! SHAK 741:4
hare-bells heath and h.-b. BRON 155:99
hare-brained every h.-b. nut SAFER 708:95
harem like eunuchs in a h. BEHAN 70:7
hares h. have no time to read BROO 156:21
little hunted h. HODG 405:46
hark H.! ah, the Nightingale! ARNO 32:12
H., h., the lark SHAK 773:61
H.! how all the welkin rings WESL 900:10
H. in thine ear SHAK 763:91
Harlem like…a son of H. OBRI 620:99
harlot h.'s cheek SHAK 753:73
h.'s cry from street BLAKE 135:70
he that cleaveth to h. BIBLE 108:55
Portia is Brutus' h. SHAK 747:85
prerogative of the h. BALD 54:46
harlots Mother Of H. BIBLE 127:73
Harlow t is silent, as in H. ASQU 36:17
harm does h. to my wit SHAK 756:51
does men great h. HESI 401:66
does no h. GILM 356:57
don't think it does any h. THOM 852:68
Fate cannot h. me SMITH 801:21
fear we'll come to h. BALL 56:85
good provoke to h. SHAK 758:41
How can it h. you CRUZ 246:87
in his sleep he does little h. SHAK 762:37
may do great h. SHAW 780:50
no h. to retool our imaginations WELD 896:38
Shall h. Macbeth SHAK 768:23
Whoop, do me no h., good man SHAK 770:91
harmful may be more h. HUXL 426:12
who say it is h. CRUZ 246:89
harming perpetual h. of somebody FORD 329:98
harmless book is not h. ELIOT 307:90
h. and even beneficial SHAW 780:50
h. as doves BIBLE 111:26
harmonies European h. GILL 356:48
h. are concealed from me FISH 324:76
h. of the body BERN 81:42
inventor of h. TENN 846:28
tranquil h. GAUG 347:66
tumult of thy mighty h. SHEL 783:47
harmony All discord, h., not understood POPE 660:15
body's h. POPE 662:77
h. comes…as a shock RAINE 677:97
h.…comes to heal WORD 923:67
h. for the honour of God BACH 46:25
H.! H.! SCHO 719:25
h. In autumn SHEL 782:21
H. in discord HORA 414:28
h. or true delight? MILT 584:2
immortal god of h. BEET 70:95
in h. with the sentiments of an assassin BIER 128:11
knew such h. alone MILT 575:96
Like h. in music WORD 925:92
may we bring h. THAT 850:16
ninefold h. MILT 576:97
notions of law and h. THOR 857:78
other h. of prose DRYD 292:43
ravish like enchanting h. SHAK 733:73
Sentimentally…disposed to h. LAMB 486:45
that famous h. YEATS 932:32
untaught h. of spring GRAY 369:3
what hope of h.? SHAK 730:54
harms bars a thousand h. SHAK 732:25
harness die in h. AMIS 14:86
joints of the h. BIBLE 92:27
Harold a masseur called H. WOOD 921:17
harp h., his sole remaining joy SCOTT 722:84
h. that once through MOORE 596:51
No h.…could so cheerily play CAMP 186:65
played everything but the h. BARR 61:1
wild h. slung behind MOORE 596:49
Harper H. smiled, well pleased SCOTT 723:89
harps h. upon the willows BIBLE 98:98
harpstring hair and h. of gold SWIN 833:34
harpy conference with this h. SHAK 744:95
harried h. man I think I be! BALL 56:79
Harris the present Mrs H. THUR 859:19
Harrison if Rex H. doesn't GRANT 366:46
to see…H. hanged PEPYS 647:28
Harrovian H. pricks up his ears ANON 21:30
Harrow H. would not be ashamed BALD 54:52
harrow beneath the h. knows KIPL 470:73
H. the house of the dead AUDEN 39:76
h. up thy soul SHAK 752:28
Harry Banish not…H.'s company SHAK 742:16
England breed again…a King H.? DRAY 286:2
grunted H. to Jack SASS 716:63
Know what I mean, H.? BRUNO 163:6
little touch of H. SHAK 746:47
harsh seem h., impertinent JONS 449:26
harshness h. which resides in your heart LABE 482:51
no h. gives offence POPE 658:59
Hart one H. that you will not leave HART 384:8
hart As the h. panteth BIBLE 95:20
Harvard chair at H. or Princeton MENC 565:60
didn't go to H. JOHN 440:89
glass flowers at H. MOORE 595:31
graduate of H. or not JOHN 440:97
H. education consists of what CONA 230:81
Yale College and my H MELV 564:28
harvest And it is h. RANS 679:23
continual spring, and h. SPEN 809:92
h. is past BIBLE 105:73
h. of a quiet eye WORD 924:84
laughs with a h. JERR 437:39
Raymond like the H. Moon FARJ 318:48
seedtime and h. BIBLE 87:67
sheaves in h. DONNE 281:88
When thou cuttest down thine h. BIBLE 89:50
white already to h. BIBLE 117:85
harvested heart has been h. BAUD 64:59
harvesting h. from existence NIET 615:9
harvests bad h., and…fluctuations ELIOT 303:87
h. bury all his pride has planned POPE 659:97
hash product is a final h. MELV 564:43
hashish puffed h.…didn't inhale RICH 686:72
hasta H. la vista, baby SCHW 721:63
haste Do nothing in h. WHYM 906:65
eat it in h. BIBLE 88:16
h. now to my setting SHAK 775:18
life and light, with envious h. ROCH 692:70
make what h. I can to be gone CROM 246:76
Married in h. CONG 231:1
marry in h. CABE 183:15
Men love in h. BYRON 182:94
repent in h. CONG 231:2
send them out of the land in h. BIBLE 88:18
shall not make h. BIBLE 103:28
such h. to be doing STEV 822:4
hasty let not thine heart be h. BIBLE 101:76
man is ever h. KORAN 479:75
need na start awa sae h. BURNS 170:71
hasty-pudding sweets of h.-p. BARL 60:58
hat All h. and no cattle CONN 232:53
as is the h. of a soldier HERB 399:24
Beneath her torn h. WHIT 906:58
can't think without his h. BECK 68:35
coat and top h. LAVER 493:82
fashion of his h. SHAK 744:84
from whose h. KIPL 473:40
get your h. FIEL 323:46

my h. is a map FIEL 322:36
No hat upon his h. SHAK 752:40
normal humble h. HERB 399:24
nowhere yet to rest my h. ARNO 32:31
off the top of your h. NEW 611:52
Off with her h.! CARR 195:74
Off with his h. SHAK 731:11
one small h. could carry all GOLD 361:55
On my defenceless h. MILT 585:26
on my h. be it BALC 53:28
Orion standing on his h. LAWR 494:5
ostrich, with its h. in the sand WILS 916:12
over h. and ears in it STER 818:88
painting in his h. MOTH 600:32
parboiled h. upon a stake MONT 593:5
pensive h. MILT 578:54
perishing never entered my h. DOUG 283:15
pops its h. into the shop FOOTE 329:94
precious jewel in his h. SHAK 749:33
punching people in the h. LEON 503:7
put things out of his h. CARY 199:62
Raindrops Keep Fallin' on my H. DAVID 253:21
raise his fiery h. WILL 914:60
repairs his drooping h. MILT 578:57
room at your h. BALL 55:72
roses at my h. ROSS 697:83
round my fallen h. TENN 842:18
Say nowt…talk your h. off CLOU 223:42
Scotch tongue in your h. SCOTT 724:37
Scratched his h. ROBI 690:32
sever h. from body WEBS 894:83
sex rears its ugly h. ALLI 12:60
shall bruise thy h. BIBLE 86:53
sharp tongue in your h. PERE 648:60
Shoot…this old grey h. WHIT 906:62
should have his h. examined GOLD 362:79
singing about her h. GRAV 368:87
smote off his h. BIBLE 90:68
Socialist after he is forty…no h. WILL 914:67
so much music in my h. RAVEL 679:36
such a h. of hair HOUS 416:90
suddenly bowed his h. JOYCE 452:83
their h. the prow DRYD 287:20
thou hast anointed my h. with oil BOOK 143:44
through the h. down to the feet ANGE 17:38
throw earth over your h. PASC 640:20
Thy h., thy sovereign SHAK 732:46
Tomorrow's vengeance on the h. SHAK 732:20
tremendous world in my h. HEWE 401:70
tumble h. over heels KING 469:57
turns no more his h. COLE 225:90
two ideas in her h. LINK 511:58
under his h. YEATS 934:63
Uneasy lies the h. SHAK 743:53
Upon his own rebellious h. MILT 582:40
violet's reclining h. DONNE 280:57
we as h., and you as members HENR 395:46
wheels go over my h. TENN 845:94
where to lay his h. BIBLE 110:16
Whose h. proud fancy never taught CRAB 242:81
with your 'ayrick h. of 'air KIPL 471:94
Words the h. does not shape ANON 19:98
would shake his h. and say LEAC 497:66
you incessantly stand on your h. CARR 194:67
headache dismal h. GILB 354:15
headaches problems…We call them h. ACHE 3:41
sex is good for h. WILB 907:79
headgear h. worn by the…world ATAT 37:32
heading h. into nut country KENN 463:39
headland All night, this h. WILB 907:77
some bold h. WORD 928:52
headlines H. pass SKEL 795:1
newspaper needs…in its h. PULI 672:4
headlong H. themselves they threw MILT 583:88
h., wild uncertain thee? DONNE 279:28
sons Hurled h. MILT 581:27
headmistress h. of a certain age JAMES 433:29
headpiece H. filled with straw ELIOT 306:69
headpieces h. stuffed with straw MACD 530:47
heads calling h. that God exists PASC 641:21
can't mess with people's h. HEND 395:37
carve h. upon cherry-stones JOHN 446:63
cut off the h. of people PEPYS 647:43
egg h. are in one basket ANON 23:87
goes to the h. of cowards MITC 588:97
hardly miss their h. SHAW 781:87
h. are green LEAR 497:79
h.…beneath their shoulders SHAK 759:61
H., h.—take care of your h. DICK 266:66
h. pass out BERR 82:61
h. replete with thoughts COWP 241:78
hover in their restless h. MARL 551:77
Hung their h. SHAK 775:13
keep their own h. MUMF 603:78
lose their h. FITZ 325:7
old h. on your young shoulders SPARK 806:21
Reared…their flourished h. MILT 583:70
sugarplums danced in their h. MOORE 594:15
tall men had ever very empty h. BACON 47:69
Tossing their h. WORD 927:41
vulgar h. that look asquint BROW 158:55
with h. on their shoulders JAMES 434:74
wooden h. may be [inherited] CONK 232:50
write plays in our h. MAMET 544:39
headstone h. s. of the corner BIBLE 97:78
headstones H. stagger BERR 82:61
h. yield their names TATE 836:3
milestones into h. LOWE 520:40
headstrong h., moody, murmuring DRYD 289:72
headway women…make some h. FALU 317:42
heal balm to h. their wounds SHAK 730:83
fame can never h. AYTO 45:18
Physician, h. thyself BIBLE 115:29
time to h. BIBLE 100:70
What wound did ever h. SHAK 760:82
healed h. by the same means SHAK 740:68
with his stripes we are h. BIBLE 104:51
healer compassion of the h.'s art ELIOT 308:21
time is no h. ELIOT 308:32
healing h. in his wings BIBLE 106:22
leaves of the tree…h. of the nations BIBLE 127:84
not heroics but h. HARD 381:42
of the most High cometh h. BIBLE 108:64
health Christian that is in h. LAW 493:85
disliked hearing about h. MITF 589:7
Drink a h. to SYNGE 834:58
drink his h. with three cheers EDGE 299:95
good to preserve the h. of Man BYRD 178:93
great deal better for the h. STEV 821:70
H. and an able body FLET 328:73
h. and plenty cheered GOLD 361:50
h. of his wife CONN 233:83
H., Wealth, Love…and Time ANON 26:91
His h., his honour BLUN 137:16
hunt in fields, for h. DRYD 292:53
implies an idea of h. TRIL 866:67
in h. wes and gladnes DUNB 294:6
in sickness and in h. BOOK 142:24
in sickness and in h. BOOK 142:25
in sickness and in h. BOOK 142:26
interest of good h. TAFT 835:78
lack of h. in the body PLATO 655:85
no h. in us BOOK 140:66
nor hope nor h. SHEL 783:32
Only do always in h. SIGI 791:27
people in the soundest h. DICK 271:17
preservation of h. SPEN 806:40
psychological h. PECK 645:7
save men of indifferent h. DOUG 283:28
saving h. among all nations BIBLE 96:37
Say that h. and wealth HUNT 423:35
simple beauty and rustic h. WHIT 906:58
spirit of h. SHAK 751:25
When you have both it's h. DONL 279:24
healths drink one another's h. JERO 437:30
healthy classical period was h. GOET 360:22
Happiness is h. for the body PROU 671:89
If you are h. FORD 330:9
makes a male h. THUR 859:29
heap all is a knot, a h. JONS 450:62
dig and h. ARNO 32:4
garbage h. GARD 346:46
H. high the…platter MACB 527:82
rude h. together hurl'd MARV 556:79
heaped H. for two days KHAY 466:94
hear can't h. what they say? SMITH 799:78
Come on and h. BERL 79:11
deaf to h. BIBLE 114:14
Do not let me h. ELIOT 308:17
ears to h. BIBLE 114:10
ears to h. BIBLE 111:35
ears to h., let him h. BIBLE 114:10
ears to h., let him h. BIBLE 111:35
h. it through their feet SOUSA 804:92
H., O Israel BIBLE 89:45
h. the soft rain RICK 686:74
If you really want to h. SALI 710:51
I h. you, I will come HOUS 415:53
I shall h. in heaven BEET 70:1
It startled him just to h. RAMOS 678:6
much to h. and see SKEL 794:89
neither see nor h. JOHN 441:4
one you cannot h. NORTH 618:68
power…to make you h. CONR 234:95
public only gets to h. STEIN 815:29
something we cannot h. SCOTT 722:78
then not h. it crying! HERB 398:13
unto you that h. shall more be given BIBLE 114:11
what they h., they repeat! SITW 794:64
what they wanted to h. SHAR 776:44
heard Ain't H. Nothin' Yet JOLS 447:82
every man that h. him JONS 450:57
fall of…civilization will not be h. READ 680:49
generally h. GILB 355:30
have ye not h.? BIBLE 103:41
I h. no longer TENN 845:83
My God, I h. this day HERB 398:3
never have been h. of HAZL 388:84
Oon ere it h. CHAU 208:61
the more h. WILD 911:89
We had h. them HEMI 393:97
hearers Be ye doers…not h. only BIBLE 124:7
maiming it to suit her h. BACON 50:70
move his h. FRAS 335:27
too deep for his h. GOLD 362:70
hearing Fall asleep, or h. die SHAK 775:15
mentioned in your h. AUST 43:70
hearings h. are just like a s. NIXON 617:41
h. will be remembered INOU 430:73
hearse h. presently arrived LAWS 495:44
h. where Lycid lies MILT 578:54
In an h. she rode SMART 796:22
laid in doleful h.? SPEN 808:90
Why does a h. horse snicker SAND 713:97
heart abundance of the h. BIBLE 111:42
actor in his h. believes WELL 897:52
adultery with her already in his h. BIBLE 109:89
affectations rise up in his h. DIDE 274:3
after Heaven's own h. DRYD 289:69
after leaving my h. on the screen QUIR 675:57
age should show your h. MARV 556:62
always knew in my h. HOPK 413:12
Ancient person of my h. ROCH 692:71
and the h. is sick TENN 843:39
artists try to break your h. RAUS 679:34
as the h. grows older HOPK 412:94
As well as want of h.! HOOD 410:50
At h. I knew THES 851:51
a trickling of h. PATC 642:48
Batter my h. DONNE 281:70
beak from out my h. POE 656:24
beanbag of a h. NOON 617:56
Because it is my H. OATES 620:94
bind the h. of man! GILM 356:55
bitter…because it is my h. CRANE 243:28
Blessed are the pure in h. WHAR 902:56
blue and white Wednesday h. HATT 385:26
books are novels at h. RABAN 675:60
breaks the h. MACD 530:46
broken and a contrite h. BIBLE 95:31
broken h. lies here MACA 526:72
bullet through his h. THAC 849:90
Bury my h. at Wounded Knee BENET 75:12
'Calais' lying in my h. MARY 559:19
Calls my h. to be his own BRID 152:26
calm sunshine of the h. CONS 235:25
captain's h. SHAK 764:9
carried in the h. of none KISS 475:93
cathedrals in my h. SASS 716:65
change of h. AUDEN 39:76
Christ in the h. PATR 643:71
Cloe…wants a h. POPE 661:46
commune with your own h. BIBLE 94:85
conversant with a Man's h. POE 656:27
corrupt the h. BYRON 179:1
Create in me a clean h. BIBLE 95:30
cry of Absence…in the h. RANS 679:25
dagger…in the h. of France QUIN 675:53
darkness of man's h. GOLD 360:28
Dead H. of Australia GREG 372:97
depths of every h. HAWT 386:47

No man is a h. JOHN 446:66
hypocrites cant of h. STER 818:83
h. austerely talk MILT 583:71
h.…in the synagogues BIBLE 109:96
scribes and Pharisees, h.! BIBLE 113:84
tongue and soul…be h. SHAK 754:98
ye h., ye can discern BIBLE 112:61
hypotheses smallest number of h. EINS 302:46
hypothesis character…to an h.? STER 817:73
conviction that a h. MEDA 563:5
discard a pet h. LORE 517:88
endeavour to construct a h. HARDY 381:54
nature of an h. STER 818:80
slaying of a beautiful h. HUXL 426:9
hyssop Purge me with h. BIBLE 95:29
sprinkle me with h. BIBLE 127:87
Hyssopps H. of the Glen ASHF 35:98
hysteria therapy of h. FREUD 336:51
hysterics blind h. of the Celt TENN 844:62

I

iacta I. est alea CAES 184:24
Iago I.'s soliloquy COLE 227:27
yet the pity of it, I. SHAK 760:98
iambics In keen i. DRYD 289:50
Iban The I., when they decide OHAN 623:45
Ibo Among the I.…conversation ACHE 2:18
Ibsen Nietzsche, I.…madmen! ONEI 625:99
These I. creatures ANON 21:38
ice bloody i. on bloody head BLAIR 132:98
cracked i. crunching STEV 820:44
Glitt'ring with i. POPE 662:66
good to break the i. BACON 49:18
hot i. and wondrous…snow SHAK 738:14
i. age ended years ago ZHAO 936:95
I. formed on the butler WODE 919:74
i. of its own indifference ROOS 696:44
i. on a hot stove FROST 339:7
i. was in the blood PIER 651:7
may not dissolve the i. SURR 829:40
skating on very thin i. CAMP 185:54
skating over thin i. EMER 312:16
sunny pleasure-dome with caves of i.! COLE 226:12
talent, a glass, and some cracked i. BARR 61:98
To curle on the i. FENE 646:19
To smooth the I. SHAK 739:30
world will end…in i. FROST 338:97
iceberg portent of an i. BROW 162:64
The i. rises BISH 131:74
icebergs like i. in the ocean GERH 350:35
icecaps blue i. on the mountains CHAI 207:49
ice-cream emperor of i.-c. STEV 819:15
enjoy your i.-c. WILD 910:79
Iceman The I. Cometh ONEI 626:2
ice pick Baby LeRoy with an i. p. ROST 699:10
ices after tea and cakes and I. ELIOT 304:19
ice-scratched I.-s. slabs SNYD 803:49
ichor perspiration was but i. BYRON 183:5
icicle hang like an i. SHAK 756:80
icicles When i. hang by the wall SHAK 734:94
White night of i. MALL 542:94
Why are there i. everywhere? ZHAO 936:95
iciness an i., a sinking POE 656:16
icing i. that detracts from the cake AUCH 39:74
id cure of the i. ANON 22:50
Ida I.'s shady brow BLAKE 133:21
idea absurd is the fundamental i. CAMUS 187:86
Alligators have the right i. MACD 531:62
always gone in for the i. that WILS 914:69
Between the i. And the reality ELIOT 306:71
charge that an i. is radical GALB 343:90
controlling i. that holds us FRID 337:57
Dying for an i. LEWIS 508:94
endowed with the i. of God DESC 263:25
entertain an i. JARR 435:85
every new i.…takes a generation FEYN 322:25
failure is not in the i. MCGO 532:92
first i. was not our own STEV 820:30
For an i. ever to be fashionable SANT 714:20
general i., of course LEAC 497:69
good i. but it won't work ROGE 695:20
had the wrong i. first FEYN 322:24
Hang your i. on a peg BRIS 153:44
hate the i. of causes FORS 331:52
his every i. rationalized PIER 651:5
i. alone is eternal FLAU 326:28
i.-bound in the past LAWR 494:99
i. for which I can live KIER 467:7
i.…has still not been said enough DELA 260:58
i. of an external cause SPIN 810:30
i. of a system GEOR 349:19
i. of death saves him FORS 331:37
i. of dying is worse PROU 671:83
i. of elder wisdom UPDI 875:96
i. of liberty SPIN 810:25
i. of weapons RUSS 705:57
i. or concept LEWI 508:7
i. that they are going to live DAVIS 255:51
innermost i. of this hue MELV 564:32
it would be a good i. GAND 345:36
let the i. soak in MILL 572:31
new i.…close to insanity MILL 571:1
nice place, inside an i. MCIL 533:2
No grand i. was ever born FITZ 325:13
Nothing is more dangerous than an i. ALAIN 9:81
possess but one i. JOHN 444:90
sacrificed…for…an i. MILL 573:57
shoot his like in the name of an i. BROD 153:57
slightest i. what they should be doing FULL 341:50
teach the young i. THOM 856:53
the i. of death must be born MACH 532:96
The man with a new i. TWAIN 872:25
to whom the i. first occurs DARW 253:19
Whatever is…perceived is an i. BERK 79:6
What redeems it is an i. only CONR 234:96
when a politician does get an i. MARQ 554:30
ideal American is an i. FRIE 337:66
An i. wife TARK 836:97
boy's i. of a manly career DISR 276:52
Christian i. has not been tried CHES 212:69
Conservative i. of freedom MADAN 538:19
Freedom is not an i. STEV 820:60
i. day for football SMITH 800:90
i. which I hope to live for MAND 544:46
i. would be to belong to none DUDEK 293:81
ideas, or on an i. LAWR 494:98
my song has an i. CHOC 214:17
nearer today to the i. HOOV 411:58
not charmed with the i. of life MILL 570:59
Religion…ultimate i. WHIT 904:8
softly sleeps the calm I. DICK 268:48
idealism grips with so-called i. MENC 566:61
i. is not uncommon ROOS 696:57
I. is the noble toga HUXL 426:2
idealistic America…only i. nation WILS 917:19
our i. pretensions OBRI 620:2
idealists I. are very apt to walk SMITH 799:82
idealized i. into powerlessness JONG 448:6
idealizer Sorrow, the great i. LOWE 520:37
ideals forever hallowed by the i. EISE 302:64
i. and visions to the past KENN 463:30
I. of a democratic…society MAND 544:46
i.…painters' techniques RENO 683:9
men without i. CAMUS 187:85
tell the i. of a nation DOUG 283:25
white man's superior i. VASC 877:39
ideas addiction…to the i. GALB 343:91
alter and exchange our i. BERN 81:36
believe in i. and die for them ANOU 26:97
borrowed i. CALL 184:38
cemetery of dead i. UNAM 873:65
dreams that have…changed my i. BRON 155:94
false i. prevail as to woman's STAN 812:63
find really marvellous i. LEON 504:19
foundation of your i. and phrases LAUT 493:77
founded not upon visionary i. GLAD 358:92
great i. are hogwash NABO 606:41
Great people talk about i. LEBO 499:12
i. about the native LESS 504:31
I. are born from hatred GENET 348:6
i. begin to destroy sex in America DOCT 277:2
i. get cloath'd STER 818:95
i. must be as broad as Nature DOYLE 285:50
i. of economists KEYN 466:89
i., or on an ideal LAWR 494:98
i. take their beginnings LOCKE 514:18
Innate i. are in every man BLAKE 135:79
isolate him, and his i. disintegrate DIDE 274:3
live in the mind, in i. MILL 572:18
machine for transmission of i. BOWL 147:33
most interesting i. SONT 804:76
new i. or fresh outlooks MACK 533:10
no i. and the ability KRAUS 480:9
no i. but in things WILL 913:50
Not many composers have i. GERS 350:36
of nasty i. SWIFT 831:87
our i. that make us UNAM 873:64
People find i. a bore POUND 665:54
publishing of his i. KAZIN 456:71
realm of i. MILL 571:1
Relations of I. HUME 422:13
share no one's i. TURG 870:65
signs of i. JOHN 442:39
two i. are more inseparable SMITH 801:9
two i. in her head LINK 511:58
two i. of government BRYAN 163:8
two opposed i. in the mind FITZ 325:8
unexpected copulation of i. JOHN 441:25
vehicle for conveying i. MACB 527:81
without any i. LOCKE 514:17
words reign over i. SAND 712:83
identical exist, but are i. FORS 331:43
identity live without an i. MCLU 536:62
mistaking…similarity for real i. PALM 635:19
questions of freedom and i. JORD 450:64
sense of personal i. STEV 822:97
short circuit in his i. ROTH 699:14
ideological i., or the abstract ROTH 699:28
ideologies i. and inventions SONT 804:73
not to have i. HOFS 406:56
ideology an i. that is warlike OBRI 620:2
more important than i. NEWM 612:67
single i. for 70 years YELT 934:70
ides Beware the i. of March SHAK 747:72
idiocy facilitate the infection of i. BIER 129:33
human…potential for i. ONET 626:12
idioms licentious i. JOHN 441:28
long words and exhausted i. ORWE 628:62
idiot artist, like the i. SITW 794:84
computer is a fast i. AMER 13:76
good loser…an i. DURO 296:36
i. who praises GILB 355:22
law is…a i. DICK 267:96
possibly an i. DALI 251:71
tale told by an i. SHAK 769:42
idiotism hundred new titles of i. NASHE 609:10
idiots fatuity of i. SMITH 801:7
I. are always in favour SHAW 781:86
play the i. in her eyes SHAK 757:4
village i., policemen MACD 530:47
your only competition is i. MANK 545:60
idle all be i. if we could JOHN 445:19
all the day i.? BIBLE 113:77
As i. as a painted ship COLE 225:84
be not i. BURT 174:83
happiest when I am i WARD 888:58
I. to hope REED 681:81
If you are i. JOHN 445:40
many a one who would be i. ELIOT 303:99
merely the art of the i. INGR 429:63
most i. and unprofitable GIBB 352:60
Most 'scruciating i. KIPL 472:38
Reputation is an i.…imposition SHAK 760:79
such i. fellows as I AUBR 39:66
idleness faculty for i. STEV 822:97
grief and sin of i. MELV 564:24
Grief is a species of i. JOHN 444:96
I., which is often becoming STEV 821:87
pains and penalties of i. POPE 662:80
reading is not i. SPEN 807:65
idlers loungers and i. of the Empire DOYLE 284:46
idling enjoy i. thoroughly JERO 437:28
idol ancient i., on his base again BROW 161:48
celestial and my soul's i. SHAK 752:44
'eathen i.'s foot KIPL 471:87
God…would be an i. BONH 140:62
i. to offend the national religion BENT 77:68
natural i. of the Anglo-Saxon BAGE 51:85
one-eyed yellow i. HAYES 387:62
plaything and their i. SHEL 782:10
idolatry contemporary man's i. MONT 591:62
on this side i. JONS 450:55
organization of i. SHAW 778:4
stubbornness is as iniquity and i. BIBLE 91:89
idols i. of consumption' LOWE 521:63
like old i. BOTT 146:17
if 'i.' is the only peacemaker SHAK 751:92
Iffucan Chieftain I. of Azcan STEV 819:20
ignis fatuus Reason, an i. f. ROCH 691:56
ignoble made i. talk TENN 846:20

there J.'s pillars stood BLAKE 135:72
Till we have built J. BLAKE 136:85
To measure J. BIBLE 106:15
was J. builded here? BLAKE 135:83
waste places of J. BIBLE 104:48
jessamine casement j. stirred TENN 845:90
Jesse rod out of the stem of J. BIBLE 102:18
Jessie J., the flower o' Dunblane TANN 836:91
jest fellow of infinite j. SHAK 755:31
glory, j., and riddle POPE 660:17
heaven admits no j. FORD 330:14
He had his j. DRYD 290:89
honour did but j. GREE 371:78
j.'s prosperity lies in the ear SHAK 734:93
jocund as to j. SHAK 734:1
Life is a j. GAY 347:76
that's no j. RALE 677:1
they do but j., poison in j. SHAK 754:93
use myself in j. DONNE 279:40
very good j. WEBS 895:96
whole wit in a j. BEAU 66:6
jester becomes a fool and j.! SHAK 743:67
Jesu J., lover of my soul WESL 900:11
J., thou art all compassion WESL 900:14
Jesus all one in Christ J. BIBLE 122:36
around when J. Christ JAGG 432:18
black people with J. GIOV 357:75
call his name J. BIBLE 108:70
come, Lord J. BIBLE 127:85
crucified J.... picture of God BAKER 53:19
dear Lord J., set me free STUA 827:99
followers of J. JOHN 441:9
for all cometh of J. LYDG 523:4
grace without J. Christ BONH 140:58
greatest Jew since J. Christ ROBB 689:13
If J. Christ were to come today CARL 193:46
J. and a nameless ape MACD 529:37
J. Christ her little child ALEX 11:24
J. Christ is a Democrat WALL 886:2
J. Christ... Word of God BARTH 62:4
J. cried with a loud voice BIBLE 114:4
J., here we are HILL 403:93
J.... I love thee still BUTL 178:84
J. increased in wisdom BIBLE 115:28
J. led up of the Spirit BIBLE 109:78
J., meek and mild WESL 900:12
J. never claims to be God ROBI 690:42
J. of Nazareth was the most scientific man EDDY 299:88
J. saw it, he was much displeased BIBLE 114:17
J. shall reign where'er WATTS 891:4
J. stretched forth his hand BIBLE 112:57
J. the author and finisher BIBLE 124:99
J., the very thought of Thee CASW 199:80
J., 'tis such a vulgar expression CONG 231:7
J. took bread BIBLE 114:96
J.... took bread BIBLE 121:6
J.... took bread BIBLE 114:96
J. was a moderniser BLAIR 133:11
J. went into the temple of God BIBLE 113:79
J. went unto them BIBLE 112:56
J. wept BIBLE 118:4
J. wept HUGO 421:97
J., when he had cried again BIBLE 114:5
J., when he was baptized BIBLE 108:77
John seeth J. BIBLE 117:75
more popular than J. Christ LENN 502:89
No man can say that J. BIBLE 121:7
none but J. heard TRUTH 869:52
recognize God without J. PASC 641:34
Sacred Heart o' J. OCAS 621:14
Stand Up For J.! DUFF 293:88
sweet reasonableness of J. ARNO 34:64
sweet the name of J. NEWT 613:78
thing that J. really would've liked SALI 711:60
When J. came to Birmingham STUD 827:5
When J. heard it, he marvelled BIBLE 110:14
when J. was born in Bethlehem BIBLE 108:72
wrong to... blame J. BENN 75:16
Jesuses trained seals, creeping J. MACD 530:47
Jew eke most lovely J. SHAK 738:2
greatest J. since Jesus Christ ROBB 689:13
Hath not a J. eyes? SHAK 740:68
I'm not really a J.... Just J.-ish MILL 573:58
In heathen, Turk or J. BLAKE 134:32
J. is only the name MILL 572:5
J. of Tarsus BIBLE 119:54
like an... assimilated J. OBRI 620:99

makes you a normal J. ROTH 699:26
neither Greek nor J. BIBLE 123:67
neither J. nor Greek BIBLE 122:36
States... the J. among the nations FERB 320:94
take my leave of the J. SHAK 740:57
jewel chastity's the j. SHAK 762:34
For your sake, j. SHAK 759:65
has yet one j. left MILT 579:78
j. in a... chest. SHAK 734:99
j. [judged] by the light ANON 23:78
j. of the kingdom SUN 829:30
j. that we find SHAK 758:21
precious j. in his head SHAK 749:33
rich j. in an Ethiope's ear SHAK 736:42
time's best j. SHAK 772:25
jewelled j. mass of millinery TENN 845:81
jewellers through most j.' hands WEBS 895:98
jewellery Don't ever wear artistic j. COLE 227:30
jewelry gigantic chunk of costume j. LAUR 492:70
hang on to her j. LOOS 517:77
rest... can rattle your j. LENN 502:88
jewels capital bosom to hang j. upon DICK 270:11
Dumb j.... move a woman's mind SHAK 729:34
Health and... body are two j. FLET 328:73
j. five-words-long TENN 841:96
j. for a set of beads SHAK 735:22
precious j. into a garret BACON 47:69
reft the j. from her hair HYDE 427:23
unvalued j. SHAK 731:8
With gold and j. cover POPE 658:55
jewel-sea love her j.-s. MACK 533:15
Jewish insights of the J. prophets NIEB 614:98
J. family was an inviolate ROTH 699:29
J.. I don't work out RIVE 688:4
J. Puritan of the middle NEME 611:39
J. Queen of Egypt TAYL 837:16
solution of the J. question GOER 360:11
Jews All men are J. MALA 541:81
don't ask employers... to like... J. BORO 145:2
fat of rendered J. and Gypsies VONN 883:56
Have mercy upon all J. BOOK 141:87
Hitler attacked the J. NIEM 614:3
J., a headstrong... race DRYD 289:72
J. and Arabs should settle AUST 44:5
J. in Palestine OROU 627:22
J. lived by... insight SACKS 707:85
J. which believeth not BIBLE 119:45
King of the J. BIBLE 118:17
King of the J. BIBLE 108:72
national home for the J. BALF 54:54
noticed that J. shout? ROTH 699:25
The Irish and the J. have a psychosis BEHAN 70:9
the last J. to die without standing up MEIR 563:12
To choose The J. EWER 316:28
university where... the J. are hosts SACH 707:83
What captivity was to the J. WILDE 908:86
Jezebel J.... painted her face BIBLE 92:35
jib cut of his j. DOUG 284:34
jilt cruel j. to me MORSE 599:11
jingle must j. in his ears WOLL 921:7
jingles trifles and j. BACON 49:38
jingling one j. padlock POPE 662:75
Jingo by J. if we do HUNT 422:21
jo For auld lang syne, my j. BURNS 171:99
John Anderson my j. BURNS 171:10
Joan If J. of Arc had been born SIMON 792:38
play Saint J. THOR 858:3
Job All books are the Book of J. ELKIN 310:69
blessed the latter end of J. BIBLE 94:80
J. open his mouth in vain BIBLE 93:68
poor as J. SHAK 742:40
job $60 GI j. EISE 302:60
difficultest j. a man can do DAVI 253:22
finish the j. CHUR 217:80
hard j. of using reason WILS 915:78
How would you like a j. PLAN 654:61
husband is a whole-time j. BENN 76:44
If they will only do their j. SELZ 727:88
It's a man's j. AESC 8:61
j., as I see it MACD 530:50
j. is likely to be ill-done KEYN 466:87
j. of the nurture of children PALEY 635:12
Keeping up... a full-time j. CRISP 244:51
loneliest j. in the world BALD 54:45
loses his j. TRUM 868:38
lost the j. JOYCE 452:89
man who wants to do a good j. ELIOT 308:12

most improper j. TOLK 862:96
Nae harder j. to mortals MACD 529:33
neighbour loses his j. REAG 680:55
only doing my j. if they do WHIT 905:25
our j. to make women unhappy PUCK 672:98
second most important j. GARN 346:51
since he has lost his j. MORG 597:80
social order... my j. to preserve FRAN 333:91
to do the j. too long SWIFT 831:75
whether my j. is a j. KNIG 476:15
will always have a j. RAVI 679:38
Jobiska Aunt J. made him drink LEAR 498:87
Aunt J.'s Runcible Cat LEAR 498:89
jobs climbing into j. REST 683:16
fewer the j. worth doing JAY 436:99
j. that pay more than others WILL 913:39
Mine is one of the j. WEAT 893:61
woman... not the top j. THAT 850:8
Jock J., when ye hae naething SCOTT 724:36
stop yer tickling, J.! LAUD 492:62
tears... For J. of Hazeldean SCOTT 724:21
Wi' J. of Hazeldean SCOTT 724:23
jocosity j. catches the crowd MARQ 554:26
jocund As gentle and as j. SHAK 734:1
j. day Stands tiptoe SHAK 736:69
Joe J., long dead SLES 796:15
Say it ain't so, J. ANON 22:48
jog As we j. on STER 817:69
J. on, j. on SHAK 770:83
jogging J. is for people WOOD 921:16
J. is very beneficial SCHU 720:49
Johannesburg No second J. PATON 643:70
John I J. saw the holy city BIBLE 127:79
J. Brown is stowed NASH 608:96
J. had his raiment of camel's hair BIBLE 108:75
J., like J. FARJ 318:48
J. seeth Jesus BIBLE 117:75
J. to the seven churches BIBLE 125:42
notorious domesticity for J. WILDE 909:33
shew J. again those things BIBLE 111:33
unto the multitudes concerning J. BIBLE 111:34
why... name your baby 'J.' GOLD 362:82
john leaning on the j. door OHARA 623:46
Johnny Little J. Head-in-Air HOFF 406:52
not despair For J. Head-in-Air PUDN 672:99
sleeps as sound As J. Underground PUDN 672:99
Johnson heroism of J. STEV 822:1
J. approached a... position MANC 544:41
J.'s morality HAWT 386:53
J. went through three years WHITE 903:98
that great man, Dr J. WESL 900:24
You are a philosopher, Dr J. EDWA 300:22
Johnsonian subtlety of J. strategy MANC 544:42
joined j. with no foot-landrakers SHAK 741:6
joiner imagination of a lodge j. MENC 566:86
j. with j. HESI 401:64
joint manacled with j. or limb MILT 581:9
The time was out of j. STRA 826:81
together every j. and member MILT 579:79
jointed It is nothing j.; it flows JAMES 434:63
joints between the j. of the harness BIBLE 92:27
fettle your fine j. SHAK 736:71
j. are stiff SHAK 737:76
joke bitter cosmic j. GELL 348:98
every j. is... a custard pie ORWE 628:65
family j. that when ROTH 699:17
funniest j. in the world SHAW 779:33
Housekeeping ain't no j. ALCO 10:4
if a j. were a charity auction MCIL 533:1
If we live inside a bad j. RABAN 675:59
j.'s a very serious thing CHUR 215:49
many a j. had he GOLD 361:54
our only j. BARR 61:87
jokes bad j. of history GUED 374:29
civil servant doesn't make j. IONE 430:75
difference of taste in j. ELIOT 304:14
don't make j. ROGE 695:29
hackneyed j. from Miller BYRON 179:97
Krishna's j. may be vapid FORS 332:57
my little j. on Thee FROST 339:13
no j.... no chance ANON 22:66
no more j. in Music-halls SASS 716:57
shouldn't make j. CARR 196:96
telling j. back there KAUF 456:60
telling j. or gossiping CABR 183:19
joking My way of j. SHAW 779:33
jollier j. than the people LUCAS 521:72

K

L

dark in l. expos'd MILT 586:47
Dark is L. Enough FRY 340:29
Darkness from l. BROW 162:73
darkness shall be the l. ELIOT 308:14
dawn's early l. KEY 465:76
Dear as the l. GRAY 370:31
dear to me as l. and life BURNS 171:5
deriving l. from each other BERL 80:24
dungeon flamed with l. WESL 899:9
eldritch l. of sundown DAY 257:85
entrance of thy words giveth l. BIBLE 97:85
every ray of God's l. DOST 283:11
everything except space and l. HEAT 390:28
face to the l. SASS 716:64
far from the l. of day ORAH 626:20
fierce l. which beats TENN 846:5
'Forward, the L. Brigade!' TENN 844:76
from far thy beauteous l. WESL 900:18
from fidelity to the l. RODR 693:95
from those flames No l. MILT 580:97
Give me a l. HASK 385:25
gives a lovely l. MILL 571:81
God called the l. Day BIBLE 85:39
golden and silver l. YEATS 933:38
Hail holy L. MILT 582:36
hands…that would l. the world MILL 571:96
happy realms of l. MILT 580:98
Heaven's l. forever shines SHEL 786:7
hours of l. return ARNO 32:4
how my l. is spent MILT 580:88
I am black…bereaved of l. BLAKE 134:30
I am the l. of the world BIBLE 117:95
infant crying for the l. TENN 843:42
In l. inaccessible SMITH 801:26
into his marvellous l. BIBLE 125:24
jewel [judged] by the l. ANON 23:78
lamps, by whose dear l. MARV 556:68
land of l. CLIN 221:91
last l. has gone THOM 854:9
laws…of l. and shade CAPO 189:27
Lead, kindly L. NEWM 612:62
leave a l.…before was dark WENT 899:5
Let there be l. BIBLE 85:38
Let there be l. MACD 529:36
Let there be l.! SHEL 786:20
level of the l. FORD 330:6
life and l., with envious haste ROCH 692:70
l. after l. well used MILT 582:44
l. and shadow never stand still WEST 900:27
l., and will aspire SHAK 732:52
l. at the end LOWE 521:60
l. beyond compare NEALE 610:28
L. dies before thy…word POPE 662:83
l. dissolved in star-showers SHEL 783:31
l. falls and fills ROET 694:1
l. fantastic round MILT 577:29
l. gleams an instant BECK 68:41
l. heart lives long SHAK 734:89
l. in manners ASCH 35:81
l. in the white mackerel sky BISH 131:77
l. in the window SPEN 807:59
l. is braying SITW 793:62
l. is in the soul MILT 586:48
l. is still ELIOT 307:99
l. of learning RALE 677:2
l. of my mind CRUZ 246:89
l. of setting suns WORD 923:71
l. of Terewth DICK 270:92
l. of the bright world dies BOUR 147:28
l. of the gospel JOHN 442:57
l. of the world BIBLE 109:85
l. of the world BIBLE 117:95
l. of thought SHEL 784:58
l. out for the territory TWAIN 871:12
L. out of darkness! MILT 585:34
l. out of darkness DONNE 281:88
l. ranged in the non-space GIBS 353:76
l., shade and perspective CONS 235:27
l., she said, not of the sky NEIL 610:30
l. shineth in darkness BIBLE 117:72
l. that is love KEND 461:95
l. that she loves TENN 845:89
L. thickens SHAK 768:16
l. to counterfeit a gloom MILT 576:17
l. to lighten the Gentiles BIBLE 115:27
l. to see that duty MACA 524:27
l. to shine upon the road COWP 240:46
l. unto my path BIBLE 97:84
l. which experience gives COLE 227:24
l. wife doth make a heavy husband SHAK 741:92
l. within his own clear breast MILT 577:35
L. wrestling…incessantly with l. CRANE 243:12
like a shaft of l. TENN 841:94
line of festal l. ARNO 32:20
lived l. in the spring ARNO 31:96
long l. shakes TENN 841:3
Lord is my l. BIBLE 94:6
lord of l. DOUG 283:18
lost to l. for evermore BYRON 181:49
lovely lady, garmented in l. SHEL 785:87
making them see the l. PLAN 654:60
married to an electric l. DIMA 275:19
mellowed to that tender l. BYRON 181:53
men loved darkness rather than l. BIBLE 117:82
More l.! GOET 360:25
morning l. creaks down again SITW 794:70
mosquitoey summer night l. ASHB 35:86
naked l. bulb WILL 912:16
Night, the shadow of l. SWIN 833:22
noose of l. FITZ 324:82
Not l. them for themselves SHAK 757:15
Of night and l. YEATS 933:38
one day, the l. MANS 547:89
On the l. fantastic MILT 576:6
out of hell leads up to l. MILT 581:29
passed away in colder l. PEAC 645:96
passion for sweetness and l. ARNO 34:60
poem is…a l. by which WARR 889:72
poets…set their own inimitable l. POUND 666:73
Prince of L. MILT 575:94
pure and endless l. VAUG 878:49
put out the l. SHAK 761:7
quality of fiery aery l. MACD 530:49
radiant l., though sun MILT 577:35
realms of l. GURN 375:45
reft the sonne his l. CHAU 209:89
remember while the l. SWIN 833:31
restore the l. DANI 252:88
river of crystal l. FIELD 322:32
round from the dark and the l. SWIN 833:47
saw great l. BIBLE 109:81
season of L. DICK 271:19
second place of air and l. FRAME 333:80
seen a great l. BIBLE 102:16
sees a green l. everywhere SCHW 721:71
severity of perfect l. TENN 846:23
sharp l. the fields did lie FREE 336:43
shed such l. before MUNRO 603:90
shew l. at Calais JOHN 443:72
slaked the l. with blood TENN 848:69
so airy and l. a quality SHAK 752:55
Some true, some l. TENN 847:42
such scant l. WHAR 901:49
sweetness and l. SWIFT 830:53
that earth lie l. WALL 886:15
That was the true L. BIBLE 117:73
the frosty l. TENN 844:60
The l. that loses SWIN 832:19
The l. that never was WORD 928:44
themes in a new l. LUCAS 522:80
the way, the truth, and the l. BIBLE 118:10
This l., this glory COLE 226:4
To l. thee thither WEBS 895:95
turned around from darkness to l. PLATO 655:1
unchanged, and universal l. POPE 658:53
University should be a place of l. DISR 277:79
waited for the l. ROBI 690:28
when my l. is low TENN 843:39
where sweetness and l. failed FORS 331:45
Where there is darkness, l. FRAN 334:98
with a l. behind her! GILB 353:90
within…all l. was contained MARTI 555:44
world of l. VAUG 878:51
lighten l. the tax burden QUINE 675:52
our own hearts SHAK 745:27
lightest l. that wear most of it SHAK 740:71
light-headed l.-h., variable men STEV 821:85
light-hearted l.-h. way…he seduces POMP 658:45
lighthouse Keeping a l.-h. with his eyes CAMP 186:62
sitivation at the l. DICK 266:86
lighting Bring in the bottled l. DICK 267:11
through its own internal l. blind SHEL 784:66
lightning beheld Satan as l. BIBLE 115:36
brilliance of a l. storm FLAU 326:33
came by a l. flash WILS 915:85
different as a moonbeam from l. BRON 155:95
I Have known the l.'s hour DAY 257:83
In the golden l. SHEL 784:56
In thunder, l., or in rain? SHAK 766:64
L. rods have had it better NEW 612:56
like flashes of l. SCHO 719:29
loosed the fatal l. HOWE 417:1
Mirth is like a flash of l. ADDI 6:20
O at l. and lashed rod HOPK 412:82
rather be a l. rod KESEY 465:72
reading Shakespeare by flashes of l. COLE 226:18
struck by l. ORWE 628:49
struck by l. five or six times JARR 435:81
thunder and l. of Desert Storm SCHW 721:67
tree On fire by l. BYRON 180:27
light-o'-love watching his luck…his l.-o.-l. SERV 728:3
lights always knew the l. were on STARR 813:77
an all-the-l.-on man REED 681:82
broken l. of thee TENN 842:21
carnival l. GREE 371:69
Father of l. BIBLE 124:6
Followed false l. DRYD 291:16
l. around the shore ROSS 698:91
l. begin to twinkle TENN 840:66
name Zimmermann in bright l.? MERM 567:15
spent l. quiver and gleam ARNO 31:84
There will be l. everywhere READ 680:49
though the l. HAWT 386:47
turn on the l. GUIM 371:32
Turn up the l. OHEN 623:57
two l. of Christendom PIUS 653:52
like as she is, I do not l. her SHAK 744:89
Besides, I l. you not SHAK 750:70
does not mean that you l. him CHUR 217:99
Do I not l. that TAYL 837:22
don't l. something GREE 370:47
get what you l. SHAW 779:24
If we are l. you SHAK 740:68
l. enough to consent SHAK 750:76
l. it or not THOM 856:48
l. or dislike them FORS 331:40
more l. my own HOPK 413:12
nothing…made me l. him less CONG 231:20
shall not look upon his l. again SHAK 751:11
What I l. about Clive BENT 77:75
what is l. to thee? BYRON 180:32
whether I l. it VAUG 877:41
Whether you l. it not KHRU 466:99
woman whom you do not l. ANOU 26:92
liked l. by only four people HOCK 405:39
like-minded company of the l.-m. DELI 261:79
likeness any l. of any thing BIBLE 88:23
l. and correct incidence of light ALBE 10:98
translate beauty into his l. SHAK 753:76
likes Agreements in l. and dislikes CATI 200:96
everyone l. you except yourself BROWN 157:50
liking Friendships begin with l. ELIOT 304:16
Thy lust and l. SKEL 795:93
lilacs l. last…bloom'd WHIT 906:47
L. out of the dead land ELIOT 305:52
lilac-time Kew in l.-t. NOYES 619:77
Lilian Airy, fairy L. TENN 838:39
lilies And a few l. blow HOPK 412:78
Beauty lives though l. die FLEC 327:45
Consider the l. of the field BIBLE 110:2
feedeth among the l. BIBLE 101:1
l. and languors of virtue SWIN 833:27
l. in her hand ROSS 698:86
l. of ambition DOUG 283:22
L. that fester SHAK 772:38
L. without, roses MARV 555:59
peacocks and l. RUSK 703:4
put thy pale, lost l. out of mind DOWS 284:44
roses overgrown, And l. MARV 555:60
Ye L. male! CRAB 242:97
Lillabullero half a dozen bars of L. STER 817:74
Lillian L. as a grown-up FEIB 319:82
L., you should have stayed a virgin CART 198:53
Lilliput Swiftian L. MCCA 528:2
lilting l. at our yowe-milking ELLI 310:78
lily Daisy and L. SITW 794:72
How sweet the l. grows HEBER 390:33
l. all her sweetness TENN 842:14
l. of the valleys BIBLE 101:96
pure as the l. in the dell LAUD 492:63
splendid…glows the l. FLEC 327:47

Self-portrait in a Convex M. ASHB 35:84
world is the m. MILL 572:20
mirrored m. themselves in my mind ELIOT 303:76
mirrors Better m. than yours JEFF 436:10
blaming m. for being untrue LAFO 485:99
cell whose walls are m. ONEI 625:89
live without m. ATWO 38:58
M. are the perfect lovers ATWO 38:56
m. of the gigantic shadows SHEL 786:17
m. of the sea FLEC 327:52
sexual pull towards m. COND 230:85
women have walked past m. ALLEN 12:38
mirth all resort of m. MILT 576:17
commended m. BIBLE 101:81
earth must borrow its m. WILC 907:80
Frame your mind to m. SHAK 732:25
he is all m. SHAK 744:10
Him serve with m. SCOT 725:64
lost all my m. SHAK 752:56
m. and fun grew fast BURNS 172:23
M. cannot move SHAK 734:92
m. hath present l. SHAK 756:61
M. is short and transient ADDI 6:20
m. of the billow CALL 185:43
m. that has no bitter springs KIPL 473:63
m., What doeth it? BIBLE 100:69
no time for m. and laughter ADE 7:45
Our m. the music RALE 677:1
red with m. SHAK 770:84
Religion does not banish m. WALT 888:53
so much wit, and m. ADDI 6:13
sunburnt m.! KEATS 459:58
swim in m., and fancy MILT 585:18
this night wi' m. and glee SKIN 795:13
With m. and laughter SHAK 739:37
mirthless heartless, m., maniacal THUR 860:51
misanthropy compounded of m. MACA 525:52
Racism…a form of m.? BROD 153:54
misbehave Even if I m. ANON 25:57
miscarriage disgraced by m. JOHN 442:38
success and m. JOHN 442:40
mischief All punishment is m. BENT 77:66
at the bottom of a' the m. SCOTT 724:33
Comet, that bodes M. MAKIN 541:76
evil…working visible m. CHUR 215:42
if any m. follow BIBLE 89:24
if m. befall him BIBLE 88:1
mean m. and break a foul gap SHAK 770:91
minds…gratified with m. COWP 241:77
mourn a m. that is past SHAK 759:66
seem like a bit of m. THUR 859:49
mischiefs intolerable M. PRYN 672:93
misconception prejudices, m. LLOY 513:6
misconduct prodigality and m. SMITH 798:46
misdeed planning any m. JUVE 453:21
miserable arise and make them m. HUXL 425:84
Heaven Knows I'm M. Now MORR 599:8
If life is m. LABR 483:70
If you are m. LAUT 493:76
Life becomes m. BAUD 64:59
life of the artist sufficiently m. BELL 71:30
live a m. life BEET 70:96
making others m. LABR 484:76
man knows that he is m. PASC 641:32
m. beyond all living things SHEL 782:12
m. have no other medicine SHAK 758:31
m. Irish Catholic childhood MCCO 528:17
m. people on earth CELI 202:38
m. sinners BOOK 140:80
m. state of mind BACON 49:17
moral once we are m. PROU 671:74
of all men most m. BIBLE 121:13
one thing is certain too, I'm m. MACI 533:4
secret of being m. SHAW 780:69
through life absolutely m. THOR 858:10
wrong decision can make me very m. DENN 262:99
miseries ambitions…on the m. CONR 234:16
bound in shallows and in m. SHAK 748:16
m. of the world KEATS 458:15
misery affluent m. GARD 346:46
Amid…the m. of nations PITT 653:47
annual expenditure…result m. DICK 269:67
can only mean a common m. COOP 236:52
departure is taken for m. BIBLE 107:31
Friends love m. JONG 448:4
greatest m. is a battle WELL 897:59
heart, all mad with m. SHAK 731:93
hopeless m. and toil STOWE 826:72
Man hands on m. LARK 491:39
Man…is full of m. BOOK 142:33
mine affliction and my m. BIBLE 105:81
M. acquaints a man SHAK 774:87
M. From this day MILT 585:26
m. of being it DRAB 286:88
m. of us, that are born great WEBS 895:4
m. peculiar to the young LESS 504:34
moral restraint, vice and m. MALT 543:16
nothing but pure m. JOHN 446:49
Oppressed…with m. CRAB 242:1
pain is perfect m. MILT 583:86
perfect in their m. MILT 577:26
poverty, vice, and m. SUMN 828:18
privileges of m. DONO 282:98
purchased by the black man's m. DOUG 284:35
supreme In m. MILT 582:56
when one is in m. DANTE 252:95
Who finds himself, loses his m. ARNO 32:6
misfits m. and precocious children MANK 545:62
strangest collection of m. REAG 680:60
misfortune m. extinguishes BALZ 57:11
m. of an old man CARY 199:62
m. of our best friends LARO 491:49
m. to ourselves BIER 129:20
m. to see all his plans JOSE 451:71
m.…to be born a woman EDGE 299:1
regarded as a m. WILDE 909:39
sour m.'s book SHAK 737:80
misfortunes boils and many other M. FLEM 327:58
heapèd with so huge m. SPEN 808:79
history is…crimes and m. VOLT 883:44
m. more bitter BACON 48:85
strong enough to bear the m. LARO 491:51
talks of his m. JOHN 446:49
misgivings Blank m. WORD 927:26
mishap know it well, your m. HEINE 391:50
mislead m. their weak minds SAYE 717:86
m. the public ASQU 36:11
misleading generate m. thoughts SPEN 807:42
m. guide to current affairs KEYN 465:81
misnomer ever was a m. TELL 838:31
This town's a m. QUIL 674:47
mispronounce men m. it MORL 598:84
misquote enough of learning to m. BYRON 179:97
misrepresentation degree of m. ELIOT 303:70
power of steady m. DARW 253:12
way to escape m. LEAV 498:2
misrepresented Science…is m. GOUR 365:27
miss could not m. 'em SHAK 767:99
I m. you HUGO 420:68
little m. HUME 422:11
missed A m. life, a m. love! HEINE 391:50
sure she'd not be m. GILB 355:22
who never would be m. GILB 355:21
missiles bombs and m. lie…buried RAND 678:14
missing M. so much and so much? CORN 237:69
years of m. each other RICH 685:53
you start m. everyone SALI 711:62
mission claim the m. workers RUNY 703:85
Complete the m. ANON 25:60
m. each time he went up HELL 392:59
m. of science will be completed PEAR 645:97
never have a m. DICK 270:95
Whate'er its m. WORD 924:88
missionary I would eat a m. WILB 907:70
more of a m. than a politician CART 198:52
Mississippi into M. Bay KIPL 474:78
missy bit of flirtation with m. SPEKE 806:36
mist clearing a m. THOM 852:55
Faustus like a foggy m. MARL 553:7
Mantled in m. AUDEN 40:11
m. and hum ARNO 32:27
m. of time THAT 850:15
m. on the sea's face MASE 559:21
rank m. they draw MILT 578:52
this fair luminous m. COLE 226:4
mistake Among all forms of m. ELIOT 304:4
Anything you make a m. about BEVIN 85:33
Cambodia was not a m. SHAW 782:6
Every great m. has a halfway BUCK 165:37
every time you make a m. PLAN 654:61
it's a m. not to JAMES 433:50
life would be a m. NIET 616:27
make a m. STEV 819:11
Many a sweet m. doth lie TRAH 864:35
m. to confound strangeness DOYLE 285:49
m. to theorize before…evidence DOYLE 284:47
Murder is always a m. WILDE 908:10
never made a m. SMIL 797:35
never made a m. in grammar SAND 713:3
never make the same m. COPE 237:60
shall be no m. WELL 898:68
under a m. SWIFT 832:3
Worst damnfool m. GARN 346:51
worst m. I made POUND 665:65
mistaken M. Identity is to Drama ABSE 1:8
M. in its assumptions REGAN 682:93
must needs be m. SWIFT 831:83
not likely that everybody is m. DESC 263:18
possible you may be m. CROM 245:72
thou wilt not often be m. PENN 647:23
mistakes America makes…m. CUMM 247:10
causes so many m. HELL 392:77
everyone makes some m. TINT 861:78
genius makes no m. JOYCE 452:90
knows some of the worst m. HEIS 391:57
learn from our m. POPP 663:98
learn from previous m. MURP 604:4
M. are a fact of life GIOV 357:72
name everyone gives to their m. WILDE 908:19
not see our own m. TELL 838:31
physician can bury his m. WRIG 929:79
result of m. which arrested MILL 573:59
the man who makes no m. PHEL 650:87
those who do nothing…make no m. CONR 234:93
to make m. THAT 850:13
too many wrong m. BERRA 82:55
whatever m. it…may condone WEBB 893:66
mister-ectomy M.-e….solution DALY 251:78
mistier and round him, m. THOM 854:7
mistress Art is a jealous m. EMER 313:41
become a man's friend…next a m. CHEK 209:12
certain m. of language JONS 450:60
finding a husband for one's m. COOP 236:57
Fortune…has made a m. DRYD 289:64
good handmaid, but the worst m. BACON 47:65
good understanding with a new m. ETHE 315:94
have no beautiful m. BELL 72:41
Maiden, and m. SWIN 832:17
make me m. to the man POPE 659:83
man can never elevate his m. BALZ 57:5
m. is nude KILP 467:19
M., know yourself SHAK 750:69
m.…little country retreat WYCH 931:7
m. of every house MILL 571:78
m. of half an island SIXT 794:88
m. of true melancholy SHAK 765:43
m. when she walks SHAK 773:51
Music is my m. ELLI 310:77
Nature…virtuous m. BEHN 71:19
never have a m. as beautiful ARLT 30:66
No casual m. TENN 843:47
O m. mine SHAK 756:60
Out of the crowd a m. SHEL 786:8
Power is my m. NAPO 607:69
proved but a mean m. JONS 450:54
smiling m. to many MORSE 599:11
teeming m. POPE 661:45
mistresses Listening…m. offer WYLIE 931:22
M. are like books WYCH 931:10
my little m. RIMB 687:90
Wives are young men's m. BACON 48:91
mistrusted m. by those who pay GOLD 361:37
mists m. of evening lie BETJ 83:90
misunderestimate new word for our press corps: m. BUSH 175:5
misunderstanding m. by marketers GITL 358:86
misunderstood being m. COCT 224:58
have m. what I said GREE 372:81
neglected and m. RABAN 675:58
so universally m. MADO 539:24
To be great is to be m. EMER 312:9
misused How often m. words SPEN 807:42
Mithridates half M. MACA 526:71
M., he died old HOUS 415:68
Mitterrand M. has 100 lovers GORB 363:4
Mitty M., the undefeated THUR 859:31
mixture creative m. of both games SHUL 789:88
m. of evil in everything COWP 241:66
m. of fact and truths FRAME 333:80
revolting m. STEV 821:76
mixtures study of the m. THEO 851:39

O

love is the gift of o.! ANOU 26:3
what is useful to o. SPIN 810:31
one-stringed old o.-s. instrument RANJ 678:16
one-trade Detroit is a o.-t. town MAIL 540:55
one-way o.-w. property of time EDDI 298:83
onion Let o. atoms lurk SMITH 801:20
tears live in an o. SHAK 764:15
only O. in America KING 468:28
o. things that are true SHAW 777:56
onward o. and outward WHIT 905:31
ooze present than in the o. NABO 606:39
opal mind is a very o. SHAK 756:66
open get these things out in the o. PULI 672:3
getting out into the o. KELM 460:77
keep the store o. nights KAUF 456:61
Never lay yourself o. HUNT 423:24
o. door, and no man can shut it BIBLE 126:50
o. thy mouth wide BIBLE 96:44
whole nation out in the o.? SIHA 791:29
opening Eyes...go on o. REID 682:95
hell of an o. REAG 681:67
No better o. anywhere DICK 269:78
o. and closing of a door SAND 713:99
opening-night o.-n. audience HIRS 403:8
opera born for o. buffa ROSS 698:4
first rule in o. MELBA 563:16
I am like an o. singer MEAT 562:4
language an o. is sung in APPL 27:23
like German o. WAUGH 892:36
No good o. plot AUDEN 41:15
o....composed by God CARD 190:43
o. isn't what it used to be COWA 239:16
o....is to music MENC 565:62
O. is where a guy gets stabbed BENC 74:6
poor man's o. HUXL 425:95
Some of the o. houses JOHN 441:4
to the o. one goes either VOLT 883:52
opera-glasses to view...take o.-g. RIDGE 687:79
operas French o. sung by Swedish WHAR 902:54
operation military-style o. CRAN 243:31
o. of separating JOHN 441:3
refused an o. GREG 372:96
operations diversities of o. BIBLE 121:8
field of o. BELL 74:91
o. of government RUNC 702:71
o. of our own minds LOCKE 514:18
performing a few simple o. SMITH 798:52
operator dial the o. TREV 865:62
operators billions of legitimate o. GIBS 353:76
Ophelia most beautified O. SHAK 752:44
much of water hast thou, poor O. SHAK 755:27
soft you, the fair O. TWAIN 871:7
Ophir Nineveh from distant O. MASE 559:26
opiate Communism is the o. LUCE 522:81
emptied some dull o. KEATS 459:57
o. of the oppressed JONG 448:99
opinion almost of o. MONT 591:64
better to have no o. of God BACON 49:14
Busy o. FORD 330:16
client asks his o. JOHN 444:99
collective o....can make history SAFI 708:2
combat...with particular o. DRYD 288:44
cost to freedom of o. SCHL 718:10
current o. MCCA 528:99
Do not despise my o. LEON 504:19
drift of public o. DAFOE 250:62
engine of temporary o. HAZL 388:76
everything else is o. DEMO 261:84
flatterer does not have a good o. LABR 484:77
fool gudgeon, this o. SHAK 739:39
form a clear o. BONH 140:61
gave it for his o. SWIFT 831:80
give him my o. DICK 270:93
God's o. that life should go on SAND 713:9
guided by o. polls THAT 851:36
have his every o. regenerated PIER 651:5
heated division of o. TYNAN 872:43
high in Mr Podsnap's o. DICK 271:42
instrument for gauging public o. GALL 344:20
laughter at their quaint o. MILT 584:97
low o. of himself TROL 866:81
mankind...of one o. MILL 570:65
man of common o. BAGE 52:96
money controls o. ORWE 628:48
north of my lady's o. SHAK 756:80
offer him an o. SPEN 807:62
of his own o. still BUTL 177:60
of the o. with the learned CONG 230:93
o. breeds ignorance HIPP 403:2
o. in good men MILT 579:66
o. is about a woman JAMES 433:45
o. of himself, having once risen BENN 76:41
o. of our best friends MARG 549:44
o. of Winston Churchill ELTON 311:95
organization of public o. LIPP 511:68
Party is organized o. DISR 276:68
poor itch of your o. SHAK 769:56
Prejudice...vagrant o. BIER 129:42
public o. will sweep them away PULI 672:3
reason the o. of others WOOLF 922:45
recurring again to Plato's o. STER 818:88
scorching world's o. FLET 328:75
was ever of the o. GOLD 361:43
whole climate of o. AUDEN 40:99
wolf remains of a different o. INGE 428:49
opinions as many o. as...people TERE 848:79
borrow other men's o. BACON 48:3
confirm and establish our o. BROW 158:57
contempt for my character and o. SHAW 778:81
don't care to give o. HERN 399:27
How long halt ye between two o.? BIBLE 92:18
Men...bad as their o. MACK 534:22
men who have no o. CHES 211:55
one truth, and many o. KURZ 482:44
o. that they...entertain PALM 636:25
o. were not acted on ELIOT 303:1
private parts...and his religious o. BUTL 178:83
Stiff in o. DRYD 290:88
takes no notice of their o. CROM 245:70
think his own o. MORE 596:58
those who have certain o. STEIN 815:29
what their o. make of them LICH 509:23
wish to spread those o. BUTL 177:64
Women were expected to have weak o. ELIOT 303:1
opium against art, as against o. RODC 693:87
antidote against the o. of time BROW 159:90
help of o. or alcohol HERZ 400:55
It is the o. of the people MARX 557:94
just, subtle, and mighty o.! DE 262:7
Music is no different from o. KHOM 466:97
o. for every conceivable mass KENN 462:4
o. has left the happiest memory GREE 371:57
o. of the West FRAN 333:84
opium-dose Bible as...an o.-d. KING 469:59
opponent an o. cannot be...honest ORWE 629:92
sound to his o. bitter MILNE 574:73
tries to best his o. PAUL 644:76
opponents pushed back...by their o. PANK 636:30
trip, hack and push their o. FRY 339:22
truth...convincing its o. PLAN 654:60
opportunist rather be an o. and float BALF 55:59
opportunities equal o. MAND 544:46
No duties, only o. ANON 24:42
o....thicker than anywhere else BALD 53:30
series of great o. GARD 346:45
wise man will make more o. BACON 50:57
woman with fair o. THAC 849:86
opportunity age of right and o. WILS 916:7
build a society of o. MAJOR 541:70
Equality of o. KENN 463:25
existence and o. TEMP 838:35
giving you the o. DICK 270:86
improving the present o. WILL 912:5
Know thine o. PITT 653:51
least o. invades it NICO 614:94
let slip an o. SHAW 781:3
maximum of o. SHAW 778:8
not time or o. AUST 42:60
o. accorded him since Adam MUGG 601:49
o. as against material interests WILS 916:8
o. cost of economic discussion GALB 343:98
o. for attacking the devil! STEAD 813:85
o. for graft BIRNS 131:72
O. makes a thief BACON 46:34
o. to rise again SARN 714:32
o. to serve our country SMITH 799:71
scarcity of o. ANGE 17:36
strong seducer, o.! DRYD 288:37
substantial equality of o. ROOS 696:55
unfettered o. MADAN 538:19
opposèd o. may beware of thee SHAK 751:18
opposite in justice and in its o. SOPH 804:84
o. of talking LEBO 499:13
opposition duty of an O. CHUR 215:58
formidable O. DISR 276:43
Her Majesty's O. BAGE 51:82
His Majesty's O. HOBH 405:31
Prime Minister or Leader of the O. DISR 277:82
war of eternal o. LYND 524:15
when it has a strong o. SWEE 830:46
young, bald Leader of the O. KINN 470:71
oppositions riven by a dozen o. ROSS 697:72
oppress o., rob, and degrade them DOUG 284:37
oppressed Christ comes to the o. RUET 701:63
friend of the o. GARI 346:47
opiate of the o. JONG 448:99
o. can find...safety ANGE 17:42
o., who wanted strength WORD 927:31
past of the o. people FANON 317:44
oppression Need and o. starveth SHAK 737:79
often a mechanical o. HEMI 394:11
o. he may heretofore have suffered MANS 547:1
proud o. will not hear me OTWAY 630:24
To make o. bitter SHAK 753:68
oppressions o. of this earth SHEL 783:26
oppressor confront the o. MAKW 541:77
day o' the O. is ended KIPL 472:23
revolutionary ends as an o. CAMUS 187:96
The o.'s wrong TWAIN 871:7
oppressors we may have our o. PUIG 672:1
optical o. flecks UPDI 875:93
o. form of thought HUGO 420:64
optimism as agreeable as o. BENN 76:49
optimist have to be an o. SAND 713:11
last o. left in Colombia GARC 345:41
o. after it, he knows too little TWAIN 872:35
o. is a guy MARQ 554:25
o. proclaims that we live in the best CABE 183:18
o....sees a green light everywhere SCHW 721:71
optimistic If I was not o. OUD 631:36
make us o. or UNAM 873:64
O. lies have...therapeutic value SHAW 780:59
options discuss your o. afterwards SHAN 776:31
opulent o. calm of angelfish ALLEN 12:35
oracle pronounces as an o. WESL 900:22
oracles o. are dumb MILT 576:99
o. of God BIBLE 124:91
orange clockwork o. BURG 167:81
Orangeman Pocket of a Stout O. ANON 21:37
oranges bowl of o., too MITC 588:90
coffee and o. STEV 819:17
orator An o. is a good man CATO 200:98
greatest o., who triumphs HUME 422:11
no o. as Brutus is SHAK 748:13
oratory Poetry...not as o. POUND 664:31
orb Cycle and epicycle, o. in o. MILT 584:97
monthly changes in her circled o. SHAK 736:51
There's not the smallest o. SHAK 741:86
orbit most beautiful sight in o. SCHW 721:69
orbits circled in their o. DICK 268:51
orbs dew her o. upon the green SHAK 737:92
o., Or dim suffusion veiled MILT 582:37
orchard fair with o. lawns TENN 847:52
hath thy o. fruit JONS 449:37
O., for a Dome DICK 272:59
orchards Not all do o. please VIRG 882:28
orchestra for o. without music RAVEL 679:37
golden rules for an o. BEEC 69:62
plays the kettle drums in the o. SALI 711:60
separates you from the o. DIDE 273:87
orchestrated Three farts...o. BARB 59:49
orchestration o. of platitudes WILD 911:83
orchid O.—breathing incense BASHO 63:43
ordeal o. of meeting me CHUR 217:96
worst possible o. BERR 82:68
order all in o. stand CRAB 242:83
And o., truth, and beauty range SMART 796:27
arranged them in alphabetical o. HELL 392:62
been a rock of o. METT 568:28
benevolence of the passive o. MERE 567:3
change the social o. FRAN 333:91
colours assembled in a certain o. DENIS 262:97
decently and in o. BIBLE 121:11
establishing a world o. EISE 302:57
explain to our sense of o. HARDY 382:62
fairest o. in the world HERA 397:71
forces working in inverse o.! CARL 192:8
Good o. is the foundation BURKE 169:44
loyalty and o. GLAD 358:92
new o. from the old WEBB 893:65
old o. changeth TENN 847:50

high p., but not a safe one BERN 80:31
if not impossible p. LEWO 508:10
in a p. to instruct us PEOP 647:24
lucidly justifying his p. AMERY 14:78
mathematical is this fundamental p. HEID 391:44
no p. more perilous TROL 867:95
only one p. for an artist THOM 853:97
p. at the summit of the world PEARY 645:2
p.…epitomized marginality ECON 298:79
p., I'd have done the same NIXON 617:50
p. of the artists of Wales THOM 853:97
p. ridiculous CHES 211:40
rose to his p. TROT 867:16
Whatever its p. or character SCOTT 722:75
positions military take p. KENN 464:53
ridiculous p. DANF 251:84
positive All satisfaction…never p. SCHO 719:28
P.…Mistaken at the top of one's voice BIER 129:41
something p. and precious PRIT 669:52
possess not enough to p. her LACL 484:85
possessed limited in order to be p. BURKE 168:19
p. by what is not LEGU 501:56
p. with murd'rous hate SHAK 770:3
possessing P. what one loves PROU 671:80
too dear for my p. SHAK 772:35
possession everlasting p. BIBLE 87:77
in the glad p. JONS 448:11
merry hart with small p. HENR 396:53
p. intended to last THUC 859:16
P. is nine points ANON 20:11
p. is the final good WHIT 904:8
p. of a bourgeois aristocracy ENGE 314:65
p. of that object conveys SMITH 797:41
secure p. of a bleak rock YOUNG 935:76
possessions concern not for…p. PLATO 654:78
for he had great p. BIBLE 113:73
jealous p. GIDE 353:81
mind is the least of p. WHITE 903:96
possessor libel on its p. SHEL 782:15
not profitable to its p. MARQ 554:29
possibilities p. of life LEAV 498:1
short of their inherent p. MUMF 603:75
To believe only in p. BROW 158:76
possibility How great a P. CARL 192:3
laws of p. REDON 681:74
life…to give it p. MILL [illegible]:47
objective p. WEBER 894:68
p. of anybody getting me out BRAD 149:78
p. of human happiness ERNST 315:90
Religion…a remote p. WHIT 904:8
Violent, vivid and of infinite p. EBER 298:72
possible art of the p. GALB 343:94
if a thing is p. CAIO 185:45
no explanation is p. SEAT 726:69
Politics is the art of the p. BUTL 176:34
p. is one of the provinces BAUD 65:71
scientist states that something is p. CLAR 220:59
thank all those who made this p. ANDR 16:29
wasn't p. for me or anyone KAVA 456:66
possum Honourable P. BERR 82:64
post boats…near the winning p. COKE 224:71
Lie follows by p. BERE 78:90
may not quit the p. TENN 847:34
p. of honour ADDI 7:37
stalked through the P. Office YEATS 934:64
postal cheque and the p. order AUDEN 39:81
desire to take p. courses BRAD 148:52
postboy keys of a p.'s horn BENET 75:10
postcard and a p. album TRAV 864:42
postcards have a set of p. printed ELLI 310:80
post-chaise driving briskly in a p.-c. JOHN 445:25
poster Kitchener…a great p. ASQU 36:12
live up to one's p. TREE 865:53
p. on the student's wall VETT 880:74
p. with the enormous face ORWE 629:98
posterior protecting his p. SAFI 708:98
posterity fear of vexing p.! ROCHE 691:47
footprints preserved for p. PATE 642:56
love of p. HAWT 386:36
People will not look forward to p. BURKE 168:30
p. be after him CROM 245:71
P. do something for us ADDI 7:40
p. talking bad grammar DISR 277:92
P. will do justice to…Gladstone DISR 277:82
protecting his posterior from p. SAFI 708:98
Thy p. shall sway COWP 241:52
To evoke p. GRAV 367:69
To invoke one's p. CELI 202:37
trustees of P. DISR 276:55
posters P. of the sea and land SHAK 766:69
post-horse contrapuntist…p. MOZA 601:46
postman hear the p.'s knock AUDEN 39:82
The P. Always Rings Twice CAIN 184:31
postmodern p.…Australia NARO 608:74
postpone p. no more WHIT 905:40
postponement Life…one long p. MILL 573:46
posts sprinkle all the p. SPEN 809:4
postscript pith is in the p. HAZL 388:86
seldom Writes…but in her P. STEE 814:98
postulate lay down as a p. WEIL 896:32
p. of objectivity MONOD 591:56
Postumus Oh, my P., P. HORA 413:21
posture died each in the despairing p. POE 656:19
postures indecent p. WILDE 910:65
post-war awash in p.-w. testosterone SCHR 720:45
posy picks a p. of daisies THOM 853:89
pot don't make them in the one p. JOYCE 452:86
Fame's luscious p. RICK 686:76
great Melting P. ZANG 936:88
Joan doth keel the p. SHAK 734:94
melting p. never worked MORR 599:3
not a melting p. CART 198:46
strawberries at the mouth of their p. ELIZ 310:64
three-hooped p. SHAK 730:63
potato any more than a p. HAWT 386:38
no more bounce than a boiled p. PORT 663:12
p. candidate ANON 25:61
You say p. GERS 351:42
potatoes Let the sky rain p. SHAK 744:81
Papa, p., poultry, prunes DICK 271:16
potent more p. than any other man STEAD 813:81
potential both as chaos and as p. POUND 665:66
p. for the disastrous rise EISE 302:58
potentialities puritanical p. LEWIS 508:96
potions p. have I drunk of siren tears SHAK 773:49
Potomac All quiet along the P. MCCL 528:15
potsherd Let the p. strive BIBLE 103:45
p. to scrape himself BIBLE 93:50
pottage bread and p. of lentiles BIBLE 87:85
mess of p. BIBLE 87:83
Potter Harry P. was a highly unusual boy ROWL 701:55
potter Hath not the p. power BIBLE 120:79
like a p.'s vessel BIBLE 94:84
P. and clay endure BROW 162:70
P. is piqued with p. HESI 401:64
poultry A p. matter MARX 557:84
foxes…prolonging the lives of the p. ELIOT 303:96
I hate pudgy p. PERD 648:52
Pound in Ezra P.'s term MACD 530:47
pound Christian on a P. a Week? HARD 381:40
give thee a silver p. CAMP 186:70
grocer puts a p. weight SPEN 807:62
hundred p. on't SHAK 773:57
pound P. a week and his keep LAWS 496:45
p.…in your pocket WILS 916:97
Take thou thy p. of flesh SHAK 740:83
two thousand p. in lead MIDD 569:38
who will p. longest WELL 897:55
pounds Fifty p.! LAWR 494:18
p. will take care LOWN 521:64
three hundred p. a year! SHAK 743:77
weight in p., shillings MILNE 575:84
pour p. on him all we can HERB 398:16
poverty abolition of p. HOOV 411:58
against hunger, p., desperation MARS 554:39
America has mitigated p. WOOL 922:25
amidst its p. and squalor ARNO 33:56
best-dressed p. HARR 383:89
between the ignorance and p. WALP 887:22
destruction of the poor is their p. BIBLE 99:20
Greed begins where p. ends BALZ 58:22
hardest thing to bear in p. JUVE 453:16
hated p. JOHN 441:14
inhibition attaches to p. HESI 401:66
In honoured p. thy voice SHEL 782:23
In p., hunger, and dirt HOOD 410:45
marry the Irish…look for p. DONL 279:23
monarchies end by p. MONT 593:95
Money is better than p. ALLEN 12:52
no…crime so shameful as p. FARQ 318:56
P. and oysters…seem to go DICK 266:76
P. has a home in Africa HEAD 388:98
p., ignorance and disease DU 293:75
P. is a great enemy JOHN 446:56
P. is…blamed on anyone OCON 622:28
P. isn't being broke WYLIE 931:24
P. makes peace ANON 19:95
p. of blackness DANG 251:85
p.'s catching BEHN 71:11
prefer p. with liberty PITT 653:42
represent p. as no evil JOHN 443:67
So shall thy p. come BIBLE 99:16
struggled with p. BALD 54:34
terrible reality of p. LEGU 501:60
there for honest P. BURNS 173:46
trouble with p. KRUG 481:24
upon p., vice, and misery SUMN 828:18
where p. is enforced DOUG 284:37
worst of crimes is p. SHAW 779:38
pow blessings on your frosty p. BURNS 171:10
powder keep her in paint and p. NIMI 616:36
keep your p. dry BLAC 132:93
take a p. and they are gone ACHE 3:41
powdered Still to be p. JONS 449:25
powders P. and liquids DOYLE 286:83
rogue gives you Love P. LAMB 486:36
power above thy p. BIBLE 108:50
according to the p. that worketh BIBLE 122:46
add reach to p. ACHE 3:51
all p. is a trust DISR 275:35
Almighty p. Hurled MILT 580:95
antithesis…is not pleasure, but p. DE 262:8
apt words have p. MILT 586:51
awful shadow of some unseen P. SHEL 782:19
beauty…hath strange p. MILT 586:59
because they confer p. RUSS 705:47
because we had p. BENET 75:14
best in his p. TROL 867:94
Black p. ANON 23:97
brute p. and human need COMM 229:66
certainty of p. DAY 257:83
changing it is within our p. REAG 680:62
charm of all p. is modesty ALCO 10:3
conceal the p. of the atom COLE 225:73
conceive a dominant p. HARDY 381:54
constructs p. structures LEGU 501:58
corridors of p. ALLEN 12:35
corruption of p. BRON 154:67
cowards…sit safe in p. OTWAY 631:28
Creator's p. display ADDI 6:76
cult…religion with no political p. WOLFE 920:94
defy P., which seems omnipotent SHEL 785:83
delightful and delighting p. MITF 588:5
depository of p. DISR 276:48
descriptive p.…literary style PULI 672:4
Desire of p. DRYD 290:84
desire of p. after p. HOBB 404:26
desire to seek p. BACON 48:1
devil hath p. SHAK 753:71
differences of speed And p. PRATT 667:1
drape over their will to p. HUXL 426:2
dream of independent p. JAY 435:96
drunk with sight of p. KIPL 472:22
During my tenure of p. PEEL 646:9
earthly p. doth then show SHAK 740:80
eat the p. out of women WEST 901:40
Eternal God of p. TENN 844:74
excessive love for the balance of p. BRIG 152:31
existence of mankind in its p. ADAMS 4:74
expression of the will to p. PAZ 644:90
fealty to those in p. MAMET 544:35
feel herself a source of p. BROO 156:27
fool, In p. of others MILT 586:47
Force is a spiritual p. LEON 503:12
fourth p.…into two p.s FERM 321:15
friend in p. is a friend lost ADAMS 4:77
full of p. TENN 844:66
gauge of their real p. LESS 505:36
given women so much p. JOHN 443:76
God…loved the People in P. PATC 642:50
good, and had no p. to see LANY 489:3
guessing p. BAGE 51:93
guilt and p. TOPL 863:15
have the p. to die TENN 846:27
history of political p. POPP 662:92
hold on to p. until then WANG 888:55
if he had the p. MILL 570:65
its source of p. KINN 470:66
Knowledge is p. BACON 46:33
lawful p. is still superior DRYD 290:98
legislative p. GIBB 351:53

Q

S

toves Twas brillig, and the slithy t. CARR 195:90
tow death will take us in t. DIBD 265:55
should'st t. me after SHAK 765:36
Tower Eyefull T. is devine LOOS 517:78
tower hawk of the t. SKEL 795:91
intending to build a t. BIBLE 116:43
name of the Lord is a strong t. BIBLE 99:40
neck is like the t. BIBLE 101:2
stony t., nor walls SHAK 747:81
tall building, with a t. and bells CRAB 242:95
Terrace or lofty T. LEAR 497:77
to the dark t. came SHAK 763:79
t. of defence ALCA 10:1
t. of my time NEME 610:38
t. of strength TENN 844:72
yonder ivy-mantled t. GRAY 369:11
towers and four grey t. TENN 839:44
branchy between t. HOPK 412:91
cloud-capped t. SHAK 774:94
hammered from a hundred t. TENN 840:72
hills and t. MUIR 601:53
Ships, t., domes WORD 926:19
thy palaces and t. BURNS 171:90
topless t. of Ilium? MARL 552:5
ye antique t. GRAY 368:92
town absent myself from the t. MARP 553:18
all the fools in t. TWAIN 871:9
anyone lived in a pretty how t. CUMM 248:19
architecture is also t. planning LECO 499:30
As the rain over the t. VERL 879:66
A T. like Alice SHUTE 790:94
Bind t. to t. CRANE 243:16
bloody t.'s a bloody cuss BLAIR 132:97
circulating library in a t. SHER 787:36
Come sounding thro' the t. BALL 55:69
Country in the t. MART 555:52
Dear old Glasgow t.! FYFFE 342:78
Detroit is a one-trade t. MAIL 540:55
direction to the t. SWIFT 832:99
drummed them out of t. CARR 197:16
Duke takes a t. POMP 658:45
foggy day in London T. GERS 351:43
girl in our t. ANON 21:28
ideal t., clean, noble LESS 505:37
in the streets of the t. PARN 639:91
Kercaldy my native t. FLEM 327:62
little marble cross below the t. HAYES 387:62
majority of the t. were otherwise LAWS 495:44
man made the t. COWP 241:68
midnight, in our little t. LIND 511:50
moonless night in the small t. THOM 853:85
necessary to destroy the t. ANON 23:2
populous railway t. THOR 858:7
streets o' the t. MACD 530:43
studies it in t. COWP 240:51
surprise of a large t. LARK 491:33
This t.'s a misnomer QUIL 674:47
toast of a' the t. BURNS 173:43
t. among the trees ROBI 690:35
t., a place JOHN 440:99
t.…buried its dead SHAW 781:1
t. has two great teams SHAN 776:33
t. is full of cozenage SHAK 733:59
t. of narrow streets THOR 858:5
t. of red brick DICK 270:3
T. small-talk flows CRAB 242:97
t. surrounded by water MOORE 595:26
transport breaks upon the t. DICK 272:55
visit the ancient t. of Crieff MCGO 531:79
wale o' ilka t. FERG 321:8
Washington is a resigning t. SHUL 789:86
Washington is a t. GERA 350:25
was the good t. once MUIR 602:58
Winkie rins through the t. MILL 574:61
town-crier as lief the t.-c. had spoke SHAK 754:85
towns elephants for want of t. SWIFT 832:98
gin joints in all the t. EPST 314:76
industrial t. MACM 536:69
London, thou art of t. DUNB 294:5
Of t. and cities WORD 923:69
run round in robot t. BRAD 149:70
t. one can safely call 'her' BETJ 83:93
t. or houses raised by poetry COWL 240:30
Winter lies too long in country t. CATH 200:87
townsmen soldiers into t. WAUGH 892:38
townspeople teach you my t. WILL 913:40
toxicologists unknown to t. THOM 853:95
toy crammed in a monster t. MACN 538:1
foolish thing was but a t. SHAK 757:92
religion but a childish t. MARL 552:82
their t. the world COWP 241:77
woman…to be the t. of man WOLL 921:7
toys all my t. beside me lay STEV 823:16
babies like such t. MORE 597:68
bundle of t. MOORE 594:18
label our t. good and bad DYSON 297:63
meddle with my t. STEV 823:14
mind with all your t. MILT 576:12
to be pretty t. THOR 857:84
t. for your delight STEV 823:32
toyshop T. of their heart POPE 658:66
trace all t.…disappeared WHIS 902:61
any t. of it in their hearts REDON 681:75
No t. of pain WORD 929:63
traces remove all t. of reality PICA 650:96
track Around the ancient t. MERE 567:8
beyond a railroad t. LOWE 519:25
Come flying on our t. THOM 856:60
forest with a golden t. LIND 511:48
Jungle star or jungle t. CULL 247:92
move us along the political t. MCNA 537:95
on earth no t. THOM 856:63
switching to their t. WALE 885:89
T. twenty nine GORD 363:8
tracks bright t. GURN 375:43
cover up all the t. FEYN 322:24
lies down on the t. of history EISE 302:50
tractates reading all manner of t. MILT 579:73
trade abolition of the slave t. PITT 653:45
accident is not my t. WORD 925:8
all is seared with t. HOPK 412:83
among…articles of t. FUSE 342:75
art…only is a t. DRYD 288:40
as much a t. to write a book LA 483:57
British t. unionist BEVIN 85:29
effect of t. and commerce HALL 378:91
fine thing for the t.! DICK 266:90
first snarl of the t. unions LLOY 513:95
functions of a t. union LENIN 502:82
homely slighted Shepherd's t. MILT 578:49
It is his t. HEINE 391:51
live by t. RUSK 704:35
master of his t. DRAY 287:7
mysterious fluctuations of t. ELIOT 303:07
no…association or t. union OAKE 619:86
North-East T. KIPL 471:7
People of the same t. SMITH 798:44
port without t. DEFOE 258:22
pride…in their daily t. PRIT 669:56
principles of t. and business HAZL 388:77
secrets of his t. ORWE 629:68
serve his time to every t. BYRON 179:97
t. and art is to live MONT 592:79
T. could not be managed JOHN 445:41
t. for the publick good SMITH 798:49
t. union for pensioners HEATH 390:18
T. Unionism of the married? SHAW 778:98
t. unionists at heart JEVO 438:47
traffic from the vulgar t. MARL 552:84
us that t. in love SHAK 765:28
War is the t. of kings DRYD 291:26
Wheel that turned the T. MAND 545:54
trader 55-year old t. GREE 372:83
traders doomed t. WRIG 930:83
free t. PALM 635:21
trades best of t., to make songs BELL 73:61
vain, superfluous t. MORE 597:66
vain title of T. Unions RUSK 704:35
tradesmen bow, ye t. GILB 354:10
trading To preserve a t. state STEU 819:8
tradition cultural t. PARS 640:1
European philosophical t. WHIT 904:12
History…It's t. FORD 330:7
no t. of moral individual MO 589:20
regard for it is a lost t. BARZ 63:32
respect t. and to innovate PEI 646:14
Science…opposed to history and t. BORN 145:98
They are a great t. ALLEN 12:35
t. Approves all forms of competition CLOU 223:40
T. does not mean MACM 536:76
T., if not constantly recreated MACI 533:5
T. means giving votes CHES 211:61
traditional atom of the t. novel LODGE 514:23
justify a t. custom TWAIN 870:86
t. and popular sport SITW 794:87
t. behavior WIEN 907:68
t. fiction GALB 343:95
t. stories and images FRYE 340:36
traditions T. are lovely things MARC 548:28
Trafalgar go to T. Square GEOR 349:17
traffic barbarous t. in slave PITT 653:45
tragedies Let us have no ranting t. AUST 43:75
t. are finished by a death BYRON 182:85
why we like t. GRAY 368:88
tragedy best actors…for t., comedy SHAK 753:62
both comedy and t. THUR 860:52
cannot balance t. in the scales BENET 75:13
Comedy…is harder to do…than t. MALA 541:82
Farce is nearer t. COLE 227:25
first time as t. BARN 60:72
first time as t. MARX 558:7
five acts of Shakespeare's t. FIELD 322:31
go, litel myn t. CHAU 208:64
great t. has ended MACA 524:23
great t. of Science HUXL 426:9
inherent t. of things STEV 823:29
most tremendous t. BEER 69:68
our only real t. PUZO 673:27
out of it is simply a t. WILDE 909:28
participate in a t. HUXL 425:92
perfect t. is the noblest production ADDI 6:12
Religion is the t. WILS 914:70
see a t. to be moved VOLT 903:52
stress and t. of it all WELLS 898:74
terrible t. and destiny of Cain JOHN 439:61
That is their t. WILDE 909:40
the food a t. POWE 666:79
the word t. means…unpleasantness BLIX 137:2
t., ecstasy, doom ROTH 700:34
t.…in the very fact of frequency ELIOT 304:9
T. is…a representation ARIS 29:54
T. is if I cut my finger BROO 157:31
t. of life is…that he almost wins BROUN 157:35
t. of the age DU 293:72
t. of the world that no one knows CARY 199:67
t. paints the passions HUGO 420:74
t. requires persons of heroic stature AMIS 15:9
t. to those that feel WALP 887:31
ultimate t. HARL 383:83
worst t. for a poet COCT 224:58
writers of t. have…insight THUR 860:55
write you a t. FITZ 325:14
tragic essentially a t. age LAWR 495:21
t. mechanisms can't work AMIS 15:9
who has experienced the t. MAMET 543:26
tragically refuse to take it t. LAWR 495:21
trail pull out on the Long T. KIPL 474:79
t. has its own stern code SERV 728:2
trails silver t. of inebriated slugs JAMES 433:28
train all her negro t. SMART 796:22
artist who has travelled on a steam t. DAVIS 255:62
car or an express t. LEGER 501:53
caught the last t. MCLE 534:27
from the t., go running by LAWS 496:46
funeral t. which the bridegroom sees CLOU 223:32
hire an express t. SPUR 811:41
in front of the…t. SHAW 778:87
light of the oncoming t. LOWE 521:60
pack, and take a t. BROO 156:12
Runs the red electric t. BETJ 84:1
shaves and takes a t. WHITE 903:89
sneak into the house in her t. LAMB 486:43
the next t. has gone PUNCH 672:10
to Vietnam to take the t. THER 851:47
t. filled the temple BIBLE 102:11
t. of events has carried him AMERY 14:78
t. of the future to run over him EISE 302:50
t. passes through stations LEWIS 507:70
T. up a child BIBLE 100:46
triumph of His t. WESL 900:16
Ultimate T. MANS 547:88
we rush in the t. THOM 856:60
whirligig wheels of the t. SITW 793:61
Winter…Affrights thy shrinking t. COLL 228:48
trained Then I t. hard HEMI 394:18
t. folly GERH 350:34
trainer animal t.…knows RYLE 707:80
training not part of our t. NORM 618:63
pitch of the highest t. ROOS 696:52
t. which fits for labour! SCHR 720:42
training-school democracy…a t.-s. WHIT 906:50

U

W

X

Y